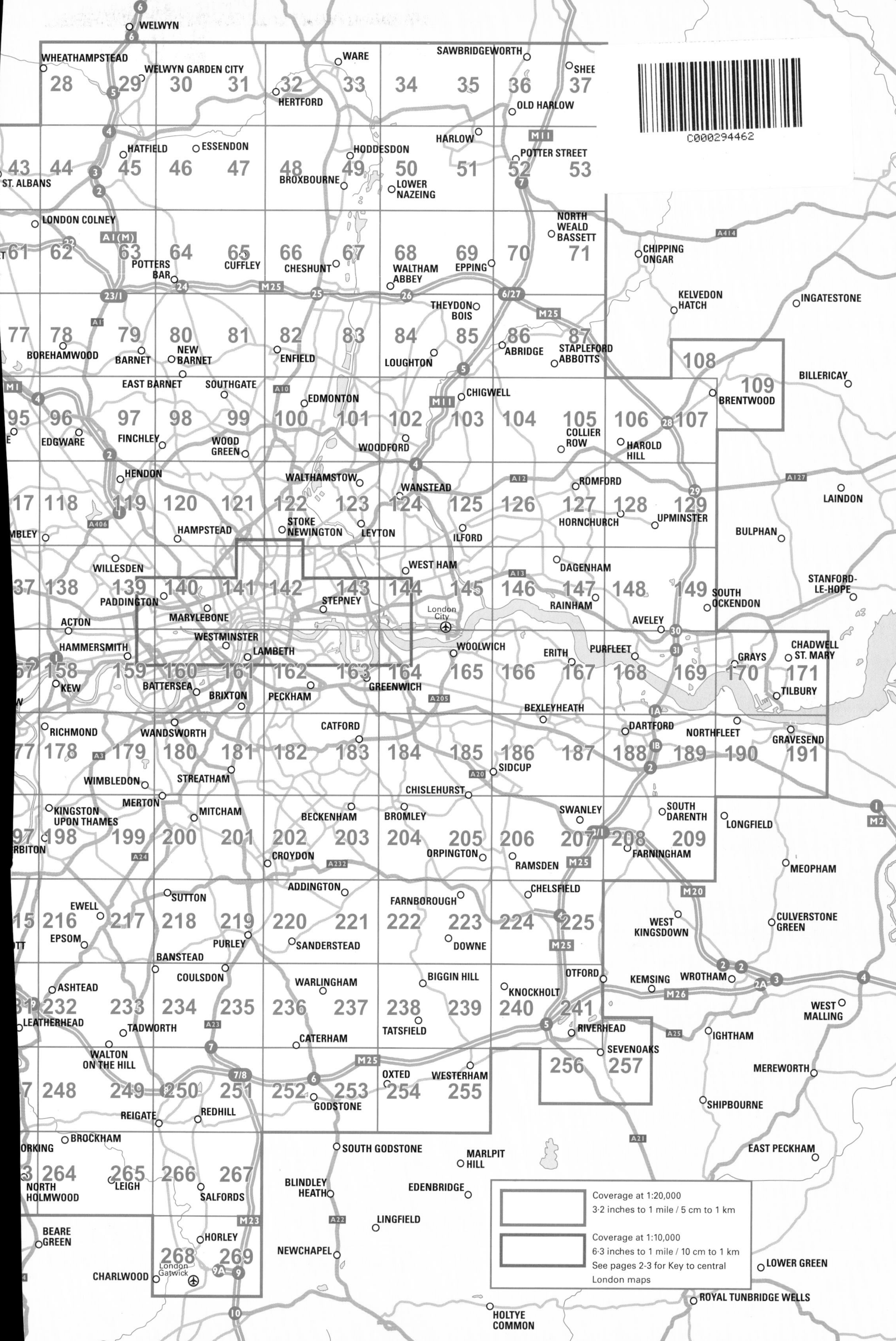

C000294462
WELWYN
WHEATHAMPSTEAD
WELWYN GARDEN CITY
WARE
SAWBRIDGEWORTH
SHEE
28
29
30
31
32
33
34
35
36
37
HERTFORD
OLD HARLOW
M11
HATFIELD
ESSENDON
HODDESDON
HARLOW
POTTER STREET
43
44
45
46
47
48
49
50
51
52
53
ST. ALBANS
BROXBOURNE
LOWER NAZEING
LONDON COLNEY
A1(M)
NORTH WEALD BASSETT
A414
CHIPPING ONGAR
61
62
63
64
65
66
67
68
69
70
71
POTTERS BAR
CUFFLEY
CHESHUNT
WALTHAM ABBEY
EPPING
M25
23/1
KELVEDON HATCH
INGATESTONE
THEYDON BOIS
6/27
A1
77
78
79
80
81
82
83
84
85
86
87
108
BOREHAMWOOD
BARNET
NEW BARNET
ENFIELD
LOUGHTON
ABRIDGE
STAPLEFORD ABBOTTS
BILLERICAY
109
BRENTWOOD
M1
EAST BARNET
SOUTHGATE
A10
EDMONTON
CHIGWELL
M11
95
96
97
98
99
100
101
102
103
104
105
106
107
EDGWARE
FINCHLEY
WOOD GREEN
WOODFORD
COLLIER ROW
HAROLD HILL
HENDON
WALTHAMSTOW
WANSTEAD
A12
ROMFORD
A127
LAINDON
117
118
119
120
121
122
123
124
125
126
127
128
129
A406
HAMPSTEAD
STOKE NEWINGTON
LEYTON
ILFORD
HORNCHURCH
UPMINSTER
BULPHAN
WEMBLEY
WILLESDEN
WEST HAM
DAGENHAM
A13
STANFORD-LE-HOPE
137
138
139
140
141
142
143
144
145
146
147
148
149
PADDINGTON
STEPNEY
RAINHAM
SOUTH OCKENDON
MARYLEBONE
London City
AVELEY
ACTON
WESTMINSTER
HAMMERSMITH
LAMBETH
WOOLWICH
ERITH
PURFLEET
GRAYS
CHADWELL ST. MARY
157
158
159
160
161
162
163
164
165
166
167
168
169
170
171
KEW
BATTERSEA
BRIXTON
PECKHAM
GREENWICH
A205
TILBURY
BEXLEYHEATH
RICHMOND
WANDSWORTH
CATFORD
DARTFORD
NORTHFLEET
GRAVESEND
177
178
179
180
181
182
183
184
185
186
187
188
189
190
191
A3
A20
SIDCUP
WIMBLEDON
STREATHAM
CHISLEHURST
MERTON
KINGSTON UPON THAMES
MITCHAM
BECKENHAM
BROMLEY
SWANLEY
SOUTH DARENTH
LONGFIELD
M2
197
198
199
200
201
202
203
204
205
206
207
208
209
SURBITON
A24
CROYDON
ORPINGTON
RAMSDEN
FARNINGHAM
A232
M25
MEOPHAM
ADDINGTON
CHELSFIELD
M20
SUTTON
FARNBOROUGH
EWELL
215
216
217
218
219
220
221
222
223
224
225
EPSOM
PURLEY
SANDERSTEAD
DOWNE
WEST KINGSDOWN
CULVERSTONE GREEN
BANSTEAD
COULSDON
WARLINGHAM
BIGGIN HILL
KNOCKHOLT
OTFORD
KEMSING
WROTHAM
M26
ASHTEAD
231
232
233
234
235
236
237
238
239
240
241
WEST MALLING
LEATHERHEAD
TADWORTH
A23
TATSFIELD
RIVERHEAD
A25
IGHTHAM
CATERHAM
SEVENOAKS
WALTON ON THE HILL
MEREWORTH
OXTED
WESTERHAM
256
257
247
248
249
250
251
252
253
254
255
REIGATE
REDHILL
GODSTONE
SHIPBOURNE
A21
BROCKHAM
DORKING
SOUTH GODSTONE
MARLPIT HILL
EAST PECKHAM
263
264
265
266
267
NORTH HOLMWOOD
LEIGH
SALFORDS
BLINDLEY HEATH
EDENBRIDGE
A22
LINGFIELD
M23
BEARE GREEN
HORLEY
NEWCHAPEL
268
269
CHARLWOOD
London Gatwick
LOWER GREEN
ROYAL TUNBRIDGE WELLS
HOLTYE COMMON
Coverage at 1:20,000
3·2 inches to 1 mile / 5 cm to 1 km
Coverage at 1:10,000
6·3 inches to 1 mile / 10 cm to 1 km
See pages 2-3 for Key to central London maps

London Underground map

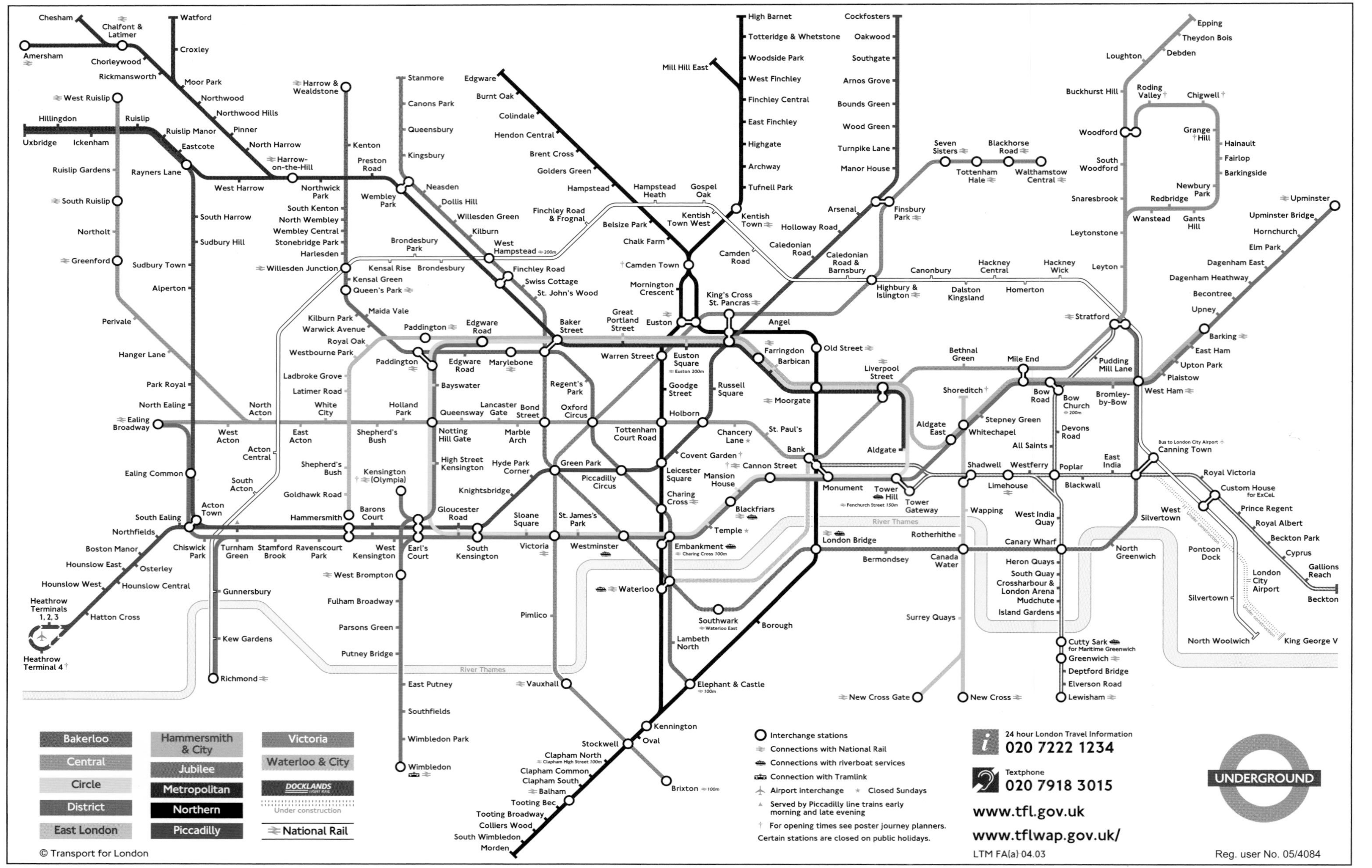

Chesham
Chalfont & Latimer
Amersham
Chorleywood
Rickmansworth
Watford
Croxley
Moor Park
Northwood
Northwood Hills
Pinner
North Harrow
Harrow-on-the-Hill
West Ruislip
Hillingdon
Ruislip
Ruislip Manor
Eastcote
Uxbridge
Ickenham
Ruislip Gardens
Rayners Lane
South Ruislip
Northolt
Greenford
Perivale
Hanger Lane
Park Royal
North Ealing
Ealing Broadway
West Harrow
South Harrow
Sudbury Hill
Sudbury Town
Alperton
Harrow & Wealdstone
Kenton
Preston Road
Northwick Park
South Kenton
North Wembley
Wembley Central
Stonebridge Park
Harlesden
Willesden Junction
Wembley Park
Stanmore
Canons Park
Queensbury
Kingsbury
Neasden
Dollis Hill
Willesden Green
Kilburn
West Hampstead
Brondesbury Park
Brondesbury
Kensal Rise
Kensal Green
Queen's Park
Finchley Road
Swiss Cottage
St. John's Wood
Edgware
Burnt Oak
Colindale
Hendon Central
Brent Cross
Golders Green
Hampstead
Hampstead Heath
Gospel Oak
Finchley Road & Frognal
Belsize Park
Chalk Farm
Kentish Town West
Camden Town
Mornington Crescent
Mill Hill East
High Barnet
Totteridge & Whetstone
Woodside Park
West Finchley
Finchley Central
East Finchley
Highgate
Archway
Tufnell Park
Kentish Town
Cockfosters
Oakwood
Southgate
Arnos Grove
Bounds Green
Wood Green
Turnpike Lane
Manor House
Arsenal
Holloway Road
Caledonian Road
Camden Road
Caledonian Road & Barnsbury
Finsbury Park
Seven Sisters
Tottenham Hale
Blackhorse Road
Walthamstow Central
Highbury & Islington
Canonbury
Dalston Kingsland
Hackney Central
Homerton
Hackney Wick
Epping
Theydon Bois
Debden
Loughton
Buckhurst Hill
Roding Valley
Chigwell
Grange Hill
Hainault
Fairlop
Barkingside
Woodford
South Woodford
Newbury Park
Snaresbrook
Redbridge
Wanstead
Gants Hill
Leytonstone
Leyton
Stratford
Upminster
Upminster Bridge
Hornchurch
Elm Park
Dagenham East
Dagenham Heathway
Becontree
Upney
Barking
East Ham
Upton Park
Plaistow
West Ham
Pudding Mill Lane
Bromley-by-Bow
Bow Church
Bow Road
Mile End
Bethnal Green
Maida Vale
Kilburn Park
Warwick Avenue
Royal Oak
Westbourne Park
Paddington
Edgware Road
Marylebone
Baker Street
Great Portland Street
Euston
King's Cross St. Pancras
Angel
Farringdon
Barbican
Old Street
Moorgate
Liverpool Street
Shoreditch
Aldgate East
Aldgate
Stepney Green
Whitechapel
Ladbroke Grove
Latimer Road
White City
North Acton
West Acton
East Acton
Acton Central
Ealing Common
South Acton
Shepherd's Bush
Goldhawk Road
Holland Park
Notting Hill Gate
Queensway
Lancaster Gate
Bond Street
Marble Arch
Bayswater
High Street Kensington
Kensington (Olympia)
Hyde Park Corner
Knightsbridge
Regent's Park
Oxford Circus
Warren Street
Euston Square
Goodge Street
Russell Square
Tottenham Court Road
Holborn
Chancery Lane
St. Paul's
Bank
Covent Garden
Leicester Square
Mansion House
Cannon Street
Monument
Tower Hill
Tower Gateway
Charing Cross
Piccadilly Circus
Green Park
Blackfriars
Temple
Embankment
Westminster
St. James's Park
Victoria
Sloane Square
Gloucester Road
South Kensington
Earl's Court
West Kensington
Barons Court
Hammersmith
Ravenscourt Park
Stamford Brook
Turnham Green
Chiswick Park
Acton Town
South Ealing
Northfields
Boston Manor
Osterley
Hounslow East
Hounslow Central
Hounslow West
Hatton Cross
Heathrow Terminals 1, 2, 3
Heathrow Terminal 4
Gunnersbury
Kew Gardens
Richmond
West Brompton
Fulham Broadway
Parsons Green
Putney Bridge
East Putney
Southfields
Wimbledon Park
Wimbledon
Pimlico
Vauxhall
Waterloo
Southwark
Lambeth North
Borough
Elephant & Castle
London Bridge
Bermondsey
Canada Water
Rotherhithe
Wapping
Surrey Quays
New Cross Gate
New Cross
Kennington
Oval
Stockwell
Brixton
Clapham North
Clapham Common
Clapham South
Balham
Tooting Bec
Tooting Broadway
Colliers Wood
South Wimbledon
Morden
Shadwell
Limehouse
Westferry
All Saints
Devons Road
Poplar
Blackwall
East India
Canning Town
West India Quay
Canary Wharf
Heron Quays
South Quay
Crossharbour & London Arena
Mudchute
Island Gardens
Cutty Sark for Maritime Greenwich
Greenwich
Deptford Bridge
Elverson Road
Lewisham
North Greenwich
West Silvertown
Pontoon Dock
London City Airport
Silvertown
North Woolwich
King George V
Royal Victoria
Custom House for ExCeL
Prince Regent
Royal Albert
Beckton Park
Cyprus
Gallions Reach
Beckton
Bus to London City Airport
River Thames
Bakerloo
Central
Circle
District
East London
Hammersmith & City
Jubilee
Metropolitan
Northern
Piccadilly
Victoria
Waterloo & City
DOCKLANDS
Under construction
National Rail
Interchange stations
Connections with National Rail
Connections with riverboat services
Connection with Tramlink
Airport interchange
Closed Sundays
Served by Piccadilly line trains early morning and late evening
For opening times see poster journey planners.
Certain stations are closed on public holidays.
24 hour London Travel Information
020 7222 1234
Textphone
020 7918 3015
www.tfl.gov.uk
www.tflwap.gov.uk/
LTM FA(a) 04.03
UNDERGROUND
Reg. user No. 05/4084
© Transport for London

GREATER LONDON

Comprehensive Edition

CONTENTS

Central London maps

Key to central London maps	2-3
Key to map symbols	3
Central area maps	4-25

London street maps

Key to London street maps	26-27
Key to map symbols	27
London street maps	28-269

Urban area maps

Key to London urban area maps	270-271
Key to map symbols	271
London urban area maps	272-283

Route planning maps

M25 London orbital motorway	284-285
Airport plans	286
Key to route planning maps	287
Key to map symbols	287
Route planning maps	288-299
Administrative areas	300-301
London congestion charging zone	302
West End theatres & cinemas	303
West End shopping	303

Index

Index to street names, places of interest, place names, stations, hospitals, schools, colleges and universities.	304-465
London Connections map	466-467

2 Key to central London maps

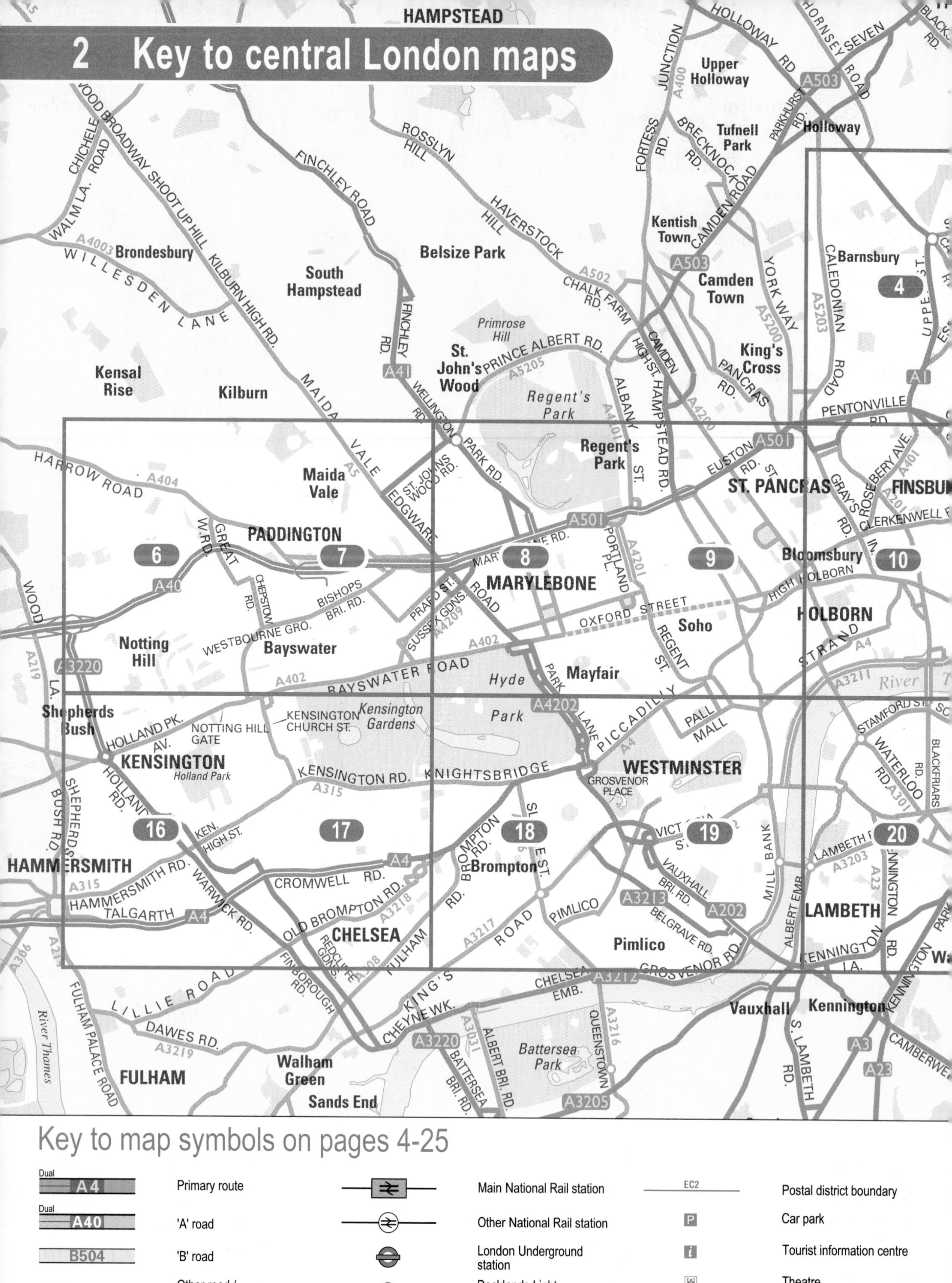
HAMPSTEAD
Upper Holloway
Tufnell Park
Holloway
Kentish Town
Camden Town
Barnsbury
King's Cross
Brondesbury
South Hampstead
Belsize Park
Primrose Hill
St. John's Wood
Regent's Park
Kensal Rise
Kilburn
Maida Vale
PADDINGTON
MARYLEBONE
ST. PANCRAS
FINSBURY
Bloomsbury
HOLBORN
Soho
Mayfair
Notting Hill
Bayswater
Hyde Park
Kensington Gardens
Shepherds Bush
KENSINGTON
Holland Park
WESTMINSTER
GROSVENOR PLACE
HAMMERSMITH
Brompton
CHELSEA
Pimlico
LAMBETH
Vauxhall
Kennington
FULHAM
Walham Green
Sands End
Battersea Park
River Thames
4
6
7
8
9
10
16
17
18
19
20
HARROW ROAD
WILLESDEN LANE
KILBURN HIGH RD.
FINCHLEY ROAD
HAVERSTOCK HILL
ROSSLYN HILL
PRINCE ALBERT RD.
CAMDEN ROAD
YORK WAY
CALEDONIAN ROAD
PENTONVILLE RD.
EUSTON RD.
OXFORD STREET
BAYSWATER ROAD
WESTBOURNE GRO.
EDGWARE RD.
PARK LANE
PICCADILLY
PALL MALL
STRAND
HIGH HOLBORN
KENSINGTON RD.
KNIGHTSBRIDGE
CROMWELL RD.
OLD BROMPTON RD.
KING'S RD.
FULHAM RD.
LILLIE ROAD
DAWES RD.
FULHAM PALACE ROAD
HAMMERSMITH RD.
TALGARTH RD.
WARWICK RD.
HOLLAND PK. AV.
NOTTING HILL GATE
KENSINGTON CHURCH ST.
REGENT ST.
PORTLAND PL.
ALBANY ST.
VAUXHALL BRI. RD.
BELGRAVE RD.
GROSVENOR RD.
MILL BANK
ALBERT EMB.
CHELSEA EMB.
CHEYNE WK.
QUEENSTOWN RD.
BATTERSEA BRI. RD.
ALBERT BRI. RD.
S. LAMBETH RD.
KENNINGTON LA.
WATERLOO RD.
BLACKFRIARS RD.
STAMFORD ST.
A5
A40
A41
A4
A402
A501
A503
A4202
A3220
A3212
A3205
A3

Key to map symbols on pages 4-25

- Dual A4 — Primary route
- Dual A40 — 'A' road
- B504 — 'B' road
- Other road / One way street
- Street market
- Pedestrian street
- Access restriction
- Track / Footpath
- Main National Rail station
- Other National Rail station
- London Underground station
- Docklands Light Railway station
- Pedestrian ferry with landing stage
- Bus / Coach station
- Extent of central London congestion charging zone
- CITY — Borough boundary
- EC2 — Postal district boundary
- P — Car park
- i — Tourist information centre
- Theatre
- Major hotel
- Historic site
- Pol — Police station
- PO — Post office
- Lib — Library

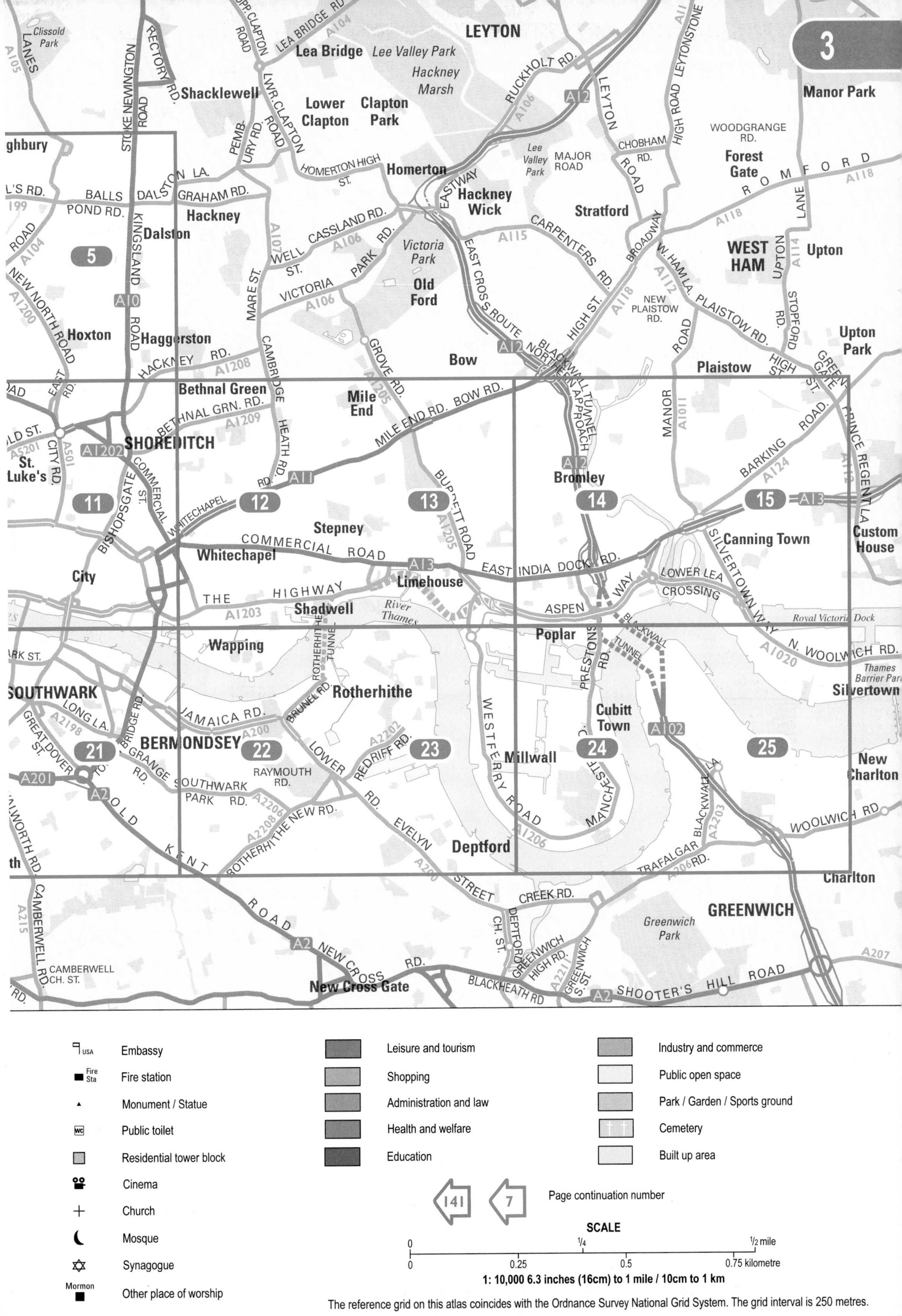
3
LEYTON
Lea Bridge
Lee Valley Park
Hackney Marsh
Manor Park
Shacklewell
Lower Clapton
Clapton Park
Homerton
Hackney Wick
Stratford
Forest Gate
WEST HAM
Upton
Hackney
Dalston
Victoria Park
Old Ford
Hoxton
Haggerston
Bow
Upton Park
Plaistow
Bethnal Green
Mile End
SHOREDITCH
St. Luke's
Bromley
Stepney
Whitechapel
City
Limehouse
Canning Town
Custom House
Shadwell
Poplar
Wapping
Rotherhithe
SOUTHWARK
BERMONDSEY
Cubitt Town
Millwall
Silvertown
New Charlton
Deptford
Charlton
GREENWICH
Greenwich Park
New Cross Gate
River Thames
Royal Victoria Dock
Thames Barrier Park
5
11
12
13
14
15
21
22
23
24
25
Embassy
Fire station
Monument / Statue
Public toilet
Residential tower block
Cinema
Church
Mosque
Synagogue
Other place of worship
Leisure and tourism
Shopping
Administration and law
Health and welfare
Education
Industry and commerce
Public open space
Park / Garden / Sports ground
Cemetery
Built up area
141
7
Page continuation number
SCALE
0
1/4
1/2 mile
0
0.25
0.5
0.75 kilometre
1: 10,000 6.3 inches (16cm) to 1 mile / 10cm to 1 km
The reference grid on this atlas coincides with the Ordnance Survey National Grid System. The grid interval is 250 metres.

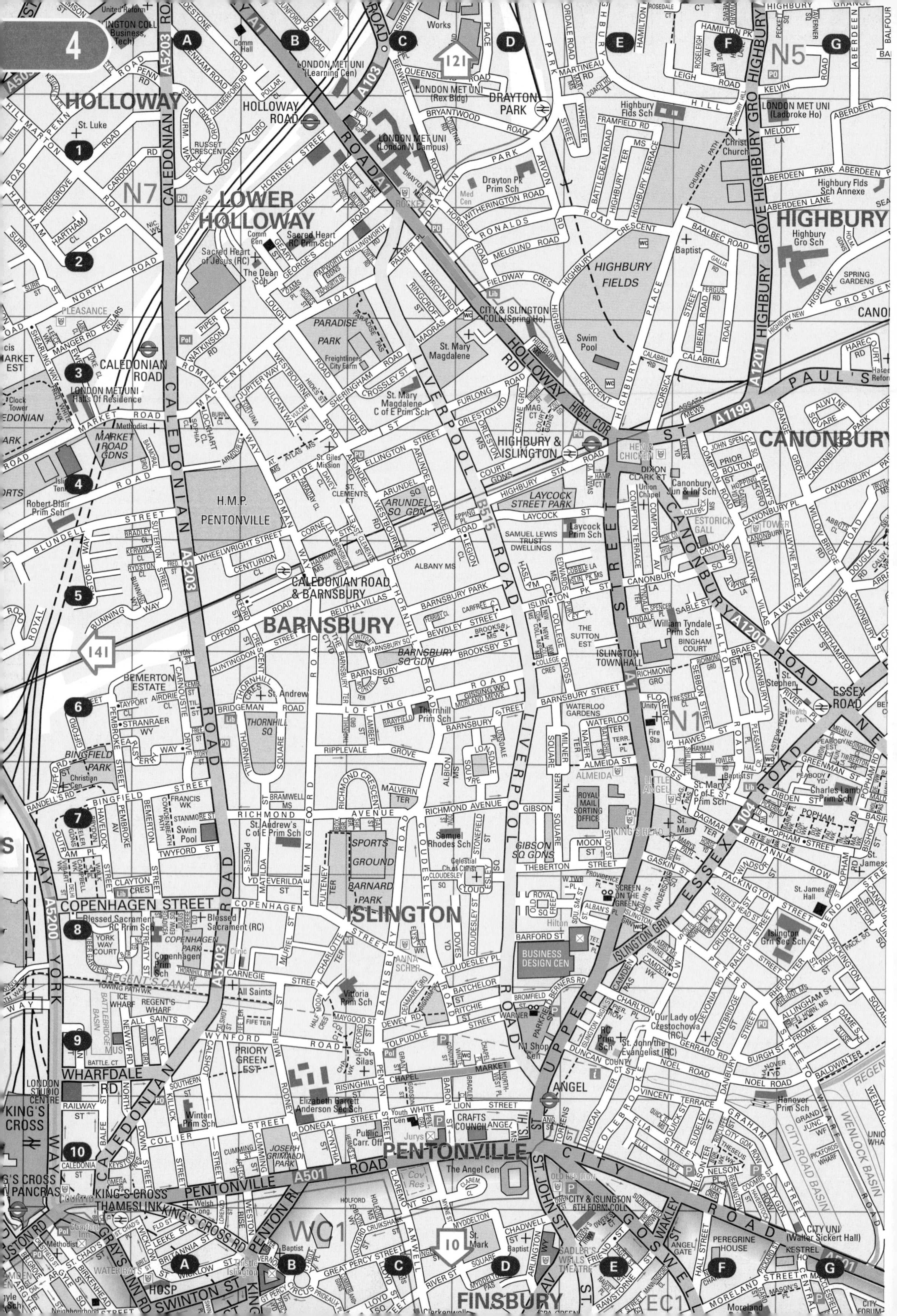
A
B
C
D
E
F
G
1
2
3
4
5
6
7
8
9
10
121
141
10
HOLLOWAY
N7
LOWER HOLLOWAY
HOLLOWAY ROAD
CALEDONIAN ROAD
DRAYTON PARK
HIGHBURY FIELDS
HIGHBURY
N5
HIGHBURY & ISLINGTON
CANONBURY
H.M.P. PENTONVILLE
CALEDONIAN ROAD & BARNSBURY
BARNSBURY
ISLINGTON
N1
ANGEL
PENTONVILLE
WC1
FINSBURY
EC1
KING'S CROSS
KING'S CROSS THAMESLINK
PARADISE PARK
THORNHILL SQ
BINGFIELD PARK
COPENHAGEN PARK
REGENT'S CANAL
BATTLEBRIDGE BASIN
JOSEPH GRIMALDI PARK
BARNARD PARK
SPORTS GROUND
LAYCOCK STREET PARK
ARUNDEL SQ GDN
BARNSBURY SQ GDN
GIBSON SQ GDNS
MARKET ROAD GDNS
CITY ROAD BASIN
WENLOCK BASIN
BUSINESS DESIGN CEN
ROYAL MAIL SORTING OFFICE
ISLINGTON TOWN HALL
LONDON MET UNI (Learning Cen)
LONDON MET UNI (Rex Bldg)
LONDON MET UNI (London N Campus)
LONDON MET UNI (Ladbroke Ho)
LONDON MET UNI - Halls Of Residence
CITY & ISLINGTON COLL (Spring Ho)
CITY & ISLINGTON 6TH FORM COLL
SADLER'S WELLS THEATRE
CRAFTS COUNCIL
The Angel Cen
N1 Shop Cen
ESTORICK GALL
ALMEIDA
LITTLE ANGEL
A1
A1199
A1200
A1201
A103
A104
A501
A5200
A5203
B515
UPPER STREET
LIVERPOOL ROAD
ESSEX ROAD
CANONBURY ROAD
HIGHBURY GROVE
CITY ROAD
GOSWELL ROAD
PENTONVILLE ROAD
YORK WAY
COPENHAGEN STREET
RICHMOND AVENUE

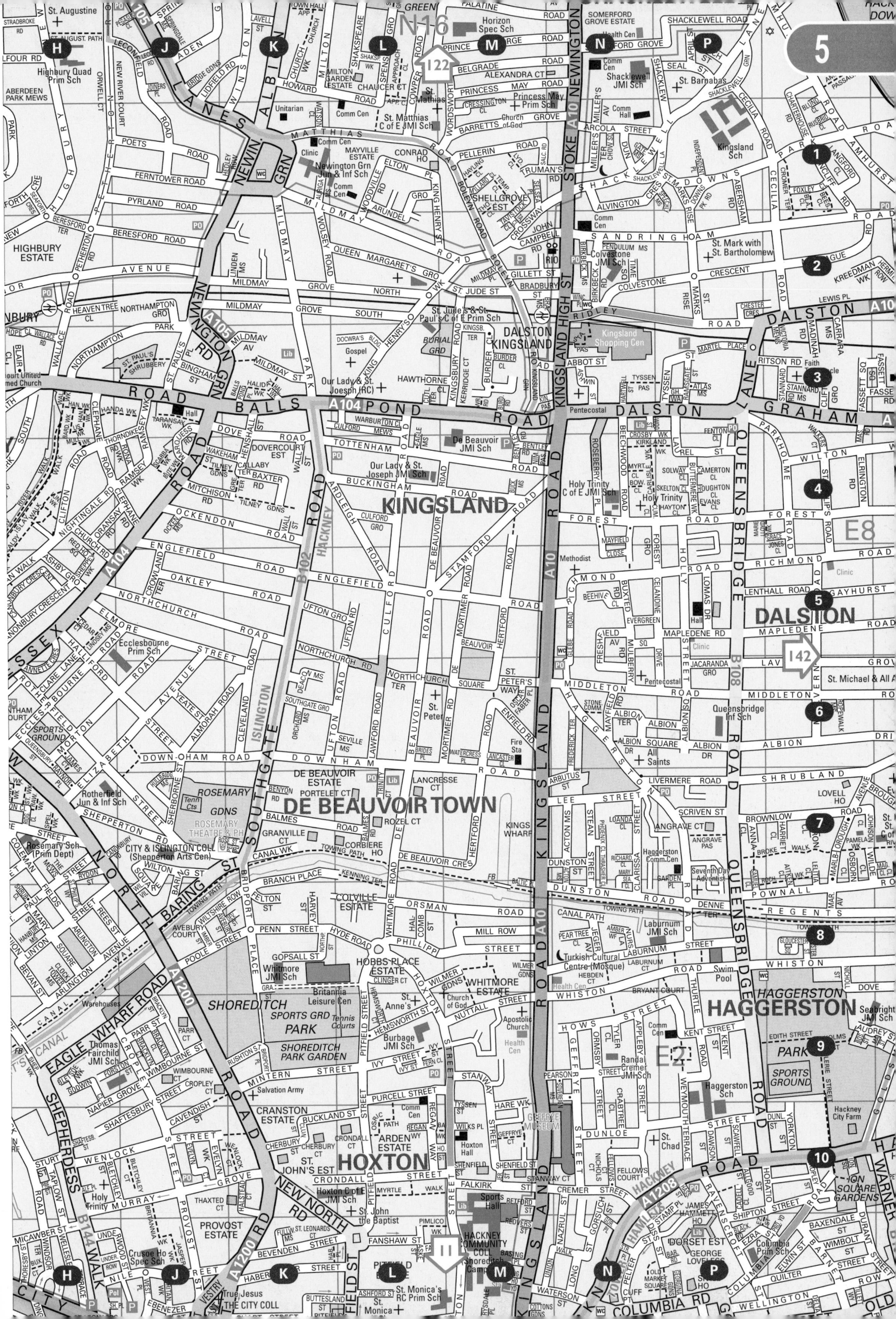
N16
122
KINGSLAND
DALSTON
E8
142
DE BEAUVOIR TOWN
HAGGERSTON
E2
HOXTON
HIGHBURY ESTATE
DALSTON KINGSLAND
SHOREDITCH SPORTS GRD PARK
SHOREDITCH PARK GARDEN
HAGGERSTON PARK
ROSEMARY GDNS
11
BALLS POND ROAD
KINGSLAND ROAD
KINGSLAND HIGH ST
STOKE NEWINGTON
SOUTHGATE ROAD
NEW NORTH ROAD
QUEENSBRIDGE ROAD
DALSTON LANE
GRAHAM ROAD
HACKNEY ROAD
MILDMAY PARK
NEWINGTON GRN
ESSEX ROAD
DOWNHAM ROAD
ENGLEFIELD ROAD
ALBION SQUARE
REGENTS CANAL
SHEPHERDESS WALK
EAGLE WHARF ROAD
Kingsland Shopping Cen
GEFFRYE MUSEUM
HACKNEY COMMUNITY COLL
Hackney City Farm
SPORTS GROUND
H
J
K
L
M
N
P
1
2
3
4
5
6
7
8
9
10
A10
A104
A105
A1200
A1208
B102
B108
B144

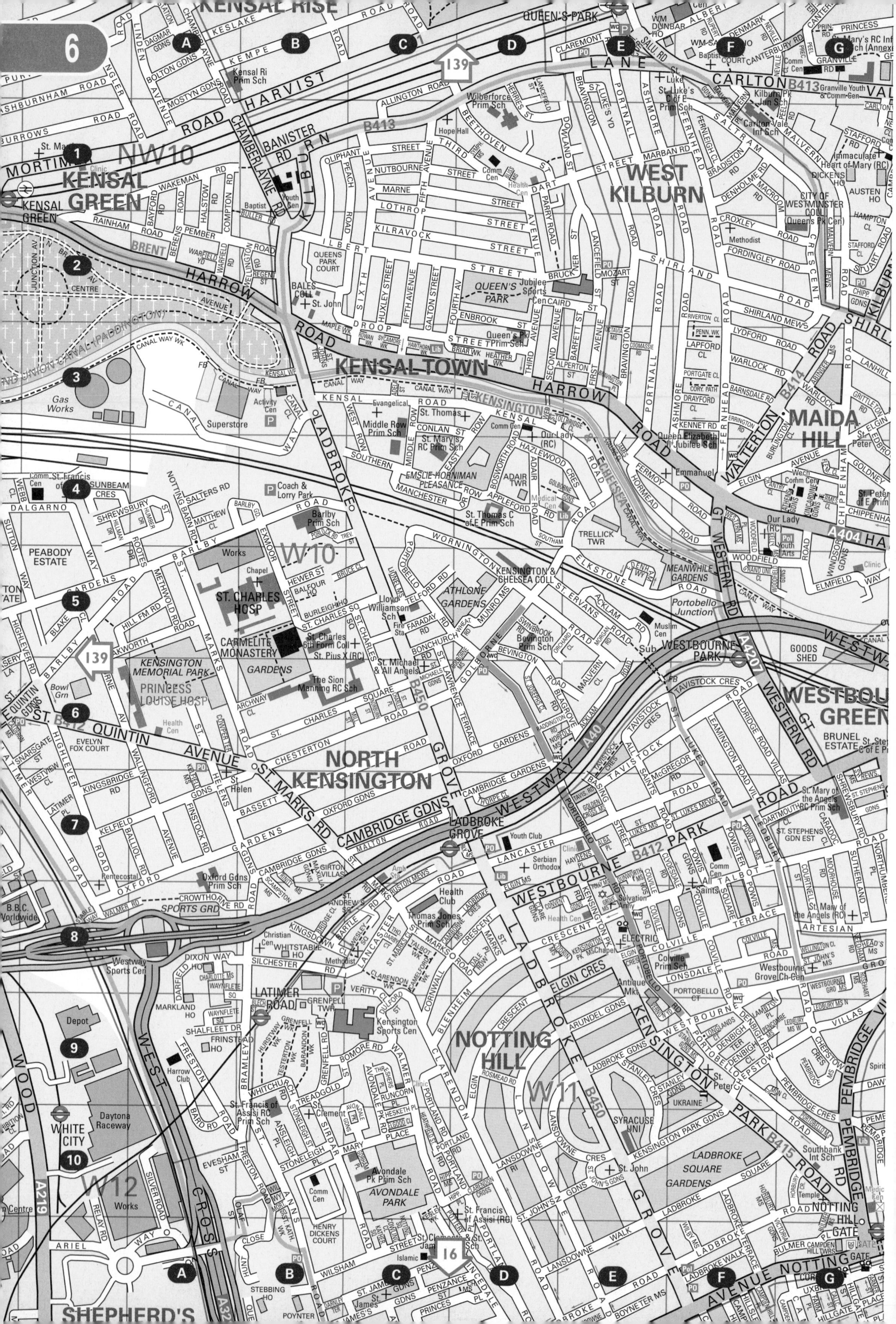
KENSAL RISE
KENSAL GREEN
NW10
WEST KILBURN
KENSAL TOWN
MAIDA HILL
W10
NORTH KENSINGTON
WESTBOURNE GREEN
NOTTING HILL
W11
W12
WHITE CITY
SHEPHERD'S
LATIMER ROAD
LADBROKE GROVE
WESTBOURNE PARK
QUEEN'S PARK
NOTTING HILL GATE
HARROW ROAD
HARVIST ROAD
LADBROKE GROVE
WESTWAY
ST. QUINTIN AVENUE
KENSINGTON PARK ROAD
QUEEN'S PARK
KENSINGTON MEMORIAL PARK
ST. CHARLES HOSP
CARMELITE MONASTERY
PRINCESS LOUISE HOSP
AVONDALE PARK
LADBROKE SQUARE GARDENS
Gas Works
Superstore
Daytona Raceway
Portobello Junction
GRAND UNION CANAL (PADDINGTON)
A B C D E F G
1 2 3 4 5 6 7 8 9 10
139
16

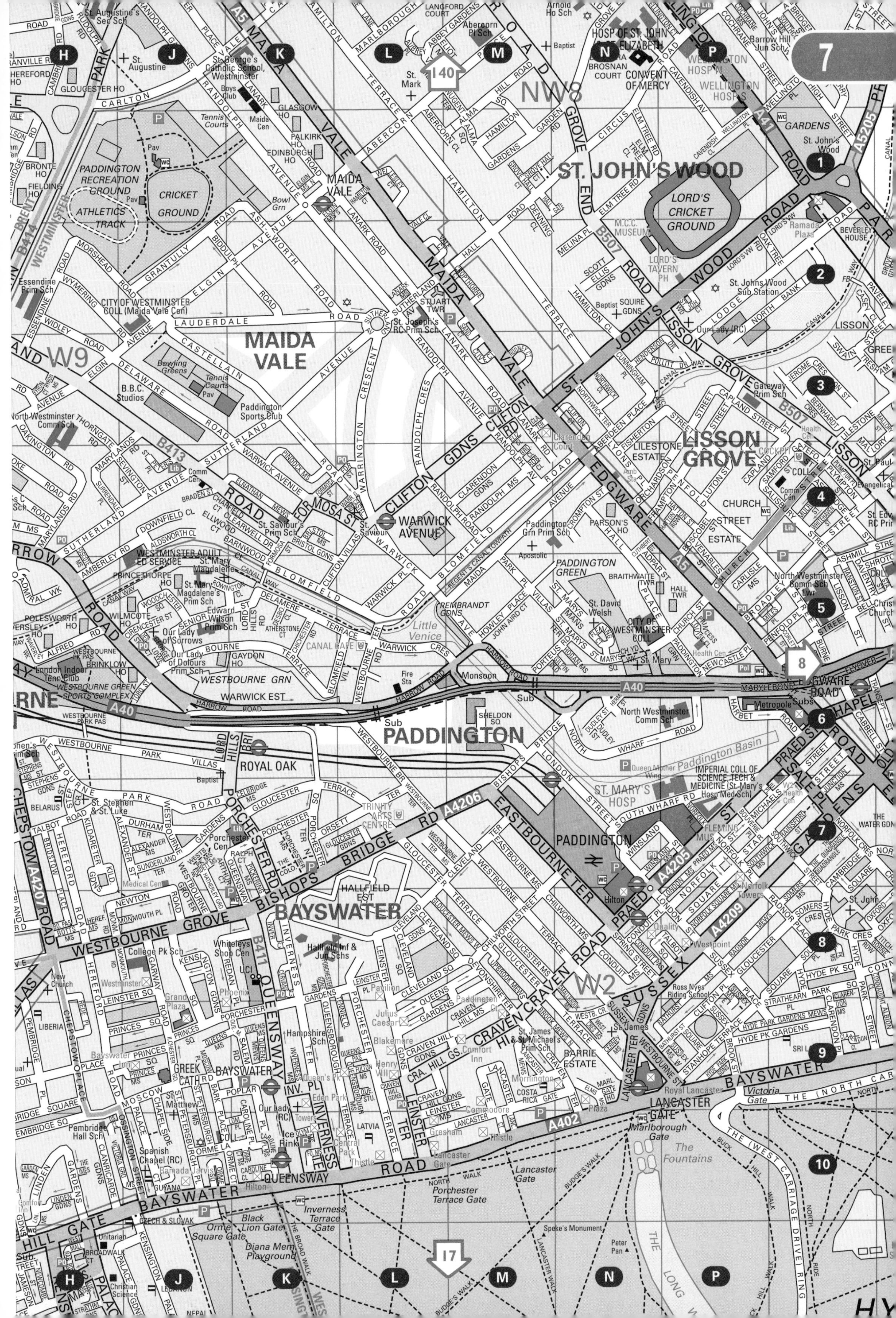

ST. JOHN'S WOOD
NW8
LORD'S CRICKET GROUND
M.C.C. MUSEUM
MAIDA VALE
W9
PADDINGTON RECREATION GROUND
CRICKET GROUND
ATHLETICS TRACK
LISSON GROVE
PADDINGTON
PADDINGTON GREEN
BAYSWATER
W2
ROYAL OAK
WARWICK AVENUE
Little Venice
ST. MARY'S HOSP
Paddington Basin
LANCASTER GATE
QUEENSWAY
The Fountains
Speke's Monument
Diana Mem Playground
Peter Pan
HOSP OF ST. JOHN & ST. ELIZABETH
WELLINGTON HOSP'N
CONVENT OF MERCY
B.B.C. Studios
Paddington Sports Club
IMPERIAL COLL OF SCIENCE, TECH & MEDICINE (St. Mary's Hosp Med Sch)
HALLFIELD EST
WESTBOURNE GREEN SPORTS COMPLEX
London Indoor Tenn Club
MAIDA VALE
EDGWARE ROAD
ST. JOHN'S WOOD ROAD
CLIFTON GDNS
BAYSWATER ROAD
WESTBOURNE GROVE
BISHOPS BRIDGE RD
EASTBOURNE TER
PRAED ST
SUSSEX GDNS
SUTHERLAND AVENUE
ELGIN AVENUE
HARROW ROAD
LONDON STREET
A5
A40
A4206
A4205
A4209
A402
A4207
A41
A5205
B507
B413
B411
B414
140
8
17
H
J
K
L
M
N
P
1
2
3
4
5
6
7
8
9
10

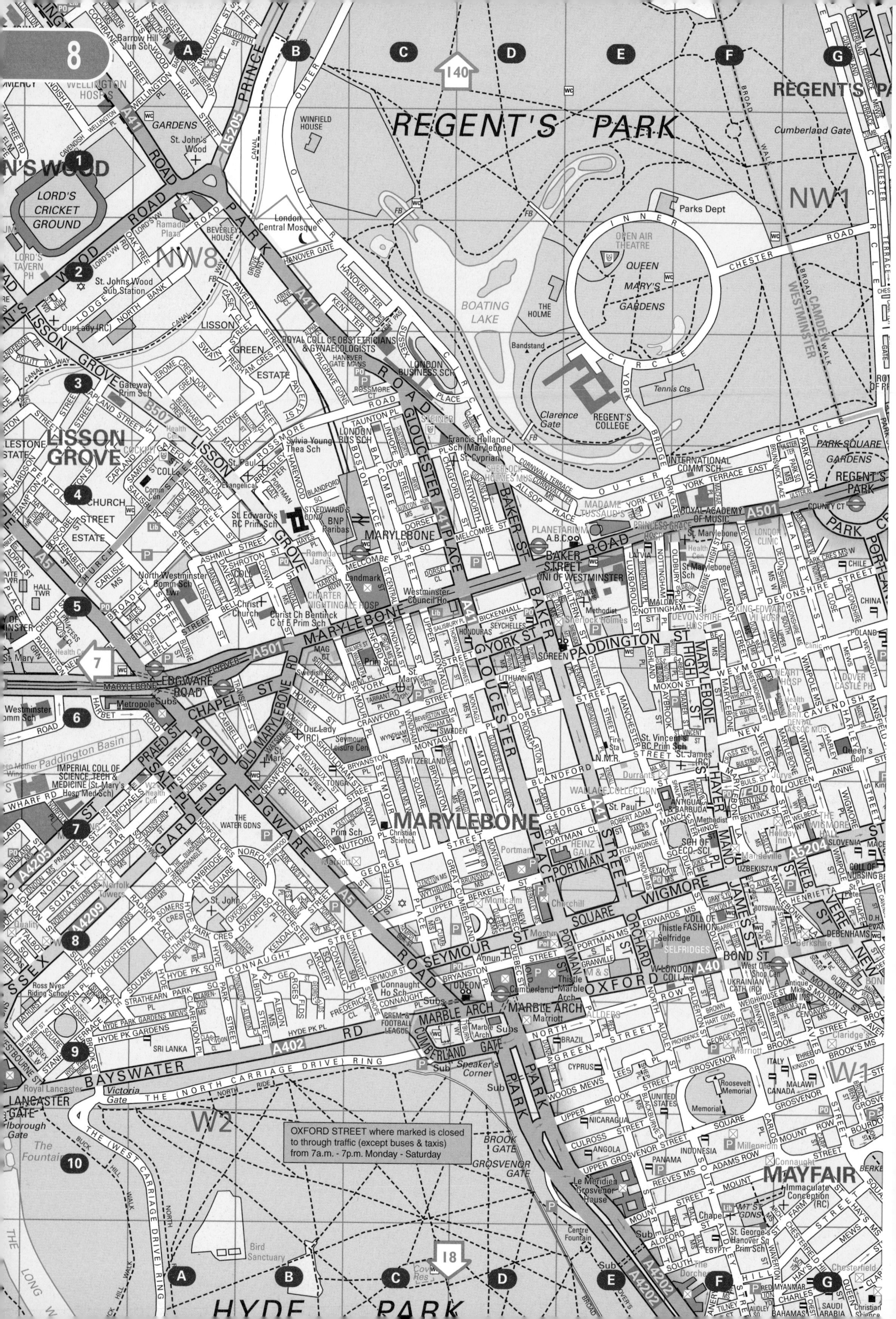
140
REGENT'S PARK
WINFIELD HOUSE
London Central Mosque
HANOVER GATE
BOATING LAKE
THE HOLME
OPEN AIR THEATRE
QUEEN MARY'S GARDENS
Parks Dept
INNER CIRCLE
Bandstand
Tennis Cts
Clarence Gate
REGENT'S COLLEGE
LONDON BUSINESS SCH
ROYAL COLL OF OBSTETRICIANS & GYNAECOLOGISTS
NW1
NW8
CHESTER ROAD
Cumberland Gate
LORD'S CRICKET GROUND
ST JOHN'S WOOD ROAD
PRINCE ALBERT ROAD
PARK ROAD
LISSON GROVE
LISSON GREEN ESTATE
CHURCH STREET ESTATE
MARYLEBONE
MARYLEBONE ROAD
BAKER STREET
MADAME TUSSAUD'S
PLANETARIUM
ROYAL ACADEMY OF MUSIC
UNI OF WESTMINSTER
INTERNATIONAL COMM SCH
Sherlock Holmes
PADDINGTON STREET
GLOUCESTER PLACE
EDGWARE ROAD
Paddington Basin
IMPERIAL COLL OF SCIENCE, TECH & MEDICINE (St Mary's Hosp Med Sch)
WALLACE COLLECTION
MARYLEBONE HIGH STREET
WIGMORE STREET
OXFORD STREET
SELFRIDGES
BOND ST
MARBLE ARCH
PORTMAN SQUARE
SEYMOUR PLACE
BAYSWATER ROAD
HYDE PARK GARDENS
CONNAUGHT STREET
W2
W1
MAYFAIR
GROSVENOR SQUARE
Roosevelt Memorial
Speaker's Corner
PARK LANE
Le Meridien Grosvenor House
OXFORD STREET where marked is closed to through traffic (except buses & taxis) from 7a.m. - 7p.m. Monday - Saturday
BROOK GATE
GROSVENOR GATE
Victoria Gate
LANCASTER GATE
The Fountains
Bird Sanctuary
18
7
HYDE PARK
A B C D E F G
1 2 3 4 5 6 7 8 9 10

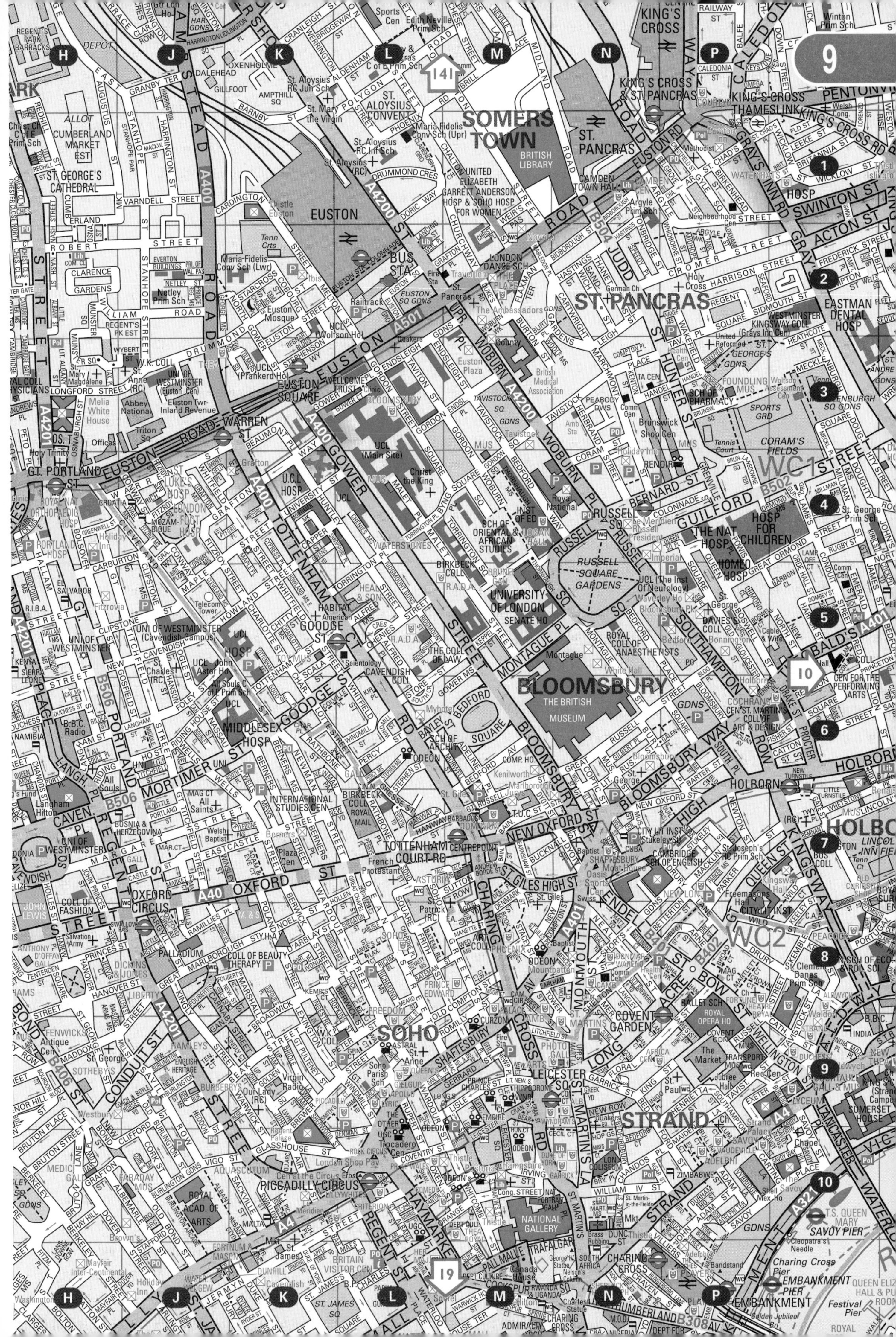
9
H
J
K
L
M
N
P
1
2
3
4
5
6
7
8
9
10
141
10
19
SOMERS TOWN
BRITISH LIBRARY
EUSTON
ST. PANCRAS
KING'S CROSS
KING'S CROSS & ST. PANCRAS
KING'S CROSS THAMESLINK
ST. PANCRAS
WC1
BLOOMSBURY
THE BRITISH MUSEUM
UNIVERSITY OF LONDON SENATE HO
RUSSELL SQUARE GARDENS
WC2
SOHO
COVENT GARDEN
STRAND
PICCADILLY CIRCUS
NATIONAL GALLERY
OXFORD CIRCUS
TOTTENHAM COURT RD
GOODGE ST
WARREN ST
EUSTON SQUARE
GT. PORTLAND ST
LEICESTER SQ
CHARING CROSS
EMBANKMENT
HOLBORN
ROYAL ACAD. OF ARTS
ROYAL OPERA HO
CORAM'S FIELDS
EUSTON ROAD
OXFORD ST
REGENT ST
TOTTENHAM COURT RD
GOWER ST
WOBURN PL
SOUTHAMPTON ROW
KINGSWAY
SHAFTESBURY AV
CHARING CROSS RD
HAYMARKET
PALL MALL
STRAND
NEW OXFORD ST
BLOOMSBURY WAY
GRAY'S INN RD
A400
A4200
A501
A40
A4201
A401
A4
B506

A
B
C
D
E
F
G
1
2
3
4
5
6
7
8
9
10
4
9
20
PENTONVILLE
PENTONVILLE ROAD
KING'S CROSS THAMESLINK
KING'S CROSS RD
GRAY'S INN RD
FINSBURY
CLERKENWELL
HOLBORN
WC1
WC2
EC4
FC1
SE1
FARRINGDON
FARRINGDON ROAD
CLERKENWELL RD
ROSEBERY AV
GOSWELL ROAD
CITY ROAD
ST. JOHN ST
SKINNER ST
PERCIVAL ST
THEOBALD'S ROAD
HOLBORN
HOLBORN VIADUCT
KINGSWAY
CHANCERY LANE
FLEET STREET
STRAND
ALDWYCH
NEW BRIDGE ST
BLACKFRIARS
BLACKFRIARS BRI
WATERLOO BRI
VICTORIA EMBANKMENT
RIVER THAMES
KING'S REACH
MOUNT PLEASANT MAIL CENTRE
CORAM'S FIELDS
LINCOLN'S INN FIELDS
GRAY'S INN GARDENS
ROYAL COURTS OF JUSTICE
SOMERSET HOUSE
ST. PAUL'S CATHEDRAL
BARTHOLOMEW'S HOSPITAL
BARBICAN
CHARTERHOUSE
Central Markets (Smithfield)
TATE MODERN
CITY THAMESLINK
TEMPLE
EMBANKMENT
MILLENNIUM BRIDGE
BANKSIDE PIER
BLACKFRIARS MILLENNIUM PIER
SAVOY PIER
SOUTHWARK

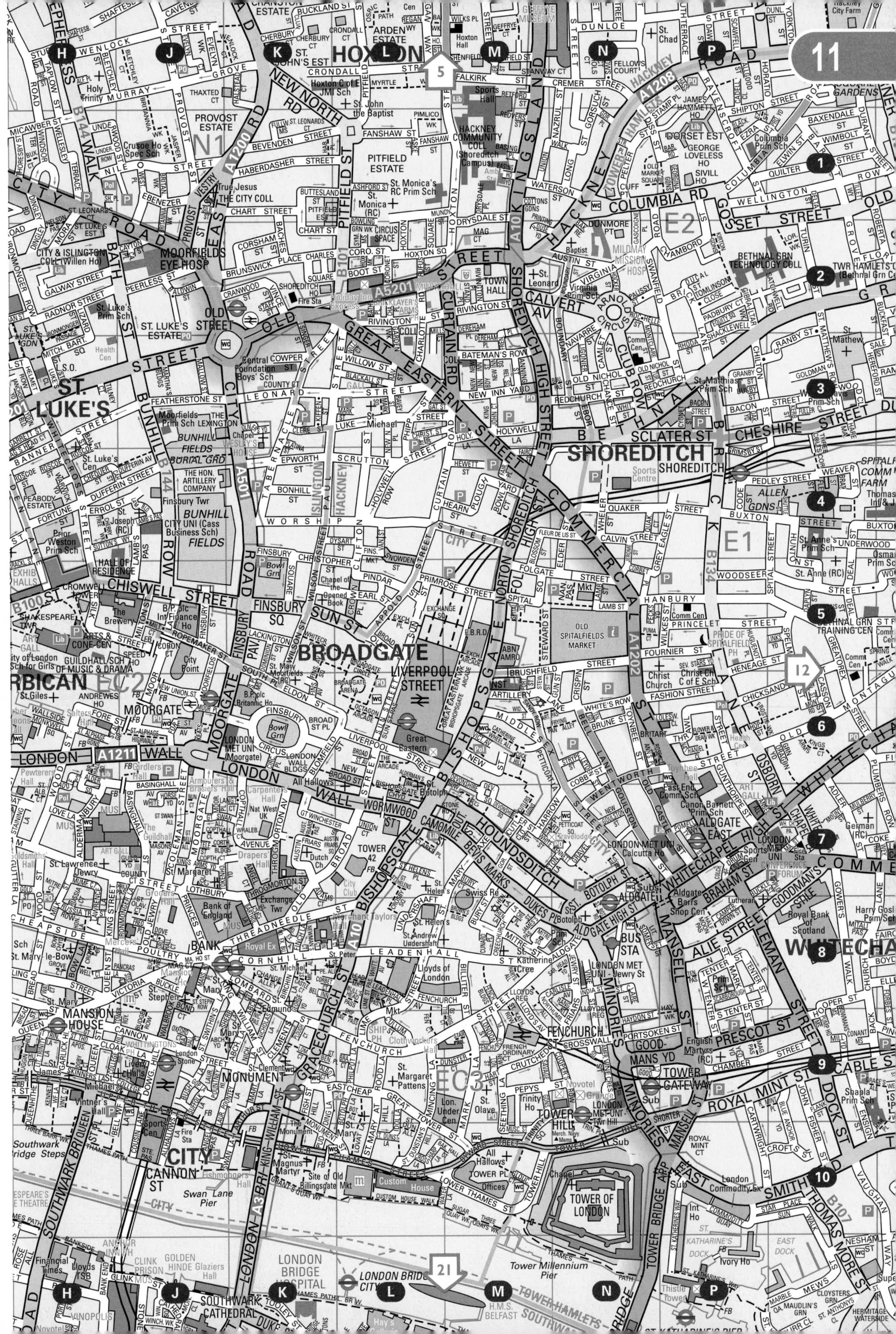
11
H
J
K
L
M
N
P
1
2
3
4
5
6
7
8
9
10
5
12
21
HOXTON
SHOREDITCH
BROADGATE
ST. LUKE'S
BARBICAN
CITY
WHITECHAPEL
N1
E2
E1
EC2
EC3
CITY ROAD
OLD STREET
GREAT EASTERN STREET
KINGSLAND ROAD
SHOREDITCH HIGH STREET
HACKNEY ROAD
COLUMBIA RD
BETHNAL GREEN ROAD
COMMERCIAL STREET
BISHOPSGATE
HOUNDSDITCH
LONDON WALL
MOORGATE
FINSBURY SQ
CHISWELL STREET
BUNHILL ROW
WHITECHAPEL HIGH ST
LEMAN STREET
MANSELL ST
MINORIES
ROYAL MINT ST
CABLE ST
LEADENHALL
FENCHURCH
CORNHILL
CHEAPSIDE
POULTRY
THREADNEEDLE
CANNON
EASTCHEAP
LOWER THAMES ST
TOWER BRIDGE APP
LONDON BRIDGE
LIVERPOOL STREET
MONUMENT
BANK
MANSION HOUSE
ALDGATE
ALDGATE EAST
TOWER GATEWAY
TOWER HILL
FENCHURCH ST
CANNON ST
OLD SPITALFIELDS MARKET
TOWER OF LONDON
LONDON BRIDGE HOSPITAL
Tower Millennium Pier
Swan Lane Pier
H.M.S. BELFAST
MOORFIELDS EYE HOSP
BUNHILL FIELDS BURIAL GRD
Tower 42
Lloyds of London
Swiss Re
Bank of England
The Guildhall
Custom House
PITFIELD ESTATE
PROVOST ESTATE
ST. LUKE'S ESTATE
A1200
A10
A5201
A501
A1202
A1211
A1208
A3
B144
B101
B134
B100
B107

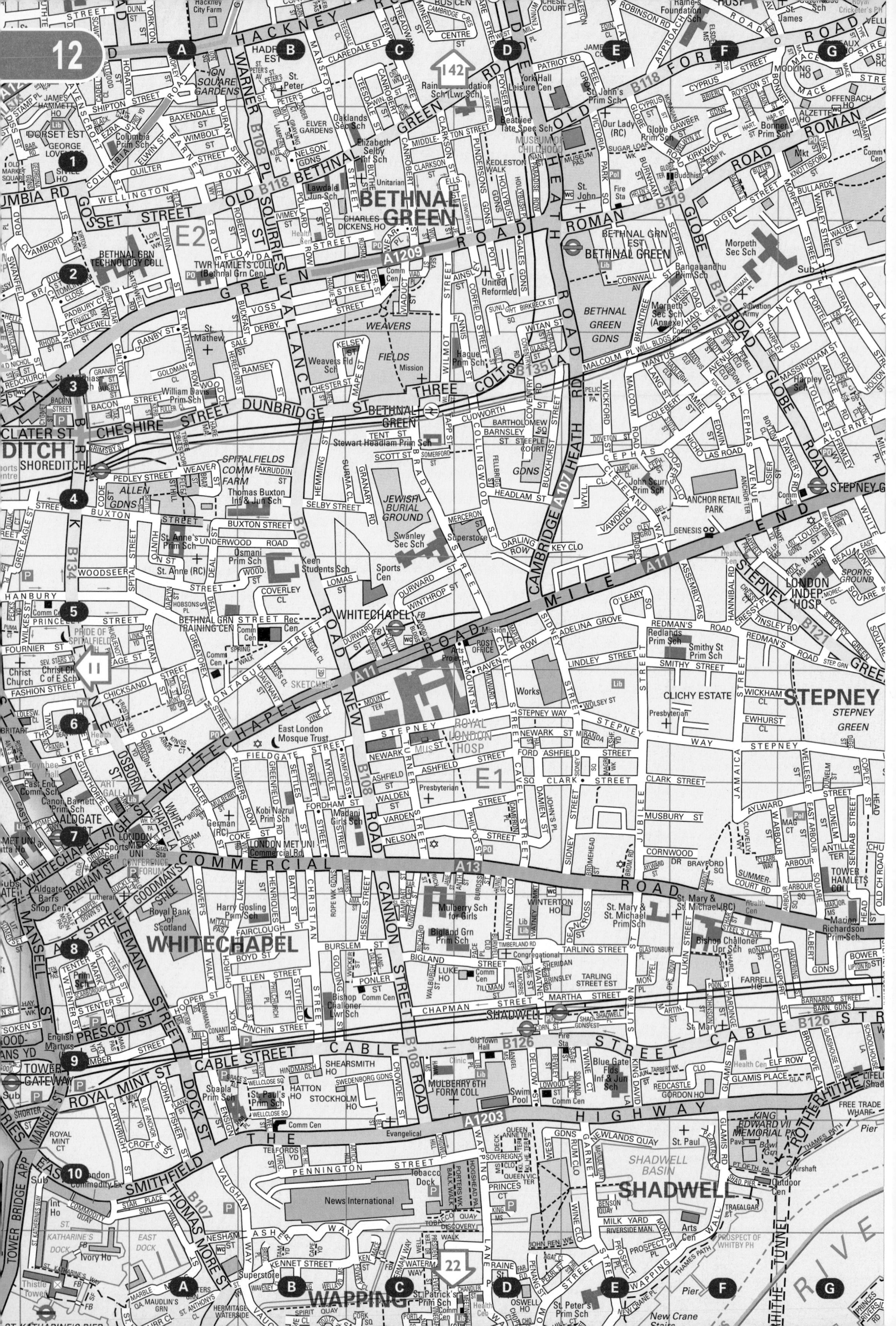
12
142
11
22
A
B
C
D
E
F
G
1
2
3
4
5
6
7
8
9
10
HACKNEY ROAD
BETHNAL GREEN
E2
E1
OLD BETHNAL GREEN ROAD
BETHNAL GREEN ROAD
ROMAN ROAD
OLD FORD ROAD
GROVE ROAD
CAMBRIDGE HEATH ROAD
MILE END ROAD
WHITECHAPEL ROAD
WHITECHAPEL HIGH ST
COMMERCIAL ROAD
COMMERCIAL STREET
CABLE STREET
THE HIGHWAY
VALLANCE ROAD
NEW ROAD
CANNON STREET ROAD
SHOREDITCH
WHITECHAPEL
STEPNEY
STEPNEY GREEN
SHADWELL
SHADWELL BASIN
WAPPING
WEAVERS FIELDS
BETHNAL GREEN GDNS
JEWISH BURIAL GROUND
ROYAL LONDON HOSP
LONDON INDEP. HOSP
News International
MULBERRY 6TH FORM COLL
KING EDWARD VII MEMORIAL PK
ROTHERHITHE TUNNEL
ALDGATE
TOWER GATEWAY
TOWER BRIDGE APP
EAST SMITHFIELD
ROYAL MINT ST
DOCK ST
LEMAN STREET
MANSELL ST
PRESCOT ST
CHESHIRE STREET
DUNBRIDGE ST
THREE COLTS LA
GLOBE ROAD
STEPNEY WAY
SIDNEY STREET
JAMAICA STREET
BRICK LANE
B108
B118
B119
B120
B121
B126
B134
B135
B107
A11
A13
A107
A1203
A1209

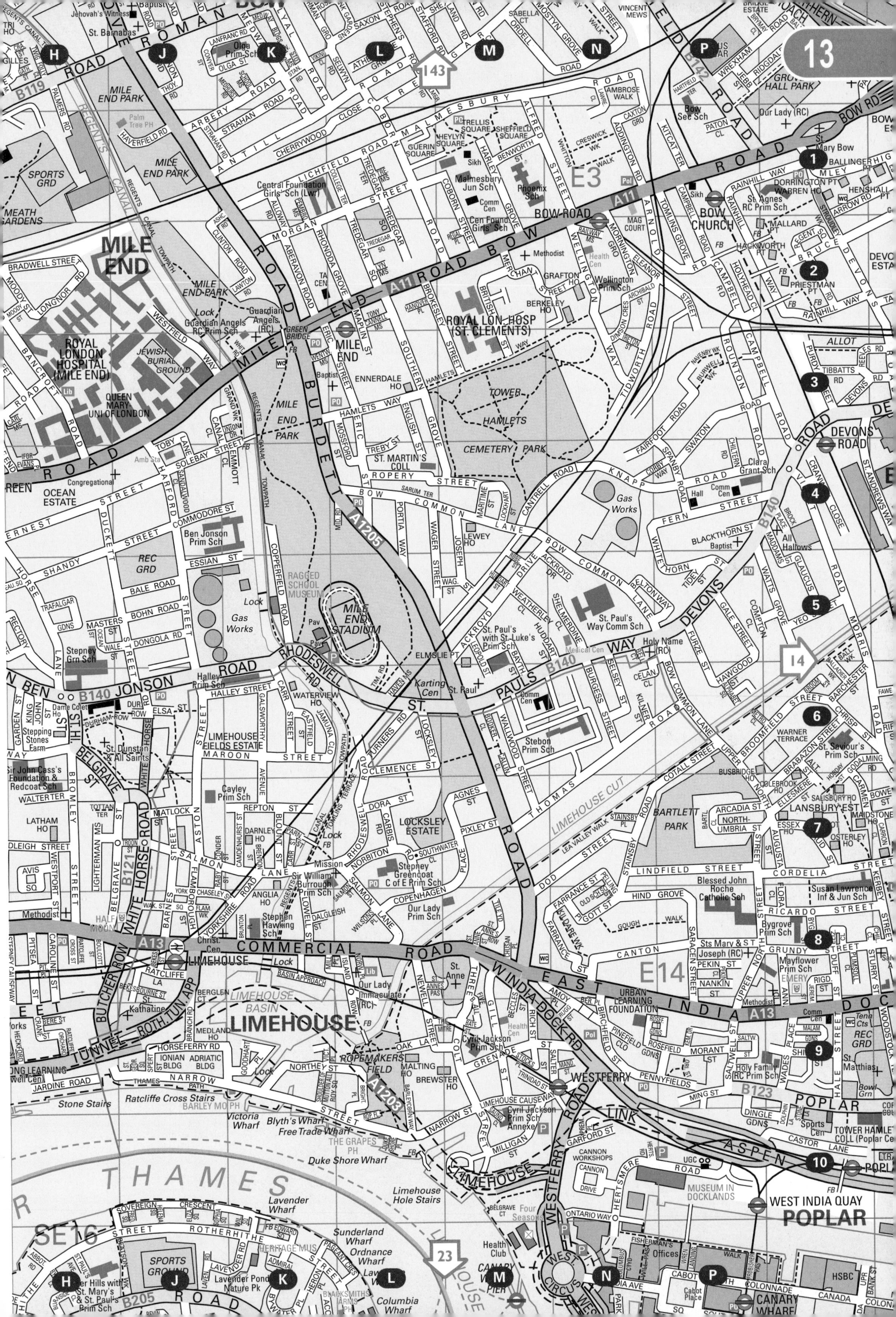
ROMAN ROAD
BOW
MILE END PARK
SPORTS GRD
MEATH GARDENS
MILE END
REGENTS CANAL
ROYAL LONDON HOSPITAL (MILE END)
JEWISH BURIAL GROUND
QUEEN MARY UNI OF LONDON
MILE END ROAD
GREEN BRIDGE
BURDETT ROAD
A1205
A11
BOW ROAD
E3
Central Foundation Girls' Sch (Lwr)
Malmesbury Jun Sch
Phoenix Sch
Cen Found. Girls' Sch
TREDEGAR SQ
ROYAL LON. HOSP (ST. CLEMENTS)
TOWER HAMLETS CEMETERY PARK
BOW CHURCH
St. Agnes RC Prim Sch
St. Mary Bow
GROVE HALL PARK
Our Lady (RC)
Bow Sec Sch
Wellington Prim Sch
Guardian Angels RC Prim Sch
ST. MARTIN'S COLL
ENNERDALE HO
HAMLETS WAY
ROPERY STREET
BOW COMMON LANE
Gas Works
Clara Grant Sch
DEVONS ROAD
All Hallows
ST. PAUL'S WAY
St. Paul's Way Comm Sch
St. Paul's with St. Luke's Prim Sch
Holy Name (RC)
OCEAN ESTATE
Ben Jonson Prim Sch
REC GRD
Stepney Grn Sch
BEN JONSON ROAD
B140
RAGGED SCHOOL MUSEUM
MILE END STADIUM
Karting Cen
St. Paul
Halley Prim Sch
LIMEHOUSE FIELDS ESTATE
St. Dunstan & All Saints
Stepping Stones Farm
Sir John Cass's Foundation & Redcoat Sch
Cayley Prim Sch
LOCKSLEY ESTATE
Stebon Prim Sch
LIMEHOUSE CUT
BARTLETT PARK
Warner Terrace
St. Saviour's Prim Sch
LANSBURY EST
Blessed John Roche Catholic Sch
Susan Lawrence Inf & Jun Sch
Bygrove Prim Sch
Mayflower Prim Sch
Stepney Greencoat C of E Prim Sch
Our Lady Prim Sch
Sir William Burrough Prim Sch
Stephen Hawking Sch
WHITE HORSE ROAD
B121
COMMERCIAL ROAD
A13
LIMEHOUSE
EAST INDIA DOCK ROAD
E14
URBAN LEARNING FOUNDATION
Our Lady Immaculate (RC)
St. Anne
LIMEHOUSE BASIN
ROTHERHITHE TUNNEL APP
Cyril Jackson Prim Sch
WESTFERRY
ROPEMAKERS FIELD
A1203
NARROW STREET
Holy Family RC Prim Sch
B123
POPLAR
TOWER HAMLETS COLL (Poplar Cen)
St. Matthias
REC GRD
Ratcliffe Cross Stairs
Victoria Wharf
Blyth's Wharf
Free Trade Wharf
THE GRAPES PH
Duke Shore Wharf
Cyril Jackson Prim Sch Annexe
LIMEHOUSE LINK
ASPEN WAY
CANNON WORKSHOPS
MUSEUM IN DOCKLANDS
WEST INDIA QUAY
POPLAR
THAMES
Stone Stairs
Lavender Wharf
Limehouse Hole Stairs
Sunderland Wharf
Ordnance Wharf
Columbia Wharf
SE16
ROTHERHITHE STREET
SPORTS GROUND
Lavender Pond Nature Pk
HERITAGE MUS
Peter Hills with St. Mary's & St. Paul's Prim Sch
B205
WESTFERRY ROAD
WEST. CIRCUS
Health Club
CANARY WHARF
HSBC
Cabot Place
Four Seasons
143
14
23
H J K L M N P
1 2 3 4 5 6 7 8 9 10

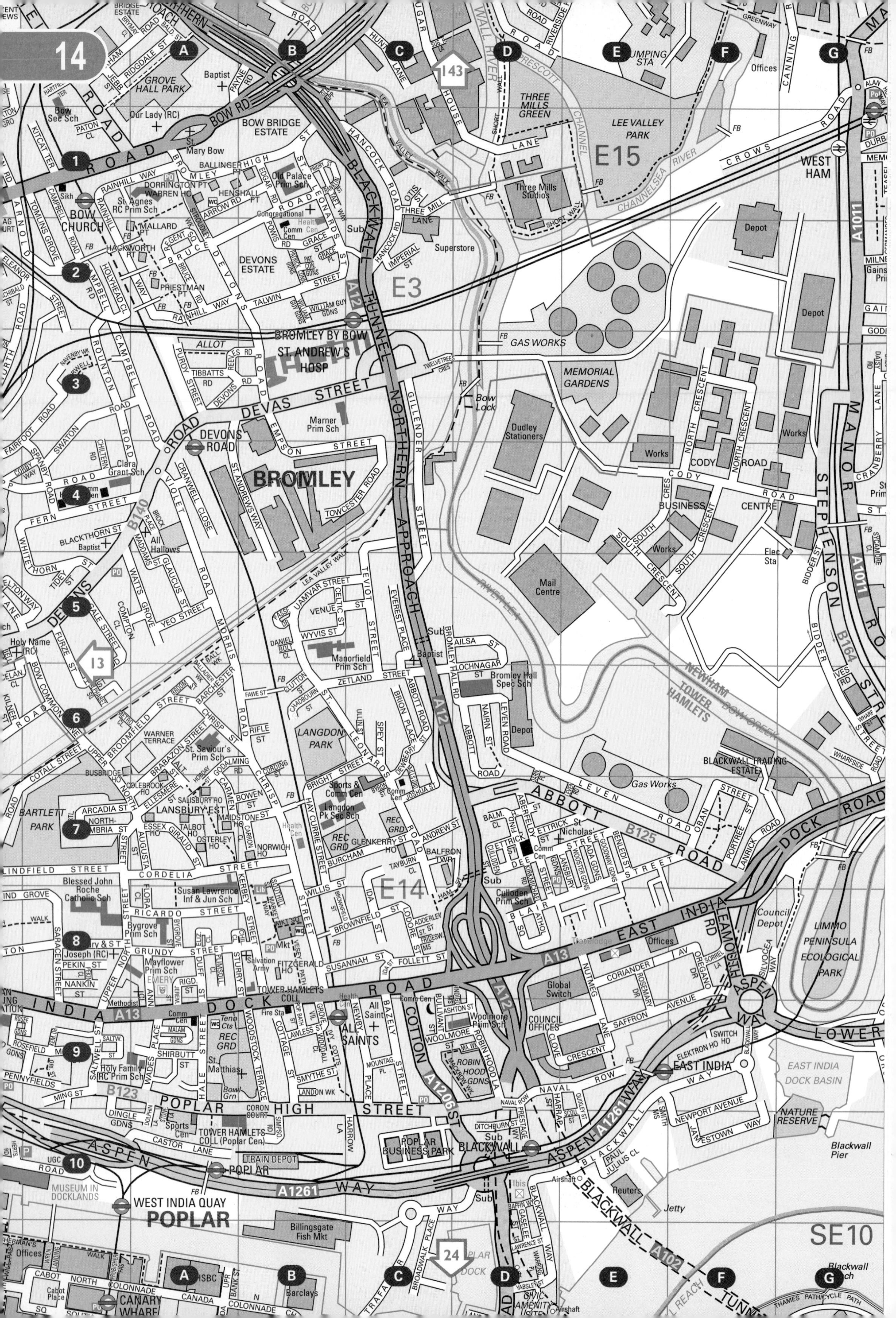
14
A
B
C
D
E
F
G
1
2
3
4
5
6
7
8
9
10
143
13
24
BOW RD
ROAD
GROVE HALL PARK
Baptist
Our Lady (RC)
Bow Sec Sch
BOW BRIDGE ESTATE
St Mary Bow
BROMLEY HIGH ST
BALLINGER PT
DORRINGTON PT
WARREN HO
HENSHALL PT
Old Palace Prim Sch
St Agnes RC Prim Sch
BOW CHURCH
Sikh
Congregational
Comm Cen
Health Cen
MALLARD PT
HACKWORTH PT
PRIESTMAN PT
DEVONS ESTATE
RAINHILL WAY
TALWIN STREET
WILLIAM GUY GDNS
BLACKWALL TUNNEL
NORTHERN APPROACH
A12
E3
E15
THREE MILLS GREEN
LEE VALLEY PARK
CHANNELSEA RIVER
Three Mills Studios
THREE MILL LANE
Superstore
PRESCOTT CHANNEL
PUMPING STA
Offices
CROWS ROAD
WEST HAM
Depot
A1011
BROMLEY BY BOW
ST. ANDREW'S HOSP
ALLOT
GAS WORKS
MEMORIAL GARDENS
TWELVETREES CRES
Bow Lock
DEVAS STREET
DEVONS ROAD
Marner Prim Sch
EMPSON STREET
BROMLEY
TOWCESTER ROAD
Clara Grant Sch
FERN STREET
BLACKTHORN ST
All Hallows
B140
Dudley Stationers
Works
NORTH CRESCENT
CODY ROAD
BUSINESS CENTRE
SOUTH CRESCENT
Mail Centre
RIVER LEA
Elec Sta
STEPHENSON ST
MANOR ROAD
B164
BIDDER ST
NEWHAM
TOWER HAMLETS
BOW CREEK
LEA VALLEY WALK
UAMVAR STREET
Manorfield Prim Sch
ZETLAND STREET
Baptist
Bromley Hall Spec Sch
Depot
LOCHNAGAR ST
LANGDON PARK
Langdon Pk Sec Sch
Sports & Comm Cen
Holy Name (RC)
BOW COMMON LANE
WARNER TERRACE
St. Saviour's Prim Sch
BROOMFIELD STREET
CHRISP STREET
BARTLETT PARK
LANSBURY EST
ABBOTT ROAD
B125
BLACKWALL TRADING ESTATE
Gas Works
St Nicholas'
Comm Cen
Culloden Prim Sch
E14
Blessed John Roche Catholic Sch
Susan Lawrence Inf & Jun Sch
CORDELIA STREET
RICARDO STREET
Bygrove Prim Sch
Mayflower Prim Sch
St Joseph (RC)
Salvation Army
EAST INDIA DOCK ROAD
A13
Travelodge
Offices
Global Switch
COUNCIL OFFICES
Council Depot
LIMMO PENINSULA ECOLOGICAL PARK
ASPEN WAY
LOWER LEA
TOWER HAMLETS COLL
Fire Sta
ALL SAINTS
All Saints
Woolmore Prim Sch
ROBIN HOOD GDNS
A1206
Holy Family RC Prim Sch
St. Matthias
B123
POPLAR HIGH STREET
Sports Cen
TOWER HAMLETS COLL (Poplar Cen)
TRAIN DEPOT
POPLAR BUSINESS PARK
BLACKWALL
EAST INDIA
EAST INDIA DOCK BASIN
NATURE RESERVE
Blackwall Pier
A1261
POPLAR
MUSEUM IN DOCKLANDS
WEST INDIA QUAY
Billingsgate Fish Mkt
Reuters
Jetty
BLACKWALL TUNNEL
A102
SE10
HSBC
Barclays
CANARY WHARF
Blackwall Reach
THAMES PATH/CYCLE PATH
CIVIC AMENITY SITE
Airshaft

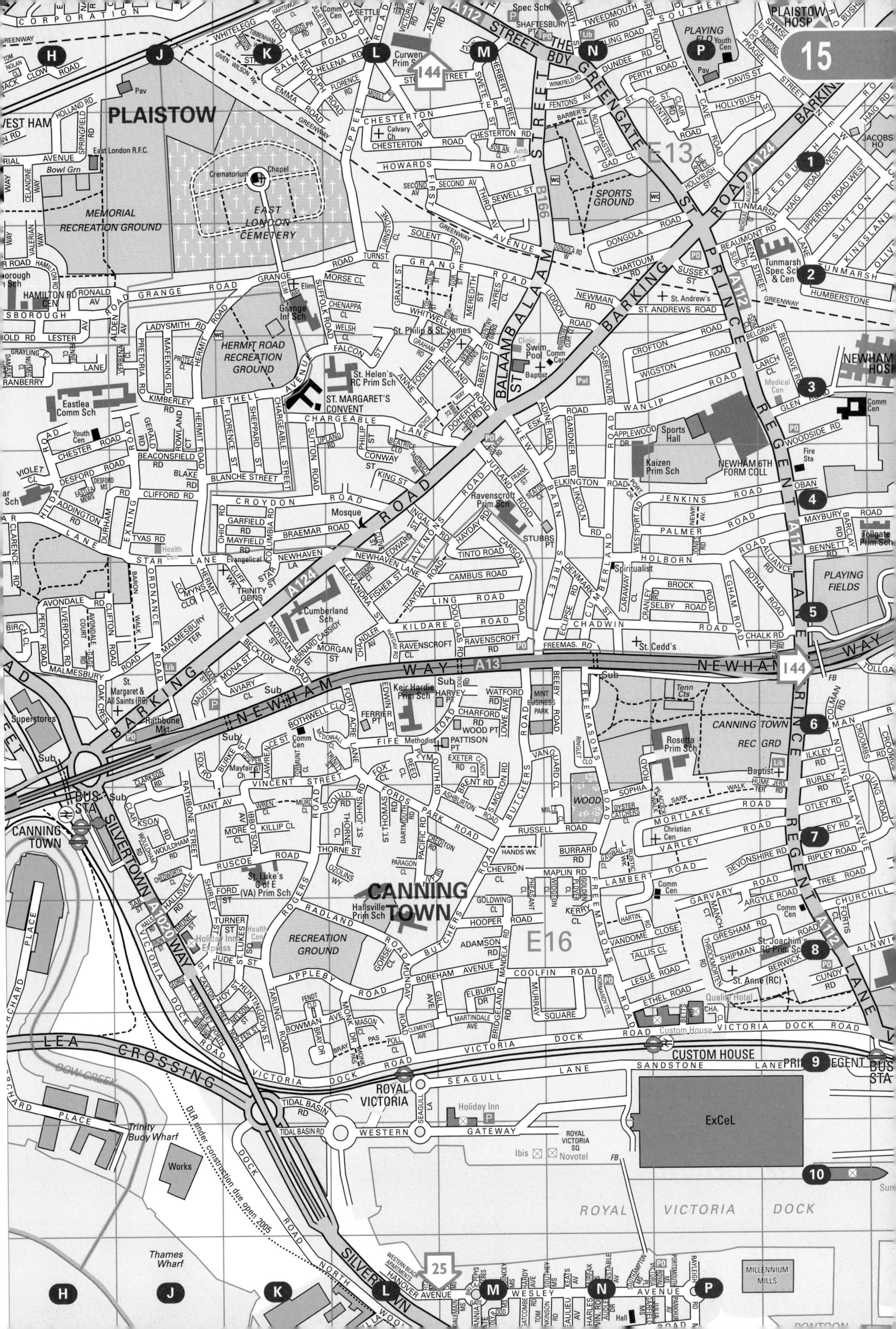
PLAISTOW
PLAISTOW HOSP
E13
E16
CANNING TOWN
CANNING TOWN
ROYAL VICTORIA
CUSTOM HOUSE
ExCeL
ROYAL VICTORIA DOCK
MEMORIAL RECREATION GROUND
EAST LONDON CEMETERY
Crematorium
Chapel
East London R.F.C.
Bowl Grn
HERMIT ROAD RECREATION GROUND
SPORTS GROUND
PLAYING FLD
PLAYING FIELDS
CANNING TOWN REC GRD
RECREATION GROUND
WOOD
ST. MARGARET'S CONVENT
St. Helen's RC Prim Sch
Grange Inf Sch
Eastlea Comm Sch
Cumberland Sch
Ravenscroft Prim Sch
Kaizen Prim Sch
NEWHAM 6TH FORM COLL
Sports Hall
Tunmarsh Spec Sch & Cen
Keir Hardie Prim Sch
Rosetta Prim Sch
Hallsville Prim Sch
St. Luke's C of E (VA) Prim Sch
St. Joachim's RC Prim Sch
Curwen Prim Sch
MINT BUSINESS PARK
Rathbone Mkt
Superstores
Holiday Inn Express
Holiday Inn
Ibis
Novotel
Quality Hotel
Custom House
Trinity Buoy Wharf
Works
Thames Wharf
MILLENNIUM MILLS
DLR under construction due open 2005
BARKING ROAD
NEWHAM WAY
A13
A124
A112
A1020
B166
PRINCE REGENT LANE
BALAAM STREET
GREENGATE STREET
SILVERTOWN WAY
VICTORIA DOCK ROAD
LEA CROSSING
WESTERN GATEWAY
SEAGULL LANE
SANDSTONE LANE
NORTH WOOLWICH ROAD
HANOVER AVENUE
WESLEY AVENUE
144
25
1
2
3
4
5
6
7
8
9
10
H
J
K
L
M
N
P

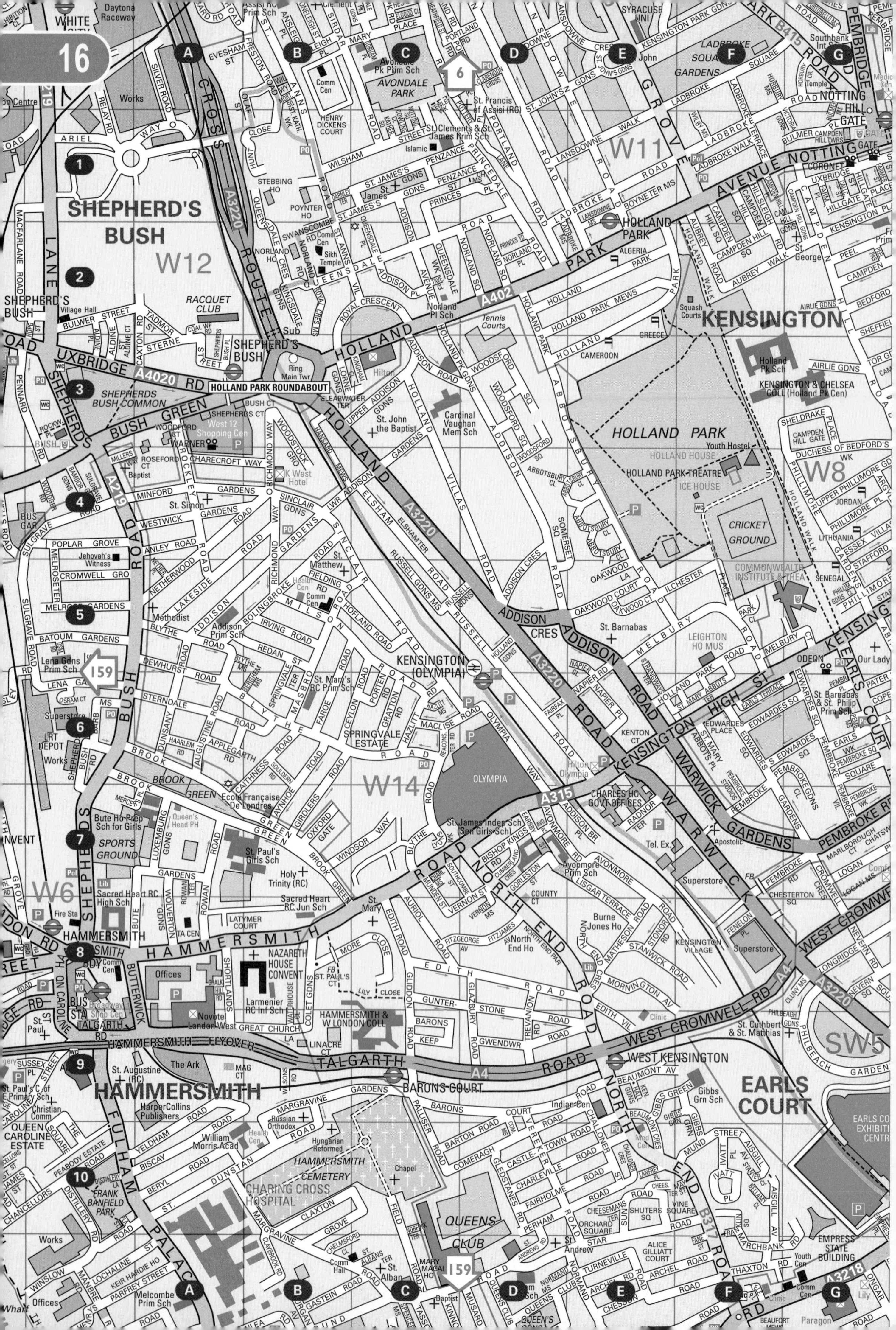
A
B
C
D
E
F
G
1
2
3
4
5
6
7
8
9
10
6
159
SHEPHERD'S BUSH
W12
W11
W14
W8
W6
SW5
KENSINGTON
HAMMERSMITH
EARLS COURT
HOLLAND PARK
HOLLAND PARK ROUNDABOUT
HOLLAND PARK
AVONDALE PARK
NOTTING HILL GATE
HOLLAND HOUSE
HOLLAND PARK THEATRE
ICE HOUSE
CRICKET GROUND
COMMONWEALTH INSTITUTE & THEA
OLYMPIA
KENSINGTON (OLYMPIA)
WEST KENSINGTON
BARONS COURT
HAMMERSMITH CEMETERY
CHARING CROSS HOSPITAL
QUEENS CLUB
SHEPHERDS BUSH COMMON
SPORTS GROUND
RACQUET CLUB
West 12 Shopping Cen
LADBROKE SQUARE GARDENS
SPRINGVALE ESTATE
QUEEN CAROLINE ESTATE
FRANK BANFIELD PARK
NAZARETH HOUSE CONVENT
HAMMERSMITH & W LONDON COLL
LEIGHTON HO MUS
KENSINGTON & CHELSEA COLL (Holland Pk Cen)
Daytona Raceway
HOLLAND
A3220
A4020
A402
A315
A219
A4
A3218
B415
B317
UXBRIDGE RD
HOLLAND PARK AVENUE
NOTTING HILL GATE
HAMMERSMITH FLYOVER
TALGARTH ROAD
WEST CROMWELL RD
KENSINGTON HIGH ST
WARWICK GARDENS
NORTH END ROAD
HOLLAND ROAD
ADDISON ROAD
SHEPHERDS BUSH ROAD
FULHAM PALACE RD
HAMMERSMITH RD
WEST CROSS ROUTE
BROOK GREEN
PEMBROKE RD
LADBROKE GROVE

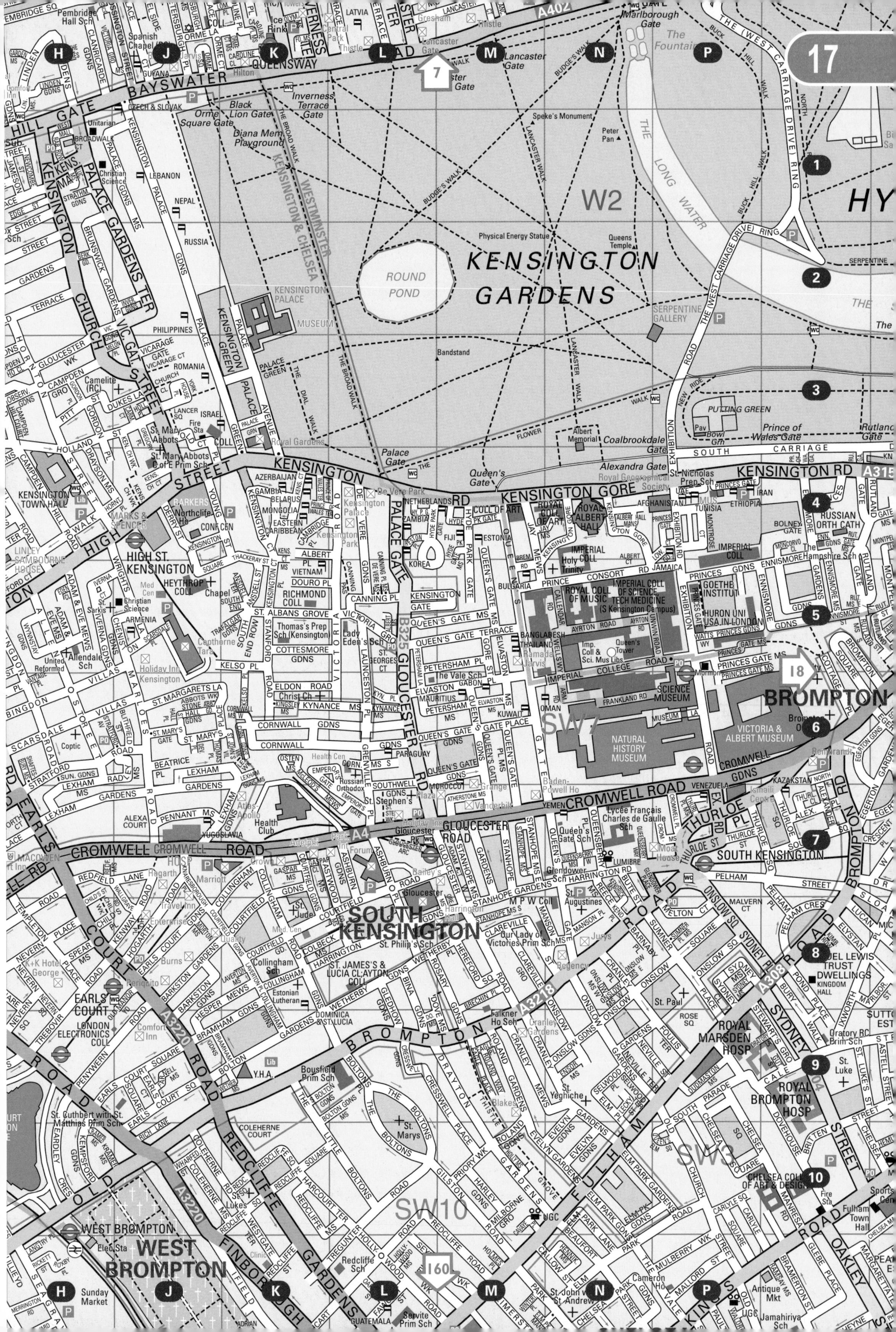
KENSINGTON GARDENS
W2
ROUND POND
THE LONG WATER
Kensington Palace
Museum
Bandstand
Physical Energy Statue
Speke's Monument
Peter Pan
Queens Temple
Serpentine Gallery
The Fountains
Marlborough Gate
Lancaster Gate
Inverness Terrace Gate
Black Lion Gate
Orme Square Gate
Diana Mem. Playground
THE BROAD WALK
LANCASTER WALK
BUDGE'S WALK
THE DIAL WALK
FLOWER WALK
THE WEST CARRIAGE DRIVE
SERPENTINE
PUTTING GREEN
Prince of Wales Gate
Rutland Gate
Albert Memorial
Coalbrookdale Gate
Alexandra Gate
Queen's Gate
Palace Gate
Royal Geographical Society
BAYSWATER ROAD
QUEENSWAY
A402
KENSINGTON RD
KENSINGTON GORE
KENSINGTON HIGH STREET
A315
HIGH ST. KENSINGTON
KENSINGTON CHURCH STREET
PALACE GARDENS TER
KENSINGTON PALACE GDNS
KENSINGTON TOWN HALL
LINLEY SAMBOURNE HOUSE
ROYAL ALBERT HALL
ROYAL COLL OF ART
ROYAL COLL OF MUSIC
IMPERIAL COLL
IMPERIAL COLL OF SCIENCE, TECH MEDICINE (S Kensington Campus)
IMPERIAL COLLEGE ROAD
SCIENCE MUSEUM
NATURAL HISTORY MUSEUM
VICTORIA & ALBERT MUSEUM
SW7
BROMPTON
Brompton Oratory
EXHIBITION RD
QUEEN'S GATE
GLOUCESTER RD
B325
CROMWELL ROAD
A4
CROMWELL HOSP
GLOUCESTER ROAD
SOUTH KENSINGTON
THURLOE PL
PELHAM STREET
HARRINGTON RD
Lycée Français Charles de Gaulle Sch
ONSLOW SQ
SYDNEY ST
A308
FULHAM ROAD
ROYAL MARSDEN HOSP
ROYAL BROMPTON HOSP
CHELSEA COLL OF ART & DESIGN
SW3
SW10
BROMPTON ROAD
A3218
OLD BROMPTON ROAD
EARLS COURT
EARLS COURT ROAD
A3220
LONDON ELECTRONICS COLL
WEST BROMPTON
REDCLIFFE GARDENS
REDCLIFFE SQUARE
THE BOLTONS
FINBOROUGH ROAD
Sunday Market
Elec.Sta
Y.H.A.
H
J
K
L
M
N
P
1
2
3
4
5
6
7
8
9
10
18
160

18
OXFORD STREET where marked is closed to through traffic (except buses & taxis) from 7a.m. - 7p.m. Monday - Saturday
8
A
B
C
D
E
F
G
1
2
3
4
5
6
7
8
9
10
HYDE PARK
W2
THE LONG WATER
THE SERPENTINE
The Lido
Pier
SERPENTINE ROAD
Bird Sanctuary
SERPENTINE GALLERY
PUTTING GREEN
Prince of Wales Gate
Rutland Gate
Edinburgh Gate
Albert Gate
Holocaust Memorial
War Memorial
Bandstand
Queen Elizabeth Gate
Achilles Statue
STANHOPE GATE
CURZON GATE
ACHILLES WAY
APSLEY HOUSE WELLINGTON MUS
HYDE PARK CORNER
ROTTEN ROW
SOUTH CARRIAGE DRIVE
NORTH RIDE
NEW RIDE
BROOK GATE
GROSVENOR GATE
Centre Fountain
PARK LANE
A4202
MAYFAIR
W1
Le Meridien Grosvenor House
The Dorchester
Inter Continental
Metropolitan
Four Seasons
Hilton
Immaculate Conception (RC)
St. George's Hanover Sq Prim Sch
Christ Church
CURZON
MOUNT ST
SOUTH ST
DEANERY ST
TILNEY ST
STANHOPE GATE
HERTFORD ST
HAMILTON PLACE
OLD PARK LANE
BUCKINGHAM PALACE GARDENS
CONSTITUTION HILL
DUKE OF WELLINGTON PL
Lanesborough
KNIGHTSBRIDGE
A4
KENSINGTON RD
A315
KNIGHTSBRIDGE BARRACKS
Mandarin Oriental Hyde Park
Sheraton
Berkeley
SW7
IMPERIAL COLL
IMPERIAL COLL SCIENCE, MEDICINE
GOETHE INSTITUT
ROYAL GEOGRAPHICAL SOCIETY
SCIENCE MUSEUM
VICTORIA & ALBERT MUSEUM
Brompton Oratory
Holy Trinity
BROMPTON
BROMPTON RD
CROMWELL RD
EXHIBITION RD
PRINCES GATE
ENNISMORE GARDENS
RUTLAND GATE
MONTPELIER SQ
TREVOR SQ
HANS RD
HARRODS
BEAUCHAMP PL
PONT STREET
B319
SLOANE STREET
A3216
CADOGAN PLACE
CADOGAN SQUARE
LOWNDES SQUARE
WILTON CRES
BELGRAVE SQUARE
B310
BELGRAVIA
EATON SQ
EATON PL
CHESTER SQ
ECCLESTON ST
A3217
GROSVENOR PL
A302
HOBART PL
SOUTH KENSINGTON
THURLOE PL
ONSLOW SQ
PELHAM ST
SYDNEY ST
A308
FULHAM ROAD
SW3
KING'S ROAD
ROYAL MARSDEN HOSP
ROYAL BROMPTON HOSP
CHELSEA COLL OF ART & DESIGN
SAMUEL LEWIS TRUST DWELLINGS
SUTTON EST
GUINNESS TRUST BLDGS
DUKE OF YORK'S HEADQUARTERS
PETER JONES
SLOANE SQ
LOWER SLOANE ST
SLOANE SQ
ROYAL COURT
PIMLICO ROAD
A3214
CHELSEA BRIDGE ROAD
BURTON'S COURT
ROYAL HOSPITAL CHELSEA
RANELAGH GARDENS
ROYAL HOSPITAL ROAD
NATIONAL ARMY MUSEUM
EMBANKMENT
EBURY BRIDGE EST
EBURY BRIDGE RD
BUCKINGHAM PALACE RD
COACH STA
LISTER HOSPITAL
CHELSEA BARRACKS
Francis Holland Sch (Belgravia)
CUNDY STREET EST
INCHBALD SCH OF DESIGN
CHELSEA
Chelsea Manor
PEABODY EST
Antique Mkt
OAKLEY ST
FLOOD ST
ST. LEONARD'S TERRACE
FRANKLIN'S ROW
17
160

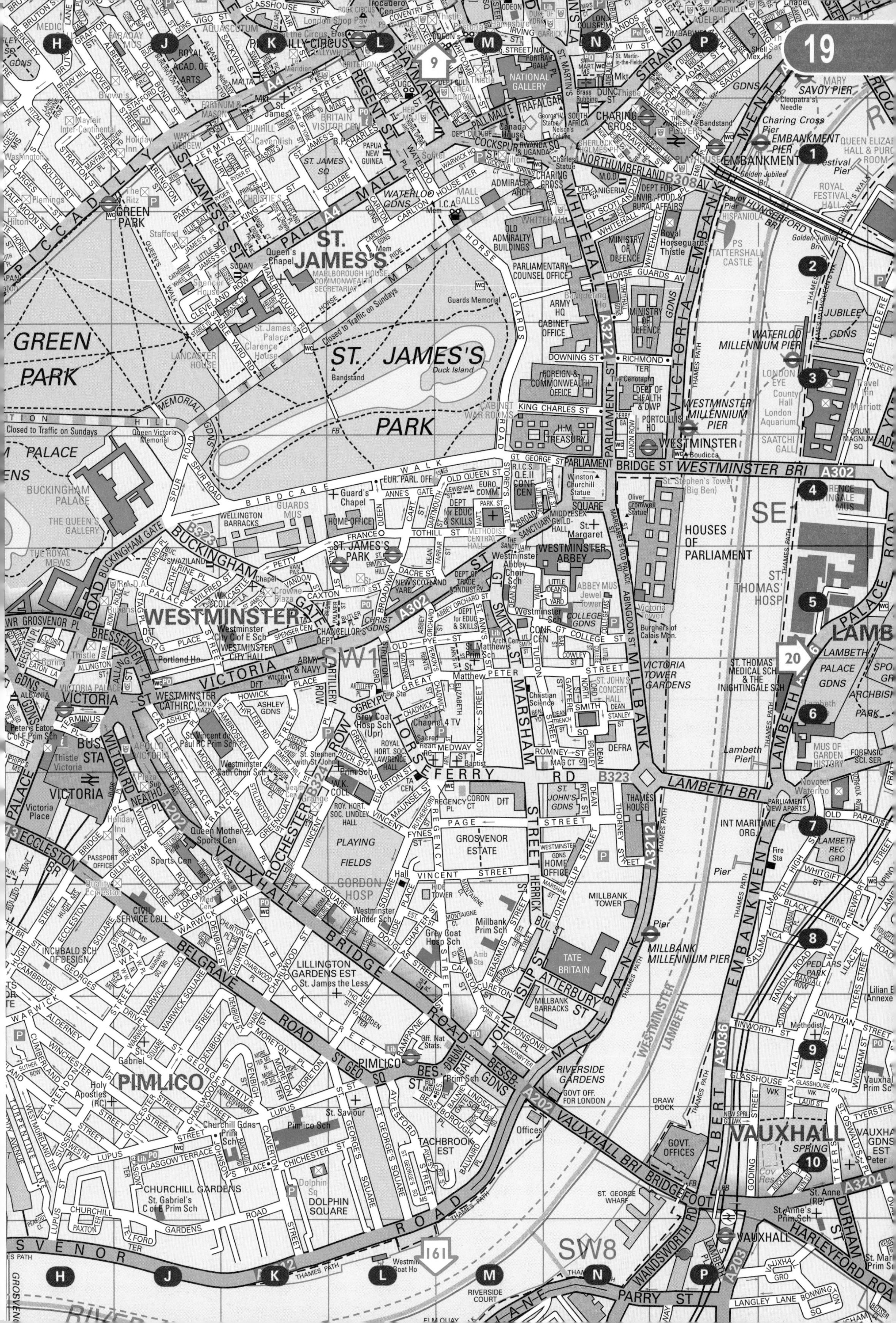
H
J
K
L
M
N
P
9
20
161
1
2
3
4
5
6
7
8
9
10
PICCADILLY
PICCADILLY CIRCUS
ROYAL ACAD. OF ARTS
REGENT ST
HAYMARKET
NATIONAL GALLERY
TRAFALGAR
STRAND
CHARING CROSS
EMBANKMENT
EMBANKMENT PIER
SAVOY PIER
Charing Cross Pier
QUEEN ELIZABETH HALL & PURCELL ROOM
ROYAL FESTIVAL HALL
Golden Jubilee Bri
HUNGERFORD BR
NORTHUMBERLAND AV
WHITEHALL
GREEN PARK
ST. JAMES'S
PALL MALL
THE MALL
Closed to Traffic on Sundays
MARLBOROUGH HOUSE COMMONWEALTH SECRETARIAT
ADMIRALTY ARCH
OLD ADMIRALTY BUILDINGS
MINISTRY OF DEFENCE
HORSE GUARDS AV
Guards Memorial
ST. JAMES'S PARK
Duck Island
Bandstand
GREEN PARK
St. James's Palace
Clarence House
LANCASTER HOUSE
Queen Victoria Memorial
BUCKINGHAM PALACE
THE QUEEN'S GALLERY
THE ROYAL MEWS
BIRDCAGE WALK
WELLINGTON BARRACKS
GUARDS MUS
HOME OFFICE
DOWNING ST
FOREIGN & COMMONWEALTH OFFICE
H.M. TREASURY
CABINET OFFICE
The Cenotaph
WESTMINSTER MILLENNIUM PIER
WESTMINSTER
WESTMINSTER BRI
PARLIAMENT SQUARE
Q.E.II CONF CEN
WESTMINSTER ABBEY
HOUSES OF PARLIAMENT
St. Stephen's Tower (Big Ben)
Victoria Tower
VICTORIA TOWER GARDENS
LONDON EYE
County Hall
London Aquarium
WATERLOO MILLENNIUM PIER
JUBILEE GDNS
ST. THOMAS' HOSP
LAMBETH PALACE
LAMBETH PALACE GDNS
ARCHBISHOP'S PARK
LAMBETH BRI
Lambeth Pier
WESTMINSTER
ST. JAMES'S PARK
BUCKINGHAM GATE
VICTORIA ST
VICTORIA
BUS STA
Victoria Place
SW1
WESTMINSTER CATH (RC)
VAUXHALL BRIDGE ROAD
HORSEFERRY RD
MILLBANK
THAMES HOUSE
PLAYING FIELDS
GROSVENOR ESTATE
TATE BRITAIN
MILLBANK TOWER
MILLBANK MILLENNIUM PIER
MILLBANK BARRACKS
ALBERT EMBANKMENT
INT MARITIME ORG.
BELGRAVE ROAD
PIMLICO
LILLINGTON GARDENS EST
Pimlico Sch
CHURCHILL GARDENS
DOLPHIN SQUARE
TACHBROOK EST
RIVERSIDE GARDENS
VAUXHALL BRI
GOVT. OFFICES
VAUXHALL
SW8
GROSVENOR RD
RIVERSIDE COURT
PARRY ST
HARLEYFORD RD
A4
A302
A3212
A202
A3036
A203
A3204
B323
B324
B308
SE1

20
A
B
C
D
E
F
G
1
2
3
4
5
6
7
8
9
10
10
19
161
RIVER THAMES
KING'S REACH
WESTMINSTER
LAMBETH
SOUTHWARK
TATE MODERN
Express Newspapers
BANKSIDE GALLERY
H.M. CUSTOMS AND EXCISE
OXO TWR WHARF
MUSEUM OF
THAMES PATH
QUEEN'S WALK
T.S. QUEEN MARY
SAVOY PIER
Charing Cross Pier
EMBANKMENT PIER
EMBANKMENT
QUEEN ELIZABETH HALL & PURCELL ROOM
Festival Pier
ROYAL FESTIVAL HALL
HAYWARD GALLERY
NAT FILM THEA
ROYAL NATIONAL
IBM
London Television Centre
The GABRIEL'S WHARF
WATERLOO BRI
STAMFORD STREET
UPPER GROUND
London Nautical Sch
PEABODY ESTATE
Colombo Cen
American Express
SOUTHWARK STREET
HOPTON STREET
Bandstand
DEPT FOR ENVIR., FOOD & RURAL AFFAIRS
Royal Horseguards Thistle
HUNGERFORD BRI
Golden Jubilee Brs
HISPANIOLA
PS TATTERSHALL CASTLE
SCHILLER INT UNI
KING'S COLL (Waterloo Campus)
IMAX
St. John the Evangelist
WATERLOO EAST
Shell Centre
JUBILEE GDNS
WATERLOO MILLENNIUM PIER
MINISTRY OF DEFENCE
VICTORIA EMBANKMENT
WATERLOO
WATERLOO INTERNATIONAL
THE YOUNG VIC
SOUTHWARK COLL (Waterloo Cen)
THE CUT
SOUTHWARK
UNION STREET
NELSON SQUARE
JERWOOD SPACE
COPPERFIELD STREET
LON. FIRE BRIGADE MUS
LONDON EYE
County Hall
London Aquarium
SAATCHI GALL
Travel Inn
Marriott
FORUM MAGNUM SQ
WESTMINSTER MILLENNIUM PIER
PORTCULLIS HO
WESTMINSTER
Boudicca
WESTMINSTER BRI
THE OLD VIC
St. Andrew with St. Thomas
Friars Prim Sch
BLACKFRIARS ROAD
THE BO
HOUSES OF PARLIAMENT
FLORENCE NIGHTINGALE MUS
ST. THOMAS' HOSP
LAMBETH NORTH
Johanna Prim Sch
TANSWELL EST
PEABODY SQUARE
WESTMINSTER BR ROAD
ST. GEORGE'S CATH (RC)
St. George's Prim Sch
ST GEORGE'S CIRCUS
BOROUGH ROAD
SOUTH BANK UNI
INST. OF OPTOMETRY
INNER LONDON CROWN COURT
LAMBETH
LAMBETH PALACE GDNS
SPORTS GRD
ARCHBISHOP'S PARK
Lambeth Palace
THOMAS' MEDICAL SCH & THE NIGHTINGALE SCH
Victoria Tower
Burghers of Calais Mon.
VICTORIA TOWER GARDENS
MILLBANK
SW1
Lambeth Pier
MUS OF GARDEN HISTORY
FORENSIC SCI. SER
LAMBETH BRI
LAMBETH ROAD
GERALDINE MARY HARMSWORTH PARK
IMPERIAL WAR MUS
IMP. WAR MUS (ANNEXE)
ST GEORGE'S ROAD
LONDON ROAD
Notre Dame Sch
St. Jude's Prim Sch
GAYWOOD EST
Charlotte Sharman Prim Sch
Salvation Army
LONDON COLL OF PRINTING
ELEPHANT & CASTLE
Shopping Cen
NEWINGTON CAUSEWAY
WALWORTH ROAD
Rec Cen
London Park
Novotel Waterloo
PARLIAMENT VIEW APARTS
INT MARITIME ORG.
LAMBETH REC GRD
Fire Sta
Walnut Tree Wk Prim Sch
LAMBETH WK OPEN SPACE
Lilian Baylis Sch
SE11
Youth Club
Archbishop Summers Prim Sch
Michael Tippett Sch
DRYDEN COURT
HURLEY HO
EBENEZER HO
FAIRFORD HO
MILLBANK MILLENNIUM PIER
ALBERT EMBANKMENT
KENNINGTON ROAD
KENNINGTON LANE
Lilian Baylis Sch (Annexe) (Lambeth)
Day Hosp
Methodist
Vauxhall Prim Sch
VAUXHALL
SPRING GDNS
VAUXHALL GDNS EST
St. Peter
GOVT. OFFICES
DRAW DOCK
St. Anne (RC)
St. Anne's Prim Sch
VAUXHALL
HARLEYFORD ROAD
GAS WORKS
St. Mark's Prim Sch
TRIANGLE EST
St. Anselm
COUNTY COURT
CLEAVER SQUARE
CITY & GUILDS OF LONDON ART SCH
KENNINGTON
St. Mary
KENNINGTON PARK ROAD
GUINNESS TRUST BUILDINGS
ALBERTA EST
Crampton Prim Sch
Keyworth Prim Sch
WALWORTH GARDEN FM
SURREY GDNS
PENROSE HOUSE
St. Paul's C of E Prim Sch
Mormon
KENNINGTON PARK
THE AMP OVAL
Fawcett Prim Sch
St. Wilfred (RC)
St. Paul
NEWINGTON BUTTS
CUMING MUS
St. John's Walworth Prim Sch

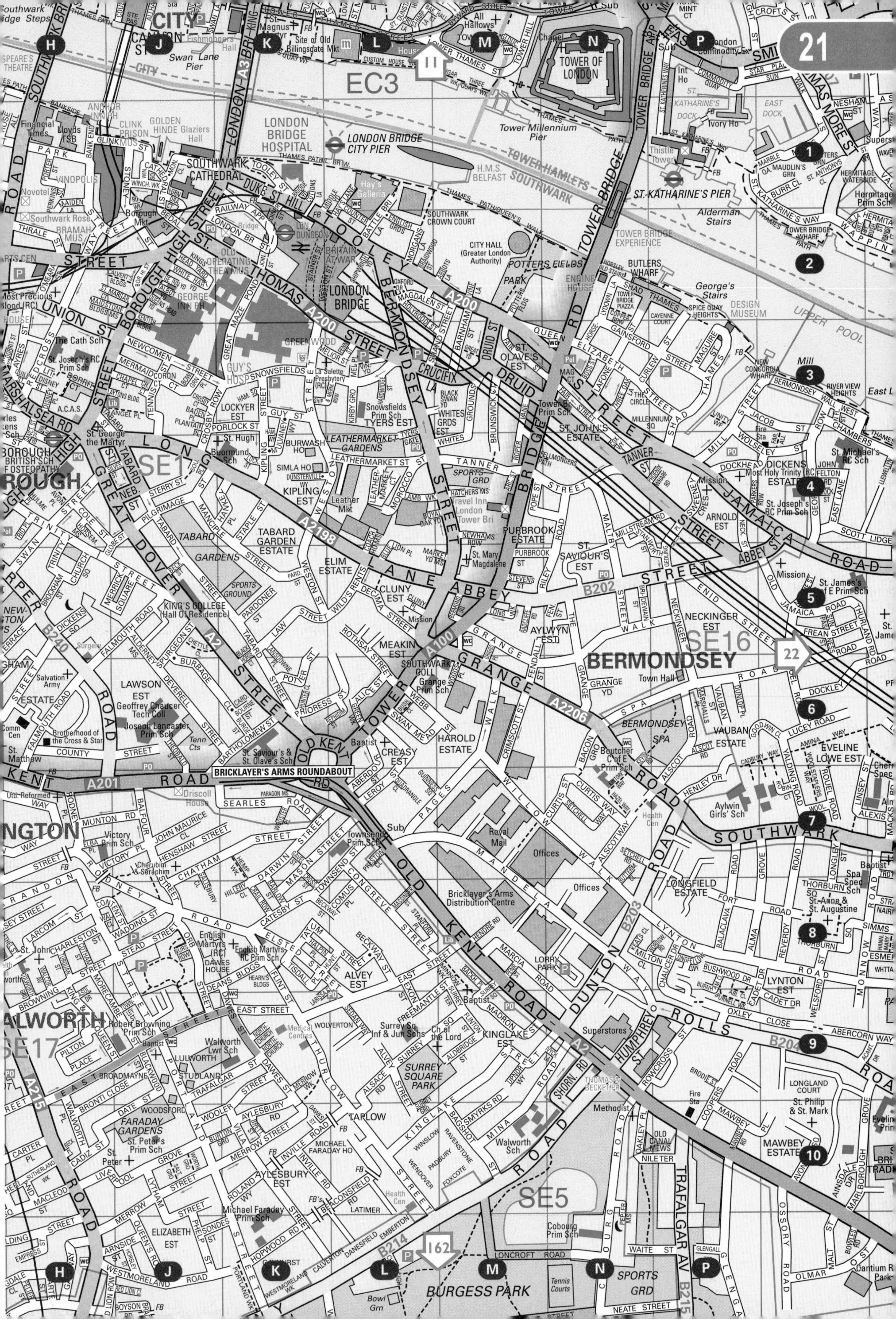
EC3
TOWER OF LONDON
LONDON BRIDGE HOSPITAL
LONDON BRIDGE CITY PIER
SOUTHWARK CATHEDRAL
Tower Millennium Pier
ST. KATHARINE'S PIER
TOWER BRIDGE
H.M.S. BELFAST
CITY HALL (Greater London Authority)
POTTERS FIELDS PARK
DESIGN MUSEUM
BUTLERS WHARF
UPPER POOL
TOOLEY STREET
BOROUGH HIGH ST.
ST. THOMAS STREET
GUY'S HOSP
LONG LANE
SE1
BOROUGH
BERMONDSEY STREET
LEATHERMARKET GARDENS
JAMAICA ROAD
ABBEY STREET
GRANGE ROAD
BERMONDSEY
SE16
BERMONDSEY SPA
SOUTHWARK PARK ROAD
TABARD GARDENS
GREAT DOVER STREET
BRICKLAYER'S ARMS ROUNDABOUT
OLD KENT ROAD
A201
A2
A100
A200
A2198
A2206
B202
B203
B204
B214
B215
A215
Bricklayer's Arms Distribution Centre
ROLLS ROAD
WALWORTH
SE17
SE5
SURREY SQUARE PARK
FARADAY GARDENS
AYLESBURY EST
BURGESS PARK
LONCROFT ROAD
WESTMORELAND ROAD
MAWBEY ESTATE
LYNTON EST
22
162
H
J
K
L
M
N
P
1
2
3
4
5
6
7
8
9
10

A
B
C
D
E
F
G
1
2
3
4
5
6
7
8
9
10
SHADWELL
SHADWELL BASIN
WAPPING
News International
Tobacco Dock
12
ST. KATHARINE'S PIER
ST. KATHARINE'S DOCK
EAST DOCK
TOWER BRIDGE EXPERIENCE
BUTLERS WHARF
DESIGN MUSEUM
UPPER POOL
THE POOL
LOWER POOL
RIVER
TOWER HAMLETS
SOUTHWARK
ROTHERHITHE TUNNEL
THAMES PATH
WAPPING HIGH STREET
WAPPING LANE
THE HIGHWAY
SMITHFIELD
THOMAS MORE ST
VAUGHAN WAY
KENNET STREET
PENNINGTON STREET
NEWLANDS QUAY
WATTS ST
GARNET ST
PROSPECT OF WHITBY PH
New Crane Stairs
Wapping Old Stairs
Wapping New Stairs
Wapping Dock Stairs
George's Stairs
Alderman Stairs
Mill Stairs
East Lane Stairs
King's Stairs
Princes Stairs
Cherry Garden Pier
John Orwell (Wapping) Sports Cen
St. Patrick (RC)
St. Peter's Prim Sch
Hermitage Prim Sch
Arts Cen
Pier
Airshaft
LEESIDE CT
MAYFLOWER PH
BRUNEL ENGINE HOUSE
St. Mary with All Saints
ROTHERHITHE
ADAMS GARDENS EST
THE ANGEL PH
KING'S STAIRS GARDENS
BERMONDSEY WALL EAST
BERMONDSEY WALL WEST
JAMAICA ROAD
A200
BERMONDSEY
DICKENS ESTATE
St. Michael's RC Sch
Most Holy Trinity (RC)
St. Joseph's RC Prim Sch
Riverside Prim Sch
MILLPOND EST
St. Peter (RC)
KIRBY ESTATE
St. Crispin
St. James's C of E Prim Sch
St. James
SOUTHWARK COLL
Africa House
SOUTHWARK PARK
Lido
CAFÉ GALLERY
SPORTS GROUND
SE16
Works
Baptist
Southwark Pk Prim Sch
SOUTHWARK PK EST
LOWER ROAD
ROTHERHITHE NEW ROAD
ROTHERHITHE OLD RD
HAWKSTONE RD
SURREY QUAYS
CANADA WATER
CANADA ESTATE
HOWLAND ESTATE
Seven Islands Leisure Cen
St. Joseph's RC Prim Sch
Swedish Seamen's
ALBION ESTATE
Albion Prim Sch
AYLTON ESTATE
Superstores
Surrey Quays Retail Centre
Rotherhithe Prim Sch
SURREY WATER
NECKINGER EST
Town Hall
21
BERMONDSEY SPA
VAUBAN ESTATE
EVELINE LOWE EST
Cherry Gdn Spec Sch
Alma Prim Sch
Aylwin Girls' Sch
SOUTHWARK PARK ROAD
RAYMOUTH RD
LONGFIELD ESTATE
St. Anne & St. Augustine
Thorburn Sch
MANOR ESTATE
TRADING ESTATE
RENNIE ESTATE
St. Gertrude (RC)
SILWOOD EST
Youth Comm Cen
LYNTON EST
LYNTON ROAD
PATERSON PARK
St. Augustine
Galleywall Prim Sch
SOUTH BERMONDSEY
NEW ROAD
A2208
ROLLS ROAD
B204
SE1
CATLIN STREET
ROTHERHITHE NEW ROAD
Lewisham Lions Cen
THE DEN MILLWALL FC
Power Station
Chimney
St. Philip & St. Mark
MAWBEY ESTATE
Eveline Lowe Prim Sch
SIX BRIDGES TRADING EST
Comm Cen
Ilderton Prim Sch
STOCKHOLM ROAD
Works
SURREY CANAL
Recycling Centre
SE15
162
Gantium Retail Park
Mountain of Fire
OLD KENT ROAD
TRAFALGAR AV
B215
Gas Works
BRIDGE MEADOWS
ROLLINS STREET

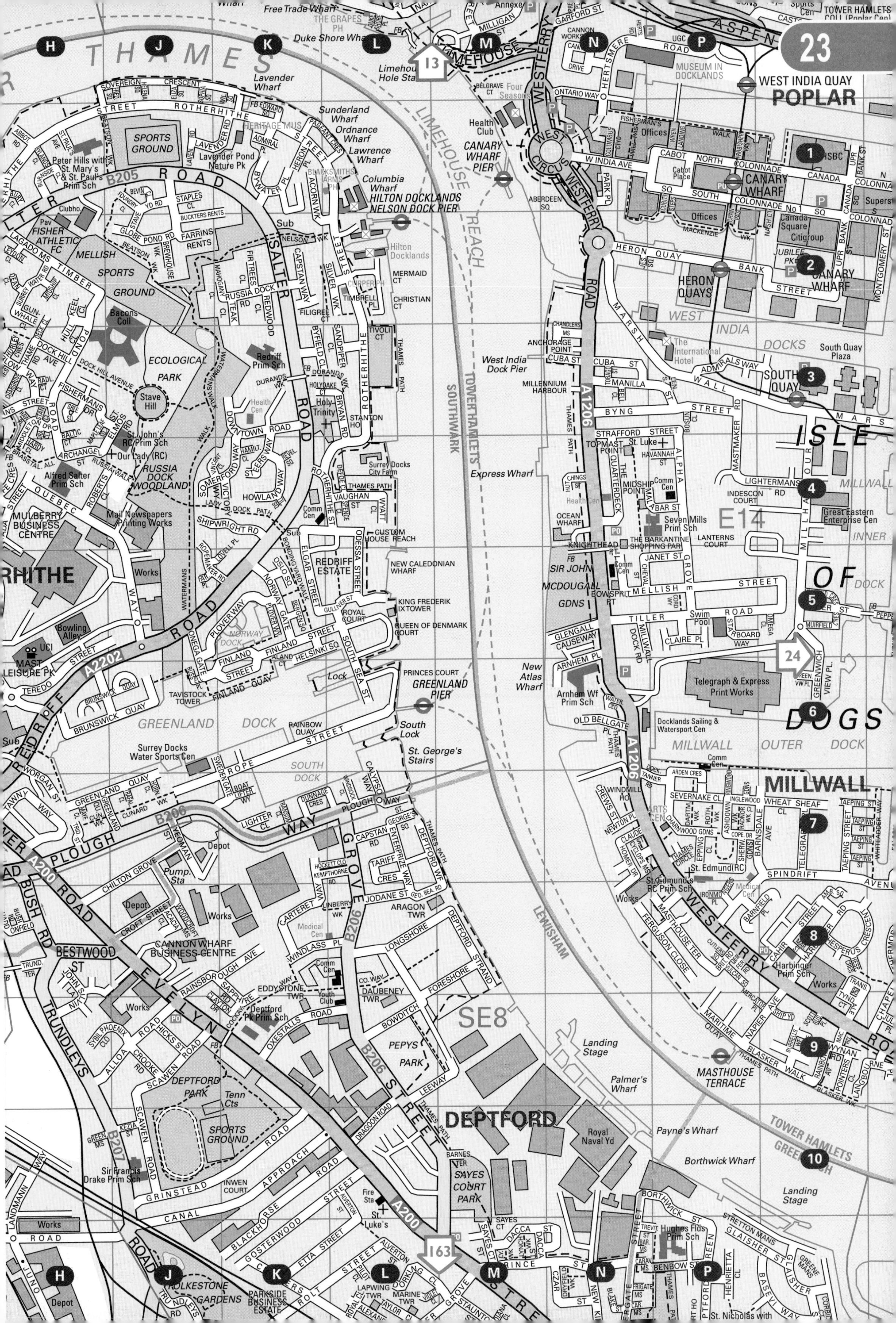

THAMES
LIMEHOUSE REACH
POPLAR
CANARY WHARF
WEST INDIA QUAY
HERON QUAYS
WEST INDIA DOCKS
SOUTH QUAY
ISLE OF DOGS
MILLWALL
E14
MILLWALL OUTER DOCK
MILLWALL INNER DOCK
SE8
DEPTFORD
Royal Naval Yd
PEPYS PARK
DEPTFORD PARK
GREENLAND DOCK
SOUTH DOCK
SOUTHWARK
TOWER HAMLETS
LEWISHAM
GREENWICH
REDRIFF ESTATE
ROTHERHITHE
RUSSIA DOCK WOODLAND
ECOLOGICAL PARK
Stave Hill
SALTER ROAD
REDRIFF ROAD
EVELYN STREET
LOWER ROAD
PLOUGH WAY
GROVE STREET
WESTFERRY ROAD
MASTHOUSE TERRACE
GREENLAND PIER
CANARY WHARF PIER
NELSON DOCK PIER
HILTON DOCKLANDS
Telegraph & Express Print Works
Docklands Sailing & Watersport Cen
Surrey Docks Water Sports Cen
Surrey Docks City Farm
Mail Newspapers Printing Works
MULBERRY BUSINESS CENTRE
CANNON WHARF BUSINESS CENTRE
FOLKESTONE GARDENS
SAYES COURT PARK
SIR JOHN MCDOUGALL GDNS
MILLENNIUM HARBOUR
West India Dock Pier
Landing Stage
Palmer's Wharf
Payne's Wharf
Borthwick Wharf
Express Wharf
New Atlas Wharf
South Lock
St. George's Stairs
H J K L M N P
13
24
163
1 2 3 4 5 6 7 8 9 10

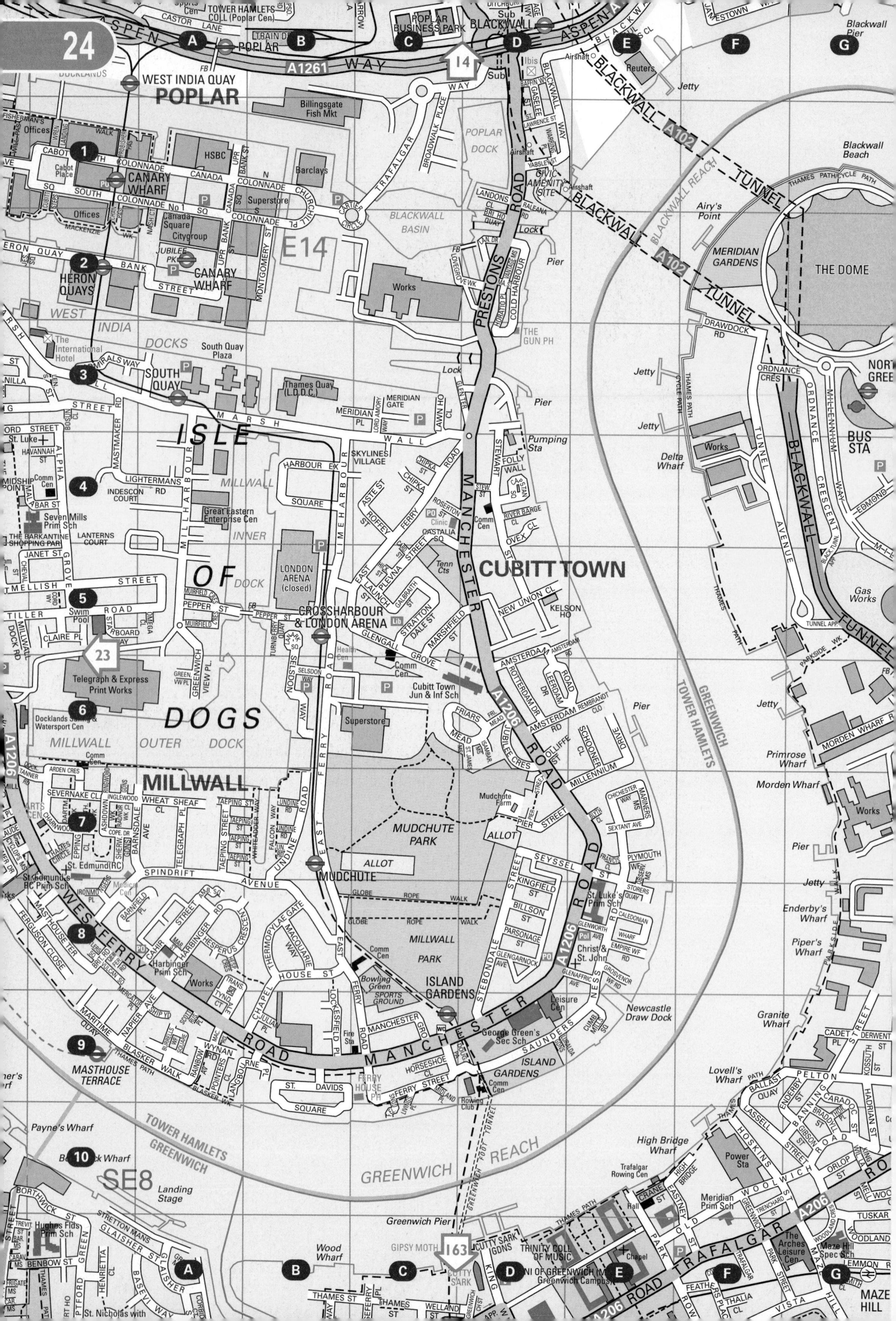

24
A
B
C
D
E
F
G
14
23
163
1
2
3
4
5
6
7
8
9
10
POPLAR
WEST INDIA QUAY
POPLAR BUSINESS PARK
BLACKWALL
A1261
ASPEN WAY
Billingsgate Fish Mkt
POPLAR DOCK
Reuters
Jetty
Blackwall Pier
Blackwall Beach
BLACKWALL TUNNEL
A102
BLACKWALL REACH
THAMES PATH/CYCLE PATH
Airy's Point
MERIDIAN GARDENS
THE DOME
CANARY WHARF
CABOT SQ
Cabot Place
HSBC
Barclays
CANADA SQ
Canada Square
Citygroup
Superstore
BLACKWALL BASIN
CARTIER CIRCLE
E14
CIVIC AMENITY SITE
HERON QUAYS
BANK STREET
MONTGOMERY ST
WEST INDIA DOCKS
The International Hotel
South Quay Plaza
SOUTH QUAY
Thames Quay (L.D.D.C.)
MERIDIAN GATE
MARSH WALL
Works
PRESTONS ROAD
COLD HARBOUR
THE GUN PH
Lock
Pier
DRAWDOCK RD
ORDNANCE CRES
MILLENNIUM WAY
NORTH GREENWICH
BUS STA
THAMES PATH
Delta Wharf
TUNNEL AVENUE
ISLE OF DOGS
MILLWALL INNER DOCK
MILLWALL OUTER DOCK
Pumping Sta
SKYLINES VILLAGE
HARBOUR EX
LIMEHARBOUR
MANCHESTER ROAD
CUBITT TOWN
LONDON ARENA (closed)
CROSSHARBOUR & LONDON ARENA
Great Eastern Enterprise Cen
LIGHTERMANS RD
MASTMAKER RD
MILLHARBOUR
Seven Mills Prim Sch
THE BARKANTINE SHOPPING PARK
MELLISH STREET
Swim Pool
Telegraph & Express Print Works
Docklands Sailing & Watersport Cen
GLENGALL GROVE
Cubitt Town Jun & Inf Sch
Superstore
NEW UNION CL
KELSON HO
AMSTERDAM RD
A1206
Gas Works
TUNNEL APP
Primrose Wharf
Morden Wharf
MORDEN WHARF RD
MILLWALL
MUDCHUTE PARK
Mudchute Farm
MUDCHUTE
ALLOT
MILLWALL PARK
ISLAND GARDENS
SPINDRIFT AVENUE
WESTFERRY ROAD
Harbinger Prim Sch
St. Luke's Prim Sch
Christ & St. John
SAUNDERS NESS RD
Leisure Cen
George Green's Sec Sch
Newcastle Draw Dock
Fire Sta
FERRY STREET
Rowing Club
GREENWICH FOOT TUNNEL
TOWER HAMLETS
GREENWICH
GREENWICH REACH
MASTHOUSE TERRACE
Payne's Wharf
SE8
Landing Stage
Greenwich Pier
Wood Wharf
GIPSY MOTH
CUTTY SARK
TRINITY COLL OF MUSIC
Greenwich Campus
Chapel
Enderby's Wharf
Piper's Wharf
Granite Wharf
Lovell's Wharf
High Bridge Wharf
Power Sta
Trafalgar Rowing Cen
Meridian Prim Sch
WOOLWICH RD
TRAFALGAR ROAD
A206
The Arches Leisure Cen
Maze Hill Spec Sch
MAZE HILL
BENBOW ST
Hughes Flds Prim Sch

ROYAL VICTORIA DOCK
MILLENNIUM MILLS
PONTOON DOCK
SILVERTOWN WAY
NORTH WOOLWICH ROAD
A1020
E16
GREENSHIELDS INDUSTRIAL ESTATE
LYLE PARK
Works
Thames Wharf
Millennium Pier
Phoenix Wharf
Manhattan Wharf
RIVER THAMES
NEWHAM
GREENWICH
Jetty
Mudlarks Pier
Slipway
Pontoon
Greenwich Yacht Club
GREENWICH PENINSULA ECOLOGY PARK
SE10
Millennium Village Sch
Holiday Inn Express Greenwich
BUGSBYS WAY
UCI
Superstores
SE7
MERIDIAN TRADING ESTATE
ANCHOR & HOPE LANE
NEW CHA
GREENWICH INDUSTRIAL ESTATE
STONE LAKE RETAIL PARK
CABLE TRADE PARK
A206
WOOLWICH ROAD
A102
BLACKWALL LANE
A2203
CITY CROSS BUSINESS PARK
COUNCIL DEPOT
Christchurch C of E Prim Sch
St Josephs RC Prim Sch
EAST GREENWICH PLEASAUNCE
Halstow Prim Sch
WESTCOMBE PARK
CHARLTON
Fossdene Prim Sch
Warehouses
SE3
Britannia Village Prim Sch
THAMES BARRIER PARK
SILVERT
15
164

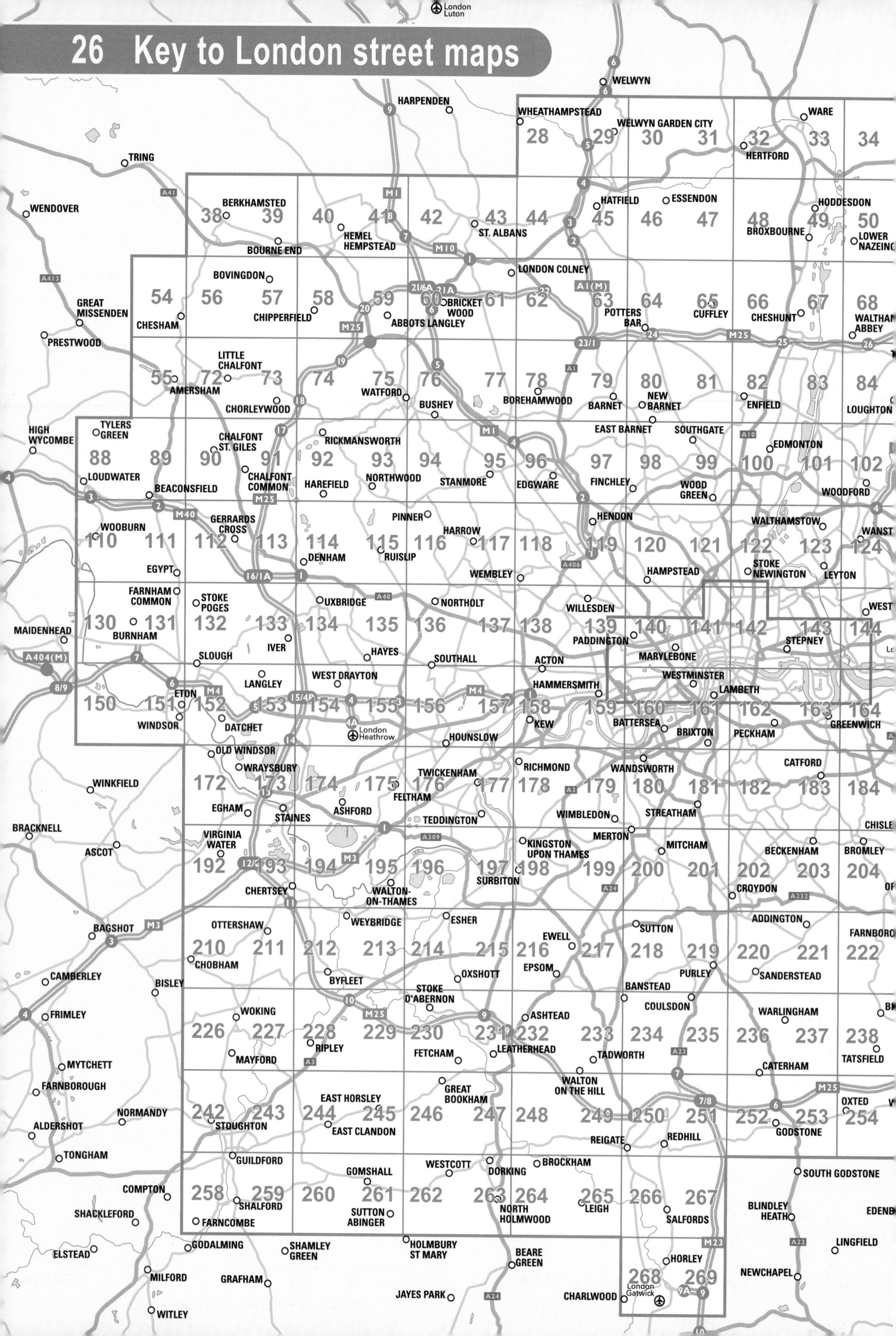

Key to London street maps

London Luton
WELWYN
HARPENDEN
WHEATHAMPSTEAD
WELWYN GARDEN CITY
WARE
HERTFORD
TRING
WENDOVER
BERKHAMSTED
HEMEL HEMPSTEAD
ST. ALBANS
HATFIELD
ESSENDON
HODDESDON
BROXBOURNE
LOWER NAZEING
BOURNE END
LONDON COLNEY
BOVINGDON
GREAT MISSENDEN
CHESHAM
CHIPPERFIELD
BRICKET WOOD
ABBOTS LANGLEY
POTTERS BAR
CUFFLEY
CHESHUNT
WALTHAM ABBEY
PRESTWOOD
LITTLE CHALFONT
AMERSHAM
WATFORD
BUSHEY
BOREHAMWOOD
BARNET
NEW BARNET
ENFIELD
LOUGHTON
CHORLEYWOOD
HIGH WYCOMBE
TYLERS GREEN
CHALFONT ST. GILES
RICKMANSWORTH
EAST BARNET
SOUTHGATE
EDMONTON
LOUDWATER
BEACONSFIELD
CHALFONT COMMON
HAREFIELD
NORTHWOOD
STANMORE
EDGWARE
FINCHLEY
WOOD GREEN
WOODFORD
GERRARDS CROSS
PINNER
HENDON
WALTHAMSTOW
WANSTEAD
WOOBURN
HARROW
DENHAM
RUISLIP
WEMBLEY
HAMPSTEAD
STOKE NEWINGTON
LEYTON
EGYPT
FARNHAM COMMON
STOKE POGES
UXBRIDGE
NORTHOLT
WILLESDEN
WEST
MAIDENHEAD
BURNHAM
IVER
PADDINGTON
MARYLEBONE
STEPNEY
SLOUGH
HAYES
SOUTHALL
ACTON
WESTMINSTER
LANGLEY
WEST DRAYTON
HAMMERSMITH
LAMBETH
ETON
WINDSOR
DATCHET
London Heathrow
KEW
BATTERSEA
BRIXTON
PECKHAM
GREENWICH
HOUNSLOW
OLD WINDSOR
WRAYSBURY
TWICKENHAM
RICHMOND
WANDSWORTH
CATFORD
WINKFIELD
FELTHAM
EGHAM
STAINES
ASHFORD
TEDDINGTON
WIMBLEDON
STREATHAM
BRACKNELL
VIRGINIA WATER
KINGSTON UPON THAMES
MERTON
MITCHAM
BECKENHAM
BROMLEY
CHISLEHURST
ASCOT
SURBITON
CHERTSEY
WALTON-ON-THAMES
CROYDON
WEYBRIDGE
ESHER
SUTTON
ADDINGTON
FARNBOROUGH
BAGSHOT
OTTERSHAW
EWELL
CHOBHAM
EPSOM
PURLEY
SANDERSTEAD
OXSHOTT
BYFLEET
CAMBERLEY
BISLEY
STOKE D'ABERNON
BANSTEAD
COULSDON
WOKING
ASHTEAD
WARLINGHAM
FRIMLEY
RIPLEY
LEATHERHEAD
TADWORTH
CATERHAM
MAYFORD
FETCHAM
TATSFIELD
MYTCHETT
GREAT BOOKHAM
WALTON ON THE HILL
FARNBOROUGH
EAST HORSLEY
OXTED
NORMANDY
ALDERSHOT
STOUGHTON
EAST CLANDON
REIGATE
REDHILL
GODSTONE
TONGHAM
GUILDFORD
WESTCOTT
DORKING
BROCKHAM
GOMSHALL
SOUTH GODSTONE
COMPTON
SHALFORD
SUTTON ABINGER
NORTH HOLMWOOD
LEIGH
SALFORDS
BLINDLEY HEATH
SHACKLEFORD
FARNCOMBE
EDENBRIDGE
GODALMING
SHAMLEY GREEN
HOLMBURY ST MARY
BEARE GREEN
HORLEY
LINGFIELD
ELSTEAD
NEWCHAPEL
MILFORD
GRAFHAM
JAYES PARK
CHARLWOOD
London Gatwick
WITLEY
M1
M10
M25
M40
M4
M3
M23
A1(M)
A404(M)
A41
A413
A1
A10
A406
A40
A309
A3
A24
A232
A23
A22
28 29 30 31 32 33 34
38 39 40 41 42 43 44 45 46 47 48 49 50
54 56 57 58 59 60 61 62 63 64 65 66 67 68
55 72 73 74 75 76 77 78 79 80 81 82 83 84
88 89 90 91 92 93 94 95 96 97 98 99 100 101 102
110 111 112 113 114 115 116 117 118 119 120 121 122 123 124
130 131 132 133 134 135 136 137 138 139 140 141 142 143 144
150 151 152 153 154 155 156 157 158 159 160 161 162 163 164
172 173 174 175 176 177 178 179 180 181 182 183 184
192 193 194 195 196 197 198 199 200 201 202 203 204
210 211 212 213 214 215 216 217 218 219 220 221 222
226 227 228 229 230 231 232 233 234 235 236 237 238
242 243 244 245 246 247 248 249 250 251 252 253 254
258 259 260 261 262 263 264 265 266 267
268 269

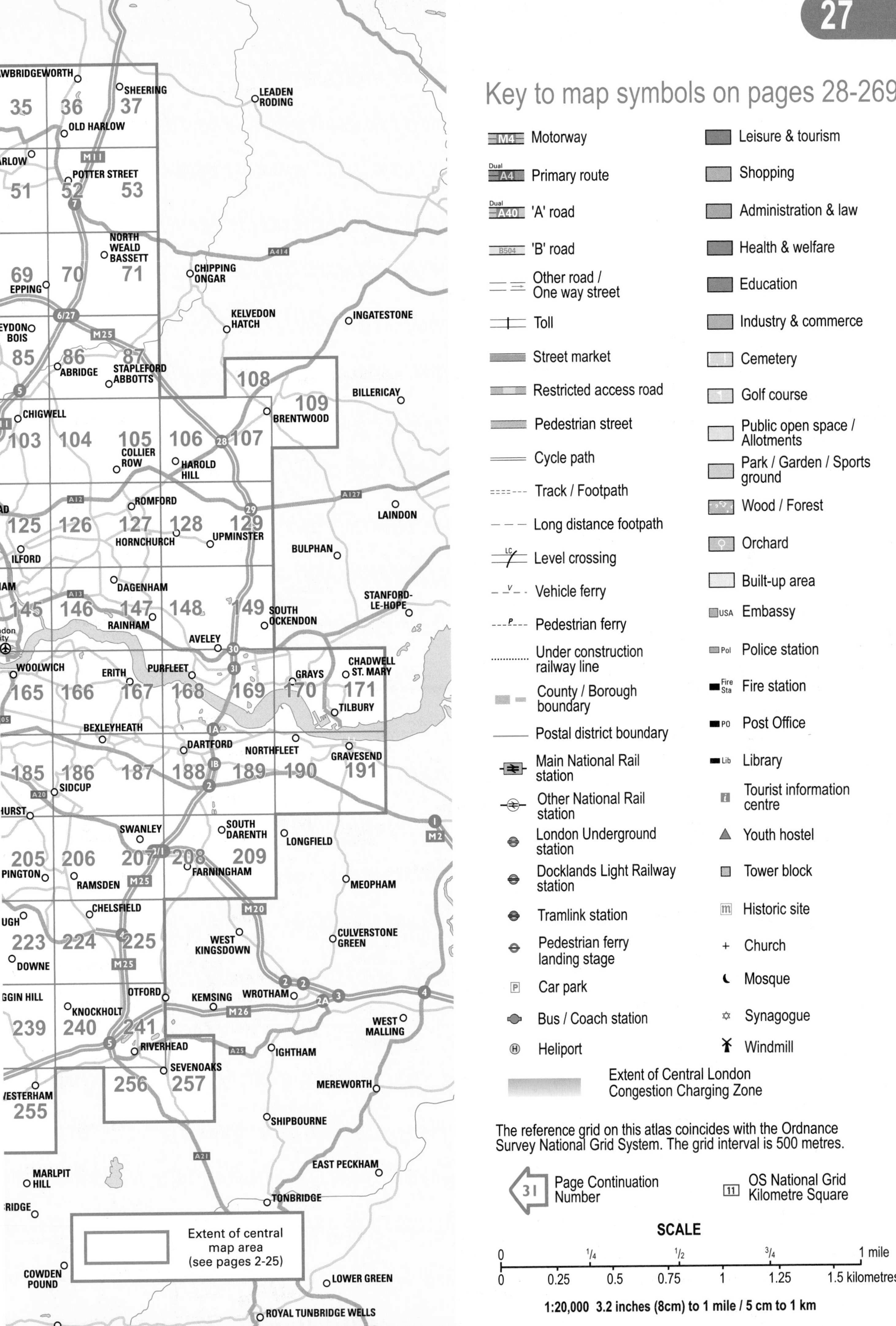
SAWBRIDGEWORTH
SHEERING
LEADEN RODING
35
36
37
OLD HARLOW
HARLOW
M11
POTTER STREET
51
52
53
NORTH WEALD BASSETT
A414
69
70
71
EPPING
CHIPPING ONGAR
6/27
THEYDON BOIS
M25
KELVEDON HATCH
INGATESTONE
85
86
87
ABRIDGE
STAPLEFORD ABBOTTS
108
109
BILLERICAY
BRENTWOOD
CHIGWELL
103
104
105
COLLIER ROW
106
HAROLD HILL
107
A12
ROMFORD
A127
LAINDON
125
126
127
128
129
HORNCHURCH
UPMINSTER
BULPHAN
ILFORD
DAGENHAM
A13
145
146
147
148
149
RAINHAM
SOUTH OCKENDON
STANFORD-LE-HOPE
AVELEY
WOOLWICH
ERITH
PURFLEET
GRAYS
CHADWELL ST. MARY
165
166
167
168
169
170
171
TILBURY
BEXLEYHEATH
DARTFORD
NORTHFLEET
GRAVESEND
185
186
187
188
189
190
191
SIDCUP
A20
SWANLEY
SOUTH DARENTH
LONGFIELD
M2
205
206
207
208
209
FARNINGHAM
RAMSDEN
M25
MEOPHAM
CHELSFIELD
M20
223
224
225
WEST KINGSDOWN
CULVERSTONE GREEN
DOWNE
M25
OTFORD
KEMSING
WROTHAM
KNOCKHOLT
M26
239
240
241
WEST MALLING
RIVERHEAD
A25
IGHTHAM
SEVENOAKS
256
257
MEREWORTH
WESTERHAM
255
SHIPBOURNE
A21
EAST PECKHAM
MARLPIT HILL
TONBRIDGE
Extent of central map area (see pages 2-25)
COWDEN POUND
LOWER GREEN
ROYAL TUNBRIDGE WELLS

Key to map symbols on pages 28-269

M4 Motorway
Dual A4 Primary route
Dual A40 'A' road
B504 'B' road
Other road / One way street
Toll
Street market
Restricted access road
Pedestrian street
Cycle path
Track / Footpath
Long distance footpath
LC Level crossing
V Vehicle ferry
P Pedestrian ferry
Under construction railway line
County / Borough boundary
Postal district boundary
Main National Rail station
Other National Rail station
London Underground station
Docklands Light Railway station
Tramlink station
Pedestrian ferry landing stage
P Car park
Bus / Coach station
H Heliport
Extent of Central London Congestion Charging Zone

Leisure & tourism
Shopping
Administration & law
Health & welfare
Education
Industry & commerce
Cemetery
Golf course
Public open space / Allotments
Park / Garden / Sports ground
Wood / Forest
Orchard
Built-up area
USA Embassy
Pol Police station
Fire Sta Fire station
PO Post Office
Lib Library
i Tourist information centre
Youth hostel
Tower block
m Historic site
+ Church
Mosque
Synagogue
Windmill

The reference grid on this atlas coincides with the Ordnance Survey National Grid System. The grid interval is 500 metres.

31 Page Continuation Number

11 OS National Grid Kilometre Square

SCALE

0 — 1/4 — 1/2 — 3/4 — 1 mile

0 — 0.25 — 0.5 — 0.75 — 1 — 1.25 — 1.5 kilometres

1:20,000 3.2 inches (8cm) to 1 mile / 5 cm to 1 km

CL
CM
CN
CP
CQ
CR
CS
19
20
21
05
06
07
08
09
10
11
12
13
14
13
12
11
Wheathampstead
Coleman Green
Cromer Hyde
Jersey Farm
AL4
AL6
AL10
LAMER PARK
Lamer Farm
SCRATCHING GROVE
THREEGROVES WOOD
CHERRYTREE SPRING
CONEYDALE SPRING
DOWDELL'S WOOD
FISH WOOD
WARREN WOOD
BLADDER WOOD
Ayot Place
Wheat-hampstead House
CODICOTE ROAD
CORY WRIGHT WAY
LOWER LUTON ROAD
SPORTS GRD
ALLOT
Marford Farm
ROBINSON'S WOOD
AYOT GREENWAY
River Lee or Lea
GRAYS WOOD
Sparrowhall Farm
BOWLE'S WOOD
WATEREND
COWPER'S SPRING
PARK MEAD SPRING
CHARLIES CROFT
MARFORD ROAD
DAVID'S DINGLE
Chalkdell Farm
BLUEBELL HILL WOOD
Flint Bridge
FB
Glasshouse
FLINT BRIDGE PLANTATION
Brocket Hall
Clubhouse
THE BROADWATER
Warren Farm
Devil's Dyke Earthworks
The Slad Earthworks
Samuels Farm
Beech Hyde Farm
BEECH HYDE LANE
COLEMAN GREEN LANE
LAMB'S GROVE
The John Bunyan PH
Meml.
PEARMAN'S SPRING
KENT'S DELL
SPRITE FIELD SPRING
Upper Cromer Hyde Farm
BROCKET PARK
Crooked Chimney PH
CROMER HYDE LANE
FLETCHER'S WICK
BENSTEAD'S WOOD
FURZEFIELD WOOD
WELWYN HATFIELD
ST. ALBANS
Nomansland Farm
DROVERS LANE
WET GROVE
LONG GROVE SPRING
LONG GROVE PLANTATION
Cromerhyde Farm
TITNOL'S WOOD
HAMMOND'S LANE
Hammond's Farm
Symondshyde Farm
DOGS HEART SPRING
CHALKDELL WOOD
SYMONDSHYDE GREAT WOOD
SYMONDSHYDE PICNIC AREA
HAMMOND'S WOOD
HARLOWDELL SPRING
HILL WOOD
FURZE FIELD
University of Hertfordshire Halls of Residence
Prim Sch
WOODCOCK HILL
PET CEM
POLICE SCIENTIFIC DEVELOPMENT BRANCH
Fairfold's Farm
Sutton's Farm
COOPERS GREEN LANE
Astwick Manor Farm
MANOR ROAD
Fielder Centre
College
HATFIELD BUSINESS PARK
Offices
44
SAND AND GRAVEL PIT
HOOK'S WOOD
SLEEVE HALL WOOD
Nashe's Farm

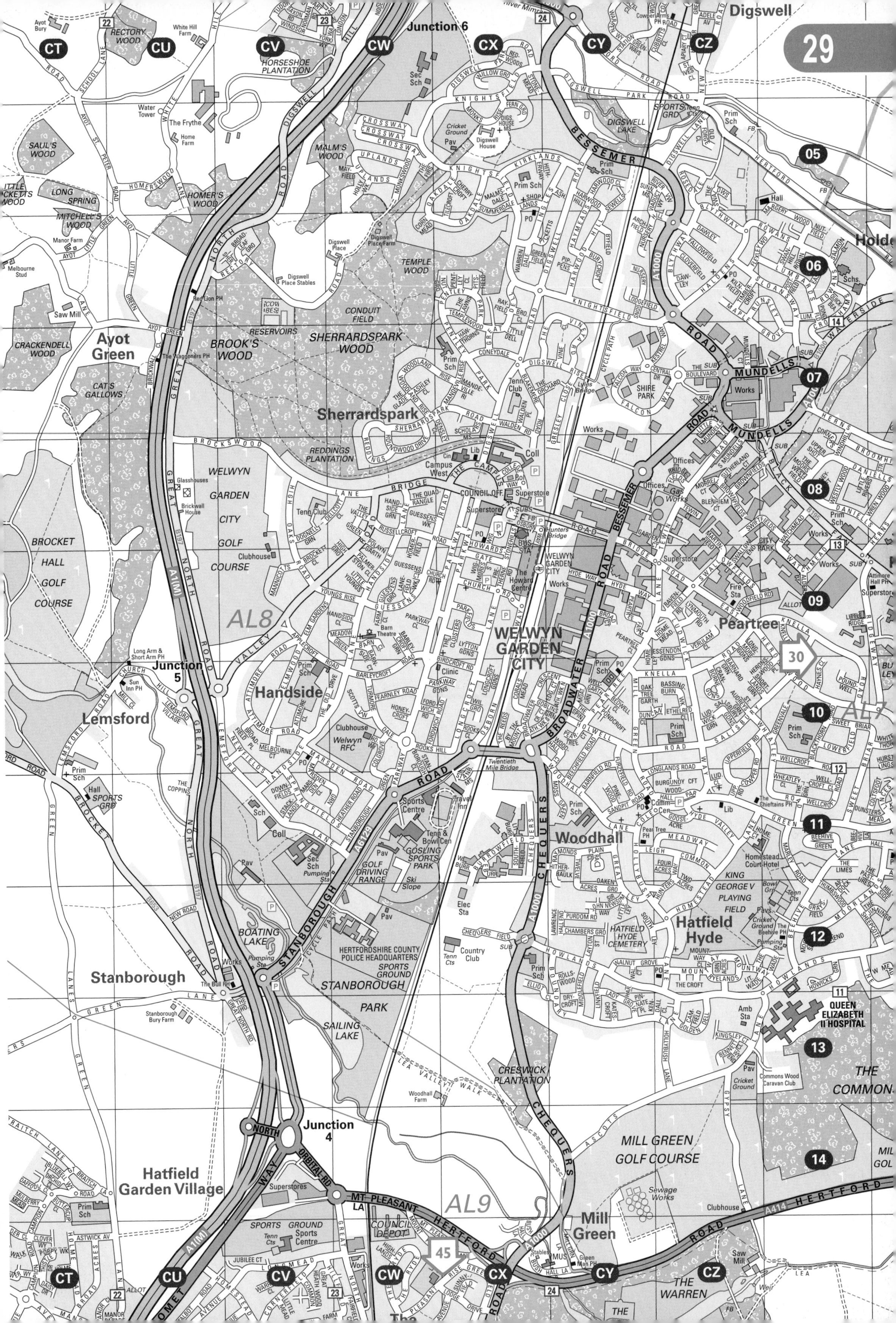
Digswell
Junction 6
Ayot Green
Sherrardspark
SHERRARDSPARK WOOD
BROOK'S WOOD
WELWYN GARDEN CITY GOLF COURSE
BROCKET HALL GOLF COURSE
Handside
Lemsford
Junction 5
WELWYN GARDEN CITY
Peartree
Woodhall
Hatfield Hyde
Stanborough
STANBOROUGH PARK
SAILING LAKE
BOATING LAKE
HERTFORDSHIRE COUNTY POLICE HEADQUARTERS
QUEEN ELIZABETH II HOSPITAL
THE COMMON
MILL GREEN GOLF COURSE
Mill Green
Junction 4
Hatfield Garden Village
THE WARREN
AL8
AL9
AL7
30
45

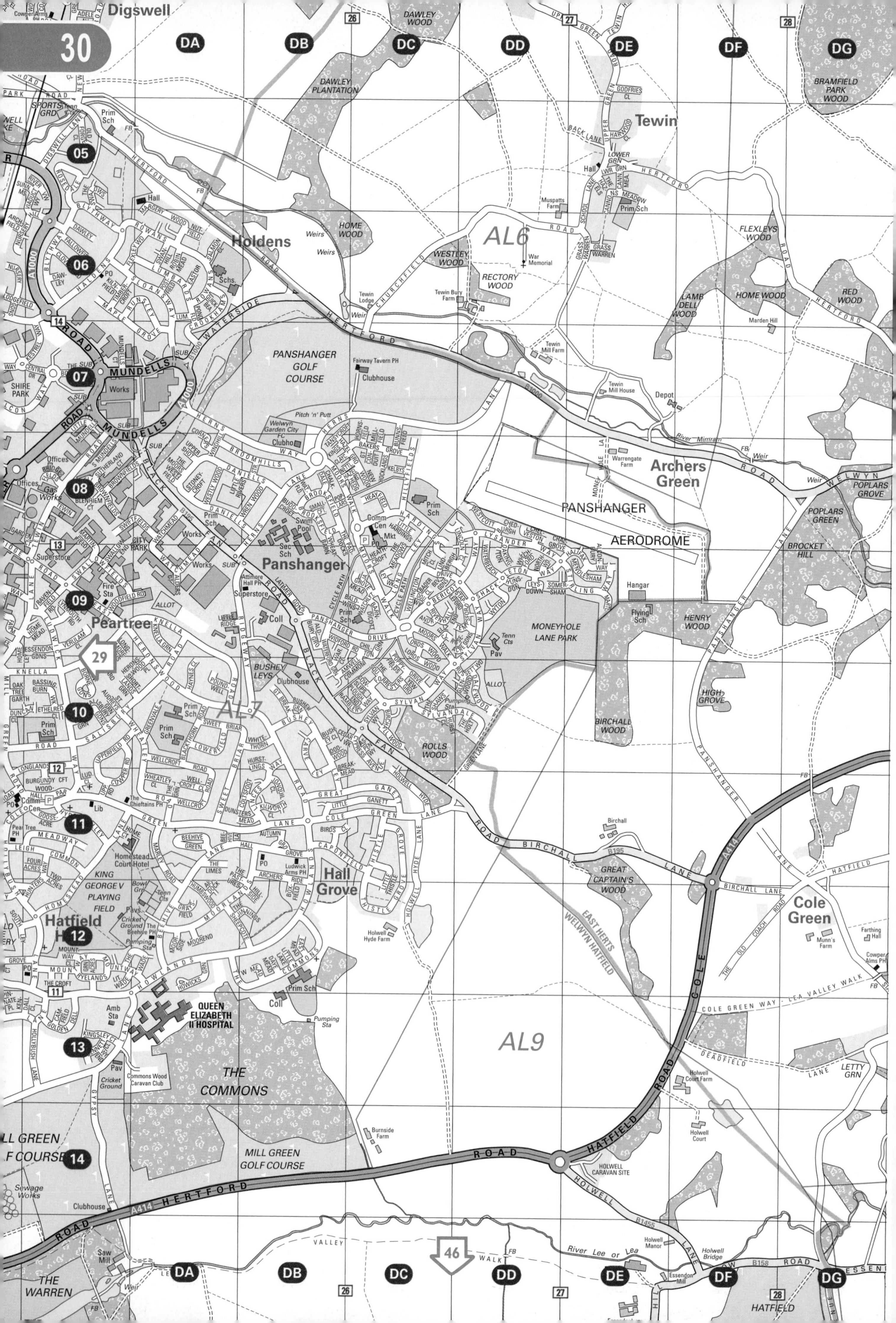

30
Digswell
DA
DB
DC
DD
DE
DF
DG
26
27
28
DAWLEY WOOD
DAWLEY PLANTATION
BRAMFIELD PARK WOOD
Tewin
GODFRIES CL
BACK LANE
UPPER GREEN
LOWER GRN
HERTFORD
Muspatts Farm
Prim Sch
SPORTS GRD
05
06
07
08
09
10
11
12
13
14
Holdens
Weirs
HOME WOOD
AL6
WESTLEY WOOD
RECTORY WOOD
War Memorial
FLEXLEYS WOOD
LAMB DELL WOOD
HOME WOOD
RED WOOD
Marden Hill
Tewin Lodge
Tewin Bury Farm
Tewin Mill Farm
Tewin Mill House
Depot
CHURCHFIELD
WATERSIDE
PANSHANGER GOLF COURSE
Fairway Tavern PH
Clubhouse
Pitch 'n' Putt
MUNDELLS
Works
SHIRE PARK
River Mimram
Warrengate Farm
Archers Green
POPLARS GROVE
POPLARS GREEN
BROCKET HILL
PANSHANGER
AERODROME
Hangar
Flying Sch
HENRY WOOD
MONEYHOLE LANE PARK
Panshanger
Peartree
29
AL7
BUSHEY LEYS
Clubhouse
ROLLS WOOD
BIRCHALL WOOD
HIGH GROVE
Birchall
BIRCHALL LANE
GREAT CAPTAIN'S WOOD
Cole Green
Farthing Hall
Munn's Farm
Cowper Alms PH
THE OLD COACH ROAD
COLE GREEN WAY - LEA VALLEY WALK
EAST HERTS
WELWYN HATFIELD
Hall Grove
Holwell Hyde Farm
KING GEORGE V PLAYING FIELD
Hatfield
QUEEN ELIZABETH II HOSPITAL
Amb Sta
Pumping Sta
Coll
AL9
THE COMMONS
Commons Wood Caravan Club
Cricket Ground
DEADFIELD LANE
LETTY GRN
Holwell Court Farm
Holwell Court
Burnside Farm
MILL GREEN GOLF COURSE
HERTFORD ROAD
A414
HATFIELD ROAD
COLE
HOLWELL CARAVAN SITE
HOLWELL LANE
Sewage Works
Clubhouse
Saw Mill
THE WARREN
46
VALLEY WALK
River Lee or Lea
Holwell Manor
Holwell Bridge
Essendon Mill
B158 ROAD
HATFIELD

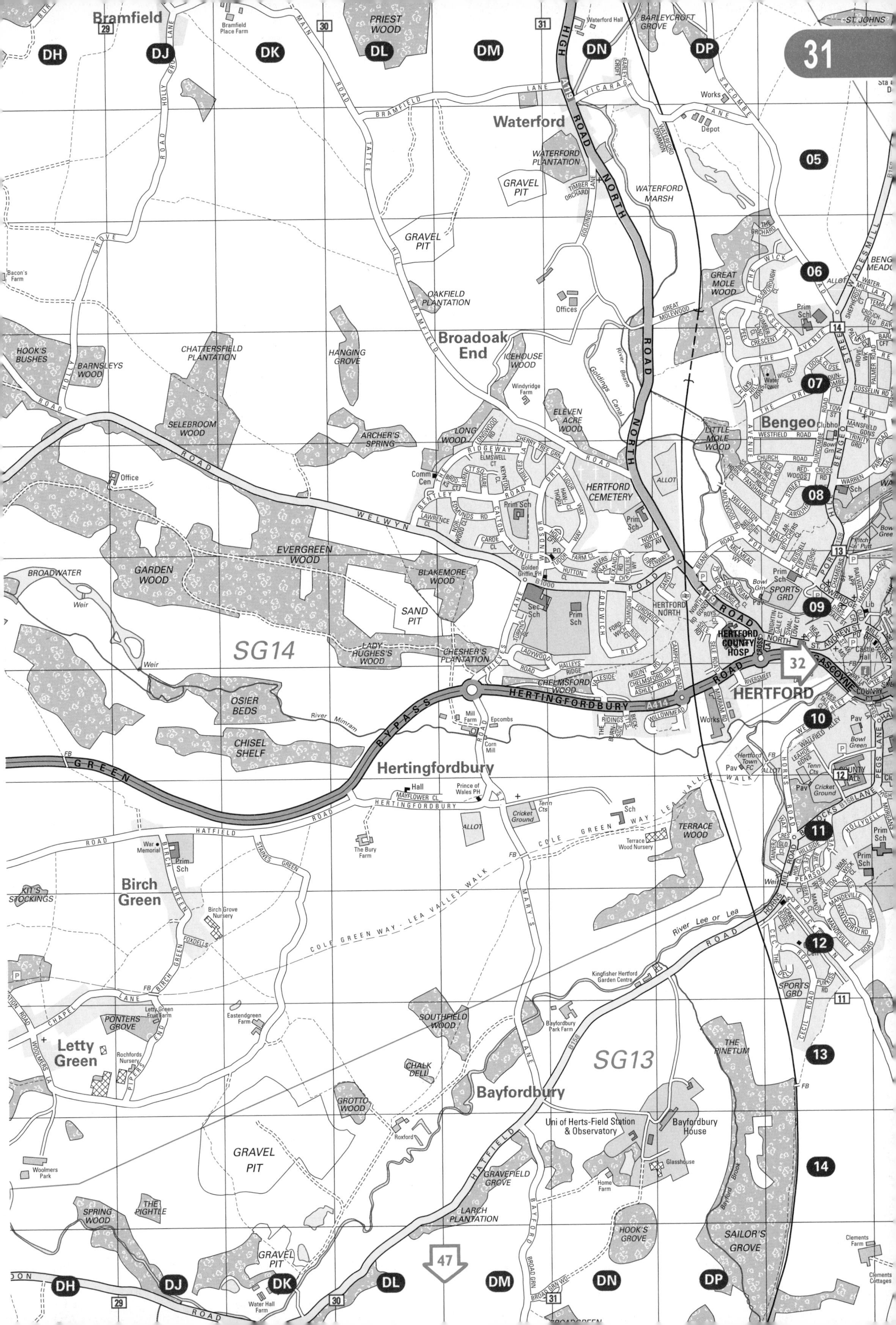
Bramfield
Bramfield Place Farm
PRIEST WOOD
Waterford Hall
BARLEYCROFT GROVE
ST. JOHNS
Waterford
WATERFORD PLANTATION
GRAVEL PIT
WATERFORD MARSH
GRAVEL PIT
Bacon's Farm
GREAT MOLE WOOD
OAKFIELD PLANTATION
Offices
Broadoak End
HOOK'S BUSHES
BARNSLEYS WOOD
CHATTERSFIELD PLANTATION
HANGING GROVE
ICEHOUSE WOOD
Windyridge Farm
ELEVEN ACRE WOOD
Bengeo
LITTLE MOLE WOOD
SELEBROOM WOOD
ARCHER'S SPRING
LONG WOOD
HERTFORD CEMETERY
Office
EVERGREEN WOOD
GARDEN WOOD
BROADWATER
Weir
BLAKEMORE WOOD
SAND PIT
SG14
LADY HUGHES'S WOOD
CHESHER'S PLANTATION
HERTFORD NORTH
HERTFORD COUNTY HOSP
HERTFORD
OSIER BEDS
CHISEL SHELF
Mill Farm
Epcombs
Corn Mill
Hertingfordbury
Hall
Prince of Wales PH
Cricket Ground
TERRACE WOOD
Terrace Wood Nursery
The Bury Farm
War Memorial
Birch Green
KIT'S STOCKINGS
Birch Grove Nursery
COLE GREEN WAY - LEA VALLEY WALK
River Lee or Lea
Kingfisher Hertford Garden Centre
PONTERS GROVE
Letty Green Fruit Farm
Eastendgreen Farm
SOUTHFIELD WOOD
Bayfordbury Park Farm
Letty Green
Rochfords Nursery
CHALK DELL
SG13
THE PINETUM
Bayfordbury
GROTTO WOOD
Uni of Herts-Field Station & Observatory
Bayfordbury House
Roxford
GRAVEL PIT
Glasshouse
Woolmers Park
GRAVEFIELD GROVE
Home Farm
THE PIGHTLE
SPRING WOOD
LARCH PLANTATION
HOOK'S GROVE
SAILOR'S GROVE
Clements Farm
Clements Cottages
GRAVEL PIT
Water Hall Farm
WELWYN ROAD
HERTINGFORDBURY ROAD
HATFIELD ROAD
HIGH ROAD NORTH
COLE GREEN BYPASS
HORNS MILL ROAD
BAYFORD LANE
32
47

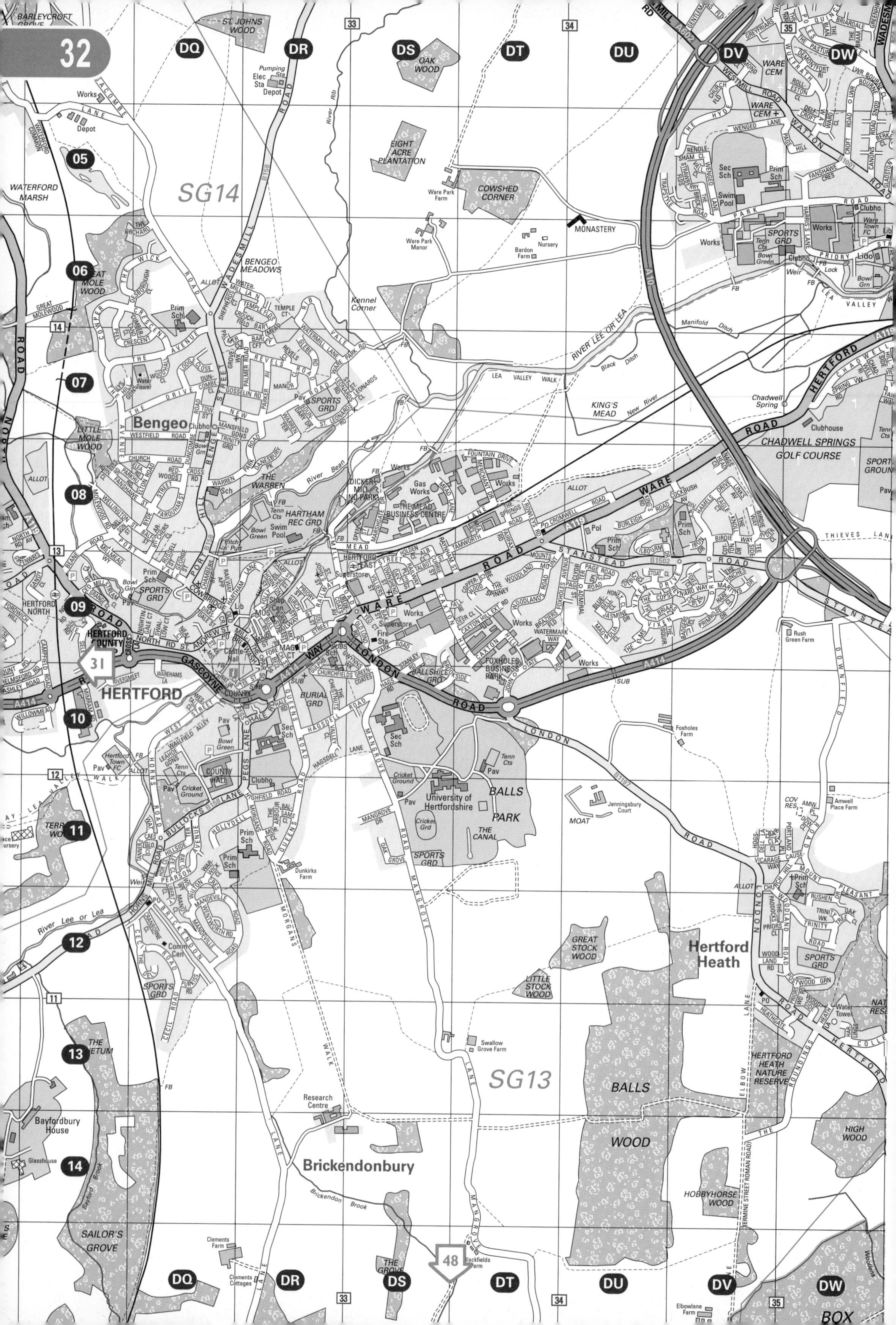
DQ
DR
DS
DT
DU
DV
DW
33
34
35
05
06
07
08
09
10
11
12
13
14
SG14
SG13
ST. JOHNS WOOD
OAK WOOD
EIGHT ACRE PLANTATION
COWSHED CORNER
Ware Park Farm
Ware Park Manor
MONASTERY
Nursery
Bardon Farm
WATERFORD MARSH
Works
Depot
Pumping Sta
Elec Sta
BENGEO MEADOWS
GREAT MOLE WOOD
Kennel Corner
River Rib
River Lee or Lea
Manifold Ditch
Black Ditch
LEA VALLEY WALK
KING'S MEAD
New River
Chadwell Spring
Clubhouse
CHADWELL SPRINGS GOLF COURSE
Bengeo
LITTLE MOLE WOOD
THE WARREN
River Beane
HARTHAM REC GRD
DICKER MILL IND PARK
Gas Works
THE MEAD BUSINESS CENTRE
FOUNTAIN DRIVE
WARE CEM
SPORTS GRD
Lido
HERTFORD NORTH
HERTFORD COUNTY
HERTFORD
Castle Hall
FOXHOLES BUSINESS PARK
BALLSHILL GRD
Superstore
HERTFORD EAST
WARE ROAD
LONDON ROAD
GASCOYNE WAY
STANSTEAD ROAD
HERTFORD ROAD
NORTH ROAD
Rush Green Farm
Foxholes Farm
University of Hertfordshire
BALLS PARK
THE CANAL
Cricket Ground
COUNTY HALL
BURIAL GRD
Hertford Town FC
Jenningsbury Court
MOAT
Amwell Place Farm
Dunkirks Farm
GREAT STOCK WOOD
LITTLE STOCK WOOD
Hertford Heath
HERTFORD HEATH NATURE RESERVE
Swallow Grove Farm
BALLS WOOD
HIGH WOOD
HOBBYHORSE WOOD
ERMINE STREET ROMAN ROAD
Research Centre
Brickendonbury
Brickendon Brook
Bayfordbury House
Glasshouse
Bayford Brook
SAILOR'S GROVE
Clements Farm
Clements Cottages
THE GROVE
Blackfields Farm
Elbowlane Farm
BOX
31
48

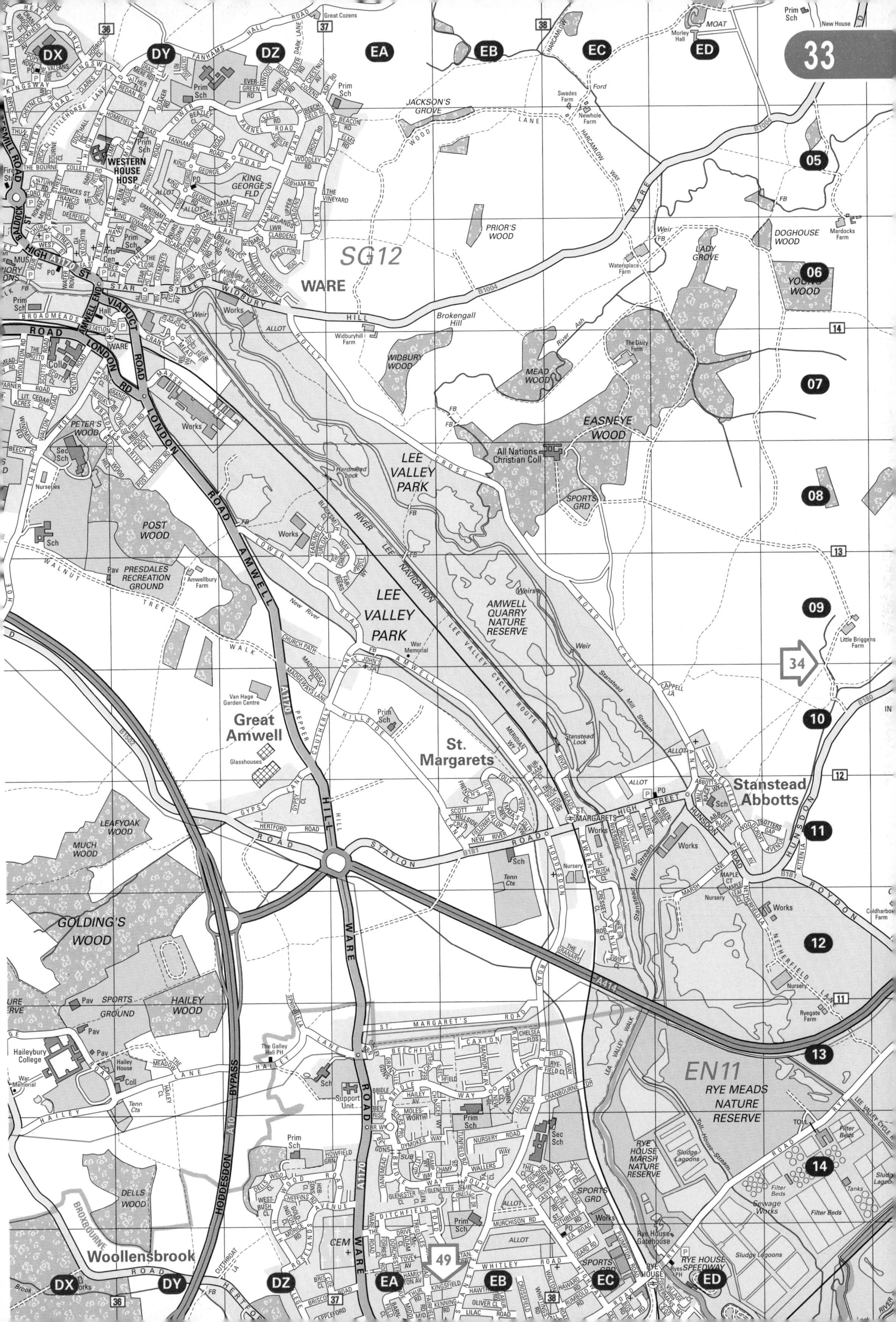
WARE
SG12
WESTERN HOUSE HOSP
KING GEORGE'S FLD
LEE VALLEY PARK
AMWELL QUARRY NATURE RESERVE
EASNEYE WOOD
All Nations Christian Coll
Great Amwell
St. Margarets
Stanstead Abbotts
EN11
RYE MEADS NATURE RESERVE
RYE HOUSE MARSH NATURE RESERVE
Haileybury College
Woollensbrook
GOLDING'S WOOD
HAILEY WOOD
DELLS WOOD
POST WOOD
PRESDALES RECREATION GROUND
WIDBURY WOOD
MEAD WOOD
PRIOR'S WOOD
JACKSON'S GROVE
LADY GROVE
DOGHOUSE WOOD
YOUNG WOOD
LEAFYOAK WOOD
MUCH WOOD
RYE HOUSE SPEEDWAY
34
49

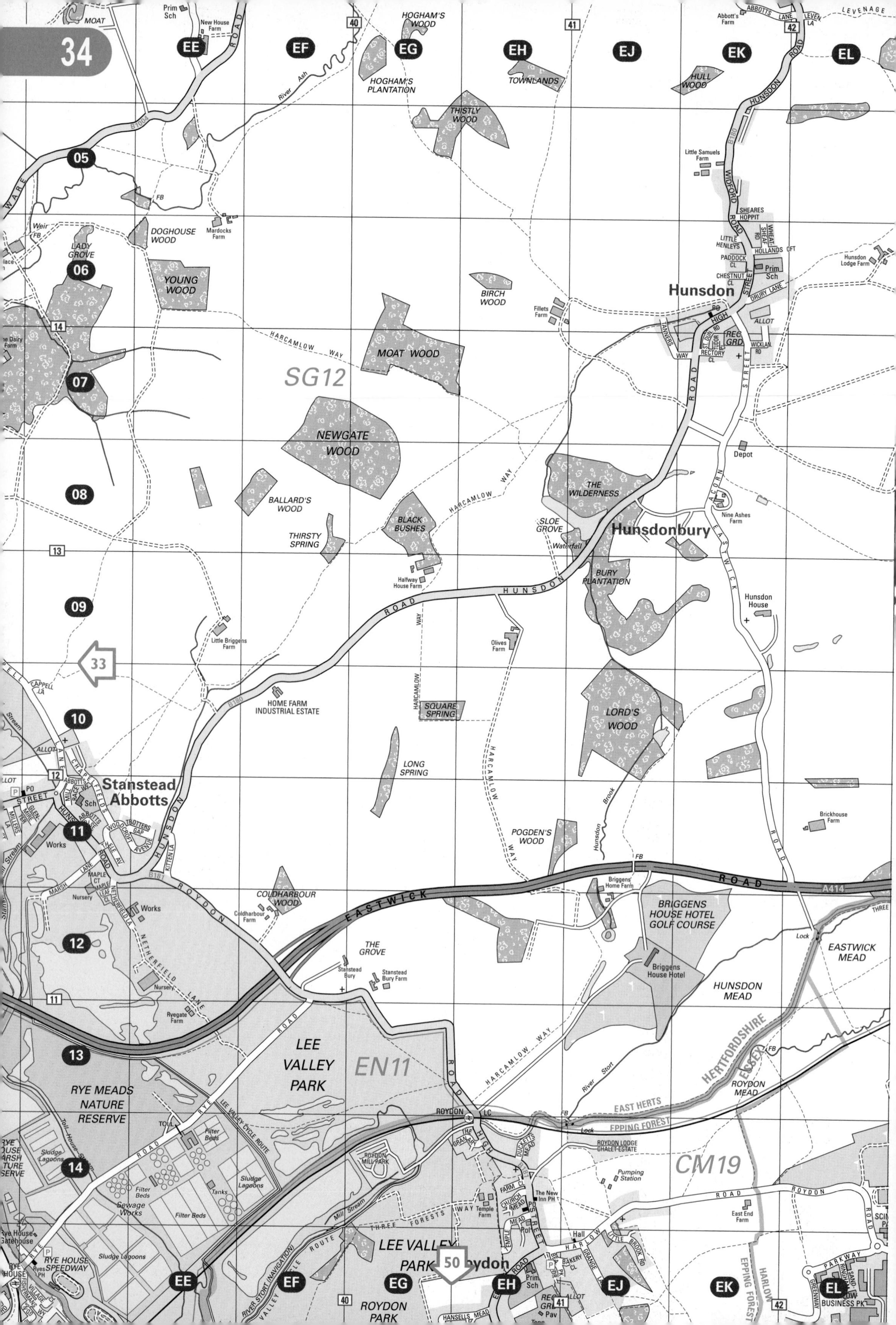
MOAT
Prim Sch
New House Farm
EE
EF
EG
EH
EJ
EK
EL
40
41
42
HOGHAM'S WOOD
HOGHAM'S PLANTATION
TOWNLANDS
Abbott's Farm
ABBOTTS LANE
LEVEN LA
LEVENAGE
HULL WOOD
River Ash
B1004
THISTLY WOOD
HUNSDON ROAD
05
WARE
FB
Weir
Little Samuels Farm
WIDFORD ROAD
B180
DOGHOUSE WOOD
Mardocks Farm
LADY GROVE
06
SHEARES HOPPIT
LITTLE HENLEYS
WHEAT SHEAF RD
HOLLANDS CFT
PADDOCK CL
CHESTNUT CL
Prim Sch
Hunsdon Lodge Farm
YOUNG WOOD
BIRCH WOOD
Hunsdon
DRURY LANE
Fillets Farm
PO
HIGH STREET
14
HARCAMLOW WAY
TANNERS WAY
ST DUNSTANS
TUDOR CL
RECTORY CL
REC GRD
ALLOT
WICKLANDS RD
MOAT WOOD
SG12
07
NEWGATE WOOD
Depot
ACORN STREET
HARCAMLOW WAY
THE WILDERNESS
BALLARD'S WOOD
BLACK BUSHES
Nine Ashes Farm
08
SLOE GROVE
Waterfall
Hunsdonbury
THIRSTY SPRING
13
Halfway House Farm
BURY PLANTATION
EASTWICK
HUNSDON ROAD
09
Hunsdon House
Little Briggens Farm
Olives Farm
33
CAPPELL LA
HARCAMLOW WAY
HOME FARM INDUSTRIAL ESTATE
SQUARE SPRING
LORD'S WOOD
Stream
10
ALLOT
12
LONG SPRING
Stanstead Abbotts
PO
STREET
Sch
HARCAMLOW WAY
Hunsdon Brook
Brickhouse Farm
POGDEN'S WOOD
11
Works
TROTTERS GAP
WOODCROFT AVENUE
HUNSDON ROAD
KITTEN LA
B181
ROAD
FB
Briggens Home Farm
EASTWICK ROAD
A414
MAPLE CT
Nursery
Works
COUDHARBOUR WOOD
Coldharbour Farm
BRIGGENS HOUSE HOTEL GOLF COURSE
THREE
Lock
EASTWICK MEAD
NETHERFIELD LANE
THE GROVE
12
Stanstead Bury
Stanstead Bury Farm
Briggens House Hotel
HUNSDON MEAD
Nursery
11
Ryegate Farm
LEE VALLEY PARK
EN11
HERTFORDSHIRE
ESSEX
13
HARCAMLOW WAY
FB
ROYDON MEAD
River Stort
RYE MEADS NATURE RESERVE
EAST HERTS
ROYDON
LC
FB
Lock
EPPING FOREST
TOLL
Filter Beds
LEE VALLEY CYCLE ROUTE
ROYDON MILL PARK
ROYDON LODGE CHALET ESTATE
CM19
Sludge Lagoons
Toll House Stream
14
Filter Beds
Sludge Lagoons
Tanks
Pumping Station
Sewage Works
Filter Beds
FARM CL
CHURCH MEAD
The New Inn PH
ROYDON ROAD
Temple Farm
East End Farm
Mill Stream
THREE FORESTS WAY
Rye House Gatehouse
Hall
HARLOW ROAD
LITTLE BROOK RD
RYE HOUSE SPEEDWAY
Sludge Lagoons
LEE VALLEY PARK
50
Roydon
Rye House PH
EE
EF
EG
EH
EJ
EK
EL
Prim Sch
BAKERY CL
GRANGE LA
HARLOW
EPPING FOREST
PARKWAY
GREENWAY
BUSINESS PK
42
40
41
ROYDON PARK
RIVER STORT (NAVIGATION)
HANSELLS MEAD
ALLOT
Pav

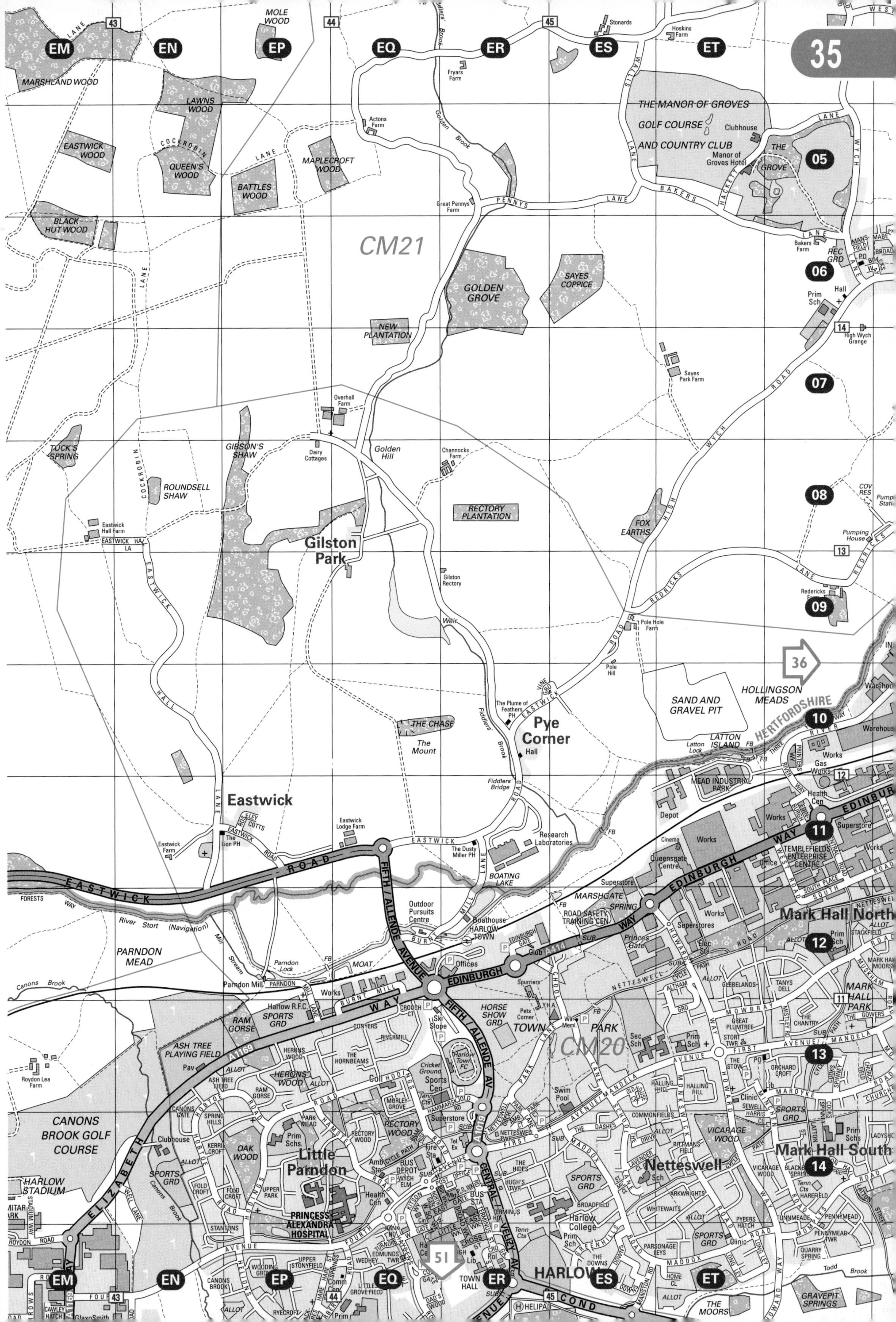
EM
EN
EP
EQ
ER
ES
ET
43
44
45
MARSHLAND WOOD
MOLE WOOD
LAWNS WOOD
EASTWICK WOOD
QUEEN'S WOOD
BATTLES WOOD
MAPLECROFT WOOD
BLACK HUT WOOD
Stonards
Hoskins Farm
Fryars Farm
Actons Farm
Golden Brook
THE MANOR OF GROVES GOLF COURSE AND COUNTRY CLUB
Clubhouse
Manor of Groves Hotel
THE GROVE
05
06
07
08
09
10
11
12
13
14
Great Pennys Farm
PENNYS LANE
BAKERS LANE
Bakers Farm
REC GRD
CM21
GOLDEN GROVE
SAYES COPPICE
NEW PLANTATION
Prim Sch
Hall
High Wych Grange
Sayes Park Farm
Overhall Farm
Dairy Cottages
Golden Hill
Channocks Farm
TUCK'S SPRING
GIBSON'S SHAW
ROUNDSELL SHAW
RECTORY PLANTATION
FOX EARTHS
Eastwick Hall Farm
Gilston Park
Gilston Rectory
Pumping House
Redericks Farm
Pole Hole Farm
Weir
Pole Hill
36
HOLLINGSON MEADS
SAND AND GRAVEL PIT
HERTFORDSHIRE
The Plume of Feathers PH
Pye Corner
Hall
THE CHASE
The Mount
Fiddlers' Bridge
Latton Lock
LATTON ISLAND
MEAD INDUSTRIAL PARK
Eastwick
Eastwick Lodge Farm
Research Laboratories
The Dusty Miller PH
BOATING LAKE
Eastwick Farm
The Lion PH
EASTWICK ROAD
FORESTS WAY
River Stort (Navigation)
Outdoor Pursuits Centre
Boathouse HARLOW TOWN
PARNDON MEAD
Parndon Lock
Parndon Mill
Canons Brook
MARSHGATE SPRING
ROAD SAFETY TRAINING CEN
EDINBURGH WAY
Princes Gate
Queensgate Centre
Cinema
Works
Depot
Superstore
TEMPLEFIELDS ENTERPRISE CENTRE
Mark Hall North
FIFTH / ALLENDE AVENUE
Harlow R.F.C.
SPORTS GRD
RAM GORSE
ASH TREE PLAYING FIELD
Roydon Lea Farm
HERONS WOOD
HORSE SHOW GRD
TOWN PARK
CM20
Sec Sch
Prim Sch
MARK HALL PARK
CANONS BROOK GOLF COURSE
Clubhouse
HARLOW STADIUM
OAK WOOD
Little Parndon
RECTORY WOOD
PRINCESS ALEXANDRA HOSPITAL
Netteswell
VICARAGE WOOD
Mark Hall South
SPORTS GRD
Harlow College
51
TOWN HALL
HARLOW
HELIPAD
THE MOORS
GRAVEPIT SPRINGS
ELIZABETH WAY
A1169
A414
A1019
FIRST AVENUE
SECOND AVENUE
HOWARD WAY
MANDELA AVENUE

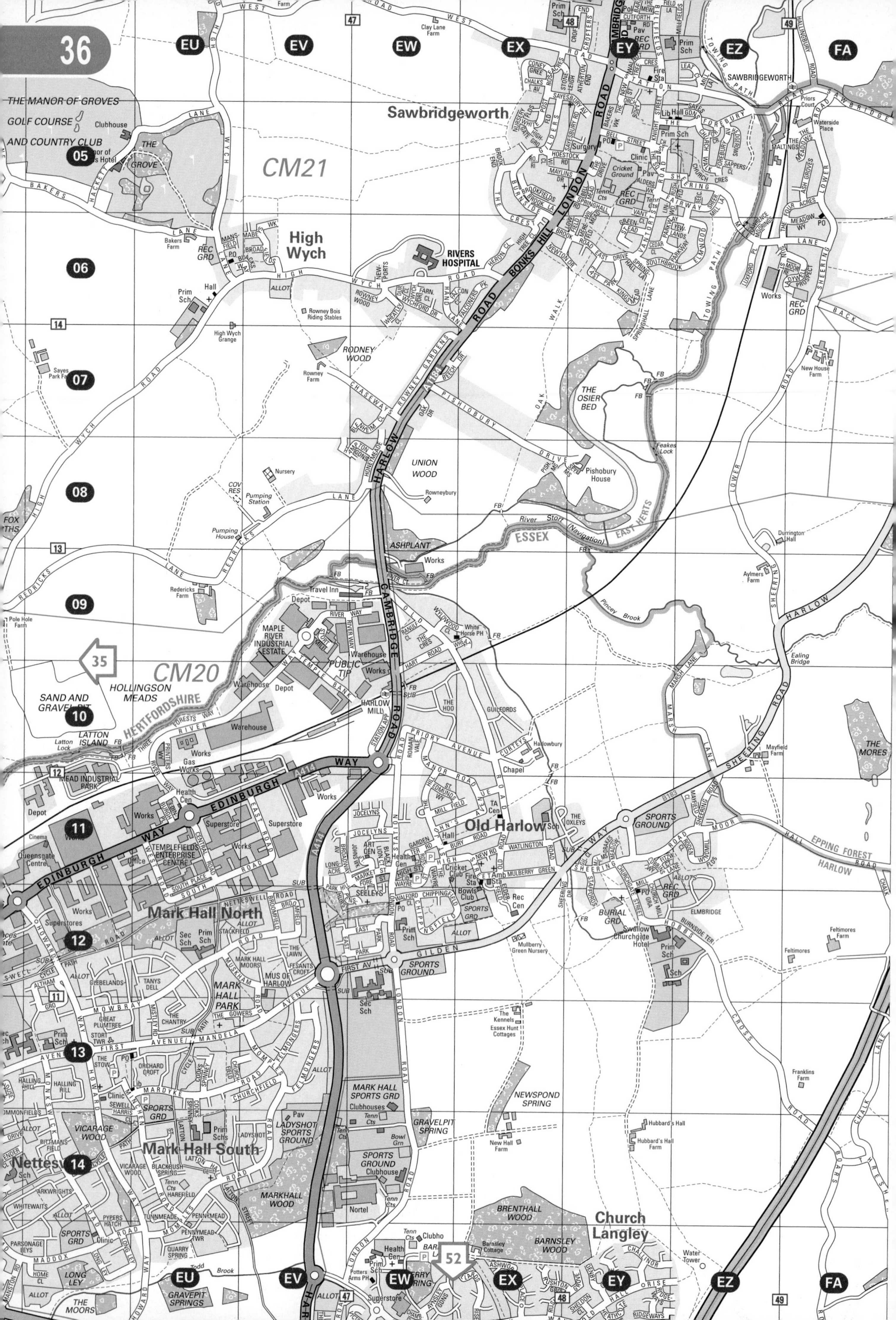
EU
EV
EW
EX
EY
EZ
FA
05
06
07
08
09
10
11
12
13
14
Sawbridgeworth
High Wych
CM21
CM20
THE MANOR OF GROVES GOLF COURSE AND COUNTRY CLUB
Clubhouse
THE GROVE
RIVERS HOSPITAL
Rowney Bois Riding Stables
RODNEY WOOD
Rowney Farm
High Wych Grange
Sayes Park Farm
UNION WOOD
Rowneybury
Nursery
Pumping Station
Pumping House
THE OSIER BED
Pishobury House
Feakes Lock
River Stort (Navigation)
ESSEX
EAST HERTS
HERTFORDSHIRE
ASHPLANT
Works
Travel Inn
Depot
MAPLE RIVER INDUSTRIAL ESTATE
PUBLIC TIP
Warehouse
HARLOW MILL
HOLLINGSON MEADS
SAND AND GRAVEL PIT
LATTON ISLAND
Latton Lock
Redericks Farm
Pole Hole Farm
Pincey Brook
Durrington Hall
Aylmers Farm
Ealing Bridge
Mayfield Farm
THE MORES
Hallowbury
Chapel
MEAD INDUSTRIAL PARK
Gas Works
Health Cen
Superstore
Queensgate Centre
Cinema
TEMPLEFIELDS ENTERPRISE CENTRE
Office
Old Harlow
SPORTS GROUND
EPPING FOREST
HARLOW
BURIAL GRD
Swallow Churchgate Hotel
ELMBRIDGE
Feltimores Farm
Feltimores
Mulberry Green Nursery
Mark Hall North
MARK HALL PARK
MUS OF HARLOW
SPORTS GROUND
The Kennels
Essex Hunt Cottages
NEWSPOND SPRING
MARK HALL SPORTS GRD
Clubhouses
LADYSHOT SPORTS GROUND
GRAVELPIT SPRING
New Hall Farm
Hubbard's Hall
Hubbard's Hall Farm
Franklins Farm
Mark Hall South
VICARAGE WOOD
Netteswell
MARKHALL WOOD
Nortel
BRENTHALL WOOD
BARNSLEY WOOD
Barnsley Cottage
Church Langley
Water Tower
LONG LEY
THE MOORS
GRAVEPIT SPRINGS
Todd Brook
Potters Arms PH
Superstore
EDINBURGH WAY
CAMBRIDGE ROAD
LONDON ROAD
HARLOW ROAD
BONKS HILL
HIGH WYCH ROAD
SHEERING ROAD
GILDEN WAY
A1184
A414
B183
47
48
49
14
13
12
11
35
52

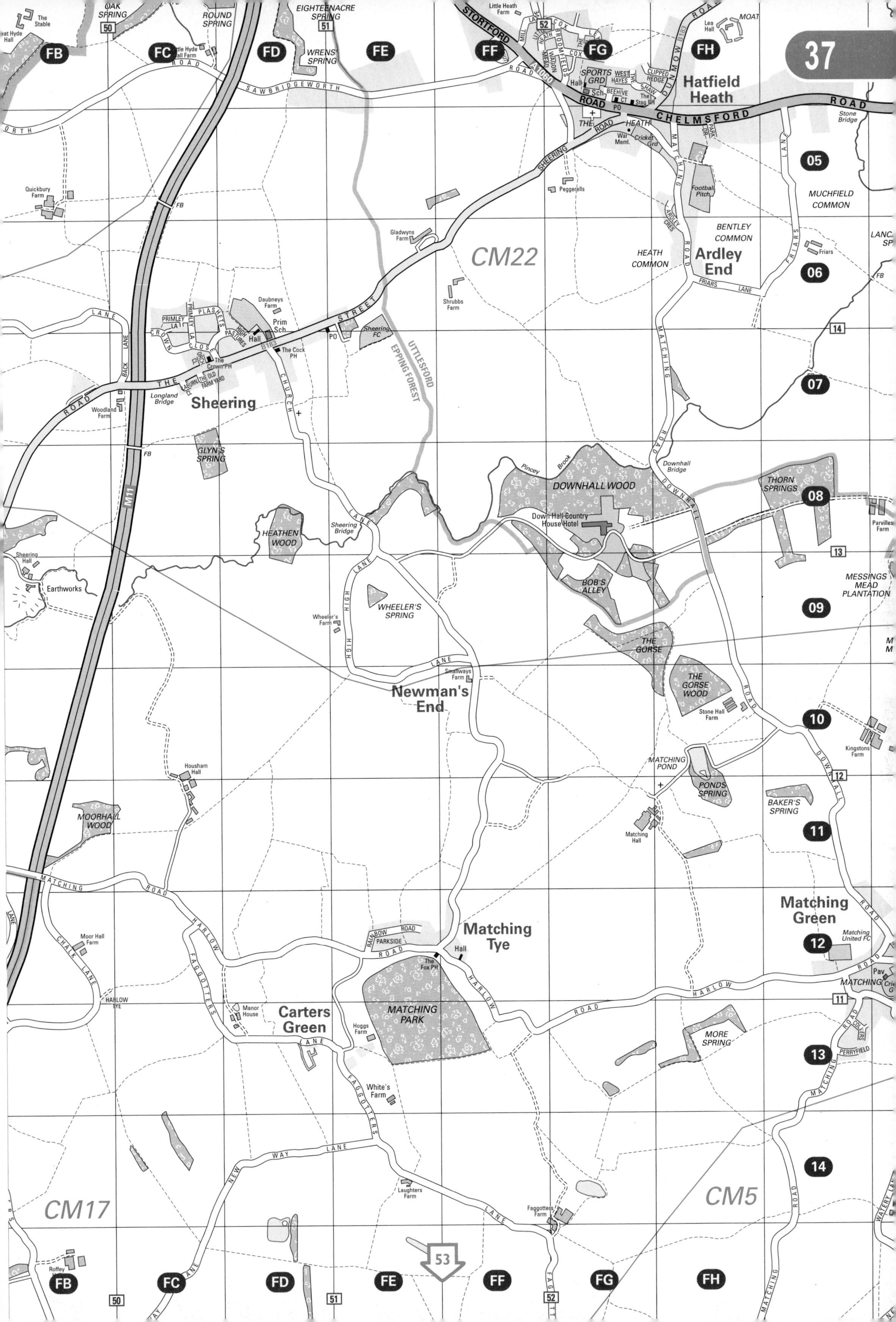
Hatfield Heath
Ardley End
Sheering
Newman's End
Matching Tye
Matching Green
Carters Green
CM22
CM17
CM5
OAK SPRING
ROUND SPRING
EIGHTEENACRE SPRING
WRENS' SPRING
Little Heath Farm
MOAT
Lea Hall
The Stable
Quickbury Farm
Gladwyns Farm
Daubneys Farm
Shrubbs Farm
Peggerells
MUCHFIELD COMMON
BENTLEY COMMON
HEATH COMMON
Friars
Stone Bridge
SAWBRIDGEWORTH ROAD
CHELMSFORD ROAD
STORTFORD ROAD
SHEERING ROAD
THE STREET
CHURCH LANE
HIGH LANE
MATCHING ROAD
DOWNHALL ROAD
FRIARS LANE
HARLOW ROAD
FAGGOTTERS LANE
NEW WAY LANE
CHALK LANE
BACK LANE
UTTLESFORD
EPPING FOREST
Sheering FC
The Cock PH
The Crown PH
Longland Bridge
Woodland Farm
GLYN'S SPRING
HEATHEN WOOD
Sheering Bridge
Sheering Hall
Earthworks
WHEELER'S SPRING
Wheeler's Farm
Smallways Farm
DOWNHALL WOOD
Down Hall Country House Hotel
Downhall Bridge
Pincey Brook
BOB'S ALLEY
THE GORSE
THE GORSE WOOD
Stone Hall Farm
THORN SPRINGS
Parvilles Farm
MESSINGS MEAD PLANTATION
Kingstons Farm
MATCHING POND
PONDS SPRING
BAKER'S SPRING
Matching Hall
Housham Hall
MOORHALL WOOD
Moor Hall Farm
HARLOW TYE
Manor House
MATCHING PARK
Hoggs Farm
The Fox PH
Hall
RAINBOW ROAD
PARKSIDE
White's Farm
MORE SPRING
Matching United FC
Laughters Farm
Faggotters Farm
Roffey
PERRYFIELD
FB
FC
FD
FE
FF
FG
FH
05
06
07
08
09
10
11
12
13
14
50
51
52
53
M11

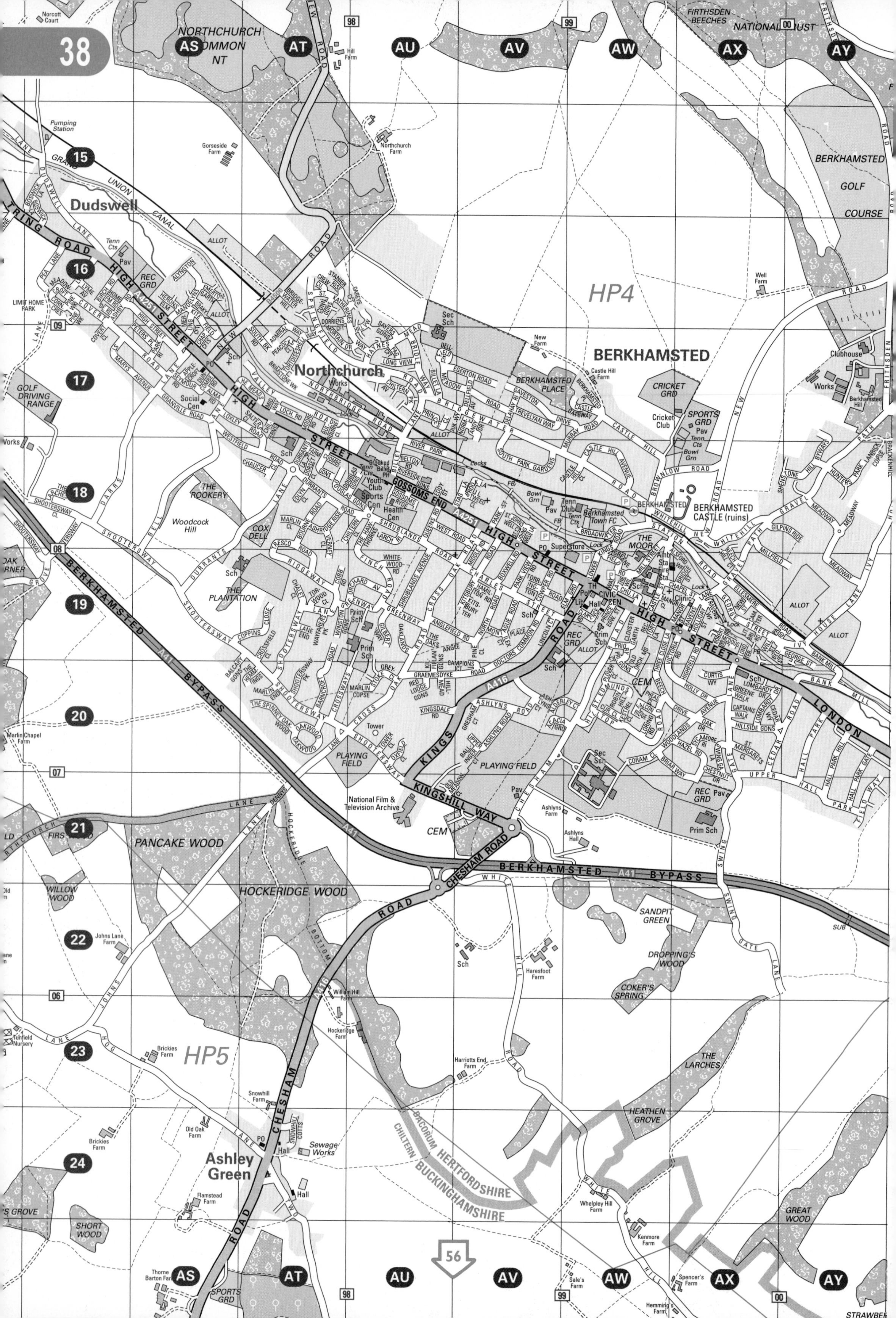
AS
AT
AU
AV
AW
AX
AY
98
99
00
Norcott Court
NORTHCHURCH COMMON NT
NEW ROAD
Hill Farm
FIRTHSDEN BEECHES
NATIONAL TRUST
FRITHSDEN
Pumping Station
Gorseside Farm
Northchurch Farm
BERKHAMSTED GOLF COURSE
15
16
17
18
19
20
21
22
23
24
09
08
07
06
GRAND UNION CANAL
Dudswell
DUDSWELL LANE
TRING ROAD
HIGH STREET
A4251
ALLOT
Tenn Cts
Pav
REC GRD
LIMIT HOME PARK
HP4
Well Farm
ROAD
Sec Sch
New Farm
BERKHAMSTED
Castle Hill Farm
BERKHAMSTED PLACE
CRICKET GRD
Cricket Club
SPORTS GRD
Clubhouse
Works
Berkhamsted Hill
Northchurch
GOLF DRIVING RANGE
Works
Social Cen
PO
Sch
GRANVILLE ROAD
WESTFIELD
LOXLEY
NEW ROAD
SOUTH BANK ROAD
BRIDGEWATER ROAD
Locks
BROWNLOW ROAD
BERKHAMSTED
BERKHAMSTED CASTLE (ruins)
CASTLE HILL
SOUTH PARK GARDENS
Bowl Grn
Tenn Club
Berkhamsted Town FC
THE MOOR
Superstore
Lock
GOSSOMS END
Youth Club
Sports Cen
Health Cen
Crooked Billet PH
RIVER PARK
THE ROOKERY
Woodcock Hill
COX DELL
SHOOTERSWAY
DURRANTS
THE PLANTATION
Sch
BERKHAMSTED A41 BY-PASS
CHAUCER
FINCH ROAD
SHRUBLANDS AVENUE
CROSS OAK ROAD
GREENWAY
Prim Sch
ANGLEFIELD RD
DOCTORS COMMON RD
KINGS ROAD
A416
TH
Lib
CIVIC CEN
Hall
Prim Sch
REC GRD
ALLOT
CEM
Sch
Clinic
HIGH STREET
LONDON ROAD
GEORGE ST
BANK MILL
ALLOT
IVY HOUSE LANE
MEADWAY
GRAVEL PATH
UPPER HALL PARK
HALL PARK
SWING GATE LANE
REC GRD
Prim Sch
Pav
Sec Sch
Ashlyns Farm
Ashlyns Hall
ASHLYNS ROAD
PLAYING FIELD
PLAYING FIELD
Tower
National Film & Television Archive
KINGSHILL WAY
CEM
CHESHAM ROAD
Marlin Chapel Farm
FIRS WOOD
PANCAKE WOOD
HOCKERIDGE WOOD
HOCKERIDGE BOTTOM
WILLOW WOOD
Johns Lane Farm
JOHNS LANE
HOG LANE
Tunfield Nursery
SANDPIT GREEN
DROPPING'S WOOD
COKER'S SPRING
SUB
Sch
Haresfoot Farm
WHITE HILL
William Hill Farm
Hockeridge Farm
Brickies Farm
HP5
Harriotts End Farm
THE LARCHES
HEATHEN GROVE
Snowhill Farm
Old Oak Farm
Brickies Farm
Sewage Works
DACORUM HERTFORDSHIRE
CHILTERN BUCKINGHAMSHIRE
Ashley Green
Hall
Hall
Flamstead Farm
SHORT WOOD
Whelpley Hill Farm
Kenmore Farm
GREAT WOOD
56
Thorne Barton Farm
SPORTS GRD
Sale's Farm
Spencer's Farm
Hemming's Farm
STRAWBERRY

AZ
BA
BB
BC
BD
BE
BF
01
02
03
09
08
07
06
15
16
17
18
19
20
21
22
23
24
40
57
HIGHPARK WOOD
Roman Farm
Nettleden Farm
NETTLEDEN ROAD
LEIGHTON
RED LION
The Red Lion PH
A4146
Grist House Farm
Watercress Beds
Gaddesden Hall
Fish Farm
Piccotts Garden Ce
FISH PONDS
GREAT FRITHDEN COPSE
NATIONAL TRUST
LITTLE FRITHSDEN COPSE
Hollybush Farm
FRITHSDEN VINES
Alford Arms PH
Crossways Farm
HERDIN'S WOOD
Strathgade Farm
HILL END ROAD
Bingham's Park Farm
Poultry Farm
BROWN'S SPRING WOOD
HOLLYBUSH WOOD
POTTEN END HILL
Rumblers Farm
Woodcroft Farm
Potten End Farm
CATSTAIL WOOD
War Memorial
BERKHAMSTED
GOLF COURSE
Grims Ditch
Potten End
DELL WOOD
SPORTS GRD
Pav
THE SQUARE
RAMBLING WAY
Martins Pond PH
HEMPSTEAD LANE
Boxted Farm
WARNERS END WOOD
COV RES
Pav
Bowling Green
BERKHAMSTED LANE
Little Heath Park
Tenn Ct
Gutteridge Farm
GUTTERIDGE WOOD
LITTLE HEATH NT
BULLBEGGARS LANE
Little Heath Farm
Boxted Pig Farm
FIELDS END LANE
POUCHEN END LANE
Gadebridge
SPORTS GROUND
Little Heath Great Farm
Lower Little Heath Farm
Fields End Farm
Warners End
WARNERS END VALLEY
BULLBEGGAR'S WOOD
HP1
Hamm
SHRUB HILL COMMON
NORTHRIDGE PARK
Chaulden
Berkhamsted Sewage Works
GRAND
River Bulbourne
A4251
Broadway Farm
LONDON ROAD
Pouchen End Hall
Pouchen End Farm
Pix Farm
PIX FARM LANE
CHAULDEN LANE
CANAL
The Three Horseshoes PH
CHAULDEN LANE PLAYING FIELD
Rugby Ground
Watercress Beds
Watermill Hotel
White Horse PH
Bourne End Farm
Bourne End
SUGAR LANE
A41
BOURNE END MILLS
KINGS LANGLEY BYPASS
BOXMOOR COMMON
HEATH PARK
Moorend Farm
HEMEL HEMPSTEAD
Lower Farm
Travel Inn
BERKHAMSTED BYPASS
STONEY LANE
Vale Farm
GREEN CROFT
HAY WOOD
Prep. Sch
ROUGHDOWN COMMON
HANGING WOOD
Clubhouse
LITTLE HAY GOLF COMPLEX
HP3
BOXMOOR GOLF CLUB
Felden
COLESHILL WOOD
SHEETHANGER COMMON
Felden Lodge
Howe's Retreat
RAMACRE WOOD
BURY WOOD
Tower Farm
Felden Grange
Felden Manor
Longcroft Farm
COVERED RESERVOIR

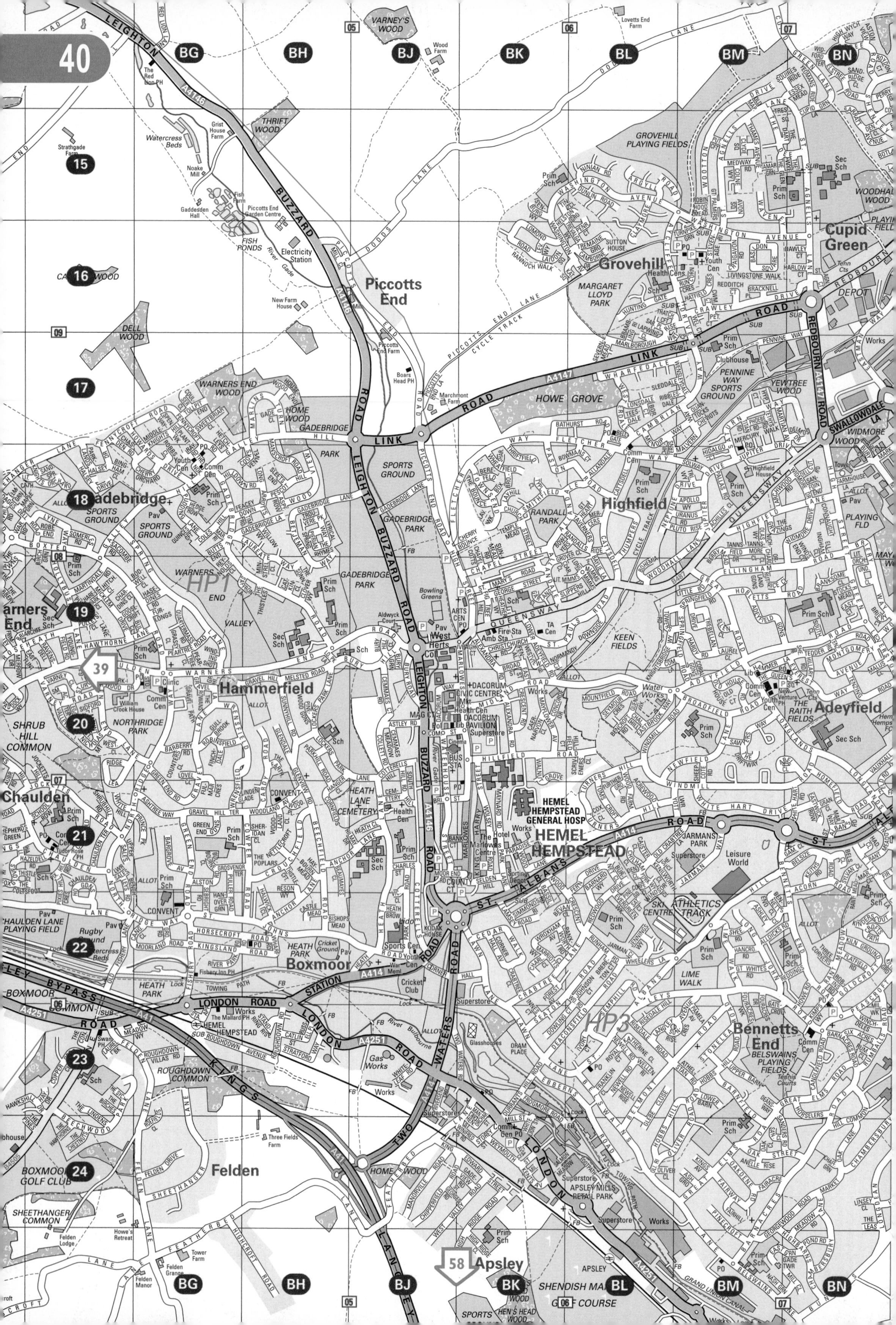

BG
BH
BJ
BK
BL
BM
BN
05
06
07
15
16
17
18
19
20
21
22
23
24
09
08
LEIGHTON BUZZARD ROAD
A4146
THRIFT WOOD
Watercress Beds
Grist House Farm
The Red Lion PH
Strathgade Farm
Noake Mill
Gaddesden Hall
Fish Farm
Piccotts End Garden Centre
FISH PONDS
River Gade
Electricity Station
New Farm House
DELL WOOD
VARNEY'S WOOD
Wood Farm
Lovetts End Farm
Piccotts End
Piccotts End Farm
Boars Head PH
Marchmont Farm
PICCOTTS END LANE
CYCLE TRACK
LINK ROAD
A4147
HOWE GROVE
GROVEHILL PLAYING FIELDS
Grovehill
MARGARET LLOYD PARK
Cupid Green
WOODHALL WOOD
DEPOT
REDBOURN ROAD
A4147
YEWTREE WOOD
PENNINE WAY SPORTS GROUND
SWALLOWDALE LA
WIDMORE WOOD
WARNERS END WOOD
HOME WOOD
GADEBRIDGE HILL
Gadebridge
SPORTS GROUND
GADEBRIDGE PARK
SPORTS GROUND
Highfield
RANDALL PARK
PLAYING FLD
HP1
WARNERS END VALLEY
Warners End
QUEENSWAY
KEEN FIELDS
Adeyfield
THE RAITH FIELDS
Hammerfield
DACORUM CIVIC CENTRE
DACORUM PAVILION
West Herts Col
SHRUB HILL COMMON
NORTHRIDGE PARK
Chaulden
HEATH LANE CEMETERY
HEMEL HEMPSTEAD GENERAL HOSP
HEMEL HEMPSTEAD
ST ALBANS ROAD
A414
Leisure World
SKI CENTRE
ATHLETICS TRACK
LIME WALK
Rugby Ground
CHAULDEN LANE PLAYING FIELD
HEATH PARK
Boxmoor
Cricket Club
STATION ROAD
LONDON ROAD
A4251
A41
BOXMOOR COMMON
ROUGHDOWN COMMON
HP3
TWO WATERS ROAD
River Bulbourne
Gas Works
Bennetts End
BELSWAINS PLAYING FIELDS
Felden
BOXMOOR GOLF CLUB
SHEETHANGER COMMON
Felden Lodge
Howe's Retreat
Tower Farm
Felden Grange
Felden Manor
Three Fields Farm
HOME WOOD
APSLEY MILLS RETAIL PARK
Apsley
SHENDISH MANOR GOLF COURSE
GRAND UNION CANAL
SPORTS
HEN'S HEAD WOOD
39
58

41
BP
BQ
BR
BS
BT
BU
BV
08
09
10
15
16
17
18
19
20
21
22
23
24
07
06
Dane End Farm
Med. Cen
Superstore
Prim Sch
Comm Cen
HEMEL HEMPSTEAD ROAD
CYCLE TRACK
Bohemia House
Hill Farm
HILL
PUNCH BOWL LANE
Wood End Farm
CHERRY TREE LANE
ST. ALBANS
DACORUM
HUNTERS
Cherry Tree Farm
LILLY LANE
Cherry Tree House
HP2
Southend Farm
Eaton Lodge
High Grange
Hogg End
HOGG
PRATTS DELL
Works
SWALLOWDALE
MAXTED ROAD
BOUNDARY ROAD
BUNCEFIELD LANE
HOGG END LANE
AL3
Old Jeromes
Butler's Farm
HEMEL HEMPSTEAD INDUSTRIAL ESTATE
MAYLANDS
EATON ROAD
BOUNDARY WY
Kettlewell's Farm
OIL DEPOT
KENTISH WOOD
WINDMILLHILL WOOD
THE VISTAS
THE WILDERNESS
CHALK DELL
GORHAMBURY
Cricket Ground
SARACEN INDUSTRIAL AREA
SPRING WAY
Diamond Point
WOOD LANE END
BOUNDARY WAY
Woodwells Farm
WOODWELLS FARM CEMETERY
BRUCE'S PLANTATION
Depot
Pol
A4147
AVENUE
LUCAS AEROSPACE SPORTS GROUND
SPORTS GRD
Breakspear Way Caravan Club
Junction 8
BREAKSPEAR WAY
Gorhambury (Ruins)
42
MARCHMONT HOUSE POND
Elec Sta
Holiday Inn
B.P. Oil Offices
BRICKKILN WOOD
CYPRESS WOOD
FB
ROAD
A414
LEVERSTOCK GRN WAY
WESTWICK
Mayers Farm Stud Cottages
M1
Prim Sch
Westwick Farm
Leverstock Green FC
Leverstock Green
Comm Cen
Lib
Cricket Ground
Pav
Westwick Row Farm
Westwick Hall
SQUARE WOOD
Hill End Farm
Junction 7
BEECHTREE LANE
Tenn Club
Sch
Corner Farm
Westwick House
HEMPSTEAD ROAD
HEMEL
M10
LONGFIELD SPRING
Prim Sch
Sports Cen
Sec Sch
CHAMBERSBURY LANE
CATSDELL BOTTOM
BLACKWATER LANE
BLACKWATER WOOD
Bunkers Farm
Well Farm
THREE RIVERS
BEDMOND ROAD
Maiden Croucher Farm
BIRCH WOOD
APPSPOND LANE
BUNKERS LANE
Highwood Hall Farm
High Herts Farm
CUMBERLAND CL
HALL
The Swan PH
POTTERS CROUCH PLANTATION
APPSPOND WOOD
LONG DEANS
HIGHWOOD
59
Bedmond House
Rose Acre
WD5
BEDMOND

BW
BX
BY
BZ
CA
CB
CC
12
13
14
15
16
17
18
09
20
21
22
23
24
09
08
07
06
Punch Bowl PH
Pumping Sta
Mill Stream
BUSH WOOD
KILMART'S SPRING WOOD
Childwick Bury
Bohemia House
Hill Farm
HILL FARM LANE
BOWL LANE
PUNCH BOWL
New Jerome Cottage
REDBOURN ROAD
A5183
WATLING STREET (ROMAN ROAD)
River Ver
Mill Race
THE PLANTATION
TOULMIN DRIVE SPORTS GROUND
Sec Sch
Pav
Woodlands
Ladygrove
LADIES GROVE WOOD
BATCH WOOD
Stafford Farm
Stafford Stud
Hogg End
HOGG END LANE
WHITEHEDGE SPRING
Tennis Centre
Tenn Cts
Bowling Green
Clubhouse
BATCHWOOD GOLF COURSE
Bow Bridge
Old Jeromes
Butler's Farm
AL3
Maynes Farm
Nash's Lodge
GORHAMBURY DRIVE
CHURCHYARD MEADOW
ST. ALBANS CITY HOSP
REC GRD
WINDMILLHILL WOOD
THE WILDERNESS
ONE ACRE
CHALK DELL
GORHAMBURY
Cricket Ground
GILPINS
HUGO'S SPINNEY
Shepherds Cottage
Course of Roman Wall
VERULAM ROAD
FOLLY
MID HERTS WING
KINGSBURY WATERMILL MUS
Gorhambury (Ruins)
41
BRICKKILN WOOD
CYPRESS WOOD
The Fosse
LORD BACON'S MOUNT
Roman Open Air Theatre
St. Michael's Bridge
BELL MEADOW
VERULAMIUM MUSEUM
TEMPLE WOOD
HEMEL HEMPSTEAD ROAD
SITE OF ROMAN VERULAMIUM
Mayers Farm Stud Cottages
Prae Wood House
Tennis Courts
PRAE WOOD
VERULAMIUM PARK
Hypocaust
Pav
THE LAKE
Ye Olde Fighting Cocks PH
Prae Wood Farm
SQUARE WOOD
River Ver
Verulam Hills
RUNNING TRACK
Leisure Centre
Hill End Farm
Superstore
Prim Sch
ABBEY VIEW GOLF COURSE
Junction 7
SPORTS GROUND
Junior Sch
Prep. Sch
HEMEL HEMPSTEAD ROAD
A4147
St. Stephens
M10
LONGFIELD SPRING
Maiden Crouch Farm
MADAM'S WOOD
Windridge Farm
PO
NETHERWAY
OPEN SPACE
Sec Sch
BIRCH WOOD
BIRCH WOOD
BEDMOND LANE
APPSPOND WOOD
M1
Holly Bush PH
PARK WOOD
Westfields Farm
WATLING STREET
A5183
RAGGED HALL LANE
Potters Crouch East Farm
Potters Crouch Farm
SQUARE WOOD
SCRUBBS WOOD
Cuckman's Farm
AL2
ALLOT
REC GRD
Prim Sch
ST. JULIAN'S WOOD
WD5
Potters Crouch
60
Plaistowes
A405
WATLING STREET CARAVAN (TRAVELLERS)
Pavs

POLICE SCIENTIFIC DEVELOPMENT BRANCH
CD
CE
CF
CG
CH
CJ
CK
15
16
17
09
08
07
06
18
19
20
21
22
23
24
TOMPKINS SPRING
WOOLLAMS PLAYING FIELD
Pav
HARPENDEN ROAD
A1081
SANDRIDGEBURY LANE
SPORTS GROUND
Sports Cen
Hall
PET CEM
Glasshouse
Jersey Farm
JERSEY FARM OPEN SPACE
Sirdane House & Kennels
Glasshouse
Carpenters Nursery
Nashe's Farm
THE GRYPHON INDUSTRIAL PARK
LONG SPRING
THE GLEN
Works
BEECH BOTTOM DYKE
Sec Sch
OLD ALBANIAN SPORTS GROUND
Compute Cen
Prim Sch
Sec Sch
SPORTS GROUND
Marshalswick
MARSHALSWICK LANE
ALLOTMENTS
Earthworks
SKYS WOOD
Oak Farm
COOPERS
Townsend
SPORTS GRD
Music Sch
CONVENT
Youth Club
SPORTS GRD
Fire Sta
Amb Sta
BERNARDS HEATH
REC GRD
Prim Sch
THE WICK
SPORTS GRD
Tennis Courts
Comm Cen
Lib
AL4
AL1
SANDPIT LANE
FAIRCROSS WAY
SPORTS FIELD
Tennis Courts
Prim Sch
Glasshouses
College Farm Buildings
Coll
Tenn Cts
HOME WOOD
44
Depot
Sec Sch
JENNINGS ROAD
Tennis Courts
Jubilee Cen
BURIAL GRD
Oakland College
St. Albans City FC
Cricket Ground
Pav
Bowl Grn
CLARENCE PARK
CIVIC OFFICES
ST. ALBANS
HATFIELD ROAD
A1057
Works
Lib
Superstore
ST. ALBANS CEMETERY
War Memorial
Prim Sch
Fleetville
Offices
SPHERE IND EST
LONGACRES PLAYING FIELD
BRICK KNOLL PARK
Coll
Sec Sch
Pav
SPORTS GRD
Council Nursery
The Maltings
Lib
ST. ALBANS CITY
Hotel
Youth Cen
Works
Offices
SPORTS GROUND
ALLOT
Sch
MUS
The Camp
Clinic
Prim Schs
Prim Sch
Caravan Site
SPORTS GROUND
Home Farm
Prim Sch
ALLOT
Lee Hall (Ruins)
ALLOT
Works
Angling Club
Clubhouse
Quality Hotel
SPORTS GROUND
SPORTS GRD
Youth Club
Sopwell Mill Farm
ALLOT
Comm Cen
SPORTS GROUND
VERULAM GOLF COURSE
Mile House PH
Sec Sch
Health & Racquet Club
SPORTS GRD
Hall
Tyttenhanger
Highfield Farm
Highfield Hall
KNIGHT'S WOOD
St. Julians
Prim Sch
Sch
River Ver
Sopwell Home Farm
Sopwell House Hotel
Mill Stream
NORTH ORBITAL TRADING ESTATE
BIRKLANDS PARK
CEM
LONDON ROAD
Junction 1
NORTH ORBITAL ROAD
A414
CHALKDELL WOOD
61
Aylett Nursery
VERULAM R.F.C.
Clubho
COLUMBANS SPORTS GRD
SPORTS GROUND
Pav
COPPICE WOOD
(SITE OF SPECIAL SCIENTIFIC INTEREST)
A5183

CL
CM
CN
CP
CQ
CR
CS
19
20
21
28
POLICE SCIENTIFIC DEVELOPMENT BRANCH
Fairfold's Farm
Sutton's Farm
WOODCOCK HILL
Jersey Farm
Astwick Manor Farm
MANOR ROAD
Fielder Centre
College
SAND AND GRAVEL PIT
HATFIELD BUSINESS PARK
Warehouse
Offices
AL10
FROBISHER WAY
HOOK'S WOOD
SLEEVE HALL WOOD
Nashe's Farm
SAND & GRAVEL PIT
BALL'S COVERT
OAK WOOD
GREEN LANE
ROUND WOOD
Beech Farm
HOME COVERT
ASH GREEN
Oak Farm
COOPERS LANE
Works
MOSQUITO WAY
BISHOP SQUARE BUSINESS PARK
WELWYN HATFIELD
ST. ALBANS
OAKLANDS LANE
NORTH DRIVE
ST. ALBANS ROAD WEST
Ramada Jarvis
Ninefields Nursery
Popefield Farm
Wilkin's Green
Ellenbrook
Tennis Courts
BAGGYMEAD SPRING
Glasshouses
College Farm Buildings
EAST DRIVE
Coll
Tenn Cts
HATFIELD ROAD
A1057
Wilkin's Green Farm
Nast Hyde Farm
Smallford
ALBAN WAY - CYCLE ROUTE
Junction 3
COMET WAY
ROEHYDE WAY
43
Depot
Smallford Nursery
PO
Superstores
Warehouse
ALBAN WAY CYCLE ROUTE
AL4
Sleaphyde
Sleapshyde Farm
COLNEY HEATH LANE
Sec Sch
Pav
SPORTS GRD
SPORTS GROUND
Council Nursery
Smallford Farm
BUTTERWICK LANE
SMALLFORD LANE
SLEAPCROSS GARDENS
A414
JOHNSON'S SPRING
Bullen's Green
BARLEY MOW CARAVAN PARK
FB
Home Farm
Prim Sch
Clubhouse
BURIAL GRD
Roundhouse Farm
Barley Mow Stables
The Barley Mow PH
Hall
Colney Heath
Pumping Sta
ROESTOCK PARK
Tyttenhanger
SAND AND GRAVEL PIT
River Colne
PARK CORNER
Queens Head PH
Colney Heath Farm
TOLLGATE ROAD
DELLSOME LANE
Roestock
Highfield Farm
KNIGHT'S WOOD
SAND AND GRAVEL PIT
Colne River
Tollgate Farm
Highfield Hall
ST. ALBANS
HERTSMERE
Warren Farm
THE WARREN
Clinic
BLOUNT SPRING
FREDERICK'S WOOD
NORTH ORBITAL ROAD
A1081 LONDON
Tyttenhanger Farm
COPPICE WOOD
62
GARDEN WOOD
Tyttenhanger House
Coursers Farm
COURSERS ROAD
15
16
17
18
19
20
21
22
23
24
09
08
07
06

Junction
Hatfield Garden Village
MILL GREEN GOLF COURSE
Mill Green
Sewage Works
Clubhouse
Superstores
MT PLEASANT LA
HERTFORD ROAD
A414
SPORTS GROUND
Sports Centre
COUNCIL DEPOT
A1(M)
COMET WAY
The Ryde
THE WARREN
THE BROADWATER
VINEYARD
HOME PARK
THE LONG RIDE
Birchwood
HATFIELD
Old Hatfield
Hillend Farm
THE FURZE FIELD
POLLARD WOOD
NEW POND
HATFIELD HOUSE
OLD BISHOP'S PALACE
HATFIELD PARK
Roe Green
BRICKKILN WOOD
CONDUIT WOOD
WELLINGTON WOOD
HOWE DELL
Meml. BURIAL GRD
Oxlease
Home Farm
RESERVOIR
COOMBE WOOD
THE ROUGHS
Park Dairy
University of Hertfordshire
OXLEYS WOOD
South Hatfield
HAZEL GROVE
SPORTS GRD
HALFWAYOAK POND
GREEN STREET
Woodside Place Farm
Woodside
MILLWARD'S PARK
SOUTHWAY
A1001
GREAT NORTH ROAD
A1000
Quality Hotel
Marshmoor Nurseries
WELWYN HATFIELD DISTRICT CEMETERY
Warehouses
AL9
Lower Woodside
Junction 2
SPORTS GROUND
Welham Green
ALPHA BUSINESS PARK
WELHAM GREEN
Marshmoor Bridge
CARAVAN PARK
TOLLGATE WOOD
BUSH WOOD
REC GRD
FOXES LANE
M.K.M. Nurseries
Nursery
Rockwater Nursery
Bell Bar Nursery
The Cock o' the North PH
BULLS LANE
Sibthorpe Arms PH
Skimpans Bridge
Potterells Farm
Comm Cen
REC GRD
PELPIN'S WOOD
THE LEGG
Tennis Courts
ROUND WOOD
Home Farm
Clubhouse
Sec Sch
BROOKMANS PARK GOLF COURSE
Med Cen
Potterells
NORTH MYMMS
DIXONS HILL ROAD

29
46
63

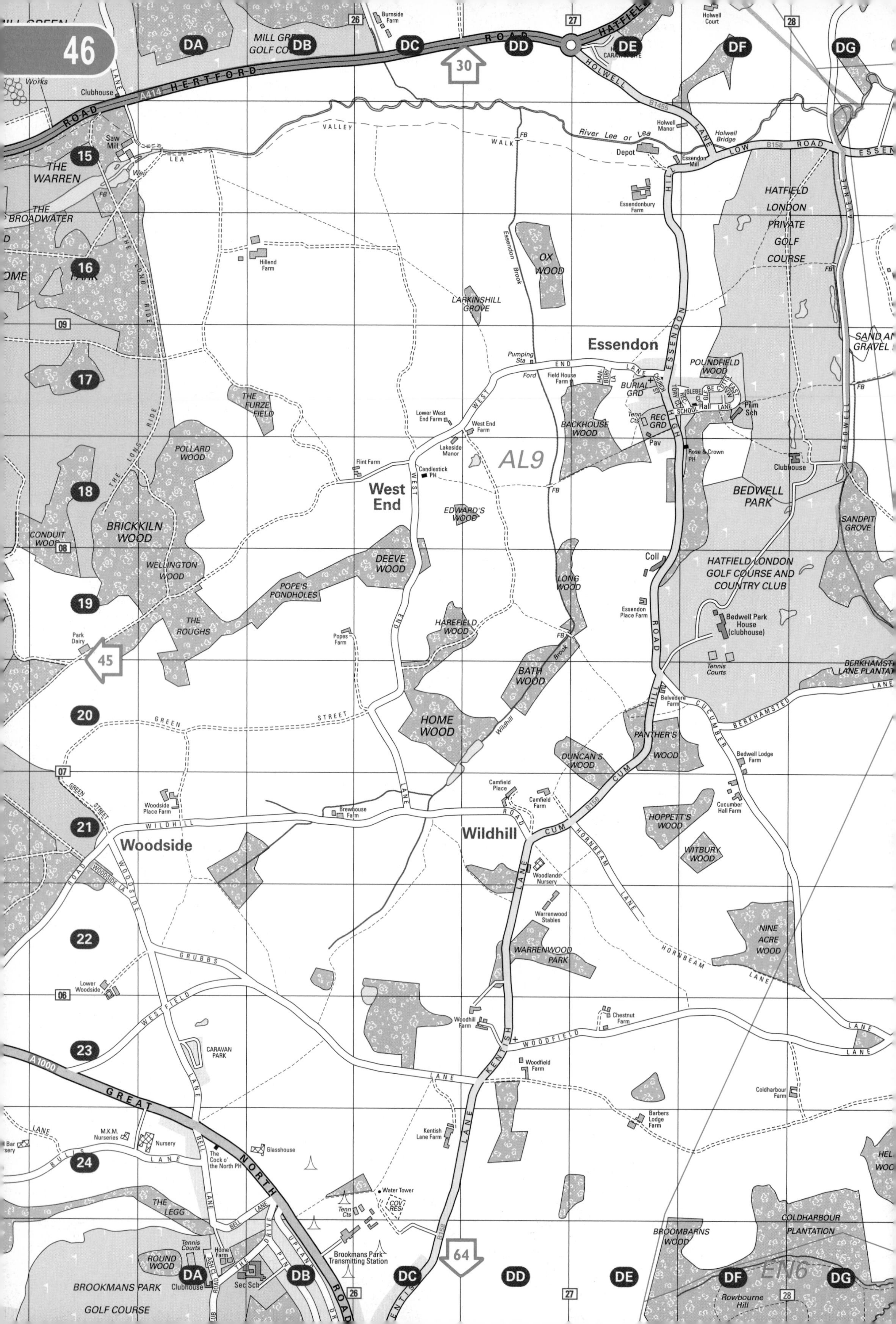
Essendon
West End
Wildhill
Woodside
AL9
EN6
HATFIELD LONDON PRIVATE GOLF COURSE
HATFIELD LONDON GOLF COURSE AND COUNTRY CLUB
BEDWELL PARK
Bedwell Park House (clubhouse)
BRICKKILN WOOD
POLLARD WOOD
WELLINGTON WOOD
CONDUIT WOOD
THE ROUGHS
POPE'S PONDHOLES
DEEVE WOOD
HAREFIELD WOOD
HOME WOOD
BATH WOOD
LONG WOOD
EDWARD'S WOOD
OX WOOD
LARKINSHILL GROVE
BACKHOUSE WOOD
POUNDFIELD WOOD
SANDPIT GROVE
PANTHER'S WOOD
DUNCAN'S WOOD
HOPPETT'S WOOD
WITBURY WOOD
NINE ACRE WOOD
WARRENWOOD PARK
BROOMBARNS WOOD
COLDHARBOUR PLANTATION
THE FURZE FIELD
THE WARREN
THE BROADWATER
THE LEGG
ROUND WOOD
BROOKMANS PARK GOLF COURSE
MILL GREEN GOLF COURSE
CARAVAN PARK
Brookmans Park Transmitting Station
HERTFORD ROAD
GREAT NORTH ROAD
River Lee or Lea
VALLEY WALK
THE LONG RIDE
GREEN STREET
WILDHILL ROAD
CUM CUM HILL
HORNBEAM LANE
CUCUMBER LANE
WOODFIELD LANE
KENTISH LANE
GRUBBS LANE
WESTFIELD LANE
BELL LANE
BULLS LANE
ESSENDON HILL
HOLWELL LANE
LOW ROAD
BEDWELL AVENUE
BERKHAMSTED LANE

30
45
64

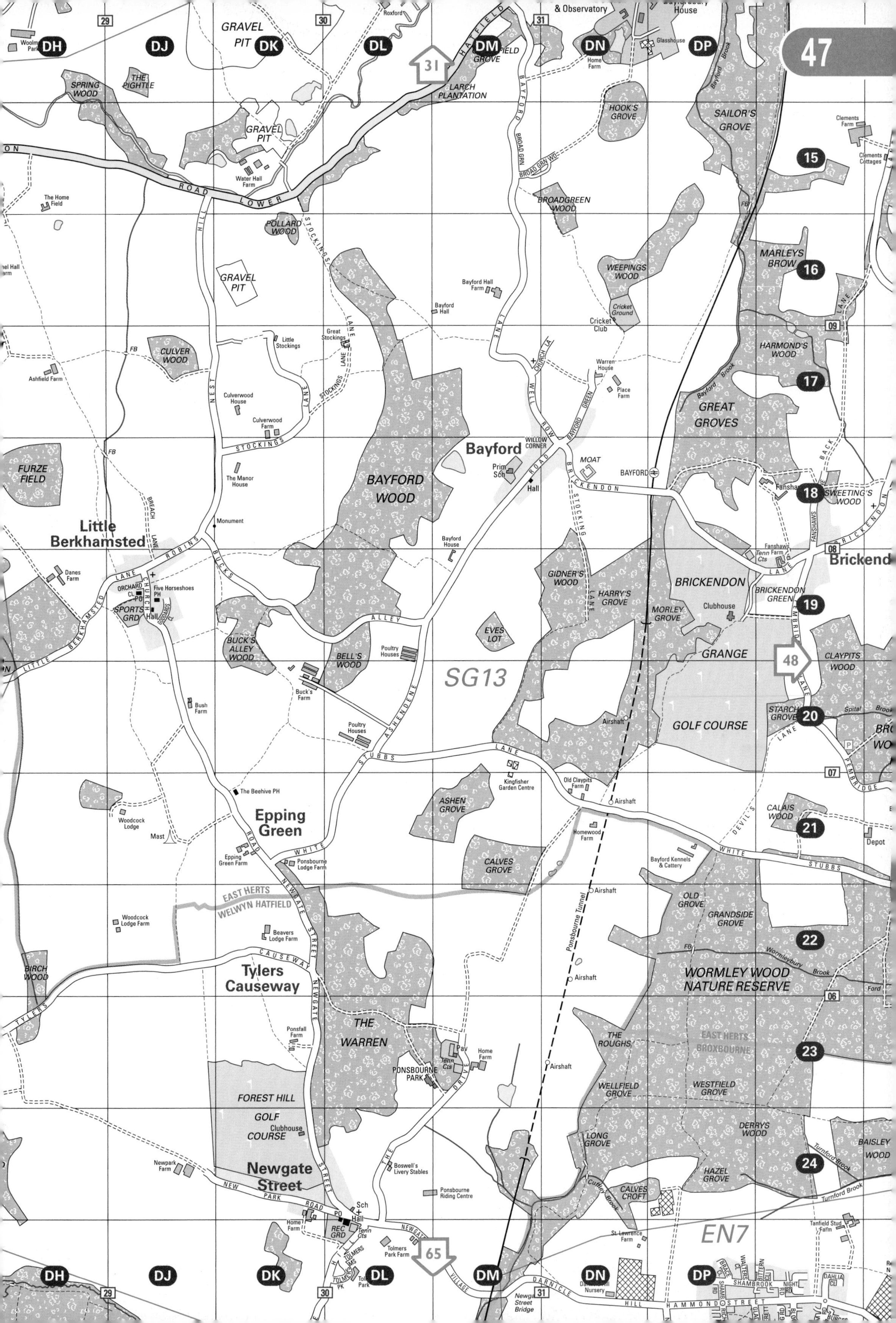
GRAVEL PIT
SPRING WOOD
THE PIGHTLE
LARCH PLANTATION
HOOK'S GROVE
SAILOR'S GROVE
Water Hall Farm
LOWER ROAD
POLLARD WOOD
BROADGREEN WOOD
WEEPINGS WOOD
MARLEYS BROW
Bayford Hall Farm
Bayford Hall
CULVER WOOD
Ashfield Farm
Culverwood House
Culverwood Farm
HARMOND'S WOOD
GREAT GROVES
FURZE FIELD
The Manor House
Bayford
BAYFORD WOOD
MOAT
BAYFORD
SWEETING'S WOOD
Little Berkhamsted
Danes Farm
Five Horseshoes PH
Bayford House
GIDNER'S WOOD
HARRY'S GROVE
BRICKENDON
Brickendon
BRICKENDON GREEN
MORLEY GROVE
GRANGE
CLAYPITS WOOD
BUCK'S ALLEY WOOD
BELL'S WOOD
EVES LOT
SG13
STARCH GROVE
GOLF COURSE
Kingfisher Garden Centre
Old Claypits Farm
ASHEN GROVE
The Beehive PH
Epping Green
Woodcock Lodge
CALAIS WOOD
CALVES GROVE
Bayford Kennels & Cattery
OLD GROVE
GRANDSIDE GROVE
EAST HERTS
WELWYN HATFIELD
Woodcock Lodge Farm
Beavers Lodge Farm
Tylers Causeway
WORMLEY WOOD NATURE RESERVE
BIRCH WOOD
THE WARREN
THE ROUGHS
PONSBOURNE PARK
FOREST HILL GOLF COURSE
WELLFIELD GROVE
WESTFIELD GROVE
LONG GROVE
DERRYS WOOD
BAISLEY WOOD
Newgate Street
HAZEL GROVE
CALVES CROFT
Boswell's Livery Stables
Ponsbourne Riding Centre
EN7
Tolmers Park Farm
Tanfield Stud Farm
Newgate Street Bridge
Ponsbourne Tunnel
BROXBOURNE

48
Brickendon
Brickendonbury
Brickendon Brook
SAILOR'S GROVE
Clements Farm
Clements Cottages
THE GROVE
Blackfields Farm
HOBBYHORSE WOOD
ERMINE STREET ROMAN ROAD
Elbowlane Farm
BOX WOOD
LIGHTS WOOD
MARLEYS BROW
Edwards Green Farm
MONKS WOOD
SG13
Jepps Farm
DALMOND'S WOOD
Water Tower
The Huntsman PH
HARMOND'S WOOD
Sewards Farm
Monks Green
Poultry Houses
JEPP'S WOOD
Highfield Farm
HODDESDON PARK WOOD NATURE RESERVE
GREAT GROVES
HIGHFIELD WOOD
Fanshaws
Bourne Orchard
Well
SWEETING'S WOOD
BRAMBLE'S WOOD
Spital Brook
Fanshaws Farm
Tenn Cts
ROUND GROVE
HAYSTACK GROVE
BOURNE WOOD
DANEMEAD WOOD
MARTIN'S GREEN
BRICKENDON
BRICKENDON GREEN
MORLEY GROVE
COWHEATH WOOD
NURSERY GROVE
CHESTNUT GROVE
CLAYPITS WOOD
BROXBOURNE COMMON
GREAT GROVE
47
BROAD RIDING WOOD
STARCH GROVE
GOLF COURSE
HEDGEROWS WOOD
LITTLE GROVE
Broxbournebury Mansion
Clubhouse
HERTFORDSHIRE GOLF COURSE
BROXBOURNE WOOD NATURE RESERVE
Hedgegrove Farm
Edgewood Farm
Home Farm
Pembridge Lane Farm
LOWER WHITE STUBBS
CALAIS WOOD
Ettridge Farm
STOCKING WOOD
UPPER WHITE STUBBS
PARADISE WILDLIFE PARK
Depot
Bayford Kennels & Cattery
Birch Farm
White Stubbs Farm
Three Farm Stables
OLD GROVE
GRANDSIDE GROVE
MORTALS WOOD
Carneles Green
BENCROFT WOOD NATURE RESERVE
BUSHY PIGHTLE
FIR GROVE
EAST HERTS
BROXBOURNE
Wormley West End
Manor Farm
Barleycroft Farm
Tudor Farm
Manor House
Bury Farm
WORMLEY WOOD NATURE RESERVE
Wormleybury Brook
Ford
The Woodman PH
Holborn Stud Farm
Brookfields Farm
Brookfields Nursery
FIRS WOOD
CONY GROVE
BIGS GROVE
WESTFIELD GROVE
BEECH GROVE
NEW PLANTATION
DERRY'S WOOD
Beaumont Manor
Beaumont Manor Farm
BAISLEY'S WOOD
BRAMBLE GROVE
THUNDERFIELD GROVE
Cheshunt Park Farm
HAZEL GROVE
Turnford Brook
Bread and Cheese Bridge
Tanfield Stud Farm
EN7
PRIESTS OSIERS
SPRING WOOD
Paradise Nursery
WATERCRESS TROT
Rosary Nursery
Doggett Hill
CROMWELL WOOD
Paradise House
Mast
HAMMOND STREET
SHAMBROOK
DAHLIA CL
APPLEBY
MANGROVE LANE
BACK LANE
BRICKENDON LANE
PEMBRIDGE LANE
WHITE STUBBS LANE
WEST END ROAD
BEAUMONT ROAD
CHEESE LANE
PARK LANE
COCK LANE
CHURCH LANE
SPRING WALK
LORD LANE
ELBOW LANE
HOLY CROSS HILL
WOOD HOUSE LANE
DEVIL'S LANE
32
66
DQ
DR
DS
DT
DU
DV
DW
33
34
35
15
16
17
18
19
20
21
22
23
24
09
08
07
06

49
DX
DY
DZ
EA
EB
EC
ED
33
50
67
36
37
38
15
16
17
18
19
20
21
22
23
24
09
08
07
06
Woollensbrook
DELLS WOOD
EN11
EN10
EN9
CM19
Rye Park
HODDESDON
Spitalbrook
BROXBOURNE
Wormley
Lower Nazeing
LEE VALLEY PARK
NAZEING MEAD
NAZEING MARSH
ADMIRALS WALK LAKE
SLURRY PIT
BOATING LAKE
RYE HOUSE MARSH NATURE RESERVE
RYE HOUSE SPEEDWAY
KART RACING
TRIDENT INDUSTRIAL EST
BELCON IND EST
HODDESDON IND CENTRE
OPTIMA BUS PK
HIGH LEIGH CONFERENCE CENTRE
BARCLAY PARK
Hoddesdon Town FC
LUCERN WARREN
CRABTREE PLANTATION
ICEHOUSE GROVE
THE FERNERY
PLAIN LARCH
COZENS GROVE
WORMLEY PLAYING FIELDS
HILLGROVE BUSINESS PARK
KEYSERS ESTATE
CARTHAGENA ESTATE
Clayton Hill
NURSERY WOOD
HELL WOOD
LANTHORNS WOOD
Baas Hill
Dobb's Weir Lock
Fielde's Weir Lock
King's Weir
Electricity Station
Power Station
Sewage Works
Filter Beds
Sludge Lagoons
RIVER LEE NAVIGATION
New River
FLOOD RELIEF CHANNEL
HERTFORDSHIRE
ESSEX
EPPING FOREST
BROXBOURNE
HODDESDON BYPASS
A10
A1170
DINANT LINK ROAD
HIGH ROAD
HIGH STREET
AMWELL ST
WARE ROAD
HERTFORD ROAD
STATION ROAD
NAZEING NEW ROAD
NAZEING ROAD
ESSEX ROAD
ST. LEONARDS ROAD
PAYNES LANE
NURSERY ROAD

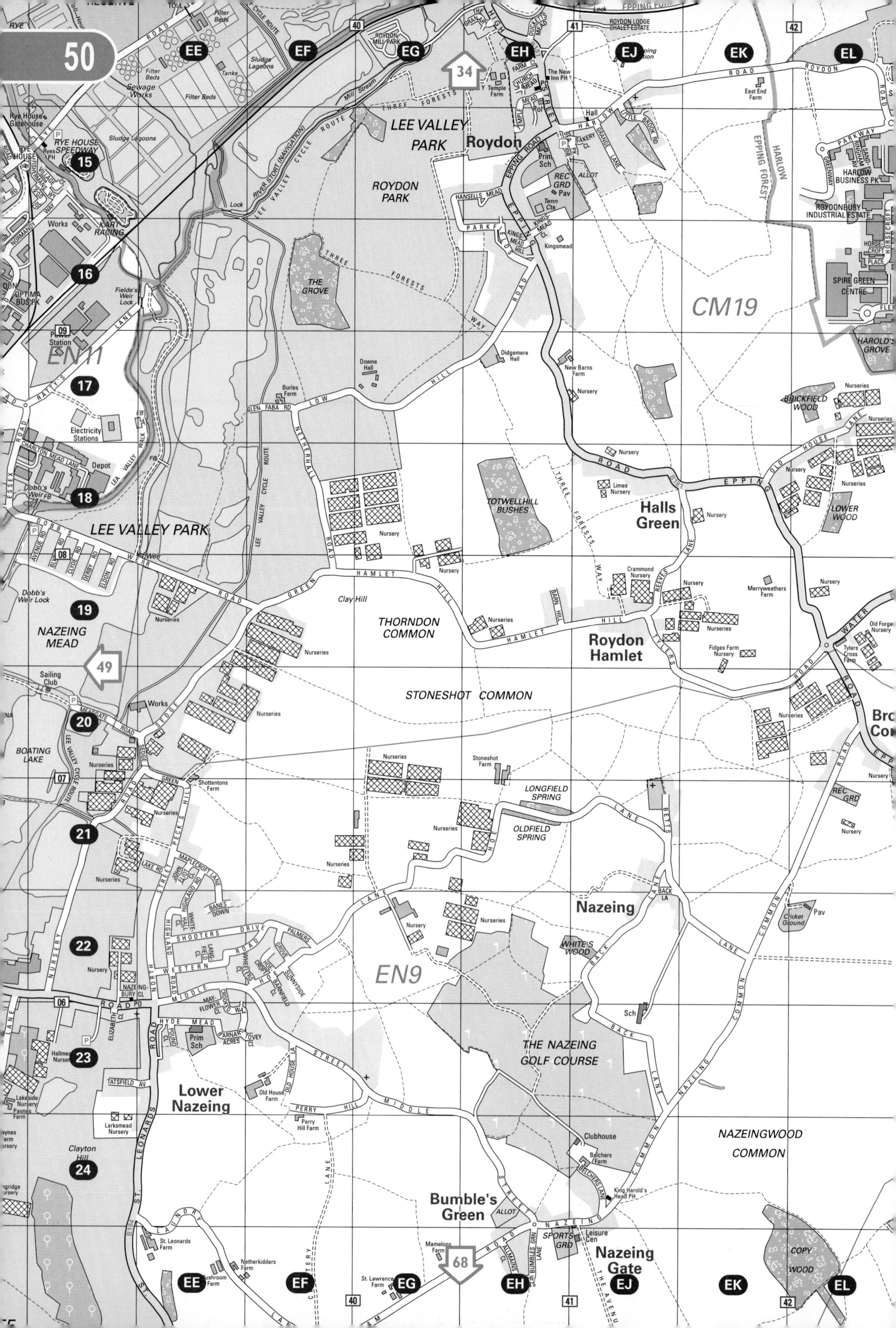

LEE VALLEY PARK
Roydon
ROYDON PARK
THE GROVE
CM19
EN11
EN9
Halls Green
Roydon Hamlet
THORNDON COMMON
STONESHOT COMMON
NAZEING MEAD
BOATING LAKE
Nazeing
THE NAZEING GOLF COURSE
Lower Nazeing
Bumble's Green
Nazeing Gate
NAZEINGWOOD COMMON
COPY WOOD
TOTWELLHILL BUSHES
LONGFIELD SPRING
OLDFIELD SPRING
BRICKFIELD WOOD
LOWER WOOD
HAROLD'S GROVE
HARLOW BUSINESS PK
ROYDONBURY INDUSTRIAL ESTATE
SPIRE GREEN CENTRE
RYE HOUSE SPEEDWAY
Sewage Works
Sludge Lagoons
Filter Beds
KART RACING
Power Station
Electricity Stations
Didgemere Hall
Downe Hall
Burles Farm
New Barns Farm
Limes Nursery
Crammond Nursery
Merryweathers Farm
Fidges Farm Nursery
Stoneshot Farm
Shottentons Farm
Old House Farm
Perry Hill Farm
Larksmead Nursery
St. Leonards Farm
Netherkidders Farm
St. Lawrence Farm
King Harold's Head PH
Clubhouse
Belchers Farm
Leisure Cen
Clay Hill
Clayton Hill
LOW HILL
HAMLET HILL
NETHERHALL ROAD
GREEN ROAD
WEIR ROAD
SEDGE GREEN
PECK'S HILL
LAUNDRY LANE
MIDDLE STREET
PERRY HILL
NAZEING COMMON
COMMON LANE
BACK LANE
BETTS LANE
HOE LANE
EPPING ROAD
HARLOW ROAD
ROYDON ROAD
THREE FORESTS WAY
LEE VALLEY CYCLE ROUTE
RIVER STORT (NAVIGATION)
34
49
68
EE EF EG EH EJ EK EL
40 41 42

CANONS BROOK GOLF COURSE
HARLOW STADIUM
EM
EN
EP
EQ
ER
ES
ET
43
44
45
35
Little Parndon
PRINCESS ALEXANDRA HOSPITAL
Harvey Centre
TOWN HALL
HARLOW
Harlow College
Netteswell
CM20
GRAVEPIT SPRINGS
THE MOORS
15
16
17
18
19
20
21
22
23
24
Pinnacles
GlaxoSmith Kline
THE COLDHARBOUR PINNACLES ESTATE
CRAMMOND PARK
HARLOW SEEDBED CENTRE
Electricity Station
ELIZABETH WAY
A1169
FOURTH AVENUE
THIRD AVENUE
SECOND AVENUE
A1025
NETTLESWELL PLANTATION
HELIPAD
COLLINS MEADOW SPORTS GRD
Hare Street
NEW FRONTIERS SCIENCE PARK
GYPSY CARAVAN PARK
PARNDON WOOD
Great Parndon
CM18
Passmores House
Passmores
Tye Green
Brays Grove
BUSH FAIR PLAYING FIELDS
TENDRING ROAD
CYCLE PATH
UPPER WOOD
Katherines
KATHERINES WAY
SOUTHERN WAY
A1169
Latton Bush
THE LATTON BUSH CENTRE
Stewards
Sumners
Leisure Centre
SPORTS GROUND
BURNETT'S WOOD
MAUND'S WOOD
PARINGDON ROAD
COMMONSIDE
52
Kingsmoor
PARNDON WOOD NATURE RESERVE
PARNDON WOOD CEM
Crem
RISDEN'S WOOD
HOSPITAL WOOD
HARLOW
EPPING FOREST
Water Tower
COV RES
RYE HILL ROAD
Dorrington Farm
Rivetts Farm
Richmonds Farm
Blake's Farm
PARSLOE ROAD
B181
EPPING ROAD
FORESTS WAY
THREE FORESTS WAY
Lodge Farm
Summers Farm
Travellers Friend PH
CM16
Marles Farm
Epping Green House
Epping Green
EPPING LONG GRN
Prim Sch
Cobbin's Brook
69
Pinch Timber Farm
Hayleys Manor Farm
BARN MEADOW
UPLAND ROAD
Rose Farm
07
06
08
09

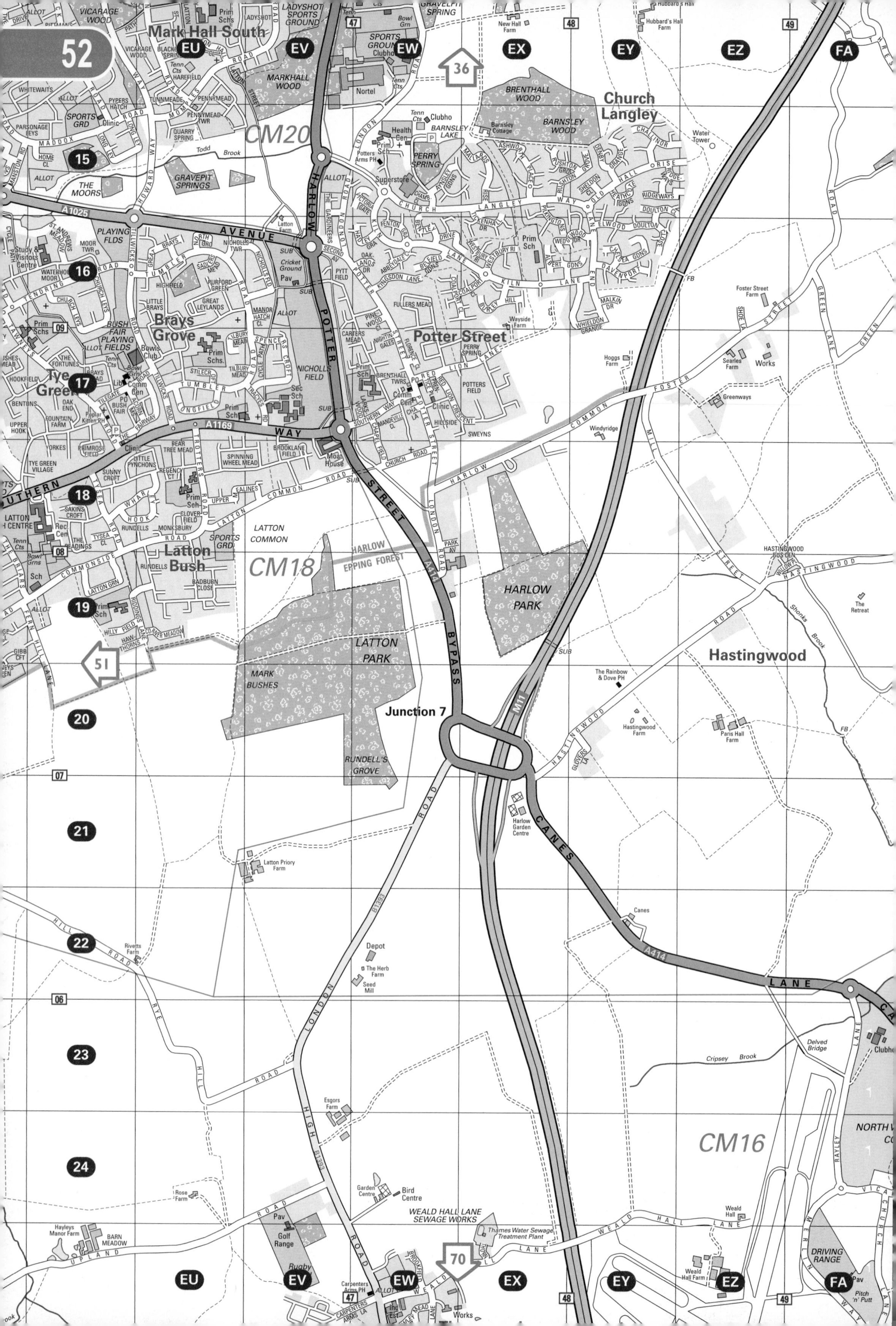
Mark Hall South
Church Langley
Brays Grove
Potter Street
Tye Green
Latton Bush
Hastingwood
CM20
CM18
CM16
BRENTHALL WOOD
BARNSLEY WOOD
MARKHALL WOOD
PERRY SPRING
GRAVEPIT SPRINGS
THE MOORS
NICHOLLS FIELD
LATTON COMMON
HARLOW PARK
LATTON PARK
MARK BUSHES
RUNDELL'S GROVE
Junction 7
HARLOW AVENUE
A1025
A1169
SOUTHERN WAY
POTTER STREET
BYPASS
A414
M1
CANES LANE
HARLOW COMMON
FOSTER STREET
HASTINGWOOD ROAD
LONDON ROAD
B1393
HIGH ROAD
HILL ROAD
RYE HILL ROAD
UPLAND ROAD
WEALD HALL LANE
WEALD HALL LANE SEWAGE WORKS
Thames Water Sewage Treatment Plant
Latton Priory Farm
Rivetts Farm
Depot
The Herb Farm
Seed Mill
Esgors Farm
Garden Centre
Bird Centre
Golf Range
Hayleys Manor Farm
BARN MEADOW
Rose Farm
Weald Hall Farm
Weald Hall
DRIVING RANGE
Cripsey Brook
Delved Bridge
Canes
Harlow Garden Centre
The Rainbow & Dove PH
Hastingwood Farm
Paris Hall Farm
The Retreat
Shonks Brook
Foster Street Farm
Searles Farm
Works
Greenways
Hoggs Farm
Windyridge
Wayside Farm
Water Tower
Hubbard's Hall Farm
New Hall Farm
Nortel
36
51
70
EU EV EW EX EY EZ FA
15 16 17 18 19 20 21 22 23 24
47 48 49
07 08 09 06

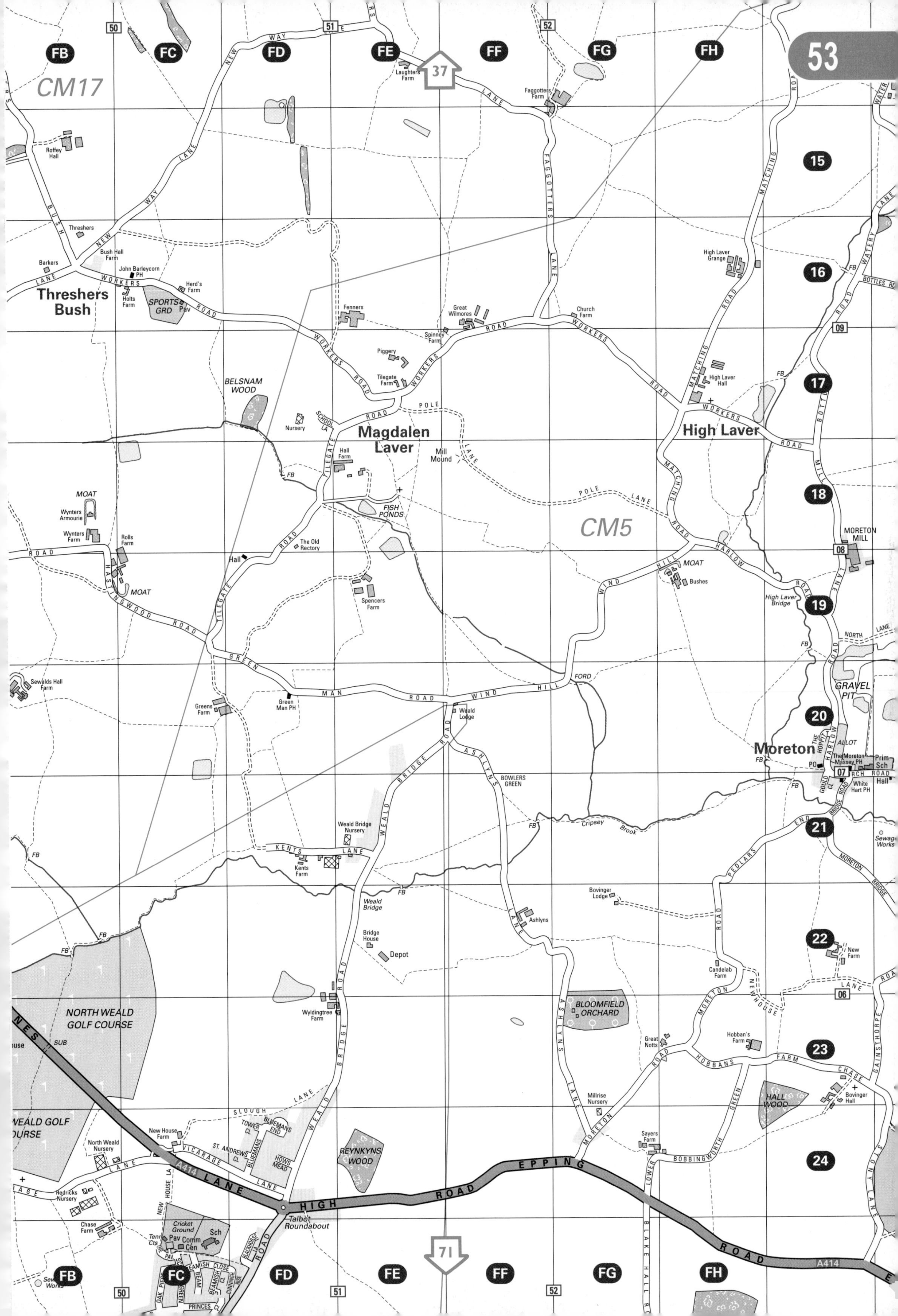
CM17
CM5
Threshers Bush
Magdalen Laver
High Laver
Moreton
Roffey Hall
Threshers
Barkers
Bush Hall Farm
John Barleycorn PH
Holts Farm
Herd's Farm
SPORTS GRD
Pav
Laughters Farm
Faggotters Farm
Fenners
Great Wilmores
Spinney Farm
Piggery
Tilegate Farm
Church Farm
High Laver Grange
High Laver Hall
BELSNAM WOOD
Nursery
Hall Farm
Mill Mound
FISH PONDS
MOAT
Wynters Armourie
Wynters Farm
Rolls Farm
The Old Rectory
Hall
Spencers Farm
Bushes
MORETON MILL
High Laver Bridge
GRAVEL PIT
Sewalds Hall Farm
Greens Farm
Green Man PH
Weald Lodge
BOWLERS GREEN
FORD
Weald Bridge Nursery
Kents Farm
Weald Bridge
Bridge House
Depot
Cripsey Brook
Bovinger Lodge
Ashlyns
Candelab Farm
New Farm
BLOOMFIELD ORCHARD
Wyldingtree Farm
NORTH WEALD GOLF COURSE
Great Notts
Hobban's Farm
HALL WOOD
Bovinger Hall
Millrise Nursery
Sayers Farm
REYNKYNS WOOD
New House Farm
North Weald Nursery
Redricks Nursery
Chase Farm
Cricket Ground
Sch
Pav
Comm Cen
Talbot Roundabout
The Moreton Massey PH
Prim Sch
PO
White Hart PH
Hall
ALLOT
Sewage Works
NEW WAY LANE
BUSH LANE
WORKERS ROAD
FAGGOTTERS LANE
MATCHING ROAD
POLE LANE
SCHOOL LA
TILEGATE ROAD
HASTINGWOOD ROAD
GREEN MAN ROAD
WIND HILL
HARLOW ROAD
BOTTLES ROAD
MILL LANE
NORTH LANE
KENTS LANE
WEALD BRIDGE ROAD
ASHLYNS LANE
PEDLARS END
MORETON BRIDGE
MORETON ROAD
HOBBANS FARM CHASE
GREEN
BOBBINGWORTH
LOWER BOBBINGWORTH
BLAKE HALL ROAD
NEWHOUSE LANE
GAINSTHORPE
EPPING ROAD
HIGH ROAD
VICARAGE LANE
SLOUGH LANE
TOWER CL
BLUEMANS END
ST. ANDREWS CL
HOWS MEAD
BLACKHORSE LA
BEAMISH CLOSE
PRINCES CL
THE HOPPIT
GOULD CL
A414
37
71
FB FC FD FE FF FG FH
50 51 52
15 16 17 18 19 20 21 22 23 24
09 08 07 06

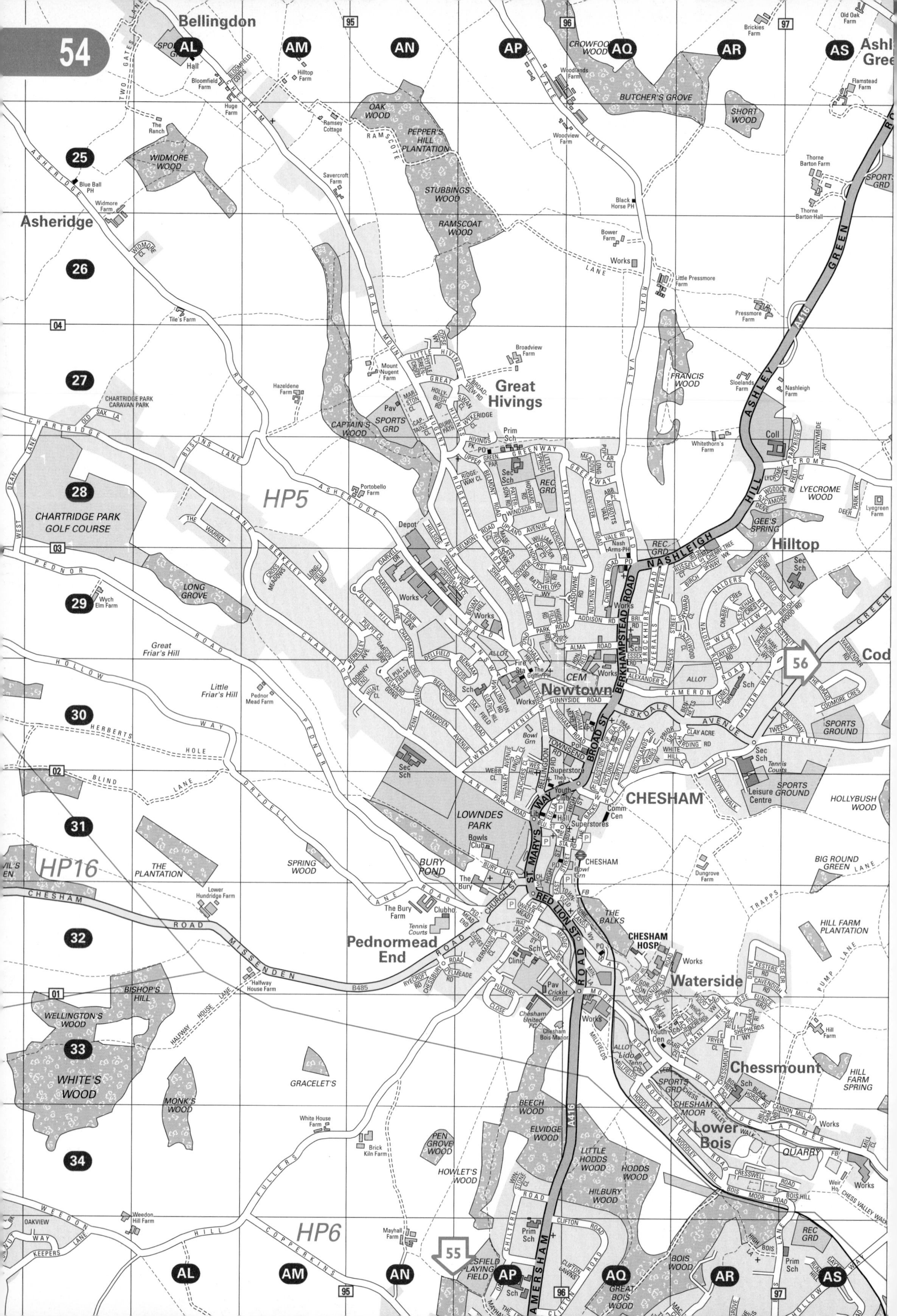

Bellingdon
Asheridge
Great Hivings
Newtown
CHESHAM
Hilltop
Pednormead End
Waterside
Chessmount
Lower Bois
HP5
HP16
HP6
CHARTRIDGE PARK GOLF COURSE
LONG GROVE
WIDMORE WOOD
OAK WOOD
PEPPER'S HILL PLANTATION
STUBBINGS WOOD
RAMSCOAT WOOD
CAPTAIN'S WOOD
BUTCHER'S GROVE
SHORT WOOD
FRANCIS WOOD
LYECROME WOOD
GEE'S SPRING
LOWNDES PARK
BURY POND
SPRING WOOD
THE PLANTATION
BISHOP'S HILL
WELLINGTON'S WOOD
WHITE'S WOOD
MONK'S WOOD
GRACELET'S
PEN GROVE WOOD
HOWLET'S WOOD
BEECH WOOD
ELVIDGE WOOD
LITTLE HODDS WOOD
HODDS WOOD
HILBURY WOOD
BOIS WOOD
GREAT BOIS WOOD
HOLLYBUSH WOOD
BIG ROUND GREEN
HILL FARM PLANTATION
HILL FARM SPRING
CHESHAM HOSP
THE BALKS
QUARRY
Great Friar's Hill
Little Friar's Hill
AL
AM
AN
AP
AQ
AR
AS
25
26
27
28
29
30
31
32
33
34

56
55

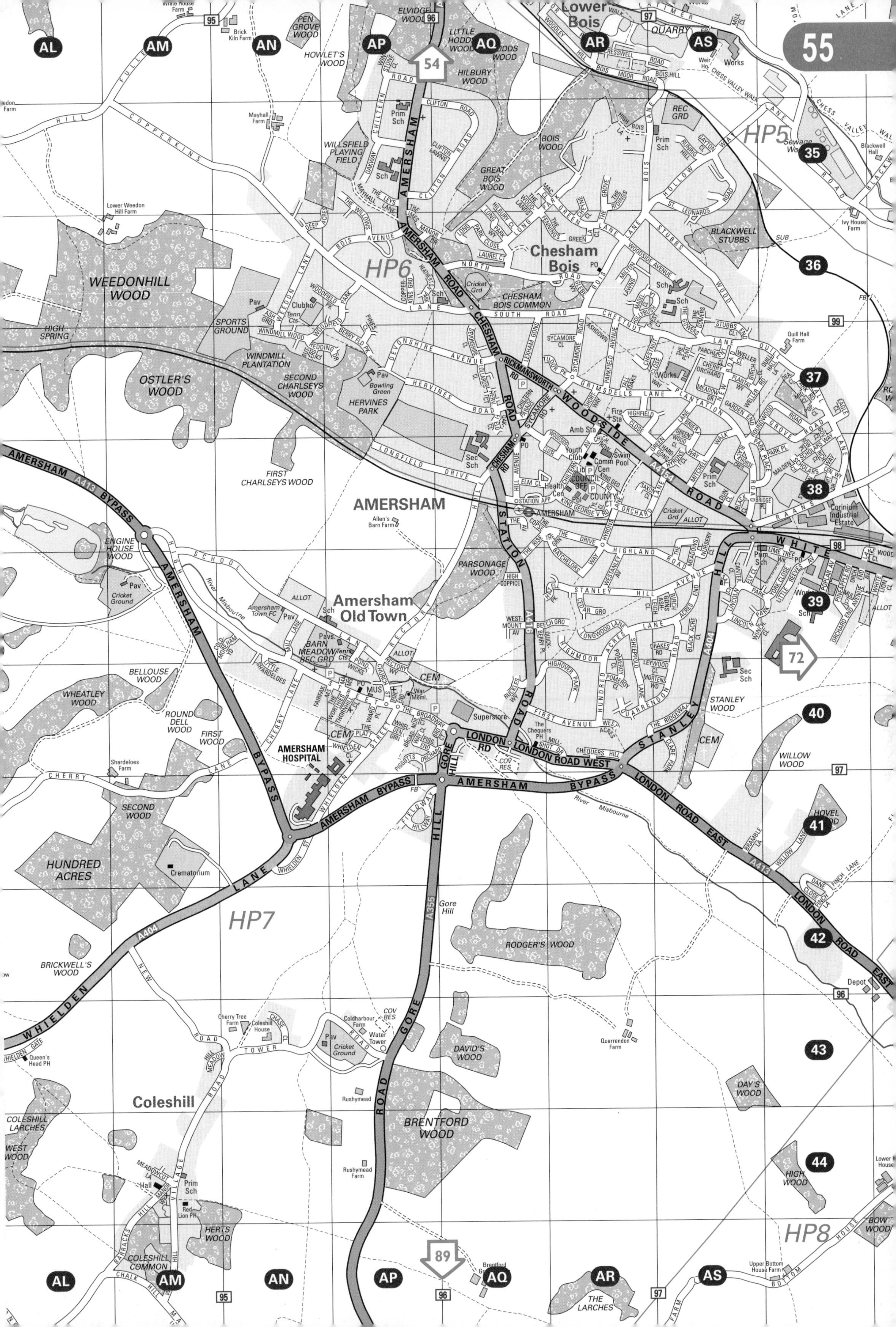
AMERSHAM
Amersham Old Town
Chesham Bois
Lower Bois
Coleshill
HP5
HP6
HP7
HP8
WEEDONHILL WOOD
OSTLER'S WOOD
HIGH SPRING
WINDMILL PLANTATION
SECOND CHARLSEYS WOOD
FIRST CHARLSEYS WOOD
HERVINES PARK
SPORTS GROUND
ENGINE HOUSE WOOD
BELLOUSE WOOD
WHEATLEY WOOD
ROUND DELL WOOD
FIRST WOOD
SECOND WOOD
HUNDRED ACRES
BRICKWELL'S WOOD
COLESHILL LARCHES
WEST WOOD
HERTS WOOD
COLESHILL COMMON
BRENTFORD WOOD
DAVID'S WOOD
RODGER'S WOOD
PARSONAGE WOOD
STANLEY WOOD
WILLOW WOOD
HOVEL WOOD
DAY'S WOOD
HIGH WOOD
BOW WOOD
THE LARCHES
GREAT BOIS WOOD
BOIS WOOD
HILBURY WOOD
HOWLET'S WOOD
PEN GROVE WOOD
ELVIDGE WOOD
LITTLE HODDS WOOD
HODDS WOOD
WILLSFIELD PLAYING FIELD
BLACKWELL STUBBS
CHESHAM BOIS COMMON
AMERSHAM HOSPITAL
AMERSHAM BYPASS
AMERSHAM ROAD
CHESHAM ROAD
WOODSIDE ROAD
STATION ROAD
LONDON ROAD WEST
LONDON ROAD EAST
GORE HILL
WHIELDEN LANE
STANLEY HILL
WHITE LION ROAD
A413
A404
A416
A355
A4154
Crematorium
Corinium Industrial Estate
Superstore
AL
AM
AN
AP
AQ
AR
AS
35
36
37
38
39
40
41
42
43
44
54
72
89
95
96
97
98
99

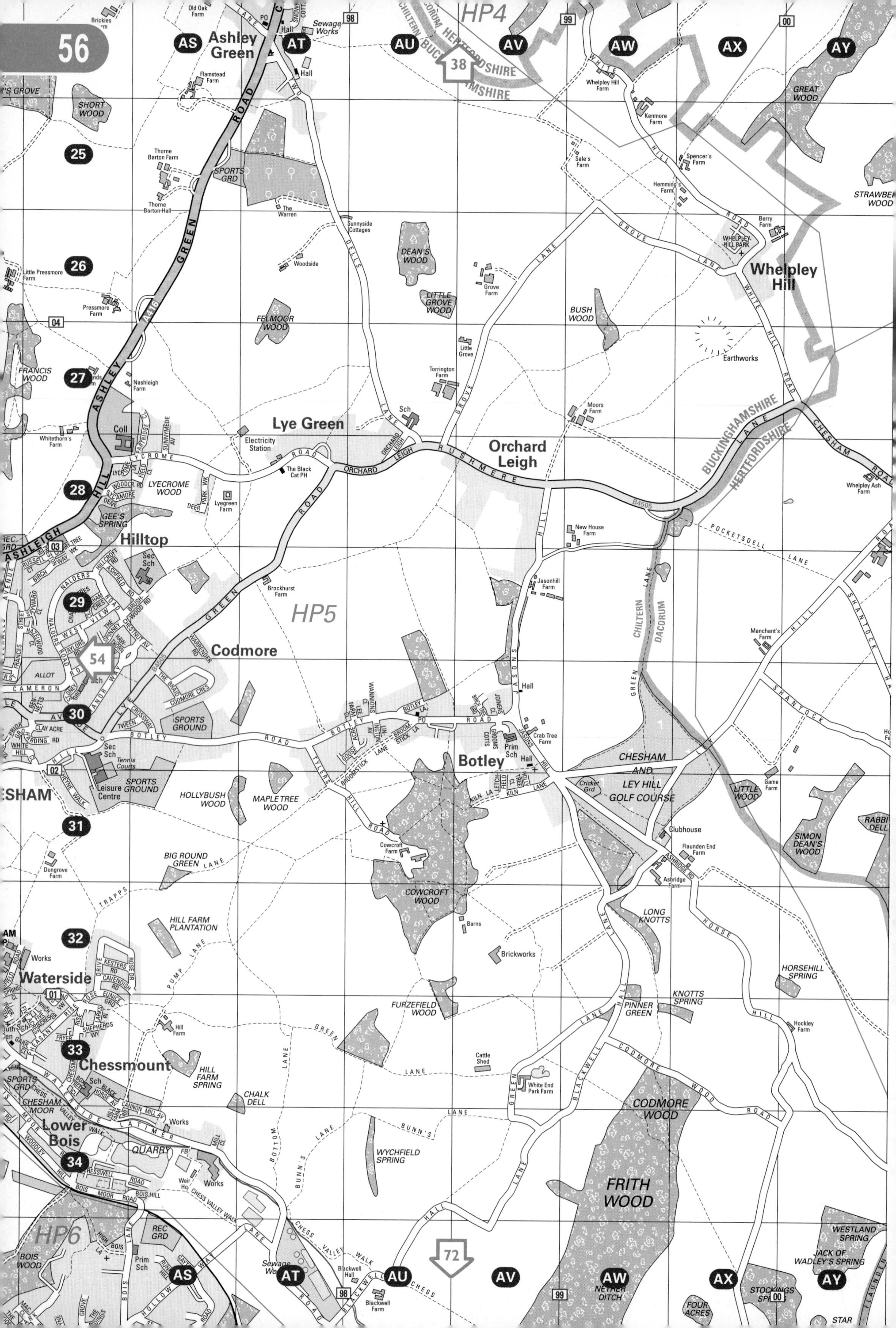
AS
AT
AU
AV
AW
AX
AY
HP4
HP5
HP6
38
54
72
Ashley Green
Whelpley Hill
Lye Green
Orchard Leigh
Hilltop
Codmore
Botley
Waterside
Chessmount
Lower Bois
CHESHAM
BUCKINGHAMSHIRE
HERTFORDSHIRE
CHILTERN
DACORUM
SHORT WOOD
FRANCIS WOOD
DEAN'S WOOD
LITTLE GROVE WOOD
FELMOOR WOOD
BUSH WOOD
GREAT WOOD
LYECROME WOOD
GEE'S SPRING
HOLLYBUSH WOOD
MAPLE TREE WOOD
COWCROFT WOOD
CHESHAM AND LEY HILL GOLF COURSE
LITTLE WOOD
SIMON DEAN'S WOOD
LONG KNOTTS
HORSEHILL SPRING
KNOTTS SPRING
PINNER GREEN
FURZEFIELD WOOD
HILL FARM PLANTATION
HILL FARM SPRING
CHALK DELL
WYCHFIELD SPRING
CODMORE WOOD
FRITH WOOD
WESTLAND SPRING
JACK OF WADLEY'S SPRING
BIG ROUND GREEN
SPORTS GROUND
Leisure Centre
Earthworks
Brickworks
Works
QUARRY
ASHLEY GREEN ROAD
A416
B4505
RUSHMERE LANE
ORCHARD LEIGH
GREEN ROAD
BOTLEY ROAD
JASONS HILL
CHILTERN LANE
GROVE LANE
WHITE HILL
CHESHAM ROAD
POCKETSDELL LANE
SHANTOCK HILL
ASHRIDGE RD
HORSE HILL
CODMORE WOOD ROAD
BLACKWELL HALL LANE
BUNN'S LANE
BOTTOM LANE
PUMP LANE
TRAPPS LANE
WATERSIDE
LATIMER RD
BOIS MOOR ROAD
CHESS VALLEY WALK
25
26
27
28
29
30
31
32
33
34
98
99
00
01
02
03
04

HANGING WOOD
LITTLE HAY GOLF COMPLEX
Clubhouse
39
HAY WOOD
BOXMOOR GOLF CLUB
SHEETHANGER COMMON
Felden Lodge
Howe's Retreat
Tower Farm
Felden Grange
Felden Manor
COLESHILL WOOD
HP1
COVERED RESERVOIR
RAMACRE WOOD
GORSEFIELD WOOD
BURY WOOD
BOX LANE
FELDEN LANE
FEATHERBED LANE
UPPER BOURNE END LANE
BURY RISE
SHOTHANGER WAY
BUSHFIELD ROAD
Longcroft Farm
LONGCROFT LANE
RAINHILL SPRING
RAINHILL DELL
KINGSHILL DELL
Bobsleigh Inn PH
Disused Airfield
H.M. THE MOUNT PRISON
HEMPSTEAD ROAD
SHORTRIDGE WOOD
OLD DEAN
FLAUNDEN LANE
BULSTRODE LANE
Duckhall Farm
Honours Farm
Random Farm
HOMEFIELD SPRING
STONEY LANE
Bury Farm
Sch
Lib
PO
Hall
Fire Sta
CHURCH ST
BELL LANE
Lane Farm
Dormers
Nuffield Farm
RUCKLERS LANE
CHESHAM ROAD
HYDE LANE
HYDE MEADOWS
CHIPPERFIELD ROAD
Bovingdon
Rent Street Farm
Darley Ash
Street Farm
Greinan Farm
Bulstrode Farm
Bovingdon Grange
Grange Farm
Pav
Bovingdon FC
Brickworks
GREEN LANE
THE GREEN
Pav
BOVINGDON GREEN
Green Farm
HP3
Cross Farm
TOWER HILL
BAKER'S WOOD
Bell Farm
Bryants Nurseries
Wyevale Garden Centre
Tenements Farm
58
Long Lane Farm
WATER LANE
Stoney Lane Nursery
The Boot PH
Tuffs Farm
Frenches Farm
SCATTERDELLS LANE
Riding School
Mast
Cottingham Farm
Chipperfield House
Meadow Way Farm
Shantock Nursery
Chiltern Farm
Shantock Farm
VENUS HILL
Venus Hill Dairy Farm
Crumlin Farm
HOLLY HEDGES LANE
WD4
Garden Centre
Works
Depot
CHAPEL CROFT
Chipperfield
New Maulden Farm
Hogpits Bottom
WOODMAN'S WOOD
Prim Sch
Hall
PO
Two Brewers PH
Pav
ALLOT
THE COMMON
War Meml
Tenn Cts
Cricket Ground
Rose Farm
FIR WOOD
HOGPITS BOTTOM
Bricklayer's Arms PH
Woodman's Farm
OLLEBERRIE LANE
WINDMILL HILL
LOWER PLANTATION
CHIPPERFIELD COMMON
Stables
Cherry Tree Farm
LITTLE WINDMILL HILL
PENMAN'S GREEN
Sharlowe's Farm
Dale Farm
WD3
Olleberrie Farm
The Plough PH
Belsize
Flaunden
Hall
FLAUNDEN SPRING
FLAUNDEN HILL
FLAUNDEN LANE
Whitedell Farm
Hillmeads Farm
Springview Farm
LIMEDELL SPRING
BRAGMANS LANE
POLES HILL
PLOUGH LANE
Newhouse Farm
Rose Hall Farm
DEBARDINE WOOD
ROSEHALL WOOD
PLOUGH WOOD
HILLMEADS SPRING
BOTTOM LANE
BRAGMANS LANE
HANGING CROFT
Moonshine Farm
Great Sarratt Hall Farm
Great Sarratt Hall
Dellfield
Mast
R.A.F. Chenies
CHENIES HILL
DACORUM
THREE RIVERS
TOP SPRING
OLDCROFT WOOD
Mast
73
LONG WOOD
Martin Top Farm
HANGINGLANE WOOD
DAFFODIL SPRING
RED LION LANE
BRAMBLE CROFT
The Boot PH
Sarratt

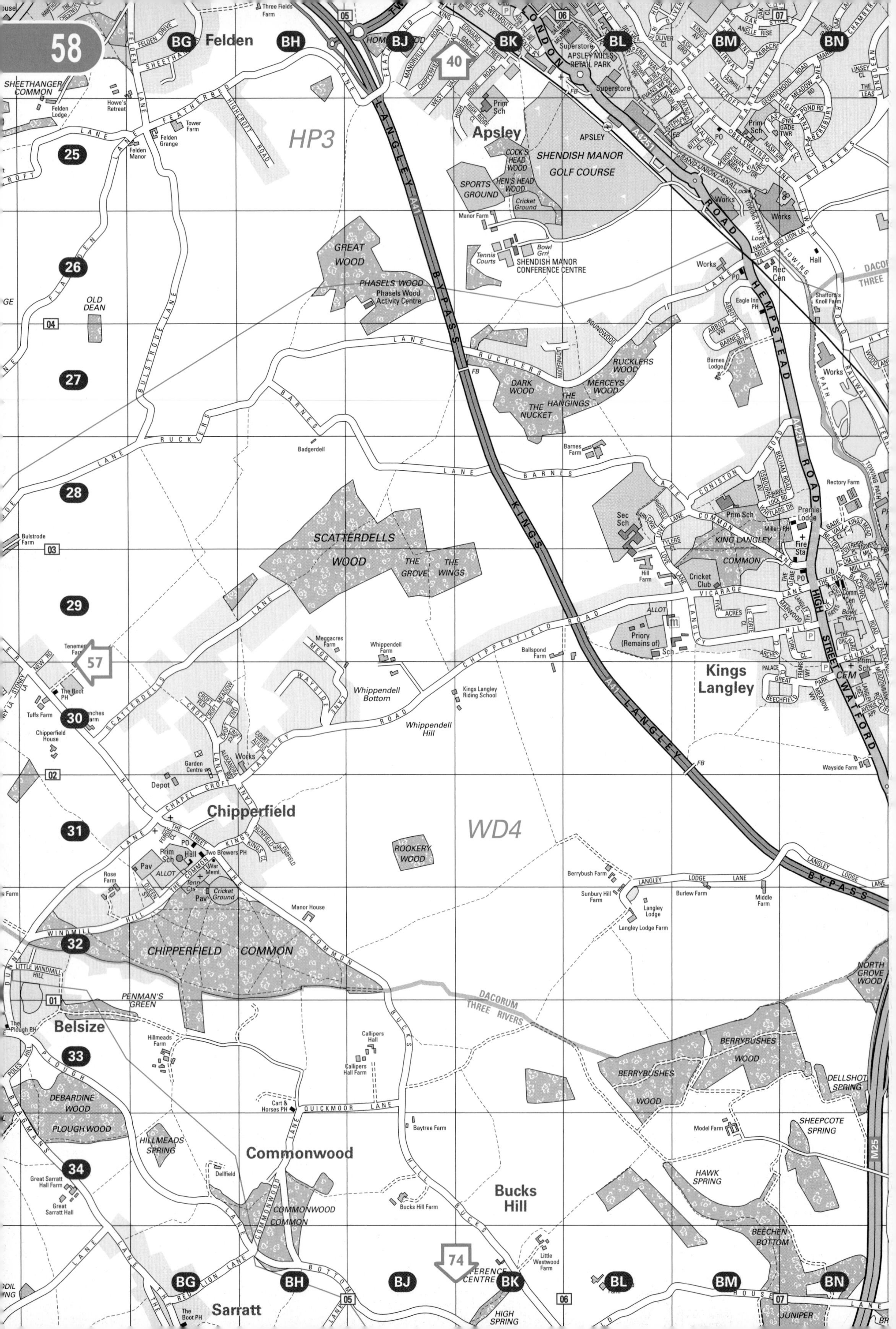
Felden
SHEETHANGER COMMON
Felden Lodge
Howe's Retreat
Tower Farm
Felden Grange
Felden Manor
FEATHERBED LANE
HIGHCROFT ROAD
BULSTRODE LANE
FLAUNDEN LANE
OLD DEAN
HP3
Apsley
APSLEY MILLS RETAIL PARK
Superstore
Prim Sch
COCK'S HEAD WOOD
HEN'S HEAD WOOD
SPORTS GROUND
SHENDISH MANOR GOLF COURSE
Manor Farm
Tennis Courts
Bowl Grn
SHENDISH MANOR CONFERENCE CENTRE
GRAND UNION CANAL
LONDON ROAD
HEMPSTEAD ROAD
Works
Rec Cen
Hall
Shafford's Knoll Farm
GREAT WOOD
PHASELS WOOD
Phasels Wood Activity Centre
LANGLEY BYPASS
A41
RUCKLERS LANE
RUCKLERS WOOD
DARK WOOD
MERCEYS WOOD
THE HANGINGS
THE NUCKET
Eagle Inn PH
Barnes Lodge
BARNES LANE
Badgerdell
Barnes Farm
Rectory Farm
Bulstrode Farm
SCATTERDELLS WOOD
THE GROVE
THE WINGS
Sec Sch
Prim Sch
Premier Lodge
KING LANGLEY COMMON
Cricket Club
Hill Farm
Fire Sta
VICARAGE LANE
Priory (Remains of)
Ballspond Farm
Kings Langley
HIGH STREET
WATFORD ROAD
Meggacres Farm
Whippendell Farm
Whippendell Bottom
Whippendell Hill
Kings Langley Riding School
CHIPPERFIELD ROAD
The Boot PH
Tuffs Farm
Chipperfield House
Garden Centre
Depot
Works
Chipperfield
Wayside Farm
WD4
ROOKERY WOOD
Prim Sch
Two Brewers PH
Rose Farm
Pav
Cricket Ground
Manor House
Berrybush Farm
Sunbury Hill Farm
Langley Lodge
Langley Lodge Farm
Burlew Farm
Middle Farm
LANGLEY LODGE LANE
CHIPPERFIELD COMMON
PENMAN'S GREEN
DACORUM
THREE RIVERS
NORTH GROVE WOOD
Belsize
The Plough PH
Hillmeads Farm
Callipers Hall
Callipers Hall Farm
BERRYBUSHES WOOD
DELLSHOT SPRING
DEBARDINE WOOD
PLOUGH WOOD
Cart & Horses PH
QUICKMOOR LANE
Baytree Farm
Model Farm
SHEEPCOTE SPRING
HILLMEADS SPRING
Commonwood
HAWK SPRING
M25
Great Sarratt Hall Farm
Great Sarratt Hall
Dellfield
COMMONWOOD COMMON
Bucks Hill Farm
Bucks Hill
BEECHEN BOTTOM
Little Westwood Farm
Sarratt
The Boot PH
HIGH SPRING
JUNIPER

POTTERS CROUCH PLANTATION
HP3
Bedmond
WD5
Junction 21 M25
Junction 6A M1
ABBOTS LANGLEY
Junction 20
Hunton Bridge
Langleybury
Woodside
Leavesden Green
Kingswood
Garston
WD25
KINGS LANGLEY
LEAVESDEN COUNTRY PARK
NORTH ORBITAL ROAD
NORTH WESTERN AVENUE

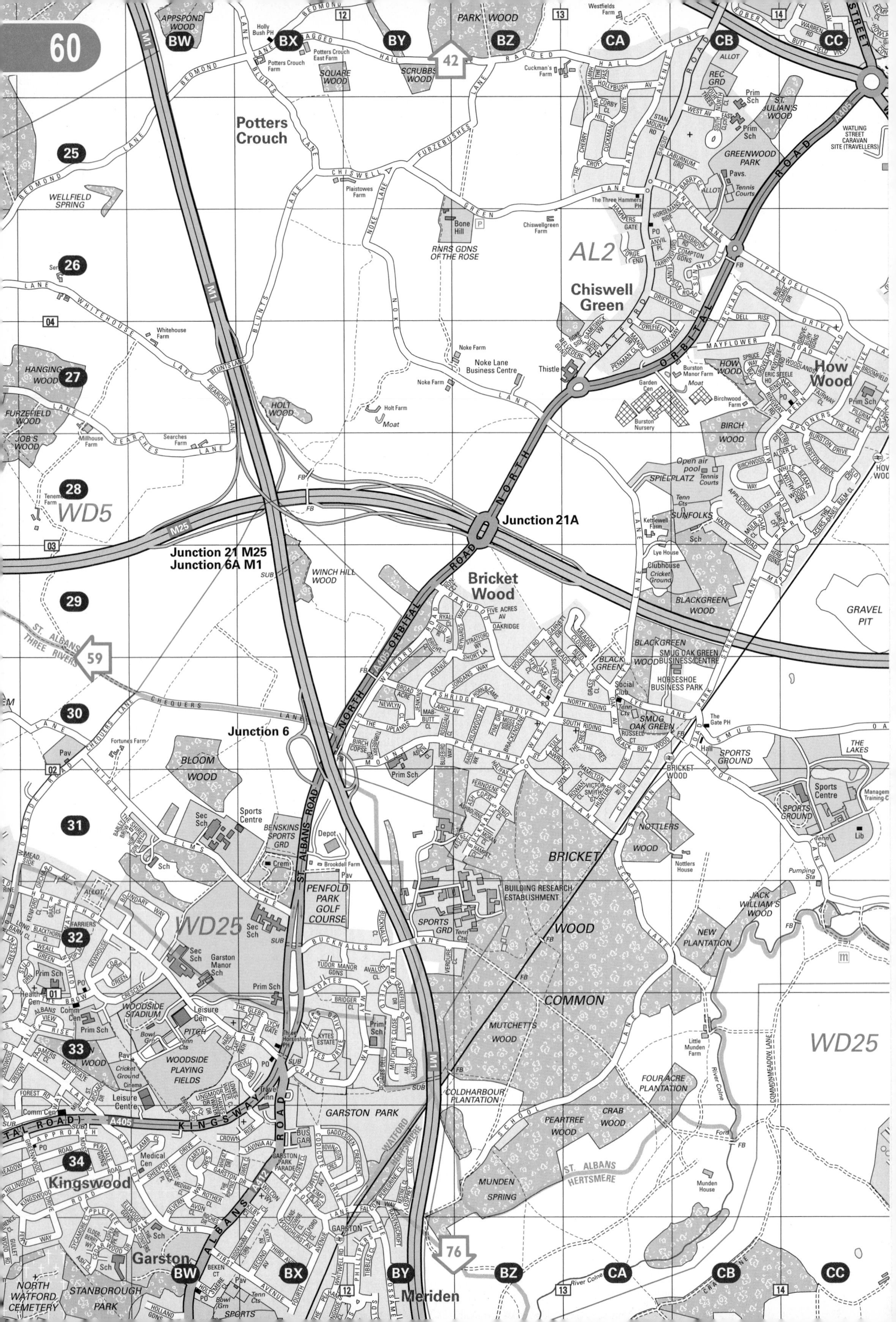
BW
BX
BY
BZ
CA
CB
CC
42
59
76
25
26
27
28
29
30
31
32
33
34
APPSPOND WOOD
PARK WOOD
SQUARE WOOD
SCRUBBS WOOD
Potters Crouch
Potters Crouch Farm
Potters Crouch East Farm
Holly Bush PH
Westfields Farm
Cuckman's Farm
ST. JULIAN'S WOOD
WATLING STREET CARAVAN SITE (TRAVELLERS)
GREENWOOD PARK
WELLFIELD SPRING
Plaistowes Farm
Bone Hill
RNRS GDNS OF THE ROSE
Chiswellgreen Farm
The Three Hammers PH
AL2
Chiswell Green
Whitehouse Farm
HANGING WOOD
FURZEFIELD WOOD
JOB'S WOOD
Millhouse Farm
Searches Farm
Noke Farm
Noke Lane Business Centre
Thistle
HOLT WOOD
Holt Farm
Moat
Burston Manor Farm
Burston Nursery
Birchwood Farm
How Wood
BIRCH WOOD
Open air pool
SPIELPLATZ
SUNFOLKS
WD5
M25
M1
Junction 21A
Junction 21 M25
Junction 6A M1
WINCH HILL WOOD
Bricket Wood
Kettlewell Farm
Lye House
Clubhouse
Cricket Ground
BLACKGREEN WOOD
GRAVEL PIT
SMUG OAK GREEN BUSINESS CENTRE
HORSESHOE BUSINESS PARK
SMUG OAK GREEN
The Gate PH
SPORTS GROUND
THE LAKES
Sports Centre
ST. ALBANS
THREE RIVERS
Junction 6
Fortunes Farm
BLOOM WOOD
Sports Centre
BENSKINS SPORTS GRD
Depot
Brookdell Farm
PENFOLD PARK GOLF COURSE
NOTTLERS WOOD
Nottlers House
BRICKET WOOD COMMON
BUILDING RESEARCH ESTABLISHMENT
JACK WILLIAM'S WOOD
NEW PLANTATION
WD25
Garston Manor Sch
WOODSIDE STADIUM
WOODSIDE PLAYING FIELDS
MUTCHETTS WOOD
Little Munden Farm
River Colne
FOUR ACRE PLANTATION
COLDHARBOUR PLANTATION
GARSTON PARK
PEARTREE WOOD
CRAB WOOD
HERTSMERE
MUNDEN SPRING
Munden House
Kingswood
Garston
NORTH WATFORD CEMETERY
STANBOROUGH PARK
Meriden
NORTH ORBITAL ROAD
ST. ALBANS ROAD
KINGSWAY
A405
A412

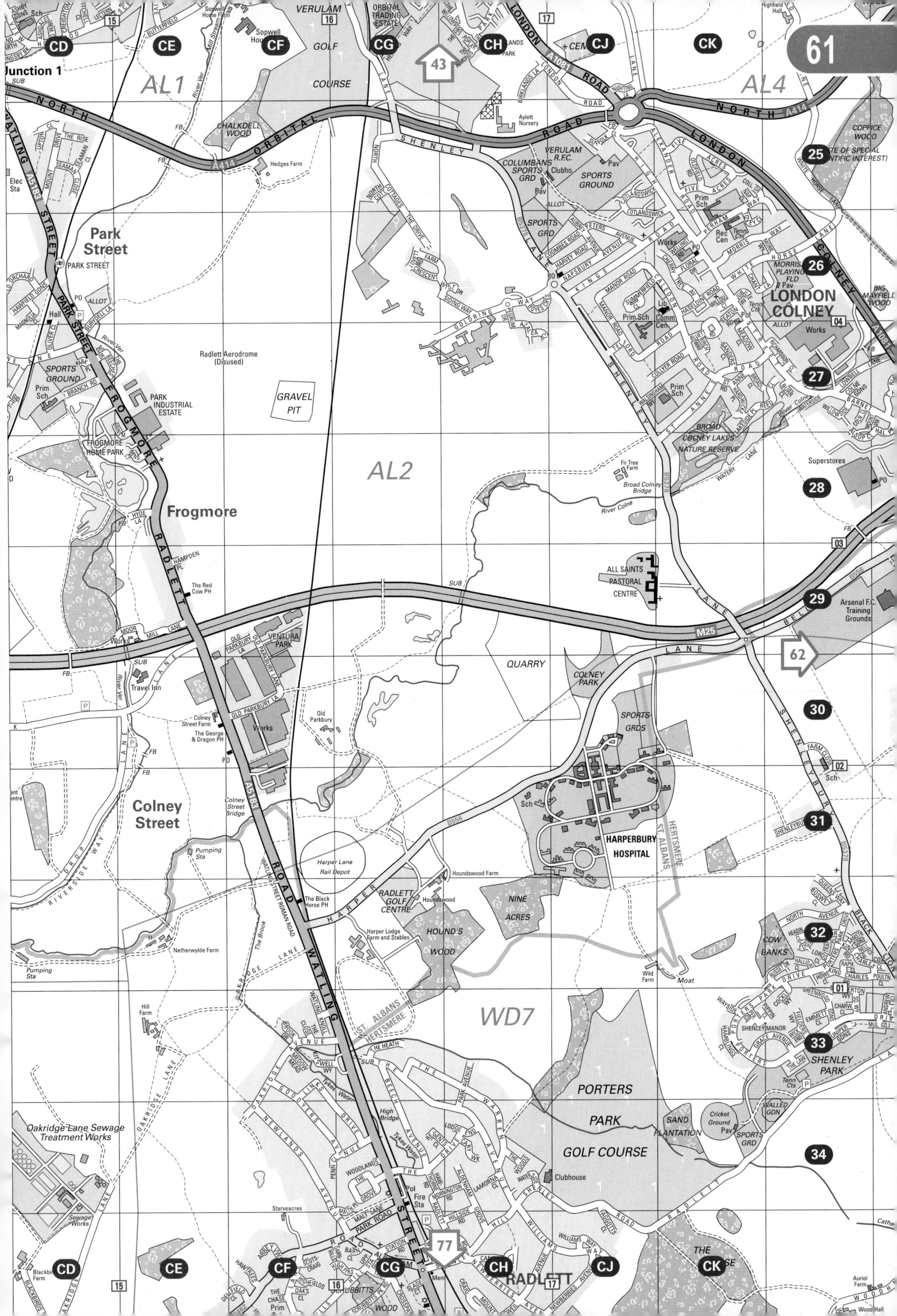

VERULAM GOLF COURSE
ORBITAL TRADING ESTATE
Sopwell House
Sopwell Home Farm
Junction 1
AL1
AL4
AL2
WD7
NORTH ORBITAL ROAD
A414
LONDON ROAD
A1081
NORTH LONDON
CHALKDELL WOOD
Hedges Farm
Aylett Nursery
COPPICE WOOD
SHENLEY LANE
VERULAM R.F.C.
COLUMBANS SPORTS GRD
SPORTS GROUND
SPORTS GRD
Park Street
PARK STREET
Elec Sta
WATLING STREET
A5183
Radlett Aerodrome (Disused)
GRAVEL PIT
PARK INDUSTRIAL ESTATE
SPORTS GROUND
FROGMORE HOME PARK
Frogmore
FROGMORE
RADLETT ROAD
The Red Cow PH
LONDON COLNEY
MORRIS PLAYING FLD
BIG MAYFIELD WOOD
BROAD COLNEY LAKES NATURE RESERVE
Fir Tree Farm
Broad Colney Bridge
River Colne
Superstores
ALL SAINTS PASTORAL CENTRE
M25
Arsenal F.C. Training Grounds
VENTURA PARK
QUARRY
COLNEY PARK
Travel Inn
Colney Street Farm
The George & Dragon PH
Old Parkbury
Works
Colney Street
Colney Street Bridge
SPORTS GRDS
HARPERBURY HOSPITAL
HERTSMERE
ST. ALBANS
Pumping Sta
Harper Lane Rail Depot
Houndswood Farm
RADLETT GOLF CENTRE
Houndswood
The Black Horse PH
HARPER LANE
NINE ACRES
HOUND'S WOOD
Harper Lodge Farm and Stables
Netherwylde Farm
RIVERSIDE WAY
COW BANKS
Wild Farm
Moat
Hill Farm
SHENLEY MANOR
SHENLEY PARK
PORTERS PARK GOLF COURSE
SAND PLANTATION
Cricket Ground
Clubhouse
Oakridge Lane Sewage Treatment Works
Sewage Works
OAKRIDGE LANE
Starveacres
RADLETT
WATLING STREET
THE CHASE
Blackbirds Farm
Auriol Farm
Wood Hall
CD
CE
CF
CG
CH
CJ
CK
43
62
77
15
16
17
25
26
27
28
29
30
31
32
33
34
01
02
03
04

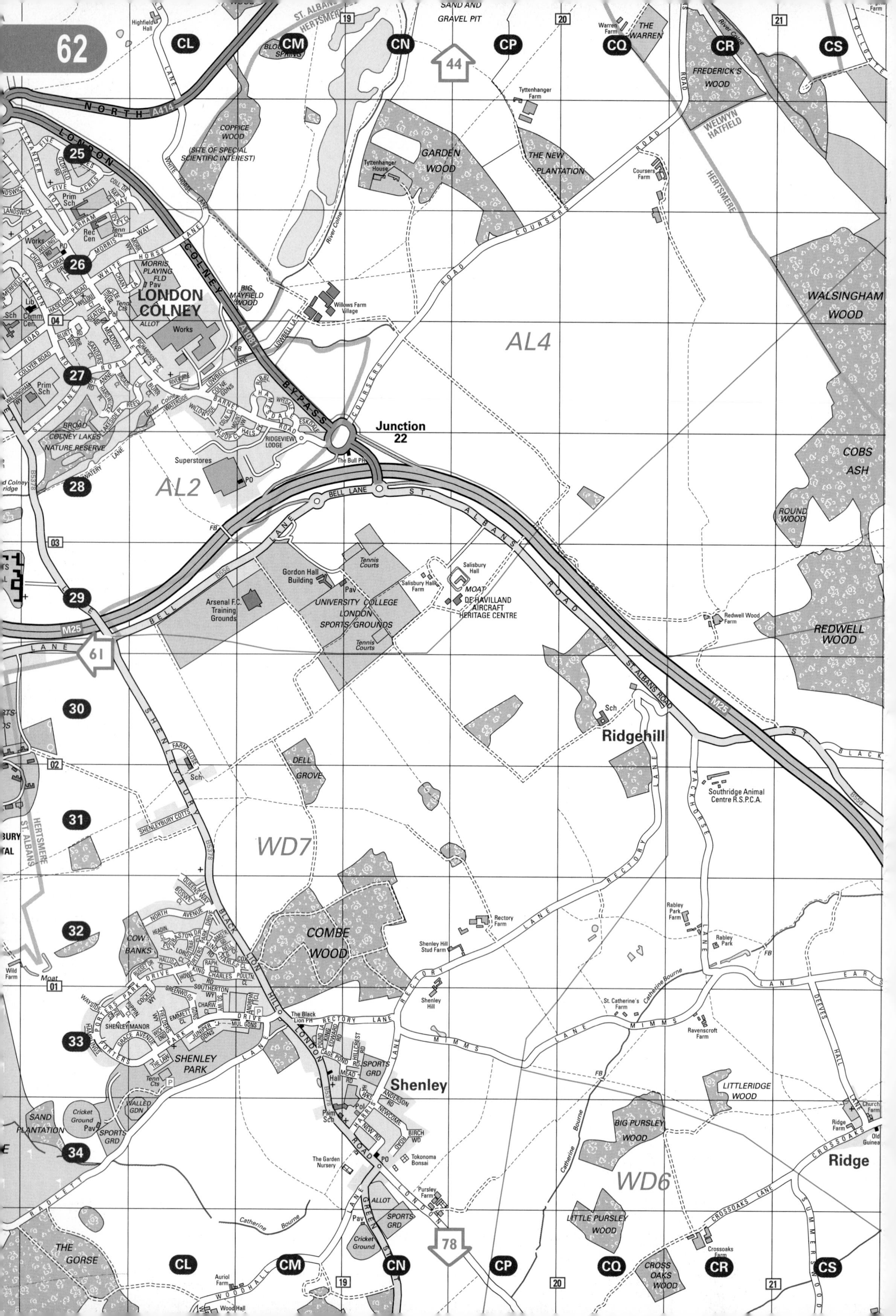
LONDON COLNEY
Junction 22
AL4
AL2
WD7
WD6
Ridgehill
Shenley
Ridge
GARDEN WOOD
THE NEW PLANTATION
FREDERICK'S WOOD
THE WARREN
WALSINGHAM WOOD
COBS ASH
ROUND WOOD
REDWELL WOOD
COPPICE WOOD (SITE OF SPECIAL SCIENTIFIC INTEREST)
BIG MAYFIELD WOOD
BROAD COLNEY LAKES NATURE RESERVE
UNIVERSITY COLLEGE LONDON SPORTS GROUNDS
Arsenal F.C. Training Grounds
Gordon Hall Building
DE HAVILLAND AIRCRAFT HERITAGE CENTRE
Southridge Animal Centre R.S.P.C.A.
DELL GROVE
COMBE WOOD
COW BANKS
SHENLEY PARK
SAND PLANTATION
THE GORSE
LITTLERIDGE WOOD
BIG PURSLEY WOOD
LITTLE PURSLEY WOOD
CROSS OAKS WOOD
NORTH ORBITAL ROAD
LONDON COLNEY BYPASS
M25
ST. ALBANS ROAD
BELL LANE
COURSERS ROAD
RECTORY LANE
MIMMS LANE
PACKHORSE LANE
SHENLEYBURY
BLACK LION HILL
LONDON ROAD
CROSSOAKS LANE
RADLETT LANE
WOODHALL LANE
HARRIS LANE
44
61
78
CL
CM
CN
CP
CQ
CR
CS
19
20
21
25
26
27
28
29
30
31
32
33
34
04
03
02
01

CT
CU
CV
CW
CX
CY
CZ
45
64
79
22
23
24
WOOD
NORTH MYMMS PARK
North Mymms Park Training Centre
Cricket Club
Cricket Ground
Home Farm
Water End
DIXONS HILL ROAD
SWANLAND ROAD
WARRENGATE ROAD
BRADMORE LANE
Potterells Farm
Comm Cen
REC GRD
Med Cen
BRICK KILN WOOD
WISE'S LANE
Pumping Sta
CANGSLEY WOOD
Royal Veterinary College (Hawkshead)
COLLEGE CLOSE
HAWKSHEAD LANE
HAWKSHEAD WOOD
WELWYN HATFIELD
HERTSMERE
MYMMSHALL WOOD
Site of Motte & Baileys
Mimmshall Brook
Pav
Tennis Courts
SPORTS GROUND
PILVAGE WOOD
Hawkshead Rail Bridge
PELPIN'S WOOD
BROOKMANS PARK GOLF COURSE
ROUND WOOD
Clubhouse
Sec Sch
BROOKMANS PARK
Prim Sch
PO
Lib
BROOKMANS AVENUE
MOFFATS LANE
BLUEBRIDGE ROAD
WESTLAND DRIVE
OAKLANDS AVENUE
THE GARDENS
GOBIONS OPEN SPACE
GOBIONS GARDEN
GOBIONS POND
AL9
Blue Bridge
Deep Bottom
SWALLOW HOLES
Royal Veterinary College (Boltons Park Farm)
POTTERS BAR GOLF COURSE
Cricket Ground
Depot
Works
FURZEFIELD WOOD
CRANBORNE INDUSTRIAL ESTATE
KING GEORGE V PLAYING FLDS
Sports Cen
Warrengate Farm
Mimms Hall Farm
MUTTON LANE
Widmore Hall
TEMPLE COURT
Prim Sch
Comm Cen
Superstore
Wyllyotts Cen & Mus
RITZ COURT
POTTERS BAR
EN6
Town Farm
CECIL ROAD
Catherine Bourne
South Mimms
Prim Sch
ST. ALBANS ROAD
Earl's Farm
Bignell's Corner
Holiday Inn South Mimms
Depot
South Mimms Services
Days Inn
Works
Cancer Research UK
Nat Inst for Biological Standards & Control
Blanche Farm
Bridgefoot
Bridgefoot House
BRIDGEFOOT LANE
Dugdale Hill
Sec Sch
Rydal Mount
Rydal Mount Stables
Prim Sch
Fire Sta
Amb Sta
War Meml
CEM
M25
A1(M)
Junction 23 (M25) Junction 1 A1(M)
BENTLEY HEATH
Elm Farm
Bentley Heath Farm
Garden Centre
Bentley Heath
Duke of York PH
Summerswood Farm

BROOKMANS PARK
GOLF COURSE
GEORGE'S WOOD
AL9
GOBIONS WOOD
LEGGATTS WOOD
WELL WOOD
GREAT
Royal Veterinary College (Boltons Park Farm)
POTTERS BAR
Northaw
EN6
HOOK WOOD
FIVE ACRE WOOD
POND WOOD
POTTERS BAR COMMUNITY HOSP
Junction 24
Bentley Heath
Ganwick Corner
46
63
80

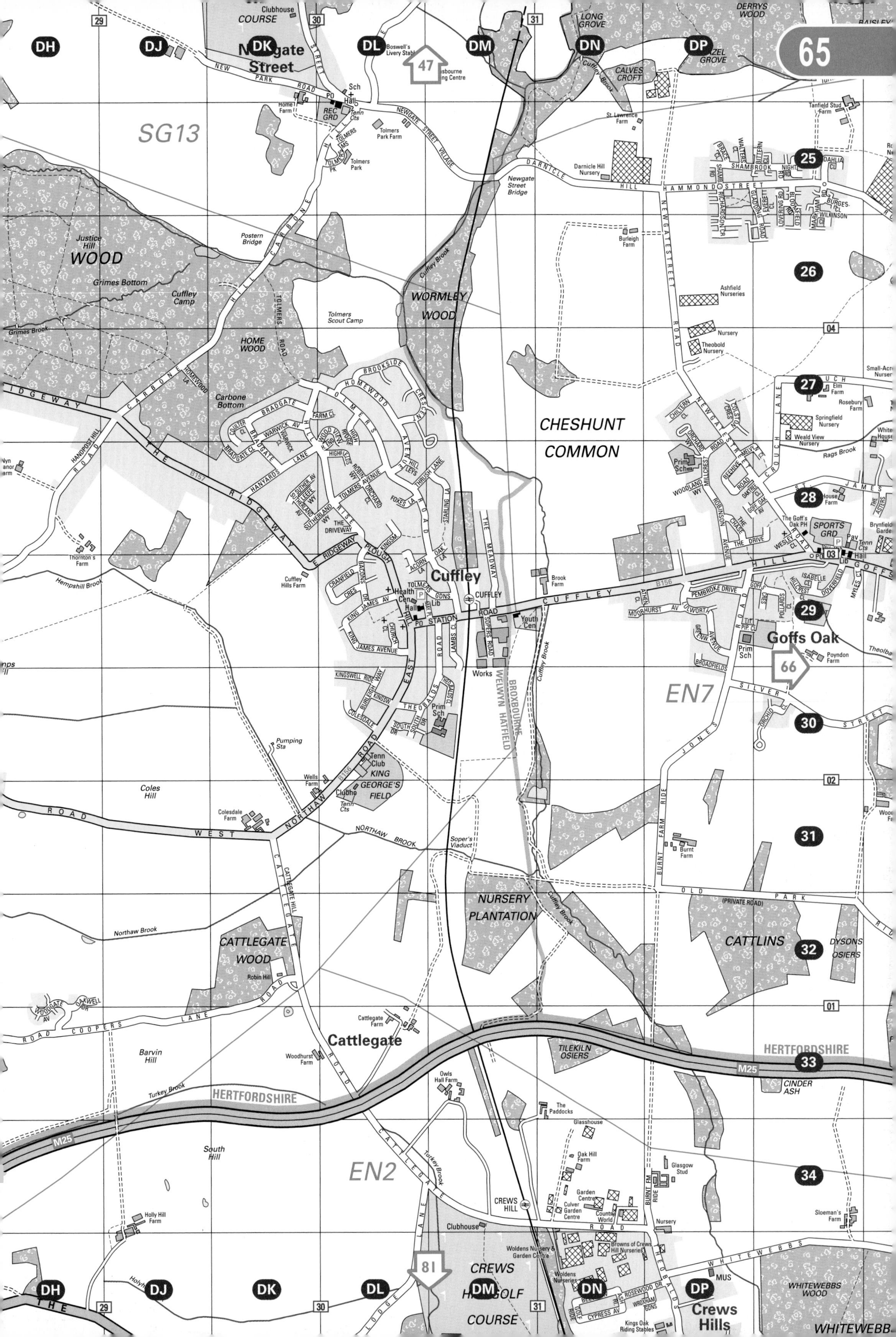

Clubhouse
COURSE
Newgate Street
NEW PARK ROAD
STREET
Sch
Hall
PO
REC GRD
Tenn Cts
Home Farm
Boswell's Livery Stables
47
NEWGATE STREET VILLAGE
Tolmers Park Farm
TOLMERS MS
TOLMERS PK
Tolmers Park
SG13
LONG GROVE
DERRYS WOOD
HAZEL GROVE
CALVES CROFT
Cuffley Brook
St Lawrence Farm
Tanfield Stud Farm
Darnicle Hill Nursery
DARNICLE HILL
Newgate Street Bridge
HAMMOND STREET
SHAMBROOK
NIGHT RD
DAHLIA CL
WALTERS
BITTERN
BURGES CL
WILKINSON
EVERETT CL
LOVERING RD
RICHARDSON CR
MARKHAM RD
NEWGATE STREET ROAD
Burleigh Farm
Ashfield Nurseries
Nursery
Theobold Nursery
Postern Bridge
CARBONE HILL
Justice Hill
WOOD
Grimes Bottom
Cuffley Camp
Grimes Brook
TOLMERS ROAD
Tolmers Scout Camp
WORMLEY WOOD
Cuffley Brook
HOME WOOD
HOMEWOOD LA
Carbone Bottom
BROOKSIDE
HOMEWOOD
CRESCENT
FARM CL
BRADGATE
WARWICK AV
WARWICK CL
COULTER CL
BRADGATE CL
HANYARDS LANE
HIGHFIELDS
ROBIN WY
TOLMERS AVENUE
ORCHARD CL
FOXES LA
HILL LEYS
THRUSH LANE
STARLING LA
SUTHERLAND WY
THE DRIVEWAY
RIDGEWAY
THE RIDGEWAY
HANDPOST HILL ROAD
B157
Thornton's Farm
Hempshill Brook
Cuffley Hills Farm
CRANFIELD CRES
BACONS DR
KINGS JAMES AV
KINGSMEAD
PLOUGH HILL
ACORN LA
OAK LA
Cuffley
Health Cen
Lib
Hall
PO
STATION ROAD
CUFFLEY
TOLMERS GDNS
THE MEADWAY
CHURCH CL
KING JAMES AVENUE
LAMBS CL
SOPERS ROAD
Works
Youth Cen
Brook Farm
CUFFLEY HILL
B156
CHESHUNT COMMON
27
Elm Farm
Rosebury Farm
Springfield Nursery
Weald View Nursery
Rags Brook
CROUCH LANE
CHILTERN CL
ORCHARD WY
NEWGATE STREET ROAD
Prim Sch
WOODLAND WY
MILLCREST
ROBINSON AVENUE
BEEHIVE
MELVILLE
THE CHASE
THE DRIVE
WESLEY CL
28
House Farm
JAMES
The Goff's Oak PH
SPORTS GRD
Pav
Tenn Cts
Hall
Lib
PO
03
GOFFS
ISABELLE CL
HILLCREST
DOVERFIELD
PEMBROKE DRIVE
MOORHURST AV
ATHEN
LUDWORTH
GREENWAY AVENUE
BROADFIELDS
POLLARDS CL
29
Goffs Oak
Prim Sch
Poyndon Farm
66
EN7
SILVER STREET
ORCHID CL
JONES ROAD
30
Theobalds
KINGSWELL RIDE
BURLEIGH WAY
KINGSW
COLESDALE
EAST RIDGEWAY
THEOBALDS ROAD
THEOBALDS CL
Prim Sch
SOUTH DR
Pumping Sta
Tenn Club
KING GEORGE'S FIELD
Clubhouse
Tenn Cts
Wells Farm
NORTHAW ROAD
Coles Hill
Colesdale Farm
WEST ROAD
NORTHAW BROOK
Soper's Viaduct
BROXBOURNE
WELWYN HATFIELD
Cuffley Brook
02
BURNT FARM RIDE
Burnt Farm
31
OLD PARK
(PRIVATE ROAD)
CATTLINS
DYSONS OSIERS
32
NURSERY PLANTATION
CATTLEGATE HILL
Northaw Brook
CATTLEGATE WOOD
Robin Hill
WOODGATE AV
OAKWELL DR
COOPERS LANE ROAD
Cattlegate Farm
Cattlegate
Barvin Hill
Woodhurst Farm
Turkey Brook
HERTFORDSHIRE
M25
TILEKILN OSIERS
HERTFORDSHIRE
33
CINDER ASH
01
Owls Hall Farm
The Paddocks
Glasshouse
Oak Hill Farm
Glasgow Stud
South Hill
EN2
CATTLEGATE ROAD
Turkey Brook
34
Garden Centre
Culver Garden Centre
Country World
CREWS HILL
BURNT FM RIDE
Nursery
Holly Hill Farm
Clubhouse
ROAD
Woldens Nursery & Garden Centre
Browns of Crews Hill Nurseries
Sloeman's Farm
WHITEWEBBS
81
CREWS HILL GOLF COURSE
Woldens Nurseries
ROSEWOOD DR
WROXHAM GDNS
CYPRESS AV
MUS
Crews Hill
WHITEWEBBS WOOD
Kings Oak Riding Stables
LODGE
THE
WHITEWEBB
DH
DJ
DK
DL
DM
DN
DP
29
30
31
04
25
26

DERRYS WOOD
BAISLEY'S WOOD
Turnford Brook
DQ
DR
DS
DT
DU
DV
DW
48
Beaumont Manor Farm
Bread and Cheese Bridge
Cheshunt Park Farm
PRIESTS OSIERS
SPRING WOOD
WATERCRES TROT
Tanfield Stud Farm
Paradise Nursery
GAMMONS LANE
Doggett Hill
CROMWELL WOOD
Paradise House
Mast
25
SHAMBROOK
HAMMOND STREET
Rosary Nursery
Gammon Farm
Francis Farm
APPLEBY STREET OPEN SPACE
Appleby Street Farm
Cheshunt Park Farm
Burleigh Farm
26
Ashfield Nurseries
ROUNDCROFT WOOD
CHESHUNT PARK
CHESHUNT GOLF COURSE
Hammond Street
04
Nursery
Theobold Nursery
27
CROUCH LANE
Small-Acre Nursery
Elm Farm
Malaya Farm
Burton Grange
Clubhouse
CHESHUNT RESERVOIR (NORTH)
Rosebury Farm
Triangle Nursery
Springfield Nursery
Weald View Nursery
White House Farm
Twelve Acres Farm
Rags Brook
Garyross Farm
Pylon Farm
POETS GATE
Prim Sch
28
White House Farm
Prince of Wales PH
ST JAMES RD
ANDREWS LANE
Flamstead End
Goff's Oak PH
SPORTS GRD
Brynfield Nursery & Garden Centre
ROSEDALE SPORTS GROUND
03
B156
Wheelwrights PH
GOFFS LANE
29
Tudor Nursery
Goffs Oak
EN7
Prim Sch
65
Poyndon Farm
Theobalds Brook
Colesgrove Manor
SPORTS GRDS
MOAT
Sec Sch
30
SILVER STREET
Kobe Nursery
Crescent Nursery
Rentokil Tropical Plants
Halstead Hill Nursery
LIEUTENANT ELLIS WAY
CIVIC OFFICES
Crocodile PH
02
ADATH YISROEL CEMETERY
Woodgreen Farm
BARROW LANE
SPORTS GROUND
CEM
Sec Sch
EN8
31
Burnt Farm
Broadfield Farm
Bury Green
Albury Farm
Sports Hall
OLD PARK (PRIVATE ROAD)
BURYGREEN PLANTATION
BROOM HILLS
RIFLE CLUB
32
CATTLINS
DYSONS OSIERS
HOME WOOD
Theobalds (Site of)
01
HANGING PLANTATION
Spring Farm
HOME PLANTATION
Temple Bar
Tesco Country Club
SPORTS GRD
WINSTON
HERTFORDSHIRE
33
M25
OLD PARK RIDE
Theobalds Park
CINDER ASH
Gunsite Farm Stables
SQUARE PLANTING
SOUTH OSIERS
Theobalds Park Farm
PARK LANE
GREAT CAMBRIDGE ROAD
A10
Bullscross Farm
Glasgow Stud
34
BULLSCROSS RIDE CEMETERY (JEWISH)
Theobalds Park Camping and Caravan Site
South Villa Nursery
BROXBOURNE
Junction 25
COUNTY BROOK PLANTATION
Aqueduct
Whitewebbs Farm
Sloeman's Farm
Nursery
Bulls Cross
Water World, Aquatic & Garden Centre
Capel Manor College
BULLSMOOR
WHITEWEBBS ROAD
82
MUS
Cricket Ground
SPORTS GROUND
CAPEL HOUSE
Crews Hill
Kings Oak Riding Stables
WHITEWEBBS
OPEN SPACE
35

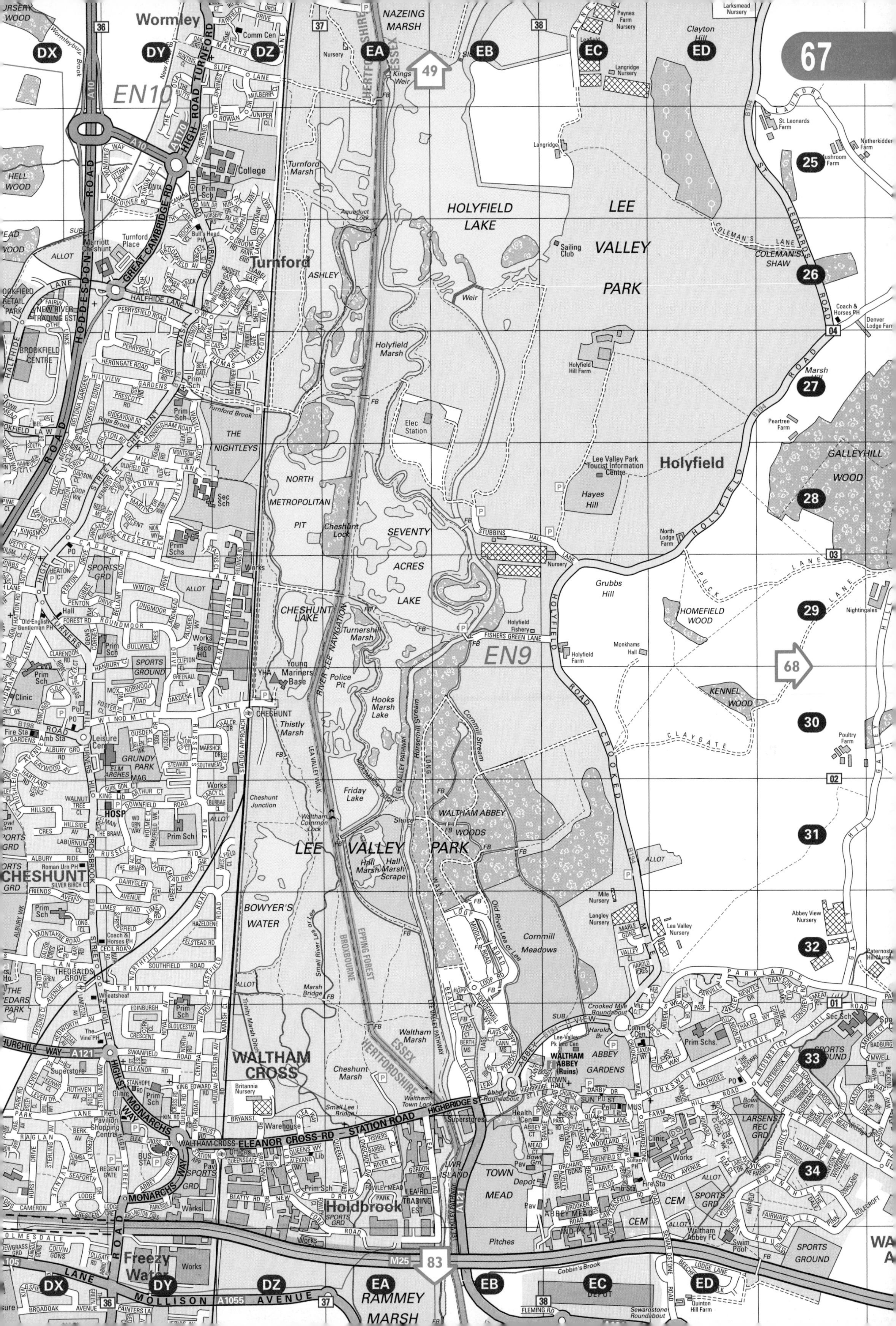

DX
DY
DZ
EA
EB
EC
ED
36
37
38
49
68
83
Wormley
EN10
EN9
Turnford
Cheshunt
CHESHUNT
Waltham Cross
WALTHAM CROSS
Holdbrook
Freezy Water
RAMMEY MARSH
NAZEING MARSH
Clayton Hill
HOLYFIELD LAKE
LEE VALLEY PARK
Holyfield
GALLEYHILL WOOD
HOMEFIELD WOOD
KENNEL WOOD
Grubbs Hill
Hayes Hill
Lee Valley Park Tourist Information Centre
Holyfield Hill Farm
Holyfield Farm
Holyfield Marsh
Turnford Marsh
ASHLEY
NORTH METROPOLITAN PIT
SEVENTY ACRES LAKE
CHESHUNT LAKE
Turnershill Marsh
Police Pit
Hooks Marsh Lake
Thistly Marsh
Friday Lake
BOWYER'S WATER
WALTHAM ABBEY WOODS
Cornmill Meadows
Hall Marsh
Hall Marsh Scrape
Waltham Marsh
Cheshunt Marsh
THE NIGHTLEYS
RIVER LEE NAVIGATION
HERTFORDSHIRE
ESSEX
BROXBOURNE
EPPING FOREST
HALFHIDE LANE
GREAT CAMBRIDGE RD
HODDESDON ROAD
HIGH ROAD TURNFORD
HOLYFIELD ROAD
CROOKED MILE
ST LEONARDS ROAD
FISHERS GREEN LANE
STUBBINS HALL LANE
ELEANOR CROSS RD
STATION ROAD
HIGHBRIDGE ST
MONKSWOOD AVENUE
MOLLISON AVENUE
MONARCHS WAY
WALTHAM ABBEY (Ruins)
ABBEY GARDENS
TOWN MEAD
LARSENS REC GRD
SPORTS GROUND
Waltham Abbey FC
M25
A10
A121
A1055
A1170
B194
25
26
27
28
29
30
31
32
33
34

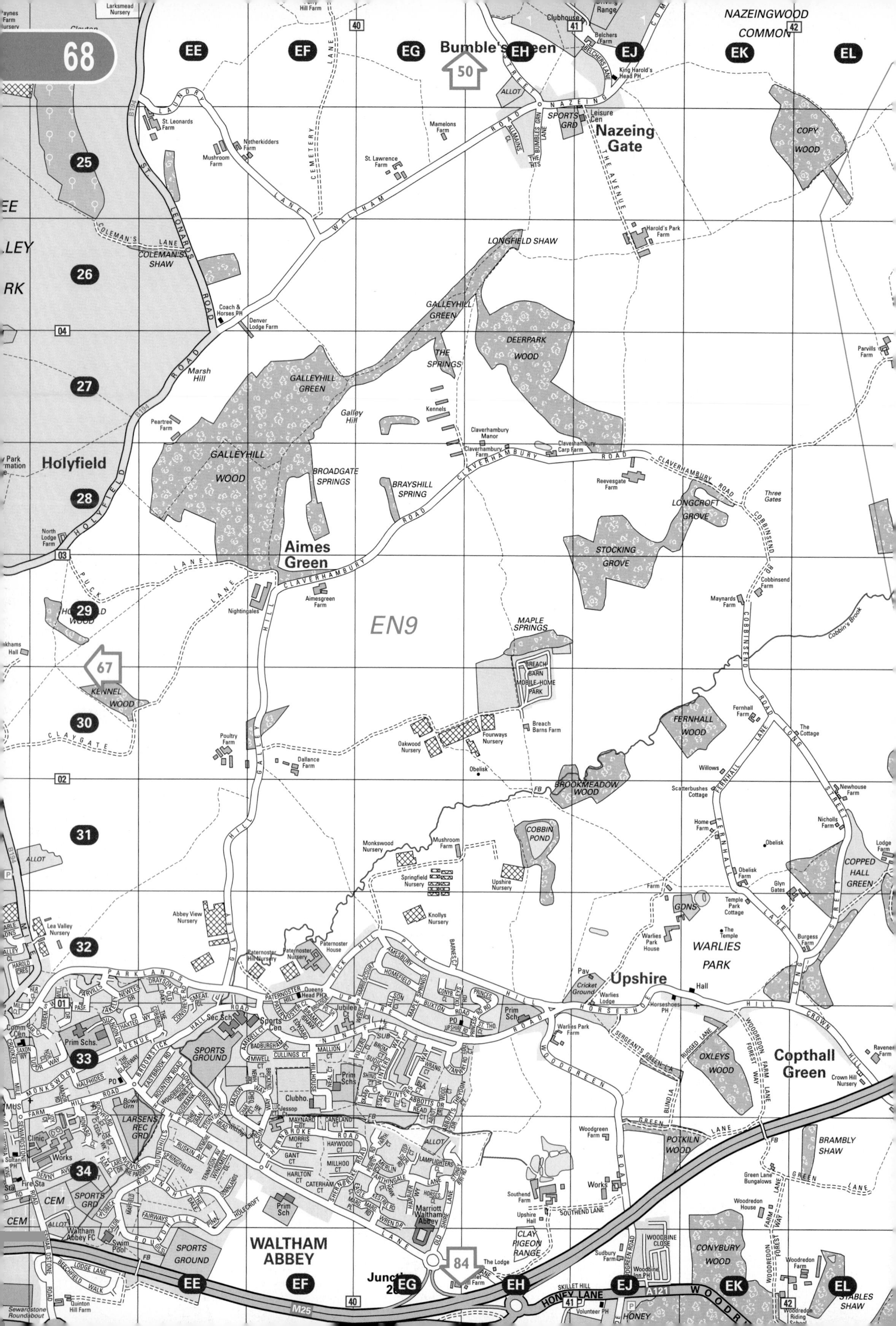
Bumble's Green
Nazeing Gate
NAZEINGWOOD COMMON
Holyfield
Aimes Green
EN9
Upshire
WARLIES PARK
Copthall Green
WALTHAM ABBEY
GALLEYHILL WOOD
DEERPARK WOOD
STOCKING GROVE
LONGCROFT GROVE
COPY WOOD
FERNHALL WOOD
BROOKMEADOW WOOD
OXLEYS WOOD
POTKILN WOOD
CONYBURY WOOD
BRAMBLY SHAW
COPPED HALL GREEN
KENNEL WOOD
LONGFIELD SHAW
MAPLE SPRINGS
BROADGATE SPRINGS
BRAYSHILL SPRING
CLAVERHAMBURY ROAD
COBBINSEND ROAD
GALLEY HILL
PICK HILL
HORSESHOE HILL
CROWN HILL
WOODGREEN ROAD
HONEY LANE
M25
Junction 26
50
67
84

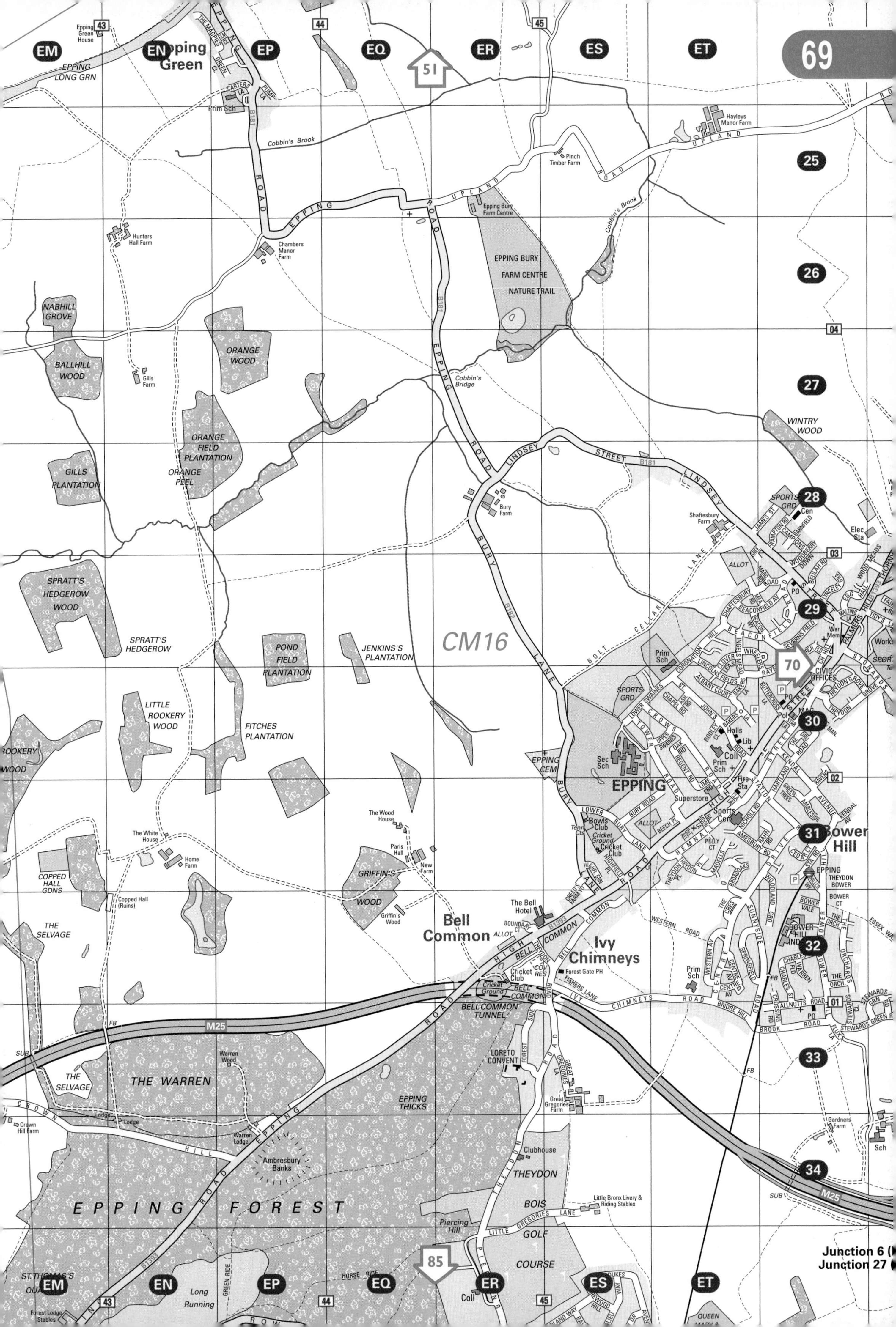

69
EM
EN
EP
EQ
ER
ES
ET
43
44
45
51
Epping Green House
Epping Green
EPPING LONG GRN
Prim Sch
Cobbin's Brook
Hayleys Manor Farm
UPLAND ROAD
Pinch Timber Farm
EPPING ROAD
Epping Bury Farm Centre
Hunters Hall Farm
Chambers Manor Farm
EPPING BURY FARM CENTRE NATURE TRAIL
25
26
27
28
29
30
31
32
33
34
04
03
02
01
NABHILL GROVE
BALLHILL WOOD
ORANGE WOOD
Gills Farm
Cobbin's Bridge
ORANGE FIELD PLANTATION
ORANGE PEEL
GILLS PLANTATION
WINTRY WOOD
LINDSEY STREET
Bury Farm
Shaftesbury Farm
SPORTS GRD
Elec Sta
ALLOT
SPRATT'S HEDGEROW WOOD
SPRATT'S HEDGEROW
POND FIELD PLANTATION
JENKINS'S PLANTATION
CM16
BURY LANE
BOLT CELLAR LANE
70
CIVIC OFFICES
LITTLE ROOKERY WOOD
FITCHES PLANTATION
ROOKERY WOOD
EPPING CEM
Sec Sch
EPPING
Superstore
Halls
Lib
Coll
Fire Sta
Bower Hill
The Wood House
The White House
Paris Hall
New Farm
Home Farm
COPPED HALL GDNS
GRIFFIN'S WOOD
Copped Hall (Ruins)
Griffin's Wood
The Bell Hotel
THE SELVAGE
Bell Common
Ivy Chimneys
Forest Gate PH
Cricket Club
BELL COMMON TUNNEL
IVY CHIMNEYS ROAD
WESTERN ROAD
M25
LORETO CONVENT
THE WARREN
Warren Wood
EPPING THICKS
Great Gregories Farm
Crown Hill Farm
Lodge
Warren Lodge
Ambresbury Banks
Clubhouse
THEYDON BOIS GOLF COURSE
Gardners Farm
Sch
EPPING FOREST
Little Bronx Livery & Riding Stables
Piercing Hill
85
Junction 6
Junction 27
ST THOMAS'S QUARTERS
Long Running
Forest Lodge Stables
Coll

EU
EV
EW
EX
EY
EZ
FA
52
47
48
49
WEALD HALL LANE SEWAGE WORKS
Thames Water Sewage Treatment Plant
Garden Centre
Bird Centre
Rose Farm
Hayleys Manor Farm
UPLAND ROAD
Pav
Golf Range
RUGBY GRD
Weald Hall Farm
Weald Hall Lane
WEALD HALL LANE
DRIVING RANGE
NORTH WEALD GOLF CEN
25
26
27
28
29
30
31
32
33
34
04
03
02
01
Thornwood
Blacksmith's Arms PH
Carpenters Arms PH
CARPENTERS ARMS LA
TEAZLE MEADE
MOAT
Hangar
NORTH WEALD AIRFIELD
Gliding Club
Pistol Club
WOODSIDE COMMERCIAL ESTATE
Works
Warehouse
Superstore
WINTRY WOOD
WOODSIDE
STUMP ROAD
EPPING ROAD
B181
B1393
HIGH ROAD
Clubhouse
NORTH WEALD PAR 3 GOLF COURSE
Norway House
BLENHEIM WAY
YORK ROAD
Piggery
THE LOWER FOREST
ROUGHTALLEY'S WOOD
Carisbrooke Farm
Wintry Park Farm
Elec Sta
EPPING PLAIN
THORNWOOD ROAD
Shaftesbury Farm
SPORTS GRD
Comm Cen
ALLOT
COOPERSALE COMMON
GERNON BUSHES
ST. MARGARET'S HOSPITAL
SPENCER CLOSE HOSPITAL
Health Cen
Amb Sta
Cricket Club
Prim Sch
Coopersale
CM16
BIRCHING COPPICE
POSTERNIANE SPRING
HAWKSHILL WOOD
MOUNT WOOD
FORTY ACRES
REDYN'S WOOD
Coopersale Farm
Coopersale House
STONARDS HILL
Stonards Farm
HOUBLONS HILL
Theydon Oak PH
Gaynes Park House
Gaynes Park
MOUNT QUARTER
ONGAR DOWN
GRAVEL PITWOOD
High Warren
69
CIVIC OFFICES
PPING
Superstore
Sports Cen
Bower Hill
EPPING
THEYDON BOWER
BOWER HILL IND EST
ESSEX WAY
STEWARDS GREEN LANE
COOPERSALE STREET
Fiddlers Hamlet
Home Farm
Merry Fiddlers PH
MOUNT ROAD
Mount End
Hornes Farm
Searles Hall
Masons Bridge Farm
STEWARDS GREEN ROAD
BROOK ROAD
Little Thorn Hall Farm
Gardners Farm
Farm
Sch
Hobbs Cross Road Sewage Works
Clubhouse
HOBBS CROSS GOLF CENTRE
HOBBS CROSS ROAD
Sawkins Farm
BEACHET WOOD
North House
Mount Hill Farm
THE ROUGH PATCH
Theydon Mount
M11
M25
Junction 6 (M11)
Junction 27 (M25)
86
BARBER'S WOOD
LONG PLANTATION
ICEHOUSE PLANTATION
Garnish Hall
SUB
QUEEN

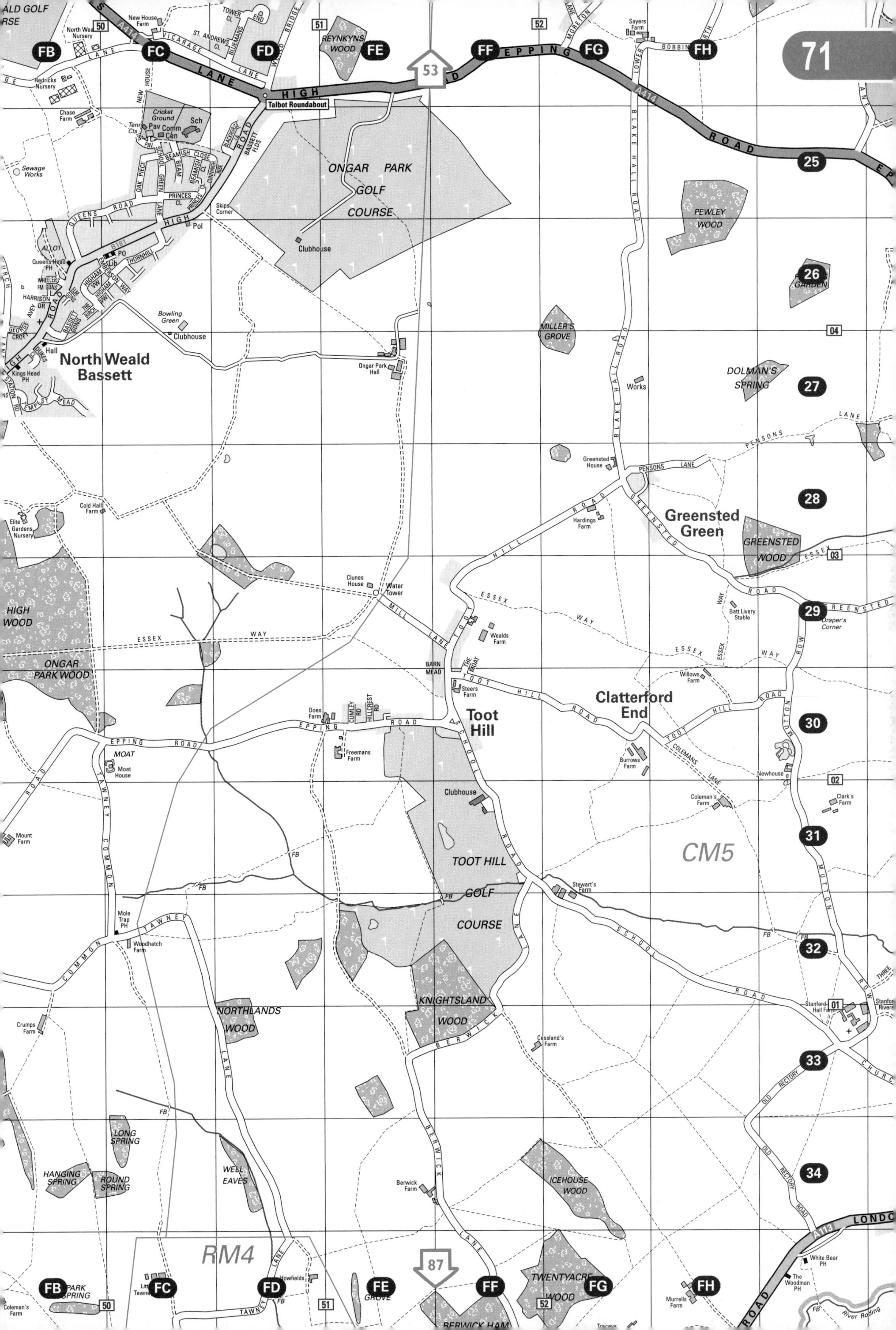
North Weald Bassett
Ongar Park Golf Course
Clubhouse
Talbot Roundabout
High Road
Epping Road
A414
Reynkyns Wood
Pewley Wood
Miller's Grove
Dolman's Spring
Greensted Green
Greensted Wood
Pensons Lane
Blake Hall Road
Toot Hill
Toot Hill Road
Clatterford End
Colemans Lane
Essex Way
High Wood
Ongar Park Wood
Moat House
Tawney Common
Mole Trap PH
Toot Hill Golf Course
Knightsland Wood
Northlands Wood
Berwick Lane
School Road
Mutton Row
Old Rectory Road
Icehouse Wood
Twentyacre Wood
Long Spring
Hanging Spring
Round Spring
Well Eaves
CM5
RM4
Stanford Rivers
White Bear PH
The Woodman PH
River Roding
Water Tower
Clunes House
Wealds Farm
Steers Farm
Does Farm
Freemans Farm
Burrows Farm
Coleman's Farm
Newhouse
Clark's Farm
Stewart's Farm
Cessland's Farm
Berwick Farm
Murrells Farm
Howfields
Woodhatch Farm
Crumps Farm
Mount Farm
Cold Hall Farm
Elite Gardens Nursery
Hardings Farm
Greensted House
Batt Livery Stable
Draper's Corner
Willows Farm
Works
Ongar Park Hall
Bowling Green
Kings Head PH
Queens Head PH
Sewage Works
Redricks Nursery
Chase Farm
North Weald Nursery
New House Farm
Sayers Farm
Skips Corner
Cricket Ground
53
87

Lower Bois
Works
QUARRY
AS
AT
AU
AV
AW
AX
AY
98
99
00
56
WYCHFIELD SPRING
FRITH WOOD
CHESS VALLEY WALK
Sewage Works
Blackwell Hall
Blackwell Farm
Weir Ho
REC GRD
Prim Sch
BOIS WOOD
35
Chesham Bois
36
37
38
39
40
41
42
43
44
BLACKWELL STUBBS
Ivy House Farm
NETHER DITCH
FOUR ACRES
STOCKINGS SPRING
WESTLAND SPRING
JACK OF WADLEY'S SPRING
STAR CLUMP
TOOLEY'S CROFT
Latimer
SPORTS GROUND
PARKFIELD WOOD
THE GROVE
RECTORY PLANTATION
LATIMER MEWS
LATIMER CONF. CEN
HP5
River Chess
DUCK COVER
Weir
MARKET READING WOOD
Quill Hall Farm
LANE WOOD
ROUND WOOD
Great Water
Latimer Park Farm
HP6
Raans Farm
WOODSIDE ROAD
A416
Amb Sta
Fire Sta
Youth Club
Swim Pool
Comm Cen
COUNCIL OFF
Health Cen
AMERSHAM
Cricket Grd
ALLOT
Corinium Industrial Estate
Prim Sch
WEST WOOD
SPORTS GROUND
Tennis Club
Boughton Business Park
WHITE LION ROAD
A404
CHALFONT & LATIMER
CHALFONT STATION RD
AMERSHAM ROAD
Coll
Sec Sch
55
STANLEY WOOD
CEM
Bendrose Farm
Works
HP7
HOBB'S DELL
Little Kimblewick Farm
Sec Sch
SNELL'S WOOD
Snell's Farm
Little Chalfont
LITTLE CHALFONT GOLF COURSE
Clubhouse
STONYDEAN WOOD
LOUDHAM'S WOOD
WILLOW WOOD
HOVEL WOOD
LONDON ROAD WEST
BYPASS
LONDON ROAD EAST
A413
River Misbourne
97
96
Coke's Farm
Burton's Farm
Nightingales
Five Diamonds
BURTON'S WOOD
DOGGETT'S WOOD
Offices
Clubhouse
NIGHTINGALES WOOD
Rowood Farm
Depot
The Gate House
The Shieling
HAREWOOD DOWNS GOLF COURSE
The Ivy House PH
POLLARDS WOOD
Pollards Park House
Elmswell House
DAY'S WOOD
Quarrendon Farm
Harewood Downs House
SPORTS GROUND
Roughwood Farm
Warren Farm
HIGH WOOD
Lower Bottom House Farm
STRATTON COPSE
HP8
BOW WOOD
BAILEY WOOD
90
Upper Bottom House Farm
RESERVOIR PLANTATION
Environmental Education Centre
THE LARCHES
BYCROFT PLANTATION
BAILEY WOOD BELT
Vache Farm
KILNPOND WOOD

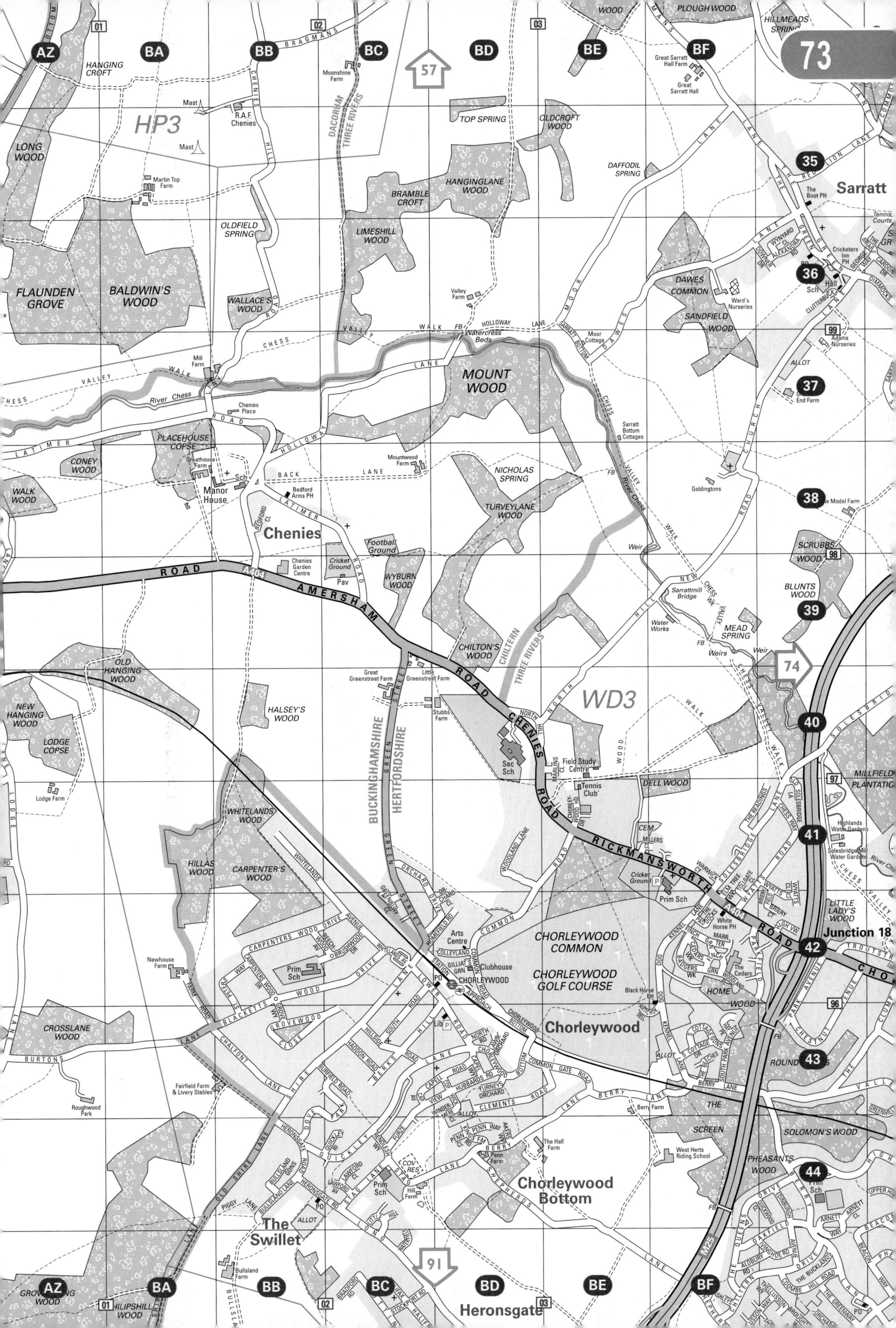

AZ
BA
BB
BC
BD
BE
BF
01
02
03
57
74
91
HP3
WD3
HANGING CROFT
BRAGMANS
Moonshine Farm
Great Sarratt Hall Farm
Great Sarratt Hall
WOOD
PLOUGH WOOD
HILLMEADS SPRING
Mast
R.A.F. Chenies
CHENIES HILL ROAD
DACORUM
THREE RIVERS
TOP SPRING
OLDCROFT WOOD
LONG WOOD
Martin Top Farm
HANGINGLANE WOOD
BRAMBLE CROFT
DAFFODIL SPRING
Sarratt
The Boot PH
Tennis Courts
OLDFIELD SPRING
LIMESHILL WOOD
Cricketers Inn PH
DAWES COMMON
Ward's Nurseries
SANDFIELD WOOD
Hall
Sch
FLAUNDEN GROVE
BALDWIN'S WOOD
WALLACE'S WOOD
Valley Farm
HOLLOWAY LANE
WALK
FB
Watercress Beds
MOOR LANE
SARRATT BOTTOM
DAWES LANE
Moor Cottage
Adams Nurseries
ALLOT
End Farm
CHESS VALLEY WALK
Mill Farm
River Chess
MOUNT WOOD
Chenies Place
LATIMER ROAD
HOLLOWAY LANE
Sarratt Bottom Cottages
CHURCH LANE
PLACEHOUSE COPSE
CONEY WOOD
Greathouse Farm
Sch
Manor House
BACK LANE
Mountwood Farm
NICHOLAS SPRING
Goldingtons
WALK WOOD
Bedford Arms PH
LATIMER ROAD
BEDFORD CL
Chenies
TURVEYLANE WOOD
Model Farm
Football Ground
Cricket Ground
Pav
Chenies Garden Centre
SCRUBBS WOOD
Weir
ROAD
A404
AMERSHAM ROAD
WYBURN WOOD
NEW HILL
Sarrattmill Bridge
BLUNTS WOOD
Water Works
MEAD SPRING
Weirs
CHILTON'S WOOD
CHILTERN
OLD HANGING WOOD
Great Greenstreet Farm
Little Greenstreet Farm
NEW HANGING WOOD
HALSEY'S WOOD
Stubbs Farm
NORTH HILL
LODGE COPSE
BUCKINGHAMSHIRE
HERTFORDSHIRE
GREEN STREET
Sec Sch
CHENIES ROAD
Field Study Centre
MARLINS CL
Tennis Club
DELL WOOD
MILLFIELD PLANTATION
Lodge Farm
LODGE LANE
WHITELANDS WOOD
WOODLAND LANE
CEM
MILLERS
Highlands Water Gardens
Solesbridge Mill Water Gardens
HILLAS WOOD
CARPENTER'S WOOD
ORCHARD DRIVE
RICKMANSWORTH ROAD
Cricket Ground
Prim Sch
White Horse PH
LITTLE LADY'S WOOD
Junction 18
Arts Centre
COMMON
CHORLEYWOOD COMMON
CHORLEYWOOD GOLF COURSE
Clubhouse
CHORLEYWOOD
Newhouse Farm
Prim Sch
CARPENTERS WOOD DRIVE
BLACKETTS WOOD DRIVE
HOME WOOD
The Cedars
Black Horse PH
CROSSLANE WOOD
GROVEWOOD CLOSE
Lib
Chorleywood
ROUND WOOD
CHALFONT LANE
BURTONS LANE
COMMON GATE ROAD
BERRY LANE
Berry Farm
THE SCREEN
SOLOMON'S WOOD
Roughwood Park
Fairfield Farm & Livery Stables
CLEMENTS ROAD
ALLOT
The Hall Farm
West Herts Riding School
PHEASANTS WOOD
HERONSGATE ROAD
QUICKLEY LANE
COV RES
Penn Farm
Prim Sch
Chorleywood Bottom
SHEPHERDS LANE
Hill Farm
OLD SHIRE LANE
PIGGY LANE
BULLSLAND LANE
PO
ALLOT
The Swillet
LONG LANE
M25
Bullsland Farm
GROVE WOOD
PHILIPSHILL WOOD
Heronsgate
STOCKPORT RD

Commonwood
Bucks Hill
Sarratt
Loudwater
Croxley Green
WD4
WD3
58
73
92
Junction 18
Junction 19
M25
BG
BH
BJ
BK
BL
BM
BN
05
06
07
35
36
37
38
39
40
41
42
43
44
99
98
97
96
PLOUGH WOOD
HILLMEADS SPRING
Dellfield
Baytree Farm
Model Farm
SHEEPCOTE SPRING
Great Sarratt Hall
COMMONWOOD COMMON
Bucks Hill Farm
HAW SPRING
BEECHEN BOTTOM
Little Westwood Farm
CONFERENCE CENTRE
Great Westwood Farm
HIGH SPRING
JUNIPER HILL
RED LION LANE
BOTTOM
HOUSE LANE
The Boot PH
Tennis Courts
SPORTS GROUND
Pav
Cricketers Inn PH
PO
Prim Sch
Hall
Poultry Houses
Newhall Farm
Buckshill Bottom
DAWS COMMON
Ward's Nurseries
SANDFIELD WOOD
TEMPLEPAN WOOD
Adams Nurseries
TEMPLEPAN LANE
GRAVE
ALLOT
Green End Business Cen
White House
Yew Court Farm
Sarratt Bottom Cottages
Mickleford Green Farm
Potten's Farm
BIRCH SPRING
DARTPATH WOOD
WHITE SHACK LANE
The Grove Lodge
Stevens Nurseries
GREAT WOOD
SHEEPYARD SPRING
Chandler's Farm
Clarendon Arms PH
River Chess
New Model Farm
SAWPIT SPRING
Country Place
Coltspring Riding Stables
Coltyard Farm
Cottage Farm
Blacketts Nurseries
Weir
SCRUBBS WOOD
BLUNTS WOOD
WILLOW WOOD
HARROCKS WOOD
Sarrattmill Bridge
Water Works
MEAD SPRING
Redhall Farm
WELLING GROVE
MERLIN'S WOOD
Micklefield Hall Farm
Micklefield Hall
MERLIN'S SPRING
Beechen Hill
BEECHENGROVE WOOD
MILLFIELD PLANTATION
LONG SPRING
UPPER PLANTATION
ROUND SPRING
Model Farm
York Ho Sch
ROUND NEWLAND SPRING
WATERDELL SPRING
FINCHES AVENUE
DELL WOOD
Highlands Water Gardens
Solesbridge Mill Water Gardens
Waterdell House
LITTLE GREEN
CEM
Cricket Ground
Prim Sch
MORNING RISE
Thurlwood House
Croxley House
Killingdown Farm
LITTLE LADY'S WOOD
White Horse PH
Loudwater House
Walden Lodge
Whitestocks Farm
PARROT'S DELL
CROXLEY GREEN
Weirs
Mont Au Source
The Cedars
HOME WOOD
Black Horse PH
Glen Chess
Loudwater Farm
COPTHORNE WOOD
BALDWINS LANE RECREATION GROUND
CHORLEYWOOD ROAD
ALLOT
ROUND SPRING
SPORTS GROUND
Watercress Beds
Coach & Horses PH
Bowl Grn
Prim Sch
Berry Farm
THE SCREEN
SOLOMON'S WOOD
Sch
Artichoke PH
West Herts Riding School
PHEASANTS WOOD
Rickmansworth Masonic Sch
HOCKEY GRD
PLAYING FIELD
CRICKET GRD
Clubhouse
FORTUNE COMMON
Scots Br
SCOTS HILL
WATFORD ROAD
CROXLEY HALL WOOD
CEM
RICKMANSWORTH PARK
RICKMANSWORTH
SPORTS GROUND

75
Langleybury
BP
BQ
BR
BS
BT
BU
BV
59
Leavesden Green
Kingswood
Garston
35
36
37
38
39
40
41
42
43
44
76
93
08
09
10
THE ROOKERY
SPORTS GROUND
Offices
Home Farm
PLAYING FIELD
Hunton Bridge Interchange
NORTH WESTERN AVENUE
A41
A405
NORTH ORBITAL ROAD
KINGSWAY
HEMPSTEAD ROAD
A411
ST. ALBANS ROAD
A412
THREE RIVERS
WATFORD
Airshafts
HEATH WOOD
GROVE
PARK
Clarendon Park Farm
Management & Conference Centre
The Grove
Poultry Houses
CHARLOTTE'S VALE
ROUGH WOOD
SPORTS GROUND
WHIPPENDELL WOOD
WEST HERTS GOLF COURSE
Jacotts Hill
DELL WOOD
LONG NEWLAND'S SPRING
GOODWOOD REC GRD
Watford Tunnels
WD24
WD17
WD18
NORTH WATFORD
CALLOWLAND REC GRD
CHESLYN GDNS
NORTH WATFORD CEMETERY
STANBOROUGH PARK
West Herts College
Sports Complex
REC GRD
British Waterways
WATFORD NORTH
MOWAT INDUSTRIAL EST
TRIDENT CENTRE
IMPERIAL PARK
WATFORD JUNCTION
British Telecom
PADDLING POOLS
CASSIOBURY PARK
WATFORD
THE COLOSSEUM
TOWN HALL
Charter Place
Harlequin Centre
WATFORD HIGH STREET
GRAND UNION CANAL
River Gade
FISH POND
RICKMANSWORTH ROAD
DURRANTS SPORTS GROUND
WEST WATFORD
VICARAGE RD CEMETERY
VICARAGE RD WATFORD FC & SARACENS RFC
WATFORD GENERAL HOSP
WATFORD ROAD
CROXLEY
CROXLEY BUSINESS PARK
WATFORD BUSINESS PARK
Holywell
HOLYWELL IND EST
Sorting Office
RIVERSIDE PARK
Electricity Transmission Station
KING GEORGE V PLAYING FIELDS
LONG VALLEY WOOD
COMMON MOOR
Moor Park Crossing
WOLSEY BUSINESS PARK
OXHEY PARK
SPORTS GROUND
Wiggenhall Bridge
TOLPITS
Brightwells Farm Cottage
EASTBURY ROAD

BW
BX
BY
BZ
CA
CB
CC
60
75
94
Garston
NORTH WATFORD CEMETERY
STANBOROUGH PARK
SPORTS GROUND
Sun Chemical
Superstore
WESTERN AVENUE
COLNE WAY (NORTH WESTERN AVENUE)
ST. ALBANS ROAD
Meriden
MUNDEN SPRING
PEARTREE WOOD
Munden House
River Colne
HERTSMERE
WATFORD
ALDENHAM GOLF COURSE & COUNTRY CLUB
Aldenham
Round Bush
WD25
Junction 5
Berrygrove Interchange
OTTERSPOOL WAY
TOP GOLF GAME CENTRE
NORTH WATFORD
WATFORD NORTH
MOWAT INDUSTRIAL EST
WD24
TRIDENT CENTRE
IMPERIAL PARK
WATFORD JUNCTION
REC GRD
Watford R.F.C.
Bushey Hall Farm
SPORTS GROUND
Hilton Watford
Superstore
ELTON WAY (NORTH WESTERN AVENUE)
Patchetts Equestrian Centre
Three Compasses PH
WINFIELD MOBILE HOME PARK
SCOTTS WOOD
BUSHEY HALL GOLF COURSE
RADLETT ROAD PLAYING FIELDS
WD17
West Herts Coll
ICEDALE WOODS
The Purcell School
METROPOLITAN POLICE BUSHEY SPORTS GROUND
BUSHEY JEWISH CEMETERY
PLAYING FIELD
The Lincolnsfields Centre
Leisure Cen
WD23
Ramada Jarvis Watford
TOWN HALL
Harlequin Centre
WATFORD HIGH STREET
Waterfields Shopping Pk
Premier Lodge
Colne Valley Water Co
Gas Works
WATFORD FLDS
Watford Arches Trading Est
WATFORD GENERAL HOSP
VICARAGE RD CEMETERY
WATFORD FC & SARACENS RFC
SPORTS GROUND
OXHEY PARK
OXHEY
Council Depot
Power Sta
Wiggenhall Bridge
DEACONS HILL
EASTBURY ROAD
PINNER ROAD
CHALK HILL
LONDON ROAD
HIGH ROAD
BUSHEY
BUSHEY GOLF COURSE & COUNTRY CLUB
BURIAL GRD
Haydon Hill House
MOAT FIELD REC GRD
KING GEORGE REC GROUND
SPARROWS HERNE
Watford Equestrian Centre
Watford Borough Council Nursery
RUNNING TRACK

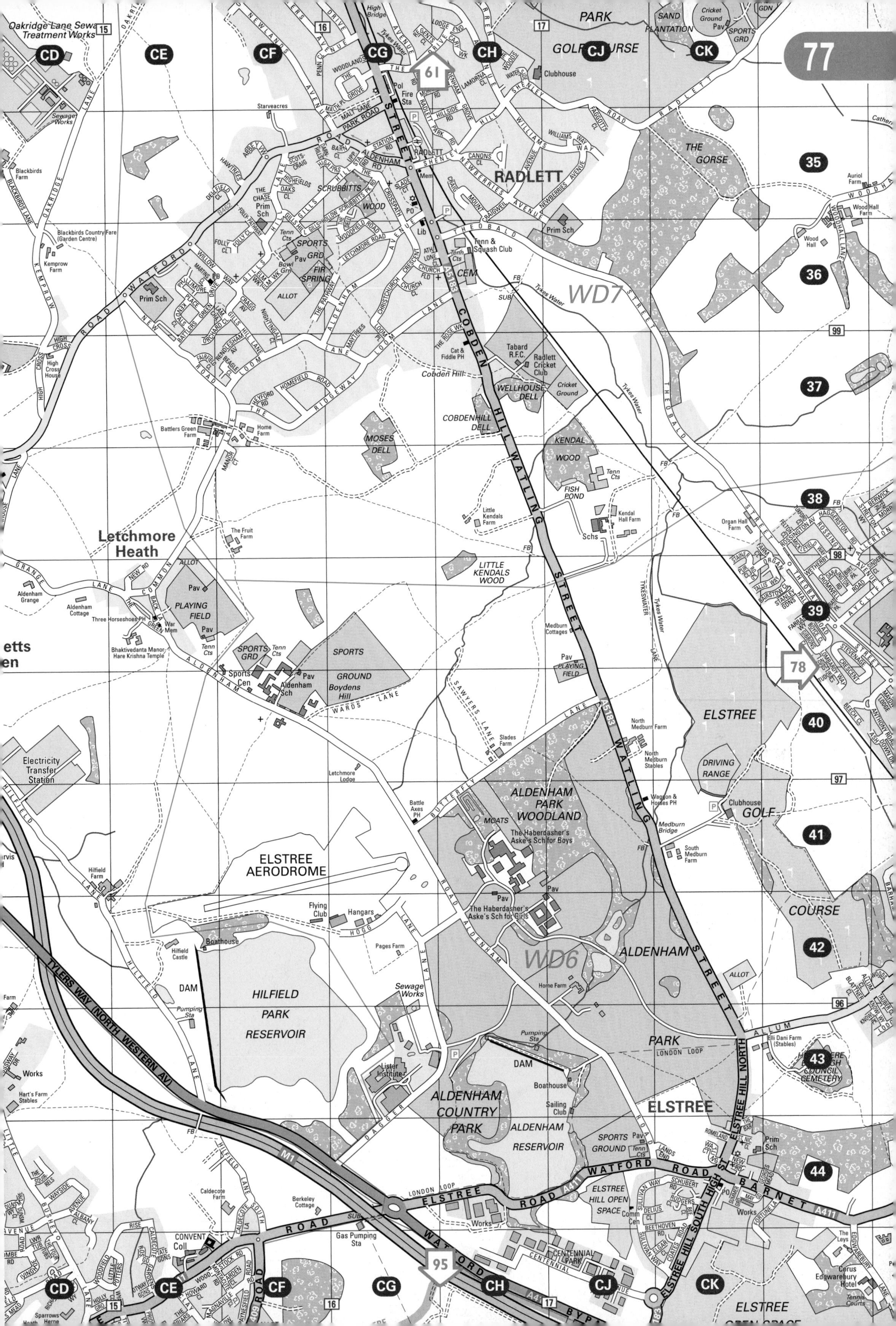
RADLETT
Letchmore Heath
ELSTREE
WD7
WD6
ELSTREE AERODROME
HILFIELD PARK RESERVOIR
ALDENHAM COUNTRY PARK
ALDENHAM RESERVOIR
ALDENHAM PARK WOODLAND
ALDENHAM PARK
ELSTREE GOLF COURSE
THE GORSE
WATLING STREET
COBDEN HILL
TYLERS WAY (NORTH WESTERN AV)
M1
WATFORD ROAD
ELSTREE ROAD
BARNET LANE
Electricity Transfer Station
The Haberdasher's Aske's Sch for Boys
The Haberdasher's Aske's Sch for Girls
Bhaktivedanta Manor Hare Krishna Temple
Lister Institute
ELSTREE HILL OPEN SPACE
CONVENT Coll
Corus Edgwarebury Hotel
HERTSMERE BOROUGH COUNCIL CEMETERY
LONDON LOOP

61
78
95

CL
CM
CN
CP
CQ
CR
CS
62
77
96
19
20
21
35
36
37
38
39
40
41
42
43
44
99
98
97
96
BIG PURSLEY WOOD
LITTLE PURSLEY WOOD
CROSS OAKS WOOD
Crossoaks Farm
BIRCH WOOD
Catherine Bourne
The Garden Nursery
Tokonoma Bonsai
Pursley Farm
SPORTS GRD
Cricket Ground
Auriol Farm
Wood Hall Farm
Wood Hall
Kitwells Farm
Villa Scalabrini
Lyndhurst
WD7
WD6
Green Street
High Canons
High Canons Farm
Holmshill House
Buckettsland Farm
Wheatsheaf Farm
Maxwelton Nurseries
Well End Farm
Holly Cottage
Well End
Strangeways Farm
Rowley Farm
Mops & Brooms PH
Cowley Hill Farm
Organ Hall Farm
AYCLIFFE ROAD PITCHES
Sec Sch
Sports Cen
Prim Schs
ABERFORD LAKE
ABERFORD PARK
SPORTS GROUND
MEADOW PARK
Borehamwood FC & Enfield FC
Oaklands College
Swimming Pool
New Horizons
BOREHAMWOOD IND PARK
G.E.C. SPORTS GROUND
Moat House Elstree
A1 DRIVING RANGE
Clubhouse
B.B.C. Elstree Studios
Imperial Studios
BOREHAMWOOD
MAXWELL PK
KING GEORGES PLAYING FLD
Boulevard 25 Retail Park
Metropolis Centre
Superstore
ELSTREE & BOREHAMWOOD
Gas Works
RIPON PARK
ROWLEY LANE SPORTS GRD
ROWLEY LANE GOLF COURSE
Furze Hill
Stirling Corner
ELSTREE
DRIVING RANGE
GOLF
COURSE
North Medburn Farm
North Medburn Stables
Waggon & Horses PH
Medburn Bridge
South Medburn Farm
DENHAM
PARK
LONDON LOOP
HERTSMERE BOROUGH COUNCIL CEMETERY
Elli Dani Farm (Stables)
ALLOT
Woodcock Hill Farm
Deacons Hill
Airshafts
DEACONS HILL OPEN SPACE
SCRATCH WOOD
FROGHALL WOOD
BOYS HILL WOOD
THISTLE WOOD
ELSTREE PARK
ARKLEY PARK
Hyver Hall
GRAVEL PIT WOOD
Elstree Manor
Penniwells Farm
Corus Edgwarebury Hotel
ELSTREE OPEN SPACE
ELSTREE TUNNEL
A411
A5135
A1
B5378
BARNET BY-PASS
BARNET LANE
ELSTREE HILL NORTH
ELSTREE HILL SOUTH
SHENLEY ROAD
THEOBALD STREET
ALLUM LANE

Junction 23
(M25)
Junction 1
A1(M)
M25
Bentley Heath
Dancers Hill
WROTHAM PARK
DYRHAM PARK GOLF COURSE
DYRHAM PARK
BRIDGEDOWN GOLF COURSE
OLD FOLD MANOR GOLF COURSE
Kitt's End
Monken Hadley
Battle of Barnet 1471
EN5
High Barnet
Hadley
BARNET
KING GEORGE'S FIELD
WROTHAM PARK OPEN SPACE
ARKLEY LANE OPEN SPACE
ARKLEY OPEN SPACE
ARKLEY GOLF COURSE
ARKLEY RISE ESTATE OPEN SPACE
Rowley Green
Arkley
Barnet Gate
CHIPPING BARNET
BARNET GENERAL HOSP
WHALEBONE PARK
Underhill
Ducks Island
WHITINGS HILL OPEN SPACE
OLD ELIZABETHANS (BARNET) MEMORIAL PLAYING FIELDS
GRANGE PLAYING FIELDS
KING GEORGE V PLAYING FIELDS
SOUTH HERTS GOLF
N20
HERTFORDSHIRE
HERTSMERE
BARNET
POOR CLARE MONASTERY
BYNG ROAD PLAYING FIELDS
South Mimms Services
Deadman's Bottom

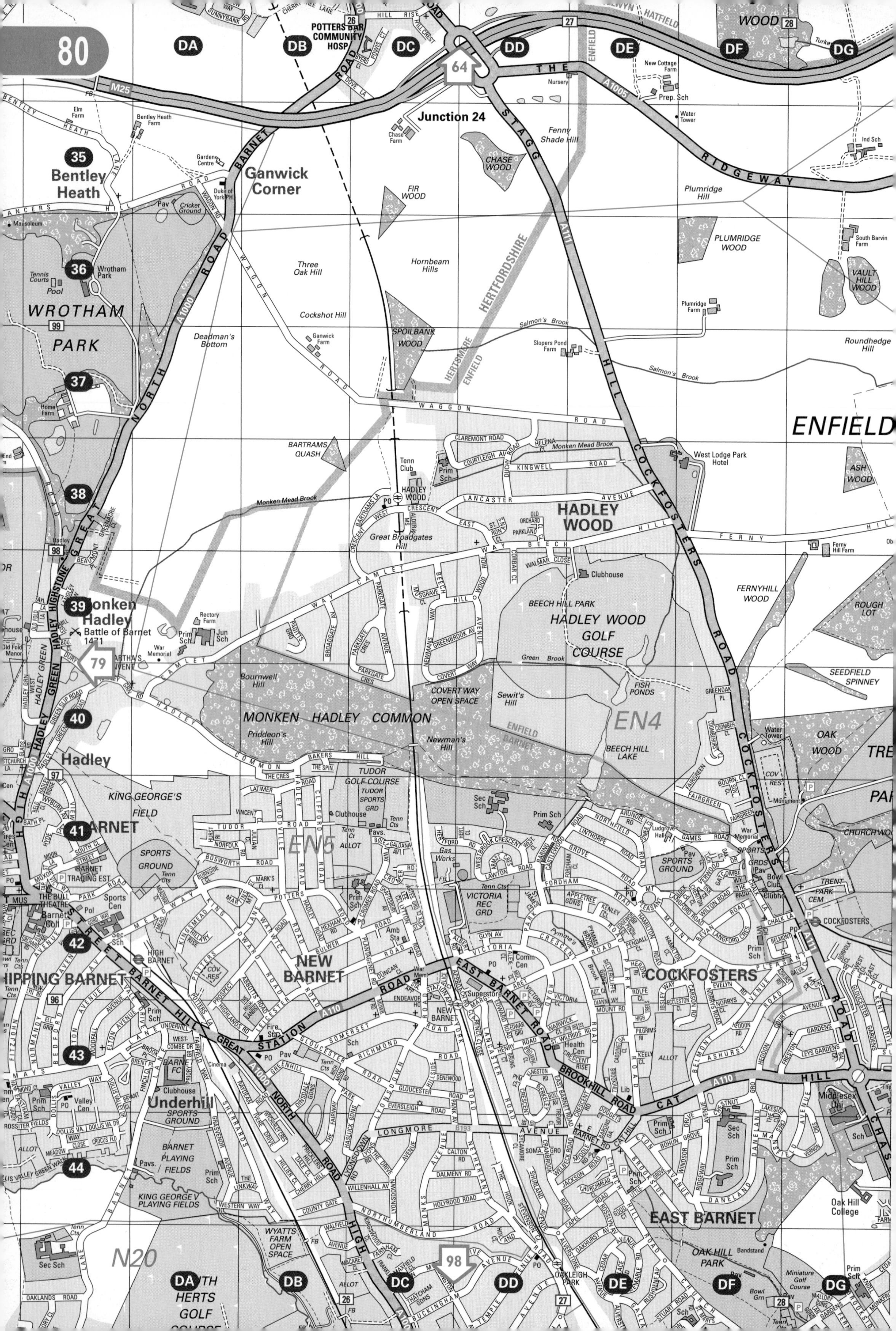

DA
DB
DC
DD
DE
DF
DG
POTTERS BAR COMMUNITY HOSP
M25
64
Junction 24
THE RIDGEWAY
A1005
HATFIELD
WOOD
New Cottage Farm
Nursery
Prep. Sch
Water Tower
Ind Sch
Elm Farm
Bentley Heath Farm
BENTLEY HEATH LANE
35
Bentley Heath
Garden Centre
Ganwick Corner
Duke of York PH
WAGON RD
Cricket Ground
Pav
Mausoleum
CHASE WOOD
Chase Farm
Fenny Shade Hill
FIR WOOD
Plumridge Hill
PLUMRIDGE WOOD
South Barvin Farm
VAULT HILL WOOD
36
Wrotham Park
Tennis Courts
Pool
WROTHAM PARK
99
Three Oak Hill
Hornbeam Hills
HERTFORDSHIRE
Cockshot Hill
Deadman's Bottom
Ganwick Farm
SPOILBANK WOOD
Plumridge Farm
Salmon's Brook
Slopers Pond Farm
Roundhedge Hill
37
Home Farm
HERTSMERE
ENFIELD
WAGGON ROAD
STAGG HILL
A111
GREAT NORTH ROAD
A1000
BARNET ROAD
ENFIELD
BARTRAMS QUASH
CLAREMONT ROAD
COURTLEIGH AV
KINGWELL ROAD
West Lodge Park Hotel
ASH WOOD
38
Monken Mead Brook
Tenn Club
Prim Sch
HADLEY WOOD
LANCASTER AVENUE
HADLEY WOOD
COCKFOSTERS ROAD
FERNY HILL
Ferny Hill Farm
Great Broadgates Hill
BEECH HILL
CAMLET WAY
Clubhouse
FERNYHILL WOOD
ROUGH LOT
98
HADLEY HIGHSTONE
39
Monken Hadley
Battle of Barnet 1471
Rectory Farm
Prim Sch
Jun Sch
War Memorial
BEECH HILL PARK
HADLEY WOOD GOLF COURSE
Green Brook
SEEDFIELD SPINNEY
79
Bournwell Hill
COVERT WAY OPEN SPACE
Sewit's Hill
FISH PONDS
40
MONKEN HADLEY COMMON
EN4
Priddeon's Hill
Newman's Hill
BEECH HILL LAKE
Water Tower
OAK WOOD
Hadley
97
HADLEY GREEN
TUDOR GOLF COURSE
TUDOR SPORTS GRD
KING GEORGE'S FIELD
Clubhouse
Sec Sch
Prim Sch
EN5
41
BARNET
SPORTS GROUND
TUDOR ROAD
Tenn Ct
ALLOT
Gas Works
VICTORIA REC GRD
Ludgrove Hall
SPORTS GROUND
Monument
CHURCH WOOD
BARNET TRADING EST
THE BULL THEATRE
Barnet Coll
Sports Cen
MEADWAY
POTTERS ROAD
FORDHAM ROAD
TRENT PARK CEM
COCKFOSTERS
42
HIGH BARNET
NEW BARNET
COV RES
Amb Sta
EAST BARNET ROAD
Comm Cen
Superstore
COCKFOSTERS
CHIPPING BARNET
96
BARNET HILL
GREAT NORTH ROAD
A1000
STATION ROAD
A110
NEW BARNET
Health Cen
43
Prim Sch
Fire Sta
Cinema
BARNET FC
Underhill
Clubhouse
SPORTS GROUND
VALLEY WAY
Prim Sch
Valley Cen
LONGMORE AVENUE
B193
BROOKHILL ROAD
CAT HILL
A110
Lib
Prim Sch
Sec Sch
Prim Sch
Middlesex Uni
44
ALLOT
BARNET PLAYING FIELDS
KING GEORGE V PLAYING FIELDS
Pavs.
Prim Sch
WESTERN WAY
WYATTS FARM OPEN SPACE
NORTHUMBERLAND ROAD
EAST BARNET
Oak Hill College
N20
Sec Sch
SOUTH HERTS GOLF COURSE
26
98
OAKLEIGH PARK
27
OAK HILL PARK
Bandstand
Miniature Golf Course
Bowl Grn
28
Prim Sch
OAKLANDS ROAD

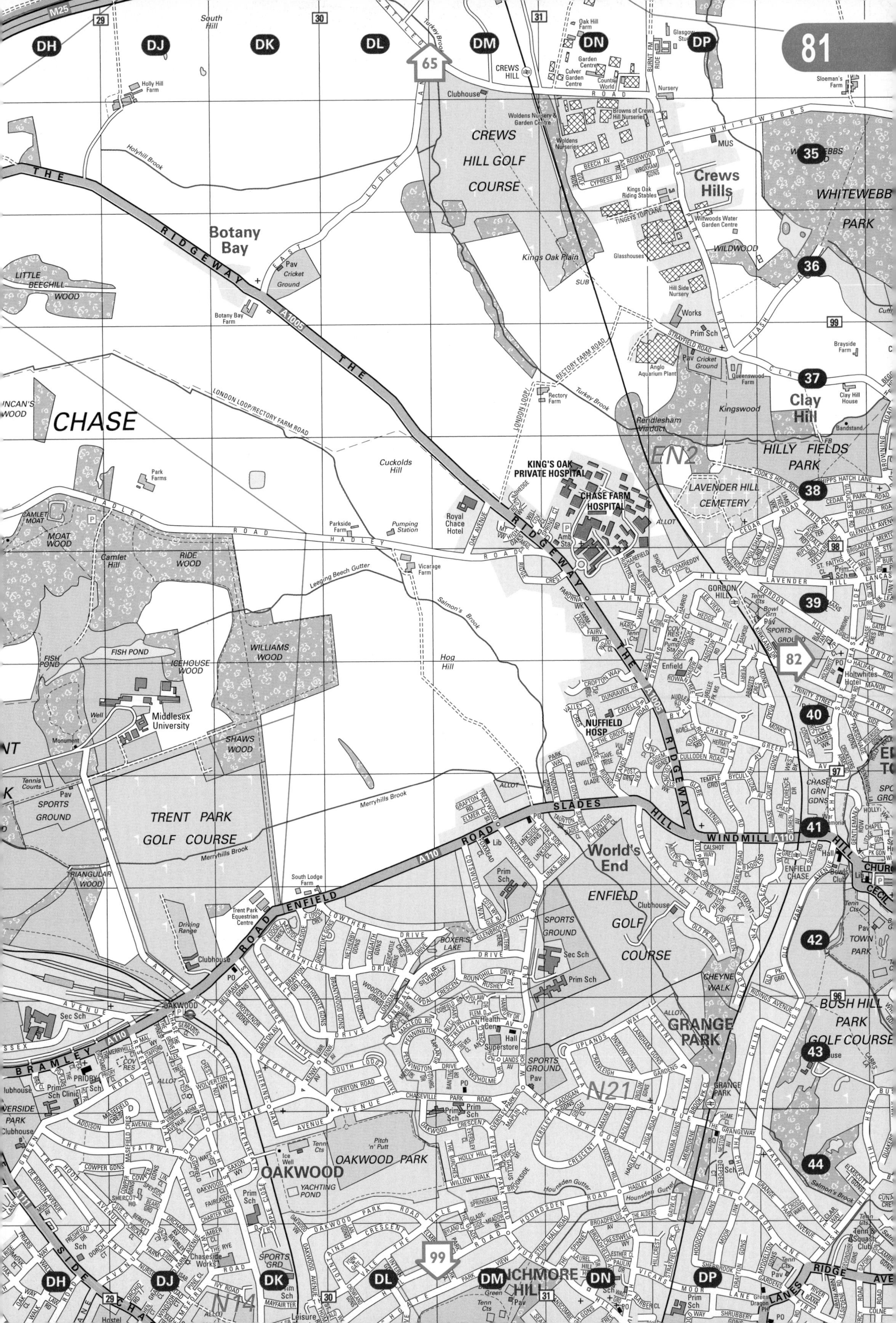
DH
DJ
DK
DL
DM
DN
DP
M25
South Hill
65
Crews Hill
Holly Hill Farm
Oak Hill Farm
Garden Centre
Culver Garden Centre
Country World
Clubhouse
Burnt Fm Ride
Nursery
Sloeman's Farm
Woldens Nursery & Garden Centre
Browns of Crews Hill Nurseries
Crews Hill Golf Course
Whitewebbs Road
Crews Hills
Whitewebbs Park
Holyhill Brook
The Ridgeway
Botany Bay
Kings Oak Riding Stables
Tingeys Top Lane
Wilwoods Water Garden Centre
Wildwood
Glasshouses
Kings Oak Plain
Hill Side Nursery
Little Beechill Wood
Pav
Cricket Ground
East Lodge Lane
Botany Bay Farm
A1005
Works
Prim Sch
Strayfield Road
Brayside Farm
Rectory Farm Road
Anglo Aquarium Plant
Queenswood Farm
Clay Hill
Clay Hill House
Kingswood
Rectory Farm
Turkey Brook
London Loop
London Loop/Rectory Farm Road
Chase
Rendlesham Viaduct
Bandstand
EN2
Hilly Fields Park
Cuckolds Hill
King's Oak Private Hospital
Chase Farm Hospital
Lavender Hill Cemetery
Park Farms
Royal Chace Hotel
Camlet Moat
Moat Wood
Hadley Road
Parkside Farm
Pumping Station
Oak Avenue
Allot
Camlet Hill
Ride Wood
Vicarage Farm
Leeging Beech Gutter
Gordon Hill
Salmon's Brook
Williams Wood
Fish Pond
Icehouse Wood
Hog Hill
Enfield
Holtwhites Hotel
82
Middlesex University
Well
Monument
Shaws Wood
Nuffield Hosp
Tennis Courts
Pav
Sports Ground
Snakes Lane
Trent Park Golf Course
Merryhills Brook
Slades Hill
Windmill Hill
A110
World's End
Enfield Golf Course
Clubhouse
Enfield Chase
Triangular Wood
South Lodge Farm
Trent Park Equestrian Centre
Driving Range
Enfield Road
Lib
Prim Sch
Sports Ground
Sec Sch
Boxer's Lake
Cheyne Walk
Town Park
Bush Hill Park Golf Course
Oakwood
Sec Sch
Bramley Road
Priory
Health Cen
Superstore
Grange Park
N21
Chaseville Park Road
Pitch 'n' Putt
Oakwood Park
Yachting Pond
Hounsden Gutter
Salmon's Brook
Green Dragon Lane
Chaseside Works
99
Winchmore Hill
N14
Leisure
Tenn & Squash Club
35
36
37
38
39
40
41
42
43
44
29
30
31
96
97
98
99

DQ
DR
DS
DT
DU
DV
DW
66
Junction 25
Bulls Cross
Crews Hill
WHITEWEBBS PARK
WHITEWEBBS GOLF COURSE
Capel Manor College
EN2
Clay Hill
HILLY FIELDS PARK
FORTY HALL COUNTRY PARK
Forty Hill
Bullsmoor
81
ENFIELD TOWN
EN1
ENFIELD
ENFIELD PLAYING FIELDS
BUSH HILL PARK GOLF COURSE
BUSH HILL PARK
GRANGE PARK
N21
JUBILEE PARK
100
35
36
37
38
39
40
41
42
43
44

Holdbrook
Freezy Water
RAMMEY MARSH
MOLLISON A1055 AVENUE
DEPOT
Sewardstone Roundabout
EN9
A121
M25
Enfield Lock
INNOVA PARK
Enfield Wash
ALBANY PARK
EN3
LEE VALLEY PARK
SEWARDSTONE MARSH
Sewardstone
KING GEORGE'S RESERVOIR
BRIMSDOWN INDUSTRIAL ESTATE
Brimsdown
DURANTS PARK
ALMA ROAD OPEN SPACE
BRIMSDOWN SPORTS GROUND
GILWELL PARK
THE QUICK
THE ROUGH
CARP LAKES
Yardley Hill
THE HAWK WOOD
ROYAL EPPING FOREST GOLF COURSE
CHINGFORD PLAIN
POLE HILL
WEST ESSEX GOLF COURSE
E4
BANCHET FIELD
NEW-FIELD
Barn Hill
THOMPSON'S WOOD
FERNHILL WOOD
WOODMAN'S GLADE
SEWARDSTONE ROAD
HERTFORD ROAD
MERIDIAN WAY
LEA VALLEY ROAD
A110
A112
River Lee Navigation
Relief Channel
Cattlegate Flood
EPPING FOREST
ENFIELD
DX DY DZ EA EB EC ED
35 36 37 38 39 40 41 42 43 44
67
84
101

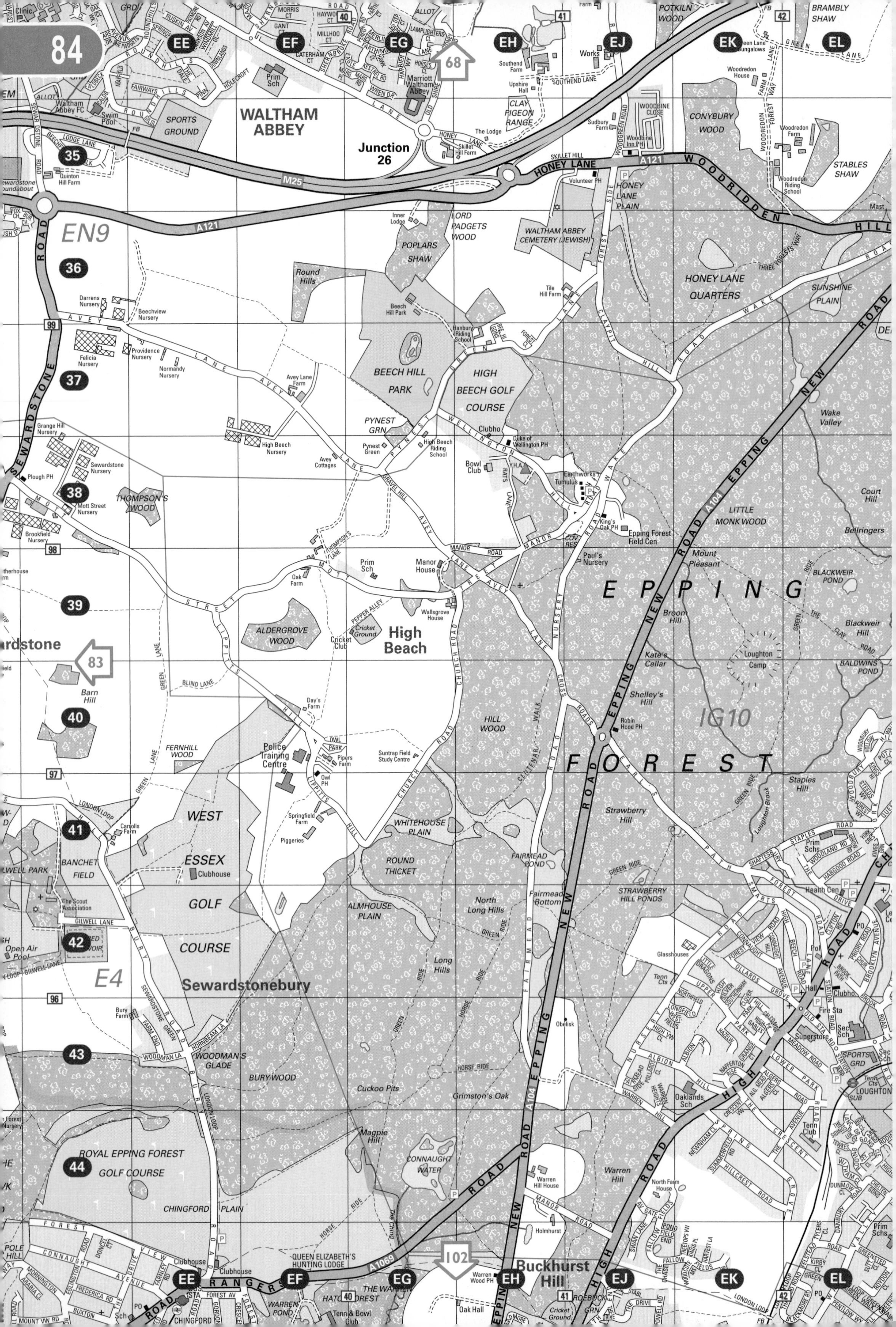

WALTHAM ABBEY
Junction 26
M25
A121
HONEY LANE
WOODRIDDEN HILL
EN9
SEWARDSTONE ROAD
AVEY LANE
BEECH HILL PARK
HIGH BEECH GOLF COURSE
LORD PADGETS WOOD
POPLARS SHAW
WALTHAM ABBEY CEMETERY (JEWISH)
HONEY LANE QUARTERS
CONYBURY WOOD
STABLES SHAW
SUNSHINE PLAIN
THOMPSON'S WOOD
ALDERGROVE WOOD
High Beach
MOTT STREET
PYNEST GRN
LITTLE MONK WOOD
EPPING FOREST
EPPING NEW ROAD
A104
HILL WOOD
FERNHILL WOOD
WEST ESSEX GOLF COURSE
Police Training Centre
Sewardstonebury
ROYAL EPPING FOREST GOLF COURSE
CHINGFORD PLAIN
CONNAUGHT WATER
QUEEN ELIZABETH'S HUNTING LODGE
Buckhurst Hill
LOUGHTON
IG10
E4
RANGERS ROAD
A1069
STRAWBERRY HILL PONDS
Loughton Camp
BLACKWEIR POND
BALDWINS POND
WHITEHOUSE PLAIN
ROUND THICKET
ALMHOUSE PLAIN
BURY WOOD
Cuckoo Pits
Grimston's Oak
Magpie Hill
Warren Hill
CHINGFORD

68
83
102

EPPING FOREST
Theydon Bois
Debden Green
Debden
LOUGHTON
THEYDON BOIS GOLF COURSE
LOUGHTON GOLF COURSE
WOOLSTON MANOR GOLF COURSE
BIRCH WOOD
RED OAK WOOD
GAUNT'S WOOD
LONG SHAW
BROADFIELD SHAW
THEYDON MEAD
HILLYFIELDS OPEN SPACE
CM16
RM4
IG7
Junction 5
Junction 6
Junction 27
M11
A121
A1168
A113
A1112
B172
B1393
69
86
103
EM
EN
EP
EQ
ER
ES
ET
35
36
37
38
39
40
41
42
43
44
96
97
98
99
43
44
45

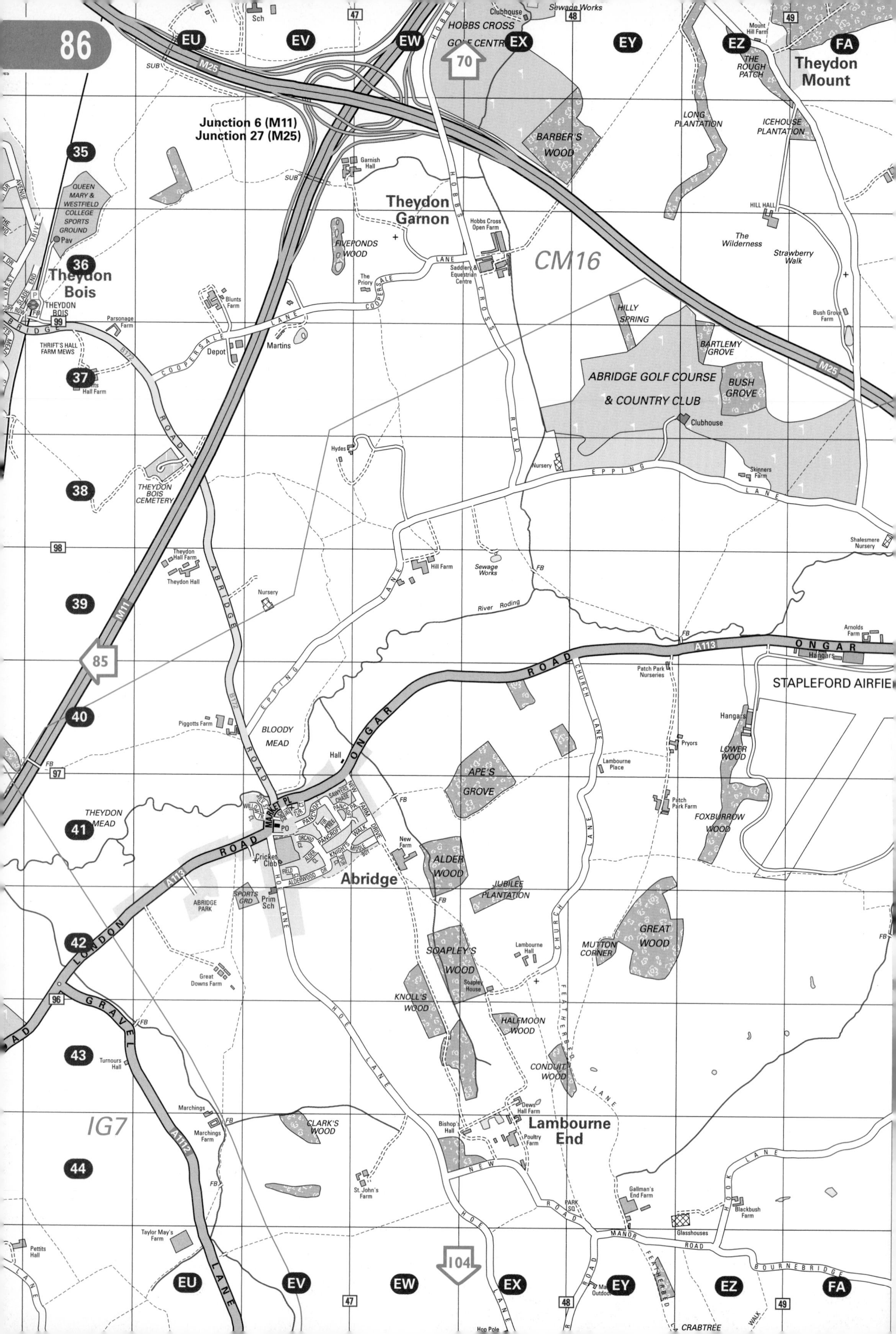

Theydon Bois
Theydon Garnon
Theydon Mount
Abridge
Lambourne End
Junction 6 (M11)
Junction 27 (M25)
CM16
IG7
HOBBS CROSS GOLF CENTRE
BARBER'S WOOD
QUEEN MARY & WESTFIELD COLLEGE SPORTS GROUND
FIVEPONDS WOOD
ABRIDGE GOLF COURSE & COUNTRY CLUB
BUSH GROVE
BARTLEMY GROVE
HILLY SPRING
LONG PLANTATION
ICEHOUSE PLANTATION
THE ROUGH PATCH
The Wilderness
Strawberry Walk
THEYDON BOIS CEMETERY
STAPLEFORD AIRFIE
LOWER WOOD
FOXBURROW WOOD
APE'S GROVE
ALDER WOOD
JUBILEE PLANTATION
GREAT WOOD
MUTTON CORNER
SOAPLEY'S WOOD
KNOLL'S WOOD
HALFMOON WOOD
CONDUIT WOOD
CLARK'S WOOD
BLOODY MEAD
THEYDON MEAD
ABRIDGE PARK
River Roding
ONGAR ROAD
LONDON ROAD
GRAVEL LANE
HOE LANE
CHURCH LANE
EPPING LANE
COOPERSALE LANE
HOBBS CROSS ROAD
ABRIDGE ROAD
MANOR ROAD
NEW ROAD
HOOK LANE
BOURNEBRIDGE
CRABTREE
M25
M11
A113
A1112
B172
70
85
104

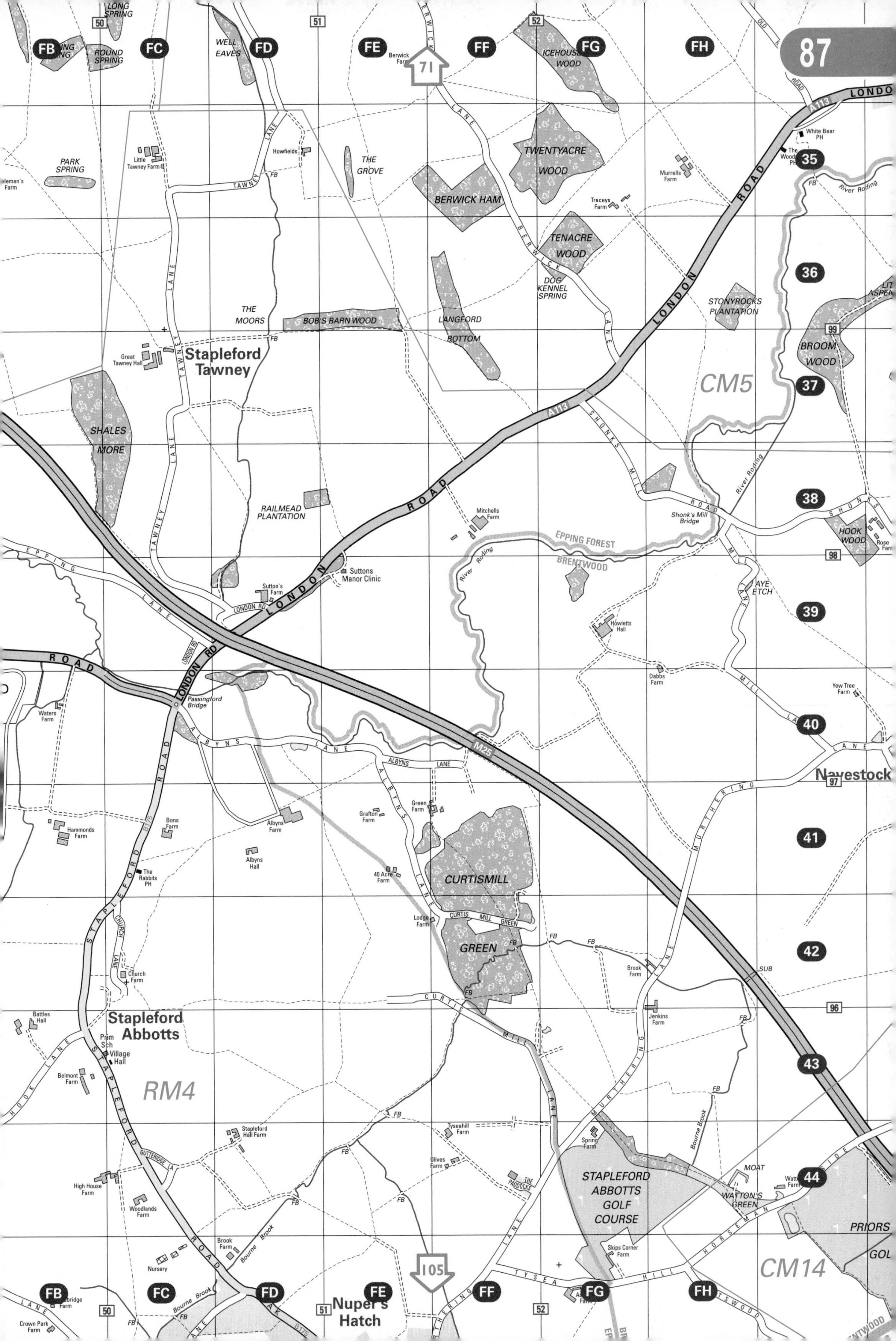

Stapleford Tawney
Stapleford Abbotts
Navestock
Nuper's Hatch
CM5
RM4
CM14
LONDON ROAD
A113
M25
TAWNEY LANE
BERWICK LANE
SHONKS MILL ROAD
MILL LANE
ALBYNS LANE
CURTIS MILL LANE
CURTIS MILL GREEN
MURTHERING LANE
STAPLEFORD ROAD
HOOK LANE
CHURCH LANE
TYSEA HILL
HORSEMAN SIDE
EPPING LANE
River Roding
Bourne Brook
EPPING FOREST
BRENTWOOD
BOB'S BARN WOOD
SHALES MORE
TWENTYACRE WOOD
BERWICK HAM
TENACRE WOOD
ICEHOUSE WOOD
CURTISMILL GREEN
STAPLEFORD ABBOTTS GOLF COURSE
STONYROCKS PLANTATION
BROOM WOOD
HOOK WOOD
RAILMEAD PLANTATION
LANGFORD BOTTOM
THE GROVE
THE MOORS
PARK SPRING
ROUND SPRING
WELL EAVES
DOG KENNEL SPRING
Suttons Manor Clinic
Passingford Bridge
Shonk's Mill Bridge
Mitchells Farm
Howletts Hall
Dabbs Farm
Great Tawney Hall
Little Tawney Farm
Howfields
Murrells Farm
Traceys Farm
White Bear PH
Albyns Farm
Albyns Hall
Hammonds Farm
Bons Farm
Waters Farm
The Rabbits PH
Church Farm
Battles Hall
Belmont Farm
Prim Sch
Village Hall
Stapleford Hall Farm
High House Farm
Woodlands Farm
Brook Farm
Nursery
Crown Park Farm
Tyseahill Farm
Olives Farm
Spring Farm
Skips Corner Farm
Jenkins Farm
Lodge Farm
Green Farm
Grafton Farm
40 Acre Farm
Yew Tree Farm
Rose Farm
Sutton's Farm
WATTON'S GREEN
MOAT
PRIORS
THE PADDOCKS
AYE ETCH
71
105

HP15
AC
AD
AE
AF
AG
AH
AJ
91
92
93
TYLERS GREEN
COMMON WOOD
THE LARCHES
CHARCOLE GROVE
THE COPSE
Penn Street Farm
Cricket Ground
Penn House
PENNHOUSE GROVE
Winchmore Hill
The Plough PH
The Potters Arms PH
Winchmore Hill Farm
Goodwins Nursery
GLORY BELT
BRANCHES WOOD
BROOK WOOD
Pennhouse Farm
ROUND WOOD
PUGH'S WOOD
COMMON WOOD LANE
HAZLEMERE ROAD
ELM ROAD
CHURCH ROAD
SCHOOL ROAD
BEACON HILL
Cricket Ground
Tennis Courts
Clubhouse
SPORTS GRD
Puttenham Place Farm
The Red Lion PH
The Old Queen's Head PH
SPORTS GROUND
KING'S WOOD
Penn
The Crown PH
VICARAGE WOOD
DOWNHAM GROVE
WESTFIELD PIECES
WITHERIDGE WOOD
WITHERIDGE LANE
PENN BOTTOM
MARRODS BOTTOM
CLAY STREET
Saucy Corner
PENBURY GROVE
CHURCH PATH WOOD
Knotty Green
Red Lion PH
GOMMS WOOD
LITTLE GOMMS WOOD
Fieldgrove Nurseries
POND WOOD
Stumpwell
MAGPIE WOOD
HP10
GATEMOOR WOOD
CORKERS WOOD
STANDERS WOOD
Town House Farm
Bottom Farm
Parsonage Farm
HP13
WYCOMBE HEIGHTS GOLF CENTRE
DRIVING RANGE
VINEYARD
COPPICE WOOD
Lude Farm
LONGFIELD WOOD
Royal Standard PH
Forty Green
THROSHERS WOOD
ROUNDHEADS WOOD
SNIGGS WOOD
CHILTERN WYCOMBE
Pitch 'n' Putt
MOBILE HOME PARK
HOGBACK WOOD
Electricity Station
Upper Derehams Farm
CEM
ALLOT
KINGS MEAD
KINGSMEAD BUSINESS PARK
FENNELL'S WOOD
Whitehouse Farm
Holtspur Bottom Farm
GREGORIES ROAD
Loudwater
KNAVES BEECH BUSINESS CENTRE
Superstore
Holtspur
CUT-THROAT WOOD
Highwayman's Farm
FLACKWELL HEATH GOLF COURSE
Superstores
Junction 3
110
LONDON ROAD
OXFORD ROAD
WYCOMBE ROAD
WHITE HILL
BOUNDARY ROAD
The Three Horseshoes PH
Clubhouse
45
46
47
48
49
50
51
52
53
54

AK
AL
AM
AN
AP
AQ
AR
55
HP7
HP8
HP9
SL9
HERTS WOOD
COLESHILL COMMON
THE LARCHES
HALES WOOD
WELPLEY'S WOOD
HILL'S WOOD
LITTLE LUCKINGS WOOD
ONGAR HILL DELLS
TALLY WOOD
GREAT LUCKINGS WOOD
HEATHFIELD GROVE
HODGEMOOR WOODS
GREAT BEARD'S WOOD
OWSLEARS WOOD
RAWLINGS DELL
STARVEACRE WOOD
BOTTOM WOOD
SANDELS WOOD
BROWN'S WOOD
NETHERLANDS WOOD
BIG COPSE
LITTLE COPSE
CLEARE CRAFT WOOD
BIRCHEN SPRING
PEGGS WOOD
BLUE CLOSE WOOD
LEDBOROUGH WOOD
OLDFIELDS FURZE
YOUNG'S WOOD
MODEL VILLAGE
Seer Green
BEACONSFIELD GOLF COURSE
THE MOUNT
WALK WOOD
WHEATSHEAF WOOD
LITTLE WALK WOOD
DEAN WOOD
THIRTY ACRE KNOLL
SPORTS GROUND
PITLANDS WOOD
BIRCHLAND WOOD
BEACONSFIELD
AMERSHAM ROAD
LONDON END
LONDON ROAD
OXFORD ROAD
WYCOMBE END
PARK LANE
LOWER PYEBUSHES
PYEBUSHES
BIRCH WOOD
45
46
47
48
49
50
51
52
53
54
90
111
94
95
96
93
92
91

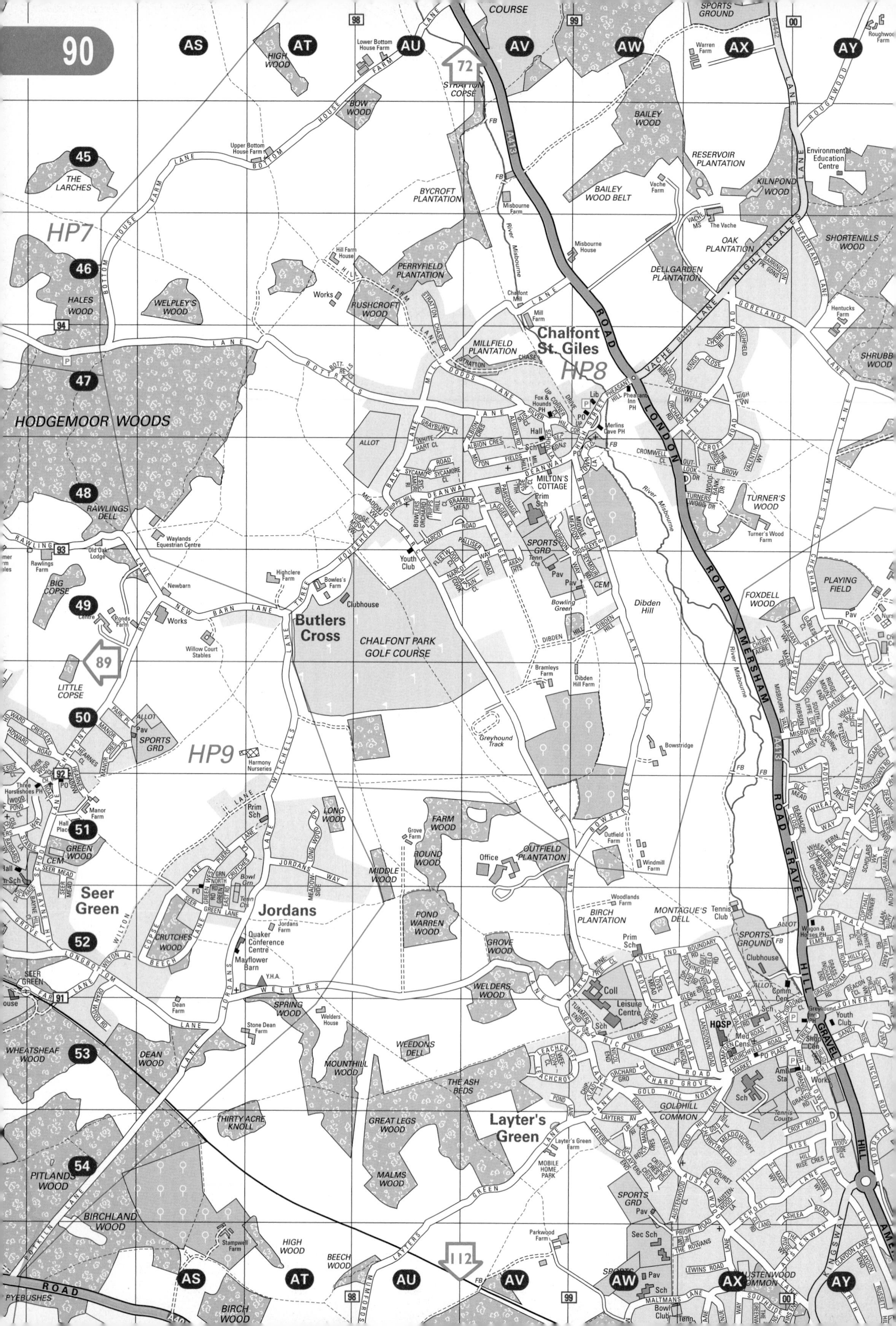

AS
AT
AU
AV
AW
AX
AY
98
99
00
72
89
112
45
46
47
48
49
50
51
52
53
54
91
92
93
94
HP7
HP8
HP9
COURSE
SPORTS GROUND
HIGH WOOD
Lower Bottom House Farm
STRATTON COPSE
Warren Farm
Roughwood Farm
BOW WOOD
BAILEY WOOD
Upper Bottom House Farm
RESERVOIR PLANTATION
Environmental Education Centre
THE LARCHES
BYCROFT PLANTATION
Misbourne Farm
BAILEY WOOD BELT
Vache Farm
KILNPOND WOOD
The Vache
OAK PLANTATION
SHORTENILLS WOOD
Hill Farm House
Misbourne House
River Misbourne
PERRYFIELD PLANTATION
DELLGARDEN PLANTATION
HALES WOOD
WELPLEY'S WOOD
Works
RUSHCROFT WOOD
Chalfont Mill
Mill Farm
Hentucks Farm
Chalfont St. Giles
MILLFIELD PLANTATION
SHRUBB WOOD
HODGEMOOR WOODS
Fox & Hounds PH
Pheasant Inn PH
Merlins Cave PH
ALLOT
Hall
Sch
MILTON'S COTTAGE
Prim Sch
TURNER'S WOOD
Turner's Wood Farm
RAWLINGS DELL
Waylands Equestrian Centre
Rawlings Farm
Old Oak Lodge
Youth Club
SPORTS GRD
Tenn Cts
Pav
CEM
Bowling Green
BIG COPSE
Highclere Farm
Bowles's Farm
Newbarn
Clubhouse
PLAYING FIELD
FOXDELL WOOD
Dibden Hill
Butlers Cross
CHALFONT PARK GOLF COURSE
Willow Court Stables
LITTLE COPSE
Bramleys Farm
Dibden Hill Farm
Greyhound Track
Bowstridge
Harmony Nurseries
Three Horseshoes PH
Manor Farm
FARM WOOD
LONG WOOD
Grove Farm
ROUND WOOD
Outfield Farm
OUTFIELD PLANTATION
Office
Windmill Farm
GREEN WOOD
CEM
MIDDLE WOOD
Seer Green
Jordans
Jordans Farm
POND WARREN WOOD
Woodlands Farm
BIRCH PLANTATION
MONTAGUE'S DELL
Tennis Club
CRUTCHES WOOD
Quaker Conference Centre
Mayflower Barn
GROVE WOOD
SPORTS GROUND
Clubhouse
Wagon & Horses PH
Y.H.A.
WELDERS WOOD
Coll
Leisure Centre
Comm Cen
Greyhound Inn PH
Youth Club
Dean Farm
SPRING WOOD
Welders House
Stone Dean Farm
HOSP
Med Cens
Shop Cen
WHEATSHEAF WOOD
DEAN WOOD
WEEDONS DELL
MOUNTHILL WOOD
Lib
Amb Sta
Works
THE ASH BEDS
GOLDHILL COMMON
Sch
Tennis Courts
THIRTY ACRE KNOLL
GREAT LEGS WOOD
Layter's Green
Layter's Green Farm
PITLANDS WOOD
MALMS WOOD
MOBILE HOME PARK
SPORTS GRD
BIRCHLAND WOOD
Stampwell Farm
HIGH WOOD
BEECH WOOD
Parkwood Farm
Sec Sch
AUSTENWOOD COMMON
PYEBUSHES
BIRCH WOOD
Bowl Club
LONDON ROAD
AMERSHAM ROAD
GRAVEL HILL
A413
B4442

The Swillet
Chorleywood Bottom
Heronsgate
Mill End
Junction 17
Maple Cross
Chalfont Common
CHALFONT ST. PETER
NEWLAND PARK
Brunel University Buckinghamshire College
Halls of Residence
CHILTERN OPEN AIR MUSEUM
SPORTS GROUND
GROVESPRING WOOD
PHILIPSHILL WOOD
NEWLAND GORSE
BOTTOM WOOD
LADYWALK WOOD
FIVE PLANTATIONS
POLLARDSHILL WOOD
KILN WOOD
BEECHEN WOOD
FRANKLINS SPRING
ROBERT'S WOOD
ROUND ROCKET PLANTATION
QUARRY & LANDFILL SITE
MIDDLE WOOD
BLOOM WOOD
GRAVEL PIT
HOGTROUGH WOOD
GERRARDS CROSS GOLF COURSE
NOCKHILL WOOD
JUNIPER WOOD
MAPLE CROSS INDUSTRIAL ESTATE
Maple Lodge Sewage Treatment Works
PLAYING FIELDS
LYNSTERS LAKE
PYNESFIELD LAKE
Horseshoe Bay
Sailing Club
SPRINGWELL CHALK PIT
SPRINGWELL LAKE
WILLIAM PENN MULTISPORTS ARENA
PARK
MOUNT PLEASANT SPORTS GRD
TRAINING CENTRE DURDENT COURT
SCREEN
SOLOMON'S WOOD
PHEASANTS WOOD
West Herts Riding School
WD3
SL9
UB9
M25
A412
A405
DENHAM (NORTH ORBITAL ROAD)
HERTFORDSHIRE
BUCKINGHAMSHIRE
THREE RIVERS
CHILTERN
SOUTH BUCKS
River Colne
73
92
113
AZ BA BB BC BD BE BF
45 46 47 48 49 50 51 52 53 54

SCREEN
SOLOMON'S WOOD
PHEASANTS WOOD
BG
BH
BJ
BK
BL
BM
BN
74
Batchworth Masonic Sch
HOCKEY GRD
PLAYING FIELD
CRICKET GRD
Clubhouse
SPORTS GROUND
CROXLEY HALL WOOD
M25
45
46
47
48
49
50
51
52
53
54
Mill End
Moneyhill
RICKMANSWORTH
RICKMANSWORTH PARK
FORTUNE COMMON
SCOTS HILL
CHALMERS COURT
Leisure Centre
Swim Pool
WILLIAM PENN MULTISPORTS ARENA
Clubho
Prim Sch
Comm Cens
Depot
Tenn Club
Amb Sta
Fire Sta
Pol
Watersmeet Cen
COUN OFF
MUS
Lib
Watercress Beds
River Colne
Lot Mead Lock
Croxley Hall Farm
Hampton Hall Farm
The Alders
Batchworth Roundabout
RIVERSIDE DRIVE
A404
Halfway House PH
Clinics
Boathouse
Weir
Works
Locks
Three Valleys Water
MOOR LANE
Clubhouse
Batchworth
RICKMANSWORTH
MOOR PARK
GOLF COURSE
BATCHWORTH PARK
GOLF COURSE
Clubhouse
Moor Park Farm
MOOR PARK MANSION
BATCHWORTH LAKE
THE AQUADROME
WD3
BURY LAKE
Superstore
White Bear PH
GRAND UNION CANAL
Boathouse
Whip & Collar PH
UXBRIDGE ROAD
A412
A405
Depot
THE GROVE
STOCKER'S LAKE (NATURE RESERVE)
Stocker's Lock
Stocker's Farm
Pumping Sta
Prim Sch
Drayton Ford
Froghall Farm
Works
GARRETT WOOD
HIGH WOOD
CHALK PIT
Watercress Beds
SPRINGWELL CHALK PIT
Lock
SPRINGWELL LAKE
HERTFORDSHIRE
THREE RIVERS
Andrews Ley Farm
Juniper Dell
Greenbroom Spring
Sandfield Spring
WOODCOCK HILL CEMETERY
HAREFIELD ROAD INDUSTRIAL ESTATE
Pipers Farm
Bush Spring
Home Farm House
Batchworth Heath
Batchworth Heath Farm
MAPLE CROSS INDUSTRIAL ESTATE
Clubhouse
91
Maple Lodge Sewage Treatment Works
Filter Beds
Sludge Beds
COCKS WOOD
LONDON LOOP
Rose & Crown PH
LONG SPRING
PARK WOOD
Lynsters Farm
Cripps House Farm
BISHOP'S WOOD
POORFIELD
LOCKWELL WOOD
Woodcock Hill Farm
HILLINGDON
Waybeards Farm
White Heath Farm
PEARSON'S WOOD
Harefield Grove
LYNSTERS LAKE
Hill End
ALLOT
WATTS COMMON
TAYLORS MEADOW
Harefield Grove Farm
COVERED RESERVOIR
Battlers Wells Farm
FRENCH GROVE
BATTLERS WELLS WOOD
Little Bourne Farm (Equestrian Stables)
PARK WOOD
Nature Reserve
PYNESFIELD LAKE
UB9
Shepherds Hill Farm
MOUNT PLEASANT SPORTS GRD
HAREFIELD HOSPITAL
Sports Cen
Sec Sch
Shepherds Hill House
FURZEFIELD
DEADMAN'S GROVE
HAREFIELD
THE GREEN
Health Cen
SPORTS GRD
Horseshoe Bay
Weir
Sailing Club
Colney Farm
Lib
Comm Cen
Prim Sch
Swan PH
Cricket Ground
Pavs.
Harefield United FC
ASHAIN SPRING
SCARLET SPRING
KILN POND
CLAYPITS
RAVENERS SPRING
DELL
Shooting School
Knightscote Farm
Langley Farm
HIGHBONES
Lock
Bourne Farm
114
BREAKSPEAR ROAD NORTH
OLD UXBRIDGE ROAD
NORTH ORBITAL WAY
05
06
07
92
93
94

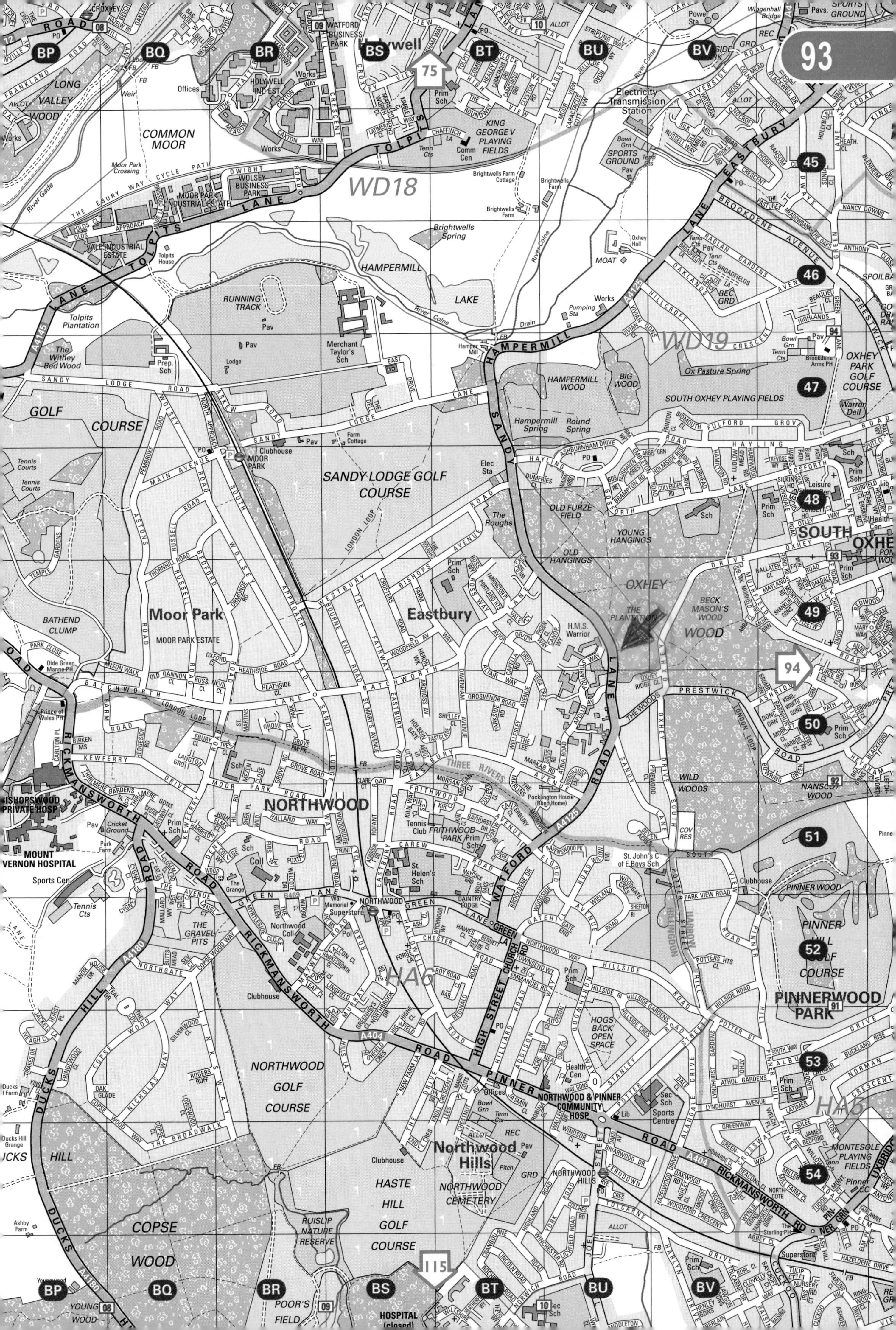
Holywell
COMMON MOOR
LONG VALLEY WOOD
WATFORD BUSINESS PARK
HOLYWELL IND EST
WOLSEY BUSINESS PARK
MOOR PARK INDUSTRIAL ESTATE
VALE INDUSTRIAL ESTATE
TOLPITS LANE
WD18
KING GEORGE V PLAYING FIELDS
SPORTS GROUND
Electricity Transmission Station
HAMPERMILL LAKE
RUNNING TRACK
Merchant Taylor's Sch
Tolpits Plantation
The Withey Bed Wood
SANDY LODGE ROAD
GOLF COURSE
MOOR PARK
SANDY LODGE GOLF COURSE
HAMPERMILL WOOD
BIG WOOD
WD19
SOUTH OXHEY PLAYING FIELDS
OXHEY PARK GOLF COURSE
OLD FURZE FIELD
YOUNG HANGINGS
OLD HANGINGS
Moor Park
MOOR PARK ESTATE
Eastbury
BATHEND CLUMP
H.M.S. Warrior
BECK MASON'S WOOD
SOUTH OXHEY
NORTHWOOD
THREE RIVERS
WILD WOODS
NANSCOT WOOD
BISHOPSWOOD PRIVATE HOSP
MOUNT VERNON HOSPITAL
PINNER WOOD
PINNER HILL GOLF COURSE
PINNERWOOD PARK
HA6
HOGS BACK OPEN SPACE
NORTHWOOD & PINNER COMMUNITY HOSP
NORTHWOOD GOLF COURSE
Northwood Hills
NORTHWOOD CEMETERY
HASTE HILL GOLF COURSE
RUISLIP NATURE RESERVE
COPSE WOOD
DUCKS HILL
HA5
MONTESOLE PLAYING FIELDS
RICKMANSWORTH ROAD
PINNER ROAD
HIGH STREET
WATFORD ROAD
SANDY LANE
HAMPERMILL LANE
EASTBURY LANE
HOSPITAL (closed)
POOR'S FIELD
YOUNG WOOD

BUSHEY
WATFORD HEATH
CARPENDERS PARK
MERRY HILL
SOUTH OXHEY
HATCH END
PINNER GREEN
PINNERWOOD PARK
BUSHEY GOLF COURSE & COUNTRY CLUB
HARTSBOURNE GOLF COURSE & COUNTRY CLUB
GRIM'S DYKE GOLF COURSE
PINNER HILL GOLF COURSE
OXHEY PARK GOLF COURSE
PINNER PARK
WD19
WD23
HA5
76
93
116

95
CD
CE
CF
CG
CH
CJ
CK
77
96
117
15
16
17
ALDENHAM RESERVOIR
SPORTS GROUND
ELSTREE HILL OPEN SPACE
ELSTREE OPEN SPACE
WD6
HERTSMERE
HARROW
M1
WATFORD BYPASS
A41
A411
A5183
A5
A4140
A409
A410
ELSTREE ROAD
WATFORD ROAD
BARNET LANE
EDGWARE WAY
BROCKLEY HILL
Junction 4
45
46
47
48
49
50
51
52
53
54
Corus Elstree Hotel
Brockley Grange
Site of Sulloniacae Roman Settlement
ROYAL NATIONAL ORTHOPAEDIC HOSP
Mike Heafey Sports & Rehabilitation Centre
Aspire Centre
HELIPAD
PEAR WOOD
BROCKLEY HILL
DRIVING RANGE
GOLF PARK
GOVT OFFICES
Canons Corner
SPUR ROAD
CLOISTERS WOOD
STANMORE COMMON
BUSHEY HEATH
B.U.P.A. HOSPITAL
CONVENT Coll
Caldecote Farm
Berkeley Cottage
Gas Pumping Sta
Centennial Park
LONDON LOOP
HEATHBOURNE ROAD
HIGH ROAD
COMMON ROAD
HARROW WEALD COMMON
BENTLEY PRIORY
BENTLEY PRIORY OPEN SPACE
BENTLEY PRIORY NATURE RESERVE
DEER PARK
HA7
HA3
HA8
STANMORE
STANMORE HILL
LITTLE COMMON
GROVE FIELDS
Harrow R.F.C.
Abercorn Arms PH
Stanmore Hall
THE BDY
LONDON ROAD
MARSH LANE
UXBRIDGE ROAD
BROOKSHILL
HARROW WEALD CEMETERY
HARROW WEALD LAKE
Harrow College
Stanmore College
STANMORE GOLF COURSE
ALLOTMENTS
N London Collegiate Sch
CANONS PARK
SPORTS GROUND
THE SPINNEY
STANMORE MARSH
HONEYPOT LANE
PLAYING FIELD
PRINCE EDWARD PLAYING FIELD
GOVT BUILDINGS
HARROW WEALD
RECREATION GROUND
BELMONT
BELMONT CIRCLE
CENTENARY PARK
QUEENSBURY
WEALDSTONE
KENTON LANE
WHITCHURCH LANE

CL
CM
CN
CP
CQ
CR
CS
19
20
21
78
A411
BARNET LANE
Superstore
Stirling Corner
Woodcock Hill Farm
Deacons Hill
DEACONS HILL
OPEN SPACE
SCRATCH WOOD
FROGHALL WOOD
ELSTREE PARK
ARKLEY PARK
Hyver Hall
BOYS HILL WOOD
THISTLE WOOD
GRAVEL PIT WOOD
CLUMP OF TREES WOOD
TARGET WOOD
LEG OF MUTTON POND
MILL HILL GOLF COURSE
NUT WOOD
HEMMINGS WOOD
STONEY WOOD LAKE
STONEY WOOD
45
46
47
48
49
50
51
52
53
54
Junction 4
ELSTREE OPEN SPACE
WD6
HERTSMERE
BARNET
M1
A5183
ELSTREE HILL SOUTH
The Leys
Elstree Manor
Penniwells Farm
Cerus Edgwarebury Hotel
Works
Brockley Grange
Site of Sulloniacae Roman Settlement
94
93
92
91
Bury Farm
EDGWAREBURY CEMETERY
REC GRD
Prim Sch
Clubhouse
SPORTS GRD
EDGWAREBURY PARK
Pav
Tennis Courts
London Gateway Services
Depot
Days Inn
FISH POND
BROCKLEY HILL
DRIVING RANGE
EDGWAREBURY GOLF COURSE
GOVT OFFICES
SPORTS GROUND
Canons Corner
A41 (WATFORD BYPASS)
EDGWARE WAY
SPUR ROAD
STONEGROVE
BROCKLEY HILL
WATLING STREET (ROMAN ROAD)
Apex Corner
SPUR RD ESTATE
STONEGROVE EST
STANMORE
95
CONVENT
EDGWARE
HA8
A5100
HALE LANE
SELVAGE LANE
DEANS LANE
STONEGROVE PARK
N London Collegiate Sch
THE LAKE
KING GEORGE V MEML GDNS
CANONS PARK
THE SPINNEY
THE BASIN
Broadwalk Shopping Centre
BUS STA
BUS DEPOT
Masons Arms PH
Premier Lodge
Wealdstone FC
CANONS PARK
SPORTS GROUND
PLAYING FIELD
STANMORE MARSH
Gas Works
GOVT BUILDINGS
CHANDOS RECREATION GROUND
PRINCE EDWARD PLAYING FIELD
DEANSBROOK ROAD
EDGWARE COMMUNITY HOSPITAL
BURNT OAK
WATLING PARK
SPORTS GROUND
LYNDHURST PARK
ADASTRAL ESTATE
GRAHAME PARK
SILKSTREAM PARK
MONTROSE PLAYING FIELDS
COLINDALE HOSP
BLOOD TRANSFUSION CENTRE
PUBLIC HEALTH LAB
COLINDALE
AEROVILLE
COLINDALE BUSINESS PK
CAPITOL IND PK
Yaohan Plaza
BRIT LIB NEWSPAPER COLLECTION
HA7
QUEENSBURY
HONEYPOT LANE
A4140
BURNT OAK BROADWAY
EDGWARE ROAD
BRIXTON EST
The Flying Eagle Tavern PH
118
Honeypot Pk
Superstore

CT
CU
CV
CW
CX
CY
CZ
22
23
24
79
Barnet Gate
Ducks Island
OLD ELIZABETHANS (BARNET) MEMORIAL PLAYING FIELDS
GRANGE PLAYING FIELDS
PLAYING FIELD
KING GEORGE PLAYING FIELDS
Brent Lodge Farm
Whitings Hill Farm
Dollis Brook
Sec Sch
OAKLANDS ROAD
N20
SOUTH HERTS GOLF COURSE
45
46
OLD CHOLMELEIAN SPORTS GROUND
TOTTERIDGE FIELDS NATURE RESERVE
TOTTERIDGE PARK
TOTTERIDGE COMMON
A5109
TOTTERIDGE
War Memorial
TOTTERIDGE VILLAGE
94
Mote End Farm
HENDON PARK WOOD
Oak Lodge
Ellern Mede Farm
The Warren
The Lynch House
Fairlawn
HIGHWOOD HILL
BEECH WOOD
HIGHWOOD PARK
Highwood House
Highwood Hill
Holcombe Dales
Orange Tree PH
Prim Sch
TOTTERIDGE GREEN
47
Cricket Grd Clubho.
Consolata Missionary Coll
Folly Brook
DARLANDS LAKE NATURE RESERVE
48
93
Folly Farm
SPORTS GROUND
Clubhouses
Belmont Riding Centre
Belmont Farm
THE MILL FIELD
NW7
Three Hammers PH
Sports Cen
Pool
Prim Sch
Mill Hill Sch
Burtonhole Farm
SPORTS GROUND Clubhouse
N12
PLAYING FIELD
SPORTS GROUND
49
Nursery
Pav
Nat Inst for Medical Research
St. Joseph's College
CHALET ESTATE
COTTAGE HOMES
Goodwyn Sch
CONV
Elec Sta
98
RIDGEWAY
Oakfields
Frith Manor Equestrian Centre
Frith Manor Farm
50
The Mount Sch
Drivers Hill
Ridgeway House
Burton Bank
MILL HILL
ARRANDENE OPEN SPACE
Milespit Hill
Watch Tower House
Wks
INGLIS BARRACKS
FINCHLEY
92
Univ of London Observatory
Featherstone Hill
Cricket Club
MILL HILL PARK
MILL HILL CEM
BITTACY HILL PARK
Depot
GOLF COURSE
Nethercourt (Clubhouse)
51
Council Depot
MILL HILL EAST
Superstore
Prim Schs.
Comm Cen
Chase Lodge
CHASE LODGE PLAYING FIELDS
METRO GOLF RANGE
Swim Pool
Clubhouse
52
HENDON
BARNET COPTHALL STADIUM
Crematorium
HENDON CEMETERY
HENDON GOLF COURSE
SPORTS GRD
91
N3
53
FINCHLEY CENTRAL
COPTHALL PLAYING FIELDS
Junction 2
Five Ways Corner
Barnet Coll (Grahame Pk Cen)
Health Cen
Comm Cen
Cricket Club
SPORTS GROUND
CHURCH END
Hendon R.F.C.
HOLDERS HILL
RAF MUSEUMS
NW4
SUNNY HILL PARK
WINDSOR OPEN SPACE
AVENUE HOUSE
54
Queens Head PH
EAST END ROAD
A504
NW9
Warehouses
Thistle Hendon Hall
119
GARDEN HOSP
Peel Cen (Metropolitan Pol Training & Driving School)
SPORTS GRD
M1
A41
A1
WATFORD WAY
GREAT NORTH WAY
HENDON LANE
REGENTS PARK ROAD
BALLARDS LANE

98
DA
DB
DC
DD
DE
DF
DG
80
97
120
EAST BARNET
OAK HILL PARK
Oak Hill College
EN4
SOUTH HERTS GOLF COURSE
N20
BROOK FARM OPEN SPACE
WYATTS FARM OPEN SPACE
KING GEORGE V PLAYING FIELDS
BARNET PLAYING FIELDS
DAME ALICE OWEN'S GRD
OAKLEIGH PARK
TOTTERIDGE VILLAGE
TOTTERIDGE LANE
A5109
TOTTERIDGE GREEN
TOTTERIDGE & WHETSTONE
WHETSTONE
SWAN LANE OPEN SPACE
BRUNSWICK PARK
NORTH MIDDLESEX GOLF COURSE
BETHUNE PARK GOLF COURSE
NEW SOUTHGATE REC GRD
FRIARY PARK
FRIERN BARNET
Consolata Missionary Coll
N12
WOODSIDE PARK
NORTH FINCHLEY
WOODHOUSE ROAD
A1003
A1000
HIGH ROAD
A598
WEST FINCHLEY
FINCHLEY
COPPETTS WOOD
GLEBELANDS OPEN SPACE
FINCHLEY MEMORIAL HOSP
NORTH CIRCULAR ROAD
A406
MUSWELL HILL SPORTS GROUND
COPPETTS WOOD HOSP
ST. PANCRAS & ISLINGTON CEMETERY
N2
COLDFALL WOOD
N3
CHURCH END
FINCHLEY CENTRAL
AVENUE HOUSE GRDS
EAST END ROAD
A504
REGENTS PARK ROAD
VICTORIA PARK
Nethercourt (Clubhouse)
FINCHLEY GOLF COURSE
45
46
47
48
49
50
51
52
53
54
26
27
28
91
92
93
94

DH
DJ
DK
DL
DM
DN
DP
OAKWOOD
OAKWOOD PARK
81
WINCHMORE HILL
GROVELANDS PARK
BOATING LAKE
PRIORY HOSPITAL
N14
N21
N13
N22
N11
OSIDGE
SOUTHGATE
SOUTHGATE CEMETERY
ARNOS PARK
NEW SOUTHGATE
BROOMFIELD PARK
PALMERS GREEN
HAZELWOOD SPORTS GRD
TOTTENHALL SPORTS GROUND
BOUNDARY PLAYING FIELDS
NEW RIVER SPORTS CENTRE
BOWES PARK
FRIERN BRIDGE RETAIL PARK
MUSWELL HILL GOLF COURSE
ALEXANDRA PALACE
ALEXANDRA PARK
MUSWELL HILL
WOOD GREEN
NOEL PARK
HORNSEY
BELMONT REC GRD
LORDSHIP RECREATION GROUND
CLOWES SPORTS GROUND
THE PAULIN GROUND
TATEM PARK REC.GRD
DOWNHILLS PARK
100
121
45
46
47
48
49
50
51
52
53
54
29
30
31
91
92
93
94

DQ
DR
DS
DT
DU
DV
DW
82
33
34
35
45
46
47
48
49
50
51
52
53
54
99
122
94
93
92
91
N21
N13
N18
N9
N17
N22
RIDGE AVENUE
GREAT CAMBRIDGE ROAD
HERTFORD ROAD
NORTH CIRCULAR ROAD
STERLING WAY
ANGEL ROAD
MERIDIAN WAY
LOWER EDMONTON
EDMONTON
UPPER EDMONTON
TOTTENHAM
TOTTENHAM HALE
TOTTENHAM MARSHES
NOEL PARK
THE PAULIN GROUND
EDMONTON CEMETERY
FIRS FARM PLAYING FIELDS
CLOWES SPORTS GROUND
CHURCH STREET REC GRD
CHURCHFIELD REC GRD
JUBILEE PARK
KING GEORGE'S FLD
PYMMES PARK
TATEM PARK REC GRD
HOLLY-WOOD GDNS
NORTH MIDDLESEX HOSPITAL
EDMONTON FEDERATION CEMETERY (JEWISH)
WESTERN SYNAGOGUE CEMETERY
TOTTENHAM PARK CEMETERY
MONTAGU RECREATION GROUND
CRAIG PARK
TOTTENHALL SPORTS GROUND
BOUNDARY PLAYING FIELDS
NEW RIVER SPORTS CENTRE
TOTTENHAM CEMETERY
BRUCE CASTLE PARK
LORDSHIP RECREATION GROUND
BROADWATER FARM EST
THE ROYAL LONDON ESTATE
WINGATE TRADING EST
WHITE HART LANE
TOTTENHAM HOTSPUR FC
LEE VALLEY TECHNOPARK
DOWN LANE REC GRD
LOCKWOOD RESERVOIR
LEE VALLEY PARK
BELMONT REC GRD
DOWNHILLS PARK
WEST

LEE VALLEY
WILLIAM GIRLING RESERVOIR
GOLF COURSE
CHINGFORD
FRIDAY HILL
CHINGFORD HATCH
SOUTH CHINGFORD
HIGHAMS PARK
HALE END
BANBURY RESERVOIR
HIGHAM HILL
WALTHAMSTOW
LLOYD PARK
CHINGFORD MOUNT CEMETERY
DEEPHAMS SEWAGE TREATMENT WORKS
LEE VALLEY PARK
EPPING FOREST
ROYAL EPPING FOREST GOLF COURSE
THE HAWK WOOD
LARKSWOOD PLAYING FIELDS
LARKS WOOD
RIDGEWAY PARK
MANSFIELD PARK
PIMP HALL PARK
JUBILEE SPORTS GRD
AINSLIE WOOD (Nat Res)
ROLLS SPORTS GRD
WALTHAMSTOW STADIUM
Cooks Wharf Roundabout
Crooked Billet Roundabout
Waterworks Cnr
E4
E17

CHINGFORD PLAIN
QUEEN ELIZABETH'S HUNTING LODGE
CHINGFORD
Buckhurst Hill
IG10
CHINGFORD GREEN
WHITEHALL PLAIN
E4
FRIDAY HILL
PIMP HALL PARK
BLUEHOUSE GROVE
HATCH FOREST
IG9
HOLLY HOUSE HOSP
LORD'S BUSHES
Knighton Wood
Woodford Wells
WOODFORD GOLF COURSE
WOODFORD GREEN
HIGHAMS PARK
THE HIGHAMS PARK
IG8
RAY PARK
ASHTON PLAYING FIELD
HALE END
WOODFORD
EPPING FOREST
WALTHAMSTOW FOREST
RODING VALLEY PARK
Waterworks Corner
SOUTH WOODFORD
E18
Junction 4
SOUTHEND ROAD
NORTH CIRCULAR ROAD

84
101
124

Chigwell
Chigwell Row
Grange Hill
HAINAULT
Fullwell Cross
CLAYHALL
BARKINGSIDE
ALDBOROUGH
Woodford Bridge
IG7
IG6
IG5
IG2
CHIGWELL GOLF COURSE
FAIRLOP WATERS GOLF COURSE
FAIRLOP WATER
HAINAULT RECREATION GROUND
FOREST ROAD PLAYING FIELD
HOSPITAL HILL WOOD
CHIGWELL ROW WATER WORKS
METROPOLITAN POLICE SPORTS GRD
WOOLSTON MANOR GOLF COURSE
ROLLS PARK
CHIGWELL CEMETERY
BARKINGSIDE CEM
85
104
125
EM
EN
EP
EQ
ER
ES
ET

Chigwell Row
IG7
HAINAULT FOREST COUNTRY PARK
HAINAULT FOREST GOLF COURSE
Havering Park
Collier Row
Mark's Gate
RM6
RM7
IG6
FAIRLOP WATER
HAINAULT RECREATION GROUND
FAIRLOP OAK PLAYING FIELD
FOREST ROAD PLAYING FIELD
GARDENS OF PEACE
SPORTS GROUND
HAINAULT INDUSTRIAL ESTATE
THE LAKE
TAYLOR'S PLAIN
WEDDRELL'S PLAIN
CABIN PLAIN
THREE CORNERS PLAIN
SPURGATE PLAIN
CRABTREE HILL
SANDHILLS
LOWER SANDHILLS
MILE PLANTATION
Dog Kennel Hill
Cabin Hill
Willoughby's Hill
Lambourne End
ROMFORD ROAD
GRAVEL LANE
MANOR ROAD
WHALEBONE LANE NORTH
FOREST ROAD
HAINAULT ROAD
FOXBURROW ROAD
FIVE OAKS LANE
PAINTERS ROAD
HOG HILL RD
COLLIER ROW
LONDON LOOP
86
103
126
EU
EV
EW
EX
EY
EZ
FA
45
46
47
48
49
50
51
52
53
54

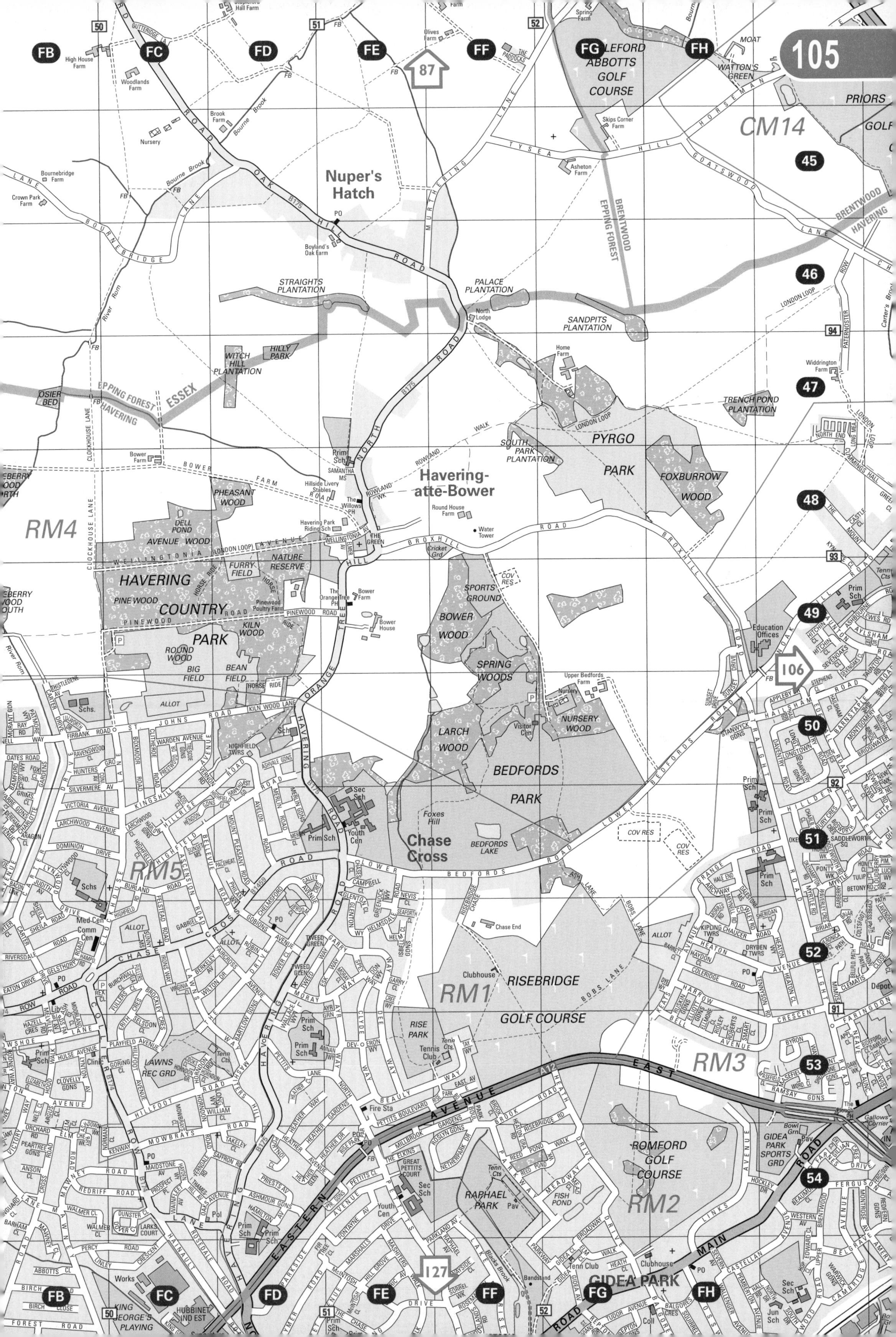
FB
FC
FD
FE
FF
FG
FH
87
106
127
CM14
RM4
RM5
RM1
RM2
RM3
45
46
47
48
49
50
51
52
53
54
Nuper's Hatch
Havering-atte-Bower
Chase Cross
GIDEA PARK
HAVERING COUNTRY PARK
PYRGO PARK
BEDFORDS PARK
RISEBRIDGE GOLF COURSE
ROMFORD GOLF COURSE
RAPHAEL PARK
RISE PARK
LAWNS REC GRD
GIDEA PARK SPORTS GRD
STRAIGHTS PLANTATION
PALACE PLANTATION
SANDPITS PLANTATION
WITCH HILL PLANTATION
HILLY PARK
TRENCH POND PLANTATION
SOUTH PARK PLANTATION
FOXBURROW WOOD
PHEASANT WOOD
DELL POND
AVENUE WOOD
FURRY FIELD
NATURE RESERVE
PINEWOOD
KILN WOOD
ROUND WOOD
BIG FIELD
BEAN FIELD
BOWER WOOD
SPRING WOODS
LARCH WOOD
NURSERY WOOD
SPORTS GROUND
BEDFORDS LAKE
Foxes Hill
EPPING FOREST
ESSEX
HAVERING
BRENTWOOD
PRIORS
MOAT
WATTON'S GREEN
Skips Corner Farm
Asheton Farm
High House Farm
Woodlands Farm
Brook Farm
Bournebridge Farm
Crown Park Farm
Boyland's Oak Farm
Bower Farm
Bower House
Home Farm
Upper Bedfords Farm
Widdrington Farm
Round House Farm
Water Tower
Education Offices
Clubhouse
Fire Sta
Bandstand
Tenn Club
Works
HUBBINET IND EST
KING GEORGE'S PLAYING
NORTH HILL
ORANGE TREE HILL
HAVERING ROAD
LOWER BEDFORDS ROAD
BROXHILL ROAD
TYSEA HILL
BOURNEBRIDGE LANE
BOWER FARM ROAD
CLOCKHOUSE LANE
EASTERN AVENUE
EAST AVENUE
MAIN ROAD
COLLIER ROW LANE
CHASE CROSS ROAD
HAINAULT ROAD
MAWNEY ROAD
RISEBRIDGE ROAD
BOBS LANE
ASH LANE
LONDON LOOP

PRIORS GOLF COURSE
ESSEX
BRENTWOOD
HAVERING
CURTIS PLANTATION
WABBING'S PLANTATION
SEVENACRE PLANTATION
CM14
LOCKSMITH WOOD
GOLDSMITH WOOD
Frieze Hall
Weald Bridge
The Chequers PH
Hou Hatch
Wright's Bridge
Old Macdonalds Farm
Wrightsbridge Farm
Wealdside
Rochetts Farm
St. Vincent's Hamlet
M25
RM4
Widdrington Farm
Pentowan Farm
SPICE PITS WOOD
Spice Pits Farm
NOAK HILL SPORTS GRD
Hill Farm
Hall
Noak Hill
TRENCH POND PLANTATION
THE OSIERS
BURNT WOOD
Weald Brook
FOXBURROW
The Bear PH
Manor Farm
DAGNAM PARK
FIR WOOD
COCK WOOD
ALDER WOOD
MAYLANDS GOLF COURSE
HATTER'S WOOD
Coll
Education Offices
Dycorts Sch
Sec Sch
DUCK WOOD NATURE RESERVE
Clubhouse
Maylands
Putwell Bridge
CENTRAL PARK
LONG WOOD
SALE WOOD
Harold Hill
Swim Pool
Health Cen
Youth Club
Comm Cen
Youth Centre
Cricket Ground
RM3
SHOULDER OF MUTTON WOOD
The Saxon King PH
Harold Park
COLCHESTER ROAD
A12
PLAYING FIELD
NAGS HEAD SEWAGE
Sludge Beds
Ingrebourne River
BATES INDUSTRIAL EST
HAROLD HILL INDUSTRIAL ESTATE
Depot
Superstore
Harold Court
Roots & Shoots Nursery
HAROLD WOOD HOSPITAL
HAROLD WOOD
AVENUE INDUSTRIAL ESTATE
Gallows Corner
The Plough PH
GIDEA PARK SPORTS GRD
ROMFORD GOLF COURSE
RM2
Ivy Lodge Farm
The Shepherd & Dog PH
Cockabourne Bridge
Pages Farm
Riding Stables
RM14
HAROLD WOOD PARK
Cricket Ground
Clinic
Comm Cen
SOUTHEND ARTERIAL ROAD
A127
MAIN ROAD
Clubhouse
Tyes Farm
Prospect Farm
Abattoir
Ingrebourne
105
128
FJ FK FL FM FN FP FQ
45 46 47 48 49 50 51 52 53 54
54 55 56
91 92 93 94

WEALD
COUNTRY
PARK
South
Weald
BRENTWOOD
Brook
Street
Warley
Great
Warley
Junction
28
CM15
CM13
LITTLE HIGHWOOD HOSP
HIGHWOOD HOSP
ESSEX NUFFIELD HOSP
BRENTWOOD COMM HOSP
MARILLAC HOSPITAL
B.U.P.A. HARTSWOOD HOSP
MASCALLS PARK
BRENTWOOD BYPASS
LONDON ROAD
HIGH STREET
SHENFIELD ROAD
INGRAVE
ONGAR ROAD
BRENTWOOD LEISURE PARK
108
109
129

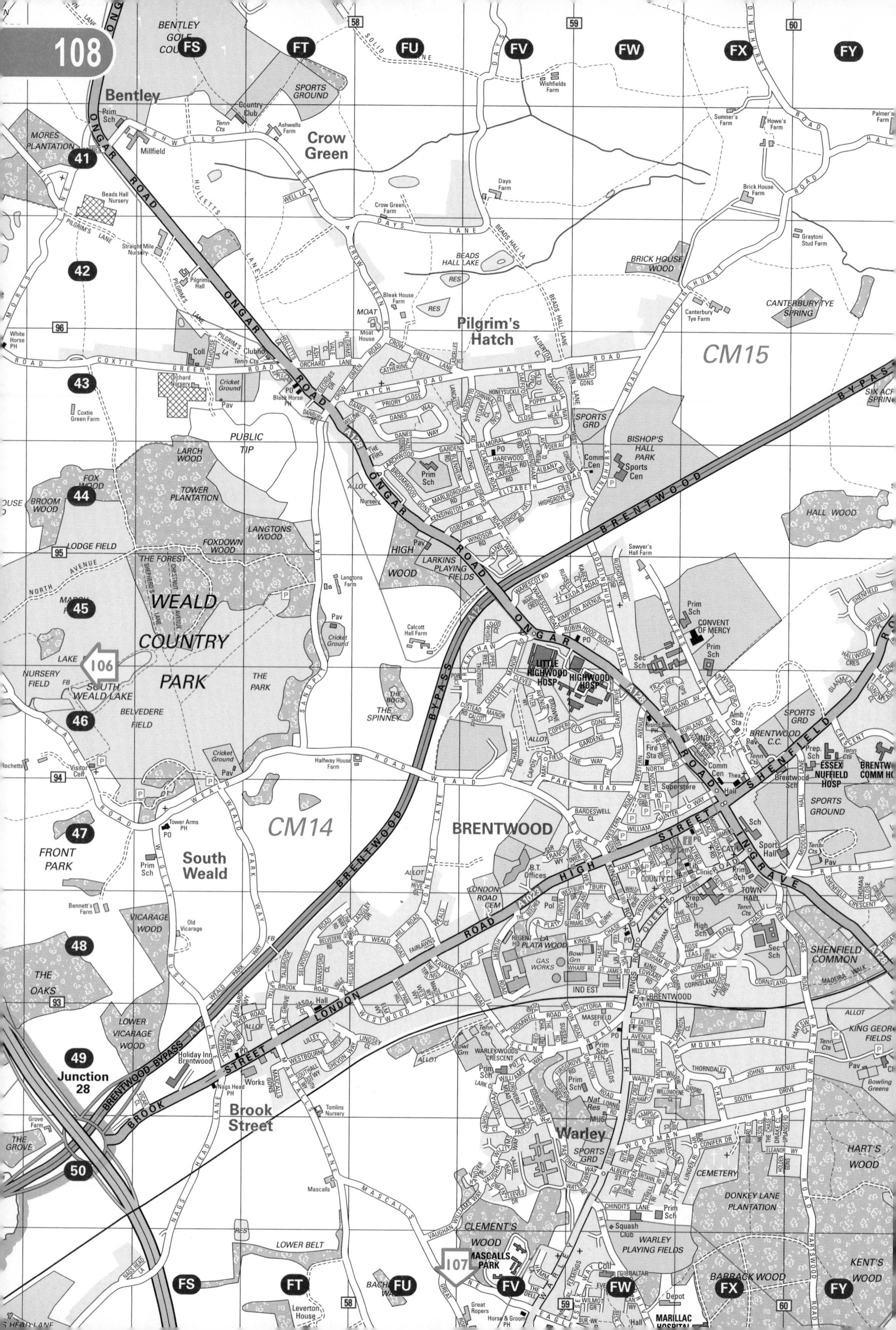
Bentley
Crow Green
Pilgrim's Hatch
CM15
WEALD COUNTRY PARK
CM14
BRENTWOOD
South Weald
Brook Street
Warley
Junction 28
ONGAR ROAD
BRENTWOOD BYPASS
SHENFIELD ROAD
INGRAVE ROAD
HIGH STREET
LONDON ROAD
WEALD ROAD
DODDINGHURST ROAD
MORES PLANTATION
LARCH WOOD
FOX WOOD
BROOM WOOD
TOWER PLANTATION
LANGTONS WOOD
FOXDOWN WOOD
HIGH WOOD
VICARAGE WOOD
LOWER VICARAGE WOOD
THE OAKS
FRONT PARK
BELVEDERE FIELD
NURSERY FIELD
SOUTH WEALD LAKE
BRICK HOUSE WOOD
HALL WOOD
CANTERBURY TYE SPRING
BISHOP'S HALL PARK
LARKINS PLAYING FIELDS
SHENFIELD COMMON
HART'S WOOD
DONKEY LANE PLANTATION
BARRACK WOOD
KENT'S WOOD
CLEMENT'S WOOD
MASCALLS PARK
WARLEY PLAYING FIELDS
LOWER BELT
LITTLE HIGHWOOD HOSP
HIGHWOOD HOSP
ESSEX NUFFIELD HOSP
CONVENT OF MERCY
BEADS HALL LAKE
PUBLIC TIP
106
107
FS FT FU FV FW FX FY
41 42 43 44 45 46 47 48 49 50
58 59 60 93 94 95 96

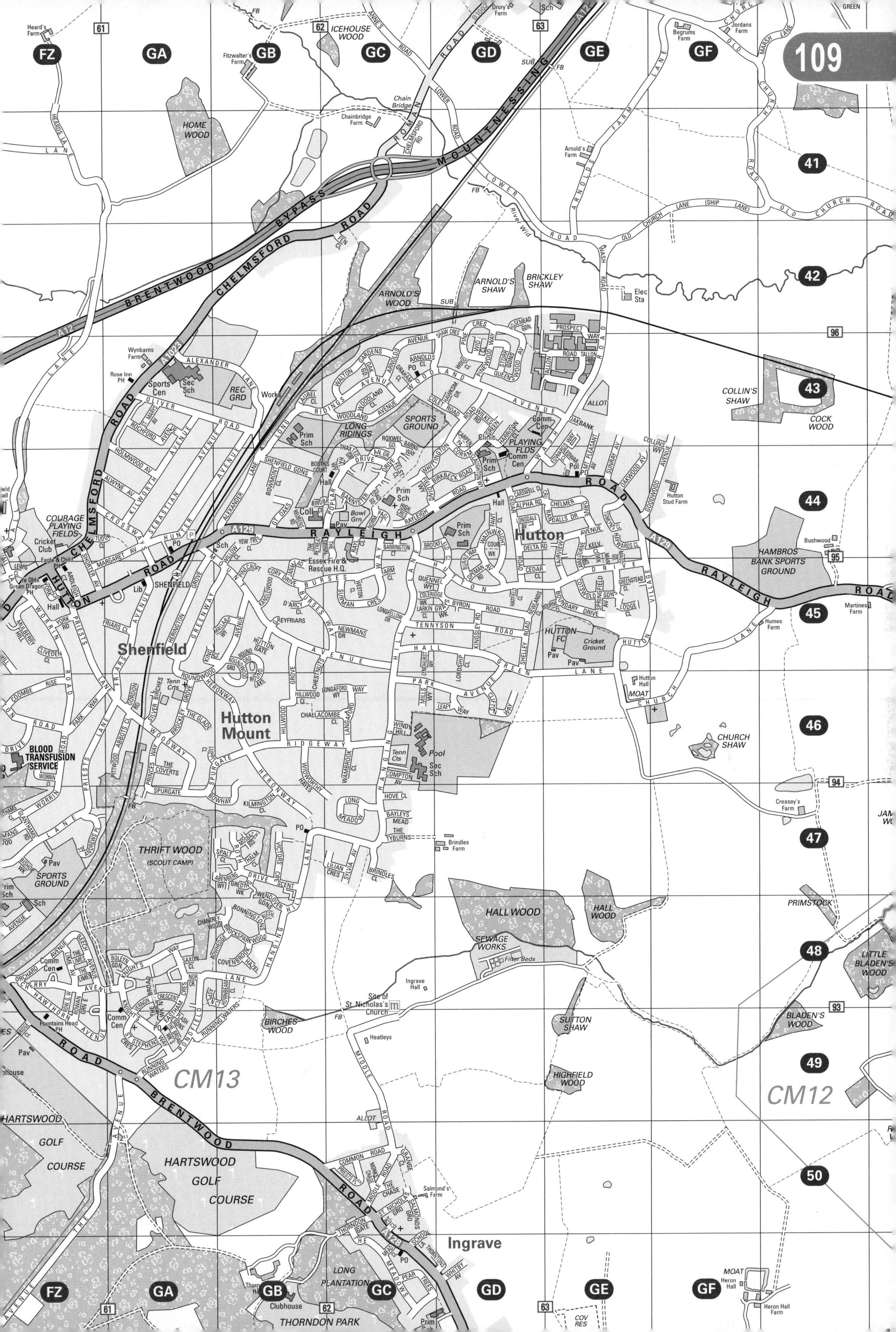

AC
AD
AE
AF
AG
AH
AJ
88
130
89
87
86
91
92
93
Holtspur
Junction 3
M40
OXFORD ROAD
LONDON ROAD
BOUNDARY ROAD
A4094
WYCOMBE ROAD
WHITE HILL
WYCOMBE END
FLACKWELL HEATH GOLF COURSE
FLACKWELL HEATH
55
56
57
58
59
60
61
62
63
64
Juniper Hill
NORTHERN WOODS
OLD MEADOWS
RONALD WOODS
Wooburn Green
Glory Hill Farm
SPORTS FIELD
CEM
QUARRY
Over's Farm
MILL WOOD
Glass Craft
Lillyfee Farm
HP10
DIPPLE WOOD
Wooburn
WOOBURN PARK
Cricket Club
SOHO MILLS IND EST
WOOBURN IND PARK
CHALKPITS CARAVAN PARK
Castleman's Farm
WOOBURN COMMON
The Royal Standard PH
SHEEPCOTE WOODS
OLDS FARM PARK
FARM WOOD
WASH HILL WOOD
THE SWILLEY
COVERED RESERVOIR
Sheepcote Farm
Meca Riding Centre
ASHEN COPPICE
Hawk's Hill
SAPPERS FIELD
The Chequers PH
Hedsor Farmhouse
BOURNE END
SL8
Hollands Farm
Tower Hill
WOOLMAN'S WOOD
White Hill
Bourne End Garden Centre
THE DENE
Priory Nursery
Hedsor Court
JOHNSON'S COPPICE
HOLLYBUSH WOOD
BRISTLES WOOD
Hedsor Wharf
Hedsor Priory
Hedsor House
PARK TOP
THE ROOKERY
HEDSOR PARK
OAKEN GROVE
BURWOOD ESTATE
Dropmore
ROOT MOUND
ABBEY WOOD
Brook End Farm
SL1
WINDSOR & MAIDENHEAD
WYCOMBE
SL6
LOCK CUT
Weir
Cookham Lock
Cookham Bridge
BUCKINGHAMSHIRE
ODNEY COMMON
ODNEY CLUB SPORTS GRD
Tennis Courts
Cricket Ground
Mill House
Formosa Court
Cliveden House & Hotel
CLIVEDEN NT
GULLEY WOOD
CADBROOK WOOD
The Feathers Inn PH
LITTLE BARNS WOOD
LAMBOURNE GOLF COURSE
Clubhouse
LAMBOURNES WOOD
Cookham
Seven Gable Cottage
Boathouse
Burwood House
WYMERS WOOD

AK
AL
AM
AN
AP
AQ
AR
89
HP9
SL9
SL2
Junction 2
Beaconsfield United FC
Beaconsfield RFC
Oak Lodge Meadows
REC GRD
LONDON END
WYCOMBE END
LONDON ROAD
OXFORD ROAD
A40
M40
A355
PITLANDS WOOD
BIRCHLAND WOOD
LOWER PYEBUSHES
PYEBUSHES
BIRCH WOOD
Bell House Hotel
Wapsey's Wood Landfill Site
SAND AND GRAVEL PIT
GREEN BROOM
Hyde Farm
Sewage Works
THE GROVE
DUKE'S UNDERWOOD
HEDGERLEY LANE
BURTLEY WOOD
BOWER WOOD
WINDSOR ROAD
CAVE WOOD
BIRCHEN SPRING COPPICE
HILLMOTTS WOOD
HILLMOTTS FURZE
Hillmotts Farm
Slade Farm
HILL WOOD
HOLLYBUSH WOOD
Woodlands Farm
HANGINGS WOOD
Downey Bottom
BROOMHILL COPPICE
JENNINGS WOOD
Jennings Farm
HICKNAHAM PLANTATION
Dorney Bottom
PENNLANDS WOOD
Pennlands Farm
Gas Works
SUTTON'S WOOD
Mount Pleasant Farm
MOLL HAYES WOOD
Hedgerley
112
RSPB NATURE RESERVE
CHURCH WOOD
The White Horse PH
Hall
KILN LANE
KILN WOOD
LITTLE WOOD
HAREHATCH LANE
COLLINSWOOD ROAD
BOVENEY WOOD
HEALY'S GORSE
Water Tower
The Yew Tree PH
HANGING WOOD
SUMMERLINS WOOD
LITTLE BURNT COPPICE
Abbey Park Farm
Boveney Wood Farm
The Jolly Woodman PH
FOOTPATH WOOD
Hollybush Corner
BLACK GROVE
PONDS WOOD
HEATHFIELD WOOD
STAPLEFURZE WOOD
PARISH LANE
COLLUM LANE
COV RES
The One Pin PH
The Blackwood Arms PH
SCHOOL WOOD
TWELVE ACRE WOOD
EGYPT WOODS
TIMBER WOOD
STOKE WOOD
Littleworth Corner
WHITESPARK WOOD
GREAT BURNT COPPICE
NINE ACRE WOOD
DORNEY WOOD
HARTLEY COURT MOAT
Clubhouse SPORTS GRD
EGYPT
BEACONSFIELD ROAD
FLEET WOOD
TOWER WOOD
BURNHAM BEECHES
INGRAM'S COPSE
BROCKHURST WOOD
DORNEYWOOD GDNS (NT)
Pumpkin Hill
SEVEN WAYS PLAIN
JUNIPER GROVE
UPPER BURNHAM COMMON
131
Farnham Common
55
56
57
58
59
60
61
62
63
64
86
87
88
94
95
96

Layter's Green
Birchland Wood
High Wood
Beech Wood
Birch Wood
Bell House Hotel
Oxford Road
Wapsey's Wood Landfill Site
Sand and Gravel Pit
Further Warren Wood
Siblet's Wood
Chantry Wood
West Plantation
SL9
Bulstrode Park
Bulstrode
Menagerie Wood
Grove Plantation
Gerrards Cross
Gerrards Cross Common
Sutton's Wood
Hedgerley
RSPB Nature Reserve
Church Wood
Leith Grove
Hanging Wood
Hedgerley Park
Mounthill Wood
Duke's Orchard
Black Grove
Footpath Wood
Parkside Cemetery
Pickeridge Wood
Timber Wood
Stoke Wood
SL2
SL3
Fulmer
Fulmer Hall (Research Laboratories)
Stoke Common
Frame Wood
Brockhurst Wood
Ingram's Copse
Penn Wood
Hay Wood
Farnham Common
M40

GERRARDS CROSS GOLF COURSE
NOCKHILL WOOD
JUNIPER WOOD
GREAT HALINGS WOOD
TRAINING CENTRE DURDENT COURT
THREE RIVERS
SOUTH BUCKS
NORTHMOOR HILL (NATURE RESERVE)
DENHAM AERODROME
DENHAM MARSH WOOD
OAKEND WOOD
QUARTERS WOOD
ROUND COPSE
SQUARE COPSE
BATTLESFORD WOOD
RANSTON COVERT
WADLEY COVERT
NIGHTINGALE WOOD
HOLLY HILL WOOD
Denham Green
DENHAM GOLF COURSE
COLLSELS WOOD
Higher Denham
UB9
MILL WOOD
GALLOWS WOOD
LITTLE GALLOWS WOOD
THE RANCHO
TOM WILLIAM'S WOOD
BRADBURY'S ISLAND
CAPS WOOD
MISBOURNE MEADOWS
BAKER'S WOOD
Tatling End
BUCKINGHAM
Denham
NABOTH
GALDWINS WOOD
BROADSPRING WOOD
HAWKS WOOD
FURZENEY WOOD
Junction 16 (M25)
Junction 1a (M40)
BROWN'S WOOD
GOSSAMS WOOD
OLDHOUSE WOOD
PARKSPRING WOOD
MOUNT FIDGET WOOD
LONG COPPICE
SL0
LANGLEY COMMON
BRIDGETTINE CONVENT
Holly Bush
AMERSHAM ROAD
OXFORD ROAD
NORTH ORBITAL ROAD
DENHAM AVENUE
DENHAM ROAD
M25
M40
A40
A412
A413
91
114
133

BG
BH
BJ
BK
BL
BM
BN
92
05
06
07
Lock
Pav
Cricket Ground
Pavs.
Harefield United FC
ASHAIN SPRING
CLAYPITS
SCARLET SPRING
DELL
Shooting School
HIGHBONES
Knightscote Farm
Langley Farm
Bourne Farm
Warren Farm
NORTH RIDING WOOD
NORTH BREAKSPEAR ROAD
BREAKSPEAR PATH
Grand Union Canal
LONDON LOOP TOWING PATH
CHURCH HILL
ST MARY'S CL
ST ANNES RD
BROADWATER LA
Broadwater Farm
FB
ALLOT
GORE CL
PRIORY AV
Comm Cen
Tenn Cts
SPORTS GRD
TRUESDALE DR
PO
Denham Lock
Widewater Lock
SOUTH HAREFIELD
Park Lodge Farm Centre
BAYHURST WOOD COUNTRY PARK
Willow Tree Farm
HARVIL ROAD
UB9
HAREFIELD MOOR
Horse & Barge PH
COV RES
Pumping Sta
MOORHALL ROAD
Green Bridge
BROADWATER PARK
Rank Film Laboratories
CIVIC AMENITY SITE
St. Leonard's Farm
NEW YEARS GREEN LANE
Highway Farm
Pylon Farm
Elm Tree Farm
High View Farm
Braemer Farm
Newyears Green
NEWYEARS GREEN COVERT
Activities Centre
Dews Farm
Savay Farm
HILLINGDON
SOUTH BUCKS
TOWING PATH
ALTCAR COVERT
CRUISE COVERT
DENHAM
55
56
57
58
59
60
61
62
63
64
89
88
87
86
NORTH ORBITAL ROAD
A412
Wyatt's Covert Caravan Site
NORTHMOOR HILL (NATURE RESERVE)
BATTLESFORD WOOD
RANSTON COVERT
WADLEY COVERT
HOLLY HILL WOOD
Denham Green
NEWSTEAD WOOD
Prim Sch
Medical Cen
MARTINSFIELD SPORTS GRD
Clubhouse
113
The Prescotts
Denham Place
Hall
VILLAGE ROAD
DENHAM AVENUE
BUCKINGHAMSHIRE GOLF COURSE
DENHAM COUNTRY PARK
FLAGMOOR COVERT
UXBRIDGE GOLF COURSE
Works
SKIP LANE
Depot
Glaxo Research Farm
COPTHALL COVERT
MOAT
RIVERSIDE WALK
Clubhouse
Harvil Farm
Copthall Farm
Denham Court
COWMOOR COVERT
Weir
ST. JOHN'S COVERT
Visitor Cen
Wellers Mead
River Misbourne
OXFORD ROAD
A40
Little Acres Farm
Prim Sch
REC Club GRD
Denham
SPORTS GROUND
DENHAM COUNTRY PARK
Denham Lock
Fray's River
The Lea
Lea Cottage
Glasshouses
Farm
Junction 1
M40
WESTERN AVENUE
WEATHERLYS COVERT
SWAKELEYS ROAD
GREEN ACRES AVENUE
KENBURY CL
SWAKELEYS DRIVE
Sec Sch
THE CLUMP
PARK WOOD
Common Plantation
Tennis Club
Bowl Grn
RIVERSIDE WALK
New House Farm
WILLETTS LANE
Cornerfields
Depot
Comm Cen
ALLOT
Ivy House Farm
Oxford Road Nursery
Denham Utd. FC
A4020
PLAYING FIELD
Works
LONDON LOOP
PLAYING FIELD
Fray's Farm
Uxbridge Alderglade Nature Reserve
Fray's Bridge
Kingcup Farm
Brickfield Farm
Copse Hill Farm
Southlands Manor
Osborne Farm
134
Tenn Cts
Works
Lock
Coll
UXBRIDGE COMMON
NORTH COMMON RD
Ski Slopes
Hillingdon Ski Centre
UXBRIDGE ATHLETICS TRACK
HILLINGDON HOUSE FARM SPORTS GROUND
UB10
Uxbridge CC
Pav
Lido (closed)
River Pinn
HILLINGDON

Northwood Hills
93
RUISLIP NATURE RESERVE
HILL GOLF COURSE
COPSE WOOD
YOUNG WOOD
HA6
MAD BESS WOOD
POOR'S FIELD
HOSPITAL (closed)
RUISLIP LIDO
PARK WOOD
RUISLIP COMMON
Breakspear Crematorium
Hillingdon Borough FC
EASTCOTE VILLAGE
EASTCOTE
HA4
RUISLIP
KINGS COLLEGE PLAYING FIELDS
GOVERNMENT OFFICES
WARRENDER PARK
116
RUISLIP MANOR
RUISLIP GOLF COURSE
CAVENDISH REC GRD
PINE GDNS
BESSINGBY FIELD
SPORTS GROUND
NEW POND FARM FIELDS
ICKENHAM
WEST RUISLIP
RUISLIP GARDENS
BRAINTREE INDUSTRIAL ESTATE
SOUTH RUISLIP
ODYSSEY BUSINESS PARK
Ickenham Marsh
RAF NORTHOLT AERODROME
135
FREEZELAND COVERT
Master Brewer Hotel
BP BQ BR BS BT BU BV
08 09 10
55 56 57 58 59 60 61 62 63 64

BW
BX
BY
BZ
CA
CB
CC
12
13
14
94
115
136
55
56
57
58
59
60
61
62
63
64
PINNER GREEN
MONTESOLE PLAYING FIELDS
LITTLE COMMON
CEM
PINNER
PINNER MEMORIAL PARK
PINNER NEW CEMETERY
Fire Training Cen
RECREATION GROUND
SPORTS GROUND
HEADSTONE
Harrow Mus & Heritage Cen
PINNER VILLAGE GARDENS
Old Lyonian Sports Club
NORTH HARROW
EASTCOTE VILLAGE
Haydon Hall
CUCKOO HILL
HA5
EASTCOTE
THE CROFT PLAYING FIELD
High Sch
WARRENDER PARK
CAVENDISH REC GRD
PINE GDNS
ROXBOURNE PARK
Streamside Reservation
RAYNERS LANE
SPORTS GRD
HA2
WEST HARROW REC GRD
WEST HARROW
NEWTON PARK WEST
NEWTON FM ECOLOGY PK
BESSINGBY FIELD
RECREATION GROUND
SOUTH HARROW
ROXETH REC GRD
PLAYING FIELD
DEANE PARK
REC GRD
ALEXANDRA PARK
Harrow Borough FC
EARLSMEAD STADIUM
BRAINTREE INDUSTRIAL ESTATE
SOUTH RUISLIP
PLAYING FIELD
VICTORIA RETAIL PARK
FROGMORE ESTATE
HA4
Civic Amenity Site
ODYSSEY BUSINESS PARK
NORTHOLT RECREATION GRD
PLAYING FIELD
Northolt Park
UB5
LORD HALSBURY MEMORIAL GRD
SPORTS GROUND
Air Traffic Radio Sta
HILLINGDON
EALING
HARROW
A404
A4090
A312
A4180
GEORGE V AVENUE
PINNER ROAD
ALEXANDRA AVENUE
WEST END ROAD
VICTORIA ROAD
PETTS HILL
NORTHOLT ROAD
EASTCOTE LANE
RAYNERS LANE

CD
CE
CF
CG
CH
CJ
CK
95
WEALDSTONE
BYRON REC GRD
QUEENSBURY
HA7
HARROW & WEALDSTONE
WAVERLEY INDUSTRIAL ESTATE
CIVIC CENTRE
HA3
KENTON RECREATION GROUND
KENTON
WOODCOCK PARK
HARROW
HARROW REC GROUND
HA1
University of Westminster
NORTHWICK PARK & ST. MARK'S HOSPITALS
NORTHWICK PARK
HARROW SCHOOL PLAYING FIELDS
HARROW SCHOOL GOLF COURSE
HARROW ON THE HILL
ST. ANDREW'S AT HARROW HOSP
CLEMENTINE CHURCHILL HOSPITAL
JOHN BILLAM SPORTS GRD
PRESTON
118
PRESTON PARK
NORTH WEMBLEY
WEMBLEY COMMERCIAL CENTRE
G.E.C. ESTATE
HA9
FORTY FARM SPORTS GROUND
VALE FARM SPORTS GROUND
KING EDWARD VII PARK
EALING NORTHERN SPORTS GRD
UB6
SUDBURY
BARHAM PARK
HA0
WEMBLEY CENTRAL
137
55
56
57
58
59
60
61
62
63
64
15
16
17
A4006
A404
A409
A4005
A4088
A4090
A312
A4140
A4089

118
CL
CM
CN
CP
CQ
CR
CS
96
HA7
HA8
QUEENSBURY
55
56
57
58
59
60
61
62
63
64
COLINDALE HOSP
BLOOD TRANSFUSION CENTRE
PUBLIC HEALTH LAB.
COLINDALE
BRIT. LIB NEWSPAPER COLLECTION
MONTROSE PLAYING FIELDS
COLINDALE BUSINESS PK
CAPITOL IND PK
Yaohan Plaza
EDGWARE
ROAD
BRIXTON EST
ETON GROVE OPEN SPACE
QUEENSBURY PARK
KINGSBURY COMMUNITY HOSPITAL
HONEYPOT
LANE
A4140
KENTON
ROAD
A4006
KINGSBURY
ROAD
ROE GREEN PARK
CHERRY TREE COURT
WOODCOCK PARK
KINGSBURY SPORTS GRD
NW9
KINGSBURY
FRYENT
COUNTRY
PARK
FRYENT COUNTRY PARK
FRYENT
WAY
SILVER JUBILEE PARK
CHURCH LANE REC GRD
KINGSBURY TRADING EST
WEST HENDON PLAYING FIELDS
WEST HENDON
WOODFIELD PARK
HA3
JOHN BILLAM SPORTS GD
PRESTON
117
PRESTON PARK
BARN HILL OPEN SPACE
WELSH HARP OPEN SPACE
Welsh Harp Environmental Education Centre
Wembley Sailing Club
WELSH
NEASDEN RECREATION GRD
Stanmore Junction
FORTY FARM SPORTS GROUND
WEMBLEY PARK
WEMBLEY COMMERCIAL CENTRE
G.E.C. ESTATE
FORTY
LANE
A4088
SALMON STREET
BRENT TOWN HALL
BLACKBIRD HILL
NEASDEN LANE
NORTH
CIRCULAR
KING EDWARD VII PARK
WEMBLEY PARK DRIVE
Palace of Industry
WEMBLEY ARENA
Sunday Market
GANNON TRADING EST
STADIUM BUS CEN
WEMBLEY STADIUM REDEVELOPMENT open 2006
HA9
NW10
NEASDEN RAIL DEPOT
GREAT CENTRAL WAY
DRURY WAY IND EST
BRENT PARK
IKEA TWR
WEMBLEY
WEMBLEY CENTRAL
SHERRINS FARM OPEN SPACE
TOKYNGTON REC GRD
TOKYNGTON
138
PLAYING FIELDS
HARROW
ROAD
HIGH
ROAD
HA0
EALING
CHURCH END
GIBBONS REC GRD
Swaminarayan Hindu Mission
NEASDEN
19
20
21

CT
CU
CV
CW
CX
CY
CZ
22
23
24
97
HILL
RAF MUSEUM
SUNNY HILL PARK
GARDEN HOSP
Thistle Hendon Hall
N3
55
56
57
58
59
60
61
62
63
64
Peel Cen Metropolitan Pol Cdg & Driving School
SPORTS GRD
A5150
THE HYDE
HENDON
Middlesex Uni
TOWN HALL
CHURCH FARM HOUSE MUS
CHURCH ROAD
FINCHLEY LANE
HENDON WAY
NORTH CIRCULAR ROAD
REGENTS PARK ROAD
FINCHLEY ROAD
BRENT STREET
Uni of London
CARMELITE MONASTERY
PRINCES PARK
NW4
HENDON PARK
HENDON CENTRAL
NW11
HOOP LANE CEMETERY (JEWISH)
GARDEN OF REMEMBRANCE
GOLDERS GREEN
Golders Green Hippodrome
89
88
87
86
120
Welsh Harp
YORK PARK
Brent Cross Shopping Centre
BRENT CROSS
Junction 1
STADIUM RD
Holiday Inn
Refuse Disposal Works
BRENT RESERVOIR
AQUARIUS BUSINESS PARK
STAPLES CORNER BUSINESS PK
WELLINGTON PARK EST
SPORTS GRD
A406
EDGWARE ROAD
BROADWAY
CLITTERHOUSE PLAYING FIELDS
Hendon FC
TRAIN DEPOT
GOLDERS GREEN ROAD
GREEK CATH
GOLDERS GREEN DEPOT
BASING HILL PK
CHILDS HILL PK
CHILDS HILL
SWAN POND
ALLOT
EVANS BUSINESS CEN
DOLLIS HILL
GLADSTONE PARK
SPORTS GRD
CRICKLEWOOD
CRICKLEWOOD BROADWAY
UNIVERSITY COLLEGE SCHOOL SPORTS GRD
HAMPSTEAD CEMETERY
Uni of London King's Coll
NW8
BARNET
CAMDEN
Open Uni Regional Cen
NW2
Coll of North West London
DOLLIS HILL
SHOOT UP HILL
CHICHELE ROAD
WALM LANE
CHAPMAN PK IND EST
CYGNUS BUS CEN
WILLESDEN
HIGH ROAD
KILBURN
WEST HAMPSTEAD
139
A4003
A4088
A407
A41
A5
A598
M1

DA
DB
DC
DD
DE
DF
DG
26
27
28
98
119
140
55
56
57
58
59
60
61
62
63
64
N3
N2
N6
NW11
NW3
EAST END ROAD
NORTH CIRCULAR ROAD
REGENTS PARK ROAD
FALLODEN WAY
LYTTELTON ROAD
AYLMER ROAD
GREAT NORTH ROAD
HIGH ROAD
FORTIS GREEN
ARCHWAY ROAD
FINCHLEY ROAD
NORTH END ROAD
NORTH END WAY
SPANIARDS ROAD
HAMPSTEAD LANE
HEATH STREET
HAVERSTOCK HILL
ROSSLYN HILL
HENDON WAY
WEST END LANE
EAST FINCHLEY
FORTIS GREEN
HAMPSTEAD GARDEN SUBURB
GOLDERS GREEN
CHILDS HILL
HAMPSTEAD
WEST HAMPSTEAD
EAST FINCHLEY CEMETERY
COLDFALL WOOD
CHERRY TREE WOOD
HIGHGATE WOOD
BIG WOOD
LITTLE WOOD
HIGHGATE GOLF COURSE
HAMPSTEAD GOLF COURSE
HAMPSTEAD HEATH EXTENSION
HOOP LANE CEMETERY (JEWISH)
GOLDERS HILL PARK
WEST HEATH
SANDY HEATH
HAMPSTEAD HEATH
KENWOOD
KENWOOD HOUSE
THE IVEAGH BEQUEST - KENWOOD HOUSE
NORTH WOOD
ATHLONE HOUSE
HIGHGATE PONDS
HIGHGATE MEN'S POND
KENWOOD LADIES POND
PARLIAMENT HILL
VALE OF HEALTH
HAMPSTEAD PONDS
LEG OF MUTTON POND
WHITESTONE POND
VIADUCT POND
QUEEN MARY'S HOSP
ROYAL FREE HOSP
HAMPSTEAD CEMETERY
ST. LUKE'S WOODSIDE HOSPITAL
LISMORE CIRCUS
MAITLAND PARK ESTATE
ST. DOMINIC'S PRIORY
TAVISTOCK CEN
WEST HAMPSTEAD (THAMESLINK)
FINCHLEY ROAD & FROGNAL
Camden Arts Centre
Golders Green Hippodrome
GOLDERS GREEN DEPOT
KILBURN
ATHLETICS TRACK
LYTTELTON PLAYING FIELDS
TURNERS WOOD
HIGHGATE

DH
DJ
DK
DL
DM
DN
DP
99
122
141
NOEL PARK
ALEXANDRA PALACE
ALEXANDRA PARK
N22
MUSWELL HILL
HORNSEY
WEST GREEN
N8
PRIORY PARK
QUEEN'S WOOD
CROUCH END
HARRINGAY
STROUD GREEN
FINSBURY PARK
N4
N19
WHITTINGTON HOSPITAL
HIGHGATE CEMETERY
WATERLOW PARK
UPPER HOLLOWAY
DARTMOUTH PARK
TUFNELL PARK
H.M. PRISON HOLLOWAY
HOLLOWAY
N7
LOWER HOLLOWAY
ARSENAL STADIUM
N5
HIGHBURY
NW5
KENTISH TOWN
CANONBURY
PENTONVILLE PRISON
ST. ANN'S HOSPITAL
CHESTNUTS PARK
DOWNHILLS PARK
BELMONT REC GRD
WEST RESERVOIR
HIGH STREET
HORNSEY ROAD
SEVEN SISTERS ROAD
HOLLOWAY ROAD
CAMDEN ROAD
CALEDONIAN ROAD
GREEN LANES
BLACKSTOCK ROAD
ARCHWAY ROAD
JUNCTION ROAD
TURNPIKE LANE
WESTBURY AVENUE
MUSWELL HILL
PRIORY ROAD
PARK ROAD
TOTTENHAM LANE
CROUCH HILL
HORNSEY RISE
STROUD GREEN ROAD
HIGHBURY PARK
HIGHBURY GROVE
BRECKNOCK ROAD
29
30
31
55
56
57
58
59
60
61
62
63
64

122
DQ
DR
DS
DT
DU
DV
DW
N22
N17
N15
N4
N16
N5
E5
E8
LORDSHIP RECREATION GROUND
BELMONT REC GRD
DOWNHILLS PARK
WEST GREEN
CHESTNUTS PARK
ST ANN'S HOSPITAL
SOUTH TOTTENHAM
TOTTENHAM MARSHES
LOCKWOOD RESERVOIR
TOTTENHAM HALE
LOCKWOOD INDUSTRIAL PARK
LOW MAYNARD RESERVOIR
DOWN LANE REC GRD
LEE VALLEY TECHNOPARK
MONUMENT WAY
FERRY LANE
MARKFIELD REC GRD
RESERVOIR NUMBER FOUR
RESERVOIR NUMBER TWO
RESERVOIR NUMBER ONE
RESERVOIR NUMBER THREE
RESERVOIR NUMBER FIVE
WARWICK RESERVOIR EAST
WARWICK RESERVOIR WEST
COPPERMILL PLAYING FIELD
SPRINGFIELD PARK
SPRINGHILL SPORTS GRD
Walthamstow Marsh
Nature Reserve
FINSBURY PARK
EAST RESERVOIR
WEST RESERVOIR
STAMFORD HILL
ABNEY PARK CEMETERY
STOKE NEWINGTON
UPPER CLAPTON
NORTH MILLFIELDS RECREATION GROUND
CLISSOLD PARK
SHACKLEWELL
HACKNEY DOWNS
ARSENAL STADIUM
HIGHBURY
CANONBURY
SEVEN SISTERS ROAD
STAMFORD HILL
STOKE NEWINGTON HIGH ST
GREEN LANES
AMHURST PARK
CLAPTON COMMON
100
121
142

DX
DY
DZ
EA
EB
EC
ED
HIGHAM HILL
LLOYD PARK
WALTHAMSTOW
WALTHAM FOREST TRACK
CHESTNUTS SHOWGROUND
TOWN HALL
ASSEMBLY HALL
THORPE COOMBE HOSP
UPLANDS BUSINESS PARK
HIGHAMS LODGE BUSINESS CEN
EPPING FOREST
CHILDREN'S BOATING POND
FOREST ROAD
A503
UPPER WALTHAMSTOW
WOOD STREET
E17
DOUGLAS EYRE PLAYING FIELDS
Flood Relief Channel
BLACKHORSE ROAD
WALTHAMSTOW CENTRAL
WALTHAMSTOW QUEENS ROAD
ST JAMES STREET
WALTHAMSTOW CEM
HOE STREET
A112
SNARESBROOK
ROUND POND
HOLLOW POND
WHIPPS CROSS ROAD
WHIPPS CROSS HOSPITAL
LEA BRIDGE ROAD
A104
COPPERMILLS TREATMENT WORKS
Filter Beds
ST. JAMES'S PARK
LOW HALL SPORTS GROUND
RECYCLING CENTRE
LEYTON IND VILLAGE
FOREST BUSINESS PK
ROXWELL TRADING PK
DORMA TRADING PK
ALLOTMENTS
MARKHOUSE ROAD
A1006
CHURCH ROAD
LEYTON
E10
LEYTONSTONE
LEYTON MIDLAND ROAD
LEYTON HIGH ROAD
ENTERPRISE PARK
SPORTS GROUND
LEYTON MARSHES
Lee Valley Ice Centre
Lee Valley Riding Cen
Gas Works
SEYMOUR ROAD PLAYING FIELD
MARSH LANE PLAYING FIELD
LEYTON BUSINESS CEN
IVE FM SPORTS GRD
LEE VALLEY PITCH & PUTT GOLF COURSE
River Lee or Lea
NATURE RESERVE
LEA BRIDGE
LEE VALLEY PARK
HACKNEY MARSH
WALTHAM FOREST
HACKNEY
LEYTON ORIENT FC
SIDMOUTH PARK
COUNCIL OFFS
ST. PATRICK'S RC CEMETERY
New Spitalfields Market
RECREATION GROUND
ETON MANOR SPORTS GROUND
Lea Valley Sports Centre
CLAPTON PARK
LOWER CLAPTON
HOMERTON HOSPITAL
HOMERTON
MABLEY GREEN
E9
WICK COMMUNITY WOODLAND
EAST CROSS ROUTE
A12
HACKNEY WICK
EASTWAY COMMERCIAL CENTRE
LEE VALLEY CYCLE CIRCUIT
Lee Valley Campsite
Cold Stores
DRAPERS FIELD REC GRD
E15
NEWHAM
LEYTON ROAD
CHOBHAM ROAD
LEYTONSTONE ROAD
STRATFORD
JEWISH CEMETERY
Uni of E London
EAST CROSS CENTRE
JOHN HOWARD CEN
101
143
124
36
37
38
55
56
57
58
59
60
61
62
63
64
86
87
88
89

124
EE
EF
EG
EH
EJ
EK
EL
NORTH CIRCULAR
Waterworks Corner
SOUTH WOODFORD
102
E18
SOUTHEND ROAD
WOODFORD NEW ROAD
EPPING FOREST
SPORTS GROUND
Junction 4
NORTH CIRCULAR ROAD
RODING HOSP
RECREATION GROUND
IG4
CHIGWELL ROAD
HERMON HILL
WOODFORD ROAD
SNARESBROOK ROAD
SNARESBROOK
EAGLE POND
SNARESBROOK CROWN COURT
HOLLOW POND
WHIPPS CROSS ROAD
WHIPPS CROSS HOSPITAL
EPPING FOREST
RUGBY FOOTBALL GROUND
EASTERN AVENUE
WANSTEAD
WANSTEAD GOLF COURSE
SPORTS GRD
REDBRIDGE
BARKING RELIEF ROAD
HOLLYBUSH HILL
NEW WANSTEAD
CAMBRIDGE PARK
GREEN MAN ROUNDABOUT
LEYTONSTONE
E11
123
WANSTEAD FLATS
BUSH ROAD
THE BASIN
WANSTEAD PARK
WANSTEAD GOLF COURSE
SHOULDER OF MUTTON POND
HERONRY POND
PERCH POND
BUSH WOOD
RESERVOIR WOOD
BLAKE HALL ROAD
ALDERSBROOK ROAD
ALDERSBROOK
CITY OF LONDON CEMETERY
LEYTONSTONE ROAD
HIGH ROAD
WANSTEAD FLATS
JUBILEE POND
CENTRE ROAD
ST. PATRICK'S RC CEMETERY
WEST HAM CEMETERY
JEWISH CEMETERY
MANOR PARK CEMETERY
MANOR PARK
WOODGRANGE ROAD
ROMFORD ROAD
E7
WOODGRANGE PARK CEMETERY
FOREST GATE
CHOBHAM ROAD
LEYTON ROAD
E15
STRATFORD
144
PLASHET JEWISH CEMETERY
55
56
57
58
59
60
61
62
63
64

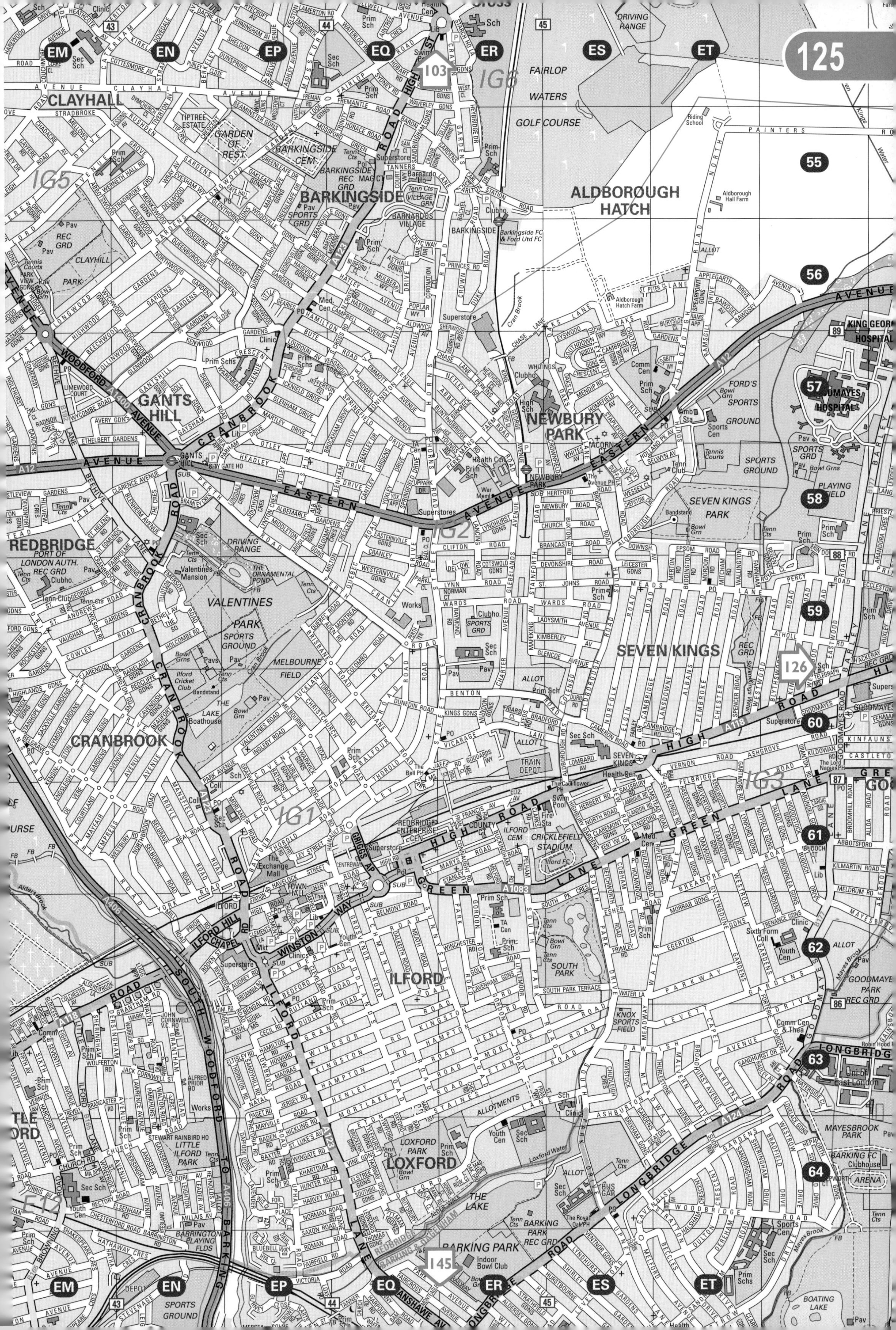
CLAYHALL
BARKINGSIDE
ALDBOROUGH HATCH
FAIRLOP WATERS GOLF COURSE
GANTS HILL
NEWBURY PARK
REDBRIDGE
VALENTINES PARK
SEVEN KINGS
SEVEN KINGS PARK
CRANBROOK
ILFORD
LOXFORD
LOXFORD PARK
SOUTH PARK
LITTLE ILFORD PARK
BARKING PARK
GOODMAYES PARK
MAYESBROOK PARK
KING GEORGE HOSPITAL
GOODMAYES HOSPITAL
MELBOURNE FIELD
KNOX SPORTS FIELD
CRICKLEFIELD STADIUM
THE LAKE
BOATING LAKE
IG1
IG2
IG3
IG5
IG6
E12
EM
EN
EP
EQ
ER
ES
ET
55
56
57
58
59
60
61
62
63
64
103
126
145

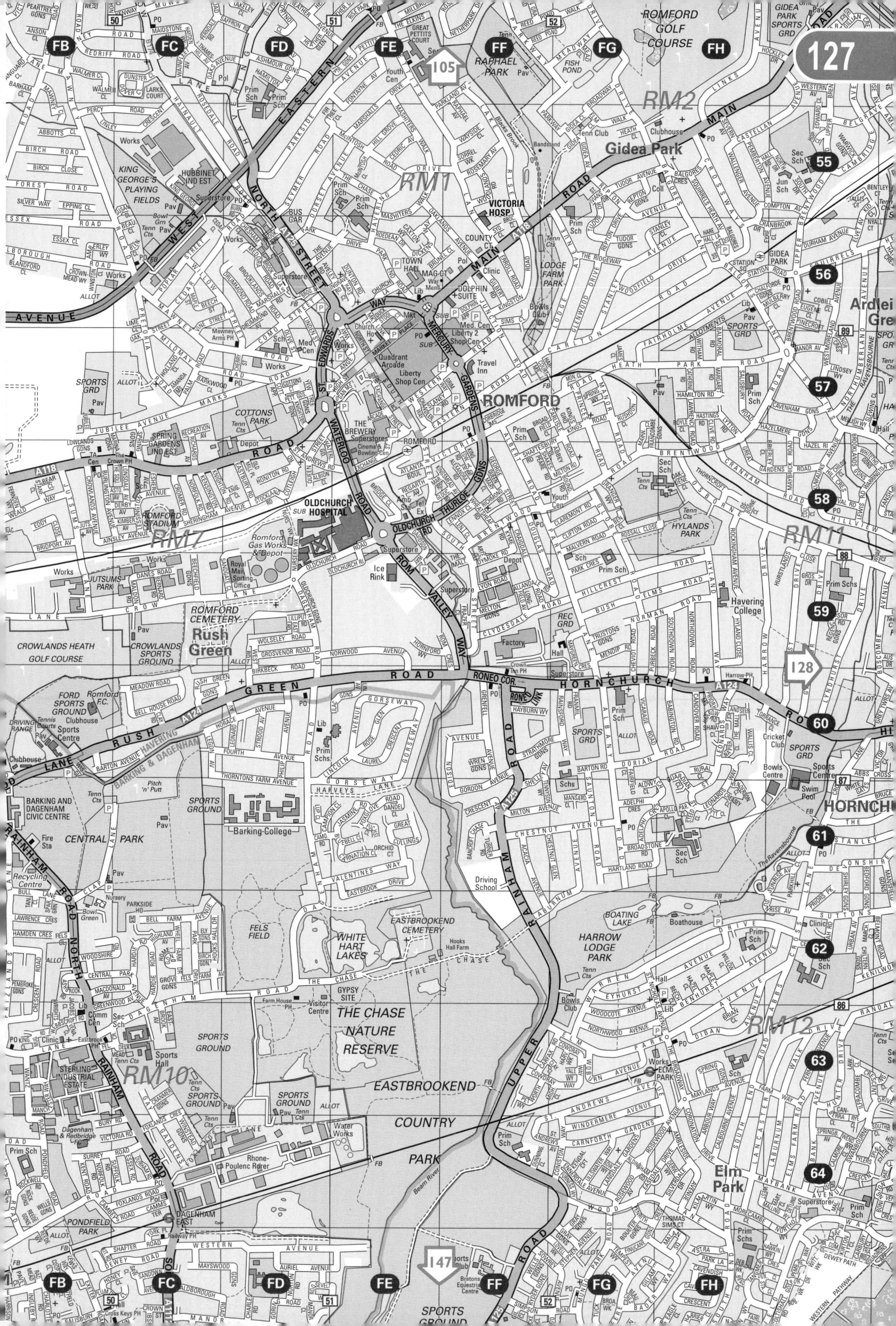
FB
FC
FD
FE
FF
FG
FH
105
128
147
ROMFORD GOLF COURSE
GIDEA PARK SPORTS GRD
RAPHAEL PARK
RM2
RM1
RM7
RM11
RM10
RM12
Gidea Park
KING GEORGE'S PLAYING FIELDS
HUBBINET IND EST
VICTORIA HOSP
LODGE FARM PARK
ROMFORD
Quadrant Arcade
Liberty Shop Cen
Liberty 2 Shop Cen
THE BREWERY Superstores
COTTONS PARK
SPRING GARDENS IND EST
ROMFORD STADIUM
OLDCHURCH HOSPITAL
Romford Gas Works & Depot
Royal Mail Sorting Office
JUTSUMS PARK
ROMFORD CEMETERY
Rush Green
CROWLANDS HEATH GOLF COURSE
CROWLANDS SPORTS GROUND
FORD SPORTS GROUND
Romford F.C.
HYLANDS PARK
Havering College
ROMFORD
RONEO COR.
HORNCHURCH ROAD
RUSH GREEN ROAD
BARKING AND DAGENHAM CIVIC CENTRE
CENTRAL PARK
Barking College
SPORTS GROUND
FELS FIELD
EASTBROOKEND CEMETERY
WHITE HART LAKES
THE CHASE NATURE RESERVE
EASTBROOKEND COUNTRY PARK
HARROW LODGE PARK
BOATING LAKE
HORNCHURCH
STERLING INDUSTRIAL ESTATE
Rhone-Poulenc Rorer
DAGENHAM EAST
PONDFIELD PARK
Elm Park
ELM PARK
RAINHAM ROAD
UPPER RAINHAM ROAD
MAIN ROAD
EASTERN AVENUE
NORTH STREET
WEST AVENUE
A118
A124
A125
Beam River
Ardleigh Green
SPORTS GROUND
55
56
57
58
59
60
61
62
63
64
50
51
52
86
87
88
89

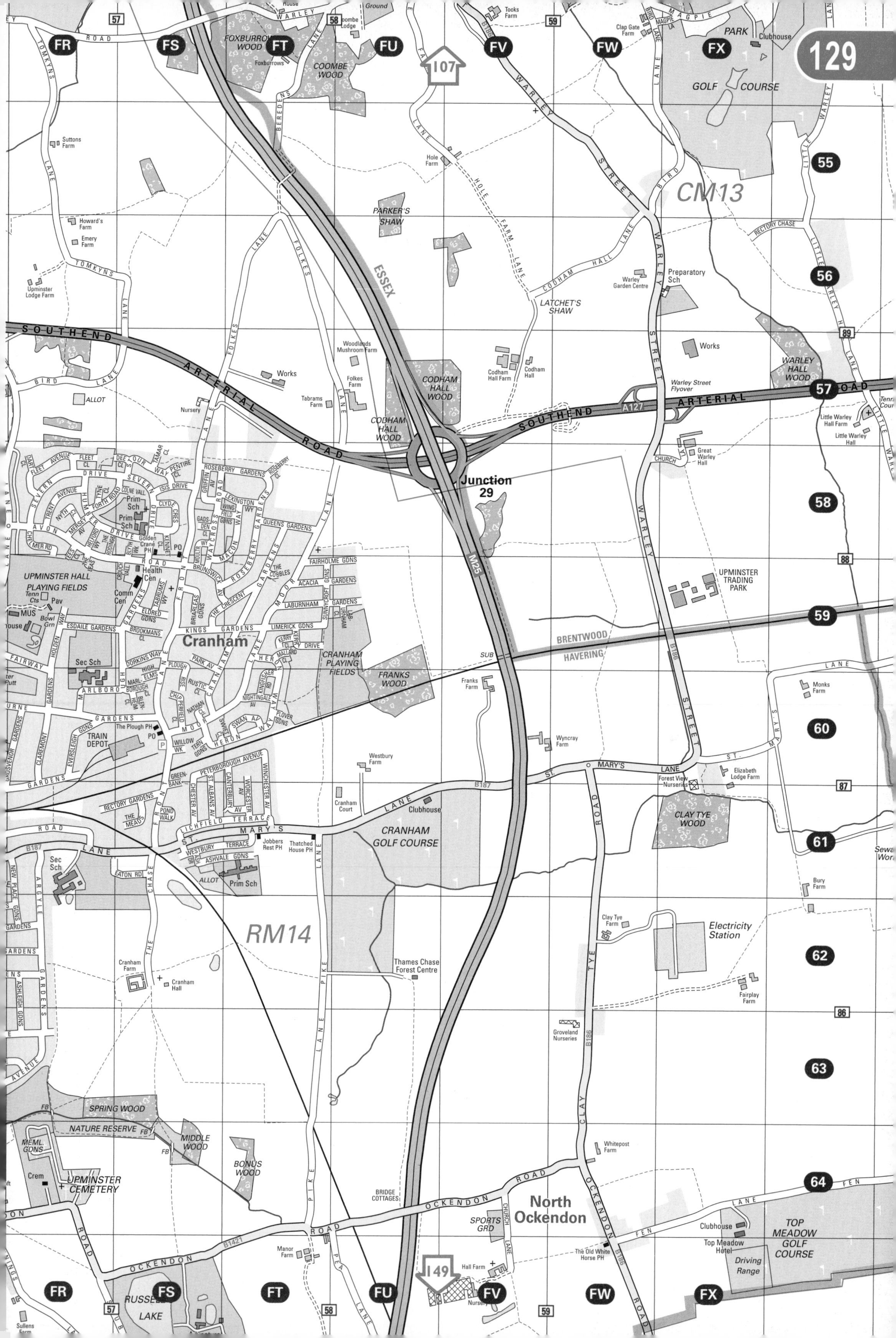
FR
FS
FT
FU
FV
FW
FX
107
149
FOXBURROW WOOD
COOMBE WOOD
Foxburrows
Tooks Farm
Clap Gate Farm
PARK
Clubhouse
GOLF COURSE
Suttons Farm
Hole Farm
CM13
PARKER'S SHAW
Howard's Farm
Emery Farm
Upminster Lodge Farm
ESSEX
LATCHET'S SHAW
Preparatory Sch
Warley Garden Centre
Codham Hall Farm
Codham Hall
Works
Woodlands Mushroom Farm
Folkes Farm
Tabrams Farm
Nursery
ALLOT
CODHAM HALL WOOD
WARLEY HALL WOOD
Warley Street Flyover
A127
Little Warley Hall Farm
Little Warley Hall
Great Warley Hall
Junction 29
M25
Cranham
UPMINSTER HALL PLAYING FIELDS
Health Cen
Comm Cen
Sec Sch
Prim Sch
TRAIN DEPOT
The Plough PH
CRANHAM PLAYING FIELDS
FRANKS WOOD
Franks Farm
BRENTWOOD
HAVERING
UPMINSTER TRADING PARK
Monks Farm
Wyncray Farm
Westbury Farm
Cranham Court
Clubhouse
CRANHAM GOLF COURSE
Elizabeth Lodge Farm
Forest View Nurseries
CLAY TYE WOOD
Jobbers Rest PH
Thatched House PH
Bury Farm
RM14
Clay Tye Farm
Electricity Station
Cranham Farm
Cranham Hall
Thames Chase Forest Centre
Fairplay Farm
Groveland Nurseries
SPRING WOOD
NATURE RESERVE
MIDDLE WOOD
BONUS WOOD
UPMINSTER CEMETERY
Crem
Whitepost Farm
North Ockendon
SPORTS GRD
BRIDGE COTTAGES
Manor Farm
Hall Farm
The Old White Horse PH
Clubhouse
Top Meadow Hotel
TOP MEADOW GOLF COURSE
Driving Range
RUSSELLS LAKE
Sullens Farm
SOUTHEND ARTERIAL ROAD
WARLEY STREET
CLAY TYE ROAD
OCKENDON ROAD
ST MARY'S LANE
PIKE LANE
FEN LANE
B186
B187
B1421
55
56
57
58
59
60
61
62
63
64
86
87
88
89

Cookham
Cliveden House & Hotel
CLIVEDEN NT
LAMBOURNE GOLF COURSE
CADBROOK WOOD
LITTLE BARNS WOOD
LAMBOURNES WOOD
WYMERS WOOD
LOWER LAMBOURNES WOOD
GULLEY WOOD
White Place Farm
WIDBROOK COMMON (NT)
RIVER THAMES
HUNTS WOOD
HUNTSWOOD GOLF COURSE
Grovefield Hotel
HITCHAM PARK
BURNHAM
Hitchambury Manor
Hitchambury Farm
GLEN ISLAND
RAY MILL ISLAND
TAPLOW COURT
Taplow
SL6
SL1
Lent Rise
BURNHAM PARK
Lent Green
Orchardville
TAPLOW LAKE
AMERDEN PONDS
Sewage Works
Superstore
HUNTERCOMBE MANOR HOSPITAL
BURNHAM ABBEY
Junction 7
SLOUGH
HUNTERCOMBE SPUR
BATH ROAD
A4
Barge Farm
Amerden House
AMERDEN CARAVAN PARK
HEADPILE EYOT
PIGEONHILL EYOT
West Town Farm
Glasshouses
Lake End Farm
BRAYWICK PARK
110
150

BURNHAM BEECHES
East Burnham
SL2
Farnham Common
EAST BURNHAM COMMON
BURNHAM BEECHES GOLF COURSE
Farnham Royal
FARNHAM PARK
FARNHAM PARK GOLF COURSE
STOKE PARK GOLF COURSE
Manor Park
KENNEDY PARK
BRITWELL ESTATE
SLOUGH TRADING ESTATE
GODOLPHIN PLAYING FIELDS
SALT HILL PARK
SLOUGH
Cippenham
MERCIAN RECREATION GROUND
VILLAGE GREEN
Haymill Valley
DEEPWOOD
SOUTH BUCKS
BUCKINGHAMSHIRE
BEACONSFIELD ROAD
FARNHAM ROAD
BATH ROAD
A4
A355
Dorneywood House
Pumpkin Hill
Hawthorn Dell
Cocksherd Wood
Thompkins Wood
George Pitcher Memorial Rec Grd
Cherry Orchard Nature Park
Granville Playing Field
Montem Rec Grd
AK
AL
AM
AN
AP
AQ
AR
65
66
67
68
69
70
71
72
73
74
132
151

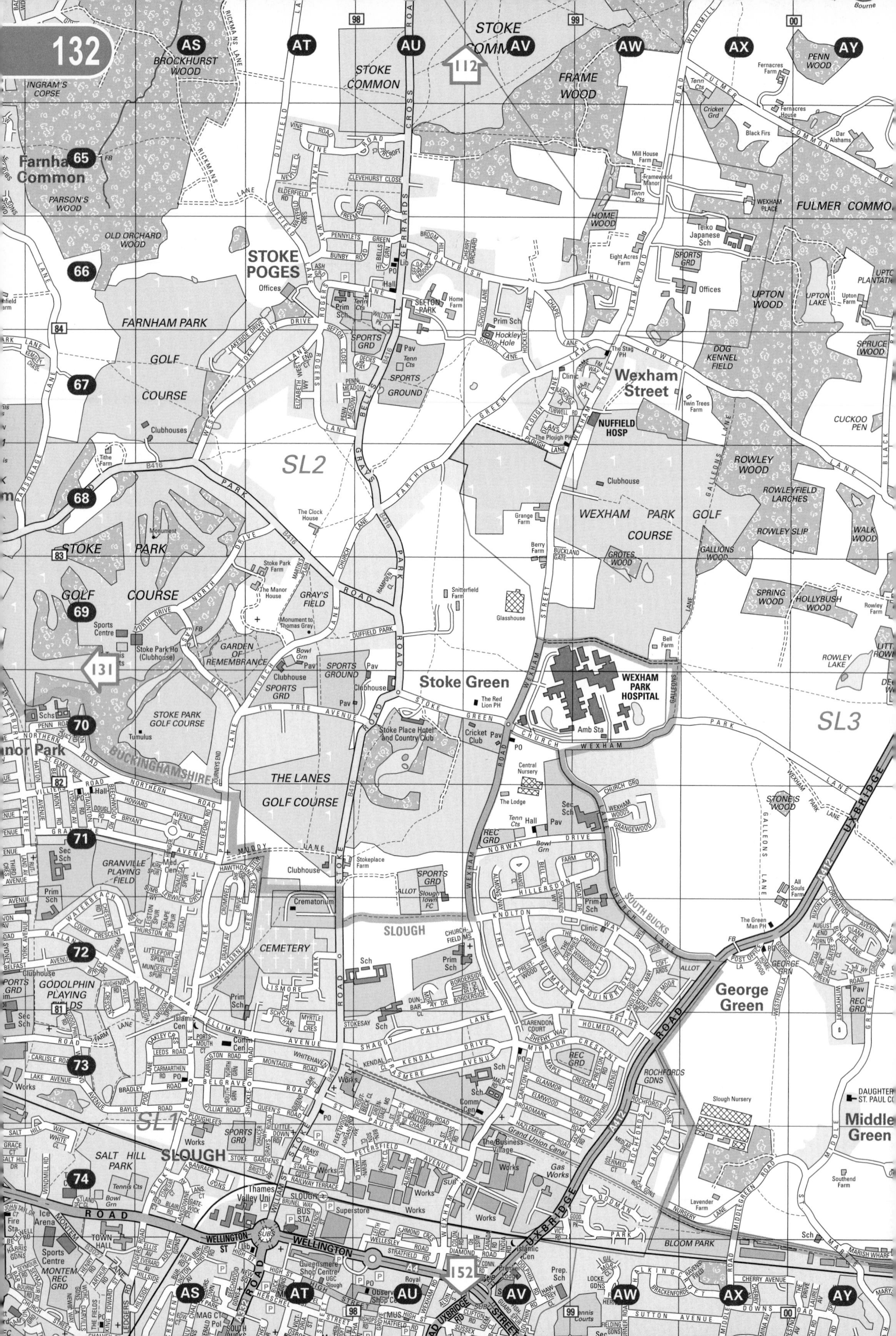

132
AS
AT
AU
AV
AW
AX
AY
112
131
152
BROCKHURST WOOD
INGRAM'S COPSE
STOKE COMMON
FRAME WOOD
PENN WOOD
Farnham Common
PARSON'S WOOD
OLD ORCHARD WOOD
STOKE POGES
FARNHAM PARK GOLF COURSE
FULMER COMMON
HOME WOOD
UPTON WOOD
DOG KENNEL FIELD
Wexham Street
NUFFIELD HOSP
SL2
ROWLEY WOOD
ROWLEYFIELD LARCHES
ROWLEY SLIP
WEXHAM PARK GOLF COURSE
GROTES WOOD
GALLIONS WOOD
SPRING WOOD
HOLLYBUSH WOOD
STOKE PARK GOLF COURSE
GRAY'S FIELD
GARDEN OF REMEMBRANCE
Stoke Park Ho (Clubhouse)
Stoke Green
WEXHAM PARK HOSPITAL
SL3
Stoke Place Hotel and Country Club
BUCKINGHAMSHIRE
THE LANES GOLF COURSE
STONE'S WOOD
GRANVILLE PLAYING FIELD
SLOUGH
CEMETERY
Crematorium
SOUTH BUCKS
George Green
GODOLPHIN PLAYING FIELDS
ROCHFORDS GDNS
Slough Nursery
Middle Green
SL1
SLOUGH
SALT HILL PARK
Grand Union Canal
Thames Valley Uni
Superstore
TOWN HALL
MONTEM REC GRD
Queensmere Shop Centre
BLOOM PARK
WELLINGTON

BROWN'S WOOD
OLDHOUSE WOOD
PARKSPRING WOOD
MOUNT FIDGET WOOD
BRIDGETTINE CONVENT
LANGLEY COMMON
LONG COPPICE
PLAYING FIELD
THE CLUMP
STRAWBERRY WOOD
HEATHFIELD PLANTATION
Pinewood Film Studios
NATURE RESERVE
Heatherden Hall
BROOM WARREN
UB9
BLACK PARK COUNTRY PARK
DIAMOND WOOD
CHANDLERS HILL
BLACKPARK LAKE
Centenary Lodge Visitors Centre
CHESTNUT WOOD
Five Points
IVER HEATH
SL0
FOXES GUTTER
COLUMN LARCHES
SPORTS GROUND
LANGLEY PARK WOOD
RHODODENDRON GARDENS
LANGLEY PARK COUNTRY PARK
Eureham Centre
Sports Centre
ROUGHGROUND WOOD
ARBORETUM
Environmental Studies Centre
Ashen Cross
Shreding Green
IVER
FARLOWS LAKE
Sewage Works
THE RIDGEWAY ESTATE
IVER GOLF COURSE
Grand Union Canal (Slough Arm)
BUCKINGHAMSHIRE
SOUTH BUCKS
SLOUGH
Chequer Bridge
THORNEY PARK GOLF COURSE
LANGLEY BUSINESS CENTRE
Water Treatment Works
SLOUGH ROAD
A4007
M25
DENHAM ROAD
CHURCH ROAD
A412
B470

113
134
153

UXBRIDGE
UXBRIDGE MOOR
COWLEY
HILLINGDON
YIEWSLEY
IVER
UB9
UB10
UB8
UB7
SL0
HILLINGDON HOUSE FARM SPORTS GROUNDS
UXBRIDGE COMMON
Uxbridge College (Uxbridge Campus)
Brunel University
HILLINGDON GOLF COURSE
HILLINGDON & UXBRIDGE CEMETERY
HILLINGDON HOSPITAL
HILLINGDON COURT PARK
HUNTSMOOR PARK
FARLOWS LAKE
LITTLE BRITAIN LAKE
COWLEY LAKE
THORNEY PARK GOLF COURSE
West Drayton Coal Depot
WEST DRAYTON
Grand Union Canal (Slough Arm)
Electricity Sub Station
Water Treatment Works
UNIVERSITY PLAYING FIELDS
Apple Tree Roundabout
Colham Roundabout
114
133
154

RAF NORTHOLT AERODROME
HA4
NORTH HILLINGDON
CUTTHROAT WOOD
NATURE RESERVE
GUTTERIDGE WOOD
WESTERN AVENUE
A40
WEST END ROAD
LONDON GOLF CENTRE
THE GORSE
HOME COVERT
POLE HILL OPEN SPACE
HARE PLANTATION
YEADING BROOK MEADOWS NATURE RESERVE
GROSVENOR PLAYING FIELD
WEST LONDON SHOOTING GROUNDS
UB5
HAYES SHRUB
HAYES PARK
YEADING
UB4
BELMORE PLAYING FIELDS
HAYES END
RECREATION GROUND
UXBRIDGE ROAD
A4020
ROSEDALE PARK
GRASSY MEADOW
HAYES STADIUM
HAYES
BARRA HALL PARK
BELL HOUSE FLD
Uxbridge College Hayes Community Campus
Lombardy Retail Park
STOCKLEY PARK GOLF COURSE
DAWLEY ROAD
UB3
E.M.I. SPORTS GROUND
Grand Union Canal
UB11
ADLER IND EST
ABERGLEN INDUSTRIAL ESTATE
PROVIDENT INDUSTRIAL ESTATE
MINET COUNTRY PARK
HAYES BYPASS
THE PARKWAY
HAYES TOWN
115
136
155

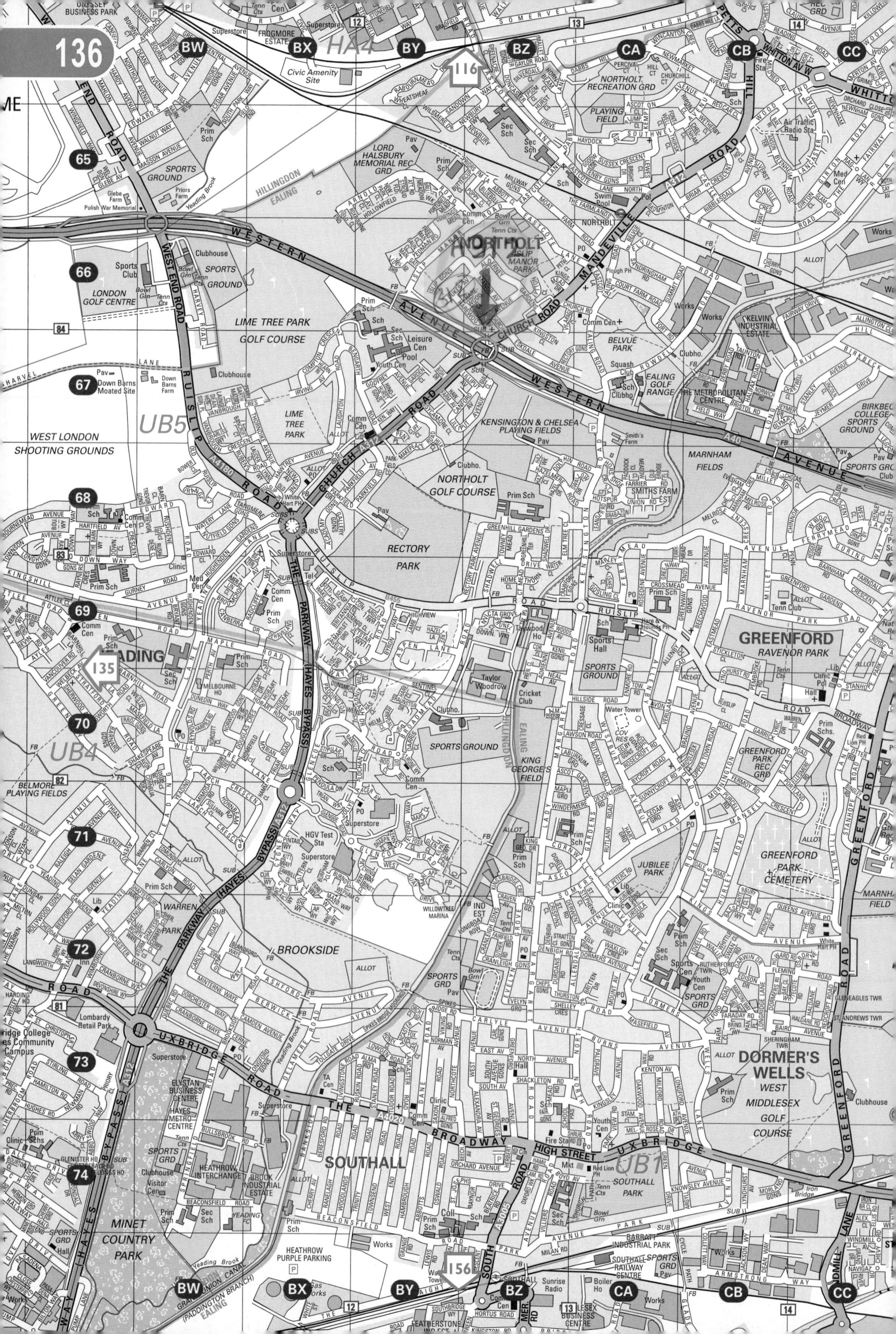
HA4
NORTHOLT
UB5
WEST LONDON SHOOTING GROUNDS
LONDON GOLF CENTRE
LIME TREE PARK GOLF COURSE
LIME TREE PARK
NORTHOLT GOLF COURSE
RECTORY PARK
KENSINGTON & CHELSEA PLAYING FIELDS
BELVUE PARK
EALING GOLF RANGE
MARNHAM FIELDS
GREENFORD
RAVENOR PARK
GREENFORD PARK CEMETERY
JUBILEE PARK
KING GEORGE'S FIELD
SPORTS GROUND
UB4
BELMORE PLAYING FIELDS
WARREN PARK
BROOKSIDE
LORD HALSBURY MEMORIAL REC GRD
NORTHOLT RECREATION GRD
SOUTHALL
SOUTHALL PARK
UB1
DORMER'S WELLS
WEST MIDDLESEX GOLF COURSE
MINET COUNTRY PARK
HEATHROW PURPLE PARKING
HILLINGDON
EALING
WESTERN AVENUE
A40
THE PARKWAY (HAYES BYPASS)
UXBRIDGE ROAD
THE BROADWAY
HIGH STREET
RUISLIP ROAD
WEST END ROAD
CHURCH ROAD
MANDEVILLE ROAD
GREENFORD ROAD
A312
A4020
A4180
A3005
116
135
156
BW
BX
BY
BZ
CA
CB
CC
65
66
67
68
69
70
71
72
73
74

137
SUDBURY
HA0
BARHAM PARK
SUDBURY GOLF COURSE
HORSENDEN HILL GOLF COURSE
HORSENDEN WOOD
HORSENDEN HILL
HOME MEAD
SPORTS GROUND
BERKELEY FIELDS
GREAT BRAMSTONES
UB6
GRAND UNION CANAL (PADDINGTON BRANCH)
ALPERTON CEMETERY
ONE TREE HILL REC GRD
PERIVALE WOOD (Nature Reserve)
PERIVALE
PERIVALE INDUSTRIAL PARK
PERIVALE NEW BUSINESS CENTRE
WADSWORTH BUSINESS CENTRE
FLEETWAY BUSINESS PARK
SHERATON BUSINESS CEN
CAPITAL BUSINESS CEN
METROPOLITAN POLICE TRAFFIC UNIT
ALPERTON SPORTS GROUND
OLDFIELD REC GRD
EALING CENTRAL SPORTS GRD
WESTERN AVENUE
A40
ATHLETICS TRACK
PERIVALE PARK SPORTS GROUND
PERIVALE PARK GOLF COURSE
EALING GOLF COURSE
PITSHANGER PARK
ALLOTMENTS
HANGER HILL PARK
River Brent
BRENT VALLEY PARK
CUCKOO PARK
CLEVELAND PARK
DRAYTON GREEN
W7
W13
W5
BRENT VALLEY GOLF COURSE
CHURCHFIELDS RECREATION GROUND
EALING
EALING BROADWAY
EALING COMMON
KENSINGTON & CHELSEA CEMETERY
HANWELL
HANWELL CEMETERY
WALPOLE PARK
PITSHANGER MANOR MUS
LAMMAS PARK
BARCLAYS BANK SPORTS GROUND
EALING HOSPITAL N.H.S. TRUST
Wharncliffe Viaduct
UXBRIDGE RD
THE BROADWAY
A4020
A4005
A4127
A4090
117
138
157
CD
CE
CF
CG
CH
CJ
CK

WEMBLEY
CL
CM
CN
CP
CQ
CR
CS
118
WEMBLEY CENTRAL
HARROW ROAD
TOKYNGTON
TOKYNGTON RECREATION GROUND
NORTH CIRCULAR ROAD
A406
CHURCH END
GIBBONS REC GRD
HA9
HA0
ONE TREE HILL REC GRD
EALING ROAD
A4089
65
66
67
68
69
70
71
72
73
74
ALPERTON
STONEBRIDGE PARK
STONEBRIDGE
BRENTFIELD
HILLSIDE
A404
CRAVEN PARK
HARLESDEN
Grand Union Canal
River Brent
PARK ROYAL
Twyford Abbey
Park Royal Guinness Brewery
CENTRAL MIDDLESEX HOSPITAL
PARK ROYAL CEN
NORTHFIELD INDUSTRIAL ESTATE
PREMIER PARK
H.J. Heinz
PUBLIC TIP
TOWNSEND INDUSTRIAL ESTATE
HANOVER W INDUSTRIAL EST
VICTORIA IND EST
WESTERN AVENUE
A40
HANGER LANE
137
HANGER HILL PARK
PLAYING FIELD
WESTERN TRADING EST
BUSH INDUSTRIAL EST
ACTON CEMETERY
NORTH ACTON
NORTH ACTON PLAYING FIELDS
Gypsy Corner
WALES FARM RD
WESTWAY IND EST
ROYAL LEISURE PARK
WESTPOINT TRADING EST
BARCLAYS BANK SPORTS GROUND
WEST ACTON
WEST ACTON
NORTH EALING
W3
HORN LANE
A4000
EALING
EALING BROADWAY
THE MALL
UXBRIDGE ROAD
A4020
EALING COMMON
GUNNERSBURY AVENUE
A406
NORTH THAMES GAS BOARD SPORTS GRD
ACTON
ACTON CENTRAL
EAST ACTON
ACTON PARK
HIGH STREET
W5
Thames Valley Uni
158
ACTON TOWN
SOUTHFIELDS
POPE'S FIELDS
19
20
21

WILLESDEN
WILLESDEN GREEN
BRONDESBURY PARK
BRONDESBURY
KILBURN
WEST KILBURN
KENSAL RISE
KENSAL GREEN
KENSAL TOWN
MAIDA HILL
NORTH KENSINGTON
NOTTING HILL
SHEPHERD'S BUSH
KENSINGTON
OLD OAK COMMON
WORMWOOD SCRUBS
NW2
NW6
NW10
W9
W10
W11
W12
W8

140
DA
DB
DC
DD
DE
DF
DG
120
27
28
26
WEST HAMPSTEAD
WEST HAMPSTEAD (THAMESLINK)
SOUTH HAMPSTEAD
BELSIZE PARK
BRONDESBURY
KILBURN
NW6
NW8
NW1
PRIMROSE HILL
REGENT'S PARK
LONDON ZOO
ST. JOHN'S WOOD
LORD'S CRICKET GROUND
LISSON GROVE
MAIDA VALE
MAIDA HILL
W9
WEST KILBURN
139
WESTBOURNE GREEN
PADDINGTON
BAYSWATER
W2
MARYLEBONE
NOTTING HILL
W11
W8
KENSINGTON
HOLLAND PARK
KENSINGTON GARDENS
ROUND POND
HYDE PARK
THE SERPENTINE
QUEEN MARY'S GARDENS
BOATING LAKE
160
FINCHLEY ROAD
MAIDA VALE
EDGWARE ROAD
BAYSWATER ROAD
WESTWAY
HARROW ROAD
KNIGHTSBRIDGE
KENSINGTON ROAD
KENSINGTON GORE
PARK LANE
OXFORD STREET
MARBLE ARCH
BAKER STREET
OXFORD STREET where marked is closed to through traffic (except buses & taxis) from 7a.m.-7p.m. Monday - Saturday
65
66
67
68
69
70
71
72
73
74

DH
DJ
DK
DL
DM
DN
DP
121
LOWER HOLLOWAY
HIGHB
KENTISH TOWN
CALEDONIAN PARK
PENTONVILLE PRISON
BARNSBURY
N7
CANONBURY
65
66
67
68
69
70
71
72
73
74
KING'S CROSS
CAMDEN TOWN
ISLINGTON
N1
SOMERS TOWN
ST. PANCRAS
PENTONVILLE
FINSBURY
EUSTON
REGENT'S PARK
142
ST. LUKE'S
EC1
WC1
CLERKENWELL
BLOOMSBURY
BRITISH MUSEUM
BARBICAN
HOLBORN
SOHO
STRAND
WC2
RIVER
SOUTHWARK
SE1
MAYFAIR
W1
ST. JAMES'S
SW1
GREEN PARK
ST. JAMES'S PARK
WATERLOO
THE BOROUGH
161
NW5
29
30
31

DQ
DR
DS
DT
DU
DV
DW
5
33
34
35
122
HIGHBURY
CANONBURY
KINGSLAND
DALSTON
HACKNEY
LONDON FIELDS
E8
SOUTH HACKNEY
DE BEAUVOIR TOWN
N1
HOXTON
HAGGERSTON
REGENT'S CANAL
E2
BETHNAL GREEN
ST. LUKE'S
EC1
SHOREDITCH
CLERKENWELL
BROADGATE
BARBICAN
STEPNEY
E1
WHITECHAPEL
EC2
EC3
EC4
RIVER THAMES
SHADWELL
WAPPING
TOWER OF LONDON
SOUTHWARK
SE1
THE BOROUGH
GUY'S HOSPITAL
LONDON BRIDGE HOSP
THE POOL
141
162
65
66
67
68
69
70
71
72
73
74
81
82
83
84
12

143
DX
DY
DZ
EA
EB
EC
ED
HOMERTON
HACKNEY WICK
MABLEY GREEN
E9
123
EAST CROSS ROUTE
STRATFORD
E15
VICTORIA PARK
OLD FORD
HERTFORD UNION CANAL
WELL STREET COMMON
BOW
MILE END
MILE END PARK
E3
TOWER HAMLETS CEMETERY PARK
BROMLEY
LIMEHOUSE
E14
POPLAR
RIVER THAMES
ISLE
WEST INDIA DOCKS
CANARY WHARF
THE DOME
NORTH GREENWICH
EAST INDIA DOCK BASIN
LIMMO PENINSULA ECOLOGICAL PARK
THREE MILLS GREEN
LEE VALLEY
WEST HAM
144
163
36
37
38
SE10
SE16
STRATFORD
BLACKWALL TUNNEL
EAST INDIA DOCK RD
COMMERCIAL ROAD
ROYAL LONDON HOSP (MILE END)
ROYAL LON. HOSP (ST. CLEMENTS)
MILE END STADIUM
BOW COMMON LA
PUDDING MILL LANE
CARPENTERS RD
WHITE POST LA
BOW RD
HIGH ST
ROMFORD RD

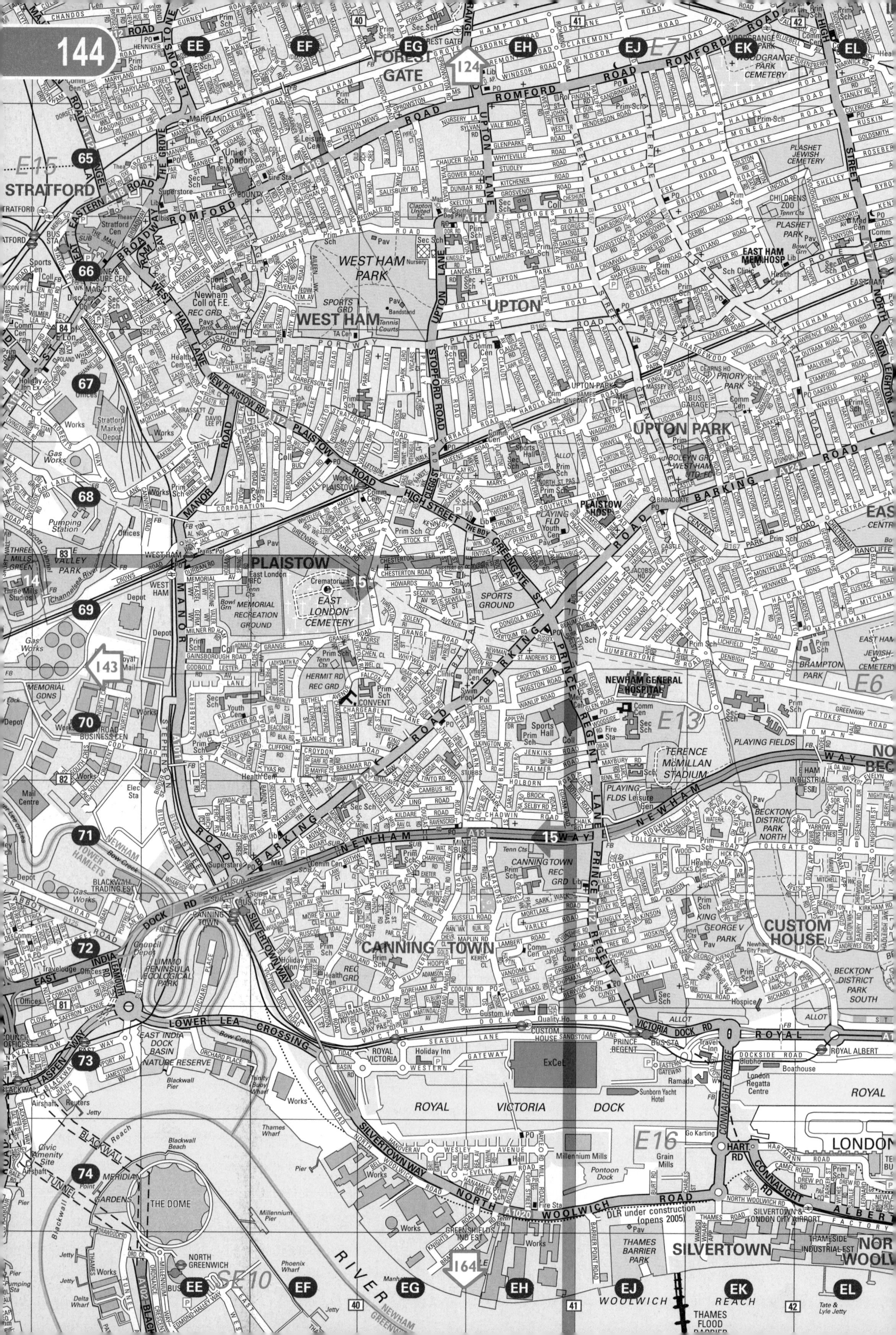
144
EE
EF
EG
EH
EJ
EK
EL
FOREST GATE
E7
124
WOODGRANGE PARK CEMETERY
ROMFORD ROAD
E15
STRATFORD
65
66
67
68
69
70
71
72
73
74
PLASHET JEWISH CEMETERY
PLASHET PARK
EAST HAM MEM HOSP
WEST HAM PARK
WEST HAM
UPTON
UPTON PARK
PRIORY PARK
BOLEYN GRD WEST HAM UTD FC
STRATFORD MARKET DEPOT
PLAISTOW
PLAISTOW HOSP
EAST LONDON CEMETERY
MEMORIAL RECREATION GROUND
SPORTS GROUND
THREE MILLS GREEN
VALLEY PARK
143
BRAMPTON PARK
E6
NEWHAM GENERAL HOSPITAL
E13
TERENCE McMILLAN STADIUM
PLAYING FIELDS
NEWHAM WAY
BECKTON DISTRICT PARK NORTH
CANNING TOWN REC GRD
CANNING TOWN
CUSTOM HOUSE
KING GEORGE V PARK
BECKTON DISTRICT PARK SOUTH
LIMMO PENINSULA ECOLOGICAL PARK
EAST INDIA DOCK BASIN NATURE RESERVE
LOWER LEA CROSSING
ROYAL VICTORIA DOCK
ExCeL
E16
LONDON
THE DOME
SILVERTOWN WAY
NORTH WOOLWICH ROAD
DLR under construction (opens 2005)
THAMES BARRIER PARK
SILVERTOWN
164
SE10
RIVER
WOOLWICH REACH
THAMES FLOOD BARRIER
40
41
42
15

LOXFORD
BARKING PARK
BARKING
IG11
BARKING HOSPITAL
UPNEY
TRIPPLESIDE BURIAL GROUND
BOATING LAKE
GREAT FIELDS PARK
BARKING INDUSTRIAL PARK
ALFREDS WAY IND ESTATE
ABBEY WHARF INDUSTRIAL ESTATE
KATELLA TRADING EST
RIVER ROAD BUSINESS PARK
TRAFALGAR BUSINESS CENTRE
BUZZARD CREEK INDUSTRIAL ESTATE
CREEKMOUTH
BARKING FLOOD BARRIER
River Roding
BECKTON REACH SEWAGE TREATMENT WORKS
Filter Beds
GALLIONS REACH
Gallions Reach Shopping Park
BECKTON
BECKTON TRIANGLE RETAIL PARK
GATEWAY RETAIL PARK
NEW BECKTON PARK
GOOSELEY'S PLAYING FIELDS
FLANDERS RD PLAYING FLDS
BARKING ROAD REC GRD
BARRINGTON PLAYING FLDS
ALBERT DOCK
CITY AIRPORT
KING GEORGE V DOCK
ALBERT BASIN
MARGARET NESS OR TRIPCOCK POINT
SE28
THAMESMEAD
NORTH WOOLWICH
H.M. PRISON
E12
BARKING & DAGENHAM
NEWHAM
125
146
165
EM
EN
EP
EQ
ER
ES
ET
65
66
67
68
69
70
71
72
73
74

DAGENHAM
BARKING HOSPITAL
PARSLOES PARK
RM9
BECONTREE
RIPPLESIDE BURIAL GROUND
CASTLE GREEN
GORESBROOK PARK
DAGENHAM LEISURE PK
FORD MOTOR WORKS
DAGENHAM DOCK
IG11
CREEKMOUTH
BARKING FLOOD BARRIER
CROSSNESS LIGHTHOUSE
THAMESMEAD NORTH
SE2
Crossness Sewage Treatment Works
RIVERSIDE GOLF COURSE
THAMESMEAD
SE28
BIRCHMERE PARK
SOUTHMERE PARK
ERITH MARSHES
DA18
H.M. PRISON

FB
FC
FD
FE
FF
FG
FH
127
148
167
PARK
DAGENHAM EAST
PONDFIELD PARK
SPORTS GROUND
MANOR ROAD SPORTS GRD
BRITTONS PLAYING FIELD
Sports Club
Bretons Equestrian Centre
RAINHAM ROAD SOUTH
RAINHAM ROAD
DAGENHAM ROAD
Newtons Corner
South Hornchurch
OLD DAGENHAM PARK
THE LEYS
RM10
RM12
RM13
DA17
HORNCHURCH COUNTRY PARK
AIRFIELD WOOD
FLIGHTWAY WOOD
FARMFIELD WOOD
LOWFIELD WOOD
RAINHAM
Dovers Corner
NEW ROAD
A1306
A125
A1112
A13
B1335
BARKING & DAGENHAM
HAVERING
Beam River
Ingrebourne River
CAR COMPOUND
HORNCHURCH MARSHES
Centre for Engineering & Manufacturing Excellence
Riverside Sewage Works
Mudlands Industrial Est
FAIRVIEW INDUSTRIAL PARK
ALBRIGHT INDUSTRIAL ESTATE
DENVER INDUSTRIAL ESTATE
CONTAINER DEPOT
Rainham Sunday Market
IMPERIAL TRADING EST
THAMES GATEWAY
Hornchurch Shoot
Old Man's Head
JENNINGTREE POINT LIGHTHOUSE
BELVEDERE INDUSTRIAL ESTATE
RAINHAM MARSHES
Silt Lagoons
WENNINGTON MARSHES
Southall Bridge
London Loop
Common Watercourse
Jetty
Wharf
Pier
Depots
Warehouses
ERITH
COLDHARBOUR LANE
FERRY LANE
MANOR WAY
50
51
52
65
66
67
68
69
70
71
72
73
74
81
82
83
84

FJ
FK
FL
FM
FN
FP
FQ
128
147
168
RM12
RM13
HORNCHURCH COUNTRY PARK
AIRFIELD WOOD
PINEWOOD
FLIGHTWAY WOOD
FARMFIELD WOOD
LOWFIELD WOOD
ABBEY WOOD
BERWICK POND
Albyns Farm
Rainham Lodge Farm
Park Corner Farm
Lodge Farm
PARKLANDS OPEN SPACE
Corbets Tey
Gardners Cor Hall
Central Farm
SAND & GRAVEL PIT
Civic Amenity Site
Gerpins Farm
Berwick Ponds Farm
SAND AND GRAVEL PIT
Berwick Manor
Berwick Manor Farm
White Post Corner
WARWICK WOOD
WHITE POST WOOD
RAINHAM CEMETERY (JEWISH)
SPRING FARM PARK
IMPERIAL TRADING EST
MOAT
Bretts Farm
Sir Henry Gurnett PH
South Hall Farm
Southall Bridge
East Hall Farm
NEW COTTAGES
Moor Hall
Travel Inn
Wennington Hall
Willow Farm
Wennington
New Farm
Sandy Lane Farm
RAINHAM MARSHES
Silt Lagoons
Common Watercourse
WENNINGTON MARSHES
AVELEY MARSHES
PURFLEET IND PARK
Works
SPORTS GROUND
NEW ROAD
A1306
A13
B1335
SANDY LANE
WENNINGTON ROAD
LAUNDERS LANE
WARWICK LANE
GERPINS LANE
PARK FARM ROAD
AVELEY ROAD
ROMFORD ROAD
UPMINSTER ROAD
NORTH ROAD
LAMBS LANE SOUTH
GATEWAY
LONDON ROAD
INGREBOURNE RIVER
WATERMEADOW
65
66
67
68
69
70
71
72
73
74
81
82
83
84
54
55
56

North Ockendon
SOUTH OCKENDON
North Stifford
Aveley
RM14
RM15
RM16
UPMINSTER CEMETERY
MIDDLE WOOD
BONUS WOOD
BRIDGE COTTAGES
Whitepost Farm
SPORTS GRD
Manor Farm
Hall Farm
Nursery
The Old White Horse PH
Clubhouse
Top Meadow Hotel
Driving Range
TOP MEADOW GOLF COURSE
RUSSELL'S LAKE
Adventure Centre
COYS LAKE
Bullens Farm
HAVERING
THURROCK
M25
Groves Barns
THE WILDERNESS
SAND AND GRAVEL PIT
FREEMAN'S SHAW
Kemp's Farm
CLAY PI
Tumulus
South Ockendon Hall
MOAT
South Ockendon Hall Farm
Prim Sch
ALLOT
Royal Oak PH
War Mem
THE GRN
Comm Cen
Pav
SOUTH OCKENDON REC GRD
Tenn Cts
Works
FORD AVELEY PLANT
WHITEHALL WOOD
BELHUS COUNTRY PARK
LITTLE BRICKKILN WOOD
BRICKKILN WOOD
BELHUS PARK
Bensons Farm
Little Mollands Farm
The Ockendon Complex
Sec Sch
LONG POND
OAK WOOD
ASH PLANTATION
ROOKERY
BONNYGATE WOOD
Prim Sch
South Ockendon Garden Centre
Jack o'Lantern PH
Lib
Hall
Health Cen
Culver Centre
DILKES PARK
SPORTS GROUND
THE SHRUBBERY
BELHUS PARK GOLF COURSE
Swimming Pool
Clubhouse
The Archer PH
The Troubadour PH
LITTLE PALMER'S SHAW
GREAT PALMER'S SHAW
Hill Farm
Clubhouse
MARDYKE VALLEY GOLF COURSE
HANGMAN'S WOOD
MILLARD'S GARDEN
BRANNETT'S WOOD
LOW WELL WOOD
Depot
Prince Albert PH
Junction 30
BRICKBARN WOOD
COMBE WOOD
LOW WELL WOOD
Stifford Bridge
The Dog & Partridge PH
SPORTS GROUND
ARENA ESSEX RACEWAY
KARTING CEN
LAKESIDE COACH PARK
PILGRIMS CARAVAN PARK
Thurrock
Mar Dyke
OCKENDON ROAD
STIFFORD ROAD
NORTH ROAD
SOUTH ROAD
STIFFORD HILL
PILGRIMS LANE
BUCKLES LANE
DENNISES LANE
THURROCK ARTERIAL ROAD
FR
FS
FT
FU
FV
FW
FX
129
169
65
66
67
68
69
70
71
72
73
74

Bray
Holyport
Fifield
Dorney Reach
Dorney
Oakley Green
SL6
WINDSOR ROAD
BRAY MARINA
GRAVEL PIT
MONKEY ISLAND
HEADPILE EYOT
PIGEONHILL EYOT
QUEEN'S EYOT
BUCKINGHAMSHIRE
WINDSOR & MAIDENHEAD
RIVER THAMES
DORNEY LAKE
SOUTH BUCKS
BRACKNELL FOREST
WINDSOR FOREST
BRAY WOOD
NOBBSCROOK
HOLLIDAY'S PLAIN
Junction 7
M4
Bray Studios
Oakley Court Hotel
Windsor Marina
WILLOWS RIVERSIDE PARK
Bullock's Hatch Bridge
New Thames Bridge
Bray Bridge
Dorney Court
Stroud Farm
Coningsby Farm
Grove House
Ledger Farm
Banham Farm
Fifield House
The Retreat Farm
The Guild House
Wayside Stables Equestrian Centre
Queen's Head PH
Kimbers Farm
Oakley Place Farm
Ye Olde Red Lion PH
Bishops Farmhouse
Nags Head PH
Gale House Farm
Tarbay Farm
Darkhole Bridge
Nightingale Corner
Braywood House
Lakeside Racing Stables
New Lodge Farm
New Lodge
Wakers Farm
Foliejon Park Farm
FISH POND
Windsor Hill
FOREST GREEN ROAD
OAKLEY GREEN ROAD
DRIFT ROAD
DARKHOLE RIDE
FORBES RIDE
FIFIELD ROAD
MONKEY ISLAND LANE
LAKE END ROAD
VILLAGE B3026 ROAD
MAIDENHEAD ROAD
DEDWORTH
TARBAY LANE
ASCOT ROAD
BURNHAM ABBEY
Glasshouses
Lake End Farm
Pigeonhouse Farm
Riding School
Court Farm
Windsor Garden Centre
Broom Farm
Prim Sch
Weir Bank Stud Farm
Amerden House
AMERDEN CARAVAN PARK
Barge Farm
Jesus Hospital
The Rising Sun PH
The White Hart PH
Hare & Hounds PH
St. Leonard's Farm
AC AD AE AF AG AH AJ
75 76 77 78 79 80 81 82 83 84
91 92 93
130

AK
AL
AM
AN
AP
AQ
AR
131
SLOUGH
SALT HILL PARK
Cippenham
SL1
MERCIAN RECREATION GROUND
WASTE WATER TREATMENT WORKS
JUBILEE RIVER
M4
Chalvey
Junction 6
75
76
77
78
79
80
81
82
83
84
152
WINDSOR & MAIDENHEAD
SLOUGH
SOUTH BUCKS
DORNEY COMMON
Eton Wick
ETON WICK COMMON
NORTH FIELD
ETON GREAT COMMON
ETON GOLF COURSE
AGARS PLOUGH PLAYING FIELDS
THE PLAYING FIELDS
ETON WICK REC GRD
SOUTH FIELD
Boveney
SL4
RIVER THAMES
ROYAL WINDSOR RACECOURSE
SOUTH FIELD
SPORTS GROUND
ETON
THE HOME PARK RECREATION GROUND
Eton College
THE BROCAS
Clewer Village
SUTHERLAND GRANGE
WINDSOR RACECOURSE PARK HOMES
MAIDENHEAD ROAD
A308
A332
WINDSOR & ETON RELIEF ROAD
WINDSOR CASTLE
Dedworth
CLEWER MEMORIAL REC GRD
Clewer Green
Clewer New Town
WINDSOR
GOLF COURSE
FROGMORE GARDENS
Royal Mausoleum
WINDSOR CEMETERY
QUEEN MARY'S PLANTATION
CAVALRY EXERCISE GROUNDS
MINIATURE RIFLE RANGE
HOG COMMON
GARRISON SPORTS GROUND
ASH PLANTATION
WITHY COVER
DININGROOM CLOSE
SPITAL MEADOW
LEGOLAND
PADDOCKHILL COPSE
NEW COVER
WINDSOR GREAT PARK
REVIEW GROUND
ALBERT ROAD
KINGS ROAD
ST. LEONARDS ROAD
WINKFIELD

SLOUGH
SALT HILL PARK
Thames Valley Uni
WELLINGTON ST
Queensmere Shop Centre
Observatory Shop Centre
UPTON HOSP
Upton Park
HERSCHEL PARK
Upton
LASCELLES PLAYING FIELD
BLOOM PARK
SL1
UPTON COURT PARK
KEDERMISTER PARK
AGARS PLOUGH PLAYING FIELDS
ETON GOLF COURSE
MOTOCROSS TRACK
SLOUGH
WINDSOR & MAIDENHEAD
B.M.X. TRACK
SLOUGH R.F.C.
DITTON PARK
ATHLETICS CENTRE
Eton College
THE HOME PARK RECREATION GROUND
DATCHET GOLF COURSE
KINGS OAK
Computer Associates
Riding Court Farm
Victoria Bri
KING EDWARD VII AVENUE
WINDSOR CASTLE
EAST LAWN
GOLF COURSE
DATCHET
DATCHET SPORTS GROUND
DATCHET CEMETERY
WINDSOR
Victoria Barracks
RIVER THAMES
THE HOME PARK
SL4
FROGMORE GARDENS
Royal Mausoleum
Southlea
Southlea Farm
PRINCESS MARGARET HOSP
GARRISON SPORTS GROUND
Albert Bridge
NICKCROFT AIT
HAM ISLAND
Sludge Lagoon
Sludge Beds
ROYAL GARDENS
NEW CUT
Sunnymead
SUNNYMEADS
Old Windsor Lock
REMENHAM PARK
GREAT
AS
AT
AU
AV
AW
AX
AY
75
76
77
78
79
80
81
82
83
84
98
99
00
132
151
172

IVER GOLF COURSE
BUCKINGHAMSHIRE
SLOUGH
SOUTH BUCKS
LANGLEY
LANGLEY BUSINESS CENTRE
LANGLEY MEMORIAL GROUND
Richings Park
RICHINGS PARK GOLF COURSE
THORNEY PARK GOLF COURSE
SL0
Junction 15 (M25)
Junction 4B (M4)
HARVEY PARK
AXIS PARK
HOME WOOD
OAK PLANTATION
OLD WOOD
M4
Sewage Works
Junction 5
Brands Hill
Quality Hotel Heathrow
COLNBROOK BYPASS
Colnbrook
REC GRD
Sailing Club
THE QUEEN MOTHER RESERVOIR
SL3
GRAVEL PIT
Poyle
SPORTS GRD
GOLF DRIVING RANGE
Longford Roundabout
BRITANNIA INDUSTRIAL EST
MCKAY TRADING ESTATE
TRIDENT INDUSTRIAL ESTATE
Horton
Arthur Jacob Nature Reserve
Junction 14
HILLINGDON
AIRPORT WAY
TW19
SURREY
WINDSOR & MAIDENHEAD
WRAYSBURY
STANWELL MOOR
M25
A4
133
154
173

THORNEY PARK GOLF COURSE
THORNEY
YIEWSLEY
WEST DRAYTON
Harmondsworth
Sipson
Longford
STANWELL MOOR
HARMONDSWORTH MOOR COUNTRY PARK
Junction 15 (M25)
Junction 4B (M4)
Sewage Works
Warehouses
Cement Works
COLNBROOK GOLF RANGE
Longford Roundabout
M25 under construction
BEDFORT COURT ESTATE
TERMINAL 3
Snow Base
CARGO TERMINAL
BRITISH AIRWAYS CARGO CENTRE
British Airways PLC
Sheraton Heathrow Hotel
Thistle Heathrow
Arora International Hotel
Holiday Inn
SIPSON WAR MEML. REC GRD
Crowne Plaza Hotel
Novotel Heathrow
Holiday Inn Heathrow
Heathrow Garden Centre
Wyevale Garden Centre
HEATHROW COACH CEN
THE CLOSES RECREATION GROUND
SOUTHLANDS ARTS CEN
West Drayton Cricket Club
COLNE PARK CARAVAN SITE
MAYFIELDS LAKE
Frays Island Nat Res
British Airways Waterside
HARMONDSWORTH CEM
HEATHPARK GOLF COURSE
SL0
SL3
UB7
TW19
TW6
SPELTHORNE
SURREY
HILLINGDON

134
153
174

HEATHROW AIRPORT
(LONDON)
HAYES TOWN
HARLINGTON
CRANFORD
CRANFORD PARK
HATTON
MINET COUNTRY PARK
UB11
UB3
TW4
TW5
TW14
Junction 4
Junction 4A
Junction 3
TERMINAL 1
TERMINAL 2
TERMINAL 4
Cherry Lane Roundabout
CHERRY LANE CEMETERY
SAM PHILIP REC GRD
IMPERIAL COLLEGE SPORTS GROUND
LITTLE HARLINGTON FIELD
SIPSON MEADOW
SPORTS GROUND
BOURNE FARM FIELD
ALLOTMENTS
GOVERNMENT BUILDINGS
PINKWELL PARK
E.M.I. SPORTS GROUND
ADLER IND EST
ABERGLEN INDUSTRIAL ESTATE
WARNFORD IND EST
PROVIDENT INDUSTRIAL ESTATE
PETER JAMES BUSINESS CENTRE
Speedmarque Centre
THE SQUIRRELS TRADING ESTATE
INTERNATIONAL TRADING EST
BULLS BRIDGE IND EST
Western International Market
HARLEQUIN CENTRE
AIR LINKS INDUSTRIAL ESTATE
BRITISH AIRWAYS SPORTS GROUND
PARKWAY TRADING ESTATE
REDWOOD ESTATE
HEATHROW ESTATE
British Airways PLC
HEATHROW INT. TRADING ESTATE
GREEN LANE OPEN SPACE
RIFLE RANGE
BALANCING RESERVOIR
HOUNSLOW HEATH GOLF COURSE
DONKEY WOOD
MERCURY CENTRE
RADIUS PARK
HATTON CROSS
CRANE MEADOW
Grand Union Canal
GRAND UNION CANAL (PADDINGTON BRANCH)
EALING
Stockley Bridge
Starveall Bridge
Bulls Bridge
Yeading Brook
RIVER CRANE
Maintenance Area
Perishable Handling Facility
Parking Express
Hangar
Heathrow Airport Visitor Cen
CUSTOM HOUSE
Renaissance Hotel
Radisson Edwardian Hotel
Marriott Hotel
Sheraton Skyline
Holiday Inn Ariel
Bowling Alley
Ibis
Cardinal Pt
Park Inn
Travel Inn
Ramada Jarvis
Europa House
STOCKLEY ROAD
STOCKLEY PARK
HAYES BY-PASS
THE PARKWAY
NORTH HYDE ROAD
STATION ROAD
HIGH STREET
BATH ROAD
GREAT SOUTH-WEST ROAD
THE CAUSEWAY
NORTHERN PERIMETER ROAD
EASTERN PERIMETER ROAD
SHEPISTON LANE
CRANFORD LANE
M4
A4
A30
A312
A437
A408
BP
BQ
BR
BS
BT
BU
BV
135
156
175
75
76
77
78
79
80
81
82
83
84

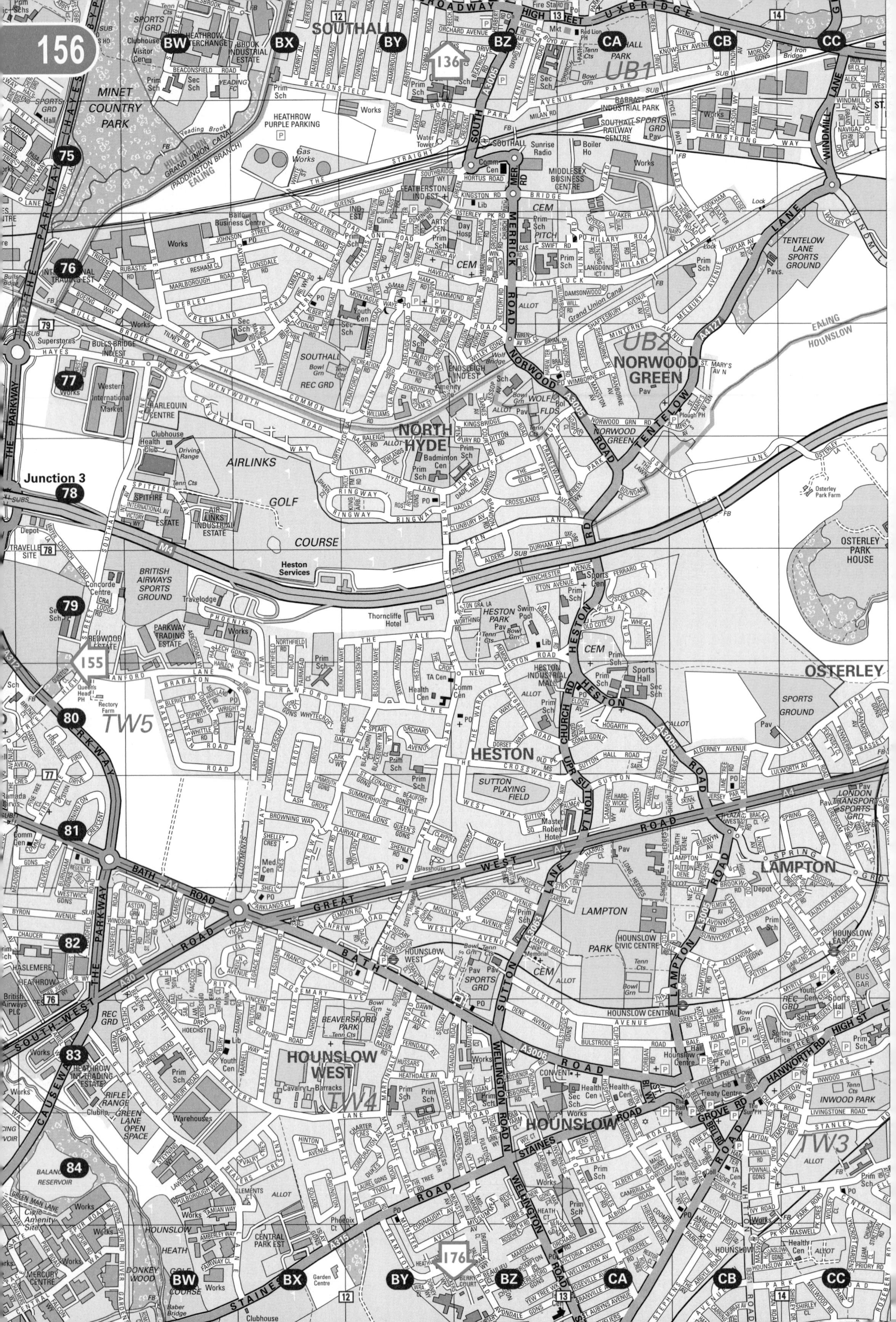

156
SOUTHALL
BW
BX
BY
BZ
CA
CB
CC
136
UB1
MINET COUNTRY PARK
HEATHROW INTERCHANGE
BROOK INDUSTRIAL ESTATE
BEACONSFIELD ROAD
HEATHROW PURPLE PARKING
Gas Works
BARRATT INDUSTRIAL PARK
SOUTHALL RAILWAY CENTRE
MIDDLESEX BUSINESS CENTRE
TENTELOW LANE SPORTS GROUND
FEATHERSTONE IND EST
Balfour Business Centre
INTERNATIONAL TRADING EST
BULLS BRIDGE IND EST
Superstores
Western International Market
HARLEQUIN CENTRE
SOUTHALL REC GRD
ENDSLEIGH IND EST
UB2
NORWOOD GREEN
NORTH HYDE
AIRLINKS GOLF COURSE
Junction 3
SPITFIRE ESTATE
AIR LINKS INDUSTRIAL ESTATE
Heston Services
BRITISH AIRWAYS SPORTS GROUND
Concorde Centre
Travelodge
PARKWAY TRADING ESTATE
REDWOOD ESTATE
155
Thorncliffe Hotel
HESTON PARK
HESTON INDUSTRIAL MALL
OSTERLEY
OSTERLEY PARK HOUSE
Osterley Park Farm
SPORTS GROUND
TW5
HESTON
SUTTON PLAYING FIELD
LONDON TRANSPORT SPORTS GRD
LAMPTON
LAMPTON PARK
HOUNSLOW CIVIC CENTRE
HOUNSLOW EAST
HOUNSLOW WEST
HOUNSLOW CENTRAL
BEAVERSFORD PARK
Cavalry Barracks
TW4
HOUNSLOW
TW3
INWOOD PARK
RIFLE RANGE
GREEN LANE OPEN SPACE
HEATHROW INT TRADING ESTATE
HOUNSLOW HEATH
HOUNSLOW HEATH GOLF COURSE
DONKEY WOOD
CENTRAL PARK EST
MERCURY CENTRE
Civic Amenity Site
BALANCING RESERVOIR
176
GREAT WEST ROAD
BATH ROAD
STAINES ROAD
THE PARKWAY
M4
A4
A30
A312
A315
A3005
A3006
A3063
A4127
Grand Union Canal
75
76
77
78
79
80
81
82
83
84
12
13
14

HANWELL
LITTLE EALING
BRENTFORD
SPRING GROVE
WOODLANDS
ISLEWORTH
OSTERLEY PARK NT
WYKE GREEN GOLF COURSE
SYON PARK
ROYAL BOTANIC GARDEN
KEW
ROYAL MID-SURREY GOLF COURSE
OLD DEER PARK RECREATION GROUND
MOGDEN WATER TREATMENT WORKS
ST. MARGARETS
RIVER THAMES
Battles of Brentford 1016 & 1642
Junction 2

CL
CM
CN
CP
CQ
CR
CS
138
W5
EALING COMMON
ACTON PARK
ACTON PK IND EST
SOUTHFIELDS PLAYING FIELDS
POPEFIELD PLAYING FIELDS
SPORTS GROUND
SOUTH ACTON
BEDFORD PARK
SOUTH EALING
SOUTH EALING CEMETERY
LITTLE EALING
CLAYPONDS HOSP
GUNNERSBURY PARK
GUNNERSBURY PARK MUSEUM
SMALL MANSION ARTS CEN
BOATING LAKE
W3
International Sch of London
KENSINGTON CEMETERY
POTOMAC (FISH POND)
GUNNERSBURY
CHISWICK PARK
GUNNERSBURY TRIANGLE NATURE RESERVE
ACTON GRN COMMON
CHISWICK COMMON
TURNHAM GREEN
Junction 1
Junction 2
CHISWICK HIGH ROAD
HEATHFIELD TER
TOWN HALL
W4
Agfa Gevaert
Glaxo SmithKline
TW8
CARVILLE HALL PARK
KEW BRIDGE STEAM MUS
BRENTFORD FC
BRENTFORD AIT
BRENTFORD
WATERMANS ARTS CEN
Herbarium & Library
OLIVER'S ISLAND
KEW GREEN
KEW
CHISWICK
CHISWICK HOUSE GROUNDS
CHISWICK HOUSE
KEW PALACE
Orangery
Kew Shop
KEW GARDENS GALLERY
The Princess of Wales Conservatory
PUBLIC RECORD OFFICE
GROVE PARK
RIVER THAMES
ROYAL BOTANIC GARDENS
THE POND
Temple of Arethusa
Victoria Gate Visitor Centre
Battles of Brentford 1016 & 1642
Sewage Works
CHISWICK CEMETERY
RIVERSIDE RECREATION GROUND
CIVIL SERVICE SPORTS GROUND
UNI WEST. SPORTS GRD
STADIUM
DUKE'S MEADOW
ARBORETUM
THE LAKE
WATER LILY POND
MARIANNE NORTH GALLERY
QUEEN'S COTTAGE GARDENS
Queen Charlotte's Cottage
Restaurant Pavilion
Pagoda
TW9
NORTH SHEEN
NORTH SHEEN CEMETERY
HAMMERSMITH CEMETERY
Crematorium
DUKE'S MEADOW GOLF COURSE
Chiswick R.F.C.
BARNES BRIDGE
HOUNSLOW
RICHMOND UPON THAMES
MORTLAKE HIGH ST
MORTLAKE
BARNES HOSP
ROYAL MID-SURREY GOLF COURSE (OLD DEER PARK)
London Welsh R.F.C. & Richmond C.C.
RICHMOND ATHLETIC GROUND
ROYAL HOSP
LOWER MORTLAKE ROAD
LOWER RICHMOND RD
UPPER RICHMOND ROAD WEST
EAST SHEEN
SW14
RICHMOND
RICHMOND GREEN
PESTHOUSE COMMON
EAST SHEEN COMMON (NT)
THE BANK OF ENGLAND'S SPORTS GROUND
PALEWELL COMMON
PALEWELL PLAYING FIELDS
157
178
75
76
77
78
79
80
81
82
83
84

159
SHEPHERD'S BUSH
139
KENSINGTON
HOLLAND PARK
HOLLAND HOUSE
W8
W14
W12
W6
HAMMERSMITH
RAVENSCOURT PARK
THE STAMFORD
STAMFORD BROOK
OLYMPIA
EARLS COURT
CASTELNAU
SW13
THE WETLANDS CENTRE
BARN ELMS PLAYING FIELDS
BARN ELMS SCHOOL SPORTS CENTRE
HARROD'S SPORTS GRD
LEG OF MUTTON NATURE RESERVE
BARNES
BARNES COMMON
PUTNEY LOWER COMMON
PUTNEY HOSP
RIVER THAMES
FULHAM
FULHAM PALACE GARDENS
BISHOP'S PARK
FULHAM CEMETERY
CHARING CROSS HOSP
SW6
PARSONS GREEN
EEL BROOK COMMON
HURLINGHAM PARK
HURLINGHAM CLUB
SOUTH PARK
SW15
SW18
WANDSWORTH PARK
PUTNEY
WANDSWORTH
ROEHAMPTON
ROEHAMPTON PRIORY HOSPITAL
160
179
CT
CU
CV
CW
CX
CY
CZ
75
76
77
78
79
80
81
82
83
84

DA
DB
DC
DD
DE
DF
DG
KENSINGTON GARDENS
HYDE PARK
ROUND POND
THE SERPENTINE
The Lido
140
KENSINGTON PALACE
SERPENTINE GALLERY
KENSINGTON
W8
HOLLAND PARK
HOLLAND HOUSE
75
76
77
78
79
80
81
82
83
84
KENSINGTON ROAD
KENSINGTON GORE
KNIGHTSBRIDGE
Royal Albert Hall
Royal Coll of Music
Imperial Coll
SCIENCE MUSEUM
NATURAL HISTORY MUSEUM
VICTORIA & ALBERT MUSEUM
HARRODS
SOUTH KENSINGTON
CROMWELL ROAD
BELGRAVIA
BROMPTON
SW7
SW5
SW10
SW3
EARLS COURT
EARLS COURT EXHIBITION CENTRE
ROYAL MARSDEN HOSP
ROYAL BROMPTON HOSP
17
18
ROYAL HOSPITAL CHELSEA
WEST BROMPTON
BROMPTON CEMETERY
CHELSEA
CHELSEA & WEST HOSP
EMBANKMENT
CHELSEA REACH
BATTERSEA PARK
159
STAMFORD BRIDGE CHELSEA FC
FULHAM BDY
KINGS ROAD
WALHAM GREEN
PARSONS GREEN
EEL BROOK COMMON
SANDS END
Gas Works
Chelsea Harbour
Chelsea Coll of Art & Design
LONDON BATTERSEA HELIPORT
HURLINGHAM PARK
HURLINGHAM CLUB GDNS
SOUTH PARK
SW6
SW11
SW15
SW18
CLAPHAM JUNCTION
LAVENDER HILL
BATTERSEA RISE
CLAPHAM COMMON
WANDSWORTH
WANDSWORTH BRIDGE
WANDSWORTH COMMON
180
BOLINGBROKE HOSP
26
27
28

DH
DJ
DK
DL
DM
DN
DP
141
ST. JAMES'S
GREEN PARK
ST. JAMES'S PARK
SW1
BUCKINGHAM PALACE
WESTMINSTER
HOUSES OF PARLIAMENT
ST. THOMAS' HOSP
LAMBETH
SOUTHWARK
SE1
THE BOROUGH
NEWINGTON
75
76
77
78
79
80
81
82
83
84
VICTORIA
PIMLICO
19
20
VAUXHALL
SE11
KENNINGTON
THE OVAL (SURREY C.C.C.)
RIVER THAMES
BATTERSEA PARK
NINE ELMS
SW8
BATTERSEA
SOUTH LAMBETH
162
CAMBERWELL
SE5
STOCKWELL
SW9
LAMBETH HOSPITAL
CLAPHAM
CLAPHAM COMMON
SW4
BRIXTON
SE24
181
RUSKIN PARK
29
30
31

DQ
DR
DS
DT
DU
DV
DW
SOUTHWARK
SE1
THE BOROUGH
NEWINGTON
WALWORTH
SE17
BERMONDSEY
WAPPING
CAMBERWELL
PECKHAM
SE15
SE5
SE22
SE24
BURGESS PARK
SOUTHWARK PARK
RUSKIN PARK
PECKHAM RYE COMMON
PECKHAM RYE PARK
KENNINGTON PARK
MYATT'S FIELDS
LONDON BRIDGE
GUY'S HOSPITAL
KING'S COLLEGE HOSPITAL
KING'S COLLEGE HOSP DULWICH
THE MAUDSLEY HOSPITAL
TOWER BRIDGE EXPERIENCE
CITY HALL
H.M.S. BELFAST
BRUNEL ENGINE HOUSE
THE POOL
LOUGHBOROUGH JUNCTION
DENMARK HILL
EAST DULWICH
PECKHAM RYE
NUNHEAD
GREEK CATHEDRAL
CAMBERWELL CH ST
PECKHAM ROAD
PECKHAM HIGH ST
QUEENS ROAD PECKHAM
OLD KENT ROAD
NEW KENT ROAD
JAMAICA ROAD
TOOLEY STREET
TOWER BRIDGE ROAD
WALWORTH ROAD
CAMBERWELL ROAD
DENMARK HILL
COLDHARBOUR LANE
EAST DULWICH ROAD
NUNHEAD LANE
EVELINA ROAD
ROTHERHITHE NEW ROAD
SOUTHWARK PARK ROAD
LOWER ROAD
142
161
182
33
34
35
75
76
77
78
79
80
81
82
83
84
21
22

DX
DY
DZ
EA
EB
EC
ED
143
ISLE
WEST INDIA DOCKS
OF
DOGS
MILLWALL
MILLWALL OUTER DOCK
MUDCHUTE PARK
E14
CUBITT TOWN
SE16
ROTHERHITHE
SURREY QUAYS
GREENLAND DOCK
SOUTH DOCK
DEPTFORD
SE8
SE14
SE10
NORTH GREENWICH
GREENWICH
GREENWICH PARK
164
BLACKHEATH
SE3
NEW CROSS
NEW CROSS GATE
ST JOHN'S
SE4
HILLY FIELDS
LEWISHAM
SE13
BROCKLEY
LADYWELL
183
LADYWELL
BROCKLEY CEMETERY
LADYWELL CEMETERY
NATIONAL MARITIME MUSEUM
CUTTY SARK
QUEEN'S HOUSE
FLAMSTEED HOUSE (Old Royal Observatory)
GOLDSMITHS College (Univ of Lon)
TELEGRAPH HILL PARK
DEPTFORD PARK
FORDHAM PARK
MANOR HOUSE GARDENS
EVELYN STREET
CREEK ROAD
LEWISHAM WAY
LOAMPIT HILL
LOAMPIT VALE
BLACKHEATH HILL
SHOOTER'S HILL
BLACKWALL TUNNEL APPROACH
MANCHESTER ROAD
WESTFERRY ROAD
36
37
38
75
76
77
78
79
80
81
82
83
84
23
24

164
THE DOME
NORTH GREENWICH
SE10
RIVER THAMES
WOOLWICH REACH
THAMES FLOOD BARRIER
SILVERTOWN
THAMES BARRIER PARK
E16
DLR under construction (opens 2005)
GREENWICH PENINSULA ECOLOGY PARK
MERIDIAN TRADING ESTATE
NEW CHARLTON
GREENWICH INDUSTRIAL ESTATE
CABLE TRADE PARK
MARYON PARK
MARYON WILSON PARK
THE VALLEY CHARLTON ATHLETIC FC
CHARLTON
SE7
CHARLTON PARK
Charlton House
EAST GREENWICH PLEASAUNCE
WESTCOMBE PARK
MAZE HILL
NATIONAL MARITIME MUSEUM
GREENWICH
GREENWICH PARK
One Tree Hill
FLAMSTEED HOUSE
The Gardens
THE WILDERNESS (DEER PARK)
RECTORY FIELD
HORNFAIR PARK
QUEEN ELIZABETH HOSPITAL
BLACKHEATH
SE3
SHOOTER'S HILL ROAD
Morden College
KIDBROOKE
BLACKHEATH PARK
SPORTS GROUND
GREENWICH CEMETERY
KIDBROOKE GREEN (NAT RES)
SE12
SE13
LEE
Lee Green
SUTCLIFFE PARK
ELTHAM
UNI OF GREENWICH ATHLETIC GRD
ROCHESTER WAY RELIEF RD
WOOLWICH ROAD
BLACKWALL TUNNEL APPROACH
EE EF EG EH EJ EK EL
144
163
184
24
25

EM
EN
EP
EQ
ER
ES
ET
43
44
45
145
166
185
KING GEORGE V DOCK
GALLIONS REACH
NEWHAM
GREENWICH
WOOLWICH FREE FERRY
WOOLWICH FOOT TUNNEL
NORTH WOOLWICH
ROYAL VICTORIA GDNS
STANDARD INDUSTRIAL ESTATE
SE28
H.M. PRISON BELMARSH
WESTERN WAY
EASTERN WAY
THAMESMEAD WEST
BROADWATER
PLUMSTEAD ROAD
PLUMSTEAD HIGH STREET
PLUMSTEAD
PLUMSTEAD COMMON
WINN'S COMMON
SE2
WOOLWICH
WOOLWICH COMMON
BARRACK FIELD
Royal Artillery Barracks
GRAND DEPOT RD
SE18
Royal Military Academy
SHREWSBURY PARK
SHOOTER'S HILL GOLF COURSE
SHOOTER'S HILL
SHOOTERS HILL
A207
BELLEGROVE ROAD
WOOLWICH CEM
WOOLWICH CEMETERY
EAST WICKHAM
EAST WICKHAM OPEN SPACE
HILLVIEW CEMETERY
ELTHAM COMMON
MEMORIAL HOSPITAL
CASTLEWOOD THERAPY CENTRE
CASTLE WOOD
JACK WOOD
OXLEAS WOOD
OXLEAS MEADOW
ELTHAM COMMON
WELLING WAY
A209
DA16
WELLING
FALCONWOOD
FALCONWOOD FIELD
SHEPHERDLEAS WOOD
ELTHAM PARK NORTH
ELTHAM PARK SOUTH
SE9
A2
ROCHESTER WAY RELIEF ROAD
ELTHAM CEMETERY
Crematorium
ELTHAM WARREN GOLF COURSE
DA15
EAST ROCHESTER WAY
75
76
77
78
79
80
81
82
83
84

EU
EV
EW
EX
EY
EZ
FA
146
SOUTHMERE PARK
ERITH MARSHES
LAKESIDE CENTRE
SOUTHMERE
BIRCHMERE PARK
SE28
DA18
WOODLAND WAY
ABBEY WOOD PARK
EASTERN WAY
H.M. PRISON BELMARSH
THISTLEBROOK INDUSTRIAL EST
Bexley Business Academy
West Thamesmead Business Park
SE18
ABBEY WOOD
EASTERN IND EST
PLUMSTEAD GARDENS
HARROW MANORWAY
KNEE HILL
A2041
ABBEY WOOD CARAVAN CLUBS SITE
SE2
BOSTALL HEATH
ABBEY WOOD
Lesnes Abbey (ruins)
GREEN CHAIN WALK
HURST ESTATE
ALBERT ROAD ESTATE
BELVEDERE SPORTS GRD
WEST HEATH
WOOLWICH ROAD
A206
BOSTALL HILL
WINN'S COMMON
CLAM FIELD RECREATION GROUND
BOSTALL WOODS
GOLDIE LEIGH HOSPITAL
BOSTALL HEATH
165
WOOLWICH CEM
WOOLWICH CEMETERY
PLUMSTEAD CEMETERY
EAST WICKHAM
EAST WICKHAM OPEN SPACE
DA16
STEVENS PARK
DA7
WELLING
WELLING HIGH STREET
A207
BEXLEYHEATH
BEXLEYHEATH CEMETERY
Broadway Shop Centre
CROOK LOG
BROADWAY
DANSON
PARK
DANSON ROAD
Danson Mansion
Bexley Grammer Sch
186
DA6
BEXLEYHEATH
ROCHESTER WAY
A2
75
76
77
78
79
80
81
82
83
84
47
48
49

ERITH
BELVEDERE
LESSNESS HEATH
NORTHUMBERLAND HEATH
BARNEHURST
BARNES CRAY
RIVER THAMES
ERITH REACH
ERITH RANDS
WENNINGTON MARSHES
CRAYFORD MARSHES
RAINHAM MARSHES
DA17
DA8
DA1
RM13
147
168
187

RAINHAM MARSHES
WENNINGTON MARSHES
RM13
AVELEY MARSHES
RIFLE RANGES
PURFLEET IND PARK
SPORTS GROUND
RM15
PURFLEET
RM19
Crayford Ness
DARENT INDUSTRIAL PARK
FLOOD BARRIER
DA8
DARTFORD SALT MARSHES
CRAYFORD MARSHES
Longreach Sewage Treatment Works
DA1
Littlebrook Power Station
HOSPITAL (closed)
BOB DUNN WAY
DARTFORD FRESH MARSHES
BARNES CRAY
Junction 1a

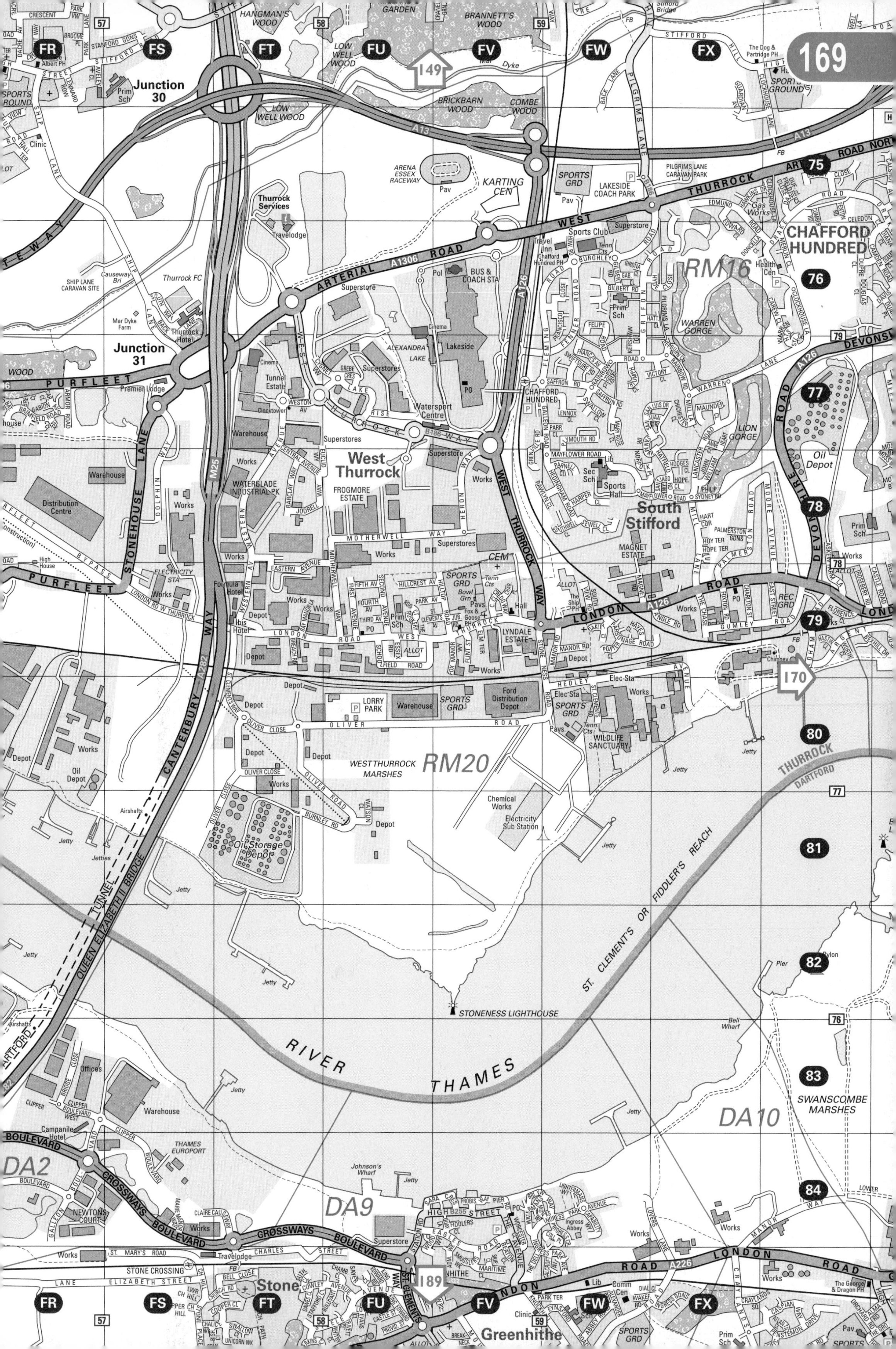

HANGMAN'S WOOD
GARDEN
BRANNETT'S WOOD
LOW WELL WOOD
149
Mar Dyke
STIFFORD
The Dog & Partridge PH
SPORTS GROUND
Junction 30
BRICKBARN WOOD
COMBE WOOD
LOW WELL WOOD
A13
ARENA ESSEX RACEWAY
KARTING CEN
SPORTS GRD
LAKESIDE COACH PARK
PILGRIMS LANE CARAVAN PARK
Thurrock Services
Travelodge
ARTERIAL ROAD
A1306
WEST THURROCK ARTERIAL ROAD NORTH
CHAFFORD HUNDRED
RM16
BUS & COACH STA
Lakeside
SHIP LANE CARAVAN SITE
Thurrock FC
Mar Dyke Farm
Thurrock Hotel
Junction 31
PURFLEET
Premier Lodge
ALEXANDRA LAKE
Watersport Centre
WARREN GORGE
LION GORGE
Oil Depot
West Thurrock
WATERGLADE INDUSTRIAL PK
FROGMORE ESTATE
South Stifford
MAGNET ESTATE
Distribution Centre
STONEHOUSE LANE
PURFLEET BYPASS
WEST THURROCK WAY
A126
LONDON ROAD
DEVONSHIRE ROAD
LYNDALE ESTATE
CANTERBURY WAY
A282
M25
LORRY PARK
Ford Distribution Depot
WILDLIFE SANCTUARY
170
WEST THURROCK MARSHES
RM20
Chemical Works
Electricity Sub Station
Oil Storage Depot
THURROCK
DARTFORD
QUEEN ELIZABETH II BRIDGE
TUNNEL
ST. CLEMENT'S OR FIDDLER'S REACH
STONENESS LIGHTHOUSE
RIVER THAMES
Bell Wharf
SWANSCOMBE MARSHES
DA10
THAMES EUROPORT
Campanile Hotel
DA2
Johnson's Wharf
DA9
CROSSWAYS BOULEVARD
NEWTONS COURT
HIGH STREET
B255
Travelodge
STONE CROSSING
Stone
189
Greenhithe
A226
The George & Dragon PH
FR FS FT FU FV FW FX
57 58 59
75 76 77 78 79 80 81 82 83 84

Stifford Interchange
Hogg Lane Roundabout
THURROCK ARTERIAL ROAD NORTH STIFFORD
A13
A1012
CHAFFORD HUNDRED
DEVONSHIRE ROAD
A126
Badgers Mere
LION GORGE
WARREN GORGE
Oil Depot
South Stifford
GRAYS
RM17
RM16
THURROCK COMMUNITY HOSPITAL
THURROCK ATHLETICS STADIUM
KING GEORGE'S FIELD
Blackshots Leisure Centre
Sockett's Heath
Little Thurrock
HANGMAN'S WOOD
GRAYS NEW CEMETERY
GLOBE IND ESTATES
CIVIC OFFICES
PALMERS AV
A1013
LONDON ROAD
ORSETT ROAD
STANFORD ROAD
LODGE LANE
EAST THURROCK RD
DOCK ROAD
Thurrock Yacht Club
Grays Beach Riverside Park
MANOR WAY IND EST
LITTLE THURROCK MARSHES
Capstan Centre
Superstore
Finnish Terminal
Grain Terminal
Warehouses
RIVER THAMES
NORTHFLEET HOPE
BROADNESS LIGHTHOUSE
Radar Mast
BROADNESS SALT MARSHES
SWANSCOMBE MARSHES
BOTANY MARSHES
DA10
DA11
TILBURY DOCKS
GALLEY HILL ROAD
A226
EBBSFLEET INDUSTRIAL ESTATE
ROBINS CREEK
Northfleet Hope
169
190
FY
FZ
GA
GB
GC
GD
GE
75
76
77
78
79
80
81
82
83
84

171
GF
GG
GH
GJ
GK
GL
GM
64
65
66
Whitecroft's Farm
Heath Place
Whittakers Nursery
The Fox PH
ORSETT GOLF COURSE
Brook Farm
Orsett Heath
Sec Sch
SPORTS GROUND
Pav
Greyhound PH
ALLOT
OLD HOUSE WOOD
GEORGE TILBURY HO
GOODERHAM HO
POOLE HO
CHADWELL ST. MARY
BRENTWOOD ROAD
HIGH HOUSE LANE
GRAVEL PIT
RAINBOW WOOD
ASHEN SHAW
Works
HOLFORD ROAD
BUCKINGHAM HILL ROAD
Sutton's Farm
Linford
SS17
Merie Loots Farm
SPORTS GRD
Muckingford
Beecksland
Ashlea Farm
75
76
77
78
79
80
81
82
83
84
TERRELS HEATH
Prim Sch
Thurrock Technical College
ST. MARY'S CEM
High House
Mill House Farm
Mill House
MUCKINGFORD ROAD
COAL ROAD
LOW STREET LANE
BLUE ANCHOR LANE
Blue Anchor Cottage
Holford Farm
Chadwell Place
Works
Poultry Farm
SHROVE HILL WOOD
TURNPIKE LANE
Hall
The Kings Head PH
Manor Farm
RECTORY ROAD
West Tilbury
Hob Hill
Hobhill Farm
Tally Ho Riding School
Broom Hill
Biggin Farm
Gunhill Farm
West Tilbury Hall
Low Street
STATION ROAD
HALLHILL COMMON
COOPERS SHAW ROAD
TILBURY MARSHES
Hutts Hill
A126
CHADWELL ROAD
Tilbury FC
PARSONAGE COMMON
RM18
TILBURY STADIUM (KARTING)
KING GEORGE'S FIELD
TILBURY
SPORTS GROUND
WEST TILBURY MARSHES
WALTHAM COMMON
Electricity Station
Works
Electricity Station
FORT ROAD
A1089
DOCK ROAD
FERRY ROAD
Offices
CUSTOM HOUSE
Warehouses
DRY DOCK
Cold Storage
Riverside Rail Terminal
Fortress Distribution Park
Tidal Basin
London International Cruise Terminal
Jetty
Pier
MOAT
Tilbury Fort
The Worlds End PH
Mercy Creek
Sewage Works
Filter Beds
Tilbury Energy & Environmental Centre
Chimney
Conveyor Belt
Tilbury B Power Station
RIVER THAMES
191
THURROCK
GRAVESHAM
GRAVESEND
REACH
Rosherville

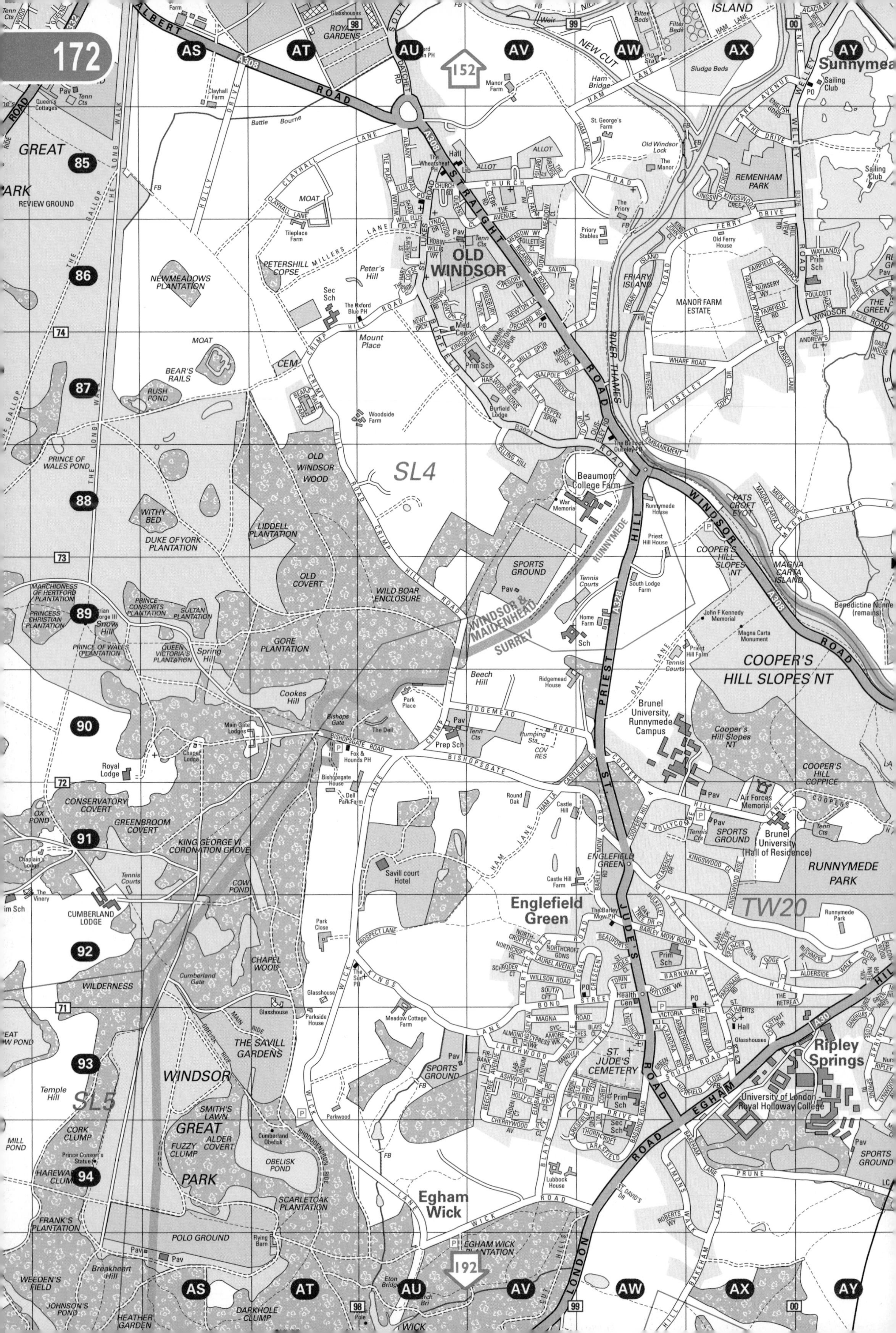

OLD WINDSOR
Englefield Green
Egham Wick
Sunnymead
Ripley Springs
SL4
SL5
TW20
GREAT PARK
WINDSOR GREAT PARK
RIVER THAMES
COOPER'S HILL SLOPES NT
RUNNYMEDE PARK
Brunel University, Runnymede Campus
University of London Royal Holloway College
Beaumont College Farm
OLD WINDSOR WOOD
WILD BOAR ENCLOSURE
GORE PLANTATION
THE SAVILL GARDENS
POLO GROUND
ALBERT ROAD
STRAIGHT ROAD
PRIEST HILL
ST. JUDE'S ROAD
EGHAM HILL
WINDSOR ROAD
LONDON ROAD
CRIMP HILL
BISHOPSGATE ROAD
WICK LANE
WINDSOR & MAIDENHEAD
SURREY
152
192

WRAYSBURY
RESERVOIR
TW19
SL3
Wraysbury
Junction 14
Junction 13
KING
GEORGE VI
RESERVOIR
STAINES MOOR
RUBBISH DUMP
HERON LAKE
QUEENSMEAD LAKE
Hythe End
RUNNYMEDE NT
RUNNYMEDE PLEASURE GROUND
WINDSOR ROAD
EGHAM
Pooley Green
Egham Hythe
Thorpe Lea
TW18
STAINES
STANWELL MOOR
THE CAUSEWAY
LONDON ROAD
STAINES BYPASS
153
174
193

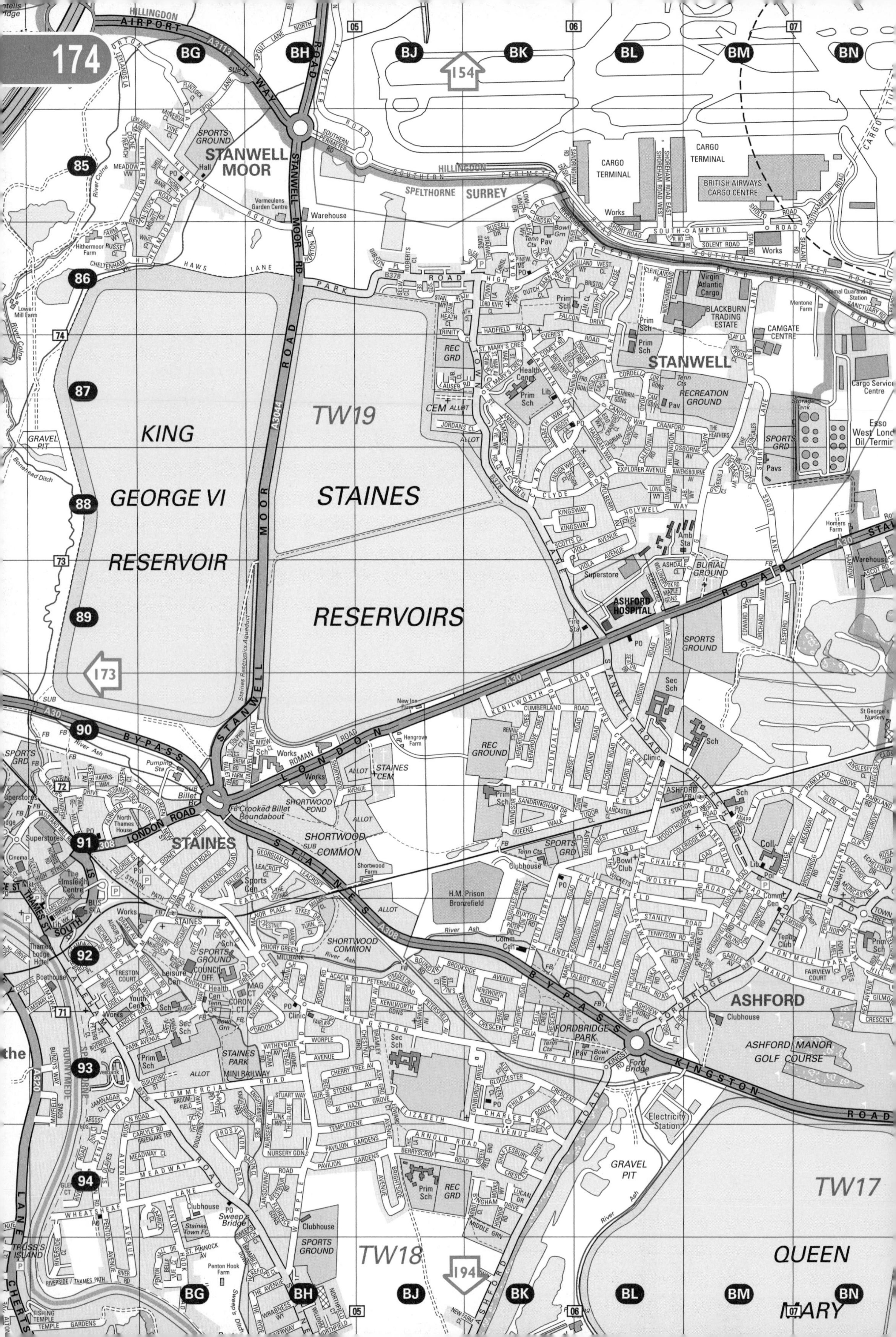
BG
BH
BJ
BK
BL
BM
BN
154
173
194
05
06
07
74
73
72
71
85
86
87
88
89
90
91
92
93
94
STANWELL MOOR
STANWELL
KING GEORGE VI RESERVOIR
STAINES RESERVOIRS
TW19
TW18
TW17
STAINES
ASHFORD
QUEEN MARY
HILLINGDON
SPELTHORNE
SURREY
CARGO TERMINAL
BRITISH AIRWAYS CARGO CENTRE
Virgin Atlantic Cargo
BLACKBURN TRADING ESTATE
CAMGATE CENTRE
Cargo Service Centre
RECREATION GROUND
ASHFORD HOSPITAL
BURIAL GROUND
SPORTS GROUND
REC GROUND
H.M. Prison Bronzefield
SHORTWOOD COMMON
SHORTWOOD POND
STAINES CEM
Crooked Billet Roundabout
ASHFORD MANOR GOLF COURSE
FORDBRIDGE PARK
STAINES PARK MINI RAILWAY
GRAVEL PIT
Electricity Station
The Elmsleigh Centre
Superstores
Sweeps Bridge
Penton Hook Farm
TRUSS'S ISLAND
STANWELL MOOR RD
STANWELL ROAD
LONDON ROAD
STAINES BYPASS
KINGSTON ROAD
CHURCH ROAD
SOUTHERN PERIMETER ROAD
PERIMETER ROAD
BEDFONT ROAD
HAWS LANE
HIGH STREET
CLARE ROAD
SHORT LANE
WOODTHORPE ROAD
CHESTERFIELD ROAD
COMMERCIAL ROAD
WHEATSHEAF LANE
MEADWAY
WORPLE AVENUE
FORDBRIDGE ROAD
LONG LANE
CHERTSEY LANE

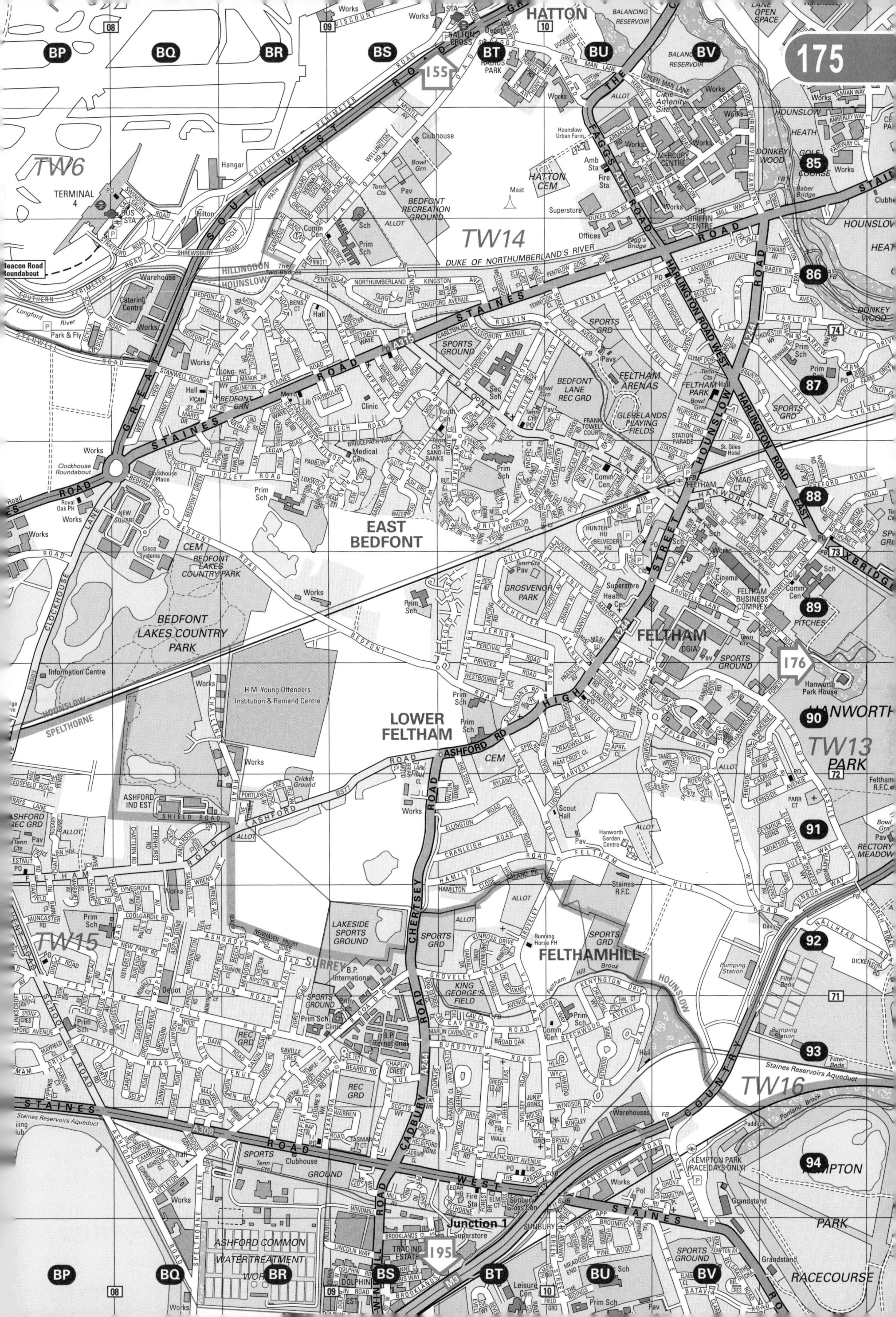

175
155
176
195
BP
BQ
BR
BS
BT
BU
BV
08
09
10
85
86
87
88
89
90
91
92
93
94
71
72
73
74
HATTON
HATTON CROSS
BALANCING RESERVOIR
TW6
TERMINAL 4
Hangar
Hilton
Beacon Road Roundabout
SOUTHERN PERIMETER ROAD
GREAT SOUTH WEST ROAD
Catering Centre
Park & Fly
Longford River
Warehouse
Clubhouse
Bowl Grn
BEDFONT RECREATION GROUND
TW14
HATTON CEM
Hounslow Urban Farm
Mast
Superstore
Offices
DUKE OF NORTHUMBERLAND'S RIVER
HILLINGDON
HOUNSLOW
The Two Bridges
Fagg's Bridge
THE FAGGS ROAD
Civic Amenity Site
MERCURY CENTRE
THE GRIFFIN CENTRE
DONKEY WOOD
HOUNSLOW HEATH GOLF COURSE
Baber Bridge
STAINES ROAD
A315
SPORTS GROUND
SPORTS GRD
BEDFONT LANE REC GRD
FELTHAM ARENAS
GLEBELANDS PLAYING FIELDS
HARLINGTON ROAD WEST
HARLINGTON ROAD EAST
HOUNSLOW ROAD
A244
FELTHAM PARK
STATION PARADE
St. Giles Hotel
Clockhouse Roundabout
Clockhouse Place
Royal Oak PH
NEW SQUARE
Cisco Systems
CEM
BEDFONT LAKES COUNTRY PARK
EAST BEDFONT
Medical Cen
Prim Sch
Sec Sch
Youth Cen
GROSVENOR PARK
Superstore
Health Cen
FELTHAM
Cinema
FELTHAM BUSINESS COMPLEX
PITCHES
Hanworth Park House
HANWORTH PARK
TW13
Information Centre
HOUNSLOW
SPELTHORNE
H.M. Young Offenders Institution & Remand Centre
LOWER FELTHAM
ASHFORD RD
HIGH STREET
ASHFORD IND EST
SHIELD ROAD
Cricket Ground
Scout Hall
Hanworth Garden Centre
Staines R.F.C.
RECTORY MEADOW
TW15
LAKESIDE SPORTS GROUND
CHERTSEY ROAD
SURREY
B.P. International
FELTHAMHILL
Running Horse PH
KING GEORGE'S FIELD
Pumping Station
Filter Beds
Staines Reservoirs Aqueduct
TW16
Portland Brook
COUNTRY WAY
KEMPTON PARK (RACE DAYS ONLY)
Grandstand
KEMPTON PARK RACECOURSE
STAINES ROAD WEST
A308
CADBURY ROAD
Junction 1
M3
SUNBURY
Sunbury Cross Cen
TRADING ESTATE
ASHFORD COMMON WATER TREATMENT WORKS
Leisure Cen
Warehouses

BW
BX
BY
BZ
CA
CB
CC
156
175
196
HOUNSLOW
TW3
TW4
TW14
TW13
TW12
TW16
HOUNSLOW HEATH
HOUNSLOW HEATH GOLF COURSE
Metropolitan Police Training Centre
WHITTON
BOROUGH CEMETERY
HEATHFIELD REC GRD
TWICKENHAM CEMETERY
CRANE PARK
FELTHAM
HANWORTH PARK
HANWORTH
TWICKENHAM PARK GOLF CENTRE
FULWELL PARK
FULWELL GOLF COURSE
KEMPTON PARK RESERVOIRS
KEMPTON PARK
HALF MOON COVERT
HAMPTON
Staines Reservoirs Aqueduct
STAINES ROAD
UXBRIDGE ROAD
HANWORTH ROAD
GREAT CHERTSEY ROAD
HAMPTON ROAD WEST
CHERTSEY RD
A316
A314
A312
A313
A311
A305
85
86
87
88
89
90
91
92
93
94

177
CD
CE
CF
CG
CH
CJ
CK
15
16
17
157
178
197
85
86
87
88
89
90
91
92
93
94
71
72
73
74
TW9
TW6
TW1
TW2
TW10
TW11
KT2
MOGDEN WATER TREATMENT WORKS
Filter Beds
TWICKENHAM
ST. MARGARETS
ST. MARGARETS ROAD
OLD DEER PARK RECREATION GROUND
RICHMOND GREEN
RICHMOND
THE SQUARE
THE QUAD
SHEEN
PARADISE RD
GEORGE ST
HILL ST
RED LION ST
IVYBRIDGE ESTATE
TWICKENHAM TRADING EST
THE RUGBY FOOTBALL UNION TWICKENHAM
Royal Military Sch of Music
CHERTSEY ROAD
WHITTON ROAD
HEATHFIELD NORTH
HEATHFIELD SOUTH
RICHMOND UPON THAMES COLLEGE
Stoop Memorial Ground Harlequins R.F.C.
PLAYING FIELD
RIFLE RANGE
KNELLER GARDENS
MOOR MEAD GRD
LONDON ROAD
RICHMOND ROAD
CROWN ROAD
MARBLE HILL PARK
MARBLE HILL HOUSE
MEADOWBANK
GLOVER'S ISLAND
PETERSHAM MEADOWS
PETERSHAM ROAD
TERRACE GDNS
TERRACE FIELD
Richmond Hill Hotel
RIVER THAMES
ORLEANS HOUSE GALLERY
YORK HOUSE
EEL PIE ISLAND
HEATH ROAD
THE GREEN
TWICKENHAM GREEN
CROSS DEEP
TWICKENHAM RIFLE CLUB
HAM HOUSE (NT)
HAM HOUSE GARDENS
Ham Polo Club
KING GEORGE'S FIELD
SPORTS GROUND
THE COPSE
PETERSHAM
KING HENRY VIII MOUND
RICHMOND GOLF COURSE
SUDBROOK PARK
HAM
HAM COMMON
ST. MICHAEL'S CONVENT
THE CASSEL HOSPITAL
UPPER HAM RD
STRAWBERRY HILL
STRAWBERRY HILL GOLF COURSE
St. Mary's Uni Coll
Thames Young Mariners Base
Ham Riverside Lands
Teddington Lock
Teddington Weir
Teddington Studios
SHELL SPORTS GRD
TROWLOCK ISLAND
BROOM ROAD REC GRD
STEVEN'S EYOT
WALDEGRAVE ROAD
STRAWBERRY VALE
TWICKENHAM RD
HAMPTON ROAD
WELLINGTON ROAD
FULWELL
TEDDINGTON CEM
HIGH STREET
BROAD STREET
TEDDINGTON
KINGSTON ROAD
PARK ROAD
NATIONAL PHYSICAL LABORATORY
BUSHY HOUSE
CANAL PLANTATION
ROUND PLANTATION
BUSHY
BROOM CLUMPS
WATERHOUSE WOODLAND GARDEN
WARREN PLANTATION
HAMPTON WICK
LEG OF MUTTON POND
HAMPTON
HAMPTON HILL
SANDY LANE
Open During Daylight Hours Only
CHESTNUT AVENUE
RICHMOND ROAD

CL
CM
CN
CP
CQ
CR
CS
158
177
198
RICHMOND
RICHMOND PARK
PETERSHAM
HAM
HAM COMMON
EAST SHEEN
SW14
TW10
KT2
COOMBE
EAST SHEEN COMMON (NT)
EAST SHEEN CEMETERY
RICHMOND CEMETERY
PESTHOUSE COMMON
PALEWELL COMMON
PALEWELL PLAYING FIELDS
THE BANK OF ENGLAND'S SPORTS GROUND
TECK PLANTATION
SHEEN WOOD
ADAM'S POND
The Bog
SHEEN CROSS WOOD
POLO FIELD
CONDUIT WOOD
BARN WOOD POND
SAW PIT PLANTATION
JUBILEE PLANTATION
WHITE LODGE PLANTATIONS
DUCHESS WOOD
The Royal Ballet Sch (White Lodge)
KIDNEY WOOD
SIDMOUTH WOOD
QUEEN ELIZABETH'S PLANTATION
LEG OF MUTTON POND
PEN PONDS
DEER PARK
KING GEORGE V JUBILEE PLANTATION
TREEBOX WOOD
SPANKER'S HILL WOOD
LAWN PLANTATION
POND PLANTATION
Tercentenary Plantation
MARTIN'S POND
PRINCE CHARLES'S SPINNEY
GIBBET WOOD
ISABELLA PLANTATION
THOMSON'S POND
PEG'S POND
STILL POND
HIGH WOOD
Deer Fold
Broomfield Hill
BROOMFIELD HILL PLANTATION
Kingston Uni (Dorich House)
HAM CROSS PLANTATION
Ham Bottom
Ham Cross
Ham Dip
CORONATION PLANTATION
DANN'S POND
Thatchedhouse Lodge
GALLOW'S POND
Kings Clump
Dark Hill
Ladderstile Gate
Kingston Gate
Robin Hood Gate
Roehampton Gate
Richmond Gate
Cambrian Gate
Bog Gate
East Sheen Gate
Ham Gate
Pond Slade
KING HENRY VIII MOUND
PETERSHAM PARK
RICHMOND GOLF COURSE SUDBROOK PARK
The Wilderness
Ormeley Lodge
PETERSHAM MEADOWS
Parkgate House
COOMBE HILL GOLF COURSE
COOMBE WOOD GOLF COURSE
Kingston University (Kingston Hill)
Kingston University (Coombe Martin)
THE CASSEL HOSPITAL
Remand Cen
STEVEN'S EYOT
GLOVER'S ISLAND
CORP ISLAND
TROWLOCK ISLAND
THAMES
KINGSTON HILL
KINGSTON VALE
ROBIN HOOD WAY
UPPER RICHMOND ROAD WEST
UPPER HAM RD
PETERSHAM ROAD
RICHMOND ROAD
SAWYER'S HILL
HAM GATE AVENUE
QUEEN'S RIDE
CYCLE PATH
HORSE RIDE
Open During Daylight Hours Only
85
86
87
88
89
90
91
92
93
94
19
20
21
71
72
73
74

179
WANDSWORTH
PUTNEY
ROEHAMPTON
ROEHAMPTON PRIORY HOSPITAL
ROEHAMPTON GOLF COURSE
Southlands College
Digby Stuart College
University of Surrey
Froebel College
QUEEN MARY'S UNI HOSP
ROEHAMPTON PLAYING FIELDS
South Thames Coll
Wandsworth Adult Ed Coll
MARYFIELD CONVENT
Whitelands College
ST. MARY'S CONVENT
ROEHAMPTON LANE
UPPER RICHMOND ROAD
PUTNEY BRIDGE ROAD
PUTNEY HILL
EAST PUTNEY
WEST HILL
SW15
SW18
SW19
SW20
PUTNEY HEATH
Tibbet's Corner
TIBBET'S RIDE
KINGSTON ROAD
ROYAL HOSPITAL
Whitelands Coll
SOUTHFIELDS
RICHMOND PARK GOLF COURSE
Kingsfarm Plantation
Silver Hill
Jerry's Hill
Crematorium
PUTNEY VALE CEMETERY
A3 VALE
WINDMILL MUSEUM
WIMBLEDON PARK SIDE
WIMBLEDON PARK
WIMBLEDON PARK GOLF COURSE
Stadium
PARKSIDE CLINIC
ALL ENGLAND LAWN TENNIS & CROQUET CLUB
Roehampton Vale Campus
PUTNEY VALE
LONDON SCOTTISH GOLF COURSE
WIMBLEDON
COMMON
BLUEGATE GRAVEL PIT (DISUSED)
HOOKHAMSLADE POND
Queen's Butt (Site off)
Gravelly Hill
Farm Bog
Farm Ravine
Caesar's Camp
CANNIZARO PARK
RUSHMERE POND
ROYAL WIMBLEDON GOLF COURSE
Shadwell Wood
Fishponds Wood Nature Reserve
Mill Corner
LADY JANE'S WOOD
HIGH ST WIMBLEDON
WIMBLEDON HILL RD
THE BROADWAY
King's Coll Sch
WOLFSON MED. REHAB CENTRE
COPSE HILL
OBERON PLAYING FIELD
SPORTS GROUND
COTTENHAM PARK
DUNDONALD REC GRD
KINGSTON ROAD
MERTON
DURNSFORD ROAD
BUCKHOLD ROAD
MERTON ROAD
159
180
199
CT CU CV CW CX CY CZ
22 23 24

DA
DB
DC
DD
DE
DF
DG
160
WANDSWORTH
SW11
BOLINGBROKE HOSP
WANDSWORTH COMMON
SPENCER PARK
H.M. PRISON WANDSWORTH
WANDSWORTH CEMETERY
EARLSFIELD
SOUTHFIELDS
SW18
SW12
BALHAM
KING GEORGE'S PARK
WIMBLEDON PARK
179
SUMMERSTOWN
GARRATT PARK
GARRATT GREEN
CENTRAL LONDON GOLF CENTRE
SPRINGFIELD HOSPITAL
STREATHAM CEMETERY
UPPER TOOTING
TOOTING BEC
SW19
WIMBLEDON STADIUM
WIMBLEDON CEMETERY
LAMBETH CEMETERY
ST. GEORGE'S HOSPITAL
SW17
FURZEDOWN
TOOTING GRAVENEY
SOUTH PARK GDNS
SOUTH WIMBLEDON
COLLIER'S WOOD
WANDLE PARK
LONDON ROAD CEMETERY
FIGGE'S MARSH
DUNDONALD REC GRD
MERTON
200
85
86
87
88
89
90
91
92
93
94

DH
DJ
DK
DL
DM
DN
DP
161
182
201
BRIXTON
CLAPHAM PARK
CLAPHAM COMMON
SW4
SW2
SE24
SE21
SE27
SW16
SE19
HERNE HILL
BROCKWELL PARK
STREATHAM HILL
TULSE HILL
TOOTING BEC COMMON
TOOTING GRAVENEY COMMON
STREATHAM PARK
STREATHAM
STREATHAM COMMON
STREATHAM VALE
WEST NORWOOD
WEST NORWOOD CEMETERY
NORWOOD GROVE RECREATION GROUND
NORWOOD NEW TOWN
NORBURY
NORBURY PARK
BIGGIN WOOD
NATIONAL WESTMINSTER BANK SPORTS GROUND
H.M. PRISON BRIXTON
CLAPHAM SOUTH
BALHAM
POYNDERS ROAD
ATKINS ROAD
STREATHAM PL
CHRISTCHURCH ROAD
BRIXTON HILL
STREATHAM HIGH ROAD
TULSE HILL
NORWOOD ROAD
KNIGHTS HILL
BEULAH HILL
CROWN LANE
STREATHAM COMMON NORTH
BEC ROAD
MITCHAM LANE
THURLOW PARK ROAD
CROXTED ROAD
DULWICH ROAD
ACRE LANE
CLAPHAM PARK ROAD
CAVENDISH ROAD
LONG ROAD

HERNE HILL
SE24
BROCKWELL PARK
TULSE HILL
DULWICH
EAST DULWICH
SE22
PECKHAM RYE COMMON
PECKHAM RYE PARK
CAMBERWELL OLD CEMETERY
DULWICH PARK
SE21
WEST DULWICH
DULWICH & SYDENHAM HILL GOLF COURSE
SYDENHAM HILL WOOD (NATURE RESERVE)
DULWICH WOOD
SE27
WEST NORWOOD CEMETERY
WEST NORWOOD
UPPER SYDENHAM
SE26
SYDENHAM
NORWOOD PARK
NORWOOD
NORWOOD NEW TOWN
CRYSTAL PALACE PARK
CRYSTAL PALACE NATIONAL SPORTS CENTRE
UPPER NORWOOD
SE19
PENGE
SE20
HORNIMAN MUS
FOREST HILL
DULWICH PICTURE GALL
KING'S COLLEGE HOSP DULWICH

183
DX
DY
DZ
EA
EB
EC
ED
163
184
203
BROCKLEY
SE4
LADYWELL
UNIVERSITY HOSPITAL LEWISHAM
LADYWELL CENTRE
SE13
HITHER GREEN
HONOR OAK PARK
SE23
FOREST HILL
CATFORD
SE6
BELL GREEN
BELLINGHAM
LOWER SYDENHAM
SOUTHEND
NEW BECKENHAM
BR3
BECKENHAM
BR2
BROMLEY PARK
LEWISHAM
HILLY FIELDS
BROCKLEY CEMETERY
LADYWELL CEMETERY
CAMBERWELL NEW CEMETERY
HONOR OAK SPORTS GRD
BLYTHE HILL FIELDS
BROCKLEY HILL PARK
LADYWELL FIELDS
CATFORD GREYHOUND STADIUM
MOUNTSFIELD PARK PLAYING FIELDS
MANOR HOUSE GARDENS
MANOR PARK
LEWISHAM PARK
FORSTER MEMORIAL PARK
MAYOW PARK
HOME PARK
SOUTHEND PARK
KENT C.C.C.
CATOR PARK
BECKENHAM PLACE PARK
GOLF COURSE
SUMMERHOUSE HILL WOOD
ASH PLANTATION
LEWISHAM BOROUGH SPORTS GROUND
MIDLAND BANK SPORTS GROUND
WARREN AVE PLAYING FIELDS
SHORTLANDS GOLF COURSE
THE SLOANE HOSPITAL
BECKENHAM JUNCTION
NATWEST BANK SPORTS GRD
H.S.B.C. GROUP SPORTS GRD
C.G.U. CUACO SPORTS GRD
PRIVATE BANKS SPORTS GRD
BROWNHILL ROAD
SOUTH CIRCULAR ROAD
STANSTEAD ROAD
BROMLEY ROAD
SOUTHEND LANE
BECKENHAM HILL ROAD
HIGH STREET
ALEXANDRA REC GRD

EE
EF
EG
EH
EJ
EK
EL
164
183
204
40
41
42
85
86
87
88
89
90
91
92
93
94
SE13
SE12
SE6
BR1
BR2
HITHER GREEN
GROVE PARK
MOTTINGHAM
ELTHAM
DOWNHAM
PLAISTOW
SUNDRIDGE
ELMSTEAD
BROMLEY PARK
Widmore Green
Lee Green
ELTHAM PALACE
SUTCLIFFE PARK
MANOR HOUSE GARDENS
MANOR PARK
OLD COLFEIANS SPORTS GROUND
CIVIL SERVICE SPORTS GROUNDS
MIDDLE PARK FIELD
QUEENSCROFT REC GRD
KING JOHN PLAYING FIELDS
UNI OF GREENWICH ATHLETIC GRD
NORTHBROOK PARK
HITHER GREEN CEMETERY
Crematorium
UNI OF WESTMINSTER SPORTS GROUND
MOTTINGHAM SPORTS GROUND
CHINBROOK MEADOWS
LOWER MARVELS WOOD
MARVELS WOOD
GROVE PARK CEMETERY
ELMSTEAD WOOD
SUNDRIDGE PARK GOLF COURSE
ELMSTEAD WOODS
ROCKPIT WOOD
LOGSHILL WOOD
FORSTER MEMORIAL PARK
DOWNHAM PLAYING FIELDS
SHAFTESBURY PARK REC GRD
KING'S MEADOW PLAYING FIELDS
LEWISHAM BOROUGH SPORTS GROUND
MIDLAND BANK SPORTS GROUND
WARREN AVE PLAYING FIELDS
SHORTLANDS GOLF COURSE
THE SLOANE HOSPITAL
BROMLEY NORTH
TRAIN DEPOT
CHILTONIAN IND ESTATE
CHINBROOK ESTATE
Colfe's Sch
Eltham Coll
Sundridge Park
S CIRCULAR ROAD
ST MILDREDS ROAD
WESTHORNE AVENUE
ELTHAM ROAD
SIDCUP ROAD
BURNT ASH HILL
BARING ROAD
BURNT ASH LANE
BROMLEY HILL
LONDON ROAD
CHINBROOK ROAD
GROVE PARK ROAD
COLLEGE RD
KIDBROOKE PARK
A20
A205
A210
A2212
A21
A2
B226
Quaggy River
Ravensbourne River

ELTHAM PARK NORTH
FALCONWOOD
DA16
EM
EN
EP
EQ
ER
ES
ET
165
ELTHAM PARK SOUTH
ELTHAM WARREN GOLF COURSE
ROCHESTER WAY RELIEF ROAD
ROCHESTER WAY
SUTHERLAND AVENUE
Crematorium
Greenwich Environment Curriculum Service
SPORTS GROUND
BEXLEY ROAD
BLACKFEN ROAD
85
AVERY HILL
AVERY HILL PARK
University of Greenwich Avery Hill Campus
HIGH ST
86
BLACKFEN
DA15
HOLLY OAK WOOD PK
87
ROYAL BLACKHEATH GOLF COURSE
TARN BIRD SANCTUARY
SE9
CAMBRIDGE MISSION SPORTS GROUND
CHARLTON ATHLETIC FC TRAINING GRD
MILLWALL FC TRAINING GRD
FOOTSCRAY PLAYING FIELDS
FOOTSCRAY ROAD
MARLBOROUGH PARK
88
LAMORBEY
FAIRY HILL REC GRD
NEW ELTHAM
PLAYING FIELD
OLD FARM PARK
89
KING GEORGE'S REC GRD
SIDCUP
186
SIDCUP ROAD
LONGLANDS
JACK NICKLAUS GOLF CENTRE
FLAMINGO PK SPORTS GRD
LONGLANDS REC GRD
90
MAIN ROAD
91
SIDCUP HIGH STREET
BELMONT LANE OPEN SPACE
Kemnal Manor Stables
DA14
SIDCUP
SPORTS GROUND
DOG RACING TRACK
CHISLEHURST CEMETERY
SIDCUP BYPASS
92
SIDCUP PLACE
CHISLEHURST WEST
WHYTES WOODLAND
Bird Sanctuary
OLD ELTHAMIANS SPORTS GRD
BR7
UNIVERSITY COLLEGE LONDON SPORTS GRD
QUEEN MARY'S HOSP
93
SCADBURY PARK NATURE RESERVE
CHISLEHURST
CAMDEN PARK
CHISLEHURST GOLF COURSE
CHISLEHURST COMMON
PERRY STREET
94
PARK WOOD
Scadbury Moated Manor House Site
205
43
44
45
BROMLEY ROAD
BROMLEY LANE
WHITEHORSE HILL
RED HILL
HIGH STREET
A20
A208
A222

EU
EV
EW
EX
EY
EZ
FA
166
DA16
DANSON
PARK
THE LAKE
The Boathouse
Bexley Grammer Sch
Danson Mansion
BROADWAY
BEXLEYHEATH
DA6
BEXLEYHEATH GOLF COURSE
PLAYING FIELD
ROCHESTER WAY
BLACKFEN ROAD
EAST ROCHESTER WAY
BEXLEY
BLACKFEN
HOLLY OAK WOOD PK
PENHILL PARK
PENHILL ROAD
BEXLEY PARK WOOD
RIVERSIDE WALK
HURST REC GRD
HURST ROAD
MARLBOROUGH PARK
SIDCUP GOLF COURSE
DA15
LAMORBEY
Rose Bruford College
LAMORBEY PARK
ABBEYHILL PARK
DA5
Bexley Cricket Club
KING GEORGE'S REC GRD
185
Sidcup Arts Cen
WARING PARK
GOLDSMITH COLLEGE SPORTS GRD
THE ALDERS
NORTH CRAY
NORTH CRAY WOOD
STABLE MEADOW
DA14
FOOTS CRAY MEADOWS
Foots Cray Place
GATTONS WOOD
GATTONS PLANTATION
LONGLANDS REC GRD
SIDCUP
SIDCUP HIGH STREET
SIDCUP PLACE
SIDCUP TECHNOLOGY CENTRE
QUEEN MARY'S HOSP
GARDEN SHAW
FOOTS CRAY
SCADBURY PARK
NATURE RESERVE
LITTLE WOOD
Crittall's Corner
Ruxley Corner
RUXLEY WOOD
BR5
SIDCUP BYPASS
MAIDSTONE ROAD
NORTH CRAY ROAD
206
RUXLEY PARK GOLF COURSE
85
86
87
88
89
90
91
92
93
94

BARNES CRAY
CRAYFORD
CRAYFORD MARSHES
DA1
OLD BEXLEY
DARTFORD HEATH
DARTFORD
Coldblow
JOYDEN'S WOOD
Joydens Wood
Hook Green
DA2
BIRCHWOOD PARK GOLF CENTRE
Hextable
BR8
SWANLEY
Swanley Village
167
188
207

DARTFORD FRESH MARSHES
CRAYFORD MARSHES
168
Junction 1a
DARTFORD
New Town
DA1
DARTFORD GOLF COURSE
OAKFIELD PARK
CENTRAL PARK
BROOKLANDS LAKE
DARTFORD TRADE PARK
North West Kent College
Leigh City Tech. Coll
LIVINGSTONE HOSP
STONE HOUSE HOSPITAL
ARCHERY HOUSE
WATLING STREET CEM
187
DARTFORD BYPASS
Junction 2
DA2
Darenth
Wilmington
Hawley
BR8
Sutton at Hone
Swanley Village
DEER PARK
ST. JOHN'S JERUSALEM
THE ALDERS
208
FJ
FK
FL
FM
FN
FP
FQ
85
86
87
88
89
90
91
92
93
94
54
55
56

Stone
Greenhithe
Knockhall
DA9
DA10
DA13
DA4
Bean
Green Street Green
South Darenth
Lane End
Betsham
CROSSWAYS BOULEVARD
LONDON ROAD
A226
WATLING STREET
A296
DARTFORD BYPASS
A2
ST. CLEMENTS WAY
B255
Bluewater Shopping Centre
BLUEWATER PARKWAY
THE VILLAGE
DARENTH VALLEY HOSPITAL
DARENTH WOOD
LADIES WOOD
LORDS WOOD
BEACON COUNTRY PARK
THE THRIFT
CHALK PIT
SWANSCOMBE HERITAGE PARK
Blue Circle Industries
Stone Castle
STONE CEM
STONE REC GRD
Travelodge
Superstore
Johnson's Wharf
Jetty
Works
Knoxfield Caravan Park
Arrow Riding & Carriage Driving Centre for the Disabled
Badger's Mount
Bean Farm
Youth Club
Prim Sch
Cherwell Farm
Manor Farm Garden Centre
The Ship PH
St. Margaret's Farm
Walnut Tree Farm
Chalkcroft
Ryecroft Farm
Gill's Farm
Westwood Farm
Wheatsheaf PH
Mates Farm
Cricket Club
QUARRY
The Royal Oak PH
The Bull PH
The George & Dragon PH
Alkerden Farm
Western Cross Farm
SANDY LANE
BETSHAM HILL
HIGHCROSS ROAD
SANDBANKS
HOOK GREEN
ST. MARGARET'S ROAD
GILL'S ROAD
DARENTH WOOD ROAD
SOUTHFLEET ROAD
MOUNTS ROAD
ALKERDEN LANE
FR
FS
FT
FU
FV
FW
FX
57
58
59
71
72
73
74
85
86
87
88
89
90
91
92
93
94
169
190
209

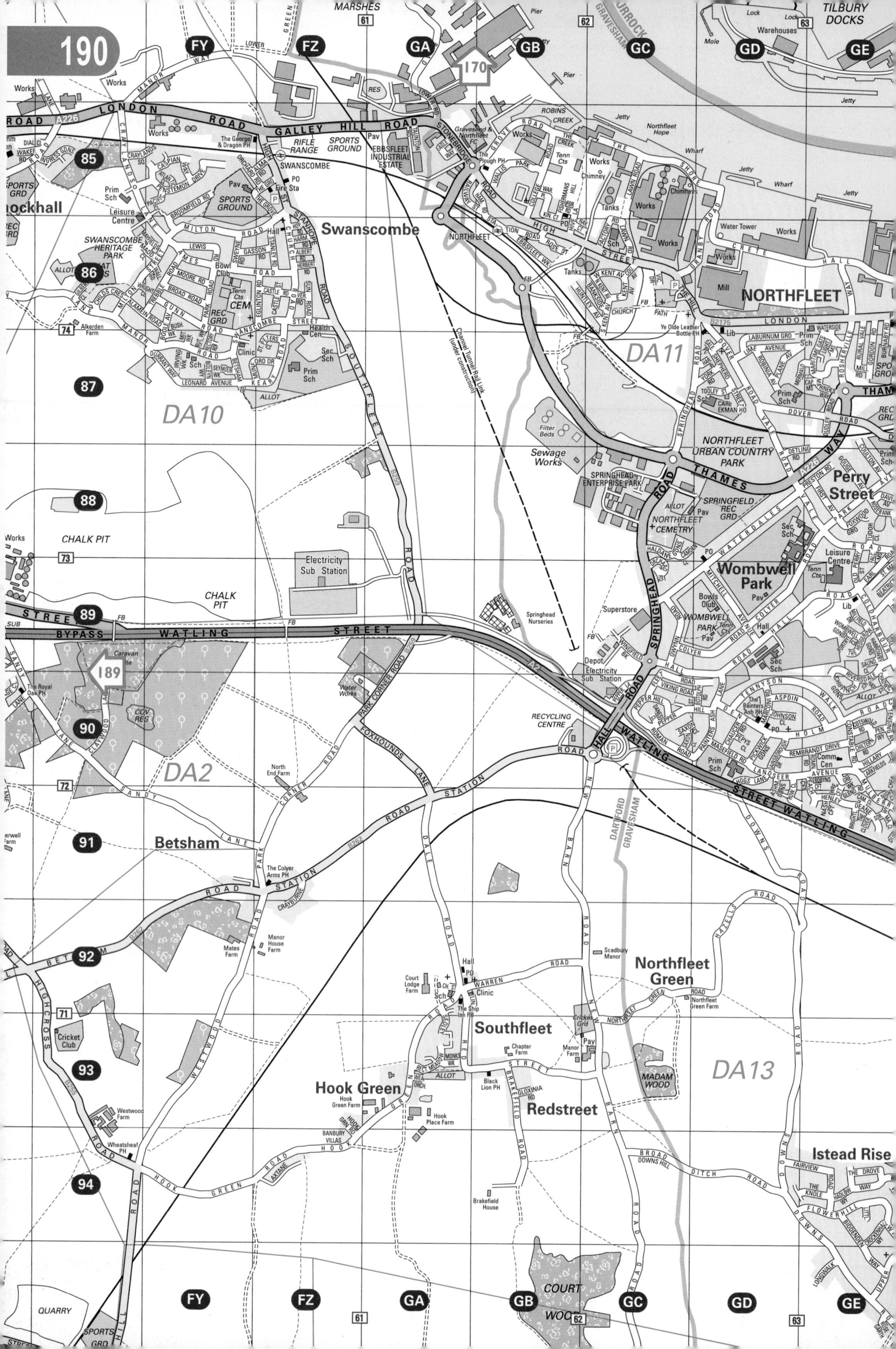
MARSHES
TILBURY DOCKS
Warehouses
Lock
Mole
Pier
170
189
LONDON ROAD
A226
GALLEY HILL ROAD
RIFLE RANGE
SPORTS GROUND
EBBSFLEET INDUSTRIAL ESTATE
SWANSCOMBE
Swanscombe
Knockhall
SWANSCOMBE HERITAGE PARK
Leisure Centre
Prim Sch
CEM
REC GRD
Clinic
Sec Sch
Health Cen
DA10
NORTHFLEET
Northfleet Hope
ROBINS CREEK
Works
Chimney
Tanks
Water Tower
Mill
Wharf
Jetty
DA11
Channel Tunnel Rail Link (under construction)
Filter Beds
Sewage Works
NORTHFLEET URBAN COUNTRY PARK
SPRINGHEAD ENTERPRISE PARK
THAMES WAY
SPRINGHEAD ROAD
SPRINGFIELD REC GRD
NORTHFLEET CEMETRY
Perry Street
Wombwell Park
Leisure Centre
Superstore
Springhead Nurseries
Depot
Electricity Sub Station
RECYCLING CENTRE
Electricity Sub Station
CHALK PIT
Works
WATLING STREET
BYPASS
A2
Caravan Site
COV RES
DA2
The Royal Oak PH
North End Farm
Water Works
PARK CORNER ROAD
FOXHOUNDS LANE
STATION ROAD
B262
Betsham
SANDY LANE
The Colyer Arms PH
BETSHAM ROAD
Mates Farm
Manor House Farm
HIGHCROSS ROAD
Cricket Club
Westwood Farm
Wheatsheaf PH
WESTWOOD
HOOK GREEN ROAD
Hook Green
Hook Green Farm
Hook Place Farm
BANBURY VILLAS
Court Lodge Farm
The Ship Inn PH
Southfleet
Chapter Farm
Black Lion PH
Redstreet
Brakefield House
DALE ROAD
NEW BARN ROAD
DARTFORD
GRAVESHAM
Scadbury Manor
Northfleet Green
Northfleet Green Farm
MADAM WOOD
DA13
Istead Rise
BROAD DITCH ROAD
DOWNS ROAD
COURT WOOD
QUARRY
FY
FZ
GA
GB
GC
GD
GE
61
62
63
71
72
73
74
85
86
87
88
89
90
91
92
93
94

RIVER THAMES
THURROCK
GRAVESHAM
GRAVESEND
Tilbury Fort
Fortress Distribution Park
Riverside Rail Terminal
London International Cruise Terminal
Tidal Basin
171
sherville
Milton
Denton
Chalk
Windmill Hill
Westcourt
Kings Farm
Parrock Farm
Riverview Park
Singlewell
Thong
DA12
MID KENT GOLF COURSE
SOUTHERN VALLEY GOLF COURSE
THAMES VIEW GOLF COURSE
DRIVING RANGE
WESTCOURT MARSHES
DENTON MARSHES
EASTCOURT MARSHES
GREAT CLAY LANE MARSHES
RIVERSIDE LEISURE AREA
OLD GRAVESENDIANS SPORTS GRD
WOODLANDS PARK
CLAYLANE WOOD
HUNTONDOWN WOOD
TWENTY ACRE WOOD
GRAVEHILL WOOD
THE BURNETT
OVERCLIFFE
MILTON ROAD
ROCHESTER ROAD
WROTHAM ROAD
WATLING STREET
OLD ROAD EAST
OLD ROAD WEST
HIGHAM ROAD
SINGLEWELL ROAD
PARROCK STREET
A226
A227
A2
GF
GG
GH
GJ
GK
GL
GM
85
86
87
88
89
90
91
92
93
94
64
65
66
71
72
73
74

172
210
AS
AT
AU
AV
AW
AX
AY
95
96
97
98
99
100
101
102
103
104
98
99
00
69
68
67
66
Egham Wick
FUZZY CLUMP
ALDER COVERT
OBELISK POND
SCARLETOAK PLANTATION
FRANK'S PLANTATION
POLO GROUND
Breakheart Hill
WEEDEN'S FIELD
JOHNSON'S POND
HEATHER GARDEN
DARKHOLE CLUMP
OXHED CLUMP
High Flyer's Hill
WINTER GARDEN
The Punch Bowl
THE VALLEY GARDENS
VIRGINIA WATER PLANTATION
EGHAM WICK PLANTATION
WICK POND
Eton Bridge
Totem Pole
Boathouse
VIRGINIA WATER
Botany Bay Point
FROSTFARM PLANTATION
BLACKNEST ROAD
LONDON ROAD
A329
A30
BELVEDERE WOOD
Fort Belvedere
SL5
GU25
GU24
Virginia Lodge
Cascade Bridge
Wheatsheaf PH
CHRISTCHURCH ROAD
KING'S COPSE
WAVERLEY COPSE
GENERAL'S COPSE
DUKE'S COPSE
Broom Hill
WENTWORTH POND
Clubhouse
Tennis Courts
WENTWORTH
Wentworth
The Dormy House
Ingliston House
Podenhale
GOLF COURSE
GREAT WOOD
BEECH WOOD
Knowle Hill
KNOWLE GROVE
KING GEORGE V PLAYING FIELD
VIRGINIA WATER
Comm Cen
Royal Holloway College
The American Comm Sch
Callow Hill
GREAT WOOD
THE DELL
Stroude Farm
Stroude Crossing
PLAYING FLD
Prep Sch
Prim Sch
The Klondyke Piggeries
Waterloo Bridge
Fairview Farm
Trumps Farm
BLUEBELLE WOOD
Burnt Hill
Little Arm
Ship Hill
Long Arm
Memorial Cross
Oystershell Hill
Rushy Pond
Staple Hill
CHOBHAM COMMON NATIONAL NATURE RESERVE
LONGCROSS
Defence Science & Technology Laboratory
Longcross
Works
Longcross House
CHERTSEY COMMON
BOG WOOD
BARROWHILLS
MILITARY GOLF COURSE
DICKEN'S WOOD
Hersham Farm
Grangewood
Hillside
Flutters Hill
Lily Pond Farm
Glasshouse
CHOBHAM LANE
CHERTSEY ROAD
LONGCROSS ROAD
B386
B383
B389
M3
ACCOMMODATION ROAD
WENTWORTH DRIVE
PORTNALL DRIVE
WEST DRIVE
EAST DRIVE
SOUTH DRIVE
WELLINGTON AVENUE
CALLOW HILL
BAKEHAM LANE
HOLLOW LANE
TRUMPS GREEN ROAD
KNOWLE HILL
STATION PAR

TW20
TW18
KT16
KT15
Stroude
Thorpe
Thorpe Green
Lyne
CHERTSEY
ADDLESTONE MOOR
THORPE PARK
MANOR LAKE
ST. ANN'S LAKE
Abbey Lake
LONGSIDE LAKE
Junction 2 (M3), Junction 12 (M25)
Junction 11
ST. ANN'S HILL PARK
FAN GROVE
FOXHILLS GOLF COURSE
RUNNYMEDE HOSP
ST. PETER'S HOSP
HOSPITAL (CLOSED)
LALEHAM GOLF COURSE
ADDLESTONE CEMETERY
ABBEY MOOR GOLF COURSE
PENTON HOOK ISLAND
PENTON HOOK MARINA
THORPE INDUSTRIAL EST
Great Fosters Hotel
Foxhills Country Club
Great Cockrow Railway
STAINES ROAD
GUILDFORD ROAD
ST. PETER'S WAY
173
194
211

BG
BH
BJ
BK
BL
BM
BN
174
TW18
QUEEN
MARY
RESERVOIR
PENTON HOOK ISLAND
PENTON HOOK
PENTON HOOK MARINA
MANOR LAKE
Abbey Lake
LALEHAM
LALEHAM GOLF COURSE
LALEHAM BURWAY
LALEHAM PARK
LALEHAM PARK SPORTS GROUND
Shepperton Studios
193
KT16
M3
CHERTSEY
CHERTSEY MEADS
RECREATION GROUND
Dumsey Eyot
Dockett Eddy
PHARAOH'S ISLAND
LOCK ISLAND
HAMHAUGH ISLAND
ADDLESTONE MOOR
ADDLESTONE CEMETERY
ABBEY MOOR GOLF COURSE
WOBURN PARK
St. George's College
KT15
Junction 11
212
WEYBRIDGE TRADING ESTATE
WEYBRIDGE BUSINESS PARK
95
96
97
98
99
100
101
102
103
104
69
68
67
66
05
06
07

BP
BQ
BR
BS
BT
BU
BV
175
Junction 1
ASHFORD COMMON WATER TREATMENT WORKS
SPORTS GROUND
STAINES ROAD
WINDMILL ROAD
M3
PARK
RACECOURSE
95
96
97
98
99
100
101
102
103
104
TW16
SUNBURY
SUNBURY PARK
LITTLETON
UPPER HALLIFORD
HAZELWOOD GOLF COURSE
SUNBURY GOLF COURSE
DRIVING RANGE
LONDON IRISH RUGBY GROUND
GAFLAC SPORTS GROUND
CEDARS REC GRD
SUNBURY CEM
SUNBURY LOCK AIT
Sunbury Locks
WATER TREATMENT WORKS
GRAVEL PIT
KT12
196
APPLE COURT GREEN
WHEATLEY'S AIT
LONGWOOD BUSINESS PARK
SHEPPERTON BUSINESS PARK
GASTON BRIDGE ROAD
UPPER HALLIFORD BYPASS
WALTON BRIDGE RD
Shepperton Moat House
Shepperton Marina
BISHOP DUPPA'S REC GRD
RIVER ASH EST
LAS PALMAS ESTATE
DESBOROUGH ISLAND
THAMES MEADOW
COWAY SALE
D'OYLY CARTE ISLAND
KT13
BROAD WATER
PLAYING FIELDS
Oatlands Park Hotel
ST. MAUR'S CONV
WALTON-ON THAMES
WALTON & HERSHAM FC
ELM GROVE REC GRD
GEORGE FROUDE PK
ASHLEY PARK
CHURCH ST
HEPWORTH WAY
NEW ZEALAND AVENUE
BRIDGE STREET
HERSHAM ROAD
OATLANDS DRIVE
MONUMENT HILL
QUEENS ROAD
213
OATLANDS PARK
RYDENS
SUNBURY CROSS
Walton-on-Thames

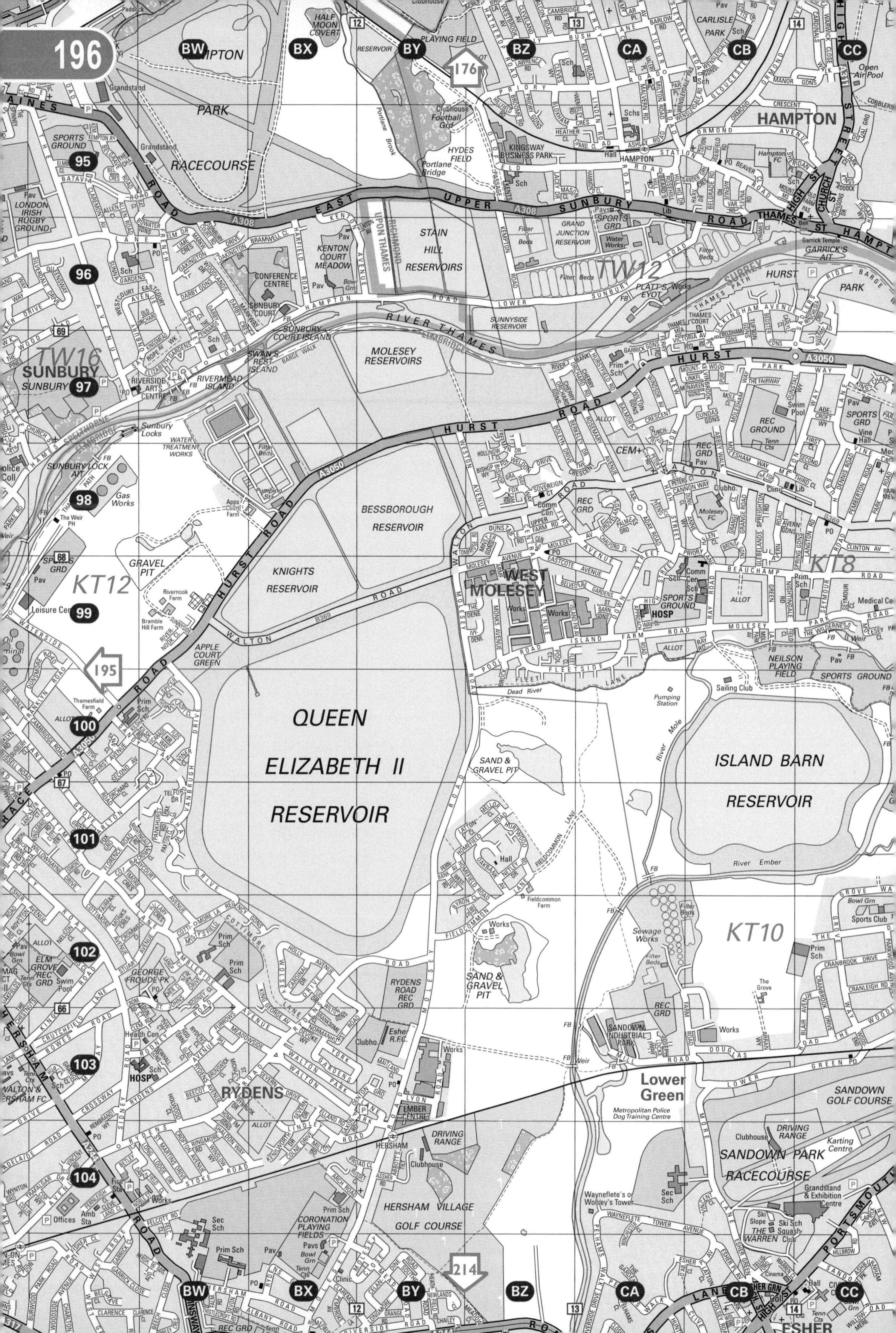
BW
BX
BY
BZ
CA
CB
CC
176
HAMPTON
PARK
RACECOURSE
HALF MOON COVERT
PLAYING FIELD
HAMPTON
KINGSWAY BUSINESS PARK
HYDES FIELD
Portlane Bridge
UPPER SUNBURY ROAD
A308
STAIN HILL RESERVOIRS
KENTON COURT MEADOW
GRAND JUNCTION RESERVOIR
TW12
PLATT'S EYOT
HURST PARK
GARRICK'S AIT
SURREY
RIVER THAMES
ELMBRIDGE
SPELTHORNE
MOLESEY RESERVOIRS
SUNNYSIDE RESERVOIR
SUNBURY COURT ISLAND
SWAN'S REST ISLAND
RIVERMEAD ISLAND
TW16
SUNBURY
LONDON IRISH RUGBY GROUND
SPORTS GROUND
CONFERENCE CENTRE
RIVERSIDE ARTS CENTRE
Sunbury Locks
SUNBURY LOCK AIT
WATER TREATMENT WORKS
Gas Works
HURST ROAD
A3050
BESSBOROUGH RESERVOIR
KNIGHTS RESERVOIR
GRAVEL PIT
KT12
Riverenook Farm
Bramble Hill Farm
APPLE COURT GREEN
WALTON ROAD
B369
WEST MOLESEY
KT8
SPORTS GROUND
NEILSON PLAYING FIELD
REC GROUND
Dead River
QUEEN ELIZABETH II RESERVOIR
ISLAND BARN RESERVOIR
River Mole
River Ember
SAND & GRAVEL PIT
Fieldcommon Farm
Sewage Works
KT10
195
RYDENS ROAD REC GRD
Esher R.F.C.
RYDENS
GEORGE FROUDE PK
ELM GROVE REC GRD
HERSHAM
EMBER CENTRE
DRIVING RANGE
HERSHAM VILLAGE GOLF COURSE
CORONATION PLAYING FIELDS
SANDOWN INDUSTRIAL PARK
Lower Green
Metropolitan Police Dog Training Centre
Wayneflete's or Wolsey's Tower
SANDOWN GOLF COURSE
SANDOWN PARK RACECOURSE
Karting Centre
Grandstand & Exhibition Centre
THE WARREN
ESHER
214
95
96
97
98
99
100
101
102
103
104

197
CD
CE
CF
CG
CH
CJ
CK
177
215
198
TW11
KT7
KT6
KT9
BUSHY PARK
HAMPTON WICK
EAST MOLESEY
HAMPTON COURT PARK
(HOME PARK)
HAMPTON COURT PALACE GOLF COURSE
THAMES DITTON
WESTON GREEN
LONG DITTON
HINCHLEY WOOD
LITTLEWORTH COMMON
KINGSTON UPON THAMES
HOOK
SURBITON
ESHER
THE ROYAL PADDOCKS
WARREN PLANTATION
HALF MOON PLANTATION
OVAL PLANTATION
HERON POND
LEG OF MUTTON POND
WATERHOUSE WOODLAND GARDEN
WATERHOUSE POND
FISHER'S POND
BROOM CLUMPS
ROUND PLANTATION
Diana Fountain
Hampton Court Gate
HAMPTON COURT GREEN
HAMPTON COURT PALACE
MAZE
The Long Water
THE RICK POND
HAMPTON WICK POND
RAVENS AIT
THAMES DITTON ISLAND
BOYLE FM ISLAND
TAGG'S ISLAND
ASH ISLAND
River Thames
River Mole
River Ember
ALBANY REACH
KINGSTON BYPASS
A308
A309
A307
A243
A240
SURBITON GENERAL HOSP
LONG DITTON REC GRD
VICTORIA REC GRD
KING EDWARD REC GRD
THAMES DITTON & ESHER GOLF COURSE
DITTON COMMON
Scilly Isles
Management Training Cen
Kingston University
Kingston Uni
Telegraph Hill
SURREY

198
CL
CM
CN
CP
CQ
CR
CS
178
197
216
95
96
97
98
99
100
101
102
103
104
COOMBE
COOMBE WOOD GOLF COURSE
KT2
KINGSTON HOSPITAL
NORBITON
KINGSTON UPON THAMES
KINGSTON CEMETERY
KT1
Crematorium
Kingstonian FC & AFC Wimbledon
NEW MALDEN
KT8
River Thames
SURBITON CEMETERY
Sewage Works
Filter Beds
Sludge Beds
GREEN LANE REC GRD
BERRYLANDS
KT3
HOGSMILL PUBLIC OPEN SPACE
KT5
SURBITON GENERAL HOSP
KT6
SURBITON
FISHPONDS OPEN SPACE
ALEXANDRA REC GRD
HOGSMILL OPEN SPACE
MALDEN MANOR
OLD MALDEN
MAORI SPORTS GROUND
G DITTON
Cockcrow Hill
TOLWORTH HOSPITAL
TOLWORTH
KINGSTON UNIVERSITY SPORTS GRD
RIVERHILL SPORTS GRD
KING GEORGES FIELD
KING GEORGE'S TRADING EST
KT9
HOOK
KING EDWARD REC GRD
WANDGAS ATHLETIC GROUND
DANCER DICKS WOOD
KING GEORGE'S FIELD AURIOL PARK
KINGSTON BYPASS
COOMBE LANE WEST
KINGSTON ROAD
KINGSTON HILL
CAMBRIDGE ROAD
EWELL ROAD
BROADWAY
MALDEN WAY
PORTSMOUTH ROAD
BRIGHTON ROAD
HOOK ROAD
SURBITON HILL RD
PENRHYN ROAD
RICHMOND ROAD
HAMPTON WICK POND
RAVENS AIT
SURREY

CT
CU
CV
CW
CX
CY
CZ
179
200
217
WOLFSON MED. REHAB CENTRE
COOMBE HILL
OBERON PLAYING FIELD
COTTENHAM PARK
COTTENHAM PK REC GRD
DUNDONALD REC GRD
NELSON HOSP
JOHN INNES REC GRD
MERTON
MERTON PARK
SW19
SW20
PRINCE GEORGE'S PLAYING FIELD
RAYNES PARK
RAYNES PARK SPORTS GRD
BEVERLEY PARK
KINGSTON UPON THAMES
MERTON
MESSINES PLAYING FLD
JOSEPH HOOD RECREATION GROUND
BUSHEY MEAD
CANNON HILL COMMON
MOSTYN GARDENS
SOUTH MERTON
MORDEN
WEST BARNES
RAYNES PARK PLAYING FIELDS
MORDEN SPORTS GROUND
MORDEN SOUTH
MORDEN PARK
SM4
OLD BLUES R.F.C.
UNIVERSITY OF LONDON ATHLETIC GROUND
THE SIR JOSEPH HOOD MEMORIAL PLAYING FIELDS
MORDEN CEMETERY
MOTSPUR PARK
B.B.C. SPORTS GRD
MANOR PARK REC GRD
MERTON & SUTTON JOINT CEMETERY
KING GEORGE'S FIELD
GARTH ROAD IND CEN
ST. ANTHONY'S HOSP
REIGATE AVENUE REC GRD
SM3
SUTTON CEMETERY
KIMPTON TRADE BUSINESS CENTRE
WORCESTER PARK
KT4
EPSOM & EWELL
SUTTON
NORTH CHEAM
CUDDINGTON REC GRD
Oldfields Trading Est
SM1
COLLINGWOOD PARK
Sutton Utd. FC
COOMBE LANE
KINGSTON ROAD
KINGSTON BY-PASS
WORPLE ROAD
BUSHEY ROAD
GRAND DRIVE
LONDON ROAD
CENTRAL ROAD
MALDEN ROAD
CHEAM COMMON ROAD
STONECOT HILL
EPSOM ROAD
ST. DUNSTAN'S HILL
OLDFIELDS ROAD

SOUTH WIMBLEDON
COLLIER'S WOOD
MERTON
MERTON PARK
MORDEN
SW19
SM4
MORDEN HALL PARK
PHIPPS BRIDGE
RAVENSBURY PARK
MITCHAM
CR4
MITCHAM GOLF COURSE
MITCHAM JUNCTION
ST. HELIER
SM5
ROSEHILL
BENHILTON
THE WRYTHE
SM3
SM1
SUTTON CEMETERY
MORDEN PARK
MORDEN REC GRD
THOMAS WALL PARK
ROSEHILL RECREATION GROUND
ST. HELIER HOSP
QUEEN MARY'S HOSP FOR CHILDREN
CARSHALTON SPORTS ARENA
ST. HELIER OPEN SPACE
WATERMEADS NT.
POULTER PARK
LONDON ROAD CEMETERY
FIGGE'S MARSH
NELSON HOSP
DUNDONALD REC GRD
MOSTYN GARDENS
MORDEN SPORTS GROUND
ROYSTON PARK
DALE PARK
WILDERNESS ISLAND
COLLINGWOOD PARK
KIMPTON TRADE CENTRE
FELNEX TRADING ESTATE
GRACE BUSINESS CENTRE
EAGLE TRADING EST
ABBEY IND EST
LOMBARD BUSINESS PARK
MERTON INDUSTRIAL PARK
NELSON TRADING EST
MORDEN ROAD
LONDON ROAD
EPSOM ROAD
REIGATE AVENUE
BISHOPSFORD ROAD
ST. HELIER AVENUE
MORDEN HALL ROAD
WESTERN ROAD
MERANTUN WAY
KINGSTON ROAD
CENTRAL ROAD
CARSHALTON ROAD
CRANMER RD
COMMONSIDE WEST
STREATHAM ROAD
OLDFIELDS ROAD
A24
A217
A297
A239
A236
A238
A237
180
199
218
DA
DB
DC
DD
DE
DF
DG
95
96
97
98
99
100
101
102
103
104
26
27
28

201
DH
DJ
DK
DL
DM
DN
DP
181
202
219
STREATHAM VALE
STREATHAM COMMON
NORBURY
NORBURY PARK
SE19
NATIONAL WESTMINSTER BANK SPORTS GROUND
STREATHAM PARK
CEMETERY
SW16
POLLARDS HILL
GREEN LANE SPORTS GROUND
CR7
THORNTON HEATH
MITCHAM
COMMON
SHERWOOD PK
PLAYING FIELD
CROYDON CEMETERY
MAYDAY HOSPITAL
BROAD GREEN
QUEEN'S ROAD CEMETERY
HACKBRIDGE
BEDDINGTON
SM6
BEDDINGTON PARK
THE GRANGE GARDENS
CR0
WADDON
WANDLE PARK
CROYDON SUB STATION
DUPPAS HILL
LONDON ROAD
MITCHAM ROAD
PURLEY WAY
CROYDON ROAD
95
96
97
98
99
100
101
102
103
104
29
30
31

202
DQ
DR
DS
DT
DU
DV
DW
UPPER NORWOOD
WESTOW PARK
182
SE19
THE LAWNS
BEAULIEU HEIGHTS
SOUTH NORWOOD GROUNDS
SPORTS GROUND
ORCHARD SCHOOL SPORTS CENTRE
SOUTH NORWOOD LAKE
SE20
ANERLEY
BETTS PARK
PENGE
SOUTH NORWOOD
GRANGEWOOD PARK
BECKENHAM CEMETERY
Crematorium
BIRKBECK
CR7
SE25
THORNTON HEATH
SELHURST PARK CRYSTAL PALACE FC
NORWOOD JUNCTION
SOUTH NORWOOD REC GRD
SOUTH NORWOOD COUNTRY PARK
CROYDON AND RYLANDS FIELDS
CROYDON SPORTS ARENA
ARENA
CROYDON DRIVING RANGE
SELHURST
RAIL DEPOT
WOOD SIDE
QUEEN'S ROAD CEMETERY
MAYDAY HOSPITAL
201
BROAD GREEN
ASHBURTON PARK
SHIRLEY OAKS HOSPITAL
WOODSIDE
BLACKHORSE LANE
CR0
ADDISCOMBE
CROYDON
EAST CROYDON
WEST CROYDON
WANDLE PARK
SANDILANDS
WHITGIFT PLAYING FIELDS
SHIRLEY PARK GOLF COURSE
LLOYD PARK
HOCKEY PITCH
COOMBE PARK
SPORTS GROUND
DUPPAS HILL
PARK HILL
220
95
96
97
98
99
100
101
102
103
104
33
34
35
66
67
68
69

BECKENHAM
ELMERS END
EDEN PARK
PARK LANGLEY
UPPER ELMERS END
MONKS ORCHARD
WEST WICKHAM
SHIRLEY
BROMLEY PARK
BETHLEM ROYAL HOSPITAL
BECKENHAM HOSPITAL
THE SLOANE HOSPITAL
LANGLEY PARK GOLF COURSE
SHORTLANDS GOLF COURSE
HARVINGTON PLAYING FIELD
CROYDON RD REC GROUND
HIGH BROOM WOOD
SPRING PARK
KELSEY PARK
BR2
BR3
BR4
CR0
183
204
221
DX
DY
DZ
EA
EB
EC
ED
36
37
38

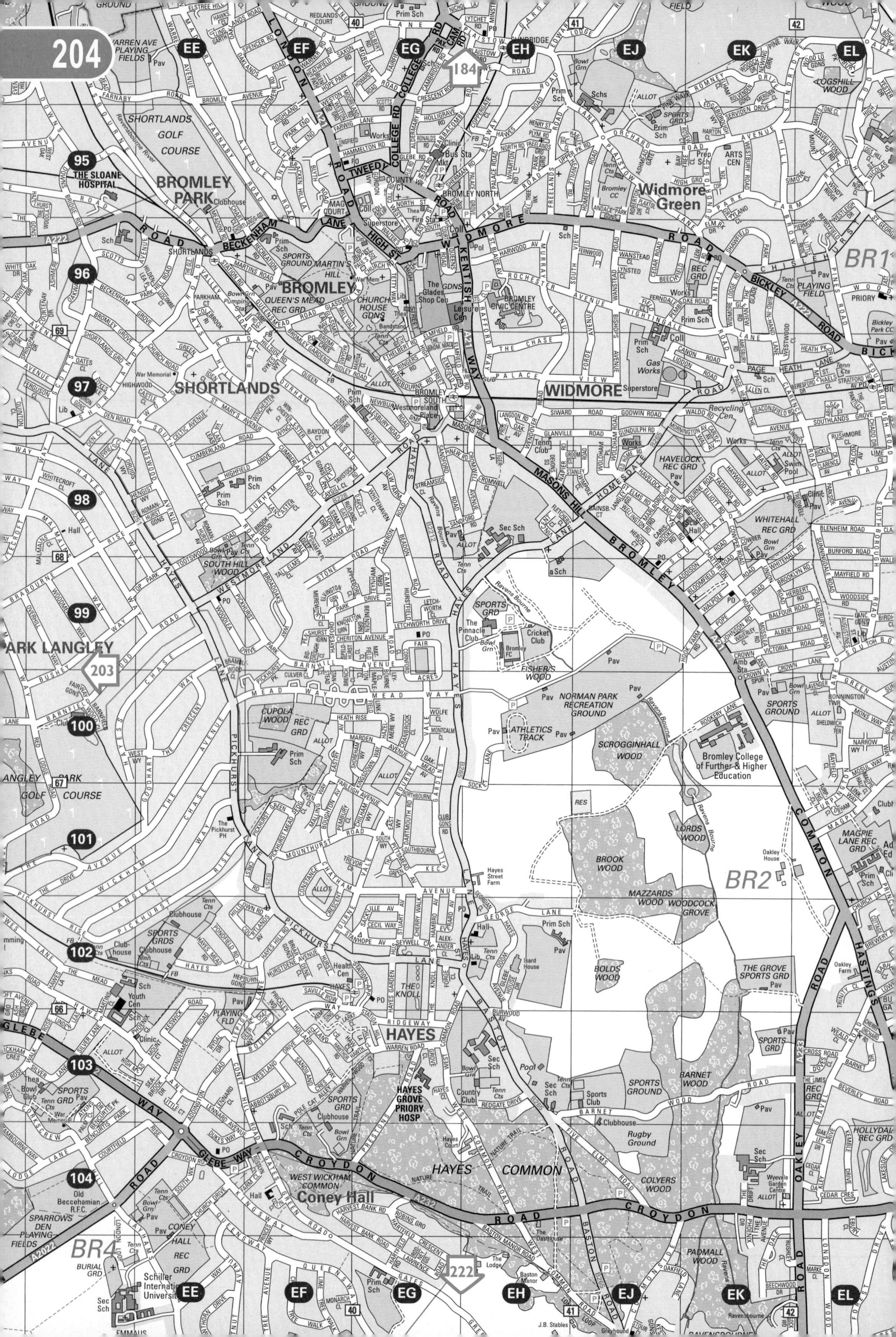
EE
EF
EG
EH
EJ
EK
EL
184
95
96
97
98
99
100
101
102
103
104
203
222
BROMLEY PARK
SHORTLANDS GOLF COURSE
THE SLOANE HOSPITAL
BROMLEY
SHORTLANDS
Widmore Green
WIDMORE
BR1
BR2
BR4
LOGSHILL WOOD
BROMLEY CIVIC CENTRE
QUEEN'S MEAD REC GRD
CHURCH HOUSE GDNS
MARTIN'S HILL
The Glades Shop Cen
HAVELOCK REC GRD
WHITEHALL REC GRD
SOUTH HILL WOOD
ARK LANGLEY
LANGLEY PARK GOLF COURSE
CUPOLA WOOD
NORMAN PARK RECREATION GROUND
ATHLETICS TRACK
SCROGGINHALL WOOD
Bromley College of Further & Higher Education
LORDS WOOD
BROOK WOOD
MAZZARDS WOOD
WOODCOCK GROVE
BOLDS WOOD
THE GROVE SPORTS GRD
BARNET WOOD
COLYERS WOOD
PADMALL WOOD
HAYES
HAYES COMMON
HAYES GROVE PRIORY HOSP
WEST WICKHAM COMMON
Coney Hall
CONEY HALL REC GRD
SPARROWS DEN PLAYING FIELDS
Schiller International University
HOLLYDALE REC GRD
MAGPIE LANE REC GRD
FISHER'S WOOD
The Pinnacle Club
Rugby Ground
Old Beccehamian R.F.C.
A21
A222
A232
A233
A2022
CROYDON ROAD
MASONS HILL
BROMLEY COMMON
OAKLEY ROAD
HASTINGS
WIDMORE ROAD
GLEBE WAY
HAYES LANE
PICKHURST LANE
WICKHAM WAY
WESTMORELAND ROAD
BECKENHAM ROAD

CAMDEN PARK
CHISLEHURST GOLF COURSE
CHISLEHURST COMMON
NATURE RESERVE
PARK WOOD
Scadbury Moated Manor House Site
Icehouse Wood
Holbrook Wood
The Larches
CHALKPIT WOOD
BANSOME WOOD
Marjorie McClure Sch
CHISLEHURST
BIRCH WOOD
GOSHILL WOOD
ST. PAUL'S CRAY COMMON
HOBLINGWELL WOOD
HOBLINGWELL WOOD REC GRD
ST. PAUL'S CRAY
BR7
HAWKWOOD ESTATE NT
POND WOOD
WALK WOOD
PETTS WOOD NT
Edlmann Memorial Wood
Willett Memorial Wood
BICKLEY
Bickley Junction
Chislehurst Junction
GREAT THRIFT
BLACKBROOK WOOD
Bickley Manor Hotel
Bromley High Sch
THORNET WOOD
JUBILEE COUNTRY PARK
Petts Wood Junction
PETTS WOOD
BR5
POVEREST
SOUTHBOROUGH OPEN SPACE
SOUTHBOROUGH
PARKFIELD
ST. LUKE'S CEM
RECREATION GROUND
BROMLEY GOLF COURSE
Bromley Common
Prince's Plain
PLAYING FIELD
SPARROW WOOD
SPARROW COMMON
ROUNDABOUT WOOD
CROFTON HEATH
PETTS WOOD REC GRD
COVET WOOD
POVEREST REC GRD
ORPINGTON
BR6
GUMPING COMMON
CLAY WOOD
NOBODY'S WOOD
KNOWLEHILL WOOD
POKERIDDEN WOOD
NEWSTEAD WOOD
DARRICK COMMON
FARNBOROUGH REC GRD
DARRICK WOOD
PRINCESS ROYAL UNI HOSP
ORPINGTON HOSPITAL
CROFTON ROAD
FARNBOROUGH ROAD
CHISLEHURST ROAD
ORPINGTON ROAD
ST. PAULS CRAY ROAD
BROMLEY LANE
SUMMER HILL
PERRY HALL ROAD
STATION ROAD
SPUR ROAD
EM EN EP EQ ER ES ET
185
206
223
43 44 45
67 68 69
95 96 97 98 99 100 101 102 103 104

NATURE RESERVE
EU
EV
EW
EX
EY
EZ
FA
186
EDGINGTON
Crittall's Corner
SIDCUP
BYPASS
A20
DA14
BROMLEY
OLD MAIDSTONE ROAD
Ruxley Manor Nursery
RUXLEY WOOD
Irish Plantation
WOOD
Scadbury Moated Manor House Site
Field-Study Centre
Youth Cen
Prim Sch
Sec Sch
SEVENOAKS
Ski Centre
Sports Club
RUXLEY PARK GOLF COURSE
DRIVING RANGE
Clubhouse
CRAY VALLEY GOLF COURSE
Barnfield Bank
Pilgrim Hill
CHAPMANS LANE
Simon's Field Shaw
Lower Hockenden Farm
Wycoomb
The Small House
PAULS CRAY HILL PARK
HIGHLANDS WOOD
BR5
Hogspring Cottages
Millewood
HOCKENDEN WOOD
HOCKENDEN LANE
95
96
97
98
99
100
101
102
103
104
HOBLINGWELL WOOD
HOBLINGWELL WOOD REC GRD
ST. PAUL'S CRAY
ST PAULS WOOD HILL
Gymnastic Cen
Lib
Clinic
Superstore
CRAYFIELD IND PARK
MURRAY BUSINESS CEN
SPRINGVALE RETAIL PARK
Gas Works
Superstores
CLARENDON
BR7
LEESONS HILL
KEVINGTON DRIVE
ST MARY CRAY
STAR LANE
CEM
BUS GARAGE
SANDWAY PK
NUGENT IND PARK
ST MARY CRAY
BLACKSMITHS LANE
THE WARREN
Sheepcote Farm
SHEEPCOTE LANE
Ringland Farm
CHILD'S WOOD
Shawcroft Sch
CROCKENHILL ROAD
B258
Blueberry Farm
Kevington Farm
Waldens Farm
Crouch Farm
POVEREST
205
POVEREST REC GRD
COVET
ST. MARY CRAY REC GRD
RIVERSIDE GDNS
Derry Downs
GRIGG'S CROSS
KYNASTON WOOD
COCKMANNINGS
Walden Manor
Depot
Heather's Holdings
Bleak House Farm
CRAY AVENUE
A224
PERRY HALL ROAD
A208
HIGH ST
COURT ROAD
PRIORY GARDENS
BROMLEY MUS
BURIAL GRD
GRASSMEADE RECREATION GROUND
ORPINGTON
RAMSDEN
Eastwood Farm
GRIFF'S WOOD
Walnuts Shop Cen
Mkt Leisure Cen
HOLLINGBOURNE TWR
BEKESBOURNE TWR
Piggery
ORPINGTON BYPASS
SPUR ROAD
A232
SAGE WENTS
Byways Nurseries
SKIBBS LANE
Crownwood Farm
BR6
Cookham Hill Farm
Cookham Farm
COOKHAM HILL
Goddington House
Goddington
GODDINGTON PARK
ROUNDS SMALLAMS
Bowling Green
LILLY'S WOOD
BLACK BUSH WOOD
CHELSFIELD LANE
Clubhouse
224
Tennis Courts
A223
ORPINGTON HOSPITAL
47
48
49
66
67
68
69

FB
FC
FD
FE
FF
FG
FH
50
51
52
187
Hextable
SPORTS GROUND
HEXTABLE GDNS
DARTFORD
SEVENOAKS
KENT
Swanley Village
95
96
Tweed Hill
SWANLEY PARK
Swanley New Barn Railway
Leisure Cen
Bowls Cen
THE WOODLANDS
White Oak Business Pk
Fire Sta
Superstore
Swanley Cen
SPORTS GROUND
Comm Cen
Sports Hall
SWANLEY
BUS DEPOT
REC GRD
MORETON IND EST
Olympic Golf Range
Broom Hill
Parkwood Hall Sch
97
98
69
68
Junction 3 (M25)
Junction 1 (M20)
99
208
TEARDROP IND EST
PEDHAM PLACE IND EST
Clubhouse
100
Pedham Place Farm
Fort Farningham (Site Of)
67
101
PEDHAM PLACE GOLF CENTRE
102
FOUNTAIN HOY
66
103
104
BIRCH WOOD
Windmill Hill Wood
BOURNE WOOD
Hook Spring
TILE KILNS WOOD
ALMA FC
BR8
SWANLEY BY-PASS
A20
M25
M20
Crockenhill
CACKETSHILL WOOD
HEATHFIELD SHAW
HORNCROSS SHAW
Hulberry
Hulberry Farm
River Darent
Lullingstone Roman Villa (Remains Of)
EYNSFORD
THE ROUGHET
ASHEN BANK
Skeet Hill
225
LULLINGSTONE PARK

FJ
FK
FL
FM
FN
FP
FQ
54
55
56
188
207
Malt House Farm
Gildenhill Place
SEVENOAKS
DARTFORD
Gildenhill Farm
CHURCH ROAD
Sutton at Hone
ST. JOHN'S JERUSALEM
DARENT VALLEY PATH
Swanley Village
Prim Sch
Works
Coldharbour Farm
SHIP LANE
SHIP STREET
SWANLEY VILLAGE ROAD
THE STABLES
Swanley Village Nursery
Lower Daltons Nursery
RES
HOMEFIELD FARM ROAD
FARNINGHAM ROAD
STATION ROAD
FARM ROAD
Homefield Farm
Works
The Bridges PH
Fire Sta
Clubho.
SPORTS GRD
Environm Ed Cen
ALLOTMENTS
DEVON ROAD
Tweed House
Tweed Hill
RAM'S WOOD
M25
BUTTON STREET
PARK LANE
Creswick Nurseries
DARTFORD ROAD
A225
Parkwood Hall Sch
Olympic Golf Range
Pavs
Bowls Club
Beechenley Nursery
Broom Hill
BR8
FARNINGHAM WOOD NATURE RESERVE
CALFSTOCK LANE
WESTMINSTER FIELD
Burial Grd
Prim Sch
Pav
BALANCING POND
The Bull PH
The Fighting Cocks PH
Oakview Stud Farm
MORETON IND EST
Junction 3 (M25)
Junction 1 (M20)
FRANKS
Franks Hall
THE FOLLY
Greenacres Nursery Group
Pav Cricket Ground
RAYS HILL
MUSSENDEN LANE
SAXON PLACE
Eglantine Farm
DA4
Hill Farm
Hill House
FARNINGHAM HILL ROAD
TEARDROP IND EST
LONDON ROAD
A20
M20
OLD DARTFORD RD
Clubhouse
GORSE HILL (MAIN ROAD)
Farningham
Mill House
PO
Hall
Pav
Cricket Ground
HORTON WAY
HIGH STREET
Pied Bull PH
EGLANTINE LANE
Charton Vale
Charton Manor
Charton Manor Farm
Pedham Place Farm
Fort Farningham (Site Of)
PEDHAM PLACE GOLF CENTRE
River Darent
Capricorn Farm
CROCKENHILL LANE
SPAREPENNY LANE
POLLY SHAW
FOUNTAIN HOY
Eynesford Hill
EYNSFORD ROAD
BEESFIELD LANE
Beesfield Farm
PRIORY LANE
Prim Sch
Hall
EYNSFORD CASTLE
Furlongs Farm
Eynsford Nursery
SPORTS GRD
Pav
Eynsford
War Memorial
DONKEY LANE
ALCHIN'S WOOD
FIREPOUND SHAW
OLIVERS SHAW
Gorse Hill Farm
Hulberry Farm
Pumping Sta
Home Farm
Ford
RIVERSIDE
ALLOT
SADDLERS PARK
POLLYHAUGH
Pollyhaugh Farm
STATION ROAD
LULLINGSTONE LANE
Lullingstone Roman Villa (Remains Of)
Newbarn Farm
Lullingstone Park Farm
EYNSFORD
ST. MARTINS DRIVE
EYNSFORD RISE
MAPLESCOMBE LANE
SANDHOLE SHAW
VINEYARD
95
96
97
98
99
100
101
102
103
104
69
68
67
66

South Darenth
Horton Kirby
Dean Bottom
Pinden
Mile End Green
Longfield
Hartley Green
New Ash Green
Fawkham Green
DA2
DA3
TN15
HORTON WOOD
GROVE WOOD
HOPKINS SPRING WOOD
HATCHFIELD WOOD
CHURCHDOWN WOOD
PENNIS WOOD
YEWFIELD SHAW
RYECROFTS WOOD
GABRIEL SPRING WOOD
CHOAKS WOOD
SAXTEN'S WOOD
SHETLEY SHAWS
FAWKHAM VALLEY GOLF COURSE
REDLIBBETS GOLF COURSE
FAWKHAM MANOR HOSPITAL
BRANDS HATCH MOTOR RACING
BRANDS HATCH KARTING
QUARRY
DARTFORD
SEVENOAKS
M20
189

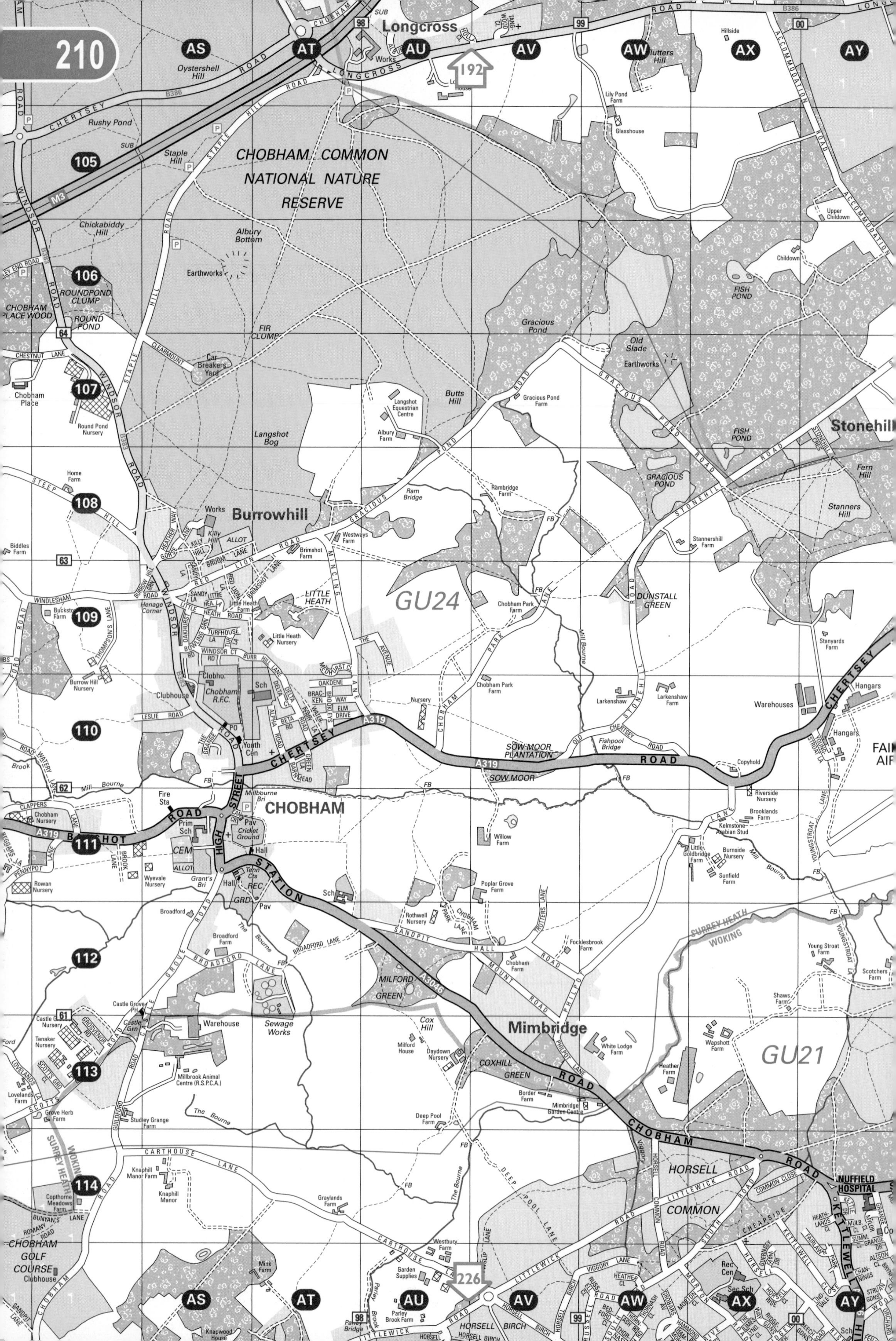
Longcross
CHOBHAM COMMON
NATIONAL NATURE
RESERVE
Oystershell Hill
Rushy Pond
Staple Hill
Chickabiddy Hill
Albury Bottom
Earthworks
ROUNDPOND CLUMP
ROUND POND
CHOBHAM PLACE WOOD
Chobham Place
Round Pond Nursery
FIR CLUMP
Car Breakers Yard
Langshot Bog
Langshot Equestrian Centre
Albury Farm
Butts Hill
Gracious Pond
Gracious Pond Farm
Old Slade
Earthworks
FISH POND
GRACIOUS POND
Stonehill
Fern Hill
Stanners Hill
Lily Pond Farm
Glasshouse
Hillside
Hutters Hill
Upper Childown
Childown
Home Farm
Burrowhill
Works
Ram Bridge
Rambridge Farm
Westways Farm
Brimshot Farm
LITTLE HEATH
Little Heath Farm
Little Heath Nursery
Biddles Farm
Buckstone Farm
Henage Corner
Burrow Hill Nursery
Clubhouse
Chobham R.F.C.
Youth Cen
GU24
Chobham Park Farm
Stannershill Farm
DUNSTALL GREEN
Stanyards Farm
Larkenshaw
Larkenshaw Farm
Warehouses
Hangars
Nursery
SOW MOOR PLANTATION
SOW MOOR
Fishpool Bridge
Copyhold
Riverside Nursery
Brooklands Farm
Kelmstone Arabian Stud
Little Goldbridge Farm
Burnside Nursery
Sunfield Farm
CHOBHAM
Millbourne Bri
Fire Sta
Chobham Nursery
Pav
Cricket Ground
Prim Sch
CEM
Wyevale Nursery
Rowan Nursery
Grant's Bri
Willow Farm
Poplar Grove Farm
Rothwell Nursery
Broadford
Broadford Farm
Chobham Farm
Focklesbrook Farm
Young Stroat Farm
Scotchers Farm
Shaws Farm
MILFORD GREEN
Castle Grove Nursery
Tenaker Nursery
Warehouse
Sewage Works
Cox Hill
Milford House
Daydown Nursery
Mimbridge
White Lodge Farm
Wapshott Farm
GU21
Heather Farm
COXHILL GREEN
Border Farm
Mimbridge Garden Centre
Millbrook Animal Centre (R.S.P.C.A.)
Lovelands Farm
Grove Herb Farm
Studley Grange Farm
Deep Pool Farm
Knaphill Manor Farm
Knaphill Manor
Copthorne Meadows Farm
Graylands Farm
HORSELL COMMON
NUFFIELD HOSPITAL
CHOBHAM GOLF COURSE
Clubhouse
Mink Farm
Westbury Farm
Garden Supplies
Parley Brook Farm
Parley Bridge
Knapwood House
HORSELL BIRCH
SURREY HEATH
WOKING
CHOBHAM ROAD
CHERTSEY ROAD
STATION ROAD
HIGH STREET
BAGSHOT ROAD
WINDSOR ROAD
STAPLE HILL
GRACIOUS POND ROAD
LONGCROSS ROAD
CARTHOUSE LANE
LITTLEWICK ROAD
A319
A3046
B386
B383
M3
192
226
AS
AT
AU
AV
AW
AX
AY
98
99
00
105
106
107
108
109
110
111
112
113
114
64
63
62
61

OTTERSHAW
ROW TOWN
WOODHAM
SHEERWATER
Pyrford
KT16
KT15
KT14
GU22
Junction 11
OTTERSHAW PARK
HORSELL COMMON
NEW ZEALAND GOLF COURSE
WEST BYFLEET GOLF COURSE
GREAT WOOD
BIRCH WOOD
HOYT WOOD
BROX COPSE
THE COMMON
ST. PETER'S HOSP
HOMEWOOD PARK
Foxhills Country Club
GOLF COURSE
MOOR GOLF COURSE
193
212
227

212
BG
BH
BJ
BK
BL
BM
BN
194
211
228
Junction 11
105
106
107
108
109
110
111
112
113
114
MOOR GOLF COURSE
ADDLESTONE
WEYBRIDGE TRADING ESTATE
WEYBRIDGE BUSINESS PARK
KT15
ROW TOWN
NEW HAW
SAYES COURT PUBLIC OPEN SPACE
SURREY GOLF AND FITNESS
CENTRAL VETERINARY LABORATORY
BROOKLANDS
BROOKLANDS MUSEUM
Brooklands College
BROOKLANDS BUSINESS PARK
AIRFIELD (DISUSED)
BROOKLANDS INDUSTRIAL PARK
Karting Centre
Paddocks Retail Pk
WOODHAM
HEATHERVALE REC GRD
CAMPHILL INDUSTRIAL ESTATE
BASINGSTOKE CANAL
DARTNELL PARK
KT14
WEST BYFLEET
BROADOAKS GOVERNMENT OFFICES
BYFLEET
GU22
GU23
COMMON MEADOWS
River Wey
Pyrford
THE ISLAND

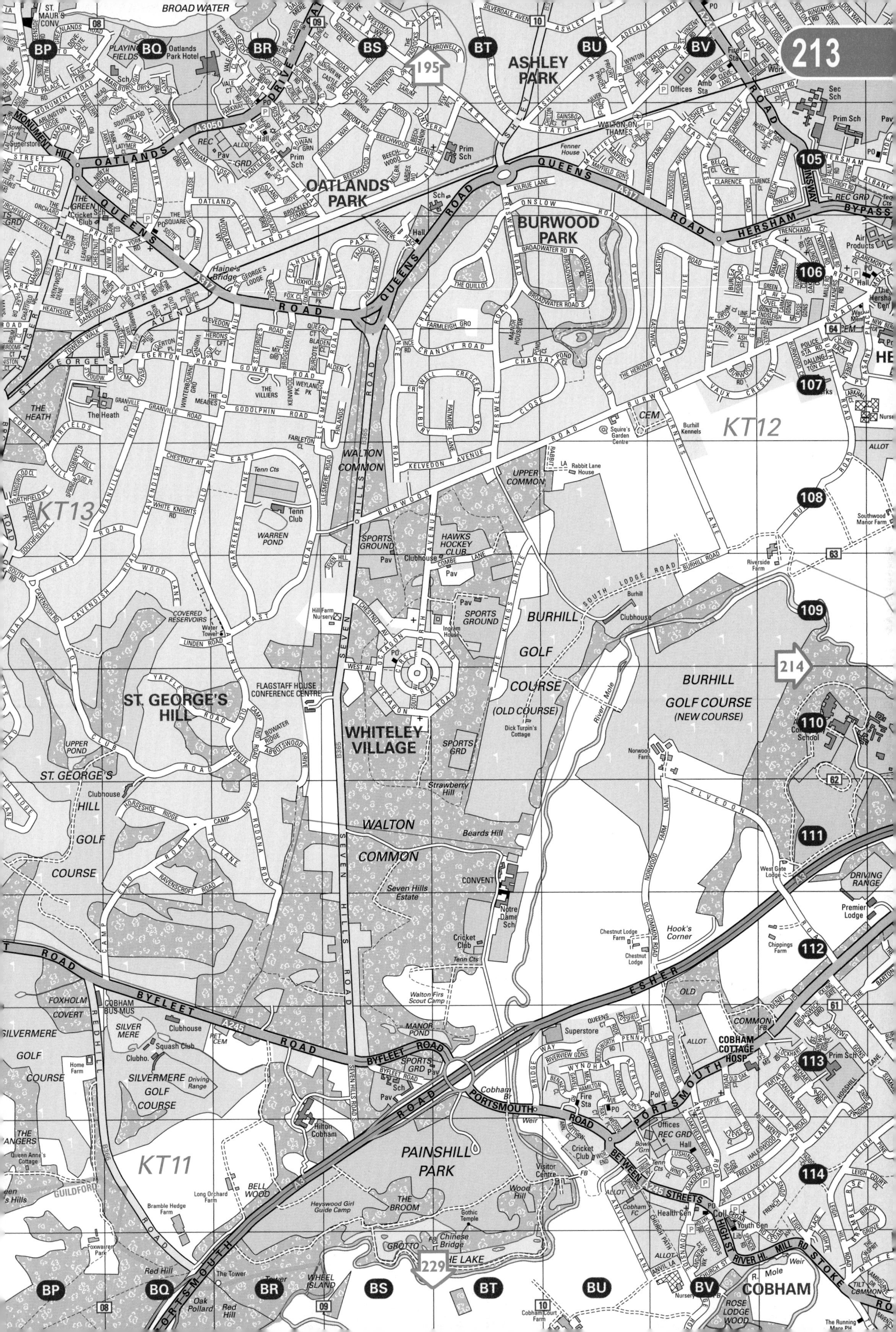
195
ASHLEY PARK
OATLANDS PARK
BURWOOD PARK
KT12
KT13
WALTON COMMON
UPPER COMMON
BURHILL GOLF COURSE
(OLD COURSE)
BURHILL GOLF COURSE
(NEW COURSE)
214
ST. GEORGE'S HILL
WHITELEY VILLAGE
ST. GEORGE'S HILL GOLF COURSE
SILVERMERE GOLF COURSE
PAINSHILL PARK
KT11
COBHAM
229

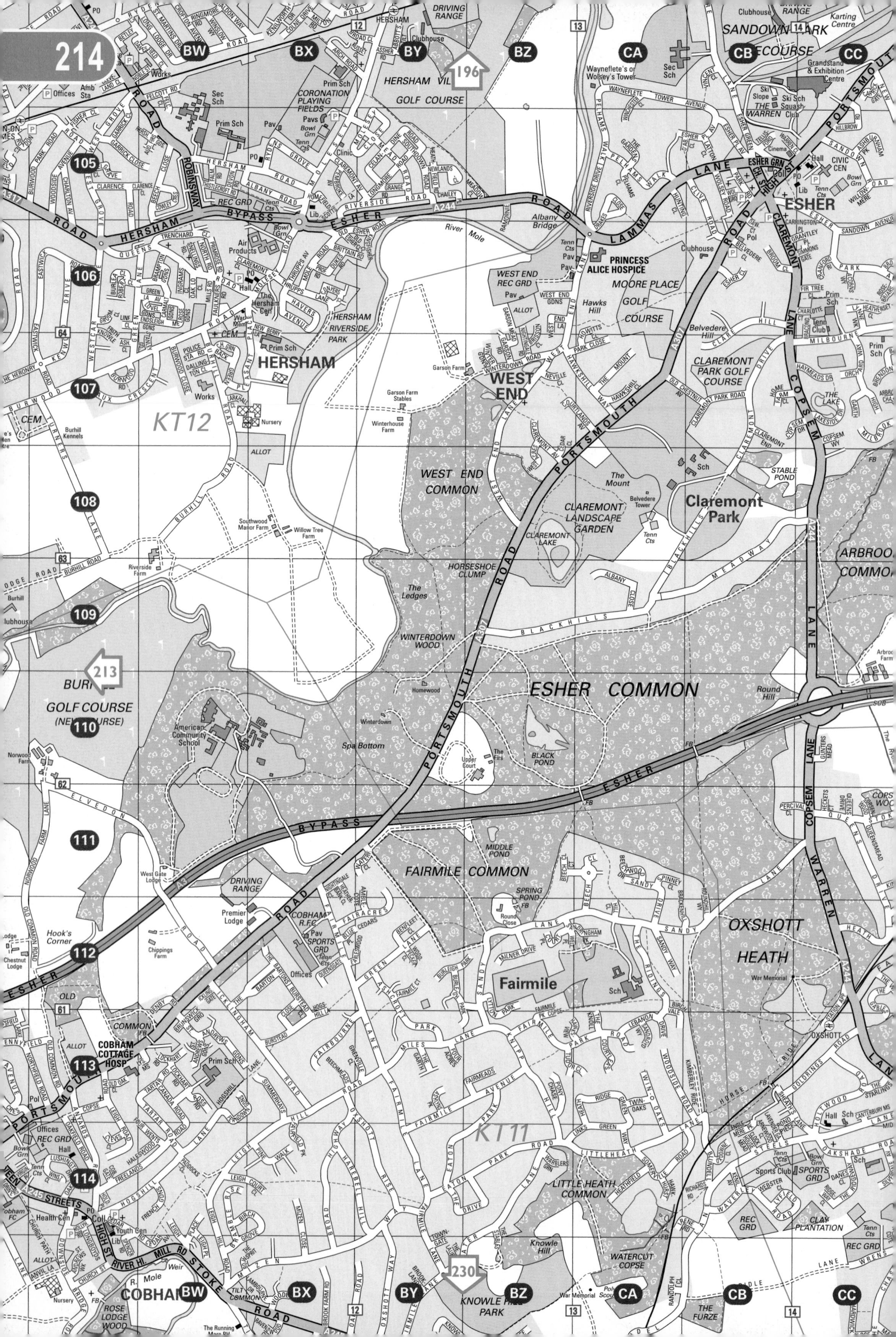
BW
BX
BY
BZ
CA
CB
CC
HERSHAM
WEST END
ESHER
ESHER COMMON
WEST END COMMON
FAIRMILE COMMON
OXSHOTT HEATH
Fairmile
Claremont Park
CLAREMONT LANDSCAPE GARDEN
SANDOWN PARK RACECOURSE
HERSHAM VILLAGE GOLF COURSE
MOORE PLACE GOLF COURSE
CLAREMONT PARK GOLF COURSE
BURHILL GOLF COURSE (NEW COURSE)
HERSHAM RIVERSIDE PARK
LITTLE HEATH COMMON
KNOWLE HILL PARK
KT12
KT11
COBHAM
OXSHOTT
PRINCESS ALICE HOSPICE
ESHER BYPASS
PORTSMOUTH ROAD
196
213
230

LITTLEWORTH COMMON
HINCHLEY WOOD
CLAYGATE
KT10
SURBITON GOLF COURSE
HOOK
CHESSINGTON
CHESSINGTON GOLF CENTRE
KT9
CHESSINGTON WORLD OF ADVENTURE
KT22
PRINCE'S COVERTS
OXSHOTT
Malden Rushett
KT21
THE FOREST
LEATHERHEAD GOLF COURSE

197
216
231

KINGSTON BYPASS
HOOK
CHESSINGTON
CHESSINGTON NORTH
CHESSINGTON SOUTH
KT9
KT19
KT18
KT21
HORTON PARK COUNTRY CLUB GOLF COURSE
HORTON COUNTRY PARK
HORTON
HOGSMILL RIVERSIDE OPEN SPACE
WEST EWELL
ST. EBBA'S HOSPITAL
EPSOM & EWELL NEW COTTAGE HOSP
WEST PARK HOSPITAL
EPSOM COMMON
EPSOM
CHESSINGTON GOLF CENTRE
BARWELL BUSINESS PARK
CHESSINGTON WOOD
FOUR ACRE WOOD
POND WOOD
GREAT WOOD
BUTCHERS GROVE
Castle Hill
GREAT POND
STEW POND
NEWTON WOOD
FOREST
KING GEORGE'S TRADING EST
HOOK RISE SOUTH IND PK
OLD HALEYBURIANS R.F.C.
KING GEORGE V REC GRD
NONSUCH INDUSTRIAL ESTATE
LONGMEAD BUSINESS PARK
COURT REC GRD
THE GREENWAY
SPA DRIVE
EPSOM GENERAL HOSP
WOODCOTE GREEN
UPPER HIGH STREET
The Quadrant
HIGH ST
SOUTH STREET
ASHLEY AV
ROSEBERY PARK
CHESSINGTON ROAD
HOOK ROAD
LEATHERHEAD ROAD
CHRIST CHURCH ROAD
HORTON LANE
LONG GROVE ROAD
RUXLEY LANE
COX LANE
CL CM CN CP CQ CR CS
198
215
232
105 106 107 108 109 110 111 112 113 114
19 20 21 61 62 63 64

CT
CU
CV
CW
CX
CY
CZ
199
NORTH CHEAM
KT4
CUDDINGTON REC GRD
STONELEIGH
SM1
COLLINGWOOD PARK
WEST SUTTON
SM3
CHEAM REC GRD
NONSUCH PARK
Nonsuch Mansion House
OAK PLANTATION
THE WOOD
Diana's Dyke
CHEAM PARK
CHEAM
Cuddington Church (Site of)
PLAYING FIELDS
Hatch Furlong
EWELL
EWELL BYPASS
EAST EWELL
SM2
OVERTON PARK REC GRD
218
SPORTS GROUND
KT17
CUDDINGTON GOLF COURSE
BANSTEAD DOWNS
GOLF COURSE
SM7
NORTH LOOE
SURREY
EPSOM & EWELL
SUTTON
REIGATE & BANSTEAD
ALEXANDRA REC GRD
Epsom College
EPSOM DOWNS
NORK
233
RIFLE RANGE
BANSTEAD
LONDON ROAD
REIGATE ROAD
CHEAM ROAD
EWELL ROAD
BRIGHTON ROAD
FIR TREE ROAD
COLLEGE ROAD
BELMONT RISE
ST. DUNSTAN'S HILL
A24
A232
A217
A240
A2022
A2043
105
106
107
108
109
110
111
112
113
114
22
23
24

SM1
COLLINGWOOD PARK
CARSHALTON
THE WRYTHE REC GRD
ROYSTON PARK
WILDERNESS ISLAND
THE GROVE
CARSHALTON PARK
CARSHALTON WAR MEMORIAL HOSP
SUTTON
SPORTS GRD
REC GRD
MANOR PARK
CARSHALTON BEECHES
OVERTON PARK REC GRD
SM2
SM5
WELLFIELD PLANTATION
PLAYING FIELD
SUTTON HOSPITAL
ROYAL MARSDEN HOSP
BELMONT
LITTLE WOODCOTE
OAKS SPORTS CENTRE GOLF COURSE
THE OAKS PARK
BANSTEAD DOWNS
BANSTEAD COMMON
GOLF COURSE
DOWNVIEW PRISON
HIGHDOWN PRISON
RIFLE RANGE
SPORTS GROUND
RIFFET WOOD
BIG WOOD
WOODMANSTERNE PARK RECREATION GROUND
CLOCKHOUSE REC GRD
SM7
WOODMANSTERNE
CARSHALTON ROAD
BRIGHTON ROAD
BELMONT RISE
WOODMANSTERNE ROAD
WOODMANSTERNE LANE
CROYDON ROAD
WINKWORTH ROAD
BANSTEAD ROAD
SUTTON LANE
DA
DB
DC
DD
DE
DF
DG
200
217
234
105
106
107
108
109
110
111
112
113
114

BEDDINGTON
PARK
WALLINGTON
SOUTH BEDDINGTON
BANDON HILL CEMETERY
MELLOWS PARK
ROUNDSHAW PLAYING FIELD
ROUNDSHAW OPEN SPACE
PURLEY WAY PLAYING FIELDS
DUPPAS HILL
SOUTH CROYDON
HALING PARK
WOODCOTE
PURLEY
WOODCOTE GROVE REC GRD
WOODCOTE PARK GOLF COURSE
FOXLEY WOOD
HIGHER DRIVE REC GRD
RIDDLESDOWN WOOD
KENLEY
SMITHAM
REEDHAM
CR0
CR2
CR5
CR8
SM6
CROYDON ROAD
PURLEY WAY
BRIGHTON ROAD
STAFFORD ROAD
WOODCOTE ROAD
FOXLEY LANE
LITTLE WOODCOTE LANE
SMITHAM BOTTOM LANE
GODSTONE ROAD
DOWNS COURT ROAD
DUPPAS HILL RD
WADDON WAY
MOLLISON DRIVE
PLOUGH LANE
BANSTEAD RD
A23
A232
A237
A235
A2022
A22
DH
DJ
DK
DL
DM
DN
DP
105
106
107
108
109
110
111
112
113
114
201
220
235

220
DQ
DR
DS
DT
DU
DV
DW
202
219
236
SOUTH CROYDON
CR0
CR2
CR8
SANDERSTEAD
SELSDON PARK HOTEL GOLF COURSE
CROHAM HURST
CROHAM HURST GOLF COURSE
PURLEY DOWNS GOLF COURSE
PURLEY BEECHES
ADDINGTON HILLS
LLOYD PARK
COOMBE PARK
COOMBE LODGE PLAYING FIELDS
COOMBE WOOD
BALLARDS PLANTATION
LITTLEHEATH WOODS
BRAMLEY BANK NATURE RESERVE
SANDERSTEAD PLANTATION
KINGS WOOD
MITCHLEY WOOD
RIDDLESDOWN WOOD
COOMBES WOOD
RAGGED WOOD
AINSLEY BERRY SHAW
NEWLANDS WOOD
FOXLEY WOOD
DUPPAS HILL
HALING GROVE
PURLEY WAY PLAYING FIELDS
SHIRLEY PARK GOLF COURSE
WHITGIFT PLAYING FIELDS
COOMBE ROAD
BRIGHTON ROAD
ADDINGTON ROAD
GODSTONE ROAD
MITCHLEY AVENUE
RECTORY PARK
DOWNS COURT ROAD
CROHAM VALLEY ROAD
UPPER SELSDON ROAD
LIMPSFIELD ROAD
105
106
107
108
109
110
111
112
113
114

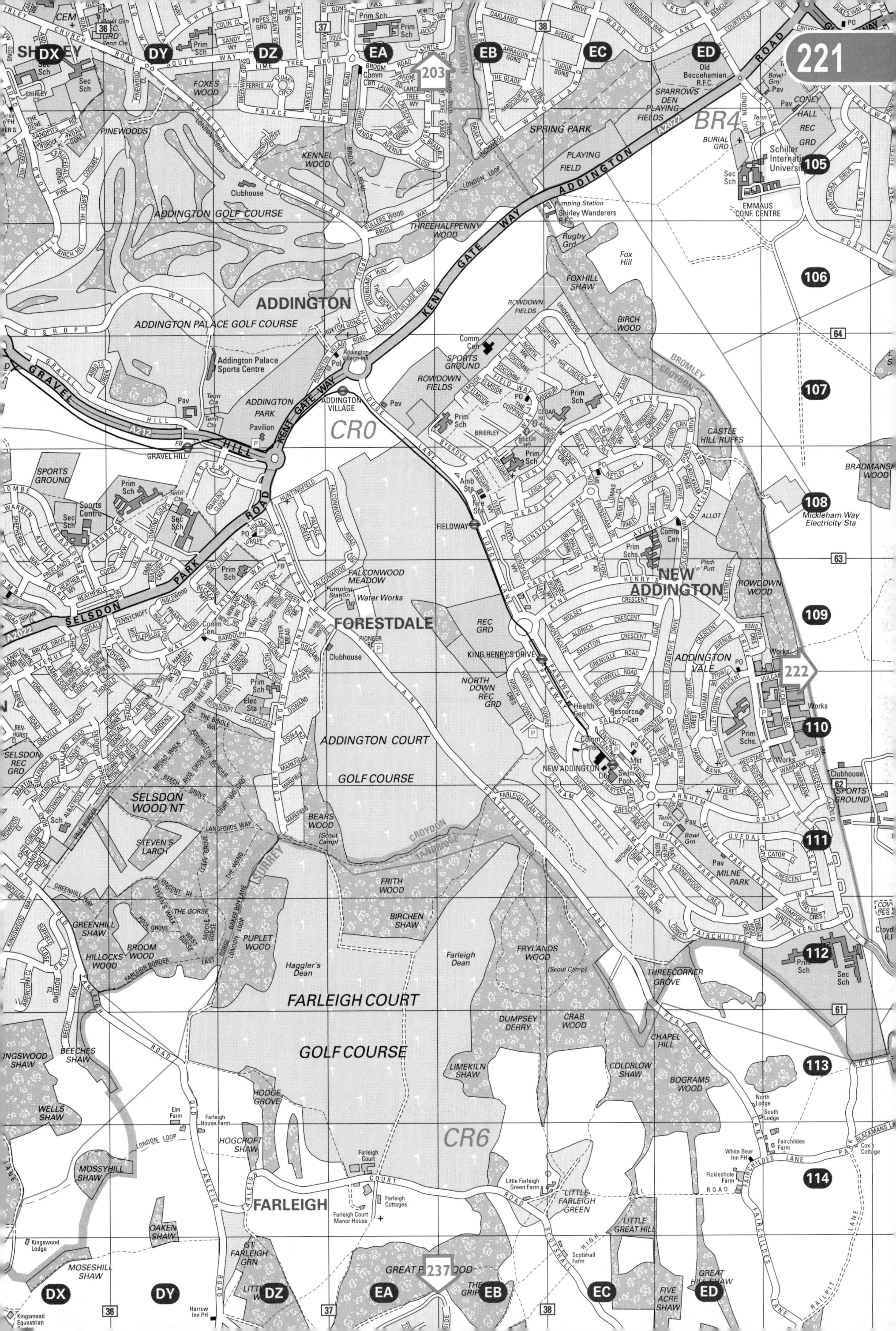
221
DX
DY
DZ
EA
EB
EC
ED
203
SHIRLEY
Prim Sch
Sec Sch
FOXES WOOD
PINEWOODS
KENNEL WOOD
SPRING PARK
PLAYING FIELD
SPARROWS DEN PLAYING FIELDS
Old Beccehamian R.F.C.
BR4
CONEY HALL REC GRD
BURIAL GRD
Schiller International University
EMMAUS CONF. CENTRE
105
Clubhouse
ADDINGTON GOLF COURSE
THREEHALFPENNY WOOD
Pumping Station
Shirley Wanderers R.F.C.
Rugby Grd
Fox Hill
106
FOXHILL SHAW
ADDINGTON
ADDINGTON PALACE GOLF COURSE
BIRCH WOOD
ROWDOWN FIELDS
SPORTS GROUND
Addington Palace Sports Centre
Addington Village Inn
Pol
ADDINGTON VILLAGE
ADDINGTON PARK
Pavilion
CR0
107
CASTLE HILL RUFFS
GRAVEL HILL
A212
A2022
BRADMANS WOOD
SPORTS GROUND
Sports Centre
Amb Sta
Fire Sta
FIELDWAY
108
Mickleham Way Electricity Sta
ALLOT
NEW ADDINGTON
ROWDOWN WOOD
FALCONWOOD MEADOW
Pumping Station
Water Works
FORESTDALE
REC GRD
109
ADDINGTON VALE
KING HENRY'S DRIVE
NORTH DOWN REC GRD
Health Cen
Resource Cen
222
Works
110
Prim Schs.
ADDINGTON COURT GOLF COURSE
NEW ADDINGTON
Swim Pool
Mkt
SELSDON REC GRD
SELSDON WOOD NT
STEVEN'S LARCH
BEARS WOOD
(Scout Camp)
Clubhouse
SPORTS GROUND
MILNE PARK
111
FRITH WOOD
BIRCHEN SHAW
GREENHILL SHAW
BROOM WOOD
HILLOCKS WOOD
PUPLET WOOD
Haggler's Dean
Farleigh Dean
FRYLANDS WOOD
(Scout Camp)
THREECORNER GROVE
112
FARLEIGH COURT GOLF COURSE
DUMPSEY DERRY
CRAB WOOD
CHAPEL HILL
113
BEECHES SHAW
LIMEKILN SHAW
COLDBLOW SHAW
BOGRAMS WOOD
WELLS SHAW
HODGE GROVE
Elm Farm
Farleigh House Farm
HOGCROFT SHAW
CR6
North Lodge
South Lodge
Fairchildes Farm
White Bear Inn PH
Fickleshole Farm
Cox's Cottage
114
MOSSYHILL SHAW
Farleigh Court
FARLEIGH
Farleigh Cottages
Farleigh Court Manor House
Little Farleigh Green Farm
LITTLE FARLEIGH GREEN
LITTLE GREAT HILL
OAKEN SHAW
Kingswood Lodge
GT FARLEIGH GRN
MOSESHILL SHAW
237
Scotshall Farm
FIVE ACRE SHAW
Harrow Inn PH
36
37
38
61
62
63
64

EE
EF
EG
EH
EJ
EK
EL
204
221
238
BR4
BR2
CR6
TN16
105
106
107
108
109
110
111
112
113
114
64
63
62
61
40
41
42
GLEBE WAY
CROYDON ROAD
Coney Hall
WICKHAM COMMON
HAYES COMMON
Rugby Ground
COLYERS WOOD
Sec Sch
OAKLEY ROAD
SPARROWS DEN PLAYING FIELDS
A2022
BURIAL GRD
Schiller International University
EMMAUS CONF. CENTRE
CONEY HALL REC GRD
KINGSWAY
QUEENSWAY
GATES GREEN ROAD
Prim Sch
HARVEST BANK RD
BASTON MANOR ROAD
Baston Manor
The Lodge
Hast Hill
PADMALL WOOD
RAVENSBOURNE OPEN SPACE
Ravensbourne
FOREST DRIVE
KESTON COMMON
SOUTH PARK
Keston
The Fox PH
Greyhound PH
J.B. Stables
WELL WOOD
Rouse Farm
NASH LANE
LONG SHAW
COOPER'S WOOD
North Pole Farm
NORTH POLE LANE
Elm Farm Cottage
Fortune Bank Farm
Nash Farm
Longfield Farm & Cottage
FULLER'S WOOD
JAMES'S WOOD
Graylings Farm
ALLOT
JACKASS SHAW
LEAFY GROVE
Foxhill Farm
War Mem
WESTERHAM ROAD
A233
Cricket Ground
Caesar's Camp
Holwood
Redwood
Seismograph Services Co H.Q.
Earthworks
Tenn Cts
Scout Camp
LONDON LOOP
War Bank
Keston Court Poultry Farm
Milchden
CHURCH ROAD
Glebe Farm
ORCHARD PLACE
BLACKNESS LANE
DOWNE ROAD
Leaves Green
Kimberley Farm
Gas Works
The Vale Farm
Crown Inn PH
LEAVES GREEN ROAD
Bradmore
High House Farm
ASHMORE LANE
Colinette Farm
Greenacres Riding School
Milking Lane Farm
MILKING LANE
The Kings Arms PH
Clubhouse
TERMINAL
HELIPAD
LONDON BIGGIN HILL AIRPORT
Hangars
SOW WOOD
CUDHAM LODGE WOODS
AIRPORT INDUSTRIAL ESTATE
BIGGIN HILL BUSINESS PARK
Hangar
MAIN ROAD
REC GRD
SUNNINGVALE
VICTORIA
OAKLANDS LANE
SALT BOX HILL
CROWN ASH
JEWELS HILL
JEWELS WOOD
SHEEPBARN LANE
Higham's Hill
Highams Hill Farm
HOPPERSNATCH SHAW
FURZE BOTTOM
Racing Circuit
Layham's Farm
LAYHAMS ROAD
Metropolitan Police Dog Training School
RUSHFIELD SHAW
BROOMFIELDBANK SHAW
BRADMANSHILL WOOD
Five Oaks Stables
Layham's Cattery
Stables
Mickleham Way Electricity Sta
CASTLE HILL RUFFS
NEW ADDINGTON
ROWDOWN WOOD
ADDINGTON VALE
VULCAN WAY
Works
Prim Schs.
SPORTS GROUND
Clubhouse
Holmshaw Farm
Greyhound Training Kennels
Croydon R.F.C.
MILNE PARK
FAIRCHILDES AVENUE
Prim Sch
Sec Sch
THREECORNER GROVE
CHAPEL HILL
BOGRAMS WOOD
North Lodge
South Lodge
Fairchildes Farm
White Bear Inn PH
FAIRCHILDES LANE
Cox's Cottage
Blackman's Cottages
BLACKMANS LANE
TANDRIDGE
SURREY
BROMLEY
SKID HILL
Skid Hill House
GREAT HILL SHAW
FIVE ACRE SHAW

FARNBOROUGH
Green Street Green
Downe
Hazelwood
Single Street
BR6
TN14
PRINCESS ROYAL UNI HOSP
ORPINGTON HOSPITAL
HIGH ELMS GOLF COURSE
HIGH ELMS COUNTRY PARK
DOWN HO-DARWIN MUSEUM
WEST KENT GOLF COURSE
FARNBOROUGH COMMON
SEVENOAKS ROAD
SEVENOAKS WAY
NEW YEARS WOOD
CUCKOO WOOD
WHITELANDS WOOD

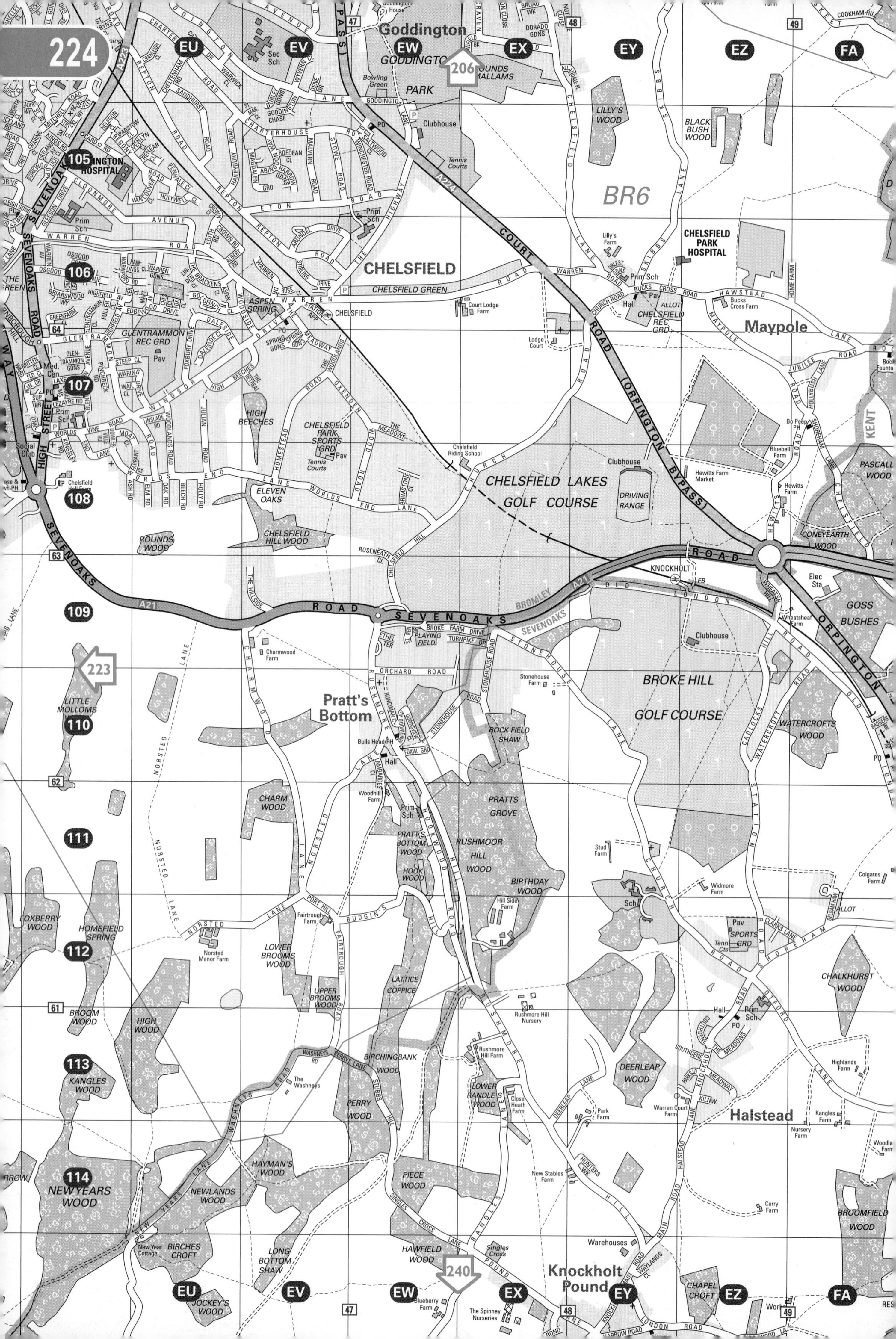
EU
EV
EW
EX
EY
EZ
FA
47
48
49
206
223
240
Goddington
GODDINGTON
PARK
Bowling Green
Clubhouse
Tennis Courts
POUNDS MALLAMS
LILLY'S WOOD
BLACK BUSH WOOD
BR6
Lilly's Farm
CHELSFIELD PARK HOSPITAL
Prim Sch
Sec Sch
CHELSFIELD
CHELSFIELD GREEN
Court Lodge Farm
Lodge Court
Hall
Pav
CHELSFIELD REC GRD
Bucks Cross Farm
Maypole
HAWSTEAD
MAYPOLE
JUBILEE
HOLLYBUSH LANE
Bo Peep PH
Bluebell Farm
Hewitts Farm Market
Hewitts Farm
KENT
PASCALL WOOD
CONEYEARTH WOOD
Elec Sta
GOSS BUSHES
Wheatsheaf Farm
WATERCROFTS WOOD
COURT ROAD
(ORPINGTON BYPASS)
A224
A223
A21
SEVENOAKS ROAD
ORPINGTON
KNOCKHOLT
FB
OLD LONDON ROAD
WARREN ROAD
CHURCH ROAD
BUCKS CROSS ROAD
SKIBBS LANE
CHELSFIELD LANE
CHELSFIELD HILL
CHURCH HILL
105
106
107
108
109
110
111
112
113
114
64
63
62
61
ORPINGTON HOSPITAL
HIGH STREET
SEVENOAKS
Med Cen
Social Club
Chelsfield Hill Farm
GLENTRAMMON REC GRD
WINDSOR DRIVE
HIGH BEECHES
CHELSFIELD PARK SPORTS GRD
Tennis Courts
THE MEADOWS
Chelsfield Riding School
Clubhouse
CHELSFIELD LAKES GOLF COURSE
DRIVING RANGE
ELEVEN OAKS
WORLDS END LANE
BRIMSTONE CL
CHELSFIELD HILL WOOD
ROUNDS WOOD
ROSENEATH CL
THE HILLSIDE
BROMLEY
SEVENOAKS
Charmwood Farm
ORCHARD ROAD
PLAYING FIELD
BROKE FARM DRIVE
TURNPIKE DR
STONEHOUSE ROAD
Stonehouse Farm
Clubhouse
BROKE HILL
GOLF COURSE
LITTLE MOLLOMS
Pratt's Bottom
Bulls Head PH
Hall
ROCK FIELD SHAW
CHARM WOOD
Woodhill Farm
PRATTS GROVE
RUSHMOOR HILL WOOD
PRATT'S BOTTOM WOOD
HOOK WOOD
BIRTHDAY WOOD
Hill Side Farm
HOOKWOOD ROAD
NORSTED LANE
CHARMWOOD LANE
Stud Farm
Widmore Farm
Sch
Colgates Farm
ALLOT
Pav
SPORTS GRD
Tenn Cts
FOXBERRY WOOD
HOMEFIELD SPRING
Fairtrough Farm
PORT HILL
BUDGIN'S HILL
Norsted Manor Farm
LOWER BROOMS WOOD
UPPER BROOMS WOOD
LATTICE COPPICE
FAIRTROUGH ROAD
SHOREHAM ROAD
CHALKHURST WOOD
BROOM WOOD
HIGH WOOD
Rushmore Hill Nursery
Rushmore Hill Farm
RUSHMORE HILL
Hall
Prim Sch
PO
THE MEADOWS
OTFORD LANE
Highlands Farm
KANGLES WOOD
WASHNEYS ROAD
PERRYS LANE
The Washneys
BIRCHINGBANK WOOD
PERRY WOOD
STUBBS HILL
LOWER RANDLE'S WOOD
Close Heath Farm
DEERLEAP WOOD
DEERLEAP LANE
Park Farm
Warren Court Farm
Halstead
Kangles Farm
Nursery Farm
HAYMAN'S WOOD
NEW YEARS WOOD
NEWLANDS WOOD
NEW YEARS LANE
PIECE WOOD
New Stables Farm
HUNTERS WK
HALSTEAD ROAD
Curry Farm
BROOMFIELD WOOD
New Year Cottage
BIRCHES CROFT
LONG BOTTOM SHAW
HAWFIELD WOOD
SINGLES CROSS LANE
RANDLES LANE
Singles Cross
Warehouses
Knockholt Pound
MAIN ROAD
CHAPEL CROFT
JOCKEY'S WOOD
Blueberry Farm
The Spinney Nurseries
LONDON ROAD

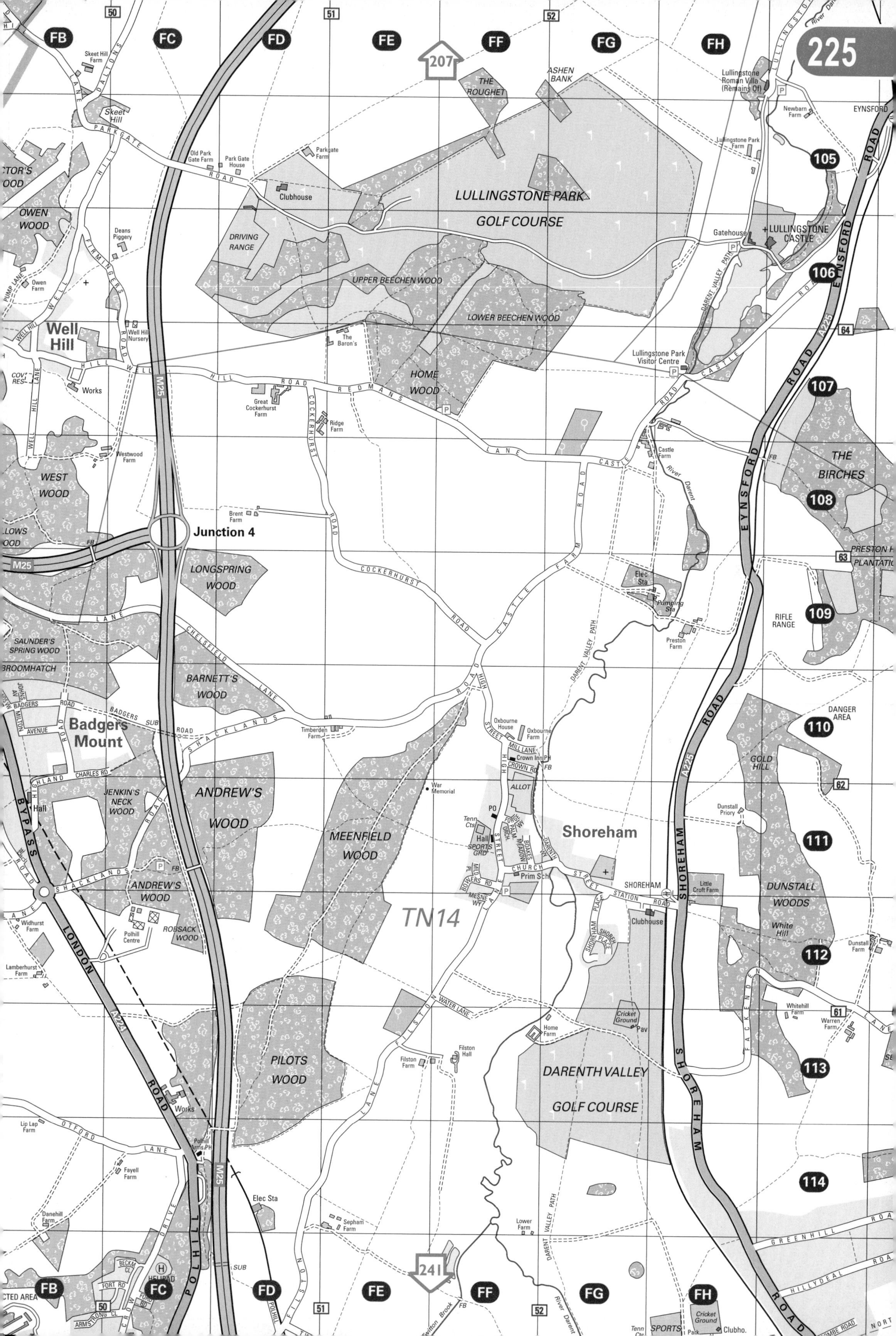

207
241
LULLINGSTONE PARK
GOLF COURSE
Clubhouse
DRIVING RANGE
UPPER BEECHEN WOOD
LOWER BEECHEN WOOD
HOME WOOD
THE ROUGHET
ASHEN BANK
Lullingstone Roman Villa (Remains Of)
LULLINGSTONE CASTLE
Gatehouse
Lullingstone Park Visitor Centre
Lullingstone Park Farm
Newbarn Farm
EYNSFORD
Well Hill
Skeet Hill
Skeet Hill Farm
Parkgate Farm
Old Park Gate Farm
Park Gate House
Deans Piggery
Owen Farm
OWEN WOOD
Well Hill Nursery
The Baron's
Great Cockerhurst Farm
Ridge Farm
Works
Westwood Farm
WEST WOOD
Brent Farm
Junction 4
LONGSPRING WOOD
Castle Farm
THE BIRCHES
Elec Sta
Pumping Sta
Preston Farm
RIFLE RANGE
SAUNDER'S SPRING WOOD
BROOMHATCH
BARNETT'S WOOD
Badgers Mount
Timberden Farm
Oxbourne House
Oxbourne Farm
Crown Inn PH
ALLOT
War Memorial
Shoreham
Prim Sch
SHOREHAM
Clubhouse
Little Croft Farm
DANGER AREA
GOLD HILL
Dunstall Priory
DUNSTALL WOODS
White Hill
Dunstall Farm
JENKIN'S NECK WOOD
ANDREW'S WOOD
MEENFIELD WOOD
TN14
Widhurst Farm
Polhill Centre
ROBSACK WOOD
Lamberhurst Farm
Cricket Ground
Home Farm
Whitehill Farm
Warren Farm
Filston Farm
Filston Hall
PILOTS WOOD
DARENTH VALLEY
GOLF COURSE
Works
Lip Lap Farm
Polhill Arms PH
Fayell Farm
Elec Sta
Danehill Farm
Sepham Farm
Lower Farm
HELIPAD
Cricket Ground
Clubho.
M25
A225
A224
LONDON ROAD
SHOREHAM ROAD
EYNSFORD ROAD
POLHILL
FILSTON LANE
WATER LANE
HIGH STREET
CHURCH STREET
STATION ROAD
CASTLE ROAD
REDMANS LANE
COCKERHURST ROAD
CASTLE FARM ROAD
CHELSFIELD LANE
SHACKLANDS ROAD
BADGERS ROAD
OTFORD LANE
GREENHILL ROAD
HILLYDEAL ROAD
DARENT VALLEY PATH
River Darent
PARKGATE ROAD
WELL HILL
FB
FC
FD
FE
FF
FG
FH
50
51
52
61
62
63
64
105
106
107
108
109
110
111
112
113
114

AS
AT
AU
AV
AW
AX
AY
210
242
98
99
00
GU21
GU24
GU3
CHOBHAM GOLF COURSE
HORSELL COMMON
LITTLEWICK COMMON
GOLDSWORTH PARK REC GRD
GOLDSWORTH PARK TRADING ESTATE
TRACIOUS COPSE
Goldsworth Park
Horsell
Knaphill
WATERERS PARK
St. John's
Mount Hermon
Hook Heath
WOKING CEMETERY
WOKING GOLF COURSE
WEST HILL GOLF COURSE
WORPLESDON GOLF COURSE
Fisher's Hill
SMART'S HEATH
PREY HEATH
Mayford
HOE VALLEY LINEAR PARK
SUTTON GREEN GOLF COURSE
BRIDLEY COPSE
WHITMOOR
WORPLESDON
Burdenshot Hill
Pye Hill
Beech Hill
Crematorium
LOCKFIELD DRIVE
A324
A320
A3046
BASINGSTOKE CANAL
CARTHOUSE LANE
LITTLEWICK ROAD
HERMITAGE ROAD
AMSTEL WAY
SMARTS LANE
SAUNDERS LANE
PREY HEATH ROAD
EGLEY ROAD
GUILDFORD ROAD
BLACKHORSE ROAD
KETTLEWELL HILL
115
116
117
118
119
120
121
122
123
124

AZ
BA
BB
BC
BD
BE
BF
211
228
243
WEST BYFLEET
GOLF COURSE
Pyrford
KINGSWEY BUSINESS CENTRE
WOKING BUSINESS PARK
GENESIS BUSINESS PARK
CHERTSEY ROAD
A245
A320
Maybury
WOKING
GU22
PYRFORD COMMON
THE ROUGH
Pyrford Court
HOEBRIDGE GOLF CENTRE
Clubhouse
Monument Hill
Fox Hill
Pyrford Village
Newark Priory (Remains)
Sewage Works
WOKING PARK
Leisure Cen
Swim Pool
LOOP ROAD SPORTS FIELD
Old Woking
HIGH STREET
A247
OLDHILL COPSE
BURIAL GRD
River Wey
WOKING
GUILDFORD
Westfield
BROADMEAD ROAD
River Wey Navigation NT
Broadmead Cut
SAND PIT
GU23
GU4
Send
SEND ROAD
Send Marsh
GARLICK'S ARCH COPSE
SEND BARNS LANE
PORTSMOUTH ROAD
Triggs Lock
Sutton Green
CEM
115
116
117
118
119
120
121
122
123
124

Pyrford
Pyrford Green
Pyrford Village
PYRFORD GOLF COURSE
THE WISLEY GOLF COURSE
Wisley
WISLEY COMMON
ROYAL HORTICULTURAL SOCIETY WISLEY GARDENS
Elm Corner
OCKHAM COMMON
Ockham
OCKHAM PARK
PARK WOOD
Ripley
RIPLEY GREEN
WALSHAM MEADOW
WALSHAM PLANTATION
Send Marsh
GU22
GU23
KT14
M25
PORTSMOUTH ROAD
RIPLEY BYPASS
NEWARK LANE
River Wey Navigation NT
River Wey
Newark Priory (Remains)
Abbey Stream
PEATMOOR WOOD
BUXTON WOOD
COMMON MEADOWS
WOOLGER'S WOOD
LOVELAND'S COPSE
ROBOROW WOOD
BRAMBLERIDE COPSE
BACHELOR'S COPSE
GARLICK'S ARCH COPSE
SHEPPARDSGROVE COPSE
Irish Hole
212
227
244
BG BH BJ BK BL BM BN
115 116 117 118 119 120 121 122 123 124
05 06 07
56 57 58 59

PAINSHILL PARK
213
THE BROOM
Heyswood Girl Guide Camp
Gothic Temple
Chinese Bridge
GROTTO
THE LAKE
Visitors Centre
Wood Hill
Long Orchard Farm
BELL WOOD
Bramble Hedge Farm
Foxwarren Park
Red Hill
The Tower
Tower Hill
WHEEL ISLAND
Oak Pollard
Red Hill
PORTSMOUTH
ROAD
A3
Junction 10
CHATLEY WOOD
Redhill Bottom
POINTERS
Cockrow Hill
Tumulus
Sandpit Hill
Chatley Farm
KT11
THE BOGS
BREACH HILL WOOD
Hut Hill Cottage
Hut Hill
CURRIE'S CLUMP
CHATLEY HEATH
Telegraph Hill
Chatley Semaphore
LODGE COPSE
River Mole
BOLDER MERE
OCKHAM COMMON
HATCHFORD WOOD
M25
HATCHFORD PARK
ELM LANE
Wilderness Farm
HUNT'S COPSE
HATCH
BRAMBLE WOOD
Poynters Farm
Pointers Green
LITTLE BRICKFIELD COPSE
BRICKFIELD COPSE
NORTON LANE
Cold Norton Farm
Hazeldene Farm
NORTON WOOD
Poultry Houses
The Black Swan PH
Martyr's Green
Bridge End Farm
Pound Farm
ELMBRIDGE
GUILDFORD
TANNERS COPSE
Upton Farm
OCKHAM LANE
Appstree Farm
Pav
SPORTS GROUND
ALMS HEATH
School Farm
SCHOOL LA
TRULLIBER COPSE
CHAFFERS COPSE
HOOK WOOD
May's Green
STUMPS GROVE
Blackmoor Farm
Barnsthorns
Slade Farm
BARNSTHORNS WOOD
Blue Ride
THE DRIFT GOLF COURSE
Clubhouse
THE DRIFT
DRIFT ROAD
THE FOREST
NORTH ROAD
OCKHAM ROAD
EVEN WOOD
GREEN
Broom House
SPORTS GRD
NIGHTINGALE CRESCENT
NIGHTINGALE AVENUE
Prim Sch
245
HIGHLANDS
Manor Farm
Cobham
BETWEEN STREETS
A245
HIGH ST
RIVER HL
MILL RD
STOKE
Cricket Club
Bowls Grn
Tenn Cts
Hall
ALLOT
Cobham FC
Health Cen
Coll
Youth Cen
Lib
CHURCH ST
ANVIL LA
ANVIL LANE
Nursery
FB
Weir
R. Mole
COBHAM
ROSE LODGE WOOD
The Running Mare PH
Cobham Court Farm
Downside Bridge
DOWNSIDE ROAD
PLOUGH LANE
Cobham Park Nursery
Works
Cobham Stud Farm
PARK WOOD
BIG POUND
COBHAM PARK ROAD
Halfpenny Cross
Cossins House
Cossins Farm
POINTERS ROAD
CHILBROOK
Downside
Pondtail Farm
DOWNSIDE COMMON
Sch
Hall
MIDDLETON RD
BOOKHAM ROAD
BEAUMONT PLANTATION
GOOSE GREEN
New Barn Farm
Highway Farm
230
Bull Riding Farm
OLD OAK COMMON
THE NEW PRESERVE
PEAKED ROUGH
ROUNDABOUT
Hurst Hill
HORSLEY ROAD
Newmarsh Farm
Gun Club
NEW BARN WOOD
CLAMP ROUGH
BUSHY THICKET
THICKET COPSE
BANKS LANE
Banks Way House
LITTLE MORNSHILL WOOD
GALLOWS GROVE
Lord Howard PH
EFFINGHAM JUNCTION
KT24
Depot
PO
Hall
Slater's Oak
Norwood Farm
EFFINGHAM COMMON
Cricket Ground
Cricket Club
LOWER FARM ROAD
Lower Farm
PIKES POOL
MALLARD MERE
Hook Farm
Indian Farm
ORCHARD CL
HEATHWAY
FOREST ROAD
HOOKE ROAD
BRIDLEWAY
BP
BQ
BR
BS
BT
BU
BV
08
09
10
56
57
58
59
115
116
117
118
119
120
121
122
123
124

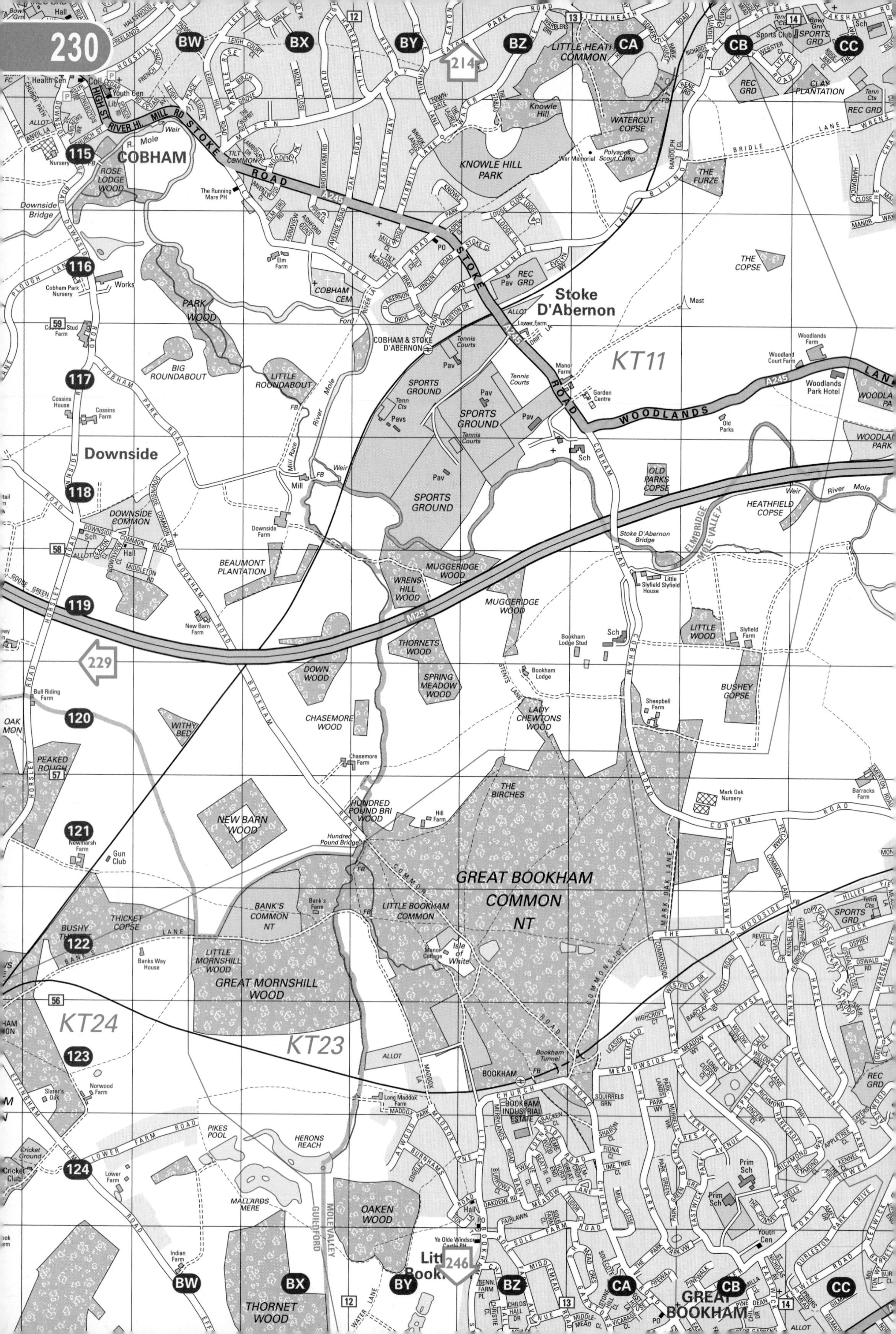

230
COBHAM
Downside
Stoke D'Abernon
KT11
KT24
KT23
GREAT BOOKHAM COMMON NT
LITTLE BOOKHAM COMMON
LITTLE HEATH COMMON
KNOWLE HILL PARK
WATERCUT COPSE
THE FURZE
THE COPSE
CLAY PLANTATION
ROSE LODGE WOOD
PARK WOOD
BIG ROUNDABOUT
LITTLE ROUNDABOUT
SPORTS GROUND
DOWNSIDE COMMON
BEAUMONT PLANTATION
WRENS HILL WOOD
MUGGERIDGE WOOD
THORNETS WOOD
SPRING MEADOW WOOD
DOWN WOOD
CHASEMORE WOOD
WITHY BED
LADY CHEWTONS WOOD
OLD PARKS COPSE
HEATHFIELD COPSE
LITTLE WOOD
BUSHEY COPSE
THE BIRCHES
PEAKED ROUGH
NEW BARN WOOD
HUNDRED POUND BRI WOOD
BANK'S COMMON NT
THICKET COPSE
LITTLE MORNSHILL WOOD
GREAT MORNSHILL WOOD
PIKES POOL
HERONS REACH
MALLARDS MERE
OAKEN WOOD
THORNET WOOD
COBHAM CEM
COBHAM & STOKE D'ABERNON
BOOKHAM
BOOKHAM INDUSTRIAL ESTATE
GREAT BOOKHAM
STOKE ROAD
WOODLANDS
A245
M25
River Mole
MOLE VALLEY
ELMBRIDGE
GUILDFORD
214
229
246
BW
BX
BY
BZ
CA
CB
CC
115
116
117
118
119
120
121
122
123
124

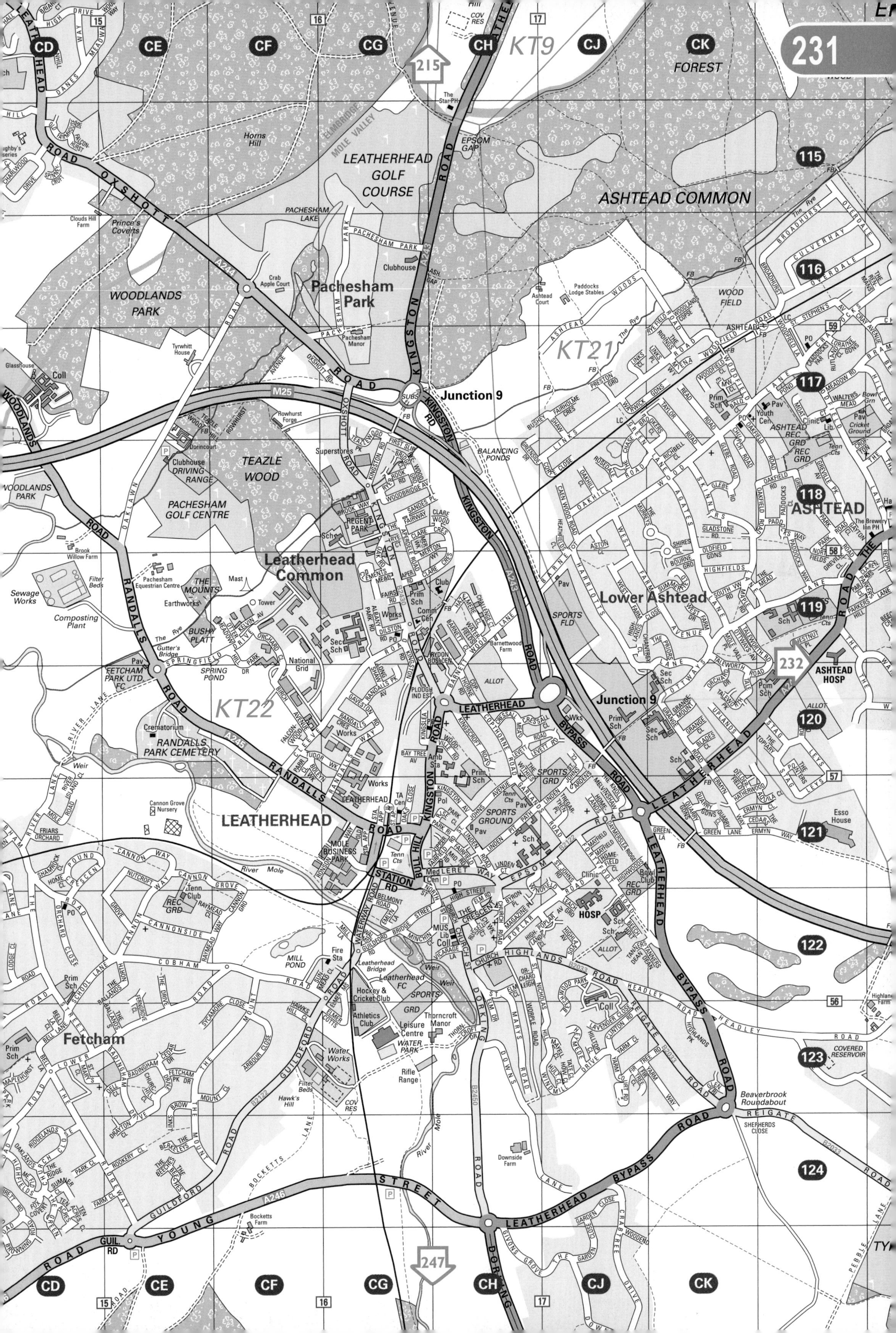

LEATHERHEAD
Leatherhead Common
Lower Ashtead
ASHTEAD
Fetcham
Pachesham Park
LEATHERHEAD GOLF COURSE
ASHTEAD COMMON
WOODLANDS PARK
TEAZLE WOOD
PACHESHAM GOLF CENTRE
RANDALLS PARK CEMETERY
Junction 9
KT9
KT21
KT22
M25
KINGSTON ROAD
OXSHOTT ROAD
RANDALLS ROAD
LEATHERHEAD BYPASS
YOUNG STREET
GUILDFORD ROAD
REIGATE ROAD
COBHAM ROAD
DORKING ROAD
Beaverbrook Roundabout
215
232
247

EPSOM COMMON
NEWTON WOOD
TEAD COMMON
WOOD FIELD
ASHTEAD
ASHTEAD PARK
Ashtead Park
City of London Freemen's School
ASHTEAD HOSP
Epsom
EPSOM GENERAL HOSP
Woodcote
WOODCOTE GREEN
WOODCOTE PARK GOLF COURSE
Woodcote Park Country Club
HALFMOON CLUMP
WORLDS END
THE GROVE
LANGLEY BOTTOM WOOD
Langley Vale
THE WARREN
KT21
KT18
KT22
EPSOM & EWELL
MOLE VALLEY
ADDLESTEAD WOOD
LITTLE HURST WOOD
Tyrrell's Wood
TYRRELL'S WOOD
HAMBLETON WOOD
HEADLEY COURT
HOOK WOOD
GREAT HURST WOOD
PIGNUT WOOD
NOWER WOOD
OYSTER HILL NT
TYRRELL'S WOOD GOLF COURSE
COSTAL WOOD
Headley
Beaverbrook Roundabout
COVERED RESERVOIR
Esso House
Chase Farm Stud
Highlands Farm
Addlestead Farm
LEATHERHEAD ROAD
LEATHERHEAD BYPASS ROAD
EPSOM ROAD
DORKING ROAD
REIGATE ROAD
M25
A24
216
231
248
CL
CM
CN
CP
CQ
CR
CS
115
116
117
118
119
120
121
122
123
124

233
217
234
249
KT17
SM7
KT20
NORK
Epsom College
EPSOM DOWNS
Drift Bridge
Drift Bridge Hotel
BUCKLE'S GAP
EPSOM DOWNS GOLF COURSE
PARK WOOD
NORK PARK
SPORTS GROUND
Toyota
TATTENHAM WAY RECREATION GROUND
EPSOM RACE COURSE
EPSOM DOWNS
The Hill
Tattenham Corner
Burgh Heath
BURGH HEATH
CANONS WOOD
PAGES ACRE
RUFFETT WOOD
LANGLEY VALE
WALTON DOWNS
PIT WOOD
Banstead Athletic FC
TADWORTH
THE CHILDRENS TRUST
KINGSWOOD
Kingswood Warren
Legal & General House
St Monica's
BANSTEAD HEATH
SANDHILL WOOD
Walton on the Hill
Police Training School
WORKHOUSE POND
MERE POND
Cricket Ground
The Clock Tower Riding Centre
BEECHEN
COPSE
BANSTEAD

BANSTEAD
WOODMANSTERNE
SM7
Banstead Place
THE SHRUBBERY
SCRATCH WOOD
GREAT SOLOM'S WOOD
PARK DOWNS
RUFFETT WOOD
PAGES ACRE
CANONS WOOD
BANSTEAD WOOD
NATURE RESERVE
DEPOT
LUNCH WOOD
FAMES ROUGH
CHIPSTEAD BOTTOM
CHIPHOUSE WOOD
WELL COPSE
Chipstead Bottom
CHIPSTEAD GOLF COURSE
Chipstead
KT20
KINGSWOOD
OUTWOOD SHAW
POORFIELD WOOD
OUTWOOD
THE LONG PLANTATION
THE BELT
Hooley
KINGSWOOD GOLF COURSE AND COUNTRY CLUB
SMUGGLERS PIT PLANTATION
TOP SHAW
ROUND WOOD
HOMEFIELD SHAWS
WELLFIELD SHAW
MILLFIELD WOOD
BEECHEN COPSE
Mugswell
HEDGELAND SHAW
STARROCK SHAW
FOURTEEN ACRE SHAW
THE RUFFETT
RUFFETTS WOOD
CHIPSTEAD MEADS REC GRD
CLOCKHOUSE REC GRD
WOODMANSTERNE PARK RECREATION GROUND
PROSPECT PLANTATION
BIG WOOD
DA
DB
DC
DD
DE
DF
DG
115
116
117
118
119
120
121
122
123
124
56
57
58
59
26
27
28
218
233
250

DH
DJ
DK
DL
DM
DN
DP
219
WOODCOTE PARK GOLF COURSE
WOODCOTE GROVE REC GRD
WOODCOTE GROVE A237
BRIGHTON ROAD
SMITHAM
WOODMANSTERNE
CHIPSTEAD VALLEY ROAD
COULSDON
COULSDON SOUTH
TWINERS WOOD
DUNSTAN'S WOOD
POSTERN WOOD
Cane Hill S.A.S.S. Unit
MARLFIELD SHAW
CR5
ULLSWATER BUSINESS PARK
STONYFIELD SHAW
COULSDON COURT PUBLIC GOLF COURSE
COULSDON MANOR GOLF COURSE
HARTLEY BUSHES
HIGHER DRIVE REC GRD
CR8
KENLEY
115
116
117
118
119
120
121
122
123
124
BETTS MEAD RECREATION GR
FARTHING OR FAIRDEAN DOWNS
GRANGE PARK
Coulsdon Coll
Old Coulsdon
SPORTS GROUND
DEVILS DEN WOOD
THE DEVILS DEN
SPARKLIE WOOD
HAPPY VALLEY PARK
236
COULSDON COMMON
STAR SHAW
THREE CORNERED SHAW
PETERSHOLE SHAW
BOXERS WOOD
DITCHES SHAW
SURREY
CROYDON
TANDRIDGE
RIFLE RANGES
Caterham Barracks (Closed)
HAPPY VALLEY GOLF COURSE
FIGGS WOOD
THE GULLET
NETHERNE WOOD
HOSPITAL (closed)
GRASSCUTS SHAW
LORD'S WOOD
ALDERSTEAD HEATH CARAVAN CLUB SITE
FURZEFIELD WOOD
ALDERSTEAD HEATH
RH1
SPARTICLES WOOD
BROAD WOOD
PILES WOOD
CHURCH GREEN
Court Farm
FRYERN BROOM WOOD
Chaldon
CR3
Rook Hill
WILLEY BROOM WOOD
BROTHERS FIELD
251
Mersham Tunnel
Junction
COVERED RESERVOIR
Alderstead Farm
Uplands Farm
29
30
31
56
57
58
59

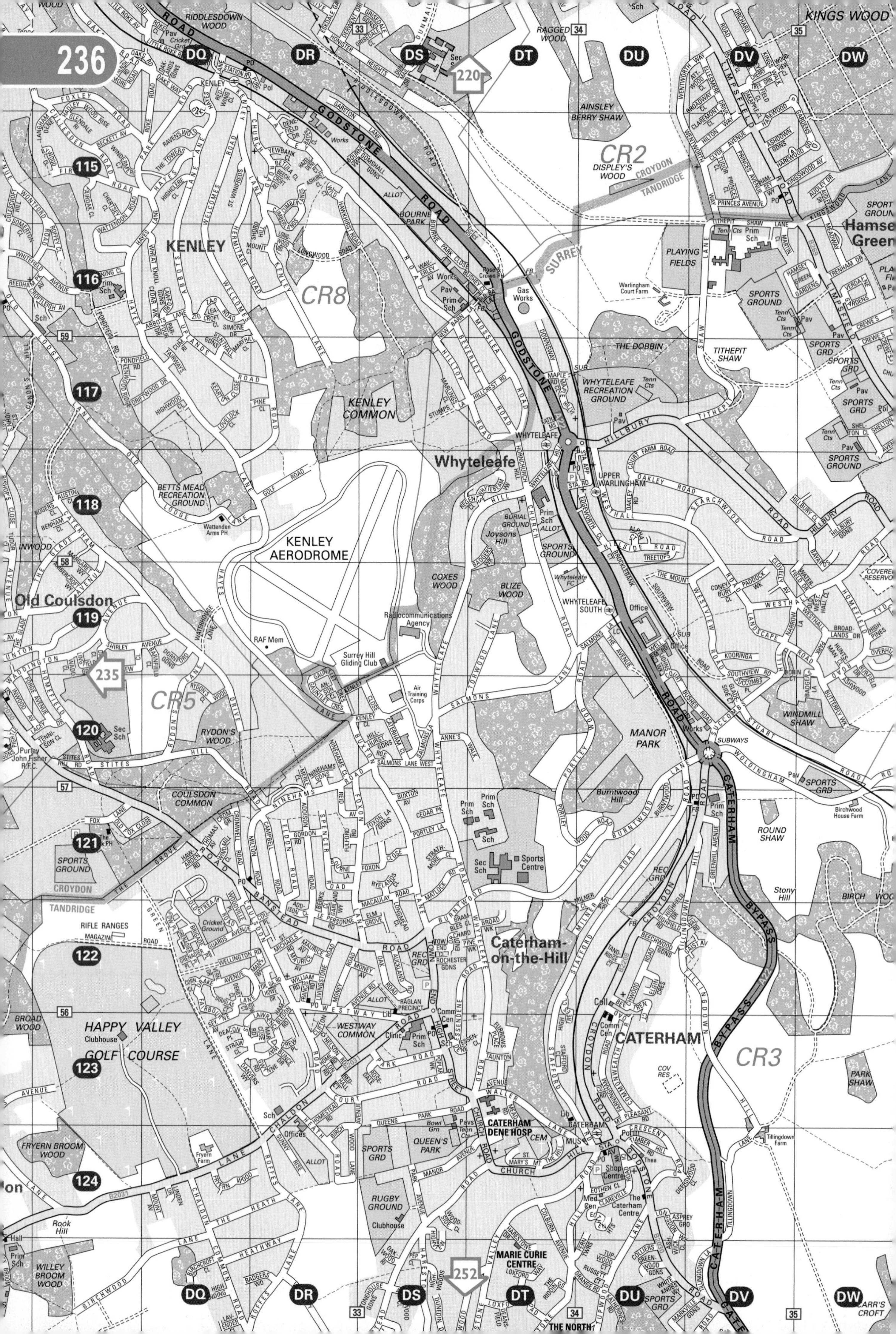

DQ
DR
DS
DT
DU
DV
DW
KINGS WOOD
RIDDLESDOWN WOOD
220
RAGGED WOOD
AINSLEY BERRY SHAW
CR2
DISPLEY'S WOOD
CROYDON
TANDRIDGE
SURREY
GODSTONE ROAD
KENLEY
115
116
117
118
119
120
121
122
123
124
CR8
BOURNE PARK
Hamsey Green
PLAYING FIELDS
Warlingham Court Farm
Gas Works
SPORTS GROUND
TITHEPIT SHAW
THE DOBBIN
WHYTELEAFE RECREATION GROUND
KENLEY COMMON
Whyteleafe
UPPER WARLINGHAM
BETTS MEAD RECREATION GROUND
Wattenden Arms PH
KENLEY AERODROME
COXES WOOD
BLIZE WOOD
Joysons Hill
WHYTELEAFE SOUTH
Old Coulsdon
Radiocommunications Agency
RAF Mem
Surrey Hill Gliding Club
Air Training Corps
235
CR5
RYDON'S WOOD
MANOR PARK
WINDMILL SHAW
Purley John Fisher R.F.C.
COULSDON COMMON
Burntwood Hill
ROUND SHAW
Birchwood House Farm
SPORTS GROUND
Stony Hill
Sports Centre
TANDRIDGE
RIFLE RANGES
MAGAZINE
Caterham-on-the-Hill
CATERHAM
CR3
BROAD WOOD
HAPPY VALLEY GOLF COURSE
Clubhouse
WESTWAY COMMON
COV RES
PARK SHAW
Tillingdown Farm
FRYERN BROOM WOOD
Fryern Farm
QUEEN'S PARK
SPORTS GRD
CATERHAM DENE HOSP
CEM
The Caterham Centre
RUGBY GROUND
Clubhouse
Rook Hill
WILLEY BROOM WOOD
MARIE CURIE CENTRE
252
CATERHAM BYPASS
A22
B2031
B2030
CARR'S CROFT
THE NORTH

FARLEIGH
Chelsham
CR6
WARLINGHAM
Woldingham Garden Village
Woldingham
GREAT PARK WOOD
HOLT WOOD
HENLEY WOOD
DUKE'S DENE GOLF COURSE
LUMBERDINE WOOD
GREENHILL SHAW
WHISTLERS WOOD
TITSEY PLANTATION
CHALK PITS
221
238
253
DX
DY
DZ
EA
EB
EC
ED
115
116
117
118
119
120
121
122
123
124

BIGGIN HILL
Tatsfield
Titsey
CR6
CR3
RH8
SURREY
TANDRIDGE
BROMLEY
MAIN ROAD
AIRPORT INDUSTRIAL ESTATE
BIGGIN HILL BUSINESS PARK
BIGGIN HILL CEM
REC GRD
The Spitfire Centre
PARK WOOD GOLF COURSE
SPORTS GROUND
BEAVER WATER WORLD
TITSEY PLANTATION
TITSEY PLACE GDNS
HONEYOAK WOOD
MOLLARDS WOOD
OWLS WOOD
LUMBERDINE WOOD
ASHEN SHAW
PITCHERS WOOD
LONG COPPICE
WESTMORE GREEN
LIMEHOUSE BOTTOM
CLARKS LANE SHAW
COLDHARBOUR BEECHES
Botley Hill
222
237
254

BR6
Single Street
Cudham
Berry's Green
TN14
Aperfield
Horns Green
CHERRY LODGE GOLF COURSE
South Street
TN16
Hawley's Corner
CUDHAM FRITH
THE GROVE
BLACKBUSH SHAW
NEW YEARS WOOD
FOXBURROW WOOD
HOOK WOOD
BIRCHES CROFT
JOCKEY'S WOOD
COPHALL WOOD
BROOM WOOD
BASTON WOOD
LITTLE JOCKEYS WOOD
KNOCKHOLT WOOD
THE NOWER
JOELAND'S WOOD
SHELLEM WOOD
GRAY'S WOOD
WITHINS WOOD
BROOMCOCKS WOOD
ROUND SHAW
WHITELANDS SHAW
HOLYWELL SHAW
PARK WOOD
HARTLEY WOOD
WESTERHAM WOOD
ROWTYE WOOD
CLACKET GREEN
Force Green
Hogtrough Hill
Betsom's Hill
TWENTY ACRE SHAW
BIRD HOUSE WOOD
BROMLEY CROFT
STRAKES SHAW
SPENCERS GROVE
LEASONS WOOD
PIMLICO WOOD
MAIN ROAD
WESTERHAM ROAD
LONDON ROAD
HILL
M25
A233
223
240
255
115
116
117
118
119
120
121
122
123
124
EM
EN
EP
EQ
ER
ES
ET
43
44
45
56
57
58
59
KENT
BROMLEY
SEVENOAKS
NORTH DOWNS WAY
PILGRIMS WAY

EU
EV
EW
EX
EY
EZ
FA
47
48
49
224
239
NEWLANDS WOOD
HAYMAN'S WOOD
New Year Cottage
BIRCHES CROFT
LONG BOTTOM SHAW
HAWFIELD WOOD
Singles Cross
New Stables Farm
Curry Farm
BROOMFIELD WOOD
Warehouses
Knockholt Pound
CHAPEL CROFT
Works
JOCKEY'S WOOD
Blueberry Farm
The Spinney Nurseries
Harrow Inn PH
Aldwyn House
Meadow Farm
Warren Farm
Rose Cottage Farm
COPHALL WOOD
Whitelegg's Garden Centre
Comm Cen
Clinic
Ivy Farm
The Grange
Bowl Grn
Mast
Football Pitch
The Mill House
LEES WOOD
DUTCHMORE WOOD
Shelleys
Letts Green
Homefield
Chine Farm
BROOM WOOD
Court Lodge
COOPER'S WOOD
Knockholt
BASTON WOOD
War Meml
Sec Sch
The Crown PH
ASHFIELD WOOD
STAR HILL WOOD
LITTLE JOCKEYS WOOD
ASHPLATT
KNOCKHOLT BEECHES
KNOCKHOLT WOOD
Masts
SAND BANKS
MINNY WOOD
COV RES
Keepers Cottage
Beeches Farm
Mountross Farm
CHEVENING PARK
The Tally Ho PH
SUMMERHOUSE WOOD
THE SPINNEY
Hazlet Wood Farm
PARK WOOD
Sundridge Hill
HAGBUSH WOOD
Chevening
ROUGHFIELDS WOOD
Well
Chevening House
BURIAL GRD
Shootfield
Home Farm
Brasted Hill Farm
SHOOTFIELD WOOD
TN14
THE NOWER
HOME WOOD
Chevening Cross
JOELAND'S WOOD
Grove House
CLAYPIT SHAW
Oveny Green Farm
Combe Bank Farm
Farm
Ovenden Lodge
Junction 5
Hogtrough Hill
Combe Bank Wood
COMBEBANK WOOD
Court Lodge Farm
TN16
COMBE WOOD
Willow Farm
PARK WOOD
Pumping Station
Sch
Council Depot
Pumping Sta
St. Martins Meadow
Tanners
Little Coombe Bank
Offices
Pav
SPORTS GROUND
Stanhope Arms PH
Mill Farm
The Old Rectory
PYM ORCHARD
Bowling Green
Warren Farm
The Lamb PH
Brasted
Mill
Depot
THE OLD YARD
Hall
White Horse PH
Sundridge
The Old Rectory
Charmans Farm
Park Farm
Tennis Courts
SPORTS GRD
Bull Inn PH
PO
White Hart Inn PH
THE CARRIAGEWAY
Orchard Farm
Brasted Place
Prim Sch
THE WARREN
THE ROOKERIES
Horizons Centre
Works
Mountwood
Fountain Cottages
Brasted Place Farm
Sundridge Place
Long Barn
NEW YEARS LANE
SHELLEYS LANE
KNOCKHOLT MAIN ROAD
HARROW ROAD
LONDON ROAD
BIRCHWOOD LA
STAR HILL
MAIN ROAD
BLUEBERRY LANE
SINGLES CROSS LANE
RANDLES LANE
POUND LANE
CHEVENING LANE
NORTH DOWNS WAY
CHATHAM'S RIDE
LORD
SUNDRIDGE ROAD
PILGRIMS WAY
OVENDEN ROAD
COMBE BANK DRIVE
CHEVENING ROAD
BRASTED HILL
BRASTED LANE
NOWER
HOGTROUGH HILL
STATION ROAD
COLES LANE
RECTORY LANE
CHURCH ROAD
HIGH STREET
MAIN ROAD
CHAPMANS ROAD
WOODSIDE ROAD
MANOR RD
CHART LANE
KENT
M25
A25
B2211
River Darent
115
116
117
118
119
120
121
122
123
124
56
57
58
59

Twitton
Otford
TN14
Dunton Green
Longford
Chipstead
Riverhead
Bessels Green
TN13
SEVENOAKS WILDFOWL RESERVE
EAST LAKE
WEST LAKE
CHIPSTEAD LAKE
OTFORD CEMETERY
GRAVEL PIT
CHALK PIT
DEFENCE SCIENCE & TECHNOLOGY LABORATORY-FORT HALSTEAD
MONTREAL PARK
SEVENOAKS HOSP
M25
M26
A224
A225
A25
A21
SEVENOAKS BYPASS
POLHILL
LONDON ROAD
STATION ROAD
PILGRIMS WAY

225
256
257

AS
AT
AU
AV
AW
AX
AY
226
GOLF COURSE
GU22
GU3
GU2
GU1
Kemishford Bridge
PREY HEATH ROAD
Burdenshot Hill
BURDENSHOT HILL
BURDENSHOT ROAD
Bonnieshott Wood Farm
Lantana Nursery
BRIDLEY COPSE
125
Hoe Stream
Blanketmill Farm
Rye Farm
GOOSE RYE ROAD
Rickford Mill
Brook Farm
Bakery
RICKFORD
126
RICKFORD COMMON
Norton Farm
Jordan Hill
Gooserye
Upper Jordan
Hockley Lands
The Jolly Farmer PH
Woodcorner Farm
Havering Farm
Suttongreen Nurseries
WHITMOOR POND
POOR JACK'S WOOD
WHITMOOR WOOD
Frog Lane Farm
Juniper Nurseries
Woodlands
Whitmoor House
Whitmoor Farm
Elm Nursery
SUTTON
Cox's Farm
St. Edward's Well
Tumulus
The Old Cottage
54
Cricket Club
Tennis Courts
THATCHERS LA
CHURCH LANE
PERRY HILL
127
Worplesdon
Worplesdon Place
BURIAL GRD
SPORTS GROUND
Pav
Coll
COOMBE LANE
Perry Hill Farm
The White Lion PH
Marylands
WHITMOOR COMMON
Hurst View
Hurst Farm
Willow Grange
CLAY LANE
128
Greenacre
PERRY HILL
A322
Sudpre
Holly Lane Nursery
BRITTEN'S POND
Stringer's Barn
SALT BOX ROAD
53
Pitmore Farm
Jacobs Well
Hall
Fairlands Farm
Clubhouse
129
ROKER PARK GOLF COURSE
LABORATORY
Tangley Place Farm
RIFLE RANGE
Pitch Place
WORPLESDON ROAD
SPORTS GROUND
Tennis Courts
STRINGER'S COMMON
Gunners Farm
Bullens Hill Farm
Stringer's Farm
Warehouse
Works
SLYFIELD INDUSTRIAL ESTATE
ALDERSHOT
130
Fairlands
KEENS LANE
CHITTY'S COMMON
Frosbury Farm
Works
RIVETT DRAKE ROAD
Depot
SPORTS GROUND
Comm Cen
WOODLANDS
WOKING ROAD
A320
52
Hunts Farm
SPORTS GROUND
LOUIS FIELDS
Prim Sch
A323
Bellfields
Sec Sch
Prim Sch
Stoughton
Clinic
Ski Slope
STOKE NEW CEMETERY
Sewage Works
ALLOT
131
Rydeshill Lodge
Liddington Lodge
Rydeshill
Hook Farm
Range Farm
The Cricketers PH
STOUGHTON ROAD
STOKE CEM
Health Cen
Depot
River Wey Navigation NT
132
BROADSTREET COMMON
BROAD STREET
Sch
REC GROUND
Comm Cen
Woodbridge Hill
ALDERSHOT ROAD
Waterside Centre
Stoke Mill House
Weir
Ice Rink
Leisure Complex
51
Prim Sch
Comm Cen
ALLOT
RIFLERANGE PLANTATION
WOODBRIDGE ROAD
GUILDFORD BYPASS
Ladymead Retail Park
LADYMEAD
Offices
Travel Inn
A25
PARK
Fire Sta
Lido
ALLOT
Bowls Club
Guildford Coll
133
Park Barn
Sec Sch
Prim Sch
CATHEDRAL HILL IND EST
GUILDFORD BUSINESS PARK
Offices
MIDLETON IND EST
Royal Mail
Depots
SPORTS GROUND
SPORTS GROUND
SPORTS GARDENS
Tennis Courts
Nursery
A3
University of Surrey
134
APPLEGARTH AVENUE
SOUTHWAY
NUFFIELD HOSP
ROYAL SURREY HOSP
Superstore
Sports Hall
Uni Coll
Surrey Research Park
Tech. Centre
Offices
STRAWBERRY GROVE
GU2
CATHEDRAL
Stag Hill
Guildford Park
Cricket Grd
BUS DEPOT
YORK ROAD
A246
LONDON ROAD
258
EGERTON ROAD
GILL AVENUE
University of Surrey
The Varsity Centre
THE PHILIP HENMAN SPORTS GROUND
Offices
Holiday
98
99
00
Prim Sch
A3100
EPSOM
MOUNT

Send
Send Marsh
Sutton Green
Sendgrove
GU23
GU4
SUTTON PARK
BURPHAM COURT FARM PARK
FRITHYS WOOD
COTTS WOOD
HIGHCOTTS WOOD
Burpham
Bushy Hill
Merrow
Abbotswood
RUNNING TRACK
STOKE PARK
MERROW COMMON
GUILDFORD GOLF COURSE
CHALK PIT
THE WILD WOOD
THE WILDERNESS
CLANDON PARK NT
WALNUT TREE BOTTOM
MERROW DOWNS
Sutton Place
Runtley Wood Farm
Cricketshill Farm
Sendholme
Wareham's Farm
Sendcourt Farm
Send Grove
Tudor Barn Farm
Sendbarns
Woodhill House Farm
Woodhill House
Sendhurst Grange
Glasshouse
Old Timbers
Nutbourne Fruit Farm
Whitehouse Farm
Nuthill Farm
Gosden Hill Farm
Tithebarns Farm
Dedswell Manor Farm
Cuckoo Farm
Onslow Inn
Clandon Park Garden Centre
Manor House Hotel
Gatehouse
Ladygrove Farm
Manor House
Sutton Park House
Sutton Green House
Burpham Court Farm
Bower's Lock
Bower's Mill
Bower's Cottages
Triggs Lock
Triggs Lock Bridge
Broadoak Bridge
Weir
River Wey
RIVER WEY NAVIGATION NT
WOKING
GUILDFORD
TOWING PATH
CEM
Prim Sch
Sec Sch
Superstore
Surrey Cricket Centre
MERROW IND EST
MERROW BUSINESS CEN
DEPOT
Depot
SPORTS GROUND
COPSE EDGE
SUTHERLAND MEMORIAL PARK
THE COPSE
RIVERSIDE PARK
Miniature Railway
Clubhouse
D.E.F.R.A.
Cricket Ground
Cricket Club
Tennis Courts
Bowling Green
Horse & Groom PH
The Bulls Head PH
REGT. MUS
SPORTS GRD
LONDON ROAD
RIPLEY BYPASS
GUILDFORD BYPASS
CLANDON ROAD
EPSOM ROAD
SEND BARNS LANE
BOUGHTON HALL AVENUE
PORTSMOUTH ROAD
VICARAGE LANE
POTTERS LANE
SEND ROAD
WOODHILL
CLAY LANE
MERROW LANE
NEW INN LANE
BOXGROVE ROAD
TRODDS LANE
THE STREET
SHERE ROAD
A3
A247
A246
A25
A3100
B2215
B2234
227
244
259
AZ
BA
BB
BC
BD
BE
BF
01
02
03
125
126
127
128
129
130
131
132
133
134
51
52
53
54

Send Marsh
GARLICK'S ARCH COPSE
OLDLANDS COPSE
Three Bridges
Nursery
Glasshouse
Tithebarns Farm
TITHEBARNS LANE
Sussex Farm
GU23
Holride Farm
August Hill
SHEPPARDSGROVE COPSE
BRAMBLERIDE COPSE
Jury Farm
FURZE COPSE
HIGHCOTTS WOOD
Hazelwood Cottage
H.M. PRISON SEND
GREEN LANE
HUMPHREY'S COPSE
FISH POND
ROAM WELLS
MARTIN FURZE
GASON WOOD
Lower Hammond's Farm
Dedswell Manor Farm
CLANDON
West Clandon
Cuckoo Farm
Onslow Arms Inn PH
SPORTS GRD
WITHYBED PLANTATION
NORCOTE WOOD
Home Farm
HATCHLANDS PARK
GREAT WIX WOOD
LITTLE WIX WOOD
Fullers Hill
Hatchlands Park (NT)
Clubhouse
CLANDON REGIS GOLF COURSE
East Clandon
Woolgars Farm
GU4
Clandon Park (NT)
THE WILDERNESS
CHALK PIT
Blake's Lane Farm
HIGH CLANDON
High Clandon Farm
COVERED RESERVOIRS
Long Acre Farm
THE WILD WOOD
CLANDON DOWNS
Sunray Farm
Wellhouse Farm
Sun Valley Farm
HARROWHILL COPSE
Old Scotland Farm
GU5
Manor House Hotel
TICKNERS COPSE
STAPLELANE COPSE
New Scotland Farm
A247
A246
A25
EPSOM ROAD
RIPLEY BY-PASS

228
243
260

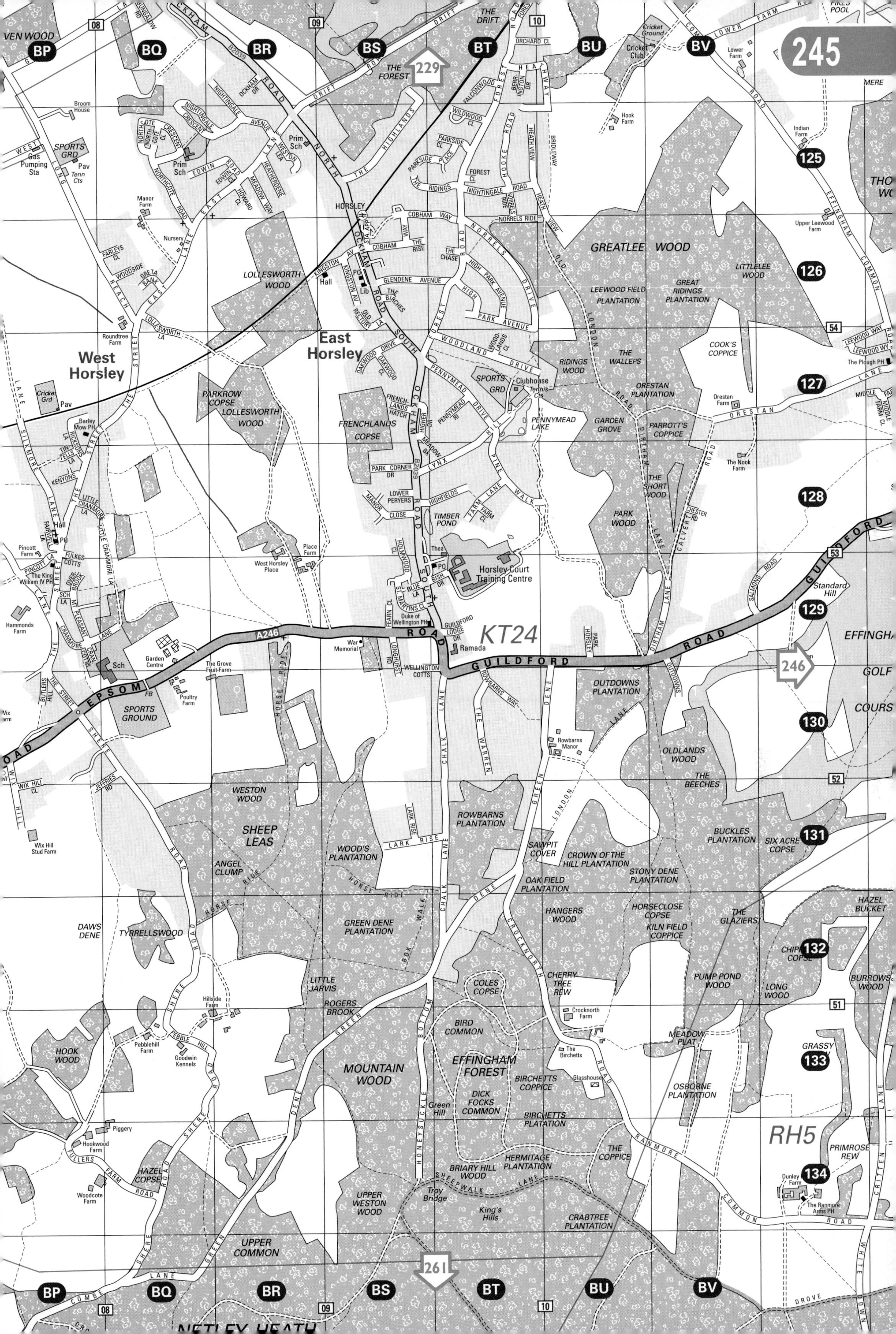
West Horsley
East Horsley
KT24
RH5
229
246
261
GREATLEE WOOD
LOLLESWORTH WOOD
FRENCHLANDS COPSE
PARKROW COPSE
Horsley Court Training Centre
GUILDFORD ROAD
EPSOM ROAD
OCKHAM ROAD NORTH
OCKHAM ROAD SOUTH
SHEEP LEAS
WESTON WOOD
MOUNTAIN WOOD
EFFINGHAM FOREST
UPPER COMMON
GREEN DENE PLANTATION
TYRRELLSWOOD
HOOK WOOD
DAWS DENE
RANMORE COMMON ROAD
CROCKNORTH ROAD
CHALK LANE
HONEYSUCKLE BOTTOM
OUTDOWNS PLANTATION
OLDLANDS WOOD
THE BEECHES
BUCKLES PLANTATION
PUMP POND WOOD
OSBORNE PLANTATION
CRABTREE PLANTATION
EFFINGHAM GOLF COURSE

BW
BX
BY
BZ
CA
CB
CC
230
245
262
12
13
14
54
53
52
51
125
126
127
128
129
130
131
132
133
134
PIKES POOL
HERONS REACH
MALLARDS MERE
OAKEN WOOD
MOLE VALLEY
GUILDFORD
Little Bookham
GREAT BOOKHAM
Hook Farm
Indian Farm
THORNET WOOD
Upper Leewood Farm
LITTLELEE WOOD
GREAT RIDINGS PLANTATION
COOK'S COPPICE
ORESTAN PLANTATION
Orestan Farm
PARROTT'S COPPICE
The Nook Farm
THE SHORT WOOD
EFFINGHAM COMMON ROAD
WATER LANE
Ye Olde Windsor Castle PH
Preston Farm
Preston Cross
REC GRD
Effingham Lodge Farm
Lower Road Nursery
Prim Sch
CONVENT
The Plough PH
Sec Sch
Effingham
KING GEORGE'S FIELD
Manor Farm
Coll
Rolls Farm
Glasshouse
Kenilworth Riding Stables
KT23
KT24
ALLOT
Sch
Club house
Tennis Courts
Wyvenhoe Riding Centre
GUILDFORD ROAD
LEATHERHEAD ROAD
A246
STRATHCONA AVENUE
WOODLANDS ROAD
CHALKPIT LANE
Goldstone Farm
POLESDEN LANE
HOGDEN LANE
CONNICUT WOOD
CROOKSFIEL WOOD
Standard Hill
Pumping Sta
Warren Farm
EFFINGHAM GOLF COURSE
BIG HIGH GROVE
Polesden Lacey
PRESERVE COPSE
ADMIRAL'S WALK
POLESDEN LACEY NT
CHAPELHI WOOD
FREEHOLD WOOD
OLDLANDS WOOD
THE BEECHES
High Barn Farm
STARS WOOD
White Hill
Polesden Farm
CHERRYTREE COPSE
ROUND COPSE
SIX ACRE COPSE
STONY DENE PLANTATION
STONYROCK COPSE
ROUND LIONS COPSE
Yewtree Farm
YEWTREE SHAW
BELCHAM'S COPSE
Y.H.A.
BAGDEN WOOD
HORSECLOSE COPSE
KILN FIELD COPPICE
THE GLAZIERS
HAZEL BUCKET
CHIPPENS COPSE
GARDEN COPSE
ST TERESA'S CONVENT
Effingham Hill Farm
Ranmore Farm
HOGDEN COPSE
LONG SHAW
PUMP POND WOOD
LONG WOOD
BURROWS WOOD
ROBINSGROVE WOOD
GARLIC STREET
RANMORE COMMON NT
MEADOW PLAT
GRASSY SHAW
Friars Elm
KESWICK PLANTATION
OSBORNE PLANTATION
Dog Kennel Green Farm
PRIMROSE REW
RANMORE COMMON ROAD
RANMORE ROUNDABOUT
LILLIES COPSE
THE SPAINS
NORTH DOWNS WAY
NATIONAL TRUST
Dunley Hill Farm
The Ranmore Arms PH
CRITTEN LANE
WHITE DOWN
HIGH BARN ROAD
STONYROCK LANE
GREAT COPSE
THE ROUNDABOUTS
Landbarn Farm
HOLE HILL LA
DROVE ROAD
BURNETTS LEAP
HORLEY'S COPSE

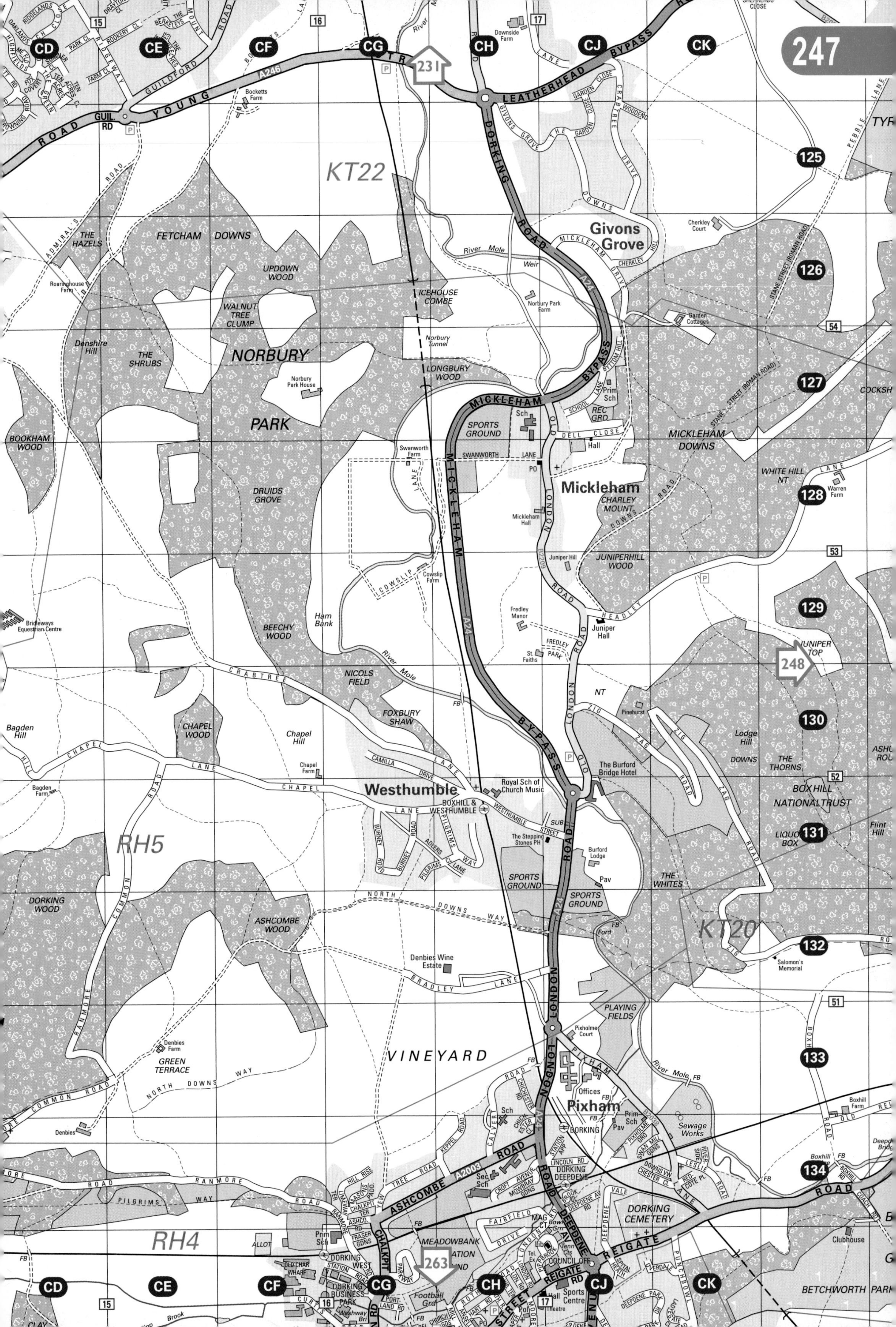

Givons Grove
Mickleham
Westhumble
Pixham
NORBURY
PARK
KT22
RH5
RH4
KT20
VINEYARD
FETCHAM DOWNS
MICKLEHAM DOWNS
BOX HILL
NATIONAL TRUST
DORKING CEMETERY

KT22
TYRRELL'S WOOD GOLF COURSE
NOWER WOOD
OYSTER HILL NT
Headley
CHERKLEY WOOD
HEADLEY WARREN NATURE RESERVE
GOODMAN'S FURZE
DEAN WOOD
COCKSHOT WOOD
MICKLEHAM DOWNS
WHITE HILL NT
KT18
HEADLEY HEATH NT
Pebble Coombe
RH5
JUNIPER TOP
HEADLEY PLANTATION
HEATH PLANTATION
BATCHELOR'S ROUGH
ASHURST ROUGH
BRAMBLE HALL WOOD
BOX HILL NATIONAL TRUST
KT20
Box Hill
CHALK PIT
BETCHWORTH CLUMP
BROCKHAM HILLS
OAK WOOD
DUKES PLANTATION
RH4
RH3
BETCHWORTH PARK GOLF COURSE
BROOKHAM BIG FIELD
Betchworth
HARTSFIELD MANOR
GREAT HURST WOOD
COSTAL WOOD
QUEEN'S WOOD
HERRING GROVE
NORTH DOWNS WAY
REIGATE ROAD
232
247
264

BANSTEAD HEATH
BANSTEAD
KT20
HEATH
WALTON HEATH GOLF COURSE
WALTON HEATH
Walton on the Hill
Lower Kingswood
Mogador
Buckland
REIGATE
RH2
REIGATE HEATH GOLF COURSE
M25
A217
A25
BRIGHTON ROAD
DORKING ROAD
BUCKLAND ROAD
Colley Hill
Juniper Hill
Mount Hill
Conybury Hill
Lady Hill
Thistle Hill
Buckland Hills
DEWRIDING PLANTATION
ROUND WOOD
MARGERY WOOD
THE HORSESHOE
THE SADDLE KNOB
QUEEN'S PARK
FOUR ACRE UPPER WOODS
THE BEECHES
NORTHLAND SHAW
BUSHY SHAW
COLLEYLAND SHAW
BUSHFIELD COPPICE
COLLEY COPSE
COLLEY WOOD
SAND AND GRAVEL PIT
ROUND ALDERS
TAP WOOD
THE ALDERS
LITTLE HEATH
Pfizer
CHUSSEX PLAIN
GAS STATION
NORTH DOWNS WAY
PILGRIMS' WAY
MOLE VALLEY
REIGATE & BANSTEAD
233
250
265

Mugswell
CR5
Lower Kingswood
KT20
Margery
Junction 8
Gatton
Coles Meads
RH2
REIGATE
REDHILL
NUTWOOD NT
GATTON PARK
THE LAKE
TEMPLE WOOD
REIGATE HILL NT
QUEEN'S PARK
WRAY COMMON
REIGATE CEMETERY
REDHILL COMMON
234
249
266
DA
DB
DC
DD
DE
DF
DG

235
252
267
Junction 7
Junction 8 (M23), Junction 7 (M25)
M23
M25
A23
A25
B2031
CR3
RH1
Merstham
South Merstham
Warwick Wold
Holmethorpe
Nutfield
Bletchingley
Coulsdon
SPARTICLES WOOD
ALDERSTEAD HEATH
FRYERN BROOM WOOD
Airshafts
Merstham Tunnel
COVERED RESERVOIR
Alderstead Farm
THE SHRUBBERY
Tollsworth Manor
Earthworks
Rook Hill
WILLEY BROOM WOOD
SIX BROTHERS FIELD
Clubhouse
Uplands Farm
RIDGEBUSHES WOOD
Hilltop Farm
Hilltop House
Masts
Willey Park Farm
GRUBS WOOD
White Hill
Ockley Hill
OCKLEY WOOD
BEDLAMS BANK
SPRING BOTTOM
QUARRY WOOD
ROCKY SHAW
BLACK BUSHES
PENDELL WOOD
FURZEFIELD WOOD
HERONSWOOD MERE
WITHY SHAW
Rockshaw Cottage
CHURCH HILL
Cricket Ground
Home Farm
GATTON PARK
Grange Court
THE GROVE
Darby House
Comm Cen
SAND PIT
SEWAGE WORKS
REIGATE & BANSTEAD
TANDRIDGE
QUARRYSIDE BUSINESS PARK
HOLMETHORPE IND EST
SAND & SILICON WORKS
MERCERS PARK COUNTRY PARK
Clubhouse
Mercers Farm
Pendell Farm
Pendell House
Lake Farm
Brewer Street Farm
Brewer Street
COCKLEY PLANTATION
Inn on the Pond PH
Chilmead Farm
PEYTON'S COTTAGES
Glebe House
Dormers Farm
Nutfield Court
SAND AND GRAVEL PIT
PUBLIC TIP
PARK WOOD
NUTFIELD CEMETERY
Capenor Nursery
Robert Denholm House
COOMBES COPPICE
STANLEY'S WOOD
Castle Hill
Castle Hill Farm
FOX HOLE
NORTH PARK
Nutfield Priory Hotel
SPORTS GRD
Furze Hill
Holmesdale
Nutfield Lodge
Stockers Hill
Priory Farm Plant Centre
Priory Farm
NUTFIELD PRIORY LAKE
STENERS HILL
Kentwyns
Sandhills
Sandhills Farm
REDSTONE CEMETERY
Bower Hill
DH DJ DK DL DM DN DP
125 126 127 128 129 130 131 132 133 134
29 30 31 51 52 53 54

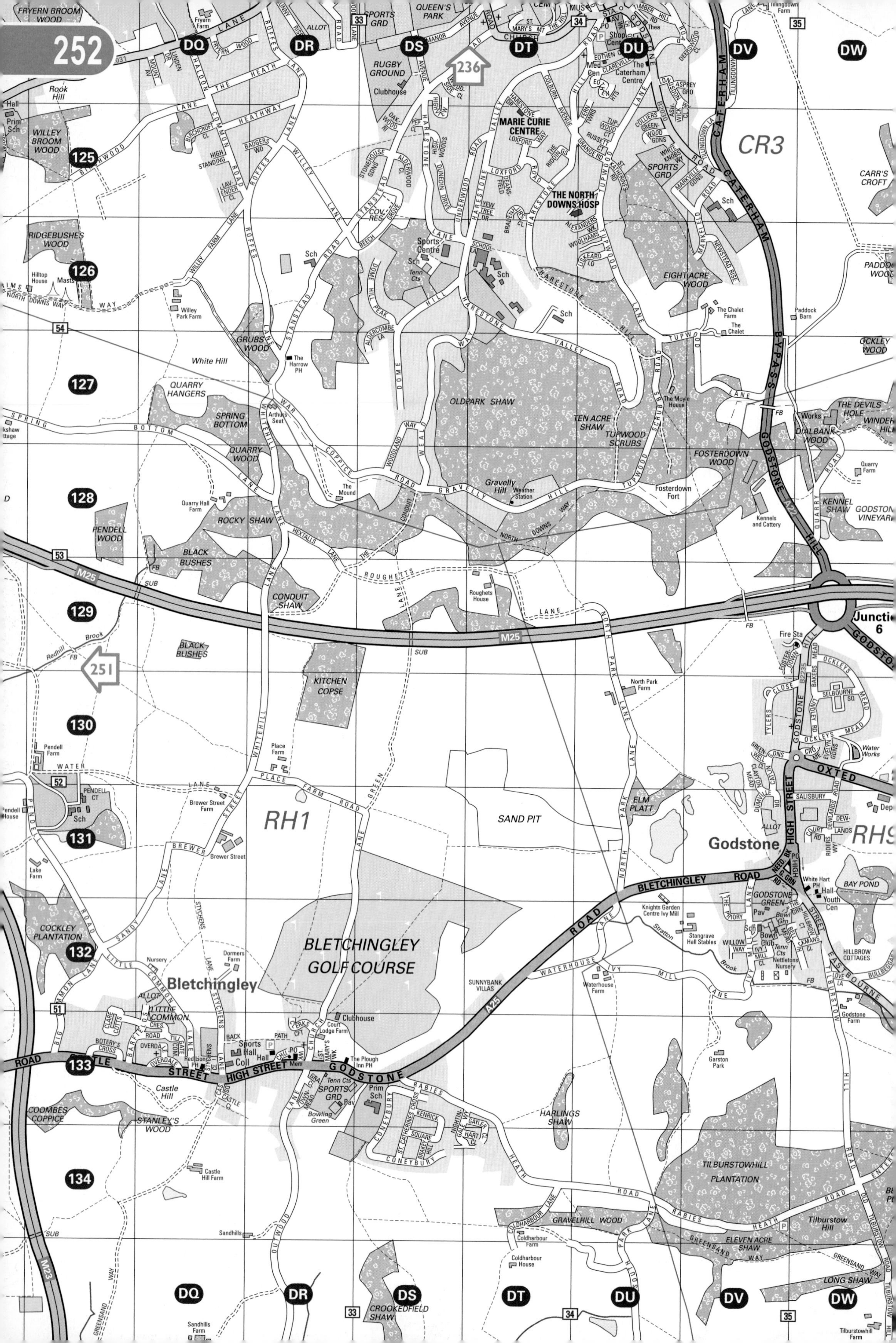

CR3
RH1
RH9
Godstone
Bletchingley
BLETCHINGLEY GOLF COURSE
SAND PIT
THE NORTH DOWNS HOSP
MARIE CURIE CENTRE
OLDPARK SHAW
TEN ACRE SHAW
TUPWOOD SCRUBS
EIGHT ACRE WOOD
FOSTERDOWN WOOD
KITCHEN COPSE
BLACK BUSHES
CONDUIT SHAW
ROCKY SHAW
PENDELL WOOD
QUARRY HANGERS
SPRING BOTTOM
QUARRY WOOD
GRUBS WOOD
RIDGEBUSHES WOOD
WILLEY BROOM WOOD
White Hill
Gravelly Hill
ELM PLATT
COCKLEY PLANTATION
COOMBES COPPICE
STANLEY'S WOOD
HARLINGS SHAW
TILBURSTOWHILL PLANTATION
GRAVELHILL WOOD
ELEVEN ACRE SHAW
CROOKEDFIELD SHAW
LONG SHAW
Tilburstow Hill
BAY POND
M25
M23
A25
A22
CATERHAM BY PASS
GODSTONE HILL
BLETCHINGLEY ROAD
HIGH STREET
OXTED
Junction 6
236
251

OXTED
Tandridge
Church Town
RH8
TANDRIDGE GOLF COURSE
NORTH DOWNS GOLF COURSE
TITSEY PLANTATION
CHALK PITS
OXTED QUARRY
CHALK PIT
BEECH PLANTATION NT
OXTED DOWNS NT
WHISTLERS WOOD
LITTLE CHURCH WOOD
TEMPLEHILL PLANTATION
GREAT CHURCH WOOD NATURE RESERVE
MARDEN PARK
STUBBS COPSE
ROOKERY
THE RUMPS
SOUTH HAWKE
WHITFIELD PLANTATION
HAZEL SHAW
HORSE SHAW
HANGING WOOD
RYE SHAW
LODGE WOOD
ARMITAGE WOOD
HAMFIELD SHAW
FIVE ACRE SHAW
RYE WOOD
ROBINS GROVE WOOD
THE ABBEYS
CHALKPIT WOOD
MASTER PARK
THE BOGS
THE MOUNT
FLOWER WOOD
PALMERS WOOD OILFIELD
SAND PIT
SPORTS GROUND
MOORE'S SHAW
GLEBE WATER
BUSHEY CROFT REC GRD
THE BIRCHES
NEW BUSTONS WOOD
BUSTONS WOOD
Beechwood Hill
ROUND WOOD
STONEPIT SHAW
OLDPARK WOOD
CASTLEHILL WOOD
THE ENTERDENT
TILBURSTOWHILL COMMON
HOPGARDEN WOOD
BRACKEY HILL
MAIZENHALL SHAW
REDDINGS WOOD
SOUTHLANDS SHAWS
SOUTHLANDS WOOD
DEAN SHAW
STOW COPPICE
BROADHAM GREEN
HELL SHAW
M25
A25
A22
B2236
GODSTONE ROAD
OXTED ROAD
EASTBOURNE ROAD
BYPASS
WEST HEATH ROAD
EAST HILL
GANGERS HILL
FLOWER LANE
TANDRIDGE HILL LANE
TANDRIDGE LANE
HOGTROUGH LANE
BARROW GREEN ROAD
SANDY LANE
CHALKPIT LANE
GORDONS WAY
STATION ROAD
BLUEHOUSE
SOUTHLANDS LANE
JACKASS LANE
LEIGH PLACE LANE
TANHOUSE ROAD
SPRING LANE
POPES LANE
BROOK LANE
NORTH DOWNS WAY
Tandridge Court
Tandridge Court Farm
Tandridge Hall
Tandridge Priory
Tandridge Hill Farm
Barrow Green Court
Barrow Green Farm
Blunt House
Little Court Farm
Round Lodge
Knights Garden Centre
The Glebe House
Leigh Place
Leigh Mill House
Sewage Works
Filter Beds
Barley Mow PH
Hall
Prim Sch
Southlands Lodge
Rose Farm
Perrysfield Farm
Stockett's Manor
Oxted Place
Mill Barn
Haycutter PH
Health Centre
Stonehall Farm
Newhouse Farm
Hollybush
Orme House
Flower Farm
Flint Hall Farm
Paddock Barn
Marden Hillboxes Farm
Whistlers Court
Flint House
Masts
Riding Centre
Works
Clubhouse
Superstore
Gas Holder
Swim Pool
HOSP (closed)
Prim Schs
Coach Depot
BURIAL GRD
Airshaft
Oxted Tunnel
DX
DY
DZ
EA
EB
EC
ED
125
126
127
128
129
130
131
132
133
134
36
37
38
51
52
53
54
237
254

EE
EF
EG
EH
EJ
EK
EL
238
CR3
HELL SHAW
TITSEY PLANTATION
TITSEY PARK
TITSEY PLACE GDNS
Titsey Place
Titsey
PILGRIMS
BROOMLANDS
ROUGHFIELD SHAW
CHURCH WOOD
CLACKET WOOD
SQUARE WOOD
Travel Inn
Clacket La Services
TITSEY WOOD
Whistlers Court
125
RIDGE
PITS
HALKPIT
BEECH PLANTATION NT
OXTED DOWNS NT
126
NORTH DOWNS WAY
Pitchfont Farm
BARTON SHAW
Limpsfield Lodge Farm
PITCHFONT
Park Farm
WATER LANE
TITSEY ROAD
River Eden
FB
M25
54
CHALKPIT WOOD
127
CENTRAL WY
SILKHAM
WESTLANDS WAY
GREENACRES
HOSP (closed)
BARNETT'S SHAW
Prim Schs
GORDONS WAY
128
CHICHELE ROAD
Tennis Courts
Sports Hall
Sec Sch
Sch
Coach Depot
BURIAL GRD
BLUEHOUSE LANE
SPORTS GROUND
ASHEN COPPICE
Broomlands Farm
SAND PIT
THRIFT WOOD
GRUBSTREET SHAW
GRUBSTREET COPSE
ROAD
RH8
Limpsfield
HIGH STREET
Hall
Pav
SPORTS GRD
Tenn Club
HOOKWOOD
LIMPSFIELD CHART
Cricket Club
Peeble Hill
Pebble Hill House
Sch
Clubhouse
GOLF COURSE
53
Blunt House
BEATRICE RD
GRESHAM
GRANVILLE
DETILLENS
PADBROOK
PO
Lib
Health Cen
COUNCIL OFF.
OXTED
MASTER PARK
Cinema
Swim Pool
Gas Holder
129
Clubhouse
MAG CT
Pol
Superstore
EAST HILL
WESTERHAM
A25
SNATTS HILL
Fire Sta
Court Langley
ALLOT
SPORTS GROUND
ANDREWS WOOD
LIMPSFIELD COMMON
NT
LOAMPIT WOOD
WATTS HILL
253
PETER
WEST HILL
130
HIGH STREET
MEADOWBROOK
Woodhurst Bridge
WOODHURST PARK
ROCKFIELD
UVEDALE ROAD
BRASSEY ROAD
Wildshaw
Swallowfield
STONESWOOD ROAD
KENT HATCH
B269
RIDLANDS
Limpsfield Chart
ST. CLAIR CL
52
QUARRY ROAD
Limpsfield Tunnel
WEST HEATH
WOLFS HILL
POLLARDS WOOD HILL
CHAPEL ROAD
BRICK KILN LANE
NED LANE
Mill Barn
SPRING LANE
131
ICEHOUSE WOOD
PARKLANDS
PASTENS ROAD
Chartfield House
LITTLE HEATH NT
CAXTON
Tenchley's Park
Crooked
THE ALDERS
TENCHLEYS
TENCHLEY'S WOOD
Champion Place
Stonehall Farm
Stonehamme
River Eden
PADDOCK
THE WALDRONS
CHURCH WAY
HOME PARK
SPORTS GROUND
GREENHURST LANE
HURST GREEN
Abbeyfield
Boulthurst Farm
132
TANHOUSE ROAD
Haycutter PH
Health Centre
Hall
Comm Cen
Prim Sch
Hurst Green
LOAMPIT WOOD
BROADHAM GREEN
51
Sch
SHORT LANE
Whitegates Farm
GRANTS LANE
Crabbett Wood
Crabbett Wood Farm
CRABBETT WOOD
Tenchleys Manor
Tenn Cts
Pav
RUNNING TRACK
REC GRD
HOLLAND
CHESTNUT
COPSE
RED LANE
Doghurst
ITCHINGWOOD COMMON
133
Perrysfield Farm
Perrysfield
Coltsford Mill
FAIRVIEW IND EST
Red Lane Farm
PARISHCROFT WOOD
Parishcroft Wood Farm
Stockett's Manor
Holland
ROSEACRE
Prim Sch
134
Depot
Sewage Works
Filter Beds
POWDERDICK SHAW
The Diamond PH
Connerton Stables
Stockenden Farm
Rose Farm
Clubhouse
Oxted R.F.C.
HONESLAND WOOD
BROOK LANE
POPES LANE
Upper Gincox Farm
40
41
42
COLLESTERS WOOD
MOLLSTONES WOOD
GUILDABLES
Hollybush

Westerham
Westerham Wood
Clacket Green
Rowtye Wood
Wet Wood
Devil of Kent
Sand Pit
Farley Common
Surrey
Kent
Moorhouse Bank
Moorhouse Bank Common NT
Cronklands
The High Chart
Goodley Stock
Kent Hatch
The Chart
Scearn Bank
Marie Curie Research Institute
Roundmead Shaw
Lodges Wood
Squerryes Court Gardens
Squerryes Park
Spring Shaw
Tower Wood
Hosey Hill
TN16
Hosey Common
Dunsdale Wood
Westerham Golf Course
Manning's Wood
Crockhamhill Common
Chartwell
Buddles Wood
Froghole
Crockham Hill
TN8
Chandler Wood
Gudge Wood
Derby Wood
Brown's Oven Wood
Ties Wood
Perry Wood
Priory Wood
Row Wood
Longcroft Wood
Hatcroft Wood
Guildables Wood
Tandridge
Sevenoaks
Westerham Road
Croydon Road
London Road
High Street
Vicarage Hill
Brasted Road
Hosey Hill
Hosey Common Road
French Street
Mapleton Road
Kent Hatch Road
Moorhouse Road
Goodley Stock Road
Main Road
Smiths Lane
Pootings Lane
Dairy Lane
Puddledock Lane
Froghole Lane
M25
A25
A233
B2026
B2024
B269
239
125
126
127
128
129
130
131
132
133
134
EM
EN
EP
EQ
ER
ES
ET
43
44
45
51
52
53
54

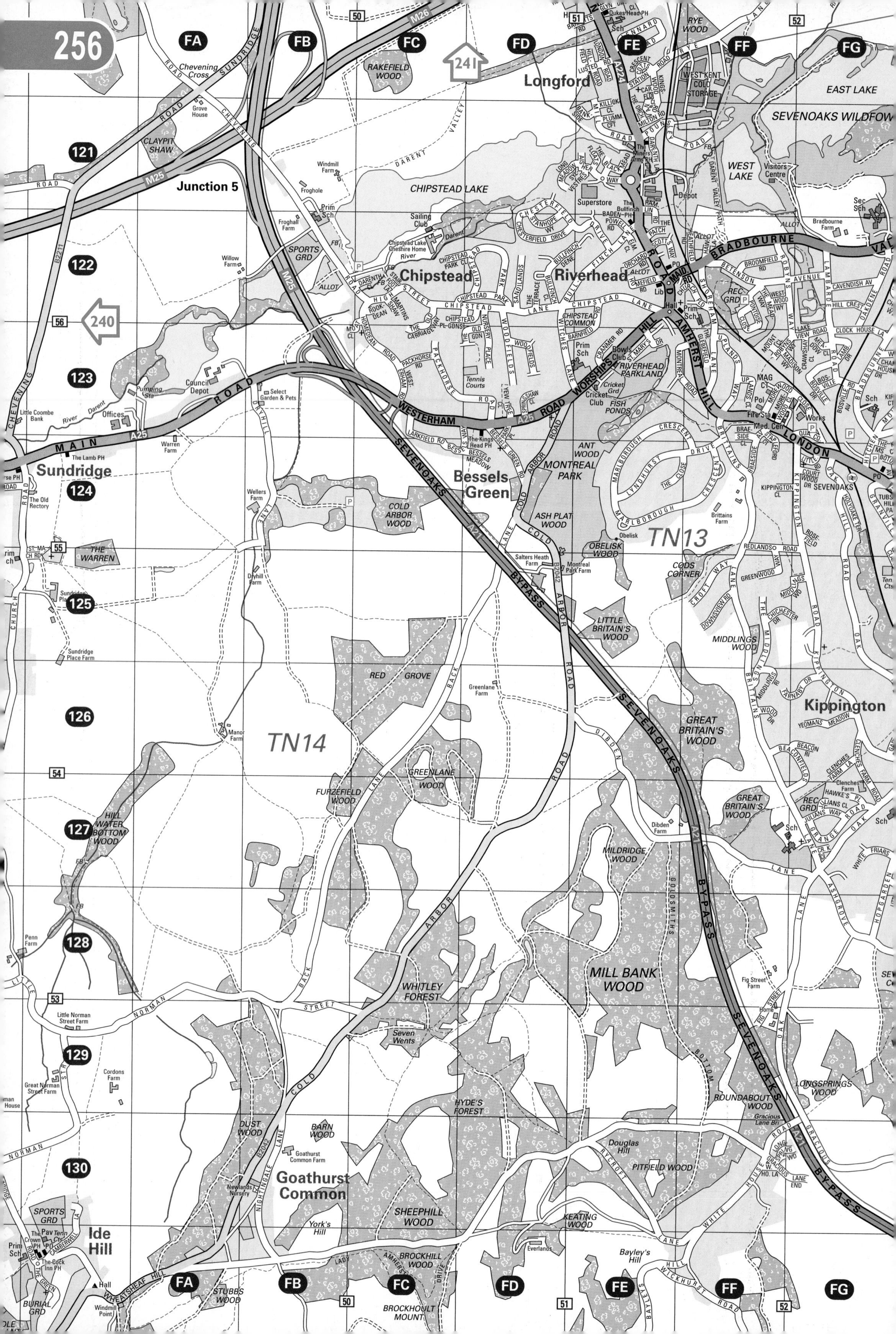

FA
FB
FC
FD
FE
FF
FG
241
240
Longford
EAST LAKE
SEVENOAKS WILDFOW
WEST LAKE
Visitors Centre
RAKEFIELD WOOD
Chevening Cross
Grove House
CLAYPIT SHAW
Junction 5
M25
M26
CHIPSTEAD LAKE
Windmill Farm
Froghole
Froghall Farm
Willow Farm
Sailing Club
Chipstead Lake Cheshire Home
SPORTS GRD
Chipstead
Riverhead
Superstore
Depot
WEST KENT COLD STORAGE
RYE WOOD
BRADBOURNE
Bradbourne Farm
Sec Sch
Council Depot
Select Garden & Pets
Pumping Sta
Little Coombe Bank
River Darent
Offices
MAIN ROAD
A25
WESTERHAM ROAD
The Lamb PH
Sundridge
The Old Rectory
Warren Farm
Wellers Farm
COLD ARBOR WOOD
THE WARREN
Dryhill Farm
Sundridge Place
Sundridge Place Farm
The Kings Head PH
Bessels Green
MONTREAL PARK
ANT WOOD
ASH PLAT WOOD
FISH PONDS
Cricket Club
RIVERHEAD PARKLAND
OBELISK WOOD
Obelisk
Salters Heath Farm
Montreal Park Farm
TN13
TN14
CODS CORNER
Brittains Farm
LITTLE BRITAIN'S WOOD
MIDDLINGS WOOD
SEVENOAKS BY-PASS
A21
RED GROVE
Greenlane Farm
Manor Farm
GREAT BRITAIN'S WOOD
Kippington
FURZEFIELD WOOD
GREENLANE WOOD
HILL WATER BOTTOM WOOD
GREAT BRITAIN'S WOOD
Dibden Farm
MILDRIDGE WOOD
Penn Farm
MILL BANK WOOD
WHITLEY FOREST
Seven Wents
Little Norman Street Farm
Cordons Farm
Great Norman Street Farm
Fig Street Farm
LONGSPRINGS WOOD
ROUNDABOUT WOOD
Gracious Lane Bri
HYDE'S FOREST
DUST WOOD
BARN WOOD
Goathurst Common Farm
Douglas Hill
PITFIELD WOOD
Goathurst Common
Newlands Nursery
SHEEPHILL WOOD
SPORTS GRD
Ide Hill
York's Hill
KEATING WOOD
Everlands
BROCKHILL WOOD
Bayley's Hill
STUBBS WOOD
BROCKHOULT MOUNT
BURIAL GRD
Windmill Point
Hall
121
122
123
124
125
126
127
128
129
130
50
51
52
53
54
55
56

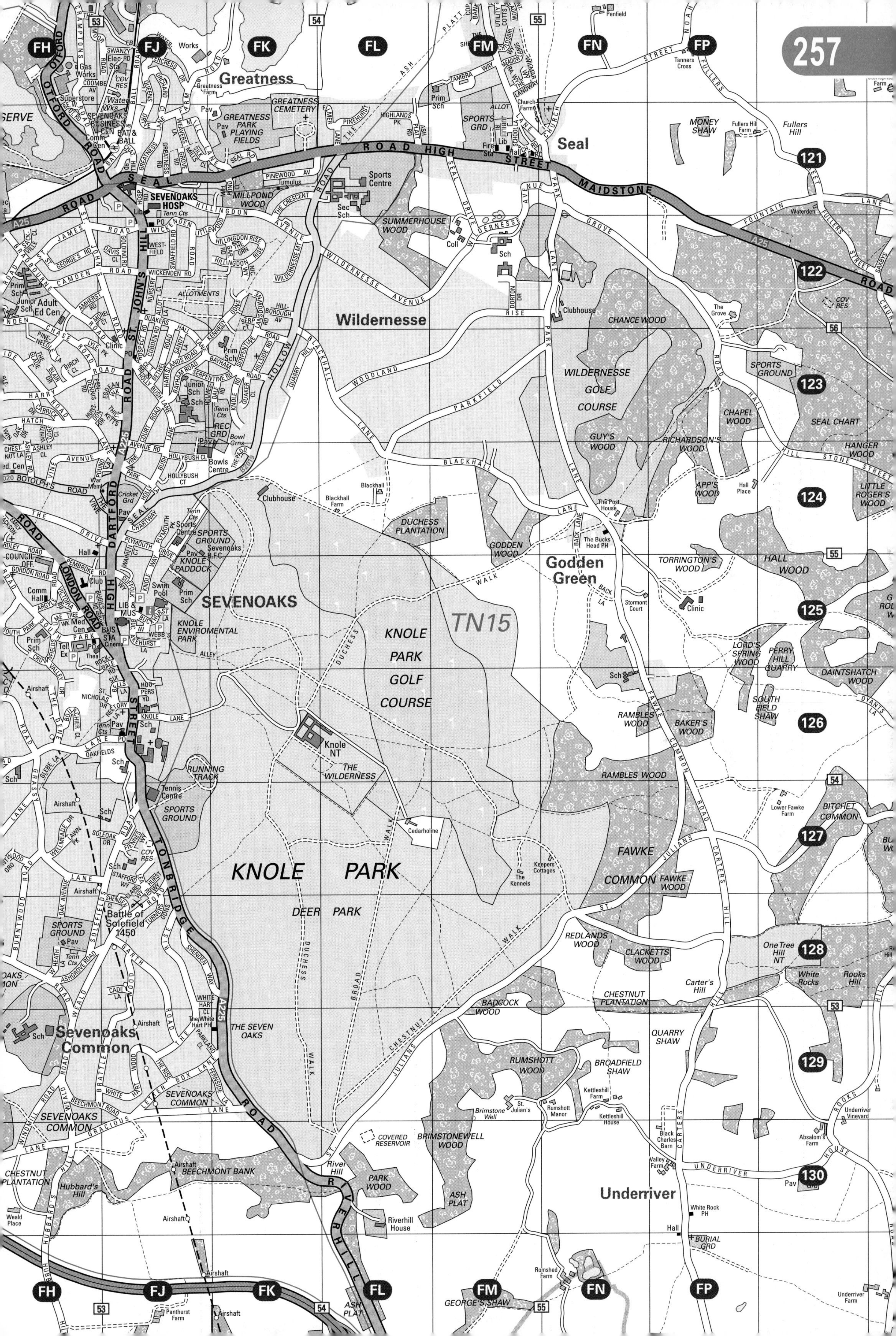
Greatness
Seal
Wildernesse
Godden Green
SEVENOAKS
TN15
KNOLE PARK
KNOLE PARK GOLF COURSE
WILDERNESSE GOLF COURSE
DEER PARK
Sevenoaks Common
SEVENOAKS COMMON
Underriver
FAWKE COMMON
SEAL CHART
HALL WOOD
RAMBLES WOOD
KNOLE PADDOCK
SEVENOAKS HOSP
Battle of Solefield 1450
Knole NT
THE WILDERNESS
THE SEVEN OAKS
RIVERHILL
TONBRIDGE ROAD
DARTFORD ROAD
HIGH STREET
SEAL ROAD
MAIDSTONE ROAD
A25
A225
FH
FJ
FK
FL
FM
FN
FP
121
122
123
124
125
126
127
128
129
130
53
54
55
56

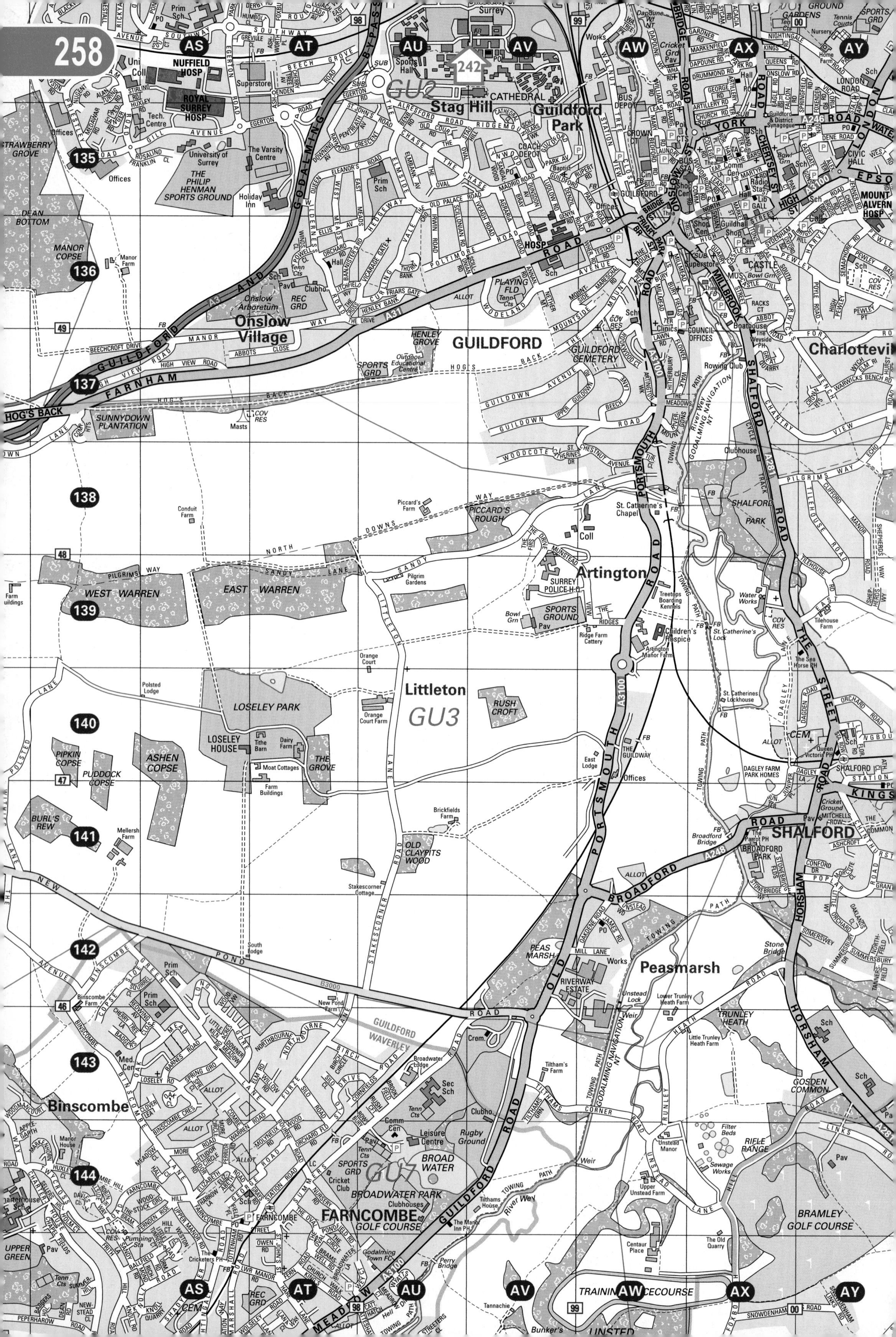
AS
AT
AU
AV
AW
AX
AY
242
GU2
GU3
GU7
NUFFIELD HOSP
ROYAL SURREY HOSP
Tech. Centre
University of Surrey
The Varsity Centre
THE PHILIP HENMAN SPORTS GROUND
Holiday Inn
STRAWBERRY GROVE
DEAN BOTTOM
MANOR COPSE
Manor Farm
Stag Hill
CATHEDRAL
Guildford Park
Onslow Arboretum
Onslow Village
REC GRD
PLAYING FLD
HENLEY GROVE
GUILDFORD
Outdoor Educational Centre
SPORTS GRD
GUILDFORD CEMETERY
COUNCIL OFFICES
Rowing Club
Charlottevil
CASTLE
MOUNT ALVERN HOSP
CIVIC HALL
HOG'S BACK
SUNNYDOWN PLANTATION
Masts
COV RES
GUILDOWN AVENUE
PORTSMOUTH ROAD
SHALFORD ROAD
River Wey GODALMING NAVIGATION NT
Clubhouse
SHALFORD PARK
St. Catherine's Chapel
Conduit Farm
Piccard's Farm
PICCARD'S ROUGH
NORTH DOWNS WAY
PILGRIMS WAY
WEST WARREN
EAST WARREN
Pilgrim Gardens
Artington
SURREY POLICE H.Q.
SPORTS GROUND
Treetops Boarding Kennels
Children's Hospice
Artington Manor Farm
Ridge Farm Cattery
St. Catherine's Lock
Water Works
Tilehouse Farm
The Sea Horse PH
St. Catherines Lockhouse
Polsted Lodge
LOSELEY PARK
LOSELEY HOUSE
Tithe Barn
Dairy Farm
THE GROVE
Moat Cottages
Farm Buildings
Orange Court
Orange Court Farm
Littleton
RUSH CROFT
THE GUILDWAY
East Lodge
Offices
PIPKIN COPSE
PUDDOCK COPSE
ASHEN COPSE
BURL'S REW
Mellersh Farm
Brickfields Farm
OLD CLAYPITS WOOD
Stakescorner Cottage
DAGLEY FARM PARK HOMES
Broadford Bridge
SHALFORD
Queen Victoria PH
Cricket Ground
BROADFORD PARK
The Parrot PH
BROADFORD ROAD
PEAS MARSH
RIVERWAY ESTATE
Peasmarsh
Unstead Lock
Lower Trunley Heath Farm
TRUNLEY HEATH
Little Trunley Heath Farm
Stone Bridge
HORSHAM ROAD
South Lodge
Binscombe Farm
New Pond Farm
Binscombe
GUILDFORD WAVERLEY
Crem.
Broadwater Lodge
Sec Sch
Leisure Centre
Rugby Ground
BROAD WATER
BROADWATER PARK
SPORTS GRD
Cricket Club
FARNCOMBE GOLF COURSE
Clubhouses
FARNCOMBE
Tiltham's Farm
Unstead Manor
Filter Beds
Sewage Works
RIFLE RANGE
GOSDEN COMMON
BRAMLEY GOLF COURSE
Upper Unstead Farm
Centaur Place
The Old Quarry
Tilthams House
The Manor Inn PH
Perry Bridge
Godalming Town FC
Tannachie
Bunker's
TRAINING RACECOURSE
UPPER GREEN
Charterhouse Sch
The Cricketers PH
Pumping Sta
B3000
A3100
A31
A281
A248
A246
FARNHAM ROAD
GUILDFORD AND GODALMING BY-PASS
135
136
137
138
139
140
141
142
143
144
49
48
47
46
98
99
00

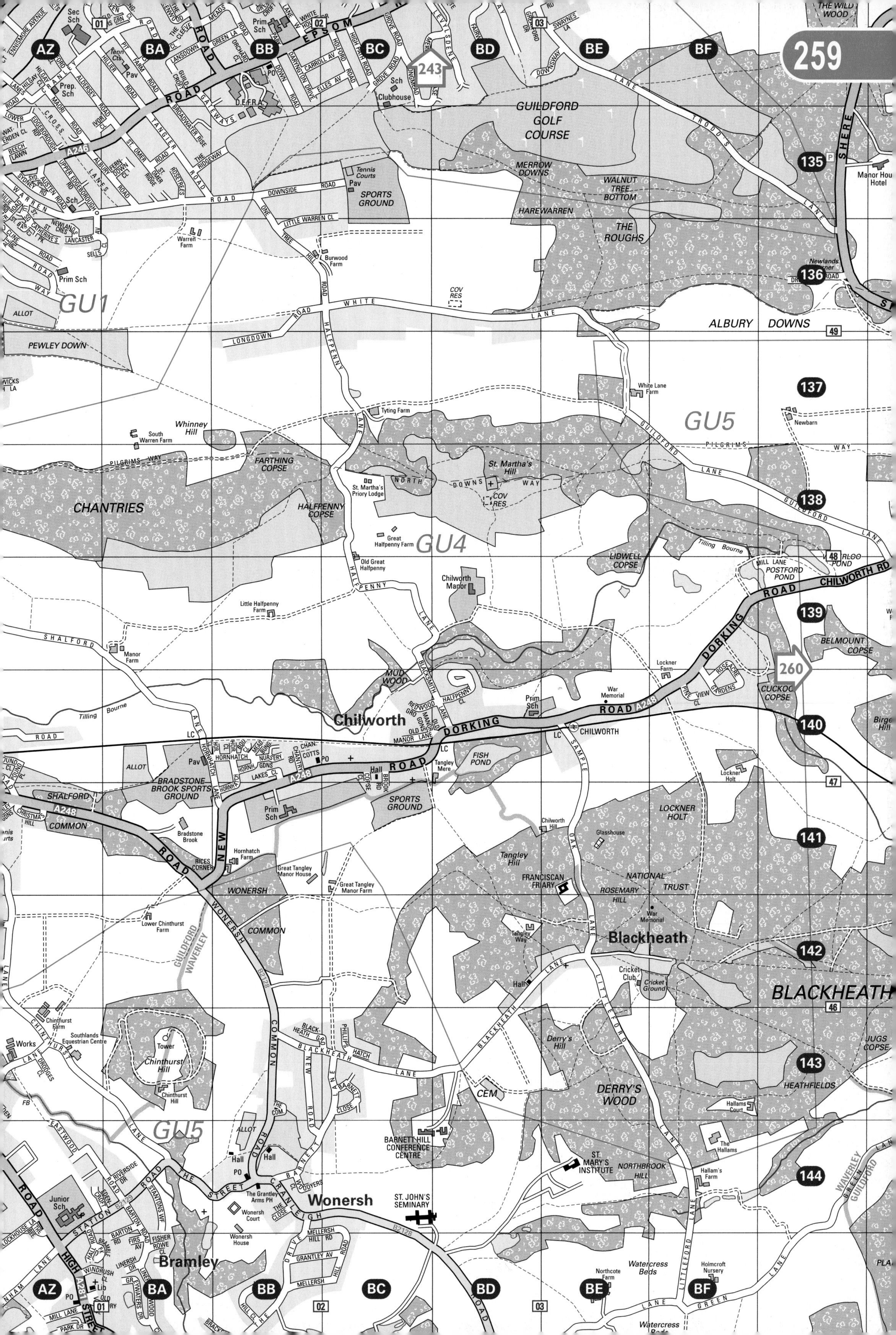
GUILDFORD GOLF COURSE
MERROW DOWNS
WALNUT TREE BOTTOM
HAREWARREN
THE ROUGHS
SPORTS GROUND
ALBURY DOWNS
PEWLEY DOWN
GU1
GU5
GU4
CHANTRIES
FARTHING COPSE
HALFPENNY COPSE
Whinney Hill
St. Martha's Hill
NORTH DOWNS WAY
PILGRIMS WAY
LIDWELL COPSE
POSTFORD POND
CHILWORTH RD
DORKING ROAD
BELMOUNT COPSE
CUCKOO COPSE
Chilworth
Chilworth Manor
MUD WOOD
FISH POND
BRADSTONE BROOK SPORTS GROUND
SHALFORD COMMON
WONERSH COMMON
LOCKNER HOLT
Tangley Hill
FRANCISCAN FRIARY
NATIONAL TRUST
ROSEMARY HILL
Blackheath
BLACKHEATH
JUGS COPSE
HEATHFIELDS
DERRY'S WOOD
Derry's Hill
Chinthurst Hill
BARNETT HILL CONFERENCE CENTRE
ST. MARY'S INSTITUTE
NORTHBROOK HILL
ST. JOHN'S SEMINARY
Wonersh
Bramley
Watercress Beds
A246
A248
A281
B2128
260
243

BG
BH
BJ
BK
BL
BM
BN
244
259
05
06
07
49
48
47
46
135
136
137
138
139
140
141
142
143
144
THE WILD WOOD
Long Acre Farm
COV RES
CLANDON DOWNS
Sunray Farm
Wellhouse Farm
Sun Valley Farm
HARROWHILL COPSE
NETHERLANDS
Old Scotland Farm
STAPLE
TROD'S LANE
SHERE
Harrowhill
Manor House Hotel
TICKNERS COPSE
STAPLELANE COPSE
New Scotland Farm
CHANTRY WOOD
COMBE
GU4
Newlands Corner
DROVE ROAD
NORTH DOWNS WAY
WEST HANGER
Mother Webb's Corner
SHERE ROAD
A25
ALBURY DOWNS
THE BOXWOOD
COMBE BOTTOM
Juniper Hill
White Lane Farm
NETLEY PLANTATION
Newbarn
GUILDFORD LANE
PILGRIMS' WAY
WATER LANE
SILENT POOL
SHERBOURNE POND
Sherbourne Farm
SHERBOURNE COTTS
Works
SAND PIT
FARM HILL WOOD
Water Lane Farm
WESTON WOOD
Manor House
SHERE REC GRD
Tilling Bourne
WATERLOO POND
MILL LANE
POSTFORD POND
SILVER WOOD
CHILWORTH RD
THE STREET
A248
SHERBOURNE
GUILDFORD LA
PO
TUPPERS CT
Weston House
Albury
GU5
The Mansion
The Old Rectory
DORKING ROAD
Weston Farm
OLD BAKERY MS
WESTON FIELDS
WESTON YD
War Memorial
Chantry Bridge
BELMOUNT COPSE
CHURCH LANE
WARREN
OAK POLLARD
Lockner Farm
Birmingham Farm
ALBURY PARK
PINE VIEW GARDENS
CUCKOO COPSE
Sher
Birget Hill
ALBURY WARREN
BLACKHEATH LANE
NEW ROAD
Lockner Holt
THE PLANTATION
PARK ROAD
SPORTS GRD
Clubho.
Mem
Albury Heath
WARNERS LANE
SHERE HEATH
LOCKNER HOLT
Ford Crossing
KILN ROUGH
ALBURY HEATH
William IV PH
Shere Heath Crossing
Parklands Farm
NATIONAL TRUST
Little Ford Farm
Watercress Beds
SANDY LANE
War Memorial
Brook Crossing
Brook Farm
BROOK LANE
PONDS LANE
Ponds Farm
Brook
Cricket Club
Cricket Ground
BLACKHEATH
BROOMFIELDS
Cotterells Farm
MUSTARD COPSE
JUGS COPSE
FOXHOLES WOOD
HEATHFIELDS
BROOK HILL
EDGELEY CARAVAN PARK
HOUND HOUSE ROAD
Hallams Court
The Hallams
AUGUST LANE
JELLEY'S COPSE
Farley Green
ROMPIN DOWNS
WAVERLEY GREEN
GUILDFORD LANE
FARLEY HEATH
SHOPHOUSE
KINGSFIELD
LOCKHURSTHATCH LANE
DILTON COPSE
RIDE LANE
Watercress Beds
Holmcroft Nursery
FAR PLANTATION
Lockhurst Hatch Farm
SKEMP
NEW FIELD
MAYORHOUSE HOLT
HURTWOOD LANE
Hound House Farm
LITTLEFORD LANE
GREEN LANE
Watercress Beds

NETLEY HEATH
OAKEN GROVE
KT24
RH5
Gomshall
Abinger Hammer
Sutton Abinger
Hoe
Smoky Hole
Peaslake
UPPER COMMON
UPPER WESTON WOOD
HERMITAGE PLANTATION
THE COPPICE
CRABTREE PLANTATION
King's Hills
GREAT KINGS WOOD
LITTLE KINGS WOOD NT
HACKHURST DOWNS
OLD SIMM'S COPSE
DUNLEY WOOD
NETLEY PARK NT
HACKHURST DOWN NT
Colkitchen Hole
ROUND DOWN
PINEY COPSE NT
GOMSHALL MARSH
FIRTREE COPSE
THE ROUGH
NATIONAL TRUST
ABINGER ROUGHS
BROOMY DOWNS
THE PLANTATION
BIRCHIN COPSE
THE PADDOCKS
Watercress Beds
ENGINE WOOD
TOWNHURST WOOD
ELLIX WOOD
ELLIX PLANTATION
HIGH COPSE
PARK REW
CONY COPSE
WOODHOUSE COPSE
WOODHOUSE POND
TENNINGSHOOK WOOD
PASTURE
RIDING COPSE
GUILDFORD ROAD
GOMSHALL ROAD
STATION ROAD
DORKING STA. RD
A25
B2126
HORSHAM ROAD
FELDAY ROAD
WONHAM WAY
RAIKES LANE
SUTTON PLACE
WATER LANE
GUILDFORD MOLE VALLEY
245
262
135
136
137
138
139
140
141
142
143
144
BP
BQ
BR
BS
BT
BU
BV

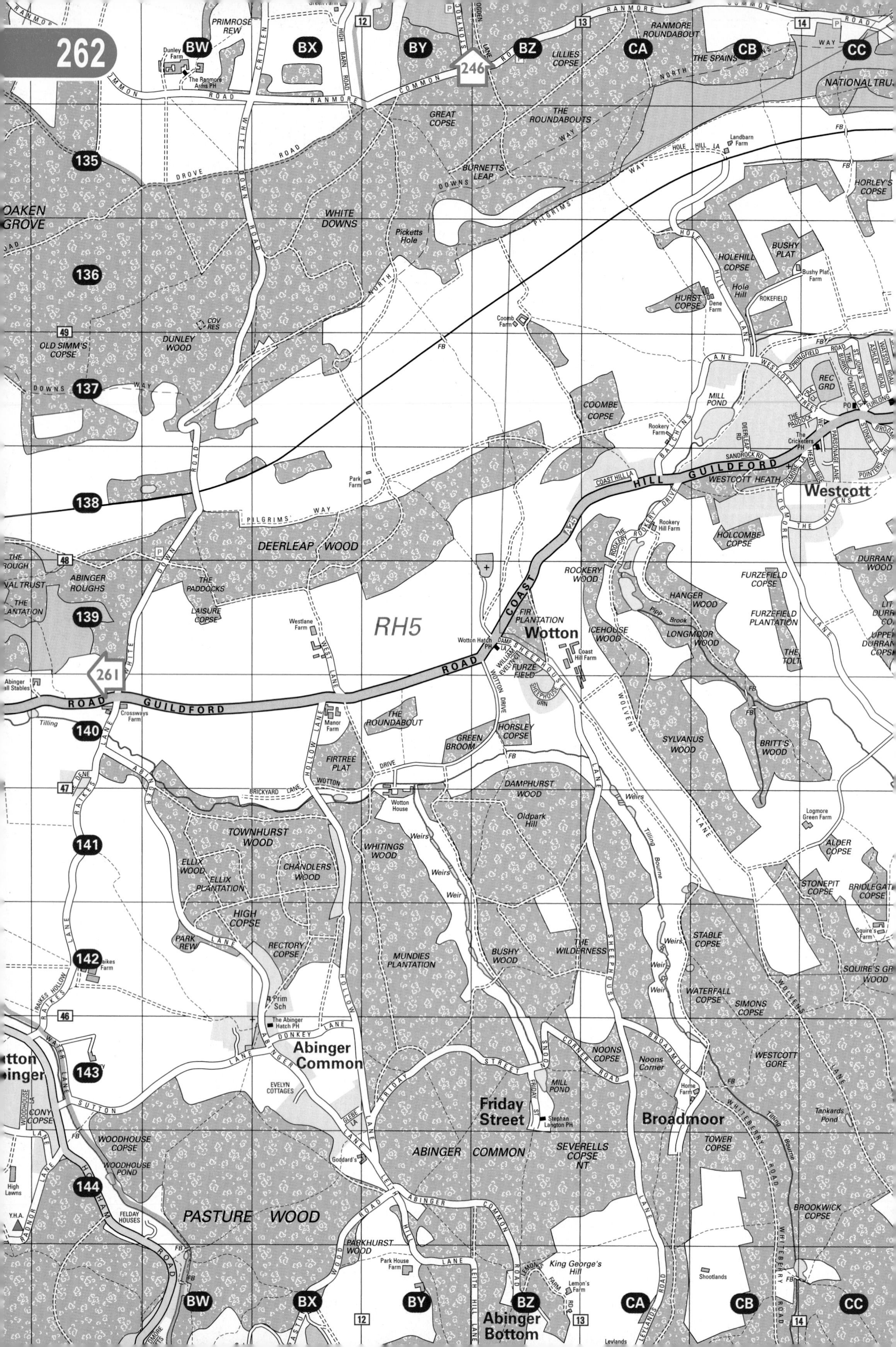

246
261
RH5
Wotton
Westcott
Abinger Common
Friday Street
Broadmoor
Abinger Bottom
PRIMROSE REW
Dunley Farm
The Ranmore Arms PH
RANMORE COMMON ROAD
LILLIES COPSE
RANMORE ROUNDABOUT
THE SPAINS
NATIONAL TRUST
GREAT COPSE
THE ROUNDABOUTS
BURNETTS LEAP
WHITE DOWNS
Picketts Hole
OAKEN GROVE
NORTH DOWNS WAY
PILGRIMS WAY
HOLE HILL LA
Landbarn Farm
HORLEY'S COPSE
HOLEHILL COPSE
BUSHY PLAT
Bushy Plat Farm
Hole Hill
HURST COPSE
Dene Farm
ROKEFIELD
Coomb Farm
COV RES
DUNLEY WOOD
OLD SIMM'S COPSE
COOMBE COPSE
MILL POND
REC GRD
Rookery Farm
The Cricketers PH
WESTCOTT HEATH
COAST HILL LA
GUILDFORD ROAD
Park Farm
DEERLEAP WOOD
THE ROUGH
ABINGER ROUGHS
THE PLANTATION
THE PADDOCKS
LAISURE COPSE
Westlane Farm
Rookery Hill Farm
HOLCOMBE COPSE
DURRANTS WOOD
ROOKERY WOOD
FURZEFIELD COPSE
FURZEFIELD PLANTATION
HANGER WOOD
LONGMOOR WOOD
FIR PLANTATION
ICEHOUSE WOOD
Coast Hill Farm
Wotton Hatch PH
FURZE FIELD
SHEEPHOUSE GRN
THE TOLT
Abinger Hall Stables
Tilling
Crossways Farm
Manor Farm
THE ROUNDABOUT
GREEN BROOM
HORSLEY COPSE
FIRTREE PLAT
SYLVANUS WOOD
BRITT'S WOOD
BRICKYARD LANE
Wotton House
DAMPHURST WOOD
Oldpark Hill
Logmore Green Farm
ALDER COPSE
TOWNHURST WOOD
ELLIX WOOD
ELLIX PLANTATION
CHANDLERS WOOD
WHITINGS WOOD
Weirs
Weir
Tilling Bourne
STONEPIT COPSE
BRIDLEGATE COPSE
HIGH COPSE
PARK REW
RECTORY COPSE
MUNDIES PLANTATION
BUSHY WOOD
THE WILDERNESS
STABLE COPSE
Squire's Farm
SQUIRE'S GREEN WOOD
Raikes Farm
Prim Sch
WATERFALL COPSE
SIMONS COPSE
The Abinger Hatch PH
NOONS COPSE
Noons Corner
WESTCOTT GORE
EVELYN COTTAGES
MILL POND
Home Farm
Tankards Pond
CONY COPSE
Stephan Langton PH
TOWER COPSE
WOODHOUSE COPSE
WOODHOUSE POND
ABINGER COMMON
SEVERELLS COPSE NT
High Lawns
Goddard's
Y.H.A.
FELDAY HOUSES
PASTURE WOOD
BROOKWICK COPSE
PARKHURST WOOD
Park House Farm
King George's Hill
Lemon's Farm
Shootlands
Leylands

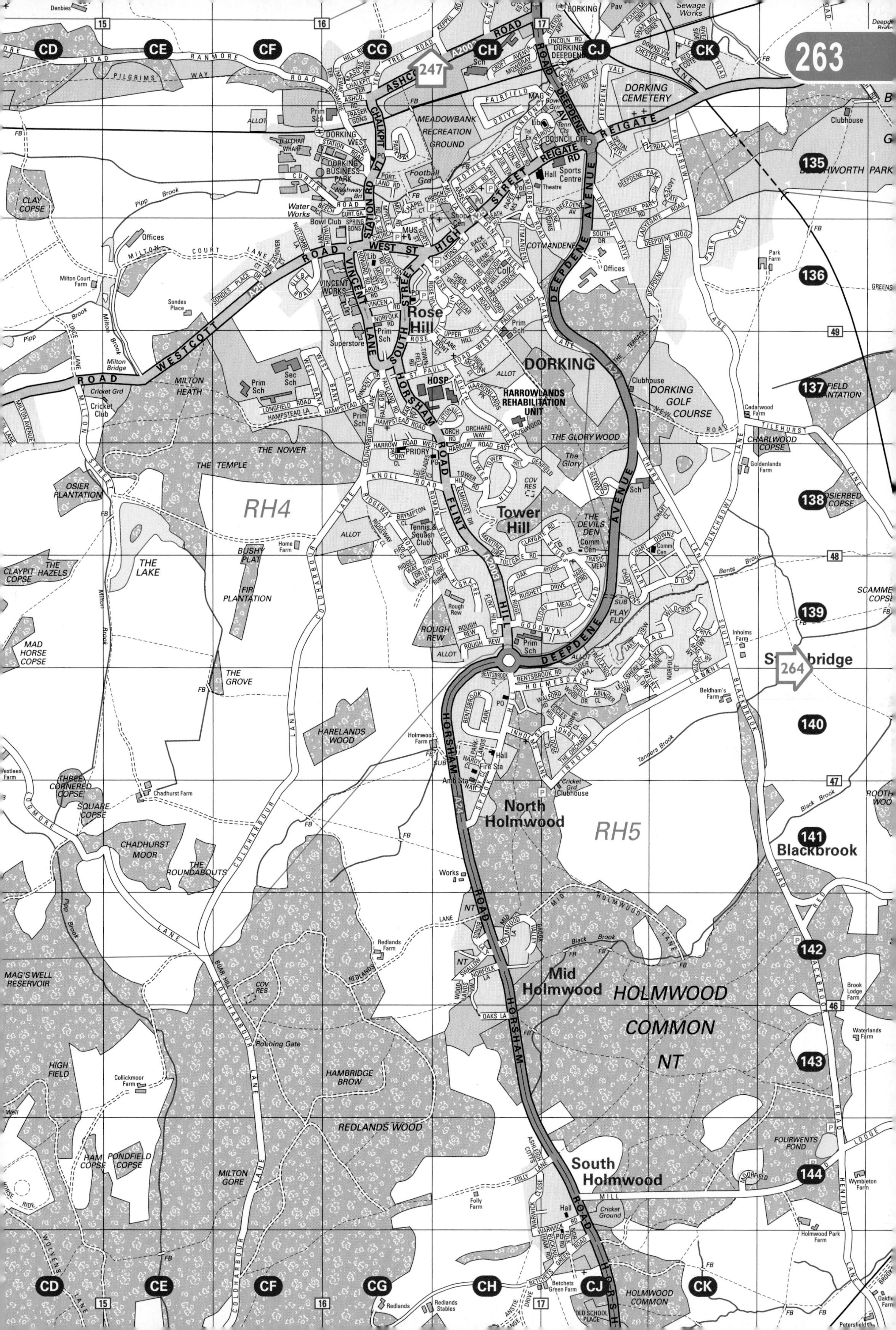
DORKING
Rose Hill
Tower Hill
North Holmwood
Mid Holmwood
South Holmwood
Blackbrook
HOLMWOOD COMMON NT
RH4
RH5
247
264
DORKING CEMETERY
MEADOWBANK RECREATION GROUND
HARROWLANDS REHABILITATION UNIT
DORKING GOLF COURSE
THE GLORY WOOD
THE NOWER
THE TEMPLE
MILTON HEATH
THE LAKE
BUSHY PLAT
FIR PLANTATION
OSIER PLANTATION
CLAYPIT COPSE
THE HAZELS
MAD HORSE COPSE
THE GROVE
HARELANDS WOOD
THREE CORNERED COPSE
SQUARE COPSE
CHADHURST MOOR
THE ROUNDABOUTS
MAG'S WELL RESERVOIR
HIGH FIELD
HAM COPSE
PONDFIELD COPSE
MILTON GORE
HAMBRIDGE BROW
REDLANDS WOOD
ROUGH REW
CLAY COPSE
BETCHWORTH PARK
CHARLWOOD COPSE
OSIERBED COPSE
FOURWENTS POND
HOLMWOOD COMMON
WESTCOTT ROAD
REIGATE ROAD
DEEPDENE AVENUE
HORSHAM ROAD
HIGH STREET
WEST ST
SOUTH STREET
VINCENT LANE
COLDHARBOUR LANE
CHART LANE
PUNCHBOWL LANE
FLINT HILL
RANMORE ROAD
PILGRIMS WAY
MILTON COURT LANE
MILTON STREET
LOGMORE LANE
INHOLMS LANE
MID HOLMWOOD LANE
SOUTH TERRACE
A24
A25
A2003
CD
CE
CF
CG
CH
CJ
CK
15
16
17
46
47
48
49
135
136
137
138
139
140
141
142
143
144

BETCHWORTH PARK GOLF COURSE
BETCHWORTH PARK
Betchworth Castle Remains
Clubhouse
DORKING CEMETERY
RH4
Betchworth
HARTSFIELD MANOR
BROOKHAM BIG FIELD
Dorking R.F.C.
Bowling Green
Borough Bridge
River Mole
Brockham Court Farm
Tanner's Bridge
Hall
Prim Sch
Brockham
SPORTS GRD
ALLOT
OLD PARK WOOD
DENDY'S WOOD
RH3
DUFFLES PLANTATION
Gadbrook Farm
Park Farm
Pondtail Farm
GREENSAND WAY
FIELD PLANTATION
DORKING GOLF COURSE
Cedarwood Farm
CHARLWOOD COPSE
Goldenlands Farm
OSIERBED COPSE
Feltons Farm
Strood Green
Stroodgreen Farm
THE ROUGH
GADBROOK COPSE
Bushbury Farm
TWEED WOOD
Gadbrook House
SCAMMELLS COPSE
Inholms Farm
Stonebridge
Beldham Farm
RH5
ROOTHILL WOOD
Root Hill
HIGHRIDGE WOOD
Hall Farm
Ashcroft Farm
Hook Farm
Root Hill Farm
ORCHARD COPSE
ROOTHILL WOOD
Great Brockhamhurst
Great Brockhamhurst Farm
Blunts Place Farm
Oakleigh Grange
HOOK COPSE
Blackbrook
KILN COPSE
Bunce Common
Westwood Farm
TWENTY ACRE SHAW
SCAMMELLS GROVE
JESSIES ROUGH
HOLMWOOD COMMON NT
Brook Lodge Farm
Waterlands Farm
Shellwood Manor
Shellwood Farm
KILN COPSE
HITHER HAWESREW
Lodge Farm
SNELLING PLANTED FIELD
FOURWENTS POND
Hawesrew Farm
NEW BARN SHAW
Wymbleton Farm
BROOKFIELD COPSE
BIRCH PLATT'S
Holmwood Park Farm
Filter Beds
SEWAGE WORKS
SIX ACRE COPSE
FURZEFIELD COPSE
BROADLANE ROUGH
HOLMWOOD COMMON
Oakfield Farm
Swires Farm
Ewood Farm
Hammond's Farm
Petersfield

248
263

265
CT
CU
CV
CW
CX
CY
CZ
22
23
24
249
266
135
136
137
138
139
140
141
142
143
144
49
47
46
SAND AND GRAVEL PIT
Dungate's Farm
Sandhills
Wonham Hill
THE ALDERS
REIGATE HEATH
GOLF COURSE
Clubhouse
Black Horse PH
Cricket Ground
SPORTS GROUND
Bowl Grn
Tenn Cts
REIGATE
Tennis Courts
Sec Sch
Site of Priory
Old Reigatians R.F.C.
ALLOT
PRIORY POND
SPORTS GROUND
Pav
Wonham Manor
Wonham Mill
MILL POND
TRUMPETS HILL ROAD
SANDY LANE
Dungate Manor
Heathfield Nursery
Heathfield Farm
Heathfield
Skimmington Castle PH
BONNY'S ROAD
FLANCHFORD ROAD
REIGATE PARK
LITTLETON LANE
Park Hill
River Mole
WILDERNESS WOOD
AGLAND COPSE
Trumpet Hill
June Farm
Little Santon Farm
Littleton Manor Stud Farm
Stepstile Meadow
GUZZLE COPSE
RICEBRIDGE LANE
Snowerhill Farm
Ricebridge Farm
Gilbert's Farm
Santon House
Wallace Brook
PARK LANE EAST
NORTH ROAD
KING GEORGE'S FIELD
Sec Sch
Clayhall Farm
Rice Bridge
FB
South Park
Comm Cen
Reigate Garden Centre
JOHN'S COPSE
RIDING'S COPSE
KNIGHT'S GORSE
SNOWERHILL ROAD
Gad Brook
CLAYHALL ROAD
SLIPSHATCH ROAD
Flanchford Farm
Little Flanchford Farm
Flanchford Bridge
MILL POND
SLIPSHATCH WOOD
WITHY WOOD
HILLY FURZE FIELD
REIGATE GRAMMAR SCHOOL
PLAYING FIELDS
Hartswood Farm
Tapner's Bridge
MARK MEAD PLANTATION
Dawesgreen
TAPNERS ROAD
MOAT
Leigh Place
LEIGH PLACE ROAD
RH2
Sch
POND FIELD PLANTATION
BIRCHETT COPSE
MOLE VALLEY
REIGATE & BANSTEAD
NINETY THREE PLANTATION
The Seven Stars PH
Prim Sch
PO
The Plough PH
Cricket Club
Leigh
Leigh Bridge
BUTLER'S SHAW
Bures Manor
ALDER COPSE
BELL COPSE
NO MAN'S LAND
Dabdon Bridge
Deanoak Brook
BROWN'S COPSE
CLAYHILL
Clayhill Farm
Lowbridge Farm
Oak Farm
SMALL'S HILL ROAD
Old Swains Farmhouse
Irons Bottom
IRONSBOTTOM
Dene Farm
Stumblehole Farm
MAGPIE WOOD
MAGPIE WOOD
Slab Castle
DULANDS COPSE
RIGDEN ROUGH
Ashurst Farm
SWAINS COPSE
DEAN OAK LANE
Dean Oak Farm
HILLY COPSE
Mynthurst
Wolvers Home Farm
Ridgewood
BUSH HOUSE COPSE
Fortune Farm
Nalderswood
PARKHOUSE COPSE
ORCHARD FOUR ACRE PLANTATION
ROOKERY WOOD
Glasshouses
Nutley Dean Farm
Duxhurst Farm
CRUTCHFIELD

REIGATE
REDHILL
Earlswood
Mead Vale
Woodhatch
South Park
Doversgreen
Sidlow
Irons Bottom
Salfords
REIGATE PARK
REDHILL COMMON
EARLSWOOD COMMON
REDHILL AND REIGATE GOLF COURSE
EARLSWOOD LAKES
REIGATE CEMETERY
REIGATE GRAMMAR SCHOOL PLAYING FIELDS
PETRIDGEWOOD COMMON
HOME GROVE
BENTING WOOD
HOLLOW SHAW
FELLAND COPSE
SAXLEY HILL
RH2
RH6
250
265
268
DA
DB
DC
DD
DE
DF
DG
135
136
137
138
139
140
141
142
143
144

South Nutfield
Ridge Green
White Bushes
Outwood
REDHILL AERODROME AND HELIPORT
RH1
M23
251
269

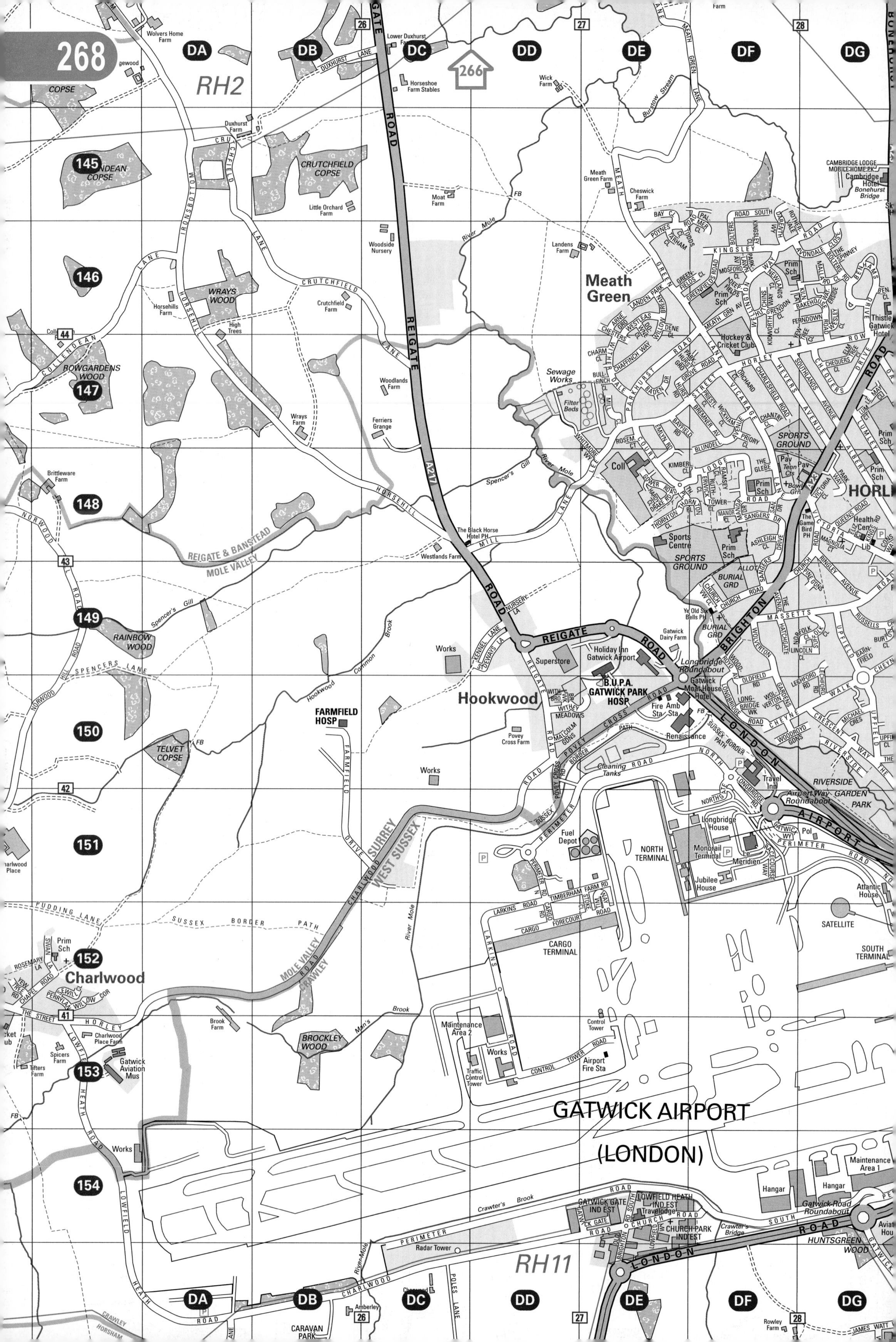

266
RH2
RH11
DA
DB
DC
DD
DE
DF
DG
26
27
28
145
146
147
148
149
150
151
152
153
154
44
43
42
41
Wolvers Home Farm
Lower Duxhurst Farm
DUXHURST LANE
Horseshoe Farm Stables
Wick Farm
Duxhurst Farm
CRUTCHFIELD
CRUTCHFIELD COPSE
Little Orchard Farm
Moat Farm
Woodside Nursery
IRONSBOTTOM
WRAYS WOOD
Horsehills Farm
High Trees
Crutchfield Farm
ROWGARDENS WOOD
COLLENDEAN LANE
Woodlands Farm
Ferriers Grange
Wrays Farm
HORSEHILL
Brittleware Farm
NORWOOD HILL ROAD
REIGATE & BANSTEAD
MOLE VALLEY
Spencer's Gill
RAINBOW WOOD
SPENCERS LANE
TELVET COPSE
The Black Horse Hotel PH
Westlands Farm
MILL LANE
REIGATE ROAD
A217
River Mole
Burstow Stream
Meath Green Farm
Cheswick Farm
Landens Farm
CAMBRIDGE LODGE MOBILE HOME PK
Cambridge Hotel
Bonehurst Bridge
Meath Green
MEATH GREEN LANE
Sewage Works
Filter Beds
Hockey & Cricket Club
Thistle Gatwick Hotel
SPORTS GROUND
Coll
Prim Sch
Sports Centre
BURIAL GRD
Ye Old Six Bells PH
BRIGHTON ROAD
A23
HORLEY
Health Cen
Lib
Gatwick Dairy Farm
Holiday Inn Gatwick Airport
Superstore
Longbridge Roundabout
Gatwick Moat House Hotel
B.U.P.A. GATWICK PARK HOSP
Fire Sta
Amb Sta
Renaissance
Hookwood
Works
FARMFIELD HOSP
FARMFIELD DRIVE
Povey Cross Farm
POVEY CROSS ROAD
Cleaning Tanks
Travel Inn
RIVERSIDE GARDEN PARK
Airport Way Roundabout
AIRPORT WAY
Longbridge House
Monorail Terminal
Le Meridien
Jubilee House
Fuel Depot
NORTH TERMINAL
PERIMETER ROAD
Atlantic House
SATELLITE
SOUTH TERMINAL
LARKINS ROAD
CARGO FORECOURT
CARGO TERMINAL
SURREY
WEST SUSSEX
CHARLWOOD ROAD
PUDDING LANE
SUSSEX BORDER PATH
Charlwood
Prim Sch
THE STREET
Charlwood Place Farm
Gatwick Aviation Mus
Spicers Farm
LOWFIELD HEATH ROAD
Brook Farm
BROCKLEY WOOD
Man's Brook
Maintenance Area 2
Works
Traffic Control Tower
Control Tower
Airport Fire Sta
CONTROL TOWER ROAD
GATWICK AIRPORT
(LONDON)
Maintenance Area 1
Hangar
Gatwick Road Roundabout
Crawter's Brook
GATWICK GATE IND EST
LOWFIELD HEATH IND EST
Travelodge
CHURCH PARK IND EST
Crawter's Bridge
HUNTSGREEN WOOD
LONDON ROAD
Radar Tower
POLES LANE
Amberley
CARAVAN PARK
Rowley Farm
CRAWLEY
HORSHAM

RH1
RH6
RH10
Smallfield
Burstow
Junction 9
Junction 9a
Airport Way Roundabout East
GATWICK AIRPORT
HORLEY
BROOK WOOD
LANGSHOTT WOOD
ALDER BED
LOST SEVENS
OAK BED
WEATHERHILL COMMON
Smallfield Grid Sub Station
THE ROOKERY
LONGYARDS SHAW
COLDLAND WOOD
ROOKERY HILL
COURTOAK GREEN
Burstow Manor
BURSTOW BUSINESS CENTRE
BRIDGEHAM WOOD
THE ROUGHS
THE PLANTATION
Site of Thunderfield Castle
Harrowsley Green Farm
Haroldslea Poultry Farm
Farney Glen Farm
Wilgers Farm
Hathersham Farm
Greatlake Farm
Tanyard Farm
The Farmhouse PH
Hunters Moon Farm
The Castle PH
MILLERS COPSE
Brightleigh Farm
Hollesley Farm
Lower Broadbridge Farm
Broadmead Farm
LARBURNUM COURT CARAVAN SITE
Gunyah Farm
Flightpath Farm
Broadbridge Stables
BELLHATCH WOOD
COLLINS WOOD
BRIDGES WOOD
Broadfield Farm
Gatwick House
Mushroom Farm
Rede Hall
Redeham Hall
EASTLANDS SHAW
KILN HEATH
Riding School
New House Farm
Burstow Park Farm
Burstow Park
The Shipley Bridge Inn PH
Courtlands
Rivington Farm
Teizers Farm
Burstow Hall
Burstow Nurseries
HORLEYLAND WOOD
UPPER PICKETT'S
ALLEN'S WOOD
Sludge Lagoons
Sewage Works
Filter Beds
Fern Court Farm
Schlumberger House
Hilton
Offices
Monorail Terminal
BUS/COACH STA
Beehive Offices
The Parsons Pig PH
Oldlands Farm
The Greyhound PH
Hollybush Farm
KING GEORGE'S FIELD
Hunters Moon Inn PH
Moorlands Farm
Triddles Farm
Green Farm
The Plough PH
PLAYING FIELD
SPORTS GRD
GATWICK METRO CENTRE
Gas Holder Sta
Prim Sch
Swim Pool
Sec Sch
Elec Sta
Depot
Sewage Works
WEST SUSSEX
SURREY
CRAWLEY
TANDRIDGE
REIGATE & BANSTEAD
SUSSEX BORDER PATH
M23
A23
B2036
B2037
LANGSHOTT
SMALLFIELD ROAD
WEATHERHILL ROAD
HATHERSHAM LANE
ROOKERY HILL
NORMANS ROAD
CHAPEL ROAD
PLOUGH LANE
WHEELERS LANE
BROADBRIDGE LANE
CHURCH ROAD
CHURCH LANE
EFFINGHAM ROAD
COPTHORNE BANK
ANTLANDS LANE
SHIPLEY BRIDGE LANE
PEEKS BROOK LANE
FERNHILL ROAD
BALCOMBE ROAD
HAROLDSLEA DRIVE
SILVERLEA GARDENS
AVENUE GARDENS
BALCOMBE GARDENS
CASTLE DRIVE
VICTORIA ROAD
REDEHALL ROAD
DH
DJ
DK
DL
DM
DN
DP
267
29
30
31
41
42
43
44
145
146
147
148
149
150
151
152
153
154

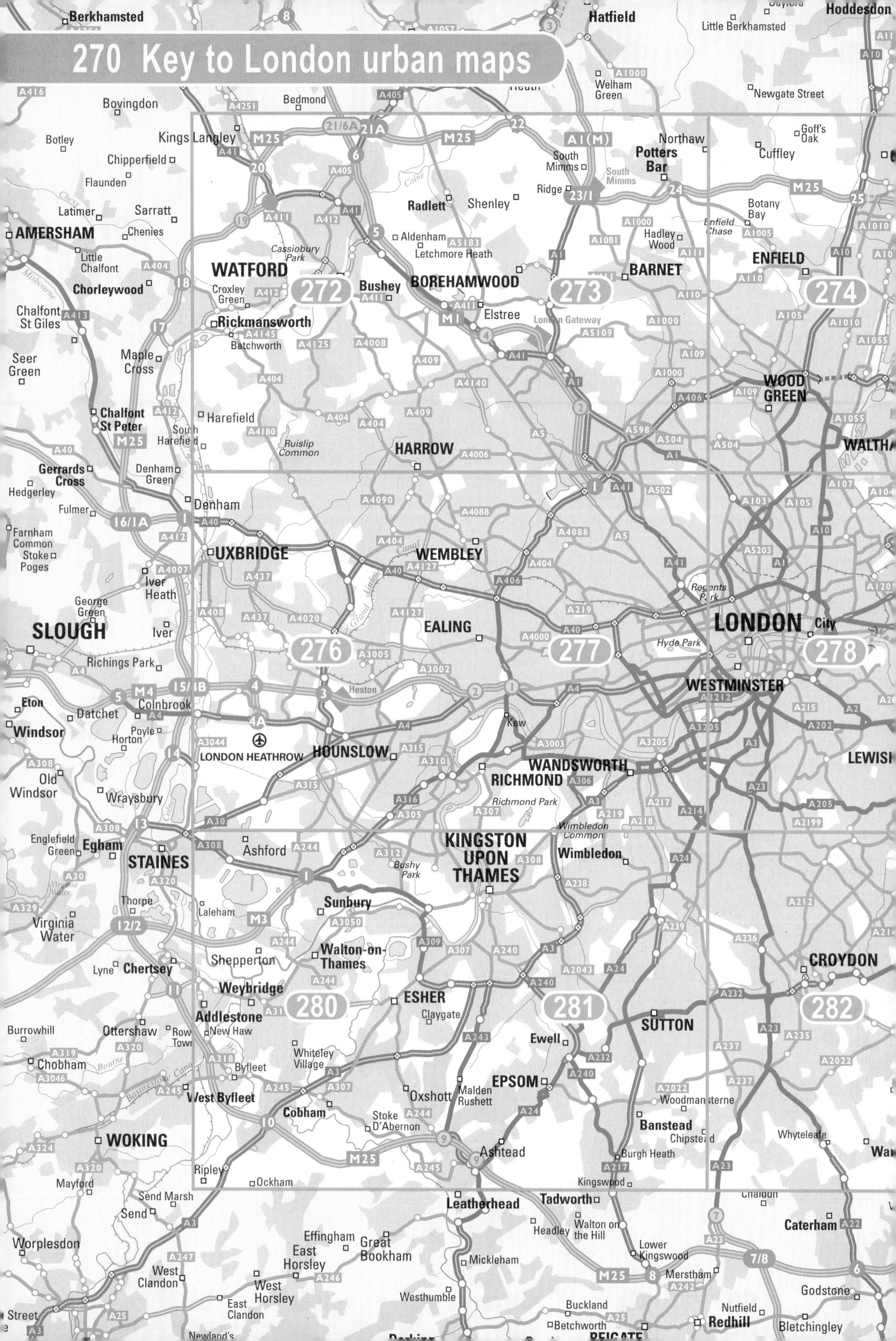

272
273
274
276
277
278
280
281
282
WATFORD
BOREHAMWOOD
BARNET
ENFIELD
HARROW
WEMBLEY
UXBRIDGE
EALING
LONDON
WESTMINSTER
HOUNSLOW
LONDON HEATHROW
WANDSWORTH
RICHMOND
KINGSTON UPON THAMES
SLOUGH
STAINES
WOKING
ESHER
EPSOM
SUTTON
CROYDON
AMERSHAM
Rickmansworth
Bushey
Elstree
Potters Bar
Radlett
Shenley
Wood Green
Windsor
Eton
Egham
Chertsey
Weybridge
Addlestone
Walton-on-Thames
Sunbury
Shepperton
Ashford
Cobham
Leatherhead
Ashtead
Banstead
Tadworth
Caterham
Redhill
Hatfield
Hoddesdon
Berkhamsted
Kings Langley
Chorleywood
Gerrards Cross
Denham
Harefield
Wimbledon
Kew
Hyde Park
Regents Park
City

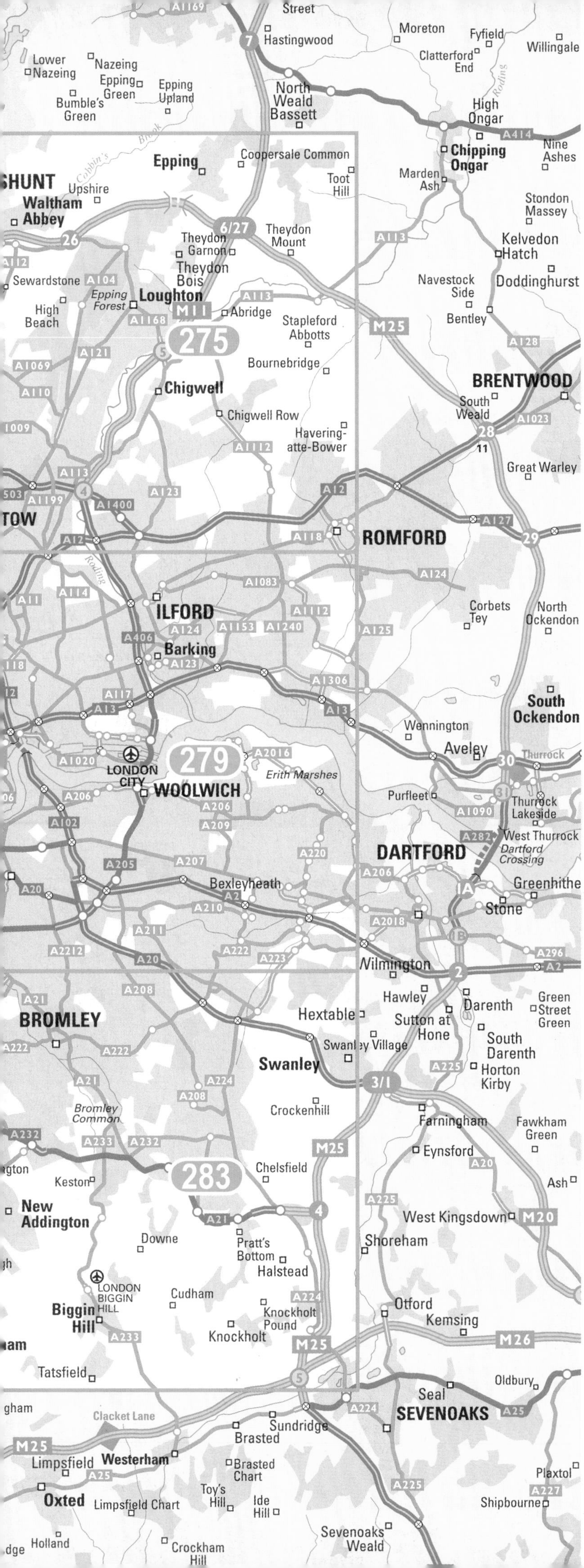

Key to map symbols

on pages 272-283

23 M25 24	Motorway junctions with full access
5 M11 4	Motorway junctions with limited access
GATEWAY SERVICES	Motorway service area
A406	Primary route with dual / single carriageway
A5	'A' road with dual / single carriageway
B552	'B' road with dual / single carriageway
	Minor road with dual / single carriageway
	Road proposed or under construction
	Road tunnel
	Roundabout
T	Toll
	One way street / Restricted access
	Level crossing
	Airport with scheduled services
	Railway line / Railway tunnel
	Railway station / Light rail station
	Underground station
Ⓗ	Heliport
	Congestion charging zone
	Public building
362 ▲	Spot height in metres
	Built up area
	Woodland / Park
CAMDEN	County / Unitary Authority boundary and name

	Football club (Major British club)		Theme park
	Garden		Wildlife park or zoo
	Historic house		Other interesting feature
	Museum	★	Landmark public house
	Racecourse	i	Information centre

SCALE

0 — 1/2 — 1 1/2 — 2 miles

0 — 1 — 2 — 3 — 4 kilometres

1:63,360 1 inch (2.5cm) to 1 mile / 1.6 cm to 1 km

Apsley
Potters Crouch
Park Street
Chiswell Green
How Wood
Frogmore
Bedmond
Great Wood
Phasels Wood
Shendish Manor Golf Course
Scatterdells Wood
KINGS LANGLEY
Chipperfield
Chipperfield Common
Belsize
The Two Brewers
ABBOTS LANGLEY
Bricket Wood
Building Research Establishment
Bricket Wood Common
Woodside
Leavesden Green
Kingswood
Garston
Hunton Bridge
The Kings Head
Berrybushes Wood
Beechen Bottom
Juniper Hill
Sarratt
Dawes Common
Sandfield Wood
Templepan Wood
Heath Wood
The Grove Park
NORTH WATFORD
Watford North
University of Hertfordshire (Watford Campus)
Aldenham Golf & Country Club
Aldenham
Letchmore Heath
Patchetts Green
The Three Compasses
The Otter
Great Wood
Whippendell Wood
Harrocks Wood
Welling Grove
Beechengrove Wood
West Herts Golf Course
Cassiobury Park
WATFORD
Watford Junction
Bushy Hall Golf Course
HERTFORD
Elstree Aerodrome
Hilfield Park Reservoir
Loudwater
CROXLEY GREEN
Croxley
Coach & Horses
The Artichoke
Chorleywood Bottom
RICKMANSWORTH
Mill End
Moneyhill
Rickmansworth Council Offices
Three Rivers Mus.
Holywell
Common Moor
Croxley Hall Wood
Hampermill Lake
Watford General Hospital
Vicarage Rd Watford FC
Watford High Street
Bushey
BUSHEY
Bushey Golf Course & Country Club
Merry Hill
Oxhey
Watford Heath
Bushey Heath
RUPA Hospital
Hartsbourne Golf & Country Club
Bentley Priory
Bentley Priory Open Space
Batchworth
Batchworth Lake
Bury Lake
Stocker's Lake
The White Bear
Batchworth Park Golf Course
Rickmansworth Golf Course
Moor Park Mansion
Moor Park
Moor Park Golf Course
Sandy Lodge Golf Course
Oxhey Park Golf Course
Carpenders Park
Oxhey Wood
South Oxhey
Grim's Dyke Golf Course
Harrow Weald Common
Eastbury
Ye Olde Green Manne
Batchworth Heath
The Rose and Crown
Prince of Wales
Bishopswood Private Hospital
Bishop's Wood
NORTHWOOD
Mount Vernon Hospital
Wild Woods
Hill End
Pearson's Wood
Park Wood
Lynsters Lake
Royal Oak
Pynesfield Lake
Harefield Hospital
Harefield
The Swan
Northwood
Pinner Hill Golf Course
Pinnerwood Park
Hatch End
Northwood & Pinner Community Hospital
Northwood Golf Course
Northwood Hills
Pinner Green
Pinner Park
HARROW
HARROW WEALD
Headstone
Harrow Museum
Harrow & Wealdstone
Civic Centre
Haste Hill Golf Course
Copse Wood
St. Vincent's Orthopaedic Hospital
Mad Bess Wood
Ruislip Lido
Park Wood
RUISLIP
Pinner
North Harrow
Grand Union Canal
South Harefield
Bayhurst Wood Country Park
HILLINGDON
Eastcote Village
Eastcote
Government Offices
Manor House
Denham Green
The Nightingale
Denham
Ruislip Common
Ruislip Golf Course
Ruislip Manor
Rayners Lane
West Harrow
HARROW
Harrow on the Hill
Buckinghamshire Golf Course
Uxbridge Golf Course
DENHAM
West Ruislip
M25
M1
A41
A405
A411
A412
A404
A4008
A409
River Gade
River Colne
River Pinn
59
73
91
276

273
LONDON COLNEY
North Mymms Park
Walsingham Wood
63
Brookmans Park Golf Course
BROOKMANS PARK
Brookmans Park
Royal Veterinary Collage
Cobs Ash
Cangsley Wood
Hawkshead Wood
Redwell Wood
Mymmshall Wood
de Havilland Aircraft Heritage Centre
Ridgehill
Harperbury Hospital
Nine Acres
Hound's Wood
Combe Wood
South Mimms
Leggatts Wood
Well Wood
Northaw
Hook Wood
POTTERS BAR
Potters Bar Golf Course
Furzefield Wood
Potters Bar Mus
Potters Bar Community Hospital
Pond Wood
Shenley
Ridge
Old Guinea
SOUTH MIMMS SERVICES
Porters Park Golf Course
Radlett
Dancers Hill
Bentley Heath
Ganwick Corner
The Duke of York
Wrotham Park
Plumridge Wood
Little Beechill Wood
Enfield Chase
Dyrham Park Golf Course
Dyrham Park
Kitt's End
Monken Hadley
Hadley Wood
Hadley Wood Golf Course
Moat Wood
Kendal Wood
The Mops & Brooms
Bridgedown Golf Course
Old Fold Manor Golf Course
Monken Hadley Common
Middlesex University
Trent Park
Elstree Studios
Hertsmere Civic Offices
Waggon & Horses
Aldenham Park Woodland
BOREHAMWOOD
High Barnet
Hadley
BARNET
The Tudor Golf Course
Beech Hill Lake
Cockfosters
Elstree Golf Course
Elstree & Borehamwood
Arkley Golf Course
Barnet Museum
Barnet Hospital
New Barnet
Cockfosters
Aldenham Country Park
Aldenham Park
Aldenham Reservoir
Rowley Lane Golf Course
Rowley Green
Arkley
Chipping Barnet
274
East Barnet
Middlesex University
Elstree
Barnet Gate
Ducks Island
Underhill
New Barnet
Oak Hill Park
Deacons Hill Open Space
Scratch Wood
Elstree Open Space
Moat Mount Open Space
South Herts Golf Course
Brook Farm Open Space
Oakleigh Park
Osidge
Royal National Orthopaedic Hospital
LONDON GATEWAY SERVICES
Mill Hill Golf Course
Highwood Hill
Nut Wood
Totteridge
Totteridge and Whetstone
Pear Wood
Brockley Hill Golf Park
Edgwarebury Park
Edgwarebury Golf Course
BARNET
Folly Brook
Whetstone
Apex Corner
Three Hammers
National Institute for Medical Research
North Middlesex Golf Course
Bethune Park Golf Course
FRIERN BARNET
Stanmore
EDGWARE
Jolly Badger
MILL HILL
Woodside Park
North Finchley
New Southgate
Canons Park
Edgware
Arandene Open Space
Mill Hill Broadway
Finchley Golf Course
Burnt Oak
Mill Hill East
West Finchley
Finchley Memorial Hospital
Coppetts Wood
Edgware Community Hospital
Government Buildings
The Masons Arms
Hendon Golf Course
Church End
Finchley Central
FINCHLEY
Coppetts Wood Hospital
Muswell Hill Golf Course
Belmont
Queensbury
RAF Museums
Colindale Hospital
Colindale
Sunny Hill Park
The Queens Head
Coldfall Wood
East Finchley
The Honeypot
Church Farm House Museum
The London Museum of Jewish Life
Kingsbury Community Hospital
Middx Uni. Town Hall
St. Luke's Woodside Hospital
Kenton
The Plough
Prince of Wales
Kingsbury
Hendon Central
Big Wood
Hampstead Garden Suburb
Highgate Wood
HORNSEY
Hendon Park
Highgate Golf Course
Queen's Wood
Northwick Park
Uni. of Westminster (Harrow Campus)
Northwick Park and St. Mark's Hospitals
Fryent Country Park
West Hendon
HENDON
Hendon
Brent Cross
Golders Green
Hampstead Golf Club
Highgate
Barn Hill Open Space
Preston Road
South Kenton
277
Brent Reservoir
Spaniards Inn
Manor House Hospital
The Iveagh Bequest Kenwood House
Athlone House
The Flask
Whittington Hospital
Brent Town Hall
Childs Hill
Jack Straw's Castle
HAMPSTEAD
Hampstead Heath
BRENT
North Wembley
Wembley
Dollis Hill
Queen Mary's Hospital
Dartmouth Park
M25
A1(M)
A1
M1
A41
A5
A406
A1000
A5109
A411
A5135
A598
A504
A502
A1003
A109
A111
A4006
A4140
A410
A5150
A5183
B556
B5378
B157
B156
B158
B193
B552
B1461
B454
B461
B519
22
23
24
4
2
1

274
66
Newgate Street
Hammond Street
Cheshunt Park
Turnford
Holyfield Lake
Cuffley
Well Wood
Cheshunt Common
Flamstead End
Holyfield
Aimes Green
Goffs Oak
Northaw
Hook Wood
Bury Green
CHESHUNT
Cattlegate
Cattlins
Waltham Cross
WALTHAM ABBEY
Holdbrook
Pond Wood
M25
25
Crews Hill
Botany Bay
Whitewebbs Park
Freezy Water
Enfield Chase
Bullsmoor
Enfield Lock
Forty Hill
Enfield Wash
ENFIELD
Sewardstone
Trent Park
Enfield Highway
Brimsdown
World's End
Grange Park
Bush Hill Park
Sewardstonebury
East Barnet
Winchmore Hill
Ponders End
Oakwood
Osidge
King George's Reservoir
William Girling Reservoir
Chingford Green
Southgate
Lower Edmonton
New Southgate
Palmers Green
EDMONTON
CHINGFORD
Friday Hill
FRIERN BARNET
Chingford Hatch
Bowes Park
Upper Edmonton
South Chingford
Highams Park
TOTTENHAM
Hale End
WOOD GREEN
Noel Park
Banbury Reservoir
Muswell Hill
West Green
Tottenham Hale
Higham Hill
WALTHAMSTOW
South Woodford
Upper Walthamstow
HORNSEY
HARRINGAY
South Tottenham
Crouch End
Stroud Green
Highgate
STOKE NEWINGTON
Upper Clapton
Leytonstone
Finsbury Park
LEYTON
273
278

Nazeing Gate
Thornwood
70
North Weald Airfield
NORTH WEALD BASSETT
Deerpark Wood
Stocking Grove
Fernhall Wood
Rookery Wood
The Lower Forest
North Weald Golf Course (9 Hole)
Roughtalley's Wood
Greensted Green
Civic Offices
EPPING
St. Margaret's Hospital
Coopersale
Toot Hill
Clatterford End
Toot Hill Golf Course
Mole Trap
Bell Common
Ivy Chimneys
Bower Hill
Fiddlers Hamlet
Mount End
Upshire
Forest Gate
The Merry Fiddlers
Beachet Wood
Copthall Green
The Warren
Epping Forest
Theydon Mount
26
27
6
Woodbine Inn
The Volunteer
Theydon Bois Golf Course
Hobbs Cross Golf Centre
Barber's Wood
Theydon Garnon
Twentyacre Wood
Berwick Ham
Honey Lane Quarters
Deer-shelter Plain
High Beech Golf Course
Red Oak Wood
Birch Wood
Theydon Bois
Abridge Golf and Country Club
Stapleford Tawney
87
Great Monk Wood
Broadstone Plain
Debden Green
The King's Oak
Little Monk Wood
Loughton Golf Course
Hill Wood
The Robin Hood
River Roding
Debden
The Plume of Feathers
Ape's Grove
Strawberry Hill
Abridge
Curtismill Green
The Sir Winston Churchill
Soapley's Wood
Great Wood
Loughton
Stapleford Abbotts
Buckhurst Hill
Woolston Manor Golf Course
5
Stapleford Abbotts Golf Course
Lambourne End
Nuper's Hatch
ESSEX
The Camelot
Three Cornered Plain
Spurgate Plain
Holly House Hospital
Lord's Bushes
Havering -atte-Bower
Pyrgo Park
Foxburrow Wood
Hainault Forest Country Park
Woodford Wells
The Mesmaams Inn
CHIGWELL
Chigwell Row
Roding Valley
Hainault Forest Golf Course
Havering Country Park
Bower Wood
Chigwell Golf Course
The Lake
Dog Kennel Hill
Bedfords
Woodford Green
The White Hart
The Bald Hind
Grange Hill
Havering Park
Chase Cross
105
Risebridge Golf Course
Old Maypole
Hainault
HAINAULT
WOODFORD
Hospital Hill Wood
Woodford Bridge
4
Fullwell Cross
Fairlop Water Country Park
Mark's Gate
Collier Row
Romford Golf Course
Raphael Park
Gidea Park
The Cocked Hat
Fairlop Water Golf Course
Roding Hospital
Clayhall
Aldborough Hatch
Barkingside
Dick Turpin
Victoria Hospital
Town Hall
ROMFORD
Snaresbrook
Gants Hill
Newbury Park
King George Hosp.
Moby Dick
Chadwell Heath
HAVERING
Golden Lion
Romford
The George
Wanstead
Redbridge
REDBRIDGE
Goodmayes Hospital
Seven Kings Park
Oldchurch Hospital
The Basin
Wanstead Golf Course
Valentine's Park
Seven Kings
Rush Green
The Crown Inn
Wanstead Park
Chadwell Heath
Becontree Heath
The Ship and Anchor
REDBRIDGE
279
Royal Oak
Aldersbrook
Ilford Golf Course
Cranbrook
Napier
Goodmayes
Goodmayes Park
Central Park
Valence House
Harrow Lodge Park
Ilford
M25
M11
A12
A113
A121
A104
A406
A118
EPPING ROAD
EASTERN AVENUE
ONGAR ROAD
LONDON ROAD
ROMFORD ROAD
MANOR ROAD
HIGH ROAD
ABRIDGE ROAD
WHALEBONE LANE NORTH
CRANBROOK ROAD
WOODFORD AVENUE
SOUTHEND ROAD
HORNCHURCH ROAD
RUSH GREEN ROAD
BOURNEBRIDGE LANE
STAPLEFORD ROAD
GRAVEL LANE
HOE LANE

HILLINGDON
HOUNSLOW
Harefield
Pinner
Ruislip Park Wood
RUISLIP
Eastcote Village
North Harrow
Civic Centre
Bayhurst Wood Country Park
272
Government Offices
Eastcote
Manor House
HARROW
Harrow on the Hill
Denham Green
The Nightingale
Denham
Ruislip Common
Ruislip Golf Course
Ruislip Manor
Rayners Lane
West Harrow
Buckinghamshire Golf Course
Uxbridge Golf Course
DENHAM
West Ruislip
Ruislip Gardens
South Ruislip
South Harrow
Ickenham
St. Andrew's at Harrow
Sudbury Hill
Sudbury Hill Harrow
M40
Hillingdon
Northolt Aerodrome
UXBRIDGE
North Hillingdon
Northolt
The Plough
Grand Union Canal
Lime Trees Park Golf Course
Greenford
New Windsor St.
Rock Rd.
St. Johns Rd.
Uxbridge Moor
Civic Centre
Northolt Golf Course
Northolt & Greenford Country Park
133
Hillingdon Golf Course
Vine Inn
HILLINGDON
Prince of Wales
Red Lion
Brunel University
Yeading
Athletics Stadium
South Greenford
Perivale Park Golf Course
Greenford
Red Lion
Castle Bar Park
Cowley
Hillingdon Hospital
Yeading Brook
Hayes End
HAYES
Iver
Paddington Packet Boat
YIEWSLEY
Stockley Park Golf Course
Dormer's Wells
West Middlesex Golf Course
Brent Valley Golf Course
Drayton Green
Hanwell
Hayes Town
Minet Country Park
SOUTHALL
West Drayton
Thorney
Tower Arms
Heathpark Golf Course
Government Buildings
Hayes & Harlington
Grand Union Canal
Southall
St. Bernard's Hospital
Ealing Hospital
WEST DRAYTON
Prospect Park
Norwood Green
North Hyde
Osterley Park
Osterley Park (NT)
Wyke Green Golf Course
M4
Airlinks Golf Course
HESTON SERVICES
Prospect Park
Harmondsworth
Sipson
Harlington
Cranford Park
Cranford
Queens Head
HESTON
Osterley
Government Buildings
Longford
Custom House
Spring Grove
Lampton
153
London Heathrow Airport
Terminal 1
Terminal 2
Terminal 3
Terminal 4
Cargo Terminal
Hounslow West
Hounslow Civic Centre
Hounslow East
Hounslow Central
Woodlands
ISLEWORTH
Hatton Cross
Hatton
HOUNSLOW
The Bell
County Arms
Stanwell Moor
Hounslow Heath Golf Course
Hounslow Heath
Twickenham R.F.U.
Museum of Rugby
King George VI Reservoir
Staines Reservoirs
Stanwell
East Bedfont
Whitton
TWICKENHAM
Ashford Hospital
Royal Oak
Bedfont Lakes Country Park
Feltham
Crane Park
FELTHAM
Strawberry Hill
Strawberry Hill Golf Course
H. M. Bronzefield Prison
Ashford
Lower Feltham
Hanworth Park
Twickenham Golf Course
Fulwell Golf Course
Fulwell
280
Staines
STAINES
Ashford
Ashford Manor Golf Course
Hanworth
Feltham Hill
Hampton Hill
M25
A4
A30
A40
A312
A4020
WESTERN AVENUE
BATH ROAD
GREAT SOUTH WEST ROAD
STAINES ROAD
LONDON ROAD
STAINES BYPASS
UXBRIDGE ROAD
THE PARKWAY
HAYES BYPASS
NORTH HYDE RD.
HIGH ROAD
OXFORD ROAD
LONG LANE
STOCKLEY ROAD
DAWLEY ROAD
GREENFORD ROAD
AIRPORT WAY
CHERTSEY ROAD

277
Kenton
Kingsbury
KINGSBURY ROAD
West Hendon
HENDON
273
Golders Green
Hampstead Garden Suburb
Highgate
BRENT
North Wembley
WEMBLEY
Wembley Park
Neasden
Dollis Hill
Childs Hill
HAMPSTEAD
Hampstead Heath
Parliament Hill
Dartmouth Park
Tokyngton
Willesden
Brondesbury
West Hampstead
South Hampstead
Belsize Park
CAMDEN
Kentish Town
Stonebridge
Perivale
Alperton
Park Royal
Harlesden
Kensal Rise
Kilburn
St John's Wood
Regent's Park
North Acton
Maida Vale
PADDINGTON
MARYLEBONE
Wormwood Scrubs
West Acton
EALING
ACTON
East Acton
Notting Hill
Bayswater
Mayfair
Hyde Park
WESTMINSTER
Shepherds Bush
KENSINGTON
Kensington Gardens
278
South Acton
Bedford Park
HAMMERSMITH
KENSINGTON & CHELSEA
Brompton
Little Ealing
Gunnersbury Park
Gunnersbury
CHELSEA
Pimlico
Brentford
CHISWICK
Castelnau
Kew
Royal Botanic Gardens Kew
Grove Park
FULHAM
Walham Green
Sands End
Battersea Park
BATTERSEA
North Sheen
BARNES
Mortlake
Putney
Parsons Green
HAMMERSMITH & FULHAM
East Sheen
WANDSWORTH
RICHMOND
Roehampton
Putney Heath
Clapham Common
RICHMOND UPON THAMES
Petersham
Richmond Park
Southfields
Earlsfield
Balham
Ham
Putney Vale
Kingston Vale
Wimbledon Park
Summerstown
Upper Tooting
281
Coombe
Furzedown
Tooting Graveney

HARRINGEY
HARRINGAY
Crouch End
Stroud Green
Highgate
STOKE NEWINGTON
Stamford Hill
Upper Clapton
Finsbury Park
LEYTON
Leytonstone
Dartmouth Park
Upper Holloway
Tufnell Park
Holloway
Lea Bridge
Lower Clapton
Clapton Park
HACKNEY
Shacklewell
Hackney Marsh
ISLINGTON
Highbury
Homerton
Hackney Wick
Forest Gate
Kentish Town
Barnsbury
Camden Town
Hackney
Dalston
Stratford
WEST HAM
Old Ford
King's Cross
Hoxton
Haggerston
Regent's Park
Bethnal Green
Mile End
Bow
Plaistow
ST. PANCRAS
FINSBURY
St. Luke's
SHOREDITCH
TOWER HAMLETS
Bloomsbury
Bromley
MARYLEBONE
HOLBORN
Soho
Stepney
Whitechapel
Limehouse
Canning Town
Mayfair
Wapping
Shadwell
Poplar
WESTMINSTER
SOUTHWARK
Rotherhithe
The Dome
BERMONDSEY
Cubitt Town
Millwall
Brompton
LAMBETH
Pimlico
Walworth
Deptford
GREENWICH
Vauxhall
Kennington
SOUTHWARK
New Cross
St. John's
Blackheath
Battersea Park
South Lambeth
CAMBERWELL
New Cross Gate
BATTERSEA
Clapham
Stockwell
Peckham
Brixton
Nunhead
Brockley
Lewisham
LEWISHAM
Clapham Common
Herne Hill
East Dulwich
Honor Oak
Honor Oak Park
Ladywell
Hither Green
Clapham Park
LAMBETH
DULWICH
Streatham Hill
Tulse Hill
Catford
Balham
West Dulwich
West Norwood
Forest Hill
Lower Sydenham
Bell Green
Bellingham
Southend
Downham
Upper Norwood
STREATHAM
SYDENHAM
Streatham Park
Furzedown
Tooting Graveney
Norwood
New Beckenham
277
274
282

ROMFORD
HAVERING
Gants Hill
Newbury Park
Seven Kings
Chadwell Heath
Goodmayes
REDBRIDGE
Redbridge
Wanstead
Wanstead Park
Wanstead Flats
Aldersbrook
Cranbrook
ILFORD
Loxford
Manor Park
Little Ilford
Upton
Upton Park
EAST HAM
BARKING
Becontree
Becontree Heath
Rush Green
Dagenham
South Hornchurch
Elm Park
Harrow Lodge Park
Central Park
Eastbrookend Country Park
Rainham
Rainham Marshes
BARKING & DAGENHAM
Creekmouth
Dagenham Dock
Ford Motor Works
River Thames
Beckton
Custom House
Gallions Reach
Royal Albert Dock
Royal Victoria Dock
Royal George V Dock
London City Airport
Silvertown
North Woolwich
Thames Barrier
Thamesmead North
Thamesmead
Thamesmead West
Erith Marshes
Jenningtree Point Lighthouse
Abbey Wood
Belvedere
Lessness Heath
Erith
Northumberland Heath
Barnehurst
Slade Green
New Charlton
Charlton
WOOLWICH
Plumstead
GREENWICH
Shooter's Hill
East Wickham
West Heath
BEXLEY
Welling
Falconwood
Bexley
Bexleyheath
Danson Park
Crayford
Eltham
Avery Hill
Blackfen
Lamorbey
Old Bexley
Coldblow
New Eltham
Mottingham
Longlands
SIDCUP
North Cray
Joydens Wood
Elmstead
Chislehurst West
Sundridge
Foots Cray
Foots Cray Meadows
Dartford Heath
275
147
167
283
A12
A13
A406
A2
A20
A205
A206
A207
A2016
A1020
EASTERN AVENUE
NORTH CIRCULAR ROAD
RIPPLE ROAD
ALFREDS WAY
NEW ROAD
THAMES GATEWAY
EASTERN WAY
WESTERN WAY
ROCHESTER WAY
EAST ROCHESTER WAY
BELLEGROVE ROAD
WOOLWICH ROAD
PLUMSTEAD HIGH ST.
SIDCUP ROAD
NORTH CRAY ROAD

Staines Reservoirs
Stanwell
East Bedfont
Feltham
TWICKENHAM
Ashford Hospital
Royal Oak
Bedfont Lakes Country Park
Crane Park
Strawberry Hill
H. M. Bronzefield Prison
Ashford
Lower Feltham
Hanworth Park
STAINES
Hanworth
Hampton Hill
Ashford Manor Golf Course
Felthamhill
Ministry of Defence
National Physical Laboratory
Queen Mary Reservoir
Kempton Park (Race days only)
Kempton Park Racecourse
Sunbury
Hampton
Bushy Park
Upper Halliford
Laleham
Sunbury
Hazelwood Golf Course
Littleton
MOLESEY RESERVOIRS
Hampton Court Palace & Maze
East Molesey
Thorpe Park
Laleham Park
Laleham Golf Course
Sunbury Golf Course
Upper Halliford
Bessborough Reservoir
Knights Reservoir
West Molesey
Shepperton
Queen Elizabeth II Reservoir
Island Barn Reservoir
Thames Ditton
Chertsey
SURREY
Weston Green
Chertsey Meads
Desborough Island
Thames Meadow
Rydens
Thames Ditton & Esher Golf Course
Lower Green
Addlestone Moor
Abbey Moor Golf Course
Woburn Park
Walton-on-Thames
Ashley Park
Walton Common Hosp.
Sandown Pk. Racecourse, Exhibition Cen & Golf Course
Hersham
Hersham Village Golf Course
Addlestone
Weybridge
Elmbridge Museum
Oatlands Park
Burwood Park
ESHER
Littleworth Common
Princess Alice Hospice
West End
Moore Place Golf Course
Clare Hill Golf Course
Claygate
Foley Arms
Row Town
Walton Common
New Haw
Central Veterinary Labs.
Brooklands Museum
Brooklands
Warren Pond
St. George's Hill
Old Burhill Golf Course
New Burhill Golf Course
Claremont Park
Claremont Landscape Garden
West End Common
Arbrook Common
Esher Common
Whiteley Village
Birch Wood
Byfleet & New Haw
St. George's Hill Golf Course
Woodham
Dartnell Park
Fairmile Common
Oxshott Heath
Prince's Coverts
West Byfleet
Byfleet
Silvermere Golf Course
Cobham Bus Museum
Fairmile
Oxshott
COBHAM
Painshill Park
Littleheath Common
Knowle Hill Park
Pyrford
Wisley
The Wisley Golf Course
Wisley Common
Stoke D'Abernon
Pachesh Park
Woodlands Park
Pyrford Green
Pyrford Golf Course
Cobham & Stoke D'abernon
Park Wood
Wisley Garden (RHS)
Ockham Common
Bolder Mere
Sports Grounds
Teazle Wood
Pyrford Village
Downside
Pachesham Golf Course
Elm Corner
Leatherhead Common
Martyr's Green
Black Swan
Ripley Green
Half Moon
Chatfers Copse
Hook Wood
New Barn Wood
Ockham
Oakham Park
Stumps Grove
Great Bookham Common (NT)
Ripley
Great Mornshill Wood
LEATHERHEAD
Fetcham
Services
Barnsthorns Wood
Effingham Junction
Bookham
Send Marsh
Jovial Sailor
Effingham Common
Oaken Wood
Little Bookham
M25
M3
A3
193
211
276
229

Petersham
Richmond Park
UPON THAMES
Ham
Putney Vale
Kingston Vale
Wimbledon Common
Wimbledon Park
Southfields
Earlsfield
Summerstown
Upper Tooting
Streatham Park
Furzedown
Tooting Graveney
Collier's Wood
Coombe
WIMBLEDON
Hampton Wick
KINGSTON upon THAMES
MERTON
Norbiton
KINGSTON
New Malden
Raynes Park
Bushey Mead
MORDEN
MITCHAM
West Barnes
Hampton Court Park
Berrylands
Morden Park
St. Helier
SURBITON
Long Ditton
Old Malden
Motspur Park
Rosehill
Hackbridge
Tolworth
Worcester Park
North Cheam
Benhilton
The Wrythe
SUTTON
CARSHALTON
Chessington
Stoneleigh
CHEAM
Nonsuch Park
West Ewell
Horton
EWELL
East Ewell
Belmont
Banstead Downs
Carshalton Beeches
Carshalton On The Hill
Malden Rushett
EPSOM
North Looe
BANSTEAD
Woodmansterne
Epsom Common
Nork
Ashtead
Tattenham Corner
Burgh Heath
Chipstead
Lower Ashtead
Ashtead Park
Langley Vale
Epsom Downs
Walton Downs
Chipstead Bottom
Tadworth
Kingswood
Hooley
Tyrrell's Wood
277
282
233

Catford
Tulse Hill
Dulwich Common
Forest Hill
West Dulwich
West Norwood
Upper Sydenham
Lower Sydenham
Bellingham
Bell Green
Southend
Downham
STREATHAM
Streatham Park
Furzedown
SYDENHAM
New Beckenham
Norwood New Town
Streatham Common
Norwood
Penge
Plaistow
Streatham Vale
BECKENHAM
Norbury
Upper Norwood
Anerley
Elmers End
South Norwood
Shortlands
Thornton Heath
Selhurst
Upper Elmers End
Eden Park
Mitcham Common
Monks Orchard
Park Langley
Woodside
West Wickham
Hackbridge
Addiscombe
BEDDINGTON
CROYDON
Shirley
WALLINGTON
Addington
South Beddington
South Croydon
NEW ADDINGTON
Carshalton On The Hill
Sanderstead
Forestdale
Purley
Selsdon
Woodcote
Farleigh
Coulsdon
Kenley
Hamsey Green
Chelsham
Whyteleafe
Chipstead
Old Coulsdon
WARLINGHAM
Woldingham Garden Village
Woldingham
Caterham-on-the-Hill
Hooley
Chaldon
CROYDON ROAD
BRIGHTON ROAD
PURLEY WAY
LONDON ROAD
ADDINGTON ROAD
LIMPSFIELD ROAD
GODSTONE ROAD
278
281
236

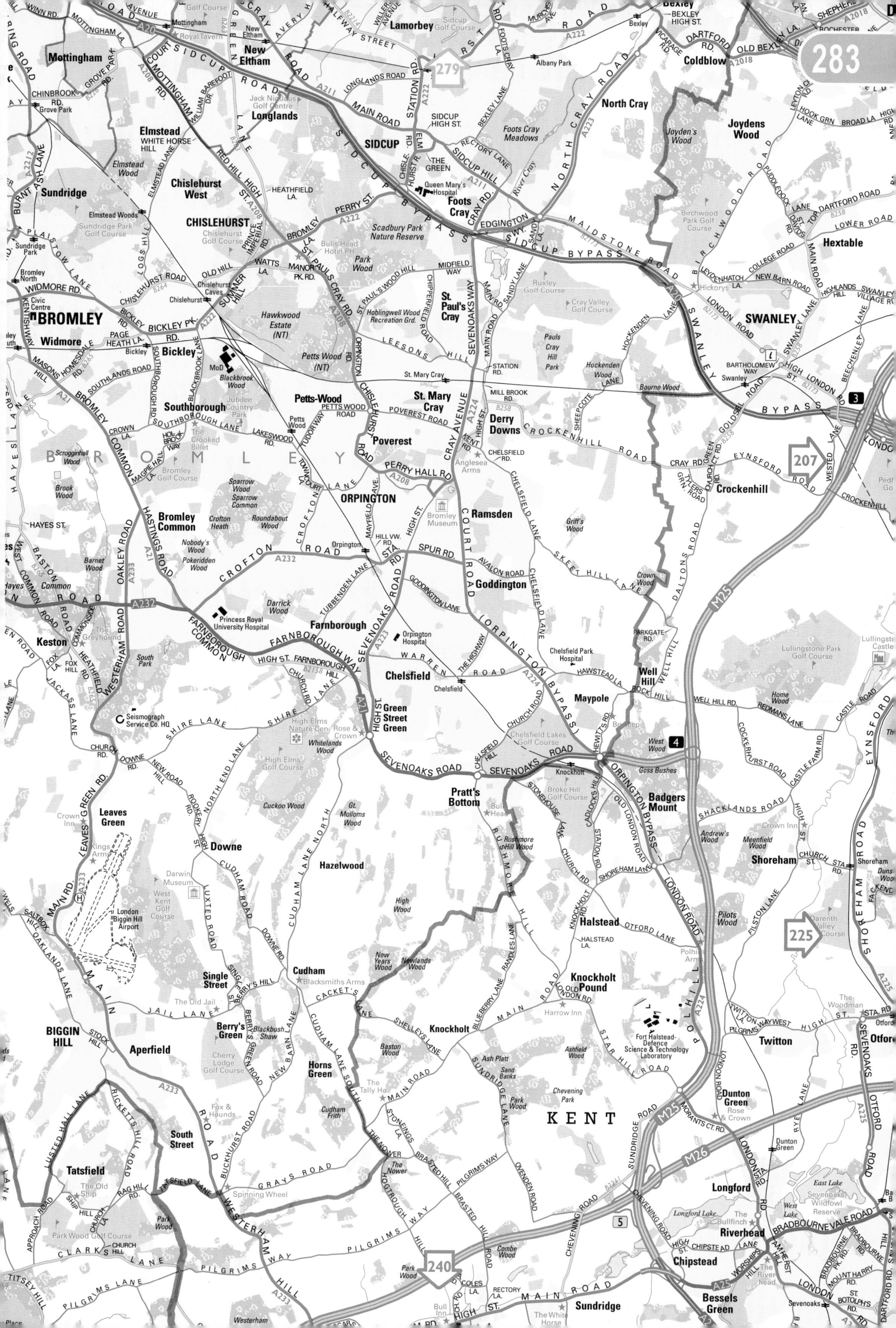

Mottingham
New Eltham
Lamorbey
Bexley
Coldblow
Longlands
Elmstead
SIDCUP
North Cray
Joydens Wood
Sundridge
Chislehurst West
CHISLEHURST
Foots Cray
Hextable
BROMLEY
Widmore
Bickley
St. Paul's Cray
SWANLEY
Southborough
Petts Wood
St. Mary Cray
Derry Downs
Poverest
ORPINGTON
Ramsden
Crockenhill
Bromley Common
Goddington
Keston
Farnborough
Chelsfield
Well Hill
Maypole
Green Street Green
Pratt's Bottom
Badgers Mount
Leaves Green
Downe
Hazelwood
Shoreham
Halstead
Cudham
Single Street
Knockholt Pound
BIGGIN HILL
Aperfield
Berry's Green
Knockholt
Twitton
Horns Green
Dunton Green
KENT
South Street
Tatsfield
Longford
Riverhead
Chipstead
Sundridge
Bessels Green

284 M25 London orbital motorway

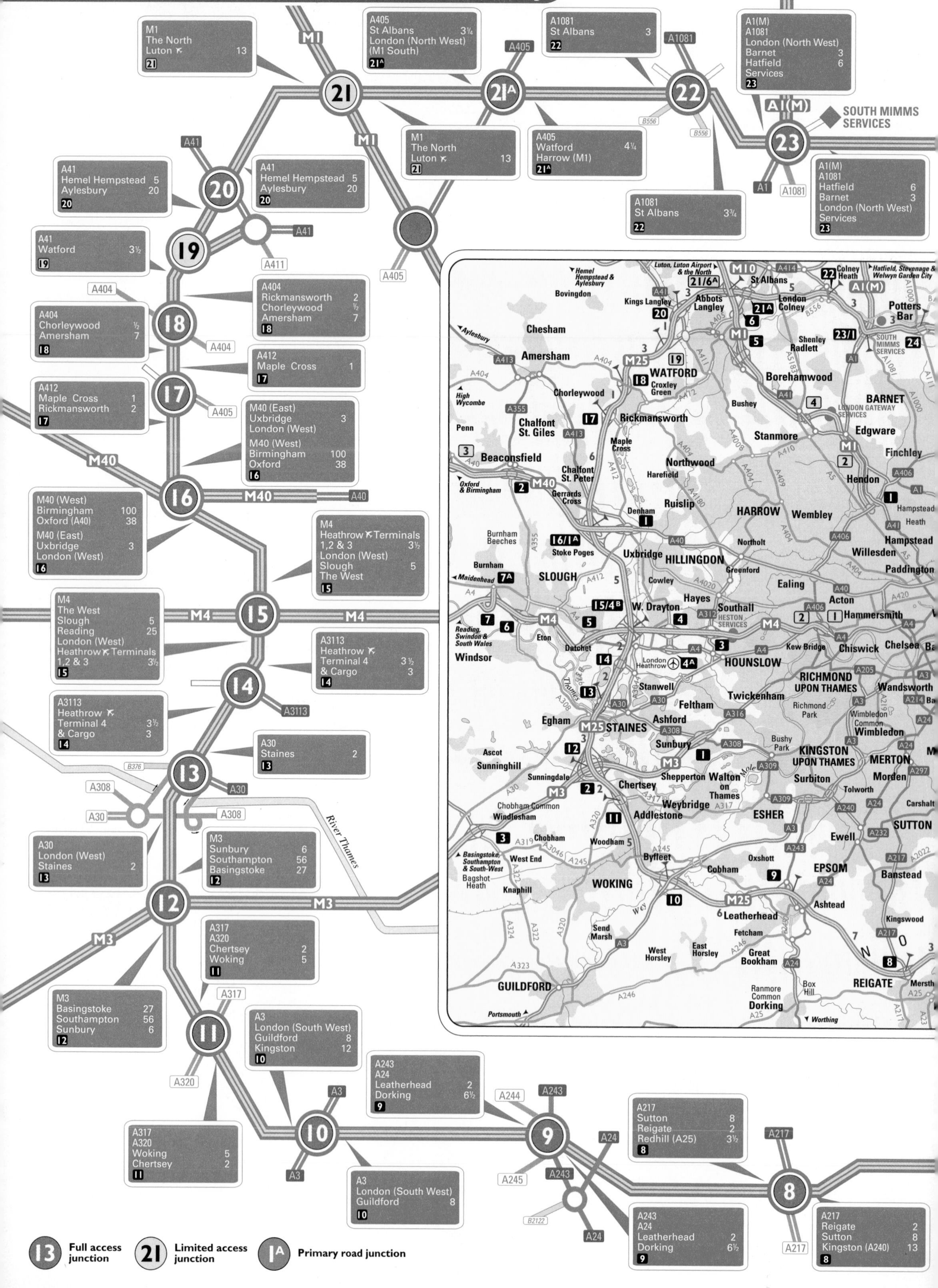

A1(M)
A1081
London (North West)
Barnet 3
Hatfield 6
Services
23

A1(M)
A1081
Hatfield 6
Barnet 3
London (North West)
Services
23

A1081
St Albans 3
22

A1081
St Albans 3¾
22

A405
St Albans 3¼
London (North West)
(M1 South)
21A

A405
Watford 4¼
Harrow (M1)
21A

M1
The North
Luton ✈ 13
21

M1
The North
Luton ✈ 13
21

A41
Hemel Hempstead 5
Aylesbury 20
20

A41
Hemel Hempstead 5
Aylesbury 20
20

A41
Watford 3½
19

A404
Rickmansworth 2
Chorleywood ½
Amersham 7
18

A404
Chorleywood ½
Amersham 7
18

A412
Maple Cross 1
17

A412
Maple Cross 1
Rickmansworth 2
17

M40 (East)
Uxbridge 3
London (West)
M40 (West)
Birmingham 100
Oxford 38
16

M40 (West)
Birmingham 100
Oxford (A40) 38
M40 (East)
Uxbridge 3
London (West)
16

M4
Heathrow ✈ Terminals 1,2 & 3 3½
London (West)
Slough 5
The West
15

M4
The West
Slough 5
Reading 25
London (West)
Heathrow ✈ Terminals 1,2 & 3 3½
15

A3113
Heathrow ✈
Terminal 4 3½
& Cargo 3
14

A3113
Heathrow ✈
Terminal 4 3½
& Cargo 3
14

A30
Staines 2
13

A30
London (West)
Staines 2
13

M3
Sunbury 6
Southampton 56
Basingstoke 27
12

M3
Basingstoke 27
Southampton 56
Sunbury 6
12

A317
A320
Chertsey 2
Woking 5
11

A317
A320
Woking 5
Chertsey 2
11

A3
London (South West)
Guildford 8
Kingston 12
10

A3
London (South West)
Guildford 8
10

A243
A24
Leatherhead 2
Dorking 6½
9

A243
A24
Leatherhead 2
Dorking 6½
9

A217
Sutton 8
Reigate 2
Redhill (A25) 3½
8

A217
Reigate 2
Sutton 8
Kingston (A240) 13
8

13 Full access junction
21 Limited access junction
1A Primary road junction

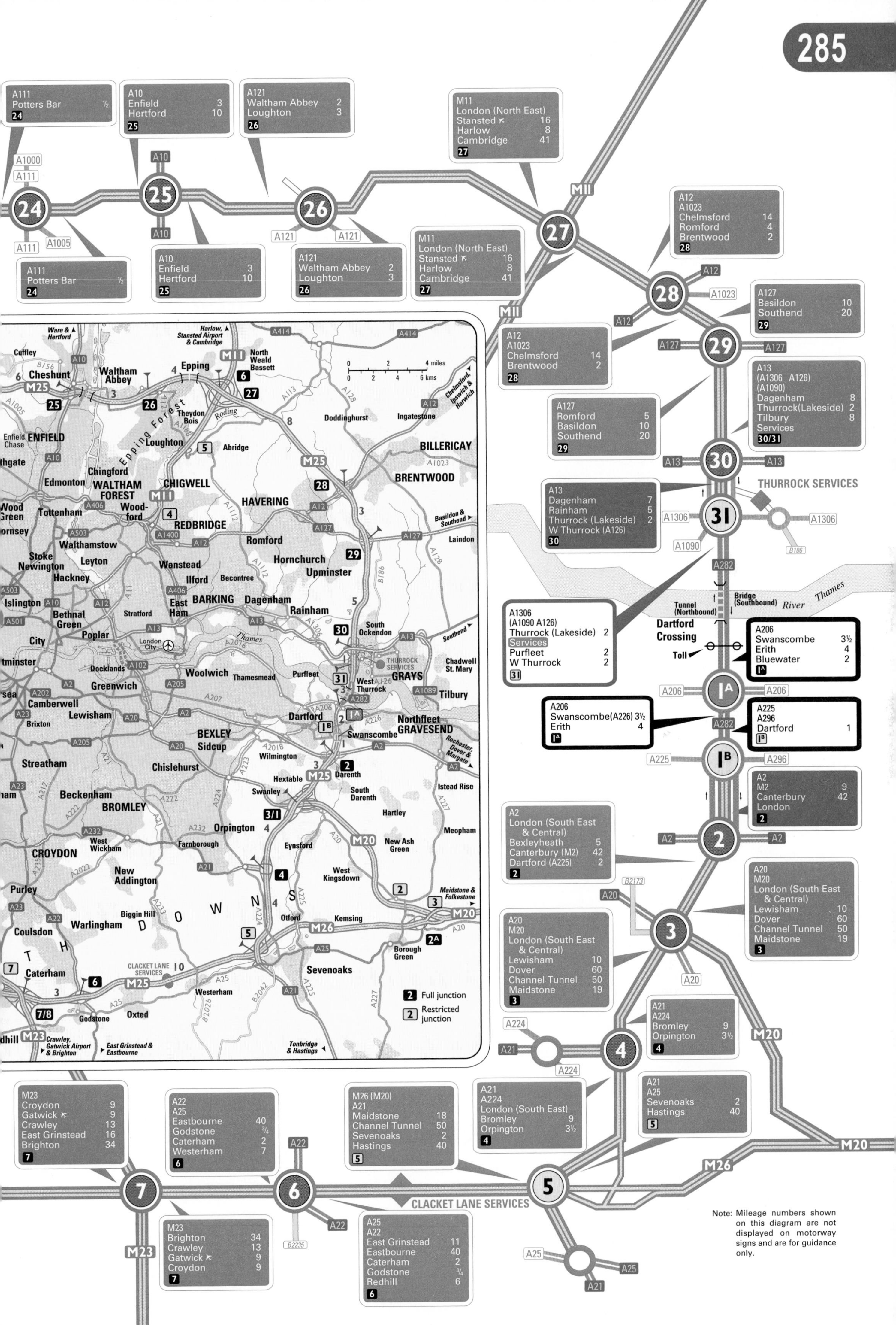
A111
Potters Bar ½
24
A10
Enfield 3
Hertford 10
25
A121
Waltham Abbey 2
Loughton 3
26
M11
London (North East)
Stansted 16
Harlow 8
Cambridge 41
27
A12
A1023
Chelmsford 14
Romford 4
Brentwood 2
28
A127
Basildon 10
Southend 20
29
A12
A1023
Chelmsford 14
Brentwood 2
28
A13
(A1306 A126)
(A1090)
Dagenham 8
Thurrock(Lakeside) 2
Tilbury 8
Services
30/31
A127
Romford 5
Basildon 10
Southend 20
29
THURROCK SERVICES
A13
Dagenham 7
Rainham 5
Thurrock (Lakeside) 2
W Thurrock (A126)
30
A1306
(A1090 A126)
Thurrock (Lakeside) 2
Services
Purfleet 2
W Thurrock 2
31
Dartford Crossing
Tunnel (Northbound)
Bridge (Southbound)
River Thames
Toll
A206
Swanscombe 3½
Erith 4
Bluewater 2
1A
A206
Swanscombe(A226) 3½
Erith 4
1A
A225
A296
Dartford 1
1B
A2
M2
Canterbury 9
London 42
2
A2
London (South East & Central)
Bexleyheath 5
Canterbury (M2) 42
Dartford (A225) 2
2
A20
M20
London (South East & Central)
Lewisham 10
Dover 60
Channel Tunnel 50
Maidstone 19
3
A20
M20
London (South East & Central)
Lewisham 10
Dover 60
Channel Tunnel 50
Maidstone 19
3
A21
A224
Bromley 9
Orpington 3½
4
A21
A224
London (South East)
Bromley 9
Orpington 3½
4
A21
A25
Sevenoaks 2
Hastings 40
5
M23
Croydon 9
Gatwick 9
Crawley 13
East Grinstead 16
Brighton 34
7
A22
A25
Eastbourne 40
Godstone ¾
Caterham 2
Westerham 7
6
M26 (M20)
A21
Maidstone 18
Channel Tunnel 50
Sevenoaks 2
Hastings 40
5
CLACKET LANE SERVICES
M23
Brighton 34
Crawley 13
Gatwick 9
Croydon 9
7
A25
A22
East Grinstead 11
Eastbourne 40
Caterham 2
Godstone ¾
Redhill 6
6
Full junction
Restricted junction
0 2 4 miles
0 2 4 6 kms
Note: Mileage numbers shown on this diagram are not displayed on motorway signs and are for guidance only.

Key to map symbols

- i Tourist information centre
- P Short stay car park
- P Long stay car park
- Railway station
- London underground station
- Bus station

Luton

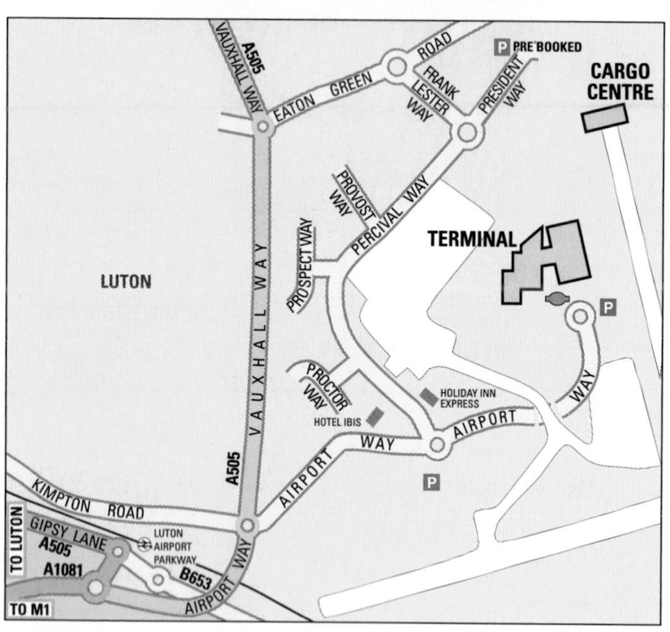

A505
VAUXHALL WAY
EATON GREEN ROAD
FRANK LESTER WAY
PRESIDENT WAY
PRE BOOKED
CARGO CENTRE
PROVOST WAY
PERCIVAL WAY
PROSPECT WAY
LUTON
TERMINAL
PROCTOR WAY
HOTEL IBIS
HOLIDAY INN EXPRESS
AIRPORT WAY
KIMPTON ROAD
GIPSY LANE
A505
A1081
LUTON AIRPORT PARKWAY
B653
TO LUTON
TO M1

Tel. 01582 405100
www.london-luton.co.uk

Stansted

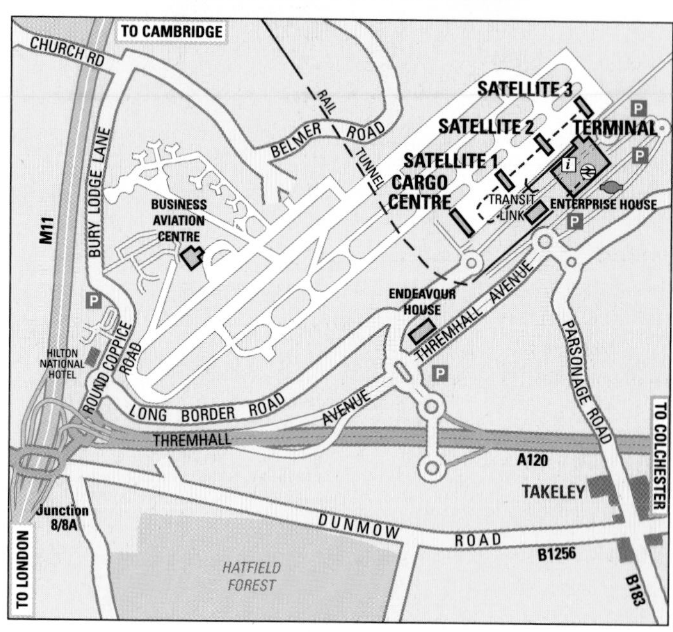

TO CAMBRIDGE
CHURCH RD
RAIL TUNNEL
BELMER ROAD
SATELLITE 3
SATELLITE 2
SATELLITE 1
TERMINAL
CARGO CENTRE
TRANSIT LINK
ENTERPRISE HOUSE
M11
BURY LODGE LANE
BUSINESS AVIATION CENTRE
ENDEAVOUR HOUSE
THREMHALL AVENUE
HILTON NATIONAL HOTEL
ROUND COPPICE ROAD
LONG BORDER ROAD
THREMHALL AVENUE
PARSONAGE ROAD
A120
TAKELEY
TO COLCHESTER
Junction 8/8A
DUNMOW ROAD
B1256
HATFIELD FOREST
TO LONDON
B183

Tel. 0870 000 0303
www.baa.co.uk/main/airports/stansted

Heathrow

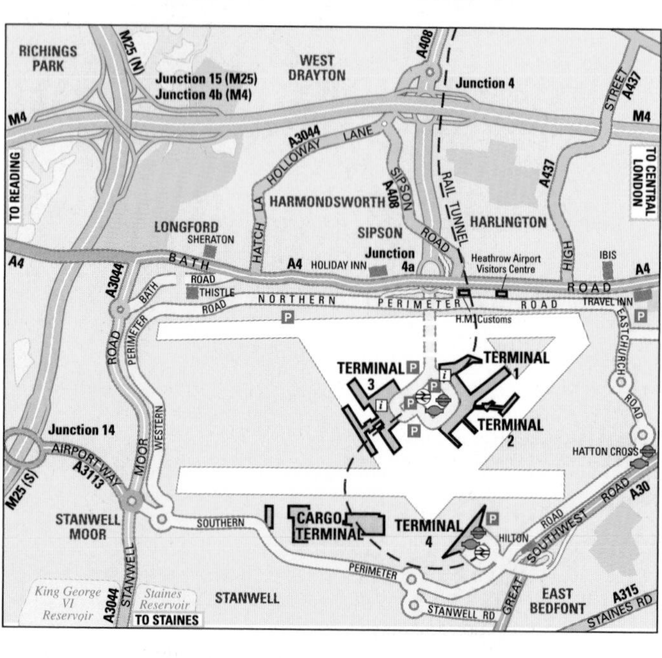

RICHINGS PARK
M25 (N)
WEST DRAYTON
Junction 15 (M25)
Junction 4b (M4)
A408
Junction 4
STREET A437
M4
A3044 HOLLOWAY LANE
TO READING
TO CENTRAL LONDON
HARMONDSWORTH
SIPSON A408
RAIL TUNNEL
A437
HARLINGTON
LONGFORD
SHERATON
HATCH LA
SIPSON
SIPSON ROAD
Junction 4a
Heathrow Airport Visitors Centre
HIGH
IBIS
A4
BATH ROAD
A4 HOLIDAY INN
THISTLE
NORTHERN PERIMETER ROAD
TRAVEL INN
H.M. Customs
A3044
TERMINAL 3
TERMINAL 1
TERMINAL 2
EASTCHURCH ROAD
Junction 14
AIRPORT WAY
A3113
MOOR
WESTERN
PERIMETER
HATTON CROSS
M25 (S)
STANWELL MOOR
SOUTHERN
CARGO TERMINAL
TERMINAL 4
HILTON
SOUTHWEST ROAD
A30
PERIMETER
STANWELL
King George VI Reservoir
Staines Reservoir
TO STAINES
STANWELL RD
GREAT
EAST BEDFONT
A315 STAINES RD

Tel. 0870 000 0123
www.baa.co.uk/main/airports/heathrow

Gatwick

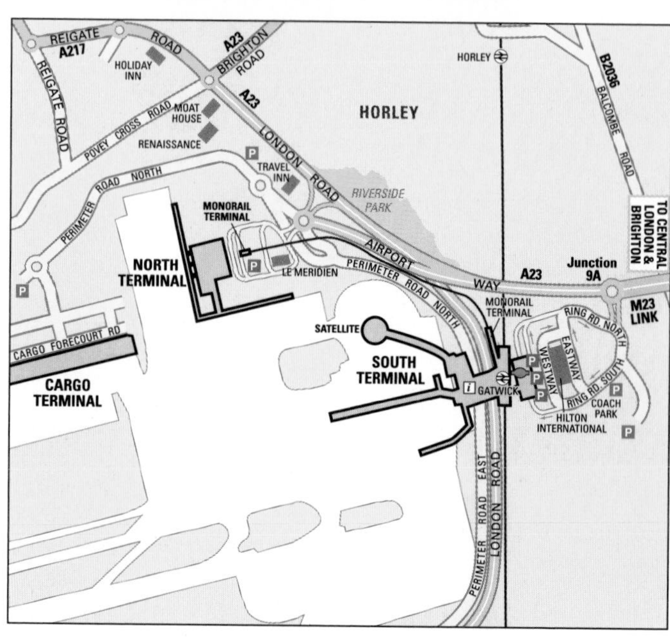

REIGATE ROAD A217
HOLIDAY INN
A23 BRIGHTON ROAD
HORLEY
B2036 BALCOMBE ROAD
HORLEY
POVEY CROSS ROAD
MOAT HOUSE
RENAISSANCE
A23
LONDON ROAD
TRAVEL INN
PERIMETER ROAD NORTH
MONORAIL TERMINAL
RIVERSIDE PARK
NORTH TERMINAL
LE MERIDIEN
AIRPORT WAY
PERIMETER ROAD NORTH
A23
Junction 9A
TO CENTRAL LONDON & BRIGHTON
M23 LINK
MONORAIL TERMINAL
RING RD NORTH
CARGO FORECOURT RD
CARGO TERMINAL
SATELLITE
SOUTH TERMINAL
GATWICK
EASTWAY
WESTWAY
RING RD SOUTH
COACH PARK
HILTON INTERNATIONAL
PERIMETER ROAD EAST
LONDON ROAD

Tel. 0870 000 2468
www.baa.co.uk/main/airports/gatwick

Key to route planning maps

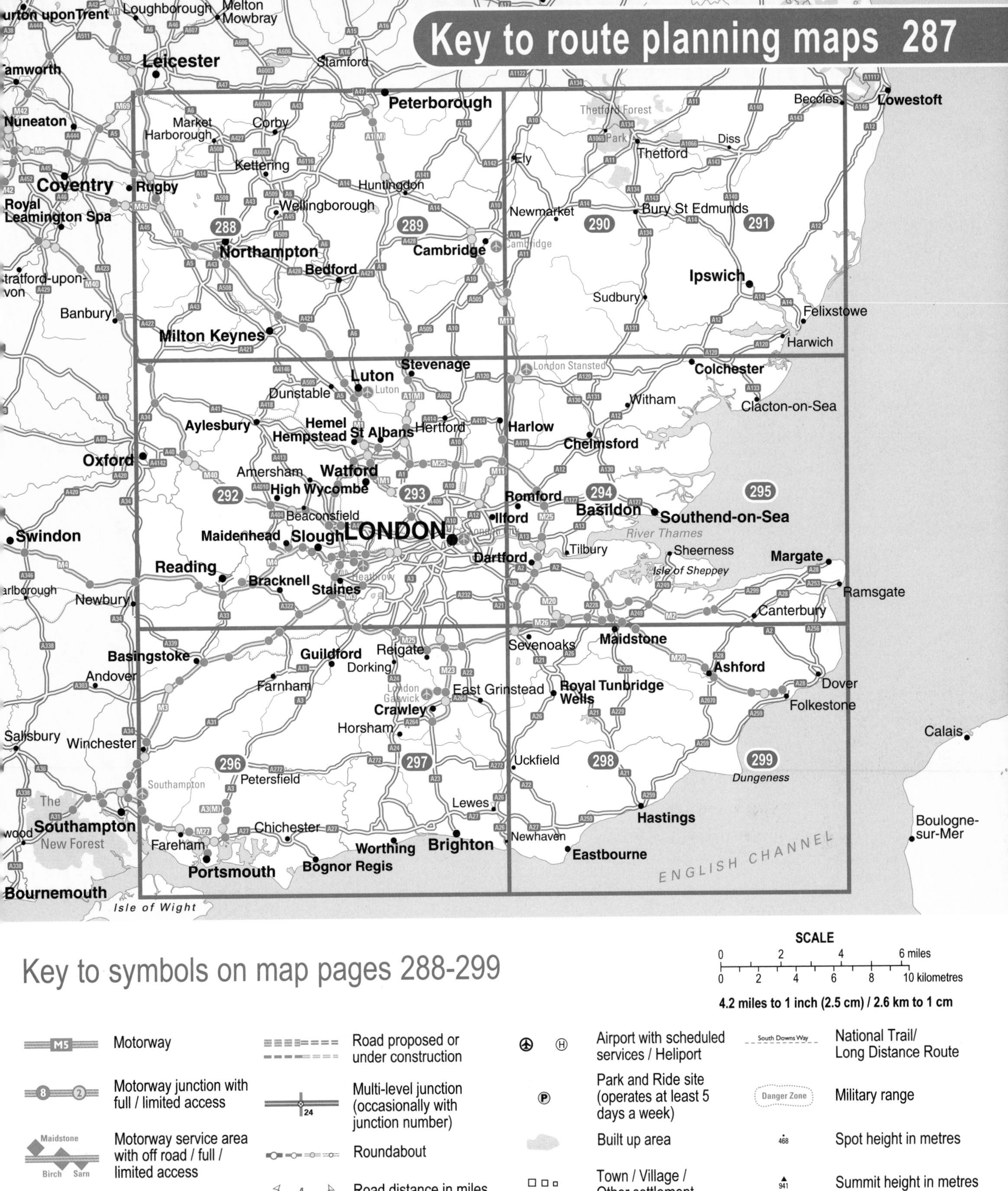
Spalding
Lynn
Loughborough
Melton Mowbray
Burton upon Trent
Leicester
Stamford
Tamworth
Peterborough
Nuneaton
Market Harborough
Corby
Beccles
Lowestoft
Thetford Forest
Thetford
Diss
Ely
Kettering
Coventry
Rugby
Royal Leamington Spa
Huntingdon
Wellingborough
Newmarket
Bury St Edmunds
288
289
290
291
Northampton
Cambridge
Bedford
Stratford-upon-Avon
Ipswich
Sudbury
Banbury
Felixstowe
Harwich
Milton Keynes
Stevenage
Luton
London Stansted
Colchester
Dunstable
Witham
Clacton-on-Sea
Aylesbury
Hemel Hempstead
St Albans
Hertford
Harlow
Chelmsford
Oxford
Amersham
Watford
High Wycombe
292
293
294
295
Romford
Basildon
Southend-on-Sea
Beaconsfield
Ilford
Swindon
Maidenhead
Slough
LONDON
River Thames
Tilbury
Sheerness
Dartford
Margate
Reading
Isle of Sheppey
Bracknell
Staines
Heathrow
Ramsgate
Marlborough
Newbury
Canterbury
Basingstoke
Guildford
Reigate
Sevenoaks
Maidstone
Andover
Dorking
Ashford
Farnham
East Grinstead
Royal Tunbridge Wells
Dover
Crawley
Folkestone
Salisbury
Winchester
Horsham
Calais
296
297
298
299
Southampton
Petersfield
Uckfield
Dungeness
The New Forest
Lewes
Hastings
Boulogne-sur-Mer
Chichester
Fareham
Worthing
Brighton
Newhaven
Eastbourne
ENGLISH CHANNEL
Portsmouth
Bognor Regis
Bournemouth
Isle of Wight

Key to symbols on map pages 288-299

SCALE

0 2 4 6 miles

0 2 4 6 8 10 kilometres

4.2 miles to 1 inch (2.5 cm) / 2.6 km to 1 cm

- M5 — Motorway
- 8 / 2 — Motorway junction with full / limited access
- Maidstone / Birch / Sarn — Motorway service area with off road / full / limited access
- A48 — Primary dual / single carriageway
- A30 — 'A' road dual / single carriageway
- B3335 — 'B' road dual / single carriageway
- Minor road
- Road with restricted access
- Road proposed or under construction
- 24 — Multi-level junction (occasionally with junction number)
- Roundabout
- 4 — Road distance in miles between markers
- Road tunnel
- Steep hill (arrows point downhill)
- Toll — Level crossing / Toll
- Car ferry route
- Railway line / Station / Tunnel
- Airport with scheduled services / Heliport
- Park and Ride site (operates at least 5 days a week)
- Built up area
- Town / Village / Other settlement
- **Peterhead** — Primary route destination

  Primary route destinations are places of major traffic importance linked by the primary route network. They are shown on a green background on direction signs.
- **St Ives** — Seaside destination
- National / Regional park
- Forest park boundary
- Woodland
- South Downs Way — National Trail/ Long Distance Route
- Danger Zone — Military range
- 468 — Spot height in metres
- 941 — Summit height in metres
- Lake / Dam / River / Waterfall
- Canal / Dry canal / Canal tunnel
- Beach
- Lighthouse
- Tourist information centre (open all year / open seasonally)

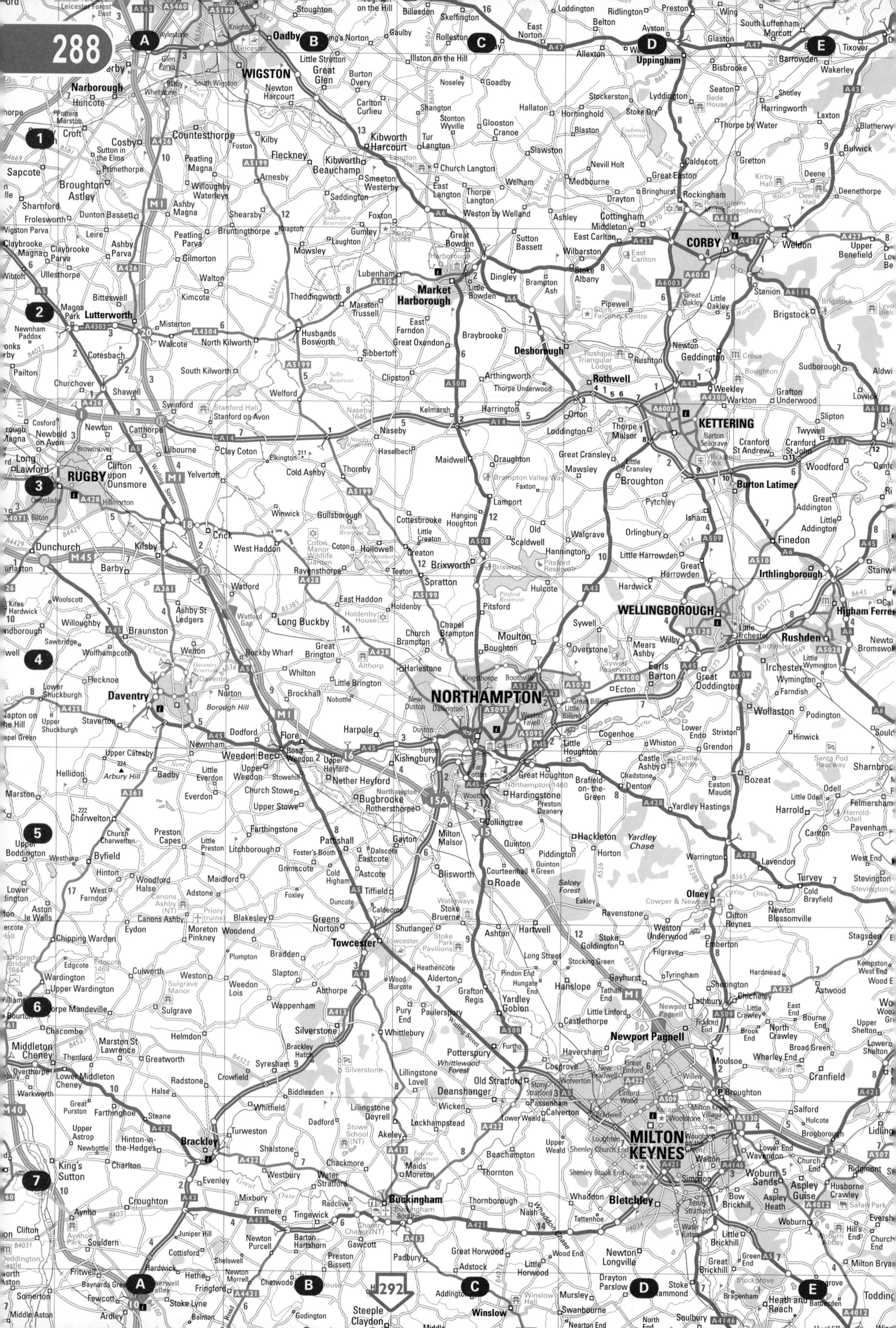
A
B
C
D
E
1
2
3
4
5
6
7
Leicester Forest East
Oadby
Stoughton
Billesdon
Skeffington
Loddington
Ridlington
Preston
Wing
South Luffenham
Morcott
Rolleston
East Norton
Belton
Ayston
Glaston
Uppingham
Tixover
Barrowden
Wakerley
Little Stretton
Great Glen
Illston on the Hill
Allexton
Bisbrooke
WIGSTON
Narborough
Huncote
Glen Parva
South Wigston
Whetstone
Newton Harcourt
Burton Overy
Carlton Curlieu
Noseley
Goadby
Seaton
Bede House
Lyddington
Stockerston
Stoke Dry
Shotley
Harringworth
Hallaton
Horninghold
Thorpe by Water
Laxton
Blatherwycke
Croft
Cosby
Countesthorpe
Kilby
Kibworth Harcourt
Tur Langton
Shangton
Stonton Wyville
Glooston
Cranoe
Blaston
Eyebrook Reservoir
Sapcote
Sutton in the Elms
Primethorpe
Peatling Magna
Foston
Fleckney
Kibworth Beauchamp
Langton Hall
Church Langton
Slawston
Nevill Holt
Caldecott
Gretton
Bulwick
Broughton Astley
Willoughby Waterleys
Arnesby
Smeeton Westerby
East Langton
Thorpe Langton
Welham
Medbourne
Great Easton
Kirby Hall
Deene
Deene Hall
Deenethorpe
Sharnford
Frolesworth
Dunton Bassett
Ashby Magna
Shearsby
Saddington
Saddington Reservoir
Weston by Welland
Drayton
Bringhurst
Rockingham
Rockingham Castle
Rockingham Motor Speedway
Wigston Parva
Claybrooke Magna
Claybrooke Parva
Leire
Ashby Parva
Peatling Parva
Bruntingthorpe
Kimcote
Walton
Gilmorton
Mowsley
Laughton
Foxton
Foxton Locks
Gumley
Great Bowden
Sutton Bassett
Ashley
Cottingham
Middleton
East Carlton
CORBY
Weldon
Upper Benefield
Ullesthorpe
Bitteswell
Lutterworth
Magna Park
Newnham Paddox
Misterton
Walcote
North Kilworth
Husbands Bosworth
Theddingworth
Lubenham
Market Harborough
Little Bowden
Dingley
Brampton Ash
Stoke Albany
Wilbarston
Pipewell
Shire Falconry Centre
Great Oakley
Little Oakley
Stanion
Brigstock
Cotesbach
Pailton
Churchover
Shawell
South Kilworth
Sulby Reservoir
Welford
Marston Trussell
East Farndon
Great Oxendon
Sibbertoft
Clipston
Braybrooke
Desborough
Rushton
Rushton Triangular Lodge
Newton
Geddington
Cross
Boughton
Sudborough
Swinford
Stanford Hall
Stanford on Avon
Catthorpe
Arthingworth
Thorpe Underwood
Rothwell
Weekley
Warkton
Grafton Underwood
Lowick
Cosford
Newbold on Avon
Long Lawford
RUGBY
Brownsover
Clifton upon Dunsmore
Hillmorton
Bilton
Overslade
Lilbourne
Clay Coton
Elkington
Yelvertoft
Cold Ashby
Naseby
Naseby 1645
Naseby Reservoir
Haselbech
Thornby
Kelmarsh
Harrington
Orton
Loddington
Thorpe Malsor
KETTERING
Barton Seagrave
Cranford St Andrew
Cranford St John
Twywell
Slipton
Woodford
Maidwell
Draughton
Brampton Valley Way
Faxton
Great Cransley
Little Cransley
Mawsley
Broughton
Pytchley
Wicksteed Park
Burton Latimer
Great Addington
Little Addington
Dunchurch
Kilsby
Barby
Crick
Winwick
West Haddon
Gullsborough
Hollowell Reservoir
Coton Manor Wildlife Garden
Coton
Hollowell
Ravensthorpe
Ravensthorpe Reservoir
Teeton
Cottesbrooke
Little Creaton
Creaton
Hanging Houghton
Lamport
Brixworth
Spratton
Old
Scaldwell
Walgrave
Hannington
Pitsford Reservoir
Orlingbury
Isham
Little Harrowden
Great Harrowden
Finedon
Irthlingborough
Woolscott
Kites Hardwick
Willoughby
Sawbridge
Wolfhampcote
Braunston
Ashby St Ledgers
Watford
Watford Gap
Long Buckby
East Haddon
Holdenby
Holdenby House
Chapel Brampton
Church Brampton
Pitsford
Hulcote
Hardwick
Sywell
Sywell Reservoir
Moulton
Boughton
Overstone
Mears Ashby
WELLINGBOROUGH
Wilby
Little Irchester
Irchester
Rushden
Higham Ferrers
Lower Shuckburgh
Upper Shuckburgh
Flecknoe
Daventry
Daventry Reservoir
Welton
Buckby Wharf
Great Brington
Althorp
Whilton
Harlestone
Little Brington
Nobottle
Brockhall
Norton
Borough Hill
Kingsthorpe
Boothville
NORTHAMPTON
Great Billing
Little Billing
Weston Favell
Ecton
Earls Barton
Great Doddington
Farndish
Wymington
Wollaston
Podington
Napton on the Hill
Staverton
Newnham
Dodford
Flore
Weedon Bec
Road Weedon
Upper Heyford
Nether Heyford
Harpole
Kislingbury
Upton
Duston
New Duston
Dallington
Cogenhoe
Whiston
Castle Ashby
Chadstone
Denton
Lower End
Grendon
Strixton
Hinwick
Bozeat
Santa Pod Raceway
Sharnbrook
Upper Catesby
Arbury Hill
Hellidon
Badby
Little Everdon
Everdon
Upper Weedon
Stowehill
Church Stowe
Upper Stowe
Bugbrooke
Rothersthorpe
Northampton
Far Cotton
Wootton
Great Houghton
Hardingstone
Preston Deanery
Brafield-on-the-Green
Easton Maudit
Yardley Hastings
Little Odell
Odell
Harrold
Harrold-Odell
Felmersham
Pavenham
Marston
Charwelton
Church Charwelton
Preston Capes
Little Preston
Farthingstone
Litchborough
Pattishall
Foster's Booth
Dalscote
Eastcote
Gayton
Milton Malsor
Collingtree
Quinton
Hackleton
Horton
Piddington
Quinton Green
Yardley Chase
Carlton
Upper Boddington
Byfield
Westhorp
Hinton
Woodford Halse
West Farndon
Adstone
Maidford
Grimscote
Cold Higham
Astcote
Tiffield
Blisworth
Courteenhall
Roade
Salcey Forest
Eakley
Warrington
Olney
Cowper & Newton
Lavendon
Turvey
Cold Brayfield
Stevington
Lower Boddington
Aston le Walls
Canons Ashby
Priory
Foxley
Duncote
Caldecote
Stoke Bruerne
Waterways
Ravenstone
Clifton Reynes
Newton Blossomville
Chipping Warden
Eydon
Moreton Pinkney
Woodend
Blakesley
Greens Norton
Towcester
Shutlanger
Stoke Park Pavilions
Ashton
Hartwell
Stoke Goldington
Weston Underwood
Emberton
Stagsden
Wardington
Upper Wardington
Edgcote
Culworth
Plumpton
Bradden
Slapton
Heathencote
Alderton
Long Street
Stocking Green
Filgrave
Tyringham
Hardmead
Kempston West End
Wood End
Thorpe Mandeville
Sulgrave
Sulgrave Manor
Weston
Weedon Lois
Abthorpe
Wood Burcote
Grafton Regis
Pindon End
Hungate End
Yardley Gobion
Hanslope
Gayhurst
Tathall End
Sherington
Chicheley
Astwood
Chacombe
Middleton Cheney
Marston St Lawrence
Helmdon
Wappenham
Silverstone
Whittlebury
Pury End
Paulerspury
Castlethorpe
Little Linford
Newport Pagnell
Lathbury
Tickford End
North Crawley
East End
Bourne End
Brook End
Upper Shelton
Overthorpe
Thenford
Greatworth
Radstone
Crowfield
Syresham
Brackley Hatch
Potterspury
Whittlewood Forest
Furtho
Haversham
Cosgrove
Broad Green
Lower Shelton
Warkworth
Lower Middleton Cheney
Halse
Biddlesden
Lillingstone Lovell
Deanshanger
Old Stratford
Stony Stratford
Wolverton
New Bradwell
Great Linford
Willen
Moulsoe
Wharley End
Cranfield
Great Purston
Farthinghoe
Steane
Whitfield
Lillingstone Dayrell
Wicken
Passenham
Calverton
Bradwell
Linford Wood
Milton Keynes Village
Broughton
Salford
Hulcote
Upper Astrop
Newbottle
Hinton-in-the-Hedges
Turweston
Brackley
Dadford
Stowe School
Akeley
Leckhampstead
Lower Weald
Upper Weald
Shenley Church End
MILTON KEYNES
Woolstone
Walton
Wavendon
Brogborough
Lidlington
King's Sutton
Charlton
Shalstone
Chackmore
Foxcote Reservoir
Maids' Moreton
Beachampton
Thornton
Shenley Brook End
Simpson
Woburn Sands
Church End
Aspley Guise
Husborne Crawley
Ridgmont
Evenley
Westbury
Water Stratford
Buckingham
Bletchley
Bow Brickhill
Aspley Heath
Safari Park
Aynho
Croughton
Mixbury
Finmere
Tingewick
Radclive
Thornborough
Whaddon
Nash
Tattenhoe
Fenny Stratford
Woburn
Hills End
Eversholt
Clifton
Aynho Park
Souldern
Juniper Hill
Newton Purcell
Barton Hartshorn
Chantry Chapel (NT)
Gawcott
Great Horwood
Whaddon Chase
Water Eaton
Little Brickhill
Woburn Abbey
Church End
Cottisford
Shelswell
Preston Bissett
Padbury
Adstock
Little Horwood
Wood End
Newton Longville
Great Brickhill
Green End
Milton Bryan
Fritwell
Hardwick
Hethe
Newton Morrell
Chetwode
Drayton Parslow
Stoke Hammond
Stockgrove
Baynards Green
Fringford
Addington
Winslow Hall
Mursley
Swanbourne
Heath and Reach
Battlesden
Somerton
Fewcott
Stoke Lyne
Steeple Claydon
Winslow
Nearton End
North End
Soulbury
Toddington
Middle Aston
Ardley
Godington
292
M1
M40
M45
A5
A6
A14
A43
A45
A361
A422
A428
A508
A509
A5199
A421
A4146
A4012

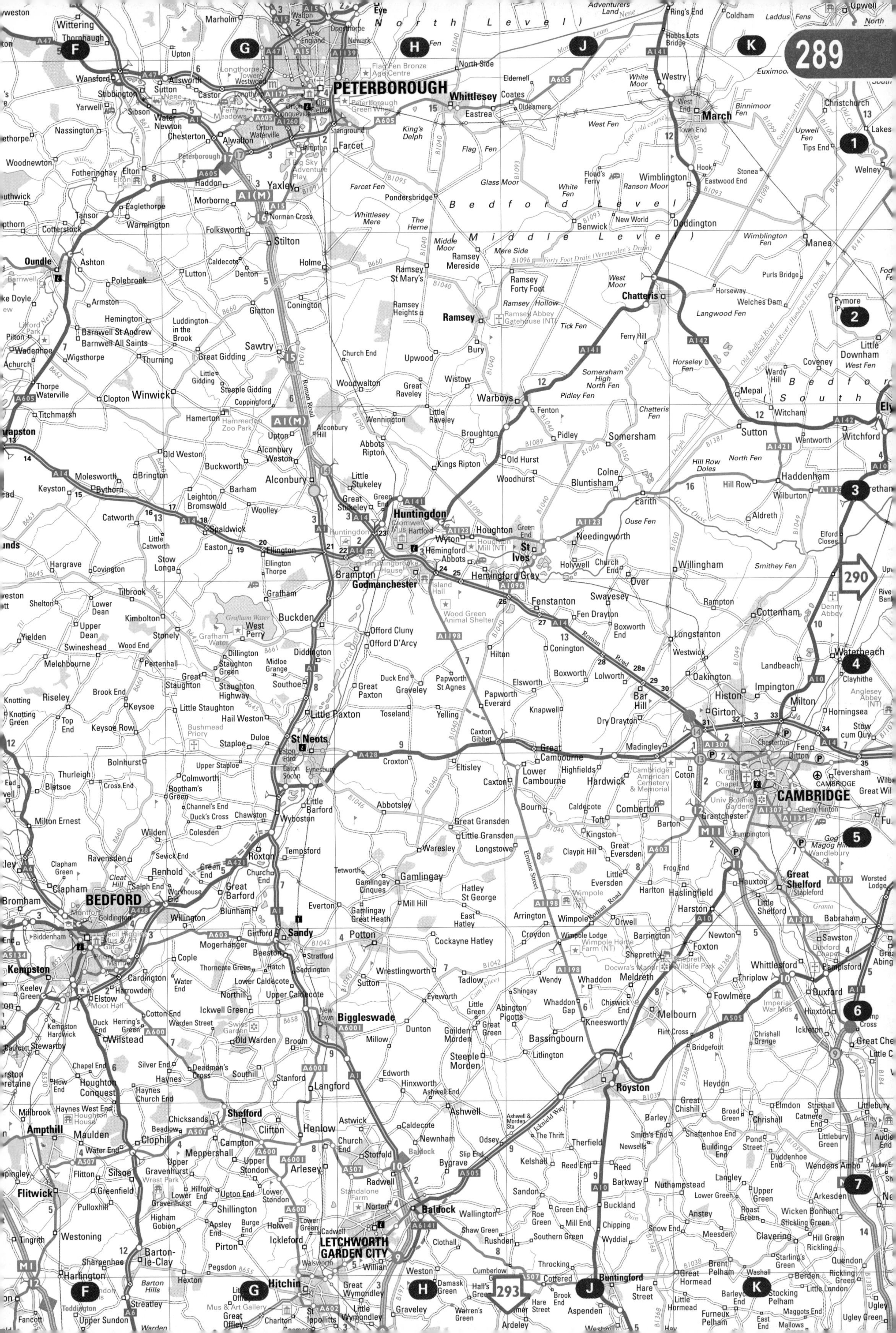

289
PETERBOROUGH
Whittlesey
March
Eye
North Level
Ring's End
Coldham
Upwell
Wittering
Thornhaugh
Marholm
Upton
Wansford
Sutton
Castor
Ailsworth
Stibbington
Yarwell
Sibson
Water Newton
Nassington
Chesterton
Alwalton
Woodnewton
Fotheringhay
Elton
Haddon
Yaxley
Farcet
Stanground
Flag Fen
Eastrea
Coates
Eldernell
Eastwood End
Westry
Euximoor
Christchurch
Upwell Fen
Tips End
Welney
Wimblington
Stonea
Doddington
Benwick
Bedford Level
Middle Level
Glassmoor
Pondersbridge
Farcet Fen
Whittlesey Mere
King's Delph
Kings Delph
Morborne
Norman Cross
Folksworth
Stilton
Holme
Caldecote
Denton
Lutton
Eaglethorpe
Warmington
Tansor
Cotterstock
Oundle
Ashton
Polebrook
Armston
Hemington
Barnwell St Andrew
Barnwell All Saints
Luddington in the Brook
Glatton
Conington
Sawtry
Great Gidding
Little Gidding
Steeple Gidding
Thurning
Wigsthorpe
Thorpe Waterville
Clopton
Winwick
Coppingford
Titchmarsh
Thrapston
Hamerton
Hamerton Zoo Park
Alconbury Hill
Upton
Old Weston
Buckworth
Brington
Molesworth
Bythorn
Keyston
Leighton Bromswold
Barham
Woolley
Alconbury
Alconbury Weston
Little Stukeley
Great Stukeley
Huntingdon
Hartford
Wyton
Houghton
Hemingford Abbots
Hemingford Grey
St Ives
Godmanchester
Brampton
Hinchingbrooke House
Catworth
Spaldwick
Little Catworth
Easton
Ellington
Ellington Thorpe
Stow Longa
Hargrave
Covington
Tilbrook
Kimbolton
Grafham
Grafham Water
West Perry
Buckden
Stonely
Lower Dean
Upper Dean
Shelton
Yielden
Swineshead
Melchbourne
Pertenhall
Dillington
Great Staughton
Staughton Highway
Little Staughton
Riseley
Keysoe
Keysoe Row
Brook End
Knotting
Knotting Green
Top End
Hail Weston
Little Paxton
Great Paxton
Diddington
Southoe
Midloe Grange
Offord Cluny
Offord D'Arcy
Duck End
Graveley
Papworth St Agnes
Papworth Everard
Toseland
Yelling
St Neots
Eaton Ford
Eaton Socon
Eynesbury
Duloe
Staploe
Bushmead Priory
Bolnhurst
Upper Staploe
Colmworth
Thurleigh
Bletsoe
Cross End
Rootham's Green
Channel's End
Duck's Cross
Chawston
Colesden
Wilden
Milton Ernest
Ravensden
Sevick End
Renhold
Clapham
Clapham Green
Bromham
BEDFORD
Goldington
Salph End
Great Barford
Roxton
Wyboston
Tempsford
Little Barford
Abbotsley
Croxton
Eltisley
Caxton
Caxton Gibbet
Great Gransden
Little Gransden
Waresley
Longstowe
Gamlingay
Gamlingay Cinques
Gamlingay Great Heath
Everton
Tetworth
Mill Hill
Hatley St George
East Hatley
Cockayne Hatley
Potton
Sandy
Blunham
Willington
Mogerhanger
Beeston
Stratford
Seddington
Cople
Cardington
Kempston
Elstow
Harrowden
Keeley Green
Wilstead
Cotton End
Northill
Ickwell Green
Upper Caldecote
Lower Caldecote
Biggleswade
Wrestlingworth
Sutton
Dunton
Millow
Tadlow
Eyeworth
Guilden Morden
Steeple Morden
Edworth
Hinxworth
Ashwell
Ashwell End
Old Warden
Broom
Southill
Stanford
Langford
Shefford
Haynes
Haynes Church End
Houghton Conquest
Ampthill
Maulden
Clophill
Chicksands
Campton
Meppershall
Upper Stondon
Henlow
Clifton
Arlesey
Astwick
Church End
Stotfold
Caldecote
Newnham
Baldock
Radwell
Norton
Bygrave
Wallington
Clothall
Rushden
Letchworth Garden City
Hitchin
Ickleford
Pirton
Holwell
Shillington
Upper Gravenhurst
Lower Gravenhurst
Silsoe
Flitton
Flitwick
Greenfield
Pulloxhill
Westoning
Barton-le-Clay
Harlington
Streatley
Hexton
Pegsdon
Tingrith
Upper Sundon
Toddington
Fancott
Great Offley
Charlton
St Ippollitts
Great Wymondley
Little Wymondley
Graveley
Weston
Willian
Cumberlow Green
Hall's Green
Ardeley
Cottered
Throcking
Buntingford
Aspenden
Hare Street
Brook End
Wyddial
Chipping
Buckland
Barkway
Reed
Reed End
Therfield
Kelshall
Sandon
Roe Green
Green End
Mill End
Southern Green
Shaw Green
Royston
Melbourn
Meldreth
Shepreth
Foxton
Barrington
Orwell
Wimpole
Wimpole Hall
Arrington
Croydon
Wendy
Whaddon
Bassingbourn
Kneesworth
Litlington
Abington Pigotts
Shingay
Litlle Chishill
Great Chishill
Barley
Heydon
Chrishall
Elmdon
Strethall
Littlebury
Nuthampstead
Langley
Anstey
Meesden
Clavering
Berden
Great Hormead
Little Hormead
Furneux Pelham
Brent Pelham
Stocking Pelham
Ugley
CAMBRIDGE
Grantchester
Trumpington
Cherry Hinton
Teversham
Fen Ditton
Chesterton
Milton
Histon
Impington
Girton
Horningsea
Waterbeach
Landbeach
Cottenham
Oakington
Longstanton
Willingham
Over
Swavesey
Fenstanton
Fen Drayton
Boxworth
Boxworth End
Conington
Lolworth
Bar Hill
Dry Drayton
Elsworth
Knapwell
Hilton
Madingley
Coton
Comberton
Barton
Toft
Hardwick
Highfields
Caldecote
Bourn
Kingston
Great Eversden
Little Eversden
Harlton
Haslingfield
Harston
Hauxton
Little Shelford
Great Shelford
Stapleford
Newton
Whittlesford
Thriplow
Fowlmere
Duxford
Pampisford
Sawston
Babraham
Hinxton
Ickleton
Great Chesterford
Little Chesterford
Chatteris
Somersham
Colne
Bluntisham
Earith
Needingworth
Holywell
Pidley
Fenton
Warboys
Broughton
Old Hurst
Woodhurst
Kings Ripton
Abbots Ripton
Wennington
Little Raveley
Great Raveley
Wistow
Woodwalton
Upwood
Bury
Ramsey
Ramsey Heights
Ramsey St Mary's
Ramsey Mereside
Ramsey Forty Foot
Ramsey Hollow
Mereside
Haddenham
Wilburton
Aldreth
Hill Row
Witcham
Sutton
Mepal
Manea
Wentworth
Witchford
Coveney
Little Downham
Pymore
Welches Dam
Purls Bridge
Horseway
Ely
Stretham
Chatteris
Ferry Hill
Stow cum Quy
Wood Green Animal Shelter
Cambridge American Cemetery & Memorial
Imperial War Mus
Duxford
Wandlebury
290
293

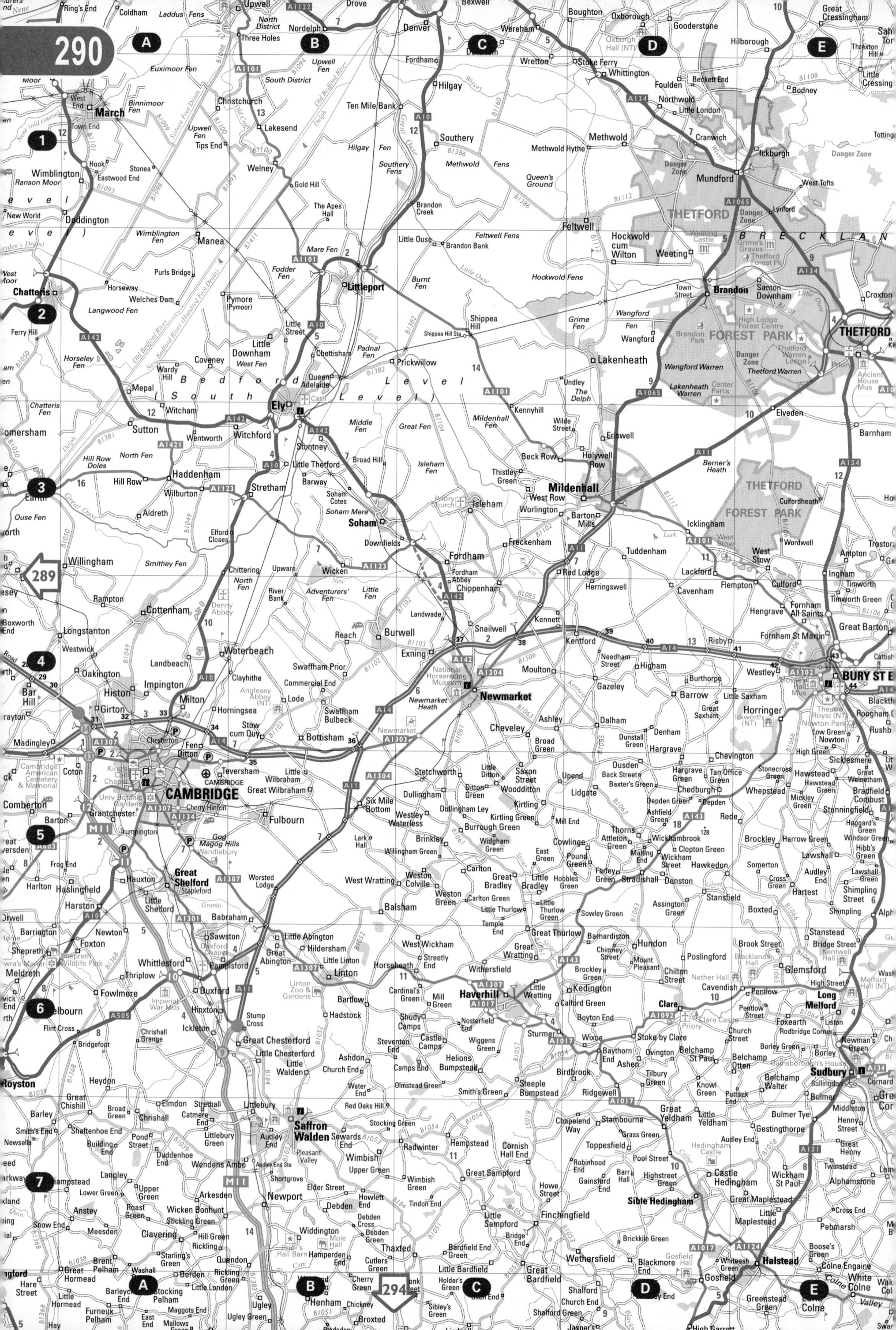

A
B
C
D
E
1
2
3
4
5
6
7
Ring's End
Coldham
Laddus Fens
Upwell
North District
Three Holes
Nordelph
Drove
Denver
Wereham
Boughton
Oxborough
Oxburgh Hall (NT)
Gooderstone
Great Cressingham
Hilborough
Threxton Hill
Little Cressing
Bodney
Euximoor Fen
Upwell Fen
South District
Fordham
Hilgay
Wretton
Stoke Ferry
Whittington
Beckett End
Foulden
Northwold
Little London
March
West End
Binnimoor Fen
Christchurch
Lakesend
Ten Mile Bank
Southery
Methwold
Methwold Hythe
Cranwich
Ickburgh
Danger Zone
Town End
Upwell Fen
Tips End
Hilgay Fen
Southery Fens
Methwold Fens
Queen's Ground
Mundford
West Tofts
Hook
Eastwood End
Stonea
Welney
Gold Hill
Wimblington
Ranson Moor
THETFORD
Lynford
New World
Doddington
The Apes Hall
Brandon Creek
Feltwell
Hockwold cum Wilton
Weeting
Weeting Castle
Grime's Graves
Thetford Forest Pk
BRECKLAND
Wimblington Fen
Manea
Mare Fen
Little Ouse
Brandon Bank
Feltwell Fens
Fodder Fen
Littleport
Burnt Fen
Hockwold Fens
Town Street
Brandon
Santon Downham
Croxton
Chatteris
Horseway
Purls Bridge
Welches Dam
Pymore (Pymoor)
Langwood Fen
Ferry Hill
Little Street
Shippea Hill
Shippea Hill Sta
Grime Fen
Wangford Fen
Wangford
Brandon Park
High Lodge Forest Centre
FOREST PARK
Thetford Warren Lodge
THETFORD
Horseley Fen
Coveney
Little Downham
West Fen
Chettisham
Padnal Fen
Prickwillow
Lakenheath
Wangford Warren
Thetford Warren
Wardy Hill
Bedford Level (South Level)
Queen Adelaide
Undley
The Delph
Lakenheath Warren
Center Parcs
Ancient House Mus
Priory
Chatteris Fen
Mepal
Witcham
Ely
Cath
Kennyhill
Elveden
Sutton
Somersham
Wentworth
Witchford
Middle Fen
Great Fen
Mildenhall Fen
Wilde Street
Eriswell
Barnham
Hill Row Doles
North Fen
Haddenham
Hill Row
Stuntney
Little Thetford
Broad Hill
Isleham Fen
Beck Row
Holywell Row
Berner's Heath
Thistley Green
Mildenhall
West Row
Earith
Wilburton
Stretham
Barway
Soham Cotes
Soham Mere
Soham
Priory Church
Isleham
Worlington
Barton Mills
Culfordheath
Ouse Fen
Aldreth
Elford Closes
Downfields
Freckenham
Icklingham
Wordwell
West Stow
Ampton
Willingham
Smithey Fen
Wicken
Fordham
Tuddenham
Lackford
Flempton
Culford
Ingham
Timworth
Chittering
Upware
North Fen
River Bank
Adventurers' Fen
Little Fen
Fordham Abbey
Chippenham
Red Lodge
Herringswell
Cavenham
Timworth Green
Rampton
Denny Abbey
Cottenham
Landwade
Kennett
Hengrave
Fornham All Saints
Boxworth End
Longstanton
Reach
Burwell
Snailwell
Kentford
Risby
Fornham St Martin
Great Barton
Westwick
Waterbeach
Landbeach
Swaffham Prior
Exning
National Horseracing Museum
Moulton
Needham Street
Higham
Westley
BURY ST EDMUNDS
Oakington
Bar Hill
Histon
Impington
Clayhithe
Anglesey Abbey (NT)
Commercial End
Lode
Newmarket
Newmarket Heath
Gazeley
Burthorpe
Barrow
Great Saxham
Little Saxham
Horringer
Ickworth (NT)
Theatre Royal (NT)
Nowton Park
Rougham
Rushbrooke
Girton
Milton
Horningsea
Swaffham Bulbeck
Stow cum Quy
Bottisham
Cheveley
Ashley
Dalham
Denham
Low Green
Nowton
Madingley
Chesterton
Fen Ditton
Teversham
Broad Green
Dunstall Green
Hargrave
Chevington
High Green
Sicklesmere
Cambridge American Cemetery & Memorial
Coton
King's Coll Chapel
Stetchworth
Little Ditton
Saxon Street
Woodditton
Upend
Ousden
Back Street
Baxter's Green
Hargrave Green
Tan Office Green
Chedburgh
Hawstead
Hawstead Green
Whepstead
Bradfield Combust
Little Wilbraham
Great Wilbraham
CAMBRIDGE
Univ Botanic Gardens
Cherry Hinton
Six Mile Bottom
Dullingham
Ditton Green
Lidgate
Depden Green
Depden
Stanningfield
Comberton
Grantchester
Fulbourn
Westley Waterless
Dullingham Ley
Kirtling
Kirtling Green
Mill End
Ashfield Green
Rede
Mickley Green
Hoggard's Green
Barton
Trumpington
Gog Magog Hills
Wandlebury
Lark Hall
Brinkley
Burrough Green
Widgham Green
Cowlinge
Thorns
Wickhambrook
Attleton Green
Clopton Green
Brockley
Harrow Green
Windsor Green
Hibb's Green
Frog End
Harlton
Haslingfield
Great Shelford
Stapleford
Hauxton
Worsted Lodge
Willingham Green
Weston Colville
West Wratting
Carlton
Great Bradley
Little Bradley
East Green
Pound Green
Hobbles Green
Farley Green
Malting End
Wickham Street
Stradishall
Hawkedon
Denston
Somerton
Lawshall
Lawshall Green
Audley End
Cross Green
Hartest
Shimpling Street
Harston
Little Shelford
Babraham
Balsham
Weston Green
Carlton Green
Little Thurlow
Little Thurlow Green
Temple End
Great Thurlow
Sowley Green
Assington Green
Stansfield
Boxted
Shimpling
Barrington
Newton
Foxton
Shepreth
Shepreth Wildlife Park
Sawston
Duxford Chapel
Pampisford
Little Abington
Great Abington
Hildersham
West Wickham
Streetly End
Great Wratting
Barnardiston
Chimney Street
Hundon
Mount Pleasant
Poslingford
Brook Street
Blacklands Hall
Stanstead
Bridge Street
Kentwell Hall
Meldreth
Whittlesford
Thriplow
Little Linton
Linton
Linton Zoo & Gardens
Horseheath
Withersfield
Brockley Green
Chilton Street
Nether Hall
Glemsford
High Street
Melford Hall (NT)
Fowlmere
Duxford
Imperial War Mus
Cardinal's Green
Mill Green
Haverhill
Little Wratting
Kedington
Calford Green
Cavendish
Pentlow
Long Melford
Melbourn
Flint Cross
Chrishall Grange
Hinxton
Ickleton
Stump Cross
Bartlow
Hadstock
Shudy Camps
Nosterfield End
Boyton End
Clare
Clare Castle
Priory
Pentlow Street
Foxearth
Rodbridge Corner
Liston
Bridgefoot
Great Chesterford
Little Chesterford
Little Walden
Ashdon
Church End
Steventon End
Castle Camps
Camps End
Helions Bumpstead
Wiggens Green
Sturmer
Wixoe
Stoke by Clare
Baythorn End
Ashen
Ovington
Belchamp St Paul
Belchamp Otten
Church Street
Borley Green
Borley
Newman's Green
Royston
Heydon
Water End
Olmstead Green
Steeple Bumpstead
Birdbrook
Tilbury Green
Knowl Green
Belchamp Walter
Gainsborough's House
Sudbury
Ballingdon
Cornard
Great Chishill
Elmdon
Strethall
Catmere End
Littlebury
Red Oaks Hill
Smith's Green
Ridgewell
Puttock End
Bulmer
Middleton
Barley
Broad Green
Chrishall
Littlebury Green
Audley End
Saffron Walden
Sewards End
Stocking Green
Hempstead
Cornish Hall End
Chapelend Way
Stambourne
Grass Green
Great Yeldham
Little Yeldham
Bulmer Tye
Henny Street
Smith's End
Shaftenhoe End
Pond Street
Building End
Duddenhoe End
Wendens Ambo
Audley End Sta
Pleasant Valley
Wimbish
Upper Green
Radwinter
Toppesfield
Hedingham Castle
Audley End
Gestingthorpe
Great Henny
Newsells
Langley
Upper Green
Shortgrove
Elder Street
Wimbish Green
Great Sampford
Robinhood End
Pool Street
Barr Hall
Gainsford End
Highstreet Green
Castle Hedingham
Wickham St Paul
Twinstead
Alphamstone
Chipping Hampstead
Lower Green
Arkesden
Newport
Howlett End
Debden
Tindon End
Howe Street
Finchingfield
Sible Hedingham
Great Maplestead
Little Maplestead
Cross End
Anstey
Roast Green
Wicken Bonhunt
Stickling Green
Debden Cross
Debden Green
Little Sampford
Bridge End
Brickkiln Green
Pebmarsh
Snow End
Meesden
Clavering
Hill Green
Rickling
Widdington
Mole Hall
Prior's Hall Barn
Thaxted
Bardfield End Green
Wethersfield
Blackmore End
Gosfield Hall
Halstead
Boose's Green
Colne Engaine
White Colne
Brent Pelham
Great Hormead
Washall
Starling's Green
Quendon
Rickling Green
Berden
Little London
Hamperden End
Cutlers Green
Cherry Green
Little Bardfield
Holder's Green
Great Bardfield
Whiteash Green
Gosfield
Hare Street
Little Hormead
Barleycroft End
Stocking Pelham
Henham
Chickney
Broxted
Sibley's Green
Shalford
Church End
Shalford Green
Jasper's Green
Greenstead Green
Earls Colne
Furneux Pelham
Maggots End
East End
Mallows Green
Ugley
Ugley Green
Hay
Broxted
High Garrett
Colne Valley
Colne
M11
A10
A14
A11
A142
A1101
A1123
A1421
A1307
A1303
A1304
A1017
A1092
A134
A143
A1065
A505
A603
A1134
A1301
A1302
A1124
A1122
B1049
B1050
B1052
B1053
B1054
B1057
B1063
B1085
B1102
B1104
B1106
B1112
B1368
B1383
B1386

289

294

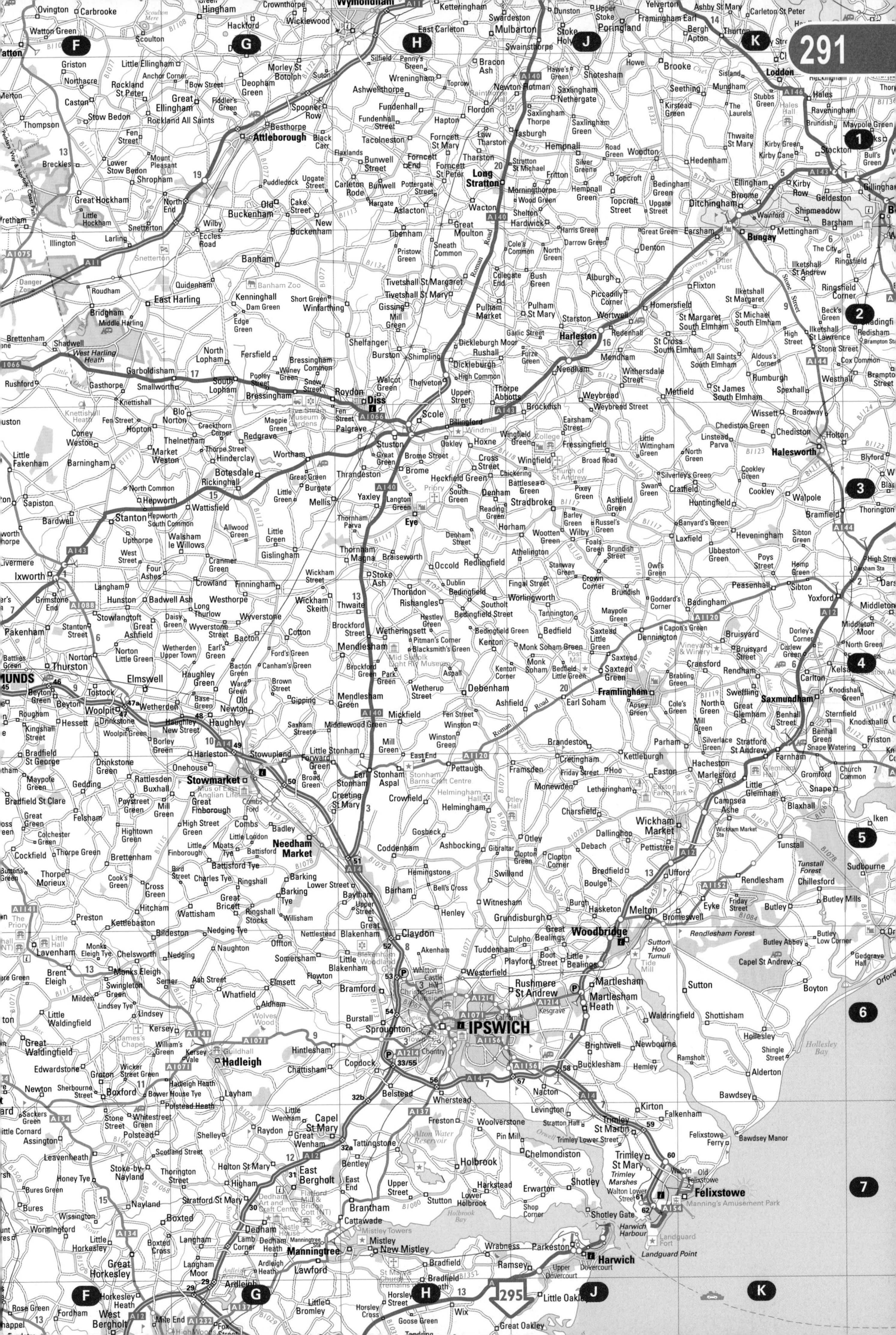
F
G
H
J
K
1
2
3
4
5
6
7
Wymondham
Attleborough
Hingham
Long Stratton
Poringland
Loddon
Ditchingham
Bungay
Halesworth
Harleston
Diss
Scole
Eye
Botesdale
Rickinghall
East Harling
Garboldisham
Thurston
Elmswell
Stowmarket
Needham Market
Debenham
Framlingham
Saxmundham
Yoxford
Wickham Market
Woodbridge
Melton
IPSWICH
Hadleigh
Lavenham
Boxford
Nayland
Dedham
Manningtree
Mistley
Harwich
Felixstowe
Trimley St Mary
Martlesham
Kesgrave
Brantham
Holbrook
Shotley
Capel St Mary
Claydon
Stradbroke
Fressingfield
Wortwell
Homersfield
Banham
Banham Zoo
Snetterton
Stanton
Ixworth
Pakenham
Woolpit
Haughley
Mendlesham
Sproughton
Bramford
Great Wenham
Little Oakley
Great Oakley
West Bergholt
Rendlesham Forest
Sutton Hoo Tumuli
Tunstall Forest
Hollesley Bay
Landguard Point
Landguard Fort
Harwich Harbour
Alton Water Reservoir
Holbrook Bay
Manning's Amusement Park
295
A11
A140
A143
A144
A146
A12
A14
A1120
A1066
A1071
A1214
A1156
A137
A134
A1141
A1152
A120

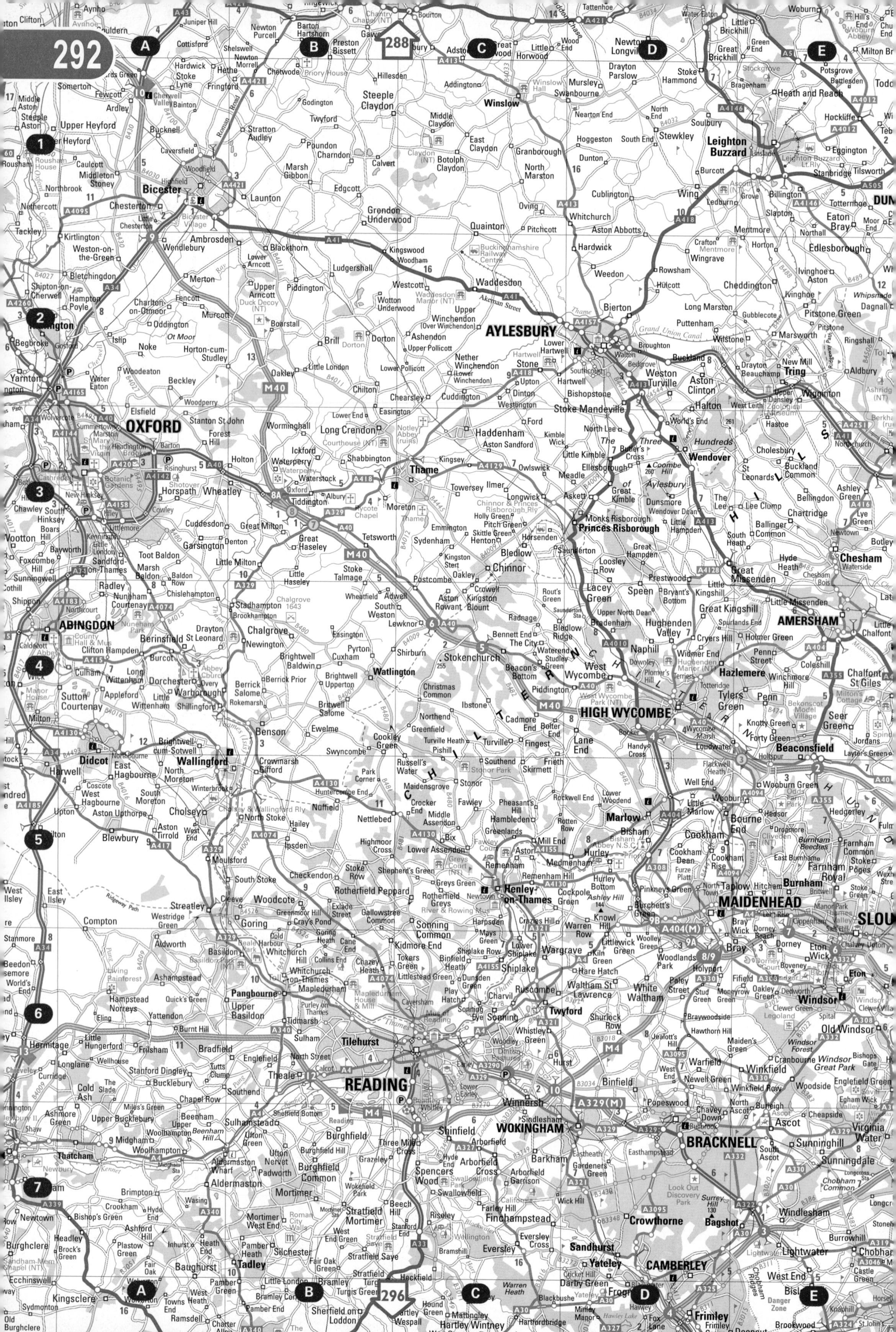

288
296
OXFORD
AYLESBURY
HIGH WYCOMBE
READING
MAIDENHEAD
WOKINGHAM
BRACKNELL
CAMBERLEY
ABINGDON
AMERSHAM
Bicester
Thame
Wallingford
Didcot
Henley-on-Thames
Marlow
Tring
Wendover
Chesham
Beaconsfield
Princes Risborough
Leighton Buzzard
Winslow
Windsor
Tilehurst
Watlington
Hazlemere

F
G
H
J
K
289
294
297
1
2
3
4
5
6
7
LETCHWORTH GARDEN CITY
Hitchin
STEVENAGE
LUTON
LONDON LUTON
Buntingford
BISHOP'S STORTFORD
Harpenden
ST ALBANS
WELWYN GARDEN CITY
HERTFORD
Ware
Sawbridgeworth
HARLOW
HEMEL HEMPSTEAD
Hatfield
Hoddesdon
CHESHUNT
Waltham Abbey
Epping
Potters Bar
Radlett
BOREHAMWOOD
WATFORD
Bushey
BARNET
ENFIELD
Loughton
Rickmansworth
Chigwell
WOOD GREEN
WALTHAMSTOW
HARROW
UXBRIDGE
WEMBLEY
ILFORD
Barking
EALING
WESTMINSTER
LONDON
WOOLWICH
HOUNSLOW
LONDON HEATHROW
RICHMOND
WANDSWORTH
LEWISHAM
Bexleyheath
KINGSTON UPON THAMES
Wimbledon
STAINES
BROMLEY
Swanley
Sunbury
Walton-on-Thames
Weybridge
ESHER
CROYDON
SUTTON
Chertsey
Addlestone
EPSOM
New Addington
West Byfleet
Cobham
WOKING
Biggin Hill
Warlingham
M1
M10
M11
M25
M4
M3
A1(M)

294
A
B
C
D
E
1
2
3
4
5
6
7
290
293
296
BISHOP'S STORTFORD
Stansted Mountfitchet
LONDON STANSTED
Great Dunmow
BRAINTREE
Halstead
Coggeshall
Witham
Tiptree
HARLOW
Sawbridgeworth
CHELMSFORD
Maldon
South Woodham Ferrers
CHESHUNT
Waltham Abbey
Epping
Chipping Ongar
Loughton
Chigwell
Ingatestone
Billericay
BRENTWOOD
Wickford
Rayleigh
Rochford
BASILDON
Hadleigh
ROMFORD
ILFORD
Barking
South Ockendon
Corringham
Stanford-le-Hope
Canvey Island
South Benfleet
SOUTHEND ON-SEA
LONDON SOUTHEND
WOOLWICH
LONDON CITY
DARTFORD
GRAYS
Tilbury
GRAVESEND
Northfleet
BROMLEY
Swanley
Rochester
CHATHAM
GILLINGHAM
Biggin Hill
West Malling
Borough Green
M11
M25
M2
M20
M26
A12
A13
A120
A130
A127
A2
THAMES

Wormingford
Little Horkesley
Boxted Cross
Langham
Dedham
Lamb Corner
Manningtree
Mistley Towers
Mistley
New Mistley
Wrabness
291
Parkeston
Harwich Harbour
Landguard Fort
Harwich
Landguard Point
Great Horkesley
Langham Moor
Lawford
St Mary's Church (remains of)
Bradfield
Bradfield Heath
Upper Dovercourt
Little Oakley
Rose Green
Horkesley Heath
Ardleigh
Little Bromley
Horsleycross Street
Horsley Cross
Goose Green
Wix
Great Oakley
Stone Point
Fordham
West Bergholt
Eight Ash Green
Fordham Heath
Fox Street
Crockleford Heath
Elmstead
Great Bromley
Cowey Green
Little Bentley
Tendring Green
Stones Green
Horsey Island
Hamford Water
The Naze
Stanway
Greenstead
Elmstead Market
Balls Green
Hare Green
Raven's Green
Goose Green
Tendring
Beaumont
Marks Tey
COLCHESTER
Stanway Green
Shrub End
St Botolph's Priory
Bourne Mill
Beth Chatto
Frating
Great Bentley
Thorpe Green
Kirby le Soken
Copford Green
Heckfordbridge
Blackheath
Rowhedge
Wivenhoe
Weeley
Thorpe-le-Soken
Kirby Cross
Walton on the Naze
New Walton Pier
Easthorpe
Maypole Green
Malting Green
Alresford
Aingers Green
Weeley Heath
Birch
Fingringhoe
High Park Corner
Thorrington
Hardy's Green
Layer de la Haye
Abberton
Row Heath
Great Holland
Frinton-on-Sea
Birch Green
South Green
Brightlingsea
Little Clacton
Clacton Common
Layer Breton
Danger Zone
Hurst Green
Great Clacton
Holland-on-Sea
Sandy Point
Layer Marney
Peldon
Tiptree Museum
Abberton Res
Mersea Island
East Mersea
Point Clear
Priory
St Osyth
St Osyth Marsh
CLACTON-ON-SEA
Tolleshunt Knights
Great Wigborough
Virley
Salcott
Jaywick
Clacton Pier
Cudmore Grove
Mersea Flats
Brightlingsea Reach
Seawick
Gunfleet Sand
Tolleshunt D'Arcy
Salcott Channel
Cobmarsh Island
West Mersea
Colne Point
Great Cob Island
Tollesbury Fleet
Virley Channel
Tollesbury
The Nass
Goldhanger
Bradwell Waterside
Sales Point
St Peter's Flat
East End
Osea Island
Blackwater
Ramsey Island
Bradwell-on-Sea
St Lawrence
Steeple
Tillingham
Dengie Flat
Maylandsea
Dengie
Mayland
Asheldham
Dengie Marshes
Southminster
Ray Sand
Mangapps Farm Railway Museum
Eves Corner
Stoneyhills
Ostend
Old Montsale
Deal Hall
Foulness Sands
Holliwell Point
Burnham-on-Crouch
Foulness Point
Crouch
Courtsend
Paglesham Churchend
Wallasea Island
Ballards Gore
Paglesham Eastend
Churchend
Foulness Island
Potton Island
Barling
Havengore Island
Little Wakering
Maplin Sands
Kid's Kingdom
Mr. B's Amusements
Great Wakering
Southchurch
North Shoebury
Thorpe Bay
Shoeburyness
Sea Life Centre
Shoebury Ness
Sheerness
Marine Town
Mile Town
West Minster
Halfway Houses
Minster
East End
Warden Point
Eastchurch
Warden
Leysdown-on-Sea
ISLE OF SHEPPEY
Swale Sta
Elmley Island
Kingshill
Eastchurch Marshes
Isle of Harty
Shell Ness
The Swale
Kemsley
Conyer
Sittingbourne & Kemsley Light Rly
Murston
Uplees
SITTINGBOURNE
Teynham
Deerton Street
Luddenham Court
Oare
Bapchild
Highsted
Rodmersham
Rodmersham Green
Lewson Street
Faversham
Preston
Ospringe
Lynsted
Dungate
Milstead
Doddington
Newnham
Whitehill
North Street
Brogdale Horticultural Trust
Sheldwich
South Channel
Long Nose Spit
Foreness Point
MARGATE
Tudor House
Cliftonville
Kingsgate
White Ness
North Foreland
Westgate on Sea
Westbrook
Salmestone Grange
Bleak House
Reculver
Towers & Roman Fort
Birchington
Quex House & Gdns
Herne Bay
Hillborough
Hampton
Beltinge
Broadstairs
Spitfire & Hurricane Memorial
Dickens House Museum
Whitstable
Tankerton
Swalecliffe
Herne
Broomfield
St Nicholas at Wade
ISLE OF THANET
Acol
Northwood
Haine
Seasalter
Chestfield
South Street
West End
Herne Common
Hunters Forstal
Highstead
Boyden Gate
Chislet
Sarre
Minster
MANSTON
Manston
Monkton
Gore Street
Yorkletts
Clapham Hill
Maypole
Hoath
Upstreet
Roman Road
Abbey
Pegwell
Ramsgate
Cliffs End
St Augustine's Cross
Graveney
Wealden Woodlands
Calcott
West Stourmouth
Plucks Gutter
Pegwell Bay
Pean Hill
Druidstone Park
Highstreet
Dargate
Broadoak
Hersden
Westbere
Grove
East Stourmouth
Westmarsh
Stour
Richborough Castle
Sandwich Flats
Goodnestone
Hernhill
Honey Hill
Blean
Tyler Hill
Sturry
Stodmarsh
Preston
Elmstone
Ware
Cop Street
Stonar Cut
Great Stonar
Sandwich Bay
Staplestreet
Boughton Street
Rough Common
Hales Place
Ford
298
Wickhambreaux
Roman Amphitheatre
Dunkirk
Upper Harbledown
Harbledown
CANTERBURY
Ickham
Ash
Salutation Gdn
Oversland
Gushmere
St Augustine's Abbey
Littlebourne
Shatterling
Wingham
Marshborough
Woodnesborough
Toll
Sandwich

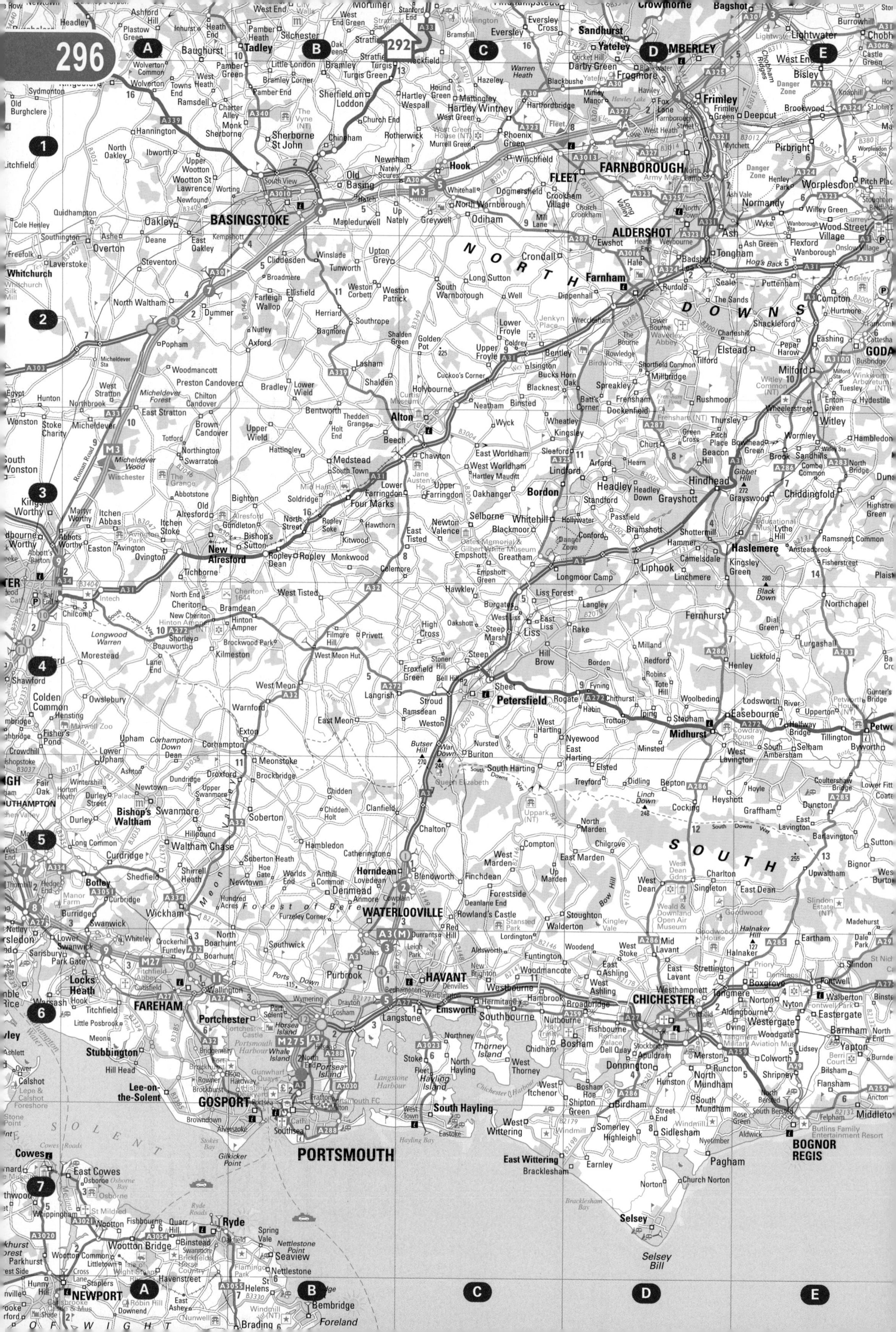
292
A
B
C
D
E
1
2
3
4
5
6
7
BASINGSTOKE
Tadley
Silchester
Sherborne St John
Oakley
Overton
Whitchurch
Hook
Odiham
Fleet
FARNBOROUGH
CAMBERLEY
Sandhurst
Yateley
Frimley
ALDERSHOT
Farnham
Crowthorne
Bagshot
Lightwater
Bisley
Pirbright
Worplesdon
Ash
Tongham
Hog's Back
Godalming
Milford
Elstead
Witley
Chiddingfold
Haslemere
Hindhead
Grayshott
Liphook
Bordon
Headley
Lindford
Alton
Chawton
Four Marks
New Alresford
Kings Worthy
Abbots Worthy
Itchen Abbas
Micheldever
Popham
Dummer
North Waltham
Medstead
Selborne
Greatham
Liss
Petersfield
Rogate
Midhurst
Easebourne
Fernhurst
Northchapel
Petworth
Bishop's Waltham
Swanmore
Droxford
Wickham
Botley
FAREHAM
Portchester
GOSPORT
PORTSMOUTH
Southsea
Lee-on-the-Solent
Stubbington
Titchfield
Locks Heath
Warsash
Horndean
WATERLOOVILLE
HAVANT
Emsworth
Southbourne
Hayling Island
South Hayling
West Wittering
East Wittering
Bracklesham
Selsey
Selsey Bill
CHICHESTER
Bosham
Sidlesham
Pagham
BOGNOR REGIS
Middleton
Barnham
Eastergate
Westergate
Boxgrove
Singleton
Cocking
Harting
Cowes
East Cowes
NEWPORT
Wootton Bridge
Ryde
Seaview
St Helens
Bembridge
Foreland
Brading
NORTH DOWNS
SOUTH DOWNS
SOLENT
Portsmouth Harbour
Langstone Harbour
Chichester Harbour
Forest of Bere
Queen Elizabeth Country Park
Butlins Family Entertainment Resort

F
G
H
J
K
1
2
3
4
5
6
7
293
298
WOKING
Byfleet
Cobham
Stoke D'Abernon
EPSOM
Ashtead
Leatherhead
Banstead
Chipstead
Tadworth
Kingswood
Woodmansterne
Whyteleafe
Warlingham
Caterham
Biggin Hill
Knockholt
Addington
Downe
Chelsham
Farleigh
Ripley
Ockham
Send
Send Marsh
Effingham
Great Bookham
East Horsley
West Horsley
West Clandon
East Clandon
Merrow
GUILDFORD
Shere
Gomshall
Abinger Hammer
Wotton
Westcott
Dorking
Brockham
REIGATE
Redhill
Merstham
Godstone
Bletchingley
South Nutfield
Oxted
Limpsfield
Westerham
Brasted
Sundridge
Sevenoaks Weald
Tatsfield
Titsey
Edenbridge
Hever
Penshurst
Chiddingstone Causeway
Four Elms
Crockham Hill
Chilworth
Shalford
Blackheath
Wonersh
Bramley
Cranleigh
Ewhurst
Holmbury St Mary
Coldharbour
Leith Hill
Capel
Ockley
Newdigate
Beare Green
Leigh
Charlwood
Horley
LONDON GATWICK
Smallfield
Lingfield
Dormansland
Felcourt
Copthorne
East Grinstead
Forest Row
Hartfield
Crowborough
CRAWLEY
Three Bridges
Crawley Down
Turners Hill
West Hoathly
Sharpthorne
Ashdown Forest
Alfold
Rudgwick
Warnham
HORSHAM
Slinfold
Broadbridge Heath
Colgate
St Leonard's Forest
Handcross
Staplefield
Balcombe
Ardingly
Horsted Keynes
Danehill
Nutley
Lower Beeding
Slaugham
Cuckfield
HAYWARDS HEATH
Lindfield
Wivelsfield
Burgess Hill
Hurstpierpoint
Keymer
Ditchling
Hassocks
Maresfield
Uckfield
Newick
Framfield
Fletching
Billingshurst
Southwater
Cowfold
Bolney
Ansty
Partridge Green
West Grinstead
Henfield
Pulborough
West Chiltington Common
Storrington
Washington
Steyning
Bramber
Upper Beeding
Ashington
Findon
Arundel
Amberley
Houghton
DOWNS
South Downs Way
Lewes
Ringmer
Falmer
Kingston near Lewes
Rodmell
Beddingham
Glynde
Alciston
Firle Beacon
Alfriston
Seaford
Bishopstone
Newhaven
Peacehaven
Telscombe
Rottingdean
Saltdean
BRIGHTON
HOVE
Portslade-by-Sea
Southwick
Shoreham-by-Sea
Lancing
Sompting
WORTHING
Goring-by-Sea
Ferring
Angmering
East Preston
Rustington
LITTLEHAMPTON
M25
M23
A23
A24
A29
A264
A272
A27
A259
A22
A26
A281
A283

298
A
B
C
D
E
1
2
3
4
5
6
7
294
297
SEVENOAKS
MAIDSTONE
ROYAL TUNBRIDGE WELLS
Tonbridge
Southborough
Crowborough
Ashdown Forest
Uckfield
Heathfield
Hailsham
Lewes
Newhaven
Peacehaven
Seaford
EASTBOURNE
Beachy Head
Pevensey Levels
Pevensey Bay
BEXHILL
HASTINGS
St Leonards
Battle
Hawkhurst
Cranbrook
Tenterden
Rye
Westerham
Oxted
Edenbridge
East Grinstead
Forest Row
Paddock Wood
West Malling
Aylesford
Wadhurst
Mayfield
Robertsbridge
Polegate
Herstmonceux
Goudhurst
Headcorn
Staplehurst
Biddenden
Lamberhurst
Brede
Fairlight
Sedlescombe
Newick
Maresfield

CANTERBURY
DOVER
FOLKESTONE
ASHFORD
Faversham
Sandwich
Deal
Hythe
New Romney
Rye
Lydd
Dymchurch
Dungeness
Romney Marsh
Walland Marsh
STRAIT OF DOVER
295

300 Administrative areas

AYLESBURY VALE
TRING
DACORUM
BERKHAMSTED
HEMEL HEMPSTEAD
HARPENDEN
WHEATHAMPSTEAD
WELWYN
WELWYN GARDEN CITY
ST. ALBANS
ST. ALBANS
LONDON COLNEY
WELWYN HATFIELD
HATFIELD
ESSENDON
WENDOVER
PRINCES RISBOROUGH
GREAT MISSENDEN
CHESHAM
ABBOTS LANGLEY
POTTERS BAR
CUFFLEY
CHILTERN
LITTLE CHALFONT
AMERSHAM
THREE RIVERS
WATFORD
WATFORD
HERTSMERE
BOREHAMWOOD
BARNET
NEW BARNET
EAST BARNET
BUSHEY
WYCOMBE
TYLERS GREEN
CHALFONT ST. GILES
RICKMANSWORTH
HIGH WYCOMBE
LOUDWATER
BEACONSFIELD
HAREFIELD
NORTHWOOD
STANMORE
EDGWARE
BARNET
FINCHLEY
HARROW
PINNER
HENDON
WOOBURN
MARLOW
GERRARDS CROSS
DENHAM
SOUTH BUCKS
RUISLIP
HARROW
HILLINGDON
WEMBLEY
BRENT
HAMPSTEAD
CAMDEN
HENLEY-ON-THAMES
MAIDENHEAD
BURNHAM
STOKE POGES
UXBRIDGE
NORTHOLT
WILLESDEN
PADDINGTON
WESTMINSTER
KENSINGTON & CHELSEA
HAMMERSMITH & FULHAM
SLOUGH
SLOUGH
IVER
LANGLEY
HAYES
EALING
EALING
SOUTHALL
ACTON
WEST DRAYTON
HAMMERSMITH
ETON
WINDSOR
TWYFORD
WINDSOR & MAIDENHEAD
DATCHET
OLD WINDSOR
HOUNSLOW
HOUNSLOW
KEW
BATTERSEA
BRIXTON
RICHMOND
WANDSWORTH
WANDSWORTH
WINKFIELD
WRAYSBURY
FELTHAM
TWICKENHAM
RICHMOND UPON THAMES
STREATHAM
EGHAM
STAINES
ASHFORD
WIMBLEDON
WOKINGHAM
WOKINGHAM
BRACKNELL
BRACKNELL FOREST
ASCOT
VIRGINIA WATER
SPELTHORNE
TEDDINGTON
KINGSTON UPON THAMES
MERTON
MERTON
MORDEN
MITCHAM
KINGSTON UPON THAMES
SURBITON
RUNNYMEDE
CHERTSEY
WALTON-ON-THAMES
OTTERSHAW
WEYBRIDGE
ESHER
SUTTON
SUTTON
SANDHURST
BAGSHOT
SURREY HEATH
CHOBHAM
ELMBRIDGE
EWELL
EPSOM
EPSOM & EWELL
CAMBERLEY
BYFLEET
OXSHOTT
STOKE D'ABERNON
BANSTEAD
FRIMLEY
WOKING
WOKING
ASHTEAD
RIPLEY
FETCHAM
LEATHERHEAD
TADWORTH
FARNBOROUGH
MYTCHETT
HART
FLEET
GREAT BOOKHAM
REIGATE & BANSTEAD
RUSHMOOR
EAST HORSLEY
NORMANDY
ALDERSHOT
EAST CLANDON
MOLE VALLEY
REIGATE
REDHILL
TONGHAM
GUILDFORD
GUILDFORD
WESTCOTT
DORKING
BROCKHAM
GOMSHALL
FARNHAM
COMPTON
SHALFORD
LEIGH
SALFORDS
SHACKLEFORD
HOLMBURY ST MARY
ELSTEAD
GODALMING
BEARE GREEN
HORLEY
EAST HANTS
MILFORD
WAVERLEY
WITLEY
CHARLWOOD
CRAWLEY

HERTFORDSHIRE
WARE
SAWBRIDGEWORTH
HERTFORD
SHEERING
UTTLESFORD
LEADEN RODING
BRAINTREE
HATFIELD PEVEREL
OLD HARLOW
HARLOW
HARLOW
HODDESDON
BROXBOURNE
BROXBOURNE
LOWER NAZEING
CHELMSFORD
CHELMSFORD
MALDON
MALDON
EPPING
NORTH WEALD BASSETT
CHIPPING ONGAR
EPPING
FOREST
WALTHAM ABBEY
CHESHUNT
INGATESTONE
KELVEDON HATCH
SOUTH WOODHAM FERRERS
THEYDON BOIS
ABRIDGE
ENFIELD
FIELD
LOUGHTON
STAPLEFORD ABBOTTS
BRENTWOOD
BRENTWOOD
BILLERICAY
WICKFORD
CHIGWELL
EDMONTON
ROCHFORD
WALTHAM FOREST
WOODFORD
COLLIER ROW
HAROLD HILL
RAYLEIGH
BASILDON
REDBRIDGE
BASILDON
CASTLE POINT
WANSTEAD
WALTHAMSTOW
ROMFORD
LAINDON
HAVERING
HACKNEY
LEYTON
ILFORD
HORNCHURCH
UPMINSTER
SOUTH BENFLEET
SOUTHEND
BARKING & DAGENHAM
DAGENHAM
HACKNEY
WEST HAM
BARKING
EAST HAM
CANVEY ISLAND
TOWER HAMLETS
NEWHAM
STANFORD-LE-HOPE
SOUTH OCKENDON
CITY
STEPNEY
RAINHAM
THURROCK
AVELEY
RIVER THAMES
SOUTHWARK
ERITH
PURFLEET
GRAYS
CHADWELL ST. MARY
WOOLWICH
PECKHAM
GREENWICH
GREENWICH
TILBURY
BEXLEY
LEWISHAM
BEXLEYHEATH
DARTFORD
NORTHFLEET
GRAVESEND
MEDWAY
CATFORD
DARTFORD
HOO
SIDCUP
GRAVESHAM
BECKENHAM
CHISLEHURST
BROMLEY
SOUTH DARENTH
LONGFIELD
SWANLEY
GILLINGHAM
CHATHAM
ORPINGTON
RAMSDEN
FARNINGHAM
CROYDON
BROMLEY
MEOPHAM
ADDINGTON
FARNBOROUGH
CHELSFIELD
WEST KINGSDOWN
SWALE
CROYDON
CULVERSTONE GREEN
DOWNE
OTFORD
KEMSING
WROTHAM
WARLINGHAM
BIGGIN HILL
KNOCKHOLT
WEST MALLING
TATSFIELD
IGHTHAM
MAIDSTONE
CATERHAM
TONBRIDGE & MALLING
SEVENOAKS
WESTERHAM
MEREWORTH
OXTED
GODSTONE
SHIPBOURNE
MAIDSTONE
SEVENOAKS
TANDRIDGE
EAST PECKHAM
TONBRIDGE
EDENBRIDGE
LINGFIELD
SOUTHBOROUGH
TUNBRIDGE WELLS
HOLTYE COMMON
ROYAL TUNBRIDGE WELLS
MID SUSSEX
EAST SUSSEX

London congestion charging zone

- London's congestion charging zone operates inside the 'Inner Ring Road' linking Marylebone Road, Euston Road, Pentonville Road, Tower Bridge, Elephant and Castle, Vauxhall Bridge and Park Lane (see map below). The 'Inner Ring Road' provides a route around the charging zone and charges do not apply to vehicles travelling on it. The daily operating time is from 7.00 am to 6.30 pm, Monday to Friday, excluding public holidays.

- Payment of the £5 congestion charge, either in advance or on the day of travel, allows the registered vehicle to enter, drive around and leave the congestion zone as many times as required on that one day. Payments can be made in a variety of ways but in all cases the vehicle registration number and the dates to be paid for must be given.
  Charges can be paid:
  - online at www.cclondon.com
  - by phone on 0845 900 1234 (charged at local rate)
  - by text message for drivers who have pre-registered on the website or telephone.
  - by post by requesting an application form from Congestion Charging, PO Box 2982, Coventry, CV7 8ZR, or downloading the form from the website and posting to the same address.
  - at self-service machines in major car parks within the congestion zone.
  - at newsagents, convenience stores or petrol stations throughout the Greater London area displaying the PayPoint logo.

- Regular drivers within the congestion zone can pay the charge weekly, monthly or yearly.
  Residents inside the congestion zone are eligible for a 90% discount upon payment of a registration fee.

- On paying the charge the car registration number is held on a database. A series of over 200 cameras around the congestion zone record all vehicle number plates and check them against the database. Drivers can pay the £5 without further penalty up until 10pm on the day of travel. Drivers paying between10pm and midnight will also have to pay a £5 surcharge. Any driver who has not paid before midnight will be sent an £80 penalty charge notice, payment within 14 days will reduce this to £40. Failure to pay within 28 days will result in the penalty being increased to £120.

- Further information, including vehicles eligible for exemption or a discount, can be found on the website www.cclondon.com or by telephoning 0845 900 1234.

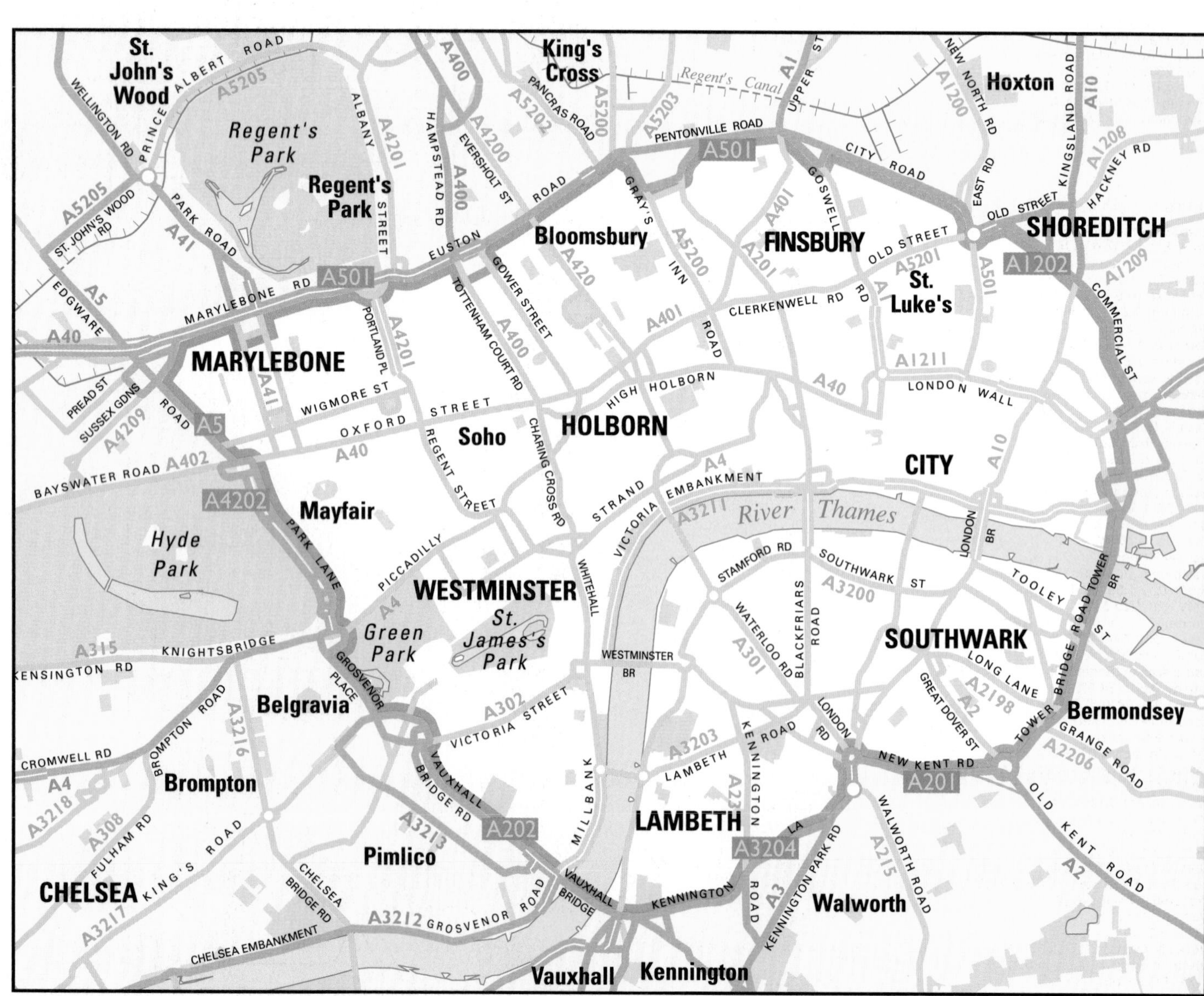
St. John's Wood
King's Cross
Hoxton
Regent's Park
Regent's Canal
PENTONVILLE ROAD
A501
Bloomsbury
FINSBURY
SHOREDITCH
St. Luke's
MARYLEBONE
EUSTON ROAD
MARYLEBONE RD
HOLBORN
Soho
CITY
Mayfair
Hyde Park
River Thames
WESTMINSTER
Green Park
St. James's Park
SOUTHWARK
Belgravia
Bermondsey
Brompton
LAMBETH
Pimlico
CHELSEA
Walworth
Vauxhall
Kennington
OXFORD STREET
HIGH HOLBORN
LONDON WALL
STRAND
VICTORIA EMBANKMENT
PARK LANE
PICCADILLY
KNIGHTSBRIDGE
BAYSWATER ROAD
VAUXHALL BRIDGE RD
NEW KENT RD
OLD KENT ROAD
TOWER BRIDGE ROAD
COMMERCIAL ST
CITY ROAD
OLD STREET
KINGS ROAD
CHELSEA EMBANKMENT
GROSVENOR ROAD
KENNINGTON ROAD
WALWORTH ROAD
A3204
A202
A201
A1202
A4202
A5

THEATRES

Adelphi *0870 403 0303*
Albery *0870 060 6621*
Aldwych *020 7379 3367*
Apollo *020 7494 5070*
Arts *020 7836 2132*
Cambridge *020 7494 5080*
Comedy *0870 060 6637*
Criterion *020 7839 8811*
Dominion *08706 077400*
Donmar Warehouse *0870 060 6624*
Duchess *020 7494 5075*
Fortune *0870 060 6626*
Garrick *020 7494 5085*
Gielgud *020 7494 5065*
Her Majesty's *020 7494 5400*
ICA *020 7930 3647*
London Coliseum *020 7632 8300*
London Palladium *020 7494 5020*
Lyceum *08706 063441*
Lyric *020 7494 5045*
New London *0870 890 0141*
New Players *0870 033 2626*
Palace *0870 895 5579*
Peacock *020 7863 8222*
Phoenix *0870 060 6629*
Piccadilly *0870 060 6630*
Playhouse *020 7839 4401*
Prince Edward *020 7447 5400*
Prince of Wales *0870 850 0393*
Queen Elizabeth Hall *020 7921 0600*
Queen's *020 7494 5040*
Royal Court Jerwood Theatre Downstairs *020 7565 5050*
Royal Court Jerwood Theatre Upstairs *020 7565 5050*
Royal Festival Hall *020 7921 0600*
Royal National *020 7452 3400*
Royal Opera House *020 7304 4000*
St. Martin's *020 7836 1443*
Savoy *020 7836 8888*
Shaftesbury *020 7379 5399*
Strand *0870 850 9170*
Theatre Royal, Drury Lane *020 7494 5060*
Theatre Royal, Haymarket *020 7930 8890*
Vaudeville *08708 900511*
Whitehall *0870 060 6632*
Wyndhams *0870 060 6633*

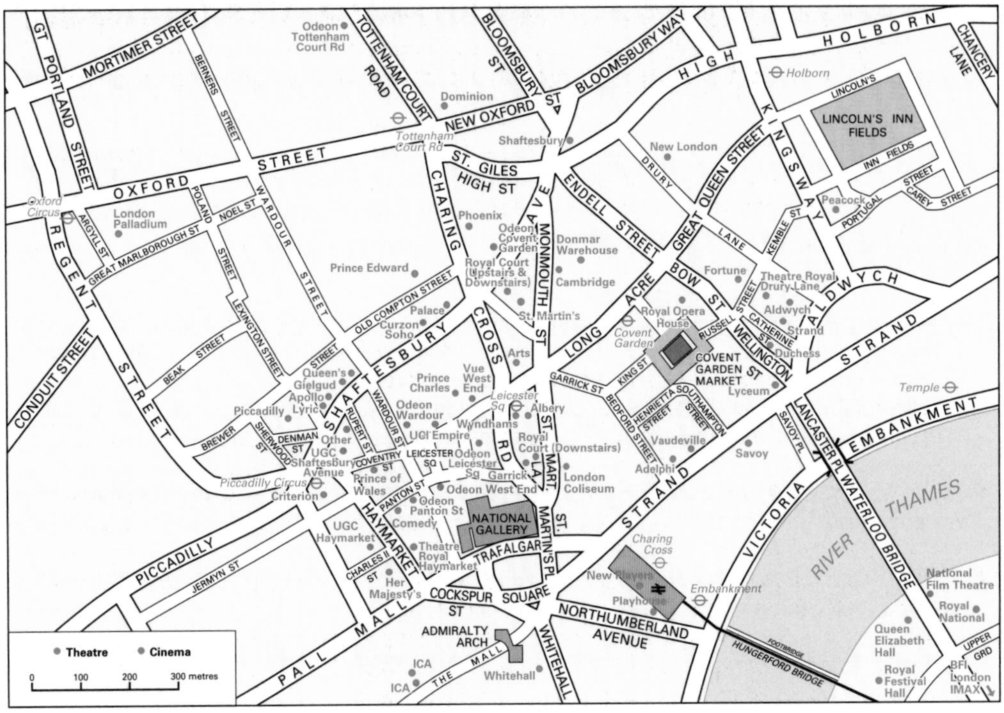

CINEMAS

BFI London IMAX *0870 787 2525*
Curzon Soho *020 7734 2255*
ICA *020 7930 3647*
National Film Theatre *020 7928 3232*
Odeon Leicester Sq *0871 224 4007*
Odeon Panton St *0871 224 4007*
Odeon Covent Garden *0871 224 4007*
Odeon Tottenham Court Rd *0871 224 4007*
Odeon Wardour Street *0871 224 4007*
Odeon West End *0871 224 4007*
Other 020 *7437 0757*
Prince Charles *020 7437 7003*
UCI Empire Leicester Sq *08700 102030*
UGC Haymarket *08709 070712*
UGC Shaftesbury Avenue *0871 200 2000*
Vue West End *0871 224 0240*

West End shopping

SHOPS

Aquascutum *020 7675 8200*
Army & Navy *020 7834 1234*
Asprey & Garrard *020 7493 6767*
Austin Reed *020 7534 7777*
BHS (Oxford St) *020 7629 2011*
Bonhams *020 7393 3900*
Burberrys *020 7968 0000*
Cartier *020 7408 5700*
Christie's *020 7839 9060*
Covent Garden Market *020 7836 9136*
Debenhams *020 7580 3000*
Dickins & Jones *020 7734 7070*
Dunhill *020 7355 9500*
Fenwick *020 7629 9161*
Fortnum & Mason *020 7734 8040*
Foyles *020 7437 5660*
Habitat (Tottenham Court Rd) *020 7631 3880*
Hamleys *08703 332455*
Harrods *020 7730 1234*
Harvey Nichols *020 7235 5000*
Hatchards *020 7439 9921*
Heal's *020 7636 1666*
HMV *020 7631 3423*
House of Fraser *0870 160 7258*
Jaeger *020 7200 4015*
John Lewis *020 7629 7711*
Laura Ashley (Regent St) *020 7355 1363*
Liberty *020 7734 1234*
Lillywhites *0870 333 9602*
London Pavilion *020 7439 1791*
Marks & Spencer (Marble Arch) *020 7935 4422*
Marks & Spencer Pantheon (Oxford St) *020 7437 7722*
Next (Regent St) *020 7434 2515*
Plaza Shopping Centre, Oxford St *020 7637 8811*
Selfridges *0870 837 7377*
Sotheby's *020 7293 5000*
Top Shop & Top Man *020 7636 7700*
Trocadero *09068 881100*
Victoria Place Shopping Centre *020 7931 8811*
Virgin Megastore *020 7631 1234*
Virgin Megastore (Piccadilly) *020 7439 2500*
Waterstones (Gower St) *020 7636 1577*
Waterstones (Piccadilly) *020 7851 2400*

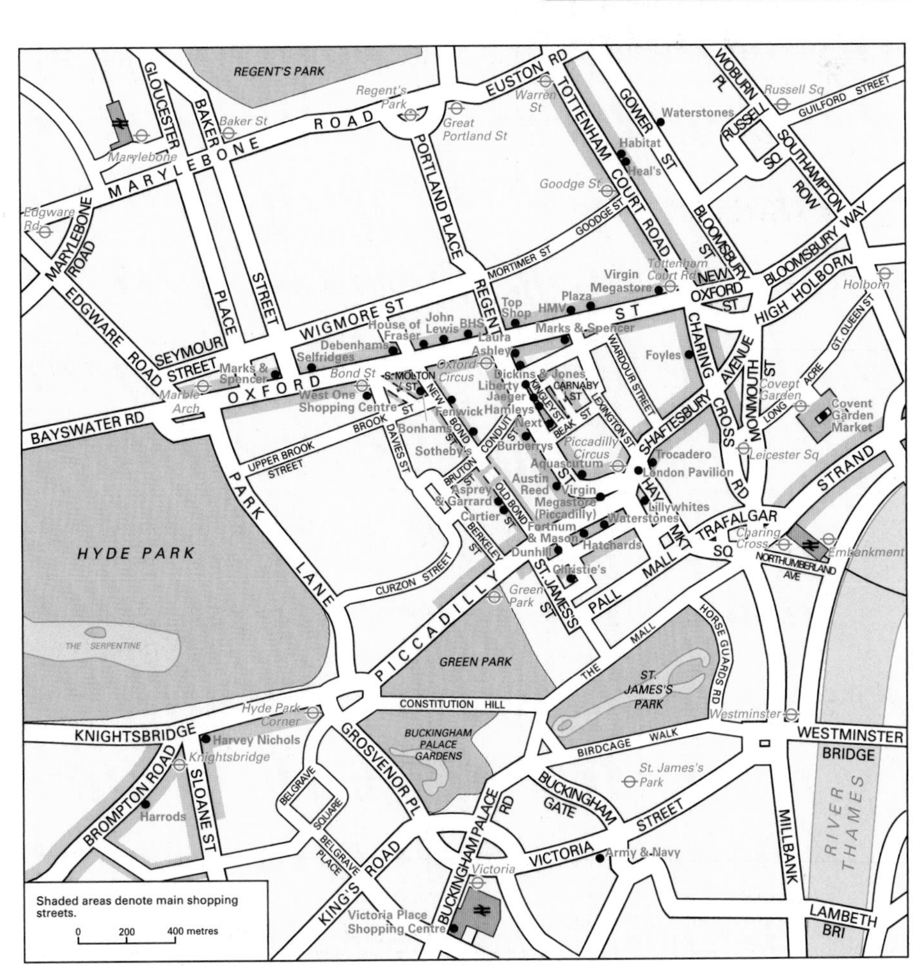
REGENT'S PARK
HYDE PARK
GREEN PARK
ST. JAMES'S PARK
BUCKINGHAM PALACE GARDENS
RIVER THAMES
OXFORD ST
REGENT ST
PICCADILLY
STRAND
Shaded areas denote main shopping streets.
0 200 400 metres

Notes on how to use the index

The index starting on page 306 combines entries for street names, place names, places of interest, stations, hospitals, schools, colleges and universities.
Place names are shown in capital letters,

e.g. **ACTON**, W3 . . . . **138** CN74

These include towns, villages and other localities within the area covered by this atlas.

Places of interest are shown with a star symbol,

e.g. ★ **British Mus**, WC1 . . . . . **9** N6

These include parks, museums, galleries, other important buildings and tourist attractions.

Hospitals, schools, colleges, universities and types of station are shown by symbols as listed :-

- H Hospital
- Sch School
- Coll College
- Uni University
- ⇌ Railway station
- ⊖ London Underground station
- DLR Docklands Light Railway station
- Tra Tramlink station
- Riv Pedestrian ferry landing stage

All other entries are for street names. When there is more than one street with exactly the same name then that name is shown only once in the index. It is then followed by a list of entries for each postal district that contains a street with that same name. For example, there are three streets called **Ardley Close** in this atlas and the index entry shows that one of these is in London postal district NW10, one is in London postal district SE6 and one is in Ruislip HA4.

e.g. **Ardley Cl**, NW10 . . . . . .**118** CS62
SE6 . . . .**183** DY90
Ruislip HA4 . . . .**115** BQ59

All entries are followed by the page number and grid reference on which the name will be found. So, in the example above, **Ardley Close,** NW10 will be found on page **118** in square CS62.
All entries are indexed to the largest scale map on which they are shown.

The index also contains some streets which are not actually named on the maps because there is not enough space. In these cases the adjoining or nearest named thoroughfare to such a street is shown in *italic.* The reference indicates where the unnamed street is located *off* the named thoroughfare.

e.g. **Baird Cl**, E10
off Marconi Rd **123** EA60

This means that **Baird Close** is not named on the map, but it is located *off Marconi Road* on page **123** in square EA60.

A strict letter-by-letter alphabetical order is followed in this index. All non-alphabetic characters such as spaces, hyphens or apostrophes have not been included in the index order. For example **Belle Vue Road** and **Bellevue Road** will be found listed together.

Standard terms such as **Avenue, Close, Rise** and **Road** are abbreviated in the index but are ordered alphabetically as if given in full. So, for example, **Abbots Ri** comes before **Abbots Rd.**

Names beginning with a definite article (i.e. **The**) are indexed from their second word onwards with the definite article being placed at the end of the name.

e.g. **Avenue, The**, E4 . . . . **101** ED51

The alphabetical order extends to include postal information so that where two or more streets have exactly the same name, London postal district references are given first in alpha-numeric order and are followed by non-London post town references in alphabetical order, e.g. **Ardley Close,** NW10 is followed by **Ardley Close,** SE6 and then **Ardley Close,** Ruislip HA4.

In cases where there are two or more streets of the same name in the same postal area, extra information is given in brackets to aid location. For example, **High St,** Orpington BR6 (Farnborough), and **High St,** Orpington BR6 (Green St Grn), distinguishes between two streets called **High Street** which are both in the post town of Orpington and within the same postal district of BR6.

Extra locational information is also given for some localities within large post towns. This is also to aid location.

e.g. **Adrian Cl**, Uxbridge (Hare.) UB9. . **92**BK53

This street is within the locality of Harefield which is part of the post town of Uxbridge, and it is within postal district UB9.
A full list of locality and post town abbreviations used in this atlas is given on the following page.

General abbreviations

Acad	Academy
All	Alley
Allot	Allotments
Amb	Ambulance
App	Approach
Arc	Arcade
Assoc	Association
Av	Avenue
Bdy	Broadway
Bk	Bank
Bldg	Building
Bldgs	Buildings
Boul	Boulevard
Bowl	Bowling
Br	Bridge
BUPA	British United Provident Association
C of E	Church of England
Cath	Cathedral
Cem	Cemetery
Cen	Central,Centre
Cft	Croft
Cfts	Crofts
Ch	Church
Chyd	Churchyard
Cin	Cinema
Circ	Circus
Cl	Close
Co	County
Coll	College
Comb	Combined
Comm	Community
Comp	Comprehensive
Conf	Conference
Cont	Continuing
Conv	Convent
Cor	Corner
Coron	Coroners
Cors	Corners
Cotts	Cottages
Cov	Covered
Crem	Crematorium
Cres	Crescent
Ct	Court
Cts	Courts
Ctyd	Courtyard
Dep	Depot
Dept	Department
Dev	Development
Dr	Drive
Dws	Dwellings
E	East
Ed	Education, Educational
Elec	Electricity
Embk	Embankment
Est	Estate
Ex	Exchange
Exhib	Exhibition
FB	Footbridge
FC	Football Club
Fld	Field
Flds	Fields
Fm	Farm
GM	Grant Maintained
Gall	Gallery
Gar	Garage
Gdn	Garden
Gdns	Gardens
Gen	General
Govt	Government
Gra	Grange
Grad	Graduate
Gram	Grammar
Grd	Ground
Grds	Grounds
Grn	Green
Grns	Greens
Gro	Grove
Gros	Groves
Gt	Great
HQ	Headquarters
Ho	House
Hos	Houses
Hosp	Hospital
Hts	Heights
Ind	Industrial
Indep	Independent
Inf	Infant(s)
Inst	Institute
Int	International
JM	Junior Mixed
JMI	Junior Mixed & Infant(s)
Jun	Junior
Junct	Junction
La	Lane
Las	Lanes
Lib	Library
Lit	Literary
Lo	Lodge
Lwr	Lower
Mag	Magistrates
Mans	Mansions
Med	Medical, Medicine
Mem	Memorial
Met	Metropolitan
Mid	Middle
Mkt	Market
Mkts	Markets
Ms	Mews
Mt	Mount
Mus	Museum
N	North
NHS	National Health Service
NT	National Trust
Nat	National
Nurs	Nursery
PH	Public House
PO	Post Office
PRU	Pupil Referral Unit
Par	Parade
Pas	Passage
Pav	Pavilion
Pk	Park
Pl	Place
Pol	Police
Poly	Polytechnic
Prec	Precinct
Prep	Preparatory
Prim	Primary
Prom	Promenade
Pt	Point
Quad	Quadrant
RC	Roman Catholic
Rd	Road
Rds	Roads
Rec	Recreation
Rehab	Rehabilitation
Res	Reservoir, Residence
Ri	Rise
S	South
SM	Secondary Mixed
Sch	School
Schs	Schools
Sec	Secondary
Sen	Senior
Shop	Shopping
Spec	Special
Sq	Square
St	Street
St.	Saint
Sta	Station
Sts	Streets
Sub	Subway
Swim	Swimming
TA	Territorial Army
TH	Town Hall
Tech	Technical, Technology
Tenn	Tennis
Ter	Terrace
Thea	Theatre
Trd	Trading
Twr	Tower
Twrs	Towers
Uni	University
Upr	Upper
VA	Voluntary Aided
VC	Voluntary Controlled
Vet	Veterinary
Vil	Villa
Vil	Villas
Vw	View
W	West
Wd	Wood
Wds	Woods
Wf	Wharf
Wk	Walk
Wks	Works
Yd	Yard

Locality & post town abbreviations

Note: In the following list of abbreviations post towns are in **bold** type.

Abb.L.	**Abbots Langley**
Abin.Com.	Abinger Common
Abin.Ham.	Abinger Hammer
Add.	**Addlestone**
Alb.Hth	Albury Heath
Ald.	Aldenham
Amer.	**Amersham**
Amer.O.T.	Amersham Old Town
Art.	Artington
Ash.Grn	Ashley Green
Ashf.	**Ashford**
Ashtd.	**Ashtead**
B.End	**Bourne End**
B.Stort.	**Bishop's Stortford**
Bad.Dene	Badgers Dene
Bad.Mt	Badgers Mount
Bans.	**Banstead**
Bark.	**Barking**
Barn.	**Barnet**
Barne.	Barnehurst
Beac.	**Beaconsfield**
Beck.	**Beckenham**
Bedd.	Beddington
Bedd.Cor.	Beddington Corner
Bell.	Bellingdon
Belv.	**Belvedere**
Berk.	**Berkhamsted**
Berry's Grn	Berry's Green
Bet.	**Betchworth**
Bex.	**Bexley**
Bexh.	**Bexleyheath**
Bigg.H.	Biggin Hill
Bkhm	Bookham
Bletch.	Bletchingley
Borwd.	**Borehamwood**
Bov.	Bovingdon
Box H.	Box Hill
Brent.	**Brentford**
Brick.Wd	Bricket Wood
Broad.Com.	Broadley Common
Brock.	Brockham
Brom.	**Bromley**
Brook.Pk	Brookmans Park
Brox.	**Broxbourne**
Brwd.	**Brentwood**
Buck.H.	**Buckhurst Hill**
Burgh Hth	Burgh Heath
Burn.	Burnham
Bushey Hth	Bushey Heath
Carp.Pk	Carpenders Park
Cars.	**Carshalton**
Cat.	**Caterham**
Ch.End	Church End
Ch.Lang.	Church Langley
Ch.St.G.	**Chalfont St. Giles**
Chad.Hth	Chadwell Heath
Chad.Spr.	Chadwell Springs
Chad.St.M.	Chadwell St. Mary
Chaff.Hun.	Chafford Hundred
Chal.St.P.	Chalfont St. Peter
Chap.End	Chapmore End
Charl.	Charlwood
Chel.	Chelsham
Chels.	Chelsfield
Cher.	**Chertsey**
Chesh.	**Chesham**
Chesh.B.	Chesham Bois
Chess.	**Chessington**
Chev.	Chevening
Chig.	**Chigwell**
Chilw.	Chilworth
Chipper.	Chipperfield
Chis.	**Chislehurst**
Chob.Com.	Chobham Common
Chorl.	Chorleywood
Chsht	Cheshunt
Cipp.	Cippenham
Clay.	Claygate
Cob.	**Cobham**
Cockfos.	Cockfosters
Cole Grn	Cole Green
Colesh.	Coleshill
Coll.Row	Collier Row
Coln.Hth	Colney Heath
Coln.St	Colney Street
Colnbr.	Colnbrook
Cooper.	Coopersale
Couls.	**Coulsdon**
Cran.	Cranford
Craw.	**Crawley**
Cray.	Crayford
Crock.	Crockenhill
Crock.H.	Crockham Hill
Crox.Grn	Croxley Green
Croy.	**Croydon**
Dag.	**Dagenham**
Dance.H.	Dancers Hill
Dart.	**Dartford**
Denh.	Denham
Dor.	**Dorking**
Dorney R.	Dorney Reach
Down.	Downside
Dunt.Grn	Dunton Green
E.Bed.	East Bedfont
E.Burn.	East Burnham
E.Clan.	East Clandon
E.Croy.	East Croydon
E.Ewell	East Ewell
E.Hors.	East Horsley
E.Mol.	**East Molesey**
E.Til.	East Tilbury
Ealing Com.	Ealing Common
Earls.	Earlswood
Eastcote Vill.	Eastcote Village
Eden.	**Edenbridge**
Edg.	**Edgware**
Eff.	Effingham
Eff.Junct.	Effingham Junction
Egh.	**Egham**
Egh.H.	Egham Hythe
Elm Pk	Elm Park
Elm.Wds	Elmstead Woods
Enf.	**Enfield**
Eng.Grn	Englefield Green
Epp.	**Epping**
Epp.Grn	Epping Green
Epsom Com.	Epsom Common
Essen.	Essendon
Ewell E.	Ewell East
Ewell W.	Ewell West
Eyns.	Eynsford
Far.Grn	Farley Green
Farn.Com.	Farnham Common
Farn.Royal	Farnham Royal
Farnboro.	Farnborough
Farnc.	Farncombe
Fawk.	Fawkham
Fawk.Grn	Fawkham Green
Felt.	**Feltham**
Fetch.	Fetcham
Flack.Hth	Flackwell Heath
Flam.	Flamstead
Flaun.	Flaunden
Fnghm	Farningham
Forest Grn	Forest Green
Forty Grn	Forty Green
Frog.	Frogmore
Gat.	**Gatwick**
Gdmg.	**Godalming**
Gdse.	**Godstone**
Geo.Grn	George Green
Ger.Cr.	**Gerrards Cross**
Gidea Pk	Gidea Park
Godden Grn	Godden Green
Goms.	Gomshall
Grav.	**Gravesend**
Green.	**Greenhithe**
Grn St Grn	Green Street Green
Grnf.	**Greenford**
Gt Amwell	Great Amwell
Gt Warley	Great Warley
Guil.	**Guildford**
H.Wyc.	**High Wycombe**
Hackbr.	Hackbridge
Had.Wd	Hadley Wood
Halst.	Halstead
Han.	Hanworth
Har.	**Harrow**
Har.Hill	Harrow on the Hill
Har.Wld	Harrow Weald
Hare.	Harefield
Harl.	**Harlow**
Harm.	Harmondsworth
Harold Wd	Harold Wood
Hast.	Hastingwood
Hat.	**Hatfield**
Hat.Hth	Hatfield Heath
Hatt.Cr.	Hatton Cross
Hav.at.Bow.	Havering-atte-Bower
Haz.	Hazlemere
Hedg.	Hedgerley
Hem.H.	**Hemel Hempstead**
Herons.	Heronsgate
Hert.	**Hertford**
Hert.Hth	Hertford Heath
Hext.	Hextable
High Barn.	High Barnet
Highams Pk	Highams Park
Hinch.Wd	Hinchley Wood
Hkwd	Hookwood
Hlgdn	Hillingdon
Hmptn H.	Hampton Hill
Hmptn W.	Hampton Wick
Hmptn.	**Hampton**
Hodd.	**Hoddesdon**
Holm.	Holmwood
Holm.St.M.	Holmbury St. Mary
Holt.	Holtspur
Holy.	Holyport
Hook Grn	Hook Green
Horl.	**Horley**
Horn.	**Hornchurch**
Hort.Kir.	Horton Kirby
Houns.	**Hounslow**
Houns.W.	Hounslow West
Hthrw Air.	Heathrow Airport
Hthrw Air.N.	Heathrow Airport North
Hutt.	Hutton
Hyde Hth	Hyde Heath
Ickhm	Ickenham
Ilf.	**Ilford**
Islw.	**Isleworth**
Ken.	**Kenley**
Kes.	**Keston**
Kgfld	Kingfield
Kgswd	Kingswood
Kings L.	**Kings Langley**
Kings.T.	**Kingston upon Thames**
Knap.	Knaphill
Knock.	Knockholt
Knock.P.	Knockholt Pound
Knot.Grn	Knotty Green
Lamb.End	Lambourne End
Let.Hth	Letchmore Heath
Letty Grn	Letty Green
Lmpfld	Limpsfield
Lmpfld Cht.	Limpsfield Chart
Lmsfd	Lemsford
Lon.Col.	London Colney
Long Dit.	Long Ditton
Long.	**Longfield**
Longcr.	Longcross
Loud.	Loudwater
Loug.	**Loughton**
Lt.Berk.	Little Berkhamsted
Lt.Chal.	Little Chalfont
Lt.Hth	Little Heath
Lt.Warley	Little Warley
Lthd.	**Leatherhead**
Lwfld Hth	Lowfield Heath
Lwr Kgswd	Lower Kingswood
Lwr Sydenham	Lower Sydenham
Lyon Pk Av	Lyon Park Avenue
Magd.Lav.	Magdalen Laver
Maid.	**Maidenhead**
Map.Cr.	Maple Cross
Mark Hall N.	Mark Hall North
Match.Tye	Matching Tye
Mdgrn	Middlegreen
Merst.	Merstham
Mick.	Mickleham
Mid Holm.	Mid Holmwood
Mimbr.	Mimbridge
Mitch.	**Mitcham**
Mitch.Com.	Mitcham Common
Mord.	**Morden**
Mots.Pk	Motspur Park
Mtnsg	Mountnessing
N.Finchley	North Finchley
N.Har.	North Harrow
N.Holm.	North Holmwood
N.Mal.	**New Malden**
N.Mymms	North Mymms
N.Ock.	North Ockendon
N.Stfd	North Stifford
N.Wld Bas.	North Weald Bassett
Nave.	Navestock
Nave.S.	Navestock Side
New Adgtn	New Addington
New Barn.	New Barnet
Norm.	Normandy
Northumb.Hth	Northumberland Heath
Norwood Junct.	Norwood Junction
Nthch	Northchurch
Nthflt	Northfleet
Nthlt.	**Northolt**
Nthwd.	**Northwood**
Nutfld	Nutfield
Oakl.	Oaklands
Oakley Grn	Oakley Green
Old Harl.	Old Harlow
Old Wind.	Old Windsor
Old Wok.	Old Woking
Ong.	**Ongar**
Ons.Vill.	Onslow Village
Orch.L.	Orchard Leigh
Orp.	**Orpington**
Ott.	Ottershaw
Oxt.	**Oxted**
Pans.	Panshanger
Peasl.	Peaslake
Peasm.	Peasmarsh
Petts Wd	Petts Wood
Picc.End	Piccotts End
Pilg.Hat.	Pilgrim's Hatch
Pnr.	**Pinner**
Port.Wd	Porters Wood
Pot.B.	**Potters Bar**
Pott.Cr.	Potters Crouch
Pott.End	Potten End
Pott.St	Potter Street
Pr.Bot.	Pratt's Bottom
Pur.	**Purley**
Purf.	**Purfleet**
Putt.	Puttenham
Rad.	**Radlett**
Rain.	**Rainham**
Ran.Com.	Ranmore Common
Red.	**Redhill**
Redbn	Redbourn
Reig.	**Reigate**
Rich.	**Richmond**
Rick.	**Rickmansworth**
Rod.Val.	Roding Valley
Roe Grn	Roe Green
Rom.	**Romford**
Rosh.	Rosherville
Ruis.	**Ruislip**
Runny.	Runnymede
Rush Grn	Rush Green
Russ.Hill	Russell Hill
Rvrhd	Riverhead
Rydes.	Rydeshill
S.Croy.	**South Croydon**
S.Darenth	South Darenth
S.Har.	South Harrow
S.Holm.	South Holmwood
S.Merst.	South Merstham
S.Mimms	South Mimms
S.Norwood	South Norwood
S.Nutfld	South Nutfield
S.Ock.	**South Ockendon**
S.Oxhey	South Oxhey
S.Park	South Park
S.Ruis.	South Ruislip
S.Stfd	South Stifford
S.Wld	South Weald
S.le H.	**Stanford-le-Hope**
Salf.	Salfords
Sand.	Sandridge
Saw.	**Sawbridgeworth**
Scad.Pk	Scadbury Park
Seer Grn	Seer Green
Send M.	Send Marsh
Sev.	**Sevenoaks**
Shalf.	Shalford
Sham.Grn	Shamley Green
Sheer.	Sheerwater
Shenf.	Shenfield
Shep.	**Shepperton**
Shore.	Shoreham
Short.	Shortlands
Sid.	**Sidcup**
Slade Grn	Slade Green
Slou.	**Slough**
St.Alb.	**St. Albans**
St.Geo.H.	St. George's Hill
St.John's	St. John's
St.M.Cray	St. Mary Cray
St.P.Cray	St. Paul's Cray
Stai.	**Staines**
Stan.	**Stanmore**
Stanboro.	Stanborough
Stans.Abb.	Stanstead Abbotts
Stanw.	Stanwell
Stap.Abb.	Stapleford Abbotts
Stap.Taw.	Stapleford Tawney
Sthflt	Southfleet
Sthl Grn	Southall Green
Sthl.	**Southall**
Stoke D'Ab.	Stoke D'Abernon
Stoke P.	Stoke Poges
Strood Grn	Strood Green
Sun.	**Sunbury-on-Thames**
Sund.	Sundridge
Surb.	**Surbiton**
Surr.Res.Pk	Surrey Research Park
Sutt.	**Sutton**
Sutt.Abin.	Sutton Abinger
Sutt.Grn	Sutton Green
Sutt.H.	Sutton at Hone
Swan.	**Swanley**
Swans.	**Swanscombe**
T.Ditt.	**Thames Ditton**
Tad.	**Tadworth**
Tand.	Tandridge
Tats.	Tatsfield
Tedd.	**Teddington**
Th.Hth.	**Thornton Heath**
They.B.	Theydon Bois
They.Gar.	Theydon Garnon
They.Mt	Theydon Mount
Thnwd	Thornwood
Thres.B.	Threshers Bush
Til.	**Tilbury**
Tkgtn	Tokyngton
Turnf.	Turnford
Twick.	**Twickenham**
Tyr.Wd	Tyrrell's Wood
Tytten.	Tyttenhanger
Undrvr	Underriver
Upmin.	**Upminster**
Uxb.	**Uxbridge**
Vir.W.	**Virginia Water**
W.Byf.	**West Byfleet**
W.Clan.	West Clandon
W.Croy.	West Croydon
W.Ealing	West Ealing
W.Ewell	West Ewell
W.Hors.	West Horsley
W.Mol.	**West Molesey**
W.Thur.	West Thurrock
W.Til.	West Tilbury
W.Wick.	**West Wickham**
Wal.Abb.	**Waltham Abbey**
Wal.Cr.	**Waltham Cross**
Wall.	**Wallington**
Walt.	**Walton-on-Thames**
Warl.	**Warlingham**
Wat.	**Watford**
Wat.Oak.	Water Oakley
Waterf.	Waterford
Wdf.Grn.	**Woodford Green**
Wdhm	Woodham
Wel.Grn	Welham Green
Well.	**Welling**
Welw.	**Welwyn**
Welw.G.C.	**Welwyn Garden City**
Wem.	**Wembley**
Wenn.	Wennington
West Dr.	**West Drayton**
West.	**Westerham**
Westc.	Westcott
Westh.	Westhumble
Wey.	**Weybridge**
Wheat.	Wheathampstead
Whel.Hill	Whelpley Hill
Whiteley Vill.	Whiteley Village
Whyt.	**Whyteleafe**
Wilm.	Wilmington
Winch.Hill	Winchmore Hill
Wind.	**Windsor**
Wldste	Wealdstone
Wok.	**Woking**
Wold.	Woldingham
Won.	Wonersh
Woob.Grn	Wooburn Green
Woodside Pk	Woodside Park
Wor.Pk.	**Worcester Park**
Worp.	Worplesdon
Wrays.	Wraysbury
Wyc.End	Wycombe End
Yiew.	Yiewsley

1 Canada Sq, E14 ... 24 A2
30 St. Mary Axe, EC3 *off St. Mary Axe* ... 142 DS72
99 Bishopsgate, EC2 *off Bishopsgate* ... 142 DS72

A

Aaron Hill Rd, E6 ... 145 EN71
Abberley Ms, SW4 *off Cedars Rd* ... 161 DH83
Abberton Wk, Rain. RM13 *off Ongar Way* ... 147 FE66
Abbess Cl, E6 *off Oliver Gdns* ... 144 EL71
SW2 ... 181 DP88
Abbeville Ms, SW4 *off Clapham Pk Rd* ... 161 DK84
Abbeville Rd, N8 *off Barrington Rd* ... 121 DK56
SW4 ... 181 DJ86
Abbey Av, St.Alb. AL3 ... 42 CA23
Wembley HA0 ... 138 CL68
Abbey Business Cen, SW8 *off Ingate Pl* ... 161 DH81
Abbey Cl, E5 ... 122 DU63
SW8 ... 161 DK81
Hayes UB3 ... 135 BV74
Northolt UB5 *off Invicta Gro* ... 136 BZ69
Pinner HA5 ... 115 BV55
Romford RM1 ... 127 FG58
Slough SL1 ... 131 AL73
Woking GU22 ... 227 BE116
Sch **Abbey C of E VA Prim Sch**, St.Alb. AL1 *off Grove Rd* ... 43 CD21
Abbey Ct, Wal.Abb. EN9 ... 67 EB34
Abbey Cres, Belv. DA17 ... 166 FA77
Abbeydale Cl, Harl. CM17 ... 52 EW16
Abbeydale Rd, Wem. HA0 ... 138 CN67
Abbey Dr, SW17 *off Church La* ... 180 DG92
Abbots Langley WD5 ... 59 BU32
Dartford DA2 ... 187 FE89
Staines TW18 ... 194 BJ98
Abbeyfield Rd, SE16 ... 22 E7
Abbeyfields Cl, NW10 ... 138 CN68
Abbeyfields Mobile Home Pk, Cher. KT16 ... 194 BK101
Abbey Gdns, NW8 ... 140 DC68
SE16 ... 22 B7
W6 ... 159 CY79
Chertsey KT16 ... 194 BG100
Chislehurst BR7 ... 205 EN95
Waltham Abbey EN9 ... 67 EC33
Abbey Grn, Cher. KT16 ... 194 BG100
Abbey Gro, SE2 ... 166 EV77
Abbeyhill Rd, Sid. DA15 ... 186 EW89
Abbey Ind Est, Mitch. CR4 ... 200 DF99
Wembley HA0 ... 138 CM67
Abbey La, E15 ... 143 EC68
Beckenham BR3 ... 183 EA94
Abbey Mead Ind Pk, Wal.Abb. EN9 ... 67 EC34
Abbey Ms, E17 *off Leamington Av* ... 123 EA57
Abbey Mill End, St.Alb. AL3 ... 42 CC21
Abbey Mill La, St.Alb. AL3 ... 42 CC21
Abbey Mills, St.Alb. AL3 ... 42 CC21
Abbey Orchard St, SW1 ... 19 M5
Abbey Par, SW19 *off Merton High St* ... 180 DC94
W5 *off Hanger La* ... 138 CM69
Abbey Pk, Beck. BR3 ... 183 EA94
Abbey Pk La, Slou. (Burn.) SL1 ... 111 AL61
Abbey Pl, Dart. DA1 *off Priory Rd N* ... 188 FK85
Sch **Abbey Prim Sch**, Mord. SM4 *off Glastonbury Rd* ... 200 DB101
Abbey Retail Pk, Bark. IG11 ... 145 EP67
Abbey Rd, E15 ... 144 EE68
NW6 ... 140 DB66
NW8 ... 140 DC68
NW10 ... 138 CP68
SE2 ... 166 EX77
SW19 ... 180 DC94
Barking IG11 ... 145 EP66
Belvedere DA17 ... 166 EX77
Bexleyheath DA7 ... 166 EY84
Chertsey KT16 ... 194 BH101
Croydon CR0 ... 201 DP104
Enfield EN1 ... 82 DS43
Gravesend DA12 ... 191 GL88
Greenhithe DA9 ... 189 FW85
Ilford IG2 ... 125 ER57
Shepperton TW17 ... 194 BN102
South Croydon CR2 ... 221 DX110
Virginia Water GU25 ... 192 AX99
Waltham Cross EN8 ... 67 DY34
Woking GU21 ... 226 AW117
Abbey Rd Est, NW8 ... 140 DB67
Abbey St, E13 ... 15 M3
SE1 ... 21 M5
Abbey Ter, SE2 ... 166 EW77
Abbey Vw, NW7 ... 97 CT48
Radlett WD7 ... 77 CF35
Waltham Abbey EN9 ... 67 EB33
Watford WD25 ... 76 BX36
Abbey Vw Rd, St.Alb. AL3 ... 42 CC20
Abbey Vw Roundabout, Wal.Abb. EN9 ... 67 EB33
Abbey Wk, W.Mol. KT8 ... 196 CB97
Abbey Way, SE2 ... 166 EX76
Abbey Wf Ind Est, Bark. IG11 ... 145 ER68
ABBEY WOOD, SE2 ... 166 EV76
⇌ **Abbey Wood** ... 166 EW76
Abbey Wd Caravan Club Site, SE2 ... 166 EW78
Abbey Wd La, Rain. RM13 ... 148 FK68
Abbey Wd Rd, SE2 ... 166 EV77
Sch **Abbey Wd SM Sch**, SE2 *off Eynsham Dr* ... 166 EU76
Abbot Cl, Stai. TW18 ... 174 BK94
West Byfleet (Byfleet) KT14 ... 212 BK110
Abbot Rd, Guil. GU1 ... 258 AX136
Abbots Av, Epsom KT19 ... 216 CN111
St. Albans AL1 ... 43 CE23
Abbots Av W, St.Alb. AL1 ... 43 CD23
Abbotsbury Cl, E15 ... 143 EC68
W14 ... 16 D4
Abbotsbury Gdns, Pnr. HA5 ... 116 BW58
Abbotsbury Ms, SE15 ... 162 DW83
Sch **Abbotsbury Prim Sch**, Mord. SM4 *off Abbotsbury Rd* ... 200 DB99
Abbotsbury Rd, W14 ... 16 D3
Bromley BR2 ... 204 EF103
Morden SM4 ... 200 DB99
Abbots Cl, N1 ... 4 G4
Brentwood (Shenf.) CM15 ... 109 GA46
Guildford GU2 ... 258 AS137
Orpington BR5 ... 205 EQ102
Rainham RM13 ... 148 FJ68
Ruislip HA4 ... 116 BX62
Abbots Dr, Har. HA2 ... 116 CA61
Virginia Water GU25 ... 192 AW98
Abbots Fld, Grav. DA12 *off Ruffets Wd* ... 191 GJ93
Sch **Abbotsfield Sch**, Uxb. UB10 *off Clifton Gdns* ... 135 BP68
Abbotsford Av, N15 ... 122 DQ56
Abbotsford Cl, Wok. GU22 *off Onslow Cres* ... 227 BA117
Abbotsford Gdns, Wdf.Grn. IG8 ... 102 EG52
Abbotsford Lo, Nthwd. HA6 ... 93 BS50
Abbotsford Rd, Ilf. IG3 ... 126 EU61
Abbots Gdns, N2 ... 120 DD56
W8 ... 17 J6
Abbots Grn, Croy. CR0 ... 221 DX107
Abbotshade Rd, SE16 ... 23 H1
Abbotshall Av, N14 ... 99 DJ48
Abbotshall Rd, SE6 ... 183 ED88
Sch **Abbot's Hill Sch**, Hem.H. HP3 *off Bunkers La* ... 59 BP25
Abbots La, SE1 ... 21 M2
Kenley CR8 ... 236 DQ116
ABBOTS LANGLEY, WD5 ... 59 BR31
Sch **Abbots Langley Sch**, Abb.L. WD5 *off Parsonage Cl* ... 59 BT30
Abbotsleigh Cl, Sutt. SM2 ... 218 DB108
Abbotsleigh Rd, SW16 ... 181 DJ91
Abbots Manor Est, SW1 ... 18 G8
Abbotsmede Cl, Twick. TW1 ... 177 CF89
Abbots Pk, SW2 ... 181 DN88
St. Albans AL1 ... 43 CF22
Abbot's Pl, NW6 ... 140 DB67
Abbots Ri, Kings L. WD4 ... 58 BM26
Redhill RH1 ... 250 DG132
Abbot's Rd, E6 ... 144 EK67
Abbots Rd, Abb.L. WD5 ... 59 BS30
Edgware HA8 ... 96 CQ52
Abbots Ter, N8 ... 121 DL58
Abbotstone Rd, SW15 ... 159 CW83
Abbot St, E8 ... 5 N3
Abbots Vw, Kings L. WD4 ... 58 BM27
Abbots Wk, W8 ... 17 J6
Caterham CR3 *off Tillingdown Hill* ... 236 DU122
Windsor SL4 ... 151 AL82
Abbots Way, Beck. BR3 ... 203 DY99
Chertsey KT16 ... 193 BF101
Guildford GU1 ... 243 BD133
Abbotsweld, Harl. CM18 ... 51 ER18
Sch **Abbotsweld Co Prim Sch**, Harl. CM18 *off Partridge Rd* ... 51 ER17
Abbotswell Rd, SE4 ... 183 DZ85
ABBOTSWOOD, Guil. GU1 ... 243 AZ132
Abbotswood, Guil. GU1 ... 243 AZ131
Abbotswood Cl, Belv. DA17 *off Coptefield Dr* ... 166 EY76
Guildford GU1 ... 243 AZ131
Abbotswood Dr, Wey. KT13 ... 213 BR110
Abbotswood Gdns, Ilf. IG5 ... 125 EM55
Abbotswood Rd, SE22 ... 162 DS84
SW16 ... 181 DK90
Abbotswood Way, Hayes UB3 ... 135 BV74
Abbott Av, SW20 ... 199 CX96
Abbott Cl, Hmptn. TW12 ... 176 BY93
Northolt UB5 ... 136 BZ65
Abbott Rd, E14 ... 14 C6
Abbotts Cl, SE28 ... 146 EW73
Romford RM7 ... 127 FB55
Swanley BR8 ... 207 FG98
Uxbridge UB8 ... 134 BK71
Abbotts Cres, E4 ... 101 ED49
Enfield EN2 ... 81 DP40
Abbotts Dr, Wal.Abb. EN9 ... 68 EG34
Wembley HA0 ... 117 CH61
Abbotts Pk Rd, E10 ... 123 EC59
Abbotts Pl, Chesh. HP5 ... 54 AQ28
Abbotts Ri, Ware (Stans.Abb.) SG12 ... 33 ED11
Abbotts Rd, Barn. EN5 ... 80 DB42
Mitcham CR4 ... 201 DJ98
Southall UB1 ... 136 BY74
Sutton SM3 ... 199 CZ104
Abbott's Tilt, Walt. KT12 ... 196 BY104
Abbotts Vale, Chesh. HP5 ... 54 AQ28
Abbotts Wk, Bexh. DA7 ... 166 EX80
Abbotts Way, Slou. SL1 ... 131 AK74
Ware (Stans.Abb.) SG12 ... 33 ED11
Abbs Cross Gdns, Horn. RM12 ... 128 FJ60
Abbs Cross La, Horn. RM12 ... 128 FJ63
Sch **Abbs Cross Sch**, Horn. RM12 *off Abbs Cross La* ... 128 FJ62
Abchurch La, EC4 ... 11 K9
Abchurch Yd, EC4 ... 11 J9
Abdale Rd, W12 ... 139 CV74
Abel Cl, Hem.H. HP2 ... 40 BM20
Sch **Abel Smith JMI Sch**, Hert. SG13 *off Churchfields* ... 32 DR09
Abenberg Way, Brwd. (Hutt.) CM13 ... 109 GB47
Aberavon Rd, E3 ... 13 K2
Abercairn Rd, SW16 ... 181 DJ94
Aberconway Rd, Mord. SM4 ... 200 DB97
Abercorn Cl, NW7 ... 97 CY52
NW8 ... 140 DC69
South Croydon CR2 ... 221 DX112
Abercorn Cres, Har. HA2 ... 116 CB60
Abercorn Gdns, Har. HA3 ... 117 CK59
Romford RM6 ... 126 EV58
Abercorn Gro, Ruis. HA4 ... 115 BR56
Abercorn Pl, NW8 ... 7 L1
Sch **Abercorn Pl Sch**, NW8 *off Abercorn Pl* ... 140 DC68
Abercorn Rd, NW7 ... 97 CY52
Stanmore HA7 ... 95 CJ52
Abercorn Way, SE1 ... 22 A9
Woking GU21 ... 226 AU118
Abercrombie Dr, Enf. EN1 *off Linwood Cres* ... 82 DU39
Abercrombie St, SW11 ... 160 DE82
Abercrombie Way, Harl. CM18 ... 51 EQ16
Aberdale Ct, SE16 *off Poolmans St* ... 163 DX75
Aberdale Gdns, Pot.B. EN6 ... 63 CZ33
Aberdare Cl, W.Wick. BR4 ... 203 EC103
Aberdare Gdns, NW6 ... 140 DB66
NW7 ... 97 CX52
Aberdare Rd, Enf. EN3 ... 82 DW42
Aberdeen Av, Slou. SL1 ... 131 AN73
Aberdeen La, N5 ... 4 F1
Aberdeen Par, N18 *off Angel Rd* ... 100 DV50
Aberdeen Pk, N5 ... 4 F1
Aberdeen Pk Ms, N5 ... 122 DQ63
Aberdeen Pl, NW8 ... 7 N4
Aberdeen Rd, N5 ... 122 DQ63
N18 ... 100 DV50
NW10 ... 119 CT64
Croydon CR0 ... 220 DQ105
Harrow HA3 ... 95 CF54
Aberdeen Sq, E14 ... 23 N1
Aberdeen Ter, SE3 ... 163 ED82
Aberdour Rd, Ilf. IG3 ... 126 EV62
Sch **Aberdour Sch**, Tad. KT20 *off Brighton Rd* ... 233 CZ118
Aberdour St, SE1 ... 21 L7
Aberfeldy St, E14 ... 14 D7
Aberford Gdns, SE18 ... 164 EL81
Aberford Rd, Borwd. WD6 ... 78 CN40
Aberfoyle Rd, SW16 ... 181 DK93
Abergeldie Rd, SE12 ... 184 EH86
Aberglen Ind Est, Hayes UB3 ... 155 BR75
Abernethy Rd, SE13 ... 164 EE84
Abersham Rd, E8 ... 5 P1
Abery St, SE18 ... 165 ES77
Abigail Ms, Rom. RM3 *off King Alfred Rd* ... 106 FM54
Abingdon Cl, NW1 *off Camden Sq* ... 141 DK65
SE1 ... 21 P9
SW19 ... 180 DC93
Uxbridge UB10 ... 134 BM67
Woking GU21 ... 226 AV118
Abingdon Pl, Pot.B. EN6 ... 64 DB32
Abingdon Rd, N3 ... 98 DC54
SW16 ... 201 DL96
W8 ... 16 G5
Abingdon St, SW1 ... 19 N5
Abingdon Vil, W8 ... 16 G6
Abingdon Way, Orp. BR6 ... 224 EV105
Abinger Av, Sutt. SM2 ... 217 CW109
Abinger Cl, Bark. IG11 ... 126 EU63
Bromley BR1 ... 204 EL97
Croydon CR0 ... 221 EC107
Dorking (N.Holm.) RH5 ... 263 CJ140
Wallington SM6 ... 219 DL106
ABINGER COMMON, Dor. RH5 ... 262 BX143
Abinger Common Rd, Dor. RH5 ... 262 BY144
Sch **Abinger Common Sch**, Dor. RH5 *off Abinger La* ... 262 BX142
Abinger Dr, Red. RH1 ... 266 DE136
Abinger Gdns, Islw. TW7 ... 157 CE83
Abinger Gro, SE8 ... 163 DZ79
ABINGER HAMMER, Dor. RH5 ... 261 BT139
Sch **Abinger Hammer Sch**, Dor. RH5 *off Hackhurst La* ... 261 BT139
Abinger La, Dor. (Abin.Com.) RH5 ... 261 BV140
Abinger Ms, W9 ... 6 G3
Abinger Rd, W4 ... 158 CS76
Abinger Way, Guil. GU4 ... 243 BB129
Ablett St, SE16 ... 22 E10
Abney Gdns, N16 *off Stoke Newington High St* ... 122 DT61
Aboyne Dr, SW20 ... 199 CU96
Aboyne Est, SW17 ... 180 DD90
Sch **Aboyne Lo Prim Sch**, St.Alb. AL3 *off Etna Rd* ... 43 CD19
Aboyne Rd, NW10 ... 118 CS62
SW17 ... 180 DD90
Abraham Cl, Wat. WD19 ... 93 BV49
ABRIDGE, Rom. RM4 ... 86 EV41
Abridge Cl, Wal.Cr. EN8 ... 83 DX35
Abridge Gdns, Rom. RM5 ... 104 FA51
Abridge Pk, Rom. (Abridge) RM4 ... 86 EU42
Abridge Rd, Chig. IG7 ... 85 ER44
Epping (They.B.) CM16 ... 85 ES36
Romford (Abridge) RM4 ... 86 EU39
Abridge Way, Bark. IG11 ... 146 EV68
Abyssinia Cl, SW11 *off Cairns Rd* ... 160 DE84
Abyssinia Rd, SW11 *off Auckland Rd* ... 160 DE84
Acacia Av, N17 ... 100 DR52
Brentford TW8 ... 157 CH80
Hayes UB3 ... 135 BT72
Hornchurch RM12 ... 127 FF61
Mitcham CR4 *off Acacia Rd* ... 201 DH96
Ruislip HA4 ... 115 BU60
Shepperton TW17 ... 194 BN99
Staines (Wrays.) TW19 ... 152 AY84
Wembley HA9 ... 118 CL64
West Drayton UB7 ... 134 BM73
Woking GU22 ... 226 AX120
Acacia Cl, SE8 ... 23 J8
SE20 *off Selby Rd* ... 202 DU96
Addlestone (Wdhm) KT15 ... 211 BF110
Orpington BR5 ... 205 ER99
Stanmore HA7 ... 95 CE51
Waltham Cross EN7 ... 66 DS27
Acacia Ct, Wal.Abb. EN9 *off Farthingale La* ... 68 EG34
Acacia Dr, Add. (Wdhm) KT15 ... 211 BF110
Banstead SM7 ... 217 CX114
Sutton SM3 ... 199 CZ102
Upminster RM14 ... 128 FN63
Acacia Gdns, NW8 *off Acacia Rd* ... 140 DD68
Upminster RM14 ... 129 FT59
West Wickham BR4 ... 203 EC103
Acacia Gro, SE21 ... 182 DR89
Berkhamsted HP4 ... 38 AV20
New Malden KT3 ... 198 CR97
Acacia Ms, West Dr. UB7 ... 154 BK79
Acacia Pl, NW8 ... 140 DD68
Acacia Rd, E11 ... 124 EE61
E17 ... 123 DY58
N22 ... 99 DN53
NW8 ... 140 DD68
SW16 ... 201 DL95
W3 ... 138 CQ73
Beckenham BR3 ... 203 DZ97
Dartford DA1 ... 188 FK88
Enfield EN2 ... 82 DR39
Greenhithe DA9 ... 189 FS86
Guildford GU1 ... 242 AX134
Hampton TW12 ... 176 CA93
Mitcham CR4 ... 201 DH96
Staines TW18 ... 174 BH92
Acacia St, Hat. AL10 ... 45 CU21
Acacia Wk, Swan. BR8 ... 207 FD96
Acacia Way, Sid. DA15 ... 185 ET88
Sch **Academy at Peckham, The**, SE15 *off Peckham Rd* ... 162 DT81
Sch **Academy at Peckham, The**, Annexe, SE15 ... 162 DT81
off Cator St ... 162 DT80
Academy Gdns, W8 *off Duchess of Bedford's Wk* ... 160 DA75
Croydon CR0 ... 202 DT102
Northolt UB5 ... 136 BX68
Coll **Academy of Live & Recorded Arts**, SW18 *off Fitzhugh Gro* ... 180 DD86
Academy Pl, SE18 ... 165 EM81
Academy Rd, SE18 ... 165 EM81
Acanthus Dr, SE1 ... 22 A9
Acanthus Rd, SW11 ... 160 DG83
Accommodation La, West Dr. UB7 ... 154 BJ79
Accommodation Rd, NW11 ... 119 CZ59
Chertsey (Longcr.) KT16 ... 192 AX104
A.C. Ct, T.Ditt. KT7 *off Harvest La* ... 197 CG100
Acer Av, Hayes UB4 ... 136 BY71
Rainham RM13 ... 148 FK69
Acer Rd, West. (Bigg.H.) TN16 ... 238 EK116
Acers, St.Alb. (Park St) AL2 ... 60 CC28
Acfold Rd, SW6 ... 160 DB81
Achilles Cl, SE1 ... 22 B9
Hemel Hempstead HP2 ... 40 BM18
Achilles Pl, Wok. GU21 ... 226 AW117
Achilles Rd, NW6 ... 120 DA64
Achilles St, SE14 ... 163 DY80
Achilles Way, W1 ... 18 F2
Acklam Rd, W10 ... 6 E6
Acklington Dr, NW9 ... 96 CS53
Ackmar Rd, SW6 ... 160 DA81
Ackroyd Dr, E3 ... 13 M5
Ackroyd Rd, SE23 ... 183 DX87
Sch **Acland Burghley Sch**, NW5 *off Burghley Rd* ... 121 DJ63
Acland Cl, SE18 *off Clothworkers Rd* ... 165 ER80
Acland Cres, SE5 ... 162 DR84
Acland Rd, NW2 ... 139 CV65
Acle Cl, Ilf. IG6 ... 103 EP52
Acme Rd, Wat. WD24 ... 75 BU38
Acock Gro, Nthlt. UB5 ... 116 CB63
Acol Cres, Ruis. HA4 ... 115 BV64
Acol Rd, NW6 ... 140 DA66
Aconbury Rd, Dag. RM9 ... 146 EV67
Acorn Cl, E4 ... 101 EA50
Chislehurst BR7 ... 185 EQ92
Enfield EN2 ... 81 DP39
Hampton TW12 ... 176 CB93
Horley RH6 ... 269 DJ147
Slough SL3 *off Tamar Way* ... 153 BB78
Stanmore HA7 ... 95 CH52
Acorn Ct, Ilf. IG2 ... 125 ES58
Acorn Gdns, SE19 ... 202 DT95
W3 ... 138 CR71
Acorn Gro, Hayes UB3 ... 155 BT80
Ruislip HA4 ... 115 BT63
Tadworth KT20 ... 233 CY124
Woking GU22 *off Old Sch Pl* ... 226 AY121
Sch **Acorn Ho Ed Dev Cen for Young Children**, Th.Hth. CR7 *off Winterbourne Rd* ... 201 DN98
Acorn Ind Pk, Dart. DA1 ... 187 FG85
Acorn La, Pot.B. (Cuffley) EN6 ... 65 DL29
Acorn Ms, Harl. CM18 ... 51 ET17
Acorn Par, SE15 *off Carlton Gro* ... 162 DV80
Acorn Pl, Wat. WD24 ... 75 BU37
Acorn Rd, Dart. DA1 ... 187 FF85
Hemel Hempstead HP3 ... 40 BN21
Acorns, The, Chig. IG7 ... 103 ES49
Horley (Smallfield) RH6 ... 269 DP148
Sch **Acorns Inf Sch, The**, Betchworth Site, Bet. RH3 *off The Street* ... 248 CR134
Leigh Site, Reig. RH2 *off Tapners Rd* ... 265 CU140
Acorn St, Ware (Hunsdon) SG12 ... 34 EK08
Acorns Way, Esher KT10 ... 214 CC106
Acorn Wk, SE16 ... 23 K1
Acorn Way, SE23 ... 183 DX90
Beckenham BR3 ... 203 EC99
Orpington BR6 ... 223 EP105
Acre Dr, SE22 ... 162 DU84
Acrefield Rd, Ger.Cr. (Chal.St.P.) SL9 ... 112 AX55
Acre La, SW2 ... 161 DL84
Carshalton SM5 ... 218 DG105
Wallington SM6 ... 218 DG105
Acre Pas, Wind. SL4 *off Madeira Wk* ... 151 AR81
Acre Path, Nthlt. UB5 *off Arnold Rd* ... 136 BY65
Acre Rd, SW19 ... 180 DD93
Dagenham RM10 ... 147 FB66
Kingston upon Thames KT2 ... 198 CL95
Acres End, Amer. HP7 ... 55 AS39
Acres Gdns, Tad. KT20 ... 233 CX119
Acre Vw, Horn. RM11 ... 128 FL56
Acre Way, Nthwd. HA6 ... 93 BT53
Acrewood, Hem.H. HP2 ... 40 BL20
Acrewood Way, St.Alb. AL4 ... 44 CM20
Acris St, SW18 ... 180 DC85
ACTON, W3 ... 138 CN74
Coll **Acton & W London Coll**, W3 *off Mill Hill Rd* ... 138 CP74
⇌ **Acton Central** ... 138 CR74
Acton Cl, N9 ... 100 DU47
Waltham Cross (Chsht) EN8 ... 67 DY31
Sch **Acton High Sch**, W3 *off Gunnersbury La* ... 158 CN75
Acton Hill Ms, W3 *off Uxbridge Rd* ... 138 CP74
Acton La, NW10 ... 138 CS68
W3 ... 158 CQ75
W4 ... 158 CR76
⇌ **Acton Main Line** ... 138 CQ72
Acton Ms, E8 ... 5 N7
Acton Pk Ind Est, W3 ... 158 CR75
Acton St, WC1 ... 10 A2
⊖ **Acton Town** ... 158 CN75
Acuba Rd, SW18 ... 180 DB89
Acworth Cl, N9 *off Turin Rd* ... 100 DW45
Ada Gdns, E14 ... 14 E7
E15 ... 144 EF67
Adair Cl, SE25 ... 202 DV97
Adair Rd, W10 ... 6 D4
Adair Twr, W10 ... 6 D4
Adam & Eve Ct, W1 ... 9 K7
Adam & Eve Ms, W8 ... 17 H5
Adam Cl, SE6 ... 183 DZ91
Adam Cl, Slough SL1 *off Telford Dr* ... 131 AN74
Adam Ct, SW7 ... 17 M7
Adam Pl, N16 *off Stoke Newington High St* ... 122 DT61
Adam Rd, E4 ... 101 DZ51
Adams Cl, N3 *off Falkland Av* ... 98 DA52
NW9 ... 118 CP61
Surbiton KT5 ... 198 CM100
Adams Ct, EC2 ... 11 K7
Adamsfield, Wal.Cr. EN7 ... 66 DU27
Adams Gdns Est, SE16 ... 22 E3
Adams Ms, N22 ... 99 DL52
SW17 ... 180 DF89
Adamson Rd, E16 ... 15 M8
NW3 ... 140 DD66
Adamson Way, Beck. BR3 *off Creswell Dr* ... 203 EB99
Adams Pl, N7 ... 4 B2
Adamsrill Cl, Enf. EN1 ... 82 DR44
Sch **Adamsrill Prim Sch**, SE26 *off Adamsrill Rd* ... 183 DY90
Adamsrill Rd, SE26 ... 183 DY91
Adams Rd, N17 ... 100 DR54
Beckenham BR3 ... 203 DY99
Adams Row, W1 ... 8 F10
Adams Sq, Bexh. DA6 *off Regency Way* ... 166 EY83
Adam St, WC2 ... 9 P10
Adams Wk, Kings.T. KT1 ... 198 CL96
Adams Way, Croy. CR0 ... 202 DT100
Adam Wk, SW6 ... 159 CW80
Ada Pl, E2 ... 142 DU67
Adare Wk, SW16 ... 181 DM90
Ada Rd, SE5 ... 162 DS80
Wembley HA0 ... 117 CK62
Adastral Est, NW9 ... 96 CS53
Ada St, E8 ... 142 DV67
Adcock Wk, Orp. BR6 *off Borkwood Pk* ... 223 ET105
Adderley Gdns, SE9 ... 185 EN91
Adderley Gro, SW11 *off Culmstock Rd* ... 180 DG85
Adderley Rd, Har. HA3 ... 95 CF53
Adderley St, E14 ... 14 C8
Sch **Addey & Stanhope Sch**, SE14 *off New Cross Rd* ... 163 EA81
ADDINGTON, Croy. CR0 ... 221 DZ106
Addington Border, Croy. CR0 ... 221 DY110
Addington Cl, Wind. SL4 ... 151 AN83
Addington Ct, SW14 ... 158 CR83
Addington Dr, N12 ... 98 DC51
Addington Gro, SE26 ... 183 DY91
Sch **Addington High Sch**, Croy. CR0 *off Fairchildes Av* ... 222 EE112
Addington Rd, E3 ... 13 N1
E16 ... 15 H4
N4 ... 121 DN58
Croydon CR0 ... 201 DN102
South Croydon CR2 ... 220 DU111
West Wickham BR4 ... 204 EE103
Addington Sq, SE5 ... 162 DQ80
Addington St, SE1 ... 20 B4
Tra **Addington Village** ... 221 EA107
Addington Village Rd, Croy. CR0 ... 221 EA106
Addis Cl, Enf. EN3 ... 83 DX39
ADDISCOMBE, Croy. CR0 ... 202 DT102
Tra **Addiscombe** ... 202 DU102
Addiscombe Av, Croy. CR0 ... 202 DU101
Addiscombe Cl, Har. HA3 ... 117 CJ57
Addiscombe Ct Rd, Croy. CR0 ... 202 DS102
Addiscombe Gro, Croy. CR0 ... 202 DR103
Addiscombe Rd, Croy. CR0 ... 202 DS103
Watford WD18 ... 75 BV42
Addison Av, N14 ... 81 DH44
W11 ... 16 C1
Hounslow TW3 ... 156 CC81
Addison Br Pl, W14 ... 16 E7
Addison Cl, Cat. CR3 ... 236 DR122
Northwood HA6 ... 93 BU53
Orpington BR5 ... 205 EQ100
Addison Ct, Epp. CM16 *off Centre Dr* ... 70 EU31
Addison Cres, W14 ... 16 D5
Addison Dr, SE12 *off Eltham Rd* ... 184 EH85
Addison Gdns, W14 ... 16 A5
Grays RM17 *off Palmers Dr* ... 170 GC77
Surbiton KT5 ... 198 CM98
Addison Gro, W4 ... 158 CS76
Addison Pl, W11 ... 16 C2
Southall UB1 *off Longford Av* ... 136 CA73
Sch **Addison Prim Sch**, W14 ... 16 A5
Addison Rd, E11 ... 124 EG58
E17 ... 123 EB57
SE25 ... 202 DU98
W14 ... 16 E5
Bromley BR2 ... 204 EJ99
Caterham CR3 ... 236 DR121
Chesham HP5 ... 54 AQ29
Enfield EN3 ... 82 DW39
Guildford GU1 ... 258 AY135
Ilford IG6 ... 103 EQ53
Teddington TW11 ... 177 CH93
Woking GU21 *off Chertsey Rd* ... 227 AZ117
Addison's Cl, Croy. CR0 ... 203 DZ103
Addison Way, NW11 ... 119 CZ56
Hayes UB3 ... 135 BU72
Northwood HA6 ... 93 BT53
Addle Hill, EC4 ... 10 F9
ADDLESTONE, KT15 ... 212 BJ106
⇌ **Addlestone** ... 212 BK105
ADDLESTONE MOOR, Add. KT15 ... 194 BG103
Addlestone Moor, Add. KT15 ... 194 BJ103
Addlestone Pk, Add. KT15 ... 212 BH106
Addlestone Rd, Add. KT15 ... 212 BL105
Addle St, EC2 ... 11 H6
Adecroft Way, W.Mol. KT8 ... 196 CC97
Adela Av, N.Mal. KT3 ... 199 CV99
Adelaide Av, SE4 ... 163 DZ84
Adelaide Cl, SW9 *off Broughton Dr* ... 161 DN84
Enfield EN1 ... 82 DT38
Slough SL1 *off Amerden Way* ... 151 AN75
Stanmore HA7 ... 95 CG49
Adelaide Cotts, W7 ... 157 CF75
Adelaide Gdns, Rom. RM6 ... 126 EY57
Adelaide Gro, W12 ... 139 CU74
Adelaide Pl, Wey. KT13 ... 213 BR105
Adelaide Rd, E10 ... 123 EB62
NW3 ... 140 DD66
SW18 *off Putney Br Rd* ... 180 DA85

★ Place of interest | H Hospital | Sch School | Coll College | Uni University | ⇌ Railway station

Adelaide Rd, W13 137 CG74
Ashford TW15 174 BK92
Chislehurst BR7 185 EP92
Hounslow TW5 156 BY81
Ilford IG1 125 EP61
Richmond TW9 158 CM84
Southall UB2 156 BY77
Surbiton KT6 198 CL99
Teddington TW11 177 CF93
Tilbury RM18 171 GF81
Walton-on-Thames KT12 195 BU104
Adelaide Sq, Wind. SL4 151 AR82
Adelaide St, WC2 9 N10
St. Albans AL3 43 CD19
Adelaide Ter, Brent. TW8 157 CK78
Adela St, W10 6 C3
Adelina Gro, E1 12 E5
Adelina Ms, SW12
off King's Av 181 DK88
Adeline Pl, WC1 9 M6
Adeliza Cl, Bark. IG11
off North St 145 EP66
Adelphi Ct, SE16
off Poolmans St 163 DX75
Adelphi Cres, Hayes UB4 135 BT69
Hornchurch RM12 127 FG61
Adelphi Gdns, Slou. SL1 152 AS75
Adelphi Rd, Epsom KT17 216 CR113
Adelphi Ter, WC2 9 P10
Adelphi Way, Hayes UB4 135 BT69
Adeney Cl, W6 159 CX79
Aden Gro, N16 122 DR63
Adenmore Rd, SE6 183 EA87
Aden Rd, Enf. EN3 83 DY42
Ilford IG1 125 EP59
Aden Ter, N16 122 DR63
ADEYFIELD, Hem.H. HP2 40 BN20
Adeyfield Gdns, Hem.H.
HP2 40 BM19
Adeyfield Rd, Hem.H. HP2 40 BM20
Sch Adeyfield Sec Sch,
Hem.H. HP2
off Longlands 40 BN20
Adhern Ct, St.Alb. AL1 43 CJ22
Adie Rd, W6 159 CW76
Adine Rd, E13 15 N3
Adler Ind Est, Hayes UB3 155 BR75
Adlers La, Dor. (Westh.)
RH5 247 CG131
Adler St, E1 12 A7
Adley St, E5 123 DY64
Adlington Cl, N18 100 DR50
Admaston Rd, SE18 165 EQ80
Admiral Cl, Orp. BR5 206 EX98
Admiral Ct, NW4
off Barton Cl 119 CU57
Admiral Ho, Tedd. TW11
off Twickenham Rd 177 CG91
Admiral Pl, SE16 23 K1
Admirals Cl, E18 124 EH56
St. Albans (Coln.Hth) AL4 44 CR23
Admirals Ct, Guil. GU1 243 BB133
Admiral Seymour Rd, SE9 165 EM84
Admirals Gate, SE10 163 EB81
Admiral Sq, SW10 160 DD81
Admiral's Rd, Lthd. KT22,
KT23 247 CD126
Admiral Stirling Ct,
Wey. KT13
off Weybridge Rd 212 BM105
Admiral St, SE8 163 EA82
Hertford SG13 32 DU09
Admirals Wk, NW3 120 DC62
Coulsdon CR5 235 DM120
Admiral's Wk, Dor. RH5 246 CB130
Admirals Wk, Green. DA9 189 FV85
Hoddesdon EN11 49 EA19
St. Albans AL1 43 CG23
Admirals Way, E14 23 P3
★ Admiralty Arch, SW1 19 M1
Admiralty Cl, SE8
off Reginald Sq 163 EA80
Admiralty Way, Tedd. TW11 177 CF93
Admiral Wk, W9 7 H5
Admiral Way, Berk. HP4 38 AT17
Adnams Wk, Rain. RM13
off Lovell Wk 147 FF65
Adolf St, SE6 183 EB91
Adolphus Rd, N4 121 DP61
Adolphus St, SE8 163 DZ80
Adomar Rd, Dag. RM8 126 EX62
Adpar St, W2 7 N4
Adrian Av, NW2
off North Circular Rd 119 CV60
Adrian Cl, Barn. EN5 79 CX44
Uxbridge (Hare.) UB9 92 BK53
Adrian Ms, SW10 160 DB79
Adrian Rd, Abb.L. WD5 59 BS31
Adrians Wk, Slou. SL2 132 AT74
Adriatic Bldg, E14 13 J9
Adrienne Av, Sthl. UB1 136 BZ70
Adstock Ms, Ger.Cr.
(Chal.St.P.) SL9
off Church La 90 AX53
Adstock Way, Grays
(Bad.Dene)
RM17 170 FZ77
Sch ADT Coll, SW15
off West Hill 179 CZ85
Coll Adult Coll of Barking &
Dagenham, The, Dag.
RM9 off Fanshawe Cres 126 EZ64
Advance Rd, SE27 182 DQ91
Advent Ct, Wdf.Grn. IG8
off Wood La 102 EF50
Advent Way, N18 101 DX50
Advice Av, Grays RM16 170 GA75
Adys Rd, SE15 162 DT83
Aerodrome Rd, NW4 97 CT54
NW9 97 CT54
Aerodrome Way, Houns.
TW5 156 BW79
Aeroville, NW9 96 CS54
Affleck St, N1 4 B10
Afghan Rd, SW11 160 DE82
★ Africa Cen, WC2 9 N9
Africa Ho, SE16 22 D5
Afton Dr, S.Ock. RM15 149 FV72
Agamemnon Rd, NW6 119 CZ64
Agar Cl, Surb. KT6 198 CM103
Agar Gro, NW1 141 DJ66
Agar Gro Est, NW1 141 DK66
Agar Pl, NW1 141 DJ66
Agars Plough, Slou. (Datchet)
SL3 152 AU79
Agar St, WC2 9 N10
Agate Cl, E16 144 EK72
Agate Rd, W6 159 CW76
Agates La, Ashtd. KT21 231 CK118
Agatha Cl, E1 22 D1
Agaton Rd, SE9 185 EQ89
Agave Rd, NW2 119 CW63
Agdon St, EC1 10 E3
Sch Agincourt Ho, PRU, NW3
off Agincourt Rd 120 DF64
Agincourt Rd, NW3 120 DF63
Agister Rd, Chig. IG7 104 EU50
Agnes Av, Ilf. IG1 125 EP63
Agnes Cl, E6 145 EN73
Agnesfield Cl, N12 98 DE51
Agnes Gdns, Dag. RM8 126 EX63
Agnes Rd, W3 139 CT74
Agnes Scott Ct, Wey. KT13
off Palace Dr 195 BP104
Agnes St, E14 13 M7
Agnew Rd, SE23 183 DX87
Agraria Rd, Guil. GU2 258 AV135
Agricola Ct, E3
off Parnell Rd 143 DZ67
Agricola Pl, Enf. EN1 82 DT43
Aidan Cl, Dag. RM8 126 EY63
Aileen Wk, E15 144 EF66
Ailsa Av, Twick. TW1 177 CG85
Ailsa Rd, Twick. TW1 177 CH85
Ailsa St, E14 14 D5
AIMES GREEN, Wal.Abb.
EN9 68 EF28
Ainger Ms, NW3
off Ainger Rd 140 DF66
Ainger Rd, NW3 140 DF66
Ainsdale Cl, Orp. BR6 205 ER102
Ainsdale Cres, Pnr. HA5 116 CA55
Ainsdale Dr, SE1 22 A10
Ainsdale Rd, W5 137 CK70
Watford WD19 94 BW48
Ainsdale Way, Wok. GU21 226 AU118
Ainsley Av, Rom. RM7 127 FB58
Ainsley Cl, N9 100 DS46
Ainsley St, E2 12 D2
Ainslie Wk, SW12 181 DH87
Ainslie Wd Cres, E4 101 EB50
Ainslie Wd Gdns, E4 101 EB49
Sch Ainslie Wd Prim Sch, E4
off Ainslie Wd Rd 101 EB50
Ainslie Wd Rd, E4 101 EA50
Ainsty Est, SE16 22 G4
Ainsworth Cl, NW2 119 CU62
SE15 off Lyndhurst Gro 162 DS82
Ainsworth Rd, E9 142 DW66
Croydon CR0 201 DP103
Ainsworth Way, NW8 140 DC67
Aintree Av, E6 144 EL67
Aintree Cl, Grav. DA12 191 GH90
Slough (Colnbr.) SL3 153 BE81
Uxbridge UB8
off Craig Dr 135 BP72
Aintree Cres, Ilf. IG6 103 EQ54
Aintree Est, SW6
off Dawes Rd 159 CY80
Aintree Gro, Upmin. RM14 128 FM62
Aintree Rd, Grnf. UB6 137 CH68
Aintree St, SW6 159 CY80
Aird Ct, Hmptn. TW12
off Oldfield Rd 196 BZ95
Airdrie Cl, N1 4 A6
Hayes UB4
off Glencoe Rd 136 BY71
Airedale, Hem.H. HP2
off Wharfedale 40 BL17
Airedale Av, W4 159 CT77
Airedale Av S, W4
off Netheravon Rd S 159 CT78
Airedale Cl, Dart. DA2 188 FQ88
Airedale Rd, SW12 180 DF87
W5 157 CJ76
Aire Dr, S.Ock. RM15 149 FV70
Airey Neave Ct, Grays RM17 170 GA75
Airfield Way, Horn. RM12 147 FH65
Watford WD25 59 BT34
★ Air Forces Mem, Egh.
TW20 172 AX91
Airlie Gdns, W8 16 G3
Ilford IG1 125 EP60
Air Links Ind Est, Houns.
TW5 156 BW78
Air Pk Way, Felt. TW13 175 BV89
Airport Ind Est, West. TN16 222 EK114
Airport Roundabout, E16
off Connaught Br 144 EK74
Airport Way, Gat. RH6 268 DG151
Staines TW19 153 BF84
Airport Way Roundabout,
Horl. RH6 268 DF151
Airport Way Roundabout E,
Horl. RH6 269 DH151
Air St, W1 9 K10
Airthrie Rd, Ilf. IG3 126 EV61
Aisgill Av, W14 16 F10
Aisher Rd, SE28 146 EW73
Aisher Way, Sev. (Rvrhd)
TN13 256 FE121
Aislibie Rd, SE12 164 EE84
Aiten Pl, W6
off Standish Rd 159 CU77
Aitken Cl, E8
off Pownall Rd 142 DU67
Mitcham CR4 200 DF101
Aitken Rd, SE6 183 EB89
Barnet EN5 79 CW43
Ajax Av, NW9 118 CS55
Slough SL1 131 AP73
Ajax Rd, NW6 120 DA64
Akabusi Cl, Croy. CR0 202 DU100
Akehurst La, Sev. TN13 257 FJ125
Akehurst St, SW15 179 CU86
Akeman Cl, St.Alb. AL3
off Meautys 42 BZ22
Akenside Rd, NW3 120 DD64
Akerman Rd, SW9 161 DP82
Surbiton KT6 197 CJ100
Akers Way, Rick. (Chorl.)
WD3 73 BD44
Sch Akiva Sch, N3
off East End Rd 98 DA54
Alabama St, SE18 165 ER80
Alacross Rd, W5 157 CJ75
Alamein Cl, Brox. EN10 49 DX20
Alamein Gdns, Dart. DA2 189 FR87
Alamein Rd, Swans. DA10 189 FX86
Alanbrooke, Grav. DA12 191 GJ87
Alan Cl, Dart. DA1 168 FJ84
Alandale Dr, Pnr. HA5 93 BV54
Aland Ct, SE16 23 K5
Alander Ms, E17 123 EC56
Alan Dr, Barn. EN5 79 CY44
Alan Gdns, Rom. RM7 126 FA59
Alan Hocken Way, E15 144 EE68
Alan Rd, SW19 179 CY92
Alanthus Cl, SE12 184 EF86
Alan Way, Slou. (Geo.Grn)
SL3 132 AY72
Alaska St, SE1 20 C2
Alba Cl, Hayes UB4
off Ramulis Dr 136 BX70
Albacore Cres, SE13 183 EB86
Alba Gdns, NW11 119 CY58
Albain Cres, Ashf. TW15 174 BL89
Alban Av, St.Alb. AL3 43 CD18
Alban Cres, Borwd. WD6 78 CP39
Dartford (Fnghm) DA4 208 FN102
Alban Highwalk, EC2
off London Wall 142 DQ71
Alban Pk, St.Alb. AL4 44 CM20
Albans Vw, Wat. WD25 59 BV33
Alban Way Cycle Route, Hat.
AL10 44 CQ20
St. Albans AL1, AL4 43 CH20
Sch Alban Wd Inf Sch, Wat.
WD25 off The Brow 59 BV32
Sch Alban Wd Jun Sch, Wat.
WD25
off Newhouse Cres 59 BV33
Albany, W1 9 J10
Albany, The, Wdf.Grn. IG8 102 EF49
Albany Cl, N15 121 DP56
SW14 158 CP84
Bexley DA5 186 EW87
Bushey WD23 77 CD44
Esher KT10 214 CA109
Reigate RH2 250 DA132
Uxbridge UB10 114 BN64
Coll Albany Coll, NW4
off Queens Rd 119 CW57
Hendry Ho, NW4
off Hendon Way 119 CV57
Albany Ct, E4
off Chelwood Cl 83 EB44
Epping CM16 69 ET30
Albany Ctyd, W1 9 K10
Albany Cres, Edg. HA8 96 CN52
Esher (Clay.) KT10 215 CE107
Albany Gate, Chesh. HP5
off Bellingdon Rd 54 AP30
Albany Mans, SW11 160 DE80
Albany Ms, N1 4 D5
SE5 off Albany Rd 162 DQ79
Bromley BR1 184 EG93
Kingston upon Thames
KT2 off Albany Pk Rd 177 CK93
St. Albans AL2
off North Orbital Rd 60 CA27
Sutton SM1
off Camden Rd 218 DB106
Ware SG12
off Albany Quay 33 DY06
⇌ Albany Park 186 EX89
Albany Pk, Slou. (Colnbr.)
SL3 153 BD81
Albany Pk Av, Enf. EN3 82 DW39
Albany Pk Rd, Kings.T.
KT2 178 CL93
Leatherhead KT22 231 CG119
Albany Pas, Rich. TW10 178 CM85
Albany Pl, Brent. TW8
off Albany Rd 158 CL79
Egham TW20 173 BA91
Albany Quay, Ware SG12 33 DY06
Albany Rd, E10 123 EA59
E12 124 EK63
E17 123 DY58
N4 121 DM58
N18 100 DV50
SE5 162 DR79
SW19 180 DB92
W13 137 CH73
Belvedere DA17 166 EZ79
Bexley DA5 186 EW87
Brentford TW8 157 CK79
Brentwood (Pilg.Hat.)
CM15 108 FV44
Chislehurst BR7 185 EP92
Enfield EN3 83 DX37
Hornchurch RM12 127 FG60
New Malden KT3 198 CR98
Richmond TW10
off Albert Rd 178 CM85
Romford RM6 126 EZ58
Walton-on-Thames KT12 214 BX105
Windsor SL4 151 AQ82
Windsor (Old Wind.) SL4 172 AU85
Albanys, The, Reig. RH2 250 DA131
Sch Albany Sch, Enf. EN3
off Bell La 83 DX38
Sch Albany Sch, The, Horn.
RM12
off Broadstone Rd 127 FG61
Albany St, NW1 141 DH68
Albany Ter, NW1
off Marylebone Rd 141 DH70
Albany Vw, Buck.H. IG9 102 EG46
Alba Pl, W11 6 E7
Alba Rd, Harl. CM17
off London Rd 36 EW14
Albatross Gdns, S.Croy.
CR2 221 DX111
Albatross St, SE18 165 ES80
Albatross Way, SE16 22 G4
Albemarle, SW19 179 CX89
Albemarle App, Ilf. IG2 125 EP58
Albemarle Av, Pot.B. EN6 64 DB33
Twickenham TW2 176 BZ88
Waltham Cross (Chsht)
EN8 66 DW28
Albemarle Cl, Grays RM17 170 GA75
Albemarle Gdns, Ilf. IG2 125 EP58
New Malden KT3 198 CR98
Albemarle Pk, Stan. HA7
off Marsh La 95 CJ50
Sch Albemarle Prim Sch,
SW19 off Princes Way 179 CY89
Albemarle Rd, Barn. EN4 98 DE45
Beckenham BR3 203 EB95
Albemarle St, W1 9 H10
Albemarle Way, EC1 10 E4
Albeny Gate, St.Alb. AL1 43 CD21
Alberon Gdns, NW11 119 CZ56
Alberta Av, Sutt. SM1 217 CY105
Alberta Dr, Horl. (Smallfield)
RH6 269 DN148
Alberta Est, SE17 20 F9
Alberta Rd, Enf. EN1 82 DT44
Erith DA8 167 FC81
Alberta St, SE17 20 E9
Albert Av, E4 101 EA49
SW8 161 DM80
Chertsey KT16 194 BG97
Albert Br, SW3 160 DE79
SW11 160 DE79
Albert Br Rd, SW11 160 DE80
Albert Carr Gdns, SW16 181 DL92
Albert Cl, E9
off Northiam St 142 DV67
N22 99 DK53
Grays RM16 170 GC76
Slough SL1
off Albert St 152 AT76
Albert Ct, SW7 17 N4
Albert Cres, E4 101 EA49
Albert Dr, SW19 179 CY89
Woking GU21 211 BD114
Albert Embk, SE1 19 P10
Albert Gdns, E1 12 G8
Harlow CM17 52 EX16
Albert Gate, SW1 17 D3
Albert Gro, SW20 199 CX95
Albert Hall Mans, SW7 17 N4
Albertine Cl, Epsom KT17 233 CV116
Albert Mans, SW11
off Albert Br Rd 160 DF81
★ Albert Mem, SW7 17 N3
Albert Ms, E14
off Narrow St 143 DY73
N4 off Albert Rd 121 DM60
SE4 off Arabin Rd 163 DY84
W8 17 L5
Redhill RH1 266 DG137
Albert Murray Cl, Grav.
DA12 off Armoury Dr 191 GJ87
Albert Pl, N3 98 DA53
N17 off High Rd 122 DT55
W8 17 K4
Windsor (Eton Wick) SL4
off Common Rd 151 AN78
Albert Rd, E10 123 EC61
E16 144 EL74
E17 123 EA57
E18 124 EH55
N4 121 DM60
N15 122 DS58
N22 99 DJ53
NW4 119 CX56
NW6 139 CZ68
NW7 97 CT50
SE9 184 EL90
SE20 183 DX94
SE25 202 DU98
W5 137 CH70
Addlestone KT15 194 BK104
Ashford TW15 174 BM92
Ashtead KT21 232 CM118
Barnet EN4 80 DC42
Belvedere DA17 166 EZ78
Bexley DA5 186 FA86
Bromley BR2 204 EK99
Buckhurst Hill IG9 102 EK47
Chesham HP5 54 AQ31
Dagenham RM8 126 FA60
Dartford DA2 188 FJ90
Egham (Eng.Grn) TW20 172 AX93
Epsom KT17 217 CT113
Hampton (Hmptn H.)
TW12 176 CC92
Harrow HA2 116 CC55
Hayes UB3 155 BS76
Horley RH6 268 DG147
Hounslow TW3 156 CA84
Ilford IG1 125 EP62
Kingston upon Thames
KT1 198 CM96
Mitcham CR4 200 DF97
New Malden KT3 199 CT98
Orpington (Chels.) BR6 224 EU106
Orpington (St.M.Cray)
BR5 206 EV100
Redhill RH1 251 DJ129
Richmond TW10 178 CL85
Romford RM1 127 FF57
Southall UB2 156 BX76
Sutton SM1 218 DD106
Swanscombe DA10 190 FZ86
Teddington TW11 177 CF93
Twickenham TW1 177 CF88
Warlingham CR6 237 DZ117
West Drayton UB7 134 BL74
Windsor SL4 152 AS84
Albert Rd Est, Belv. DA17 166 EZ78
Albert Rd N, Reig. RH2 249 CZ133
Watford WD17 75 BV41
Albert Rd S, Wat. WD17 75 BV41
Albert Sq, E15 124 EE64
SW8 161 DM80
Albert St, N12 98 DC50
NW1 141 DH67
Brentwood (Warley)
CM14 108 FW50
St. Albans AL1 43 CD21
Slough SL1 152 AT76
Windsor SL4 151 AP81
Albert Ter, NW1 140 DG67
NW10 138 CR67
Buckhurst Hill IG9 102 EK47
Albert Ter Ms, NW1
off Regents Pk Rd 140 DG67
Albert Way, SE15 162 DV80
Albion Av, N10 98 DG53
SW8 161 DK82
Albion Bldgs, EC1
off Bartholomew Cl 142 DQ71
Albion Cl, W2 8 B9
Hertford SG13 32 DS08
Romford RM7 127 FD58
Slough SL2 132 AU74
Albion Cres, Ch.St.G. HP8 90 AV48
Albion Dr, E8 5 N6
Albion Est, SE16 22 G4
Albion Gro, N16 122 DS63
Albion Hill, Hem.H. HP2
off Wolsey Rd 40 BK21
Loughton IG10 84 EJ43
Albion Ho, Slou. SL3 153 BB78
Woking GU21 227 AZ117
Albion Ms, N1 4 C7
NW6 off Kilburn High Rd 139 CZ66
W2 8 B8
W6 off Galena Rd 159 CV77
Albion Par, N16
off Albion Rd 122 DR63
Gravesend DA12 191 GK86
Albion Pk, Loug. IG10 84 EK43
Albion Pl, EC1 10 E5
SE25 off High St 202 DU97
W6 159 CV77
Sch Albion Prim Sch, SE16 22 F4
Albion Riverside Bldg,
SW11 off Hester Rd 160 DE80
Albion Rd, E17 123 EC55
N16 5 K1
N17 100 DT54
Bexleyheath DA6 166 EZ84
Chalfont St. Giles HP8 90 AV47
Gravesend DA12 191 GJ87
Hayes UB3 135 BS72
Hounslow TW3 156 CA84
Kingston upon Thames
KT2 198 CQ95
Reigate RH2 266 DC135
St. Albans AL1 43 CF20
Sutton SM2 218 DD107
Twickenham TW2 177 CE88
Albion Sq, E8 5 N6
Albion St, SE16 22 F4
W2 8 B8
Croydon CR0 201 DP102
Albion Ter, E8 5 N6
Gravesend DA12 191 GJ86
Albion Vil Rd, SE26 182 DW90
Albion Wk, N1
off York Way 141 DL68
Albion Way, EC1 10 G6
SE13 163 EC84
Albion Way, Wem. HA9
off North End Rd 118 CP62
Albion Yd, N1 off Balfe St 141 DL68
Albon Ho, SW18
off Neville Gill Cl 180 DB86
Albright Ind Est, Rain.
RM13 147 FF71
Albrighton Rd, SE22 162 DS83
Albuhera Cl, Enf. EN2 81 DN39
ALBURY, Guil. GU5 260 BJ139
Albury Av, Bexh. DA7 166 EY82
Isleworth TW7 157 CF80
Sutton SM2 217 CW109
Albury Cl, Cher. (Longcr.)
KT16 192 AU104
Epsom KT19 216 CP109
Hampton TW12 176 CA93
Albury Ct, Sutt. SM1
off Ripley Gdns 218 DC105
Albury Dr, Pnr. HA5 94 BX52
Albury Gro Rd, Wal.Cr. (Chsht)
EN8 67 DX30
ALBURY HEATH, Guil. GU5 260 BL141
Albury Heath, Guil. (Albury)
GU5 260 BL141
Albury Ms, E12 124 EJ60
Albury Pk, Guil. (Albury)
GU5 260 BL140
Albury Ride, Wal.Cr. (Chsht)
EN8 67 DX31
Albury Rd, Chess. KT9 216 CL106
Guildford GU1 259 AZ135
Redhill RH1 251 DJ129
Walton-on-Thames KT12 213 BS107
Albury St, SE8 163 EA79
Albury Wk, Wal.Cr. (Chsht)
EN8 67 DX32
Albyfield, Brom. BR1 205 EM97
Albyn Ho, Hem.H. HP2
off Alexandra Rd 40 BK19
Albyn Rd, SE8 163 EA81
Albyns Cl, Rain. RM13 147 FG66
Albyns La, Rom. RM4 87 FC40
Alcester Cres, E5 122 DV61
Alcester Rd, Wall. SM6 219 DH105
Alcock Cl, Wall. SM6 219 DK108
Alcock Rd, Houns. TW5 156 BX80
Alcocks Cl, Tad. KT20 233 CY120
Alcocks La, Tad. (Kgswd)
KT20 233 CY120
Alconbury, Welw.G.C. AL7 30 DE09
Alconbury Rd, E5 122 DU61
Alcorn Cl, Sutt. SM3 200 DA103
Alcott Cl, W7
off Westcott Cres 137 CF71
Alcuin Ct, Stan. HA7
off Old Ch La 95 CJ52
ALDBOROUGH HATCH, Ilf.
IG2 125 ES55
Aldborough Rd, Dag. RM10 147 FC65
Upminster RM14 128 FM61
Aldborough Rd N, Ilf. IG2 125 ET57
Aldborough Rd S, Ilf. IG3 125 ES60
Aldborough Spur, Slou.
SL1 132 AS72
Aldbourne Rd, W12 139 CT74
Slough (Burn.) SL1 130 AH71
Aldbridge St, SE17 21 M9
Aldburgh Ms, W1 8 F7
Aldbury Av, Wem. HA9 138 CP66
Aldbury Cl, St.Alb. AL4
off Sandringham Cres 43 CJ15
Watford WD25 76 BX36
Aldbury Gro, Welw.G.C. AL7 30 DB09
Aldbury Ms, N9 100 DR45
Aldbury Rd, Rick. (Mill End)
WD3 91 BF45
Aldebert Ter, SW8 161 DL80
Aldeburgh Cl, E5
off Southwold Rd 122 DV61
Aldeburgh Pl, SE10 25 M8
Woodford Green IG8 102 EG49
Aldeburgh St, SE10 25 L9
Alden Av, E15 15 J2
ALDENHAM, Wat. WD25 76 CB38
Aldenham Av, Rad. WD7 77 CG36
★ Aldenham Country Pk,
Borwd. WD6 77 CH43
Aldenham Dr, Uxb. UB8 135 BP70
Aldenham Gro, Rad. WD7 61 CH34
Aldenham Rd, Borwd.
(Elstree) WD6 77 CH42
Bushey WD23 76 BZ42
Radlett WD7 77 CG35
Watford WD19 76 BX44
Watford (Let.Hth) WD25 77 CE39
Sch Aldenham Sch, Borwd.
WD6
off Aldenham Rd 77 CF40
Aldenham St, NW1 141 DK68
Aldenholme, Wey. KT13 213 BS107
Aldensley Rd, W6 159 CV76
Alden Vw, Wind. SL4 151 AK81
Alder Av, Upmin. RM14 128 FM63
Alderbourne La, Iver SL0 113 BA64
Slough (Fulmer) SL3 112 AX63
Sch Alderbrook Prim Sch,
SW12 off Oldridge Rd 181 DH87
Alderbrook Rd, SW12 181 DH86
Alderbury Rd, SW13 159 CU79
Slough SL3 153 AZ75
Alderbury Rd W, Slou. SL3 153 AZ75
Alder Cl, SE15 162 DT79
Egham (Eng.Grn) TW20 172 AY92
Hoddesdon EN11 49 EB15
St. Albans (Park St) AL2 60 CB28
Slough SL1 131 AM74
Aldercombe La, Cat. CR3 252 DS127
Aldercroft, Couls. CR5 235 DM116
Alder Dr, S.Ock. RM15
off Laburnum Gro 149 FW70
Alder Gro, NW2 119 CV61
Aldergrove Gdns, Houns.
TW3 off Bath Rd 156 BY82
Aldergrove Wk, Horn. RM12
off Airfield Way 148 FJ65
Alderholt Way, SE15
off Blakes Rd 162 DS80
Alderley Ct, Berk. HP4 38 AV20
Alderman Av, Bark. IG11 146 EU69
Aldermanbury, EC2 11 H7
Aldermanbury Sq, EC2 11 H6
Alderman Cl, Dart. DA1 187 FE87
Hatfield (N.Mymms) AL9 45 CW24
Alderman Judge Mall,
Kings.T. KT1 off Eden St 198 CL96
Aldermans Hill, N13 99 DL49
Alderman's Wk, EC2 11 L6
Aldermary Rd, Brom. BR1 204 EG95

⊖ London Underground station   DLR Docklands Light Railway station   Tra Tramlink station   Riv Pedestrian ferry landing stage

Alder Ms, N19
off Bredgar Rd 121 DJ61
Aldermoor Rd, SE6 183 DZ90
Alderney Av, Houns. TW5 156 CB80
Alderney Gdns, Nthlt. UB5 136 BZ66
Alderney Ms, SE1 21 J5
Alderney Rd, E1 12 G3
Erith DA8 167 FG80
Alderney St, SW1 19 H9
Alder Rd, SW14 158 CR83
Iver SL0 133 BC68
Sidcup DA14 185 ET90
Uxbridge (Denh.) UB9 134 BJ65
Alders, The, N21 81 DN44
Feltham TW13 176 BY91
Hounslow TW5 156 BZ79
West Byfleet KT14 212 BJ112
West Wickham BR4 203 EB102
Alders Av, Wdf.Grn. IG8 102 EE51
ALDERSBROOK, E12 124 EH61
Aldersbrook Av, Enf. EN1 82 DS40
Aldersbrook Dr, Kings.T.
KT2 178 CM93
Aldersbrook La, E12 125 EM62
Sch Aldersbrook Prim Sch,
E12 off Ingatestone Rd 124 EJ60
Aldersbrook Rd, E11 124 EH61
E12 124 EK62
Alders Cl, E11
off Aldersbrook Rd 124 EH61
W5 157 CK76
Edgware HA8 96 CQ50
Alders Ct, Welw.G.C. AL7 30 DA09
Aldersey Gdns, Bark. IG11 145 ER65
Aldersey Rd, Guil. GU1 243 AZ134
Aldersford Cl, SE4 183 DX85
Aldersgate St, EC1 10 G7
Alders Gro, E.Mol. KT8
off Esher Rd 197 CD99
Aldersgrove, Wal.Abb. EN9
off Roundhills 68 EE34
Aldersgrove Av, SE9 184 EJ90
Aldershot Rd, NW6 139 CZ67
Guildford GU2, GU3 242 AT132
Alderside Wk, Egh. (Eng.Grn)
TW20 172 AY92
Aldersmead Av, Croy. CR0 203 DX100
Aldersmead Rd, Beck. BR3 183 DY94
Alderson Pl, Sthl. UB2 136 CC74
Alderson St, W10 6 D3
Alders Rd, Edg. HA8 96 CQ50
Reigate RH2 250 DB132
Alderstead Heath, Red. RH1 235 DK124
Alderstead Heath Caravan
Club, Red. RH1 235 DL123
Alderstead La, Red. RH1 251 DK126
Alders Wk, Saw. CM21 36 EY05
Alderton Cl, NW10 118 CR62
Brentwood (Pilg.Hat.)
CM15 108 FV43
Loughton IG10 85 EN42
Sch Alderton Co Inf Sch, The,
Loug. IG10
off Alderton Hall La 85 EN42
Sch Alderton Co Jun Sch, The,
Loug. IG10
off Alderton Hall La 85 EN42
Alderton Cres, NW4 119 CV57
Alderton Hall La, Loug. IG10 85 EN42
Alderton Hill, Loug. IG10 84 EL43
Alderton Ms, Loug. IG10
off Alderton Hall La 85 EN42
Alderton Ri, Loug. IG10 85 EN42
Alderton Rd, SE24 162 DQ83
Croydon CR0 202 DT101
Alderton Way, NW4 119 CV57
Loughton IG10 85 EM43
Alderville Rd, SW6 159 CZ82
Alder Wk, Ilf. IG1 125 EQ64
Watford WD25
off Aspen Pk Dr 75 BV35
Alder Way, Swan. BR8 207 FD96
Alderwick Dr, Houns. TW3 157 CD83
Alderwood Cl, Cat. CR3 252 DS125
Romford (Abridge) RM4 86 EV41
Alderwood Dr, Rom. (Abridge)
RM4 86 EV41
Alderwood Ms, Barn. EN4 80 DC38
Sch Alderwood Prim Sch, SE9
off Rainham Cl 185 ES86
Alderwood Rd, SE9 185 ER86
Aldford St, W1 18 E1
⊖ Aldgate 11 N7
Aldgate, EC3 11 N8
Aldgate Av, E1 11 N7
Aldgate Barrs Shop Cen, E1 11 P7
⊖ Aldgate East 11 P7
Aldgate High St, EC3 11 N8
Aldham Dr, S.Ock. RM15 149 FW71
Aldin Av N, Slou. SL1 152 AU75
Aldin Av S, Slou. SL1 152 AU75
Aldine Ct, W12
off Aldine St 139 CW74
Aldine Pl, W12
off Uxbridge Rd 139 CW74
Aldine St, W12 159 CW75
Aldingham Ct, Horn. RM12
off Easedale Dr 127 FG64
Aldingham Gdns, Horn.
RM12 127 FG64
Aldington Cl, Dag. RM8 126 EW59
Aldington Rd, SE18 164 EK76
Aldis Ms, SW17 off Aldis St 180 DE92
Enfield EN3
off Martini Dr 83 EA37
Aldis St, SW17 180 DE92
Aldock, Welw.G.C. AL7 30 DA12
Aldred Rd, NW6 120 DA64
Aldren Rd, SW17 180 DC90
Aldrich Cres, Croy.
(New Adgtn) CR0 221 EC109
Aldriche Way, E4 101 EC51
Aldrich Gdns, Sutt. SM3 199 CZ104
Aldrich Ter, SW18
off Lidiard Rd 180 DC89
Aldridge Av, Edg. HA8 96 CP48
Enfield EN3 83 EA38
Ruislip HA4 116 BX61
Stanmore HA7 96 CL53
Aldridge Ri, N.Mal. KT3 198 CS101
Aldridge Rd, Slou. SL2 131 AN70
Aldridge Rd Vil, W11 6 F6
Aldridge Wk, N14 99 DL45
Aldrington Rd, SW16 181 DJ92
Aldsworth Cl, W9 7 J4
Aldwick, St.Alb. AL1 43 CH22
Aldwick Cl, SE9 185 ER90
Aldwick Rd, Croy. CR0 201 DM104
Aldworth Gro, SE13 183 EC86
Aldworth Rd, E15 144 EE66
Aldwych, WC2 10 A9
Aldwych Av, Ilf. IG6 125 EQ56
Aldwych Cl, Horn. RM12 127 FG61
Aldwych Underpass, WC2
off Kingsway 141 DM72
Aldwyk Ct, Hem.H. HP1
off Leighton Buzzard Rd 40 BJ19
Aldykes, Hat. AL10 45 CT18
Alers Rd, Bexh. DA6 186 EX85
Alesia Cl, N22
off Nightingale Rd 99 DL52
Alestan Beck Rd, E16 144 EK71
Alexa Ct, W8 17 J7
Sutton SM2
off Mulgrave Rd 218 DA107
Alexander Av, NW10 139 CV66
Alexander Cl, Barn. EN4 80 DD42
Bromley BR2 204 EG102
Sidcup DA15 185 ES85
Southall UB2 136 CC74
Twickenham TW2 177 CF89
Alexander Ct, Wal.Cr. (Chsht)
EN8 67 DX30
Alexander Cres, Cat. CR3
off Coulsdon Rd 236 DQ122
Alexander Evans Ms, SE23
off Sunderland Rd 183 DX88
Sch Alexander First Sch, Wind.
SL4 off Kenneally Rd 150 AJ83
★ Alexander Fleming
Laboratory Mus, W2 7 P7
Alexander Godley Cl, Ashtd.
KT21 232 CM119
Alexander Ho, Kings.T. KT2
off Kingsgate Rd 198 CL95
Alexander La, Brwd. (Hutt.)
CM13, CM15 109 GB44
Sch Alexander McLeod JMI Sch,
SE2 off Fuchsia St 166 EV78
Alexander Ms, W2 7 J7
Alexander Pl, SW7 18 A7
Oxted RH8
off Barrow Grn Rd 254 EE128
Alexander Rd, N19 121 DL62
Bexleyheath DA7 166 EX82
Chislehurst BR7 185 EP92
Coulsdon CR5 235 DH115
Egham TW20 173 BB92
Greenhithe DA9 189 FW85
Hertford SG14 31 DN09
Reigate RH2 266 DA137
St. Albans (Lon.Col.) AL2 61 CJ25
Alexander Sq, SW3 18 A7
Alexander St, W2 7 H7
Chesham HP5 54 AQ30
Alexanders Wk, Cat. CR3 252 DT126
Alexandra Av, N22 99 DK53
SW11 160 DG81
W4 158 CR80
Harrow HA2 116 BZ60
Southall UB1 136 BZ73
Sutton SM1 200 DA104
Warlingham CR6 237 DZ117
Alexandra Cl, SE8 163 DZ79
Ashford TW15
off Alexandra Rd 175 BR94
Grays RM16 171 GH75
Harrow HA2
off Alexandra Av 116 CA62
Staines TW18 174 BK93
Swanley BR8 207 FE96
Walton-on-Thames KT12 195 BU103
Alexandra Cotts, SE14 163 DZ81
Alexandra Ct, N14 81 DJ43
N16 off Belgrade Rd 122 DT63
Ashford TW15
off Alexandra Rd 175 BR93
Wembley HA9 118 CM63
Alexandra Cres, Brom. BR1 184 EF93
Alexandra Dr, SE19 182 DS92
Surbiton KT5 198 CN101
Alexandra Gdns, N10 121 DH56
W4 158 CR80
Carshalton SM5 218 DG109
Hounslow TW3 156 CB82
Alexandra Gro, N4 121 DP60
N12 98 DB50
Sch Alexandra Inf Sch, Beck.
BR3 off Kent Ho Rd 183 DX93
Kingston upon Thames
KT2 off Alexandra Rd 178 CN94
Sch Alexandra Inf Sch (Spec Unit),
Beck. BR3
off Kent Ho Rd 183 DY94
Sch Alexandra Jun Sch,
SE26 off Cator Rd 183 DX93
Hounslow TW3
off Denbigh Rd 156 CB82
Alexandra Ms, N2
off Fortis Grn 120 DF55
SW19 off Alexandra Rd 180 DA93
Sch Alexandra Nurs & Inf Sch,
Houns. TW3
off Denbigh Rd 156 CB82
★ Alexandra Palace, N22 99 DK54
⇌ Alexandra Palace 99 DL54
Alexandra Palace Way, N22 121 DJ55
Alexandra Pk Rd, N10 99 DH54
N22 99 DK54
Sch Alexandra Pk Sec Sch,
N11 off Bidwell Gdns 99 DJ53
Alexandra Pl, NW8 140 DC67
SE25 202 DR99
Croydon CR0
off Alexandra Rd 202 DS102
Guildford GU1 259 AZ136
Sch Alexandra Prim Sch,
N22 off Western Rd 99 DM54
Alexandra Rd, E6 145 EN69
E10 123 EC62
E17 123 DZ58
E18 124 EH55
N8 121 DN55
N9 100 DV45
N10 99 DH51
N15 122 DR57
NW4 119 CX56
NW8 140 DC66
SE26 183 DX93
SW14 158 CR83
SW19 179 CZ93
W4 158 CR75
Addlestone KT15 212 BK105
Ashford TW15 175 BR94
Borehamwood WD6 78 CR38
Brentford TW8 157 CK79
Brentwood CM14 108 FW48
Croydon CR0 202 DS102
Egham (Eng.Grn) TW20 172 AW93
Enfield EN3 83 DX42
Epsom KT17 217 CT113
Erith DA8 167 FF79
Gravesend DA12 191 GL87
Hemel Hempstead HP2 40 BK20
Alexandra Rd, Houns. TW3 156 CB82
Kings Langley WD4 58 BN29
Kings Langley (Chipper.)
WD4 58 BG30
Kingston upon Thames
KT2 178 CN94
Mitcham CR4 180 DE94
Rainham RM13 147 FF67
Richmond TW9 158 CM82
Rickmansworth (Sarratt)
WD3 74 BG36
Romford RM1 127 FF58
Romford (Chad.Hth) RM6 126 EX58
St. Albans AL1 43 CE20
Slough SL1 151 AR76
Thames Ditton KT7 197 CF99
Tilbury RM18 171 GF82
Twickenham TW1 177 CJ86
Uxbridge UB8 134 BK68
Warlingham CR6 237 DY117
Watford WD17 75 BU40
Westerham (Bigg.H.)
TN16 238 EH119
Windsor SL4 151 AR82
Sch Alexandra Sch, Har. HA2
off Alexandra Av 116 CA61
Alexandra Sq, Mord. SM4 200 DA99
Alexandra St, E16 15 L5
SE14 163 DY80
Alexandra Ter, Guil. GU1 258 AY135
Alexandra Wk, SE19 182 DS92
Dartford (S.Darenth) DA4 209 FS96
Alexandra Way, Epsom
KT19 216 CN111
Waltham Cross EN8 67 DZ34
Alexandria Rd, W13 137 CG73
Alex Ct, Hem.H. HP2
off Alexandra Rd 40 BK19
Alexis St, SE16 22 A7
Alfan La, Dart. DA2 187 FD92
Alfearn Rd, E5 122 DW63
Alford Grn, Croy. (New Adgtn)
CR0 221 ED107
Alford Pl, N1 5 H10
Alford Rd, Erith DA8 167 FD78
Alfoxton Av, N15 121 DP56
Alfreda St, SW11 161 DH81
Alfred Cl, W4
off Belmont Rd 158 CR77
Alfred Gdns, Sthl. UB1 136 BY73
Alfred Ms, W1 9 L5
Alfred Pl, WC1 9 L5
Gravesend (Nthflt) DA11 191 GF88
Alfred Prior Ho, E12 125 EN63
Alfred Rd, E15 124 EF64
SE25 202 DU99
W2 7 H5
W3 138 CQ74
Belvedere DA17 166 EZ78
Brentwood CM14 108 FX47
Buckhurst Hill IG9 102 EK47
Dartford (Hawley) DA2 188 FL91
Feltham TW13 176 BW89
Gravesend DA11 191 GH89
Kingston upon Thames
KT1 198 CL97
South Ockendon (Aveley)
RM15 148 FQ74
Sutton SM1 218 DC106
Sch Alfred Salter Prim Sch,
SE16 23 H4
Alfred's Gdns, Bark. IG11 145 ES68
Alfred St, E3 143 DZ69
Grays RM17 170 GC79
Alfreds Way, Bark. IG11 145 EQ69
Alfreds Way Ind Est, Bark.
IG11 146 EU67
Alfreton Cl, SW19 179 CX90
Alfriston Av, Croy. CR0 201 DL101
Harrow HA2 116 CA58
Alfriston Cl, Dart. DA1 187 FE86
Surbiton KT5 198 CM99
Alfriston Rd, SW11 180 DF85
Sch Alfriston Sch, Beac. HP9
off Penn Rd 88 AJ49
Algar Cl, Islw. TW7
off Algar Rd 157 CG83
Stanmore HA7 95 CF50
Algar Rd, Islw. TW7 157 CG83
Algarve Rd, SW18 180 DB88
Algernon Rd, NW4 119 CU58
NW6 140 DA67
SE13 163 EB84
Algers Cl, Loug. IG10 84 EK43
Algers Mead, Loug. IG10 84 EK43
Algers Rd, Loug. IG10 84 EK43
Algiers Rd, SE13 163 EA84
Alibon Gdns, Dag. RM10 126 FA64
Alibon Rd, Dag. RM9,
RM10 126 EZ64
Alice Cl, Barn. EN5 80 DC42
Alice Ct, SW15
off Deodar Rd 159 CZ84
Alice Gilliatt Ct, W14 159 CZ79
Alice La, E3 143 DZ67
Slough (Burn.) SL1 130 AH70
Alice Ms, Tedd. TW11
off Luther Rd 177 CF92
Alice Ruston Pl, Wok.
GU22 226 AW119
Alice St, SE1 21 L6
Alice Thompson Cl, SE12 184 EJ89
Alice Walker Cl, SE24
off Shakespeare Rd 161 DP84
Alice Way, Houns. TW3 156 CB84
Alicia Av, Har. HA3 117 CH56
Alicia Cl, Har. HA3 117 CJ56
Alicia Gdns, Har. HA3 117 CH56
Alie St, E1 11 P8
Alington Cres, NW9 118 CQ60
Alington Gro, Wall. SM6 219 DJ109
Alison Cl, E6 145 EN72
Croydon CR0
off Shirley Oaks Rd 203 DX102
Woking GU21 226 AY115
Aliwal Rd, SW11 160 DE84
Alkerden La, Green. DA9 189 FW86
Swanscombe DA10 189 FW86
Alkerden Rd, W4 158 CS78
Alkham Rd, N16 122 DT61
Allan Barclay Cl, N15
off High Rd 122 DT58
Allan Cl, N.Mal. KT3 198 CR99
Allandale, Hem.H. HP2 40 BK18
St. Albans AL3 42 CB23
Allandale Av, N3 119 CY55
Allandale Cres, Pot.B. EN6 63 CY32
Allandale Pl, Orp. BR6 206 EX104
Allandale Rd, Enf. EN3 83 DX36
Hornchurch RM11 127 FF59
Allan Way, W3 138 CQ71
Allard Cl, Orp. BR5 206 EW101
Waltham Cross (Chsht)
EN7 66 DT27
Allard Cres, Bushey
(Bushey Hth) WD23 94 CC46
Allard Gdns, SW4 181 DK85
Allard Way, Brox. EN10 49 DY21
Allardyce St, SW4 161 DM84
Allbrook Cl, Tedd. TW11 177 CE92
Allcot Cl, Felt. TW14 175 BT88
Allcroft Rd, NW5 120 DG64
Allder Way, S.Croy. CR2 219 DP108
Alldicks Rd, Hem.H. HP3 40 BM22
Allenby Av, S.Croy. CR2 220 DQ109
Allenby Cl, Grnf. UB6 136 CA69
Allenby Cres, Grays RM17 170 GB78
Allenby Dr, Horn. RM11 128 FL60
Sch Allenby Inf Sch, Sthl.
UB1 off Allenby Rd 136 CA72
Allenby Rd, SE23 183 DY90
Southall UB1 136 CA72
Westerham (Bigg.H.)
TN16 238 EL117
Allen Cl, Mitch. CR4 201 DH95
Radlett (Shenley) WD7
off Russet Dr 62 CL32
Sunbury-on-Thames
TW16 195 BV95
Allen Ct, Dor. RH4
off High St 263 CH136
Greenford UB6 117 CF64
Hatfield AL10
off Drakes Way 45 CV20
Allendale Av, Sthl. UB1 136 CA72
Allendale Cl, SE5
off Daneville Rd 162 DR81
SE26 183 DX92
Dartford DA2
off Princes Rd 189 FR88
Allendale Rd, Grnf. UB6 137 CH65
Sch Allendale Sch, W8 17 H5
Allende Av, Harl. CM20 35 ER13
Allen Edwards Dr, SW8 161 DL81
Sch Allen Edwards Prim Sch,
SW4 off Studley Rd 161 DL81
Allenford Ho, SW15
off Tunworth Cres 179 CT86
Allen Ho Pk, Wok. GU22 226 AW120
Allen Pl, Twick. TW1
off Church St 177 CG88
Allen Rd, E3 143 DZ68
N16 122 DS63
Beckenham BR3 203 DX96
Croydon CR0 201 DM101
Leatherhead (Bkhm)
KT23 246 CB126
Rainham RM13 148 FJ69
Sunbury-on-Thames
TW16 195 BV95
Allensbury Pl, NW1 141 DK66
Allens Mead, Grav. DA12
off Marsh Vw 191 GM88
Allens Rd, Enf. EN3 82 DW43
Allen St, W8 17 H5
Allenswood Rd, SE9 164 EL83
Allerds Rd, Slou. (Farn.Royal)
SL2 131 AM67
Allerford Ct, Har. HA2 116 CB57
Allerford Rd, SE6 183 EB91
Allerton Cl, Borwd. WD6 78 CM38
Allerton Ct, NW4
off Holders Hill Rd 97 CX54
Allerton Rd, N16 122 DQ61
Borehamwood WD6 78 CL38
Allerton Wk, N7
off Durham Rd 121 DM61
Allestree Rd, SW6 159 CY80
Alleyn Cres, SE21 182 DR89
Alleyndale Rd, Dag. RM8 126 EW61
Alleyn Pk, SE21 182 DR89
Southall UB2 156 BZ77
Alleyn Rd, SE21 182 DR90
Sch Alleyn's Sch, SE22
off Townley Rd 182 DS85
Allfarthing La, SW18 180 DB86
Sch Allfarthing Prim Sch,
SW18 off St. Ann's Cres 180 DC86
Allgood Cl, Mord. SM4 199 CX100
Allgood St, E2 5 P10
Allhallows La, EC4 11 J10
★ All Hallows-on-the-Wall
C of E Ch, EC2 11 K6
Allhallows Rd, E6 144 EL71
All Hallows Rd, N17 100 DS53
Allhusen Gdns, Slou. (Fulmer)
SL3 off Alderbourne La 112 AY63
Alliance Cl, Wem. HA0 117 CK63
Alliance Ct, W3
off Alliance Rd 138 CP70
Alliance Rd, E13 144 EJ70
SE18 166 EU79
W3 138 CP70
Allied Way, W3
off Larden Rd 158 CS75
Allingham Cl, W7 137 CF73
Allingham Ct, Gdmg. GU7
off Summers Rd 258 AT144
Allingham Ms, N1 4 G9
Allingham Rd, Reig. RH2 266 DA137
Allingham St, N1 4 G9
Allington Av, N17 100 DS51
Allington Cl, SW19
off High St Wimbledon 179 CX92
Gravesend DA12
off Farley Rd 191 GM88
Greenford UB6 136 CC66
Allington Ct, Enf. EN3 83 DX43
Slough SL2
off Myrtle Cres 132 AT73
Allington Rd, NW4 119 CV57
W10 6 C1
Harrow HA2 116 CC57
Orpington BR6 205 ER103
Allington St, SW1 19 J6
Allis Ms, Harl. CM17
off London Rd 36 EW14
Allison Cl, SE10
off Dartmouth Hill 163 EC81
Waltham Abbey EN9 68 EG33
Allison Gro, SE21 182 DS88
Allison Rd, N8 121 DN57
W3 138 CQ72
Allitsen Rd, NW8 140 DE68
Allmains Cl, Wal.Abb. EN9 68 EH25
Coll All Nations Christian Coll,
Ware (Easneye) SG12 33 EC08
Allnutts Rd, Epp. CM16 70 EU33
Allnutt Way, SW4 181 DK85
Alloa Rd, SE8 23 H9
Ilford IG3 126 EU61
Allonby Dr, Ruis. HA4 115 BP59
Allonby Gdns, Wem. HA9 117 CJ60
Allotment La, Sev. TN13 257 FJ122
Allotment Way, NW2
off Midland Ter 119 CX62
Alloway Cl, Wok. GU21
off Inglewood 226 AV118
Alloway Rd, E3 13 K1
Allports Ms, E1 12 F4
DLR All Saints 14 C9
Sch All Saints Benhilton C of E
Prim Sch, Sutt. SM1
off All Saints Rd 200 DB104
Sch All Saints Carshalton C of E
Prim Sch, Cars. SM5
off Rotherfield Rd 218 DG106
Sch All Saints Catholic Sch -
Tech Coll, Dag. RM8
off Terling Rd 126 FA61
All Saints Cl, N9 100 DT47
SW8 off Lansdowne Way 161 DL81
Chigwell IG7 104 EU48
Swanscombe DA10
off High St 190 FZ85
Sch All Saints C of E (Inf & Nurs)
Sch, Lthd. KT22
off Aperdele Rd 231 CG119
Sch All Saints C of E Jun Sch,
SE19
off Upper Beulah Hill 202 DS95
Sch All Saints C of E Prim Sch,
N20 off Oakleigh Rd N 98 DD47
NW2 off Cricklewood La 119 CZ62
SE3 off Blackheath Vale 164 EE82
SW6 off Bishop's Av 159 CY82
SW15
off Putney Common 159 CW83
SW19 off East Rd 180 DC94
Sch All Saints Co Inf Sch,
SE19
off Upper Beulah Hill 202 DS95
All Saints Cres, Wat. WD25 60 BX33
All Saints Dr, SE3 164 EE82
South Croydon CR2 220 DT112
All Saints La, Rick. (Crox.Grn)
WD3 74 BN44
All Saints Ms, Har. HA3 95 CE51
All Saints Pas, SW18
off Wandsworth High St 180 DB85
All Saints Rd, SW19 180 DC94
W3 158 CQ76
W11 6 E6
Gravesend (Nthflt) DA11 191 GF88
Sutton SM1 200 DB104
All Saints St, N1 4 A9
All Saints Twr, E10 123 EB59
Allsop Pl, NW1 8 D4
All Souls Av, NW10 139 CV68
Sch All Souls C of E Prim Sch,
W1 9 J6
All Souls Pl, W1 9 H6
Allum Cl, Borwd. (Elstree)
WD6 78 CL42
Allum Gro, Tad. KT20
off Preston La 233 CV121
Allum La, Borwd. (Elstree)
WD6 78 CM42
Allum Way, N20 98 DC46
Allwood Cl, SE26 183 DX91
Allwood Rd, Wal.Cr. EN7 66 DT27
Allyn Cl, Stai. TW18
off Penton Rd 173 BF93
Alma Av, E4 101 EC52
Hornchurch RM12 128 FL63
Almack Rd, E5 122 DW63
Alma Cl, Wok. (Knap.) GU21 226 AS118
Alma Cres, Sutt. SM1 217 CY106
Alma Cut, St.Alb. AL1 43 CE21
Alma Gro, SE1 21 P8
Alma Pl, NW10
off Harrow Rd 139 CV69
SE19 182 DT94
Thornton Heath CR7 201 DN99
Sch Alma Prim Sch, SE16 22 B7
Enfield EN3 off Alma Rd 83 DX43
Alma Rd, N10 98 DG52
SW18 180 DC85
Berkhamsted HP4 38 AS17
Carshalton SM5 218 DE106
Chesham HP5 54 AQ29
Enfield EN3 83 DY43
Esher KT10 197 CE102
Orpington BR5 206 EX103
Reigate RH2 250 DB133
St. Albans AL1 43 CE21
Sidcup DA14 186 EU90
Southall UB1 136 BY73
Swanscombe DA10 190 FZ85
Windsor SL4 151 AQ82
Windsor (Eton Wick) SL4 151 AM77
Alma Row, Har. HA3 95 CD53
Alma Sq, NW8 7 M1
Alma St, E15 143 ED65
NW5 141 DH65
Alma Ter, SW18 180 DD87
W8 off Allen St 160 DA76
Almeida St, N1 4 E6
Almeric Rd, SW11 160 DF84
Almer Rd, SW20 179 CU94
Almington St, N4 121 DM60
Almners Rd, Cher. (Lyne)
KT16 193 BC100
Almond Av, W5 158 CL76
Carshalton SM5 200 DF103
Uxbridge UB10 115 BP62
West Drayton UB7 154 BN76
Woking GU22 226 AX121
Almond Cl, SE15 162 DU82
Bromley BR2 205 EN101
Egham (Eng.Grn) TW20 172 AV93
Feltham TW13
off Highfield Rd 175 BU88
Grays RM16 171 GG76
Guildford GU1 242 AX130
Hayes UB3 135 BS73
Ruislip HA4
off Roundways 115 BT62
Shepperton TW17 195 BQ96
Windsor SL4 151 AP82
Almond Dr, Swan. BR8 207 FD96
Almond Gro, Brent. TW8 157 CH80
Almond Rd, N17 100 DU52
SE16 22 D7
Dartford DA2 188 FQ87
Epsom KT19 216 CR111
Slough (Burn.) SL1 130 AH68
Almonds, The, St.Alb. AL1 43 CH24
Almonds Av, Buck.H. IG9 102 EG47
Almond Wk, Hat. AL10
off Southdown Rd 45 CU21
Almond Way, Borwd. WD6 78 CP42
Bromley BR2 205 EN101
Harrow HA2 94 CB54
Mitcham CR4 201 DK99
Almons Way, Slou. SL2 132 AV71
Almorah Rd, N1 5 J6
Hounslow TW5 156 BX81
Alms Heath, Wok. (Ockham)
GU23 229 BP121
Almshouse La, Chess. KT9 215 CJ109
Enfield EN1 82 DV37
Almshouses, The, Dor. RH4
off Cotmandene 263 CH135

★ Place of interest | H Hospital | Sch School | Coll College | Uni University | ⇌ Railway station

Alnwick Gro, Mord. SM4
off Bordesley Rd 200 DB98
Alnwick Rd, E16 144 EJ72
SE12 184 EH87
ALPERTON, Wem. HA0 138 CM67
⊖ Alperton 138 CL67
Sch Alperton Comm Sch,
Lwr Sch, Wem. HA0
off Ealing Rd 138 CL67
Upr Sch & 6th Form Cen,
Wem. HA0
off Stanley Av 138 CL66
Alperton La, Grnf. UB6 137 CK69
Wembley HA0 137 CK69
Alperton St, W10 6 D3
Alphabet Gdns, Cars. SM5 200 DD100
Alphabet Sq, E3 13 P6
Alpha Business Pk, Hat. AL9 45 CW23
Alpha Cl, NW1 8 B2
Alpha Ct, Whyt. CR3 236 DU118
Alpha Gro, E14 23 P4
Alpha Pl, NW6 140 DA68
SW3 160 DE79
Sch Alpha Prep Sch, Har. HA1
off Hindes Rd 117 CE57
Alpha Rd, E4 101 EB48
N18 100 DU51
SE14 163 DZ81
Brentwood (Hutt.) CM13 109 GD44
Croydon CR0 202 DS102
Enfield EN3 83 DY42
Surbiton KT5 198 CM100
Teddington TW11 177 CD92
Uxbridge UB10 135 BP70
Woking GU22 227 BB116
Woking (Chobham) GU24 210 AT110
Alpha St, SE15 162 DU82
Alpha St N, Slou. SL1 152 AU75
Alpha St S, Slou. SL1 152 AT76
Alpha Way, Egh. TW20 193 BC95
Alphea Cl, SW19
off Courtney Rd 180 DE94
Alpine Av, Surb. KT5 198 CQ103
Alpine Business Cen, E6 145 EN71
Alpine Cl, Croy. CR0 202 DS104
Alpine Copse, Brom. BR1 205 EN96
Alpine Gro, E9 142 DW66
Alpine Rd, E10 123 EB61
SE16 22 F8
Redhill RH1 250 DG131
Walton-on-Thames KT12 195 BU101
Alpine Vw, Cars. SM5 218 DE106
Alpine Wk, Stan. HA7 95 CE47
Alpine Way, E6 145 EN71
Alresford Rd, Guil. GU2 258 AU135
Alric Av, NW10 138 CR66
New Malden KT3 198 CS97
Alroy Rd, N4 121 DN59
Alsace Rd, SE17 21 L9
Alscot Rd, SE1 21 P7
Alscot Way, SE1 21 N7
Alsford Wf, Berk. HP4 38 AX19
Alsike Rd, SE2 166 EX76
Erith DA18 166 EY76
Alsom Av, Wor.Pk. KT4 217 CU105
Alsop Cl, St.Alb. (Lon.Col.)
AL2 62 CL27
Alston Cl, Surb. KT6 197 CH101
Alston Rd, N18 100 DV50
SW17 180 DD91
Barnet EN5 79 CY41
Hemel Hempstead HP1 40 BG21
Altair Cl, N17 100 DT51
Altair Way, Nthwd. HA6 93 BT49
Altash Way, SE9 185 EM89
Altenburg Av, W13 157 CH76
Altenburg Gdns, SW11 160 DF84
Alterton Cl, Wok. GU21 226 AU117
Alt Gro, SW19
off St. George's Rd 179 CZ94
Altham Gdns, Wat. WD19 94 BX49
Altham Gro, Harl. CM20 35 ET12
Altham Rd, Pnr. HA5 94 BY52
Althea St, SW6 160 DB83
Althorne Gdns, E18 124 EF56
Althorne Rd, Red. RH1 266 DG136
Althorne Way, Dag. RM10 126 FA61
Althorp Cl, Barn. EN5 97 CU45
Althorpe Gro, SW11
off Westbridge Rd 160 DD81
Althorpe Ms, SW11
off Battersea High St 160 DD81
Althorpe Rd, Har. HA1 116 CC57
Althorp Rd, SW17 180 DF88
St. Albans AL1 43 CE19
Altmore Av, E6 145 EM66
Sch Altmore Inf Sch, E6
off Altmore Av 145 EM67
Altona Rd, H.Wyc. (Loud.)
HP10 88 AC52
Alton Av, Stan. HA7 95 CF52
Altona Way, Slou. SL1 131 AP72
Alton Cl, Bex. DA5 186 EY88
Isleworth TW7 157 CF82
Alton Ct, Stai. TW18 193 BE95
Alton Gdns, Beck. BR3 183 EA94
Twickenham TW2 177 CD87
Alton Rd, N17 122 DR55
SW15 179 CU88
Croydon CR0 201 DN104
Richmond TW9 158 CL84
Sch Alton Sch, The, SW15
off Danebury Av 178 CS86
Alton St, E14 14 A6
Altwood Cl, Slou. SL1
off Burnham La 131 AL71
Altyre Cl, Beck. BR3 203 DZ99
Altyre Rd, Croy. CR0 202 DR103
Altyre Way, Beck. BR3 203 DZ99
Aluric Cl, Grays RM16 171 GH77
Alvanley Gdns, NW6 120 DB64
Alva Way, Wat. WD19 94 BX47
Alverstoke Rd, Rom. RM3 106 FL52
Alverstone Av, SW19 180 DA89
Barnet EN4 98 DE45
Alverstone Gdns, SE9 185 EQ88
Alverstone Rd, E12 125 EN63
NW2 139 CW66
New Malden KT3 199 CT98
Wembley HA9 118 CM60
Alverston Gdns, SE25 202 DS99
Alverton, St.Alb. AL3
off Green La 42 CC17
Alverton St, SE8 23 L10
Alveston Av, Har. HA3 117 CH55
Alvey Est, SE17 21 L8
Alvey St, SE17 21 L9
Alvia Gdns, Sutt. SM1 218 DC105
Alvington Cres, E8 5 N1
Alvista Av, Maid. (Taplow)
SL6 130 AH72
Alway Av, Epsom KT19 216 CQ106
Alwen Gro, S.Ock. RM15 149 FV71
Alwold Cres, SE12 184 EH86
Alwyn Av, W4 158 CR78
Alwyn Cl, Borwd. (Elstree)
WD6 78 CM44
Croydon (New Adgtn)
CR0 221 EB108
Alwyne Av, Brwd. (Shenf.)
CM15 109 GA44
Alwyne Ct, Wok. GU21 226 AY116
Alwyne La, N1 4 F5
Alwyne Pl, N1 4 G4
Alwyne Rd, N1 4 F5
SW19 179 CZ93
W7 137 CE73
Alwyne Sq, N1 4 G3
Alwyne Vil, N1 4 F5
Alwyn Gdns, NW4 119 CU56
W3 138 CP72
Alwyns Cl, Cher. KT16
off Alwyns La 194 BG100
Alwyns La, Cher. KT16 193 BF100
Alyngton, Berk. HP4 38 AS16
Alyth Gdns, NW11 120 DA58
Alzette Ho, E2 12 G1
Amalgamated Dr, Brent.
TW8 157 CG79
Amanda Cl, Chig. IG7 103 ER51
Amanda Ct, Slou. SL3 152 AX76
Amanda Ms, Rom. RM7 127 FC57
Amazon St, E1 12 C8
Ambassador Cl, Houns.
TW3 156 BY82
Ambassador Gdns, E6 145 EM71
Ambassador's Ct, SW1 19 K2
Ambassador Sq, E14 24 A8
Amber Av, E17 101 DY53
Amber Ct, SW17
off Brudenell Rd 180 DG91
Staines TW18
off Laleham Rd 173 BF92
Ambercroft Way, Couls.
CR5 235 DP119
Amberden Av, N3 120 DA55
Ambergate St, SE17 20 F9
Amber Gro, NW2
off Prayle Gro 119 CX60
Amber La, Ilf. IG6 103 EP52
Amberley Cl, Orp. BR6
off Warnford Rd 223 ET106
Pinner HA5 116 BZ55
Woking (Send) GU23 243 BF125
Amberley Ct, Maid. SL6 130 AC69
Sidcup DA14 186 EW92
Amberley Dr, Add. (Wdhm)
KT15 211 BF110
Amberley Gdns, Enf. EN1 100 DS45
Epsom KT19 217 CT105
Amberley Gro, SE26 182 DV91
Croydon CR0 202 DT101
Amberley Rd, E10 123 EB59
N13 99 DM47
SE2 166 EX79
W9 7 H5
Buckhurst Hill IG9 102 EJ46
Enfield EN1 100 DT45
Slough SL2 131 AL71
Amberley Way, Houns.
TW4 176 BW85
Morden SM4 199 CZ101
Romford RM7 127 FB56
Uxbridge UB10 134 BL69
Amber Ms, N22
off Brampton Pk Rd 121 DN55
Amberry Ct, Harl. CM20 35 ER14
Amberside Cl, Islw. TW7 177 CD86
Amber St, E15
off Great Eastern Rd 143 ED65
Amber Wf, E2 5 N8
Amberwood Cl, Wall. SM6
off The Chase 219 DL106
Amberwood Ri, N.Mal. KT3 198 CS100
Amblecote, Cob. KT11 214 BY111
Amblecote Cl, SE12 184 EH90
Amblecote Meadows, SE12 184 EH90
Amblecote Rd, SE12 184 EH90
Sch Ambler Prim Sch, N4
off Blackstock Rd 121 DP61
Ambler Rd, N4 121 DP62
Ambleside, Brom. BR1 183 ED93
Epping CM16 70 EU31
Ambleside Av, SW16 181 DK91
Beckenham BR3 203 DY99
Hornchurch RM12 127 FH64
Walton-on-Thames KT12 196 BW102
Ambleside Cl, E9
off Churchill Wk 122 DW64
E10 123 EB59
Redhill RH1 267 DH139
Ambleside Cres, Enf. EN3 83 DX41
Ambleside Dr, Felt. TW14 175 BT88
Ambleside Gdns, SW16 181 DK92
Ilford IG4 124 EL56
South Croydon CR2 221 DX109
Sutton SM2 218 DC107
Wembley HA9 117 CK60
Sch Ambleside Jun Sch,
Walt. KT12
off Ambleside Av 196 BW102
Ambleside Pt, SE15
off Ilderton Rd 162 DW80
Ambleside Rd, NW10 139 CT66
Bexleyheath DA7 166 FA82
Ambleside Wk, Uxb. UB8
off High St 134 BK67
Ambleside Way, Egh. TW20 173 BB94
Ambrey Way, Wall. SM6 219 DK109
Ambrooke Rd, Belv. DA17 166 FA76
Ambrosden Av, SW1 19 K6
Ambrose Av, NW11 119 CY59
Ambrose Cl, E6
off Lovage App 144 EL71
Dartford (Cray.) DA1 167 FF84
Orpington BR6
off Stapleton Rd 205 ET104
Ambrose Ms, SW11 160 DE82
Ambrose St, SE16 22 C7
Ambrose Wk, E3
off Malmesbury Rd 143 EA68
Amelia Cl, W3 138 CP74
Amelia St, SE17 20 F9
Amen Cor, EC4 10 F8
SW17 180 DF93
Amen Ct, EC4 10 F7
Amenity Way, Mord. SM4 199 CW101
Amerden Caravan Pk, Maid.
SL6 150 AE75
Amerden Cl, Maid. (Taplow)
SL6 130 AD72
Amerden La, Maid. (Taplow)
SL6 130 AD74
Amerden Way, Slou. SL1 151 AN75
Sch American Comm Cen,
The, Egh. TW20
off London Rd 192 AW96
Sch American Comm Sch,
Uxb. UB10
off Vine La 134 BM67
Sch American Comm Sch,
The, Cob. KT11
off Portsmouth Rd 214 BW110
Sch American Sch in London,
The, NW8
off Waverley Pl 140 DD68
America Sq, EC3 11 N9
America St, SE1 20 G2
Amerland Rd, SW18 179 CZ86
AMERSHAM, HP6 & HP7 55 AP38
⇌ Amersham 55 AQ38
⊖ Amersham 55 AQ38
Coll Amersham & Wycombe Coll,
Amersham Campus,
Amer. HP7
off Stanley Hill 72 AT39
Chesham Campus, Chesh.
HP5 off Lycrome Rd 54 AR28
Amersham Av, N18 100 DR51
Amersham Bypass, Amer.
HP7 55 AN41
Amersham Cl, Rom. RM3 106 FM51
Amersham Dr, Rom. RM3 106 FL51
Amersham Gro, SE14 163 DZ80
H Amersham Hosp, Amer.
HP7 55 AN41
★ Amersham Mus, Amer.
HP7 55 AP40
AMERSHAM OLD TOWN,
Amer. HP7 55 AP39
Amersham Pl, Amer. HP7 72 AW39
Amersham Rd, SE14 163 DZ80
Amersham (Chesh.B.)
HP6 55 AP36
Amersham (Colesh.) HP7 89 AP46
Amersham (Lt.Chal.) HP6 72 AX39
Beaconsfield HP9 89 AM53
Chalfont St. Giles HP8 72 AU43
Chesham HP5 55 AP35
Croydon CR0 202 DQ100
Gerrards Cross SL9 113 BB59
Gerrards Cross (Chal.St.P.)
SL9 90 AX49
Rickmansworth WD3 73 BB39
Romford RM3 106 FM51
Sch Amersham Sch, The,
Amer. HP7
off Stanley Hill 55 AS40
Amersham Vale, SE14 163 DZ80
Amersham Wk, Rom. RM3 106 FM51
Amersham Way, Amer. HP6 72 AX39
Amery Gdns, NW10 139 CV67
Romford RM2 128 FK55
Amery Rd, Har. HA1 117 CG61
Amesbury, Wal.Abb. EN9 68 EG32
Amesbury Av, SW2 181 DL89
Amesbury Cl, Epp. CM16
off Amesbury Rd 69 ET31
Worcester Park KT4 199 CW102
Amesbury Dr, E4 83 EB44
Amesbury Rd, Brom. BR1 204 EK97
Dagenham RM9 146 EX66
Epping CM16 69 ET31
Feltham TW13 176 BX89
Amesbury Twr, SW8
off Westbury St 161 DJ82
Ames Rd, Swans. DA10 190 FY86
Amethyst Cl, N11 99 DK52
Amethyst Rd, E15 123 ED63
Amey Dr, Lthd. (Bkhm)
KT23 230 CC124
Amherst Av, W13 137 CJ72
Amherst Cl, Orp. BR5 206 EU98
Amherst Dr, Orp. BR5 205 ET98
Amherst Hill, Sev. TN13 256 FE122
Sch Amherst JMI Sch, E8
off Sigdon Rd 122 DU64
Amherst Rd, W13 137 CJ72
Sevenoaks TN13 257 FH122
Sch Amherst Sch, Sev. TN13
off Witches La 256 FE123
Amhurst Gdns, Islw. TW7 157 CF81
Amhurst Par, N16
off Amhurst Pk 122 DT59
Amhurst Pk, N16 122 DR59
Amhurst Pas, E8 122 DU63
Amhurst Rd, E8 122 DV64
N16 122 DT63
Amhurst Ter, E8 122 DU63
Amhurst Wk, SE28
off Pitfield Cres 146 EU74
Amidas Gdns, Dag. RM8 126 EV63
Amiel St, E1 12 F3
Amies St, SW11 160 DF83
Amina Way, SE16 22 A6
Amis Av, Add. (New Haw)
KT15 212 BG111
Epsom KT19 216 CP107
Amis Rd, Wok. GU21 226 AS119
Amity Gro, SW20 199 CW95
Amity Rd, E15 144 EF67
Ammanford Grn, NW9
off Ruthin Cl 118 CS58
Amner Rd, SW11 180 DG86
Amor Rd, W6 159 CW76
Amott Rd, SE15 162 DU83
Amoy Pl, E14 13 N8
Tra Ampere Way 201 DM101
Ampere Way, Croy. CR0 201 DL101
Ampleforth Rd, SE2 166 EV75
Ampthill Sq, NW1
off Eversholt St 141 DJ68
Ampton Pl, WC1 10 A2
Ampton St, WC1 10 A2
Amroth Cl, SE23 182 DV88
Amroth Grn, NW9
off Fryent Gro 118 CS58
Amstel Way, Wok. GU21 226 AT118
Amsterdam Rd, E14 24 D6
Amundsen Ct, E14
off Napier Av 163 EA78
Amwell Cl, Enf. EN2 82 DR43
Watford WD25
off Phillipers 76 BY35
Amwell Common, Welw.G.C.
AL7 30 DB10
Amwell Ct, Hodd. EN11 49 EA16
Waltham Abbey EN9 68 EF33
Amwell Ct Est, N4 122 DQ60
Amwell End, Ware SG12 33 DX06
Amwell Hill, Ware
(Gt Amwell) SG12 33 DZ08
Amwell La, Ware SG12 33 EA09
Amwell Pl, Hert. (Hert.Hth)
SG13 32 DW11
Amwell St, EC1 10 C1
Hoddesdon EN11 49 EA17
Sch Amwell Vw Sch, Ware
SG12 off Station Rd 33 EB11
Amyand Cotts, Twick. TW1
off Amyand Pk Rd 177 CH86
Amyand La, Twick. TW1
off Marble Hill Gdns 177 CH87
Amyand Pk Gdns, Twick. TW1
off Amyand Pk Rd 177 CH87
Amyand Pk Rd, Twick. TW1 177 CG87
Amy Cl, Wall. SM6
off Mollison Dr 219 DL108
Sch Amy Johnson Prim Sch,
Wall. SM6
off Mollison Dr 219 DL108
Amy La, Chesh. HP5 54 AP32
Amy Rd, Oxt. RH8 254 EE129
Amyruth Rd, SE4 183 EA85
Amy Warne Cl, E6
off Evelyn Denington Rd 144 EL70
Anatola Rd, N19
off Dartmouth Pk Hill 121 DH61
Ancaster Cres, N.Mal. KT3 199 CU100
Ancaster Ms, Beck. BR3 203 DX97
Ancaster Rd, Beck. BR3 203 DX97
Ancaster St, SE18 165 ES80
Anchorage Cl, SW19 180 DA92
Anchorage Pt, E14 23 N3
Anchorage Pt Ind Est, SE7 164 EJ76
Anchor & Hope La, SE7 25 P6
Anchor Bay Ind Est, Erith
DA8 167 FG79
Anchor Boul, Dart. DA2 168 FQ84
Anchor Cl, Bark. IG11 146 EV69
Waltham Cross (Chsht)
EN8 67 DX28
Anchor Dr, Rain. RM13 147 FH69
Anchor La, Hem.H. HP1 40 BH21
Anchor Ms, SW12
off Hazelbourne Rd 181 DH86
Anchor Retail Pk, E1 12 F4
Anchor St, SE16 22 C7
Anchor Ter, E1 12 F4
Anchor Wf, E3 off Watts Gro 143 EB71
Anchor Yd, EC1 11 H3
Ancill Cl, W6 159 CY79
Ancona Rd, NW10 139 CU68
SE18 165 ER78
Andace Pk Gdns, Brom.
BR1 204 EJ95
Andalus Rd, SW9 161 DL83
Ander Cl, Wem. HA0 117 CK63
Andermans, Wind. SL4 151 AK81
Anderson Cl, N21 81 DM43
W3 138 CR72
Epsom KT19 216 CP112
Guildford GU2
off Tylehost 242 AU130
Sutton SM3 200 DA102
Uxbridge (Hare.) UB9 92 BG53
Anderson Ct, Red. RH1
off Royal Earlswood Pk 266 DG137
Anderson Dr, Ashf. TW15 175 BQ91
Anderson Ho, Bark. IG11
off The Coverdales 145 ER68
Anderson Pl, Houns. TW3 156 CB84
Anderson Rd, E9 143 DX65
Radlett (Shenley) WD7 62 CN33
Weybridge KT13 195 BR104
Woodford Green IG8 124 EK55
Andersons Sq, N1 4 E8
Anderson St, SW3 18 C9
Anderson Way, Belv. DA17 167 FB75
Anderton Cl, SE5 162 DR83
Andmark Ct, Sthl. UB1
off Herbert Rd 136 BZ74
Andover Av, E16
off King George Av 144 EK72
Andover Cl, Epsom KT19 216 CR111
Feltham TW14 175 BT88
Greenford UB6
off Ruislip Rd 136 CB70
Uxbridge UB8 134 BH68
Andover Pl, NW6 140 DB68
Andover Rd, N7 121 DM61
Orpington BR6 205 ER102
Twickenham TW2 177 CD88
Andrea Av, Grays RM16 170 GA75
Andre St, E8 122 DU64
Andrew Borde St, WC2 9 M7
Andrew Cl, Dart. DA1 187 FD85
Ilford IG6 103 ER51
Radlett (Shenley) WD7 62 CM33
Andrewes Gdns, E6 144 EL72
Andrewes Ho, EC2 11 H6
Sch Andrew Ewing Junior,
Inf & Nurs Sch, Houns.
TW5 off Westbrook Rd 156 BZ80
Andrew Hill La, Slou. (Hedg.)
SL2 111 AQ61
Andrew Pl, SW8
off Cowthorpe Rd 161 DK81
Andrew Reed Ho, SW18
off Linstead Way 179 CY87
Andrews Cl, E6
off Linton Gdns 144 EL72
Buckhurst Hill IG9 102 EJ47
Epsom KT17 217 CT114
Harrow HA1
off Bessborough Rd 117 CD59
Hemel Hempstead HP2
off Church St 40 BK18
Orpington BR5 206 EX96
Worcester Park KT4 199 CX103
Andrews Crosse, WC2 10 C8
Andrewsfield, Welw.G.C.
AL7 30 DC09
Andrews La, Wal.Cr. (Chsht)
EN7 66 DU28
Sch Andrews La Prim Sch,
Wal.Cr. EN7
off Andrews La 66 DU28
Andrews Pl, SE9 185 EP86
Dartford DA2 187 FE89
Andrew's Rd, E8 142 DV67
Andrew St, E14 14 C7
Andrews Wk, SE17
off Dale Rd 161 DP79
Andwell Cl, SE2 166 EV75
Anelle Ri, Hem.H. HP3 40 BM24
ANERLEY, SE20 202 DV95
⇌ Anerley 182 DV94
Anerley Gro, SE19 182 DT94
Anerley Hill, SE19 182 DT93
Anerley Pk, SE20 182 DU94
Anerley Pk Rd, SE20 182 DV94
Anerley Rd, SE19 182 DU94
SE20 182 DU94
Sch Anerley Sch Spec
Opportunity Unit, SE20
off William Booth Rd 202 DU95
Anerley Sta Rd, SE20 202 DV95
Anerley St, SW11 160 DF82
Anerley Vale, SE19 182 DT94
Anfield Cl, SW12
off Belthorn Cres 181 DJ87
Angas Ct, Wey. KT13 213 BQ106
⊖ Angel 4 D9
Angel All, E1 11 P7
Angel Cl, N18 100 DT49
Angel Cor Par, N18
off Fore St 100 DU50
Angel Ct, EC2 11 K7
SW1 19 K2
Angel Ct, SW17 180 DF91
Angel Edmonton, N18
off Angel Rd 100 DU50
Angelfield, Houns. TW3 156 CB84
Angel Gate, EC1 10 F1
Guildford GU1
off High St 258 AX135
Angel Hill, Sutt. SM1
off Sutton Common Rd 200 DB104
Angel Hill Dr, Sutt. SM1 200 DB104
Angelica Cl, West Dr. UB7
off Lovibonds Av 134 BL72
Angelica Dr, E6 145 EN71
Angelica Gdns, Croy. CR0 203 DX102
Angelica Rd, Guil. GU2 242 AU130
Angelis Apartments, N1
off Graham St 141 DP68
Angel La, E15 143 ED65
Hayes UB3 135 BR71
Angell Pk Gdns, SW9 161 DN83
Angell Rd, SW9 161 DN83
Angell Town Est, SW9 161 DN82
Angel Ms, E1 12 D9
N1 4 D10
SW15
off Roehampton High St 179 CU87
Angel Pas, EC4 11 J10
Angel Pl, N18 100 DU50
SE1 21 J3
Reigate RH2
off Cockshot Hill 266 DB137
⇌ Angel Road 100 DW50
Angel Rd, N18 100 DV50
Harrow HA1 117 CE58
Thames Ditton KT7 197 CG101
Angel Rd Wks, N18 100 DW50
Angel Sq, EC1 4 D10
Angel St, EC1 10 G7
Angel Wk, W6 159 CW77
Angel Way, Rom. RM1 127 FE57
Angerstein La, SE3 164 EF80
Angle Cl, Uxb. UB10 134 BN67
Anglefield Rd, Berk. HP4 38 AU19
Angle Grn, Dag. RM8 126 EW60
Angle Pl, Berk. HP4 38 AU19
Angle Rd, Grays RM20 169 FX79
Anglers Cl, Rich. TW10
off Locksmeade Rd 177 CJ91
Angler's La, NW5 141 DH65
Anglers Reach, Surb. KT6 197 CK99
Anglesea Av, SE18 165 EP77
Anglesea Cen, Grav. DA11
off New Rd 191 GH86
Anglesea Ms, SE18
off Anglesea Av 165 EP77
Anglesea Pl, Grav. DA11
off Clive Rd 191 GH86
Anglesea Rd, SE18 165 EP77
Kingston upon Thames
KT1 197 CK98
Orpington BR5 206 EW100
Anglesea Ter, W6
off Wellesley Av 159 CV76
Anglesey Cl, Ashf. TW15 174 BN90
Anglesey Ct Rd, Cars. SM5 218 DG107
Anglesey Dr, Rain. RM13 147 FG70
Anglesey Gdns, Cars. SM5 218 DG107
Anglesey Rd, Enf. EN3 82 DV42
Watford WD19 94 BW50
Anglesmede Cres, Pnr. HA5 116 CA55
Anglesmede Way, Pnr. HA5 116 BZ55
Angles Rd, SW16 181 DL91
Anglia Cl, N17 off Park La 100 DV52
Anglia Ct, Dag. RM8
off Spring Cl 126 EX60
Anglia Ho, E14 13 K8
Anglian Cl, Wat. WD24 76 BW40
Anglian Rd, E11 123 ED62
Anglia Wk, E6 145 EM67
Anglo Rd, E3 143 DZ68
Anglo Way, Red. RH1 250 DG132
Angrave Ct, E8 5 P7
Angrave Pas, E8 5 P7
Angus Cl, Chess. KT9 216 CN106
Angus Dr, Ruis. HA4 116 BW63
Angus Gdns, NW9 96 CR53
Angus Home, Sev.
(Cudham) TN14
off Cudham La S 239 ER115
Angus Rd, E13 144 EJ69
Angus St, SE14 163 DY80
Anhalt Rd, SW11 160 DE80
Anisdowne Cl, Dor.
(Abin.Ham.) RH5 261 BT142
Ankerdine Cres, SE18 165 EN80
Ankerwycke Priory, Stai.
(Wrays.) TW19 173 AZ89
Anlaby Rd, Tedd. TW11 177 CE92
Anley Rd, W14 16 A4
Anmersh Gro, Stan. HA7 95 CK53
Annabel Cl, E14 14 A9
Anna Cl, E8 5 P7
Annalee Gdns, S.Ock.
RM15 149 FV71
Annalee Rd, S.Ock. RM15 149 FV71
Annandale Gro, Uxb. UB10
off Thorpland Av 115 BQ62
Annandale Rd, SE10 25 J10
W4 158 CS77
Croydon CR0 202 DU103
Guildford GU2 258 AV136
Sidcup DA15 185 ES87
Annan Dr, Cars. SM5 218 DG109
Anna Neagle Cl, E7
off Dames Rd 124 EG63
Annan Way, Rom. RM1 105 FD53
Anne Boleyn's Wk, Kings.T.
KT2 178 CL92
Sutton SM3 217 CX108
Anne Case Ms, N.Mal. KT3
off Sycamore Gro 198 CR97
Anne Compton Ms, SE12 184 EF87
Anne Heart Cl, Grays
(Chaff.Hun.) RM16 169 FX77
Anne of Cleves Rd, Dart.
DA1 188 FK85
Anners Cl, Egh. TW20 193 BC97
Annesley Av, NW9 118 CR55
Annesley Cl, NW10 118 CS62
Annesley Dr, Croy. CR0 203 DZ104
Annesley Rd, SE3 164 EH81
Annesley Wk, N19 121 DJ61
Anne St, E13 15 L3
Anne's Wk, Cat. CR3 236 DS120
Annett Cl, Shep. TW17 195 BS98
Annette Cl, Har. HA3
off Spencer Rd 95 CE54
Annette Cres, N1 5 H6
Annette Rd, N7 121 DM63

A B C D E F G H I J K L M N O P Q R S T U V W X Y Z

⊖ London Underground station DLR Docklands Light Railway station Tra Tramlink station Riv Pedestrian ferry landing stage

Annett Rd, Walt. KT12 195 BU101
Anne Way, Ilf. IG6 103 EQ51
West Molesey KT8 196 CB98
Annie Besant Cl, E3 143 DZ67
Annie Brooks Cl, Stai.
TW18 173 BD90
Annie Taylor Ho, E12
off Walton Rd 125 EN63
Annifer Way, S.Ock. RM15 149 FV71
Anning St, EC2 11 M3
Annington Rd, N2 120 DF55
Annis Rd, E9 143 DY65
Ann La, SW10 160 DD80
Ann Moss Way, SE16 22 E5
Ann's Cl, SW1 18 D4
Ann's Pl, E1 11 N6
Ann St, SE18 165 ER77
Annsworthy Av, Th.Hth. CR7
off Grange Pk Rd 202 DR97
Annsworthy Cres, SE25
off Grange Rd 202 DR96
Sch Annunciation Jun Sch, The, Edg. HA8
off The Meads 96 CR51
Sch Annunciation RC Inf Sch, The, Edg. HA8
off Thirleby Rd 96 CR53
Ansculf Rd, Slou. SL2 131 AN69
Ansdell Rd, SE15 162 DW82
Ansdell St, W8 17 K5
Ansdell Ter, W8 17 K5
Ansell Gro, Cars. SM5 200 DG102
Ansell Rd, SW17 180 DE90
Dorking RH4 263 CH135
Anselm Cl, Croy. CR0
off Park Hill Ri 202 DT104
Anselm Rd, SW6 160 DA79
Pinner HA5 94 BZ52
Ansford Rd, Brom. BR1 183 EC92
Ansleigh Pl, W11 6 B10
Ansley Cl, S.Croy. CR2 220 DV114
Anslow Gdns, Iver SL0 133 BD68
Anslow Pl, Slou. SL1 130 AJ71
Anson Cl, Hem.H. (Bov.)
HP3 57 AZ27
Kenley CR8 236 DR120
Romford RM7 105 FB54
St. Albans AL1 43 CH22
Anson Pl, SE28 165 ER75
Sch Anson Prim Sch, NW2
off Anson Rd 119 CX64
Anson Rd, N7 121 DJ63
NW2 119 CX64
Anson Ter, Nthlt. UB5 136 CB65
Anson Wk, Nthwd. HA6 93 BQ49
Anstead Dr, Rain. RM13 147 FG68
Anstey Rd, SE15 162 DU83
Anstey Wk, N15 121 DP56
Anstice Cl, W4 158 CS80
Anston Cl, Guil. GU2
off Southway 242 AS134
Anstridge Path, SE9 185 ER86
Anstridge Rd, SE9 185 ER86
Antelope Av, Grays RM16
off Hogg La 170 GA76
Antelope Rd, SE18 165 EM76
Anthony Cl, NW7 96 CS49
Sevenoaks (Dunt.Grn)
TN13 256 FE121
Watford WD19 94 BW46
★ Anthony d'Offay Gall,
W1 9 H8
Anthony La, Swan. BR8 207 FG95
Anthony Rd, SE25 202 DU100
Borehamwood WD6 78 CM40
Greenford UB6 137 CE68
Welling DA16 166 EU81
Sch Anthony Roper Prim Sch, Dart. DA4 off High St 208 FL103
Anthonys, Wok. GU21 211 BB112
Anthony St, E1 12 D7
Anthony Way, N18 101 DX51
Slough SL1 131 AK73
Anthorne Cl, Pot.B. EN6 64 DB31
Anthus Ms, Nthwd. HA6 93 BS52
Antigua Cl, SE19
off Salters Hill 182 DR92
Antigua Wk, SE19 182 DR92
Antill Rd, E3 13 J1
N15 122 DT56
Antill Ter, E1 12 G7
Antlands La, Horl. RH6 269 DK153
Antlands La E, Horl. RH6 269 DL153
Antlands La W, Horl. RH6 269 DL153
Antlers Hill, E4 83 EB43
Antoinette Ct, Abb.L. WD5
off Dairy Way 59 BT29
Anton Cres, Sutt. SM1 200 DA104
Antoneys Cl, Pnr. HA5 94 BX54
Antonine Gate, St.Alb. AL3 42 CA21
Anton Pl, Wem. HA9 118 CP62
Anton Rd, S.Ock. RM15 149 FV70
Anton St, E8 122 DU64
Antrim Gro, NW3 140 DF65
Antrim Mans, NW3 140 DE65
Antrim Rd, NW3 140 DF65
Antrobus Cl, Sutt. SM1 217 CZ106
Antrobus Rd, W4 158 CQ77
Anvil Cl, SW16 181 DJ94
Hemel Hempstead (Bov.)
HP3 off Yew Tree Dr 57 BB28
Anvil Cl, Slou. (Langley) SL3
off Blacksmith Row 153 BA77
Anvil La, Cob. KT11 213 BU114
Anvil Pl, St.Alb. AL2 60 CA26
Anvil Rd, Sun. TW16 195 BU97
Anvil Ter, Dart. DA2
off Pinewood Pl 187 FE89
Anworth Cl, Wdf.Grn. IG8 102 EH51
Anyards Rd, Cob. KT11 213 BV113
Apeldoorn Dr, Wall. SM6 219 DL109
Aperdele Rd, Lthd. KT22 231 CG118
APERFIELD, West. TN16 239 EM117
Aperfield Rd, Erith DA8 167 FF79
Westerham (Bigg.H.)
TN16 238 EL117
Apers Av, Wok. GU22 227 AZ121
Apex Cl, Beck. BR3 203 EB95
Apex Cor, NW7 96 CR49
Apex Ind Est, NW10
off Hythe Rd 139 CU69
Apex Retail Pk, Felt. TW13 176 BZ90
Apex Twr, N.Mal. KT3 198 CS97
Apley Rd, Reig. RH2 266 DA137
Aplin Way, Islw. TW7 157 CE81
Apollo Av, Brom. BR1
off Rodway Rd 204 EH95
Northwood HA6 93 BU50
Apollo Cl, Horn. RM12 127 FH61
★ Apollo Hammersmith,
W6 159 CW78
Apollo Pl, E11 124 EE62
SW10 160 DD80
Woking (St.John's) GU21
off Church Rd 226 AU119
★ Apollo Thea, W1 9 L9
★ Apollo Victoria Thea,
SW1 19 J6
Apollo Way, SE28
off Broadwater Rd 165 ER76
Hemel Hempstead HP2 40 BM18
Apostle Way, Th.Hth. CR7 201 DP96
Apothecary St, EC4 10 E8
Appach Rd, SW2 181 DN86
Apperlie Dr, Horl. RH6 269 DJ150
Apple Blossom Ct, SW8
off Pascal St 161 DK80
Appleby Cl, E4 101 EC51
N15 122 DR57
Twickenham TW2 177 CD89
Appleby Dr, Rom. RM3 106 FJ50
Appleby Gdns, Felt. TW14 175 BT88
Appleby Grn, Rom. RM3
off Appleby Dr 106 FJ50
Appleby Rd, E8 142 DU66
E16 15 K8
Appleby St, E2 5 N9
Waltham Cross (Chsht)
EN7 66 DT26
Apple Cotts, Hem.H. (Bov.)
HP3 57 BA27
Applecroft, Berk. HP4 38 AS17
St. Albans (Park St) AL2 60 CB28
Applecroft Rd, Welw.G.C.
AL8 29 CV09
Sch Applecroft Sch, Welw.G.C. AL8 off Applecroft Rd 29 CV10
Appledore Av, Bexh. DA7 167 FC81
Ruislip HA4 115 BV62
Appledore Cl, SW17 180 DF89
Bromley BR2 204 EF99
Edgware HA8 96 CN53
Romford RM3 106 FJ53
Appledore Cres, Sid. DA14 185 ES90
Appledore Way, NW7
off Tavistock Av 97 CX52
Appledown Ri, Couls. CR5 235 DJ115
Applefield, Amer. HP7 72 AW39
Appleford Cl, Hodd. EN11 49 DZ15
Appleford Rd, W10 6 D4
Apple Garth, Brent. TW8 157 CK77
Applegarth, Croy.
(New Adgtn) CR0 221 EB108
Esher (Clay.) KT10 215 CF106
Applegarth Dr, Dart. DA1 188 FL89
Ilford IG2 125 ET56
Applegarth Ho, Erith DA8 167 FF82
Sch Applegarth Inf Sch, Croy. CR0 off Bygrove 221 EB107
Sch Applegarth Jun Sch, Croy. CR0 off Bygrove 221 EB107
Applegarth Rd, SE28 146 EV74
W14 16 A6
Applegate, Brwd. CM14 108 FT43
Apple Gro, Chess. KT9 216 CL105
Enfield EN1 82 DS41
Apple Mkt, Kings.T. KT1
off Eden St 197 CK96
Apple Orchard, Swan. BR8 207 FD98
Apple Orchard, The, Hem.H.
HP2 off Highfield La 40 BM18
Apple Rd, E11 124 EE62
Appleshaw Cl, Grav. DA11 191 GG92
Appleton Cl, Amer. HP7 72 AV40
Bexleyheath DA7 167 FC82
Harlow CM19 51 EQ16
Appleton Dr, Dart. DA2 187 FH90
Appleton Gdns, N.Mal.
KT3 199 CU100
Appleton Rd, SE9 164 EL83
Loughton IG10 85 EP41
Appleton Sq, Mitch. CR4
off Silbury Av 200 DE95
Appleton Way, Horn. RM12 128 FK60
Appletree Av, Uxb. UB8 134 BM71
West Drayton UB7 134 BM71
Appletree Cl, SE20
off Jasmine Gro 202 DV95
Leatherhead KT22 230 CC124
Appletree Ct, Guil. GU4
off Old Merrow St 243 BD131
Appletree Gdns, Barn. EN4 80 DE42
Appletree La, Slou. SL3 152 AW76
Apple Tree Roundabout,
West Dr. UB7 134 BM73
Appletree Wk, Chesh. HP5
off Cresswell Rd 54 AR34
Watford WD25 59 BV34
Apple Tree Yd, SW1 19 K1
Applewood Cl, N20 98 DE46
NW2 119 CV62
Uxbridge (Ickhm) UB10 114 BL63
Applewood Dr, E13 15 N3
Appold St, EC2 11 L5
Erith DA8 167 FF79
Apprentice Way, E5
off Clarence Rd 122 DV63
Approach, The, NW4 119 CX57
W3 138 CR72
Enfield EN1 82 DV40
Orpington BR6 205 ET103
Potters Bar EN6 63 CZ32
Upminster RM14 128 FP62
Approach Cl, N16 5 L1
Approach Rd, E2 142 DW68
SW20 199 CW96
Ashford TW15 175 BQ93
Barnet EN4 80 DD42
Maidenhead (Taplow)
SL6 130 AE72
Purley CR8 219 DP112
St. Albans AL1 43 CE21
West Molesey KT8 196 CA99
Appspond La, St.Alb.
(Pott.Cr.) AL2 41 BV23
Aprey Gdns, NW4 119 CW56
April Cl, W7 137 CE73
Ashtead KT21 232 CM117
Feltham TW13 175 BU90
Orpington BR6
off Briarswood Way 223 ET106
April Glen, SE23 183 DX90
April St, E8 122 DT63
Aprilwood Cl, Add. (Wdhm)
KT15 211 BF111
Apsledene, Grav. DA12
off Miskin Way 191 GK93
APSLEY, Hem.H. HP3 58 BK25
⇌ Apsley 58 BL25
Apsley Cl, Har. HA2 116 CC57
Apsley Gra, Hem.H. HP3
off London Rd 58 BL25
★ Apsley Ho, Wellington
Mus, W1 18 E3
Apsley Mills Retail Pk,
Hem.H. HP3 40 BL24
Apsley Rd, SE25 202 DV98
New Malden KT3 198 CQ97
Apsley Way, NW2 119 CU61
W1 18 F3
Aquarius Business Pk, NW2 119 CU60
Aquarius Way, Nthwd. HA6 93 BU50
★ Aquatic Experience,
Brent. TW8 157 CH81
Aquila Cl, Lthd. KT22 232 CL121
Aquila St, NW8 140 DD68
Aquinas St, SE1 20 D2
Aquis Ct, St.Alb. AL3 42 CC20
Arabella Dr, SW15 158 CS84
Arabia Cl, E4 101 ED45
Arabin Rd, SE4 163 DY84
Araglen Av, S.Ock. RM15 149 FV71
Aragon Av, Epsom KT17 217 CV109
Thames Ditton KT7 197 CF99
Aragon Cl, Brom. BR2 205 EM102
Croydon (New Adgtn)
CR0 222 EE110
Enfield EN2 81 DM38
Hemel Hempstead HP2 41 BQ15
Loughton IG10 84 EL44
Romford RM5 105 FB51
Sunbury-on-Thames
TW16 175 BT94
Aragon Dr, Ilf. IG6 103 EQ52
Ruislip HA4 116 BX60
Sch Aragon Prim Sch, Mord. SM4 off Aragon Rd 199 CY101
Aragon Rd, Kings.T. KT2 178 CL92
Morden SM4 199 CX100
Aragon Twr, SE8 23 L8
Aragon Wk, W.Byf. (Byfleet)
KT14 212 BM113
Aragorn Ct, Guil. GU2
off South Rd 242 AV132
Aran Ct, Wey. KT13
off Mallards Reach 195 BR103
Arandora Cres, Rom. RM6 126 EV59
Aran Dr, Stan. HA7 95 CJ49
Aran Hts, Ch.St.G. HP8 90 AV49
Arbery Rd, E3 13 J1
Arbor Cl, Beck. BR3 203 EB96
Arbor Ct, N16
off Lordship Rd 122 DR61
Arborfield Cl, SW2 181 DM88
Slough SL1 152 AS76
Arbor Rd, E4 101 ED48
Arbour, The, Hert. SG13 32 DR11
Arbour Cl, Brwd. CM14 108 FW50
Leatherhead (Fetch.)
KT22 231 CF123
Arbour Rd, Enf. EN3 83 DX42
Arbour Sq, E1 12 G8
Sch Arbour Vale Sch, Slou. SL2 off Stoke Rd 132 AU72
Arbour Vw, Amer. HP7 72 AV39
Arbour Way, Horn. RM12 127 FH64
Arbroath Grn, Wat. WD19 93 BU48
Arbroath Rd, SE9 164 EL83
Arbrook Chase, Esher KT10 214 CC107
Arbrook Cl, Orp. BR5 206 EU97
Arbrook La, Esher KT10 214 CC107
Arbury Ter, SE26
off Oaksford Av 182 DV90
Arbuthnot La, Bex. DA5 186 EY86
Arbuthnot Rd, SE14 163 DX82
Arbutus Cl, Red. RH1 266 DC136
Arbutus Rd, Red. RH1 266 DC136
Arbutus St, E8 5 N7
Arcade, The, EC2 11 L6
Croydon CR0 off High St 202 DQ104
Hatfield AL10
off Kennelwood La 45 CV17
Romford RM3
off Farnham Rd 106 FK50
Arcade Pl, Rom. RM1 127 FE57
Arcadia Av, N3 98 DA53
Arcadia Caravans, Stai.
TW18 194 BH95
Arcadia Cl, Cars. SM5 218 DG105
Arcadian Av, Bex. DA5 186 EY86
Arcadian Cl, Bex. DA5 186 EY86
Arcadian Gdns, N22 99 DM52
Arcadian Pl, SW18
off Sutherland Gro 179 CZ87
Arcadian Rd, Bex. DA5 186 EY86
Arcadia Shop Cen, W5 137 CK73
Arcadia St, E14 13 P7
Arcany Rd, S.Ock. RM15 149 FV70
Archangel St, SE16 23 H4
Archates Av, Grays RM16 170 GA76
Sch Archbishop Lanfranc High Sch, The, Croy. CR0
off Mitcham Rd 201 DL100
Sch Archbishop Michael Ramsey Tech Coll, SE5
off Farmers Rd 162 DQ80
Archbishops Pl, SW2 181 DM86
Sch Archbishop Summers' C of E Prim Sch, SE11 20 D8
Sch Archbishop Tenison's CE Sch, Croy. CR0
off Selborne Rd 202 DT104
Sch Archbishop Tenison's Sch, SE11
off Kennington Oval 161 DM79
Archdale Pl, N.Mal. KT3 198 CP97
Archdale Rd, SE22 182 DT85
Sch Archdeacon Cambridge's C of E Prim Sch, Twick.
TW2 off The Green 177 CE89
Archel Rd, W14 159 CZ79
Archer Cl, Kings L. WD4 58 BM29
Kingston upon Thames
KT2 178 CL94
Archer Ho, SW11
off Vicarage Cres 160 DD81
Archer Ms, Hmptn.
(Hmptn H.) TW12
off Windmill Rd 176 CC93
Archer Rd, SE25 202 DV98
Orpington BR5 206 EU99
Archers, Harl. CM19 51 EP20
Archers Cl, Hert. SG14 32 DQ08
Archers Ct, S.Ock. RM15 149 FV71
Archers Dr, Enf. EN3 82 DW40
Archers Fld, St.Alb. AL1 43 CF18
ARCHERS GREEN, Welw.
AL6 30 DE08
Archer Sq, SE14
off Knoyle St 163 DY79
Archers Ride, Welw.G.C.
AL7 30 DB11
Archer St, W1 9 L9
Archer Ter, West Dr. UB7
off Yew Av 134 BL73
Archer Way, Swan. BR8 207 FF96
Archery Cl, W2 8 B8
Harrow HA3 117 CF55
H Archery Ho, Dart. DA2 188 FP86
Archery Rd, SE9 185 EM85
Arches, The, SW6
off Munster Rd 159 CZ82
WC2 19 P1
Harrow HA2 116 CB61
Archfield, Welw.G.C. AL7 29 CY06
Archibald Ms, W1 8 F10
Archibald Rd, N7 121 DK63
Romford RM3 106 FN53
Archibald St, E3 13 N2
Archie Cl, West Dr. UB7 154 BN75
Archie St, SE1 21 M4
Coll Architectural Assoc Sch of Architecture, WC1 9 M6
Arch Rd, Walt. KT12 196 BX104
Arch St, SE1 20 G6
⊖ Archway 121 DJ61
Archway, Rom. RM3 105 FH51
Uni Archway Campus, The, N19 off Highgate Hill 121 DJ61
Archway Cl, N19
off St. Johns Way 121 DJ61
SW19 180 DB91
W10 6 A6
Wallington SM6 201 DK104
Archway Mall, N19
off Magdala Av 121 DJ61
Archway Ms, SW15
off Putney Br Rd 159 CY84
Dorking RH4
off Chapel Ct 263 CG135
Archway Pl, Dor. RH4
off Chapel Ct 263 CG135
Archway Rd, N6 120 DF58
N19 121 DJ60
Archway St, SW13 158 CS83
Arcola St, E8 5 N1
Arctic St, NW5
off Gillies St 120 DG64
Arcus Rd, Brom. BR1 184 EE93
Ardbeg Rd, SE24 182 DR86
Arden Cl, SE28
off Redbourne Dr 146 EX72
Bushey (Bushey Hth)
WD23 95 CF45
Harrow HA1 117 CD62
Hemel Hempstead (Bov.)
HP3 57 BA28
Reigate RH2 266 DB138
Arden Ct Gdns, N2 120 DD58
Arden Cres, E14 23 P7
Dagenham RM9 146 EW66
Arden Est, N1 5 L10
Arden Gro, Orp. BR6 223 EP105
Arden Ho, SW9
off Grantham Rd 161 DL82
Arden Ms, E17 123 EB57
Arden Mhor, Pnr. HA5 115 BV56
Arden Rd, N3 119 CY55
W13 137 CJ73
Ardens Way, St.Alb. AL4 43 CK18
Ardent Cl, SE25 202 DS97
Ardesley Wd, Wey. KT13 213 BS105
Ardfern Av, SW16 201 DN97
Ardfillan Rd, SE6 183 ED88
Ardgowan Rd, SE6 184 EE87
Ardilaun Rd, N5 122 DQ63
Ardingly Cl, Croy. CR0 203 DX104
Ardleigh Cl, Horn. RM11 128 FK55
Ardleigh Ct, Brwd. (Shenf.)
CM15 109 FZ45
Ardleigh Gdns, Brwd. (Hutt.)
CM13 off Fairview Av 109 GE44
Sutton SM3 200 DA101
ARDLEIGH GREEN, Horn.
RM11 128 FJ56
Sch Ardleigh Grn Inf Sch, Horn. RM11
off Ardleigh Grn Rd 128 FK56
Sch Ardleigh Grn Jun Sch, Horn. RM11
off Ardleigh Grn Rd 128 FK56
Ardleigh Grn Rd, Horn.
RM11 128 FK57
Ardleigh Ho, Bark. IG11
off St. Ann's 145 EQ67
Ardleigh Ms, Ilf. IG1
off Bengal Rd 125 EP62
Ardleigh Rd, E17 101 DZ53
N1 5 K4
Ardleigh Ter, E17 101 DZ53
Ardley Cl, NW10 118 CS62
SE6 183 DY90
Ruislip HA4 115 BQ59
Ardley Cres, B.Stort.
(Hat.Hth) CM22 37 FH05
ARDLEY END, B.Stort.
CM22 37 FH06
Ardlui Rd, SE27 182 DQ89
Ardmay Gdns, Surb. KT6 198 CL99
Ardmere Rd, SE13 183 ED86
Ardmore Av, Guil. GU2 242 AV132
Ardmore La, Buck.H. IG9 102 EH45
Ardmore Pl, Buck.H. IG9 102 EH45
Ardmore Rd, S.Ock. RM15 149 FV70
Ardmore Way, Guil. GU2 242 AV132
Ardoch Rd, SE6 183 ED89
Ardra Rd, N9 101 DX48
Ardrossan Cl, Slou. SL2 131 AQ70
Ardrossan Gdns, Wor.Pk.
KT4 199 CU104
Ardross Av, Nthwd. HA6 93 BS50
Ardshiel Cl, SW15
off Bemish Rd 159 CX83
Ardshiel Dr, Red. RH1 266 DE136
Ardwell Av, Ilf. IG6 125 EQ57
Ardwell Rd, SW2 181 DL89
Ardwick Rd, NW2 120 DA63
Arena 202 DW99
Arena, The, Enf. EN3 83 DZ38
Arewater Grn, Loug. IG10 85 EM39
Argali Ho, Erith DA18
off Kale Rd 166 EY76
Argall Av, E10 123 DX59
Argall Way, E10 123 DX60
Argenta Way, NW10 138 CP66
Argent Cl, Egh. TW20
off Holbrook Meadow 173 BC93
Argent St, Grays RM17 170 FY79
Argent Way, Wal.Cr. (Chsht)
EN7 66 DR26
Argles Cl, Green. DA9
off Cowley Av 189 FU85
Argon Ms, SW6 160 DA80
Argon Rd, N18 100 DW50
Argosy Gdns, Stai. TW18 173 BF93
Argosy La, Stai. (Stanw.)
TW19 174 BK87
Argus Cl, Rom. RM7 105 FB53
Argus Way, Nthlt. UB5 136 BY69
Argyle Av, Houns. TW3 176 CA86
Argyle Cl, W13 137 CG70
Argyle Gdns, Upmin. RM14 129 FR61
Argyle Pas, N17 100 DT53
Argyle Pl, W6 159 CV77
Sch Argyle Prim Sch, WC1 9 N1
Argyle Rd, E1 12 G3
E15 124 EE63
E16 144 EJ72
N12 98 DA50
N17 100 DU53
N18 100 DU49
W13 137 CG71
Barnet EN5 79 CW42
Greenford UB6 137 CF69
Harrow HA2 116 CB58
Hounslow TW3 176 CB85
Ilford IG1 125 EN61
Sevenoaks TN13 257 FH125
Teddington TW11 177 CE92
Argyle Sq, WC1 9 P1
Argyle St, WC1 9 N1
Argyle Wk, WC1 9 P2
Argyle Way, SE16 22 B10
Argyll Av, Slou. SL1 131 AN73
Southall UB1 136 CB74
Argyll Cl, SW9
off Dalyell Rd 161 DM83
Argyll Gdns, Edg. HA8 96 CP54
Argyll Rd, SE18 165 EQ76
W8 16 G4
Grays RM17 170 GA78
Hemel Hempstead HP2 40 BL15
Argyll St, W1 9 J8
Arica Rd, SE4 163 DY84
Ariel Cl, Grav. DA12 191 GM91
Ariel Rd, NW6 140 DA65
Ariel Way, W12 139 CW74
Hounslow TW4 155 BV83
Arisdale Av, S.Ock. RM15 149 FV71
Aristotle Rd, SW4 161 DK83
Ark Av, Grays RM16 170 GA76
Arkell Gro, SE19 181 DP94
Arkindale Rd, SE6 183 EC90
Arklay Cl, Uxb. UB8
off Royal La 134 BM70
ARKLEY, Barn. EN5 79 CU43
Arkley Ct, Hem.H. HP2
off Arkley Rd 41 BP15
Arkley Cres, E17 123 DZ57
Arkley Dr, Barn. EN5 79 CU42
Arkley La, Barn. EN5 79 CU41
Arkley Pk, Barn. EN5 78 CR44
Arkley Rd, E17 123 DZ57
Hemel Hempstead HP2 41 BP15
Arkley Vw, Barn. EN5 79 CV42
Arklow Ct, Rick. (Chorl.) WD3
off Station App 73 BC42
Arklow Ms, Surb. KT6
off Vale Rd S 198 CL103
Arklow Rd, SE14 163 DZ79
Arkwright Rd, NW3 120 DC64
Slough (Colnbr.) SL3 153 BE82
South Croydon CR2 220 DT110
Tilbury RM18 171 GG82
Arkwrights, Harl. CM20 35 ET14
Arlesey Cl, SW15
off Lytton Gro 179 CY86
Arlesford Rd, SW9 161 DL83
Arlingford Rd, SW2 181 DN85
Arlingham Ms, Wal.Abb.
EN9 off Sun St 67 EC33
Arlington, N12 98 DA48
Arlington Av, N1 5 H8
Arlington Cl, SE13 183 ED86
Sidcup DA15 185 ES87
Sutton SM1 200 DA103
Twickenham TW1 177 CJ86
Arlington Ct, Hayes UB3
off Shepiston La 155 BR78
Reigate RH2
off Oakfield Dr 250 DB132
Arlington Cres, Wal.Cr. EN8 67 DY34
Arlington Dr, Cars. SM5 200 DF103
Ruislip HA4 115 BR58
Arlington Gdns, W4 158 CQ78
Ilford IG1 125 EN60
Romford RM3 106 FL53
Arlington Grn, NW7 97 CX52
Arlington Lo, SW2 161 DM84
Weybridge KT13 213 BP105
Arlington Ms, Twick. TW1
off Arlington Rd 177 CJ86
Arlington Pl, SE10
off Greenwich S St 163 EC80
Arlington Rd, N14 99 DH47
NW1 141 DH67
W13 137 CH72
Ashford TW15 174 BM92
Richmond TW10 177 CK89
Surbiton KT6 197 CK100
Teddington TW11 177 CF91
Twickenham TW1 177 CJ86
Woodford Green IG8 102 EG53
Arlington Sq, N1 5 H8
Arlington St, SW1 19 J1
Arlington Way, EC1 10 D1
Arliss Way, Nthlt. UB5 136 BW67
Arlow Rd, N21 99 DN46
Armada Ct, SE8
off Watergate St 163 EA79
Grays RM16 off Hogg La 170 GA76
Armadale Cl, N17 122 DV56
Armadale Rd, SW6 160 DA80
Feltham TW14 175 BU85
Woking GU21 226 AU117
Armada Way, E6 145 EP71
Armagh Rd, E3 143 DZ67
Armand Cl, Wat. WD17 75 BT38
Armfield Cl, W.Mol. KT8 196 BZ99
Armfield Cres, Mitch. CR4 200 DF96
Armfield Rd, Enf. EN2 82 DR39
Arminger Rd, W12 139 CV74
Armistice Gdns, SE25
off Penge Rd 202 DU97
Armitage Cl, Rick. (Loud.)
WD3 74 BK42
Armitage Rd, NW11 119 CZ60
SE10 25 J9
Armor Rd, Purf. RM19 169 FR77
Armour Cl, N7 4 A4
Armoury Dr, Grav. DA12 191 GJ87
Armoury Rd, SE8 163 EB82
Armoury Way, SW18 180 DA85
Armstead Wk, Dag. RM10 146 FA66
Armstrong Av, Wdf.Grn.
IG8 102 EE51
Armstrong Cl, E6
off Porter Rd 145 EM72
Borehamwood WD6 78 CQ41
Dagenham RM8
off Palmer Rd 126 EX60
Pinner HA5 115 BU58
St. Albans (Lon.Col.) AL2
off Willowside 62 CL27
Sevenoaks (Halst.)
TN14 241 FB115
Walton-on-Thames KT12
off Sunbury La 195 BU100
Armstrong Cres, Barn. EN4 80 DD41

★ Place of interest H Hospital Sch School Coll College Uni University ⇌ Railway station

Armstrong Gdns, Rad. (Shenley) WD7 62 CL32
Armstrong Pl, Hem.H. HP1 off High St 40 BK19
Armstrong Rd, SE18 165 EQ76
SW7 17 N6
W3 139 CT74
Egham (Eng.Grn) TW20 172 AW93
Feltham TW13 176 BY92
Armstrong Way, Sthl. UB2 156 CB75
Armytage Rd, Houns. TW5 156 BX80
Arnal Cres, SW18 179 CY87
Arncliffe Cl, N11 off Kettlewell Cl 98 DG51
Arncroft Ct, Bark. IG11 off Renwick Rd 146 EV69
Arndale Wk, SW18 off Garratt La 180 DB85
Arndale Way, Egh. TW20 off Church Rd 173 BA92
Arne Gro, Horl. RH6 268 DE146
Orpington BR6 205 ET104
Arne St, WC2 9 P8
Arnett Cl, Rick. WD3 74 BG44
Arnett Hills JMI Sch, Rick. WD3 off Berry La 74 BG44
Arnett Sq, E4 101 DZ51
Arnett Way, Rick. WD3 74 BG44
Arne Wk, SE3 164 EF84
Arneways Av, Rom. RM6 126 EX55
Arneway St, SW1 19 M6
Arnewood Cl, SW15 179 CU88
Leatherhead (Oxshott) KT22 214 CB113
Arney's La, Mitch. CR4 200 DG100
Arngask Rd, SE6 183 ED87
Arnhem Av, S.Ock. (Aveley) RM15 148 FQ74
Arnhem Dr, Croy. (New Adgtn) CR0 221 ED111
Arnhem Pl, E14 23 N6
Arnhem Way, SE22 off East Dulwich Gro 182 DS85
Arnhem Wf, E14 off Arnhem Pl 163 EA76
Arnhem Wf Prim Sch, E14 23 N6
Arnison Rd, E.Mol. KT8 197 CD98
Arnold Av E, Enf. EN3 83 EA38
Arnold Av W, Enf. EN3 83 DZ38
Arnold Circ, E2 11 N2
Arnold Cl, Har. HA3 118 CM59
Arnold Cres, Islw. TW7 177 CD85
Arnold Dr, Chess. KT9 215 CK107
Arnold Est, SE1 21 P4
Arnold Gdns, N13 99 DP50
Arnold Ho Sch, NW8 off Loudoun Rd 140 DD68
Arnold Pl, Til. RM18 171 GJ81
Arnold Rd, E3 13 N1
N15 122 DT55
SW17 180 DF94
Dagenham RM9, RM10 146 EZ66
Gravesend DA12 191 GJ89
Northolt UB5 136 BX65
Staines TW18 174 BJ94
Waltham Abbey EN9 83 EC35
Woking GU21 227 BB116
Arnolds Av, Brwd. (Hutt.) CM13 109 GC43
Arnolds Cl, Brwd. (Hutt.) CM13 109 GC43
Arnolds Fm La, Brwd. (Mtnsg) CM13 109 GE41
Arnolds La, Dart. (Sutt.H.) DA4 188 FM93
⊖ Arnos Grove 99 DJ49
Arnos Gro, N14 99 DK49
Arnos Rd, N11 99 DJ50
Arnott Cl, SE28 off Applegarth Rd 146 EW73
W4 off Fishers La 158 CR77
Arnould Av, SE5 162 DR84
Arnsberg Way, Bexh. DA7 166 FA84
Arnside Gdns, Wem. HA9 117 CK60
Arnside Rd, Bexh. DA7 166 FA81
Arnside St, SE17 162 DQ79
Arnulf St, SE6 183 EB91
Arnulls Rd, SW16 181 DN93
Arodene Rd, SW2 181 DM86
Arosa Rd, Twick. TW1 177 CK86
Arpley Sq, SE20 off High St 182 DW94
Arragon Gdns, SW16 181 DL94
West Wickham BR4 203 EB104
Arragon Rd, E6 144 EK67
SW18 180 DB88
Twickenham TW1 177 CG87
Arran Cl, Erith DA8 167 FD79
Hemel Hempstead HP3 41 BP22
Wallington SM6 219 DH105
Arran Dr, E12 124 EK60
Arran Grn, Wat. WD19 off Prestwick Rd 94 BW46
Arran Ms, W5 138 CM74
Arranmore Ct, Bushey WD23 off Bushey Hall Rd 76 BY42
Arran Rd, SE6 183 EB89
Arran Wk, N1 4 G5
Arran Way, Esher KT10 196 CB103
Arras Av, Mord. SM4 200 DC99
Arretine Cl, St.Alb. AL3 42 BZ22
Arreton Mead, Wok. (Horsell) GU21 210 AY114
Arrol Rd, Beck. BR3 202 DW97
Arrow Rd, E3 14 A1
Arrowscout Wk, Nthlt. UB5 off Argus Way 136 BY69
Arrowsmith Cl, Chig. IG7 103 ET50
Arrowsmith Path, Chig. IG7 103 ET50
Arrowsmith Rd, Chig. IG7 103 ES50
Loughton IG10 84 EL41
⊖ Arsenal 121 DN62
★ Arsenal FC, N5 121 DP62
Arsenal Rd, SE9 165 EM82
Arsenal Way, SE18 165 EQ76
Artemis Cl, Grav. DA12 191 GL87
Arterberry Rd, SW20 179 CW94
Arterial Av, Rain. RM13 147 FH70
Arterial Rd N Stifford, Grays RM17 170 FY75
Arterial Rd Purfleet, Purf. RM19 168 FN76
Arterial Rd W Thurrock, Grays RM16, RM20 169 FU76
Artesian Cl, NW10 138 CR66
Hornchurch RM11 127 FF58
Artesian Gro, Barn. EN5 80 DC42
Artesian Rd, W2 6 G8
Artesian Wk, E11 124 EE62
Arthingworth St, E15 144 EE67
Arthur Ct, W2 7 J7
Arthurdon Rd, SE4 183 EA85
Arthur Gro, SE18 165 EQ77
Arthur Henderson Ho, SW6 159 CZ82
Arthur Horsley Wk, E7 off Magpie Cl 124 EF64
★ Arthur Jacob Nature Reserve, Slou. SL3 153 BC83
Arthur Rd, E6 145 EM68
N7 121 DM63
N9 100 DT47
SW19 180 DA90
Kingston upon Thames KT2 178 CN94
New Malden KT3 199 CV99
Romford RM6 126 EW59
St. Albans AL1 43 CH20
Slough SL1 151 AR75
Westerham (Bigg.H.) TN16 238 EJ115
Windsor SL4 151 AP81
Arthur's Br Rd, Wok. GU21 226 AW117
Arthur St, EC4 11 K10
Bushey WD23 76 BX42
Erith DA8 167 FF80
Gravesend DA11 191 GG87
Grays RM17 170 GC79
Arthur St W, Grav. DA11 191 GG87
Arthur Toft Ho, Grays RM17 off New Rd 170 GB79
Arthur Walls Ho, E12 off Grantham Rd 125 EN62
Artichoke Dell, Rick. (Chorl.) WD3 73 BE43
Artichoke Hill, E1 12 C10
Artichoke Pl, SE5 off Camberwell Ch St 162 DR81
Artillery Cl, Ilf. IG2 off Horns Rd 125 EQ58
Artillery La, E1 11 M6
W12 139 CU72
Artillery Pas, E1 11 M6
Artillery Pl, SE18 165 EM78
SW1 19 L6
Harrow HA3 off Chicheley Rd 94 CC52
Artillery Rd, Guil. GU1 258 AX135
Artillery Row, SW1 19 L6
Gravesend DA12 191 GJ87
Artillery Ter, Guil. GU1 242 AX134
ARTINGTON, Guil. GU3 258 AW139
Artington Cl, Orp. BR6 223 EQ105
Artington Wk, Guil. GU2 258 AW137
Artisan Cl, E6 off Ferndale St 145 EP72
Artisan Cres, St.Alb. AL3 42 CC19
Artizan St, E1 11 M7
Arts Ed Sch London, The, W4 off Bath Rd 158 CS77
Arundel Av, Epsom KT17 217 CV110
Morden SM4 199 CZ98
South Croydon CR2 220 DU110
Arundel Cl, E15 124 EE63
SW11 off Chivalry Rd 180 DE85
Bexley DA5 186 EZ86
Croydon CR0 201 DP104
Hampton (Hmptn H.) TW12 176 CB92
Hemel Hempstead HP2 41 BP19
Waltham Cross (Chsht) EN8 66 DW29
Arundel Ct, N12 98 DE51
Harrow HA2 116 CA63
Slough SL3 152 AX77
Arundel Dr, Borwd. WD6 78 CQ43
Harrow HA2 116 BZ63
Orpington BR6 224 EV106
Woodford Green IG8 102 EG52
Arundel Gdns, N21 99 DN46
W11 6 E9
Edgware HA8 96 CR52
Ilford IG3 126 EU61
Arundel Gt Ct, WC2 10 B9
Arundel Gro, N16 5 L1
St. Albans AL3 43 CD15
Arundel Pl, N1 4 C4
Arundel Rd, Abb.L. WD5 59 BU32
Barnet EN4 80 DE41
Croydon CR0 202 DR100
Dartford DA1 168 FJ84
Dorking RH4 263 CG136
Hounslow TW4 156 BW83
Kingston upon Thames KT1 198 CP96
Romford RM3 106 FM53
Sutton SM2 217 CZ108
Uxbridge UB8 134 BH68
Arundel Sq, N7 4 C4
Arundel St, WC2 10 B9
Arundel Ter, SW13 159 CV79
Arvon Rd, N5 4 D1
Asbaston Ter, Ilf. IG1 off Buttsbury Rd 125 EQ64
Ascalon St, SW8 161 DJ80
Ascension Rd, Rom. RM5 105 FC51
Ascent Pk, Harl. CM20 off Edinburgh Way 36 EU11
Ascham Dr, E4 off Rushcroft Rd 101 EB52
Ascham End, E17 101 DY53
Ascham St, NW5 121 DJ64
Aschurch Rd, Croy. CR0 202 DT101
Ascot Cl, Borwd. (Elstree) WD6 78 CN43
Ilford IG6 103 ES51
Northolt UB5 116 CA64
Ascot Gdns, Enf. EN3 82 DW37
Hornchurch RM12 128 FL63
Southall UB1 136 BZ71
Ascot Ms, Wall. SM6 219 DJ109
Ascot Rd, E6 145 EM69
N15 122 DR57
N18 100 DU49
SW17 180 DG93
Feltham TW14 174 BN88
Gravesend DA12 191 GH90
Orpington BR5 205 ET98
Watford WD18 75 BS43
Ascots La, Welw.G.C. AL7 29 CY14
Ascott Av, W5 158 CL75
Ashanti Ms, E8 off Lower Clapton Rd 122 DV64
Ashbeam Cl, Brwd. CM13 off Canterbury Way 107 FW51
Ashbourne, St.Alb. AL2 60 BZ31
Ashbourne Av, E18 124 EH56
N20 98 DF47
NW11 119 CZ57
Bexleyheath DA7 166 EY80
Harrow HA2 117 CD61
Ashbourne Cl, N12 98 DB49
W5 138 CN71
Coulsdon CR5 235 DJ118
Ashbourne Ct, E5 off Daubeney Rd 123 DY63
Ashbourne Gro, NW7 96 CR50
SE22 182 DT85
W4 158 CS78
Ashbourne Indep 6th Form Coll, W8 17 J3
Ashbourne Par, W5 off Ashbourne Rd 138 CM70
Ashbourne Ri, Orp. BR6 223 ER105
Ashbourne Rd, W5 138 CM71
Broxbourne EN10 49 DZ21
Mitcham CR4 180 DG93
Romford RM3 106 FJ49
Ashbourne Sq, Nthwd. HA6 93 BS51
Ashbourne Ter, SW19 180 DA94
Ashbourne Way, NW11 off Ashbourne Av 119 CZ57
Ashbridge Rd, E11 124 EF59
Ashbridge St, NW8 8 A4
Ashbrook Rd, N19 121 DK60
Dagenham RM10 127 FB62
Windsor (Old Wind.) SL4 172 AV87
Ashburn Gdns, SW7 17 L7
Ashburnham Av, Har. HA1 117 CF58
Ashburnham Cl, N2 120 DD55
Sevenoaks TN13 off Fiennes Way 257 FJ127
Watford WD19 off Ashburnham Dr 93 BU48
Ashburnham Dr, Wat. WD19 93 BU48
Ashburnham Gdns, Har. HA1 117 CF58
Upminster RM14 128 FP60
Ashburnham Gro, SE10 163 EB80
Ashburnham Pk, Esher KT10 214 CC105
Ashburnham Pl, SE10 163 EB80
Ashburnham Prim Sch, SW10 off Blantyre St 160 DD80
Ashburnham Retreat, SE10 163 EB80
Ashburnham Rd, NW10 139 CW69
SW10 160 DC80
Belvedere DA17 167 FC77
Richmond TW10 177 CH90
Ashburn Pl, SW7 17 L7
Ashburton Av, Croy. CR0 202 DV102
Ilford IG3 125 ES63
Ashburton Cl, Croy. CR0 202 DU102
Ashburton Ct, Pnr. HA5 116 BX55
Ashburton Gdns, Croy. CR0 202 DU103
Ashburton High Sch, Croy. CR0 off Shirley Rd 202 DV101
Ashburton Jun & Inf Sch, Croy. CR0 off Long La 202 DV100
Ashburton Rd, E16 15 M7
Croydon CR0 202 DU102
Ruislip HA4 115 BU61
Ashburton Ter, E13 off Grasmere Rd 144 EG68
Ashbury Cl, Hat. AL10 44 CS18
Ashbury Cres, Guil. GU4 243 BC132
Ashbury Dr, Uxb. UB10 115 BP61
Ashbury Gdns, Rom. RM6 126 EX57
Ashbury Pl, SW19 180 DC93
Ashbury Rd, SW11 160 DF83
Ashby Av, Chess. KT9 216 CN107
Ashby Cl, Horn. RM11 off Holme Rd 128 FN60
Ashby Gdns, St.Alb. AL1 43 CD24
Ashby Gro, N1 5 H5
Ashby Ms, SE4 163 DZ82
SW2 off Prague Pl 181 DL85
Ashby Rd, N15 122 DU57
SE4 163 DZ82
Watford WD24 75 BU38
Ashby St, EC1 10 F2
Ashby Wk, Croy. CR0 202 DQ100
Ashby Way, West Dr. UB7 154 BN80
Ashchurch Gro, W12 159 CU75
Ashchurch Pk Vil, W12 159 CU76
Ashchurch Ter, W12 159 CU76
Ash Cl, SE20 202 DW96
Abbots Langley WD5 59 BR32
Brentwood (Pilg.Hat.) CM15 108 FT43
Carshalton SM5 200 DF103
Edgware HA8 96 CQ49
Hatfield AL9 64 DA25
New Malden KT3 198 CR96
Orpington BR5 205 ER99
Redhill RH1 251 DJ130
Romford RM5 105 FB52
Sidcup DA14 186 EV90
Slough SL3 153 BB76
Stanmore HA7 95 CG51
Swanley BR8 207 FC96
Uxbridge (Hare.) UB9 92 BK53
Watford WD25 75 BV35
Woking GU22 226 AY120
Woking (Pyrford) GU22 228 BG115
Ashcombe, Welw.G.C. AL8 29 CY05
Ashcombe Av, Surb. KT6 197 CK101
Ashcombe Gdns, Edg. HA8 96 CN49
Ashcombe Ho, Enf. EN3 83 DX41
Ashcombe Pk, NW2 118 CS62
Ashcombe Rd, SW19 180 DA92
Carshalton SM5 218 DG107
Dorking RH4 247 CG134
Redhill RH1 251 DJ127
Ashcombe Sch, The, Dor. RH4 off Ashcombe Rd 247 CH134
Ashcombe Sq, N.Mal. KT3 198 CQ97
Ashcombe St, SW6 160 DB82
Ashcombe Ter, Tad. KT20 233 CV120
Ash Copse, St.Alb. (Brick.Wd) AL2 60 BZ31
Ash Ct, Epsom KT19 216 CQ105
Ashcroft, Guil. (Shalf.) GU4 258 AY141
Pinner HA5 94 CA51
Ashcroft Av, Sid. DA15 186 EU86
Ashcroft Ct, N20 off Oakleigh Rd N 98 DD47
Broxbourne EN10 off Winford Dr 49 DZ22
Slough (Burn.) SL1 130 AH68
Ashcroft Cres, Sid. DA15 186 EU86
Ashcroft Dr, Uxb. (Denh.) UB9 113 BF58
Ashcroft Pk, Cob. KT11 214 BY112
Ashcroft Ri, Couls. CR5 235 DL116
Ashcroft Rd, E3 13 K1
Chessington KT9 198 CM104
Ashcroft Sq, W6 off King St 159 CW77
Ashdale, Lthd. (Bkhm) KT23 246 CC126
Ashdale Cl, Stai. TW19 174 BL89
Twickenham TW2 176 CC87
Ashdale Gro, Stan. HA7 95 CF51
Ashdale Rd, SE12 184 EH88
Ashdales, St.Alb. AL1 43 CD24
Ashdale Way, Twick. TW2 off Ashdale Cl 176 CC87
Ashdene, SE15 162 DV81
Pinner HA5 116 BW55
Ashdene Cl, Ashf. TW15 175 BQ94
Ashdon Cl, Brwd. (Hutt.) CM13 off Poplar Dr 109 GC44
Ashdon Cl, S. Ock. RM15 off Afton Dr 149 FV72
Woodford Green IG8 102 EH51
Ashdon Rd, NW10 138 CS67
Bushey WD23 76 BX41
Ashdown Cl, Beck. BR3 203 EB96
Bexley DA5 187 FC87
Reigate RH2 266 DB138
Ashdown Cres, NW5 off Queen's Cres 120 DG64
Waltham Cross (Chsht) EN8 67 DY28
Ashdown Dr, Borwd. WD6 78 CM40
Ashdown Est, E11 off High Rd Leytonstone 124 EE63
Ashdown Gdns, S.Croy. CR2 236 DV115
Ashdown Pl, T.Ditt. KT7 197 CG101
Ashdown Rd, Enf. EN3 82 DW41
Epsom KT17 217 CT113
Kingston upon Thames KT1 198 CL96
Reigate RH2 266 DB138
Uxbridge UB10 134 BN68
Ashdown Wk, E14 23 P7
Romford RM7 105 FB54
Ashdown Way, SW17 180 DG89
Amersham HP6 55 AR37
Ash Dr, Hat. AL10 45 CU21
Redhill RH1 267 DH136
Ashen, E6 off Downings 145 EN72
Ashen Cross, Slou. SL3 133 BB71
Ashendene Rd, Hert. (Bayford) SG13 47 DL20
Ashenden Rd, E5 123 DX64
Guildford GU2 258 AT135
Ashenden Wk, Slou. (Farn.Com.) SL2 111 AR63
Ashen Dr, Dart. DA1 187 FG86
Ashen Gro, SW19 180 DA90
Ashentree Ct, EC4 10 D8
Ashen Vale, S.Croy. CR2 221 DX109
Asheridge Rd, Chesh. HP5 54 AM28
Asher Loftus Way, N11 98 DF51
Asher Way, E1 22 B1
Ashfield Av, Bushey WD23 76 CB44
Feltham TW13 175 BV88
Ashfield Cl, Beck. BR3 183 EA94
Richmond TW10 178 CL88
Ashfield Jun Sch, Bushey WD23 off School La 94 CB45
Ashfield La, Chis. BR7 185 EQ93
Ashfield Par, N14 99 DK46
Ashfield Rd, N4 122 DQ58
N14 99 DJ48
W3 139 CT74
Chesham HP5 54 AR29
Ashfields, Loug. IG10 85 EM40
Reigate RH2 250 DB132
Watford WD25 75 BT35
Ashfield St, E1 12 C6
Ashfield Yd, E1 12 E6
ASHFORD, TW15 174 BM92
⇌ Ashford 174 BL91
Ashford Av, N8 121 DL56
Ashford TW15 175 BP93
Brentwood CM14 108 FV48
Hayes UB4 136 BX72
Ashford Cl, E17 123 DZ58
Ashford TW15 174 BL91
Ashford C of E Prim Sch, Ashf. TW15 off School Rd 175 BP93
Ashford Cres, Ashf. TW15 174 BL90
Enfield EN3 82 DW40
Ashford Gdns, Cob. KT11 230 BX116
Ashford Grn, Wat. WD19 94 BX50
Ashford High Sch, The, Ashf. TW15 off Stanwell Rd 174 BL90
H Ashford Hosp, Ashf. TW15 174 BL89
Ashford Ind Est, Ashf. TW15 175 BQ91
Ashford La, Maid. SL6 150 AG75
Windsor (Dorney) SL4 150 AH75
Ashford Ms, N17 off Vicarage Rd 100 DU53
Ashford Pk Prim Sch, Ashf. TW15 off Station Cres 174 BK91
Ashford Rd, E6 145 EN65
E18 102 EH54
NW2 119 CX63
Ashford TW15 175 BQ94
Feltham TW13 175 BT90
Iver SL0 133 BC66
Staines TW18 194 BK95
Ashford St, N1 11 L1
Ash Grn, Uxb. (Denh.) UB9 134 BH65
Ash Gro, E8 142 DV67
N13 100 DQ48
NW2 119 CX63
SE20 202 DW96
W5 158 CL75
Amersham HP6 55 AN36
Enfield EN1 100 DS45
Feltham TW14 175 BS88
Guildford GU2 242 AU134
Hayes UB3 135 BR73
Hemel Hempstead HP3 40 BM24
Hounslow TW5 156 BX81
Slough (Stoke P.) SL2 132 AT66
Southall UB1 136 CA71
Staines TW18 174 BJ93
Uxbridge (Hare.) UB9 92 BK53
Wembley HA0 117 CG63
West Drayton UB7 134 BM73
West Wickham BR4 203 EC103
Ashgrove Rd, Ashf. TW15 175 BQ92
Bromley BR1 183 ED93
Ilford IG3 125 ET60
Sevenoaks TN13 256 FG127
Ash Gros, Saw. CM21 36 FA05
Ashgrove Sch, Brom. BR1 off Widmore Rd 204 EH96
Ash Hill Cl, Bushey WD23 94 CB46
Ash Hill Dr, Pnr. HA5 116 BW55
Ash Ind Est, Harl. CM19 off Flex Meadow 51 EM16
Ashingdon Cl, E4 101 EC48
Ashington Rd, SW6 159 CZ82
Ash Island, E.Mol. KT8 197 CD97
Ashlake Rd, SW16 181 DL91
Ashland Pl, W1 8 E5
Ash La, Horn. RM11 off Southend Arterial Rd 128 FN56
Romford RM1 105 FG51
Windsor SL4 151 AK82
Ashlar Pl, SE18 off Masons Hill 165 EP77
Ashlea Rd, Ger.Cr. (Chal.St.P.) SL9 90 AX54
Ashleigh Av, Egh. TW20 173 BC94
Ashleigh Cl, Amer. HP7 55 AS39
Horley RH6 268 DF148
Ashleigh Cotts, Dor. RH5 263 CH144
Ashleigh Ct, Wal.Abb. EN9 off Lamplighters Cl 68 EG34
Ashleigh Gdns, Sutt. SM1 200 DB103
Upminster RM14 129 FR62
Ashleigh Pt, SE23 off Dacres Rd 183 DX90
Ashleigh Rd, SE20 202 DV97
SW14 158 CS83
Ashley Av, Epsom KT18 216 CR113
Ilford IG6 103 EP54
Morden SM4 200 DA99
Ashley Cen, Epsom KT18 216 CR113
Ashley Cl, NW4 97 CW54
Hemel Hempstead HP3 40 BM22
Leatherhead (Bkhm) KT23 246 BZ125
Pinner HA5 93 BV54
Sevenoaks TN13 257 FH124
Walton-on-Thames KT12 195 BT102
Welwyn Garden City AL8 29 CW07
Ashley C of E (Aided) Prim Sch, Walt. KT12 off Ashley Rd 195 BU102
Ashley Ct, Epsom KT18 216 CR113
Hatfield AL10 45 CV17
Woking GU21 226 AT118
Ashley Cres, N22 99 DN54
SW11 160 DG83
Ashley Dr, Bans. SM7 218 DA114
Borehamwood WD6 78 CQ43
High Wycombe (Penn) HP10 88 AC45
Isleworth TW7 157 CE79
Twickenham TW2 176 CB87
Walton-on-Thames KT12 195 BU104
Ashley Gdns, N13 100 DQ49
SW1 19 K6
Guildford (Shalf.) GU4 259 AZ141
Orpington BR6 223 ES106
Richmond TW10 177 CK90
Wembley HA9 118 CL61
ASHLEY GREEN, Chesh. HP5 38 AS24
Ashley Grn Rd, Chesh. HP5 54 AR27
Ashley Gro, Loug. IG10 off Staples Rd 84 EL41
Ashley La, NW4 97 CW54
Croydon CR0 219 DP105
ASHLEY PARK, Walt. KT12 195 BT104
Ashley Pk Av, Walt. KT12 195 BT103
Ashley Pk Cres, Walt. KT12 195 BT102
Ashley Pk Rd, Walt. KT12 195 BU103
Ashley Pl, SW1 19 J6
Ashley Ri, Walt. KT12 213 BU105
Ashley Rd, E4 101 EA50
E7 144 EJ66
N17 122 DU55
N19 121 DL60
SW19 180 DB93
Dorking (Westc.) RH4 262 CC137
Enfield EN3 82 DW40
Epsom KT18 216 CR114
Hampton TW12 196 CA95
Hertford SG14 31 DN10
Richmond TW9 off Jocelyn Rd 158 CL83
St. Albans AL1 43 CJ20
Sevenoaks TN13 257 FH123
Thames Ditton KT7 197 CF100
Thornton Heath CR7 201 DM98
Uxbridge UB8 134 BH68
Walton-on-Thames KT12 195 BU102
Woking GU21 226 AT118
Ashleys, Rick. WD3 91 BF45
Ashley Sq, Epsom KT18 216 CR113
Ashley Wk, NW7 97 CW52
Ashling Rd, Croy. CR0 202 DU102
Ashlin Rd, E15 123 ED63
Ashlone Rd, SW15 159 CW83
Ashlyn Cl, Bushey WD23 76 BY42
Ashlyn Gro, Horn. RM11 128 FK55
Ashlyns Ct, Berk. HP4 38 AV20
Ashlyns La, Ong. CM5 53 FG23
Ashlyns Pk, Cob. KT11 214 BY113
Ashlyns Rd, Berk. HP4 38 AV20
Epping CM16 69 ET30
Ashlyns Sch, Berk. HP4 off Chesham Rd 38 AW21
Ashlyns Way, Chess. KT9 215 CK107
Ashmead, N14 81 DJ43
Ashmead Dr, Uxb. (Denh.) UB9 114 BG61
Ashmead Gate, Brom. BR1 204 EJ95
Ashmead Ho, E9 off Kingsmead Way 123 DY64
Ashmead Jun Sch, SE8 off Ashmead Rd 163 EA82
Ashmead La, Uxb. (Denh.) UB9 114 BG61
Ashmead Rd, SE8 163 EA82
Feltham TW14 175 BU88
Ashmeads Ct, Rad. (Shenley) WD7 off Porters Pk Dr 61 CK33
Ashmere Av, Beck. BR3 203 ED96
Ashmere Cl, Sutt. SM3 217 CW106
Ashmere Gro, SW2 161 DL84
Ash Ms, Epsom KT18 216 CS113
Ashmill St, NW1 8 A5
Ashmole Pl, SW8 161 DM79
Ashmole Prim Sch, SW8 off Ashmole St 161 DM79
Ashmole Sec Sch, N14 off Cecil Rd 99 DJ46
Ashmole St, SW8 161 DM79
Ashmore Ct, Houns. TW5 off Wheatlands 156 CA79
Ashmore Gdns, Grav. (Nthflt) DA11 190 GD91
Hemel Hempstead HP3 41 BP21
Ashmore Gro, Well. DA16 165 ER83
Ashmore La, Kes. BR2 222 EH111
Ashmore Rd, W9 6 F3
Ashmount Est, N19 off Ashmount Rd 121 DK59
Ashmount Rd, N15 122 DT57
N19 121 DJ59
Ashmount Sch, N19 off Ashmount Rd 121 DJ59
Ashmount Ter, W5 off Murray Rd 157 CK77
Ashmour Gdns, Rom. RM1 105 FD54
Ashneal Gdns, Har. HA1 117 CD62
Ashness Gdns, Grnf. UB6 137 CH65
Ashness Rd, SW11 180 DF85

Ash Platt, The, Sev. (Seal) TN14,TN15 257 FL121
Ash Platt Rd, Sev. (Seal) TN15 257 FL121
Ash Ride, Enf. EN2 81 DN35
Ashridge Cl, Har. HA3 117 CJ58
Hemel Hempstead (Bov.) HP3 57 BA28
Ashridge Cres, SE18 165 EQ80
Ashridge Dr, St.Alb. (Brick.Wd) AL2 60 BY30
Watford WD19 94 BW50
Ashridge Gdns, N13 99 DK50
Pinner HA5 116 BY56
Ashridge Ri, Berk. HP4 38 AT18
Ashridge Rd, Chesh. HP5 56 AW31
Ashridge Way, Mord. SM4 199 CZ97
Sunbury-on-Thames TW16 175 BU93
Ash Rd, E15 124 EE64
Croydon CR0 203 EA103
Dartford DA1 188 FK88
Dartford (Hawley) DA2 188 FM91
Gravesend DA12 191 GJ91
Orpington BR6 223 ET108
Shepperton TW17 194 BN98
Sutton SM3 199 CY101
Westerham TN16 255 ER125
Woking GU22 226 AX120
Ash Row, Brom. BR2 205 EN101
ASHTEAD, KT21 232 CL118
⇌ Ashtead 231 CK117
Ashtead Gap, Lthd. KT22 231 CH116
H Ashtead Hosp, Ashtd. KT21 232 CL119
ASHTEAD PARK, Ashtd. KT21 232 CN118
Ashtead Rd, E5 122 DU59
Ashtead Wds Rd, Ashtd. KT21 231 CJ117
Ashton Cl, Sutt. SM1 218 DA105
Walton-on-Thames KT12 213 BV107
Ashton Gdns, Houns. TW4 156 BZ84
Romford RM6 126 EY58
Sch Ashton Ho Sch, Islw. TW7 off Eversley Cres 157 CD81
Ashton Rd, E15 123 ED64
Enfield EN3 83 DY36
Romford RM3 106 FK52
Woking GU21 226 AT117
Ashton St, E14 14 D9
Ashtree Av, Mitch. CR4 200 DE96
Ash Tree Cl, Croy. CR0 203 DY100
Ashtree Cl, Orp. BR6 off Broadwater Gdns 223 EP105
Ash Tree Cl, Surb. KT6 198 CL102
Ashtree Ct, St.Alb. AL1 off Granville Rd 43 CF20
Waltham Abbey EN9 off Farthingale La 68 EG34
Ash Tree Dell, NW9 118 CQ57
Ash Tree Fld, Harl. CM20 35 EN13
Ash Tree Rd, Wat. WD24 75 BV36
Ash Tree Way, Croy. CR0 203 DY99
Ashtree Way, Hem.H. HP1 40 BG21
Ashurst Cl, SE20 202 DV95
Dartford DA1 167 FF83
Kenley CR8 236 DR115
Northwood HA6 93 BS52
Ashurst Dr, Ilf. IG2, IG6 125 EP58
Shepperton TW17 194 BL99
Tadworth (Box H.) KT20 248 CP130
Ashurst Pl, Dor. RH4 off Reigate Rd 263 CJ135
Ashurst Rd, N12 98 DE50
Barnet EN4 80 DF43
Tadworth KT20 233 CV121
Ashurst Wk, Croy. CR0 202 DV103
Ash Vale, Rick. (Map.Cr.) WD3 91 BD50
Ashvale Dr, Upmin. RM14 129 FS61
Ashvale Gdns, Rom. RM5 105 FD50
Upminster RM14 129 FS61
Ashvale Rd, SW17 180 DF92
Ashview Cl, Ashf. TW15 174 BL93
Ashview Gdns, Ashf. TW15 174 BL92
Ashville Rd, E11 123 ED61
Ash Wk, SW2 181 DM88
South Ockendon RM15 149 FX69
Wembley HA0 117 CJ63
Ashwater Rd, SE12 184 EG88
Ashwell Cl, E6 off Northumberland Rd 144 EL72
Ashwells Manor Dr, H.Wyc. (Penn) HP10 88 AC47
Ashwells Rd, Brwd. (Pilg.Hat.) CM15 108 FS41
Ashwell St, St.Alb. AL3 43 CD19
Ashwells Way, Ch.St.G. HP8 90 AW47
Ashwick Cl, Cat. CR3 252 DU125
Ashwindham Ct, Wok. GU21 226 AS118
Ashwin St, E8 5 N3
Ashwood, Warl. CR6 236 DW120
Ashwood Av, Rain. RM13 147 FH70
Uxbridge UB8 134 BN72
Ashwood Gdns, Croy. (New Adgtn) CR0 221 EB107
Hayes UB3 off Cranford Dr 155 BT77
Ashwood Ms, St.Alb. AL1 off Prospect Rd 43 CD22
Ashwood Pk, Lthd. (Fetch.) KT22 230 CC124
Woking GU22 227 BA118
Ashwood Pl, Dart. (Bean) DA2 off Bean La 189 FV90
Ashwood Rd, E4 101 ED48
Egham (Eng.Grn) TW20 172 AV93
Potters Bar EN6 64 DB33
Woking GU22 227 AZ118
Ashworth Cl, SE5 off Love Wk 162 DR82
Ashworth Pl, Guil. GU2 242 AT134
Harlow CM17 52 EX15
Ashworth Rd, W9 7 K1
Askern Cl, Bexh. DA6 166 EX84
Aske St, N1 11 L1
Askew Cres, W12 159 CT75
Askew Fm La, Grays RM17 170 FY78
Askew Rd, W12 139 CT74
Northwood HA6 93 BR47
Askham Ct, W12 139 CU74
Askham Rd, W12 139 CU74
Askill Dr, SW15 off Keswick Rd 179 CY85
Askwith Rd, Rain. RM13 147 FD69
Asland Rd, E15 144 EE67
Aslett St, SW18 180 DB87
Asmara Rd, NW2 119 CY64
Asmar Cl, Couls. CR5 235 DL115
Asmuns Hill, NW11 120 DA57
Asmuns Pl, NW11 119 CZ57
Asolando Dr, SE17 21 H8
Aspasia Cl, St.Alb. AL1 43 CF21
Aspdin Rd, Grav. (Nthflt) DA11 190 GD90
Aspen Cl, N19 off Hargrave Pk 121 DJ61
W5 158 CM75
Cobham (Stoke D'Ab.) KT11 230 BY116
Guildford GU4 243 BD131
Orpington BR6 224 EU106
St. Albans (Brick.Wd) AL2 60 BY30
Slough SL2 off Birch Gro 131 AP71
Staines TW18 173 BF90
Swanley BR8 207 FD95
West Drayton UB7 154 BM74
Aspen Copse, Brom. BR1 205 EM96
Aspen Ct, Brwd. CM13 109 GA48
Hayes UB3 155 BS77
Virginia Water GU25 192 AY98
Aspen Dr, Wem. HA0 117 CG63
Aspen Gdns, W6 159 CV78
Ashford TW15 175 BQ92
Mitcham CR4 200 DG99
Aspen Grn, Erith DA18 166 EZ76
Aspen Gro, Upmin. RM14 128 FN63
Aspen La, Nthlt. UB5 136 BY69
Aspenlea Rd, W6 159 CX79
Aspen Pk Dr, Wat. WD25 75 BV35
Aspen Sq, Wey. KT13 off Oatlands Dr 195 BR104
Aspen Vale, Whyt. CR3 off Whyteleafe Hill 236 DT118
Aspen Way, E14 14 P10
Banstead SM7 217 CX114
Enfield EN3 83 DX35
Feltham TW13 175 BV90
South Ockendon RM15 149 FX69
Welwyn Garden City AL7 30 DC10
Aspern Gro, NW3 120 DE64
Aspfield Row, Hem.H. HP1 40 BH18
Aspinall Rd, SE4 163 DX83
Aspinden Rd, SE16 22 D7
Aspley Rd, SW18 180 DB85
Asplins Rd, N17 100 DU53
Asprey Gro, Cat. CR3 236 DU124
Asprey Ms, Beck. BR3 203 DZ99
Asprey Pl, Brom. BR1 off Chislehurst Rd 204 EK96
Asquith Cl, Dag. RM8 126 EW60
Assam St, E1 12 A7
Assata Ms, N1 4 F3
Assembly Pas, E1 12 F5
Assembly Wk, Cars. SM5 200 DE101
Assher Rd, Walt. KT12 196 BY104
Assheton Rd, Beac. HP9 89 AK51
Ass Ho La, Har. HA3 94 CB49
Assurance Cotts, Belv. DA17 off Heron Hill 166 EZ78
Astall Cl, Har. HA3 95 CE53
Astbury Business Pk, SE15 off Station Pas 162 DW81
Astbury Rd, SE15 162 DW81
Astede Pl, Ashtd. KT21 232 CM118
Astell St, SW3 18 B9
Asters, The, Wal.Cr. EN7 66 DR28
Aste St, E14 24 C4
Asteys Row, N1 4 F6
Asthall Gdns, Ilf. IG6 125 EQ56
Astleham Rd, Shep. TW17 194 BL97
Astle St, SW11 160 DG82
Astley, Grays RM17 170 FZ79
Astley Av, NW2 119 CW64
Sch Astley Cen, Brom. BR2 off Holbrook Way 205 EM100
Sch Astley Cooper Sec Sch, The, Hem.H. HP2 off St. Agnells La 40 BN15
Astley Rd, Hem.H. HP1 40 BJ20
Aston Av, Har. HA3 117 CJ59
Aston Cl, Ashtd. KT21 231 CJ118
Bushey WD23 76 CC44
Sidcup DA14 186 EU90
Watford WD24 76 BW40
Aston Grn, Houns. TW4 156 BW82
Sch Aston Ho Sch, W5 off Montpelier Rd 137 CK71
Aston Mead, Wind. SL4 151 AL80
Aston Ms, Rom. RM6 126 EW59
Aston Pl, SW16 off Averil Gro 181 DP93
Aston Rd, SW20 199 CW96
W5 137 CK72
Esher (Clay.) KT10 215 CE106
Astons Rd, Nthwd. HA6 93 BQ48
Aston St, E14 13 J7
Aston Ter, SW12 off Cathles Rd 181 DH86
Astonville St, SW18 180 DA88
Aston Way, Epsom KT18 233 CT115
Potters Bar EN6 64 DD32
Astor Av, Rom. RM7 127 FC58
Astor Cl, Add. KT15 212 BK105
Kingston upon Thames KT2 178 CP93
Astoria Wk, SW9 161 DN83
Astra Business Cen, The, Red. RH1 267 DH144
Astra Cen, Harl. CM20 off Edinburgh Way 35 ET11
Astra Cl, Horn. RM12 147 FH65
Astra Dr, Grav. DA12 191 GL92
Astrop Ms, W6 159 CW76
Astrop Ter, W6 159 CW76
Astwick Av, Hat. AL10 45 CT15
Astwood Ms, SW7 17 L7
Asylum Arch Rd, Red. RH1 266 DF137
Asylum Rd, SE15 162 DV80
Atalanta Cl, Pur. CR8 219 DN110
Atalanta St, SW6 159 CX81
Atbara Ct, Tedd. TW11 177 CH93
Atbara Rd, Tedd. TW11 177 CH93
Atcham Rd, Houns. TW3 156 CC84
Atcost Rd, Bark. IG11 146 EU71
Atheldene Rd, SW18 180 DB88
Sch Athelney Prim Sch, SE6 off Athelney St 183 EA90
Athelney St, SE6 183 EA90
Athelstan Cl, Rom. RM3 106 FM54
Athelstane Gro, E3 143 DZ68
Athelstane Ms, N4 off Stroud Grn Rd 121 DN60
Athelstan Ho, E9 off Kingsmead Way 123 DZ64
Sch Athelstan Ho Sch, Hmptn. TW12 off Percy Rd 196 CA95
Athelstan Rd, Hem.H. HP3 40 BM23
Kingston upon Thames KT1 198 CM98
Romford RM3 106 FM53
Athelstan Wk N, Welw.G.C. AL7 29 CY10
Athelstan Wk S, Welw.G.C. AL7 29 CX10
Athelstan Way, Orp. BR5 206 EU95
Athelstone Rd, Har. HA3 95 CD54
Athena Cl, Har. HA2 off Byron Hill Rd 117 CE61
Kingston upon Thames KT1 198 CM97
Athenaeum Pl, N10 off Fortis Grn Rd 121 DH55
Athenaeum Rd, N20 98 DC46
Athena Pl, Nthwd. HA6 off The Drive 93 BT53
Athenia Cl, Wal.Cr. (Goffs Oak) EN7 65 DP29
Athenlay Rd, SE15 183 DX85
Athens Gdns, W9 6 G4
Atherden Rd, E5 122 DW63
Atherfield Rd, Reig. RH2 266 DC137
Atherfold Rd, SW9 161 DL83
Atherley Way, Houns. TW4 176 BZ87
Atherstone Ct, W2 7 K5
Atherstone Ms, SW7 17 M7
Atherton Cl, Guil. (Shalf.) GU4 258 AY140
Staines (Stanw.) TW19 174 BK86
Atherton Ct, Wind. (Eton) SL4 off Meadow La 151 AR80
Atherton Dr, SW19 179 CX91
Atherton Gdns, Grays RM16 171 GJ77
Atherton Hts, Wem. HA0 137 CJ65
Atherton Ms, E7 144 EF65
Atherton Pl, Har. HA2 117 CD55
Southall UB1 136 CB73
Atherton Rd, E7 124 EF64
SW13 159 CU80
Ilford IG5 102 EL54
Atherton St, SW11 160 DE82
Athlone, Esher (Clay.) KT10 215 CE107
Athlone Cl, E5 off Goulton Rd 122 DV63
Radlett WD7 77 CH36
H Athlone Ho, N6 120 DF60
Athlone Rd, SW2 181 DM87
Athlone Sq, Wind. SL4 off Alma Rd 151 AQ81
Athlone St, NW5 140 DG65
Athlon Rd, Wem. HA0 137 CK68
Athol Cl, Pnr. HA5 93 BV53
Athole Gdns, Enf. EN1 82 DS43
Athol Gdns, Pnr. HA5 93 BV53
Atholl Rd, Ilf. IG3 126 EU59
Athol Rd, Erith DA8 167 FC78
Athol Sq, E14 14 D8
Athol Way, Uxb. UB10 134 BN69
Atkins Cl, Wok. GU21 off Greythorne Rd 226 AU118
Atkins Dr, W.Wick. BR4 203 ED103
Atkinson Cl, Orp. BR6 off Martindale Av 224 EU106
Atkinson Rd, E16 144 EJ71
Atkins Rd, E10 123 EB58
SW12 181 DK87
Atlanta Boul, Rom. RM1 127 FE58
Atlantic Cl, Swans. DA10 190 FY85
Atlantic Rd, SW9 161 DN84
Atlantis Cl, Bark. IG11 146 EV69
Atlas Gdns, SE7 164 EJ77
Atlas Ms, E8 5 P3
N7 4 B4
Atlas Rd, E13 144 EG68
N11 99 DH51
NW10 138 CS69
Dartford DA1 off Cornwall Rd 168 FM83
Wembley HA9 118 CQ63
Atley Rd, E3 143 EA67
Atlip Rd, Wem. HA0 138 CL67
Atney Rd, SW15 159 CY84
Atria Rd, Nthwd. HA6 93 BU50
Attenborough Cl, Wat. WD19 off Harrow Way 94 BY48
Atterbury Cl, West. TN16 255 ER126
Atterbury Rd, N4 121 DN58
Atterbury St, SW1 19 M8
Attewood Av, NW10 118 CS62
Attewood Rd, Nthlt. UB5 136 BY65
Attfield Cl, N20 98 DD47
Attimore Cl, Welw.G.C. AL8 29 CV10
Attimore Rd, Welw.G.C. AL8 29 CV10
Attle Cl, Uxb. UB10 134 BN68
Attlee Cl, Hayes UB4 135 BV69
Thornton Heath CR7 202 DQ100
Attlee Ct, Grays RM17 170 GA76
Attlee Dr, Dart. DA1 188 FN85
Attlee Rd, SE28 146 EV73
Hayes UB4 135 BU69
Attlee Ter, E17 123 EB56
Attneave St, WC1 10 C2
Attwood Cl, S.Croy. CR2 220 DV114
Atwater Cl, SW2 181 DN88
Atwell Cl, E10 off Belmont Pk Rd 123 EB58
Atwell Pl, T.Ditt. KT7 197 CF102
Atwell Rd, SE15 off Rye La 162 DU82
Atwood, Lthd. (Bkhm) KT23 230 BY124
Atwood Av, Rich. TW9 158 CN82
Sch Atwood Co Prim Sch, S.Croy. CR2 off Limpsfield Rd 220 DU113
Atwood Rd, W6 159 CV77
Atwoods All, Rich. TW9 off Leyborne Pk 158 CN81
Aubert Pk, N5 121 DP63
Aubert Rd, N5 121 DP63
Aubretia Cl, Rom. RM3 106 FL53
Aubrey Av, St.Alb. (Lon.Col.) AL2 61 CJ26
Aubrey Pl, NW8 off Violet Hill 140 DC68
Aubrey Rd, E17 123 EA55
N8 121 DL57
W8 16 F1
Aubreys Rd, Hem.H. HP1 39 BE21
Aubrey Wk, W8 16 F2
Auburn Cl, SE14 163 DY80
Aubyn Hill, SE27 182 DQ91
Aubyn Sq, SW15 159 CU84
Auckland Av, Rain. RM13 147 FF69
Auckland Cl, SE19 202 DT95
Enfield EN1 82 DV37
Tilbury RM18 171 GG82
Auckland Gdns, SE19 202 DS95
Auckland Hill, SE27 182 DQ91
Auckland Ri, SE19 202 DS95
Auckland Rd, E10 123 EB62
SE19 202 DT95
SW11 160 DE84
Caterham CR3 236 DS122
Ilford IG1 125 EP60
Kingston upon Thames KT1 198 CM98
Auckland Rd, Pot. B. EN6 63 CY32
Auckland St, SE11 20 A10
Auden Pl, NW1 140 DG67
Sutton SM3 off Wordsworth Dr 217 CW105
Audleigh Pl, Chig. IG7 103 EN51
Audley Cl, N10 99 DH52
SW11 160 DG83
Addlestone KT15 212 BH106
Borehamwood WD6 78 CN41
Audley Ct, E18 124 EF56
Pinner HA5 off Rickmansworth Rd 94 BW54
Audley Dr, E16 25 N1
Warlingham CR6 236 DW115
Audley Firs, Walt. KT12 214 BW105
Audley Gdns, Ilf. IG3 125 ET61
Loughton IG10 85 EQ40
Waltham Abbey EN9 67 EC34
Audley Pl, Sutt. SM2 218 DA108
Sch Audley Prim Sch, Cat. CR3 off Whyteleafe Rd 236 DT121
Audley Rd, NW4 119 CV58
W5 138 CM71
Enfield EN2 81 DP40
Richmond TW10 178 CM85
Audley Sq, W1 18 F1
Audley Wk, Orp. BR5 206 EW100
Audrey Cl, Beck. BR3 203 EB100
Audrey Gdns, Wem. HA0 117 CH61
Audrey Rd, Ilf. IG1 125 EP62
Audrey St, E2 142 DU68
Audric Cl, Kings.T. KT2 198 CN95
Audwick Cl, Wal.Cr. (Chsht) EN8 67 DX28
Augur Cl, Stai. TW18 173 BF92
Augurs La, E13 15 P1
Augusta Cl, W.Mol. KT8 off Freeman Dr 196 BZ97
Augusta Rd, Twick. TW2 176 CC89
Augusta St, E14 14 A7
August End, Slou. (Geo.Grn) SL3 132 AY72
Augustine Cl, Slou. (Colnbr.) SL3 153 BE83
Augustine Ct, Wal.Abb. EN9 off Beaulieu Dr 67 EB33
Augustine Rd, W14 16 A6
Gravesend DA12 191 GJ87
Harrow HA3 94 CB53
Orpington BR5 206 EX97
August La, Guil. (Albury) GU5 260 BK144
Augustus Cl, W12 off Goldhawk Rd 159 CV75
Brentford TW8 157 CJ80
St. Albans AL3 42 CA22
Augustus La, Orp. BR6 206 EU103
Augustus Rd, SW19 179 CY88
Augustus St, NW1 141 DH68
Aultone Way, Cars. SM5 200 DF104
Sutton SM1 200 DB103
Aulton Pl, SE11 20 D10
Aurelia Gdns, Croy. CR0 201 DM99
Aurelia Rd, Croy. CR0 201 DL100
Auriel Av, Dag. RM10 147 FD65
Auriga Ms, N16 5 K1
Auriol Cl, Wor.Pk. KT4 off Auriol Pk Rd 198 CS104
Auriol Dr, Grnf. UB6 137 CD66
Uxbridge UB10 134 BN65
Sch Auriol Jun Sch, Epsom KT19 off Vale Rd 217 CT105
Auriol Pk Rd, Wor.Pk. KT4 198 CS104
Auriol Rd, W14 16 C8
Aurum Cl, Horl. RH6 269 DH149
Austell Gdns, NW7 96 CS48
Austen Cl, SE28 146 EV74
Greenhithe DA9 189 FW85
Loughton IG10 85 ER41
Tilbury RM18 off Coleridge Rd 171 GJ82
Austen Gdns, Dart. DA1 168 FM84
Austen Ho, NW6 6 G1
Austen Rd, Erith DA8 167 FB80
Guildford GU1 259 AZ135
Harrow HA2 116 CB61
Austenway, Ger.Cr. (Chal.St.P.) SL9 112 AX55
Austen Way, Slou. SL3 off Ditton Rd 153 AZ79
Austenwood Cl, Ger.Cr. (Chal.St.P.) SL9 90 AW54
Austenwood La, Ger.Cr. (Chal.St.P.) SL9 90 AX54
Austin Av, Brom. BR2 204 EL99
Austin Cl, SE23 183 DZ87
Coulsdon CR5 235 DP118
Twickenham TW1 177 CJ85
Austin Ct, E6 off Kings Rd 144 EJ67
Austin Friars, EC2 11 K7
Austin Friars Pas, EC2 11 K7
Austin Friars Sq, EC2 11 K7
Austin Rd, SW11 160 DG81
Gravesend (Nthflt) DA11 191 GF88
Hayes UB3 155 BT75
Orpington BR5 206 EU100
Austin's La, Uxb. UB10 115 BR63
Austins Mead, Hem.H. (Bov.) HP3 57 BB28
Austins Pl, Hem.H. HP2 off St. Mary's Rd 40 BK19
Austin St, E2 11 N2
Austin Waye, Uxb. UB8 134 BJ67
Austral Cl, Sid. DA15 185 ET90
Austral Dr, Horn. RM11 128 FK59
Australia Rd, W12 139 CV73
Slough SL1 152 AV75
Austral St, SE11 20 E7
Austyn Gdns, Surb. KT5 198 CP102
Autumn Cl, SW19 180 DC93
Enfield EN1 82 DU39
Slough SL1 131 AM74
Autumn Dr, Sutt. SM2 218 DB109
Autumn Glades, Hem.H. HP3 41 BQ22
Autumn Gro, Welw.G.C. AL7 30 DB11
Autumn St, E3 143 EA67
Auxiliaries Way, Uxb. UB9 113 BF57
Avalon Cl, SW20 199 CY96
W13 137 CG71
Enfield EN2 81 DN40
Orpington BR6 206 EX104
Watford WD25 60 BY32
Avalon Rd, SW6 160 DB81
W13 137 CG70
Orpington BR6 206 EW103
Avard Gdns, Orp. BR6 223 EQ105
Avarn Rd, SW17 180 DF93
Avebury, Slou. SL1 131 AN74
Avebury Ct, N1 5 J8
Hemel Hempstead HP2 40 BN17
Avebury Pk, Surb. KT6 197 CK101
Avebury Rd, E11 off Southwest Rd 123 ED60
SW19 199 CZ95
Orpington BR6 205 ER104
Avebury St, N1 5 J8
AVELEY, S.Ock. RM15 149 FR73
Aveley Bypass, S.Ock. RM15 148 FQ73
Aveley Cl, Erith DA8 167 FF79
South Ockendon (Aveley) RM15 149 FR74
Sch Aveley Prim Sch, S.Ock. RM15 off Stifford Rd 149 FS74
Aveley Rd, Rom. RM1 127 FD56
Upminster RM14 148 FP65
Sch Aveley Sch, The, S.Ock. RM15 off Nethan Dr 149 FR73
Aveline St, SE11 20 C9
Aveling Cl, Pur. CR8 219 DM113
Aveling Pk Rd, E17 101 EA54
Sch Aveling Pk Sch, E17 off Aveling Pk Rd 101 EA54
Avelon Rd, Rain. RM13 147 FG67
Romford RM5 105 FD51
Ave Maria La, EC4 10 F8
Avenell Rd, N5 121 DP62
Avening Rd, SW18 off Brathway Rd 180 DA87
Avening Ter, SW18 180 DA86
Avenons Rd, E13 15 L4
Avenue, The, E4 101 ED51
E11 (Leytonstone) 124 EF61
E11 (Wanstead) 124 EH58
N3 98 DA54
N8 121 DN55
N10 99 DJ54
N11 99 DH49
N17 100 DS54
NW6 139 CX67
SE10 163 ED80
SW4 180 DG85
SW11 180 DF87
SW18 180 DE87
W4 158 CS76
W13 137 CH73
Addlestone (New Haw) KT15 212 BG110
Amersham HP7 55 AQ38
Barnet EN5 79 CY41
Beckenham BR3 203 EB95
Betchworth (Brock.) RH3 248 CN134
Bexley DA5 186 EX87
Brentwood CM13 107 FX51
Bromley BR1 204 EK97
Bushey WD23 76 BZ42
Carshalton SM5 218 DG108
Coulsdon CR5 235 DK115
Croydon CR0 202 DS104
Egham TW20 173 BB91
Epsom KT17 217 CV108
Esher (Clay.) KT10 215 CE107
Gravesend DA11 191 GG88
Greenhithe DA9 169 FV84
Guildford (Worp.) GU3 242 AS127
Hampton TW12 176 BZ93
Harrow HA3 95 CF53
Hemel Hempstead HP1 39 BE19
Hertford SG14 31 DP07
Hoddesdon EN11 49 DZ19
Horley RH6 268 DF149
Hornchurch RM12 128 FJ61
Hounslow TW3 176 CB85
Hounslow (Cran.) TW5 155 BU81
Isleworth TW7 157 CD79
Keston BR2 204 EK104
Leatherhead KT22 215 CF112
Loughton IG10 84 EK44
Northwood HA6 93 BQ51
Orpington BR6 205 ET103
Orpington (St.P.Cray) BR5 186 EV94
Pinner HA5 116 BZ58
Pinner (Hatch End) HA5 94 CA52
Potters Bar EN6 63 CZ30
Radlett WD7 61 CG33
Redhill (S.Nutfld) RH1 267 DL137
Richmond TW9 158 CM82
Romford RM1 127 FD56
Slough (Datchet) SL3 152 AV81
Slough (Farn.Com.) SL2 111 AP63
Staines TW18 194 BH95
Staines (Wrays.) TW19 152 AX83
Sunbury-on-Thames TW16 195 BV95
Surbiton KT5 198 CM100
Sutton SM2 217 CZ109
Sutton (Cheam) SM3 217 CW108
Tadworth KT20 233 CV122
Twickenham TW1 177 CJ85
Uxbridge (Cowley) UB8 134 BK70
Uxbridge (Ickhm) UB10 114 BN63
Waltham Abbey (Nazeing) EN9 68 EJ25
Watford WD17 75 BU40
Wembley HA9 118 CM61
West Drayton UB7 154 BL76
West Wickham BR4 203 EC101
Westerham TN16 239 EM122
Whyteleafe CR3 236 DU119
Windsor (Old Wind.) SL4 172 AV85
Woking (Chobham) GU24 210 AT109
Worcester Park KT4 199 CT103
Avenue App, Kings L. WD4 58 BN30
Coll Avenue Cen, Tedd. TW11 off Normansfield Av 177 CK94
Avenue Cl, N14 81 DJ44
NW8 140 DE67
Hounslow TW5 off The Avenue 155 BU81
Romford RM3 106 FM52
Tadworth KT20 233 CV122
West Drayton UB7 154 BK76
Avenue Ct, Tad. KT20 off The Avenue 233 CV123
Avenue Cres, W3 158 CP75
Hounslow TW5 155 BV80
Avenue Dr, Slou. SL3 133 AZ71
Avenue Elmers, Surb. KT6 198 CL99
Avenue Gdns, SE25 202 DU97
SW14 158 CS83
W3 158 CP75
Horley RH6 269 DJ149
Hounslow TW5 off The Avenue 155 BU80
Teddington TW11 177 CF94
Avenue Gate, Loug. IG10 84 EJ44
Avenue Ind Est, E4 101 DZ51
Romford RM3 106 FK54
Avenue Ms, N10 121 DH55
Avenue Pk Rd, SE27 181 DP89
Sch Avenue Prim Sch, E12 off Meanley Rd 124 EL64
Sch Avenue Prim Sch, The, NW6 off The Avenue 139 CY66
Sutton SM2 off Avenue Rd 218 DA110

Avenue Ri, Bushey WD23 .76 CA43
[Tra] Avenue Road .203 DX96
Avenue Rd, E7 .124 EH64
N6 .121 DJ59
N12 .98 DC49
N14 .99 DH45
N15 .122 DR57
NW3 .140 DD66
NW8 .140 DD66
NW10 .139 CT68
SE20 .202 DW95
SE25 .202 DU96
SW16 .201 DK96
SW20 .199 CV96
W3 .158 CP75
Banstead SM7 .234 DB115
Beckenham BR3 .202 DW95
Belvedere DA17 .167 FC77
Bexleyheath DA7 .166 EY83
Brentford TW8 .157 CJ78
Brentwood CM14 .108 FW49
Caterham CR3 .236 DR122
Cobham KT11 .230 BX116
Epping (They.B.) CM16 .85 ER36
Epsom KT18 .216 CR114
Erith DA8 .167 FC80
Feltham TW13 .175 BT90
Hampton TW12 .196 CB95
Hoddesdon EN11 .49 ED19
Isleworth TW7 .157 CF81
Kingston upon Thames
KT1 .198 CL97
New Malden KT3 .198 CS98
Pinner HA5 .116 BY55
Romford (Chad.Hth) RM6 .126 EV59
Romford (Harold Wd)
RM3 .106 FM52
St. Albans AL1 .43 CE19
Sevenoaks TN13 .257 FJ123
Southall UB1 .156 BZ75
Staines TW18 .173 BD92
Sutton SM2 .218 DA110
Teddington TW11 .177 CG94
Wallington SM6 .219 DJ108
Westerham (Tats.) TN16 .238 EL120
Woodford Green IG8 .102 EJ51
Avenue S, Surb. KT5 .198 CM101
Avenue Ter, N.Mal. KT3
off Kingston Rd .198 CQ97
Watford WD19 .76 BY44
Averil Ct, Maid. SL6 .130 AJ72
Averil Gro, SW16 .181 DP93
Averill St, W6 .159 CX79
Avern Gdns, W.Mol. KT8 .196 CB98
Avern Rd, W.Mol. KT8 .196 CB99
Avery Fm Row, SW1 .18 F8
Avery Gdns, Ilf. IG2 .125 EM57
AVERY HILL, SE9 .185 EQ86
★ Avery Hill Pk, SE9 .185 EQ86
Avery Hill Rd, SE9 .185 ER86
Avery Row, W1 .8 G9
Avey La, Loug. IG10 .84 EH39
Waltham Abbey EN9 .83 ED36
Avia Cl, Hem.H. HP3 .40 BK24
Aviary Cl, E16 .15 K6
Aviary Rd, Wok. GU22 .228 BG116
Aviator Pk, Add. KT15 .194 BK104
Aviemore Cl, Beck. BR3 .203 DZ99
Aviemore Way, Beck. BR3 .203 DY99
[Sch] Avigdor JMI Sch, N16
off Lordship Rd .122 DR61
Avignon Rd, SE4 .163 DX83
Avington Cl, Guil. GU1
off London Rd .242 AY134
Avington Ct, SE1
off Old Kent Rd .162 DS77
Avington Gro, SE20 .182 DW94
Avington Way, SE15
off Daniel Gdns .162 DT80
Avion Cres, NW9 .97 CU53
Avior Dr, Nthwd. HA6 .93 BT49
Avis Gro, Croy. CR0 .221 DY110
Avis Sq, E1 .13 H7
Avoca Rd, SW17 .180 DG91
Avocet Ms, SE28 .165 ER76
Avon Cl, Add. KT15 .212 BG107
Gravesend DA12 .191 GK89
Hayes UB4 .136 BW70
Slough SL1 .131 AL73
Sutton SM1 .218 DC105
Watford WD25 .60 BW34
Worcester Park KT4 .199 CU103
Avon Ct, Grnf. UB6
off Braund Av .136 CB70
Avondale Av, N12 .98 DB50
NW2 .118 CS62
Barnet EN4 .98 DF46
Esher KT10 .197 CG104
Staines TW18 .173 BF94
Worcester Park KT4 .199 CT102
Avondale Cl, Horl. RH6 .268 DF146
Loughton IG10 .103 EM45
Walton-on-Thames KT12
off Pleasant Pl .214 BW106
Avondale Ct, E11 .124 EE60
E16 .15 H5
E18 .102 EH53
Avondale Cres, Enf. EN3 .83 DY41
Ilford IG4 .124 EK57
Avondale Dr, Hayes UB3 .135 BU74
Loughton IG10 .103 EM45
Avondale Gdns, Houns.
TW4 .176 BZ85
Avondale Ms, Brom. BR1
off Avondale Rd .184 EG93
Avondale Pk Gdns, W11 .6 C10
[Sch] Avondale Pk Prim Sch,
W11 .6 C10
Avondale Pk Rd, W11 .6 C9
Avondale Pavement, SE1
off Avondale Sq .162 DU78
Avondale Ri, SE15 .162 DT83
Avondale Rd, E16 .15 H5
E17 .123 EA59
N3 .98 DC53
N13 .99 DN47
N15 .121 DP57
SE9 .184 EL89
SW14 .158 CR83
SW19 .180 DB92
Ashford TW15 .174 BK90
Bromley BR1 .184 EE93
Harrow HA3 .117 CF55
South Croydon CR2 .220 DQ107
Welling DA16 .166 EW82
Avondale Sq, SE1 .22 A10
Avon Grn, S.Ock. RM15 .149 FV72
[Sch] Avon Ho Sch,
Wdf.Grn. IG8
off High Rd Woodford Grn .102 EG49
Avonley Rd, SE14 .162 DW80
Avonmead, Wok. GU21
off Silversmiths Way .226 AW118
Avon Ms, Pnr. HA5 .94 BZ53
Avonmore Av, Guil. GU1 .243 AZ133
Avonmore Gdns, W14
off Avonmore Rd .159 CZ77
Avonmore Pl, W14 .16 D7
[Sch] Avonmore Prim Sch,
W14 .16 D7
Avonmore Rd, W14 .16 E7
Avonmouth Rd, Dart. DA1 .188 FK85
Avonmouth St, SE1 .20 G5
Avon Path, S.Croy. CR2 .220 DQ107
Avon Pl, SE1 .21 H4
Avon Rd, E17 .123 ED55
SE4 .163 EA83
Greenford UB6 .136 CA70
Sunbury-on-Thames
TW16 .175 BT94
Upminster RM14 .129 FR58
Avon Sq, Hem.H. HP2 .40 BM15
Avonstowe Cl, Orp. BR6 .205 EQ104
Avontar Rd, S.Ock. RM15 .149 FV70
Avon Way, E18 .124 EG55
Avonwick Rd, Houns. TW3 .156 CB82
Avril Way, E4 .101 EC50
Avro Way, Wall. SM6 .219 DL108
Weybridge KT13 .212 BL110
Awlfield Av, N17 .100 DR53
Awliscombe Rd, Well. DA16 .165 ET82
Axes La, Red. RH1 .267 DJ141
Axe St, Bark. IG11 .145 EQ67
Axholme Av, Edg. HA8 .96 CN53
Axis Pk, Slou. (Langley)
SL3 .153 BB77
Axminster Cres, Well. DA16 .166 EW81
Axminster Rd, N7 .121 DL62
Axtaine Rd, Orp. BR5 .206 EX101
Axtane, Grav. (Sthflt) DA13 .190 FZ94
Axtane Cl, Dart. (Sutt.H.)
DA4 .208 FQ96
Axwood, Epsom KT18 .232 CQ115
Aybrook St, W1 .8 E6
Aycliffe Cl, Brom. BR1 .205 EM98
Aycliffe Dr, Hem.H. HP2 .40 BL16
[Sch] Aycliffe Dr JMI Sch,
Hem.H. HP2
off Aycliffe Dr .40 BL16
Aycliffe Rd, W12 .139 CT74
Borehamwood WD6 .78 CL39
Ayebridges Av, Egh. TW20 .173 BC94
Aylands Cl, Wem. HA9
off Preston Rd .118 CL61
Aylands Rd, Enf. EN3 .82 DW36
[Sch] Aylands Sch, Enf. EN3
off Keswick Dr .82 DW36
Aylesbury Cl, E7
off Atherton Rd .144 EF65
Aylesbury Ct, Sutt. SM1
off Benhill Wd Rd .200 DC104
Aylesbury Cres, Slou. SL1 .131 AR72
Aylesbury End, Beac. HP9 .89 AL54
Aylesbury Est, SE17 .21 K10
Aylesbury Rd, SE17 .21 K10
Bromley BR2 .204 EG97
[Coll] Aylesbury Rd Adult Ed
Service, Brom. BR2
off Aylesbury Rd .204 EG97
Aylesbury St, EC1 .10 E4
NW10 .118 CR62
Aylesford Av, Beck. BR3 .203 DY99
Aylesford St, SW1 .19 L9
Aylesham Cen, The, SE15 .162 DU81
Aylesham Cl, NW7 .97 CU52
Aylesham Rd, Orp. BR6 .205 ET101
Ayles Rd, Hayes UB4 .135 BV69
Aylestone Av, NW6 .139 CX67
Aylesworth Av, Slou. SL2
off Doddsfield Rd .131 AN69
Aylesworth Spur, Wind.
(Old Wind.) SL4 .172 AV87
Aylets Fld, Harl. CM18 .51 ES19
Aylett Rd, SE25 .202 DV98
Isleworth TW7 .157 CE82
Upminster RM14 .128 FQ61
Ayley Cft, Enf. EN1 .82 DU43
Ayliffe Cl, Kings.T. KT1
off Cambridge Gdns .198 CN96
Aylmer Cl, Stan. HA7 .95 CG49
Aylmer Dr, Stan. HA7 .95 CG49
Aylmer Par, N2 .120 DF57
Aylmer Rd, E11 .124 EF60
N2 .120 DE57
W12 .158 CS75
Dagenham RM8 .126 EY62
Ayloffe Rd, Dag. RM9 .146 EZ65
[Sch] Ayloff Prim Sch, Horn.
RM12 off South End Rd .127 FH63
Ayloffs Cl, Horn. RM11 .128 FL57
Ayloffs Wk, Horn. RM11 .128 FK57
Aylsham Dr, Uxb. UB10 .115 BR62
Aylsham La, Rom. RM3 .106 FJ49
Aylsham Rd, Hodd. EN11 .49 EC15
Aylton Est, SE16 .22 F4
[Sch] Aylward First & Mid Sch,
Stan. HA7
off Pangbourne Dr .95 CK50
Aylward Gdns, Chesh. HP5 .54 AN30
Aylward Rd, SE23 .183 DX89
SW20 .199 CZ96
[Sch] Aylward Sch, N18
off Windmill Rd .100 DR49
Aylwards Ri, Stan. HA7 .95 CG49
Aylward St, E1 .12 E7
[Sch] Aylwin Girls' Sch, SE16 .21 P7
Aylwyn Est, SE1 .21 N5
Aymer Cl, Stai. TW18 .193 BE95
Aymer Dr, Stai. TW18 .193 BE95
Aynhoe Rd, W14 .16 B7
Aynho St, Wat. WD18 .75 BV43
Aynscombe Angle,
Orp. BR6 .206 EV101
Aynscombe La, SW14 .158 CQ83
Aynscombe Path, SW14
off Thames Bk .158 CQ82
Aynsley Gdns, Harl. CM17 .52 EW15
AYOT GREEN, Welw. AL6 .29 CT07
Ayot Grn, Welw. AL6 .29 CU06
Ayot Greenway, St.Alb. AL4 .28 CN06
Ayot Little Grn, Welw. AL6 .29 CT06
Ayot Path, Borwd. WD6 .78 CN37
Ayot St. Peter Rd, Welw. AL6 .29 CT05
Ayr Ct, W3 off Monks Dr .138 CN71
Ayres Cl, E13 .15 M2
Ayres Cres, NW10 .138 CR66
Ayres St, SE1 .21 H3
Ayr Grn, Rom. RM1 .105 FE52
Ayron Rd, S.Ock. RM15 .149 FV70
Ayrsome Rd, N16 .122 DS62
Ayrton Rd, SW7 .17 N5
Ayr Way, Rom. RM1 .105 FE52
Aysgarth Ct, Sutt. SM1
off Sutton Common Rd .200 DB104
Aysgarth Rd, SE21 .182 DS86
Aytoun Pl, SW9 .161 DM82
Aytoun Rd, SW9 .161 DM82
Azalea Cl, W7 .137 CF74
Ilford IG1 .125 EP64
St. Albans (Lon.Col.) AL2 .61 CH27
Azalea Ct, Wok. GU22 .226 AX119
Woodford Green IG8
off The Bridle Path .102 EE52
Azalea Dr, Swan. BR8 .207 FD98
Azalea Wk, Pnr. HA5 .115 BV57
Southall UB2
off Navigator Dr .156 CC75
Azalea Way, Slou. (Geo.Grn)
SL3 off Blinco La .132 AY72
Azania Ms, NW5 .121 DH64
Azenby Rd, SE15 .162 DT82
Azile Everitt Ho, SE18
off Blendon Ter .165 EQ78
Azof St, SE10 .25 H8
[Coll] B6 6th Form Coll, E5
off Kenninghall Rd .122 DV62

B

Baalbec Rd, N5 .4 F2
Baas Hill, Brox. EN10 .49 DX21
Baas Hill Cl, Brox. EN10 .49 DY21
Baas La, Brox. EN10 .49 DY21
Babbacombe Cl, Chess.
KT9 .215 CK106
Babbacombe Gdns, Ilf. IG4 .124 EL56
Babbacombe Rd, Brom.
BR1 .204 EG95
Baber Dr, Felt. TW14 .176 BW86
[Sch] Babington Ho Sch, Chis.
BR7 off Grange Dr .185 EM93
Babington Ri, Wem. HA9 .138 CN65
Babington Rd, NW4 .119 CV56
SW16 .181 DK92
Dagenham RM8 .126 EW64
Hornchurch RM12 .127 FH60
Babmaes St, SW1 .9 K10
Babylon La, Tad.
(Lwr Kgswd) KT20 .250 DA127
Bacchus Wk, N1 .5 L10
Bachelors Acre, Wind. SL4 .151 AR81
Bachelor's La, Wok. GU23 .228 BN124
Baches St, N1 .11 K2
Back, The, Berk. (Pott.End)
HP4 .39 BB16
Back All, Dor. RH4 .263 CH136
Back Ch La, E1 .12 A9
Back Grn, Walt. KT12 .214 BW107
Back Hill, EC1 .10 C4
Backhouse Pl, SE17 .21 M8
Back La, N8 .121 DL57
NW3 off Heath St .120 DC63
Bexley DA5 .186 FA87
Bishop's Stortford
(Sheering) CM22 .36 FA06
Brentford TW8 .157 CK79
Chalfont St. Giles HP8 .90 AU48
Edgware HA8 .96 CQ53
Grays (N.Stfd) RM16 .149 FW74
Guildford (E.Clan.) GU4 .244 BK130
Hertford SG13 .48 DQ18
Purfleet RM19 .169 FS76
Richmond TW10 .177 CJ90
Rickmansworth (Chenies)
WD3 .73 BB38
Romford RM6
off St. Chad's Rd .126 EY59
Sevenoaks (Godden Grn)
TN15 .257 FN124
Sevenoaks (Ide Hill) TN14 .256 FC126
Waltham Abbey EN9 .50 EJ23
Watford (Let.Hth) WD25 .77 CE39
Welwyn (Tewin) AL6 .30 DD05
Backley Gdns, SE25 .202 DU100
Back Path, Red. RH1 .252 DQ133
Back Rd, Sid. DA14 .186 EU91
Backs, The, Chesh. HP5 .54 AQ31
Back St, Harl. CM17
off Broadway Av .36 EW11
Bacon Gro, SE1 .21 N6
Bacon La, NW9 .118 CP56
Edgware HA8 .96 CN53
Bacon Link, Rom. RM5 .105 FB51
[Sch] Bacons Coll, SE16 .23 J3
Bacons Dr, Pot.B. (Cuffley)
EN6 .65 DL29
Bacons La, N6 .120 DG60
Bacons Mead, Uxb. (Denh.)
UB9 .114 BG61
Bacon St, E1 .11 P3
E2 .11 P3
Bacon Ter, Dag. RM8
off Fitzstephen Rd .126 EV64
Bacton, NW5 .120 DG64
Bacton St, E2 .12 F1
Badburgham Ct, Wal.Abb.
EN9 .68 EF33
Baddeley Cl, Enf. EN3
off Burton Dr .83 EA37
Baddow Cl, Dag. RM10 .146 FA67
Woodford Green IG8 .102 EK51
Baddow Wk, N1 .4 G7
Baden Cl, Stai. TW18 .174 BG94
Baden Dr, Horl. RH6 .268 DE147
Baden Pl, SE1 .21 J3
Baden Powell Cl, Dag. RM9 .146 EY67
Surbiton KT6 .198 CM103
[Sch] Baden-Powell JMI Sch,
E5 off Ferron Rd .122 DV62
Baden Powell Rd, Sev.
TN13 .256 FE121
Baden Rd, N8 .121 DK56
Guildford GU2 .242 AV132
Ilford IG1 .125 EP64
Bader Cl, Ken. CR8 .236 DR115
Welwyn Garden City AL7 .30 DC09
Bader Gdns, Slou. SL1 .151 AN75
Bader Wk, Grav. (Nthflt)
DA11 .190 GE90
Bader Way, Rain. RM13 .147 FG65
Badger Cl, Felt. TW13
off Sycamore Cl .175 BU90
Guildford GU2 .242 AV131
Hounslow TW4 .156 BW83
Ilford IG2 .125 EQ59
Badgers Cl, Ashf. TW15
off Fordbridge Rd .174 BM92
Borehamwood WD6
off Kingsley Av .78 CM40
Enfield EN2 .81 DP41
Harrow HA1 .117 CD58
Hayes UB3 .135 BS73
Hertford SG13 .32 DV09
Woking GU21 .226 AW118
Badgers Copse, Orp. BR6 .205 ET103
Worcester Park KT4 .199 CT103
Badgers Cft, N20 .97 CY46
SE9 .185 EN90
Broxbourne EN10 .49 DY21
Hemel Hempstead HP2 .41 BR21
Badgers Hill, Vir.W. GU25 .192 AW99
Badgers Hole, Croy. CR0 .221 DX105
Badgers La, Warl. CR6 .236 DW120
BADGERS MOUNT, Sev.
TN14 .225 FB110
Badgers Mt, Grays (Orsett)
RM16 .171 GF75
Badgers Ri, Sev. (Bad.Mt)
TN14 .224 FA110
Badgers Rd, Sev. (Bad.Mt)
TN14 .225 FB110
Badgers Wk, N.Mal. KT3 .198 CS96
Purley CR8 .219 DK111
Rickmansworth (Chorl.)
WD3 .73 BF42
Whyteleafe CR3 .236 DT119
Badgers Wd, Cat. CR3 .252 DQ125
Slough (Farn.Com.) SL2 .111 AQ64
Badger Way, Hat. AL10 .45 CV20
Badingham Dr, Lthd. (Fetch.)
KT22 .231 CE123
Badlis Rd, E17 .101 EA54
Badlow Cl, Erith DA8 .167 FE80
Badma Cl, N9
off Hudson Way .100 DW48
Badminton Cl, Borwd. WD6 .78 CN40
Harrow HA1 .117 CE56
Northolt UB5 .136 CA65
Badminton Ms, E16 .25 M1
Badminton Pl, Brox. EN10 .49 DY20
Badminton Rd, SW12 .180 DG86
Badric Ct, SW11
off Yelverton Rd .160 DD82
Badsworth Rd, SE5 .162 DQ80
Baffin Way, E14 .14 D10
Bagden Hill, Dor. (Westh.)
RH5 .247 CD130
Bagley Cl, West Dr. UB7 .154 BL75
Bagley's La, SW6 .160 DB81
Bagleys Spring, Rom. RM6 .126 EY56
Bagot Cl, Ashtd. KT21 .232 CM116
Bagshot Ct, SE18
off Prince Imperial Rd .165 EN81
Bagshot Rd, Egh. (Eng.Grn)
TW20 .172 AW94
Enfield EN1 .100 DT45
Bagshot St, SE17 .21 M10
Bahram Rd, Epsom KT19 .216 CR110
Baildon St, SE8 .163 DZ80
Bailey Cl, E4 .101 EC49
N11 .99 DK52
Purfleet RM19
off Gabion Av .169 FR77
Windsor SL4 .151 AN82
Bailey Cres, Chess. KT9
off Nigel Fisher Way .215 CK107
Bailey Ms, SW2 .181 DN85
Bailey Pl, SE26 .183 DX93
Bailey Rd, Dor. (Westc.) RH4 .262 CC137
Baillie Cl, Rain. RM13 .147 FH70
Baillie Rd, Guil. GU1 .259 AZ135
Baillies Wk, W5
off Liverpool Rd .157 CK75
Bainbridge Cl, Rich. (Ham)
TW10 off Latchmere Cl .178 CL92
Bainbridge Rd, Dag. RM9 .126 EZ63
Bainbridge St, WC1 .9 M7
Baines Cl, S.Croy. CR2
off Brighton Rd .220 DQ106
Bainton Mead, Wok. GU21 .226 AU117
Baird Av, Sthl. UB1 .136 CB73
Baird Cl, E10
off Marconi Rd .123 EA60
NW9 .118 CQ58
Bushey WD23
off Ashfield Av .76 CB44
Slough SL1 .151 AP75
Baird Gdns, SE19 .182 DS91
Baird Rd, Enf. EN1 .82 DV42
Baird St, EC1 .11 H3
Bairny Wd App, Wdf.Grn.
IG8 off Broadway Cl .102 EH51
Bairstow Cl, Borwd. WD6 .78 CL39
Baizdon Rd, SE3 .164 EE82
Bakeham La, Egh. (Eng.Grn)
TW20 .172 AW94
Bakehouse Rd, Horl. RH6 .268 DF146
Baker Boy La, Croy. CR0 .221 DZ112
Baker Hill Cl, Grav. (Nthflt)
DA11 .191 GF91
Baker La, Mitch. CR4 .200 DG96
Baker Pas, NW10
off Acton La .138 CS67
Baker Rd, NW10 .138 CS67
SE18 .164 EL80
Bakers Av, E17 .123 EB58
Bakers Cl, Ken. CR8 .220 DQ114
Bakers Ct, SE25 .202 DS97
Bakers End, SW20 .199 CY96
Bakers Fld, N7
off Crayford Rd .121 DK63
Bakers Gdns, Cars. SM5 .200 DE103
Bakers Gro, Welw.G.C. AL7 .30 DC08
Bakers Hall Ct, EC3 .11 M10
Bakers Hill, E5 .122 DW60
Barnet EN5 .80 DB40
Bakers La, N6 .120 DF57
Epping CM16 .69 ET30
Sawbridgeworth
(High Wych) CM21 .35 ET05
Bakers Mead, Gdse. RH9 .252 DW130
Baker's Ms, W1 .8 E7
Bakers Ms, Orp. BR6 .223 ET107
Bakers Orchard, H.Wyc.
(Woob.Grn) HP10 .110 AE58
Bakers Pas, NW3
off Heath St .120 DC63
Baker's Rents, E2 .11 N2
Bakers Rd, Uxb. UB8 .134 BK66
Waltham Cross (Chsht)
EN7 .66 DV30
Bakers Row, E15 .144 EE68
Baker's Row, EC1 .10 C4
⊖ Baker Street .8 D5
Baker St, NW1 .8 D4
W1 .8 D5
Enfield EN1 .82 DR41
Hertford SG13 .32 DS09
Potters Bar EN6 .79 CY35
Weybridge KT13 .212 BN105
Bakers Wk, Saw. CM21 .36 EY05
Bakers Wd, Uxb. (Denh.)
UB9 .113 BD60
Baker's Yd, EC1
off Baker's Row .141 DN70
Uxbridge UB8
off Bakers Rd .134 BK66
Bakery Cl, SW9 .161 DM81
Harlow (Roydon) CM19 .50 EJ15
Bakery Path, Edg. HA8
off Station Rd .96 CP51
Bakery Pl, SW11
off Altenburg Gdns .160 DF84
Bakewell Way, N.Mal. KT3 .198 CS96
Balaams La, N14 .99 DK47
Balaam St, E13 .15 M3
Balaclava Rd, SE1 .21 P8
Surbiton KT6 .197 CJ101
Bala Grn, NW9
off Snowdon Dr .118 CS58
Balcary Gdns, Berk. HP4 .38 AS20
Balcaskie Rd, SE9 .185 EM85
Balchen Rd, SE3 .164 EK82
Balchier Rd, SE22 .182 DV86
Balchins La, Dor. (Westc.)
RH4 .262 CA138
Balcombe Cl, Bexh. DA6 .166 EX84
Balcombe Gdns, Horl. RH6 .269 DJ149
Balcombe Rd, Horl. RH6 .269 DH147
Balcombe St, NW1 .8 C4
Balcon Ct, W5
off Boileau Rd .138 CM72
Balcon Way, Borwd. WD6 .78 CQ39
Balcorne St, E9 .142 DW66
Balder Ri, SE12 .184 EH89
Balderton St, W1 .8 F8
Baldocks Rd, Epp. (They.B.)
CM16 .85 ES35
Baldock St, E3 .143 EB68
Ware SG12 .33 DX06
Baldock Way, Borwd. WD6 .78 CM39
Baldry Gdns, SW16 .181 DL93
Baldwin Cres, SE5 .162 DQ81
Guildford GU4 .243 BC132
Baldwin Gdns, Houns. TW3
off Chamberlain Gdns .156 CC81
Baldwin Rd, Beac. HP9 .89 AP54
Slough (Burn.) SL1 .130 AJ69
Baldwins, Welw.G.C. AL7 .30 DB09
Baldwin's Gdns, EC1 .10 C5
Baldwins Hill, Loug. IG10 .85 EM40
Baldwins La, Rick.
(Crox.Grn) WD3 .74 BN42
Baldwins Shore, Wind.
(Eton) SL4 .151 AR79
Baldwin St, EC1 .11 J2
Baldwin Ter, N1 .4 G9
Baldwyn Gdns, W3 .138 CQ73
Baldwyns Pk, Bex. DA5 .187 FD89
Baldwyns Rd, Bex. DA5 .187 FD89
Bale Rd, E1 .13 J5
[Coll] Bales Coll, W10 .6 B2
Balfern Gro, W4 .158 CS78
Balfern St, SW11 .160 DE81
Balfe St, N1 .141 DL68
Balfont Cl, S.Croy. CR2 .220 DU113
Balfour Av, W7 .137 CF74
Woking GU22 .226 AY122
Balfour Business Cen, Sthl.
UB2 .156 BX76
Balfour Gro, N20 .98 DF48
Balfour Ho, W10 .6 B5
Balfour Ms, N9
off The Broadway .100 DU48
W1 .18 F1
Balfour Pl, SW15 .159 CV84
W1 .8 F10
Balfour Rd, N5 .122 DQ63
SE25 .202 DU98
SW19 .180 DB94
W3 .138 CQ71
W13 .157 CG75
Bromley BR2 .204 EK99
Carshalton SM5 .218 DF108
Grays RM17 .170 GC77
Harrow HA1 .117 CD57
Hounslow TW3 .156 CB83
Ilford IG1 .125 EP61
Southall UB2 .156 BX76
Weybridge KT13 .212 BN105
Balfour St, SE17 .21 J7
Hertford SG14 .32 DQ08
Balfron Twr, E14 .14 C7
Balgonie Rd, E4 .101 ED46
Balgores Cres, Rom. RM2 .127 FH55
Balgores La, Rom. RM2 .127 FH55
Balgores Sq, Rom. RM2 .127 FH56
Balgowan Cl, N.Mal. KT3 .198 CS99
[Sch] Balgowan Prim Sch,
Beck. BR3
off Balgowan Rd .203 DY96
Balgowan Rd, Beck. BR3 .203 DY97
Balgowan St, SE18 .165 ET77
BALHAM, SW12 .180 DF88
⇌ Balham .181 DH88
⊖ Balham .181 DH88
Balham Continental Mkt,
SW12 off Shipka Rd .181 DH88
Balham Gro, SW12 .180 DG87
Balham High Rd, SW12 .180 DG88
SW17 .180 DG89
Balham Hill, SW12 .181 DH87
Balham New Rd, SW12 .181 DH87
Balham Pk Rd, SW12 .180 DF88
Balham Rd, N9 .100 DU47
Balham Sta Rd, SW12 .181 DH88
Balkan Wk, E1 .12 C10
Balladier Wk, E14 .14 A6
Ballamore Rd, Brom. BR1 .184 EG90
Ballance Rd, E9 .143 DX65
Ballands N, The, Lthd. KT22 .231 CE122
Ballands S, The, Lthd. KT22 .231 CE123
Ballantine St, SW18 .160 DC84
Ballantyne Dr, Tad. (Kgswd)
KT20 .233 CZ121
Ballard Cl, Kings.T. KT2 .178 CR94
Ballard Grn, Wind. SL4 .151 AL80
Ballards Cl, Dag. RM10 .147 FB67
Ballards Fm Rd, Croy. CR0 .220 DU107
South Croydon CR2 .220 DU107
Ballards Grn, Tad. KT20 .233 CY119
Ballards La, N3 .98 DA53
N12 .98 DA53
Oxted RH8 .254 EJ129
Ballards Ms, Edg. HA8 .96 CN51
Ballards Ri, S.Croy. CR2 .220 DU107
Ballards Rd, NW2 .119 CU61
Dagenham RM10 .147 FB67
Ballards Way, Croy. CR0 .220 DV107
South Croydon CR2 .220 DU107
Ballast Quay, SE10 .24 F9
Ballater Cl, Wat. WD19 .94 BW49
Ballater Rd, SW2 .161 DL84
South Croydon CR2 .220 DT106
Ball Ct, EC3 off Cornhill .142 DR72
Ballenger Ct, Wat. WD18 .75 BV41
Ballina St, SE23 .183 DX86
Ballingdon Rd, SW11 .180 DG86
Ballinger Ct, Berk. HP4 .38 AV20
Ballinger Pt, E3 .14 B1
Balliol Av, E4 .101 ED49
Balliol Rd, N17 .100 DS53
W10 .139 CW72
Welling DA16 .166 EV82
Balloch Rd, SE6 .183 ED88
Ballogie Av, NW10 .118 CS63
Ballow Cl, SE5 off Harris St .162 DS80

⊖ London Underground station [DLR] Docklands Light Railway station [Tra] Tramlink station [Riv] Pedestrian ferry landing stage

Balls Pk, Hert. SG13 32 DT11
Balls Pond Pl, N1 5 K3
Balls Pond Rd, N1 5 K3
Balmain Cl, W5 137 CK74
Balmer Rd, E3 143 DZ68
Balmes Rd, N1 5 K7
Balmoral Apartments, W2
off Praed St 140 DE71
Balmoral Av, N11 98 DG50
Beckenham BR3 203 DY98
Balmoral Cl, SW15
off Westleigh Av 179 CX86
St. Albans (Park St) AL2 60 CC28
Slough SL1 131 AL72
Balmoral Ct, Wor.Pk. KT4 199 CV103
Balmoral Cres, W.Mol. KT8 196 CA97
Balmoral Dr, Borwd. WD6 78 CR43
Hayes UB4 135 BT71
Southall UB1 136 BZ70
Woking GU22 227 BC116
Balmoral Gdns, W13 157 CG76
Bexley DA5 186 EZ87
Ilford IG3 125 ET60
South Croydon CR2 220 DR110
Windsor SL4 151 AR83
Balmoral Gro, N7 4 A4
Balmoral Ms, W12 159 CT75
Balmoral Rd, E7 124 EJ63
E10 123 EB61
NW2 139 CV65
Abbots Langley WD5 59 BU32
Brentwood (Pilg.Hat.)
CM15 108 FV44
Dartford (Sutt.H.) DA4 188 FP94
Enfield EN3 83 DX36
Harrow HA2 116 CA63
Hornchurch RM12 128 FK62
Kingston upon Thames
KT1 198 CM98
Romford RM2 127 FH56
Watford WD24 76 BW38
Worcester Park KT4 199 CV104
Balmoral Way, Sutt. SM2 218 DA110
Balmore Cl, E14 14 D7
Balmore Cres, Barn. EN4 80 DG43
Balmore St, N19 121 DH61
Balmuir Gdns, SW15 159 CW84
Balnacraig Av, NW10 118 CS63
Balniel Gate, SW1 19 M9
Balquhain Cl, Ashtd. KT21 231 CK117
Balsams Cl, Hert. SG13 32 DR11
Baltic Cl, SW19 180 DD94
Baltic Ct, SE16 23 H3
Baltic Pl, N1 5 M8
Baltic St E, EC1 10 G4
Baltic St W, EC1 10 G4
Baltic Wf, Grav. DA11
off West St 191 GG86
Baltimore Pl, Well. DA16 165 ET82
Balvaird Pl, SW1 19 M10
Balvernie Gro, SW18 179 CZ87
Bamber Ho, Bark. IG11
off St. Margarets 145 EQ67
Bamborough Gdns, W12 159 CW75
Bamford Av, Wem. HA0 138 CM67
Bamford Ct, E15
off Clays La 123 EB64
Bamford Rd, Bark. IG11 145 EQ65
Bromley BR1 183 EC92
Bamford Way, Rom. RM5 105 FB50
Bampfylde Cl, Wall. SM6 201 DJ104
Bampton Dr, NW7 97 CU52
Bampton Rd, SE23 183 DX90
Romford RM3 106 FL53
Bampton Way, Wok. GU21 226 AU118
Banavie Gdns, Beck. BR3 203 EC95
Banbury Av, Slou. SL1 131 AM71
Banbury Cl, Enf. EN2
off Holtwhites Hill 81 DP39
Banbury Ct, WC2 9 N9
Sutton SM2 218 DA108
Banbury Enterprise Cen, Croy.
CR0 off Factory La 201 DP103
Banbury Rd, E9 143 DX66
E17 101 DX52
Banbury St, SW11 160 DE82
Watford WD18 75 BU43
Banbury Vil, Grav. DA13 190 FZ94
Banbury Wk, Nthlt. UB5
off Brabazon Rd 136 CA68
Banchory Rd, SE3 164 EH80
Bancroft Av, N2 120 DE57
Buckhurst Hill IG9 102 EG47
Bancroft Chase, Horn. RM12 127 FF61
Bancroft Cl, Ashf. TW15
off Feltham Hill Rd 174 BN92
Bancroft Ct, Nthlt. UB5 136 BW67
Reigate RH2 250 DB134
Bancroft Gdns, Har. HA3 94 CC53
Orpington BR6 205 ET102
Bancroft Rd, E1 12 F2
Harrow HA3 94 CC54
Reigate RH2 250 DA134
[Sch] Bancrofts Sch, Wdf.Grn.
IG8 off High Rd
Woodford Grn 102 EG48
Banders Ri, Guil. GU1 243 BC133
Band La, Egh. TW20 173 AZ92
Bandon Cl, Uxb. UB10 134 BM67
[Sch] Bandon Hill Prim Sch, Wall.
SM6 off Sandy La S 219 DK107
Bandon Ri, Wall. SM6 219 DK106
Banes Down, Wal.Abb. EN9 50 EE22
Banfield Rd, SE15 162 DV84
[Sch] Bangabandhu Prim Sch,
E2 12 F2
Bangalore St, SW15 159 CW83
Bangor Cl, Nthlt. UB5 116 CB64
Bangors Cl, Iver SL0 133 BE72
Bangors Rd N, Iver SL0 133 BD67
Bangors Rd S, Iver SL0 133 BE71
Banim St, W6 159 CV76
Banister Rd, W10 6 B1
⊖ Bank 11 J8
[DLR] Bank 11 J8
Bank, The, N6
off Cholmeley Pk 121 DH60
Bank Av, Mitch. CR4 200 DD96
Bank Ct, Dart. DA1
off High St 188 FL86
Hemel Hempstead HP1 40 BJ21
Bank End, SE1 21 H1
Bankfoot, Grays (Bad.Dene)
RM17 170 FZ77
Bankfoot Rd, Brom. BR1 184 EE91
Bankhurst Rd, SE6 183 DZ87
Bank La, SW15 178 CS85
Kingston upon Thames
KT2 178 CL94
Bank Ms, Sutt. SM1
off Sutton Ct Rd 218 DC107
Bank Mill, Berk. HP4 38 AY19
Bank Mill La, Berk. HP4 38 AY20
★ Bank of England, EC2 11 J8
★ Bank of England Mus,
EC2 11 K8
Bank Pl, Brwd. CM14
off High St 108 FW47
Bank Rd, H.Wyc. (Penn)
HP10 88 AC47
Banksian Wk, Islw. TW7 157 CE81
Banksia Rd, N18 100 DW50
Bankside, SE1 10 G10
Enfield EN2 81 DP39
Gravesend (Nthflt) DA11 190 GC86
Sevenoaks (Dunt.Grn)
TN13 256 FE121
South Croydon CR2 220 DT107
Southall UB1 136 BX74
Woking GU21
off Wyndham Rd 226 AV118
Bankside Av, Nthlt. UB5
off Townson Av 135 BU68
Bankside Cl, Bex. DA5 187 FD91
Carshalton SM5 218 DE107
Isleworth TW7 157 CF84
Uxbridge (Hare.) UB9 92 BG51
Westerham (Bigg.H.)
TN16 238 EJ118
Bankside Dr, T.Ditt. KT7 197 CH102
★ Bankside Gall, SE1 10 F10
[Pier] Bankside Pier 10 G10
Bankside Rd, Ilf. IG1 125 EQ64
Bankside Way, SE19
off Lunham Rd 182 DS93
Banks La, Bexh. DA6 166 EZ84
Epping CM16 70 EY32
Bank's La, Lthd. (Eff.) KT24 229 BV122
Banks Rd, Borwd. WD6 78 CQ40
Banks Spur, Slou. SL1
off Cooper Way 151 AP75
Bank St, E14 23 P2
Gravesend DA12 191 GH86
Sevenoaks TN13 257 FH125
Banks Way, E12
off Grantham Rd 125 EN63
Guildford GU4 243 AZ131
Bankton Rd, SW2 161 DN84
Bankwell Rd, SE13 164 EE84
Bann Cl, S.Ock. RM15 149 FV73
Banner Cl, Purf. RM19 169 FR77
Bannerman Ho, SW8 161 DM79
Banner St, EC1 11 H4
Banning St, SE10 24 G10
Bannister Cl, SW2
off Ewen Cres 181 DN88
Greenford UB6 117 CD64
Slough SL3 152 AY75
Bannister Dr, Brwd. (Hutt.)
CM13 109 GC44
Bannister Gdns, Orp. BR5
off Main Rd 206 EW97
Bannister Ho, E9
off Homerton High St 123 DX64
Bannister's Rd, Guil. GU2 258 AT136
[Sch] Bannockburn Prim Sch,
SE18
off Plumstead High St 165 ET77
Bannockburn Rd, SE18 165 ES77
Bannow Cl, Epsom KT19 216 CS105
★ Banqueting Ho, SW1 19 N2
BANSTEAD, SM7 234 DB115
⇌ Banstead 217 CY114
[Sch] Banstead Comm Jun Sch,
Bans. SM7
off The Horseshoe 233 CZ115
Banstead Gdns, N9 100 DS48
[Sch] Banstead Inf Sch, Bans.
SM7 off The Horseshoe 233 CZ115
Banstead Pl, Bans. SM7 234 DC116
Banstead Rd, Bans. SM7 217 CX112
Carshalton SM5 218 DE107
Caterham CR3 236 DR121
Epsom KT17 217 CV110
Purley CR8 219 DN111
Banstead Rd S, Sutt. SM2 218 DD110
Banstead St, SE15 162 DW83
Banstead Way, Wall. SM6 219 DL106
Banstock Rd, Edg. HA8 96 CP51
Banting Dr, N21 81 DM43
Banton Cl, Enf. EN1
off Central Av 82 DV40
Bantry St, SE5 162 DR80
Banwell Rd, Bex. DA5
off Woodside La 186 EX86
Banyard Rd, SE16 22 D6
Banyards, Horn. RM11 128 FL56
Bapchild Pl, Orp. BR5 206 EW98
Baptist Gdns, NW5
off Queen's Cres 140 DG65
Barandon Wk, W11 6 B9
Barbara Brosnan Ct, NW8
off Grove End Rd 140 DD68
Barbara Cl, Shep. TW17 195 BP99
Barbara Hucklesby Cl, N22
off The Sandlings 99 DP54
[Sch] Barbara Speake Stage Sch,
W3 off East Acton La 138 CS73
Barbauld Rd, N16 122 DS62
Barbel Cl, Wal.Cr. EN8 67 EA34
Barber Cl, N21 99 DN45
Barberry Cl, Rom. RM3 106 FJ52
Barberry Rd, Hem.H. HP1 40 BG20
Barber's All, E13 15 N1
Barbers Rd, E15 143 EB68
BARBICAN, EC2 10 G6
⇌ Barbican 10 F5
⊖ Barbican 10 F5
★ Barbican Arts & Conf Cen,
EC2 11 H5
Barbican Rd, Grnf. UB6 136 CB72
Barb Ms, W6 159 CW76
Barbon Cl, WC1 10 A5
Barbot Cl, N9 100 DU48
Barchard St, SW18 180 DB85
Barchester Cl, W7 137 CF74
Uxbridge UB8 134 BJ70
Barchester Rd, Har. HA3 95 CD54
Slough SL3 153 AZ75
Barchester St, E14 14 A6
Barclay Cl, SW6 160 DA80
Hertford (Hert.Hth) SG13 32 DV11
Leatherhead (Fetch.)
KT22 230 CB123
Watford WD18 75 BU44
Barclay Ct, Hodd. EN11 49 EA18
Slough SL1 151 AQ75
[Sch] Barclay Inf Sch, E10
off Canterbury Rd 123 ED58
[Sch] Barclay Jun Sch, E10
off Canterbury Rd 123 ED58
Barclay Oval, Wdf.Grn. IG8 102 EG49
Barclay Path, E17 123 EC57
Barclay Rd, E11 124 EE60
Barclay Rd, E13 144 EJ70
E17 123 EC57
N18 100 DR51
SW6 160 DA80
Croydon CR0 202 DR104
Barclay Way, SE22
off Lordship La 182 DU87
Grays (W.Thur.) RM20 169 FT78
Barcombe Av, SW2 181 DL89
Barcombe Cl, Orp. BR5 205 ET97
Barden Cl, Uxb. (Hare.) UB9 92 BJ52
Barden St, SE18 165 ES80
Bardeswell Cl, Brwd. CM14 108 FW47
Bardfield Av, Rom. RM6 126 EX55
Bardney Rd, Mord. SM4 200 DB98
Bardolph Av, Croy. CR0 221 DZ109
Bardolph Rd, N7 121 DL63
Richmond TW9
off St. Georges Rd 158 CM83
Bardon Wk, Wok. GU21
off Bampton Way 226 AV117
Bard Rd, W10 6 A10
Bards Cor, Hem.H. HP1
off Laureate Way 40 BH19
Bardsey Pl, E1 12 E4
Bardsey Wk, N1 5 H4
Bardsley Cl, Croy. CR0 202 DT104
Bardsley La, SE10 163 EC79
Bardwell Ct, St.Alb. AL1 43 CD21
Bardwell Rd, St.Alb. AL1 43 CD21
Barfett St, W10 6 E3
Barfield, Dart. (Sutt.H.) DA4 208 FP95
Barfield Av, N20 98 DE47
Barfield Rd, E11 124 EF60
Bromley BR1 205 EN97
Barfields, Loug. IG10 85 EN42
Redhill (Bletch.) RH1 251 DP133
Barfields Gdns, Loug. IG10
off Barfields 85 EN42
Barfields Path, Loug. IG10 85 EN42
Barfolds, Hat. AL9
off Dixons Hill Rd 45 CW23
Barford Cl, NW4 97 CU53
Barford St, N1 4 D8
Barforth Rd, SE15 162 DV83
Barfreston Way, SE20 202 DV95
Bargate Cl, SE18 165 ET78
New Malden KT3 199 CU100
Bargate Ct, Guil. GU2
off Park Barn Dr 242 AS134
Barge Ho Rd, E16 145 EP74
Barge Ho St, SE1 20 D1
Bargery Rd, SE6 183 EB88
Barge Wk, E.Mol. KT8 197 CK96
Kingston upon Thames
KT1 197 CK95
Walton-on-Thames KT12 196 BX97
Bargrove Av, Hem.H. HP1 40 BG21
Bargrove Cl, SE20 182 DU94
Bargrove Cres, SE6
off Elm La 183 DZ89
Barham Av, Borwd. (Elstree)
WD6 78 CM41
Barham Cl, Brom. BR2 204 EL102
Chislehurst BR7 185 EP92
Gravesend DA12 191 GM88
Romford RM7 105 FB54
Wembley HA0 137 CH65
Weybridge KT13 213 BQ105
[Sch] Barham Prim Sch, Wem.
HA0 off Danethorpe Rd 137 CJ65
Barham Rd, SW20 179 CU94
Chislehurst BR7 185 EP92
Dartford DA1 188 FN87
South Croydon CR2 220 DQ106
Baring Cl, SE12 184 EG89
Baring Cres, Beac. HP9 88 AJ52
[Sch] Baring Prim Sch, SE12
off Linchmere Rd 184 EG87
Baring Rd, SE12 184 EG87
Barnet EN4 80 DD41
Beaconsfield HP9 88 AJ52
Croydon CR0 202 DU102
Baring St, N1 5 J8
Barkantine Shop Par, The,
E14 23 N4
Bark Burr Rd, Grays RM16 170 FZ75
Barker Cl, Cher. KT16
off Barker Rd 193 BE101
New Malden KT3 198 CP98
Northwood HA6 93 BT52
Barker Dr, NW1 141 DJ66
Barker Ms, SW4 161 DH84
Barker Rd, Cher. KT16 193 BE101
Barker St, SW10 160 DC79
Barker Wk, SW16 181 DK90
Barker Way, SE22
off Dulwich Common 182 DU88
Barkham Rd, N17 100 DR52
Barkham Ter, SE1 20 D5
Bark Hart Rd, Orp. BR6 206 EV102
BARKING, IG11 145 EP67
⇌ Barking 145 EQ66
⊖ Barking 145 EQ66
[Sch] Barking Abbey Comp Sch,
Lwr Sch, Bark. IG11
off Longbridge Rd 125 ES64
Upr Sch, Bark. IG11
off Sandringham Rd 145 ET65
[Coll] Barking Adult Training Cen,
Bark. IG11
off The Shaftesburys 145 EQ67
[Coll] Barking Coll, Rom. RM7
off Dagenham Rd 127 FD61
[H] Barking Hosp, Bark. IG11 145 ET66
Barking Ind Pk, Bark. IG11 145 ET67
Barking Rd, E6 144 EK68
E13 15 N2
E16 15 J6
BARKINGSIDE, Ilf. IG6 125 EP55
⊖ Barkingside 125 ER56
Bark Pl, W2 7 J9
Barkston Gdns, SW5 17 J9
Barkston Path, Borwd. WD6 78 CN37
Barkwood Cl, Rom. RM7 127 FC57
Barkworth Rd, SE16 22 D10
Barlborough St, SE14 162 DW80
Barlby Gdns, W10 6 A4
[Sch] Barlby Prim Sch, W10 6 B4
Barlby Rd, W10 6 A5
Barlee Cres, Uxb. UB8 134 BJ71
Barle Gdns, S.Ock. RM15 149 FV72
Barley Brow, Wat. WD25 59 BV31
Barley Cl, Bushey WD23 76 CB43
Barleycorn Way, E14 13 L9
Hornchurch RM11 128 FM58
Barley Cft, Harl. CM18 51 ES19
Hemel Hempstead HP2 41 BQ20
Hertford SG14 32 DR07
Barleycroft Grn, Welw.G.C.
AL8 29 CW09
Barleycroft Rd, Welw.G.C.
AL8 29 CW10
Barley Flds, H.Wyc.
(Woob.Grn) HP10 110 AE55
Barleyfields Cl, Rom. RM6 126 EV59
Barley La, Ilf. IG3 126 EU60
Romford RM6 126 EV58
[Sch] Barley La Prim Sch, Rom.
RM6 off Huxley Dr 126 EV59
Barleymead, Horl. RH6
off Oatlands 269 DH147
Barley Mow Caravan Pk,
St.Alb. AL4 44 CM22
Barley Mow Ct, Bet. RH3 248 CQ134
Barley Mow La, St.Alb. AL4 44 CL23
Barley Mow Pas, EC1 10 F6
W4 158 CR78
Barley Mow Rd, Egh.
(Eng.Grn) TW20 172 AW92
Barley Mow Way, Shep.
TW17 194 BN98
Barley Ponds Cl, Ware SG12 33 DZ06
Barley Ponds Rd, Ware
SG12 33 DZ06
Barley Shotts Business Pk,
W10 off St. Ervans Rd 139 CZ71
Barlow Cl, Wall. SM6 219 DL108
Barlow Dr, SE18 164 EL81
Barlow Pl, W1 9 H10
Barlow Rd, NW6 139 CZ65
W3 138 CP74
Hampton TW12 176 CA94
Barlow St, SE17 21 K8
Barlow Way, Rain. RM13 147 FD71
Barmeston Rd, SE6 183 EB89
Barmor Cl, Har. HA2 94 CB54
Barmouth Av, Grnf. UB6 137 CF68
Barmouth Rd, SW18 180 DC86
Croydon CR0 203 DX103
Barnabas Ct, N21
off Cheyne Wk 81 DN43
Barnabas Rd, E9 123 DX64
Barnaby Cl, Har. HA2 116 CC61
Barnaby Pl, SW7 17 N8
Barnaby Way, Chig. IG7 103 EP48
Barnacre Cl, Uxb. UB8
off New Peachey La 134 BK72
Barnacres Rd, Hem.H. HP3 58 BM25
Barnard Acres, Wal.Abb.
EN9 50 EE23
Barnard Cl, SE18 165 EN77
Chislehurst BR7 205 ER95
Sunbury-on-Thames
TW16 off Oak Gro 175 BV94
Wallington SM6 219 DK108
Barnard Ct, Wok. GU21
off Raglan Rd 226 AS118
Barnard Gdns, Hayes UB4 135 BV70
New Malden KT3 199 CU98
Barnard Grn, Welw.G.C.
AL7 29 CZ10
Barnard Gro, E15
off Vicarage La 144 EF66
Barnard Hill, N10 98 DG54
Barnard Ms, SW11 160 DE84
Barnardo Dr, Ilf. IG6 125 EQ56
Barnardo Gdns, E1 12 G8
Barnardo St, E1 12 G8
Barnardos Village, Ilf. IG6 125 EQ55
Barnard Rd, SW11 160 DE84
Enfield EN1 82 DV40
Mitcham CR4 200 DG97
Warlingham CR6 237 EB119
Barnard's Inn, EC1 10 D7
Barnards Pl, S.Croy. CR2 219 DP109
Barnard Way, Hem.H. HP3 40 BL21
Barnato Cl, W.Byf. KT14
off Viscount Gdns 212 BL112
Barnby Sq, E15
off Barnby St 144 EE67
Barnby St, E15 144 EE67
NW1 141 DJ68
Barn Cl, Ashf. TW15 175 BP92
Banstead SM7 234 DD115
Epsom KT18 232 CQ115
Hemel Hempstead HP3
off Barnfield 40 BM23
Northolt UB5 136 BW68
Radlett WD7 77 CG35
Slough (Farn.Com.) SL2 111 AP63
Welwyn Garden City AL8 29 CW09
Barn Cres, Pur. CR8 220 DR113
Stanmore HA7 95 CJ51
Barncroft Cl, Loug. IG10 85 EN43
Uxbridge UB8 135 BP71
Barncroft Grn, Loug. IG10 85 EN43
[Sch] Barncroft JMI & Nurs Sch,
Hem.H. HP2
off Washington Av 40 BK15
[Sch] Barn Cft Prim Sch, E17
off Brunel Rd 123 DY58
Barncroft Rd, Berk. HP4 38 AT20
Loughton IG10 85 EN43
Barncroft Way, St.Alb. AL1 43 CG21
Barndicott, Welw.G.C. AL7 30 DC09
Barneby Cl, Twick. TW2
off Rowntree Rd 177 CE88
BARNEHURST, Bexh. DA7 167 FD83
⇌ Barnehurst 167 FC82
Barnehurst Av, Bexh. DA7 167 FC81
Erith DA8 167 FC81
Barnehurst Cl, Erith DA8 167 FC81
[Sch] Barnehurst Inf Sch, Erith
DA8 off Barnehurst Cl 167 FC81
[Sch] Barnehurst Jun Sch, Erith
DA8 off Barnehurst Cl 167 FC81
Barnehurst Rd, Bexh. DA7 167 FC82
Barn Elms Pk, SW15 159 CW82
[Sch] Barn End Cen, Dart. DA2
off High Rd 188 FJ90
Barn End Dr, Dart. DA2 188 FJ90
Barn End La, Dart. DA2 188 FJ92
BARNES, SW13 159 CU82
⇌ Barnes 159 CU83
Barnes All, Hmptn. TW12
off Hampton Ct Rd 196 CC96
Barnes Av, SW13 159 CU80
Chesham HP5 54 AQ30
Southall UB2 156 BZ77
⇌ Barnes Bridge 158 CS82
Barnes Br, SW13 158 CS82
W4 158 CS82
Barnesbury Ho, SW4 181 DK85
Barnes Cl, E12 124 EK63
★ Barnes Common, SW13 159 CU83
Barnes Ct, E16
off Ridgwell Rd 144 EJ71
Woodford Green IG8 102 EK50
BARNES CRAY, Dart. DA1 167 FH84
Barnes Cray Cotts, Dart. DA1
off Maiden La 187 FG85
[Sch] Barnes Cray Prim Sch,
Dart. DA1
off Iron Mill La 167 FG84
Barnes Cray Rd, Dart. DA1 167 FG84
Barnesdale Cres, Orp. BR5 206 EU100
Barnes End, N.Mal. KT3 199 CU99
Barnes High St, SW13 159 CT82
[H] Barnes Hosp, SW14 158 CS83
Barnes Ho, Bark. IG11
off St. Marys 145 ER67
Barnes La, Kings L. WD4 58 BH27
Barnes Pikle, W5 137 CK73
[Sch] Barnes Prim Sch, SW13
off Cross St 159 CT83
Barnes Ri, Kings L. WD4 58 BM27
Barnes Rd, N18 100 DW49
Godalming GU7 258 AS143
Ilford IG1 125 EQ64
Barnes St, E14 13 J8
Barnes Ter, SE8 23 M10
Barnes Wallis Dr, Wey. KT13 212 BL111
Barnes Way, Iver SL0 133 BF73
BARNET, EN4 & EN5 79 CZ41
Barnet Bypass, Barn. EN5 78 CS41
[Coll] Barnet Coll, Grahame Pk
Cen, NW9 97 CT53
Montagu Rd Cen, NW4 119 CU58
Russell La Cen, N20 98 DF46
Stanhope Rd Cen, N12 98 DD50
Wood St Cen, Barn. EN5 79 CZ42
Barnet Dr, Brom. BR2 204 EL103
BARNET GATE, Barn. EN5 79 CT44
Barnet Gate La, Barn. EN5 79 CT44
[H] Barnet Gen Hosp, Barn.
EN5 79 CX42
Barnet Gro, E2 12 A1
Barnet Hill, Barn. EN5 80 DA42
[Sch] Barnet Hill Prim Sch, Barn.
EN5 off Hammond Cl 79 CZ43
Barnet Ho, N20 98 DC47
Barnet La, N20 97 CZ46
Barnet EN5 79 CZ44
Borehamwood WD6 77 CK44
★ Barnet Mus, Barn. EN5
off Wood St 79 CY42
Barnet Rd, Barn. EN5 79 CV43
Potters Bar EN6 80 DA35
St. Albans (Lon.Col.) AL2 62 CL27
Barnett Cl, Erith DA8 167 FF82
Guildford (Won.) GU5 259 BC143
Leatherhead KT22 231 CH119
Barnett La, Guil. (Won.)
GU5 259 BB144
Barnet Trd Est, Barn. EN5 79 CZ41
Barnett Row, Guil. GU4 242 AX129
Barnetts Shaw, Oxt. RH8 253 ED127
Barnett St, E1 12 C7
[Sch] Barnett Wd Inf Sch,
Ashtd. KT21
off Barnett Wd La 231 CK117
Barnett Wd La, Ashtd. KT21 231 CJ119
Leatherhead KT22 231 CH120
Barnet Way, NW7 96 CR45
Barnet Wd Rd, Brom. BR2 204 EJ103
Barney Cl, SE7 164 EJ78
Barnfield, Bans. SM7 218 DB114
Epping CM16 70 EU28
Gravesend DA11 191 GG89
Hemel Hempstead HP3 40 BM23
Horley RH6 268 DG149
Iver SL0 133 BE72
New Malden KT3 198 CS100
Slough SL1 131 AK74
Barnfield Av, Croy. CR0 202 DW103
Kingston upon Thames
KT2 178 CL92
Mitcham CR4 201 DH98
Barnfield Cl, N4
off Crouch Hill 121 DL59
SW17 180 DC90
Coulsdon CR5 236 DQ119
Greenhithe DA9 189 FT86
Hoddesdon EN11 49 EA15
Swanley BR8 207 FC101
Waltham Abbey EN9 50 EF22
Barnfield Gdns, SE18
off Plumstead
Common Rd 165 EP79
Kingston upon Thames
KT2 178 CL91
Barnfield Pl, E14 23 P8
[Sch] Barnfield Prim Sch, Edg.
HA8 off Silkstream Rd 96 CQ53
Barnfield Rd, SE18 165 EP79
W5 137 CJ70
Belvedere DA17 166 EZ79
Edgware HA8 96 CQ53
Orpington BR5 206 EX97
St. Albans AL4 43 CJ17
Sevenoaks TN13 256 FD123
South Croydon CR2 220 DS109
Welwyn Garden City AL7 29 CY11
Westerham (Tats.) TN16 238 EK120
Barnfield Way, Oxt. RH8 254 EG133
Barnfield Wd Cl, Beck. BR3 203 ED100
Barnfield Wd Rd, Beck. BR3 203 ED100
Barnham Dr, SE28 145 ET74
Barnham Rd, Grnf. UB6 136 CC69
Barnham St, SE1 21 M3
Barn Hill, Harl. (Roydon)
CM19 50 EH19
Barnhill, Pnr. HA5 116 BW57
Barn Hill, Wem. HA9 118 CP61
Barnhill Av, Brom. BR2 204 EF99
[Sch] Barnhill Comm High Sch,
Hayes UB4
off Owen Rd 136 BW69
Barnhill La, Hayes UB4 135 BV69
Barnhill Rd, Hayes UB4 135 BV70
Wembley HA9 118 CQ62
Barnhurst Path, Wat. WD19 94 BW50
Barningham Way, NW9 118 CR58
Barn Lea, Rick. (Mill End)
WD3 92 BG46
Barnlea Cl, Felt. TW13 176 BY89
Barn Mead, Epp. (They.B.)
CM16 85 ES36
Harlow CM18 51 ER17
Ongar CM5 71 FE29
Barnmead, Wok. (Chobham)
GU24 210 AT110
Barnmead Gdns, Dag. RM9 126 EZ64
Barn Meadow, Epp. CM16
off Upland Rd 69 ET25
Barn Meadow La, Lthd.
(Bkhm) KT23 230 BZ124
Barnmead Rd, Beck. BR3 203 DY95
Dagenham RM9 126 EZ64
Barnock Cl, Dart. DA1 187 FE87
Barn Ri, Wem. HA9 118 CN60
BARNSBURY, N1 4 B5
Barnsbury Cl, N.Mal. KT3 198 CQ98
Barnsbury Cres, Surb. KT5 198 CQ102
Barnsbury Est, N1
off Barnsbury Rd 141 DN67
Barnsbury Gro, N7 4 B4
[Sch] Barnsbury Inf Sch, Wok.
GU22 off Hawthorn Rd 226 AX121
[Sch] Barnsbury Jun Sch, Wok.
GU22 off Almond Av 226 AX121
Barnsbury La, Surb. KT5 198 CP103
Barnsbury Pk, N1 4 C5
Barnsbury Rd, N1 4 C9

Barnsbury Sq, N1 . . . . 4 C6
Barnsbury St, N1 . . . . 4 C6
Barnsbury Ter, N1 . . . . 4 B6
Barns Ct, Harl. CM19 . . . . 51 EN20
Waltham Abbey EN9 . . . . 68 EG32
Barnscroft, SW20 . . . . 199 CV97
Barnsdale Av, E14 . . . . 23 P7
Barnsdale Cl, Borwd. WD6 . . 78 CM39
Barnsdale Rd, W9 . . . . 6 F3
Barnsfield Pl, Uxb. UB8 . . . 134 BJ66
Barnside Ct, Welw.G.C. AL8 . . 29 CW09
Barnsley Rd, Rom. RM3 . . 106 FM52
Barnsley St, E1 . . . . 12 D3
Barnstaple Path, Rom. RM3 . 106 FJ50
Barnstaple Rd, Rom. RM3 . . 106 FJ50
Ruislip HA4 . . . . 116 BW62
Barnston Wk, N1 . . . . 4 G7
Barnston Way, Brwd. (Hutt.)
CM13 . . . . 109 GC43
Barn St, N16
off Stoke Newington Ch St . 122 DS62
Barnsway, Kings L. WD4 . . . 58 BL28
Barnway, Egh. (Eng.Grn)
TW20 . . . . 172 AW92
Barn Way, Wem. HA9 . . . . 118 CN60
Barnwell Rd, SW2 . . . . 181 DN85
Dartford DA1 . . . . 168 FM83
Barnwood Cl, N20 . . . . 97 CZ46
W9 . . . . 7 J4
Guildford GU2 . . . . 242 AS132
Ruislip HA4
off Lysander Rd 115 BR61
Barnwood Rd, Guil. GU2 . . 242 AS133
Sch Barnwood Sch, Guil. GU2
off Barnwood Rd 242 AS133
Barnyard, The, Tad. KT20 . . 233 CU124
Baron Cl, N11
off Balmoral Av 98 DG50
Sutton SM2 . . . . 218 DB110
Baroness Rd, E2 . . . . 11 P1
Baronet Gro, N17
off St. Paul's Rd 100 DU53
Baronet Rd, N17 . . . . 100 DU53
Baron Gdns, Ilf. IG6 . . . . 125 EQ55
Baron Gro, Mitch. CR4 . . . . 200 DE98
Baron Rd, Dag. RM8 . . . . 126 EX60
Barons, The, Twick. TW1 . . . 177 CH86
⊖ Barons Court 16 B9
Barons Ct, Wall. SM6
off Whelan Way 201 DK104
Barons Ct Rd, W14 . . . . 16 C9
Baronsfield Rd, Twick. TW1 . . 177 CH86
Barons Gate, Barn. EN4 . . . 80 DE44
Barons Hurst, Epsom KT18 . 232 CQ116
Barons Keep, W14 . . . . 16 C9
Barons Mead, Har. HA1 . . . 117 CE56
Baronsmead Rd, SW13 . . . 159 CU81
Baronsmede, W5 . . . . 158 CM75
Baronsmere Rd, N2 . . . . 120 DE56
Barons Pl, SE1 . . . . 20 D4
Baron St, N1 . . . . 4 C9
Barons Wk, Croy. CR0 . . . 203 DY100
Barons Way, Egh. TW20 . . . 173 BD93
Reigate RH2 . . . . 266 DA138
Baron Wk, E16 . . . . 15 J5
Mitcham CR4 . . . . 200 DE98
Barque Ms, SE8
off Watergate St 163 EA79
Barrack La, Wind. SL4 . . . 151 AR81
Barrack Path, Wok. GU21 . . 226 AT118
Barrack Rd, Guil. GU2 . . . 242 AU132
Hounslow TW4 . . . . 156 BX84
Barrack Row, Grav. DA11 . . 191 GH86
Barracks, The, Add. KT15 . . 194 BH104
Barracks Hill, Amer. HP7 . . . 89 AM45
Barracks La, Barn. EN5
off High St 79 CY41
Barra Cl, Hem.H. HP3 . . . . 41 BP23
Barra Hall Circ, Hayes UB3 . 135 BS72
Barra Hall Rd, Hayes UB3 . . 135 BS73
Barrards Way, Beac.
(Seer Grn) HP9 . . . . 89 AQ51
Barrass Cl, Enf. EN3 . . . . 83 EA37
Barratt Av, N22 . . . . 99 DM54
Barratt Ind Pk, Sthl. UB1 . . 156 CA75
Barratt Way, Har. HA3
off Tudor Rd 117 CD55
Barrenger Rd, N10 . . . . 98 DF53
Barrens Brae, Wok. GU22 . . 227 BA118
Barrens Cl, Wok. GU22 . . . 227 BA118
Barrens Pk, Wok. GU22 . . . 227 BA118
Barrett Cl, Rom. RM3 . . . . 105 FH52
Barrett Rd, E17 . . . . 123 EC56
Leatherhead (Fetch.)
KT22 . . . . 230 CC124
Barretts Grn Rd, NW10 . . . 138 CQ68
Barretts Gro, N16 . . . . 5 M1
Barretts Rd, Sev. (Dunt.Grn)
TN13 . . . . 241 FD120
Barrett St, W1 . . . . 8 F8
Barrhill Rd, SW2 . . . . 181 DL89
Barricane, Wok. GU21 . . . 226 AV119
Barrie Cl, Couls. CR5 . . . . 235 DJ115
Barriedale, SE14 . . . . 163 DY81
Barrie Est, W2 . . . . 7 N9
Barrier App, SE7 . . . . 164 EK76
Barrier Pt Rd, E16 . . . . 144 EJ74
Barrier Pt Twr, E16
off Barrier Pt Rd 164 EJ75
Barringer Sq, SW17 . . . . 180 DG91
Barrington Cl, NW5 . . . . 120 DG64
Ilford IG5 . . . . 103 EM53
Loughton IG10
off Barrington Rd 85 EQ42
Barrington Ct, Brwd. (Hutt.)
CM13 . . . . 109 GC44
Dorking RH4
off Barrington Rd 263 CG137
Barrington Dr, Uxb. (Hare.)
UB9 . . . . 92 BG52
Barrington Grn, Loug. IG10 . . 85 EQ42
Barrington Lo, Wey. KT13 . . 213 BQ106
Barrington Ms, Welw.G.C.
AL7 off Black Fan Rd . . . 30 DB10
Barrington Pk Gdns, Ch.St.G.
HP8 . . . . 90 AX46
Sch Barrington Prim Sch, Bexh.
DA7 off Barrington Rd . . 166 EX82
Barrington Rd, E12 . . . . 145 EN65
N8 . . . . 121 DK57
SW9 . . . . 161 DP83
Bexleyheath DA7 . . . . 166 EX82
Dorking RH4 . . . . 263 CG137
Loughton IG10 . . . . 85 EQ41
Purley CR8 . . . . 219 DJ112
Sutton SM3 . . . . 200 DA102
Barrington Vil, SE18 . . . . 165 EN81
Barrow Av, Cars. SM5 . . . . 218 DF108
Barrow Cl, N21 . . . . 99 DP48
Barrowdene Cl, Pnr. HA5
off Paines La 94 BY54
Barrowell Grn, N21 . . . . 99 DP47
Barrowfield Cl, N9 . . . . 100 DV48
Barrowgate Rd, W4 . . . . 158 CQ78
Barrow Grn Rd, Oxt. RH8 . . 253 EC128
Barrow Hedges Cl, Cars.
SM5 . . . . 218 DE108
Sch Barrow Hedges Prim Sch,
Cars. SM5
off Harbury Rd 218 DE108
Barrow Hedges Way, Cars.
SM5 . . . . 218 DE108
Barrow Hill, Wor.Pk. KT4 . . 198 CS103
Barrow Hill Cl, Wor.Pk. KT4
off Barrow Hill 198 CS103
Barrow Hill Est, NW8
off Barrow Hill Rd 140 DE68
Sch Barrow Hill Jun Sch,
NW8 off Bridgeman St . 140 DE68
Barrow Hill Rd, NW8 . . . . 140 DE68
Barrow La, Wal.Cr. (Chshf)
EN7 . . . . 66 DT30
Barrow Pt Av, Pnr. HA5 . . . 94 BY54
Barrow Pt La, Pnr. HA5 . . . 94 BY54
Barrow Rd, SW16 . . . . 181 DK93
Croydon CR0 . . . . 219 DN106
Barrowsfield, S.Croy. CR2 . . 220 DT112
Barrows Rd, Harl. CM19 . . . 51 EM15
Barrow Wk, Brent. TW8
off Glenhurst Rd 157 CJ78
Barr Rd, Grav. DA12 . . . . 191 GM89
Potters Bar EN6 . . . . 64 DC33
Barrsbrook Fm Rd, Cher.
KT16 off Guildford Rd . . 193 BE102
Barrs Rd, NW10 . . . . 138 CR66
Barr's Rd, Maid. (Taplow)
SL6 . . . . 130 AH72
Barry Av, N15
off Craven Pk Rd 122 DT58
Bexleyheath DA7 . . . . 166 EY80
Windsor SL4 . . . . 151 AQ80
Barry Cl, Grays RM16 . . . . 171 GG75
Orpington BR6 . . . . 205 ES104
St. Albans AL2 . . . . 60 CB25
Barry Rd, E6 . . . . 144 EL72
NW10 . . . . 138 CQ66
SE22 . . . . 182 DU86
Bars, The, Guil. GU1 . . . . 258 AX135
Barset Rd, SE15 . . . . 162 DW83
Barson Cl, SE20 . . . . 182 DW94
Barston Rd, SE27 . . . . 182 DQ90
Barstow Cres, SW2 . . . . 181 DM88
Bartel Cl, Hem.H. HP3 . . . . 41 BR22
Bartelotts Rd, Slou. SL2 . . 131 AK70
Barter St, WC1 . . . . 9 P6
Barters Wk, Pnr. HA5
off High St 116 BY55
Bartholomew Cl, EC1 . . . . 10 G6
SW18 . . . . 160 DC84
Bartholomew Ct, Dor. RH4
off South St 263 CG137
Bartholomew Dr, Rom.
(Harold Wd) RM3 . . . . 106 FK54
Bartholomew La, EC2 . . . . 11 K8
Bartholomew Pl, EC1 . . . . 10 G6
Bartholomew Rd, NW5 . . . 141 DJ65
Bartholomew Sq, E1 . . . . 12 D3
EC1 . . . . 11 H3
Bartholomew St, SE1 . . . . 21 J6
Bartholomew Vil, NW5 . . . 141 DJ65
Bartholomew Way, Swan.
BR8 . . . . 207 FE97
Barth Rd, SE18 . . . . 165 ES77
Bartle Av, E6 . . . . 144 EL68
Bartle Rd, W11 . . . . 6 B8
Bartlett Cl, E14 . . . . 13 P7
Bartlett Ct, EC4 . . . . 10 D7
Bartlett Rd, Grav. DA11 . . . 191 GG88
Westerham TN16 . . . . 255 EQ126
Bartletts Mead, Hert. SG14 . 32 DR06
Bartletts Pas, EC4 . . . . 10 D7
Bartlett St, S.Croy. CR2 . . 220 DR106
Bartlow Gdns, Rom. RM5 . . 105 FD53
Barton, The, Cob. KT11 . . . 214 BX112
Barton Av, Rom. RM7 . . . . 127 FB60
Barton Cl, E6 . . . . 145 EM72
E9 off Churchill Wk 122 DW64
NW4 . . . . 119 CU57
SE15 off Kirkwood Rd . . . 162 DV83
Addlestone KT15 . . . . 212 BG107
Bexleyheath DA6 . . . . 186 EY85
Chigwell IG7 . . . . 103 EQ47
Shepperton TW17 . . . . 195 BP100
Barton Grn, N.Mal. KT3 . . . 198 CR96
Barton Ho, SW6
off Wandsworth Br Rd . . 160 DB83
Barton Meadows, Ilf. IG6 . . 125 EQ56
Barton Pl, Guil. GU4
off London Rd 243 BB131
Barton Rd, W14 . . . . 16 C10
Dartford (Sutt.H.) DA4 . . . 208 FP95
Guildford (Bramley) GU5 . 259 BA144
Hornchurch RM12 . . . . 127 FG60
Sidcup DA14 . . . . 186 EY93
Slough SL3 . . . . 153 AZ75
Bartons, The, Borwd.
(Elstree) WD6 . . . . 77 CK44
Barton St, SW1 . . . . 19 N5
Bartonway, NW8
off Queen's Ter 140 DD68
Barton Way, Borwd. WD6 . . 78 CN40
Rickmansworth (Crox.Grn)
WD3 . . . . 75 BP43
Bartram Cl, Uxb. UB8
off Lees Rd 135 BP70
Bartram Rd, SE4 . . . . 183 DY85
Bartrams La, Barn. EN4 . . . 80 DC38
Bartrop Cl, Wal.Cr. EN7
off Poppy Wk 66 DR28
Barts Cl, Beck. BR3 . . . . 203 EA99
Barville Cl, SE4
off St. Norbert Rd 163 DY84
Barwell Business Pk, Chess.
KT9 . . . . 215 CK109
Barwick Dr, Uxb. UB8 . . . 135 BP71
Barwick Rd, E7 . . . . 124 EH63
Barwood Av, W.Wick. BR4 . 203 EB102
Bascombe Gro, Dart. DA1 . . 187 FE87
Bascombe St, SW2 . . . . 181 DN86
Basden Gro, Felt. TW13 . . . 176 CA89
Basedale Rd, Dag. RM9 . . . 146 EV66
Baseing Cl, E6 . . . . 145 EN73
Basevi Way, SE8 . . . . 163 EB79
Basford Way, Wind. SL4 . . . 151 AK83
Bashley Rd, NW10 . . . . 138 CR70
Basil Av, E6 . . . . 144 EL68
Basildene Rd, Houns. TW4 . 156 BX82
Basildon Av, Ilf. IG5 . . . . 103 EN53
Basildon Cl, Sutt. SM2 . . . 218 DB109
Watford WD18 . . . . 75 BQ44
Basildon Rd, SE2 . . . . 166 EU78
Basildon Sq, Hem.H. HP2 . . 40 BM16
Basil Gdns, SE27 . . . . 182 DQ92
Croydon CR0
off Primrose La 203 DX102
Basil Ms, Harl. CM17
off London Rd 36 EW14
Basilon Rd, Bexh. DA7 . . . 166 EY82
Basil St, SW3 . . . . 18 C5
Basin App, E14 . . . . 13 K8
Basing Cl, T.Ditt. KT7 . . . . 197 CF101
Basing Ct, SE15 . . . . 162 DT81
Basingdon Way, SE5 . . . . 162 DR84
Basing Dr, Bex. DA5 . . . . 186 EZ86
Basingfield Rd, T.Ditt. KT7 . 197 CF101
Basinghall Av, EC2 . . . . 11 J6
Basinghall Gdns, Sutt. SM2 . 218 DB109
Basinghall St, EC2 . . . . 11 J7
Basing Hill, NW11 . . . . 119 CZ60
Wembley HA9 . . . . 118 CM61
Basing Ho, Bark. IG11
off St. Margarets 145 ER67
Basing Ho Yd, E2 . . . . 11 M1
Basing Pl, E2 . . . . 11 M1
Basing Rd, Bans. SM7 . . . . 217 CZ114
Rickmansworth (Mill End)
WD3 . . . . 91 BF46
Basing St, W11 . . . . 6 E7
Basing Way, N3 . . . . 120 DA55
Thames Ditton KT7 . . . . 197 CF101
Basire St, N1 . . . . 4 G7
Baskerville Rd, SW18 . . . . 180 DE87
Basket Gdns, SE9 . . . . 184 EL85
Baslow Cl, Har. HA3 . . . . 95 CD53
Baslow Wk, E5
off Overbury St 123 DX63
Basnett Rd, SW11 . . . . 160 DG83
Basque Ct, SE16 . . . . 22 G4
Bassano St, SE22 . . . . 182 DT85
Bassant Rd, SE18 . . . . 165 ET79
Bassein Pk Rd, W12 . . . . 159 CT75
Basset Cl, Add. (New Haw)
KT15 . . . . 212 BH110
Bassett Cl, Sutt. SM2 . . . . 218 DB109
Bassett Dr, Reig. RH2 . . . . 250 DA133
Bassett Flds, Epp.
(N.Wld Bas.) CM16 . . . . 71 FD25
Bassett Gdns, Epp.
(N.Wld Bas.) CM16 . . . . 71 FB26
Isleworth TW7 . . . . 156 CC80
Bassett Ho, Dag. RM9 . . . . 146 EV67
Bassett Rd, W10 . . . . 6 B7
Uxbridge UB8
off New Windsor St . . . 134 BJ66
Woking GU22 . . . . 227 BC116
Bassetts Cl, Orp. BR6 . . . . 223 EP105
H Bassetts Day Cen, Orp.
BR6 . . . . 223 EP105
Bassett St, NW5 . . . . 140 DG65
Bassetts Way, Orp. BR6 . . . 223 EP105
Bassett Way, Grnf. UB6 . . . 136 CB72
Slough SL2
off Pemberton Rd 131 AL70
Bassil Rd, Hem.H. HP2 . . . . 40 BK21
Bassingbourne Cl, Brox.
EN10 . . . . 49 DZ20
Bassingburn Wk, Welw.G.C.
AL7 . . . . 29 CZ10
Bassingham Rd, SW18 . . . 180 DC87
Wembley HA0 . . . . 137 CK65
Bassishaw Highwalk, EC2
off London Wall 142 DQ71
Bastable Av, Bark. IG11 . . . 145 ES68
Bastion Highwalk, EC2
off London Wall 142 DQ71
Bastion Ho, EC2
off London Wall 142 DQ71
Bastion Rd, SE2 . . . . 166 EU78
Baston Manor Rd, Brom.
BR2 . . . . 204 EH104
Baston Rd, Brom. BR2 . . . . 204 EH102
Sch Baston Sch, Brom. BR2
off Baston Rd 204 EH103
Bastwick St, EC1 . . . . 10 G3
Basuto Rd, SW6 . . . . 160 DA81
⇌ Bat & Ball 257 FJ121
Bat & Ball Junct, Sev. TN14
off Bradbourne Rd 257 FJ121
Bat & Ball Rd, Sev. TN14 . . 257 FJ121
Batavia Cl, Sun. TW16 . . . 196 BW95
Batavia Ms, SE14
off Goodwood Rd 163 DY80
Batavia Rd, SE14 . . . . 163 DY80
Sunbury-on-Thames
TW16 . . . . 195 BV95
Batchelor St, N1 . . . . 4 C9
Batchelors Way, Amer. HP7 . 55 AR39
Chesham HP5 . . . . 54 AP29
Batchwood Dr, St.Alb. AL3 . 42 CC17
Batchwood Gdns, St.Alb.
AL3 . . . . 43 CD17
Batchwood Grn, Orp. BR5 . 206 EU97
Sch Batchwood Sch, St.Alb.
AL3 off Townsend Dr . . . 43 CD17
Batchwood Vw, St.Alb. AL3 . 42 CC18
BATCHWORTH, Rick. WD3 . . 92 BM47
BATCHWORTH HEATH, Rick.
WD3 . . . . 92 BN49
Batchworth Heath Hill, Rick.
WD3 . . . . 92 BN49
Batchworth Hill, Rick. WD3 . 92 BM48
Batchworth La, Nthwd.
HA6 . . . . 93 BS50
Batchworth Roundabout,
Rick. WD3 . . . . 92 BK46
Bateman Cl, Bark. IG11
off Glenny Rd 145 EQ65
Bateman Ho, SE17
off Otto St 161 DP79
Bateman Rd, E4 . . . . 101 EA51
Rickmansworth (Crox.Grn)
WD3 . . . . 74 BN44
Bateman's Bldgs, W1 . . . . 9 L8
Batemans Ms, Brwd.
(Warley) CM14
off Vaughan Williams Way . 108 FV49
Bateman's Row, EC2 . . . . 11 M3
Bateman St, W1 . . . . 9 L8
Bates Cl, Slou. (Geo.Grn)
SL3 . . . . 132 AY72
Bates Cres, SW16 . . . . 181 DJ94
Croydon CR0 . . . . 219 DN106
Bates Ind Est, Rom.
(Harold Wd) RM3 . . . . 106 FP52
Bateson St, SE18 . . . . 165 ES77
Bateson Way, Wok. GU21 . . 211 BC114
Bates Pt, E13 off Pelly Rd . . 144 EG67
Bates Rd, Rom. RM3 . . . . 106 FN52
Bate St, E14 . . . . 13 M9
Bates Wk, Add. KT15 . . . . 212 BJ108
B.A.T. Export Ho, Wok.
GU21 . . . . 226 AY117
Batford Cl, Welw.G.C. AL7
off Waterford Grn 30 DB10
Bath Cl, SE15
off Asylum Rd 162 DV80
Bath Ct, EC1 . . . . 10 C4
Bathgate Rd, SW19 . . . . 179 CX90
Bath Ho Rd, Croy. CR0 . . . 201 DL102
Bath Pas, Kings.T. KT1
off St. James Rd 197 CK96
Bath Pl, EC2 . . . . 11 L2
Barnet EN5 . . . . 79 CZ41
Bath Rd, E7 . . . . 144 EK65
N9 . . . . 100 DV47
Bath Rd, W4 . . . . 158 CS77
Dartford DA1 . . . . 187 FH87
Hayes UB3 . . . . 155 BQ81
Hounslow TW3, TW4,
TW5, TW6 . . . . 156 BX82
Maidenhead (Taplow)
SL6 . . . . 130 AF72
Mitcham CR4 . . . . 200 DD97
Romford RM6 . . . . 126 EY58
Slough SL1 . . . . 131 AP74
Slough (Colnbr.) SL3 . . . . 153 BB79
West Drayton UB7 . . . . 154 BK81
Baths Rd, Brom. BR2 . . . . 204 EK98
Bath St, EC1 . . . . 11 H2
Gravesend DA11 . . . . 191 GH86
Bath Ter, SE1 . . . . 20 G6
Bathurst Av, SW19
off Brisbane Av 200 DB95
Bathurst Cl, Iver SL0 . . . . 153 BF75
Bathurst Gdns, NW10 . . . . 139 CV68
Bathurst Ms, W2 . . . . 7 N9
Bathurst Rd, Hem.H. HP2 . . 40 BK17
Ilford IG1 . . . . 125 EP60
Bathurst St, W2 . . . . 7 N9
Bathurst Wk, Iver SL0 . . . . 153 BE75
Bathway, SE18 . . . . 165 EN77
Batley Cl, Mitch. CR4 . . . . 200 DF101
Batley Pl, N16 . . . . 122 DT62
Batley Rd, N16
off Stoke Newington
High St 122 DT62
Enfield EN2 . . . . 82 DQ39
Batman Cl, W12 . . . . 139 CV74
Baton Cl, Purf. RM19 . . . . 169 FR77
Batoum Gdns, W6 . . . . 159 CW76
Batson St, W12 . . . . 159 CU75
Batsworth Rd, Mitch. CR4 . . 200 DD97
Batten Av, Wok. GU21 . . . . 226 AS119
Battenburg Wk, SE19
off Brabourne Cl 182 DS92
Batten Cl, E6
off Savage Gdns 145 EM72
Batten St, SW11 . . . . 160 DE83
Batterdale, Hat. AL9 . . . . 45 CW17
Battersby Rd, SE6 . . . . 183 ED89
BATTERSEA, SW11 . . . . 161 DH81
Battersea Br, SW3 . . . . 160 DD80
SW11 . . . . 160 DD80
Battersea Br Rd, SW11 . . . . 160 DE80
Battersea Ch Rd, SW11 . . . 160 DD81
★ Battersea Dogs Home,
SW8 . . . . 161 DH80
Battersea High St, SW11 . . 160 DD81
★ Battersea Park, SW11 . . 160 DF80
⇌ Battersea Park 161 DH80
Battersea Pk, SW11 . . . . 160 DF80
Battersea Pk Rd, SW8 . . . . 161 DH81
SW11 . . . . 160 DE82
Battersea Ri, SW11 . . . . 180 DE85
Battersea Sq, SW11
off Battersea High St . . . 160 DD81
Sch Battersea Tech Coll, SW11
off Battersea Pk Rd 160 DF81
Battery Rd, SE28 . . . . 165 ES75
Battis, The, Rom. RM1
off Waterloo Rd 127 FE58
Battishill Gdns, N1
off Waterloo Ter 141 DP66
Battishill St, N1 . . . . 4 E6
Battlebridge Ct, N1
off Wharfdale Rd 141 DL68
Battle Br La, SE1 . . . . 21 L2
Battlebridge La, Red. RH1 . 251 DH130
Battle Br Rd, NW1 . . . . 141 DL68
Battle Cl, SW19
off North Rd 180 DC93
Battledean Rd, N5 . . . . 4 E1
Battlefield Rd, St.Alb. AL1 . . 43 CF18
Battlemead Cl, Maid. SL6 . . 130 AC68
Battle Rd, Belv. DA17 . . . . 167 FC77
Erith DA8 . . . . 167 FC77
Battlers Grn Dr, Rad. WD7 . . 77 CE37
Batts Hill, Red. RH1 . . . . 250 DE132
Reigate RH2 . . . . 250 DD132
Batty St, E1 . . . . 12 B7
Baudwin Rd, SE6 . . . . 184 EE89
Baugh Rd, Sid. DA14 . . . . 186 EW92
Baulk, The, SW18 . . . . 180 DA87
Bavant Rd, SW16 . . . . 201 DL96
Bavaria Rd, N19 . . . . 121 DL61
Bavdene Ms, NW4
off The Burroughs 119 CV56
Bavent Rd, SE5 . . . . 162 DQ82
Bawdale Rd, SE22 . . . . 182 DT85
Bawdsey Av, Ilf. IG2 . . . . 125 ET56
Bawtree Cl, Sutt. SM2 . . . . 218 DC110
Bawtree Rd, SE14 . . . . 163 DY80
Uxbridge UB8 . . . . 134 BK65
Bawtry Rd, N20 . . . . 98 DF48
Baxendale, N20 . . . . 98 DC47
Baxendale St, E2 . . . . 12 A1
Baxter Av, Red. RH1 . . . . 250 DE134
Baxter Cl, Slou. SL1 . . . . 152 AS76
Southall UB2 . . . . 156 CB75
Uxbridge UB10 . . . . 135 BP69
Baxter Gdns, Rom.
(Noak Hill) RM3
off Cummings Hall La . . 106 FJ48
Baxter Rd, E16 . . . . 144 EJ72
N1 . . . . 5 K4
N18 . . . . 100 DV49
NW10 . . . . 138 CS70
Ilford IG1 . . . . 125 EP64
Bayards, Warl. CR6 . . . . 236 DW118
Bay Cl, Horl. RH6 . . . . 268 DE145
Bay Ct, W5 off Popes La . . . 158 CL76
Baycroft Cl, Pnr. HA5 . . . . 116 BW55
Baydon Ct, Brom. BR2 . . . . 204 EF97
Bayes Cl, SE26 . . . . 182 DW92
Bayeux, Tad. KT20 . . . . 233 CX122
Bayfield Rd, SE9 . . . . 164 EK84
Horley RH6 . . . . 268 DE147
BAYFORD, Hert. SG13 . . . . 47 DM18
⇌ Bayford 47 DN18
BAYFORDBURY, Hert. SG13 . 31 DM13
Bayford Cl, Hem.H. HP2 . . . 41 BQ15
Hertford SG13 . . . . 32 DQ11
Bayford Grn, Hert. (Bayford)
SG13 . . . . 47 DN18
Bayford La, Hert. (Bayford)
SG13 . . . . 31 DM14
Bayford Ms, E8
off Bayford St 142 DV66
Sch Bayford Prim Sch, Hert.
SG13 off Ashendene Rd . . 47 DM18
Bayford Rd, NW10 . . . . 6 A2
Bayford St, E8 . . . . 142 DV66
Bayham Pl, NW1 . . . . 141 DJ67
Bayham Rd, W4 . . . . 158 CR76
W13 . . . . 137 CH73
Morden SM4 . . . . 200 DB98
Sevenoaks TN13 . . . . 257 FJ123
Bayham St, NW1 . . . . 141 DJ67
Bayhorne La, Horl. RH6 . . . 269 DJ150
Bayhurst Dr, Nthwd. HA6 . . . 93 BT51
★ Bayhurst Wood Country
Pk, Uxb. UB9 . . . . 114 BM56
Bayley Cres, Slou. (Burn.)
SL1 . . . . 130 AG71
Bayleys Mead, Brwd. (Hutt.)
CM13 . . . . 109 GC47
Bayley St, WC1 . . . . 9 L6
Bayley Wk, SE2
off Woolwich Rd 166 EY78
Baylie Ct, Hem.H. HP2
off Baylie La 40 BL19
Baylie La, Hem.H. HP2 . . . . 40 BL18
Baylin Rd, SW18
off Garratt La 180 DB86
Sch Baylis Ct Sch, Slou. SL1
off Gloucester Av 131 AR71
Baylis Ms, Twick. TW1
off Amyand Pk Rd 177 CG87
Baylis Par, Slou. SL1
off Oatlands Dr 132 AS72
Baylis Rd, SE1 . . . . 20 C4
Slough SL1 . . . . 131 AR73
Bayliss Av, SE28 . . . . 146 EX73
Bayliss Cl, N21 . . . . 81 DL43
Southall UB1 . . . . 136 CB72
Bayliss Ct, Guil. GU1
off Mary Rd 258 AW135
Bayly Rd, Dart. DA1 . . . . 188 FN86
Bay Manor La, Grays RM20 . 169 FT79
Baymans Wd, Brwd. (Shenf.)
CM15 . . . . 108 FY47
Bayne Cl, E6
off Savage Gdns 145 EM72
Bayne Hill, Beac. HP9 . . . . 89 AR52
Bayne Hill Cl, Beac.
(Seer Grn) HP9 . . . . 89 AR52
Baynes Cl, Enf. EN1 . . . . 82 DU40
Baynes Ms, NW3
off Belsize La 140 DD65
Baynes St, NW1 . . . . 141 DJ66
Baynham Cl, Bex. DA5 . . . . 186 EZ86
Bayonne Rd, W6 . . . . 159 CY79
Bays Fm Ct, West Dr. UB7 . 154 BJ81
Bayshill Ri, Nthlt. UB5 . . . . 136 CB65
Bayston Rd, N16 . . . . 122 DT62
BAYSWATER, W2 . . . . 7 K8
⊖ Bayswater 7 J9
Bayswater Rd, W2 . . . . 7 P9
Baythorne St, E3 . . . . 13 M5
Bay Tree Av, Lthd. KT22 . . . 231 CG120
Bay Tree Cl, Brom. BR1 . . . 204 EJ95
Ilford IG6 off Hazel La . . . 103 EP52
Baytree Cl, St.Alb. (Park St)
AL2 . . . . 60 CB27
Sidcup DA15 . . . . 185 ET88
Waltham Cross EN7 . . . . 66 DT27
Bay Tree Ct, Slou. (Burn.)
SL1 . . . . 130 AJ69
Baytree Ho, E4 off Dells Cl . 101 EB45
Baytree Rd, SW2 . . . . 161 DM84
Baytree Wk, Wat. WD17 . . . 75 BT38
Baywood Sq, Chig. IG7 . . . 104 EV49
Bazalgette Cl, N.Mal. KT3 . . 198 CR99
Bazalgette Gdns, N.Mal.
KT3 . . . . 198 CR99
Bazely St, E14 . . . . 14 C9
Bazile Rd, N21 . . . . 81 DN44
Beacham Cl, SE7 . . . . 164 EK78
Beachamps, Welw.G.C. AL7
off Black Fan Rd 30 DB10
Beachborough Rd, Brom.
BR1 . . . . 183 EC91
Beachcroft Rd, E11 . . . . 124 EE62
Beachcroft Way, N19 . . . . 121 DK60
Beach Gro, Felt. TW13 . . . . 176 CA89
Beachy Rd, E3 . . . . 143 EA66
Beacon Cl, Bans. SM7 . . . . 233 CX116
Beaconsfield HP9 . . . . 88 AG54
Gerrards Cross (Chal.St.P.)
SL9 . . . . 90 AY52
Uxbridge UB8 . . . . 114 BK64
★ Beacon Country Pk,
Dart. DA2 . . . . 189 FV91
Beacon Dr, Dart. (Bean)
DA2 . . . . 189 FV90
Beaconfield Av, Epp. CM16 . . 69 ET29
Beaconfield Rd, Epp. CM16 . . 69 ET29
Beaconfields, Sev. TN13 . . 256 FF126
Beaconfield Way, Epp.
CM16 . . . . 69 ET29
Beacon Gate, SE14 . . . . 163 DX83
Beacon Gro, Cars. SM5 . . . 218 DG105
Beacon Hill, N7 . . . . 121 DL64
High Wycombe (Penn)
HP10 . . . . 88 AD48
Purfleet RM19 . . . . 168 FP78
Woking GU21 . . . . 226 AW118
Sch Beacon Ho Sch, W5
off Gunnersbury Av 138 CM74
Beacon Ri, Sev. TN13 . . . . 256 FG126
Beacon Rd, SE13 . . . . 183 ED86
Erith DA8 . . . . 167 FH80
Hounslow (Hthrw Air.)
TW6 . . . . 174 BN86
Ware SG12 . . . . 33 EA05
Beacon Rd Roundabout,
Houns. (Hthrw Air.) TW6 . 175 BP86
Beacons, The, Hat. AL10
off Beaconsfield Cl 45 CW17
Loughton IG10 . . . . 85 EN38
Sch Beacon Sch, The, Amer.
HP6 off Amersham Rd . . . 55 AP35
Banstead SM7
off Picquets Way 233 CY117
Beacons Cl, E6
off Oliver Gdns 144 EL71
BEACONSFIELD, HP9 . . . . 88 AJ53
⇌ Beaconsfield 89 AL52
Beaconsfield Cl, N11 . . . . 98 DG49
SE3 . . . . 164 EG79
W4 . . . . 158 CQ78
Hatfield AL10 . . . . 45 CW17
Beaconsfield Common La,
Slou. SL2 . . . . 111 AQ57
Beaconsfield Gdns, Esher
(Clay.) KT10 . . . . 215 CE108
Sch Beaconsfield High Sch,
Beac. HP9
off Wattleton Rd 89 AL54
Beaconsfield Par, SE9
off Beaconsfield Rd 184 EL91
Beaconsfield Pl, Epsom
KT17 . . . . 216 CS112
Sch Beaconsfield Prim Sch,
Sthl. UB1
off Beaconsfield Rd 156 BY75
Beaconsfield Rd, E10 . . . . 123 EC61
E16 . . . . 15 J4
E17 . . . . 123 DZ58

Beaconsfield Rd, N9 100 DU49
N11 98 DG48
N15 122 DS56
NW10 139 CT65
SE3 164 EF80
SE9 184 EL89
SE17 21 K10
W4 158 CR76
W5 157 CJ75
Bexley DA5 187 FE88
Bromley BR1 204 EK97
Croydon CR0 202 DR100
Enfield EN3 83 DX37
Epsom KT18 232 CR119
Esher (Clay.) KT10 215 CE108
Hatfield AL10 45 CW17
Hayes UB4 136 BW74
New Malden KT3 198 CR96
St. Albans AL1 43 CE20
Slough SL2 131 AQ68
Southall UB1 136 BX74
Surbiton KT5 198 CM101
Twickenham TW1 177 CH86
Woking GU22 227 AZ120
Sch **Beaconsfield Sch, The**, Beac. HP9
off Wattleton Rd 89 AL54
Beaconsfield Ter, Rom. RM6 126 EX58
Beaconsfield Ter Rd, W14 16 C6
Beaconsfield Wk, E6
off East Ham Manor Way 145 EN72
SW6 159 CZ81
Beacontree Av, E17 101 ED53
Beacontree Rd, E11 124 EF59
Beacon Way, Bans. SM7 233 CX116
Rickmansworth WD3 92 BG45
Beadles La, Oxt. RH8 253 ED130
Beadlow Cl, Cars. SM5
off Olveston Wk 200 DD100
Beadman Pl, SE27
off Norwood High St 181 DP91
Beadman St, SE27 181 DP91
Beadnell Rd, SE23 183 DX88
Beadon Rd, W6 159 CW77
Bromley BR2 204 EG98
Beads Hall La, Brwd.
(Pilg.Hat.) CM15 108 FV42
Beaford Gro, SW20 199 CY97
Beagle Cl, Felt. TW13 175 BV91
Radlett WD7 77 CF37
Beagles Cl, Orp. BR5 206 EX103
Beak St, W1 9 K9
Beal Cl, Well. DA16 166 EU81
Beale Cl, N13 99 DP50
Beale Pl, E3 143 DZ68
Beale Rd, E3 143 DZ67
Beales La, Wey. KT13 194 BN104
Beales Rd, Lthd. (Bkhm)
KT23 246 CB127
Sch **Beal High Sch**, Ilf. IG4
off Woodford Br Rd 124 EL56
Bealings End, Beac. HP9 89 AK50
Beal Rd, Ilf. IG1 125 EN61
Beam Av, Dag. RM10 147 FB67
Beaminster Gdns, Ilf. IG6 103 EP54
Beamish Cl, Epp.
(N.Wld Bas.) CM16 71 FC25
Beamish Dr, Bushey
(Bushey Hth) WD23 94 CC46
Beamish Rd, N9 100 DU46
Orpington BR5 206 EW101
Sch **Beam Prim Sch**, Dag.
RM10 off Oval Rd N 147 FC68
Beam Way, Dag. RM10 147 FD66
BEAN, Dart. DA2 189 FV90
Beanacre Cl, E9 143 DZ65
Sch **Bean Co Prim Sch**, Dart.
DA2 off School La 189 FW91
Beane Cft, Grav. DA12 191 GM88
Beane Rd, Hert. SG14 31 DP09
Bean La, Dart. (Bean) DA2 189 FV89
Bean Rd, Bexh. DA6 166 EX84
Greenhithe DA9 189 FV85
Beanshaw, SE9 185 EN91
Beansland Gro, Rom. RM6 104 EY54
Bear All, EC4 10 E7
Bear Cl, Rom. RM7 127 FB58
Beardell St, SE19 182 DT93
Beardow Gro, N14 81 DJ44
Beard Rd, Kings.T. KT2 178 CM92
Beardsfield, E13
off Valetta Gro 144 EG67
Beard's Hill, Hmptn. TW12 196 CA95
Beard's Hill Cl, Hmptn. TW12
off Beard's Hill 196 CA95
Beardsley Ter, Dag. RM8
off Fitzstephen Rd 126 EV64
Beardsley Way, W3 158 CR75
Beards Rd, Ashf. TW15 175 BS93
Bearfield Rd, Kings.T. KT2 178 CL94
Bear Gdns, SE1 20 G1
Bearing Cl, Chig. IG7 104 EU49
Bearing Way, Chig. IG7 104 EU49
Bear La, SE1 20 F1
Bear Rd, Felt. TW13 176 BX92
Bears Den, Tad. (Kgswd)
KT20 233 CZ122
Bears Rails Pk, Wind.
(Old Wind.) SL4 172 AT87
Bearstead Ri, SE4 183 DZ85
Bearsted Ter, Beck. BR3 203 EA95
Bear St, WC2 9 M9
Bearswood End, Beac. HP9 89 AL51
Bearwood Cl, Add. KT15
off Ongar Pl 212 BG107
Potters Bar EN6 64 DD31
Beasley's Ait La, Sun. TW16 195 BT100
Beasleys Yd, Uxb. UB8
off Warwick Pl 134 BJ66
Beaton Cl, SE15 162 DT81
Greenhithe DA9 169 FV84
Beatrice Av, SW16 201 DM97
Wembley HA9 118 CL64
Beatrice Cl, E13 15 L3
Pinner HA5 off Reid Cl 115 BU56
Beatrice Ct, Buck.H. IG9 102 EK47
Beatrice Gdns, Grav. (Nthflt)
DA11 190 GE89
Beatrice Pl, W8 17 J6
Beatrice Rd, E17 123 EA57
N4 121 DN59
N9 100 DW45
SE1 22 B8
Oxted RH8 254 EE129
Richmond TW10
off Albert Rd 178 CM85
Southall UB1 136 BZ74
Sch **Beatrice Tate Spec Sch**,
E2 12 D1
Sch **Beatrix Potter Prim Sch**,
SW18 off Magdalen Rd 180 DC88
Beatson Wk, SE16 23 J1
Beattie Cl, Felt. TW14 175 BT88
Leatherhead (Bkhm)
KT23 230 BZ124
Beattock Ri, N10 121 DH56
Beatty Av, Guil. GU1 243 BA133
Beatty Rd, N16 122 DS63
Stanmore HA7 95 CJ51
Waltham Cross EN8 67 DZ34
Beatty St, NW1 141 DJ68
Beattyville Gdns, Ilf. IG6 125 EN55
Beauchamp Cl, W4
off Church Path 158 CQ76
Beauchamp Ct, Stan. HA7
off Hardwick Cl 95 CJ50
Beauchamp Gdns, Rick.
(Mill End) WD3 92 BG46
Beauchamp Pl, SW3 18 B5
Beauchamp Rd, E7 144 EH66
SE19 202 DR95
SW11 160 DE84
East Molesey KT8 196 CB99
Sutton SM1 218 DA106
Twickenham TW1 177 CG87
West Molesey KT8 196 CB99
Beauchamp St, EC1 10 C6
Beauchamp Ter, SW15
off Dryburgh Rd 159 CV83
Beauclare Cl, Lthd. KT22
off Hatherwood 231 CK121
Sch **Beauclerc Inf Sch**, Sun.
TW16
off French St 196 BW97
Beauclerc Rd, W6 159 CV76
Beauclerk Cl, Felt. TW13
off Florence Rd 175 BV88
Beaudesert Ms, West Dr.
UB7 154 BL75
Beaufort, E6
off Newark Knok 145 EN71
Beaufort Av, Har. HA3 117 CG56
Beaufort Cl, E4
off Higham Sta Av 101 EB51
SW15 179 CV87
W5 138 CM71
Epping (N.Wld Bas.)
CM16 70 FA27
Grays (Chaff.Hun.) RM16
off Clifford Rd 170 FZ76
Reigate RH2 249 CZ133
Romford RM7 127 FC56
Woking GU22 227 BC116
Sch **Beaufort Comm Prim Sch**,
Wok. GU21
off Kirkland Av 226 AT116
Beaufort Ct, Rich. TW10
off Beaufort Rd 177 CJ91
Beaufort Dr, NW11 120 DA56
Beaufort Gdns, NW4 119 CW58
SW3 18 B5
SW16 181 DM94
Hounslow TW5 156 BY81
Ilford IG1 125 EN60
Beaufort Ms, SW6
off Lillie Rd 159 CZ79
Beaufort Pk, NW11 120 DA56
Beaufort Pl, Maid. SL6 150 AD75
Beaufort Rd, W5 138 CM71
Kingston upon Thames
KT1 198 CL98
Reigate RH2 249 CZ133
Richmond TW10 177 CJ91
Ruislip HA4
off Lysander Rd 115 BR61
Twickenham TW1 177 CJ87
Woking GU22 227 BC116
Beauforts, Egh. (Eng.Grn)
TW20 172 AW92
Beaufort St, SW3 160 DD79
Beaufort Way, Epsom KT17 217 CU108
Beaufoy Rd, N17 100 DS52
Beaufoy Wk, SE11 20 B8
Beaulieu Av, E16 25 N1
SE26 182 DV91
Beaulieu Cl, NW9 118 CS56
SE5 162 DR83
Hounslow TW4 176 BZ85
Mitcham CR4 200 DG95
Slough (Datchet) SL3 152 AV81
Twickenham TW1 177 CK87
Watford WD19 94 BW46
Beaulieu Dr, Pnr. HA5 116 BX58
Waltham Abbey EN9 67 EB32
Beaulieu Gdns, N21 100 DQ45
Beaulieu Pl, W4
off Rothschild Rd 158 CQ76
Beauly Way, Rom. RM1 105 FE53
Beaumanor Gdns, SE9 185 EN91
Beaumaris Dr, Wdf.Grn. IG8 102 EK52
Beaumaris Grn, NW9
off Goldsmith Av 118 CS58
Beaumayes Cl, Hem.H. HP1 40 BH21
Beaumont Av, W14 16 E9
Harrow HA2 116 CB58
Richmond TW9 158 CM83
St. Albans AL1 43 CH18
Wembley HA0 117 CJ64
Beaumont Cl, Kings.T. KT2 178 CN94
Romford RM2 106 FJ54
Beaumont Cres, W14 16 E9
Rainham RM13 147 FG65
Beaumont Dr, Ashf. TW15 175 BR92
Gravesend (Nthflt) DA11 190 GE87
Beaumont Gdns, NW3 120 DA62
Brentwood (Hutt.) CM13
off Bannister Dr 109 GC44
Beaumont Gate, Rad. WD7
off Shenley Hill 77 CH35
Beaumont Gro, E1 12 G4
Beaumont Ms, W1 8 F5
Pinner HA5 116 BY55
Beaumont Pk Dr, Harl.
(Roydon) CM19 50 EH15
Beaumont Pl, W1 9 K3
Barnet EN5 79 CZ39
Isleworth TW7 177 CF85
Sch **Beaumont Prim Sch**, E10
off Burchell Rd 123 EB60
Purley CR8 off Old Lo La 219 DN114
Beaumont Ri, N19 121 DK60
Beaumont Rd, E10 123 EB59
E13 15 P2
SE19 182 DQ93
SW19 179 CY87
W4 158 CQ76
Broxbourne EN10 48 DR24
Orpington BR5 205 ER100
Purley CR8 219 DN113
Slough SL2 131 AR70
Windsor SL4 151 AQ82
Beaumonts, Red. RH1 266 DF143
Sch **Beaumont Sch**, St.Alb.
AL4 off Oakwood Dr 43 CJ19
Beaumont Sq, E1 12 G5
Beaumont St, W1 8 F5
Beaumont Vw, Wal.Cr.
(Chsht) EN7 66 DR26
Beaumont Wk, NW3 140 DF66
Beauvais Ter, Nthlt. UB5 136 BX69
Beauval Rd, SE22 182 DT86
Beaverbank Rd, SE9 185 ER88
Beaverbrook Roundabout,
Lthd. KT22 232 CL123
Beaver Cl, SE20
off Lullington Rd 182 DU94
Hampton TW12 196 CB95
Beaver Gro, Nthlt. UB5
off Jetstar Way 136 BY69
Beaver Rd, Ilf. IG6 104 EW50
Beavers Cl, Guil. GU3 242 AS133
Sch **Beavers Comm Prim Sch**,
Houns. TW4
off Arundel Rd 156 BW83
Beavers Cres, Houns. TW4 156 BW84
Beavers La, Houns. TW4 156 BW83
Beavers La Camp, Houns.
TW4 off Beavers La 156 BW83
Beaverwood Rd, Chis. BR7 185 ES93
Sch **Beaverwood Sec Sch for Girls**, Chis. BR7
off Beaverwood Rd 185 ES93
Beavor Gro, W6
off Beavor La 159 CU77
Beavor La, W6 159 CU77
Beazley Cl, Ware SG12 33 DY05
Bebbington Rd, SE18 165 ES77
Bebletts Cl, Orp. BR6 223 ET106
Beccles Dr, Bark. IG11 145 ES65
Beccles St, E14 13 M9
Bec Cl, Ruis. HA4 116 BX62
Beck Cl, SE13 163 EB81
Beck Ct, Beck. BR3 203 DX97
BECKENHAM, BR3 203 EA95
Beckenham Business Cen,
Beck. BR3 183 DY93
Beckenham Gdns, N9 100 DS48
Beckenham Gro, Brom. BR2 203 ED96
⇌ **Beckenham Hill** 183 EC92
Beckenham Hill Rd, SE6 183 EB92
Beckenham BR3 183 EB92
H **Beckenham Hosp**, Beck.
BR3 203 DZ96
⇌ **Beckenham Junction** 203 EA95
Tram **Beckenham Junction** 203 EA95
Beckenham La, Brom. BR2 204 EE96
Beckenham Pl Pk, Beck.
BR3 183 EB94
Tram **Beckenham Road** 203 DY95
Beckenham Rd, Beck. BR3 203 DX95
West Wickham BR4 203 EB101
Beckenshaw Gdns, Bans.
SM7 234 DE115
Beckers, The, N16
off Rectory Rd 122 DU62
Becket Av, E6 145 EN69
Becket Cl, SE25 202 DU100
Brentwood CM13 107 FW51
Becket Fold, Har. HA1
off Courtfield Cres 117 CF57
Becket Rd, N18 100 DW49
Beckets Sq, Berk. HP4
off Bridle Way 38 AU17
Becket St, SE1 21 J5
Beckett Av, Ken. CR8 235 DP115
Beckett Chase, Slou. SL3
off Ditton Rd 153 AZ78
Beckett Cl, NW10 138 CR65
SW16 181 DK89
Belvedere DA17
off Tunstock Way 166 EY76
Beckett Rd, Couls. CR5
off Blue Leaves Av 235 DK122
Becketts, Hert. SG14 31 DN10
Beckett's Av, St.Alb. AL3 42 CC17
Becketts Cl, Bex. DA5 187 FC88
Feltham TW14 175 BV86
Orpington BR6 205 ET104
Becketts Pl, Kings.T.
(Hmptn W.) KT1 197 CK95
Beckett Wk, Beck. BR3 183 DY93
Beckford Dr, Orp. BR5 205 ER101
Beckford Pl, SE17 21 H10
Sch **Beckford Prim Sch**, NW6
off Dornfell St 119 CZ64
Beckford Rd, Croy. CR0 202 DT100
Beckingham Rd, Guil. GU2 242 AU132
Beckings Way, H.Wyc.
(Flack.Hth) HP10 110 AC56
Beck La, Beck. BR3 203 DX97
Becklow Gdns, W12
off Becklow Rd 159 CU75
Becklow Ms, W12
off Becklow Rd 159 CT75
Becklow Rd, W12 159 CU75
Beckman Cl, Sev. (Halst.)
TN14 241 FC115
Beck River Pk, Beck. BR3 203 DZ95
Beck Rd, E8 142 DV67
Becks Rd, Sid. DA14 186 EU90
BECKTON, E6 145 EN71
DLR **Beckton** 145 EN71
Coll **Beckton Globe**, E6
off Kingsford Way 145 EM71
DLR **Beckton Park** 145 EM73
Beckton Pk Roundabout, E16
off Royal Albert Way 145 EM73
Beckton Retail Pk, E6 145 EN71
Beckton Rd, E16 15 K5
Beckton Triangle Retail Pk,
E6 145 EN70
Beck Way, Beck. BR3 203 DZ97
Beckway Rd, SW16 201 DK96
Beckway St, SE17 21 K8
Beckwell Rd, Slou. SL1 151 AQ75
Beckwith Rd, SE24 182 DR86
Beclands Rd, SW17 180 DG93
Becmead Av, SW16 181 DK91
Harrow HA3 117 CH57
Becondale Rd, SE19 182 DS92
BECONTREE, Dag. RM8 126 EY62
⊖ **Becontree** 146 EW66
Becontree Av, Dag. RM8 126 EV63
BECONTREE HEATH, Dag.
RM8 126 FA60
Sch **Becontree Prim Sch**, Dag.
RM8 off Stevens Rd 126 EV62
Bective Pl, SW15
off Bective Rd 159 CZ84
Bective Rd, E7 124 EG63
SW15 159 CZ84
Becton Pl, Erith DA8 167 FB80
Bedale Rd, Enf. EN2 82 DQ38
Romford RM3 106 FN50
Bedale St, SE1 21 J2
Bedale Wk, Dart. DA2 188 FP88
BEDDINGTON, Croy. CR0 201 DK103
BEDDINGTON CORNER,
Mitch. CR4 200 DG101
Beddington Cross, Croy.
CR0 201 DK102
Beddington Fm Rd, Croy.
CR0 201 DL102
Beddington Gdns, Cars.
SM5 218 DG107
Wallington SM6 219 DH107
Beddington Grn, Orp. BR5 205 ET95
Beddington Gro, Wall. SM6 219 DK106
Sch **Beddington Inf Sch**, Wall.
SM6 off Croydon Rd 219 DJ105
Tram **Beddington Lane** 201 DJ100
Beddington La, Croy. CR0 201 DJ99
Sch **Beddington Pk Prim Sch**,
Croy. CR0 off Derry Rd 201 DK104
Beddington Path, Orp. BR5 205 ET95
Beddington Rd, Ilf. IG3 125 ET59
Orpington BR5 205 ES96
Beddington Trd Pk W, Croy.
CR0 201 DL102
Beddlestead La, Warl. CR6 238 EF117
Bede Cl, Pnr. HA5 94 BX53
Sch **Bedelsford Sch**, Kings.T.
KT1 off Grange Rd 198 CL97
Bedenham Way, SE15
off Daniel Gdns 162 DT80
Bedens Rd, Sid. DA14 186 EY93
Bede Rd, Rom. RM6 126 EW58
Bedevere Rd, N9
off Salisbury Rd 100 DU48
Bedfont Cl, Felt. TW14 175 BQ86
Mitcham CR4 200 DG96
Bedfont Ct, Stai. TW19 154 BH84
Bedfont Ct Est, Stai. TW19 154 BG83
Bedfont Grn Cl, Felt. TW14 175 BQ88
Sch **Bedfont Inf & Nurs Sch**,
Felt. TW14
off Hatton Rd 175 BS86
Sch **Bedfont Jun Sch**, Felt.
TW14 off Hatton Rd 175 BS86
Bedfont La, Felt. TW13,
TW14 175 BT87
Bedfont Rd, Felt. TW13,
TW14 175 BS89
Staines (Stanw.) TW19 174 BL86
Bedford Av, WC1 9 M6
Amersham HP6 72 AW39
Barnet EN5 79 CZ43
Hayes UB4 135 BV72
Slough SL1 131 AM72
Bedfordbury, WC2 9 N9
Bedford Cl, N10 98 DG52
W4 158 CS79
Rickmansworth (Chenies)
WD3 73 BB38
Woking GU21 226 AW115
Bedford Cor, W4
off The Avenue 158 CS77
Bedford Ct, WC2 9 N10
Bedford Cres, Enf. EN3 83 DY35
Bedford Dr, Slou. (Farn.Com.)
SL2 111 AP64
Bedford Gdns, W8 16 G2
Hornchurch RM12 128 FJ61
Bedford Hill, SW12 181 DH88
SW16 181 DH88
Bedford Ho, SW4 161 DL84
Bedford Ms, N2
off Bedford Rd 120 DE55
SE6 off Aitken Rd 183 EB89
BEDFORD PARK, W4 158 CR76
Bedford Pk, Croy. CR0 202 DQ102
Bedford Pk Cor, W4
off Bath Rd 158 CS77
Bedford Pk Rd, St.Alb. AL1 43 CE20
Bedford Pas, SW6
off Dawes Rd 159 CY80
Bedford Pl, WC1 9 N5
Croydon CR0 202 DR102
Bedford Rd, E6 145 EN67
E17 101 EA54
E18 102 EG54
N2 120 DE55
N8 121 DK58
N9 100 DV45
N15 122 DS56
N22 99 DL53
NW7 96 CS48
SW4 161 DL83
W4 158 CR76
W13 137 CH73
Dartford DA1 188 FN87
Gravesend (Nthflt) DA11 191 GF89
Grays RM17 170 GB78
Guildford GU1 258 AW135
Harrow HA1 116 CC58
Ilford IG1 125 EP62
Northwood HA6 93 BQ48
Orpington BR6 206 EV103
Ruislip HA4 115 BT63
St. Albans AL1 43 CE21
Sidcup DA15 185 ES90
Twickenham TW2 177 CD90
Worcester Park KT4 199 CW103
Bedford Row, WC1 10 B5
Bedford Sq, WC1 9 M6
Bedford St, WC2 9 N9
Berkhamsted HP4 38 AX19
Watford WD24 75 BV39
Bedford Ter, SW2
off Lyham Rd 181 DL85
Bedford Way, WC1 9 M4
Bedgebury Gdns, SW19 179 CY89
Bedgebury Rd, SE9 164 EK84
Bedivere Rd, Brom. BR1 184 EG90
Bedlam Ms, SE11 20 B7
Bedlow Way, Croy. CR0 219 DM105
BEDMOND, Abb.L. WD5 59 BS27
Bedmond La, Abb.L. WD5 59 BV25
St. Albans AL2, AL3 42 BX24
Bedmond Rd, Abb.L. WD5 59 BT29
Hemel Hempstead HP3 41 BS23
Sch **Bedmond Village Prim & Nurs Sch**, Abb.L. WD5
off Meadow Way 59 BT28
Sch **Bedonwell Jun Sch**, Belv.
DA17 off Bedonwell Rd 166 EY79
Sch **Bedonwell Prim Inf & Nurs Sch**, Belv. DA17
off Bedonwell Rd 166 EY79
Bedonwell Rd, SE2 166 EY79
Belvedere DA17 166 FA79
Bexleyheath DA7 166 FA79
Bedser Cl, SE11
off Harleyford Rd 161 DM79
Thornton Heath CR7 202 DQ97
Woking GU21 227 BA116
Bedser Dr, Grnf. UB6 117 CD64
Bedster Gdns, W.Mol. KT8 196 CB96
Bedwardine Rd, SE19 182 DS94
Bedwell Av, Hat. AL9 46 DG18
Bedwell Cl, Welw.G.C. AL7 29 CY10
Bedwell Gdns, Hayes UB3 155 BS78
Bedwell Pk, Hat. AL9 46 DF18
Bedwell Rd, N17 100 DS53
Bedwell Rd, Belv. DA17 166 FA78
Beeby Rd, E16 15 N6
Beech Av, N20 98 DE46
W3 138 CS74
Brentford TW8 157 CH80
Brentwood CM13 109 FZ48
Buckhurst Hill IG9 102 EH47
Enfield EN2 81 DN35
Leatherhead (Eff.) KT24 246 BX129
Radlett WD7 61 CG33
Ruislip HA4 115 BV60
Sidcup DA15 186 EU87
South Croydon CR2 220 DR111
Swanley BR8 207 FF98
Upminster RM14 128 FP62
Westerham (Tats.) TN16 238 EK119
Beech Bottom, St.Alb. AL3 43 CD17
Beech Cl, N9 82 DU44
SE8 off Clyde St 163 DZ79
SW15 179 CU87
SW19 179 CW93
Ashford TW15 175 BR92
Carshalton SM5 200 DF103
Cobham KT11 214 CA112
Dorking RH4 263 CF135
Hatfield AL10 45 CU19
Hornchurch RM12 127 FH62
Leatherhead (Eff.) KT24 246 BX128
Loughton IG10
off Cedar Dr 85 EP40
Staines (Stanw.) TW19
off St. Mary's Cres 174 BK87
Sunbury-on-Thames
TW16 off Harfield Rd 196 BX96
Walton-on-Thames KT12 214 BW105
Ware SG12 33 DX08
West Byfleet (Byfleet)
KT14 212 BL112
West Drayton UB7 154 BN76
Beech Cl Ct, Cob. KT11 214 BZ111
Beech Copse, Brom. BR1 205 EM96
South Croydon CR2 220 DS106
Beech Ct, E17 123 ED55
SE9 184 EL86
Ilford IG1
off Riverdene Rd 125 EN62
Beech Cres, Tad. (Box H.)
KT20 248 CQ130
Beechcroft, Ashtd. KT21 232 CM119
Chislehurst BR7 185 EN94
Beechcroft Av, NW11 119 CZ59
Bexleyheath DA7 167 FD81
Harrow HA2 116 CA59
Kenley CR8 236 DR115
New Malden KT3 198 CQ95
Rickmansworth (Crox.Grn)
WD3 75 BQ44
Southall UB1 136 BZ74
Beechcroft Cl, Houns. TW5 156 BY80
Orpington BR6 223 ER105
Beechcroft Gdns, Wem.
HA9 118 CM62
Beechcroft Lo, Sutt. SM2
off Devonshire Rd 218 DC108
Beechcroft Manor, Wey.
KT13 195 BR104
Beechcroft Rd, E18 102 EH54
SW14 off Elm Rd 158 CQ83
SW17 180 DE89
Bushey WD23 76 BY43
Chesham HP5 54 AN30
Chessington KT9 198 CM104
Orpington BR6 223 ER105
Sch **Beechcroft Sch**, SW17
off Beechcroft Rd 180 DE89
Beechdale, N21 99 DM47
Beechdale Rd, SW2 181 DM86
Beech Dell, Kes. BR2 223 EM105
Beechdene, Tad. KT20 233 CV122
Beech Dr, N2 120 DF55
Berkhamsted HP4 38 AW20
Borehamwood WD6 78 CM40
Reigate RH2 250 DD134
Sawbridgeworth CM21 36 EW07
Tadworth (Kgswd) KT20 233 CZ122
Woking (Ripley) GU23 228 BG124
Beechen Cliff Way, Islw. TW7
off Henley Cl 157 CF81
Beechen Gro, Pnr. HA5 116 BZ55
Watford WD17 76 BW42
Beechen La, Tad. KT20 249 CZ125
Beechenlea La, Swan. BR8 207 FH97
Beeches, The, Amer. HP6
off Woodfield Pk 55 AN36
Banstead SM7 234 DB116
Beaconsfield HP9 88 AH54
Brentwood CM14 108 FV48
Guildford (Bramley) GU5 259 AZ144
Hounslow TW3 156 CB81
Leatherhead (Fetch.)
KT22 231 CE124
Rickmansworth (Chorl.)
WD3 73 BF43
St. Albans (Park St) AL2 61 CE27
Swanley BR8 187 FF94
Tilbury RM18 171 GH82
Beeches Av, Cars. SM5 218 DE108
Coll **Beeches Cen, The**, Belv.
DA17
off Halt Robin Rd 167 FB77
Beeches Cl, SE20
off Genoa Rd 202 DW95
Tadworth (Kgswd) KT20 234 DA123
Beeches Dr, Slou.
(Farn.Com.) SL2 111 AP64
Beeches Pk, Beac. HP9 89 AK53
Beeches Rd, SW17 180 DE90
Slough (Farn.Com.) SL2 111 AP64
Sutton SM3 199 CY102
Beeches Wk, Cars. SM5 218 DD109
Beeches Way, B.End SL8 110 AD61
Beeches Wd, Tad. KT20 234 DA122
Beech Fm Rd, Warl. CR6 237 EC120
Beechfield, Bans. SM7 218 DB113
Hoddesdon EN11 33 EA13
Kings Langley WD4 58 BM30
Sawbridgeworth CM21 36 EZ05
Beechfield Cl, Borwd. WD6 78 CL40
Beechfield Cotts, Brom. BR1
off Widmore Rd 204 EJ96
Beechfield Gdns, Rom. RM7 127 FC59
Beechfield Rd, N4 122 DQ58
SE6 183 DZ88
Bromley BR1 204 EJ96
Erith DA8 167 FE80
Hemel Hempstead HP1 40 BH21
Welwyn Garden City AL7 29 CY11
Sch **Beechfield Sch**, Wat.
WD24 off Gammons La 75 BU37
Beechfield Wk, Wal.Abb.
EN9 83 ED35
Beech Gdns, EC2
off Aldersgate St 142 DQ71
W5 158 CL75
Dagenham RM10 147 FB66

Beech Gdns, Wok. GU21 226 AY115
Beech Gro, Add. KT15 212 BH105
Amersham HP7 55 AQ39
Caterham CR3 252 DS126
Croydon CR0 221 DY110
Epsom KT18 233 CV117
Guildford GU2 242 AT134
Ilford IG6 103 ES51
Leatherhead (Bkhm) KT23 246 CA127
Mitcham CR4 201 DK98
New Malden KT3 198 CR97
South Ockendon (Aveley) RM15 148 FQ74
Woking (Mayford) GU22 226 AX123
Beech Hall, Cher. (Ott.) KT16 211 BC108
Beech Hall Cres, E4 101 ED52
Beech Hall Rd, E4 101 EC52
Beech Hill, Barn. EN4 80 DD38
Woking GU22 226 AX123
Beech Hill Av, Barn. EN4 80 DC39
Beech Hill Ct, Berk. HP4 38 AX18
Beech Hill Gdns, Wal.Abb. EN9 84 EH37
Beechhill Rd, SE9 185 EN85
Beech Holt, Lthd. KT22 231 CJ122
Beech Ho, Croy. CR0 221 EB107
Beech Ho Rd, Croy. CR0 202 DR104
Beech Hyde La, St.Alb. (Wheat.) AL4 28 CM07
Beech La, Beac. (Jordans) HP9 90 AS52
Buckhurst Hill IG9 102 EH47
Guildford GU2 258 AW137
Beech Lawn, Guil. GU1 259 AZ135
Beech Lawns, N12 98 DD50
Beech Lo, Stai. TW18 *off Farm Cl* 173 BE92
Beechmeads, Cob. KT11 214 BX113
Beechmont Av, Vir.W. GU25 192 AX99
Beechmont Cl, Brom. BR1 184 EE92
Beechmont Rd, Sev. TN13 257 FH129
Beechmore Gdns, Sutt. SM3 199 CX103
Beechmore Rd, SW11 160 DF81
Beechmount Av, W7 137 CD71
Beecholme, Bans. SM7 217 CY114
Beecholme Av, Mitch. CR4 201 DH95
Beecholme Est, E5 *off Prout Rd* 122 DV62
Sch **Beecholme Prim Sch**, Mitch. CR4 *off Edgehill Rd* 201 DH95
Beecholm Ms, Wal.Cr. EN8 67 DX28
Beech Pk, Amer. HP6 72 AV39
Beechpark Way, Wat. WD17 75 BS37
Beech Pl, Epp. CM16 69 ET31
St. Albans AL3 43 CD17
Beech Rd, N11 99 DL51
SW16 201 DL96
Dartford DA1 188 FK88
Epsom KT17 233 CT115
Feltham TW14 175 BS87
Orpington BR6 224 EU108
Redhill RH1 251 DJ126
Reigate RH2 250 DA131
St. Albans AL3 43 CE17
Sevenoaks TN13 *off Victoria Rd* 257 FH125
Slough SL3 152 AY75
Watford WD24 75 BU37
Westerham (Bigg.H.) TN16 238 EH118
Weybridge KT13 *off St. Marys Rd* 213 BR105
Beech Row, Rich. TW10 178 CL91
Beech St, EC2 10 G5
Romford RM7 127 FC56
Beechtree Av, Egh. (Eng.Grn) TW20 172 AV93
Beech Tree Cl, Stan. HA7 95 CJ50
Beech Tree Glade, E4 *off Forest Side* 102 EF46
Beechtree La, St.Alb. AL3 41 BV22
Beech Tree La, Stai. TW18 *off Staines Rd* 194 BH96
Beech Tree Pl, Sutt. SM1 *off St. Nicholas Way* 218 DB106
Beech Vale, Wok. GU22 *off Hill Vw Rd* 227 AZ118
Beechvale Cl, N12 98 DE50
Beech Wk, NW7 96 CS51
Dartford DA1 167 FG84
Epsom KT17 217 CU111
Hoddesdon EN11 49 DZ17
Beech Way, NW10 138 CR66
Beechway, Bex. DA5 186 EX86
Beech Way, Epsom KT17 233 CT115
Beechway, Guil. GU1 243 BB133
Beech Way, S.Croy. CR2 221 DX113
Twickenham TW2 176 CA90
Beech Waye, Ger.Cr. SL9 113 AZ59
Beechwood Av, N3 119 CZ55
Amersham HP6 72 AW38
Coulsdon CR5 235 DH115
Greenford UB6 136 CB69
Harrow HA2 116 CB62
Hayes UB3 135 BR73
Orpington BR6 223 ES106
Potters Bar EN6 64 DB33
Richmond TW9 158 CN81
Rickmansworth (Chorl.) WD3 73 BB42
Ruislip HA4 115 BT61
St. Albans AL1 43 CH18
Staines TW18 174 BH93
Sunbury-on-Thames TW16 175 BU93
Tadworth (Kgswd) KT20 234 DA121
Thornton Heath CR7 201 DP98
Uxbridge UB8 134 BN72
Weybridge KT13 213 BS105
Beechwood Circle, Har. HA2 *off Beechwood Gdns* 116 CB62
Beechwood Cl, NW7 96 CR50
Amersham HP6 72 AW39
Hertford SG13 32 DT09
Surbiton KT6 197 CJ101
Waltham Cross (Chsht) EN7 66 DS26
Weybridge KT13 213 BS105
Woking (Knap.) GU21 226 AS117
Beechwood Ct, Cars. SM5 218 DF105
Sunbury-on-Thames TW16 175 BU93
Beechwood Cres, Bexh. DA7 166 EX83
Beechwood Dr, Cob. KT11 214 CA111
Keston BR2 222 EK105
Woodford Green IG8 102 EF50
Beechwood Gdns, NW10 *off St. Annes Gdns* 138 CM69
Caterham CR3 236 DU122
Harrow HA2 116 CB62
Ilford IG5 125 EM57
Beechwood Gdns, Rain. RM13 147 FH71
Slough SL1 152 AS75
Beechwood Gro, W3 *off East Acton La* 138 CS73
Surbiton KT6 197 CJ101
Beechwood La, Warl. CR6 237 DX119
Beechwood Manor, Wey. KT13 213 BS105
Beechwood Ms, N9 100 DU47
Beechwood Pk, E18 124 EG55
Hemel Hempstead HP3 39 BF24
Leatherhead KT22 231 CJ123
Rickmansworth (Chorl.) WD3 73 BF42
Beechwood Ri, Chis. BR7 185 EP91
Watford WD24 75 BV36
Beechwood Rd, E8 5 N3
N8 121 DK56
Beaconsfield HP9 88 AJ53
Caterham CR3 236 DU122
Slough SL2 131 AR71
South Croydon CR2 220 DS109
Virginia Water GU25 192 AU101
Woking (Knap.) GU21 226 AS117
Sch **Beechwood Sch**, SW16 *off Leigham Ct Rd* 181 DL90
Slough SL2 *off Long Readings La* 131 AP69
Beechwoods Ct, SE19 *off Crystal Palace Par* 182 DT92
Beechwood Vil, Red. RH1 266 DG144
Beechworth Cl, NW3 120 DA61
Beecot La, Walt. KT12 196 BW103
Beecroft La, SE4 *off Beecroft Rd* 183 DY85
Beecroft Ms, SE4 *off Beecroft Rd* 183 DY85
Beecroft Rd, SE4 183 DY85
Beehive Cl, E8 5 N5
Borehamwood (Elstree) WD6 77 CK44
Uxbridge UB10 *off Honey Hill* 134 BM66
Beehive Ct, Rom. RM3 *off Arundel Rd* 106 FM52
Beehive Grn, Welw.G.C. AL7 30 DA11
Beehive La, Ilf. IG1, IG4 125 EM58
Welwyn Garden City AL7 30 DA12
Beehive Pas, EC3 11 L8
Beehive Pl, SW9 161 DN83
Beehive Rd, Stai. TW18 173 BF92
Waltham Cross (Chsht) EN7 65 DP28
Beehive Way, Reig. RH2 266 DB138
Beeken Dene, Orp. BR6 *off Isabella Dr* 223 EQ105
Beel Cl, Amer. HP7 72 AW39
Beeleigh Rd, Mord. SM4 200 DB98
Beesfield La, Dart. (Fnghm) DA4 208 FN101
Beeston Cl, E8 *off Ferncliff Rd* 122 DU64
Watford WD19 94 BX49
Beeston Dr, Wal.Cr. EN8 67 DX27
Beeston Pl, SW1 19 H6
Beeston Rd, Barn. EN4 80 DD44
Beeston Way, Felt. TW14 176 BW86
Beethoven Rd, Borwd. (Elstree) WD6 77 CK44
Beethoven St, W10 6 D1
Beeton Cl, Pnr. HA5 94 CA52
Begbie Rd, SE3 164 EJ81
Beggars Bush La, Wat. WD18 75 BR43
Beggars Hill, Epsom KT17 217 CT108
Beggars Hollow, Enf. EN2 82 DR37
Beggars La, Dor. (Abin.Ham.) RH5 261 BT137
Westerham TN16 255 ER125
Beggars Roost La, Sutt. SM1 218 DA107
Begonia Cl, E6 144 EL71
Begonia Pl, Hmptn. TW12 *off Gresham Rd* 176 CA93
Begonia Wk, W12 *off Du Cane Rd* 139 CT72
Beira St, SW12 181 DH87
Sch **Beis Chinuch Lebonos Girls Sch**, N4 *off Woodberry Gro* 122 DQ59
Sch **Beis Malka Sch**, N16 *off Amhurst Pk* 122 DR59
Sch **Beis Rochel D'Satmar Girls' Sch**, N16 *off Amhurst Pk* 122 DS59
Beken Ct, Wat. WD25 76 BW35
Bekesbourne St, E14 13 J8
Bekesbourne Twr, Orp. BR5 206 EY102
★ **Bekonscot Model Village**, Beac. HP9 89 AK51
Belcher Rd, Hodd. EN11 *off Amwell St* 49 EA16
Belchers La, Wal.Abb. EN9 50 EJ24
Belcon Ind Est, Hodd. EN11 49 EC17
Belcroft Cl, Brom. BR1 *off Hope Pk* 184 EF94
Beldam Haw, Sev. (Halst.) TN14 224 FA112
Beldham Gdns, W.Mol. KT8 196 CB97
Belfairs Dr, Rom. RM6 126 EW59
Belfairs Grn, Wat. WD19 *off Heysham Dr* 94 BX50
Belfast Av, Slou. SL1 131 AQ72
Belfast Rd, N16 122 DT61
SE25 202 DV98
Belfield Gdns, Harl. CM17 52 EW16
Belfield Rd, Epsom KT19 216 CR109
Belfont Wk, N7 121 DL63
Belford Gro, SE18 165 EN77
Belford Rd, Borwd. WD6 78 CM38
Belfort Rd, SE15 162 DW82
Belfour Ter, N3 98 DB54
Belfry Av, Uxb. (Hare.) UB9 92 BG53
Belfry Cl, SE16 22 D9
Belfry La, Rick. WD3 92 BJ46
Belfry Shop Cen, The, Red. RH1 250 DF133
Belgrade Rd, N16 122 DS63
Hampton TW12 196 CB95
Belgrave Av, Rom. RM2 128 FJ55
Watford WD18 75 BT43
Belgrave Cl, N14 *off Prince George Av* 81 DJ43
NW7 96 CR50
W3 *off Avenue Rd* 158 CQ75
Orpington BR5 206 EW98
St. Albans AL4 43 CJ16
Walton-on-Thames KT12 213 BV105
Belgrave Ct, E14 13 M10
Belgrave Cres, Sun. TW16 195 BV95
Belgrave Dr, Kings L. WD4 59 BQ28
Belgrave Gdns, N14 81 DK43
NW8 140 DB67
Belgrave Gdns, Stan. HA7 *off Copley Rd* 95 CJ50
Belgrave Hts, E11 124 EG60
Belgrave Manor, Wok. GU22 226 AY119
Belgrave Ms, Uxb. UB8 134 BK70
Belgrave Ms N, SW1 18 E4
Belgrave Ms S, SW1 18 F5
Belgrave Ms W, SW1 18 E5
Belgrave Pl, SW1 18 F5
Slough SL1 *off Clifton Rd* 152 AV75
Belgrave Rd, E10 123 EC60
E11 124 EG61
E13 15 P3
E17 123 EA57
SE25 202 DT98
SW1 19 J8
SW13 159 CT80
Hounslow TW4 156 BZ83
Ilford IG1 125 EM60
Mitcham CR4 200 DD97
Slough SL1 132 AS73
Sunbury-on-Thames TW16 195 BV95
Belgrave Sq, SW1 18 E5
Belgrave St, E1 13 H8
Belgrave Ter, Wdf.Grn. IG8 102 EG48
Tra **Belgrave Walk** 200 DD97
Belgrave Wk, Mitch. CR4 200 DD97
Belgrave Yd, SW1 18 G6
BELGRAVIA, SW1 18 E6
Belgravia Cl, Barn. EN5 79 CZ41
Belgravia Gdns, Brom. BR1 184 EE93
Belgravia Ho, SW4 181 DK86
Belgravia Ms, Kings.T. KT1 197 CK98
Belgrove St, WC1 9 N1
Belham Rd, Kings L. WD4 58 BM28
Belham Wk, SE5 *off D'Eynsford Rd* 162 DR81
Belhaven Ct, Borwd. WD6 78 CM39
Belhus Pk, S.Ock. (Aveley) RM15 149 FR71
Belinda Rd, SW9 161 DP83
Belitha Vil, N1 4 B5
Bellamy Cl, E14 23 N3
W14 16 F10
Edgware HA8 96 CQ48
Uxbridge UB10 114 BN62
Watford WD17 75 BU39
Bellamy Dr, Stan. HA7 95 CH53
Bellamy Rd, E4 101 EB51
Enfield EN2 82 DR40
Waltham Cross (Chsht) EN8 67 DY29
Bellamy St, SW12 181 DH87
Bellarmine Cl, SE28 165 ET75
Bellasis Av, SW2 181 DL89
Bell Av, Rom. RM3 105 FH53
West Drayton UB7 154 BM77
Bell Br Rd, Cher. KT16 193 BF102
Bell Cl, Abb.L. (Bedmond) WD5 59 BT27
Beaconsfield HP9 89 AM53
Greenhithe DA9 189 FT85
Pinner HA5 116 BW55
Ruislip HA4 115 BT62
Slough SL2 132 AV71
Bellclose Rd, West Dr. UB7 154 BL75
BELL COMMON, Epp. CM16 69 ER32
Bell Common, Epp. CM16 69 ES32
Bell Common Tunnel, Epp. CM16 69 ER33
Bell Ct, Surb. KT5 *off Barnsbury La* 198 CP103
Bell Cres, Couls. CR5 *off Maple Way* 235 DH121
Bell Dr, SW18 179 CY87
Bellefield Rd, Orp. BR5 206 EV99
Bellefields Rd, SW9 161 DM83
Bellegrove Cl, Well. DA16 165 ET82
Bellegrove Par, Well. DA16 *off Bellegrove Rd* 165 ET83
Bellegrove Rd, Well. DA16 165 ER82
Sch **Bellenden Prim Sch**, SE15 *off Reedham St* 162 DU83
Bellenden Rd, SE15 162 DT82
Coll **Bellerbys Coll London**, SW15 *off Roehampton La* 179 CU86
Bellestaines Pleasaunce, E4 101 EA47
Sch **Belleville Prim Sch**, SW11 *off Webbs Rd* 180 DF85
Belleville Rd, SW11 180 DF85
Belle Vue, Grnf. UB6 137 CD67
Belle Vue Cl, Stai. TW18 194 BG95
Belle Vue Est, NW4 *off Bell La* 119 CW56
Belle Vue La, Bushey (Bushey Hth) WD23 95 CD46
Bellevue Ms, N11 *off Bellevue Rd* 98 DG50
Bellevue Par, SW17 *off Bellevue Rd* 180 DE88
Belle Vue Pk, Th.Hth. CR7 202 DQ97
Bellevue Pl, E1 12 E4
Slough SL1 *off Albert St* 152 AT76
Belle Vue Rd, E17 101 ED54
Bellevue Rd, N11 98 DG49
Belle Vue Rd, NW4 *off Bell La* 119 CW56
Bellevue Rd, SW13 159 CU82
SW17 180 DE88
W13 137 CH70
Bexleyheath DA6 186 EZ85
Hornchurch RM11 128 FM60
Kingston upon Thames KT1 198 CL97
Belle Vue Rd, Orp. BR6 *off Standard Rd* 223 EN110
Bellevue Rd, Rom. RM5 105 FC51
Belle Vue Rd, Ware SG12 33 DZ06
Bellevue Ter, Uxb. (Hare.) UB9 92 BG52
Bellew St, SW17 180 DC90
Bell Fm Av, Dag. RM10 127 FC62
Sch **Bell Fm Jun Sch**, Walt. KT12 *off Hersham Rd* 214 BW105
Bellfield, Croy. CR0 221 DY109
Bellfield Av, Har. HA3 94 CC51
BELLFIELDS, Guil. GU1 242 AW131
Bellfields Ct, Guil. GU1 *off Oak Tree Dr* 242 AW130
Bellfields Rd, Guil. GU1 242 AX132
Bellflower Cl, E6 *off Sorrel Gdns* 144 EL71
Bellflower Path, Rom. RM3 106 FJ52
Bell Gdns, E10 *off Church Rd* 123 EA60
E17 *off Markhouse Rd* 123 DZ57
Orpington BR5 206 EW99
Bellgate, Hem.H. HP2 40 BL17
Sch **Bellgate JMI Sch**, Hem.H. HP2 *off Fletcher Way* 40 BL18
Bellgate Ms, NW5 *off York Ri* 121 DH62
BELL GREEN, SE6 183 DZ90
Bell Grn, SE26 183 DZ90
Hemel Hempstead (Bov.) HP3 57 BB27
Bell Grn La, SE26 183 DY92
Bell Hill, Croy. CR0 *off Surrey St* 202 DQ104
Bellhouse La, Brwd. CM14 108 FS43
Bell Ho Rd, Rom. RM7 127 FC60
Bellingdon Rd, Chesh. HP5 54 AP31
BELLINGHAM, SE6 183 EB90
⇌ **Bellingham** 183 EB90
Bellingham Ct, Bark. IG11 *off Renwick Rd* 146 EV69
Bellingham Grn, SE6 183 EA90
Bellingham Rd, SE6 183 EB90
Bell Inn Yd, EC3 11 K8
Bell La, E1 11 N6
E16 25 L1
NW4 119 CX56
Abbots Langley (Bedmond) WD5 59 BT27
Amersham HP6, HP7 72 AV39
Berkhamsted HP4 38 AS18
Broxbourne EN10 49 DY21
Enfield EN3 83 DX38
Hatfield (Brook.Pk) AL9 64 DA25
Hertford SG14 32 DR09
Hoddesdon EN11 49 EA17
Leatherhead (Fetch.) KT22 231 CD123
St. Albans (Lon.Col.) AL2 62 CL29
Twickenham TW1 *off The Embankment* 177 CG88
Wembley HA9 *off Magnet Rd* 117 CK61
Windsor (Eton Wick) SL4 151 AM77
Bell La Cl, Lthd. (Fetch.) KT22 231 CD123
Sch **Bell La Comb Sch**, Amer. HP6 *off Bell La* 72 AV38
Sch **Bell La Prim Sch**, NW4 *off Bell La* 119 CX56
Bellmaker Ct, E3 13 N5
Bellman Av, Grav. DA12 191 GL88
Bellmarsh Rd, Add. KT15 212 BH105
Bell Mead, Saw. CM21 36 EY05
Bell Meadow, SE19 *off Dulwich Wd Av* 182 DS91
Godstone RH9 252 DV132
Bellmount Wd Av, Wat. WD17 75 BS39
Bello Cl, SE24 181 DP87
Bellot Gdns, SE10 25 H9
Bellot St, SE10 25 H9
Bell Par, Wind. SL4 *off St. Andrews Av* 151 AM82
Bellring Cl, Belv. DA17 166 FA79
Bell Rd, E.Mol. KT8 197 CD99
Enfield EN1 82 DR39
Hounslow TW3 156 CB84
Bells All, SW6 160 DA82
Bells Gdn Est, SE15 *off Buller Cl* 162 DU80
Bells Hill, Barn. EN5 79 CX43
Bell's Hill, Slou. (Stoke P.) SL2 132 AU67
Bells Hill Grn, Slou. (Stoke P.) SL2 132 AU66
Bells La, Slou. (Horton) SL3 153 BB83
Bell St, NW1 8 A5
SE18 164 EL81
Reigate RH2 250 DA134
Sawbridgeworth CM21 36 EY05
Bellswood La, Iver SL0 133 BB71
Belltrees Gro, SW16 181 DM92
Bell Vw, St.Alb. AL4 43 CK20
Windsor SL4 151 AM83
Bell Vw Cl, Wind. SL4 151 AM82
Bell Water Gate, SE18 165 EN76
Bell Weir Cl, Stai. TW19 173 BB89
Bellwether La, Red. (Outwood) RH1 267 DP143
Bell Wf La, EC4 11 H9
Bellwood Rd, SE15 163 DX84
Bell Yd, WC2 10 C7
Belmarsh Rd, SE28 *off Western Way* 165 ES75
BELMONT, Har. HA3 95 CG54
BELMONT, Sutt. SM2 218 DB111
⇌ **Belmont** 218 DA110
Belmont, Slou. SL2 131 AN71
Belmont Av, N9 100 DU46
N13 99 DL50
N17 122 DQ55
Barnet EN4 80 DF43
Guildford GU2 242 AT131
New Malden KT3 199 CU99
Southall UB2 156 BY76
Upminster RM14 128 FM61
Welling DA16 165 ES83
Wembley HA0 138 CM67
Belmont Circle, Har. HA3 95 CH53
Belmont Cl, E4 101 ED50
N20 98 DB46
SW4 161 DJ83
Barnet EN4 80 DF42
Uxbridge UB8 134 BK65
Woodford Green IG8 102 EH49
Belmont Cotts, Slou. (Colnbr.) SL3 *off High St* 153 BC80
Belmont Ct, NW11 119 CZ57
Sch **Belmont First Sch**, Har. HA3 *off Hibbert Rd* 95 CF54
Belmont Gro, SE13 163 ED83
W4 *off Belmont Rd* 158 CR77
Belmont Hall Ct, SE13 *off Belmont Gro* 163 ED83
Belmont Hill, SE13 163 ED83
St. Albans AL1 43 CD21
Sch **Belmont Inf Sch**, N22 *off Rusper Rd* 122 DQ55
Sch **Belmont Jun Sch**, N22 *off Rusper Rd* 122 DQ55
Belmont La, Chis. BR7 185 EQ92
Stanmore HA7 95 CJ52
Belmont Ms, SW19 *off Chapman Sq* 179 CX89
Sch **Belmont Mid Sch**, Har. HA3 *off Hibbert Rd* 95 CF54
Belmont Pk, SE13 163 ED84
Belmont Pk Cl, SE13 *off Belmont Pk* 163 ED84
Belmont Pk Rd, E10 123 EB58
Sch **Belmont Pk Sch**, E10 *off Leyton Grn Rd* 123 EC58
Sch **Belmont Prim Sch**, W4 *off Belmont Rd* 158 CR77
Erith DA8 *off Belmont Rd* 166 FA80
Belmont Ri, Sutt. SM2 217 CZ107
Belmont Rd, N15 122 DQ56
N17 122 DQ56
SE25 202 DV99
SW4 161 DJ83
W4 158 CR77
Beckenham BR3 203 DZ96
Belmont Rd, Bushey WD23 76 BY43
Chesham HP5 54 AP29
Chislehurst BR7 185 EP92
Erith DA8 166 FA80
Grays RM17 170 FZ78
Harrow HA3 117 CF55
Hemel Hempstead HP3 40 BL24
Hornchurch RM12 128 FK62
Ilford IG1 125 EQ62
Leatherhead KT22 231 CG122
Reigate RH2 266 DC135
Sutton SM2 218 DA110
Twickenham TW2 177 CD89
Uxbridge UB8 134 BK66
Wallington SM6 219 DH106
Belmont St, NW1 140 DG66
Belmont Ter, W4 *off Belmont Rd* 158 CR77
Sch **Belmont, The Mill Hill Jun Sch**, NW7 *off The Ridgeway* 97 CU48
Belmor, Borwd. (Elstree) WD6 78 CN43
Belmore Av, Hayes UB4 135 BU72
Woking GU22 227 BD116
Belmore La, N7 121 DK64
Sch **Belmore Prim Sch**, Hayes UB4 *off Owen Rd* 135 BV69
Belmore St, SW8 161 DK81
Beloe Cl, SW15 159 CU83
Belper Ct, E5 *off Pedro St* 123 DX63
Belsham St, E9 142 DW65
BELSIZE, Rick. WD3 57 BF33
Belsize Av, N13 99 DM51
NW3 140 DD65
W13 157 CH76
Belsize Cl, Hem.H. HP3 40 BN21
St. Albans AL4 43 CJ15
Belsize Ct, NW3 *off Belsize La* 120 DE64
Belsize Cres, NW3 120 DD64
Belsize Gdns, Sutt. SM1 218 DB105
Belsize Gro, NW3 140 DE65
Belsize La, NW3 140 DD65
Belsize Ms, NW3 *off Belsize La* 140 DD65
BELSIZE PARK, NW3 140 DE65
⊖ **Belsize Park** 120 DE64
Belsize Pk, NW3 140 DD65
Belsize Pk Gdns, NW3 140 DE65
Belsize Pk Ms, NW3 *off Belsize La* 140 DD65
Belsize Pl, NW3 *off Belsize La* 140 DD65
Belsize Rd, NW6 140 DB67
Harrow HA3 95 CD52
Hemel Hempstead HP3 40 BN21
Belsize Sq, NW3 140 DD65
Belsize Ter, NW3 140 DD65
Belson Rd, SE18 165 EM77
Belswains Grn, Hem.H. HP3 *off Belswains La* 40 BL23
Belswains La, Hem.H. HP3 58 BM25
Sch **Belswains Prim Sch**, Hem.H. HP3 *off Barnfield* 40 BM24
Beltana Dr, Grav. DA12 191 GL91
Beltane Dr, SW19 179 CX90
Belthorn Cres, SW12 181 DJ87
Beltinge Rd, Rom. RM3 128 FM55
Beltona Gdns, Wal.Cr. (Chsht) EN8 67 DX27
Belton Rd, E7 144 EH66
E11 124 EE63
N17 122 DS55
NW2 139 CU65
Berkhamsted HP4 38 AU18
Sidcup DA14 186 EU91
Belton Way, E3 13 N5
Beltran Rd, SW6 160 DB82
Beltwood Rd, Belv. DA17 167 FC77
BELVEDERE, DA17 167 FB77
⇌ **Belvedere** 166 FA76
Belvedere Av, SW19 179 CY92
Ilford IG5 103 EP54
Belvedere Bldgs, SE1 20 F4
Belvedere Cl, Esher KT10 214 CB106
Gravesend DA12 191 GJ88
Guildford GU2 242 AV132
Teddington TW11 177 CE92
Weybridge KT13 212 BN106
Belvedere Ct, N2 120 DD57
Belvedere Dr, SW19 179 CY92
Belvedere Gdns, St.Alb. AL2 60 CA27
West Molesey KT8 196 BZ99
Belvedere Gro, SW19 179 CY92
Belvedere Ho, Felt. TW13 175 BU88
H **Belvedere Ho Day Hosp**, NW10 139 CU67
Belvedere Ind Est, Belv. DA17 167 FC76
Sch **Belvedere Inf Sch**, Belv. DA17 *off Mitchell Cl* 167 FB76
Sch **Belvedere Jun Sch**, Belv. DA17 *off Mitchell Cl* 167 FB76
Belvedere Ms, SE3 *off Langton Way* 164 EF81
SE15 162 DV83
Belvedere Pl, SE1 20 F4
SW2 *off Acre La* 161 DM84
Belvedere Rd, E10 123 DY60
SE1 20 B3
SE2 146 EX74
SE19 182 DT94
W7 157 CF76
Bexleyheath DA7 166 EZ83
Brentwood CM14 108 FT48
Westerham (Bigg.H.) TN16 239 EM118
Belvedere Sq, SW19 179 CY92
Belvedere Strand, NW9 97 CT54
Belvedere Twr, The, SW10 160 DC81
Belvedere Way, Har. HA3 118 CL58
Belvoir Cl, SE9 184 EL90
Belvoir Rd, SE22 182 DU87
Belvue Cl, Nthlt. UB5 136 CA66
Belvue Rd, Nthlt. UB5 136 CA66
Sch **Belvue (Spec) Sch**, Nthlt. UB5 *off Rowdell Rd* 136 CA67
Bembridge Cl, NW6 139 CY66
Bembridge Ct, Slou. SL1 *off Park St* 152 AT76
Bembridge Gdns, Ruis. HA4 115 BR61
Bemerton Est, N1 4 A6
Bemerton St, N1 4 A7
Bemish Rd, SW15 159 CX83
Bempton Dr, Ruis. HA4 115 BV61
Bemsted Rd, E17 123 DZ55

Benares Rd, SE18 165 ET77
Benbow Cl, St.Alb. AL1 43 CH22
Benbow Rd, W6 159 CV76
Benbow St, SE8 163 EA79
Benbow Waye, Uxb. UB8 134 BJ71
Benbrick Rd, Guil. GU2 258 AU135
Benbury Cl, Brom. BR1 183 EC92
Bence, The, Egh. TW20 193 BB97
Bench Fld, S.Croy. CR2 220 DT107
Benchleys Rd, Hem.H. HP1 39 BF21
Bench Manor Cres, Ger.Cr.
(Chal.St.P.) SL9 90 AW54
Bencombe Rd, Pur. CR8 219 DN114
Bencroft, Wal.Cr. (Chsht) EN7 66 DU26
Bencroft Rd, SW16 181 DJ94
Hemel Hempstead HP2 40 BL20
Bencurtis Pk, W.Wick. BR4 203 ED104
Bendall Ms, NW1 8 B5
Bendemeer Rd, SW15 159 CX83
Bendish Rd, E6 144 EL66
Bendmore Av, SE2 166 EU78
Bendon Valley, SW18 180 DB87
Bendysh Rd, Bushey WD23 76 BY41
Benedict Cl, Belv. DA17
off Tunstock Way 166 EY76
Orpington BR6 205 ES104
Benedict Dr, Felt. TW14 175 BR87
Benedictine Gate, Wal.Cr.
EN8 67 DY27
Sch Benedict Prim Sch, Mitch.
CR4 off Church Rd 200 DD97
Benedict Rd, SW9 161 DM83
Mitcham CR4 200 DD97
Benedict Way, N2 120 DC55
Benenden Grn, Brom. BR2 204 EG99
Benen-Stock Rd, Stai. TW19 173 BF85
Benets Rd, Horn. RM11 128 FN60
Benett Gdns, SW16 201 DL96
Benfleet Cl, Cob. KT11 214 BY112
Sutton SM1 200 DC104
Benfleet Way, N11 98 DG47
Benford Rd, Hodd. EN11 49 DY19
Bengal Ct, EC3
off Birchin La 142 DR72
Bengal Rd, Ilf. IG1 125 EP63
Bengarth Dr, Har. HA3 95 CD54
Bengarth Rd, Nthlt. UB5 136 BX67
BENGEO, Hert. SG14 32 DQ07
Sch Bengeo Co Prim Sch, Hert.
SG14 off The Avenue 32 DQ06
Bengeo Meadows, Hert.
SG14 32 DR06
Bengeo Ms, Hert. SG14
off Bengeo St 32 DQ06
Bengeo St, Hert. SG14 32 DQ08
Bengeworth Rd, SE5 162 DQ83
Harrow HA1 117 CG61
Ben Hale Cl, Stan. HA7 95 CH49
Benham Cl, SW11 160 DD83
Chesham HP5 54 AP29
Chessington KT9
off Merritt Gdns 215 CJ107
Coulsdon CR5 235 DP118
Benham Gdns, Houns. TW4 176 BZ85
Benham Rd, W7 137 CE71
Benhams Cl, Horl. RH6 268 DG146
Benhams Dr, Horl. RH6 268 DG146
Benhams Pl, NW3
off Holly Wk 120 DC63
Benhill Av, Sutt. SM1 218 DB105
Benhill Rd, SE5 162 DR80
Sutton SM1 200 DC104
Benhill Wd Rd, Sutt. SM1 200 DC104
BENHILTON, Sutt. SM1 200 DB103
Benhilton Gdns, Sutt. SM1 200 DB104
Benhurst Av, Horn. RM12 127 FH62
Benhurst Cl, S.Croy. CR2 221 DX110
Benhurst Ct, SW16 181 DN92
Benhurst Gdns, S.Croy. CR2 220 DW110
Benhurst La, SW16 181 DN92
Sch Benhurst Prim Sch, Horn.
RM12 off Benhurst Av 127 FH62
Benin St, SE13 183 ED87
Benison Ct, Slou. SL1
off Osborne St 152 AT76
Benjafield Cl, N18
off Brettenham Rd 100 DV49
Benjamin Cl, E8 142 DU67
Hornchurch RM11 127 FG58
Benjamin St, EC1 10 E5
Sch Ben Jonson Prim Sch, E1 13 K4
Ben Jonson Rd, E1 13 H6
Benledi St, E14 14 E7
Benn Cl, Oxt. RH8 254 EG134
Bennelong Cl, W12 139 CV73
Bennerley Rd, SW11 180 DE85
Bennetsfield Rd, Uxb. UB11 135 BP74
Bennet's Hill, EC4 10 F9
Bennett Cl, Cob. KT11 213 BU113
Kingston upon Thames
(Hmptn W.) KT1 197 CJ95
Northwood HA6 93 BT52
Welling DA16 166 EU82
Welwyn Garden City AL7 29 CZ13
Bennett Gro, SE13 163 EB81
Bennett Pk, SE3 164 EF83
Bennett Rd, E13 144 EJ70
N16 122 DS63
Romford RM6 126 EY58
Bennetts, Chesh. HP5 54 AR30
Bennetts Av, Croy. CR0 203 DY103
Greenford UB6 137 CE67
Bennetts Castle La, Dag.
RM8 126 EW63
Bennetts Cl, N17 100 DT51
Mitcham CR4 201 DH95
St. Albans (Coln.Hth) AL4
off Meadway 44 CR23
Slough SL1 131 AN74
Bennetts Copse, Chis. BR7 184 EL93
BENNETTS END, Hem.H.
HP3 40 BM23
Bennetts End Cl, Hem.H.
HP3 40 BM21
Bennetts End Rd, Hem.H.
HP3 40 BM21
Bennetts Fm Pl, Lthd. (Bkhm)
KT23 246 BZ125
Bennetts Gate, Hem.H. HP3
off Bennetts End Rd 40 BN23
Bennett St, SW1 19 J1
W4 158 CS79
Bennetts Way, Croy. CR0 203 DY103
Bennetts Yd, SW1 19 M6
Uxbridge UB8
off High St 134 BJ66
Bennett Way, Dart. (Lane End)
DA2 189 FR91
Guildford (W.Clan.) GU4 244 BG129
Benning Cl, Wind. SL4 151 AK83
Benningfield Gdns, Berk. HP4
off Frithsden Rd 38 AY17
Benningholme Rd, Edg. HA8 96 CS51
Bennington Rd, N17 100 DS53
Woodford Green IG8 102 EE52
Bennions Cl, Horn. RM12
off Franklin Rd 148 FK65
Bennison Dr, Rom.
(Harold Wd) RM3 106 FK54
Benn St, E9 143 DY65
Benn's Wk, Rich. TW9
off Rosedale Rd 158 CL84
Benrek Cl, Ilf. IG6 103 EQ53
Bensbury Cl, SW15 179 CV87
Bensham Cl, Th.Hth. CR7 202 DQ98
Bensham Gro, Th.Hth. CR7 202 DQ96
Bensham La, Croy. CR0 201 DP101
Thornton Heath CR7 201 DP98
Bensham Manor Rd, Th.Hth.
CR7 202 DQ98
Sch Bensham Manor Sch
(Spec), Th.Hth. CR7
off Ecclesbourne Rd 202 DQ99
Bensington Ct, Felt. TW14 175 BR86
Benskin Rd, Wat. WD18 75 BU43
Benskins La, Rom. (Noak Hill)
RM4 106 FK46
Bensley Cl, N11 98 DF50
Ben Smith Way, SE16 22 B5
Benson Av, E6 144 EJ68
Benson Cl, Houns. TW3 156 CA84
Slough SL2 132 AU74
Uxbridge UB8 134 BL71
Sch Benson Prim Sch, Croy.
CR0 off West Way 203 DY104
Benson Quay, E1 12 E10
Benson Rd, SE23 182 DW88
Croydon CR0 201 DN104
Grays RM17 170 GB79
Bentalls Cen, Kings.T. KT1 197 CK96
Bentfield Gdns, SE9
off Aldersgrove Av 184 EJ90
Sch Benthal Inf Sch, N16
off Benthal Rd 122 DU62
Sch Benthal Jun Sch, N16
off Benthal Rd 122 DU62
Benthall Gdns, Ken. CR8 236 DQ116
Benthal Rd, N16 122 DU61
Bentham Av, Wok. GU21 227 BC115
Bentham Ct, N1 5 H6
Bentham Rd, E9 143 DX65
SE28 146 EV73
Bentham Wk, NW10 118 CQ64
Ben Tillet Cl, Bark. IG11 146 EU66
Ben Tillett Cl, E16
off Newland St 145 EM74
Bentinck Cl, Ger.Cr. SL9 112 AX57
Bentinck Ms, W1 8 F7
Bentinck Rd, West Dr. UB7 134 BK74
Bentinck St, W1 8 F7
Bentley Ct, Rom. (Gidea Pk)
RM2 128 FJ55
Bentley Dr, NW2 119 CZ62
Harlow CM17 52 EW16
Ilford IG2 125 EQ58
Weybridge KT13 212 BN109
BENTLEY HEATH, Barn. B93 79 CZ35
Bentley Heath La, Barn. EN5 63 CY34
Bentley Ms, Enf. EN1 82 DR44
Bentley Pk, Slou. (Burn.)
SL1 131 AK68
★ Bentley Priory, Stan. HA7 95 CE48
Bentley Rd, N1 5 M4
Hertford SG14 31 DL08
Slough SL1 131 AN74
Bentley St, Grav. DA12 191 GJ86
Bentley Way, Stan. HA7 95 CG50
Woodford Green IG8 102 EG48
Sch Bentley Wd High Sch for
Girls, Stan. HA7
off Bridges Rd 95 CF50
Benton Rd, Ilf. IG1 125 ER60
Watford WD19 94 BX50
Bentons, Harl. CM18 51 ES17
Bentons La, SE27 182 DQ91
Bentons Ri, SE27 182 DR92
Bentry Cl, Dag. RM8 126 EY61
Bentry Rd, Dag. RM8 126 EY61
Bentsbrook Cl, Dor. (N.Holm.)
RH5 263 CH140
Bentsbrook Pk, Dor. (N.Holm.)
RH5 263 CH140
Bentsbrook Rd, Dor. (N.Holm.)
RH5 263 CH140
Bentsley Cl, St.Alb. AL4 43 CJ16
Sch Bentworth Prim Sch, W12
off Bentworth Rd 139 CV72
Bentworth Rd, W12 139 CV72
Benwell Ct, Sun. TW16 195 BU95
Benwell Rd, N7 121 DN63
Benwick Cl, SE16 22 D7
Benworth St, E3 13 M1
Benyon Path, S.Ock. RM15
off Tyssen Pl 149 FW68
Sch Benyon Prim Sch, S.Ock.
RM15 off West Rd 149 FW68
Benyon Rd, N1 5 K7
Beomonds Row, Cher. KT16
off Heriot Rd 194 BG101
Sch Beormund Sch, SE1 21 K4
Berberis Cl, Guil. GU1 242 AW132
Berberis Wk, West Dr. UB7 154 BL77
Berber Pl, E14 13 N9
Berber Rd, SW11 180 DF85
Berberry Cl, Edg. HA8
off Larkspur Gro 96 CQ49
Berceau Wk, Wat. WD17 75 BS39
Bercta Rd, SE9 185 EQ89
Bere Cl, Green. DA9
off Ingress Pk Av 189 FW85
Berecroft, Harl. CM18 51 ER20
Beredens La, Brwd. CM13 129 FT55
Berefeld, Hem.H. HP2 40 BK18
Berenger Wk, SW10
off Blantyre St 160 DD80
Berens Rd, NW10 6 A2
Orpington BR5 206 EX99
Berens Way, Chis. BR7 205 ET98
Beresford Av, N20 98 DF47
W7 137 CD71
Slough SL2 132 AW74
Surbiton KT5 198 CP102
Twickenham TW1 177 CJ86
Wembley HA0 138 CM67
Beresford Dr, Brom. BR1 204 EK97
Woodford Green IG8 102 EJ49
Beresford Gdns, Enf. EN1 82 DS42
Hounslow TW4 176 BZ85
Romford RM6 126 EY57
Sch Beresford Ho Sch, Brom.
BR1 off College Rd 184 EG94
Beresford Rd, E4 102 EE46
E17 101 EB53
N2 120 DE55
Beresford Rd, N5 5 J2
N8 121 DN57
Dorking RH4 263 CH136
Gravesend (Nthflt) DA11 190 GE87
Harrow HA1 117 CD57
Kingston upon Thames
KT2 198 CM95
New Malden KT3 198 CQ98
Rickmansworth (Mill End)
WD3 91 BF46
St. Albans AL1 43 CH21
Southall UB1 136 BX74
Sutton SM2 217 CZ108
Beresford Sq, SE18 165 EP77
Beresford St, SE18 165 EP76
Beresford Ter, N5 5 H2
Berestede Rd, W6 159 CT78
Bere St, E1 13 H9
Bergen Sq, SE16 23 K5
Berger Cl, Orp. BR5 205 ER100
Sch Berger JMI Sch, E9
off Anderson Rd 143 DX65
Berger Rd, E9 143 DX65
Berghem Ms, W14 16 B6
Berghers Hill, H.Wyc.
(Woob.Grn) HP10 110 AF59
Bergholt Av, Ilf. IG4 124 EL57
Bergholt Cres, N16 122 DS59
Bergholt Ms, NW1
off Rossendale Way 141 DJ66
Berglen Ct, E14 13 J8
Bericot Way, Welw.G.C. AL7 30 DC09
Bering Sq, E14 off Napier Av 163 EA78
Bering Wk, E16 144 EK72
Berisford Ms, SW18 180 DC86
Berkeley Av, Bexh. DA7 166 EX81
Chesham HP5 54 AN30
Greenford UB6 137 CE65
Hounslow TW4 155 BU82
Ilford IG5 103 EN54
Romford RM5 105 FC52
Berkeley Cl, Abb.L. WD5 59 BT32
Borehamwood (Elstree)
WD6 78 CN43
Chesham HP5
off Berkeley Av 54 AN30
Hornchurch RM11 128 FP61
Kingston upon Thames
KT2 178 CL94
Orpington BR5 205 ES101
Potters Bar EN6 63 CY32
Ruislip HA4 115 BU62
Staines TW19 173 BD89
Ware SG12 32 DW05
Berkeley Ct, N14 81 DJ44
Guildford GU1
off London Rd 242 AY134
Rickmansworth (Crox.Grn)
WD3 off Mayfare 75 BR43
Wallington SM6 201 DJ104
Weybridge KT13 195 BR103
Berkeley Cres, Barn. EN4 80 DD43
Dartford DA1 188 FM88
Berkeley Dr, Horn. RM11 128 FN60
West Molesey KT8 196 BZ97
Berkeley Gdns, N21 100 DR45
W8 17 H2
Esher (Clay.) KT10 215 CG107
Walton-on-Thames KT12 195 BT101
West Byfleet KT14 211 BF114
Berkeley Ho, E3 13 N2
Berkeley Ms, W1 8 D7
Berkeley Pl, SW19 179 CX93
Epsom KT18 232 CR115
Sch Berkeley Prim Sch, Houns.
TW5 off Cranford La 156 BX80
Berkeley Rd, E12 124 EL64
N8 121 DK57
N15 122 DR58
NW9 118 CN56
SW13 159 CU81
High Wycombe (Loud.)
HP10 88 AC53
Uxbridge UB10 135 BQ66
Berkeleys, The, Lthd. (Fetch.)
KT22 231 CE124
Berkeley Sq, W1 9 H10
Berkeley St, W1 9 H10
Berkeley Twr, E14
off Westferry Circ 143 DZ74
Berkeley Wk, N7
off Durham Rd 121 DM61
Berkeley Waye, Houns. TW5 156 BX80
Berkhampstead Rd, Belv.
DA17 166 FA78
Chesham HP5 54 AQ30
BERKHAMSTED, HP4 38 AW17
⇌ Berkhamsted 38 AW18
Berkhamsted Av, Wem. HA9 138 CM65
Berkhamsted Bypass, Berk.
HP4 38 AV21
Hemel Hempstead HP1 39 BB23
★ Berkhamsted Castle, Berk.
HP4 38 AX18
Sch Berkhamsted Collegiate Sch,
Berk. HP4 off Castle St 38 AW19
Berkhamsted Hill, Berk. HP4 38 AY17
Berkhamsted La, Hat. (Essen.)
AL9 46 DF20
Berkhamsted Pl, Berk. HP4 38 AW17
Berkhamsted Rd, Hem.H.
HP1 39 BD17
Sch Berkhamsted Sch for Girls,
Berk. HP4 off Kings Rd 38 AV19
Berkley Av, Wal.Cr. EN8 67 DX34
Berkley Cl, St.Alb. AL4 43 CJ16
Berkley Ct, Berk. HP4
off Mill St 38 AW19
Berkley Cres, Grav. DA12
off Milton Rd 191 GJ86
Berkley Gro, NW1
off Berkley Rd 140 DF66
Berkley Rd, NW1 140 DF66
Beaconsfield HP9 89 AK49
Gravesend DA12 191 GH86
Berks Hill, Rick. (Chorl.) WD3 73 BC43
Berkshire Av, Slou. SL1 131 AP72
Berkshire Cl, Cat. CR3 236 DR122
Berkshire Gdns, N13 99 DN51
N18 100 DV50
Berkshire Rd, E9 143 DZ65
Berkshire Sq, Mitch. CR4
off Berkshire Way 201 DL98
Berkshire Way, Horn. RM11 128 FN57
Mitcham CR4 201 DL98
★ Berkshire Yeomanry Mus,
Windsor TA Cen,
Wind. SL4 151 AR83
Bermans Cl, Brwd. (Hutt.)
CM13
off Hanging Hill La 109 GB47
Bermans Way, NW10 118 CS63
BERMONDSEY, SE1 21 N6
⊖ Bermondsey 22 B5
Bermondsey Sq, SE1 21 M5
Bermondsey St, SE1 21 L2
Bermondsey Wall E, SE16 22 B4
Bermondsey Wall W, SE16 22 A3
Bermuda Rd, Til. RM18 171 GG82
Bernal Cl, SE28
off Haldane Rd 146 EX73
Bernard Ashley Dr, SE7 25 N10
Bernard Av, W13 157 CH76
Bernard Cassidy St, E16 15 K5
Bernard Gdns, SW19 179 CZ92
Bernard Gro, Wal.Abb. EN9
off Beaulieu Dr 67 EB33
Bernard Rd, N15 122 DT57
Romford RM7 127 FC59
Wallington SM6 219 DH105
Bernards Cl, Ilf. IG6 103 EQ51
Sch Bernard's Heath Inf Sch,
St.Alb. AL1
off Sandridge Rd 43 CF18
Bernard St, WC1 9 N4
Gravesend DA12 191 GH86
St. Albans AL3 43 CD19
Bernays Cl, Stan. HA7 95 CJ51
Bernays Gro, SW9 161 DM84
Bernel Dr, Croy. CR0 203 DZ104
Berne Rd, Th.Hth. CR7 202 DQ99
Berners Cl, Slou. SL1 131 AL73
Berners Dr, W13 137 CG72
Broxbourne EN10
off Berners Way 49 DZ23
St. Albans AL1 43 CD23
Bernersmede, SE3
off Blackheath Pk 164 EG83
Berners Ms, W1 9 K6
Berners Pl, W1 9 K7
Berners Rd, N1 4 D9
N22 99 DN53
Berners St, W1 9 K6
Berners Way, Brox. EN10 49 DZ23
Berney Rd, Croy. CR0 202 DR101
Bernhardt Cres, NW8 8 A3
Bernhart Cl, Edg. HA8 96 CQ52
Bernice Cl, Rain. RM13 148 FJ70
Bernville Way, Har. HA3
off Kenton Rd 118 CM57
Bernwell Rd, E4 102 EE48
Berridge Grn, Edg. HA8 96 CN52
Berridge Ms, NW6
off Hillfield Rd 120 DA64
Berridge Rd, SE19 182 DR92
Berries, The, St.Alb. (Sand.)
AL4 43 CG16
Berriman Rd, N7 121 DM62
Berrington Dr, Lthd. (E.Hors.)
KT24 229 BT124
Berriton Rd, Har. HA2 116 BZ60
Berry Av, Wat. WD24 75 BU36
Berrybank Cl, E4
off Greenbank Cl 101 EC47
Berry Cl, N21 99 DP46
NW10 138 CS66
Dagenham RM10 126 FA64
Hornchurch RM12
off Airfield Way 128 FJ64
Rickmansworth WD3 92 BH45
Berry Ct, Houns. TW4 176 BZ85
Berrydale Rd, Hayes UB4 136 BY70
Berryfield, Slou. SL2 132 AW72
Berryfield Cl, E17 123 EB56
Bromley BR1 204 EL95
Berry Fld Pk, Amer. HP6 55 AP37
Berryfield Rd, SE17 20 F9
Berry Gro La, Wat. WD25 76 CA39
Berryhill, SE9 165 EP84
Berry Hill, Maid. (Taplow)
SL6 130 AD71
Stanmore HA7 95 CK49
Berry Hill Ct, Maid. (Taplow)
SL6 130 AD71
Berryhill Gdns, SE9 165 EP84
BERRYLANDS, Surb. KT5 198 CM99
⇌ Berrylands 198 CN98
Berrylands, SW20 199 CW97
Orpington BR6 206 EW104
Surbiton KT5 198 CN99
Berrylands Rd, Surb. KT5 198 CM100
Berry La, SE21 182 DR91
Rickmansworth WD3 92 BH46
Walton-on-Thames KT12
off Burwood Rd 214 BX106
Berryman Cl, Dag. RM8
off Bennetts Castle La 126 EW62
Berrymans La, SE26 183 DX91
Berrymead, Hem.H. HP2 40 BM19
Berry Meade, Ashtd. KT21 232 CM117
Berry Meade Cl, Ashtd. KT21
off Berry Meade 232 CM117
Berrymead Gdns, W3 138 CQ74
Sch Berrymede Inf Sch, W3
off Park Rd N 158 CP75
Sch Berrymede Jun Sch, W3
off Osborne Rd 158 CP75
Berrymede Rd, W4 158 CR76
Berry Pl, EC1 10 F2
Berryscroft Ct, Stai. TW18
off Berryscroft Rd 174 BJ94
Berryscroft Rd, Stai. TW18 174 BJ94
BERRY'S GREEN, West.
TN16 239 EP116
Berry's Grn Rd, West.
(Berry's Grn) TN16 239 EP116
Berry's Hill, West.
(Berry's Grn) TN16 239 EP115
Berrys La, W.Byf. (Byfleet)
KT14 212 BK111
Berry St, EC1 10 F3
Berry Wk, Ashtd. KT21 232 CM119
Berry Way, W5 158 CL76
Rickmansworth WD3 92 BH45
Bersham La, Grays
(Bad.Dene) RM17 170 FZ77
Bertal Rd, SW17 180 DD91
Berther Rd, Horn. RM11 128 FK59
Berthold Ms, Wal.Abb. EN9 67 EB33
Berthon St, SE8 163 EA80
Bertie Rd, NW10 139 CU65
SE26 183 DX93
Bertram Cotts, SW19
off Hartfield Rd 180 DA94
Bertram Rd, NW4 119 CU58
Enfield EN1 82 DU42
Kingston upon Thames
KT2 178 CN94
Bertram St, N19 121 DH61
Bertram Way, Enf. EN1 82 DT42
Bertrand St, SE13 163 EB83
Bertrand Way, SE28 146 EV73
Bert Rd, Th.Hth. CR7 202 DQ99
Berwick Av, Hayes UB4 136 BX72
Slough SL1 131 AP73
Berwick Cl, Beac. HP9 89 AP54
Stanmore HA7
off Gordon Av 95 CF52
Twickenham TW2 176 CA88
Waltham Cross EN8 67 EA34
Berwick Cres, Sid. DA15 185 ES86
Berwick La, Ong. CM5 87 FF36
Berwick Pond Cl, Rain.
RM13 148 FK68
Berwick Pond Rd, Rain.
RM13 148 FL68
Upminster RM14 148 FM66
Berwick Rd, E16 144 EH72
N22 99 DP53
Borehamwood WD6 78 CM38
Rainham RM13 148 FK68
Welling DA16 166 EV81
Berwick St, W1 9 L8
Berwick Way, Orp. BR6 206 EU102
Sevenoaks TN14 257 FH121
Berwyn Av, Houns. TW3 156 CB81
Berwyn Rd, SE24 181 DP88
Richmond TW10 158 CP84
Beryl Av, E6 144 EL71
Beryl Ho, SE18 off Spinel Cl 165 ET78
Beryl Rd, W6 16 A10
Berystede, Kings.T. KT2 178 CP94
Besant Ct, N1
off Newington Grn Rd 122 DR64
Besant Rd, NW2 119 CY63
Besant Wk, N7
off Newington Barrow Way 121 DM61
Besant Way, NW10 118 CQ64
Besley St, SW16 181 DJ93
Bessant Dr, Rich. TW9 158 CP81
Bessborough Gdns, SW1 19 M9
Bessborough Pl, SW1 19 L9
Bessborough Rd, SW15 179 CU88
Harrow HA1 117 CD60
Bessborough St, SW1 19 L9
BESSELS GREEN, Sev. TN13 256 FC124
Bessels Grn Rd, Sev. TN13 256 FD123
Bessels Meadow, Sev. TN13 256 FD124
Bessels Way, Sev. TN13 256 FC124
Bessemer Cl, Slou. SL3
off Ditton Pk Rd 153 AZ78
Sch Bessemer Gra Prim Sch,
SE5 off Dylways 162 DR84
Bessemer Rd, SE5 162 DQ82
Welwyn Garden City AL7,
AL8 29 CY05
Bessie Lansbury Cl, E6 145 EN72
Bessingby Rd, Ruis. HA4 115 BU61
Bessingham Wk, SE4
off Frendsbury Rd 163 DX84
Besson St, SE14 162 DW81
Bessy St, E2 12 F1
Bestobell Rd, Slou. SL1 131 AQ72
Bestwood St, SE8 23 H8
Beswick Ms, NW6
off Lymington Rd 140 DB65
Betam Rd, Hayes UB3 155 BR75
Beta Pl, SW4 off Santley St 161 DL84
Beta Rd, Wok. GU22 227 BB116
Woking (Chobham) GU24 210 AT110
Beta Way, Egh. TW20 193 BC95
BETCHWORTH, RH3 248 CR134
⇌ Betchworth 248 CR132
Betchworth Cl, Sutt. SM1
off Turnpike La 218 DD106
Betchworth Rd, Ilf. IG3 125 ES61
Betchworth Way, Croy.
(New Adgtn) CR0 221 EC109
Betenson Av, Sev. TN13 256 FF122
Betham Rd, Grnf. UB6 137 CD69
Bethany Waye, Felt. TW14 175 BS87
Bethecar Rd, Har. HA1 117 CE57
Bethell Av, E16 15 J3
Ilford IG1 125 EN59
Bethel Rd, Sev. TN13 257 FJ123
Welling DA16 166 EW83
Bethersden Cl, Beck. BR3 183 DZ94
H Bethlem Royal Hosp,
Beck. BR3 203 EA101
BETHNAL GREEN, E2 12 C1
⇌ Bethnal Green 12 C3
⊖ Bethnal Green 12 E2
Bethnal Grn Est, E2 12 E2
★ Bethnal Green Mus of
Childhood, E2 12 D1
Bethnal Grn Rd, E1 11 N3
E2 11 N3
Sch Bethnal Grn Tech Coll, E2 11 P2
Coll Bethnal Grn Training Cen,
E1 12 A5
Bethune Av, N11 98 DF49
Bethune Rd, N16 122 DR59
NW10 138 CR70
Bethwin Rd, SE5 161 DP80
Betjeman Cl, Couls. CR5 235 DM117
Pinner HA5 116 CA56
Waltham Cross EN7
off Rosedale Way 66 DU28
Betjeman Way, Hem.H. HP1 40 BH18
Betley Ct, Walt. KT12 195 BV104
Betony Cl, Croy. CR0
off Primrose La 203 DX102
Betony Rd, Rom. RM3 106 FK51
Betoyne Av, E4 102 EE49
BETSHAM, Dart. DA13 190 FY91
BETSHAM, Grav. DA13 190 FY91
Betsham Rd, Erith DA8 167 FF80
Gravesend (Sthflt) DA13 189 FX92
Swanscombe DA10 190 FY87
Betstyle Circ, N11 99 DH49
Betstyle Rd, N11 99 DH49
Betterton Dr, Sid. DA14 186 EY89
Betterton Rd, Rain. RM13 147 FE69
Betterton St, WC2 9 N8
Bettles Cl, Uxb. UB8
off Wescott Way 134 BJ68
Bettons Pk, E15 144 EE67
Bettridge Rd, SW6 159 CZ82
Betts Cl, Beck. BR3
off Kendall Rd 203 DY96
Betts La, Wal.Abb. EN9 50 EJ21
Betts Ms, E17
off Queen's Rd 123 DZ58
Betts Rd, E16 15 P8
Betts St, E1 12 C10
Betts Way, SE20 202 DV95
Surbiton KT6 197 CH102
Sch Betty Layward Prim Sch,
The, N16
off Clissold Rd 122 DR62
Betula Cl, Ken. CR8 236 DR115
Betula Wk, Rain. RM13 148 FK69
Between Sts, Cob. KT11 213 BU114
Beulah Av, Th.Hth. CR7
off Beulah Rd 202 DQ96
Beulah Cl, Edg. HA8 96 CP48
Beulah Cres, Th.Hth. CR7 202 DQ96
Beulah Gro, Croy. CR0 202 DQ100
Beulah Hill, SE19 181 DP93
Sch Beulah Inf Sch, Th.Hth.
CR7 off Furze Rd 202 DQ97
Sch Beulah Jun Sch, Th.Hth.
CR7 off Beulah Rd 202 DQ97
Beulah Path, E17
off Addison Rd 123 EB57

Beulah Rd, E17 123 EB57
SW19 179 CZ94
Epping CM16 70 EU29
Hornchurch RM12 128 FJ62
Sutton SM1 218 DA105
Thornton Heath CR7 202 DQ97
Beulah Wk, Cat. (Wold.) CR3 237 DY120
Beult Rd, Dart. DA1 167 FG83
Bevan Av, Bark. IG11 146 EU66
Bevan Cl, Hem.H. HP3 40 BK22
Bevan Ct, Croy. CR0 219 DN106
Bevan Hill, Chesh. HP5 54 AP29
Bevan Ho, Grays RM16 off Laird Av 170 GD75
Bevan Pk, Epsom KT17 217 CT110
Bevan Pl, Swan. BR8 207 FF98
Bevan Rd, SE2 166 EV78
Barnet EN4 80 DF42
Bevans Cl, Green. DA9 off Johnsons Way 189 FW86
Bevan St, N1 5 H8
Bevan Way, Horn. RM12 128 FM63
Bev Callender Cl, SW8 off Daley Thompson Way 161 DH83
Bevenden St, N1 11 K1
Bevercote Wk, Belv. DA17 off Osborne Rd 166 EZ79
Beveridge Rd, NW10 off Curzon Cres 138 CS66
Beverley Av, SW20 199 CT95
Hounslow TW4 156 BZ84
Sidcup DA15 185 ET87
Beverley Cl, N21 100 DQ46
SW11 off Maysoule Rd 160 DD84
SW13 159 CT82
Addlestone KT15 212 BK106
Broxbourne EN10 49 DY21
Chessington KT9 215 CJ105
Enfield EN1 82 DS42
Epsom KT17 217 CW111
Hornchurch RM11 128 FM59
Weybridge KT13 195 BS103
Beverley Cotts, SW15 off Kingston Vale 178 CR91
Beverley Ct, N14 99 DJ45
N20 off Farnham Cl 98 DC45
SE4 163 DZ83
Slough SL1 off Dolphin Rd 152 AV75
Beverley Cres, Wdf.Grn. IG8 102 EH53
Beverley Dr, Edg. HA8 118 CP55
Beverley Gdns, NW11 119 CY59
SW13 159 CT83
Hornchurch RM11 128 FM59
St. Albans AL4 43 CK16
Stanmore HA7 95 CG53
Waltham Cross (Chsht) EN7 66 DT30
Welwyn Garden City AL7 30 DC09
Wembley HA9 118 CM60
Worcester Park KT4 off Green La 199 CU102
Beverley Hts, Reig. RH2 250 DB132
Beverley Ho, NW8 8 A2
Beverley La, SW15 179 CT90
Kingston upon Thames KT2 178 CS94
Beverley Ms, E4 off Beverley Rd 101 ED51
Beverley Path, SW13 159 CT82
Beverley Rd, E4 101 ED51
E6 144 EK69
SE20 off Wadhurst Cl 202 DV96
SW13 159 CT83
W4 159 CT78
Bexleyheath DA7 167 FC82
Bromley BR2 204 EL103
Dagenham RM9 126 EY63
Kingston upon Thames KT1 197 CJ95
Mitcham CR4 201 DK98
New Malden KT3 199 CU98
Ruislip HA4 115 BU61
Southall UB2 156 BY76
Sunbury-on-Thames TW16 195 BT95
Whyteleafe CR3 236 DS116
Worcester Park KT4 199 CW103
Sch Beverley Sch, N.Mal. KT3 off College Gdns 199 CU99
Beverley Trd Est, Mord. SM4 off Garth Rd 199 CX101
Beverley Way, SW20 199 CT95
New Malden KT3 199 CT95
Beversbrook Rd, N19 121 DK62
Beverstone Rd, SW2 181 DM85
Thornton Heath CR7 201 DN98
Beverston Ms, W1 8 C6
Bevil Ct, Hodd. EN11 off Molesworth 33 EA14
Bevill Allen Cl, SW17 180 DF92
Bevill Cl, SE25 202 DU97
Bevin Cl, SE16 23 J1
Bevin Ct, WC1 off Holford St 141 DN69
Bevington Path, SE1 off Tanner St 162 DT75
Sch Bevington Prim Sch, W10 6 D5
Bevington Rd, W10 6 D5
Beckenham BR3 203 EB96
Bevington St, SE16 22 B4
Bevin Rd, Hayes UB4 135 BU69
Bevin Sq, SW17 180 DF90
Bevin Way, WC1 10 C1
Bevis Cl, Dart. DA2 188 FQ87
Bevis Marks, EC3 11 M7
Bewcastle Gdns, Enf. EN2 81 DL42
Bewdley St, N1 4 C5
Bewick Ms, SE15 162 DV80
Bewick St, SW8 161 DH82
Bewley Cl, Wal.Cr. (Chsht) EN8 67 DX31
Bewley St, E1 12 D9
SW19 180 DC93
Bewlys Rd, SE27 181 DP92
Bexhill Cl, Felt. TW13 176 BY89
Bexhill Dr, Grays RM17 170 FY79
Bexhill Rd, N11 99 DK50
SE4 183 DZ87
SW14 158 CQ83
Bexhill Wk, E15 off Mitre Rd 144 EE68
BEXLEY, DA5 186 FA86
⇌ Bexley 186 FA88
Coll Bexley Adult Ed Cen, Bexh. DA7 off Brampton Rd 166 EX83
Sch Bexley Business Acad, Erith DA18 off Yarnton Way 166 EY75
Bexley Cl, Dart. DA1 187 FE85
Coll Bexley Coll, Erith Rd Campus, Belv. DA17 167 FB78
St. Joseph's Campus, SE2 off Woolwich Rd 166 EX79
The Oaks, SE2 off Woolwich Rd 166 EX79
Tower Rd Campus, Belv. DA17 167 FC77
Sch Bexley-Erith Tech High Sch for Boys, Bex. DA5 off Hartford Rd 187 FB86
Bexley Gdns, N9 100 DR48
Romford (Chad.Hth) RM6 126 EV57
Sch Bexley Gram Sch, Well. DA16 off Danson La 166 EV84
BEXLEYHEATH, DA6 & DA7 186 EZ85
⇌ Bexleyheath 166 EY82
Sch Bexleyheath Sch, Bexh. DA6 off Graham Rd 166 EZ83
Bexley High St, Bex. DA5 186 FA87
Bexley La, Dart. DA1 187 FE85
Sidcup DA14 186 EW90
Coll Bexley Professional Dev Cen (Music & Arts), Sid. DA15 off Station Rd 186 EU90
Bexley Rd, SE9 185 EP85
Erith DA8 167 FC80
Bexley St, Wind. SL4 151 AQ81
Beyers Gdns, Hodd. EN11 33 EA14
Beyers Prospect, Hodd. EN11 33 EA13
Beyers Ride, Hodd. EN11 33 EA13
Beynon Rd, Cars. SM5 218 DF106
Sch Bhois Jerusholaim (London) Sch, N16 off Amhurst Pk 122 DS59
Bianca Ho, N1 off Crondall St 142 DS68
Bianca Rd, SE15 162 DT79
Bibsworth Rd, N3 97 CZ54
Bibury Cl, SE15 162 DS79
Bicester Rd, Rich. TW9 158 CN83
Bickenhall St, W1 8 D5
Bickersteth Rd, SW17 180 DF93
Bickerton Rd, N19 121 DJ61
BICKLEY, Brom. BR1 205 EM97
⇌ Bickley 204 EL97
Bickley Cres, Brom. BR1 204 EL98
Bickley Pk Rd, Brom. BR1 204 EL97
Sch Bickley Pk Sch, Brom. BR1 off Page Heath La 204 EK97
Sch Bickley Prim Sch, Brom. BR1 off Nightingale La 204 EJ96
Bickley Rd, E10 123 EB59
Bromley BR1 204 EK96
Bickley St, SW17 180 DE92
Bicknell Cl, Guil. GU1 off Stocton Rd 242 AW133
Bicknell Rd, SE5 162 DQ83
Bickney Way, Lthd. (Fetch.) KT22 230 CC122
Bicknoller Cl, Sutt. SM2 218 DB110
Bicknoller Rd, Enf. EN1 82 DT39
Bicknor Rd, Orp. BR6 205 ES101
Bidborough Cl, Brom. BR2 204 EF99
Bidborough St, WC1 9 N2
Biddenden Way, SE9 185 EN91
Gravesend (Istead Rise) DA13 190 GE94
Biddenham Turn, Wat. WD25 76 BW35
Bidder St, E16 14 G5
Biddestone Rd, N7 121 DM63
Biddles Cl, Slou. SL1 131 AL74
Biddulph Rd, W9 7 J2
South Croydon CR2 220 DQ109
Bideford Av, Grnf. UB6 137 CH68
Bideford Cl, Edg. HA8 96 CN53
Feltham TW13 176 BZ90
Romford RM3 106 FJ53
Bideford Gdns, Enf. EN1 100 DS45
Bideford Rd, Brom. BR1 184 EF90
Enfield EN3 83 DZ38
Ruislip HA4 115 BV62
Welling DA16 166 EV80
Bideford Spur, Slou. SL2 131 AP69
Bidhams Cres, Tad. KT20 233 CW121
Bidwell Gdns, N11 99 DJ52
Bidwell St, SE15 162 DV81
★ Big Ben (St. Stephens Tower), SW1 19 P4
Bigbury Cl, N17 100 DS52
Big Common La, Red. (Bletch.) RH1 251 DP133
Biggerstaff Rd, E15 143 EC67
Biggerstaff St, N4 121 DN61
Biggin Av, Mitch. CR4 200 DF95
BIGGIN HILL, West. TN16 238 EH116
Biggin Hill, SE19 181 DP94
Biggin Hill Business Pk, West. TN16 238 EK115
Biggin Hill Cl, Kings.T. KT2 177 CJ92
Sch Biggin Hill Inf Sch, West. TN16 off Old Tye Av 238 EL116
Sch Biggin Hill Jun Sch, West. TN16 off Old Tye Av 238 EL116
Biggin La, Grays RM16 171 GH79
Biggin Way, SE19 181 DP94
Bigginwood Rd, SW16 181 DP94
Biggs Gro Rd, Wal.Cr. (Chsht) EN7 66 DR27
Biggs Row, SW15 off Felsham Rd 159 CX83
Big Hill, E5 122 DV60
Sch Bigland Grn Prim Sch, E1 12 C8
Bigland St, E1 12 C8
Bignell Rd, SE18 165 EP78
Bignell's Cor, Pot.B. (S.Mimms) EN6 63 CV33
Bignold Rd, E7 124 EG63
Bigwood Rd, NW11 120 DB57
Biko Cl, Uxb. UB8 off Sefton Way 134 BJ72
Billet Cl, Rom. RM6 126 EX55
Billet La, Berk. HP4 38 AU18
Hornchurch RM11 128 FK60
Iver SL0 133 BB69
Slough SL3 133 BB73
Billet Rd, E17 101 DX54
Romford RM6 126 EV55
Staines TW18 174 BG90
Billets Hart Cl, W7 157 CE75
Billet Wks, E17 101 DZ53
Bill Hamling Cl, SE9 185 EM89
Billingford Cl, SE4 163 DX84
Billing Pl, SW10 160 DB80
Billing Rd, SW10 160 DB80
Billings Cl, Dag. RM9 off Ellerton Rd 146 EW66
★ Billingsgate Fish Mkt, E14 24 B1
Billing St, SW10 160 DB80
Billington Rd, SE14 163 DX80
Billiter Sq, EC3 11 M9
Billiter St, EC3 11 M8
Bill Nicholson Way, N17 off High Rd 100 DT52
Billockby Cl, Chess. KT9 216 CM107
Billson St, E14 24 D8
Billy Lows La, Pot.B. EN6 64 DA31
Bilsby Gro, SE9 184 EK91
Bilton Cl, Slou. (Poyle) SL3 153 BE82
Bilton Rd, Erith DA8 167 FG80
Greenford UB6 137 CH67
Bilton Way, Enf. EN3 83 DY39
Bilton Way, Hayes UB3 155 BV75
Bina Gdns, SW5 17 L8
Bincote Rd, Enf. EN2 81 DM41
Binden Rd, W12 159 CT76
Bindon Grn, Mord. SM4 200 DB98
Binfield Rd, SW4 161 DL81
South Croydon CR2 220 DT106
West Byfleet (Byfleet) KT14 212 BL112
Bingfield St, N1 141 DL67
Bingham Cl, Hem.H. HP1 39 BF18
South Ockendon RM15 149 FV72
Bingham Ct, N1 4 F5
Bingham Dr, Stai. TW18 174 BK94
Woking GU21 226 AT118
Bingham Pl, W1 8 E5
Bingham Pt, SE18 off Whitworth Pl 165 EP77
Bingham Rd, Croy. CR0 202 DU102
Slough (Burn.) SL1 130 AG71
Bingham St, N1 5 J3
Bingley Rd, E16 144 EJ72
Greenford UB6 136 CC71
Hoddesdon EN11 49 EC17
Sunbury-on-Thames TW16 175 BU94
Binley Ho, SW15 off Highcliffe Dr 179 CU86
Binney St, W1 8 F9
Binns Rd, W4 158 CS78
Binns Ter, W4 off Binns Rd 158 CS78
Binscombe Cres, Gdmg. GU7 258 AS144
Sch Binscombe Jun Sch, Gdmg. GU7 off Green La 258 AS143
Binsey Wk, SE2 146 EW74
Binstead Cl, Hayes UB4 136 BY71
Binyon Cres, Stan. HA7 95 CF50
Birbetts Rd, SE9 185 EM89
Birchall La, Hert. SG14 30 DF12
Birchall Wd, Welw.G.C. AL7 30 DC10
Bircham Path, SE4 off St. Norbert Rd 163 DX84
Birchanger Rd, SE25 202 DU99
Birch Av, N13 100 DQ48
Caterham CR3 236 DR124
Leatherhead KT22 231 CF120
West Drayton UB7 134 BM72
Birch Circle, Gdmg. GU7 258 AT143
Birch Cl, E16 15 H5
N19 off Hargrave Pk 121 DJ61
SE15 off Bournemouth Rd 162 DU82
Addlestone (New Haw) KT15 212 BK109
Amersham HP6 55 AS37
Brentford TW8 157 CH80
Buckhurst Hill IG9 102 EK48
Dartford (Eyns.) DA4 208 FK104
Hounslow TW3 157 CD83
Iver SL0 133 BD68
Romford RM7 127 FB55
Sevenoaks TN13 257 FH123
South Ockendon RM15 149 FX69
Teddington TW11 177 CG92
Woking GU21 226 AW119
Woking (Send M.) GU23 243 BF125
Birch Copse, St.Alb. (Brick.Wd) AL2 60 BY30
Birch Ct, Nthwd. HA6 off Rickmansworth Rd 93 BQ51
Birch Cres, Horn. RM11 128 FL56
South Ockendon RM15 149 FX69
Uxbridge UB10 134 BM67
Birchcroft Cl, Cat. CR3 252 DQ125
Birchdale, Ger.Cr. SL9 112 AX60
Birchdale Cl, W.Byf. KT14 212 BJ111
Birchdale Gdns, Rom. RM6 126 EX59
Birchdale Rd, E7 124 EJ64
Birchdene Dr, SE28 166 EU75
Birch Dr, Hat. AL10 45 CU19
Rickmansworth (Map.Cr.) WD3 91 BD50
Birchen Cl, NW9 118 CR61
Birchend Cl, S.Croy. CR2 220 DR107
Birchen Gro, NW9 118 CR61
Bircherley Ct, Hert. SG14 off Priory St 32 DR09
Bircherley Grn Cen, The, Hert. SG14 off Green St 32 DR09
Bircherley St, Hert. SG14 32 DR09
Birches, The, N21 81 DM44
SE7 164 EH79
Beaconsfield HP9 88 AH53
Brentwood CM13 108 FY48
Bushey WD23 76 CC43
Epping (N.Wld Bas.) CM16 71 FB26
Hemel Hempstead HP3 39 BF23
Leatherhead (E.Hors.) KT24 245 BS126
Orpington BR6 223 EN105
Swanley BR8 207 FE96
Waltham Abbey EN9 off Honey La 68 EF34
Woking GU22 off Heathside Rd 227 AZ118
Birches Cl, Epsom KT18 232 CS115
Mitcham CR4 200 DF97
Pinner HA5 116 BY57
Birchfield Cl, Add. KT15 212 BH105
Coulsdon CR5 235 DM116
Birchfield Gro, Epsom KT17 217 CW110
Birchfield Rd, Wal.Cr. (Chsht) EN8 66 DV29
Birchfield St, E14 13 N9
Birch Gdns, Amer. HP7 55 AS39
Dagenham RM10 127 FC62
Birchgate Ms, Tad. KT20 off Bidhams Cres 233 CW121
BIRCH GREEN, Hert. SG14 31 DJ11
Birch Grn, NW9 off Clayton Fld 96 CS52
Hemel Hempstead HP1 39 BF19
Hertford SG14 31 DJ12
Staines TW18 174 BG91
Birch Gro, E11 124 EE62
SE12 184 EF87
W3 138 CN74
Cobham KT11 214 BW114
Potters Bar EN6 64 DA32
Shepperton TW17 195 BS96
Slough SL2 131 AP71
Tadworth KT20 233 CY124
Welling DA16 166 EU84
Windsor SL4 151 AK81
Woking GU22 227 BD115
★ Birch Hall, Epp. CM16 85 EQ36
Birch Hill, Croy. CR0 221 DX106
Birchington Cl, Bexh. DA7 167 FB81
Orpington BR5 off Hart Dyke Rd 206 EW102
Birchington Rd, N8 121 DK58
NW6 140 DA67
Surbiton KT5 198 CM101
Windsor SL4 151 AN82
Birchin La, EC3 11 K8
Birchlands Av, SW12 180 DF87
Birch La, Hem.H. (Flaun.) HP3 57 BB33
Purley CR8 219 DL111
Birch Leys, Hem.H. HP2 off Hunters Oak 41 BQ15
Birch Mead, Orp. BR6 205 EN103
Birchmead, Wat. WD17 75 BT38
Birchmead Av, Pnr. HA5 116 BW56
Birchmead Cl, St.Alb. AL3 43 CD17
Birchmere Business Pk, SE28 off Eastern Way 166 EU75
Birchmere Row, SE3 164 EF82
Birchmore Wk, N5 122 DQ62
Birch Pk, Har. HA3 94 CC52
Birch Pl, Green. DA9 189 FS86
Birch Rd, Felt. TW13 176 BX92
Godalming GU7 258 AT143
Romford RM7 127 FB55
Birch Row, Brom. BR2 205 EN101
Birch Tree Av, W.Wick. BR4 222 EF106
Birch Tree Gro, Chesh. (Ley Hill) HP5 56 AV30
Birch Tree Wk, Wat. WD17 75 BT37
Birch Tree Way, Croy. CR0 202 DV103
Birch Vale, Cob. KT11 214 CA112
Birch Vw, Epp. CM16 70 EV29
Birchville Ct, Bushey (Bushey Hth) WD23 off Heathbourne Rd 95 CE46
Birch Wk, Borwd. WD6 78 CN39
Erith DA8 167 FC79
Mitcham CR4 201 DH95
West Byfleet KT14 212 BG112
Birch Way, Chesh. HP5 54 AR29
Hatfield AL10 off Crawford Rd 45 CV16
Birchway, Hayes UB3 135 BU74
Redhill RH1 267 DH136
Birch Way, St.Alb. (Lon.Col.) AL2 61 CK27
Warlingham CR6 237 DY118
BIRCHWOOD, Hat. AL10 45 CU16
Birch Wd, Rad. (Shenley) WD7 62 CN34
Birchwood, Wal.Abb. EN9 off Roundhills 68 EE34
Birchwood Av, N10 120 DG55
Beckenham BR3 203 DZ98
Hatfield AL10 45 CU16
Sidcup DA14 186 EV89
Wallington SM6 200 DG104
Sch Birchwood Av Prim Sch, Hat. AL10 off Birchwood Av 45 CV16
Birchwood Cl, Brwd. CM13 off Canterbury Way 107 FW51
Hatfield AL10 45 CU16
Horley RH6 269 DH147
Morden SM4 200 DB98
Birchwood Ct, N13 99 DP50
Edgware HA8 96 CQ54
Birchwood Dr, NW3 120 DB62
Dartford DA2 187 FE91
West Byfleet KT14 212 BG112
Birchwood Gro, Hmptn. TW12 176 CA93
Birchwood La, Cat. CR3 251 DP125
Esher KT10 215 CD110
Leatherhead KT22 215 CD110
Sevenoaks (Knock.) TN14 240 EZ115
Birchwood Pk Av, Swan. BR8 207 FE97
Sch Birchwood Prim Sch, Swan. BR8 off Russett Way 207 FD95
Birchwood Rd, SW17 181 DH92
Dartford DA2 187 FE92
Orpington BR5 205 ER98
Swanley BR8 207 FC95
West Byfleet KT14 212 BG112
Birchwood Ter, Swan. BR8 off Birchwood Rd 207 FC95
Birchwood Way, St.Alb. (Park St) AL2 60 CB28
Birdbrook Cl, Brwd. (Hutt.) CM13 109 GB44
Dagenham RM10 147 FC66
Birdbrook Rd, SE3 164 EJ83
Birdcage Wk, SW1 19 K4
Harlow CM20 35 EQ14
Birdcroft Rd, Welw.G.C. AL8 29 CW09
Birdham Cl, Brom. BR1 204 EL99
Birdhouse La, Orp. BR6 239 EN115
Birdhurst Av, S.Croy. CR2 220 DR105
Birdhurst Gdns, S.Croy. CR2 220 DR105
Birdhurst Ri, S.Croy. CR2 220 DS106
Birdhurst Rd, SW18 160 DC84
SW19 180 DE93
South Croydon CR2 220 DS106
Birdie Way, Hert. SG13 32 DV08
Bird in Bush Rd, SE15 162 DU80
Bird-in-Hand La, Brom. BR1 204 EK96
Bird-in-Hand Pas, SE23 off Dartmouth Rd 182 DW89
Bird La, Brwd. (Gt Warley) CM13 129 FX55
Upminster RM14 129 FR57
Uxbridge (Hare.) UB9 92 BJ54
Birds Cl, Welw.G.C. AL7 30 DB11
Birds Fm Av, Rom. RM5 105 FB53
Birdsfield La, E3 143 DZ67
Birds Hill Dr, Lthd. (Oxshott) KT22 215 CD113
Birds Hill Ri, Lthd. (Oxshott) KT22 215 CD113
Birds Hill Rd, Lthd. (Oxshott) KT22 215 CD112
Bird St, W1 8 F8
Birdswood Dr, Wok. GU21 226 AS119
Bird Wk, Twick. TW2 176 BZ88
Birdwood Cl, S.Croy. CR2 221 DX111
Teddington TW11 177 CE91
Birfield Rd, H.Wyc. (Loud.) HP10 88 AC53
⇌ Birkbeck 202 DW97
Tra Birkbeck 202 DW97
Birkbeck Av, W3 138 CQ73
Greenford UB6 136 CC67
Uni Birkbeck Coll, Main Bldg, WC1 9 M4
Russell Sq, WC1 9 M5
Birkbeck Gdns, Wdf.Grn. IG8 102 EF47
Birkbeck Gro, W3 158 CR75
Birkbeck Hill, SE21 181 DP89
Birkbeck Ms, E8 5 N2
W3 off Birkbeck Rd 138 CR74
Birkbeck Pl, SE21 182 DQ88
Sch Birkbeck Prim Sch, Sid. DA14 off Alma Rd 186 EV90
Birkbeck Rd, E8 5 N2
N8 121 DL56
N12 98 DC50
N17 100 DT53
NW7 97 CT50
SW19 180 DB92
W3 138 CR74
Birkbeck Rd, W5 157 CJ77
Beckenham BR3 202 DW96
Brentwood (Hutt.) CM13 109 GD44
Enfield EN2 82 DR39
Ilford IG2 125 ER57
Romford RM7 127 FD60
Sidcup DA14 186 EU90
Birkbeck St, E2 12 D2
Birkbeck Way, Grnf. UB6 136 CC67
Birkdale Av, Pnr. HA5 116 CA55
Romford RM3 106 FM52
Birkdale Cl, SE16 22 C10
SE28 off Redbourne Dr 146 EX72
Orpington BR6 205 ER101
Birkdale Gdns, Croy. CR0 221 DX105
Watford WD19 94 BX48
Birkdale Rd, SE2 166 EU77
W5 138 CL70
Birkenhead Av, Kings.T. KT2 198 CM96
Birkenhead St, WC1 9 P1
Birken Ms, Nthwd. HA6 93 BP50
Birkett Way, Ch.St.G. HP8 72 AX41
Birkhall Rd, SE6 183 ED88
Birkheads Rd, Reig. RH2 250 DA133
Birklands La, St.Alb. AL1 61 CH25
Birklands Pk, St.Alb. AL1 43 CH24
Birkwood Cl, SW12 181 DK87
Birley Rd, N20 98 DC47
Slough SL1 131 AR72
Birley St, SW11 160 DG82
Birling Rd, Erith DA8 167 FD80
Birnam Rd, N4 121 DM61
Birnham Cl, Wok. (Send M.) GU23 228 BG123
Birrell Ho, SW9 off Stockwell Rd 161 DM82
Birse Cres, NW10 118 CS63
Birstall Grn, Wat. WD19 94 BX49
Birstall Rd, N15 122 DS57
Birtley Path, Borwd. WD6 78 CL39
Biscay Rd, W6 16 A10
Biscoe Cl, Houns. TW5 156 CA79
Biscoe Way, SE13 163 ED83
Bisenden Rd, Croy. CR0 202 DS103
Bisham Cl, Cars. SM5 200 DF102
Bisham Gdns, N6 120 DG60
Bishop Butt Cl, Orp. BR6 off Stapleton Rd 205 ET104
Bishop Cen, Maid. (Taplow) SL6 130 AF72
Sch Bishop Challoner Lwr Sch, E1 12 B8
Sch Bishop Challoner Sch, Brom. BR2 off Bromley Rd 203 EC96
Sch Bishop Challoner Upr Sch, E1 12 F8
Bishop Cl, W4 158 CQ78
Sch Bishop David Brown Sch, Wok. GU21 off Albert Dr 211 BD113
Sch Bishop Douglass RC Sec Sch, N2 off Hamilton Rd 120 DC55
Bishop Duppa's Pk, Shep. TW17 195 BR101
Bishop Fox Way, W.Mol. KT8 196 BZ98
Sch Bishop Gilpin C of E Prim Sch, SW19 off Lake Rd 179 CZ92
Sch Bishop John Robinson C of E Prim Sch, SE28 off Hoveton Rd 146 EW73
Bishop Ken Rd, Har. HA3 95 CF54
Bishop Kings Rd, W14 16 D7
Sch Bishop Perrin C of E Prim Sch, Twick. TW2 off Hospital Br Rd 176 CB88
Sch Bishop Ramsey C of E Sch, Lwr Sch, Ruis. HA4 off Eastcote Rd 115 BT59
Upr Sch, Ruis. HA4 off Warrender Way 115 BU59
Sch Bishop Reindorp C of E Sch, Guil. GU1 off Larch Av 242 AW131
Bishop Rd, N14 99 DH45
Bishop's Av, E13 144 EH67
SW6 159 CX82
Bishops Av, Borwd. (Elstree) WD6 78 CM43
Bromley BR1 204 EJ96
Northwood HA6 93 BS49
Romford RM6 126 EW58
Bishops Av, The, N2 120 DD59
Bishops Br, W2 7 M7
Bishops Br Rd, W2 7 K8
Bishops Cl, E17 123 EB56
N19 off Wyndham Cres 121 DJ62
SE9 185 EQ89
Barnet EN5 79 CX44
Bishop's Cl, Couls. CR5 235 DN118
Bishops Cl, Enf. EN1 off Central Av 82 DV40
Hatfield AL10 45 CT18
Richmond TW10 177 CK90
St. Albans AL4 43 CG16
Bishop's Cl, Sutt. SM1 200 DA104
Bishops Cl, Uxb. UB10 134 BN68
Bishop's Ct, EC4 10 E7
WC2 10 C7
Bishops Ct, Abb.L. WD5 59 BT31
Greenhithe DA9 189 FS85
Waltham Cross EN8 off Churchgate 66 DV30
Bishops Dr, Felt. TW14 175 BR86
Northolt UB5 136 BY67
Bishops Fm Cl, Wind. (Oakley Grn) SL4 150 AH82
Bishopsfield, Harl. CM18 51 ES18
Sch Bishopsford Comm Sch, Mord. SM4 off Lilleshall Rd 200 DD100
Bishopsford Rd, Mord. SM4 200 DC101
Bishops Garth, St.Alb. AL4 off Bishops Cl 43 CG16
Bishopsgate, EC2 11 L8
Bishopsgate Arc, EC2 11 M6
Bishopsgate Chyd, EC2 11 L6
Coll Bishopsgate Inst, EC2 11 M6
Bishopsgate Rd, Egh. (Eng.Grn) TW20 172 AT90
Sch Bishopsgate Sch, Egh. TW20 off Bishopsgate Rd 172 AU90
Bishops Gro, N2 120 DD58
Hampton TW12 176 BZ91
Bishop's Hall, Kings.T. KT1 197 CK96
Bishops Hall Rd, Brwd. (Pilg.Hat.) CM15 108 FV44
Sch Bishopshalt Sch, Uxb. UB8 off Royal La 134 BM69

Bishop's Hatfield Girls' Sch, Hat. AL10
off Woods Av 45 CU18
Bishops Hill, Walt. KT12 195 BU101
Bishops Mead, Hem.H. HP1 40 BH22
Bishopsmead Cl, Epsom KT19 216 CS110
Leatherhead (E.Hors.) KT24 off Ockham Rd S 245 BS128
Bishopsmead Dr, Lthd. (E.Hors.) KT24 245 BT129
Bishopsmead Par, Lthd. (E.Hors.) KT24 off Ockham Rd S 245 BS129
Bishops Orchard, Slou. (Farn.Royal) SL2 131 AP69
Bishop's Pk, SW6 159 CX82
Bishop's Pk Rd, SW6 159 CX82
Bishops Pk Rd, SW16 201 DL95
Bishops Pl, Sutt. SM1 off Lind Rd 218 DC106
Bishop Sq Business Pk, Hat. AL10 44 CS17
Bishops Ri, Hat. AL10 45 CT22
Bishops Rd, N6 120 DG58
SW6 159 CZ81
Bishop's Rd, SW11 160 DE80
Bishops Rd, W7 157 CE75
Croydon CR0 201 DP101
Hayes UB3 135 BQ71
Slough SL1 152 AU75
Bishops Ter, SE11 20 D7
Bishopsthorpe Rd, SE26 183 DX91
Bishop Stopford's Sch, Enf. EN1 off Brick La 82 DV40
Bishop St, N1 4 G7
Bishops Wk, Chis. BR7 205 EQ95
Croydon CR0 221 DX106
High Wycombe (Woob.Grn) HP10 110 AE58
Bishop's Wk, Pnr. HA5 off High St 116 BY55
Bishops Way, E2 142 DV68
Egham TW20 173 BD93
Bishops Wd, Wok. GU21 226 AT117
Bishopswood Private Hosp, Nthwd. HA6 93 BP51
Bishopswood Rd, N6 120 DF59
Bishop Thomas Grant Sch, SW16 off Belltrees Gro 181 DM92
Bishop Wk, Brwd. (Shenf.) CM15 109 FZ47
Bishop Wand C of E Sch, The, Sun. TW16 off Laytons La 195 BT96
Bishop Way, NW10 138 CS66
Bishop Wilfred Wd Cl, SE15 off Moncrieff St 162 DU82
Bishop Winnington-Ingram C of E Prim Sch, Ruis. HA4 off Southcote Ri 115 BR59
Biskra, Wat. WD17 75 BU39
Bisley Cl, Wal.Cr. EN8 67 DX33
Worcester Park KT4 199 CW102
Bisley Ho, SW19 179 CX89
Bispham Rd, NW10 138 CM69
Bisson Rd, E15 143 EC68
Bisterne Av, E17 123 ED55
Bittacy Cl, NW7 97 CX51
Bittacy Hill, NW7 97 CX51
Bittacy Pk Av, NW7 97 CX51
Bittacy Ri, NW7 97 CW51
Bittacy Rd, NW7 97 CX51
Bittams La, Cher. KT16 211 BE105
Bittern Cl, Hayes UB4 136 BX71
Hemel Hempstead HP3 58 BM25
Waltham Cross (Chsht) EN7 66 DQ25
Bitterne Dr, Wok. GU21 226 AT117
Bittern St, SE1 20 G4
Bittoms, The, Kings.T. KT1 197 CK97
Bixley Cl, Sthl. UB2 156 BZ77
Black Acre Cl, Amer. HP7 55 AS39
Blackacre Rd, Epp. (They.B.) CM16 85 ES37
Blackall St, EC2 11 L3
Blackberry Cl, Guil. GU1 242 AV131
Shepperton TW17 off Cherry Way 195 BS98
Blackberry Fm Cl, Houns. TW5 156 BY80
Blackberry Fld, Orp. BR5 206 EU95
Blackbird Hill, NW9 118 CQ61
Blackbirds La, Wat. (Ald.) WD25 77 CD35
Blackbird Yd, E2 11 P1
Blackborne Rd, Dag. RM10 146 FA65
Blackborough Cl, Reig. RH2 250 DC134
Blackborough Rd, Reig. RH2 266 DC135
Black Boy La, N15 122 DQ57
Black Boy Wd, St.Alb. (Brick.Wd) AL2 60 CA30
Blackbridge Rd, Wok. GU22 226 AX119
BLACKBROOK, Dor. RH5 264 CL141
Blackbrook La, Brom. BR1, BR2 205 EN97
Blackbrook Rd, Dor. RH5 263 CK140
Blackburn, The, Lthd. (Bkhm) KT23 off Little Bookham St 230 BZ124
Blackburne's Ms, W1 8 E9
Blackburn Rd, NW6 140 DB65
Blackburn Trd Est, Stai. (Stanw.) TW19 174 BM86
Blackbury Cl, Pot.B. EN6 64 DC31
Blackbush Av, Rom. RM6 126 EX57
Blackbush Cl, Sutt. SM2 218 DB108
Blackbush Spring, Harl. CM20 36 EU14
Black Cut, St.Alb. AL1 43 CE21
Blackdale, Wal.Cr. (Chsht) EN7 66 DU27
Blackdown Av, Wok. GU22 227 BE115
Blackdown Cl, N2 98 DC54
Woking GU22 227 BC116
Blackdown Ter, SE18 off Prince Imperial Rd 165 EN80
Black Eagle Cl, West. TN16 255 EQ127
Blackett Cl, Stai. TW18 193 BE96
Blackett St, SW15 159 CX83
Blacketts Wd Dr, Rick. (Chorl.) WD3 73 BB43
Black Fan Cl, Enf. EN2 82 DQ39
Black Fan Rd, Welw.G.C. AL7 30 DB09
BLACKFEN, Sid. DA15 185 ET87
Blackfen Rd, Sid. DA15 185 ES85
Blackfen Sch For Girls, Sid. DA15 off Blackfen Rd 186 EV86
Blackford Cl, S.Croy. CR2 219 DP109
Blackford Rd, Wat. WD19 94 BX50
Blackford's Path, SW15 off Roehampton High St 179 CU87
⇌ Blackfriars 10 F9
⊖ Blackfriars 10 F9
Blackfriars Br, EC4 10 E9
SE1 10 E9
Blackfriars Ct, EC4 10 E9
Black Friars La, EC4 10 E9
Blackfriars Millennium Pier 10 D9
Blackfriars Pas, EC4 10 E9
Blackfriars Rd, SE1 20 E4
Black Gates, Pnr. HA5 off Church La 116 BZ55
Blackhall La, Sev. TN15 257 FK123
Blackhall Pl, Sev. TN15 off Blackhall La 257 FL124
BLACKHEATH, SE3 164 EE81
BLACKHEATH, Guil. GU4 259 BE142
★ Blackheath, SE3 163 ED81
⇌ Blackheath 164 EE83
Blackheath Av, SE10 163 ED80
Blackheath Bluecoat C of E Sec Sch, SE3 off Old Dover Rd 164 EH80
Blackheath Conservatoire of Music, SE3 off Lee Rd 164 EF83
Blackheath Gro, SE3 164 EF82
Guildford (Won.) GU5 259 BB143
Blackheath High Sch, SE3 off Vanbrugh Pk 164 EG80
Blackheath Hill, SE10 163 EC81
Blackheath Hosp, The, SE3 164 EE83
Blackheath La, Guil. GU4, GU5 259 BD143
BLACKHEATH PARK, SE3 164 EF84
Blackheath Pk, SE3 164 EF83
Blackheath Prep Sch (Jun Dept), SE3 off Wemyss Rd 164 EF82
Blackheath Ri, SE13 163 EC82
Blackheath Rd, SE10 163 EB81
Blackheath Vale, SE3 164 EE82
Blackheath Village, SE3 164 EF82
Blackhills, Esher KT10 214 CA109
Black Horse Av, Chesh. HP5 54 AR33
Blackhorse Cl, Amer. HP6 55 AS38
Black Horse Cl, Wind. SL4 151 AK82
Black Horse Ct, SE1 21 K5
Blackhorse Cres, Amer. HP6 55 AS38
Blackhorse Lane 202 DU101
Blackhorse La, E17 123 DX56
Croydon CR0 202 DU101
Epping (N.Wld Bas.) CM16 71 FD25
Potters Bar EN6 62 CS30
Reigate RH2 250 DB129
Blackhorse Ms, E17 off Blackhorse La 123 DX55
Black Horse Pl, Uxb. UB8 off Waterloo Rd 134 BJ67
⇌ Blackhorse Road 123 DX56
⊖ Blackhorse Road 123 DX56
Blackhorse Rd, E17 123 DX56
SE8 163 DY78
Sidcup DA14 186 EU91
Woking GU22 226 AS122
Black Lake Cl, Egh. TW20 193 BA95
Blacklands Dr, Hayes UB4 135 BQ70
Blacklands Meadow, Red. (Nutfld) RH1 251 DL133
Blacklands Rd, SE6 183 EC91
Blacklands Ter, SW3 18 C8
Blackley Cl, Wat. WD17 75 BT37
Black Lion Ct, Harl. CM17 36 EW11
Black Lion Hill, Rad. (Shenley) WD7 62 CL32
Black Lion La, W6 159 CU77
Black Lion Ms, W6 off Black Lion La 159 CU77
Blackmans Cl, Dart. DA1 188 FJ88
Blackmans La, Warl. CR6 222 EE114
Blackmead, Sev. (Rvrhd) TN13 256 FE121
Blackmoor La, Wat. WD18 75 BR43
Blackmore Av, Sthl. UB1 137 CD74
Blackmore Cl, Grays RM17 170 GC78
Blackmore Ct, Wal.Abb. EN9 68 EG33
Blackmore Cres, Wok. GU21 227 BB115
Blackmore Rd, Buck.H. IG9 102 EL45
Blackmores, Harl. CM19 51 EP15
Blackmores Gro, Tedd. TW11 177 CG93
Blackmore Twr, W3 158 CQ75
Blackmore Way, Uxb. UB8 134 BK65
Blackness La, Kes. BR2 222 EK109
Woking GU22 226 AY119
★ Black Park Country Pk, Slou. SL3 133 AZ67
Black Pk Rd, Slou. SL3 133 AZ68
Black Path, E10 123 DX59
Blackpond La, Slou. (Farn.Com.) SL2 131 AP66
Blackpool Gdns, Hayes UB4 135 BS70
Blackpool Rd, SE15 162 DV82
Black Prince Cl, W.Byf. (Byfleet) KT14 212 BM114
Black Prince Rd, SE1 20 A8
SE11 20 B8
Black Rod Cl, Hayes UB3 155 BT76
Blackshaw Pl, N1 off Hertford Rd 142 DS66
Blackshaw Rd, SW17 180 DC91
Blackshots La, Grays RM16 170 GD75
Blacksmith Cl, Ashtd. KT21 off Rectory La 232 CM119
Ware (Gt Amwell) SG12 33 DZ08
Blacksmith La, Guil. (Chilw.) GU4 259 BC139
Blacksmith Row, Slou. SL3 153 BA77
Blacksmiths Cl, Rom. RM6 126 EW58
Blacksmiths Hill, S.Croy. CR2 220 DU113
Blacksmiths La, Cher. KT16 194 BG101
Orpington BR5 206 EW99
Rainham RM13 147 FF67
St. Albans AL3 42 CB20
Staines TW18 194 BH97
Uxbridge (Denh.) UB9 113 BC61
Blacksmiths Way, Saw. (High Wych) CM21 36 EU06
Blacks Rd, W6 off Queen Caroline St 159 CW77
Blackstock Ms, N4 off Blackstock Rd 121 DP61
Blackstock Rd, N4 121 DP61
N5 121 DP61
Blackstone Cl, Red. RH1 266 DE135
Blackstone Est, E8 142 DV66
Blackstone Hill, Red. RH1 266 DE135
Blackstone Rd, NW2 119 CW64
Black Swan Ct, Ware SG12 off Baldock St 33 DX06
Black Swan Yd, SE1 21 M3
Black's Yd, Sev. TN13 off Bank St 257 FJ125
Blackthorn Av, West Dr. UB7 154 BN77
Blackthorn Cl, Reig. RH2 266 DC136
St. Albans AL4 43 CJ17
Watford WD25 59 BV32
Blackthorn Ct, Houns. TW5 156 BY80
Blackthorn Dell, Slou. SL3 152 AW76
Blackthorne Av, Croy. CR0 202 DW101
Blackthorne Cl, Hat. AL10 45 CT21
Blackthorne Cres, Slou. (Colnbr.) SL3 153 BE83
Blackthorne Dr, E4 101 ED49
Blackthorne Rd, Lthd. (Bkhm) KT23 246 CC126
Slough (Colnbr.) SL3 153 BE83
Westerham (Bigg.H.) TN16 238 EK116
Blackthorn Gro, Bexh. DA7 166 EX83
Blackthorn Rd, Reig. RH2 266 DC136
Welwyn Garden City AL7 30 DA10
Blackthorn St, E3 13 P4
Blackthorn Way, Brwd. CM14 108 FX50
Blacktree Ms, SW9 161 DN83
DLR Blackwall 14 D10
Blackwall La, SE10 25 H9
Blackwall Pier, E14 14 G10
Blackwall Trd Est, E14 14 F6
Blackwall Tunnel, E14 14 E10
Blackwall Tunnel App, SE10 24 G4
Blackwall Tunnel Northern App, E3 143 EA68
E14 14 C1
Blackwall Way, E14 14 D10
Blackwater Cl, E7 124 EF63
Rainham RM13 147 FD71
Blackwater La, Hem.H. HP3 41 BS23
Blackwater Rd, Sutt. SM1 off High St 218 DB105
Blackwater St, SE22 182 DT85
Blackwell Cl, E5 123 DX63
Harrow HA3 95 CD52
Blackwell Dr, Wat. WD19 76 BW44
Blackwell Gdns, Edg. HA8 96 CN48
Blackwell Hall La, Chesh. HP5 56 AW33
Blackwell Rd, Kings L. WD4 58 BN29
Blackwood Av, N18 off Harbet Rd 101 DX50
Blackwood Cl, W.Byf. KT14 212 BJ112
Blackwood Ct, Brox. EN10 off Groom Rd 67 DZ26
Blackwood St, SE17 21 J9
Blade Ms, SW15 off Deodar Rd 159 CZ84
Bladen Cl, Wey. KT13 213 BR107
Blades Cl, Lthd. KT22 231 CK120
Blades Ct, SW15 off Deodar Rd 159 CZ84
Bladindon Dr, Bex. DA5 186 EW87
Bladon Cl, Guil. GU1 243 BA133
Bladon Gdns, Har. HA2 116 CB58
Blagdens Cl, N14 99 DJ47
Blagdens La, N14 99 DK47
Blagdon Rd, SE13 183 EB86
New Malden KT3 199 CT98
Blagdon Wk, Tedd. TW11 177 CJ93
Blagrove Rd, W10 6 D6
Blair Av, NW9 118 CS59
Esher KT10 196 CC103
Blair Cl, N1 5 H3
Hayes UB3 155 BU77
Sidcup DA15 185 ES85
Blairderry Rd, SW2 181 DL89
Blair Dr, Sev. TN13 257 FH123
Blairhead Dr, Wat. WD19 93 BV48
Blair Peach Prim Sch, Sthl. UB1 off Beaconsfield Rd 136 BX74
Blair Rd, Slou. SL1 132 AS74
Blair St, E14 14 D8
Blake Av, Bark. IG11 145 ES67
Blakeborough Dr, Rom. (Harold Wd) RM3 106 FL54
Blake Cl, W10 139 CW71
Carshalton SM5 200 DE101
Rainham RM13 147 FF67
St. Albans AL1 43 CG23
Welling DA16 165 ES81
Blakeden Dr, Esher (Clay.) KT10 215 CF107
Blake Gdns, SW6 160 DB81
Dartford DA1 168 FM84
Blake Hall Cres, E11 124 EG60
Blake Hall Rd, E11 124 EG59
Blakehall Rd, Cars. SM5 218 DF107
Blake Hall Rd, Ong. CM5 71 FG25
Blake Ho, Beck. BR3 183 EA93
Blakemere Rd, Welw.G.C. AL8 29 CX07
Blake Ms, Rich. TW9 off High Pk Rd 158 CN81
Blakemore Rd, SW16 181 DL90
Thornton Heath CR7 201 DM99
Blakemore Way, Belv. DA17 166 EY76
Blakeney Av, Beck. BR3 203 DZ95
Blakeney Cl, E8 off Ferncliff Rd 122 DU64
N20 98 DC46
NW1 off Rossendale Way 141 DK66
Epsom KT19 216 CR111
Blakeney Rd, Beck. BR3 183 DZ94
Blakenham Rd, SW17 180 DF91
Blaker Ct, SE7 off Fairlawn 164 EJ80
Blake Rd, E16 15 J4
N11 99 DJ52
Croydon CR0 202 DS103
Mitcham CR4 200 DE97
Blaker Rd, E15 143 EC67
Blakes Av, N.Mal. KT3 199 CT99
Blakes Cl, Saw. CM21 off Church St 36 EY05
Blake's Grn, W.Wick. BR4 203 EC102
Blakes La, Guil. (E.Clan.) GU4 244 BL132
Leatherhead (W.Hors.) KT24 244 BM131
New Malden KT3 199 CT99
Blakesley Av, W5 137 CJ72
Blakesley Ho, E12 off Grantham Rd 125 EN62
Blakesley Wk, SW20 off Kingston Rd 199 CZ96
Blakes Rd, SE15 162 DS80
Blakes Ter, N.Mal. KT3 199 CU99
Blake St, SE8 off Watergate St 163 EA79
Blakesware Gdns, N9 100 DR45
Blakes Way, Til. RM18 off Coleridge Rd 171 GJ82
Blakewood Cl, Felt. TW13 176 BW91
Blanchard Cl, SE9 184 EL90
Blanchard Gro, Enf. EN3 83 EA38
Blanchard Ms, Rom. (Harold Wd) RM3 off Avenue Rd 106 FM52
Blanchards Hill, Guil. GU4 242 AY128
Blanchard Way, E8 142 DU65
Blanch Cl, SE15 off Culmore Rd 162 DW80
Blanchedowne, SE5 162 DR84
Blanche La, Pot.B. EN6 63 CT34
Blanche St, E16 15 J4
Blanchland Rd, Mord. SM4 200 DB99
Blanchmans Rd, Warl. CR6 237 DY118
Blandfield Rd, SW12 180 DG86
Blandford Av, Beck. BR3 203 DY96
Twickenham TW2 176 CB88
Blandford Cl, N2 120 DC56
Croydon CR0 201 DL104
Romford RM7 127 FB56
Slough SL3 152 AX76
Woking GU22 227 BB117
Blandford Ct, Slou. SL3 off Blandford Rd S 152 AX76
Blandford Cres, E4 101 EC45
Blandford Rd, W4 158 CS76
W5 157 CK75
Beckenham BR3 202 DW96
St. Albans AL1 43 CG20
Southall UB2 156 CA77
Teddington TW11 177 CD92
Blandford Rd N, Slou. SL3 152 AX76
Blandford Rd S, Slou. SL3 152 AX76
Blandford Sq, NW1 8 B4
Blandford St, W1 8 D7
Blandford Waye, Hayes UB4 136 BW72
Bland St, SE9 164 EK84
Blaney Cres, E6 145 EP69
Blanford Ms, Reig. RH2 off Blackborough Rd 250 DD134
Blanford Rd, Reig. RH2 266 DC135
Blanmerle Rd, SE9 185 EP88
Blann Cl, SE9 184 EK86
Blantyre St, SW10 160 DD80
Blantyre Wk, SW10 off Blantyre St 160 DD80
Blashford, NW3 140 DF66
Blashford St, SE13 183 ED87
Blasker Wk, E14 23 P9
Blattner Cl, Borwd. (Elstree) WD6 78 CL42
Blawith Rd, Har. HA1 117 CE56
Blaxland Ter, Wal.Cr. (Chsht) EN8 off Davison Dr 67 DX28
Blaydon Cl, N17 100 DV52
Ruislip HA4 115 BS59
Blaydon Wk, N17 100 DV52
Blays Cl, Egh. (Eng.Grn) TW20 172 AW93
Blays La, Egh. (Eng.Grn) TW20 172 AV94
Bleak Hill La, SE18 165 ET79
Blean Gro, SE20 182 DW94
Bleasdale Av, Grnf. UB6 137 CG68
Blechynden St, W10 6 B9
Bleddyn Cl, Sid. DA15 186 EW86
Bledlow Cl, SE28 146 EW73
Bledlow Ri, Grnf. UB6 136 CC68
Bleeding Heart Yd, EC1 10 D6
Blegborough Rd, SW16 181 DJ93
Blencarn Cl, Wok. GU21 226 AT116
Blendon Dr, Bex. DA5 186 EX86
Blendon Path, Brom. BR1 184 EF94
Blendon Rd, Bex. DA5 186 EX86
Blendon Ter, SE18 165 EQ78
Blendworth Pt, SW15 off Wanborough Dr 179 CV88
Blendworth Way, SE15 off Blakes Rd 162 DS80
Blenheim Av, Ilf. IG2 125 EN58
Blenheim Cl, N21 off Elm Pk Rd 100 DQ46
SE12 184 EH88
SW20 199 CW97
Dartford DA1 188 FJ86
Greenford UB6 off Leaver Gdns 137 CD68
Romford RM7 127 FC56
Sawbridgeworth CM21 36 EW07
Slough SL3 133 AZ74
Upminster RM14 129 FS60
Wallington SM6 219 DJ108
Watford WD19 94 BX45
West Byfleet KT14 off Madeira Rd 211 BF113
Blenheim Ct, N19 off Marlborough Rd 121 DL61
Sidcup DA14 185 ER90
Sutton SM2 off Wellesley Rd 218 DC107
Woodford Green IG8 off Navestock Cres 102 EJ52
Blenheim Cres, W11 6 C9
Ruislip HA4 115 BR61
South Croydon CR2 220 DQ108
Blenheim Dr, Well. DA16 165 ET81
Blenheim Gdns, NW2 119 CW64
SW2 181 DM86
Kingston upon Thames KT2 178 CP94
South Croydon CR2 220 DU112
South Ockendon (Aveley) RM15 148 FP74
Wallington SM6 219 DJ107
Wembley HA9 118 CL62
Woking GU22 226 AV119
Blenheim Gro, SE15 162 DU82
Blenheim High Sch, Epsom KT19 off Longmead Rd 216 CR110
Blenheim Inf Sch, Orp. BR6 off Blenheim Rd 206 EW103
Blenheim Jun Sch, Orp. BR6 off Blenheim Rd 206 EW103
Blenheim Pk Rd, S.Croy. CR2 220 DQ109
Blenheim Pas, NW8 off Blenheim Ter 140 DC68
Blenheim Pl, Tedd. TW11 177 CF92
Blenheim Ri, N15 off Talbot Rd 122 DT56
Blenheim Rd, E6 144 EK69
E15 124 EE63
E17 123 DX55
NW8 140 DC68
SE20 off Maple Rd 182 DW94
SW20 199 CW97
W4 158 CS76
Abbots Langley WD5 59 BU33
Barnet EN5 79 CX41
Brentwood (Pilg.Hat.) CM15 108 FU44
Blenheim Rd, Brom. BR1 204 EL98
Dartford DA1 188 FJ86
Epsom KT19 216 CR111
Harrow HA2 116 CB58
Northolt UB5 136 CB65
Orpington BR6 206 EW103
St. Albans AL1 43 CF19
Sidcup DA15 186 EW88
Slough SL3 152 AX77
Sutton SM1 200 DA104
Blenheim Shop Cen, SE20 182 DW94
Blenheim St, W1 8 G8
Blenheim Ter, NW8 140 DC68
Blenheim Way, Epp. (N.Wld Bas.) CM16 70 FA27
Isleworth TW7 157 CG81
Blenhiem Ct, Welw.G.C. AL7 29 CZ08
Blenkarne Rd, SW11 180 DF86
Blenkin Cl, St.Alb. AL3 42 CC16
Bleriot Rd, Houns. TW5 156 BW80
Blessbury Rd, Edg. HA8 96 CQ53
Blessed Dominic RC Prim Sch, NW9 off Lanacre Av 97 CT54
Blessed John Roche Catholic Sch, The, E14 13 P8
Blessed Sacrament RC Prim Sch, N1 4 A8
Blessington Cl, SE13 163 ED83
Blessington Rd, SE13 163 ED83
Blessing Way, Bark. IG11 146 EW69
BLETCHINGLEY, Red. RH1 252 DQ132
Bletchingley Adult Ed Cen, Red. RH1 off Stychens La 252 DQ133
Bletchingley Cl, Red. RH1 251 DJ129
Thornton Heath CR7 201 DP98
Bletchingley Rd, Gdse. RH9 252 DU131
Redhill (Bletch.) RH1 251 DN133
Redhill (S.Merst.) RH1 251 DJ129
Bletchley Ct, N1 5 J10
Bletchley St, N1 5 H10
Bletchmore Cl, Hayes UB3 155 BR78
Bletsoe Wk, N1 5 H9
Blewbury Ho, SE2 off Yarnton Way 166 EX75
Bligh Rd, Grav. DA11 191 GG86
Bligh's Rd, Sev. TN13 257 FH125
Blincoe Cl, SW19 179 CX89
Blinco La, Slou. (Geo.Grn) SL3 132 AY72
Blind La, Bans. SM7 234 DE115
Betchworth RH3 264 CQ137
Loughton (High Beach) IG10 84 EE40
Waltham Abbey EN9 68 EJ33
Blindman's La, Wal.Cr. (Chsht) EN8 67 DX30
Bliss Cres, SE13 163 EB82
Blissett St, SE10 163 EC81
Bliss Ms, W10 6 D1
Blisworth Cl, Hayes UB4 off Braunston Dr 136 BY70
Blithbury Rd, Dag. RM9 146 EV65
Blithdale Rd, SE2 166 EU77
Blithfield St, W8 17 J6
Blockhouse Rd, Grays RM17 170 GC79
Blockley Rd, Wem. HA0 117 CH61
Bloemfontein Av, W12 139 CV74
Bloemfontein Rd, W12 139 CV73
Blomfield Rd, W9 7 L5
Blomfield St, EC2 11 K6
Blomfield Vil, W2 7 K6
Blomville Rd, Dag. RM8 126 EY62
Blondell Cl, West Dr. UB7 154 BK79
Blondel St, SW11 160 DG82
Blondin Av, W5 157 CJ77
Blondin St, E3 143 EA68
Bloomburg St, SW1 19 K8
Bloomfield Cl, Wok. (Knap.) GU21 226 AS118
Bloomfield Cres, Ilf. IG2 125 EP58
Bloomfield Pl, W1 9 H9
Bloomfield Rd, N6 120 DG58
SE18 165 EP78
Bromley BR2 204 EK99
Kingston upon Thames KT1 198 CL98
Waltham Cross (Chsht) EN7 66 DQ25
Bloomfield Ter, SW1 18 F9
Westerham TN16 255 ES125
Bloom Gro, SE27 181 DP90
Bloomhall Rd, SE19 182 DR92
Bloom Pk Rd, SW6 159 CZ80
BLOOMSBURY, WC1 9 M6
Bloomsbury Cl, NW7 97 CU52
W5 138 CM73
Epsom KT19 216 CR110
Bloomsbury Ct, WC1 9 P6
Guildford GU1 off St. Lukes Sq 259 AZ135
Pinner HA5 116 BZ55
Bloomsbury Ho, SW4 181 DK86
Bloomsbury Pl, SW18 off Fullerton Rd 180 DC85
WC1 9 P5
Bloomsbury Sq, WC1 9 P6
Bloomsbury St, WC1 9 M6
Bloomsbury Way, WC1 9 N7
Blore Cl, SW8 off Thessaly Rd 161 DK81
Blore Ct, W1 9 L8
Blossom Cl, W5 off Almond Av 158 CL75
Dagenham RM9 146 EZ67
South Croydon CR2 220 DT106
Blossom Ho Sch, SW20 off The Drive 179 CW94
Blossom La, Enf. EN2 82 DQ39
Blossom St, E1 11 M5
Blossom Way, Uxb. UB10 134 BM66
West Drayton UB7 154 BN77
Blossom Waye, Houns. TW5 156 BY80
Blount St, E14 13 K7
Bloxam Gdns, SE9 184 EL85
Bloxhall Rd, E10 123 DZ60
Bloxham Cres, Hmptn. TW12 176 BZ94
Bloxworth Cl, Wall. SM6 201 DJ104
Blucher Rd, SE5 162 DQ80
Blucher St, Chesh. HP5 54 AP31
Blue Anchor All, Rich. TW9 off Kew Rd 158 CL84
Blue Anchor La, SE16 22 B7
Tilbury (W.Til.) RM18 171 GL77
Blue Anchor Yd, E1 12 A9
Blue Ball La, Egh. TW20 173 AZ92
Blue Ball Yd, SW1 19 J2
Blue Barn La, Wey. KT13 212 BN111
Bluebell Av, E12 124 EK64
Bluebell Cl, E9 off Moulins Rd 142 DW67
SE26 182 DT91

A B C D E F G H I J K L M N O P Q R S T U V W X Y Z

★ Place of interest | H Hospital | Sch School | Coll College | Uni University | ⇌ Railway station

Bluebell Cl, Hem. H. HP1
off Sundew Rd 39 BE21
Hertford SG13 32 DU09
Northolt UB5 136 BZ65
Orpington BR6 205 EQ103
Romford (Rush Grn) RM7 127 FE61
Wallington SM6 201 DH102
Bluebell Ct, Wok. GU22 226 AX119
Bluebell Dr, Abb.L.
(Bedmond) WD5 59 BT27
Waltham Cross EN7 66 DR28
Bluebell La, Lthd. (E.Hors.)
KT24 245 BS129
Bluebell Way, Hat. AL10 29 CT14
Ilford IG1 145 EP65
Blueberry Cl, St.Alb. AL3 43 CD16
Woodford Green IG8 102 EG51
Blueberry Gdns, Couls. CR5 235 DM116
Blueberry La, Sev. (Knock.)
TN14 240 EW116
Bluebird La, Dag. RM10 146 FA66
Bluebird Way, SE28 165 ER75
St. Albans AL2 60 BY30
Bluebridge Av, Hat. AL9 63 CZ27
Bluebridge Rd, Hat.
(Brook.Pk) AL9 63 CY26
Blue Cedars, Bans. SM7 217 CX114
Blue Cedars Pl, Cob. KT11 214 BX112
Bluecoat Ct, Hert. SG14
off Railway St 32 DR09
Bluecoats Av, Hert. SG14 32 DS09
Bluecoat Yd, Ware SG12 33 DX06
Sch **Blue C of E Sch, The**, Islw.
TW7 *off North St* 157 CG83
Bluefield Cl, Hmptn. TW12 176 CA92
Sch **Blue Gate Flds Inf & Jun Sch**, E1 12 E9
Bluegates, Epsom (Ewell)
KT17 217 CU108
Bluehouse Gdns, Oxt. RH8 254 EG128
Blue Ho Hill, St.Alb. AL3 42 CA20
Bluehouse La, Oxt. RH8 254 EG127
Bluehouse Rd, E4 102 EE48
Blue Leaves Av, Couls. CR5 235 DK121
Bluelion Pl, SE1 21 L5
Bluemans, Epp. CM16 53 FD24
Bluemans End, Epp. CM16 53 FD24
Bluett Rd, St.Alb. (Lon.Col.)
AL2 61 CK27
Bluewater Ho, SW18
off Smugglers Way 160 DB84
Bluewater Parkway, Green.
(Bluewater) DA9 189 FS87
Bluewater Shop Cen, Green.
DA9 189 FT88
Blumfield Ct, Slou. SL1 131 AK70
Blumfield Cres, Slou. SL1 131 AK70
Blundel La, Cob. (Stoke D'Ab.)
KT11 214 CB114
Blundell Av, Horl. RH6 268 DF148
Blundell Cl, E8
off Amhurst Rd 122 DU64
St. Albans AL3 43 CD16
Blundell Rd, Edg. HA8 96 CR53
Blundell St, N7 141 DL66
Blunden Cl, Dag. RM8 126 EW60
Blunden Dr, Slou. SL3 153 BB77
Blunesfield, Pot.B. EN6 64 DD31
Blunt Rd, S.Croy. CR2 220 DR106
Blunts Av, West Dr. UB7 154 BN80
Blunts La, St.Alb. AL2 60 BW27
Blunts Rd, SE9 185 EN85
Blurton Rd, E5 122 DW63
Blyth Cl, E14 24 E7
Borehamwood WD6 78 CM39
Twickenham TW1
off Grimwood Rd 177 CF86
Blythe Cl, SE6 183 DZ87
Iver SL0 133 BF72
Blythe Hill, SE6 183 DZ87
Orpington BR5 205 ET95
Blythe Hill La, SE6 183 DZ87
Blythe Hill Pl, SE23
off Brockley Pk 183 DY87
Blythe Ms, W14 16 B5
Blythe Rd, W14 16 C7
Hoddesdon EN11 49 ED19
Blythe St, E2 12 C1
Blytheswood, Hem.H. HP3
off Sheethanger La 40 BG23
Blythe Vale, SE6 183 DZ88
Blyth Rd, E17 123 DZ59
SE28 146 EW73
Bromley BR1 204 EF95
Hayes UB3 155 BS75
Blyth's Wf, E14 13 K10
Blythswood Rd, Ilf. IG3 126 EU60
Blyth Wk, Upmin. RM14 129 FS58
Blythway, Welw.G.C. AL7 29 CZ06
Blyth Wd Pk, Brom. BR1
off Blyth Rd 204 EF95
Blythwood Rd, N4 121 DL59
Pinner HA5 94 BX53
Blyton Cl, Beac. HP9 89 AK51
Boades Ms, NW3
off New End 120 DD63
Boadicea Cl, Slou. SL1 131 AK74
Boadicea St, N1 4 A8
Boakes Cl, NW9 118 CQ56
Boakes Meadow, Sev.
(Shore.) TN14 225 FF111
Boar Cl, Chig. IG7 104 EU50
Boardman Av, E4 83 EB43
Boardman Cl, Barn. EN5 79 CY43
Board Sch Rd, Wok. GU21 227 AZ116
Boar Hill, Dor. RH5 263 CF142
Boarlands Cl, Slou. SL1 131 AM73
Boarlands Path, Slou. SL1
off Brook Path 131 AM73
Boar's Head Yd, Brent. TW8
off Brent Way 157 CK80
Boars Rd, Harl. CM17 36 FA14
Boathouse Wk, SE15 162 DT80
Richmond TW9 158 CL81
Boat Lifter Way, SE16 23 K7
Boat Quay, E16
off Royal Albert Way 144 EJ73
Bob Anker Cl, E13 15 M1
Sch **Bobath Cen**, N2
off East End Rd 120 DE56
Bobbin Cl, SW4 161 DJ83
Bobby Moore Way, N10 98 DF52
Bob Dunn Way, Dart. DA1 168 FJ84
Bob Marley Way, SE24
off Mayall Rd 161 DN84
Sch **Bobov Foundation**, N16
off Egerton Rd 122 DT59
Bobs La, Rom. RM1 105 FG52
Bocketts La, Lthd. KT22 231 CF124
Bockhampton Rd, Kings.T.
KT2 178 CM94
Bocking St, E8 142 DV67
Boddicott Cl, SW19 179 CY89
Bodell Cl, Grays RM16 170 GB76
Bodiam Cl, Enf. EN1 82 DR40
Bodiam Rd, SW16 181 DK94
Bodicea Ms, Houns. TW4 176 BZ87
Bodle Av, Swans. DA10 190 FY87
Bodley Cl, Epp. CM16 69 ET30
New Malden KT3 198 CS99
Bodley Manor Way, SW2
off Papworth Way 181 DN87
Bodley Rd, N.Mal. KT3 198 CR100
Bodmin Av, Slou. SL2 131 AN71
Bodmin Cl, Har. HA2 116 BZ62
Orpington BR5 206 EW102
Bodmin Gro, Mord. SM4 200 DB99
Bodmin St, SW18 180 DA88
Bodnant Gdns, SW20 199 CU97
Bodney Rd, E8 122 DV64
Bodwell Cl, Hem.H. HP1 39 BF19
Boeing Way, Sthl. UB2 155 BV76
Boevey Path, Belv. DA17 166 EZ79
Bogey La, Orp. BR6 223 EN108
Bognor Gdns, Wat. WD19
off Bowring Grn 94 BW50
Bognor Rd, Well. DA16 166 EX81
Bohemia, Hem.H. HP2 40 BL19
Bohemia Pl, E8 142 DV65
Bohn Rd, E1 13 J5
Bohun Gro, Barn. EN4 80 DE44
Boileau Par, W5
off Boileau Rd 138 CM72
Boileau Rd, SW13 159 CU80
W5 138 CM72
Bois Av, Amer. HP6 55 AP36
Bois Hall Rd, Add. KT15 212 BK105
Bois Hill, Chesh. HP5 54 AS34
Bois La, Amer. HP6 55 AR35
Bois Moor Rd, Chesh. HP5 54 AQ33
Boissy Cl, St.Alb. AL4 44 CL21
Bolden St, SE8 163 EB82
Bolderwood Way, W.Wick.
BR4 203 EB103
Boldmere Rd, Pnr. HA5 116 BW59
Boleyn Av, Enf. EN1 82 DV39
Epsom KT17 217 CV110
Boleyn Cl, E17 123 EA56
Grays (Chaff.Hun.) RM16
off Clifford Rd 170 FZ76
Hemel Hempstead HP2
off Parr Cres 41 BQ15
Loughton IG10
off Roding Gdns 84 EL44
Staines TW18
off Chertsey La 173 BE92
Boleyn Ct, Brox. EN10 49 DY21
Buckhurst Hill IG9 102 EG46
Boleyn Dr, Ruis. HA4 116 BX61
St. Albans AL1 43 CD22
West Molesey KT8 196 BZ97
Boleyn Gdns, Brwd. CM13 109 GA48
Dagenham RM10 147 FC66
West Wickham BR4 203 EB103
Boleyn Gro, W.Wick. BR4 203 EC103
Boleyn Rd, E6 144 EK68
E7 144 EG66
N16 5 M2
Boleyn Wk, Lthd. KT22 231 CF120
Boleyn Way, Barn. EN5 80 DC41
Ilford IG6 103 EQ51
Swanscombe DA10 190 FY87
Bolina Rd, SE16 22 F9
Bolingbroke Gro, SW11 160 DE84
H **Bolingbroke Hosp**,
SW11 180 DE85
Bolingbroke Rd, W14 16 B5
Bolingbroke Wk, SW11 160 DD80
Bolingbroke Way, Hayes
UB3 135 BR74
Bolingbrook, St.Alb. AL4 43 CG16
Bolliger Ct, NW10
off Park Royal Rd 138 CQ70
Bollo Br Rd, W3 158 CP76
Bollo La, W3 158 CP75
W4 158 CQ77
Bolney Gate, SW7 18 A4
Bolney St, SW8 161 DM80
Bolney Way, Felt. TW13 176 BY90
Bolsover Gro, Red. RH1 251 DL129
Bolsover St, W1 9 H4
Bolstead Rd, Mitch. CR4 201 DH95
Bolt Cellar La, Epp. CM16 69 ES29
Bolt Ct, EC4 10 D8
Bolters La, Bans. SM7 217 CZ114
Bolters Rd, Horl. RH6 268 DG146
Bolters Rd S, Horl. RH6 268 DF146
Boltmore Cl, NW4 119 CX55
Bolton Av, Wind. SL4 151 AQ83
Bolton Cl, SE20
off Selby Rd 202 DU96
Chessington KT9 215 CK107
Bolton Cres, SE5 161 DP79
Windsor SL4 151 AQ83
Bolton Gdns, NW10 139 CX68
SW5 17 J9
Bromley BR1 184 EF93
Teddington TW11 177 CG93
Bolton Gdns Ms, SW10 17 L9
Bolton Rd, E15 144 EF65
N18 100 DT50
NW8 140 DB67
NW10 138 CS67
W4 158 CQ80
Chessington KT9 215 CK107
Harrow HA1 116 CC56
Windsor SL4 151 AQ83
Boltons, The, SW10 17 L9
Wembley HA0 117 CF63
Woodford Green IG8 102 EG49
Boltons Cl, Wok. GU22 228 BG116
Boltons La, Hayes UB3 155 BQ80
Woking GU22 228 BG116
Boltons Pl, SW5 17 L9
Bolton St, W1 19 H1
Bolton Wk, N7
off Durham Rd 121 DM61
Bombay St, SE16 22 C7
Bombers La, West. TN16 239 ER119
Bomer Cl, West Dr. UB7 154 BN80
Bomore Rd, W11 6 B9
Bonar Pl, Chis. BR7 184 EL94
Bonar Rd, SE15 162 DU80
Bonaventure Ct, Grav. DA12 191 GM91
Bonchester Cl, Chis. BR7 185 EN94
Bonchurch Cl, Sutt. SM2 218 DB108
Bonchurch Rd, W10 6 C5
W13 137 CH74
Bond Cl, Sev. (Knock.) TN14 240 EX115
West Drayton UB7 134 BM72
Bond Ct, EC4 11 J8
Bondfield Av, Hayes UB4 135 BU69
Bondfield Rd, E6
off Lovage App 144 EL71
Bondfield Wk, Dart. DA1 168 FM84
Bond Gdns, Wall. SM6 219 DJ105
Bonding Yd Wk, SE16 23 K4
Sch **Bond Prim Sch**, Mitch.
CR4 *off Bond Rd* 200 DF96
Bond Rd, Mitch. CR4 200 DE96
Bond Rd, Surb. KT6 198 CM103
Warlingham CR6 237 DX118
Bonds La, Dor. (Mid Holm.)
RH5 263 CH142
⊖ **Bond Street** 8 F8
Bond St, E15 124 EE64
W4 158 CS77
W5 137 CK73
Egham (Eng.Grn) TW20 172 AV92
Grays RM17 170 GC79
Bondway, SW8 161 DL79
Bonehurst Rd, Horl. RH6 266 DG144
Redhill (Salf.) RH1 266 DG142
Bone Mill La, Gdse. RH9
off Eastbourne Rd 253 DY134
Boneta Rd, SE18 165 EM76
Bonfield Rd, SE13 163 EC84
Bonham Gdns, Dag. RM8 126 EX61
Bonham Rd, SW2 181 DM85
Dagenham RM8 126 EX61
Bonheur Rd, W4 158 CR75
Bonhill St, EC2 11 K4
Boniface Gdns, Har. HA3 94 CB52
Boniface Rd, Uxb. UB10 115 BP62
Boniface Wk, Har. HA3 94 CB52
Bonington Ho, Enf. EN1
off Ayley Cft 82 DU43
Bonington Rd, Horn. RM12 128 FK64
Bonita Ms, SE4 163 DX83
Bonks Hill, Saw. CM21 36 EX06
Bon Marche Ter Ms, SE27
off Gipsy Rd 182 DS91
Bonner Hill Rd, Kings.T. KT1 198 CM97
Sch **Bonner Prim Sch**, E2 12 G1
Bonner Rd, E2 142 DW68
Bonners Cl, Wok. GU22 226 AY122
Bonnersfield Cl, Har. HA1 117 CF58
Bonnersfield La, Har. HA1 117 CG58
Bonner St, E2 142 DW68
Bonner Wk, Grays RM16
off Clifford Rd 170 FZ76
Bonnett Ms, Horn. RM11 128 FL60
Bonneville Gdns, SW4 181 DJ86
Sch **Bonneville Prim Sch**, SW4
off Bonneville Gdns 181 DJ86
Bonney Gro, Wal.Cr. (Chsht)
EN7 66 DU30
Sch **Bonneygrove Co Prim Sch**, Wal.Cr. EN7
off Dark La 66 DU30
Bonney Way, Swan. BR8 207 FE96
Bonningtons, Brwd. CM13 109 GB48
Bonnington Sq, SW8 161 DM79
Bonnington Twr, Brom.
BR2 204 EL100
Sch **Bonnygate Prim Sch**, S.Ock.
RM15 *off Arisdale Av* 149 FV71
Bonny's Rd, Reig. RH2 265 CX135
Bonny St, NW1 141 DJ66
Bonser Rd, Twick. TW1 177 CF89
Bonsey Cl, Wok. GU22 226 AY121
Bonsey La, Wok. GU22 226 AY121
Bonseys La, Wok. (Chobham)
GU24 211 AZ110
Bonsor Dr, Tad. KT20 233 CY122
Bonsor St, SE5 162 DS80
Sch **Bonus Pastor RC Sch**,
Brom. BR1
off Winlaton Rd 184 EE91
Churchdown Annexe,
Brom. BR1
off Churchdown 184 EE91
Bonville Gdns, NW4
off Handowe Cl 119 CU56
Bonville Rd, Brom. BR1 184 EF92
Bookbinders' Cotts, N20
off Manor Dr 98 DF48
Booker Cl, E14 13 M6
Booker Rd, N18 100 DU50
⇌ **Bookham** 230 BZ123
Bookham Ct, Lthd. KT23
off Church Rd 230 BZ123
Bookham Gro, Lthd. (Bkhm)
KT23 246 CB126
Bookham Ind Est, Lthd.
(Bkhm) KT23 230 BZ123
Bookham Rd, Cob. (Down.)
KT11 230 BW119
Book Ms, WC2 9 M8
Boone Ct, N9 100 DW48
Boones Rd, SE13 164 EE84
Boone St, SE13 164 EE84
Boord St, SE10 25 H5
Boothby Rd, N19 121 DK61
Booth Cl, E9
off Victoria Pk Rd 142 DV67
SE28 146 EV73
Booth Dr, Stai. TW18 174 BK93
Booth Rd, NW9 96 CS54
Croydon CR0
off Waddon New Rd 201 DP103
Booths Cl, Hat. (N.Mymms)
AL9 45 CX24
Booth's Ct, Brwd. (Hutt.)
CM13 109 GB44
Booth's Pl, W1 9 K6
Boot St, N1 11 L2
Bordars Rd, W7 137 CE71
Bordars Wk, W7 137 CE71
Borden Av, Enf. EN1 82 DR44
Border Cres, SE26 182 DV92
Border Gdns, Croy. CR0 221 EB105
Bordergate, Mitch. CR4 200 DE95
Border Rd, SE26 182 DV92
Borderside, Slou. SL2 132 AU72
Borders La, Loug. IG10 85 EN42
Bordesley Rd, Mord. SM4 200 DB98
Bordon Wk, SW15 179 CU87
Boreas Wk, N1 4 F10
Boreham Av, E16 15 L8
Boreham Cl, E11
off Hainault Rd 123 EC60
Boreham Holt, Borwd.
(Elstree) WD6 78 CM42
Boreham Rd, N22 100 DQ54
BOREHAMWOOD, WD6 78 CP41
Borehamwood Ind Pk,
Borwd. WD6 78 CR40
Borgard Rd, SE18 165 EM77
Borkwood Pk, Orp. BR6 223 ET105
Borkwood Way, Orp. BR6 223 ES105
Borland Cl, Green. DA9
off Steele Av 189 FU85
Borland Rd, SE15 162 DW84
Teddington TW11 177 CH93
Bornedene, Pot.B. EN6 63 CY31
Borneo St, SW15 159 CW83
⊖ **Borough** 21 H4
BOROUGH, THE, SE1 20 G4
Borough, The, Bet. (Brock.)
RH3 264 CN135
Borough High St, SE1 20 G4
Borough Hill, Croy. CR0 201 DP104
★ **Borough Mkt**, SE1 21 J2
Borough Rd, SE1 20 E5
Borough Rd, Islw. TW7 157 CE81
Kingston upon Thames
KT2 198 CN95
Mitcham CR4 200 DE96
Westerham (Tats.) TN16 238 EK121
Borough Sq, SE1 20 G4
Borough Way, Pot.B. EN6 63 CY32
Borrell Cl, Brox. EN10 49 DZ20
Borrett Cl, SE17 20 G10
Borrodaile Rd, SW18 180 DB86
Borrowdale Av, Har. HA3 95 CG54
Borrowdale Cl, Egh. TW20
off Derwent Rd 173 BB94
Ilford IG4 124 EL56
South Croydon CR2 220 DT113
Borrowdale Ct, Enf. EN2 82 DQ39
Hemel Hempstead HP2 40 BL17
Borrowdale Dr, S.Croy.
CR2 220 DT112
Borthwick Ms, E15
off Borthwick Rd 124 EE63
Borthwick Rd, E15 124 EE63
NW9
off West Hendon Bdy 119 CT58
Borthwick St, SE8 23 N10
Borwick Av, E17 123 DZ55
Bosanquet Cl, Uxb. UB8 134 BK70
Bosanquet Rd, Hodd. EN11 49 EC15
Bosbury Rd, SE6 183 EC90
Boscastle Rd, NW5 121 DH62
Boscobel Cl, Brom. BR1 205 EM96
Boscobel Pl, SW1 18 F7
Boscobel St, NW8 7 P4
Bosco Cl, Orp. BR6
off Strickland Way 223 ET105
Boscombe Av, E10 123 ED59
Grays RM17 170 GD77
Hornchurch RM11 128 FK60
Boscombe Cl, E5 123 DY64
Egham TW20 193 BC95
Boscombe Gdns, SW16 181 DL93
Boscombe Rd, SW17 180 DG93
SW19 200 DB95
W12 139 CU74
Worcester Park KT4 199 CW102
Bose Cl, N3
off Claremont Pk 97 CY53
Bosgrove, E4 101 EC46
Boshers Gdns, Egh. TW20 173 AZ93
Boss Ho, SE1 21 N3
Boss St, SE1 21 N3
Bostall Heath, SE2 166 EW78
Bostall Hill, SE2 166 EU78
Bostall La, SE2 166 EV78
Bostall Manorway, SE2 166 EV77
Bostall Pk Av, Bexh. DA7 166 EY80
Bostall Rd, Orp. BR5 186 EV94
Bostal Row, Bexh. DA7
off Harlington Rd 166 EZ83
Boston Gdns, W4 158 CS79
W7 157 CG77
Brentford TW8 157 CG77
Boston Gro, Ruis. HA4 115 BQ58
Slough SL1 131 AQ72
★ **Boston Manor**, Brent.
TW8 157 CH78
⊖ **Boston Manor** 157 CG77
Boston Manor Rd, Brent.
TW8 157 CH77
Boston Pk Rd, Brent. TW8 157 CJ78
Boston Pl, NW1 8 C4
Boston Rd, E6 144 EL69
E17 123 EA58
W7 137 CE74
Croydon CR0 201 DM100
Edgware HA8 96 CQ52
Boston St, E2 *off Audrey St* 142 DU68
Bostonthorpe Rd, W7 157 CE75
Boston Vale, W7 157 CG77
Bosun Cl, E14 23 P3
Bosville Av, Sev. TN13 256 FG123
Bosville Dr, Sev. TN13 256 FG123
Bosville Rd, Sev. TN13 256 FG123
Boswell Cl, Orp. BR5
off Killewarren Way 206 EW100
Radlett (Shenley) WD7 62 CL32
Boswell Ct, WC1 9 P5
Boswell Path, Hayes UB3
off Croyde Av 155 BT77
Boswell Rd, Th.Hth. CR7 202 DQ98
Boswell St, WC1 9 P5
Bosworth Cl, E17 101 DZ53
Bosworth Cres, Rom. RM3 106 FJ51
Bosworth Ho, Erith DA8
off Saltford Cl 167 FE78
Bosworth Rd, N11 99 DK51
W10 6 D4
Barnet EN5 80 DA41
Dagenham RM10 126 FA63
BOTANY BAY, Enf. EN2 81 DK36
Botany Bay La, Chis. BR7 205 EQ97
Botany Cl, Barn. EN4 80 DE42
Botany Rd, Grav. (Nthflt)
DA11 170 GA83
Botany Way, Purf. RM19 168 FP78
Boteley Cl, E4 101 ED47
Botery's Cross, Red. RH1 251 DP133
Botham Cl, Edg. HA8
off Pavilion Way 96 CQ52
Botham Dr, Slou. SL1 152 AS76
Botha Rd, E13 144 EH71
Bothwell Cl, E16 15 K6
Bothwell Rd, Croy.
(New Adgtn) CR0 221 EC110
Bothwell St, W6
off Delorme St 159 CX79
BOTLEY, Chesh. HP5 56 AV30
Botley La, Chesh. HP5 56 AU30
Botley Rd, Chesh. HP5 56 AT30
Hemel Hempstead HP2 40 BN15
Botolph All, EC3 11 L9
Botolph La, EC3 11 L9
Botsford Rd, SW20 199 CY96
Bottom Ho Fm La, Ch.St.G.
HP8 90 AT45
Bottom La, Beac. (Seer Grn)
HP9 89 AP51
Chesham HP5 56 AT34
Kings Langley WD4 74 BH35
Bottrells Cl, Ch.St.G. HP8 90 AT47
Bottrells La, Amer. (Colesh.)
HP7 89 AP46
Chalfont St. Giles HP8 90 AT47
Bott Rd, Dart. (Hawley)
DA2 188 FM91
Botts Ms, W2 7 H8
Botts Pas, W2 7 H8
Botwell Common Rd, Hayes
UB3 135 BR73
Botwell Cres, Hayes UB3 135 BS72
Sch **Botwell Ho RC Prim Sch**,
Hayes UB3
off Botwell La 155 BT75
Botwell La, Hayes UB3 135 BS74
Boucher Cl, Tedd. TW11 177 CF92
Boucher Dr, Grav. (Nthflt)
DA11 191 GF90
Bouchier Wk, Rain. RM13
off Deere Av 147 FG65
Boughton Av, Brom. BR2 204 EF101
Boughton Business Pk,
Amer. HP6 72 AV39
Boughton Hall Av, Wok.
(Send) GU23 227 BF124
Boughton Rd, SE28 165 ES76
Boughton Way, Amer. HP6 72 AW38
Boulcott St, E1 13 H8
Boulevard, The, SW6 160 DC81
SW17
off Balham High Rd 180 DG89
SW18 *off Smugglers Way* 160 DB84
Greenhithe DA9 169 FW84
Pinner HA5 *off Pinner Rd* 116 CA56
Watford WD18 75 BR43
Welwyn Garden City AL7 29 CZ07
Woodford Green IG8 103 EN52
Boulevard 25 Retail Pk,
Borwd. WD6 78 CN41
Boulmer Rd, Uxb. UB8 134 BJ69
Boulogne Rd, Croy. CR0 202 DQ100
Boulter Gdns, Rain. RM13 147 FG65
Boulters Cl, Maid. SL6 130 AC70
Slough SL1
off Amerden Way 151 AN75
Boulters Ct, Maid. SL6 130 AC70
Boulters Gdns, Maid. SL6 130 AC70
Boulters La, Maid. SL6 130 AC70
Boulters Lock Island, Maid.
SL6 130 AC69
Boulthurst Way, Oxt. RH8 254 EH132
Boulton Ho, Brent. TW8
off Green Dragon La 158 CL78
Boulton Rd, Dag. RM8 126 EY62
Boultwood Rd, E6 144 EL72
Bounce, The, Hem.H. HP2 40 BK18
Bounce Hill, Rom. (Nave.)
RM4 *off Mill La* 87 FH38
Bounces La, N9 100 DV47
Bounces Rd, N9 100 DV46
Boundaries Rd, SW12 180 DF89
Feltham TW13 176 BW88
Boundary Av, E17 123 DZ59
Boundary Cl, SE20
off Haysleigh Gdns 202 DU96
Barnet EN5 79 CZ39
Ilford IG3 *off Loxford La* 125 ES63
Kingston upon Thames
KT1 198 CP97
Southall UB2 156 CA78
Boundary Ct, Epp. CM16 69 ER32
Welwyn Garden City AL7
off Boundary La 29 CZ13
Boundary Dr, Brwd. (Hutt.)
CM13 109 GE45
Hertford SG14 32 DR07
Boundary La, E13 144 EK69
SE17 162 DQ79
Welwyn Garden City AL7 29 CY12
Boundary Pas, E2 11 N3
Boundary Pl, H.Wyc.
(Woob.Grn) HP10 110 AD55
Boundary Rd, E13 144 EJ68
E17 123 DZ59
N9 82 DW44
N22 121 DP55
NW8 140 DB67
SW19 180 DD93
Ashford TW15 174 BJ92
Barking IG11 145 EQ68
Carshalton SM5 219 DH107
Gerrards Cross
(Chal.St.P) SL9 90 AX52
High Wycombe (Loud.)
HP10 88 AC54
Maidenhead (Taplow)
SL6 130 AE70
Pinner HA5 116 BX58
Romford RM1 127 FG58
St. Albans AL1 43 CE18
Sidcup DA15 185 ES85
Upminster RM14 128 FN62
Wallington SM6 219 DH107
Wembley HA9 118 CL62
Woking GU21 227 BA116
Boundary Row, SE1 20 E3
Boundary St, E2 11 N2
Erith DA8 167 FF80
Boundary Way, Croy. CR0 221 EA106
Hemel Hempstead HP2 41 BQ18
Watford WD25 59 BV32
Woking GU21 227 BA115
Boundary Yd, Wok. GU21
off Boundary Rd 227 BA116
Boundfield Rd, SE6 184 EE90
⊖ **Bounds Green** 99 DK51
Sch **Bounds Grn Inf Sch**,
N11 *off Bounds Grn Rd* 99 DK52
Sch **Bounds Grn Jun Sch**,
N11 *off Bounds Grn Rd* 99 DL52
Bounds Grn Rd, N11 99 DJ51
N22 99 DJ51
Bourchier Cl, Sev. TN13 257 FH126
Bourchier St, W1 9 L9
Bourdon Pl, W1 9 H9
Bourdon Rd, SE20 202 DW96
Bourdon St, W1 9 H9
Bourke Cl, NW10
off Mayo Rd 138 CS65
SW4 181 DL86
Bourke Hill, Couls. CR5 234 DF118
Bourlet Cl, W1 9 J6
Bourn Av, N15 122 DR56
Barnet EN4 80 DD43
Uxbridge UB8 134 BN70
Bournbrook Rd, SE3 164 EK83
Bourne, The, N14 99 DK46
Hemel Hempstead (Bov.)
HP3 57 BA27
Ware SG12 33 DX05
Bourne Av, N14 99 DL47
Chertsey KT16 194 BG97
Hayes UB3 155 BQ76
Ruislip HA4 116 BW64
Windsor SL4 151 AQ84
Bournebridge Cl, Brwd.
(Hutt.) CM13 109 GE45
Bournebridge La, Rom.
(Stap.Abb.) RM4 104 EZ45
Bourne Cl, Brox. EN10 49 DZ20
Guildford (Chilw.) GU4 259 BB140
Thames Ditton KT7 197 CF103
Ware SG12 33 DX05
West Byfleet KT14 212 BH113
Bourne Ct, Ruis. HA4 115 BV64

⊖ London Underground station DLR Docklands Light Railway station Tm Tramlink station Riv Pedestrian ferry landing stage

Bourne Dr, Mitch. CR4 200 DD96
BOURNE END, Hem.H. HP1 39 BC22
Bourne End, Horn. RM11 128 FN59
Bourne End La, Hem.H. HP1 39 BC22
Bourne End Mills, Hem.H. HP1 39 BB22
Bourne End Rd, Maid. SL6 110 AD62
Northwood HA6 93 BS49
Bourne Est, EC1 10 C5
Bournefield Rd, Whyt. CR3 off Godstone Rd 236 DT118
Bourne Gdns, E4 101 EB49
Bourne Gro, Ashtd. KT21 231 CK119
Bournehall Av, Bushey WD23 76 CA43
Sch Bournehall JM & Inf Sch, Bushey WD23 off Bournehall Av 76 CB43
Bournehall La, Bushey WD23 76 CA44
★ Bourne Hall Mus, Epsom KT17 217 CT109
Bournehall Rd, Bushey WD23 76 CA44
Bourne Hill, N13 99 DL46
Bourne Hill Cl, N13 off Bourne Hill 99 DM47
Bourne Ind Pk, Dart. DA1 off Bourne Rd 187 FE85
Bourne La, Cat. CR3 236 DR121
Bourne Mead, Bex. DA5 187 FD85
Bournemead Av, Nthlt. UB5 135 BU68
Bournemead Cl, Nthlt. UB5 135 BU68
Bourne Meadow, Egh. TW20 193 BB98
Bournemead Way, Nthlt. UB5 135 BV68
Bournemouth Cl, SE15 162 DU82
Bournemouth Rd, SE15 162 DU82
SW19 200 DA95
Bourne Pk Cl, Ken. CR8 236 DS115
Bourne Pl, W4 off Dukes Av 158 CR78
Sch Bourne Prim Sch, Ruis. HA4 off Cedar Av 136 BW65
Bourne Rd, E7 124 EF62
N8 121 DL58
Berkhamsted HP4 38 AT18
Bexley DA5 187 FB86
Bromley BR2 204 EK98
Bushey WD23 76 CA43
Dartford DA1 187 FC86
Godalming GU7 258 AT143
Gravesend DA12 191 GM89
Redhill RH1 251 DJ130
Slough SL1 151 AQ75
Virginia Water GU25 192 AX99
Bourneside, Vir.W. GU25 192 AU101
Bourneside Cres, N14 99 DK46
Bourneside Gdns, SE6 183 EC92
Bourneside Rd, Add. KT15 212 BK105
Bourne St, SW1 18 E8
Croydon CR0 off Waddon New Rd 201 DP103
Bourne Ter, W2 7 J5
Bourne Vale, Brom. BR2 204 EG101
Bournevale Rd, SW16 181 DL91
Bourne Vw, Grnf. UB6 137 CF65
Kenley CR8 236 DR115
Bourne Way, Add. KT15 212 BJ106
Bromley BR2 204 EF103
Epsom KT19 216 CQ105
Sutton SM1 217 CZ106
Swanley BR8 207 FC97
Woking GU22 226 AX122
Bournewood Rd, SE18 166 EU80
Orpington BR5 206 EV101
Bournville Rd, SE6 183 EA87
Bournwell Cl, Barn. EN4 80 DF41
Bourton Cl, Hayes UB3 135 BU74
Sch Bousfield Prim Sch, SW5 17 L9
Bousfield Rd, SE14 163 DX82
Bousley Ri, Cher. (Ott.) KT16 211 BD108
Sch Boutcher C of E Prim Sch, SE1 21 N7
Boutflower Rd, SW11 160 DE84
Bouverie Gdns, Har. HA3 117 CK58
Purley CR8 219 DL114
Bouverie Ms, N16 off Bouverie Rd 122 DS61
Bouverie Pl, W2 7 P7
Bouverie Rd, N16 122 DS61
Coulsdon CR5 234 DG118
Harrow HA1 116 CC59
Bouverie St, EC4 10 D8
Bouverie Way, Slou. SL3 152 AY78
Bouvier Rd, Enf. EN3 82 DW38
BOVENEY, Wind. SL4 151 AK79
Boveney Cl, Slou. SL1 off Amerden Way 151 AN75
Boveney New Rd, Wind. (Eton Wick) SL4 151 AL77
Boveney Rd, SE23 183 DX87
Windsor (Dorney) SL4 150 AJ77
Boveney Wd La, Slou. (Burn.) SL1 110 AJ62
Bovey Way, S.Ock. RM15 149 FV71
Bovill Rd, SE23 183 DX87
BOVINGDON, Hem.H. HP3 57 BA28
Bovingdon Av, Wem. HA9 138 CN65
Bovingdon Cl, N19 off Brookside Rd 121 DJ61
Bovingdon Cres, Wat. WD25 60 BX34
Sch Bovingdon Inf Sch, Hem.H. HP3 off St. Lawrence Cl 57 BB27
Sch Bovingdon Jun Sch, Hem.H. HP3 off High St 57 BB27
Bovingdon La, NW9 96 CS53
Bovingdon Rd, SW6 160 DB81
Bovingdon Sq, Mitch. CR4 off Leicester Av 201 DL98
BOW, E3 143 DZ68
Bow Arrow La, Dart. DA1, DA2 188 FN86
Bowater Cl, NW9 118 CR57
SW2 181 DL86
Bowater Gdns, Sun. TW16 195 BV96
Bowater Pl, SE3 164 EH80
Bowater Ridge, Wey. KT13 213 BR110
Bowater Rd, SE18 164 EK76
Wembley HA9 off Chalkhill Rd 118 CP62
Bow Back Rivers Wk, E15 143 EB66
Bow Br Est, E3 143 EB69
DLR Bow Church 13 P1
Bow Chyd, EC4 11 H8
Bow Common La, E3 13 L4
Bowden Cl, Felt. TW14 175 BS88
Bowden Dr, Horn. RM11 128 FL60
Bowden St, SE11 20 D10
Bowditch, SE8 23 L9
Bowdon Rd, E17 123 EA59
Bowen Dr, SE21 182 DS90
Bowen Rd, Har. HA1 116 CC59
Bowen St, E14 14 B7
Bowens Wd, Croy. CR0 221 DZ109
Bowen Way, Couls. CR5 off Netherne Dr 235 DK121
Bower Av, SE10 164 EE81
Bower Cl, Nthlt. UB5 136 BW68
Romford RM5 105 FD52
Bower Ct, Epp. CM16 70 EU32
Woking GU22 off Princess Rd 227 BB116
Bowerdean St, SW6 160 DB81
Bower Fm Rd, Rom. (Hav.at.Bow.) RM4 105 FC48
BOWER HILL, Epp. CM16 70 EU31
Bower Hill, Epp. CM16 70 EU32
Bower Hill Cl, Red. (S.Nutfld) RH1 267 DL137
Bower Hill Ind Est, Epp. CM16 70 EU32
Bower Hill La, Red. (S.Nutfld) RH1 267 DK135
Bower La, Dart. (Eyns.) DA4 208 FL103
Bowerman Av, SE14 163 DY79
Bowerman Rd, Grays RM16 171 GG77
Sch Bower Pk Sch, Rom. RM1 off Havering Rd 105 FE51
Bower Rd, Swan. BR8 187 FG94
Bowers Av, Grav. (Nthflt) DA11 191 GF91
Bowers Cl, Guil. GU4 off Cotts Wd Dr 243 BA130
Bowers Fm Dr, Guil. GU4 243 BA130
Bowers La, Guil. GU4 243 BA129
Bowers Rd, Sev. (Shore.) TN14 225 FF111
Bower St, E1 12 G8
Bowers Wk, E6 144 EL72
Bower Ter, Epp. CM16 off Bower Hill 70 EU32
Bower Vale, Epp. CM16 70 EU32
Bower Way, Slou. SL1 131 AM73
Bowes Cl, Sid. DA15 186 EV86
Bowes-Lyon Cl, Wind. SL4 off Alma Rd 151 AQ81
Bowes-Lyon Ms, St.Alb. AL3 43 CD20
BOWES PARK, N22 99 DL51
⇌ Bowes Park 99 DL51
Sch Bowes Prim Sch, N11 off Bowes Rd 99 DK50
Bowes Rd, N11 99 DH50
N13 99 DL50
W3 138 CS73
Dagenham RM8 126 EW63
Staines TW18 173 BE92
Walton-on-Thames KT12 195 BV103
Bowfell Rd, W6 159 CW79
Bowford Av, Bexh. DA7 166 EY81
Bowgate, St.Alb. AL1 43 CE19
Bowhay, Brwd. (Hutt.) CM13 109 GA47
Bowhill Cl, SW9 161 DN80
Bowie Cl, SW4 181 DK87
Bow Ind Pk, E15 143 EA66
Bowland Rd, SW4 161 DK84
Woodford Green IG8 102 EJ51
Bowland Yd, SW1 18 D4
Bow La, EC4 11 H8
N12 98 DC53
Morden SM4 199 CY100
Bowl Ct, EC2 11 M4
Bowlers Grn, Ong. CM5 53 FF21
Bowlers Orchard, Ch.St.G. HP8 90 AU48
Bowles Grn, Enf. EN1 82 DV36
Bowles Rd, SE1 off Old Kent Rd 162 DU79
Bowley Cl, SE19 182 DT93
Bowley La, SE19 182 DT92
Bowling Cl, Uxb. UB10 off Birch Cres 134 BM67
Bowling Ct, Wat. WD18 75 BU42
Bowling Grn Cl, SW15 179 CV87
Bowling Grn La, EC1 10 D3
Bowling Grn Pl, SE1 21 J3
Bowling Grn Rd, Wok. (Chobham) GU24 210 AS109
Bowling Grn Row, SE18 off Samuel St 165 EM76
Bowling Grn St, SE11 161 DN79
Bowling Grn Wk, N1 11 L1
Bowling Rd, Ware SG12 33 DY06
Bowls, The, Chig. IG7 103 ES49
Bowls Cl, Stan. HA7 95 CH50
Bowman Av, E16 15 K9
Bowman Ms, SW18 179 CZ88
Bowmans Cl, W13 137 CH74
Potters Bar EN6 64 DD32
Slough (Burn.) SL1 130 AH67
Bowmans Ct, Hem.H. HP2 40 BK18
Bowmans Grn, Wat. WD25 76 BX36
Sch Bowmansgreen Prim Sch, St.Alb. AL2 off Telford Rd 61 CJ27
Bowmans Lea, SE23 182 DW87
Bowmans Meadow, Wall. SM6 201 DH104
Bowmans Ms, E1 12 A9
N7 off Seven Sisters Rd 121 DL62
Bowmans Pl, N7 off Holloway Rd 121 DL62
Bowmans Rd, Dart. DA1 187 FF87
Bowman's Trd Est, NW9 off Westmoreland Rd 118 CM55
Bowmead, SE9 185 EM89
Bowmont Cl, Brwd. (Hutt.) CM13 109 GB44
Bowmore Wk, NW1 off St. Paul's Cres 141 DK66
Bown Cl, Til. RM18 171 GH82
Bowness Cl, E8 5 N4
Bowness Cres, SW15 178 CS92
Bowness Dr, Houns. TW4 156 BY84
Bowness Rd, SE6 183 EB87
Bexleyheath DA7 167 FB82
Bowness Way, Horn. RM12 127 FG64
Bowood Rd, SW11 160 DG84
Enfield EN3 83 DX40
Bowring Grn, Wat. WD19 94 BW50
⊖ Bow Road 13 M1
Bow Rd, E3 13 M2
Bowrons Av, Wem. HA0 137 CK66
Bowry Dr, Stai. (Wrays.) TW19 173 AZ86
Sch Bow Sec Sch, E3 13 P1
Bowsley Ct, Felt. TW13 off Highfield Rd 175 BU88
Bowsprit, The, Cob. KT11 230 BW115
Bowsprit Pt, E14 23 N5
Bow St, E15 124 EE64
WC2 9 P8
Bowstridge La, Ch.St.G. HP8 90 AW51
Bowyer Cl, E6 145 EM71
Bowyer Cres, Uxb. (Denh.) UB9 113 BF58
Bowyer Dr, Slou. SL1 131 AL74
Bowyer Pl, SE5 162 DR80
Bowyers, Hem.H. HP2 40 BK18
Bowyers Cl, Ashtd. KT21 232 CM118
Bowyer St, SE5 162 DQ80
Boxall Rd, SE21 182 DS86
Boxfield, Welw.G.C. AL7 30 DB12
Boxford Cl, S.Croy. CR2 221 DX112
Boxgrove Av, Guil. GU1 243 BA132
Boxgrove La, Guil. GU1 243 BA133
Sch Boxgrove Prim Sch, SE2 off Boxgrove Rd 166 EW76
Guildford GU1 off Boxgrove La 243 BB133
Boxgrove Rd, SE2 166 EW76
Guildford GU1 243 BA133
BOX HILL, Tad. KT20 248 CP131
Boxhill, Hem.H. HP2 40 BK18
⇌ Boxhill & Westhumble 247 CH131
Boxhill Rd, Dor. RH4 248 CL133
Tadworth (Box H.) KT20 248 CP131
Sch Box Hill Sch, Dor. (Mick.) RH5 247 CH127
Boxhill Way, Bet. (Strood Grn) RH3 264 CP138
Box La, Bark. IG11 146 EV68
Hemel Hempstead HP3 39 BE24
Hoddesdon EN11 49 DX16
Boxley Rd, Mord. SM4 200 DC98
Boxley St, E16 25 N2
BOXMOOR, Hem.H. HP1 40 BH22
Sch Boxmoor Ho Sch, Hem.H. HP3 off Box La 39 BF23
Sch Boxmoor Prim Sch, Hem.H. HP1 off Cowper Rd 40 BG21
Boxmoor Rd, Har. HA3 117 CH56
Romford RM5 105 FC50
Boxoll Rd, Dag. RM9 126 EZ63
Box Ridge Av, Pur. CR8 219 DM112
Boxted Cl, Buck.H. IG9 102 EL46
Boxted Rd, Hem.H. HP1 39 BF18
Box Tree Cl, Chesh. HP5 54 AR33
Boxtree La, Har. HA3 94 CC53
Boxtree Rd, Har. HA3 95 CD52
Boxtree Wk, Orp. BR5 206 EX102
Box Tree Wk, Red. RH1 266 DC136
Box Wk, Lthd. KT24 245 BS132
Boxwell Rd, Berk. HP4 38 AV19
Boxwood Cl, West Dr. UB7 off Hawthorne Cres 154 BM75
Boxwood Way, Warl. CR6 237 DX117
Boxworth Cl, N12 98 DD50
Boxworth Gro, N1 4 B7
Boyard Rd, SE18 165 EP78
Boyce Cl, Borwd. WD6 78 CL39
Boyce St, SE1 20 B2
Boyce Way, E13 15 L3
Boycroft Av, NW9 118 CQ58
Boyd Av, Sthl. UB1 136 BZ74
Boyd Cl, Kings.T. KT2 off Crescent Rd 178 CN94
Boydell Ct, NW8 off St. John's Wd Pk 140 DD66
Boyd Rd, SW19 180 DD93
Boyd St, E1 12 A8
Boyes Cres, St.Alb. (Lon.Col.) AL2 61 CH26
Boyfield St, SE1 20 F4
Boyland Rd, Brom. BR1 184 EF92
Boyle Av, Stan. HA7 95 CG51
Boyle Cl, Uxb. UB10 134 BM68
Boyle Fm Island, T.Ditt. KT7 197 CG100
Boyle Fm Rd, T.Ditt. KT7 197 CG100
Boyle St, W1 9 J9
Boyne Av, NW4 119 CX56
Boyne Rd, SE13 163 EC83
Dagenham RM10 126 FA62
Boyne Ter Ms, W11 16 E1
Boyseland Ct, Edg. HA8 96 CQ47
Boyson Rd, SE17 162 DR79
Boyton Cl, E1 12 F3
N8 121 DL55
Boyton Rd, N8 121 DL55
Brabant Ct, EC3 11 L9
Brabant Rd, N22 99 DM54
Brabazon Av, Wall. SM6 219 DL108
Brabazon Rd, Houns. TW5 156 BW80
Northolt UB5 136 CA68
Brabazon St, E14 14 A7
Brabourne Cl, SE19 182 DS92
Brabourne Cres, Bexh. DA7 166 EZ79
Brabourne Hts, NW7 96 CS48
Brabourne Ri, Beck. BR3 203 EC99
Brabourn Gro, SE15 162 DW82
Brace Cl, Wal.Cr. (Chsht) EN7 65 DP25
Bracewell Av, Grnf. UB6 117 CF64
Bracewell Rd, W10 139 CW71
Bracewood Gdns, Croy. CR0 202 DT104
Bracey Ms, N4 off Bracey St 121 DL61
Bracey St, N4 121 DL61
Bracken, The, E4 off Hortus Rd 101 EC47
Bracken Av, SW12 180 DG86
Croydon CR0 203 EB104
Brackenbridge Dr, Ruis. HA4 116 BX62
Brackenbury Gdns, W6 159 CV76
Sch Brackenbury Prim Sch, W6 off Dalling Rd 159 CV76
Brackenbury Rd, N2 120 DC55
W6 159 CV76
Bracken Cl, E6 145 EM71
Borehamwood WD6 78 CP39
Leatherhead (Bkhm) KT23 230 BZ124
Slough (Farn.Com.) SL2 111 AR63
Sunbury-on-Thames TW16 off Cavendish Rd 175 BT93
Twickenham TW2 off Hedley Rd 176 CA87
Woking GU22 227 AZ118
Brackendale, N21 99 DM47
Potters Bar EN6 64 DA33
Brackendale Cl, Houns. TW3 156 CB81
Brackendale Gdns, Upmin. RM14 128 FQ63
Brackendene, Dart. DA2 187 FE91
St. Albans (Brick.Wd) AL2 60 BZ30
Brackendene Cl, Wok. GU21 227 BA115
Bracken Dr, Chig. IG7 103 EP51
Bracken End, Islw. TW7 177 CD85
Brackenfield Cl, E5 off Tiger Way 122 DV63
Brackenforde, Slou. SL3 152 AW75
Bracken Gdns, SW13 159 CU82
Brackenhill, Berk. HP4 38 AY17
Cobham KT11 214 CA111
Bracken Hill Cl, Brom. BR1 off Bracken Hill La 204 EF95
Bracken Hill La, Brom. BR1 204 EF95
Bracken Ind Est, Ilf. IG6 103 ET52
Bracken Ms, E4 off Hortus Rd 101 EC47
Romford RM7 126 FA58
Bracken Path, Epsom KT18 216 CP113
Brackens, The, Enf. EN1 100 DS45
Hemel Hempstead HP2 off Heather Way 40 BK19
Orpington BR6 224 EU106
Brackens Dr, Brwd. CM14 108 FW50
Brackenside, Horl. RH6 off Stockfield 269 DH147
Bracken Way, Guil. GU3 242 AS132
Woking (Chobham) GU24 210 AT110
Brackenwood, Sun. TW16 195 BU95
Brackley, Wey. KT13 213 BR106
Brackley Cl, Wall. SM6 219 DL108
Brackley Rd, W4 158 CS78
Beckenham BR3 183 DZ94
Brackley Sq, Wdf.Grn. IG8 102 EK52
Brackley St, EC1 10 G5
Brackley Ter, W4 158 CS78
Bracklyn Cl, N1 5 J9
Bracklyn Ct, N1 5 J9
Bracklyn St, N1 5 J9
Bracknell Cl, N22 99 DN53
Bracknell Gdns, NW3 120 DB63
Bracknell Gate, NW3 120 DB64
Bracknell Pl, Hem.H. HP2 40 BM16
Bracknell Way, NW3 120 DB63
Bracondale, Esher KT10 214 CC107
Bracondale Rd, SE2 166 EU77
H Bracton Cen, The, Dart. DA2 187 FF89
Bradbery, Rick. (Map.Cr.) WD3 91 BD50
Bradbourne Pk Rd, Sev. TN13 256 FG123
Bradbourne Rd, Bex. DA5 186 FA87
Grays RM17 170 GB79
Sevenoaks TN13 257 FH122
Sch Bradbourne Sch, Sev. TN13 off Bradbourne Vale Rd 256 FG121
Bradbourne St, SW6 160 DA82
Bradbourne Vale Rd, Sev. TN13 256 FF122
Bradbury Cl, Borwd. WD6 78 CP39
Southall UB2 156 BZ77
Bradbury Gdns, Slou. (Fulmer) SL3 112 AX63
Bradbury Ms, N16 5 M2
Bradbury St, N16 5 M2
Bradd Cl, S.Ock. RM15 149 FW69
Braddock Cl, Islw. TW7 157 CF83
Romford (Coll.Row) RM5 105 FC51
Braddon Rd, Rich. TW9 158 CM83
Braddyll St, SE10 24 G10
Bradenham Av, Well. DA16 166 EU84
Bradenham Cl, SE17 162 DR79
Bradenham Rd, Har. HA3 117 CH56
Hayes UB4 135 BS69
Bradenhurst Cl, Cat. CR3 252 DT126
Braden St, W9 7 J4
Bradfield Cl, Guil. GU4 243 BA131
Woking GU22 226 AY118
Bradfield Dr, Bark. IG11 126 EU64
Bradfield Rd, E16 25 M3
Ruislip HA4 116 BY64
Bradford Cl, N17 off Commercial Rd 100 DS51
SE26 off Coombe Rd 182 DV91
Bromley BR2 205 EM102
Bradford Dr, Epsom KT19 217 CT107
Bradford Rd, W3 off Warple Way 158 CS75
Ilford IG1 125 ER60
Rickmansworth (Herons.) WD3 91 BC45
Slough SL1 131 AN72
Bradgate, Pot.B. (Cuffley) EN6 65 DK27
Bradgate Cl, Pot.B. (Cuffley) EN6 65 DK28
Bradgate Rd, SE6 183 EA86
Brading Cres, E11 124 EH61
Brading Rd, SW2 181 DM87
Croydon CR0 201 DM100
Brading Ter, W12 159 CV76
Bradiston Rd, W9 6 F1
Bradleigh Av, Grays RM17 170 GC77
Bradley Cl, N1 4 D9
N7 off Sutterton St 141 DM65
Sutton (Belmont) SM2 off Station Rd 218 DA110
Bradley Gdns, W13 137 CH72
Bradley La, Dor. RH5 247 CG132
Bradley Ms, SW17 off Bellevue Rd 180 DF88
Bradley Rd, N22 99 DM54
SE19 182 DQ93
Enfield EN3 83 DY38
Slough SL1 131 AR73
Waltham Abbey EN9 83 EC35
Bradley Stone Rd, E6 145 EM71
Bradman Row, Edg. HA8 off Pavilion Way 96 CQ52
Bradmead, SW8 161 DH80
Bradmore Grn, Couls. CR5 off Coulsdon Rd 235 DM118
Hatfield (Brook.Pk) AL9 63 CY26
Bradmore La, Hat. (Brook.Pk) AL9 63 CW27
Bradmore Pk Rd, W6 159 CV76
Bradmore Way, Couls. CR5 235 DL117
Hatfield (Brook.Pk) AL9 63 CY26
Bradshaw Cl, SW19 180 DA93
Windsor SL4 151 AL81
Bradshaw Dr, NW7 97 CX52
Bradshawe Waye, Uxb. UB8 134 BL71
Bradshaw Rd, Wat. WD24 76 BW39
Bradshaws, Hat. AL10 45 CT22
Bradshaws Cl, SE25 202 DU97
Bradstock Rd, E9 143 DX65
Epsom KT17 217 CU106
Brad St, SE1 20 D2
Bradwell Av, Dag. RM10 126 FA61
Bradwell Cl, E18 124 EF56
Hornchurch RM12 147 FH65
Bradwell Grn, Brwd. (Hutt.) CM13 109 GC44
Bradwell Ms, N18 off Lyndhurst Rd 100 DU49
Bradwell Rd, Buck.H. IG9 102 EL46
Bradwell St, E1 13 H2
Brady Av, Loug. IG10 85 EQ40
Bradymead, E6 145 EN72
Sch Brady Prim Sch, Rain. RM13 off Wennington Rd 148 FJ71
Brady St, E1 12 C4
Braemar Av, N22 99 DL53
Braemar Av, NW10 118 CR62
SW19 180 DA89
Bexleyheath DA7 167 FC84
South Croydon CR2 220 DQ109
Thornton Heath CR7 201 DN97
Wembley HA0 137 CK66
Braemar Cl, SE16 22 C9
Braemar Gdns, NW9 96 CR53
Hornchurch RM11 128 FN58
Sidcup DA15 185 ER90
Slough SL1 151 AN75
West Wickham BR4 203 EC102
Braemar Rd, E13 15 K4
N15 122 DS57
Brentford TW8 158 CL79
Worcester Park KT4 199 CV104
Braeside, Add. (New Haw) KT15 212 BH111
Beckenham BR3 183 EA92
Braeside Av, SW19 199 CY95
Sevenoaks TN13 256 FF124
Braeside Cl, Pnr. HA5 off The Avenue 94 CA52
Sevenoaks TN13 256 FF123
Braeside Cres, Bexh. DA7 167 FC84
Sch Braeside Jun Sch, Buck.H. IG9 off Palmerston Rd 102 EJ47
Braeside Rd, SW16 181 DJ94
Sch Braeside Sch for Girls, Buck.H. IG9 off High Rd 102 EH46
Braes Mead, Red. (S.Nutfld) RH1 267 DL135
Braes St, N1 4 F5
Braesyde Cl, Belv. DA17 166 EZ77
Brafferton Rd, Croy. CR0 220 DQ105
Braganza St, SE17 20 E9
Bragg Cl, Dag. RM8 off Porters Av 146 EV65
Bragmans La, Hem.H. (Flaun.) HP3 57 BB34
Rickmansworth (Sarratt) WD3 57 BE33
Braham St, E1 11 P8
Braid, The, Chesh. HP5 54 AS30
Braid Av, W3 138 CS72
Braid Cl, Felt. TW13 176 BZ89
Braid Ct, W4 off Lawford Rd 158 CQ80
Braidwood Pas, EC1 off Aldersgate St 142 DQ71
Braidwood Rd, SE6 183 ED88
Braidwood St, SE1 21 L2
Brailsford Cl, Mitch. CR4 180 DE94
Brailsford Rd, SW2 181 DN85
Brain Cl, Hat. AL10 45 CV18
Sch Braintcroft Prim Sch, NW2 off Warren Rd 119 CT61
Brainton Av, Felt. TW14 175 BV87
Braintree Av, Ilf. IG4 124 EL56
Braintree Ind Est, Ruis. HA4 115 BV63
Braintree Rd, Dag. RM10 126 FA62
Ruislip HA4 115 BV63
Braintree St, E2 12 E3
Braithwaite Av, Rom. RM7 126 FA59
Braithwaite Gdns, Stan. HA7 95 CJ53
Braithwaite Rd, Enf. EN3 83 DZ41
Braithwaite Twr, W2 7 N5
Brakefield Rd, Grav. (Sthflt) DA13 190 GB93
Brakey Hill, Red. (Bletch.) RH1 252 DS134
Brakynbery, Berk. HP4 38 AS16
Bramah Grn, SW9 161 DN81
★ Bramah Mus, SE1 21 H2
Bramalea Cl, N6 120 DG58
Bramall Cl, E15 off Idmiston Rd 124 EF64
Bramber Ct, Brent. TW8 off Sterling Pl 158 CL77
Slough SL1 131 AN74
Bramber Ho, Kings.T. KT2 off Kingsgate Rd 198 CL95
Bramber Rd, N12 98 DE50
W14 159 CZ79
Brambleacres Cl, Sutt. SM2 218 DA108
Bramble Av, Dart. (Bean) DA2 189 FW90
Bramble Banks, Cars. SM5 218 DG109
Bramblebury Rd, SE18 165 EQ78
Bramble Cl, N15 off Broad La 122 DU56
Beckenham BR3 203 EC99
Chigwell IG7 off High Rd 103 EQ46
Croydon CR0 221 EA105
Guildford GU3 242 AS132
Redhill RH1 266 DG136
Shepperton TW17 off Halliford Cl 195 BR98
Stanmore HA7 95 CK52
Uxbridge UB8 134 BM71
Watford WD25 59 BU34
Bramble Cft, Erith DA8 167 FC77
Brambledene Cl, Wok. GU21 226 AW118
Brambledown, Stai. TW18 194 BG95
Brambledown Cl, W.Wick. BR4 204 EE99
Brambledown Rd, Cars. SM5 218 DG108
South Croydon CR2 220 DS108
Wallington SM6 219 DH108
Bramblefield Cl, Long. DA3 209 FX97
Bramble Gdns, W12 off Wallflower St 139 CT73
Bramble Hall La Mobile Home Pk, Tad. (Box H.) KT20 248 CM132
Bramble La, Amer. HP7 55 AS41
Hampton TW12 176 BZ93
Hoddesdon EN11 49 DY17
Sevenoaks TN13 257 FH128
Upminster RM14 148 FQ67
Bramble Mead, Ch.St.G. HP8 90 AU48
Bramble Ri, Cob. KT11 230 BW115
Harlow CM20 35 EQ14
Bramble Rd, Hat. AL10 44 CR18
Brambles, The, Chig. IG7 off Clayside 103 EQ50
St. Albans AL1 43 CD22
Waltham Cross EN8 67 DX31
West Drayton UB7 154 BL77
Brambles Cl, Cat. CR3 236 DS122
Isleworth TW7 157 CH80
Brambles Fm Dr, Uxb. UB10 134 BN69
Sch Brambletye Jun Sch, Red. RH1 off Brambletye Pk Rd 266 DG136
Brambletye Pk Rd, Red. RH1 266 DG135
Bramble Wk, Epsom KT18 216 CP114
Bramble Way, Wok. (Ripley) GU23 227 BF124
Bramblewood, Red. RH1 251 DH129

★ Place of interest | H Hospital | Sch School | Coll College | Uni University | ⇌ Railway station

Bramblewood Cl, Cars. SM5 200 DE102
Brambling Cl, Bushey WD23 76 BY42
Brambling Ri, Hem.H. HP2 40 BL17
Bramblings, The, E4 101 ED49
Bramcote Av, Mitch. CR4 200 DF98
Bramcote Ct, Mitch. CR4
off Bramcote Av 200 DF98
Bramcote Gro, SE16 22 E9
Bramcote Rd, SW15 159 CV84
Bramdean Cres, SE12 184 EG88
Bramdean Gdns, SE12 184 EG88
Bramerton Rd, Beck. BR3 203 DZ97
Bramerton St, SW3 160 DE79
Bramfield, Wat. WD25
off Garston La 60 BY34
Bramfield Ct, N4
off Queens Dr 122 DQ61
Hertford SG14
off Windsor Dr 31 DN08
Bramfield La, Hert. SG14 31 DL05
Bramfield Rd, SW11 180 DE86
Hertford SG14 31 DL06
Bramford Ct, N14 99 DK47
Bramford Rd, SW18 160 DC84
Bramham Gdns, SW5 17 J9
Chessington KT9 215 CK105
Bramhope La, SE7 164 EH79
Bramlands Cl, SW11 160 DE83
Bramleas, Wat. WD18 75 BT42
Bramley Av, Couls. CR5 235 DJ115
Bramley Cl, E17 101 DY54
N14 81 DH43
Chertsey KT16 194 BH102
Gravesend (Istead Rise) DA13 191 GF94
Hayes UB3 135 BU73
Orpington BR6 205 EP102
Pinner HA5
off Wiltshire La 115 BT55
Redhill RH1
off Abinger Dr 266 DE136
South Croydon CR2 219 DP106
Staines TW18 174 BJ93
Swanley BR8 207 FE98
Twickenham TW2 176 CC86
Woodford Green IG8
off Orsett Ter 102 EJ52
Bramley Ct, Wat. WD25
off Orchard Av 59 BV31
Welling DA16 166 EV81
Bramley Cres, SW8
off Pascal St 161 DK80
Ilford IG2 125 EN58
Bramley Gdns, Wat. WD19 94 BW50
Bramley Gdns, Ashtd. KT21
off Ottways La 232 CL119
Bramley Hill, S.Croy. CR2 219 DP106
Bramley Ho, SW15
off Tunworth Cres 179 CT86
Bramley Ho Ct, Enf. EN2 82 DR37
Bramley Pl, Dart. DA1 167 FG84
Bramley Rd, N14 81 DH43
W5 157 CJ76
W10 6 B9
Sutton SM1 218 DD106
Sutton (Cheam) SM2 217 CX109
Sch Bramley Sch, Tad. KT20
off Chequers La 249 CU125
Bramley Shaw, Wal.Abb. EN9 68 EF33
Bramley Wk, Horl. RH6 269 DJ148
Bramley Way, Ashtd. KT21 232 CM117
Hounslow TW4 176 BZ85
St. Albans AL4 43 CJ21
West Wickham BR4 203 EB103
Brammas Cl, Slou. SL1 151 AQ76
Brampton Cl, E5 122 DV61
Waltham Cross (Chsht) EN7 66 DU28
Brampton Gdns, N15
off Brampton Rd 122 DQ57
Walton-on-Thames KT12 214 BW106
Brampton Gro, NW4 119 CV56
Harrow HA3 117 CG56
Wembley HA9 118 CN60
Brampton La, NW4 119 CW56
Sch Brampton Manor Sch, E6 off Roman Rd 144 EK70
Brampton Pk Rd, N22 121 DN55
Sch Brampton Prim Sch, E6
off Brampton Rd 144 EK69
Bexleyheath DA7
off Brampton Rd 166 EX82
Brampton Rd, E6 144 EK69
N15 122 DQ57
NW9 118 CN56
SE2 166 EW79
Bexleyheath DA7 166 EX80
Croydon CR0 202 DT101
St. Albans AL1 43 CG19
Uxbridge UB10 135 BP68
Watford WD19 93 BU48
Brampton Ter, Borwd. WD6 78 CN38
Bramshaw Gdns, Wat. WD19 94 BX50
Bramshaw Ri, N.Mal. KT3 198 CS100
Bramshaw Rd, E9 143 DX65
Bramshill Cl, Chig. IG7
off Tine Rd 103 ES50
Bramshill Gdns, NW5 121 DH62
Bramshill Rd, NW10 139 CT68
Bramshot Av, SE7 25 M10
Bramshot Way, Wat. WD19 93 BU47
Bramston Cl, Ilf. IG6 103 ET51
Bramston Rd, NW10 139 CU68
SW17 180 DC90
Bramwell Cl, Sun. TW16 196 BX96
Bramwell Ms, N1 4 B7
Brancaster Dr, NW7 97 CT52
Brancaster La, Pur. CR8 220 DQ112
Brancaster Pl, Loug. IG10 85 EM41
Brancaster Rd, E12 125 EM63
SW16 181 DL90
Ilford IG2 125 ER58
Brancepeth Gdns, Buck.H. IG9 102 EG47
Branch Cl, Hat. AL10 45 CW16
Branch Hill, NW3 120 DC62
Branch Pl, N1 5 K7
Branch Rd, E14 13 J9
Ilford IG6 104 EV50
St. Albans AL3 42 CB19
St. Albans (Park St) AL2 61 CD27
Branch St, SE15 162 DS80
Brancker Cl, Wall. SM6
off Brown Cl 219 DL108
Brancker Rd, Har. HA3 117 CK55
Brancroft Way, Enf. EN3 83 DY39
Brand Cl, N4 121 DP60
Brandesbury Sq, Wdf.Grn. IG8 103 EN52
Sch Brandlehow Prim Sch, SW15
off Brandlehow Rd 159 CZ84
Brandlehow Rd, SW15 159 CZ84
Brandon Cl, Grays (Chaff.Hun.) RM16 170 FZ75
Waltham Cross (Chsht) EN7 66 DS26
Brandon Est, SE17 161 DP79
Brandon Gros Av, S.Ock. RM15 149 FW69
Brandon Ms, EC2
off The Barbican 142 DQ71
Brandon Rd, E17 123 EC55
N7 141 DL66
Dartford DA1 188 FN87
Southall UB2 156 BZ78
Sutton SM1 218 DB105
Brandon St, SE17 20 G8
Gravesend DA11 191 GH87
Brandram Ms, SE13
off Brandram Rd 164 EE83
Brandram Rd, SE13 164 EE83
Brandreth Rd, E6 145 EM72
SW17 181 DH89
Brandries, The, Wall. SM6 201 DK104
BRANDS HILL, Slou. SL3 153 BB79
Brandsland, Reig. RH2 266 DB138
Brands Rd, Slou. SL3 153 BB79
Brand St, SE10 163 EC80
Brandville Gdns, Ilf. IG6 125 EP56
Brandville Rd, West Dr. UB7 154 BL75
Brandy Way, Sutt. SM2 218 DA108
Sch Branfil Inf Sch, Upmin. RM14 off Cedar Av 128 FN63
Sch Branfil Jun Sch, Upmin. RM14 off Cedar Av 128 FN63
Branfill Rd, Upmin. RM14 128 FP61
Brangbourne Rd, Brom. BR1 183 EC92
Brangton Rd, SE11 20 B10
Brangwyn Cres, SW19 200 DD95
Branksea St, SW6 159 CY80
Branksome Av, N18 100 DT50
Branksome Cl, Hem.H. HP2 40 BN19
Teddington TW11 177 CD91
Walton-on-Thames KT12 196 BX103
Branksome Rd, SW2 181 DL85
SW19 200 DA95
Branksome Way, Har. HA3 118 CL58
New Malden KT3 198 CQ95
Bransby Rd, Chess. KT9 216 CL107
Branscombe Gdns, N21 99 DN45
Branscombe St, SE13 163 EB83
Bransdale Cl, NW6
off West End La 140 DB67
Bransell Cl, Swan. BR8 207 FC100
Bransgrove Rd, Edg. HA8 96 CM53
Branston Cres, Orp. BR5 205 ER102
Branstone Rd, Rich. TW9 158 CM81
Branton Rd, Green. DA9 189 FT86
Brants Wk, W7 137 CE70
Brantwood Av, Erith DA8 167 FC80
Isleworth TW7 157 CG84
Brantwood Cl, E17 123 EB55
West Byfleet KT14
off Brantwood Gdns 212 BG113
Brantwood Ct, W.Byf. KT14
off Brantwood Dr 211 BF113
Brantwood Dr, W.Byf. KT14 211 BF113
Brantwood Gdns, Enf. EN2 81 DL42
Ilford IG4 124 EL56
West Byfleet KT14 211 BF113
Brantwood Rd, N17 100 DT51
SE24 182 DQ85
Bexleyheath DA7 167 FB82
South Croydon CR2 220 DQ109
Brantwood Way, Orp. BR5 206 EW97
Brasenose Dr, SW13 159 CW79
Brasher Cl, Grnf. UB6 117 CD64
Brassett Pt, E15 144 EE67
Brassey Cl, Felt. TW14 175 BU88
Oxted RH8
off Westerham Rd 254 EG129
Brassey Hill, Oxt. RH8 254 EG130
Brassey Rd, NW6 139 CZ65
Oxted RH8 254 EF130
Brassey Sq, SW11 160 DG83
Brassie Av, W3 138 CS72
Brass Tally All, SE16 23 H4
BRASTED, West. TN16 240 EW124
Brasted Cl, SE26 182 DW91
Bexleyheath DA6 186 EX85
Orpington BR6 206 EU103
Sutton SM2 218 DA110
Brasted Hill, Sev. (Knock.) TN14 240 EU120
Brasted Hill Rd, West. (Brasted) TN16 240 EV121
Brasted La, Sev. (Knock.) TN14 240 EU119
Brasted Rd, Erith DA8 167 FE80
Westerham TN16 255 ES126
Brathway Rd, SW18 180 DA87
Bratley St, E1 12 A4
Brattle Wd, Sev. TN13 257 FH129
Braund Av, Grnf. UB6 136 CB70
Braundton Av, Sid. DA15 185 ET88
Braunston Dr, Hayes UB4 136 BY70
Bravington Cl, Shep. TW17 194 BM99
Bravington Pl, W9 6 E3
Bravington Rd, W9 6 E3
Bravingtons Wk, N1
off Pentonville Rd 141 DL68
Brawlings La, Ger.Cr. (Chal.St.P.) SL9 91 BA49
Brawne Ho, SE17
off Hillingdon St 161 DP79
Braxfield Rd, SE4 163 DY84
Braxted Pk, SW16 181 DM93
BRAY, Maid. SL6 150 AC76
Bray, NW3 140 DE66
Brayards Rd, SE15 162 DV82
Braybank, Maid. SL6 150 AC75
Braybourne Cl, Uxb. UB8 134 BJ65
Braybourne Dr, Islw. TW7 157 CF80
Braybrooke Gdns, SE19
off Fox Hill 182 DT94
Braybrook St, W12 139 CT71
Brayburne Av, SW4 161 DJ82
Bray Cl, Borwd. WD6 78 CQ39
Bray Ct, Maid. SL6 150 AC77
Braycourt Av, Walt. KT12 195 BV101
Bray Cres, SE16 22 G3
Braydon Rd, N16 122 DT60
Bray Dr, E16 15 K9
Brayfield Rd, Maid. SL6 150 AC75
Brayfield Ter, N1 4 C6
Brayford Sq, E1 12 F7
Bray Gdns, Wok. GU22 227 BE116
Bray Pas, E16 15 L9
Bray Pl, SW3 18 C8
Bray Rd, NW7 97 CX51
Cobham (Stoke D'Ab.) KT11 230 BY116
Guildford GU2 258 AV135
BRAYS GROVE, Harl. CM18 52 EU16
Sch Brays Gro Comp Sch, Harl. CM18 off Tracyes Rd 52 EV17
Brays Mead, Harl. CM18 51 ET17
Bray Springs, Wal.Abb. EN9
off Roundhills 68 EE34
Brayton Gdns, Enf. EN2 81 DK42
Braywood Av, Egh. TW20 173 AZ93
Sch Braywood C of E First Sch, Wind. SL4
off Oakley Grn Rd 150 AE82
Braywood Rd, SE9 165 ER84
Braziers Fld, Hert. SG13 32 DT09
Brazil Cl, Croy. (Bedd.) CR0 201 DL101
Breach Barn Mobile Home Pk, Wal.Abb. EN9 68 EH29
Breach Barns La, Wal.Abb. EN9 off Galley Hill 68 EF30
Breach La, Dag. RM9 146 FA69
Hertford (Lt.Berk.) SG13 47 DJ18
Breach Rd, Grays RM20 169 FT79
Bread & Cheese La, Wal.Cr. (Chsht) EN7 66 DR25
Bread St, EC4 11 H8
Breakfield, Couls. CR5 235 DL116
Breakmead, Welw.G.C. AL7 30 DB10
Breakneck Hill, Green. DA9 189 FV85
Breakspear Av, St.Alb. AL1 43 CF21
Breakspear Ct, Abb.L. WD5 59 BT30
Breakspeare Cl, Wat. WD24 75 BV38
Breakspeare Rd, Abb.L. WD5 59 BS31
Sch Breakspeare Sch, Abb.L. WD5 off Gallows Hill La 59 BS31
Sch Breakspear Inf Sch, Uxb. UB10
off Bushey Rd 114 BN61
Sch Breakspear Jun Sch, Uxb. UB10
off Bushey Rd 114 BN61
Breakspear Path, Uxb. (Hare.) UB9 114 BJ55
Breakspear Rd, Ruis. HA4 115 BP59
Breakspear Rd N, Uxb. (Hare.) UB9 114 BN57
Breakspear Rd S, Uxb. (Ickhm) UB9, UB10 114 BM62
Breakspears Dr, Orp. BR5 206 EU95
Breakspears Ms, SE4
off Breakspears Rd 163 EA82
Breakspears Rd, SE4 163 DZ83
Breakspear Way, Hem.H. HP2 41 BQ20
Breakspear Way Caravan Club, Hem.H. HP2 41 BR19
Breaks Rd, Hat. AL10 45 CV18
Bream Cl, N17 122 DV56
Bream Gdns, E6 145 EN69
Breamore Cl, SW15 179 CU88
Breamore Rd, Ilf. IG3 125 ET61
Bream's Bldgs, EC4 10 C7
Bream St, E3 143 EA66
Breamwater Gdns, Rich. TW10 177 CH90
Brearley Cl, Edg. HA8
off Pavilion Way 96 CQ52
Uxbridge UB8 134 BL65
Sch Breaside Prep Sch, Brom. BR1 off Orchard Rd 204 EJ95
Breasley Cl, SW15 159 CV84
Brechin Pl, SW7 17 M8
Brecken Cl, St.Alb. AL4 43 CG16
Sch Brecknock Prim Sch, N7
off York Way 141 DK65
Brecknock Rd, N7 121 DJ63
N19 121 DJ63
Brecknock Rd Est, N7 121 DJ63
Breckonmead, Brom. BR1
off Wanstead Rd 204 EJ96
Brecon Cl, Mitch. CR4 201 DL97
Worcester Park KT4 199 CW103
Brecon Grn, NW9
off Goldsmith Av 118 CS58
Brecon Rd, W6 159 CY79
Enfield EN3 82 DW42
Brede Cl, E6 145 EN69
Bredgar, SE13 183 EC85
Bredgar Rd, N19 121 DJ61
Bredhurst Cl, SE20 182 DW93
Sch Bredinghurst Sch, SE15
off Stuart Rd 163 DX84
Bredon Rd, Croy. CR0 202 DT101
Bredune, Ken. CR8 236 DR115
Bredward Cl, Slou. (Burn.) SL1 130 AH69
Breech La, Tad. KT20 233 CU124
Breer St, SW6 160 DB83
Breezers Hill, E1 12 B10
Breeze Ter, Wal.Cr. (Chsht) EN8 off Collet Cl 67 DX28
Brember Rd, Har. HA2 116 CC61
Bremer Ms, E17
off Church La 123 EB56
Bremer Rd, Stai. TW18 174 BG90
Bremner Av, Horl. RH6 268 DF147
Bremner Cl, Swan. BR8 207 FG98
Bremner Rd, SW7 17 M4
Brenchley Av, Grav. DA11 191 GH92
Brenchley Cl, Brom. BR2 204 EF100
Chislehurst BR7 205 EN95
Brenchley Gdns, SE23 182 DW86
Brenchley Rd, Orp. BR5 205 ET95
Bren Ct, Enf. EN3
off Colgate Pl 83 EA37
Brendans Cl, Horn. RM11 128 FL60
Brenda Rd, SW17 180 DF89
Brenda Ter, Swans. DA10
off Manor Rd 190 FY87
Brende Gdns, W.Mol. KT8 196 CB98
Brendon Av, NW10 118 CS63
Brendon Cl, Erith DA8 167 FE81
Esher KT10 214 CC107
Hayes UB3 155 BQ80
Brendon Ct, Rad. WD7
off The Avenue 61 CH34
Brendon Dr, Esher KT10 214 CC107
Brendon Gdns, Har. HA2 116 CB63
Ilford IG2 125 ES57
Brendon Gro, N2 98 DC54
Brendon Rd, SE9 185 ER89
Dagenham RM8 126 EZ60
Brendon St, W1 8 B7
Brendon Way, Enf. EN1 100 DS45
Brenley Cl, Mitch. CR4 200 DG97
Brenley Gdns, SE9 164 EK84
Brennan Rd, Til. RM18 171 GH82
Brent, The, Dart. DA1, DA2 188 FN87
Brent Cl, Bex. DA5 186 EY88
Dartford DA2 188 FP86
Brentcot Cl, W13 137 CH70
Sch Brent Co Jun Sch, The, Dart. DA2 off London Rd 188 FQ87
Brent Cres, NW10 138 CM68
⊖ Brent Cross 119 CX59
Brent Cross Gdns, NW4
off Haley Rd 119 CX58
Brent Cross Shop Cen, NW4 119 CW59
Brentfield, NW10 138 CP66
Brentfield Cl, NW10
off Normans Mead 138 CR65
Brentfield Gdns, NW2
off Hendon Way 119 CX59
Sch Brentfield Prim Sch, NW10
off Meadow Garth 138 CR65
Brentfield Rd, NW10 138 CR65
Dartford DA1 188 FN86
BRENTFORD, TW8 157 CK79
⇌ Brentford 157 CJ79
Brentford Business Cen, Brent. TW8 157 CJ80
Brentford Cl, Hayes UB4 136 BX70
★ Brentford FC, Brent. TW8 157 CK79
Sch Brentford Sch for Girls, Brent. TW8
off Boston Manor Rd 157 CK79
Brent Grn, NW4 119 CW57
Brent Grn Wk, Wem. HA9 118 CQ62
Brenthall Twrs, Harl. CM17 52 EW17
Brentham Way, W5 137 CK70
Brenthouse Rd, E9 142 DV66
Brenthurst Rd, NW10 119 CT64
Sch Brent Knoll Spec Sch, SE23 off Mayow Rd 183 DX90
Brentlands Dr, Dart. DA1 188 FN88
Brent La, Dart. DA1 188 FM87
Brent Lea, Brent. TW8 157 CJ80
Brentmead Cl, W7 137 CE73
Brentmead Gdns, NW10 138 CM68
Brentmead Pl, NW11
off North Circular Rd 119 CX58
Brenton St, E14 13 K7
Brent Pk, NW10 118 CR64
Brent Pk Rd, NW4 119 CV59
NW9 119 CU60
Brent Pl, Barn. EN5 80 DA43
Brent Rd, E16 15 M7
SE18 165 EP80
Brentford TW8 157 CJ79
South Croydon CR2 220 DV109
Southall UB2 156 BW76
Brent Side, Brent. TW8 157 CJ79
Brentside Cl, W13 137 CG70
Brentside Executive Cen, Brent. TW8 157 CH79
Sch Brentside High Sch, W7
off Greenford Av 137 CE70
Sch Brentside Prim Sch, W7
off Laurie Rd 137 CE71
Brent St, NW4 119 CW56
Brent Ter, NW2 119 CW61
Brentvale Av, Sthl. UB1 137 CD74
Wembley HA0 138 CM67
Brent Vw Rd, NW9 119 CU59
Brent Way, N3 98 DA51
Brentford TW8 157 CK80
Dartford DA2 188 FP86
Wembley HA9 138 CP65
Brentwick Gdns, Brent. TW8 158 CL77
BRENTWOOD, CM13 - CM15 108 FV47
⇌ Brentwood 108 FW48
Brentwood Bypass, Brwd. CM14, CM15 107 FR49
Brentwood Cl, SE9 185 EQ88
H Brentwood Comm Hosp & Minor Injuries Unit, Brwd. CM15 108 FY46
Sch Brentwood Co High Sch, Brwd. CM14
off Seven Arches Rd 108 FX48
Brentwood Ct, Add. KT15 212 BH105
Brentwood Ho, SE18
off Shooter's Hill Rd 164 EK80
★ Brentwood Mus, Brwd. CM14 108 FW49
Brentwood Pl, Brwd. CM15 108 FX46
Sch Brentwood Prep Sch, Brwd. CM15
off Middleton Hall La 108 FY46
Brentwood Rd, Brwd. CM13 109 GA49
Grays RM16 171 GH77
Romford RM1, RM2 127 FF58
Sch Brentwood Sch, Brwd. CM15 off Ingrave Rd 108 FX47
Girls' Sch, Brwd. CM15
off Ingrave Rd 108 FX47
Sch Brentwood Ursuline High Sch, Brwd. CM14
off Queens Rd 108 FX48
Brereton Ct, Hem.H. HP3 40 BL22
Brereton Rd, N17 100 DT52
Bressenden Pl, SW1 19 H5
Bressey Av, Enf. EN1 82 DU39
Bressey Gro, E18 102 EF54
Sch Bretby Ho Sch, N.Mal. KT3 off Woodlands Av 198 CR95
Bretlands Rd, Cher. KT16 193 BE103
Brett Cl, N16 off Yoakley Rd 122 DS61
Northolt UB5
off Broomcroft Av 136 BX69
Brett Ct, N9 100 DW47
Brett Cres, NW10 138 CR66
Brettell St, SE17 21 K10
Brettenham Av, E17 101 EA53
Sch Brettenham Prim Sch, N18 off Brettenham Rd 100 DU49
Brettenham Rd, E17 101 EA54
N18 100 DV49
Brett Gdns, Dag. RM9 146 EY66
Brettgrave, Epsom KT19 216 CQ110
Brett Ho Cl, SW15
off Putney Heath La 179 CX86
Brett Pas, E8
off Kenmure Rd 122 DV64
Brett Pl, Wat. WD24
off The Harebreaks 75 BU37
Brett Rd, E8 122 DV64
Barnet EN5 79 CW43
Brevet Cl, Purf. RM19 169 FR77
Brewer's Fld, Dart. DA2 188 FJ91
Brewer's Grn, SW1 19 L5
Brewers Hall Gdns, EC2 11 H6
Brewers La, Rich. TW9 177 CK85
Brewer St, W1 9 K9
Redhill (Bletch.) RH1 252 DQ131
★ Brewery, The, EC1 11 H5
Brewery, The, Rom. RM1
off Waterloo Rd 127 FE57
Brewery Cl, Wem. HA0 117 CG64
Brewery La, Sev. TN13
off High St 257 FJ125
Twickenham TW1 177 CF87
West Byfleet (Byfleet) KT14 212 BL113
Brewery Rd, N7 141 DL66
SE18 165 ER78
Bromley BR2 204 EL102
Hoddesdon EN11 49 EA17
Woking GU21 226 AX117
Brewery Sq, EC1 10 F3
SE1 off Horselydown La 142 DT74
Brewery Wk, Rom. RM1 127 FE57
Brewhouse La, E1 22 D2
SW15 159 CY83
Hertford SG14
off St. Andrew St 32 DQ09
Brewhouse Rd, SE18 165 EM77
Brew Ho Rd, Bet. (Strood Grn) RH3
off Tanners Meadow 264 CQ138
Brewhouse Wk, SE16 23 J2
Brewhouse Yd, EC1 10 F3
Gravesend DA12
off Queen St 191 GH86
Brewood Rd, Dag. RM8 146 EV65
Brewster Gdns, W10 139 CW71
Brewster Ho, E14 13 M9
Brewster Rd, E10 123 EB60
Brian Av, S.Croy. CR2 220 DS112
Brian Cl, Horn. RM12 127 FH63
Briane Rd, Epsom KT19 216 CQ110
Brian Rd, Rom. RM6 126 EW57
Briants Cl, Pnr. HA5 94 BZ54
Briant St, SE14 163 DX81
Briar Av, SW16 181 DM94
Briarbank Rd, W13 137 CG72
Briar Banks, Cars. SM5 218 DG109
Briarcliff, Hem.H. HP1 39 BE19
Briar Cl, N2 120 DB55
N13 100 DQ48
Berkhamsted (Pott.End) HP4 39 BA16
Buckhurst Hill IG9 102 EK47
Hampton TW12 176 BZ92
Isleworth TW7 177 CF85
Maidenhead (Taplow) SL6 130 AH72
Waltham Cross (Chsht) EN8 66 DW29
Warlingham CR6 237 EA116
West Byfleet KT14 212 BJ111
Briar Ct, Sutt. SM3 217 CW105
Briar Cres, Nthlt. UB5 136 CB65
Briardale Gdns, NW3 120 DA62
Briarfield Av, N3 98 DB54
Briarfield Cl, Bexh. DA7
off Palmar Rd 166 FA82
Briar Gdns, Brom. BR2 204 EF102
Briar Gro, S.Croy. CR2 220 DU113
Briar Hill, Pur. CR8 219 DL111
Briaris Cl, N17 100 DV52
Briar La, Cars. SM5 218 DG109
Croydon CR0 221 EB105
Briarleas Gdns, Upmin. RM14 129 FS59
Briarley Cl, Brox. EN10 49 DZ22
Briar Pas, SW16 201 DL97
Briar Pl, SW16 201 DM97
Briar Rd, NW2 119 CW63
SW16 201 DL97
Bexley DA5 187 FD90
Harrow HA3 117 CJ57
Romford RM3 106 FJ52
St. Albans AL4 43 CJ17
Shepperton TW17 194 BM99
Twickenham TW2 177 CE88
Watford WD25 59 BU34
Woking (Send) GU23 227 BB123
Briars, The, Bushey (Bushey Hth) WD23 95 CE45
Harlow CM18 51 ES18
Hertford SG13 32 DU09
Rickmansworth (Sarratt) WD3 74 BH36
Slough SL3 153 AZ78
Waltham Cross (Chsht) EN8 67 DY31
Briars Cl, Hat. AL10 45 CU18
Briars Ct, Lthd. KT22 215 CD114
Briars La, Hat. AL10 45 CU18
Briars Wk, Rom. RM3 106 FL54
Briars Wd, Hat. AL10 45 CT18
Horley RH6 269 DJ147
Briarswood, Wal.Cr. EN7 66 DS28
Briarswood Way, Orp. BR6 223 ET106
Briar Wk, SW15 159 CV84
W10 6 C3
Edgware HA8 96 CQ52
West Byfleet KT14 212 BG112
Briar Way, Berk. HP4 38 AW20
Guildford GU4 243 BB130
Slough SL2 131 AQ71
West Drayton UB7 154 BN75
Briarwood, Bans. SM7
off High St 234 DA115
Briarwood Cl, NW9 118 CQ58
Feltham TW13 175 BS90
Briarwood Dr, Nthwd. HA6 93 BU54
Briarwood Rd, SW4 181 DK85
Epsom KT17 217 CU107
Briary Cl, NW3
off Fellows Rd 140 DE66
Briary Ct, E16 off Turner St 144 EF72
Sidcup DA14 186 EV92
Briary Gdns, Brom. BR1 184 EH92
Briary Gro, Edg. HA8 96 CP54
Briary La, N9 100 DT48
Brick Ct, EC4 10 C8
Grays RM17
off Columbia Wf Rd 170 GA79
Brickcroft, Brox. EN10 67 DY26
Brickenden Ct, Wal.Abb. EN9 68 EF33
BRICKENDON, Hert. SG13 48 DQ19
BRICKENDONBURY, Hert. SG13 32 DR14
Brickendon Grn, Hert. SG13 48 DQ19
Brickendon La, Hert. SG13 48 DQ18
Bricket Rd, St.Alb. AL1 43 CD20
Brickett Cl, Ruis. HA4 115 BQ57
BRICKET WOOD, St.Alb. AL2 60 BZ29
⇌ Bricket Wood 60 CA30
Brick Fm Cl, Rich. TW9 158 CP81
Brickfield, Hat. AL10 45 CU21
Brickfield Av, Hem.H. HP3 41 BP21
Brickfield Cl, Brent. TW8 157 CJ80
Brickfield Cotts, SE18 165 ET79
Brickfield Fm Gdns, Orp. BR6 223 EQ105
Brickfield La, Barn. EN5 79 CT44
Hayes UB3 155 BR79
Horley RH6
off Reigate Rd 268 DD149
Slough (Burn.) SL1 130 AG67
Brickfield Rd, SW19 180 DB91
Epping (Cooper.) CM16 70 EX29
Redhill (Outwood) RH1 267 DN142

⊖ London Underground station   DLR Docklands Light Railway station   Tra Tramlink station   Riv Pedestrian ferry landing stage

Brickfield Rd, Th.Hth. CR7 201 DP95
Brickfields, Har. HA2 117 CD61
Brickfields, The, Ware SG12 32 DV05
Brickfields La, Epp. (Cooper.) CM16 off Brickfield Rd 70 EX29
Brickfields Way, West Dr. UB7 154 BM76
Brick Kiln Cl, Wat. WD19 76 BY44
Brick Kiln La, Oxt. RH8 254 EJ131
Brick Knoll Pk, St.Alb. AL1 43 CJ21
Brick La, E1 11 P3
E2 11 P2
Enfield EN1, EN3 82 DV40
Stanmore HA7 off Honeypot La 95 CK52
Bricklayer's Arms Distribution Cen, SE1 21 M8
Bricklayer's Arms Roundabout, SE1 21 J7
Brickmakers La, Hem.H. HP3 41 BP21
Brick St, W1 18 G2
Brickwall Cl, Welw. AL6 29 CU07
Brickwall La, Ruis. HA4 115 BS60
Brickwood Cl, SE26 182 DV90
Brickwood Rd, Croy. CR0 202 DS103
Brickyard La, Dor. (Wotton) RH5 262 BW141
Brideale Cl, SE15 off Colegrove Rd 162 DT79
Bride Ct, EC4 10 E8
Bride La, EC4 10 E8
Bridel Ms, N1 4 E8
Brides Pl, N1 5 L6
Bride St, N7 4 B4
Bridewain St, SE1 21 N5
Bridewell Pl, E1 22 D2
EC4 10 E8
Bridford Ms, W1 9 H5
Bridge, The, Har. HA3 117 CE55
Bridge App, NW1 140 DG66
Bridge Av, W6 159 CW78
W7 137 CD71
Upminster RM14 128 FN61
Bridge Barn La, Wok. GU21 226 AW117
Bridge Cl, W10 6 B8
Brentwood CM13 109 FZ49
Dartford DA2 169 FR83
Enfield EN1 82 DV40
Romford RM7 127 FE58
Slough SL1 131 AM73
Staines TW18 173 BE91
Teddington TW11 off Shacklegate La 177 CF91
Walton-on-Thames KT12 195 BT101
West Byfleet (Byfleet) KT14 212 BM112
Woking GU21 226 AW117
Bridge Cotts, Upmin. RM14 129 FU64
Bridge Ct, Welw.G.C. AL7 off Bridge Rd E 29 CZ09
Woking GU21 226 AX117
Bridge Dr, N13 99 DM49
Bridge End, E17 101 EC53
Bridgefield Cl, Bans. SM7 233 CW115
Bridgefield Rd, Sutt. SM1 218 DA107
Bridgefields, Welw.G.C. AL7 29 CZ08
Bridgefoot, SE1 19 N10
Ware SG12 off High St 33 DX06
Bridgefoot La, Pot.B. EN6 63 CX33
Bridge Gdns, N16 off Green Las 122 DR63
Ashford TW15 175 BQ94
East Molesey KT8 197 CD98
Bridge Gate, N21 off Ridge Av 100 DQ45
Bridgeham Cl, Wey. KT13 off Mayfield Rd 212 BN106
Bridgeham Way, Horl. (Smallfield) RH6 269 DP148
Bridge Hill, Epp. CM16 69 ET33
Bridgehill Cl, Guil. GU2 242 AU133
Bridge Ho Quay, E14 24 D2
Bridgeland Rd, E16 15 M9
Bridge La, NW11 119 CY57
SW11 160 DE81
Virginia Water GU25 192 AY99
Bridgeman Dr, Wind. SL4 151 AN82
Bridgeman Rd, N1 4 A6
Teddington TW11 177 CG93
Bridgeman St, NW8 140 DE68
Bridge Meadows, SE14 163 DX79
Bridge Ms, Wok. GU21 off Bridge Barn La 226 AX117
Bridgend Rd, SW18 160 DC84
Enfield EN1 82 DW35
Bridgenhall Rd, Enf. EN1 82 DT39
Bridgen Rd, Bex. DA5 186 EY86
Bridge Pk, SW18 180 DA85
Guildford GU4 243 BC131
Bridge Pl, SW1 19 H7
Amersham HP6 72 AT38
Croydon CR0 202 DR101
Bridgeport Pl, E1 22 B1
Bridger Cl, Wat. WD25 60 BX33
Bridge Rd, E6 145 EM66
E15 143 ED66
E17 123 DZ59
N9 off The Broadway 100 DU48
N22 99 DL53
NW10 138 CS65
Beckenham BR3 183 DZ94
Bexleyheath DA7 166 EY82
Chertsey KT16 194 BH101
Chessington KT9 216 CL106
East Molesey KT8 197 CE98
Epsom KT17 217 CT112
Erith DA8 167 FF81
Grays RM17 170 GB78
Hounslow TW3 157 CD82
Isleworth TW7 157 CD83
Kings Langley WD4 59 BQ33
Orpington BR5 206 EV100
Rainham RM13 147 FF70
Southall UB2 156 BZ75
Sutton SM2 218 DB107
Twickenham TW1 177 CH86
Uxbridge UB8 134 BJ68
Wallington SM6 219 DJ106
Welwyn Garden City AL7, AL8 29 CW08
Wembley HA9 118 CN62
Weybridge KT13 212 BM105
Bridge Rd E, Welw.G.C. AL7 29 CY08
Bridge Row, Croy. CR0 off Cross Rd 202 DR102
Sch Bridge Sch, The, EC1 10 E3
N1 5 H7
Sch Bridge Sch, The, N19 off Elthorne Rd 121 DK61
Bridges Cl, Horl. RH6 269 DK148
Bridges Ct, SW11 160 DD83
Bridges Dr, Dart. DA1 188 FP85
Bridges La, Croy. CR0 219 DL105
Bridges Pl, SW6 159 CZ81
Bridges Rd, SW19 180 DB93
Stanmore HA7 95 CF50
Bridges Rd Ms, SW19 off Bridges Rd 180 DB93
Bridge St, SW1 19 N4
W4 158 CR77
Berkhamsted HP4 38 AX19
Guildford GU1 258 AW135
Hemel Hempstead HP1 40 BJ21
Leatherhead KT22 231 CG122
Pinner HA5 116 BX55
Richmond TW9 177 CK85
Slough (Colnbr.) SL3 153 BD80
Staines TW18 173 BE91
Walton-on-Thames KT12 195 BT102
Bridge Ter, E15 off Bridge Rd 143 ED66
SE13 off Mercator Rd 163 ED84
Bridgetown Cl, SE19 off St. Kitts Ter 182 DS92
Bridge Vw, W6 159 CW78
Greenhithe DA9 169 FV84
Bridgeview Ct, Ilf. IG6 103 ER51
Bridgewater Cl, Chis. BR7 205 ES97
Bridgewater Ct, Slou. SL3 153 BA78
Bridgewater Gdns, Edg. HA8 96 CM54
Bridgewater Hill, Berk. (Nthch) HP4 38 AT16
Bridgewater Rd, Berk. HP4 38 AU17
Ruislip HA4 115 BU63
Wembley HA0 137 CJ66
Weybridge KT13 213 BR107
Sch Bridgewater Sch, Berk. HP4 off Bridle Way 38 AU17
Bridgewater Sq, EC2 10 G5
Bridgewater St, EC2 10 G5
Bridgewater Ter, Wind. SL4 151 AR81
Bridgewater Way, Bushey WD23 76 CB44
Bridge Way, N11 off Pymmes Grn Rd 99 DJ48
NW11 119 CZ57
Bridgeway, Bark. IG11 145 ET66
Bridge Way, Cob. KT11 213 BT113
Coulsdon CR5 234 DE119
Twickenham TW2 176 CC87
Uxbridge UB10 115 BP64
Bridgeway, Wem. HA0 138 CL66
Bridgeway St, NW1 141 DJ68
Bridge Wf, Cher. KT16 194 BJ102
Bridge Wf Rd, Islw. TW7 off Church St 157 CH83
Bridgewood Cl, SE20 182 DV94
Bridgewood Rd, SW16 181 DK94
Worcester Park KT4 217 CU105
Bridge Wks, Uxb. UB8 134 BJ70
Bridge Yd, SE1 21 K1
Bridgford St, SW18 180 DC90
Bridgman Rd, W4 158 CQ76
Bridgwater Cl, Rom. RM3 106 FK50
Bridgwater Rd, E15 143 EC67
Romford RM3 106 FJ50
Bridgwater Wk, Rom. RM3 106 FK50
Bridle Cl, Enf. EN3 83 DZ37
Epsom KT19 216 CR106
Hoddesdon EN11 33 EA13
Kingston upon Thames KT1 197 CK98
St. Albans AL3 43 CE18
Sunbury-on-Thames TW16 off Forge La 195 BU97
Bridle End, Epsom KT17 217 CT114
Bridle La, W1 9 K9
Cobham KT11 230 CB115
Leatherhead KT22 230 CB115
Rickmansworth (Loud.) WD3 74 BK41
Twickenham TW1 off Crown Rd 177 CH86
Bridle Path, Croy. CR0 201 DM104
Watford WD17 75 BV40
Bridle Path, The, Epsom KT17 217 CV110
Woodford Green IG8 102 EE52
Bridlepath Way, Felt. TW14 175 BS88
Bridle Rd, Croy. CR0 203 EA104
Epsom KT17 217 CT113
Esher (Clay.) KT10 215 CH107
Pinner HA5 116 BW58
Bridle Rd, The, Pur. CR8 219 DL110
Bridle Way, Berk. HP4 38 AU17
Croydon CR0 221 EA106
Hoddesdon EN11 33 EA14
Orpington BR6 223 EQ105
Ware (Gt Amwell) SG12 33 EA09
Bridle Way, The, Croy. CR0 221 DY110
Bridleway, The, Wall. SM6 219 DJ105
Bridleway Cl, Epsom KT17 217 CW110
Bridle Way N, Hodd. EN11 33 EA13
Bridle Way S, Hodd. EN11 33 EA14
Bridlington Cl, West. (Bigg.H.) TN16 238 EH119
Bridlington Rd, N9 100 DV45
Watford WD19 94 BX48
Bridlington Spur, Slou. SL1 151 AP76
Bridport Av, Rom. RM7 127 FB58
Bridport Pl, N1 5 K9
Bridport Rd, N18 100 DS50
Greenford UB6 136 CB67
Thornton Heath CR7 201 DN97
Bridport Ter, SW8 off Wandsworth Rd 161 DK81
Bridport Way, Slou. SL2 131 AP70
Bridstow Pl, W2 7 H7
Brief St, SE5 161 DP81
Brier Lea, Tad. (Lwr Kgswd) KT20 249 CZ126
Brierley, Croy. (New Adgtn) CR0 221 EB107
Brierley Av, N9 100 DW46
Brierley Cl, SE25 202 DU98
Hornchurch RM11 128 FJ58
Brierley Rd, E11 123 ED63
SW12 181 DJ89
Brierly Cl, Guil. GU2 242 AU132
Brierly Gdns, E2 12 F1
Brier Rd, Tad. KT20 233 CV119
Briery Ct, Hem.H. HP2 40 BN19
Rickmansworth (Chorl.) WD3 74 BG42
Briery Fld, Rick. (Chorl.) WD3 74 BG42
Briery Way, Amer. HP6 55 AS37
Hemel Hempstead HP2 40 BN18
Brigade Cl, Har. HA2 117 CD61
Brigade Pl, Cat. CR3 236 DQ122
Brigade St, SE3 off Royal Par 164 EF82
Brigadier Av, Enf. EN2 82 DQ39
Brigadier Hill, Enf. EN2 82 DQ38
Briggeford Cl, E5 off Geldeston Rd 122 DU61
Briggs Cl, Mitch. CR4 201 DH95
Bright Cl, Belv. DA17 166 EX77
Brightfield Rd, SE12 184 EF85
Bright Hill, Guil. GU1 258 AX136
Brightlands, Grav. (Nthflt) DA11 190 GE91
Brightlands Rd, Reig. RH2 250 DC132
Brightling Rd, SE4 183 DZ86
Brightlingsea Pl, E14 13 L9
Brightman Rd, SW18 180 DD88
Brighton Av, E17 123 DZ57
Brighton Cl, Add. KT15 212 BJ106
Uxbridge UB10 135 BP66
Brighton Dr, Nthlt. UB5 136 CA65
Brighton Gro, SE14 off Harts La 163 DY81
Brighton Rd, E6 145 EN69
N2 98 DC54
N16 122 DS63
Addlestone KT15 212 BJ105
Banstead SM7 217 CZ114
Coulsdon CR5 235 DJ119
Horley RH6 268 DF149
Purley CR8 220 DQ110
Redhill RH1 266 DF135
South Croydon CR2 220 DQ106
Surbiton KT6 197 CJ100
Sutton SM2 218 DB109
Tadworth KT20 233 CY119
Watford WD24 75 BU38
Brighton Spur, Slou. SL2 131 AP70
Brighton Ter, SW9 161 DM84
Redhill RH1 off Hooley La 266 DF135
Brights Av, Rain. RM13 147 FH70
Brightside, The, Enf. EN3 83 DX39
Brightside Av, Stai. TW18 174 BJ94
Brightside Rd, SE13 183 ED86
Bright St, E14 14 B6
Brightview Cl, St.Alb. (Brick.Wd) AL2 60 BY29
Brightwell Cl, Croy. CR0 off Sumner Rd 201 DN102
Brightwell Cres, SW17 180 DF92
Brightwell Rd, Wat. WD18 75 BU43
Sch Brigidine Conv Sch, Wind. SL4 off King's Rd 151 AR83
Brig Ms, SE8 off Watergate St 163 EA79
Brigstock Rd, Belv. DA17 167 FB77
Coulsdon CR5 235 DH115
Thornton Heath CR7 201 DN99
Brill Pl, NW1 141 DK68
Brimfield Rd, Purf. RM19 169 FR77
Brim Hill, N2 120 DC56
Brimpsfield Cl, SE2 166 EV76
BRIMSDOWN, Enf. EN3 83 DY41
⇌ Brimsdown 83 DY41
Brimsdown Av, Enf. EN3 83 DY40
Brimsdown Ind Est, Enf. EN3 83 DZ40
Sch Brimsdown Inf Sch, Enf. EN3 off Green St 83 DX41
Sch Brimsdown Jun Sch, Enf. EN3 off Green St 83 DX41
Brimshot La, Wok. (Chobham) GU24 210 AS109
Brimstone Cl, Orp. BR6 224 EW108
Brimstone La, Dor. RH5 264 CM143
Brimstone Wk, Berk. HP4 38 AT17
Sch Brindishe Prim Sch, SE12 off Wantage Rd 184 EF85
Brindle Gate, Sid. DA15 185 ES88
Brindle La, Beac. (Forty Grn) HP9 88 AG51
Brindles, Horn. RM11 128 FL56
Brindles, The, Bans. SM7 233 CZ117
Brindles Cl, Brwd. (Hutt.) CM13 109 GC47
Brindley Cl, Bexh. DA7 167 FB83
Wembley HA0 137 CJ67
Brindley Ho, SW2 off New Pk Rd 181 DL87
Brindley St, SE14 163 DZ81
Brindley Way, Brom. BR1 184 EG92
Hemel Hempstead HP3 off London Rd 58 BM25
Southall UB1 136 CB73
Brindwood Rd, E4 101 DZ48
Brinkburn Cl, SE2 166 EU77
Edgware HA8 96 CP54
Brinkburn Gdns, Edg. HA8 118 CN55
Brinkley, Kings.T. KT1 off Burritt Rd 198 CN96
Brinkley Rd, Wor.Pk. KT4 199 CV103
Brinklow Cl, St.Alb. AL3 42 CB23
Brinklow Cres, SE18 165 EP80
Brinklow Ho, W2 7 J5
Brinkworth Rd, Ilf. IG5 124 EL55
Brinkworth Way, E9 143 DZ65
Brinley Cl, Wal.Cr. (Chsht) EN8 67 DX31
Brinsdale Rd, NW4 119 CX56
Brinsley Rd, Har. HA3 95 CD54
Brinsley St, E1 12 D8
Brinsmead, St.Alb. (Park St) AL2 61 CD27
Brinsmead Rd, Rom. RM3 106 FN54
Brinsworth Cl, Twick. TW2 177 CD89
Brinton Wk, SE1 20 E2
Brion Pl, E14 14 C6
Brisbane Av, SW19 200 DB95
Brisbane Ct, N10 off Sydney Rd 99 DH52
Brisbane Ho, Til. RM18 off Leicester Rd 171 GF81
Brisbane Rd, E10 123 EB61
W13 157 CG75
Ilford IG1 125 EP59
Brisbane St, SE5 162 DR80
Briscoe Cl, E11 124 EF61
Hoddesdon EN11 49 DZ15
Briscoe Rd, SW19 180 DD93
Hoddesdon EN11 49 DZ15
Rainham RM13 148 FJ68
Briset Rd, SE9 164 EK83
Briset St, EC1 10 E5
Briset Way, N7 121 DM61
Brisson Cl, Esher KT10 214 BZ107
Bristol Cl, Stai. (Stanw.) TW19 174 BL86
Wallington SM6 219 DL108
Bristol Gdns, SW15 off Portsmouth Rd 179 CW87
W9 7 K4
Bristol Ms, W9 7 K4
Bristol Pk Rd, E17 123 DY56
Bristol Rd, E7 144 EJ65
Gravesend DA12 191 GK90
Greenford UB6 136 CB67
Morden SM4 200 DC99
Bristol Way, Slou. SL1 132 AT74
Briston Gro, N8 121 DL58
Briston Ms, NW7 97 CU52
Bristowe Cl, SW2 off Tulse Hill 181 DN86
Bristow Rd, SE19 182 DS92
Bexleyheath DA7 166 EY81
Croydon CR0 219 DL105
Hounslow TW3 156 CC83
★ Britain at War Experience, SE1 21 L2
Britannia Cl, SW4 off Bowland Rd 161 DK84
Erith DA8 167 FF79
Northolt UB5 136 BX69
Britannia Dr, Grav. DA12 191 GM92
Britannia Gate, E16 25 M1
Britannia Ind Est, Slou. (Colnbr.) SL3 153 BE82
Britannia La, Twick. TW2 176 CC87
Britannia Rd, E14 23 P8
N12 98 DC48
SW6 160 DB80
Brentwood (Warley) CM14 108 FW50
Chesham HP5 54 AQ29
Ilford IG1 125 EP62
Surbiton KT5 198 CM101
Waltham Cross EN8 67 DZ34
Britannia Row, N1 4 F7
Britannia St, WC1 10 A1
Sch Britannia Village Prim Sch, E16 25 N2
Britannia Wk, N1 11 J1
Britannia Way, NW10 138 CP70
SW6 off Britannia Rd 160 DB81
Staines (Stanw.) TW19 174 BK87
★ British Dental Assoc Mus, W1 8 G6
British Gro, W4 159 CT78
British Gro Pas, W4 159 CT78
British Gro S, W4 off British Gro Pas 159 CT78
British Legion Rd, E4 102 EF47
★ British Lib, NW1 9 M1
★ British Lib Newspaper Collection, NW9 118 CS55
★ British Med Assoc, WC1 9 M3
★ British Mus, WC1 9 N6
★ British Red Cross Mus & Archives, SW1 18 E4
Coll British Sch of Osteopathy, SE1 21 H4
British St, E3 13 M2
Coll British Transport Pol Training Sch, Tad. KT20 off Sandlands Gro 233 CU123
Briton Cl, S.Croy. CR2 220 DS111
Briton Cres, S.Croy. CR2 220 DS111
Briton Hill Rd, S.Croy. CR2 220 DS110
Coll BRIT Sch for Performing Arts & Tech, The, Croy. CR0 off The Crescent 202 DR100
Brittain Rd, Dag. RM8 126 EY62
Walton-on-Thames KT12 214 BX106
Brittains La, Sev. TN13 256 FF123
Britten Cl, NW11 120 DB60
Borehamwood (Elstree) WD6 off Rodgers Cl 77 CK44
Brittenden Cl, Orp. BR6 223 ES107
Brittenden Par, Orp. BR6 off Glentrammon Rd 223 ET107
Britten Dr, Sthl. UB1 136 CA72
Brittens Cl, Guil. GU2 242 AU129
Britten St, SW3 18 A10
Britton Av, St.Alb. AL3 43 CD20
Britton Cl, SE6 off Brownhill Rd 183 ED87
Sch Brittons Sch, Rain. RM13 off Ford La 147 FF66
Britton St, EC1 10 E4
Britwell Dr, Berk. HP4 off Frithsden Rd 38 AY17
Britwell Est, Slou. SL2 131 AM70
Britwell Rd, Slou. SL1 131 AK69
Brixham Cres, Ruis. HA4 115 BU60
Brixham Gdns, Ilf. IG3 125 ES64
Brixham Rd, Well. DA16 166 EX81
Brixham St, E16 145 EM74
BRIXTON, SW2 161 DL84
⇌ Brixton 161 DN84
⊖ Brixton 161 DN84
★ Brixton Acad, The, SW9 161 DM83
Brixton Est, Edg. HA8 96 CP54
Brixton Hill, SW2 181 DL87
Brixton Hill Pl, SW2 off Brixton Hill 181 DL87
Brixton Oval, SW2 161 DN84
Brixton Rd, SW9 161 DN82
Watford WD24 75 BV39
Brixton Sta Rd, SW9 161 DN84
Brixton Water La, SW2 181 DM85
Broad Acre, St.Alb. (Brick.Wd) AL2 60 BY30
Broadacre, Stai. TW18 174 BG92
Broadacre Cl, Uxb. UB10 115 BP62
Broad Acres, Gdmg. GU7 258 AS143
Broadacres, Guil. GU3 242 AS132
Broad Acres, Hat. AL10 45 CT15
Broadbent Cl, N6 121 DH60
Broadbent St, W1 8 G9
Broadberry Ct, N18 100 DV50
Broadbridge Cl, SE3 164 EG80
Broadbridge La, Horl. (Smallfield) RH6 269 DN148
Broad Cl, Walt. KT12 196 BX104
Broadcoombe, S.Croy. CR2 220 DW108
Broad Ct, WC2 9 P8
Welwyn Garden City AL7 29 CY09
Broadcroft, Hem.H. HP2 40 BK18
Broadcroft Av, Stan. HA7 95 CK54
Broadcroft Rd, Orp. BR5 205 ER101
Broad Ditch Rd, Grav. (Sthflt) DA13 190 GC94
Broadeaves Cl, S.Croy. CR2 220 DS106
Broadfield, Harl. CM20 35 ES14
Broadfield Cl, NW2 119 CW62
Croydon CR0 off Progress Way 201 DM103
Romford RM1 127 FF57
Tadworth KT20 233 CW120
Broadfield Ct, Bushey (Bushey Hth) WD23 95 CE47
Sch Broadfield Inf Sch, Hem.H. HP2 off Broadfield Rd 40 BM20
Sch Broadfield Jun Sch, Hem.H. HP2 off Windmill Rd 40 BM20
Broadfield La, NW1 141 DL66
Broadfield Pl, Welw.G.C. AL8 29 CV10
Broadfield Rd, SE6 184 EE87
Guildford (Peasl.) GU5 261 BR142
Hemel Hempstead HP2 40 BM20
Broadfields, E.Mol. KT8 197 CD100
Harrow HA2 94 CB54
Broadfields, Saw. (High Wych) CM21 36 EV06
Waltham Cross (Chsht) EN7 65 DP29
Broadfields Av, N21 99 DN45
Edgware HA8 96 CP49
Sch Broadfields Co Prim Sch, Harl. CM20 off Freshwaters 35 ES14
Broadfields Hts, Edg. HA8 96 CP49
Sch Broadfields Inf Sch, Edg. HA8 off Hartland Dr 96 CN47
Sch Broadfields JM Sch, Edg. HA8 off Broadfields Av 96 CP47
Broadfields La, Wat. WD19 93 BV46
Broadfield Sq, Enf. EN1 82 DV40
Broadfields Way, NW10 119 CT64
Broadfield Way, Buck.H. IG9 102 EJ48
Broadford La, Wok. (Chobham) GU24 210 AT112
Broadford Pk, Guil. (Shalf.) GU4 258 AX141
Sch Broadford Prim Sch, Rom. RM3 off Faringdon Av 106 FK51
Broadford Rd, Guil. (Peasm.) GU3 258 AW142
BROADGATE, EC2 11 K5
Broadgate, E13 144 EJ68
EC2 off Liverpool St 142 DS71
Waltham Abbey EN9 68 EF33
Broadgate Circle, EC2 11 L5
Broadgate Rd, E16 144 EK72
Broadgates Av, Barn. EN4 80 DB39
Broadgates Rd, SW18 off Ellerton Rd 180 DD88
BROAD GREEN, Croy. CR0 201 DN100
Broad Grn, Hert. SG13 47 DM15
Broad Grn Av, Croy. CR0 201 DP101
Broadgreen Rd, Wal.Cr. (Chsht) EN7 66 DR26
Broad Grn Wd, Hert. SG13 47 DM15
Broadham Grn Rd, Oxt. RH8 253 ED132
Broadham Pl, Oxt. RH8 253 ED131
Broadhead Strand, NW9 97 CT53
Broadheath Dr, Chis. BR7 185 EM92
Broad Highway, Cob. KT11 214 BX114
Broadhinton Rd, SW4 161 DH83
Broadhurst, Ashtd. KT21 232 CL116
Broadhurst Av, Edg. HA8 96 CP49
Ilford IG3 125 ET63
Broadhurst Cl, NW6 off Broadhurst Gdns 140 DC65
Richmond TW10 off Lower Gro Rd 178 CM85
Broadhurst Gdns, NW6 140 DB65
Chigwell IG7 103 EQ49
Reigate RH2 266 DB137
Ruislip HA4 116 BW61
Broadhurst Wk, Rain. RM13 147 FG65
Broadlake Cl, St.Alb. (Lon.Col.) AL2 61 CK27
Broadlands, Felt. TW13 176 BZ90
Grays (Bad.Dene) RM17 off Bankfoot 170 FZ78
Horley RH6 269 DJ147
Broadlands Av, SW16 181 DL89
Chesham HP5 54 AQ31
Enfield EN3 82 DV41
Shepperton TW17 195 BQ100
Broadlands Cl, N6 120 DG59
SW16 181 DL89
Enfield EN3 82 DV41
Waltham Cross EN8 67 DX34
Broadlands Dr, Warl. CR6 236 DW119
Broadlands Rd, N6 120 DF59
Bromley BR1 184 EH91
Broadlands Way, N.Mal. KT3 199 CT100
Broad La, EC2 11 L5
N8 off Tottenham La 121 DM57
N15 122 DT56
Beaconsfield HP9 110 AH55
Dartford DA2 187 FG91
Hampton TW12 176 CA93
High Wycombe (Woob.Grn) HP10 110 AG58
Broad Lawn, SE9 185 EN89
Broadlawns Ct, Har. HA3 95 CF53
Broadleaf Gro, Welw.G.C. AL8 29 CV06
BROADLEY COMMON, Wal.Abb. EN9 50 EL20
Broadley Gdns, Rad. (Shenley) WD7 off Queens Way 62 CL32
Broadley Rd, Harl. CM19 51 EM19
Broadley St, NW8 7 P5
Broadley Ter, NW1 8 B4
Waltham Abbey EN9 off Common Rd 50 EL20
Broadmark Rd, Slou. SL2 132 AV73
Broadmayne, SE17 21 J9
Broadmead, SE6 183 EA90
Broad Mead, Ashtd. KT21 232 CM117
Broadmead, Horl. RH6 269 DJ147
Broadmead Av, Wor.Pk. KT4 199 CU101
Broadmead Cl, Hmptn. TW12 176 CA93
Pinner HA5 94 BY52
Sch Broadmead Jun & Inf Sch, Croy. CR0 off Sydenham Rd 202 DR101
Broadmead Rd, Hayes UB4 136 BY70
Northolt UB5 136 BY70
Woking (Send) GU22, GU23 227 BB122
Woodford Green IG8 102 EG51
Broadmeads, Ware SG12 33 DX06
Woking (Send) GU23 off Broadmead Rd 227 BB122
Sch Broadmere Comm Prim Sch, The, Wok. GU21 off Devonshire Av 211 BD113
BROADMOOR, Dor. RH5 262 CA143
Broadmoor, Dor. RH5 262 CA143
Broad Oak, Slou. SL2 131 AQ70
Sunbury-on-Thames TW16 175 BT93
Woodford Green IG8 102 EH50
Broadoak Av, Enf. EN3 83 DX35
Broad Oak Cl, E4 101 EA50
Broadoak Cl, Dart. (Sutt.H.) DA4 188 FN93
Broad Oak Cl, Orp. BR5 206 EU96
Broadoak Ct, Slou. SL2 131 AQ70
BROADOAK END, Hert. SG14 31 DM07
Broadoak Rd, Erith DA8 167 FD80
Broadoaks, Epp. CM16 69 ET31
Surbiton KT6 198 CP102
Broadoaks Cres, W.Byf. KT14 212 BH114
Broadoaks Way, Brom. BR2 204 EF99
Broad Platts, Slou. SL3 152 AX76
Broad Ride, Egh. TW20 192 AU96
Virginia Water GU25 192 AU96

★ Place of interest | H Hospital | Sch School | Coll College | Uni University | ⇌ Railway station

Broad Rd, Swans. DA10 190 FY86
Broad Sanctuary, SW1 19 M4
Broadstone Pl, W1 8 E6
Broadstone Rd, Horn. RM12 127 FG61
Broad St, Chesh. HP5 54 AQ30
Dagenham RM10 146 FA66
Hemel Hempstead HP2 40 BK19
Teddington TW11 177 CF93
Broad St Av, EC2 11 L6
Broad St Pl, EC2 11 K6
Broadstrood, Loug. IG10 85 EN38
Broad Vw, NW9 118 CN58
Broadview Av, Grays RM16 170 GD75
Broadview Rd, SW16 181 DK94
Chesham HP5 54 AP27
Broadwalk, E18 124 EF55
Broad Wk, N21 99 DM47
NW1 8 G2
SE3 164 EJ83
W1 18 E1
Caterham CR3 236 DT122
Coulsdon CR5 234 DG123
Croydon CR0 221 DY110
Epsom KT18 off Chalk La 232 CS117
Epsom (Burgh Hth) KT18 233 CX119
Harlow CM20 35 ER14
Broadwalk, Har. HA2 116 CA57
Broad Wk, Houns. TW5 156 BX81
Orpington BR6 206 EX104
Richmond TW9 158 CM80
Sevenoaks TN15 257 FL128
Broad Wk, The, W8 7 K10
East Molesey KT8 197 CF97
Broadwalk, The, Nthwd. HA6 93 BQ54
Broadwalk Ct, W8 17 H1
Broad Wk La, NW11 119 CZ59
Broad Wk N, The, Brwd. CM13 109 GA49
Broadwalk Pl, E14 24 C1
Broadwalk Shop Cen, Edg. HA8 96 CP51
Broad Wk S, The, Brwd. CM13 109 GA49
Broadwall, SE1 20 D1
Broadwater, Berk. HP4 38 AW18
Potters Bar EN6 64 DB30
Broadwater Cl, Stai. (Wrays.) TW19 173 AZ87
Walton-on-Thames KT12 213 BU106
Woking GU21 211 BD112
Broadwater Cres, Welw.G.C. AL7 29 CX10
Broad Water Cres, Wey. KT13 off Churchill Dr 195 BQ104
Broadwater Fm Est, N17 100 DR54
Sch Broadwater Fm Prim Sch, N17 off Moira Cl 100 DR54
Broadwater Gdns, Orp. BR6 223 EP105
Uxbridge (Hare.) UB9 114 BH56
Broadwater La, Uxb. (Hare.) UB9 114 BH56
Broadwater Pk, Maid. SL6 150 AE78
Uxbridge (Denh.) UB9 114 BG58
Broadwater Pl, Wey. KT13 off Oatlands Dr 195 BS103
Sch Broadwater Prim Sch, SW17 off Broadwater Rd 180 DE91
Broadwater Ri, Guil. GU1 243 BA134
Broadwater Rd, N17 100 DS53
SE28 165 ER76
SW17 180 DE91
Welwyn Garden City AL7 29 CY10
Broadwater Rd N, Walt. KT12 213 BT106
Broadwater Rd S, Walt. KT12 213 BT106
Sch Broadwater Sch, Gdmg. GU7 off Summers Rd 258 AU143
Broadway, E15 143 ED66
SW1 19 L5
Barking IG11 145 EQ66
Bexleyheath DA6 166 EY84
Grays RM17 170 GC79
Rainham RM13 147 FG70
Romford RM2 127 FG55
Staines TW18 off Kingston Rd 174 BH92
Swanley BR8 207 FC100
Tilbury RM18 171 GF82
Broadway, The, E4 101 EC51
E13 144 EH68
N8 121 DL58
N9 100 DU48
N14 off Winchmore Hill Rd 99 DK46
N22 99 DN54
NW7 96 CS50
SW13 off The Terrace 158 CS82
SW19 179 CZ93
W5 137 CK73
W7 off Cherington Rd 137 CE74
W7 (W.Ealing) 137 CG74
W13 137 CG74
Addlestone (New Haw) KT15 212 BG110
Amersham HP7 55 AP40
Beaconsfield HP9 off Penn Rd 89 AK52
Beaconsfield (Wyc.End) HP9 89 AL54
Chesham HP5 54 AP31
Croydon CR0 off Croydon Rd 219 DL105
Dagenham RM8 126 EZ61
Greenford UB6 136 CC70
Harrow HA2 95 CE54
Hatfield AL9 45 CW17
Hornchurch RM12 127 FH63
Loughton IG10 85 EQ42
Pinner HA5 94 BZ52
Slough (Farn.Com.) SL2 131 AQ65
Southall UB1 136 BX73
Staines (Laleham) TW18 194 BJ97
Stanmore HA7 95 CJ50
Sutton SM1 off Manor La 218 DC106
Sutton (Cheam) SM3 217 CY107
Thames Ditton KT7 off Hampton Ct Way 197 CE102
Watford WD17 76 BW41
Wembley HA9 off East La 118 CL62
Woking GU21 227 AZ117
Woodford Green IG8 102 EH51
Broadway Av, Croy. CR0 202 DR99
Harlow CM17 36 EV11
Twickenham TW1 177 CH86
Broadway Cl, Amer. HP7 55 AP40
South Croydon CR2 220 DV114
Woodford Green IG8 102 EH51
Broadway Ct, SW19 off The Broadway 180 DA93
Amersham HP7 55 AP40
Broadway E, Uxb. (Denh.) UB9 114 BG58
Broadway Gdns, Mitch. CR4 200 DE98
Broadway Ho, Brom. BR1 off Elmfield Pk 204 EG97
Broadway Mkt, E8 142 DV67
Broadway Mkt Ms, E8 off Regents Row 142 DU67
Broadway Ms, E5 122 DT59
N13 off Elmdale Rd 99 DM50
N21 off Compton Rd 99 DP46
Broadway Par, N8 121 DL58
Hayes UB3 off Coldharbour La 135 BU74
Hornchurch RM12 off The Broadway 127 FH63
Broadway Pl, SW19 off Hartfield Rd 179 CZ93
Broadway Shop Cen, W6 off Hammersmith Bdy 159 CW77
Bexleyheath DA6 166 FA84
Broadwick St, W1 9 K9
Broadwood, Grav. DA11 191 GH92
Broadwood Av, Ruis. HA4 115 BS58
Broadwood Rd, Couls. CR5 off Netherne Dr 235 DK121
Broadwood Ter, W8 off Pembroke Rd 159 CZ77
Broad Yd, EC1 10 E4
Brocas Cl, NW3 off Fellows Rd 140 DE66
Brocas St, Wind. (Eton) SL4 151 AR80
Brockbridge Ho, SW15 off Tangley Gro 179 CT86
Brockdish Av, Bark. IG11 125 ET64
Brockenhurst, W.Mol. KT8 196 BZ100
Brockenhurst Av, Wor.Pk. KT4 198 CS102
Brockenhurst Cl, Wok. GU21 211 AZ114
Brockenhurst Gdns, NW7 96 CS50
Ilford IG1 125 EQ64
Brockenhurst Ms, N18 off Lyndhurst Rd 100 DU49
Brockenhurst Rd, Croy. CR0 202 DV101
Brockenhurst Way, SW16 201 DK96
Brocket Cl, Chig. IG7 off Burrow Rd 103 ET50
Brocket Pk, Welw.G.C. (Lmsfd) AL8 28 CS10
Brocket Rd, Grays RM16 171 GG76
Hoddesdon EN11 49 EA17
Welwyn Garden City AL8 29 CT11
Brockett Cl, Welw.G.C. AL8 29 CV09
Brocket Way, Chig. IG7 103 ES50
Brock Grn, S.Ock. RM15 off Cam Grn 149 FV72
BROCKHAM, Bet. RH3 264 CP136
Brockham Cl, SW19 179 CZ92
Brockham Cres, Croy. (New Adgtn) CR0 221 ED108
Brockham Dr, SW2 off Fairview Pl 181 DM87
Ilford IG2 125 EP58
Brockham Grn, Bet. (Brock.) RH3 264 CP135
Brockham Hill Pk, Tad. (Box H.) KT20 248 CQ131
Brockhamhurst Rd, Bet. RH3 264 CN141
Brockham La, Bet. (Brock.) RH3 248 CN134
Sch Brockham Sch, Bet. RH3 off Wheelers La 264 CP136
Brockham St, SE1 21 H5
Brockhurst Cl, Stan. HA7 95 CF51
Brockhurst Rd, Chesh. HP5 54 AQ30
Brockill Cres, SE4 163 DY84
Brocklebank Ct, Whyt. CR3 236 DU118
Brocklebank Rd, SE7 25 N8
SW18 180 DC87
Brocklehurst St, SE14 163 DX80
Brocklesbury Cl, Wat. WD24 76 BW41
Brocklesby Rd, SE25 202 DV98
Brockles Mead, Harl. CM19 51 EQ19
BROCKLEY, SE4 183 DY85
⇌ Brockley 163 DY83
Brockley Av, Stan. HA7 96 CL48
Brockley Cl, Stan. HA7 96 CL49
Brockley Combe, Wey. KT13 213 BR105
Brockley Cres, Rom. RM5 105 FC52
Brockley Cross, SE4 off Endwell Rd 163 DY83
Brockley Footpath, SE15 162 DW84
Brockley Gdns, SE4 163 DZ82
Brockley Gro, SE4 183 DZ85
Brentwood (Hutt.) CM13 109 GA46
Brockley Hall Rd, SE4 183 DY86
Brockley Hill, Stan. HA7 95 CJ46
Brockley Ms, SE4 183 DY85
Brockley Pk, SE23 183 DY87
Sch Brockley Prim Sch, SE4 off Brockley Rd 183 DZ85
Brockley Ri, SE23 183 DY86
Brockley Rd, SE4 163 DZ83
Brockleyside, Stan. HA7 95 CK49
Brockley Vw, SE23 183 DY87
Brockley Way, SE4 183 DX85
Brockman Ri, Brom. BR1 183 ED91
Brock Pl, E3 14 A4
Brock Rd, E13 15 P5
Brocks Dr, Sutt. SM3 199 CY104
Brockshot Cl, Brent. TW8 157 CK79
Brocksparkwood, Brwd. CM13 109 GB48
Brock St, SE15 off Evelina Rd 162 DW83
Brockswood La, Welw.G.C. AL8 29 CU08
Brockton Cl, Rom. RM1 127 FF56
Brock Way, Vir.W. GU25 192 AW99
Brockway Cl, E11 124 EE60
Guildford GU1 243 BB132
Brockway Ho, Slou. SL3 153 BB78
Brockwell Av, Beck. BR3 203 EB99
Brockwell Cl, Orp. BR5 205 ET99
★ Brockwell Park, SE24 181 DP86
Brockwell Pk Gdns, SE24 181 DN87
Brockwell Pk Row, SW2 181 DN86
Broderick Gro, Lthd. (Bkhm) KT23 off Lower Shott 246 CA126
Brodewater Rd, Borwd. WD6 78 CP40
Brodia Rd, N16 122 DS62
Brodie Rd, E4 101 EC46
Enfield EN2 82 DQ38
Guildford GU1 258 AY135
Brodie St, SE1 21 P9
Brodlove La, E1 12 G9
Brodrick Gro, SE2 166 EV77
Brodrick Rd, SW17 180 DE89
Brograve Gdns, Beck. BR3 203 EB96
Broke Ct, Guil. GU4 off Speedwell Cl 243 BC131
Broke Fm Dr, Orp. BR6 224 EW109
Broken Furlong, Wind. (Eton) SL4 151 AP78
Brokengate La, Uxb. (Denh.) UB9 113 BC60
Broken Wf, EC4 10 G9
Brokes Cres, Reig. RH2 250 DA132
Brokesley St, E3 13 L2
Brokes Rd, Reig. RH2 250 DA132
Broke Wk, E8 5 P7
Bromar Rd, SE5 162 DS83
Bromborough Grn, Wat. WD19 94 BW50
Bromefield, Stan. HA7 95 CJ53
Bromefield Ct, Wal.Abb. EN9 68 EG33
Bromehead Rd, E1 12 E7
Bromehead St, E1 12 E7
Bromell's Rd, SW4 161 DJ84
Brome Rd, SE9 165 EM83
Bromet Cl, Wat. WD17 75 BT38
Sch Bromet Prim Sch, Wat. WD19 off Oxhey Rd 94 BX45
Bromfelde Rd, SW4 161 DK82
Bromfelde Wk, SW4 161 DK82
Bromfield St, N1 4 D9
Bromford Cl, Oxt. RH8 254 EG133
Bromhall Rd, Dag. RM8, RM9 146 EV65
Bromhedge, SE9 185 EM90
Bromholm Rd, SE2 166 EV76
Bromleigh Cl, Wal.Cr. (Chsht) EN8 off Martins Dr 67 DY28
Bromleigh Ct, SE23 off Lapse Wd Wk 182 DV89
BROMLEY, E3 14 B4
BROMLEY, BR1 & BR2 204 EF96
Bromley, Grays RM17 170 FZ79
Coll Bromley Adult Ed Coll, Brom. BR2 off Princes Plain 204 EL101
Bromley Av, Brom. BR1 184 EE94
⊖ Bromley-by-Bow 14 B3
Coll Bromley Coll of Further & Higher Ed, SE20 (Anerley) off Hawthorn Gro 202 DW95
Brom. BR2 off Rookery La 204 EK100
BROMLEY COMMON, Brom. BR2 205 EM101
Bromley Common, Brom. BR2 204 EJ98
Bromley Cres, Brom. BR2 204 EF97
Ruislip HA4 115 BT63
Bromley Gdns, Brom. BR2 204 EF97
Bromley Gro, Brom. BR2 203 ED96
Bromley Hall Rd, E14 14 C5
Sch Bromley Hall Spec Sch, E14 14 D6
Sch Bromley High Sch, Brom. BR1 off Blackbrook La 205 EN95
Jun Section, Brom. BR1 off Blackbrook La 205 EN98
Bromley High St, E3 14 A1
Bromley Hill, Brom. BR1 184 EE92
Bromley La, Chis. BR7 185 EQ94
Bromley Mall, The, Brom. BR1 204 EG97
★ Bromley Mus, Orp. BR6 206 EV101
⇌ Bromley North 204 EG95
BROMLEY PARK, Brom. BR1 204 EE95
Bromley Pk, Brom. BR1 off London Rd 204 EF95
Bromley Pl, W1 9 J5
Bromley Rd, E10 123 EB58
E17 101 EA54
N17 100 DT53
N18 100 DR48
SE6 183 EB88
Beckenham BR3 203 EB95
Bromley (Downham) BR1 183 EC91
Bromley (Short.) BR2 203 EC96
Chislehurst BR7 205 EP95
Sch Bromley Rd Inf Sch, Beck. BR3 off St. George's Rd 203 EB95
⇌ Bromley South 204 EG97
Bromley St, E1 13 H7
BROMPTON, SW3 18 A6
Brompton Arc, SW3 18 C4
Brompton Cl, SE20 off Selby Rd 202 DU96
Hounslow TW4 176 BZ85
Brompton Dr, Erith DA8 167 FH80
Brompton Gro, N2 120 DE56
★ Brompton Oratory, SW7 18 A6
Brompton Pk Cres, SW6 160 DB79
Brompton Pl, SW3 18 B5
Brompton Rd, SW1 18 B5
SW3 18 A7
SW7 18 B5
Brompton Sq, SW3 18 A5
Brompton Ter, SE18 off Prince Imperial Rd 165 EN81
Bromwich Av, N6 120 DG61
Bromyard Av, W3 138 CS74
Bromyard Ho, SE15 162 DV80
Bromycroft Rd, Slou. SL2 131 AN69
BRONDESBURY, NW2 139 CY66
⇌ Brondesbury 139 CZ66
Brondesbury Ct, NW2 139 CW65
Brondesbury Ms, NW6 off Willesden La 140 DA66
BRONDESBURY PARK, NW6 139 CW66
⇌ Brondesbury Park 139 CX67
Brondesbury Pk, NW2 139 CV65
NW6 139 CX66
Brondesbury Rd, NW6 139 CZ68
Brondesbury Vil, NW6 139 CZ68
Bronsart Rd, SW6 159 CY80
Bronsdon Way, Uxb. (Denh.) UB9 113 BF61
Bronson Rd, SW20 199 CX96
Bronte Cl, E7 off Bective Rd 124 EG63
Erith DA8 167 FB80
Ilford IG2 125 EN57
Tilbury RM18 171 GJ82
Bronte Gro, Dart. DA1 168 FM84
Bronte Ho, NW6 7 H1
Sch Bronte Sch, Grav. DA11 off Pelham Rd 191 GG87
Bronte Vw, Grav. DA12 191 GJ88
Bronti Cl, SE17 21 H10
Bronze Age Way, Belv. DA17 167 FC76
Erith DA8 167 FC76
Bronze St, SE8 163 EA80
BROOK, Guil. GU5 260 BL142
Brook Av, Dag. RM10 147 FB66
Edgware HA8 96 CP51
Wembley HA9 118 CN62
Brookbank, H.Wyc. (Woob.Grn) HP10 110 AC60
Brookbank Av, W7 137 CD71
Brookbank Rd, SE13 163 EA83
Brook Cl, NW7 off Frith Ct 97 CY52
SW17 180 DG89
SW20 199 CV97
W3 off West Lo Av 138 CN74
Borehamwood WD6 78 CP41
Dorking RH4 247 CJ134
Epsom KT19 216 CS109
Brook Cl, Rom. RM2 105 FF53
Ruislip HA4 115 BS59
Staines (Stanw.) TW19 174 BM87
Brook Ct, Buck.H. IG9 102 EH46
Brook Cres, E4 101 EA49
N9 100 DV49
Slough SL1 131 AL72
Brookdale, N11 99 DJ49
Brookdale Av, Upmin. RM14 128 FN62
Brookdale Cl, Upmin. RM14 128 FP62
Brookdale Rd, E17 123 EA55
SE6 183 EB86
Bexley DA5 186 EY86
Brookdene Av, Wat. WD19 93 BV45
Brookdene Dr, Nthwd. HA6 93 BT52
Brookdene Rd, SE18 165 ET77
Brook Dr, SE11 20 D6
Harrow HA1 116 CC56
Radlett WD7 61 CF33
Ruislip HA4 115 BS58
Sunbury-on-Thames TW16 off Chertsey Rd 175 BS92
Brooke Av, Har. HA2 116 CC62
Brooke Cl, Bushey WD23 94 CC45
Brookehowse Rd, SE6 183 EB90
Brook End, Saw. CM21 36 EX05
Brookend Rd, Sid. DA15 185 ES88
Brooke Rd, E5 122 DU62
E17 123 EC56
N16 122 DT62
Grays RM17 170 GA78
Brooker Rd, Wal.Abb. EN9 67 EC34
Brookers Cl, Ashtd. KT21 231 CJ117
Brooke's Ct, EC1 10 C5
Brookes Mkt, EC1 10 D5
Brooke St, EC1 10 C6
Brooke Way, Bushey WD23 off Richfield Rd 94 CC45
Brook Fm Rd, Cob. KT11 230 BX115
Brookfield, N6 120 DG62
Epping (Thnwd) CM16 70 EW25
Godalming GU7 258 AU143
Woking GU21 226 AV116
Brookfield Av, E17 123 EC56
NW7 97 CV51
W5 137 CK70
Sutton SM1 218 DD105
Brookfield Cen, Wal.Cr. (Chsht) EN8 67 DX27
Brookfield Cl, NW7 97 CV51
Ashtead KT21 off Leatherhead Rd 232 CL120
Brentwood (Hutt.) CM13 109 GC44
Chertsey (Ott.) KT16 211 BD107
Redhill RH1 266 DG140
Brookfield Ct, Grnf. UB6 136 CC69
Harrow HA3 117 CK57
Brookfield Cres, NW7 97 CV51
Harrow HA3 118 CL57
Brookfield Gdns, Esher (Clay.) KT10 215 CF107
Waltham Cross (Chsht) EN8 67 DX27
Sch Brookfield Ho Sch, Wdf.Grn. IG8 off Alders Av 102 EE51
Brookfield La, Wal.Cr. (Chsht) EN8 67 DX27
Brookfield La W, Wal.Cr. (Chsht) EN8 66 DV28
Brookfield Pk, NW5 121 DH62
Brookfield Path, Wdf.Grn. IG8 102 EE51
Sch Brookfield Prim Sch, N19 off Chester Rd 121 DH61
Sutton SM3 off Ridge Rd 199 CY102
Brookfield Retail Pk, Wal.Cr. (Chsht) EN8 67 DX26
Brookfield Rd, E9 143 DY65
N9 100 DU48
W4 158 CR75
High Wycombe (Woob.Grn) HP10 110 AD60
Brookfields, Enf. EN3 83 DX42
Sawbridgeworth CM21 36 EX05
Brookfields Av, Mitch. CR4 200 DE99
Brook Gdns, E4 101 EB49
SW13 159 CT83
Kingston upon Thames KT2 198 CQ95
Brook Gate, W1 8 D10
Brook Grn, W6 16 B7
Woking (Chobham) GU24 off Brookleys 210 AT110
Brook Hill, Guil. (Far.Grn) GU5 260 BK143
Oxted RH8 253 EC130
Brookhill Cl, SE18 165 EP78
Barnet EN4 80 DE43
Brookhill Rd, SE18 165 EP78
Barnet EN4 80 DE43
Brookhouse Dr, H.Wyc. (Woob.Grn) HP10 110 AC60
Brookhouse Gdns, E4 102 EE49
Brookhurst Rd, Add. KT15 212 BH107
Brook Ind Est, Hayes UB4 136 BX74
Brooking Cl, Dag. RM8 126 EW62
Brooking Rd, E7 124 EG64
Brookland Cl, NW11 120 DA56
Brookland Garth, NW11 120 DB56
Brookland Hill, NW11 120 DA56
Sch Brookland Inf Sch, NW11 off Hill Top 120 DB56
Waltham Cross EN8 off Elm Dr 67 DY28
Sch Brookland Jun Sch, NW11 off Hill Top 120 DB56
Waltham Cross EN8 off Elm Dr 67 DY28
Brookland Ri, NW11 120 DA56
BROOKLANDS, Wey. KT13 212 BM109
Brooklands, Dart. DA1 188 FL88
Brooklands App, Rom. RM1 127 FD56
Brooklands Av, SW19 180 DB89
Sidcup DA15 185 ER89
Brooklands Business Pk, Wey. KT13 212 BN110
Brooklands Cl, Cob. KT11 230 BY115
Romford RM7 off Marshalls Rd 127 FD56
Sunbury-on-Thames TW16 195 BS95
Coll Brooklands Coll, Wey. KT13 off Heath Rd 212 BM107
Brooklands Ct, Add. (New Haw) KT15 212 BK110
Weybridge KT13 off Northfield Pl 213 BP108
Brooklands Dr, Grnf. UB6 137 CK67
Brooklands Gdns, Horn. RM11 128 FJ57
Potters Bar EN6 63 CY32
Brooklands Ind Pk, Wey. KT13 212 BL110
Sch Brooklands JMI Sch, SE3 off Medebourne Cl 164 EG83
Brooklands La, Rom. RM7 127 FD56
Weybridge KT13 212 BM107
★ Brooklands Mus, Wey. KT13 212 BN109
Brooklands Pk, SE3 164 EG83
Brooklands Rd, Rom. RM7 127 FD56
Thames Ditton KT7 197 CF102
Weybridge KT13 213 BP107
Sch Brooklands Sch, Reig. RH2 off Wray Pk Rd 250 DB132
Brooklands Way, Red. RH1 250 DE132
Brook La, SE3 164 EH82
Berkhamsted HP4 38 AV18
Bexley DA5 186 EX86
Bromley BR1 184 EG93
Guildford (Albury) GU5 260 BL142
Sawbridgeworth CM21 36 EX05
Woking (Send) GU23 227 BE122
Brooklane Fld, Harl. CM18 52 EV18
Brook La N, Brent. TW8 157 CK78
Brooklea Cl, NW9 96 CS53
Brookleys, Wok. (Chobham) GU24 210 AT110
Brooklyn Av, SE25 202 DV98
Loughton IG10 84 EL42
Brooklyn Cl, Cars. SM5 200 DE103
Woking GU22 226 AY119
Brooklyn Ct, Wok. GU22 off Brooklyn Rd 226 AY119
Brooklyn Gro, SE25 202 DV98
Brooklyn Rd, SE25 202 DV98
Bromley BR2 204 EK99
Woking GU22 226 AY118
Brooklyn Way, West Dr. UB7 154 BK76
Brookmans Av, Hat. (Brook.Pk) AL9 63 CY26
Brookmans Cl, Upmin. RM14 129 FS59
BROOKMANS PARK, Hat. AL9 63 CY26
⇌ Brookmans Park 63 CX27
Sch Brookmans Pk Prim Sch, Hat. AL9 off Bradmore Way 63 CY26
Brookmarsh Ind Est, SE10 off Norman Rd 163 EB80
Brook Mead, Epsom KT19 216 CS107
Brookmead Av, Brom. BR1 205 EM99
Brookmead Cl, Orp. BR5 206 EV101
Brook Meadow, N12 98 DB49
Brook Meadow Cl, Wdf.Grn. IG8 102 EE51
Brookmeadow Way, Wal.Abb. EN9 off Breach Barn Mobile Home Pk 68 EH30
Brookmead Rd, Croy. CR0 201 DJ100
Brookmeads Est, Mitch. CR4 200 DE99
Brookmead Way, Orp. BR5 206 EV100
Brook Ms N, W2 7 M9
Brookmill Cl, Wat. WD19 off Brookside Rd 93 BV45
Brookmill Rd, SE8 163 EA81
Brook Par, Chig. IG7 off High Rd 103 EP48
Brook Pk, Dart. DA1 188 FN89
Brook Pk Cl, N21 81 DP44
Brook Path, Loug. IG10 84 EL42
Slough SL1 131 AM73
Brook Pl, Barn. EN5 80 DA43
Brook Ri, Chig. IG7 103 EN48
Brook Rd, N8 121 DL56
N22 121 DM55
NW2 119 CU61
Borehamwood WD6 78 CN40
Brentwood CM14 108 FT48
Buckhurst Hill IG9 102 EG47
Epping CM16 70 EU33
Gravesend (Nthflt) DA11 190 GE88
Guildford (Chilw.) GU4 259 BC140
Ilford IG2 125 ES58
Loughton IG10 84 EL43
Redhill RH1 266 DF135
Redhill (Merst.) RH1 251 DJ129
Romford RM2 105 FF53
Sawbridgeworth CM21 36 EX06
Surbiton KT6 198 CL103
Swanley BR8 207 FD97
Thornton Heath CR7 202 DQ98
Twickenham TW1 177 CG86
Waltham Cross EN8 67 DZ34
Brook Rd S, Brent. TW8 157 CK79
Brooks Av, E6 145 EM70
Brooksbank St, E9 142 DW65
Brooksby Ms, N1 4 D5
Brooksby St, N1 4 D6
Brooksby's Wk, E9 123 DX64
Brooks Cl, SE9 185 EN89
Weybridge KT13 212 BN110
Brooks Ct, E15 off Clays La 123 EB64
Hertford SG14 31 DM08
Brookscroft, Croy. CR0 221 DY110
Brookscroft Rd, E17 101 EB53
Brooksfield, Welw.G.C. AL7 30 DB08
Brookshill, Har. HA3 95 CD50
Brookshill Av, Har. HA3 95 CD50
Brookshill Dr, Har. HA3 95 CD50
Brookshill Gate, Har. (Har.Wld) HA3 95 CD50
Brookside, N21 81 DM44
Barnet EN4 80 DE44
Carshalton SM5 218 DG106
Chertsey KT16 193 BE101
Guildford GU4 242 AX129
Harlow CM19 51 EM17
Hatfield AL10 44 CR18
Hertford SG13 32 DS09
Hoddesdon EN11 49 DZ17
Hornchurch RM11 128 FL57
Ilford IG6 103 EQ51
Orpington BR6 205 ET101
Potters Bar EN6 63 CU32
Slough (Colnbr.) SL3 153 BC80
Uxbridge UB10 134 BM66
Waltham Abbey EN9 off Broomstick Hall Rd 68 EE33
Brookside Av, Ashf. TW15 174 BJ92
Staines (Wrays.) TW19 152 AY83
Brookside Cl, Barn. EN5 79 CY44
Feltham TW13 off Sycamore Cl 175 BU90
Harrow (Kenton) HA2 117 CK57
Harrow (S.Har.) HA3 116 BY63
Brookside Cres, Pot.B. (Cuffley) EN6 65 DL27

Brookside Cres, Worcester Park KT4 off Green La ... 199 CU102
Brookside Gdns, Enf. EN1 ... 82 DV37
Sch Brookside Jun & Inf Sch, Rom. RM3 off Dagnam Pk Dr ... 106 FL50
Sch Brookside Prim Sch, Hayes UB4 off Perth Av ... 136 BW69
Brookside Rd, N9 ... 100 DV49
N19 ... 121 DJ61
NW11 ... 119 CY58
Gravesend (Istead Rise) DA13 ... 191 GF94
Hayes UB4 ... 136 BW73
Watford WD19 ... 93 BV45
Brookside S, Barn. EN4 ... 98 DG45
Sch Brookside Unit, Ilf. IG3 off Barley La ... 126 EU57
Brookside Wk, N3 ... 97 CY54
N12 ... 98 DA51
NW4 ... 119 CY56
NW11 ... 119 CY56
Brookside Way, Croy. CR0 ... 203 DX100
Brooks La, W4 ... 158 CN79
Brook's Ms, W1 ... 8 G9
Brook Sq, SE18 off Shooter's Hill Rd ... 164 EL81
Brooks Rd, E13 ... 144 EG67
W4 ... 158 CN78
BROOK STREET, Brwd. CM14 ... 108 FS49
Brook St, N17 off High Rd ... 100 DT54
W1 ... 8 F9
W2 ... 7 P9
Belvedere DA17 ... 167 FB78
Brentwood CM14 ... 108 FS50
Erith DA8 ... 167 FB79
Kingston upon Thames KT1 ... 198 CL96
Windsor SL4 ... 151 AR82
Brooksville Av, NW6 ... 139 CY67
Brooks Way, Orp. BR5 ... 206 EW96
Brook Vale, Erith DA8 ... 167 FB81
Brook Valley, Dor. (Mid Holm.) RH5 ... 263 CH142
Brookview Rd, SW16 ... 181 DJ92
Brookville Rd, SW6 ... 159 CZ80
Brook Wk, N2 ... 98 DD53
Edgware HA8 ... 96 CR51
Brookway, SE3 ... 164 EG83
Brook Way, Chig. IG7 ... 103 EN48
Leatherhead KT22 ... 231 CG118
Rainham RM13 ... 147 FH71
Brookwood, Horl. RH6 off Stockfield ... 269 DH147
Brookwood Av, SW13 ... 159 CT83
Brookwood Cl, Brom. BR2 ... 204 EF98
Brookwood Rd, SW18 ... 179 CZ88
Hounslow TW3 ... 156 CB81
Broom Av, Orp. BR5 ... 206 EV96
Broom Cl, Brom. BR2 ... 204 EL100
Esher KT10 ... 214 CB106
Hatfield AL10 ... 45 CT21
Teddington TW11 ... 177 CK94
Waltham Cross (Chsht) EN7 ... 66 DU27
Broomcroft Av, Nthlt. UB5 ... 136 BW69
Broomcroft Cl, Wok. GU22 ... 227 BD116
Broomcroft Dr, Wok. GU22 ... 227 BD115
Broome Cl, Epsom (Headley) KT18 ... 248 CQ126
Broome Pl, S.Ock. (Aveley) RM15 ... 149 FR74
Broome Rd, Hmptn. TW12 ... 176 BZ94
Broomer Pl, Wal.Cr. EN8 ... 66 DW29
Broome Way, SE5 ... 162 DQ80
Broomfield, E17 ... 123 DZ59
Guildford GU2 ... 242 AS133
Harlow CM20 ... 36 EV12
St. Albans (Park St) AL2 ... 60 CC27
Staines TW18 ... 174 BG93
Sunbury-on-Thames TW16 ... 195 BU95
Broomfield Av, N13 ... 99 DM50
Broxbourne EN10 ... 67 DY26
Loughton IG10 ... 85 EM44
Broomfield Cl, Guil. GU3 ... 242 AS132
Romford RM5 ... 105 FD52
Broomfield Ct, Wey. KT13 ... 213 BP107
Broomfield Gate, Slou. SL2 off Crofthill Rd ... 131 AP70
Sch Broomfield Ho Sch, Rich. TW9 off Broomfield Rd ... 158 CM81
Broomfield La, N13 ... 99 DM49
Broomfield Pk, Dor. (Westc.) RH4 ... 262 CC137
Broomfield Pl, W13 off Broomfield Rd ... 137 CH74
Broomfield Ride, Lthd. (Oxshott) KT22 ... 215 CD112
Broomfield Ri, Abb.L. WD5 ... 59 BR32
Broomfield Rd, N13 ... 99 DL50
W13 ... 137 CH74
Addlestone (New Haw) KT15 ... 212 BH111
Beckenham BR3 ... 203 DY97
Bexleyheath DA6 ... 186 FA85
Richmond TW9 ... 158 CM81
Romford RM6 ... 126 EX59
Sevenoaks TN13 ... 256 FF122
Surbiton KT5 ... 198 CM102
Swanscombe DA10 ... 190 FY86
Teddington TW11 off Melbourne Rd ... 177 CJ93
Broomfields, Esher KT10 ... 214 CC106
Sch Broomfield Sch, N14 off Wilmer Way ... 99 DK50
Broomfield St, E14 ... 13 P6
Broom Gdns, Croy. CR0 ... 203 EA104
Broom Gro, Wat. WD17 ... 75 BU38
Broomgrove Gdns, Edg. HA8 ... 96 CN53
Broomgrove Rd, SW9 ... 161 DM82
Broom Hall, Lthd. (Oxshott) KT22 ... 215 CD114
Broomhall End, Wok. GU21 off Broomhall La ... 226 AY116
Broomhall La, Wok. GU21 ... 226 AY116
Broomhall Rd, S.Croy. CR2 ... 220 DR109
Woking GU21 ... 226 AY116
Broom Hill, Hem.H. HP1 ... 39 BE21
Slough (Stoke P.) SL2 ... 132 AU66
Broomhill Ct, Wdf.Grn. IG8 off Broomhill Rd ... 102 EG51
Broomhill Ri, Bexh. DA6 ... 186 FA85
Broomhill Rd, SW18 ... 180 DA85
Dartford DA1 ... 187 FH86
Ilford IG3 ... 126 EU61
Orpington BR6 ... 206 EU101
Broomhill Rd, Wdf.Grn. IG8 ... 102 EG51
Broomhills, Grav. (Sthflt) DA13 off Betsham Rd ... 190 FY91
Welwyn Garden City AL7 ... 30 DA08
Broomhill Wk, Wdf.Grn. IG8 ... 102 EF52
Broomhouse La, SW6 ... 160 DA82
Broomhouse Rd, SW6 ... 160 DA82
Broomlands La, Oxt. RH8 ... 254 EJ125
Broom La, Wok. (Chobham) GU24 ... 210 AS109
Broom Leys, St.Alb. AL4 ... 43 CK17
Broomloan La, Sutt. SM1 ... 200 DA103
Broom Lock, Tedd. TW11 ... 177 CJ93
Broom Mead, Bexh. DA6 ... 186 FA85
Broom Pk, Tedd. TW11 ... 177 CK94
Broom Rd, Croy. CR0 ... 203 EA104
Teddington TW11 ... 177 CJ93
Brooms Cl, Welw.G.C. AL8 ... 29 CX06
Broomsleigh St, NW6 ... 119 CZ64
Broomstick Hall Rd, Wal.Abb. EN9 ... 68 EE33
Broomstick La, Chesh. HP5 ... 56 AU30
Broom Water, Tedd. TW11 ... 177 CJ93
Broom Water W, Tedd. TW11 ... 177 CJ92
Broom Way, Wey. KT13 ... 213 BS105
Broomwood Cl, Croy. CR0 ... 203 DX99
Broomwood Gdns, Brwd. (Pilg.Hat.) CM15 ... 108 FU44
Sch Broomwood Hall Prep Sch, SW12 off Nightingale La ... 180 DG87
Broomwood Rd, SW11 ... 180 DF86
Orpington BR5 ... 206 EV96
Broseley Gdns, Rom. RM3 ... 106 FL49
Broseley Gro, SE26 ... 183 DY92
Broseley Rd, Rom. RM3 ... 106 FL49
Broster Gdns, SE25 ... 202 DT97
Brougham Rd, E8 ... 142 DU67
W3 ... 138 CQ72
Brougham St, SW11 ... 160 DF82
Brough Cl, SW8 off Kenchester Cl ... 161 DL80
Kingston upon Thames KT2 ... 177 CK92
Broughinge Rd, Borwd. WD6 ... 78 CP40
Broughton Av, N3 ... 119 CY55
Richmond TW10 ... 177 CH90
Broughton Dr, SW9 ... 161 DN84
Broughton Gdns, N6 ... 121 DJ58
Broughton Rd, SW6 ... 160 DB82
W13 ... 137 CH73
Orpington BR6 ... 205 ER103
Sevenoaks (Otford) TN14 ... 241 FG116
Thornton Heath CR7 ... 201 DN100
Broughton Rd App, SW6 off Wandsworth Br Rd ... 160 DB82
Broughton St, SW8 ... 160 DG82
Broughton Way, Rick. WD3 ... 92 BG45
Brouncker Rd, W3 ... 158 CQ75
Brow, The, Ch.St.G. HP8 ... 90 AX48
Redhill RH1 off Spencer Way ... 266 DG139
Watford WD25 ... 59 BV33
Brow Cl, Orp. BR5 off Brow Cres ... 206 EX101
Brow Cres, Orp. BR5 ... 206 EW102
Browells La, Felt. TW13 ... 175 BV89
Brownacres Towpath, Wey. KT13 ... 195 BP102
Brown Cl, Wall. SM6 ... 219 DL108
Browne Cl, Brwd. CM14 ... 108 FV46
Romford RM5 ... 105 FB50
Brownfields, Welw.G.C. AL7 ... 29 CZ08
Brownfields Ct, Welw.G.C. AL7 off Brownfields ... 30 DA08
Brownfield St, E14 ... 14 B8
Browngraves Rd, Hayes UB3 ... 155 BQ80
Brown Hart Gdns, W1 ... 8 F9
Brownhill Rd, SE6 ... 183 EB87
Browning Av, W7 ... 137 CF72
Sutton SM1 ... 218 DE105
Worcester Park KT4 ... 199 CV102
Browning Cl, E17 ... 123 EC56
W9 ... 7 M4
Hampton TW12 ... 176 BZ91
Romford (Coll.Row) RM5 ... 104 EZ52
Welling DA16 ... 165 ES81
Browning Ho, W12 off Wood La ... 139 CW72
Browning Ms, W1 ... 8 G6
Browning Rd, E11 ... 124 EF59
E12 ... 145 EM65
Dartford DA1 ... 168 FM84
Enfield EN2 ... 82 DR38
Leatherhead (Fetch.) KT22 ... 247 CD125
Browning St, SE17 ... 21 H9
Browning Wk, Til. RM18 off Coleridge Rd ... 171 GJ82
Browning Way, Houns. TW5 ... 156 BX81
Brownlea Gdns, Ilf. IG3 ... 126 EU61
Brownlow Cl, Barn. EN4 ... 80 DD43
Brownlow Ms, WC1 ... 10 B4
Brownlow Rd, E7 off Woodford Rd ... 124 EH63
E8 ... 5 P7
N3 ... 98 DB52
N11 ... 99 DL51
NW10 ... 138 CS66
W13 ... 137 CG74
Berkhamsted HP4 ... 38 AW18
Borehamwood WD6 ... 78 CN42
Croydon CR0 ... 220 DS105
Redhill RH1 ... 250 DE134
Brownlow St, WC1 ... 10 B6
Brownrigg Rd, Ashf. TW15 ... 174 BN91
Brown Rd, Grav. DA12 ... 191 GL88
Brown's Bldgs, EC3 ... 11 M8
Brownsea Wk, NW7 off Sanders La ... 97 CX51
Browns La, NW5 ... 121 DH64
Leatherhead (Eff.) KT24 ... 246 BX127
Brownspring Dr, SE9 ... 185 EP91
Browns Rd, E17 ... 123 EA55
Surbiton KT5 ... 198 CM101
Browns Spring, Berk. (Pott.End) HP4 ... 39 BC16
Brown St, W1 ... 8 C7
Brownswell Rd, N2 ... 98 DD54
Brownswood Rd, N4 ... 121 DP62
Beaconsfield HP9 ... 89 AK51
Broxash Rd, SW11 ... 180 DG86
BROXBOURNE, EN10 ... 49 DZ21
⇌ Broxbourne ... 49 EA20
Broxbourne Av, E18 ... 124 EH56
Broxbournebury Ms, Brox. EN10 off White Stubbs La ... 48 DW21
Sch Broxbourne C of E Prim Sch, Brox. EN10 off Mill La ... 49 DZ21
Broxbourne Common, Brox. EN10 ... 48 DU19
Broxbourne Rd, E7 ... 124 EG62
Broxbourne Rd, Orp. BR6 ... 205 ET101
Sch Broxbourne Sch, The, Brox. EN10 off High Rd ... 49 DZ21
Broxburn Dr, S.Ock. RM15 ... 149 FV73
Broxburn Par, S.Ock. RM15 off Broxburn Dr ... 149 FV73
Broxhill Rd, Rom. (Hav.at.Bow.) RM4 ... 105 FH48
Broxholm Rd, SE27 ... 181 DN90
Brox La, Cher. (Ott.) KT16 ... 211 BD109
Brox Rd, Cher. (Ott.) KT16 ... 211 BC107
Broxted Ms, Brwd. (Hutt.) CM13 off Bannister Dr ... 109 GC44
Broxted Rd, SE6 ... 183 DZ89
Broxwood Way, NW8 ... 140 DE67
Bruce Av, Horn. RM12 ... 128 FK61
Shepperton TW17 ... 195 BQ100
★ Bruce Castle Mus, N17 ... 100 DS53
Bruce Castle Rd, N17 ... 100 DT53
Bruce Cl, W10 ... 6 B5
Slough SL1 ... 131 AN74
Welling DA16 ... 166 EV81
West Byfleet (Byfleet) KT14 ... 212 BK113
Bruce Dr, S.Croy. CR2 ... 221 DX109
Bruce Gdns, N20 off Balfour Gro ... 98 DF48
⇌ Bruce Grove ... 100 DT54
Bruce Gro, N17 ... 100 DS53
Orpington BR6 ... 206 EU102
Watford WD24 ... 76 BW38
Sch Bruce Gro Prim Sch, N17 off Sperling Rd ... 100 DT54
Bruce Hall Ms, SW17 off Brudenell Rd ... 180 DG91
Bruce Rd, E3 ... 14 A2
NW10 ... 138 CR66
SE25 ... 202 DR98
Barnet EN5 off St. Albans Rd ... 79 CY41
Harrow HA3 ... 95 CE54
Mitcham CR4 ... 180 DG94
Bruce's Wf Rd, Grays RM17 ... 170 GA79
Bruce Wk, Wind. SL4 off Tinkers La ... 151 AK82
Bruce Way, Wal.Cr. EN8 ... 67 DX33
Bruckner St, W10 ... 6 D2
Brudenell, Wind. SL4 ... 151 AM83
Brudenell Rd, SW17 ... 180 DF90
Coll Brudenell Sch of English, W5 off The Mall ... 137 CK73
Bruffs Meadow, Nthlt. UB5 ... 136 BY65
Bruges Pl, NW1 off Randolph St ... 141 DJ66
Brumana Cl, Wey. KT13 ... 213 BP107
Brumfield Rd, Epsom KT19 ... 216 CQ106
Brummel Cl, Bexh. DA7 ... 167 FC83
★ Brunei Gall, WC1 ... 9 M5
Brunel Cl, SE19 ... 182 DT93
Hounslow TW5 ... 155 BV80
Northolt UB5 ... 136 BZ69
Romford RM1 ... 127 FE56
Tilbury RM18 ... 171 GH83
★ Brunel Engine Ho, SE16 ... 22 E3
Brunel Est, W2 ... 6 G6
Brunel Pl, Sthl. UB1 ... 136 CB72
Brunel Rd, E17 ... 123 DY58
SE16 ... 22 E4
W3 ... 138 CS71
Woodford Green IG8 ... 103 EM50
Brunel St, E16 ... 15 J8
Uni Brunel Uni, Osterley Campus, Islw. TW7 off Borough Rd ... 157 CE80
Runnymede Campus, Egh. TW20 off Coopers Hill La ... 172 AW90
Twickenham Campus, Twick. TW1 off St. Margarets Rd ... 157 CH84
Uxbridge Campus, Uxb. UB8 off Kingston La ... 134 BK69
Brunel Wk, N15 ... 122 DS56
Twickenham TW2 off Stephenson Rd ... 176 CA87
Brunel Way, Slou. SL1 ... 132 AT74
Brune St, E1 ... 11 N6
Brunner Cl, NW11 ... 120 DC57
Brunner Ct, Cher. (Ott.) KT16 ... 211 BC106
Brunner Rd, E17 ... 123 DZ57
W5 ... 137 CK70
Bruno Pl, NW9 ... 118 CQ61
Brunswick Av, N11 ... 98 DG48
Upminster RM14 ... 129 FS59
Brunswick Cl, Bexh. DA6 ... 166 EX84
Pinner HA5 ... 116 BY58
Thames Ditton KT7 ... 197 CF102
Twickenham TW2 ... 177 CD90
Walton-on-Thames KT12 ... 196 BW103
Brunswick Ct, EC1 off Northampton Sq ... 141 DP69
SE1 ... 21 M4
Barnet EN4 ... 80 DD43
Upminster RM14 off Waycross Rd ... 129 FS59
Brunswick Cres, N11 ... 98 DG48
Brunswick Gdns, W5 ... 138 CL69
W8 ... 17 H2
Ilford IG6 ... 103 EQ52
Brunswick Gro, N11 ... 98 DG48
Cobham KT11 ... 214 BW113
Brunswick Ind Pk, N11 ... 99 DH49
Brunswick Ms, SW16 off Potters La ... 181 DK93
W1 ... 8 D7
BRUNSWICK PARK, N11 ... 98 DF47
Brunswick Pk, SE5 ... 162 DR81
Sch Brunswick Pk Comm Prim Sch, SE5 off Picton St ... 162 DR80
Brunswick Pk Gdns, N11 ... 98 DG47
Sch Brunswick Pk Prim Sch, N14 off Osidge La ... 98 DG47
Brunswick Pk Rd, N11 ... 98 DG47
Brunswick Pl, N1 ... 11 K2
NW1 ... 8 F3
SE19 ... 182 DU94
Brunswick Quay, SE16 ... 23 H6
Brunswick Rd, E10 ... 123 EC60
E14 off Blackwall Tunnel Northern App ... 143 EC72
N15 ... 122 DS57
W5 ... 137 CK70
Bexleyheath DA6 ... 166 EX84
Enfield EN3 ... 83 EA38
Kingston upon Thames KT2 ... 198 CN95
Sutton SM1 ... 218 DB105
Brunswick Shop Cen, WC1 ... 9 N3
Brunswick Sq, N17 ... 100 DT51
WC1 ... 9 P4
Brunswick St, E17 ... 123 EC57
Brunswick Vil, SE5 ... 162 DS81
Brunswick Wk, Grav. DA12 ... 191 GK87
Brunswick Way, N11 ... 99 DH49
Brunton Pl, E14 ... 13 K8
Brushfield St, E1 ... 11 M6
Brushrise, Wat. WD24 ... 75 BU36
Brushwood Dr, Rick. (Chorl.) WD3 ... 73 BC42
Sch Brushwood Mid Sch, Chesh. HP5 off Brushwood Rd ... 54 AS29
Brushwood Rd, Chesh. HP5 ... 54 AR29
Brussels Rd, SW11 ... 160 DD84
Bruton Cl, Chis. BR7 ... 185 EM94
Bruton La, W1 ... 9 H10
Bruton Pl, W1 ... 9 H10
Bruton Rd, Mord. SM4 ... 200 DC99
Bruton St, W1 ... 9 H10
Bruton Way, W13 ... 137 CG71
Bryan Av, NW10 ... 139 CV66
Bryan Cl, Sun. TW16 ... 175 BU94
Bryan Rd, SE16 ... 23 L3
Bryan's All, SW6 off Wandsworth Br Rd ... 160 DB82
Bryanston Av, Twick. TW2 ... 176 CB88
Bryanston Cl, Sthl. UB2 ... 156 BZ77
Bryanstone Av, Guil. GU2 ... 242 AU131
Bryanstone Cl, Guil. GU2 ... 242 AT131
Bryanstone Ct, Sutt. SM1 off Oakhill Rd ... 218 DC105
Bryanstone Gro, Guil. GU2 ... 242 AT130
Bryanstone Rd, N8 ... 121 DK57
Waltham Cross EN8 ... 67 DZ34
Bryanston Ms E, W1 ... 8 C6
Bryanston Ms W, W1 ... 8 C6
Bryanston Pl, W1 ... 8 C6
Bryanston Rd, Til. RM18 ... 171 GJ82
Bryanston Sq, W1 ... 8 C6
Bryanston St, W1 ... 8 C8
Bryant Av, Rom. RM3 ... 106 FK53
Slough SL2 ... 131 AR71
Bryant Cl, Barn. EN5 ... 79 CZ43
Bryant Ct, E2 ... 5 N9
Bryant Rd, Nthlt. UB5 ... 136 BW69
Bryant Row, Rom. (Noak Hill) RM3 off Cummings Hall La ... 106 FJ48
Bryant St, E15 ... 143 ED66
Bryantwood Rd, N7 ... 4 C1
Brycedale Cres, N14 ... 99 DK49
Bryce Rd, Dag. RM8 ... 126 EW63
Bryden Cl, SE26 ... 183 DY92
Brydges Pl, WC2 ... 9 N10
Brydges Rd, E15 ... 123 ED64
Brydon Wk, N1 off Outram Pl ... 141 DL67
Bryer Ct, EC2 off Aldersgate St ... 142 DQ71
Bryer Pl, Wind. SL4 ... 151 AK83
Bryett Rd, N7 ... 121 DL62
Brymay Cl, E3 ... 143 EA68
Brympton Cl, Dor. RH4 ... 263 CG138
Brynford Cl, Wok. GU21 ... 226 AY115
Brynmaer Rd, SW11 ... 160 DF81
Bryn-y-Mawr Rd, Enf. EN1 ... 82 DT42
Bryony Cl, Loug. IG10 ... 85 EP42
Uxbridge UB8 ... 134 BM71
Bryony Rd, W12 ... 139 CU73
Guildford GU1 ... 243 BB131
Bryony Way, Sun. TW16 ... 175 BT93
Bubblestone Rd, Sev. (Otford) TN14 ... 241 FH116
Buccleuch Rd, Slou. (Datchet) SL3 ... 152 AU80
Buchanan Cl, N21 ... 81 DM43
South Ockendon (Aveley) RM15 ... 148 FQ74
Buchanan Ct, Borwd. WD6 ... 78 CQ40
Buchanan Gdns, NW10 ... 139 CV68
Buchan Cl, Uxb. UB8 ... 134 BJ69
Buchan Rd, SE15 ... 162 DW83
Bucharest Rd, SW18 ... 180 DC87
Buckbean Path, Rom. RM3 off Clematis Cl ... 106 FJ52
Buckden Cl, N2 off Southern Rd ... 120 DF56
SE12 off Upwood Rd ... 184 EF86
Buckettsland La, Borwd. WD6 ... 78 CR38
Buckfast Ct, W13 off Romsey Rd ... 137 CG73
Buckfast Rd, Mord. SM4 ... 200 DB98
Buckfast St, E2 ... 12 B2
Buckham Thorns Rd, West. TN16 ... 255 EQ126
Buck Hill Wk, W2 ... 7 P10
Buckhold Rd, SW18 ... 180 DA86
Buckhurst Av, Cars. SM5 ... 200 DE102
Sevenoaks TN13 ... 257 FJ125
Buckhurst Cl, Red. RH1 ... 250 DE132
BUCKHURST HILL, IG9 ... 102 EH45
⊖ Buckhurst Hill ... 102 EK47
Sch Buckhurst Hill Prim Sch, Buck.H. IG9 off Lower Queens Rd ... 102 EL47
Buckhurst La, Sev. TN13 ... 257 FJ125
Buckhurst Rd, West. TN16 ... 239 EN121
Buckhurst St, E1 ... 12 D4
Buckhurst Way, Buck.H. IG9 ... 102 EK49
Buckingham Arc, WC2 ... 9 P10
Buckingham Av, N20 ... 98 DC45
Feltham TW14 ... 175 BV86
Greenford UB6 ... 137 CG67
Slough SL1 ... 131 AN72
Thornton Heath CR7 ... 201 DN95
Welling DA16 ... 165 ES84
West Molesey KT8 ... 196 CB97
Buckingham Av E, Slou. SL1 ... 131 AQ72
Buckingham Cl, W5 ... 137 CJ71
Enfield EN1 ... 82 DS40
Guildford GU1 ... 243 AZ133
Hampton TW12 ... 176 BZ92
Hornchurch RM11 ... 128 FK58
Orpington BR5 ... 205 ES101
Coll Buckingham Coll Sch, Har. HA1 off Hindes Rd ... 117 CE57
Buckingham Ct, NW4 ... 119 CU55
Loughton IG10 off Rectory La ... 85 EN40
Buckingham Dr, Chis. BR7 ... 185 EP92
Buckingham Gdns, Edg. HA8 ... 96 CM52
Slough SL1 ... 152 AT75
Thornton Heath CR7 ... 201 DN96
West Molesey KT8 off Buckingham Av ... 196 CB96
Buckingham Gate, SW1 ... 19 J4
Gatwick RH6 ... 269 DJ152
Buckingham Gro, Uxb. UB10 ... 134 BN68
Buckingham La, SE23 ... 183 DY87
Buckingham Ms, N1 ... 5 M4
NW10 off Buckingham Rd ... 139 CT68
SW1 ... 19 J5
★ Buckingham Palace, SW1 ... 19 H4
Buckingham Palace Rd, SW1 ... 18 G8
Buckingham Pl, SW1 ... 19 J5
Sch Buckingham Prim Sch, Hmptn. TW12 off Buckingham Rd ... 176 BZ92
Buckingham Rd, E10 ... 123 EB62
E11 ... 124 EJ57
E15 ... 124 EF64
E18 ... 102 EF53
N1 ... 5 L4
N22 ... 99 DL53
NW10 ... 139 CT68
Borehamwood WD6 ... 78 CR42
Edgware HA8 ... 96 CM52
Gravesend DA11 off Dover Rd ... 190 GD87
Hampton TW12 ... 176 BZ91
Harrow HA1 ... 117 CD57
Ilford IG1 ... 125 ER61
Kingston upon Thames KT1 ... 198 CM98
Mitcham CR4 ... 201 DL99
Richmond TW10 ... 177 CK89
Watford WD24 ... 76 BW37
Uni Buckinghamshire Chilterns Uni Coll, Chalfont Campus, Ch.St.G. HP8 off Gorelands La ... 91 BA47
Chalfont Campus Halls of Res, Ch.St.G. HP8 off Gorelands La ... 91 BA46
Buckingham St, WC2 ... 9 P10
Buckingham Way, Wall. SM6 ... 219 DJ109
BUCKLAND, Bet. RH3 ... 249 CU133
Buckland Av, Slou. SL3 ... 152 AV77
Buckland Ct Gdns, Bet. RH3 ... 249 CU133
Buckland Cres, NW3 ... 140 DD66
Windsor SL4 ... 151 AM81
Buckland Gate, Slou. (Wexham) SL2 ... 132 AV68
Sch Buckland Inf Sch, Chess. KT9 off Buckland Rd ... 216 CM105
Staines TW18 off Berryscroft Rd ... 174 BJ94
Sch Buckland Jun Sch, Stai. TW18 off Berryscroft Rd ... 174 BJ94
Buckland La, Bet. RH3 ... 249 CT129
Tadworth KT20 ... 249 CT129
Buckland Ri, Pnr. HA5 ... 94 BW53
Buckland Rd, E10 ... 123 EC61
Chessington KT9 ... 216 CM106
Orpington BR6 ... 223 ES105
Reigate RH2 ... 249 CX133
Sutton SM2 ... 217 CW110
Tadworth (Lwr Kgswd) KT20 ... 249 CZ128
Bucklands, The, Rick. WD3 ... 92 BG45
Bucklands Rd, Tedd. TW11 ... 177 CJ93
Buckland St, N1 ... 5 K10
Buckland Wk, W3 ... 158 CQ75
Morden SM4 ... 200 DC98
Buckland Way, Wor.Pk. KT4 ... 199 CW102
Buck La, NW9 ... 118 CR57
Bucklebury Cl, Maid. SL6 ... 150 AC78
Buckleigh Av, SW20 ... 199 CY97
Buckleigh Rd, SW16 ... 181 DK93
Buckleigh Way, SE19 ... 202 DT95
Buckler Gdns, SE9 off Southold Ri ... 185 EM90
Bucklers All, SW6 ... 159 CZ79
Bucklersbury, EC4 ... 11 J8
Bucklersbury Pas, EC4 ... 11 J8
Bucklers Cl, Brox. EN10 ... 49 DZ22
Bucklers Ct, Brwd. CM14 ... 108 FW50
Bucklers Way, Cars. SM5 ... 200 DF104
Buckles Ct, Belv. DA17 off Fendyke Rd ... 166 EX76
Buckles La, S.Ock. RM15 ... 149 FW71
Buckle St, E1 ... 11 P7
Buckles Way, Bans. SM7 ... 233 CY116
Buckley Cl, SE23 ... 182 DV87
Dartford DA1 ... 167 FF82
Buckley Rd, NW6 ... 139 CZ66
Buckley St, SE1 off Mepham St ... 141 DN74
Buckmaster Cl, SW9 off Stockwell Pk Rd ... 161 DM83
Buckmaster Rd, SW11 ... 160 DE84
Bucknalls Cl, Wat. WD25 ... 60 BY32
Bucknalls Dr, St.Alb. (Brick.Wd) AL2 ... 60 BZ31
Bucknalls La, Wat. WD25 ... 60 BX32
Bucknall St, WC2 ... 9 M7
Bucknall Way, Beck. BR3 ... 203 EB98
Bucknell Cl, SW2 ... 161 DM84
Buckner Rd, SW2 ... 161 DM84
Bucknills Cl, Epsom KT18 ... 216 CP114
Buckrell Rd, E4 ... 101 ED47
Bucks All, Hert. SG13 ... 47 DK19
Bucks Av, Wat. WD19 ... 94 BY45
Bucks Cl, W.Byf. KT14 ... 212 BH114
Bucks Cross Rd, Grav. (Nthflt) DA11 ... 191 GF90
Orpington BR6 ... 224 EY106
BUCKS HILL, Kings L. WD4 ... 58 BK34
Bucks Hill, Kings L. WD4 ... 58 BK34
Buckstone Cl, SE23 ... 182 DW86
Buckstone Rd, N18 ... 100 DU51
Buck St, NW1 ... 141 DH66
Buckters Rents, SE16 ... 23 J2
Buckthorne Ho, Chig. IG7 ... 104 EV49
Buckthorne Rd, SE4 ... 183 DY86
Buckton Rd, Borwd. WD6 ... 78 CM38
Buck Wk, E17 off Wood St ... 123 ED56
Budd Cl, N12 ... 98 DB49
Buddcroft, Welw.G.C. AL7 ... 30 DB08
Buddings Circle, Wem. HA9 ... 118 CQ62
Budd's All, Twick. TW1 off Arlington Cl ... 177 CJ85
Budebury Rd, Stai. TW18 ... 174 BG92
Bude Cl, E17 ... 123 DZ57
Budge La, Mitch. CR4 ... 200 DF101
Budgen Dr, Red. RH1 ... 250 DG131
Budge Row, EC4 ... 11 J9
Budge's Wk, W2 ... 17 L1
Budgin's Hill, Orp. BR6 ... 224 EW112
Budleigh Cres, Well. DA16 ... 166 EW81
Budoch Ct, Ilf. IG3 ... 126 EU61
Budoch Dr, Ilf. IG3 ... 126 EU61
Buer Rd, SW6 ... 159 CY82
Buff Av, Bans. SM7 ... 218 DB114
Buffers La, Lthd. KT22 off Kingston Rd ... 231 CG119
Buffins, Maid. (Taplow) SL6 ... 130 AE69
Bug Hill, Cat. (Wold.) CR3 ... 237 DX120
Bugsby's Way, SE7 ... 25 M8
SE10 ... 25 J7
Coll Building Crafts Coll, E15 off Kennard Rd ... 143 ED66
Bulbourne Cl, Berk. HP4 ... 38 AT17
Hemel Hempstead HP1 ... 40 BG21
Bulganak Rd, Th.Hth. CR7 ... 202 DQ98
Bulinga St, SW1 ... 19 M8

Bulkeley Av, Wind. SL4 ....151 AP82
Bulkeley Cl, Egh. (Eng.Grn)
TW20 ....172 AW91
Bullace Cl, Hem.H. HP1 ....40 BG19
Bullace La, Dart. DA1
off High St 188 FL86
Bullace Row, SE5 ....162 DR80
Bull All, Well. DA16
off Welling High St 166 EV83
Bullards Pl, E2 ....12 G1
Bullbanks Rd, Belv. DA17 ....167 FC77
Bullbeggars La, Berk. HP4 ....39 AZ20
Godstone RH9 ....252 DW132
Woking GU21 ....226 AV116
Bull Cl, Grays RM16 ....170 FZ75
BULLEN'S GREEN, St.Alb.
AL4 ....44 CS22
Bullens Grn La, St.Alb.
(Coln.Hth) AL4 ....44 CS23
Bullen St, SW11 ....160 DE82
Buller Cl, SE15 ....162 DU80
Buller Rd, N17 ....100 DU54
N22 ....99 DN54
NW10 ....6 B2
Barking IG11 ....145 ES66
Thornton Heath CR7 ....202 DR96
Bullers Cl, Sid. DA14 ....186 EY92
Bullers Wd Dr, Chis. BR7 ....184 EL94
Sch Bullers Wd Sch, Chis.
BR7 off Logs Hill 204 EL95
Bullescroft Rd, Edg. HA8 ....96 CN48
Bullfinch Cl, Horl. RH6 ....268 DE147
Sevenoaks TN13 ....256 FD122
Bullfinch Dene, Sev. TN13 ....256 FD122
Bullfinch La, Sev. TN13 ....256 FD122
Bullfinch Rd, S.Croy. CR2 ....221 DX110
Bullhead Rd, Borwd. WD6 ....78 CQ41
Bull Hill, Dart. (Hort.Kir.)
DA4 ....208 FQ98
Leatherhead KT22 ....231 CG121
Bullied Way, SW1 ....19 H8
Bull Inn Ct, WC2 ....9 P10
Bullivant Cl, Green. DA9 ....189 FU85
Bullivant St, E14 ....14 C8
Bull La, N18 ....100 DS50
Chislehurst BR7 ....185 ER94
Dagenham RM10 ....127 FB62
Gerrards Cross (Chal.St.P.)
SL9 ....112 AX55
Guildford (Sutt.Grn) GU4 ....243 AZ126
Bullocks La, Hert. SG13 ....32 DQ11
Bull Plain, Hert. SG14 ....32 DR09
Bull Rd, E15 ....144 EF68
Bullrush Cl, Croy. CR0 ....202 DS100
Hatfield AL10 ....45 CV19
Bullrush Gro, Uxb. UB8 ....134 BJ70
Bull's All, SW14 ....158 CR82
Bulls Br Ind Est, Sthl. UB2 ....155 BV77
Bulls Br Rd, Sthl. UB2 ....155 BV76
Bullsbrook Rd, Hayes UB4 ....136 BW74
BULLS CROSS, Wal.Cr. EN7 ....82 DT35
Bulls Cross, Enf. EN2 ....82 DU37
Bulls Cross Ride, Wal.Cr.
EN7 ....82 DU35
Bulls Gdns, SW3 ....18 B7
Bull's Head Pas, EC3 ....11 L8
Bullsland Gdns, Rick.
(Chorl.) WD3 ....73 BB44
Bullsland La, Ger.Cr. SL9 ....91 BB45
Rickmansworth (Chorl.)
WD3 ....73 BB44
Bulls La, Hat. AL9 ....45 CZ24
BULLSMOOR, Enf. EN1 ....82 DV37
Bullsmoor Cl, Wal.Cr. EN8 ....82 DW35
Bullsmoor Gdns, Wal.Cr.
EN8 ....82 DV35
Bullsmoor La, Enf. EN1, EN3 ....82 DW35
Waltham Cross EN7 ....82 DU35
Bullsmoor Ride, Wal.Cr. EN8 ....82 DW35
Bullsmoor Way, Wal.Cr. EN8 ....82 DV35
Bull Stag Grn, Hat. AL9 ....45 CW15
Bullwell Cres, Wal.Cr. (Chsht)
EN8 ....67 DY29
Bull Yd, SE15
off Peckham High St 162 DU81
Gravesend DA12
off High St 191 GH86
Bulmer Gdns, Har. HA3 ....117 CK59
Bulmer Ms, W11 ....16 G1
Bulmer Pl, W11 ....16 G1
Bulmer Wk, Rain. RM13 ....148 FJ68
Bulow Est, SW6
off Broughton Rd 160 DB82
Bulrush Cl, Cars. SM5 ....200 DE103
Bulstrode Av, Houns. TW3 ....156 BZ82
Bulstrode Ct, Ger.Cr. SL9 ....112 AX58
Bulstrode Gdns, Houns.
TW3 ....156 BZ83
Bulstrode La, Hem.H.
(Felden) HP3 ....58 BG27
Kings Langley (Chipper.)
WD4 ....57 BE29
Bulstrode Pl, W1 ....8 F6
Slough SL1 ....152 AT76
Bulstrode Rd, Houns. TW3 ....156 CA83
Bulstrode St, W1 ....8 F7
Bulstrode Way, Ger.Cr. SL9 ....112 AX57
Bulwer Ct Rd, E11 ....123 ED60
Bulwer Gdns, Barn. EN5
off Bulwer Rd 80 DC42
Bulwer Rd, E11 ....123 ED59
N18 ....100 DS49
Barnet EN5 ....80 DB42
Bulwer St, W12 ....139 CW74
BUMBLE'S GREEN, Wal.Abb.
EN9 ....50 EG24
Bumbles Grn La, Wal.Abb.
EN9 ....68 EH25
Bunbury Way, Epsom KT17 ....233 CV116
Bunby Rd, Slou. (Stoke P.)
SL2 ....132 AT66
BUNCE COMMON, Reig.
RH2 ....264 CR141
Bunce Common Rd, Reig.
(Leigh) RH2 ....264 CR141
Bunce Dr, Cat. CR3 ....236 DR123
Buncefield La, Hem.H. HP2 ....41 BR20
Buncefield Terminal, Hem.H.
HP2 off Green La 41 BR18
Bunces Cl, Wind. (Eton Wick)
SL4 ....151 AP78
Bunces La, Wdf.Grn. IG8 ....102 EF52
Bundys Way, Stai. TW18 ....173 BF93
Bungalow Rd, SE25 ....202 DS98
Woking GU23 ....229 BQ124
Bungalows, The, SW16 ....181 DH94
Wallington SM6 ....219 DH106
Bunhill Row, EC1 ....11 J3
Bunhouse Pl, SW1 ....18 E9
Bunkers Hill, NW11 ....120 DC59
Belvedere DA17 ....166 FA77
Sidcup DA14 ....186 EZ90
Bunkers La, Hem.H. HP3 ....41 BQ24
Bunning Way, N7 ....141 DL66
Bunnsfield, Welw.G.C. AL7 ....30 DC08
Bunns La, NW7 ....97 CT51
Bunn's La, Chesh. HP5 ....56 AU34
Bunsen St, E3
off Kenilworth Rd 143 DY68
Bunten Meade, Slou. SL1 ....131 AP74
Buntingbridge Rd, Ilf. IG2 ....125 ER57
Bunting Cl, N9
off Dunnock Cl 101 DX46
Mitcham CR4 ....200 DF99
Bunton St, SE18 ....165 EN76
Bunyan Ct, EC2
off Beech St 142 DQ71
Bunyan Rd, E17 ....123 DY55
Bunyard Dr, Wok. GU21 ....211 BC114
Bunyons Cl, Brwd. CM13
off Essex Way 107 FW51
Buonaparte Ms, SW1 ....19 L9
H BUPA Bushey Hosp,
Bushey WD23 ....95 CF46
H BUPA Gatwick Pk Hosp,
Horl. RH6 ....268 DE149
H BUPA Hartswood Hosp,
Brwd. CM13 ....107 FV51
H BUPA Redwood Hosp,
Red. RH1 ....266 DG138
H BUPA Roding Hosp, Ilf.
IG4 ....124 EK55
Burbage Cl, SE1 ....21 J6
Hayes UB3 ....135 BR72
Waltham Cross (Chsht)
EN8 ....67 DZ31
Sch Burbage JMI Sch, N1 ....5 L9
Burbage Rd, SE21 ....182 DR86
SE24 ....182 DQ86
Burberry Cl, N.Mal. KT3 ....198 CS96
Burbidge Rd, Shep. TW17 ....194 BN98
Burbridge Way, N17 ....100 DT54
Burcham St, E14 ....14 B7
Burcharbro Rd, SE2 ....166 EX79
Burchell Ct, Bushey WD23
off Catsey La 94 CC45
Burchell Rd, E10 ....123 EB60
SE15 ....162 DV81
Burchets Hollow, Guil.
(Peasl.) GU5 ....261 BR144
Burchetts Way, Shep. TW17 ....195 BP100
Burchett Way, Rom. RM6 ....126 EZ58
Burch Rd, Grav. (Nthflt)
DA11 ....191 GF86
Burchwall Cl, Rom. RM5 ....105 FC52
Burcote, Wey. KT13 ....213 BR107
Burcote Rd, SW18 ....180 DD88
Burcott Gdns, Add. KT15 ....212 BJ107
Burcott Rd, Pur. CR8 ....219 DN114
Burden Cl, Brent. TW8 ....157 CJ78
Burdenshott Hill, Guil.
(Worp.) GU3 ....242 AU125
Burdenshott Av, Rich. TW10 ....158 CP84
Burdenshott Rd, Guil.
(Worp.) GU3 ....242 AU125
Woking GU22 ....242 AU125
Burden Way, E11
off Brading Cres 124 EH61
Guildford GU2 ....242 AV129
Burder Cl, N1 ....5 M3
Burder Rd, N1 ....5 M3
Burdett Av, SW20 ....199 CU95
Burdett Cl, W7
off Cherington Rd 157 CF75
Sidcup DA14 ....186 EY92
Sch Burdett Coutts C of E
Prim Sch, SW1 ....19 L6
Burdett Ms, NW3
off Belsize Cres 140 DD65
W2 ....7 J7
Burdett Rd, E3 ....13 K3
E14 ....13 K3
Croydon CR0 ....202 DR100
Richmond TW9 ....158 CM83
Burdetts Rd, Dag. RM9 ....146 EZ67
Burdett St, SE1 ....20 C5
Burdock Cl, Croy. CR0 ....203 DX102
Burdock Rd, N17 ....122 DU55
Burdon La, Sutt. SM2 ....217 CY108
Burdon Pk, Sutt. SM2 ....217 CZ109
Burfield Cl, SW17 ....180 DD91
Hatfield AL10 ....45 CU16
Burfield Dr, Warl. CR6 ....236 DW119
Burfield Rd, Rick. (Chorl.)
WD3 ....73 BB43
Windsor (Old Wind.) SL4 ....172 AU86
Burford Cl, Dag. RM8 ....126 EW62
Ilford IG6 ....125 EQ56
Uxbridge UB10 ....114 BL63
Burford Gdns, N13 ....99 DM48
Hoddesdon EN11 ....49 EB16
Slough SL1
off Buttermere Av 130 AJ71
Burford La, Epsom KT17 ....217 CW111
Burford Ms, Hodd. EN11
off Burford St 49 EA16
Burford Pl, Hodd. EN11 ....49 EB16
Burford Rd, E6 ....144 EL69
E15 ....143 ED66
SE6 ....183 DZ89
Brentford TW8 ....158 CL78
Bromley BR1 ....204 EL98
Sutton SM1 ....200 DA103
Worcester Park KT4 ....199 CT101
Burford St, Hodd. EN11 ....49 EA17
Burford Wk, SW6
off Cambria St 160 DB80
Burford Way, Croy.
(New Adgtn) CR0 ....221 EC107
Burgage La, Ware SG12 ....33 DX06
Burgate Cl, Dart. DA1 ....167 FF83
Burges Cl, Horn. RM11 ....128 FM58
Burges Ct, E6 ....145 EN66
Burges Gro, SW13 ....159 CV80
Burges Rd, E6 ....144 EL66
Burgess Av, NW9 ....118 CR58
Burgess Cl, Felt. TW13 ....176 BY91
Waltham Cross (Chsht)
EN7 ....66 DQ25
Burgess Ct, Borwd. WD6
off Belford Rd 78 CM38
Burgess Hill, NW2 ....120 DA63
Burgess Rd, E15 ....124 EE63
Sutton SM1 ....218 DB105
Burgess St, E14 ....13 N6
Burgess Wd Gro, Beac. HP9 ....88 AH53
Burgess Wd Rd, Beac. HP9 ....88 AH53
Burgess Wd Rd S, Beac. HP9 ....110 AH55
Burge St, SE1 ....21 K6
Burges Way, Stai. TW18 ....174 BG92
Burgett Rd, Slou. SL1 ....151 AP76
Burghfield, Epsom KT17 ....233 CT115
Burghfield Rd, Grav.
(Istead Rise) DA13 ....191 GF94
BURGH HEATH, Tad. KT20 ....233 CX119
Burgh Heath Rd, Epsom
KT17 ....216 CS114
★ Burgh Ho (Hampstead Mus),
NW3 off New End Sq 120 DD63
Burghill Rd, SE26 ....183 DY91
Burghley Av, Borwd. WD6 ....78 CQ43
Burghley Av, N. Mal. KT3 ....198 CR95
Burghley Hall Cl, SW19 ....179 CY87
Burghley Ho, SW19 ....179 CY90
Burghley Pl, Mitch. CR4 ....200 DG99
Burghley Rd, E11 ....124 EE60
N8 ....121 DN55
NW5 ....121 DH64
SW19 ....179 CX91
Grays (Chaff.Hun.) RM16 ....169 FW76
Burghley Twr, W3 ....139 CT73
Burgh Mt, Bans. SM7 ....233 CZ115
Burgh St, N1 ....4 F9
Burgh Wd, Bans. SM7 ....233 CY115
Burgon St, EC4 ....10 F8
Burgos Cl, Croy. CR0 ....219 DN107
Burgos Gro, SE10 ....163 EB81
Burgoyne Hatch, Harl.
CM20 off Momples Rd 36 EU14
Burgoyne Rd, N4 ....121 DP58
SE25 ....202 DT98
SW9 ....161 DM83
Sunbury-on-Thames
TW16 ....175 BT93
Burgundy Cft, Welw.G.C.
AL7 ....29 CZ11
Burham Cl, SE20
off Maple Rd 182 DW94
Sch Burhill Comm Inf Sch, Walt.
KT12 off Pleasant Pl 214 BX107
Burhill Gro, Pnr. HA5 ....94 BY54
Burhill Rd, Walt. KT12 ....214 BW107
Burke Cl, SW15 ....158 CS84
Burkes Cl, Beac. HP9 ....110 AH55
Burkes Cres, Beac. HP9 ....89 AK53
Burkes Par, Beac. HP9
off Station Rd 89 AK52
Burkes Rd, Beac. HP9 ....88 AJ54
Burke St, E16 ....15 K6
Burket Cl, Sthl. UB2
off Kingsbridge Rd 156 BZ77
Burland Rd, SW11 ....180 DF85
Brentwood CM15 ....108 FX46
Romford RM5 ....105 FC51
Burlea Cl, Walt. KT12 ....213 BV106
Burleigh Av, Sid. DA15 ....185 ET85
Wallington SM6 ....200 DG104
Burleigh Cl, Add. KT15 ....212 BH106
Sch Burleigh Co Prim Sch,
Wal.Cr. EN8
off Blindman's La 67 DX29
Burleigh Gdns, N14 ....99 DJ46
Ashford TW15 ....175 BQ92
Burleigh Ho, W10 ....6 B5
Burleigh Mead, Hat. AL9 ....45 CW16
Burleigh Pk, Cob. KT11 ....214 BY112
Burleigh Pl, SW15 ....179 CX85
Burleigh Rd, Add. KT15 ....212 BH105
Enfield EN1 ....82 DS42
Hemel Hempstead HP2 ....41 BQ21
Hertford SG13 ....32 DU08
St. Albans AL1 ....43 CH20
Sutton SM3 ....199 CY102
Uxbridge UB10 ....135 BP67
Waltham Cross (Chsht)
EN8 ....67 DY32
Burleigh St, WC2 ....10 A9
Burleigh Wk, SE6
off Muirkirk Rd 183 EC88
Burleigh Way, Enf. EN2
off Church St 82 DR41
Potters Bar (Cuffley) EN6 ....65 DL30
Burley Cl, E4 ....101 EA50
SW16 ....201 DK96
Burley Hill, Harl. CM17 ....52 EX16
Burley Orchard, Cher. KT16 ....194 BG100
Burley Rd, E16 ....144 EJ72
Burlingham Cl, Guil. GU4
off Gilliat Dr 243 BD132
Burlings La, Sev. (Knock.)
TN14 ....239 ET118
Burlington Arc, W1 ....9 J10
Burlington Av, Rich. TW9 ....158 CN81
Romford RM7 ....127 FB58
Slough SL1 ....152 AS75
Burlington Cl, E6
off Northumberland Rd 144 EL72
W9 ....6 F4
Feltham TW14 ....175 BR87
Orpington BR6 ....205 EP103
Pinner HA5 ....115 BV55
Sch Burlington Danes Sch,
W12 off Wood La 139 CV72
Burlington Gdns, W1 ....9 J10
W3 ....138 CQ74
W4 ....158 CQ78
Romford RM6 ....126 EY59
Sch Burlington Inf Sch, N.Mal.
KT3 off Burlington Rd 199 CT98
Sch Burlington Jun Sch, N.Mal.
KT3 off Burlington Rd 199 CT98
Burlington La, W4 ....158 CS80
Burlington Ms, SW15 ....179 CZ85
W3 ....138 CQ74
Burlington Pl, SW6
off Burlington Rd 159 CY82
Reigate RH2 ....250 DA134
Woodford Green IG8 ....102 EG48
Burlington Ri, Barn. EN4 ....98 DE46
Burlington Rd, N10
off Tetherdown 98 DG54
N17 ....100 DU53
SW6 ....159 CY82
W4 ....158 CQ78
Enfield EN2 ....82 DR39
Isleworth TW7 ....157 CD81
New Malden KT3 ....199 CU98
Slough SL1 ....152 AS75
Slough (Burn.) SL1 ....130 AH70
Thornton Heath CR7 ....202 DQ96
Burman Cl, Dart. DA2 ....188 FQ87
Burma Rd, N16 ....122 DR63
Chertsey (Longcr.) KT16 ....192 AT104
Burmester Rd, SW17 ....180 DC90
Burnaby Cres, W4 ....158 CP79
Burnaby Gdns, W4 ....158 CQ79
Burnaby Rd, Grav. (Nthflt)
DA11 ....190 GE87
Burnaby St, SW10 ....160 DC80
Burnbrae Cl, N12 ....98 DB51
Burnbury Rd, SW12 ....181 DJ88
Burn Cl, Add. KT15 ....212 BK105
Leatherhead (Oxshott)
KT22 ....230 CC115
Burncroft Av, Enf. EN3 ....82 DW40
Burndell Way, Hayes UB4 ....136 BY71
Burne Jones Ho, W14 ....16 E8
Burnell Av, Rich. TW10 ....177 CJ92
Welling DA16 ....166 EU82
Burnell Gdns, Stan. HA7 ....95 CK53
Burnell Rd, Sutt. SM1 ....218 DB105
Burnell Wk, SE1 ....21 P9
Brentwood CM13 ....107 FW51
Burnels Av, E6 ....145 EN69
Burness Cl, N7 ....4 A3
Burness Cl, Uxb. UB8
off Whitehall Rd 134 BK68
Burne St, NW1 ....8 A5
Burnet Av, Guil. GU1 ....243 BB131
Burnet Cl, Hem.H. HP3 ....40 BL21
Burnet Gro, Epsom KT19 ....216 CQ113
Burnett Cl, E9 ....122 DW64
Burnett Pk, Harl. CM19 ....51 EP20
Burnett Rd, Erith DA8 ....168 FK79
Burnett Sq, Hert. SG14 ....31 DM08
Burnetts Rd, Wind. SL4 ....151 AL81
Burney Av, Surb. KT5 ....198 CM99
Burney Cl, Lthd. (Fetch.)
KT22 ....246 CC125
Burney Dr, Loug. IG10 ....85 EP40
Burney Rd, Dor. (Westh.)
RH5 ....247 CG131
Burney St, SE10 ....163 EC80
Burnfoot Av, SW6 ....159 CY81
Burnfoot Ct, SE22 ....182 DV88
BURNHAM, Slou. SL1 ....130 AJ68
⇌ Burnham 131 AK72
Burnham, NW3 ....140 DE66
Burnham Av, Beac. HP9 ....111 AN55
Uxbridge UB10 ....115 BQ63
Burnham Cl, NW7 ....97 CU52
SE1 ....21 P8
Enfield EN1 ....82 DS38
Harrow (Wldste) HA3 ....117 CG56
Windsor SL4 ....151 AK82
Burnham Ct, NW4 ....119 CW56
Burnham Cres, E11 ....124 EJ56
Dartford DA1 ....168 FJ84
Burnham Dr, Reig. RH2 ....250 DA133
Worcester Park KT4 ....199 CX103
Burnham Gdns, Croy. CR0 ....202 DT101
Hayes UB3 ....155 BR76
Hounslow TW4 ....155 BV81
Sch Burnham Gram Sch, Slou.
SL1 off Hogfair La 131 AK70
Burnham Hts, Slou. SL1
off Goldsworthy Way 130 AJ72
Burnham La, Slou. SL1 ....131 AL72
Burnham Rd, E4 ....101 DZ50
Beaconsfield HP9 ....111 AL58
Dagenham RM9 ....146 EV66
Dartford DA1 ....168 FJ84
Morden SM4 ....200 DB99
Romford RM7 ....127 FD55
St. Albans AL1 ....43 CG20
Sidcup DA14 ....186 EY89
Burnhams Rd, Lthd. (Bkhm)
KT23 ....230 BY124
Burnham St, E2 ....12 E1
Kingston upon Thames
KT2 ....198 CN95
Sch Burnham Upr Sch, Slou.
SL1 off Opendale Rd 130 AH71
Burnham Wk, Slou. SL2 ....111 AN64
Burnham Way, SE26 ....183 DZ92
W13 ....157 CH77
Burnhill Cl, SE15
off Gervase St 162 DV80
Burnhill Rd, Beck. BR3 ....203 EA96
Burnley Cl, Wat. WD19 ....94 BW50
Burnley Rd, NW10 ....119 CU64
SW9 ....161 DM82
Grays RM20 ....169 FT81
Burnsall St, SW3 ....18 B9
Burns Av, Felt. TW14 ....175 BU86
Romford (Chad.Hth) RM6 ....126 EW59
Sidcup DA15 ....186 EV86
Southall UB1 ....136 CA73
Burns Cl, E17 ....123 EC56
SW19 ....180 DD93
Carshalton SM5 ....218 DG109
Erith DA8 ....167 FF81
Hayes UB4 ....135 BT71
Welling DA16 ....165 ET81
Burns Dr, Bans. SM7 ....217 CY114
Burnside, Ashtd. KT21 ....232 CM118
Hertford SG14 ....31 DN10
Hoddesdon EN11 ....49 DZ17
St. Albans AL1 ....43 CH22
Sawbridgeworth CM21 ....36 EX05
Burnside Av, E4 ....101 DZ51
Burnside Cl, SE16 ....23 H1
Barnet EN5 ....80 DA41
Hatfield AL10
off Homestead Rd 45 CU15
Twickenham TW1 ....177 CG86
Burnside Cres, Wem. HA0 ....137 CK67
Burnside Rd, Dag. RM8 ....126 EW61
Burnside Ter, Harl. CM17 ....36 EZ12
Burns Pl, Til. RM18 ....171 GH81
Burns Rd, NW10 ....139 CT67
SW11 ....160 DF82
W13 ....157 CH75
Wembley HA0 ....137 CK68
Burns Way, Brwd. (Hutt.)
CM13 ....109 GD45
Hounslow TW5 ....156 BX82
Burnt Ash Hill, SE12 ....184 EF86
Burnt Ash La, Brom. BR1 ....184 EG93
Sch Burnt Ash Prim Sch, Brom.
BR1 off Rangefield Rd 184 EG92
Burnt Ash Rd, SE12 ....184 EF85
Burnt Common Cl, Wok.
(Ripley) GU23 ....243 BF125
Burnt Common La, Wok.
(Ripley) GU23 ....244 BG125
Burnt Fm Ride, Enf. EN2 ....65 DP34
Waltham Cross EN7 ....65 DP31
Burnt Ho La, Dart. (Hawley)
DA2 ....188 FL91
Burnthwaite Rd, SW6 ....160 DA80
Burnt Mill, Harl. CM20 ....35 EQ13
Burnt Mill Cl, Harl. CM20
off Burnt Mill La 35 EQ12
Burntmill Cor, Harl. CM20
off Eastwick Rd 35 EQ11
Burnt Mill La, Harl. CM20 ....35 EQ12
Sch Burnt Mill Sch, Harl.
CM20 off First Av 35 ES13
BURNT OAK, Edg. HA8 ....96 CQ52
⊖ Burnt Oak 96 CQ53
Burnt Oak Bdy, Edg. HA8 ....96 CP52
Burnt Oak Flds, Edg. HA8 ....96 CQ53
Burnt Oak La, Sid. DA15 ....186 EU86
Sch Burnt Oak Sch, Sid.
DA15 off Burnt Oak La 186 EU88
Burntwood, Brwd. CM14 ....108 FW48
Burntwood Av, Horn. RM11 ....128 FK58
Burntwood Cl, SW18 ....180 DD88
Caterham CR3 ....236 DU121
Burntwood Gra Rd, SW18 ....180 DD88
Burntwood Gro, Sev. TN13 ....257 FH127
Burntwood La, SW17 ....180 DE89
Caterham CR3 ....236 DU121
Burntwood Rd, Sev. TN13 ....257 FH128
Sch Burntwood Sch, SW17
off Burntwood La 180 DD89
Burntwood Vw, SE19
off Bowley La 182 DT92
Burn Wk, Slou. (Burn.) SL1 ....130 AH70
Burnway, Horn. RM11 ....128 FL59
Buross St, E1 ....12 D7
BURPHAM, Guil. GU1 ....243 BB130
Burpham Cl, Hayes UB4 ....136 BX71
★ Burpham Court Fm Pk,
Guil. GU4 ....243 AZ128
Burpham La, Guil. GU4 ....243 BA129
Sch Burpham Prim Sch, Guil.
GU4 off Burpham La 243 BA130
Burrage Gro, SE18 ....165 EQ77
Burrage Pl, SE18 ....165 EP78
Burrage Rd, SE18 ....165 EQ79
Burrard Rd, E16 ....15 N7
NW6 ....120 DA64
Burr Cl, E1 ....22 A1
Bexleyheath DA7 ....166 EZ83
St. Albans (Lon.Col.) AL2 ....62 CL27
Burrell, The, Dor. (Westc.)
RH4 ....262 CC137
Burrell Cl, Croy. CR0 ....203 DY100
Edgware HA8 ....96 CP47
Burrell Row, Beck. BR3
off High St 203 EA96
Burrell St, SE1 ....20 E1
Burrells Wf Sq, E14 ....24 A9
Burrell Twr, E10 ....123 EA59
Burrfield Dr, Orp. BR5 ....206 EX99
Burr Hill La, Wok.
(Chobham) GU24 ....210 AS109
Burritt Rd, Kings.T. KT1 ....198 CN96
Burroughs, The, NW4 ....119 CV57
Burroughs Gdns, NW4 ....119 CV56
Burroughs Par, NW4
off The Burroughs 119 CV56
Burroway Rd, Slou. SL3 ....153 BB76
Burrow Cl, Chig. IG7
off Burrow Rd 103 ET50
Burrowfield, Welw.G.C.
AL7 ....29 CX11
Burrow Grn, Chig. IG7 ....103 ET50
BURROWHILL, Wok. GU24 ....210 AS108
Burrow Rd, SE22 ....162 DS84
Chigwell IG7 ....103 ET50
Burrows Chase, Wal.Abb.
EN9 ....83 ED36
Burrows Cl, Guil. GU2 ....242 AT133
High Wycombe (Penn)
HP10 ....88 AC45
Leatherhead (Bkhm)
KT23 ....230 BZ124
Burrows Cross, Guil.
(Goms.) GU5 ....261 BQ141
Burrows La, Guil. (Goms.)
GU5 ....261 BQ140
Burrows Ms, SE1 ....20 E3
Burrows Rd, NW10 ....139 CW69
Burrow Wk, SE21
off Rosendale Rd 182 DQ87
Burr Rd, SW18 ....180 DA87
Bursdon Cl, Sid. DA15 ....185 ET89
Burses Way, Brwd. (Hutt.)
CM13 ....109 GB45
Bursland Rd, Enf. EN3 ....83 DX42
Burslem Av, Ilf. IG6 ....104 EU51
Burslem St, E1 ....12 B8
Burstead Cl, Cob. KT11 ....214 BX113
Sch Bursted Wd Prim Sch,
Bexh. DA7
off Swanbridge Rd 167 FB82
Burstock Rd, SW15 ....159 CY84
Burston Dr, St.Alb.
(Park St) AL2 ....60 CC28
Burston Rd, SW15 ....179 CX85
Burston Vil, SW15
off St. John's Av 179 CX85
BURSTOW, Horl. RH6 ....269 DN152
Burstow Business Cen,
Horl. RH6 ....269 DP146
Sch Burstow Prim Sch, Horl.
RH6 off Wheelers La 269 DP148
Burstow Rd, SW20 ....199 CY95
Burtenshaw Rd, T.Ditt. KT7 ....197 CG101
Burtley Cl, N4 ....122 DQ60
Burton Av, Wat. WD18 ....75 BU42
Burton Cl, Chess. KT9 ....215 CK108
Horley RH6 ....268 DG149
Thornton Heath CR7 ....202 DR97
Burton Ct, SW3
off Franklin's Row 160 DF78
Burton Dr, Enf. EN3 ....83 EA37
Burton Gdns, Houns. TW5 ....156 BZ81
Burton Gro, SE17 ....21 J10
Burtonhole Cl, NW7 ....97 CX49
Burtonhole La, NW7 ....97 CY49
Burton La, SW9 ....161 DN82
Waltham Cross (Chsht)
EN7 ....66 DS29
Burton Ms, SW1 ....18 F8
Burton Pl, WC1 ....9 M2
Burton Rd, E18 ....124 EH55
NW6 ....139 CZ66
SW9 ....161 DP82
Kingston upon Thames
KT2 ....178 CL94
Loughton IG10 ....85 EQ42
Burtons La, Ch.St.G. HP8 ....73 AZ43
Rickmansworth WD3 ....73 AZ43
Burtons Rd, Hmptn.
(Hmptn H.) TW12 ....176 CB91
Burton St, WC1 ....9 M2
Burtons Way, Ch.St.G. HP8 ....72 AW40
Burton Way, Wind. SL4 ....151 AL83
Burt Rd, E16 ....144 EJ74
Burtwell La, SE27 ....182 DR91
Burwash Ct, Orp. BR5
off Rookery Gdns 206 EW99
Burwash Ho, SE1 ....21 K4
Burwash Rd, SE18 ....165 ER78
Burway Cres, Cher. KT16 ....194 BG97
Burwell Av, Grnf. UB6 ....137 CE65
Burwell Cl, E1 ....12 D8
Burwell Rd, E10 ....123 DY60
Burwell Wk, E3 ....13 P3
Burwood Av, Brom. BR2 ....204 EH103
Kenley CR8 ....219 DP114
Pinner HA5 ....116 BW57
Burwood Cl, Guil. GU1 ....243 BD133
Reigate RH2 ....250 DD134
Surbiton KT6 ....198 CN102
Walton-on-Thames
KT12 ....214 BW107
Burwood Gdns, Rain. RM13 ....147 FF69
BURWOOD PARK, Walt.
KT12 ....213 BT106
Burwood Pk Rd, Walt. KT12 ....213 BV105
Burwood Pl, W2 ....8 B7
Burwood Rd, Walt. KT12 ....213 BV107
Sch Burwood Sch, Orp. BR6
off Avalon Rd 206 EX103

⊖ London Underground station   DLR Docklands Light Railway station   Tra Tramlink station   Riv Pedestrian ferry landing stage

Bury,The, Chesh. HP5
off Church St 54 AP31
Hemel Hempstead HP1
off Queensway 40 BJ19
Bury Av, Hayes UB4 135 BS68
Ruislip HA4 115 BQ58
Bury Cl, SE16 23 H1
Woking GU21 226 AX116
Bury Ct, EC3 11 M7
Burycroft, Welw.G.C. AL8 29 CY06
Burydell La, St.Alb. (Park St)
AL2 61 CD27
Bury Fm, Amer. HP7
off Gore Hill 55 AP40
Bury Flds, Guil. GU2 258 AW136
BURY GREEN, Wal.Cr. EN7 66 DV31
Bury Grn, Hem.H. HP1 40 BJ19
Bury Grn Rd, Wal.Cr. (Chshtt)
EN7 66 DU31
Bury Gro, Mord. SM4 200 DB99
Bury Hill, Hem.H. HP1 40 BH19
Bury Hill Cl, Hem.H. HP1 40 BJ19
Buryholme, Brox. EN10 49 DZ23
Bury La, Chesh. HP5 54 AP31
Epping CM16 69 ES31
Rickmansworth WD3 92 BK46
Woking GU21 226 AW116
Bury Meadows, Rick. WD3 92 BK46
Bury Pl, WC1 9 N6
Bury Ri, Hem.H. HP3 57 BD25
Bury Rd, E4 84 EE43
N22 121 DN55
Dagenham RM10 127 FB64
Epping CM16 69 ES31
Harlow CM17 36 EW11
Hatfield AL10 45 CW17
Hemel Hempstead HP1 40 BJ19
Sch Burys Ct Sch, Reig. RH2
off Flanchford Rd 265 CX140
Buryside Cl, Ilf. IG2 125 ET56
Bury St, EC3 11 M8
N9 100 DU46
SW1 19 J1
Guildford GU2 258 AW136
Ruislip HA4 115 BQ57
Bury St W, N9 100 DR45
Bury Wk, SW3 18 A8
Busbridge Ho, E14 13 P7
Busby Pl, NW5 141 DK65
Busby St, E2 11 P3
Bushbaby Cl, SE1 21 L6
Bushbarns, Wal.Cr. (Chshtt)
EN7 66 DU29
Bushberry Rd, E9 143 DY65
Bushbury La, Bet. RH3 264 CN139
Bushby Av, Brox. EN10 49 DZ22
Bush Cl, Add. KT15 212 BJ106
Ilford IG2 125 ER57
Bush Cotts, SW18
off Putney Br Rd 180 DA85
Bush Ct, W12 16 B3
Bushell Cl, SW2 181 DM89
Bushell Grn, Bushey
(Bushey Hth) WD23 95 CD47
Bushell St, E1 22 B2
Bushell Way, Chis. BR7 185 EN92
Bush Elms Rd, Horn. RM11 127 FG59
Bushetts Gro, Red. RH1 251 DH129
BUSHEY, WD23 94 CA45
⇌ Bushey 76 BX44
Bushey Av, E18 124 EF55
Orpington BR5 205 ER101
Bushey Cl, E4 101 EC48
Kenley CR8 236 DS116
Uxbridge UB10 115 BP61
Welwyn Garden City AL7 30 DB10
Bushey Ct, SW20 199 CV96
Bushey Cft, Harl. CM18 51 ES17
Oxted RH8 253 EC130
Bushey Down, SW12
off Bedford Hill 181 DH89
Bushey Grn, Welw.G.C. AL7 30 DB10
Bushey Gro Rd, Bushey
WD23 76 BX42
Bushey Hall Dr, Bushey
WD23 76 BY42
Bushey Hall Rd, Bushey
WD23 76 BX42
Sch Bushey Hall Sch, Bushey
WD23
off London Rd 76 BZ44
BUSHEY HEATH, Bushey
WD23 95 CE46
Sch Bushey Heath Prim Sch,
Bushey WD23
off The Rutts 95 CD46
Bushey Hill Rd, SE5 162 DS81
Bushey La, Sutt. SM1 218 DA105
Bushey Lees, Sid. DA15
off Fen Gro 185 ET86
Bushey Ley, Welw.G.C. AL7 30 DB10
Sch Bushey Manor JM Sch,
Bushey WD23
off Grange Rd 76 BY44
BUSHEY MEAD, SW20 199 CX97
Sch Bushey Meads Sec Sch,
Bushey WD23
off Coldharbour La 76 CC43
Bushey Mill Cres, Wat.
WD24 76 BW37
Bushey Mill La, Bushey
WD23 76 BZ40
Watford WD24 76 BW37
Bushey Rd, E13 144 EJ68
N15 122 DS58
SW20 199 CV97
Croydon CR0 203 EA103
Hayes UB3 155 BS77
Sutton SM1 218 DB105
Uxbridge UB10 114 BN61
Bushey Shaw, Ashtd. KT21 231 CH117
Bushey Vw Wk, Wat. WD24 76 BX40
Bushey Way, Beck. BR3 203 ED100
Bush Fair, Harl. CM18 51 ET17
Bushfield Cl, Edg. HA8 96 CP47
Bushfield Cres, Edg. HA8 96 CP47
Bushfield Dr, Red. RH1 266 DG139
Bushfield Rd, Hem.H. (Bov.)
HP3 57 BC25
Bushfields, Loug. IG10 85 EN43
Bushfield Wk, Swans. DA10 190 FY86
Bush Gro, NW9 118 CQ59
Stanmore HA7 95 CK53
Bushgrove Rd, Dag. RM8 126 EX63
Bush Hall Fm, Harl. CM17 53 FB16
Bush Hall La, Hat. AL9 45 CX15
Bush Hill, N21 100 DQ45
BUSH HILL PARK, Enf. EN1 82 DS43
⇌ Bush Hill Park 82 DT44
Sch Bush Hill Pk Prim Sch, Enf.
EN1 off Main Av 82 DU43
Bush Hill Rd, N21 82 DR44
Harrow HA3 118 CM58
Bush Ind Est, NW10 138 CR70
Bush La, EC4 11 J9
Woking (Send) GU23 227 BD124
Bushmead Cl, N15
off Copperfield Dr 122 DT56
Bushmoor Cres, SE18 165 EQ80
Bushnell Rd, SW17 181 DH89
Bush Rd, E8 142 DV67
E11 124 EF59
SE8 23 H7
Buckhurst Hill IG9 102 EK49
Richmond TW9 158 CM79
Shepperton TW17 194 BM99
Bushway, Dag. RM8 126 EX63
Bushwood, E11 124 EF60
Bushwood Cl, Hat. AL9
off Dellsome La 45 CV23
Bushwood Dr, SE1 21 P8
Bushwood Rd, Rich. TW9 158 CN79
BUSHY HILL, Guil. GU1 243 BC132
Bushy Hill Dr, Guil. GU1 243 BB132
Sch Bushy Hill Sch, Guil. GU1
off Sheeplands Av 243 BD133
★ Bushy Park, Tedd. TW11 197 CF95
Bushy Pk, Hmptn. (Hmptn H.)
TW12 197 CF95
Teddington TW11 197 CF95
Bushy Pk Gdns, Tedd. TW11 177 CD92
Bushy Pk Rd, Tedd. TW11 177 CH94
Bushy Rd, Lthd. (Fetch.)
KT22 230 CB122
Teddington TW11 177 CF93
★ Business Design Cen, N1 4 D8
Business Village, The, Slou.
SL2 132 AV74
Buslins La, Chesh. HP5 54 AL28
Butcher Row, E1 13 H9
E14 13 H9
Butchers La, Sev. TN15 209 FX103
Butchers Rd, E16 15 M7
Butcher Wk, Swans. DA10 190 FY87
Bute Av, Rich. TW10 178 CL89
Bute Ct, Wall. SM6
off Bute Rd 219 DJ106
Bute Gdns, W6 16 A8
Wallington SM6 219 DJ106
Bute Gdns W, Wall. SM6 219 DJ106
Sch Bute Ho Prep Sch
for Girls, W6 16 A7
Bute Ms, NW11
off Northway 120 DB57
Bute Rd, Croy. CR0 201 DN102
Ilford IG6 125 EP57
Wallington SM6 219 DJ105
Bute St, SW7 17 N7
Bute Wk, N1 5 J4
Butler Av, Har. HA1 117 CD59
Butler Ct, Wem. HA0
off Harrow Rd 117 CG63
Butler Ho, Grays RM17
off Argent St 170 GB79
Butler Pl, SW1 19 L5
Butler Rd, NW10
off Curzon Cres 139 CT66
Dagenham RM8 126 EV63
Harrow HA1 116 CC59
Butlers Cl, Amer. HP6 55 AN37
Windsor SL4 151 AK82
Butlers Ct, Beac. HP9 89 AK54
Waltham Cross EN8
off Trinity La 67 DY32
Sch Butlers Ct Comb Sch, Beac.
HP9 off Wattleton Rd 89 AK54
Butlers Ct Rd, Beac. HP9 89 AK54
BUTLERS CROSS, Beac.
HP9 90 AT49
Butlers Dene Rd, Cat.
(Wold.) CR3 237 DZ120
Butlers Dr, E4 83 EC38
Butlers Hill, Lthd. (W.Hors.)
KT24 245 BP130
Butler St, E2 12 F1
Uxbridge UB10 135 BP70
Butlers Wf, SE1 21 P2
Butler Wk, Grays RM17
off Palmers Dr 170 GD77
Buttell Cl, Grays RM17 170 GD78
Buttercross La, Epp. CM16 70 EU30
Buttercup Cl, Hat. AL10 29 CT14
Northolt UB5 136 BZ65
Romford RM3
off Copperfields Way 106 FK53
Buttercup Sq, Stai. (Stanw.)
TW19 off Diamedes Av 174 BK88
Butterfield, H.Wyc.
(Woob.Grn) HP10 110 AD59
Butterfield Cl, N17
off Devonshire Rd 100 DQ51
SE16 22 C4
Twickenham TW1
off Rugby Rd 177 CF86
Butterfield La, St.Alb. AL1 43 CE24
Butterfields, E17 123 EC57
Butterfield Sq, E6
off Harper Rd 145 EM72
Butterfly La, SE9 185 EP86
Borehamwood (Elstree)
WD6 77 CG41
Butterfly Wk, SE5
off Denmark Hill 162 DR81
Warlingham CR6 236 DW120
Butter Hill, Cars. SM5 200 DG104
Dorking RH4 off South St 263 CG136
Wallington SM6 200 DG104
Butteridges Cl, Dag. RM9 146 EZ67
Butterly Av, Dart. DA1 188 FM89
Buttermere Av, Slou. SL1 130 AJ71
Buttermere Cl, E15 123 ED63
SE1 21 N7
Feltham TW14 175 BT88
Morden SM4 199 CX100
St. Albans AL1 43 CH21
Buttermere Dr, SW15 179 CY85
Buttermere Gdns, Pur. CR8 220 DR113
Buttermere Rd, Orp. BR5 206 EX98
Buttermere Wk, E8 5 P4
Buttermere Way, Egh. TW20
off Keswick Rd 173 BB94
Buttersweet Ri, Saw. CM21
off Brook Rd 36 EY06
Butterwick, W6 159 CW77
Watford WD25 76 BY36
Butterwick La, St.Alb. AL4 44 CN22
Butterworth Gdns, Wdf.Grn.
IG8 102 EG51
Buttesland St, N1 11 K1
Buttfield Cl, Dag. RM10 147 FB65
Butt Fld Vw, St.Alb. AL1 42 CC24
Buttlehide, Rick. (Map.Cr.)
WD3 91 BD50
Buttmarsh Cl, SE18 165 EP78
Buttondene Cres, Brox.
EN10 49 EB22
Button Rd, Grays RM17 170 FZ77
Button St, Swan. BR8 208 FJ96
Butts,The, Brent. TW8 157 CK79
Broxbourne EN10 49 DY24
Sevenoaks (Otford) TN14 241 FH116
Sunbury-on-Thames TW16
off Elizabeth Gdns 196 BW97
Buttsbury Rd, Ilf. IG1 125 EQ64
Butts Cotts, Felt. TW13 176 BZ90
Butts Cres, Felt. TW13 176 CA90
Butts End, Hem.H. HP1 40 BG18
Butts Grn Rd, Horn. RM11 128 FK58
Buttsmead, Nthwd. HA6 93 BQ52
Butts Piece, Nthlt. UB5
off Longhook Gdns 135 BV68
Butts Rd, Brom. BR1 184 EE92
Woking GU21 226 AY117
Buxhall Cres, E9 143 DZ65
Sch Buxlow Prep Sch, Wem.
HA9 off Castleton Gdns 118 CL62
Buxted Rd, E8 5 N5
N12 98 DE50
SE22 162 DS84
Buxton Av, Cat. CR3 236 DS121
Buxton Cl, N9 100 DW47
St. Albans AL4 43 CK17
Woodford Green IG8 102 EK51
Buxton Ct, N1 11 H1
Buxton Cres, Sutt. SM3 217 CY105
Buxton Dr, E11 124 EE56
New Malden KT3 198 CR96
Buxton Gdns, W3 138 CP73
Buxton La, Cat. CR3 236 DR120
Buxton Path, Wat. WD19 94 BW48
Buxton Rd, E4 101 ED45
E6 144 EL69
E15 124 EE64
E17 123 DY56
N19 121 DK60
NW2 139 CV65
SW14 158 CS83
Ashford TW15 174 BK92
Epping (They.B.) CM16 85 ES36
Erith DA8 167 FD80
Grays RM16 170 GE75
Ilford IG2 125 ES58
Thornton Heath CR7 201 DP99
Waltham Abbey EN9 68 EG32
Buxton St, E1 11 P4
Buzzard Creek Ind Est, Bark.
IG11 145 ET71
Coll Byam Shaw Sch of Art,
N19 off Elthorne Rd 121 DK61
Byam St, SW6 160 DC82
Byards Cft, SW16 201 DK95
Byatt Wk, Hmptn. TW12
off Victors Dr 176 BY93
Bybend Cl, Slou.
(Farn.Royal) SL2 131 AP67
Bychurch End, Tedd. TW11
off Church Rd 177 CF92
Bycliffe Ter, Grav. DA11 191 GF87
Bycroft Rd, Sthl. UB1 136 CA70
Bycroft St, SE20
off Parish La 183 DX94
Bycullah Av, Enf. EN2 81 DP41
Bycullah Rd, Enf. EN2 81 DP41
Byde St, Hert. SG14 32 DQ08
Bye, The, W3 138 CS72
Byegrove Rd, SW19 180 DD93
Byers Cl, Pot.B. EN6 64 DC34
Byewaters, Wat. WD18 75 BQ44
Byeway, The, SW14 158 CQ83
Bye Way, The, Har. HA3 95 CE53
Byeway, The, Rick. WD3 92 BL47
Byeways, Twick. TW2 176 CB90
Byeways, The, Ashtd. KT21
off Skinners La 231 CK118
Surbiton KT5 198 CN99
Byfeld Gdns, SW13 159 CU81
Byfield, Welw.G.C. AL8 29 CY06
Byfield Cl, SE16 23 K3
Byfield Pas, Islw. TW7 157 CG83
Byfield Rd, Islw. TW7 157 CG83
BYFLEET, W.Byf. KT14 212 BM113
⇌ Byfleet & New Haw 212 BK110
Sch Byfleet Prim Sch, W.Byf.
KT14 off Kings Head La 212 BK111
Byfleet Rd, Add. (New Haw)
KT15 212 BK108
Cobham KT11 213 BS113
West Byfleet (Byfleet)
KT14 212 BN112
Byfleet Tech Cen, W.Byf.
(Byfleet) KT14 212 BK111
Byford Cl, E15 144 EE66
Bygrove, Croy. (New Adgtn)
CR0 221 EB107
Sch Bygrove Prim Sch, E14 14 A8
Bygrove St, E14 14 A8
Byland Cl, N21 99 DM45
Bylands, Wok. GU22 227 BA119
Bylands Cl, SE2
off Finchale Rd 166 EV76
SE16 23 H1
Byne Rd, SE26 182 DW93
Carshalton SM5 200 DE103
Bynes Rd, S.Croy. CR2 220 DR108
Byng Dr, Pot.B. EN6 64 DA31
Bynghams, Harl. CM19 51 EM17
Byng Pl, WC1 9 L4
Byng Rd, Barn. EN5 79 CX41
Byng St, E14 23 N3
Bynon Av, Bexh. DA7 166 EY83
Byre, The, N14 off Farm La 81 DH44
Byrefield Rd, Guil. GU2 242 AT131
Byre Rd, N14 off Farm La 80 DG44
Byrne Rd, SW12 181 DH88
Byron Av, E12 144 EL65
E18 124 EF55
NW9 118 CP56
Borehamwood WD6 78 CN43
Coulsdon CR5 235 DL115
Hounslow TW4 155 BU82
New Malden KT3 199 CU99
Sutton SM1 218 DD105
Watford WD24 76 BX39
Byron Av E, Sutt. SM1 218 DD105
Byron Cl, E8 142 DU67
SE26 off Porthcawe Rd 183 DY91
SE28 146 EW74
Hampton TW12 176 BZ91
Waltham Cross EN7
off Allard Cl 66 DT27
Walton-on-Thames KT12 196 BY102
Woking (Knap.) GU21 226 AS117
Byron Ct, W9 7 H3
Enfield EN2
off Bycullah Rd 81 DP40
Harrow HA1 117 CE58
Sch Byron Ct Prim Sch, Wem.
HA0 off Spencer Rd 117 CJ61
Byron Dr, N2 120 DD58
Byron Dr, Erith DA8 167 FB80
Byron Gdns, Sutt. SM1 218 DD105
Tilbury RM18 171 GJ81
Byron Hill Rd, Har. HA2 117 CD60
Byron Ho, Beck. BR3 183 EA93
Slough SL3 153 BB78
Byron Ms, NW3 120 DE64
W9 7 H3
Byron Pl, Lthd. KT22 231 CH122
Sch Byron Prim Sch, Couls.
CR5 off St. Davids 235 DM117
Byron Rd, E10 123 EB60
E17 123 EA55
NW2 119 CV61
NW7 97 CU50
W5 138 CM74
Addlestone KT15 212 BL105
Brentwood (Hutt.) CM13 109 GD45
Dartford DA1 168 FP84
Harrow HA1 117 CE58
Harrow (Wldste) HA3 95 CF54
South Croydon CR2 220 DV110
Wembley HA0 117 CJ62
Byron St, E14 14 C7
Byron Ter, N9 100 DW45
Byron Way, Hayes UB4 135 BT70
Northolt UB5 136 BY69
Romford RM3 106 FJ53
West Drayton UB7 154 BM77
Bysouth Cl, N15 122 DR56
Ilford IG5 103 EP53
By the Mt, Welw.G.C. AL7 29 CX10
By the Wd, Wat. WD19 94 BX47
Bythorn St, SW9 161 DM83
Byton Rd, SW17 180 DF93
Byttom Hill, Dor. (Mick.)
RH5 247 CJ127
Byward Av, Felt. TW14 176 BW86
Byward St, EC3 11 M10
Bywater Pl, SE16 23 K1
Bywater St, SW3 18 C9
Byway, The, Epsom KT19 217 CT105
Potters Bar EN6 64 DA33
Sutton SM2 218 DD109
Byways, Berk. HP4 38 AY18
Slough (Burn.) SL1 130 AG71
Bywell Pl, W1 9 J6
Bywood Av, Croy. CR0 202 DW100
Bywood Cl, Ken. CR8 235 DP115
By-Wood End, Ger.Cr.
(Chal.St.P.) SL9 91 AZ50
Byworth Wk, N19
off Courtauld Rd 121 DK60

C

Cabbell Pl, Add. KT15 212 BJ105
Cabbell St, NW1 8 A6
Cabell Rd, Guil. GU2 242 AS133
Caberfeigh Pl, Red. RH1 250 DE134
★ Cabinet War Rooms,
SW1 19 M3
Cabinet Way, E4 101 DZ51
Sch Cable Ho Sch, Wok.
GU21 off Horsell Ri 226 AY115
Cable Pl, SE10
off Diamond Ter 163 EC81
Cable St, E1 12 A9
Cable Trade Pk, SE7 164 EJ77
Cabot Pl, E14 23 P1
Cabot Sq, E14 23 P1
Cabot Way, E6 off Parr Rd 144 EK67
Cabrera Av, Vir.W. GU25 192 AW100
Cabrera Cl, Vir.W. GU25 192 AX100
Cabul Rd, SW11 160 DE82
Cacket's Cotts, Sev. (Cudham)
TN14 off Cackets La 239 ES115
Cackets La, Sev. (Cudham)
TN14 239 ER115
Cactus Cl, SE15
off Lyndhurst Gro 162 DS82
Cactus Wk, W12
off Du Cane Rd 139 CT72
Cadbury Cl, Islw. TW7 157 CG81
Sunbury-on-Thames
TW16 175 BS94
Cadbury Rd, Sun. TW16 175 BS94
Cadbury Way, SE16 21 P6
Caddington Cl, Barn. EN4 80 DE43
Caddington Rd, NW2 119 CY62
Caddis Cl, Stan. HA7
off Daventer Dr 95 CF52
Caddy Cl, Egh. TW20 173 BA92
Cade La, Sev. TN13 257 FJ128
Cadell Cl, E2 5 P10
Cade Rd, SE10 163 ED81
Cader Rd, SW18 180 DC86
Cadet Dr, SE1 21 P9
Cadet Pl, SE10 24 G9
Cadiz Ct, Dag. RM10
off Rainham Rd S 147 FD66
Cadiz Rd, Dag. RM10 147 FC66
Cadiz St, SE17 21 H10
Cadley Ter, SE23 182 DW89
Cadlocks Hill, Sev. (Halst.)
TN14 224 EZ110
Cadman Cl, SW9
off Langton Rd 161 DP80
Cadmer Cl, N.Mal. KT3 198 CS98
Cadmore Ct, Hert. SG14
off The Ridgeway 31 DM07
Cadmore La, Wal.Cr. (Chshtt)
EN8 67 DX28
Cadmus Cl, SW4
off Aristotle Rd 161 DK83
Cadnam Pt, SW15
off Dilton Gdns 179 CV88
Cadogan Av, Dart. DA2 189 FR87
Cadogan Cl, E9
off Cadogan Ter 143 DZ66
Beckenham BR3
off Albemarle Rd 203 ED95
Harrow HA2 116 CB63
Teddington TW11 177 CE92
Cadogan Ct, Sutt. SM2 218 DB107
Cadogan Gdns, E18 124 EH55
N3 98 DB53
N21 81 DN43
SW3 18 D7
Cadogan Gate, SW1 18 D7
Cadogan La, SW1 18 E6
Pier Cadogan Pier 160 DE79
Cadogan Pl, SW1 18 D5
Cadogan Rd, SE18 165 EQ76
Surbiton KT6 197 CK99
Cadogan Sq, SW1 18 D6
Cadogan St, SW3 18 C8
Cadogan Ter, E9 143 DZ65
Cadoxton Av, N15 122 DT58
Cadwallon Rd, SE9 185 EP89
Caedmon Rd, N7 121 DM63
Caenshill Rd, Wey. KT13 212 BN108
Caenwood Cl, Wey. KT13 212 BN107
Caen Wd Rd, Ashtd. KT21 231 CJ118
Caerleon Cl, Esher (Clay.)
KT10 215 CH108
Sidcup DA14 186 EW92
Caerleon Ter, SE2
off Blithdale Rd 166 EV77
Caernarvon Cl, Hem.H. HP2 40 BK20
Hornchurch RM11 128 FN60
Mitcham CR4 201 DL97
Caernarvon Dr, Ilf. IG5 103 EN53
Caesars Wk, Mitch. CR4 200 DF99
Caesars Way, Shep. TW17 195 BR100
Cage Pond Rd, Rad. (Shenley)
WD7 62 CM33
Cages Wd Dr, Slou.
(Farn.Com.) SL2 111 AP63
Cage Yd, Reig. RH2
off High St 250 DA134
Cahill St, EC1 11 H4
Cahir St, E14 24 A8
Caillard Rd, W.Byf. (Byfleet)
KT14 212 BL111
Cains La, Felt. TW14 175 BS85
Caird St, W10 6 D2
Cairn Av, W5 137 CK74
Cairndale Cl, Brom. BR1 184 EF94
Cairnes Ms, SE18
off Shooter's Hill Rd 164 EL81
Cairnfield Av, NW2 118 CS62
Cairngorm Cl, Tedd. TW11
off Vicarage Rd 177 CG92
Cairngorm Pl, Slou. SL2 131 AR70
Cairns Av, Wdf.Grn. IG8 102 EL51
Cairns Cl, Dart. DA1 188 FK85
St. Albans AL4 43 CK21
Cairns Rd, SW11 180 DE85
Cairn Way, Stan. HA7 95 CF51
Cairo New Rd, Croy. CR0 201 DP103
Cairo Rd, E17 123 EA56
Caishowe Rd, Borwd. WD6 78 CP39
Caister Cl, Hem.H. HP2 40 BL21
Caistor Ms, SW12
off Caistor Rd 181 DH87
Caistor Pk Rd, E15 144 EF67
Caistor Rd, SW12 181 DH87
Caithness Dr, Epsom KT18 216 CR114
Caithness Gdns, Sid. DA15 185 ET86
Caithness Rd, W14 16 A7
Mitcham CR4 181 DH94
Calabria Rd, N5 4 E3
Calais Cl, Wal.Cr. EN7
off Argent Way 66 DR26
Calais Gate, SE5
off Calais St 161 DP81
Calais St, SE5 161 DP81
Calbourne Av, Horn. RM12 127 FH64
Calbourne Rd, SW12 180 DF87
Calbroke Ct, Slou. SL2
off Calbroke Rd 131 AM69
Calbroke Rd, Slou. SL2 131 AM70
Calcott Cl, Brwd. CM14 108 FV46
Calcott Wk, SE9 184 EK91
Calcroft Av, Green. DA9 189 FW85
Calcutta Rd, Til. RM18 171 GF82
Caldbeck, Wal.Abb. EN9 67 ED34
Caldbeck Av, Wor.Pk. KT4 199 CU103
Caldecot Av, Wal.Cr. EN7 66 DT29
Caldecote Gdns, Bushey
WD23 77 CE44
Caldecote La, Bushey WD23 95 CF45
Caldecot Rd, SE5 162 DQ82
Caldecott Way, E5 123 DX62
Caldecot Way, Brox. EN10 49 DZ22
Calder Av, Grnf. UB6 137 CF68
Hatfield (Brook.Pk) AL9 64 DB26
Calder Cl, Enf. EN1 82 DS41
Calder Ct, Slou. SL3 153 AZ78
Calder Gdns, Edg. HA8 118 CN55
Calderon Pl, W10
off St. Quintin Gdns 139 CW71
Calderon Rd, E11 123 EC63
Calder Rd, Mord. SM4 200 DC99
Caldervale Rd, SW4 181 DK85
Calder Way, Slou. (Colnbr.)
SL3 153 BF83
Calderwood, Grav. DA12 191 GL92
Calderwood St, SE18 165 EN77
Caldicot Grn, NW9
off Snowdon Dr 118 CS58
Sch Caldicott Sch, Slou. SL2
off Crown La 131 AP66
Caldwell Rd, Wat. WD19 94 BX49
Caldwell St, SW9 161 DM80
Caldwell Yd, EC4
off Upper Thames St 142 DQ73
Caldy Rd, Belv. DA17 167 FB76
Caldy Wk, N1 4 G5
Caleb St, SE1 20 G3
Caledon Cl, Beac. HP9 89 AK52
Caledonian Cl, Ilf. IG3 126 EV60
⊖ Caledonian Road 141 DL65
Caledonian Rd, N1 141 DM68
N7 4 A3
⇌ Caledonian Road &
Barnsbury 4 B5
Caledonian Way, Gat. RH6
off Queen's Gate 269 DH151
Caledonian Wf, E14 24 E8
Caledonia Rd, Stai. TW19 174 BL88
Caledonia St, N1 141 DL68
Caledon Pl, Guil. GU4
off Darfield Rd 243 BA131
Caledon Rd, E6 144 EL67
Beaconsfield HP9 89 AL52
St. Albans (Lon.Col.) AL2 61 CK26
Wallington SM6 218 DG105
Cale St, SW3 18 A9
Caletock Way, SE10 25 J9
Calfstock La, Dart.
(S.Darenth) DA4 208 FL98
Calico Row, SW11
off York Pl 160 DC83
Calidore Cl, SW2
off Endymion Rd 181 DM86
California Cl, Sutt. SM2
off Station Rd 218 DA110
California La, Bushey
(Bushey Hth) WD23 95 CD46
California Rd, N.Mal. KT3 198 CQ98
Caliph Cl, Grav. DA12 191 GM90
Callaby Ter, N1 5 K4
Callaghan Cl, SE13
off Glenton Rd 164 EE84
Callander Rd, SE6 183 EB89
Callan Gro, S.Ock. RM15 149 FV73
Callard Av, N13 99 DP50
Callcott Rd, NW6 139 CZ66
Callcott St, W8 16 G1
Callendar Rd, SW7 17 N5
Calley Down Cres, Croy.
(New Adgtn) CR0 221 ED110
Callingham Cl, E14 13 M6
Callis Fm Cl, Stai. (Stanw.)
TW19
off Bedford Rd 174 BL86

Callis Rd, E17 . . . . .123 DZ58
Callisto Ct, Hem.H. HP2
off Jupiter Dr 40 BM17
Callow Fld, Pur. CR8 . . . . . .219 DN113
Callow Hill, Vir.W. GU25 . . . .192 AW97
Callowland Cl, Wat. WD24 . . .75 BV38
Callow St, SW3 . . . . .160 DD79
Calluna Ct, Wok. GU22
off Heathside Rd 227 AZ118
Calmont Rd, Brom. BR1 . . . .183 ED93
Calmore Cl, Horn. RM12 . . .128 FJ64
Calne Av, Ilf. IG5 . . . . .103 EP53
Calonne Rd, SW19 . . . . .179 CX91
Calshot Av, Grays
(Chaff.Hun.) RM16 . . . . . .170 FZ75
Calshot Rd, Houns.
(Hthrw Air.) TW6 . . . . . . .154 BN82
Calshot St, N1 . . . . .4 A9
Calshot Way, Enf. EN2 . . . . . .81 DP41
Hounslow (Hthrw Air.)
TW6 *off Calshot Rd* 155 BP82
Calthorpe Gdns, Edg. HA8
off Jesmond Way 96 CL50
Sutton SM1 . . . . .200 DC104
Calthorpe St, WC1 . . . . .10 B3
Calton Av, SE21 . . . . .182 DS85
Hertford SG14 . . . . .31 DM08
Calton Ct, Hert. SG14
off Calton Av 31 DM09
Calton Rd, Barn. EN5 . . . . . . .80 DC44
Calverley Cl, Beck. BR3 . . . .183 EB93
Calverley Cres, Dag. RM10 . .126 FA61
Calverley Gdns, Har. HA3 . . .117 CK59
Calverley Gro, N19 . . . . . . .121 DK60
Calverley Rd, Epsom KT17 . .217 CU107
Calvert Av, E2 . . . . .11 M2
Calvert Cl, Belv. DA17 . . . . .166 FA77
Sidcup DA14 . . . . .186 EY93
Calvert Cres, Dor. RH4
off Calvert Rd 247 CH134
Calvert Dr, Dart. DA2 . . . . . .187 FD89
Calverton, SE5 . . . . .162 DS79
Sch **Calverton Prim Sch**, E16
off King George Av 144 EK72
Calverton Rd, E6 . . . . .145 EN67
Calvert Rd, SE10 . . . . .25 J10
Barnet EN5 . . . . .79 CX40
Dorking RH4 . . . . .247 CH134
Leatherhead (Eff.) KT24 . .245 BV128
Calvert's Bldgs, SE1 . . . . . . .21 J2
Calvert St, NW1
off Chalcot Rd 140 DG67
Calvin Cl, Orp. BR5 . . . . . . .206 EX97
Calvin St, E1 . . . . .11 N4
Calydon Rd, SE7 . . . . .25 P10
Calypso Way, SE16 . . . . .23 L6
Camac Rd, Twick. TW2 . . . . .177 CD88
Cambalt Rd, SW15 . . . . .179 CX85
Sch **Cambell Inf Sch**, Dag.
RM9 *off Langley Cres* . . .146 EX66
Sch **Cambell Jun Sch**, Dag.
RM9 *off Langley Cres* . . .146 EX66
Camberley Av, SW20 . . . . . .199 CV96
Enfield EN1 . . . . .82 DS42
Camberley Cl, Sutt. SM3 . . .199 CX104
Camberley Rd, Houns.
(Hthrw Air.) TW6 . . . . . . .154 BN83
Cambert Way, SE3 . . . . .164 EH84
CAMBERWELL, SE5 . . . . . . .162 DQ80
Camberwell Ch St, SE5 . . . .162 DR81
Uni **Camberwell Coll of Arts**,
Peckham Rd, SE5 . . . . . . .162 DS81
Sumner Rd, SE15 . . . . . . .162 DT80
Wilson Rd, SE5 . . . . .162 DS81
Camberwell Glebe, SE5 . . . .162 DR81
Camberwell Grn, SE5 . . . . . .162 DR81
Camberwell Gro, SE5 . . . . . .162 DR81
Camberwell New Rd, SE5 . . .161 DN80
Camberwell Pas, SE5
off Camberwell Grn 162 DQ81
Camberwell Rd, SE5 . . . . . .162 DQ79
Camberwell Sta Rd, SE5 . . . .162 DQ81
Cambeys Rd, Dag. RM10 . . .127 FB64
Camborne Av, W13 . . . . . . .157 CH75
Romford RM3 . . . . .106 FL52
Camborne Cl, Houns.
(Hthrw Air.) TW6
off Camborne Rd S 154 BN83
Camborne Dr, Hem.H. HP2 . .40 BL16
Camborne Ms, W11 . . . . .6 D8
Camborne Rd, SW18 . . . . . .180 DA87
Croydon CR0 . . . . .202 DU101
Morden SM4 . . . . .199 CX99
Sidcup DA14 . . . . .186 EW90
Sutton SM2 . . . . .218 DA108
Welling DA16 . . . . .165 ET82
Camborne Rd N, Houns.
(Hthrw Air.) TW6
off Camborne Rd S 154 BN83
Camborne Rd S, Houns.
(Hthrw Air.) TW6 . . . . . . .154 BN83
Camborne Way, Houns. TW5 .156 CA81
Hounslow (Hthrw Air.) TW6
off Camborne Rd S 154 BN83
Romford RM3 . . . . .106 FL52
Cambourne Av, N9 . . . . .101 DX45
Cambray Rd, SW12 . . . . .181 DJ88
Orpington BR6 . . . . .205 ET101
Cambria Cl, Houns. TW3 . . . .156 CA84
Sidcup DA15 . . . . .185 ER88
Cambria Ct, Felt. TW14
off Hounslow Rd 175 BV87
Slough SL3 *off Turner Rd* .152 AW75
Cambria Cres, Grav. DA12 . . .191 GL91
Cambria Gdns, Stai. TW19 . .174 BL87
Cambria Ho, SE26
off High Level Dr 182 DU91
Erith DA8 *off Larner Rd* . .167 FE80
Cambrian Av, Ilf. IG2 . . . . . .125 ES57
Cambrian Cl, SE27 . . . . .181 DP90
Cambrian Grn, NW9
off Snowdon Dr 118 CS57
Cambrian Gro, Grav. DA11 . .191 GG87
Cambrian Rd, E10 . . . . .123 EA59
Richmond TW10 . . . . .178 CM86
Cambrian Way, Hem.H. HP2 . .40 BL17
Cambria Rd, SE5 . . . . .162 DQ83
Cambria St, SW6 . . . . .160 DB80
Cambridge Av, NW6 . . . . . . .140 DA68
Greenford UB6 . . . . .117 CF64
New Malden KT3 . . . . . . .199 CT96
Romford RM2 . . . . .128 FJ55
Slough SL1 . . . . .131 AM72
Slough (Burn.) SL1 . . . . . .130 AH68
Welling DA16 . . . . .165 ET84
Cambridge Barracks Rd,
SE18 . . . . .165 EM77
Cambridge Circ, WC2 . . . . .9 M8
Cambridge Cl, E17 . . . . .123 DZ58
N22 *off Pellatt Gro* 99 DN53
NW10 *off Lawrence Way* .118 CQ62
SW20 . . . . .199 CV95
Hounslow TW4 . . . . .156 BY84
Waltham Cross (Chsht)
EN8 . . . . .66 DW29
Cambridge Cl, West Dr. UB7 .154 BK79
Woking GU21
off Bingham Dr 226 AT118
Cambridge Cotts, Rich. TW9 158 CN79
Cambridge Cres, E2 . . . . . . .142 DV68
Teddington TW11 . . . . . . .177 CG92
Cambridge Dr, SE12 . . . . . . .184 EG85
Potters Bar EN6 . . . . .63 CX31
Ruislip HA4 . . . . .116 BW61
Cambridge Gdns, N10 . . . . . .99 DH53
N13 . . . . .99 DN50
N17
off Great Cambridge Rd .100 DR52
N21 . . . . .100 DR45
NW6 . . . . .140 DA68
W10 .6 D7
Enfield EN1 . . . . .82 DU40
Grays RM16 . . . . .171 GG77
Kingston upon Thames
KT1 . . . . .198 CN96
Cambridge Gate, NW1 . . . . . . .9 H2
Cambridge Gate Ms, NW1 . . . .9 H2
Cambridge Grn, SE9 . . . . . . .185 EP88
Cambridge Gro, SE20 . . . . . .202 DV95
W6 . . . . .159 CV77
Cambridge Gro Rd, Kings.T.
KT1 . . . . .198 CN96
⇌ **Cambridge Heath** 142 DV68
Cambridge Heath Rd, E1 . . . .12 D5
E2 .12 D5
**Cambridge Lo Mobile
Home Pk**, Horl. RH6 . . . .268 DG145
Cambridge Mans, SW11
off Cambridge Rd 160 DF81
Cambridge Par, Enf. EN1
off Great Cambridge Rd . .82 DU39
Cambridge Pk, E11 . . . . .124 EG59
Twickenham TW1 . . . . . . .177 CK87
Cambridge Pk Rd, E11
off Cambridge Pk 124 EF59
Cambridge Pl, W8 . . . . .17 K4
Cambridge Rd, E4 . . . . .101 ED46
E11 . . . . .124 EF58
NW6 . . . . .6 G1
SE20 . . . . .202 DV97
SW11 . . . . .160 DF81
SW13 . . . . .159 CT82
SW20 . . . . .199 CU95
W7 . . . . .157 CF75
Ashford TW15 . . . . .175 BQ94
Barking IG11 . . . . .145 EQ66
Beaconsfield HP9 . . . . .88 AJ53
Bromley BR1 . . . . .184 EG94
Carshalton SM5 . . . . .218 DE107
Hampton TW12 . . . . .176 BZ94
Harlow CM20 . . . . .36 EW09
Harrow HA2 . . . . .116 CA57
Hounslow TW4 . . . . .156 BY84
Ilford IG3 . . . . .125 ES60
Kingston upon Thames
KT1 . . . . .198 CM96
Mitcham CR4 . . . . .201 DJ97
New Malden KT3 . . . . . . .198 CS98
Richmond TW9 . . . . .158 CN80
St. Albans AL1 . . . . .43 CH21
Sidcup DA14 . . . . .185 ES91
Southall UB1 . . . . .136 BZ74
Teddington TW11 . . . . . . .177 CF91
Twickenham TW1 . . . . . . .177 CK86
Uxbridge UB8 . . . . .134 BK65
Walton-on-Thames KT12 . .195 BV100
Watford WD18 . . . . .76 BW42
West Molesey KT8 . . . . . .196 BZ98
Cambridge Rd N, W4 . . . . . .158 CP78
Cambridge Rd S, W4 . . . . . .158 CP78
Cambridge Row, SE18 . . . . .165 EP78
Sch **Cambridge Sch & Resource
Base**, W6
off Cambridge Gro 159 CV77
Coll **Cambridge Sch of English,
The**, WC2 . . . . .9 P7
Cambridge Sq, W2 . . . . .8 A7
Redhill RH1 . . . . .266 DG137
Cambridge St, SW1 . . . . .19 H8
Cambridge Ter, N13 . . . . .99 DN50
NW1 . . . . .9 H2
Berkhamsted HP4 . . . . .38 AX19
Cambridge Ter Ms, NW1 . . . . .9 H2
Coll **Cambridge Tutors Coll**,
Croy. CR0
off Water Twr Hill 220 DS105
Cambstone Cl, N11 . . . . .98 DG47
Cambus Cl, Hayes UB4 . . . . .136 BY71
Cambus Rd, E16 . . . . .15 M5
Camdale Rd, SE18 . . . . .165 ET80
★ **Camden Arts Cen**, NW3 .120 DC64
Camden Av, Felt. TW13 . . . . .176 BW89
Hayes UB4 . . . . .136 BW73
Camden Cl, Chis. BR7 . . . . . .185 EQ94
Gravesend DA11 . . . . .190 GC88
Grays RM16 . . . . .171 GH77
Camden Gdns, NW1
off Kentish Town Rd 141 DH66
Sutton SM1 . . . . .218 DB106
Thornton Heath CR7 . . . . .201 DP97
Camden Gro, Chis. BR7 . . . . .185 EP93
Camden High St, NW1 . . . . . .141 DH67
Camden Hill Rd, SE19 . . . . . .182 DS93
Camdenhurst St, E14 . . . . . . .13 K7
Sch **Camden Jun Sch**, Cars.
SM5 *off Camden Rd* 218 DF105
Camden La, N7
off Rowstock Gdns 141 DK65
★ **Camden Lock Mkt &
Waterbuses**, NW1 . . . . . .141 DH66
Camden Lock Pl, NW1
off Chalk Fm Rd 141 DH66
Camden Ms, NW1 . . . . .141 DK65
H **Camden Ms Day Hosp**,
NW1 . . . . .141 DJ66
Camden Pk Rd, NW1 . . . . . .141 DK65
Chislehurst BR7 . . . . .185 EM94
Camden Pas, N1 . . . . .4 E8
⇌ **Camden Road** 141 DJ66
Camden Rd, E11 . . . . .124 EH58
E17 . . . . .123 DZ58
N7 . . . . .121 DK64
NW1 . . . . .141 DJ67
Bexley DA5 . . . . .186 EZ88
Carshalton SM5 . . . . .218 DF105
Grays RM16 . . . . .170 FY76
Sevenoaks TN13 . . . . .257 FH122
Sutton SM1 . . . . .218 DA106
Camden Row, SE3 . . . . .164 EE82
Sch **Camden Sch for Girls**,
NW5 *off Sandall Rd* 141 DJ65
Camden Sq, NW1 . . . . .141 DK65
SE15 *off Watts St* 162 DT81
Camden St, NW1 . . . . .141 DH66
Camden Ter, NW1
off North Vil 141 DK65
CAMDEN TOWN, NW1 . . . . . .141 DJ67
⊖ **Camden Town** 141 DH67
Camden Wk, N1 . . . . .4 E8
Camden Way, Chis. BR7 . . . .185 EM94
Camden Way, Th. Hth. CR7 . .201 DP97
Camelford Wk, W11 . . . . .6 C8
Camel Gro, Kings.T. KT2 . . . .177 CK92
Camellia Cl, Rom. RM3 . . . . .106 FL53
Camellia Ct, Wdf.Grn. IG8
off The Bridle Path 102 EE52
Camellia Pl, Twick. TW2 . . . .176 CB87
Camellia St, SW8 . . . . .161 DL80
Camelot Cl, SE28 . . . . .165 ER75
SW19 . . . . .180 DA91
Westerham (Bigg.H.)
TN16 . . . . .238 EJ116
Sch **Camelot Prim Sch**, SE15
off Bird in Bush Rd 162 DV79
Camelot St, SE15
off Bird in Bush Rd 162 DV80
Camel Rd, E16 . . . . .144 EK74
Camera Pl, SW10 . . . . .160 DD79
Cameron Cl, N18 . . . . .100 DV49
N20 *off Myddelton Pk* 98 DE47
Bexley DA5 . . . . .187 FD90
Brentwood CM14 . . . . . . .108 FW49
Cameron Ct, Ware SG12
off Crib St 33 DX05
Cameron Dr, Wal.Cr. EN8 . . . .67 DX34
Sch **Cameron Ho**, SW3
off The Vale 160 DD79
Cameron Pl, E1 . . . . .12 D7
Cameron Rd, SE6 . . . . .183 DZ89
Bromley BR2 . . . . .204 EG98
Chesham HP5 . . . . .54 AQ30
Croydon CR0 . . . . .201 DP100
Ilford IG3 . . . . .125 ES60
Cameron Sq, Mitch. CR4 . . . .200 DE95
Camerton Cl, E8 . . . . .5 P4
Camfield, Welw.G.C. AL7 . . . .29 CZ13
Camfield Pl, Hat. (Essen.)
AL9 . . . . .46 DD21
Camgate Cen, Stai. (Stanw.)
TW19 . . . . .174 BM86
Cam Grn, S.Ock. RM15 . . . . .149 FV72
Camilla Cl, Lthd. (Bkhm)
KT23 . . . . .246 CB125
Sunbury-on-Thames
TW16 . . . . .175 BS93
Camilla Dr, Dor. (Westh.)
RH5 . . . . .247 CG130
Camilla Rd, SE16 . . . . .22 C8
Camille Cl, SE25 . . . . .202 DU97
Camlan Rd, Brom. BR1 . . . . .184 EF91
Camlet St, E2 . . . . .11 N3
Camlet Way, Barn. EN4 . . . . .80 DA40
St. Albans AL3 . . . . .42 CB19
Camley St, NW1 . . . . .141 DK66
★ **Camley St Natural Pk**,
NW1 . . . . .141 DL68
Camm Av, Wind. SL4 . . . . . . .151 AL83
Camm Gdns, Kings.T. KT1
off Church Rd 198 CM96
Thames Ditton KT7 . . . . . .197 CE101
Camms Ter, Dag. RM10 . . . . .127 FC64
Camomile Av, Mitch. CR4 . . .200 DF95
Camomile Rd, Rom.
(Rush Grn) RM7 . . . . .127 FD61
Camomile St, EC3 . . . . .11 L7
Camomile Way, West Dr.
UB7 . . . . .134 BL72
CAMP, THE, St.Alb. AL1 . . . . .43 CH21
Campana Rd, SW6 . . . . .160 DA81
Campbell Av, Ilf. IG6 . . . . . . .125 EQ56
Woking GU22 . . . . .227 AZ121
Campbell Cl, SE18
off Moordown 165 EN81
SW16 . . . . .181 DK91
Romford (Hav.at.Bow.)
RM1 . . . . .105 FE51
Ruislip HA4 . . . . .115 BU58
Twickenham TW2 . . . . . . .177 CD89
West Byfleet (Byfleet)
KT14 . . . . .212 BK112
Campbell Ct, N17 . . . . .100 DT53
Campbell Cft, Edg. HA8 . . . . .96 CN50
Campbell Dr, Beac. HP9 . . . . .88 AJ51
Campbell Gordon Way,
NW2 . . . . .119 CV63
Campbell Rd, E3 . . . . .13 P1
E6 . . . . .144 EL67
E15 *off Trevelyan Rd* 124 EF63
E17 . . . . .123 DZ56
N17 . . . . .100 DU53
W7 . . . . .137 CE73
Caterham CR3 . . . . .236 DR121
Croydon CR0 . . . . .201 DP101
East Molesey KT8
off Hampton Ct Rd 197 CF97
Gravesend DA11 . . . . .191 GF88
Twickenham TW2 . . . . . . .177 CD89
Weybridge KT13 . . . . .212 BN108
Campbells Cl, Harl. CM17
off Carters Mead 52 EV16
Campbell Wk, N1
off Outram Pl 141 DL67
Campdale Rd, N7 . . . . .121 DK62
Campden Cres, Dag. RM8 . . .126 EV63
Wembley HA0 . . . . .117 CH61
Campden Gro, W8 . . . . .17 H3
Campden Hill Ct, W8 . . . . . . .17 H3
Campden Hill Gdns, W8 . . . . .16 F1
Campden Hill Gate, W8 . . . . .16 G3
Campden Hill Pl, W11 . . . . . . .16 F1
Campden Hill Rd, W8 . . . . . . .17 H4
Campden Hill Sq, W8 . . . . . . .16 F2
Campden Hill Twrs, W11 . . . . .16 G1
Campden Ho Cl, W8 . . . . .16 G3
Campden Rd, S.Croy. CR2 . .220 DS106
Uxbridge UB10 . . . . .114 BM62
Campden St, W8 . . . . .16 G2
Campen Cl, SW19 . . . . .179 CY89
Camp End Rd, Wey. KT13 . . .213 BR110
Camperdown St, E1 . . . . .11 P8
Campfield Rd, SE9 . . . . .184 EK87
Hertford SG14 . . . . .31 DP09
St. Albans AL1 . . . . .43 CG21
Camphill Ct, W.Byf. KT14 . . .212 BG112
Camphill Ind Est, W.Byf.
KT14 . . . . .212 BH111
Camphill Rd, W.Byf. KT14 . . .212 BG112
Campine Cl, Wal.Cr. (Chsht)
EN8
off Welsummer Way 67 DX28
Campion Cl, E6 . . . . .145 EM73
Croydon CR0 . . . . .220 DS105
Gravesend (Nthflt) DA11 . .190 GE91
Harrow HA3 . . . . .118 CM58
Romford (Rush Grn) RM7 127 FD61
Uxbridge (Denh.) UB9
off Lindsey Rd 114 BG62
Uxbridge (Hlgdn) UB8 . . .134 BM71
Watford WD25 . . . . .59 BU33
Campion Ct, Grays RM17 . . .170 GD79
Campion Dr, Tad. KT20 . . . . .233 CV120
Campion Gdns, Wdf.Grn.
IG8 . . . . .102 EG50
Campion Pl, SE28 . . . . .146 EV74
Campion Rd, SW15 . . . . .159 CW84
Campion Rd, Hat. AL10 . . . . . .45 CT15
Hemel Hempstead HP1 . . . .39 BE21
Isleworth TW7 . . . . .157 CF81
Campions, Epp. CM16 . . . . . . .70 EU28
Loughton IG10 . . . . .85 EN38
Campions, The, Borwd. WD6 .78 CN38
Sch **Campion Sch, The**, Horn.
RM11 *off Wingletye La* . .128 FM60
Campions Cl, Borwd. WD6 . . .78 CP37
Campions Ct, Berk. HP4 . . . . .38 AU20
Campion Ter, NW2 . . . . .119 CX62
Campion Way, Edg. HA8 . . . . .96 CQ49
Sch **Camp JMI Sch**, St.Alb.
AL1 *off Camp Rd* 43 CH21
Cample La, S.Ock. RM15 . . . .149 FU73
Camplin Rd, Har. HA3 . . . . . .118 CL57
Camplin St, SE14 . . . . .163 DX80
Camp Rd, SW19 . . . . .179 CW92
Caterham (Wold.) CR3 . . .237 DY120
Gerrards Cross SL9 . . . . .112 AX59
St. Albans AL1 . . . . .43 CJ21
Campsbourne, The, N8
off High St 121 DL56
Sch **Campsbourne Inf Sch**,
N8 *off Nightingale La* . . .121 DL55
Sch **Campsbourne Jun Sch**,
N8 *off Nightingale La* . . .121 DL55
Campsbourne Rd, N8 . . . . . . .121 DL55
Campsey Gdns, Dag. RM9 . . .146 EV66
Campsey Rd, Dag. RM9 . . . . .146 EV66
Campsfield Rd, N8
off Campsbourne Rd . . .121 DL55
Campshill Pl, SE13
off Campshill Rd 183 EC85
Campshill Rd, SE13 . . . . . . .183 EC85
Campus, The, Welw.G.C.
AL8 . . . . .29 CX08
Campus Rd, E17 . . . . .123 DZ58
Campus Way, NW4
off Greyhound Hill 119 CV55
Camp Vw, SW19 . . . . .179 CV92
Camp Vw Rd, St.Alb. AL1 . . . .43 CH21
Cam Rd, E15 . . . . .143 ED67
Camrose Av, Edg. HA8 . . . . . .96 CM53
Erith DA8 . . . . .167 FB79
Feltham TW13 . . . . .175 BV91
Camrose Cl, Croy. CR0 . . . . .203 DY101
Morden SM4 . . . . .200 DA98
Camrose St, SE2 . . . . .166 EU78
Canada Av, N18 . . . . .100 DQ51
Redhill RH1 . . . . .266 DG138
Canada Cres, W3 . . . . .138 CQ71
Canada Dr, Red. RH1 . . . . . .266 DG138
Canada Est, SE16 . . . . .22 F5
Canada Fm Rd, Dart.
(S.Darenth) DA4 . . . . . . .209 FU98
Longfield DA3 . . . . .209 FU99
Canada Gdns, SE13 . . . . . . .183 EC85
Canada La, Brox. EN10 . . . . . .67 DY25
Canada Rd, W3 . . . . .138 CQ70
Cobham KT11 . . . . .214 BW113
Erith DA8 . . . . .167 FH80
Slough SL1 . . . . .152 AV75
West Byfleet (Byfleet)
KT14 . . . . .212 BK111
Canadas, The, Brox. EN10 . . .67 DY25
Canada Sq, E14 . . . . .24 A1
Canada St, SE16 . . . . .22 G4
⊖ **Canada Water** 22 F4
Canada Way, W12 . . . . .139 CV73
Canadian Av, SE6 . . . . .183 EB88
Canadian Mem Av, Egh.
TW20 . . . . .192 AT96
Canal App, SE8 . . . . .23 J10
Canal Basin, Grav. DA12 . . . .191 GK86
Canal Cl, E1 . . . . .13 J3
W10 . . . . .6 B3
Canal Ct, Berk. HP4
off George St 38 AY19
Canal Est, Slou. (Langley)
SL3 . . . . .153 BA75
Canal Gro, SE15 . . . . .162 DU79
Canal Path, E2 . . . . .5 N8
Canal Rd, Grav. DA12 . . . . . .191 GJ86
Canal St, SE5 . . . . .162 DR79
Canal Wk, N1 . . . . .5 K7
SE26 . . . . .182 DW92
Croydon CR0 . . . . .202 DS100
Canal Way, N1 . . . . .5 H9
NW1 . . . . .8 B1
NW8 . . . . .8 A2
NW10 . . . . .139 CT70
W10 . . . . .6 F5
Uxbridge (Hare.) UB9 . . . . .92 BG51
Canal Way Wk, W10 . . . . .6 A3
Canal Wf, Slou. SL3 . . . . .153 BA75
⊖ **Canary Wharf** 24 A2
DLR **Canary Wharf** 23 P1
Riv **Canary Wharf Pier** 23 M1
Canberra Cl, NW4 . . . . .119 CU55
Dagenham RM10 . . . . . . .147 FD66
Hornchurch RM12 . . . . . . .128 FJ63
St. Albans AL3 . . . . .43 CF16
Canberra Cres, Dag. RM10 . .147 FD66
Canberra Dr, Hayes UB4 . . . .136 BW69
Northolt UB5 . . . . .136 BW69
Sch **Canberra Prim Sch**,
W12 *off Australia Rd* 139 CV73
Canberra Rd, E6
off Barking Rd 145 EM67
SE7 . . . . .164 EJ79
W13 . . . . .137 CG74
Bexleyheath DA7 . . . . . . .166 EX79
Hounslow (Hthrw Air.)
TW6 . . . . .154 BN83
Canberra Sq, Til. RM18 . . . . .171 GG82
Canbury Av, Kings.T. KT2 . . .198 CM95
Canbury Ms, SE26
off Wells Pk Rd 182 DU90
Canbury Pk Rd, Kings.T.
KT2 . . . . .198 CL95
Canbury Pas, Kings.T. KT2 . .197 CK95
Canbury Path, Orp. BR5 . . . .206 EU98
Sch **Canbury Sch**, Kings.T.
KT2
off Kingston Hill 178 CP93
Cancell Rd, SW9 . . . . .161 DN81
Candahar Rd, SW11 . . . . . . .160 DE82
Cander Way, S.Ock. RM15 . . .149 FV73
Candlefield Cl, Hem.H. HP3
off Candlefield Rd 40 BN23
Candlefield Rd, Hem.H. HP3 .40 BN23
Candlefield Wk, Hem.H. HP3
off Candlefield Rd 40 BN23
Candle Gro, SE15 . . . . .162 DV83
Candlemakers Apartments,
SW18
off York Rd 160 DD83
Candlemas La, Beac. HP9 . . . .89 AL53
Candlemas Mead, Beac.
HP9 . . . . .89 AL53
Candler St, N15 . . . . .122 DR58
Candlerush Cl, Wok. GU22 . .227 BB117
Candlestick La, Wal.Cr. EN7
off Park La 66 DV27
Candover Cl, West Dr. UB7 . .154 BK80
Candover Rd, Horn. RM12 . . .127 FH60
Candover St, W1 . . . . .9 J6
Candy Cft, Lthd. (Bkhm)
KT23 . . . . .246 CB126
Candy St, E3 . . . . .143 DZ67
Cane Hill, Rom. (Harold Wd)
RM3 *off Bennison Dr* . . .106 FK54
Caneland Ct, Wal.Abb. EN9 . .68 EF34
Canes La, Epp. (N.Wld Bas.)
CM16 . . . . .52 FA23
Harlow (Hast.) CM17 . . . . .52 EX21
Canewdon Cl, Wok. GU22
off Guildford Rd 226 AY119
Caney Ms, NW2
off Claremont Rd 119 CX61
Canfield Dr, Ruis. HA4 . . . . .115 BV64
Canfield Gdns, NW6 . . . . . . .140 DC66
Canfield Pl, NW6
off Canfield Gdns 140 DC65
Canfield Rd, Rain. RM13 . . . .147 FF67
Woodford Green IG8 . . . . .102 EL52
Canford Av, Nthlt. UB5 . . . . .136 BY67
Canford Cl, Enf. EN2 . . . . . . .81 DN40
Canford Dr, Add. KT15 . . . . .194 BH103
Canford Gdns, N.Mal. KT3 . .198 CR100
Canford Pl, Tedd. TW11 . . . .177 CH93
Canford Rd, SW11 . . . . .180 DG85
Cangels Cl, Hem.H. HP1 . . . . .39 BF22
Canham Rd, SE25 . . . . .202 DS97
W3 . . . . .158 CS75
Can Hatch, Tad. KT20 . . . . . .233 CY118
Canmore Gdns, SW16 . . . . . .181 DJ94
Sch **Cann Hall Prim Sch**,
E11 *off Cann Hall Rd* 124 EF62
Cann Hall Rd, E11 . . . . .124 EE63
Canning Cres, N22 . . . . .99 DM53
Canning Cross, SE5 . . . . . . .162 DS82
Canning Pas, W8 . . . . .17 L5
Canning Pl, W8 . . . . .17 L5
Canning Pl Ms, W8 . . . . .17 L4
Canning Rd, E15 . . . . .144 EE68
E17 . . . . .123 DY56
N5 . . . . .121 DP62
Croydon CR0 . . . . .202 DT103
Harrow HA3 . . . . .117 CF55
Cannington Rd, Dag. RM9 . . .146 EW65
CANNING TOWN, E16 . . . . . . .15 L7
⇌ **Canning Town** 15 H7
⊖ **Canning Town** 15 H7
DLR **Canning Town** 15 H7
Cannizaro Rd, SW19 . . . . . . .179 CW93
Cannonbury Av, Pnr. HA5 . . .116 BX58
Cannon Cl, SW20 . . . . .199 CW97
Hampton TW12
off Hanworth Rd 176 CB93
Cannon Ct, EC1
off St. John St 141 DP70
Cannon Cres, Wok.
(Chobham) GU24 . . . . . . .210 AS111
Cannon Dr, E14 . . . . .13 N10
Cannon Gate, Slou. SL2
off The Frithe 132 AW73
Cannon Gro, Lthd. (Fetch.)
KT22 . . . . .231 CE121
Cannon Hill, N14 . . . . .99 DK48
NW6 . . . . .120 DA64
Cannon Hill Cl, Maid. SL6 . . .150 AC77
Cannon Hill La, SW20 . . . . . .199 CY97
Cannon La, NW3 . . . . .120 DD62
Pinner HA5 . . . . .116 BY60
Sch **Cannon La First Sch**,
Pnr. HA5
off Cannonbury Av 116 BX58
Sch **Cannon La Mid Sch**,
Pnr. HA5
off Cannonbury Av 116 BX58
Cannon Ms, Wal.Abb. EN9 . . .67 EB33
Cannon Mill Av, Chesh. HP5 . .54 AR33
Cannon Pl, NW3 . . . . .120 DD62
SE7 . . . . .164 EL78
Cannon Rd, N14 . . . . .99 DL48
Bexleyheath DA7 . . . . . . .166 EY81
Watford WD18 . . . . .76 BW43
Cannonside, Lthd. (Fetch.)
KT22 . . . . .231 CE122
Cannons Meadow, Welw.
(Tewin) AL6 . . . . .30 DE06
⇌ **Cannon Street** 11 J10
⊖ **Cannon Street** 11 J10
Cannon St, EC4 . . . . .10 G8
St. Albans AL3 . . . . .43 CD19
Cannon St Rd, E1 . . . . .12 C7
Cannon Trd Est, Wem. HA9 . .118 CP63
Cannon Way, Lthd. (Fetch.)
KT22 . . . . .231 CE121
West Molesey KT8 . . . . . .196 CA98
Cannon Wf Business Cen,
SE8 . . . . .23 J8
Cannon Workshops, E14 . . . .13 N10
Canon Av, Rom. RM6 . . . . . .126 EW57
Sch **Canon Barnett Prim Sch**,
E1 . . . . .11 P7
Canon Beck Rd, SE16 . . . . . . .22 F3
Canonbie Rd, SE23 . . . . .182 DW87
CANONBURY, N1 . . . . .4 F4
⇌ **Canonbury** 4 G2
Canonbury Cres, N1 . . . . .4 G5
Canonbury Gro, N1 . . . . .4 G5
Sch **Canonbury Jun &
Inf Sch**, N1 . . . . .4 F4
Canonbury La, N1 . . . . .4 E5
Canonbury Pk N, N1 . . . . .4 G4
Canonbury Pk S, N1 . . . . .4 G4
Canonbury Pl, N1 . . . . .4 F4
Canonbury Rd, N1 . . . . .4 E4
Enfield EN1 . . . . .82 DS39
Canonbury Sq, N1 . . . . .4 F5
Canonbury St, N1 . . . . .4 G5
Canonbury Vil, N1 . . . . .4 F5
Canonbury Yd, N1 . . . . .5 J7
Canonbury Yd W, N1 . . . . .4 F4
Canon Mohan Cl, N14
off Farm La 81 DH44
Sch **Canon Palmer RC High
Sch**, Ilf. IG3
off Aldborough Rd S . . .125 ES60
Canon Rd, Brom. BR1 . . . . . .204 EJ97
Canon Row, SW1 . . . . .19 N4
Canons Brook, Harl. CM19 . . .51 EN15
Canons Cl, N2 . . . . .120 DD59
Edgware HA8 . . . . .96 CM51
Radlett WD7 . . . . .77 CH35
Reigate RH2 . . . . .249 CZ133
Canons Cor, Edg. HA8 . . . . . .96 CL49
Canons Dr, Edg. HA8 . . . . . . .96 CL51
Canons Gate, Harl. CM20 . . . .35 EN13
Waltham Cross (Chsht)
EN8 . . . . .67 DZ26

⊖ London Underground station DLR Docklands Light Railway station Tra Tramlink station Riv Pedestrian ferry landing stage

Sch Canons High Sch, Edg.
HA8 off Shaldon Rd 96 CM54
Canon's Hill, Couls. CR5 235 DN117
Canons La, Tad. KT20 233 CY118
Canonsleigh Rd, Dag. RM9 146 EV66
CANONS PARK, Edg. HA8 96 CL52
⊖ Canons Park 96 CL52
Canons Pk Cl, Edg. HA8
off Donnefield Av 96 CL52
Canons Rd, Ware SG12 32 DW05
Canon St, N1 4 G8
Canons Wk, Croy. CR0 203 DX104
Canopus Way, Nthwd. HA6 93 BU49
Staines TW19 174 BL87
Canopy La, Harl. CM17
off London Rd 36 EW14
Canrobert St, E2 12 C1
Cantelowes Rd, NW1 141 DK65
Canterbury Av, Ilf. IG1 124 EL59
Sidcup DA15 186 EW89
Slough SL2 131 AQ70
Upminster RM14 129 FT60
Canterbury Cl, E6
off Harper Rd 145 EM72
Amersham HP7 55 AS39
Beckenham BR3 203 EB95
Chigwell IG7 103 ET48
Dartford DA1 188 FN87
Greenford UB6 136 CB72
Northwood HA6 93 BT51
Canterbury Cres, SW9 161 DN83
Canterbury Gro, SE27 181 DP90
Canterbury Ho, Borwd. WD6 78 CN40
Erith DA8 off Arthur St 167 FF80
Canterbury Ms, Lthd.
(Oxshott) KT22 214 CC113
Windsor SL4 off Green La 151 AN82
Canterbury Par, S.Ock.
RM15 149 FW69
Canterbury Pl, SE17 20 F8
Canterbury Rd, E10 123 EC59
NW6 140 DA68
Borehamwood WD6 78 CN40
Croydon CR0 201 DM101
Feltham TW13 176 BY90
Gravesend DA12 191 GJ89
Guildford GU2 242 AT132
Harrow HA1, HA2 116 CB57
Morden SM4 200 DC99
Watford WD17 75 BV40
Canterbury Ter, NW6 140 DA68
Canterbury Way, Brwd.
(Gt Warley) CM13 107 FW51
Purfleet RM19 169 FS80
Rickmansworth (Crox.Grn)
WD3 75 BQ41
Cantium Retail Pk, SE1 162 DU79
Cantley Gdns, SE19 202 DT95
Ilford IG2 125 EQ58
Cantley Rd, W7 157 CG76
Canton St, E14 13 N8
Cantrell Rd, E3 13 M4
Cantwell Rd, SE18 165 EP80
Canute Gdns, SE16 22 G7
Canvey St, SE1 20 F1
Capability Way, Green. DA9 169 FW84
Cape Cl, Bark. IG11
off North St 145 EQ65
Capel Av, Wall. SM6 219 DM106
Capel Cl, N20 98 DC48
Bromley BR2 204 EL102
Capel Ct, EC2 11 K8
SE20 off Melvin Rd 202 DW95
Capel Gdns, Ilf. IG3 125 ET63
Pinner HA5 116 BZ56
Capella Rd, Nthwd. HA6 93 BT50
Capell Av, Rick. (Chorl.)
WD3 73 BC43
Capell Rd, Rick. (Chorl.)
WD3 73 BC43
Capell Way, Rick. (Chorl.)
WD3 73 BD43
Coll Capel Manor Coll & Gdns,
Enf. EN1
off Bullsmoor La 82 DU35
Sch Capel Manor Prim Sch, Enf.
EN1 off Bullsmoor La 82 DV35
Capel Pl, Dart. DA2 188 FJ91
Capel Pt, E7 124 EH63
Capel Rd, E7 124 EH63
E12 124 EJ63
Barnet EN4 80 DE44
Enfield EN1 82 DV36
Watford WD19 76 BY44
Capel Vere Wk, Wat. WD17 75 BS39
Capener's Cl, SW1 18 E4
Capern Rd, SW18
off Cargill Rd 180 DC88
Cape Rd, N17
off High Cross Rd 122 DU55
St. Albans AL1 43 CH20
Cape Yd, E1 22 B1
Capital Business Cen, Wem.
HA0 137 CK68
Sch Capital City Acad, NW10
off Doyle Gdns 139 CU67
Coll Capital Coll (C.I.F.E.)
London Sch of Insurance,
WC1 10 A5
Capital Ind Est, Mitch. CR4
off Willow La 200 DF99
Capital Interchange Way,
Brent. TW8 158 CN78
Capital Pk, Wok. (Old Wok.)
GU22 227 BB121
Capitol Pl, Harl. CM19
off Lovet Rd 51 EN16
Capitol Ind Pk, NW9 118 CQ55
Capitol Way, NW9 118 CQ55
Capland St, NW8 7 P3
Caple Par, NW10
off Harley Rd 138 CS68
Caple Rd, NW10 139 CT68
Capon Cl, Brwd. CM14 108 FV46
Caponfield, Welw.G.C. AL7 30 DB11
Cappell La, Ware SG12 33 ED10
Capper St, WC1 9 K4
Caprea Cl, Hayes UB4
off Triandra Way 136 BX71
Capri Rd, Croy. CR0 202 DT102
Capstan Cen, Til. RM18 170 GD80
Capstan Cl, Rom. RM6 126 EV58
Capstan Ct, Dart. DA2 168 FQ84
Capstan Ms, Grav. DA11 190 GE87
Capstan Ride, Enf. EN2 81 DN40
Capstan Rd, SE8 23 L7
Capstan Sq, E14 24 D4
Capstan's Wf, Wok.
(St.John's) GU21 226 AT118
Capstan Way, SE16 23 K2
Capstone Rd, Brom. BR1 184 EF91
Captain Cook Cl, Ch.St.G.
HP8 90 AU49
Captains Cl, Chesh. HP5 54 AN27
Captains Wk, Berk. HP4 38 AX20
Capthorne Av, Har. HA2 116 BY60
Capuchin Cl, Stan. HA7 95 CH51
Capulet Ms, E16 25 M1
Capworth St, E10 123 EA60
Caractacus Cottage Vw, Wat.
WD18 93 BU45
Caractacus Grn, Wat. WD18 75 BT44
Caradoc Cl, W2 6 G7
Caradoc St, SE10 24 G9
Caradon Cl, E11
off Brockway Cl 124 EE61
Woking GU21 226 AV118
Caradon Way, N15 122 DR56
Caravan La, Rick. WD3 92 BL45
Caravel Cl, E14
off Tiller Rd 163 EA76
Grays RM16 170 FZ76
Caravelle Gdns, Nthlt. UB5
off Javelin Way 136 BX69
Caravel Ms, SE8
off Watergate St 163 EA79
Caraway Cl, E13 15 N5
Caraway Pl, Guil. GU2 242 AU129
Wallington SM6 201 DH104
Carberry Rd, SE19 182 DS93
Carbery Av, W3 158 CM75
Carbis Cl, E4 101 ED46
Carbis Rd, E14 13 L7
Carbone Hill, Hert.
(Newgate St) SG13 65 DK26
Potters Bar (Cuffley) EN6 65 DJ27
Carbuncle Pas Way, N17 100 DU54
Carburton St, W1 9 H5
Carbury Cl, Horn. RM12 148 FJ65
Cardale St, E14 24 C5
Carde Cl, Hert. SG14 31 DM08
Carden Rd, SE15 162 DV83
Cardiff Rd, W7 157 CG76
Enfield EN3 82 DV42
Watford WD18 75 BV44
Cardiff St, SE18 165 ES80
Cardiff Way, Abb.L. WD5 59 BU32
Cardigan Cl, Slou. SL1 131 AM73
Woking GU21
off Bingham Dr 226 AS118
Cardigan Gdns, Ilf. IG3 126 EU61
Cardigan Rd, E3 143 DZ68
SW13 159 CU82
SW19 off Haydons Rd 180 DC93
Richmond TW10 178 CL86
Cardigan St, SE11 20 C9
Cardigan Wk, N1
off Ashby Gro 142 DQ66
Cardinal Av, Borwd. WD6 78 CP41
Kingston upon Thames
KT2 178 CL92
Morden SM4 199 CY100
Cardinal Bourne St, SE1 21 K6
Cardinal Cl, Chis. BR7 205 ER95
Edgware HA8
off Abbots Rd 96 CR52
Morden SM4 199 CY101
South Croydon CR2 220 DU113
Waltham Cross (Chsht)
EN7 off Adamsfield 66 DT26
Worcester Park KT4 217 CU105
Cardinal Ct, Borwd. WD6
off Cardinal Av 78 CP41
Cardinal Cres, N.Mal. KT3 198 CQ96
Cardinal Dr, Ilf. IG6 103 EQ51
Walton-on-Thames KT12 196 BX102
Cardinal Gro, St.Alb. AL3 42 CB22
Cardinal Hinsley Cl, NW10 139 CU68
Sch Cardinal Hinsley RC
High Sch, NW10
off Harlesden Rd 139 CU67
Sch Cardinal Newman Catholic
Prim Sch, Walt. KT12
off Arch Rd 196 BX104
Cardinal Pl, SW15 159 CX84
Sch Cardinal Pole RC Sec Sch,
E9 off Kenworthy Rd 123 DY64
Annexe, E9
off Victoria Pk Rd 143 DX66
Cardinal Rd, Felt. TW13 175 BV88
Ruislip HA4 116 BX60
Sch Cardinal Rd Inf & Nurs
Sch, Felt. TW13
off Cardinal Rd 175 BV88
Cardinals Wk, Hmptn. TW12 176 CC94
Maidenhead SL6 130 AJ72
Sunbury-on-Thames
TW16 175 BS93
Cardinals Way, N19 121 DK60
Sch Cardinal Vaughan Mem
Sch, W14 16 C3
Cardinal Way, Har. HA3
off Wolseley Rd 117 CE55
Rainham RM13 148 FK68
Sch Cardinal Wiseman RC
High Sch, Grnf. UB6
off Greenford Rd 136 CC71
Cardine Ms, SE15 162 DV80
Cardingham, Wok. GU21 226 AU117
Cardington Sq, Houns. TW4 156 BX84
Cardington St, NW1 9 J1
Cardinham Rd, Orp. BR6 223 ET105
Cardozo Rd, N7 121 DL64
Cardrew Av, N12 98 DD50
Cardrew Cl, N12 98 DE50
Cardross St, W6 159 CV76
Sch Cardwell Prim Sch, SE18
off Frances St 165 EM77
Cardwell Rd, N7 121 DL63
Cardwells Keep, Guil. GU2 242 AU131
Cardy Rd, Hem.H. HP1 40 BH21
Carew Cl, N7 121 DM61
Coulsdon CR5 235 DP119
Grays (Chaff.Hun.) RM16 170 FY76
Carew Ct, Sutt. SM2 218 DB109
Sch Carew Manor Sch, Wall.
SM6 off Church Rd 201 DK104
Carew Rd, N17 100 DU54
W13 157 CJ75
Ashford TW15 175 BQ93
Mitcham CR4 200 DG96
Northwood HA6 93 BS51
Thornton Heath CR7 201 DP97
Wallington SM6 219 DJ107
Carew St, SE5 162 DQ82
Carew Way, Wat. WD19 94 BZ48
Carey Cl, Wind. SL4 151 AP83
Carey Ct, Bexh. DA6 187 FB85
Carey Gdns, SW8 161 DJ81
Carey La, EC2 10 G7
Carey Pl, SW1 19 L8
Carey Rd, Dag. RM9 126 EY63
Careys Cft, Berk. HP4 38 AU16
Carey's Fld, Sev. (Dunt.Grn)
TN13 241 FE120
Carey St, WC2 10 B8
Careys Wd, Horl. (Smallfield)
RH6 269 DP148
Carfax Pl, SW4
off Holwood Pl 161 DK84
Carfax Rd, Hayes UB3 155 BT78
Hornchurch RM12 127 FF63
Carfree Cl, N1 4 D5
Cargill Rd, SW18 180 DB88
Cargo Forecourt Rd, Gat.
RH6 268 DD152
Cargo Rd, Gat. RH6 268 DD152
Cargreen Pl, SE25
off Cargreen Rd 202 DT98
Cargreen Rd, SE25 202 DT98
Carholme Rd, SE23 183 DZ88
Carisbrooke Av, Bex. DA5 186 EX88
Watford WD24 76 BX39
Carisbrooke Cl, Enf. EN1 82 DT39
Hornchurch RM11 128 FN60
Stanmore HA7 95 CK54
Carisbrooke Ct, Slou. SL1 132 AT73
Carisbrooke Gdns, SE15
off Commercial Way 162 DT80
Carisbrooke Ho, Kings.T.
KT2 off Kingsgate Rd 198 CL95
Carisbrooke Rd, E17 123 DY56
Bromley BR2 204 EJ98
Mitcham CR4 201 DK98
St. Albans AL2 60 CB26
Carisbrook Rd, Brwd.
(Pilg.Hat.) CM15 108 FV44
Carker's La, NW5 121 DH64
Carlbury Cl, St.Alb. AL1 43 CH21
Carl Ekman Ho, Grav. DA11 190 GD87
Carleton Av, Wall. SM6 219 DK109
Carleton Cl, Esher KT10 197 CD102
Carleton Pl, Dart. (Hort.Kir.)
DA4 208 FQ98
Carleton Rd, N7 121 DK64
Dartford DA1 188 FN87
Waltham Cross (Chsht)
EN8 67 DX28
Carleton Vil, NW5
off Leighton Gro 121 DJ64
Carlile Cl, E3 143 DZ68
Carlina Gdns, Wdf.Grn. IG8 102 EH50
Carlingford Gdns, Mitch.
CR4 180 DF94
Carlingford Rd, N15 121 DP55
NW3 120 DD63
Morden SM4 199 CX100
Carlisle Av, EC3 11 M8
W3 138 CS72
St. Albans AL1, AL3 43 CD18
Carlisle Cl, Kings.T. KT2 198 CN95
Pinner HA5 116 BY59
Carlisle Gdns, Har. HA3 117 CK59
Ilford IG1 124 EL58
Sch Carlisle Inf Sch, Hmptn.
TW12 off Broad La 176 CB93
Carlisle La, SE1 20 B6
Carlisle Ms, NW8 7 P5
Carlisle Pl, N11 99 DH49
SW1 19 J6
Carlisle Rd, E10 123 EA61
N4 121 DN59
NW6 139 CY67
NW9 118 CQ55
Dartford DA1 188 FN86
Hampton TW12 176 CB94
Romford RM1 127 FG57
Slough SL1 131 AR73
Sutton SM1 217 CZ106
Carlisle St, W1 9 L8
Carlisle Wk, E8 5 N4
Carlisle Way, SW17 180 DG92
Carlos Pl, W1 8 F10
Carlow St, NW1
off Arlington Rd 141 DJ68
Carlton Av, N14 81 DK43
Feltham TW14 176 BW86
Greenhithe DA9 189 FS86
Harrow HA3 117 CH57
Hayes UB3 155 BS77
South Croydon CR2 220 DS108
Carlton Av E, Wem. HA9 118 CL60
Carlton Av W, Wem. HA0 117 CH61
Carlton Cl, NW3 120 DA61
Borehamwood WD6 78 CR42
Chessington KT9 215 CK107
Edgware HA8 96 CN50
Northolt UB5
off Whitton Av W 116 CC64
Upminster RM14 128 FP61
Woking GU21 211 AZ114
Carlton Ct, SW9 161 DP81
Ilford IG6 125 ER55
Uxbridge UB8 134 BK71
Carlton Cres, Sutt. SM3 217 CY105
Carlton Dr, SW15 179 CY85
Ilford IG6 125 ER55
Carlton Gdns, SW1 19 L2
W5 137 CJ72
Carlton Grn, Red. RH1 250 DE131
Carlton Gro, SE15 162 DV81
Carlton Hill, NW8 140 DB68
Carlton Ho, Felt. TW14 175 BT87
Carlton Ho Ter, SW1 19 L2
Carlton Par, Orp. BR6 206 EV101
Sevenoaks TN13
off St. John's Hill 257 FJ122
Carlton Pk Av, SW20 199 CW96
Carlton Pl, Nthwd. HA6 93 BP50
Weybridge KT13
off Castle Vw Rd 213 BP105
Sch Carlton Prim Sch, NW5
off Grafton Rd 120 DG64
Coll Carlton Resource Cen
(Adult Ed Inst for the Mentally
Handicapped), Sid. DA14
off Carlton Rd 185 ET91
Carlton Rd, E11 124 EF60
E12 124 EK63
E17 101 DY53
N4 121 DN59
N11 98 DG50
SW14 158 CQ83
W4 158 CR75
W5 137 CJ73
Erith DA8 167 FB79
Grays RM16 171 GF75
New Malden KT3 198 CS96
Redhill RH1 250 DF131
Reigate RH2 250 DD132
Romford RM2 127 FG57
Sidcup DA14 185 ET92
Slough SL2 132 AV73
South Croydon CR2 220 DR107
Sunbury-on-Thames
TW16 175 BT94
Walton-on-Thames KT12 195 BV101
Carlton Rd, Well. DA16 166 EV83
Woking GU21 211 BA114
Carlton Sq, E1 12 G3
Carlton St, SW1 9 L10
Carlton Ter, E11 124 EH57
N18 100 DR48
SE26 182 DW90
Carlton Twr Pl, SW1 18 D5
Carlton Tye, Horl. RH6 269 DJ148
Carlton Vale, NW6 140 DB68
Sch Carlton Vale Inf Sch,
NW6 6 F1
Carlton Vil, SW15
off St. John's Av 179 CW85
Carlwell St, SW17 180 DE92
Carlyle Av, Brom. BR1 204 EK97
Southall UB1 136 BZ73
Carlyle Cl, N2 120 DC58
West Molesey KT8 196 CB96
Carlyle Gdns, Sthl. UB1 136 BZ73
Carlyle Lo, Barn. (New Barn.)
EN5 off Richmond Rd 80 DC43
Carlyle Ms, E1 13 H3
Carlyle Pl, SW15 159 CX84
Carlyle Rd, E12 124 EL63
NW10 138 CR67
SE28 146 EV73
W5 157 CJ78
Croydon CR0 202 DU103
Staines TW18 173 BF94
★ Carlyle's Ho, SW3 160 DE79
Carlyle Sq, SW3 17 P10
Carlyon Av, Har. HA2 116 BZ63
Carlyon Cl, Wem. HA0 138 CL67
Carlyon Rd, Hayes UB4 136 BW72
Wembley HA0 138 CL68
Carmalt Gdns, SW15 159 CW84
Walton-on-Thames KT12 214 BW106
Carmarthen Grn, NW9
off Snowdon Dr 118 CS58
Carmarthen Rd, Slou. SL1 132 AS73
Carmel Cl, Wok. GU22 226 AY118
Carmel Ct, W8 17 J3
Wembley HA9 118 CP61
Carmelite Cl, Har. HA3 94 CC53
Carmelite Rd, Har. HA3 94 CC53
Carmelite St, EC4 10 D9
Carmelite Wk, Har. HA3 94 CC53
Carmelite Way, Har. HA3 94 CC54
Carmen Ct, Borwd. WD6
off Belford Rd 78 CM38
Carmen St, E14 14 A7
Carmichael Cl, SW11
off Darien Rd 160 DD83
Ruislip HA4 115 BU63
Carmichael Ms, SW18 180 DD87
Carmichael Rd, SE25 202 DU99
Carminia Rd, SW17 181 DH89
Carnaby Rd, Brox. EN10 49 DY20
Carnaby St, W1 9 J8
Carnach Grn, S.Ock. RM15 149 FV73
Carnac St, SE27 182 DR91
Carnanton Rd, E17 101 ED53
Carnarvon Av, Enf. EN1 82 DT41
Carnarvon Dr, Hayes UB3 155 BQ76
Carnarvon Rd, E10 123 EC58
E15 144 EF65
E18 102 EF53
Barnet EN5 79 CY41
Carnation Cl, Rom.
(Rush Grn) RM7 127 FE61
Carnation St, SE2 166 EV78
Carnbrook Rd, SE3 164 EK83
Carnecke Gdns, SE9 184 EL85
Carnegie Cl, Enf. EN3 83 EB38
Surbiton KT6
off Fullers Av 198 CM103
Carnegie Pl, SW19 179 CX90
Carnegie Rd, St.Alb. AL3 43 CD16
Carnegie St, N1 4 A8
CARNELES GREEN, Brox.
EN10 48 DV22
Carnet Cl, Dart. DA1 187 FE87
Carnforth Cl, Epsom KT19 216 CP107
Carnforth Gdns, Horn.
RM12 127 FG64
Carnforth Rd, SW16 181 DK94
Carnie Lo, SW17
off Manville Rd 181 DH90
Carnoustie Cl, SE28
off Redbourne Dr 146 EX72
Carnoustie Dr, N1 4 A6
Carnwath Rd, SW6 160 DA83
Caro La, Hem.H. HP3 40 BN22
Carol Cl, NW4 119 CX56
Carolina Cl, E15 124 EE64
Carolina Rd, Th.Hth. CR7 201 DP96
Caroline Cl, N10
off Alexandra Pk Rd 99 DH54
SW16 181 DM91
W2 7 K10
Croydon CR0 220 DS105
Isleworth TW7 157 CD80
West Drayton UB7 154 BK75
Caroline Ct, Ashf. TW15 175 BP93
Stanmore HA7
off The Chase 95 CG51
Caroline Gdns, SE15 162 DV80
Caroline Pl, SW11 160 DG82
W2 7 K9
Hayes UB3 155 BS80
Watford WD19 76 BY44
Caroline Pl Ms, W2 7 K10
Caroline Rd, SW19 179 CZ94
Caroline St, E1 13 H8
Caroline Ter, SW1 18 E8
Caroline Wk, W6 159 CY79
Carol St, NW1 141 DJ67
Carolyn Cl, Wok. GU21 226 AT119
Carolyn Dr, Orp. BR6 206 EU104
Caroon Dr, Rick. (Sarratt)
WD3 74 BH36
Carpenders Av, Wat. WD19 94 BY48
CARPENDERS PARK, Wat.
WD19 94 BZ47
⇌ Carpenders Park 94 BX48
Carpenders Pk, Wat. WD19 94 BY47
Carpenter Cl, Epsom KT17
off West St 217 CT109
Carpenter Gdns, N21 99 DP47
Carpenter Path, Brwd.
(Hutt.) CM13 109 GD43
Carpenters Arms La, Epp.
(Thnwd) CM16 70 EV25
Carpenters Arms Path, SE9
off Eltham High St 185 EM86
Carpenters Ct, Twick. TW2 177 CE89
Carpenters Pl, SW4 161 DK84
Sch Carpenters Prim Sch,
E15 off Friendship Way 143 EC67
Carpenters Rd, E15 143 EB65
Enfield EN1 82 DW36
Carpenter St, W1 8 G10
Carpenters Wd Dr, Rick.
(Chorl.) WD3 73 BB42
Carpenter Way, Pot.B. EN6 64 DC33
Carrack Ho, Erith DA8
off Saltford Cl 167 FE78
Carrara Cl, SW9
off Eaton Dr 161 DP84
Carrara Ms, E8 122 DU64
Carrara Wf, SW6 159 CY83
Carr Cl, Stan. HA7 95 CH51
Carr Gro, SE18 164 EL77
Carriage Dr E, SW11 160 DG80
Carriage Dr N, SW11 160 DG79
Carriage Dr S, SW11 160 DF81
Carriage Dr W, SW11 160 DF80
Carriage Ms, Ilf. IG1 125 EQ61
Carriage Pl, N16 122 DR62
SW16 off Eardley Rd 181 DJ92
Carriage St, SE18 165 EP76
Carriageway, The, West.
TN16 240 EX124
Carrick Cl, Islw. TW7 157 CG83
Carrick Dr, Ilf. IG6 103 EQ53
Sevenoaks TN13 257 FH123
Carrick Gdns, N17
off Flexmere Rd 100 DS52
Carrick Gate, Esher KT10 196 CC104
Carrick Ms, SE8
off Watergate St 163 EA79
Carriden Ct, Hert. SG14
off The Ridgeway 31 DM07
Carrill Way, Belv. DA17 166 EX77
Carrington Av, Borwd. WD6 78 CP43
Hounslow TW3 176 CB85
Carrington Cl, Barn. EN5 79 CU43
Borehamwood WD6 78 CQ43
Croydon CR0 203 DY101
Kingston upon Thames
KT2 178 CQ92
Redhill RH1 250 DF133
Carrington Gdns, E7
off Woodford Rd 124 EH63
Carrington Pl, Esher KT10 214 CC105
Carrington Rd, Dart. DA1 188 FM86
Richmond TW10 158 CN84
Slough SL1 132 AS73
Carrington Sq, Har. HA3 94 CC52
Carrington St, W1 18 G2
Carrol Cl, NW5 121 DH63
Carroll Av, Guil. GU1 243 BB134
Carroll Cl, E15 124 EF64
Carroll Hill, Loug. IG10 85 EM41
Carronade Pl, SE28 165 EQ76
Carron Cl, E14 14 B7
Carroun Rd, SW8 161 DM80
Carroway La, Grnf. UB6
off Cowgate Rd 137 CD69
Carrow Rd, Dag. RM9 146 EV66
Walton-on-Thames KT12
off Kenilworth Dr 196 BX104
Carr Rd, E17 101 DZ54
Northolt UB5 136 CA65
Carrs La, N21 82 DQ43
Carr St, E14 13 K7
CARSHALTON, SM5 218 DD105
⇌ Carshalton 218 DF105
H Carshalton, Beddington &
Wallington War Mem
Hosp, Cars. SM5 218 DF107
CARSHALTON BEECHES,
Cars. SM5 218 DD109
⇌ Carshalton Beeches 218 DF107
Coll Carshalton Coll, Cars.
SM5
off Nightingale Rd 200 DF104
Carshalton Gro, Sutt. SM1 218 DD105
Sch Carshalton High Sch
for Boys, Cars. SM5
off Winchcombe Rd 200 DE103
Sch Carshalton High Sch for
Girls, Cars. SM5
off West St 200 DF104
CARSHALTON ON THE HILL,
Cars. SM5 218 DG109
Carshalton Pk Rd, Cars.
SM5 218 DF106
Carshalton Pl, Cars. SM5 218 DG105
Carshalton Rd, Bans. SM7 218 DF114
Carshalton SM5 218 DC106
Mitcham CR4 200 DG98
Sutton SM1 218 DC106
Carsington Gdns, Dart. DA1 188 FK89
Carslake Rd, SW15 179 CW86
Carson Rd, E16 15 M4
SE21 182 DR89
Barnet EN4 80 DF42
Carstairs Rd, SE6 183 EC90
Carston Cl, SE12 184 EF85
Carswell Cl, Brwd. (Hutt.)
CM13 109 GD44
Ilford IG4
off Roding La S 124 EK56
Carswell Rd, SE6 183 EC87
Cartbridge Cl, Wok. (Send)
GU23 off Send Rd 227 BB123
Cartel Cl, Purf. RM19 169 FR77
Carter Cl, Rom. RM5 105 FB52
Wallington SM6 219 DK108
Windsor SL4 151 AN82
Carter Ct, EC4 off Carter La 141 DP72
Carter Dr, Rom. RM5 105 FB52
Carteret St, SW1 19 L4
Carteret Way, SE8 23 K8
Sch Carterhatch Inf Sch, Enf.
EN1 off Carterhatch La 82 DV39
Sch Carterhatch Jun Sch, Enf.
EN1 off Carterhatch La 82 DV39
Carterhatch La, Enf. EN1 82 DU40
Carterhatch Rd, Enf. EN3 82 DW40
Carter La, EC4 10 F8
Carter Pl, SE17 21 H10
Carter Rd, E13 144 EH67
SW19 180 DD93
Carters Cl, Guil. GU1
off Slyfield Grn 242 AY130
Worcester Park KT4 199 CX103
Carters Cotts, Red. RH1
off Kings Av 266 DE136
Cartersfield Rd, Wal.Abb.
EN9 67 EC34
CARTERS GREEN, Harl.
CM17 37 FD13
Carters Hill, Sev. (Undrvr)
TN15 257 FP127
Carters Hill Cl, SE9 184 EJ88
Carters La, SE23 183 DY89
Epping CM16 51 EP24
Woking GU22 227 BC120
Carters Mead, Harl. CM17 52 EW17
Cartersmead Cl, Horl. RH6
off Wheatfield Way 269 DH147
Carters Rd, Epsom KT17 233 CT115
Carters Row, Grav. (Nthflt)
DA11 191 GF88
Carter St, SE17 162 DQ79
Carters Yd, SW18
off Wandsworth High St 180 DA85

★ Place of interest | H Hospital | Sch School | Coll College | Uni University | ⇌ Railway station

Carter Wk, H.Wyc. (Penn) HP10 **88** AC47
Carthagena Est, Brox. EN10 **49** EC20
Carthew Rd, W6 **159** CV76
Carthew Vil, W6 **159** CV76
Carthouse La, Wok. GU21 **210** AS114
Carthusian St, EC1 **10** G5
Cartier Circle, E14 **24** B2
Carting La, WC2 **9** P10
Cart La, E4 **101** ED45
Cartmel Cl, N17
off Heybourne Rd **100** DV52
Reigate RH2 **250** DE133
Cartmel Gdns, Mord. SM4 **200** DC99
Cartmel Rd, Bexh. DA7 **166** FA81
Carton St, W1 **8** D7
Cart Path, Wat. WD25 **60** BW33
Cartridge Pl, SE18 **165** EP76
Cartwright Gdns, WC1 **9** N2
Cartwright Rd, Dag. RM9 **146** EZ66
Cartwright St, E1 **11** P9
Cartwright Way, SW13 **159** CV80
Carve Ley, Welw.G.C. AL7 **30** DB10
Carver Cl, W4 **158** CQ76
Carver Rd, SE24 **182** DQ86
Carville Cres, Brent. TW8 **158** CL77
Cary Rd, E11 **124** EE63
Carysfort Rd, N8 **121** DK57
N16 **122** DR62
Cary Wk, Rad. WD7 **61** CH34
Cascade Av, N10 **121** DJ56
Cascade Cl, Buck.H. IG9
off Cascade Rd **102** EK47
Orpington BR5 **206** EW97
Cascade Rd, Buck.H. IG9 **102** EK47
Cascades, Croy. CR0 **221** DZ110
Caselden Cl, Add. KT15 **212** BJ106
Casella Rd, SE14 **163** DX80
Casewick Rd, SE27 **181** DP91
Casey Cl, NW8 **8** A2
Casimir Rd, E5 **122** DV62
Casino Av, SE24 **182** DQ85
Caspian St, SE5 **162** DR80
Caspian Wk, E16 **144** EK72
Caspian Way, Swans. DA10 **190** FY85
Caspian Wf, E3 *off Violet Rd* **143** EB71
Cassandra Cl, Nthlt. UB5 **117** CD63
Cassandra Gate, Wal.Cr. EN8 **67** DZ27
Casselden Rd, NW10 **138** CR66
H **Cassel Hosp, The**, Rich. TW10 **177** CK91
Cassidy Rd, SW6 **160** DA80
Cassilda Rd, SE2 **166** EU77
Cassilis Rd, Twick. TW1 **177** CH85
Cassiobridge, Wat. WD18 **75** BR42
Cassiobridge Rd, Wat. WD18 **75** BS42
Cassiobury Av, Felt. TW14 **175** BT86
Cassiobury Ct, Wat. WD17 **75** BT40
Cassiobury Dr, Wat. WD17 **75** BT40
Sch **Cassiobury Inf Sch**, Wat. WD17
off Bellmount Wd Av **75** BS39
Sch **Cassiobury Jun Sch**, Wat. WD17
off Bellmount Wd Av **75** BS39
★ **Cassiobury Park**, Wat. WD18 **75** BS41
Cassiobury Pk, Wat. WD18 **75** BS41
Cassiobury Pk Av, Wat. WD18 **75** BS41
Cassiobury Rd, E17 **123** DX57
Cassio Rd, Wat. WD18 **75** BV41
Cassis Ct, Loug. IG10 **85** EQ42
Cassland Rd, E9 **142** DW66
Thornton Heath CR7 **202** DR98
Casslee Rd, SE6 **183** DZ87
Cassocks Sq, Shep. TW17 **195** BR100
Casson St, E1 **12** A6
Castaine Cl, Swan. BR8 **187** FF94
Castalia Sq, E14 **24** C4
Castalia St, E14
off Plevna St **163** EC75
Castano Ct, Abb.L. WD5 **59** BS31
Castellain Rd, W9 **7** L4
Castellan Av, Rom. RM2 **127** FH55
Castellane Cl, Stan. HA7
off Daventer Dr **95** CF52
Castello Av, SW15 **179** CW85
Castell Rd, Loug. IG10 **85** EQ39
CASTELNAU, SW13 **159** CU79
Castelnau, SW13 **159** CV79
Castelnau Gdns, SW13
off Arundel Ter **159** CV79
Castelnau Pl, SW13
off Castelnau **159** CV79
Castelnau Row, SW13
off Lonsdale Rd **159** CV79
Casterbridge, NW6 **140** DB67
Casterbridge Rd, SE3 **164** EG83
Casterton St, E8
off Wilton Way **142** DV65
Castile Rd, SE18 **165** EN77
Sch **Castilion Prim Sch**, SE28
off Copperfield Rd **146** EW72
Castillon Rd, SE6 **184** EE89
Castlands Rd, SE6 **183** DZ89
Castle Av, E4 **101** ED50
Epsom KT17 **217** CU109
Rainham RM13 **147** FE66
Slough (Datchet) SL3 **152** AU79
West Drayton UB7 **134** BL73
Castlebar Hill, W5 **137** CH71
Castlebar Ms, W5 **137** CJ71
⇌ **Castle Bar Park** **137** CF71
Castlebar Pk, W5 **137** CH70
Castlebar Rd, W5 **137** CJ71
Sch **Castlebar (Spec) Sch**, W13 *off Hathaway Gdns* **137** CF71
Castle Baynard St, EC4 **10** F9
Castlebrook Cl, SE11 **20** E7
Castle Cl, E9
off Swinnerton St **123** DY64
SW19 **179** CX90
W3 **158** CP75
Bromley BR2 **204** EE97
Bushey WD23 **76** CB44
Hoddesdon EN11 **33** EC14
Redhill (Bletch.) RH1 **252** DQ133
Reigate RH2 **266** DB138
Romford RM3 **106** FJ48
Sunbury-on-Thames TW16 *off Mill Fm Av* **175** BS94
Castlecombe Dr, SW19 **179** CX87
Sch **Castlecombe Prim Sch**, SE9 *off Castlecombe Rd* **184** EL92
Castlecombe Rd, SE9 **184** EL91
Castle Ct, EC3 **11** K8
SE26 *off Champion Rd* **183** DY91
SW15 *off Brewhouse La* **159** CY83
Castledine Rd, SE20 **182** DV94
Castle Dr, Horl. RH6 **269** DJ150
Ilford IG4 **124** EL58
Reigate RH2 **266** DA138
Castle Fm Rd, Sev. (Shore.) TN14 **225** FF109
Castlefield Rd, Reig. RH2 **250** DA133
Castleford Av, SE9 **185** EP88
Castleford Cl, N17 **100** DT51
Borehamwood WD6 **78** CM38
Castle Gdns, Dor. RH4 **248** CM134
Castlegate, Rich. TW9 **158** CM83
Castle Gateway, Berk. HP4 **38** AW17
Castle Grn, Wey. KT13 **195** BS104
Castle Gro Rd, Wok. (Chobham) GU24 **210** AS113
Castlehaven Rd, NW1 **141** DH66
Castle Hill, Berk. HP4 **38** AW17
Guildford GU1 **258** AX136
Longfield (Fawk.) DA3 **209** FX99
Windsor SL4 **151** AR81
Castle Hill Av, Berk. HP4 **38** AW18
Croydon (New Adgtn) CR0 **221** EB109
Castle Hill Cl, Berk. HP4 **38** AV18
Sch **Castle Hill Prim Sch**, Croy. CR0 *off Dunley Dr* **221** EC107
Castle Hill Rd, Egh. TW20 **172** AV91
Castle La, SW1 **19** K5
Castleleigh Ct, Enf. EN2 **82** DR43
Castlemaine Av, Epsom KT17 **217** CV109
South Croydon CR2 **220** DT106
Castlemaine Twr, SW11 **160** DF81
Castle Mead, Hem.H. HP1 **40** BH22
Castle Ms, N12
off Castle Rd **98** DC50
NW1 *off Castle Rd* **141** DH65
Hampton TW12
off Station Rd **196** CB95
Castle Par, Epsom KT17
off Ewell Bypass **217** CU108
Castle Pl, NW1 **141** DH65
W4 *off Windmill Rd* **158** CS77
Castle Pt, E13 **144** EJ68
Castlereagh St, W1 **8** C7
Castle Rd, N12 **98** DC50
NW1 **141** DH65
Coulsdon CR5 **234** DE120
Dagenham RM9 **146** EV67
Dartford (Eyns.) DA4 **225** FH107
Enfield EN3 **83** DY39
Epsom KT18 **232** CP115
Grays RM17 **170** FZ79
Hoddesdon EN11 **33** EB14
Isleworth TW7 **157** CF82
Northolt UB5 **136** CB65
St. Albans AL1 **43** CH20
Sevenoaks (Shore.) TN14 **225** FG108
Southall UB2 **156** BZ76
Swanscombe DA10 **190** FZ86
Weybridge KT13 **195** BS104
Woking GU21 **211** AZ114
Castle Sq, Guil. GU1 **258** AX136
Redhill (Bletch.) RH1 **252** DQ133
Castle St, E6 **144** EJ68
Berkhamsted HP4 **38** AW19
Greenhithe DA9 **189** FU85
Guildford GU1 **258** AX136
Hertford SG14 **32** DQ10
Kingston upon Thames KT1 **198** CL96
Redhill (Bletch.) RH1 **251** DP133
Slough SL1 **152** AT76
Swanscombe DA10 **190** FZ86
Castleton Av, Bexh. DA7 **167** FD81
Wembley HA9 **118** CL63
Castleton Cl, Bans. SM7 **234** DA115
Croydon CR0 **203** DY100
Castleton Dr, Bans. SM7 **234** DA115
Castleton Gdns, Wem. HA9 **118** CL62
Castleton Rd, E17 **101** ED54
SE9 **184** EK91
Ilford IG3 **126** EU60
Mitcham CR4 **201** DK98
Ruislip HA4 **116** BX60
Castletown Rd, W14 **16** D10
Castle Vw, Epsom KT18 **216** CP114
Castleview Cl, N4 **122** DQ60
Sch **Castleview Comb Sch**, Slou. SL3
off Woodstock Av **152** AX77
Castleview Gdns, Ilf. IG1 **124** EL58
Castleview Rd, Slou. SL3 **152** AW77
Castle Vw Rd, Wey. KT13 **213** BP105
Castle Wk, Reig. RH2
off High St **250** DA134
Sunbury-on-Thames TW16
off Elizabeth Gdns **196** BW97
Castle Way, SW19 **179** CX90
Epsom KT17
off Castle Av **217** CU109
Feltham TW13 **176** BW91
Castlewood Dr, SE9 **165** EM82
Castlewood Rd, N15 **122** DU58
N16 **122** DU59
Barnet EN4 **80** DD41
H **Castlewood Therapy Cen**, SE18 **165** EN81
Castle Yd, N6 *off North Rd* **120** DG59
SE1 **20** F1
Richmond TW10
off Hill St **177** CK85
Castor La, E14 **14** A10
Catalina Av, Grays (Chaff.Hun.) RM16 **170** FZ75
Catalin Ct, Wal.Abb. EN9
off Howard Cl **67** ED33
Catalpa Cl, Guil. GU1
off Cedar Way **242** AW132
Cater Gdns, Guil. GU3 **242** AT132
CATERHAM, CR3 **236** DU123
⇌ **Caterham** **236** DU124
Caterham Av, Ilf. IG5 **103** EM54
Caterham Bypass, Cat. CR3 **236** DV120
Caterham Cl, Cat. CR3 **236** DS120
Caterham Ct, Wal.Abb. EN9 **68** EF34
H **Caterham Dene Hosp**, Cat. CR3 **236** DT123
Caterham Dr, Couls. CR5 **235** DP118
Sch **Caterham High Sch**, Ilf. IG5
off Caterham Av **103** EM54
CATERHAM-ON-THE-HILL, Cat. CR3 **236** DT122
Caterham Rd, SE13 **163** EC83
Sch **Caterham Sch**, Cat. CR3
off Harestone Valley Rd **252** DT126
Coll **Caterham Valley Comm Learning Cen**, Cat. CR3
off Beechwood Rd **236** DU122
Catesby St, SE17 **21** K8
CATFORD, SE6 **183** EB88
⇌ **Catford** **183** EA87
⇌ **Catford Bridge** **183** EA87
Catford Bdy, SE6 **183** EB87
Sch **Catford Girls Sch**, SE6
off Bellingham Rd **183** EC90
Catford Hill, SE6 **183** DZ89
Catford Ms, SE6
off Holbeach Rd **183** EB87
Catford Rd, SE6 **183** EA88
Cathall Rd, E11 **123** ED62
Catham Cl, St.Alb. AL1 **43** CH22
Cathay St, SE16 **22** D4
Cathay Wk, Nthlt. UB5
off Brabazon Rd **136** CA68
Cathcart Dr, Orp. BR6 **205** ES103
Cathcart Hill, N19 **121** DJ62
Cathcart Rd, SW10 **160** DC79
Cathcart St, NW5 **141** DH65
Cathedral Ct, Guil. GU2 **258** AV135
Cathedral Ct, St.Alb. AL3 **42** CB22
Cathedral Hill Ind Est, Guil. GU2 **242** AU133
Cathedral Piazza, SW1 **19** J6
Sch **Cathedral Sch of St. Saviours & St. Mary Overie C of E, The**, SE1 **21** H3
Cathedral St, SE1 **21** J1
Cathedral Vw, Guil. GU2 **242** AT134
Catherall Rd, N5 **122** DQ62
Catherine Cl, Brwd. (Pilg.Hat.) CM15 **108** FU43
Grays RM16 **170** FZ75
Hemel Hempstead HP2
off Parr Cres **41** BP15
Loughton IG10
off Roding Gdns **85** EM44
West Byfleet (Byfleet) KT14 **212** BL114
Catherine Ct, N14
off Conisbee Ct **81** DJ43
Catherine Dr, Rich. TW9 **158** CL84
Sunbury-on-Thames TW16 **175** BT93
Catherine Gdns, Houns. TW3 **157** CD84
Catherine Griffiths Ct, EC1 **10** D3
Catherine Gro, SE10 **163** EB81
Catherine Howard Ct, Wey. KT13
off Old Palace Rd **195** BP104
Catherine Pl, SW1 **19** J5
Harrow HA1 **117** CF57
Catherine Rd, Enf. EN3 **83** DY36
Romford RM2 **127** FH57
Surbiton KT6 **197** CK99
Catherine's Cl, West Dr. UB7
off Money La **154** BK76
Catherine St, WC2 **10** A9
St. Albans AL3 **43** CD19
Catherine Wheel All, E1 **11** M6
Catherine Wheel Rd, Brent. TW8 **157** CK80
Catherine Wheel Yd, SW1 **19** J2
Cat Hill, Barn. EN4 **80** DE44
Cathles Rd, SW12 **181** DH86
Cathnor Rd, W12 **159** CV75
Catisfield Rd, Enf. EN3 **83** DY37
Catkin Cl, Hem.H. HP1 **40** BH19
Catlin Cres, Shep. TW17 **195** BR99
Catlin Gdns, Gdse. RH9 **252** DV130
Catling Cl, SE23 **182** DW90
Catlins La, Pnr. HA5 **115** BV55
Catlin St, SE16 **22** B10
Hemel Hempstead HP3 **40** BH23
Cator Cl, Croy. (New Adgtn) CR0 **222** EE111
Cator Cres, Croy. (New Adgtn) CR0 **221** ED111
Cator La, Beck. BR3 **203** DZ96
Cato Rd, SW4 **161** DK83
Sch **Cator Pk Sch for Girls**, Beck. BR3
off Lennard Rd **183** DY94
Cator Rd, SE26 **183** DX93
Carshalton SM5 **218** DF106
Cator St, SE15 **162** DT79
Cato St, W1 **8** B6
Catsey La, Bushey WD23 **94** CC45
Catsey Wds, Bushey WD23 **94** CC45
Catterick Cl, N11 **98** DG51
Catterick Way, Borwd. WD6 **78** CM39
Cattistock Rd, SE9 **184** EL92
CATTLEGATE, Enf. EN2 **65** DL33
Cattlegate Hill, Pot.B. (Northaw) EN6 **65** DK31
Cattlegate Rd, Enf. EN2 **65** DL34
Potters Bar EN6 **65** DK31
Cattley Cl, Barn. EN5
off Wood St **79** CY42
Cattlins Cl, Wal.Cr. EN7 **66** DT29
Catton St, WC1 **10** A6
Cattsdell, Hem.H. HP2 **40** BL18
Caulfield Rd, E6 **145** EM66
SE15 **162** DV82
Causeway, The, N2 **120** DE56
SW18 **160** DB84
SW19 **179** CX92
Carshalton SM5 **200** DG104
Chessington KT9 **216** CL105
Esher (Clay.) KT10 **215** CF108
Feltham TW14 **155** BU84
Hounslow TW4 **155** BU84
Maidenhead (Bray) SL6 **150** AC75
Potters Bar EN6 **64** DC31
Staines TW18 **173** BC91
Sutton SM2 **218** DC109
Teddington TW11
off Broad St **177** CF93
Causeway Cl, Pot.B. EN6 **64** DD31
Causeway Ct, Wok. GU21
off Bingham Dr **226** AT118
Causeyware Rd, N9 **100** DV45
Causton Rd, N6 **121** DH59
Causton Sq, Dag. RM10 **146** FA66
Causton St, SW1 **19** M8
Cautherly La, Ware (Gt Amwell) SG12 **33** DZ10
Cautley Av, SW4 **181** DJ85
Cavalier Cl, Rom. RM6 **126** EX56
Cavalier Gdns, Hayes UB3
off Hanover Circle **135** BR72
Cavalry Barracks, Houns. TW4 **156** BX83
Cavalry Cres, Houns. TW4 **156** BX84
Windsor SL4 **151** AQ83
Cavalry Gdns, SW15 **179** CY85
Cavan Dr, St.Alb. AL3 **43** CD15
Cavan Pl, Pnr. HA5 **94** BZ53
Cavaye Pl, SW10 **17** M10
Cavell Cres, Dart. DA1 **168** FN84
Romford (Harold Wd) RM3 **106** FL54
Cavell Dr, Enf. EN2 **81** DN40
Cavell Rd, N17 **100** DR52
Waltham Cross (Chsht) EN7 **66** DT27
Cavell St, E1 **12** D5
Cavell Way, Epsom KT19 **216** CN111
Cavendish Av, N3 **98** DA54
NW8 **140** DD68
Cavendish Av, W13 **137** CG71
Erith DA8 **167** FC79
Harrow HA1 **117** CD63
Hornchurch RM12 **147** FH65
New Malden KT3 **199** CV99
Ruislip HA4 **115** BV64
Sevenoaks TN13 **256** FG122
Sidcup DA15 **186** EU87
Welling DA16 **165** ET83
Woodford Green IG8 **102** EH53
Cavendish Cl, N18 **100** DV50
NW6 *off Cavendish Rd* **139** CZ66
NW8 **7** P1
Amersham HP6 **72** AV39
Hayes UB4 *off Westacott* **135** BS71
Maidenhead (Taplow) SL6 **130** AG72
Sunbury-on-Thames TW16 **175** BT93
Coll **Cavendish Coll**, WC1 **9** L5
Cavendish Ct, EC3 **11** M7
Rickmansworth (Crox.Grn) WD3 *off Mayfare* **75** BR43
Sunbury-on-Thames TW16 **175** BT93
Cavendish Cres, Borwd. (Elstree) WD6 **78** CN42
Hornchurch RM12 **147** FH65
Cavendish Dr, E11 **123** ED60
Edgware HA8 **96** CM51
Esher (Clay.) KT10 **215** CE106
Cavendish Gdns, Bark. IG11 **125** ES64
Ilford IG1 **125** EN60
Redhill RH1 **250** DG133
Romford RM6 **126** EY57
Cavendish Ms N, W1 **9** H5
Cavendish Ms S, W1 **9** H6
Cavendish Par, Houns. TW4
off Bath Rd **156** BY82
Cavendish Pl, W1 **9** H7
Sch **Cavendish Prim Sch**, W4
off Edensor Rd **158** CS80
Cavendish Rd, E4 **101** EC51
N4 **121** DN58
N18 **100** DV50
NW6 **139** CY66
SW12 **181** DH86
SW19 **180** DD94
W4 **158** CQ81
Barnet EN5 **79** CW41
Chesham HP5 **54** AR32
Croydon CR0 **201** DP102
New Malden KT3 **199** CT99
Redhill RH1 **250** DG134
St. Albans AL1 **43** CF20
Sunbury-on-Thames TW16 **175** BT93
Sutton SM2 **218** DC108
Weybridge KT13 **213** BQ108
Woking GU22 **226** AX119
Sch **Cavendish Sch, The**, NW1 *off Arlington Rd* **141** DH67
Hemel Hempstead HP1
off Warners End Rd **40** BH19
Sch **Cavendish (Spec) Sch**, W13 *off Compton Cl* **137** CG72
Cavendish Sq, W1 **9** H7
Longfield DA3 **209** FX97
Cavendish St, N1 **5** J10
Cavendish Ter, Felt. TW13
off High St **175** BU89
Cavendish Way, Hat. AL10 **45** CT18
West Wickham BR4 **203** EB102
Cavenham Cl, Wok. GU22 **226** AY119
Cavenham Gdns, Horn. RM11 **128** FJ57
Ilford IG1 **125** ER62
Caverleigh Way, Wor.Pk. KT4 **199** CU102
Cave Rd, E13 **144** EH68
Richmond TW10 **177** CJ91
Caversham Av, N13 **99** DN48
Sutton SM3 **199** CY103
Caversham Ct, N11 **98** DG48
Caversham Flats, SW3
off Caversham St **160** DF79
Caversham Rd, N15 **122** DQ56
NW5 **141** DJ65
Kingston upon Thames KT1 **198** CM96
Caversham St, SW3 **160** DF79
Caverswall St, W12 **139** CW72
Caveside Cl, Chis. BR7 **205** EN95
Cavill's Wk, Chig. IG7 **104** EW47
Romford RM4 **104** EX47
Cawcott Dr, Wind. SL4 **151** AL81
Cawdor Av, S.Ock. RM15 **149** FU73
Cawdor Cres, W7 **157** CG77
Cawley Hatch, Harl. CM19 **51** EM15
Cawnpore St, SE19 **182** DS92
Cawsey Way, Wok. GU21 **226** AY117
Caxton Av, Add. KT15 **212** BG107
Caxton Dr, Uxb. UB8
off Chiltern Vw Rd **134** BK68
Caxton Gdns, Guil. GU2 **242** AV133
Caxton Gro, E3 **13** N1
Caxton Hill, Hert. SG13 **32** DT09
Caxton Hill Extension Rd, Hert. SG13 **32** DT09
Caxton La, Oxt. RH8 **254** EL131
Caxton Ms, Brent. TW8
off The Butts **157** CK79
Caxton Ri, Red. RH1 **250** DG133
Caxton Rd, N22 **99** DM54
SW19 **180** DC92
W12 **16** A3
Hoddesdon EN11 **33** EB13
Southall UB2 **156** BX76
Caxtons Ct, Guil. GU1 **243** BA132
Caxton St, SW1 **19** K5
Caxton St N, E16 **15** J9
Caxton Way, Rom. RM1 **127** FE56
Watford WD18 **75** BR44
Cayenne Ct, SE1 **21** P2
Caygill Cl, Brom. BR2 **204** EF98
Cayley Cl, Wall. SM6 **219** DL108
Sch **Cayley Prim Sch**, E14 **13** J7
Cayley Rd, Sthl. UB2
off McNair Rd **156** CB76
Cayton Pl, EC1 **11** J2
Cayton Rd, Couls. CR5 **235** DJ122
Greenford UB6 **137** CE68
Cayton St, EC1 **11** J2
Cazenove Rd, E17 **101** EA53
N16 **122** DT61
Cearns Ho, E6 **144** EK67
Cearn Way, Couls. CR5 **235** DM115
Cecil Av, Bark. IG11 **145** ER66
Enfield EN1 **82** DT42
Grays RM16 **170** FZ75
Hornchurch RM11 **128** FL55
Wembley HA9 **118** CM64
Cecil Cl, W5 *off Helena Rd* **137** CK71
Ashford TW15 **175** BQ93
Chessington KT9 **215** CK105
Cecil Ct, WC2 **9** M10
Barnet EN5 **79** CX41
Cecil Cres, Hat. AL10 **45** CV16
Cecile Pk, N8 **121** DL58
Cecilia Cl, N2 **120** DC55
★ **Cecilia Coleman Gall**, NW8 *off St. John's Wd High St* **140** DD68
Cecilia Rd, E8 **122** DU64
Cecil Pk, Pnr. HA5 **116** BY56
Cecil Pl, Mitch. CR4 **200** DF99
Cecil Rd, E11 **124** EE62
E13 **144** EG67
E17 **101** EA53
N10 **99** DH54
N14 **99** DJ46
NW9 **118** CS55
NW10 **138** CS67
SW19 **180** DB94
W3 **138** CQ71
Ashford TW15 **175** BQ94
Croydon CR0 **201** DM100
Enfield EN2 **82** DR42
Gravesend DA11 **191** GF88
Harrow HA3 **117** CE55
Hertford SG13 **32** DQ12
Hoddesdon EN11 **49** EC15
Hounslow TW3 **156** CC82
Ilford IG1 **125** EP63
Iver SL0 **133** BE72
Potters Bar EN6 **63** CU32
Romford RM6 **126** EX59
St. Albans AL1 **43** CF20
Sutton SM1 **217** CZ107
Waltham Cross (Chsht) EN8 **67** DX32
Sch **Cecil Rd Prim Sch**, Grav. DA11 *off Cecil Rd* **191** GF88
★ **Cecil Sharp Ho**, NW1 **140** DG67
Cecil St, Wat. WD24 **75** BV38
Cecil Way, Brom. BR2 **204** EG102
Slough SL2 **131** AM70
Cedar Av, Barn. EN4 **98** DE45
Cobham KT11 **230** BW115
Enfield EN3 **82** DW40
Gravesend DA12 **191** GJ91
Hayes UB3 **135** BU72
Romford RM6 **126** EY57
Ruislip HA4 **136** BW65
Sidcup DA15 **186** EU87
Twickenham TW2 **176** CB86
Upminster RM14 **128** FN63
Waltham Cross EN8 **67** DX33
West Drayton UB7 **134** BM74
Cedar Chase, Maid. (Taplow) SL6 **130** AD70
Cedar Cl, E3 **143** DZ67
SE21 **182** DQ88
SW15 **178** CR91
Borehamwood WD6 **78** CP42
Brentwood (Hutt.) CM13 **109** GD45
Bromley BR2 **204** EL104
Buckhurst Hill IG9 **102** EK47
Carshalton SM5 **218** DF107
Chesham HP5
off Lye Grn Rd **54** AS30
Dorking RH4 **263** CH136
East Molesey KT8
off Cedar Rd **197** CE98
Epsom KT17 **217** CT114
Esher KT10 **214** BZ108
Hertford SG14 **31** DP09
Iver SL0
off Thornbridge Rd **133** BC66
Potters Bar EN6 **64** DA30
Reigate RH2 **266** DC136
Romford RM7 **127** FC56
Sawbridgeworth CM21 **36** EY06
Staines TW18 **194** BJ97
Swanley BR8 **207** FC96
Ware SG12 **33** DX07
Warlingham CR6 **237** DY118
Cedar Copse, Brom. BR1 **205** EM96
Cedar Ct, E11
off Grosvenor Rd **124** EH57
N1 **5** H5
SE9 **184** EL86
SW19 **179** CX90
Egham TW20 **173** BA91
Epping CM16 **70** EU31
St. Albans AL4 **43** CK20
Cedar Cres, Brom. BR2 **204** EL104
Cedarcroft Rd, Chess. KT9 **216** CM105
Cedar Dr, N2 **120** DE56
Dartford (Sutt.H.) DA4 **208** FP96
Leatherhead (Fetch.) KT22 **231** CE123
Loughton IG10 **85** EP40
Pinner HA5 **94** CA51
Cedar Gdns, Sutt. SM2 **218** DC107
Upminster RM14 **128** FQ62
Woking GU21
off St. John's Rd **226** AV118
Cedar Grn, Hodd. EN11 **49** EA18
Cedar Gro, W5 **158** CL76
Amersham HP7 **55** AR39
Bexley DA5 **186** EW86
Southall UB1 **136** CA71
Weybridge KT13 **213** BQ105
Cedar Hts, Rich. TW10 **178** CL88
Cedar Hill, Epsom KT18 **232** CQ116
Cedar Ho, Croy. CR0 **221** EB107
Sunbury-on-Thames TW16 **175** BT94
Cedarhurst, Brom. BR1
off Elstree Hill **184** EE94
Cedarhurst Dr, SE9 **184** EJ85
Cedar Lawn Av, Barn. EN5 **79** CY43
Cedar Mt, SE9 **184** EK88
Cedarne Rd, SW6 **160** DB80
Cedar Pk, Cat. CR3 **236** DS121
Chigwell IG7 *off High Rd* **103** EP49
Cedar Pk Gdns, Rom. RM6 **126** EX59
Cedar Pk Rd, Enf. EN2 **82** DQ38
Cedar Pl, SE7 *off Floyd Rd* **164** EJ78
Northwood HA6 **93** BQ51
Cedar Ri, N14 **98** DG45
South Ockendon RM15
off Sycamore Way **149** FX70
Cedar Rd, N17 **100** DT53
NW2 **119** CW63
Berkhamsted HP4 **38** AX20
Brentwood (Hutt.) CM13 **109** GD44
Bromley BR1 **204** EJ96
Cobham KT11 **213** BV114
Croydon CR0 **202** DS103
Dartford DA1 **188** FK88
East Molesey KT8 **197** CE98
Enfield EN2 **81** DP38

⊖ London Underground station   DLR Docklands Light Railway station   Tra Tramlink station   Riv Pedestrian ferry landing stage

Cedar Rd, Erith DA8 **167** FG81
Feltham TW14 **175** BR88
Grays RM16 **171** GG76
Hatfield AL10 **45** CU19
Hornchurch RM12 **128** FJ62
Hounslow TW4 **156** BW82
Romford RM7 **127** FC56
Sutton SM2 **218** DC107
Teddington TW11 **177** CG92
Watford WD19 **76** BW44
Weybridge KT13 **212** BN105
Woking GU22 **226** AV120
Cedars, Bans. SM7 **218** DF114
Cedars, The, E15 *off Portway* **144** EF67
W13 *off Heronsforde* **137** CJ72
Buckhurst Hill IG9 **102** EG46
Guildford GU4 **243** BA131
Leatherhead KT22 **232** CL121
Reigate RH2 **250** DD134
Slough SL2 *off Calbroke Rd* **131** AM69
Teddington TW11 *off Adelaide Rd* **177** CF93
West Byfleet (Byfleet) KT14 **212** BM112
Cedars Av, E17 **123** EA57
Mitcham CR4 **200** DG98
Rickmansworth WD3 **92** BJ46
Cedars Cl, NW4 **119** CX55
SE13 **163** ED83
Gerrards Cross (Chal.St.P.) SL9 **90** AY50
Cedars Ct, N9 *off Church St* **100** DS47
Cedars Dr, Uxb. UB10 **134** BM68
[Sch] **Cedars First Sch**, Har. HA3 *off Whittlesea Rd* **94** CC53
Cedars Ms, SW4 *off Cedars Rd* **161** DH84
[Sch] **Cedars Mid Sch**, Har. HA3 *off Whittlesea Rd* **94** CC53
[Sch] **Cedars Prim Sch, The**, Houns. TW5 *off High St* **155** BV80
Cedars Rd, E15 **144** EE65
N9 *off Church St* **100** DU47
N21 **99** DP47
SW4 **161** DH83
SW13 **159** CT82
W4 **158** CQ78
Beckenham BR3 **203** DY96
Croydon CR0 **201** DL104
Kingston upon Thames (Hmptn W.) KT1 **197** CJ95
Morden SM4 **200** DA98
Cedars Wk, Rick. (Chorl.) WD3 **73** BF42
Cedar Ter, Rich. TW9 **158** CL84
Cedar Ter Rd, Sev. TN13 **257** FJ123
Cedar Tree Gro, SE27 **181** DP92
Cedarville Gdns, SW16 **181** DM93
Cedar Vista, Rich. TW9 *off Kew Rd* **158** CL81
Cedar Wk, Esher (Clay.) KT10 **215** CF107
Hemel Hempstead HP3 **40** BK22
Kenley CR8 **236** DQ116
Tadworth (Kgswd) KT20 **233** CY120
Waltham Abbey EN9 **67** ED34
Welwyn Garden City AL7 **30** DB10
Cedar Way, NW1 **141** DK66
Berkhamsted HP4 **38** AX20
Guildford GU1 **242** AW132
Slough SL3 **152** AY78
Sunbury-on-Thames TW16 **175** BS94
Cedarwood Dr, St.Alb. AL4 **43** CK20
Cedar Wd Dr, Wat. WD25 **75** BV35
Cedra Ct, N16 **122** DU60
Cedric Av, Rom. RM1 **127** FE55
Cedric Rd, SE9 **185** EQ90
Celadon Cl, Enf. EN3 **83** DY41
Celandine Cl, E14 **13** N6
South Ockendon RM15 **149** FW70
Celandine Dr, E8 **5** P5
SE28 **146** EV74
Celandine Rd, Walt. KT12 **214** BY105
Celandine Way, E15 **15** H1
Celbridge Ms, W2 **7** K7
Celedon Cl, Grays RM16 **170** FY75
Celestial Gdns, SE13 **163** ED84
Celia Cres, Ashf. TW15 **174** BK93
Celia Rd, N19 **121** DJ63
Cell Barnes Cl, St.Alb. AL1 *off Cell Barnes La* **43** CH22
Cell Barnes La, St.Alb. AL1 **43** CH23
Cell Fm Av, Wind. (Old Wind.) SL4 **172** AV85
Celtic Av, Brom. BR2 **204** EE97
Celtic Rd, W.Byf. (Byfleet) KT14 **212** BL114
Celtic St, E14 **14** B5
Cement Block Cotts, Grays RM17 **170** GC79
Cemetery Hill, Hem.H. HP1 **40** BJ21
Cemetery La, SE7 **164** EL79
Shepperton TW17 **195** BP101
Waltham Abbey EN9 **68** EF25
Cemetery Rd, E7 **124** EF63
N17 **100** DS52
SE2 **166** EV80
Cemmaes Ct Rd, Hem.H. HP1 **40** BJ20
Cemmaes Meadow, Hem.H. HP1 **40** BJ20
Cenacle Cl, NW3 **120** DA62
★ **Cenotaph, The**, SW1 **19** N3
Centaurs Business Cen, Islw. TW7 **157** CG79
Centaur St, SE1 **20** B5
Centaury Ct, Grays RM17 **170** GD79
Centenary Est, Enf. EN3 **83** DZ42
Centenary Rd, Enf. EN3 **83** DZ42
Centenary Wk, Loug. IG10 **84** EH41
Centenary Way, Amer. HP6 **72** AT38
Centennial Av, Borwd. (Elstree) WD6 **95** CH45
Centennial Pk, Borwd. (Elstree) WD6 **95** CJ45
Central Av, E11 **123** ED61
N2 **98** DD54
N9 **100** DS48
SW11 **160** DF80
Enfield EN1 **82** DV40
Gravesend DA12 **191** GH89
Grays RM20 **169** FT77
Harlow CM20 **35** ER14
Hayes UB3 **135** BU73
Hounslow TW3 **156** CC84
Pinner HA5 **116** BZ58
Central Av, S. Ock. (Aveley) RM15 **168** FQ75
Tilbury RM18 **171** GG81
Wallington SM6 **219** DL106
Waltham Cross EN8 **67** DY33
Welling DA16 **165** ET82
West Molesey KT8 **196** BZ98
Central Circ, NW4 *off Hendon Way* **119** CV57
★ **Central Criminal Ct (Old Bailey)**, EC4 **10** F7
Central Dr, Horn. RM12 **128** FL62
St. Albans AL4 **43** CJ19
Slough SL1 **131** AM73
Welwyn Garden City AL7 **29** CZ07
[Sch] **Central Foundation Boys' Sch**, EC2 **11** K3
[Sch] **Central Foundation Girls' Sch**, Lwr Sch, E3 **13** K1
Upr Sch, E3 **13** M2
Central Gdns, Mord. SM4 *off Central Rd* **200** DB99
Central Hill, SE19 **182** DR92
Central Ho, E15 *off High St* **143** EC68
[H] **Central Middlesex Hosp**, NW10 **138** CQ69
Central Par, Croy. (New Adgtn) CR0 **221** EC110
Feltham TW14 **176** BW87
Greenford UB6 **137** CG69
Hounslow TW5 *off Heston Rd* **156** CA80
Surbiton KT6 *off St. Mark's Hill* **198** CL100
Central Pk Av, Dag. RM10 **127** FB62
Central Pk Est, Houns. TW4 **176** BX85
[Sch] **Central Pk Prim Sch**, E6 *off Central Pk Rd* **144** EK68
Central Pk Rd, E6 **144** EK68
Central Pl, SE25 *off Portland Rd* **202** DV98
[Sch] **Central Prim Sch**, Wat. WD17 *off Derby Rd* **76** BW42
Central Rd, Dart. DA1 **188** FL85
Harlow CM20 **36** EU11
Morden SM4 **200** DA99
Wembley HA0 **117** CH64
Worcester Park KT4 **199** CU103
[Uni] **Central St. Martins Coll of Art & Design**, Catton St, WC1 **141** DM71
Charing Cross Rd, WC2 **9** M8
Eagle Ct, EC1 **10** E5
Southampton Row, WC1 **10** A6
Central Sch Footpath, SW14 **158** CQ83
[Coll] **Central Sch of Ballet**, EC1 **10** D4
[Coll] **Central Sch of Speech & Drama**, NW3 *off Eton Av* **140** DD66
Central Sq, NW11 **120** DB58
Wembley HA9 *off Station Gro* **118** CL64
West Molesey KT8 **196** BZ98
Central St, EC1 **10** G2
Central Wk, Epsom KT19 *off Station App* **216** CR113
Central Way, NW10 **138** CQ69
SE28 **146** EU74
Carshalton SM5 **218** DE108
Feltham TW14 **175** BV85
Oxted RH8 **253** ED127
Centre, The, Felt. TW13 **175** BU89
Walton-on-Thames KT12 **195** BT102
Centre at the Circ, W1 **9** K10
Centre Av, W3 **138** CR74
W10 *off Harrow Rd* **139** CW69
Epping CM16 **69** ET32
Centre Cl, Epp. CM16 *off Centre Av* **69** ET32
Centre Common Rd, Chis. BR7 **185** EQ93
Centre Ct Shop Cen, SW19 **179** CZ93
Centre Dr, Epp. CM16 **69** ET32
[Coll] **Centre for Engineering & Manufacturing Excellence**, Ceme Campus, Rain. RM13 *off Marsh Way* **147** FD70
Centre Grn, Epp. CM16 *off Centre Av* **69** ET32
Centrepoint, WC1 **9** M7
Centre Rd, E7 **124** EG61
E11 **124** EG61
Dagenham RM10 **147** FB68
Centre St, E2 **142** DV68
Centre Way, E17 **101** EC52
N9 **100** DW47
Centreway, Ilf. IG1 **125** EQ61
Centric Cl, NW1 *off Oval Rd* **141** DH67
Centurion Cl, N7 **4** B5
Centurion Ct, St.Alb. AL1 *off Camp Rd* **43** CG21
Wallington SM6 *off Wandle Rd* **201** DH103
Centurion La, E3 *off Libra Rd* **143** DZ68
Centurion Way, Erith DA18 **166** FA76
Purfleet RM19 **168** FM77
Century Cl, NW4 **119** CX57
St. Albans AL3 **42** CC19
Century Ct, Wok. GU21 **227** AZ116
Century Ms, E5 *off Lower Clapton Rd* **122** DW63
Century Pk, Wat. WD17 **76** BW43
Century Rd, E17 **123** DY55
Hoddesdon EN11 **49** EA16
Staines TW18 **173** BC92
Ware SG12 **33** DX05
Century Yd, SE23 **182** DW89
Cephas Av, E1 **12** F3
Cephas St, E1 **12** E4
Ceres Rd, SE18 **165** ET77
Cerise Rd, SE15 **162** DU81
Cerne Cl, Hayes UB4 **136** BX73
Cerne Rd, Grav. DA12 **191** GL91
Morden SM4 **200** DC100
Cerney Ms, W2 **7** N9
Cerotus Pl, Cher. KT16 **193** BF101
Cervantes Ct, W2 **7** K8
Northwood HA6 *off Green La* **93** BT52
Cervia Way, Grav. DA12 **191** GM90
Cester St, E2 *off Whiston Rd* **142** DU67
Cestreham Cres, Chesh. HP5 **54** AR29
Ceylon Rd, W14 **16** B6
Chace Av, Pot.B. EN6 **64** DD32
[Sch] **Chace Comm Sch**, Enf. EN1 *off Churchbury La* **82** DS39
Chacombe Pl, Beac. HP9 **89** AK50
Chadacre Av, Ilf. IG5 **125** EM55
Chadacre Rd, Epsom KT17 **217** CV107
Chadbourn St, E14 **14** B6
Chad Cres, N9 **100** DW48
Chadd Dr, Brom. BR1 **204** EL97
Chadd Grn, E13 **144** EG67
Chadfields, Til. RM18 **171** GG80
Chadhurst Cl, Dor. (N.Holm.) RH5 *off Wildcroft Dr* **263** CK139
Chadview Ct, Rom. (Chad.Hth) RM6 **126** EX59
Chadville Gdns, Rom. RM6 **126** EX57
Chadway, Dag. RM8 **126** EW60
Chadwell, Ware SG12 **32** DW07
Chadwell Av, Rom. RM6 **126** EV59
Waltham Cross (Chsht) EN8 **66** DW28
Chadwell Bypass, Grays RM16 **171** GF78
CHADWELL HEATH, Rom. RM6 **126** EX58
⇌ **Chadwell Heath** **126** EX59
[Sch] **Chadwell Heath High Sch**, Rom. RM6 *off Christie Gdns* **126** EV58
Grove Centre, Rom. RM6 *off Christie Gdns* **126** EV58
[H] **Chadwell Heath Hosp**, Rom. RM6 **126** EV57
Chadwell Heath La, Rom. RM6 **126** EV57
Chadwell Hill, Grays RM16 **171** GH78
[Sch] **Chadwell Prim Sch**, Rom. RM6 *off High Rd* **126** EW59
Chadwell Ri, Ware SG12 **32** DW07
Chadwell Rd, Grays RM17 **170** GC77
CHADWELL ST. MARY, Grays RM16 **171** GJ76
[Sch] **Chadwell St. Mary Prim Sch**, Grays RM16 *off River Vw* **171** GH77
Chadwell St, EC1 **10** D1
Chadwick Av, E4 **101** ED49
N21 *off Laidlaw Dr* **81** DM43
SW19 **180** DA93
Chadwick Cl, SW15 **179** CT87
W7 *off Westcott Cres* **137** CF71
Gravesend (Nthflt) DA11 **190** GE89
Teddington TW11 **177** CG93
Chadwick Dr, Rom. (Harold Wd) RM3 **106** FK54
Chadwick Ms, W4 *off Thames Rd* **158** CP79
Chadwick Pl, Surb. KT6 **197** CJ101
Chadwick Rd, E11 **124** EE59
NW10 **139** CT67
SE15 **162** DT82
Ilford IG1 **125** EP62
Chadwick St, SW1 **19** M6
Chadwick Way, SE28 **146** EX73
Chadwin Rd, E13 **15** N5
Chadworth Way, Esher (Clay.) KT10 **215** CD106
Chaffers Mead, Ashtd. KT21 **232** CM116
Chaffinch Av, Croy. CR0 **203** DX100
Chaffinch Cl, N9 **101** DX46
Croydon CR0 **203** DX100
Surbiton KT6 **198** CN104
Chaffinches Grn, Hem.H. HP3 **40** BN24
Chaffinch La, Wat. WD18 **93** BT45
Chaffinch Rd, Beck. BR3 **203** DY95
Chaffinch Way, Horl. RH6 **268** DE147
CHAFFORD HUNDRED, Grays RM16 **170** FY76
⇌ **Chafford Hundred** **169** FV77
[Sch] **Chafford Hundred Campus**, Grays RM16 *off Mayflower Rd* **169** FW78
[Sch] **Chafford Sch**, Rain. RM13 *off Lambs La S* **148** FJ71
Chafford Wk, Rain. RM13 **148** FJ68
Chafford Way, Rom. RM6 **126** EW56
Chagford St, NW1 **8** C4
Chailey Av, Enf. EN1 **82** DT40
Chailey Cl, Houns. TW5 *off Springwell Rd* **156** BX81
Chailey Pl, Walt. KT12 **214** BY105
Chailey St, E5 **122** DW62
Chairmans Av, Uxb. (Denh.) UB9 **113** BF58
Chalbury Wk, N1 **4** B9
Chalcombe Rd, SE2 **166** EV76
Chalcot Cl, Sutt. SM2 **218** DA108
Chalcot Cres, NW1 **140** DF67
Chalcot Gdns, NW3 **140** DF65
Chalcot Ms, SW16 **181** DL90
Chalcot Rd, NW1 **140** DG66
[Sch] **Chalcot Sch**, NW1 *off Harmood St* **141** DH66
Chalcot Sq, NW1 **140** DG66
Chalcott Gdns, Surb. KT6 **197** CJ102
Chalcroft Rd, SE13 **184** EE85
CHALDON, Cat. CR3 **235** DN124
Chaldon Cl, Red. RH1 **266** DE136
Chaldon Common Rd, Cat. CR3 **236** DQ124
Chaldon Path, Th.Hth. CR7 **201** DP98
Chaldon Rd, SW6 **159** CY80
Caterham CR3 **236** DR124
Chaldon Way, Couls. CR5 **235** DL117
Chale Rd, SW2 **181** DL86
Chalet Cl, Berk. HP4 **38** AT19
Bexley DA5 **187** FD91
Chalet Est, NW7 **97** CU49
Chale Wk, Sutt. SM2 *off Hulverston Cl* **218** DB109
⇌ **Chalfont & Latimer** **72** AW39
⊖ **Chalfont & Latimer** **72** AW39
Chalfont Av, Amer. HP6 **72** AX39
Wembley HA9 **138** CP65
Chalfont Cl, Hem.H. HP2 **41** BP15
CHALFONT COMMON, Ger.Cr. SL9 **91** AZ49
Chalfont Ct, NW9 **119** CT55
Chalfont Grn, N9 **100** DS48
Chalfont Gro, Ger.Cr. SL9 *off Narcot La* **90** AV51
Chalfont La, Ger.Cr. SL9 **91** BC51
Rickmansworth (Chorl.) WD3 **73** BB43
Rickmansworth (Map.Cr.) WD3 **91** BC51
Chalfont Ms, SW19 *off Augustus Rd* **179** CZ88
Chalfont Pk, Ger.Cr. (Chal.St.P.) SL9 **113** AZ55
Chalfont Rd, N9 **100** DS48
SE25 **202** DT97
Beaconsfield (Seer Grn) HP9 **89** AR50
Gerrards Cross SL9 **91** BB48
Hayes UB3 **155** BU75
Rickmansworth (Map.Cr.) WD3 **91** BD49
CHALFONT ST. GILES, HP8 **90** AV47
[Sch] **Chalfont St. Giles Co First Sch**, Ch.St.G. HP8 *off School La* **90** AV48
[Sch] **Chalfont St. Giles Mid Sch**, Ch.St.G. HP8 *off Parsonage Rd* **90** AV48
CHALFONT ST. PETER, Ger.Cr. SL9 **91** AZ53
[Sch] **Chalfont St. Peter C of E Mid Sch**, Ger.Cr. SL9 *off Penn Rd* **90** AX53
[Sch] **Chalfont St. Peter Co First Sch**, Ger.Cr. SL9 *off Lovel End* **90** AW52
[H] **Chalfonts & Gerrards Cross Hosp**, Ger.Cr. SL9 **90** AX53
[Sch] **Chalfonts Comm Coll, The**, Ger.Cr. SL9 *off Narcot La* **90** AW52
Chalfont Sta Rd, Amer. HP7 **72** AW40
Chalfont Wk, Pnr. HA5 *off Willows Cl* **94** BW54
Chalfont Way, W13 **157** CH76
Chalford Cl, W.Mol. KT8 **196** CA98
Chalforde Gdns, Rom. RM2 **127** FH56
Chalford Flats, H.Wyc. (Woob.Grn) HP10 **110** AE57
Chalford Rd, SE21 **182** DR91
Chalford Wk, Wdf.Grn. IG8 **102** EK53
Chalgrove, Welw.G.C. AL7 **30** DD08
Chalgrove Av, Mord. SM4 **200** DA99
Chalgrove Cres, Ilf. IG5 **102** EL54
Chalgrove Gdns, N3 **119** CY55
[Sch] **Chalgrove Prim Sch**, N3 *off Chalgrove Gdns* **119** CY55
Chalgrove Rd, N17 **100** DV53
Sutton SM2 **218** DD108
Chalice Cl, Wall. SM6 *off Lavender Vale* **219** DK107
Chalice Way, Green. DA9 **189** FS85
Chalkdale, Welw.G.C. AL7 **30** DB08
Chalkdell Flds, St.Alb. AL4 **43** CG16
Chalkdell Hill, Hem.H. HP2 **40** BL20
[Sch] **Chalk Dell Inf Sch**, Hert. SG13 *off Wilton Cres* **32** DQ11
Chalkenden Cl, SE20 **182** DV94
⊖ **Chalk Farm** **140** DG66
Chalk Fm Rd, NW1 **140** DG66
Chalk Hill, Amer. (Colesh.) HP7 **89** AM45
Chesham HP5 **54** AP29
Watford WD19 **76** BX44
[Sch] **Chalkhill Prim Sch**, Wem. HA9 *off Barnhill Rd* **118** CP62
Chalk Hill Rd, W6 **16** A8
Chalkhill Rd, Wem. HA9 **118** CP62
Chalklands, Wem. HA9 **118** CQ62
Chalk La, Ashtd. KT21 **232** CM119
Barnet EN4 **80** DF42
Epsom KT18 **232** CR115
Harlow CM17 **36** FA14
Leatherhead (E.Hors.) KT24 **245** BT130
Chalkley Cl, Mitch. CR4 **200** DF96
Chalkmill Dr, Enf. EN1 **82** DV41
Chalk Paddock, Epsom KT18 **232** CR115
Chalk Pit Av, Orp. BR5 **206** EW97
Chalkpit La, Bet. RH3 **248** CP133
Dorking RH4 **263** CG135
Leatherhead (Bkhm) KT23 **246** BZ128
Oxted RH8 **253** EC125
Chalk Pit La, Slou. (Burn.) SL1 **130** AH66
Chalk Pit Rd, Bans. SM7 **234** DA117
Epsom KT18 **232** CQ119
Chalkpits Caravan Pk, H.Wyc. (Woob.Grn) HP10 **110** AE57
Chalkpit Ter, Dor. RH4 **247** CG134
Chalk Pit Way, Sutt. SM1 **218** DC106
Chalkpit Wd, Oxt. RH8 **253** ED127
Chalk Rd, E13 **15** P5
Chalkstone Cl, Well. DA16 **166** EU81
Chalkstream Way, H.Wyc. HP10 *off Glory Mill La* **110** AE56
Chalkwell Pk Av, Enf. EN1 **82** DS42
Chalky Bk, Grav. DA11 **191** GG91
Chalky La, Chess. KT9 **215** CK109
Challacombe Cl, Brwd. (Hutt.) CM13 **109** GB46
Challenge Cl, Grav. DA12 **191** GM91
Challenge Ct, Lthd. KT22 **231** CH119
Challenge Rd, Ashf. TW15 **175** BQ90
Challice Way, SW2 **181** DM88
Challinor, Harl. CM17 **52** EY15
Challin St, SE20 **202** DW95
Challis Rd, Brent. TW8 **157** CK78
Challock Cl, West. (Bigg.H.) TN16 **238** EJ116
Challoner Cl, N2 **98** DD54
Challoner Cres, W14 **16** E10
Challoners Cl, E.Mol. KT8 **197** CD98
Challoner St, W14 **16** E9
Chalmers Ct, Rick. (Crox.Grn) WD3 **74** BM44
Chalmers Ho, SW11 *off York Rd* **160** DC83
Chalmers Rd, Ashf. TW15 **175** BP91
Banstead SM7 **234** DD115
Chalmers Rd E, Ashf. TW15 **175** BP91
Chalmers Wk, SE17 *off Hillingdon St* **161** DP79
Chalmers Way, Felt. TW14 **175** BU85
Chaloner Ct, SE1 **21** J3
Chalsey Rd, SE4 **163** DZ84
Chalton Dr, N2 **120** DC58
Chalton St, NW1 **9** M1
CHALVEY, Slou. SL1 **151** AQ76
Chalvey Gdns, Slou. SL1 **152** AS75
Chalvey Gro, Slou. SL1 **151** AP75
Chalvey Pk, Slou. SL1 **152** AS75
Chalvey Rd E, Slou. SL1 **152** AS75
Chalvey Rd W, Slou. SL1 **151** AR75
Chamberlain Cl, SE28 *off Broadwater Rd* **165** ER76
Harlow CM17 **52** EW15
Chamberlain Cotts, SE5 *off Camberwell Gro* **162** DR81
Chamberlain Cres, W.Wick. BR4 **203** EB102
Chamberlain Gdns, Houns. TW3 **156** CC81
Chamberlain La, Pnr. HA5 **115** BU56
Chamberlain Pl, E17 **123** DY55
Chamberlain Rd, N2 **98** DC54
N9 **100** DU48
W13 *off Midhurst Rd* **157** CG75
Chamberlain St, NW1 *off Regents Pk Rd* **140** DF66
Chamberlain Wk, Felt. TW13 *off Burgess Cl* **176** BY91
Chamberlain Way, Pnr. HA5 **115** BV55
Surbiton KT6 **198** CL101
Chamberlayne Av, Wem. HA9 **118** CL61
Chamberlayne Rd, NW10 **6** A1
Chambersbury La, Hem.H. HP3 **58** BN25
[Sch] **Chambersbury Prim Sch**, Hem.H. HP3 *off Hill Common* **40** BN23
Chambers Cl, Green. DA9 **189** FU85
Chambers Gdns, N2 **98** DD53
Chambers Gro, Welw.G.C. AL7 **29** CY12
Chambers La, NW10 **139** CV66
Chambers Pl, S.Croy. CR2 *off Rolleston Rd* **220** DR108
Chambers Rd, N7 **121** DL63
Chambers St, SE16 **22** A3
Hertford SG14 **32** DQ09
Chamber St, E1 **11** P9
Chambers Wk, Stan. HA7 **95** CH51
Chambon Pl, W6 *off Beavor La* **159** CU77
Chambord St, E2 **11** P2
Champion Cres, SE26 **183** DY91
Champion Down, Lthd. KT24 *off Norwood Cl* **246** BY128
Champion Gro, SE5 **162** DR83
Champion Hill, SE5 **162** DR83
Champion Hill Est, SE5 **162** DS83
Champion Pk, SE5 **162** DR82
Champion Pk Est, SE5 *off Denmark Hill* **162** DR83
Champion Rd, SE26 **183** DY91
Upminster RM14 **128** FP61
Champions Grn, Hodd. EN11 **33** EA14
Champions Way, Hodd. EN11 **33** EA14
Champness Cl, SE27 *off Rommany Rd* **182** DR91
Champness Rd, Bark. IG11 **145** ET65
Champney Cl, Slou. SL3 *off Stanwell Rd* **153** BA83
Champneys Cl, Sutt. SM2 **217** CZ108
Chance Cl, Grays RM16 **170** FZ76
Chancellor Gdns, S.Croy. CR2 **219** DP109
Chancellor Gro, SE21 **182** DQ89
Chancellor Pas, E14 **23** P2
Chancellor Pl, NW9 **97** CT54
Chancellors Rd, W6 **159** CW78
[Sch] **Chancellor's Sch**, Hat. AL9 *off Pine Gro* **64** DB25
Chancellors St, W6 **159** CW78
Chancellor Way, Sev. TN13 **256** FG122
Chancelot Rd, SE2 **166** EV77
Chancel St, SE1 **20** E1
Chancery Cl, St.Alb. AL4 **43** CK15
Chancery Ct, Dart. DA1 *off Downs Av* **188** FN87
⊖ **Chancery Lane** **10** C6
Chancery La, WC2 **10** C7
Beckenham BR3 **203** EB96
Chancery Ms, SW17 **180** DE89
Chance St, E1 **11** N3
E2 **11** N3
Chanctonbury Chase, Red. RH1 **251** DH134
Chanctonbury Cl, SE9 **185** EP90
Chanctonbury Gdns, Sutt. SM2 **218** DB108
Chanctonbury Way, N12 **97** CZ49
Chandler Av, E16 **15** L5
Chandler Cl, Hmptn. TW12 **196** CA95
Chandler Ms, Twick. TW1 **177** CG87
Chandler Rd, Loug. IG10 **85** EP39
Chandlers Cl, Felt. TW14 **175** BT87
Chandlers Dr, Erith DA8 **167** FD77
[Sch] **Chandlers Fld Prim Sch**, W.Mol. KT8 *off High St* **196** CA99
Chandler's La, Rick. WD3 **74** BL37
Chandlers Ms, E14 **23** N3
Chandlers Rd, St.Alb. AL4 **43** CJ17
Chandler St, E1 **22** D1
Chandlers Way, SW2 **181** DN87
Hertford SG14 **31** DN09
Romford RM1 **127** FE57
Chandler Way, SE15 **162** DT80
Chandon Lo, Sutt. SM2 *off Devonshire Rd* **218** DC108
Chandos Av, E17 **101** EA54
N14 **99** DJ48
N20 **98** DC46
W5 **157** CJ77
Chandos Cl, Amer. HP6 **72** AW38
Buckhurst Hill IG9 **102** EH47
Chandos Ct, Stan. HA7 **95** CH51
Chandos Cres, Edg. HA8 **96** CM52
Chandos Mall, Slou. SL1 *off High St* **152** AT75
Chandos Par, Edg. HA8 *off Chandos Cres* **96** CM52
Chandos Pl, WC2 **9** N10
Chandos Rd, E15 **123** ED64
N2 **98** DD54
N17 **100** DS54
NW2 **119** CW64
NW10 **138** CS70
Borehamwood WD6 **78** CM40
Harrow HA1 **116** CC57
Pinner HA5 **116** BW59
Staines TW18 **173** BD92
Chandos St, W1 **9** H6
Chandos Way, NW11 **120** DB60
Change All, EC3 **11** K8
Chanlock Path, S.Ock. RM15 *off Carnach Grn* **149** FV73
Channel Cl, Houns. TW5 **156** CA81
Channel Gate Rd, NW10 *off Old Oak La* **139** CT69
Channelsea Rd, E15 **143** ED67
Channing Cl, Horn. RM11 **128** FM59
[Sch] **Channing Jun Sch**, N6 *off Highgate High St* **121** DH60
Channings, Wok. (Horsell) GU21 **226** AY115
[Sch] **Channing Sch**, N6 *off Highgate High St* **121** DH60
Chanton Dr, Epsom KT17 **217** CW110
Sutton SM2 **217** CW110
Chantress Cl, Dag. RM10 **147** FC67
Chantrey Cl, Ashtd. KT21 **231** CJ119
Chantrey Rd, SW9 **161** DM83
Chantreywood, Brwd. CM13 **109** GA48
Chantry, The, Harl. CM20 **36** EU13
Uxbridge UB8 **134** BM69
Chantry Cl, NW7 *off Hendon Wd La* **79** CT44
SE2 *off Felixstowe Rd* **166** EW76
W9 **6** F4
Enfield EN2 *off Bedale Rd* **82** DQ38
Harrow HA3 **118** CM57
Horley RH6 **268** DF147
Kings Langley WD4 **58** BN29
Sidcup DA14 *off Ellenborough Rd* **186** EY92
Sunbury-on-Thames TW16 **175** BU94
West Drayton UB7 **134** BK73
Windsor SL4 **151** AN81

★ Place of interest | [H] Hospital | [Sch] School | [Coll] College | [Uni] University | ⇌ Railway station

Chantry Cotts, Guil. (Chilw.) GU4 ... 259 BB140
Chantry Ct, Cars. SM5 ... 200 DE104
Hatfield AL10 ... 45 CU19
Chantry Ho, Rain. RM13
off Chantry Way ... 147 FD68
Chantry Hurst, Epsom KT18 ... 232 CR115
Chantry La, Brom. BR2
off Bromley Common ... 204 EK99
Guildford (Shere) GU5 ... 260 BM138
Hatfield AL10 ... 45 CT19
St. Albans (Lon.Col.) AL2 ... 61 CK26
Chantry Pl, Har. HA3 ... 94 CB53
Chantry Prim Sch, Grav. DA12 off Ordnance Rd ... 191 GJ86
Chantry Rd, Cher. KT16 ... 194 BJ101
Chessington KT9 ... 216 CM106
Guildford (Chilw.) GU4 ... 259 BB140
Harrow HA3 ... 94 CB53
Chantry Sch, The, West Dr. UB7 off Falling La ... 134 BL73
Chantry Sq, W8
off St. Mary's Pl ... 160 DB76
Chantry St, N1 ... 4 F8
Chantry Vw Rd, Guil. GU1 ... 258 AX137
Chantry Way, Mitch. CR4 ... 200 DD97
Rainham RM13 ... 147 FD68
Chant Sq, E15 ... 143 ED66
Chant St, E15 ... 143 ED66
Chapel Av, Add. KT15 ... 212 BH105
Chapel Cl, Dart. DA1 ... 187 FE85
Grays RM20 ... 169 FV79
Hatfield AL9 ... 64 DD27
Watford WD25 ... 59 BT34
Chapel Cotts, Hem.H. HP2 ... 40 BK18
Chapel Ct, N2 ... 120 DE55
SE1 ... 21 J3
Dorking RH4 ... 263 CG135
Chapel Cft, Kings L. (Chipper.) WD4 ... 58 BG31
Chapel Cfts, Berk. (Nthch) HP4 ... 38 AS17
Chapel End, Ger.Cr. (Chal.St.P.) SL9
off Austenwood La ... 90 AX54
Hoddesdon EN11 ... 49 EA18
Chapel End Inf Sch, E17 off Beresford Rd ... 101 EB53
Chapel End Jun Sch, E17 off Roberts Rd ... 101 EB53
Chapel Fm Rd, SE9 ... 185 EM90
Chapel Fld, Harl. CM17 ... 52 EW17
Chapelfields, Ware (Stans.Abb.) SG12 ... 33 ED10
Chapel Gate Ms, SW4
off Bedford Rd ... 161 DL83
Chapel Gro, Add. KT15 ... 212 BH105
Epsom KT18 ... 233 CW119
Chapel High Shop Prec, Brwd. CM14 ... 108 FW47
Chapel Hill, Dart. DA1 ... 187 FE85
Leatherhead (Eff.) KT24
off The Street ... 246 BX127
Chapelhouse Cl, Guil. GU2
off Park Barn Dr ... 242 AS134
Chapel Ho St, E14 ... 24 B9
Chapelier Ho, SW18
off Point Pleasant ... 160 DA84
Chapel La, Chig. IG7 ... 103 ET48
Dorking (Westc.) RH4 ... 262 CC137
Dorking (Westh.) RH5 ... 247 CD130
Harlow CM17 ... 52 EW17
Hertford (Letty Grn) SG14 ... 31 DH13
Leatherhead (Bkhm) KT23 ... 246 CC128
Pinner HA5 ... 116 BX55
Romford RM6 ... 126 EX59
Slough (Stoke P.) SL2 ... 132 AV66
Uxbridge UB8 ... 134 BN72
Chapel Mkt, N1 ... 4 C9
Chapel Ms, Wdf.Grn. IG8 ... 103 EN51
Chapelmount Rd, Wdf.Grn. IG8 ... 103 EM51
Chapel Pk Rd, Add. KT15 ... 212 BH105
Chapel Path, E11 ... 124 EG58
Chapel Pl, EC2 ... 11 L2
N1 ... 4 D9
N17 off White Hart La ... 100 DT52
W1 ... 8 G8
Chapel Rd, SE27 ... 181 DP91
W13 ... 137 CH74
Bexleyheath DA7 ... 166 FA84
Epping CM16 ... 69 ET30
Horley (Smallfield) RH6 ... 269 DP148
Hounslow TW3 ... 156 CB83
Ilford IG1 ... 125 EN62
Oxted RH8 ... 254 EJ130
Redhill RH1 ... 250 DF134
Tadworth KT20 ... 233 CW123
Twickenham TW1 ... 177 CH87
Warlingham CR6 ... 237 DX118
Chapel Row, Uxb. (Hare.) UB9 ... 92 BJ53
Chapels Cl, Slou. SL1 ... 131 AL74
Chapel Side, W2 ... 7 J9
Chapel Sq, Vir.W. GU25 ... 192 AY98
Chapel Stones, N17 ... 100 DT53
Chapel St, NW1 ... 8 A6
SW1 ... 18 F5
Berkhamsted HP4 ... 38 AW19
Enfield EN2 ... 82 DQ41
Guildford GU1
off Castle St ... 258 AX136
Hemel Hempstead HP2 ... 40 BK19
Slough SL1 ... 152 AT75
Uxbridge UB8
off Trumper Way ... 134 BJ67
Woking GU21 ... 227 AZ117
Chapel Ter, Loug. IG10
off Forest Rd ... 84 EL42
Chapel Vw, S.Croy. CR2 ... 220 DV107
Chapel Wk, NW4 ... 119 CV56
Coulsdon CR5
off Netherne La ... 235 DK122
Croydon CR0
off Wellesley Rd ... 202 DQ103
Dartford DA2 ... 187 FE89
Chapel Way, N7
off Sussex Way ... 121 DM62
Abbots Langley (Bedmond) WD5 ... 59 BT27
Epsom KT18 ... 233 CW119
Chapel Yd, SW18
off Wandsworth High St ... 180 DA85
Chaplaincy Gdns, Horn. RM11 ... 128 FL60
Chaplin Cl, SE1 ... 20 D3
Chaplin Cres, Sun. TW16 ... 175 BS93
Chaplin Ms, Slou. SL3
off Ditton Rd ... 153 AZ78
Chaplin Rd, E15 ... 144 EE68
N17 ... 122 DT55
NW2 ... 139 CU65
Dagenham RM9 ... 146 EY66
Wembley HA0 ... 137 CJ65
Chaplin Sq, N12 ... 98 DD52
Chapman Cl, West Dr. UB7 ... 154 BM76
Chapman Cres, Har. HA3 ... 118 CL57
Chapman Pk Ind Est, NW10 ... 139 CT65
Chapman Pl, N4 ... 121 DP61
Chapman Rd, E9 ... 143 DZ65
Belvedere DA17 ... 166 FA78
Croydon CR0 ... 201 DN102
Chapmans Cres, Chesh. HP5 ... 54 AN29
Chapman's La, SE2 ... 166 EW77
Belvedere DA17 ... 166 EX77
Chapmans La, Orp. BR5 ... 206 EX96
Chapman Sq, SW19 ... 179 CX89
Chapmans Rd, Sev. (Sund.) TN14 ... 240 EY124
Chapman St, E1 ... 12 C9
Chapone Pl, W1 ... 9 L8
Chapter Cl, W4
off Beaumont Rd ... 158 CQ76
Uxbridge UB10 ... 134 BM66
Chapter Ho Ct, EC4 ... 10 G8
Chapter Rd, NW2 ... 119 CU64
SE17 ... 20 F10
Chapter St, SW1 ... 19 L8
Chapter Way, Hmptn. TW12 ... 176 CA91
Chaptree Ms, Wind. SL4 ... 151 AR80
Chara Pl, W4 ... 158 CR79
Charcot Ho, SW15
off Highcliffe Dr ... 179 CT86
Charcroft Gdns, Enf. EN3 ... 83 DX42
Chardin Rd, W4
off Elliott Rd ... 158 CS77
Chardins Cl, Hem.H. HP1 ... 39 BF19
Chardmore Rd, N16 ... 122 DU60
Chard Rd, Houns. (Hthrw Air.) TW6
off Heathrow Tunnel App ... 154 BN83
Chardwell Cl, E6
off Northumberland Rd ... 144 EL72
Charecroft Way, W12 ... 16 A4
Charfield Ct, W9 ... 7 J4
Charford Rd, E16 ... 15 N8
Chargate Cl, Walt. KT12 ... 213 BT107
Chargeable La, E13 ... 15 K3
Chargeable St, E16 ... 15 K3
Chargrove Cl, SE16 ... 23 H3
Charing Cl, Orp. BR6 ... 223 ET105
⇌ Charing Cross ... 19 N1
⊖ Charing Cross ... 19 N1
Charing Cross, SW1 ... 19 N1
Charing Cross Hosp, W6 ... 159 CX79
Charing Cross Rd, WC2 ... 9 M7
Chariotts Pl, Wind. SL4
off Victoria St ... 151 AR81
Charkham Ms, Hat. (N.Mymms) AL9
off Dixons Hill Rd ... 45 CW24
Charlbert St, NW8 ... 140 DE68
Charlbury Av, Stan. HA7 ... 95 CK50
Charlbury Cl, Rom. RM3 ... 106 FJ51
Charlbury Cres, Rom. RM3 ... 106 FJ51
Charlbury Gdns, Ilf. IG3 ... 125 ET61
Charlbury Gro, W5 ... 137 CJ72
Charlbury Ho, E12
off Grantham Rd ... 125 EN62
Charlbury Rd, Uxb. UB10 ... 114 BM62
Charldane Rd, SE9 ... 185 EP90
Charlecote Gro, SE26 ... 182 DV90
Charlecote Rd, Dag. RM8 ... 126 EY62
Charlemont Rd, E6 ... 145 EM69
Charles Babbage Cl, Chess. KT9 ... 215 CJ108
Charles Barry Cl, SW4 ... 161 DJ83
Charles Burton Ct, E5
off Ashenden Rd ... 123 DY64
Charles Cl, Sid. DA14 ... 186 EV91
Charles Cobb Gdns, Croy. CR0 ... 219 DN106
Charles Coveney Rd, SE15 ... 162 DT81
Charles Cres, Har. HA1 ... 117 CD59
Charles Darwin Sch, West. TN16 off Jail La ... 239 EM116
Charles Dickens Ho, E2 ... 12 C2
Charles Dickens Prim Sch, SE1 ... 20 G4
Charles Dickens Ter, SE20
off Maple Rd ... 182 DW94
Charles Edward Brooke C of E Sec Girls' Sch, Lwr Sch, SE5
off Cormont Rd ... 161 DP81
Upr Sch, SW9
off Langton Rd ... 161 DP81
Charlesfield, SE9 ... 184 EJ90
Charlesfield Rd, Horl. RH6 ... 268 DF147
Charles Flemwell Ms, E16 ... 25 M2
Charles Gdns, Slou. SL2 ... 132 AV72
Charles Grinling Wk, SE18 ... 165 EN77
Charles Haller St, SW2
off Tulse Hill ... 181 DN87
Charles Ho, N17 off Love La ... 100 DT52
Windsor SL4 off Alma Rd ... 151 AQ81
Charles Lamb Prim Sch, N1 ... 4 G7
Charles La, NW8
off St. John's Wd High St ... 140 DD68
Charles Pl, NW1 ... 9 K2
Charles Rd, E7 off Lens Rd ... 144 EJ66
SW19 ... 200 DA95
W13 ... 137 CG72
Dagenham RM10 ... 147 FD65
Romford RM6 ... 126 EX59
Sevenoaks (Bad.Mt) TN14 ... 225 FB110
Staines TW18 ... 174 BK93
Charles II Pl, SW3
off King's Rd ... 160 DF78
Charles II St, SW1 ... 19 L1
Charles Sevright Dr, NW7 ... 97 CX50
Charles Sq, N1 ... 11 K2
Charles Sq Est, N1
off Pitfield St ... 142 DR69
Charles St, E16 ... 144 EK74
SW13 ... 158 CS82
W1 ... 18 G1
Berkhamsted HP4 ... 38 AV19
Chertsey KT16 ... 193 BF102
Croydon CR0 ... 202 DQ104
Enfield EN1 ... 82 DT43
Epping CM16 ... 70 EU32
Grays RM17 ... 170 GB79
Greenhithe DA9 ... 189 FT85
Hemel Hempstead HP1 ... 40 BJ21
Hounslow TW3 ... 156 BZ82
Uxbridge UB10 ... 135 BP70
Windsor SL4 ... 151 AQ81
Charleston Cl, Felt. TW13
off Vineyard Rd ... 175 BU90
Charleston St, SE17 ... 21 H8
Charles Townsend Ho, EC1 ... 10 D2
Charles Whincup Rd, E16 ... 25 N1
Charlesworth Cl, Hem.H. HP3 ... 40 BK22
Charleville Circ, SE26 ... 182 DU92
Charleville Ms, Islw. TW7
off Railshead Rd ... 157 CH84
Charleville Rd, W14 ... 16 D10
Charlie Chaplin Wk, SE1
off Waterloo Rd ... 141 DN74
Charlieville Rd, Erith DA8
off Northumberland Pk ... 167 FC80
Charlmont Rd, SW17 ... 180 DF93
Charlock Way, Guil. GU1 ... 243 BB131
Watford WD18 ... 75 BT44
Charlotte Av, Slou. SL2 ... 132 AT73
Charlotte Cl, Bexh. DA6 ... 186 EY85
Ilford IG6 off Connor Cl ... 103 EQ53
Charlotte Ct, Esher KT10 ... 214 CC106
Charlotte Despard Av, SW11 ... 160 DG81
Charlotte Gdns, Rom. RM5 ... 105 FB51
Charlotte Gro, Horl. (Smallfield) RH6 ... 269 DN147
Charlotte Ms, W1 ... 9 K5
W10 ... 6 A8
W14 ... 16 C7
Charlotte Pl, NW9
off Uphill Dr ... 118 CQ57
SW1 ... 19 J8
W1 ... 9 K6
Grays RM20 ... 169 FV79
Charlotte Rd, EC2 ... 11 L3
SW13 ... 159 CT81
Dagenham RM10 ... 147 FB65
Wallington SM6 ... 219 DJ107
Charlotte Row, SW4 ... 161 DJ83
Charlotte Sharman Prim Sch, SE11 ... 20 E6
Charlotte Sq, Rich. TW10
off Greville Rd ... 178 CM86
Charlotte St, W1 ... 9 K5
Charlotte Ter, N1 ... 4 B8
CHARLOTTEVILLE, Guil. GU1 ... 258 AY137
Charlow Cl, SW6
off Townmead Rd ... 160 DC82
CHARLTON, SE7 ... 164 EJ79
⇌ Charlton ... 164 EH78
★ Charlton Athletic FC, SE7 ... 164 EJ78
Charlton Av, Walt. KT12 ... 213 BV105
Charlton Ch La, SE7 ... 164 EJ78
Charlton Cl, Hodd. EN11 ... 49 EA17
Slough SL1 ... 151 AP75
Uxbridge UB10 ... 115 BP61
Charlton Cres, Bark. IG11 ... 145 ET68
Charlton Dene, SE7 ... 164 EJ80
Charlton Dr, West. (Bigg.H.) TN16 ... 238 EK117
Charlton Gdns, Couls. CR5 ... 235 DJ118
Charlton Kings, Wey. KT13 ... 195 BS104
Charlton Kings Rd, NW5 ... 121 DK64
Charlton La, SE7 ... 164 EK78
Shepperton TW17 ... 195 BS98
Charlton Manor Prim Sch, SE7 off Indus Rd ... 164 EK80
Charlton Mead La, Hodd. EN11 ... 49 EC18
Charlton Mead La S, Hodd. EN11
off Charlton Mead La ... 49 ED18
Charlton Pk La, SE7 ... 164 EK80
Charlton Pk Rd, SE7 ... 164 EK79
Charlton Pk Spec Sch, SE7 off Charlton Pk Rd ... 164 EL79
Charlton Pl, N1 ... 4 E9
Windsor SL4
off Charlton Row ... 150 AJ82
Charlton Rd, N9 ... 101 DX46
NW10 ... 138 CS67
SE3 ... 164 EG80
SE7 ... 164 EH80
Harrow HA3 ... 117 CK56
Shepperton TW17 ... 195 BQ97
Wembley HA9 ... 118 CM60
Charlton Row, Wind. SL4 ... 150 AJ82
Charlton Sch, SE10
off Royal Hill ... 163 EC80
Charlton Sq, Wind. SL4
off Charlton Row ... 150 AJ82
Charlton St, Grays RM20 ... 169 FX79
Charlton Wk, Wind. SL4
off Charlton Row ... 150 AJ82
Charlton Way, SE3 ... 164 EE81
Hoddesdon EN11 ... 49 EA17
Windsor SL4 ... 150 AJ82
Charlwood, Croy. CR0 ... 221 DZ109
Charlwood Cl, Har. HA3
off Kelvin Cres ... 95 CE52
Charlwood Dr, Lthd. (Oxshott) KT22 ... 231 CD115
Charlwood Pl, SW1 ... 19 K8
Charlwood Rd, SW15 ... 159 CX83
Horley RH6 ... 268 DB152
Charlwood Sq, Mitch. CR4 ... 200 DD97
Charlwood St, SW1 ... 19 K8
Charlwood Ter, SW15
off Cardinal Pl ... 159 CX84
Charman Rd, Red. RH1 ... 250 DE134
Charm Cl, Horl. RH6 ... 268 DE147
Charmian Av, Stan. HA7 ... 117 CK55
Charminster Av, SW19 ... 200 DB96
Charminster Ct, Surb. KT6 ... 197 CK101
Charminster Rd, SE9 ... 184 EK91
Worcester Park KT4 ... 199 CX102
Charmouth Ct, St.Alb. AL1 ... 43 CG17
Charmouth Rd, St.Alb. AL1 ... 43 CG18
Welling DA16 ... 166 EW81
Charmwood La, Orp. BR6 ... 224 EV109
Charne, The, Sev. (Otford) TN14 ... 241 FG117
Charnock, Swan. BR8 ... 207 FE98
Charnock Rd, E5 ... 122 DV62
Charnwood Av, SW19 ... 200 DA96
Charnwood Cl, N.Mal. KT3 ... 198 CS98
Charnwood Dr, E18 ... 124 EH55
Charnwood Gdns, E14 ... 23 P7
Charnwood Pl, N20 ... 98 DC48
Charnwood Rd, SE25 ... 202 DR99
Enfield EN1 ... 82 DV36
Uxbridge UB10 ... 134 BN68
Charnwood St, E5 ... 122 DU61
Charrington Rd, Croy. CR0
off Drayton Rd ... 201 DP103
Charrington St, NW1 ... 141 DK68
Charsley Cl, Amer. HP6 ... 72 AW39
Charsley Rd, SE6 ... 183 EB89
Charta Rd, Egh. TW20 ... 173 BC92
Chart Cl, Brom. BR2 ... 204 EE95
Croydon CR0
off Stockbury Rd ... 202 DW100
Dorking RH5 ... 263 CK138
Chart Downs, Dor. RH5 ... 263 CJ139
Charter Av, Ilf. IG2 ... 125 ER60
Charter Cl, St.Alb. AL1
off Bricket Rd ... 43 CE20
Slough SL1 off Osborne St ... 152 AT76
Charter Ct, N.Mal. KT3 ... 198 CS97
Charter Cres, Houns. TW4 ... 156 BY84
Charter Dr, Amer. HP6 ... 72 AT38
Bexley DA5 ... 186 EY87
★ Chartered Insurance Institutes Mus, EC2
off Aldermanbury ... 11 H7
★ Charterhouse, EC1 ... 10 F5
Charterhouse Av, Wem. HA0 ... 117 CJ63
Charterhouse Bldgs, EC1 ... 10 F4
Charterhouse Dr, Sev. TN13 ... 256 FG123
Charterhouse Ms, EC1 ... 10 F5
Charterhouse Rd, E8 ... 122 DU63
Orpington BR6 ... 206 EU104
Charterhouse Sq, EC1 ... 10 F5
Charterhouse Sq Sch, EC1 ... 10 G5
Charterhouse St, EC1 ... 10 D6
Charteris Rd, N4 ... 121 DN60
NW6 ... 139 CZ67
Woodford Green IG8 ... 102 EH52
Charter Nightingale Hosp, NW1 ... 8 B5
Charter Pl, Stai. TW18 ... 174 BG93
Uxbridge UB8 ... 134 BK66
Watford WD17 ... 76 BW41
Charter Rd, Kings.T. KT1 ... 198 CP97
Slough SL1 ... 131 AL73
Charter Rd, The, Wdf.Grn. IG8 ... 102 EE51
Charter Sch, The, SE24
off Red Post Hill ... 182 DR85
Charters Cl, SE19 ... 182 DS92
Charters Cross, Harl. CM18 ... 51 ER18
Charter Sq, Kings.T. KT1 ... 198 CP96
Charter Way, N3 ... 119 CZ56
N14 ... 81 DJ44
Chartfield Av, SW15 ... 179 CV85
Chartfield Pl, Wey. KT13 ... 213 BP106
Chartfield Rd, Reig. RH2 ... 266 DC135
Chartfield Sch, SW15
off St. Margaret's Cres ... 179 CV85
Chartfield Sq, SW15 ... 179 CX85
Chart Gdns, Dor. RH5 ... 263 CJ139
Chartham Gro, SE27
off Royal Circ ... 181 DN90
Chartham Rd, SE25 ... 202 DV97
Chart Hills Cl, SE28
off Fairway Dr ... 146 EY72
Chart La, Dor. RH4 ... 263 CH136
Reigate RH2 ... 250 DB134
Chart La S, Dor. RH5 ... 263 CJ138
Chartley Av, NW2 ... 118 CS62
Stanmore HA7 ... 95 CF51
Charton Cl, Belv. DA17
off Nuxley Rd ... 166 EZ79
Chartridge Cl, Barn. EN5 ... 79 CU43
Bushey WD23 ... 76 CC44
Chartridge La, Chesh. HP5 ... 54 AM29
Chartridge Way, Hem.H. HP2 ... 41 BQ20
Chart St, N1 ... 11 K1
Chartway, Reig. RH2 ... 250 DB133
Sevenoaks TN13 ... 257 FJ124
★ Chartwell, West. TN16 ... 255 ET132
Chartwell Cl, SE9 ... 185 EQ89
Croydon CR0 ... 202 DR102
Greenford UB6 ... 136 CB67
Waltham Abbey EN9 ... 68 EE33
Chartwell Dr, Orp. BR6 ... 223 ER106
Chartwell Gdns, Sutt. SM3 ... 217 CY105
Chartwell Gate, Beac. HP9 ... 89 AK53
Chartwell Pl, Epsom KT18 ... 216 CS114
Harrow HA2 ... 117 CD61
Sutton SM3 ... 217 CZ105
Chartwell Rd, Nthwd. HA6 ... 93 BT51
Chartwell Way, SE20 ... 202 DV95
Chartwood Pl, Dor. RH4
off South St ... 263 CG136
Charville La, Hayes UB4 ... 135 BS68
Charville La W, Uxb. UB10 ... 135 BP69
Charville Prim Sch, Hayes UB4 off Bury Av ... 135 BS68
Charwood, SW16 ... 181 DN91
Charwood Cl, Rad. (Shenley) WD7 ... 62 CL33
Chasden Rd, Hem.H. HP1 ... 39 BF17
Chase, The, E12 ... 124 EK63
SW4 ... 161 DH83
SW16 ... 181 DM94
SW20 ... 199 CY95
Ashtead KT21 ... 231 CJ118
Bexleyheath DA7 ... 167 FB83
Brentwood (Cromwell Rd) CM14 ... 108 FV49
Brentwood (Ingrave) CM13 ... 109 GC50
Brentwood (Seven Arches Rd) CM14 ... 108 FX48
Brentwood (Woodman Rd) CM14 ... 108 FX50
Bromley BR1 ... 204 EH97
Chesham HP5
off Chalk Hill ... 54 AP29
Chigwell IG7 ... 103 EQ49
Coulsdon CR5 ... 219 DJ114
Edgware HA8 ... 96 CP53
Grays RM20 ... 169 FX79
Guildford GU2 ... 258 AU135
Harlow CM17
off London Rd ... 36 EW14
Hemel Hempstead HP2
off Turners Hill ... 40 BL21
High Wycombe (Penn) HP10 ... 88 AC46
High Wycombe (Woob.Grn) HP10 ... 110 AF59
Hornchurch RM12 ... 127 FE62
Leatherhead (E.Hors.) KT24 ... 245 BT126
Leatherhead (Oxshott) KT22 ... 230 CC115
Loughton IG10 ... 102 EJ45
Pinner HA5 ... 116 BZ56
Pinner (Eastcote) HA5 ... 116 BW58
Radlett WD7 ... 77 CF35
Reigate RH2 ... 266 DD135
Romford RM1 ... 127 FE55
Romford (Chad.Hth) RM6 ... 126 EY58
Romford (Rush Grn) RM7 ... 127 FD62
Stanmore HA7 ... 95 CG50
Sunbury-on-Thames TW16 ... 195 BV95
Tadworth (Kgswd) KT20 ... 234 DA122
Upminster RM14 ... 129 FS62
Uxbridge UB10 ... 114 BN64
Wallington SM6 ... 219 DL106
Waltham Cross (Goffs Oak) EN7 ... 65 DP28
Ware (Gt Amwell) SG12 ... 33 EA09
Watford WD18 ... 75 BS42
Chase Br Prim Sch, Twick. TW2
off Kneller Rd ... 177 CE86
Chase Cl, Amer. (Colesh.) HP7 ... 55 AN43
High Wycombe (Penn) HP10 ... 88 AC46
Chase Ct Gdns, Enf. EN2 ... 82 DQ41
CHASE CROSS, Rom. RM1 ... 105 FE51
Chase Cross Rd, Rom. RM5 ... 105 FC52
Chase End, Epsom KT19 ... 216 CR112
Chase Fm Hosp, Enf. EN2 ... 81 DN38
Chasefield Cl, Guil. GU4 ... 243 BA131
Chasefield Rd, SW17 ... 180 DF91
Chase Gdns, E4 ... 101 EA49
Twickenham TW2 ... 177 CD86
Chase Grn, Enf. EN2 ... 82 DQ41
Chase Grn Av, Enf. EN2 ... 81 DP40
Chase Hill, Enf. EN2 ... 82 DQ41
Chase Ho Gdns, Horn. RM11
off Great Nelmes Chase ... 128 FM57
Chase La, Chig. IG7 ... 104 EU48
Ilford IG6 ... 125 ER57
Chase La Inf Sch, E4
off York Rd ... 101 DZ49
Chase La Jun Sch, E4
off York Rd ... 101 DZ49
Chaseley Dr, W4 ... 158 CP78
South Croydon CR2 ... 220 DR110
Chaseley St, E14 ... 13 J8
Chasemore Cl, Mitch. CR4 ... 200 DF101
Chasemore Gdns, Croy. CR0
off Thorneloe Gdns ... 219 DP106
Chase Ridings, Enf. EN2 ... 81 DN40
Chase Rd, N14 ... 81 DJ44
NW10 ... 138 CR70
W3 ... 138 CR70
Brentwood CM14 ... 108 FW48
Epsom KT19 ... 216 CR112
Chase Side, N14 ... 80 DG44
Enfield EN2 ... 82 DQ41
Chase Side Av, SW20 ... 199 CY95
Enfield EN2 ... 82 DQ40
Chaseside Cl, Rom. RM1 ... 105 FE51
Chase Side Cres, Enf. EN2 ... 82 DQ39
Chaseside Gdns, Cher. KT16 ... 194 BH101
Chase Side Pl, Enf. EN2
off Chase Side ... 82 DQ40
Chase Side Prim Sch, Enf. EN2 off Trinity St ... 82 DQ40
Chase Sq, Grav. DA11
off High St ... 191 GH86
Chaseville Pk Rd, N21 ... 81 DL43
Chase Way, N14 ... 99 DH47
Chaseways, Saw. CM21 ... 36 EW07
Chasewood Av, Enf. EN2 ... 81 DP40
Chasewood Pk, Har. HA1 ... 117 CF62
Chastilian Rd, Dart. DA1 ... 187 FF87
Chatelet Cl, Horl. RH6 ... 269 DH147
Chater Inf Sch, Wat. WD18 off Southsea Av ... 75 BU42
Chater Jun Sch, Wat. WD18
off Addiscombe Rd ... 75 BV42
Chatfield, Slou. SL2 ... 131 AN71
Chatfield Ct, Cat. CR3
off Yorke Gate Rd ... 236 DR122
Chatfield Dr, Guil. GU4 ... 243 BC132
Chatfield Rd, SW11 ... 160 DC83
Croydon CR0 ... 201 DP102
Chatham Av, Brom. BR2 ... 204 EF101
Chatham Cl, NW11 ... 120 DA57
Sutton SM3 ... 199 CZ101
Chatham Hill Rd, Sev. TN14 ... 257 FJ121
Chatham Ms, Guil. GU2
off Stoughton Rd ... 242 AU131
Chatham Pl, E9 ... 142 DW65
Chatham Rd, E17 ... 123 DY55
E18 off Grove Hill ... 102 EF54
SW11 ... 180 DF86
Kingston upon Thames KT1 ... 198 CN96
Orpington BR6 ... 223 EQ106
Chatham St, SE17 ... 21 J7
Chatsfield, Epsom KT17 ... 217 CU110
Chatsfield Pl, W5 ... 138 CL72
Chatsworth Av, NW4 ... 97 CW54
SW20 ... 199 CY95
Bromley BR1 ... 184 EH91
Sidcup DA15 ... 186 EU88
Wembley HA9 ... 118 CM64
Chatsworth Cl, NW4 ... 97 CW54
Borehamwood WD6 ... 78 CN41
West Wickham BR4 ... 204 EF103
Chatsworth Ct, W8 ... 16 G7
Stanmore HA7
off Marsh La ... 95 CJ50
Chatsworth Cres, Houns. TW3 ... 157 CD84
Chatsworth Dr, Enf. EN1 ... 100 DU45
Chatsworth Est, E5
off Elderfield Rd ... 123 DX63
Chatsworth Gdns, W3 ... 138 CP73
Harrow HA2 ... 116 CB60
New Malden KT3 ... 199 CT99
Chatsworth Inf & Nurs Sch, Houns. TW3
off Heath Rd ... 156 CC84
Chatsworth Jun Sch, Houns. TW3
off Heath Rd ... 156 CC84
Chatsworth Ms, Wat. WD24 ... 75 BU38
Chatsworth Par, Orp. BR5
off Queensway ... 205 EQ99
Chatsworth Pl, Lthd. (Oxshott) KT22 ... 215 CD112
Mitcham CR4 ... 200 DF97
Teddington TW11 ... 177 CG91
Chatsworth Prim Inf Sch, Sid. DA15
off Burnt Oak La ... 186 EU88
Chatsworth Ri, W5 ... 138 CM70
Chatsworth Rd, E5 ... 122 DW62
E15 ... 124 EF64
NW2 ... 139 CX65
W4 ... 158 CQ79
W5 ... 138 CM70
Croydon CR0 ... 220 DR105
Dartford DA1 ... 188 FJ85
Hayes UB4 ... 135 BV70
Sutton SM3 ... 217 CX106
Chatsworth Way, SE27 ... 181 DP90
Chatteris Av, Rom. RM3 ... 106 FJ51
Chattern Hill, Ashf. TW15 ... 175 BP91
Chattern Rd, Ashf. TW15 ... 175 BQ91
Chatterton Ms, N4
off Chatterton Rd ... 121 DP62
Chatterton Rd, N4 ... 121 DP62
Bromley BR2 ... 204 EK98
Chatto Rd, SW11 ... 180 DF85
Chaucer Av, Hayes UB4 ... 135 BU71
Hounslow TW4 ... 155 BV82
Richmond TW9 ... 158 CN82
Weybridge KT13 ... 212 BN108
Chaucer Cen, Mord. SM4
off Canterbury Rd ... 200 DB101

Chaucer Cl, N11 ... 99 DJ50
Banstead SM7 ... 217 CY114
Berkhamsted HP4 ... 38 AT18
Tilbury RM18 ... 171 GJ82
Chaucer Ct, N16 ... 122 DS63
Guildford GU2 off Lawn Rd ... 258 AW137
Chaucer Dr, SE1 ... 21 P8
Chaucer Gdns, Sutt. SM1 ... 200 DA104
Chaucer Grn, Croy. CR0 ... 202 DV101
Chaucer Ho, Sutt. SM1 ... 200 DA104
Chaucer Pk, Dart. DA1 ... 188 FM87
Chaucer Rd, E7 ... 144 EG65
E11 ... 124 EG58
E17 ... 101 EC54
SE24 ... 181 DN85
W3 ... 138 CQ74
Ashford TW15 ... 174 BL91
Gravesend (Nthflt) DA11 ... 190 GD90
Romford RM3 ... 105 FH52
Sidcup DA15 ... 186 EW88
Sutton SM1 ... 218 DA105
Welling DA16 ... 165 ES81
Chaucer Way, SW19 ... 180 DD93
Addlestone KT15 ... 212 BG107
Dartford DA1 ... 168 FN84
Hoddesdon EN11 ... 33 EA13
Slough SL1 ... 132 AT74
CHAULDEN, Hem.H. HP1 ... 39 BE21
Chaulden Ho Gdns, Hem.H. HP1 ... 39 BF21
Sch Chaulden Infant, Nurs & Jun Sch, Hem.H. HP1 off School Row ... 39 BF21
Chaulden La, Hem.H. HP1 ... 39 BD22
Chaulden Ter, Hem.H. HP1 ... 39 BF21
Chauncey Cl, N9 ... 100 DU48
Chauncy Av, Pot.B. EN6 ... 64 DC33
Chauncy Ct, Hert. SG14 off Bluecoats Av ... 32 DR09
Sch Chauncy Sch, The, Ware SG12 off Park Rd ... 32 DV05
Chaundrye Cl, SE9 ... 185 EM86
Chauntler Cl, E16 ... 15 P9
Chauntry Cl, Maid. SL6 ... 130 AC73
Chavecroft Ter, Epsom KT18 ... 233 CW119
Chave Rd, Dart. DA2 ... 188 FL90
Chaworth Cl, Cher. KT16 ... 211 BC107
Chaworth Rd, Cher. (Ott.) KT16 ... 211 BC107
CHEAM, Sutt. SM3 ... 217 CX107
⇌ Cheam ... 217 CY108
Cheam Cl, Tad. KT20 off Waterfield ... 233 CV121
Sch Cheam Common Inf Sch, Wor.Pk. KT4 off Balmoral Rd ... 199 CV103
Sch Cheam Common Jun Sch, Wor.Pk. KT4 off Kingsmead Av ... 199 CV103
Cheam Common Rd, Wor.Pk. KT4 ... 199 CV103
Sch Cheam Flds Prim Sch, Sutt. SM3 off Stoughton Av ... 217 CY106
Sch Cheam High Sch, Sutt. SM3 off Chatsworth Rd ... 217 CY105
Cheam Mans, Sutt. SM3 ... 217 CY108
Sch Cheam Pk Fm Inf Sch, Sutt. SM3 off Molesey Dr ... 199 CY104
Sch Cheam Pk Fm Jun Sch, Sutt. SM3 off Kingston Av ... 199 CY104
Cheam Pk Way, Sutt. SM3 ... 217 CY107
Cheam Rd, Epsom KT17 ... 217 CU109
Sutton SM1 ... 217 CZ107
Sutton (E.Ewell) SM2 ... 217 CX110
Cheam St, SE15 off Evelina Rd ... 162 DV83
Cheapside, EC2 ... 11 H8
N13 off Taplow Rd ... 100 DQ49
Woking GU21 ... 210 AX114
Cheapside La, Uxb. (Denh.) UB9 ... 113 BF61
Chedburgh, Welw.G.C. AL7 ... 30 DD08
Cheddar Cl, N11 off Martock Gdns ... 98 DG51
Cheddar Rd, Houns. (Hthrw Air.) TW6 off Cromer Rd ... 154 BN82
Cheddar Waye, Hayes UB4 ... 135 BV72
Cheddington Rd, N18 ... 100 DS48
Chedworth Cl, E16 ... 15 J7
Cheelson Rd, S.Ock. RM15 ... 149 FW68
Cheeseman Cl, Hmptn. TW12 ... 176 BY93
Cheesemans Ter, W14 ... 16 E10
Cheffins Rd, Hodd. EN11 ... 33 DZ14
Cheldon Av, NW7 ... 97 CX52
Chelford Rd, Brom. BR1 ... 183 ED92
Chelmer Cres, Bark. IG11 ... 146 EV68
Chelmer Dr, Brwd. (Hutt.) CM13 ... 109 GE44
South Ockendon RM15 ... 149 FW73
Chelmer Rd, E9 ... 123 DX64
Grays RM16 ... 171 GG78
Upminster RM14 ... 129 FR58
Chelmsford Av, Rom. RM5 ... 105 FD52
Chelmsford Cl, E6 off Guildford Rd ... 145 EM72
W6 ... 159 CX79
Sutton SM2 ... 218 DA109
Chelmsford Dr, Upmin. RM14 ... 128 FM62
Chelmsford Gdns, Ilf. IG1 ... 124 EL59
Chelmsford Rd, E11 ... 123 ED60
E17 ... 123 EA58
E18 ... 102 EF53
N14 ... 99 DJ45
Bishop's Stortford (Hat.Hth) CM22 ... 37 FH05
Brentwood (Shenf.) CM15 ... 109 FZ44
Hertford SG14 ... 31 DN10
Chelmsford Sq, NW10 ... 139 CW67
CHELSEA, SW3 ... 160 DD79
H Chelsea & Westminster Hosp, SW10 ... 160 DC79
★ Chelsea Antique Mkt, SW3 ... 160 DD79
Chelsea Br, SW1 ... 161 DH79
SW8 ... 161 DH79
Chelsea Br Rd, SW1 ... 18 E9
Chelsea Cloisters, SW3 off Lucan Pl ... 160 DE77
Chelsea Cl, NW10 off Winchelsea Rd ... 138 CR67
Edgware HA8 ... 96 CN54
Hampton (Hmptn H.) TW12 ... 176 CC92
Chelsea Cl, Wor. Pk. KT4 ... 199 CU101
Uni Chelsea Coll of Art & Design, SW1 off Atterbury St ... 161 DL78
Chelsea Cres, SW10 off Harbour Av ... 160 DC81
Chelsea Embk, SW3 ... 160 DE79
Chelsea Flds, Hodd. EN11 ... 33 EB13
★ Chelsea FC, SW6 ... 160 DB80
Chelsea Gdns, W13 off Hathaway Gdns ... 137 CF71
Harlow CM17 ... 52 EY16
Sutton SM3 ... 217 CY105
Chelsea Harbour, SW10 ... 160 DC81
Chelsea Harbour Dr, SW10 ... 160 DC81
Chelsea Harbour Pier ... 160 DD81
Chelsea Manor Ct, SW3 off Chelsea Manor St ... 160 DE79
Chelsea Manor Gdns, SW3 ... 160 DE79
Chelsea Manor St, SW3 ... 18 A10
Chelsea Ms, Horn. RM11 off St. Leonards Way ... 127 FH60
Chelsea Pk Gdns, SW3 ... 160 DD79
★ Chelsea Physic Gdn, SW3 ... 160 DF79
Chelsea Sq, SW3 ... 17 P9
Chelsea Vista, SW6 off The Boulevard ... 160 DC81
Chelsea Wf, SW10 ... 160 DD80
CHELSFIELD, Orp. BR6 ... 224 EW106
⇌ Chelsfield ... 224 EV106
Chelsfield Av, N9 ... 101 DX45
Chelsfield Gdns, SE26 ... 182 DW90
Chelsfield Grn, N9 off Chelsfield Av ... 101 DX45
Chelsfield Hill, Orp. BR6 ... 224 EW109
Chelsfield La, Orp. BR5, BR6 ... 206 EX101
Orpington (Maypole) BR6 ... 224 FA108
Sevenoaks TN14 ... 225 FC109
H Chelsfield Pk Hosp, Orp. BR6 ... 224 EZ106
Sch Chelsfield Prim Sch, Orp. BR6 off Warren Rd ... 224 EY106
Chelsfield Rd, Orp. BR5 ... 206 EW100
CHELSHAM, Warl. CR6 ... 237 EA117
Chelsham Cl, Warl. CR6 ... 237 DY118
Chelsham Common Rd, Warl. CR6 ... 237 EA117
Chelsham Ct Rd, Warl. CR6 ... 237 ED118
Chelsham Rd, SW4 ... 161 DK83
South Croydon CR2 ... 220 DR107
Warlingham CR6 ... 237 EA117
Chelsing Ri, Hem.H. HP2 ... 41 BQ21
Chelston App, Ruis. HA4 ... 115 BU61
Chelston Rd, Ruis. HA4 ... 115 BU60
Chelsworth Cl, Rom. RM3 off Chelsworth Dr ... 106 FM53
Chelsworth Dr, SE18 ... 165 ER79
Romford RM3 ... 106 FL53
Cheltenham Av, Twick. TW1 ... 177 CG87
Cheltenham Cl, Grav. DA12 ... 191 GJ92
New Malden KT3 off Northcote Rd ... 198 CQ97
Northolt UB5 ... 136 CB65
Cheltenham Gdns, E6 ... 144 EL68
Loughton IG10 ... 84 EL44
Cheltenham Pl, W3 ... 138 CP74
Harrow HA3 ... 118 CL56
Cheltenham Rd, E10 ... 123 EC58
SE15 ... 162 DW84
Orpington BR6 ... 206 EU104
Cheltenham Ter, SW3 ... 18 D9
Cheltenham Vil, Stai. TW19 ... 173 BF86
Chelverton Rd, SW15 ... 159 CX84
Chelveston, Welw.G.C. AL7 ... 30 DD08
Chelwood, N20 off Oakleigh Rd N ... 98 DD47
Chelwood Av, Hat. AL10 ... 45 CU16
Chelwood Cl, E4 ... 83 EB44
Coulsdon CR5 off Starrock Rd ... 235 DJ119
Epsom KT17 ... 217 CT112
Northwood HA6 ... 93 BQ52
Chelwood Gdns, Rich. TW9 ... 158 CN82
Chelwood Gdns Pas, Rich. TW9 off Chelwood Gdns ... 158 CN82
Chelwood Wk, SE4 ... 163 DY84
Chenappa Cl, E13 ... 15 K2
Chenduit Way, Stan. HA7 ... 95 CF50
Chene Dr, St.Alb. AL3 ... 43 CD18
Chene Ms, St.Alb. AL3 off Waverley Rd ... 43 CD18
Cheney Row, E17 ... 101 DZ53
Cheneys Rd, E11 ... 124 EE62
Cheney St, Pnr. HA5 ... 116 BW57
CHENIES, Rick. WD3 ... 73 BB38
Chenies, The, Dart. DA2 ... 187 FE91
Orpington BR6 ... 205 ES100
Chenies Av, Amer. HP6 ... 72 AW39
Sch Chenies Comb Sch, Rick. WD3 off Latimer Rd ... 73 BB38
Chenies Ct, Hem.H. HP2 off Datchet Cl ... 41 BP15
Chenies Hill, Hem.H. (Flaun.) HP3 ... 57 BB34
★ Chenies Manor, Rick. WD3 ... 73 BA38
Chenies Ms, WC1 ... 9 L4
Chenies Par, Amer. HP7 ... 72 AW40
Chenies Pl, NW1 ... 141 DK68
Chenies Rd, Rick. (Chorl.) WD3 ... 73 BD40
Chenies St, WC1 ... 9 L5
Chenies Way, Wat. WD18 ... 93 BS45
Cheniston Cl, W.Byf. KT14 ... 212 BG113
Cheniston Gdns, W8 ... 17 J5
Chennells, Hat. AL10 ... 45 CT19
Sch Chennestone Prim Comm Sch, Sun. TW16 off Manor La ... 195 BV96
Chepstow Av, Horn. RM12 ... 128 FL62
Chepstow Cl, SW15 off Lytton Gro ... 179 CY86
Chepstow Cres, W11 ... 6 G9
Ilford IG3 ... 125 ES58
Chepstow Gdns, Sthl. UB1 ... 136 BZ72
Chepstow Pl, W2 ... 7 H9
Chepstow Ri, Croy. CR0 ... 202 DS104
Chepstow Rd, W2 ... 7 H7
W7 ... 157 CG76
Croydon CR0 ... 202 DS104
Chepstow Vil, W11 ... 6 F9
Chepstow Way, SE15 ... 162 DT80
Chequers, Buck.H. IG9 off Hills Rd ... 102 EH46
Hatfield AL9 ... 29 CX13
Welwyn Garden City AL7 ... 29 CX11
Chequers Cl, NW9 ... 118 CS55
Horley RH6 ... 268 DG147
Orpington BR5 ... 205 ET98
Tadworth KT20 ... 249 CU125
Chequers Dr, Horl. RH6 ... 268 DG147
Chequers Fld, Welw.G.C. AL7 ... 29 CX12
Chequers Gdns, N13 ... 99 DP50
Chequers Hill, Amer. HP7 ... 55 AR40
Chequers La, Dag. RM9 ... 146 EZ70
Tadworth KT20 ... 249 CU125
Watford WD25 ... 60 BW30
Chequers Orchard, Iver SL0 ... 133 BF72
Chequers Par, SE9 off Eltham High St ... 185 EM86
Chequers Pl, Dor. RH4 ... 263 CH136
Chequers Rd, Brwd. CM14 ... 106 FM46
Loughton IG10 ... 85 EN43
Romford RM3 ... 106 FL47
Chequers Sq, Uxb. UB8 off High St ... 134 BJ66
Chequer St, EC1 ... 11 H4
St. Albans AL1 ... 43 CD20
Chequers Wk, Wal.Abb. EN9 ... 68 EF33
Chequers Way, N13 ... 100 DQ50
Chequers Yd, Dor. RH4 off Chequers Pl ... 263 CH136
Chequer Tree Cl, Wok. (Knap.) GU21 ... 226 AS116
Cherbury Cl, SE28 ... 146 EX72
Cherbury Ct, N1 ... 5 K10
Cherbury St, N1 ... 5 K10
Cherchefelle Ms, Stan. HA7 ... 95 CH50
Cherimoya Gdns, W.Mol. KT8 off Kelvinbrook ... 196 CB97
Cherington Rd, W7 ... 137 CF74
Cheriton Av, Brom. BR2 ... 204 EF99
Ilford IG5 ... 103 EM54
Cheriton Cl, W5 ... 137 CJ71
Barnet EN4 ... 80 DF41
St. Albans AL4 ... 43 CK16
Cheriton Ct, Walt. KT12 ... 196 BW102
Cheriton Dr, SE18 ... 165 ER80
Cheriton Sq, SW17 ... 180 DG89
Cherkley Hill, Lthd. KT22 ... 247 CJ126
Cherries, The, Slou. SL2 ... 132 AV72
Cherry Acre, Ger.Cr. (Chal.St.P.) SL9 ... 90 AX49
Cherry Av, Brwd. CM13 ... 109 FZ48
Slough SL3 ... 152 AX75
Southall UB1 ... 136 BX74
Swanley BR8 ... 207 FD97
Cherry Blossom Cl, N13 ... 99 DP50
Cherry Bounce, Hem.H. HP1 ... 40 BK18
Cherry Cl, E17 off Eden Rd ... 123 EB56
NW9 ... 96 CS54
SW2 off Tulse Hill ... 181 DN87
W5 ... 157 CK76
Banstead SM7 ... 217 CX114
Carshalton SM5 ... 200 DF103
Morden SM4 ... 199 CY98
Ruislip HA4 off Roundways ... 115 BT62
Cherrycot Hill, Orp. BR6 ... 223 ER105
Cherrycot Ri, Orp. BR6 ... 223 EQ105
Cherry Cres, Brent. TW8 ... 157 CH80
Cherry Cft, Rick. (Crox.Grn) WD3 ... 74 BN44
Welwyn Garden City AL8 ... 29 CX05
Cherrycroft Gdns, Pnr. HA5 off Westfield Pk ... 94 BZ52
Cherrydale, Wat. WD18 ... 75 BT42
Cherrydown Av, E4 ... 101 DZ48
Cherrydown Cl, E4 ... 101 DZ48
Cherrydown Rd, Sid. DA14 ... 186 EX89
Cherrydown Wk, Rom. RM7 ... 105 FB54
Cherry Dr, Beac. (Forty Grn) HP9 ... 88 AH51
Cherry Gdns, Dag. RM9 ... 126 EZ64
Northolt UB5 ... 136 CB66
Sch Cherry Gdn Spec Sch, SE16 ... 22 B7
Cherry Gdn St, SE16 ... 22 C4
Cherry Garth, Brent. TW8 ... 157 CK77
Cherry Grn Cl, Red. RH1 ... 267 DH136
Cherry Gro, Hayes UB3 ... 135 BV74
Uxbridge UB8 ... 135 BP71
Cherry Hill, Barn. EN5 ... 80 DB44
Harrow HA3 ... 95 CE51
Rickmansworth (Loud.) WD3 ... 74 BH41
St. Albans AL2 ... 60 CA25
Cherry Hill Gdns, Croy. CR0 ... 219 DM105
Cherry Hills, Wat. WD19 ... 94 BY50
Cherry Hollow, Abb.L. WD5 ... 59 BT31
Cherrylands Cl, NW9 ... 118 CQ61
Cherry La, Amer. HP7 ... 55 AN40
West Drayton UB7 ... 154 BM77
Sch Cherry La Prim Sch, West Dr. UB7 off Sipson Rd ... 154 BM77
Cherry La Roundabout, West Dr. UB7 ... 155 BP77
Cherry Laurel Wk, SW2 off Beechdale Rd ... 181 DM86
Cherry Orchard, Amer. HP6 ... 55 AS37
Ashtead KT21 ... 232 CP118
Hemel Hempstead HP1 ... 40 BG18
Slough (Stoke P.) SL2 ... 132 AV66
Staines TW18 ... 174 BG92
West Drayton UB7 ... 154 BL75
Sch Cherry Orchard Cen, Croy. CR0 off St. James's Rd ... 202 DR101
Cherry Orchard Cl, Orp. BR5 ... 206 EW99
Cherry Orchard Gdns, Croy. CR0 off Oval Rd ... 202 DR103
West Molesey KT8 ... 196 BZ97
Sch Cherry Orchard Prim Sch, SE7 off Rectory Fld Cres ... 164 EJ80
Cherry Orchard Rd, Brom. BR2 ... 204 EL103
Croydon CR0 ... 202 DR103
West Molesey KT8 ... 196 CA97
Cherry Ri, Ch.St.G. HP8 ... 90 AX47
Cherry Rd, Enf. EN3 ... 82 DW38
Cherry St, Rom. RM7 ... 127 FD57
Woking GU21 ... 226 AY118
Cherry Tree Av, Guil. GU2 ... 242 AT134
St. Albans (Lon.Col.) AL2 ... 61 CK26
Staines TW18 ... 174 BH93
West Drayton UB7 ... 134 BM72
Cherry Tree Cl, E9 off Moulins Rd ... 142 DW67
Grays RM17 ... 170 GC79
Rainham RM13 ... 147 FG68
Wembley HA0 ... 117 CF63
Cherry Tree Ct, NW9 ... 118 CQ56
Coulsdon CR5 ... 235 DM117
Cherry Tree Dr, SW16 ... 181 DL90
South Ockendon RM15 ... 149 FX70
Cherry Tree Grn, Hert. SG14 ... 31 DM07
South Croydon CR2 ... 220 DV114
Cherry Tree La, Dart. DA2 ... 187 FF90
Epsom KT19 off Christ Ch Rd ... 216 CN112
Cherrytree La, Ger.Cr. (Chal.St.P.) SL9 ... 90 AX54
Cherry Tree La, Harl. CM20 off Hamstel Rd ... 35 EP14
Hemel Hempstead HP2 ... 41 BQ17
Iver SL0 ... 134 BG67
Potters Bar EN6 ... 64 DB34
Cherry Tree La, Rain. RM13 ... 147 FE69
Rickmansworth (Herons.) WD3 ... 91 BC46
Slough (Fulmer) SL3 ... 133 AZ65
Sch Cherry Tree Prim Sch, Wat. WD24 off Berry Av ... 75 BU36
Cherry Tree Ri, Buck.H. IG9 ... 102 EJ49
Cherry Tree Rd, E15 off Wingfield Rd ... 124 EE63
N2 ... 120 DF56
Beaconsfield HP9 ... 88 AH54
Hoddesdon EN11 ... 49 EA16
Slough (Farn.Royal) SL2 ... 131 AQ66
Watford WD24 ... 75 BV36
Cherrytrees, Couls. CR5 off Blue Leaves Av ... 235 DK121
Cherry Tree Wk, EC1 ... 11 H4
Beckenham BR3 ... 203 DZ98
Chesham HP5 ... 54 AR29
West Wickham BR4 ... 222 EF105
Cherry Tree Way, H.Wyc. (Penn) HP10 ... 88 AC46
Stanmore HA7 ... 95 CH51
Cherry Wk, Brom. BR2 ... 204 EG102
Grays RM16 ... 171 GG76
Rainham RM13 ... 147 FF68
Rickmansworth (Loud.) WD3 ... 74 BJ40
Cherry Way, Epsom KT19 ... 216 CR107
Hatfield AL10 ... 45 CU21
Shepperton TW17 ... 195 BR98
Slough (Horton) SL3 ... 153 BC83
Cherrywood Av, Egh. (Eng.Grn) TW20 ... 172 AV93
Cherrywood Cl, E3 ... 13 K1
Cherry Wd Cl, Beac. (Seer Grn) HP9 ... 89 AR50
Cherrywood Cl, Kings.T. KT2 ... 178 CN94
Cherrywood Dr, SW15 ... 179 CX85
Gravesend (Nthflt) DA11 ... 190 GE90
Cherrywood La, Mord. SM4 ... 199 CY98
Cherry Wd Way, W5 off Hanger Vale La ... 138 CN71
Cherston Gdns, Loug. IG10 off Cherston Rd ... 85 EN42
Cherston Rd, Loug. IG10 ... 85 EN42
CHERTSEY, KT16 ... 194 BG102
⇌ Chertsey ... 193 BF102
Chertsey Br Rd, Cher. KT16 ... 194 BK101
Chertsey Cl, Ken. CR8 ... 235 DP115
Chertsey Cres, Croy. (New Adgtn) CR0 ... 221 EC110
Chertsey Dr, Sutt. SM3 ... 199 CY103
Chertsey La, Cher. KT16 ... 193 BE95
Epsom KT19 ... 216 CN112
Staines TW18 ... 173 BE92
★ Chertsey Mus, Cher. KT16 off Windsor St ... 194 BG100
Chertsey Rd, E11 ... 123 ED61
Addlestone KT15 ... 194 BH103
Ashford TW15 ... 175 BR94
Feltham TW13 ... 175 BS92
Ilford IG1 ... 125 ER63
Shepperton TW17 ... 194 BN101
Sunbury-on-Thames TW16 ... 175 BR94
Twickenham TW1, TW2 ... 177 CF86
West Byfleet (Byfleet) KT14 ... 212 BK111
Woking GU21 ... 211 BA113
Woking (Chobham) GU24 ... 210 AY110
Chertsey St, SW17 ... 180 DG92
Guildford GU1 ... 258 AX135
Cherubs, The, Slou. (Farn.Com.) SL2 ... 131 AQ65
Chervil Cl, Felt. TW13 ... 175 BU90
Chervil Ms, SE28 ... 146 EV74
Cherwell Cl, Rick. (Crox.Grn) WD3 ... 74 BN43
Slough SL3 off Tweed Rd ... 153 BB79
Cherwell Ct, Epsom KT19 ... 216 CQ105
Cherwell Gro, S.Ock. RM15 ... 149 FV73
Cherwell Way, Ruis. HA4 ... 115 BQ58
Cheryls Cl, SW6 ... 160 DB81
Cheselden Rd, Guil. GU1 ... 258 AY135
Cheseman St, SE26 ... 182 DV90
Chesfield Rd, Kings.T. KT2 ... 178 CL94
CHESHAM, HP5 ... 54 AQ31
⊖ Chesham ... 54 AQ31
Chesham Av, Orp. BR5 ... 205 EP100
CHESHAM BOIS, Amer. HP6 ... 55 AQ36
Sch Chesham Bois C of E Comb Sch, Amer. HP6 off Bois La ... 55 AS35
Chesham Cl, SW1 ... 18 E6
Romford RM7 ... 127 FD56
Sutton SM2 ... 217 CY110
Chesham Ct, Nthwd. HA6 off Frithwood Av ... 93 BT51
Chesham Cres, SE20 ... 202 DW96
Sch Chesham High Sch, Chesh. HP5 off White Hill ... 54 AR30
H Chesham Hosp, Chesh. HP5 ... 54 AQ32
Chesham La, Ch.St.G. HP8 ... 90 AY48
Gerrards Cross (Chal.St.P.) SL9 ... 90 AY49
Chesham Ms, SW1 ... 18 E5
Guildford GU1 off Chesham Rd ... 259 AZ135
Sch Chesham Pk Sch, Chesh. HP5 off Chartridge La ... 54 AN30
Chesham Pl, SW1 ... 18 E6
Sch Chesham Prep Sch, Chesh. HP5 off Orchard Leigh ... 56 AU27
Chesham Rd, SE20 ... 202 DW96
SW19 ... 180 DD92
Amersham HP6 ... 55 AQ38
Berkhamsted HP4 ... 38 AV21
Chesham (Ash.Grn) HP5 ... 38 AT24
Guildford GU1 ... 258 AY135
Hemel Hempstead (Bov.) HP3 ... 56 AY27
Kingston upon Thames KT1 ... 198 CN95
Chesham St, NW10 ... 118 CR62
SW1 ... 18 E6
Chesham Ter, W13 ... 157 CH75
Chesham Way, Wat. WD18 ... 75 BS44
Cheshire Cl, E17 ... 101 EB53
SE4 ... 163 DZ82
Chertsey (Ott.) KT16 ... 211 BC107
Hornchurch RM11 ... 128 FN57
Mitcham CR4 ... 201 DL97
Cheshire Ct, EC4 ... 10 D8
Slough SL1 off Clements Cl ... 152 AV75
Cheshire Dr, Wat. (Lvsdn) WD25 ... 59 BT34
Cheshire Gdns, Chess. KT9 ... 215 CK107
Cheshire Ho, N18 ... 100 DV49
Cheshire Rd, N22 ... 99 DM52
Cheshire St, E2 ... 11 P3
Chesholm Rd, N16 ... 122 DS62
CHESHUNT, Wal.Cr. EN8 ... 67 DX31
⇌ Cheshunt ... 67 DZ30
H Cheshunt Comm Hosp, Wal.Cr. EN8 ... 67 DY31
Cheshunt Pk, Wal.Cr. (Chsht) EN7 ... 66 DV26
Cheshunt Rd, E7 ... 144 EH65
Belvedere DA17 ... 166 FA78
Sch Cheshunt Sch, Wal.Cr. EN8 off College Rd ... 66 DW30
Cheshunt Wash, Wal.Cr. (Chsht) EN8 ... 67 DY27
Chesil Ct, E2 ... 142 DW68
Chesilton Rd, SW6 ... 159 CZ81
Chesil Way, Hayes UB4 ... 135 BT69
Chesley Gdns, E6 ... 144 EK68
Cheslyn Gdns, Wat. WD17 ... 75 BT37
Chesney Cres, Croy. (New Adgtn) CR0 ... 221 EC108
Chesney St, SW11 ... 160 DG81
Chesnut Est, N17 ... 122 DT55
Chesnut Gro, N17 off Chesnut Rd ... 122 DT55
Chesnut Rd, N17 ... 122 DT55
Chessbury Cl, Chesh. HP5 off Missenden Rd ... 54 AP32
Chessbury Rd, Chesh. HP5 ... 54 AN32
Chess Cl, Chesh. (Latimer) HP5 ... 72 AX36
Rickmansworth (Loud.) WD3 ... 74 BK42
Chessell Cl, Th.Hth. CR7 ... 201 DP98
Chessfield Pk, Amer. HP6 ... 72 AY39
Chess Hill, Rick. (Loud.) WD3 ... 74 BK42
Chessholme Ct, Sun. TW16 off Scotts Av ... 175 BS94
Chessholme Rd, Ashf. TW15 ... 175 BQ93
Chessinghams, The, Epsom KT18 ... 216 CR113
CHESSINGTON, KT9 ... 216 CL107
Chessington Av, N3 ... 119 CY55
Bexleyheath DA7 ... 166 EY80
Chessington Cl, Epsom KT19 ... 216 CQ107
Coll Chessington Comm Coll, Chess. KT9 off Garrison La ... 215 CK108
Chessington Ct, Pnr. HA5 ... 116 BZ56
Chessington Hall Gdns, Chess. KT9 ... 215 CK108
Chessington Hill Pk, Chess. KT9 ... 216 CN106
Chessington Lo, N3 ... 119 CZ55
⇌ Chessington North ... 216 CL106
Chessington Rd, Epsom KT17, KT19 ... 217 CT109
⇌ Chessington South ... 215 CK108
Chessington Way, W.Wick. BR4 ... 203 EB103
★ Chessington World of Adventure, Chess. KT9 ... 215 CJ110
Chess La, Rick. (Loud.) WD3 ... 74 BK42
CHESSMOUNT, Chesh. HP5 ... 54 AR33
Chessmount Ri, Chesh. HP5 ... 54 AR33
Chesson Rd, W14 ... 159 CZ79
Chess Vale Ri, Rick. (Crox.Grn) WD3 ... 74 BM44
Chess Valley Wk, Chesh. HP5 ... 72 AU35
Rickmansworth WD3 ... 74 BL44
Chess Way, Rick. (Chorl.) WD3 ... 74 BG41
Chesswood Way, Pnr. HA5 ... 94 BX54
Chester Av, Rich. TW10 ... 178 CM85
Twickenham TW2 ... 176 BZ88
Upminster RM14 ... 129 FS61
Chester Cl, SW1 ... 18 F4
SW13 ... 159 CV83
Ashford TW15 ... 175 BR92
Dorking RH4 ... 247 CJ134
Guildford GU2 ... 242 AT132
Loughton IG10 ... 85 EQ39
Potters Bar EN6 ... 64 DB29
Sutton SM1 ... 200 DA103
Uxbridge UB8 off Dawley Av ... 135 BP72
Chester Cl N, NW1 ... 9 H1
Chester Cl S, NW1 ... 9 H2
Chester Cotts, SW1 ... 18 E8
Chester Ct, NW1 ... 9 H1
SE5 ... 162 DR80
Chester Cres, E8 ... 5 P2
Chester Dr, Har. HA2 ... 116 BZ58
Chesterfield Cl, Orp. BR5 ... 206 EX98
Chesterfield Dr, Dart. DA1 ... 187 FH85
Esher KT10 ... 197 CG103
Sevenoaks TN13 ... 256 FD122
Chesterfield Gdns, N4 ... 121 DP57
SE10 off Crooms Hill ... 163 ED80
W1 ... 18 G1
Chesterfield Gro, SE22 ... 182 DT85
Chesterfield Hill, W1 ... 8 G10
Sch Chesterfield Inf Sch, Enf. EN3 off Chesterfield Rd ... 83 DY37
Sch Chesterfield Jun Sch, Enf. EN3 off Chesterfield Rd ... 83 DY37
Chesterfield Ms, N4 off Chesterfield Gdns ... 121 DP57
Ashford TW15 off Chesterfield Rd ... 174 BL91
Chesterfield Rd, E10 ... 123 EC58
N3 ... 98 DA51
W4 ... 158 CQ79
Ashford TW15 ... 174 BL91
Barnet EN5 ... 79 CX43
Enfield EN3 ... 83 DY37
Epsom KT19 ... 216 CR108
Chesterfield St, W1 ... 18 G1
Chesterfield Wk, SE10 ... 163 ED81
Chesterfield Way, SE15 ... 162 DW80
Hayes UB3 ... 155 BU75
Chesterford Gdns, NW3 ... 120 DB63
Chesterford Ho, SE18 off Shooter's Hill Rd ... 164 EK80
Chesterford Rd, E12 ... 125 EM64
Chester Gdns, W13 ... 137 CG72
Enfield EN3 ... 82 DV44
Morden SM4 ... 200 DC100
Chester Gate, NW1 ... 8 G2
Chester Gibbons Grn, St.Alb. (Lon.Col.) AL2 off High St ... 61 CK26
Chester Grn, Loug. IG10 ... 85 EQ39
Chester Ms, E17 off Chingford Rd ... 101 EA54
SW1 ... 18 G5
Chester Path, Loug. IG10 ... 85 EQ39
Chester Pl, NW1 ... 8 G1
Chester Rd, E7 ... 144 EK66
E11 ... 124 EH58
E16 ... 15 H3
E17 ... 123 DX57
N9 ... 100 DV46
N17 ... 122 DR55
N19 ... 121 DH61

★ Place of interest · H Hospital · Sch School · Coll College · Uni University · ⇌ Railway station

Chester Rd, NW1 8 F2
SW19 179 CW93
Borehamwood WD6 78 CQ41
Chigwell IG7 103 EN48
Hounslow TW4 155 BV83
Hounslow (Hthrw Air.)
TW6 154 BN83
Ilford IG3 125 ET60
Leatherhead (Eff.) KT24 245 BV128
Loughton IG10 85 EP40
Northwood HA6 93 BS52
Sidcup DA15 185 ES85
Slough SL1 131 AR72
Watford WD18 75 BU43
Chester Row, SW1 18 E8
Chesters, Horl. RH6 268 DE146
Chesters, The, N.Mal. KT3 198 CS95
Chester Sq, SW1 18 G7
Chester Sq Ms, SW1 18 G6
Chester St, E2 12 B3
SW1 18 F5
Chester Ter, NW1 8 G1
Chesterton Cl, SW18
off Ericcson Cl 180 DA85
Chesham HP5
off Milton Rd 54 AP29
Greenford UB6 136 CB68
Chesterton Dr, Red. RH1 251 DL128
Staines TW19 174 BM88
Chesterton Grn, Beac. HP9 89 AL52
Chesterton Ho, SW11
off Ingrave St 160 DD83
Sch Chesterton Prim Sch,
SW11 off Dagnall St 160 DG81
Chesterton Rd, E13 15 M1
W10 6 B6
Chesterton Sq, W8 16 G7
Chesterton Ter, E13 15 L1
Kingston upon Thames
KT1 198 CN96
Chester Way, Til. RM18 171 GJ82
Chester Way, SE11 20 D8
Chesthunte Rd, N17 100 DQ53
Chestnut All, SW6
off Lillie Rd 159 CZ79
Chestnut Av, E7 124 EH63
N8 121 DL57
SW14 off Thornton Rd 158 CR83
Brentford TW8 157 CK77
Brentwood CM14 108 FS45
Buckhurst Hill IG9 102 EK48
Chesham HP5 54 AR29
East Molesey KT8 197 CF97
Edgware HA8 96 CL51
Epsom KT19 216 CS105
Esher KT10 197 CD101
Grays RM16 170 GB75
Greenhithe (Bluewater)
DA9 189 FT87
Guildford GU2 258 AW138
Hampton TW12 176 CA94
Hornchurch RM12 127 FF61
Northwood HA6 93 BT54
Rickmansworth WD3 74 BG43
Slough SL3 152 AY75
Teddington TW11 197 CF96
Virginia Water GU25 192 AT98
Walton-on-Thames
(Whiteley Vill.) KT12 213 BS109
Wembley HA0 117 CH64
West Drayton UB7 134 BM73
West Wickham BR4 222 EE106
Westerham TN16 238 EK122
Weybridge KT13 213 BQ108
Chestnut Av N, E17 123 EC56
Chestnut Av S, E17 123 EC56
Chestnut Cl, N14 81 DJ43
N16 off Lordship Gro 122 DR61
SE6 183 EC92
SE14 163 DZ81
SW16 181 DN91
Addlestone KT15 212 BK106
Amersham HP6 55 AR37
Ashford TW15 175 BP91
Berkhamsted (Pott.End)
HP4 39 BB17
Buckhurst Hill IG9 102 EK47
Carshalton SM5 200 DF102
Egham (Eng.Grn) TW20 172 AW93
Gerrards Cross (Chal.St.P.)
SL9 91 AZ52
Gravesend (Nthflt) DA11
off Burch Rd 191 GF86
Hayes UB3 135 BS73
Hornchurch RM12
off Lancaster Dr 128 FJ63
Orpington BR6 224 EU106
Redhill RH1
off Haigh Cres 267 DH136
Sidcup DA15 186 EU88
Sunbury-on-Thames
TW16 175 BT93
Tadworth KT20 234 DA123
Ware (Hunsdon) SG12 34 EK06
West Drayton UB7 155 BP80
Woking (Ripley) GU23 228 BG124
Chestnut Copse, Oxt. RH8 254 EG132
Chestnut Ct, SW6
off North End Rd 159 CZ79
Amersham HP6 55 AS37
Surbiton KT6
off Penners Gdns 198 CL101
Chestnut Cres, Walt.
(Whiteley Vill.) KT12
off Chestnut Av 213 BS109
Chestnut Dr, E11 124 EG58
Berkhamsted HP4 38 AX20
Bexleyheath DA7 166 EX83
Egham (Eng.Grn) TW20 172 AX93
Harrow HA3 95 CF52
Pinner HA5 116 BX58
St. Albans AL4 43 CH18
Windsor SL4 151 AL84
Chestnut Glen, Horn. RM12 127 FF61
Chestnut Gro, SE20 182 DV94
SW12 180 DG87
W5 157 CK76
Barnet EN4 80 DF43
Brentwood CM14 108 FW47
Dartford DA2 187 FD91
Ilford IG6 103 ES51
Isleworth TW7 157 CG84
Mitcham CR4 201 DK98
New Malden KT3 198 CR97
South Croydon CR2 220 DV108
Staines TW18 174 BJ93
Wembley HA0 117 CH64
Woking GU22 226 AY120
Sch Chestnut Gro Sch, SW12
off Chestnut Gro 180 DG88
Chestnut La, N20 97 CY46
Amersham HP6 55 AR36
Harlow CM20
off Hamstel Rd 35 EP14
Sevenoaks TN13 257 FH124
Chestnut La, Wey. KT13 213 BP106
Sch Chestnut La Co First Sch,
Amer. HP6
off Chestnut La 55 AS36
Chestnut Manor Cl, Stai.
TW18 174 BH92
Chestnut Mead, Red. RH1
off Oxford Rd 250 DE133
Chestnut Pl, SE26 182 DT91
Ashtead KT21 232 CL119
Epsom KT17 217 CU111
Chestnut Ri, SE18 165 ER79
Bushey WD23 94 CB45
Chestnut Rd, SE27 181 DP90
SW20 199 CX96
Ashford TW15 175 BP91
Beaconsfield HP9 88 AH54
Dartford DA1 188 FK88
Enfield EN3 83 DY36
Guildford GU1 242 AX134
Horley RH6 268 DG146
Kingston upon Thames
KT2 178 CL94
Twickenham TW2 177 CE89
Chestnut Row, N3
off Nether St 98 DA52
Chestnuts, Brwd. (Hutt.)
CM13 109 GB46
Chestnuts, The, Hem.H. HP3 39 BF24
Hertford SG13 32 DR10
Horley RH6 269 DH146
Romford (Abridge) RM4 86 EV41
Walton-on-Thames KT12 195 BU102
Chestnut Wk, Epp. CM16
off Epping Rd 51 EP24
Gerrards Cross (Chal.St.P.)
SL9 90 AY52
Sevenoaks TN15 257 FL129
Shepperton TW17 195 BS99
Walton-on-Thames
(Whiteley Vill.) KT12
off Octagon Rd 213 BS109
Watford WD24 75 BU37
West Byfleet (Byfleet)
KT14 off Royston Rd 212 BL112
Woodford Green IG8 102 EG50
Chestnut Way, Felt. TW13 175 BV90
Cheston Av, Croy. CR0 203 DY103
Chestwood Gro, Uxb. UB10 134 BM66
Cheswick Cl, Dart. DA1 167 FF84
Chesworth Cl, Erith DA8 167 FE81
Chettle Cl, SE1 21 J5
Chettle Ct, N8 121 DN58
Chetwode Dr, Epsom KT18 233 CX118
Chetwode Rd, SW17 180 DF90
Tadworth KT20 233 CW119
Chetwood Wk, E6 144 EL72
Chetwynd Av, Barn. EN4 98 DF46
Chetwynd Dr, Uxb. UB10 134 BM68
Chetwynd Rd, NW5 121 DH63
Chevalier Cl, Stan. HA7 96 CL49
Cheval Pl, SW7 18 B5
Cheval St, E14 23 N5
Cheveley Cl, Rom. RM3
off Chelsworth Dr 106 FM53
Cheveley Gdns, Slou. (Burn.)
SL1 130 AJ68
Chevely Cl, Epp. (Cooper.)
CM16 70 EX29
Cheveney Wk, Brom. BR2
off Marina Cl 204 EG97
CHEVENING, Sev. TN14 240 EZ119
Chevening Cross, Sev.
(Chev.) TN14 240 FA120
Chevening La, Sev. (Knock.)
TN14 240 EY115
Chevening Rd, NW6 139 CX68
SE10 25 K10
SE19 182 DR93
Sevenoaks TN13, TN14 240 EZ119
Sevenoaks (Sund.) TN14 240 EY123
Chevenings, The, Sid. DA14 186 EW90
Sch Chevening St. Botolph's
C of E Prim Sch, Sev.
TN13 off Chevening Rd 256 FB122
Cheverton Rd, N19 121 DK60
Chevet St, E9
off Kenworthy Rd 123 DY64
Chevington Pl, Horn. RM12
off Chevington Way 128 FK64
Chevington Way, Horn.
RM12 128 FK63
Cheviot Cl, Bans. SM7 234 DB115
Bexleyheath DA7 167 FE82
Bushey WD23 76 CC44
Enfield EN1 82 DR40
Hayes UB3 155 BR80
Sutton SM2 218 DD109
Cheviot Gdns, NW2 119 CX61
SE27 181 DP91
Cheviot Gate, NW2 119 CY61
Cheviot Rd, SE27 181 DN92
Hornchurch RM11 127 FG60
Slough SL3 153 BA78
Cheviots, Hat. AL10 45 CU21
Hemel Hempstead HP2 40 BM17
Cheviot Way, Ilf. IG2 125 ES56
Chevron Cl, E16 15 M7
Chevy Rd, Sthl. UB2 156 CC75
Chewton Rd, E17 123 DY56
Cheyham Gdns, Sutt. SM2 217 CX110
Cheyham Way, Sutt. SM2 217 CY110
Cheyne Av, E18 124 EF55
Twickenham TW2 176 BZ88
Cheyne Cl, NW4 119 CW57
Amersham HP6 55 AR36
Bromley BR2
off Cedar Cres 204 EL104
Gerrards Cross SL9 112 AY60
Ware SG12 33 DX05
Cheyne Ct, SW3
off Flood St 160 DF79
Banstead SM7
off Park Rd 234 DB115
Cheyne Gdns, SW3 160 DE79
Cheyne Hill, Surb. KT5 198 CM98
Cheyne Ms, SW3 160 DE79
Cheyne Path, W7 137 CF71
Cheyne Pl, SW3 160 DF79
Cheyne Rd, Ashf. TW15 175 BR93
Cheyne Row, SW3 160 DE79
Cheyne Wk, N21 81 DP43
NW4 119 CW58
SW3 160 DE79
SW10 160 DD80
Chesham HP5 54 AR31
Croydon CR0 202 DU103
Horley RH6 268 DG149
Longfield DA3
off Cavendish Sq 209 FX97
Cheyneys Av, Edg. HA8 95 CK51
Chichele Gdns, Croy. CR0 220 DS105
Chichele Rd, NW2 119 CX64
Oxted RH8 254 EE128
Chicheley Gdns, Har. HA3 94 CC52
Chicheley Rd, Har. HA3 94 CC52
Chicheley St, SE1 20 B3
Chichester Av, Ruis. HA4 115 BR61
Chichester Cl, E6 144 EL72
SE3 164 EJ81
Dorking RH4 247 CH134
Grays (Chaff.Hun.) RM16 169 FX77
Hampton TW12
off Maple Cl 176 BZ93
South Ockendon (Aveley)
RM15 148 FQ74
Chichester Ct, Epsom KT17 217 CT109
Slough SL1 152 AV75
Stanmore HA7 118 CL55
Chichester Dr, Pur. CR8 219 DM112
Sevenoaks TN13 256 FF125
Chichester Gdns, Ilf. IG1 124 EL59
Chichester Ms, SE27 181 DN91
Chichester Rents, WC2 10 C7
Chichester Ri, Grav. DA12 191 GK91
Chichester Rd, E11 124 EE62
N9 100 DU46
NW6 140 DA68
W2 7 K5
Croydon CR0 202 DS104
Dorking RH4 247 CH133
Greenhithe DA9 189 FT85
Chichester Row, Amer. HP6 55 AR38
Chichester St, SW1 19 K10
Chichester Way, E14 24 E7
Feltham TW14 175 BV87
Watford WD25 60 BY33
Chichester Wf, Erith DA8 167 FE78
Chicksand St, E1 11 P6
Chiddingfold, N12 98 DA48
Chiddingstone Av, Bexh.
DA7 166 EZ80
Chiddingstone Cl, Sutt.
SM2 218 DA110
Chiddingstone St, SW6 160 DA82
Chieftan Dr, Purf. RM19 168 FM77
Chieveley Rd, Bexh. DA7 167 FB84
Chiffinch Gdns, Grav.
(Nthflt) DA11 190 GE90
Chignell Pl, W13
off The Broadway 137 CG74
CHIGWELL, IG7 103 EP48
⊖ Chigwell 103 EP49
Sch Chigwell Co Prim Sch,
Chig. IG7 off High Rd 103 EQ47
Chigwell Hill, E1 12 C10
Chigwell Hurst Ct, Pnr.
HA5 116 BX55
Chigwell La, Loug. IG10 85 EQ43
Chigwell Pk, Chig. IG7 103 EP49
Chigwell Pk Dr, Chig. IG7 103 EN48
Chigwell Ri, Chig. IG7 103 EN47
Chigwell Rd, E18 124 EH55
Woodford Green IG8 102 EJ54
CHIGWELL ROW, Chig. IG7 104 EU47
Sch Chigwell Row Co
Prim Sch, Chig. IG7
off Lambourne Rd 104 EV47
Sch Chigwell Sch, Chig. IG7
off High Rd 103 EQ47
Chigwell Vw, Rom. RM5
off Lodge La 104 FA51
Sch Chilbec Cen, Chesh.
HP5 off Five Acres 54 AR33
Chilberton Dr, Red. RH1 251 DJ130
Chilbrook Rd, Cob. (Down.)
KT11 229 BU118
Chilcombe Ho, SW15
off Fontley Way 179 CU87
Chilcot Cl, E14 14 B8
Chilcote La, Amer. (Lt.Chal.)
HP7 72 AV39
Chilcott Cl, Wem. HA0 117 CJ63
Chilcott Rd, Wat. WD24 75 BS36
Childebert Rd, SW17 181 DH89
Sch Childeric Prim Sch, SE14
off Childeric Rd 163 DY80
Childeric Rd, SE14 163 DY80
Childerley, Kings.T. KT1
off Burritt Rd 198 CN97
Childerley St, SW6
off Fulham Palace Rd 159 CX81
Childers, The, Wdf.Grn. IG8 103 EM50
Childers St, SE8 163 DY79
Child La, SE10 25 K6
H Children's Trust, The, Tad.
KT20 233 CX121
Childs Av, Uxb. (Hare.) UB9 92 BJ54
Childs Cl, Horn. RM11 128 FJ58
Childs Cres, Swans. DA10 189 FX86
Childs Hall Cl, Lthd. (Bkhm)
KT23 off Childs Hall Rd 246 BZ125
Childs Hall Dr, Lthd. (Bkhm)
KT23 246 BZ125
Childs Hall Rd, Lthd. (Bkhm)
KT23 246 BZ125
CHILDS HILL, NW2 120 DA61
Sch Childs Hill Prim Sch, NW2
off Dersingham Rd 119 CY62
Childs Hill Wk, NW2 119 CZ62
Childs La, SE19
off Westow St 182 DS93
Child's Ms, SW5
off Child's Pl 160 DA77
Child's Pl, SW5 17 H8
Child's St, SW5 17 H8
Child's Wk, SW5 17 H8
Childs Way, NW11 119 CZ57
Childwick Ct, Hem.H. HP3
off Rumballs Rd 40 BN23
Chilham Cl, Bex. DA5 186 EZ87
Greenford UB6 137 CG68
Hemel Hempstead HP2 40 BL21
Chilham Rd, SE9 184 EL91
Chilham Way, Brom. BR2 204 EG101
Chillerton Rd, SW17 180 DG92
Chillington Dr, SW11
off Wynter St 160 DC84
Chillingworth Gdns, Twick.
TW1 off Tower Rd 177 CF90
Chillingworth Rd, N7 4 C2
Chilmans Dr, Lthd. (Bkhm)
KT23 246 CB125
Chilmark Gdns, N.Mal. KT3 199 CT101
Redhill RH1 251 DL129
Chilmark Rd, SW16 201 DK96
Chilmead La, Red. (Nutfld)
RH1 251 DK132
Chilsey Grn Rd, Cher. KT16 193 BE100
Chiltern Av, Amer. HP6 55 AR38
Bushey WD23 76 CC44
Twickenham TW2 176 CA88
Chiltern Business Village,
Uxb. UB8 134 BH68
Chiltern Cl, Berk. HP4 38 AT18
Bexleyheath DA7 167 FE81
Borehamwood WD6 78 CM40
Bushey WD23 76 CB44
Croydon CR0 202 DS104
Uxbridge (Ickhm) UB10 115 BP61
Chiltern Cl, Wal. Cr. (Chsht)
EN7 65 DP27
Woking GU22 226 AW122
Worcester Park KT4
off Cotswold Way 199 CW103
Chiltern Cor, Berk. HP4
off Durrants Rd 38 AU18
Chiltern Dene, Enf. EN2 81 DM42
Chiltern Dr, Rick. (Mill End)
WD3 91 BF45
Surbiton KT5 198 CP99
Chiltern Gdns, NW2 119 CX62
Bromley BR2 204 EF98
Hornchurch RM12 128 FJ62
Chiltern Hts, Amer. HP7 72 AU39
Chiltern Hill, Ger.Cr.
(Chal.St.P.) SL9 90 AY53
Chiltern Hills Rd, Beac. HP9 88 AJ53
★ Chiltern Open Air Mus,
Ch.St.G. HP8 91 AZ47
Chiltern Par, Amer. HP6 55 AQ37
Chiltern Pk Av, Berk. HP4 38 AU17
Chiltern Rd, E3 13 P4
Amersham HP6 55 AP35
Gravesend (Nthflt) DA11 190 GE90
Ilford IG2 125 ES56
Pinner HA5 116 BW57
St. Albans AL4 43 CJ16
Slough (Burn.) SL1 130 AH71
Sutton SM2 218 DB109
Chilterns, Berk. HP4 38 AT17
Hatfield AL10 45 CU21
Hemel Hempstead HP2 40 BL18
Chilterns, The, Sutt. SM2
off Gatton Cl 218 DB109
Chiltern St, W1 8 E5
Chiltern Vw Rd, Uxb. UB8 134 BJ68
Chiltern Way, Wdf.Grn. IG8 102 EG48
Chilthorne Cl, SE6
off Ravensbourne Pk Cres 183 DZ87
Chilton Av, W5 157 CK77
Chilton Cl, H.Wyc. (Penn)
HP10 88 AC45
Chilton Ct, Hert. SG14
off The Ridgeway 31 DM07
Walton-on-Thames KT12 213 BU105
Chilton Grn, Welw.G.C. AL7 30 DC09
Chilton Gro, SE8 23 H8
Chiltonian Ind Est, SE12 184 EF86
Chilton Rd, Chesh. HP5 54 AQ29
Edgware HA8
off Manor Pk Cres 96 CN51
Grays RM16 171 GG76
Richmond TW9 158 CN83
Chiltons, The, E18
off Grove Hill 102 EG54
Chiltons Cl, Bans. SM7
off High St 234 DB115
Chilton St, E2 11 P3
Chilver St, SE10 25 K9
Chilwell Gdns, Wat. WD19 94 BW49
Chilwick Rd, Slou. SL2 131 AM69
CHILWORTH, Guil. GU4 259 BC140
⇌ Chilworth 259 BE140
Sch Chilworth C of E Sch,
Guil. GU4
off Dorking Rd 259 BD140
Chilworth Ct, SW19
off Windlesham Gro 179 CX88
Chilworth Gdns, Sutt. SM1 200 DC104
Chilworth Ms, W2 7 M8
Chilworth Rd, Guil. (Albury)
GU5 260 BG139
Chilworth St, W2 7 M8
Chimes Av, N13 99 DN50
Chime Sq, St.Alb. AL1 43 CE19
Chimes Shop Cen, The,
Uxb. UB8 134 BK66
Chimney La, H.Wyc. HP10
off Glory Mill La 110 AE56
China Ms, SW2
off Craster Rd 181 DM87
★ Chinatown, W1
off Gerrard St 9 L9
Chinbrook Cres, SE12 184 EH90
Chinbrook Est, SE9 184 EK90
Chinbrook Rd, SE12 184 EH90
Chinchilla Dr, Houns. TW4 156 BW82
Chindit Cl, Brox. EN10 49 DY20
Chindits La, Brwd. CM14 108 FW50
Chine, The, N10 121 DJ56
N21 81 DP44
Dorking RH4 off High St 263 CH135
Wembley HA0 117 CH64
Chine Fm Pl, Sev. TN14
off Main Rd 240 EX116
Ching Ct, WC2 9 N8
Chingdale Rd, E4 102 EE48
CHINGFORD, E4 101 EB46
⇌ Chingford 102 EE45
Chingford Av, E4 101 EB48
Sch Chingford C of E Inf Sch,
E4 off Kings Rd 101 ED46
Sch Chingford C of E (VC)
Jun Sch, E4
off Cambridge Rd 101 ED46
CHINGFORD GREEN, E4 102 EF46
Sch Chingford Hall Prim Sch,
E4 off Burnside Av 101 DZ51
CHINGFORD HATCH, E4 101 EC49
Chingford Ind Cen, E4 101 DY50
Chingford La, Wdf.Grn. IG8 102 EE49
Chingford Mt Rd, E4 101 EA49
Chingford Rd, E4 101 EA51
E17 101 EB53
Sch Chingford Sch, E4
off Nevin Dr 101 EC46
Chingley Cl, Brom. BR1 184 EE93
Ching Way, E4 101 DZ51
Chinnery Cl, Enf. EN1
off Garnault Rd 82 DT39
Chinnor Cres, Grnf. UB6 136 CB68
Chinthurst La, Guil. GU4,
GU5 258 AY141
Chinthurst Pk, Guil. (Shalf.)
GU4 258 AY142
Sch Chinthurst Sch, Tad.
KT20, off Tadworth St 233 CW123
Chipka St, E14 24 C4
Chipley St, SE14 163 DY79
Chipmunk Chase, Hat. AL10
off Mosquito Way 44 CR16
Chipmunk Gro, Nthlt. UB5
off Argus Way 136 BY69
Chippendale All, Uxb. UB8
off Chippendale Waye 134 BK66
Chippendale St, E5 123 DX62
Chippendale Waye, Uxb.
UB8 134 BK66
Chippenham Av, Wem. HA9 118 CP64
Chippenham Cl, Pnr. HA5 115 BT56
Romford RM3
off Chippenham Rd 106 FK50
Chippenham Gdns, NW6 6 G2
Romford RM3 106 FK50
Chippenham Ms, W9 6 G4
Chippenham Rd, W9 6 G4
Romford RM3 106 FK51
Chippenham Wk, Rom. RM3
off Chippenham Rd 106 FK51
CHIPPERFIELD, Kings L.
WD4 58 BG31
Chipperfield Cl, Upmin.
RM14 129 FS60
Chipperfield Rd, Hem.H.
HP3 40 BJ24
Hemel Hempstead (Bov.)
HP3 57 BB27
Kings Langley WD4 58 BK30
Orpington BR5 206 EU95
CHIPPING BARNET, Barn.
EN5 79 CY42
Chipping Cl, Barn. EN5
off St. Albans Rd 79 CY41
Chippingfield, Harl. CM17 36 EW12
CHIPSTEAD, Couls. CR5 234 DF118
CHIPSTEAD, Sev. TN13 256 FC122
⇌ Chipstead 234 DF118
Chipstead, Ger.Cr.
(Chal.St.P.) SL9 90 AW53
Chipstead Av, Th.Hth. CR7 201 DP98
CHIPSTEAD BOTTOM, Couls.
CR5 234 DE121
Chipstead Cl, SE19 182 DT94
Coulsdon CR5 234 DG116
Redhill RH1 266 DF136
Sutton SM2 218 DB109
Chipstead Ct, Wok. (Knap.)
GU21 off Creston Av 226 AS117
Chipstead Gdns, NW2 119 CV61
Chipstead Gate, Couls. CR5
off Woodfield Cl 235 DJ119
Chipstead La, Couls. CR5 234 DB124
Sevenoaks TN13 256 FC122
Tadworth KT20 249 CZ125
Chipstead Pk, Sev. TN13 256 FD122
Chipstead Pk Cl, Sev. TN13 256 FC122
Chipstead Pl Gdns, Sev.
TN13 256 FC122
Chipstead Rd, Bans. SM7 233 CZ117
Erith DA8 167 FE80
Chipstead Sta Par, Couls.
(Chipstead) CR5
off Station App 234 DF118
Chipstead St, SW6 160 DA81
Sch Chipstead Valley Prim
Sch, Couls. CR5
off Chipstead Valley Rd 234 DG116
Chipstead Valley Rd, Couls.
CR5 235 DH116
Chipstead Way, Bans. SM7 234 DF115
Chip St, SW4 161 DK83
Chirk Cl, Hayes UB4
off Braunston Dr 136 BY70
Chirton Wk, Wok. GU21
off Shilburn Way 226 AU118
Sch Chisenhale Prim Sch,
E3 off Chisenhale Rd 143 DY68
Chisenhale Rd, E3 143 DY68
Chisholm Rd, Croy. CR0 202 DS103
Richmond TW10 178 CM86
Chisledon Wk, E9
off Southmoor Way 143 DZ65
CHISLEHURST, BR7 185 EN94
⇌ Chislehurst 205 EN96
Sch Chislehurst & Sidcup
Gram Sch, Sid. DA15
off Hurst Rd 186 EV89
Chislehurst Av, N12 98 DC52
★ Chislehurst Caves, Chis.
BR7 off Caveside Cl 205 EN95
Sch Chislehurst C of E
Prim Sch, Chis. BR7
off School Rd 185 EQ94
Chislehurst Rd, Brom. BR1 204 EK96
Chislehurst BR7 204 EK96
Orpington BR5, BR6 205 ES98
Richmond TW10 178 CL86
Sidcup DA14 186 EU92
CHISLEHURST WEST, Chis.
BR7 185 EM92
Chislet Cl, Beck. BR3
off Abbey La 183 EA94
Chisley Rd, N15 122 DS58
Chiswell Ct, Wat. WD24 76 BW38
CHISWELL GREEN, St.Alb.
AL2 60 CA26
Chiswell Grn La, St.Alb.
AL2 60 BX25
Chiswell Sq, SE3
off Brook La 164 EH82
Chiswell St, EC1 11 H5
CHISWICK, W4 158 CR79
⇌ Chiswick 158 CQ80
Coll Chiswick Adult Ed &
Training Cen, W4
off Burlington La 158 CR80
Sch Chiswick & Bedford Pk
Prep Sch, W4
off Priory Av 158 CS77
Chiswick Br, SW14 158 CQ82
W4 158 CQ82
Chiswick Cl, Croy. CR0 201 DM104
Chiswick Common Rd, W4 158 CR77
Sch Chiswick Comm Sch, W4
off Burlington La 158 CR80
Chiswick Ct, Pnr. HA5 116 BZ55
Chiswick Grn Studios, W4
off Evershed Wk 158 CQ77
Chiswick High Rd, W4 158 CP78
Brentford TW8 158 CM78
★ Chiswick Ho, W4 158 CS79
Chiswick Ho Grds, W4 158 CR79
Chiswick La, W4 158 CS78
Chiswick La S, W4 159 CT78
H Chiswick Lo, W4 159 CT78
Chiswick Mall, W4 159 CT79
W6 159 CT79
⊖ Chiswick Park 158 CQ77
Chiswick Pk, W4 158 CP77
Chiswick Quay, W4 158 CQ81
Chiswick Rd, N9 100 DU47
W4 158 CQ77
Chiswick Roundabout, W4
off Chiswick High Rd 158 CN78
Chiswick Sq, W4
off Hogarth Roundabout 158 CS79
Chiswick Staithe, W4 158 CQ81
Chiswick Ter, W4
off Acton La 158 CQ77
Chiswick Village, W4 158 CP78
Chiswick Wf, W4 159 CT79
Chittenden Cl, Hodd. EN11
off Founders Rd 33 EB14

⊖ London Underground station   DLR Docklands Light Railway station   Tramlink station   Pedestrian ferry landing stage

Chittenden Cotts, Wok. (Wisley) GU23 228 BL116
Chitterfield Gate, West Dr. UB7 154 BN80
Chitty's Common, Guil. GU2 242 AT130
Chitty's La, Dag. RM8 126 EX61
Chitty St, W1 9 K5
Chittys Wk, Guil. GU3 242 AT130
Chivalry Rd, SW11 180 DE85
Chivenor Gro, Kings.T. KT2 177 CK92
Chivenor Pl, St.Alb. AL4 43 CJ22
Chivers Rd, E4 101 EB48
Choats Manor Way, Dag. RM9 146 EY68
Choats Rd, Bark. IG11 146 EW68
Dagenham RM9 146 EW68
CHOBHAM, Wok. GU24 210 AT111
Chobham Cl, Cher. (Ott.) KT16 211 BB107
★ **Chobham Common National Nature Reserve**, Wok. GU24 210 AS105
Chobham Gdns, SW19 179 CX89
Chobham La, Cher. (Longcr.) KT16 192 AV102
Chobham Pk La, Wok. (Chobham) GU24 210 AU110
Chobham Rd, E15 123 ED64
Chertsey (Ott.) KT16 211 BA108
Woking GU21 226 AY116
Woking (Horsell) GU21 210 AW113
Sch **Chobham St. Lawrence's C of E Prim Sch**, Wok. GU24 off Bagshot Rd 210 AS111
Choir Grn, Wok. (Knap.) GU21 off Semper Cl 226 AS117
Cholmeley Cres, N6 121 DH59
Cholmeley Pk, N6 121 DH60
Cholmley Gdns, NW6 off Fortune Grn Rd 120 DA64
Cholmley Rd, T.Ditt. KT7 197 CH100
Cholmondeley Av, NW10 139 CU68
Cholmondeley Wk, Rich. TW9 177 CJ85
Choppins Ct, E1 22 D1
Chopwell Cl, E15 off Bryant St 143 EE66
CHORLEYWOOD, Rick. WD3 73 BE43
⇌ **Chorleywood** 73 BD42
⊖ **Chorleywood** 73 BD42
CHORLEYWOOD BOTTOM, Rick. WD3 73 BD44
Chorleywood Bottom, Rick. (Chorl.) WD3 73 BD43
Chorleywood Cl, Rick. WD3 92 BK45
Chorleywood Common, Rick. (Chorl.) WD3 73 BE42
Chorleywood Cres, Orp. BR5 205 ET96
Chorleywood Ho Dr, Rick. (Chorl.) WD3 73 BE41
Chorleywood Lo La, Rick. (Chorl.) WD3 off Rickmansworth Rd 73 BF41
Sch **Chorleywood Prim Sch**, Rick. WD3 off Stag La 73 BC44
Chorleywood Rd, Rick. WD3 74 BG42
Choumert Gro, SE15 162 DU82
Choumert Ms, SE15 162 DU82
Choumert Rd, SE15 162 DT83
Choumert Sq, SE15 162 DU82
Chow Sq, E8 5 N1
Chrislaine Cl, Stai. (Stanw.) TW19 174 BK86
Chrisp St, E14 14 A6
Christabel Cl, Islw. TW7 157 CE83
Christchurch Av, N12 98 DC51
NW6 139 CY66
Erith DA8 167 FD79
Harrow HA3 117 CH56
Rainham RM13 147 FF68
Teddington TW11 177 CG92
Wembley HA0 138 CL65
Sch **Christ Ch Bentinck C of E Prim Sch**, NW1 8 B5
Sch **Christchurch (Brixton) C of E Prim Sch**, SW9 off Cancell Rd 161 DN81
Sch **Christ Ch Brondesbury C of E Prim Sch**, NW6 off Clarence Rd 139 CZ66
Christchurch Cl, N12 off Summers La 98 DD52
SW19 180 DD94
Enfield EN2 82 DQ40
St. Albans AL3 42 CC19
Sch **Christ Ch C of E Inf Sch**, N.Mal. KT3 off Lime Gro 198 CS97
Sch **Christchurch C of E Inf Sch**, Vir.W. GU25 off Christchurch Rd 192 AV97
Sch **Christ Ch C of E Jun Sch**, W5 off New Bdy 137 CK73
New Malden KT3 off Elm Rd 198 CR97
Sch **Christ Ch C of E Prim Sch**, NW1 9 H1
NW3 off Christchurch Hill 120 DD62
SE10 25 H9
SE23 off Perry Vale 183 DX89
SW3 off Robinson St 160 DF79
Sch **Christchurch C of E Prim Sch**, SW11 off Este Rd 160 DE83
Sch **Christ Ch C of E Prim Sch**, Barn. EN5 off Byng Rd 79 CX40
Purley CR8 off Montpelier Rd 219 DP110
Rickmansworth WD3 off Rickmansworth Rd 73 BF41
Surbiton KT5 off Pine Gdns 198 CN100
Sch **Christ Ch C of E Sch**, E1 11 P5
N12 off Warnham Rd 98 DD50
SE18 off Shooter's Hill 165 EN81
Chertsey KT16 off Fletcher Rd 211 BD107
Christchurch Ct, NW6 139 CY66
Christchurch Cres, Grav. DA12 off Christchurch Rd 191 GJ87
Radlett WD7 77 CG36
Christchurch Gdns, Epsom KT19 216 CP111
Harrow HA3 117 CG56
Christchurch Grn, Wem. HA0 138 CL65
Christchurch Hill, NW3 120 DD62
Christchurch La, Barn. EN5 79 CY40
Christ Ch Mt, Epsom KT19 216 CP112
Christchurch Pk, Sutt. SM2 218 DC108
Christ Ch Pas, EC1 10 F7
Christchurch Pas, NW3 120 DC62
Barnet EN5 79 CY41
Christ Ch Path, Hayes UB3 155 BQ76
Christchurch Pl, Epsom KT19 216 CP111
Sch **Christchurch Prim Sch**, Ilf. IG1 off Wellesley Rd 125 ER60
Sch **Christ Ch Prim Sch**, Ware SG12 off New Rd 33 DY06
Christchurch Rd, N8 121 DL58
SW2 181 DM88
SW14 178 CP85
SW19 200 DD95
Christ Ch Rd, Beck. BR3 off Fairfield Rd 203 EA96
Christchurch Rd, Dart. DA1 188 FJ87
Christ Ch Rd, Epsom KT19 216 CL112
Christchurch Rd, Grav. DA12 191 GJ88
Hemel Hempstead HP2 40 BK19
Hounslow (Hthrw Air.) TW6 off Courtney Rd 154 BN83
Ilford IG1 125 EP60
Purley CR8 219 DP110
Sidcup DA15 185 ET91
Christ Ch Rd, Surb. KT5 198 CM100
Christchurch Rd, Til. RM18 171 GG81
Virginia Water GU25 192 AU97
Christchurch Sq, E9 off Victoria Pk Rd 142 DW67
Sch **Christ Ch (Streatham) C of E Prim Sch**, SW2 off Cotherstone Rd 181 DM88
Christchurch St, SW3 160 DF79
Christchurch Ter, SW3 off Christchurch St 160 DF79
Christchurch Way, SE10 25 H8
Woking GU21 off Church St E 227 AZ117
Christian Ct, SE16 23 L2
Christian Flds, SW16 181 DN94
Christian Flds Av, Grav. DA12 191 GJ91
Christian Sq, Wind. SL4 off Alma Rd 151 AQ81
Christian St, E1 12 B7
Christie Cl, Brox. EN10 49 DZ21
Guildford GU1 off Waterside Rd 242 AX131
Leatherhead (Bkhm) KT23 246 BZ125
Christie Dr, Croy. CR0 202 DU99
Christie Gdns, Rom. RM6 126 EV58
Christie Rd, E9 143 DY65
Waltham Abbey EN9 off Deer Pk Way 83 EB36
Christies Av, Sev. (Bad.Mt) TN14 224 FA110
Coll **Christie's Ed**, W1 9 H5
Christie Wk, Cat. CR3 off Hambledon Rd 236 DR122
Christina Sq, N4 off Adolphus Rd 121 DP60
Christina St, EC2 11 L3
Christine Worsley Cl, N21 off Highfield Rd 99 DP47
Christmas Hill, Guil. (Shalf.) GU4 259 AZ141
Christmas La, Slou. (Farn.Com.) SL2 111 AQ62
Christopher Av, W7 157 CG76
Christopher Cl, SE16 22 G3
Hornchurch RM12 off Chevington Way 128 FK63
Sidcup DA15 185 ET85
Christopher Ct, Hem.H. HP3 off Seaton Rd 40 BK23
Tadworth KT20 off High St 233 CW123
Christopher Gdns, Dag. RM9 off Wren Rd 126 EX64
Sch **Christopher Hatton Prim Sch**, EC1 10 C4
Christopher Pl, NW1 9 M2
St. Albans AL3 off Market Pl 43 CD20
Christopher Rd, Sthl. UB2 155 BV77
Christopher's Ms, W11 16 D1
Christopher St, EC2 11 K4
Sch **Christ's Coll**, SE3 off St. German's Pl 164 EG81
Sch **Christ's Coll Finchley**, N2 off East End Rd 120 DB55
Sch **Christ's Coll Sec Sch**, N2 off East End Rd 120 DB55
Sch **Christ's Sch**, Rich. TW10 off Queens Rd 178 CN85
Sch **Christ the King RC Prim Sch**, N4 off Tollington Pk 121 DM61
Staines TW19 off Falcon Dr 174 BL86
Coll **Christ the King 6th Form Coll**, SE13 off Belmont Hill 163 ED83
Christy Rd, West. (Bigg.H.) TN16 238 EJ115
Chryssell Rd, SW9 161 DN80
Chrystie La, Lthd. (Bkhm) KT23 246 CB126
Chubworthy St, SE14 163 DY79
Chucks La, Tad. KT20 233 CV124
Chudleigh Cres, Ilf. IG3 125 ES63
Chudleigh Gdns, Sutt. SM1 200 DC104
Chudleigh Rd, NW6 139 CX66
SE4 183 DZ85
Romford RM3 106 FL49
Twickenham TW2 177 CF87
Chudleigh St, E1 12 G7
Chudleigh Way, Ruis. HA4 115 BU60
Chulsa Rd, SE26 182 DV92
Chumleigh St, SE5 162 DS79
Chumleigh Wk, Surb. KT5 198 CM98
Church All, Croy. CR0 201 DN102
Gravesend DA11 off High St 191 GH86
Watford (Ald.) WD25 76 CC38
Church App, SE21 182 DR90
Egham TW20 193 BC97
Sevenoaks (Cudham) TN14 off Cudham La S 239 EQ115
Staines (Stanw.) TW19 174 BK86
Church Av, E4 101 ED51
NW1 off Kentish Town Rd 141 DH65
SW14 158 CR83
Beckenham BR3 203 EA95
Northolt UB5 136 BZ66
Pinner HA5 116 BY58
Ruislip HA4 115 BR60
Sidcup DA14 186 EU92
Southall UB2 156 BY76
Churchbury Cl, Enf. EN1 82 DS40
Churchbury La, Enf. EN1 82 DR41
Churchbury Rd, SE9 184 EK87
Enfield EN1 82 DR40
Church Cl, N20 98 DE48
W8 17 J3
Addlestone KT15 212 BH105
Edgware HA8 96 CQ50
Hayes UB4 135 BR71
Hertford (Lt.Berk.) SG13 off Goddards Cl 47 DJ19
Hounslow TW3 off Bath Rd 156 BZ83
Leatherhead (Fetch.) KT22 231 CD124
Loughton IG10 85 EM40
Northwood HA6 93 BT52
Potters Bar (Cuffley) EN6 65 DL29
Radlett WD7 77 CG36
Staines TW18 off The Broadway 194 BJ97
Tadworth KT20 off Buckland Rd 249 CZ127
Uxbridge UB8 134 BH68
West Drayton UB7 154 BL76
Windsor (Eton) SL4 151 AR79
Woking (Horsell) GU21 226 AX116
Church Ct, Reig. RH2 250 DB134
Richmond TW9 off George St 177 CK85
Church Cres, E9 143 DX66
N3 97 CZ53
N10 121 DH56
N20 98 DE48
St. Albans AL3 42 CC19
Sawbridgeworth CM21 36 EZ05
South Ockendon RM15 149 FW69
Church Cft, St.Alb. AL4 43 CJ22
Churchcroft Cl, SW12 off Endlesham Rd 180 DG87
Churchdown, Brom. BR1 184 EE91
Church Dr, NW9 118 CR60
Harrow HA2 116 BZ58
Maidenhead (Bray) SL6 150 AC75
West Wickham BR4 204 EE104
Church Elm La, Dag. RM10 146 FA65
CHURCH END, N3 97 CZ53
CHURCH END, NW10 138 CS65
Church End, E17 123 EB56
NW4 119 CV55
Harlow CM19 51 EN17
Church Entry, EC4 10 F8
Church Fm Cl, Swan. BR8 207 FC100
★ **Church Farm Ho Mus**, NW4 119 CV55
Church Fm La, Sutt. SM3 217 CY107
Church Fm Way, Wat. (Ald.) WD25 76 CB38
Church Fld, Dart. DA2 188 FK89
Epping CM16 70 EU29
Church Fld, Rad. WD7 77 CG36
Sevenoaks TN13 256 FE122
Churchfield Av, N12 98 DC51
Churchfield Cl, Har. HA2 116 CC56
Hayes UB3 off West Av 135 BT73
Churchfield Ms, Slou. SL2 132 AU72
Churchfield Path, Wal.Cr. (Chsht) EN8 66 DW29
Churchfield Pl, Shep. TW17 off Chertsey Rd 195 BP101
Sch **Churchfield Prim Sch**, N9 off Latymer Rd 100 DT46
Churchfield Rd, W3 138 CQ74
W7 157 CE75
W13 137 CH74
Gerrards Cross (Chal.St.P.) SL9 90 AX53
Reigate RH2 249 CZ133
Walton-on-Thames KT12 195 BU102
Welling DA16 166 EU83
Welwyn AL6 30 DC06
Weybridge KT13 212 BN105
Churchfields, E18 102 EG53
SE10 off Roan St 163 EC79
Broxbourne EN10 49 EA21
Guildford GU4 off Burpham La 243 BA130
Hertford SG13 32 DR10
Loughton IG10 84 EL42
West Molesey KT8 196 CA97
Woking (Horsell) GU21 226 AY116
Churchfields Av, Felt. TW13 176 BZ90
Weybridge KT13 213 BP105
Sch **Churchfield Sch**, SE2 off Church Manorway 166 EU77
Sch **Churchfields Inf Sch**, E18 off Churchfields 102 EG53
Sch **Churchfields Jun Sch**, E18 off Churchfields 102 EG53
Churchfields La, Brox. EN10 off Station Rd 49 EA20
Sch **Churchfields Prim Sch**, Beck. BR3 off Churchfields Rd 203 DX96
Churchfields Rd, Beck. BR3 203 DX96
Watford WD24 75 BT36
Church Gdns, W5 157 CK75
Dorking RH4 263 CG135
Wembley HA0 117 CG63
Church Gate, SW6 159 CY83
Churchgate, Wal.Cr. (Chsht) EN8 66 DV30
Sch **Churchgate C of E Prim Sch**, Harl. CM17 off Hobbs Cross Rd 36 EZ12
Churchgate Gdns, Harl. CM17 off Sheering Rd 36 EZ11
Churchgate Rd, Wal.Cr. (Chsht) EN8 66 DV29
Churchgate St, Harl. CM17 36 EY11
Church Grn, Hayes UB3 135 BT72
St. Albans AL1 off Hatfield Rd 43 CD19
Walton-on-Thames KT12 214 BW107
Church Gro, SE13 163 EB84
Amersham HP6 72 AY39
Kingston upon Thames KT1 197 CJ95
Slough (Wexham) SL3 132 AW71
Church Hill, E17 123 EA56
N21 99 DM45
SE18 165 EM76
SW19 179 CZ92
Abbots Langley (Bedmond) WD5 59 BT26
Carshalton SM5 218 DF106
Caterham CR3 236 DT124
Dartford DA2 188 FK90
Dartford (Cray.) DA2 167 FE84
Epping CM16 70 EU29
Greenhithe DA9 189 FS85
Guildford (Shere) GU5 260 BN139
Harrow HA1 117 CE60
Hertford (Hert.Hth) SG13 32 DV11
Loughton IG10 84 EL41
Church Hill, Orp. BR6 206 EU101
Purley CR8 219 DL110
Redhill (Merst.) RH1 251 DH126
Redhill (Nutfld) RH1 251 DM133
Sevenoaks (Cudham) TN14 239 EQ115
Uxbridge (Hare.) UB9 114 BJ55
Welwyn Garden City (Lmsfd) AL8 29 CU10
Westerham (Tats.) TN16 238 EK122
Woking (Horsell) GU21 226 AX116
Woking (Pyrford) GU22 227 BF117
Sch **Church Hill Prim Sch**, Barn. EN4 off Burlington Ri 98 DF45
Church Hill Rd, E17 123 EB56
Barnet EN4 98 DF45
Surbiton KT6 198 CL99
Sutton SM3 217 CX105
Church Hill Wd, Orp. BR5 205 ET99
Church Hollow, Purf. RM19 168 FN78
Church Hyde, SE18 off Old Mill Rd 165 ES79
Churchill Av, Har. HA3 117 CH58
Uxbridge UB10 135 BP69
Churchill Cl, Dart. DA1 188 FP88
Feltham TW14 175 BT88
Leatherhead (Fetch.) KT22 231 CE123
Uxbridge UB10 135 BP69
Warlingham CR6 236 DW117
Sch **Churchill C of E Prim Sch**, West. TN16 off Rysted La 255 EQ125
Churchill Ct, W5 138 CM70
Northolt UB5 116 CA64
Staines TW18 off Chestnut Gro 174 BJ93
Churchill Cres, Hat. AL9 off Dixons Hill Rd 45 CW23
Churchill Dr, Beac. (Knot.Grn) HP9 88 AJ50
Weybridge KT13 195 BQ104
Churchill Gdns, SW1 19 J10
W3 138 CN72
Sch **Churchill Gdns Prim Sch**, SW1 19 K10
Churchill Gdns Rd, SW1 19 H10
Churchill Ms, Wdf.Grn. IG8 off High Rd Woodford Grn 102 EF51
Churchill Pl, E14 24 B1
Harrow HA1 off Sandridge Cl 117 CE56
Churchill Rd, E16 144 EJ72
NW2 139 CV65
NW5 121 DH63
Dartford (Hort.Kir.) DA4 208 FQ98
Edgware HA8 96 CM51
Epsom KT19 216 CN111
Gravesend DA11 191 GF88
Grays RM17 170 GD79
Guildford GU1 258 AY135
Horley (Smallfield) RH6 269 DP148
St. Albans AL1 43 CG18
Slough SL3 153 AZ77
South Croydon CR2 220 DQ109
Churchill Ter, E4 101 EA49
Churchill Wk, E9 122 DW64
Churchill Way, Brom. BR1 off Ethelbert Rd 204 EG97
Sunbury-on-Thames TW16 175 BU92
Westerham (Bigg.H.) TN16 222 EK113
Church Island, Stai. TW18 173 BD91
Church La, E11 124 EE60
E17 123 EB56
N2 120 DD55
N8 121 DM56
N9 100 DU47
N17 100 DS53
NW9 118 CQ61
SW17 181 DH91
SW19 199 CZ95
W5 157 CJ75
Banstead (Nork) SM7 233 CX117
Berkhamsted HP4 38 AW19
Bishop's Stortford (Sheering) CM22 37 FD07
Brentwood (Gt Warley) CM13 129 FW58
Brentwood (Hutt.) CM13 109 GE46
Bromley BR2 204 EL102
Broxbourne EN10 48 DW22
Caterham CR3 235 DN123
Chessington KT9 216 CM107
Chislehurst BR7 205 EQ95
Coulsdon CR5 234 DG122
Dagenham RM10 147 FB65
Enfield EN1 82 DR41
Epping (N.Wld Bas.) CM16 71 FB26
Epsom (Headley) KT18 232 CQ124
Gerrards Cross (Chal.St.P.) SL9 90 AX53
Godstone RH9 253 DX132
Guildford (Albury) GU5 260 BH139
Guildford (Worp.) GU3 242 AS127
Harrow HA3 95 CF53
Hatfield AL9 45 CW18
Hemel Hempstead (Bov.) HP3 57 BB27
Hertford (Bayford) SG13 47 DM17
Horley RH6 269 DL153
Kings Langley WD4 58 BN29
Loughton IG10 85 EM41
Maidenhead (Bray) SL6 150 AC75
Oxted RH8 254 EE129
Pinner HA5 116 BY55
Potters Bar (Northaw) EN6 64 DG30
Purfleet RM19 168 FN78
Rainham (Wenn.) RM13 148 FK72
Redhill (Bletch.) RH1 252 DR133
Richmond TW10 178 CL88
Rickmansworth (Mill End) WD3 92 BG46
Rickmansworth (Sarratt) WD3 73 BF38
Romford RM1 127 FE56
Romford (Abridge) RM4 86 EY40
Romford (Stap.Abb.) RM4 87 FC42
St. Albans (Coln.Hth) AL4 44 CP22
Slough (Stoke P.) SL2 132 AT69
Slough (Wexham) SL3 132 AW71
Teddington TW11 177 CF92
Thames Ditton KT7 197 CF100
Twickenham TW1 177 CG88
Upminster (N.Ock.) RM14 129 FV64
Uxbridge UB8 134 BH68
Wallington SM6 201 DK104
Waltham Cross (Chsht) EN8 66 DV29
Warlingham CR6 237 DX117
Warlingham (Chel.) CR6 237 EC116
Watford (Ald.) WD25 76 CB38
Westerham TN16 238 EK122
Weybridge KT13 212 BN105
Windsor SL4 151 AR81
Church La, Wok. (Send) GU23 243 BB126
Church La Av, Couls. CR5 235 DH122
Church La Dr, Couls. CR5 235 DH122
CHURCH LANGLEY, Harl. CM17 36 EW14
Sch **Church Langley Co Prim Sch**, Harl. CM17 off Church Langley Way 52 EW15
Church Langley Way, Harl. CM17 52 EW15
Churchley Rd, SE26 182 DV91
Church Leys, Harl. CM18 51 ET16
Church Manor Est, SW9 off Vassall Rd 161 DN80
Church Manorway, SE2 165 ET77
Erith DA8 167 FD76
Church Manorway Ind Est, Erith DA8 167 FC76
Church Mead, Harl. (Roydon) CM19 34 EH14
Churchmead Cl, Barn. EN4 80 DE44
Sch **Church Mead Inf Sch**, E10 off Grange Rd 123 EA60
Sch **Church Mead Jun Sch**, E10 off Church Rd 123 EA60
Church Meadow, Surb. KT6 197 CJ103
Churchmead Rd, NW10 139 CU65
Sch **Churchmead Sch**, Slou. SL3 off Priory Way 152 AV80
Church Ms, Add. KT15 212 BJ105
Ware SG12 off Church St 33 DX06
Church Mill Gra, Harl. CM17 36 EY12
Churchmore Rd, SW16 201 DJ95
Church Mt, N2 120 DD57
Church Paddock Ct, Wall. SM6 201 DK104
Church Pk Ind Est, Craw. RH11 268 DF154
Church Pas, EC2 off Gresham St 142 DQ72
Barnet EN5 off Wood St 79 CZ42
Surbiton KT6 198 CL99
Church Path, E11 124 EG57
E17 off St. Mary Rd 123 EB56
N5 4 F1
N12 98 DC50
N17 off White Hart La 100 DS52
N20 98 DC49
NW10 138 CS66
SW14 158 CR83
SW19 200 DA96
W4 158 CQ76
W7 137 CE74
Cobham KT11 213 BV114
Coulsdon CR5 235 DN118
Gravesend (Nthflt) DA11 190 GC86
Grays RM17 170 GA79
Greenhithe DA9 189 FT85
Maidenhead (Bray) SL6 150 AC75
Mitcham CR4 200 DE97
Southall UB1 136 CA74
Southall (Sthl Grn) UB2 156 BZ76
Ware (Gt Amwell) SG12 33 DZ09
Woking GU21 off High St 227 AZ117
Church Pl, SW1 9 K10
W5 off Church Gdns 157 CK75
Mitcham CR4 200 DE97
Twickenham TW1 off Church St 177 CH88
Uxbridge (Ickhm) UB10 115 BQ62
Church Ri, SE23 183 DX88
Chessington KT9 216 CM107
Church Rd, E10 123 EB61
E12 124 EL64
E17 101 DY54
N1 5 H4
N6 120 DG58
N17 100 DS53
NW4 119 CV56
NW10 138 CS65
SE19 202 DS95
SW13 159 CT82
SW19 (Wimbledon) 179 CY91
W3 158 CQ75
W7 137 CF74
Addlestone KT15 212 BG106
Ashford TW15 174 BM90
Ashtead KT21 231 CK117
Barking IG11 145 EQ65
Beaconsfield (Seer Grn) HP9 89 AR51
Berkhamsted (Pott.End) HP4 39 BB16
Bexleyheath DA7 166 EZ82
Bourne End SL8 110 AD62
Bromley BR2 204 EG96
Bromley (Short.) BR2 204 EE97
Buckhurst Hill IG9 102 EH46
Caterham CR3 236 DT123
Caterham (Wold.) CR3 237 DX122
Crawley RH11 268 DE154
Croydon CR0 201 DP104
Dartford (Sutt.H.) DA4 188 FL94
East Molesey KT8 197 CD98
Egham TW20 173 BA92
Enfield EN3 82 DW44
Epsom KT17 216 CS112
Epsom (W.Ewell) KT19 216 CR108
Erith DA8 167 FD78
Esher (Clay.) KT10 215 CF107
Feltham TW13 176 BX92
Gravesend (Cobham) DA12, DA13 191 GJ94
Greenhithe DA9 189 FS85
Guildford GU1 258 AX135
Harlow CM17 52 EW18
Hayes UB3 135 BT72
Hemel Hempstead HP3 41 BQ21
Hertford SG14 31 DP08
Hertford (Lt.Berk.) SG13 47 DJ19
High Wycombe HP10 88 AD47
High Wycombe (Penn) HP10 88 AC47
Horley RH6 268 DF149
Horley (Burstow) RH6 269 DN151
Hounslow (Cran.) TW5 155 BV78
Hounslow (Heston) TW5 156 CA80
Ilford IG2 125 ER58
Isleworth TW7 157 CD81
Iver SL0 133 BC69
Kenley CR8 236 DR115
Keston BR2 222 EK108
Kingston upon Thames KT1 198 CM96
Leatherhead KT22 231 CH122
Leatherhead (Bkhm) KT23 230 BZ123
Loughton (High Beach) IG10 84 EH40
Mitcham CR4 200 DD96
Northolt UB5 136 BZ66
Northwood HA6 93 BT52
Orpington (Chels.) BR6 224 EY106
Orpington (Farnboro.) BR6 223 EQ106

★ Place of interest H Hospital Sch School Coll College Uni University ⇌ Railway station

Church Rd, Pot. B. EN6 .....64 DB30
Purley CR8 .....219 DL110
Redhill RH1 .....266 DE136
Reigate RH2 .....266 DA136
Reigate (Leigh) RH2 .....265 CU141
Richmond TW9, TW10 .....178 CL85
Richmond (Ham) TW10 .....178 CM92
Romford (Harold Wd) RM3 .....106 FN53
Romford (Noak Hill) RM4 .....106 FK46
Sevenoaks (Halst.) TN14 .....224 EY111
Sevenoaks (Seal) TN15 .....257 FM121
Shepperton TW17 .....195 BP101
Sidcup DA14 .....186 EU91
Slough (Farn.Royal) SL2 .....131 AQ69
Southall UB2 .....156 BZ76
Stanmore HA7 .....95 CH50
Surbiton KT6 .....197 CJ103
Sutton SM3 .....217 CY107
Swanley BR8 .....208 FK95
Swanley (Crock.) BR8 .....207 FD101
Swanscombe DA10 .....190 FZ86
Teddington TW11 .....177 CE91
Tilbury RM18 .....171 GF81
Tilbury (W.Til.) RM18 .....171 GL79
Uxbridge (Cowley) UB8 .....134 BK70
Uxbridge (Hare.) UB9 .....114 BJ55
Wallington SM6 .....201 DJ104
Warlingham CR6 .....236 DW117
Watford WD17 .....75 BU39
Welling DA16 .....166 EV82
Welwyn Garden City AL8 .....29 CX09
West Byfleet (Byfleet) KT14 .....212 BM113
West Drayton UB7 .....154 BK76
Westerham (Bigg.H.) TN16 .....238 EK117
Westerham (Brasted) TN16 .....240 EV124
Whyteleafe CR3 .....236 DT118
Windsor (Old Wind.) SL4 .....172 AV85
Woking (Horsell) GU21 .....226 AY116
Woking (St.John's) GU21 .....226 AU119
Worcester Park KT4 .....198 CS102
Church Rd Merton, SW19 .....200 DD95
Church Rd Twr Block, Stan. HA7 *off Church Rd* 95 CJ50
Church Row, NW3 .....120 DC63
Chislehurst BR7 .....185 EQ94
Church Row Ms, Ware SG12 *off Church St* 33 DX06
Church Side, Epsom KT18 .....216 CP113
Churchside Cl, West. (Bigg.H.) TN16 .....238 EJ117
Church Sq, Shep. TW17 .....195 BP101
Tra **Church Street** 201 DP103
Church St, E15 .....144 EE67
E16 .....145 EP74
N9 .....100 DS47
NW8 .....7 P5
W2 .....7 P5
W4 .....158 CS79
Amersham HP7 .....55 AP40
Betchworth RH3 .....264 CS135
Chesham HP5 .....54 AP31
Cobham KT11 .....229 BV115
Croydon CR0 .....202 DQ103
Dagenham RM10 .....147 FB65
Dorking RH4 .....263 CG136
Enfield EN2 .....82 DR41
Epsom KT17 .....216 CS113
Epsom (Ewell) KT17 .....217 CU109
Esher KT10 .....214 CB105
Gravesend DA11 .....191 GH86
Gravesend (Sthflt) DA13 .....190 GA92
Grays RM17 .....170 GC79
Hampton TW12 .....196 CC95
Hatfield AL9 .....45 CW17
Hatfield (Essen.) AL9 .....46 DE17
Hemel Hempstead HP2 .....40 BK18
Hemel Hempstead (Bov.) HP3 .....57 BB27
Hertford SG14 .....32 DR09
Isleworth TW7 .....157 CH83
Kingston upon Thames KT1 .....197 CK96
Leatherhead KT22 .....231 CH122
Leatherhead (Eff.) KT24 .....246 BX127
Reigate RH2 .....250 DA134
Rickmansworth WD3 .....92 BL46
St. Albans AL3 .....43 CD19
Sawbridgeworth CM21 .....36 EY05
Sevenoaks (Seal) TN15 .....257 FN121
Sevenoaks (Shore.) TN14 .....225 FF111
Slough SL1 .....152 AT76
Slough (Burn.) SL1 .....130 AJ70
Slough (Chalvey) SL1 .....151 AQ75
Staines TW18 .....173 BE91
Sunbury-on-Thames TW16 .....195 BV97
Sutton SM1 *off High St* 218 DB106
Twickenham TW1 .....177 CG88
Waltham Abbey EN9 .....67 EC33
Walton-on-Thames KT12 .....195 BU102
Ware SG12 .....33 DX06
Watford WD18 .....76 BW42
Weybridge KT13 .....212 BN105
Windsor SL4 *off Castle Hill* 151 AR81
Woking (Old Wok.) GU22 .....227 BC121
Church St E, Wok. GU21 .....227 AZ117
Church St Est, NW8 .....7 P4
Church St N, E15 .....144 EE67
Church St Pas, E15 *off Church St* 144 EE67
Church St W, Wok. GU21 .....226 AY117
Church Stretton Rd, Houns. TW3 .....176 CC85
Church Ter, NW4 .....119 CV55
SE13 .....164 EE83
SW8 .....161 DK82
Richmond TW10 .....177 CK85
Windsor SL4 .....151 AL82
CHURCH TOWN, Gdse. RH9 .....253 DX131
Church Trd Est, The, Erith DA8 .....167 FG80
Church Vale, N2 .....120 DF55
SE23 .....182 DW89
Church Vw, Brox. EN10 .....49 DZ20
South Ockendon (Aveley) RM15 .....168 FQ75
Swanley BR8 *off Lime Rd* 207 FD97
Upminster RM14 .....128 FN61
Church Vw Cl, Horl. RH6 .....268 DF149
Churchview Rd, Twick. TW2 .....177 CD88
Church Vil, Sev. TN13 *off Church Fld* 256 FE122
Church Wk, N6 *off Swains La* 120 DG62
N16 .....122 DR63
NW2 .....119 CZ62
NW4 .....119 CW55
NW9 .....118 CR61
SW13 .....159 CU81
Church Wk, SW15 .....179 CV85
SW16 .....201 DJ96
SW20 .....199 CW97
Brentford TW8 .....157 CJ79
Bushey WD23 *off High St* 76 CA44
Caterham CR3 .....236 DU124
Chertsey KT16 .....194 BG101
Dartford DA2 .....188 FK90
Dartford (Eyns.) DA4 .....208 FL104
Enfield EN2 *off Church La* 82 DR41
Gravesend DA12 .....191 GK88
Hayes UB3 .....135 BT72
Horley RH6 *off Woodroyd Av* 268 DF149
Leatherhead KT22 .....231 CH122
Redhill (Bletch.) RH1 .....252 DR133
Reigate RH2 *off Reigate Rd* 250 DC134
Richmond TW9 *off Red Lion St* 177 CK85
Sawbridgeworth CM21 .....36 EZ05
Slough (Burn.) SL1 .....130 AH70
Thames Ditton KT7 .....197 CF100
Walton-on-Thames KT12 .....195 BU102
Weybridge KT13 *off Beales La* 195 BP103
Church Wk Shop Cen, Cat. CR3 *off Church Wk* 236 DU124
Church Way, N20 .....98 DD48
Churchway, NW1 .....9 M1
Church Way, Barn. EN4 .....80 DF42
Edgware HA8 .....96 CN51
Oxted RH8 .....254 EF132
South Croydon CR2 .....220 DT110
Churchwell Path, E9 .....122 DW64
Churchwood Gdns, Wdf.Grn. IG8 .....102 EG49
Churchyard Row, SE11 .....20 F7
Church Yd Wk, W2 .....7 N5
Churston Av, E13 .....144 EH67
Churston Cl, SW2 *off Tulse Hill* 181 DP88
Churston Dr, Mord. SM4 .....199 CX99
Churston Gdns, N11 .....99 DJ51
Churton Pl, SW1 .....19 K8
Churton St, SW1 .....19 K8
Chusan Pl, E14 .....13 M8
Chuters Cl, W.Byf. (Byfleet) KT14 .....212 BL112
Chuters Gro, Epsom KT17 .....217 CT112
Chyne, The, Ger.Cr. SL9 .....113 AZ57
Chyngton Cl, Sid. DA15 .....185 ET90
Cibber Rd, SE23 .....183 DX89
Cicada Rd, SW18 .....180 DC85
Cicely Rd, SE15 .....162 DU81
Cillocks Cl, Hodd. EN11 .....49 EA16
Cimba Wd, Grav. DA12 .....191 GL91
Cinderella Path, NW11 *off North End Rd* 120 DB60
Cinderford Way, Brom. BR1 .....184 EE91
Cinder Path, Wok. GU22 .....226 AW119
Cinema Par, W5 *off Ashbourne Rd* 138 CM70
Cinnabar Wf, E1 .....22 B2
Cinnamon Cl, Croy. CR0 .....201 DL101
Cinnamon Gdns, Guil. GU2 .....242 AU129
Cinnamon Row, SW11 .....160 DC83
Cinnamon St, E1 .....22 D2
Cintra Pk, SE19 .....182 DT94
CIPPENHAM, Slou. SL1 .....151 AM75
Cippenham Cl, Slou. SL1 .....131 AM73
Sch **Cippenham Inf Sch**, Slou. SL1 *off Dennis Way* 131 AK73
Sch **Cippenham Jun Sch**, Slou. SL1 *off Elmshott La* 131 AL73
Cippenham La, Slou. SL1 .....131 AM73
Circle, The, NW2 .....118 CS62
NW7 .....96 CR50
SE1 .....21 N3
Tilbury RM18 *off Toronto Rd* 171 GG81
Circle Gdns, SW19 .....200 DA96
West Byfleet (Byfleet) KT14 .....212 BM113
Circle Rd, Walt. (Whiteley Vill.) KT12 .....213 BS110
Circuits, The, Pnr. HA5 .....116 BW56
Circular Rd, N17 .....122 DT55
Circular Way, SE18 .....165 EM79
Circus Ms, W1 .....8 C5
Circus Pl, EC2 .....11 K6
Circus Rd, NW8 .....7 N1
Coll **Circus Space**, N1 .....11 L2
Circus St, SE10 .....163 EC80
Cirencester St, W2 .....7 J5
Cirrus Cl, Wall. SM6 .....219 DL108
Cirrus Cres, Grav. DA12 .....191 GL92
Cissbury Ring N, N12 .....97 CZ50
Cissbury Ring S, N12 .....97 CZ50
Cissbury Rd, N15 .....122 DR57
Citadel Pl, SE11 .....20 A9
Citizen Ho, N7 *off Harvist Est* 121 DN63
Citizen Rd, N7 .....121 DN63
C.I. Twr, N.Mal. KT3 .....198 CS97
Citron Ter, SE15 *off Nunhead La* 162 DV83
Coll **City & Guilds of London Art Sch**, SE11 .....20 D10
Coll **City & Islington Coll**, Cen for Applied Sciences, EC1 .....10 E1
Cen for Business, Arts & Tech, N7 *off Camden Rd* 121 DL63
Cen for Health, Social & Child Care, N7 *off Holloway Rd* 121 DL63
Cen for Lifelong Learning, N4 *off Blackstock Rd* 121 DP61
Shepperton Arts Cen, N1 .....5 J7
Spring Ho, N7 .....4 D3
Willen Ho, EC1 .....11 H2
Coll **City & Islington 6th Form Coll**, EC1 *off Goswell Rd* 141 DP69
Coll **City Business Coll**, EC1 .....10 F2
Coll **City Coll, The**, N1 .....11 J1
City Cross Business Pk, SE10 .....25 H7
City Forum, EC1 .....10 G1
City Gdn Row, N1 .....4 F10
City Gate Ho, Ilf. IG2 .....125 EP58
City Ho, Croy. CR0 .....201 DP101
Coll **City Learning Cen**, NW10 *off Tiverton Rd* 139 CX67
Coll **City Lit Inst, The**, Bolt Ct Cen, EC4 .....10 D8
Keeley Ho, WC2 .....10 A8
Stukeley St, WC2 .....9 P7
City Mill River Towpath, E15 .....143 EB66
Sch **City of London Acad, The**, SE1 *off Lynton Rd* 162 DU79
Coll **City of London Coll of Higher Ed (inc. London Coll of Tourism)**, SW4 *off The Pavement* 161 DJ84
Sch **City of London Freemen's Sch**, Ashtd. KT21 *off Park La* 232 CN119
Sch **City of London Sch**, EC4 .....10 G9
Sch **City of London Sch for Girls**, EC2 .....11 H5
★ **City of Westminster Archives Cen**, SW1 .....19 M5
Coll **City of Westminster Coll**, NW8 .....8 A4
Cosway St Cen, NW1 .....8 B5
Maida Vale Cen, W9 .....7 J2
Paddington Grn Cen, W2 .....7 N5
Queens Pk Cen, W9 .....6 G2
City Pk, Welw.G.C. AL7 .....30 DA08
City Pt, EC2 .....11 J5
City Rd, EC1 .....4 E10
⇌ **City Thameslink** 10 E8
Uni **City Uni**, Cass Business Sch, EC1 .....11 J4
College Bldg, EC1 .....10 E2
Drysdale Bldg, EC1 .....10 E2
Gloucester Bldg, EC1 .....10 E2
Halls of Res & Saddlers Sports Cen, EC1 .....10 G3
Health Cen, EC1 .....10 F2
Innovation Cen, EC1 *off Whiskin St* 141 DP69
Social Sciences Bldg, EC1 .....10 E2
Tait Bldg, EC1 .....10 E2
Uni Bldg, EC1 .....10 E2
Walmsley Bldg, EC1 .....10 E3
Walter Sickert Hall, N1 .....10 G1
Uni **City Uni - Inns of Ct Sch of Law**, Atkin Bldg, WC1 *off Gray's Inn* 141 DM71
Gray's Inn Pl, WC1 .....141 DM71
Princeton St, WC1 .....141 DM71
Civic Cl, St.Alb. AL1 .....43 CD20
Civic Offices, St.Alb. AL1 .....43 CE20
Civic Sq, Harl. CM20 *off South Gate* 51 ER15
Tilbury RM18 .....171 GG82
Civic Way, Ilf. IG6 .....125 EQ56
Ruislip HA4 .....116 BX64
Coll **Civil Service Coll**, SW1 .....19 J8
Clabon Ms, SW1 .....18 C6
Clacket La, West. TN16 .....238 EL124
Clack La, Ruis. HA4 .....115 BQ60
Clack St, SE16 .....22 F4
Clacton Rd, E6 .....144 EK69
E17 .....123 DY58
N17 *off Sperling Rd* 100 DT54
Claigmar Gdns, N3 .....98 DB53
Claire Causeway, Dart. DA2 .....169 FT84
Claire Ct, N12 .....98 DC48
Bushey (Bushey Hth) WD23 .....95 CD46
Pinner HA5 *off Westfield Pk* 94 BZ52
Claire Gdns, Stan. HA7 .....95 CJ50
Claire Pl, E14 .....23 P5
Clairvale, Horn. RM11 .....128 FL59
Clairvale Rd, Houns. TW5 .....156 BX81
Clairview Rd, SW16 .....181 DH92
Clairville Ct, Reig. RH2 .....250 DD134
Clairville Gdns, W7 .....137 CF74
Clairville Pt, SE23 .....183 DX90
Clammas Way, Uxb. UB8 .....134 BJ71
Clamp Hill, Stan. HA7 .....95 CD49
Clancarty Rd, SW6 .....160 DA82
⇌ **Clandon** 244 BH129
Clandon Av, Egh. TW20 .....173 BC94
Clandon Cl, W3 *off Avenue Rd* 158 CP75
Epsom KT17 .....217 CT107
Sch **Clandon C of E Inf Sch**, Guil. GU4 *off The Street* 244 BG131
Clandon Gdns, N3 .....120 DA55
★ **Clandon Park**, Guil. GU4 .....244 BG132
Clandon Pk, Guil. (W.Clan.) GU4 .....244 BG132
Clandon Rd, Guil. GU1 .....258 AY135
Guildford (W.Clan.) GU4 .....243 BF125
Ilford IG3 .....125 ES61
Woking (Send) GU23 .....243 BF125
Clandon St, SE8 .....163 EA82
Clandon Way, Wok. (Send M.) GU23 *off Clandon Rd* 243 BF125
Clanfield Way, SE15 *off Blakes Rd* 162 DS80
Clanricarde Gdns, W2 .....7 H10
Clapgate Rd, Bushey WD23 .....76 CB44
CLAPHAM, SW4 .....161 DH83
★ **Clapham Common**, SW4 .....160 DG84
⊖ **Clapham Common** 161 DJ84
Clapham Common N Side, SW4 .....161 DH84
Clapham Common S Side, SW4 .....181 DH86
Clapham Common W Side, SW4 .....160 DG84
Clapham Cres, SW4 .....161 DK84
Clapham Est, SW11 .....160 DE84
⇌ **Clapham High Street** 161 DK83
Clapham High St, SW4 .....161 DK84
⇌ **Clapham Junction** 160 DD84
Sch **Clapham Manor Prim Sch**, SW4 *off Belmont Rd* 161 DJ83
Clapham Manor St, SW4 .....161 DJ83
⊖ **Clapham North** 161 DL83
CLAPHAM PARK, SW4 .....181 DK86
Clapham Pk Est, SW4 .....181 DK86
Clapham Pk Rd, SW4 .....161 DK84
Clapham Rd, SW9 .....161 DL83
Clapham Rd Est, SW4 .....161 DK83
⊖ **Clapham South** 181 DH86
Clap La, Dag. RM10 .....127 FB62
Claps Gate La, E6 .....145 EP70
⇌ **Clapton** 122 DV61
Clapton App, H.Wyc. (Woob.Grn) HP10 .....110 AD55
Clapton Common, E5 .....122 DT59
Sch **Clapton Girls' Tech Coll**, E5 *off Laura Pl* 122 DW63
CLAPTON PARK, E5 .....123 DY63
Clapton Pk Est, E5 *off Blackwell Cl* 123 DY63
Clapton Pas, E5 .....122 DW64
Clapton Sq, E5 .....122 DW64
Clapton Ter, N16 *off Oldhill St* 122 DU60
Clapton Way, E5 .....122 DU63
Sch **Clara Grant Sch**, E3 .....13 P4
Clara Pl, SE18 .....165 EN77
Clare Cl, N2 *off Thomas More Way* 120 DC55
Borehamwood (Elstree) WD6 .....78 CM44
West Byfleet KT14 .....212 BG113
Clare Cor, SE9 .....185 EP87
Clare Cotts, Red. (Bletch.) RH1 .....251 DP133
Clare Ct, Cat. (Wold.) CR3 .....237 EA123
Northwood HA6 .....93 BS50
Clare Cres, Lthd. KT22 .....231 CG118
Claredale, Wok. GU22 *off Claremont Av* 226 AY119
Claredale St, E2 .....142 DU68
Clare Dr, Slou. (Farn.Com.) SL2 .....111 AP63
Clare Gdns, E7 .....124 EG63
W11 .....6 D8
Barking IG11 .....145 ET65
Egham TW20 *off Mowbray Cres* 173 BA92
Clare Hill, Esher KT10 .....214 CB107
Clare Ho, E3 .....143 DZ67
Sch **Clare Ho Prim Sch**, Beck. BR3 *off Oakwood Av* 203 EC96
Clare La, N1 .....5 H6
Clare Lawn Av, SW14 .....178 CR85
Clare Mkt, WC2 .....10 A8
Clare Ms, SW6 *off Waterford Rd* 160 DB80
Claremont, St.Alb. (Brick.Wd) AL2 .....60 CA31
Waltham Cross (Chsht) EN7 .....66 DT29
Claremont Av, Esher KT10 .....214 BZ107
Harrow HA3 .....118 CL57
New Malden KT3 .....199 CU99
Sunbury-on-Thames TW16 .....195 BV95
Walton-on-Thames KT12 .....214 BX105
Woking GU22 .....226 AY119
Claremont Cl, E16 .....145 EN74
N1 .....4 D10
SW2 *off Streatham Hill* 181 DL88
Grays RM16 *off Premier Av* 170 GC76
Orpington BR6 .....223 EN105
South Croydon CR2 .....236 DV115
Walton-on-Thames KT12 .....214 BW106
Claremont Ct, Dor. RH4 .....263 CH137
Surbiton KT6 *off St. James Rd* 197 CK100
Claremont Cres, Dart. DA1 .....167 FE84
Rickmansworth (Crox.Grn) WD3 .....75 BQ43
Claremont Dr, Esher KT10 .....214 CB108
Shepperton TW17 .....195 BP100
Woking GU22 .....226 AY119
Claremont End, Esher KT10 .....214 CB107
Sch **Claremont Fan Ct Sch**, Esher KT10 *off Claremont Dr* 214 CB108
Claremont Gdns, Ilf. IG3 .....125 ES61
Surbiton KT6 .....198 CL99
Upminster RM14 .....129 FR60
Claremont Gro, W4 *off Edensor Gdns* 158 CS80
Woodford Green IG8 .....102 EJ51
Sch **Claremont High Sch**, Har. HA3 *off Claremont Av* 118 CL57
★ **Claremont Landscape Gdns**, Esher KT10 .....214 BZ108
Claremont La, Esher KT10 .....214 CB105
CLAREMONT PARK, Esher KT10 .....214 CB108
Claremont Pk, N3 .....97 CY53
Claremont Pk Rd, Esher KT10 .....214 CB107
Claremont Pl, Grav. DA11 *off Cutmore St* 191 GH87
Claremont Rd, E7 .....124 EH64
E17 .....101 DY54
N6 .....121 DJ59
NW2 .....119 CX62
W9 .....139 CY68
W13 .....137 CG71
Barnet EN4 .....80 DD37
Bromley BR1 .....204 EL98
Croydon CR0 .....202 DU102
Esher (Clay.) KT10 .....215 CE108
Harrow HA3 .....95 CE54
Hornchurch RM11 .....127 FG58
Redhill RH1 .....250 DG131
Staines TW18 .....173 BD92
Surbiton KT6 .....198 CL100
Swanley BR8 .....187 FE94
Teddington TW11 .....177 CF92
Twickenham TW1 .....177 CJ86
West Byfleet KT14 .....212 BG112
Windsor SL4 .....151 AQ82
Claremont Sq, N1 .....4 C10
Claremont St, E16 .....145 EN74
N18 .....100 DU51
SE10 .....163 EB79
Claremont Way, NW2 .....119 CW60
Claremount Cl, Epsom KT18 .....233 CW117
Claremount Gdns, Epsom KT18 .....233 CW117
Clarence Av, SW4 .....181 DK86
Bromley BR1 .....204 EL98
Ilford IG2 .....125 EN58
New Malden KT3 .....198 CQ96
Upminster RM14 .....128 FN61
Clarence Cl, Barn. EN4 .....80 DD43
Bushey (Bushey Hth) WD23 .....95 CF45
Walton-on-Thames KT12 .....214 BW105
Clarence Ct, Egh. TW20 *off Clarence St* 173 AZ93
Horley RH6 *off Clarence Way* 269 DK147
Clarence Cres, SW4 .....181 DK86
Sidcup DA14 .....186 EV90
Windsor SL4 .....151 AQ81
Clarence Dr, Egh. (Eng.Grn) TW20 .....172 AW91
Clarence Gdns, NW1 .....9 H2
Clarence Gate, Wdf.Grn. IG8 .....103 EN51
Clarence Gate Gdns, NW1 *off Glentworth St* 140 DF70
★ **Clarence Ho**, SW1 .....19 K3
Clarence La, SW15 .....178 CS86
Clarence Ms, E5 .....122 DV64
SE16 .....22 G2
SW12 .....181 DH87
Clarence Pl, E5 .....122 DV64
Gravesend DA12 .....191 GH87
Clarence Rd, E5 .....122 DV63
E12 .....124 EK64
E16 .....15 H4
E17 .....101 DX54
N15 .....122 DQ57
N22 .....99 DL52
NW6 .....139 CZ66
SE8 .....163 EB79
SE9 .....184 EL89
SW19 .....180 DB93
W4 .....158 CN78
Berkhamsted HP4 .....38 AW19
Bexleyheath DA6 .....166 EY84
Clarence Rd, Brwd. (Pilg.Hat.) CM15 .....108 FV44
Bromley BR1 .....204 EK97
Croydon CR0 .....202 DR101
Enfield EN3 .....82 DV43
Grays RM17 .....170 GA79
Redhill RH1 .....266 DD137
Richmond TW9 .....158 CM81
St. Albans AL1 .....43 CF20
Sidcup DA14 .....186 EV90
Sutton SM1 .....218 DB105
Teddington TW11 .....177 CF93
Wallington SM6 .....219 DH106
Walton-on-Thames KT12 .....213 BV105
Westerham (Bigg.H.) TN16 .....239 EM118
Windsor SL4 .....151 AP81
Clarence Row, Grav. DA12 .....191 GH87
Clarence St, Egh. TW20 .....173 AZ93
Kingston upon Thames KT1 .....198 CL96
Richmond TW9 .....158 CL84
Southall UB2 .....156 BX76
Staines TW18 .....173 BE91
Clarence Ter, NW1 .....8 D3
Hounslow TW3 .....156 CB84
Clarence Wk, SW4 .....161 DL82
Redhill RH1 .....266 DD137
Clarence Way, NW1 .....141 DH66
Horley RH6 .....269 DK147
Clarence Way Est, NW1 .....141 DH66
Clarenden Pl, Dart. DA2 .....187 FD92
Clarendon Cl, E9 .....142 DW66
W2 .....8 A9
Hemel Hempstead HP2 .....40 BK19
Orpington BR5 .....206 EU97
Clarendon Ct, Slou. SL2 .....132 AV73
Clarendon Cres, Twick. TW2 .....177 CD90
Clarendon Cross, W11 .....6 D10
Clarendon Dr, SW15 .....159 CW84
Clarendon Gdns, NW4 .....119 CV55
W9 .....7 M4
Dartford DA2 .....189 FR87
Ilford IG1 .....125 EM60
Wembley HA9 .....118 CL63
Clarendon Gate, Cher. (Ott.) KT16 .....211 BD107
Clarendon Grn, Orp. BR5 .....206 EU98
Clarendon Gro, NW1 .....9 L1
Mitcham CR4 .....200 DF97
Orpington BR5 .....206 EU97
Clarendon Ms, W2 .....8 A8
Ashtead KT21 .....232 CL119
Bexley DA5 .....187 FB88
Borehamwood WD6 *off Clarendon Rd* 78 CN41
Clarendon Path, Orp. BR5 .....206 EU97
Clarendon Pl, W2 .....8 A9
Sevenoaks TN13 *off Clarendon Rd* 256 FG125
Sch **Clarendon Prim Sch**, Ashf. TW15 *off Knapp Rd* 174 BM91
Clarendon Ri, SE13 .....163 EC83
Clarendon Rd, E11 .....123 ED60
E17 .....123 EB58
E18 .....124 EG55
N8 .....121 DM55
N15 .....121 DP56
N18 .....100 DU51
N22 .....99 DM54
SW19 .....180 DE94
W5 .....138 CL70
W11 .....6 C9
Ashford TW15 .....174 BM91
Borehamwood WD6 .....78 CN41
Croydon CR0 .....201 DP103
Gravesend DA12 .....191 GJ86
Harrow HA1 .....117 CE58
Hayes UB3 .....155 BT75
Redhill RH1 .....250 DF133
Sevenoaks TN13 .....256 FG124
Wallington SM6 .....219 DJ107
Waltham Cross (Chsht) EN8 .....67 DX29
Watford WD17 .....75 BV40
Sch **Clarendon Sch**, Hmptn. TW12 *off Hanworth Rd* 176 CB93
Clarendon St, SW1 .....19 H10
Clarendon Ter, W9 .....7 M3
Clarendon Wk, W11 .....6 C8
Clarendon Way, N21 .....82 DQ44
Chislehurst BR7 .....205 ET97
Orpington BR5 .....205 ET97
Clarens St, SE6 .....183 DZ89
Clare Pk, Amer. HP7 .....55 AS40
Clare Pl, SW15 *off Minstead Gdns* 179 CT87
Clare Pt, NW2 *off Claremont Rd* 119 CX60
Clare Rd, E11 .....123 ED58
NW10 .....139 CU66
SE14 .....163 DZ81
Greenford UB6 .....137 CD65
Hounslow TW4 .....156 BZ83
Maidenhead (Taplow) SL6 .....130 AJ72
Staines (Stanw.) TW19 .....174 BL87
Clare St, E2 .....142 DV68
Claret Gdns, SE25 .....202 DS98
Clareville Gro, SW7 .....17 M8
Clareville Rd, Cat. CR3 .....236 DU124
Orpington BR5 .....205 EQ103
Clareville St, SW7 .....17 M8
Clare Way, Bexh. DA7 .....166 EY81
Sevenoaks TN13 .....257 FJ127
Clare Wd, Lthd. KT22 .....231 CH118
Clarewood Wk, SW9 .....161 DP84
Clarges Ms, W1 .....18 G1
Clarges St, W1 .....19 H1
Claribel Rd, SW9 .....161 DP82
Clarice Way, Wall. SM6 .....219 DL109
Claridge Rd, Dag. RM8 .....126 EX60
Clarina Rd, SE20 *off Evelina Rd* 183 DX94
Clarissa Rd, Rom. RM6 .....126 EX59
Clarissa St, E8 .....5 N8
Clark Cl, Erith DA8 *off Forest Rd* 167 FG81
Clarkebourne Dr, Grays RM17 .....170 GD79
Clarke Grn, Wat. WD25 .....75 BU35
Clarke Ms, N9 *off Plevna Rd* 100 DV48
Clarke Path, N16 .....122 DU60
Clarkes Av, Wor.Pk. KT4 .....199 CX102
Clarkes Dr, Uxb. UB8 .....134 BL71
Clarke's Ms, W1 .....8 F5
Clarkes Rd, Hat. AL10 .....45 CV17
Clarke Way, Wat. WD25 .....75 BU35

A B C D E F G H I J K L M N O P Q R S T U V W X Y Z

⊖ London Underground station   DLR Docklands Light Railway station   Tra Tramlink station   Riv Pedestrian ferry landing stage

Clarkfield, Rick. (Mill End) WD3 . . . 92 BH46
Clark Lawrence Ct, SW11 off Winstanley Rd . . . 160 DD83
Clarks La, Epp. CM16 . . . 69 ET31
Sevenoaks (Halst.) TN14 . . . 224 EZ112
Warlingham CR6 . . . 238 EF123
Westerham TN16 . . . 238 EK123
Clarks Mead, Bushey WD23 . . . 94 CC45
Clarkson Rd, E16 . . . 15 J7
Clarkson Row, NW1 . . . 141 DJ68
Clarksons, The, Bark. IG11 . . . 145 EQ68
Clarkson St, E2 . . . 12 C1
Clarks Pl, EC2 . . . 11 L7
Clarks Rd, Ilf. IG1 . . . 125 ER61
Clark St, E1 . . . 12 D6
Clark Way, Houns. TW5 . . . 156 BX80
Classon Cl, West Dr. UB7 . . . 154 BL75
Claston Cl, Dart. DA1 off Iron Mill La . . . 167 FE84
CLATTERFORD END, Ong. CM5 . . . 71 FG30
Claude Rd, E10 . . . 123 EC61
E13 . . . 144 EH67
SE15 . . . 162 DV82
Claude St, E14 . . . 23 N7
Claudia Jones Way, SW2 . . . 181 DL86
Claudian Pl, St.Alb. AL3 . . . 42 CA22
Claudian Way, Grays RM16 . . . 171 GH76
Claudia Pl, SW19 . . . 179 CY88
Claughton Rd, E13 . . . 144 EJ68
Claughton Way, Brwd. (Hutt.) CM13 . . . 109 GD44
Clauson Av, Nthlt. UB5 . . . 116 CB64
Clavell St, SE10 . . . 163 EC79
Claverdale Rd, SW2 . . . 181 DM87
Claverhambury Rd, Wal.Abb. EN9 . . . 68 EF29
Clavering Av, SW13 . . . 159 CV79
Clavering Cl, Twick. TW1 . . . 177 CG91
Clavering Rd, E12 . . . 124 EK60
Claverings Ind Est, N9 . . . 101 DX47
Clavering Way, Brwd. (Hutt.) CM13 off Poplar Dr . . . 109 GC44
Claverley Gro, N3 . . . 98 DA52
Claverley Vil, N3 off Claverley Gro . . . 98 DB52
Claverton Cl, Hem.H. (Bov.) HP3 . . . 57 BA28
Claverton St, SW1 . . . 19 K10
Clave St, E1 . . . 22 E2
Claxton Gro, W6 . . . 16 B10
Clay Acre, Chesh. HP5 . . . 54 AR30
Clay Av, Mitch. CR4 . . . 201 DH96
Claybank Gro, SE13 off Algernon Rd . . . 163 EB83
Claybourne Ms, SE19 off Church Rd . . . 182 DS94
Claybridge Rd, SE12 . . . 184 EJ91
Claybrook Cl, N2 . . . 120 DD55
Claybrook Rd, W6 . . . 159 CX79
Clayburn Gdns, S.Ock. RM15 . . . 149 FV73
Claybury, Bushey WD23 . . . 94 CB45
Claybury Bdy, Ilf. IG5 . . . 124 EL55
Claybury Hall, Wdf.Grn. IG8 off Regents Dr . . . 103 EM52
Claybury Rd, Wdf.Grn. IG8 . . . 102 EL52
Sch Claycots Prim Sch, Slou. SL2 off Monksfield Way . . . 131 AN69
Claycroft, Welw.G.C. AL7 . . . 30 DB08
Claydon Dr, Croy. CR0 . . . 219 DL105
Claydon End, Ger.Cr. (Chal.St.P.) SL9 . . . 112 AY55
Claydon La, Ger.Cr. (Chal.St.P.) SL9 . . . 112 AY55
Claydon Rd, Wok. GU21 . . . 226 AU116
Claydown Ms, SE18 off Woolwich New Rd . . . 165 EN78
Clayfarm Rd, SE9 . . . 185 EQ89
Clayfields, H.Wyc. (Penn) HP10 . . . 88 AC45
CLAYGATE, Esher KT10 . . . 215 CE108
⇌ Claygate . . . 215 CD107
Claygate Cl, Horn. RM12 . . . 127 FG63
Claygate Cres, Croy. (New Adgtn) CR0 . . . 221 EC107
Claygate La, Esher KT10 . . . 197 CG103
Thames Ditton KT7 . . . 197 CG102
Waltham Abbey EN9 . . . 67 ED30
Claygate Lo Cl, Esher (Clay.) KT10 . . . 215 CE108
Sch Claygate Prim Sch, Esher KT10 off Foley Rd . . . 215 CE108
Claygate Rd, W13 . . . 157 CH76
Dorking RH4 . . . 263 CH138
CLAYHALL, Ilf. IG5 . . . 103 EM54
Clayhall Av, Ilf. IG5 . . . 124 EL55
Clayhall La, Reig. RH2 . . . 265 CX138
Windsor (Old Wind.) SL4 . . . 172 AT85
Clayhanger, Guil. GU4 off Chatfield Dr . . . 243 BC132
CLAY HILL, Enf. EN2 . . . 82 DQ37
Clay Hill, Enf. EN2 . . . 82 DQ37
Clayhill, Surb. KT5 . . . 198 CN99
Clayhill Cl, Reig. (Leigh) RH2 . . . 265 CU141
Clayhill Cres, SE9 . . . 184 EK91
Clayhill Rd, Reig. (Leigh) RH2 . . . 265 CT142
Claylands Pl, SW8 . . . 161 DN80
Claylands Rd, SW8 . . . 161 DM79
Clay La, Bushey (Bushey Hth) WD23 . . . 95 CE45
Edgware HA8 . . . 96 CN46
Epsom (Headley) KT18 . . . 232 CP124
Guildford GU4 . . . 242 AY128
Redhill (S.Nutfld) RH1 . . . 267 DJ135
Staines (Stanw.) TW19 . . . 174 BM87
Claymill Ho, SE18 . . . 165 EQ78
Claymore, Hem.H. HP2 . . . 40 BL16
Claymore Cl, Mord. SM4 . . . 200 DA101
Claymore Ct, E17 off Billet Rd . . . 101 DY53
Claypit Hill, Wal.Abb. EN9 . . . 84 EJ36
Claypole Dr, Houns. TW5 . . . 156 BY81
Claypole Rd, E15 . . . 143 EC68
Clayponds Av, Brent. TW8 . . . 158 CL77
Clayponds Gdns, W5 . . . 157 CK77
H Clayponds Hosp, W5 . . . 158 CL77
Clayponds La, Brent. TW8 . . . 158 CL78
Clay Rd, The, Loug. IG10 . . . 84 EL39
Clayside, Chig. IG7 . . . 103 EQ51
Clays La, E15 . . . 123 EB64
Clay's La, Loug. IG10 . . . 85 EN39
Clays La Cl, E15 . . . 123 EB64
Clay St, W1 . . . 8 D6
Beaconsfield HP9 . . . 88 AJ48
Clayton Av, Upmin. RM14 . . . 128 FP64
Wembley HA0 . . . 138 CL66
Clayton Cl, E6 off Brandreth Rd . . . 145 EM72
Clayton Cres, N1 . . . 4 A8
Brentford TW8 . . . 157 CK78
Clayton Cft Rd, Dart. DA2 . . . 187 FG89
Clayton Dr, SE8 . . . 23 J9
Guildford GU2 . . . 242 AT131
Clayton Fld, NW9 . . . 96 CS52
Clayton Mead, Gdse. RH9 . . . 252 DV130
Clayton Ms, SE10 . . . 163 ED81
Clayton Rd, SE15 . . . 162 DU81
Chessington KT9 . . . 215 CJ105
Epsom KT17 . . . 216 CS113
Hayes UB3 . . . 155 BS75
Isleworth TW7 . . . 157 CE83
Romford RM7 . . . 127 FC60
Clayton St, SE11 . . . 161 DN79
Clayton Ter, Hayes UB4 off Jollys La . . . 136 BX71
Clayton Wk, Amer. HP7 . . . 72 AW39
Clayton Way, Uxb. UB8 . . . 134 BK70
Clay Tye Rd, Upmin. RM14 . . . 129 FW63
Claywood Cl, Orp. BR6 . . . 205 ES101
Claywood La, Dart. (Bean) DA2 . . . 189 FX90
Clayworth Cl, Sid. DA15 . . . 186 EV86
Cleall Av, Wal.Abb. EN9 off Quaker La . . . 67 EC34
Cleanthus Cl, SE18 off Cleanthus Rd . . . 165 EP81
Cleanthus Rd, SE18 . . . 165 EP81
Clearbrook Way, E1 . . . 12 F7
Cleardene, Dor. RH4 . . . 263 CH136
Cleardown, Wok. GU22 . . . 227 BB118
Cleares Pasture, Slou. (Burn.) SL1 . . . 130 AH69
Clearmount, Wok. (Chobham) GU24 . . . 210 AS107
Clears, The, Reig. RH2 . . . 249 CY132
Clearwater Ter, W11 . . . 16 B3
Clearwell Dr, W9 . . . 7 J4
Cleave Av, Hayes UB3 . . . 155 BS77
Orpington BR6 . . . 223 ES107
Cleaveland Rd, Surb. KT6 . . . 197 CK99
Cleave Prior, Couls. CR5 . . . 234 DE119
Cleaverholme Cl, SE25 . . . 202 DV100
Cleaver Sq, SE11 . . . 20 D9
Cleaver St, SE11 . . . 20 D9
Cleeve, The, Guil. GU1 . . . 243 BA134
Cleeve Ct, Felt. TW14 off Kilross Rd . . . 175 BS88
Cleeve Hill, SE23 . . . 182 DV88
Cleeve Pk Gdns, Sid. DA14 . . . 186 EV89
Sch Cleeve Pk Sch, Sid. DA14 off Bexley La . . . 186 EW90
Cleeve Rd, Lthd. KT22 . . . 231 CF120
Cleeve Way, SW15 off Danebury Av . . . 179 CT87
Clegg Ho, SE3 off Pinto Way . . . 164 EH84
Clegg St, E1 . . . 22 D1
E13 . . . 144 EG68
Cleland Path, Loug. IG10 . . . 85 EP39
Cleland Rd, Ger.Cr. (Chal.St.P.) SL9 . . . 90 AX54
Clematis Cl, Rom. RM3 . . . 106 FJ52
Clematis Gdns, Wdf.Grn. IG8 . . . 102 EG50
Clematis St, W12 . . . 139 CT73
Clem Attlee Ct, SW6 . . . 159 CZ79
Clem Attlee Est, SW6 off Lillie Rd . . . 159 CZ79
Clem Attlee Par, SW6 off North End Rd . . . 159 CZ79
Clemence Rd, Dag. RM10 . . . 147 FC67
Clemence St, E14 . . . 13 L6
Clement Atlee Sq, Harl. CM20 off South Gate . . . 51 ER15
Clement Av, SW4 . . . 161 DK84
Clement Cl, NW6 . . . 139 CW66
W4 off Acton La . . . 158 CR77
Purley CR8 off Croftleigh Av . . . 235 DP116
Clement Gdns, Hayes UB3 . . . 155 BS77
Clementhorpe Rd, Dag. RM9 . . . 146 EW65
Clementina Rd, E10 . . . 123 DZ60
H Clementine Churchill Hosp, Har. HA1 . . . 117 CF62
Clementine Cl, W13 off Balfour Rd . . . 157 CH75
Clementine Wk, Wdf.Grn. IG8 off Salway Cl . . . 102 EG52
Clement Rd, SW19 . . . 179 CY92
Beckenham BR3 . . . 203 DX96
Waltham Cross (Chshт) EN8 . . . 67 DY27
Clements Av, E16 . . . 15 L9
Clements Cl, Slou. SL1 . . . 152 AV75
Clements Ct, Houns. TW4 . . . 156 BX84
Ilford IG1 off Clements La . . . 125 EP62
Clement's Inn, WC2 . . . 10 B8
Clement's Inn Pas, WC2 . . . 10 B8
Clements La, EC4 . . . 11 K9
Ilford IG1 . . . 125 EP62
Clements Mead, Lthd. KT22 . . . 231 CG119
Clements Pl, Brent. TW8 . . . 157 CK78
Clements Rd, E6 . . . 145 EM66
SE16 . . . 22 B6
Ilford IG1 . . . 125 EP62
Rickmansworth (Chorl.) WD3 . . . 73 BD43
Walton-on-Thames KT12 . . . 195 BV103
Clements St, Ware SG12 . . . 33 DY06
Clement St, Swan. BR8 . . . 188 FK93
Clement Way, Upmin. RM14 . . . 128 FM62
Clenches Fm La, Sev. TN13 . . . 256 FG126
Clenches Fm Rd, Sev. TN13 . . . 256 FG126
Clendon Way, SE18 off Polthorne Gro . . . 165 ER77
Clennam St, SE1 . . . 21 H3
Clensham Ct, Sutt. SM1 off Sutton Common Rd . . . 200 DA103
Clensham La, Sutt. SM1 . . . 200 DA103
Clenston Ms, W1 . . . 8 C7
★ Cleopatra's Needle, WC2 . . . 20 A1
Clephane Rd, N1 . . . 5 J4
Clere St, EC2 . . . 11 K3
Clerics Wk, Shep. TW17 off Gordon Rd . . . 195 BR100
CLERKENWELL, EC1 . . . 10 E4
Clerkenwell Cl, EC1 . . . 10 D3
Clerkenwell Grn, EC1 . . . 10 D4
Sch Clerkenwell Parochial C of E Prim Sch, EC1 . . . 10 C1
Clerkenwell Rd, EC1 . . . 10 C4
Clerks Cft, Red. (Bletch.) RH1 . . . 252 DR133
Clerks Piece, Loug. IG10 . . . 85 EM41
Clermont Rd, E9 . . . 142 DW67
Clevedon, Wey. KT13 . . . 213 BQ106
Clevedon Cl, N16 off Smalley Cl . . . 122 DT62
Clevedon Gdns, Hayes UB3 . . . 155 BR76
Hounslow TW5 . . . 155 BV81
Clevedon Rd, SE20 . . . 203 DX95
Kingston upon Thames KT1 . . . 198 CN96
Twickenham TW1 . . . 177 CK86
Clevehurst Cl, Slou. (Stoke P.) SL2 . . . 132 AT65
Cleveland Av, SW20 . . . 199 CZ96
W4 . . . 159 CT77
Hampton TW12 . . . 176 BZ94
Cleveland Cl, H.Wyc. (Woob.Grn) HP10 off Wootton Dr . . . 110 AE55
Walton-on-Thames KT12 . . . 195 BV104
Cleveland Cres, Borwd. WD6 . . . 78 CQ43
Cleveland Dr, Stai. TW18 . . . 194 BH96
Cleveland Gdns, N4 . . . 122 DQ57
NW2 . . . 119 CX61
SW13 . . . 159 CT82
W2 . . . 7 L8
Worcester Park KT4 . . . 198 CS103
Cleveland Gro, E1 . . . 12 E4
Sch Cleveland Inf Sch, Ilf. IG1 off Cleveland Rd . . . 125 EP63
Sch Cleveland Jun Sch, Ilf. IG1 off Cleveland Rd . . . 125 EP63
Cleveland Ms, W1 . . . 9 J5
Cleveland Pk, Stai. TW19 . . . 174 BL86
Cleveland Pk Av, E17 . . . 123 EA56
Cleveland Pk Cres, E17 . . . 123 EA56
Cleveland Pl, SW1 . . . 19 K1
Cleveland Ri, Mord. SM4 . . . 199 CX101
Cleveland Rd, E18 . . . 124 EG55
N1 . . . 5 K6
N9 . . . 100 DV45
SW13 . . . 159 CT82
W4 off Antrobus Rd . . . 158 CQ76
W13 . . . 137 CH71
Hemel Hempstead HP2 . . . 41 BP18
Ilford IG1 . . . 125 EP62
Isleworth TW7 . . . 157 CG84
New Malden KT3 . . . 198 CS98
Uxbridge UB8 . . . 134 BK68
Welling DA16 . . . 165 ET82
Worcester Park KT4 . . . 198 CS103
Cleveland Row, SW1 . . . 19 J2
Cleveland Sq, W2 . . . 7 L8
Cleveland St, W1 . . . 9 J4
Cleveland Ter, W2 . . . 7 M7
Cleveland Way, E1 . . . 12 E4
Hemel Hempstead HP2 . . . 41 BP18
Cleveley Cl, SE7 . . . 164 EK77
Cleveley Cres, W5 . . . 138 CL68
Cleveleys Rd, E5 . . . 122 DV62
Cleverly Est, W12 . . . 139 CU74
Cleve Rd, NW6 . . . 140 DA66
Sidcup DA14 . . . 186 EX90
Cleves Av, Brwd. CM14 . . . 108 FV46
Epsom KT17 . . . 217 CV109
Cleves Cl, Cob. KT11 . . . 213 BV114
Loughton IG10 . . . 84 EL44
Cleves Ct, Wind. SL4 . . . 151 AM83
Cleves Cres, Croy. (New Adgtn) CR0 . . . 221 EC111
Cleves Rd, E6 . . . 144 EK67
Hemel Hempstead HP2 . . . 41 BP15
Richmond TW10 . . . 177 CJ90
Sch Cleves Sch, E6 off Arragon Rd . . . 144 EK67
Weybridge KT13 off Oatlands Av . . . 213 BT105
Cleves Wk, Ilf. IG6 . . . 103 EQ52
Cleves Way, Hmptn. TW12 . . . 176 BZ94
Ruislip HA4 . . . 116 BX60
Sunbury-on-Thames TW16 . . . 175 BT93
Cleves Wd, Wey. KT13 . . . 213 BS105
Clewer Av, Wind. SL4 . . . 151 AN82
Clewer Ct Rd, Wind. SL4 . . . 151 AP80
Clewer Cres, Har. HA3 . . . 95 CD53
Clewer Flds, Wind. SL4 . . . 151 AQ81
CLEWER GREEN, Wind. SL4 . . . 151 AM82
Sch Clewer Grn C of E First Sch, Wind. SL4 off Hatch La . . . 151 AN83
Clewer Hill Rd, Wind. SL4 . . . 151 AL82
Clewer Ho, SE2 off Wolvercote Rd . . . 166 EX75
CLEWER NEW TOWN, Wind. SL4 . . . 151 AN82
Clewer New Town, Wind. SL4 . . . 151 AN82
Clewer Pk, Wind. SL4 . . . 151 AN80
CLEWER VILLAGE, Wind. SL4 . . . 151 AM80
Clichy Est, E1 . . . 12 F6
Clifden Rd, E5 . . . 122 DW64
Brentford TW8 . . . 157 CK79
Twickenham TW1 . . . 177 CF88
Cliff End, Pur. CR8 . . . 219 DP112
Cliffe Rd, S.Croy. CR2 . . . 220 DR106
Cliffe Wk, Sutt. SM1 off Turnpike La . . . 218 DC106
Clifford Av, SW14 . . . 158 CP83
Chislehurst BR7 . . . 185 EM93
Ilford IG5 . . . 103 EP53
Wallington SM6 . . . 219 DJ105
Clifford Cl, Nthlt. UB5 . . . 136 BY67
Clifford Dr, SW9 . . . 161 DP84
Clifford Gdns, NW10 . . . 139 CW68
Hayes UB3 . . . 155 BR77
Clifford Gro, Ashf. TW15 . . . 174 BN91
Clifford Manor Rd, Guil. GU4 . . . 258 AY138
Clifford Rd, E16 . . . 15 J4
E17 . . . 101 EC54
N9 . . . 82 DW44
SE25 . . . 202 DU98
Barnet EN5 . . . 80 DB41
Grays (Chaff.Hun.) RM16 . . . 170 FZ75
Hounslow TW4 . . . 156 BX83
Richmond TW10 . . . 177 CK89
Wembley HA0 . . . 137 CK67
Clifford's Inn Pas, EC4 . . . 10 C8
Clifford St, W1 . . . 9 J10
Clifford Way, NW10 . . . 119 CT63
Cliff Pl, S.Ock. RM15 . . . 149 FX69
Cliff Reach, Green. (Bluewater) DA9 . . . 189 FS87
Cliff Rd, NW1 . . . 141 DK65
Cliff Ter, SE8 . . . 163 EA82
Cliffview Rd, SE13 . . . 163 EA83
Cliff Vil, NW1 . . . 141 DK65
Cliff Wk, E16 . . . 15 K5
Clifton Av, E17 . . . 123 DX55
N3 . . . 97 CZ53
W12 . . . 139 CT74
Feltham TW13 . . . 176 BW90
Stanmore HA7 . . . 95 CH54
Sutton SM2 . . . 218 DB111
Wembley HA9 . . . 138 CM65
Clifton Cl, Add. KT15 . . . 194 BH103
Caterham CR3 . . . 236 DR123
Horley RH6 . . . 269 DK148
Clifton Cl, Orp. BR6 . . . 223 EQ106
Waltham Cross (Chsht) EN8 off Maxwell Rd . . . 67 DY29
Clifton Ct, N4 off Biggerstaff St . . . 121 DN61
NW8 . . . 7 N3
Woodford Green IG8 off Snakes La W . . . 102 EG51
Clifton Cres, SE15 . . . 162 DV80
Clifton Est, SE15 off Consort Rd . . . 162 DV81
Clifton Gdns, N15 . . . 122 DT58
NW11 . . . 119 CZ58
W4 off Dolman Rd . . . 158 CR77
W9 . . . 7 L4
Enfield EN2 . . . 81 DL42
Uxbridge UB10 . . . 135 BP68
Clifton Gro, E8 . . . 142 DU65
Gravesend DA11 . . . 191 GH87
Clifton Hatch, Harl. CM18 off Trotters Rd . . . 52 EU18
Clifton Hill, NW8 . . . 140 DB68
Sch Clifton Hill Sch, Cat. CR3 off Chaldon Rd . . . 236 DR123
Clifton Lawns, Amer. HP6 . . . 55 AQ35
Sch Clifton Lo Boys' Prep Sch, W5 off Florence Rd . . . 138 CL73
Clifton Marine Par, Grav. DA11 . . . 191 GF86
Clifton Pk Av, SW20 . . . 199 CW96
Clifton Pl, SE16 . . . 22 F3
W2 . . . 7 P9
Banstead SM7 off Court Rd . . . 234 DA116
Sch Clifton Prim Sch, Sthl. UB2 off Talbot Rd . . . 156 BY77
Clifton Ri, SE14 . . . 163 DY80
Windsor SL4 . . . 151 AK81
Clifton Rd, E7 . . . 144 EK65
E16 . . . 15 H5
N1 . . . 5 H4
N3 . . . 98 DC53
N8 . . . 121 DK58
N22 . . . 99 DJ53
NW10 . . . 139 CU68
SE25 . . . 202 DS98
SW19 . . . 179 CX93
W9 . . . 7 M3
Amersham HP6 . . . 55 AP35
Coulsdon CR5 . . . 235 DH115
Gravesend DA11 . . . 191 GG86
Greenford UB6 . . . 136 CC70
Harrow HA3 . . . 118 CM57
Hornchurch RM11 . . . 127 FG58
Hounslow (Hthrw Air.) TW6 off Inner Ring E . . . 155 BP83
Ilford IG2 . . . 125 ER58
Isleworth TW7 . . . 157 CD82
Kingston upon Thames KT2 . . . 178 CM94
Loughton IG10 . . . 84 EL42
Sidcup DA14 . . . 185 ES91
Slough SL1 . . . 152 AV75
Southall UB2 . . . 156 BY77
Teddington TW11 . . . 177 CE91
Wallington SM6 . . . 219 DH106
Watford WD18 . . . 75 BV43
Welling DA16 . . . 166 EW83
Cliftons La, Reig. RH2 . . . 249 CX131
Clifton St, EC2 . . . 11 L5
St. Albans AL1 . . . 43 CE19
Clifton Ter, N4 . . . 121 DN61
Clifton Vil, W9 . . . 7 K5
Cliftonville, Dor. RH4 . . . 263 CH137
Clifton Wk, E6 . . . 144 EL72
W6 off Galena Rd . . . 159 CV77
Dartford DA2 off Osbourne Rd . . . 188 FP86
Clifton Way, SE15 . . . 162 DV80
Borehamwood WD6 . . . 78 CN39
Brentwood (Hutt.) CM13 . . . 109 GD46
Wembley HA0 . . . 138 CL67
Woking GU21 . . . 226 AT117
Climb, The, Rick. WD3 . . . 74 BH44
Clinch Ct, E16 . . . 15 M6
Cline Rd, N11 . . . 99 DJ51
Guildford GU1 . . . 259 AZ136
Clinger Ct, N1 . . . 5 L8
★ Clink Prison Mus, SE1 . . . 21 J1
Clink St, SE1 . . . 21 H1
Clinton Av, E.Mol. KT8 . . . 196 CC98
Welling DA16 . . . 165 ET84
Clinton Cl, Wey. KT13 . . . 195 BP104
Clinton Cres, Ilf. IG6 . . . 103 ES51
Clinton End, Hem.H. HP2 . . . 41 BQ20
Clinton Rd, E3 . . . 13 J2
E7 . . . 124 EG63
N15 . . . 122 DR56
Leatherhead KT22 . . . 231 CJ123
Clinton Ter, Sutt. SM1 off Manor La . . . 218 DC105
Clipper Boul, Dart. DA2 . . . 169 FS83
Clipper Boul W, Dart. DA2 . . . 169 FR83
Clipper Cl, SE16 . . . 22 G3
Clipper Cres, Grav. DA12 . . . 191 GM91
Clipper Way, SE13 . . . 163 EC84
Clippesby Cl, Chess. KT9 . . . 216 CM108
Clipstone Ms, W1 . . . 9 J4
Clipstone Rd, Houns. TW3 . . . 156 CA83
Clipstone St, W1 . . . 9 H5
Clissold Cl, N2 . . . 120 DF55
Clissold Ct, N4 . . . 122 DQ61
Clissold Cres, N16 . . . 122 DR62
Clissold Rd, N16 . . . 122 DR62
Clitheroe Av, Har. HA2 . . . 116 CA60
Clitheroe Gdns, Wat. WD19 . . . 94 BX48
Clitheroe Rd, SW9 . . . 161 DL82
Romford RM5 . . . 105 FC50
Clitherow Av, W7 . . . 157 CG76
Clitherow Pas, Brent. TW8 . . . 157 CJ78
Clitherow Rd, Brent. TW8 . . . 157 CJ78
Clitterhouse Cres, NW2 . . . 119 CW60
Sch Clitterhouse Inf Sch, NW2 off Claremont Rd . . . 119 CX61
Sch Clitterhouse Jun Sch, NW2 off Claremont Rd . . . 119 CX61
Clitterhouse Rd, NW2 . . . 119 CW60
Clive Av, N18 off Claremont St . . . 100 DU51
Dartford DA1 . . . 187 FF86
Clive Cl, Pot.B. EN6 . . . 63 CZ31
Clive Ct, W9 . . . 7 M3
Slough SL1 . . . 151 AR75
★ Cliveden, Maid. SL6 . . . 110 AD64
Cliveden Cl, N12 off Woodside Av . . . 98 DC49
Brentwood (Shenf.) CM15 . . . 109 FZ45
Cliveden Pl, SW1 . . . 18 E7
Shepperton TW17 . . . 195 BP100
Cliveden Rd, SW19 . . . 199 CZ95
Maidenhead (Taplow) SL6 . . . 130 AE65
Slough (Burn.) SL1 . . . 130 AE65
Clivedon Ct, W13 . . . 137 CH71
Clivedon Rd, E4 . . . 102 EE50
Clive Par, Nthwd. HA6 off Maxwell Rd . . . 93 BS52
Clive Pas, SE21 off Clive Rd . . . 182 DR90
Clive Rd, SE21 . . . 182 DR90
SW19 . . . 180 DE93
Belvedere DA17 . . . 166 FA77
Brentwood CM13 . . . 107 FW52
Enfield EN1 . . . 82 DU42
Esher KT10 . . . 214 CB105
Feltham TW14 . . . 175 BU86
Gravesend DA11 . . . 191 GH86
Romford RM2 . . . 127 FH57
Twickenham TW1 . . . 177 CF91
Clivesdale Dr, Hayes UB3 . . . 135 BV74
Clive Way, Enf. EN1 . . . 82 DU42
Watford WD24 . . . 76 BW39
Cloak La, EC4 . . . 11 H9
⇌ Clock House . . . 203 DY96
Clockhouse Av, Bark. IG11 . . . 145 EQ67
Clockhouse Cl, SW19 . . . 179 CW90
Clock Ho Cl, W.Byf. (Byfleet) KT14 . . . 212 BM112
Sch Clockhouse Inf Sch, Rom. RM5 off Clockhouse La . . . 105 FB52
Sch Clockhouse Jun Sch, Rom. RM5 off Clockhouse La . . . 105 FB51
Clockhouse La, Ashf. TW15 . . . 174 BN91
Feltham TW14 . . . 175 BP89
Grays RM16 . . . 149 FX74
Romford RM5 . . . 105 FB52
Clock Ho La, Sev. TN13 . . . 256 FG123
Clockhouse La E, Egh. TW20 . . . 173 BB94
Clockhouse La W, Egh. TW20 . . . 173 BA94
Clock Ho Mead, Lthd. (Oxshott) KT22 . . . 214 CB114
Clockhouse Ms, Rick. (Chorl.) WD3 off Chorleywood Ho Dr . . . 73 BE41
Clockhouse Pl, SW15 . . . 179 CY85
Feltham TW14 . . . 175 BQ88
Clock Ho Rd, Beck. BR3 . . . 203 DY97
Clockhouse Roundabout, Felt. TW14 . . . 175 BP88
★ Clockmakers Company Collection, The, Guildhall Lib, EC2 . . . 11 H7
Clock Twr Ms, N1 . . . 5 H8
SE28 . . . 146 EV73
Clock Twr Pl, N7 . . . 141 DL65
Clock Twr Rd, Islw. TW7 . . . 157 CF83
Cloister Cl, Rain. RM13 . . . 147 FH70
Teddington TW11 . . . 177 CH92
Cloister Gdns, SE25 . . . 202 DV100
Edgware HA8 . . . 96 CQ50
Cloister Garth, Berk. HP4 . . . 38 AW19
St. Albans AL1 . . . 43 CE24
Cloister Rd, NW2 . . . 119 CZ62
W3 . . . 138 CQ71
Cloisters, The, Bushey WD23 . . . 76 CB44
Rickmansworth WD3 . . . 92 BL45
Welwyn Garden City AL8 . . . 29 CX09
Woking GU22 . . . 227 BB121
Cloisters Av, Brom. BR2 . . . 205 EM99
Cloisters Business Cen, SW8 off Battersea Pk Rd . . . 161 DH80
Cloisters Mall, Kings.T. KT1 off Union St . . . 197 CK96
Cloister Wk, Hem.H. HP2 off Townsend . . . 40 BK18
Clonard Way, Pnr. HA5 . . . 94 CA51
Clonbrock Rd, N16 . . . 122 DS63
Cloncurry St, SW6 . . . 159 CX82
Clonmel Cl, Har. HA2 . . . 117 CD60
Clonmell Rd, N17 . . . 122 DR55
Clonmel Rd, SW6 . . . 159 CZ80
Teddington TW11 . . . 177 CD91
Clonmel Way, Slou. (Burn.) SL1 . . . 130 AH69
Clonmore St, SW18 . . . 179 CZ88
Cloonmore Av, Orp. BR6 . . . 223 ET105
Clorane Gdns, NW3 . . . 120 DA62
Sch Clore Shalom Sch, Rad. WD7 off Hugo Gryn Way . . . 62 CL30
Sch Clore Tikva Prim Sch, Ilf. IG6 off Fullwell Av . . . 103 EQ54
Close, The, E4 off Beech Hall Rd . . . 101 EC52
N14 . . . 99 DK47
N20 . . . 97 CZ47
SE3 off Heath La . . . 163 ED82
Barnet EN4 . . . 80 DF44
Beckenham BR3 . . . 203 DY98
Betchworth (Strood Grn) RH3 . . . 264 CP138
Bexley DA5 . . . 186 FA86
Brentwood CM14 . . . 108 FW48
Bushey WD23 . . . 76 CB43
Carshalton SM5 . . . 218 DE109
Dartford DA2 . . . 188 FJ90
Grays RM16 . . . 170 GC75
Guildford (Won.) GU5 . . . 259 BB144
Harrow HA2 . . . 94 CC54
Hatfield AL9 . . . 63 CY26
Horley RH6 . . . 269 DJ150
Isleworth TW7 . . . 157 CD82
Iver SL0 . . . 133 BC69
Mitcham CR4 . . . 200 DF98
New Malden KT3 . . . 198 CQ96
Orpington BR5 . . . 205 ES100
Pinner (Eastcote) HA5 . . . 116 BW59
Pinner (Rayners La) HA5 . . . 116 BZ59
Potters Bar EN6 . . . 64 DA32
Purley (Pampisford Rd) CR8 . . . 219 DP110
Purley (Russ.Hill) CR8 . . . 219 DM110
Radlett WD7 . . . 61 CF33
Reigate RH2 . . . 266 DB135
Richmond TW9 . . . 158 CP83
Rickmansworth WD3 . . . 92 BJ46
Romford RM6 . . . 126 EY58
Sevenoaks TN13 . . . 256 FE124
Sidcup DA14 . . . 186 EV92
Slough SL1 off St. George's Cres . . . 131 AK73
Sutton SM3 . . . 199 CZ101
Uxbridge UB10 . . . 134 BL66
Uxbridge (Hlgdn) UB10 . . . 134 BN67
Virginia Water GU25 . . . 192 AW99
Ware SG12 . . . 33 DY06
Wembley (Barnhill Rd) HA9 . . . 118 CQ62
Wembley (Lyon Pk Av) HA0 . . . 138 CL65
West Byfleet KT14 . . . 212 BG113
Westerham (Berry's Grn) TN16 . . . 239 EP116
Closemead Cl, Nthwd. HA6 . . . 93 BQ51
Cloth Ct, EC1 . . . 10 F6
Cloth Fair, EC1 . . . 10 F6
Clothier St, E1 . . . 11 M7
Cloth St, EC1 . . . 10 G5
Clothworkers Rd, SE18 . . . 165 ER80

★ Place of interest | H Hospital | Sch School | Coll College | Uni University | ⇌ Railway station

Cloudberry Rd, Rom. RM3 . . 106 FK51
Cloudesdale Rd, SW17 . . . . 181 DH89
Cloudesley Pl, N1 . . . . 4 C8
Cloudesley Rd, N1 . . . . 4 C7
Bexleyheath DA7 . . . . 166 EZ81
Erith DA8 . . . . 167 FF81
Cloudesley Sq, N1 . . . . 4 C8
Cloudesley St, N1 . . . . 4 D8
Clouston Cl, Wall. SM6 . . . . 219 DL106
Clova Rd, E7 . . . . 144 EF65
Clove Cres, E14 . . . . 14 D9
Clove Hitch Quay, SW11 . . . 160 DC83
Clovelly Av, NW9 . . . . 119 CT56
Uxbridge UB10 . . . . 115 BQ63
Warlingham CR6 . . . . 236 DV118
Clovelly Cl, Pnr. HA5 . . . . 115 BV55
Uxbridge UB10 . . . . 115 BQ63
Clovelly Ct, Horn. RM11 . . . 128 FN61
Clovelly Gdns, SE19 . . . . 202 DT95
Enfield EN1 . . . . 100 DS45
Romford RM7 . . . . 105 FB53
Clovelly Rd, N8 . . . . 121 DK56
W4 . . . . 158 CQ75
W5 . . . . 157 CJ75
Bexleyheath DA7 . . . . 166 EY79
Hounslow TW3 . . . . 156 CA82
Clovelly Way, E1 . . . . 12 F7
Harrow HA2 . . . . 116 BZ61
Orpington BR6 . . . . 205 ET100
Clover Cl, E11
off Norman Rd 123 ED61
Clover Ct, Grays RM17
off Churchill Rd 170 GD79
Woking GU22 . . . . 226 AX118
Cloverdale Gdns, Sid. DA15 . 185 ET86
Clover Fld, Harl. CM18 . . . . 52 EU18
Cloverfield, Welw.G.C. AL7 . . 29 CZ06
Clover Fld, The, Bushey
WD23 . . . . 76 BZ44
Cloverfields, Horl. RH6 . . . 269 DH147
Clover Hill, Couls. CR5 . . . 235 DH121
Cloverland, Hat. AL10 . . . . 45 CT21
Clover Lea, Gdmg. GU7 . . . 258 AS143
Clover Leas, Epp. CM16 . . . . 69 ET30
Cloverleys, Loug. IG10 . . . . 84 EK43
Clover Ms, SW3 off Dilke St . 160 DF79
Clover Rd, Guil. GU2 . . . . 242 AS132
Clovers, The, Grav. (Nthflt)
DA11 . . . . 190 GE91
Clover Way, Hat. AL9 . . . . 45 CT15
Hemel Hempstead HP1 . . 40 BH19
Wallington SM6 . . . . 200 DG102
Clove St, E13 . . . . 15 L4
Clowders Rd, SE6 . . . . 183 DZ90
Clowser Cl, Sutt. SM1
off Turnpike La 218 DC106
Cloysters Grn, E1 . . . . 22 A1
Cloyster Wd, Edg. HA8 . . . . 95 CK52
Club Gdns Rd, Brom. BR2 . . 204 EG101
Club Row, E1 . . . . 11 N3
E2 . . . . 11 N3
Clump, The, Rick. WD3 . . . . 74 BG43
Clump Av, Tad. (Box H.)
KT20 . . . . 248 CQ131
Clumps, The, Ashf. TW15 . . . 175 BR91
Clunas Gdns, Rom. RM2 . . . 128 FK55
Clunbury Av, Sthl. UB2 . . . 156 BZ78
Clunbury St, N1 . . . . 5 K10
Cluny Est, SE1 . . . . 21 L5
Cluny Ms, SW5 . . . . 16 G8
Cluny Pl, SE1 . . . . 21 L5
Cluse Ct, N1 . . . . 4 G9
Clutterbucks, Rick. (Sarratt)
WD3 . . . . 74 BG36
Clutton St, E14 . . . . 14 B6
Clydach Rd, Enf. EN1 . . . . 82 DT42
Clyde Av, S.Croy. CR2 . . . 236 DV115
Clyde Circ, N15 . . . . 122 DS56
Clyde Cl, Red. RH1 . . . . 250 DG133
Clyde Ct, Red. RH1
off Clyde Cl 250 DG133
Clyde Cres, Upmin. RM14 . . 129 FS58
Clyde Pl, E10 . . . . 123 EB59
Clyde Rd, N15 . . . . 122 DS56
N22 . . . . 99 DK53
Croydon CR0 . . . . 202 DT102
Hoddesdon EN11 . . . . 49 ED19
Staines (Stanw.) TW19 . . . 174 BK88
Sutton SM1 . . . . 218 DA106
Wallington SM6 . . . . 219 DJ106
Clydesdale, Enf. EN3 . . . . 83 DX42
Clydesdale Av, Stan. HA7 . . 117 CK55
Clydesdale Cl, Borwd. WD6 . . 78 CR43
Isleworth TW7 . . . . 157 CF83
Clydesdale Gdns, Rich.
TW10 . . . . 158 CP84
Clydesdale Ho, Erith DA18
off Kale Rd 166 EY75
Clydesdale Rd, W11 . . . . 6 F7
Hornchurch RM11 . . . . 127 FF59
Clydesdale Wk, Brox. EN10
off Tarpan Way 67 DZ25
Clyde Sq, Hem.H. HP2 . . . . 40 BM15
Clyde St, SE8 . . . . 163 DZ79
Clyde Ter, SE23 . . . . 182 DW89
Hertford SG13 . . . . 32 DU09
Clyde Vale, SE23 . . . . 182 DW89
Clyde Way, Rom. RM1 . . . . 105 FE53
Clydon Cl, Erith DA8 . . . . 167 FE79
Clyfford Rd, Ruis. HA4 . . . . 115 BT63
Clyfton Cl, Brox. EN10 . . . . 49 DZ23
Clymping Dene, Felt. TW14 . 175 BV87
Clyston Rd, Wat. WD18 . . . . 75 BT44
Clyston St, SW8 . . . . 161 DJ82
Clyve Way, Stai. TW18 . . . 193 BE95
Coach All, H.Wyc.
(Woob.Grn) HP10 . . . . 110 AF60
Coach & Horses Yd, W1 . . . . 9 H9
Coach Ho La, N5
off Highbury Hill 121 DP63
SW19 . . . . 179 CX91
Coach Ho Ms, SE1 . . . . 21 L5
SE14 off Waller Rd 163 DX82
Coachhouse Ms, SE20 . . . . 182 DV94
Coach Ho Ms, SE23 . . . . 183 DX86
Redhill RH1 off Mill St . . 266 DF135
Coach Ho Yd, SW18
off Ebner St 160 DB84
Coachlads Av, Guil. GU2 . . 242 AT134
Coachmaker Ms, SW4
off Fenwick Pl 161 DL83
Coach Rd, Bet. (Brock.) RH3 . 248 CL134
Chertsey (Ott.) KT16 . . . 211 BC107
Coach Yd Ms, N19
off Trinder Rd 121 DL60
Coal Ct, Grays RM17
off Columbia Wf Rd . . . 170 GA79
Coaldale Wk, SE21
off Lairdale Cl 182 DQ87
Coalecroft Rd, SW15 . . . . 159 CW84
Coalmans Way, Slou. (Burn.)
SL1 . . . . 130 AH72
Coalport Cl, Harl. CM17 . . . 52 EW16
Coal Rd, Til. RM18 . . . . 171 GL77
Coal Wf Rd, W12 . . . . 16 A2
Coast Hill, Dor. (Westc.)
RH4 . . . . 262 BZ139
Coast Hill La, Dor. (Westc.)
RH4 . . . . 262 CA138
Coaters La, H.Wyc. HP10
off Glory Mill La 110 AE56
Coates Av, SW18 . . . . 180 DE86
Coates Dell, Wat. WD25 . . . 60 BY33
Coates Hill Rd, Brom. BR1 . 205 EN96
Coates Rd, Borwd. (Elstree)
WD6 . . . . 95 CK45
Coate St, E2 . . . . 142 DU68
Coates Wk, Brent. TW8 . . . 158 CL78
Coates Way, Wat. WD25 . . . 60 BX33
Sch Coates Way JMI &
Nurs Sch, Wat. WD25
off Coates Way 60 BY33
Coat Wicks, Beac. (Seer Grn)
HP9 . . . . 89 AQ51
Cobb Cl, Borwd. WD6 . . . . 78 CQ43
Slough (Datchet) SL3 . . . 152 AX81
Cobbett Cl, Enf. EN3 . . . . 82 DW36
Cobbett Rd, SE9 . . . . 164 EL83
Guildford GU2 . . . . 242 AS133
Twickenham TW2 . . . . 176 CA88
Cobbetts Av, Ilf. IG4 . . . . 124 EK57
Cobbetts Cl, Wok. GU21 . . . 226 AV117
Cobbetts Hill, Wey. KT13 . . 213 BP107
Cobbett St, SW8 . . . . 161 DM80
Cobb Grn, Wat. WD25 . . . . 59 BV32
Cobbins, The, Wal.Abb. EN9 . 68 EE33
Cobbinsend Rd, Wal.Abb.
EN9 . . . . 68 EK29
Cobbins Way, Harl. CM17 . . . 36 EY11
Cobble La, N1 . . . . 4 E5
Cobble Ms, N5 . . . . 122 DQ62
Cobblers Cl, Slou.
(Farn.Royal) SL2 . . . . 131 AP68
Cobblers Wk, E.Mol. KT8 . . 197 CG95
Hampton TW12 . . . . 176 CC94
Kingston upon Thames
KT2 . . . . 197 CG95
Teddington TW11 . . . . 197 CG95
Cobbles, The, Brwd. CM15 . 108 FY47
Upminster RM14 . . . . 129 FT59
Cobblestone Pl, Croy. CR0
off Oakfield Rd 202 DQ102
Cobbold Est, NW10 . . . . 139 CT65
Cobbold Ms, W12
off Cobbold Rd 159 CT75
Cobbold Rd, E11 . . . . 124 EF62
NW10 . . . . 139 CT65
W12 . . . . 158 CS75
Cobb Rd, Berk. HP4 . . . . 38 AT19
Cobb's Ct, EC4
off Ludgate Hill 141 DP72
Cobb's Rd, Houns. TW4 . . . 156 BZ84
Cobb St, E1 . . . . 11 N6
Cobden Cl, Uxb. UB8 . . . . 134 BJ67
Cobden Hill, Rad. WD7 . . . . 77 CH36
Cobden Rd, E11 . . . . 124 EE62
SE25 . . . . 202 DU99
Orpington BR6 . . . . 223 ER105
Sevenoaks TN13 . . . . 257 FJ123
COBHAM, KT11 . . . . 229 BV115
Cobham, Grays RM16 . . . . 170 GB75
Coll Cobham Adult Ed Cen,
Cob. KT11 off Cedar Rd . 213 BV114
⇌ Cobham & Stoke
D'Abernon 230 BY117
Cobham Av, N.Mal. KT3 . . . 199 CU99
★ Cobham Bus Mus, Cob.
KT11 . . . . 213 BQ112
Cobham Cl, SW11 . . . . 180 DE86
Bromley BR2 . . . . 204 EL101
Edgware HA8 . . . . 96 CP54
Enfield EN1 . . . . 82 DU41
Greenhithe DA9 . . . . 189 FV86
Sidcup DA15
off Park Mead 186 EV86
Slough SL1 . . . . 151 AM75
Wallington SM6 . . . . 219 DL107
Cobham Gate, Cob. KT11 . . 213 BV114
H Cobham Hosp, Cob.
KT11 . . . . 213 BV113
Cobham Ho, Bark. IG11
off St. Margarets 145 EQ67
Erith DA8 off Boundary St . 167 FF80
Cobham Ms, NW1
off Agar Gro 141 DK66
Cobham Pk, Cob. KT11
off Downside Rd 229 BV116
Cobham Pk Rd, Cob. KT11 . . 229 BV117
Cobham Pl, Bexh. DA6 . . . . 186 EX85
Cobham Rd, E17 . . . . 101 EC53
N22 . . . . 121 DP55
Cobham (Stoke D'Ab.)
KT11 . . . . 230 CA118
Hounslow TW5 . . . . 156 BW80
Ilford IG3 . . . . 125 ES61
Kingston upon Thames
KT1 . . . . 198 CN95
Leatherhead (Fetch.) KT22 . 231 CE122
Ware SG12 . . . . 33 DZ05
Cobham St, Grav. DA11 . . . 191 GG87
Cobham Ter, Green. DA9
off Bean Rd 189 FV85
Cobham Way, Lthd. (E.Hors.)
KT24 . . . . 245 BS126
Cobill Cl, Horn. RM11 . . . . 128 FJ56
Cobland Rd, SE12 . . . . 184 EJ91
Cob Mead, Hat. AL10 . . . . 45 CV16
Coborn Rd, E3 . . . . 143 DZ69
Coborn St, E3 . . . . 13 M1
Sch Cobourg Prim Sch, SE5
off Cobourg Rd 162 DT79
Cobourg Rd, SE5 . . . . 162 DT79
Cobourg St, NW1 . . . . 9 K2
Cobsdene, Grav. DA12 . . . . 191 GK93
Cobs Way, Add. (New Haw)
KT15 . . . . 212 BJ110
Coburg Cl, SW1 . . . . 19 K7
Coburg Cres, SW2 . . . . 181 DM88
Coburg Gdns, Ilf. IG5 . . . . 102 EK54
Coburg Rd, N22 . . . . 121 DM55
Cochrane Ms, NW8
off Circus Rd 140 DD68
Cochrane Rd, SW19 . . . . 179 CZ94
Cochrane St, NW8 . . . . 140 DD68
Cockayne Way, SE8 . . . . 23 K9
Cockbush Av, Hert. SG13 . . . 32 DU08
Cockerell Rd, E17 . . . . 123 DY59
Cockerhurst Rd, Sev.
(Shore.) TN14 . . . . 225 FD107
Cocker Rd, Enf. EN1 . . . . 82 DV36
Cockett Rd, Slou. SL3 . . . . 152 AY76
COCKFOSTERS, Barn. EN4 . . 80 DE42
⊖ Cockfosters 80 DG42
Cockfosters Par, Barn. EN4
off Cockfosters Rd 80 DG42
Cockfosters Rd, Barn. EN4 . . 80 DF40
Cock Grn, Harl. CM19 . . . . 51 EP17
Cock Hill, E1 . . . . 11 M6
Cock La, EC1 . . . . 10 E6
Broxbourne EN10 . . . . 48 DU20
Cock La, Hodd. EN11 . . . . 49 DY19
Leatherhead (Fetch.)
KT22 . . . . 230 CC122
Cockle Way, Rad. (Shenley)
WD7 . . . . 62 CL33
Cockmannings La, Orp. BR5 . 206 EX102
Cockmannings Rd, Orp. BR5 . 206 EX101
Cockpit Steps, SW1 . . . . 19 M4
Cockpit Yd, WC1 . . . . 10 B5
Cockrobin La, Harl. CM20 . . . 35 EN08
Ware SG12 . . . . 35 EN05
Cocks Cres, N.Mal. KT3 . . . 199 CT98
Cocksett Av, Orp. BR6 . . . . 223 ES107
Cockshot Hill, Reig. RH2 . . 266 DB136
Cockshot Rd, Reig. RH2 . . . 266 DB135
Cockspur Ct, SW1 . . . . 19 M1
Cockspur St, SW1 . . . . 19 M1
Cocksure La, Sid. DA14 . . . 186 FA90
Cock's Yd, Uxb. UB8
off Bakers Rd 134 BJ66
Coda Cen, The, SW6 . . . . 159 CY81
Code St, E1 . . . . 11 P4
Codham Hall La, Brwd.
(Gt Warley) CM13 . . . . 129 FV56
Codicote Dr, Wat. WD25 . . . 60 BX34
Codicote Rd, St.Alb.
(Wheat.) AL4 . . . . 28 CL05
Welwyn AL6 . . . . 28 CL05
Codicote Ter, N4
off Green Las 122 DQ61
Codling Cl, E1 . . . . 22 B1
Codling Way, Wem. HA0 . . . 117 CK63
CODMORE, Chesh. HP5 . . . . 54 AS29
Codmore Cres, Chesh. HP5 . . 54 AS30
Codmore Wd Rd, Chesh.
HP5 . . . . 56 AW33
Codrington Ct, Wok. GU21
off Raglan Rd 226 AS118
Codrington Cres, Grav.
DA12 . . . . 191 GJ92
Codrington Gdns, Grav.
DA12 . . . . 191 GK92
Codrington Hill, SE23 . . . . 183 DY87
Codrington Ms, W11 . . . . 6 D8
Cody Cl, Har. HA3 . . . . 117 CK55
Wallington SM6
off Alcock Cl 219 DK108
Cody Rd, E16 . . . . 14 F4
Cody Rd Business Cen, E16 . . 14 F4
Coe Av, SE25 . . . . 202 DU100
Coe's All, Barn. EN5
off Wood St 79 CY42
Coe Spur, Slou. SL1 . . . . 151 AP75
Coftards, Slou. SL2 . . . . 132 AW72
Cogan Av, E17 . . . . 101 DY53
Cohen Cl, Wal.Cr. EN8 . . . . 67 DY31
Coin St, SE1 . . . . 20 C1
Coity Rd, NW5 . . . . 140 DG65
Cokers La, SE21
off Perifield 182 DR88
Coke's Fm La, Ch.St.G. HP8 . 72 AV41
Coke's La, Amer. HP7 . . . . 72 AW41
Chalfont St. Giles HP8 . . . 72 AU42
Coke St, E1 . . . . 12 A7
Colas Ms, NW6
off Birchington Rd 140 DA67
Colbeck Ms, SW7 . . . . 17 K8
Colbeck Rd, Har. HA1 . . . . 116 CC59
Colberg Pl, N16 . . . . 122 DS59
Colborne Way, Wor.Pk. KT4 . 199 CW104
Colbrook Av, Hayes UB3 . . . 155 BR76
Colbrook Cl, Hayes UB3 . . . 155 BR76
Colburn Av, Cat. CR3 . . . . 236 DT124
Pinner HA5 . . . . 94 BY51
Colburn Cres, Guil. GU4
off Sutherland Dr 243 BA131
Colburn Way, Sutt. SM1 . . . 200 DD104
Colby Ms, SE19
off Gipsy Hill 182 DS92
Colby Rd, SE19 . . . . 182 DS92
Walton-on-Thames KT12
off Winchester Rd 195 BU102
Colchester Av, E12 . . . . 125 EM62
Colchester Dr, Pnr. HA5 . . . 116 BX57
Colchester Rd, E10 . . . . 123 EC59
E17 . . . . 123 EA58
Edgware HA8 . . . . 96 CQ52
Northwood HA6 . . . . 93 BU54
Romford RM3 . . . . 106 FK53
Colchester St, E1 . . . . 11 P7
Colcokes Rd, Bans. SM7 . . . 234 DA116
Cold Arbor Rd, Sev. TN13 . . 256 FD124
Coldbath Sq, EC1 . . . . 10 C3
Coldbath St, SE13 . . . . 163 EB81
COLDBLOW, Bex. DA5 . . . . 187 FC89
Cold Blow Cres, Bex. DA5 . . 187 FD88
Cold Blow La, SE14 . . . . 163 DX80
Cold Blows, Mitch. CR4 . . . 200 DG97
Coldershaw Rd, W13 . . . . 137 CG74
Coldfall Av, N10 . . . . 98 DF54
Sch Coldfall Prim Sch, N10
off Coldfall Av 98 DF54
Coldham Gro, Enf. EN3 . . . . 83 DY37
Cold Harbour, E14 . . . . 24 D2
Coldharbour Cl, Egh. TW20 . 193 BC97
Coldharbour Crest, SE9
off Great Harry Dr 185 EN90
Coldharbour La, SE5 . . . . 161 DN84
SW9 . . . . 161 DN84
Bushey WD23 . . . . 76 CB44
Dorking RH4, RH5 . . . . 263 CG138
Egham TW20 . . . . 193 BC97
Hayes UB3 . . . . 135 BU73
Purley CR8 . . . . 219 DN110
Rainham RM13 . . . . 147 FE72
Redhill (Bletch.) RH1 . . . . 252 DT134
Woking GU22 . . . . 227 BF115
Coldharbour Pinnacles Est,
The, Harl. CM19 . . . . 51 EN16
Coldharbour Pl, SE5
off Denmark Hill 162 DQ82
Coldharbour Rd, Croy. CR0 . 219 DN106
Gravesend (Nthflt) DA11 . 190 GE89
Harlow CM19 . . . . 51 EM16
West Byfleet KT14 . . . . 211 BF114
Woking GU22 . . . . 227 BF115
Coldharbour Way, Croy.
CR0 . . . . 219 DN106
Coldmoreham Yd, Amer.
HP7 . . . . 55 AM39
Coldshott, Oxt. RH8 . . . . 254 EG133
Coldstream Gdns, SW18 . . . 179 CZ86
Coldstream Rd, Cat. CR3 . . 236 DQ121
Cole Av, Grays RM16 . . . . 171 GJ77
Colebeck Ms, N1 . . . . 4 F4
Colebert Av, E1 . . . . 12 E3
Colebrook, Cher. (Ott.) KT16 . 211 BD107
Colebrook Cl, NW7 . . . . 97 CX52
SW15 off West Hill 179 CX87
Colebrooke Av, W13 . . . . 137 CH72
Colebrooke Dr, E11 . . . . 124 EH59
Colebrooke Pl, N1 . . . . 4 F8
Colebrooke Ri, Brom. BR2 . . 204 EE96
Colebrooke Rd, Red. RH1 . . 250 DE132
Colebrooke Row, N1 . . . . 4 E10
Colebrook Gdns, Loug. IG10 . . 85 EP40
Colebrook Ho, E14 . . . . 14 A7
Colebrook La, Loug. IG10 . . . 85 EP40
Colebrook Path, Loug. IG10 . . 85 EP40
Colebrook Pl, Cher. (Ott.)
KT16 . . . . 211 BB108
Colebrook Rd, SW16 . . . . 201 DL95
Colebrook St, Erith DA8 . . . 167 FF79
Colebrook Way, N11 . . . . 99 DH50
Coleby Path, SE5
off Harris St 162 DR80
Cole Cl, SE28 . . . . 146 EV74
Coledale Dr, Stan. HA7 . . . . 95 CJ53
Coleford Rd, SW18 . . . . 180 DC85
Cole Gdns, Houns. TW5 . . . 155 BU80
Sch Colegrave Prim Sch,
E15 off Henniker Rd 123 ED64
Colegrave Rd, E15 . . . . 123 ED64
COLE GREEN, Hert. SG14 . . . 30 DG12
Cole Grn Bypass, Hert. SG14 . 30 DF13
Cole Grn La, Welw.G.C. AL7 . . 30 DB11
Cole Grn Way, Hert. SG14 . . . 31 DK12
Colegrove Rd, SE15 . . . . 162 DT80
Coleherne Ct, SW5 . . . . 17 K10
Coleherne Ms, SW10 . . . . 17 J10
Coleherne Rd, SW10 . . . . 17 J10
Colehill Gdns, SW6
off Fulham Palace Rd . . . 159 CY82
Colehill La, SW6 . . . . 159 CY81
Colekitchen La, Guil.
(Goms.) GU5 . . . . 261 BR136
Coleman Cl, SE25 . . . . 202 DU96
Coleman Flds, N1 . . . . 5 H7
COLEMAN GREEN, St.Alb.
AL4 . . . . 28 CM10
Coleman Grn La, St.Alb.
(Wheat.) AL4 . . . . 28 CM10
Coleman Rd, SE5 . . . . 162 DS80
Belvedere DA17 . . . . 166 FA77
Dagenham RM9 . . . . 146 EY65
Colemans Heath, SE9 . . . . 185 EP90
Colemans La, Ong. CM5 . . . . 71 FH30
Coleman's La, Wal.Abb. EN9 . 67 ED26
Coleman St, EC2 . . . . 11 J7
Colenorton Cres, Wind.
(Eton Wick) SL4 . . . . 151 AL77
Colenso Dr, NW7 . . . . 97 CU52
Colenso Rd, E5 . . . . 122 DW63
Ilford IG2 . . . . 125 ES60
Cole Pk Gdns, Twick. TW1 . . 177 CG86
Cole Pk Rd, Twick. TW1 . . . 177 CG86
Cole Pk Vw, Twick. TW1
off Hill Vw Rd 177 CG86
Colepits Wd Rd, SE9 . . . . 185 EQ85
Sch Coleraine Pk Prim Sch,
N17 off Glendish Rd 100 DV53
Coleraine Rd, N8 . . . . 121 DN55
SE3 . . . . 164 EF79
Coleridge Av, E12 . . . . 144 EL65
Sutton SM1 . . . . 218 DE105
Coleridge Cl, SW8 . . . . 161 DH82
Waltham Cross (Chsht)
EN7 off Peakes La 66 DT27
Coleridge Cres, Slou.
(Colnbr.) SL3 . . . . 153 BE81
Coleridge Gdns, NW6
off Fairhazel Gdns 140 DC66
SW10 . . . . 160 DB80
Coleridge La, N8
off Coleridge Rd 121 DL58
Sch Coleridge Prim Sch, N8
off Crescent Rd 121 DK59
Coleridge Rd, E17 . . . . 123 DZ56
N4 . . . . 121 DN61
N8 . . . . 121 DK58
N12 . . . . 98 DC50
Ashford TW15 . . . . 174 BL91
Croydon CR0 . . . . 202 DW101
Dartford DA1 . . . . 168 FN84
Romford RM3 . . . . 105 FH52
Tilbury RM18 . . . . 171 GJ82
Coleridge Sq, SW10 . . . . 160 DC80
W13 off Berners Dr 137 CG72
Coleridge Wk, NW11 . . . . 120 DA56
Brentwood (Hutt.) CM13 . 109 GC45
Coleridge Way, Hayes UB4 . 135 BU72
Orpington BR6 . . . . 206 EU100
West Drayton UB7 . . . . 154 BM77
Cole Rd, Twick. TW1 . . . . 177 CG86
Watford WD17
off Stamford Rd 75 BV39
Colesburg Rd, Beck. BR3 . . 203 DZ97
Coles Cres, Har. HA2 . . . . 116 CB61
Colescroft Hill, Pur. CR8 . . . 235 DN115
Colesdale, Pot.B. (Cuffley)
EN6 . . . . 65 DL30
Coles Grn, Bushey
(Bushey Hth) WD23 . . . . 94 CC46
Loughton IG10 . . . . 85 EN39
Coles Grn Ct, NW2 . . . . 119 CU61
Coles Grn Rd, NW2 . . . . 119 CU60
COLESHILL, Amer. HP7 . . . . 55 AM43
Coles Hill, Hem.H. HP1 . . . . 40 BG18
Sch Coleshill C of E First Sch,
Amer. HP7
off Village Rd 55 AM44
Coleshill La, Amer. (Colesh.)
HP7 . . . . 88 AJ45
Coleshill Rd, Tedd. TW11 . . . 177 CE93
Coles La, West. (Brasted)
TN16 . . . . 240 EW123
Colesmead Rd, Red. RH1 . . 250 DF131
COLES MEADS, Red. RH1 . . 250 DF131
Colestown St, SW11 . . . . 160 DE82
Cole St, SE1 . . . . 21 H4
Colet Cl, N13 . . . . 99 DP51
Colet Gdns, W14 . . . . 16 B9
Colet Rd, Brwd. (Hutt.)
CM13 . . . . 109 GC43
Colets Orchard, Sev.
(Otford) TN14 . . . . 241 FH116
Coley Av, Wok. GU22 . . . . 227 BA118
Coley St, WC1 . . . . 10 B4
Colfe Rd, SE23 . . . . 183 DY88
Sch Colfe's Sch, SE12
off Horn Pk La 184 EH86
Colgate Pl, Enf. EN3 . . . . 83 EA37
Colgrove, Welw.G.C. AL8 . . . 29 CW10
Colham Av, West Dr. UB7 . . 134 BL74
Colham Grn Rd, Uxb. UB8 . . 134 BN71
Sch Colham Manor Jun Sch,
Uxb. UB8
off Violet Av 134 BN72
Sch Colham Manor Nurs &
Inf Sch, Uxb. UB8
off Violet Av 134 BN72
Colham Mill Rd, West Dr.
UB7 . . . . 154 BK75
Colham Rd, Uxb. UB8 . . . . 134 BM70
Colham Roundabout, Uxb.
UB8 . . . . 134 BN73
Colina Ms, N15
off Harringay Rd 121 DP57
Colina Rd, N15 . . . . 121 DP57
Colin Cl, NW9 . . . . 118 CS56
Colin Cl, Croy. CR0 . . . . 203 DZ104
Dartford DA2 . . . . 188 FP86
West Wickham BR4 . . . . 204 EF104
Colin Cres, NW9 . . . . 119 CT56
⊖ Colindale 118 CS55
Colindale Av, NW9 . . . . 118 CR55
St. Albans AL1 . . . . 43 CF22
Colindale Business Pk,
NW9 . . . . 118 CQ55
H Colindale Hosp, NW9 . . . . 96 CS54
Sch Colindale Prim Sch,
NW9 off Poolsford Rd . . . 119 CT56
Colindeep Gdns, NW4 . . . . 119 CU57
Colindeep La, NW4 . . . . 118 CS55
NW9 . . . . 118 CS55
Colin Dr, NW9 . . . . 119 CT57
Colinette Rd, SW15 . . . . 159 CW84
Colin Gdns, NW9 . . . . 119 CT57
Colin Par, NW9
off Edgware Rd 118 CS56
Colin Pk Rd, NW9 . . . . 118 CS56
Colin Rd, NW10 . . . . 139 CU65
Caterham CR3 . . . . 236 DU123
Colinton Rd, Ilf. IG3 . . . . 126 EV61
Colin Way, Slou. SL1 . . . . 151 AP76
★ Coliseum, The, WC2 . . . . 9 N10
Coliston Pas, SW18
off Coliston Rd 180 DA87
Coliston Rd, SW18 . . . . 180 DA87
Collamore Av, SW18 . . . . 180 DE88
Collapit Cl, Har. HA1 . . . . 116 CB57
Collard Av, Loug. IG10 . . . . 85 EQ40
Collard Grn, Loug. IG10
off Collard Av 85 EQ40
Collard Pl, NW1
off Harmood St 141 DH66
College App, SE10 . . . . 163 EC79
College Av, Egh. TW20 . . . . 173 BB93
Epsom KT17 . . . . 217 CT114
Grays RM17 . . . . 170 GB77
Harrow HA3 . . . . 95 CE53
Slough SL1 . . . . 152 AS76
College Cl, E9
off Median Rd 122 DW64
N18 . . . . 100 DT50
Addlestone KT15 . . . . 194 BK104
Grays RM17 . . . . 170 GC77
Harrow HA3 . . . . 95 CE52
Hatfield (N.Mymms) AL9 . . 63 CX28
Twickenham TW2
off Meadway 177 CD88
Ware SG12 . . . . 33 DX07
College Ct, Wal.Cr. (Chsht)
EN8 . . . . 66 DW30
College Cres, NW3 . . . . 140 DD65
Redhill RH1 . . . . 250 DG131
Windsor SL4 . . . . 151 AP82
College Cross, N1 . . . . 4 D6
College Dr, Ruis. HA4 . . . . 115 BU59
Thames Ditton KT7 . . . . 197 CE101
College Gdns, E4 . . . . 101 EB45
N18 . . . . 100 DT50
SE21 . . . . 182 DS88
SW17 . . . . 180 DE89
Enfield EN2 . . . . 82 DR39
Ilford IG4 . . . . 124 EL57
New Malden KT3 . . . . 199 CT99
College Gate, Harl. CM20 . . . 51 EQ15
College Grn, SE19 . . . . 182 DS94
College Gro, NW1
off St. Pancras Way 141 DK67
College Hill, EC4 . . . . 11 H9
College Hill Rd, Har. HA3 . . . 95 CF53
College La, NW5 . . . . 121 DH63
Hatfield AL10 . . . . 44 CS20
Woking GU22 . . . . 226 AW119
College Ms, SW1 . . . . 19 N5
SW18 off St. Ann's Hill . . . 180 DB85
★ College of Arms, EC4 . . . . 10 F9
Coll College of Law, The, WC1 . 9 L5
Guildford GU3
off Portsmouth Rd 258 AW138
Coll College of N E London,
The, Tottenham Cen, N15
off High Rd 122 DT56
Tottenham Grn Cen, N15
off Town Hall App Rd . . . 122 DT56
Coll College of N W London,
Kilburn Cen, NW6
off Priory Pk Rd 140 DA67
Wembley Pk Cen, Wem.
HA9 off North End Rd . . . 118 CN62
Willesden Cen, NW10
off Dudden Hill La 119 CT64
College Pk Cl, SE13 . . . . 163 ED84
College Pk Rd, N17
off College Rd 100 DT51
Sch College Pk Sch, W2 . . . . 7 J8
College Pl, E17 . . . . 124 EE56
NW1 . . . . 141 DJ67
SW10 off Hortensia Rd . . . 160 DC80
Greenhithe DA9 . . . . 169 FW84
St. Albans AL3 . . . . 42 CC20
College Pt, E15 . . . . 144 EF65
College Rd, E17 . . . . 123 EC57
N17 . . . . 100 DT51
N21 . . . . 99 DN47
NW10 . . . . 139 CW68
SE19 . . . . 182 DT92
SE21 . . . . 182 DS87
SW19 . . . . 180 DD93
W13 . . . . 137 CH72
Abbots Langley WD5 . . . . 59 BT31
Bromley BR1 . . . . 184 EG94
Croydon CR0 . . . . 202 DR103
Enfield EN2 . . . . 82 DR40
Epsom KT17 . . . . 217 CU114
Gravesend (Nthflt) DA11 . 190 GB85
Grays RM17 . . . . 170 GC77
Guildford GU1 . . . . 258 AX135
Harrow (Har.Hill) HA1 . . . 117 CE58
Harrow (Har.Wld) HA3 . . . . 95 CE53
Hertford (Hert.Hth) SG13 . . 32 DW13
Hoddesdon EN11 . . . . 49 DZ15
Isleworth TW7 . . . . 157 CF81
St. Albans AL1 . . . . 43 CH21
Slough SL1 . . . . 131 AM74
Swanley BR8 . . . . 207 FE95
Waltham Cross (Chsht)
EN8 . . . . 66 DV30
Wembley HA9 . . . . 117 CK60
Woking GU22 . . . . 227 BB116
Coll College Rd Training Cen,
NW10 off College Rd . . . 139 CW68
College Row, E9 . . . . 123 DX64
College Slip, Brom. BR1 . . . 204 EG95
College Sq, Harl. CM20
off College Gate 51 EQ15
College St, EC4 . . . . 11 H9

⊖ London Underground station | DLR Docklands Light Railway station | Tra Tramlink station | Riv Pedestrian ferry landing stage

College St, St. Alb. AL3 ....43 CD20
College Ter, E3 ....13 L1
N3 *off Hendon La* 97 CZ54
College Vw, SE9 ....184 EK88
College Wk, Kings.T. KT1
off Grange Rd 198 CL96
College Way, Ashf. TW15 ....174 BM91
Hayes UB3 ....135 BU73
Northwood HA6 ....93 BR51
Welwyn Garden City AL8 ..29 CX08
College Yd, NW5
off College La 121 DH63
Watford WD24
off Gammons La 75 BV38
Collent St, E9 ....142 DW65
Coller Cres, Dart. (Lane End)
DA2 ....189 FS91
Colless Rd, N15 ....122 DT57
Collet Cl, Wal.Cr. (Chsht) EN8 .67 DX28
Collet Gdns, Wal.Cr. (Chsht)
EN8 *off Collet Cl* 67 DX28
Collett Rd, SE16 ....22 B6
Hemel Hempstead HP1 ...40 BJ20
Ware SG12 ....33 DX05
Sch Collett Sch, The, Hem.H.
HP1 *off Lockers Pk La* ...40 BH19
Collett Way, Sthl. UB2 ....136 CB74
Colley Hill La, Slou. (Hedg.)
SL2 ....112 AT62
Colleyland, Rick. (Chorl.)
WD3 ....73 BD42
Colley La, Reig. RH2 ....249 CY132
Colley Manor Dr, Reig. RH2 .249 CX133
Colley Way, Reig. RH2 ....249 CY131
Collier Cl, E6 *off Trader Rd* ..145 EP72
Epsom KT19 ....216 CN107
Collier Dr, Edg. HA8 ....96 CN54
COLLIER ROW, Rom. RM5 ..104 FA53
Collier Row La, Rom. RM5 ..105 FB52
Collier Row Rd, Rom. RM5 .104 EZ53
Colliers, Cat. CR3 ....252 DU125
Colliers Cl, Wok. GU21 ....226 AV117
Colliers Shaw, Kes. BR2 ...222 EK105
Collier St, N1 ....4 A10
Colliers Water La, Th.Hth.
CR7 ....201 DN99
COLLIER'S WOOD, SW19 ..180 DD94
⊖ **Colliers Wood** 180 DD94
Collier Way, Guil. GU4 ....243 BD132
Collindale Av, Erith DA8 ...167 FB79
Sidcup DA15 ....186 EU88
Collingbourne Rd, W12 ....139 CV74
Collingham Gdns, SW5 ....17 K8
H Collingham Gdns Hosp,
SW5 ....17 K8
Collingham Pl, SW5 ....17 J8
Collingham Rd, SW5 ....17 K7
Sch Collingham Sch, SW5 ...17 K8
Collings Cl, N22
off Whittington Rd 99 DM51
Collington Cl, Grav. (Nthflt)
DA11 *off Beresford Rd* ..190 GE87
Collington St, SE10
off Hoskins St 163 ED78
Collingtree Rd, SE26 ....182 DW91
Collingwood Av, N10 ....120 DG55
Surbiton KT5 ....198 CQ102
Collingwood Cl, SE20 ....202 DV95
Horley RH6 ....269 DH147
Twickenham TW2 ....176 CA86
Collingwood Cres, Guil.
GU1 ....243 BA133
Collingwood Dr, St.Alb.
(Lon.Col.) AL2 ....61 CK25
Collingwood Pl, Walt. KT12 .195 BU104
Collingwood Rd, E17 ....123 EA58
N15 ....122 DS56
Mitcham CR4 ....200 DE96
Rainham RM13 ....147 FF68
Sutton SM1 ....200 DA104
Uxbridge UB8 ....135 BP70
Sch Collingwood Sch, Wall.
SM6 *off Springfield Rd* .219 DH106
Collingwood St, E1 ....12 D3
Collins Av, Stan. HA7 ....96 CL54
Collins Dr, Ruis. HA4 ....116 BW61
Collins Meadow, Harl. CM19 .51 EP15
Collinson St, SE1 ....20 G4
Collinson Wk, SE1 ....20 G4
Collins Rd, N5 ....122 DQ63
Collins Sq, SE3
off Tranquil Vale 164 EF82
Collins St, SE3 ....164 EE82
Collins Way, Brwd. (Hutt.)
CM13 ....109 GE43
Collinswood Rd, Slou.
(Farn.Com.) SL2 ....111 AN60
Collin's Yd, N1 ....4 E8
Collinwood Av, Enf. EN3 ...82 DW41
Collinwood Gdns, Ilf. IG5 ...125 EM57
Collis All, Twick. TW2
off The Green 177 CE88
Collison Pl, N16 ....122 DS61
Sch Collis Prim Sch, Tedd.
TW11 *off Fairfax Rd* 177 CH93
Colls Rd, SE15 ....162 DW81
Collum Grn Rd, Slou. SL2 ..111 AR62
Collyer Av, Croy. CR0 ....219 DL105
Collyer Pl, SE15
off Peckham High St ...162 DU81
Collyer Rd, Croy. CR0 ....219 DL105
St. Albans (Lon.Col.) AL2 ..61 CJ27
Colman Cl, Epsom KT18 ...233 CW117
Colman Rd, E16 ....144 EJ71
Colmans Hill, Guil. (Peasl.)
GU5 ....261 BS144
Colman Way, Red. RH1 ....250 DE132
Colmar Cl, E1 ....12 G3
Colmer Pl, Har. HA3 ....95 CD52
Colmer Rd, SW16 ....201 DL95
Colmore Ms, SE15 ....162 DV81
Colmore Rd, Enf. EN3 ....82 DW42
COLNBROOK, Slou. SL3 ...153 BD80
Colnbrook Bypass, Slou.
SL3 ....153 BF80
West Drayton UB7 ....153 BF80
Colnbrook Cl, St.Alb.
(Lon.Col.) AL2 ....62 CL28
**Sch Colnbrook C of E Comb
Sch**, Slou. SL3
off High St 153 BD80
Colnbrook Ct, Slou. SL3 ...153 BF81
Sch Colnbrook Sch, Wat.
WD19 *off Hayling Rd* 94 BW48
Colnbrook St, SE1 ....20 E6
Colndale Rd, Slou. (Colnbr.)
SL3 ....153 BE82
Colne Av, Rick. (Mill End)
WD3 ....92 BG47
Colne Av, Wat. WD19 ....75 BV44
West Drayton UB7 ....154 BJ75
Colne Bk, Slou. (Horton)
SL3 ....153 BC83
Colnebridge Cl, Stai. TW18
off Clarence St 173 BE91
Colne Br Retail Pk, Wat.
WD17 *off Lower High St* ..76 BX44
Colne Cl, S.Ock. RM15 ....149 FW73
Colne Ct, Epsom KT19 ....216 CQ105
Colnedale Rd, Uxb. UB8 ....114 BK64
Colne Dr, Rom. RM3 ....106 FM51
Walton-on-Thames KT12 .196 BX104
Colne Gdns, St.Alb.
(Lon.Col.) AL2 ....62 CL27
Colne Ho, Bark. IG11 ....145 EP65
Colne Mead, Rick. (Mill End)
WD3 *off Uxbridge Rd* ...92 BG47
Colne Orchard, Iver SL0 ....133 BF72
Colne Pk Caravan Site,
West Dr. UB7 ....154 BJ77
Colne Reach, Stai. TW19 ...173 BF85
Colne Rd, E5 ....123 DY63
N21 ....100 DR45
Twickenham TW1, TW2 ...177 CE88
Colne St, E13 ....15 L2
Colne Valley, Upmin. RM14 .129 FS58
Colne Way, Hem.H. HP2 ....40 BM15
Staines TW19 ....173 BB90
Watford WD24, WD25 ....76 BY37
Colney Hatch La, N10 ....98 DG52
N11 ....98 DF51
COLNEY HEATH, St.Alb. AL4 .44 CR22
**Sch Colney Heath JM &
Inf Sch**, St.Alb. AL4
off High St 44 CQ22
Colney Heath La, St.Alb.
AL4 ....44 CL20
Colney Rd, Dart. DA1 ....188 FM86
COLNEY STREET, St.Alb.
AL2 ....61 CE31
Cologne Rd, SW11 ....160 DD84
Sch Coloma Conv Sch, Croy.
CR0 *off Upper Shirley Rd* .203 DX104
Colombo Rd, Ilf. IG1 ....125 EQ60
Colombo St, SE1 ....20 E2
Colomb St, SE10 ....25 H10
Colonels La, Cher. KT16 ....194 BG100
Colonels Wk, Enf. EN2 ....81 DP41
Colonial Av, Twick. TW2 ....176 CC85
Colonial Dr, W4 ....158 CQ77
Colonial Rd, Felt. TW14 ....175 BS87
Slough SL1 ....152 AU75
Colonial Way, Wat. WD24 ....76 BX39
Colonnade, WC1 ....9 N4
Colonnades, The, W2 ....7 K7
Colonnade Wk, SW1 ....18 G8
Colonsay, Hem.H. HP3 ....41 BQ22
Colosseum Ter, NW1
off Albany St 141 DH70
Colson Gdns, Loug. IG10
off Colson Rd 85 EP42
Colson Path, Loug. IG10 ....85 EN42
Colson Rd, Croy. CR0 ....202 DS103
Loughton IG10 ....85 EP42
Colson Way, SW16 ....181 DJ91
Colsterworth Rd, N15 ....122 DT56
Colston Av, Cars. SM5 ....218 DE105
Colston Cl, Cars. SM5
off West St 218 DF105
Colston Cres, Wal.Cr. (Chsht)
EN7 ....65 DP27
Colston Rd, E7 ....144 EK65
SW14 ....158 CQ84
Colt Hatch, Harl. CM20
off Hobtoe Rd 35 EP14
Colthurst Cres, N4 ....122 DQ61
Colthurst Dr, N9 ....100 DV48
Colthurst Gdns, Hodd. EN11 .49 ED15
Coltishall Rd, Horn. RM12 ..148 FJ65
Colt Ms, Enf. EN3
off Martini Dr 83 EA37
Coltness Cres, SE2 ....166 EV78
Colton Gdns, N17 ....122 DQ55
Colton Rd, Har. HA1 ....117 CE57
Coltsfoot, Welw.G.C. AL7 ....30 DB11
Coltsfoot, The, Hem.H. HP1 ..39 BE21
Coltsfoot Ct, Grays RM17 ..170 GD79
Coltsfoot Dr, Guil. GU1 ....243 BA131
West Drayton UB7 ....134 BL72
Coltsfoot La, Oxt. RH8 ....254 EF133
Coltsfoot Path, Rom. RM3 ..106 FJ52
Columbia Av, Edg. HA8 ....96 CP53
Ruislip HA4 ....115 BV60
Worcester Park KT4 ....199 CT101
Columbia Pt, SE16 ....22 F5
Sch Columbia Prim Sch, E2 ..11 P1
Columbia Rd, E2 ....11 N1
E13 ....15 K5
Columbia Sq, SW14
off Upper Richmond Rd W .158 CQ84
Columbia Wf Rd, Grays
RM17 ....170 GA79
Columbine Av, E6 ....144 EL71
South Croydon CR2 ....219 DP108
Columbine Way, SE13 ....163 EC82
Romford RM3 ....106 FL53
Columbus Ct, SE16
off Rotherhithe St 142 DW74
Columbus Ctyd, E14 ....23 N1
Columbus Gdns, Nthwd.
HA6 ....93 BU53
Columbus Sq, Erith DA8 ...167 FF79
Colva Wk, N19
off Chester Rd 121 DH61
Colvestone Cres, E8 ....5 N2
Sch Colvestone JMI Sch, E8 ..5 N2
Colview Ct, SE9
off Mottingham La 184 EK88
Colville Est, N1 ....5 L8
Colville Gdns, W11 ....6 F8
Colville Hos, W11 ....6 E7
Colville Ms, W11 ....6 F8
Colville Pl, W1 ....9 K6
Sch Colville Prim Sch, W11 ...6 F8
Colville Rd, E11 ....123 EC62
E17 ....101 DY54
N9 ....100 DW46
W3 ....158 CP76
W11 ....6 F8
Colville Sq, W11 ....6 E8
Colville Ter, W11 ....6 E8
Colvin Cl, SE26 ....182 DW92
Colvin Gdns, E4 ....101 EC48
E11 ....124 EH56
Ilford IG6 ....103 EQ53
Waltham Cross EN8 ....83 DX35
Colvin Rd, E6 ....144 EL66
Thornton Heath CR7 ....201 DN99
Colwall Gdns, Wdf.Grn. IG8 .102 EG50
Colwell Rd, SE22 ....182 DT85
Colwick Cl, N6 ....121 DK59
Colwith Rd, W6 ....159 CW79
Colwood Gdns, SW19 ....180 DD94
Colworth Gro, SE17 ....21 H8
Colworth Rd, E11 ....124 EE58
Croydon CR0 ....202 DU102
Colwyn Av, Grnf. UB6 ....137 CF68
Colwyn Cl, SW16 ....181 DJ92
Colwyn Cres, Houns. TW3 ..156 CC81
Colwyn Grn, NW9
off Snowdon Dr 118 CS58
Colwyn Rd, NW2 ....119 CV62
Colyer Cl, N1 ....4 B9
SE9 ....185 EP89
Colyer Rd, Grav. (Nthflt)
DA11 ....190 GC89
Colyers Cl, Erith DA8 ....167 FD81
Colyers La, Erith DA8 ....167 FC81
Sch Colyers Prim Sch, Erith
DA8 *off Colyers La* 167 FD81
Colyers Wk, Erith DA8
off Colyers La 167 FE81
Colyton Cl, Well. DA16 ....166 EX81
Wembley HA0
off Bridgewater Rd 137 CJ65
Woking GU21 ....226 AW118
Colyton La, SW16 ....181 DN92
Colyton Rd, SE22 ....182 DV85
Colyton Way, N18 ....100 DU50
Combe Av, SE3 ....164 EF80
Combe Bk Dr, Sev. (Sund.)
TN14 ....240 EY122
Sch Combe Bk Sch, Sev.
TN14 *off Combe Bk Dr* ..240 EY123
Combe Bottom, Guil. GU5 .260 BM137
Combedale Rd, SE10 ....25 L9
Combe La, Guil. GU5 ....261 BP135
Walton-on-Thames
(Whiteley Vill.) KT12 ...213 BT109
Combe Lo, SE7
off Elliscombe Rd 164 EJ79
Combemartin Rd, SW18 ...179 CY87
Combe Ms, SE3 ....164 EF80
Comber Cl, NW2 ....119 CV62
Comber Gro, SE5 ....162 DQ81
Sch Comber Gro Prim Sch,
SE5 *off Comber Gro* ...162 DQ80
Combermere Rd, SW9 ....161 DM83
Morden SM4 ....200 DB100
Combe Rd, Gdmg. GU7 ....258 AS143
Watford WD18 ....75 BT44
Comberton Rd, E5 ....122 DV61
Combeside, SE18 ....165 ET80
Combe St, Hem.H. HP1 ....40 BJ20
Combwell Cres, SE2 ....166 EU76
Comely Bk Rd, E17 ....123 EC57
Comeragh Cl, Wok. GU22 ..226 AU120
Comeragh Ms, W14 ....16 D9
Comeragh Rd, W14 ....16 C10
Comer Cres, Sthl. UB2
off Windmill Av 156 CC75
Comerford Rd, SE4 ....163 DY84
Comet Cl, E12 ....124 EK63
Purfleet RM19 ....168 FN77
Watford WD25 ....59 BT34
Comet Pl, SE8 ....163 EA80
Comet Rd, Hat. AL10 ....45 CT18
Staines (Stanw.) TW19 ...174 BK87
Comet St, SE8 ....163 EA80
Comet Way, Hat. AL9, AL10 ..44 CS19
Comforts Fm Av, Oxt. RH8 ..254 EF133
Comfort St, SE15 ....162 DS79
Comfrey Ct, Grays RM17 ...170 GD79
Commerce Rd, N22 ....99 DM53
Brentford TW8 ....157 CJ80
Commerce Way, Croy. CR0 .201 DM103
Commercial Pl, Grav. DA12 .191 GJ86
Commercial Rd, E1 ....12 A7
E14 ....13 K8
N17 ....100 DS51
N18 ....100 DS50
Guildford GU1 ....258 AX135
Staines TW18 ....174 BG93
Commercial St, E1 ....11 N4
Commercial Way, NW10 ....138 CP68
SE15 ....162 DT80
Woking GU21 ....227 AZ117
Commerell St, SE10 ....25 H9
Commodity Quay, E1 ....11 P10
Commodore St, E1 ....13 J4
Common, The, E15 ....144 EE65
W5 ....138 CL73
Berkhamsted HP4 ....39 AZ17
Guildford (Shalf.) GU4 ...258 AY141
Guildford (Won.) GU5 ....259 BB143
Hatfield AL10 ....45 CU17
Kings Langley (Chipper.)
WD4 ....58 BG32
Richmond TW10 ....177 CK90
Southall UB2 ....156 BW77
Stanmore HA7 ....95 CE47
West Drayton UB7 ....154 BJ77
Common Cl, Wok. GU21 ....210 AX114
Commondale, SW15 ....159 CW83
Commonfield Rd, Bans.
SM7 ....218 DA114
Commonfields, Harl. CM20 ..35 ES14
Common Gdns, Berk.
(Pott.End) HP4 ....39 BB17
Common Gate Rd, Rick.
(Chorl.) WD3 ....73 BD43
Common La, Add.
(New Haw) KT15 ....212 BJ109
Dartford DA2 ....187 FG89
Esher (Clay.) KT10 ....215 CG108
Kings Langley WD4 ....58 BM28
Radlett WD7 ....77 CE39
Slough (Burn.) SL1 ....111 AK62
Watford (Let.Hth) WD25 ...77 CE39
Windsor (Eton) SL4 ....151 AQ78
Commonmeadow La, Wat.
(Ald.) WD25 ....60 CB33
Common Mile Cl, SW4 ....181 DK85
Common Rd, SW13 ....159 CU83
Brentwood (Ingrave)
CM13 ....109 GC50
Esher (Clay.) KT10 ....215 CG107
Leatherhead KT23 ....230 BY121
Redhill RH1 ....266 DF136
Rickmansworth (Chorl.)
WD3 ....73 BD42
Slough (Langley) SL3 ....153 BA77
Stanmore HA7 ....95 CD49
Waltham Abbey EN9 ....50 EK22
Windsor (Dorney) SL4 ....150 AJ77
Windsor (Eton Wick) SL4 .151 AM78
Commons, The, Welw.G.C.
AL7 ....30 DA12
Commonside, Epsom KT18 .232 CN115
Harlow CM18
off Fern Hill La 51 ES19
Keston BR2 ....222 EJ105
Leatherhead (Bkhm) KT23 .230 CA122
Commonside Cl, Couls.
CR5 *off Coulsdon Rd* 235 DP120
Sutton SM2 *off Downs Rd* .218 DB110
Commonside E, Mitch. CR4 .200 DF97
Commonside Rd, Harl.
CM18 ....51 ES19
Sch Commonside Sch, The,
Harl. CM18
off Commonside Rd 51 ET19
Commonside W, Mitch. CR4 .200 DF97
Commons La, Hem.H. HP2 ..40 BL19
Commons Wd Caravan Club,
Welw.G.C. AL7 ....30 DA13
Sch Commonswood Sch,
Welw.G.C. AL7
off The Commons 30 DB12
Sch Commonweal Lo Sch, Pur.
CR8 *off Woodcote La* ...219 DK112
Commonwealth Av, W12 ....139 CV73
Hayes UB3 ....135 BR72
★ **Commonwealth Inst**, W8 .16 F5
Commonwealth Rd, N17 ....100 DU52
Caterham CR3 ....236 DU123
Commonwealth Way, SE2 ..166 EV78
COMMONWOOD, Kings L.
WD4 ....58 BH34
Common Wd, Slou.
(Farn.Com.) SL2 ....111 AQ63
Common Wd La, H.Wyc.
(Penn) HP10 ....88 AD46
Commonwood La, Kings L.
WD4 ....74 BH35
Community Cl, Houns. TW5 .155 BV81
Uxbridge UB10 ....115 BQ62
Coll Community Coll Hackney,
London Fields, E8
off Mare St 142 DV67
Shoreditch Campus, N1 ...11 M1
Coll Community Ed Lewisham,
Brockley Ri Cen, SE23 ..183 DY88
Grove Pk Cen, SE12
off Pragnell Rd 184 EH89
Holbeach Centre, SE6
off Doggett Rd 183 EA87
Mornington Cen, SE8
off Stanley St 163 DZ80
Community La, N7 ....121 DK64
Community Rd, E15 ....123 ED64
Greenford UB6 ....136 CC67
Community Wk, Esher
KT10 *off High St* 214 CC105
Community Way, Rick.
(Crox.Grn) WD3
off Barton Way 75 BP43
Como Rd, SE23 ....183 DY89
Como St, Rom. RM7 ....127 FD57
Compass Cl, Ashf. TW15 ...175 BQ94
Compass Hill, Rich. TW10 ...177 CK86
Compass Ho, SW18
off Smugglers Way 160 DB84
Compass Pt, Berk. (Nthch)
HP4 *off Chapel Crfts* 38 AS17
Compayne Gdns, NW6 ....140 DB66
Comport Grn, Croy.
(New Adgtn) CR0 ....222 EE112
Compton Av, E6 ....144 EK68
N1 ....4 E4
N6 ....120 DE59
Brentwood (Hutt.) CM13 .109 GC46
Romford RM2 ....127 FH55
Wembley HA0 ....117 CJ63
Compton Cl, E3 ....13 P5
NW1 ....9 H2
NW11 *off The Vale* 119 CX62
W13 ....137 CG72
Edgware HA8
off Pavilion Way 96 CQ52
Esher KT10 ....214 CC106
Compton Ct, SE19
off Victoria Cres 182 DS92
Slough SL1 *off Brook Cres* .131 AL72
Compton Cres, N17 ....100 DQ52
W4 ....158 CQ79
Chessington KT9 ....216 CL107
Northolt UB5 ....136 BX67
Compton Gdns, Add. KT15
off Monks Cres 212 BH106
St. Albans AL2 ....60 CB26
Compton Ho, SW11
off Parkham St 160 DE81
Compton Pas, EC1 ....10 F3
Compton Pl, WC1 ....9 N3
Erith DA8 ....167 FF79
Watford WD19 ....94 BY48
Compton Ri, Pnr. HA5 ....116 BY57
Compton Rd, N1 ....4 F4
N21 ....99 DN46
NW10 ....6 A2
SW19 ....179 CZ93
Croydon CR0 ....202 DV102
Hayes UB3 ....135 BS73
Sch Compton Sec Sch, N12
off Summers La 98 DE51
Compton St, EC1 ....10 E3
Compton Ter, N1 ....4 E4
Computer Ho, Brent. TW8 ..157 CJ79
Comreddy Cl, Enf. EN2 ....81 DP39
Comus Pl, SE17 ....21 L8
Comyne Rd, Wat. WD24 ....75 BT36
Comyn Rd, SW11 ....160 DE84
Comyns, The, Bushey
(Bushey Hth) WD23 ....94 CC46
Comyns Cl, E16 ....15 J5
Comyns Rd, Dag. RM9 ....146 FA66
Conant Ms, E1 ....12 A9
Conaways Cl, Epsom KT17 .217 CU110
Concanon Rd, SW2 ....161 DM84
Concert Hall App, SE1 ....20 B2
Concord Cl, Nthlt. UB5 ....136 BY69
Concorde Cl, Houns. TW3 ..156 CB82
Uxbridge UB10 ....134 BL68
Concorde Ct, Wind. SL4
off Green La 151 AN82
Concorde Dr, E6 ....145 EM71
Hemel Hempstead HP2 ...40 BK20
Concorde Way, Slou. SL1 ...151 AQ75
Concord Rd, W3 ....138 CP70
Enfield EN3 ....82 DW43
Concord Ter, Har. HA2
off Coles Cres 116 CB61
Concourse, The, N9
off New Rd 100 DU47
NW9 ....97 CT53
Concrete Cotts, Wok.
(Wisley) GU23
off Wisley La 228 BL116
Condell Rd, SW8 ....161 DJ81
Conder St, E14 ....13 J7
Condor Ct, Guil. GU2
off Millmead Ter 258 AW136
Condor Path, Nthlt. UB5
off Brabazon Rd 136 CA68
Condor Rd, Stai. TW18 ....194 BH97
Condor Wk, Horn. RM12
off Heron Flight Av 147 FH66
Condover Cres, SE18 ....165 EP80
Condray Pl, SW11 ....160 DE80
Sch Conductive Ed Cen, N10
off Dukes Av 121 DH55
Conduit, The, Red. (Bletch.)
RH1 ....252 DS129
Conduit Av, SE10
off Crooms Hill 163 ED81
Conduit Ct, WC2 ....9 N9
Conduit La, N18 ....100 DW50
Croydon CR0 ....220 DU106
Enfield EN3
off Morson Rd 83 DY44
South Croydon CR2 ....220 DU106
Conduit La E, Hodd. EN11 ..49 EB17
Conduit La W, Hodd. EN11 ..49 EA17
Conduit Ms, SE18 ....165 EP78
W2 ....7 N8
Conduit Pas, W2 ....7 N8
Conduit Pl, W2 ....7 N8
Conduit Rd, SE18 ....165 EP78
Slough SL3 ....152 AY78
Conduit St, W1 ....9 H9
Conduit Way, NW10 ....138 CQ66
Conegar Ct, Slou. SL1 ....132 AS74
Conewood St, N5 ....121 DP62
Coney Acre, SE21 ....182 DQ88
Coneyberry, Reig. RH2 ....266 DC138
Coney Burrows, E4
off Wyemead Cres 102 EE47
Coneybury, Red. (Bletch.)
RH1 ....252 DS134
Coneybury Cl, Warl. CR6 ...236 DV119
Coney Cl, Hat. AL10 ....45 CV19
Coneydale, Welw.G.C. AL8 ..29 CX07
Coney Gro, Uxb. UB8 ....134 BN69
Coneygrove Path, Nthlt.
UB5 *off Arnold Rd* 136 BY65
CONEY HALL, W.Wick. BR4 .204 EF104
Coney Hill Rd, W.Wick. BR4 .204 EE103
Sch Coney Hill Spec Sch, Brom.
BR2 *off Croydon Rd* 204 EF104
Coney Way, SW8 ....161 DM79
Conference Cl, E4
off Greenbank Cl 101 EC47
★ **Conference Forum, The**,
E1 ....12 A7
Conference Rd, SE2 ....166 EW77
Conford Dr, Guil. (Shalf.)
GU4 ....258 AY141
Congleton Gro, SE18 ....165 EQ78
Congo Dr, N9 ....100 DW48
Congo Rd, SE18 ....165 ER78
Congress Rd, SE2 ....166 EW77
Congreve Rd, SE9 ....165 EM83
Waltham Abbey EN9 ....68 EE33
Congreve St, SE17 ....21 L7
Congreve Wk, E16 ....144 EK71
Conical Cor, Enf. EN2 ....82 DQ40
Coniers Way, Guil. GU4 ....243 BB131
Conifer Av, Rom. RM5 ....105 FB50
Conifer Cl, Orp. BR6 ....223 ER105
Reigate RH2 ....250 DA132
Waltham Cross EN7 ....66 DT29
Conifer Dr, Brwd. CM14 ....108 FX50
Conifer Gdns, SW16 ....181 DL90
Enfield EN1 ....82 DS44
Sutton SM1 ....200 DB103
Conifer La, Egh. TW20 ....173 BC92
Conifer Pk, Epsom KT17 ...216 CS111
Conifers, Wey. KT13 ....213 BS105
Conifers, The, Hem.H. HP3 ..39 BF23
Watford WD25 ....76 BW35
Conifers Cl, Tedd. TW11 ...177 CH94
Conifer Way, Hayes UB3
off Longmead Rd 135 BU73
Swanley BR8 ....207 FC95
Wembley HA0 ....117 CJ62
Coniger Rd, SW6 ....160 DA82
Coningesby Dr, Wat. WD17 ..75 BS39
Coningham Ms, W12
off Percy Rd 139 CU74
Coningham Rd, W12 ....159 CV75
Coningsby Bk, St.Alb. AL1 ..42 CC24
Coningsby Cl, Hat. AL9 ....45 CX24
Coningsby Cotts, W5
off Coningsby Rd 157 CK75
Coningsby Dr, Pot.B. EN6 ...64 DD33
Coningsby Gdns, E4 ....101 EB51
Coningsby La, Maid. SL6 ...150 AC81
Coningsby Rd, N4 ....121 DP59
W5 ....157 CJ75
South Croydon CR2 ....220 DQ109
Conington Rd, SE13 ....163 EB82
Conisbee Ct, N14 ....81 DJ43
Conisborough Cres, SE6 ...183 EC90
Coniscliffe Cl, Chis. BR7 ...205 EN95
Coniscliffe Rd, N13 ....100 DQ48
Conista Ct, Wok. GU21
off Roundthorn Way 226 AT116
Coniston Av, Bark. IG11 ....145 ES66
Greenford UB6 ....137 CH69
Upminster RM14 ....128 FQ63
Welling DA16 ....165 ES83
Coniston Cl, N20 ....98 DC48
SW13 *off Lonsdale Rd* ...159 CT80
SW20 ....199 CX100
W4 ....158 CQ81
Barking IG11
off Coniston Av 145 ES66
Bexleyheath DA7 ....167 FC81
Dartford DA1 ....187 FH88
Erith DA8 ....167 FE80
Hemel Hempstead HP3 ...41 BQ21
Coniston Ct, Wey. KT13 ....213 BP107
Coniston Cres, Slou. SL1 ...130 AJ71
Conistone Way, N7 ....141 DL66
Coniston Gdns, N9 ....100 DW46
NW9 ....118 CR57
Ilford IG4 ....124 EL56
Pinner HA5 ....115 BU56
Sutton SM2 ....218 DD107
Wembley HA9 ....117 CJ60
Coniston Ho, SE5 ....162 DQ80
Coniston Rd, N10 ....99 DH54
N17 ....100 DU51
Bexleyheath DA7 ....167 FC81
Bromley BR1 ....184 EE93
Coulsdon CR5 ....235 DJ116
Croydon CR0 ....202 DU101
Kings Langley WD4 ....58 BM28
Twickenham TW2 ....176 CB86
Woking GU22 ....227 BB120
Coniston Wk, E9
off Clifden Rd 122 DW64
Coniston Way, Chess. KT9 ..198 CL104
Egham TW20 ....173 BB94
Hornchurch RM12 ....127 FG64
Reigate RH2 ....250 DE133
Conlan St, W10 ....6 C3
Conley Rd, NW10 ....138 CS65
Conley St, SE10 ....25 H9
Connaught Av, E4 ....101 ED45
SW14 ....158 CQ83
Ashford TW15 ....174 BL91
Barnet EN4 ....98 DF46
Enfield EN1 ....82 DS40
Grays RM16 ....170 GB75
Hounslow TW4 ....176 BY85
Loughton IG10 ....84 EK42
Connaught Br, E16 ....144 EK74

★ Place of interest   H Hospital   Sch School   Coll College   Uni University   ⇄ Railway station

Connaught Business Cen, Mitch. CR4
off Wandle Way .200 DF99
Connaught Cl, E10 .123 DY61
W2 .8 A8
Enfield EN1 .82 DS40
Hemel Hempstead HP2 .40 BN18
Sutton SM1 .200 DD103
Uxbridge UB8 off New Rd .135 BQ70
Connaught Ct, E17
off Orford Rd .123 EB56
Buckhurst Hill IG9 .165 EH46
Connaught Dr, NW11 .120 DA56
Weybridge KT13 .212 BN111
Connaught Gdns, N10 .121 DH57
N13 .99 DP49
Berkhamsted HP4 .38 AT16
Morden SM4 .200 DC98
Sch Connaught Girls' High Sch, E11 off Connaught Rd .124 EE60
Annexe, E11
off Dyers Hall Rd .124 EE61
Connaught Hts, Uxb. UB10
off Uxbridge Rd .135 BQ70
Connaught Hill, Loug. IG10 .84 EK42
Sch Connaught Ho Sch, W2 .8 C8
Connaught La, Ilf. IG1
off Connaught Rd .125 ER61
Connaught Ms, SE18 .165 EN78
Ilford IG1
off Connaught Rd .125 ER61
Connaught Pl, W2 .8 C9
Connaught Rd, E4 .102 EE45
E11 .123 ED60
E16 .144 EK74
E17 .123 EA57
N4 .121 DN59
NW10 .138 CS67
SE18 .165 EN78
W13 .137 CH73
Barnet EN5 .79 CX44
Harrow HA3 .95 CF53
Hornchurch RM12 .128 FK62
Ilford IG1 .125 ER61
New Malden KT3 .198 CS98
Richmond TW10
off Albert Rd .178 CM85
St. Albans AL3 .42 CC17
Slough SL1 .152 AV75
Sutton SM1 .200 DD103
Teddington TW11 .177 CD92
Connaught Roundabout,
E16 off Connaught Br .144 EK73
Connaught Sq, W2 .8 C8
Connaught St, W2 .8 A8
Connaught Way, N13 .99 DP49
Connell Cres, W5 .138 CM70
Connemara Cl, Borwd. WD6
off Percheron Rd .78 CR44
Connicut La, Lthd. KT23 .246 CB128
Connington Cres, E4 .101 ED48
Connop Rd, Enf. EN3 .83 DX38
Connor Cl, E11 .124 EE59
Ilford IG6 .103 EP53
Connor Rd, Dag. RM9 .126 EZ63
Connor St, E9
off Lauriston Rd .143 DX67
Conolly Rd, W7 .137 CE74
Conquerors Hill, St.Alb. (Wheat.) AL4 .28 CL07
Conquest Rd, Add. KT15 .212 BG106
Conrad Cl, Grays RM16 .170 GB75
Conrad Dr, Wor.Pk. KT4 .199 CW102
Conrad Gdns, Grays RM16 .170 GA75
Conrad Ho, N16 .5 L1
Consfield Av, N.Mal. KT3 .199 CU98
Coll Consolata Missionary Coll, N20 off Totteridge Grn .98 DA48
Consort Cl, Brwd. CM14 .108 FW50
Consort Ms, Islw. TW7 .177 CD85
Consort Rd, SE15 .162 DV81
Consort Way, Horl. RH6 .268 DG148
Uxbridge (Denh.) UB9
off Knowland Way .113 BF58
Consort Way E, Horl. RH6 .269 DH149
Cons St, SE1 .20 D3
Constable Av, E16 .25 N1
Constable Cl, NW11 .120 DB58
Hayes UB4
off Charville La .135 BQ69
Constable Cres, N15 .122 DU57
Constable Gdns, Edg. HA8 .96 CN53
Isleworth TW7 .177 CD85
Constable Ms, Dag. RM8
off Stonard Rd .126 EV63
Constable Rd, Grav. (Nthflt) DA11 .190 GE90
Constable Wk, SE21 .182 DT90
Constance Cres, Brom. BR2 204 EF101
Constance Rd, Croy. CR0 .201 DP101
Enfield EN1 .82 DS44
Sutton SM1 .218 DC105
Twickenham TW2 .176 CB87
Constance St, E16
off Albert Rd .144 EL74
Constantine Pl, Uxb. (Hlgdn) UB10 .134 BM67
Constantine Rd, NW3 .120 DE63
Constitution Hill, SW1 .18 G3
Gravesend DA12 .191 GJ88
Woking GU22 .226 AY119
Constitution Ri, SE18 .165 EN81
Consul Av, Dag. RM9 .147 FC69
Consul Gdns, Swan. BR8 .187 FG94
Content St, SE17 .21 H8
Contessa Cl, Orp. BR6 .223 ES106
Control Twr Rd, Gat. RH6 .268 DD153
Hounslow (Hthrw Air.) TW6 .154 BN83
Convair Wk, Nthlt. UB5
off Kittiwake Rd .136 BX69
Convent Cl, Beck. BR3 .183 EC94
Convent Gdns, W5 .157 CJ77
W11 .6 D8
Convent Hill, SE19 .182 DQ93
Convent La, Cob. KT11
off Seven Hills Rd .213 BS111
Sch Convent of Jesus & Mary RC High Sch, NW10
off Crownhill Rd .139 CT67
Sch Convent of Jesus & Mary RC Inf Sch, NW2
off Park Av .139 CW65
Convent Rd, Ashf. TW15 .174 BN92
Windsor SL4 .151 AN82
Convent Way, Sthl. UB2 .156 BW77
Conway Cl, H.Wyc. (Loud.) HP10 .88 AC53
Rainham RM13 .147 FG66
Stanmore HA7 .95 CG51
Conway Cres, Grnf. UB6 .137 CE68
Romford RM6 .126 EW59
Conway Dr, Ashf. TW15 .175 BQ93
Hayes UB3 .155 BQ76
Sutton SM2 .218 DB107
Conway Gdns, Enf. EN2 .82 DS38
Grays RM17 .170 GB80
Mitcham CR4 .201 DK98
Wembley HA9 .117 CJ59
Conway Gro, W3 .138 CR71
Conway Ms, W1 .9 J4
Sch Conway Prim Sch, SE18
off Gallosson Rd .165 ES77
Conway Rd, N14 .99 DL48
N15 .121 DP57
NW2 .119 CW61
SE18 .165 ER77
SW20 .199 CW95
Feltham TW13 .176 BX92
Hounslow TW4 .176 BZ87
Hounslow (Hthrw Air.)
TW6 off Inner Ring E .155 BP83
Maidenhead (Taplow) SL6 .130 AH72
Conway St, E13 .15 L4
W1 .9 J4
Conway Wk, Hmptn. TW12
off Fearnley Cres .176 BZ93
Conybeare, NW3
off King Henry's Rd .140 DE66
Conybury Cl, Wal.Abb. EN9 .68 EG32
Cony Cl, Wal.Cr. (Chsht) EN7 .66 DS26
Conyers, Harl. CM20 .35 EQ13
Conyers Cl, Walt. KT12 .214 BX106
Woodford Green IG8 .102 EE51
Conyers Rd, SW16 .181 DK92
Conyer St, E3 .143 DY68
Conyers Way, Loug. IG10 .85 EP41
Cooden Cl, Brom. BR1
off Plaistow La .184 EH94
Cook Ct, SE16
off Rotherhithe St .142 DW74
Cooke Cl, E14 off Cabot Sq .143 EA74
Cookes Cl, E11 .124 EF61
Cookes La, Sutt. SM3 .217 CY107
Cookham Cl, Sthl. UB2 .156 CB75
Cookham Cres, SE16 .22 G3
Cookham Dene Cl, Chis. BR7 .205 ER95
Cookham Hill, Orp. BR6 .206 FA104
Cookham Rd, Sid. DA14 .186 FA94
Swanley BR8 .206 FA95
Cookhill Rd, SE2 .166 EV75
Cook Rd, Dag. RM9 .146 EY67
Cooks Cl, Rom. RM5 .105 FC53
Cook's Hole Rd, Enf. EN2 .81 DP38
Cooks Mead, Bushey WD23 .76 CB44
Cookson Gro, Erith DA8 .167 FB80
Cook Sq, Erith DA8 .167 FF80
Cook's Rd, E15 .143 EB68
Cooks Rd, SE17 .161 DP79
Cooks Spinney, Harl. CM20 .36 EU13
Cooks Vennel, Hem.H. HP1 .40 BG18
Cooks Way, Hat. AL10 .45 CV20
Cooks Wf Roundabout, N18 .101 DX50
Coolfin Rd, E16 .15 N8
Coolgardie Av, E4 .101 EC50
Chigwell IG7 .103 EN48
Coolgardie Rd, Ashf. TW15 .175 BQ92
Coolhurst Rd, N8 .121 DK58
Cool Oak La, NW9 .118 CS59
Coomassie Rd, W9 .6 E3
COOMBE, Kings.T. KT2 .178 CQ94
Coombe, The, Bet. RH3 .248 CR131
Coombe Av, Croy. CR0 .220 DS105
Sevenoaks TN14 .241 FH120
Coombe Bk, Kings.T. KT2 .198 CS95
Coll Coombe Cliff Cont Ed Training Cen, Croy. CR0
off Coombe Rd .220 DR105
Coombe Cl, Edg. HA8 .96 CM54
Hounslow TW3 .156 CA84
Coombe Cor, N21 .99 DP46
Coombe Cres, Hmptn. TW12 176 BY94
Coombe Dr, Add. KT15 .211 BF107
Kingston upon Thames KT2 .178 CR94
Ruislip HA4 .115 BV60
Coombe End, Kings.T. KT2 .178 CR94
Coombefield Cl, N.Mal. KT3 .198 CS99
Coombe Gdns, SW20 .199 CU96
Berkhamsted HP4 .38 AT18
New Malden KT3 .199 CT98
Sch Coombe Girls' Sch, N.Mal. KT3 off Clarence Av .198 CR96
Coombe Hts, Kings.T. KT2 .178 CS94
Coombe Hill Ct, Wind. SL4 .151 AL83
Coombe Hill Glade, Kings.T. KT2 .178 CS94
Sch Coombe Hill Inf Sch, Kings.T. KT2
off Coombe La W .198 CR95
Sch Coombe Hill Jun Sch, Kings.T. KT2
off Coombe La W .198 CR95
Coombe Hill Rd, Kings.T. KT2 .178 CS94
Rickmansworth (Mill End) WD3 .92 BG45
Coombe Ho Chase, N.Mal. KT3 .198 CR95
Coombehurst Cl, Barn. EN4 .80 DF40
Coombelands La, Add. KT15 .212 BG107
Tra Coombe Lane .220 DW106
Coombe La, SW20 .199 CU95
Croydon CR0 .220 DV106
Coombe La W, Kings.T. KT2 .178 CS94
Coombe Lea, Brom. BR1 .204 EL97
Coombe Neville, Kings.T. KT2 .178 CR94
Coombe Pk, Kings.T. KT2 .178 CR92
Coombe Ridings, Kings.T. KT2 .178 CQ92
Coombe Ri, Brwd. (Shenf.) CM15 .109 FZ46
Kingston upon Thames KT2 .198 CQ95
Coombermere Cl, Wind. SL4 151 AP82
Coombe Rd, N22 .99 DN53
NW10 .118 CR62
SE26 .182 DV91
W4 .158 CS78
W13 off Northcroft Rd .157 CH76
Bushey WD23 .94 CC45
Croydon CR0 .220 DR105
Gravesend DA12 .191 GJ89
Hampton TW12 .176 BZ93
Kingston upon Thames KT2 .198 CN95
New Malden KT3 .198 CS96
Romford RM3 .128 FM55
Coomber Way, Croy. CR0 .201 DK101
Coombes Rd, Dag. RM9 .146 EZ67
St. Albans (Lon.Col.) AL2 .61 CH26
Coombe Vale, Ger.Cr. SL9 .112 AY60
Coombe Wk, Sutt. SM1 .200 DB104
Coombe Way, W.Byf. (Byfleet) KT14 .212 BM112
Coombewood Dr, Rom. RM6 .126 EZ58
Coombe Wd Hill, Pur. CR8 .220 DQ112
Coombe Wd Rd, Kings.T. KT2 .178 CQ92
Coombfield Dr, Dart. (Lane End) DA2 .189 FR91
Coombs St, N1 .4 F10
Coomer Ms, SW6
off Coomer Pl .159 CZ79
Coomer Pl, SW6 .159 CZ79
Coomer Rd, SW6
off Coomer Pl .159 CZ79
Cooms Wk, Edg. HA8
off East Rd .96 CQ53
Cooperage Cl, N17
off Brantwood Rd .100 DT51
Cooper Av, E17 .101 DX53
Cooper Cl, SE1 .20 D4
Greenhithe DA9 .189 FT85
Horley (Smallfield) RH6 .269 DN148
Cooper Ct, E15 off Clays La .123 EB64
Cooper Cres, Cars. SM5 .200 DF104
Cooper Rd, NW4 .119 CX58
NW10 .119 CT64
Croydon CR0 .219 DN105
Guildford GU1 .258 AY136
COOPERSALE, Epp. CM16 .70 EX29
Sch Coopersale & Theydon Garnon C of E Prim Sch, Epp. CM16
off Brickfields La .70 EX29
Coopersale Cl, Wdf.Grn. IG8
off Navestock Cres .102 EJ52
Coopersale Common, Epp. (Cooper.) CM16 .70 EX28
Sch Coopersale Hall Sch, Epp. CM16 off Flux's La .70 EV34
Coopersale La, Epp. CM16 .86 EU37
Coopersale Rd, E9 .123 DX64
Coopersale St, Epp. CM16 .70 EW32
Coopers Cl, E1 .12 E4
Chigwell IG7 .104 EV47
Dagenham RM10 .147 FB65
Dartford (S.Darenth) DA4 .208 FQ95
Staines TW18 .173 BE92
Sch Coopers' Company & Coborn Sch, Upmin. RM14
off St. Mary's La .128 FP61
Coopers Ct, Rom. (Gidea Pk) RM2 off Kidman Cl .128 FJ55
Cooper's Ct, Ware SG12 .33 DY06
Coopers Cres, Borwd. WD6 .78 CQ39
Coopers Dr, Dart. DA2 .187 FE89
Coopers Gate, St.Alb. AL4
off Church La .44 CP22
Coopers Grn La, Hat. AL10 .28 CS13
St. Albans AL4 .44 CL17
Welwyn Garden City AL8 .28 CQ14
Coopers Hill La, Egh. TW20 .172 AY91
Coopers Hill Rd, Red. (Nutfld) RH1 .251 DM133
Coopers La, E10 .123 EB60
NW1 .141 DK68
Cooper's La, SE12 .184 EH89
Coopers La, Pot.B. EN6 .64 DD31
Sch Cooper's La Prim Sch, SE12 off Pragnell Rd .184 EH89
Coopers La Rd, Pot.B. EN6 .64 DE31
Coopers Ms, Wat. WD25
off High Elms La .60 BW31
Coopers Rd, SE1 .21 P10
Gravesend (Nthflt) DA11 .190 GE88
Potters Bar EN6 .64 DC30
Cooper's Row, EC3 .11 N9
Coopers Row, Iver SL0 .133 BC70
Sch Coopers Sec Sch, Chis. BR7 off Hawkwood La .205 EQ95
Coopers Shaw Rd, Til. RM18 .171 GK80
Cooper St, E16 .15 K6
Coopers Wk, E15
off Maryland St .123 ED64
Waltham Cross (Chsht) EN8 .67 DX28
Coopers Yd, N1 off Upper St .141 DP66
Cooper's Yd, SE19
off Westow Hill .182 DS93
Cooper Way, Berk. HP4
off Robertson Rd .38 AX19
Slough SL1 .151 AP76
Coll Co-op Hall (Streatham & Tooting Adult Ed Inst), The, SW16 off Greyhound La .181 DL93
Coote Gdns, Dag. RM8 .126 EZ62
Coote Rd, Bexh. DA7 .166 EZ81
Dagenham RM8 .126 EZ62
Copeland Dr, E14 .23 P7
Copeland Rd, E17 .123 EB57
SE15 .162 DU82
Copeman Cl, SE26 .182 DW92
Copeman Rd, Brwd. (Hutt.) CM13 .109 GD45
Copenhagen Gdns, W4 .158 CQ75
Copenhagen Pl, E14 .13 L8
Sch Copenhagen Prim Sch, N1 .4 A8
Copenhagen St, N1 .141 DL67
Copenhagen Way, Walt. KT12 .195 BV104
Cope Pl, W8 .16 G6
Copers Cope Rd, Beck. BR3 .183 DZ93
Cope St, SE16 .22 G7
Copford Cl, Wdf.Grn. IG8 .102 EL51
Copford Wk, N1 .4 G7
Copgate Path, SW16 .181 DM93
Copinger Wk, Edg. HA8
off North Rd .96 CP53
Copland Av, Wem. HA0 .117 CK64
Copland Cl, Wem. HA0 .117 CJ64
Sch Copland Comm Sch & Tech Cen, Wem. HA9
off Cecil Av .118 CM64
Copland Ms, Wem. HA0
off Copland Rd .138 CL65
Copland Rd, Wem. HA0 .138 CL65
Copleigh Dr, Tad. KT20 .233 CY120
Copleston Ms, SE15
off Copleston Rd .162 DT82
Copleston Pas, SE15 .162 DT83
Copleston Rd, SE15 .162 DT83
Copley Cl, SE17
off Hillingdon St .161 DP79
W7 .137 CF71
Redhill RH1 .250 DE132
Woking GU21 .226 AS119
Copley Dene, Brom. BR1 .204 EK95
Copley Pk, SW16 .181 DM93
Copley Rd, Stan. HA7 .95 CJ50
Copley St, E1 .12 G6
Copley Way, Tad. KT20 .233 CX120
Copmans Wick, Rick. (Chorl.) WD3 .73 BD43
Copnor Way, SE15
off Blakes Rd .162 DS80
Coppard Gdns, Chess. KT9 .215 CJ107
Copped Hall, SE21
off Glazebrook Cl .182 DR89
Coppelia Rd, SE3 .164 EF84
Coppen Rd, Dag. RM8 .126 EZ59
Copperas St, SE8 .163 EB79
Copper Beech Cl, Grav. DA12 .191 GK87
Hemel Hempstead HP3 .39 BF23
Ilford IG5 .103 EN53
Orpington BR5
off Rookery Gdns .206 EW99
Windsor SL4 .151 AK81
Woking GU22 .226 AV121
Copper Beech Ct, Loug. IG10 .85 EN39
Copper Beeches, Islw. TW7
off Eversley Cres .157 CD81
Copper Beech Rd, S.Ock. RM15 .149 FW69
Copper Cl, SE19
off Auckland Rd .182 DT94
Copper Ct, Saw. CM21
off Brook Rd .36 EX06
Copperdale Rd, Hayes UB3 .155 BU75
Copperfield, Chig. IG7 .103 ER51
Copperfield App, Chig. IG7 .103 ER51
Copperfield Av, Uxb. UB8 .134 BN71
Copperfield Cl, S.Croy. CR2 .220 DQ111
Copperfield Ct, Lthd. KT22
off Kingston Rd .231 CG121
Pinner HA5
off Copperfield Way .116 BZ56
Copperfield Dr, N15 .122 DT56
Copperfield Gdns, Brwd. CM14 .108 FV46
Copperfield Ms, N18 .100 DS50
Copperfield Ri, Add. KT15 .211 BF106
Copperfield Rd, E3 .13 K5
SE28 .146 EW72
Copperfields, Beac. HP9 .89 AL50
Dartford DA1
off Spital St .188 FL86
Leatherhead (Fetch.) KT22 .230 CC122
Welwyn Garden City AL7
off Forresters Dr .30 DC10
Copperfield St, SE1 .20 F3
Copperfields Way, Rom. RM3 .106 FK53
Copperfield Ter, Slou. SL2
off Mirador Cres .132 AV73
Copperfield Way, Chis. BR7 .185 EQ93
Pinner HA5 .116 BZ56
Coppergate Cl, Brom. BR1 .204 EH95
Coppergate Ct, Wal.Abb. EN9 off Farthingale La .68 EG34
Copperkins Gro, Amer. HP6 .55 AP36
Copperkins La, Amer. HP6 .55 AM35
Copper Mead Cl, NW2 .119 CW62
Copper Mill Dr, Islw. TW7 .157 CF82
Coppermill La, E17 .122 DW58
Copper Mill La, SW17 .180 DC91
Coppermill La, Rick. WD3 .91 BE52
Uxbridge (Hare.) UB9 .91 BE52
Sch Coppermill Prim Sch, E17 off Edward Rd .123 DX57
Coppermill Rd, Stai. (Wrays.) TW19 .153 BC84
Copper Ridge, Ger.Cr. (Chal.St.P.) SL9 .91 AZ50
Copper Row, SE1 .21 N2
Copperwood, Hert. SG13 .32 DT09
Coppetts Cl, N12 .98 DE52
Coppetts Rd, N10 .98 DG54
H Coppetts Wd Hosp, N10 .98 DF53
Sch Coppetts Wd Prim Sch, N10 off Coppetts Rd .98 DG53
Coppice, The, Ashf. TW15
off School Rd .175 BP93
Beaconsfield HP9
off School La .89 AR51
Enfield EN2 .81 DP42
Hemel Hempstead HP2 .41 BP19
Watford WD19 .76 BW44
West Drayton UB7 .134 BL72
Coppice Cl, SW20 .199 CW97
Beckenham BR3 .203 EB98
Hatfield AL10 .45 CT22
Ruislip HA4 .115 BR58
Stanmore HA7 .95 CF51
Coppice Dr, SW15 .179 CV86
Staines (Wrays.) TW19 .172 AX87
Coppice End, Wok. GU22 .227 BE116
Coppice Fm Rd, H.Wyc. (Penn) HP10 .88 AC45
Coppice Hatch, Harl. CM18 .51 ER17
Coppice La, Reig. RH2 .249 CZ132
Coppice Path, Chig. IG7 .104 EV49
Sch Coppice Prim Sch, Chig. IG7 off Manford Way .104 EU50
Coppice Row, Epp. CM16 .85 EM36
Coppice Wk, N20 .98 DA48
Coppice Way, E18 .124 EF56
Slough (Hedg.) SL2 .111 AR61
Coppies Gro, N11 .98 DG49
Copping Cl, Croy. CR0 .220 DS105
Coppings, The, Hodd. EN11
off Danemead .33 EA14
Coppins, The, Croy. (New Adgtn) CR0 .221 EB107
Harrow HA3 .95 CE51
Welwyn Garden City AL8 .29 CU11
Coppins Cl, Berk. HP4 .38 AS19
Coppins La, Iver SL0 .133 BF71
Coppock Cl, SW11 .160 DE82
Coppsfield, W.Mol. KT8
off Hurst Rd .196 CA97
Copse, The, E4 .102 EF46
Amersham HP7 .55 AQ38
Beaconsfield HP9 .88 AJ51
Caterham CR3
off Tupwood La .252 DU126
Hemel Hempstead HP1 .39 BE18
Hertford SG13 .32 DU09
Leatherhead (Fetch.) KT22 .230 CB123
Redhill (S.Nutfld) RH1 .267 DL136
Copse Av, W.Wick. BR4 .203 EB104
Copse Cl, SE7 .164 EH79
Guildford (Chilw.) GU4 .259 BC140
Northwood HA6 .93 BQ54
Slough SL1 .131 AM74
West Drayton UB7 .154 BK76
Copse Edge Av, Epsom KT17 .217 CT113
Copse Glade, Surb. KT6 .197 CK102
COPSE HILL, SW20 .179 CU94
Copse Hill, SW20 .179 CV94
Harlow CM19 .51 EP18
Purley CR8 .219 DL113
Sutton SM2 .218 DB108
Copse La, Beac. (Jordans) HP9 .90 AS52
Horley RH6 .269 DJ147
Copsem Dr, Esher KT10 .214 CB107
Copsem La, Esher KT10 .214 CB107
Leatherhead (Oxshott) KT22 .214 CC111
Copsem Way, Esher KT10 .214 CC107
Copsen Wd, Lthd. KT22 .214 CC111
Copse Rd, Cob. KT11 .213 BV113
Redhill RH1 .266 DC136
Woking GU21 .226 AT118
Copse Vw, S.Croy. CR2 .221 DX109
Copse Way, Chesh. HP5 .54 AN27
Copse Wd, Iver SL0 .133 BD67
Copsewood Cl, Sid. DA15 .185 ES86
Copse Wd Ct, Reig. RH2
off Green La .250 DE132
Copsewood Rd, Wat. WD24 .75 BV39
Copse Wd Way, Nthwd. HA6 .93 BQ52
Copshall Cl, Harl. CM18 .51 ES19
Copsleigh Av, Red. RH1 .266 DG141
Copsleigh Cl, Red. (Salf.) RH1 .266 DG140
Copsleigh Way, Red. RH1 .266 DG140
Coptefield Dr, Belv. DA17 .166 EX76
Coptfold Rd, Brwd. CM14 .108 FW47
Copthall Av, EC2 .11 K7
Copthall Bldgs, EC2 .11 J7
Copthall Cl, EC2 .11 J7
Gerrards Cross (Chal.St.P.) SL9 .91 AZ52
Copthall Cor, Ger.Cr. (Chal.St.P.) SL9 .90 AY52
Copthall Ct, EC2 .11 J7
Copthall Dr, NW7 .97 CU52
Copthall Gdns, NW7 .97 CU52
Twickenham TW1 .177 CF88
COPTHALL GREEN, Wal.Abb. EN9 .68 EK33
Copthall La, Ger.Cr. (Chal.St.P.) SL9 .90 AY52
Copthall Rd E, Uxb. UB10 .114 BN61
Copthall Rd W, Uxb. UB10 .114 BN61
Sch Copthall Sch, NW7
off Pursley Rd .97 CV52
Copthall Way, Add. (New Haw) KT15 .211 BF110
Copt Hill La, Tad. KT20 .233 CY120
Copthorn Av, Brox. EN10 .49 DZ21
Copthorne Av, SW12 .181 DK87
Bromley BR2 .205 EM103
Ilford IG6 .103 EP51
Copthorne Chase, Ashf. TW15
off Ford Rd .174 BM91
Copthorne Cl, Rick. (Crox.Grn) WD3 .74 BM43
Shepperton TW17 .195 BQ100
Copthorne Gdns, Horn. RM11 .128 FN57
Copthorne Ms, Hayes UB3 .155 BS77
Copthorne Ri, S.Croy. CR2 .220 DR113
Copthorne Rd, Lthd. KT22 .231 CH120
Rickmansworth (Crox.Grn) WD3 .74 BM44
Coptic St, WC1 .9 N6
Copwood Cl, N12 .98 DD49
Coral Cl, Rom. RM6 .126 EW56
Coral Gdns, Hem.H. HP2 .40 BM19
Coraline Cl, Sthl. UB1 .136 BZ69
Coralline Wk, SE2 .166 EW75
Coral Row, SW11
off Gartons Way .160 DC83
Corals Mead, Welw.G.C. AL7 .29 CX10
Coral St, SE1 .20 D4
Coram Cl, Berk. HP4 .38 AW20
Coram Grn, Brwd. (Hutt.) CM13 .109 GD44
Coram St, WC1 .9 N4
Coran Cl, N9 .101 DX45
Corban Rd, Houns. TW3 .156 CA83
Corbar Cl, Barn. EN4 .80 DD38
Corbden Cl, SE15 .162 DT81
Corbet Cl, Wall. SM6 .200 DG102
Corbet Ct, EC3 .11 K8
Corbet Pl, E1 .11 N5
Corbet Rd, Epsom KT17 .216 CS110
Corbets Av, Upmin. RM14 .128 FP64
CORBETS TEY, Upmin. RM14 .148 FQ65
Corbets Tey Rd, Upmin. RM14 .128 FP63
Sch Corbets Tey Sch, Upmin. RM14
off Harwood Hall La .128 FQ64
Corbett Cl, Croy. CR0 .221 ED112
Corbett Gro, N22 .99 DL52
Corbett Ho, Wat. WD19 .94 BW48
Corbett Rd, E11 .124 EJ58
E17 .123 EC55
Corbetts La, SE16 .22 E8
Corbetts Pas, SE16 .22 E8
Corbicum, E11 .124 EE59
Corbidge Ct, SE8
off Glaisher St .163 EB79
Corbiere Ct, SW19
off Thornton Rd .179 CX93
Corbiere Ho, N1 .5 L7
Corbins La, Har. HA2 .116 CB62
Corbridge Cres, E2 .142 DV68
Corbridge Ms, Rom. RM1 .127 FF57
Corby Cl, Egh. (Eng.Grn) TW20 .172 AW93
St. Albans AL2 .60 CA25
Corby Cres, Enf. EN2 .81 DL42
Corby Dr, Egh. (Eng.Grn) TW20 .172 AV93
Corbylands Rd, Sid. DA15 .185 ES87
Corbyn St, N4 .121 DL60
Corby Rd, NW10 .138 CR68
Corby Way, E3 .13 P4
Corcorans, Brwd. (Pilg.Hat.) CM15 .108 FV44
Cordelia Cl, SE24 .161 DP84
Cordelia Gdns, Stai. TW19 .174 BL87
Cordelia Rd, Stai. TW19 .174 BL87
Cordelia St, E14 .14 A7
Cordell Cl, Wal.Cr. (Chsht) EN8 .67 DY28
Cordell Ho, N15
off Newton Rd .122 DT57
Corder Cl, St.Alb. AL3 .42 CA23
Corderoy Pl, Cher. KT16 .193 BE100
Cordingley Rd, Ruis. HA4 .115 BR61
Cording St, E14 .14 B6
Cordons Cl, Ger.Cr. (Chal.St.P.) SL9 .90 AX53
Cordrey Gdns, Couls. CR5 .235 DL115
Uni Cordwainers at London Coll of Fashion, Golden La, EC1 .10 G4
Cordwainers Wk, E13
off Richmond St .144 EG68
Cord Way, E14 .23 P5
Cordwell Rd, SE13 .184 EE85

Corefield Cl, N11
off Benfleet Way 98 DG47
Corelli Rd, SE3 164 EL82
Corfe Av, Har. HA2 116 CA63
Corfe Cl, Ashtd. KT21 231 CJ118
Borehamwood WD6
off Chester Rd 78 CR41
Hayes UB4 136 BW72
Hemel Hempstead HP2 40 BL21
Corfe Gdns, Slou. SL1
off Avebury 131 AN73
Corfe Twr, W3 158 CP75
Corfield Rd, N21 81 DM43
Corfield St, E2 12 D2
Corfton Rd, W5 138 CL72
Coriander Av, E14 14 E8
Coriander Cres, Guil. GU2 242 AU129
Cories Cl, Dag. RM8 126 EX61
Corinium Cl, Wem. HA9 118 CM63
Corinium Gate, St.Alb. AL3 42 CA22
Corinium Ind Est, Amer. HP6 72 AT38
Corinne Rd, N19 121 DJ63
Corinthian Manorway, Erith
DA8 167 FD77
Corinthian Rd, Erith DA8 167 FD77
Corinthian Way, Stai. (Stanw.)
TW19 off Clare Rd 174 BK87
Corker Wk, N7 121 DM61
Corkran Rd, Surb. KT6 197 CK101
Corkscrew Hill, W.Wick. BR4 203 ED103
Cork Sq, E1 22 C1
Cork St, W1 9 J10
Cork St Ms, W1 9 J10
Cork Tree Way, E4 101 DY50
Corlett St, NW1 8 A5
Cormongers La, Red.
(Nutfld) RH1 251 DK131
Cormont Rd, SE5 161 DP81
Cormorant Cl, E17
off Banbury Rd 101 DX53
Cormorant Ho, Enf. EN3
off Alma Rd 83 DX43
Cormorant Pl, Sutt. SM1
off Sandpiper Rd 217 CZ106
Cormorant Rd, E7 124 EF63
Cormorant Wk, Horn. RM12
off Heron Flight Av 147 FH65
Cornbury Rd, Edg. HA8 95 CK52
Corncroft, Hat. AL10 45 CV16
Cornelia Dr, Hayes UB4 136 BW70
Cornelia Pl, Erith DA8
off Queen St 167 FE79
Cornelia St, N7 4 B4
Cornell Cl, Sid. DA14 186 EY93
Cornell Way, Rom. RM5 104 FA50
Corner, The, W.Byf. KT14 212 BG113
Corner Fm Cl, Tad. KT20 233 CW122
Cornerfield, Hat. AL10 45 CV15
Corner Grn, SE3 164 EG83
Corner Hall, Hem.H. HP3 40 BJ22
Corner Hall Av, Hem.H. HP3 40 BK22
Corner Ho St, WC2 19 N1
Corner Mead, NW9 97 CT52
Corner Meadow, Harl. CM18 52 EU19
Corners, Welw.G.C. AL7 30 DA07
Cornerside, Ashf. TW15 175 BQ94
Corner Vw, Hat. AL9 45 CW24
Corney Reach Way, W4 158 CS80
Corney Rd, W4 158 CS79
Cornfield Cl, Uxb. UB8
off The Greenway 134 BK68
Cornfield Rd, Bushey WD23 76 CB42
Reigate RH2 266 DC135
Cornfields, Gdmg. GU7 258 AT143
Hemel Hempstead HP1 40 BH21
Cornflower La, Croy. CR0 203 DX102
Cornflower Ter, SE22 182 DV86
Cornflower Way, Hat. AL9 45 CS15
Romford RM3 106 FL53
Cornford Cl, Brom. BR2 204 EG99
Cornford Gro, SW12 181 DH89
Cornhill, EC3 11 K8
Cornhill Cl, Add. KT15 194 BH103
Cornhill Dr, Enf. EN3
off Ordnance Rd 83 DY37
Cornish Ct, N9 100 DV45
Cornish Gro, SE20 182 DV94
Cornish Ho, SE17 off Otto St 161 DP79
Brentford TW8
off Green Dragon La 158 CM78
Corn Mead, Welw.G.C. AL8 29 CW06
Cornmill, Wal.Abb. EN9 67 EB33
Corn Mill Dr, Orp. BR6 205 ET101
Cornmill La, SE13 163 EB83
Cornmill Ms, Wal.Abb. EN9
off Highbridge St 67 EB33
Cornmow Dr, NW10 119 CT64
Cornshaw Rd, Dag. RM8 126 EX60
Cornsland, Brwd. CM14 108 FX48
Cornsland Ct, Brwd. CM14 108 FW48
Cornthwaite Rd, E5 122 DW62
Cornwall Av, E2 12 E2
N3 98 DA52
N22 99 DL53
Esher (Clay.) KT10
off The Causeway 215 CF108
Slough SL2 131 AQ70
Southall UB1 136 BZ71
Welling DA16 165 ES83
West Byfleet (Byfleet)
KT14 212 BM114
Cornwall Cl, Bark. IG11 145 ET65
Hornchurch RM11 128 FN56
Waltham Cross EN8 67 DY33
Windsor (Eton Wick) SL4 151 AL78
Cornwall Cres, W11 6 C9
Cornwall Dr, Orp. BR5 186 EW94
Cornwall Gdns, NW10 139 CV65
SW7 17 K6
Cornwall Gdns Wk, SW7 17 K6
Cornwall Gate, Purf. RM19
off Fanns Ri 168 FN77
Cornwall Gro, W4 158 CS78
Cornwallis Av, N9 100 DV47
SE9 185 ER89
Cornwallis Cl, Cat. CR3 236 DQ122
Erith DA8 167 FF79
Cornwallis Gro, N9 100 DV47
Cornwallis Rd, E17 123 DX56
N9 100 DV47
N19 121 DL61
Dagenham RM9 126 EX63
Cornwallis Sq, N19 121 DL61
Cornwallis Wk, SE9 165 EM83
Cornwall Ms S, SW7 17 L6
Cornwall Ms W, SW7 17 K6
Cornwall Rd, N4 121 DN59
N15 122 DR57
N18 off Fairfield Rd 100 DU50
Cornwall Rd, SE1 20 C1
Brentwood (Pilg.Hat.)
CM15 108 FV43
Croydon CR0 201 DP103
Dartford DA1 168 FM83
Esher (Clay.) KT10 215 CG108
Harrow HA1 116 CC58
Pinner HA5 94 BZ52
Ruislip HA4 115 BT62
St. Albans AL1 43 CE22
Sutton SM2 217 CZ108
Twickenham TW1 177 CG88
Uxbridge UB8 134 BK65
Windsor SL4 172 AU86
Cornwall Sq, SE11 20 E9
Cornwall St, E1 12 D9
Cornwall Ter, NW1 8 D4
Cornwall Ter Ms, NW1 8 D4
Cornwall Way, Stai. TW18 173 BE93
Corn Way, E11 123 ED62
Cornwell Av, Grav. DA12 191 GJ90
Cornwood Cl, N2 120 DD57
Cornwood Dr, E1 12 E7
Cornworthy Rd, Dag. RM8 126 EW64
Corona Rd, SE12 184 EG87
Coronation Av, N16
off Victorian Rd 122 DT62
Slough (Geo.Grn) SL3 132 AY72
Windsor SL4 152 AT81
Coronation Cl, Bex. DA5 186 EX86
Ilford IG6 125 EQ56
Coronation Dr, Horn. RM12 127 FH63
Coronation Hill, Epp. CM16 69 ET30
Coronation Rd, E13 144 EJ69
NW10 138 CM69
Hayes UB3 155 BT77
Ware SG12 33 DX05
Coronation Wk, Twick. TW2 176 BZ88
Coronet, The, Horl. RH6 269 DJ150
Coronet St, N1 11 L2
Corporation Av, Houns. TW4 156 BY84
Corporation Row, EC1 10 D3
Corporation St, E15 144 EE68
N7 121 DL64
Sch Corpus Christi RC Prim Sch,
SW2 off Trent Rd 181 DM85
Annexe, SW2 off Trent Rd 181 DM85
New Malden KT3
off Chestnut Gro 198 CQ97
Corrance Rd, SW2 161 DL84
Corran Way, S.Ock. RM15 149 FV73
Corri Av, N14 99 DK49
Corrib Dr, Sutt. SM1 218 DE106
Corrie Gdns, Vir.W. GU25 192 AW101
Corrie Rd, Add. KT15 212 BK105
Woking GU22 227 BC120
Corrigan Av, Couls. CR5 218 DG114
Corrigan Cl, NW4 119 CW55
Corringham Ct, NW11
off Corringham Rd 120 DB59
St. Albans AL1
off Lemsford Rd 43 CF19
Corringham Rd, NW11 120 DA59
Wembley HA9 118 CN61
Corringway, NW11 120 DB59
W5 138 CN70
Corris Grn, NW9
off Snowdon Dr 118 CS58
Corry Dr, SW9 161 DP84
Corsair Cl, Stai. TW19 174 BK87
Corsair Rd, Stai. TW19 174 BL87
Corscombe Cl, Kings.T. KT2 178 CQ92
Corsehill St, SW16 181 DJ93
Corsham St, N1 11 K2
Corsica St, N5 4 E3
Cortayne Rd, SW6 159 CZ82
Cortina Dr, Dag. RM9 147 FC69
Cortis Rd, SW15 179 CV86
Cortis Ter, SW15 179 CV86
Cortland Cl, Dart. DA1 187 FE86
Corunna Rd, SW8 161 DJ81
Corunna Ter, SW8 161 DJ81
Corve La, S.Ock. RM15 149 FV73
Corvette Sq, SE10
off Feathers Pl 163 ED79
Corwell Gdns, Uxb. UB8 135 BQ72
Corwell La, Uxb. UB8 135 BQ72
Cory Dr, Brwd. (Hutt.) CM13 109 GB45
Coryton Path, W9 6 F3
Cory Wright Way, St.Alb.
(Wheat.) AL4 28 CL06
Cosbycote Av, SE24 182 DQ85
Cosdach Av, Wall. SM6 219 DK108
Cosedge Cres, Croy. CR0 219 DN106
Cosgrove Cl, N21 100 DQ47
Hayes UB4
off Kingsash Dr 136 BY70
Cosmo Pl, WC1 9 P5
Cosmur Cl, W12 159 CT76
Cossall Wk, SE15 162 DV81
Cossar Ms, SW2
off Tulse Hill 181 DN86
Cosser St, SE1 20 C5
Costa St, SE15 162 DU82
Costead Manor Rd, Brwd.
CM14 108 FV46
Costell's Meadow, West.
TN16 255 ER126
Costins Wk, Berk. HP4
off Robertson Rd 38 AX19
Sch Coston Prim Sch, Grnf.
UB6 off Oldfield La S 136 CC69
Costons Av, Grnf. UB6 137 CD69
Costons La, Grnf. UB6 137 CD69
Coston Wk, SE4
off Hainford Cl 163 DX84
Cosway St, NW1 8 B5
Cotall St, E14 13 P6
Coteford Cl, Loug. IG10 85 EP40
Pinner HA5 115 BU57
Sch Coteford Inf Sch, Pnr.
HA5 off Fore St 115 BU58
Sch Coteford Jun Sch, Pnr.
HA5 off Fore St 115 BT57
Coteford St, SW17 180 DF91
Cotelands, Croy. CR0 202 DS104
Cotesbach Rd, E5 122 DW62
Cotesmore Gdns, Dag. RM8 126 EW63
Cotesmore Rd, Hem.H. HP1 39 BE21
Cotford Rd, Th.Hth. CR7 202 DQ98
Cotham St, SE17 21 H8
Cotherstone, Epsom KT19 216 CR110
Cotherstone Rd, SW2 181 DM88
Cotland Acres, Red. RH1 266 DD136
Cotlandswick, St.Alb.
(Lon.Col.) AL2 61 CJ26
Cotleigh Av, Bex. DA5 186 EX89
Cotleigh Rd, NW6 140 DA66
Romford RM7 127 FD58
Cotman Cl, NW11 120 DC58
SW15 off Westleigh Av 179 CX86
Cotmandene, Dor. RH4 263 CH136
Cotmandene Cres, Orp.
BR5 206 EU96
Cotman Gdns, Edg. HA8 96 CN54
Cotman Ms, Dag. RM8
off Highgrove Rd 126 EW64
Cotmans Cl, Hayes UB3 135 BU74
Coton Rd, Well. DA16 166 EU83
Cotsford Av, N.Mal. KT3 198 CQ99
Cotswold, Hem.H. HP2
off Mendip Way 40 BL17
Cotswold Av, Bushey WD23 76 CC44
Cotswold Cl, Bexh. DA7 167 FE82
Esher KT10 197 CF104
Kingston upon Thames
KT2 178 CP93
St. Albans AL4
off Chiltern Rd 43 CJ15
Slough SL1 151 AP76
Staines TW18 174 BG92
Uxbridge UB8 134 BJ67
Cotswold Ct, EC1 10 G3
N11 98 DG49
Cotswold Gdns, E6 144 EK69
NW2 119 CX61
Brentwood (Hutt.) CM13 109 GE45
Ilford IG2 125 ER59
Cotswold Gate, NW2
off Cotswold Gdns 119 CY60
Cotswold Grn, Enf. EN2
off Cotswold Way 81 DM42
Cotswold Ms, SW11
off Battersea High St 160 DD81
Cotswold Ri, Orp. BR6 205 ET100
Cotswold Rd, Grav. (Nthflt)
DA11 190 GE90
Hampton TW12 176 CA93
Romford RM3 106 FM54
Sutton SM2 218 DB110
Cotswolds, Hat. AL10 45 CU20
Cotswold St, SE27
off Norwood High St 181 DP91
Cotswold Way, Enf. EN2 81 DM42
Worcester Park KT4 199 CW103
Cottage Av, Brom. BR2 204 EL102
Cottage Cl, Cher. (Ott.) KT16 211 BC107
Rickmansworth (Crox.Grn)
WD3 74 BM44
Ruislip HA4 115 BR60
Watford WD17 75 BT40
Cottage Fm Way, Egh. TW20
off Green Rd 193 BC97
Cottage Fld Cl, Sid. DA14 186 EW88
Cottage Gdns, Wal.Cr. EN8 66 DW29
Cottage Grn, SE5 162 DR80
Cottage Gro, SW9 161 DL83
Surbiton KT6 197 CK100
Cottage Homes, NW7 97 CU49
Cottage Pk Rd, Slou. (Hedg.)
SL2 111 AR61
Cottage Pl, SW3 18 A5
Cottage Rd, Epsom KT19 216 CR108
Cottage St, E14 14 B9
Cottage Wk, N16
off Smalley Cl 122 DT62
Cottenham Dr, NW9 119 CT55
SW20 179 CV94
Cottenham Par, SW20
off Durham Rd 199 CV96
COTTENHAM PARK, SW20 199 CV95
Cottenham Pk Rd, SW20 179 CV94
Cottenham Pl, SW20 179 CV94
Cottenham Rd, E17 123 DZ56
Cotterells, Hem.H. HP1 40 BJ21
Cotterells Hill, Hem.H. HP1 40 BJ20
Cotterill Rd, Surb. KT6 198 CL103
Cottesbrooke Cl, Slou.
(Colnbr.) SL3 153 BD81
Cottesbrook St, SE14
off Nynehead St 163 DY80
Cottesloe Ms, SE1 20 D5
Cottesmore Av, Ilf. IG5 103 EN54
Cottesmore Gdns, W8 17 K5
Cottimore Av, Walt. KT12 195 BV102
Cottimore Cres, Walt. KT12 195 BV101
Cottimore La, Walt. KT12 196 BW102
Cottimore Ter, Walt. KT12 195 BV101
Cottingham Chase, Ruis.
HA4 115 BU62
Cottingham Rd, SE20 183 DX94
SW8 161 DM80
Cottington Rd, Felt. TW13 176 BX91
Cottington St, SE11 20 D9
Cottle Way, SE16 22 D4
Cotton Av, W3 138 CR72
Cotton Cl, Dag. RM9
off Flamstead Rd 146 EW66
Cotton Dr, Hert. SG13 32 DV08
Cotton Fld, Hat. AL10 45 CV16
Cottongrass Cl, Croy. CR0
off Cornflower La 203 DX102
Cotton Hill, Brom. BR1 183 ED91
Cotton La, Dart. DA2 188 FQ86
Greenhithe DA9 188 FQ85
Cottonmill Cres, St.Alb. AL1 43 CD21
Cottonmill La, St.Alb. AL1 43 CE23
Cotton Rd, Pot.B. EN6 64 DC31
Cotton Row, SW11 160 DC83
Cottons App, Rom. RM7 127 FD57
Cottons Ct, Rom. RM7 127 FD57
Cottons Gdns, E2 11 M1
Cottons La, SE1 21 K1
Cotton St, E14 14 C9
Cottrell Ct, SE10
off Greenroof Way 164 EF76
Cotts Cl, W7
off Westcott Cres 137 CF71
Cotts Wd Dr, Guil. GU4 243 BA129
Couchmore Av, Esher KT10 197 CE103
Ilford IG5 103 EM54
Coulgate St, SE4 163 DY83
COULSDON, CR5 235 DJ116
Sch Coulsdon C of E Prim
Sch, Couls. CR5
off Bradmore Grn 235 DM118
Coll Coulsdon Coll, Couls.
CR5 off Placehouse La 235 DN119
Coulsdon Common, Cat.
CR3 236 DQ121
Coulsdon Ct Rd, Couls.
CR5 235 DM116
Sch Coulsdon High Sch, Couls.
CR5 off Homefield Rd 235 DP120
Coulsdon La, Couls. CR5 234 DF119
Coulsdon N Ind Est, Couls.
CR5 off Station App 235 DK115
Coulsdon Pl, Cat. CR3 236 DR122
Coulsdon Ri, Couls. CR5 235 DL117
Coulsdon Rd, Cat. CR3 236 DQ122
Coulsdon CR5 235 DM115
⇌ Coulsdon South 235 DK116
Coulser Cl, Hem.H. HP1 40 BG17
Coulson Cl, Dag. RM8 126 EW59
Coulson St, SW3 18 C9
Coulson Way, Slou. (Burn.)
SL1 130 AH71
Coulter Cl, Hayes UB4
off Berrydale Rd 136 BY70
Potters Bar (Cuffley) EN6 65 DK27
Coulter Rd, W6 159 CV76
Coulton Av, Grav. (Nthflt)
DA11 190 GE87
Council Av, Grav. (Nthflt)
DA11 190 GC86
Council Cotts, Wok. (Wisley)
GU23 off Wisley La 228 BK115
Councillor St, SE5 162 DQ80
Counter Ct, SE1
off Southwark St 142 DR74
Counters Cl, Hem.H. HP1 40 BG20
Counter St, SE1 21 L2
Sch Countess Anne C of E
Prim Sch, Hat. AL10
off School La 45 CW17
Countess Cl, Uxb. (Hare.)
UB9 92 BJ54
Countess Rd, NW5 121 DJ64
Countisbury Av, Enf. EN1 100 DT45
Countisbury Gdns, Add.
KT15 off Addlestone Pk 212 BH106
Country Way, Felt. TW13 175 BV94
Sunbury-on-Thames
TW16 175 BV94
County Gate, SE9 185 EQ90
Barnet EN5 80 DB44
County Gro, SE5 162 DQ81
★ County Hall, SE1 20 A3
County Rd, E6 145 EP71
Thornton Heath CR7 201 DP96
County St, SE1 21 H6
Coupland Pl, SE18 165 EQ78
Courage Cl, Horn. RM11 128 FJ58
Courage Wk, Brwd. (Hutt.)
CM13 109 GD44
Courcy Rd, N8 121 DN55
Courier Rd, Dag. RM9 147 FC70
Courland Gro, SW8 161 DK81
Courland Gro Hall, SW8 161 DK81
Courland Rd, Add. KT15 194 BH104
Courland St, SW8 161 DK81
Course, The, SE9 185 EN90
Coursers Rd, St.Alb.
(Coln.Hth) AL4 62 CN27
Court, The, Ruis. HA4 116 BY63
Warlingham CR6 237 DY118
Courtauld Cl, SE28
off Pitfield Cres 146 EU74
★ Courtauld Inst of Art,
WC2 10 A9
Courtauld Rd, N19 121 DK60
Courtaulds, Kings L.
(Chipper.) WD4 58 BH30
Court Av, Belv. DA17 166 EZ78
Coulsdon CR5 235 DN118
Romford RM3 106 FN52
Court Bushes Rd, Whyt.
CR3 236 DU120
Court Cl, Har. HA3 118 CL55
Maidenhead SL6 150 AC77
Twickenham TW2 176 CB90
Wallington SM6 219 DK108
Court Cl Av, Twick. TW2 176 CB90
Court Cres, Chess. KT9 215 CK106
Slough SL1 131 AR72
Swanley BR8 207 FE98
Court Downs Rd, Beck. BR3 203 EB96
★ Court Dress Collection,
Kensington Palace, W8 17 K2
Court Dr, Croy. CR0 219 DM105
Maidenhead SL6 130 AC68
Stanmore HA7 96 CL49
Sutton SM1 218 DE105
Uxbridge UB10 134 BM67
Courtenay Av, N6 120 DE58
Harrow HA3 94 CC53
Sutton SM2 218 DA109
Courtenay Dr, Beck. BR3 203 ED96
Grays (Chaff.Hun.) RM16
off Clifford Rd 170 FZ76
Courtenay Gdns, Har. HA3 94 CC54
Upminster RM14 128 FQ60
Courtenay Ms, E17
off Cranbrook Ms 123 DY57
Courtenay Pl, E17 123 DY57
Courtenay Rd, E11 124 EF62
E17 123 DX56
SE20 183 DX94
Wembley HA9 117 CK62
Woking GU21 227 BA116
Worcester Park KT4 199 CW104
Courtenay Sq, SE11 20 C10
Courtenay St, SE11 20 C9
Courtens Ms, Stan. HA7 95 CJ52
Court Fm Av, Epsom KT19 216 CR106
Court Fm Rd, SE9 184 EK89
Northolt UB5 136 CA66
Warlingham CR6 236 DU118
Courtfield, W5
off Castlebar Hill 137 CJ71
Courtfield Av, Har. HA1 117 CF57
Courtfield Cl, Brox. EN10 49 EA20
Courtfield Cres, Har. HA1 117 CF57
Courtfield Gdns, SW5 17 K7
W13 137 CG72
Ruislip HA4 115 BT61
Uxbridge (Denh.) UB9 114 BG62
Courtfield Ms, SW5 17 L8
Courtfield Ri, W.Wick. BR4 204 ED104
Courtfield Rd, SW7 17 K8
Ashford TW15 175 BP93
Court Gdns, N7 4 D4
Courtgate Cl, NW7 97 CT51
Court Grn Hts, Wok. GU22 226 AW120
Court Haw, Bans. SM7 234 DE115
Court Hill, Couls. CR5 234 DE118
South Croydon CR2 220 DS112
Courthill Rd, SE13 163 EC84
Courthope Rd, NW3 120 DF63
SW19 179 CY92
Greenford UB6 137 CD68
Courthope Vil, SW19 179 CY94
Court Ho Gdns, N3 98 DA51
Courthouse Rd, N12 98 DB51
Courtland Av, E4 102 EF47
NW7 96 CR48
SW16 181 DM94
Ilford IG1 125 EM61
Courtland Cl, Wdf.Grn. IG8 102 EJ53
Courtland Dr, Chig. IG7 103 EP48
Courtland Gro, SE28 146 EX73
Sch Courtland JMI Sch, NW7
off Courtland Av 96 CS47
Courtland Rd, E6
off Harrow Rd 144 EL67
Courtlands, Rich. TW10 158 CN84
Courtlands Av, SE12 184 EH85
Bromley BR2 204 EF102
Esher KT10 214 BZ107
Hampton TW12 176 BZ93
Richmond TW9 158 CP82
Slough SL3 152 AX77
Courtlands Cl, Ruis. HA4 115 BT59
South Croydon CR2 220 DT110
Watford WD24 75 BS35
Courtlands Cres, Bans.
SM7 234 DA116
Courtlands Dr, Epsom KT19 216 CS107
Watford WD17, WD24 75 BS37
Courtlands Rd, Surb. KT5 198 CN101
Court La, SE21 182 DS86
Epsom KT19 216 CQ113
Iver SL0 134 BG74
Slough (Burn.) SL1 131 AK69
Windsor (Dorney) SL4 150 AG76
Court La Gdns, SE21 182 DS87
Court Lawns, H.Wyc. (Penn)
HP10 88 AC46
Courtleas, Cob. KT11 214 CA113
Courtleet Dr, Erith DA8 167 FB81
Courtleigh Av, Barn. EN4 80 DD38
Courtleigh Gdns, NW11 119 CY56
Sch Court Lo Inf Sch, Horl.
RH6 off Court Lo Rd 268 DF148
Court Lo Rd, Horl. RH6 268 DE147
Courtman Rd, N17 100 DQ52
Court Mead, Nthlt. UB5 136 BZ69
Courtmead Cl, SE24 182 DQ86
Courtnell St, W2 6 G7
Courtney Cl, SE19 182 DS93
Courtney Cres, Cars. SM5 218 DF108
Courtney Pl, Cob. KT11 214 BZ112
Croydon CR0 201 DN104
Courtney Rd, N7 4 C1
SW19 180 DE94
Croydon CR0 201 DN104
Grays RM16 171 GJ75
Hounslow (Hthrw Air.)
TW6 154 BN83
Courtney Way, Houns.
(Hthrw Air.) TW6
off Courtney Rd 154 BN82
Court Par, Wem. HA0 117 CH62
Courtrai Rd, SE23 183 DY86
Court Rd, SE9 184 EL89
SE25 202 DT96
Banstead SM7 234 DA116
Caterham CR3 236 DR123
Dartford (Lane End) DA2 189 FS92
Godstone RH9 252 DW131
Maidenhead SL6 130 AC69
Orpington BR6 206 EV101
Southall UB2 156 BZ77
Uxbridge UB10 115 BP64
Courtside, N8 121 DK58
Court St, E1 12 C5
Bromley BR1 204 EG96
Court Way, NW9 118 CS56
W3 138 CQ71
Ilford IG6 125 EQ55
Romford RM3 106 FL54
Twickenham TW2 177 CF87
Courtway, Wdf.Grn. IG8 102 EJ50
Courtway, The, Wat. WD19 94 BY47
Court Wd Dr, Sev. TN13 256 FG124
Court Wd Gro, Croy. CR0 221 DZ111
Court Wd La, Croy. CR0 221 DZ111
Sch Courtwood Prim Sch, Croy.
CR0 off Court Wd La 221 DZ110
Court Yd, SE9 184 EL86
Courtyard, The, N1 4 B5
Courtyards, The, Slou. SL3
off Waterside Dr 153 BA75
Cousin La, EC4 11 J10
Cousins Cl, West Dr. UB7 134 BL73
Couthurst Rd, SE3 164 EH79
Coutts Av, Chess. KT9 216 CL106
Coutts Cres, NW5 120 DG62
Coval Gdns, SW14 158 CP84
Coval La, SW14 158 CP84
Coval Rd, SW14 158 CP84
Coveham Cres, Cob. KT11 213 BU113
Covelees Wall, E6 145 EN72
Covell Ct, SE8
off Reginald Sq 163 EA80
Covenbrook, Brwd. CM13 109 GB48
★ Covent Garden, WC2 9 P9
⊖ Covent Garden 9 N9
Coventry Cl, E6
off Harper Rd 145 EM72
NW6 off Kilburn High Rd 140 DA67
Coventry Cross, E3
off Gillender St 143 EC70
Coventry Rd, E1 12 D3
E2 12 D3
SE25 202 DU98
Ilford IG1 125 EP60
Coventry St, W1 9 L10
Coverack Cl, N14 81 DJ44
Croydon CR0 203 DY101
Coverdale, Hem.H. HP2
off Wharfedale 40 BL17
Coverdale Cl, Stan. HA7 95 CH50
Coverdale Ct, Enf. EN3
off Raynton Rd 83 DY37
Coverdale Gdns, Croy. CR0
off Park Hill Ri 202 DT104
Coverdale Rd, N11 98 DG51
NW2 139 CX66
W12 139 CV74
Coverdales, The, Bark. IG11 145 EQ68
Coverdale Way, Slou. SL2 131 AL70
Coverley Cl, E1 12 B5
Brentwood (Gt Warley)
CM13 off Wilmot Grn 107 FW51
Covert, The, Nthwd. HA6 93 BQ53
Orpington BR6 205 ES100
Coverton Rd, SW17 180 DE92
Covert Rd, Ilf. IG6 103 ET51
Coverts, The, Brwd. (Hutt.)
CM13 109 GA46
Coverts Rd, Esher (Clay.)
KT10 215 CF109
Covert Way, Barn. EN4 80 DC40
Covesfield, Grav. DA11 191 GF87
Covet Wd Cl, Orp. BR5
off Lockesley Dr 205 ET100
Covey Cl, SW19 200 DB96
Covington Gdns, SW16 181 DP94
Covington Way, SW16 181 DM93
Cowan Cl, E6
off Oliver Gdns 144 EL71
Cowbridge, Hert. SG14 32 DQ09
Cowbridge La, Bark. IG11 145 EP66
Cowbridge Rd, Har. HA3 118 CM56
Cowcross St, EC1 10 E5
Cowdenbeath Path, N1 4 A7
Cowden Rd, Orp. BR6 205 ET101
Cowden St, SE6 183 EA91
Cowdray Rd, Uxb. UB10 135 BQ67
Cowdray Way, Horn. RM12 127 FF63
Cowdrey Cl, Enf. EN1 82 DS40
Cowdrey Ct, Dart. DA1 187 FH87
Cowdrey Rd, SW19 180 DB92
Cowdry Rd, E9 off Wick Rd 143 DY65
Cowen Av, Har. HA2 116 CC61
Cowgate Rd, Grnf. UB6 137 CD68
Cowick Rd, SW17 180 DF91
Cowings Mead, Nthlt. UB5 136 BY66
Cowland Av, Enf. EN3 82 DW42

★ Place of interest | H Hospital | Sch School | Coll College | Uni University | ⇌ Railway station

Cow La, Grnf. UB6 ....137 CD68
Watford WD25 ....76 BW36
Cow Leaze, E6 ....145 EN72
Cowleaze Rd, Kings.T. KT2 ....198 CL95
Cowles, Wal.Cr. (Chsht) EN7 ....66 DT27
COWLEY, Uxb. UB8 ....134 BJ70
Cowley Av, Cher. KT16 ....193 BF101
Greenhithe DA9 ....189 FT85
Cowley Business Pk, Uxb. UB8 ....134 BJ69
Cowley Cl, S.Croy. CR2 ....220 DW109
Cowley Cres, Uxb. UB8 ....134 BJ71
Walton-on-Thames KT12 ....214 BW105
Cowley Hill, Borwd. WD6 ....78 CP37
Sch Cowley Hill First Sch, Borwd. WD6 off Winstre Rd 78 CN39
Sch Cowley Inf Sch, Uxb. UB8 off Worcester Rd 134 BJ71
Cowley La, E11 off Cathall Rd 124 EE62
Chertsey KT16 ....193 BF101
Cowley Mill Rd, Uxb. UB8 ....134 BH68
Cowley Pl, NW4 ....119 CW57
Cowley Rd, E11 ....124 EH57
SW9 ....161 DN81
SW14 ....158 CS83
W3 ....139 CT74
Ilford IG1 ....125 EM59
Romford RM3 ....105 FH52
Uxbridge UB8 ....134 BJ68
Cowley St, SW1 ....19 N5
Cowling Cl, W11 ....6 C10
Cowlins, Harl. CM17 off New Rd 36 EX11
Cowper Av, E6 ....144 EL66
Sutton SM1 ....218 DD105
Tilbury RM18 ....171 GH81
Cowper Cl, Brom. BR2 ....204 EK98
Chertsey KT16 ....193 BF100
Welling DA16 ....186 EU85
Cowper Ct, Wat. WD24 ....75 BU37
Cowper Cres, Hert. SG14 ....31 DP07
Cowper Gdns, N14 ....81 DJ44
Wallington SM6 ....219 DJ107
Cowper Rd, N14 ....99 DH46
N16 ....5 L1
N18 ....100 DU50
SW19 ....180 DC93
W3 ....138 CR74
W7 ....137 CF73
Belvedere DA17 ....166 FA77
Berkhamsted HP4 ....38 AV19
Bromley BR2 ....204 EK98
Chesham HP5 ....54 AP29
Hemel Hempstead HP1 ....40 BH21
Kingston upon Thames KT2 ....178 CM92
Rainham RM13 ....147 FG70
Slough SL2 ....131 AN70
Welwyn Garden City AL7 ....29 CZ11
Cowpers Ct, EC3 off Birchin La 142 DR72
Cowper St, EC2 ....11 K3
Cowper Ter, W10 ....6 A6
Cowslip Cl, Uxb. UB10 ....134 BL66
Cowslip La, Dor. (Mick.) RH5 ....247 CG129
Woking GU21 ....226 AV115
Cowslip Rd, E18 ....102 EH54
Cowslips, Welw.G.C. AL7 ....30 DC10
Cowthorpe Rd, SW8 ....161 DK81
Cox Cl, Rad. (Shenley) WD7 ....62 CM32
Coxdean, Epsom KT18 ....233 CW119
Coxe Pl, Har. (Wldste) HA3 ....117 CG56
Coxfield Cl, Hem.H. HP2 ....40 BL21
Cox La, Chess. KT9 ....216 CM105
Epsom KT19 ....216 CP106
Coxley Ri, Pur. CR8 ....220 DQ113
Coxmount Rd, SE7 ....164 EK78
Coxson Way, SE1 ....21 N4
Cox's Wk, SE21 ....182 DU88
Coxwell Rd, SE18 ....165 ER78
SE19 ....182 DS94
Coxwold Path, Chess. KT9 off Garrison La 216 CL108
Cozens La E, Brox. EN10 ....49 DZ23
Cozens La W, Brox. EN10 ....49 DY22
Cozens Rd, Ware SG12 ....33 DZ06
Crabbe Cres, Chesh. HP5 ....54 AR29
Crabbs Cft Cl, Orp. BR6 off Ladycroft Way 223 EQ106
Crab Hill, Beck. BR3 ....183 ED94
Crab Hill La, Red. RH1 ....267 DM138
Crab La, Wat. (Ald.) WD25 ....76 CB35
Crabtree Av, Rom. RM6 ....126 EX56
Wembley HA0 ....138 CL68
Crabtree Cl, E2 ....5 N10
Beaconsfield HP9 ....88 AH54
Bushey WD23 ....76 CB43
Hemel Hempstead HP3 ....40 BK22
Leatherhead (Bkhm) KT23 ....246 CC126
Crabtree Cor, Egh. TW20 ....193 BB95
Crabtree Ct, E15 off Clays La 123 EB64
Hemel Hempstead HP3 off Crabtree La 40 BL22
Crabtree Dr, Lthd. KT22 ....231 CJ124
Crabtree Hill, Rom. (Abridge) RM4 ....104 EZ45
Crabtree La, SW6 ....159 CX80
Dorking (Westh.) RH5 ....247 CF130
Hemel Hempstead HP3 ....40 BK22
Leatherhead (Bkhm) KT23 ....246 CC126
Crabtree Manorway Ind Est, Belv. DA17 ....167 FB76
Crabtree Manorway N, Belv. DA17 ....167 FC75
Crabtree Manorway S, Belv. DA17 ....167 FC76
Crabtree Rd, Egh. TW20 ....193 BC96
Crabtree Wk, Brox. EN10 ....49 DY19
Crackley Meadow, Hem.H. HP2 ....41 BP15
Craddock Rd, Enf. EN1 ....82 DT41
Craddocks Av, Ashtd. KT21 ....232 CL117
Craddocks Par, Ashtd. KT21 ....232 CL117
Cradock St, NW5 off Prince of Wales Rd 140 DG65
Cradhurst Cl, Dor. (Westc.) RH4 ....262 CC137
Cradley Rd, SE9 ....185 ER88
★ Crafts Council, N1 ....4 D10
Cragg Av, Rad. WD7 ....77 CF36
Craigavon Rd, Hem.H. HP2 ....40 BM16
Craigdale Rd, Horn. RM11 ....127 FF58
Craig Dr, Uxb. UB8 ....135 BP72
Craigen Av, Croy. CR0 ....202 DV102
Craigerne Rd, SE3 ....164 EH80
Craig Gdns, E18 ....102 EF54
Craigholm, SE18 ....165 EN82
Craiglands, St.Alb. AL4 ....43 CK16
Craigmore Twr, Wok. GU22 off Guildford Rd 226 AY119
Craig Mt, Rad. WD7 ....77 CH35
Craigmuir Pk, Wem. HA0 ....138 CM67
Craignair Rd, SW2 ....181 DN87
Craignish Av, SW16 ....201 DM96
Craig Pk Rd, N18 ....100 DV50
Craig Rd, Rich. TW10 ....177 CJ91
Craigs Ct, SW1 ....19 N1
Craigs Wk, Wal.Cr. (Chsht) EN8 off Davison Dr 67 DX28
Craigton Rd, SE9 ....165 EM84
Craigweil Av, Rad. WD7 ....77 CH35
Craigweil Cl, Stan. HA7 ....95 CK50
Craigweil Dr, Stan. HA7 ....95 CK50
Craigwell Av, Felt. TW13 ....175 BU90
Craigwell Cl, Stai. TW18 ....193 BE95
Craik Ct, NW6 off Carlton Vale 139 CZ68
Crail Row, SE17 ....21 K8
Crakell Rd, Reig. RH2 ....266 DC135
Cramer Ct, N.Mal. KT3 off Warwick Rd 198 CQ97
Cramer St, W1 ....8 F6
Crammerville Wk, Rain. RM13 ....147 FH70
Crammond Pk, Harl. CM19 ....51 EN16
Cramond Cl, W6 ....159 CY79
Cramond Ct, Felt. TW14 ....175 BS88
Crampshaw La, Ashtd. KT21 ....232 CM119
Sch Crampton Prim Sch, SE17 ....20 F9
Crampton Rd, SE20 ....182 DW93
Cramptons Rd, Sev. TN14 ....241 FH120
Crampton St, SE17 ....20 G8
Cranberry Cl, Nthlt. UB5 off Parkfield Av 136 BX68
Cranberry La, E16 ....14 G4
Cranborne Av, Sthl. UB2 ....156 CA77
Surbiton KT6 ....198 CN104
Cranborne Cl, Hert. SG13 ....32 DQ12
Potters Bar EN6 ....63 CY31
Cranborne Cres, Pot.B. EN6 ....63 CY31
Cranborne Gdns, Upmin. RM14 ....128 FP61
Welwyn Garden City AL7 ....29 CZ10
Cranborne Ind Est, Pot.B. EN6 ....63 CY30
Sch Cranborne Prim Sch, Pot.B. EN6 off Laurel Flds 63 CZ31
Cranborne Rd, Bark. IG11 ....145 ER67
Hatfield AL10 ....45 CV17
Hoddesdon EN11 ....49 EB16
Potters Bar EN6 ....63 CY30
Waltham Cross (Chsht) EN8 ....67 DX32
Cranborne Waye, Hayes UB4 ....136 BW73
Cranbourn All, WC2 ....9 M9
Cranbourne Av, E11 ....124 EH56
Windsor SL4 ....151 AM82
Cranbourne Cl, SW16 ....201 DL97
Horley RH6 ....269 DH146
Slough SL1 ....131 AQ74
Cranbourne Dr, Hodd. EN11 ....33 EB13
Pinner HA5 ....116 BX57
Cranbourne Gdns, NW11 ....119 CY57
Ilford IG6 ....125 EQ55
Cranbourne Pas, SE16 ....22 C4
Sch Cranbourne Prim Sch, Hodd. EN11 off Bridle Way N 33 EB13
Cranbourne Rd, E12 off High St N 124 EL64
E15 ....123 EC63
N10 ....99 DH54
Northwood HA6 ....115 BT55
Slough SL1 ....131 AQ74
Cranbourn St, WC2 ....9 M9
CRANBROOK, Ilf. IG1 ....125 EM60
Cranbrook Cl, Brom. BR2 ....204 EG100
Sch Cranbrook Coll, Ilf. IG1 off Mansfield Rd 125 EN61
Cranbrook Dr, Esher KT10 ....196 CC102
Romford RM2 ....127 FH56
St. Albans AL4 ....44 CL20
Twickenham TW2 ....176 CB88
Cranbrook Ho, Erith DA8 off Boundary St 167 FF80
Cranbrook Ms, E17 ....123 DY57
Cranbrook Pk, N22 ....99 DM53
Cranbrook Ri, Ilf. IG1 ....125 EM59
Cranbrook Rd, SE8 ....163 EA81
SW19 ....179 CY94
W4 ....158 CS78
Barnet EN4 ....80 DD44
Bexleyheath DA7 ....166 EZ81
Hounslow TW4 ....156 BZ84
Ilford IG1, IG2, IG6 ....125 EN59
Thornton Heath CR7 ....202 DQ96
Cranbrook St, E2 off Mace St 143 DX68
Cranbury Rd, SW6 ....160 DB82
Crandon Wk, Dart. (S.Darenth) DA4 ....209 FS96
Crane Av, W3 ....138 CQ73
Isleworth TW7 ....177 CG85
Cranebank Ms, Twick. TW1 ....157 CG84
Cranebrook, Twick. TW2 off Manor Rd 176 CC89
Crane Cl, Dag. RM10 ....146 FA65
Harrow HA2 ....116 CC62
Crane Ct, EC4 ....10 D8
Epsom KT19 ....216 CQ105
Cranefield Dr, Wat. WD25 ....60 BY32
Craneford Cl, Twick. TW2 ....177 CF87
Craneford Way, Twick. TW2 ....177 CE87
Crane Gdns, Hayes UB3 ....155 BT77
Crane Gro, N7 ....4 D3
Cranell Grn, S.Ock. RM15 ....149 FV74
Crane Lo Rd, Houns. TW5 ....155 BV79
Crane Mead, SE16 ....22 G8
Ware SG12 ....33 DY07
Sch Crane Pk Prim Sch, Felt. TW13 off Norman Av 176 BZ89
Crane Pk Rd, Twick. TW2 ....176 CB89
Crane Rd, Twick. TW2 ....177 CE88
Cranesbill Cl, NW9 off Colindale Av 118 CR55
Cranes Dr, Surb. KT5 ....198 CL98
Cranes Pk, Surb. KT5 ....198 CL98
Cranes Pk Av, Surb. KT5 ....198 CL98
Cranes Pk Cres, Surb. KT5 ....198 CM98
Crane St, SE10 ....24 E10
SE15 ....162 DT81
Craneswater, Hayes UB3 ....155 BT80
Craneswater Pk, Sthl. UB2 ....156 BZ78
Cranes Way, Borwd. WD6 ....78 CQ43
Crane Way, Twick. TW2 ....176 CC87
Cranfield Cl, SE27 off Dunelm Gro 182 DQ90
Cranfield Ct, Wok. GU21 off Martindale Rd 226 AU118
Cranfield Cres, Pot.B. (Cuffley) EN6 ....65 DL29
Cranfield Dr, NW9 ....96 CS52
Cranfield Rd, SE4 ....163 DZ83
Cranfield Rd E, Cars. SM5 ....218 DG109
Cranfield Rd W, Cars. SM5 ....218 DF109
Cranfield Row, SE1 ....20 D5
CRANFORD, Houns. TW5 ....155 BU80
Cranford Av, N13 ....99 DL50
Staines TW19 ....174 BL87
Cranford Cl, SW20 ....199 CV95
Purley CR8 ....220 DQ113
Staines TW19 ....174 BL87
Sch Cranford Comm Coll, Houns. TW5 off High St 155 BV79
Cranford Cotts, E1 off Cranford St 143 DX73
Cranford Ct, Hert. SG14 off The Ridgeway 31 DM07
Cranford Dr, Hayes UB3 ....155 BT77
Sch Cranford Inf & Nurs Sch, Houns. TW4 off Berkeley Av 155 BV82
Sch Cranford Jun Sch, Houns. TW4 off Woodfield Rd 155 BV82
Cranford La, Hayes UB3 ....155 BR79
Hounslow (Hthrw Air.) TW6 ....155 BT83
Hounslow (Hthrw Air.N.) TW6 ....155 BT81
Hounslow (Heston) TW5 ....156 BX80
Sch Cranford Pk Prim Sch, Hayes UB3 off Phelps Way 155 BT77
Cranford Pk Rd, Hayes UB3 ....155 BT77
Cranford Ri, Esher KT10 ....214 CC106
Cranford Rd, Dart. DA1 ....188 FL88
Cranford St, E1 ....13 H9
Cranford Way, N8 ....121 DM57
CRANHAM, Upmin. RM14 ....129 FS59
Cranham Gdns, Upmin. RM14 ....129 FS60
Cranham Rd, Horn. RM11 ....127 FH58
Cranhurst Rd, NW2 ....119 CW64
Cranleigh Cl, SE20 ....202 DV96
Bexley DA5 ....187 FB86
Orpington BR6 ....206 EU104
South Croydon CR2 ....220 DU112
Waltham Cross (Chsht) EN7 ....66 DU28
Cranleigh Dr, Swan. BR8 ....207 FE98
Cranleigh Gdns, N21 ....81 DN43
SE25 ....202 DS97
Barking IG11 ....145 ER66
Harrow HA3 ....118 CL57
Kingston upon Thames KT2 ....178 CM93
Loughton IG10 ....85 EM44
South Croydon CR2 ....220 DU112
Southall UB1 ....136 BZ72
Sutton SM1 ....200 DB103
Cranleigh Gdns Ind Est, Sthl. UB1 off Cranleigh Gdns 136 BZ72
Cranleigh Ms, SW11 ....160 DE82
Cranleigh Rd, N15 ....122 DQ57
SW19 ....200 DA97
Esher KT10 ....196 CC102
Feltham TW13 ....175 BT91
Guildford (Won.) GU5 ....259 BB144
Cranleigh St, NW1 ....141 DJ68
Cranley Cl, Guil. GU1 ....243 BA134
Cranley Dene, Guil. GU1 off Cranley Rd 243 BA134
Cranley Dene Ct, N10 ....121 DH56
Cranley Dr, Ilf. IG2 ....125 EQ59
Ruislip HA4 ....115 BT61
Cranley Gdns, N10 ....121 DJ56
N13 ....99 DM48
SW7 ....17 M9
Wallington SM6 ....219 DJ108
Cranley Ms, SW7 ....17 M9
Cranley Par, SE9 off Beaconsfield Rd 184 EL91
Cranley Pl, SW7 ....17 N8
Cranley Rd, E13 ....15 N5
Guildford GU1 ....243 AZ134
Ilford IG2 ....125 EQ58
Walton-on-Thames KT12 ....213 BS106
Cranmer Av, W13 ....157 CH76
Cranmer Cl, Mord. SM4 ....199 CX100
Potters Bar EN6 ....64 DB30
Ruislip HA4 ....116 BX60
Stanmore HA7 ....95 CJ52
Warlingham CR6 ....237 DY117
Weybridge KT13 ....212 BN108
Cranmer Ct, SW3 ....18 B8
SW4 ....161 DK83
Hampton (Hmptn H.) TW12 off Cranmer Rd 176 CB92
Sch Cranmere Prim Sch, Esher KT10 off The Drive 196 CC102
Cranmer Fm Cl, Mitch. CR4 ....200 DF98
Cranmer Gdns, Dag. RM10 ....127 FC63
Warlingham CR6 ....237 DY117
Cranmer Ho, SW11 off Surrey La 160 DE81
Sch Cranmer Prim Sch, Mitch. CR4 off Cranmer Rd 200 DF98
Cranmer Rd, E7 ....124 EH63
SW9 ....161 DN80
Croydon CR0 ....201 DP104
Edgware HA8 ....96 CP48
Hampton (Hmptn H.) TW12 ....176 CB92
Hayes UB3 ....135 BR72
Kingston upon Thames KT2 ....178 CL92
Mitcham CR4 ....200 DF98
Sevenoaks TN13 ....256 FE123
Cranmer Ter, SW17 ....180 DD92
Cranmore Av, Islw. TW7 ....156 CC80
Cranmore Cotts, Lthd. KT24 ....245 BP129
Cranmore Ct, St.Alb. AL1 ....43 CF19
Cranmore La, Lthd. (W.Hors.) KT24 ....245 BP129
Cranmore Rd, Brom. BR1 ....184 EE90
Chislehurst BR7 ....185 EM92
Sch Cranmore Sch, Lthd. KT24 off Cranmore La 245 BQ130
Cranmore Way, N10 ....121 DJ56
Cranston Cl, Houns. TW3 ....156 BY82
Reigate RH2 ....266 DB135
Uxbridge UB10 ....115 BR61
Cranston Est, N1 ....5 K10
Cranston Gdns, E4 ....101 EB50
Cranston Pk Av, Upmin. RM14 ....128 FP63
Cranston Rd, SE23 ....183 DY88
Cranstoun Cl, Guil. GU3 ....242 AT130
Cranswick Rd, SE16 ....22 D9
Crantock Rd, SE6 ....183 EB89
Cranwell Cl, E3 ....14 A4
St. Albans AL4 ....43 CJ22
Cranwell Gro, Shep. TW17 ....194 BM98
Cranwich Av, N21 ....100 DR45
Cranwich Rd, N16 ....122 DR59
Cranwood St, EC1 ....11 J2
Cranworth Cres, E4 ....101 ED46
Cranworth Gdns, SW9 ....161 DN81
Craster Rd, SW2 ....181 DM87
Crathie Rd, SE12 ....184 EH86
Cravan Av, Felt. TW13 ....175 BU89
Craven Av, W5 ....137 CJ73
Southall UB1 ....136 BZ71
Craven Cl, Hayes UB4 ....135 BU72
Craven Gdns, SW19 ....180 DA92
Barking IG11 ....145 ES68
Ilford IG6 ....103 ER54
Romford (Coll.Row) RM5 ....104 FA50
Romford (Harold Wd) RM3 ....106 FQ51
Craven Hill, W2 ....7 M9
Craven Hill Gdns, W2 ....7 L9
Craven Hill Ms, W2 ....7 M9
Craven Ms, SW11 off Taybridge Rd 160 DG83
Craven Pk, NW10 ....138 CS67
Sch Craven Pk JMI Sch, N16 off Castlewood Rd 122 DU58
Craven Pk Ms, NW10 ....138 CS67
Craven Pk Rd, N15 ....122 DT58
NW10 ....138 CS67
Craven Pas, WC2 ....19 N1
Craven Rd, NW10 ....138 CR67
W2 ....7 M9
W5 ....137 CJ73
Croydon CR0 ....202 DV102
Kingston upon Thames KT2 ....198 CM95
Orpington BR6 ....206 EX104
Cravens, The, Horl. (Smallfield) RH6 ....269 DN148
Craven St, WC2 ....19 N1
Craven Ter, W2 ....7 M9
Craven Wk, N16 ....122 DU59
Crawford Av, Wem. HA0 ....117 CK64
Crawford Cl, Islw. TW7 ....157 CE82
Crawford Compton Cl, Horn. RM12 ....148 FJ65
Crawford Est, SE5 ....162 DQ82
Crawford Gdns, N13 ....99 DP48
Northolt UB5 ....136 BZ69
Crawford Ms, W1 ....8 C6
Crawford Pas, EC1 ....10 C4
Crawford Pl, W1 ....8 B7
Sch Crawford Prim Sch, SE5 off Crawford Rd 162 DQ81
Crawford Rd, SE5 ....162 DQ81
Hatfield AL10 ....45 CU16
Crawfords, Swan. BR8 ....187 FE94
Crawford St, NW10 off Fawood Av 138 CR66
W1 ....8 C6
Crawley Dr, Hem.H. HP2 ....40 BM16
Crawley Rd, E10 ....123 EB60
N22 ....100 DQ54
Enfield EN1 ....100 DS45
Crawshaw Rd, Cher. (Ott.) KT16 ....211 BD107
Crawshay Cl, Sev. TN13 ....256 FG123
Crawshay Ct, SW9 off Eythorne Rd 161 DN81
Crawthew Gro, SE22 ....162 DT84
Cray Av, Ashtd. KT21 ....232 CL116
Orpington BR5 ....206 EV99
Craybrooke Rd, Sid. DA14 ....186 EV91
Crayburne, Grav. (Sthflt) DA13 ....190 FZ92
Craybury End, SE9 ....185 EQ89
Cray Cl, Dart. DA1 ....167 FG84
Craydene Rd, Erith DA8 ....167 FF81
Crayfield Ind Pk, Orp. BR5 ....206 EW96
CRAYFORD, Dart. DA1 ....187 FD85
⇌ Crayford 187 FE86
Crayford Cl, E6 off Neatscourt Rd 144 EL71
Crayford High St, Dart. DA1 ....167 FE84
Coll Crayford Manor Ho (Adult Ed Cen), Dart. DA1 off Mayplace Rd E 167 FE83
Crayford Rd, N7 ....121 DK63
Dartford DA1 ....187 FF85
Crayford Way, Dart. DA1 ....187 FF85
Crayke Hill, Chess. KT9 ....216 CL108
Craylands, Orp. BR5 ....206 EW97
Craylands La, Swans. DA10 ....189 FX85
Sch Craylands Sch, The, Swans. DA10 off Craylands La 189 FX85
Craylands Sq, Swans. DA10 ....189 FX85
Crayle St, Slou. SL2 ....131 AN69
Craymill Sq, Dart. DA1 ....167 FF82
Crayonne Cl, Sun. TW16 ....195 BS95
Cray Riverway, Dart. DA1 ....187 FG85
Cray Rd, Belv. DA17 ....166 FA79
Sidcup DA14 ....186 EW94
Swanley BR8 ....207 FB100
Crayside Ind Est, Dart. DA1 off Thames Rd 167 FH84
Cray Valley Rd, Orp. BR5 ....206 EU99
Crealock Gro, Wdf.Grn. IG8 ....102 EF50
Crealock St, SW18 ....180 DB86
Creasey Cl, Horn. RM11 ....127 FH61
Creasy Cl, Abb.L. WD5 ....59 BT31
Creasy Est, SE1 ....21 L6
Crebor St, SE22 ....182 DU86
Credenhall Dr, Brom. BR2 ....205 EM102
Credenhill St, SW16 ....181 DJ93
Crediton Hill, NW6 ....120 DB64
Crediton Rd, E16 ....15 M7
NW10 ....139 CX67
Crediton Way, Esher (Clay.) KT10 ....215 CG106
Credon Rd, E13 ....144 EJ68
SE16 ....22 D9
Credo Way, Grays RM20 ....169 FV79
Creechurch La, EC3 ....11 M8
Creechurch Pl, EC3 ....11 M8
Creed Ct, EC4 off Ludgate Hill 141 DP72
Creed La, EC4 ....10 F8
Creed's Fm Yd, Epp. CM16 ....69 ES31
Creek, The, Grav. DA11 ....190 GB85
Sunbury-on-Thames TW16 ....195 BU99
CREEKMOUTH, Bark. IG11 ....146 EU70
Creek Rd, SE8 ....163 EA79
SE10 ....163 EA79
Barking IG11 ....145 ET69
East Molesey KT8 ....197 CE98
Creekside, SE8 ....163 EB80
Rainham RM13 ....147 FE70
Creeland Gro, SE6 off Catford Hill 183 DZ88
Cree Way, Rom. RM1 ....105 FE52
Crefeld Cl, W6 ....159 CX79
Creffield Rd, W3 ....138 CM73
W5 ....138 CM73
Creighton Av, E6 ....144 EK68
N2 ....120 DE55
N10 ....98 DG54
St. Albans AL1 ....43 CD24
Creighton Cl, W12 ....139 CV73
Creighton Rd, N17 ....100 DS52
Creighton Rd, NW6 ....139 CX68
W5 ....157 CK76
Cremer St, E2 ....5 N10
Cremorne Est, SW10 off Milman's St 160 DD79
Cremorne Gdns, Epsom KT19 ....216 CR109
Cremorne Rd, SW10 ....160 DC80
Gravesend (Nthflt) DA11 ....191 GF87
Crescent, EC3 ....11 N9
Crescent, The, E17 ....123 DY57
N11 ....98 DF49
NW2 ....119 CV62
SW13 ....159 CT82
SW19 ....180 DA90
W3 ....138 CS72
Abbots Langley WD5 ....59 BT30
Ashford TW15 ....174 BM92
Barnet EN5 ....80 DB41
Beckenham BR3 ....203 EA95
Bexley DA5 ....186 EW87
Caterham CR3 ....237 EA123
Chertsey KT16 off Western Av 194 BG97
Croydon CR0 ....202 DR99
Egham TW20 ....172 AY93
Epping CM16 ....69 ET32
Epsom KT18 ....216 CN114
Gravesend (Nthflt) DA11 ....191 GF89
Greenhithe DA9 ....189 FW85
Guildford GU2 ....242 AU132
Harlow CM17 ....36 EW09
Harrow HA2 ....117 CD60
Hayes UB3 ....155 BQ80
Horley RH6 ....269 DH150
Ilford IG2 ....125 EN58
Leatherhead KT22 ....231 CH122
Loughton IG10 ....84 EK43
New Malden KT3 ....198 CQ96
Reigate RH2 off Chartway 250 DB134
Rickmansworth (Crox.Grn) WD3 ....75 BP44
St. Albans (Brick.Wd) AL2 ....60 CA30
Sevenoaks TN13 ....257 FK121
Shepperton TW17 ....195 BT101
Sidcup DA14 ....185 ET91
Slough SL1 ....152 AS75
Southall UB1 ....156 BZ75
Surbiton KT6 ....198 CL99
Sutton SM1 ....218 DD105
Sutton (Belmont) SM2 ....218 DA111
Upminster RM14 ....129 FS59
Watford WD18 ....76 BW42
Watford (Ald.) WD25 ....76 CB37
Wembley HA0 ....117 CH61
West Molesey KT8 ....196 CA98
West Wickham BR4 ....204 EE100
Weybridge KT13 ....194 BN104
Crescent Arc, SE10 off Creek Rd 163 EC79
Crescent Av, Grays RM17 ....170 GD78
Hornchurch RM12 ....127 FF61
Crescent Cotts, Sev. TN13 ....241 FE120
Crescent Ct, Surb. KT6 ....197 CK99
Crescent Dr, Brwd. (Shenf.) CM15 ....108 FY46
Orpington BR5 ....205 EP100
Crescent E, Barn. EN4 ....80 DC38
Crescent Gdns, SW19 ....180 DA90
Ruislip HA4 ....115 BV58
Swanley BR8 ....207 FC96
Crescent Gro, SW4 ....161 DJ84
Mitcham CR4 ....200 DE98
Crescent Ho, SE13 off Ravensbourne Pl 163 EB82
Crescent La, SW4 ....181 DK85
Crescent Ms, N22 off Palace Gates Rd 99 DL53
Crescent Pl, SW3 ....18 A7
Crescent Ri, N22 ....99 DK53
Barnet EN4 ....80 DE43
Crescent Rd, E4 ....102 EE45
E6 ....144 EJ67
E10 ....123 EB61
E13 ....144 EG67
E18 ....102 EJ54
N3 ....97 CZ53
N8 ....121 DK59
N9 ....100 DU46
N11 ....98 DF49
N15 off Carlingford Rd 121 DP55
N22 ....99 DK53
SE18 ....165 EP78
SW20 ....199 CX95
Barnet EN4 ....80 DE43
Beckenham BR3 ....203 EB96
Brentwood CM14 ....108 FV49
Bromley BR1 ....184 EG94
Caterham CR3 ....236 DU124
Dagenham RM10 ....127 FB63
Enfield EN2 ....81 DP41
Erith DA8 ....167 FF79
Hemel Hempstead HP2 ....40 BK20
Kingston upon Thames KT2 ....178 CN94
Redhill (Bletch.) RH1 ....252 DQ133
Reigate RH2 ....266 DA136
Shepperton TW17 ....195 BQ99
Sidcup DA15 ....185 ET90
South Ockendon (Aveley) RM15 ....168 FQ75
Crescent Row, EC1 ....10 G4
Crescent Stables, SW15 off Upper Richmond Rd 159 CY84
Crescent St, N1 ....4 B5
Crescent Vw, Loug. IG10 ....84 EK44
Crescent Wk, S.Ock. (Aveley) RM15 ....168 FQ75
Crescent Way, N12 ....98 DE51
SE4 ....163 EA83
SW16 ....181 DM94
Horley RH6 ....268 DG150
Orpington BR6 ....223 ES106
South Ockendon (Aveley) RM15 ....149 FR74
Crescent W, Barn. EN4 ....80 DC38
Crescent Wd Rd, SE26 ....182 DU90
Cresford Rd, SW6 ....160 DB81
Crespigny Rd, NW4 ....119 CV58
Cressage Cl, Sthl. UB1 ....136 CA70
Cressall Cl, Lthd. KT22 ....231 CH120
Cressall Mead, Lthd. KT22 ....231 CH120
Cress End, Rick. WD3 off Springwell Av 92 BG46
Cresset Cl, Ware (Stans.Abb.) SG12 ....33 EC12
Cresset Rd, E9 ....142 DW65
Cresset St, SW4 ....161 DK83
Cressfield Cl, NW5 ....120 DG64

⊖ London Underground station   DLR Docklands Light Railway station   Tra Tramlink station   Riv Pedestrian ferry landing stage

Cressida Rd, N19 121 DJ60
Cressingham Gro, Sutt. SM1 218 DC105
Cressingham Rd, SE13 163 EC83
Edgware HA8 96 CR51
Cressington Cl, N16 5 M1
Cress Ms, Brom. BR1 183 ED92
Cress Rd, Slou. SL1 151 AP75
Cresswell Gdns, SW5 17 L9
Cresswell Pk, SE3 164 EF83
Cresswell Pl, SW10 17 L9
Cresswell Rd, SE25 202 DU98
Chesham HP5 54 AR34
Feltham TW13 176 BY91
Twickenham TW1 177 CK86
Cresswell Way, N21 99 DN45
Cressy Ct, E1 12 F5
W6 159 CV76
Cressy Pl, E1 12 F5
Cressy Rd, NW3 120 DF64
Crest, The, N13 99 DN49
NW4 119 CW57
Beaconsfield HP9 88 AG54
Sawbridgeworth CM21 36 EX05
Surbiton KT5 198 CN99
Waltham Cross (Chsht) EN7 off Orchard Way 65 DP27
Cresta Dr, Add. (Wdhm) KT15 211 BF110
Crest Av, Grays RM17 170 GB80
Crestbrook Av, N13 99 DP48
Crestbrook Pl, N13 99 DP48
Crest Cl, Sev. (Bad.Mt)TN14 225 FB111
Crest Dr, Enf. EN3 82 DW38
Crestfield St, WC1 9 P1
Crest Gdns, Ruis. HA4 116 BW62
Crest Hill, Guil. (Peasl.) GU5 261 BR142
Cresthill Av, Grays RM17 170 GC77
Creston Av, Wok. (Knap.) GU21 226 AS116
Creston Way, Wor.Pk. KT4 199 CX102
Crest Pk, Hem.H. HP2 41 BQ19
Crest Rd, NW2 119 CT62
Bromley BR2 204 EF101
South Croydon CR2 220 DV108
Crest Vw, Green. DA9 off Woodland Way 169 FU84
Pinner HA5 116 BX56
Crest Vw Dr, Orp. BR5 205 EP99
Crestway, SW15 179 CV86
Crestwood Way, Houns. TW4 176 BZ85
Creswell Dr, Beck. BR3 203 EB99
Creswick Ct, Welw.G.C. AL7 29 CX10
Sch Creswick JMI Sch, Welw.G.C. AL7 off Chequers 29 CX12
Creswick Rd, W3 138 CP73
Creswick Wk, E3 13 N1
NW11 119 CZ56
Crete Hall Rd, Grav. DA11 190 GD86
Creton St, SE18 165 EN76
Crewdson Rd, SW9 161 DN80
Horley RH6 269 DH148
Crewe Curve, Berk. HP4 38 AT16
Crewe Pl, NW10 139 CT69
Crewe's Av, Warl. CR6 236 DW116
Crewe's Cl, Warl. CR6 236 DW116
Crewe's Fm La, Warl. CR6 237 DX116
Crewe's La, Warl. CR6 237 DX116
CREWS HILL, Enf. EN2 81 DP35
⇌ Crews Hill 65 DM34
Crews St, E14 23 N7
Crewys Rd, NW2 119 CZ61
SE15 162 DV82
Crib St, Ware SG12 33 DX05
Crichton Av, Wall. SM6 219 DK106
Crichton Rd, Cars. SM5 218 DF107
Crichton St, SW8 off Westbury St 161 DJ82
Cricketers Arms Rd, Enf. EN2 82 DQ40
Cricketers Cl, N14 99 DJ45
Chessington KT9 215 CK105
Erith DA8 167 FE78
St. Albans AL3 off Stonecross 43 CE19
Cricketers Ct, SE11 20 E8
Cricketers Ms, SW18 off East Hill 180 DB85
Cricketers Ter, Cars. SM5 off Wrythe La 200 DE104
Cricketfield Rd, E5 122 DV63
Cricket Fld Rd, Uxb. UB8 134 BK67
Cricketfield Rd, West Dr. UB7 154 BJ77
Cricket Grn, Mitch. CR4 200 DF97
Sch Cricket Grn Sch, Mitch. CR4 off Lower Grn W 200 DE97
Cricket Grd Rd, Chis. BR7 205 EP95
Cricket Hill, Red. (S.Nutfld) RH1 267 DM136
Cricket La, Beck. BR3 183 DY93
Cricket Way, Wey. KT13 195 BS103
Cricklade Av, SW2 181 DL89
Romford RM3 106 FK51
CRICKLEWOOD, NW2 119 CX62
⇌ Cricklewood 119 CX63
Cricklewood Bdy, NW2 119 CW62
Cricklewood La, NW2 119 CX63
Cridland St, E15 off Church St 144 EF67
Crieff Ct, Tedd. TW11 177 CJ94
Crieff Rd, SW18 180 DC86
Criffel Av, SW2 181 DK89
Crimp Hill, Egh. (Eng.Grn) TW20 172 AU90
Crimp Hill Rd, Wind. (Old Wind.) SL4 172 AU88
Crimscott St, SE1 21 M6
Crimsworth Rd, SW8 161 DK81
Crinan St, N1 141 DL68
Cringle St, SW8 161 DJ80
Cripplegate St, EC2 10 G5
Cripps Grn, Hayes UB4 off Stratford Rd 135 BV70
Crispe Ho, Bark. IG11 off Dovehouse Mead 145 ER68
Crispen Rd, Felt. TW13 176 BY91
Crispian Cl, NW10 118 CS63
Crispin Cl, Ashtd. KT21 232 CM118
Beaconsfield HP9 88 AJ51
Croydon CR0 off Harrington Cl 201 DL103
Crispin Cres, Croy. CR0 201 DK104
Crispin Rd, Edg. HA8 96 CQ51
Crispin St, E1 11 N6
Crispin Way, Slou. (Farn.Com.) SL2 111 AR63
Crispin Way, Uxb. UB8 off Pield Heath Rd 134 BM70
Crisp Rd, W6 159 CW78
Criss Cres, Ger.Cr. (Chal.St.P.) SL9 90 AW54
Criss Gro, Ger.Cr. (Chal.St.P.) SL9 90 AW54
Cristowe Rd, SW6 159 CZ82
Criterion Ms, N19 121 DK61
Crittall's Cor, Sid. DA14 186 EW94
Critten La, Dor. RH5 246 BX132
Crockenhall Way, Grav. (Istead Rise) DA13 190 GE94
CROCKENHILL, Swan. BR8 207 FD101
Sch Crockenhill Co Prim Sch, Swan. BR8 off Stones Cross Rd 207 FC100
Crockenhill La, Dart. (Eyns.) DA4 208 FJ102
Swanley BR8 207 FG101
Crockenhill Rd, Orp. BR5 206 EX99
Swanley BR8 206 EZ100
Crockerton Rd, SW17 180 DF89
Crockery La, Guil. (E.Clan.) GU4 244 BL129
Crockford Cl, Add. KT15 212 BJ105
Crockford Pk Rd, Add. KT15 212 BJ106
CROCKHAM HILL, Eden. TN8 255 EQ133
Sch Crockham Hill C of E Prim Sch, Eden. TN8 off Main Rd 255 EQ133
Crockham Way, SE9 185 EN91
Crocknorth Rd, Lthd. (E.Hors.) KT24 245 BT132
Crocus Cl, Croy. CR0 off Cornflower La 203 DX102
Crocus Fld, Barn. EN5 79 CZ44
Croffets, Tad. KT20 233 CX121
Croft, The, E4 102 EE47
NW10 139 CT68
W5 138 CL71
Barnet EN5 79 CX42
Broxbourne EN10 49 DY23
Hounslow TW5 156 BY79
Loughton IG10 85 EN40
Pinner HA5 off Rayners La 116 BZ59
Ruislip HA4 116 BW63
St. Albans AL2 60 CA25
Swanley BR8 207 FC97
Welwyn Garden City AL7 29 CZ12
Wembley HA0 117 CJ64
Croft Av, Dor. RH4 247 CH134
West Wickham BR4 203 EC102
Croft Cl, NW7 96 CS48
Belvedere DA17 166 EZ78
Chislehurst BR7 185 EM91
Hayes UB3 155 BQ80
Kings Langley (Chipper.) WD4 58 BG30
Uxbridge UB10 134 BN66
Croft Ct, Borwd. WD6 off Kensington Way 78 CR41
Croftdown Rd, NW5 120 DG62
Croft End Cl, Chess. KT9 off Ashcroft Rd 198 CM104
Croft End Rd, Kings L. (Chipper.) WD4 58 BG30
Crofters, The, Wind. SL4 172 AU86
Crofters Cl, Islw. TW7 off Ploughmans End 177 CD85
Redhill RH1 off Oaklands Dr 267 DH136
Crofters Ct, SE8 off Croft St 163 DY77
Crofters Mead, Croy. CR0 221 DZ109
Crofters Rd, Nthwd. HA6 93 BS49
Crofters Way, NW1 141 DK67
Croft Fld, Hat. AL10 45 CU18
Kings Langley (Chipper.) WD4 58 BG30
Croft Gdns, W7 157 CG75
Ruislip HA4 115 BT60
Crofthill Rd, Slou. SL2 131 AP70
Croft La, Kings L. (Chipper.) WD4 58 BG30
Croftleigh Av, Pur. CR8 235 DN116
Croft Lo Cl, Wdf.Grn. IG8 102 EH51
Croft Meadow, Kings L. (Chipper.) WD4 58 BG30
Croft Ms, N12 98 DC48
Crofton, Ashtd. KT21 232 CL118
Crofton Av, W4 158 CR80
Bexley DA5 186 EX87
Orpington BR6 205 EQ103
Walton-on-Thames KT12 196 BW104
Crofton Cl, Cher. (Ott.) KT16 211 BC108
Croftongate Way, SE4 183 DY85
Crofton Gro, E4 101 ED49
Sch Crofton Inf Sch, Orp. BR5 off Towncourt La 205 ER101
Sch Crofton Jun Sch, Orp. BR5 off Towncourt La 205 ER101
Crofton La, Orp. BR5, BR6 205 ER101
⇌ Crofton Park 183 DZ85
Crofton Pk Rd, SE4 183 DZ86
Crofton Rd, E13 15 N3
SE5 162 DS81
Grays RM16 170 GE76
Orpington BR6 205 EN104
Sch Crofton Sec Sch, SE4 off Manwood Rd 183 EA86
Crofton Ter, E5 off Studley Cl 123 DY64
Richmond TW9 158 CM84
Crofton Way, Barn. EN5 off Wycherley Cres 80 DB44
Enfield EN2 81 DN40
Croft Rd, SW16 201 DN95
SW19 180 DC94
Bromley BR1 184 EG93
Caterham (Wold.) CR3 237 DZ122
Enfield EN3 83 DY39
Gerrards Cross (Chal.St.P.) SL9 90 AY54
Sutton SM1 218 DE106
Ware SG12 32 DW05
Westerham TN16 255 EP126
Crofts, The, Hem.H. HP3 41 BP21
Shepperton TW17 195 BS98
Croftside, SE25 off Sunny Bk 202 DU97
Crofts La, N22 off Glendale Av 99 DN52
Crofts Path, Hem.H. HP3 41 BP22
Crofts Rd, Har. HA1 117 CG58
Crofts St, E1 12 A10
Croft St, SE8 23 J8
Croft Wk, Brox. EN10 49 DY23
Croftway, NW3 120 DA63
Richmond TW10 177 CH90
Croft Way, Sev. TN13 256 FF125
Sidcup DA15 185 ES90
Crogsland Rd, NW1 140 DG66
Croham Cl, S.Croy. CR2 220 DS107
Sch Croham Hurst Sch, S.Croy. CR2 off Croham Rd 220 DT107
South Croydon CR2 off Melville Av 220 DT106
Croham Manor Rd, S.Croy. CR2 220 DS106
Croham Mt, S.Croy. CR2 220 DS108
Croham Pk Av, S.Croy. CR2 220 DT106
Croham Rd, S.Croy. CR2 220 DR106
Croham Valley Rd, S.Croy. CR2 220 DT107
Croindene Rd, SW16 201 DL95
Cromartie Rd, N19 121 DK59
Cromarty Rd, Edg. HA8 96 CP47
Crombie Cl, Ilf. IG4 125 EM57
Crombie Rd, Sid. DA15 185 ER88
Cromer Cl, Uxb. UB8 off Dawley Av 135 BQ72
CROMER HYDE, Welw.G.C. AL8 28 CS10
Cromer Hyde La, Welw.G.C. AL8 28 CR11
Crome Rd, NW10 138 CS65
Cromer Pl, Orp. BR6 off Andover Rd 205 ER102
Cromer Rd, E10 off James La 123 ED58
N17 100 DU54
SE25 202 DV97
SW17 180 DG93
Barnet EN5 80 DC42
Hornchurch RM11 128 FK59
Hounslow (Hthrw Air.) TW6 154 BN83
Romford RM7 127 FC58
Romford (Chad.Hth) RM6 126 EY58
Watford WD24 76 BW38
Woodford Green IG8 102 EG49
Sch Cromer Rd Prim Sch, Barn. EN5 off Cromer Rd 80 DC41
Cromer Rd W, Houns. (Hthrw Air.) TW6 154 BN83
Cromer St, WC1 9 P2
Cromer Ter, E8 off Ferncliff Rd 122 DU64
Cromer Vil Rd, SW18 179 CZ86
Cromford Cl, Orp. BR6 205 ES104
Cromford Path, E5 off Overbury St 123 DX63
Cromford Rd, SW18 180 DA85
Cromford Way, N.Mal. KT3 198 CR95
Cromlix Cl, Chis. BR7 205 EP96
Crompton Pl, Enf. EN3 off Brunswick Rd 83 EA38
Crompton St, W2 7 N4
Cromwell Av, N6 121 DH60
W6 159 CV78
Bromley BR2 204 EH98
New Malden KT3 199 CT99
Waltham Cross (Chsht) EN7 66 DU30
Cromwell Cl, E1 off Vaughan Way 142 DU74
N2 120 DD56
W3 off High St 138 CQ74
Bromley BR2 204 EH98
Chalfont St. Giles HP8 90 AW48
St. Albans AL4 43 CK15
Walton-on-Thames KT12 195 BV102
Cromwell Cres, SW5 16 G7
Cromwell Dr, Slou. SL1 132 AS72
Cromwell Gdns, SW7 17 P6
Cromwell Gro, W6 159 CW76
Caterham CR3 236 DQ121
Cromwell Highwalk, EC2 off Beech St 142 DQ71
H Cromwell Hosp, The, SW5 17 J7
Cromwell Ind Est, E10 123 DY60
Cromwell Ms, SW7 17 P7
Cromwell Pl, N6 121 DH60
SW7 17 P7
SW14 158 CQ83
W3 off Grove Pl 138 CQ74
Cromwell Rd, E7 144 EJ66
E17 123 EC57
N3 98 DC53
N10 98 DG52
SW5 17 H7
SW7 17 N7
SW9 161 DP81
SW19 180 DA92
Beckenham BR3 203 DY96
Borehamwood WD6 78 CL39
Brentwood (Warley) CM14 108 FV49
Caterham CR3 236 DQ121
Croydon CR0 202 DR101
Feltham TW13 175 BV88
Grays RM17 170 GA77
Hayes UB3 135 BR72
Hertford SG13 32 DT08
Hounslow TW3 156 CA84
Kingston upon Thames KT2 198 CL95
Redhill RH1 250 DF133
Teddington TW11 177 CG93
Waltham Cross (Chsht) EN7 66 DV28
Walton-on-Thames KT12 195 BV102
Ware SG12 33 DZ06
Wembley HA0 138 CL68
Worcester Park KT4 198 CR104
Cromwells Mere, Rom. RM1 off Havering Rd 105 FD51
Cromwell St, Houns. TW3 156 CA84
Cromwell Twr, EC2 11 H5
Cromwell Wk, Red. RH1 250 DF134
Crondace Rd, SW6 160 DA81
Crondall Ct, N1 5 L10
Crondall Ho, SW15 off Fontley Way 179 CU88
Crondall St, N1 5 K10
Cronin St, SE15 162 DT80
Cronks Hill, Red. RH1 266 DC135
Reigate RH2 266 DC135
Cronks Hill Cl, Red. RH1 266 DD136
Cronks Hill Rd, Red. RH1 266 DD136
Crooked Billet, SW19 off Woodhayes Rd 179 CW93
Crooked Billet Roundabout, E17 101 EA52
Staines TW18 174 BG91
Crooked Billet Yd, E2 off Kingsland Rd 142 DS69
Crooked La, Grav. DA12 191 GH86
Crooked Mile, Wal.Abb. EN9 67 EC33
Crooked Mile Roundabout, Wal.Abb. EN9 67 EC33
Crooked Usage, N3 119 CY55
Crooked Way, Wal.Abb. EN9 50 EE22
Crooke Rd, SE8 23 J9
Crookham Rd, SW6 159 CZ81
Crookhams, Welw.G.C. AL7 30 DA07
Crook Log, Bexh. DA6 166 EX83
Sch Crook Log JMI Sch, Bexh. DA6 off Crook Log 166 EX84
Crookston Rd, SE9 165 EN83
Croombs Rd, E16 144 EJ71
Crooms Hill, SE10 163 ED80
Crooms Hill Gro, SE10 163 EC80
Crop Common, Hat. AL10 45 CV16
Cropley Ct, N1 5 J9
Cropley St, N1 5 J9
Croppath Rd, Dag. RM10 126 FA63
Cropthorne Ct, W9 7 M2
Crosby Cl, Beac. HP9 111 AM55
Feltham TW13 176 BY91
St. Albans AL4 43 CJ23
Crosby Ct, SE1 21 J3
Crosby Rd, E7 144 EG65
Dagenham RM10 147 FB68
Crosby Row, SE1 21 J4
Crosby Sq, EC3 11 L8
Crosby Wk, E8 5 N4
SW2 181 DN87
Crosier Cl, SE3 164 EL81
Crosier Rd, Uxb. (Ickhm) UB10 115 BQ63
Crosier Way, Ruis. HA4 115 BS62
Crosland Pl, SW11 off Taybridge Rd 160 DG83
Crossacres, Wok. GU22 227 BE115
Cross Av, SE10 163 ED79
Crossbow Rd, Chig. IG7 103 ET50
Crossbrook, Hat. AL10 44 CS19
Crossbrook Rd, SE3 164 EL82
Crossbrook St, Wal.Cr. (Chsht) EN8 67 DX31
Cross Cl, SE15 off Gordon Rd 162 DV81
Cross Deep, Twick. TW1 177 CF89
Cross Deep Gdns, Twick. TW1 177 CF89
Crossett Grn, Hem.H. HP3 41 BQ22
Crossfell Rd, Hem.H. HP3 41 BQ22
Crossfield Cl, Berk. HP4 38 AT19
Crossfield Pl, Wey. KT13 213 BP108
Crossfield Rd, N17 122 DQ55
NW3 140 DD66
Hoddesdon EN11 49 EB15
Crossfields, Loug. IG10 85 EP43
St. Albans AL3 42 CB23
Crossfield St, SE8 163 EA80
Crossford St, SW9 161 DM82
Crossgate, Edg. HA8 96 CN48
Greenford UB6 137 CH65
DLR Crossharbour & London Arena 24 B5
Crossing Rd, Epp. CM16 70 EU32
Cross Keys Cl, N9 off Balham Rd 100 DU47
W1 8 F6
Sevenoaks TN13 256 FG127
Cross Keys Sq, EC1 10 G6
Cross Lances Rd, Houns. TW3 156 CB84
Crossland Rd, Red. RH1 250 DG134
Thornton Heath CR7 201 DP100
Crosslands, Cher. KT16 193 BE104
Crosslands Av, W5 138 CM74
Southall UB2 156 BZ78
Crosslands Rd, Epsom KT19 216 CR107
Cross La, EC3 11 L10
N8 121 DM55
Beaconsfield HP9 111 AM55
Bexley DA5 186 EZ87
Chertsey (Ott.) KT16 211 BB107
Hertford SG14 31 DP09
Cross La E, Grav. DA12 191 GH89
Cross Las, Ger.Cr. (Chal.St.P.) SL9 90 AY50
Guildford GU1 259 AZ135
Cross Las Cl, Ger.Cr. (Chal.St.P.) SL9 off Cross Las 91 AZ50
Cross La W, Grav. DA11 191 GH89
Crosslet St, SE17 21 K7
Crosslet Vale, SE10 163 EB81
Crossley Cl, West. (Bigg.H.) TN16 238 EK115
Crossleys, Ch.St.G. HP8 90 AW49
Crossley St, N7 4 C3
Crossmead, SE9 185 EM88
Watford WD19 75 BV44
Crossmead Av, Grnf. UB6 136 CA69
Cross Meadow, Chesh. HP5 54 AM29
Crossmount Ho, SE5 162 DQ80
Crossness La, SE28 146 EX73
★ Crossness Pumping Sta, SE2 146 EY72
Crossness Rd, Bark. IG11 145 ET69
Cross Oak, Wind. SL4 151 AN82
Crossoak La, Red. RH1 267 DH144
Cross Oak Rd, Berk. HP4 38 AU20
Crossoaks La, Borwd. WD6 78 CR35
Potters Bar (S.Mimms) EN6 62 CS34
Crosspath, The, Rad. WD7 77 CG35
Cross Rd, E4 102 EE46
N11 99 DH50
N22 99 DN52
SE5 162 DS82
SW19 180 DA94
Bromley BR2 204 EL103
Croydon CR0 202 DR102
Dartford DA1 188 FJ86
Dartford (Hawley) DA2 188 FM91
Enfield EN1 82 DS42
Feltham TW13 176 BY91
Gravesend (Nthflt) DA11 191 GF86
Harrow HA1 117 CD56
Harrow (S.Har.) HA2 116 CB62
Harrow (Wldste) HA3 95 CG54
Hertford SG14 32 DQ08
Kingston upon Thames KT2 178 CM94
Orpington BR5 206 EV99
Purley CR8 219 DP113
Romford RM7 126 FA55
Romford (Chad.Hth) RM6 126 EW59
Sidcup DA14 off Sidcup Hill 186 EV91
Sutton SM2 218 DD106
Sutton (Belmont) SM2 218 DA110
Tadworth KT20 233 CW122
Uxbridge UB8 off New Windsor St 134 BJ66
Waltham Cross EN8 67 DY33
Watford WD19 76 BY44
Weybridge KT13 195 BR104
Woodford Green IG8 103 EM51
Cross Rds, Loug. (High Beach) IG10 84 EH40
Crossroads, The, Lthd. (Eff.) KT24 246 BX128
Cross St, N1 4 E7
SW13 158 CS82
Erith DA8 off Bexley Rd 167 FE78
Cross St, Hampton (Hmptn H.) TW12 176 CC92
Harlow CM20 51 ER15
St. Albans AL3 off Spencer St 43 CD20
Uxbridge UB8 134 BJ66
Ware SG12 33 DY06
Watford WD17 76 BW41
Cross Ter, Wal.Abb. EN9 off Stonyshotts 68 EE34
Crossthwaite Av, SE5 162 DR84
Crosswall, EC3 11 N9
Crossway, N12 98 DD51
N16 5 M2
NW9 119 CT56
SE28 146 EW72
SW20 199 CW98
W13 137 CG70
Chesham HP5 54 AS30
Dagenham RM8 126 EW62
Enfield EN1 100 DS45
Harlow CM17 off London Rd 36 EX14
Hayes UB3 135 BU74
Orpington BR5 205 ER98
Pinner HA5 93 BV54
Ruislip HA4 116 BW63
Walton-on-Thames KT12 195 BV103
Welwyn Garden City AL8 29 CW05
Woodford Green IG8 102 EJ49
Crossway, The, N22 99 DP52
SE9 184 EK89
Cross Way, The, Har. HA3 95 CE54
Crossway, The, Uxb. UB10 134 BM68
Crossways, N21 82 DQ44
Beaconsfield HP9 89 AM54
Berkhamsted HP4 38 AT20
Brentwood (Shenf.) CM15 109 GA44
Egham TW20 173 BD93
Hemel Hempstead HP3 41 BP20
Leatherhead KT24 off The Street 246 BX127
Romford RM2 127 FH55
South Croydon CR2 221 DY108
Sunbury-on-Thames TW16 175 BT94
Sutton SM2 218 DD109
Westerham (Tats.) TN16 238 EJ120
Crossways, The, Couls. CR5 235 DM119
Guildford GU2 258 AU135
Hounslow TW5 156 BZ80
Redhill RH1 251 DJ130
Wembley HA9 118 CN61
Coll Crossways Acad, SE4 off Sprules Rd 163 DY82
Crossways Boul, Dart. DA2 168 FQ84
Greenhithe DA9 169 FT84
Crossways Business Pk, Dart. DA2 168 FQ84
Crossways La, Reig. RH2 250 DC128
Crossways Rd, Beck. BR3 203 EA98
Mitcham CR4 201 DH97
Crosswell Cl, Shep. TW17 195 BQ96
Crosthwaite Way, Slou. SL1 131 AK71
Croston St, E8 142 DU67
Crothall Cl, N13 99 DM48
Crouch Av, Bark. IG11 146 EV68
Crouch Cl, Beck. BR3 off Abbey La 183 EA93
Crouch Ct, Harl. CM20 35 EQ13
Crouch Cft, SE9 185 EN90
CROUCH END, N8 121 DJ58
Crouch End Hill, N8 121 DK59
Crouchfield, Hem.H. HP1 40 BH21
Hertford SG14 32 DQ06
Crouch Hall Rd, N8 121 DK58
⇌ Crouch Hill 121 DM59
Crouch Hill, N4 121 DL58
N8 121 DL58
Crouch La, Wal.Cr. (Chsht) EN7 66 DQ28
Crouchman's Cl, SE26 182 DT90
Crouch Oak La, Add. KT15 212 BJ105
Crouch Rd, NW10 138 CR66
Grays RM16 171 GG78
Crouch Valley, Upmin. RM14 129 FS59
Crowborough Cl, Warl. CR6 237 DY117
Crowborough Dr, Warl. CR6 237 DY118
Crowborough Path, Wat. WD19 off Prestwick Rd 94 BX49
Crowborough Rd, SW17 180 DG93
Crowcroft Cl, Guil. GU2 off Grange Rd 242 AV130
Crowden Way, SE28 146 EW73
Crowder St, E1 12 C9
Crow Dr, Sev. (Halst.) TN14 241 FC115
Crowfoot Cl, E9 off Lee Conservancy Rd 123 DZ64
CROW GREEN, Brwd. CM15 108 FT41
Crow Grn La, Brwd. (Pilg.Hat.) CM15 108 FU43
Crow Grn Rd, Brwd. (Pilg.Hat.) CM15 108 FT43
Crowhurst Cl, SW9 161 DN82
Crowhurst Mead, Gdse. RH9 252 DW130
Crowhurst Way, Orp. BR5 206 EW99
Crowland Av, Hayes UB3 155 BS77
Crowland Gdns, N14 99 DL45
Sch Crowland Prim Sch, N15 off Crowland Rd 122 DU57
Crowland Rd, N15 122 DT57
Thornton Heath CR7 202 DR98
Crowlands Av, Rom. RM7 127 FB58
Sch Crowlands Inf Sch, Rom. RM7 off London Rd 127 FC58
Sch Crowlands Jun Sch, Rom. RM7 off London Rd 127 FC58
Crowland Ter, N1 5 J5
Crowland Wk, Mord. SM4 200 DB100
Crow La, Rom. RM7 126 EZ59
Crowley Cres, Croy. CR0 219 DN106
Crowline Wk, N1 off St. Paul's Rd 142 DR65
Crowmarsh Gdns, SE23 off Tyson Rd 182 DW87
Crown Arc, Kings.T. KT1 off Union St 197 CK96
Crown Ash Hill, West. TN16 222 EH114
Crown Ash La, Warl. CR6 238 EG116
Westerham TN16 238 EG116
Crown Cl, E3 143 EA67
N22 off Winkfield Rd 99 DN53
NW6 140 DB65
NW7 97 CT47
Bishop's Stortford (Sheering) CM22 37 FC07
Hayes UB3 155 BT75
Orpington BR6 224 EU105
Slough (Colnbr.) SL3 153 BC80
Walton-on-Thames KT12 196 BW101
Crown Ct, EC2 11 H8
SE12 184 EH86
WC2 9 P8

★ Place of interest | H Hospital | Sch School | Coll College | Uni University | ⇌ Railway station

Crown Ct, Brom. BR2
off Victoria Rd 204 EK99
Crown Dale, SE19 181 DP93
Crowndale Rd, NW1 141 DJ68
Crownfield, Brox. EN10 49 EA21
Crownfield Av, Ilf. IG2 125 ES57
Sch Crownfield Inf Sch, Rom.
RM7 off White Hart La 104 FA54
Sch Crownfield Jun Sch, Rom.
RM7 off White Hart La 104 FA54
Crownfield Rd, E15 123 ED64
Crownfields, Sev. TN13 257 FH125
Crown Gate, Harl. CM20 51 ER15
Crown Hts, Guil. GU1 258 AY137
Crown Hill, Croy. CR0
off Church St 202 DQ103
Epping CM16 69 EM33
Waltham Abbey EN9 69 EM33
Crownhill Rd, NW10 139 CT67
Woodford Green IG8 102 EL52
Crown Ho, Bark. IG11
off Linton Rd 145 EQ66
Crown La, N14 99 DJ46
SW16 181 DN92
Bromley BR2 204 EK99
Chislehurst BR7 205 EQ95
High Wycombe HP11 88 AF48
Morden SM4 200 DB97
Slough (Farn.Royal) SL2 131 AN68
Virginia Water GU25 192 AX100
Crown La Gdns, SW16
off Crown La 181 DN92
Sch Crown La Prim Sch,
SE2 off Gipsy Rd 182 DQ91
Crown La Spur, Brom. BR2 204 EK100
Crown Meadow, Slou.
(Colnbr.) SL3 153 BB80
Crownmead Way, Rom.
RM7 127 FB56
Crown Ms, E13
off Waghorn Rd 144 EJ67
W6 159 CU77
Crown Office Row, EC4 10 C9
Crown Pas, SW1 19 K2
Kingston upon Thames
KT1 off Church St 197 CK96
Watford WD18
off The Crescent 76 BW42
Crown Pl, EC2 11 L5
NW5 off Kentish Town Rd 141 DH65
Crown Pt Par, SE19
off Beulah Hill 181 DP93
Crown Reach, SW1
off Grosvenor Rd 161 DK78
Crown Ri, Cher. KT16 193 BF102
Watford WD25 60 BW34
Crown Rd, N10 98 DG52
Borehamwood WD6 78 CN39
Enfield EN1 82 DV42
Grays RM17 170 GA79
Ilford IG6 125 ER56
Morden SM4 200 DB98
New Malden KT3 198 CQ95
Orpington BR6 224 EU106
Ruislip HA4 116 BX64
Sevenoaks (Shore.) TN14 225 FF110
Sutton SM1 218 DB105
Twickenham TW1 177 CH86
Virginia Water GU25 192 AW100
Crown Sq, Wok. GU21
off Commercial Way 227 AZ117
Crownstone Rd, SW2 181 DN85
Crown St, SE5 162 DQ80
W3 138 CP74
Brentwood CM14 108 FW47
Dagenham RM10 147 FC65
Egham TW20 173 BA92
Harrow HA2 117 CD60
Crown Ter, Rich. TW9 158 CM84
Crowntree Cl, Islw. TW7 157 CF79
Crown Wk, Hem.H. HP3 40 BL24
Uxbridge UB8
off Oxford Rd 134 BJ66
Wembley HA9 118 CM62
Crown Way, West Dr. UB7 134 BM74
Crown Wds La, SE9 165 EP82
SE18 165 EP82
Sch Crown Wds Sch, SE9
off Riefield Rd 185 EQ85
Crown Wds Way, SE9 185 ER85
Crown Wks, E2
off Temple St 142 DV68
Crown Yd, Houns. TW3
off High St 156 CC83
Crow Piece La, Slou. SL2 131 AM66
Crowshott Av, Stan. HA7 95 CJ53
Crows Rd, E15 14 F1
Barking IG11 145 EP65
Epping CM16 69 ET30
Crowstone Rd, Grays RM16 170 GC75
Crowther Av, Brent. TW8 158 CL77
Crowther Rd, SE25 202 DU98
Crowthorne Cl, SW18 179 CZ88
Crowthorne Rd, W10 6 A8
Croxdale Rd, Borwd. WD6 78 CM40
Croxden Cl, Edg. HA8 118 CM55
Croxden Wk, Mord. SM4 200 DC100
Croxford Gdns, N22 99 DP52
Croxford Way, Rom. RM7
off Horace Av 127 FD60
⊖ Croxley 75 BP44
Croxley Business Pk, Wat.
WD18 75 BR43
Croxley Cl, Orp. BR5 206 EV96
CROXLEY GREEN, Rick.
WD3 74 BN43
⇌ Croxley Green (closed) 75 BR43
Croxley Grn, Orp. BR5 206 EV95
Croxley Rd, W9 6 F2
Croxley Vw, Wat. WD18 75 BS44
Croxted Cl, SE21 182 DQ87
Croxted Ms, SE24
off Croxted Rd 182 DQ86
Croxted Rd, SE21 182 DQ87
SE24 182 DQ87
Croyde Av, Grnf. UB6 136 CC69
Hayes UB3 155 BS77
Croyde Cl, Sid. DA15 185 ER87
CROYDON, CR0 202 DR103
Coll Croydon Coll, Croy.
CR0 off College Rd 202 DR103
Coll Croydon English Language
Scheme, SE25
off Sandown Rd 202 DV99
Coll Croydon Evangelical Ch,
Croy. CR0
off Cranmer Rd 201 DP104
Croydon Flyover, Croy. CR0 219 DP105
Croydon Gro, Croy. CR0 201 DP102
Sch Croydon High Sch GPDST,
S.Croy. CR2
off Old Farleigh Rd 220 DW110
Croydon La, Bans. SM7 218 DB114
Croydon La S, Bans. SM7 218 DB114
★ Croydon Mus, Croy. CR0 202 DQ104
Croydon Rd, E13 15 K4
SE20 202 DV96
Beckenham BR3 203 DY98
Bromley BR2 204 EF104
Caterham CR3 236 DU122
Croydon (Bedd.) CR0 219 DL105
Croydon (Mitch.Com.)
CR0 200 DG98
Hounslow (Hthrw Air.)
TW6 155 BP82
Keston BR2 204 EJ104
Mitcham CR4 200 DG98
Reigate RH2 250 DB134
Wallington SM6 219 DH105
Warlingham CR6 237 ED122
West Wickham BR4 204 EE104
Westerham TN16 239 EM123
Croyland Rd, N9 100 DU46
Croylands Dr, Surb. KT6 198 CL101
Croysdale Av, Sun. TW16 195 BU97
Crozier Dr, S.Croy. CR2 220 DV110
Crozier Ho, SE3
off Ebdon Way 164 EH83
Crozier Ter, E9 123 DX64
Crucible Cl, Rom. RM6 126 EV58
Crucifix La, SE1 21 L3
Cruden Ho, SE17
off Hillingdon St 161 DP79
Cruden Rd, Grav. DA12 191 GM90
Cruden St, N1 4 F8
Cruick Av, S.Ock. RM15 149 FW73
Cruikshank Rd, E15 124 EE63
Cruikshank St, WC1 10 C1
Crummock Cl, Slou. SL1 130 AJ72
Crummock Gdns, NW9 118 CS57
Crumpsall St, SE2 166 EW77
Crundale Av, NW9 118 CN57
Crundal Twr, Orp. BR5 206 EW102
Crunden Rd, S.Croy. CR2 220 DR108
Crusader Cl, Purf. RM19
off Centurion Way 168 FN77
Crusader Gdns, Croy. CR0
off Cotelands 202 DS104
Crusader Way, Wat. WD18 75 BT44
Crushes Cl, Brwd. (Hutt.)
CM13 109 GE44
Sch Crusoe Ho Spec Sch, N1 11 J1
Crusoe Ms, N16 122 DR61
Crusoe Rd, Erith DA8 167 FD78
Mitcham CR4 180 DF94
Crutched Friars, EC3 11 M9
Crutches La, Beac. (Jordans)
HP9 90 AS51
Crutchfield La, Horl. (Hkwd)
RH6 268 DA145
Walton-on-Thames KT12 195 BV103
Crutchley Rd, SE6 184 EE89
Crystal Av, Horn. RM12 128 FL63
Crystal Ct, SE19
off College Rd 182 DT92
Crystal Ho, SE18
off Spinel Cl 165 ET78
⇌ Crystal Palace 182 DU93
Crystal Palace Caravan Club,
SE19 182 DT92
★ Crystal Palace FC, SE25 202 DS98
★ Crystal Palace Nat Sport
Cen, SE19 182 DU93
Crystal Palace Par, SE19 182 DT93
★ Crystal Palace Pk, SE19 182 DT92
Crystal Palace Pk Rd, SE26 182 DU92
Crystal Palace Rd, SE22 162 DU84
Crystal Palace Sta Rd, SE19 182 DU93
Crystal Ter, SE19 182 DR93
Crystal Vw Ct, Brom. BR1
off Winlaton Rd 183 ED91
Crystal Way, Dag. RM8 126 EW60
Harrow HA1 117 CF57
Crystal Wf, N1
off Graham St 141 DP68
Cuba Dr, Enf. EN3 82 DW40
Cuba St, E14 23 N3
Cubitt Sq, Sthl. UB2
off Windmill Av 136 CC74
Cubitt Steps, E14 23 P1
Cubitt St, WC1 10 A2
Croydon CR0 219 DM106
Cubitts Yd, WC2 9 P9
Cubitt Ter, SW4 161 DJ83
CUBITT TOWN, E14 24 D5
Sch Cubitt Town Jun &
Inf Sch, E14 24 D6
Cublands, Hert. SG13 32 DV09
Cuckmans Dr, St.Alb. AL2 60 CA25
Cuckoo Av, W7 137 CE70
Cuckoo Dene, W7 137 CD71
Cuckoo Hall La, N9 100 DW45
Sch Cuckoo Hall Prim Sch,
N9 off Cuckoo Hall La 101 DX45
Cuckoo Hill, Pnr. HA5 116 BW55
Cuckoo Hill Dr, Pnr. HA5 116 BW55
Cuckoo Hill Rd, Pnr. HA5 116 BW56
Cuckoo La, W7 137 CE73
Cuckoo Pound, Shep. TW17 195 BS99
Cucumber La, Hat. (Essen.)
AL9 46 DF20
Hertford SG13 46 DF20
Cudas Cl, Epsom KT19 217 CT105
Cuddington Av, Wor.Pk. KT4 199 CT104
Cuddington Cl, Tad. KT20 233 CW120
Sch Cuddington Comm Prim
Sch, Wor.Pk. KT4
off Salisbury Rd 199 CT104
Sch Cuddington Cft Prim Sch,
Sutt. SM2 off West Dr 217 CX109
Cuddington Glade, Epsom
KT19 216 CN112
Cuddington Pk Cl, Bans.
SM7 217 CZ113
Cuddington Way, Sutt. SM2 217 CX112
CUDHAM, Sev. TN14 239 ER115
Cudham Cl, Sutt. (Belmont)
SM2 218 DA110
Sch Cudham C of E Prim Sch,
West. TN16 off Jail La 239 EN116
Cudham Dr, Croy.
(New Adgtn) CR0 221 EC110
Cudham La N, Orp. BR6 223 ES110
Sevenoaks (Cudham)
TN14 223 ER112
Cudham La S, Sev. (Cudham)
TN14 239 EQ115
Cudham Pk Rd, Sev.
(Cudham) TN14 223 ES110
Cudham Rd, Orp. BR6 223 EN111
Westerham (Tats.) TN16 238 EL120
Cudham St, SE6 183 EC87
Cudworth St, E1 12 D3
Cuff Cres, SE9 184 EK86
CUFFLEY, Pot.B. EN6 65 DM29
⇌ Cuffley 65 DM29
Cuffley Av, Wat. WD25 60 BX34
Cuffley Ct, Hem.H. HP2 41 BQ15
Cuffley Hill, Wal.Cr. (Chsht)
EN7 65 DN29
Sch Cuffley Sch, Pot.B. EN6
off Theobalds Rd 65 DM30
Cuff Pt, E2 11 N1
Cugley Rd, Dart. DA2 188 FQ87
Culford Gdns, SW3 18 D8
Culford Gro, N1 5 L4
Culford Ms, N1 5 L3
Culford Rd, N1 5 L5
Grays RM16 170 GC75
Culgaith Gdns, Enf. EN2 81 DL42
Cullen Sq, S.Ock. RM15 149 FW73
Cullen Way, NW10 138 CQ70
Cullera Cl, Nthwd. HA6 93 BT51
Cullerne Cl, Epsom (Ewell)
KT17 217 CT110
Cullesden Rd, Ken. CR8 235 DP115
Culling Rd, SE16 22 E5
Cullings Ct, Wal.Abb. EN9 68 EF33
Cullington Cl, Har. HA3 117 CG56
Cullingworth Rd, NW10 119 CU64
Culloden Cl, SE16 22 B10
Sch Culloden Prim Sch, E14 14 D8
Culloden Rd, Enf. EN2 81 DP40
Culloden St, E14 14 D7
Cullum St, EC3 11 L9
Culmington Rd, W13 157 CJ75
South Croydon CR2 220 DQ109
Culmore Rd, SE15 162 DV80
Culmstock Rd, SW11 180 DG85
Culpeper Cl, Ilf. IG6 103 EP51
Culpepper Cl, N18
off Dysons Rd 100 DV50
Culross Cl, N15 122 DQ56
Culross St, W1 8 E10
Culsac Rd, Surb. KT6 198 CL103
Culverden Rd, SW12 181 DJ89
Watford WD19 93 BV48
Culver Dr, Oxt. RH8 254 EE130
Culver Gro, Stan. HA7 95 CJ54
Culverhay, Ashtd. KT21 232 CL116
Culverhouse Gdns, SW16 181 DM90
Culverlands Cl, Stan. HA7 95 CH49
Culverley Rd, SE6 183 EB88
Culver Rd, St.Alb. AL1 43 CE19
Culvers Av, Cars. SM5 200 DF103
Culvers Cft, Beac. (Seer Grn)
HP9 89 AQ51
Sch Culvers Ho Prim Sch, Mitch.
CR4 off Orchard Av 200 DG102
Culvers Retreat, Cars. SM5 200 DF102
Culverstone Cl, Brom. BR2 204 EF100
Culvers Way, Cars. SM5 200 DF103
Culvert La, Uxb. UB8 134 BH68
Culvert Pl, SW11 160 DG82
Culvert Rd, N15 122 DS57
SW11 160 DF82
Culworth St, NW8
off Prince Albert Rd 140 DE68
Cumberland Av, NW10 138 CP69
Gravesend DA12 191 GJ87
Guildford GU2 242 AU129
Hornchurch RM12 128 FL62
Slough SL2 131 AQ70
Welling DA16 165 ES83
Cumberland Cl, E8 5 N4
SW20 off Lansdowne Rd 179 CX94
Amersham HP7 72 AV39
Epsom KT19 216 CS110
Hemel Hempstead HP3 41 BS24
Hertford SG14 31 DP06
Hornchurch RM12 128 FL62
Ilford IG6 103 EQ53
Twickenham TW1
off Westmorland Cl 177 CH86
Cumberland Cres, W14 16 D7
Cumberland Dr, Bexh. DA7 166 EY80
Chessington KT9 198 CM104
Dartford DA1 188 FM87
Esher KT10 197 CG103
Cumberland Gdns, NW4 97 CY54
WC1 10 B1
Cumberland Gate, W1 8 C9
Cumberland Mkt, NW1 9 H1
Cumberland Mkt Est, NW1 9 H1
Cumberland Mills Sq, E14 24 E9
Cumberland Pk, NW10 139 CU69
W3 138 CQ73
Cumberland Pl, NW1 8 G1
SE6 184 EF88
Sunbury-on-Thames
TW16 195 BU98
Cumberland Rd, E12 124 EK63
E13 15 N5
E17 101 DY54
N9 100 DW46
N22 99 DM54
SE25 202 DV100
SW13 159 CT81
W3 138 CQ73
W7 157 CF75
Ashford TW15 174 BK90
Bromley BR2 204 EE98
Grays (Chaff.Hun.) RM16 170 FY75
Harrow HA1 116 CB57
Richmond TW9 158 CN80
Stanmore HA7 118 CM55
Cumberlands, Ken. CR8 236 DR115
Sch Cumberland Sch, E16 15 K6
Cumberland St, SW1 19 H9
Staines TW18 173 BD92
Cumberland Ter, NW1
off Outer Circle 141 DH68
Cumberland Ter Ms, NW1
off Albany St 141 DH68
Cumberland Vil, W3
off Cumberland Rd 138 CQ73
Cumberlow Av, SE25 202 DT97
Cumberlow Pl, Hem.H. HP2 41 BQ21
Cumbernauld Gdns, Sun.
TW16 175 BT92
Cumberton Rd, N17 100 DR53
Cumbrae Cl, Slou. SL2
off St. Pauls Av 132 AU74
Cumbrae Gdns, Surb. KT6 197 CK103
Cumbrian Av, Bexh. DA7 167 FE81
Cumbrian Gdns, NW2 119 CX61
Cumbrian Way, Uxb. UB8
off Chippendale Waye 134 BK66
Cum Cum Hill, Hat. AL9 46 DD21
★ Cuming Mus, SE17 20 G8
Cumley Rd, Ong. CM5 71 FE30
Cummings Hall La, Rom.
(Noak Hill) RM3 106 FJ48
Cumming St, N1 4 A10
Cumnor Gdns, Epsom KT17 217 CU107
Sch Cumnor Ho Sch, S.Croy.
CR2 off Pampisford Rd 219 DP109
Cumnor Ri, Ken. CR8 236 DQ117
Cumnor Rd, Sutt. SM2 218 DC107
Cunard Cres, N21 82 DR44
Cunard Pl, EC3 11 M8
Cunard Rd, NW10 138 CR69
Cunard St, SE5
off Albany Rd 162 DS79
Cunard Wk, SE16 23 H7
Cundalls Rd, Ware SG12 33 DY05
Cundy Rd, E16 144 EJ72
Cundy St, SW1 18 F8
Cundy St Est, SW1 18 F8
Cunliffe Cl, Epsom (Headley)
KT18 232 CP124
Cunliffe Rd, Epsom KT19 217 CT105
Cunliffe St, SW16 181 DJ93
Cunningham Av, Enf. EN3 83 DY36
Guildford GU1 243 BA133
Hatfield AL10
off Mosquito Way 44 CR17
St. Albans AL1 43 CF22
Cunningham Cl, Rom. RM6 126 EW57
West Wickham BR4 203 EB103
Sch Cunningham Hill Inf Sch,
St.Alb. AL1
off Cell Barnes La 43 CG21
Sch Cunningham Hill Jun Sch,
St.Alb. AL1
off Cell Barnes La 43 CG22
Cunningham Hill Rd, St.Alb.
AL1 43 CF22
Cunningham Pk, Har. HA1 116 CC57
Cunningham Pl, NW8 7 N3
Cunningham Ri, Epp.
(N.Wld Bas.) CM16 71 FC25
Cunningham Rd, N15 122 DU56
Banstead SM7 234 DD115
Waltham Cross (Chsht)
EN8 67 DY27
Cunnington St, W4 158 CQ76
Cupar Rd, SW11 160 DG81
CUPID GREEN, Hem.H. HP2 40 BN16
Cupid Grn La, Hem.H. HP2 40 BN15
Cupola Cl, Brom. BR1 184 EH92
Curates Wk, Dart. DA1 188 FK90
Cureton St, SW1 19 M8
Curfew Bell Rd, Cher. KT16 193 BF101
Curfew Ho, Bark. IG11
off St. Ann's 145 EQ67
Curfew Yd, Wind. SL4
off Thames St 151 AR81
Curie Gdns, NW9
off Pasteur Cl 96 CS54
Curlew Cl, SE28 146 EX73
Berkhamsted HP4 38 AW20
South Croydon CR2 221 DX111
Curlew Ct, Brox. EN10 49 DZ23
Surbiton KT6 198 CM104
Curlew Gdns, Guil. GU4 243 BD132
Curlew Ho, Enf. EN3
off Allington Ct 83 DX43
Curlews, The, Grav. DA12 191 GK89
Curlew St, SE1 21 N3
Curlew Ter, Ilf. IG5
off Tiptree Cres 125 EN55
Curlew Way, Hayes UB4 136 BX71
Curling Cl, Couls. CR5 235 DM120
Curling La, Grays
(Bad.Dene) RM17 170 FZ78
Curling Vale, Guil. GU2 258 AU136
Curnick's La, SE27
off Chapel Rd 182 DQ91
Curnock Est, NW1
off Plender St 141 DJ67
Curran Av, Sid. DA15 185 ET85
Wallington SM6 200 DG104
Curran Cl, Uxb. UB8 134 BJ70
Currey Rd, Grnf. UB6 137 CD65
Curricle St, W3 138 CS74
Currie Hill Cl, SW19 179 CZ91
Curries La, Slou. SL1 111 AK64
Currie St, Hert. SG13 32 DS09
Curry Ri, NW7 97 CX51
Cursitor St, EC4 10 C7
Curtain Pl, EC2
off Curtain Rd 142 DS69
Curtain Rd, EC2 11 L4
Curteys, Harl. CM17 36 EX10
Curthwaite Gdns, Enf. EN2 81 DK42
Curtis Cl, Rick. (Mill End)
WD3 92 BG46
Curtis Dr, W3 138 CR72
Curtis Fld Rd, SW16 181 DM91
Curtis Gdns, Dor. RH4 263 CG135
Curtis La, Wem. HA0
off Montrose Cres 138 CL65
Curtismill Cl, Orp. BR5 206 EV97
Curtis Mill Grn, Rom.
(Nave.) RM4 87 FF42
Curtis Mill La, Rom. (Nave.)
RM4 87 FF42
Curtismill Way, Orp. BR5 206 EV97
Curtis Rd, Dor. RH4 263 CF135
Epsom KT19 216 CQ105
Hemel Hempstead HP3 41 BQ21
Hornchurch RM11 128 FM60
Hounslow TW4 176 BZ87
Curtiss Dr, Wat. (Lvsdn)
WD25 59 BT34
Curtis St, SE1 21 N7
Curtis Way, SE1 21 N7
SE28 off Tawney Rd 146 EV73
Berkhamsted HP4 38 AX20
Curvan Cl, Epsom KT17 217 CT110
Curve, The, W12 139 CU73
Curwen Av, E7
off Woodford Rd 124 EH63
Sch Curwen Prim Sch, E13
off Atlas Rd 144 EG68
Curwen Rd, W12 159 CU75
Curzon Av, Beac. HP9 89 AK51
Enfield EN3 83 DX43
High Wycombe (Haz.)
HP15 88 AC45
Stanmore HA7 95 CG53
Curzon Cl, H.Wyc. (Haz.)
HP15 88 AC45
Orpington BR6 223 ER105
Weybridge KT13
off Curzon Rd 212 BN105
Curzon Cres, NW10 139 CT66
Barking IG11 145 ET68
Curzon Dr, Grays RM17 170 GC80
Curzon Gate, W1 18 F2
Curzon Mall, Slou. SL1
off High St 152 AT75
Curzon Pl, Pnr. HA5 116 BW57
Curzon Rd, N10 99 DH54
W5 137 CH70
Thornton Heath CR7 201 DN100
Weybridge KT13 212 BN105
Curzon Sq, W1 18 F2
Curzon St, W1 18 F2
Cusack Cl, Twick. TW1
off Waldegrave Rd 177 CF91
Cussons Cl, Wal.Cr. (Chsht)
EN7 66 DU29
CUSTOM HOUSE, E16 144 EK72
⇌ Custom House 15 P9
DLR Custom House 15 P9
Custom Ho Reach, SE16 23 L4
Custom Ho Wk, EC3 11 L10
Cut, The, SE1 20 D3
Cut, The, Slough SL2 131 AN70
Cutcombe Rd, SE5 162 DQ82
Cuthberga Cl, Bark. IG11
off George St 145 EQ66
Cuthbert Gdns, SE25 202 DS97
Cuthbert Rd, E17 123 EC55
N18 off Fairfield Rd 100 DU50
Croydon CR0 201 DP103
Cuthberts Cl, Wal.Cr. EN7 66 DT29
Cuthbert St, W2 7 N5
Cut Hills, Egh. TW20 192 AV95
Virginia Water GU25 192 AU96
Cuthill Wk, SE5 162 DR81
Cutlers Gdns, EC2 11 M7
Cutlers Gdns Arc, EC2
off Cutler St 142 DS72
Cutlers Sq, E14 23 P8
Cutlers Ter, N1 5 L3
Cutler St, E1 11 M7
Cutmore Dr, St.Alb.
(Coln.Hth) AL4 44 CP22
Cutmore St, Grav. DA11 191 GH87
Cutthroat All, Rich. TW10
off Ham St 177 CJ89
Cutthroat La, Hodd. EN11 49 DZ15
Cutting, The, Red. RH1 266 DF136
Cuttsfield Ter, Hem.H. HP1 39 BF21
★ Cutty Sark, SE10 163 EC79
DLR Cutty Sark 163 EC79
Cutty Sark Ct, Green. DA9
off Low Cl 189 FU85
Cutty Sark Gdns, SE10
off King William Wk 163 EC79
Cuxton Cl, Bexh. DA6 186 EY85
Cwmbran Ct, Hem.H. HP2 40 BM16
Cyclamen Cl, Hmptn. TW12
off Gresham Rd 176 CA93
Cyclamen Rd, Swan. BR8 207 FD98
Cyclamen Way, Epsom
KT19 216 CP106
Cyclops Ms, E14 23 N7
Cygnet Av, Felt. TW14 176 BW87
Cygnet Cl, NW10 118 CR64
Borehamwood WD6 78 CQ39
Northwood HA6 93 BQ52
Woking GU21 226 AV116
Cygnet Gdns, Grav. (Nthflt)
DA11 191 GF89
Cygnets, The, Felt. TW13 176 BY91
Staines TW18
off Edgell Rd 173 BF92
Cygnets Cl, Red. RH1 250 DG132
Cygnet St, E1 11 P3
Cygnet Vw, Grays RM20 169 FT77
Cygnet Way, Harl. (Roydon)
CM19 off Roydon Mill Pk 34 EG14
Hayes UB4 136 BX71
Cygnus Business Cen,
NW10 139 CT65
Cymbeline Ct, Har. HA1 117 CF58
Cynthia St, N1 4 B10
Cyntra Pl, E8 142 DV66
Cypress Av, Enf. EN2 81 DN35
Twickenham TW2 176 CC87
Welwyn Garden City AL7 30 DC10
Cypress Cl, Wal.Abb. EN9 67 ED34
Cypress Ct, Vir.W. GU25 192 AY98
Cypress Gdns, SE4 183 DY85
Cypress Gro, Ilf. IG6 103 ES51
Sch Cypress Inf Sch, SE25
off Cypress Rd 202 DS96
Sch Cypress Jun Sch, SE25
off Cypress Rd 202 DS96
Cypress Path, Rom. RM3 106 FK52
Cypress Pl, W1 9 K4
Cypress Rd, SE25 202 DS96
Guildford GU1 242 AW132
Harrow HA3 95 CD54
Cypress Tree Cl, Sid. DA15
off White Oak Gdns 185 ET87
Cypress Wk, Egh. (Eng.Grn)
TW20 172 AV93
Watford WD25
off Cedar Wd Dr 75 BV35
Cypress Way, Bans. SM7 217 CX114
DLR Cyprus 145 EN73
Cyprus Av, N3 97 CY54
Cyprus Cl, N4
off Atterbury Rd 121 DP58
Cyprus Gdns, N3 97 CY54
Cyprus Pl, E2 142 DW68
E6 145 EN73
Cyprus Rd, N3 97 CZ54
N9 100 DT47
Cyprus Roundabout, E16
off Royal Albert Way 145 EN73
Cyprus St, E2 142 DW68
Cyrena Rd, SE22 182 DT86
Sch Cyril Jackson Prim Sch,
E14 13 M9
Annexe, E14 13 M10
Cyril Mans, SW11 160 DF81
Cyril Rd, Bexh. DA7 166 EY82
Orpington BR6 206 EU101
Cyrils Way, St.Alb. AL1
off Maynard Dr 43 CD23
Cyrus St, EC1 10 F3
Czar St, SE8 163 EA79

D

Dabbling Cl, Erith DA8 167 FH80
Dabbs Hill La, Nthlt. UB5 116 CB64
D'Abernon Cl, Esher KT10 214 CA105
D'Abernon Dr, Cob.
(Stoke D'Ab.) KT11 230 BY116
Dabin Cres, SE10 163 EC81
Dacca St, SE8 163 DZ79
Dace Rd, E3 143 EA66
Dacorum Way, Hem.H. HP1 40 BJ20
Dacre Av, Ilf. IG5 103 EN54
South Ockendon (Aveley)
RM15 149 FR74
Dacre Cl, Chig. IG7 103 EQ49
Greenford UB6 136 CB68
Dacre Cres, S.Ock. (Aveley)
RM15 149 FR74
Dacre Gdns, SE13 164 EE84
Borehamwood WD6 78 CR43
Chigwell IG7 103 EQ49
Dacre Pk, SE13 164 EE83
Dacre Pl, SE13 164 EE83
Dacre Rd, E11 124 EF60
E13 144 EH67
Croydon CR0 201 DL101
Dacres Rd, SE23 183 DX90
Dacre St, SW1 19 L5

⊖ London Underground station DLR Docklands Light Railway station Tra Tramlink station Riv Pedestrian ferry landing stage

Dade Way, Sthl. UB2 156 BZ78
Dad's Wd, Harl. CM20 51 EQ15
Daerwood Cl, Brom. BR2 205 EM102
Daffodil Av, Brwd. (Pilg.Hat.)
CM15 108 FV43
Daffodil Cl, Croy. CR0
off Primrose La 203 DX102
Hatfield AL10 29 CT14
Daffodil Gdns, Ilf. IG1 125 EP64
Daffodil Pl, Hmptn. TW12
off Gresham Rd 176 CA93
Daffodil St, W12 139 CT73
Dafforne Rd, SW17 180 DG90
Dagden Rd, Guil. (Shalf.)
GU4 258 AY140
DAGENHAM, RM8 - RM10 146 FA65
Dagenham Av, Dag. RM9 146 EY67
≠ Dagenham Dock 146 EZ68
⊖ Dagenham East 127 FC64
⊖ Dagenham Heathway 146 EZ65
Sch Dagenham Priory Comp Sch, Dag. RM10 *off School Rd* 146 FA67
Dagenham Rd, E10 123 DZ60
Dagenham RM10 127 FC63
Rainham RM13 147 FD66
Romford RM7 127 FD62
Dagger La, Borwd. (Elstree)
WD6 77 CG44
Daggs Dell Rd, Hem.H. HP1 39 BE18
Dagley Fm Pk Homes, Guil. (Shalf.) GU4 258 AX140
Dagley La, Guil. (Shalf.)
GU4 258 AX140
Dagmar Av, Wem. HA9 118 CM63
Dagmar Gdns, NW10 139 CX68
Dagmar Ms, Sthl. UB2
off Dagmar Rd 156 BY76
Dagmar Pas, N1 4 F7
Dagmar Rd, N4 121 DN59
N15 *off Cornwall Rd* 122 DR56
N22 99 DK53
SE5 162 DS81
SE25 202 DS99
Dagenham RM10 147 FC66
Kingston upon Thames
KT2 198 CM95
Southall UB2 156 BY76
Windsor SL4 151 AR82
Dagmar Ter, N1 4 F7
Dagnall Cres, Uxb. UB8 134 BJ71
Dagnall Pk, SE25 202 DS100
Dagnall Rd, SE25 202 DS99
Dagnall St, SW11 160 DF82
Dagnam Pk Cl, Rom. RM3 106 FN50
Dagnam Pk Dr, Rom. RM3 106 FL50
Dagnam Pk Gdns, Rom.
RM3 106 FN51
Dagnam Pk Sq, Rom. RM3 106 FP51
Dagnan Rd, SW12 181 DH87
Dagonet Gdns, Brom. BR1 184 EG90
Dagonet Rd, Brom. BR1 184 EG90
Dahlia Cl, Wal.Cr. (Chsht)
EN7 66 DQ25
Dahlia Dr, Swan. BR8 207 FF96
Dahlia Gdns, Ilf. IG1 145 EP65
Mitcham CR4 201 DK98
Dahlia Rd, SE2 166 EV77
Dahomey Rd, SW16 181 DJ93
Daiglen Dr, S.Ock. RM15 149 FU73
Sch Daiglen Sch, The, Buck.H. IG9 *off Palmerston Rd* 102 EJ47
Daimler Way, Wall. SM6 219 DL108
Daines Cl, E12
off Colchester Av 125 EM62
South Ockendon RM15 149 FU70
Dainford Cl, Brom. BR1 183 ED92
Dainton Cl, Brom. BR1 204 EH95
Daintry Cl, Har. HA3 117 CG56
Daintry Lo, Nthwd. HA6 93 BT52
Daintry Way, E9
off Osborne Rd 143 DZ65
Sch Dair Ho Sch, Slou. SL2
off Beaconsfield Rd 131 AQ67
Dairsie Rd, SE9 165 EN83
Dairy Cl, NW10 139 CU67
Dartford (Sutt.H.) DA4 188 FP94
Thornton Heath CR7 202 DQ96
Dairyglen Av, Wal.Cr. EN8 67 DY31
Dairy La, SE18 165 EM77
Edenbridge (Crock.H.)
TN8 255 EN134
Dairyman Cl, NW2
off Claremont Rd 119 CY62
Dairyman's Wk, Guil. GU4 243 BB129
Sch Dairy Meadow Prim Sch, Sthl. UB2 *off Swift Rd* 156 BZ76
Dairy Ms, SW9 161 DL83
Dairy Wk, SW19 179 CY91
Dairy Way, Abb.L. WD5 59 BT29
Daisy Cl, Croy. CR0
off Primrose La 203 DX102
Daisy Dobbins Wk, N19
off Hillrise Rd 121 DL59
Daisy Dr, Hat. AL9 45 CT15
Daisy La, SW6 160 DA83
Daisy Rd, E16 14 G3
E18 102 EH54
Dakota Cl, Wall. SM6 219 DM108
Dakota Gdns, E6 144 EL70
Northolt UB5
off Argus Way 136 BY69
Dalberg Rd, SW2 161 DN84
Dalberg Way, SE2
off Lanridge Rd 166 EX76
Dalby Rd, SW18 160 DC84
Dalby St, NW5 141 DH65
Dalcross Rd, Houns. TW4 156 BY82
Dale, The, Kes. BR2 222 EK105
Waltham Abbey EN9 68 EE34
Dale Av, Edg. HA8 96 CM53
Hounslow TW4 156 BY83
Dalebury Rd, SW17 180 DE89
Dale Cl, SE3 164 EG83
Addlestone KT15 212 BH106
Barnet EN5 80 DB44
Dartford DA1 187 FF86
Pinner HA5 93 BV53
South Ockendon RM15 149 FU72
Dale Ct, Saw. CM21
off The Crest 36 EX06
Slough SL1 *off Tuns La* 151 AQ75
Dale Dr, Hayes UB4 135 BT70
Dale End, Dart. DA1
off Dale Rd 187 FF86
Dalefield Way, Grav. DA12
off Marsh Vw 191 GM88
Dale Gdns, Wdf.Grn. IG8 102 EH49
Dalegarth Gdns, Pur. CR8 220 DR113
Dale Grn Rd, N11 99 DH48
Dale Gro, N12 98 DC50
Daleham Av, Egh. TW20 173 BA93
Daleham Dr, Uxb. UB8 135 BP72
Daleham Gdns, NW3 120 DD64
Daleham Ms, NW3 140 DD65
Dalehead, NW1 141 DJ68
Dalemain Ms, E16 25 M1
Dale Pk Av, Cars. SM5 200 DF103
Dale Pk Rd, SE19 202 DQ95
Dale Rd, NW5 *off Grafton Rd* 120 DG64
SE17 161 DP79
Dartford DA1 187 FF86
Gravesend (Sthflt) DA13 190 GA91
Greenford UB6 136 CB71
Purley CR8 219 DN112
Sunbury-on-Thames
TW16 175 BT94
Sutton SM1 217 CZ105
Swanley BR8 207 FC96
Walton-on-Thames KT12 195 BT101
Dale Row, W11 6 D8
Daleside, Ger.Cr. SL9 112 AY60
Orpington BR6 224 EU106
Daleside Cl, Orp. BR6 224 EU107
Daleside Dr, Pot.B. EN6 63 CZ32
Daleside Gdns, Chig. IG7 103 EQ48
Daleside Rd, SW16 181 DH92
Epsom KT19 216 CR107
Dales Path, Borwd. WD6
off Farriers Way 78 CR43
Dales Rd, Borwd. WD6 78 CR43
Dalestone Ms, Rom. RM3 105 FH51
Dale St, W4 158 CS78
Dale Vw, Epsom (Headley)
KT18 232 CP123
Erith DA8 167 FF82
Woking GU21 226 AU118
Dale Vw Av, E4 101 EC47
Dale Vw Cres, E4 101 EC47
Dale Vw Gdns, E4 101 ED48
Daleview Rd, N15 122 DS58
Dale Wk, Dart. DA2 188 FQ88
Dalewood, Welw.G.C. AL7 30 DD10
Dalewood Cl, Horn. RM11 128 FM59
Dalewood Gdns, Wor.Pk.
KT4 199 CV103
Dale Wd Rd, Orp. BR6 205 ES101
Daley St, E9 143 DX65
Daley Thompson Way, SW8 161 DH82
Dalgarno Gdns, W10 139 CW71
Dalgarno Way, W10 139 CW70
Dalgleish St, E14 13 K8
Daling Way, E3 143 DY67
Dalkeith Gro, Stan. HA7 95 CK50
Dalkeith Rd, SE21 182 DQ88
Ilford IG1 125 EQ62
Dallas Rd, NW4 119 CU59
SE26 182 DV91
W5 138 CM71
Sutton SM3 217 CY107
Dallas Ter, Hayes UB3 155 BT76
Dallega Cl, Hayes UB3
off Dawley Rd 135 BR73
Dallinger Rd, SE12 184 EF86
Dalling Rd, W6 159 CV76
Dallington Cl, Walt. KT12 214 BW107
Sch Dallington Sch, EC1 10 F3
Dallington Sq, EC1
off Dallington St 141 DP70
Dallington St, EC1 10 F3
Dallin Rd, SE18 165 EP80
Bexleyheath DA6 166 EX84
Sch Dalmain Prim Sch, SE23
off Grove Cl 183 DY88
Dalmain Rd, SE23 183 DX88
Dalmally Rd, Croy. CR0 202 DT101
Dalmeny Av, N7 121 DK63
SW16 201 DN96
Dalmeny Cl, Wem. HA0 137 CJ65
Dalmeny Cres, Houns. TW3 157 CD84
Dalmeny Rd, N7 121 DK62
Barnet EN5 80 DC44
Carshalton SM5 218 DG108
Erith DA8 167 FB81
Worcester Park KT4 199 CV104
Dalmeyer Rd, NW10 139 CT65
Dalmore Av, Esher (Clay.)
KT10 215 CF107
Dalmore Rd, SE21 182 DQ89
Dalroy Cl, S.Ock. RM15 149 FU72
Dalrymple Cl, N14 99 DK45
Dalrymple Rd, SE4 163 DY84
DALSTON, E8 142 DU66
Dalston Gdns, Stan. HA7 96 CL53
≠ Dalston Kingsland 5 M3
Dalston La, E8 5 N3
Dalton Av, Mitch. CR4 200 DE96
Dalton Cl, Hayes UB4 135 BR70
Orpington BR6 205 ES104
Purley CR8 220 DQ112
Dalton Grn, Slou. SL3
off Ditton Rd 153 AZ78
Dalton Rd, Har. (Har.Wld)
HA3 95 CD54
Daltons Rd, Orp. BR6 207 FB104
Swanley BR8 207 FC102
Dalton St, SE27 181 DP89
St. Albans AL3 43 CD19
Dalton Way, Wat. WD17 76 BX43
Dalwood St, SE5 162 DS81
Daly Ct, E15 *off Clays La* 123 EC64
Dalyell Rd, SW9 161 DM83
Damascene Wk, SE21
off Lovelace Rd 182 DQ88
Damask Cres, E16 15 H3
Damask Grn, Hem.H. HP1 39 BE21
Sch Dame Alice Owen's Sch, Pot.B. EN6
off Dugdale Hill La 63 CY33
Damer Ter, SW10
off Tadema Rd 160 DC80
Dames Rd, E7 124 EG62
Dame St, N1 4 G9
Dameswick Vw, St.Alb. AL2 60 CA27
Sch Dame Tipping C of E Prim Sch, Rom. RM4
off North Rd 105 FE48
Damien St, E1 12 D7
Damigos Rd, Grav. DA12 191 GM88
Damon Cl, Sid. DA14 186 EV90
Damphurst La, Dor. RH5 262 BZ139
Damson Ct, Swan. BR8 207 FD98
Damson Dr, Hayes UB3 135 BU73
Damson Gro, Slou. SL1 151 AQ75
Damson Way, Cars. SM5 218 DF110
St. Albans AL4 43 CJ18
Damsonwood Rd, Sthl. UB2 156 CA76
Danbrook Rd, SW16 201 DL95
Danbury Cl, Brwd. (Pilg.Hat.)
CM15 108 FT43
Romford RM6 126 EX55
Danbury Cres, S.Ock. RM15 149 FV72
Danbury Ms, Wall. SM6 219 DH105
Danbury Rd, Loug. IG10 102 EL45
Rainham RM13 147 FF67
Danbury St, N1 4 F9
Danbury Way, Wdf.Grn. IG8 102 EJ51
Danby St, SE15 162 DT83
Dancer Rd, SW6 159 CZ81
Richmond TW9 158 CN83
DANCERS HILL, Barn. EN5 79 CW35
Dancers Hill Rd, Barn. EN5 79 CY36
Dancers La, Barn. EN5 79 CW35
Dandelion Cl, Rom.
(Rush Grn) RM7 127 FE61
Dando Cres, SE3 164 EH83
Dandridge Cl, SE10 25 K9
Slough SL3 152 AX77
Dandridge Dr, B.End SL8
off Millside 110 AC60
Danebury, Croy. (New Adgtn)
CR0 221 EB107
Danebury Av, SW15 178 CS86
Daneby Rd, SE6 183 EB90
Dane Cl, Amer. HP7 72 AT41
Bexley DA5 186 FA87
Orpington BR6 223 ER106
Dane Ct, Wok. GU22 227 BF115
Danecourt Gdns, Croy. CR0 202 DT104
Danecroft Rd, SE24 182 DQ85
Sch Danegrove Prim Sch, Inf Dept, Barn. EN4
off Ridgeway Av 80 DF44
Jun Dept, Barn. EN4
off Windsor Dr 80 DE44
Danehill Wk, Sid. DA14
off Hatherley Rd 186 EU90
Danehurst Cl, Egh. TW20 172 AY93
Danehurst Gdns, Ilf. IG4 124 EL57
Danehurst St, SW6 159 CY81
Daneland, Barn. EN4 80 DF44
Danemead, Hodd. EN11 33 EA14
Danemead Gro, Nthlt. UB5 116 CB64
Danemere St, SW15 159 CW83
Dane Pl, E3 *off Roman Rd* 143 DY68
Dane Rd, N18 100 DW48
SW19 200 DC95
W13 137 CJ74
Ashford TW15 175 BQ93
Ilford IG1 125 EQ64
Sevenoaks (Otford) TN14 241 FE117
Southall UB1 136 BY73
Warlingham CR6 237 DX117
Danes, The, St.Alb. (Park St)
AL2 60 CC28
Danesbury Pk, Hert. SG14 32 DR08
Danesbury Rd, Felt. TW13 175 BV88
Danes Cl, Grav. (Nthflt) DA11 190 GC90
Leatherhead (Oxshott)
KT22 214 CC114
Danescombe, SE12
off Winn Rd 184 EG88
Danes Ct, Wem. HA9 118 CP62
Danescourt Cres, Sutt. SM1 200 DC103
Danescroft, NW4 119 CX57
Danescroft Av, NW4 119 CX57
Danescroft Gdns, NW4 119 CX57
Danesdale Rd, E9 143 DY65
Danesfield, SE5 162 DS79
Woking GU23
off Polesden La 227 BF123
Danesfield Cl, Walt. KT12 195 BV104
Sch Danesfield Manor Sch, Walt. KT12
off Rydens Av 196 BW103
Danes Gate, Har. HA1 117 CE55
Daneshill, Red. RH1 250 DE133
Danes Hill, Wok. GU22 227 BA118
Daneshill Cl, Red. RH1 250 DE133
Sch Danes Hill Jun Sch, Lthd. KT22 *off Steels La* 214 CC113
Sch Danes Hill Sch, Lthd. KT22 *off Leatherhead Rd* 215 CD114
Danes Rd, Rom. RM7 127 FC59
Danesrood, Guil. GU1
off Lower Edgeborough Rd 259 AZ135
Dane St, WC1 10 A6
Danes Way, Brwd. (Pilg.Hat.)
CM15 108 FU43
Leatherhead (Oxshott)
KT22 215 CD114
Daneswood Av, SE6 183 EC90
Daneswood Cl, Wey. KT13 213 BP106
Danethorpe Rd, Wem. HA0 137 CK65
Danetree Cl, Epsom KT19 216 CQ108
Sch Danetree Jun Sch, Epsom KT19 *off Danetree Rd* 216 CQ108
Danetree Rd, Epsom KT19 216 CQ108
Danette Gdns, Dag. RM10 126 EZ61
Daneville Rd, SE5 162 DR81
Dangan Rd, E11 124 EG58
Daniel Bolt Cl, E14 14 B5
Daniel Cl, N18 100 DW49
SW17 180 DE93
Grays RM16 171 GH76
Grays (Chaff.Hun.) RM16 170 FY75
Hounslow TW4
off Harvey Rd 176 BZ87
Daniel Gdns, SE15 162 DT80
Daniells, Welw.G.C. AL7 30 DA08
Daniell Way, Croy. CR0 201 DL102
Daniel Pl, NW4 119 CV58
Daniel Rd, W5 138 CM73
Daniels La, Warl. CR6 237 DZ116
Daniels Rd, SE15 162 DW83
Daniel Way, Bans. SM7 218 DB114
Dan Leno Wk, SW6
off Britannia Rd 160 DB80
Dan Mason Dr, W4
off Great Chertsey Rd 158 CQ82
Danses Cl, Guil. GU4 243 BD132
Dansey Pl, W1 9 L9
Dansington Rd, Well. DA16 166 EU84
Danson Cres, Well. DA16 166 EV83
Danson La, Well. DA16 166 EU84
Danson Mead, Well. DA16 166 EW83
★ Danson Park, Well. DA16 166 EW84
Danson Pk, Bexh. DA6 166 EW84
Sch Danson Prim Sch, Well. DA16 *off Danson La* 166 EU84
Danson Rd, Bex. DA5 186 EX85
Bexleyheath DA6 186 EX85
Danson Underpass, Sid.
DA15 *off Danson Rd* 186 EW86
Dante Pl, SE11 20 F7
Dante Rd, SE11 20 E7
Danube St, SW3 18 B9
Danvers Rd, N8 121 DK56
Danvers St, SW3 160 DD79
Danvers Way, Cat. CR3 236 DQ123
Danyon Cl, Rain. RM13 148 FJ68
Danziger Way, Borwd. WD6 78 CQ39
Dapdune Ct, Guil. GU1 242 AW134
Dapdune Rd, Guil. GU1 242 AW134
Dapdune Wf, Guil. GU1 242 AW134
Daphne Gdns, E4
off Gunners Gro 101 EC48
Daphne St, SW18 180 DC86
Daplyn St, E1 12 A5
Darblay Cl, St.Alb. (Sand.)
AL4 28 CM10
D'Arblay St, W1 9 K8
Darby Cl, Cat. CR3 236 DQ122
Darby Cres, Sun. TW16 196 BW96
Darby Dr, Wal.Abb. EN9 67 EC33
Darby Gdns, Sun. TW16 196 BW96
Darcy Av, Wall. SM6 219 DJ105
Darcy Cl, N20 98 DD47
D'Arcy Cl, Brwd. (Hutt.)
CM13 109 GB45
Darcy Cl, Couls. CR5 235 DP119
Waltham Cross (Chsht)
EN8 67 DY31
D'Arcy Dr, Har. HA3 117 CK56
Darcy Gdns, Dag. RM9 146 EZ67
D'Arcy Gdns, Har. HA3 118 CL56
D'Arcy Pl, Ashtd. KT21 232 CM117
Bromley BR2 204 EG98
Darcy Rd, SW16 201 DL96
D'Arcy Rd, Ashtd. KT21 232 CM117
Darcy Rd, Islw. TW7
off London Rd 157 CG81
D'Arcy Rd, Sutt. SM3 217 CX105
Dare Gdns, Dag. RM8
off Grafton Rd 126 EY62
Sch Darell Prim Sch, Rich. TW9 *off Darell Rd* 158 CN83
Darell Rd, Rich. TW9 158 CN83
DARENTH, Dart. DA2 188 FQ91
Darenth Cl, Sev. TN13 256 FC122
Sch Darenth Co Prim Sch, Dart. DA2
off Green St Grn Rd 189 FT93
Darenth Gdns, West. TN16
off Quebec Av 255 ER126
Darenth Hill, Dart. (Darenth)
DA2 188 FQ92
Darenth La, Sev. (Dunt.Grn)
TN13 256 FE121
South Ockendon RM15 149 FU72
Darenth Pk Av, Dart. DA2 189 FR89
Darenth Rd, N16 122 DT59
Dartford DA1 188 FM87
Dartford (Darenth) DA2 188 FP91
Welling DA16 166 EU81
Darenth Way, Horl. RH6 268 DF145
Sevenoaks (Shore.) TN14 225 FG111
Darenth Wd Rd, Dart. DA2 189 FS89
Darent Ind Pk, Erith DA8 168 FJ79
Darent Mead, Dart. (Sutt.H.)
DA4 208 FP95
H Darent Valley Hosp, Dart. DA2 189 FS88
Darent Valley Path, Dart.
DA1, DA2, DA4 188 FM89
Sevenoaks TN13, TN14 241 FG115
Darfield Rd, SE4 183 DZ85
Guildford GU4 243 BA131
Darfield Way, W10 6 A9
Darfur St, SW15 159 CX83
Dargate Cl, SE19
off Chipstead Cl 182 DT94
Darien Rd, SW11 160 DD83
Darkes La, Pot.B. EN6 64 DA32
Darkhole Ride, Wind. SL4 150 AH84
Dark Ho Wk, EC3
off King William St 142 DS73
Dark La, Brwd. (Gt Warley)
CM14 107 FU52
Guildford (Putt.) GU3 260 BM139
Waltham Cross (Chsht)
EN7 66 DU31
Ware (Musley La) SG12 33 DY05
Darlands Dr, Barn. EN5 79 CX43
Darlan Rd, SW6 159 CZ80
Darlaston Rd, SW19 179 CX94
Darley Cl, Add. KT15 212 BJ106
Croydon CR0 203 DY100
Darley Cft, St.Alb. AL2 60 CB28
Sch Darley Dene Inf Sch, Add. KT15 *off Garfield Rd* 212 BJ106
Darley Dr, N.Mal. KT3 198 CR96
Darley Gdns, Mord. SM4 200 DB100
Darley Rd, N9 100 DT46
SW11 180 DF86
Darling Rd, SE4 163 EA83
Darling Row, E1 12 D4
Darlington Cl, Amer. HP6
off King George V Rd 55 AR38
Darlington Gdns, Rom. RM3 106 FK50
Darlington Path, Rom. RM3
off Darlington Gdns 106 FK50
Darlington Rd, SE27 181 DP92
Darlton Cl, Dart. DA1 167 FF83
Darmaine Cl, S.Croy. CR2
off Churchill Rd 220 DQ108
Darnaway Pl, E14 14 D6
Darndale Cl, E17 101 DZ54
Darnets Fld, Sev. (Otford)
TN14 241 FF117
Darnhills, Rad. WD7 77 CG35
Darnicle Hill, Wal.Cr. (Chsht)
EN7 65 DM25
Darnley Ho, E14 13 K7
Darnley Pk, Wey. KT13 195 BP104
Darnley Rd, E9 142 DV65
Gravesend DA11 191 GG88
Grays RM17
off Stanley Rd 170 GB79
Woodford Green IG8 102 EG53
Darnley St, Grav. DA11 191 GG87
Darnley Ter, W11 16 B1
Darns Hill, Swan. BR8 207 FC101
Darrell Cl, Slou. SL3 153 AZ77
Darrell Rd, SE22 182 DU85
Darren Cl, N4 121 DM59
Sch Darrick Wd Inf Sch, Orp. BR6 *off Lovibonds Av* 223 EP105
Sch Darrick Wd Jun Sch, Orp. BR6 *off Lovibonds Av* 223 EP105
Darrick Wd Rd, Orp. BR6 205 ER103
Sch Darrick Wd Sch, Orp. BR6
off Lovibonds Av 205 EP104
Darrington Rd, Borwd. WD6 78 CL39
Darris Cl, Hayes UB4 136 BY70
Darsley Dr, SW8 161 DL81
Dart, The, Hem.H. HP2 40 BN15
Dart Cl, Slou. SL3 153 BB79
Upminster RM14 129 FR58
Dartfields, Rom. RM3 106 FK51
DARTFORD, DA1 &
DA2; DA4 188 FJ87
≠ Dartford 188 FL86
Coll Dartford Adult Ed Cen, Dart. DA1 *off East Hill Dr* 188 FM87
Dartford DA1
off Lowfield St 188 FL87
Dartford Av, N9 82 DW44
Dartford Bypass, Dart. DA2 187 FE88
Dartford Gdns, Rom.
(Chad.Hth) RM6
off Heathfield Pk Dr 126 EV58
Sch Dartford Gram Sch, Dart. DA1 *off West Hill* 188 FJ86
Sch Dartford Gram Sch for Girls, Dart. DA1
off Shepherds La 188 FJ87
★ Dartford Heath, Dart.
DA1 187 FG88
★ Dartford Mus, Dart. DA1 188 FL87
Dartford Rd, Bex. DA5 187 FC88
Dartford DA1 187 FG86
Dartford (Fnghm) DA4 208 FP95
Sevenoaks TN13 257 FJ124
Coll Dartford Social Ed Cen, Dart. DA2 *off Brent Way* 188 FP86
Dartford St, SE17 162 DQ79
Sch Dartford Tech Coll, Dart. DA1 *off Heath La* 188 FJ87
Dartford Trade Pk, Dart. DA1 188 FL89
Dartford Tunnel, Dart. DA1 169 FR83
Purfleet RM19 169 FR83
Dartford Tunnel App Rd, Dart.
DA1 188 FN86
Sch Dartford W High Sch for Boys, Dart. DA1
off Highfield Rd 188 FK87
Dart Grn, S.Ock. RM15 149 FV71
Dartmoor Wk, E14 23 P7
Dartmouth Av, Wok. GU21 211 BC114
Dartmouth Cl, W11 6 F7
Dartmouth Grn, Wok. GU21 211 BD114
Dartmouth Gro, SE10 163 EC81
Dartmouth Hill, SE10 163 EC81
Dartmouth Ho, Kings.T. KT2
off Kingsgate Rd 198 CL95
DARTMOUTH PARK, NW5 121 DH62
Dartmouth Pk Av, NW5 121 DH62
Dartmouth Pk Hill, N19 121 DH60
NW5 121 DH60
Dartmouth Pk Rd, NW5 121 DH63
Dartmouth Path, Wok. GU21 211 BD114
Dartmouth Pl, SE23
off Dartmouth Rd 182 DW89
W4 158 CS79
Dartmouth Rd, E16 15 L7
NW2 139 CX65
NW4 119 CU58
SE23 182 DW90
SE26 182 DW90
Bromley BR2 204 EG101
Ruislip HA4 115 BU62
Dartmouth Row, SE10 163 EC82
Dartmouth St, SW1 19 L4
Dartmouth Ter, SE10 163 ED81
Dartnell Av, W.Byf. KT14 212 BH112
Dartnell Cl, W.Byf. KT14 212 BH112
Dartnell Ct, W.Byf. KT14 212 BJ112
Dartnell Cres, W.Byf. KT14 212 BH112
DARTNELL PARK, W.Byf.
KT14 212 BJ112
Dartnell Pk Rd, W.Byf. KT14 212 BJ111
Dartnell Pl, W.Byf. KT14 212 BH112
Dartnell Rd, Croy. CR0 202 DT101
Dartrey Wk, SW10
off World's End Est 160 DD80
Dart St, W10 6 D1
Dartview Cl, Grays RM17 170 GE77
Darvel Cl, Wok. GU21 226 AU116
Darvell Dr, Chesh. HP5 54 AN29
Darville Rd, N16 122 DT62
Darvills La, Slou. SL1 151 AR75
Darwell Cl, E6 145 EN68
Darwin Cl, N11 99 DH48
Orpington BR6 223 ER106
St. Albans AL3 43 CE16
Darwin Ct, Guil. GU1 242 AX130
Darwin Dr, Sthl. UB1 136 CB72
Darwin Gdns, Wat. WD19
off Barnhurst Path 94 BW50
Darwin Rd, N22 99 DP53
W5 157 CJ78
Slough SL3 153 AZ75
Tilbury RM18 171 GF81
Welling DA16 165 ET83
Darwin St, SE17 21 K7
Daryngton Dr, Grnf. UB6 137 CD68
Guildford GU1 243 BB134
Dashes, The, Harl. CM20 35 ES14
Dashwood Cl, Bexh. DA6 186 FA85
Slough SL3 152 AW77
West Byfleet KT14 212 BJ112
Dashwood Rd, N8 121 DM58
Gravesend DA11 191 GG89
Dassett Rd, SE27 181 DP92
Datchelor Pl, SE5 162 DR81
DATCHET, Slou. SL3 152 AW81
≠ Datchet 152 AV81
Datchet Cl, Hem.H. HP2 41 BP15
Datchet Pl, Slou. (Datchet)
SL3 152 AV81
Datchet Rd, SE6 183 DZ90
Slough SL3 152 AT77
Slough (Horton) SL3 153 AZ83
Windsor SL4 151 AR80
Windsor (Old Wind.) SL4 152 AU84
Sch Datchet St. Mary's C of E Comb Sch, Slou. SL3
off The Green 152 AV81
Datchworth Ct, N4
off Queens Dr 122 DQ62
Datchworth Turn, Hem.H.
HP2 41 BQ20
Date St, SE17 21 J10
Daubeney Gdns, N17 100 DQ52
Sch Daubeney JMI Sch, E5
off Daubeney Rd 123 DY63
Daubeney Rd, E5 123 DY63
N17 100 DQ52
Daubeney Twr, SE8 23 L8
Dault Rd, SW18 180 DC86
Davall Ho, Grays RM17
off Argent St 170 GB79
Davema Cl, Chis. BR7
off Brenchley Cl 205 EN95
Sch Davenant Foundation Sch, Loug. IG10
off Chester Rd 85 EQ39
Davenant Rd, N19 121 DK61
Croydon CR0
off Duppas Hill Rd 219 DP105
Davenant St, E1 12 B6
Davenham Av, Nthwd. HA6 93 BT49
Sch Davenies Sch, Beac. HP9 *off Station Rd* 89 AL53
Davenport, Harl. (Ch.Lang.)
CM17 52 EY16
Davenport Cl, Tedd. TW11 177 CG93
Davenport Rd, SE6 183 EB86
Sidcup DA14 186 EX89
Daventer Dr, Stan. HA7 95 CF52
Daventry Av, E17 123 EA57
Daventry Cl, Slou. (Colnbr.)
SL3 153 BF81
Daventry Gdns, Rom. RM3 106 FJ50
Daventry Grn, Rom. RM3
off Hailsham Rd 106 FJ50
Daventry Rd, Rom. RM3 106 FJ50
Daventry St, NW1 8 A5

★ Place of interest   H Hospital   Sch School   Coll College   Uni University   ≠ Railway station

Davern Cl, SE10 . . . 25 J8
Davey Cl, N7 . . . 4 B4
Davey Rd, E9 . . . 143 EA66
Davey St, SE15 . . . 162 DT79
David Av, Grnf. UB6 . . . 137 CE69
David Cl, Hayes UB3 . . . 155 BR80
David Dr, Rom. RM3 . . . 106 FN51
Coll David Game Coll, W5 off New Bdy . . . 137 CJ73
Davidge St, SE1 . . . 20 E4
David Lee Pt, E15 . . . 144 EE67
Sch David Livingstone Prim Sch, Th.Hth. CR7 off Northwood Rd . . . 202 DQ95
David Ms, W1 . . . 8 D5
David Rd, Dag. RM8 . . . 126 EY61
Slough (Colnbr.) SL3 . . . 153 BF82
Coll Davidson Cen (Schs Advisory Cen), Croy. CR0 off Brampton Rd . . . 202 DT100
Davidson Gdns, SW8 . . . 161 DL80
Sch Davidson Jun & Inf Sch, Croy. CR0 off Dartnell Rd . . . 202 DT101
Davidson La, Har. HA1 off Grove Hill . . . 117 CF59
Davidson Rd, Croy. CR0 . . . 202 DT100
Davidson Way, Rom. RM7 . . . 127 FE58
Davids Rd, SE23 . . . 182 DW88
David St, E15 . . . 143 ED65
David's Way, Ilf. IG6 . . . 103 ES52
David Twigg Cl, Kings.T. KT2 . . . 198 CL95
Davies Cl, Croy. CR0 . . . 202 DU100
Rainham RM13 . . . 148 FJ69
Sch Davies Jun & Inf Sch, E11 off Davies La . . . 124 EF61
Coll Davies Laing & Dick Indep Coll, W1 . . . 8 F7
Davies La, E11 . . . 124 EE61
Davies Ms, W1 . . . 8 G9
Davies St, W1 . . . 8 G9
Hertford SG13 . . . 32 DS09
Davies Way, H.Wyc. (Loud.) HP10 . . . 88 AC54
Davington Gdns, Dag. RM8 . . . 126 EV64
Davington Rd, Dag. RM8 . . . 146 EV65
Davinia Cl, Wdf.Grn. IG8 off Deacon Way . . . 103 EM51
Davis Av, Grav. (Nthflt) DA11 . . . 190 GE88
Davis Cl, Sev. TN13 . . . 257 FJ122
Davison Cl, Wal.Cr. EN8 . . . 67 DX28
Davison Dr, Wal.Cr. (Chsht) EN8 . . . 67 DX28
Davison Rd, Slou. SL3 off Ditton Rd . . . 153 AZ78
Davis Rd, W3 . . . 139 CT74
Chessington KT9 . . . 216 CN105
Grays (Chaff.Hun.) RM16 . . . 170 FZ76
South Ockendon (Aveley) RM15 . . . 149 FR74
Weybridge KT13 . . . 212 BM110
Davis St, E13 . . . 144 EH68
Davisville Rd, W12 . . . 159 CU75
Davos Cl, Wok. GU22 . . . 226 AY119
Davys Cl, St.Alb. (Wheat.) AL4 . . . 28 CL08
Davys Pl, Grav. DA12 . . . 191 GL93
Dawell Dr, West. (Bigg.H.) TN16 . . . 238 EJ117
Dawes Av, Horn. RM12 . . . 128 FK62
Isleworth TW7 . . . 177 CG85
Dawes Cl, Chesh. HP5 . . . 54 AP32
Greenhithe DA9 . . . 189 FT85
Dawes Ct, Esher KT10 . . . 214 CB105
Dawes E Rd, Slou. (Burn.) SL1 . . . 130 AJ70
DAWESGREEN, Reig. RH2 . . . 265 CT140
Dawes Ho, SE17 . . . 21 K8
Dawes La, Rick. (Sarratt) WD3 . . . 73 BE37
Dawes Moor Cl, Slou. SL2 . . . 132 AW72
Dawes Rd, SW6 . . . 159 CY80
Uxbridge UB10 . . . 134 BL68
Dawes St, SE17 . . . 21 K9
Dawley, Welw.G.C. AL7 . . . 29 CZ06
Dawley Av, Uxb. UB8 . . . 135 BQ71
Dawley Ct, Hem.H. HP2 . . . 40 BM16
Dawley Grn, S.Ock. RM15 . . . 149 FU72
Dawley Par, Hayes UB3 off Dawley Rd . . . 135 BQ73
Dawley Ride, Slou. (Colnbr.) SL3 . . . 153 BE81
Dawley Rd, Hayes UB3 . . . 135 BR73
Uxbridge UB8 . . . 135 BQ73
Dawlish Av, N13 . . . 99 DL49
SW18 . . . 180 DB89
Greenford UB6 . . . 137 CG68
Dawlish Dr, Ilf. IG3 . . . 125 ES63
Pinner HA5 . . . 116 BY57
Ruislip HA4 . . . 115 BU61
Sch Dawlish Prim Sch, E10 off Jesse Rd . . . 123 EC60
Dawlish Rd, E10 . . . 123 EC61
N17 . . . 122 DU55
NW2 . . . 139 CX65
Dawlish Wk, Rom. RM3 . . . 106 FJ53
Dawnay Gdns, SW18 . . . 180 DD89
Dawnay Rd, SW18 . . . 180 DC89
Leatherhead (Bkhm) KT23 . . . 246 CB126
Sch Dawnay Sch, The, Lthd. KT23 off Griffin Way . . . 246 CA126
Dawn Cl, Houns. TW4 . . . 156 BY83
Dawn Cres, E15 off Bridge Rd . . . 143 ED67
Dawn Redwood Cl, Slou. (Horton) SL3 . . . 153 BA83
Dawpool Rd, NW2 . . . 119 CT61
Daws Hill, E4 . . . 83 EC41
Daws La, NW7 . . . 97 CT50
Dawson Av, Bark. IG11 . . . 145 ES66
Orpington BR5 . . . 206 EV96
Dawson Cl, SE18 . . . 165 EQ77
Hayes UB3 . . . 135 BR71
Windsor SL4 . . . 151 AN82
Dawson Dr, Rain. RM13 . . . 147 FH66
Swanley BR8 . . . 187 FE94
Dawson Gdns, Bark. IG11 off Dawson Av . . . 145 ET66
Dawson Hts Est, SE22 . . . 182 DU87
Dawson Pl, W2 . . . 6 G9
Dawson Rd, NW2 . . . 119 CW64
Kingston upon Thames KT1 . . . 198 CM97
West Byfleet (Byfleet) KT14 . . . 212 BK111
Dawson St, E2 . . . 5 P10
Dax Ct, Sun. TW16 off Thames St . . . 196 BW97
Daybrook Rd, SW19 . . . 200 DB96
Daye Mead, Welw.G.C. AL7 . . . 30 DB12
Daylesford Av, SW15 . . . 159 CU84
Daylop Dr, Chig. IG7 . . . 104 EV48
Daymer Gdns, Pnr. HA5 . . . 115 BV56
Daymerslea Ridge, Lthd. KT22 . . . 231 CJ121
Days Acre, S.Croy. CR2 . . . 220 DT110
Daysbrook Rd, SW2 . . . 181 DM89
Days Cl, Hat. AL10 . . . 45 CT18
Dayseys Hill, Red. (Outwood) RH1 . . . 267 DN143
Days La, Brwd. (Pilg.Hat.) CM15 . . . 108 FU42
Sidcup DA15 . . . 185 ES87
Sch Days La Prim Sch, Sid. DA15 off Days La . . . 185 ET86
Days Mead, Hat. AL10 . . . 45 CT18
Dayspring, Guil. GU2 . . . 242 AV130
Dayton Dr, Erith DA8 . . . 168 FK78
Dayton Gro, SE15 . . . 162 DW81
Deacon Cl, Cob. (Down.) KT11 . . . 229 BV119
Purley CR8 . . . 219 DL109
St. Albans AL1 off Creighton Av . . . 43 CD24
Deacon Fld, Guil. GU2 off Midleton Rd . . . 242 AV133
Deacon Ms, N1 . . . 5 K6
Deacon Pl, Cat. CR3 . . . 236 DQ123
Deacon Rd, NW2 . . . 119 CU64
Kingston upon Thames KT2 . . . 198 CM95
Deacons Cl, Borwd. (Elstree) WD6 . . . 78 CN42
Pinner HA5 . . . 93 BV54
Deaconsfield Rd, Hem.H. HP3 . . . 40 BK23
Deacons Hill, Wat. WD19 . . . 76 BW44
Deacon's Hill Rd, Borwd. (Elstree) WD6 . . . 78 CM42
Deacons Leas, Orp. BR6 . . . 223 ER105
Deacons Ri, N2 . . . 120 DD57
Deacons Wk, Hmptn. TW12 off Bishops Gro . . . 176 BZ91
Deacon Way, SE17 . . . 20 G7
Woodford Green IG8 . . . 103 EM52
Deadfield La, Hert. SG14 . . . 30 DF13
Deadhearn La, Ch.St.G. HP8 . . . 90 AY46
Deadman's Ash La, Rick. (Sarratt) WD3 . . . 74 BH36
Deakin Cl, Wat. WD18 off Chenies Way . . . 93 BS45
Deal Av, Slou. SL1 . . . 131 AM72
Deal Ms, W5 off Darwin Rd . . . 157 CK77
Deal Porters Way, SE16 . . . 22 F5
Deal Rd, SW17 . . . 180 DG93
Deal's Gateway, SE10 off Blackheath Rd . . . 163 EB81
Deal St, E1 . . . 12 A5
Dealtry Rd, SW15 . . . 159 CW84
Deal Wk, SW9 off Mandela St . . . 161 DN80
Deanacre Cl, Ger.Cr. (Chal.St.P.) SL9 . . . 90 AY51
Dean Av, Hodd. EN11 . . . 49 DX17
DEAN BOTTOM, Dart. DA4 . . . 209 FV97
Dean Bradley St, SW1 . . . 19 N6
Dean Cl, E9 off Churchill Wk . . . 122 DW64
SE16 . . . 23 H2
Uxbridge UB10 . . . 134 BM66
Windsor SL4 . . . 151 AK83
Woking GU22 . . . 227 BE115
Dean Ct, Wem. HA0 . . . 117 CH62
Deancroft Rd, Ger.Cr. (Chal.St.P.) SL9 . . . 90 AY51
Deancross St, E1 . . . 12 E8
Dean Dr, Stan. HA7 . . . 96 CL54
Deane Av, Ruis. HA4 . . . 116 BW64
Deane Cft Rd, Pnr. HA5 . . . 115 BV58
Deanery Cl, N2 . . . 120 DE56
Deanery Ms, W1 . . . 18 F1
Deanery Rd, E15 . . . 144 EE65
Edenbridge (Crock.H.) TN8 . . . 255 EQ134
Deanery St, W1 . . . 18 F1
Sch Deanesfield Prim Sch, Ruis. HA4 off Queens Wk . . . 116 BX63
Deane Way, Ruis. HA4 . . . 115 BV58
Dean Farrar St, SW1 . . . 19 L5
Dean Fld, Hem.H. (Bov.) HP3 . . . 57 BA27
Dean Gdns, E17 . . . 123 ED56
W13 off Northfield Av . . . 137 CH74
Deanhill Rd, SW14 . . . 158 CP84
Dean La, Red. RH1 . . . 235 DH123
Dean Moore Cl, St.Alb. AL1 . . . 43 CD21
Dean Oak La, Reig. (Leigh) RH2 . . . 265 CW144
Dean Rd, NW2 . . . 139 CW65
SE28 . . . 146 EU73
Croydon CR0 . . . 220 DR105
Hampton TW12 . . . 176 CA92
Hounslow TW3 . . . 176 CB85
Dean Ryle St, SW1 . . . 19 N7
Deansbrook Cl, Edg. HA8 . . . 96 CQ52
Sch Deansbrook Inf Sch, NW7 off Hale Dr . . . 96 CQ51
Sch Deansbrook Jun Sch, NW7 off Hale Dr . . . 96 CQ51
Deansbrook Rd, Edg. HA8 . . . 96 CQ51
Deans Bldgs, SE17 . . . 21 J8
Sch Dean Sch, The, N7 . . . 4 B2
Deans Cl, W4 . . . 158 CP79
Abbots Langley WD5 . . . 59 BR32
Amersham HP6 . . . 72 AT37
Dean's Cl, Croy. CR0 . . . 202 DT104
Deans Cl, Edg. HA8 . . . 96 CQ51
Slough (Stoke P.) SL2 . . . 132 AV67
Tadworth KT20 off Deans La . . . 233 CV124
Deans Ct, EC4 . . . 10 F8
Deanscroft Av, NW9 . . . 118 CQ61
Deans Dr, N13 . . . 99 DP51
Edgware HA8 . . . 96 CR50
Deansfield, Cat. CR3 . . . 252 DT125
Sch Deansfield Jun & Inf Sch, SE9 off Dairsie Rd . . . 165 EN83
Deans Gdns, St.Alb. AL4 . . . 43 CG16
Dean's Gate Cl, SE23 . . . 183 DX90
Deans La, W4 . . . 158 CP79
Edgware HA8 . . . 96 CQ51
Redhill (Nutfld) RH1 . . . 251 DN133
Tadworth KT20 . . . 233 CV124
Deans Ms, W1 . . . 9 H7
Deans Rd, W7 . . . 137 CF74
Brentwood CM14 . . . 108 FV49
Redhill RH1 . . . 251 DJ130
Sutton SM1 . . . 200 DB104
Dean Stanley St, SW1 . . . 19 N6
Dean St, E7 . . . 124 EG64
W1 . . . 9 L7
Deans Wk, Couls. CR5 . . . 235 DN118
Deansway, N2 . . . 120 DD56
N9 . . . 100 DS48
Chesham HP5 . . . 54 AP29
Deans Way, Edg. HA8 . . . 96 CQ50
Deansway, Hem.H. HP3 . . . 40 BM23
Dean's Yd, SW1 . . . 19 M5
Dean Trench St, SW1 . . . 19 N6
Dean Wk, Edg. HA8 off Deansbrook Rd . . . 96 CQ51
Leatherhead (Bkhm) KT23 . . . 246 CB126
Deanway, Ch.St.G. HP8 . . . 90 AU48
Dean Way, Sthl. UB2 . . . 156 CB75
Dean Wd Rd, Beac. (Jordans) HP9 . . . 89 AR52
Dearne Cl, Stan. HA7 . . . 95 CG50
De'Arn Gdns, Mitch. CR4 . . . 200 DE97
Dearsley Ho, Rain. RM13 . . . 147 FD68
Dearsley Rd, Enf. EN1 . . . 82 DU41
Deason St, E15 off High St . . . 143 EC67
De Barowe Ms, N5 off Leigh Rd . . . 121 DP63
DEBDEN, Loug. IG10 . . . 85 ER41
⊖ Debden . . . 85 EQ42
Debden Cl, Kings.T. KT2 . . . 177 CK92
Woodford Green IG8 . . . 102 EJ52
DEBDEN GREEN, Loug. IG10 . . . 85 EQ38
Debden Grn, Loug. IG10 . . . 85 EP38
Coll Debden Ho Cen, Loug. IG10 off Debden Rd . . . 85 EP38
Debden La, Loug. IG10 . . . 85 EP38
Sch Debden Pk High Sch, Loug. IG10 off Willingale Rd . . . 85 ER40
Debden Rd, Loug. IG10 . . . 85 EP38
Debden Wk, Horn. RM12 . . . 147 FH65
De Beauvoir Cres, N1 . . . 5 L7
De Beauvoir Est, N1 . . . 5 K7
Sch De Beauvoir JMI Sch, N1 . . . 5 M4
De Beauvoir Rd, N1 . . . 5 L5
De Beauvoir Sq, N1 . . . 5 M6
DE BEAUVOIR TOWN, N1 . . . 5 K7
Debenham Rd, Wal.Cr. (Chsht) EN7 . . . 66 DV27
Debnams Rd, SE16 . . . 22 E8
De Bohun Av, N14 . . . 81 DH44
Sch De Bohun Prim Sch, N14 off Green Rd . . . 81 DH43
Deborah Cl, Islw. TW7 . . . 157 CE81
Deborah Cres, Ruis. HA4 . . . 115 BR59
Debrabant Cl, Erith DA8 . . . 167 FD79
De Brome Rd, Felt. TW13 . . . 176 BW88
De Burgh Gdns, Tad. KT20 . . . 233 CX119
De Burgh Pk, Bans. SM7 . . . 234 DB115
Deburgh Rd, SW19 . . . 180 DC94
Decies Way, Slou. (Stoke P.) SL2 . . . 132 AU67
Decima St, SE1 . . . 21 L5
Deck Cl, SE16 . . . 23 H3
Decoy Av, NW11 . . . 119 CY57
De Crespigny Pk, SE5 . . . 162 DR82
Dedswell Dr, Guil. (W.Clan.) GU4 . . . 244 BG128
DEDWORTH, Wind. SL4 . . . 151 AL81
Dedworth Dr, Wind. SL4 . . . 151 AL81
Sch Dedworth Grn First Sch, Wind. SL4 off Smiths La . . . 151 AL82
Sch Dedworth Mid Sch, Wind. SL4 off Smiths La . . . 151 AL82
Dedworth Rd, Wind. SL4 . . . 151 AL82
Dee, The, Hem.H. HP2 . . . 40 BM15
Dee Cl, Upmin. RM14 . . . 129 FS58
Deeley Rd, SW8 . . . 161 DK81
Deena Cl, W3 . . . 138 CM72
Slough SL1 . . . 131 AL73
Deep Acres, Amer. HP6 . . . 55 AN36
Deepdale, SW19 . . . 179 CX91
Deepdale Av, Brom. BR2 . . . 204 EF98
Deepdale Cl, N11 off Ribblesdale Av . . . 98 DG51
Deepdene, W5 . . . 138 CM70
Potters Bar EN6 . . . 63 CX31
Deepdene Av, Croy. CR0 . . . 202 DT104
Dorking RH4, RH5 . . . 247 CJ134
Deepdene Av Rd, Dor. RH4 . . . 247 CJ134
Deepdene Cl, E11 . . . 124 EG56
Deepdene Ct, N21 . . . 81 DP44
Deepdene Dr, Dor. RH5 . . . 263 CJ135
Deepdene Gdns, SW2 . . . 181 DM87
Dorking RH4 . . . 263 CH135
Deepdene Pk Rd, Dor. RH5 . . . 263 CJ135
Deepdene Path, Loug. IG10 . . . 85 EN42
Deepdene Pt, SE23 off Dacres Rd . . . 183 DX90
Deepdene Rd, SE5 . . . 162 DR84
Loughton IG10 . . . 85 EN42
Welling DA16 . . . 166 EU83
Deepdene Vale, Dor. RH4 . . . 263 CJ135
Deepdene Wd, Dor. RH5 . . . 263 CJ136
Deep Fld, Slou. (Datchet) SL3 . . . 152 AV80
Deepfields, Horl. RH6 . . . 268 DF146
Deepfield Way, Couls. CR5 . . . 235 DL116
Deep Pool La, Wok. (Chobham) GU24 . . . 210 AV114
Deeprose Cl, Guil. GU2 . . . 242 AV130
Deepwell Cl, Islw. TW7 . . . 157 CG81
Deepwood La, Grnf. UB6 off Cowgate Rd . . . 137 CD69
Deerbarn Rd, Guil. GU2 . . . 242 AV133
Deerbrook Rd, SE24 . . . 181 DP88
Deer Cl, Hert. SG13 . . . 32 DT09
Deerdale Rd, SE24 . . . 162 DQ84
Deere Av, Rain. RM13 . . . 147 FG65
Deerfield Cl, NW9 off Rookery Cl . . . 119 CT57
Ware SG12 . . . 33 DX05
Deerhurst Cl, Felt. TW13 . . . 175 BU91
Deerhurst Cres, Hmptn. (Hmptn H.) TW12 . . . 176 CC92
Deerhurst Rd, NW2 . . . 139 CX65
SW16 . . . 181 DM92
Deerings Dr, Pnr. HA5 . . . 115 BU57
Deerings Rd, Reig. RH2 . . . 250 DB134
Deerleap Gro, E4 . . . 83 EB43
Deerleap La, Sev. TN14 . . . 224 EX113
Deerleap Rd, Dor. (Westc.) RH4 . . . 262 CB137
Dee Rd, Rich. TW9 . . . 158 CM84
Deer Pk, Harl. CM19 . . . 51 EN18
Deer Pk Cl, Kings.T. KT2 . . . 178 CP94
Deer Pk Gdns, Mitch. CR4 . . . 200 DD97
Deer Pk Rd, SW19 . . . 200 DB96
Deer Pk Wk, Chesh. HP5 . . . 54 AS28
Deer Pk Way, Wal.Abb. EN9 . . . 83 EC36
West Wickham BR4 . . . 204 EF103
Deers Fm Cl, Wok. (Wisley) GU23 . . . 228 BL116
Deerswood Av, Hat. AL10 . . . 45 CV20
Deerswood Cl, Cat. CR3 . . . 236 DU124
Deeside Rd, SW17 . . . 180 DD90
Dee St, E14 . . . 14 D7
Deeves Hall La, Pot.B. EN6 . . . 62 CS33
Dee Way, Epsom KT19 . . . 216 CS110
Romford RM1 . . . 105 FE53
Coll Defence Sch of Languages, Beac. HP9 off Maude Rd . . . 89 AN54
Beaconsfield HP9 off Wilton Pk . . . 89 AP54
Defiance Wk, SE18 . . . 165 EM76
Defiant Way, Wall. SM6 . . . 219 DL108
Defoe Av, Rich. TW9 . . . 158 CN80
Defoe Cl, SE16 . . . 23 L4
SW17 . . . 180 DE93
Erith DA8 off Selkirk Dr . . . 167 FE81
Defoe Ho, EC2 . . . 11 H5
Defoe Par, Grays RM16 . . . 171 GH76
Defoe Pl, EC2 off Beech St . . . 142 DQ71
SW17 off Lessingham Av . . . 180 DF91
Defoe Rd, N16 . . . 122 DS61
Defoe Way, Rom. RM5 . . . 105 FB51
De Frene Rd, SE26 . . . 183 DX91
De Gama Pl, E14 off Maritime Quay . . . 163 EA78
Degema Rd, Chis. BR7 . . . 185 EP92
Dehar Cres, NW9 . . . 119 CT59
De Havilland Cl, Hat. AL10 . . . 45 CT17
Dehavilland Cl, Nthlt. UB5 . . . 136 BX69
De Havilland Ct, Rad. (Shenley) WD7 off Armstrong Gdns . . . 62 CL32
De Havilland Dr, Wey. KT13 . . . 212 BL111
★ De Havilland Mosquito Aircraft Mus, St.Alb. AL2 . . . 62 CP29
De Havilland Rd, Edg. HA8 . . . 96 CP54
Hounslow TW5 . . . 156 BW80
De Havilland Way, Abb.L. WD5 . . . 59 BT32
Staines (Stanw.) TW19 . . . 174 BK86
Deimos Dr, Hem.H. HP2 . . . 40 BN17
Dekker Rd, SE21 . . . 182 DS86
Delabole Rd, Red. RH1 . . . 251 DL129
Delacourt Rd, SE3 off Old Dover Rd . . . 164 EH80
Delafield Rd, SE7 . . . 25 P9
Grays RM17 . . . 170 GD78
Delaford Cl, Iver SL0 . . . 133 BF72
Delaford Rd, SE16 . . . 22 D9
Delaford St, SW6 . . . 159 CY80
Delagarde Rd, West. TN16 . . . 255 EQ126
Delahay Ri, Berk. HP4 . . . 38 AV17
Delamare Cres, Croy. CR0 . . . 202 DW100
Delamare Rd, Wal.Cr. (Chsht) EN8 . . . 67 DZ30
Delamere Gdns, NW7 . . . 96 CR51
Delamere Rd, SW20 . . . 199 CX95
W5 . . . 138 CL74
Borehamwood WD6 . . . 78 CP39
Hayes UB4 . . . 136 BX73
Reigate RH2 . . . 266 DB138
Delamere Ter, W2 . . . 7 K5
Delancey Pas, NW1 off Delancey St . . . 141 DH67
Delancey St, NW1 . . . 141 DH67
Delaporte Cl, Epsom KT17 . . . 216 CS112
De Lapre Cl, Orp. BR5 . . . 206 EX101
De Lara Way, Wok. GU21 . . . 226 AX118
Delargy Cl, Grays RM16 . . . 171 GH76
De Laune St, SE17 . . . 20 E10
Delaware Rd, W9 . . . 7 J3
Delawyk Cres, SE24 . . . 182 DQ86
Delcombe Av, Wor.Pk. KT4 . . . 199 CW102
Delderfield, Lthd. KT22 . . . 231 CK120
Delft Way, SE22 off East Dulwich Gro . . . 182 DS85
Delhi Rd, Enf. EN1 . . . 100 DT45
Delhi St, N1 . . . 141 DL67
Delia St, SW18 . . . 180 DB87
Delisle Rd, SE28 . . . 145 ES74
Delius Cl, Borwd. (Elstree) WD6 . . . 77 CJ44
Delius Gro, E15 . . . 143 ED68
Dell, The, SE2 . . . 166 EU78
SE19 . . . 202 DT95
Bexley DA5 . . . 187 FE88
Brentford TW8 . . . 157 CJ79
Brentwood (Gt Warley) CM13 . . . 107 FV51
Feltham TW14 off Harlington Rd W . . . 175 BV87
Gerrards Cross (Chal.St.P.) SL9 . . . 90 AY51
Greenhithe DA9 . . . 189 FV85
Hertford SG13 . . . 32 DQ12
High Wycombe (Penn) HP10 . . . 88 AC46
Horley RH6 . . . 269 DH147
Northwood HA6 . . . 93 BS47
Pinner HA5 . . . 94 BX54
Radlett WD7 . . . 77 CG36
Reigate RH2 . . . 250 DA133
St. Albans AL1 . . . 43 CG18
Tadworth KT20 . . . 233 CW121
Waltham Abbey EN9 off Greenwich Way . . . 83 EC36
Wembley HA0 . . . 117 CH64
Woking GU21 . . . 226 AW118
Woodford Green IG8 . . . 102 EH48
Della Path, E5 off Napoleon Rd . . . 122 DV62
Dellbow Rd, Felt. TW14 off Central Way . . . 175 BV85
Dell Cl, E15 . . . 143 ED67
Dorking (Mick.) RH5 . . . 247 CJ127
Leatherhead (Fetch.) KT22 . . . 231 CE123
Slough (Farn.Com.) SL2 . . . 111 AQ64
Wallington SM6 . . . 219 DK105
Woodford Green IG8 . . . 102 EH48
Dellcott Cl, Welw.G.C. AL8 . . . 29 CV08
Dellcut Rd, Hem.H. HP2 . . . 40 BN18
Dell Fm Rd, Ruis. HA4 . . . 115 BR57
Dellfield, Chesh. HP5 . . . 54 AN29
St. Albans AL1 . . . 43 CF21
Dellfield Av, Berk. HP4 . . . 38 AV17
Dellfield Cl, Beck. BR3 off Foxgrove Rd . . . 183 EC94
Berkhamsted HP4 . . . 38 AU17
Radlett WD7 . . . 77 CE35
Watford WD17 . . . 75 BU40
Dellfield Cres, Uxb. UB8 . . . 134 BJ70
Dellfield Par, Uxb. (Cowley) UB8 off High St . . . 134 BJ70
Dellfield Rd, Hat. AL10 . . . 45 CU18
Dell La, Epsom KT17 . . . 217 CU106
Dell Lees, Beac. (Seer Grn) HP9 . . . 89 AQ51
Dellmeadow, Abb.L. WD5 . . . 59 BS30
Dell Meadow, Hem.H. HP3 . . . 40 BL24
Dellors Cl, Barn. EN5 . . . 79 CX43
Dellow Cl, Ilf. IG2 . . . 125 ER59
Dellow St, E1 . . . 12 D9
Dell Ri, St.Alb. (Park St) AL2 . . . 60 CB26
Dell Rd, Enf. EN3 . . . 82 DW38
Epsom KT17 . . . 217 CU107
Grays RM17 . . . 170 GB77
Watford WD24 . . . 75 BU37
West Drayton UB7 . . . 154 BM76
Dells, The, Hem.H. HP3 . . . 41 BP21
Dells Cl, E4 . . . 101 EB45
Teddington TW11 off Middle La . . . 177 CF93
Dellside, Uxb. (Hare.) UB9 . . . 114 BJ57
Dell Side, Wat. WD24 off The Harebreaks . . . 75 BU37
Dell's Ms, SW1 . . . 19 K8
Dellsome La, Hat. (N.Mymms) AL9 . . . 45 CV23
St. Albans (Coln.Hth) AL4 . . . 44 CS23
Dellswood Cl, Hert. SG13 off Hagsdell Rd . . . 32 DS10
Dells Wd Cl, Hodd. EN11 . . . 33 DZ14
Dell Wk, N.Mal. KT3 . . . 198 CS96
Dell Way, W13 . . . 137 CJ72
Dellwood, Rick. WD3 . . . 92 BH46
Dellwood Gdns, Ilf. IG5 . . . 125 EN55
Delmar Av, Hem.H. HP2 . . . 41 BR21
Delmare Cl, SW9 off Brighton Ter . . . 161 DM84
Delmeade Rd, Chesh. HP5 . . . 54 AN32
Delme Cres, SE3 . . . 164 EH82
Delmey Cl, Croy. CR0 off Radcliffe Rd . . . 202 DT104
Deloraine St, SE8 . . . 163 EA81
Delorme St, W6 . . . 159 CX79
Delta Bungalows, Horl. RH6 off Michael Cres . . . 268 DG150
Delta Cl, Wok. (Chobham) GU24 . . . 210 AT110
Worcester Park KT4 . . . 199 CT104
Delta Ct, NW2 . . . 119 CU61
Delta Dr, Horl. RH6 off Cheyne Wk . . . 268 DG150
Delta Gain, Wat. WD19 . . . 94 BX47
Delta Gro, Nthlt. UB5 . . . 136 BX69
Delta Rd, Brwd. (Hutt.) CM13 . . . 109 GD44
Woking GU21 . . . 227 BA116
Woking (Chobham) GU24 . . . 210 AT110
Worcester Park KT4 . . . 198 CS104
Delta St, E2 . . . 12 A1
Delta Way, Egh. TW20 . . . 193 BC95
De Luci Rd, Erith DA8 . . . 167 FC78
Sch De Lucy Prim Sch, SE2 off Cookhill Rd . . . 166 EV75
De Lucy St, SE2 . . . 166 EV77
Delvan Cl, SE18 off Ordnance Rd . . . 165 EN80
Delvers Mead, Dag. RM10 . . . 127 FC63
Delverton Rd, SE17 . . . 20 F10
Delves, Tad. KT20 off Heathcote . . . 233 CX121
Delvino Rd, SW6 . . . 160 DA81
De Mandeville Gate, Enf. EN1 off Southbury Rd . . . 82 DU42
De Mel Cl, Epsom KT19 . . . 216 CP112
Demesne Rd, Wall. SM6 . . . 219 DK106
Demeta Cl, Wem. HA9 . . . 118 CQ62
De Montfort Par, SW16 off Streatham High Rd . . . 181 DL90
De Montfort Rd, SW16 . . . 181 DL90
De Morgan Rd, SW6 . . . 160 DB83
Dempster Cl, Surb. KT6 . . . 197 CJ102
Dempster Rd, SW18 . . . 180 DC85
Denbar Par, Rom. RM7 off Mawney Rd . . . 127 FC56
Denberry Dr, Sid. DA14 . . . 186 EV90
Denbigh Cl, NW10 . . . 138 CS66
W11 . . . 6 F9
Chislehurst BR7 . . . 185 EM93
Hemel Hempstead HP2 . . . 40 BL21
Hornchurch RM11 . . . 128 FN56
Ruislip HA4 . . . 115 BT61
Southall UB1 . . . 136 BZ72
Sutton SM1 . . . 217 CZ106
Denbigh Dr, Hayes UB3 . . . 155 BQ75
Denbigh Gdns, Rich. TW10 . . . 178 CM85
Denbigh Ms, SW1 . . . 19 J8
Denbigh Pl, SW1 . . . 19 J9
Denbigh Rd, E6 . . . 144 EK69
W11 . . . 6 F9
W13 . . . 137 CH73
Hounslow TW3 . . . 156 CB82
Southall UB1 . . . 136 BZ72
Denbigh St, SW1 . . . 19 J8
Denbigh Ter, W11 . . . 6 F9
Denbridge Rd, Brom. BR1 . . . 205 EM96
Denby Gra, Harl. CM17 . . . 52 EY15
Denby Rd, Cob. KT11 . . . 214 BW113
Den Cl, Beck. BR3 . . . 203 ED97
Dendridge Cl, Enf. EN1 . . . 82 DV37
Dene, The, W13 . . . 137 CH71
Croydon CR0 . . . 221 DX105
Dorking (Abin.Ham.) RH5 . . . 261 BV141
Sevenoaks TN13 . . . 257 FH126
Sutton SM2 . . . 217 CZ111
Wembley HA9 . . . 118 CL63
West Molesey KT8 . . . 196 BZ99
Dene Av, Houns. TW3 . . . 156 BZ83
Sidcup DA15 . . . 186 EV87
Dene Cl, SE4 . . . 163 DY83
Bromley BR2 . . . 204 EF102
Coulsdon CR5 . . . 234 DE119
Dartford DA2 . . . 187 FE91
Guildford GU1 . . . 243 BB132
Horley RH6 . . . 268 DE146
Worcester Park KT4 . . . 199 CT103
Dene Ct, Stan. HA7 off Marsh La . . . 95 CJ50
Denecroft Cres, Uxb. UB10 . . . 135 BP67
Denecroft Gdns, Grays RM17 . . . 170 GD76
Dene Dr, Orp. BR6 . . . 206 EV104
Denefield Dr, Ken. CR8 . . . 236 DR115
Dene Gdns, Stan. HA7 . . . 95 CJ50
Thames Ditton KT7 . . . 197 CG103
Sch Deneholm Prim Sch, Grays RM16 off Culford Rd . . . 170 GC75
Dene Holm Rd, Grav. (Nthflt) DA11 . . . 190 GD90
Denehurst Gdns, NW4 . . . 119 CW58
W3 . . . 138 CP74
Richmond TW10 . . . 158 CN84
Twickenham TW2 . . . 177 CD87
Woodford Green IG8 . . . 102 EH49
Dene Path, S.Ock. RM15 . . . 149 FU72
Dene Pl, Wok. GU21 . . . 226 AV118
Dene Rd, N11 . . . 98 DF46
Ashtead KT21 . . . 232 CM119
Buckhurst Hill IG9 . . . 102 EK46
Dartford DA1 . . . 188 FM87
Guildford GU1 . . . 258 AY135
Northwood HA6 . . . 93 BS51
Denes, The, Hem.H. HP3 off Barnacres Rd . . . 40 BM24
Dene St, Dor. RH4 . . . 263 CH136
Dene St Gdns, Dor. RH4 . . . 263 CH136
Denewood, Barn. EN5 . . . 80 DC43
Denewood Cl, Wat. WD17 . . . 75 BT37
Denewood Rd, N6 . . . 120 DF58
Denfield, Dor. RH4 . . . 263 CH138
Denford St, SE10 . . . 25 J9
Dengie Wk, N1 . . . 4 G7
DENHAM, Uxb. UB9 . . . 114 BG62
⇌ Denham . . . 114 BG59

⊖ London Underground station DLR Docklands Light Railway station Tra Tramlink station Riv Pedestrian ferry landing stage

★ Denham Aerodrome, Uxb. UB9 .....113 BD57
Denham Av, Uxb. (Denh.) UB9 .....113 BF61
Denham Cl, Hem.H. HP2 ....40 BN15
Uxbridge (Denh.) UB9 ...114 BG62
Welling DA16
off Park Vw Rd 166 EW83
Denham Ct Dr, Uxb. (Denh.) UB9 .....114 BH63
Denham Cres, Mitch. CR4 ..200 DF98
Denham Dr, Ilf. IG2 .....125 EQ58
Denham Gdn Village, Uxb. UB9 off Denham Grn La .113 BF58
⇌ Denham Golf Club 113 BD59
DENHAM GREEN, Uxb. UB9 .113 BE58
Denham Grn Cl, Uxb. (Denh.) UB9 .....114 BG59
Denham Grn La, Uxb. (Denh.) UB9 .....113 BE57
Denham La, Ger.Cr. (Chal.St.P.) SL9 .....91 BA53
Denham Lo, Uxb. UB9 .....134 BJ65
Denham Rd, N20 .....98 DF48
Egham TW20 .....173 BA91
Epsom KT17 .....217 CT112
Feltham TW14 .....176 BW86
Iver SL0 .....133 BD67
Uxbridge (Denh.) UB9 ...133 BE65
Denham St, SE10 .....25 L9
Sch Denham Village Inf Sch, Uxb. UB9
off Cheapside La 113 BF61
Denham Wk, Ger.Cr. (Chal.St.P.) SL9 .....91 AZ51
Denham Way, Bark. IG11 ...145 ES67
Borehamwood WD6 .....78 CR39
Rickmansworth (Map.Cr.) WD3 .....91 BE50
Uxbridge (Denh.) UB9 ...114 BG62
Denholme Rd, W9 .....6 F1
Denholme Wk, Rain. RM13
off Ryder Gdns 147 FF65
Denholm Gdns, Guil. GU4 ..243 BA131
Denison Cl, N2 .....120 DC55
Denison Rd, SW19 .....180 DD93
W5 .....137 CJ70
Feltham TW13 .....175 BT91
Deniston Av, Bex. DA5 .....186 EY88
Denis Way, SW4
off Gauden Rd 161 DK83
Denleigh Gdns, N21 .....99 DN46
Thames Ditton KT7 .....197 CE100
Denman Dr, NW11 .....120 DA57
Ashford TW15 .....175 BP93
Esher (Clay.) KT10 .....215 CG106
Denman Dr N, NW11 .....120 DA57
Denman Dr S, NW11 .....120 DA57
Denman Pl, W1
off Great Windmill St ...141 DK73
Denman Rd, SE15 .....162 DT81
Denman St, W1 .....9 L10
Denmark Av, SW19 .....179 CY94
Denmark Ct, Mord. SM4 ...200 DA99
Denmark Gdns, Cars. SM5 .200 DF104
Denmark Gro, N1 .....4 C9
⇌ Denmark Hill 162 DR82
Denmark Hill, SE5 .....162 DR81
Denmark Hill Dr, NW9 .....119 CT56
Denmark Hill Est, SE5 .....162 DR84
Denmark Pl, WC2 .....9 M7
Denmark Rd, N8 .....121 DN56
NW6 .....139 CZ68
SE5 .....162 DQ81
SE25 .....202 DU99
SW19 .....179 CX93
W13 .....137 CH73
Bromley BR1 .....204 EH95
Carshalton SM5 .....200 DF104
Guildford GU1 .....258 AY135
Kingston upon Thames KT1 .....198 CL97
Twickenham TW2 .....177 CD90
Denmark St, E11
off High Rd Leytonstone .124 EE62
E13 .....15 N5
N17 .....100 DV53
WC2 .....9 M8
Watford WD17 .....75 BV40
Denmark Wk, SE27 .....182 DQ91
Denmead Cl, Ger.Cr. SL9 ..112 AY59
Denmead Ho, SW15
off Highcliffe Dr 179 CT86
Denmead Rd, Croy. CR0 ...201 DP102
Sch Denmead Sch, Hmptn. TW12
off Wensleydale Rd 176 CB94
Denmead Way, SE15
off Pentridge St 162 DT80
Dennan Rd, Surb. KT6 .....198 CM102
Dennard Way, Orp. BR6 ....223 EP105
Denner Rd, E4 .....101 EA47
Denne Ter, E8 .....5 P8
Dennett Rd, Croy. CR0 ....201 DN102
Dennetts Gro, SE14
off Dennetts Rd 163 DX82
Dennettsland Rd, Eden. (Crock.H.) TN8 .....255 EQ134
Dennetts Rd, SE14 .....162 DW81
Denning Av, Croy. CR0 .....219 DN105
Denning Cl, NW8 .....7 M1
Hampton TW12 .....176 BZ93
Denning Rd, NW3 .....120 DD63
Dennington Cl, E5
off Detmold Rd 122 DV61
Dennington Pk Rd, NW6 ...140 DA65
Denningtons, The, Wor.Pk. KT4 .....198 CS103
Dennis Av, Wem. HA9 .....118 CM64
Dennis Cl, Ashf. TW15 .....175 BR93
Redhill RH1 .....250 DE132
Dennises La, Upmin. RM14 .149 FS67
Dennis Gdns, Stan. HA7 ....95 CJ50
Dennis La, Stan. HA7 .....95 CH48
Dennison Pt, E15 .....143 EC66
Dennis Pk Cres, SW20 .....199 CY95
Dennis Reeve Cl, Mitch. CR4 .....200 DF95
Dennis Rd, E.Mol. KT8 .....196 CC98
Gravesend DA11 .....191 GG90
South Ockendon RM15 ..149 FU66
Dennis Way, Guil. GU1 .....242 AY129
Slough SL1 .....131 AK73
Denny Av, Wal.Abb. EN9 ....67 ED34
Denny Cl, E6
off Linton Gdns 144 EL71
Denny Cres, SE11 .....20 D8
Denny Gdns, Dag. RM9
off Canonsleigh Rd 146 EV66
Denny Gate, Wal.Cr. EN8 ....67 DZ27
Denny Rd, N9 .....100 DV46
Slough SL3 .....153 AZ77
Dennys La, Berk. HP4 .....38 AT21
Denny St, SE11 .....20 D9
Den Rd, Brom. BR2 .....203 ED97
Densham Dr, Pur. CR8 .....219 DN114
Densham Rd, E15 .....144 EE67
Densley Cl, Welw.G.C. AL8 ..29 CX07
Densole Cl, Beck. BR3
off Kings Hall Rd 203 DY95
Densworth Gro, N9 .....100 DW47
Dent Cl, S.Ock. RM15 .....149 FU72
DENTON, Grav. DA12 .....191 GL87
Denton Cl, Barn. EN5 .....79 CW43
Redhill RH1 .....266 DG139
Denton Ct Rd, Grav. DA12 ..191 GL87
Denton Gro, Walt. KT12 ...196 BX103
Denton Rd, N8 .....121 DM57
N18 .....100 DS49
Bexley DA5 .....187 FE89
Dartford DA1 .....187 FE88
Twickenham TW1 .....177 CK86
Welling DA16 .....166 EW80
Denton St, SW18 .....180 DB86
Gravesend DA12 .....191 GL87
Denton Ter, Bex. DA5
off Denton Rd 187 FE89
Denton Way, E5 .....123 DX62
Woking GU21 .....226 AT118
Dents Gro, Tad. KT20 .....249 CZ128
Dents Rd, SW11 .....180 DF86
Denvale Wk, Wok. GU21 ...226 AU118
Denver Cl, Orp. BR6 .....205 ES100
Denver Ind Est, Rain. RM13 .147 FF71
Denver Rd, N16 .....122 DS59
Dartford DA1 .....187 FG87
Denyer St, SW3 .....18 B8
Denziloe Av, Uxb. UB10 ....135 BP69
Denzil Rd, NW10 .....119 CT64
Guildford GU2 .....258 AV135
Deodara Cl, N20 .....98 DE48
Deodar Rd, SW15 .....159 CY84
★ Department for Environment, Food & Rural Affairs (D.E.F.R.A.), SW1 .....19 N1
★ Department for Transport (D.f.T.), SW1 .....19 M7
★ Department of Health & Dept for Work & Pensions (D.W.P.), SW1 .....19 N3
Depot App, NW2 .....119 CX63
Depot Rd, Epsom KT17 ....216 CS113
Hounslow TW3 .....157 CD83
DEPTFORD, SE8 .....23 M10
⇌ Deptford 163 DZ80
DLR Deptford Bridge 163 EA81
Deptford Br, SE8 .....163 EA81
Deptford Bdy, SE8 .....163 EA81
Deptford Ch St, SE8 .....163 EA79
Deptford Ferry Rd, E14 .....23 P8
Deptford Grn, SE8 .....163 EA79
Sch Deptford Grn Sch, SE14
off Amersham Vale 163 DZ80
Annexe, SE14
off Angus St 163 DY80
Deptford High St, SE8 .....163 EA79
Sch Deptford Pk Prim Sch, SE8 .....23 K9
Deptford Strand, SE8 .....23 M8
Deptford Wf, SE8 .....23 L7
De Quincey Ms, E16 .....25 M1
De Quincey Rd, N17 .....100 DR53
Derby Arms Rd, Epsom KT18 .....233 CT117
Derby Av, N12 .....98 DC50
Harrow HA3 .....95 CD53
Romford RM7 .....127 FC58
Upminster RM14 .....128 FM62
Derby Cl, Epsom KT18 .....233 CV119
Derby Ct, E5 off Overbury St .123 DX63
Derby Gate, SW1 .....19 N3
Derby Hill, SE23 .....182 DW89
Derby Hill Cres, SE23 .....182 DW89
Derby Rd, E7 .....144 EJ66
E9 .....143 DX67
E18 .....102 EF53
N18 .....100 DW50
SW14 .....158 CP84
SW19 off Russell Rd 180 DA94
Croydon CR0 .....201 DP103
Enfield EN3 .....82 DV43
Grays RM17 .....170 GB78
Greenford UB6 .....136 CB67
Guildford GU2 .....242 AS134
Hoddesdon EN11 .....49 ED19
Hounslow TW3 .....156 CB84
Surbiton KT5 .....198 CN102
Sutton SM1 .....217 CZ107
Uxbridge UB8 .....134 BJ68
Watford WD17 .....76 BW41
Derby Rd Br, Grays RM17 ..170 GB79
Derby Rd Ind Est, Houns. TW3 off Derby Rd 156 CB84
Derbyshire St, E2 .....12 B2
Derby Sq, The, Epsom KT19
off High St 216 CR113
Derby Stables Rd, Epsom KT18 .....232 CS117
Derby St, W1 .....18 F2
Dereham Pl, EC2 .....11 M2
Romford RM5 .....105 FB51
Dereham Rd, Bark. IG11 ...145 ET65
Derehams Av, H.Wyc. (Loud.) HP10 .....88 AC52
Derehams La, H.Wyc. (Loud.) HP10 .....88 AC53
Derek Av, Epsom KT19 .....216 CN106
Wallington SM6 .....219 DH105
Wembley HA9 .....138 CP66
Derek Cl, Epsom (Ewell) KT19 .....216 CP106
Derek Walcott Cl, SE24
off Shakespeare Rd 181 DP85
Derham Gdns, Upmin. RM14 .....128 FQ62
Deri Av, Rain. RM13 .....147 FH70
Dericote St, E8 .....142 DU67
Deridene Cl, Stai. (Stanw.) TW19 off Bedfont Rd ...174 BL86
Derifall Cl, E6 .....145 EM71
Dering Pl, Croy. CR0 .....220 DQ105
Dering Rd, Croy. CR0 .....220 DQ105
Dering St, W1 .....8 G8
Dering Way, Grav. DA12 ...191 GM87
Derinton Rd, SW17 .....180 DF91
Derley Rd, Sthl. UB2 .....156 BW76
Dermody Gdns, SE13 .....183 ED85
Dermody Rd, SE13 .....183 ED85
Deronda Rd, SE24 .....181 DP88
De Ros Pl, Egh. TW20 .....173 BA93
Deroy Cl, Cars. SM5 .....218 DF107
Derrick Av, S.Croy. CR2 ...220 DQ110
Derrick Gdns, SE7
off Anchor & Hope La ..164 EJ77
Derrick Rd, Beck. BR3 .....203 DZ97
Derry Av, S.Ock. RM15 .....149 FU72
Derrydown, Wok. GU22 ....226 AW121
DERRY DOWNS, Orp. BR5 ..206 EX100
Derry Downs, Orp. BR5 ...206 EW100
Derry Leys, Hat. AL10
off Mosquito Way 44 CS16
Derry Rd, Croy. CR0 .....201 DL104
Derry St, W8 .....17 J4
Dersingham Av, E12 .....125 EN64
Sch Dersingham Inf Sch, E12
off Dersingham Av 125 EN64
Dersingham Rd, NW2 .....119 CY62
Derwent Av, N18 .....100 DR50
NW7 .....96 CR50
SW15 .....178 CS91
Barnet EN4 .....98 DF46
Pinner HA5 .....94 BY51
Uxbridge UB10 .....114 BN62
Derwent Cl, Add. KT15 .....212 BK106
Amersham HP7 .....72 AV39
Dartford DA1 .....187 FH88
Esher (Clay.) KT10 .....215 CE107
Feltham TW14 .....175 BT88
Watford WD25 .....60 BW34
Derwent Cres, N20 .....98 DC48
Bexleyheath DA7 .....166 FA82
Stanmore HA7 .....95 CJ54
Derwent Dr, NW9 .....118 CS57
Hayes UB4 .....135 BS71
Orpington BR5 .....205 ER101
Purley CR8 .....220 DR113
Slough SL1 .....130 AJ71
Derwent Gdns, Ilf. IG4 .....124 EL56
Wembley HA9 .....117 CJ59
Derwent Gro, SE22 .....162 DT84
Derwent Par, S.Ock. RM15 ..149 FV72
Derwent Ri, NW9 .....118 CS58
Derwent Rd, N13 .....99 DM49
SE20 .....202 DU96
SW20 .....199 CX100
W5 .....157 CJ76
Egham TW20 .....173 BB94
Hemel Hempstead HP3 ...41 BQ21
Southall UB1 .....136 CA72
Twickenham TW2 .....176 CB86
Derwent St, SE10 .....24 G9
Derwent Wk, Wall. SM6 ....219 DH108
Sch Derwentwater Prim Sch, W3 off Shakespeare Rd .138 CQ74
Derwentwater Rd, W3 .....138 CQ74
Derwent Way, Horn. RM12 .127 FH64
Derwent Yd, W5
off Northfield Av 157 CJ76
De Salis Rd, Uxb. UB10 ....135 BQ70
Desborough Cl, W2 .....7 K5
Hertford SG14 .....31 DP06
Shepperton TW17 .....194 BN101
Welwyn Garden City AL7
off Howlands 30 DB12
Desborough St, W2 .....7 J5
Desenfans Rd, SE21 .....182 DS86
Desford Ct, Ashf. TW15
off Desford Way 174 BM89
Desford Ms, E16 .....15 H4
Desford Rd, E16 .....15 H4
Desford Way, Ashf. TW15 ...174 BM89
★ Design Mus, SE1 .....21 P2
Desmond Rd, Wat. WD24 ....75 BT36
Desmond St, SE14 .....163 DY79
Despard Rd, N19 .....121 DJ60
Sch De Stafford Coll of Tech & The Arts, Cat. CR3
off Burntwood La 236 DT121
De Tany Ct, St.Alb. AL1 .....43 CD21
Detillens La, Oxt. RH8 .....254 EG129
Detling Cl, Horn. RM12 .....128 FJ64
Detling Rd, Brom. BR1 .....184 EG92
Erith DA8 .....167 FD80
Gravesend (Nthflt) DA11 .190 GD88
Detmold Rd, E5 .....122 DW61
Deva Cl, St.Alb. AL3 .....42 CA22
Devalls Cl, E6 .....145 EN73
Devana End, Cars. SM5 ....200 DF104
Devas Rd, SW20 .....199 CW95
Devas St, E3 .....14 B3
Devenay Rd, E15 .....144 EF66
Devenish Rd, SE2 .....166 EU75
Deventer Cres, SE22 .....182 DS85
Deveraux Cl, Beck. BR3
off Creswell Dr 203 EB99
De Vere Cotts, W8
off Canning Pl 160 DC76
De Vere Gdns, W8 .....17 L4
Ilford IG1 .....125 EM61
Deverell St, SE1 .....21 J6
De Vere Ms, W8 .....17 L5
Devereux Ct, WC2 .....10 C8
Devereux Dr, Wat. WD17 ....75 BS38
Devereux La, SW13 .....159 CV80
Devereux Rd, SW11 .....180 DF86
Grays RM16 .....170 FZ76
Windsor SL4 .....151 AR82
De Vere Wk, Wat. WD17 .....75 BS40
Deverill Ct, SE20 .....202 DW95
Deverills Way, Slou. SL3 ...153 BC77
Deveron Gdns, S.Ock. RM15 .149 FU71
Deveron Way, Rom. RM1 ...105 FE53
Devey Cl, Kings.T. KT2 .....178 CS94
Devils La, Egh. TW20 .....173 BD94
Devil's La, Hert. SG13 .....47 DP21
Devitt Cl, Ashtd. KT21 .....232 CN116
Devizes St, N1 .....5 K8
Devoil Cl, Guil. GU4 .....243 BB130
Devoke Way, Walt. KT12 ....196 BX103
Devon Av, Slou. SL1 .....131 AQ72
Twickenham TW2 .....176 CC88
Devon Bk, Guil. GU2
off Portsmouth Rd 258 AW137
Devon Cl, N17 .....122 DT55
Buckhurst Hill IG9 .....102 EH47
Greenford UB6 .....137 CJ67
Kenley CR8 .....236 DT116
Devon Ct, Buck.H. IG9 .....102 EH46
Dartford (Sutt.H.) DA4 ...208 FP95
St. Albans AL1 .....43 CE21
Devon Cres, Red. RH1 .....250 DD134
Devoncroft Gdns, Twick. TW1 .177 CG87
Devon Gdns, N4 .....121 DP58
Devonhurst Pl, W4
off Heathfield Ter 158 CR78
Devonia Gdns, N18 .....100 DQ51
Devonia Rd, N1 .....4 F9
Devon Mead, Hat. AL10
off Mosquito Way 44 CR16
Devonport Gdns, Ilf. IG1 ...125 EM58
Devonport Ms, W12
off Devonport Rd 139 CV74
Devonport Rd, W12 .....159 CV75
Devonport St, E1 .....12 G8
Devon Ri, N2 .....120 DD56
Devon Rd, Bark. IG11 .....145 ES67
Dartford (Sutt.H.) DA4 ...208 FP95
Redhill RH1 .....251 DJ130
Sutton SM2 .....217 CY109
Devon Rd, Walt. KT12 .....214 BW105
Watford WD24 .....76 BX39
Devons Est, E3 .....14 B2
Devonshire Av, Amer. HP6 ...55 AP37
Dartford DA1 .....187 FH86
Sutton SM2 .....218 DC108
Tadworth (Box H.) KT20 ..248 CQ131
Woking GU21 .....211 BC114
Devonshire Cl, E15 .....124 EE63
N13 .....99 DN49
W1 .....8 G5
Amersham HP6 .....55 AQ37
Slough (Farn.Royal) SL2 .131 AP68
Devonshire Cres, NW7 .....97 CX52
Devonshire Dr, SE10 .....163 EB80
Surbiton KT6 .....197 CK102
Devonshire Gdns, N17 .....100 DQ51
N21 .....100 DQ45
W4 .....158 CQ80
Devonshire Grn, Slou. (Farn.Royal) SL2 .....131 AP68
Devonshire Gro, SE15 .....162 DV79
Devonshire Hill La, N17 ....100 DQ51
Sch Devonshire Hill Prim Sch, N17 off Weir Hall Rd ...100 DR51
H Devonshire Hosp, W1 .....8 F5
Devonshire Ho, Sutt. SM2
off Devonshire Av 218 DC108
Devonshire Ms, SW10
off Park Wk 160 DD79
W4 off Glebe St 158 CS78
Devonshire Ms N, W1 .....8 G5
Devonshire Ms S, W1 .....8 G5
Devonshire Ms W, W1 .....8 G4
Devonshire Pas, W4 .....158 CS78
Devonshire Pl, NW2 .....120 DA62
W1 .....8 F4
W8 .....17 J6
Devonshire Pl Ms, W1 .....8 F4
Sch Devonshire Prim Sch, Sutt. SM2 off Devonshire Av .218 DC108
Devonshire Rd, E16 .....15 P7
E17 .....123 EA58
N9 .....100 DW46
N13 .....99 DM49
N17 .....100 DQ51
NW7 .....97 CX52
SE9 .....184 EL89
SE23 .....182 DW88
SW19 .....180 DE94
W4 .....158 CS78
W5 .....157 CJ76
Bexleyheath DA6 .....166 EY84
Carshalton SM5 .....218 DG105
Croydon CR0 .....202 DR101
Feltham TW13 .....176 BY90
Gravesend DA12 .....191 GH88
Grays RM16 .....170 FY77
Harrow HA1 .....117 CD58
Hornchurch RM12 .....128 FJ61
Ilford IG2 .....125 ER59
Orpington BR6 .....206 EU101
Pinner (Eastcote) HA5 ....116 BW58
Pinner (Hatch End) HA5 ...94 BZ53
Southall UB1 .....136 CA71
Sutton SM2 .....218 DC108
Weybridge KT13 .....212 BN105
Devonshire Row, EC2 .....11 M6
Devonshire Row Ms, W1 .....9 H4
Devonshire Sq, EC2 .....11 M7
Bromley BR2 .....204 EH98
Devonshire St, W1 .....8 F5
W4 .....158 CS78
Devonshire Ter, W2 .....7 M8
Devonshire Way, Croy. CR0 .203 DY103
Hayes UB4 .....135 BV72
DLR Devons Road 14 A3
Devons Rd, E3 .....13 P5
Devon St, SE15 .....162 DV79
Devon Way, Chess. KT9 .....215 CJ106
Epsom KT19 .....216 CP106
Uxbridge UB10 .....134 BM68
Devon Waye, Houns. TW5 ...156 BZ80
De Walden St, W1 .....8 F6
Dewar Spur, Slou. SL3
off Ditton Rd 153 AZ78
Dewar St, SE15 .....162 DU83
Dewberry Gdns, E6 .....144 EL71
Dewberry St, E14 .....14 C6
Dewey Path, Horn. RM12 ...148 FJ65
Dewey Rd, N1 .....4 C9
Dagenham RM10 .....147 FB65
Dewey St, SW17 .....180 DF92
Dewgrass Gro, Wal.Cr. EN8 ..83 DX35
Dewhurst Rd, W14 .....16 A5
Waltham Cross (Chsht) EN8 .....66 DW29
Sch Dewhurst St. Mary C of E Prim Sch, Wal.Cr. EN8
off Churchgate 66 DW28
Dewlands, Gdse. RH9 .....252 DW131
Dewlands Av, Dart. DA2 ....188 FP87
Dewlands Ct, NW4
off Holders Hill Rd 97 CX54
Dewsbury Cl, Pnr. HA5 .....116 BZ58
Romford RM3 .....106 FL51
Dewsbury Ct, W4
off Chiswick Rd 158 CQ77
Dewsbury Gdns, Rom. RM3 .....106 FK51
Worcester Park KT4 .....199 CU104
Dewsbury Rd, NW10 .....119 CU64
Romford RM3 .....106 FK51
Dewsbury Ter, NW1
off Camden High St 141 DH67
Dexter Cl, Grays RM17 .....170 GA76
St. Albans AL1
off Camp Rd 43 CG21
Dexter Ho, Erith DA18
off Kale Rd 166 EY76
Dexter Rd, Barn. EN5 .....79 CX44
Uxbridge (Hare.) UB9 .....92 BJ54
Deyncourt Gdns, Upmin. RM14 .....128 FQ61
Deyncourt Rd, N17 .....100 DQ53
Deynecourt Gdns, E11 .....124 EJ56
D'Eynsford Rd, SE5 .....162 DR81
Diadem Ct, W1 .....9 L8
Dial Cl, Green. DA9 .....189 FW85
Dialmead, Pot.B. EN6
off Crossoaks La 63 CT34
Dial Wk, The, W8 .....17 K3
Diamedes Av, Stai. (Stanw.) TW19 .....174 BK87
Diameter Rd, Orp. BR5 .....205 EP101
Diamond Cl, Dag. RM8 .....126 EW60
Grays RM16 .....170 FZ76
Diamond Rd, Ruis. HA4 .....116 BX63
Slough SL1 .....152 AU75
Watford WD24 .....75 BU38
Diamond St, NW10 .....138 CR66
SE15 .....162 DS80
Diamond Ter, SE10 .....163 EC81
Diamond Way, SE8
off Deptford High St 163 EA80
Diana Cl, E18 .....102 EH53
SE8 off Staunton St 163 DZ79
Grays (Chaff.Hun.) RM16 .170 FZ76
Slough (Geo.Grn) SL3 ....132 AY72
Diana Gdns, Surb. KT6 .....198 CM103
Diana Ho, SW13 .....159 CT81
Diana Rd, E17 .....123 DZ55
Diana Wk, Horl. RH6
off High St 269 DH148
Dianne Way, Barn. EN4 .....80 DE43
Dianthus Cl, SE2
off Carnation St 166 EV78
Chertsey KT16 .....193 BE101
Dianthus Ct, Wok. GU22 ...226 AX118
Diban Av, Horn. RM12 .....127 FH63
Dibden Hill, Ch.St.G. HP8 ...90 AW49
Dibden La, Sev. (Ide Hill) TN14 .....256 FE126
Dibden Row, SE1
off Gerridge St 161 DN76
Dibden St, N1 .....4 F7
Dibdin Cl, Sutt. SM1 .....200 DA104
Dibdin Rd, Sutt. SM1 .....200 DA104
Diceland Rd, Bans. SM7 ...233 CZ116
Dicey Av, NW2 .....119 CW64
Dickens Av, N3 .....98 DC53
Dartford DA1 .....168 FN84
Tilbury RM18 .....171 GH81
Uxbridge UB8 .....135 BP72
Dickens Cl, Erith DA8 .....167 FB80
Hayes UB3 off Croyde Av ..155 BS77
Richmond TW10 .....178 CL89
St. Albans AL3 .....43 CD19
Waltham Cross EN7 .....66 DU26
Dickens Ct, Hat. AL10 .....45 CV16
Dickens Dr, Add. KT15 .....211 BF107
Chislehurst BR7 .....185 EQ93
Dickens Est, SE1 .....22 A4
SE16 .....22 A4
★ Dickens Ho, WC1 .....10 B4
Dickens La, N18 .....100 DS50
Dickenson Cl, N9
off Croyland Rd 100 DU46
Dickenson Rd, N8 .....121 DL59
Feltham TW13 .....176 BW92
Dickensons La, SE25 .....202 DU99
Dickensons Pl, SE25 .....202 DU100
Dickenson St, NW5
off Dalby St 141 DH65
Dickens Pl, Slou. SL3
off Bath Rd 153 BE81
Dickens Ri, Chig. IG7 .....103 EN48
Dickens Rd, E6 .....144 EK68
Gravesend DA12 .....191 GL88
Dickens Sq, SE1 .....21 H5
Dickens St, SW8 .....161 DH82
Dickens Way, Rom. RM1 ...127 FE56
Dickenswood Cl, SE19 .....181 DP94
Dickerage La, N.Mal. KT3 ..198 CQ97
Dickerage Rd, Kings.T. KT1 .198 CQ95
New Malden KT3 .....198 CQ95
Dicker Mill Ind Pk, Hert. SG13 .....32 DS08
Dickinson Av, Rick. (Crox.Grn) WD3 .....74 BN44
Dickinson Ct, EC1
off St. John St 141 DP70
Dickinson Quay, Hem.H. HP3 .40 BM24
Dickinson Sq, Rick. (Crox.Grn) WD3 .....74 BN44
Dickson, Wal.Cr. (Chsht) EN7 ..66 DT27
Dickson Fold, Pnr. HA5 .....116 BX56
Dickson Rd, SE9 .....164 EL83
Dick Turpin Way, Felt. TW14 .155 BT84
Didsbury Cl, E6
off Barking Rd 145 EM67
Dieppe Cl, W14
off Gibbs Grn 159 CZ78
Digby Cres, N4 .....122 DQ61
Digby Gdns, Dag. RM10 .....146 FA67
Digby Pl, Croy. CR0 .....202 DT104
Digby Rd, E9 .....143 DX65
Barking IG11 .....145 ET66
Digby St, E2 .....12 F2
Digby Wk, Horn. RM12
off Pembrey Way 148 FJ65
Digby Way, W.Byf. (Byfleet) KT14 off High Rd 212 BM112
Dig Dag Hill, Wal.Cr. (Chsht) EN7 .....66 DT27
Digdens Ri, Epsom KT18 ...232 CQ115
Diggon St, E1 .....12 G6
Dighton Ct, SE5 .....162 DQ79
Dighton Rd, SW18 .....180 DC85
Dignum St, N1 .....4 C9
Digswell Cl, Borwd. WD6 ....78 CN38
Digswell Hill, Welw. AL6 ....29 CV05
Digswell Ho, Welw.G.C. AL8 ..29 CX05
Digswell Ho Ms, Welw.G.C. AL8 .....29 CX05
Digswell La, Welw.G.C. AL7 ..29 CZ05
Digswell Pl, Welw.G.C. AL8 ..29 CW06
Digswell Ri, Welw.G.C. AL8 ..29 CX07
Digswell Rd, Welw.G.C. AL8 ..29 CY06
Digswell St, N7 .....4 D3
Dilhorne Cl, SE12 .....184 EH90
Sch Dilkes Prim Sch, S.Ock. RM15 off Garron La 149 FT72
Dilke St, SW3 .....160 DF79
Dilloway Yd, Sthl. UB2
off The Green 156 BY75
Dillwyn Cl, SE26 .....183 DY91
Dilston Cl, Nthlt. UB5
off Yeading La 136 BW69
Dilston Gro, SE16 .....22 E7
Dilston Rd, Lthd. KT22 .....231 CG119
Dilton Gdns, SW15 .....179 CU88
Dilwyn Ct, E17
off Hillyfield 123 DY55
Dimes Pl, W6 off King St ...159 CV77
Dimmock Dr, Grnf. UB6 .....117 CD64
Dimmocks La, Rick. (Sarratt) WD3 .....74 BH36
Dimond Cl, E7 .....124 EG63
Dimsdale Dr, NW9 .....118 CQ60
Enfield EN1 .....82 DU44
Slough SL2 .....111 AM63
Dimsdale St, Hert. SG14 ....32 DQ09
Dimsdale Wk, E13
off Stratford Rd 144 EG67
Dimson Cres, E3 .....13 N3
Dinant Link Rd, Hodd. EN11 .49 DY16
Dingle, The, Uxb. UB10 .....135 BP68
Dingle Cl, Barn. EN5 .....79 CT44
Dingle Gdns, E14 .....13 P10
Dingle Rd, Ashf. TW15 .....175 BP92
Dingley La, SW16 .....181 DK89
Dingley Pl, EC1 .....11 H2
Dingley Rd, EC1 .....10 G2
Dingwall Av, Croy. CR0 .....202 DQ103
Dingwall Gdns, NW11 .....120 DA58
Dingwall Rd, SW18 .....180 DC87
Carshalton SM5 .....218 DF109
Croydon CR0 .....202 DR103
Dinmont St, E2 off Coate St .142 DV68

★ Place of interest | H Hospital | Sch School | Coll College | Uni University | ⇌ Railway station

Dinmore, Hem.H. (Bov.) HP3 .57 AZ28
Dinsdale Cl, Wok. GU22 . . . .227 BA118
Dinsdale Gdns, SE25 . . . . . .202 DS99
Barnet EN5 . . . . .80 DB43
Dinsdale Rd, SE3 . . . . .164 EF79
Dinsmore Rd, SW12 . . . . . . .181 DH87
Dinton Rd, SW19 . . . . .180 DD93
Kingston upon Thames
KT2 . . . . .178 CM94
Dione Rd, Hem.H. HP2
off Saturn Way 40 BM17
Diploma Av, N2 . . . . .120 DE56
Diploma Ct, N2
off Diploma Av 120 DE56
Dirdene Cl, Epsom KT17 . . .217 CT112
Dirdene Gdns, Epsom KT17 .217 CT112
Dirdene Gro, Epsom KT17 . .216 CS112
Dirleton Rd, E15 . . . . .144 EF67
Dirtham La, Lthd. (Eff.)
KT24 . . . . .245 BU127
Disbrowe Rd, W6 . . . . .159 CY79
Discovery Business Pk, SE16
off St. James's Rd 162 DU76
Discovery Wk, E1 . . . . .12 C10
Dishforth La, NW9 . . . . .96 CS53
Disney Ms, N4
off Chesterfield Gdns . . .121 DP57
Disney Pl, SE1 . . . . .21 H3
Disney St, SE1 . . . . .21 H3
Dison Cl, Enf. EN3 . . . . .83 DX39
Disraeli Cl, SE28 . . . . .146 EW74
W4 *off Acton La* 158 CR77
Disraeli Ct, Slou. SL3
off Sutton Pl 153 BB79
Disraeli Gdns, SW15
off Fawe Pk Rd 159 CZ84
Disraeli Pk, Beac. HP9 . . . . . .89 AK50
Disraeli Rd, E7 . . . . .144 EG65
NW10 . . . . .138 CQ68
SW15 . . . . .159 CY84
W5 . . . . .137 CK74
Diss St, E2 . . . . .11 N1
Distaff La, EC4 . . . . .10 G9
Distillery La, W6
off Fulham Palace Rd . . .159 CW78
Distillery Rd, W6 . . . . .159 CW78
Distillery Wk, Brent. TW8 . . .158 CL79
Distin St, SE11 . . . . .20 C8
District Rd, Wem. HA0 . . . . .117 CH64
Ditch All, SE10 . . . . .163 EB81
Ditchburn St, E14 . . . . .14 D10
Ditches La, Cat. CR3 . . . . . .235 DM122
Coulsdon CR5 . . . . .235 DL120
Ditches Ride, The, Loug.
IG10 . . . . .85 EN37
Ditchfield Rd, Hayes UB4 . . .136 BY70
Hoddesdon EN11 . . . . .33 EA14
Dittisham Rd, SE9 . . . . .184 EL91
Ditton Cl, T.Ditt. KT7 . . . . . .197 CG101
Dittoncroft Cl, Croy. CR0 . . .220 DS105
Ditton Gra Cl, Surb. KT6 . . .197 CK102
Ditton Gra Dr, Surb. KT6 . . .197 CK102
Ditton Hill, Surb. KT6 . . . . . .197 CJ102
Ditton Hill Rd, Surb. KT6 . . . .197 CJ102
Ditton Lawn, T.Ditt. KT7 . . . .197 CG102
Ditton Pk, Slou. SL3 . . . . . . .152 AX78
Ditton Pk Rd, Slou. SL3 . . . .152 AY79
Ditton Pl, SE20 . . . . .202 DV95
Ditton Reach, T.Ditt. KT7 . . . .197 CH100
Ditton Rd, Bexh. DA6 . . . . . .186 EX85
Slough SL3 . . . . .153 AZ79
Slough (Datchet) SL3 . . . .152 AX81
Southall UB2 . . . . .156 BZ77
Surbiton KT6 . . . . .198 CL102
Sch Divine Saviour RC Prim Sch, The, Abb.L. WD5
off Broomfield Ri 59 BR32
Divis Way, SW15 . . . . .179 CV86
Divot Pl, Hert. SG13 . . . . .32 DV08
Dixon Clark Ct, N1 . . . . .4 E4
Dixon Cl, E6
off Brandreth Rd 145 EM72
Dixon Dr, Wey. KT13 . . . . . .212 BM110
Dixon Ho, W10 . . . . .6 A8
Dixon Pl, W.Wick. BR4 . . . . .203 EB102
Dixon Rd, SE14 . . . . .163 DY81
SE25 . . . . .202 DS97
Dixon's All, SE16 . . . . .22 C4
Dixon's Ct, Ware SG12
off Crane Mead 33 DY06
Dixons Hill Cl, Hat.
(N.Mymms) AL9 . . . . .63 CV25
Dixons Hill Rd, Hat.
(N.Mymms) AL9 . . . . .63 CU25
Dobbin Cl, Har. HA3 . . . . .95 CG54
Dobb's Weir, Hodd. EN11 . . . .49 ED18
Dobb's Weir Caravan Pk,
Hodd. EN11 . . . . .49 EC19
Dobb's Weir Rd, Hodd. EN11 .49 ED18
Dobell Path, SE9
off Dobell Rd 185 EM85
Dobell Rd, SE9 . . . . .185 EM85
Dobree Av, NW10 . . . . .139 CV66
Dobson Cl, NW6 . . . . .140 DD66
Dobson Rd, Grav. DA12 . . . . .191 GL92
Doby Ct, EC4 . . . . .11 H9
Dockers Tanner Rd, E14 . . . . .23 N6
Dockett Eddy La, Shep.
TW17 . . . . .194 BM102
Dockhead, SE1 . . . . .21 P4
Dock Hill Av, SE16 . . . . .23 H3
Dockland St, E16 . . . . .145 EN74
Dockley Rd, SE16 . . . . .22 A6
Dock Rd, E16 . . . . .15 K10
Brentford TW8 . . . . .157 CK80
Grays RM17 . . . . .170 GD79
Tilbury RM18 . . . . .171 GF82
Dockside Rd, E16 . . . . .144 EK73
Dock St, E1 . . . . .12 A9
Dockwell Cl, Felt. TW14 . . . .155 BU84
Dockyard Ind Est, SE18
off Woolwich Ch St 164 EL76
Sch Doctor Challoner's Gram Sch, Amer. HP6
off Chesham Rd 55 AQ38
Sch Doctor Challoner's High Sch, Amer. HP7
off Coke's La 72 AV40
Doctor Johnson Av, SW17 . .181 DH90
★ **Doctor Johnson's Ho**,
EC4 . . . . .10 D8
Doctors Cl, SE26 . . . . .182 DW92
Doctors Commons Rd, Berk.
HP4 . . . . .38 AV20
Doctors La, Cat. CR3 . . . . . .235 DN123
Sch Doctor Triplett's C of E Prim Sch, Hayes UB3
off Hemmen La 135 BT72
Docwra's Bldgs, N1 . . . . .5 L3
Dodbrooke Rd, SE27 . . . . . . .181 DN90
Doddinghurst Rd, Brwd.
CM15 . . . . .108 FW44
Doddington Gro, SE17 . . . . . .161 DP79
Doddington Pl, SE17 . . . . . . .161 DP79
Dodd's Cres, W.Byfl. KT14 . . .212 BH114
Doddsfield Rd, Slou. SL2 . . .131 AN69
Dodds La, Ch.St.G. HP8 . . . . . .90 AU47
Hemel Hempstead
(Picc.End) HP2 . . . . .40 BJ16
Dodd's La, Wok. GU22 . . . . .212 BG114
Dodds Pk, Bet. (Brock.) RH3 . .264 CP136
Dodsley Pl, N9 . . . . .100 DW48
Dodson St, SE1 . . . . .20 D4
Dod St, E14 . . . . .13 N7
Dodwood, Welw.G.C. AL7 . . .30 DB10
Doebury Wk, SE18
off Prestwood Cl 166 EU79
Doel Cl, SW19 . . . . .180 DC94
Doggets Ct, Barn. EN4 . . . . . .80 DE43
Doggett Rd, SE6 . . . . .183 EA87
Doggetts Fm Rd, Uxb.
(Denh.) UB9 . . . . .113 BC59
Doggetts Way, St.Alb. AL1 . . .42 CC22
Doggetts Wd Cl, Ch.St.G.
HP8 . . . . .72 AV42
Doggetts Wd La, Ch.St.G.
HP8 . . . . .72 AV41
Doghurst Av, Hayes UB3 . . .155 BP80
Doghurst Dr, West Dr. UB7 .155 BP80
Doghurst La, Couls. CR5 . . .234 DF120
Dog Kennel Hill, SE22 . . . . .162 DS83
Dog Kennel Hill Est, SE22 . .162 DS83
Sch Dog Kennel Hill Prim Sch,
SE22 *off Dog Kennel Hill* . .162 DS83
Dog Kennel La, Hat. AL10 . . .45 CU17
Rickmansworth (Chorl.)
WD3 . . . . .73 BF42
Dog La, NW10 . . . . .118 CS63
Doggell Grn, Welw.G.C. AL8 .29 CV08
Dogwood Cl, Grav. (Nthflt)
DA11 . . . . .190 GE91
Doherty Rd, E13 . . . . .15 M3
Dokal Ind Est, Sthl. UB2
off Hartington Rd 156 BY76
Dolben St, SE1 . . . . .20 E2
Dolby Rd, SW6 . . . . .159 CZ82
Dolland St, SE11 . . . . .20 B10
Dollis Av, N3 . . . . .97 CZ53
Dollis Brook Wk, Barn. EN5 . .79 CY44
Dollis Cres, Ruis. HA4 . . . . .116 BW60
DOLLIS HILL, NW2 . . . . .119 CV62
⊖ **Dollis Hill** 119 CU64
Dollis Hill Av, NW2 . . . . .119 CV62
Dollis Hill La, NW2 . . . . .119 CV62
Sch Dollis Inf Sch, NW7
off Pursley Rd 97 CW52
Sch Dollis Jun Sch, NW7
off Pursley Rd 97 CW52
Dollis Ms, N3 *off Dollis Pk* . . .97 CZ53
Dollis Pk, N3 . . . . .97 CZ53
Dollis Rd, N3 . . . . .97 CY52
NW7 . . . . .97 CY52
Dollis Valley Dr, Barn. EN5 . .79 CZ44
Dollis Valley Grn Wk, N20
off Totteridge La 98 DC47
Barnet EN5 . . . . .79 CY44
Dollis Valley Way, Barn. EN5 . .79 CZ44
Dolman Cl, N3
off Avondale Rd 98 DC54
Dolman Rd, W4 . . . . .158 CR77
Dolman St, SW4 . . . . .161 DM84
Dolphin App, Rom. RM1 . . . .127 FF56
Dolphin Cl, SE16 . . . . .22 G3
SE28 . . . . .146 EX72
Surbiton KT6 . . . . .197 CK100
Dolphin Ct, NW11 . . . . .119 CY58
Slough SL1
off Dolphin Rd 152 AV75
Staines TW18 . . . . .174 BG90
Dolphin Ct N, Stai. TW18 . . .174 BG90
Dolphin Est, Sun. TW16 . . . .195 BS95
Dolphin Ho, SW18
off Smugglers Way 160 DB84
Dolphin La, E14 . . . . .14 A10
Dolphin Rd, Nthlt. UB5 . . . . .136 BZ68
Slough SL1 . . . . .152 AV75
Sunbury-on-Thames
TW16 . . . . .195 BS95
Dolphin Rd N, Sun. TW16 . . .195 BS95
Dolphin Rd S, Sun. TW16 . . .195 BR95
Dolphin Rd W, Sun. TW16 . . .195 BR95
Dolphin Sq, SW1 . . . . .19 K10
W4 . . . . .158 CS80
Dolphin St, Kings.T. KT1 . . . .198 CL95
Dolphin Twr, SE8
off Abinger Gro 163 DZ79
Dolphin Way, Purf. RM19 . . .169 FS78
Dolphin Yd, St.Alb. AL1 . . . . .43 CD20
Ware SG12 *off East St* 33 DX06
Dombey St, WC1 . . . . .10 A5
★ **Dome, The**, SE10 . . . . .24 G2
Dome Hill, Cat. CR3 . . . . . . .252 DS127
Dome Hill Pk, SE26 . . . . .182 DT91
Dome Hill Peak, Cat. CR3 . . .252 DS126
Domett Cl, SE5 . . . . .162 DR84
Dome Way, Red. RH1 . . . . . .250 DF133
Domfe Pl, E5
off Rushmore Rd 122 DW63
Domingo St, EC1 . . . . .10 G3
Dominica Cl, E13 . . . . .144 EJ68
Dominic Ct, Wal.Abb. EN9 . . .67 EB33
Dominion Dr, Rom. RM5 . . . .105 FB51
Dominion Rd, Croy. CR0 . . . .202 DT101
Southall UB2 . . . . .156 BY76
Dominion St, EC2 . . . . .11 K5
★ **Dominion Thea**, W1 . . . . . . .9 M7
Dominion Way, Rain. RM13 .147 FG69
Domonic Dr, SE9 . . . . .185 EP91
Domville Cl, N20 . . . . .98 DD47
Donald Biggs Dr, Grav.
DA12 . . . . .191 GK87
Donald Dr, Rom. RM6 . . . . . .126 EW57
Donald Rd, E13 . . . . .144 EH67
Croydon CR0 . . . . .201 DM100
Donaldson Rd, NW6 . . . . . . .139 CZ67
SE18 . . . . .165 EN81
Donald Wds Gdns, Surb.
KT5 . . . . .198 CP103
Doncaster Dr, Nthlt. UB5 . . .116 BZ64
Doncaster Gdns, N4
off Stanhope Gdns 122 DQ58
Northolt UB5 . . . . .116 BZ64
Doncaster Grn, Wat. WD19 . . .94 BW50
Doncaster Rd, N9 . . . . .100 DV45
Doncaster Way, Upmin.
RM14 . . . . .128 FM62
Doncel Ct, E4 . . . . .101 ED45
Doncella Cl, Grays
(Chaff.Hun.) RM16 . . . . .169 FX76
Donegal St, N1 . . . . .4 B10
Doneraile St, SW6 . . . . .159 CX82
Dongola Rd, E1 . . . . .13 J5
E13 . . . . .15 N2
N17 . . . . .122 DS55
Dongola Rd W, E13 . . . . .15 N2
Donington Av, Ilf. IG6 . . . . . .125 EQ57
Donkey All, SE22 . . . . .182 DU87
Donkey La, Dart. (Fnghm)
DA4 . . . . .208 FP103
Dorking (Abin.Com.) RH5 262 BX143
Donkey La, Enf. EN1 . . . . . . .82 DU40
Horley RH6 . . . . .269 DK152
West Drayton UB7 . . . . . .154 BJ77
Donnay Cl, Ger.Cr. SL9 . . . . .112 AX58
Donne Ct, SE24 . . . . .182 DQ86
Donnefield Av, Edg. HA8 . . . .96 CL52
Donne Gdns, Wok. GU22 . . . .227 BE115
Donne Pl, SW3 . . . . .18 B7
Mitcham CR4 . . . . .201 DH98
Donne Rd, Dag. RM8 . . . . . . .126 EW61
Sch Donnington Prim Sch,
NW10 *off Uffington Rd* . .139 CV66
Donnington Rd, NW10 . . . . .139 CV66
Harrow HA3 . . . . .117 CK57
Sevenoaks (Dunt.Grn)
TN13 . . . . .241 FD120
Worcester Park KT4 . . . . .199 CU103
Donnybrook Rd, SW16 . . . . .181 DJ94
Donovan Av, N10 . . . . .99 DH54
Donovan Cl, Epsom KT19
off Nimbus Rd 216 CR110
Don Phelan Cl, SE5 . . . . . . .162 DR81
Don Way, Rom. RM1 . . . . . . .105 FE52
Doods Pk Rd, Reig. RH2 . . . .250 DC133
Doods Rd, Reig. RH2 . . . . . .250 DC133
Doods Way, Reig. RH2 . . . . .250 DD133
Doone Cl, Tedd. TW11 . . . . . .177 CG93
Doon St, SE1 . . . . .20 C2
Dorado Gdns, Orp. BR6 . . . .206 EX104
Doral Way, Cars. SM5 . . . . . .218 DF106
Dorando Cl, W12 . . . . .139 CV73
Doran Dr, Red. RH1 . . . . . . .250 DD134
Doran Gdns, Red. RH1 . . . . .250 DD134
Doran Gro, SE18 . . . . .165 ES80
Doran Wk, E15 . . . . .143 EC66
Dora Rd, SW19 . . . . .180 DA92
Dora St, E14 . . . . .13 L7
Dorcas Ct, St.Alb. AL1 . . . . . .43 CE21
Dorchester Av, N13 . . . . . . .100 DQ49
Bexley DA5 . . . . .186 EX88
Harrow HA2 . . . . .116 CC58
Hoddesdon EN11 . . . . .49 EA15
Dorchester Cl, Dart. DA1 . . .188 FM87
Northolt UB5 . . . . .116 CB64
Orpington BR5
off Grovelands Rd 186 EU94
Dorchester Ct, N14 . . . . .99 DH45
SE24 . . . . .182 DQ85
Rickmansworth (Crox.Grn)
WD3
off Mayfare 75 BR43
Woking GU22 . . . . .227 BA116
Dorchester Dr, SE24 . . . . . .182 DQ85
Feltham TW14 . . . . .175 BS86
Dorchester Gdns, E4 . . . . . .101 EA49
NW11 . . . . .120 DA56
Dorchester Gro, W4 . . . . . . .158 CS78
Dorchester Ms, N.Mal. KT3
off Elm Rd 198 CR98
Twickenham TW1 . . . . .177 CJ87
Sch Dorchester Prim Sch,
Wor.Pk. KT4
off Dorchester Rd 199 CW102
Dorchester Rd, Grav. DA12 .191 GK90
Morden SM4 . . . . .200 DB101
Northolt UB5 . . . . .116 CB64
Weybridge KT13 . . . . .195 BP104
Worcester Park KT4 . . . . .199 CW102
Dorchester Way, Har. HA3 . .118 CM58
Dorchester Waye, Hayes
UB4 . . . . .136 BW72
Dorcis Av, Bexh. DA7 . . . . . .166 EY82
Dordrecht Rd, W3 . . . . .138 CS74
Dore Av, E12 . . . . .125 EN64
Doreen Av, NW9 . . . . .118 CR60
Coll Doreen Bird Coll (Theatre & Dance), Sid.
DA14 *off Clarence Cres* . .186 EU90
Dore Gdns, Mord. SM4 . . . . .200 DB101
Dorell Cl, Sthl. UB1 . . . . . . .136 BZ71
Doria Dr, Grav. DA12 . . . . . .191 GL90
Dorian Rd, Horn. RM12 . . . . .127 FG60
Doria Rd, SW6 . . . . .159 CZ82
Doric Dr, Tad. KT20 . . . . . . .233 CZ120
Doric Way, NW1 . . . . .9 L1
Dorien Rd, SW20 . . . . .199 CX96
Dorin Ct, Warl. CR6 . . . . . . .236 DV119
Dorincourt, Wok. GU22 . . . . .227 BE115
Doris Av, Erith DA8 . . . . . . .167 FC81
Doris Rd, E7 . . . . .144 EG66
Ashford TW15 . . . . .175 BR93
DORKING, RH4 & RH5 . . . . . .263 CH137
⇌ **Dorking** 247 CJ134
Coll Dorking Adult Learning Cen, Dor. RH4
off Dene St 263 CH136
★ **Dorking & District Mus**,
Dor. RH4 . . . . .263 CG136
Dorking Business Pk, Dor.
RH4 . . . . .263 CG135
Dorking Cl, SE8 . . . . .163 DZ79
Worcester Park KT4 . . . . .199 CX103
⇌ **Dorking Deepdene** 247 CJ134
Dorking Gdns, Rom. RM3 . . .106 FK50
Dorking Glen, Rom. RM3 . . .106 FK49
H Dorking Hosp, Dor. RH4 .263 CH137
Dorking Ri, Rom. RM3 . . . . .106 FK49
Dorking Rd, Dor. (Abin.Ham.)
RH5 . . . . .261 BS139
Epsom KT18 . . . . .232 CN116
Guildford (Chilw.) GU4,
GU5 . . . . .259 BF139
Leatherhead KT22 . . . . . .231 CH122
Leatherhead (Bkhm) KT23 .246 CB126
Romford RM3 . . . . .106 FK49
Tadworth KT20 . . . . .233 CX123
Dorking Wk, Rom. RM3 . . . . .106 FK49
⇌ **Dorking West** 263 CG135
Dorkins Way, Upmin. RM14 .129 FS59
Dorlcote Rd, SW18 . . . . .180 DD87
Dorling Dr, Epsom KT17 . . . .217 CT112
Dorly Cl, Shep. TW17 . . . . . .195 BS99
Dorman Pl, N9
off Balham Rd 100 DU47
Dormans Cl, Nthwd. HA6 . . . .93 BR52
Dorman Wk, NW10
off Garden Way 118 CR64
Dorman Way, NW8 . . . . .140 DD67
Dorma Trd Pk, E10 . . . . .123 DX60
Dormay St, SW18 . . . . .180 DB85
Dormer Cl, E15 . . . . .144 EF65
Barnet EN5 . . . . .79 CX43
Dormers Av, Sthl. UB1 . . . . .136 CA72
Dormers Ri, Sthl. UB1 . . . . .136 CB72
DORMER'S WELLS, Sthl.
UB1 . . . . .136 CB73
Sch Dormers Wells High Sch,
Sthl. UB1
off Dormers Wells La . . .136 CA72
Sch Dormers Wells Inf Sch,
Sthl. UB1
off Dormers Wells La . . .136 CB73
Sch Dormers Wells Jun Sch,
Sthl. UB1
off Dormers Wells La . . .136 CB73
Dormers Wells La, Sthl. UB1 .136 CA72
Dormie Cl, St.Alb. AL3 . . . . . .42 CC18
Dormywood, Ruis. HA4 . . . . .115 BT57
Dornberg Cl, SE3 . . . . .164 EG80
Dornberg Rd, SE3
off Banchory Rd 164 EH80
Dorncliffe Rd, SW6 . . . . .159 CY82
Dornels, Slou. SL2 . . . . .132 AW72
DORNEY, Wind. SL4 . . . . . .150 AH76
Dorney, NW3 . . . . .140 DE66
Sch Dorney Comb Sch, Maid.
SL6 *off Harcourt Cl* 150 AF76
★ **Dorney Ct**, Wind. SL4 . . . .150 AG77
Dorney End, Chesh. HP5 . . . .54 AN30
Dorney Gro, Wey. KT13 . . . . .195 BP103
DORNEY REACH, Maid. SL6 .150 AF76
Dorney Reach Rd, Maid.
(Dorney R.) SL6 . . . . .150 AF76
Dorney Ri, Orp. BR5 . . . . . . .205 ET98
Dorney Way, Houns. TW4 . . . .176 BY85
Dorney Wd Rd, Slou. (Burn.)
SL1 . . . . .111 AK63
Dornfell St, NW6 . . . . .119 CZ64
Dornford Gdns, Couls. CR5 . .236 DQ119
Dornton Rd, SW12 . . . . .181 DH89
South Croydon CR2 . . . . .220 DR106
Dorothy Av, Wem. HA0 . . . . .138 CL66
Sch Dorothy Barley Inf Sch,
Dag. RM8
off Davington Rd 126 EV64
Sch Dorothy Barley Jun Sch,
Dag. RM8
off Ivinghoe Rd 126 EV64
Dorothy Evans Cl, Bexh.
DA7 . . . . .167 FB84
Dorothy Gdns, Dag. RM8 . . .126 EV63
Dorothy Rd, SW11 . . . . .160 DF83
Dorrell Pl, SW9
off Brixton Rd 161 DN84
Dorriens Cft, Berk. HP4 . . . . .38 AT16
Dorrien Wk, SW16 . . . . .181 DK89
Dorrington Ct, SE25 . . . . . . .202 DS96
Dorrington Gdns, Horn.
RM12 . . . . .128 FK60
Dorrington Pt, E3 . . . . .14 A1
Dorrington St, EC1 . . . . .10 C5
Dorrington Way, Beck. BR3
off Creswell Dr 203 EB99
Dorrit Cres, Guil. GU3 . . . . .242 AS132
Dorrit Ms, N18 . . . . .100 DS49
Dorrit St, SE1 . . . . .21 H3
Dorrit Way, Chis. BR7 . . . . . .185 EQ93
Dorrofield Cl, Rick.
(Crox.Grn) WD3 . . . . .75 BQ43
Dors Cl, NW9 . . . . .118 CR60
Dorset Av, Hayes UB4 . . . . .135 BS69
Romford RM1 . . . . .127 FD55
Southall UB2 . . . . .156 CA77
Welling DA16 . . . . .165 ET84
Dorset Bldgs, EC4 . . . . .10 E8
Dorset Cl, NW1 . . . . .8 C5
Berkhamsted HP4 . . . . .38 AT18
Hayes UB4 . . . . .135 BS69
Dorset Cres, Grav. DA12 . . . .191 GL91
Dorset Dr, Edg. HA8 . . . . .96 CM51
Woking GU22 . . . . .227 BB117
Dorset Est, E2 . . . . .11 P1
Dorset Gdns, Mitch. CR4 . . .201 DM98
Dorset Ho, Enf. EN3 . . . . .83 DX37
Dorset Ms, N3 . . . . .98 DA53
SW1 . . . . .18 G5
Dorset Pl, E15 . . . . .143 ED65
Dorset Ri, EC4 . . . . .10 E8
Dorset Rd, E7 . . . . .144 EJ66
N15 . . . . .122 DR56
N22 . . . . .99 DL53
SE9 . . . . .184 EL89
SW8 . . . . .161 DM80
SW19 . . . . .200 DA95
W5 . . . . .157 CJ76
Ashford TW15 . . . . .174 BK90
Beckenham BR3 . . . . .203 DX97
Harrow HA1 . . . . .116 CC58
Mitcham CR4 . . . . .200 DE96
Sutton SM2 . . . . .218 DA110
Windsor SL4 . . . . .151 AQ82
Sch Dorset Rd Inf Sch, SE9
off Dorset Rd 185 EM90
Dorset Sq, NW1 . . . . .8 C4
Epsom KT19 . . . . .216 CR110
Dorset St, W1 . . . . .8 D6
Sevenoaks TN13
off High St 257 FH125
Dorset Way, Twick. TW2 . . . .177 CD88
Uxbridge UB10 . . . . .134 BM68
West Byfleet (Byfleet)
KT14 . . . . .212 BK110
Dorset Waye, Houns. TW5 . .156 BZ80
Dorton Cl, SE15
off Chandler Way 162 DT80
Coll Dorton Coll of Further Ed,
Sev. TN15 *off Seal Dr* . . .257 FM122
Dorton Dr, Sev. TN15 . . . . . .257 FM122
Sch Dorton Ho, Sev. TN15
off Wildernesse Av 257 FM122
Dorton Way, Wok. (Ripley)
GU23 . . . . .228 BH121
Dorville Cres, W6 . . . . .159 CV76
Dorville Rd, SE12 . . . . .184 EF85
Dothill Rd, SE18 . . . . .165 ER80
Douai Gro, Hmptn. TW12 . . .196 CC95
Sch Douay Martyrs Sch, The,
Lwr Sch, Uxb. UB10
off Long La 115 BP64
Upr Sch, Uxb. UB10
off Edinburgh Dr 115 BP63
Doubleday Rd, Loug. IG10 . . .85 EQ41
Doughty Ms, WC1 . . . . .10 A4
Doughty St, WC1 . . . . .10 A3
Douglas Av, E17 . . . . .101 EA53
New Malden KT3 . . . . .199 CV98
Romford RM3 . . . . .106 FL54
Watford WD24 . . . . .76 BX37
Wembley HA0 . . . . .138 CL66
Douglas Cl, Grays
(Chaff.Hun.) RM16 . . . . .170 FY76
Guildford GU4 . . . . .242 AX128
Stanmore HA7 . . . . .95 CG50
Wallington SM6 . . . . .219 DL108
Douglas Ct, Cat. CR3 . . . . . .236 DQ122
Westerham TN16 . . . . .238 EL117
Douglas Cres, Hayes UB4 . . .136 BW70
Douglas Dr, Croy. CR0 . . . . .203 EA104
Douglas Gdns, Berk. HP4 . . . .38 AT18
Douglas La, Stai. (Wrays.)
TW19 . . . . .173 AZ85
Douglas Ms, NW2 . . . . .119 CY62
Banstead SM7
off North Acre 233 CZ116
Douglas Path, E14 . . . . .24 D9
Douglas Rd, E4 . . . . .102 EE45
E16 . . . . .15 M6
N1 . . . . .4 G5
N22 . . . . .99 DN53
NW6 . . . . .139 CZ67
Douglas Rd, Add. KT15 . . . .194 BH104
Esher KT10 . . . . .196 CB103
Hornchurch RM11 . . . . .127 FF58
Hounslow TW3 . . . . .156 CB83
Ilford IG3 . . . . .126 EU58
Kingston upon Thames
KT1 . . . . .198 CP96
Reigate RH2 . . . . .250 DA133
Slough SL2 . . . . .131 AR71
Staines (Stanw.) TW19 . . . .174 BK86
Surbiton KT6 . . . . .198 CM103
Welling DA16 . . . . .166 EV81
Douglas Sq, Mord. SM4 . . . .200 DA100
Douglas St, SW1 . . . . .19 L8
Douglas Ter, E17
off Douglas Av 101 EA53
Douglas Way, SE8 . . . . .163 DZ80
Welwyn Garden City AL7 . .30 DC09
Doug Siddons Ct, Grays
RM17 *off Elm Rd* 170 GC79
Doulton Cl, Harl. CM17 . . . . .52 EY16
Doulton Ms, NW6
off Lymington Rd 140 DB65
Doultons, The, Stai. TW18 . .174 BG94
Dounesforth Gdns, SW18 . . .180 DB88
Dounsell Ct, Brwd. (Pilg.Hat.)
CM15 *off Ongar Rd* 108 FU44
Douro Pl, W8 . . . . .17 K5
Douro St, E3 . . . . .143 EA68
Douthwaite Sq, E1 . . . . .22 B1
Dove App, E6 . . . . .144 EL71
Dove Cl, NW7 *off Bunns La* . .97 CT52
Northolt UB5
off Wayfarer Rd 136 BX70
South Croydon CR2 . . . . .221 DX111
Wallington SM6 . . . . .219 DM108
Dovecot Cl, Pnr. HA5 . . . . . .115 BV57
Dovecote Av, N22 . . . . .121 DN55
Dovecote Cl, Wey. KT13 . . . .195 BP104
Dovecote Gdns, SW14
off Avondale Rd 158 CR83
Dove Ct, EC2 . . . . .11 J8
Beaconsfield HP9 . . . . .89 AK52
Hatfield AL10 . . . . .45 CU19
Dovedale Av, Har. HA3 . . . . .117 CJ58
Ilford IG5 . . . . .103 EN54
Dovedale Cl, Guil. GU4
off Weylea Av 243 BA131
Uxbridge (Hare.) UB9 . . . . .92 BJ54
Welling DA16 . . . . .166 EU82
Dovedale Ri, Mitch. CR4 . . . .180 DF94
Dovedale Rd, SE22 . . . . .182 DV85
Dartford DA2 . . . . .188 FQ88
Dovedon Cl, N14 . . . . .99 DL47
Dove Ho Cres, Slou. SL2 . . . .131 AL69
Dovehouse Cft, Harl. CM20
off Mistley Rd 36 EU13
Dove Ho Gdns, E4 . . . . .101 EA47
Dovehouse Grn, Wey. KT13
off Rosslyn Pk 213 BR105
Dovehouse Mead, Bark.
IG11 . . . . .145 ER68
Dovehouse St, SW3 . . . . .18 A9
Dove La, Pot.B. EN6 . . . . .64 DB34
Dove Ms, SW5 . . . . .17 L8
Doveney Cl, Orp. BR5 . . . . . .206 EW97
Dove Pk, Pnr. HA5 . . . . .94 CA52
Rickmansworth (Chorl.)
WD3 . . . . .73 BB44
Dover Cl, NW2 *off Brent Ter* . .119 CX61
Romford RM5 . . . . .105 FC54
Dovercourt Av, Th.Hth. CR7 .201 DN98
Dovercourt Est, N1 . . . . .5 K4
Dovercourt Gdns, Stan. HA7 .96 CL50
Dovercourt La, Sutt. SM1 . . .200 DC104
Dovercourt Rd, SE22 . . . . . . .182 DS86
Doverfield, Wal.Cr. EN7 . . . . .66 DQ29
Doverfield Rd, SW2 . . . . .181 DL86
Guildford GU4 . . . . .243 BA131
Dover Flats, SE1
off Old Kent Rd 162 DS77
Dover Gdns, Cars. SM5 . . . . .200 DF104
Dover Ho Rd, SW15 . . . . .159 CU84
Doveridge Gdns, N13 . . . . . . .99 DP49
Dove Rd, N1 . . . . .5 J3
Dove Row, E2 . . . . .142 DU67
Dover Pk Dr, SW15 . . . . .179 CV86
Dover Patrol, SE3
off Kidbrooke Way 164 EH82
Dover Rd, E12 . . . . .124 EJ61
N9 . . . . .100 DW47
SE19 . . . . .182 DR93
Gravesend (Nthflt) DA11 . .190 GD87
Romford RM6 . . . . .126 EY58
Slough SL1 . . . . .131 AM72
Sch Dover Rd Comm Prim Sch, Grav. DA11
off Dover Rd E 190 GE88
Dover Rd E, Grav. DA11 . . . . .190 GE87
DOVERSGREEN, Reig. RH2 .266 DB139
Sch Dovers Grn Inf Sch, Reig.
RH2 *off Rushetts Rd* 266 DC138
Dovers Grn Rd, Reig. RH2 . . .266 DB139
Doversmead, Wok. (Knap.)
GU21 . . . . .226 AS116
Dover St, W1 . . . . .9 H10
Dover Way, Rick. (Crox.Grn)
WD3 . . . . .75 BQ42
Dover Yd, W1 . . . . .19 J1
Doves Cl, Brom. BR2 . . . . . . .204 EL103
Doves Yd, N1 . . . . .4 D8
Doveton Rd, S.Croy. CR2 . . . .220 DR106
Doveton St, E1 . . . . .12 E3
Dove Wk, SW1 . . . . .18 E9
Hornchurch RM12
off Heron Flight Av 147 FH65
Dowanhill Rd, SE6 . . . . .183 ED88
Dowdeswell Cl, SW15 . . . . . .158 CS84
Dowding Pl, Stan. HA7 . . . . . .95 CG51
Dowding Rd, Uxb. UB10 . . . .134 BM66
Westerham (Bigg.H.)
TN16 . . . . .238 EK115
Dowding Wk, Grav. (Nthflt)
DA11 . . . . .190 GE90
Dowding Way, Horn. RM12 .147 FH66
Waltham Abbey EN9
off Sewardstone Rd 83 ED35
Watford (Lvsdn) WD25 . . . .59 BT34
Dowdney Cl, NW5 . . . . .121 DJ64
Dower Av, Wall. SM6 . . . . . . .219 DH109
Dower Cl, Beac. (Knot.Grn)
HP9 . . . . .88 AJ50
Dower Pk, Wind. SL4 . . . . . . .151 AL84
Dowgate Hill, EC4 . . . . .11 J9
Dowland St, W10 . . . . .6 E1
Dowlans Cl, Lthd. (Bkhm)
KT23 . . . . .246 CA127
Dowlans Rd, Lthd. (Bkhm)
KT23 . . . . .246 CB127

A B C D E F G H I J K L M N O P Q R S T U V W X Y Z

⊖ London Underground station
DLR Docklands Light Railway station
Tra Tramlink station
Riv Pedestrian ferry landing stage

Dowlas Est, SE5
off Dowlas St 162 DS80
Dowlas St, SE5 162 DS80
Dowlerville Rd, Orp. BR6 223 ET107
Dowling Ct, Hem.H. HP3 40 BK23
Dowman Cl, SW19
off Nelson Gro Rd 200 DB95
Downage, NW4 119 CW55
Downage, The, Grav. DA11 191 GG89
Downalong, Bushey
(Bushey Hth) WD23 95 CD46
Downbank Av, Bexh. DA7 167 FD81
Downbarns Rd, Ruis. HA4 116 BX62
Downbury Ms, SW18
off Merton Rd 180 DA86
Down Cl, Nthlt. UB5 135 BV68
Sch **Downderry Prim Sch**,
Brom. BR1
off Downderry Rd 184 EE91
Downderry Rd, Brom. BR1 183 ED90
DOWNE, Orp. BR6 223 EM111
Downe Av, Sev. (Cudham)
TN14 223 EQ112
Downe Cl, Horl. RH6 268 DE146
Welling DA16 166 EW80
Downedge, St.Alb. AL3 42 CB19
Sch **Downe Manor Prim Sch**,
Nthlt. UB5
off Rayners Cres 135 BV69
Downend, SE18
off Moordown 165 EP80
Sch **Downe Prim Sch**, Orp.
BR6 off High Elms Rd 223 EN111
Downer Dr, Rick. (Sarratt)
WD3 74 BG36
Downer Meadow, Gdmg.
GU7 258 AS143
Downe Rd, Kes. BR2 222 EK109
Mitcham CR4 200 DF96
Sevenoaks (Cudham)
TN14 223 EQ114
Downers Cotts, SW4
off The Pavement 161 DJ84
Downes Cl, Twick. TW1
off St. Margarets Rd 177 CH86
Downes Ct, N21 99 DN46
Downes Rd, St.Alb. AL4 43 CH16
Downfield, Wor.Pk. KT4 199 CT102
Downfield Cl, W9 7 J4
Hertford (Hert.Hth) SG13 32 DW11
Sch **Downfield JMI Sch**, Wal.Cr.
EN8 off Downfield Rd 67 DY31
Downfield Rd, Hert.
(Hert.Hth) SG13 32 DW09
Waltham Cross (Chsht)
EN8 67 DY31
Downfields, Welw.G.C. AL8 29 CV11
Downhall Rd, B.Stort.
(Hat.Hth) CM22 37 FH08
Harlow CM17 37 FH08
Down Hall Rd, Kings.T. KT2 197 CK95
DOWNHAM, Brom. BR1 184 EF92
Downham Cl, Rom. RM5 104 FA52
Downham La, Brom. BR1
off Downham Way 183 ED92
Downham Rd, N1 5 J6
Downham Way, Brom. BR1 183 ED92
Downhills Av, N17 122 DR55
Downhills Pk Rd, N17 122 DQ55
Sch **Downhills Prim Sch**,
N15 off Philip La 122 DR56
Downhills Way, N17 122 DQ55
★ **Down Ho - Darwin Mus**,
Orp. BR6 223 EN112
Downhurst Av, NW7 96 CR50
Downing Av, Guil. GU2 258 AT135
Downing Cl, Har. HA2 116 CC55
Downing Dr, Grnf. UB6 137 CD67
Downing Path, Slou. SL2 131 AL70
Downing Rd, Dag. RM9 146 EZ67
Downings, E6 145 EN72
Downing St, SW1 19 N3
Downings Wd, Rick.
(Map.Cr.) WD3 91 BD50
Downland Cl, N20 98 DC46
Coulsdon CR5 219 DH114
Epsom KT18 233 CV118
Downland Gdns, Epsom
KT18 233 CV118
Downlands, Wal.Abb. EN9 68 EE34
Downlands Rd, Pur. CR8 219 DL113
Downland Way, Epsom
KT18 233 CV118
Sch **Down La Jun Sch**, N17
off Parkhurst Rd 100 DU54
Downleys Cl, SE9 184 EL89
Downman Rd, SE9 164 EL83
Down Pl, W6 159 CV77
Windsor (Wat.Oak.) SL4 150 AG79
Down Rd, Guil. GU1 243 BB134
Teddington TW11 177 CH93
Downs, The, SW20 179 CX94
Harlow CM20 51 ES15
Hatfield AL10 45 CU20
Leatherhead KT22 247 CJ125
Downs Av, Chis. BR7 185 EM92
Dartford DA1 188 FN87
Epsom KT18 216 CS114
Pinner HA5 116 BZ58
Downs Br Rd, Beck. BR3 203 ED95
Downsbury Ms, SW18
off Merton Rd 180 DA85
Sch **Downs Co Prim Sch, The**,
Harl. CM20 off The Hides 51 ES15
Downs Ct, Sutt. SM2 218 DB111
Downs Ct Rd, Pur. CR8 219 DP112
Sch **Downsell Jun & Inf Sch**,
E15 off Downsell Rd 123 ED63
Downsell Rd, E15 123 EC63
Sch **Downsend Sch**, Lthd.
KT22
off Leatherhead Rd 231 CK120
Downsfield, Hat. AL10
off Sandifield 45 CV21
Downsfield Rd, E17 123 DY58
Downshall Av, Ilf. IG3 125 ES58
Sch **Downshall Prim Sch**, Ilf.
IG3 off Meads La 125 ES59
Downs Hill, Beck. BR3 183 ED94
Gravesend (Sthflt) DA13 190 GC94
Downs Hill Rd, Epsom KT18 216 CS114
Downshire Hill, NW3 120 DD63
Downs Ho Rd, Epsom KT18 233 CT118
DOWNSIDE, Cob. KT11 229 BV118
Downside, Cher. KT16 193 BF102
Epsom KT18 216 CS114
Hemel Hempstead HP2 40 BL19
Sunbury-on-Thames
TW16 195 BU95
Downside, Twick. TW1 177 CF90
Downside Br Rd, Cob. KT11 229 BV115
Downside Cl, SW19 180 DC93
Downside Common, Cob.
(Down.) KT11 229 BV118
Downside Common Rd, Cob.
(Down.) KT11 229 BV118
Downside Cres, NW3 120 DE64
W13 137 CG70
Downside Orchard, Wok.
GU22 off Park Rd 227 BA117
Downside Rd, Cob. (Down.)
KT11 229 BV116
Guildford GU4 259 BB135
Sutton SM2 218 DD107
Sch **Downside Sch**, Pur. CR8
off Woodcote La 219 DK112
Downside Wk, Nthlt. UB5 136 BZ69
Downsland Dr, Brwd. CM14 108 FW48
Downs La, E5 off Downs Rd 122 DV63
Hatfield AL10 45 CU20
Leatherhead KT22 231 CH123
Downs Pk Rd, E5 122 DU64
E8 5 P1
Downs Rd, E5 122 DU63
Beckenham BR3 203 EB96
Coulsdon CR5 235 DK118
Dorking RH5 247 CJ128
Enfield EN1 82 DS42
Epsom KT18 232 CS115
Gravesend (Istead Rise)
DA13 190 GD91
Purley CR8 219 DP111
Slough SL3 152 AX75
Sutton SM2 218 DB110
Thornton Heath CR7 202 DQ95
Downs Side, Sutt. SM2 217 CZ111
Down St, W1 18 G2
West Molesey KT8 196 CA99
Down St Ms, W1 18 G2
Downs Vw, Dor. RH4 247 CJ134
Isleworth TW7 157 CF80
Tadworth KT20 233 CV121
Downsview Av, Wok. GU22 227 AZ121
Downsview Cl, Orp. BR6 224 EW110
Swanley BR8 207 FF97
Downsview Ct, Guil. GU1
off Hazel Av 242 AW130
Downsview Gdns, SE19 181 DP94
Dorking RH4 off South Ter 263 CH137
Sch **Downsview Inf Sch**,
Swan. BR8 off Beech Av 207 FG97
Sch **Downsview Jun Sch**,
Swan. BR8 off Beech Av 207 FG97
Sch **Downsview Prim Sch**,
SE19 off Biggin Way 182 DQ94
Downsview Rd, SE19 182 DQ94
Downs Vw Rd, Lthd. (Bkhm)
KT23 246 CC126
Downsview Rd, Sev. TN13 256 FF125
Sch **Downsview Spec Sch**,
E5 off Downs Rd 122 DV63
Downs Way, Epsom KT18 233 CT116
Downsway, Guil. GU1 243 BD134
Downs Way, Lthd. (Bkhm)
KT23 246 CC126
Downsway, Orp. BR6 223 ES106
Downs Way, Oxt. RH8 254 EE127
Downsway, S.Croy. CR2 220 DS111
Downs Way, Tad. KT20 233 CV121
Downsway, Whyt. CR3 236 DT116
Downsway, The, Sutt. SM2 218 DC109
Downs Way Cl, Tad. KT20 233 CU121
Sch **Downs Way Prim Sch**, Oxt.
RH8 off Downs Way 254 EE128
Downs Wd, Epsom KT18 233 CV117
Downswood, Reig. RH2 250 DE131
Downton Av, SW2 181 DL89
Downtown Rd, SE16 23 K3
Downview Cl, Cob. (Down.)
KT11 229 BV119
Down Way, Nthlt. UB5 135 BV69
Dowrey St, N1 4 C7
Dowry Wk, Wat. WD17 75 BT38
Dowsett Rd, N17 100 DT54
Dowson Cl, SE5 162 DR84
Doyce St, SE1 20 G3
Doyle Cl, Erith DA8 167 FE81
Doyle Gdns, NW10 139 CU67
Doyle Rd, SE25 202 DU98
Doyle Way, Til. RM18
off Coleridge Rd 171 GJ82
D'Oyley St, SW1 18 E7
D'Oyly Carte Island, Wey.
KT13 195 BP102
Doynton St, N19 121 DH61
Draco St, SE17 162 DQ79
Dragonfly Cl, E13 15 P1
Dragon La, Wey. KT13 212 BN110
Dragon Rd, SE15 162 DS79
Hatfield AL10
off Mosquito Way 44 CS17
Dragoon Rd, SE8 23 L10
Dragor Rd, NW10 138 CQ70
Drake Av, Cat. CR3 236 DQ122
Slough SL3 152 AX77
Staines TW18 173 BF92
Drake Cl, SE16 23 H3
Brentwood CM14 108 FX50
Drake Ct, SE19 182 DT92
W12 159 CW75
Harrow HA2 116 BZ60
Drake Cres, SE28 146 EW72
Drakefell Rd, SE4 163 DX82
SE14 163 DX82
Drakefield Rd, SW17 180 DG90
Drakeley Ct, N5
off Highbury Hill 121 DP63
Drake Ms, Horn. RM12
off Fulmar Rd 147 FG66
Drake Rd, SE4 163 EA83
Chessington KT9 216 CN106
Croydon CR0 201 DM101
Grays (Chaff.Hun.) RM16 170 FY75
Harrow HA2 116 BZ61
Horley RH6 268 DE148
Mitcham CR4 200 DG100
Drakes Cl, Esher KT10 214 CA106
Waltham Cross (Chsht)
EN8 67 DX28
Drakes Ctyd, NW6 139 CZ66
Drakes Dr, Nthwd. HA6 93 BP53
St. Albans AL1 43 CH23
Drakes Meadow, Harl. CM17 36 EY11
Drakes Rd, Amer. HP7 55 AR39
Drake St, WC1 10 A6
Enfield EN2 82 DR39
Drakes Wk, E6 145 EM67
Drakes Way, Hat. AL10 45 CV20
Woking GU22 226 AX122
Drakewood Rd, SW16 181 DK94
Sch **Drama Cen London**, NW5
off Prince of Wales Rd 140 DG65
Draper Cl, Belv. DA17 166 EZ77
Isleworth TW7 157 CD82
Draper Ct, Horn. RM12 128 FL61
Draper Ho, SE1
off Newington Butts 161 DP77
Draper Pl, N1 off Dagmar Ter 141 DP67
Drapers Gdns, EC2
off Copthall Av 142 DR72
Drapers Rd, E15 123 ED63
N17 122 DT55
Enfield EN2 81 DP40
Drappers Way, SE16 22 B7
Draven Cl, Brom. BR2 204 EF101
Drawdock Rd, SE10 24 F2
Drawell Cl, SE18 165 ES78
Drax Av, SW20 179 CV94
Draxmont, SW19 179 CY93
Draycot Rd, E11 124 EH58
Surbiton KT6 198 CN102
Draycott Av, SW3 18 B7
Harrow HA3 117 CH58
Draycott Cl, NW2 119 CX62
Harrow HA3 117 CH58
Draycott Ms, SW6
off New Kings Rd 159 CZ82
Draycott Pl, SW3 18 C8
Draycott Ter, SW3 18 D7
Dray Ct, Guil. GU2
off The Chase 258 AV135
Drayford Cl, W9 6 F3
Dray Gdns, SW2 181 DM85
Draymans Way, Islw. TW7 157 CF83
Drayside Ms, Sthl. UB2
off Kingston Rd 156 BZ75
Drayson Cl, Wal.Abb. EN9 68 EE32
Drayson Ms, W8 17 H4
Drayton Av, W13 137 CG73
Loughton IG10 85 EM44
Orpington BR6 205 EP102
Potters Bar EN6 63 CY32
Drayton Br Rd, W7 137 CF73
W13 137 CF73
Drayton Cl, Houns. TW4 176 BZ85
Ilford IG1 125 ER60
Leatherhead (Fetch.)
KT22 231 CE124
Drayton Ford, Rick. WD3 92 BG48
Drayton Gdns, N21 99 DP45
SW10 17 M9
W13 137 CG73
West Drayton UB7 154 BL75
⇌ **Drayton Green** 137 CF72
Drayton Grn, W13 137 CG73
Drayton Grn Rd, W13 137 CH73
Drayton Gro, W13 137 CG73
Sch **Drayton Ho Sch**, Guil.
GU1 off Austen Rd 259 AZ135
Sch **Drayton Manor High Sch**,
W7 off Drayton Br Rd 137 CF73
⇌ **Drayton Park** 4 D1
Drayton Pk, N5 4 C2
Drayton Pk Ms, N5 4 C1
Sch **Drayton Pk Prim Sch**, N5 4 D1
Sch **Drayton Prim Sch**, W13
off Drayton Gro 137 CG73
Drayton Rd, E11 123 ED60
N17 100 DS54
NW10 139 CT67
W13 137 CG73
Borehamwood WD6 78 CN42
Croydon CR0 201 DP103
Drayton Waye, Har. HA3 117 CH58
Drenon Sq, Hayes UB3 135 BT73
Dresden Cl, NW6 140 DB65
Dresden Rd, N19 121 DK60
Dresden Way, Wey. KT13 213 BQ106
Dressington Av, SE4 183 EA86
Drew Av, NW7 97 CY51
Drew Gdns, Grnf. UB6 137 CF65
Drew Meadow, Slou.
(Farn.Com.) SL2 111 AQ63
Drew Pl, Cat. CR3 236 DR123
Sch **Drew Prim Sch**, E16
off Wythes Rd 144 EL74
Drew Rd, E16 144 EL74
Drews Pk, Beac. (Knot.Grn)
HP9 88 AH49
Drewstead Rd, SW16 181 DK89
Drey, The, Ger.Cr. (Chal.St.P.)
SL9 90 AY50
Driffield Rd, E3 143 DY68
Drift, The, Brom. BR2 204 EK104
Drift La, Cob. KT11 230 BZ117
Drift Rd, Lthd. KT24 229 BT124
Windsor SL4 150 AD84
Drift Way, Rich. TW10 178 CM88
Slough (Colnbr.) SL3 153 BC81
Driftway, The, Bans. SM7 233 CW115
Hemel Hempstead HP2 40 BM20
Leatherhead KT22
off Downs La 231 CH123
Mitcham CR4 200 DG95
Driftwood Av, St.Alb. AL2 60 CA26
Driftwood Dr, Ken. CR8 235 DP117
Drill Hall Rd, Cher. KT16 194 BG101
Dorking RH4
off Westcott Rd 263 CG136
Drinkwater Rd, Har. HA2 116 CB61
Drive, The, E4 101 ED45
E17 123 EB56
E18 124 EG56
N3 98 DA52
N6 120 DF57
N11 99 DJ51
NW10 off Longstone Av 139 CT67
NW11 119 CY59
SW6 off Fulham Rd 159 CY82
SW16 201 DM97
SW20 179 CW94
W3 138 CQ72
Amersham HP7 55 AR38
Ashford TW15 175 BR94
Banstead SM7 233 CY117
Barking IG11 145 ET66
Barnet (High Barn.) EN5 79 CY41
Barnet (New Barn.) EN5 80 DC44
Beckenham BR3 203 EA96
Bexley DA5 186 EW86
Brentwood CM13 108 FW50
Buckhurst Hill IG9 102 EJ45
Chislehurst BR7 205 ET97
Chislehurst (Scad.Pk) BR7 205 ES95
Cobham KT11 214 BY114
Coulsdon CR5 219 DL114
Edgware HA8 96 CN50
Enfield EN2 82 DR39
Epsom KT19 217 CT107
Epsom (Headley) KT18 232 CN124
Erith DA8 167 FB80
Esher KT10 196 CC102
Feltham TW14 176 BW87
Gerrards Cross (Chal.St.P.)
SL9 90 AY52
Gravesend DA12 191 GK91
Guildford GU2
off Beech Gro 242 AT134
Guildford (Art.) GU3 258 AV138
Drive, The, Guil. (Ons.Vill.)
GU2 258 AT136
Harlow CM20 35 ES14
Harrow HA2 116 CA59
Hatfield (Brook.Pk) AL9 64 DA25
Hertford SG14 32 DQ07
Hertford (Newgate St)
SG13 47 DL24
Hoddesdon EN11 49 EA15
Horley RH6 269 DH149
Hounslow TW3 157 CD82
Ilford IG1 125 EM60
Isleworth TW7 157 CD82
Kingston upon Thames
KT2 178 CQ94
Leatherhead (Fetch.)
KT22 231 CE122
Leatherhead (Tyr.Wd)
KT22 232 CN124
Loughton IG10 84 EL41
Morden SM4 200 DD99
Northwood HA6 93 BS54
Orpington BR6 205 ET103
Potters Bar EN6 63 CZ33
Radlett WD7 61 CG34
Rickmansworth WD3 74 BJ44
Romford (Coll.Row) RM5 105 FC53
Romford (Harold Wd) RM3 106 FL53
St. Albans (Lon.Col.) AL2 61 CG26
Sawbridgeworth CM21 36 EY05
Sevenoaks TN13 257 FH124
Sidcup DA14 186 EV90
Slough SL3 152 AY75
Slough (Datchet) SL3 152 AV81
Staines (Wrays.) TW19 172 AX85
Surbiton KT6 198 CL101
Sutton SM2 217 CZ112
Thornton Heath CR7 202 DR98
Uxbridge UB10 114 BL63
Virginia Water GU25 193 AZ99
Wallington SM6 219 DJ110
Waltham Cross (Chsht)
EN7 65 DP28
Watford WD17 75 BR37
Wembley HA9 118 CQ61
West Wickham BR4 203 ED101
Woking GU22 226 AV120
Drive Mead, Couls. CR5 219 DL114
Drive Rd, Couls. CR5 235 DM119
Drive Spur, Tad. KT20 234 DB121
Driveway, The, E17
off Hoe St 123 EB58
Potters Bar (Cuffley) EN6 65 DL28
Drodges Cl, Guil. (Bramley)
GU5 259 AZ143
Droitwich Cl, SE26 182 DU90
Dromey Gdns, Har. HA3 95 CF52
Dromore Rd, SW15 179 CY86
Dronfield Gdns, Dag. RM8 126 EW64
Droop St, W10 6 C3
Drop La, St.Alb. (Brick.Wd)
AL2 60 CB30
Sch **Dropmore Co First Sch**,
Slou. SL1
off Littleworth Rd 110 AJ62
Dropmore Rd, Slou. (Burn.)
SL1 130 AJ67
Drove Rd, Dor. RH5 262 BW135
Guildford GU4 260 BG136
Drovers Mead, Brwd.
(Warley) CM14 108 FV49
Drovers Pl, SE15 162 DV80
Drovers Rd, S.Croy. CR2 220 DR106
Drovers Way, Beac.
(Seer Grn) HP9 89 AQ51
Hatfield AL10 45 CV15
St. Albans AL3 43 CD20
Droveway, Loug. IG10 85 EP40
Drove Way, The, Grav.
(Istead Rise) DA13 190 GE94
Druce Rd, SE21 182 DS86
Drudgeon Way, Dart. (Bean)
DA2 189 FV90
Druids Cl, Ashtd. KT21 232 CM120
Druid St, SE1 21 M3
Druids Way, Brom. BR2 203 ED98
Drumaline Ridge, Wor.Pk.
KT4 198 CS103
Drummond Av, Rom. RM7 127 FD56
Drummond Cen, Croy.
CR0 202 DQ103
Drummond Cl, Erith DA8 167 FE81
Drummond Cres, NW1 9 L1
Drummond Dr, Stan. HA7 95 CF52
Drummond Gdns, Epsom
KT19 216 CP111
Drummond Gate, SW1 19 M9
Drummond Ho, Wind. SL4
off Balmoral Gdns 151 AR83
Drummond Pl, Twick. TW1 177 CH86
Drummond Rd, E11 124 EH58
SE16 22 C5
Croydon CR0 202 DQ103
Guildford GU1 242 AX134
Romford RM7 127 FD56
Drummonds, The, Buck.H.
IG9 102 EH47
Epping CM16 70 EU30
Drummonds Pl, Rich. TW9 158 CL84
Drummond St, NW1 9 J3
Drum St, E1 11 P7
Drury Cres, Croy. CR0 201 DN103
Drury La, WC2 9 P8
Ware (Hunsdon) SG12 34 EK06
Drury Rd, Har. HA1 116 CC59
Drury Way, NW10 118 CR64
Drury Way Ind Est, NW10 118 CQ64
Dryad St, SW15 159 CX83
Dryburgh Gdns, NW9 118 CN55
Dryburgh Rd, SW15 159 CV83
Drycroft, Welw.G.C. AL7 29 CY13
Drydell La, Chesh. HP5 54 AM31
Dryden Av, W7 137 CF72
Dryden Cl, Ilf. IG6 103 ET51
Dryden Ct, SE11 20 D8
Dryden Pl, Til. RM18
off Fielding Av 171 GH81
Dryden Rd, SW19 180 DC93
Enfield EN1 82 DS44
Harrow HA3 95 CF53
Welling DA16 165 ES81
Dryden St, WC2 9 P8
Dryden Twrs, Rom. RM3 105 FH52
Dryden Way, Orp. BR6 206 EU102
Dryfield Cl, NW10 138 CQ65
Dryfield Rd, Edg. HA8 96 CQ51
Dryfield Wk, SE8
off New King St 163 EA79
Dryhill La, Sev. (Sund.)
TN14 256 FB123
Dryhill Rd, Belv. DA17 166 EZ79
Dryland Av, Orp. BR6 223 ET105
Drylands Rd, N8 121 DL58
Drynham Pk, Wey. KT13 195 BS104
Drysdale Av, E4 101 EB45
Drysdale Cl, Nthwd. HA6
off Northbrook Dr 93 BS52
Drysdale Pl, N1 11 M1
Drysdale St, N1 11 M2
Duarte Pl, Grays RM16 170 FZ76
Dublin Av, E8 142 DU67
Dubrae Cl, St.Alb. AL3 42 CA22
Du Burstow Ter, W7 157 CE75
Ducal St, E2 11 P2
Du Cane Cl, W12 139 CW72
Du Cane Ct, SW17 180 DG88
Du Cane Rd, W12 139 CT72
Duchess Cl, N11 99 DH50
Sutton SM1 218 DC105
Duchess Ct, Wey. KT13 195 BR104
Duchess Gro, Buck.H. IG9 102 EH47
Duchess Ms, W1 9 H6
Duchess of Bedford's Wk,
W8 16 G4
Duchess of Kent Cl, Guil.
GU2 off Tylehost 242 AV130
Duchess St, W1 9 H6
Slough SL1 131 AL74
Duchess Wk, Sev. TN15 257 FL125
Duchy Rd, Barn. EN4 80 DD38
Duchy St, SE1 20 D1
Ducie St, SW4 161 DM84
Duckett Ms, N4
off Duckett Rd 121 DP58
Duckett Rd, N4 121 DP58
Ducketts Mead, Harl.
(Roydon) CM19 34 EH14
Ducketts Rd, Dart. DA1 187 FF85
Duckett St, E1 13 J5
Ducking Stool Ct, Rom.
RM1 127 FE56
Duck La, W1 9 L8
Epping (Thnwd) CM16 70 EW26
Duck Lees La, Enf. EN3 83 DY42
Duckling La, Saw. CM21
off Vantorts Rd 36 EY05
Ducks Hill, Nthwd. HA6 93 BP54
Ducks Hill Rd, Nthwd. HA6 93 BP54
Ruislip HA4 93 BP54
DUCKS ISLAND, Barn. EN5 79 CX44
Ducks Wk, Twick. TW1 177 CJ85
Du Cros Dr, Stan. HA7 95 CK51
Du Cros Rd, W3
off The Vale 138 CS74
Dudden Hill La, NW10 119 CT63
Duddington Cl, SE9 184 EK91
Dudley Av, Har. HA3 117 CJ55
Waltham Cross EN8 67 DX32
Dudley Cl, Add. KT15 194 BJ104
Grays (Chaff.Hun.) RM16 170 FY75
Hemel Hempstead (Bov.)
HP3 57 BA27
Dudley Ct, NW11 119 CZ56
Slough SL1 off Upton Rd 152 AU76
Dudley Dr, Mord. SM4 199 CY101
Ruislip HA4 115 BV64
Dudley Gdns, W13 157 CH75
Harrow HA2 117 CD60
Romford RM3 106 FK51
Dudley Gro, Epsom KT18 216 CQ114
Dudley Ms, SW2
off Bascombe St 181 DN86
Dudley Pl, Hayes UB3 155 BR77
Dudley Rd, E17 101 EA54
N3 98 DB54
NW6 139 CY68
SW19 180 DA93
Ashford TW15 174 BM92
Feltham TW14 175 BQ88
Gravesend (Nthflt) DA11 190 GE87
Harrow HA2 116 CC61
Ilford IG1 125 EP63
Kingston upon Thames
KT1 198 CM97
Richmond TW9 158 CM82
Romford RM3 106 FK51
Southall UB2 156 BX75
Walton-on-Thames KT12 195 BU100
Dudley St, W2 7 N6
Dudlington Rd, E5 122 DW61
Dudmaston Ms, SW3 17 P9
Dudrich Ms, SE22
off Melbourne Gro 182 DT85
Dudsbury Rd, Dart. DA1 187 FG86
Sidcup DA14 186 EV93
Dudset La, Houns. TW5 155 BU81
Dufferin Av, EC1 11 J4
Dufferin St, EC1 11 H4
Duffield Cl, Grays (Daniel Cl)
RM16 170 FY75
Grays (Davis Rd) RM16 170 FZ76
Harrow HA1 117 CF57
Duffield Dr, N15
off Copperfield Dr 122 DT56
Duffield La, Slou. (Stoke P.)
SL2 132 AT65
Duffield Pk, Slou. (Stoke P.)
SL2 132 AU69
Duffield Rd, Tad. KT20 233 CV124
Duffins Orchard, Cher. (Ott.)
KT16 211 BC108
Duff St, E14 14 A8
Dufour's Pl, W1 9 K8
Dugard Way, SE11 20 E7
Dugdale Hill La, Pot.B. EN6 63 CY33
Dugdales, Rick. (Crox.Grn)
WD3 74 BN42
Duggan Dr, Chis. BR7
off Wood Dr 184 EL93
Dugolly Av, Wem. HA9
off Chalkhill Rd 118 CP62
Duke Gdns, Ilf. IG6
off Duke Rd 125 ER56
Duke Humphrey Rd, SE3 164 EE81
Duke of Cambridge Cl, Twick.
TW2 177 CD86
Duke of Edinburgh Rd, Sutt.
SM1 200 DD103
Duke of Wellington Av,
SE18 165 EP76
Duke of Wellington Pl, SW1 18 F3
Duke of York Sq, SW3 18 D8
Duke of York St, SW1 19 K1
Duke Rd, W4 158 CR78
Ilford IG6 125 ER56
Dukes Av, N3 98 DB53
N10 121 DJ55
W4 158 CR78
Edgware HA8 96 CM51
Epping (They.B.) CM16 85 ES35
Grays RM17 170 GA75
Harrow HA1 117 CE56
Harrow (N.Har.) HA2 116 BZ58
Hounslow TW4 156 BY84
Kingston upon Thames
KT2 177 CJ91
New Malden KT3 199 CT97
Northolt UB5 136 BY66
Richmond TW10 177 CJ91
Dukes Cl, Ashf. TW15 175 BQ91

Dukes Cl, Epp. (N.Wld Bas.)
CM16 71 FB27
Gerrards Cross SL9 112 AX60
Hampton TW12 176 BZ92
Dukes Ct, E6 145 EN67
Woking GU21 227 AZ117
Dukes Dr, Slou. SL2 111 AM64
Dukes Gate, W4
off Acton La 158 CQ77
Dukes Grn Av, Felt. TW14 175 BU85
Dukes Head Yd, N6
off Highgate High St 121 DH60
Dukes Hill, Cat. (Wold.) CR3 237 DY120
Duke Shore Pl, E14 13 L10
Duke Shore Wf, E14 13 L10
Dukes Kiln Dr, Ger.Cr. SL9 112 AW60
Dukes La, W8 17 H3
Gerrards Cross SL9 112 AY59
Dukes Lo, Nthwd. HA6
off Eastbury Av 93 BS50
Duke's Meadows, W4
off Great Chertsey Rd 158 CQ82
Dukes Ms, N10 off Dukes Av 121 DH55
Duke's Ms, W1 8 F7
Dukes Orchard, Bex. DA5 187 FC88
Duke's Pas, E17 123 EC56
Dukes Pl, EC3 11 M8
Dukes Ride, Dor. (N.Holm.)
RH5 263 CK139
Gerrards Cross SL9 112 AY60
Uxbridge UB10 114 BL63
Dukes Rd, E6 145 EN67
W3 138 CN71
Duke's Rd, WC1 9 M2
Dukes Rd, Walt. KT12 214 BX106
Dukesthorpe Rd, SE26 183 DX91
Duke St, SW1 19 K1
W1 8 F7
Hoddesdon EN11 49 EA16
Richmond TW9 157 CK84
Sutton SM1 218 DD105
Watford WD17 76 BW41
Windsor SL4 151 AP80
Woking GU21 227 AZ117
Duke St Hill, SE1 21 K1
Dukes Valley, Ger.Cr. SL9 112 AV61
Dukes Way, Berk. HP4 38 AU17
Uxbridge UB8
off Waterloo Rd 134 BJ67
West Wickham BR4 204 EE104
Dukes Wd Av, Ger.Cr. SL9 112 AY60
Dukes Wd Dr, Ger.Cr. SL9 112 AW60
Duke's Yd, W1 8 F9
Dulas St, N4
off Everleigh St 121 DM60
Dulford St, W11 6 C9
Dulka Rd, SW11 180 DF85
Sch Dulverton Prim Sch,
SE9 off Dulverton Rd 185 ER89
Dulverton Rd, SE9 185 EQ89
Romford RM3 106 FK51
Ruislip HA4 115 BU60
South Croydon CR2 220 DW110
DULWICH, SE21 182 DS87
Sch Dulwich Coll, SE21
off College Rd 182 DS89
★ Dulwich Coll Picture Gall,
SE21 182 DS87
Sch Dulwich Coll Prep Sch,
SE21 off Alleyn Pk 182 DS90
Dulwich Common, SE21 182 DS88
SE22 182 DS88
Sch Dulwich Hamlet Jun Sch,
SE21 off Dulwich Village 182 DS86
Dulwich Lawn Cl, SE22
off Colwell Rd 182 DT85
Dulwich Oaks, The, SE21 182 DS90
Dulwich Rd, SE24 181 DN85
Dulwich Village, SE21 182 DS86
Sch Dulwich Village C of E
Inf Sch, SE21
off Dulwich Village 182 DS86
Dulwich Way, Rick.
(Crox.Grn) WD3 74 BN43
Dulwich Wd Av, SE19 182 DS91
Dulwich Wd Pk, SE19 182 DS91
Dumbarton Av, Wal.Cr. EN8 67 DX34
Dumbarton Rd, SW2 181 DL86
Dumbleton Cl, Kings.T. KT1
off Gloucester Rd 198 CP95
Dumbletons, The, Rick.
(Map.Cr.) WD3 91 BE49
Dumbreck Rd, SE9 165 EM84
Dumfries Cl, Wat. WD19 93 BT48
Dumont Rd, N16 122 DS62
Dumpton Pl, NW1
off Gloucester Av 140 DG66
Dumville Dr, Gdse. RH9 252 DV131
Dunally Pk, Shep. TW17 195 BR101
Dunbar Av, SW16 201 DN96
Beckenham BR3 203 DY98
Dagenham RM10 126 FA62
Dunbar Cl, Hayes UB4 135 BU71
Slough SL2 132 AU72
Dunbar Ct, Sutt. SM1 218 DD106
Walton-on-Thames KT12 196 BW103
Dunbar Gdns, Dag. RM10 126 FA64
Dunbar Rd, E7 144 EG65
N22 99 DN53
New Malden KT3 198 CQ98
Dunbar St, SE27 182 DQ90
Dunblane Cl, Edg. HA8
off Tayside Dr 96 CP47
Dunblane Rd, SE9 164 EL83
Dunboe Pl, Shep. TW17 195 BQ101
Dunboyne Rd, NW3 120 DF64
Dunbridge Ho, SW15
off Highcliffe Dr 179 CT86
Dunbridge St, E2 12 B3
Duncan Cl, Barn. EN5 80 DC42
Welwyn Garden City AL7 29 CY10
Duncan Dr, Guil. GU1 243 BA133
Duncan Gdns, Stai. TW18
off Burges Way 174 BG92
Duncan Gro, W3 138 CS72
Duncannon Cres, Wind. SL4 151 AK83
Duncannon St, WC2 9 N10
Duncan Rd, E8 142 DV67
Richmond TW9 158 CL84
Tadworth KT20 233 CY119
Duncan St, N1 4 E9
Duncan Ter, N1 4 E10
Duncan Way, Bushey WD23 76 BZ40
Dunch St, E1 12 D8
Duncombe Cl, Amer. HP6 55 AS38
Hertford SG14 32 DQ07
Duncombe Ct, Stai. TW18 173 BF94
Duncombe Hill, SE23 183 DY87
Sch Duncombe Prim Sch,
N19 off Sussex Way 121 DL60
Duncombe Rd, N19 121 DK60
Berkhamsted HP4 38 AS17
Hertford SG14 32 DQ08
Sch Duncombe Sch, Hert.
SG14 off Warren Pk Rd 32 DQ08
Duncrievie Rd, SE13 183 ED86
Duncroft, SE18 165 ES80
Windsor SL4 151 AM83
Duncroft Cl, Reig. RH2 249 CZ133
Dundalk Rd, SE4 163 DY83
Dundas Gdns, W.Mol. KT8 196 CB97
Dundas Ms, Enf. EN3 83 EA37
Dundas Rd, SE15 162 DW82
Dundee Rd, E13 144 EH68
SE25 202 DV99
Slough SL1 131 AM72
Dundee St, E1 22 C2
Dundee Way, Enf. EN3 83 DY41
Dundela Gdns, Wor.Pk. KT4 217 CV105
Dundonald Cl, E6
off Northumberland Rd 144 EL72
Sch Dundonald Prim Sch,
SW19
off Dundonald Rd 179 CZ94
Tra Dundonald Road 179 CZ94
Dundonald Rd, NW10 139 CX67
SW19 179 CY94
Dundrey Cres, Red. RH1 251 DL129
Dunedin Dr, Cat. CR3 252 DS125
Dunedin Ho, E16
off Manwood St 145 EM74
Dunedin Rd, E10 123 EB62
Ilford IG1 125 EQ60
Rainham RM13 147 FF69
Dunedin Way, Hayes UB4 136 BW70
Dunelm Gro, SE27 182 DQ91
Dunelm St, E1 12 G7
Dunfee Way, W.Byf. KT14 212 BL112
Dunfield Gdns, SE6 183 EB91
Dunfield Rd, SE6 183 EB92
Dunford Rd, N7 121 DM63
Dungarvan Av, SW15 159 CU84
Dungates La, Bet.
(Buckland) RH3 249 CU133
Dunheved Cl, Th.Hth. CR7 201 DN100
Dunheved Rd N, Th.Hth.
CR7 201 DN100
Dunheved Rd S, Th.Hth.
CR7 201 DN100
Dunheved Rd W, Th.Hth.
CR7 201 DN100
Dunhill Pt, SW15
off Dilton Gdns 179 CV88
Dunholme Grn, N9 100 DT48
Dunholme La, N9
off Dunholme Rd 100 DT48
Dunholme Rd, N9 100 DT48
Dunkeld Rd, SE25 202 DR98
Dagenham RM8 126 EV61
Dunkellin Gro, S.Ock. RM15
off Dunkellin Way 149 FU72
Dunkellin Way, S.Ock. RM15 149 FU72
Dunkery Rd, SE9 184 EK91
Dunkin Rd, Dart. DA1 168 FN84
Dunkirk Cl, Grav. DA12 191 GJ92
Dunkirks Ms, Hert. SG13
off Queens Rd 32 DR11
Dunkirk St, SE27
off Waring St 182 DQ91
Dunlace Rd, E5 122 DW63
Dunleary Cl, Houns. TW4 176 BZ87
Dunley Dr, Croy.
(New Adgtn) CR0 221 EB108
Dunlin Cl, Red. RH1 266 DE139
Dunlin Ho, W13 137 CF70
Dunlin Ri, Guil. GU4 243 BD132
Dunlin Rd, Hem.H. HP2 40 BL15
Dunloe Av, N17 122 DR55
Dunloe St, E2 5 N10
Dunlop Cl, Dart. DA1 168 FL83
Dunlop Pl, SE16 21 P6
Dunlop Rd, Til. RM18 171 GF81
Dunmail Dr, Pur. CR8 220 DS114
Dunmore Pt, E2 11 N2
Dunmore Rd, NW6 139 CY67
SW20 199 CW95
Dunmow Cl, Felt. TW13 176 BY91
Loughton IG10 84 EL44
Romford RM6 126 EW57
Dunmow Dr, Rain. RM13 147 FF67
Dunmow Ho, Dag. RM9 146 EV67
Dunmow Rd, E15 123 ED63
Dunmow Wk, N1 4 G7
Dunnage Cres, SE16 23 K7
Dunnets, Wok. (Knap.) GU21 226 AS117
Dunning Cl, S.Ock. RM15 149 FU72
Dunningford Cl, Horn.
RM12 127 FF64
Sch Dunningford Prim Sch,
Horn. RM12
off Upper Rainham Rd 127 FF63
Dunn Mead, NW9
off Field Mead 97 CT52
Dunnock Cl, N9 101 DX46
Borehamwood WD6 78 CN42
Dunnock Rd, E6 144 EL72
Dunns Pas, WC1 9 P7
Dunn St, E8 5 N1
Dunny La, Kings L.
(Chipper.) WD4 57 BE32
Dunnymans Rd, Bans. SM7 233 CZ115
Dunollie Pl, NW5
off Dunollie Rd 121 DJ64
Dunollie Rd, NW5 121 DJ64
Dunoon Rd, SE23 182 DW87
Dunottar Cl, Red. RH1 266 DD136
Sch Dunottar Sch, Reig. RH2
off High Trees Rd 266 DD135
Dunraven Av, Red. RH1 267 DH141
Dunraven Dr, Enf. EN2 81 DN40
Dunraven Rd, W12 139 CU74
Sch Dunraven Sch, Lwr Sch,
SW16 off Mount Nod Rd 181 DM90
Upr Sch, SW16
off Leigham Ct Rd 181 DM90
Dunraven St, W1 8 D9
Dunsany Rd, W14 16 A6
Dunsborough Pk, Wok.
(Ripley) GU23 228 BJ120
Dunsbury Cl, Sutt. SM2
off Nettlecombe Cl 218 DB109
Dunsdon Av, Guil. GU2 258 AV135
Dunsfold Ri, Couls. CR5 219 DK113
Dunsfold Way, Croy.
(New Adgtn) CR0 221 EB108
Dunsford Way, SW15
off Dover Pk Dr 179 CV86
Dunsmore Cl, Bushey WD23 77 CD44
Hayes UB4 136 BX70
Dunsmore Rd, Walt. KT12 195 BV100
Dunsmore Way, Bushey
WD23 77 CD44
Dunsmure Rd, N16 122 DS60
Dunspring La, Ilf. IG5 103 EP54
Dunstable Cl, Rom. RM3
off Dunstable Rd 106 FK51
Dunstable Ms, W1 8 F5
Dunstable Rd, Rich. TW9 158 CL84
Romford RM3 106 FK51
West Molesey KT8 196 BZ98
Dunstall Grn, Wok.
(Chobham) GU24 210 AW109
Dunstall Rd, SW20 179 CV93
Dunstalls, Harl. CM19 51 EN19
Dunstall Way, W.Mol. KT8 196 CB97
Dunstan Cl, N2
off Thomas More Way 120 DC55
Dunstan Rd, NW11 119 CZ60
Coulsdon CR5 235 DK117
Dunstans Gro, SE22 182 DV86
Dunstans Rd, SE22 182 DU87
Dunster Av, Mord. SM4 199 CX102
Dunster Cl, Barn. EN5 79 CX42
Romford RM5 105 FC54
Uxbridge (Hare.) UB9 92 BH53
Dunster Ct, EC3 11 L9
Borehamwood WD6
off Kensington Way 78 CR41
Dunster Cres, Horn. RM11 128 FN61
Dunster Dr, NW9 118 CQ60
Dunster Gdns, NW6 139 CZ66
Slough SL1 off Avebury 131 AN73
Dunsters Mead, Welw.G.C.
AL7 30 DA11
Dunsterville Way, SE1 21 K4
Dunster Way, Har. HA2 116 BY62
Wallington SM6
off Helios Rd 200 DG102
Dunston Rd, E8 5 N8
SW11 160 DG82
Dunston St, E8 5 N7
Dunton Cl, Surb. KT6 198 CL102
DUNTON GREEN, Sev.
TN13 241 FC119
⇌ Dunton Green 241 FF119
Sch Dunton Grn Prim Sch, Sev.
TN13 off London Rd 241 FE120
Dunton Rd, E10 123 EB59
SE1 21 N9
Romford RM1 127 FE56
Duntshill Rd, SW18 180 DB88
Dunvegan Cl, W.Mol. KT8 196 CB98
Dunvegan Rd, SE9 165 EM84
Dunwich Rd, Bexh. DA7 166 EZ81
Dunworth Ms, W11 6 E7
Duplex Ride, SW1 18 D4
Dupont Rd, SW20 199 CX96
Duppas Av, Croy. CR0
off Violet La 219 DP105
Duppas Cl, Shep. TW17 195 BR99
Duppas Hill La, Croy. CR0
off Duppas Hill Rd 219 DP105
Duppas Hill Rd, Croy. CR0 219 DP105
Duppas Hill Ter, Croy. CR0 201 DP104
Sch Duppas Jun Sch, Croy.
CR0 off Goodwin Rd 219 DP106
Duppas Rd, Croy. CR0 201 DN104
Dupre Cl, Grays (Chaff.Hun.)
RM16 170 FY76
Slough SL1 151 AL75
Dupre Cres, Beac. HP9 89 AP54
Dupree Rd, SE7 25 N9
Du Pre Wk, H.Wyc. (Woob.Grn)
HP10 off Stratford Dr 110 AD59
Dura Den Cl, Beck. BR3 183 EB94
Durand Cl, Cars. SM5 200 DF102
Durand Gdns, SW9 161 DM81
Sch Durand Prim Sch, SW9
off Hackford Rd 161 DM81
Annexe, SW9
off Cowley Rd 161 DN81
Durands Wk, SE16 23 K3
Durand Way, NW10 138 CQ66
Durant Rd, Swan. BR8 187 FG93
Durants Pk Av, Enf. EN3 83 DX42
Durants Rd, Enf. EN3 82 DW42
Sch Durants Sch, Enf. EN3
off Pitfield Way 82 DW39
Durant St, E2 12 A1
Durban Gdns, Dag. RM10 147 FC66
Durban Rd, E15 14 G1
E17 101 DZ53
N17 100 DS51
SE27 182 DQ91
Beckenham BR3 203 DZ96
Ilford IG2 125 ES60
Durban Rd E, Wat. WD18 75 BU42
Durban Rd W, Wat. WD18 75 BU42
Durbin Rd, Chess. KT9 216 CL105
Sch Durdans Pk Prim Sch,
Sthl. UB1
off King Georges Dr 136 BZ71
Durdans Rd, Sthl. UB1 136 BZ72
Durell Gdns, Dag. RM9 126 EX64
Durell Rd, Dag. RM9 126 EX64
Durfold Dr, Reig. RH2 250 DC134
Durford Cres, SW15 179 CU88
Durham Av, Brom. BR2 204 EF98
Hounslow TW5 156 BZ78
Romford RM2 128 FJ56
Slough SL1 131 AN72
Woodford Green IG8 102 EK50
Durham Cl, SW20
off Durham Rd 199 CV96
Guildford GU2 242 AT132
Sawbridgeworth CM21 36 EW06
Ware (Stans.Abb.) SG12 33 EB10
Durham Hill, Brom. BR1 184 EF91
Durham Ho St, WC2 9 P10
Durham Pl, SW3 18 C10
Ilford IG1 off Eton Rd 125 EQ63
Durham Ri, SE18 165 EQ78
Durham Rd, E12 124 EK63
E16 15 H4
N2 120 DE55
N7 121 DM61
N9 100 DU47
SW20 199 CV95
W5 157 CK76
Borehamwood WD6 78 CQ41
Bromley BR2 204 EF97
Dagenham RM10 127 FC64
Feltham TW14 176 BW87
Harrow HA1 116 CB57
Sidcup DA14 186 EV92
Durham Row, E1 13 H6
Durham St, SE11 20 A10
Durham Ter, W2 7 J7
Durham Wf, Brent. TW8
off London Rd 157 CJ80
Durham Yd, E2 12 C1
Duriun Way, Erith DA8 167 FH80
Durleston Pk Dr, Lthd.
(Bkhm) KT23 246 CC125
Durley Av, Pnr. HA5 116 BY59
Durley Gdns, Orp. BR6 224 EV105
Durley Rd, N16 122 DS59
Durlston Rd, E5 122 DU61
Kingston upon Thames
KT2 178 CL93
Durndale La, Grav. (Nthflt)
DA11 191 GF91
Durnell Way, Loug. IG10 85 EN41
Durnford St, N15 122 DS57
SE10 off Greenwich Ch St 163 EC79
Durning Rd, SE19 182 DR92
Durnsford Av, SW19 180 DA89
Durnsford Rd, N11 99 DK53
SW19 180 DA89
Durrant Path, Chesh. HP5 54 AN27
Durrants Cl, Rain. RM13 148 FJ68
Durrants Dr, Rick. (Crox.Grn)
WD3 75 BQ42
Durrants Hill Rd, Hem.H.
HP3 40 BK23
Durrants La, Berk. HP4 38 AT18
Durrants Rd, Berk. HP4 38 AT18
Durrant Way, Orp. BR6 223 ER106
Swanscombe DA10 190 FY87
Durrell Rd, SW6 159 CZ81
Durrell Way, Shep. TW17 195 BR100
Durrington Av, SW20 199 CW95
Durrington Pk Rd, SW20 179 CW94
Durrington Rd, E5 123 DY63
Durrington Twr, SW8
off Westbury St 161 DJ82
Dursley Cl, SE3 164 EJ82
Dursley Gdns, SE3 164 EK81
Dursley Rd, SE3 164 EJ82
Sch Durston Ho Sch, W5
off Castlebar Rd 137 CK72
Durward St, E1 12 C5
Durweston Ms, W1 8 D5
Durweston St, W1 8 D5
Dury Falls Cl, Horn. RM11 128 FM60
Dury Rd, Barn. EN5 79 CZ39
Dutch Barn Cl, Stai.
(Stanw.) TW19 174 BK86
Dutch Elm Av, Wind. SL4 152 AT80
Dutch Gdns, Kings.T. KT2
off Windmill Ri 178 CP93
Dutch Yd, SW18
off Wandsworth High St 180 DA85
Dutton St, SE10 163 EC81
Dutton Way, Iver SL0 133 BE72
Duxberry Cl, Brom. BR2
off Southborough La 204 EL99
Duxford Cl, Horn. RM12 147 FH65
Duxford Ho, SE2
off Wolvercote Rd 166 EX75
Duxhurst La, Reig. RH2 266 DB144
Duxons Turn, Hem.H. HP2
off Maylands Av 41 BP19
Dwight Ct, SW6
off Burlington Rd 159 CY82
Dwight Rd, Wat. WD18 93 BR45
Sch Dycorts Sch, Rom.
RM3 off Settle Rd 106 FN49
Dye Ho La, E3 143 EA67
Dyer's Bldgs, EC1 10 C6
Dyers Fld, Horl. (Smallfield)
RH6 269 DP148
Dyers Hall Rd, E11 124 EE60
Dyers La, SW15 159 CV84
Dyers Way, Rom. RM3 105 FH52
Dyke Dr, Orp. BR5 206 EW102
Dykes Path, Wok. GU21
off Bentham Av 227 BC115
Dykes Way, Brom. BR2 204 EF97
Dykewood Cl, Bex. DA5 187 FE90
Dylan Cl, Borwd. (Elstree)
WD6 off Coates Rd 95 CK45
Dylan Rd, SE24 161 DP84
Belvedere DA17 166 FA76
Dylways, SE5 162 DR84
Dymchurch Cl, Ilf. IG5 103 EN54
Orpington BR6 223 ES105
Dymes Path, SW19
off Queensmere Rd 179 CX89
Dymock St, SW6 160 DB83
Dymoke Grn, St.Alb. AL4 43 CG16
Dymoke Rd, Horn. RM11 127 FF59
Dymokes Way, Hodd. EN11 33 EA14
Dymond Est, SW17
off Glenburnie Rd 180 DE90
Dyneley Rd, SE12 184 EJ91
Dyne Rd, NW6 139 CZ66
Dynevor Rd, N16 122 DS62
Richmond TW10 178 CL85
Dynham Rd, NW6 140 DA66
Dyott St, WC1 9 N7
Dyrham La, Barn. EN5 79 CU36
Dysart Av, Kings.T. KT2 177 CJ92
Sch Dysart Sch, Surb. KT6
off Ewell Rd 198 CM101
Dysart St, EC2 11 L4
Dyson Cl, Wind. SL4 151 AP83
Dyson Rd, E11 124 EE58
E15 144 EF65
Dysons Cl, Wal.Cr. EN8 67 DX33
Dysons Rd, N18 100 DV50

E

Eade Rd, N4 122 DQ59
Eagans Cl, N2 off Market Pl 120 DE55
Eagle Av, Rom. RM6 126 EY58
Eagle Cl, SE16 22 E10
Amersham HP6 72 AT37
Enfield EN3 82 DW42
Hornchurch RM12 147 FH65
Wallington SM6 219 DL107
Waltham Abbey EN9 68 EG34
Eagle Ct, EC1 10 E5
Hertford SG13 32 DV08
Eagle Dr, NW9 96 CS54
Eagle Hts, SW11
off Bramlands Cl 160 DE83
Eagle Hill, SE19 182 DR93
Eagle La, E11 124 EG56
Eagle Ms, N1 5 L4
Eagle Pl, SW1 9 K10
SW7 17 M9
Eagle Rd, Guil. GU1 258 AX135
Wembley HA0 137 CK66
Eagles Dr, West. (Tats.)
TN16 238 EK118
Eaglesfield Rd, SE18 165 EP80
Sch Eaglesfield Sec Sch,
SE18 off Red Lion La 165 EN80
Eagles Rd, Green. DA9 169 FV84
Eagle St, WC1 10 A6
Eagle Ter, Wdf.Grn. IG8 102 EH52
Eagle Trd Est, Mitch. CR4
off Willow La 200 DF100
Eagle Way, Brwd. CM13 107 FV51
Gravesend (Nthflt) DA11 190 GA85
Hatfield AL10 45 CU20
Eagle Wf, E14
off Broomfield St 143 EB71
Eagle Wf Rd, N1 5 H9
Sch Ealdham Prim Sch,
SE9 off Ealdham Sq 164 EJ84
Ealdham Sq, SE9 164 EJ84
EALING, W5 137 CJ73
Coll Ealing & W London Coll,
W5 off Ealing Grn 137 CK74
⇌ Ealing Broadway 137 CK73
⊖ Ealing Broadway 137 CK73
Ealing Bdy Shop Cen, W5 137 CK73
Ealing Cl, Borwd. WD6 78 CR39
Sch Ealing Coll Upr Sch,
W13 off The Avenue 137 CH72
★ Ealing Common, W5 138 CL74
⊖ Ealing Common 138 CM74
Sch Ealing Dean Anglo-French
Sch, W5 off Mattock La 137 CK73
Ealing Downs Ct, Grnf.
UB6 off Perivale La 137 CG69
Coll Ealing Ed Cen (Elthorne
Complex - Adult Ed),
W7 off Boston Rd 157 CF76
Ealing Grn, W5 137 CK74
H Ealing Hosp, Sthl. UB1 157 CD75
Ealing Pk Gdns, W5 157 CJ77
Ealing Rd, Brent. TW8 157 CK78
Northolt UB5 136 CA66
Wembley HA0 137 CK67
Coll Ealing Tutorial Coll, W5
off New Bdy 137 CJ73
Ealing Village, W5 138 CL72
Eamont Cl, Ruis. HA4
off Allonby Dr 115 BP59
Eamont St, NW8 140 DE68
Eardemont Cl, Dart. DA1 167 FF84
Eardley Cres, SW5 17 H10
Eardley Pt, SE18
off Wilmount St 165 EP77
Sch Eardley Prim Sch,
SW16 off Cunliffe St 181 DJ93
Eardley Rd, SW16 181 DJ92
Belvedere DA17 166 FA78
Sevenoaks TN13 257 FH124
Earl Cl, N11 99 DH50
Earldom Rd, SW15 159 CW84
Earle Gdns, Kings.T. KT2 178 CL93
Earleswood, Cob. KT11 214 BX112
Earlham Gro, E7 124 EF64
N22 99 DM52
Sch Earlham Prim Sch, E7
off Earlham Gro 124 EF64
N22 off Earlham Gro 99 DN52
Earlham St, WC2 9 M8
Earl Ri, SE18 165 ER77
Earl Rd, SW14 off Elm Rd 158 CQ84
Gravesend (Nthflt) DA11 190 GE89
Earlsbrook Rd, Red. RH1 266 DF136
EARLS COURT, SW5 16 F9
⊖ Earls Court 17 H8
★ Earls Court Exhib Cen,
SW5 16 G9
Earls Ct Gdns, SW5 17 J8
Earls Ct Rd, SW5 17 H7
W8 17 H7
Earls Ct Sq, SW5 17 J9
Earls Cres, Har. HA1 117 CE56
Earlsdown Ho, Bark. IG11
off Wheelers Cross 145 ER68
Earlsferry Way, N1 141 DM66
EARLSFIELD, SW18 180 DC88
⇌ Earlsfield 180 DC88
Earlsfield, Maid. SL6 150 AC77
Earlsfield Ho, Kings.T. KT2
off Kingsgate Rd 198 CL95
Sch Earlsfield Prim Sch,
SW18
off Tranmere Rd 180 DC89
Earlsfield Rd, SW18 180 DC88
Earlshall Rd, SE9 165 EM84
Earls La, Pot.B. EN6 62 CS32
Slough SL1 131 AL74
Earlsmead, Har. HA2 116 BZ63
Sch Earlsmead First & Mid
Sch, Har. HA2
off Arundel Dr 116 BZ63
Sch Earlsmead Prim Sch,
N15 off Broad La 122 DT56
Earlsmead Rd, N15 122 DT57
NW10 139 CW68
Earl's Path, Loug. IG10 84 EJ40
Earls Ter, W8 16 F6
Earlsthorpe Ms, SW12 180 DG86
Earlsthorpe Rd, SE26 183 DX91
Earlstoke St, EC1 10 E1
Earlston Gro, E9 142 DV67
Earl St, EC2 11 L5
Watford WD17 76 BW41
Earls Wk, W8 16 G6
Dagenham RM8 126 EV63
Earls Way, Orp. BR6
off Station Rd 205 ET103
EARLSWOOD, Red. RH1 266 DF136
⇌ Earlswood 266 DF136
Earlswood Av, Th.Hth. CR7 201 DN99
Earlswood Gdns, Ilf. IG5 125 EN55
Sch Earlswood Inf & Nurs
Sch, Red. RH1
off St. John's Rd 266 DG135
Earlswood Rd, Red. RH1 266 DF135
Earlswood St, SE10 25 H10
Early Ms, NW1
off Arlington Rd 141 DH67
Earnshaw St, WC2 9 M7
Earsby St, W14 16 D7
Easby Cres, Mord. SM4 200 DB100
Easebourne Rd, Dag. RM8 126 EW64
Easedale Dr, Horn. RM12 127 FG64
Easedale Ho, Islw. TW7
off Summerwood Rd 177 CF85
Eashing Pt, SW15
off Wanborough Dr 179 CV88
Easington Pl, Guil. GU1
off Maori Rd 259 AZ135
Easington Way, S.Ock.
RM15 149 FU71
Easley's Ms, W1 8 F7
EAST ACTON, W3 138 CR74
⊖ East Acton 139 CT72
East Acton La, W3 138 CS73
Sch East Acton Prim Sch,
W3 off East Acton La 138 CS73
East Arbour St, E1 12 G7
East Av, E12 144 EL66
E17 123 EB56
Hayes UB3 155 BT75
Southall UB1 136 BZ73
Wallington SM6 219 DM106
Walton-on-Thames
(Whiteley Vil.) KT12
off Octagon Rd 213 BT110
East Bk, N16 122 DS59
Eastbank Rd, Hmptn.
(Hmptn H.) TW12 176 CC92
EAST BARNET, Barn. EN4 80 DE44
East Barnet Rd, Barn. EN4 80 DE44
Sch East Barnet Sch, Barn.
EN4 off Chestnut Gro 80 DF44

⊖ London Underground station · DLR Docklands Light Railway station · Tra Tramlink station · Riv Pedestrian ferry landing stage

Sch East Barnet Sch, 5th & 6th Form Cen, Barn. EN4 off Westbrook Cres 80 DD41
EAST BEDFONT, Felt. TW14 175 BS88
Coll East Berkshire Coll,
Langley Campus, Slou. SL3 off Station Rd 153 BA76
Windsor Campus, Wind. SL4 off Claremont Rd 151 AQ82
Eastbourne Av, W3 138 CR72
Eastbourne Gdns, SW14 158 CQ83
Eastbourne Ms, W2 7 M7
Eastbourne Rd, E6 145 EN69
E15 144 EE67
N15 122 DS58
SW17 180 DG93
W4 158 CQ79
Brentford TW8 157 CJ78
Feltham TW13 176 BX89
Godstone RH9 252 DW132
Slough SL1 131 AM72
Eastbourne Ter, W2 7 M7
Eastbournia Av, N9 100 DV48
Eastbridge, Slou. SL2 off Victoria Rd 132 AV74
Eastbrook Av, N9 100 DW45
Dagenham RM10 127 FC63
Eastbrook Cl, Wok. GU21 227 BA116
Sch Eastbrook Comp Sch, Dag. RM10 off Dagenham Rd 127 FC63
Eastbrook Dr, Rom. RM7 127 FE62
Sch Eastbrook JMI Sch, Hem.H. HP2 off St. Agnells La 40 BN15
Eastbrook Rd, SE3 164 EH80
Waltham Abbey EN9 68 EE33
Eastbrook Way, Hem.H. HP2 40 BL20
EAST BURNHAM, Slou. SL2 131 AN67
East Burnham La, Slou. (Farn.Royal) SL2 131 AN67
East Burrowfield, Welw.G.C. AL7 29 CX11
EASTBURY, Nthwd. HA6 93 BS49
Eastbury Av, Bark. IG11 145 ES67
Enfield EN1 82 DS39
Northwood HA6 93 BS50
Sch Eastbury Comp Sch,
Lwr Sch, Bark. IG11 off Rosslyn Rd 145 ES65
Upr Sch, Bark. IG11 off Dawson Av 145 ET66
Eastbury Ct, Bark. IG11 145 ES67
St. Albans AL1 43 CF19
Sch Eastbury Fm JMI Sch, Nthwd. HA6 off Bishops Av 93 BT49
Eastbury Gro, W4 158 CS78
★ Eastbury Ho, Bark. IG11 145 ET67
Sch Eastbury Inf Sch, Bark. IG11 off Dawson Av 145 ET66
Eastbury Pl, Nthwd. HA6 off Eastbury Av 93 BT50
Eastbury Rd, E6 145 EN70
Kingston upon Thames KT2 178 CL94
Northwood HA6 93 BS51
Orpington BR5 205 ER100
Romford RM7 127 FD58
Watford WD19 93 BV45
Eastbury Sq, Bark. IG11 145 ET67
Eastbury Ter, E1 12 G4
Eastcastle St, W1 9 J7
Eastcheap, EC3 11 K9
East Churchfield Rd, W3 138 CR74
Eastchurch Rd, Houns. (Hthrw Air.) TW6 155 BS82
EAST CLANDON, Guil. GU4 244 BL131
East Cl, W5 138 CN70
Barnet EN4 80 DG42
Greenford UB6 136 CC68
Rainham RM13 147 FH70
St. Albans AL2 60 CB25
Eastcombe Av, SE7 164 EH79
East Common, Ger.Cr. SL9 112 AY58
EASTCOTE, Pnr. HA5 116 BW58
⊖ Eastcote 116 BW59
Eastcote, Orp. BR6 205 ET102
Eastcote Av, Grnf. UB6 117 CG64
Harrow HA2 116 CB61
West Molesey KT8 196 BZ99
Eastcote La, Har. HA2 116 CA62
Northolt UB5 136 CA66
Eastcote La N, Nthlt. UB5 136 BZ65
Eastcote Pl, Pnr. HA5 115 BV58
Sch Eastcote Prim Sch, Well. DA16 off Eastcote Rd 165 ER83
Eastcote Rd, Har. HA2 116 CC62
Pinner HA5 116 BX57
Pinner (Eastcote Vill.) HA5 115 BU58
Ruislip HA4 115 BS59
Welling DA16 165 ER82
Eastcote St, SW9 161 DM82
Eastcote Vw, Pnr. HA5 116 BW56
EASTCOTE VILLAGE, Pnr. HA5 115 BV57
Eastcourt, Sun. TW16 196 BW96
East Ct, Wem. HA0 117 CJ61
Sch Eastcourt Sch, Ilf. IG3 off Eastwood Rd 126 EU60
East Cres, N11 98 DF49
Enfield EN1 82 DT43
Windsor SL4 151 AM81
East Cres Rd, Grav. DA12 191 GJ86
Eastcroft, Slou. SL2 131 AP70
Eastcroft Rd, Epsom KT19 216 CS108
East Cross Cen, E15 143 EA65
East Cross Route, E3 143 DZ66
E9 143 DZ66
⇌ East Croydon 202 DR103
Tra East Croydon 202 DR103
Eastdean Av, Epsom KT18 216 CP113
East Dene Dr, Rom. (Harold Hill) RM3 106 FK50
Eastdown Pk, SE13 163 ED84
East Dr, Cars. SM5 218 DE109
Northwood HA6 93 BS47
Orpington BR5 206 EV100
St. Albans (Oakl.) AL4 44 CL19
Sawbridgeworth CM21 36 EY06
Slough (Stoke P.) SL2 132 AS69
Virginia Water GU25 192 AU101
Watford WD25 75 BV35
East Duck Lees La, Enf. EN3 83 DY42
EAST DULWICH, SE22 182 DU86
⇌ East Dulwich 162 DS84
East Dulwich Gro, SE22 182 DS86
East Dulwich Rd, SE15 162 DT84
SE22 162 DT84
Sch East End Comm Sch, E1 11 P7
East End Rd, N2 120 DC55
East End Rd, N3 98 DA54
East End Way, Pnr. HA5 116 BY55
East Entrance, Dag. RM10 147 FB68
Eastergate, Beac. HP9 88 AJ51
Eastern Av, E11 124 EJ58
Chertsey KT16 194 BG97
Grays (W.Thur.) RM20 169 FT78
Ilford IG2, IG4 124 EL58
Pinner HA5 116 BX59
Romford RM6 126 EW56
South Ockendon (Aveley) RM15 148 FQ74
Waltham Cross EN8 67 DY33
Eastern Av E, Rom. RM1, RM2, RM3 127 FD55
Eastern Av W, Rom. RM1, RM5, RM6, RM7 126 EY56
Eastern Dr, B.End SL8 110 AC59
Eastern Gateway, E16 144 EJ73
Eastern Ind Est, Erith DA18 166 FA75
Eastern Pathway, Horn. RM12 148 FJ67
Eastern Perimeter Rd, Houns. (Hthrw Air.) TW6 155 BT83
Eastern Quay Apartments, E16 off Rayleigh Rd 144 EH74
Eastern Rd, E13 144 EH68
E17 123 EC57
N2 120 DF55
N22 99 DL53
SE4 163 EA84
Grays RM17 170 GD77
Romford RM1 127 FE57
Eastern Vw, West. (Bigg.H.) TN16 238 EJ117
Easternville Gdns, Ilf. IG2 125 EQ58
Eastern Way, SE2 146 EX74
SE28 166 EU75
Belvedere DA17 167 FB75
Erith DA18 146 EX74
Grays RM17 170 GA79
EAST EWELL, Sutt. SM2 217 CX110
East Ferry Rd, E14 24 B7
Eastfield Av, Wat. WD24 76 BX39
Eastfield Cl, Slou. SL1 off St. Laurence Way 152 AU76
Eastfield Cotts, Hayes UB3 155 BS78
Eastfield Ct, St.Alb. AL4 off Southfield Way 43 CK17
Eastfield Gdns, Dag. RM10 126 FA63
Eastfield Par, Pot.B. EN6 64 DD32
Sch Eastfield Prim Sch, Enf. EN3 off Eastfield Rd 83 DX38
Eastfield Rd, E17 123 EA56
N8 121 DL55
Brentwood CM14 108 FX47
Dagenham RM9, RM10 126 FA63
Enfield EN3 83 DX38
Redhill RH1 267 DJ135
Slough (Burn.) SL1 130 AG71
Waltham Cross EN8 67 DY32
Eastfields, Pnr. HA5 116 BW57
Eastfields Rd, W3 138 CQ71
Mitcham CR4 200 DG96
Eastfield St, E14 13 K6
Eastfileds Av, SW18 off Point Pleasant 160 DA84
EAST FINCHLEY, N2 120 DD56
⊖ East Finchley 120 DE56
East Flint, Hem.H. HP1 39 BF19
East Gdns, SW17 180 DE93
Woking GU22 227 BC117
Eastgate, Bans. SM7 217 CY114
East Gate, Harl. CM20 35 EQ14
Eastgate Cl, SE28 146 EX72
Eastgate Gdns, Guil. GU1 258 AY135
Eastglade, Nthwd. HA6 93 BS50
Pinner HA5 116 BY55
East Gorse, Croy. CR0 221 DY112
East Grn, Hem.H. HP3 58 BM25
East Hall La, Rain. (Wenn.) RM13 148 FK72
East Hall Rd, Orp. BR5 206 EY101
EAST HAM, E6 144 EL68
⊖ East Ham 144 EL66
Eastham Cl, Barn. EN5 79 CY43
Eastham Cres, Brwd. CM13 109 GA49
East Ham Ind Est, E6 144 EL70
East Ham Manor Way, E6 145 EN72
H East Ham Mem Hosp, E7 144 EK66
East Ham Shop Hall, E6 off Myrtle Rd 144 EL67
East Harding St, EC4 10 D7
East Heath Rd, NW3 120 DD62
East Hill, SW18 180 DB85
Dartford DA1 188 FM87
Dartford (S.Darenth) DA4 208 FQ95
Oxted RH8 254 EE129
South Croydon CR2 220 DS110
Wembley HA9 118 CN61
Westerham (Bigg.H.) TN16 238 EH118
Woking GU22 227 BC116
East Hill Dr, Dart. DA1 188 FM87
East Hill Rd, Oxt. RH8 254 EE129
Eastholm, NW11 120 DB56
East Holme, Erith DA8 167 FD81
Eastholme, Hayes UB3 135 BU74
EAST HORSLEY, Lthd. KT24 245 BS127
DLR East India 14 F9
East India Dock Rd, E14 13 M8
East India Way, Croy. CR0 202 DT102
East Kent Av, Grav. (Nthflt) DA11 190 GC86
Eastlake Rd, SE5 161 DP82
Eastlands Cl, Oxt. RH8 off Eastlands Way 253 ED127
Eastlands Cres, SE21 182 DT86
Eastlands Way, Oxt. RH8 253 ED127
East La, SE16 22 A4
Abbots Langley WD5 59 BU29
Dartford (S.Darenth) DA4 209 FR96
Kingston upon Thames KT1 off High St 197 CK97
Leatherhead (W.Hors.) KT24 245 BQ125
Wembley HA0, HA9 117 CK62
Eastlea Av, Wat. WD25 76 BY37
Sch Eastlea Comm Sch, E16 15 H3
Eastlea Ms, E16 15 H4
Eastleigh Av, Har. HA2 116 CB61
Eastleigh Cl, NW2 118 CS62
Sutton SM2 218 DB108
Eastleigh Rd, E17 101 DZ54
Bexleyheath DA7 167 FC82
Hounslow (Hthrw Air.) TW6 off Cranford La 155 BT83
Eastleigh Wk, SW15 179 CU87
Eastleigh Way, Felt. TW14 175 BU88
East Lo La, Enf. EN2 81 DK36
H Eastman Dental Hosp, WC1 10 A2
Eastman Rd, W3 138 CR74
Eastman Way, Hem.H. HP2 40 BN17
East Mascalls, SE7 off Mascalls Rd 164 EJ79
East Mead, Ruis. HA4 116 BX62
Welwyn Garden City AL7 30 DB12
Eastmead, Wok. GU21 226 AV117
Eastmead Av, Grnf. UB6 136 CB69
Eastmead Cl, Brom. BR1 204 EL96
East Meads, Guil. GU2 258 AT135
Eastmearn Rd, SE21 182 DQ89
East Mill, Grav. DA11 191 GF86
East Milton Rd, Grav. DA12 191 GK87
East Mimms, Hem.H. HP2 40 BL19
EAST MOLESEY, KT8 197 CD98
Eastmont Rd, Esher KT10 197 CE103
Eastmoor Pl, SE7 off Eastmoor St 164 EK76
Eastmoor St, SE7 164 EK76
East Mt St, E1 12 D5
Eastney Rd, Croy. CR0 201 DP102
Eastney St, SE10 24 E10
Eastnor, Hem.H. (Bov.) HP3 57 BA28
Eastnor Cl, Reig. RH2 265 CZ137
Eastnor Rd, SE9 185 EQ88
Reigate RH2 266 DA136
Easton Gdns, Borwd. WD6 78 CR42
Easton St, WC1 10 C2
Eastor, Welw.G.C. AL7 30 DA06
East Pk, Harl. CM17 36 EV12
Sawbridgeworth CM21 36 EY06
East Pk Cl, Rom. RM6 126 EX57
East Parkside, SE10 25 J4
Warlingham CR6 237 EA116
East Pas, EC1 10 F5
East Pier, E1 22 C2
East Pl, SE27 off Pilgrim Hill 182 DQ91
East Poultry Av, EC1 10 E6
⊖ East Putney 179 CY85
East Ramp, Houns. (Hthrw Air.) TW6 155 BP81
East Ridgeway, Pot.B. (Cuffley) EN6 65 DK29
East Rd, E15 144 EG67
N1 11 J2
SW19 180 DC93
Barnet EN4 98 DG46
Edgware HA8 96 CP53
Enfield EN3 82 DW38
Feltham TW14 175 BR87
Harlow CM20 36 EV11
Kingston upon Thames KT2 198 CL95
Reigate RH2 249 CZ133
Romford (Chad.Hth) RM6 126 EY57
Romford (Rush Grn) RM7 127 FD59
Welling DA16 166 EV82
West Drayton UB7 154 BM77
Weybridge KT13 213 BR108
East Rochester Way, SE9 165 ES84
Bexley DA5 186 EX86
Sidcup DA15 165 ES84
East Row, E11 124 EG58
W10 6 C4
Eastry Av, Brom. BR2 204 EF100
Eastry Rd, Erith DA8 166 FA80
East Shalford La, Guil. GU4 258 AY139
EAST SHEEN, SW14 158 CR84
East Sheen Av, SW14 158 CR84
Sch East Sheen Prim Sch, SW14 off Upper Richmond Rd W 158 CS84
Eastside Rd, NW11 119 CZ56
East Smithfield, E1 11 P10
East St, SE17 21 H9
Barking IG11 145 EQ66
Bexleyheath DA7 166 FA84
Brentford TW8 157 CJ80
Bromley BR1 204 EG96
Chertsey KT16 194 BG101
Chesham HP5 54 AP32
Epsom KT17 216 CS113
Grays RM17 170 GC79
Grays (S.Stfd) RM20 170 FY79
Hemel Hempstead HP2 40 BK20
Leatherhead (Bkhm) KT23 246 CB125
Ware SG12 33 DX06
Coll East Surrey Coll,
Gatton Pt, Red. RH1 off Claremont Rd 250 DG131
Gatton Pt S, Red. RH1 off College Cres 250 DG130
East Surrey Gro, SE15 162 DT80
H East Surrey Hosp, Red. RH1 266 DG137
★ East Surrey Mus, Cat. CR3 236 DU124
East Tenter St, E1 11 P8
East Ter, Grav. DA12 191 GJ86
East Thurrock Rd, Grays RM17 170 GB79
East Twrs, Pnr. HA5 116 BX57
East Vw, E4 101 EC50
Barnet EN5 79 CZ41
Hatfield AL9 46 DF17
Eastview Av, SE18 165 ES80
Eastville Av, NW11 119 CZ58
East Wk, Barn. EN4 98 DG45
Harlow CM20 35 ER14
Hayes UB3 135 BU74
Reigate RH2 250 DB134
Eastway, E9 143 DZ65
East Way, E11 124 EH57
Beaconsfield HP9 88 AG54
Bromley BR2 204 EG101
Croydon CR0 203 DY103
Eastway, Epsom KT19 216 CQ112
Gatwick RH6 269 DH152
East Way, Guil. GU2 242 AT134
Hayes UB3 135 BU74
Eastway, Mord. SM4 199 CX99
East Way, Ruis. HA4 115 BU60
Eastway, Wall. SM6 219 DJ105
Eastway Commercial Cen, E9 123 EA64
Eastway Cres, Har. HA2 off Eliot Dr 116 CB61
Eastwell Cl, Beck. BR3 203 DY95
EASTWICK, Harl. CM20 35 EP11
Eastwick Ct, SW19 off Victoria Dr 179 CX88
Eastwick Cres, Rick. (Mill End) WD3 91 BF47
Eastwick Dr, Lthd. (Bkhm) KT23 230 CA123
Eastwick Hall La, Harl. CM20 35 EN09
EAST WICKHAM, Well. DA16 166 EU80
Sch East Wickham Inf Sch, Well. DA16 off Wickham St 165 ET81
Sch East Wickham Jun Sch, Well. DA16 off Wickham St 166 EU81
Sch Eastwick Inf Sch, Lthd. KT23 off Eastwick Dr 230 CB124
Sch Eastwick Jun Sch, Lthd. KT23 off Eastwick Dr 230 CB124
Eastwick Pk Av, Lthd. (Bkhm) KT23 230 CB124
Eastwick Rd, Harl. CM20 35 EM11
Leatherhead (Bkhm) KT23 246 CB125
Walton-on-Thames KT12 213 BV106
Ware (Hunsdon) SG12 34 EK08
Ware (Stans.Abb.) SG12 34 EF12
Eastwick Row, Hem.H. HP2 40 BN21
Eastwood Cl, E18 off George La 102 EG54
N7 4 B1
N17 off Northumberland Gro 100 DV52
Eastwood Ct, Hem.H. HP2 40 BN19
Eastwood Dr, Rain. RM13 147 FH72
Eastwood Rd, E18 102 EG54
N10 98 DG54
Guildford (Bramley) GU5 259 AZ144
Ilford IG3 126 EU59
West Drayton UB7 154 BN75
East Woodside, Bex. DA5 186 EY88
Eastwood St, SW16 181 DJ93
Eastworth Rd, Cher. KT16 194 BG102
Eatington Rd, E10 123 ED57
Eaton Cl, SW1 18 E8
Stanmore HA7 95 CH49
Eaton Ct, Guil. GU1 243 BA132
Eaton Dr, SW9 161 DP84
Kingston upon Thames KT2 178 CN94
Romford RM5 105 FB52
Eaton Gdns, Dag. RM9 146 EY66
Eaton Gate, SW1 18 E7
Northwood HA6 93 BQ51
Eaton Ho, E14 off Westferry Circ 143 EA74
Eaton La, SW1 19 H6
Eaton Ms N, SW1 18 E7
Eaton Ms S, SW1 18 F7
Eaton Ms W, SW1 18 F7
Eaton Pk, Cob. KT11 214 BY114
Eaton Pk Rd, N13 99 DN47
Cobham KT11 214 BY114
Eaton Pl, SW1 18 E6
Eaton Ri, E11 124 EJ57
W5 137 CK72
Eaton Rd, NW4 119 CW57
Enfield EN1 82 DS41
Hemel Hempstead HP2 41 BP17
Hounslow TW3 157 CD84
St. Albans AL1 43 CH20
Sidcup DA14 186 EX89
Sutton SM2 218 DD107
Upminster RM14 129 FS61
Eaton Row, SW1 18 G6
Eatons Mead, E4 101 EA47
Eaton Sq, SW1 18 G5
Longfield DA3 off Bramblefield Cl 209 FX97
Eaton Ter, SW1 18 E7
Eaton Ter Ms, SW1 18 E7
Eatonville Rd, SW17 180 DF89
Eatonville Vil, SW17 off Eatonville Rd 180 DF89
Ebbas Way, Epsom KT18 232 CP115
Ebberns Rd, Hem.H. HP3 40 BK23
Ebbisham Cen, The, Epsom KT19 216 CR113
Ebbisham Cl, Dor. RH4 off Nower Rd 263 CG136
Ebbisham Dr, SW8 161 DM79
Ebbisham La, Tad. KT20 233 CT121
Ebbisham Rd, Epsom KT18 216 CP114
Worcester Park KT4 199 CW103
Ebbsfleet Ind Est, Grav. (Nthflt) DA11 190 GA85
Ebbsfleet Rd, NW2 119 CY63
Ebbsfleet Wk, Grav. (Nthflt) DA11 190 GB86
Ebdon Way, SE3 164 EH83
Ebenezer Ho, SE11 20 D8
Ebenezer St, N1 11 J1
Ebenezer Wk, SW16 201 DJ95
Ebley Cl, SE15 162 DT79
Ebner St, SW18 180 DB85
Ebor St, E1 11 N3
Ebrington Rd, Har. HA3 117 CK58
Ebsworth Cl, Maid. SL6 130 AC68
Ebsworth St, SE23 183 DX87
Eburne Rd, N7 121 DL62
Ebury App, Rick. WD3 92 BK46
Ebury Br, SW1 18 G9
Ebury Br Est, SW1 18 G9
Ebury Br Rd, SW1 18 F10
Ebury Cl, Kes. BR2 204 EL104
Northwood HA6 93 BQ50
Ebury Ms, SE27 181 DP90
SW1 18 F7
Ebury Ms E, SW1 18 G7
Ebury Rd, Rick. WD3 92 BK46
Watford WD17 76 BW41
Ebury Sq, SW1 18 F8
Ebury St, SW1 18 G7
Ebury Way Cycle Path, The, Rick. WD3 93 BP45
Watford WD18 93 BP45
Ecclesbourne Cl, N13 99 DN50
Ecclesbourne Gdns, N13 99 DN50
Sch Ecclesbourne Inf Sch, Th.Hth. CR7 off Bensham La 202 DQ99
Sch Ecclesbourne Jun Sch, Th.Hth. CR7 off Bensham La 202 DQ99
Sch Ecclesbourne Prim Sch, N1 5 J6
Ecclesbourne Rd, N1 5 H6
Thornton Heath CR7 202 DQ99
Eccles Hill, Dor. (N.Holm.) RH5 263 CJ140
Eccles Rd, SW11 160 DF84
Eccleston Br, SW1 19 H7
Eccleston Cl, Barn. EN4 80 DF42
Orpington BR6 205 ER102
Eccleston Cres, Rom. RM6 126 EU59
Ecclestone Ct, Wem. HA9 off St. John's Rd 118 CL64
Ecclestone Pl, Wem. HA9 118 CM64
Eccleston Ms, SW1 18 F6
Eccleston Pl, SW1 18 G7
Eccleston Rd, W13 137 CG73
Eccleston Sq, SW1 19 H8
Eccleston Sq Ms, SW1 19 J8
Eccleston St, SW1 18 G6
Echelforde Dr, Ashf. TW15 174 BN91
Sch Echelford Prim Sch, The, Ashf. TW15 off Park Rd 175 BP92
Echo Hts, E4 off Mount Echo Dr 101 EB46
Echo Pit Rd, Guil. GU1 258 AY138
Echo Sq, Grav. DA12 off Old Rd E 191 GJ89
Eckersley St, E1 off Buxton St 142 DU70
Eckford St, N1 4 C9
Eckington Ho, N15 off Fladbury Rd 122 DR58
Eckstein Rd, SW11 160 DE84
Eclipse Rd, E13 15 N5
Ecob Cl, Guil. GU3 242 AT130
Sch Ecole Française de Londres, W6 16 B7
Ecton Rd, Add. KT15 212 BH105
Ector Rd, SE6 184 EE89
Edbrooke Rd, W9 6 G3
Eddiscombe Rd, SW6 159 CZ82
Eddy Cl, Rom. RM7 127 FB58
Eddystone Rd, SE4 183 DY85
Eddystone Twr, SE8 23 K8
Eddystone Wk, Stai. TW19 174 BL87
Eddy St, Berk. HP4 38 AU18
Ede Cl, Houns. TW3 156 BZ83
Edenbridge Cl, SE16 22 D10
Orpington BR5 206 EX98
Edenbridge Rd, E9 143 DX66
Enfield EN1 82 DS44
Eden Cl, NW3 120 DA61
W8 17 H5
Addlestone (New Haw) KT15 212 BH110
Bexley DA5 187 FD91
Enfield EN3 83 EA38
Slough SL3 153 BA78
Wembley HA0 137 CK67
Edencourt Rd, SW16 181 DH93
Edencroft, Guil. (Bramley) GU5 259 AZ144
Edendale Rd, Bexh. DA7 167 FD81
Edenfield Gdns, Wor.Pk. KT4 199 CT104
Eden Grn, S.Ock. RM15 149 FV71
Eden Gro, E17 123 EB57
N7 4 B2
Eden Gro Rd, W.Byf. (Byfleet) KT14 212 BL113
Edenhall Cl, Hem.H. HP2 41 BR21
Romford RM3 106 FJ50
Edenhall Glen, Rom. RM3 106 FJ50
Edenhall Rd, Rom. RM3 106 FJ50
Sch Edenham High Sch, Croy. CR0 off Orchard Way 203 DZ101
Edenham Way, W10 6 E5
Edenhurst Av, SW6 159 CZ83
Eden Ms, SW17 off Huntspill St 180 DC90
EDEN PARK, Beck. BR3 203 EA99
⇌ Eden Park 203 EA99
Eden Pk Av, Beck. BR3 203 DY98
Eden Pl, Grav. DA12 off Lord St 191 GH87
Eden Rd, E17 123 EB57
SE27 181 DP92
Beckenham BR3 203 DY98
Bexley DA5 187 FC91
Croydon CR0 220 DR105
Edenside Rd, Lthd. (Bkhm) KT23 230 BZ124
Edensor Gdns, W4 158 CS80
Edensor Rd, W4 158 CS80
Eden St, Kings.T. KT1 197 CK96
Edenvale Cl, Mitch. CR4 off Edenvale Rd 180 DG94
Edenvale Rd, Mitch. CR4 180 DG94
Edenvale St, SW6 160 DB82
Eden Wk, Kings.T. KT1 off Eden St 198 CL96
Eden Wk Shop Cen, Kings.T. KT1 198 CL96
Eden Way, Beck. BR3 203 DZ99
Warlingham CR6 237 DY118
Ederline Av, SW16 201 DM97
Edes Flds, Reig. RH2 265 CY136
Edgar Cl, Swan. BR8 207 FF97
Edgar Kail Way, SE22 162 DS84
Edgarley Ter, SW6 159 CY81
Edgar Rd, E3 14 B1
Hounslow TW4 176 BZ87
Romford RM6 126 EX59
South Croydon CR2 220 DR109
West Drayton UB7 134 BL73
Westerham (Tats.) TN16 238 EK121
Edgars Ct, Welw.G.C. AL7 29 CY10
Edgbaston Dr, Rad. (Shenley) WD7 62 CL32
Edgbaston Rd, Wat. WD19 93 BV48
Edgeborough Way, Brom. BR1 184 EK94
Edgebury, Chis. BR7 185 EP91
Sch Edgebury Prim Sch, Chis. BR7 off Belmont La 185 EQ91
Edgebury Wk, Chis. BR7 185 EQ91
Edge Cl, Wey. KT13 212 BN108
Edgecombe Ho, SW19 179 CY88
Edgecoombe, S.Croy. CR2 220 DW108
Edgecoombe Cl, Kings.T. KT2 178 CR94
Edgecote Cl, W3 off Cheltenham Pl 138 CQ74
Edgecot Gro, N15 off Oulton Rd 122 DR57
Edgefield Av, Bark. IG11 145 ET66
Edgefield Cl, Dart. DA1 188 FP88
Redhill RH1 266 DG139
Edge Hill, SE18 165 EP79
SW19 179 CX94
Edge Hill Av, N3 120 DA55
Edge Hill Ct, SW19 179 CX94
Edgehill Ct, Walt. KT12 off St. Johns Dr 196 BW102
Edgehill Gdns, Dag. RM10 126 FA63
Edgehill Rd, W13 137 CJ71
Chislehurst BR7 185 EQ90
Mitcham CR4 201 DH95
Purley CR8 219 DN110
Edgeley, Lthd. (Bkhm) KT23 230 BY124
Edgeley Caravan Pk, Guil. (Far.Grn) GU5 260 BL143
Edgeley La, SW4 off Edgeley Rd 161 DK83
Edgeley Rd, SW4 161 DK83
Edgell Cl, Vir.W. GU25 193 AZ97
Edgell Rd, Stai. TW18 173 BF92
Edgel St, SW18 off Ferrier St 160 DB84
Edgepoint Cl, SE27 off Knights Hill 181 DP92
Edge St, W8 17 H1
Edgewood Dr, Orp. BR6 223 ET106
Edgewood Grn, Croy. CR0 203 DX102
Edgeworth Av, NW4 119 CU57
Edgeworth Cl, NW4 119 CU57
Whyteleafe CR3 236 DU118
Edgeworth Cres, NW4 119 CU57
Edgeworth Rd, SE9 164 EJ84
Barnet EN4 80 DE42
Edgington Rd, SW16 181 DK93
Edgington Way, Sid. DA14 186 EW94

★ Place of interest   H Hospital   Sch School   Coll College   Uni University   ⇌ Railway station

EDGWARE, HA8 96 CP50
⊖ Edgware 96 CP51
Edgwarebury Gdns, Edg. HA8 96 CN50
Edgwarebury La, Borwd. (Elstree) WD6 96 CL45
Edgware HA8 96 CN49
H Edgware Comm Hosp, Edg. HA8 96 CP52
Edgware Ct, Edg. HA8 off Cavendish Dr 96 CN51
Sch Edgware Inf Sch, Edg. HA8 off High St 96 CN51
Sch Edgware Jun Sch, Edg. HA8 off Heming Rd 96 CN51
⊖ Edgware Road 8 A6
Edgware Rd, NW2 119 CV60
NW9 118 CR55
W2 8 B7
Edgware Rd Sub, W2 off Edgware Rd 140 DE71
Sch Edgware Sch, Edg. HA8 off Green La 96 CM49
Edgware Way, Edg. HA8 96 CM49
Edinburgh Av, Rick. (Mill End) WD3 74 BG44
Slough SL1 131 AN71
Edinburgh Cl, E2 off Russia La 142 DW68
Pinner HA5 116 BX59
Uxbridge UB10 115 BP63
Edinburgh Ct, SW20 199 CX99
Edinburgh Cres, Wal.Cr. EN8 67 DY33
Edinburgh Dr, Abb.L. WD5 59 BU32
Romford RM7 off Eastern Av W 127 FC56
Staines TW18 174 BK93
Uxbridge (Denh.) UB9 113 BF58
Uxbridge (Ickhm) UB10 115 BP63
Edinburgh Gdns, Wind. SL4 151 AR83
Edinburgh Gate, SW1 18 C3
Harlow CM20 35 ER12
Edinburgh Ho, W9 7 K1
Edinburgh Ms, Til. RM18 171 GH82
Edinburgh Pl, Harl. CM20 36 EU11
Sch Edinburgh Prim Sch, E17 off Edinburgh Rd 123 DZ57
Edinburgh Rd, E13 144 EH68
E17 123 EA57
N18 100 DU50
W7 157 CF75
Sutton SM1 200 DC103
Edinburgh Way, Harl. CM20 35 ER12
Edington Rd, SE2 166 EV76
Enfield EN3 82 DW40
Edison Av, Horn. RM12 127 FF61
Edison Cl, E17 off Exeter Rd 123 EA57
Hornchurch RM12 off Edison Av 127 FF60
St. Albans AL4 43 CJ21
Edison Ct, SE10 25 K7
Edison Dr, Sthl. UB1 136 CB72
Wembley HA9 118 CL61
Edison Gro, SE18 165 ET80
Edison Rd, N8 121 DK58
Bromley BR2 204 EG96
Enfield EN3 83 DZ40
Welling DA16 165 ET81
Edis St, NW1 140 DG67
Edith Cavell Cl, N19 off Hornsey Ri Gdns 121 DK59
Edith Gdns, Surb. KT5 198 CP101
Edith Gro, SW10 160 DC79
Edithna St, SW9 161 DL83
Sch Edith Neville Prim Sch, NW1 off Ossulston St 141 DK68
Edith Rd, E6 144 EK66
E15 off Chandos Rd 123 ED64
N11 99 DK52
SE25 202 DR99
SW19 180 DB93
W14 16 C8
Orpington BR6 224 EU106
Romford RM6 126 EX58
Edith Row, SW6 160 DB81
Edith St, E2 142 DU68
Edith Summerskill Ho, SW6 off Clem Attlee Ct 159 CZ80
Edith Ter, SW10 160 DC80
Edith Vil, SW15 off Bective Rd 159 CY84
W14 16 E8
Edith Yd, SW10 off World's End Est 160 DC80
Edlyn Cl, Berk. HP4 38 AT18
Edmansons Cl, N17 off Bruce Gro 100 DS53
Edmeston Cl, E9 143 DY65
Edmond Beaufort Dr, St.Alb. AL3 43 CD18
Edmond Halley Way, SE10 24 G4
Edmonds Ct, W.Mol. KT8 off Avern Rd 196 CB98
EDMONTON, N9 100 DU49
Sch Edmonton Co Sch, Lwr Sch, N9 off Little Bury St 100 DS46
Upr Sch, Enf. EN1 off Great Cambridge Rd 100 DT45
⇌ Edmonton Green 100 DU47
Edmonton Grn, N9 off Hertford Rd 100 DV47
Edmonton Grn Shop Cen, N9 100 DV47
Edmund Gro, Felt. TW13 176 BZ89
Edmund Hurst Dr, E6 145 EP71
Edmund Rd, Grays (Chaff.Hun.) RM16 169 FX75
Mitcham CR4 200 DE97
Orpington BR5 206 EW100
Rainham RM13 147 FE68
Welling DA16 166 EU83
Edmunds Av, Orp. BR5 206 EX97
Edmunds Cl, Hayes UB4 136 BW71
Edmunds Rd, Hert. SG14 31 DM08
Edmunds Twr, Harl. CM19 51 EQ15
Edmund St, SE5 162 DR80
Edmunds Wk, N2 120 DE56
Edmunds Way, Slou. SL2 132 AV71
Sch Edmund Waller Prim Sch, SE14 off Waller Rd 163 DX82
Edna Rd, SW20 199 CX96
Edna St, SW11 160 DE81
Edrich Ho, SW4 161 DL81
Edrick Rd, Edg. HA8 96 CQ51
Edrick Wk, Edg. HA8 96 CQ51
Edric Rd, SE14 163 DX80
Edridge Cl, Bushey WD23 76 CC43
Hornchurch RM12 128 FK64
Edridge Rd, Croy. CR0 202 DQ104
Sch Education Support Cen, The, SE15 off St. Mary's Rd 162 DW81
Edulf Rd, Borwd. WD6 78 CP39
Edward Amey Cl, Wat. WD25 76 BW36
Edward Av, E4 101 EB51
Edward Av, Mord. SM4 200 DD99
Sch Edward Betham C of E Prim Sch, Grnf. UB6 off Oldfield La S 136 CC68
Edward Cl, N9 100 DT45
NW2 119 CX63
Abbots Langley WD5 59 BT32
Grays (Chaff.Hun.) RM16 169 FX76
Hampton (Hmptn H.) TW12 off Edward Rd 176 CC92
Northolt UB5 136 BW68
Romford RM2 128 FJ55
St. Albans AL1 43 CF21
Edward Ct, E16 15 L5
Hemel Hempstead HP3 off King Edward St 40 BK24
Staines TW18 174 BJ93
Waltham Abbey EN9 68 EF33
Edwardes Pl, W8 16 F6
Edwardes Sq, W8 16 G5
Edward Gro, Barn. EN4 80 DD43
Edward Ho, Red. RH1 off Royal Earlswood Pk 266 DG137
Edward Ms, NW1 off Redhill St 141 DH68
Edward Pauling Ho, Felt. TW14 off Westmacott Dr 175 BT87
Sch Edward Pauling Prim Sch, Felt. TW13 off Redford Cl 175 BS89
Edward Pl, SE8 163 DZ79
Sch Edward Redhead Inf Sch, E17 off Higham Hill Rd 123 DY55
Sch Edward Redhead Jun Sch, E17 off Higham Hill Rd 123 DY55
Edward Rd, E17 123 DX56
SE20 183 DX94
Barnet EN4 80 DD43
Bromley BR1 184 EH94
Chislehurst BR7 185 EP92
Coulsdon CR5 235 DK115
Croydon CR0 202 DS101
Feltham TW14 175 BR85
Hampton (Hmptn H.) TW12 176 CC92
Harrow HA2 116 CC55
Northolt UB5 136 BW68
Romford RM6 126 EY58
Westerham (Bigg.H.) TN16 238 EL118
Edward's Av, Ruis. HA4 135 BV65
Edwards Cl, Brwd. (Hutt.) CM13 109 GE44
Worcester Park KT4 199 CX103
Edwards Cotts, N1 4 E4
Edwards Ct, Slou. SL1 152 AS75
Waltham Cross EN8 off Turners Hill 67 DX31
Edwards Dr, N11 off Gordon Rd 99 DK52
Edward II Av, W.Byf. (Byfleet) KT14 212 BM114
Edwards Gdns, Swan. BR8 off Ladds Way 207 FD98
Edwards La, N16 122 DR61
Edwards Ms, N1 4 D5
W1 8 E8
Edward Sq, N1 off Caledonian Rd 141 DM67
SE16 23 K1
Edwards Rd, Belv. DA17 166 FA77
Edward St, E16 15 L4
SE8 163 DZ79
SE14 163 DY80
Edwards Way, Brwd. (Hutt.) CM13 109 GE44
Edwards Yd, Wem. HA0 off Mount Pleasant 138 CL67
Edward Temme Av, E15 144 EF66
Edward Tyler Rd, SE12 184 EH89
Edward Way, Ashf. TW15 174 BM89
Sch Edward Wilson Prim Sch, W2 7 J5
Edwina Gdns, Ilf. IG4 124 EL57
Edwin Av, E6 145 EN68
Edwin Cl, Bexh. DA7 166 EZ79
Leatherhead (W.Hors.) KT24 245 BR125
Rainham RM13 147 FF69
Sch Edwin Lambert Jun & Inf Sch, Horn. RM11 off Malvern Rd 127 FG59
Edwin Pl, Croy. CR0 off Cross Rd 202 DR102
Edwin Rd, Dart. DA2 187 FH90
Edgware HA8 96 CR51
Leatherhead (W.Hors.) KT24 245 BQ125
Twickenham TW1, TW2 177 CF88
Edwin's Mead, E9 off Lindisfarne Way 123 DY63
Edwin St, E1 12 F3
E16 15 L6
Gravesend DA12 191 GH87
Edwyn Cl, Barn. EN5 79 CW44
Edwyn Ho, SW18 off Neville Gill Cl 180 DB86
Eel Brook Studios, SW6 off Moore Pk Rd 160 DA80
Eel Pie Island, Twick. TW1 177 CH88
Effie Pl, SW6 160 DA80
Effie Rd, SW6 160 DA80
EFFINGHAM, Lthd. KT24 246 BY127
Effingham Cl, Sutt. SM2 218 DB108
Effingham Common, Lthd. (Eff.) KT24 229 BU123
Effingham Common Rd, Lthd. (Eff.) KT24 229 BU123
Effingham Ct, Wok. GU22 off Constitution Hill 226 AY118
Effingham Hill, Dor. RH5 off Critten La 246 BX132
⇌ Effingham Junction 229 BU123
Effingham Pl, Lthd. (Eff.) KT24 246 BX127
Effingham Rd, N8 121 DN57
SE12 184 EE85
Croydon CR0 201 DM101
Reigate RH2 266 DB135
Surbiton KT6 197 CH101
Effort St, SW17 180 DE92
Effra Par, SW2 181 DN85
Effra Rd, SW2 161 DN84
SW19 180 DB93
Egan Way, Hayes UB3 135 BS73
Egbert St, NW1 140 DG67
Egbury Ho, SW15 off Tangley Gro 179 CT86
Egdean Wk, Sev. TN13 257 FJ123
Egerton Av, Swan. BR8 187 FF94
Egerton Cl, Dart. DA1 187 FH88
Pinner HA5 115 BU56
Egerton Ct, Guil. GU2 off Egerton Rd 242 AS134
Egerton Cres, SW3 18 B7
Egerton Dr, SE10 163 EB81
Egerton Gdns, NW4 119 CV56
NW10 139 CW67
SW3 18 A6
W13 137 CH72
Ilford IG3 125 ET62
Egerton Gdns Ms, SW3 18 B6
Egerton Pl, SW3 18 B6
Weybridge KT13 213 BQ107
Egerton Rd, N16 122 DT59
SE25 202 DS97
Berkhamsted HP4 38 AU17
Guildford GU2 242 AS134
New Malden KT3 199 CT98
Slough SL2 131 AL70
Twickenham TW2 177 CE87
Wembley HA0 138 CM66
Weybridge KT13 213 BQ107
Sch Egerton-Rothesay Lwr Sch, Berk. HP4 off Charles St 38 AV19
Sch Egerton-Rothesay Sch, Berk. HP4 off Durrants La 38 AT19
Egerton Ter, SW3 18 B6
Egerton Way, Hayes UB3 155 BP80
Eggardon Ct, Nthlt. UB5 off Lancaster Rd 136 CC65
Egg Fm La, Kings L. WD4 59 BP30
Egg Hall, Epp. CM16 70 EU29
EGHAM, TW20 173 BA93
⇌ Egham 173 BA92
Egham Bypass, Egh. TW20 173 AZ92
Egham Cl, SW19 off Winterfold Cl 179 CY89
Sutton SM3 199 CY103
Egham Cres, Sutt. SM3 199 CX104
Egham Hill, Egh. TW20 172 AX93
EGHAM HYTHE, Stai. TW18 173 BE93
★ Egham Mus, Egh. TW20 173 BA92
Egham Rd, E13 15 P5
Eghams Cl, Beac. (Knot.Grn) HP9 88 AJ51
Eghams Wd Rd, Beac. HP9 88 AH51
EGHAM WICK, Egh. TW20 172 AU94
Eglantine La, Dart. (Hort.Kir.) DA4 208 FN101
Eglantine Rd, SW18 180 DC85
Egleston Rd, Mord. SM4 200 DB100
Egley Dr, Wok. GU22 226 AX122
Egley Rd, Wok. GU22 226 AX122
Eglington Ct, SE17 off Carter St 162 DQ79
Eglington Rd, E4 101 ED45
Eglinton Hill, SE18 165 EP79
Sch Eglinton Inf Sch, SE18 off Paget Ri 165 EN80
Sch Eglinton Jun Sch, SE18 off Whitworth Rd 165 EN79
Eglinton Rd, SE18 165 EN79
Swanscombe DA10 190 FZ86
Eglise Rd, Warl. CR6 237 DY117
Egliston Ms, SW15 159 CW83
Egliston Rd, SW15 159 CW83
Eglon Ms, NW1 off Berkley Rd 140 DF66
Egmont Av, Surb. KT6 198 CM102
Egmont Pk Rd, Tad. KT20 249 CU125
Egmont Rd, N.Mal. KT3 199 CT98
Surbiton KT6 198 CM102
Sutton SM2 218 DC108
Walton-on-Thames KT12 195 BV101
Egmont St, SE14 163 DX80
Egmont Way, Tad. KT20 off Oatlands Rd 233 CY119
Egremont Gdns, Slou. SL1 131 AN74
Egremont Ho, SE13 off Conington Rd 163 EB82
Egremont Rd, SE27 181 DN90
Egret Way, Hayes UB4 136 BX71
EGYPT, Slou. SL2 111 AQ63
Egypt La, Slou. (Farn.Com.) SL2 111 AP61
Eider Cl, E7 124 EF64
Hayes UB4 off Cygnet Way 136 BX71
Eight Acres, Slou. (Burn.) SL1 130 AH70
Eighteenth Rd, Mitch. CR4 201 DL98
Eighth Av, E12 125 EM63
Hayes UB3 135 BU74
Eileen Rd, SE25 202 DR99
Eindhoven Cl, Cars. SM5 200 DG102
Eisenhower Dr, E6 144 EL71
Elaine Gro, NW5 120 DG64
Elam Cl, SE5 161 DP82
Elam St, SE5 161 DP82
Eland Pl, Croy. CR0 off Eland Rd 201 DP104
Eland Rd, SW11 160 DF83
Croydon CR0 201 DP104
Sch Elangeni Mid Sch, Amer. HP6 off Woodside Av 55 AS36
Elan Rd, S.Ock. RM15 149 FU71
Elba Pl, SE17 21 H7
Elberon Av, Croy. CR0 201 DJ100
Elbe St, SW6 160 DC82
Elborough Rd, SE25 202 DU99
Elborough St, SW18 180 DA88
Elbow La, Hert. (Hert.Hth) SG13 48 DV17
Elbow Meadow, Slou. (Colnbr.) SL3 153 BF81
Elbury Dr, E16 15 M8
Elcho St, SW11 160 DE80
Elcot Av, SE15 162 DV80
Elder Av, N8 121 DL57
Elderbek Cl, Wal.Cr. EN7 66 DU28
Elderberry Cl, Ilf. IG6 off Hazel La 103 EP52
Elderberry Gro, SE27 off Linton Gro 182 DQ92
Elderberry Rd, W5 158 CL75
Elderberry Way, E6 off Vicarage La 145 EM69
Watford WD25 75 BV35
Elder Cl, N20 98 DB47
Guildford GU4 243 BA131
Sidcup DA15 185 ET88
West Drayton UB7 off Yew Av 134 BL73
Elder Ct, Bushey (Bushey Hth) WD23 95 CE47
Elderfield, Harl. CM17 36 EX11
Elderfield Pl, SW17 181 DH91
Elderfield Rd, E5 122 DW63
Slough (Stoke P.) SL2 132 AT65
Elderfield Wk, E11 124 EH57
Elderflower Way, E15 144 EE66
Elder Gdns, SE27 182 DQ91
Elder Oak Cl, SE20 202 DV95
Elder Rd, SE27 182 DQ92
Eldersley Cl, Red. RH1 250 DF132
Elderslie Cl, Beck. BR3 203 EB99
Elderslie Rd, SE9 185 EN85
Elder St, E1 11 N5
Elderton Rd, SE26 183 DY91
Eldertree Pl, Mitch. CR4 off Eldertree Way 201 DJ95
Eldertree Way, Mitch. CR4 201 DH95
Elder Wk, N1 4 F7
Elder Way, Dor. (N.Holm.) RH5 263 CJ140
Rainham RM13 148 FK69
Slough (Langley) SL3 153 AZ75
Elderwood Pl, SE27 off Elder Rd 182 DQ92
Eldon Av, Borwd. WD6 78 CN40
Croydon CR0 202 DW103
Hounslow TW5 156 CA80
Eldon Gro, NW3 120 DD64
Sch Eldon Inf Sch, N9 off Eldon Rd 100 DW46
Sch Eldon Jun Sch, N9 off Eldon Rd 100 DW46
Eldon Pk, SE25 202 DV98
Eldon Rd, E17 123 DZ56
N9 100 DW47
N22 99 DP53
W8 17 K6
Caterham CR3 236 DR121
Hoddesdon EN11 49 ED19
Eldon St, EC2 11 K6
Eldon Way, NW10 138 CP68
Eldred Dr, Orp. BR5 206 EW103
Eldred Gdns, Upmin. RM14 129 FS59
Eldred Rd, Bark. IG11 145 ES67
Eldrick Ct, Felt. TW14 175 BR88
Eldridge Cl, Felt. TW14 175 BU88
Eleanor Av, Epsom KT19 216 CR110
St. Albans AL3 43 CD18
Eleanor Cl, N15 off Arnold Rd 122 DT55
SE16 22 G3
Eleanor Cres, NW7 97 CX49
Eleanor Cross Rd, Wal.Cr. EN8 67 DY34
Eleanor Gdns, Barn. EN5 79 CX43
Dagenham RM8 126 EZ62
Eleanor Gro, SW13 158 CS83
Uxbridge (Ickhm) UB10 115 BP62
Sch Eleanor Palmer Prim Sch, NW5 off Lupton St 121 DJ63
Eleanor Rd, E8 142 DV66
E15 144 EF65
N11 99 DL51
Gerrards Cross (Chal.St.P.) SL9 90 AW53
Hertford SG14 32 DQ08
Waltham Cross EN8 67 DY33
Sch Eleanor Smith Spec Sch, E13 off North St 144 EH68
Eleanor St, E3 13 N2
Eleanor Wk, SE18 off Samuel St 165 EM77
Eleanor Way, Brwd. CM14 108 FX50
Waltham Cross EN8 67 DZ34
Electric Av, SW9 161 DN84
Enfield EN3 83 DZ36
Electric La, SW9 161 DN84
Electric Par, E18 off George La 102 EG54
Surbiton KT6 197 CK100
Elektron Ho, E14 14 F9
⇌ Elephant & Castle 20 G7
⊖ Elephant & Castle 20 G7
Elephant & Castle, SE1 20 F6
Elephant & Castle Shop Cen, SE1 off Elephant & Castle 162 DQ77
Elephant La, SE16 22 E3
Elephant Rd, SE17 20 G7
Elers Rd, W13 157 CJ75
Hayes UB3 155 BR77
Eleven Acre Ri, Loug. IG10 85 EM41
Eley Est, N18 100 DW50
Eley Rd, N18 101 DX50
Elfindale Rd, SE24 182 DQ85
Elfin Gro, Tedd. TW11 off Broad St 177 CF92
Elford Cl, SE3 164 EH84
Elfort Rd, N5 121 DN63
Elfrida Cres, SE6 183 EA91
Sch Elfrida Prim Sch, SE6 off Elfrida Cres 183 EB91
Elfrida Rd, Wat. WD18 76 BW43
Elf Row, E1 12 F9
Elfwine Rd, W7 137 CE71
Elgal Cl, Orp. BR6 off Orchard Rd 223 EP106
Elgar Av, NW10 off Mitchellbrook Way 138 CR65
SW16 201 DL97
W5 158 CL75
Surbiton KT5 198 CP101
Elgar Cl, E13 off Bushey Rd 144 EJ68
SE8 off Comet St 163 EA80
Borehamwood (Elstree) WD6 95 CK45
Buckhurst Hill IG9 102 EK47
Uxbridge UB10 114 BN61
Elgar Gdns, Til. RM18 171 GH81
Elgar St, SE16 23 K5
Elgin Av, W9 7 J2
W12 159 CU75
Ashford TW15 175 BQ93
Harrow HA3 95 CH54
Romford RM3 106 FP52
Elgin Cl, W12 159 CV75
Elgin Cres, W11 6 E8
Caterham CR3 236 DU122
Hounslow (Hthrw Air.) TW6 off Eastern Perimeter Rd 155 BS82
Elgin Dr, Nthwd. HA6 93 BS52
Elgin Gdns, Guil. GU1 243 BA133
Elgin Ms, W11 6 D8
Elgin Ms N, W9 7 K1
Elgin Ms S, W9 7 K1
Elgin Pl, Wey. KT13 213 BQ107
Elgin Rd, N22 99 DJ54
Broxbourne EN10 49 DZ24
Croydon CR0 202 DT102
Ilford IG3 125 ES60
Sutton SM1 200 DC104
Wallington SM6 219 DJ107
Waltham Cross (Chsht) EN8 66 DW30
Weybridge KT13 212 BN106
Elgiva La, Chesh. HP5 54 AP31
Elgood Av, Nthwd. HA6 93 BU51
Elgood Cl, W11 6 C10
Elham Cl, Brom. BR1 184 EK94
Elia Ms, N1 4 E10
Elias Pl, SW8 161 DN79
Elia St, N1 4 E10
Elibank Rd, SE9 165 EN84
Elim Est, SE1 21 L5
Elim Way, E13 15 K2
Eliot Bk, SE23 182 DV89
Sch Eliot Bk Prim Sch, SE26 off Thorpewood Av 182 DV89
Eliot Cotts, SE3 off Eliot Pl 164 EE82
Eliot Ct, N15 off Tynemouth Rd 122 DT56
Eliot Dr, Har. HA2 116 CB61
Eliot Gdns, SW15 159 CU84
Eliot Hill, SE13 163 EC82
Eliot Ms, NW8 140 DC68
Eliot Pk, SE13 163 EC83
Eliot Pl, SE3 164 EE82
Eliot Rd, Dag. RM9 126 EX63
Dartford DA1 188 FP85
Eliot Vale, SE3 163 ED82
Elizabethan Cl, Stai. (Stanw.) TW19 off Elizabethan Way 174 BK87
Elizabethan Way, Stai. (Stanw.) TW19 174 BK87
Elizabeth Av, N1 5 H7
Amersham HP6 72 AV39
Enfield EN2 81 DP41
Ilford IG1 125 ER61
Staines TW18 174 BJ93
Elizabeth Blackwell Ho, N22 off Progress Way 99 DN53
Elizabeth Br, SW1 18 G8
Elizabeth Cl, E14 14 A8
W9 7 M3
Barnet EN5 79 CX41
Romford RM7 105 FB53
Sutton SM1 217 CZ105
Tilbury RM18 171 GH82
Waltham Abbey EN9 49 ED23
Welwyn Garden City AL7 30 DC09
Elizabeth Clyde Cl, N15 122 DS56
Elizabeth Cotts, Rich. TW9 158 CM81
Elizabeth Ct, SW1 19 M6
Godalming GU7 258 AS144
Gravesend DA11 off St. James's Rd 191 GG86
Horley RH6 268 DG148
St. Albans AL4 off Villiers Cres 43 CK17
Watford WD17 75 BT38
Woodford Green IG8 off Navestock Cres 102 EJ52
Elizabeth Dr, Epp. (They.B.) CM16 85 ES36
Elizabeth Est, SE17 162 DR79
Elizabeth Fry Pl, SE18 164 EL81
Elizabeth Fry Rd, E8 off Lamb La 142 DV66
Elizabeth Gdns, W3 139 CT74
Isleworth TW7 157 CG84
Stanmore HA7 95 CJ51
Sunbury-on-Thames TW16 196 BW97
Sch Elizabeth Garrett Anderson Sec Sch, N1 4 B9
Elizabeth Huggins Cotts, Grav. DA11 191 GG89
Elizabeth Ms, NW3 140 DE65
Elizabeth Pl, N15 122 DR56
Elizabeth Ride, N9 100 DV45
Elizabeth Rd, E6 144 EK67
N15 122 DS57
Brentwood (Pilg.Hat.) CM15 108 FV44
Godalming GU7 258 AS144
Grays RM16 170 FZ76
Rainham RM13 147 FH71
Sch Elizabeth Selby Inf Sch, E2 12 B1
Elizabeth Sq, SE16 13 J10
Elizabeth St, SW1 18 F7
Greenhithe DA9 189 FS85
Elizabeth Ter, SE9 185 EM86
Elizabeth Way, SE19 182 DR94
Feltham TW13 176 BW91
Harlow CM19, CM20 51 EM16
Orpington BR5 206 EW99
Slough (Stoke P.) SL2 132 AT67
Eliza Cook Cl, Green. DA9 off Watermans Way 169 FV84
Elkanette Ms, N20 off Ridgeview Rd 98 DC47
Elkington Rd, E13 15 N4
Elkins, The, Rom. RM1 105 FE54
Elkins Gdns, Guil. GU4 243 BA131
Elkins Rd, Slou. (Hedg.) SL2 112 AS61
Elkstone Rd, W10 6 E5
Ellaline Rd, W6 159 CX79
Ellanby Cres, N18 100 DV50
Elland Rd, SE15 162 DW84
Walton-on-Thames KT12 196 BX103
Ella Rd, N8 121 DL59
Ellement Cl, Pnr. HA5 116 BX57
Ellenborough Pl, SW15 159 CU84
Ellenborough Rd, N22 100 DQ53
Sidcup DA14 186 EX92
Ellenbridge Way, S.Croy. CR2 220 DS109
ELLENBROOK, Hat. AL10 44 CR19
Ellenbrook Cl, Wat. WD24 off Hatfield Rd 75 BV39
Ellenbrook Cres, Hat. AL10 off Ellenbrook La 44 CR18
Ellenbrook La, Hat. AL10 44 CS19
Ellen Cl, Brom. BR1 204 EK97
Hemel Hempstead HP2 40 BM19
Ellen Ct, N9 off Densworth Gro 100 DW47
Ellen St, E1 12 B8
Ellen Webb Dr, Har. (Wldste) HA3 117 CE55
Sch Ellen Wilkinson High Sch, W3 off Queens Dr 138 CM72
Sch Ellen Wilkinson Jun & Inf Sch, E6 off Tollgate Rd 144 EL71
Elleray Rd, Tedd. TW11 177 CF93
Ellerby St, SW6 159 CX81
Ellerdale Cl, NW3 off Ellerdale Rd 120 DC63
Ellerdale Rd, NW3 120 DC64
Ellerdale St, SE13 163 EB84
Ellerdine Rd, Houns. TW3 156 CC84
Ellerker Gdns, Rich. TW10 178 CL86
Ellerman Av, Twick. TW2 176 BZ88
Ellerman Rd, Til. RM18 171 GF82
Ellerslie, Grav. DA12 191 GK87
Ellerslie Gdns, NW10 139 CU67
Ellerslie Rd, W12 139 CV74
Ellerslie Sq Ind Est, SW2 181 DL85
Ellerton Gdns, Dag. RM9 146 EW66
Ellerton Rd, SW13 159 CU81
SW18 180 DD88
SW20 179 CU94
Dagenham RM9 146 EW66

Ellerton Rd, Surb. KT6 198 CM103
Ellery Rd, SE19 182 DR94
Ellery St, SE15 162 DV82
Elles Av, Guil. GU1 243 BB134
Ellesborough Cl, Wat. WD19 94 BW50
Ellesmere Av, NW7 96 CR48
Beckenham BR3 203 EB96
Ellesmere Cl, E11 124 EF57
Ruislip HA4 115 BQ59
Ellesmere Dr, S.Croy. CR2 220 DV114
Ellesmere Gdns, Ilf. IG4 124 EL57
Ellesmere Gro, Barn. EN5 79 CZ43
Ellesmere Pl, Walt. KT12 213 BS106
Ellesmere Rd, E3 143 DY68
NW10 119 CU64
W4 158 CR79
Berkhamsted HP4 38 AX19
Greenford UB6 136 CC70
Twickenham TW1 177 CJ86
Weybridge KT13 213 BR107
Ellesmere St, E14 14 A7
Ellice Rd, Oxt. RH8 254 EF129
Elliman Av, Slou. SL2 132 AS73
Ellingfort Rd, E8 142 DV66
Ellingham Cl, Hem.H. HP2 40 BN18
Sch **Ellingham Prim Sch**, Chess. KT9 *off Ellingham Rd* 215 CK108
Ellingham Rd, E15 123 ED63
W12 159 CU75
Chessington KT9 215 CK107
Hemel Hempstead HP2 40 BM19
Ellington Ct, Maid. (Taplow) SL6 *off Ellington Rd* 130 AC72
Ellington Gdns, Maid. (Taplow) SL6 130 AC72
Ellington Rd, N10 121 DH56
Feltham TW13 175 BT91
Hounslow TW3 156 CB82
Maidenhead (Taplow) SL6 130 AC72
Ellington St, N7 4 C4
Ellington Way, Epsom KT18 233 CV117
Elliot Cl, E15 144 EE66
Welwyn Garden City AL7 29 CX12
Elliot Rd, NW4 119 CV58
Stanmore HA7 95 CG51
Sch **Elliot Sch**, SW15 *off Pullman Gdns* 179 CW86
Elliott Av, Ruis. HA4 115 BV61
Elliott Cl, Wem. HA9 118 CM62
Elliott Gdns, Rom. RM3 105 FH53
Shepperton TW17 194 BN98
Elliott Rd, SW9 161 DP80
W4 158 CS77
Bromley BR2 204 EK98
Thornton Heath CR7 201 DP98
Elliotts Cl, Uxb. (Cowley) UB8 134 BJ71
Elliotts La, West. (Brasted) TN16 240 EW124
Elliott's Pl, N1 4 F8
Elliott Sq, NW3 140 DE66
Elliotts Row, SE11 20 E7
Elliott St, Grav. DA12 191 GK87
Ellis Av, Ger.Cr. (Chal.St.P.) SL9 91 AZ53
Guildford (Ons.Vill.) GU2 258 AT136
Rainham RM13 147 FG71
Slough SL1 152 AS75
Ellis Cl, NW10 *off High Rd* 139 CV65
SE9 185 EQ89
Coulsdon CR5 235 DM120
Elliscombe Rd, SE7 164 EJ78
Ellis Ct, W7 137 CF71
Ellis Fm Cl, Wok. GU22 226 AX122
Ellisfield Dr, SW15 179 CT87
Ellison Cl, Wind. SL4 151 AM83
Ellison Gdns, Sthl. UB2 156 BZ77
Ellison Ho, SE13 *off Lewisham Rd* 163 EC82
Ellison Rd, SW13 159 CT82
SW16 181 DK94
Sidcup DA15 185 ER88
Ellis Rd, Couls. CR5 235 DM120
Mitcham CR4 200 DF100
Southall UB2 136 CC74
Ellis St, SW1 18 D7
Elliston Ho, SE18 165 EN77
Ellis Way, Dart. DA1 188 FM89
Ellmore Cl, Rom. RM3 105 FH53
Ellora Rd, SW16 181 DK92
Ellsworth St, E2 12 C1
Ellwood Ct, W9 7 J4
Ellwood Gdns, Wat. WD25 59 BY34
Ellwood Ri, Ch.St.G. HP8 90 AW47
Ellwood Rd, Beac. HP9 88 AH54
Elmar Grn, Slou. SL2 131 AN69
Elmar Rd, N15 122 DR56
Elm Av, W5 138 CL74
Carshalton SM5 218 DF110
Ruislip HA4 115 BU60
Upminster RM14 128 FP62
Watford WD19 94 BY45
Elmbank, N14 99 DL45
Elmbank Av, Barn. EN5 79 CW42
Egham (Eng.Grn) TW20 172 AV93
Guildford GU2 258 AU135
Elm Bk Dr, Brom. BR1 204 EK96
Elm Bk Gdns, SW13 158 CS82
Elmbank Way, W7 137 CD71
Elmbourne Dr, Belv. DA17 167 FB77
Elmbourne Rd, SW17 180 DG90
Elmbridge, Harl. CM17 36 EZ12
Elmbridge Av, Surb. KT5 198 CP99
Elmbridge Cl, Ruis. HA4 115 BU58
Elmbridge Dr, Ruis. HA4 115 BT57
Elmbridge La, Wok. GU22 227 AZ119
★ **Elmbridge Mus**, Wey. KT13 212 BN105
Elmbridge Rd, Ilf. IG6 104 EU51
Elmbridge Wk, E8 *off Wilman Gro* 142 DU66
Elmbrook Cl, Sun. TW16 195 BV95
Elmbrook Gdns, SE9 164 EL84
Elmbrook Rd, Sutt. SM1 217 CZ105
Elm Cl, E11 124 EH58
N19 *off Hargrave Pk* 121 DJ61
NW4 119 CX57
SW20 *off Grand Dr* 199 CW98
Amersham HP6 55 AQ38
Buckhurst Hill IG9 102 EK47
Carshalton SM5 200 DF102
Dartford DA1 188 FJ88
Epping (Epp.Grn) CM16 51 EP24
Harrow HA2 116 CB58
Hayes UB3 135 BU72
Leatherhead KT22 231 CH122
Romford RM7 105 FB54
Slough (Farn.Com.) SL2 131 AQ65
Elm Cl, S. Croy. CR2 220 DS107
Staines (Stanw.) TW19 174 BK88
Surbiton KT5 198 CQ101
Tadworth (Box H.) KT20 248 CQ130
Twickenham TW2 176 CB89
Waltham Abbey EN9 67 ED34
Warlingham CR6 237 DX117
Woking GU21 226 AX115
Woking (Send M.) GU23 228 BG124
ELM CORNER, Wok. GU23 228 BN119
Elmcote Way, Rick. (Crox.Grn) WD3 74 BM44
Elm Ct, EC4 10 C9
Mitcham CR4 *off Armfield Cres* 200 DF96
Sunbury-on-Thames TW16 175 BT94
Elmcourt Rd, SE27 181 DP89
Sch **Elm Ct Sch**, SE27 *off Elmcourt Rd* 182 DQ89
Elm Cres, W5 138 CL74
Kingston upon Thames KT2 198 CL95
Elmcroft, N8 121 DM57
Leatherhead KT23 230 CA124
Elm Cft, Slou. (Datchet) SL3 152 AW81
Elmcroft Av, E11 124 EH57
N9 82 DV44
NW11 119 CZ59
Sidcup DA15 185 ET86
Elmcroft Cl, E11 124 EH56
W5 137 CK72
Chessington KT9 198 CL104
Feltham TW14 175 BT86
Elmcroft Cres, NW11 119 CY59
Harrow HA2 116 CA55
Elmcroft Dr, Ashf. TW15 174 BN92
Chessington KT9 198 CL104
Elmcroft Gdns, NW9 118 CN57
Elmcroft Rd, Orp. BR6 206 EU101
Elmcroft St, E5 122 DW63
Elmdale Rd, N13 99 DM50
Elmdene, Surb. KT5 198 CQ102
Elmdene Av, Horn. RM11 128 FM57
Elmdene Cl, Beck. BR3 203 DZ99
Elmdene Ct, Wok. GU22 *off Constitution Hill* 226 AY118
Elmdene Rd, SE18 165 EP78
Elmdon Rd, Houns. TW4 156 BX82
Hounslow (Hatt.Cr.) TW6 155 BT83
South Ockendon RM15 149 FU71
Elm Dr, Har. HA2 116 CB58
Hatfield AL10 45 CU19
Leatherhead KT22 231 CH122
St. Albans AL4 43 CJ20
Sunbury-on-Thames TW16 196 BW96
Swanley BR8 207 FD96
Waltham Cross (Chsht) EN8 67 DY28
Woking (Chobham) GU24 210 AT110
Elmer Av, Rom. (Hav.at.Bow.) RM4 105 FE48
Elmer Cl, Enf. EN2 81 DM41
Rainham RM13 147 FG66
Elmer Cotts, Lthd. KT22 231 CG123
Elmer Gdns, Edg. HA8 96 CP52
Isleworth TW7 157 CD83
Rainham RM13 147 FG66
Elmer Ms, Lthd. (Fetch.) KT22 231 CG123
Elmer Rd, SE6 183 EC87
Elmers Dr, Tedd. TW11 *off Kingston Rd* 177 CH93
ELMERS END, Beck. BR3 203 DY97
⇌ **Elmers End** 203 DX98
Tra **Elmers End** 203 DX98
Elmers End Rd, SE20 202 DW96
Beckenham BR3 202 DW96
Elmerside Rd, Beck. BR3 203 DY98
Elmers Rd, SE25 202 DU101
Sch **Elmer White Inf Sch**, NW4 *off Brent St* 119 CX57
Elm Fm Caravan Pk, Cher. (Lyne) KT16 193 BC101
Elmfield, Lthd. (Bkhm) KT23 230 CA123
Elmfield Av, N8 121 DL57
Mitcham CR4 200 DG95
Teddington TW11 177 CF92
Elmfield Cl, Grav. DA11 191 GH88
Harrow HA1 117 CE61
Potters Bar EN6 63 CY33
Elmfield Pk, Brom. BR1 204 EG97
Elmfield Rd, E4 101 EC47
E17 123 DX58
N2 120 DD55
SW17 180 DG89
Bromley BR1 204 EG97
Potters Bar EN6 63 CY33
Southall UB2 156 BY76
Elmfield Way, W9 6 G5
South Croydon CR2 220 DT109
Elm Friars Wk, NW1 141 DK66
Elm Gdns, N2 120 DC55
Enfield EN2 82 DR38
Epping (N.Wld Bas.) CM16 71 FB26
Epsom KT18 233 CW119
Esher (Clay.) KT10 215 CF107
Mitcham CR4 201 DK98
Welwyn Garden City AL8 29 CV09
Elmgate Av, Felt. TW13 175 BV90
Elmgate Gdns, Edg. HA8 96 CR50
Elm Grn, W3 138 CS72
Hemel Hempstead HP1 39 BE18
Elmgreen Cl, E15 *off Church St N* 144 EE67
Elm Gro, N8 121 DL58
NW2 119 CX63
SE15 162 DT82
SW19 179 CY94
Berkhamsted HP4 38 AV19
Caterham CR3 236 DS122
Epsom KT18 216 CQ114
Erith DA8 167 FD80
Harrow HA2 116 CA59
Hornchurch RM11 128 FL58
Kingston upon Thames KT2 198 CL95
Orpington BR6 205 ET102
Sutton SM1 218 DB105
Watford WD24 75 BU37
West Drayton UB7 *off Willow Av* 134 BM73
Woodford Green IG8 102 EF50
Coll **Elmgrove Adult Ed Cen**, Walt. KT12 *off Hersham Rd* 195 BU102
Elmgrove Cres, Har. HA1 117 CF57
Sch **Elmgrove First Sch**, Har. HA3 *off Kenmore Av* 117 CG56
Elmgrove Gdns, Har. HA1 117 CG57
Sch **Elmgrove Mid Sch**, Har. HA3 *off Kenmore Av* 117 CG56
Elm Gro Par, Wall. SM6 *off Butter Hill* 200 DG104
Elm Gro Rd, SW13 159 CU82
W5 158 CL75
Cobham KT11 230 BX116
Elmgrove Rd, Croy. CR0 202 DV101
Harrow HA1 117 CF57
Weybridge KT13 212 BN105
Elm Hall Gdns, E11 124 EH57
Elm Hatch, Harl. CM18 *off St. Andrews Meadow* 51 ET16
Elmhurst, Belv. DA17 166 EY79
Elmhurst Av, N2 120 DD55
Mitcham CR4 181 DH94
Elmhurst Ct, Guil. GU1 *off Lower Edgeborough Rd* 259 AZ135
Elmhurst Dr, E18 102 EG54
Dorking RH4 263 CH138
Hornchurch RM11 128 FJ60
Elmhurst Gdns, E18 *off Elmhurst Dr* 102 EH53
Elmhurst Mans, SW4 *off Edgeley Rd* 161 DK83
Sch **Elmhurst Prim Sch**, E7 *off Upton Pk Rd* 144 EH66
Elmhurst Rd, E7 144 EH66
N17 100 DT54
SE9 184 EL89
Enfield EN3 82 DW37
Slough SL3 153 BA76
Sch **Elmhurst Sch**, S.Croy. CR2 *off South Pk Hill Rd* 220 DR106
Elmhurst St, SW4 161 DK83
Elmhurst Vil, SE15 *off Cheltenham Rd* 162 DW84
Elmhurst Way, Loug. IG10 103 EM45
Elmington Cl, Bex. DA5 187 FB86
Elmington Est, SE5 162 DR80
Elmington Rd, SE5 162 DR81
Elmira St, SE13 163 EB83
Elm La, SE6 183 DZ89
Woking GU23 229 BP118
Elm Lawn Cl, Uxb. UB8 *off Park Rd* 134 BL66
Elmlea Dr, Hayes UB3 *off Grange Rd* 135 BS71
Elmlee Cl, Chis. BR7 185 EM93
Elmley Cl, E6 *off Northumberland Rd* 144 EL71
Elmley St, SE18 165 ER77
Elm Ms, Rich. TW10 *off Grove Rd* 178 CM86
Elmore Cl, Wem. HA0 138 CL68
Elmore Rd, E11 123 EC62
Coulsdon CR5 234 DF121
Enfield EN3 83 DX39
Elmores, Loug. IG10 85 EN41
Elmore St, N1 5 H5
Elm Par, Horn. RM12 *off St. Nicholas Av* 127 FH63
ELM PARK, Horn. RM12 127 FH64
⊖ **Elm Park** 127 FH63
Elm Pk, SW2 181 DM86
Stanmore HA7 95 CH50
Elm Pk Av, N15 122 DT57
Hornchurch RM12 127 FG63
Elm Pk Ct, Pnr. HA5 116 BW55
Elm Pk Gdns, NW4 119 CX57
SW10 17 N10
Elmpark Gdns, S.Croy. CR2 220 DW110
Elm Pk La, SW3 17 N10
Elm Pk Mans, SW10 *off Park Wk* 160 DC79
Elm Pk Rd, E10 123 DY60
N3 97 CZ52
N21 100 DQ45
SE25 202 DT97
SW3 160 DD79
Pinner HA5 94 BW54
Elm Pl, SW7 17 N9
Elm Quay Ct, SW8 161 DK79
Elm Rd, E7 144 EF65
E11 123 ED61
E17 123 EC57
N22 *off Granville Rd* 99 DP53
SW14 158 CQ83
Barnet EN5 79 CZ42
Beckenham BR3 203 DZ96
Chessington KT9 216 CL105
Dartford DA1 188 FK88
Epsom KT17 217 CT107
Erith DA8 167 FG81
Esher (Clay.) KT10 215 CF107
Feltham TW14 175 BR88
Godalming GU7 258 AT143
Gravesend DA12 191 GJ90
Grays RM17 170 GC79
Greenhithe DA9 189 FS86
High Wycombe (Penn) HP10 88 AD46
Hoddesdon EN11 *off Taverners Way* 49 EA17
Kingston upon Thames KT2 198 CM95
Leatherhead KT22 231 CH122
New Malden KT3 198 CR98
Orpington BR6 224 EU108
Purley CR8 219 DP113
Redhill RH1 250 DE134
Romford RM7 105 FB54
Sidcup DA14 186 EU91
South Ockendon (Aveley) RM15 148 FQ74
Thornton Heath CR7 202 DR98
Wallington SM6 200 DG102
Warlingham CR6 237 DX117
Wembley HA9 118 CL64
Westerham TN16 255 ES125
Windsor SL4 151 AP83
Woking GU21 226 AX118
Woking (Horsell) GU21 227 AZ115
Elm Rd W, Sutt. SM3 199 CZ101
Elm Row, NW3 120 DC62
Elmroyd Av, Pot.B. EN6 63 CZ33
Elmroyd Cl, Pot.B. EN6 63 CZ33
Elms, The, SW13 159 CT83
Hertford SG13 32 DU09
Elms Av, N10 121 DH55
NW4 119 CX57
Elmscott Gdns, N21 82 DQ44
Elmscott Rd, Brom. BR1 184 EF92
Elms Ct, Wem. HA0 117 CF63
Elms Cres, SW4 181 DJ86
Elmscroft Gdns, Pot.B. EN6 63 CY32
Elmsdale Rd, E17 123 DZ56
Elms Fm Rd, Horn. RM12 128 FJ64
Elms Gdns, Dag. RM9 126 EZ63
Wembley HA0 117 CG63
Elmshaw Rd, SW15 179 CU85
Elmshorn, Epsom KT17 233 CW116
Elmshott La, Slou. SL1 131 AL73
Elmshurst Cres, N2 120 DD56
Elmside, Croy. (New Adgtn) CR0 221 EB107
Guildford GU2 258 AU135
Elmside Rd, Wem. HA9 118 CN62
Elms La, Wem. HA0 117 CG63
Elmsleigh Av, Har. HA3 117 CH56
Elmsleigh Cen, The, Stai. TW18 173 BF91
Elmsleigh Ct, Sutt. SM1 200 DB104
Elmsleigh Rd, Stai. TW18 173 BF92
Twickenham TW2 177 CD89
Elmslie Cl, Epsom KT18 216 CQ114
Woodford Green IG8 103 EM51
Elmslie Pt, E3 13 L5
Elms Ms, W2 7 N9
Elms Pk Av, Wem. HA0 117 CG63
Elms Rd, SW4 181 DJ85
Gerrards Cross (Chal.St.P.) SL9 90 AY52
Harrow HA3 95 CE52
Ware SG12 33 EA05
ELMSTEAD, Chis. BR7 184 EK92
Elmstead Av, Chis. BR7 185 EM92
Wembley HA9 118 CL60
Elmstead Cl, N20 98 DA47
Epsom KT19 216 CS106
Sevenoaks TN13 256 FE122
Elmstead Cres, Well. DA16 166 EW79
Elmstead Gdns, Wor.Pk. KT4 199 CU104
Elmstead Glade, Chis. BR7 185 EM93
Elmstead La, Chis. BR7 185 EM92
Elmstead Rd, Erith DA8 167 FE81
Ilford IG3 125 ES61
West Byfleet KT14 212 BG113
⇌ **Elmstead Woods** 184 EL93
Elmstone Rd, SW6 160 DA81
Elm St, WC1 10 B4
Elmsway, Ashf. TW15 174 BM92
Elmswell Ct, Hert. SG14 31 DM08
Elmswood, Lthd. (Bkhm) KT23 230 BZ124
Elmsworth Av, Houns. TW3 156 CB82
Elm Ter, NW2 120 DA62
SE9 185 EN86
Grays RM20 169 FV79
Harrow HA3 95 CD52
Elmton Way, E5 *off Rendlesham Rd* 122 DU62
Elm Tree Av, Esher KT10 197 CD101
Elm Tree Cl, NW8 7 N1
Ashford TW15 *off Convent Rd* 175 BP92
Chertsey KT16 193 BE103
Horley RH6 268 DG147
Northolt UB5 136 BZ68
Elmtree Cl, W.Byf. (Byfleet) KT14 212 BL113
Sch **Elmtree Co First Sch**, Chesh. HP5 *off Elmtree Hill* 54 AP30
Elmtree Hill, Chesh. HP5 54 AP30
Elm Tree Rd, NW8 7 N1
Elmtree Rd, Tedd. TW11 177 CE91
Elm Tree Wk, Rick. (Chorl.) WD3 73 BF42
Elm Wk, NW3 120 DA61
SW20 199 CW98
Orpington BR6 205 EM104
Radlett WD7 77 CF36
Romford RM2 127 FG55
Elm Way, N11 98 DG51
NW10 118 CS63
Brentwood CM14 108 FU48
Epsom KT19 216 CR106
Rickmansworth WD3 92 BH46
Worcester Park KT4 199 CW104
Elmwood, Saw. CM21 36 EZ06
Welwyn Garden City AL8 29 CV10
Elmwood Av, N13 99 DL50
Borehamwood WD6 78 CP42
Feltham TW13 175 BU89
Harrow HA3 117 CG57
Elmwood Cl, Ashtd. KT21 231 CK117
Epsom KT17 217 CU108
Wallington SM6 200 DG103
Elmwood Ct, SW11 161 DH81
Ashtead KT21 *off Elmwood Cl* 231 CK117
Wembley HA0 117 CG62
Elmwood Cres, NW9 118 CQ56
Elmwood Dr, Bex. DA5 186 EY87
Epsom KT17 217 CU107
Elmwood Gdns, W7 137 CE72
Sch **Elmwood Inf Sch**, Croy. CR0 *off Lodge Rd* 201 DP100
Sch **Elmwood Jun Sch**, Croy. CR0 *off Lodge Rd* 201 DP101
Elmwood Pk, Ger.Cr. SL9 112 AY60
Sch **Elm Wd Prim Sch**, SE27 *off Carnac St* 182 DR90
Elmwood Rd, SE24 182 DR85
W4 158 CQ79
Croydon CR0 201 DP101
Mitcham CR4 200 DF97
Redhill RH1 250 DG130
Slough SL2 132 AV73
Elmworth Gro, SE21 182 DR89
Elnathan Ms, W9 7 K4
Elphinstone Rd, E17 101 DZ54
Elphinstone St, N5 *off Avenell Rd* 121 DP63
Elppin Ct, Brox. EN10 49 DZ20
Elrick Cl, Erith DA8 *off Queen St* 167 FE79
Elrington Rd, E8 142 DU65
Woodford Green IG8 102 EG50
Elruge Cl, West Dr. UB7 154 BK76
Elsa Rd, Well. DA16 166 EV82
Elsa St, E1 13 J6
Elsdale St, E9 142 DW65
Elsden Ms, E2 *off Old Ford Rd* 142 DW68
Elsden Rd, N17 100 DT53
Elsdon Rd, Wok. GU21 226 AU117
Elsenham Rd, E12 125 EN64
Elsenham St, SW18 179 CZ88
Elsham Rd, E11 124 EE62
W14 16 C4
Elsham Ter, W14 16 C4
Elsiedene Rd, N21 100 DQ45
Elsiemaud Rd, SE4 183 DZ85
Elsie Rd, SE22 162 DT84
Elsinge Rd, Enf. EN1 82 DV36
Elsinore Av, Stai. TW19 174 BL87
Elsinore Gdns, NW2 119 CY62
Elsinore Rd, SE23 183 DY88
Elsinore Way, Rich. TW9 *off Lower Richmond Rd* 158 CP83
Sch **Elsley Prim Sch**, Wem. HA9 *off Tokyngton Av* 138 CM65
Elsley Rd, SW11 160 DF83
Sch **Elsley Sch**, SW11 *off Elsley Rd* 160 DG83
Elspeth Rd, SW11 160 DF84
Wembley HA0 118 CL64
Elsrick Av, Mord. SM4 200 DA99
Elstan Way, Croy. CR0 203 DY101
Elstead Ct, Sutt. SM3 *off Stonecot Hill* 199 CY102
Elsted St, SE17 21 K8
Elstow Cl, SE9 185 EN85
Ruislip HA4 116 BX59
Elstow Gdns, Dag. RM9 146 EY67
Elstow Rd, Dag. RM9 146 EY66
ELSTREE, Borwd. WD6 77 CK43
★ **Elstree Aerodrome**, Borwd. WD6 77 CF41
⇌ **Elstree & Borehamwood** 78 CM42
Elstree Cl, Horn. RM12 *off Airfield Way* 147 FH65
Elstree Gdns, N9 100 DV46
Belvedere DA17 166 EY77
Ilford IG1 125 EQ64
Elstree Hill, Brom. BR1 184 EE94
Elstree Hill N, Borwd. (Elstree) WD6 77 CK44
Elstree Hill S, Borwd. (Elstree) WD6 95 CJ45
Elstree Pk, Borwd. WD6 78 CR44
Elstree Rd, Borwd. (Elstree) WD6 77 CG44
Bushey (Bushey Hth) WD23 95 CD45
Elstree Way, Borwd. WD6 78 CP41
Elswick Rd, SE13 163 EB82
Elswick St, SW6 160 DC82
Elsworth Cl, Felt. TW14 175 BS88
Elsworthy, T.Ditt. KT7 197 CE100
Elsworthy Ri, NW3 140 DE66
Elsworthy Rd, NW3 140 DE67
Elsworthy Ter, NW3 140 DE66
Elsynge Rd, SW18 180 DD85
ELTHAM, SE9 184 EK86
⇌ **Eltham** 185 EM85
Eltham Av, Slou. SL1 151 AL75
Sch **Eltham C of E Prim Sch**, SE9 *off Roper St* 185 EM85
Sch **Eltham Coll Jun Sch**, SE9 *off Mottingham La* 184 EK88
Sch **Eltham Coll Sen Sch**, SE9 *off Grove Pk Rd* 184 EK89
Eltham Grn, SE9 184 EJ85
Eltham Grn Rd, SE9 164 EJ84
Sch **Eltham Grn Sch**, SE9 *off Queenscroft Rd* 184 EK86
Eltham High St, SE9 185 EM86
Eltham Hill, SE9 184 EK85
Sch **Eltham Hill Tech Coll for Girls**, SE9 *off Eltham Hill* 184 EL86
★ **Eltham Palace**, SE9 184 EL87
Eltham Palace Rd, SE9 184 EJ86
Eltham Pk Gdns, SE9 165 EN84
Eltham Rd, SE9 184 EJ85
SE12 184 EF85
Elthiron Rd, SW6 160 DA81
Elthorne Av, W7 157 CF75
Elthorne Ct, Felt. TW13 176 BW88
Elthorne Pk Rd, W7 157 CF75
Elthorne Rd, N19 121 DK61
NW9 118 CR59
Uxbridge UB8 134 BK68
Elthorne Way, NW9 118 CR58
Elthruda Rd, SE13 183 ED86
Eltisley Rd, Ilf. IG1 125 EP63
Elton Av, Barn. EN5 79 CZ43
Greenford UB6 137 CF65
Wembley HA0 117 CH64
Elton Cl, Kings.T. KT1 177 CJ94
Elton Ho, E3 143 DZ67
Elton Pk, Wat. WD17 75 BV40
Elton Pl, N16 5 L1
Elton Rd, Hert. SG14 32 DQ08
Kingston upon Thames KT2 198 CM95
Purley CR8 219 DJ112
Elton Way, Wat. WD25 76 CB40
Eltringham St, SW18 160 DC84
Elvaston Ms, SW7 17 M5
Elvaston Pl, SW7 17 L6
Elveden Cl, Wok. GU22 228 BH117
Elveden Pl, NW10 138 CN68
Elveden Rd, NW10 138 CN68
Elvedon Rd, Cob. KT11 213 BV111
Feltham TW13 *off Ashford Rd* 175 BT90
Elvendon Rd, N13 99 DL51
Elver Gdns, E2 12 B1
Elverson Ms, SE8 163 EB82
DLR **Elverson Road** 163 EB82
Elverson Rd, SE8 163 EB82
Elverton St, SW1 19 L7
Elvet Av, Rom. RM2 128 FJ56
Elvington Grn, Brom. BR2 204 EF99
Elvington La, NW9 96 CS53
Elvino Rd, SE26 183 DY92
Elvis Rd, NW2 139 CW65
Elwell Cl, Egh. TW20 *off Mowbray Cres* 173 BA92
Elwick Rd, S.Ock. RM15 149 FW72
Elwill Way, Beck. BR3 203 EC98
Elwin St, E2 12 A1
Elwood, Harl. CM17 52 EY16
Elwood St, N5 121 DP62
Elwyn Gdns, SE12 184 EG87
Ely Av, Slou. SL1 131 AQ71
Ely Cl, Amer. HP7 55 AS39
Erith DA8 167 FF82
Hatfield AL10 45 CT17
New Malden KT3 199 CT96
Ely Ct, EC1 10 D6
Ely Gdns, Borwd. WD6 78 CR43
Dagenham RM10 127 FC62
Ilford IG1 *off Canterbury Av* 124 EL59
Elyne Rd, N4 121 DN58
Ely Pl, EC1 10 D6
Guildford GU2 *off Canterbury Rd* 242 AT132
Woodford Green IG8 103 EN51
Ely Rd, E10 123 EC58
Croydon CR0 202 DR99
Hounslow (Hthrw Air.) TW6 *off Eastern Perimeter Rd* 155 BT82
Hounslow (Houns.W.) TW4 156 BW83
St. Albans AL1 43 CH21
Elysian Av, Orp. BR5 205 ET100
Elysium Pl, SW6 *off Fulham Pk Gdns* 159 CZ82
Elysium St, SW6 *off Fulham Pk Gdns* 159 CZ82
Elystan Business Cen, Hayes UB4 136 BW73
Elystan Cl, Wall. SM6 219 DH109
Elystan Pl, SW3 18 B9
Elystan St, SW3 18 A8
Elystan Wk, N1 4 C8
Emanuel Av, W3 138 CQ72
Emanuel Dr, Hmptn. TW12 176 BZ92
Sch **Emanuel Sch**, SW11 *off Battersea Ri* 180 DE85

★ Place of interest | H Hospital | Sch School | Coll College | Uni University | ⇌ Railway station

⊖ Embankment 19 P1
Embankment, SW15 159 CX82
Embankment, The, Stai. (Wrays.) TW19 172 AW87
Twickenham TW1 177 CG88
Embankment Gdns, SW3 160 DF79
Embankment Pier 20 A1
Embankment Pl, WC2 19 P1
Embassy Ct, Sid. DA14 186 EV90
Welling DA16 off Welling High St 166 EV83
Embassy Gdns, Beck. BR3 off Blakeney Rd 203 DZ95
Emba St, SE16 22 B4
Ember Cen, Walt. KT12 196 BY103
Ember Cl, Add. KT15 212 BK106
Orpington BR5 205 EQ101
Embercourt Rd, T.Ditt. KT7 197 CE100
Ember Fm Av, E.Mol. KT8 197 CD100
Ember Fm Way, E.Mol. KT8 197 CD100
Ember Gdns, T.Ditt. KT7 197 CE101
Ember La, E.Mol. KT8 197 CD101
Esher KT10 197 CD101
Ember Rd, Slou. SL3 153 BB76
Emberson Way, Epp. (N.Wld Bas.) CM16 71 FC26
Emberton, SE5 162 DS79
Embleton Rd, SE13 163 EB83
Watford WD19 93 BU48
Embleton Wk, Hmptn. TW12 off Fearnley Cres 176 BZ93
Embry Cl, Stan. HA7 95 CG49
Embry Dr, Stan. HA7 95 CG51
Embry Way, Stan. HA7 95 CG50
Emden Cl, West Dr. UB7 154 BN75
Emden St, SW6 160 DB81
Emerald Cl, E16 144 EL72
Emerald Ct, Slou. SL1 152 AS75
Emerald Gdns, Dag. RM8 126 FA60
Emerald Sq, Sthl. UB2 156 BX76
Emerald St, WC1 10 A5
Emerson Dr, Horn. RM11 128 FK59
Emerson Gdns, Har. HA3 118 CM58
EMERSON PARK, Horn. RM11 128 FL58
⇌ Emerson Park 128 FL59
Emerson Pk Sch, Horn. RM11 off Wych Elm Rd 128 FP59
Emerson Rd, Ilf. IG1 125 EN59
Emersons Av, Swan. BR8 187 FF94
Emerson St, SE1 20 G1
Emerton Cl, Bexh. DA6 166 EY84
Emerton Ct, Berk. HP4 off Emerton Garth 38 AS16
Emerton Garth, Berk. HP4 38 AS16
Emerton Rd, Lthd. KT22 230 CC120
Emery Hill St, SW1 19 K6
Emery St, SE1 20 D5
Emes Rd, Erith DA8 167 FC80
Emilia Cl, Enf. EN3 82 DV43
Emily Davidson Dr, Epsom KT18 233 CV118
Emily Jackson Cl, Sev. TN13 257 FH124
Emley Rd, Add. KT15 194 BG104
Emlyn Gdns, W12 158 CS75
Emlyn La, Lthd. KT22 231 CG122
Emlyn Rd, W12 158 CS75
Horley RH6 268 DE147
Redhill RH1 266 DG136
Emmanuel Ct, Guil. GU2 242 AU131
Emmanuel C of E Prim Sch, NW6 off Mill La 120 DA64
Emmanuel Lo, Wal.Cr. (Chsht) EN8 off College Rd 66 DW30
Emmanuel Rd, SW12 181 DJ88
Northwood HA6 93 BT52
Emma Rd, E13 144 EF68
Emma's Cres, Ware (Stans.Abb.) SG12 33 EB11
Emma St, E2 142 DV68
Emmaus Way, Chig. IG7 103 EN50
Emmett Cl, Rad. (Shenley) WD7 62 CL33
Emmetts Cl, Wok. GU21 226 AW117
Emmott Av, Ilf. IG6 125 EQ57
Emmott Cl, E1 13 K4
NW11 120 DC58
Emms Pas, Kings.T. KT1 off High St 197 CK96
Emperor Cl, Berk. HP4 off Springfield Rd 38 AT16
Emperor's Gate, SW7 17 K6
Empire Av, N18 100 DQ50
Empire Ct, Wem. HA9 118 CP62
Empire Rd, Grnf. UB6 137 CJ67
Empire Sq, N7 121 DL62
SE20 off High St 183 DX94
Empire Vil, Red. RH1 266 DG144
Empire Way, Wem. HA9 118 CM63
Empire Wf Rd, E14 24 E8
Empress Av, E4 101 EA52
E12 124 EJ61
Ilford IG1 125 EM61
Woodford Green IG8 102 EF52
Empress Dr, Chis. BR7 185 EP93
Empress Ms, SE5 162 DQ82
Empress Pl, SW6 16 G10
Empress Rd, Grav. DA12 191 GL87
Empress St, SE17 162 DQ79
Empson St, E3 14 B3
Emsworth Cl, N9 100 DW46
Emsworth Rd, Ilf. IG6 103 EP54
Emsworth St, SW2 181 DM89
Emu Rd, SW8 161 DH82
Ena Rd, SW16 201 DL97
Enborne Grn, S.Ock. RM15 149 FU71
Enbrook St, W10 6 D2
Endale Cl, Cars. SM5 200 DF103
Endeavour Ho, Barn. EN5 80 DC42
Endeavour Rd, Wal.Cr. (Chsht) EN8 67 DY27
Endeavour Sch, The, Brwd. CM15 off Hogarth Av 109 FZ48
Endeavour Way, SW19 180 DB91
Barking IG11 146 EU68
Croydon CR0 201 DK101
Endell St, WC2 9 N7
Enderby St, SE10 24 F10
Enderley Cl, Har. HA3 off Enderley Rd 95 CE53
Enderley Rd, Har. HA3 95 CE53
Endersby Rd, Barn. EN5 79 CW43
Endersleigh Gdns, NW4 119 CU56
Endlebury Rd, E4 101 EB47
Endlesham Rd, SW12 180 DG87
Endsleigh Cl, S.Croy. CR2 220 DW110
Endsleigh Gdns, WC1 9 L3
Ilford IG1 125 EM61
Surbiton KT6 197 CJ100
Walton-on-Thames KT12 214 BW106
Endsleigh Ind Est, Sthl. UB2 156 BZ77
Endsleigh Pl, WC1 9 M3
Endsleigh Rd, W13 137 CG73
Redhill RH1 251 DJ129
Endsleigh Rd, Sthl. UB2 156 BY77
Endsleigh St, WC1 9 L3
Endway, Surb. KT5 198 CN101
Endwell Rd, SE4 163 DY82
Endymion Ct, Hat. AL10 off Endymion Rd 45 CW17
Endymion Ms, Hat. AL10 off Endymion Rd 45 CW17
Endymion Rd, N4 121 DN59
SW2 181 DM86
Hatfield AL10 45 CW17
Energen Cl, NW10 138 CS65
ENFIELD, EN1 - EN3 82 DT41
⇌ Enfield Chase 82 DQ41
Enfield Cl, Uxb. UB8 off Villier St 134 BK68
Enfield Coll, Enf. EN3 off Hertford Rd 82 DW41
Enfield Co Sch, Lwr Sch, Enf. EN2 off Rosemary Av 82 DS39
Upr Sch, Enf. EN2 off Holly Wk 82 DR41
Enfield Gram Sch, Boys Lwr Sch, Enf. EN1 off Baker St 82 DR40
Boys Upr Sch, Enf. EN2 off Market Pl 82 DR41
ENFIELD HIGHWAY, Enf. EN3 82 DW41
ENFIELD LOCK, Enf. EN3 83 DZ37
⇌ Enfield Lock 83 DY37
Enfield Retail Pk, Enf. EN1 82 DV41
Enfield Rd, N1 5 M6
W3 158 CP75
Brentford TW8 157 CK78
Enfield EN2 81 DK42
Hounslow (Hthrw Air.) TW6 off Eastern Perimeter Rd 155 BS82
ENFIELD TOWN, Enf. EN2 82 DR40
⇌ Enfield Town 82 DS42
Enfield Wk, Brent. TW8 157 CK78
ENFIELD WASH, Enf. EN3 83 DX38
Enford St, W1 8 C5
Engadine Cl, Croy. CR0 202 DT104
Engadine St, SW18 179 CZ88
Engate St, SE13 163 EC84
Engayne Gdns, Upmin. RM14 128 FP60
Engayne Prim Sch, Upmin. RM14 off Severn Dr 129 FS58
Engel Pk, NW7 97 CW51
Engineer Cl, SE18 165 EN79
Engineers Way, Wem. HA9 118 CN63
Englands La, NW3 140 DF65
Loughton IG10 85 EN40
England Way, N.Mal. KT3 198 CP98
Englefield Cl, Croy. CR0 off Queen's Rd 202 DQ100
Egham (Eng.Grn) TW20 off Alexandra Rd 172 AW93
Enfield EN2 81 DN40
Orpington BR5 205 ET98
Englefield Cres, Orp. BR5 205 ET98
ENGLEFIELD GREEN, Egh. TW20 172 AV92
Englefield Grn, Egh. (Eng.Grn) TW20 172 AW91
Englefield Grn Inf Sch, Egh. TW20 off Barley Mow Rd 172 AW92
Englefield Path, Orp. BR5 205 ET98
Englefield Rd, N1 5 J4
Orpington BR5 206 EU98
Engleheart Dr, Felt. TW14 175 BT86
Engleheart Rd, SE6 183 EB87
Englehurst, Egh. (Eng.Grn) TW20 172 AW93
Englemere Pk, Lthd. (Oxshott) KT22 214 CB114
Englewood Rd, SW12 181 DH86
Engliff La, Wok. GU22 227 BF116
English Gdns, Stai. (Wrays.) TW19 152 AX84
English Grds, SE1 21 L2
English Martyrs RC Prim Sch, E1 11 P8
SE17 21 K8
English St, E3 13 L3
Enid Cl, St.Alb. (Brick.Wd) AL2 60 BZ31
Enid St, SE16 21 P5
Enmore Av, SE25 202 DU99
Enmore Gdns, SW14 178 CR85
Enmore Rd, SE25 202 DU99
SW15 159 CW84
Southall UB1 136 CA70
Ennerdale Av, Horn. RM12 127 FG64
Stanmore HA7 117 CJ55
Ennerdale Cl, Felt. TW14 175 BT88
St. Albans AL1 43 CH22
Sutton SM1 217 CZ105
Ennerdale Cres, Slou. SL1 130 AJ71
Ennerdale Dr, NW9 118 CS57
Watford WD25 60 BW34
Ennerdale Gdns, Wem. HA9 117 CK60
Ennerdale Ho, E3 13 L3
Ennerdale Rd, Bexh. DA7 166 FA81
Richmond TW9 158 CM82
Ennersdale Rd, SE13 183 ED85
Ennismore Av, W4 159 CT77
Greenford UB6 137 CE65
Guildford GU1 243 AZ134
Ennismore Gdns, SW7 18 A4
Thames Ditton KT7 197 CE100
Ennismore Gdns Ms, SW7 18 A5
Ennismore Ms, SW7 18 A5
Ennismore St, SW7 18 A5
Ennis Rd, N4 121 DN60
SE18 165 EQ79
Ensign Cl, Pur. CR8 219 DN110
Staines (Stanw.) TW19 174 BK88
Ensign Dr, N13 100 DQ48
Ensign St, E1 12 A9
Ensign Way, Stai. (Stanw.) TW19 174 BK88
Wallington SM6 219 DL108
Enslin Rd, SE9 185 EN86
Ensor Ms, SW7 17 N9
Enstone Rd, Enf. EN3 83 DY41
Uxbridge UB10 114 BM62
Enterdent Rd, Gdse. RH9 252 DW134
Enterprise Cl, Croy. CR0 201 DN102
Enterprise Pk, E10 123 DY60
Enterprise Way, NW10 139 CU69
SW18 160 DA84
Teddington TW11 177 CF92
Enterprize Way, SE8 23 L7
Eothen Cl, Cat. CR3 236 DU124
Eothen Hts, Cat. CR3 236 DU124
Epirus Ms, SW6 160 DA80
Epirus Rd, SW6 159 CZ80
EPPING, CM16 69 ES31
⊖ Epping 70 EU31
Epping Cen for Comm Ed, Epp. CM16 off St. John's Rd 69 ET30
Epping Cl, E14 23 P7
Romford RM7 127 FB55
Epping Co Inf Sch, Epp. CM16 off Coronation Hill 69 ET29
Epping Co Jun Sch, Epp. CM16 off St. John's Rd 69 ET30
★ Epping Forest, Epp. & Loug. 84 EJ39
Epping Forest Coll of Further Ed, Loug. IG10 off Borders La 85 EP42
★ Epping Forest District Mus, Wal.Abb. EN9 off Sun St 67 EC33
Epping Forest Fld Cen, Loug. IG10 off Wake Rd 84 EJ38
Epping Glade, E4 83 EC44
EPPING GREEN, Epp. CM16 51 EN24
EPPING GREEN, Hert. SG13 47 DK21
Epping Grn, Hem.H. HP2 40 BN15
Epping La, Rom. (Stap.Taw.) RM4 86 EV40
Epping Long Grn, Epp. (Epp.Grn) CM16 51 EM24
Epping New Rd, Buck.H. IG9 102 EH47
Loughton IG10 84 EH43
Epping Pl, N1 4 C4
Epping Rd, Epp. CM16 85 EM36
Epping (Epp.Grn) CM16 69 ER27
Epping (N.Wld Bas.) CM16 70 EW28
Harlow CM19 50 EK18
Ongar CM5 53 FF24
Ongar (Toot Hill) CM5 71 FC30
Waltham Abbey EN9 50 EK18
Epping Upland C of E Prim Sch, Epp. CM16 off Carters La 51 EP24
Epping Way, E4 83 EB44
Epple Rd, SW6 159 CZ81
EPSOM, KT17 - KT19 216 CQ114
⇌ Epsom 216 CR113
Epsom & Ewell Comm Hosp, Epsom KT19 216 CL111
Epsom & Ewell High Sch, Epsom KT19 off Ruxley La 216 CQ106
Epsom Cl, Bexh. DA7 167 FB83
Northolt UB5 116 BZ64
Epsom Coll, Epsom KT17 off Longdown La S 217 CU114
Epsom Co Prim Sch, Epsom KT19 off Pound La 216 CR111
⇌ Epsom Downs 233 CV115
Epsom Downs, Epsom KT18 233 CU118
Epsom Downs Metro Cen, Tad. KT20 off Waterfield 233 CV120
Epsom Gap, Lthd. KT22 231 CH115
Epsom Gen Hosp, Epsom KT18 232 CQ115
Epsom La N, Epsom KT18 233 CV118
Tadworth KT20 233 CV118
Epsom La S, Tad. KT20 233 CW121
★ Epsom Racecourse, Epsom KT18 233 CT118
Epsom Rd, E10 123 EC58
Ashtead KT21 232 CM118
Croydon CR0 219 DN105
Epsom KT17 217 CT110
Guildford GU1 243 BD133
Guildford (E.Clan.) GU4 244 BM131
Ilford IG3 125 ET58
Leatherhead KT22 231 CH121
Leatherhead (W.Hors.) KT24 245 BP130
Morden SM4 199 CZ101
Sutton SM3 199 CZ101
Epsom Sch of Art & Design, Epsom KT18 off Ashley Rd 216 CS114
Epsom KT17 off Lintons La 216 CS112
Epsom Sq, Houns. (Hthrw Air.) TW6 off Eastern Perimeter Rd 155 BT82
Epsom Way, Horn. RM12 128 FM63
Epstein Rd, SE28 146 EU74
Epworth Rd, Islw. TW7 157 CH80
Epworth St, EC2 11 K4
Equity Sq, E2 11 P2
Erasmus St, SW1 19 M8
Erconwald St, W12 139 CT72
Erebus Dr, SE28 165 EQ76
Eresby Dr, Beck. BR3 203 EA102
Eresby Pl, NW6 140 DA66
Erica Cl, Slou. SL1 131 AL73
Erica Ct, Swan. BR8 off Azalea Dr 207 FE98
Woking GU22 226 AX118
Erica Gdns, Croy. CR0 221 EB105
Erica St, W12 139 CU73
Eric Clarke La, Bark. IG11 145 EP70
Eric Cl, E7 124 EG63
Ericcson Cl, SW18 180 DA85
Eric Rd, E7 124 EG63
NW10 off Church Rd 139 CT65
Romford RM6 126 EX59
Eric Steele Ho, St.Alb. AL2 60 CB27
Eric St, E3 13 L3
Eridge Grn Cl, Orp. BR5 off Petten Gro 206 EW102
Eridge Rd, W4 158 CR76
Erin Cl, Brom. BR1 184 EE94
Ilford IG3 126 EU58
Erindale, SE18 165 ER79
Erindale Ter, SE18 165 ER79
Eriswell Cres, Walt. KT12 213 BS107
Eriswell Rd, Walt. KT12 213 BT105
ERITH, DA8 & DA18 167 FD79
⇌ Erith 167 FE78
Erith & District Hosp, Erith DA8 167 FD79
Erith Ct, Purf. RM19 168 FN77
Erith Cres, Rom. RM5 105 FC53
Erith High St, Erith DA8 167 FE78
★ Erith Lib & Mus, Erith DA8 off Walnut Tree Rd 167 FE78
Erith Rd, Belv. DA17 166 FA78
Bexleyheath DA7 167 FB84
Erith DA8 167 FB84
Erith Sch, Erith DA8 off Avenue Rd 167 FD80
West, Erith DA8 off Avenue Rd 167 FD80
Erkenwald Cl, Cher. KT16 193 BE101
Erlanger Rd, SE14 163 DX81
Erlesmere Gdns, W13 157 CG76
Ermine Cl, Houns. TW4 156 BW82
St. Albans AL3 42 CA21
Waltham Cross (Chsht) EN7 66 DV31
Ermine Ho, N17 off Moselle St 100 DT52
Ermine Rd, N15 122 DT58
SE13 163 EB83
Ermine Side, Enf. EN1 82 DU43
Ermington Rd, SE9 185 EQ89
Ermyn Cl, Lthd. KT22 231 CK121
Ermyn Way, Lthd. KT22 231 CK121
Ernald Av, E6 144 EL68
Ernan Cl, S.Ock. RM15 149 FU71
Ernan Rd, S.Ock. RM15 149 FU71
Erncroft Way, Twick. TW1 177 CF86
Ernest Av, SE27 181 DP91
Ernest Bevin Coll, SW17 off Beechcroft Rd 180 DE89
Ernest Cl, Beck. BR3 203 EA99
Ernest Gdns, W4 158 CP79
Ernest Gro, Beck. BR3 203 DZ99
Ernest Rd, Horn. RM11 128 FL58
Kingston upon Thames KT1 198 CP96
Ernest Sq, Kings.T. KT1 198 CP96
Ernest St, E1 13 H4
Ernle Rd, SW20 179 CV94
Ernshaw Pl, SW15 off Carlton Dr 179 CY85
★ Eros, W1 9 L10
Erpingham Rd, SW15 159 CW83
Erridge Rd, SW19 200 DA96
Erriff Dr, S.Ock. RM15 149 FT71
Errington Cl, Grays RM16 off Cedar Rd 171 GH76
Errington Dr, Wind. SL4 151 AN81
Errington Rd, W9 6 F3
Errol Gdns, Hayes UB4 135 BV70
New Malden KT3 199 CU98
Erroll Rd, Rom. RM1 127 FF56
Errol St, EC1 11 H4
Erskine Cl, Sutt. SM1 200 DE104
Erskine Cres, N17 122 DV56
Erskine Hill, NW11 120 DA57
Erskine Ms, NW3 off Erskine Rd 140 DF66
Erskine Rd, E17 123 DZ56
NW3 140 DF66
Sutton SM1 218 DD105
Watford WD19 94 BW48
Erwood Rd, SE7 164 EL78
Esam Way, SW16 181 DN92
Escombe Dr, Guil. GU2 242 AV129
Escott Gdns, SE9 184 EL91
Escott Pl, Cher. (Ott.) KT16 211 BC107
Escot Way, Barn. EN5 79 CW43
Escreet Gro, SE18 165 EN77
Esdaile Gdns, Upmin. RM14 129 FR59
Esdaile La, Hodd. EN11 49 EA18
ESHER, KT10 214 CB105
⇌ Esher 197 CD103
Esher Av, Rom. RM7 127 FC58
Sutton SM3 199 CX104
Walton-on-Thames KT12 195 BU101
Esher Bypass, Chess. KT9 215 CH108
Cobham KT11 213 BU112
Esher KT10 215 CH108
Esher Cl, Bex. DA5 186 EY88
Esher KT10 214 CB106
Esher C of E (Aided) Prim Sch, Esher KT10 off Milbourne La 214 CC106
Esher C of E High Sch, Esher KT10 off More La 196 CA104
Esher Cres, Houns. (Hthrw Air.) TW6 off Eastern Perimeter Rd 155 BS82
Esher Gdns, SW19 179 CX89
Esher Grn, Esher KT10 214 CB105
Esher Grn Cen - Adult Ed Cen, Esher KT10 off Esher Grn 214 CB105
Esher Ms, Mitch. CR4 200 DF97
Esher Pk Av, Esher KT10 214 CC105
Esher Pl Av, Esher KT10 214 CB105
Esher Rd, E.Mol. KT8 197 CD100
Ilford IG3 125 ES62
Walton-on-Thames KT12 214 BX106
Esher 6th Form Coll, T.Ditt. KT7 off Weston Grn Rd 197 CE101
Eskdale, St.Alb. (Lon.Col.) AL2 62 CM27
Eskdale Av, Chesh. HP5 54 AQ30
Northolt UB5 136 BZ67
Eskdale Cl, Dart. DA2 188 FQ89
Wembley HA9 117 CK61
Eskdale Ct, Hem.H. HP2 off Lonsdale 40 BL17
Eskdale Gdns, Pur. CR8 220 DR114
Eskdale Rd, Bexh. DA7 166 FA82
Uxbridge UB8 134 BH68
Eskley Gdns, S.Ock. RM15 149 FV70
Eskmont Ridge, SE19 182 DS94
Esk Rd, E13 15 M3
Esk Way, Rom. RM1 105 FD52
Esmar Cres, NW9 119 CU59
Esme Ho, SW15 159 CT84
Esmeralda Rd, SE1 22 B8
Esmond Cl, Rain. RM13 off Dawson Dr 147 FH66
Esmond Rd, NW6 139 CZ67
W4 158 CR77
Esmond St, SW15 159 CY84
Esparto St, SW18 180 DB87
Essendene Cl, Cat. CR3 236 DS123
Essendene Lo Sch, Cat. CR3 off Essendene Rd 236 DS123
Essendene Rd, Cat. CR3 236 DS123
Essenden Rd, Belv. DA17 166 FA78
South Croydon CR2 220 DS108
Essendine Prim Sch, W9 7 H2
Essendine Rd, W9 7 H3
ESSENDON, Hat. AL9 46 DE17
Essendon C of E Prim Sch, Hat. AL9 off School La 46 DF17
Essendon Gdns, Welw.G.C. AL7 29 CZ09
Essendon Hill, Hat. AL9 46 DE17
Essendon Rd, Hert. SG13 46 DG15
Essex Av, Islw. TW7 157 CE83
Slough SL2 131 AQ71
Essex Cl, E17 123 DY56
Addlestone KT15 212 BJ105
Morden SM4 199 CX101
Romford RM7 127 FB56
Ruislip HA4 116 BX60
Essex Ct, EC4 10 C8
SW13 159 CT82
Essex Gdns, N4 121 DP58
Hornchurch RM11 128 FM57
Essex Gro, SE19 182 DR93
Essex Ho, E14 14 A7
Essex La, Kings L. WD4 59 BS33
Essex Nuffield Hosp, Brwd. CM15 108 FY46
Essex Pk, N3 98 DB51
Essex Pk Ms, W3 138 CS74
Essex Pl, W4 158 CQ77
Essex Pl Sq, W4 off Chiswick High Rd 158 CR77
Essex Prim Sch, E12 off Sheridan Rd 125 EM64
⇌ Essex Road 4 G6
Essex Rd, E4 102 EE46
E10 123 EC58
E12 124 EL64
E17 123 DY58
E18 102 EH54
N1 4 G6
NW10 138 CS66
W3 138 CQ73
W4 off Belmont Rd 158 CR77
Barking IG11 145 ER66
Borehamwood WD6 78 CN41
Chesham HP5 54 AQ29
Dagenham RM10 127 FC64
Dartford DA1 188 FK86
Enfield EN2 82 DR42
Gravesend DA11 191 GG88
Grays RM20 169 FU79
Hoddesdon EN11 49 EC18
Longfield DA3 209 FX96
Romford RM7 127 FB56
Romford (Chad.Hth) RM6 126 EW59
Watford WD17 75 BU40
Essex Rd S, E11 123 ED59
Essex St, E7 124 EG64
WC2 10 C9
St. Albans AL1 43 CE19
Essex Twr, SE20 202 DV95
Essex Vil, W8 16 G4
Essex Way, Brwd. CM13 107 FW51
Epping CM16 70 EV32
Ongar CM5 71 FF29
Essex Wf, E5 122 DW61
Essian St, E1 13 J5
Essoldo Way, Edg. HA8 118 CM55
Estate Way, E10 123 DZ60
Estcourt Rd, SE25 202 DV100
SW6 159 CZ80
Watford WD17 76 BW41
Estella Av, N.Mal. KT3 199 CV98
Estelle Rd, NW3 120 DF63
Esterbrooke St, SW1 19 L8
Este Rd, SW11 160 DE83
Estfeld Cl, Hodd. EN11 33 EB14
Esther Cl, N21 99 DN45
Esther Rd, E11 124 EE59
Estoria Cl, SW2 181 DN87
★ Estorick Collection of Modern Italian Art, N1 4 F4
Estreham Rd, SW16 181 DK93
Estridge Cl, Houns. TW3 156 CA84
Estuary Cl, Bark. IG11 146 EV69
Eswyn Rd, SW17 180 DF91
Etchingham Pk Rd, N3 98 DB52
Etchingham Rd, E15 123 EC63
Eternit Wk, SW6 159 CW81
Etfield Gro, Sid. DA14 186 EV92
Ethel Bailey Cl, Epsom KT19 216 CN112
Ethelbert Cl, Brom. BR1 204 EG97
Ethelbert Gdns, Ilf. IG2 125 EM57
Ethelbert Rd, SW20 199 CX95
Bromley BR1 204 EG97
Dartford (Hawley) DA2 188 FL91
Erith DA8 167 FC80
Orpington BR5 206 EX97
Ethelbert St, SW12 off Fernlea Rd 181 DH88
Ethelburga Rd, Rom. RM3 106 FM53
Ethelburga St, SW11 160 DE81
Ethel Davis Spec Sch, Ilf. IG3 off Barley La 126 EV57
Etheldene Av, N10 121 DJ56
Ethelden Rd, W12 139 CV74
Ethelred Cl, Welw.G.C. AL7 29 CZ10
Ethel Rd, E16 15 N8
Ashford TW15 174 BL92
Ethel St, SE17 20 G8
Ethel Ter, Orp. BR6 224 EW109
Ethelwine Pl, Abb.L. WD5 off The Crescent 59 BT30
Etheridge Grn, Loug. IG10 off Etheridge Rd 85 EQ41
Etheridge Rd, NW2 119 CW59
Loughton IG10 85 EP40
Etherley Rd, N15 122 DQ57
Etherow St, SE22 182 DU86
Etherstone Grn, SW16 181 DN91
Etherstone Rd, SW16 181 DN91
Ethnard Rd, SE15 162 DV79
Ethorpe Cl, Ger.Cr. SL9 112 AY57
Ethorpe Cres, Ger.Cr. SL9 112 AY57
Ethronvi Rd, Bexh. DA7 166 EY83
Etloe Rd, E10 123 EA61
Etna Rd, St.Alb. AL3 43 CD19
ETON, Wind. SL4 151 AQ80
Eton Av, N12 98 DC52
NW3 140 DD66
Barnet EN4 80 DE44
Hounslow TW5 156 BZ79
New Malden KT3 198 CR99
Wembley HA0 117 CH63
Eton Cl, SW18 180 DB87
Slough (Datchet) SL3 152 AU79
Eton Coll, Wind. SL4 off High St 151 AR79
Eton Coll Rd, NW3 140 DF65
Eton Ct, NW3 off Eton Av 140 DD66
Staines TW18 off Richmond Rd 173 BF92
Wembley HA0 off Eton Av 117 CJ63
Windsor (Eton) SL4 151 AR80
Eton End P.N.E.U. Sch, Slou. SL3 off Eton Rd 152 AU79
Eton Garages, NW3 off Lambolle Pl 140 DE65
Eton Gro, NW9 118 CN55
SE13 164 EE83
Eton Hall, NW3 off Eton Coll Rd 140 DF65
Eton Ho, SW4 off Clapham Common N Side 161 DH84
Eton Pl, NW3 off Haverstock Hill 140 DG66
Eton Porny C of E First Sch, Wind. SL4 off High St 151 AR79
Eton Ri, NW3 off Eton Coll Rd 140 DF65
Eton Rd, NW3 140 DF66
Hayes UB3 155 BT80
Ilford IG1 125 EQ64
Orpington BR6 224 EV105

Eton Rd, Slou. (Datchet) SL3 .152 AT78
Eton Sq, Wind. (Eton) SL4 . .151 AR80
Eton St, Rich.TW9 .178 CL85
Eton Vil, NW3 .140 DF65
Eton Way, Dart. DA1 .168 FJ84
ETON WICK, Wind. SL4 . . .151 AM77
Sch Eton Wick C of E First Sch, Wind. SL4
off Sheepcote Rd .151 AN78
Eton Wick Rd, Wind. (Eton Wick) SL4 .151 AL77
Etta St, SE8 .163 DY79
Etton Cl, Horn. RM12 .128 FL61
Ettrick St, E14 .14 D7
Etwell Pl, Surb. KT5 .198 CM100
Euclid Way, Grays RM20 . .169 FU78
Euesden Cl, N9 .100 DV48
Eugene Cl, Rom. RM2 .128 FJ56
Eugenia Rd, SE16 .22 F8
Eunice Gro, Chesh. HP5 . . . .54 AR32
Eureka Rd, Kings.T. KT1
off Washington Rd .198 CN96
Coll Eurocentres Lee Grn, SE3 *off Meadowcourt Rd* .164 EF84
Coll Europa Cen for Modern Languages, Horn. RM11
off The Walk .128 FM61
Europa Pk Rd, Guil. GU1 . . .242 AW133
Europa Pl, EC1 .10 G2
Europa Rd, Hem.H. HP2
off Jupiter Dr .40 BM17
Europa Trd Est, Erith DA8 . .167 FD78
Europe Rd, SE18 .165 EM76
Eustace Rd, E6 .144 EL69
SW6 .160 DA80
Guildford GU4 .243 BD132
Romford RM6 .126 EX59
⇌ Euston .9 K1
⊖ Euston .9 K1
Euston Av, Wat. WD18 .75 BT43
Euston Cen, NW1
off Triton Sq .141 DJ70
Euston Gro, NW1 .9 L2
Euston Rd, N1 .9 N1
NW1 .9 H4
Croydon CR0 .201 DN102
⊖ Euston Square .9 K3
Euston Sq, NW1 .9 L2
Euston Sta Colonnade, NW1 . .9 L2
Euston St, NW1 .9 K3
Euston Twr, NW1 .9 J3
Evandale Rd, SW9 .161 DN82
Evangelist Rd, NW5 .121 DH63
Evans Av, Wat. WD25 .75 BT35
Evans Business Cen, NW2 . .119 CU62
Evans Cl, E8 .5 P4
Greenhithe DA9 .189 FU85
Rickmansworth (Crox.Grn) WD3 *off New Rd* .74 BN43
Evansdale, Rain. RM13
off New Zealand Way . . .147 FF69
Evans Gro, Felt.TW13 .176 CA89
St. Albans AL4 .43 CJ16
Evans Rd, SE6 .184 EE89
Evanston Av, E4 .101 EC52
Evanston Gdns, Ilf. IG4 .124 EL58
Evans Wf, Hem.H. HP3 .40 BL24
Eva Rd, Rom. RM6 .126 EW59
H Evelina Children's Hosp, St. Thomas' Hosp, SE1 . .20 A5
Evelina Rd, SE15 .162 DW83
SE20 .183 DX94
Eveline Lowe Est, SE16 .22 A6
Sch Eveline Lowe Prim Sch, SE1 .22 B10
Eveline Rd, Mitch. CR4 .200 DF95
Evelyn Av, NW9 .118 CR56
Ruislip HA4 .115 BT58
Evelyn Cl, Twick. TW2 .176 CB87
Woking GU22 .226 AX120
Evelyn Cotts, Dor. RH5 . . .262 BX143
Evelyn Ct, N1 .5 J10
Evelyn Cres, Sun.TW16 . . .195 BT95
Evelyn Denington Rd, E6 . .144 EL70
Evelyn Dr, Pnr. HA5 .94 BX52
Evelyn Fox Ct, W10 .139 CW71
Evelyn Gdns, SW7 .17 N10
Godstone RH9 .252 DW130
Richmond TW9
off Kew Rd .158 CL84
Evelyn Gro, W5 .138 CM74
Southall UB1 .136 BZ72
Evelyn Rd, E16 .25 N1
E17 .123 EC56
SW19 .180 DB92
W4 .158 CR76
Barnet EN4 .80 DF42
Richmond TW9 .158 CL83
Richmond (Ham) TW10 . . .177 CJ90
Evelyns Cl, Uxb. UB8 .134 BN72
Sch Evelyns Comm Sch, West Dr. UB7
off Appletree Av .134 BM72
Evelyn Sharp Cl, Rom. RM2
off Amery Gdns .128 FK55
Evelyn St, SE8 .23 J8
Evelyn Ter, Rich.TW9 .158 CL83
Evelyn Wk, N1 .5 J10
Brentwood CM13 .107 FW51
Evelyn Way, Cob. (Stoke D'Ab.) KT11 .230 BZ116
Epsom KT19 .216 CN111
Sunbury-on-Thames TW16 .195 BT95
Wallington SM6 .219 DK105
Evelyn Yd, W1 .9 L7
Evening Hill, Beck. BR3 . . .183 EC94
Evensyde, Wat. WD18 .75 BR44
Evenwood Cl, SW15 .179 CY85
Everard Av, Brom. BR2 .204 EG102
Slough SL1 .152 AS75
Everard Cl, St.Alb. AL1 .43 CD22
Everard La, Cat. CR3
off Tillingdown Hill .236 DU122
Everard Way, Wem. HA9 . . .118 CL62
Everatt Cl, SW18
off Amerland Rd .179 CZ86
Everdon Rd, SW13 .159 CU79
Everest Cl, Grav. (Nthflt) DA11 .190 GE90
Everest Ct, Wok. GU21
off Langmans Way .226 AS116
Everest Pl, E14 .14 C5
Swanley BR8 .207 FD98
Everest Rd, SE9 .185 EM85
Staines (Stanw.) TW19 . . .174 BK87
Everest Way, Hem.H. HP2 . .40 BN19
Everett Cl, Bushey (Bushey Hth) WD23 .95 CE46
Everett Cl, Pnr. HA5 .115 BT55
Waltham Cross (Chsht) EN7 .66 DQ25
Everett Wk, Belv. DA17
off Osborne Rd .166 EZ78
Everglade, West. (Bigg.H.) TN16 .238 EK118
Everglade Strand, NW9 .97 CT53
Evergreen Cl, Stai. (Stanw.) TW19 *off Evergreen Way* .174 BK87
Evergreen Oak Av, Wind. SL4 .152 AU83
Evergreen Sq, E8 .5 N5
Evergreen Wk, Hem.H. HP3 . .40 BL22
Evergreen Way, Hayes UB3 .135 BT73
Staines (Stanw.) TW19 . . .174 BK87
Everilda St, N1 .4 B8
Evering Rd, E5 .122 DT62
N16 .122 DT62
Everington Rd, N10 .98 DF54
Everington St, W6 .159 CX79
Everitt Rd, NW10 .138 CR69
Everlands Cl, Wok. GU22 . . .226 AY118
Everlasting La, St.Alb. AL3 . .42 CC19
Everleigh St, N4 .121 DM60
Eve Rd, E11 .124 EE63
E15 .144 EE68
N17 .122 DS55
Isleworth TW7 .157 CG84
Woking GU21 .227 BB115
Eversfield Gdns, NW7 .96 CS52
Eversfield Rd, Reig. RH2 . . .250 DB134
Richmond TW9 .158 CM82
Evershed Wk, W4 .158 CR77
Eversholt St, NW1 .141 DJ68
Evershot Rd, N4 .121 DM60
Eversleigh Gdns, Upmin. RM14 .129 FR60
Eversleigh Rd, E6 .144 EK67
N3 .97 CZ52
SW11 .160 DF83
Barnet EN5 .80 DC43
Eversley Av, Bexh. DA7 .167 FD82
Wembley HA9 .118 CN61
Eversley Cl, N21 .81 DM44
Loughton IG10 .85 EQ41
Eversley Cres, N21 .81 DM44
Isleworth TW7 .157 CD81
Ruislip HA4 .115 BS61
Eversley Cross, Bexh. DA7 . .167 FE82
Eversley Mt, N21 .81 DM44
Eversley Pk, SW19 .179 CV92
Eversley Pk Rd, N21 .81 DM44
Sch Eversley Prim Sch, N21
off Chaseville Pk Rd .81 DM43
Eversley Rd, SE7 .164 EH79
SE19 .182 DR94
Surbiton KT5 .198 CM98
Eversley Way, Croy. CR0 . . .221 EA105
Egham TW20 .193 BC96
Everthorpe Rd, SE15 .162 DT83
Everton Bldgs, NW1 .9 J2
Everton Dr, Stan. HA7 .118 CM55
Everton Rd, Croy. CR0 .202 DU102
Evesham Av, E17 .101 EA54
Evesham Cl, Grnf. UB6 .136 CB68
Reigate RH2 .249 CZ133
Sutton SM2 .218 DA108
Evesham Ct, W13
off Tewkesbury Rd .137 CG74
Evesham Grn, Mord. SM4 . .200 DB100
Evesham Rd, E15 .144 EF67
N11 .99 DJ50
Gravesend DA12 .191 GK89
Morden SM4 .200 DB100
Reigate RH2 .249 CZ134
Evesham Rd N, Reig. RH2 . .249 CZ133
Evesham St, W11 .6 A10
Evesham Wk, SE5
off Love Wk .162 DR82
SW9 .161 DN82
Evesham Way, SW11 .160 DG83
Ilford IG5 .125 EN55
Evreham Rd, Iver SL0 .133 BE72
Evron Pl, Hert. SG14
off Fore St .32 DR09
Evry Rd, Sid. DA14 .186 EW93
Ewald Rd, SW6 .159 CZ82
Ewanrigg Ter, Wdf.Grn. IG8 .102 EJ50
Ewan Rd, Rom. (Harold Wd) RM3 .106 FK54
Ewart Gro, N22 .99 DN53
Ewart Pl, E3 *off Roman Rd* .143 DZ68
Ewart Rd, SE23 .183 DX87
Ewe Cl, N7 .141 DL65
Ewelands, Horl. RH6 .269 DJ147
EWELL, Epsom KT17 .217 CU110
Ewell Bypass, Epsom KT17 .217 CU108
Sch Ewell Castle Sch, Epsom KT17 *off Church St* .217 CU109
Ewell Ct Av, Epsom KT19 . .216 CS106
Ewell Downs Rd, Epsom KT17 .217 CU111
⇌ Ewell East .217 CV110
Sch Ewell Gro Inf Sch, Epsom KT17 *off West St* .217 CT109
Ewell Ho Gro, Epsom KT17 .217 CT110
Ewellhurst Rd, Ilf. IG5 .102 EL54
Ewell Pk Gdns, Epsom KT17 .217 CU108
Ewell Pk Way, Epsom (Ewell) KT17 .217 CU107
Ewell Rd, Surb. KT6 .198 CL100
Surbiton (Long Dit.) KT6 .197 CH101
Sutton SM3 .217 CY107
⇌ Ewell West .216 CS109
Ewelme Rd, SE23 .182 DW88
Ewen Cres, SW2 .181 DN87
Ewer St, SE1 .20 G2
Ewhurst Av, S.Croy. CR2 . .220 DT109
Ewhurst Cl, E1 .12 F6
Sutton SM2 .217 CW109
Ewhurst Rd, SE4 .183 DZ86
Exbury Rd, SE6 .183 EA89
★ ExCeL, E16 .15 P9
Excel Ct, WC2 .9 M10
ExCeL Marina, E16
off Western Gateway . . .144 EH73
Excelsior Cl, Kings.T. KT1
off Washington Rd .198 CN96
Excelsior Gdns, SE13 .163 EC82
ExCeL Waterfront, E16
off Western Gateway . . .144 EH73
Exchange Arc, EC2 .11 M5
Exchange Bldgs, E1
off Cutler St .142 DS72
Exchange Cl, N11
off Benfleet Way .98 DG47
Exchange Ct, WC2 .9 P10
Exchange Ho, N8
off Crouch End Hill .121 DL58
Exchange Mall, The, Ilf. IG1 .125 EP61
Exchange Pl, EC2 .11 L5
Exchange Rd, Wat. WD18 . . .75 BV42
Exchange Sq, EC2 .11 L5
Exchange St, Rom. RM1 . . .127 FE57
Exchange Wk, Pnr. HA5 .116 BY59
Exeforde Av, Ashf.TW15 . . .174 BN91
Exeter Cl, E6 *off Harper Rd* .145 EM72
Watford WD24 .76 BW40
Exeter Gdns, Ilf. IG1 .124 EL60
Exeter Ho, SW15
off Putney Heath .179 CW86
Exeter Ms, NW6
off West Hampstead Ms . .140 DB65
SW6 *off Farm La* .160 DA80
Exeter Pl, Guil. GU2 .242 AT132
Exeter Rd, E16 .15 M6
E17 .123 EA57
N9 .100 DW47
N14 .99 DH46
NW2 .119 CY64
Croydon CR0 .202 DS101
Dagenham RM10 .147 FB65
Enfield EN3 .83 DX41
Feltham TW13 .176 BZ90
Gravesend DA12 .191 GK90
Harrow HA2 .116 BY61
Hounslow (Hthrw Air.) TW6 .155 BS82
Welling DA16 .165 ET82
Exeter St, WC2 .9 P9
Exeter Way, SE14 .163 DZ80
Hounslow (Hthrw Air.) TW6 .155 BS83
Exford Gdns, SE12 .184 EH88
Exford Rd, SE12 .184 EH89
Exhibition Cl, W12 .139 CW73
Exhibition Rd, SW7 .17 P4
Exmoor Cl, Ilf. IG6 .103 EQ53
Exmoor St, W10 .6 B4
Exmouth Mkt, EC1 .10 C3
Exmouth Ms, NW1 .9 K2
Exmouth Pl, E8 .142 DV66
Exmouth Rd, E17 .123 DZ57
Bromley BR2 .204 EH97
Grays RM17 .170 GB79
Hayes UB4 .135 BS69
Ruislip HA4 .116 BW62
Welling DA16 .166 EW81
Exmouth St, E1 .12 F7
Exning Rd, E16 .15 J4
Exon St, SE17 .21 L9
Explorer Av, Stai.TW19 .174 BL88
Explorer Dr, Wat. WD18 .75 BT44
Express Dr, Ilf. IG3 .126 EV60
Exton Cres, NW10 .138 CQ66
Exton Gdns, Dag. RM8 .126 EW64
Exton Rd, NW10 .138 CQ66
Exton St, SE1 .20 C2
Eyebright Cl, Croy. CR0
off Primrose La .203 DX102
Eyhurst Av, Horn. RM12 . . .127 FG62
Eyhurst Cl, NW2 .119 CU61
Tadworth (Kgswd) KT20 . .233 CZ123
Eyhurst Pk, Tad. KT20 .234 DC123
Eyhurst Spur, Tad. KT20 . . .233 CZ124
Eylewood Rd, SE27 .182 DQ92
Eynella Rd, SE22 .182 DT87
Eynham Rd, W12 .139 CW72
EYNSFORD, Dart. DA4 .208 FL103
★ Eynsford Castle, Dart. DA4 .208 FK103
Eynsford Cl, Orp. BR5 .205 EQ101
Eynsford Cres, Bex. DA5 . .186 EW88
Eynsford Rd, Dart. (Fnghm) DA4 .208 FM102
Greenhithe DA9 .189 FW85
Ilford IG3 .125 ES61
Sevenoaks TN14 .225 FH108
Swanley BR8 .207 FD100
Eynsham Dr, SE2 .166 EU77
Eynswood Dr, Sid. DA14 . . .186 EV92
Eyot Gdns, W6 .159 CT78
Eyot Grn, W4
off Chiswick Mall .159 CT79
Eyre Cl, Rom. RM2 .127 FH56
Eyre Ct, NW8
off Finchley Rd .140 DD68
Eyre Grn, Slou. SL2 .131 AN69
Eyre St Hill, EC1 .10 C4
Eyston Dr, Wey. KT13 .212 BN110
Eythorne Rd, SW9 .161 DN81
Eywood Rd, St.Alb. AL1 .42 CC22
Ezra St, E2 .11 P1

F

Faber Gdns, NW4 .119 CU57
Fabian Rd, SW6 .159 CZ80
Fabian St, E6 .145 EM70
Fackenden La, Sev. (Shore.) TN14 .225 FH113
Factory La, N17 .100 DT54
Croydon CR0 .201 DN102
Factory Rd, E16 .144 EL74
Gravesend (Nthflt) DA11 .190 GC86
Factory Sq, SW16 .181 DL93
Factory Yd, W7
off Uxbridge Rd .137 CE74
Faesten Way, Bex. DA5 .187 FE90
Faggotters La, Harl. CM17 . .37 FE13
Ongar CM5 .53 FF15
Faggotts Cl, Rad. WD7 .77 CJ35
Faggs Rd, Felt.TW14 .175 BU85
Fagnall La, Amer. (Winch.Hill) HP7 .88 AJ45
Fagus Av, Rain. RM13 .148 FK69
Faints Cl, Wal.Cr. EN7 .66 DT29
Fairacre, Hem.H. HP3 .40 BM24
New Malden KT3 .198 CS97
Fairacres, SW15 .159 CU84
Fair Acres, Brom. BR2 .204 EG99
Fairacres, Cob. KT11 .214 BX112
Croydon CR0 .221 DZ109
Redhill RH1 .267 DJ142
Ruislip HA4 .115 BT59
Tadworth KT20 .233 CW121
Windsor SL4 .151 AK82
Fairacres Cl, Pot.B. EN6 . . .63 CZ33
Fairbairn Cl, Pur. CR8 .219 DN113
Fairbairn Grn, SW9 .161 DN81
Fairbank Av, Orp. BR6 .205 EP103
Fairbank Est, N1 *off East Rd* .142 DR68
Fairbanks Rd, N17 .122 DT55
Fairborne Way, Guil. GU2 . .242 AU131
Fairbourne, Cob. KT11 .214 BX113
Fairbourne Cl, Wok. GU21
off Abercorn Way .226 AU118
Fairbourne La, Cat. CR3 . . .236 DQ122
Fairbourne Rd, N17 .122 DS55
Fairbridge Rd, N19 .121 DK61
Fairbrook Cl, N13 .99 DN50
Fairbrook Rd, N13 .99 DN51
Fairburn Cl, Borwd. WD6 . . .78 CN39
Fairburn Ct, SW15
off Mercier Rd .179 CY85
Fairby Rd, SE12 .184 EH85
Faircharm Trd Est, SE8 .163 EB80
Fairchild Cl, SW11
off Wye St .160 DD82
Fairchildes Av, Croy. (New Adgtn) CR0 .221 ED112
Fairchildes La, Warl. CR6 . .221 ED114
Sch Fairchildes Prim Sch, Croy. CR0 *off Fairchildes Av* .222 EE112
Fairchild Pl, EC2 .11 M4
Fairchild St, EC2 .11 M4
Fair Cl, Bushey WD23
off Claybury .94 CB45
Fairclough St, E1 .12 B8
Faircroft, Slou. SL2 .131 AP70
Faircross Av, Bark. IG11 . . .145 EQ65
Romford RM5 .105 FD52
Faircross Way, St.Alb. AL1 . .43 CG18
Fairdale Gdns, SW15 .159 CV84
Hayes UB3 .135 BU74
Fairdene Rd, Couls. CR5 . . .235 DK117
Fairey Av, Hayes UB3 .155 BT77
Fairfax Av, Epsom KT17 .217 CV109
Redhill RH1 .250 DE133
Fairfax Cl, Walt. KT12 .195 BV102
Fairfax Gdns, SE3 .164 EK81
Fairfax Ms, E16 .25 N1
SW15 .159 CW84
Amersham HP7 .55 AN40
Fairfax Pl, NW6 .140 DC66
W14 .16 D6
Fairfax Rd, N8 .121 DN56
NW6 .140 DC66
W4 .158 CS76
Grays RM17 .170 GB78
Hertford SG13 .32 DT08
Teddington TW11 .177 CG93
Tilbury RM18 .171 GF81
Woking GU22 .227 BB120
Fairfax Way, N10
off Cromwell Rd .98 DG52
Fairfield App, Stai. (Wrays.) TW19 .172 AX86
Fairfield Av, NW4 .119 CV58
Edgware HA8 .96 CP51
Horley RH6 .268 DG149
Ruislip HA4 .115 BQ59
Slough (Datchet) SL3 .152 AW80
Staines TW18 .173 BF91
Twickenham TW2 .176 CB88
Upminster RM14 .128 FQ62
Watford WD19 .94 BW48
Fairfield Cl, N12 .98 DC49
Dorking RH4
off Fairfield Dr .247 CH134
Enfield EN3
off Scotland Grn Rd N . . .83 DY42
Epsom (Ewell) KT19 .216 CS106
Guildford GU2 .242 AU133
Hatfield AL10 .45 CW15
Hornchurch RM12 .127 FG60
Mitcham CR4 .180 DE94
Northwood HA6
off Thirlmere Gdns .93 BP50
Radlett WD7 .77 CE37
Sidcup DA15 .185 ET86
Slough (Datchet) SL3 .152 AX80
Fairfield Cotts, Lthd. KT23 . .246 CB125
Fairfield Ct, NW10 .139 CU67
Northwood HA6
off Windsor Cl .93 BU54
Fairfield Cres, Edg. HA8 . . . .96 CP51
Fairfield Dr, SW18 .180 DB85
Broxbourne EN10 .49 DZ24
Dorking RH4 .247 CH134
Greenford UB6 .137 CJ67
Harrow HA2 .116 CC55
Fairfield E, Kings.T. KT1 . . .198 CL96
Fairfield Gdns, N8
off Elder Av .121 DL57
Fairfield Gro, SE7 .164 EK78
★ Fairfield Halls, Croy. CR0 .202 DR104
Sch Fair Fld Jun Sch, Rad. WD7 *off Watford Rd* .77 CE36
Fairfield La, Slou. (Farn.Royal) SL2 .131 AP68
Fairfield N, Kings.T. KT1 . .198 CL96
Fairfield Pk, Cob. KT11 .214 BX114
Fairfield Path, Croy. CR0 . .202 DR104
Fairfield Pathway, Horn. RM12 .148 FJ66
Fairfield Pl, Kings.T. KT1 . .198 CL97
Fairfield Ri, Guil. GU2 .242 AT133
Fairfield Rd, E3 .143 EA68
E17 .123 DY54
N8 .121 DL57
N18 .100 DU49
W7 .157 CG76
Beckenham BR3 .203 EA96
Bexleyheath DA7 .166 EZ82
Brentwood CM14 .108 FW48
Bromley BR1 .184 EG94
Croydon CR0 .202 DS104
Epping CM16 .70 EV29
Hoddesdon EN11 .49 EA15
Ilford IG1 .145 EP65
Kingston upon Thames KT1 .198 CL96
Leatherhead KT22 .231 CH121
Orpington BR5 .205 ER100
Slough (Burn.) SL1 .130 AJ69
Southall UB1 .136 BZ72
Staines (Wrays.) TW19 . . .172 AX86
Uxbridge UB8 .134 BK65
West Drayton UB7 .134 BL74
Woodford Green IG8 .102 EG51
Fairfields, Cher. KT16 .194 BG102
Gravesend DA12 .191 GL92
Fairfields Cl, NW9 .118 CQ57
Fairfields Cres, NW9 .118 CQ56
Fairfield S, Kings.T. KT1 . .198 CL96
Sch Fairfields Prim Sch, Wal.Cr. EN7
off Rosedale Way .66 DU27
Fairfields Rd, Houns.TW3 . .156 CC83
Fairfield St, SW18 .180 DB85
Fairfield Trade Pk, Kings.T. KT1 .198 CM97
Fairfield Wk, Lthd. KT22
off Fairfield Rd .231 CH121
Waltham Cross (Chsht) EN8 .67 DY28
Fairfield Way, Barn. EN5 . . .80 DA43
Coulsdon CR5 .219 DK114
Epsom KT19 .216 CS106
Fairfield W, Kings.T. KT1 . .198 CL96
Fairfolds, Wat. WD25 .76 BY36
Fairfoot Rd, E3 .13 N4
Fairford Av, Bexh. DA7 .167 FD81
Croydon CR0 .203 DX99
Fairford Cl, Croy. CR0 .203 DY99
Reigate RH2 .250 DC132
Romford RM3
off Fairford Way .106 FP51
West Byfleet KT14 .211 BF114
Fairford Ct, Sutt. SM2
off Grange Rd .218 DB108
Fairford Gdns, Wor.Pk. KT4 .199 CT104
Fairford Ho, SE11 .20 D8
Fairford Way, Rom. RM3 . . .106 FP51
Fairgreen, Barn. EN4 .80 DF41
Fair Grn, Saw. CM21
off The Square .36 EY05
Fairgreen E, Barn. EN4 .80 DF41
Fairgreen Par, Mitch. CR4
off London Rd .200 DF97
Fairgreen Rd, Th.Hth. CR7 . .201 DP99
Fairham Av, S.Ock. RM15 . .149 FU73
Fairhaven, Egh.TW20 .173 AZ92
Fairhaven Av, Croy. CR0 . . .203 DX100
Fairhaven Cres, Wat. WD19 . .93 BU48
Fairhaven Rd, Red. RH1 .250 DG130
Fairhazel Gdns, NW6 .140 DB65
Fairhill, Hem.H. HP3 .40 BM24
Fairholme, Felt.TW14 .175 BR87
Fairholme Av, Rom. RM2 . . .127 FG57
Fairholme Cl, N3 .119 CY56
Fairholme Cres, Ashtd. KT21 .231 CJ117
Hayes UB4 .135 BT70
Fairholme Gdns, N3 .119 CY55
Upminster RM14 .129 FT59
Sch Fairholme Prim Sch, Felt.TW14
off Peacock Av .175 BR88
Fairholme Rd, W14 .16 D10
Ashford TW15 .174 BL92
Croydon CR0 .201 DN101
Harrow HA1 .117 CF57
Ilford IG1 .125 EM59
Sutton SM1 .217 CZ107
Fairholt Cl, N16 .122 DS60
Fairholt Rd, N16 .122 DR60
Fairholt St, SW7 .18 B5
Fairkytes Av, Horn. RM11 . .128 FK60
Fairland Rd, E15 .144 EF65
Fairlands Av, Buck.H. IG9 . .102 EG47
Sutton SM1 .200 DA103
Thornton Heath CR7 .201 DM98
Fairlands Ct, SE9
off North Pk .185 EN86
Fair La, Couls. CR5 .250 DC125
Fairlawn, SE7 .164 EJ79
Leatherhead (Bkhm) KT23 .230 BZ124
Fairlawn Av, N2 .120 DE56
W4 .158 CQ77
Bexleyheath DA7 .166 EX82
Fairlawn Cl, N14 .81 DJ44
Esher (Clay.) KT10 .215 CF107
Feltham TW13 .176 BZ91
Kingston upon Thames KT2 .178 CQ93
Fairlawn Dr, Red. RH1 .266 DE136
Woodford Green IG8 .102 EG52
Fairlawnes, Wall. SM6
off Maldon Rd .219 DH106
Fairlawn Gdns, Sthl. UB1 . .136 BZ73
Fairlawn Gro, W4 .158 CQ77
Banstead SM7 .218 DD113
Fairlawn Pk, SE26 .183 DY92
Windsor SL4 .151 AL84
Woking GU21 .210 AY114
Sch Fairlawn Prim Sch, SE23
off Honor Oak Rd .182 DW87
Sch Fairlawn Prim Sch Annexe, SE23 *off Waldenshaw Rd* .182 DW88
Fairlawn Rd, SW19 .179 CZ94
Banstead SM7 .218 DD112
Carshalton SM5 .218 DC111
Fairlawns, Add. (Wdhm) KT15 .211 BF111
Brentwood CM14 .108 FU48
Horley RH6 .269 DH149
Pinner HA5 .94 BW54
Sunbury-on-Thames TW16 .195 BU97
Twickenham TW1 .177 CJ86
Watford WD17 .75 BT38
Weybridge KT13 .213 BS106
Fairlawns Cl, Horn. RM11 . .128 FM59
Staines TW18 .174 BH93
Fairlea Pl, W5 .137 CK70
Fair Leas, Chesh. HP5 .54 AN29
Fairley Way, Wal.Cr. (Chsht) EN7 .66 DV28
Fairlie Gdns, SE23 .182 DW87
Fairlie Rd, Slou. SL1 .131 AN72
Fairlight Av, E4 .101 ED47
NW10 .138 CS68
Windsor SL4 .151 AR82
Woodford Green IG8 .102 EG51
Fairlight Cl, E4 .101 ED47
Worcester Park KT4 .217 CW105
Fairlight Dr, Uxb. UB8 .134 BK65
Fairlight Rd, SW17 .180 DD91
⊖ Fairlop .103 ER53
Fairlop Cl, Horn. RM12 .147 FH65
Fairlop Gdns, Ilf. IG6 .103 EQ52
Sch Fairlop Prim Sch, Ilf. IG6
off Colvin Gdns .103 EQ53
Fairlop Rd, E11 .123 ED59
Ilford IG6 .103 EQ54
Fairmark Dr, Uxb. UB10 . . .134 BN65
Fairmead, Brom. BR1 .205 EM98
Surbiton KT5 .198 CP102
Woking GU21 .226 AW118
Fairmead Cl, Brom. BR1 . . .205 EM98
Hounslow TW5 .156 BX80
New Malden KT3 .198 CR97
Fairmead Cres, Edg. HA8 . . .96 CQ48
Fairmead Gdns, Ilf. IG4 .124 EL57
Fairmead Ho, E9
off Kingsmead Way .123 DY63
Fairmead Rd, N19 .121 DK62
Croydon CR0 .201 DM102
Loughton IG10 .84 EH42
Fairmeads, Cob. KT11 .214 BZ113
Loughton IG10 .85 EP40
Fairmead Side, Loug. IG10 . .84 EJ43
FAIRMILE, Cob. KT11 .214 BZ112
Fairmile Av, SW16 .181 DK92
Cobham KT11 .214 BY114
Fairmile Ct, Cob. KT11 .214 BY112
Fairmile Ho, Tedd. TW11
off Twickenham Rd .177 CG91
Fairmile La, Cob. KT11 .214 BX112
Fairmile Pk Copse, Cob. KT11 .214 BZ112
Fairmile Pk Rd, Cob. KT11 . .214 BZ113
Fairmont Av, E14
off Blackwall Way .143 ED74
Fairmont Cl, Belv. DA17 . . .166 EZ78
Fairmount Rd, SW2 .181 DM86
Fairoak Cl, Ken. CR8 .235 DP115
Leatherhead (Oxshott) KT22 .215 CD112
Orpington BR5 .205 EP101
Fairoak Dr, SE9 .185 ER85
Fairoak Gdns, Rom. RM1 . . .105 FE54
Fairoak La, Chess. KT9 .215 CF111

Fairoak La, Lthd. (Oxshott) KT22 . . . 215 CF111
Fairseat Cl, Bushey (Bushey Hth) WD23 off Hive Rd . . . 95 CE47
Fairs Rd, Lthd. KT22 . . . 231 CG119
Fairstead Wk, N1 . . . 4 G7
Fairstone Ct, Horl. RH6 off Tanyard Way . . . 269 DH147
Fair St, SE1 . . . 21 M3
Hounslow TW3 off High St . . . 156 CC83
Fairthorn Rd, SE7 . . . 25 M9
Fairtrough Rd, Orp. BR6 . . . 224 EV112
Fairview, Epsom KT17 . . . 217 CW111
Erith DA8 off Guild Rd . . . 167 FF80
Potters Bar EN6 off Hawkshead Rd . . . 64 DB29
Fairview Av, Brwd. (Hutt.) CM13 . . . 109 GE45
Rainham RM13 . . . 148 FK68
Wembley HA0 . . . 137 CK65
Woking GU22 . . . 226 AY118
Fairview Cl, E17 . . . 101 DY53
Chigwell IG7 . . . 103 ES49
Woking GU22 off Fairview Av . . . 227 AZ118
Fairview Ct, Ashf. TW15 . . . 174 BN92
Fairview Cres, Har. HA2 . . . 116 CA60
Fairview Dr, Chig. IG7 . . . 103 ES49
Orpington BR6 . . . 223 ER105
Shepperton TW17 . . . 194 BM99
Watford WD17 . . . 75 BS36
Fairview Gdns, Wdf.Grn. IG8 . . . 102 EH53
Fairview Ind Est, Oxt. RH8 . . . 254 EG133
Fairview Ind Pk, Rain. RM13 . . . 147 FD71
Fairview Pl, SW2 . . . 181 DM87
Fairview Rd, N15 . . . 122 DT57
SW16 . . . 201 DM95
Chigwell IG7 . . . 103 ES49
Enfield EN2 . . . 81 DN39
Epsom KT17 . . . 217 CT111
Gravesend (Istead Rise) DA13 . . . 190 GD94
Maidenhead (Taplow) SL6 . . . 130 AG72
Slough SL2 . . . 131 AM70
Sutton SM1 . . . 218 DD106
Fairview Way, Edg. HA8 . . . 96 CN49
Fairwater Av, Well. DA16 . . . 166 EU84
Fairwater Dr, Add. (New Haw) KT15 . . . 212 BK109
Fairway, SW20 . . . 199 CW97
Bexleyheath DA6 . . . 186 EY85
Carshalton SM5 . . . 218 DC111
Chertsey KT16 . . . 194 BH102
Guildford GU1 . . . 243 BD133
Hemel Hempstead HP3 . . . 40 BM24
Orpington BR5 . . . 205 ER99
Sawbridgeworth CM21 . . . 36 EY05
Virginia Water GU25 . . . 192 AV100
Ware SG12 . . . 32 DW07
Woodford Green IG8 . . . 102 EJ50
Fairway, The, N13 . . . 100 DQ48
N14 . . . 81 DH44
NW7 . . . 96 CR48
W3 . . . 138 CS72
Abbots Langley WD5 . . . 59 BR32
Barnet EN5 . . . 80 DB44
Bromley BR1 . . . 205 EM99
Gravesend DA11 . . . 191 GG89
Harlow CM18 . . . 51 ET17
High Wycombe (Flack.Hth) HP10 . . . 110 AC56
Leatherhead KT22 . . . 231 CG118
New Malden KT3 . . . 198 CR95
Northolt UB5 . . . 136 CC65
Northwood HA6 . . . 93 BS49
Ruislip HA4 . . . 116 BX62
Slough (Burn.) SL1 . . . 130 AJ68
Upminster RM14 . . . 128 FQ59
Uxbridge UB10 . . . 134 BM68
Wembley HA0 . . . 117 CH62
West Molesey KT8 . . . 196 CB97
Weybridge KT13 . . . 212 BN111
Fairway Av, NW9 . . . 118 CP55
Borehamwood WD6 . . . 78 CP40
West Drayton UB7 . . . 134 BJ74
Fairway Cl, NW11 . . . 120 DC59
Croydon CR0 . . . 203 DY99
Epsom KT19 . . . 216 CQ105
Hounslow TW4 . . . 176 BW85
St. Albans (Park St) AL2 . . . 60 CC27
West Drayton UB7 off Fairway Av . . . 134 BK74
Woking GU22 . . . 226 AU119
Fairway Ct, NW7 off The Fairway . . . 96 CR48
Hemel Hempstead HP3 off Fairway . . . 40 BM24
Fairway Dr, SE28 . . . 146 EX72
Dartford DA2 . . . 188 FP87
Greenford UB6 . . . 136 CB66
Fairway Gdns, Beck. BR3 . . . 203 ED100
Ilford IG1 . . . 125 EQ64
Sch Fairway Prim Sch, The, NW7 off The Fairway . . . 96 CR47
Fairways, Ashf. TW15 . . . 175 BP93
Kenley CR8 . . . 236 DQ117
Stanmore HA7 . . . 96 CL54
Teddington TW11 . . . 177 CK94
Waltham Abbey EN9 . . . 68 EE34
Waltham Cross (Chsht) EN8 . . . 67 DX26
Fairways, The, Red. RH1 . . . 266 DD137
Fairweather Cl, N15 . . . 122 DS56
Fairweather Rd, N16 . . . 122 DU58
Fairwell La, Lthd. (W.Hors.) KT24 . . . 245 BP128
Fairwyn Rd, SE26 . . . 183 DY91
Fakenham Cl, NW7 . . . 97 CU52
Northolt UB5 off Goodwood Dr . . . 136 CA65
Fakruddin St, E1 . . . 12 B4
Falaise, Egh. TW20 . . . 172 AY92
Falcon Av, Brom. BR1 . . . 204 EL98
Grays RM17 . . . 170 GB79
Falconberg Ct, W1 . . . 9 M7
Falconberg Ms, W1 . . . 9 L7
Sch Falconbrook Prim Sch, SW11 off Wye St . . . 160 DD83
Falcon Cl, SE1 . . . 20 F1
W4 off Sutton La S . . . 158 CQ79
Dartford DA1 . . . 188 FM85
Hatfield AL10 . . . 45 CU20
Northwood HA6 . . . 93 BS52
Sawbridgeworth CM21 . . . 36 EW06
Waltham Abbey EN9 off Kestrel Rd . . . 68 EG34
Falcon Ct, EC4 . . . 10 C8
Woking GU21 . . . 211 BC113
Falcon Cres, Enf. EN3 . . . 83 DX43
Falcon Dr, Stai. (Stanw.) TW19 . . . 174 BK86
Falconer Rd, Bushey WD23 . . . 76 BZ44
Ilford IG6 . . . 104 EV50
Sch Falconer Sch, The, Bushey WD23 off Falconer Rd . . . 76 CA43
Falconers Pk, Saw. CM21 . . . 36 EX06
Falconer Wk, N7 off Newington Barrow Way . . . 121 DM61
Falcon Gro, SW11 . . . 160 DE83
Falcon Ho, W13 . . . 137 CF70
Falconhurst, Lthd. (Oxshott) KT22 . . . 231 CD115
Falcon La, SW11 . . . 160 DE83
Falcon Ms, Grav. DA11 . . . 190 GE88
Falcon Pk Ind Est, NW10 . . . 119 CT64
Falcon Ridge, Berk. HP4 . . . 38 AW20
Falcon Rd, SW11 . . . 160 DE82
Enfield EN3 . . . 83 DX43
Guildford GU1 . . . 242 AX134
Hampton TW12 . . . 176 BZ94
Falcons Cl, West. (Bigg.H.) TN16 . . . 238 EK117
Falcons Cft, H.Wyc. HP10 . . . 110 AE55
Sch Falcon's Pre-Preparatory Sch, The, W4 off Burnaby Gdns . . . 158 CQ79
Falcon St, E13 . . . 15 L3
Falcon Ter, SW11 . . . 160 DE83
Falcon Way, E11 . . . 124 EG56
E14 . . . 24 B7
NW9 . . . 96 CS54
Feltham TW14 . . . 175 BV85
Harrow HA3 . . . 118 CL57
Hornchurch RM12 . . . 147 FG66
Sunbury-on-Thames TW16 . . . 195 BS96
Watford WD25 . . . 60 BY34
Welwyn Garden City AL7 . . . 29 CY07
FALCONWOOD, Well. DA16 . . . 165 ER83
⇌ Falconwood . . . 165 EQ84
Falconwood, Egh. TW20 . . . 172 AY92
Leatherhead (E.Hors.) KT24 . . . 231 CF120
Falconwood Av, Well. DA16 . . . 165 ER82
Falconwood Par, Well. DA16 . . . 165 ES84
Falconwood Rd, Croy. CR0 . . . 221 EA108
Falcourt Cl, Sutt. SM1 . . . 218 DB106
Falkirk Cl, Horn. RM11 . . . 128 FN60
Falkirk Gdns, Wat. WD19 off Blackford Rd . . . 94 BX50
Falkirk Ho, W9 . . . 7 K1
Falkirk St, N1 . . . 5 M10
Falkland Av, N3 . . . 98 DA52
N11 . . . 98 DG49
Coll Falkland Cen, N8 off Falkland Rd . . . 121 DN56
Falkland Gdns, Dor. RH4 off Harrow Rd W . . . 263 CG137
Falkland Gro, Dor. RH4 . . . 263 CG137
Falkland Pk Av, SE25 . . . 202 DS97
Falkland Pl, NW5 off Falkland Rd . . . 121 DJ64
Falkland Rd, N8 . . . 121 DN56
NW5 . . . 121 DJ64
Barnet EN5 . . . 79 CY40
Dorking RH4 . . . 263 CG137
Sch Falkner Ho Sch, SW7 . . . 17 M8
Fallaize Av, Ilf. IG1 off Riverdene Rd . . . 125 EP63
Falling La, West Dr. UB7 . . . 134 BL73
Falloden Way, NW11 . . . 120 DA56
Fallow Cl, Chig. IG7 . . . 103 ET50
Fallow Ct, SE16 . . . 22 B10
Fallow Ct Av, N12 . . . 98 DC52
Fallowfield, Dart. (Bean) DA2 . . . 189 FV90
Stanmore HA7 . . . 95 CG48
Welwyn Garden City AL7 . . . 29 CZ06
Fallowfield Cl, Uxb. (Hare.) UB9 . . . 92 BJ53
Fallowfield Ct, Stan. HA7 . . . 95 CG48
Fallow Flds, Loug. IG10 . . . 102 EJ45
Fallowfields Dr, N12 . . . 98 DE51
Fallowfield Wk, Hem.H. HP1 off Tollpit End . . . 40 BG17
Fallowfield Way, Horl. RH6 . . . 269 DH147
Fallow Ri, Hert. SG13 . . . 32 DS09
Fallows Cl, N2 . . . 98 DC54
Fallsbrook Rd, SW16 . . . 181 DJ94
Falman Cl, N9 off Croyland Rd . . . 100 DU46
Falmer Rd, E17 . . . 123 EB55
N15 . . . 122 DQ57
Enfield EN1 . . . 82 DS42
Falmouth Av, E4 . . . 101 ED50
Falmouth Cl, N22 off Truro Rd . . . 99 DM52
SE12 . . . 184 EF85
Falmouth Ct, St.Alb. AL3 . . . 43 CD18
Falmouth Gdns, Ilf. IG4 . . . 124 EL57
Falmouth Ho, Kings.T. KT2 off Kingsgate Rd . . . 198 CL95
Falmouth Rd, SE1 . . . 21 H5
Slough SL1 . . . 131 AN72
Walton-on-Thames KT12 . . . 214 BW105
Falmouth St, E15 . . . 123 ED64
Falmouth Way, E17 off Gosport Rd . . . 123 DZ57
Falstaff Cl, Dart. DA1 . . . 187 FE87
Falstaff Gdns, St.Alb. AL1 . . . 42 CB23
Falstaff Ms, Hmptn. (Hmptn H.) TW12 off Hampton Rd . . . 177 CD92
Falstone, Wok. GU21 . . . 226 AV118
Fambridge Cl, SE26 . . . 183 DZ91
Fambridge Rd, Dag. RM8 . . . 126 FA60
Famet Av, Pur. CR8 . . . 220 DQ113
Famet Cl, Pur. CR8 . . . 220 DQ113
Famet Wk, Pur. CR8 . . . 220 DQ113
★ Family Records Cen, Public Record Office, EC1 . . . 10 D2
Fane St, W14 off North End Rd . . . 159 CZ79
Fangrove Pk, Cher. (Lyne) KT16 . . . 193 BB102
Fanhams Rd, Ware SG12 . . . 33 DY05
★ Fan Mus, SE10 . . . 163 EC80
Fanns Ri, Purf. RM19 . . . 168 FN77
Fann St, EC1 . . . 10 G4
EC2 . . . 10 G4
Fanshawe Av, Bark. IG11 . . . 145 EQ65
Fanshawe Ct, Hert. SG14 off Byde St . . . 32 DQ08
Fanshawe Cres, Dag. RM9 . . . 126 EY64
Hornchurch RM11 . . . 128 FK58
Ware SG12 . . . 32 DW05
Fanshawe Rd, Grays RM16 . . . 171 GG76
Richmond TW10 . . . 177 CJ91
Fanshawe St, Hert. SG14 . . . 31 DP08
Fanshaws La, Hert. SG13 . . . 48 DQ18
Fanshaw St, N1 . . . 11 L1
Fanthorpe St, SW15 . . . 159 CW83
Faraday Av, Sid. DA14 . . . 186 EU89
Faraday Cl, N7 . . . 4 B4
Slough SL2 . . . 131 AP71
Watford WD18 . . . 75 BR44
★ Faraday Mus, W1 . . . 9 J10
Faraday Rd, E15 . . . 144 EF65
SW19 . . . 180 DA93
W3 . . . 138 CQ73
W10 . . . 6 C5
Guildford GU1 off Woodbridge Rd . . . 242 AW133
Slough SL2 . . . 131 AP71
Southall UB1 . . . 136 CB73
Welling DA16 . . . 166 EU83
West Molesey KT8 . . . 196 CA98
Faraday Way, SE18 . . . 164 EK76
Croydon CR0 off Ampere Way . . . 201 DM102
Orpington BR5 . . . 206 EV98
Fareham Rd, Felt. TW14 . . . 176 BW87
Fareham St, W1 . . . 9 L7
Far End, Hat. AL10 . . . 45 CV21
Farewell Pl, Mitch. CR4 . . . 200 DE95
Faringdon Av, Brom. BR2 . . . 205 EP100
Romford RM3 . . . 106 FJ53
Faringford Cl, Pot.B. EN6 . . . 64 DD31
Faringford Rd, E15 . . . 144 EE66
Farington Acres, Wey. KT13 . . . 195 BR104
Faris Barn Dr, Add. (Wdhm) KT15 . . . 211 BF112
Faris La, Add. (Wdhm) KT15 . . . 211 BF111
Farjeon Rd, SE3 . . . 164 EK81
Farland Rd, Hem.H. HP2 . . . 40 BN21
FARLEIGH, Warl. CR6 . . . 221 DZ114
Farleigh Av, Brom. BR2 . . . 204 EF100
Farleigh Border, Croy. CR0 . . . 221 DY112
Farleigh Ct, Guil. GU2 off Park Barn Dr . . . 242 AS134
Farleigh Ct Rd, Warl. CR6 . . . 221 DZ114
Farleigh Dean Cres, Croy. CR0 . . . 221 EB111
Farleigh Pl, N16 off Farleigh Rd . . . 122 DT63
Sch Farleigh Prim Sch, Warl. CR6 off Farleigh Rd . . . 237 DY117
Farleigh Rd, N16 . . . 122 DT63
Addlestone (New Haw) KT15 . . . 212 BG111
Warlingham CR6 . . . 237 DX118
Farleton Cl, Wey. KT13 . . . 213 BR107
Farley Common, West. TN16 . . . 255 EP126
Farleycroft, West. TN16 . . . 255 EQ126
Farley Dr, Ilf. IG3 . . . 125 ES60
FARLEY GREEN, Guil. GU5 . . . 260 BK144
Farley Heath, Guil. (Albury) GU5 . . . 260 BJ144
Farley La, West. TN16 . . . 255 EP127
Farley Ms, SE6 . . . 183 EC87
Farley Nurs, West. TN16 . . . 255 EQ127
Farley Pk, Oxt. RH8 . . . 253 ED130
Farley Pl, SE25 . . . 202 DU98
Farley Rd, SE6 . . . 183 EB87
Gravesend DA12 . . . 191 GM88
South Croydon CR2 . . . 220 DV108
Farleys Cl, Lthd. (W.Hors.) KT24 . . . 245 BQ126
Farlington Pl, SW15 off Roehampton La . . . 179 CV87
Farlow Cl, Grav. (Nthflt) DA11 . . . 191 GF90
Farlow Rd, SW15 . . . 159 CX83
Farlton Rd, SW18 . . . 180 DB87
Farman Gro, Nthlt. UB5 off Wayfarer Rd . . . 136 BX69
Farm Av, NW2 . . . 119 CY62
SW16 . . . 181 DL91
Harrow HA2 . . . 116 BZ59
Swanley BR8 . . . 207 FC97
Wembley HA0 . . . 137 CJ65
Farmborough Cl, Har. HA1 off Pool Rd . . . 117 CD59
Farm Cl, SW6 off Farm La . . . 160 DA80
Amersham HP6 . . . 72 AX39
Barnet EN5 . . . 79 CW43
Borehamwood WD6 . . . 77 CK38
Brentwood (Hutt.) CM13 . . . 109 GC45
Buckhurst Hill IG9 . . . 102 EJ48
Chertsey (Lyne) KT16 . . . 193 BA100
Coulsdon CR5 . . . 234 DF120
Dagenham RM10 . . . 147 FC66
Guildford GU1 . . . 242 AX131
Harlow (Roydon) CM19 . . . 34 EH14
Hertford SG14 . . . 31 DN09
Leatherhead (E.Hors.) KT24 . . . 245 BT128
Leatherhead (Fetch.) KT22 . . . 231 CD124
Maidenhead (Holy.) SL6 . . . 150 AC78
Potters Bar (Cuffley) EN6 . . . 65 DK27
Radlett WD7 . . . 62 CL30
Shepperton TW17 . . . 194 BN101
Southall UB1 . . . 136 CB73
Staines TW18 . . . 173 BE92
Sutton SM2 . . . 218 DD108
Uxbridge UB10 . . . 115 BP61
Wallington SM6 . . . 219 DJ110
Waltham Cross (Chsht) EN8 . . . 66 DW30
Welwyn Garden City AL8 . . . 29 CW09
West Byfleet (Byfleet) KT14 . . . 212 BM112
West Wickham BR4 . . . 204 EE104
Farmcote Rd, SE12 . . . 184 EG88
Farm Ct, NW4 . . . 119 CU55
Farm Cres, St.Alb. (Lon.Col.) AL2 . . . 61 CG26
Slough SL2 . . . 132 AV71
Farmcroft, Grav. DA11 . . . 191 GG89
Farmdale Rd, SE10 . . . 25 M9
Carshalton SM5 . . . 218 DE108
Farm Dr, Croy. CR0 . . . 203 DZ103
Purley CR8 . . . 219 DK112
Farm End, E4 . . . 84 EE43
Northwood HA6 off Drakes Dr . . . 93 BP53
Farmer Rd, E10 . . . 123 EB60
Farmers Cl, Wat. WD25 . . . 59 BV33
Farmers Ct, Wal.Abb. EN9 off Winters Way . . . 68 EG33
Farmers Rd, SE5 . . . 161 DP80
Staines TW18 . . . 173 BE92
Farmer St, W8 . . . 16 G1
Farmers Way, Beac. (Seer Grn) HP9 . . . 89 AQ51
Farmery Ct, Berk. HP4 off Frithsden Rd . . . 38 AY17
Farm Fld, Wat. WD17 . . . 75 BS38
Farmfield Dr, Horl. (Charl.) RH6 . . . 268 DB150
H Farmfield Hosp, Horl. RH6 . . . 268 DB150
Farmfield Rd, Brom. BR1 . . . 184 EE92
Farm Flds, S.Croy. CR2 . . . 220 DS111
Farm Gro, Beac. (Knot.Grn) HP9 . . . 88 AJ50
Farm Hill Rd, Wal.Abb. EN9 . . . 67 EC34
Farm Ho Cl, Brox. EN10 . . . 67 DZ25
Farmhouse Cl, Wok. GU22 . . . 227 BD115
Farmhouse La, Hem.H. HP2 . . . 40 BN18
Farmhouse Rd, SW16 . . . 181 DJ94
Farmilo Rd, E17 . . . 123 DZ59
Farmington Av, Sutt. SM1 . . . 200 DD104
Farmlands, Enf. EN2 . . . 81 DN39
Pinner HA5 . . . 115 BU56
Farmlands, The, Nthlt. UB5 . . . 136 BZ65
Farmland Wk, Chis. BR7 . . . 185 EP92
Farm La, N14 . . . 80 DG44
SW6 . . . 160 DA79
Addlestone KT15 . . . 212 BG107
Ashtead KT21 . . . 232 CN116
Beaconsfield (Jordans) HP9 . . . 89 AR52
Carshalton SM5 . . . 218 DF110
Croydon CR0 . . . 203 DZ103
Epsom KT18 . . . 232 CP119
Hoddesdon EN11 . . . 49 EC15
Leatherhead (E.Hors.) KT24 . . . 245 BT128
Purley CR8 . . . 219 DJ110
Rickmansworth (Loud.) WD3 . . . 74 BH41
Slough SL1 . . . 131 AR73
Woking (Send) GU23 . . . 227 BC124
Farm Lea, H.Wyc. (Woob.Grn) HP10 . . . 110 AF56
Farmleigh, N14 . . . 99 DJ45
Farmleigh Gro, Walt. KT12 . . . 213 BT106
Farm Pl, W8 . . . 16 G1
Berkhamsted HP4 . . . 38 AT18
Dartford DA1 . . . 167 FG84
Farm Rd, N21 . . . 99 DP46
NW10 . . . 138 CR67
Edgware HA8 . . . 96 CP51
Esher KT10 . . . 196 CB102
Grays (Orsett) RM16 . . . 171 GF75
Hoddesdon EN11 . . . 49 EC16
Hounslow TW4 . . . 176 BY88
Maidenhead (Taplow) SL6 . . . 130 AG72
Morden SM4 . . . 200 DB99
Northwood HA6 . . . 93 BQ50
Rainham RM13 . . . 148 FJ69
Rickmansworth (Chorl.) WD3 . . . 73 BA42
St. Albans AL1 . . . 43 CH19
Sevenoaks TN14 . . . 257 FJ121
Staines TW18 . . . 174 BH93
Sutton SM2 . . . 218 DD108
Warlingham CR6 . . . 237 DY119
Woking GU22 . . . 227 BB120
Farmstead Rd, SE6 . . . 183 EB91
Harrow HA3 . . . 95 CD53
Farm St, W1 . . . 8 G10
Farm Vale, Bex. DA5 . . . 187 FB86
Farmview, Cob. KT11 . . . 230 BX116
Farm Vw, Tad. (Lwr Kgswd) KT20 . . . 249 CZ127
Farm Wk, NW11 . . . 119 CZ57
Guildford GU2 off Wilderness Rd . . . 258 AT136
Horley RH6 off Court Lo Rd . . . 268 DF148
Farm Way, Buck.H. IG9 . . . 102 EJ49
Bushey WD23 . . . 76 CB42
Farmway, Dag. RM8 . . . 126 EW63
Farm Way, Hat. AL10 . . . 45 CV15
Hornchurch RM12 . . . 127 FH63
Northwood HA6 . . . 93 BS49
Staines TW19 . . . 173 BF86
Worcester Park KT4 . . . 199 CW104
Farm Yd, Wind. SL4 . . . 151 AR80
Farnaby Dr, Sev. TN13 . . . 256 FF126
Farnaby Rd, SE9 . . . 164 EJ84
Bromley BR1, BR2 . . . 183 ED94
Farnan Av, E17 . . . 101 EA54
Farnan Rd, SW16 . . . 181 DL92
FARNBOROUGH, Orp. BR6 . . . 223 EP106
Farnborough Av, E17 . . . 123 DY55
South Croydon CR2 . . . 221 DX108
Farnborough Cl, Wem. HA9 off Chalkhill Rd . . . 118 CP61
Farnborough Common, Orp. BR6 . . . 205 EM104
Farnborough Cres, Brom. BR2 off Saville Row . . . 204 EF102
South Croydon CR2 . . . 221 DY109
Farnborough Hill, Orp. BR6 . . . 223 ER106
Farnborough Ho, SW15 off Fontley Way . . . 179 CU88
Sch Farnborough Prim Sch, Orp. BR6 off Farnborough Hill . . . 223 EQ106
Farnborough Way, SE15 off Blakes Rd . . . 162 DS80
Orpington BR6 . . . 223 EQ105
Farnburn Av, Slou. SL1 . . . 131 AP71
FARNCOMBE, Gdmg. GU7 . . . 258 AT144
⇌ Farncombe . . . 258 AT144
Sch Farncombe C of E Inf Sch, Gdmg. GU7 off Grays Rd . . . 258 AS144
Farncombe St, SE16 . . . 22 B4
Godalming GU7 . . . 258 AS144
Farndale Av, N13 . . . 99 DP48
Farndale Cres, Grnf. UB6 . . . 136 CC69
Farnell Ms, SW5 . . . 17 J9
Farnell Pl, W3 . . . 138 CP73
Farnell Rd, Islw. TW7 . . . 157 CD83
Staines TW18 . . . 174 BG90
Farnes Dr, Rom. RM2 . . . 106 FJ54
Farney Fld, Guil. (Peasl.) GU5 . . . 261 BR142
Farnham Cl, N20 . . . 98 DC45
Hemel Hempstead (Bov.) HP3 . . . 57 BA28
Sawbridgeworth CM21 . . . 36 EW06
FARNHAM COMMON, Slou. SL2 . . . 111 AQ65
Sch Farnham Common Co Inf Sch, Slou. SL2 off Beaconsfield Rd . . . 111 AQ63
Sch Farnham Common Co Jun Sch, Slou. SL2 off Sherbourne Wk . . . 111 AQ63
Farnham Gdns, SW20 . . . 199 CV96
Sch Farnham Grn Prim Sch, Ilf. IG3 off Royal Cl . . . 126 EU58
Farnham La, Slou. SL2 . . . 131 AN68
Farnham Pk La, Slou. (Farn.Royal) SL2 . . . 131 AQ66
Farnham Pl, SE1 . . . 20 F2
Farnham Rd, Guil. GU1, GU2 . . . 258 AS137
Ilford IG3 . . . 125 ET59
Romford RM3 . . . 106 FK50
Slough SL1, SL2 . . . 131 AQ71
Welling DA16 . . . 166 EW82
H Farnham Rd Hosp, Guil. GU2 . . . 258 AV136
FARNHAM ROYAL, Slou. SL2 . . . 131 AQ68
Farnham Royal, SE11 . . . 20 B10
Sch Farnham Royal C of E Comb Sch, Slou. SL2 off Church Rd . . . 131 AQ69
FARNINGHAM, Dart. DA4 . . . 208 FN100
Farningham Cres, Cat. CR3 off Commonwealth Rd . . . 236 DU123
Farningham Hill Rd, Dart. (Fnghm) DA4 . . . 208 FJ99
⇌ Farningham Road . . . 208 FP96
Farningham Rd, N17 . . . 100 DU52
Caterham CR3 . . . 236 DU123
Farnley, Wok. GU21 . . . 226 AT117
Farnley Rd, E4 . . . 102 EE45
SE25 . . . 202 DR98
Farnol Rd, Dart. DA1 . . . 168 FN84
Faro Cl, Brom. BR1 . . . 205 EN96
Faroe Rd, W14 . . . 16 B6
Faroma Wk, Enf. EN2 . . . 81 DN39
Farquhar Rd, SE19 . . . 182 DT92
SW19 . . . 180 DA90
Farquharson Rd, Croy. CR0 . . . 202 DQ102
Farquhar St, Hert. SG14 . . . 32 DQ08
Farraline Rd, Wat. WD18 . . . 75 BV42
Farrance Rd, Rom. RM6 . . . 126 EY58
Farrance St, E14 . . . 13 M8
Farrans Ct, Har. HA3 . . . 117 CH59
Farrant Av, N22 . . . 99 DN54
Farrant Cl, Orp. BR6 . . . 224 EU108
Farrant Way, Borwd. WD6 . . . 78 CL39
Farr Av, Bark. IG11 . . . 146 EU68
Farrell Ho, E1 . . . 12 F8
Farren Rd, SE23 . . . 183 DY89
Farrer Ms, N8 off Farrer Rd . . . 121 DJ56
Farrer Rd, N8 . . . 121 DJ56
Harrow HA3 . . . 118 CL57
Farrer's Pl, Croy. CR0 . . . 221 DX105
Farriday Cl, St.Alb. AL3 . . . 43 CE16
Farrier Cl, Sun. TW16 . . . 195 BU98
Uxbridge UB8 off Horseshoe Dr . . . 134 BN72
Farrier Rd, Nthlt. UB5 . . . 136 CA68
Farriers, Ware (Gt Amwell) SG12 . . . 33 EA09
Farriers Cl, Epsom KT17 . . . 216 CS111
Gravesend DA12 . . . 191 GM88
Hemel Hempstead (Bov.) HP3 off Chipperfield Rd . . . 57 BB28
Farriers Ct, Sutt. SM3 off Forge La . . . 217 CY108
Watford WD25 . . . 59 BV32
Farriers End, Brox. EN10 . . . 67 DZ26
Farriers Ms, SE15 off Machell Rd . . . 162 DW83
Farriers Rd, Epsom KT17 . . . 216 CS112
Farrier St, NW1 . . . 141 DH66
Farriers Way, Borwd. WD6 . . . 78 CQ44
Farrier Wk, SW10 . . . 160 DC79
⇌ Farringdon . . . 10 D5
⊖ Farringdon . . . 10 D5
Farringdon La, EC1 . . . 10 D4
Farringdon Rd, EC1 . . . 10 C3
Farringdon St, EC4 . . . 10 E7
Farringford Cl, St.Alb. AL2 . . . 60 CA26
Farrington Av, Orp. BR5 . . . 206 EV97
Farrington Pl, Chis. BR7 . . . 185 ER94
Northwood HA6 . . . 93 BT49
Sch Farringtons & Stratford Ho, Chis. BR7 off Perry St . . . 185 ER94
Farrins Rents, SE16 . . . 23 J2
Farrow La, SE14 . . . 162 DW80
Farrow Pl, SE16 . . . 23 J5
Farr Rd, Enf. EN2 . . . 82 DR39
Farthingale Ct, Wal.Abb. EN9 . . . 68 EG34
Farthingale La, Wal.Abb. EN9 . . . 68 EG34
Farthingale Wk, E15 . . . 143 ED66
Farthing All, SE1 . . . 22 A4
Farthing Cl, Dart. DA1 . . . 168 FM84
Farthing Flds, E1 . . . 22 D1
Farthing Grn La, Slou. (Stoke P.) SL2 . . . 132 AU68
Farthings, Wok. (Knap.) GU21 . . . 226 AS116
Farthings, The, Amer. HP6 off Milton Lawns . . . 55 AR36
Hemel Hempstead HP1 . . . 40 BH20
Kingston upon Thames KT2 off Brunswick Rd . . . 198 CN95
Farthings Cl, E4 . . . 102 EE48
Pinner HA5 . . . 115 BV58
Farthing St, Orp. BR6 . . . 223 EM108
Farwell Rd, Sid. DA14 . . . 186 EV90
Farwig La, Brom. BR1 . . . 204 EF95
Fashion St, E1 . . . 11 N6
Fashoda Rd, Brom. BR2 . . . 204 EK98
Fassett Rd, E8 . . . 142 DU65
Kingston upon Thames KT1 . . . 198 CL98
Fassett Sq, E8 . . . 142 DU65
Fassnidge Way, Uxb. UB8 off Oxford Rd . . . 134 BJ66
Fauconberg Rd, W4 . . . 158 CQ79
Faulkner Cl, Dag. RM8 . . . 126 EX59
Faulkner's All, EC1 . . . 10 E5
Faulkners Rd, Walt. KT12 . . . 214 BW106
Faulkner St, SE14 . . . 162 DW81
Fauna Cl, Rom. RM6 . . . 126 EW59
Faunce St, SE17 off Harmsworth St . . . 161 DP78
Favart Rd, SW6 . . . 160 DA81
Faverolle Grn, Wal.Cr. EN8 . . . 67 DX28
Faversham Av, E4 . . . 102 EE46
Enfield EN1 . . . 82 DR44
Faversham Cl, Chig. IG7 . . . 104 EV47
Faversham Rd, SE6 . . . 183 DZ87
Beckenham BR3 . . . 203 DZ96
Morden SM4 . . . 200 DB100
Sch Fawbert & Barnard Co Inf Sch, Saw. CM21 off Knight St . . . 36 EY05
Sch Fawbert & Barnard's Prim Sch, Harl. CM17 off London Rd . . . 36 EW12
Fawcett Cl, SW11 . . . 160 DD82
SW16 . . . 181 DN91
Fawcett Est, E5 . . . 122 DU60
Fawcett Rd, NW10 . . . 139 CT67
Croydon CR0 . . . 202 DQ104
Windsor SL4 . . . 151 AP81
Fawcett St, SW10 . . . 160 DC79
Fawcus Cl, Esher (Clay.) KT10 off Dalmore Av . . . 215 CF107
Fawe Pk Rd, SW15 . . . 159 CZ84
Fawe St, E14 . . . 14 B6
Fawke Common, Sev. (Undrvr) TN15 . . . 257 FP127
Fawke Common Rd, Sev. TN15 . . . 257 FP126
Fawkes Av, Dart. DA1 . . . 188 FM89
Sch Fawkham C of E Prim Sch, Long. DA3 off Valley Rd . . . 209 FV102

⊖ London Underground station   DLR Docklands Light Railway station   Tra Tramlink station   Riv Pedestrian ferry landing stage

FAWKHAM GREEN, Long. DA3 209 FV104
Fawkham Grn Rd, Long. (Fawk.Grn) DA3 209 FV104
[H] Fawkham Manor Hosp, Long. DA3 209 FW102
Fawkham Rd, Long. DA3 209 FX97
Fawkon Wk, Hodd. EN11 off Taverners Way 49 EA17
Fawley Rd, NW6 120 DB64
Fawnbrake Av, SE24 181 DP85
Fawn Ct, Hat. AL9 45 CW16
Fawn Rd, E13 144 EJ68
Chigwell IG7 103 ET50
Fawns Manor Cl, Felt. TW14 175 BQ88
Fawns Manor Rd, Felt. TW14 175 BR88
Fawood Av, NW10 138 CR66
Fawsley Cl, Slou. (Colnbr.) SL3 153 BE80
Fawters Cl, Brwd. (Hutt.) CM13 109 GD44
Fayerfield, Pot.B. EN6 64 DD31
Faygate Cres, Bexh. DA6 186 FA85
Faygate Rd, SW2 181 DM89
Fay Grn, Abb.L. WD5 59 BR33
Fayland Av, SW16 181 DJ92
Faymore Gdns, S.Ock. RM15 149 FU72
Feacey Down, Hem.H. HP1 40 BG18
Fearn Cl, Lthd. (E.Hors.) KT24 245 BS129
Fearney Mead, Rick. (Mill End) WD3 92 BG46
Fearnley Cres, Hmptn. TW12 176 BY92
Fearnley Rd, Welw.G.C. AL8 29 CW10
Fearnley St, Wat. WD18 75 BV42
Fearns Mead, Brwd. CM14 off Bucklers Ct 108 FW50
Fearon St, SE10 25 L9
Featherbed La, Abb.L. (Bedmond) WD5 off Sergehill La 59 BV26
Croydon CR0 221 DZ108
Hemel Hempstead HP3 40 BJ24
Romford RM4 104 EY45
Warlingham CR6 221 ED113
Feather Dell, Hat. AL10 45 CT18
Feathers La, Stai. (Wrays.) TW19 173 BA89
Feathers Pl, SE10 163 ED79
Featherstone Av, SE23 182 DV89
Featherstone Gdns, Borwd. WD6 78 CQ42
[Sch] Featherstone High Sch, Sthl. UB2 off Montague Waye 156 BY76
Western Annexe, Sthl. UB2 off Western Rd 156 BX77
Featherstone Ind Est, Sthl. UB2 156 BY75
[Sch] Featherstone Prim Sch, Sthl. UB2 off Featherstone Rd 156 BY76
Featherstone Rd, NW7 97 CV51
Southall UB2 156 BY76
Featherstone St, EC1 11 J3
Featherstone Ter, Sthl. UB2 156 BY76
Featley Rd, SW9 161 DP83
Federal Rd, Grnf. UB6 137 CJ68
Federal Way, Wat. WD24 76 BW38
Federation Rd, SE2 166 EV77
Fee Fm Rd, Esher (Clay.) KT10 215 CF108
Feenan Highway, Til. RM18 171 GH80
Felbridge Av, Stan. HA7 95 CG53
Felbridge Cl, SW16 181 DN91
Sutton SM2 218 DC109
Felbrigge Rd, Ilf. IG3 125 ET61
Felcott Cl, Walt. KT12 196 BW104
Felcott Rd, Walt. KT12 196 BW104
Felday Hos, Dor. (Holm.St.M.) RH5 261 BV144
Felday Rd, SE13 183 EB86
Dorking (Abin.Ham.) RH5 261 BT140
FELDEN, Hem.H. HP3 40 BG24
Felden Cl, Pnr. HA5 94 BY52
Watford WD25 60 BX34
Felden Dr, Hem.H. (Felden) HP3 40 BG24
Felden La, Hem.H. (Felden) HP3 40 BG24
Felden St, SW6 159 CZ81
Feldman Cl, N16 122 DU60
Felgate Ms, W6 159 CV77
Felhampton Rd, SE9 185 EP89
Felhurst Cres, Dag. RM10 127 FB63
Felicia Way, Grays RM16 171 GH77
Felipe Rd, Grays (Chaff.Hun.) RM16 169 FW76
Felix Av, N8 121 DL58
Felix Dr, Guil. (W.Clan.) GU4 244 BG128
Felix La, Shep. TW17 195 BS100
Felix Rd, W13 137 CG73
Walton-on-Thames KT12 195 BU100
Felixstowe Ct, E16 off Fishguard Way 165 EP75
Felixstowe Rd, N9 100 DU49
N17 122 DT55
NW10 139 CV69
SE2 166 EV76
Felland Way, Reig. RH2 266 DC138
Fellbrigg Rd, SE22 182 DT85
Fellbrigg St, E1 12 D4
Fellbrook, Rich. TW10 177 CH90
Fellmongers Path, SE1 21 M4
Fellmongers Yd, Croy. CR0 off Surrey St 202 DQ103
Fellowes Cl, Hayes UB4 off Paddington Cl 136 BX70
Fellowes La, St.Alb. (Coln.Hth) AL4 44 CS23
Fellowes Rd, Cars. SM5 200 DE104
Fellows Ct, E2 5 N10
Fellows Rd, NW3 140 DD66
Fell Rd, Croy. CR0 202 DQ104
Felltram Way, SE7 25 M9
Fell Wk, Edg. HA8 off East Rd 96 CP53
Felmersham Cl, SW4 off Haselrigge Rd 161 DK84
Felmingham Rd, SE20 202 DW96
Felmongers, Harl. CM20 36 EV13
Felnex Trd Est, Wall. SM6 200 DG103
Felsberg Rd, SW2 181 DL86
Fels Cl, Dag. RM10 127 FB62
Fels Fm Av, Dag. RM10 127 FC62
Felsham Rd, SW15 159 CX83
Felspar Cl, SE18 165 ET78
Felstead Av, Ilf. IG5 103 EN53
Felstead Cl, Brwd. (Hutt.) CM13 109 GC44
Felstead Gdns, E14 24 C10
Felstead Rd, E11 124 EG59
Epsom KT19 216 CR111
Loughton IG10 102 EL45
Orpington BR6 206 EU103
Romford RM5 105 FC51
Waltham Cross EN8 67 DY32
Felstead St, E9 143 DZ65
Felsted Rd, E16 144 EK72
FELTHAM, TW13 & TW14 175 BU89
⇌ Feltham 175 BV88
Feltham Av, E.Mol. KT8 197 CE98
Felthambrook Way, Felt. TW13 175 BV90
Feltham Business Complex, Felt. TW13 175 BV89
[Coll] Feltham City Learning Cen, Felt. TW13 off Browells La 176 BW89
[Sch] Feltham Comm Coll, Felt. TW13 off Browells La 176 BW89
FELTHAMHILL, Felt. TW13 175 BT92
[Sch] Feltham Hill Inf & Nurs Sch, Felt. TW13 off Bedfont Rd 175 BT90
[Sch] Feltham Hill Jun Sch, Felt. TW13 off Ashford Rd 175 BT90
Feltham Hill Rd, Ashf. TW15 175 BP92
Feltham TW13 175 BU91
Feltham Rd, Ashf. TW15 175 BP91
Mitcham CR4 200 DF96
Redhill RH1 266 DF139
Feltham Wk, Red. RH1 266 DF139
Felton Cl, Borwd. WD6 78 CL38
Broxbourne EN10 67 DZ25
Orpington BR5 205 EP100
[Sch] Feltonfleet Sch, Cob. KT11 off Byfleet Rd 213 BS113
Felton Gdns, Bark. IG11 off Sutton Rd 145 ES67
Felton Ho, SE3 off Ryan Cl 164 EH84
Felton Lea, Sid. DA14 185 ET92
Felton Rd, W13 off Camborne Av 157 CJ75
Barking IG11 off Sutton Rd 145 ES68
Felton St, N1 5 K8
Fencepiece Rd, Chig. IG7 103 EQ50
Ilford IG6 103 EQ50
Fenchurch Av, EC3 11 L8
Fenchurch Bldgs, EC3 11 M8
Fenchurch Pl, EC3 11 M9
⇌ Fenchurch Street 11 M9
Fenchurch St, EC3 11 L9
Fen Cl, Brwd. (Shenf.) CM15 109 GC42
Fen Ct, EC3 11 L9
Fendall Rd, Epsom KT19 216 CQ106
Fendall St, SE1 21 M6
Fendt Cl, E16 15 K8
Fendyke Rd, Belv. DA17 166 EX76
Fenelon Pl, W14 16 F8
Fengates Rd, Red. RH1 250 DE134
Fen Gro, Sid. DA15 185 ET86
Fenham Rd, SE15 162 DU80
Fen La, Upmin. (N.Ock.) RM14 129 FW64
Fenman Ct, N17 off Shelbourne Rd 100 DV53
Fenman Gdns, Ilf. IG3 126 EV60
Fenn Cl, Brom. BR1 184 EG93
Fennel Cl, E16 15 H3
Croydon CR0 off Primrose La 203 DX102
Guildford GU1 243 BB131
Fennells, Harl. CM19 51 EQ20
Fennells Mead, Epsom KT17 217 CT109
Fennel St, SE18 165 EN79
Fenner Cl, SE16 22 D7
Fenner Ho, Walt. KT12 213 BU105
Fenner Rd, Grays RM16 169 FW77
Fenners Marsh, Grav. DA12 191 GM88
Fenner Sq, SW11 off Thomas Baines Rd 160 DD83
Fennings, The, Amer. HP6 55 AR36
Fenning St, SE1 21 L3
Fenn St, E9 122 DW64
Fenns Way, Wok. GU21 226 AY115
Fennycroft Rd, Hem.H. HP1 40 BG17
Fensomes All, Hem.H. HP2 40 BK19
Fensomes Cl, Hem.H. HP2 off Broad St 40 BK19
Fenstanton Av, N12 98 DD50
[Sch] Fenstanton Prim Sch, SW2 off Abbots Pk 181 DN88
Fen St, E16 15 K9
Fens Way, Swan. BR8 187 FG93
Fenswood Cl, Bex. DA5 186 FA85
Fentiman Rd, SW8 161 DL79
Fentiman Way, Horn. RM11 128 FL60
Fenton Av, Stai. TW18 174 BJ93
Fenton Cl, E8 5 P3
SW9 161 DM82
Chislehurst BR7 185 EM92
Redhill RH1 250 DG134
Fenton Gra, Harl. CM17 52 EW16
★ Fenton Ho, NW3 120 DC62
Fenton Rd, N17 100 DQ52
Grays (Chaff.Hun.) RM16 170 FY75
Redhill RH1 250 DG134
Fentons Av, E13 144 EH68
Fentum Rd, Guil. GU2 242 AU132
Fenwick Cl, SE18 off Ritter St 165 EN79
Woking GU21 226 AV118
Fenwick Gro, SE15 162 DU83
Fenwick Path, Borwd. WD6 78 CM38
Fenwick Pl, SW9 161 DL83
South Croydon CR2 off Columbine Av 219 DP108
Fenwick Rd, SE15 162 DU83
Ferdinand Pl, NW1 off Ferdinand St 140 DG66
Ferdinand St, NW1 140 DG65
Ferguson Av, Grav. DA12 191 GJ91
Romford RM2 106 FJ54
Surbiton KT5 198 CM99
Ferguson Cl, E14 23 N8
Bromley BR2 203 EC97
Ferguson Ct, Rom. RM2 106 FK54
Ferguson Dr, W3 138 CR72
Fergus Rd, N5 4 F2
Ferme Pk Rd, N4 121 DL57
N8 121 DL57
Fermor Rd, SE23 183 DY88
Fermoy Rd, W9 6 E4
Greenford UB6 136 CB70
Fern Av, Mitch. CR4 201 DK98
Fernbank, Buck.H. IG9 102 EH46
Fernbank Av, Horn. RM12 128 FJ63
Walton-on-Thames KT12 196 BY101
Fernbank Av, Wem. HA0 117 CF63
Fernbank Ms, SW12 181 DJ86
Fernbank Rd, Add. KT15 212 BG106
Fernbrook Av, Sid. DA15 off Blackfen Rd 185 ES85
Fernbrook Cres, SE13 184 EE86
Fernbrook Dr, Har. HA2 116 CB59
Fernbrook Rd, SE13 184 EE86
Ferncliff Rd, E8 122 DU64
Fern Cl, N1 5 L9
Broxbourne EN10 49 DZ23
Erith DA8 off Hollywood Way 167 FH81
Warlingham CR6 237 DY118
Ferncroft Av, N12 98 DE51
NW3 120 DA62
Ruislip HA4 116 BW61
Ferndale, Brom. BR1 204 EJ96
Guildford GU3 242 AS132
Ferndale Av, E17 123 ED57
Chertsey KT16 193 BE104
Hounslow TW4 156 BY83
Ferndale Cl, Bexh. DA7 166 EY81
Ferndale Ct, SE3 164 EF80
Ferndale Cres, Uxb. UB8 134 BJ69
Ferndale Rd, E7 144 EH66
E11 124 EE61
N15 122 DT58
SE25 202 DV99
SW4 161 DL84
SW9 161 DM83
Ashford TW15 174 BK92
Banstead SM7 233 CZ116
Enfield EN3 83 DY37
Gravesend DA12 191 GH89
Romford RM5 105 FC54
Woking GU21 227 AZ116
Ferndale St, E6 145 EP73
Ferndale Ter, Har. HA1 117 CF56
Ferndale Way, Orp. BR6 223 ER106
Ferndell Av, Bex. DA5 187 FD90
Fern Dells, Hat. AL10 45 CT19
Fern Dene, W13 off Templewood 137 CH71
Ferndene, St.Alb. (Brick.Wd) AL2 60 BZ31
Ferndene Rd, SE24 162 DQ84
Fernden Ri, Gdmg. GU7 258 AS144
Fernden Way, Rom. RM7 127 FB58
Ferndown, Horl. RH6 268 DF146
Hornchurch RM11 128 FM58
Northwood HA6 93 BU54
Ferndown Av, Orp. BR6 205 ER102
Ferndown Cl, Guil. GU1 259 BA135
Pinner HA5 94 BY52
Sutton SM2 218 DD107
Ferndown Ct, Guil. GU1 242 AW133
Ferndown Gdns, Cob. KT11 214 BW113
Ferndown Rd, SE9 184 EK87
Watford WD19 94 BW48
Fern Dr, Hem.H. HP3 40 BL21
Maidenhead (Taplow) SL6 130 AH72
Fernecroft, St.Alb. AL1 43 CD23
Fernery, The, Stai. TW18 173 BE92
Fernes Cl, Uxb. UB8 134 BJ72
Ferney Ct, W.Byf. (Byfleet) KT14 off Ferney Rd 212 BK112
Ferney Meade Way, Islw. TW7 157 CG82
Ferney Rd, Barn. EN4 98 DG45
Waltham Cross (Chsht) EN7 66 DR26
West Byfleet (Byfleet) KT14 212 BK112
Fern Gro, Felt. TW14 175 BV87
Welwyn Garden City AL8 29 CX05
Ferngrove Cl, Lthd. (Fetch.) KT22 231 CE123
Fernhall Dr, Ilf. IG4 124 EK57
Fernhall La, Wal.Abb. EN9 68 EK31
Fernham Rd, Th.Hth. CR7 202 DQ97
Fernhead Rd, W9 6 F1
Fernheath Way, Dart. DA2 187 FD92
Fernhill, Lthd. (Oxshott) KT22 215 CD114
Fernhill Cl, Wok. GU22 226 AW120
Fernhill Ct, E17 101 ED54
Fernhill Gdns, Kings.T. KT2 177 CK92
Fern Hill La, Harl. CM18 51 ES19
Fernhill La, Wok. GU22 226 AW120
Fernhill Pk, Wok. GU22 226 AW120
[Sch] Fern Hill Prim Sch, Kings.T. KT2 off Richmond Rd 178 CL93
Fernhill Rd, Horl. RH6 269 DK152
Fernhills, Kings L. WD4 59 BR33
Fernhill St, E16 145 EM74
Fernholme Rd, SE15 183 DX85
Fernhurst Cl, Beac. HP9 89 AM53
Fernhurst Gdns, Edg. HA8 96 CN51
Fernhurst Rd, SW6 159 CY81
Ashford TW15 175 BQ91
Croydon CR0 202 DU101
Fernie Cl, Chig. IG7 104 EU50
Fernihough Cl, Wey. KT13 212 BN111
Fernlands Cl, Cher. KT16 193 BE104
Fern La, Houns. TW5 156 BZ78
Fernlea, Lthd. (Bkhm) KT23 230 CB124
Fernlea Rd, SW12 181 DH88
Mitcham CR4 200 DG96
Fernleigh Cl, W9 6 F1
Croydon CR0 off Stafford Rd 219 DN105
Walton-on-Thames KT12 195 BV104
Fernleigh Ct, Har. HA2 94 CB54
Wembley HA9 118 CL61
Fernleigh Rd, N21 99 DN47
Fern Leys, St.Alb. AL4 43 CJ17
Ferns, The, Beac. HP9 89 AM54
Hatfield AL10 off Campion Rd 45 CT15
Fernsbury St, WC1 10 C2
Ferns Cl, Enf. EN3 83 DY36
South Croydon CR2 220 DV110
Fernshaw Rd, SW10 160 DC79
Fernside, NW11 off Finchley Rd 120 DA61
Buckhurst Hill IG9 102 EH46
Fernside Av, NW7 96 CR48
Feltham TW13 175 BV91
Fernside La, Sev. TN13 257 FJ129
Fernside Rd, SW12 180 DF88
Fernsleigh Cl, Ger.Cr. (Chal.St.P.) SL9 90 AY51
Ferns Rd, E15 144 EF65
Fern St, E3 13 P4
Fernthorpe Rd, SW16 181 DJ93
Ferntower Rd, N5 5 J1
Fern Twrs, Cat. CR3 252 DU125
Fernville La, Hem.H. HP2 off Midland Rd 40 BK20
Fern Wk, SE16 22 B10
Ashford TW15 off Ferndale Rd 174 BK92
Fern Way, Wat. WD25 75 BU35
Fernways, Ilf. IG1 off Cecil Rd 125 EP63
Fernwood Av, SW16 181 DK91
Wembley HA0 off Bridgewater Rd 117 CJ64
Fernwood Cl, Brom. BR1 204 EJ96
Fernwood Cres, N20 98 DF48
Ferny Hill, Barn. EN4 80 DF38
Ferranti Cl, SE18 164 EK76
Ferraro Cl, Houns. TW5 156 CA79
Ferrers Av, Wall. SM6 219 DK105
West Drayton UB7 154 BK75
Ferrers Cl, Slou. SL1 131 AL74
Ferrers Rd, SW16 181 DK92
Ferrestone Rd, N8 121 DM56
Ferrey Ms, SW9 161 DN82
Ferriby Cl, N1 4 C5
Ferrier Pt, E16 15 L6
Ferrier St, SW18 160 DB84
Ferriers Way, Epsom KT18 233 CW119
Ferring Cl, Har. HA2 116 CC60
Ferrings, SE21 182 DS89
Ferris Av, Croy. CR0 203 DZ104
Ferris Rd, SE22 162 DU84
Ferron Rd, E5 122 DV62
Ferro Rd, Rain. RM13 147 FG70
Ferrour Ct, N2 120 DD55
Ferry Av, Stai. TW18 173 BE94
Ferryhills Cl, Wat. WD19 94 BW48
Ferry La, N17 122 DU56
SW13 159 CT79
Brentford TW8 158 CL79
Chertsey KT16 194 BH98
Guildford GU2 off Portsmouth Rd 258 AW138
Rainham RM13 147 FE72
Richmond TW9 158 CM79
Shepperton TW17 194 BN102
Staines (Laleham) TW18 194 BJ97
Staines (Wrays.) TW19 173 BB89
[Sch] Ferry La Prim Sch, N17 off Jarrow Rd 122 DV56
Ferryman's Quay, SW6 160 DC82
Ferrymead Av, Grnf. UB6 136 CA69
Ferrymead Dr, Grnf. UB6 136 CA68
Ferrymead Gdns, Grnf. UB6 136 CC68
Ferrymoor, Rich. TW10 177 CH90
Ferry Pl, SE18 off Woolwich High St 165 EN76
Ferry Rd, SW13 159 CU80
Maidenhead SL6 150 AC75
Teddington TW11 177 CH92
Thames Ditton KT7 197 CH100
Tilbury RM18 171 GG83
Twickenham TW1 177 CH88
West Molesey KT8 196 CA97
Ferry Sq, Brent. TW8 158 CL79
Shepperton TW17 195 BP101
Ferry St, E14 24 C9
Feryby Rd, Grays RM16 171 GH76
Feryngs Cl, Harl. CM17 off Watlington Rd 36 EX11
Fesants Cft, Harl. CM20 36 EV12
Festing Rd, SW15 159 CX83
Festival Cl, Bex. DA5 186 EX88
Erith DA8 off Betsham Rd 167 FF80
Uxbridge UB10 135 BP67
Festival Path, Wok. GU21 226 AT119
Festival Wk, Cars. SM5 218 DF106
Festoon Way, E16 144 EK73
FETCHAM, Lthd. KT22 231 CD123
Fetcham Common La, Lthd. (Fetch.) KT22 230 CB121
Fetcham Downs, Lthd. (Fetch.) KT22 247 CE126
Fetcham Pk Dr, Lthd. (Fetch.) KT22 231 CE123
[Sch] Fetcham Village Inf Sch, Lthd. KT22 off The Street 231 CD122
Fetherstone Cl, Pot.B. EN6 64 DD32
Fetter La, EC4 10 D8
Ffinch St, SE8 163 EA80
Fiddicroft Av, Bans. SM7 218 DB114
Fiddlebridge La, Hat. AL10 45 CT17
Fiddlers Cl, Green. DA9 169 FV84
FIDDLERS HAMLET, Epp. CM16 70 EW32
Fidler Pl, Bushey WD23 off Ashfield Av 76 CB44
Field Cl, E4 101 EB51
NW2 119 CU61
Bromley BR1 204 EJ96
Buckhurst Hill IG9 102 EJ48
Chesham HP5 54 AS28
Chessington KT9 215 CJ106
Guildford GU4 243 BD132
Hayes UB3 155 BQ80
Hounslow TW4 155 BV81
Romford (Abridge) RM4 86 EV41
Ruislip HA4 off Field Way 115 BQ60
St. Albans (Sand.) AL4 43 CG16
South Croydon CR2 220 DV114
West Molesey KT8 196 CB99
Fieldcommon La, Walt. KT12 196 BZ101
Field Ct, WC1 10 B6
Oxted RH8 off Silkham Rd 254 EE127
Field End, Barn. EN5 79 CV42
Coulsdon CR5 219 DK114
Northolt UB5 136 BX65
Ruislip HA4 136 BW65
Fieldend, Twick. TW1 177 CF91
Field End Cl, Wat. WD19 94 BY45
[Sch] Field End Inf Sch, Ruis. HA4 off Field End Rd 116 BX61
[Sch] Field End Jun Sch, Ruis. HA4 off Field End Rd 116 BX61
Field End Ms, Wat. WD19 off Field End Cl 94 BY45
Fieldend Rd, SW16 201 DJ95
Field End Rd, Pnr. HA5 115 BV58
Ruislip HA4 116 BY63
Fielders Cl, Enf. EN1 off Woodfield Cl 82 DS42
Harrow HA2 116 CC60
Fielders Grn, Guil. GU1 243 AZ134
Fielders Way, Rad. (Shenley) WD7 62 CL33
Fieldfare Rd, SE28 146 EW73
Fieldgate La, Mitch. CR4 200 DE97
Fieldgate St, E1 12 B6
Fieldhouse Cl, E18 102 EG53
Fieldhouse Rd, SW12 181 DJ88
Fieldhurst, Slou. SL3 153 AZ78
Fieldhurst Cl, Add. KT15 212 BH106
[Sch] Field Inf Sch, Wat. WD18 off Neal St 76 BW43
Fielding Av, Til. RM18 171 GH81
Twickenham TW2 176 CC90
[Sch] Fielding Co Prim Sch, W13 off Wyndham Rd 157 CH76
Fielding Gdns, Slou. SL3 152 AW75
Fielding Ho, NW6 7 H1
Fielding Ms, SW13 off Castelnau 159 CV79
Fielding Rd, W4 158 CR76
W14 16 B5
Fieldings, The, SE23 182 DW88
Banstead SM7 233 CZ117
Horley RH6 269 DH147
Woking GU21 226 AT116
Fieldings Rd, Wal.Cr. (Chsht) EN8 67 DZ29
Fielding St, SE17 162 DQ79
Fielding Wk, W13 157 CH76
Fielding Way, Brwd. (Hutt.) CM13 109 GC44
[Sch] Field Jun Sch, Wat. WD18 off Watford Fld Rd 76 BW43
Field La, Brent. TW8 157 CJ80
Godalming GU7 off The Oval 258 AT144
Teddington TW11 177 CG92
Field Mead, NW7 96 CS52
NW9 96 CS52
Field Pl, Gdmg. GU7 258 AS144
New Malden KT3 199 CT100
Field Rd, E7 124 EF63
N17 122 DR55
W6 16 C10
Feltham TW14 175 BV86
Hemel Hempstead HP2 40 BN21
South Ockendon (Aveley) RM15 148 FQ74
Uxbridge (Denh.) UB9 113 BE63
Watford WD19 76 BY44
Fields, The, Slou. SL1 151 AR75
Fields Ct, Pot.B. EN6 64 DD33
Fields End La, Hem.H. HP1 39 BE18
Fieldsend Rd, Sutt. SM3 217 CY106
Fields Est, E8 142 DU66
Fieldside Cl, Orp. BR6 off State Fm Av 223 EQ105
Fieldside Rd, Brom. BR1 183 ED92
Fields Pk Cres, Rom. RM6 126 EX57
Field St, WC1 10 A1
Fieldview, SW18 180 DD88
Field Vw, Egh. TW20 173 BC92
Feltham TW13 175 BR91
Fieldview, Horl. RH6 off Stockfield 269 DH147
Fieldview Ct, Stai. TW18 off Burges Way 174 BG93
Field Vw Ri, St.Alb. (Brick.Wd) AL2 60 BY29
Field Vw Rd, Pot.B. EN6 64 DA33
[Tra] Fieldway 221 EB108
Field Way, NW10 off Twybridge Way 138 CQ66
Fieldway, Amer. HP7 55 AP41
Field Way, Berk. HP4 38 AY21
Croydon CR0 221 EB107
Fieldway, Dag. RM8 126 EV63
Field Way, Ger.Cr. (Chal.St.P.) SL9 90 AX52
Greenford UB6 136 CB67
Hemel Hempstead (Bov.) HP3 57 BA27
Hoddesdon EN11 33 EC13
Fieldway, Orp. BR5 205 ER100
Field Way, Rick. WD3 92 BH46
Ruislip HA4 115 BQ60
Uxbridge UB8 134 BK70
Fieldway, Ware (Stans.Abb.) SG12 33 EB11
Field Way, Wok. (Ripley) GU23 243 BF125
Fieldway Cres, N5 4 D2
Fiennes Cl, Dag. RM8 126 EW60
Fiennes Way, Sev. TN13 257 FJ127
Fiesta Dr, Dag. RM9 147 FC70
Fifehead Cl, Ashf. TW15 174 BL93
Fife Rd, E16 15 L6
N22 99 DP52
SW14 178 CQ85
Kingston upon Thames KT1 198 CL96
Fife Ter, N1 4 B9
Fifeway, Lthd. KT23 246 CA125
FIFIELD, Maid. SL6 150 AD81
Fifield La, Wind. SL4 150 AD84
Fifield Path, SE23 off Bampton Rd 183 DX90
Fifield Rd, Maid. SL6 150 AD80
Fifth Av, E12 125 EM63
W10 6 C2
Grays RM20 169 FU79
Harlow CM20 35 ER13
Hayes UB3 135 BT74
Watford WD25 76 BX35
Fifth Cross Rd, Twick. TW2 177 CD89
Fifth Way, Wem. HA9 118 CP63
Figges Rd, Mitch. CR4 180 DG94
Figgs Wd, Couls. CR5 off Jennys Way 235 DJ122
Fig St, Sev. TN14 256 FF129
Fig Tree Cl, NW10 off Craven Pk 138 CS67
Fig Tree Hill, Hem.H. HP2 40 BK19
Filby Rd, Chess. KT9 216 CM107
Filey Av, N16 122 DU60
Filey Cl, Sutt. SM2 218 DC108
Westerham (Bigg.H.) TN16 238 EH119
Filey Spur, Slou. SL1 151 AP75
Filey Waye, Ruis. HA4 115 BU61
Filigree Ct, SE16 23 K2
Fillebrook Av, Enf. EN1 82 DS40
Fillebrook Rd, E11 123 ED60
Fillingham Way, Hat. AL10 off Mosquito Way 44 CS16
Filmer La, Sev. TN14 257 FL121
Filmer Rd, SW6 159 CY81
Windsor SL4 151 AK82
Filston La, Sev. TN14 225 FE113
Filston Rd, Erith DA8 off Riverdale Rd 167 FB78
Finborough Rd, SW10 160 DB78
SW17 180 DF93
Finchale Rd, SE2 166 EU76
Fincham Cl, Uxb. UB10 off Aylsham Dr 115 BQ61
Finch Av, SE27 182 DR91
Finch Cl, NW10 118 CR64
Barnet EN5 80 DA43
Hatfield AL10 off Eagle Way 45 CU20
Finchdale, Hem.H. HP1 40 BG20
Finchdean Ho, SW15 off Tangley Gro 179 CT87
Finch Dr, Felt. TW14 176 BX87
Finch End, H.Wyc. (Penn) HP10 88 AC47
Finches, The, Hert. SG13 32 DV09
Finches Av, Rick. (Crox.Grn) WD3 74 BM41
Finches Ri, Guil. GU1 243 BC132
Finch Gdns, E4 101 EA50

★ Place of interest | [H] Hospital | [Sch] School | [Coll] College | [Uni] University | ⇌ Railway station

Finch Grn, Rick. (Chorl.)
WD3 73 BF42
Finchingfield Av, Wdf.Grn.
IG8 102 EJ52
Finch La, EC3 11 K8
Amersham HP7 72 AV40
Beaconsfield (Knot.Grn)
HP9 88 AJ50
Bushey WD23 76 CA43
FINCHLEY, N3 98 DB53
Sch Finchley Catholic High Sch,
N12 off Woodside La 98 DB48
⊖ Finchley Central 98 DA53
Finchley Cl, Dart. DA1 188 FN86
Finchley Ct, N3 98 DB51
Finchley La, NW4 119 CW56
H Finchley Mem Hosp, N12 98 DC52
Finchley Pk, N12 98 DC49
Finchley Pl, NW8 140 DD68
⊖ Finchley Road 140 DC65
Finchley Rd, NW2 120 DA62
NW3 140 DC65
NW8 140 DD67
NW11 119 CZ58
Grays RM17 170 GB79
⇌ Finchley Road & Frognal 120 DC64
Finchley Way, N3 98 DA52
Finch Ms, SE15 162 DT80
Finchmoor, Harl. CM18 51 ER18
Finch Rd, Berk. HP4 38 AU19
Guildford GU1 242 AX134
Finden Rd, E7 124 EH64
Findhorn Av, Hayes UB4 135 BV71
Findhorn St, E14 14 D7
Findlay Dr, Guil. GU3 242 AT130
Findon Cl, SW18
off Wimbledon Pk Rd 180 DA86
Harrow HA2 116 CB62
Findon Ct, Add. KT15 211 BF106
Findon Gdns, Rain. RM13 147 FG71
Findon Rd, N9 100 DV46
W12 159 CU75
Fine Bush La, Uxb. (Hare.)
UB9 115 BP58
Fingal St, SE10 25 K9
Finglesham Cl, Orp. BR5
off Westwell Cl 206 EX102
Finians Cl, Uxb. UB10 134 BM66
Finland Quay, SE16 23 K6
Finland Rd, SE4 163 DY83
Finland St, SE16 23 K5
Finlay Gdns, Add. KT15 212 BJ105
Finlays Cl, Chess. KT9 216 CN106
Finlay St, SW6 159 CX81
Finnart Cl, Wey. KT13 213 BQ105
Finnart Ho Dr, Wey. KT13
off Vaillant Rd 213 BQ105
Finney La, Islw. TW7 157 CG81
Finnis St, E2 12 D2
Finnymore Rd, Dag. RM9 146 EY66
FINSBURY, EC1 10 D1
Finsbury Av, EC2 11 K6
Finsbury Av Sq, EC2 11 K6
Finsbury Circ, EC2 11 K6
Finsbury Cotts, N22
off Clarence Rd 99 DL52
Finsbury Ct, Wal.Cr. EN8
off Parkside 67 DY34
Finsbury Est, EC1 10 E2
Finsbury Ho, N22 99 DL53
Finsbury Mkt, EC2 11 L4
FINSBURY PARK, N4 121 DN60
★ Finsbury Park, N4 121 DP59
⇌ Finsbury Park 121 DN61
⊖ Finsbury Park 121 DN61
Finsbury Pk Av, N4 122 DQ58
Finsbury Pk Rd, N4 121 DP61
Finsbury Pavement, EC2 11 K5
Finsbury Rd, N22 99 DM53
Finsbury Sq, EC2 11 K5
Finsbury St, EC2 11 J5
Finsbury Twr, EC1 11 J4
Finsbury Way, Bex. DA5 186 EZ86
Finsen Rd, SE5 162 DQ83
Finstock Rd, W10 6 A7
Finucane Dr, Orp. BR5 206 EW101
Finucane Gdns, Rain. RM13 147 FG65
Finucane Ri, Bushey
(Bushey Hth) WD23 94 CC47
Finway Ct, Wat. WD18
off Whippendell Rd 75 BT43
Finway Rd, Hem.H. HP2 41 BP16
Fiona Cl, Lthd. (Bkhm)
KT23 230 CA124
Firbank Cl, E16 144 EK71
Enfield EN2
off Gladbeck Way 82 DQ42
Firbank Dr, Wat. WD19 94 BY45
Woking GU21 226 AV119
Firbank La, Wok. GU21 226 AV119
Firbank Pl, Egh. (Eng.Grn)
TW20 172 AV93
Firbank Rd, SE15 162 DV82
Romford RM5 105 FB50
St. Albans AL3 43 CF16
Fir Cl, Walt. KT12 195 BU101
Fircroft Cl, Slou. (Stoke P.)
SL2 132 AU65
Woking GU22 227 AZ118
Fircroft Ct, Wok. GU22
off Fircroft Cl 227 AZ118
Fircroft Gdns, Har. HA1 117 CE62
Sch Fircroft Prim Sch, SW17
off Fircroft Rd 180 DF90
Fircroft Rd, SW17 180 DF89
Chessington KT9 216 CM105
Fir Dene, Orp. BR6 205 EM104
Firdene, Surb. KT5 198 CQ102
Fire Bell All, Surb. KT6 198 CL100
Firecrest Dr, NW3 120 DB62
Firefly Cl, Wall. SM6 219 DL108
Firefly Gdns, E6
off Jack Dash Way 144 EL70
★ Firepower, SE18 165 EP76
Fire Sta All, Barn. EN5
off Christchurch La 79 CZ40
Firethorn Cl, Edg. HA8
off Larkspur Gro 96 CQ49
Firfield Rd, Add. KT15 212 BG105
Firfields, Wey. KT13 213 BP107
Fir Gra Av, Wey. KT13 213 BP106
Fir Gro, N.Mal. KT3 199 CT100
Woking GU21 226 AU119
Fir Gro Rd, SW9
off Marcella Rd 161 DN82
Firham Pk Av, Rom. RM3 106 FN52
Firhill Rd, SE6 183 EA91
Firlands, Horl. RH6
off Stockfield 269 DH147
Weybridge KT13 213 BS107
Firmingers Rd, Orp. BR6 225 FB106
Firmin Rd, Dart. DA1 188 FJ85
Fir Pk, Harl. CM19 51 EP18
Fir Rd, Felt. TW13 176 BX92
Sutton SM3 199 CZ102
Firs, The, E17 off Leucha Rd 123 DY57
N20 98 DD46
W5 137 CK71
Bexley DA5
off Dartford Rd 187 FD88
Brentwood (Pilg.Hat.)
CM15 108 FU44
Caterham CR3
off Yorke Gate Rd 236 DR122
Guildford (Art.) GU3 258 AV138
Leatherhead (Bkhm)
KT23 230 CC124
St. Albans AL1 43 CH24
Tadworth KT20
off Brighton Rd 249 CZ126
Waltham Cross (Chsht)
EN7 66 DS27
Welwyn Garden City AL8 29 CW05
Firs Av, N10 120 DG55
N11 98 DG51
SW14 158 CQ84
Windsor SL4 151 AM83
Firsby Av, Croy. CR0 203 DX102
Firsby Rd, N16 122 DT60
Firs Cl, N10 off Firs Av 120 DG55
SE23 183 DX87
Dorking RH4 263 CG138
Esher (Clay.) KT10 215 CE107
Hatfield AL10 45 CV19
Iver SL0
off Thornbridge Rd 133 BC67
Mitcham CR4 201 DH96
Firscroft, N13 100 DQ48
Firsdene Cl, Cher. (Ott.)
KT16
off Slade Rd 211 BD107
Firs Dr, Houns. TW5 155 BV80
Loughton IG10 85 EN39
Slough SL3 133 AZ74
Firs End, Ger.Cr. (Chal.St.P.)
SL9 112 AY55
Sch Firs Fm Prim Sch, N13
off Rayleigh Rd 100 DR48
Firsgrove Cres, Brwd. CM14 108 FV49
Firsgrove Rd, Brwd. CM14 108 FV49
Firside Gro, Sid. DA15 185 ET88
Firs La, N13 100 DQ48
N21 100 DQ47
Potters Bar EN6 64 DB33
Firs Pk Av, N21 100 DR46
Firs Pk Gdns, N21 100 DQ46
Firs Rd, Ken. CR8 235 DP115
First Av, E12 124 EL63
E13 15 L1
E17 123 EA57
N18 100 DW49
NW4 119 CW56
SW14 158 CS83
W3 139 CT74
W10 6 E3
Amersham HP7 55 AQ40
Bexleyheath DA7 166 EW80
Dagenham RM10 147 FB68
Enfield EN1 82 DT44
Epsom KT19 216 CS109
Gravesend (Nthflt) DA11 190 GE88
Grays RM20 169 FU79
Greenford UB6 137 CD66
Harlow CM17, CM20 35 ER14
Hayes UB3 135 BT74
Romford RM6 126 EW57
Tadworth (Lwr Kgswd)
KT20 249 CY125
Waltham Abbey EN9
off Breach Barn Mobile
Home Pk 68 EH30
Walton-on-Thames KT12 195 BV100
Watford WD25 76 BW35
Wembley HA9 117 CK61
West Molesey KT8 196 BZ98
First Cl, W.Mol. KT8 196 CC97
First Cres, Slou. SL1 131 AQ71
First Cross Rd, Twick. TW2 177 CE89
First Dr, NW10 138 CQ66
First Slip, Lthd. KT22 231 CG118
First St, SW3 18 B7
Firstway, SW20 199 CW96
First Way, Wem. HA9 118 CP63
Firs Wk, Nthwd. HA6 93 BR51
Woodford Green IG8 102 EG50
Firsway, Guil. GU2 242 AT133
Firswood Av, Epsom KT19 217 CT106
Firs Wd Cl, Pot.B. EN6 64 DF32
Firth Gdns, SW6 159 CY81
Fir Tree Av, Mitch. CR4 200 DG96
Slough (Stoke P.) SL2 132 AT70
West Drayton UB7 154 BN76
Fir Tree Cl, SW16 181 DJ92
W5 138 CL72
Epsom KT17 233 CW115
Epsom (Ewell) KT19 217 CT105
Esher KT10 214 CC106
Grays RM17 170 GD79
Hemel Hempstead HP3 40 BN21
Leatherhead KT22 231 CJ123
Orpington BR6
off Highfield Av 223 ET106
Romford RM1 127 FD55
Firtree Ct, Borwd. (Elstree)
WD6 78 CM42
Fir Tree Gdns, Croy. CR0 221 EA105
Fir Tree Gro, Cars. SM5 218 DF108
Fir Tree Hill, Rick. WD3 74 BM38
Fir Tree Pl, Ashf. TW15
off Percy Av 174 BN92
Fir Tree Rd, Bans. SM7 217 CW114
Epsom KT17 233 CV116
Guildford GU1 242 AX131
Hounslow TW4 156 BY84
Leatherhead KT22 231 CJ123
Fir Trees, Rom. (Abridge)
RM4 86 EV41
Fir Trees Cl, SE16 23 K2
Fir Tree Wk, Dag. RM10
off Wheel Fm Dr 127 FC62
Enfield EN1 82 DR41
Reigate RH2 250 DD134
Firwood Av, St.Alb. AL4 44 CL20
Firwood Cl, Wok. GU21 226 AS119
Firwood Rd, Vir.W. GU25 192 AS100
Fisher Cl, Croy. CR0
off Grant Rd 202 DT102
Enfield EN3 83 EA37
Greenford UB6 136 CA69
Kings Langley WD4 58 BN29
Walton-on-Thames KT12 213 BV105
Fisherman Cl, Rich. TW10
off Locksmeade Rd 177 CJ91
Fishermans Dr, SE16 23 H3
Fishermans Hill, Grav. DA11 190 GB85
Fisherman's Wk, E14 23 N1
Fishermans Wk, SE28
off Tugboat St 165 ES75
Fishermans Way, Hodd.
EN11 49 ED15
Fisher Rd, Har. HA3 95 CF54
Fishers, Horl. RH6
off Ewelands 269 DJ147
Fishers Cl, SW16
off Garrad's Rd 181 DK90
Bushey WD23 76 BY41
Waltham Cross EN8 67 EA34
Fishers Ct, SE14
off Besson St 163 DX81
Brentwood (Warley)
CM14 108 FV50
Fishersdene, Esher (Clay.)
KT10 215 CG108
Fishers Grn La, Wal.Abb.
EN9 67 EB29
Fishers Hatch, Harl. CM20
off School La 35 ES14
Fishers La, W4 158 CR77
Epping CM16 69 ES32
Fisher St, E16 15 L5
WC1 9 P6
Fishers Way, Belv. DA17 147 FC74
Fisherton St, NW8 7 N4
Fishery Pas, Hem.H. HP1
off Fishery Rd 40 BG22
Fishery Rd, Hem.H. HP1 40 BG22
Maidenhead SL6 130 AC74
Fishguard Spur, Slou. SL1 152 AV75
Fishguard Way, E16 165 EP75
Fishing Temple, Stai. TW18 193 BF95
Fishponds Rd, SW17 180 DE91
Keston BR2 222 EK106
Fishpool St, St.Alb. AL3 42 CB20
Fish St Hill, EC3 11 K9
Fitzalan Rd, N3 119 CY55
Esher (Clay.) KT10 215 CE108
Fitzalan St, SE11 20 C7
Fitzgeorge Av, W14 16 C8
New Malden KT3 198 CR95
Fitzgerald Av, SW14 158 CS83
Fitzgerald Cl, E11
off Fitzgerald Rd 124 EG57
Fitzgerald Ho, E14 14 B8
Hayes UB3 135 BV74
Fitzgerald Rd, E11 124 EG57
SW14 158 CR83
Thames Ditton KT7 197 CG100
Fitzhardinge St, W1 8 E7
Fitzherbert Ho, Rich. TW10
off Kingsmead 178 CM86
Fitzhugh Gro, SW18 180 DD86
Fitzilian Av, Rom. RM3 106 FM53
Fitzjames Av, W14 16 D8
Croydon CR0 202 DU103
Fitzjohn Av, Barn. EN5 79 CY43
Fitzjohn Cl, Guil. GU4 243 BC131
Fitzjohn's Av, NW3 120 DC64
Sch Fitzjohn's Prim Sch,
NW3 off Fitzjohn's Av 120 DD64
Fitzmaurice Pl, W1 19 H1
Fitzneal St, W12 139 CT72
Fitzrobert Pl, Egh. TW20 173 BA93
Fitzroy Cl, N6 120 DF60
Fitzroy Ct, W1 9 K4
Fitzroy Cres, W4 158 CR80
Fitzroy Gdns, SE19 182 DS94
Fitzroy Ms, W1 9 J4
Fitzroy Pk, N6 120 DF60
Fitzroy Rd, NW1 140 DG67
Fitzroy Sq, W1 9 J4
Fitzroy St, W1 9 J4
Fitzroy Yd, NW1
off Fitzroy Rd 140 DG67
Fitzstephen Rd, Dag. RM8 126 EV64
Fitzwarren Gdns, N19 121 DJ60
Fitzwilliam Av, Rich. TW9 158 CM82
Fitzwilliam Cl, Harl. CM17 36 EY11
Fitzwilliam Ms, E16 25 L1
Fitzwilliam Rd, SW4 161 DJ83
Fitzwygram Cl, Hmptn.
(Hmptn H.) TW12 176 CC92
Five Acre, NW9 97 CT53
Fiveacre Cl, Th.Hth. CR7 201 DN100
Five Acres, Chesh. HP5 54 AR33
Harlow CM18 51 ES18
High Wycombe
(Woob.Grn) HP10 110 AF56
Kings Langley WD4 58 BM29
St. Albans (Lon.Col.) AL2 61 CK25
Five Acres Av, St.Alb.
(Brick.Wd) AL2 60 BZ29
Fiveash Rd, Grav. DA11 191 GF87
Five Bell All, E14 13 M8
Sch Five Elms Prim Sch, Dag.
RM9 off Wood La 126 EZ62
Five Elms Rd, Brom. BR2 204 EH104
Dagenham RM9 126 EZ62
Five Flds Cl, Wat. WD19 94 BZ48
Five Oaks, Add. KT15 211 BF107
Five Oaks La, Chig. IG7 104 EY51
Sch Five Oaks Prim & Nurs
Sch, Hat. AL10
off Travellers La 45 CU20
Five Points, Iver SL0 133 BC69
Fives Ct, SE11 20 E7
Five Ways Cor, NW4 97 CV53
Fiveways Rd, SW9 161 DN82
Five Wents, Swan. BR8 207 FG96
Fladbury Rd, N15 122 DR58
Fladgate Rd, E11 124 EE58
Flag Cl, Croy. CR0 203 DX102
Flags, The, Hem.H. HP2 41 BP20
Flagstaff Cl, Wal.Abb. EN9 67 EB33
Flagstaff Rd, Wal.Abb. EN9 67 EB33
Flag Wk, Pnr. HA5
off Eastcote Rd 115 BU58
Flambard Rd, Har. HA1 117 CG58
Flamborough Cl, West.
(Bigg.H.) TN16 238 EH119
Flamborough Rd, Ruis. HA4 115 BU62
Flamborough Spur, Slou.
SL1 151 AN75
Flamborough St, E14 13 J7
Flamborough Wk, E14 13 J8
Flamingo Cl, Hat. AL10
off Mosquito Way 44 CR17
Flamingo Gdns, Nthlt. UB5
off Jetstar Way 136 BY69
Flamingo Wk, Horn. RM12 147 FG65
FLAMSTEAD END, Wal.Cr.
EN7 66 DU28
Sch Flamstead End Inf Sch,
Wal.Cr. EN7
off Longfield La 66 DU27
Sch Flamstead End Jun Sch,
Wal.Cr. EN7
off Longfield La 66 DU27
Flamstead End Rd, Wal.Cr.
(Chsht) EN8 66 DV28
Flamstead Gdns, Dag. RM9
off Flamstead Rd 146 EW66
Flamstead Rd, Dag. RM9 146 EW66
Flamsted Av, Wem. HA9 138 CN65
★ Flamsteed Ho Mus,
SE10 163 ED80
Flamsteed Rd, SE7 164 EL78
Flanchford Rd, W12 159 CT76
Reigate RH2 249 CX134
Flanders Ct, Egh. TW20 173 BC92
Flanders Cres, SW17 180 DF94
Flanders Rd, E6 145 EM68
W4 158 CS77
Flanders Way, E9 143 DX65
Flank St, E1 12 A9
Flash La, Enf. EN2 81 DP37
Flask Cotts, NW3
off New End Sq 120 DD63
Flask Wk, NW3 120 DD63
Flatfield Rd, Hem.H. HP3 40 BN22
Flat Iron Sq, SE1
off Union St 142 DQ74
FLAUNDEN, Hem.H. HP3 57 BB33
Flaunden Bottom, Chesh.
HP5 72 AY36
Hemel Hempstead (Flaun.)
HP3 72 AY35
Flaunden Hill, Hem.H. (Flaun.)
HP3 57 AZ33
Flaunden La, Hem.H. (Bov.)
HP3 57 BB32
Rickmansworth WD3 57 BD33
Flaunden Pk, Hem.H. (Flaun.)
HP3 57 BA32
Flavell Ms, SE10 25 H9
Flavian Cl, St.Alb. AL3 42 BZ22
Flaxen Cl, E4 off Flaxen Rd 101 EB48
Flaxen Rd, E4 101 EB48
Flaxley Rd, Mord. SM4 200 DB100
Flaxman Ct, W1 9 L8
Flaxman Rd, SE5 161 DP82
Flaxman Ter, WC1 9 M2
Flaxton Rd, SE18 165 ER81
Flecker Cl, Stan. HA7 95 CF50
Fleece Dr, N9 100 DU49
Sch Fleecefield Prim Sch,
N18 off Brettenham Rd 100 DU49
Fleece Rd, Surb. KT6 197 CJ102
Fleece Wk, N7
off Manger Rd 141 DL65
Fleeming Cl, E17
off Pennant Ter 101 DZ54
Fleeming Rd, E17 101 DZ54
Fleet Av, Dart. DA2 188 FQ88
Upminster RM14 129 FR58
Fleet Cl, Ruis. HA4 115 BQ58
Upminster RM14 129 FR58
West Molesey KT8 196 BZ99
Fleetdale Par, Dart. DA2
off Fleet Av 188 FQ88
Sch Fleetdown Co Prim Sch,
Dart. DA2 off Lunedale Rd 188 FQ89
Fleet La, W.Mol. KT8 196 BZ100
Fleet Pl, EC4
off Farringdon St 141 DN72
Sch Fleet Prim Sch, NW3
off Fleet Rd 120 DF64
Fleet Rd, NW3 120 DE64
Dartford DA2 188 FQ88
Gravesend (Nthflt) DA11 190 GC90
Fleetside, W.Mol. KT8 196 BZ100
Fleet Sq, WC1 10 A2
Fleet St, EC4 10 C8
Fleet St Hill, E1 12 A4
FLEETVILLE, St.Alb. AL1 43 CG20
Sch Fleetville Inf Sch, St.Alb.
AL1 off Woodstock Rd S 43 CH20
Sch Fleetville Jun Sch,
St.Alb. AL1
off Hatfield Rd 43 CG20
Fleetway, Egh. TW20 193 BC97
Fleetway Business Pk, Grnf.
UB6 137 CH68
Fleetwood Cl, E16 144 EK71
Chalfont St. Giles HP8 90 AU49
Chessington KT9 215 CK108
Croydon CR0 202 DT104
Tadworth KT20 233 CW120
Fleetwood Ct, E6
off Evelyn Denington Rd 145 EM71
West Byfleet KT14 212 BG113
Fleetwood Gro, W3
off East Acton La 138 CS73
Fleetwood Rd, NW10 119 CU64
Kingston upon Thames
KT1 198 CP97
Slough SL2 132 AT74
Fleetwood Sq, Kings.T. KT1 198 CP97
Fleetwood St, N16
off Stoke Newington Ch St 122 DS61
Fleetwood Way, Wat. WD19 94 BW49
Fleming Cl, W9 6 G4
Waltham Cross (Chsht)
EN7 66 DU26
Fleming Ct, W2 7 N5
Croydon CR0 219 DN106
Fleming Cres, Hert. SG14
off Windsor Dr 31 DN09
Fleming Dr, N21 81 DM43
Fleming Gdns, Rom.
(Harold Wd) RM3
off Bartholomew Dr 106 FK54
Tilbury RM18
off Fielding Av 171 GJ81
Fleming Mead, Mitch. CR4 180 DE94
Fleming Rd, SE17 161 DP79
Grays (Chaff.Hun.) RM16 169 FW77
Southall UB1 136 CB72
Waltham Abbey EN9 83 EB35
Flemings, Brwd. CM13 107 FW51
Fleming Wk, NW9
off Pasteur Cl 96 CS54
Fleming Way, SE28 146 EX73
Isleworth TW7 157 CF83
Flemish Flds, Cher. KT16 194 BG101
Flemming Av, Ruis. HA4 115 BV60
Flempton Rd, E10 123 DY59
Fletcher Cl, E6
off Trader Rd 145 EP72
Chertsey (Ott.) KT16 211 BE107
Fletcher La, E10 123 EC59
Fletcher Path, SE8
off New Butt La 163 EA80
Fletcher Rd, W4 158 CQ76
Chertsey (Ott.) KT16 211 BD107
Chigwell IG7 103 ET50
Fletchers Cl, Brom. BR2 204 EH98
Fletcher St, E1 12 B9
Fletcher Way, Hem.H. HP2 40 BJ18
Fletching Rd, E5 122 DW62
SE7 164 EJ79
Fletton Rd, N11 99 DL52
Fleur de Lis St, E1 11 M4
Fleur Gates, SW19
off Princes Way 179 CX87
Sch Flexlands Sch, Wok.
GU24 off Station Rd 210 AT111
Flexley Wd, Welw.G.C. AL7 29 CZ06
Flex Meadow, Harl. CM19 50 EL16
Flexmere Gdns, N17
off Flexmere Rd 100 DR53
Flexmere Rd, N17 100 DR53
Flight App, NW9 97 CT54
Flimwell Cl, Brom. BR1 184 EE92
Flinders Cl, St.Alb. AL1 43 CG22
Flint Cl, Bans. SM7 218 DB114
Leatherhead (Bkhm)
KT23 246 CC126
Redhill RH1 250 DF133
Flint Down Cl, Orp. BR5 206 EU95
Flint Hill, Dor. RH4 263 CH138
Flint Hill Cl, Dor. RH4 263 CH139
Flintlock Cl, Stai. TW19 154 BG84
Flintmill Cres, SE3 164 EL82
Flinton St, SE17 21 M9
Flint St, SE17 21 K8
Grays RM20 169 FV79
Flint Way, St.Alb. AL3 42 CC15
Flitcroft St, WC2 9 M7
Floathaven Cl, SE28 146 EU74
Floats, The, Sev. (Rvrhd)
TN13 256 FE121
Flock Mill Pl, SW18 180 DB88
Flockton St, SE16 22 A4
Flodden Rd, SE5 162 DQ81
Flood La, Twick. TW1
off Church La 177 CG88
Flood Pas, SE18
off Samuel St 165 EM77
Flood St, SW3 18 B10
Flood Wk, SW3 160 DE79
Flora Cl, E14 14 A8
Flora Gdns, W6 159 CV77
Croydon CR0 221 EC111
Romford RM6 126 EW58
Sch Flora Gdns Prim Sch,
W6 off Dalling Rd 159 CV77
Flora Gro, St.Alb. AL1 43 CF21
Floral Ct, Ashtd. KT21
off Rosedale 231 CJ118
Floral Dr, St.Alb. (Lon.Col.)
AL2 61 CK26
Floral St, WC2 9 N9
Flora St, Belv. DA17
off Victoria St 166 EZ78
Florence Av, Add.
(New Haw) KT15 212 BG111
Enfield EN2 82 DQ41
Morden SM4 200 DC99
Florence Cantwell Wk, N19
off Hillrise Rd 121 DL59
Florence Cl, Grays RM20 170 FY79
Harlow CM17 52 EW17
Hornchurch RM12 128 FL61
Walton-on-Thames KT12
off Florence Rd 195 BV101
Watford WD25 75 BU35
Florence Dr, Enf. EN2 82 DQ41
Florence Elson Cl, E12
off Grantham Rd 125 EN63
Florence Gdns, W4 158 CQ79
Romford RM6
off Roxy Av 126 EW59
Staines TW18 174 BH94
★ Florence Nightingale
Mus, SE1 20 A4
Florence Rd, E6 144 EJ67
E13 144 EF68
N4 121 DN60
SE2 166 EW76
SE14 163 DZ81
SW19 180 DB93
W4 158 CR76
W5 138 CL73
Beckenham BR3 203 DX96
Bromley BR1 204 EG95
Feltham TW13 175 BV88
Kingston upon Thames
KT2 178 CM94
South Croydon CR2 220 DR109
Southall UB2 156 BX77
Walton-on-Thames KT12 195 BV101
Florence St, E16 15 K3
N1 4 E6
NW4 119 CW56
Florence Ter, SE14 163 DZ81
Florence Way, SW12 180 DF88
Uxbridge UB8
off Wyvern Way 134 BJ67
Florey Sq, N21
off Highlands Av 81 DM43
Florfield Pas, E8
off Reading La 142 DV65
Florfield Rd, E8
off Reading La 142 DV65
Florian Av, Sutt. SM1 218 DD105
Florian Rd, SW15 159 CY84
Florida Cl, Bushey
(Bushey Hth) WD23 95 CD47
Florida Rd, Guil. (Shalf.)
GU4 258 AY140
Thornton Heath CR7 201 DP95
Florida St, E2 12 A2
Florin Ct, SE1
off Tanner St 162 DT75
Floris Pl, SW4
off Fitzwilliam Rd 161 DJ83
Floriston Av, Uxb. UB10 135 BQ66
Floriston Cl, Stan. HA7 95 CH53
Floriston Ct, Nthlt. UB5 116 CB64
Floriston Gdns, Stan. HA7 95 CH53
Floss St, SW15 159 CW82
Flower & Dean Wk, E1 11 P6
Flower Cres, Cher. (Ott.)
KT16 211 BB107
Flowerfield, Sev. (Otford)
TN14 241 FF117
Flowerhill Way, Grav.
(Istead Rise) DA13 190 GE94
Flower La, NW7 97 CT50
Godstone RH9 253 DY128
Flower Ms, NW11 119 CY58
Flower Pot Cl, N15
off St. Ann's Rd 122 DT58
Flowers Cl, NW2 119 CU62
Flowersmead, SW17 180 DG89
Flowers Ms, N19
off Archway Rd 121 DJ61
Flower Wk, Guil. GU2 258 AW137
Flower Wk, The, SW7 17 L4
Floyd Rd, SE7 164 EJ78
Floyds La, Wok. GU22 228 BG116
Floyer Cl, Rich. TW10
off Queens Rd 178 CM85
Fludyer St, SE13 164 EE84
Flux's La, Epp. CM16 70 EU33
Flyer's Way, The, West. TN16 255 ER126
Fogerty Cl, Enf. EN3 83 EB37
Fold Cft, Harl. CM20 35 EN14
Foley Cl, Beac. HP9 88 AJ51

Fol - Fox

Foley Ms, Esher (Clay.) KT10 215 CE108
Foley Rd, Esher (Clay.) KT10 215 CE108
 Westerham (Bigg.H.) TN16 238 EK118
Foley St, W1 9 J6
Folgate St, E1 11 M5
Foliot St, W12 139 CT72
Folkes La, Upmin. RM14 129 FT57
Folkestone Ct, Slou. SL3 153 BA78
Folkestone Rd, E6 145 EN68
 E17 123 EB56
 N18 100 DU49
Folkingham La, NW9 96 CR53
Folkington Cor, N12 97 CZ50
Follet Dr, Abb.L. WD5 59 BT31
Follett Cl, Wind. (Old Wind.) SL4 172 AV86
Follett St, E14 14 C8
Folly, The, Hert. SG14 32 DR09
Folly Av, St.Alb. AL3 42 CC19
Folly Cl, Rad. WD7 77 CF36
Follyfield Rd, Bans. SM7 218 DA114
Folly La, E4 101 DZ52
 E17 101 DY53
 Dorking (Holm.) RH5 263 CH144
 St. Albans AL3 42 CC19
Folly Ms, W11 6 E8
Folly Pathway, Rad. WD7 77 CF35
Folly Vw, Ware (Stans.Abb.) SG12 33 EB10
Folly Wall, E14 24 D4
Fontaine Rd, SW16 181 DM94
Fontarabia Rd, SW11 160 DG84
Fontayne Av, Chig. IG7 103 EQ49
 Rainham RM13 147 FE66
 Romford RM1 105 FE54
Fontenoy Rd, SW12 181 DH89
Fonteyne Gdns, Wdf.Grn. IG8 *off Lechmere Av* 102 EK54
Fonthill Cl, SE20 *off Selby Rd* 202 DU96
Fonthill Ms, N4 *off Lennox Rd* 121 DN61
Fonthill Rd, N4 121 DM60
Font Hills, N2 98 DC54
Fontigarry Fm Business Pk, Reig. RH2 266 DC143
Fontley Way, SW15 179 CU87
Fontmell Cl, Ashf. TW15 174 BN92
 St. Albans AL3 43 CE18
Fontmell Pk, Ashf. TW15 174 BM92
Fontwell Cl, Har. HA3 95 CE52
 Northolt UB5 136 CA65
Fontwell Dr, Brom. BR2 205 EN99
Fontwell Pk Gdns, Horn. RM12 128 FL63
Foord Cl, Dart. DA2 189 FS89
Football La, Har. HA1 117 CE60
Footbury Hill Rd, Orp. BR6 206 EU101
Footpath, The, SW15 179 CU85
FOOTS CRAY, Sid. DA14 186 EV93
Foots Cray High St, Sid. DA14 186 EW93
Foots Cray La, Sid. DA14 185 EW88
Footscray Rd, SE9 185 EN86
Forbench Cl, Wok. (Ripley) GU23 228 BH122
Forbes Av, Pot.B. EN6 64 DD33
Forbes Cl, NW2 119 CU62
 Hornchurch RM11 *off St. Leonards Way* 127 FH60
Forbes Ct, SE19 182 DS92
Forbe's Ride, Wind. SL4 150 AG84
Forbes St, E1 12 B8
Forbes Way, Ruis. HA4 115 BV61
Forburg Rd, N16 122 DU60
FORCE GREEN, West. TN16 239 ER124
Force Grn La, West. TN16 239 ER124
Fordbridge Cl, Cher. KT16 194 BH102
Fordbridge Rd, Ashf. TW15 174 BL93
 Shepperton TW17 195 BS100
 Sunbury-on-Thames TW16 195 BS100
Ford Cl, E3 *off Roman Rd* 143 DY68
 Ashford TW15 174 BL93
 Bushey WD23 76 CC42
 Harrow HA1 117 CD59
 Rainham RM13 147 FF66
 Shepperton TW17 194 BN98
 Thornton Heath CR7 201 DP100
Fordcroft Rd, Orp. BR5 206 EV99
Forde Av, Brom. BR1 204 EJ97
Fordel Rd, SE6 183 ED88
Ford End, Uxb. (Denh.) UB9 113 BF61
 Woodford Green IG8 102 EH51
Fordham Cl, Barn. EN4 80 DE41
 Hornchurch RM11 128 FN59
Fordham Rd, Barn. EN4 80 DD41
Fordham St, E1 12 B7
Fordhook Av, W5 138 CM73
Fordingley Rd, W9 6 F2
Fordington Ho, SE26 *off Sydenham Hill* 182 DU90
Fordington Rd, N6 120 DF57
Ford La, Iver SL0 134 BG72
 Rainham RM13 147 FF66
Fordmill Rd, SE6 183 EA89
Ford Rd, E3 143 DY67
 Ashford TW15 174 BM91
 Chertsey KT16 194 BH102
 Dagenham RM9, RM10 146 EZ66
 Gravesend (Nthflt) DA11 190 GB85
 Woking (Old Wok.) GU22 227 BB120
Fords Gro, N21 100 DQ46
Fords Pk Rd, E16 15 L7
Ford Sq, E1 12 D6
Ford St, E3 143 DY67
 E16 15 K7
Fordwater Rd, Cher. KT16 194 BH102
Fordwater Trd Est, Cher. KT16 194 BJ102
Fordwich Cl, Hert. SG14 31 DN09
 Orpington BR6 205 ET101
Fordwich Hill, Hert. SG14 31 DN09
Fordwich Ri, Hert. SG14 31 DN09
Fordwich Rd, Welw.G.C. AL8 29 CW10
Fordwych Rd, NW2 119 CY63
Fordyce Cl, Horn. RM11 128 FM59
Fordyce Ho, SW16 *off Colson Way* 181 DJ91
Fordyce Rd, SE13 183 EC86
Fordyke Rd, Dag. RM8 126 EZ61
Forebury, The, Saw. CM21 36 EY05
Forebury Av, Saw. CM21 36 EZ05
Forebury Cres, Saw. CM21 36 EZ05
Forefield, St.Alb. AL2 60 CA27
★ Foreign & Commonwealth Office, SW1 19 N3
Foreign St, SE5 161 DP82
Foreland Ct, NW4 97 CY53
Foreland St, SE18 *off Plumstead Rd* 165 ER77
Forelands Way, Chesh. HP5 54 AQ32
Foreman Ct, W6 *off Hammersmith Bdy* 159 CW77
Foremark Cl, Ilf. IG6 103 ET50
Foreshore, SE8 23 M8
Forest, The, E11 124 EE56
Forest App, E4 102 EE45
 Woodford Green IG8 102 EF52
Forest Av, E4 102 EE45
 Chigwell IG7 103 EN50
 Hemel Hempstead HP3 40 BK22
Forest Business Pk, E17 123 DX59
Forest Cl, E11 124 EF57
 Chislehurst BR7 205 EN95
 Leatherhead (E.Hors.) KT24 245 BT125
 Waltham Abbey EN9 84 EH37
 Woking GU22 227 BD115
 Woodford Green IG8 102 EH48
Forest Ct, E4 102 EF46
 E11 124 EE56
Forest Cres, Ashtd. KT21 232 CN116
Forest Cft, SE23 182 DV89
FORESTDALE, Croy. CR0 221 EA109
Forestdale, N14 99 DK49
Sch Forestdale Prim Sch, Croy. CR0 *off Pixton Way* 221 DZ109
Forest Dr, E12 124 EK62
 Epping (They.B.) CM16 85 ES36
 Keston BR2 222 EL105
 Sunbury-on-Thames TW16 175 BT94
 Tadworth (Kgswd) KT20 233 CZ121
 Woodford Green IG8 101 ED52
Forest Dr E, E11 123 ED59
Forest Dr W, E11 123 EC59
Forest Edge, Buck.H. IG9 102 EJ49
Forester Rd, SE15 162 DV84
Foresters Cl, Wall. SM6 219 DK108
 Waltham Cross EN7 66 DS27
 Woking GU21 226 AT118
Foresters Cres, Bexh. DA7 167 FB84
Foresters Dr, E17 123 ED56
 Wallington SM6 219 DK108
Sch Foresters Prim Sch, Wall. SM6 *off Redford Av* 219 DK107
Forest Gdns, N17 100 DT54
FOREST GATE, E7 124 EG64
≠ Forest Gate 124 EG64
Forest Gate, NW9 118 CS57
Sch Forest Gate Comm Sch, E7 *off Forest St* 124 EG64
Forest Glade, E4 102 EE49
 E11 124 EE58
 Epping (N.Wld Bas.) CM16 70 EY27
Forest Grn Rd, Wind. SL4 150 AE82
Forest Gro, E8 5 N4
Forest Hts, Buck.H. IG9 102 EG47
FOREST HILL, SE23 183 DX88
≠ Forest Hill 182 DW89
Forest Hill Business Cen, SE23 182 DW89
Forest Hill Ind Est, SE23 *off Perry Vale* 182 DW89
Forest Hill Rd, SE22 182 DV85
 SE23 182 DV85
Sch Forest Hill Sch, SE23 *off Dacres Rd* 183 DX90
Forestholme Cl, SE23 182 DW89
Forest Ind Pk, Ilf. IG6 103 ES53
Forest La, E7 124 EE64
 E15 124 EE64
 Chigwell IG7 103 EN50
 Leatherhead (E.Hors.) KT24 229 BT124
Forest Mt Rd, Wdf.Grn. IG8 101 ED52
Fore St, EC2 11 H6
 N9 100 DU50
 N18 100 DT51
 Harlow CM17 36 EW11
 Hatfield AL9 45 CW17
 Hertford SG14 32 DR09
 Pinner HA5 115 BU57
Fore St Av, EC2 11 J6
Forest Ridge, Beck. BR3 203 EA97
 Keston BR2 222 EL105
Forest Ri, E17 123 ED57
Forest Rd, E7 124 EG63
 E8 5 N4
 E11 123 ED59
 E17 122 DW56
 N9 100 DV46
 N17 122 DW56
 Enfield EN3 83 DY36
 Erith DA8 167 FG81
 Feltham TW13 176 BW89
 Ilford IG6 103 ES53
 Leatherhead (E.Hors.) KT24 229 BU123
 Loughton IG10 84 EK41
 Richmond TW9 158 CN80
 Romford RM7 127 FB55
 Sutton SM3 200 DA102
 Waltham Cross (Chsht) EN8 67 DX29
 Watford WD25 59 BV33
 Windsor SL4 151 AK82
 Woking GU22 227 BD115
 Woodford Green IG8 102 EG48
Sch Forest Sch, E17 *off College Pl* 124 EE56
Forest Side, E4 102 EF45
 E7 *off Capel Rd* 124 EH63
 Buckhurst Hill IG9 102 EJ46
 Epping CM16 69 ER33
 Waltham Abbey EN9 84 EJ36
 Worcester Park KT4 199 CT102
Forest St, E7 124 EG64
Forest Vw, E4 101 ED45
 E11 *off High Rd Leytonstone* 124 EF59
Forest Vw Av, E10 123 ED57
Forest Vw Rd, E12 124 EL63
 E17 101 EC53
 Loughton IG10 84 EK42
Forest Wk, N10 99 DH53
 Bushey WD23 *off Millbrook Rd* 76 BZ39
Forest Way, N19 *off Hargrave Pk* 121 DJ61
 Ashtead KT21 232 CM117
 Loughton IG10 84 EL41
 Orpington BR5 205 ET99
 Sidcup DA15 185 ER87
 Waltham Abbey EN9 84 EK35
 Woodford Green IG8 102 EH49
Forfar Rd, N22 99 DP53
 SW11 160 DG81
Forge, The, Pot.B. (Northaw) EN6 64 DE30
Forge Av, Couls. CR5 235 DN120
Forge Br La, Couls. CR5 235 DH121
Forge Cl, Brom. BR2 204 EG102
 Hayes UB3 *off High St* 155 BR79
 Kings Langley (Chipper.) WD4 58 BG31
Forge Cotts, W5 *off Ealing Grn* 137 CK74
Forge Dr, Esher (Clay.) KT10 215 CG108
 Slough (Farn.Com.) SL2 131 AQ65
Forge End, Amer. HP7 55 AP40
 St. Albans AL2 60 CA26
 Woking GU21 226 AY117
Forgefield, West. (Bigg.H.) TN16 *off Main Rd* 238 EK116
Forge La, Dart. (Hort.Kir.) DA4 208 FQ98
 Feltham TW13 176 BY92
 Gravesend DA12 191 GM89
 Northwood HA6 93 BS52
 Sunbury-on-Thames TW16 195 BU97
 Sutton SM3 217 CY108
Sch Forge La Prim Sch, Felt. TW13 *off Forge La* 176 BY92
Forge Ms, Croy. CR0 *off Addington Village Rd* 221 EA106
 Sunbury-on-Thames TW16 *off Forge La* 195 BU97
Forge Pl, NW1 *off Malden Cres* 140 DG65
 Horley RH6 *off Povey Cross Rd* 268 DE150
Forge Way, Sev. (Shore.) TN14 225 FF111
Forlong Path, Nthlt. UB5 *off Arnold Rd* 136 BY65
Forman Pl, N16 *off Farleigh Rd* 122 DT63
Formation, The, E16 *off Woolwich Manor Way* 165 EP75
Formby Av, Stan. HA7 117 CJ55
Formby Cl, Slou. SL3 153 BC77
Formosa St, W9 7 L4
Formunt Cl, E16 15 K6
Forres Cl, Hodd. EN11 49 EA15
Sch Forres Co Prim Sch, Hodd. EN11 *off Stanstead Rd* 33 EB14
Forres Gdns, NW11 120 DA58
Forrester Path, SE26 183 DX91
Forresters Dr, Welw.G.C. AL7 30 DC10
Forrest Gdns, SW16 201 DM97
Forris Av, Hayes UB3 135 BT74
Forset St, W1 8 B7
Forstal Cl, Brom. BR2 *off Ridley Rd* 204 EG97
Forster Cl, E17 101 ED52
Sch Forster Pk Prim Sch, SE6 *off Boundfield Rd* 184 EE90
Forster Rd, E17 123 DY58
 N17 122 DT55
 SW2 181 DL87
 Beckenham BR3 203 DY97
 Croydon CR0 *off Windmill Rd* 202 DQ101
 Guildford GU2 *off Tylehost* 242 AU130
Forsters Cl, Rom. RM6 126 EZ58
Forster's Way, SW18 180 DB88
Forsters Way, Hayes UB4 135 BV72
Forston St, N1 5 J9
Forsyte Cres, SE19 202 DS95
Forsyth Gdns, SE17 161 DP79
Forsythia Cl, Ilf. IG1 125 EP64
Forsythia Gdns, Slou. SL3 152 AY76
Forsythia Pl, Guil. GU1 *off Larch Av* 242 AW132
Forsyth Path, Wok. GU21 211 BD113
Forsyth Pl, Enf. EN1 82 DS43
Forsyth Rd, Wok. GU21 211 BC114
Forterie Gdns, Ilf. IG3 126 EU62
Fortescue Av, E8 *off Mentmore Ter* 142 DV66
 Twickenham TW2 176 CC90
Fortescue Rd, SW19 180 DD94
 Edgware HA8 96 CR53
 Weybridge KT13 212 BM105
Fortess Gro, NW5 *off Fortess Rd* 121 DH64
Fortess Rd, NW5 121 DH64
Fortess Wk, NW5 *off Fortess Rd* 121 DH64
Forthbridge Rd, SW11 160 DG84
Forth Rd, Upmin. RM14 129 FR58
Fortin Cl, S.Ock. RM15 149 FU73
Fortin Path, S.Ock. RM15 149 FU73
Fortin Way, S.Ock. RM15 149 FU73
Fortis Cl, E16 144 EJ72
FORTIS GREEN, N2 120 DF56
Fortis Grn, N2 120 DE56
 N10 120 DE56
Fortis Grn Av, N2 120 DF55
Fortis Grn Rd, N10 120 DG55
Fortismere Av, N10 120 DG55
Sch Fortismere Sec Sch, N10 *off Tetherdown* 120 DG55
Fort La, Reig. RH2 250 DB130
Fortnam Rd, N19 121 DK61
★ Fortnum & Mason, W1 19 J1
Fortnums Acre, Stan. HA7 95 CF51
Fortress Distribution Pk, Til. RM18 171 GH84
Fort Rd, SE1 21 P8
 Guildford GU1 258 AY137
 Northolt UB5 136 CA66
 Sevenoaks (Halst.) TN14 241 FC115
 Tadworth (Box H.) KT20 248 CP131
 Tilbury RM18 171 GH84
Fortrose Gdns, SW2 *off New Pk Rd* 181 DK88
Fortrye Cl, Grav. (Nthflt) DA11 190 GE89
Fort St, E1 11 M6
 E16 25 P2
Fortuna Cl, N7 4 B3
Fortune Gate Rd, NW10 138 CS67
Fortune Grn Rd, NW6 120 DA63
Fortune La, Borwd. (Elstree) WD6 77 CK44
Fortunes, The, Harl. CM18 51 ET17
Fortunes Mead, Nthlt. UB5 136 BY65
Fortune St, EC1 11 H4
Fortune Wk, SE28 *off Broadwater Rd* 165 ER76
Fortune Way, NW10 139 CU69
Forty Acre La, E16 15 L6
Forty Av, Wem. HA9 118 CM62
Forty Cl, Wem. HA9 118 CM61
Forty Footpath, SW14 158 CQ83
Fortyfoot Rd, Lthd. KT22 231 CJ121
FORTY GREEN, Beac. HP9 88 AH50
Forty Grn Rd, Beac. (Knot.Grn) HP9 88 AH51
★ Forty Hall & Mus, Enf. EN2 82 DT38
FORTY HILL, Enf. EN2 82 DS37
Forty Hill, Enf. EN2 82 DT38
Sch Forty Hill C of E Prim Sch, Enf. EN2 *off Forty Hill* 82 DU37
Forty La, Wem. HA9 118 CP61
Forum, The, W.Mol. KT8 196 CB98
★ Forum Club, NW5 121 DH64
Forum Magnum Sq, SE1 20 A3
Forum Pl, Hat. AL10 45 CU17
Forumside, Edg. HA8 *off High St* 96 CN51
Forum Way, Edg. HA8 *off High St* 96 CN51
Forval Cl, Mitch. CR4 200 DF99
Forward Dr, Har. HA3 117 CF56
Fosbury Ms, W2 7 K10
Foscote Ms, W9 7 H4
Foscote Rd, NW4 119 CV58
Foskett Rd, SW6 159 CZ82
Foss Av, Croy. CR0 219 DN106
Sch Fossdene Prim Sch, SE7 25 P10
Fossdene Rd, SE7 25 P10
Fossdyke Cl, Hayes UB4 136 BY71
Fosse Way, W13 137 CG71
 West Byfleet KT14 *off Brantwood Dr* 211 BF113
Fossil Rd, SE13 163 EA83
Fossington Rd, Belv. DA17 166 EX77
Foss Rd, SW17 180 DD91
Fossway, Dag. RM8 126 EW61
Foster Av, Wind. SL4 151 AL83
Foster Cl, Wal.Cr. (Chsht) EN8 67 DX30
Fosterdown, Gdse. RH9 252 DV129
Foster La, EC2 10 G7
Foster Rd, E13 15 L3
 W3 138 CS73
 W4 158 CR78
 Hemel Hempstead HP1 40 BG22
Fosters Cl, E18 102 EH53
 Chislehurst BR7 185 EM92
Fosters Path, Slou. SL2 *off Vermont Rd* 131 AM70
Sch Foster's Prim Sch, Well. DA16 *off Westbrooke Rd* 166 EW83
Foster St, NW4 119 CW56
 Harlow CM17 52 EY17
Foster Wk, NW4 *off New Brent St* 119 CW56
Fothergill Cl, E13 144 EG68
Fothergill Dr, N21 81 DL43
Fotheringay Gdns, Slou. SL1 131 AN73
Fotheringham Rd, Enf. EN1 82 DT42
Fotherley Rd, Rick. (Mill End) WD3 91 BF47
Foubert's Pl, W1 9 J8
Foulden Rd, N16 122 DT63
Foulden Ter, N16 *off Foulden Rd* 122 DT63
Sch Foulds Prim Sch, Barn. EN5 *off Byng Rd* 79 CX41
Foulis Ter, SW7 17 P9
Foulser Rd, SW17 180 DF90
Foulsham Rd, Th.Hth. CR7 202 DQ97
Founder Cl, E6 *off Trader Rd* 145 EP72
Founders Ct, EC2 11 J7
Founders Dr, Uxb. (Denh.) UB9 113 BF58
Founders Gdns, SE19 182 DQ94
Founders Rd, Hodd. EN11 33 EB14
★ Foundling Mus, WC1 9 P3
Foundry Cl, SE16 23 J1
Foundry Gate, Wal.Cr. EN8 *off York Rd* 67 DY34
Foundry La, Slou. (Horton) SL3 153 BB83
Foundry Ms, NW1 9 K3
Fountain Cl, Uxb. UB8 *off New Rd* 135 BQ71
Fountain Ct, EC4 10 C9
Fountain Dr, SE19 182 DT91
 Carshalton SM5 218 DF109
 Hertford SG13 32 DT08
Fountain Fm, Harl. CM18 51 ET17
Fountain Gdns, Wind. SL4 151 AR83
Fountain Grn Sq, SE16 22 B3
Fountain La, Sev. TN15 257 FP122
Fountain Ms, N5 *off Highbury Gra* 122 DQ63
 NW3 140 DF65
Fountain Pl, SW9 161 DN81
 Waltham Abbey EN9 67 EC34
Fountain Rd, SW17 180 DD92
 Redhill RH1 266 DE136
 Thornton Heath CR7 202 DQ96
Fountains, The, Loug. IG10 *off Fallow Flds* 102 EK45
Fountains Av, Felt. TW13 176 BZ90
Fountains Cl, Felt. TW13 176 BZ89
Fountains Cres, N14 99 DL45
Fountain Sq, SW1 18 G7
Fountain St, E2 *off Columbia Rd* 142 DT69
Fountain Wk, Grav. (Nthflt) DA11 190 GE86
Fountayne Rd, N15 122 DU56
 N16 122 DU61
Fount St, SW8 161 DK80
Fouracres, SW12 *off Little Dimocks* 181 DH89
Four Acres, Cob. KT11 214 BY113
Fouracres, Enf. EN3 83 DY39
Four Acres, Guil. GU1 243 BC132
 Welwyn Garden City AL7 29 CZ11
Four Acres, The, Saw. CM21 36 EZ06
Fouracres Dr, Hem.H. HP3 40 BM22
Fouracres Wk, Hem.H. HP3 40 BM22
Fourland Wk, Edg. HA8 96 CQ51
Fournier St, E1 11 N5
Four Oaks, Chesh. HP5 *off Great Hivings* 54 AN27
Four Seasons Cl, E3 143 EA68
Four Seasons Cres, Sutt. SM3 199 CZ103
Sch Four Swannes Prim Sch, Wal.Cr. EN8 *off King Edward Rd* 67 DY33
Fourth Av, E12 125 EM63
 W10 6 C2
 Grays RM20 169 FU79
 Harlow CM19, CM20 51 EM15
 Hayes UB3 135 BT74
 Romford RM7 127 FD60
 Watford WD25 76 BX35
Fourth Cross Rd, Twick. TW2 177 CD89
Fourth Dr, Couls. CR5 235 DK116
Fourth Way, Wem. HA9 118 CQ63
Four Trees, St.Alb. AL2 42 CB24
Four Tubs, The, Bushey WD23 95 CD45
Fourways, St.Alb. AL4 *off Hatfield Rd* 44 CM20
Four Wents, Cob. KT11 213 BV113
Four Wents, The, E4 *off Kings Rd* 101 ED47
Fowey Av, Ilf. IG4 124 EK57
Fowey Cl, E1 22 C1
Fowler Cl, SW11 160 DD83
Fowler Rd, E7 124 EG63
 N1 4 F6
 Ilford IG6 104 EV51
 Mitcham CR4 200 DG96
Fowlers Cl, Sid. DA14 *off Thursland Rd* 186 EY92
Fowlers Mead, Wok. (Chobham) GU24 *off Windsor Rd* 210 AS109
Fowlers Wk, W5 137 CK70
Fowley Cl, Wal.Cr. EN8 67 DZ34
Fowley Mead Pk, Wal.Cr. EN8 67 EA34
Fownes St, SW11 160 DE83
Foxacre, Cat. CR3 *off Town End Cl* 236 DS122
Fox & Knot St, EC1 10 F5
Foxberry Rd, SE4 163 DY83
Foxberry Wk, Grav. (Nthflt) DA11 *off Rowmarsh Cl* 190 GD91
Foxborough Cl, Slou. SL3 153 BA78
Sch Foxborough Comb Sch, Slou. SL3 *off Common Rd* 153 BA78
Foxborough Gdns, SE4 183 EA86
Foxbourne Rd, SW17 180 DG89
Foxburrow Rd, Chig. IG7 104 EX50
Foxburrows Av, Guil. GU2 242 AT134
Foxbury Av, Chis. BR7 185 ER93
Foxbury Cl, Brom. BR1 184 EH93
 Orpington BR6 *off Foxbury Dr* 224 EU106
Foxbury Dr, Orp. BR6 224 EU107
Foxbury Rd, Brom. BR1 184 EG93
Fox Cl, E1 12 F3
 E16 15 L6
 Borehamwood (Elstree) WD6 *off Rodgers Cl* 77 CK44
 Bushey WD23 76 CB42
 Orpington BR6 224 EU106
 Romford RM5 105 FB50
 Weybridge KT13 213 BR106
 Woking GU22 227 BD115
Foxcombe, Croy. (New Adgtn) CR0 221 EB107
Foxcombe Cl, E6 *off Boleyn Rd* 144 EK68
Foxcombe Rd, SW15 *off Alton Rd* 179 CU88
Foxcote, SE5 21 M10
Fox Covert, Lthd. (Fetch.) KT22 231 CD124
Foxcroft, St.Alb. AL1 43 CG22
Foxcroft Rd, SE18 165 EP81
Foxdell, Nthwd. HA6 93 BR51
Foxdells, Hert. SG14 31 DJ12
Foxdell Way, Ger.Cr. (Chal.St.P.) SL9 90 AY50
Foxearth Cl, West. (Bigg.H.) TN16 238 EL118
Foxearth Rd, S.Croy. CR2 220 DW110
Foxearth Spur, S.Croy. CR2 220 DW109
Foxenden Rd, Guil. GU1 258 AY135
Foxes Cl, Hert. SG13 32 DV09
Foxes Dale, SE3 164 EG83
 Bromley BR2 203 ED97
Foxes Dr, Wal.Cr. EN7 66 DU29
Foxes Grn, Grays (Orsett) RM16 171 GG75
Foxes La, Hat. AL9 45 CY23
 Potters Bar (Cuffley) EN6 65 DL28
Foxes Path, Guil. (Sutt.Grn) GU4 243 AZ126
Foxfield Cl, Nthwd. HA6 93 BT51
Sch Foxfield Prim Sch, SE18 *off Sandbach Pl* 165 EQ78
Foxfield Rd, Orp. BR6 205 ER103
Foxglove Cl, Hat. AL10 45 CV19
 Hoddesdon EN11 *off Castle Cl* 33 EC14
 Sidcup DA15 *off Wellington Av* 186 EU86
 Southall UB1 136 BY73
 Staines (Stanw.) TW19 174 BK88
Foxglove Gdns, E11 124 EJ56
 Guildford GU4 243 BC132
 Purley CR8 219 DL111
Foxglove La, Chess. KT9 216 CN105
Foxglove Rd, Rom. (Rush Grn) RM7 127 FE61
 South Ockendon RM15 149 FW71
Foxgloves, The, Hem.H. HP1 39 BE21
Foxglove St, W12 139 CT73
Foxglove Way, Wall. SM6 201 DH102
Foxgrove, N14 99 DL48
Fox Gro, Walt. KT12 195 BV101
Foxgrove Av, Beck. BR3 183 EB94
Foxgrove Dr, Wok. GU21 227 BA115
Foxgrove Path, Wat. WD19 94 BX50
Foxgrove Rd, Beck. BR3 183 EB94
Foxhall Rd, Upmin. RM14 128 FQ64
Foxham Rd, N19 121 DK62
Foxhanger Gdns, Wok. GU22 *off Oriental Rd* 227 BA116
Foxherne, Slou. SL3 152 AW75
Fox Hill, SE19 182 DT94
 Keston BR2 222 EJ106
Foxhill, Wat. WD24 75 BU36
Fox Hill Gdns, SE19 182 DT94
Foxhills, Wok. GU21 226 AW117
Foxhills Cl, Cher. (Ott.) KT16 211 BB107
Foxhills Ms, Cher. KT16 193 BB104
Foxhills Rd, Cher. (Ott.) KT16 211 BA105
Foxhole Rd, SE9 184 EL85
Foxholes, Wey. KT13 213 BR106
Foxholes Av, Hert. SG13 32 DT09
Foxholes Business Pk, Hert. SG13 32 DT09
Fox Hollow Cl, SE18 165 ES78
Fox Hollow Dr, Bexh. DA7 166 EX83
Foxhollow Dr, Slou. (Farn.Com.) SL2 111 AQ64
Foxhollows, Hat. AL10 45 CV16
Foxholt Gdns, NW10 138 CQ66
Foxhome Cl, Chis. BR7 185 EN93
Foxhounds La, Grav. DA13 190 GA90
Fox Ho Rd, Belv. DA17 167 FB77
Foxlake Rd, W.Byf. (Byfleet) KT14 212 BM112
Foxlands Cl, Wat. WD25 59 BU34
Foxlands Cres, Dag. RM10 127 FC64
Foxlands La, Dag. RM10 127 FC64
Foxlands Rd, Dag. RM10 127 FC64
Fox La, N13 99 DM48

★ Place of interest   H Hospital   Sch School   Coll College   Uni University   ≠ Railway station

Fox La, W5 138 CL70
Caterham CR3 235 DP121
Keston BR2 222 EH106
Leatherhead (Bkhm)
KT23 230 BY124
Reigate RH2 250 DB131
Fox La N, Cher. KT16 193 BF102
Fox La S, Cher. KT16
off Guildford St 193 BF102
Foxlees, Wem. HA0 117 CG63
Foxley Cl, E8
off Ferncliff Rd 122 DU64
Loughton IG10 85 EP40
Redhill RH1 266 DG139
Foxley Ct, Sutt. SM2 218 DC108
Foxley Gdns, Pur. CR8 219 DP113
Foxley Hill Rd, Pur. CR8 219 DN112
Foxley La, Pur. CR8 219 DK111
Foxley Rd, SW9 161 DN80
Kenley CR8 219 DP114
Thornton Heath CR7 201 DP98
Foxleys, Wat. WD19 94 BY48
Foxley Sq, SW9
off Cancell Rd 161 DP80
Fox Manor Way, Grays
RM20 169 FV79
Foxmead Cl, Enf. EN2 81 DM41
Foxmoor Ct, Uxb. (Denh.)
UB9 off North Orbital Rd 114 BG58
Foxmore St, SW11 160 DF81
Foxon Cl, Cat. CR3 236 DS121
Foxon La, Cat. CR3 236 DR121
Foxon La Gdns, Cat. CR3 236 DS121
Sch Fox Prim Sch, W8 16 G1
Fox Rd, E16 15 J6
Slough SL3 152 AX77
Fox's Path, Mitch. CR4 200 DE96
Foxton Gro, Mitch. CR4 200 DD96
Foxton Rd, Grays RM20 169 FX79
Hoddesdon EN11 49 DZ17
Foxwarren, Esher (Clay.)
KT10 215 CF109
Foxwell Ms, SE4
off Foxwell St 163 DY83
Foxwell St, SE4 163 DY83
Foxwood Chase, Wal.Abb.
EN9 83 ED35
Foxwood Cl, NW7 96 CS49
Feltham TW13 175 BV90
Foxwood Grn Cl, Enf. EN1 82 DS44
Foxwood Gro, Grav. (Nthflt)
DA11 190 GE88
Orpington BR6 224 EW110
Foxwood Rd, SE3 164 EF84
Dartford (Bean) DA2 189 FV90
Foyle Dr, S.Ock. RM15 149 FU71
Foyle Rd, N17 100 DU53
SE3 164 EF79
Frailey Cl, Wok. GU22 227 BB116
Frailey Hill, Wok. GU22 227 BB116
Framewood Rd, Slou. SL2,
SL3 132 AW66
Framfield Cl, N12 98 DA48
Framfield Ct, Enf. EN1 82 DS44
Framfield Rd, N5 4 E1
W7 137 CE72
Mitcham CR4 180 DG94
Framlingham Cl, E5
off Detmold Rd 122 DW61
Framlingham Cres, SE9 184 EL91
Frampton Cl, Sutt. SM2 218 DA108
Frampton Pk Rd, E9 142 DW65
Frampton Rd, Epp. CM16 70 EU28
Hounslow TW4 176 BY85
Potters Bar EN6 64 DC30
Frampton St, NW8 7 N4
Hertford SG14 32 DR09
Francemary Rd, SE4 183 EA85
Frances Av, Grays
(Chaff.Hun.) RM16 169 FW77
Maidenhead SL6 130 AC70
Sch Frances Bardsley Sch for
Girls, The, Rom. RM1
off Brentwood Rd 127 FH58
Frances Gdns, S.Ock. RM15 149 FT72
Sch Frances King Sch of
English, Victoria, SW1 19 H5
Frances Rd, E4 101 EA51
Windsor SL4 151 AR82
Frances St, SE18 165 EM77
Chesham HP5 54 AQ30
Franche Ct Rd, SW17 180 DC90
Franchise St, Chesh. HP5 54 AQ30
Francis Av, Bexh. DA7 166 FA82
Feltham TW13 175 BU90
Ilford IG1 125 ER61
St. Albans AL3 42 CC17
Sch Francis Bacon Sch,
St.Alb. AL1 off Drakes Dr 43 CH23
Francis Barber Cl, SW16
off Well Cl 181 DM91
Sch Franciscan Prim Sch,
SW17 off Franciscan Rd 180 DG92
Franciscan Rd, SW17 180 DF92
Francis Chichester Way,
SW11 160 DG81
Francis Cl, E14 24 E7
Epsom KT19 216 CR105
Shepperton TW17 194 BN98
Francisco Cl, Grays
(Chaff.Hun.) RM16 169 FW76
Sch Francis Combe Sch &
Comm Coll, Wat. WD25
off Horseshoe La 60 BW32
Francis Gro, SW19 179 CZ93
Sch Francis Holland Sch,
NW1 (Marylebone) 8 C3
SW1 (Belgravia) 18 F8
Francis Rd, E10 123 EC60
N2 off Lynmouth Rd 120 DF56
Caterham CR3 236 DR122
Croydon CR0 201 DP101
Dartford DA1 188 FK85
Greenford UB6 137 CJ67
Harrow HA1 117 CG57
Hounslow TW4 156 BX82
Ilford IG1 125 ER61
Orpington BR5 206 EX97
Pinner HA5 116 BW57
Wallington SM6 219 DJ107
Ware SG12 33 DX05
Watford WD18 75 BV42
Francis St, E15 124 EE64
SW1 19 J7
Ilford IG1 125 ER61
Francis Ter, N19
off Junction Rd 121 DJ62
Francis Wk, N1 4 A7
Francis Way, Slou. SL1 131 AK73
Francklyn Gdns, Edg. HA8 96 CN48
Francombe Gdns, Rom.
RM1 127 FG58
Franconia Rd, SW4 181 DJ85
Frank Bailey Wk, E12
off Gainsborough Av 125 EN64
Sch Frank Barnes Sch,
NW3 off Harley Rd 140 DD66
Frank Burton Cl, SE7 25 P10
Frank Dixon Cl, SE21 182 DS88
Frank Dixon Way, SE21 182 DS88
Frankfurt Rd, SE24 182 DQ85
Frankham St, SE8 163 EA80
Frankland Cl, SE16 22 D6
Rickmansworth (Crox.Grn)
WD3 92 BN45
Woodford Green IG8 102 EJ50
Frankland Rd, E4 101 EA50
SW7 17 N6
Rickmansworth (Crox.Grn)
WD3 75 BP44
Franklands Dr, Add. KT15 211 BF108
Franklin Av, Slou. SL2 131 AP71
Waltham Cross (Chsht) E
N7 66 DV30
Franklin Cl, N20 98 DC45
SE13 163 EB81
SE27 181 DP90
Hemel Hempstead HP3 40 BL23
Kingston upon Thames
KT1 198 CN97
St. Albans (Coln.Hth) AL4 44 CS22
Franklin Cres, Mitch. CR4 201 DJ98
Franklin Ho, NW9 119 CT59
Franklin Pas, SE9 164 EL83
Franklin Pl, SE13 163 EB81
Franklin Rd, SE20 182 DW94
Bexleyheath DA7 166 EY81
Dartford DA2 187 FE89
Gravesend DA12 191 GK92
Hornchurch RM12 148 FJ65
Watford WD17 75 BV40
Franklins Ms, Har. HA2 116 CC61
Franklin Sq, W14 16 F10
Franklin's Row, SW3 18 D9
Franklin St, E3 14 B1
N15 122 DS58
Franklin Way, Croy. CR0 201 DL101
Frank Lunnon Cl, B.End SL8 110 AC60
Franklyn Ct, Guil. GU2
off Humbolt Cl 242 AT134
Franklyn Cres, Wind. SL4 151 AK83
Franklyn Gdns, Ilf. IG6 103 ER51
Franklyn Rd, NW10 139 CT66
Walton-on-Thames KT12 195 BU100
Frank Martin Ct, Wal.Cr. EN7 66 DU30
Franks Av, N.Mal. KT3 198 CQ98
Franksfield, Guil. (Peasl.)
GU5 261 BS144
Franks La, Dart. (Hort.Kir.)
DA4 208 FN98
Franks Rd, Guil. GU2 242 AU132
Frank St, E13 15 M4
Frank Sutton Way, Slou. SL1
off Whitby Rd 131 AR73
Frankswood Av, Orp. BR5 205 EP99
West Drayton UB7 134 BM72
Frank Towell Ct, Felt. TW14
off Glebelands Rd 175 BU88
Franlaw Cres, N13 100 DQ49
Franmil Rd, Horn. RM12 127 FG60
Fransfield Gro, SE26 182 DV90
Frant Cl, SE20 182 DW94
Franthorne Way, SE6 183 EB89
Frant Rd, Th.Hth. CR7 201 DP99
Fraser Cl, E6
off Linton Gdns 144 EL72
Bexley DA5
off Dartford Rd 187 FC88
Fraser Gdns, Dor. RH4 263 CG135
Fraser Ho, Brent. TW8
off Green Dragon La 158 CM78
Fraser Rd, E17 123 EB57
N9 100 DV48
Erith DA8 167 FC78
Greenford UB6 137 CH67
Waltham Cross (Chsht)
EN8 67 DY28
Fraser St, W4 158 CS78
Frating Cres, Wdf.Grn. IG8 102 EG51
Coll Frays Adult Ed Cen, Uxb
UB8 off Harefield Rd 134 BJ65
Frays Av, West Dr. UB7 154 BK75
Frays Cl, West Dr. UB7 154 BK76
Frays Lea, Uxb. UB8 134 BJ68
Frays Waye, Uxb. UB8 134 BJ67
Frazer Av, Ruis. HA4 116 BW64
Frazer Cl, Rom. RM1 127 FF59
Frazier St, SE1 20 C4
Frean St, SE16 22 A5
Freda Corbett Cl, SE15
off Bird in Bush Rd 162 DU80
Frederica Rd, E4 101 ED45
Frederica St, N7 4 A5
Frederick Andrews Ct,
Grays RM17 170 GD79
Frederick Cl, W2 8 C9
Sutton SM1 217 CZ105
Frederick Ct, NW2
off Douglas Ms 119 CY62
Frederick Cres, SW9 161 DP80
Enfield EN3 82 DW40
Frederick Gdns, Croy. CR0 201 DP100
Sutton SM1 217 CZ106
Frederick Pl, SE18 165 EP78
Frederick Rd, SE17
off Chapter Rd 161 DP78
Rainham RM13 147 FD68
Sutton SM1 217 CZ106
Frederick's Pl, EC2 11 J8
Fredericks Pl, N12 98 DC49
Frederick Sq, SE16 13 J10
Frederick's Row, EC1 10 E1
Frederick St, WC1 10 A2
Frederick Ter, E8 5 N6
Frederick Vil, W7
off Lower Boston Rd 137 CE74
Frederic Ms, SW1 18 D4
Frederic St, E17 123 DY57
Fredley Pk, Dor. (Mick.) RH5 247 CJ129
Fredora Av, Hayes UB4 135 BT70
Fred White Wk, N7
off Market Rd 141 DL65
Fred Wigg Twr, E11 124 EF61
Freeborne Gdns, Rain.
RM13 off Mungo Pk Rd 147 FG65
Freedom Cl, E17 123 DY56
Freedom Rd, N17 100 DR54
Freedom St, SW11 160 DF82
Freedown La, Sutt. SM2 218 DC113
Freegrove Rd, N7 121 DL64
Freeland Pk, NW4 97 CY54
Freeland Rd, W5 138 CM73
Freelands Av, S.Croy. CR2 221 DX109
Freelands Gro, Brom. BR1 204 EH95
Freelands Rd, Brom. BR1 204 EH95
Cobham KT11 213 BV114
Freeland Way, Erith DA8
off Slade Grn Rd 167 FG81
Freeling St, N1 4 A6
Freeman Cl, Nthlt. UB5 136 BY66
Freeman Cl, Shep. TW17 195 BS98
Freeman Ct, N7
off Tollington Way 121 DL62
Chesham HP5
off Barnes Av 54 AQ30
Freeman Dr, W.Mol. KT8 196 BZ97
Freeman Rd, Grav. DA12 191 GL90
Morden SM4 200 DD99
Freemans Cl, Slou.
(Stoke P.) SL2 132 AT65
Freemans La, Hayes UB3 135 BS73
Freemantle Av, Enf. EN3 83 DX43
Sch Freemantles Sch, Cher.
KT16 off Pyrcroft Rd 193 BE101
Freemantle St, SE17 21 L9
Freeman Way, Horn. RM11 128 FL58
★ Freemason's Hall (United
Grand Lo of England),
WC2 9 P7
Freemasons Rd, E16 15 N6
Croydon CR0 202 DS102
Free Prae Rd, Cher. KT16 194 BG102
Freesia Cl, Orp. BR6
off Briarswood Way 223 ET106
Freethorpe Cl, SE19 202 DR95
Free Trade Wf, E1 12 G9
Freezeland Way, Uxb. UB10
off Western Av 134 BN65
FREEZY WATER, Wal.Cr. EN8 83 DY35
Sch Freezywater St. George's
Prim Sch, Enf. EN3
off Hertford Rd 83 DX36
★ Freightliners City Fm,
N7 4 B3
Freightmaster Est, Rain.
RM13 167 FG76
Freke Rd, SW11 160 DG83
Fremantle Ho, Til. RM18
off Leicester Rd 171 GF81
Fremantle Rd, Belv. DA17 166 FA77
Ilford IG6 103 EQ54
Fremont St, E9 142 DW67
French Apartments, The, Pur.
CR8 off Lansdowne Rd 219 DN112
Frenchaye, Add. KT15 212 BJ106
Frenches, The, Red. RH1 250 DG132
Frenches Ct, Red. RH1
off Frenches Rd 250 DG132
Frenches Dr, Red. RH1
off The Frenches 250 DG132
Frenches Rd, Red. RH1 250 DG132
French Gdns, Cob. KT11 214 BW114
French Horn La, Hat. AL10 45 CV17
Frenchlands Hatch, Lthd.
(E.Hors.) KT24 245 BS127
French Ordinary Ct, EC3 11 M9
French Pl, E1 11 M3
French Row, St.Alb. AL3
off Market Pl 43 CD20
French's Cl, Ware
(Stans.Abb.) SG12 33 EB11
French St, Sun. TW16 196 BW96
Westerham TN16 255 ES128
French's Wells, Wok. GU21 226 AV117
Frenchum Gdns, Slou. SL1 131 AL73
Frendsbury Rd, SE4 163 DY84
Frensham, Wal.Cr. (Chsht)
EN7 66 DT27
Frensham Cl, Sthl. UB1 136 BZ70
Frensham Ct, Mitch. CR4
off Phipps Br Rd 200 DD97
Frensham Dr, SW15 179 CU89
Croydon (New Adgtn)
CR0 221 EC108
Frensham Rd, SE9 185 ER89
Kenley CR8 219 DP114
Frensham St, SE15 162 DU79
Frensham Wk, Slou.
(Farn.Com.) SL2 111 AQ64
Frensham Way, Epsom
KT17 233 CW116
Frere St, SW11 160 DE82
Freshborough Ct, Guil. GU1
off Lower
Edgeborough Rd 259 AZ135
Freshfield Av, E8 5 N6
Freshfield Cl, SE13
off Marischal Rd 163 ED84
Freshfield Dr, N14 99 DH45
Freshfields, Croy. CR0 203 DZ101
Freshfields Av, Upmin.
RM14 128 FP64
Freshford St, SW18 180 DC90
Freshmount Gdns, Epsom
KT19 216 CP111
Freshwater Cl, SW17 180 DG93
Freshwater Rd, SW17 180 DG93
Dagenham RM8 126 EX60
Freshwaters, Harl. CM20
off School La 35 ES14
Freshwell Av, Rom. RM6 126 EW56
Fresh Wf Rd, Bark. IG11 145 EP67
Freshwood Cl, Beck. BR3 203 EB95
Freshwood Way, Wall. SM6 219 DH109
Freston Gdns, Barn. EN4 80 DG43
Freston Pk, N3 97 CZ54
Freston Rd, W10 6 A9
W11 6 B10
Freta Rd, Bexh. DA6 186 EZ85
Fretherne Rd, Welw.G.C.
AL8 29 CX09
★ Freud Mus, NW3 140 DC65
Frewin Rd, SW18 180 DD88
Friar Ms, SE27
off Prioress Rd 181 DP90
Friar Rd, Hayes UB4 136 BX70
Orpington BR5 206 EU99
Friars, The, Chig. IG7 103 ES49
Harlow CM19 51 EN17
Friars Av, N20 98 DE48
SW15 179 CT90
Brentwood (Shenf.) CM15 109 GA46
Friars Cl, E4 101 EC48
N2 120 DD56
SE1 20 F2
Brentwood (Shenf.) CM15 109 FZ45
Ilford IG1 126 ER60
Northolt UB5
off Broomcroft Av 136 BX69
Friarscroft, Brox. EN10 49 EA20
Friars Fld, Berk. HP4
off Herons Elm 38 AS16
Friars Gdns, W3
off St. Dunstans Av 138 CR72
Friars Gate, Guil. GU2 258 AU136
Friars Gate Cl, Wdf.Grn. IG8 102 EG49
Friars La, B.Stort. (Hat.Hth)
CM22 37 FH06
Richmond TW9 177 CK85
Friars Mead, E14 24 C6
Friars Ms, SE9 185 EN85
Friars Orchard, Lthd. (Fetch.)
KT22 231 CD121
Friars Pl La, W3 138 CR73
Sch Friars Prim Sch, SE1 20 F3
Friars Ri, Wok. GU22 227 BA118
Friars Rd, E6 144 EK67
Virginia Water GU25 192 AX98
Friars Stile Pl, Rich. TW10
off Friars Stile Rd 178 CL86
Friars Stile Rd, Rich. TW10 178 CL86
Friar St, EC4 10 F8
Friars Wk, N14 99 DH46
SE2 166 EX78
Friars Way, W3 138 CR72
Bushey WD23 76 BZ39
Chertsey KT16 194 BG100
Kings Langley WD4 58 BN30
Friars Wd, Croy. CR0 221 DY109
Friary, The, Wind.
(Old Wind.) SL4 172 AW86
Friary Br, Guil. GU1 258 AW135
Friary Cl, N12 98 DE50
Friary Ct, SW1 19 K2
Woking GU21 226 AT118
Friary Est, SE15 162 DU79
Friary Island, Stai. (Wrays.)
TW19 172 AW86
Friary La, Wdf.Grn. IG8 102 EG49
Friary Pas, Guil. GU1
off Friary St 258 AW136
Friary Rd, N12 98 DD49
SE15 162 DU80
W3 138 CR72
Staines (Wrays.) TW19 172 AW86
Friary Shop Cen, The, Guil.
GU1 off Onslow St 258 AW135
Friary St, Guil. GU1 258 AW136
Friary Way, N12 98 DE49
FRIDAY HILL, E4 101 ED47
Friday Hill, E4 102 EE47
Coll Friday Hill Adult Ed Cen,
E4 off Simmons La 102 EE47
Friday Hill E, E4 102 EE48
Friday Hill W, E4 102 EE47
Friday Rd, Erith DA8 167 FD78
Mitcham CR4 180 DF94
FRIDAY STREET, Dor. RH5 262 BZ143
Friday St, EC4 10 G8
Dorking (Abin.Com.) RH5 262 BZ143
Frideswide Pl, NW5
off Islip St 121 DJ64
Friendly Pl, SE13
off Lewisham Rd 163 EB81
Friendly St, SE8 163 EA81
Friendly St Ms, SE8
off Friendly St 163 EA82
Friends Av, Wal.Cr. EN8 67 DX31
Friendship Wk, Nthlt. UB5
off Wayfarer Rd 136 BX69
Friendship Way, E15
off Carpenters Rd 143 EC67
Friends Rd, Croy. CR0 202 DR104
Purley CR8 219 DP112
Friend St, EC1 10 E1
Friends Wk, Stai. TW18 173 BF92
Uxbridge UB8
off Bakers Rd 134 BK66
FRIERN BARNET, N11 98 DE49
Sch Friern Barnet Co Sch,
N11 off Hemington Av 98 DF50
Friern Barnet La, N11 98 DE49
N20 98 DE49
Friern Barnet Rd, N11 98 DF50
Friern Br Retail Pk, N11 99 DH51
Friern Cl, Wal.Cr. EN7 66 DS26
Friern Ct, N20 98 DD48
Friern Mt Dr, N20 98 DC45
Friern Pk, N12 98 DC50
Friern Rd, SE22 182 DU86
Friern Watch Av, N12 98 DC49
Frigate Ms, SE8
off Watergate St 163 EA79
Frimley Av, Horn. RM11 128 FN60
Wallington SM6 219 DL106
Frimley Cl, SW19 179 CY89
Croydon (New Adgtn)
CR0 221 EC108
Frimley Ct, Sid. DA14 186 EV92
Frimley Cres, Croy.
(New Adgtn) CR0 221 EC108
Frimley Gdns, Mitch. CR4 200 DE97
Frimley Rd, Chess. KT9 216 CL106
Hemel Hempstead HP1 39 BE19
Ilford IG3 125 ES62
Frimley Vw, Wind. SL4 151 AK81
Frimley Way, E1 12 G4
Fringewood Cl, Nthwd. HA6 93 BP53
Frinstead Gro, Orp. BR5 206 EX98
Frinstead Ho, W10 6 A9
Frinsted Rd, Erith DA8 167 FD80
Frinton Cl, Wat. WD19 93 BV47
Frinton Dr, Wdf.Grn. IG8 101 ED52
Frinton Ms, Ilf. IG2
off Bramley Cres 125 EN58
Frinton Rd, E6 144 EK69
N15 122 DS58
SW17 180 DG93
Romford RM5 104 EZ52
Sidcup DA14 186 EY89
Friston Path, Chig. IG7 103 ES50
Friston St, SW6 160 DB82
Friswell Pl, Bexh. DA6 166 FA84
Fritham Cl, N.Mal. KT3 198 CS100
Frith Ct, NW7 97 CY52
Frithe, The, Slou. SL2 132 AV72
Frith Knowle, Walt. KT12 213 BV106
Frith La, NW7 97 CY52
Sch Frith Manor Prim Sch,
N12 off Lullington Garth 97 CZ50
Frith Rd, E11 123 EC63
Croydon CR0 202 DQ103
Frithsden Copse, Berk. HP4 39 AZ15
Frithsden Rd, Berk. HP4 38 AY17
Friths Dr, Reig. RH2 250 DB131
Frith St, W1 9 L8
Frithville Gdns, W12 139 CW74
Frithwald Rd, Cher. KT16 193 BF101
Frithwood Av, Nthwd. HA6 93 BS51
Sch Frithwood Prim Sch,
Nthwd. HA6
off Carew Rd 93 BT51
Frizlands La, Dag. RM10 127 FB63
Frobisher Cl, Bushey WD23 76 CA44
Kenley CR8 off Hayes La 236 DR117
Pinner HA5 116 BX59
Frobisher Cres, EC2
off Beech St 142 DQ71
Staines TW19 174 BL87
Frobisher Gdns, Guil. GU1 243 BA133
Staines TW19 174 BL87
Frobisher Pas, E14 23 P1
Frobisher Rd, E6 145 EM72
N8 121 DN56
Erith DA8 167 FF80
St. Albans AL1 43 CJ22
Frobisher St, SE10 164 EE79
Frobisher Way, Grav. DA12 191 GL92
Greenhithe DA9 169 FV84
Hatfield AL10 44 CR15
Froggy La, Uxb. (Denh.)
UB9 113 BD62
Froghall La, Chig. IG7 103 ER49
FROGHOLE, Eden. TN8 255 ER133
Froghole La, Eden. TN8 255 ER132
Frog La, Guil. (Sutt.Grn)
GU4 242 AY125
Frogley Rd, SE22 162 DT84
Frogmoor La, Rick. WD3 92 BK47
FROGMORE, St.Alb. AL2 61 CE28
Frogmore, SW18 180 DA85
St. Albans AL2 61 CD27
Frogmore Av, Hayes UB4 135 BS69
Frogmore Cl, Slou. SL1 151 AN75
Sutton SM3 199 CX104
Frogmore Dr, Wind. SL4 152 AS81
Frogmore Est, Ruis. HA4 116 BX64
Frogmore Gdns, Hayes UB4 135 BS70
Sutton SM3 217 CY105
Frogmore Home Pk, St.Alb.
AL2 61 CD28
Frogmore Ind Est, NW10 138 CQ69
Frogmore Rd, Hem.H. HP3 40 BK23
Frognal, NW3 120 DC64
Frognal Av, Har. HA1 117 CF56
Sidcup DA14 186 EU92
Frognal Cl, NW3 120 DC64
Frognal Ct, NW3 140 DC65
Frognal Gdns, NW3 120 DC63
Frognal La, NW3 120 DB64
Frognal Par, NW3
off Frognal Ct 140 DC65
Frognal Pl, Sid. DA14 186 EU93
Frognal Ri, NW3 120 DC63
Frognal Way, NW3 120 DC63
Froissart Rd, SE9 184 EK85
Frome Rd, N22
off Westbury Av 121 DP55
Fromer Rd, H.Wyc.
(Woob.Grn) HP10 110 AD59
Frome Sq, Hem.H. HP2
off Waveney 40 BN15
Frome St, N1 4 G9
Fromondes Rd, Sutt. SM3 217 CY106
Front, The, Berk. (Pott.End)
HP4 39 BB16
Front La, Upmin. RM14 129 FS59
Frostic Wk, E1 11 P6
Froude St, SW8 161 DH82
Frowick Cl, Hat. AL9 45 CW23
Frowyke Cres, Pot.B. EN6 63 CU32
Fruen Rd, Felt. TW14 175 BT87
Fruiterers Pas, EC4
off Southwark Br 142 DQ73
Fryatt Rd, N17 100 DR52
Fry Cl, Rom. RM5 104 FA50
Fryday Gro Ms, SW12
off Weir Rd 181 DJ87
Fryent Cl, NW9 118 CN58
Fryent Cres, NW9 118 CS58
Fryent Flds, NW9 118 CS58
Fryent Gro, NW9 118 CS58
Sch Fryent Prim Sch, NW9
off Church La 118 CQ59
Fryent Way, NW9 118 CN57
Fryer Cl, Chesh. HP5 54 AR33
Fryern Wd, Cat. CR3 236 DQ124
Frying Pan All, E1 11 N6
Fry Rd, E6 144 EK66
NW10 139 CT67
Fryston Av, Couls. CR5 219 DH114
Croydon CR0 202 DU103
Frythe, The, Welw. AL6 29 CU05
Fryth Mead, St.Alb. AL3 42 CB19
Fuchsia Cl, Rom.
(Rush Grn) RM7 127 FE61
Fuchsia St, SE2 166 EV78
Fulbeck Dr, NW9 96 CS53
Fulbeck Wk, Edg. HA8
off Knightswood Cl 96 CP47
Fulbeck Way, Har. HA2 94 CC54
Fulbourne Cl, Red. RH1
off Dennis Cl 250 DE132
Fulbourne Rd, E17 101 EC53
Fulbourne St, E1 12 C5
Fulbrook Av, Add.
(New Haw) KT15 212 BG111
Fulbrook La, S.Ock. RM15 149 FT73
Fulbrook Rd, N19
off Junction Rd 121 DJ63
Fulford Gro, Wat. WD19 93 BV47
Fulford Rd, Cat. CR3 236 DR121
Epsom KT19 216 CR108
Fulford St, SE16 22 D4
FULHAM, SW6 159 CY82
⊖ Fulham Broadway 160 DA80
Fulham Bdy, SW6 160 DA80
Fulham Cl, Uxb. UB10
off Uxbridge Rd 135 BQ70
Fulham Ct, SW6
off Shottendane Rd 160 DA80
Sch Fulham Cross Sec Sch,
SW6 off Munster Rd 159 CY80
★ Fulham FC, SW6 159 CX81
Fulham High St, SW6 159 CY82
★ Fulham Palace Mus,
SW6 159 CX82
Fulham Palace Rd, SW6 159 CX80
W6 159 CW78
Fulham Pk Gdns, SW6 159 CZ82
Fulham Pk Rd, SW6 159 CZ82
Sch Fulham Prep Sch, SW6
off Fulham High St 159 CY82
W14 off Greyhound Rd 159 CY79
Sch Fulham Prim Sch, SW6
off Halford Rd 160 DA79
Fulham Rd, SW3 17 N10
SW6 159 CY82
SW10 17 N10
Fulkes Cotts, Lthd. KT24 245 BP128
Fullarton Cres, S.Ock. RM15 149 FT72
Fullbrooks Av, Wor.Pk. KT4 199 CT102
Sch Fullbrook Sec Sch, Add.
KT15 off Selsdon Rd 212 BG111
Fuller Cl, E2 12 A3
Orpington BR6 223 ET106
Fuller Gdns, Wat. WD24
off Fuller Rd 75 BV37
Fuller Rd, Dag. RM8 126 EV62
Watford WD24 75 BV37
Fullers Av, Surb. KT6 198 CM103
Woodford Green IG8 102 EF52
Fullers Cl, Chesh. HP5 54 AP32
Romford RM5 105 FC52
Waltham Abbey EN9 68 EG33
Fullers Fm Rd, Lthd.
(W.Hors.) KT24 245 BP134
★ Fuller's Griffin Brewery,
W4 159 CT79

A B C D E F G H I J K L M N O P Q R S T U V W X Y Z

Fullers Hill, Amer.
(Hyde Hth) HP6 ...54 AM34
Chesham HP5 ...54 AM34
Westerham TN16
off High St ...255 ER126
Fullers La, Rom. RM5 ...105 FC52
Fullers Mead, Harl. CM17 ...52 EW16
Fullers Rd, E18 ...102 EF53
Fuller St, NW4 ...119 CW56
Fullers Way N, Surb. KT6 ...198 CM104
Fullers Way S, Chess. KT9 ...216 CL105
Fullers Wd, Croy. CR0 ...221 EA106
Fullers Wd La, Red. (S.Nutfld)
RH1 ...251 DJ134
Fuller Ter, Ilf. IG1
off Oaktree Gro ...125 EQ64
Fullerton Cl, W.Byf. (Byfleet)
KT14 ...212 BM114
Fullerton Dr, W.Byf. (Byfleet)
KT14 ...212 BL114
Fullerton Rd, SW18 ...180 DC85
Carshalton SM5 ...218 DE109
Croydon CR0 ...202 DT101
West Byfleet (Byfleet)
KT14 ...212 BM114
Fullerton Way, W.Byf.
(Byfleet) KT14 ...212 BL114
Fuller Way, Hayes UB3 ...155 BT78
Rickmansworth
(Crox.Grn) WD3 ...74 BN43
Fullmer Way, Add. (Wdhm)
KT15 ...211 BF110
Fullwell Av, Ilf. IG5, IG6 ...103 EM53
FULLWELL CROSS, Ilf. IG6 ...103 ER53
Fullwell Cross Roundabout,
Ilf. IG6 off High St ...103 ER54
Sch Fullwood Prim Sch, Ilf.
IG6 off Burford Cl ...125 EQ56
Fullwoods Ms, N1 ...11 K1
Fulmar Cl, Surb. KT5 ...198 CM100
Fulmar Cres, Hem.H. HP1 ...40 BG21
Fulmar Rd, Horn. RM12 ...147 FG66
Fulmead St, SW6 ...160 DB81
FULMER, Slou. SL3 ...112 AX63
Fulmer Cl, Hmptn. TW12 ...176 BY92
Fulmer Common Rd, Iver
SL0 ...133 AZ65
Slough (Fulmer) SL3 ...133 AZ65
Sch Fulmer Co First Sch,
Slou. SL3
off Alderbourne La ...112 AY63
Fulmer Dr, Ger.Cr. SL9 ...112 AY61
Fulmer La, Ger.Cr. SL9 ...113 BB60
Slough (Fulmer) SL3 ...112 AY62
Fulmer Ri Est, Slou. SL3 ...133 AZ65
Fulmer Rd, E16 ...144 EK71
Gerrards Cross SL9 ...112 AY59
Slough (Fulmer) SL3 ...112 AY63
Fulmer Way, W13 ...157 CH76
Gerrards Cross SL9 ...112 AY58
Fulready Rd, E10 ...123 ED57
Fulstone Cl, Houns. TW4 ...156 BZ84
Fulthorp Rd, SE3 ...164 EF82
Fulton Ms, W2 ...7 L9
Fulton Rd, Wem. HA9 ...118 CN62
Fulvens, Guil. (Peasl.) GU5 ...261 BS143
Fulvens Cotts, Guil. (Peasl.)
GU5 ...261 BS142
⇌ Fulwell ...177 CD91
Fulwell Pk Av, Twick. TW2 ...176 CB89
Fulwell Rd, Tedd. TW11 ...177 CD91
Fulwich Rd, Dart. DA1 ...188 FM86
Fulwood Av, Wem. HA0 ...138 CM67
Fulwood Cl, Hayes UB3 ...135 BT72
Fulwood Gdns, Twick. TW1 ...177 CF86
Fulwood Pl, WC1 ...10 B6
Fulwood Wk, SW19 ...179 CY88
Furber St, W6 ...159 CV76
Furham Feild, Pnr. HA5 ...94 CA52
Furley Rd, SE15 ...162 DU80
Furlong Cl, Wall. SM6 ...200 DG102
Furlong Rd, N7 ...4 D3
Dorking (Westc.) RH4 ...262 CC137
Furlongs, Hem.H. HP1 ...40 BG19
Furlong Way, Ware
(Gt Amwell) SG12 ...33 DZ09
Furlough, The, Wok. GU22
off Pembroke Rd ...227 BA117
Furmage St, SW18 ...180 DB87
Furneaux Av, SE27 ...181 DP92
Furner Cl, Dart. DA1 ...167 FF83
Furness, Grays RM16 ...171 GH78
Furness Pl, Wind. SL4
off Furness Row ...150 AJ82
Furness Rd, NW10 ...139 CU68
SW6 ...160 DB82
Harrow HA2 ...116 CB59
Morden SM4 ...200 DB101
Furness Row, Wind. SL4 ...150 AJ82
Sch Furness Sch, Swan. BR8
off Rowhill Rd ...187 FF93
Furness Sq, Wind. SL4
off Furness Row ...150 AJ82
Furness Wk, Wind. SL4
off Furness Row ...150 AJ82
Furness Way, Horn. RM12 ...127 FG64
Windsor SL4 ...150 AJ82
Furnival Av, Slou. SL2 ...131 AP71
Furnival Cl, Vir.W. GU25 ...192 AX100
Furnival St, EC4 ...10 C7
Furrowfield, Hat. AL10
off Cob Mead ...45 CV16
Furrow La, E9 ...122 DW64
Furrows, The, Uxb. (Hare.)
UB9 ...114 BJ57
Walton-on-Thames KT12 ...196 BW103
Furrows Pl, Cat. CR3 ...236 DT123
Fursby Av, N3 ...98 DA51
Furse Av, St.Alb. AL4 ...43 CG17
Further Acre, NW9 ...97 CT54
Furtherfield, Abb.L. WD5 ...59 BS32
Furtherfield Cl, Croy. CR0 ...201 DN100
Further Grn Rd, SE6 ...184 EE87
Furtherground, Hem.H. HP2 ...40 BL21
Furzebushes La, St.Alb.
AL2 ...60 BY25
Furze Cl, Horl. RH6 ...269 DK148
Redhill RH1 ...250 DF133
Watford WD19 ...94 BW50
FURZEDOWN, SW17 ...180 DG92
Furzedown Cl, Egh. TW20 ...172 AY93
Furzedown Dr, SW17 ...181 DH92
Furzedown Hall, SW17
off Spalding Rd ...181 DH92
Sch Furzedown Prim Sch,
SW17 off Beclands Rd ...180 DG93
Furzedown Rd, SW17 ...181 DH92
Sutton SM2 ...218 DC111
Furze Fm Cl, Rom. RM6 ...104 EY54
Furze Fld, Lthd. (Oxshott)
KT22 ...215 CD113
Furzefield, Wal.Cr. (Chsht)
EN8 ...66 DV28
Furzefield Cl, Chis. BR7 ...185 EP93
Sch Furzefield Co Prim Inf
Sch, Red. RH1
off Delabole Rd ...251 DK128
Furzefield Cres, Reig. RH2 ...266 DC136
Furzefield Rd, SE3 ...164 EH79
Beaconsfield HP9 ...88 AJ53
Reigate RH2 ...266 DC136
Welwyn Garden City AL7 ...29 CY10
Furzeground Way, Uxb.
UB11 ...135 BQ74
Furze Gro, Tad. KT20 ...233 CZ121
Furzeham Rd, West Dr. UB7 ...154 BL75
Furze Hill, Pur. CR8 ...219 DL111
Redhill RH1
off Linkfield La ...250 DE133
Tadworth (Kgswd) KT20 ...233 CZ120
Furzehill Rd, Borwd. WD6 ...78 CN42
Furzehill Sq, Orp.
(St.M.Cray) BR5 ...206 EV98
Sch Furze Inf Sch, Rom.
RM6 off Bennett Rd ...126 EY58
Furze La, Gdmg. GU7 ...258 AT143
Purley CR8 ...219 DL111
Furzen Cl, Slou. SL2 ...131 AN69
Furzen Cres, Hat. AL10 ...45 CT21
Furze Rd, Add. KT15 ...211 BF107
Hemel Hempstead HP1 ...39 BE21
Thornton Heath CR7 ...202 DQ97
Furze St, E3 ...13 P5
Furze Vw, Rick. (Chorl.) WD3 ...73 BC44
Furzewood, Sun. TW16 ...195 BU95
Fuschia Ct, Wdf.Grn. IG8
off The Bridle Path ...102 EE52
Fusedale Way, S.Ock. RM15 ...149 FT73
Fuzzens Wk, Wind. SL4 ...151 AL82
Fyfe Way, Brom. BR1
off Widmore Rd ...204 EG96
Fyfield Cl, Brom. BR2 ...203 ED98
Fyfield Ct, E7 ...144 EG65
Fyfield Rd, E17 ...123 ED55
SW9 ...161 DN83
Enfield EN1 ...82 DS41
Rainham RM13 ...147 FF67
Woodford Green IG8 ...102 EJ52
Fynes St, SW1 ...19 L7

G

Gabion Av, Purf. RM19 ...169 FR77
Gable Cl, Abb.L. WD5 ...59 BS32
Dartford DA1 ...187 FG85
Pinner HA5 ...94 CA52
Gable Ct, SE26
off Lawrie Pk Av ...182 DV92
Gables, The, Bans. SM7 ...233 CZ117
Hemel Hempstead HP2
off Chapel St ...40 BK19
Leatherhead (Oxshott)
KT22 ...214 CC112
Wembley HA9 ...118 CM62
Gables Av, Ashf. TW15 ...174 BM92
Borehamwood WD6 ...78 CM41
Gables Cl, SE5 ...162 DS81
SE12 ...184 EG88
Gerrards Cross (Chal.St.P.)
SL9 ...90 AY49
Slough (Datchet) SL3 ...152 AU79
Woking (Kgfld) GU22
off Kingfield Rd ...227 AZ120
Gables Ct, Wok. (Kgfld)
GU22 off Kingfield Rd ...227 AZ120
Gables Way, Bans. SM7 ...233 CZ117
Gabriel Cl, Felt. TW13 ...176 BX91
Grays (Chaff.Hun.) RM16 ...169 FW76
Romford RM5 ...105 FC52
Gabrielle Cl, Wem. HA9 ...118 CM62
Gabrielle Ct, NW3 ...140 DD65
Gabriels Gdns, Grav. DA12 ...191 GL92
Gabriel Spring Rd, Long.
(Fawk.Grn) DA3 ...209 FR103
Gabriel Spring Rd (East),
Long. (Fawk.Grn) DA3 ...209 FS103
Gabriel St, SE23 ...183 DX87
Gabriel's Wf, SE1 ...20 C1
Gadbrook Rd, Bet. RH3 ...264 CS139
Gad Cl, E13 ...15 N1
Gaddesden Av, Wem. HA9 ...138 CM65
Gaddesden Cres, Wat. WD25 ...60 BX34
Gaddesdon Gro, Welw.G.C.
AL7 off Widford Rd ...30 DC09
Gade Av, Wat. WD18 ...75 BS42
Gade Bk, Rick. (Crox.Grn)
WD3 ...75 BR42
GADEBRIDGE, Hem.H. HP1 ...39 BF18
Gadebridge La, Hem.H. HP1 ...40 BJ18
Gadebridge Rd, Hem.H. HP1 ...40 BG18
Gade Cl, Hayes UB3 ...135 BV74
Hemel Hempstead HP1 ...40 BH17
Watford WD18 ...75 BS42
Gadesden Rd, Epsom KT19 ...216 CQ107
Gadeside, Wat. WD25 ...75 BS35
Gade Twr, Hem.H. HP3 ...58 BN25
Gade Valley Cl, Kings L. WD4 ...58 BN28
Sch Gade Valley JMI Sch,
Hem.H. HP1
off Gadebridge Rd ...40 BH19
Gade Vw Gdns, Kings L.
WD4 ...59 BQ32
Gadeview Rd, Hem.H. HP3 ...40 BK24
Gadsbury Cl, NW9 ...119 CT58
Gadsden Cl, Upmin. RM14 ...129 FS58
Gadswell Cl, Wat. WD25 ...76 BX36
Gadwall Cl, E16 ...15 N7
Gadwall Way, SE28 ...165 ER75
Gage Rd, E16 ...15 H5
Gage St, WC1 ...9 P5
Gainford St, N1 ...4 C7
Gainsboro Gdns, Grnf. UB6 ...117 CE64
Gainsborough Av, E12 ...125 EN64
Dartford DA1 ...188 FJ85
St. Albans AL1 ...43 CF19
Tilbury RM18 ...171 GG81
Gainsborough Cl, Beck. BR3 ...183 EA94
Esher KT10
off Lime Tree Av ...197 CE102
Gainsborough Ct, N12 ...98 DB50
W12 off Lime Gro ...159 CW75
Bromley BR2 ...204 EJ98
Walton-on-Thames KT12 ...213 BU105
Gainsborough Dr, Grav.
(Nthflt) DA11 ...190 GD90
South Croydon CR2 ...220 DU113
Gainsborough Gdns, NW3 ...120 DD62
NW11 ...119 CZ59
Edgware HA8 ...96 CM54
Isleworth TW7 ...177 CD85
Gainsborough Ho, Enf.
EN1 off Ayley Cft ...82 DU43
Sch Gainsborough JMI Sch,
E9 off Berkshire Rd ...143 EA65
Gainsborough Ms, SE26
off Panmure Rd ...182 DV90
Gainsborough Pl, Chig. IG7 ...103 ET48
Sch Gainsborough Prim Sch,
E15 ...13 H2
Gainsborough Rd, E11 ...124 EE59
E15 ...14 G2
N12 ...98 DB50
W4 ...159 CT77
Dagenham RM8 ...126 EV63
Epsom KT19 ...216 CQ110
Hayes UB4 ...135 BQ68
New Malden KT3 ...198 CR101
Rainham RM13 ...147 FG67
Richmond TW9 ...158 CM83
Woodford Green IG8 ...102 EL51
Gainsborough Sq, Bexh.
DA6 off Regency Way ...166 EX83
Gainsborough St, E9
off Trowbridge Rd ...143 DZ65
Gainsborough Studios, N1
off Poole St ...142 DR67
Gainsford Rd, E17 ...123 DZ56
Gainsford St, SE1 ...21 N3
Gainswood, Welw.G.C. AL7
off Mill Grn Rd ...29 CY10
Gairloch Rd, SE5 ...162 DS82
Gaisford St, NW5 ...141 DJ65
Gaist Av, Cat. CR3 ...236 DU122
Gaitskell Ct, SW11 ...160 DE82
Gaitskell Rd, SE9 ...185 EQ88
Galahad Cl, Slou. SL1 ...151 AN75
Galahad Rd, N9
off Salisbury Rd ...100 DU48
Bromley BR1 ...184 EG90
Galata Rd, SW13 ...159 CU80
Galatea Sq, SE15
off Scylla Rd ...162 DV83
Galba Ct, Brent. TW8
off Augustus Cl ...157 CK80
Galbraith St, E14 ...24 C5
Galdana Av, Barn. EN5 ...80 DC41
Galeborough Av, Wdf.Grn.
IG8 ...101 ED52
Gale Cl, Hmptn. TW12
off Stewart Cl ...176 BY93
Mitcham CR4 ...200 DD97
Gale Cres, Bans. SM7 ...234 DA117
Galena Ho, SE18
off Grosmont Rd ...165 ET78
Galena Rd, W6 ...159 CV77
Galen Cl, Epsom KT19 ...216 CN111
Galen Pl, WC1 ...9 P6
Galesbury Rd, SW18 ...180 DC86
Gales Cl, Guil. GU4
off Gilliat Dr ...243 BD132
Gales Gdns, E2 ...12 D2
Gale St, E3 ...13 P5
Dagenham RM9 ...146 EX67
Gales Way, Wdf.Grn. IG8 ...102 EL52
Galey Grn, S.Ock. RM15
off Bovey Way ...149 FV71
Galgate Cl, SW19 ...179 CY88
Gallants Fm Rd, Barn. EN4 ...98 DE45
Galleon Boul, Dart. DA2 ...169 FR84
Galleon Cl, SE16 ...22 F3
Erith DA8 ...167 FD77
Galleon Ms, Grav. DA11
off Maritime Gate ...190 GE87
Galleon Rd, Grays
(Chaff.Hun.) RM16 ...169 FW77
Galleons Dr, Bark. IG11 ...146 EU69
Galleons La, Slou. (Geo.Grn)
SL3 ...132 AX71
Galleria Shop Mall, The, Hat.
AL10 ...44 CS18
Gallery Gdns, Nthlt. UB5 ...136 BX68
Gallery Rd, SE21 ...182 DR88
Galley Grn, Hert. (Hailey)
SG13 ...33 EA13
Galley Hill, Hem.H. HP1 ...39 BF18
Waltham Abbey EN9 ...68 EF30
Galley Hill Rd, Grav. (Nthflt)
DA11 ...190 FZ85
Swanscombe DA10 ...190 FZ85
Galley La, Barn. EN5 ...79 CV41
Galleymead Rd, Slou.
(Colnbr.) SL3 ...153 BF81
Sch Galleywall Prim Sch,
SE16 ...22 D8
Galleywall Rd, SE16 ...22 C8
Galleywood Cres, Rom.
RM5 ...105 FD51
Galliard Cl, N9 ...82 DW44
Sch Galliard Prim Sch, N9
off Galliard Rd ...82 DU44
Galliard Rd, N9 ...100 DU46
Gallia Rd, N5 ...4 F2
Gallions Cl, Bark. IG11 ...146 EU69
Sch Gallions Mt Prim Sch,
SE18 off Purrett Rd ...165 ET78
Sch Gallions Prim Sch, E6
off Warwall ...145 EP72
[DLR] Gallions Reach ...145 EP72
Gallions Reach Shop Pk, E6 ...145 EQ71
Gallions Rd, SE7 ...25 P8
Gallions Roundabout, E16 ...145 EP73
Gallions Vw Rd, SE28
off Goldfinch Rd ...165 ES75
Gallon Cl, SE7 ...164 EJ77
Gallop, The, S.Croy. CR2 ...220 DV108
Sutton SM2 ...218 DC108
Gallops, The, Tad. KT20 ...249 CV126
Gallosson Rd, SE18 ...165 ES77
Galloway Chase, Slou. SL2 ...132 AU73
Galloway Cl, Brox. EN10 ...67 DZ26
Galloway Dr, Dart. DA1 ...187 FE87
Galloway Path, Croy. CR0 ...220 DR105
Galloway Rd, W12 ...139 CU74
Gallows Cor, Rom.
(Harold Wd) RM3 ...106 FK53
Gallows Hill, Kings L. WD4 ...59 BQ31
Gallows Hill La, Abb.L. WD5 ...59 BQ32
Gallus Cl, N21 ...81 DM44
Gallus Sq, SE3 ...164 EH83
Gallys Rd, Wind. SL4 ...151 AK82
Galpins Rd, Th.Hth. CR7 ...201 DM98
Galsworthy Av, E14 ...13 K6
Romford RM6 ...126 EV59
Galsworthy Cl, SE28 ...146 EV74
Galsworthy Cres, SE3
off Merriman Rd ...164 EJ81
Galsworthy Rd, NW2 ...119 CY63
Chertsey KT16 ...194 BG101
Kingston upon Thames
KT2 ...178 CP94
Tilbury RM18 ...171 GJ81
Galsworthy Ter, N16
off Hawksley Rd ...122 DS62
Galton St, W10 ...6 C3
Galva Cl, Barn. EN4 ...80 DG42
Galvani Way, Croy. CR0
off Ampere Way ...201 DM102
Galveston Rd, SW15 ...179 CZ85
Galvin Rd, Slou. SL1 ...131 AQ74
Galvins Cl, Guil. GU2 ...242 AU131
Galway Cl, SE16 ...22 D10
Galway St, EC1 ...11 H2
Gambetta St, SW8 ...161 DH82
Gambia St, SE1 ...20 F2
Gambles La, Wok. (Ripley)
GU23 ...228 BJ124
Gambole Rd, SW17 ...180 DE91
Games Rd, Barn. EN4 ...80 DF41
Gamlen Rd, SW15 ...159 CX84
Gammon Cl, Hem.H. HP3 ...40 BN21
Gammons Fm Cl, Wat. WD24 ...75 BT36
Gammons La, Brox. EN10 ...66 DT25
Watford WD24 ...75 BV38
Gamuel Cl, E17 ...123 EA58
Gander Grn Cres, Hmptn.
TW12 ...196 CA95
Gander Grn La, Sutt. SM1,
SM3 ...199 CY103
Ganders Ash, Wat. WD25 ...59 BU33
Gandhi Cl, E17 ...123 EA58
Gandolfi St, SE15
off St. Georges Way ...162 DS79
Gangers Hill, Cat. (Wold.)
CR3 ...253 EA127
Godstone RH9 ...253 EA127
Ganghill, Guil. GU1 ...243 BA132
Gant Ct, Wal.Abb. EN9 ...68 EF34
Ganton St, W1 ...9 J9
Ganton Wk, Wat. WD19
off Woodhall La ...94 BY49
GANTS HILL, Ilf. IG2 ...125 EN57
⊖ Gants Hill ...125 EN58
Gants Hill, Ilf. IG2
off Eastern Av ...125 EN58
Gantshill Cres, Ilf. IG2 ...125 EN57
GANWICK CORNER, Barn.
EN5 ...80 DB35
Ganymede Pl, Hem.H. HP2
off Jupiter Dr ...40 BM18
Gap Rd, SW19 ...180 DA92
Garage Rd, W3 ...138 CN72
Garbrand Wk, Epsom KT17 ...217 CT109
Garbutt Pl, W1 ...8 F5
Garbutt Rd, Upmin. RM14 ...128 FQ61
Garden Av, Bexh. DA7 ...166 FA83
Hatfield AL10 ...45 CU22
Mitcham CR4 ...181 DH94
Garden City, Edg. HA8 ...96 CN51
Garden Cl, E4 ...101 EA50
SE12 ...184 EH90
SW15 ...179 CV87
Addlestone KT15 ...212 BK105
Ashford TW15 ...175 BQ93
Banstead SM7 ...234 DA115
Barnet EN5 ...79 CW42
Hampton TW12 ...176 BZ92
Leatherhead KT22 ...231 CJ124
Northolt UB5 ...136 BY67
Ruislip HA4 ...115 BS61
St. Albans AL1 ...43 CH19
Wallington SM6 ...219 DL106
Watford WD17 ...75 BT40
Garden Cotts, Orp. BR5
off Main Rd ...206 EW96
Garden Ct, EC4 ...10 C9
N12 off Holden Rd ...98 DB50
Richmond TW9
off Lichfield Rd ...158 CM81
Stanmore HA7
off Marsh La ...95 CJ50
Welwyn Garden City AL7 ...29 CY08
West Molesey KT8
off Avern Rd ...196 CB98
Garden End, Amer. HP6 ...55 AS37
Gardeners Cl, N11 ...98 DG47
SE9 ...184 EL90
Gardeners Rd, Croy. CR0 ...201 DP102
Gardeners Wk, Lthd. (Bkhm)
KT23 ...246 CB126
Garden Fld La, Berk. HP4 ...39 AZ21
Sch Garden Flds JMI Sch,
St.Alb. AL3
off Townsend Dr ...43 CD17
[H] Garden Hosp, The, NW4 ...119 CW55
Sch Garden Ho Prep Sch,
SW1 ...18 D6
Gardenia Rd, Enf. EN1 ...82 DS44
Gardenia Way, Wdf.Grn. IG8 ...102 EG50
Garden La, SW2
off Christchurch Rd ...181 DM88
Bromley BR1 ...184 EH93
Garden Ms, W2 ...7 H10
Slough SL1
off Littledown Rd ...132 AT74
Garden Pl, E8 ...5 N7
Dartford DA2 ...188 FK90
Sch Garden Prim Sch, Mitch.
CR4 off Abbotts Rd ...201 DK97
Garden Reach, Ch.St.G. HP8 ...72 AX41
Garden Rd, NW8 ...7 M1
SE20 ...202 DW95
Abbots Langley WD5 ...59 BS31
Bromley BR1 ...184 EH94
Richmond TW9 ...158 CN83
Sevenoaks TN13 ...257 FK122
Walton-on-Thames KT12 ...195 BV100
Garden Row, SE1 ...20 E6
Gravesend (Nthflt) DA11 ...191 GF90
Gardens, The, SE22 ...162 DU84
Beckenham BR3 ...203 EC96
Esher KT10 ...214 CA105
Feltham TW14 ...175 BR85
Harrow HA1 ...116 CC58
Hatfield (Brook.Pk) AL9 ...63 CY27
Pinner HA5 ...116 BZ58
Watford WD17 ...75 BT40
★ Gardens of the Rose,
St.Alb. AL2 ...60 BY26
Garden St, E1 ...13 H6
Sch Garden Suburb Inf Sch,
NW11 off Childs Way ...119 CZ57
Sch Garden Suburb Jun Sch,
NW11 off Childs Way ...119 CZ57
Garden Ter, SW1 ...19 L9
Garden Ter Rd, Harl. CM17 ...36 EW11
Garden Wk, EC2 ...11 L2
Beckenham BR3
off Hayne Rd ...203 DZ95
Coulsdon CR5 ...235 DH123
Garden Way, NW10 ...138 CQ65
Loughton IG10 ...85 EN38
Gardiner Av, NW2 ...119 CW64
Gardiner Cl, Dag. RM8 ...126 EX63
Enfield EN3 ...83 DX44
Orpington BR5 ...206 EW96
[H] Gardiner Hill Unit,
SW17 ...180 DE89
Gardiners, The, Harl. CM17 ...52 EV15
Gardner Cl, E11 ...124 EH58
Gardner Ct, EC1
off St. John St ...141 DP70
Gardner Gro, Felt. TW13 ...176 BZ89
Gardner Pl, Felt. TW14 ...175 BV86
Gardner Rd, E13 ...15 N3
Guildford GU1 ...242 AW134
Gardners La, EC4 ...10 G9
Gardnor Rd, NW3
off Flask Wk ...120 DD63
Gard St, EC1 ...10 F1
Garendon Gdns, Mord.
SM4 ...200 DB101
Garendon Rd, Mord. SM4 ...200 DB101
Gareth Cl, Wor.Pk. KT4
off Burnham Dr ...199 CX103
Gareth Gro, Brom. BR1 ...184 EG91
Garfield Ms, SW11
off Garfield Rd ...160 DG83
Garfield Pl, Wind. SL4
off Albany Rd ...151 AR82
Sch Garfield Prim Sch, N11
off Springfield Rd ...99 DJ50
SW19 off Garfield Rd ...180 DC93
Garfield Rd, E4 ...101 ED46
E13 ...15 K4
SW11 ...160 DG83
SW19 ...180 DC92
Addlestone KT15 ...212 BJ106
Enfield EN3 ...82 DW42
Twickenham TW1 ...177 CG88
Garfield St, Wat. WD24 ...75 BV38
Garford St, E14 ...13 N10
Garganey Wk, SE28 ...146 EX73
Gargery Cl, Grav. DA12 ...191 GM88
Garibaldi Rd, Red. RH1 ...266 DF135
Garibaldi St, SE18 ...165 ES77
Garland Cl, Hem.H. HP2 ...40 BK19
Waltham Cross EN8 ...67 DY31
Garland Dr, Houns. TW3 ...156 CC82
Garland Ho, Kings.T. KT2
off Kingsgate Rd ...198 CL95
Garland Rd, SE18 ...165 ER80
Stanmore HA7 ...96 CL53
Ware SG12 ...33 DY06
Garlands Ct, Croy. CR0
off Chatsworth Rd ...220 DR105
Garlands Rd, Lthd. KT22 ...231 CH121
Redhill RH1 ...266 DF135
Garland Way, Cat. CR3 ...236 DR122
Hornchurch RM11 ...128 FL56
Garlichill Rd, Epsom KT18 ...233 CV117
Garlick Hill, EC4 ...11 H9
Garlic St, Dor. RH5 ...246 BZ133
Garlies Rd, SE23 ...183 DY90
Garlinge Rd, NW2 ...139 CZ65
Garman Cl, N18 ...100 DR50
Garman Rd, N17 ...100 DW52
Garnault Ms, EC1 ...10 D2
Garnault Pl, EC1 ...10 D2
Garnault Rd, Enf. EN1 ...82 DT38
Garner Cl, Dag. RM8 ...126 EX60
Garner Dr, Brox. EN10 ...67 DY26
Garner Rd, E17 ...101 EC53
Garners Cl, Ger.Cr.
(Chal.St.P.) SL9 ...90 AY51
Garners End, Ger.Cr.
(Chal.St.P.) SL9 ...90 AY51
Garners Rd, Ger.Cr.
(Chal.St.P.) SL9 ...90 AY51
Garner St, E2 off Coate St ...142 DU68
Garnet Cl, Slou. SL1 ...151 AN75
Garnet Rd, NW10 ...138 CS65
Thornton Heath CR7 ...202 DR98
Garnet St, E1 ...12 E10
Garnett Cl, SE9 ...165 EM83
Watford WD24 ...76 BX37
Garnett Dr, St.Alb.
(Brick.Wd) AL2 ...60 BZ29
Garnett Rd, NW3 ...120 DF64
Garnett Way, E17
off McEntee Av ...101 DY53
Garnet Wk, E6
off Kingfisher St ...144 EL71
Garnham Cl, N16
off Garnham St ...122 DT61
Garnham St, N16 ...122 DT61
Garnies Cl, SE15 ...162 DT80
Garnon Mead, Epp.
(Cooper.) CM16 ...70 EX28
Garrad's Rd, SW16 ...181 DK90
Garrard Cl, Bexh. DA7 ...166 FA83
Chislehurst BR7 ...185 EP92
Garrard Rd, Bans. SM7 ...234 DA116
Slough SL2 ...131 AL70
Garrard Wk, NW10
off Garnet Rd ...138 CS65
Garratt Cl, Croy. CR0 ...219 DL105
Garratt La, SW17 ...180 DD91
SW18 ...180 DB85
Sch Garratt Pk Sch, SW18
off Waldron Rd ...180 DC90
Garratt Rd, Edg. HA8 ...96 CN52
Garratts La, Bans. SM7 ...233 CZ116
Garratts Rd, Bushey WD23 ...94 CC45
Garratt Ter, SW17 ...180 DE91
Garrett Cl, W3 off Jenner Av ...138 CR71
Chesham HP5 ...54 AQ33
Garrett St, EC1 ...11 H3
Garrick Av, NW11 ...119 CY58
Garrick Cl, SW18 ...160 DC84
W5 ...138 CL70
Richmond TW9
off The Green ...177 CK85
Staines TW18 ...174 BG94
Walton-on-Thames KT12 ...213 BV105
Garrick Cres, Croy. CR0 ...202 DS103
Garrick Dr, NW4 ...97 CW54
SE28 off Broadwater Rd ...165 ER76
Garrick Gdns, W.Mol. KT8 ...196 CA97
Garrick Pk, NW4 ...97 CX54
Garrick Rd, NW9 ...119 CT58
Greenford UB6 ...136 CB70
Richmond TW9 ...158 CN82
Garricks Ho, Kings.T. KT1
off Wadbrook St ...197 CK96
Garrick St, WC2 ...9 N9
Gravesend DA11
off Barrack Row ...191 GH86
Garrick Way, NW4 ...119 CX56
Garrison Cl, SE18
off Red Lion La ...165 EN80
Hounslow TW4 ...176 BZ85
Garrison La, Chess. KT9 ...215 CK108
Garrison Par, Purf. RM19
off Comet Cl ...168 FN77
Garrolds Cl, Swan. BR8 ...207 FD96
Garron La, S.Ock. RM15 ...149 FT72
Garry Cl, Rom. RM1 ...105 FE52
Garry Way, Rom. RM1 ...105 FE52
Garsdale Cl, N11 ...98 DG51
Garside Cl, SE28
off Goosander Way ...165 ER76
Hampton TW12 ...176 CB93
Garsington Ms, SE4 ...163 DZ83
Garsmouth Way, Wat. WD25 ...76 BX36
Garson Cl, Esher KT10
off Garson Rd ...214 BZ107
Garson Gro, Chesh. HP5 ...54 AN29

★ Place of interest [H] Hospital Sch School Coll College Uni University ⇌ Railway station

Garson La, Stai. (Wrays.) TW19 172 AX87
Garson Mead, Esher KT10 214 BZ106
Garson Rd, Esher KT10 214 BZ107
GARSTON, Wat. WD25 76 BW35
⇌ Garston 76 BX35
Garston Cres, Wat. WD25 60 BW34
Garston Dr, Wat. WD25 60 BW34
Garston Gdns, Ken. CR8 off Godstone Rd 236 DR115
Sch Garston Inf Sch, Wat. WD25 off Fourth Av 76 BX35
Garston La, Ken. CR8 220 DR114
Watford WD25 60 BX34
Sch Garston Manor Sch, Wat. WD25 off Horseshoe La 60 BW32
Garston Pk Par, Wat. WD25 60 BX34
Garstons, The, Lthd. (Bkhm) KT23 246 CA125
Garter Way, SE16 22 G4
Garth, The, N12 off Holden Rd 98 DB50
Abbots Langley WD5 59 BR33
Cobham KT11 214 BY113
Hampton (Hmptn H.) TW12 off Uxbridge Rd 176 CB93
Harrow HA3 118 CM58
Garth Cl, W4 158 CR78
Kingston upon Thames KT2 178 CM92
Morden SM4 199 CX101
Ruislip HA4 116 BX60
Garth Ct, W4 off Garth Rd 158 CR78
Garthland Dr, Barn. EN5 79 CV43
Garth Ms, W5 off Greystoke Gdns 138 CL70
Garthorne Rd, SE23 183 DX87
Garth Rd, NW2 119 CZ61
W4 158 CR79
Kingston upon Thames KT2 178 CM92
Morden SM4 199 CW100
Sevenoaks TN13 257 FJ128
South Ockendon RM15 149 FW70
Garth Rd Ind Cen, Mord. SM4 199 CX101
Garthside, Rich. TW10 178 CL92
Garthway, N12 98 DE51
Gartlett Rd, Wat. WD17 76 BW41
Gartmoor Gdns, SW19 179 CZ88
Gartmore Rd, Ilf. IG3 125 ET60
Garton Pl, SW18 180 DC86
Gartons Cl, Enf. EN3 82 DW43
Gartons Way, SW11 160 DC83
Garvary Rd, E16 15 P7
Garvin Av, Beac. HP9 89 AL52
Garvock Dr, Sev. TN13 256 FG126
Garway Rd, W2 7 J8
Garwood Cl, N17 100 DV53
Gascoigne Gdns, Wdf.Grn. IG8 102 EE52
Sch Gascoigne Jun & Inf Sch, Bark. IG11 off Gascoigne Rd 145 EQ67
Gascoigne Pl, E2 11 N2
Gascoigne Rd, Bark. IG11 145 EQ67
Croydon (New Adgtn) CR0 221 EC110
Weybridge KT13 195 BP104
Gascons Gro, Slou. SL2 131 AN70
Gascony Av, NW6 140 DA66
Gascoyne Cl, Pot.B. EN6 63 CU32
Romford RM3 106 FK52
Gascoyne Dr, Dart. DA1 167 FF82
Gascoyne Rd, E9 143 DX66
Gascoyne Way, Hert. SG13, SG14 32 DQ09
Gaselee St, E14 14 D10
Gasholder Pl, SE11 20 B10
Gaskarth Rd, SW12 181 DH86
Edgware HA8 96 CQ53
Gaskell Rd, N6 120 DF58
Gaskell St, SW4 161 DL82
Gaskin St, N1 4 E7
Gaspar Cl, SW5 17 K7
Gaspar Ms, SW5 17 K7
Gassiot Rd, SW17 180 DF91
Gassiot Way, Sutt. SM1 200 DD104
Gasson Rd, Swans. DA10 190 FY86
Gastein Rd, W6 159 CX79
Gaston Bell Cl, Rich. TW9 158 CM83
Gaston Br Rd, Shep. TW17 195 BS99
Gaston Rd, Mitch. CR4 200 DG97
Gaston Way, Shep. TW17 195 BR99
Gas Wks La, Brox. EN10 49 EA19
Gataker St, SE16 22 D5
Gatcombe Ms, W5 138 CM73
Gatcombe Rd, E16 25 M1
N19 121 DK62
Gatcombe Way, Barn. EN4 80 DF41
Gate Cl, Borwd. WD6 78 CQ39
Gatecroft, Hem.H. HP3 40 BM22
Gate End, Nthwd. HA6 93 BU52
Gateforth St, NW8 8 A4
Gatehill Rd, Nthwd. HA6 93 BT52
Gatehope Dr, S.Ock. RM15 149 FT72
Gatehouse Cl, Kings.T. KT2 178 CQ94
Sch Gatehouse Sch, The, E2 off Sewardstone Rd 143 DX68
Gatehouse Sq, SE1 off Southwark Br Rd 142 DQ74
Gateley Rd, SW9 161 DM83
Gate Ms, SW7 18 B4
Gater Dr, Enf. EN2 82 DR39
Gatesborough St, EC2 11 L3
Gatesden Cl, Lthd. (Fetch.) KT22 230 CC123
Gatesden Rd, Lthd. (Fetch.) KT22 230 CC123
Gates Grn Rd, Kes. BR2 222 EG105
West Wickham BR4 204 EF104
Gateshead Rd, Borwd. WD6 78 CM39
Gateside Rd, SW17 180 DF90
Gatestone Rd, SE19 182 DS93
Gate St, WC2 10 A7
Gateway, SE17 162 DQ79
Weybridge KT13 off Palace Dr 195 BP104
Gateway, The, Wok. GU21 211 BB114
Gateway Arc, N1 off Islington High St 141 DP68
Gateway Cl, Nthwd. HA6 93 BQ51
Sch Gateway Comm Coll, The, N Site, Grays RM16 off Buxton Rd 171 GF75
S Site, Til. RM18 off St. Chad's Rd 171 GG81
Gateway Ho, Bark. IG11 off St. Ann's 145 EQ67
Gateway Ind Est, NW10 139 CT69
Gateway Ms, E8 5 N1
Sch Gateway Prim Sch, NW8 7 P3
Dartford DA2 off Milestone Rd 188 FP86
Gateway Retail Pk, E6 145 EP70
Gateway Rd, E10 123 EB62
Gateways, Guil. GU1 243 BA134
Gateways, The, SW3 18 B8
Waltham Cross EN7 66 DR28
Gatewick Cl, Slou. SL1 132 AS74
Gatfield Gro, Felt. TW13 176 CA89
Gathorne Rd, N22 99 DN54
Gathorne St, E2 off Mace St 143 DX68
Gatley Av, Epsom KT19 216 CP106
Gatley Dr, Guil. GU4 243 AZ131
Gatliff Rd, SW1 18 F10
Gatling Rd, SE2 166 EU78
Gatonby St, SE15 162 DT81
Gatting Cl, Edg. HA8 off Pavilion Way 96 CQ52
Gatting Way, Uxb. UB8 134 BL65
GATTON, Reig. RH2 250 DF128
Gatton Bottom, Red. RH1 251 DH127
Reigate RH2 250 DE128
Gatton Cl, Reig. RH2 250 DC131
Sutton SM2 218 DB109
Gatton Pk, Reig. RH2 250 DF129
Gatton Pk Rd, Red. RH1 250 DD132
Reigate RH2 250 DD132
Gatton Rd, SW17 180 DE91
Reigate RH2 250 DC131
Gattons Way, Sid. DA14 186 EZ91
Sch Gatton VA Muslim Prim Sch, SW17 off Gatton Rd 180 DE91
Gatward Cl, N21 81 DP44
Gatward Grn, N9 100 DS47
★ Gatwick Airport, Gat. RH6 268 DD153
⇌ Gatwick Airport 269 DH152
Gatwick Gate, Craw. RH11 268 DD154
Gatwick Gate Ind Est, Craw. (Lwfld Hth) RH11 268 DE154
Gatwick Metro Cen, Horl. RH6 269 DH147
Gatwick Rd, SW18 179 CZ87
Gatwick RH6 268 DG154
Gravesend DA12 191 GH90
Gatwick Rd Roundabout, Horl. RH6 268 DG154
Gatwick Way, Gat. RH6 268 DF151
Hornchurch RM12 off Haydock Cl 128 FM63
Gauden Cl, SW4 161 DK83
Gauden Rd, SW4 161 DK82
Gaumont App, Wat. WD17 75 BV41
Gaumont Ter, W12 off Lime Gro 159 CW75
Gauntlet Cl, Nthlt. UB5 136 BY66
Gauntlet Cres, Ken. CR8 236 DR120
Gauntlett Ct, Wem. HA0 117 CH64
Gauntlett Rd, Sutt. SM1 218 DD106
Gaunt St, SE1 20 F5
Gautrey Rd, SE15 162 DW82
Gautrey Sq, E6 145 EM72
Gavell Rd, Cob. KT11 213 BU113
Gavel St, SE17 21 K7
Gavenny Path, S.Ock. RM15 149 FT72
Gaveston Cl, W.Byf. (Byfleet) KT14 212 BM113
Gaveston Dr, Berk. HP4 38 AV17
Gavestone Cres, SE12 184 EH87
Gavestone Rd, SE12 184 EH87
Gaveston Rd, Lthd. KT22 231 CG120
Slough SL2 131 AL69
Gaviller Pl, E5 off Clarence Rd 122 DV63
Gavina Cl, Mord. SM4 200 DE99
Gavin St, SE18 165 ES77
Gaviots Cl, Ger.Cr. SL9 113 AZ60
Gaviots Grn, Ger.Cr. SL9 112 AY60
Gaviots Way, Ger.Cr. SL9 112 AY59
Gawain Wk, N9 off Salisbury Rd 100 DU48
Gawber St, E2 12 F1
Gawdrey Cl, Chesh. HP5 off Five Acres 54 AR33
Gawsworth Cl, E15 off Ash Rd 124 EE64
Gawthorne Av, NW7 off Lane App 97 CY50
Gawthorne Ct, E3 off Mostyn Gro 143 EA68
Gay Cl, NW2 119 CV64
Gaydon Ho, W2 7 K5
Gaydon La, NW9 96 CS53
Gayfere Rd, Epsom KT17 217 CU106
Ilford IG5 125 EM55
Gayfere St, SW1 19 N6
Gayford Rd, W12 159 CT75
Gay Gdns, Dag. RM10 127 FC63
Gayhurst, SE17 off Hopwood Rd 162 DR79
Sch Gayhurst JMI Sch, E8 off Gayhurst Rd 142 DU66
Gayhurst Rd, E8 142 DU66
Sch Gayhurst Sch, Ger.Cr. SL9 off Bull La 112 AW56
Jun Dept, Ger.Cr. SL9 off Maltmans La 112 AW56
Gayler Cl, Red. (Bletch.) RH1 252 DT133
Gaylor Rd, Nthlt. UB5 116 BZ64
Tilbury RM18 170 GE81
Gaynes Ct, Upmin. RM14 128 FP63
Gaynesford Rd, SE23 183 DX89
Carshalton SM5 218 DF108
Gaynes Hill Rd, Wdf.Grn. IG8 102 EL51
Gaynes Pk, Epp. (Cooper.) CM16 70 EY31
Gaynes Pk Rd, Upmin. RM14 128 FN63
Gaynes Rd, Upmin. RM14 128 FP61
Sch Gaynes Sch, Upmin. RM14 off Brackendale Gdns 128 FQ64
Gay Rd, E15 143 ED68
Gaysham Av, Ilf. IG2 125 EN57
Gaysham Hall, Ilf. IG5 125 EP55
Gay St, SW15 159 CX83
Gayton Cl, Amer. HP6 55 AS35
Ashtead KT21 232 CL118
Gayton Ct, Har. HA1 117 CF58
Gayton Cres, NW3 120 DD63
Gayton Ho, E3 off Blackthorn St 143 EA70
Gayton Rd, NW3 120 DD63
SE2 off Florence Rd 166 EW76
Harrow HA1 117 CF58
Gayville Rd, SW11 180 DF86
Gaywood Av, Wal.Cr. (Chsht) EN8 67 DX30
Gaywood Cl, SW2 181 DM88
Gaywood Est, SE1 20 F6
Gaywood Rd, E17 123 EA55
Ashtead KT21 232 CM118
Gaywood St, SE1 20 F6
Gaza St, SE17 20 E10
Gazelle Glade, Grav. DA12 191 GM92
Gean Wk, Hat. AL10 45 CU21
Sch Geariies Inf Sch, Ilf. IG2 off Waremead Rd 125 EP57
Sch Gearies Jun Sch, Ilf. IG2 off Gantshill Cres 125 EP57
Geariesville Gdns, Ilf. IG6 125 EP56
Geary Cl, Horl. (Smallfield) RH6 269 DP150
Geary Dr, Brwd. CM14, CM15 108 FW46
Geary Rd, NW10 119 CU64
Geary St, N7 4 B2
G.E.C. Est, Wem. HA9 117 CK62
Geddes Pl, Bexh. DA6 off Market Pl 166 FA84
Geddes Rd, Bushey WD23 76 CC42
Geddings Rd, Hodd. EN11 49 EB17
Gedeney Rd, N17 100 DQ53
Gedling Pl, SE1 21 P5
Geere Rd, E15 144 EF67
Gees Ct, W1 8 F8
Gee St, EC1 10 G3
Geffrye Ct, N1 5 M10
Geffrye Est, N1 off Stanway St 142 DS68
★ Geffrye Mus, E2 5 M10
Geffrye St, E2 5 N9
Geisthorp Ct, Wal.Abb. EN9 off Winters Way 68 EG33
Geldart Rd, SE15 162 DV80
Geldeston Rd, E5 122 DU61
Gellatly Rd, SE14 162 DW82
Gell Cl, Uxb. UB10 114 BM62
Gelsthorpe Rd, Rom. RM5 105 FB52
Gemini Gro, Nthlt. UB5 off Javelin Way 136 BY69
General Gordon Pl, SE18 165 EP77
Generals Wk, The, Enf. EN3 83 DY37
General Wolfe Rd, SE10 163 ED81
Genesis Business Pk, Wok. GU21 227 BC115
Genesis Cl, Stai. (Stanw.) TW19 174 BM88
Genesta Rd, SE18 165 EP79
Geneva Cl, Shep. TW17 195 BS96
Geneva Dr, SW9 161 DN84
Geneva Gdns, Rom. RM6 126 EY57
Geneva Rd, Kings.T. KT1 198 CL98
Thornton Heath CR7 202 DQ99
Genever Cl, E4 101 EA50
Genista Rd, N18 100 DV50
Genoa Av, SW15 179 CW85
Genoa Rd, SE20 202 DW95
Genotin Ms, Horn. RM12 128 FJ64
Genotin Rd, Enf. EN1 82 DR41
Genotin Ter, Enf. EN1 off Genotin Rd 82 DR41
Gentian Row, SE13 off Sparta St 163 EC81
Gentlemans Row, Enf. EN2 82 DQ41
Gentry Gdns, E13 15 M3
Genyn Rd, Guil. GU2 258 AV136
Geoffrey Av, Rom. RM3 106 FN51
Sch Geoffrey Chaucer Tech Coll, SE1 21 J6
Geoffrey Cl, SE5 162 DQ82
Geoffrey Gdns, E6 144 EL68
Geoffrey Rd, SE4 163 DZ83
Sch Geo Abbot Sch, Guil. GU1 off Woodruff Av 243 BB132
George Avey Cft, Epp. (N.Wld Bas.) CM16 71 FB26
George Beard Rd, SE8 23 L8
George Comberton Wk, E12 off Gainsborough Av 125 EN64
George Ct, WC2 9 P10
George Cres, N10 98 DG52
George Crook's Ho, Grays RM17 off New Rd 170 GB79
George Downing Est, N16 off Cazenove Rd 122 DT61
Sch George Eliot Inf Sch, NW8 off Marlborough Hill 140 DD67
Sch George Eliot Jun Sch, NW8 off Marlborough Hill 140 DD67
George V Av, Pnr. HA5 116 CA55
George V Cl, Pnr. HA5 off George V Av 116 CA55
George V Way, Grnf. UB6 137 CH67
Rickmansworth (Sarratt) WD3 74 BG36
George Gange Way, Har. (Wldste) HA3 117 CE55
GEORGE GREEN, Slou. SL3 132 AX72
George Grn Dr, Slou. (Geo.Grn) SL3 133 AZ71
George Grn Rd, Slou. (Geo.Grn) SL3 132 AX72
Sch George Green's Sec Sch, E14 24 D9
George Gro Rd, SE20 202 DU95
★ George Inn, SE1 21 J2
George Inn Yd, SE1 21 J2
Georgelands, Wok. (Ripley) GU23 228 BH121
George La, E18 102 EG54
SE13 183 EC86
Bromley BR2 204 EH102
George Lansbury Ho, N22 off Progress Way 99 DN53
George Loveless Ho, E2 11 P1
George Lovell Dr, Enf. EN3 83 EA37
George Lowe Ct, W2 7 J5
George Mathers Rd, SE11 20 E7
George Ms, NW1 9 J2
Enfield EN2 off Sydney Rd 82 DR41
Sch George Mitchell Sec Sch, E10 off Farmer Rd 123 EB60
George Pl, N17 off Dongola Rd 122 DS55
George Rd, E4 101 EA51
Godalming GU7 258 AS144
Guildford GU1 242 AX134
Kingston upon Thames KT2 178 CP94
New Malden KT3 199 CT98
George Row, SE16 22 A4
Georges Cl, Orp. BR5 206 EW97
Georges Dr, Brwd. (Pilg.Hat.) CM15 108 FT43
High Wycombe (Flack.Hth) HP10 110 AC56
Georges Mead, Borwd. (Elstree) WD6 77 CK44
Sch George Spicer Prim Sch, Enf. EN1 off Southbury Rd 82 DT41
George Sq, SW19 off Mostyn Rd 199 CZ97
George's Rd, N7 4 B2
Georges Rd, West. (Tats.) TN16 238 EK120
Georges Sq, SW6 off North End Rd 159 CZ79
Georges Ter, Cat. CR3 off Coulsdon Rd 236 DQ122
Tra George Street 202 DQ103
George St, E16 15 J8
W1 8 D7
W7 off The Broadway 137 CE74
Barking IG11 145 EQ66
Berkhamsted HP4 38 AY19
Chesham HP5 off Berkhampstead Rd 54 AQ30
Croydon CR0 202 DR103
Grays RM17 170 GA79
Hemel Hempstead HP2 40 BK19
Hertford SG14 32 DQ09
Hounslow TW3 156 BZ82
Richmond TW9 177 CK85
Romford RM1 127 FF58
St. Albans AL3 42 CC20
Southall UB2 156 BY77
Staines TW18 173 BF91
Uxbridge UB8 134 BK66
Watford WD18 76 BW42
Sch George St JMI Sch, Hem.H. HP2 off George St 40 BK19
George's Wd Rd, Hat. (Brook.Pk) AL9 64 DA26
George Tilbury Ho, Grays RM16 171 GH75
Sch George Tomlinson Prim Sch, E11 off Harrington Rd 124 EE60
Georgetown Cl, SE19 off St. Kitts Ter 182 DR92
Georgette Pl, SE10 off King George St 163 EC80
Georgeville Gdns, Ilf. IG6 125 EP56
Georgewood Rd, Hem.H. HP3 58 BM25
George Wyver Cl, SW19 off Beaumont Rd 179 CY87
George Yd, EC3 11 K8
W1 8 F9
Georgiana St, NW1 141 DJ67
Georgian Cl, Brom. BR2 204 EH101
Staines TW18 174 BH91
Stanmore HA7 95 CG52
Uxbridge UB10 114 BL63
Georgian Ct, SW16 off Gleneldon Rd 181 DL91
Wembley HA9 138 CN65
Georgian Way, Har. HA1 117 CD61
Georgia Rd, N.Mal. KT3 198 CQ98
Thornton Heath CR7 201 DP95
Georgina Gdns, E2 11 P1
Coll GEOS English Acad, W5 off New Bdy 137 CK73
Geraint Rd, Brom. BR1 184 EG91
Geraldine Rd, SW18 180 DC85
W4 158 CN79
Geraldine St, SE11 20 E6
Gerald Ms, SW1 18 F7
Gerald Rd, E16 15 J3
SW1 18 F7
Dagenham RM8 126 EZ61
Gravesend DA12 191 GL87
Geralds Gro, Bans. SM7 217 CX114
Gerard Av, Houns. TW4 176 CA87
Gerard Gdns, Rain. RM13 147 FE68
Gerard Rd, SW13 159 CT81
Harrow HA1 117 CG58
Gerards Cl, SE16 22 E10
Gerda Rd, SE9 185 EQ89
Gerdview Dr, Dart. DA2 188 FJ91
Germains Cl, Chesh. HP5 54 AP32
Germain St, Chesh. HP5 54 AP32
Germander Way, E15 15 H2
Sch German Sch, The, Rich. TW10 off Petersham Rd 177 CK88
Gernigan Ho, SW18 off Fitzhugh Gro 180 DD86
Gernon Cl, Rain. RM13 off Jordans Way 148 FK68
Gernon Rd, E3 143 DY68
Geron Way, NW2 119 CV60
Gerpins La, Upmin. RM14 148 FM68
Gerrard Cres, Brwd. CM14 108 FV48
Gerrard Gdns, Pnr. HA5 115 BU57
Gerrard Pl, W1 9 M9
Gerrard Rd, N1 4 F9
Gerrards Cl, N14 81 DJ43
GERRARDS CROSS, SL9 112 AX58
⇌ Gerrards Cross 112 AY57
Sch Gerrards Cross C of E Sch, Ger.Cr. SL9 off Moreland Dr 113 AZ59
Gerrards Cross Rd, Slou. (Stoke P.) SL2 132 AU66
Gerrards Mead, Bans. SM7 off Garratts La 233 CZ117
Gerrard St, W1 9 L9
Gerridge St, SE1 20 D4
Gerry Raffles Sq, E15 off Great Eastern Rd 143 ED65
Gertrude Rd, Belv. DA17 166 FA77
Gertrude St, SW10 160 DC79
Gervaise Cl, Slou. SL1 131 AM74
Gervase Cl, Wem. HA9 118 CQ62
Gervase Rd, Edg. HA8 96 CQ53
Gervase St, SE15 162 DV80
Gews Cor, Wal.Cr. (Chsht) EN8 67 DX29
Ghent St, SE6 183 EA89
Ghent Way, E8 5 P3
Giant Arches Rd, SE24 182 DQ87
Giant Tree Hill, Bushey (Bushey Hth) WD23 95 CD46
Gibbard Ms, SW19 179 CX92
Gibb Cft, Harl. CM18 51 ES19
Gibbfield Cl, Rom. RM6 126 EY55
Gibbins Rd, E15 143 EC66
Gibbon Rd, SE15 162 DW82
W3 138 CS73
Kingston upon Thames KT2 198 CL95
Gibbons Cl, Borwd. WD6 78 CL39
Gibbons Ms, NW11 off Hayes Cres 119 CZ57
Gibbons Rents, SE1 off Magdalen St 142 DS74
Gibbons Rd, NW10 138 CR65
Gibbon Wk, SW15 off Swinburne Rd 159 CU84
Gibbs Av, SE19 182 DR92
Gibbs Cl, SE19 182 DR92
Waltham Cross (Chsht) EN8 67 DX29
Gibbs Couch, Wat. WD19 94 BX48
Gibbs Grn, W14 16 F9
Edgware HA8 96 CQ50
Sch Gibbs Grn Sch, W14 16 F9
Gibbs Rd, N18 100 DW49
Gibbs Sq, SE19 182 DR92
Gibraltar Cl, Brwd. CM13 off Essex Way 107 FW51
Gibraltar Cres, Epsom KT19 216 CS110
Gibraltar Ho, Brwd. CM13 107 FW51
Gibraltar Wk, E2 11 P2
Gibson Cl, E1 12 F3
N21 81 DN44
Chessington KT9 215 CJ107
Epping (N.Wld Bas.) CM16 off Beamish Cl 71 FC25
Gravesend (Nthflt) DA11 191 GF90
Isleworth TW7 157 CD83
Gibson Ct, Rom. RM1 off Regarth Av 127 FE58
Slough SL3 153 AZ78
Gibson Gdns, N16 off Northwold Rd 122 DT61
Gibson Ms, Twick. TW1 off Richmond Rd 177 CJ87
Gibson Pl, Stai. (Stanw.) TW19 174 BJ86
Gibson Rd, SE11 20 B8
Dagenham RM8 126 EW60
Sutton SM1 218 DB106
Uxbridge UB10 114 BM63
Gibson's Hill, SW16 181 DN93
Gibson Sq, N1 4 D7
Gibson St, SE10 24 G10
Gidd Hill, Couls. CR5 234 DG116
Gidea Av, Rom. RM2 127 FG55
Gidea Cl, Rom. RM2 127 FG55
South Ockendon RM15 off Tyssen Pl 149 FW69
GIDEA PARK, Rom. RM2 127 FG55
⇌ Gidea Park 128 FJ56
Sch Gidea Pk Coll, Rom. RM2 off Balgores La 127 FH55
Sch Gidea Pk Prim Sch, Rom. RM2 off Lodge Av 127 FG55
Gideon Cl, Belv. DA17 167 FB77
Gideon Ms, W5 157 CK75
Gideon Rd, SW11 160 DG83
Gidian Ct, St.Alb. AL2 61 CD27
Giesbach Rd, N19 121 DJ61
Giffard Rd, N18 100 DS50
Giffard Way, Guil. GU2 242 AU131
Giffin St, SE8 163 EA80
Gifford Gdns, W7 137 CD71
Gifford Pl, Brwd. CM14 off Blackthorn Way 108 FX50
Sch Gifford Prim Sch, Nthlt. UB5 off Greenhill Gdns 136 BZ68
Giffordside, Grays RM16 171 GH78
Gifford St, N1 141 DL66
Gift La, E15 144 EE67
Giggs Hill, Orp. BR5 206 EU96
Giggs Hill Gdns, T.Ditt. KT7 197 CG102
Giggs Hill Rd, T.Ditt. KT7 197 CG101
Gilbert Cl, SE18 165 EM81
Swanscombe DA10 189 FX86
Sch Gilbert Colvin Prim Sch, Ilf. IG5 off Strafford Av 103 EN54
Gilbert Gro, Edg. HA8 96 CR53
Gilbert Ho, EC2 off The Barbican 142 DQ71
SE8 off McMillan St 163 EA79
Gilbert Pl, WC1 9 N6
Gilbert Rd, SE11 20 D8
SW19 180 DC94
Belvedere DA17 166 FA76
Bromley BR1 184 EG94
Grays (Chaff.Hun.) RM16 169 FW76
Pinner HA5 116 BX56
Romford RM1 127 FF56
Uxbridge (Hare.) UB9 92 BK54
Gilbert Scott Ct, Amer. HP7 off Whielden St 55 AP40
Sch Gilbert Scott Prim Sch, S.Croy. CR2 off Farnborough Av 221 DY108
Gilbert St, E15 124 EE63
W1 8 F8
Enfield EN3 82 DW37
Hounslow TW3 off High St 156 CC83
Gilbert Way, Berk. HP4 38 AU19
Croydon CR0 off Beddington Fm Rd 201 DL102
Slough SL3 off Ditton Rd 153 AZ78
Gilbey Cl, Uxb. UB10 115 BP63
Gilbey Rd, SW17 180 DE91
Gilbeys Yd, NW1 140 DG66
Gilbey Wk, H.Wyc. (Woob.Grn) HP10 off Stratford Dr 110 AD59
Gilbourne Rd, SE18 165 ET79
Gilda Av, Enf. EN3 83 DY43
Gilda Cres, N16 122 DU60
Gildea Cl, Pnr. HA5 94 CA52
Gildea St, W1 9 H6
Gilden Cl, Harl. CM17 36 EY11
Gilden Cres, NW5 120 DG64
Gildenhill Rd, Swan. BR8 188 FJ94
Gilden Way, Harl. CM17 36 EW12
Gilders, Saw. CM21 36 EX05
Gildersome St, SE18 off Nightingale Vale 165 EN79
Gilders Rd, Chess. KT9 216 CM107
Giles Cl, Rain. RM13 148 FK68
Giles Coppice, SE19 182 DT91
Giles Fld, Grav. DA12 off Damigos Rd 191 GM88
Giles Travers Cl, Egh. TW20 193 BC97
Gilfrid Cl, Uxb. UB8 off Craig Dr 135 BP72
Gilhams Av, Bans. SM7 217 CY112
Gilkes Cres, SE21 182 DS86
Gilkes Pl, SE21 182 DS86
Gillam Way, Rain. RM13 147 FG65
Gillan Grn, Bushey (Bushey Hth) WD23 94 CC47
Gillards Ms, E17 off Gillards Way 123 EA56
Gillards Way, E17 123 EA56
Gill Av, E16 15 M8
Guildford GU2 258 AS135
Gill Cl, Wat. WD18 75 BQ44
Gill Cres, Grav. (Nthflt) DA11 191 GF90
Gillender St, E3 14 C3
E14 14 C3
Sch Gillespie Prim Sch, N5 off Gillespie Rd 121 DP62
Gillespie Rd, N5 121 DN62
Gillett Av, E6 144 EL68
Gillette Cor, Islw. TW7 157 CG80
Gillett Pl, N16 off Gillett St 142 DS64
Gillett Rd, Th.Hth. CR7 202 DR98
Gillett St, N16 5 M2
Gillfoot, NW1 141 DJ68
Gillham Ter, N17 100 DU51
Gilliam Gro, Pur. CR8 219 DN110

Gillian Av, St.Alb. AL1 42 CC24
Gillian Cres, Rom. RM2 106 FJ54
Gillian Pk Rd, Sutt. SM3 199 CZ102
Gillian St, SE13 183 EB85
Gilliat Cl, Iver SL0
 off Dutton Way 133 BE72
Gilliat Dr, Guil. GU4 243 BD132
Gilliat Rd, Slou. SL1 132 AS73
Gilliat's Grn, Rick. (Chorl.)
 WD3 73 BD42
Gillies St, NW5 120 DG64
Gilling Ct, NW3 140 DE65
Gillingham Ms, SW1 19 J7
Gillingham Rd, NW2 119 CY62
Gillingham Row, SW1 19 J7
Gillingham St, SW1 19 H7
Gillison Wk, SE16 22 B5
Gillman Dr, E15 144 EF67
Gillmans Rd, Orp. BR5 206 EV102
Gills Hill, Rad. WD7 77 CF35
Gills Hill La, Rad. WD7 77 CF36
Gills Hollow, Rad. WD7 77 CF36
Gill's Rd, Dart. (S.Darenth)
 DA2, DA4 209 FS95
Gill St, E14 13 M9
Gillum Cl, Barn. EN4 98 DF46
Gilmais, Lthd. (Bkhm) KT23 246 CC125
Gilman Cres, Wind. SL4 151 AK83
Gilmore Cl, Slou. SL3 152 AW75
 Uxbridge UB10 114 BN62
Gilmore Cres, Ashf. TW15 174 BN92
Gilmore Rd, SE13 163 ED84
Gilmour Cl, Wal.Cr. EN7 82 DU35
Gilpin Av, SW14 158 CR84
Gilpin Cl, W2 7 N5
 Mitcham CR4 200 DE96
Gilpin Cres, N18 100 DT50
 Twickenham TW2 176 CB87
Gilpin Rd, E5 123 DY63
 Ware SG12 33 DY07
Gilpin's Gallop, Ware
 (Stans.Abb.) SG12 33 EB11
Gilpins Ride, Berk. HP4 38 AX18
Gilpin Way, Hayes UB3 155 BR80
Gilroy Cl, Rain. RM13 147 FF65
Gilroy Way, Orp. BR5 206 EV101
Gilsland, Wal.Abb. EN9 84 EE35
Gilsland Rd, Th.Hth. CR7 202 DR98
Gilstead Ho, Bark. IG11 146 EV68
Gilstead Rd, SW6 160 DB82
GILSTON PARK, Harl. CM20 35 EQ08
Gilston Rd, SW10 17 M10
Gilton Rd, SE6 184 EE90
Giltspur St, EC1 10 F7
Gilwell Cl, E4
 off Antlers Hill 83 EB42
Gilwell La, E4 83 EC42
Gilwell Pk, E4 83 EC41
Gimcrack Hill, Lthd. KT22
 off Dorking Rd 231 CH123
Gippeswyck Cl, Pnr. HA5
 off Uxbridge Rd 94 BX53
≠ Gipsy Hill 182 DS92
Gipsy Hill, SE19 182 DS91
Gipsy La, SW15 159 CU83
 Grays RM17 170 GC79
★ Gipsy Moth IV, SE10 163 EC79
Gipsy Rd, SE27 182 DQ91
 Welling DA16 166 EX81
Gipsy Rd Gdns, SE27 182 DQ91
Giralda Cl, E16
 off Fulmer Rd 144 EK71
Giraud St, E14 14 A7
Girdlers Rd, W14 16 B7
Girdlestone Wk, N19 121 DJ61
Girdwood Rd, SW18 179 CY87
Girling Way, Felt. TW14 155 BU83
Girona Cl, Grays
 (Chaff.Hun.) RM16 169 FW76
Gironde Rd, SW6 159 CZ80
Girtin Rd, Bushey WD23 76 CB43
Girton Av, NW9 118 CN55
Girton Cl, Nthlt. UB5 136 CC65
Girton Ct, Wal.Cr. EN8 67 DY30
Girton Gdns, Croy. CR0 203 EA104
Girton Rd, SE26 183 DX92
 Northolt UB5 136 CC65
Girton Vil, W10 6 B7
Girton Way, Rick. (Crox.Grn)
 WD3 75 BQ43
Gisborne Gdns, Rain. RM13 147 FF69
Gisbourne Cl, Wall. SM6 201 DK104
Gisburne Way, Wat. WD24 75 BU37
Gisburn Rd, N8 121 DM56
Gissing Wk, N1 4 D6
Gittens Cl, Brom. BR1 184 EF91
Given Wilson Wk, E13 144 EF68
GIVONS GROVE, Lthd.
 KT22 247 CJ126
Givons Gro, Lthd. KT22 247 CH125
Glacier Way, Wem. HA0 137 CK68
Gladbeck Way, Enf. EN2 81 DP42
Gladding Rd, E12 124 EK63
 Waltham Cross (Chsht)
 EN7 65 DP25
Glade, The, N21 81 DM44
 SE7 164 EJ80
 Brentwood (Hutt.) CM13 109 GA46
 Bromley BR1 204 EK96
 Coulsdon CR5 235 DN119
 Croydon CR0 203 DX99
 Enfield EN2 81 DN41
 Epsom KT17 217 CU106
 Gerrards Cross SL9 112 AX60
 High Wycombe (Penn)
 HP10 88 AC46
 Ilford IG5 103 EM53
 Leatherhead (Fetch.) KT22 230 CA122
 Sevenoaks TN13 257 FH123
 Staines TW18 174 BH94
 Sutton SM2 217 CY109
 Tadworth KT20 234 DA121
 Upminster RM14 128 FQ64
 Welwyn Garden City AL8 29 CW07
 West Byfleet KT14 211 BE113
 West Wickham BR4 203 EB104
 Woodford Green IG8 102 EH48
Glade Cl, Surb. KT6 197 CK103
Glade Ct, Ilf. IG5
 off The Glade 103 EM53
Glade Gdns, Croy. CR0 203 DY101
Glade La, Sthl. UB2 156 CB75
Sch Glade Prim Sch, Ilf. IG5
 off Atherton Rd 103 EM54
Glades, The, Grav. DA12 191 GK93
 Hemel Hempstead HP1 39 BE19
Gladeside, N21 81 DM44
 Croydon CR0 203 DX100
 St. Albans AL4 43 CK17
Gladeside Cl, Chess. KT9
 off Leatherhead Rd 215 CK108
Gladeside Ct, Warl. CR6 236 DV120
Sch Gladesmore Comm Sch,
 N15 off Crowland Rd 122 DU57
Gladesmore Rd, N15 122 DT58
Glade Spur, Tad. KT20 234 DB121
Glades Shop Cen, The,
 Brom. BR1 204 EG96
Gladeswood Rd, Belv. DA17 167 FB77
Gladeway, The, Wal.Abb.
 EN9 67 ED33
Gladiator St, SE23 183 DY86
Glading Ter, N16 122 DT62
Gladioli Cl, Hmptn. TW12
 off Gresham Rd 176 CA93
Gladsdale Dr, Pnr. HA5 115 BU56
Gladsmuir Cl, Walt. KT12 196 BW103
Gladsmuir Rd, N19 121 DJ60
 Barnet EN5 79 CY40
Gladstone Av, E12 144 EL66
 N22 99 DN54
 Feltham TW14 175 BU86
 Twickenham TW2 177 CD87
Gladstone Ct, SW19
 off Gladstone Rd 180 DA94
Gladstone Gdns, Houns.
 TW3 off Palmerston Rd 156 CC81
Gladstone Ms, N22
 off Pelham Rd 99 DN54
 NW6 off Cavendish Rd 139 CZ66
 SE20 182 DW94
Gladstone Par, NW2
 off Edgware Rd 119 CV60
Gladstone Pk Gdns, NW2 119 CV62
Sch Gladstone Pk Prim Sch,
 NW10 off Sherrick Grn Rd 119 CV64
Gladstone Pl, E3
 off Roman Rd 143 DZ68
 Barnet EN5 79 CX42
Gladstone Rd, SW19 180 DA94
 W4 off Acton La 158 CR76
 Ashtead KT21 231 CK118
 Buckhurst Hill IG9 102 EH46
 Chesham HP5 54 AQ31
 Croydon CR0 202 DR101
 Dartford DA1 188 FM86
 Hoddesdon EN11 49 EB16
 Kingston upon Thames
 KT1 198 CN97
 Orpington BR6 223 EQ106
 Southall UB2 156 BY76
 Surbiton KT6 197 CK103
 Ware SG12 32 DW05
 Watford WD17 76 BW41
Gladstone St, SE1 20 E5
Gladstone Ter, SE27
 off Bentons La 182 DQ91
Gladstone Way, Har.
 (Wldste) HA3 117 CE55
 Slough SL1 151 AN75
Gladwell Rd, N8 121 DM58
 Bromley BR1 184 EG93
Gladwyn Rd, SW15 159 CX83
Gladys Rd, NW6 140 DA66
Sch Glaisdale Sch, Sutt.
 SM2 off Arundel Rd 217 CZ108
Glaisher St, SE8 163 EA79
Glaisyer Way, Iver SL0 133 BC68
Glamis Cl, Wal.Cr. (Chsht)
 EN7 66 DU29
Glamis Cres, Hayes UB3 155 BQ76
Glamis Dr, Horn. RM11 128 FL60
Glamis Pl, E1 12 F9
Glamis Rd, E1 12 F9
Glamis Way, Nthlt. UB5 136 CC65
Glamorgan Cl, Mitch. CR4 201 DL97
Glamorgan Rd, Kings.T. KT1 177 CJ94
Glanfield, Hem.H. HP2
 off Bathurst Rd 40 BL17
Glanfield Rd, Beck. BR3 203 DZ98
Glanleam Rd, Stan. HA7 95 CK49
Glanmead, Brwd. (Shenf.)
 CM15 108 FY46
Glanmor Rd, Slou. SL2 132 AV73
Glanthams Cl, Brwd.
 (Shenf.) CM15 108 FY47
Glanthams Rd, Brwd.
 (Shenf.) CM15 109 FZ47
Glanty, The, Egh. TW20 173 BB91
Glanville Dr, Horn. RM11 128 FM60
Glanville Ms, Stan. HA7 95 CG50
Glanville Rd, SW2 181 DL85
 Bromley BR2 204 EH97
Glasbrook Av, Twick. TW2 176 BZ88
Glasbrook Rd, SE9 184 EK87
Glaserton Rd, N16 122 DS59
Glasford St, SW17 180 DF93
Glasgow Ho, W9 7 K1
Glasgow Rd, E13 144 EH68
 N18 off Aberdeen Rd 100 DV50
 Slough SL1 131 AN72
Glasgow Ter, SW1 19 J10
Glasse Cl, W13 137 CG73
Glasshill St, SE1 20 F3
Glasshouse Cl, Uxb. UB8 135 BP71
Glasshouse Flds, E1 12 G9
Glasshouse St, W1 9 K10
Glasshouse Wk, SE11 19 P9
Glasshouse Yd, EC1 10 G4
Glasslyn Rd, N8 121 DK57
Glassmill La, Brom. BR2 204 EF96
Glass St, E2 12 D3
Glass Yd, SE18
 off Woolwich High St 165 EN76
Glastonbury Av, Wdf.Grn.
 IG8 102 EK52
Glastonbury Cl, Orp. BR5 206 EW102
Glastonbury Pl, E1 12 E8
Glastonbury Rd, N9 100 DU46
 Morden SM4 200 DA101
Glastonbury St, NW6 119 CZ64
Glaucus St, E3 14 A5
Glazbury Rd, W14 16 D8
Glazebrook Cl, SE21 182 DR89
Glazebrook Rd, Tedd. TW11 177 CF94
Gleave Cl, St.Alb. AL1 43 CH19
Glebe, The, SE3 164 EE83
 SW16 181 DK91
 Chislehurst BR7 205 EQ95
 Harlow CM20
 off School La 35 ES14
 Horley RH6 268 DF148
 Kings Langley WD4 58 BN29
 Reigate (Leigh) RH2 265 CU141
 Watford WD25 60 BW33
 West Drayton UB7 154 BM77
 Worcester Park KT4 199 CT102
Glebe Av, Enf. EN2 81 DP41
 Harrow HA3 118 CL55
 Mitcham CR4 200 DE96
 Ruislip HA4 135 BV65
 Uxbridge UB10 115 BQ63
 Woodford Green IG8 102 EG51
Glebe Cl, W4 off Glebe St 158 CS78
Glebe Cl, Ger. Cr. (Chal.St.P.)
 SL9 90 AX52
 Hatfield (Essen.) AL9 46 DF17
 Hemel Hempstead HP3 40 BL24
 Leatherhead (Bkhm) KT23 246 CA126
 Maidenhead (Taplow) SL6 150 AF75
 South Croydon CR2 220 DT111
 Uxbridge UB10 115 BQ63
Glebe Cotts, Guil. (W.Clan.)
 GU4 244 BH132
 Hatfield (Essen.) AL9 46 DF17
 Sutton SM1 off Vale Rd 218 DB105
 Westerham (Brasted)
 TN16 240 EV123
Glebe Ct, W7 137 CD73
 Coulsdon CR5 235 DH115
 Guildford GU1 243 AZ134
 Mitcham CR4 200 DF97
 Sevenoaks TN13
 off Oak La 257 FH126
 Stanmore HA7 95 CJ50
Glebe Cres, NW4 119 CW56
 Harrow HA3 118 CL55
Glebefield, The, Sev. TN13 256 FF123
Sch Glebe First & Mid Sch,
 Har. HA3
 off D'Arcy Gdns 118 CL56
Glebe Gdns, N.Mal. KT3 198 CS101
 West Byfleet (Byfleet)
 KT14 212 BK114
Glebe Ho Dr, Brom. BR2 204 EH102
Glebe Hyrst, SE19
 off Giles Coppice 182 DT91
 South Croydon CR2 220 DT112
Glebeland, Hat. AL10
 off St. Ethelredas Dr 45 CW18
Glebeland Gdns, Shep.
 TW17 195 BQ100
Glebelands, Chig. IG7 104 EV48
 Dartford DA1 167 FF84
 Esher (Clay.) KT10 215 CF109
 Harlow CM20 35 ET12
 High Wycombe (Penn)
 HP10 88 AC47
 West Molesey KT8 196 CB99
Glebelands Av, E18 102 EG54
 Ilford IG2 125 ER59
Glebelands Cl, SE5
 off Grove Hill Rd 162 DS83
Glebelands Rd, Felt. TW14 175 BU87
Glebe La, Barn. EN5 79 CU43
 Dorking (Abin.Com.) RH5 262 BX143
 Harrow HA3 118 CL56
 Sevenoaks TN13 257 FH126
Glebe Path, Mitch. CR4 200 DE97
Glebe Pl, SW3 160 DE79
 Dartford (Hort.Kir.) DA4 208 FQ98
Sch Glebe Prim Sch, Uxb.
 UB10 off Sussex Rd 115 BQ63
Glebe Rd, E8 5 N6
 N3 98 DC53
 N8 121 DM56
 NW10 139 CT65
 SW13 159 CU82
 Ashtead KT21 231 CK118
 Bromley BR1 204 EG95
 Carshalton SM5 218 DF107
 Dagenham RM10 147 FB65
 Dorking RH4 263 CF136
 Egham TW20 173 BC93
 Gerrards Cross (Chal.St.P.)
 SL9 90 AW53
 Gravesend DA11 191 GF88
 Hayes UB3 135 BT74
 Hertford SG14 32 DR07
 Rainham RM13 148 FJ69
 Redhill RH1 235 DH124
 Staines TW18 174 BH93
 Stanmore HA7 95 CJ50
 Sutton SM2 217 CY109
 Uxbridge UB8 134 BJ68
 Warlingham CR6 237 DX117
 Windsor (Old Wind.) SL4 172 AV85
Sch Glebe Sch, W.Wick.
 BR4 off Hawes La 203 ED103
Glebe Side, Twick. TW1 177 CF86
Glebe St, W4 158 CS78
Glebe Ter, E3 off Bow Rd 143 EA69
Glebe Way, Amer. HP6 55 AR36
 Erith DA8 167 FE79
 Feltham TW13 176 CA90
 Hornchurch RM11 128 FL59
 South Croydon CR2 220 DT111
 West Wickham BR4 203 EC103
Glebeway, Wdf.Grn. IG8 102 EJ50
Gledhow Gdns, SW5 17 L8
Gledhow Wd, Tad. KT20 234 DB121
Gledstanes Rd, W14 16 D10
Gledwood Av, Hayes UB4 135 BT71
Gledwood Cres, Hayes UB4 135 BT71
Gledwood Dr, Hayes UB4 135 BT71
Gledwood Gdns, Hayes
 UB4 135 BT71
Gleed Av, Bushey
 (Bushey Hth) WD23 95 CD47
Gleeson Dr, Orp. BR6 223 ET106
Gleeson Ms, Add. KT15 212 BJ105
Glegg Pl, SW15 159 CX84
Glen, The, Add. KT15 211 BF106
 Bromley BR2 204 EE96
 Croydon CR0 203 DX103
 Enfield EN2 81 DP42
 Hemel Hempstead HP2 40 BM15
 Northwood HA6 93 BR52
 Orpington BR6 205 EM104
 Pinner HA5 116 BY59
 Pinner (Eastcote) HA5 115 BV57
 Rainham RM13 148 FJ70
 Slough SL3 152 AW77
 Southall UB2 156 BZ78
 Wembley HA9 117 CK63
Glenaffric Av, E14 24 E8
Glen Albyn Rd, SW19 179 CX89
Glenalla Rd, Ruis. HA4 115 BT59
Glenalmond Rd, Har. HA3 118 CL56
Glenalvon Way, SE18 164 EL77
Glena Mt, Sutt. SM1 218 DC105
Coll Glenarm Coll, Ilf. IG1
 off Coventry Rd 125 EN61
Glenarm Rd, E5 122 DW64
Glen Av, Ashf. TW15 174 BN91
Glenavon Cl, Esher (Clay.)
 KT10 215 CG108
Glenavon Gdns, Slou. SL3 152 AW77
Glenavon Rd, E15 144 EE66
Glenbarr Cl, SE9
 off Dumbreck Rd 165 EP83
Glenbow Rd, Brom. BR1 184 EE93
Sch Glenbrook Inf Sch,
 SW4 off Clarence Av 181 DK86
Sch Glenbrook Jun Sch,
 SW4 off Clarence Av 181 DK86
Glenbrook N, Enf. EN2 81 DM42
Glenbrook Rd, NW6 120 DA64
Glenbrook S, Enf. EN2 81 DM42
Glenbuck Ct, Surb. KT6
 off Glenbuck Rd 197 CK100
Glenbuck Rd, Surb. KT6 197 CK100
Glenburnie Rd, SW17 180 DF90
Glencairn Dr, W5 137 CH70
Glencairne Cl, E16 144 EK71
Glencairn Rd, SW16 201 DL95
Glen Cl, Shep. TW17 194 BN98
 Tadworth (Kgswd) KT20 233 CY123
Glencoe Av, Ilf. IG2 125 ER59
Glencoe Dr, Dag. RM10 126 FA63
Glencoe Rd, Bushey WD23 76 CA44
 Hayes UB4 136 BX71
 Weybridge KT13 194 BN104
Glencorse Grn, Wat. WD19
 off Caldwell Rd 94 BX49
Glen Ct, Stai. TW18 173 BF94
Glen Cres, Wdf.Grn. IG8 102 EH51
Glendale, Hem.H. HP1 40 BH20
 Swanley BR8 207 FF99
Glendale Av, N22 99 DN52
 Edgware HA8 96 CM49
 Romford RM6 126 EW59
Glendale Cl, SE9
 off Dumbreck Rd 165 EN83
 Brentwood (Shenf.) CM15 108 FY45
 Woking GU21 226 AW118
Glendale Dr, SW19 179 CZ92
 Guildford GU4 243 BB130
Glendale Gdns, Wem. HA9 117 CK60
Glendale Ms, Beck. BR3 203 EB95
Glendale Ri, Ken. CR8 235 DP115
Glendale Rd, Erith DA8 167 FC77
 Gravesend (Nthflt) DA11 190 GE91
Glendale Wk, Wal.Cr. (Chsht)
 EN8 67 DY30
Glendale Way, SE28 146 EW73
Glendall St, SW9 161 DM84
Glendarvon St, SW15 159 CX83
Glendene Av, Lthd. (E.Hors.)
 KT24 245 BS126
Glendevon Cl, Edg. HA8
 off Tayside Dr 96 CP48
Glendish Rd, N17 100 DU53
Glendor Gdns, NW7 96 CR49
Glendower Cres, Orp. BR6 206 EU100
Glendower Gdns, SW14
 off Glendower Rd 158 CR83
Glendower Pl, SW7 17 N7
Glendower Rd, E4 101 ED46
 SW14 158 CR83
Sch Glendower Sch, SW7 17 N7
Glendown Rd, SE2 166 EU78
Glendun Rd, W3 138 CS73
Gleneagle Ms, SW16
 off Ambleside Av 181 DK92
Gleneagle Rd, SW16 181 DK92
Gleneagles, Stan. HA7 95 CH51
Gleneagles Cl, SE16 22 C10
 Orpington BR6 205 ER102
 Romford RM3 106 FM52
 Staines (Stanw.) TW19 174 BK86
 Watford WD19 94 BX49
Gleneagles Grn, Orp. BR6
 off Tandridge Dr 205 ER102
Gleneagles Twr, Sthl. UB1 136 CC72
Gleneldon Ms, SW16 181 DL91
Gleneldon Rd, SW16 181 DL91
Glenelg Rd, SW2 181 DL85
Glenesk Rd, SE9 165 EN83
Sch Glenesk Sch, Lthd.
 KT24 off Ockham Rd N 245 BR125
Glenester Cl, Hodd. EN11 33 EA14
Glen Faba Rd, Harl.
 (Roydon) CM19 50 EF17
Glenfarg Rd, SE6 183 ED88
Glenferrie Rd, St.Alb. AL1 43 CG20
Glenfield Cl, Bet. (Brock.)
 RH3 264 CP138
Glenfield Cres, Ruis. HA4 115 BR59
Glenfield Rd, SW12 181 DJ88
 W13 157 CH75
 Ashford TW15 175 BP93
 Banstead SM7 234 DB115
 Betchworth (Brock.) RH3 264 CP138
Glenfield Ter, W13 157 CH75
Glenfinlas Way, SE5 161 DP80
Glenforth St, SE10 25 K9
Glengall Causeway, E14 23 N5
Glengall Gro, E14 24 C5
Glengall Rd, NW6 139 CZ67
 SE15 162 DT79
 Bexleyheath DA7 166 EY83
 Edgware HA8 96 CP48
 Woodford Green IG8 102 EG51
Glengall Ter, SE15 162 DT79
Glen Gdns, Croy. CR0 201 DN104
Glengarnock Av, E14 24 D8
Glengarry Rd, SE22 182 DS85
Glenham Dr, Ilf. IG2 125 EP57
Glenhaven Av, Borwd. WD6 78 CN41
Glenhead Cl, SE9
 off Dumbreck Rd 165 EP83
Glenheadon Cl, Lthd. KT22
 off Glenheadon Ri 231 CK123
Glenheadon Ri, Lthd.
 KT22 231 CK123
Glenhill Cl, N3 98 DA54
Glenhouse Rd, SE9 185 EN85
Glenhurst Av, NW5 120 DG63
 Bexley DA5 186 EZ88
 Ruislip HA4 115 BQ59
Glenhurst Ct, SE19 182 DT92
Glenhurst Ri, SE19 182 DQ94
Glenhurst Rd, N12 98 DD50
 Brentford TW8 157 CJ79
Glenilla Rd, NW3 140 DE65
Glenister Ho, Hayes UB3 135 BV74
Glenister Pk Rd, SW16 181 DK94
Glenister Rd, SE10 25 J9
 Chesham HP5 54 AQ28
Glenister St, E16 145 EN74
Glenkerry Ho, E14 14 C7
Glenlea Path, SE9
 off Well Hall Rd 185 EM85
Glenlea Rd, SE9 185 EM85
Glenlion Ct, Wey. KT13 195 BS104
Glenloch Rd, NW3 140 DE65
 Enfield EN3 82 DW40
Glen Luce, Wal.Cr. EN8
 off Turners Hill 67 DX30
Glenluce Rd, SE3 164 EG80
Glenlyn Av, St.Alb. AL1 43 CH21
Glenlyon Rd, SE9 185 EN85
Glenmere Av, NW7 97 CU52
Glen Ms, E17 off Glen Rd 123 DZ57
Glenmill, Hmptn. TW12 176 BZ92
Glenmire Ter, Ware
 (Stans.Abb.) SG12 33 ED11
Glenmore Cl, Add. KT15 194 BH104
Glenmore Gdns, Abb.L.
 WD5 off Stewart Cl 59 BU32
Glenmore Rd, NW3 140 DE65
 Welling DA16 165 ET81
Glenmore Way, Bark. IG11 146 EU69
Glenmount Path, SE18
 off Raglan Rd 165 EQ78
Glenn Av, Pur. CR8 219 DP111
Glennie Rd, SE27 181 DN90
Glenny Rd, Bark. IG11 145 EQ65
Glenorchy Cl, Hayes UB4 136 BY71
Glenparke Rd, E7 144 EH65
Glen Ri, Wdf.Grn. IG8 102 EH51
Glen Rd, E13 144 EJ70
 E17 123 DZ57
 Chessington KT9 198 CL104
Glen Rd End, Wall. SM6 219 DH109
Glenrosa Gdns, Grav. DA12 191 GM92
Glenrosa St, SW6 160 DC82
Glenrose Ct, Sid. DA14 186 EV92
Glenroy St, W12 139 CW72
Glensdale Rd, SE4 163 DZ83
Glenshee Cl, Nthwd. HA6
 off Rickmansworth Rd 93 BQ51
Glenshiel Rd, SE9 185 EN85
Glenside, Chig. IG7 103 EP51
Glenside Cotts, Slou. SL1 152 AT76
Glentanner Way, SW17
 off Aboyne Rd 180 DD90
Glen Ter, E14 24 D3
Glentham Gdns, SW13
 off Glentham Rd 159 CV79
Glentham Rd, SW13 159 CU79
Glenthorne Av, Croy. CR0 202 DV102
Glenthorne Cl, Sutt. SM3 200 DA102
 Uxbridge UB10
 off Uxbridge Rd 134 BN69
Glenthorne Gdns, Ilf. IG6 125 EN55
 Sutton SM3 200 DA102
Sch Glenthorne High Sch,
 Sutt. SM3
 off Sutton Common Rd 200 DA102
Glenthorne Ms, W6
 off Glenthorne Rd 159 CV77
Glenthorne Rd, E17 123 DY57
 N11 98 DF50
 W6 159 CW77
 Kingston upon Thames
 KT1 198 CM98
Glenthorpe Rd, Mord. SM4 199 CX99
Glenton Cl, Rom. RM1 105 FE51
Glenton Rd, SE13 164 EE84
Glenton Way, Rom. RM1 105 FE52
Glentrammon Av, Orp. BR6 223 ET107
Glentrammon Cl, Orp. BR6 223 ET107
Glentrammon Gdns, Orp.
 BR6 223 ET107
Glentrammon Rd, Orp. BR6 223 ET107
Glentworth Pl, Slou. SL1 131 AQ74
Glentworth St, NW1 8 D4
Glenure Rd, SE9 185 EN85
Glenview, SE2 166 EX79
Glen Vw, Grav. DA12 191 GJ88
Glenview Gdns, Hem.H.
 HP1 off Glenview Rd 40 BH20
Glenview Rd, Brom. BR1 204 EK96
 Hemel Hempstead HP1 40 BH20
Glenville Av, Enf. EN2 82 DQ38
Glenville Gro, SE8 163 DZ80
Glenville Ms, SW18 180 DB87
Glenville Rd, Kings.T. KT2 198 CN95
Glen Wk, Islw. TW7 177 CD85
Glen Way, Wat. WD17 75 BS38
Glenwood, Brox. EN10 49 DZ19
 Dorking RH5 263 CJ138
 Welwyn Garden City AL7 30 DD10
Glenwood Av, NW9 118 CS60
 Rainham RM13 147 FH70
Glenwood Cl, Har. HA1 117 CF57
Glenwood Ct, E18
 off Clarendon Rd 124 EG55
Glenwood Dr, Rom. RM2 127 FG56
Glenwood Gdns, Ilf. IG2 125 EN57
Glenwood Gro, NW9 118 CQ60
Glenwood Rd, N15 121 DP57
 NW7 96 CS48
 SE6 183 DZ88
 Epsom KT17 217 CU107
 Hounslow TW3 157 CD83
Glenwood Way, Croy. CR0 203 DX100
Glenworth Av, E14 24 E8
Glevum Cl, St.Alb. AL3 42 BZ22
Gliddon Dr, E5 122 DV63
Gliddon Rd, W14 16 C8
Glimpsing Grn, Erith DA18 166 EY76
Glisson Rd, Uxb. UB10 134 BN68
Gload Cres, Orp. BR5 206 EX103
Global App, E3
 off Hancock Rd 143 EB68
Globe Ct, Hert. SG14
 off Grove Wk 32 DQ07
Globe Ind Estates, Grays
 RM17 170 GC78
Globe Pond Rd, SE16 23 J2
Sch Globe Prim Sch, E2 12 F1
Globe Rd, E1 12 F1
 E2 142 DW69
 E15 124 EF64
 Hornchurch RM11 127 FG58
 Woodford Green IG8 102 EJ51
Globe Rope Wk, E14 24 C8
Globe St, SE1 21 H5
Globe Ter, E2 12 E1
Globe Yd, W1 8 G8
Glory Cl, H.Wyc. (Woob.Grn)
 HP10 110 AF56
Glory Hill La, Beac. HP9 110 AF55
Glory Mead, Dor. RH4 263 CH139
Glory Mill La, H.Wyc.
 (Woob.Grn) HP10 110 AE56
Glossop Rd, S.Croy. CR2 220 DR109
Gloster Rd, N.Mal. KT3 198 CS98
 Woking GU22 227 BA120
Gloucester Arc, SW7 17 L7
Gloucester Av, NW1 140 DG66
 Grays RM16 170 GC75
 Hornchurch RM11 128 FN56
 Sidcup DA15 185 ES89
 Slough SL1 131 AQ71
 Waltham Cross EN8 67 DY33
 Welling DA16 165 ET84
Gloucester Circ, SE10 163 EC80
Gloucester Cl, NW10 138 CR66
 Thames Ditton KT7 197 CG102
Gloucester Ct, EC3 11 M10
 Richmond TW9 158 CN80
 Tilbury RM18 off Dock Rd 171 GF82
 Uxbridge (Denh.) UB9
 off Moorfield Rd 114 BG58
Gloucester Cres, NW1 141 DH67
 Staines TW18 174 BK93
Gloucester Dr, N4 121 DP61
 NW11 120 DA56
 Staines TW18 173 BC90
Gloucester Gdns, NW11 119 CZ59
 W2 7 K7
 Barnet EN4 80 DG42
 Ilford IG1 124 EL59
 Sutton SM1 200 DB103
Gloucester Gate, NW1 141 DH68

★ Place of interest | H Hospital | Sch School | Coll College | Uni University | ≠ Railway station

Gloucester Gate Ms, NW1 off Gloucester Gate 141 DH68
Gloucester Gro, Edg. HA8 96 CR53
Gloucester Gro Est, SE15 162 DS79
Gloucester Ho, NW6 140 DA68
Gloucester Ms, E10 off Gloucester Rd 123 EA59
W2 7 M8
Gloucester Ms W, W2 7 L8
Gloucester Par, Sid. DA15 186 EU85
Gloucester Pk, SW7 17 L7
Gloucester Pl, NW1 8 C3
W1 8 D5
Windsor SL4 151 AR82
Gloucester Pl Ms, W1 8 D6
Sch Gloucester Prim Sch, SE15 off Daniel Gdns 162 DT80
⊖ Gloucester Road 17 M7
Gloucester Rd, E10 123 EA59
E11 124 EH57
E12 125 EM62
E17 101 DX54
N17 100 DR54
N18 100 DT50
SW7 17 L5
W3 158 CQ75
W5 157 CJ75
Barnet EN5 80 DC43
Belvedere DA17 166 EZ78
Brentwood (Pilg.Hat.) CM15 108 FV43
Croydon CR0 202 DR100
Dartford DA1 187 FH87
Enfield EN2 82 DQ38
Feltham TW13 176 BW88
Gravesend DA12 191 GJ91
Guildford GU2 242 AT132
Hampton TW12 176 CB94
Harrow HA1 116 CB57
Hounslow TW4 156 BY84
Kingston upon Thames KT1 198 CP96
Redhill RH1 250 DF133
Richmond TW9 158 CN80
Romford RM1 127 FE58
Teddington TW11 177 CE92
Twickenham TW2 176 CC88
Gloucester Sq, E2 off Whiston Rd 142 DU67
W2 7 P8
Woking GU21 off Church St E 226 AY117
Gloucester St, SW1 19 J10
Gloucester Ter, W2 7 L7
Gloucester Wk, W8 17 H3
Woking GU21 227 AZ117
Gloucester Way, EC1 10 D2
Glover Cl, SE2 166 EW77
Waltham Cross EN7 off Allwood Rd 66 DT27
Glover Dr, N18 100 DW51
Glover Rd, Pnr. HA5 116 BX58
Glovers Cl, Hert. SG13 32 DQ11
Westerham TN16 off Norheads La 238 EH116
Glovers Gro, Ruis. HA4 115 BP59
Glovers La, Harl. CM17 52 EY20
Glovers Rd, Reig. RH2 266 DB135
Gloxinia Rd, Grav. (Sthflt) DA13 190 GB93
Gloxinia Wk, Hmptn. TW12 176 CA93
Glycena Rd, SW11 160 DF83
Glyn Av, Barn. EN4 80 DD42
Glyn Cl, SE25 202 DS96
Epsom KT17 217 CU109
Glyn Ct, SW16 181 DN90
Stanmore HA7 95 CH51
Glyn Davies Cl, Sev. (Dunt.Grn) TN13 241 FE120
Glyndebourne Pk, Orp. BR6 205 EP103
Glynde Ms, SW3 18 B6
Glynde Rd, Bexh. DA7 166 EX83
Glynde St, SE4 183 DZ86
Glyndon Rd, SE18 165 EQ77
Glyn Dr, Sid. DA14 186 EV91
Glynfield Rd, NW10 138 CS66
Glynne Rd, N22 99 DN54
Glyn Rd, E5 123 DX62
Enfield EN3 82 DW42
Worcester Park KT4 199 CX103
Glyn St, SE11 20 A10
Glynswood, Ger.Cr. (Chal.St.P.) SL9 91 AZ52
Sch Glyn Tech Sch, Epsom KT17 off The Kingsway 217 CT111
Glynwood Ct, SE23 182 DW89
Goaters All, SW6 159 CZ80
GOATHURST COMMON, Sev. TN14 256 FB130
Goat La, Enf. EN1 82 DT38
Surbiton KT6 197 CJ103
Goat Rd, Mitch. CR4 200 DG101
Goatsfield Rd, West. (Tats.) TN16 238 EJ120
Goatswood La, Rom. (Nave.) RM4 105 FH45
Goat Wf, Brent. TW8 158 CL79
Gobions Av, Rom. RM5 105 FD52
Sch Gobions Prim Sch, Rom. RM1 off Havering Rd 105 FD51
Gobions Way, Pot.B. EN6 off Swanley Bar La 64 DB28
Goblins Grn, Welw.G.C. AL7 29 CX10
Godalming Av, Wall. SM6 219 DL106
Godalming Rd, E14 14 A6
Godbold Rd, E15 15 H2
Goddard Cl, Guil. GU2 off Tylehost 242 AU130
Shepperton TW17 off Magdalene Rd 194 BM97
Goddard Pl, N19 121 DJ62
Goddard Rd, Beck. BR3 203 DX98
Goddards Cl, Hert. SG13 47 DJ19
Goddards Way, Ilf. IG1 125 ER60
GODDEN GREEN, Sev. TN15 257 FN125
H Godden Grn Clinic, Sev. (Godden Grn) TN15 257 FP125
GODDINGTON, Orp. BR6 206 EW104
Goddington Chase, Orp. BR6 224 EV105
Goddington La, Orp. BR6 206 EU104
Godfrey Av, Nthlt. UB5 136 BY67
Twickenham TW2 177 CD87
Godfrey Hill, SE18 164 EL77
Godfrey Rd, SE18 165 EM77
Godfrey St, E15 143 EC68
SW3 18 B9
Godfrey Way, Houns. TW4 176 BY87
Goding St, SE11 19 P10
Godley Cl, SE14 off Kender St 162 DW81
Godley Rd, SW18 180 DD88
West Byfleet (Byfleet) KT14 212 BM113
Godliman St, EC4 10 G8
Godman Rd, SE15 162 DV82
Grays RM16 171 GG76
Sch Godolphin & Latymer Sch, The, W6 off Iffley Rd 159 CV77
Godolphin Cl, N13 99 DP51
Sutton SM2 217 CZ111
Sch Godolphin Inf Sch, Slou. SL1 off Warrington Av 131 AQ72
Sch Godolphin Jun Sch, Slou. SL1 off Oatlands Dr 131 AR72
Godolphin Pl, W3 off Vyner Rd 138 CR73
Godolphin Rd, W12 159 CV75
Beaconsfield (Seer Grn) HP9 89 AQ51
Slough SL1 131 AR73
Weybridge KT13 213 BR107
Godric Cres, Croy. (New Adgtn) CR0 221 ED110
Godson Rd, Croy. CR0 201 DN104
Godson St, N1 4 C9
GODSTONE, RH9 252 DV131
Godstone Bypass, Gdse. RH9 252 DW129
Godstone Grn, Gdse. RH9 252 DV131
Godstone Grn Rd, Gdse. RH9 252 DV131
Godstone Hill, Gdse. RH9 252 DV127
Godstone Rd, Cat. CR3 236 DU124
Kenley CR8 236 DR115
Oxted RH8 253 EA131
Purley CR8 219 DN112
Redhill (Bletch.) RH1 252 DR133
Sutton SM1 218 DC105
Twickenham TW1 177 CG86
Whyteleafe CR3 236 DT116
Sch Godstone Village Sch, Gdse. RH9 off Ivy Mill La 252 DV132
Godstow Rd, SE2 166 EW75
Godwin Cl, E4 83 EC38
N1 5 H9
Epsom KT19 216 CQ107
Godwin Ct, NW1 off Crowndale Rd 141 DJ68
Sch Godwin Inf & Jun Sch, Dag. RM9 off Hatfield Rd 146 EY66
Sch Godwin Jun Sch, E7 off Cranmer Rd 124 EH63
Godwin Rd, E7 124 EH63
Bromley BR2 204 EJ97
Coll Goethe Inst, SW7 17 P5
Goffers Rd, SE3 163 ED81
Goffs Cres, Wal.Cr. (Chsht) EN7 65 DP29
Goffs La, Wal.Cr. (Chsht) EN7 66 DU29
GOFFS OAK, Wal.Cr. EN7 66 DQ29
Goffs Oak Av, Wal.Cr. (Chsht) EN7 65 DP28
Sch Goffs Oak Prim Sch, Wal.Cr. EN7 off Millcrest Rd 65 DP28
Goffs Rd, Ashf. TW15 175 BR93
Sch Goffs Sch, Wal.Cr. EN7 off Goffs La 66 DU29
Gogmore Fm Cl, Cher. KT16 193 BF101
Gogmore La, Cher. KT16 194 BG101
Goidel Cl, Wall. SM6 219 DK105
Golborne Gdns, W10 6 D4
Golborne Ms, W10 6 C6
Golborne Rd, W10 6 D6
Goldace, Grays RM17 170 FZ79
Golda Cl, Barn. EN5 79 CX44
Goldbeaters Gro, Edg. HA8 96 CS51
Sch Goldbeaters JMI Sch, Edg. HA8 off Thirleby Rd 96 CR53
Goldcliff Cl, Mord. SM4 200 DA100
Gold Cl, Brox. EN10 49 DY20
Goldcrest Cl, E16 off Sheerwater Rd 144 EK71
SE28 146 EW73
Horley RH6 off Wither Dale 268 DE147
Goldcrest Ms, W5 off Montpelier Av 137 CK71
Goldcrest Way, Bushey WD23 94 CC46
Croydon (New Adgtn) CR0 221 ED109
Purley CR8 219 DK110
Goldcroft, Hem.H. HP3 40 BN22
Golden Ct, Rich. TW9 off George St 177 CK85
Golden Cres, Hayes UB3 135 BT74
Golden Cross Ms, W11 6 E7
Golden Dell, Welw.G.C. AL7 29 CZ13
★ Golden Hinde, SE1 21 J1
Golden Jubilee Br, SE1 20 A2
WC2 20 A1
Golden La, EC1 10 G4
Golden La Est, EC1 10 G4
Golden Manor, W7 137 CE73
Golden Oak Cl, Slou. (Farn.Com.) SL2 131 AQ65
Golden Plover Cl, E16 15 N7
Golden Sq, W1 9 K9
Golden Yd, NW3 off Heath St 120 DC63
Golders Cl, Edg. HA8 96 CP50
Golders Gdns, NW11 119 CY59
GOLDERS GREEN, NW11 120 DA59
⊖ Golders Green 120 DA59
Golders Grn Cres, NW11 119 CZ59
Golders Grn Rd, NW11 119 CY58
Sch Golders Hill Sch, NW11 off Finchley Rd 120 DA59
Golders Manor Dr, NW11 119 CX58
Golders Pk Cl, NW11 120 DB60
Golders Ri, NW4 119 CX57
Golders Way, NW11 119 CZ59
Goldfinch Cl, Orp. BR6 224 EU106
Goldfinch Gdns, Guil. GU4 243 BD133
Goldfinch Rd, SE28 165 ER76
South Croydon CR2 221 DY110
Goldfinch Way, Borwd. WD6 78 CN42
Goldfort Wk, Wok. GU21 off Langmans Way 226 AS116
Goldhawk Ms, W12 off Devonport Rd 159 CV75
⊖ Goldhawk Road 159 CW75
Goldhawk Rd, W6 159 CT77
W12 159 CU76
Goldhaze Cl, Wdf.Grn. IG8 102 EK52
Gold Hill, Edg. HA8 96 CR51
Gold Hill E, Ger.Cr. (Chal.St.P.) SL9 90 AX54
Gold Hill N, Ger.Cr. (Chal.St.P.) SL9 90 AW53
Gold Hill W, Ger.Cr. (Chal.St.P.) SL9 90 AW53
Goldhurst Ter, NW6 140 DB66
H Goldie Leigh Hosp, SE2 166 EW79
Golding Cl, Chess. KT9 off Coppard Gdns 215 CJ107
Goldingham Av, Loug. IG10 85 EQ40
Golding Rd, Sev. TN13 257 FJ122
Goldings, The, Wok. GU21 226 AT116
Goldings Cres, Hat. AL10 45 CV17
Goldings Hill, Loug. IG10 85 EN39
Goldings La, Hert. (Waterf.) SG14 31 DN06
Goldings Ri, Loug. IG10 85 EN39
Goldings Rd, Loug. IG10 85 EN39
Golding St, E1 12 B8
Golding Ter, SW11 off Longhedge St 160 DG82
Goldington Cl, Hodd. EN11 33 DZ14
Goldington Cres, NW1 141 DK68
Goldington St, NW1 141 DK68
Gold La, Edg. HA8 96 CR51
Goldman Cl, E2 12 A3
Goldmark Ho, SE3 off Lebrun Sq 164 EH83
Goldney Rd, W9 6 G4
Goldrill Dr, N11 98 DG47
Goldrings Rd, Lthd. (Oxshott) KT22 214 CC113
Goldring Way, St.Alb. (Lon.Col.) AL2 61 CG27
Goldsboro Rd, SW8 161 DK81
Goldsborough Cres, E4 101 EC47
H Goldsborough Indep Hosp, Red. RH1 266 DG138
Goldsdown Cl, Enf. EN3 83 DY40
Goldsdown Rd, Enf. EN3 83 DX40
Goldsel Rd, Swan. BR8 207 FD99
Goldsmid St, SE18 off Sladedale Rd 165 ES78
Goldsmith, Grays RM17 170 FZ79
Goldsmith Av, E12 144 EL65
NW9 119 CT58
W3 138 CR73
Romford RM7 126 FA59
Goldsmith Cl, W3 off East Acton La 138 CS74
Harrow HA2 116 CB60
Goldsmith La, NW9 118 CP56
Goldsmith Rd, E10 123 EA60
E17 101 DX54
N11 98 DF50
SE15 162 DU81
W3 138 CR74
Goldsmiths Bottom, Sev. TN14 256 FE127
Goldsmiths Cl, Wok. GU21 226 AW118
Uni Goldsmiths Coll, SE14 off Lewisham Way 163 DY81
★ Goldsmiths' Hall, EC2 11 H7
Goldsmith's Row, E2 142 DU68
Goldsmith's Sq, E2 142 DU68
Goldsmith St, EC2 11 H7
Goldsmith Way, St.Alb. AL3 42 CC19
Goldstone Cl, Ware SG12 off High Oak Rd 33 DX05
Goldstone Fm Vw, Lthd. KT23 246 CA127
Goldsworth Orchard, Wok. GU21 off St. John's Rd 226 AU118
GOLDSWORTH PARK, Wok. GU21 226 AU117
Goldsworth Pk Trd Est, Wok. GU21 226 AV116
Sch Goldsworth Prim Sch, Wok. GU21 off Bridge Barn La 226 AW118
Goldsworth Rd, Wok. GU21 226 AW118
Goldsworthy Gdns, SE16 22 F8
Goldsworthy Way, Slou. SL1 130 AJ72
Goldwell Rd, Th.Hth. CR7 201 DM98
Goldwin Cl, SE14 162 DW81
Goldwing Cl, E16 15 M8
Golf Cl, Bushey WD23 76 BX41
Stanmore HA7 95 CJ52
Thornton Heath CR7 off Kensington Av 201 DN95
Woking GU22 211 BE114
Golf Club Dr, Kings.T. KT2 178 CR94
Golf Club Rd, Hat. AL9 64 DA26
Weybridge KT13 213 BP109
Woking GU22 226 AU120
Golfe Rd, Ilf. IG1 125 ER62
Golf Ho Rd, Oxt. RH8 254 EJ129
Golf Links Av, Grav. DA11 191 GH92
Golf Ride, Enf. EN2 81 DN35
Golf Rd, W5 off Boileau Rd 138 CM72
Bromley BR1 205 EN97
Kenley CR8 236 DR118
Golf Side, Sutt. SM2 217 CY111
Twickenham TW2 177 CD90
Golfside Cl, N20 98 DE48
New Malden KT3 198 CS96
Goliath Cl, Wall. SM6 219 DL108
Gollogly Ter, SE7 164 EJ78
Gombards, St.Alb. AL3 43 CD19
Gombards All, St.Alb. AL3 off Worley Rd 43 CD19
Gomer Gdns, Tedd. TW11 177 CG93
Gomer Pl, Tedd. TW11 177 CG93
Gomm Rd, SE16 22 E6
Gomms Wd Cl, Beac. (Forty Grn) HP9 88 AH51
GOMSHALL, Guil. GU5 261 BR139
≠ Gomshall 261 BR139
Gomshall Av, Wall. SM6 219 DL106
Gomshall Gdns, Ken. CR8 236 DS115
Gomshall La, Guil. (Shere) GU5 260 BN139
Gomshall Rd, Guil. (Goms.) GU5 261 BP138
Sutton SM2 217 CW110
Gondar Gdns, NW6 119 CZ64
Gonnerston, St.Alb. AL3 off Kings Rd 42 CB19
Gonson St, SE8 163 EB79
Gonston Cl, SW19 179 CY89
Gonville Av, Rick. (Crox.Grn) WD3 75 BP44
Gonville Cres, Nthlt. UB5 136 CB65
Sch Gonville Prim Sch, Th.Hth. CR7 off Gonville Rd 201 DM99
Gonville Rd, Th.Hth. CR7 201 DM99
Gonville St, SW6 off Putney Br App 159 CY83
Gooch Ho, E5 122 DV62
Goodall Rd, E11 123 EC62
Gooden Ct, Har. HA1 117 CE62
Goodenough Cl, Couls. CR5 235 DN120
Goodenough Rd, SW19 179 CZ94
Goodenough Way, Couls. CR5 235 DM120
Gooderham Ho, Grays RM16 171 GH75
Goodey Rd, Bark. IG11 145 ET66
Goodge Pl, W1 9 K6
⊖ Goodge Street 9 K5
Goodge St, W1 9 K6
Goodhall Cl, Stan. HA7 95 CH51
Goodhall St, NW10 138 CS69
Goodhart Pl, E14 13 K9
Goodhart Way, W.Wick. BR4 204 EE101
Goodhew Rd, Croy. CR0 202 DU100
Gooding Cl, N.Mal. KT3 198 CQ98
Goodinge Cl, N7 141 DL65
Goodlake Ct, Uxb. (Denh.) UB9 113 BF59
GOODLEY STOCK, West. TN16 255 EP130
Goodley Stock, West. TN16 255 EP129
Goodley Stock Rd, Eden. (Crock.H.) TN8 255 EP131
Westerham TN16 255 EP128
Goodman Cres, SW2 181 DK89
Goodman Pk, Slou. SL2 132 AW74
Goodman Pl, Stai. TW18 173 BF91
Goodman Rd, E10 123 EC59
Goodmans Ct, E1 11 N9
Wembley HA0 117 CK63
Goodman's Stile, E1 12 A8
Goodmans Yd, E1 11 N9
GOODMAYES, Ilf. IG3 126 EV61
≠ Goodmayes 126 EU60
Goodmayes Av, Ilf. IG3 126 EU60
H Goodmayes Hosp, Ilf. IG3 126 EU57
Goodmayes La, Ilf. IG3 126 EU63
Sch Goodmayes Prim Sch, Ilf. IG3 off Airthrie Rd 126 EV60
Goodmayes Rd, Ilf. IG3 126 EU60
Goodmead Rd, Orp. BR6 206 EU101
Goodrich Cl, Wat. WD25 75 BU35
Sch Goodrich Prim Sch, SE22 off Dunstans Rd 182 DU86
Goodrich Rd, SE22 182 DT86
Sch Good Shepherd RC Prim Sch, Brom. BR1 off Moorside Rd 184 EF91
Croydon CR0 off Dunley Dr 221 EB108
Goodson Rd, NW10 138 CS66
Goods Way, NW1 141 DL68
Goodway Gdns, E14 14 E7
Goodwin Cl, SE16 21 P6
Mitcham CR4 200 DD97
Goodwin Ct, Barn. EN4 80 DE44
Waltham Cross EN8 67 DY28
Goodwin Dr, Sid. DA14 186 EX90
Goodwin Gdns, Croy. CR0 219 DP107
Goodwin Meadows, H.Wyc. (Woob.Grn) HP10 110 AE57
Goodwin Rd, N9 100 DW46
W12 159 CU75
Croydon CR0 219 DP106
Slough SL2 131 AM69
Goodwins Ct, WC2 9 N9
Goodwin St, N4 off Fonthill Rd 121 DN61
Goodwood Av, Brwd. (Hutt.) CM13 109 GE44
Enfield EN3 82 DW37
Hornchurch RM12 128 FL63
Watford WD24 75 BS35
Goodwood Cl, Hodd. EN11 49 DZ16
Morden SM4 200 DA98
Stanmore HA7 95 CJ50
Goodwood Cres, Grav. DA12 191 GJ93
Goodwood Dr, Nthlt. UB5 136 CA65
Goodwood Path, Borwd. WD6 off Stratfield Rd 78 CN41
Goodwood Rd, SE14 163 DY80
Redhill RH1 250 DF132
Goodwyn Av, NW7 96 CS50
Sch Goodwyn Sch, NW7 off Hammers La 97 CU50
Goodwyns Rd, Dor. RH4 263 CH139
Goodwyns Vale, N10 98 DG53
Goodyers Av, Rad. WD7 61 CF33
Goodyers Gdns, NW4 119 CX57
Goosander Way, SE28 165 ER76
Goose Acre, Chesh. HP5 54 AT30
Gooseacre, Welw.G.C. AL7 29 CZ11
Gooseacre La, Har. HA3 117 CK57
Goosecroft, Hem.H. HP1 39 BF19
Goosefields, Rick. WD3 74 BJ44
Goose Grn, Cob. KT11 229 BU119
Guildford (Goms.) GU5 261 BQ139
Hoddesdon EN11 off Lord St 49 DY17
Slough (Farn.Royal) SL2 131 AP68
Goose Grn Cl, Orp. BR5 206 EU96
Sch Goose Grn Prim Sch, SE22 off Tintagel Cres 162 DT84
Goose La, Wok. GU22 226 AV122
Gooseley La, E6 145 EN69
Goosens Cl, Sutt. SM1 off Turnpike La 218 DC106
Goose Rye Rd, Guil. (Worp.) GU3 242 AT125
Goose Sq, E6 off Harper Rd 145 EM72
Gooshays Dr, Rom. RM3 106 FL50
Gooshays Gdns, Rom. RM3 106 FL51
Gophir La, EC4 11 J9
Gopsall St, N1 5 K8
Goral Mead, Rick. WD3 92 BK46
Gordon Av, E4 102 EE51
SW14 158 CS84
Hornchurch RM12 127 FF61
South Croydon CR2 220 DQ110
Stanmore HA7 95 CH51
Twickenham TW1 177 CG85
Sch Gordonbrock Prim Sch, SE4 off Gordonbrock Rd 183 EA85
Gordonbrock Rd, SE4 183 EA85
Gordon Cl, E17 123 EA58
N19 off Highgate Hill 121 DJ60
Chertsey KT16 193 BE104
St. Albans AL1 off Kitchener Cl 43 CH21
Staines TW18 174 BH93
Gordon Ct, W12 139 CW72
Gordon Cres, Croy. CR0 202 DS102
Hayes UB3 155 BU76
Gordondale Rd, SW19 180 DA89
Gordon Dr, Cher. KT16 193 BE104
Shepperton TW17 195 BR100
Gordon Gdns, Edg. HA8 96 CP54
Gordon Gro, SE5 161 DP82
≠ Gordon Hill 81 DP39
Gordon Hill, Enf. EN2 82 DQ39
H Gordon Hosp, SW1 19 L8
Gordon Ho, E1 12 E9
Gordon Ho Rd, NW5 120 DG63
Sch Gordon Inf Sch, Ilf. IG1 off Golfe Rd 125 ER62
Gordon Pl, W8 17 H3
Gravesend DA12 off East Ter 191 GJ86
Sch Gordon Prim Sch, SE9 off Earlshall Rd 165 EM84
Gordon Prom, Grav. DA12 191 GJ86
Gordon Prom E, Grav. DA12 191 GJ86
Gordon Rd, E4 102 EE45
E11 124 EG58
E15 123 EC63
E18 102 EH53
Gordon Rd, N3 97 CZ52
N9 100 DV47
N11 99 DK52
SE15 162 DV82
W4 158 CP79
W5 137 CJ73
W13 137 CH73
Ashford TW15 174 BL90
Barking IG11 145 ES67
Beckenham BR3 203 DZ97
Belvedere DA17 167 FC77
Brentwood (Shenf.) CM15 109 GA46
Carshalton SM5 218 DF107
Caterham CR3 236 DR121
Chesham HP5 54 AQ32
Dartford DA1 188 FK87
Enfield EN2 82 DQ39
Esher (Clay.) KT10 215 CE107
Gravesend (Nthflt) DA11 190 GE87
Grays RM16 171 GF75
Harrow HA3 117 CE55
Hounslow TW3 156 CC84
Ilford IG1 125 ER62
Kingston upon Thames KT2 198 CM95
Redhill RH1 250 DG131
Richmond TW9 158 CM82
Romford RM6 126 EZ58
Sevenoaks TN13 257 FH125
Shepperton TW17 195 BR100
Sidcup DA15 185 ES85
Southall UB2 156 BY77
Staines TW18 173 BC91
Surbiton KT5 198 CM101
Waltham Abbey EN9 67 EA34
West Drayton UB7 134 BL73
Windsor SL4 151 AM82
Gordon Sq, WC1 9 M4
Gordon St, E13 15 M2
WC1 9 L3
Gordons Way, Oxt. RH8 253 ED128
Gordon Way, Barn. EN5 79 CZ42
Bromley BR1 204 EG95
Chalfont St. Giles HP8 90 AV48
Gore, The, Slou. (Burn.) SL1 130 AG69
Gore Cl, Uxb. (Hare.) UB9 114 BH56
Gore Ct, NW9 118 CN57
Gorefield Pl, NW6 140 DA68
Gore Hill, Amer. HP7 55 AP43
Gorelands La, Ch.St.G. HP8 91 AZ47
Gorell Rd, Beac. HP9 89 AP54
Gore Rd, E9 142 DW67
SW20 199 CW96
Dartford DA2 188 FQ90
Slough (Burn.) SL1 130 AH69
Goresbrook Rd, Dag. RM9 146 EV67
Goresbrook Village, Dag. RM9 off Goresbrook Rd 146 EV67
Gore St, SW7 17 M5
★ Gorhambury, St.Alb. AL3 42 BW19
Gorhambury Dr, St.Alb. AL3 42 BW19
Gorham Dr, St.Alb. AL1 43 CE23
Gorham Pl, W11 6 C10
Goring Cl, Rom. RM5 105 FC53
Goring Gdns, Dag. RM8 126 EW63
Goring Rd, N11 99 DL51
Dagenham RM10 147 FD65
Staines TW18 173 BD92
Gorings Sq, Stai. TW18 173 BE91
Goring St, EC3 11 M7
Goring Way, Grnf. UB6 136 CC68
Gorle Cl, Wat. WD25 59 BU34
Gorleston Rd, N15 122 DR57
Gorleston St, W14 16 D7
Gorman Rd, SE18 165 EM77
Gorringe Av, Dart. (S.Darenth) DA4 209 FR96
Gorringe Pk Av, Mitch. CR4 180 DF94
Sch Gorringe Pk Prim Sch, Mitch. CR4 off Sandy La 200 DG95
Gorse Cl, E16 15 L8
Hatfield AL10 45 CT21
Tadworth KT20 233 CV120
Gorse Ct, Guil. GU4 off Kingfisher Dr 243 BC132
Gorse Hill, Dart. (Fnghm) DA4 208 FL100
Gorse Hill La, Vir.W. GU25 192 AX98
Gorse Hill Rd, Vir.W. GU25 192 AX98
Gorselands Cl, W.Byf. KT14 212 BJ111
Gorse La, Wok. (Chobham) GU24 210 AS108
Gorse Meade, Slou. SL1 131 AP74
Gorse Ri, SW17 180 DG92
Gorse Rd, Croy. CR0 221 EA105
Orpington BR5 206 FA103
Gorse Wk, West Dr. UB7 134 BL72
Gorseway, Rom. RM7 127 FD61
Gorst Rd, NW10 138 CQ70
SW11 180 DF86
Gorsuch Pl, E2 11 N1
Gorsuch St, E2 11 N1
Gosberton Rd, SW12 180 DG88
Gosbury Hill, Chess. KT9 216 CL105
Gosden Cl, Guil. (Bramley) GU5 258 AY143
Gosden Common, Guil. (Bramley) GU5 258 AY143
Gosden Hill Rd, Guil. GU4 243 BC130
Sch Gosden Ho Sch, Guil. GU5 off Gosden Common 258 AY143
Gosfield Rd, Dag. RM8 126 FA61
Epsom KT19 216 CR112
Gosfield St, W1 9 J5
Gosford Gdns, Ilf. IG4 125 EM57
Gosforth La, Wat. WD19 94 BW48
Gosforth Path, Wat. WD19 93 BU48
Goshawk Gdns, Hayes UB4 135 BS69
Goslar Way, Wind. SL4 151 AP82
Goslett Ct, Bushey WD23 off Bournehall Av 76 CA43
Goslett Yd, WC2 9 M8
Gosling Cl, Grnf. UB6 136 CA69
Gosling Grn, Slou. SL3 152 AY76
Gosling Rd, Slou. SL3 152 AY76
Gosling Way, SW9 161 DN81
Gospatrick Rd, N17 100 DQ52
GOSPEL OAK, NW5 120 DG63
≠ Gospel Oak 120 DG63
Gospel Oak Est, NW5 120 DF64
Sch Gospel Oak Jun & Inf Sch, NW3 off Mansfield Rd 120 DG63
Gosport Dr, Horn. RM12 148 FJ65
Gosport Rd, E17 123 DZ57
Gosport Wk, N17 off Yarmouth Cres 122 DV57

⊖ London Underground station   DLR Docklands Light Railway station   Tra Tramlink station   Riv Pedestrian ferry landing stage

Gosport Way, SE15
off Blakes Rd 162 DT80
Gossage Rd, SE18
off Ancona Rd 165 ER78
Uxbridge UB10 ....134 BM66
Gossamers, The, Wat. WD25 . .76 BY36
Gosselin Rd, Hert. SG14 ....32 DQ07
Gosset St, E2 ....11 P1
Goss Hill, Dart. DA2 ....188 FJ93
Swanley BR8 ....188 FJ93
Gosshill Rd, Chis. BR7 .....205 EN96
Gossington Cl, Chis. BR7
off Beechwood Ri 185 EP91
Gossoms End, Berk. HP4 ....38 AU18
Gossoms Ryde, Berk. HP4 ...38 AU18
Gosterwood St, SE8 ....163 DY79
Gostling Rd, Twick. TW2 ....176 CA88
Goston Gdns, Th.Hth. CR7 ..201 DN97
Goswell Hill, Wind. SL4 .....151 AR81
Goswell Rd, EC1 ....10 G4
Windsor SL4 ....151 AR81
Gothic Cl, Dart. DA1 ....188 FK90
Gothic Ct, Hayes UB3
off Sipson La 155 BR79
Gothic Rd, Twick. TW2 ......177 CD89
Gottfried Ms, NW5
off Fortess Rd 121 DJ63
Goudhurst Rd, Brom. BR1 ..184 EE92
Gouge Av, Grav. (Nthflt)
DA11 ....190 GE88
Gough Rd, E15 ....124 EF63
Enfield EN1 ....82 DV40
Gough Sq, EC4 ....10 D7
Gough St, WC1 ....10 B3
Gough Wk, E14 ....13 N8
Gould Cl, Hat. AL9 ....45 CV24
Gould Ct, SE19 ....182 DT92
Guildford GU4
off Eustace Rd 243 BD132
Goulden Ho App, SW11 ....160 DE82
Goulding Gdns, Th.Hth. CR7 .201 DP96
Gould Rd, Felt. TW14 ....175 BS87
Twickenham TW2 ....177 CE88
Goulds Grn, Uxb. UB8 ......135 BP72
Gould Ter, E8
off Kenmure Rd 122 DV64
Goulston St, E1 ....11 N7
Goulton Rd, E5 ....122 DV63
Gourley Pl, N15
off Gourley St 122 DS57
Gourley St, N15 ....122 DS57
Gourock Rd, SE9 ....185 EN85
Govan St, E2
off Whiston Rd 142 DU67
Government Row, Enf. EN3 . .83 EA38
Governors Av, Uxb. (Denh.)
UB9 ....113 BF57
Governors Cl, Amer. HP6 ....72 AT37
Govett Av, Shep. TW17 .....195 BQ99
Govier Cl, E15 ....144 EE66
Gowan Av, SW6 ....159 CY81
Gowan Rd, NW10 ....139 CV65
Gowar Fld, Pot.B. EN6 ....63 CU32
Gower, The, Egh. TW20 .....193 BB97
Gower Cl, SW4 ....181 DJ86
Gower Ct, WC1 ....9 L3
Sch **Gower Ho Sch**, NW9
off Blackbird Hill 118 CQ61
Gower Ms, WC1 ....9 L6
Gower Pl, WC1 ....9 K3
Gower Rd, E7 ....144 EG65
Horley RH6 ....268 DE148
Isleworth TW7 ....157 CF79
Weybridge KT13 ....213 BR107
Gowers, The, Amer. HP6 ....55 AS36
Harlow CM20 ....36 EU13
Gowers La, Grays (Orsett)
RM16 ....171 GF75
Gower St, WC1 ....9 K3
Gower's Wk, E1 ....12 A7
Gowings Grn, Slou. SL1 ....151 AL75
Gowland Pl, Beck. BR3 .....203 DZ96
Gowlett Rd, SE15 ....162 DU83
Gowlland Cl, Croy. CR0 ....202 DU101
Gowrie Pl, Cat. CR3 ....236 DQ122
Gowrie Rd, SW11 ....160 DG83
Graburn Way, E.Mol. KT8 ...197 CD97
Grace Av, Bexh. DA7 ....166 EZ82
Radlett (Shenley) WD7 ....61 CK33
Grace Business Cen, Mitch.
CR4 ....200 DF99
Gracechurch St, EC3 ....11 K9
Grace Cl, SE9 ....184 EK90
Borehamwood WD6 ....78 CR39
Edgware HA8
off Pavilion Way 96 CQ52
Ilford IG6 ....103 ET51
Grace Ct, Slou. SL1 ....131 AQ74
Gracedale Rd, SW16 ....181 DH92
Gracefield Gdns, SW16 .....181 DL90
Grace Jones Cl, E8
off Parkholme Rd 142 DU65
Grace Path, SE26 ....182 DW91
Grace Pl, E3 ....14 B2
Grace Rd, Croy. CR0 ....202 DQ100
Grace's All, E1 ....12 A9
Graces Ms, SE5 ....162 DS82
Graces Rd, SE5 ....162 DS82
Grace St, E3 ....14 B2
Gracious La, Sev. TN13 ....256 FG130
Gracious La End, Sev. TN14 .256 FF130
Gracious Pond Rd, Wok.
(Chobham) GU24 ....210 AT108
Gradient, The, SE26 ....182 DU91
Graduate Pl, SE1
off Long La 162 DS76
Graeme Rd, Enf. EN1 ....82 DR40
Graemesdyke Av, SW14 ....158 CP83
Graemesdyke Rd, Berk. HP4 ..38 AU20
Grafton Cl, W13 ....137 CG72
Hounslow TW4 ....176 BY88
St. Albans AL4
off Princess Diana Dr 43 CK21
Slough (Geo.Grn) SL3 ....132 AY72
West Byfleet KT14
off Madeira Rd 211 BF113
Worcester Park KT4 .....198 CS104
Grafton Ct, Felt. TW14 ......175 BR88
Grafton Cres, NW1 ....141 DH65
Grafton Gdns, N4 ....122 DQ58
Dagenham RM8 ....126 EY61
Grafton Ho, E3 ....13 N2
Sch **Grafton Inf Sch**, Dag.
RM8 off Grafton Rd 126 EZ61
Sch **Grafton Jun Sch**, Dag.
RM8 off Grafton Rd 126 EZ61
Grafton Ms, W1 ....9 J4
Grafton Pk Rd, Wor.Pk. KT4 .198 CS103
Grafton Pl, NW1 ....9 L2
Sch **Grafton Prim Sch**, N7
off Eburne Rd 121 DL62
Grafton Rd, NW5 ....120 DG64
W3 ....138 CQ73
Croydon CR0 ....201 DN102
Dagenham RM8 ....126 EY61
Enfield EN2 ....81 DM41
Harrow HA1 ....116 CC57
New Malden KT3 ....198 CS97
Worcester Park KT4 .....198 CR104
Graftons, The, NW2
off Hermitage La 120 DA62
Grafton Sq, SW4 ....161 DJ83
Grafton St, W1 ....9 H10
Grafton Ter, NW5 ....120 DF64
Grafton Way, W1 ....9 J4
WC1 ....9 J4
West Molesey KT8 ....196 BZ98
Grafton Yd, NW5
off Prince of Wales Rd ..141 DH65
Graham Av, W13 ....157 CH75
Broxbourne EN10 ....49 DY20
Mitcham CR4 ....200 DG95
Graham Cl, Brwd. (Hutt.)
CM13 ....109 GC43
Croydon CR0 ....203 EA103
St. Albans AL1 ....43 CD23
Grahame Pk Est, NW9 ......96 CS53
Grahame Pk Way, NW7 .....97 CT52
NW9 ....97 CT54
Graham Gdns, Surb. KT6 ...198 CL102
Graham Rd, E8 ....142 DT65
E13 ....15 L3
N15 ....121 DP55
NW4 ....119 CV58
SW19 ....179 CZ94
W4 ....158 CR76
Bexleyheath DA6 ....166 FA84
Hampton TW12 ....176 CA91
Harrow HA3 ....117 CE55
Mitcham CR4 ....200 DG95
Purley CR8 ....219 DN113
Graham St, N1 ....4 F10
Graham Ter, SW1 ....18 E8
Grainger Cl, Nthlt. UB5
off Lancaster Rd 116 CC64
Grainger Rd, N22 ....100 DQ53
Isleworth TW7 ....157 CF82
Grainge's Yd, Uxb. UB8
off Cross St 134 BJ66
Gramer Cl, E11
off Norman Rd 123 ED61
Grampian Cl, Hayes UB3 ...155 BR80
Orpington BR6
off Cotswold Ri 205 ET100
Sutton SM2
off Devonshire Rd 218 DC108
Grampian Gdns, NW2 ....119 CY60
Grampian Ho, N9
off Plevna Rd 100 DV47
Grampian Way, Slou. SL3 ...153 BA78
Granard Av, SW15 ....179 CV85
Sch **Granard Prim Sch**,
SW15 off Cortis Rd 179 CV86
Granard Rd, SW12 ....180 DF87
Granaries, The, Wal.Abb. EN9 .68 EE34
Granary, The, Harl. (Roydon)
CM19 ....34 EH14
Ware (Stans.Abb.) SG12 ..33 EC12
Granary Cl, N9 off Turin Rd .100 DW45
Horley RH6 off Waterside .268 DG146
Granary Rd, E1 ....12 C4
Granary Sq, N1
off Liverpool Rd 141 DN65
Granary St, NW1 ....141 DK67
Granby Pk Rd, Wal.Cr.
(Chsht) EN7 ....66 DT28
Granby Pl, SE1 ....20 C4
Granby Rd, SE9 ....165 EM82
Gravesend DA11 ....190 GC86
Granby St, E2 ....11 P3
Granby Ter, NW1 ....141 DJ68
Grand Arc, N12
off Ballards La 98 DC50
Grand Av, EC1 ....10 F5
N10 ....120 DG56
Surbiton KT5 ....198 CP99
Wembley HA9 ....118 CN64
Grand Av E, Wem. HA9 .....118 CP64
Sch **Grand Av Prim Sch**, Surb.
KT5 off Grand Av 198 CQ101
Grand Dep Rd, SE18 ....165 EN78
Grand Dr, SW20 ....199 CW96
Southall UB2 ....156 CC75
Granden Rd, SW16 ....201 DL96
Grandfield Av, Wat. WD17 ....75 BT39
Grandis Cotts, Wok. (Ripley)
GU23 ....228 BH122
Grandison Rd, SW11 ....180 DF85
Worcester Park KT4 .....199 CW103
Grand Junct Wf, N1 ....4 G10
Grand Par Ms, SW15
off Upper Richmond Rd .179 CY85
Grand Stand Rd, Epsom
KT18 ....233 CT117
Grand Union Canal Wk, W7 .157 CE76
Grand Union Cl, W9 ....6 F5
Grand Union Cres, E8 ....142 DU66
Grand Union Ind Est, NW10 .138 CP68
Grand Union Wk, NW1 ......141 DH66
Grand Vw Av, West. (Bigg.H.)
TN16 ....238 EJ117
Grand Wk, E1 ....13 K3
Granfield St, SW11 ....160 DD81
Grange, The, N2
off Central Av 98 DD54
N20 ....98 DC46
SE1 ....21 N5
SW19 ....179 CX93
Croydon CR0 ....203 DZ103
Dartford (S.Darenth) DA4 .209 FR95
Walton-on-Thames KT12 .195 BV103
Wembley HA0 ....138 CN66
Windsor (Old Wind.) SL4 .172 AV85
Woking (Chobham) GU24 .210 AS110
Worcester Park KT4 .....198 CR104
Grange Av, N12 ....98 DC50
N20 ....97 CY45
SE25 ....202 DS96
Barnet EN4 ....98 DE46
Stanmore HA7 ....95 CH54
Twickenham TW2 ....177 CE89
Woodford Green IG8 .....102 EG51
Grangecliffe Gdns, SE25 ...202 DS96
Grange Cl, Brwd. (Ingrave)
CM13 ....109 GC50
Edgware HA8 ....96 CQ50
Gerrards Cross (Chal.St.P.)
SL9 ....90 AY53
Guildford GU2 ....242 AV130
Hayes UB3 ....135 BS71
Hemel Hempstead HP2 ....40 BN21
Hertford SG14 ....31 DP09
Hounslow TW5 ....156 BZ79
Leatherhead KT22 ....231 CK120
Grange Cl, Red. (Bletch.)
RH1 ....252 DR133
Redhill (Merst.) RH1 .....251 DH128
Sidcup DA15 ....186 EU90
Staines (Wrays.) TW19 ...172 AY86
Watford WD17 ....75 BU39
West Molesey KT8 ....196 CB98
Westerham TN16 ....255 EQ126
Woodford Green IG8 .....102 EG52
Sch **Grange Comm Inf Sch**,
The, Add. KT15
off The Avenue 212 BG110
Grange Ct, WC2 ....10 B8
Chigwell IG7 ....103 EQ47
Loughton IG10 ....84 EK43
Northolt UB5 ....136 BW68
Staines TW18 ....174 BG92
Waltham Abbey EN9 ......67 EC34
Walton-on-Thames KT12 .195 BU103
Grangecourt Rd, N16 ....122 DS60
Grange Cres, SE28 ....146 EW72
Chigwell IG7 ....103 ER50
Dartford DA2 ....188 FP86
Grangedale Cl, Nthwd. HA6 ..93 BS53
Grange Dr, Chis. BR7 ....184 EL93
High Wycombe
(Woob.Grn) HP10 ....110 AD60
Orpington BR6
off Rushmore Hill 224 EW109
Redhill (Merst.) RH1
off London Rd S 251 DH128
Woking GU21 ....210 AY114
Grange End, Horl.
(Smallfield) RH6 ....269 DN148
Grange Fm Cl, Har. HA2 ....116 CC61
Grange Flds, Ger.Cr.
(Chal.St.P.) SL9
off Lower Rd 90 AY53
Grangefields Rd, Guil. GU4 .242 AX128
Sch **Grange First Sch**, Har.
HA2 off Welbeck Rd 116 CB60
Grange Gdns, N14 ....99 DK46
NW3 ....120 DB62
SE25 ....202 DS96
Banstead SM7 ....218 DB113
Pinner HA5 ....116 BZ56
Slough (Farn.Com.) SL2 ..111 AR64
Ware SG12 ....33 DY07
Grange Gro, N1 ....4 F3
GRANGE HILL, Chig. IG7 ...103 ER51
⊖ **Grange Hill** 103 ER49
Grange Hill, SE25 ....202 DS96
Edgware HA8 ....96 CQ50
Grangehill Pl, SE9
off Westmount Rd 165 EM83
Grangehill Rd, SE9 ....165 EM83
Grange Ho, Bark. IG11
off St. Margarets 145 ER67
Erith DA8 ....167 FG82
Grange La, SE21 ....182 DT89
Harlow (Roydon) CM19 ....50 EJ15
Watford (Let.Hth) WD25 ...77 CD39
Grange Mans, Epsom KT17 .217 CT108
Grange Meadow, Bans.
SM7 ....218 DB113
Sch **Grange Mid Sch**, Har.
HA2 off Welbeck Rd 116 CB60
Grangemill Rd, SE6 ....183 EA90
Grangemill Way, SE6 ....183 EA89
Grangemount, Lthd. KT22 ..231 CK120
★ **Grange Mus of Comm**
History, NW10
off Neasden La 118 CS63
GRANGE PARK, N21 ....81 DP43
⇌ **Grange Park** 81 DP43
Grange Pk, W5 ....138 CL74
Woking GU21 ....226 AY115
Grange Pk Av, N21 ....81 DP44
Sch **Grange Pk Inf Sch**, Hayes
UB4 off Lansbury Dr 135 BT70
Sch **Grange Pk Jun Sch**, Hayes
UB4 off Lansbury Dr 135 BT70
Grange Pk Pl, SW20 ....179 CV94
Sch **Grange Pk Prep Sch**, N21
off The Chine 81 DP44
Sch **Grange Pk Prim Sch**,
N21 off Worlds End La 81 DN42
Grange Pk Rd, E10 ....123 EB60
Thornton Heath CR7 .....202 DR98
Grange Pl, NW6 ....140 DA66
Staines TW18 ....194 BJ96
Walton-on-Thames KT12 .195 BU103
Sch **Grange Prim Sch**, E13 ....15 K2
SE1 ....21 L6
W5 off Church Pl 157 CK75
Grange Rd, E10 ....123 EA60
E13 ....15 J2
E17 ....123 DY57
N6 ....120 DG58
N17 ....100 DU51
N18 ....100 DU51
NW10 ....139 CV65
SE1 ....21 M5
SE19 ....202 DR98
SE25 ....202 DR98
SW13 ....159 CU81
W4 ....158 CP78
W5 ....137 CK74
Addlestone (New Haw)
KT15 ....212 BG110
Borehamwood (Elstree)
WD6 ....78 CM43
Bushey WD23 ....76 BY43
Caterham CR3 ....252 DU125
Chessington KT9 ....216 CL105
Edgware HA8 ....96 CR51
Egham TW20 ....173 AZ92
Gerrards Cross (Chal.St.P.)
SL9 ....90 AY53
Gravesend DA11 ....191 GG87
Grays RM17 ....170 GB79
Guildford GU2 ....242 AV129
Harrow HA1 ....117 CG58
Harrow (S.Har.) HA2 .....117 CD61
Hayes UB3 ....135 BS72
Ilford IG1 ....125 EP63
Kingston upon Thames
KT1 ....198 CL97
Leatherhead KT22 ....231 CK120
Orpington BR6 ....205 EQ103
Romford RM3 ....105 FH51
Sevenoaks TN13 ....256 FG127
South Croydon CR2 ......220 DQ110
South Ockendon (Aveley)
RM15 ....148 FQ74
Southall UB1 ....156 BY75
Sutton SM2 ....218 DA108
Thornton Heath CR7 .....202 DR98
Walton-on-Thames KT12 .214 BY105
West Molesey KT8 ....196 CB98
Woking GU21 ....210 AY114
Granger Way, Rom. RM1 ....127 FG58
Grange St, N1 ....5 K8
St. Albans AL3 ....43 CD19
Grange Vale, Sutt. SM2 .....218 DB108
Grange Vw Rd, N20 ....98 DC46
Grange Wk, SE1 ....21 M5
Grangeway, N12 ....98 DB49
NW6 off Messina Av 140 DA66
Grange Way, Erith DA8 .....167 FH80
Grangeway, Horl.
(Smallfield) RH6 ....269 DN148
Grange Way, Iver SL0 ....133 BF72
Grangeway, Wdf.Grn. IG8 ..102 EJ49
Grangeway, The, N21 ....81 DP44
Grangeway Gdns, Ilf. IG4 ...124 EL57
Grangeways Cl, Grav.
(Nthflt) DA11 ....191 GF91
Grangewood, Bex. DA5
off Hurst Rd 186 EZ88
Potters Bar EN6 ....64 DB30
Slough (Wexham) SL3 ...132 AW71
Grangewood Av, Grays
RM16 ....170 GE76
Rainham RM13 ....148 FJ70
Grangewood Cl, Brwd.
CM13 off Knight's Way ..109 GA48
Pinner HA5 ....115 BU57
Grangewood Dr, Sun.
TW16 off Forest Dr 175 BT94
Sch **Grangewood Indep Sch**,
E7 off Chester Rd 144 EK66
Grangewood La, Beck. BR3 .183 DZ93
Sch **Grangewood Sch**, Pnr.
HA5 off Fore St 115 BT57
Grangewood St, E6 ....144 EJ67
Grangewood Ter, SE25
off Grange Rd 202 DR97
Grange Yd, SE1 ....21 N6
Granham Gdns, N9 ....100 DT47
Granite St, SE18 ....165 ET78
Granleigh Rd, E11 ....124 EE61
Gransden Av, E8 ....142 DV66
Gransden Rd, W12
off Wendell Rd 159 CT75
Grant Av, Slou. SL1 ....132 AS72
Grantbridge St, N1 ....4 F9
Grantchester Cl, Har. HA1 ..117 CF62
Grant Cl, N14 ....99 DJ45
Shepperton TW17 ....195 BP100
Grantham Cen, The, SW9 ...161 DL82
Grantham Cl, Edg. HA8 .....96 CL48
Grantham Gdns, Rom. RM6 .126 EZ58
Ware SG12 ....33 DY05
Grantham Grn, Borwd. WD6 .78 CQ43
Grantham Pl, W1 ....18 G2
Grantham Rd, E12 ....125 EN63
SW9 ....161 DL82
W4 ....158 CS80
Grantley Cl, Guil. (Shalf.)
GU4 ....258 AY141
Grantley Gdns, Guil. GU2 ..242 AU133
Grantley Pl, Esher KT10 ....214 CB106
Grantley Rd, Guil. GU2 .....242 AU133
Hounslow TW4 ....156 BW82
Grantley St, E1 ....12 G2
Grantock Rd, E17 ....101 ED53
Granton Av, Upmin. RM14 ..128 FM61
Sch **Granton Prim Sch**,
SW16 off Granton Rd ...181 DJ94
Granton Rd, SW16 ....201 DJ95
Ilford IG3 ....126 EU60
Sidcup DA14 ....186 EW93
Grant Pl, Croy. CR0 ....202 DT102
Grant Rd, SW11 ....160 DD84
Croydon CR0 ....202 DT102
Harrow HA3 ....117 CE55
Grants Cl, N17 ....100 DS54
NW7 ....97 CW52
Grants La, Oxt. RH8 ....254 EJ132
Grant's Quay Wf, EC3 ....11 K10
Grant St, E13 ....15 L2
N1 ....4 C9
Grantully Rd, W9 ....7 J2
Grant Way, Islw. TW7 ......157 CG79
Grantwood Cl, Red. RH1
off Bushfield Dr 267 DH139
Granville Av, N9 ....100 DW48
Feltham TW13 ....175 BU89
Hounslow TW3 ....176 CA85
Slough SL2 ....131 AR71
Granville Cl, Croy. CR0 .....202 DS103
West Byfleet (Byfleet)
KT14 off Church Rd 212 BM113
Weybridge KT13 ....213 BQ107
Granville Ct, N1 ....5 K7
Granville Dene, Hem.H.
(Bov.) HP3 ....57 BA27
Granville Gdns, SW16 ......201 DM95
W5 ....138 CM74
Hoddesdon EN11 ....33 EA13
Granville Gro, SE13 ....163 EC83
Granville Ms, Sid. DA14 .....186 EU91
Granville Pk, SE13 ....163 EC83
Granville Pl, N12 (N.Finchley)
off High Rd 98 DC52
SW6 off Maxwell Rd 160 DB80
W1 ....8 E8
Pinner HA5 ....116 BX55
Granville Rd, E17 ....123 EB58
E18 ....102 EH54
N4 ....121 DM58
N12 ....98 DB52
N13 off Russell Rd 99 DM51
N22 ....99 DP53
NW2 ....119 CZ61
NW6 ....140 DA68
SW18 ....180 DA87
SW19 off Russell Rd 180 DA94
Barnet EN5 ....79 CW42
Berkhamsted HP4 ....38 AS17
Epping CM16 ....70 EV29
Gravesend DA11 ....191 GF87
Hayes UB3 ....155 BT77
Ilford IG1 ....125 EP60
Oxted RH8 ....254 EF129
St. Albans AL1 ....43 CF20
Sevenoaks TN13 ....256 FG124
Sidcup DA14 ....186 EU91
Uxbridge UB10 ....135 BP65
Watford WD18 ....76 BW42
Welling DA16 ....166 EW83
Westerham TN16 ....255 EQ126
Weybridge KT13 ....213 BQ107
Woking GU22 ....227 AZ120
Sch **Granville Sch, The**, Sev.
TN13
off Bradbourne Pk Rd ..256 FG123
Granville Sq, SE15 ....162 DS80
WC1 ....10 B2
Granville St, WC1 ....10 B2
Grape St, WC2 ....9 N7
Graphite Sq, SE11 ....20 A9
Grapsome Cl, Chess. KT9
off Nigel Fisher Way 215 CJ108
Grasdene Rd, SE18 ....166 EU80
Grasgarth Cl, W3
off Creswick Rd 138 CQ73
Grasholm Way, Slou. SL3 ...153 BC77
Grasmere Av, SW15 ....178 CR91
Grasmere Av, SW19 ....200 DA97
W3 ....138 CQ73
Hounslow TW3 ....176 CB86
Orpington BR6 ....205 EP104
Ruislip HA4 ....115 BQ59
Slough SL2 ....132 AU73
Wembley HA9 ....117 CK59
Grasmere Cl, Egh. TW20
off Keswick Rd 173 BB94
Feltham TW14 ....175 BT88
Guildford GU1 ....243 BB133
Hemel Hempstead HP3 ....41 BP22
Loughton IG10 ....85 EM40
Watford WD25 ....59 BV32
Grasmere Ct, N22
off Palmerston Rd 99 DM51
Grasmere Gdns, Har. HA3 ...95 CG54
Ilford IG4 ....125 EM57
Orpington BR6 ....205 EP104
Sch **Grasmere JMI Sch**,
N16 off Albion Rd 122 DR63
Grasmere Pt, SE15
off Ilderton Rd 162 DW80
Grasmere Rd, E13 ....144 EG68
N10 ....99 DH53
N17 ....100 DU51
SE25 ....202 DV100
SW16 ....181 DM92
Bexleyheath DA7 ....167 FC81
Bromley BR1 ....204 EF95
Orpington BR6 ....205 EP104
Purley CR8 ....219 DP111
St. Albans AL1 ....43 CH22
Grasmere Way, W.Byf.
(Byfleet) KT14 ....212 BM112
Grassfield Cl, Couls. CR5 ...235 DH119
Grasshaven Way, SE28 ......145 ET74
Grassingham End, Ger.Cr.
(Chal.St.P.) SL9 ....90 AY52
Grassingham Rd, Ger.Cr.
(Chal.St.P.) SL9 ....90 AY52
Grassington Cl, N11
off Ribblesdale Av 98 DG51
St. Albans (Brick.Wd) AL2 ..60 CA30
Grassington Rd, Sid. DA14 .186 EU91
Grasslands, Horl.
(Smallfield) RH6 ....269 DN148
Grassmere, Horl. RH6 ......269 DH147
Grassmere Rd, Horn. RM11 .128 FM56
Grassmount, SE23 ....182 DV89
Purley CR8 ....219 DJ110
Grass Pk, N3 ....97 CZ53
Grass Warren, Welw. AL6 ....30 DE06
Grassway, Wall. SM6 ....219 DJ105
Grassy Cl, Hem.H. HP1 ......40 BG19
Grassy La, Sev. TN13 ....257 FH126
Grasvenor Av, Barn. EN5 ....80 DA44
Grately Way, SE15
off Daniel Gdns 162 DT80
Gratton Dr, Wind. SL4 ......151 AL84
Gratton Rd, W14 ....16 C6
Gratton Ter, NW2 ....119 CX62
Gravel Cl, Chig. IG7 ....104 EU47
Graveley, Kings.T. KT1
off Willingham Way 198 CN96
Graveley Av, Borwd. WD6 ....78 CQ42
Graveley Ct, Hem.H. HP2 .....41 BQ21
Graveley Dell, Welw.G.C.
AL7 off Waterford Grn 30 DB10
Uni **Gravel Hill** 221 DY108
Gravel Hill, N3 ....97 CZ54
Bexleyheath DA6 ....187 FB85
Croydon CR0 ....221 DX107
Gerrards Cross (Chal.St.P.)
SL9 ....90 AY53
Hemel Hempstead HP1 ....40 BH20
Leatherhead KT22
off North St 231 CH121
Loughton (High Beach)
IG10 ....84 EG38
Uxbridge UB8 ....114 BK64
Gravel Hill Cl, Bexh. DA6 ...187 FB85
Sch **Gravel Hill Prim Sch**,
Bexh. DA6 off Watling St .167 FB84
Gravel Hill Ter, Hem.H. HP1 ..40 BG21
Gravel La, E1 ....11 N7
Chigwell IG7 ....104 EU46
Hemel Hempstead HP1 ....40 BG21
Gravelly Hill, Cat. CR3 .....252 DS128
Gravelly Ride, SW19 ....179 CV91
Gravel Path, Berk. HP4 ......38 AX19
Hemel Hempstead HP1 ....40 BG20
Gravel Pit La, SE9 ....185 EQ85
Gravelpits La, Guil. (Goms.)
GU5 ....261 BQ139
Gravel Pit Way, Orp. BR6 ...206 EU103
Gravel Rd, Brom. BR2 ......204 EL103
Dartford (Sutt.H.) DA4 ...188 FP94
Twickenham TW2 ....177 CE88
Gravelwood Cl, Chis. BR7 ..185 EQ90
Gravely Way, H.Wyc. (Penn)
HP10 ....88 AF45
Graveney Gro, SE20 ....182 DW94
Graveney Rd, SW17 ....180 DE91
Sch **Graveney Sch**, SW17
off Welham Rd 181 DH92
GRAVESEND, DA11 - DA13 .191 GJ85
⇌ **Gravesend** 191 GG87
H **Gravesend & N Kent**
Hosp, Grav. DA11 ......191 GG86
Sch **Gravesend Gram Sch for**
Boys, Grav. DA12
off Church Wk 191 GK87
Sch **Gravesend Gram Sch for**
Girls, Grav. DA11
off Pelham Rd 191 GG88
Gravesend Rd, W12 ....139 CU73
Coll **Gravesend Social Ed Cen**,
Grav. DA12
off Haig Gdns 191 GK87
Gravesham Ct, Grav. DA12
off Clarence Row 191 GH87
★ **Gravesham Mus**, Grav.
DA11 ....191 GH86
Gravetts La, Guil. GU3 .....242 AS131
Gray Av, Dag. RM8 ....126 EZ60
Grayburn Cl, Ch.St.G. HP8 ...90 AU47
Gray Gdns, Rain. RM13 .....147 FG65
Grayham Cres, N.Mal. KT3 ..198 CR98
Grayham Rd, N.Mal. KT3 ....198 CR98
Grayland Cl, Brom. BR1 .....204 EK95
Graylands, Epp. (They.B.)
CM16 ....85 ER37
Woking GU21 ....226 AY116
Graylands Cl, Wok. GU21 ...226 AY116
Grayling Cl, E16 ....15 H3
Grayling Ct, Berk. HP4
off Admiral Way 38 AT17
Grayling Rd, N16 ....122 DR61
Graylings, The, Abb.L. WD5 ..59 BR33
Grayling Sq, E2 ....12 B1
Gray Pl, Cher. (Ott.) KT16
off Clarendon Gate 211 BD106
GRAYS, RM16 & RM17;
RM20 ....170 GA78

★ Place of interest H Hospital Sch School Coll College Uni University ⇌ Railway station

⇌ Grays ... 170 GA79
Coll Grays Adult Ed Cen, Grays RM17 off Bridge Rd ... 170 GB78
Sch Grays Conv High Sch, Grays RM17 off College Av ... 170 GB77
Grayscroft Rd, SW16 ... 181 DK94
Grays End Cl, Grays RM17 ... 170 GA76
Sch Gray's Fm Prim Sch, Orp. BR5 off Grays Fm Rd ... 206 EV95
Grays Fm Rd, Orp. BR5 ... 206 EV95
Graysfield, Welw.G.C. AL7 ... 30 DA12
Grayshott Rd, SW11 ... 160 DG82
★ Gray's Inn, WC1 ... 10 B5
Gray's Inn Pl, WC1 ... 10 B6
Gray's Inn Rd, WC1 ... 10 A2
Gray's Inn Sq, WC1 ... 10 C5
Grays La, Ashf. TW15 ... 175 BP91
Gray's La, Ashtd. KT21 ... 232 CM119
Epsom KT18 ... 232 CN120
Grays Pk Rd, Slou. (Stoke P.) SL2 ... 132 AU68
Grays Pl, Slou. SL2 ... 132 AT74
Grays Rd, Gdmg. GU7 ... 258 AT144
Slough SL1 ... 132 AT74
Uxbridge UB10 ... 134 BL67
Westerham TN16 ... 239 EP121
Sch Grays Sch, The, Grays RM17 off Hathaway Rd ... 170 GB76
Grays Town Shop Cen, Grays RM17 off High St ... 170 GA79
Gray St, SE1 ... 20 D4
Grays Wk, Brwd. (Hutt.) CM13 ... 109 GD45
Chesham HP5 ... 54 AP29
Grays Wd, Horl. RH6 ... 269 DJ148
Grayswood Gdns, SW20 off Farnham Gdns ... 199 CV96
Grayswood Pt, SW15 off Norley Vale ... 179 CU88
Gray's Yd, W1 ... 8 F8
Graywood Ct, N12 ... 98 DC52
Sch Grazebrook JMI Sch, N16 off Lordship Rd ... 122 DR61
Grazebrook Rd, N16 ... 122 DR61
Grazeley Cl, Bexh. DA6 ... 187 FC85
Grazeley Ct, SE19 off Gipsy Hill ... 182 DS91
Grazings, The, Hem.H. HP2 ... 40 BM18
Great Acre Ct, SW4 off St. Alphonsus Rd ... 161 DK84
GREAT AMWELL, Ware SG12 ... 33 DZ10
Great Arthur Ho, EC1 off Fann St ... 142 DQ70
Great Bell All, EC2 ... 11 J7
Great Benty, West Dr. UB7 ... 154 BL77
Great Bois Wd, Amer. HP6 off Bois Av ... 55 AP36
GREAT BOOKHAM, Lthd. KT23 ... 246 CB125
★ Great Bookham Common, Lthd. KT23 ... 230 BZ121
Great Braitch La, Hat. AL10 ... 29 CT14
Great Brays, Harl. CM18 ... 52 EU16
Great Break, Welw.G.C. AL7 ... 30 DB10
Great Brownings, SE21 ... 182 DT91
Great Bushey Dr, N20 ... 98 DB46
Great Cambridge Junct, N18 off North Circular Rd ... 100 DR49
Great Cambridge Rd, N9 ... 100 DS46
N17 ... 100 DR50
N18 ... 100 DR50
Broxbourne (Turnf.) EN10 ... 67 DY26
Enfield EN1 ... 82 DU42
Waltham Cross (Chsht) EN8 ... 66 DW34
Great Castle St, W1 ... 9 H7
Great Cen Av, Ruis. HA4 ... 116 BW64
Great Cen St, NW1 ... 8 C5
Great Cen Way, NW10 ... 118 CS64
Wembley HA9 ... 118 CQ63
Great Chapel St, W1 ... 9 L7
Great Chart St, SW11 off Wynter St ... 160 DC84
Great Chertsey Rd, W4 ... 158 CQ82
Feltham TW13 ... 176 CA90
Great Ch La, W6 ... 16 B9
Great Coll St, SW1 ... 19 N5
Great Conduit, Welw.G.C. AL7 ... 30 DC08
Great Cross Av, SE10 ... 164 EE80
Great Cullings, Rom. RM7 ... 127 FE61
Great Cumberland Ms, W1 ... 8 C8
Great Cumberland Pl, W1 ... 8 C7
Great Dell, Welw.G.C. AL8 ... 29 CX07
Great Dover St, SE1 ... 21 H4
Greatdown Rd, W7 ... 137 CF70
Great Eastern Rd, E15 ... 143 ED66
Brentwood CM14 ... 108 FW49
Great Eastern St, EC2 ... 11 L2
Great Eastern Wk, EC2 ... 11 M6
Great Ellshams, Bans. SM7 ... 234 DA116
Great Elms Rd, Brom. BR2 ... 204 EJ98
Hemel Hempstead HP3 ... 40 BM24
Great Fld, NW9 ... 96 CS53
Greatfield Av, E6 ... 145 EM70
Greatfield Cl, N19 off Warrender Rd ... 121 DJ63
SE4 ... 163 EA84
Greatfields Dr, Uxb. UB8 ... 134 BN71
Greatfields Rd, Bark. IG11 ... 145 ER67
Great Fleete Way, Bark. IG11 off Choats Rd ... 146 EW68
Greatford Dr, Guil. GU1 ... 243 BD134
Great Galley Cl, Bark. IG11 ... 146 EV69
Great Ganett, Welw.G.C. AL7 ... 30 DB11
Great Gdns Rd, Horn. RM11 ... 127 FH58
Great Gatton Cl, Croy. CR0 ... 203 DY101
Great George St, SW1 ... 19 M4
Great Goodwin Dr, Guil. GU1 ... 243 BB132
Great Gregories La, Epp. CM16 ... 69 ES33
Great Gro, Bushey WD23 ... 76 CB42
Great Gros, Wal.Cr. EN7 ... 66 DS28
Great Guildford St, SE1 ... 20 G1
Greatham Rd, Bushey WD23 ... 76 BX41
Greatham Wk, SW15 ... 179 CU88
Great Harry Dr, SE9 ... 185 EN90
Great Heart, Hem.H. HP2 ... 40 BL18
Great Heath, Hat. AL10 ... 45 CV15
GREAT HIVINGS, Chesh. HP5 ... 54 AP27
Great Hivings, Chesh. HP5 ... 54 AN27
Greathurst End, Lthd. (Bkhm) KT23 ... 230 BZ124
Great James St, WC1 ... 10 A4
Great Julians, Rick. WD3 off Grove Cres ... 74 BN42
Great Lake Ct, Horl. RH6 off Tanyard Way ... 269 DH147
Great Ley, Welw.G.C. AL7 ... 29 CY11
Great Leylands, Harl. CM18 ... 52 EU16
Great Marlborough St, W1 ... 9 J8
Great Maze Pond, SE1 ... 21 K3
Great Meadow, Brox. EN10 ... 49 EB22
Great Molewood, Hert. SG14 ... 31 DP06
Great Nelmes Chase, Horn. RM11 ... 128 FM57
Greatness La, Sev. TN14 ... 257 FJ121
Greatness Rd, Sev. TN14 ... 257 FJ121
Great Newport St, WC2 off Cranbourn St ... 141 DK73
Great New St, EC4 ... 10 D7
Great N Leisure Pk, N12 ... 98 DD52
Great N Rd, N2 ... 120 DE56
N6 ... 120 DE56
Barnet EN5 ... 79 CZ38
Barnet (New Barn.) EN5 ... 80 DA43
Hatfield AL9, AL10 ... 45 CZ23
Potters Bar EN6 ... 64 DB27
Welwyn Garden City AL8 ... 29 CV13
Great N Way, NW4 ... 97 CW54
Great Oaks, Brwd. (Hutt.) CM13 ... 109 GB44
Chigwell IG7 ... 103 EQ49
Great Oaks Pk, Guil. GU4 ... 243 BB129
Greatorex St, E1 ... 12 A5
Great Ormond St, WC1 ... 9 P5
H Great Ormond St Hosp for Children, The, WC1 ... 9 P4
Great Owl Rd, Chig. IG7 ... 103 EN48
Great Palmers, Hem.H. HP2 ... 40 BM15
Great Pk, Kings L. WD4 ... 58 BM30
GREAT PARNDON, Harl. CM19 ... 51 EP17
Great Percy St, WC1 ... 10 B1
Great Peter St, SW1 ... 19 L6
Great Pettits Ct, Rom. RM1 ... 105 FE54
Great Plumtree, Harl. CM20 ... 35 ET13
⊖ Great Portland Street ... 9 H4
Great Portland St, W1 ... 9 H5
Great Pulteney St, W1 ... 9 K9
Great Quarry, Guil. GU1 ... 258 AX137
Great Queen St, WC2 ... 9 P8
Dartford DA1 ... 188 FM87
Great Rd, Hem.H. HP2 ... 40 BM19
Great Ropers La, Brwd. CM13 ... 107 FU51
Great Russell St, WC1 ... 9 M7
Great St. Helens, EC3 ... 11 L7
Great St. Thomas Apostle, EC4 ... 11 H9
Great Scotland Yd, SW1 ... 19 N2
Great Slades, Pot.B. EN6 ... 63 CZ33
Great Smith St, SW1 ... 19 M5
Great South-West Rd, Felt. TW14 ... 175 BQ87
Hounslow TW4 ... 155 BT84
Great Spilmans, SE22 ... 182 DS85
Great Stockwood Rd, Wal.Cr. (Chsht) EN7 ... 66 DR26
Great Strand, NW9 ... 97 CT53
Great Sturgess Rd, Hem.H. HP1 ... 39 BF20
Great Suffolk St, SE1 ... 20 F2
Great Sutton St, EC1 ... 10 F4
Great Swan All, EC2 ... 11 J7
Great Tattenhams, Epsom KT18 ... 233 CV118
Great Thrift, Orp. BR5 ... 205 EQ98
Great Till Cl, Sev. (Otford) TN14 ... 241 FE116
Great Titchfield St, W1 ... 9 J7
Great Twr St, EC3 ... 11 L9
Great Trinity La, EC4 ... 11 H9
Great Turnstile, WC1 ... 10 B6
GREAT WARLEY, Brwd. CM14 ... 107 FV53
Great Warley St, Brwd. (Gt Warley) CM13 ... 107 FU53
Great Western Rd, W2 ... 6 G6
W9 ... 6 F4
W11 ... 6 G6
Great W Rd, W4 ... 158 CP78
W6 ... 159 CT78
Brentford TW8 ... 158 CP78
Hounslow TW5 ... 156 BX82
Isleworth TW7 ... 157 CE80
Great Wf Rd, E14 off Churchill Pl ... 143 EB74
Great Whites Rd, Hem.H. HP3 ... 40 BM22
Great Winchester St, EC2 ... 11 K7
Great Windmill St, W1 ... 9 L9
Greatwood, Chis. BR7 ... 185 EN94
Greatwood Cl, Cher. (Ott.) KT16 ... 211 BC109
Great Woodcote Dr, Pur. CR8 ... 219 DK110
Great Woodcote Pk, Pur. CR8 ... 219 DK110
Great Yd, SE1 ... 21 M3
Greaves Cl, Bark. IG11 off Norfolk Rd ... 145 ES66
Greaves Pl, SW17 ... 180 DE91
Grebe Av, Hayes UB4 off Cygnet Way ... 136 BX72
Grebe Cl, E7 off Cormorant Rd ... 124 EF64
E17 ... 101 DY52
Barking IG11 ... 146 EU70
Grebe Ct, Sutt. SM1 ... 217 CZ106
Grebe Crest, Grays RM20 ... 169 FU77
Grecian Cres, SE19 ... 181 DP93
Greding Wk, Brwd. (Hutt.) CM13 ... 109 GB47
Gredo Ho, Bark. IG11 ... 146 EV69
Greek Ct, W1 ... 9 M8
★ Greek Orthodox Cath of the Divine Wisdom (St. Sophia), W2 ... 7 J9
Greek St, W1 ... 9 M8
Greek Yd, WC2 ... 9 N9
Green, The, E4 ... 101 EC46
E11 ... 124 EH58
E15 ... 144 EE65
N9 ... 100 DU47
N14 ... 99 DK48
N21 ... 99 DN45
SW14 ... 158 CQ83
SW19 ... 179 CX92
W3 ... 138 CS72
W5 off High St ... 137 CK74
Amersham HP7 ... 55 AR38
Berkhamsted (Pott.End) HP4 ... 39 BB17
Bexleyheath DA7 ... 166 FA81
Bromley BR1 off Downham Way ... 184 EG90
Bromley (Hayes) BR2 ... 204 EG101
Carshalton SM5 ... 218 DG105
Caterham (Wold.) CR3 ... 237 EA123
Chalfont St. Giles HP8 off High St ... 90 AW47
Croydon CR0 ... 221 DZ109
Dartford DA2 ... 189 FR89
Epping (They.B.) CM16 ... 85 ES37
Green, The, Epsom KT17 ... 217 CU111
Esher (Clay.) KT10 ... 215 CF107
Feltham TW13 ... 175 BV89
Hayes UB3 off Wood End ... 135 BS72
Hemel Hempstead (Bov.) HP3 ... 57 BA29
High Wycombe (Woob.Grn) HP10 ... 110 AE58
Hounslow TW5 off Heston Rd ... 156 CA79
Leatherhead (Fetch.) KT22 ... 231 CD124
Morden SM4 ... 199 CY98
New Malden KT3 ... 198 CQ97
Orpington (Pr.Bot.) BR6 off Rushmore Hill ... 224 EW110
Orpington (St.P.Cray) BR5 off The Avenue ... 186 EV94
Rainham (Wenn.) RM13 ... 148 FL73
Richmond TW9 ... 177 CK85
Rickmansworth (Crox.Grn) WD3 ... 74 BN44
Rickmansworth (Sarratt) WD3 ... 74 BG35
Romford (Hav.at.Bow.) RM4 ... 105 FE48
Sevenoaks TN13 ... 257 FK122
Shepperton TW17 ... 195 BS98
Sidcup DA14 ... 186 EU91
Slough (Burn.) SL1 ... 130 AH70
Slough (Chalvey) SL1 ... 151 AR75
Slough (Datchet) SL3 ... 152 AV80
South Ockendon RM15 ... 149 FW69
Southall UB2 ... 156 BY76
Staines (Wrays.) TW19 ... 172 AY86
Sutton SM1 ... 200 DB104
Tadworth (Burgh Hth) KT20 ... 233 CY119
Tilbury (W.Til.) RM18 ... 171 GL79
Twickenham TW2 ... 177 CE88
Uxbridge (Hare.) UB9 ... 92 BJ53
Uxbridge (Ickhm) UB10 ... 115 BQ61
Waltham Abbey EN9 off Sewardstone Rd ... 67 EC34
Waltham Cross (Chsht) EN8 ... 66 DW28
Walton-on-Thames (Whiteley Vill.) KT12 off Octagon Rd ... 213 BS110
Warlingham CR6 ... 237 DX117
Watford (Let.Hth) WD25 ... 77 CE39
Welling DA16 ... 165 ES84
Welwyn Garden City AL7 ... 30 DA11
Wembley HA0 ... 117 CG61
West Drayton UB7 ... 154 BK76
Westerham TN16 ... 255 ER126
Woking (Ripley) GU23 ... 228 BH121
Woodford Green IG8 ... 102 EG50
Greenacre, Dart. DA1 off Oakfield La ... 188 FL89
Windsor SL4 ... 151 AL82
Woking (Knap.) GU21 off Mead Ct ... 226 AS116
Greenacre Cl, Barn. EN5 ... 79 CZ38
Northolt UB5 ... 116 BZ64
Swanley BR8 ... 207 FE98
Greenacre Ct, Egh. (Eng.Grn) TW20 ... 172 AW93
Greenacre Gdns, E17 ... 123 EC56
Greenacre Pl, Wall. (Hackbr.) SM6 off Park Rd ... 201 DH103
Greenacres, N3 ... 97 CY54
SE9 ... 185 EN86
Bushey (Bushey Hth) WD23 ... 95 CD47
Green Acres, Croy. CR0 ... 202 DT104
Greenacres, Epp. CM16 ... 69 ET29
Green Acres, Hem.H. HP2 ... 41 BR22
Greenacres, Lthd. (Bkhm) KT23 ... 230 CB124
Oxted RH8 ... 254 EE127
Green Acres, Welw.G.C. AL7 ... 29 CZ12
Greenacres Av, Uxb. UB10 ... 114 BM62
Sch Greenacre Sch, Bans. SM7 off Sutton La ... 218 DB113
Greenacres Cl, Orp. BR6 ... 223 EQ105
Rainham RM13 ... 148 FL69
Greenacres Dr, Stan. HA7 ... 95 CH52
Sch Greenacres Prim Sch, SE9 off Witherston Way ... 185 EN89
Greenacre Sq, SE16 ... 23 H3
Greenacre Wk, N14 ... 99 DL48
Greenall Cl, Wal.Cr. (Chsht) EN8 ... 67 DY30
Green Arbour Ct, EC1 ... 10 E7
Green Av, NW7 ... 96 CR49
W13 ... 157 CH76
Greenaway Av, N18 ... 101 DX51
Greenaway Gdns, NW3 ... 120 DB63
Green Bk, E1 ... 22 C2
N12 ... 98 DB49
Greenbank, Wal.Cr. (Chsht) EN8 ... 66 DV28
Greenbank Av, Wem. HA0 ... 117 CG64
Greenbank Cl, E4 ... 101 EC47
Romford RM3 ... 106 FK48
Greenbank Cres, NW4 ... 119 CY56
Greenbank Rd, Wat. WD17 ... 75 BR36
Greenbanks, Dart. DA1 ... 188 FL89
St. Albans AL1 off Colindale Av ... 43 CF22
Upminster RM14 ... 129 FS60
Greenbay Rd, SE7 ... 164 EK80
Greenberry St, NW8 ... 140 DE68
Greenbrook Av, Barn. EN4 ... 80 DC39
Greenbury Cl, Rick. (Chorl.) WD3 ... 73 BC42
Green Cl, NW9 ... 118 CQ58
NW11 ... 120 DC59
Bromley BR2 ... 204 EE97
Carshalton SM5 ... 200 DF103
Epping CM16 ... 51 EP24
Feltham TW13 ... 176 BY92
Hatfield AL9 off Station Rd ... 63 CY26
Maidenhead (Taplow) SL6 ... 130 AG72
Waltham Cross (Chsht) EN8 ... 67 DY32
Greencoates, Hert. SG13 ... 32 DS10
Greencoat Pl, SW1 ... 19 K7
Greencoat Row, SW1 ... 19 K6
Sch Green C of E Prim Sch, The, N17 off Somerset Rd ... 122 DT55
Green Common La, H.Wyc. (Woob.Grn) HP10 ... 110 AG59
Greencourt Av, Croy. CR0 ... 202 DV103
Edgware HA8 ... 96 CP53
Greencourt Gdns, Croy. CR0 ... 202 DV102
Greencourt Rd, Orp. BR5 ... 205 ER99
Green Ct Rd, Swan. BR8 ... 207 FD99
Green Cres, H.Wyc. (Flack.Hth) HP10 ... 110 AC56
Greencrest Pl, NW2 off Dollis Hill La ... 119 CU62
Green Cft, Edg. HA8 off Deans La ... 96 CQ50
Greencroft, Guil. GU1 ... 243 BB134
Green Cft, Hat. AL10 off Talbot Rd ... 45 CU15
Greencroft Av, Ruis. HA4 ... 116 BW61
Greencroft Cl, E6 off Neatscourt Rd ... 144 EL71
Greencroft Gdns, NW6 ... 140 DB66
Enfield EN1 ... 82 DS41
Greencroft Rd, Houns. TW5 ... 156 BZ81
Green Curve, Bans. SM7 ... 217 CZ114
Green Dale, SE5 ... 162 DR84
SE22 ... 182 DS85
Green Dale Cl, SE22 off Green Dale ... 182 DS85
Greendale Ms, Slou. SL2 ... 132 AU73
Greendale Wk, Grav. (Nthflt) DA11 ... 190 GE90
Green Dell Way, Hem.H. HP3 ... 41 BP20
Green Dene, Lthd. (E.Hors.) KT24 ... 245 BT131
Green Dragon Ct, SE1 ... 21 J1
Green Dragon La, N21 ... 81 DP44
Brentford TW8 ... 158 CL78
Sch Green Dragon Prim Sch, Brent. TW8 off North Rd ... 158 CL79
Green Dragon Yd, E1 ... 12 A6
Green Dr, Maid. SL6 ... 130 AE65
Slough SL3 ... 152 AY77
Southall UB1 ... 136 CA74
Woking (Ripley) GU23 ... 227 BF123
Green E Rd, Beac. (Jordans) HP9 ... 90 AS52
Green Edge, Wat. WD25 off Clarke Grn ... 75 BU35
Greene Fielde End, Stai. TW18 ... 174 BK94
Greene Fld Rd, Berk. HP4 ... 38 AW19
Green End, N21 ... 99 DP47
Chessington KT9 ... 216 CL105
Green End Business Cen, Rick. (Sarratt) WD3 ... 74 BG37
Green End Gdns, Hem.H. HP1 ... 40 BG21
Green End La, Hem.H. HP1 ... 39 BF20
Greenend Rd, W4 ... 158 CS75
Green End Rd, Hem.H. HP1 ... 40 BG21
Greenes Ct, Berk. HP4 off Lower Kings Rd ... 38 AW18
Greene Wk, Berk. HP4 ... 38 AX20
Greenfarm Cl, Orp. BR6 ... 223 ET106
Greenfell Mans, SE8 off Glaisher St ... 163 EB79
Greenfern Av, Slou. SL1 ... 130 AJ72
Greenfield, Hat. AL9 ... 45 CX15
Welwyn Garden City AL8 ... 29 CX06
Greenfield Av, Surb. KT5 ... 198 CP101
Watford WD19 ... 94 BX47
Greenfield Dr, N2 ... 120 DF56
Greenfield End, Ger.Cr. (Chal.St.P.) SL9 ... 90 AY51
Greenfield Gdns, NW2 ... 119 CY61
Dagenham RM9 ... 146 EX67
Orpington BR5 ... 205 ER101
Greenfield Link, Couls. CR5 ... 235 DL115
Greenfield Rd, E1 ... 12 B6
N15 ... 122 DS57
Dagenham RM9 ... 146 EW67
Dartford DA2 ... 187 FD92
Greenfields, Loug. IG10 ... 85 EN42
Potters Bar (Cuffley) EN6 off South Dr ... 65 DL30
Greenfields Cl, Brwd. CM13 off Essex Way ... 107 FW51
Horley RH6 ... 268 DE146
Loughton IG10 ... 85 EN42
Sch Greenfields JMI Sch, Wat. WD19 off Ellesborough Cl ... 94 BW50
Greenfields Rd, Horl. RH6 ... 268 DE146
Sch Greenfields Spec Sch, N10 off Coppetts Rd ... 98 DF53
Greenfield St, Wal.Abb. EN9 ... 67 EC34
Greenfield Way, Har. HA2 ... 116 CB55
GREENFORD, UB6 ... 136 CB69
⇌ Greenford ... 137 CD67
⊖ Greenford ... 137 CD67
Greenford Av, W7 ... 137 CE70
Southall UB1 ... 136 BZ73
Greenford Gdns, Grnf. UB6 ... 136 CB69
Sch Greenford High Sch, Grnf. UB6 off Ruislip Rd ... 136 CA69
Greenford Rd, Grnf. UB6 ... 136 CC71
Harrow HA1 ... 117 CE64
Southall UB1 ... 136 CC74
Sutton SM1 ... 218 DB105
Green Gdns, Orp. BR6 ... 223 EQ106
Greengate, Grnf. UB6 ... 137 CH65
Greengate St, E13 ... 144 EH68
Green Glade, Epp. (They.B.) CM16 ... 85 ES37
Green Glades, Horn. RM11 ... 128 FM58
Greenhalgh Wk, N2 ... 120 DC56
Greenham Cl, SE1 ... 20 C4
Greenham Cres, E4 ... 101 DZ51
Greenham Rd, N10 ... 98 DG54
Greenham Wk, Wok. GU21 ... 226 AW118
Greenhaven Dr, SE28 ... 146 EV72
Greenhayes Av, Bans. SM7 ... 218 DA114
Greenhayes Cl, Reig. RH2 ... 250 DC134
Greenhayes Gdns, Bans. SM7 ... 234 DA115
Greenheys Cl, Nthwd. HA6 ... 93 BS53
Greenheys Dr, E18 ... 124 EF55
Greenheys Pl, Wok. GU22 off White Rose La ... 227 AZ118
Greenhill, NW3 off Hampstead High St ... 120 DD63
SE18 ... 165 EM78
Green Hill, Buck.H. IG9 ... 102 EJ46
Orpington BR6 ... 222 EL112
Greenhill, Sutt. SM1 ... 200 DC103
Wembley HA9 ... 118 CP61
Greenhill Av, Cat. CR3 ... 236 DV121
Greenhill Cres, Wat. WD18 ... 75 BS44
Greenhill Gdns, Guil. GU4 ... 243 BC131
Northolt UB5 ... 136 BZ68
Greenhill Gro, E12 ... 124 EL63
Green Hill La, Warl. CR6 ... 237 DY117
Greenhill Pk, NW10 ... 138 CS67
Barnet EN5 ... 80 DB43
Greenhill Rd, NW10 ... 138 CS67
Gravesend (Nthflt) DA11 ... 191 GF89
Harrow HA1 ... 117 CE58
Greenhills, Harl. CM20 ... 51 ES15
Greenhills Cl, Rick. WD3 ... 74 BH43
Greenhill's Rents, EC1 ... 10 F5
Greenhills Ter, N1 ... 5 K4
Greenhill Ter, SE18 ... 165 EM78
Northolt UB5 ... 136 BZ68
Greenhill Way, Croy. CR0 ... 221 DX111
Harrow HA1 ... 117 CE58
Wembley HA9 ... 118 CP61
GREENHITHE, DA9 ... 189 FV85
⇌ Greenhithe ... 189 FU85
Greenhithe Cl, Sid. DA15 ... 185 ES87
Greenholm Rd, SE9 ... 185 EP85
Green Hundred Rd, SE15 ... 162 DU79
Greenhurst La, Oxt. RH8 ... 254 EG132
Greenhurst Rd, SE27 ... 181 DN92
Greening St, SE2 ... 166 EW77
Greenlake Ter, Stai. TW18 ... 173 BF94
Greenland Cres, Sthl. UB2 ... 156 BW76
Greenland Ms, SE8 ... 23 H10
Riv Greenland Pier ... 23 L6
Greenland Pl, NW1 off Greenland Rd ... 141 DH67
Greenland Quay, SE16 ... 23 H7
Greenland Rd, NW1 ... 141 DJ67
Barnet EN5 ... 79 CW44
Greenlands, Cher. KT16 ... 193 BC104
Greenlands Rd, Stai. TW18 ... 174 BG91
Weybridge KT13 ... 195 BP104
Greenland St, NW1 off Camden High St ... 141 DH67
Green La, E4 ... 84 EE41
NW4 ... 119 CX57
SE9 ... 185 EN89
SE20 ... 183 DX94
SW16 ... 181 DM94
W7 ... 157 CE75
Addlestone KT15 ... 194 BG104
Amersham HP6 ... 55 AS38
Amersham (Chesh.B.) HP6 ... 55 AR35
Ashtead KT21 ... 231 CJ117
Brentwood (Pilg.Hat.) CM15 ... 108 FV43
Brentwood (Warley) CM14 ... 107 FU52
Broxbourne EN10 ... 49 EB23
Caterham CR3 ... 236 DQ122
Chertsey KT16 ... 193 BE103
Chesham HP5 ... 56 AV33
Chessington KT9 ... 216 CL109
Chigwell IG7 ... 103 ER47
Chislehurst BR7 ... 185 EP91
Cobham KT11 ... 214 BY112
Coulsdon CR5 ... 250 DA125
Dagenham RM8 ... 126 EU60
Edgware HA8 ... 96 CN50
Egham TW20 ... 173 BB91
Egham (Thorpe) TW20 ... 193 BD95
Feltham TW13 ... 176 BY92
Godalming GU7 ... 258 AS142
Guildford GU1 ... 243 BB134
Guildford (Sham.Grn) GU5 ... 260 BG144
Guildford (W.Clan.) GU4 ... 244 BG127
Harlow (Thres.B.) CM17 ... 52 FA16
Harrow HA1 ... 117 CE62
Hemel Hempstead HP2 ... 41 BQ21
Hemel Hempstead (Bov.) HP3 ... 57 AZ28
Horley RH6 ... 269 DM152
Hounslow TW4 ... 155 BV83
Ilford IG1, IG3 ... 125 EQ61
Leatherhead KT22 ... 231 CK121
Maidenhead (Fifield) SL6 ... 150 AC81
Morden SM4 ... 200 DB100
New Malden KT3 ... 198 CQ99
Northwood HA6 ... 93 BT52
Purley CR8 ... 219 DJ111
Redhill RH1 ... 250 DE132
Redhill (Bletch.) RH1 ... 252 DS131
Redhill (Outwood) RH1 ... 267 DL141
Redhill (White Bushes) RH1 ... 266 DG139
Reigate RH2 ... 249 CZ134
Rickmansworth (Crox.Grn) WD3 ... 74 BM43
St. Albans AL3 ... 43 CD16
Shepperton TW17 ... 195 BQ100
Slough (Burn.) SL1 ... 131 AK66
Slough (Datchet) SL3 ... 152 AV81
Slough (Farn.Com.) SL2 ... 111 AP64
South Ockendon RM15 ... 149 FR69
Staines TW18 ... 193 BE95
Stanmore HA7 ... 95 CH49
Sunbury-on-Thames TW16 ... 175 BT94
Tadworth KT20 ... 249 CZ126
Thornton Heath CR7 ... 201 DN95
Upminster RM14 ... 149 FR68
Uxbridge UB8 ... 135 BQ71
Waltham Abbey EN9 ... 68 EJ34
Walton-on-Thames KT12 ... 213 BV107
Warlingham CR6 ... 237 DY116
Watford WD19 ... 94 BW46
Welwyn Garden City (Pans.) AL7 ... 30 DD10
West Byfleet (Byfleet) KT14 ... 212 BM112
West Molesey KT8 ... 196 CB99
Windsor SL4 ... 151 AP82
Woking (Chobham) GU24 ... 210 AT110
Woking (Mayford) GU24 off Copper Beech Cl ... 226 AV121
Woking (Ockham) GU23 ... 229 BP124
Worcester Park KT4 ... 199 CU102
Green La Av, Walt. KT12 ... 214 BW106
Green La Caravan Pk, Red. (Outwood) RH1 ... 267 DL141
Green La Cl, Amer. HP6 ... 55 AR36
Chertsey KT16 ... 193 BE103
West Byfleet (Byfleet) KT14 ... 212 BM112
Green La Gdns, Th.Hth. CR7 ... 202 DQ96
Sch Green La Inf Sch, Gdmg. GU7 off Green La ... 258 AS142
Sch Green Las Prim Sch, Wor.Pk. KT4 off Green La ... 199 CV101
Green Las, N4 ... 122 DQ60
N8 ... 121 DP55
N13 ... 99 DM51
N15 ... 121 DP55
N16 ... 122 DQ62
N21 ... 99 DP46
Epsom KT19 ... 216 CS109
Hatfield AL10 ... 29 CT13
Welwyn Garden City (Lmsfd) AL8 ... 29 CT11
Sch Green Las Prim Sch, Hat. AL10 off Green Las ... 29 CT14
Green La W, Wok. GU23 ... 244 BN125
Greenlaw Gdns, N.Mal. KT3 ... 199 CT101
Greenlawn La, Brent. TW8 off Ealing Rd ... 157 CK77
Green Lawns, Ruis. HA4 ... 116 BW60
Greenlaw St, SE18 ... 165 EN76
Green Leaf Av, Wall. SM6 ... 219 DK105
Greenleaf Cl, SW2 off Tulse Hill ... 181 DN87

⊖ London Underground station   DLR Docklands Light Railway station   Tra Tramlink station   Riv Pedestrian ferry landing stage

Greenleafe Dr, Ilf. IG6 125 EP56
Sch Greenleaf Prim Sch, E17 off Greenleaf Rd 123 DZ55
Greenleaf Rd, E6
off Redclyffe Rd 144 EJ67
E17 123 DZ55
Greenlea Pk, SW19 200 DD95
Green Leas, Sun.TW16 175 BT93
Waltham Abbey EN9
off Roundhills 67 ED34
Green Leas Cl, Sun.TW16
off Green Leas 175 BT93
Greenleaves Ct, Ashf.TW15
off Redleaves Av 175 BP93
Greenleigh Av, Orp. BR5 206 EV98
Green Man Gdns, W13 137 CG73
Green Man La, W13 137 CG74
Feltham TW14 155 BU84
Green Manor Way, Grav.
DA11 170 FZ84
Green Man Pas, W13 137 CG73
Green Man Rd, Ong. CM5 53 FD19
Green Man Roundabout,
E11 124 EF59
Greenman St, N1 4 G6
Green Mead, Esher KT10
off Winterdown Gdns 214 BZ107
Greenmead Cl, SE25 202 DU99
Green Meadow, Pot.B. EN6 64 DA30
Greenmeads, Wok. GU22 226 AY122
Sch Greenmead Sch, SW15
off St. Margaret's Cres 179 CV85
Green Moor Link, N21 99 DP45
Greenmoor Rd, Enf. EN3 82 DW40
Green N Rd, Beac. (Jordans)
HP9 90 AS51
Greenoak Pl, Barn. EN4 80 DF40
Greenoak Ri, West. (Bigg.H.)
TN16 238 EJ118
Greenoak Way, SW19 179 CX91
Greenock Rd, SW16 201 DK95
W3 158 CP76
Slough SL1 131 AN72
Greenock Way, Rom. RM1 105 FE51
Greeno Cres, Shep.TW17 194 BN99
★ Green Park, SW1 19 H3
⊖ Green Park 19 J2
Green Pk, Harl. CM20
off Greenhills 51 ES15
Staines TW18 173 BE90
Greenpark Ct, Wem. HA0 137 CJ66
Green Pk Way, Grnf. UB6 137 CE67
Green Pl, Dart. DA1 187 FE85
Green Pt, E15 144 EE65
Green Pond Cl, E17 123 DZ55
Green Pond Rd, E17 123 DY55
Green Ride, Epp. CM16 85 EP35
Loughton IG10 84 EG43
Green Rd, N14 81 DH44
N20 98 DC48
Egham (Thorpe) TW20 193 BB98
Greenroof Way, SE10 25 K6
Greensand Cl, Red. (S.Merst.)
RH1 251 DK128
Green Sand Rd, Red. RH1 250 DG133
Greensand Way, Bet. RH3
off Old Sch La 264 CM136
Dorking RH5 264 CM136
Godstone RH9 252 DV134
Redhill (S.Nutfld) RH1 267 DP135
Sch Green Sch for Girls (C of E), The, Islw. TW7
off London Rd 157 CG81
Greens Cl, The, Loug. IG10 85 EN40
Green's Ct, W1 9 L9
Green's End, SE18 165 EP77
Greenshank Cl, E17
off Banbury Rd 101 DY52
Greenshaw, Brwd. CM14 108 FV46
Sch Greenshaw High Sch, Sutt.
SM1 off Grennell Rd 200 DD103
Greenshields Ind Est, E16 25 N2
Greenside, Bex. DA5 186 EY88
Borehamwood WD6 78 CN38
Dagenham RM8 126 EW60
Slough SL2 131 AN71
Swanley BR8 207 FD96
Greenside Cl, N20 98 DD47
SE6 183 ED89
Guildford GU4
off Foxglove Gdns 243 BC132
Greenside Dr, Ashtd. KT21 231 CH118
Sch Greenside Prim Sch,
W12 off Westville Rd 159 CU75
Greenside Rd, W12 159 CU76
Croydon CR0 201 DN101
Weybridge KT13 195 BP104
Greenside Wk, West. (Bigg.H.)
TN16 off Kings Rd 238 EH118
Greenslade Av, Ashtd. KT21 232 CP119
Sch Greenslade Prim Sch,
SE18 off Erindale 165 ER79
Greenslade Rd, Bark. IG11 145 ER66
Greensleeves Cl, St.Alb. AL4 43 CJ21
Greensleeves Dr, Brwd.
(Warley) CM14 108 FV50
Green Slip Rd, Barn. EN5 79 CZ40
Greenstead, Saw. CM21 36 EY06
Greenstead Av, Wdf.Grn.
IG8 102 EJ52
Greenstead Cl, Brwd. (Hutt.)
CM13 109 GE45
Woodford Green IG8
off Greenstead Gdns 102 EJ51
Greenstead Gdns, SW15 179 CU85
Woodford Green IG8 102 EJ51
GREENSTED GREEN, Ong.
CM5 71 FH28
Greensted Rd, Loug. IG10 102 EL45
Ongar CM5 71 FG28
Greenstone Ms, E11 124 EG58
GREEN STREET, Borwd.
WD6 78 CP37
Green St, E7 144 EH65
E13 144 EJ67
W1 8 D9
Borehamwood WD6 78 CN36
Enfield EN3 82 DW40
Harlow CM17
off London Rd 36 EX14
Hatfield AL9 45 CZ21
Hertford SG14 32 DR09
Radlett (Shenley) WD7 78 CN36
Rickmansworth (Chorl.)
WD3 73 BC40
Sunbury-on-Thames
TW16 195 BU95
GREEN STREET GREEN,
Dart. DA2 189 FU93
GREEN STREET GREEN,
Orp. BR6 223 ES107
Sch Green St Grn Prim Sch,
Orp. BR6 off Vine Rd 223 ET107
Green St Grn Rd, Dart. DA1,
DA2 188 FP88
Greensward, Bushey WD23 76 CB44
Green Ter, EC1 10 D2
Green Tiles La, Uxb. (Denh.)
UB9 113 BF58
Greentrees, Epp. CM16 70 EU31
Green Vale, W5 138 CM72
Bexleyheath DA6 186 EX85
Greenvale, Welw.G.C. AL7 30 DA10
Sch Greenvale Prim Sch, S.Croy.
CR2 off Sandpiper Rd 221 DX111
Greenvale Rd, SE9 165 EM84
Sch Greenvale Spec Sch,
SE23 off Perry Ri 183 DY90
Green Valley, H.Wyc.
(Woob.Grn) HP10 88 AE54
Green Verges, Stan. HA7 95 CK52
Green Vw, Chess. KT9 216 CM108
Greenview Av, Beck. BR3 203 DY100
Croydon CR0 203 DY100
Greenview Cl, W3 138 CS74
Green Vw Cl, Hem.H. (Bov.)
HP3 57 BA29
Greenview Ct, Ashf.TW15
off Village Way 174 BM91
Green Wk, NW4 119 CX57
SE1 21 L6
Buckhurst Hill IG9 102 EL45
Dartford DA1 167 FF84
Hampton TW12
off Orpwood Cl 176 BZ93
Ruislip HA4 115 BT60
Southall UB2 156 CA78
Woodford Green IG8 102 EL51
Green Wk, The, E4 101 EC46
Greenway, N14 99 DL47
N20 98 DA47
Green Way, SE9 184 EK85
Greenway, SW20 199 CW98
Berkhamsted HP4 38 AU19
Brentwood (Hutt.) CM13 109 GA45
Green Way, Brom. BR2 204 EL100
Greenway, Chesh. HP5 54 AP28
Chislehurst BR7 185 EN92
Dagenham RM8 126 EW61
Harlow CM19 50 EL15
Harrow HA3 118 CL57
Hayes UB4 135 BV70
Hemel Hempstead HP2 41 BP20
Leatherhead (Bkhm)
KT23 230 CB123
Pinner HA5 93 BV54
Green Way, Red. RH1 250 DE132
Greenway, Rom. RM3 106 FP51
Green Way, Slou. (Burn.)
SL1 130 AH69
Sunbury-on-Thames
TW16 195 BU98
Greenway, Wall. SM6 219 DJ105
Westerham (Tats.) TN16 238 EJ120
Woodford Green IG8 102 EJ50
Greenway, The, NW9 96 CR54
Enfield EN3 83 DX35
Epsom KT18 232 CN115
Gerrards Cross (Chal.St.P.)
SL9 112 AX55
Harrow HA3 95 CE53
Hounslow TW4 156 BZ84
Orpington BR5 206 EV100
Oxted RH8 254 EH133
Pinner HA5 116 BZ58
Potters Bar EN6 64 DA33
Rickmansworth (Mill End)
WD3 92 BG45
Slough SL1 131 AK74
Uxbridge UB8 134 BJ68
Uxbridge (Ickhm) UB10 115 BQ61
Greenway Av, E17 123 ED56
Greenway Cl, N4 122 DQ61
N11 98 DG51
N15 off Copperfield Dr 122 DT56
N20 98 DA47
NW9 96 CR54
West Byfleet KT14 212 BG113
Greenway Dr, Stai. TW18 194 BK95
Sch Greenway First Sch, Berk.
HP4 off Crossways 38 AU19
Greenway Gdns, NW9 96 CR54
Croydon CR0 203 DZ104
Greenford UB6 136 CA69
Harrow HA3 95 CE54
Greenway Par, Chesh. HP5 54 AP28
Greenways, Abb.L. WD5 59 BS32
Beckenham BR3 203 EA96
Egham TW20 172 AY92
Esher KT10 215 CE105
Hertford SG14 31 DN09
Tadworth KT20 249 CV125
Waltham Cross (Chsht)
EN7 65 DP29
Woking GU22
off Pembroke Rd 227 BA117
Greenways, The, Twick. TW1
off South Western Rd 177 CG86
Greenwell Cl, Gdse. RH9 252 DV130
Greenwell St, W1 9 H4
Green W Rd, Beac. (Jordans)
HP9 90 AS52
GREENWICH, SE10 163 ED79
⇌ Greenwich 163 EB80
DLR Greenwich 163 EB80
Greenwich Ch St, SE10 163 EC79
Coll Greenwich Comm Coll,
Burrage Cen, SE18
off Burrage Gro 165 EQ77
Haimo Cen, SE9
off Haimo Rd 184 EK85
Kidbrooke Cen, SE3
off Corelli Rd 164 EK82
King's Pk Cen, SE9
off Eltham Palace Rd 184 EK86
London Leisure Coll, SE7
off Harvey Gdns 164 EK78
New Horizon Cen, SE3
off Telemann Sq 164 EH83
Plumstead Cen, SE18
off Plumstead Rd 165 EQ77
Greenwich Ct, Wal.Cr. EN8
off Parkside 67 DY34
Greenwich Cres, E6
off Swan App 144 EL71
Greenwich Foot Tunnel, E14 24 D10
SE10 24 D10
Greenwich High Rd, SE10 163 EB81
Greenwich Ind Est, SE7 25 N8
Greenwich Mkt, SE10
off King William Wk 163 EC79
★ Greenwich Park, SE10 163 ED80
Greenwich Pk, SE10 164 EE80
Greenwich Pk St, SE10 24 F10
★ Greenwich Pier, SE10 163 EC79
Greenwich Quay, SE8 163 EB79
Coll Greenwich Sch of Management, SE10
off Royal Hill 163 EC80
Greenwich S St, SE10 163 EB81
Greenwich Vw Pl, E14 24 A6
Greenwich Way, Wal.Abb.
EN9 83 EC36
Sch Greenwich Young Peoples Cen, SE9
off Newhaven Gdns 164 EK84
Greenwood, The, Guil. GU1 243 BA134
Greenwood Av, Dag. RM10 127 FB63
Enfield EN3 83 DY40
Waltham Cross (Chsht)
EN7 66 DV31
Greenwood Cl, Add.
(Wdhm) KT15 211 BF111
Amersham HP6 55 AS37
Beaconsfield (Seer Grn)
HP9 off Farmers Way 89 AQ51
Bushey (Bushey Hth)
WD23 off Langmead Dr 95 CE45
Morden SM4 199 CY98
Orpington BR5 205 ES100
Sidcup DA15 off Hurst Rd 186 EU89
Thames Ditton KT7 197 CG102
Waltham Cross (Chsht)
EN7 off Greenwood Av 66 DV31
Greenwood Ct, SW1 19 J9
Greenwood Dr, E4
off Avril Way 101 EC50
Redhill RH1 266 DG139
Watford WD25 59 BV34
Greenwood Gdns, N13 99 DP48
Caterham CR3 252 DU125
Ilford IG6 103 EQ52
Oxted RH8 254 EG134
Radlett (Shenley) WD7 62 CL33
Greenwood Ho, Grays
RM17 off Argent St 170 GB79
Greenwood La, Hmptn.
(Hmptn H.) TW12 176 CB92
Greenwood Pk, Kings.T. KT2 178 CS94
Greenwood Pl, NW5
off Highgate Rd 121 DH64
Sch Greenwood Prim Sch, Nthlt.
UB5 off Wood End Way 117 CD64
Greenwood Rd, E8 142 DU65
E13 off Valetta Gro 144 EF68
Bexley DA5 187 FD91
Chigwell IG7 104 EV49
Croydon CR0 201 DP101
Isleworth TW7 157 CE83
Mitcham CR4 201 DK97
Thames Ditton KT7 197 CG102
Woking GU21 226 AS120
Greenwoods, The, Har.
(S.Har.) HA2 116 CC61
Sch Greenwood Sch, SE18
off Welton Rd 165 ES81
Greenwood Ter, NW10 138 CR67
Greenwood Way, Sev. TN13 256 FF125
Green Wrythe Cres, Cars.
SM5 200 DE102
Green Wrythe La, Cars.
SM5 200 DD100
Sch Green Wrythe Prim Sch,
Cars. SM5
off Green Wrythe La 200 DD100
Greenyard, Wal.Abb. EN9 67 EC33
Greer Rd, Har. HA3 94 CC53
Greet St, SE1 20 D2
Greg Cl, E10 123 EC58
Gregories Fm La, Beac. HP9 89 AK53
Gregories Rd, Beac. HP9 88 AH53
Gregor Ms, SE3 164 EG80
Gregory Av, Pot.B. EN6 64 DC33
Gregory Cl, Wok. GU21 226 AW117
Gregory Cres, SE9 184 EK87
Gregory Dr, Wind.
(Old Wind.) SL4 172 AV86
Gregory Ms, Wal.Abb.
EN9 off Beaulieu Dr 67 EB33
Gregory Pl, W8 17 J3
Gregory Rd, Rom. RM6 126 EX56
Slough (Hedg.) SL2 111 AR61
Southall UB2 156 CA76
Gregson Cl, Borwd. WD6 78 CQ39
Gregson's Ride, Loug. IG10 85 EN38
Sch Greig City Acad, N8
off High St 121 DL56
Greig Cl, N8 121 DL57
Greig Ter, SE17
off Lorrimore Sq 161 DP79
Grenaby Av, Croy. CR0 202 DR101
Grenaby Rd, Croy. CR0 202 DR101
Grenada Rd, SE7 164 EJ80
Grenade St, E14 13 M9
Grenadier Cl, St.Alb. AL4 43 CJ21
Grenadier Pl, Cat. CR3 236 DQ122
Grenadier St, E16 145 EN74
Grenadine Cl, Wal.Cr. EN7
off Allwood Rd 66 DT27
Grena Gdns, Rich. TW9 158 CM84
Grena Rd, Rich. TW9 158 CM84
Grendon Cl, Horl. RH6 268 DF146
Grendon Gdns, Wem. HA9 118 CN61
Grendon St, NW8 8 A3
Grenfell Av, Horn. RM12 127 FF60
Grenfell Cl, Borwd. WD6 78 CQ39
Grenfell Gdns, Har. HA3 118 CL59
Grenfell Rd, W11 6 B9
Beaconsfield HP9 89 AL52
Mitcham CR4 180 DF93
Grenfell Twr, W11 6 B9
Grenfell Wk, W11 6 B9
Grennell Cl, Sutt. SM1 200 DD103
Grennell Rd, Sutt. SM1 200 DC103
Grenoble Gdns, N13 99 DN51
Grenville Av, Brox. EN10 49 DZ21
Grenville Cl, N3 97 CZ53
Cobham KT11 214 BX113
Slough (Burn.) SL1 130 AH68
Surbiton KT5 198 CQ102
Waltham Cross EN8 67 DX32
Grenville Ct, SE19
off Lymer Av 182 DT92
Grenville Gdns, Wdf.Grn.
IG8 102 EJ53
Grenville Ms, SW7 17 M7
Hampton TW12 176 CB92
Grenville Pl, NW7 96 CR50
SW7 17 L6
Grenville Rd, N19 121 DL60
Croydon (New Adgtn)
CR0 221 EC109
Grays (Chaff.Hun.) RM16 169 FV78
Grenville St, WC1 9 P4
Gresford Cl, St.Alb. AL4 43 CK20
Gresham Av, N20 98 DF49
Warlingham CR6 237 DY118
Gresham Cl, Bex. DA5 186 EY86
Brentwood CM14 108 FW48
Gresham Cl, Enf. EN2 82 DQ41
Oxted RH8 254 EF128
Gresham Ct, Berk. HP4 38 AV20
Gresham Dr, Rom. RM6 126 EV57
Gresham Gdns, NW11 119 CY60
Gresham Pl, N19 121 DK61
Sch Gresham Prim Sch, S.Croy.
CR2 off Limpsfield Rd 220 DU112
Gresham Rd, E6 145 EM68
E16 15 P8
NW10 118 CR64
SE25 202 DU98
SW9 161 DN83
Beckenham BR3 203 DY96
Brentwood CM14 108 FW48
Edgware HA8 96 CM51
Hampton TW12 176 CA93
Hounslow TW3 156 CC81
Oxted RH8 254 EF128
Slough SL1 131 AN72
Staines TW18 173 BF92
Uxbridge UB10 134 BN68
Gresham St, EC2 10 G7
Gresham Way, SW19 180 DA90
Gresley Cl, E17 123 DY58
N15 off Clinton Rd 122 DR56
Welwyn Garden City AL8 29 CY08
Gresley Ct, Pot.B. EN6 64 DC29
Gresley Rd, N19 121 DJ60
Gressenhall Rd, SW18 179 CZ86
Gresse St, W1 9 L6
Gresswell Cl, Sid. DA14 186 EU90
Greswell St, SW6 159 CX81
Greta Bk, Lthd. (W.Hors.)
KT24 245 BQ126
Gretton Rd, N17 100 DS52
Greville Av, S.Croy. CR2 221 DX110
Greville Cl, Ashtd. KT21 232 CL119
Guildford GU2 242 AT134
Hatfield (N.Mymms) AL9 45 CV24
Twickenham TW1 177 CH87
Greville Ct, Lthd. (Bkhm)
KT23 off Keswick Rd 246 CC125
Greville Hall, NW6 140 DB68
Greville Ms, NW6
off Greville Rd 140 DB68
Greville Pk Av, Ashtd. KT21 232 CL118
Greville Pk Rd, Ashtd. KT21 232 CL118
Greville Pl, NW6 140 DB68
Sch Greville Prim Sch, The,
Ashtd. KT21
off Stonny Cft 232 CM117
Greville Rd, E17 123 EC56
NW6 140 DB67
Richmond TW10 178 CM86
Greville St, EC1 10 D6
Grey Alders, Bans. SM7
off High Beeches 217 CW114
Greycaine Rd, Wat. WD24 76 BX37
Grey Cl, NW11 120 DC58
Sch Grey Coat Hosp Sch,
SW1 19 L8
Upr Sch, SW1 19 L6
Greycoat Pl, SW1 19 L6
Greycoat St, SW1 19 L6
Greycot Rd, Beck. BR3 183 EA92
Sch Grey Ct Sch, Rich.
TW10 off Ham St 177 CJ90
Grey Eagle St, E1 11 N5
Greyfell Cl, Stan. HA7
off Coverdale Cl 95 CH50
Greyfields Cl, Pur. CR8 219 DP113
Greyfriars, Brwd. (Hutt.)
CM13 109 GB45
Greyfriars Pas, EC1 10 F7
Greyfriars Rd, Wok. (Ripley)
GU23 228 BG124
Greygoose Pk, Harl. CM19 51 EN18
Greyhound Hill, NW4 119 CU55
Greyhound La, SW16 181 DK93
Grays (Orsett) RM16 171 GG75
Potters Bar EN6 63 CU33
Greyhound Rd, N17 122 DS55
NW10 139 CV69
W6 159 CX79
W14 159 CY79
Sutton SM1 218 DC106
Greyhound Ter, SW16 201 DJ95
Greyhound Way, Dart. DA1 187 FE86
Greys Pk Cl, Kes. BR2 222 EJ106
Greystead Rd, SE23 182 DW87
Greystoke Av, Pnr. HA5 116 CA55
Greystoke Cl, Berk. HP4 38 AU20
Greystoke Dr, Ruis. HA4 115 BP58
Greystoke Gdns, W5 138 CL70
Enfield EN2 81 DK42
Greystoke Pk Ter, W5 137 CK69
Greystoke Pl, EC4 10 C7
Greystoke Rd, Slou. SL2 131 AM71
Greystone Cl, S.Croy. CR2 220 DW111
Greystone Gdns, Har. HA3 117 CJ58
Ilford IG6 103 EQ54
Greystone Path, E11
off Grove Rd 124 EF59
Greystones Cl, Red. RH1
off Hardwick Rd 266 DD136
Greystones Dr, Reig. RH2 250 DC132
Greyswood Av, N18 101 DX51
Greyswood St, SW16 181 DH93
Greythorne Rd, Wok. GU21 226 AU118
Grey Twrs Av, Horn. RM11 128 FK60
Grey Twrs Gdns, Horn.
RM11 off Grey Twrs Av 128 FK60
Grice Av, West. (Bigg.H.)
TN16 222 EH113
Gridiron Pl, Upmin. RM14 128 FP62
Grierson Rd, SE23 183 DX87
Grieves Rd, Grav. (Nthflt)
DA11 191 GF90
Griffetts Yd, Chesh. HP5
off Bellingdon Rd 54 AP30
Griffin Av, Upmin. RM14 129 FS58
Griffin Cen, The, Felt. TW14 175 BV85
Griffin Cl, NW10 119 CV64
Slough SL1 151 AQ75
Griffin Ct, Lthd. (Bkhm)
KT23 off Griffin Way 246 CA126
Sch Griffin Manor Sch,
SE18 off Welton Rd 165 ES81
Griffin Manor Way, SE28 165 ER76
Griffin Rd, N17 100 DS54
SE18 165 ER78
Griffins, The, Grays RM16 170 GB75
Griffins Cl, N21 100 DR45
Griffin Wk, Green. DA9
off Church Rd 189 FT85
Griffin Way, Lthd. (Bkhm)
KT23 246 CA126
Sunbury-on-Thames
TW16 195 BU96
Griffith Cl, Dag. RM8
off Gibson Rd 126 EW60
Griffiths Cl, Wor.Pk. KT4 199 CV103
Griffiths Rd, SW19 180 DA94
Griffiths Way, St.Alb. AL1 42 CC22
Griffon Way, Wat. (Lvsdn)
WD25 59 BT34
Grifon Rd, Grays (Chaff.Hun.)
RM16 169 FW76
Griggs App, Ilf. IG1 125 EQ61
Griggs Gdns, Horn. RM12
off Tylers Cres 128 FJ64
Griggs Pl, SE1 21 M6
Griggs Rd, E10 123 EC58
Grilse Cl, N9 100 DV49
Grimsby Gro, E16 145 EP74
Grimsby St, E2 11 P4
Grimsdells La, Amer. HP6 55 AR37
Grimsdyke Cres, Barn. EN5 79 CW41
Sch Grimsdyke First & Mid Sch,
Pnr. HA5 off Sylvia Av 94 BZ51
Grimsdyke Rd, Pnr. HA5 94 BY52
Grimsel Path, SE5
off Laxley Cl 161 DP80
Grimshaw Cl, N6 120 DG59
Grimshaw Way, Rom. RM1 127 FF57
Grimstone Cl, Rom. RM5 105 FB51
Grimston Rd, SW6 159 CZ82
St. Albans AL1 43 CF21
Grimthorpe Cl, St.Alb. AL3 43 CD17
Grimwade Av, Croy. CR0 202 DU104
Grimwade Cl, SE15 162 DW83
Grimwood Rd, Twick. TW1 177 CF87
Grindall Cl, Croy. CR0
off Hillside Rd 219 DP105
Grindal St, SE1 20 C4
Grindcobbe, St.Alb. AL1 43 CD23
Grindleford Av, N11 98 DG47
Grindley Gdns, Croy. CR0 202 DT100
Sch Grinling Gibbons Prim
Sch, SE8 off Clyde St 163 DZ79
Grinling Pl, SE8 163 EA79
Grinstead Rd, SE8 23 J10
Grisedale Cl, Pur. CR8 220 DS114
Grisedale Gdns, Pur. CR8 220 DS114
Grittleton Av, Wem. HA9 138 CP65
Grittleton Rd, W9 6 G3
Grizedale Ter, SE23 182 DV89
Grobars Av, Wok. GU21 226 AW115
Grocer's Hall Ct, EC2 11 J8
Grogan Cl, Hmptn. TW12 176 BZ93
Groombridge Cl, Walt. KT12 213 BV106
Welling DA16 186 EU85
Groombridge Rd, E9 143 DX66
Groom Cl, Brom. BR2 204 EH98
Groom Cres, SW18 180 DD87
Groomfield Cl, SW17 180 DG91
Groom Pl, SW1 18 F5
Groom Rd, Brox. EN10 67 DZ26
Grooms Cotts, Chesh. HP5 56 AV30
Grooms Dr, Pnr. HA5 115 BU57
Groom Wk, Guil. GU1 242 AY131
Grosmont Rd, SE18 165 ET78
Grosse Way, SW15 179 CV86
Grosvenor Av, N5 4 G2
SW14 158 CS83
Carshalton SM5 218 DF107
Harrow HA2 116 CB58
Hayes UB4 135 BS68
Kings Langley WD4 59 BQ28
Richmond TW10
off Grosvenor Rd 178 CL85
Sch Grosvenor Av Inf Sch,
Barn. EN5
off Grasvenor Av 80 DA44
Grosvenor Cl, Horl. RH6
off Upfield 268 DG150
Iver SL0 133 BD69
Loughton IG10 85 EP39
Grosvenor Cotts, SW1 18 E7
Grosvenor Ct, N14 99 DJ45
NW6 139 CX67
Guildford GU4
off London Rd 243 BA132
Rickmansworth (Crox.Grn)
WD3 off Mayfare 75 BR43
Slough SL1
off Stoke Poges La 132 AS72
Grosvenor Cres, NW9 118 CN56
SW1 18 F4
Dartford DA1 188 FK85
Uxbridge UB10 135 BP66
Grosvenor Cres Ms, SW1 18 E4
Grosvenor Dr, Horn. RM11 128 FJ60
Loughton IG10 85 EP39
Maidenhead SL6 130 AC71
Grosvenor Est, SW1 19 M7
Grosvenor Gdns, E6 144 EK69
N10 121 DJ55
N14 81 DK43
NW2 119 CW64
NW11 119 CZ58
SW1 18 G5
SW14 158 CS83
Kingston upon Thames
KT2 177 CK93
Upminster RM14 129 FR60
Wallington SM6 219 DJ108
Woodford Green IG8 102 EG51
Grosvenor Gdns Ms E, SW1 19 H5
Grosvenor Gdns Ms N, SW1 18 G6
Grosvenor Gdns Ms S, SW1 19 H6
Grosvenor Gate, W1 8 D10
Grosvenor Hill, SW19 179 CY93
W1 8 G9
Grosvenor Ms, Reig. RH2 266 DB137
Grosvenor Pk, SE5 162 DQ79
Grosvenor Pk Rd, E17 123 EA57
Grosvenor Path, Loug. IG10 85 EP39
Grosvenor Pl, SW1 18 F4
Weybridge KT13
off Vale Rd 195 BR104
Grosvenor Ri E, E17 123 EB57
Grosvenor Rd, E6 144 EK67
E7 144 EH65
E10 123 EC60
E11 124 EG57
N3 97 CZ52
N9 100 DV46
N10 99 DH53
SE25 202 DU98
SW1 161 DH79
W4 158 CP78
W7 137 CG74
Belvedere DA17 166 FA79
Bexleyheath DA6 186 EX85
Borehamwood WD6 78 CN41
Brentford TW8 157 CK79
Broxbourne EN10 49 DZ20
Dagenham RM8 126 EZ60
Epsom KT18 232 CR119
Hounslow TW3 156 BZ83
Ilford IG1 125 EQ62
Northwood HA6 93 BT50
Orpington BR5 205 ES100
Richmond TW10 178 CL85
Romford RM7 127 FD59
St. Albans AL1 43 CE21
Southall UB2 156 BZ76
Staines TW18 174 BG94

★ Place of interest | H Hospital | Sch School | Coll College | Uni University | ⇌ Railway station

Grosvenor Rd, Twick. TW1 177 CG87
Wallington SM6 219 DH107
Watford WD17 76 BW42
West Wickham BR4 203 EB102
Grosvenor Sq, W1 8 F9
Kings Langley WD4
off Grosvenor Av 59 BQ28
Grosvenor St, W1 8 G9
Grosvenor Ter, SE5 161 DP80
Hemel Hempstead HP1 40 BG21
Grosvenor Vale, Ruis. HA4 115 BT61
Grosvenor Way, E5 122 DW61
Grosvenor Wf Rd, E14 24 E8
Grote's Bldgs, SE3 164 EE82
Grote's Pl, SE3 164 EE82
Groton Rd, SW18 180 DB89
Grotto, The, Ware SG12 33 DX07
Grotto Pas, W1 8 F5
Grotto Rd, Twick. TW1 177 CF89
Weybridge KT13 195 BP104
Ground La, Hat. AL10 45 CV16
Grove, The, E15 144 EE65
N3 98 DA53
N4 121 DM59
N6 120 DG60
N8 121 DK57
N13 99 DN50
N14 81 DJ43
NW9 118 CR57
NW11 119 CY59
W5 137 CK74
Addlestone KT15 212 BH106
Amersham HP6 55 AR36
Bexleyheath DA6 166 EX84
Brentwood CM14 108 FT49
Caterham CR3 235 DP121
Chesham HP5 72 AX36
Coulsdon CR5 235 DK115
Edgware HA8 96 CP49
Egham TW20 173 BA92
Enfield EN2 81 DN40
Epsom KT17 216 CS113
Epsom (Ewell) KT17 217 CT110
Esher KT10 196 CB102
Gravesend DA12 191 GH87
Greenford UB6 136 CC72
Hatfield (Brook.Pk) AL9 64 DA27
Horley RH6 269 DH149
Isleworth TW7 157 CE81
Potters Bar EN6 64 DC32
Radlett WD7 61 CG34
Sidcup DA14 186 EY91
Slough SL1 152 AU75
Stanmore HA7 95 CG47
Swanley BR8 207 FF97
Swanscombe DA10 190 FZ85
Teddington TW11 177 CG91
Twickenham TW1
off Bridge Rd 177 CH86
Upminster RM14 128 FP63
Uxbridge UB10 114 BN64
Walton-on-Thames KT12 195 BV101
Watford WD17 75 BQ37
West Wickham BR4 203 EB104
Westerham (Bigg.H.) TN16 238 EK118
Woking GU21 227 AZ116
Grove Av, N3 98 DA52
N10 99 DJ54
W7 137 CE72
Epsom KT17 216 CS113
Pinner HA5 116 BY56
Sutton SM1 218 DA107
Twickenham TW1 177 CF88
Grove Bk, Wat. WD19 94 BX46
Grovebarns, Stai. TW18 174 BG93
Grovebury Cl, Erith DA8 167 FD79
Grovebury Gdns, St.Alb.
(Park St) AL2 60 CC27
Grovebury Rd, SE2 166 EV75
Grove Cl, N14 off Avenue Rd 99 DH45
SE23 183 DX88
Bromley BR2 204 EG103
Epsom KT19 216 CN110
Feltham TW13 176 BY91
Gerrards Cross (Chal.St.P.)
SL9 off Grove La 90 AW53
Kingston upon Thames
KT1 198 CM98
Slough SL1
off Alpha St S 152 AU76
Uxbridge UB10 114 BN64
Windsor (Old Wind.) SL4 172 AV87
Grove Cor, Lthd. (Bkhm)
KT23 off Lower Shott 246 CA126
Grove Cotts, SW3 160 DE79
Grove Ct, SE3 164 EG81
Barnet EN5 off High St 79 CZ41
Beaconsfield HP9
off Station Rd 89 AK53
East Molesey KT8
off Walton Rd 197 CD99
Waltham Abbey EN9
off Highbridge St 67 EB33
Grove Cres, E18 102 EF54
NW9 118 CQ56
Feltham TW13 176 BY91
Kingston upon Thames
KT1 198 CL97
Rickmansworth (Crox.Grn)
WD3 74 BN42
Walton-on-Thames KT12 195 BV101
Grove Cres Rd, E15 143 ED65
Grovedale Cl, Wal.Cr. (Chsht)
EN7 66 DT30
Grovedale Rd, N19 121 DK61
Grove End, E18
off Grove Hill 102 EF54
NW5 off Chetwynd Rd 121 DH63
Gerrards Cross (Chal.St.P.)
SL9 90 AW53
Grove End Gdns, NW8
off Grove End Rd 140 DD68
Grove End La, Esher KT10 197 CD102
Grove End Rd, NW8 140 DD69
Grove Fm Ct, Mitch. CR4
off Brookfields Av 200 DF98
Grove Fm Pk, Nthwd. HA6 93 BR50
Grove Footpath, Surb. KT5 198 CL98
Grove Gdns, NW4 119 CU56
NW8 8 B2
Dagenham RM10 127 FC62
Enfield EN3 83 DX39
Teddington TW11 177 CG91
Grove Grn Rd, E11 123 EC62
Grove Hall Ct, NW8 7 M1
Grove Hall Rd, Bushey
WD23 76 BY42
Grove Heath, Wok. (Ripley)
GU23 228 BJ124
Grove Heath Ct, Wok. (Ripley)
GU23 228 BJ124
Grove Heath N, Wok. (Ripley)
GU23 228 BH122
Grove Heath Rd, Wok. (Ripley)
GU23 228 BJ123
Groveherst Rd, Dart. DA1 168 FM83
GROVEHILL, Hem.H. HP2 40 BL16
Grove Hill, E18 102 EF54
Gerrards Cross (Chal.St.P.)
SL9 90 AW52
Harrow HA1 117 CE59
Grove Hill Rd, SE5 162 DS83
Harrow HA1 117 CE59
Grovehill Rd, Red. RH1 250 DE134
Grove Ho Rd, N8 121 DL56
Groveland Av, SW16 181 DM94
Groveland Ct, EC4 11 H8
Groveland Rd, Beck. BR3 203 DZ97
Grovelands, Hem.H. HP2 41 BQ18
St. Albans (Park St) AL2 60 CB27
West Molesey KT8 196 CA98
Grovelands Cl, SE5 162 DS82
Harrow HA2 116 CB62
Grovelands Ct, N14 99 DK45
Grovelands Rd, N13 99 DM49
N15 122 DU58
Orpington BR5 186 EU94
Purley CR8 219 DL112
[Sch] Grovelands Sch, Walt.
KT12 off Terrace Rd 195 BV100
Grovelands Way, Grays
RM17 170 FZ78
Groveland Way, N.Mal. KT3 198 CQ99
Grove La, SE5 162 DR81
Chesham HP5 56 AV27
Chigwell IG7 103 ET48
Coulsdon CR5 218 DG113
Epping CM16
off High St 70 EU30
Gerrards Cross (Chal.St.P.)
SL9 90 AW53
Kingston upon Thames
KT1 198 CL98
Uxbridge UB8 134 BM70
Grove La Ter, SE5
off Grove La 162 DS83
Grove Lea, Hat. AL10 45 CU21
Groveley Rd, Sun. TW16 175 BT92
Grove Mkt Pl, SE9 185 EM86
Grove Mead, Hat. AL10 45 CT18
Grove Meadow, Welw.G.C.
AL7 30 DC09
Grove Ms, W6 159 CW76
W11 6 E8
Grove Mill La, Wat. WD17 75 BP37
Grove Mill Pl, Cars. SM5 200 DG104
GROVE PARK, SE12 184 EG89
GROVE PARK, W4 158 CP80
⇌ Grove Park 184 EG90
Grove Pk, E11 124 EH58
NW9 118 CQ56
SE5 162 DS82
Grove Pk Av, E4 101 EB52
Grove Pk Br, W4 158 CQ80
Grove Pk Gdns, W4 158 CP79
Grove Pk Ms, W4 158 CQ80
[Sch] Grove Pk Prim Sch,
W4 off Nightingale Cl 158 CQ79
Grove Pk Rd, N15 122 DS56
SE9 184 EJ90
W4 158 CP80
Rainham RM13 147 FG67
[Sch] Grove Pk Spec Sch,
NW9 off Grove Pk 118 CQ56
Grove Pk Ter, W4 158 CP79
Grove Pas, E2 142 DV68
Teddington TW11 177 CG92
Grove Path, Wal.Cr. (Chsht)
EN7 66 DU31
Grove Pl, NW3
off Christchurch Hill 120 DD63
SW12 off Cathles Rd 181 DH86
W3 138 CQ74
W5 off The Grove 137 CK74
Banstead SM7 218 DF112
Barking IG11
off Clockhouse Av 145 EQ67
Hatfield AL9
off Dixons Hill Rd 45 CW24
Watford WD25 76 CB39
Weybridge KT13 213 BQ106
[Sch] Grove Prim Sch,
Rom. RM6
off Chadwell Heath La 126 EW57
Grover Cl, Hem.H. HP2 40 BK19
Grove Rd, E3 143 DX67
E4 101 EB49
E11 124 EF59
E17 123 EB58
E18 102 EF54
N11 99 DH50
N12 98 DD50
N15 122 DS57
NW2 139 CW65
SW13 159 CT82
SW19 180 DC94
W3 138 CQ74
W5 137 CK73
Amersham HP6 72 AT37
Ashtead KT21 232 CM118
Barnet EN4 80 DE41
Beaconsfield HP9 89 AK53
Belvedere DA17 166 EZ79
Bexleyheath DA7 167 FC84
Borehamwood WD6 78 CN39
Brentford TW8 157 CJ78
Chertsey KT16 193 BF100
East Molesey KT8 197 CD98
Edgware HA8 96 CN51
Epsom KT17 216 CS113
Gravesend (Nthflt) DA11 190 GB85
Grays RM17 170 GC79
Guildford GU1 243 BC134
Hemel Hempstead HP1 40 BG22
Horley RH6 268 DE147
Hounslow TW3 156 CB84
Isleworth TW7 157 CE81
Mitcham CR4 201 DH96
Northwood HA6 93 BR50
Oxted RH8
off Southlands La 253 EC134
Pinner HA5 116 BZ57
Richmond TW10 178 CM86
Rickmansworth (Mill End)
WD3 92 BG47
Romford RM6 126 EV59
St. Albans AL1 43 CD21
Sevenoaks TN14 257 FJ121
Sevenoaks (Seal) TN15 257 FN122
Shepperton TW17 195 BQ100
Slough (Burn.) SL1 131 AL67
Surbiton KT6 197 CK99
Sutton SM1 218 DB107
Thornton Heath CR7 201 DN98
Twickenham TW2 177 CD90
Uxbridge UB8 134 BK66
Ware SG12 33 DZ05
Westerham (Tats.) TN16 238 EJ120
Windsor SL4 151 AQ82
Woking GU21 227 AZ116
[Sch] Grove Rd Prim Sch,
Houns. TW3
off Cromwell Rd 156 CA84
Grove Rd W, Enf. EN3 82 DW37
Grover Rd, Wat. WD19 94 BX45
[Sch] Grove Sch, Wat. WD25
off High Cross 76 CC37
Groves Cl, B.End SL8 110 AC60
Grove Shaw, Tad. (Kgswd)
KT20 233 CY124
Groveside, Lthd. (Bkhm)
KT23 246 CA127
Groveside Cl, W3 138 CN72
Carshalton SM5 200 DE103
Leatherhead (Bkhm) KT23 246 CA127
Groveside Rd, E4 102 EE47
Grovestile Waye, Felt. TW14 175 BR87
Grove St, N18 100 DT51
SE8 23 L7
Grove Ter, NW5 121 DH62
Teddington TW11 177 CG91
Grove Ter Ms, NW5
off Grove Ter 121 DH62
Grove Vale, SE22 162 DS84
Chislehurst BR7 185 EN93
Grove Vil, E14 14 B9
Grove Wk, Hert. SG14 32 DQ07
Groveway, SW9 161 DM81
Dagenham RM8 126 EX63
Grove Way, Esher KT10 196 CC101
Rickmansworth (Chorl.)
WD3 73 BB42
Uxbridge UB8 134 BK66
Wembley HA9 118 CP64
Grovewood, Rich. TW9
off Sandycombe Rd 158 CN81
Grovewood Cl, Rick. (Chorl.)
WD3 73 BB43
Grove Wd Hill, Couls. CR5 219 DK114
Grovewood Pl, Wdf.Grn. IG8 103 EM51
Grubbs La, Hat. AL9 46 DA22
Grubb St, Oxt. RH8 254 EJ128
Grummant Rd, SE15 162 DT81
Grundy St, E14 14 A8
Gruneisen Rd, N3 98 DB52
Gryphon Ind Pk, The, St.Alb.
(Port.Wd) AL3 43 CF15
[Coll] GSA Conservatoire, Guil.
GU2 off Millmead Ter 258 AW136
[Sch] Guardian Angels RC
Prim Sch, E3 13 K3
Guardian Av, Grays (N.Stfd)
RM16 169 FX75
Guardian Cl, Horn. RM11 127 FH60
Guards Av, Cat. CR3 236 DQ122
Guards Club Rd, Maid. SL6 130 AC72
Guardsman Cl, Brwd. CM14 108 FX50
★ Guards Mus, SW1 19 K4
Guards Rd, Wind. SL4 150 AJ82
Guards Wk, Wind. SL4
off Guards Rd 150 AJ82
Gubbins La, Rom. RM3 106 FM52
Gubyon Av, SE24 181 DP85
Guerin Sq, E3 13 L1
Guernsey Cl, Guil. GU4
off Cotts Wd Dr 243 BA129
Hounslow TW5 156 CA81
Guernsey Fm Dr, Wok.
GU21 226 AX115
Guernsey Gro, SE24 182 DQ87
Guernsey Ho, Enf. EN3
off Eastfield Rd 83 DX38
Guernsey Rd, E11 123 ED60
Guessens Ct, Welw.G.C.
AL8 29 CW09
Guessens Gro, Welw.G.C.
AL8 29 CW09
Guessens Rd, Welw.G.C.
AL8 29 CW09
Guessens Wk, Welw.G.C.
AL8 29 CW08
Guibal Rd, SE12 184 EH87
Guildcroft, Guil. GU1 243 BA134
Guildersfield Rd, SW16 181 DL94
GUILDFORD, GU1 - GU5 258 AU137
⇌ Guildford 258 AW135
[Coll] Guildford Adult Learning
Cen, Guil. GU1
off Sydenham Rd 258 AY135
Guildford & Godalming
Bypass, Guil. GU3 258 AS137
Guildford Av, Felt. TW13 175 BT89
Guildford Business Pk, Guil.
GU2 242 AV133
Guildford Bypass, Guil. GU1,
GU2, GU4 243 AZ131
★ Guildford Castle, Guil.
GU1 258 AX136
★ Guildford Cath, Guil.
GU2 242 AV134
[Coll] Guildford Coll of Further
& Higher Ed, Stoke Park
Campus, Guil. GU1
off Stoke Rd 242 AX133
[Sch] Guildford Co Sch, The, Guil.
GU2 off Farnham Rd 258 AV136
Guildford Gdns, Rom. RM3 106 FL51
Guildford Gro, SE10 163 EB81
[Sch] Guildford High Sch for Girls,
Guil. GU1 off London Rd 242 AY134
★ Guildford House Gall,
Guil. GU1 off High St 258 AX135
Guildford La, Guil. (Albury)
GU5 260 BH139
Woking GU22 226 AX120
Guildford Lo Dr, Lthd.
(E.Hors.) KT24 245 BT129
★ Guildford Mus, Guil.
GU1 258 AX136
[H] Guildford Nuffield Hosp,
Guil. GU2 242 AS134
GUILDFORD PARK, Guil.
GU2 258 AV135
Guildford Pk Av, Guil. GU2 258 AV135
Guildford Pk Rd, Guil. GU2 258 AV135
Guildford Rd, E6 144 EL72
E17 101 EC53
SW8 161 DL81
Chertsey KT16 193 BE102
Croydon CR0 202 DR100
Dorking (Abin.Ham.) RH5 262 BW140
Dorking (Westc.) RH4 262 CA138
Godalming GU7 258 AU144
Guildford (Norm.) GU3 242 AX127
Ilford IG3 125 ES61
Leatherhead (Bkhm)
KT23 246 BZ127
Leatherhead (E.Hors.)
KT24 246 BW129
Leatherhead (Fetch.)
KT22 231 CG122
Romford RM3 106 FL51
St. Albans AL1 43 CH21
Woking GU22 226 AY119
Woking (Mayford) GU22 226 AX122
Guildford St, Cher. KT16 194 BG101
Staines TW18 174 BG93
Guildford Way, Wall. SM6 219 DL106
★ Guildhall, The, EC2 11 J7
★ Guildhall Art Gall,
Guildhall Lib, EC2 11 H7
Guildhall Bldgs, EC2
off Basinghall St 142 DR72
[Coll] Guildhall Sch of Music
& Drama, EC2 11 H5
Hall of Res, EC1 11 J5
Guildhall Yd, EC2 11 J7
Guildhouse St, SW1 19 J7
Guildown Av, N12 98 DB49
Guildford GU2 258 AV137
Guildown Rd, Guil. GU2 258 AV137
Guild Rd, SE7 164 EK78
Erith DA8 167 FF80
Guildsway, E17 101 DZ53
Guileway, The, Guil. GU3 258 AW140
Guileshill La, Wok. (Ockham)
GU23 228 BL123
Guilford Av, Surb. KT5 198 CM99
Guilford Pl, WC1 10 A4
Guilfords, Harl. CM17 36 EX10
Guilford St, WC1 9 P4
Guilford Vil, Surb. KT5
off Alpha Rd 198 CM100
Guilsborough Cl, NW10 138 CS66
Guinevere Gdns, Wal.Cr.
EN8 67 DY31
Guinness Cl, E9 143 DY66
Hayes UB3 155 BR76
Guinness Ct, Wok. GU21
off Iveagh Rd 226 AT118
Guinness Sq, SE1 21 L7
Guinness Trust Bldgs, SE1
off Snowsfields 162 DS75
SE11 20 F9
SW3 18 C8
SW9 161 DP84
Guinness Trust Est, N16
off Holmleigh Rd 122 DS60
Guion Rd, SW6 159 CZ82
Gulland Cl, Bushey WD23 76 CC43
Gulland Wk, N1
off Clephane Rd 142 DQ65
Gullbrook, Hem.H. HP1 40 BG20
Gull Cl, Wall. SM6 219 DL108
Gullet Wd Rd, Wat. WD25 75 BU35
Gulliver Cl, Nthlt. UB5 136 BZ67
Gulliver Rd, Sid. DA15 185 ES89
Gulliver St, SE16 23 L5
Gull Wk, Horn. RM12
off Heron Flight Av 147 FH66
Gulphs, The, Hert. SG13 32 DR10
Gulston Wk, SW3 18 D8
Gumleigh Rd, W5 157 CJ77
Gumley Gdns, Islw. TW7 157 CG83
[Sch] Gumley Ho RC Conv
Sch, Islw. TW7
off St. John's Rd 157 CG83
Gumley Rd, Grays RM20 169 FX79
Gumping Rd, Orp. BR5 205 EQ103
Gundulph Rd, Brom. BR2 204 EJ97
Gunfleet Cl, Grav. DA12 191 GL87
Gun Hill, Til. (W.Til.) RM18 171 GK79
Gunmakers La, E3 143 DY67
Gunnell Cl, SE26 182 DU92
Croydon CR0 202 DU100
Gunner Dr, Enf. EN3 83 EA37
Gunner La, SE18 165 EN78
GUNNERSBURY, W4 158 CP77
⇌ Gunnersbury 158 CP78
⊖ Gunnersbury 158 CP78
Gunnersbury Av, W3 158 CN76
W4 158 CN76
W5 138 CM74
[Sch] Gunnersbury Catholic
Sch for Boys, Brent. TW8
off The Ride 157 CJ78
Gunnersbury Cl, W4
off Grange Rd 158 CP78
Gunnersbury Ct, W3
off Bollo La 158 CP75
Gunnersbury Cres, W3 158 CN75
Gunnersbury Dr, W5 158 CM75
Gunnersbury Gdns, W3 158 CN75
Gunnersbury La, W3 158 CN76
Gunnersbury Ms, W4
off Chiswick High Rd 158 CP78
★ Gunnersbury Park, W3 158 CM77
Gunnersbury Pk, W3 158 CM77
W5 158 CM77
★ Gunnersbury Park Mus
& Art Cen, W3 158 CN76
Gunners Gro, E4 101 EC48
Gunners Rd, SW18 180 DD89
Gunnery Ter, SE18 165 EQ77
Gunning Rd, Grays RM17 170 GD78
Gunning St, SE18 165 ES77
Gunn Rd, Swans. DA10 190 FY86
Gunpowder Sq, EC4 10 D7
Gunstor Rd, N16 122 DS63
Gun St, E1 11 N6
Gunter Gro, SW10 160 DC79
Edgware HA8 96 CR53
Gunters Mead, Esher
KT10 214 CC110
Gunterstone Rd, W14 16 C8
Gunthorpe St, E1 11 P6
Gunton Rd, E5 122 DV62
SW17 180 DG93
Gunwhale Cl, SE16 23 H2
Gurdon Rd, SE7 25 M10
Gurnard Cl, West Dr. UB7
off Trout Rd 134 BK73
Gurnell Gro, W13 137 CF70
Gurnells Rd, Beac.
(Seer Grn) HP9 89 AQ51
Gurney Cl, E15
off Gurney Rd 124 EE64
E17 101 DX53
Barking IG11 145 EP65
Beaconsfield HP9 88 AJ53
Gurney Ct Rd, St.Alb. AL1 43 CF18
Gurney Cres, Croy. CR0 201 DM102
Gurney Dr, N2 120 DC57
Gurney Rd, E15 124 EE64
SW6 160 DC83
Carshalton SM5 218 DG105
Northolt UB5 135 BV69
Gurney's Cl, Red. RH1 266 DF135
[Sch] Guru Nanak Prim Sch,
Hayes UB4
off Springfield Rd 136 BW74
[Sch] Guru Nanak Sec Sch,
Hayes UB4
off Springfield Rd 136 BW74
Guthrie St, SW3 18 A9
Gutteridge La, Rom.
(Stap.Abb.) RM4 87 FC44
Gutter La, EC2 11 H7
Guyatt Gdns, Mitch. CR4
off Ormerod Gdns 200 DG96
Guy Barnett Gro, SE3
off Casterbridge Rd 164 EG83
Guy Rd, Wall. SM6 201 DK104
Guyscliff Rd, SE13 183 EC85
Guysfield Cl, Rain. RM13 147 FG67
Guysfield Dr, Rain. RM13 147 FG67
[H] Guy's Hosp, SE1 21 K3
Guy St, SE1 21 K3
Gwalior Rd, SW15
off Felsham Rd 159 CX83
Gwendolen Av, SW15 179 CX85
Gwendolen Cl, SW15 179 CX85
Gwendoline Av, E13 144 EH67
Gwendwr Rd, W14 16 D9
Gwent Cl, Wat. WD25 60 BX34
Gwillim Cl, Sid. DA15 186 EU85
Gwydor Rd, Beck. BR3 203 DX98
Gwydyr Rd, Brom. BR2 204 EF97
Gwyn Cl, SW6 160 DC80
[Sch] Gwyn Jones Prim Sch,
E11 off Hainault Rd 123 ED59
Gwynne Av, Croy. CR0 203 DX101
Gwynne Cl, W4
off Pumping Sta Rd 159 CT79
Windsor SL4 151 AL81
Gwynne Ct, Guil. GU2
off Grange Rd 242 AV130
Gwynne Pk Av, Wdf.Grn.
IG8 103 EM51
Gwynne Pl, WC1 10 B2
Gwynne Rd, SW11 160 DD82
Caterham CR3 236 DR123
Gwynne Vaughan Av, Guil.
GU2 242 AU130
Gwynn Rd, Grav. (Nthflt)
DA11 190 GC89
Gwynns Wk, Hert. SG13 32 DR09
Gyfford Wk, Wal.Cr. EN7 66 DV31
Gylcote Cl, SE5 162 DR84
Gyles Pk, Stan. HA7 95 CJ53
Gyllyngdune Gdns, Ilf. IG3 125 ET61
Gypsy Cl, Ware (Gt Amwell)
SG12 33 DZ11
Gypsy Cor, W3 138 CR71
Gypsy La, Kings L. WD4 75 BR35
Slough (Stoke P.) SL2 131 AS63
Ware (Gt Amwell) SG12 33 DZ11
Welwyn Garden City AL7 29 CZ13
Gypsy Moth Av, Hat. AL10 44 CS16

H

Haarlem Rd, W14 16 A6
Haberdasher Est, N1
off Haberdasher St 142 DR69
Haberdasher Pl, N1 11 K1
[Sch] Haberdashers' Aske's
Hatcham Coll, Boys,
SE14 off Pepys Rd 163 DY82
Girls, SE14
off Jerningham Rd 163 DY81
[Sch] Haberdashers' Aske's Sch,
Borwd. WD6
off Butterfly La 77 CH41
[Sch] Haberdashers' Aske's
Sch for Girls, Borwd. WD6
off Aldenham Rd 77 CH42
Haberdasher St, N1 11 K1
Habgood Rd, Loug. IG10 84 EL41
Haccombe Rd, SW19
off Haydons Rd 180 DC93
HACKBRIDGE, Wall. SM6 201 DH103
⇌ Hackbridge 201 DH103
Hackbridge Grn, Wall. SM6 200 DG103
Hackbridge Pk Gdns, Cars.
SM5 200 DG103
[Sch] Hackbridge Prim Sch, Wall.
SM6 off Hackbridge Rd 200 DG103
Hackbridge Rd, Wall. SM6 200 DG103
Hackett La, Saw. CM21 35 ET05
Hacketts La, Wok. GU22 211 BF114
Hackford Rd, SW9 161 DM81
Hackford Wk, SW9 161 DM81
Hackforth Cl, Barn. EN5 79 CV43
Hackhurst La, Dor.
(Abin.Ham.) RH5 261 BT138
Hackington Cres, Beck. BR3 183 EA93
HACKNEY, E8 142 DV65
⇌ Hackney Central 142 DV65
★ Hackney City Fm, E2 142 DU68
Hackney Cl, Borwd. WD6 78 CR43
⇌ Hackney Downs 122 DV64
[Sch] Hackney Free & Parochial
C of E Sec Sch (Lwr), E9
off Paragon Rd 142 DW65
Hackney Gro, E8
off Reading La 142 DV65
★ Hackney Marsh, E9 123 DY62
★ Hackney Mus, E8 142 DV65
Hackney Rd, E2 11 N2
HACKNEY WICK, E9 123 EA64
⇌ Hackney Wick 143 EA65
Hackworth Pt, E3 14 A2
HACTON, Rain. RM13 128 FM64
Hacton Dr, Horn. RM12 128 FK63
Hacton La, Horn. RM12 128 FM62
Upminster RM14 128 FM64
[Sch] Hacton Prim Sch, Horn.
RM12 off Chepstow Av 127 FD55
Hadar Cl, N20 98 DB46
Hadden Rd, SE28 165 ES76
Hadden Way, Grnf. UB6 137 CD65
Haddestoke Gate, Wal.Cr.
(Chsht) EN8 67 DZ26
Haddington Rd, Brom. BR1 183 ED90
Haddon Cl, Borwd. WD6 78 CN41
Enfield EN1 82 DU44
Hemel Hempstead HP3 40 BN21
New Malden KT3 199 CT99
Weybridge KT13 195 BR104
Haddonfield, SE8 23 H8
Haddon Gro, Sid. DA15 186 EU87
Haddon Rd, Orp. BR5 206 EW99
Rickmansworth (Chorl.)
WD3 73 BC43
Sutton SM1 218 DB105
Haddo St, SE10 163 EB79
Hadfield Cl, Sthl. UB1
off Adrienne Av 136 BZ69
Hadfield Rd, Stai. (Stanw.)
TW19 174 BK86
Hadlands Cl, Hem.H. (Bov.)
HP3 57 AZ26
Hadleigh Cl, E1 12 F3
SW20 199 CZ96
Hadleigh Ct, Brox. EN10 49 DZ22
Hadleigh Dr, Sutt. SM2 218 DA109

⊖ London Underground station — [DLR] Docklands Light Railway station — [Tra] Tramlink station — [Riv] Pedestrian ferry landing stage

Hadleigh Rd, N9 100 DV45
Hadleigh St, E2 12 F2
Hadleigh Wk, E6 144 EL72
HADLEY, Barn. EN5 79 CZ40
Hadley Cl, N21 81 DN44
Borehamwood (Elstree) WD6 78 CM44
Hadley Common, Barn. EN5 80 DA40
Hadley Gdns, W4 158 CR78
Southall UB2 178 BZ78
Hadley Gra, Harl. CM17 52 EW16
Hadley Grn, Barn. EN5 79 CZ40
Hadley Grn Rd, Barn. EN5 79 CZ40
Hadley Grn W, Barn. EN5 79 CZ40
Hadley Gro, Barn. EN5 79 CY40
Hadley Highstone, Barn. EN5 79 CZ39
Hadley Pl, Wey. KT13 212 BN108
Hadley Ridge, Barn. EN5 79 CZ41
Hadley Rd, Barn. (Had.Wd) EN4 81 DH38
Barnet (New Barn.) EN5 80 DB42
Belvedere DA17 166 EZ77
Enfield EN2 81 DL38
Mitcham CR4 201 DK98
Hadley St, NW1 141 DH65
Hadley Way, N21 81 DN44
HADLEY WOOD, Barn. EN4 80 DD38
⇌ Hadley Wood 80 DC38
Sch Hadley Wd Prim Sch, Barn. EN4 off Courtleigh Av 80 DC38
Hadley Wd Ri, Ken. CR8 235 DP115
Hadlow Ct, Slou. SL1 131 AQ73
Hadlow Pl, SE19 182 DU94
Hadlow Rd, Sid. DA14 186 EU91
Welling DA16 166 EW80
Hadlow Way, Grav. (Istead Rise) DA13 190 GE94
Hadrian Cl, St.Alb. AL3 42 BZ22
Staines TW19 174 BL88
Hadrian Ct, Sutt. SM2 off Stanley Rd 218 DB108
Hadrian Est, E2 142 DU68
Hadrian Ms, N7 4 B5
Hadrians Ride, Enf. EN1 82 DT43
Hadrian St, SE10 24 G10
Hadrian Way, Stai. (Stanw.) TW19 174 BL87
Hadyn Pk Rd, W12 159 CU75
Hafer Rd, SW11 160 DF84
Hafton Rd, SE6 184 EE88
Hagden La, Wat. WD18 75 BT43
Haggard Rd, Twick. TW1 177 CH87
HAGGERSTON, E2 5 P9
Haggerston Rd, E8 5 N6
Borehamwood WD6 78 CL38
Sch Haggerston Sch, E2 5 P9
Hag Hill La, Maid. (Taplow) SL6 130 AG72
Hag Hill Ri, Maid. (Taplow) SL6 130 AG72
Hagsdell La, Hert. SG13 32 DR10
Hagsdell Rd, Hert. SG13 32 DR10
Sch Hague Prim Sch, E2 12 D3
Hague St, E2 12 B2
Ha-Ha Rd, SE18 165 EM79
Haig Cl, St.Alb. AL1 off Kitchener Cl 43 CH21
Haig Dr, Slou. SL1 151 AP75
Haig Gdns, Grav. DA12 191 GJ87
Haigh Cres, Red. RH1 267 DH136
Haig Pl, Mord. SM4 off Green La 200 DA100
Haig Rd, Grays RM16 171 GG76
Stanmore HA7 95 CJ50
Uxbridge UB8 135 BP71
Westerham (Bigg.H.) TN16 238 EL117
Haig Rd E, E13 144 EJ69
Haig Rd W, E13 144 EJ69
Haigville Gdns, Ilf. IG6 125 EP56
Hailes Cl, SW19 off North Rd 180 DC93
Hailey Av, Hodd. EN11 33 EA13
Haileybury Av, Enf. EN1 82 DT44
Sch Haileybury Coll, Hert. SG13 off College Rd 33 DX13
Haileybury Rd, Orp. BR6 224 EU105
Hailey Cl, Hert. (Hailey) SG13 33 DY13
Sch Hailey Hall Sch, Hert. SG13 off Hailey La 33 DZ13
Hailey La, Hert. (Hailey) SG13 33 DX14
Hailey Rd, Erith DA18 166 FA75
Hailsham Av, SW2 181 DM89
Hailsham Cl, Rom. RM3 106 FJ50
Surbiton KT6 197 CK101
Hailsham Dr, Har. HA1 117 CD55
Hailsham Gdns, Rom. RM3 106 FJ50
Hailsham Rd, SW17 180 DG93
Romford RM3 106 FJ50
Hailsham Ter, N18 100 DQ50
Sch Haimo Prim Sch, SE9 off Haimo Rd 184 EK85
Haimo Rd, SE9 184 EK85
HAINAULT, Ilf. IG6 103 ES52
⊖ Hainault 103 ES52
Hainault Ct, E17 123 ED56
★ Hainault Forest Country Pk, Chig. IG7 104 EW47
Sch Hainault Forest High Sch, Ilf. IG6 off Harbourer Rd 104 EV50
Hainault Gore, Rom. RM6 126 EY57
Hainault Gro, Chig. IG7 103 EQ49
Hainault Ind Est, Ilf. IG6 104 EW50
Hainault Rd, E11 123 EC60
Chigwell IG7 103 EP48
Romford RM5 105 FC54
Romford (Chad.Hth) RM6 126 EZ58
Romford (Lt.Hth) RM6 126 EV55
Hainault St, SE9 185 EP88
Ilford IG1 125 EP61
Haines Ct, Wey. KT13 off St. George's Lo 213 BR106
Haines Wk, Mord. SM4 off Dorchester Rd 200 DB101
Haines Way, Wat. WD25 59 BU34
Hainford Cl, SE4 163 DX84
Haining Cl, W4 off Wellesley Rd 158 CN78
Hainthorpe Rd, SE27 181 DP90
Hainton Cl, E1 12 D8
Halberd Ms, E5 off Knightland Rd 122 DV61
Halbutt Gdns, Dag. RM9 126 EZ62
Halbutt St, Dag. RM9 126 EZ63
Halcomb St, N1 5 L8
Halcot Av, Bexh. DA6 187 FB85
Halcrow St, E1 12 D6
Halcyon Way, Horn. RM11 128 FM60
Haldane Cl, N10 99 DH52
Enfield EN3 83 EB38
Haldane Gdns, Grav. DA11 190 GC88
Haldane Pl, SW18 180 DB88
Haldane Rd, E6 144 EK69
SE28 146 EX73
SW6 159 CZ80
Southall UB1 136 CC72
Haldan Rd, E4 101 EC51
Haldens, Welw.G.C. AL7 29 CZ06
Haldon Cl, Chig. IG7 off Arrowsmith Rd 103 ES50
Haldon Rd, SW18 179 CZ85
Hale, The, E4 101 ED52
N17 122 DU55
Hale Cl, E4 101 EC48
Edgware HA8 96 CQ50
Orpington BR6 223 EQ105
Hale Dr, NW7 96 CQ51
HALE END, E4 101 ED51
Hale End, Rom. RM3 105 FH51
Woking GU22 226 AV121
Hale End Cl, Ruis. HA4 115 BU58
Hale End Rd, E4 101 ED51
E17 101 ED53
Woodford Green IG8 101 ED52
Halefield Rd, N17 100 DU53
Hale Gdns, N17 122 DU55
W3 138 CN74
Hale Gro Gdns, NW7 96 CR50
Hale La, NW7 96 CR50
Edgware HA8 96 CP50
Sevenoaks (Otford) TN14 241 FE117
Hale Path, SE27 181 DP91
Hale Pit Rd, Lthd. (Bkhm) KT23 246 CC126
Hale Rd, E6 144 EL70
N17 122 DU55
Hertford SG13 32 DR10
Hales Oak, Lthd. (Bkhm) KT23 246 CC126
Halesowen Rd, Mord. SM4 200 DB101
Hales Pk, Hem.H. HP2 41 BQ19
Hales Pk Cl, Hem.H. HP2 41 BQ19
Hales St, SE8 off Deptford High St 163 EA80
Hale St, E14 14 A9
Staines TW18 173 BE91
Haleswood, Cob. KT11 213 BV114
Haleswood Rd, Hem.H. HP2 40 BN19
Halesworth Cl, E5 off Theydon Rd 122 DW61
Romford RM3 106 FL52
Halesworth Rd, SE13 163 EB83
Romford RM3 106 FL51
Hale Wk, W7 137 CE71
Haley Rd, NW4 119 CW58
Half Acre, Brent. TW8 157 CK79
Halfacre Hill, Ger.Cr. (Chal.St.P.) SL9 90 AY53
Half Acre Rd, W7 137 CE74
Halfhide La, Brox. (Turnf.) EN10 67 DY26
Waltham Cross (Chsht) EN8 67 DX27
Halfhides, Wal.Abb. EN9 67 ED33
Half Moon Ct, EC1 10 G6
Half Moon Cres, N1 4 B9
Half Moon La, SE24 182 DQ86
Epping CM16 69 ET31
Half Moon Meadow, Hem.H. HP2 41 BQ15
Half Moon Ms, St.Alb. AL1 off London Rd 43 CD20
Half Moon Pas, E1 11 P8
Half Moon St, W1 19 H1
Half Moon Yd, St.Alb. AL1 off Chequer St 43 CD20
Halford Cl, Edg. HA8 96 CP54
Halford Ct, Hat. AL10 off Mosquito Way 44 CS17
Halford Rd, E10 123 ED57
SW6 160 DA79
Richmond TW10 178 CL85
Uxbridge UB10 114 BN64
Halfpenny Cl, Guil. (Chilw.) GU4 259 BD140
Halfpenny La, Guil. (Chilw.) GU4 259 BC136
Halfway Ct, Purf. RM19 168 FN77
Halfway Grn, Walt. KT12 195 BV104
Halfway Ho La, Amer. HP6 54 AL33
Halfway St, Sid. DA15 185 ER87
Haliburton Rd, Twick. TW1 177 CG85
Haliday Wk, N1 5 K3
Halidon Cl, E9 off Urswick Rd 122 DW64
Halidon Ri, Rom. RM3 106 FP51
Halifax Cl, St.Alb. AL2 60 BZ30
Watford (Lvsdn) WD25 59 BT34
Halifax Rd, Enf. EN2 82 DQ40
Greenford UB6 136 CB67
Rickmansworth (Herons.) WD3 91 BC45
Halifax St, SE26 182 DV91
Halifax Way, Welw.G.C. AL7 30 DE09
Halifield Dr, Belv. DA17 166 EY76
Haling Down Pas, S.Croy. CR2 220 DQ109
Haling Gro, S.Croy. CR2 220 DQ108
Sch Haling Manor High Sch, S.Croy. CR2 off Kendra Hall Rd 219 DP108
Haling Pk, S.Croy. CR2 220 DQ107
Haling Pk Gdns, S.Croy. CR2 219 DP107
Haling Pk Rd, S.Croy. CR2 219 DP106
Haling Rd, S.Croy. CR2 220 DR107
Halings La, Uxb. (Denh.) UB9 113 BE56
Halkin Arc, SW1 18 E5
Halkingcroft, Slou. SL3 152 AW75
Halkin Ms, SW1 18 E5
Halkin Pl, SW1 18 E5
Halkin St, SW1 18 F4
Hall, The, SE3 164 EG83
Hallam Cl, Chis. BR7 185 EM92
Watford WD24 76 BW40
Hallam Gdns, Pnr. HA5 94 BY52
Hallam Ms, W1 9 H5
Hallam Rd, N15 121 DP56
SW13 159 CV83
Hallam St, W1 9 H4
Halland Way, Nthwd. HA6 93 BR51
Hall Av, N18 off Weir Hall Av 100 DR51
South Ockendon (Aveley) RM15 148 FQ74
Hall Cl, W5 138 CL71
Godalming GU7 258 AS144
Rickmansworth (Mill End) WD3 92 BG46
Hall Ct, Slou. (Datchet) SL3 152 AV80
Teddington TW11 177 CF92
Hall Cres, S.Ock. (Aveley) RM15 168 FQ75
Hall Dene Cl, Guil. GU1 243 BC133
Hall Dr, SE26 182 DW92
W7 137 CE72
Uxbridge (Hare.) UB9 92 BJ53
Halley Gdns, SE13 163 ED84
Sch Halley Prim Sch, E14 13 K6
Halley Rd, E7 144 EJ65
E12 144 EK65
Waltham Abbey EN9 83 EB36
Halleys App, Wok. GU21 226 AU118
Halleys Ct, Wok. GU21 off Halleys App 226 AU118
Halleys Ridge, Hert. SG14 31 DN10
Halley St, E14 13 J6
Halleys Wk, Add. KT15 212 BJ108
Hall Fm Cl, Stan. HA7 95 CH49
Hall Fm Dr, Twick. TW2 177 CD87
Hallfield Est, W2 7 L8
Sch Hallfield Inf Sch, W2 7 K8
Sch Hallfield Jun Sch, W2 7 K8
Hallford Way, Dart. DA1 188 FJ85
Hall Gdns, E4 101 DZ49
St. Albans (Coln.Hth) AL4 44 CR23
Hall Gate, NW8 7 M1
Hall Grn La, Brwd. (Hutt.) CM13 109 GC45
HALL GROVE, Welw.G.C. AL7 30 DB11
Hall Gro, Welw.G.C. AL7 30 DB11
Hall Heath Cl, St.Alb. AL1 43 CH18
Hall Hill, Oxt. RH8 253 ED131
Sevenoaks (Seal) TN15 257 FP123
Halliards, The, Walt. KT12 off Felix Rd 195 BU100
Halliday Cl, Rad. (Shenley) WD7 62 CL32
Halliday Sq, Sthl. UB2 137 CD74
Halliford Cl, Shep. TW17 195 BR98
Halliford Rd, Shep. TW17 195 BS99
Sunbury-on-Thames TW16 195 BS99
Sch Halliford Sch, Shep. TW17 off Russell Rd 195 BQ101
Halliford St, N1 5 H5
Halliloo Valley Rd, Cat. (Wold.) CR3 237 DZ119
Hallingbury Ct, E17 123 EB55
Halling Hill, Harl. CM20 35 ET13
Hallington Cl, Wok. GU21 226 AV117
Halliwell Rd, SW2 181 DM86
Halliwick Rd, N10 98 DG53
Hall La, E4 101 DY50
E4 (Junct) 101 DY50
NW4 97 CU53
Brentwood (Shenf.) CM15 109 FZ44
Hayes UB3 155 BR80
South Ockendon RM15 149 FX68
Upminster RM14 128 FQ60
Hallmark Trd Est, NW10 off Great Cen Way 118 CQ63
Hall Meadow, Slou. SL1 130 AJ68
Hallmead Rd, Sutt. SM1 200 DB104
Sch Hall Mead Sch, Upmin. RM14 off Marlborough Gdns 129 FR60
Hallmores, Brox. EN10 49 EA19
Hall Oak Wk, NW6 off Barlow Rd 139 CZ65
Hallowell Av, Croy. CR0 219 DL105
Hallowell Cl, Mitch. CR4 200 DG97
Hallowell Rd, Nthwd. HA6 93 BS52
Hallowes Cl, Guil. GU2 off Grange Rd 242 AV129
Hallowes Cres, Wat. WD19 off Hayling Rd 93 BU48
Hallowfield Way, Mitch. CR4 200 DD98
Hallows Gro, Sun. TW16 off Groveley Rd 175 BT92
Hall Pk, Berk. HP4 38 AY20
Hall Pk Gate, Berk. HP4 38 AY21
Hall Pk Hill, Berk. HP4 38 AY21
Hall Pk Rd, Upmin. RM14 128 FQ64
★ Hall Pl, Bex. DA5 187 FC86
Hall Pl, W2 7 N4
Woking GU21 227 BA116
Hall Pl Cl, St.Alb. AL1 43 CE19
Hall Pl Cres, Bex. DA5 187 FC85
Hall Pl Dr, Wey. KT13 213 BS106
Hall Pl Gdns, St.Alb. AL1 43 CE19
Hall Rd, E6 145 EM67
E15 123 ED63
NW8 7 M2
Dartford DA1 168 FM84
Gravesend (Nthflt) DA11 190 GC90
Hemel Hempstead HP2 41 BP18
Isleworth TW7 177 CD85
Romford (Chad.Hth) RM6 126 EW58
Romford (Gidea Pk) RM2 127 FH55
South Ockendon (Aveley) RM15 168 FQ75
Wallington SM6 219 DH109
Sch Hall Sch, The, NW3 off Crossfield Rd 140 DD65
SW15 off Stroud Cres 179 CU90
SW20 off The Downs 199 CX95
HALLS GREEN, Harl. CM19 50 EJ18
Hallside Rd, Enf. EN1 82 DT38
Hallsland Way, Oxt. RH8 254 EF133
Hall St, EC1 10 F1
N12 98 DC50
Sch Hallsville Prim Sch, E16 15 L8
Hallsville Rd, E16 15 J8
Hallswelle Rd, NW11 119 CZ57
Hall Ter, Rom. RM3 106 FN52
South Ockendon (Aveley) RM15 169 FR75
Hall Twr, W2 7 P5
Hall Vw, SE9 184 EK89
Hall Way, Pur. CR8 219 DP113
Hallwood Cres, Brwd. (Shenf.) CM15 108 FY45
Hallywell Cres, E6 145 EM71
Halons Rd, SE9 185 EN87
Halpin Pl, SE17 21 K8
Halsbrook Rd, SE3 164 EK83
Halsbury Cl, Stan. HA7 95 CH49
Halsbury Rd, W12 139 CV74
Halsbury Rd E, Nthlt. UB5 116 CC63
Halsbury Rd W, Nthlt. UB5 116 CB64
Halse Dr, Slou. SL2 111 AM64
Halsend, Hayes UB3 135 BV74
Halsey Dr, Hem.H. HP1 39 BF18
Halsey Ms, SW3 18 C7
Halsey Pk, St.Alb. (Lon.Col.) AL2 62 CM27
Halsey Pl, Wat. WD24 75 BV38
Halsey Rd, Wat. WD18 75 BV41
Halsey St, SW3 18 C7
Halsham Cres, Bark. IG11 145 ET65
Halsmere Rd, SE5 161 DP81
HALSTEAD, Sev. TN14 224 EZ113
Halstead Cl, Croy. CR0 off Charles St 202 DQ104
Sch Halstead Comm Prim Sch, Sev. TN14 off Otford La 224 EZ112
Halstead Ct, N1 5 K10
Halstead Gdns, N21 100 DR46
Halstead Hill, Wal.Cr. (Chsht) EN7 66 DS29
Halstead La, Sev. (Knock.) TN14 224 EZ114
Sch Halstead Pl Sch, Sev. TN14 off Church Rd 224 EY111
Sch Halstead Prep Sch, Wok. GU21 off Woodham Ri 211 BA114
Halstead Rd, E11 124 EG57
N21 100 DQ46
Enfield EN1 82 DS42
Erith DA8 167 FE81
Halstead Way, Brwd. (Hutt.) CM13 109 GC44
Halston Cl, SW11 180 DF86
Sch Halstow Prim Sch, SE10 25 L10
Halstow Rd, NW10 6 A2
SE10 25 L9
Halsway, Hayes UB3 135 BU74
Halter Cl, Borwd. WD6 off Clydesdale Cl 78 CR43
Halton Cl, N11 off Colney Hatch La 98 DF51
Halton Cross St, N1 4 F7
Halton Pl, N1 4 G7
Halton Rd, N1 4 F5
Grays RM16 171 GJ76
Halt Robin La, Belv. DA17 off Halt Robin Rd 167 FB77
Halt Robin Rd, Belv. DA17 166 FA77
Haltside, Hat. AL10 44 CS19
Halwick Cl, Hem.H. HP1 40 BH21
HAM, Rich. TW10 177 CK90
Ham, The, Brent. TW8 157 CJ80
Hambalt Rd, SW4 181 DJ85
Hamble Cl, Ruis. HA4 off Chichester Av 115 BS61
Woking GU21 226 AU117
Hamble Ct, Tedd. TW11 177 CK94
Hambledon Cl, Uxb. UB8 off Aldenham Dr 135 BP71
Hambledon Gdns, SE25 202 DT97
Hambledon Hill, Epsom KT18 232 CQ116
Hambledon Pl, SE21 182 DS88
Hambledon Rd, SW18 179 CZ87
Caterham CR3 236 DR123
Hambledon Vale, Epsom KT18 232 CQ116
Hambledown Rd, Sid. DA15 185 ER87
Hamble La, S.Ock. RM15 149 FT71
Hamble St, SW6 160 DB83
Hambleton Cl, Wor.Pk. KT4 off Cotswold Way 199 CW103
Hamble Wk, Nthlt. UB5 off Brabazon Rd 136 CA68
Woking GU21 226 AU118
Hamblings Cl, Rad. (Shenley) WD7 61 CK33
Hambridge Way, SW2 181 DN87
Hambro Av, Brom. BR2 204 EG102
Hambrook Rd, SE25 202 DV97
Hambro Rd, SW16 181 DK93
Brentwood CM14 108 FX47
Sch Hambrough Prim Sch, Sthl. UB1 off South Rd 136 BZ74
Hambrough Rd, Sthl. UB1 136 BY74
Hamburgh Ct, Wal.Cr. EN8 67 DX28
Ham Cl, Rich. TW10 177 CJ90
Ham Common, Rich. TW10 178 CM91
Ham Cft Cl, Felt. TW13 175 BU90
Hamden Cres, Dag. RM10 127 FB62
Hamel Cl, Har. HA3 117 CK55
Hamelin St, E14 14 C8
Hamels Dr, Hert. SG13 32 DV08
Hamer Cl, Hem.H. (Bov.) HP3 57 BA28
Hamerton Rd, Grav. (Nthflt) DA11 190 GB85
Hameway, E6 145 EN70
Ham Fm Rd, Rich. TW10 177 CK91
Hamfield Cl, Oxt. RH8 253 EC127
Hamfrith Rd, E15 144 EF65
Ham Gate Av, Rich. TW10 177 CK90
Hamhaugh Island, Shep. TW17 194 BN103
★ Ham Ho, Rich. TW10 177 CJ88
Hamilton Av, N9 100 DU45
Cobham KT11 213 BU113
Hoddesdon EN11 49 EA15
Ilford IG6 125 EP56
Romford RM1 105 FD54
Surbiton KT6 198 CP102
Sutton SM3 199 CY103
Woking GU22 227 BE115
Hamilton Cl, N17 122 DT55
NW8 7 N2
SE16 23 K4
Barnet EN4 80 DE42
Chertsey KT16 193 BF102
Epsom KT19 216 CQ112
Feltham TW13 175 BT92
Guildford GU2 242 AU129
Potters Bar EN6 63 CU33
Purley CR8 219 DP112
St. Albans (Brick.Wd) AL2 60 CA30
Stanmore HA7 95 CF47
Hamilton Ct, W5 138 CM73
W9 7 L1
Hatfield AL10 off Cooks Way 45 CV20
Leatherhead (Bkhm) KT23 off Eastwick Pk Av 246 CB125
Hamilton Cres, N13 99 DN49
Brentwood CM14 108 FW49
Harrow HA2 116 BZ62
Hounslow TW3 176 CB85
Hamilton Dr, Guil. GU2 242 AU129
Romford RM3 106 FL54
Hamilton Gdns, NW8 7 M1
Slough (Burn.) SL1 130 AH69
Hamilton Gordon Ct, Guil. GU1 off Langley Cl 242 AW133
Hamilton La, N5 off Hamilton Pk 121 DP63
Hamilton Mead, Hem.H. (Bov.) HP3 57 BA27
Hamilton Ms, SW18 off Merton Rd 180 DA88
W1 18 G3
Hamilton Pk, N5 121 DP63
Hamilton Pk W, N5 121 DP63
Hamilton Pl, N19 off Wedmore St 121 DK62
W1 18 F2
Guildford GU2 242 AU129
Sunbury-on-Thames TW16 175 BV94
Tadworth (Kgswd) KT20 233 CZ122
Hamilton Rd, E15 15 H2
Hamilton Rd, E17 101 DY54
N2 120 DC55
N9 100 DU45
NW10 119 CU64
NW11 119 CX59
SE27 182 DR91
SW19 180 DB94
W4 158 CS75
W5 138 CL73
Barnet EN4 80 DE42
Berkhamsted HP4 38 AV19
Bexleyheath DA7 166 EY82
Brentford TW8 157 CK79
Feltham TW13 175 BT91
Harrow HA1 117 CE57
Hayes UB3 135 BV73
Ilford IG1 125 EP63
Kings Langley WD4 59 BQ33
Romford RM2 127 FH57
St. Albans AL1 43 CG19
Sidcup DA15 186 EU91
Slough SL1 131 AN72
Southall UB1 136 BZ74
Thornton Heath CR7 202 DR97
Twickenham TW2 177 CE88
Uxbridge UB8 134 BK71
Watford WD19 93 BV48
Coll Hamilton Rd Cen, E15 15 H2
Hamilton Rd Ind Est, SE27 182 DR91
Hamilton Sq, N12 off Sandringham Gdns 98 DD51
SE1 21 K3
Hamilton St, SE8 off Deptford High St 163 EA79
Watford WD18 76 BW43
Hamilton Ter, NW8 7 M1
Hamilton Wk, Erith DA8 167 FF80
Hamilton Way, N3 98 DA51
N13 99 DP49
Wallington SM6 219 DK109
Ham Island, Wind. (Old Wind.) SL4 152 AX84
Ham La, Egh. (Eng.Grn) TW20 172 AV91
Windsor (Old Wind.) SL4 152 AX84
Hamlea Cl, SE12 184 EF85
Hamlet, The, SE5 162 DR83
Berkhamsted (Pott.End) HP4 39 BA16
Hamlet Cl, SE13 off Old Rd 164 EE84
Romford RM5 104 FA52
St. Albans AL2 60 BZ30
Hamlet Gdns, W6 159 CU77
Hamlet Hill, Harl. (Roydon) CM19 50 EG19
Hamlet Ho, Erith DA8 off Waterhead Cl 167 FE80
Hamleton Ter, Dag. RM9 off Flamstead Rd 146 EW66
Hamlet Rd, SE19 182 DT94
Romford RM5 104 FA52
Hamlet Sq, NW2 119 CY62
Hamlets Way, E3 13 L3
Hamlet Way, SE1 21 K3
★ Hamleys, W1 9 J9
Hamlin Cres, Pnr. HA5 116 BW57
Hamlin Rd, Sev. TN13 256 FE121
Hamlyn Cl, Edg. HA8 96 CL48
Hamlyn Gdns, SE19 182 DS94
Hammarskjold Rd, Harl. CM20 35 EQ14
Hamm Ct, Wey. KT13 194 BL103
Hammelton Grn, SW9 off Cromwell Rd 161 DP81
Hammelton Rd, Brom. BR1 204 EF95
HAMMERFIELD, Hem.H. HP1 40 BG20
Hammerfield Dr, Dor. (Abin.Ham.) RH5 261 BT140
Hammer La, Hem.H. HP2 40 BM19
Hammer Par, Wat. WD25 59 BU33
Hammers Gate, St.Alb. AL2 60 CA25
Hammers La, NW7 97 CU50
Hammersley La, H.Wyc. HP10, HP13 88 AC49
HAMMERSMITH, W6 159 CW78
⊖ Hammersmith 159 CW77
Coll Hammersmith & W London Coll, W14 16 C9
Hammersmith Br, SW13 159 CV79
W6 159 CV79
Hammersmith Br Rd, W6 159 CW78
Hammersmith Bdy, W6 159 CW77
Hammersmith Flyover, W6 159 CW78
Hammersmith Gro, W6 159 CW76
H Hammersmith Hosp, W12 139 CT72
Hammersmith Rd, W6 16 A8
W14 16 A8
Hammersmith Ter, W6 159 CU78
Hammet Cl, Hayes UB4 136 BX71
Hammett St, EC3 11 N9
Hamm Moor La, Add. KT15 212 BL106
Hammond Av, Mitch. CR4 201 DH96
Hammond Cl, Barn. EN5 79 CY43
Greenford UB6 off Lilian Board Way 117 CD64
Hampton TW12 196 CA95
Waltham Cross (Chsht) EN7 66 DS26
Woking GU21 226 AW115
Hammond End, Slou. (Farn.Com.) SL2 111 AP63
Sch Hammond JMI Sch, Hem.H. HP2 off Cambrian Way 40 BM17
Hammond Rd, Enf. EN1 82 DV40
Southall UB2 156 BY76
Woking GU21 226 AW115
Hammonds Cl, Dag. RM8 126 EW62
Hammonds La, Brwd. CM13 107 FV51
Hammond's La, Hat. AL10 28 CQ13
St. Albans (Sand.) AL4 28 CN12
HAMMOND STREET, Wal.Cr. EN7 66 DR26
Hammond St, NW5 141 DJ65
Hammondstreet Rd, Wal.Cr. (Chsht) EN7 66 DR26
Hammond Way, SE28 off Oriole Way 146 EV73
Hamond Cl, S.Croy. CR2 219 DP109
Hamonde Cl, Edg. HA8 96 CP47
Ham Pk Rd, E7 144 EF66
E15 144 EF66
Hampden Av, Beck. BR3 203 DY96
Chesham HP5 54 AN30
Hampden Cl, NW1 off Coopers La 141 DK68
Epping (N.Wld Bas.) CM16 70 FA27
Slough (Stoke P.) SL2 132 AU69
Hampden Cres, Brwd. CM14 108 FW49
Waltham Cross (Chsht) EN7 66 DV31
Sch Hampden Gurney C of E Prim Sch, W1 8 B7
Hampden Gurney St, W1 8 C8
Hampden Hill, Beac. HP9 88 AH53
Ware SG12 33 DZ06

★ Place of interest | H Hospital | Sch School | Coll College | Uni University | ⇌ Railway station

Hampden Hill Cl, Ware SG12 . 33 DZ05
Hampden La, N17 . . . . 100 DT53
Hampden Pl, St.Alb. (Frog.)
AL2 . . . . 61 CE29
Hampden Rd, N8 . . . . 121 DN56
N10 . . . . 98 DG52
N17 . . . . 100 DU53
N19 off Holloway Rd 121 DK61
Beckenham BR3 . . . . 203 DY96
Gerrards Cross (Chal.St.P.)
SL9 . . . . 90 AX53
Grays RM17 . . . . 170 GB78
Harrow HA3 . . . . 94 CC53
Kingston upon Thames
KT1 . . . . 198 CN97
Romford RM5 . . . . 105 FB52
Slough SL3 . . . . 153 AZ76
Hampden Sq, N14
off Osidge La 99 DH46
Hampden Way, N14 . . . . 99 DH47
Watford WD17 . . . . 75 BS36
Hampermill La, Wat. WD19 . . 93 BT47
Hampshire Av, Slou. SL1 . . . 131 AQ71
Hampshire Cl, N18
off Berkshire Gdns 100 DV50
Hampshire Hog La, W6
off King St 159 CV77
Hampshire Rd, N22 . . . . 99 DM52
Hornchurch RM11 . . . . 128 FN56
Sch Hampshire Sch, The, SW7 .
(Knightsbridge Upr Sch) . 18 A4
W2 (Bayswater) 7 L9
Hampshire St, NW5
off Torriano Av 141 DK65
Hampson Way, SW8 . . . . 161 DM81
HAMPSTEAD, NW3 . . . . 120 DD63
⊖ Hampstead 120 DC63
Hampstead Av, Wdf.Grn.
IG8 . . . . 103 EN52
Hampstead Cl, SE28 . . . . . . 146 EV74
St. Albans (Brick.Wd) AL2 . . 60 BZ31
Hampstead Gdns, NW11 . . . 120 DA58
Romford (Chad.Hth) RM6 . 126 EV57
HAMPSTEAD GARDEN SUBURB,
N2 . . . . 120 DC57
Hampstead Grn, NW3 . . . . . 120 DE64
Hampstead Gro, NW3 . . . . . 120 DC62
★ Hampstead Heath, NW3 120 DD61
⇌ Hampstead Heath 120 DE63
Hampstead Hts, N2 . . . . 120 DC56
Hampstead High St, NW3 . . 120 DC63
Hampstead Hill Gdns, NW3 . 120 DD63
Sch Hampstead Hill
Pre-Preparatory Sch,
NW3 off Courthope Rd . . 120 DF63
Hampstead La, N6 . . . . 120 DD59
NW3 . . . . 120 DD59
Dorking RH4 . . . . 263 CG137
Sch Hampstead Parochial C of E
Prim Sch, NW3
off Holly Bush Vale 120 DC63
Hampstead Rd, NW1 . . . . . . 141 DJ68
Dorking RH4 . . . . 263 CG137
Sch Hampstead Sec Sch,
NW2 off Westbere Rd . . . 119 CY63
Hampstead Sq, NW3 . . . . . . 120 DC62
Hampstead Wk, E3
off Waterside Cl 143 DZ67
Hampstead Way, NW11 . . . . 120 DC60
HAMPTON, TW12 . . . . 196 CB95
⇌ Hampton 196 CA95
Hampton Cl, N11
off Balmoral Av 99 DH50
NW6 . . . . 6 G2
SW20 . . . . 179 CW94
Sch Hampton Comm Coll,
Hmptn. TW12
off Hanworth Rd 176 CA92
⇌ Hampton Court 197 CE98
Hampton Ct, N1 . . . . 4 E4
Hampton Ct Av, E.Mol. KT8 . 197 CD99
Hampton Ct Cres, E.Mol.
KT8 . . . . 197 CD97
★ Hampton Court Palace &
Pk, E.Mol. KT8 . . . . 197 CE97
Hampton Ct Par, E.Mol.
KT8 off Creek Rd 197 CE98
Hampton Ct Rd, E.Mol. KT8 . 197 CF97
Hampton TW12 . . . . 196 CC96
Kingston upon Thames
KT1 . . . . 197 CF97
Hampton Ct Way, E.Mol.
KT8 . . . . 197 CE100
Thames Ditton KT7 . . . . . . 197 CE103
Hampton Cres, Grav. DA12 . 191 GL89
Hampton Fm Ind Est, Felt.
TW13 . . . . 176 BZ90
Hampton Gdns, Saw. CM21 . 36 EV08
Hampton Gro, Epsom KT17 . 217 CT111
HAMPTON HILL, Hmptn.
TW12 . . . . 176 CC93
Hampton Hill Business Pk,
Hmptn. TW12
off Wellington Rd 176 CC92
Sch Hampton Hill Jun Sch,
Hmptn. TW12
off St. James's Av 176 CC92
Sch Hampton Inf Sch, Hmptn.
TW12 off Ripley Rd 176 CA94
Sch Hampton Jun Sch, Hmptn.
TW12 off Percy Rd 196 CA95
Hampton La, Felt. TW13 . . . 176 BY91
Hampton Mead, Loug. IG10 . 85 EP41
Hampton Ms, NW10
off Minerva Rd 138 CR69
Hampton Ri, Har. HA3 . . . . 118 CL58
Hampton Rd, E4 . . . . 101 DZ50
E7 . . . . 124 EH64
E11 . . . . 123 ED60
Croydon CR0 . . . . 202 DQ100
Hampton (Hmptn H.)
TW12 . . . . 177 CD92
Ilford IG1 . . . . 125 EP63
Redhill RH1 . . . . 266 DF139
Teddington TW11 . . . . 177 CD92
Twickenham TW2 . . . . 177 CD90
Worcester Park KT4 . . . . . 199 CU103
Hampton Rd E, Felt. TW13 . 176 BZ90
Hampton Rd W, Felt. TW13 . 176 BY89
Sch Hampton Sch, Hmptn.
TW12 off Hanworth Rd . . 176 CA92
Hampton St, SE1 . . . . 20 F8
SE17 . . . . 20 F8
HAMPTON WICK, Kings.T.
KT1 . . . . 197 CH95
⇌ Hampton Wick 197 CJ95
Sch Hampton Wick Inf & Nurs
Sch, Tedd. TW11
off Normansfield Av 177 CK94
Ham Ridings, Rich. TW10 . . . 178 CM92
HAMSEY GREEN, Warl. CR6 . 236 DW116
Hamsey Grn Gdns, Warl.
CR6 . . . . 236 DV116
Sch Hamsey Grn Inf Sch, Warl.
CR6 off Tithepit Shaw La . 236 DV116
Sch Hamsey Grn Jun Sch,
Warl. CR6
off Tithepit Shaw La 236 DV116
Hamsey Way, S.Croy. CR2 . . 236 DV115
Hamshades Cl, Sid. DA15 . . 185 ET90
Hamstel Rd, Harl. CM20 . . . . 35 EP14
Ham St, Rich. TW10 . . . . . . 177 CJ89
Ham Vw, Croy. CR0 . . . . 203 DY100
Ham Yd, W1 . . . . 9 L9
Hanah Ct, SW19 . . . . 179 CX94
Hanameel St, E16 . . . . 25 M1
Hana Ms, E5 off Goulton Rd . 122 DW63
Hanbury Cl, NW4 . . . . 119 CW55
Slough (Burn.) SL1 . . . . . . 130 AG71
Waltham Cross (Chsht)
EN8 . . . . 67 DX29
Ware SG12 . . . . 33 DY06
Hanbury Dr, E11
off High Rd Leytonstone 124 EF59
N21 . . . . 81 DM43
Westerham (Bigg.H.)
TN16 . . . . 222 EH113
Hanbury La, Hat. (Essen.)
AL9 . . . . 46 DE17
Hanbury Ms, N1 . . . . 5 H8
Hanbury Path, Wok. GU21 . 211 BD114
Hanbury Rd, N17 . . . . 100 DV54
W3 . . . . 158 CP75
Hanbury St, E1 . . . . 11 N5
Hanbury Wk, Bex. DA5 . . . . 187 FE90
Hancock Ct, Borwd. WD6 . . . 78 CQ39
Hancock Rd, E3 . . . . 14 C2
SE19 . . . . 182 DR93
Hancroft Rd, Hem.H. HP3 . . . 40 BM22
Handa Cl, Hem.H. HP3 . . . . . 41 BP23
Handa Wk, N1 . . . . 5 H3
Hand Ct, WC1 . . . . 10 B6
Handcroft Rd, Croy. CR0 . . . 201 DP101
Handel Cl, Edg. HA8 . . . . 96 CM51
Handel Cres, Til. RM18 . . . . 171 GG80
Handel Pl, NW10
off Mitchellbrook Way . . 138 CR65
Handel St, WC1 . . . . 9 N3
Handel Way, Edg. HA8 . . . . . 96 CN52
Handen Rd, SE12 . . . . 184 EE85
Handforth Rd, SW9 . . . . 161 DN80
Ilford IG1
off Winston Way 125 EP62
Hand La, Saw. CM21 . . . . 36 EW06
Handley Gro, NW2 . . . . 119 CX62
Handley Page Rd, Wall. SM6 . 219 DM108
Handley Rd, E9 . . . . 142 DW66
Handowe Cl, NW4 . . . . 119 CU56
Handpost Hill, Pot.B.
(Northaw) EN6 . . . . 65 DH28
HANDSIDE, Welw.G.C. AL8 . . 29 CV10
Handside Cl, Welw.G.C. AL8 . 29 CW09
Worcester Park KT4
off Carters Cl 199 CX102
Handside Grn, Welw.G.C.
AL8 . . . . 29 CW08
Handside La, Welw.G.C. AL8 . 29 CV11
Hands Wk, E16 . . . . 15 M7
Handsworth Av, E4 . . . . 101 ED51
Sch Handsworth Prim Sch,
E4 off Handsworth Av . . . 101 ED51
Handsworth Rd, N17 . . . . . . 122 DR55
Handsworth Way, Wat.
WD19 off Hayling Rd 93 BU48
Handtrough Way, Bark. IG11
off Fresh Wf Rd 145 EP68
Hanford Cl, SW18 . . . . 180 DA88
Hanford Rd, S.Ock. (Aveley)
RM15 . . . . 148 FQ74
Hanford Row, SW19 . . . . . . 179 CW93
Hangar Ruding, Wat. WD19 . . 94 BZ48
Hanger Cl, Hem.H. HP1 . . . . . 40 BH21
Hanger Grn, W5 . . . . 138 CN70
Hanger Hill, Wey. KT13 . . . . 213 BP107
⊖ Hanger Lane 138 CM69
Hanger La, W5 . . . . 138 CM70
Hanger Vale La, W5 . . . . . . 138 CM72
Hanger Vw Way, W3 . . . . . . 138 CN72
Hanging Hill La, Brwd.
CM13 . . . . 109 GB48
Hanging Sword All, EC4 . . . . . 10 D8
Hangrove Hill, Orp. BR6 . . . 223 EP113
Hankey Pl, SE1 . . . . 21 K4
Hankins La, NW7 . . . . 96 CS48
Hanley Cl, Wind. SL4 . . . . . . 151 AK81
Hanley Gdns, N4 . . . . 121 DM60
Hanley Pl, Beck. BR3 . . . . . . 183 EA94
Hanley Rd, N4 . . . . 121 DL60
Hanmer Wk, N7
off Newington
Barrow Way 121 DM62
Hannah Cl, NW10 . . . . 118 CQ63
Beckenham BR3 . . . . 203 EC97
Hannah Ct, N13 . . . . 99 DM47
Hannah Mary Way, SE1 . . . . . 22 B8
Hannah Ms, Wall. SM6 . . . . . 219 DJ108
Hannards Way, Ilf. IG6 . . . . 104 EV50
Hannay La, N8 . . . . 121 DK59
Hannay Wk, SW16 . . . . 181 DK89
Hannell Rd, SW6 . . . . 159 CY80
Hannen Rd, SE27
off Norwood High St . . . 181 DP90
Hannibal Rd, E1 . . . . 12 F5
Staines (Stanw.) TW19 . . . 174 BK87
Hannibal Way, Croy. CR0 . . . 219 DM106
Hannington Rd, SW4 . . . . . . 161 DH83
Hanover Av, E16 . . . . 25 L1
Feltham TW13 . . . . 175 BU88
Hanover Circle, Hayes UB3 . 135 BQ72
Hanover Cl, Egh. (Eng.Grn)
TW20 . . . . 172 AV93
Redhill RH1 . . . . 251 DJ128
Richmond TW9 . . . . 158 CN80
Slough SL1 . . . . 152 AU76
Sutton SM3 . . . . 217 CZ105
Windsor SL4
off Hanover Way 151 AM81
Hanover Ct, SE19
off Anerley Rd 182 DU94
W12 off Uxbridge Rd 139 CU74
Dorking RH4 . . . . 263 CF136
Guildford GU1
off Riverside 242 AX132
Hoddesdon EN11
off Jersey Cl 49 EA16
Woking GU22
off Midhope Rd 226 AY119
Hanover Dr, Chis. BR7 . . . . . 185 EQ91
Hanover Gdns, SE11 . . . . . . 161 DN79
Abbots Langley WD5 . . . . . 59 BT30
Ilford IG6 . . . . 103 EQ52
Hanover Gate, NW1 . . . . 8 B2
Slough SL1
off Cippenham La 131 AN74
Hanover Gate Mans, NW1 . . . 8 B3
Hanover Grn, Hem.H. HP1 . . . 40 BG22
Hanover Ho, Surb. KT6
off Lenelby Rd 198 CN102
Hanover Mead, Maid. SL6 . . 150 AC76
Hanover Pk, SE15 . . . . 162 DU81
Hanover Pl, E3 . . . . 13 L2
WC2 . . . . 9 P8
Brentwood (Warley)
CM14 . . . . 108 FV50
Sch Hanover Prim Sch, N1 . . . . 4 F9
Hanover Rd, N15 . . . . 122 DT56
NW10 . . . . 139 CW66
SW19 . . . . 180 DC94
Hanover Sq, W1 . . . . 9 H8
Hanover St, W1 . . . . 9 H8
Croydon CR0
off Abbey Rd 201 DP104
Hanover Ter, NW1 . . . . 8 B2
Hanover Ter Ms, NW1 . . . . . . 8 B2
Hanover Wk, Hat. AL10 . . . . . 45 CT21
Weybridge KT13 . . . . 195 BS104
Hanover Way, Bexh. DA6 . . . 166 EX83
Windsor SL4 . . . . 151 AM82
Hanover W Ind Est, NW10 . . 138 CR68
Hanover Yd, N1 . . . . 4 F9
Hansard Ms, W14 . . . . 16 B3
Hansart Way, Enf. EN2
off The Ridgeway 81 DN39
Hanscomb Ms, SW4
off Bromell's Rd 161 DJ84
Hans Cres, SW1 . . . . 18 C5
Hanselin Cl, Stan. HA7 . . . . . 95 CF50
Hansells Mead, Harl.
(Roydon) CM19 . . . . 50 EG15
Hansen Dr, N21 . . . . 81 DM43
Hanshaw Dr, Edg. HA8 . . . . . 96 CR53
Hansler Gro, E.Mol. KT8 . . . 197 CD98
Hansler Rd, SE22 . . . . 182 DT85
Hansol Rd, Bexh. DA6 . . . . . 186 EY85
Hanson Cl, SW12 . . . . 181 DH87
SW14 . . . . 158 CQ83
Beckenham BR3 . . . . 183 EB93
Guildford GU4 . . . . 243 AZ131
Loughton IG10
off Hanson Dr 85 EQ40
West Drayton UB7 . . . . . . 154 BM76
Hanson Dr, Loug. IG10 . . . . . . 85 EQ40
Hanson Gdns, Sthl. UB1 . . . 156 BY75
Hanson Grn, Loug. IG10
off Hanson Dr 85 EQ40
Hanson St, W1 . . . . 9 J5
Hans Pl, SW1 . . . . 18 D5
Hans Rd, SW3 . . . . 18 C5
Hans St, SW1 . . . . 18 D6
Hanway Pl, W1 . . . . 9 L7
Hanway Rd, W7 . . . . 137 CD72
Hanway St, W1 . . . . 9 L7
HANWELL, W7 . . . . 137 CF74
⇌ Hanwell 137 CE73
HANWORTH, Felt. TW13 . . . 176 BX91
Hanworth La, Cher. KT16 . . . 193 BF102
Hanworth Rd, Felt. TW13 . . . 175 BV88
Hampton TW12 . . . . 176 CB93
Hounslow TW3, TW4 . . . . . 156 CB83
Redhill RH1 . . . . 266 DF139
Sunbury-on-Thames
TW16 . . . . 175 BU94
Hanworth Ter, Houns. TW3 . 156 CB84
Hanworth Trd Est, Felt.
TW13 . . . . 176 BY90
Hanyards End, Pot.B.
(Cuffley) EN6 . . . . 65 DL28
Hanyards La, Pot.B.
(Cuffley) EN6 . . . . 65 DK28
Hapgood Cl, Grnf. UB6 . . . . . 117 CD64
Harads Pl, E1 . . . . 12 B10
Harben Rd, NW6 . . . . 140 DC66
Harberson Rd, E15 . . . . 144 EF67
SW12 . . . . 181 DH88
Harberton Rd, N19 . . . . 121 DJ60
Harberts Rd, Harl. CM19 . . . . 51 EP16
Harbet Rd, E4 . . . . 101 DX50
N18 . . . . 101 DX50
W2 . . . . 7 P6
Harbex Cl, Bex. DA5 . . . . . . 187 FB87
Sch Harbinger Prim Sch, E14 . 24 A8
Harbinger Rd, E14 . . . . 24 A8
Harbledown Pl, Orp. BR5 . . 206 EW98
Harbledown Rd, SW6 . . . . . 160 DA81
South Croydon CR2 . . . . . 220 DU111
Harbord Cl, SE5
off De Crespigny Pk 162 DR82
Harbord St, SW6 . . . . 159 CX81
Harborne Cl, Wat. WD19 . . . . 94 BW50
Harborough Av, Sid. DA15 . . 185 ES87
Harborough Cl, Slou. SL1
off West Pt 131 AK74
Harborough Rd, SW16 . . . . 181 DM91
Harbour Av, SW10 . . . . 160 DC81
Harbourer Cl, Ilf. IG6 . . . . . 104 EV50
Harbourer Rd, Ilf. IG6 . . . . . 104 EV50
Harbour Ex Sq, E14 . . . . 24 B4
Harbourfield Rd, Bans. SM7 . 234 DB115
Harbour Reach, SW6
off The Boulevard 160 DC81
Harbour Rd, SE5 . . . . 162 DQ83
Harbour Yd, SW10
off Harbour Av 160 DC81
Harbridge Av, SW15 . . . . . . 179 CT87
Harbury Rd, Cars. SM5 . . . . 218 DE109
Harbut Rd, SW11 . . . . 160 DD84
Harcamlow Way, Ware SG12 . 34 EH10
Harcombe Rd, N16 . . . . 122 DS62
Harcourt, Stai. (Wrays.)
TW19 . . . . 172 AY86
Harcourt Av, E12 . . . . 125 EM63
Edgware HA8 . . . . 96 CQ48
Sidcup DA15 . . . . 186 EW86
Wallington SM6 . . . . 219 DH105
Harcourt Cl, Egh. TW20 . . . . 173 BC93
Isleworth TW7 . . . . 157 CG83
Maidenhead (Dorney R.)
SL6 . . . . 150 AF76
Harcourt Fld, Wall. SM6 . . . 219 DH105
Harcourt Lo, Wall. SM6
off Croydon Rd 219 DH105
Harcourt Ms, Rom. RM2 . . . 127 FF57
Harcourt Rd, E15 . . . . 144 EF68
N22 . . . . 99 DK53
SE4 . . . . 163 DY84
SW19 off Russell Rd 180 DA94
Bexleyheath DA6 . . . . 166 EY84
Bushey WD23 . . . . 76 CC43
Maidenhead (Dorney R.)
SL6 . . . . 150 AF76
Thornton Heath CR7 . . . . 201 DM100
Wallington SM6 . . . . 219 DH105
Windsor SL4 . . . . 151 AL81
Harcourt St, W1 . . . . 8 B6
Harcourt Ter, SW10 . . . . 17 K10
Hardcastle Cl, Croy. CR0 . . . 202 DU100
Hardcourts Cl, W.Wick. BR4 . 203 EB104
Hardell Cl, Egh. TW20 . . . . . 173 BA92
Hardel Ri, SW2 . . . . 181 DP89
Hardel Wk, SW2
off Papworth Way 181 DN87
Harden Fm Cl, Couls. CR5 . . 235 DJ121
Harden Rd, Grav. (Nthflt)
DA11 . . . . 191 GF90
Hardens Manorway, SE7 . . . 164 EK76
Harders Rd, SE15 . . . . 162 DV82
Hardess St, SE24
off Herne Hill Rd 162 DQ83
Hardie Cl, NW10 . . . . 118 CR64
Hardie Rd, Dag. RM10 . . . . . 127 FC62
Harding Cl, SE17
off Hillingdon St 162 DQ79
Croydon CR0 . . . . 202 DT104
Watford WD25 . . . . 60 BW33
Hardinge Cl, Uxb. UB8
off Dawley Av 135 BP72
Hardinge Rd, N18 . . . . 100 DS50
NW10 . . . . 139 CV67
Hardinge St, E1 . . . . 12 F8
Harding Ho, Hayes UB3 . . . . 135 BV72
Harding Rd, Bexh. DA7 . . . . 166 EZ82
Chesham HP5 . . . . 54 AR30
Epsom KT18 . . . . 232 CS119
Grays RM16 . . . . 171 GG76
Hardings, Welw.G.C. AL7 . . . . 30 DC08
Hardings Cl, Iver SL0 . . . . . . 133 BB69
Harding's Cl, Kings.T. KT2 . . 198 CM95
Hardings La, SE20 . . . . 183 DX93
Harding Spur, Slou. SL3
off Ditton Rd 153 AZ78
Hardings Row, Iver SL0 . . . . 133 BC69
Hardley Cres, Horn. RM11 . . 128 FK56
Hardman Rd, SE7 . . . . 25 N9
Kingston upon Thames
KT2 . . . . 198 CL96
Hardwick Cl, Lthd. (Oxshott)
KT22 . . . . 230 CC115
Stanmore HA7 . . . . 95 CJ50
Hardwick Cres, Dart. DA2 . . 188 FP86
Hardwicke Av, Houns. TW5 . 156 CA81
Hardwicke Gdns, Amer. HP6 . 55 AS38
Hardwicke Ms, WC1 . . . . 10 B2
Hardwicke Pl, St.Alb.
(Lon.Col.) AL2 . . . . 61 CK27
Hardwicke Rd, N13 . . . . 99 DL51
W4 . . . . 158 CR77
Reigate RH2 . . . . 250 DA133
Richmond TW10 . . . . 177 CJ91
Hardwicke St, Bark. IG11 . . . 145 EQ67
Hardwick Grn, W13 . . . . 137 CH71
Hardwick La, Cher. (Lyne)
KT16 . . . . 193 BC101
Hardwick Rd, Red. RH1 . . . . 266 DD136
Hardwick St, EC1 . . . . 10 D2
Hardwicks Way, SW18
off Buckhold Rd 180 DA85
Hardwidge St, SE1 . . . . 21 L3
Hardy Av, E16 . . . . 25 M1
Gravesend (Nthflt) DA11 . 190 GE89
Ruislip HA4 . . . . 115 BV64
Hardy Cl, SE16 . . . . 23 H4
Barnet EN5 . . . . 79 CY44
Dorking (N.Holm.) RH5 . . 263 CH140
Horley RH6 . . . . 268 DE148
Pinner HA5 . . . . 116 BX59
Slough SL1 . . . . 131 AN74
Hardy Gro, Dart. DA1 . . . . . 168 FN84
Hardy Rd, E4 . . . . 101 DZ51
SE3 . . . . 164 EF80
SW19 . . . . 180 DB94
Hemel Hempstead HP2 . . . 40 BM19
Hardys Cl, E.Mol. KT8
off Feltham Av 197 CE98
Hardy Way, Enf. EN2 . . . . 81 DN39
Hare & Billet Rd, SE3 . . . . . 163 ED81
Harebell, Welw.G.C. AL7 . . . . 29 CY13
Harebell Cl, Hert. SG13 . . . . . 32 DV09
Harebell Dr, E6 . . . . 145 EN71
Harebell Hill, Cob. KT11 . . . 214 BX114
Harebell Way, Rom. RM3 . . . 106 FK52
Harebreaks, The, Wat. WD24 . . 75 BV38
Harecastle Cl, Hayes UB4 . . 136 BY70
Hare Ct, EC4 . . . . 10 C8
Harecourt Rd, N1 . . . . 4 G3
Hare Cres, Wat. WD25 . . . . . . 59 BU32
Harecroft, Dor. RH4 . . . . . . 263 CJ139
Leatherhead (Fetch.) KT22 . 230 CB123
Haredale Rd, SE24 . . . . 162 DQ84
Haredon Cl, SE23 . . . . 182 DW87
HAREFIELD, Uxb. UB9 . . . . . . 92 BL53
Harefield, Esher KT10 . . . . . 215 CE105
Harlow CM20 . . . . 36 EU14
Harefield Av, Sutt. SM2 . . . 217 CY109
Harefield Cl, Enf. EN2 . . . . . . 81 DN39
H Harefield Hosp, Uxb.
UB9 . . . . 92 BJ53
Sch Harefield Inf Sch, Uxb.
UB9 off Park La 92 BJ53
Sch Harefield Jun Sch, Uxb.
UB9 off Park La 92 BJ53
Harefield Ms, SE4 . . . . 163 DZ83
Harefield Pl, St.Alb. AL4 . . . . 43 CK17
Harefield Rd, N8 . . . . 121 DK57
SE4 . . . . 163 DZ83
SW16 . . . . 181 DM94
Rickmansworth WD3 . . . . . 92 BK50
Sidcup DA14 . . . . 186 EX89
Uxbridge UB8 . . . . 134 BK65
Harefield Rd Ind Est, Rick.
WD3 . . . . 92 BL49
Hare Hall La, Rom. RM2 . . . . 127 FH56
Harehatch La, Slou. SL2 . . . . 111 AL60
Hare Hill, Add. KT15 . . . . . . 211 BF107
Hare Hill Cl, Wok. (Pyrford)
GU22 . . . . 228 BG115
Harelands Cl, Wok. GU21 . . 226 AW117
Harelands La, Wok. GU21 . . 226 AW117
Hare La, Esher (Clay.) KT10 . 215 CE107
Hatfield AL10 . . . . 45 CU20
Hare Marsh, E2 . . . . 12 A3
Sch Harenc Sch, Sid. DA14
off Rectory La 186 EW92
Harendon, Tad. KT20 . . . . . 233 CW121
Harepark Cl, Hem.H. HP1 . . . . 39 BF19
Hare Pl, EC4 . . . . 10 D8
Hare Row, E2 . . . . 142 DV68
Hares Bk, Croy.
(New Adgtn) CR0 . . . . . . 221 ED110
Haresfield Rd, Dag. RM10 . . 146 FA65
Sch Haresfoot Sch, Berk.
HP4 off Chesham Rd 38 AV22
Harestone Dr, Cat. CR3 . . . . 236 DT124
Harestone Hill, Cat. CR3 . . . 252 DT126
Harestone La, Cat. CR3 . . . . 252 DS125
H Harestone Marie Curie
Cen, Cat. CR3 . . . . 252 DT125
Harestone Valley Rd, Cat.
CR3 . . . . 252 DT126
HARE STREET, Harl. CM19 . . 51 EP16
Hare St, SE18 . . . . 165 EN76
Harlow CM19 . . . . 51 EP15
Sch Hare St Co Jun Sch, Harl.
CM19 off Little Gro Fld . . . 51 EQ15
Sch Hare St Inf Sch, Harl.
CM19 off Little Gro Fld . . . 51 EQ15
Hare St Springs, Harl.
CM19 . . . . 51 EP15
Hare Ter, Grays RM20
off Mill La 169 FX78
Hare Wk, N1 . . . . 5 M10
Hareward Rd, Guil. GU4 . . . 243 BC132
Harewood, Rick. WD3 . . . . . . 74 BH43
Harewood Av, NW1 . . . . 8 B4
Northolt UB5 . . . . 136 BY66
Harewood Cl, Nthlt. UB5 . . . 136 BZ66
Reigate RH2 . . . . 250 DC132
Harewood Dr, Ilf. IG5 . . . . . 103 EM54
Harewood Gdns, S.Croy.
CR2 . . . . 236 DV115
Harewood Hill, Epp.
(They.B.) CM16 . . . . 85 ES35
Harewood Pl, W1 . . . . 9 H8
Slough SL1 . . . . 152 AU76
Harewood Rd, SW19 . . . . . . 180 DE93
Brentwood (Pilg.Hat.)
CM15 . . . . 108 FV44
Chalfont St. Giles HP8 . . . . 72 AW41
Isleworth TW7 . . . . 157 CF80
South Croydon CR2 . . . . . 220 DS107
Watford WD19 . . . . 93 BV48
Harewood Row, NW1 . . . . 8 B5
Harewood Ter, Sthl. UB2 . . . 156 BZ77
Harfield Gdns, SE5 . . . . 162 DS83
Harfield Rd, Sun. TW16 . . . . 196 BX96
Harford Cl, E4 . . . . 101 EB45
Harford Dr, Wat. WD17 . . . . . 75 BS38
Harford Ms, N19
off Wedmore St 121 DK62
Harford Rd, E4 . . . . 101 EB45
Harford St, E1 . . . . 13 J4
Harford Wk, N2 . . . . 120 DD57
Harfst Way, Swan. BR8 . . . . 207 FC95
Hargood Cl, Har. HA3 . . . . . 118 CL58
Hargood Rd, SE3 . . . . 164 EJ81
Hargrave Pk, N19 . . . . 121 DJ61
Sch Hargrave Pk Prim Sch,
N19 off Hargrave Pk 121 DJ61
Hargrave Pl, N7
off Brecknock Rd 121 DK64
Hargrave Rd, N19 . . . . 121 DJ61
Hargreaves Av, Wal.Cr.
(Chsht) EN7 . . . . 66 DV30
Hargreaves Cl, Wal.Cr.
(Chsht) EN7 . . . . 66 DV31
Hargwyne St, SW9 . . . . 161 DM83
Haringey Pk, N8 . . . . 121 DL58
Haringey Pas, N4 . . . . 121 DP58
N8 . . . . 121 DN56
Haringey Rd, N8 . . . . 121 DL56
Harington Ter, N9 . . . . 100 DR48
N18 . . . . 100 DR48
Harkett Cl, Har. HA3
off Byron Rd 95 CF54
Harkett Ct, Har. HA3 . . . . 95 CF54
Harkness, Wal.Cr. (Chsht)
EN7 . . . . 66 DU29
Harkness Cl, Epsom KT17 . . 233 CW116
Romford RM3 . . . . 106 FM50
Harkness Rd, Slou. (Burn.)
SL1 . . . . 130 AH71
Harland Av, Croy. CR0 . . . . . 202 DT104
Sidcup DA15 . . . . 185 ER90
Harland Cl, SW19 . . . . 200 DB97
Harland Rd, SE12 . . . . 184 EG88
Harlands Gro, Orp. BR6
off Pinecrest Gdns 223 EP105
Harlech Gdns, Houns. TW5 . 156 BW79
Pinner HA5 . . . . 116 BX59
Harlech Rd, N14 . . . . 99 DL48
Abbots Langley WD5 . . . . . 59 BU31
Harlech Twr, W3 . . . . 158 CP75
Harlequin Av, Brent. TW8 . . . 157 CG79
Harlequin Cen, Wat. WD17 . . 76 BW42
Harlequin Cl, Hayes UB4
off Cygnet Way 136 BX71
Isleworth TW7 . . . . 177 CE85
Harlequin Ho, Erith DA18
off Kale Rd 166 EY76
Harlequin Rd, Tedd. TW11 . . 177 CH94
★ Harlequins F.C. (Rugby),
Twick. TW2 . . . . 177 CE87
Harlescott Rd, SE15 . . . . . . 163 DX84
HARLESDEN, NW10 . . . . 138 CS68
⇌ Harlesden 138 CR68
⊖ Harlesden 138 CR68
Harlesden Cl, Rom. RM3 . . . 106 FM52
Harlesden Gdns, NW10 . . . . 139 CT67
Harlesden La, NW10 . . . . . . 139 CU67
Sch Harlesden Prim Sch,
NW10 off Acton La 138 CS68
Harlesden Rd, NW10 . . . . . . 139 CU67
Romford RM3 . . . . 106 FM51
St. Albans AL1 . . . . 43 CG20
Harlesden Wk, Rom. RM3 . . 106 FM52
Harleston Cl, E5
off Theydon Rd 122 DW61
Harley Cl, Wem. HA0 . . . . . . 137 CK65
Harley Ct, E11
off Blake Hall Rd 124 EG59
St. Albans AL4
off Villiers Cres 43 CK16
Harley Cres, Har. HA1 . . . . . 117 CD56
Harleyford, Brom. BR1 . . . . . 204 EH95
Harleyford Rd, SE11 . . . . . . 161 DM79
Harleyford St, SE11 . . . . 161 DN79
Harley Gdns, SW10 . . . . 17 M10
Orpington BR6 . . . . 223 ES105
Harley Gro, E3 . . . . 13 M1
Harley Pl, W1 . . . . 8 G6
Harley Rd, NW3 . . . . 140 DD66
NW10 . . . . 138 CS68
Harrow HA1 . . . . 117 CD56
Harley St, W1 . . . . 8 G6
Harling Ct, SW11
off Latchmere Rd 160 DF82
Harlinger St, SE18 . . . . 164 EL76
Harlings, Hert. (Hert.Hth)
SG13 . . . . 32 DW13
HARLINGTON, Hayes UB3 . . 155 BQ79
Harlington Cl, Hayes UB3
off New Rd 155 BQ80
Sch Harlington Comm Sch,
Hayes UB3
off Pinkwell La 155 BR77
Harlington Rd, Bexh. DA7 . . 166 EY83
Hounslow (Hthrw Air.)
TW6 . . . . 155 BT84
Uxbridge UB8 . . . . 135 BP71
Harlington Rd E, Felt. TW13,
TW14 . . . . 175 BV87
Harlington Rd W, Felt. TW14 . 175 BV86
HARLOW, CM17 - CM20 . . . . 51 ER15
Sch Harlowbury Co Prim Sch,
Harl. CM17
off Watlington Rd 36 EX11
Harlow Business Pk, Harl.
CM19 . . . . 50 EL15
Sch Harlow Coll, Harl.
CM20 off Velizy Av 35 ES14

Harlow Common, Harl. CM17 52 EW18
Harlow Ct, Hem.H. HP2 40 BM16
Harlow Gdns, Rom. RM5 105 FC51
⇌ Harlow Mill 36 EW10
Harlow Potter St Bypass, Harl. CM17, CM20 52 EV15
Harlow Rd, N13 100 DR48
  Bishop's Stortford (Sheering) CM22 36 FA09
  Harlow CM20 36 EW08
  Harlow (Match.Tye) CM17 37 FC12
  Harlow (Old Harl.) CM17 36 FA09
  Harlow (Roydon) CM19 50 EJ15
  Rainham RM13 147 FF67
  Sawbridgeworth CM21 36 EW08
Sch Harlow Sec Tutorial Unit, Harl. CM20 off Mowbray Rd 36 EU12
Harlow Seedbed Cen, Harl. CM19 51 EN16
⇌ Harlow Town 35 ER12
Harlow Tye, Harl. CM17 37 FC12
Harlton Ct, Wal.Abb. EN9 68 EF34
Harlyn Dr, Pnr. HA5 115 BV55
Sch Harlyn Prim Sch, Pnr. HA5 off Tolcarne Dr 115 BV55
Harman Av, Grav. DA11 191 GH92
  Woodford Green IG8 102 EF52
Harman Cl, E4 101 ED49
  NW2 119 CY62
Harman Dr, NW2 119 CY62
  Sidcup DA15 185 ET86
Harman Pl, Pur. CR8 219 DP111
Harman Rd, Enf. EN1 82 DT43
Harmer Rd, Swans. DA10 190 FZ86
Harmer St, Grav. DA12 191 GJ86
HARMONDSWORTH, West Dr. UB7 154 BK79
Harmondsworth La, West Dr. UB7 154 BL79
Sch Harmondsworth Prim Sch, West Dr. UB7 off School Rd 154 BK79
Harmondsworth Rd, West Dr. UB7 154 BL78
Harmony Cl, NW11 119 CY57
  Hatfield AL10 45 CU16
  Wallington SM6 219 DL109
Harmony Ter, Har. HA2 off Goldsmith Cl 116 CB60
Harmony Way, NW4 off Victoria Rd 119 CW56
Harmood Gro, NW1 off Clarence Way 141 DH66
Harmood Pl, NW1 off Harmood St 141 DH66
Harmood St, NW1 141 DH66
Harms Gro, Guil. GU4 243 BC131
Harmsworth Ms, SE11 20 E6
Harmsworth St, SE17 20 E10
Harmsworth Way, N20 97 CZ46
Harness Rd, SE28 166 EU75
Harness Way, St.Alb. AL4 43 CK17
Harnetts Cl, Swan. BR8 207 FD100
Harold Av, Belv. DA17 166 EZ78
  Hayes UB3 155 BT76
Sch Harold Ct Prim Sch, Rom. RM3 off Church Rd 106 FN53
Harold Ct Rd, Rom. RM3 106 FP51
Harold Cres, Wal.Abb. EN9 67 EC32
Harold Est, SE1 21 M6
Harold Gibbons Ct, SE7 164 EJ79
HAROLD HILL, Rom. RM3 106 FL50
Harold Hill Ind Est, Rom. RM3 106 FK52
Harold Laski Ho, EC1 10 E2
HAROLD PARK, Rom. RM3 106 FN51
Harold Pl, SE11 20 C10
Harold Rd, E4 101 EC49
  E11 124 EE60
  E13 144 EH67
  N8 121 DM57
  N15 122 DT57
  NW10 138 CR69
  SE19 182 DS93
  Dartford (Hawley) DA2 188 FM91
  Sutton SM1 218 DD105
  Woodford Green IG8 102 EG53
Harolds Cl, Harl. CM19 51 EM16
Haroldslea, Horl. RH6 269 DK150
Haroldslea Cl, Horl. RH6 269 DJ150
Haroldslea Dr, Horl. RH6 269 DJ150
Harolds Rd, Harl. CM19 50 EL16
Haroldstone Rd, E17 123 DX57
Harold Vw, Rom. RM3 106 FM54
HAROLD WOOD, Rom. RM3 106 FL54
⇌ Harold Wood 106 FM53
H Harold Wd Hosp, Rom. RM3 106 FL54
Sch Harold Wd Prim Sch, Rom. RM3 off Recreation Av 128 FN55
Harp All, EC4 10 E7
Harpenden Rd, E12 124 EJ61
  SE27 181 DP90
  St. Albans AL3 43 CD17
Harpenmead Pt, NW2 off Granville Rd 119 CZ61
H Harperbury Hosp, Rad. WD7 61 CJ31
Harper Cl, N14 off Alexandra Ct 81 DJ43
  Grays (Chaff.Hun.) RM16 189 FW78
Harper La, Rad. WD7 61 CG32
Harper Ms, SW17 180 DC90
Harper Rd, E6 145 EM72
  SE1 20 G5
Harpers Yd, N17 off Ruskin Rd 100 DT53
Harpesford Av, Vir.W. GU25 192 AV99
Harp Island Cl, NW10 118 CR61
Harp La, EC3 11 L10
Sch Harpley Sch, E1 12 G3
Harpley Sq, E1 12 F2
Harpour Rd, Bark. IG11 145 EQ65
Harp Rd, W7 137 CF70
Harpsden St, SW11 160 DG81
Harpsfield Bdy, Hat. AL10 45 CT17
Harps Oak La, Red. RH1 250 DF125
Harpswood Cl, Couls. CR5 off Jennys Way 235 DJ122
Harptree Way, St.Alb. AL1 43 CG18
Harpur Ms, WC1 10 A5
Harpurs, Tad. KT20 233 CX122
Harpur St, WC1 10 A5
Harraden Rd, SE3 164 EJ81
Harrap Chase, Grays (Bad.Dene) RM17 170 FZ78
Harrap St, E14 14 D9
Harrier Av, E11 off Eastern Av 124 EH58
Harrier Cl, Horn. RM12 147 FH65
Harrier Ms, SE28 165 ER76
Harrier Rd, NW9 96 CS54
Harriers Cl, W5 138 CL73
Harrier Way, E6 145 EM70
  Waltham Abbey EN9 68 EG34
Harries Cl, Chesh. HP5 off Deansway 54 AP30
Harriescourt, Wal.Abb. EN9 68 EG32
Harries Rd, Hayes UB4 136 BW70
Harriet Cl, E8 142 DU67
Harriet Gdns, Croy. CR0 202 DU103
Harriet St, SW1 18 D4
Harriet Tubman Cl, SW2 181 DN87
Harriet Wk, SW1 18 D4
Harriet Walker Way, Rick. WD3 91 BF45
Harriet Way, Bushey WD23 95 CD45
HARRINGAY, N8 121 DN57
⇌ Harringay 121 DN58
Harringay Gdns, N8 121 DP56
⇌ Harringay Green Lanes 121 DP58
Harringay Rd, N15 121 DP57
Harrington Cl, NW10 118 CR62
  Croydon CR0 201 DL103
  Reigate (Leigh) RH2 265 CU141
  Windsor SL4 151 AM84
Harrington Ct, W10 off Dart St 139 CZ69
  Hertford (Hert.Hth) SG13 off Trinity Rd 32 DW12
Harrington Gdns, SW7 17 K8
Harrington Hill, E5 122 DV60
Sch Harrington Hill JMI Sch, E5 off Harrington Hill 122 DV60
Tram Harrington Road 202 DW97
Harrington Rd, E11 124 EE60
  SE25 202 DU98
  SW7 17 N7
Harrington Sq, NW1 141 DJ68
Harrington St, NW1 9 J1
Harrington Way, SE18 164 EK76
Harriott Cl, SE10 25 J8
Harriotts Cl, Ashtd. KT21 off Harriotts La 231 CJ120
Harriotts La, Ashtd. KT21 231 CJ119
Sch Harris City Tech Sch, SE19 off Maberley Rd 202 DT95
Harris Cl, Enf. EN2 81 DP39
  Gravesend (Nthflt) DA11 190 GE90
  Hounslow TW3 156 CA81
  Romford RM3 106 FL52
Harris Gdns, Slou. SL1 151 AQ75
Harris La, Rad. (Shenley) WD7 62 CN34
Harrison Cl, N20 98 DE46
  Brentwood (Hutt.) CM13 109 GD43
  Northwood HA6 93 BQ51
  Reigate RH2 266 DB135
Harrison Ct, Shep. TW17 off Greeno Cres 195 BP99
Harrison Dr, Epp. (N.Wld Bas.) CM16 71 FB26
Harrison Rd, Dag. RM10 147 FB65
Harrisons Ri, Croy. CR0 201 DP104
Harrison St, WC1 9 P2
Harrisons Wf, Purf. RM19 168 FN78
Harrison Wk, Wal.Cr. (Chsht) EN8 67 DX30
Harrison Way, Sev. TN13 256 FG122
  Slough SL1 131 AK74
  Waltham Abbey EN9 off Greenwich Way 83 EC36
Harris Rd, Bexh. DA7 166 EY81
  Dagenham RM9 126 EZ64
  Watford WD25 75 BU35
Harris's La, Ware SG12 32 DW05
Harris St, E17 123 DZ59
  SE5 162 DR80
Harris Way, Sun. TW16 195 BS95
Sch Harrodian Sch, The, SW13 off Lonsdale Rd 159 CT80
★ Harrods, SW1 18 C5
Harrogate Ct, N11 off Coverdale Rd 98 DG51
  Slough SL3 153 BA78
Harrogate Rd, Wat. WD19 94 BW48
Harrold Rd, Dag. RM8 126 EV64
HARROW, HA1 - HA3 117 CD59
⇌ Harrow & Wealdstone 117 CE56
⊖ Harrow & Wealdstone 117 CE56
★ Harrow Arts Cen, Pnr. HA5 94 CB52
Harrow Av, Enf. EN1 82 DT44
Harroway Rd, SW11 160 DD82
Harrow Bottom Rd, Vir.W. GU25 193 AZ100
Harrowby Gdns, Grav. (Nthflt) DA11 190 GE89
Harrowby St, W1 8 B7
Harrow Cl, Add. KT15 194 BH103
  Chessington KT9 215 CK108
  Dorking RH4 off Harrow Rd W 263 CG137
  Hornchurch RM11 127 FH60
Coll Harrow Coll, Adult Learners Cen, Pnr. HA5 off Uxbridge Rd 94 CA52
  Harrow-on-the-Hill Campus, Har. HA1 off Lowlands Rd 117 CE59
  Harrow Weald Campus, Har. HA3 off Brookshill 95 CE51
Harrow Cres, Rom. RM3 105 FH52
Harrowdene Cl, Wem. HA0 117 CK63
Harrowdene Gdns, Tedd. TW11 177 CG93
Harrowdene Rd, Wem. HA0 117 CK62
Harrow Dr, N9 100 DT46
  Hornchurch RM11 127 FH60
Harrowes Meade, Edg. HA8 96 CN48
Harrow Flds Gdns, Har. HA1 117 CE62
Coll Harrow Fire Training Cen, Pnr. HA5 off Pinner Rd 116 CA56
Harrow Gdns, Orp. BR6 224 EV105
  Warlingham CR6 237 DZ115
Harrow Gate Gdns, Dor. RH4 off Horsham Rd 263 CH138
Harrowgate Rd, E9 143 DY65
Harrow Grn, E11 off Harrow Rd 124 EE62
Sch Harrow High Sch, Har. HA1 off Gayton Rd 117 CF58
Harrowlands Pk, Dor. RH4 263 CH137
H Harrowlands Rehab Unit, Dor. RH4 263 CH137
Harrow La, E14 14 C10
  Godalming GU7 258 AS144
Harrow Manorway, SE2 146 EW74
Harrow Mkt, Slou. SL3 153 BA76
★ Harrow Mus & Heritage Cen, Har. HA2 116 CC55
HARROW ON THE HILL, Har. HA1 117 CE61
⇌ Harrow on the Hill 117 CE58
⊖ Harrow on the Hill 117 CE58
Harrow Pk, Har. HA1 117 CE61
Harrow Pas, Kings.T. KT1 off Market Pl 197 CK96
Harrow Pl, E1 11 M7
Harrow Rd, E6 144 EL67
  E11 124 EE62
  NW10 6 A2
  W2 7 J6
  W9 6 G4
  W10 6 D3
  Barking IG11 145 ES67
  Carshalton SM5 218 DE106
  Feltham TW14 174 BN88
  Ilford IG1 125 EQ63
  Sevenoaks (Knock.) TN14 240 EY115
  Slough SL3 153 AZ76
  Warlingham CR6 237 DZ115
  Wembley HA0 117 CJ64
  Wembley (Tkgtn) HA9 118 CM64
Harrow Rd E, Dor. RH4 263 CH138
Harrow Rd W, Dor. RH4 263 CG138
Sch Harrow Sch, Har. HA1 off High St 117 CE60
Harrowsley Ct, Horl. RH6 off Tanyard Way 269 DH147
Harrowsley Grn La, Horl. RH6 269 DJ149
Harrow Vw, Har. HA1, HA2 117 CD56
  Hayes UB3 135 BU72
  Uxbridge UB10 135 BQ69
Harrow Vw Rd, W5 137 CH70
Harrow Way, Shep. TW17 195 BQ96
  Watford WD19 94 BY48
HARROW WEALD, Har. HA3 95 CD53
Harrow Weald Pk, Har. HA3 95 CD51
Sch Harry & Abe Sherman Prim Sch, Edg. HA8 off Glengall Rd 96 CP48
Sch Harry Gosling Prim Sch, E1 12 B8
Harston Dr, Enf. EN3 83 EA38
Hart Cl, Red. (Bletch.) RH1 252 DT134
Hart Cor, Grays RM20 169 FX78
Hart Cres, Chig. IG7 103 ET50
Hart Dyke Cres, Swan. BR8 off Hart Dyke Rd 207 FD97
Hart Dyke Rd, Orp. BR5 206 EW102
  Swanley BR8 207 FD97
Harte Rd, Houns. TW3 156 BZ82
Hartfield Av, Borwd. (Elstree) WD6 78 CN43
  Northolt UB5 135 BV68
Hartfield Cl, Borwd. (Elstree) WD6 78 CN43
Hartfield Ct, Ware SG12 33 DX05
Hartfield Cres, SW19 179 CZ94
  West Wickham BR4 204 EG104
Hartfield Gro, SE20 202 DV95
Hartfield Pl, Grav. (Nthflt) DA11 190 GD87
Hartfield Rd, SW19 179 CZ94
  Chessington KT9 215 CK106
  West Wickham BR4 222 EG105
Hartfield Ter, E3 143 EA68
Hartford Av, Har. HA3 117 CG55
Hartforde Rd, Borwd. WD6 78 CN40
Hartford Rd, Bex. DA5 186 FA86
  Epsom KT19 216 CN107
Hart Gdns, Dor. RH4 off Hart Rd 263 CH135
Hart Gro, W5 138 CN74
  Southall UB1 136 CA71
Harthall La, Hem.H. HP3 59 BS26
  Kings Langley WD4 59 BP28
Hartham Cl, N7 121 DL64
  Isleworth TW7 157 CG81
Hartham La, Hert. SG14 32 DQ09
Hartham Rd, N7 121 DL64
  N17 100 DT54
  Isleworth TW7 157 CF81
Harting Rd, SE9 184 EL91
Hartington Cl, Har. HA1 117 CE63
Hartington Ct, W4 158 CP80
Hartington Pl, Reig. RH2 250 DA132
Hartington Rd, E16 15 N8
  E17 123 DY58
  SW8 161 DL81
  W4 158 CP80
  W13 137 CH73
  Southall UB2 156 BY75
  Twickenham TW1 177 CH87
Hartismere Rd, SW6 159 CZ80
Hartlake Rd, E9 143 DX65
Hartland Cl, N21 off Elmscott Gdns 82 DQ44
  Addlestone (New Haw) KT15 212 BJ110
  Edgware HA8 96 CN47
  Slough SL1 131 AR74
Hartland Dr, Edg. HA8 96 CN47
  Ruislip HA4 115 BV62
Hartland Rd, E15 144 EF66
  N11 98 DF50
  NW1 141 DH66
  NW6 139 CZ68
  Addlestone KT15 212 BG108
  Epping CM16 70 EU31
  Hampton (Hmptn H.) TW12 176 CB91
  Hornchurch RM12 127 FG61
  Isleworth TW7 157 CG83
  Morden SM4 200 DA101
  Waltham Cross (Chsht) EN8 67 DX30
Hartlands Cl, Bex. DA5 186 EZ86
Hartland Way, Croy. CR0 203 DY103
  Morden SM4 199 CZ101
Hartlepool Ct, E16 off Fishguard Way 165 EP75
Hartley Av, E6 144 EL67
  NW7 97 CT50
Hartley Cl, NW7 97 CT50
  Bromley BR1 205 EM96
  Slough (Stoke P.) SL3 132 AW67
Hartley Copse, Wind. (Old Wind.) SL4 172 AU86
Hartley Down, Pur. CR8 219 DM113
Hartley Fm Est, Pur. CR8 235 DM115
HARTLEY GREEN, Long. DA3 209 FX99
Hartley Hill, Pur. CR8 235 DM115
Hartley Old Rd, Pur. CR8 219 DM114
Sch Hartley Prim Sch, E6 off Hartley Av 144 EL67
Hartley Rd, E11 124 EF60
  Croydon CR0 201 DP101
  Welling DA16 166 EW80
  Westerham TN16 255 ER125
Hartley St, E2 12 F1
Hartley Way, Pur. CR8 235 DM115
Hartmann Rd, E16 144 EK74
Hartmoor Ms, Enf. EN3 83 DX37
Hartnoll St, N7 4 B1
Harton Cl, Brom. BR1 204 EK95
Harton Rd, N9 100 DV47
Harton St, SE8 163 EA81
Hart Rd, Dor. RH4 263 CH135
  Harlow CM17 36 EW10
  St. Albans AL1 43 CD21
  West Byfleet (Byfleet) KT14 212 BL113
Hartsbourne Av, Bushey (Bushey Hth) WD23 94 CC47
Hartsbourne Cl, Bushey (Bushey Hth) WD23 95 CD47
Sch Hartsbourne Prim Sch, Bushey WD23 off Hartsbourne Rd 95 CD47
Hartsbourne Rd, Bushey (Bushey Hth) WD23 95 CD47
Hartsbourne Way, Hem.H. HP2 41 BQ21
Harts Cl, Bushey WD23 76 CA40
Hartscroft, Croy. CR0 221 DY109
Harts Gdns, Guil. GU2 242 AV131
Harts Gro, Wdf.Grn. IG8 102 EG50
Hartshill Cl, Uxb. UB10 134 BN65
Hartshill Rd, Grav. (Nthflt) DA11 191 GF89
Hartshill Wk, Wok. GU21 226 AV116
Hartshorn All, EC3 11 M8
Hartshorn Gdns, E6 145 EN70
Hartslands Rd, Sev. TN13 257 FJ123
Harts La, SE14 163 DY80
  Barking IG11 145 EP65
Hartslock Dr, SE2 166 EX75
Hartsmead Rd, SE9 185 EM89
Hartspiece Rd, Red. RH1 266 DG136
Hartspring La, Bushey WD23 76 CA39
  Watford WD25 76 CA39
Hart St, EC3 11 M9
  Brentwood CM14 108 FW47
Hartsway, Enf. EN3 82 DW42
Hartswood, Dor. (N.Holm.) RH5 off Wildcroft Dr 263 CK139
Hartswood Av, Reig. RH2 266 DA138
Hartswood Cl, Brwd. CM14 108 FY49
Hartswood Gdns, W12 159 CT76
Hartswood Grn, Bushey (Bushey Hth) WD23 95 CD47
Hartswood Rd, W12 159 CT75
  Brentwood CM14 108 FY49
Hartsworth Cl, E13 144 EF68
Hartville Rd, SE18 165 ES77
Hartwell Cl, H.Wyc. (Penn) HP10 88 AC45
Hartwell Dr, E4 101 EC51
  Beaconsfield HP9 89 AK52
Hartwell St, E8 5 N3
Harvard Hill, W4 158 CP79
Harvard La, W4 158 CP78
Harvard Rd, SE13 183 EC85
  W4 158 CP78
  Isleworth TW7 157 CE81
Harvard Wk, Horn. RM12 127 FG63
Harvel Cl, Orp. BR5 206 EU97
Harvel Cres, SE2 166 EX78
Harvest Bk Rd, W.Wick. BR4 204 EF104
Harvest Ct, St.Alb. AL4 off Harvesters 43 CK16
  Shepperton TW17 194 BN98
Harvest End, Wat. WD25 76 BX36
Harvester Rd, Epsom KT19 216 CR110
Harvesters, St.Alb. AL4 43 CK16
Harvesters Cl, Islw. TW7 177 CD85
Harvest Hill, B.End SL8 110 AD61
Harvest La, Loug. IG10 102 EK45
  Thames Ditton KT7 197 CG100
Harvest Mead, Hat. AL10 45 CV16
Harvest Rd, Bushey WD23 76 CB42
  Egham (Eng.Grn) TW20 172 AX92
  Feltham TW13 175 BU91
Harvestside, Horl. RH6 269 DJ147
Harvest Way, Swan. BR8 207 FD101
Harvey, Grays RM16 170 GB75
Harvey Cen, Harl. CM20 51 EQ15
Harvey Dr, Hmptn. TW12 196 CB95
Harveyfields, Wal.Abb. EN9 67 EC34
Harvey Gdns, E11 off Harvey Rd 124 EF60
  SE7 164 EJ78
  Loughton IG10 85 EP41
Harvey Ho, Brent. TW8 off Green Dragon La 158 CL78
Harvey Orchard, Beac. HP9 88 AJ52
Harvey Pt, E16 15 M6
Harvey Rd, E11 124 EE60
  N8 121 DM57
  SE5 162 DR81
  Guildford GU1 258 AY136
  Hounslow TW4 176 BZ87
  Ilford IG1 125 EP64
  Northolt UB5 136 BW66
  Rickmansworth (Crox.Grn) WD3 74 BN44
  St. Albans (Lon.Col.) AL2 61 CJ26
  Slough SL3 153 BB76
  Uxbridge UB10 134 BN68
  Walton-on-Thames KT12 195 BU101
Sch Harvey Rd Prim Sch, Rick. WD3 off Harvey Rd 74 BN44
Harveys La, Rom. RM7 127 FD61
Harvey St, N1 5 K8
Harvill Rd, Sid. DA14 186 EX92
Harvil Rd, Uxb. (Hare.) UB9 114 BK58
  Uxbridge (Ickhm) UB10 114 BL60
Sch Harvington Sch, W5 off Castlebar Rd 137 CK72
Harvington Wk, E8 off Wilman Gro 142 DU66
Harvist Est, N7 121 DN63
Harvist Rd, NW6 6 B1
Harwater Dr, Loug. IG10 85 EM40
Harwell Cl, Ruis. HA4 115 BR60
Harwell Pas, N2 120 DF56
Harwich Rd, Slou. SL1 131 AN72
Harwood Av, Brom. BR1 204 EH96
  Hornchurch RM11 128 FL55
  Mitcham CR4 200 DE97
Harwood Cl, N12 off Summerfields Av 98 DE51
  Welwyn (Tewin) AL6 30 DE05
  Welwyn Garden City AL8 29 CY05
  Wembley HA0 off Harrowdene Rd 117 CK63
Harwood Dr, Uxb. UB10 134 BM67
Harwood Gdns, Wind. (Old Wind.) SL4 172 AV87
Harwood Hall La, Upmin. RM14 148 FP65
Harwood Hill, Welw.G.C. AL8 29 CY06
Sch Harwood Hill JMI & Nurs Sch, Welw.G.C. AL8 off Harwood Hill 29 CY05
Harwood Pk, Red. RH1 266 DG143
Harwood Rd, SW6 160 DA80
Harwoods Rd, Wat. WD18 75 BU42
Harwoods Yd, N21 off Wades Hill 99 DN45
Harwood Ter, SW6 160 DB81
Hascombe Ter, SE5 off Love Wk 162 DR82
Hasedines Rd, Hem.H. HP1 40 BG19
Haselbury Rd, N9 100 DS49
  N18 100 DS49
Haseldine Meadows, Hat. AL10 45 CT19
Haseldine Rd, St.Alb. (Lon.Col.) AL2 61 CK26
Haseley End, SE23 off Tyson Rd 182 DW87
Haselrigge Rd, SW4 161 DK84
Sch Haseltine Prim Sch, SE26 off Haseltine Rd 183 DZ91
Haseltine Rd, SE26 183 DZ91
Haselwood Dr, Enf. EN2 81 DP42
Haskard Rd, Dag. RM9 126 EX63
Hasker St, SW3 18 B7
Haslam Av, Sutt. SM3 199 CY102
Haslam Cl, N1 4 D5
  Uxbridge UB10 115 BQ61
Haslam St, SE15 162 DT80
Haslemere Av, NW4 119 CX58
  SW18 180 DB89
  W7 157 CG76
  W13 157 CG76
  Barnet EN4 98 DF46
  Hounslow TW5 156 BW82
  Mitcham CR4 200 DD96
Haslemere Cl, Hmptn. TW12 176 BZ92
  Wallington SM6 off Stafford Rd 219 DL106
Haslemere Gdns, N3 119 CZ55
Haslemere Heathrow Est, Houns. TW4 155 BV82
Sch Haslemere Prim Sch, Mitch. CR4 off Haslemere Av 200 DD96
Haslemere Rd, N8 121 DK59
  N21 99 DP47
  Bexleyheath DA7 166 EZ82
  Ilford IG3 125 ET61
  Thornton Heath CR7 201 DP99
  Windsor SL4 151 AN81
Hasler Cl, SE28 146 EV73
Haslett Rd, Shep. TW17 195 BS96
Haslewood Av, Hodd. EN11 49 EA17
Hasluck Gdns, Barn. EN5 80 DC44
Sch Hasmonean High Sch, Boys, NW4 off Holders Hill Rd 97 CX54
  Girls, NW7 off Page St 97 CU53
Sch Hasmonean Prep Sch, NW4 off Shirehall La 119 CX57
Hassard St, E2 5 P10
Hassendean Rd, SE3 164 EH79
Hassett Rd, E9 143 DX65
Hassocks Cl, SE26 182 DV90
Hassocks Rd, SW16 201 DK95
Hassock Wd, Kes. BR2 222 EK105
Hassop Rd, NW2 119 CX63
Hassop Wk, SE9 184 EL91
Hasted Cl, Green. DA9 189 FW86
Hasted Rd, SE7 164 EK78
Hastings Av, Ilf. IG6 125 EQ56
Hastings Cl, SE15 162 DU80
  Barnet EN5 off Leicester Rd 80 DC42
  Grays RM17 170 FY79
  Maidenhead (Bray) SL6 150 AC77
  Wembley HA0 117 CJ63
Hastings Dr, Surb. KT6 197 CJ100
Hastings Ho, SE18 165 EM77
Hastings Rd, N11 99 DJ50
  N17 122 DR55
  W13 137 CH73
  Bromley BR2 204 EL102
  Croydon CR0 202 DT102
  Romford RM2 127 FH57
Hastings St, SE18 165 EQ76
  WC1 9 N2
Hastings Way, Bushey WD23 76 BY42
  Rickmansworth (Crox.Grn) WD3 75 BP42
HASTINGWOOD, Harl. CM17 52 EZ19
Hastingwood Business Cen, Harl. (Hast.) CM17 52 EZ18
Hastingwood Rd, Harl. (Hast.) CM17 52 EX20
Hastingwood Trd Est, N18 101 DX51
Hastoe Cl, Hayes UB4 136 BY70
Hat & Mitre Ct, EC1 10 F4
Hatch, The, Enf. EN3 83 DX39
  Windsor SL4 150 AJ80
Hatcham Pk Ms, SE14 off Hatcham Pk Rd 163 DX81
Hatcham Pk Rd, SE14 163 DX81
Hatcham Rd, SE15 162 DW79
Hatchard Rd, N19 121 DK61
Hatch Cl, Add. KT15 194 BH104
Hatchcroft, NW4 119 CV55
HATCH END, Pnr. HA5 94 BY51
⇌ Hatch End 94 BZ52
Sch Hatch End High Sch, Har. HA3 off Headstone La 94 CB53
Hatchers Ms, SE1 21 M4
Hatchett Rd, Felt. TW14 175 BQ88
Hatch Gdns, Tad. KT20 233 CX120
Hatchgate, Horl. RH6 268 DF149
Hatchgate Gdns, Slou. (Burn.) SL1 131 AK69
Hatch Gro, Rom. RM6 126 EY56
★ Hatchlands Ho & Pk, Guil. GU4 244 BM131
Hatchlands Rd, Red. RH1 250 DE134
Hatch La, E4 101 ED49
  Cobham KT11 229 BP119
  Coulsdon CR5 234 DG115
  Redhill RH1 267 DM142
  West Drayton UB7 154 BK80
  Windsor SL4 151 AN83
  Woking (Ockham) GU23 229 BP120
Hatch Pl, Kings.T. KT2 178 CM92
Hatch Rd, SW16 201 DL96
  Brentwood (Pilg.Hat.) CM15 108 FU43
Hatch Side, Chig. IG7 103 EN50
Hatchwood Cl, Wdf.Grn. IG8 off Sunset Av 102 EF49
Hatcliffe Cl, SE3 164 EF83
Hatcliffe St, SE10 25 J9
HATFIELD, AL9 & AL10 45 CV17
⇌ Hatfield 45 CW17
Hatfield Av, Hat. AL10 44 CS15
Hatfield Business Pk, Hat. AL10 44 CS15
Hatfield Cl, SE14 off Reaston St 163 DX80

★ Place of interest | H Hospital | Sch School | Coll College | Uni University | ⇌ Railway station

Hatfield Cl, Brent. (Hutt.) CM13 109 GD45
Hornchurch RM12 128 FK64
Ilford IG6 125 EP55
Mitcham CR4 200 DD98
Sutton SM2 218 DA109
West Byfleet KT14 212 BH112
Hatfield Cres, Hem.H. HP2 40 BM16
HATFIELD GARDEN VILLAGE, Hat. AL10 29 CU14
★ Hatfield Ho & Pk, Hat. AL9 45 CX18
HATFIELD HYDE, Welw.G.C. AL7 29 CZ12
Hatfield Mead, Mord. SM4 off Central Rd 200 DA99
Hatfield Pk, Hat. AL9 45 CX18
Sch Hatfield Prim Sch, Mord. SM4 off Lower Morden La 199 CY100
Hatfield Rd, E15 124 EE64
W4 158 CR75
W13 137 CG74
Ashtead KT21 232 CM119
Dagenham RM9 146 EY65
Grays (Chaff.Hun.) RM16 169 FX77
Hatfield AL9 30 DE14
Hertford SG14 30 DG11
Potters Bar EN6 30 DC30
St. Albans AL1, AL4 44 CN20
Slough SL1 152 AU75
Watford WD24 75 BV39
Hatfields, SE1 20 D1
Loughton IG10 85 EP41
Hatfield Tunnel, Hat. AL10 45 CT17
Hathaway Cl, Brom. BR2 205 EM102
Ruislip HA4 off Stafford Rd 115 BT63
Stanmore HA7 95 CG50
Hathaway Ct, St.Alb. AL4 44 CL20
Hathaway Cres, E12 145 EM65
Hathaway Gdns, W13 137 CF71
Grays RM17 off Hathaway Rd 170 GB76
Romford RM6 126 EX57
Sch Hathaway Prim Sch, W13 off Hathaway Gdns 137 CF71
Hathaway Rd, Croy. CR0 201 DP101
Grays RM17 170 GB77
Hatherleigh Cl, NW7 97 CX52
Chessington KT9 215 CK106
Morden SM4 200 DA98
Hatherleigh Gdns, Pot.B. EN6 64 DD32
Hatherleigh Rd, Ruis. HA4 115 BU61
Hatherleigh Way, Rom. RM3 106 FK53
Hatherley Cres, Sid. DA14 186 EU89
Hatherley Gdns, E6 144 EK68
N8 121 DL58
Hatherley Gro, W2 7 J7
Hatherley Ms, E17 123 EA56
Hatherley Rd, E17 123 DZ56
Richmond TW9 158 CM82
Sidcup DA14 186 EU91
Hatherley St, SW1 19 K7
Hathern Gdns, SE9 185 EN91
Hatherop Rd, Hmptn. TW12 176 BZ94
Hathersham Cl, Horl. (Smallfield) RH6 269 DN147
Hathersham La, Horl. (Smallfield) RH6 267 DK144
Hatherwood, Lthd. KT22 231 CK121
Hathorne Cl, SE15 162 DV82
Hathway St, SE15 off Gibbon Rd 162 DW82
Hathway Ter, SE14 off Kitto Rd 162 DW82
Hatley Av, Ilf. IG6 125 EQ56
Hatley Cl, N11 98 DF50
Hatley Rd, N4 121 DM61
Hatteraick St, SE16 22 F3
Hattersfield Cl, Belv. DA17 166 EZ77
Hatters La, Wat. WD18 75 BR44
HATTON, Felt. TW14 155 BT84
Hatton Av, Slou. SL2 131 AR70
Hatton Cl, SE18 165 ER80
Gravesend (Nthflt) DA11 190 GE90
Grays (Chaff.Hun.) RM16 169 FX76
Hatton Ct, E5 off Gilpin Rd 123 DY63
⊖ Hatton Cross 155 BT84
Hatton Gdn, EC1 10 D5
Hatton Gdns, Mitch. CR4 200 DF99
Hatton Grn, Felt. TW14 155 BU84
Hatton Gro, West Dr. UB7 154 BK75
Hatton Ho, E1 12 B9
Hatton Pl, EC1 10 D4
Hatton Rd, Croy. CR0 201 DN102
Feltham TW14 175 BS85
Waltham Cross (Chsht) EN8 67 DX29
Hatton Row, NW8 7 P4
Sch Hatton Sch, Wdf.Grn. IG8 off Roding La S 124 EK55
Hatton St, NW8 7 P4
Hatton Wall, EC1 10 C5
Haul Rd, NW1 141 DL68
Haunch of Venison Yd, W1 8 G8
Havana Cl, Rom. RM1 off Exchange St 127 FE57
Havana Rd, SW19 180 DA89
Havannah St, E14 23 P4
Havant Rd, E17 123 EC55
Havant Way, SE15 off Daniel Gdns 162 DT80
Havelock Pl, Har. HA1 117 CE58
Sch Havelock Prim Sch, Sthl. UB2 off Havelock Rd 156 BZ76
Havelock Rd, N17 100 DU54
SW19 180 DC92
Belvedere DA17 166 EZ77
Bromley BR2 204 EJ98
Croydon CR0 202 DT102
Dartford DA1 187 FH87
Gravesend DA11 191 GF88
Harrow HA3 117 CE55
Kings Langley WD4 58 BN28
Southall UB2 156 BZ76
Havelock St, N1 141 DL67
Ilford IG1 125 EP61
Havelock Ter, SW8 161 DH80
Havelock Wk, SE23 182 DW88
Haven, The, SE26 off Springfield Rd 182 DV92
Grays RM16 171 GF78
Richmond TW9 158 CN83
Sunbury-on-Thames TW16 175 BU94
Havenbury Ind Est, Dor. RH4 off Station Rd 263 CG135
Haven Cl, SE9 185 EM90
SW19 179 CX90
Gravesend (Istead Rise) DA13 191 GF94
Hatfield AL10 45 CT17
Hayes UB4 135 BS71
Sidcup DA14 186 EW93
Haven Cl, Swan. BR8 207 FF96
Haven Ct, Esher KT10 197 CE10
Havengore Av, Grav. DA12 191 GL87
Haven Grn, W5 137 CK72
Haven Grn Ct, W5 off Haven Grn 137 CK72
Havenhurst Ri, Enf. EN2 81 DN40
Haven La, W5 138 CL72
Haven Ms, E3 13 L6
N1 off Liverpool Rd 141 DN66
Haven Pl, W5 off The Broadway 137 CK73
Grays RM16 170 GC75
Haven Rd, Ashf. TW15 175 BP91
Havensfield, Kings L. (Chipper.) WD4 58 BH31
Haven St, NW1 off Castlehaven Rd 141 DH66
Haven Ter, W5 off The Broadway 137 CK73
Havenwood, Wem. HA9 118 CP62
Havenwood Cl, Brwd. CM13 off Wilmot Grn 107 FW51
Havercroft Cl, St.Alb. AL3 off King Harry La 42 CB22
Haverfield Gdns, Rich. TW9 158 CN80
Haverfield Rd, E3 13 J1
Haverford Way, Edg. HA8 96 CM53
Haverhill Rd, E4 101 EC46
SW12 181 DJ88
HAVERING-ATTE-BOWER, Rom. RM4 105 FE48
Coll Havering Coll of Further & Higher Ed, Horn. RM11 off Ardleigh Grn Rd 128 FL56
Harrow Lodge Site, Horn. RM11 off Hyland Way 127 FH59
Quarles Campus, Rom. RM3 off Tring Gdns 106 FL49
Havering Dr, Rom. RM1 127 FE56
Havering Gdns, Rom. RM6 126 EW57
Sch Havering Music Cen, Horn. RM11 off The Walk 128 FM61
HAVERING PARK, Rom. RM5 104 FA50
Havering Rd, Rom. RM1 127 FD55
Coll Havering 6th Form Coll, Horn. RM11 off Wingletye La 128 FM60
Havering St, E1 12 G8
Havering Way, Bark. IG11 146 EV69
Havers Av, Walt. KT12 214 BX106
Haversfield Est, Brent. TW8 158 CL78
Haversham Cl, Twick. TW1 177 CK86
Haversham Pl, N6 120 DF61
Haverstock Ct, Orp. BR5 206 EU96
Haverstock Hill, NW3 120 DE64
Haverstock Pl, N1 off Haverstock St 141 DP68
Haverstock Rd, NW5 120 DG64
Sch Haverstock Sch, NW1 off Crogsland Rd 140 DG65
Haverstock St, N1 4 F10
Haverthwaite Rd, Orp. BR6 205 ER103
Havil St, SE5 162 DS80
Havisham Pl, SE19 181 DP93
Hawarden Gro, SE24 182 DQ87
Hawarden Hill, NW2 119 CU62
Hawarden Rd, E17 123 DX56
Caterham CR3 236 DQ121
Haward Rd, Hodd. EN11 49 EC15
Hawbridge Rd, E11 123 ED60
Hawes Cl, Nthwd. HA6 93 BT52
Sch Hawes Down Inf Sch, W.Wick. BR4 off The Mead 203 ED102
Sch Hawes Down Jun Sch, W.Wick. BR4 off The Mead 203 ED102
Hawes La, E4 83 EC38
West Wickham BR4 203 ED102
Hawes Rd, N18 100 DV51
Bromley BR1 204 EH95
Tadworth KT20 off Hatch Gdns 233 CX120
Hawes St, N1 4 F6
Haweswater Dr, Wat. WD25 60 BW33
Haweswater Ho, Islw. TW7 off Summerwood Rd 177 CF85
Hawfield Bk, Orp. BR6 206 EX104
Hawfield Gdns, St.Alb. (Park St) AL2 61 CD26
Hawgood St, E3 13 P6
Hawk Cl, Wal.Abb. EN9 68 EG34
Hawkdene, E4 83 EB44
Sch Hawkedale Inf - A Foundation Sch, Sun. TW16 off Stratton Rd 195 BT97
Hawkenbury, Harl. CM19 51 EP17
Hawke Pk Rd, N22 121 DP55
Hawke Pl, SE16 23 H3
Hawke Rd, SE19 182 DS93
Hawkesbury Rd, SW15 179 CV85
Hawkes Cl, Grays RM17 off New Rd 170 GB79
Hawkesfield Rd, SE23 183 DY89
Hawkesley Cl, Twick. TW1 177 CG91
Hawke's Pl, Sev. TN13 256 FG127
Hawkes Rd, Felt. TW14 175 BU87
Mitcham CR4 200 DE95
Hawkesworth Cl, Nthwd. HA6 93 BS52
Hawke Twr, SE14 off Nynehead St 163 DY79
Hawkewood Rd, Sun. TW16 195 BU97
Hawkhirst Rd, Ken. CR8 236 DR115
Hawkhurst, Cob. KT11 214 CA114
Hawkhurst Gdns, Chess. KT9 216 CL105
Romford RM5 105 FD51
Hawkhurst Rd, SW16 201 DK95
Hawkhurst Way, N.Mal. KT3 198 CR99
West Wickham BR4 203 EB103
Hawkinge Wk, Orp. BR5 206 EV97
Hawkinge Way, Horn. RM12 148 FJ65
Hawkins Av, Grav. DA12 191 GJ91
Hawkins Cl, NW7 off Hale La 96 CR50
Borehamwood WD6 off Banks Rd 78 CQ40
Harrow HA1 117 CD59
Hawkins Dr, Grays (Chaff.Hun.) RM16 169 FX75
Hawkins Rd, Tedd. TW11 177 CH93
Hawkins Way, SE6 183 EA92
Hemel Hempstead (Bov.) HP3 57 BA26
Hawkley Gdns, SE27 181 DP89
Hawkridge Cl, Rom. RM6 126 EW59
Hawkridge Dr, Grays RM17 170 GD78
Hawksbrook La, Beck. BR3 203 EB100
Hawkshaw Cl, SW2 off Tierney Rd 181 DL87
Hawkshead Cl, Brom. BR1 184 EE94
Hawkshead La, Hat. (N.Mymms) AL9 63 CW28
Hawkshead Rd, NW10 139 CT66
W4 158 CS75
Potters Bar EN6 64 DB29
Hawks Hill, B.End SL8 110 AC61
Epping (N.Wld Bas.) CM16 70 FA27
Hawk's Hill, Lthd. KT22 231 CF123
Hawkshill, St.Alb. AL1 43 CG21
Hawkshill Cl, Esher KT10 214 CA107
Hawks Hill Cl, Lthd. (Fetch.) KT22 231 CF122
Hawkshill Dr, Hem.H. (Felden) HP3 39 BE23
Hawkshill Rd, Slou. SL2 131 AN69
Hawkshill Way, Esher KT10 214 BZ107
Hawkslade Rd, SE15 183 DX85
Hawksley Rd, N16 122 DS62
Hawksmead Cl, Enf. EN3 83 DX35
Hawks Ms, SE10 off Luton Pl 163 EC80
Hawksmoor, Rad. (Shenley) WD7 62 CN33
Hawksmoor Cl, E6 off Allhallows Rd 144 EL72
SE18 165 ES78
Hawksmoor Grn, Brwd. (Hutt.) CM13 109 GD43
Hawksmoor Ms, E1 12 C9
Sch Hawksmoor Prim Sch, SE28 off Bentham Rd 146 EV74
Hawksmoor St, W6 159 CX79
Hawksmouth, E4 101 EB45
Hawks Rd, Kings.T. KT1 198 CM96
Hawkstone Rd, SE16 22 F8
Hawksview, Cob. KT11 214 BZ113
Hawksway, Stai. TW18 173 BF90
Hawkswell Cl, Wok. GU21 226 AT117
Hawkswell Wk, Wok. GU21 off Lockfield Dr 226 AS117
Hawkswood Gro, Slou. (Fulmer) SL3 133 AZ65
Hawkswood La, Ger.Cr. SL9 113 AZ64
Sch Hawkswood Sch & Cen, E4 off Antlers Hill 83 EC43
Hawk Ter, Ilf. IG5 off Tiptree Cres 125 EN55
Hawkwell Ct, E4 off Colvin Gdns 101 EC48
Hawkwell Ho, Dag. RM8 126 FA60
Hawkwell Wk, N1 5 H7
Hawkwood Cres, E4 83 EB44
Hawkwood Dell, Lthd. (Bkhm) KT23 246 CA126
Hawkwood La, Chis. BR7 205 EQ95
Hawkwood Mt, E5 122 DV60
Hawkwood Ri, Lthd. (Bkhm) KT23 246 CA126
Hawlands Dr, Pnr. HA5 116 BY59
HAWLEY, Dart. DA2 188 FM92
Hawley Cl, Hmptn. TW12 176 BZ93
Hawley Cres, NW1 141 DH66
Sch Hawley Inf Sch, NW1 off Buck St 141 DH66
Hawley Ms, NW1 off Hawley St 141 DH66
Hawley Mill, Dart. DA2 188 FN91
Hawley Rd, N18 101 DX50
NW1 141 DH66
Dartford DA1, DA2 188 FL89
HAWLEY'S CORNER, West. TN16 239 EN121
Hawley St, NW1 141 DH66
Hawley Ter, Dart. DA2 off Hawley Rd 188 FN92
Hawley Vale, Dart. DA2 188 FN92
Hawley Way, Ashf. TW15 174 BN92
Haws La, Stai. TW19 174 BG86
Hawstead La, Orp. BR6 224 EZ106
Hawstead Rd, SE6 183 EB86
Hawsted, Buck.H. IG9 102 EH45
Hawthorn Av, E3 143 DZ67
N13 99 DL50
Brentwood CM13 109 FZ48
Carshalton SM5 218 DG108
Rainham RM13 147 FH70
Richmond TW9 off Kew Rd 158 CL82
Thornton Heath CR7 201 DP95
Hawthorn Cen, Har. HA1 117 CF56
Hawthorn Cl, Abb.L. WD5 59 BU32
Banstead SM7 217 CY114
Gravesend DA12 191 GH91
Hampton TW12 176 CA92
Hertford SG14 31 DN08
Hounslow TW5 155 BV80
Iver SL0 133 BD68
Orpington BR5 205 ER100
Redhill RH1 off Bushfield Dr 266 DG139
Watford WD17 75 BT38
Woking GU22 226 AY120
Hawthorn Cotts, Well. DA16 off Hook La 166 EU83
Hawthorn Ct, Rich. TW9 off West Hall Rd 158 CP81
Hawthorn Cres, SW17 180 DG92
South Croydon CR2 220 DW111
Hawthornden Cl, N12 off Fallowfields Dr 98 DE51
Hawthorndene Cl, Brom. BR2 204 EF103
Hawthorndene Rd, Brom. BR2 204 EF103
Hawthorn Dr, Har. HA2 116 BZ58
Uxbridge (Denh.) UB9 134 BJ65
West Wickham BR4 222 EE105
Hawthorne Av, Har. HA3 117 CG58
Mitcham CR4 200 DD96
Ruislip HA4 115 BV58
Waltham Cross (Chsht) EN7 66 DV31
Westerham (Bigg.H.) TN16 238 EK115
Hawthorne Cl, N1 5 L3
Bromley BR1 205 EM97
Sutton SM1 off Aultone Way 200 DB103
Waltham Cross (Chsht) EN7 66 DV31
Hawthorne Ct, Nthwd. HA6 off Ryefield Cres 93 BU54
Walton-on-Thames KT12 off Ambleside Av 196 BX103
Hawthorne Cres, Slou. SL1 132 AS71
West Drayton UB7 154 BM75
Hawthorne Fm Av, Nthlt. UB5 136 BY67
Hawthorne Gro, NW9 118 CQ59
Hawthorne La, Hem.H. HP1 39 BF19
Hawthorne Ms, Grnf. UB6 off Greenford Rd 136 CC72
Hawthorne Pl, Epsom KT17 216 CS112
Hayes UB3 135 BT73
Hawthorne Rd, E17 123 EA55
Bromley BR1 204 EL97
Radlett WD7 61 CG34
Hawthorne Rd, Stai. TW18 173 BC92
Hawthornes, Hat. AL10 45 CT20
Hawthorne Way, N9 100 DS47
Guildford GU4 243 BB130
Staines (Stanw.) TW19 174 BK87
Hawthorn Gdns, W5 157 CK76
Hawthorn Gro, SE20 182 DV94
Barnet EN5 79 CT44
Enfield EN2 82 DR38
Hawthorn Hatch, Brent. TW8 157 CH80
Hawthorn La, Sev. TN13 256 FF122
Slough (Farn.Com.) SL2 131 AP65
Hawthorn Ms, NW7 off Holders Hill Rd 97 CY53
Hawthorn Pl, Erith DA8 167 FC78
Guildford GU4 off Merrow St 243 BD132
High Wycombe (Penn) HP10 88 AC47
Hawthorn Rd, N8 121 DK55
N18 100 DT50
NW10 139 CU66
Bexleyheath DA6 166 EZ84
Brentford TW8 157 CH80
Buckhurst Hill IG9 102 EK49
Dartford DA1 188 FK88
Hoddesdon EN11 49 EB15
Sutton SM1 218 DE107
Wallington SM6 219 DH108
Woking GU22 226 AX120
Woking (Send M.) GU23 228 BG124
Hawthorns, Harl. CM18 51 ET19
Welwyn Garden City AL8 29 CX07
Woodford Green IG8 102 EG48
Hawthorns, The, Berk. HP4 38 AU18
Chalfont St. Giles HP8 72 AW40
Epsom KT17 off Ewell Bypass 217 CT107
Hemel Hempstead HP3 39 BF24
Loughton IG10 85 EN42
Oxted RH8 254 EG133
Rickmansworth (Map.Cr.) WD3 91 BD50
Slough (Colnbr.) SL3 153 BF81
Sch Hawthorns Sch, The, Red. RH1 off Pendell Rd 251 DP131
Hawthorn Wk, W10 6 C3
Hawthorn Way, Add. (New Haw) KT15 212 BJ110
Chesham HP5 54 AR29
Redhill RH1 267 DH136
St. Albans AL2 42 CA24
Shepperton TW17 195 BR98
Hawtrees, Rad. WD7 77 CF35
Hawtrey Av, Nthlt. UB5 136 BX68
Hawtrey Cl, Slou. SL1 152 AV75
Hawtrey Dr, Ruis. HA4 115 BU59
Hawtrey Rd, NW3 140 DE66
Windsor SL4 151 AQ82
Haxted Rd, Brom. BR1 off North Rd 204 EH95
Haybourn Mead, Hem.H. HP1 40 BH21
Hayburn Way, Horn. RM12 127 FF60
Hay Cl, E15 144 EE66
Borehamwood WD6 78 CQ40
Haycroft Cl, Couls. CR5 off Caterham Dr 235 DP118
Haycroft Gdns, NW10 139 CU67
Haycroft Rd, SW2 181 DL85
Surbiton KT6 198 CL104
Hay Currie St, E14 14 B7
Hayday Rd, E16 15 L5
Hayden Ct, Add. (New Haw) KT15 212 BH111
Hayden Rd, Wal.Abb. EN9 83 EC35
Haydens Cl, Orp. BR5 206 EV100
Haydens Pl, W11 6 E7
Haydens Rd, Harl. CM20 51 EQ15
Hayden Way, Rom. RM5 105 FC54
Haydn Av, Pur. CR8 219 DN114
Haydns Ms, W3 off Emanuel Av 138 CQ72
Haydock Av, Nthlt. UB5 136 CA65
Haydock Cl, Horn. RM12 128 FM63
Haydock Grn, Nthlt. UB5 off Haydock Av 136 CA65
Haydon Cl, NW9 118 CQ56
Enfield EN1 off Mortimer Dr 82 DS44
Romford RM3 105 FH52
Haydon Dr, Pnr. HA5 115 BU56
Haydon Pk Rd, SW19 180 DB92
Haydon Pl, Guil. GU1 258 AX135
Haydon Rd, Dag. RM8 126 EW61
Watford WD19 76 BY44
Sch Haydon Sch, Pnr. HA5 off Wiltshire La 115 BT55
⇌ Haydons Road 180 DC92
Haydons Rd, SW19 180 DB92
Haydon St, EC3 11 N9
Haydon Wk, E1 11 P9
Haydon Way, SW11 160 DD84
HAYES, Brom. BR2 204 EG103
HAYES, UB3 & UB4 135 BS72
⇌ Hayes 204 EF102
Hayes, The, Epsom KT18 232 CR119
⇌ Hayes & Harlington 155 BT76
Hayes Barton, Wok. GU22 227 BD116
Hayes Bypass, Hayes UB3, UB4 136 BX70
Hayes Chase, W.Wick. BR4 204 EE99
Hayes Cl, Brom. BR2 204 EG103
Grays RM20 169 FW79
Hayes Ct, SW2 181 DL88
Hayes Cres, NW11 119 CZ57
Sutton SM3 217 CX105
Hayes Dr, Rain. RM13 147 FH66
HAYES END, Hayes UB3 135 BQ71
Hayes End Cl, Hayes UB4 135 BR70
Hayes End Dr, Hayes UB4 135 BR70
Hayes End Rd, Hayes UB4 135 BR70
Hayesford Pk Dr, Brom. BR2 204 EF99
Hayes Gdn, Brom. BR2 204 EG103
Hayes Gro, SE15 162 DT84
H Hayes Gro Priory Hosp, Brom. BR2 204 EG103
Hayes Hill, Brom. BR2 204 EE102
Hayes Hill Rd, Brom. BR2 204 EF102
Hayes La, Beck. BR3 203 EC97
Bromley BR2 204 EG99
Kenley CR8 220 DQ114
Sch Hayes Manor Sch, Hayes UB3 off Wood End Grn Rd 135 BS72
Hayes Mead Rd, Brom. BR2 204 EE102
Hayes Metro Cen, Hayes UB4 136 BW73
Hayes Pk, Hayes UB4 135 BS70
Sch Hayes Pk Sch, Hayes UB4 off Raynton Dr 135 BT70
Hayes Pl, NW1 8 B4
Sch Hayes Prim Sch, Brom. BR2 off George La 204 EH102
Sch Hayes Prim Sch, The, Ken. CR8 off Hayes La 235 DP116
Hayes Rd, Brom. BR2 204 EG98
Greenhithe DA9 189 FS87
Southall UB2 155 BV77
Sch Hayes Sch, Brom. BR2 off West Common Rd 204 EH103
Hayes St, Brom. BR2 204 EH102
HAYES TOWN, Hayes UB3 155 BS75
Hayes Wk, Brox. EN10 off Landau Way 67 DZ25
Horley (Smallfield) RH6 269 DN147
Potters Bar EN6 off Hyde Av 64 DB33
Hayes Way, Beck. BR3 203 EC98
Hayes Wd Av, Brom. BR2 204 EH102
Hayfield Cl, Bushey WD23 76 CB42
Hayfield Pas, E1 12 F4
Hayfield Rd, Orp. BR5 206 EU99
Hayfields, Horl. RH6 off Ryelands 269 DJ147
Hayfield Yd, E1 12 F4
Haygarth Pl, SW19 179 CX92
Haygreen Cl, Kings.T. KT2 178 CP93
Hay Hill, W1 9 H10
Hayland Cl, NW9 118 CR56
Hay La, NW9 118 CR56
Slough (Fulmer) SL3 112 AX63
Hayles St, SE11 20 E7
Haylett Gdns, Kings.T. KT1 off Anglesea Rd 197 CK98
Hayling Av, Felt. TW13 175 BU90
Hayling Cl, N16 5 M1
Hayling Rd, Wat. WD19 93 BV47
Haymaker Cl, Uxb. UB10 off Honey Hill 134 BM66
Hayman Cres, Hayes UB4 135 BR68
Hayman St, N1 4 F6
Haymarket, SW1 9 L10
Haymarket Arc, SW1 9 L10
Haymeads, Welw.G.C. AL8 29 CY06
Haymeads Dr, Esher KT10 214 CC107
Haymer Gdns, Wor.Pk. KT4 199 CU104
Haymerle Rd, SE15 162 DU79
Sch Haymerle Spec Sch, SE15 off Haymerle Rd 162 DU79
Haymill Cl, Grnf. UB6 137 CF69
Haymill Rd, Slou. SL1, SL2 131 AK70
Hayne Rd, Beck. BR3 203 DZ96
Haynes Cl, N11 98 DG48
N17 100 DV52
SE3 164 EE83
Slough SL3 153 AZ78
Welwyn Garden City AL7 30 DA10
Woking (Ripley) GU23 228 BH122
Haynes Dr, N9 100 DV48
Haynes La, SE19 182 DS93
Haynes Mead, Berk. HP4 38 AU17
Haynes Pk Ct, Horn. RM11 off Slewins Cl 128 FJ57
Haynes Rd, Grav. (Nthflt) DA11 191 GF90
Hornchurch RM11 128 FK57
Wembley HA0 138 CL66
Hayne St, EC1 10 F5
Haynt Wk, SW20 199 CY97
Hayse Hill, Wind. SL4 151 AK81
★ Hay's Galleria, SE1 21 L1
Hay's La, SE1 21 L2
Haysleigh Gdns, SE20 202 DU96
Hay's Ms, W1 8 G10
Haysoms Cl, Rom. RM1 127 FE56
Haystall Cl, Hayes UB4 135 BS68
Hay St, E2 142 DU67
Hays Wk, Sutt. SM2 217 CX110
Hayter Ct, E11 124 EH61
Hayter Rd, SW2 181 DL85
Hayton Cl, E8 5 P4
Haywain, Oxt. RH8 253 ED130
Hayward Cl, SW19 200 DB95
Dartford DA1 187 FD85
Hayward Dr, Dart. DA1 188 FM89
★ Hayward Gall, SE1 20 B1
Hayward Gdns, SW15 179 CW86
Hayward Rd, N20 98 DC47
Thames Ditton KT7 197 CG102
Haywards Cl, Brwd. (Hutt.) CM13 109 GE44
Romford (Chad.Hth) RM6 126 EV57
Haywards Mead, Wind. (Eton Wick) SL4 151 AM78
Hayward's Pl, EC1 10 E4
Haywood Cl, Pnr. HA5 94 BX54
Haywood Ct, Wal.Abb. EN9 68 EF34
Haywood Dr, Hem.H. HP3 39 BF23
Rickmansworth (Chorl.) WD3 73 BF43
Haywood Pk, Rick. (Chorl.) WD3 73 BF43
Haywood Ri, Orp. BR6 223 ES105
Haywood Rd, Brom. BR2 204 EK98
Hayworth Cl, Enf. EN3 off Green St 83 DY40
Hazel Av, Guil. GU1 242 AW130
West Drayton UB7 154 BN76
Hazelbank, Surb. KT5 198 CQ102
Hazelbank Ct, Cher. KT16 194 BJ102
Hazelbank Rd, SE6 183 ED89
Chertsey KT16 194 BJ102
Hazelbourne Rd, SW12 181 DH86
Hazelbrouck Gdns, Ilf. IG6 103 ER52
Hazelbury Av, Abb.L. WD5 59 BQ32
Hazelbury Cl, SW19 200 DA96
Hazelbury Grn, N9 100 DS48
Sch Hazelbury Inf Sch, N9 off Haselbury Rd 100 DS48
Sch Hazelbury Jun Sch, N9 off Haselbury Rd 100 DS48
Hazelbury La, N9 100 DS48
Hazel Cl, N13 100 DR48
N19 off Hargrave Pk 121 DJ61
NW9 96 CS54
SE15 162 DU82
Brentford TW8 157 CH80
Croydon CR0 203 DX101
Egham (Eng.Grn) TW20 172 AV93
Hornchurch RM12 127 FH62
Mitcham CR4 201 DK98
Reigate RH2 266 DC136
Twickenham TW2 176 CC87
Waltham Cross EN7 off The Laurels 66 DS26
Hazelcroft, Pnr. HA5 94 CA51
Hazelcroft Cl, Uxb. UB10 134 BM66
Hazeldean Rd, NW10 138 CR66
Hazeldell Link, Hem.H. HP1 39 BF21
Hazeldell Rd, Hem.H. HP1 39 BE21
Hazeldene, Add. KT15 212 BJ106
Waltham Cross EN8 67 DY32

⊖ London Underground station DLR Docklands Light Railway station Tra Tramlink station Riv Pedestrian ferry landing stage

Hazeldene Ct, Ken. CR8 236 DR115
Hazeldene Dr, Pnr. HA5 116 BW55
Hazeldene Gdns, Uxb.
UB10 135 BQ67
Hazeldene Rd, Ilf. IG3 126 EV61
Welling DA16 166 EW82
Hazeldon Rd, SE4 183 DY85
Hazel Dr, Erith DA8 167 FH81
South Ockendon RM15 149 FW69
Woking (Ripley) GU23 243 BF125
Hazeleigh, Brwd. CM13 109 GB48
Hazeleigh Gdns, Wdf.Grn.
IG8 102 EL50
Hazel End, Swan. BR8 207 FE99
Hazel Gdns, Edg. HA8 96 CP49
Grays RM16 170 GE76
Sawbridgeworth CM21
off Sun St 36 EZ06
Hazelgreen Cl, N21 99 DP46
Hazel Gro, SE26 183 DX91
Enfield EN1
off Dimsdale Dr 82 DU44
Hatfield AL10 45 CT21
Orpington BR6 205 EP103
Romford RM6 126 EY55
Staines TW18 174 BH93
Watford WD25
off Cedar Wd Dr 75 BV35
Welwyn Garden City AL7 30 DB08
Wembley HA0
off Carlyon Rd 138 CL67
Hazel Gro Est, SE26 183 DX91
[Sch] Hazel Gro Sch, Hat.
AL10 off Hazel Gro 45 CT21
Hazelhurst, Beck. BR3 203 ED95
Horley RH6 269 DJ146
Hazelhurst Cl, Guil. GU4
off Weybrook Dr 243 BB129
Hazelhurst Rd, SW17 180 DC91
Slough (Burn.) SL1 130 AJ68
Hazel La, Ilf. IG6 103 EP52
Richmond TW10 178 CL89
Hazell Cres, Rom. RM5 105 FB53
Hazell Pk, Amer. HP7 55 AR39
Hazells Rd, Grav. DA13 190 GD92
Hazellville Rd, N19 121 DK59
Hazell Way, Slou. (Stoke P.)
SL2 132 AT65
Hazel Mead, Barn. EN5 79 CV43
Epsom KT17 217 CU110
Hazelmere Cl, Felt. TW14 175 BR86
Leatherhead KT22 231 CH119
Northolt UB5 136 BZ68
Hazelmere Dr, Nthlt. UB5 136 BZ68
Hazelmere Gdns, Horn.
RM11 127 FH57
Hazelmere Rd, NW6 140 DA67
Northolt UB5 136 BZ68
Orpington BR5 205 EQ98
St. Albans AL4 43 CJ17
Hazelmere Wk, Nthlt. UB5 136 BZ68
Hazelmere Way, Brom. BR2 204 EG100
Hazel Ms, N22
off Alexandra Rd 121 DN55
Hazel Ri, Horn. RM11 128 FJ58
Hazel Rd, E15
off Wingfield Rd 124 EE64
NW10 139 CW69
Berkhamsted HP4 38 AX20
Dartford DA1 188 FK89
Erith DA8 167 FG81
Reigate RH2 266 DC136
St. Albans (Park St) AL2 60 CB28
West Byfleet KT14 212 BG114
Hazels, The, Welw. AL6 30 DE05
Hazeltree La, Nthlt. UB5 136 BY69
Hazel Tree Rd, Wat. WD24 75 BV37
Hazel Wk, Brom. BR2 205 EN100
Dorking (N.Holm.) RH5
off Lake Vw 263 CJ139
Hazel Way, E4 101 DZ51
SE1 21 N7
Coulsdon CR5 234 DF119
Leatherhead (Fetch.)
KT22 230 CC122
HAZELWOOD, Sev. TN14 223 ER111
Hazelwood, Dor. RH4 263 CH137
Loughton IG10 84 EK43
Hazelwood Av, Mord. SM4 200 DB98
Hazelwood Cl, W5 158 CL75
Chesham HP5 54 AR29
Harrow HA2 116 CB56
Hazelwood Ct, NW10
off Neasden La N 118 CS62
Hazelwood Cres, N13 99 DN49
Hazelwood Cft, Surb. KT6 198 CL100
Hazelwood Dr, Pnr. HA5 93 BV54
St. Albans AL4 43 CJ19
Hazelwood Gdns, Brwd.
(Pilg.Hat.) CM15 108 FU44
Hazelwood Gro, S.Croy.
CR2 220 DV113
Hazelwood Hts, Oxt. RH8 254 EG131
[Sch] Hazelwood Inf Sch,
N13 off Hazelwood La 99 DN49
[Sch] Hazelwood Jun Sch,
N13 off Hazelwood La 99 DN49
Hazelwood La, N13 99 DN49
Abbots Langley WD5 59 BQ32
Coulsdon CR5 234 DF119
Hazelwood Pk Cl, Chig.
IG7 103 ES50
Hazelwood Rd, E17 123 DY57
Enfield EN1 82 DT44
Oxted RH8 254 EH132
Rickmansworth (Crox.Grn)
WD3 75 BQ44
Sevenoaks (Cudham)
TN14 223 ER112
Woking (Knap.) GU21 226 AS118
[Sch] Hazelwood Sch, Oxt.
RH8 off Wolfs Hill 254 EG131
Hazlebury Rd, SW6 160 DB82
Hazledean Rd, Croy. CR0 202 DR103
Hazledene Rd, W4 158 CQ79
Hazlemere Gdns, Wor.Pk.
KT4 199 CV102
Hazlemere Rd, H.Wyc.
(Penn) HP10 88 AC45
Slough SL2 132 AW74
Hazlewell Rd, SW15 179 CV85
Hazlewood Cl, E5
off Mandeville St 123 DY62
Hazlewood Cres, W10 6 D4
Hazlitt Cl, Felt. TW13 176 BY91
Hazlitt Ms, W14 16 C6
Hazlitt Rd, W14 16 C6
Hazon Way, Epsom KT19 216 CR112
Heacham Av, Uxb. UB10 115 BQ62
Headcorn Pl, Th.Hth. CR7
off Headcorn Rd 201 DM98
Headcorn Rd, N17 100 DT52
Bromley BR1 184 EF92
Thornton Heath CR7 201 DM98
Headfort Pl, SW1 18 F4
Headingley Cl, Ilf. IG6 103 ET51
Radlett (Shenley) WD7 62 CL32
Waltham Cross (Chsht)
EN7 66 DT26
Headington Rd, SW18 180 DC89
Headlam Rd, SW4 181 DK86
Headlam St, E1 12 D4
Headlands Dr, Berk. HP4
off Byways 38 AY18
HEADLEY, Epsom KT18 248 CQ125
Headley App, Ilf. IG2 125 EN57
Headley Av, Wall. SM6 219 DM106
Headley Chase, Brwd. CM14 108 FW49
Headley Cl, Epsom KT19 216 CN107
Headley Common, Brwd.
CM13 off Warley Gap 107 FV52
Headley Common Rd,
Epsom (Headley) KT18 248 CR127
Tadworth KT20 248 CR127
Headley Ct, SE26 182 DV92
Headley Dr, Croy.
(New Adgtn) CR0 221 EB108
Epsom KT18 233 CV119
Ilford IG2 125 EP58
Headley Gro, Tad. KT20 233 CV120
★ Headley Heath, Epsom
KT18 248 CP128
Headley Heath App, Dor. (Mick.)
RH5 off Ashurst Dr 248 CP130
Tadworth (Box H.) KT20 248 CP130
Headley La, Dor. (Mick.) RH5 247 CJ129
Headley Rd, Epsom (Tyr.Wd)
KT18 232 CN123
Epsom (Woodcote) KT18 232 CP118
Leatherhead KT22 231 CK123
Head's Ms, W11 6 G8
HEADSTONE, Har. HA2 116 CC56
Headstone Dr, Har. HA1,
HA3 117 CE55
Headstone Gdns, Har. HA2 116 CC56
⇌ Headstone Lane 94 CB53
Headstone La, Har. HA2,
HA3 116 CB56
Headstone Rd, Har. HA1 117 CE57
Head St, E1 12 G8
Headway, The, Epsom KT17 217 CT109
Headway Cl, Rich. TW10
off Locksmeade Rd 177 CJ91
Heald St, SE14 163 DZ81
Healey Dr, Orp. BR6 223 ET105
Healey Rd, Wat. WD18 75 BT44
Healey St, NW1 141 DH65
Heanor Ct, E5 off Pedro St 123 DX62
Heards La, Brwd. (Shenf.)
CM15 109 FZ41
Hearne Ct, Ch.St.G. HP8
off Gordon Way 90 AV48
Hearne Rd, W4 158 CN79
Hearnes Cl, Beac. (Seer Grn)
HP9 89 AR50
Hearnes Meadow, Beac.
(Seer Grn) HP9 89 AR50
Hearn Ri, Nthlt. UB5 136 BX67
Hearn Rd, Rom. RM1 127 FF58
Hearn's Bldgs, SE17 21 K8
Hearn's Rd, Orp. BR5 206 EW98
Hearn St, EC2 11 M4
Hearnville Rd, SW12 180 DG88
[H] Heart Hosp, The, W1 8 F6
Heath, The, W7
off Lower Boston Rd 137 CE74
Bishop's Stortford
(Hat.Hth) CM22 37 FG05
Caterham CR3 236 DQ124
Radlett WD7 61 CG33
Heathacre, Slou. (Colnbr.)
SL3 off Park St 153 BE81
Heatham Pk, Twick. TW2 177 CF87
Heath Av, Bexh. DA7 166 EX79
St. Albans AL3 43 CD18
Heathbourne Rd, Bushey
(Bushey Hth) WD23 95 CE47
Stanmore HA7 95 CE47
Heathbridge, Wey. KT13 212 BN108
[Sch] Heathbrook Prim Sch,
SW8 off St. Rule St 161 DJ82
Heath Brow, NW3
off North End Way 120 DC62
Hemel Hempstead HP1 40 BJ22
Heath Business Cen, The,
Red. (Salf.) RH1 267 DH143
Heath Cl, NW11 120 DB59
W5 138 CM70
Banstead SM7 218 DB114
Hayes UB3 155 BR80
Hemel Hempstead HP1 40 BJ21
Orpington BR5
off Sussex Rd 206 EW100
Potters Bar EN6 64 DB30
Romford RM2 127 FG55
Staines (Stanw.) TW19 174 BJ86
Heathclose, Swan. BR8
off Bonney Way 207 FE96
Heath Cl, Vir.W. GU25 192 AX98
Heathclose Av, Dart. DA1 187 FH87
Heathclose Rd, Dart. DA1 187 FG88
Heathcock Ct, WC2
off Strand 141 DL73
Heathcote, Tad. KT20 233 CX121
Heathcote Av, Hat. AL10 45 CU16
Ilford IG5 103 EM54
Heathcote Ct, Ilf. IG5
off Heathcote Av 103 EM54
Heathcote Gdns, Harl. CM17 52 EY15
Heathcote Gro, E4 101 EC48
Heathcote Pt, E9
off Wick Rd 143 DX65
Heathcote Rd, Epsom KT18 216 CR114
Twickenham TW1 177 CH86
[Sch] Heathcote Sch, E4
off Normanton Pk 102 EE47
Heathcote St, WC1 10 A3
Heathcote Way, West Dr.
UB7 off Tavistock Rd 134 BK74
Heath Cotts, Pot.B. EN6
off Heath Rd 64 DB30
Heath Ct, Hert. SG14
off The Ridgeway 31 DM08
Hounslow TW4 156 BZ84
Uxbridge UB8 134 BL66
Heathcroft, NW11 120 DB60
W5 138 CM70
Welwyn Garden City AL7 30 DC09
Heathcroft Av, Sun. TW16 175 BT94
Heathcroft Gdns, E17 101 ED53
Heathdale Av, Houns. TW4 156 BY83
Heathdene, Tad. KT20
off Canons La 233 CY119
Heathdene Dr, Belv. DA17 167 FB77
Heathdene Rd, SW16 181 DM94
Wallington SM6 219 DH108
Heathdown Rd, Wok. GU22 227 BD115
Heath Dr, NW3 120 DB63
SW20 199 CW98
Epping (They.B.) CM16 85 ES35
Potters Bar EN6 64 DA30
Romford RM2 105 FG53
Sutton SM2 218 DC109
Tadworth KT20 249 CU125
Woking (Send) GU23 227 BB122
Heathedge, SE26 182 DV89
Heath End Rd, Bex. DA5 187 FE88
Heather Av, Rom. RM1 105 FD54
Heatherbank, SE9 165 EM82
Chislehurst BR7 205 EN96
Heatherbank Cl, Cob. KT11 214 BX111
Dartford DA1 187 FE86
Heather Cl, E6 145 EP72
N7
off Newington Barrow Way 121 DM62
SE13 183 ED86
SW8 161 DH83
Abbots Langley WD5 59 BU32
Addlestone (New Haw)
KT15 212 BH110
Brentwood (Pilg.Hat.)
CM15 108 FV43
Guildford GU2 242 AV132
Hampton TW12 196 BZ95
Isleworth TW7
off Harvesters Cl 177 CD85
Redhill RH1 251 DH130
Romford RM1 105 FD53
Tadworth KT20 233 CY122
Uxbridge UB8
off Violet Av 134 BM71
Woking GU21 226 AW115
Heatherdale Cl, Kings.T. KT2 178 CN93
Heatherdene, Lthd. (W.Hors.)
KT24 245 BR125
Heatherdene Cl, N12
off Bow La 98 DC53
Mitcham CR4 200 DE98
Heatherden Grn, Iver SL0 133 BC67
Heather Dr, Dart. DA1 187 FG87
Enfield EN2
off Chasewood Av 81 DP40
Romford RM1 105 FD54
Heather End, Swan. BR8 207 FD98
Heatherfields, Add.
(New Haw) KT15 212 BH110
Heatherfold Way, Pnr. HA5 115 BT55
Heather Gdns, NW11 119 CY58
Romford RM1 105 FD54
Sutton SM2 218 DA107
Waltham Abbey EN9 83 EC36
Heather Glen, Rom. RM1 105 FD54
Heatherlands, Horl. RH6
off Stockfield 269 DH147
Sunbury-on-Thames
TW16 175 BU93
Heather La, Wat. WD24 75 BT35
West Drayton UB7 134 BL72
Heatherley Dr, Ilf. IG5 124 EL55
[Coll] Heatherley Sch of Fine Art,
SW10 off Upcerne Rd 160 DC80
Heather Pk Dr, Wem. HA0 138 CN66
Heather Pl, Esher KT10
off Park Rd 214 CB105
Heather Ri, Bushey WD23 76 BZ40
Heather Rd, E4 101 DZ51
NW2 119 CT61
SE12 184 EG89
Welwyn Garden City AL8 29 CW11
Heathers, The, Stai. TW19 174 BM87
Heatherset Cl, Esher KT10 214 CC106
Heatherset Gdns, SW16 181 DM94
Heatherside Cl, Lthd. KT23
off Little Bookham St 246 BZ125
Heatherside Dr, Vir.W. GU25 192 AU100
Heatherside Gdns, Slou.
(Farn.Com.) SL2 111 AR62
Heatherside Rd, Epsom
KT19 216 CR108
Sidcup DA14 off Wren Rd 186 EX90
Heathersland, Dor. RH4
off Goodwyns Rd 263 CJ139
[Sch] Heatherton Ho Sch, Amer.
HP6 off Copperkins La 55 AQ36
Heatherton Pk, Amer. HP6 55 AP36
Heatherton Ter, N3 98 DB54
Heathervale Caravan Pk, Add.
(New Haw) KT15 212 BJ110
Heathervale Rd, Add.
(New Haw) KT15 212 BH110
Heather Wk, W10 6 D3
Edgware HA8 96 CP50
Twickenham TW2
off Stephenson Rd 176 CA87
Walton-on-Thames
(Whiteley Vill.) KT12
off Octagon Rd 213 BT110
Heather Way, Hem.H. HP2 40 BK19
Potters Bar EN6 63 CZ32
Romford RM1 105 FD54
South Croydon CR2 221 DX109
Stanmore HA7 95 CF51
Woking (Chobham) GU24 210 AS108
Heatherwood Cl, E12 124 EJ61
Heatherwood Dr, Hayes
UB4 off Charville La 135 BR68
Heath Fm Ct, Wat. WD17
off Grove Mill La 75 BR37
Heath Fm La, St.Alb. AL3 43 CE18
Heathfield, E4 101 EC48
Chislehurst BR7 185 EQ93
Cobham KT11 214 CA114
Heathfield Av, SW18
off Heathfield Rd 180 DD87
South Croydon CR2 221 DY109
Heathfield Cl, E16 144 EK71
Keston BR2 222 EJ106
Potters Bar EN6 64 DB30
Watford WD19 94 BW45
Woking GU22 227 BA118
Heathfield Ct, St.Alb. AL1
off Avenue Rd 43 CE19
Heathfield Dr, Mitch. CR4 200 DE95
Redhill RH1 266 DE139
Heathfield Gdns, NW11 119 CX58
SE3 164 EE82
SW18 off Heathfield Rd 180 DD86
W4 158 CQ78
Croydon CR0
off Coombe Rd 220 DR105
Heathfield La, Chis. BR7 185 EP93
Heathfield N, Twick. TW2 177 CF87
[Sch] Heathfield Nurs & Inf Sch,
Twick. TW2 off Cobbett Rd 176 CA88
Heathfield Pk, NW2 139 CW65
Heathfield Pk Dr, Rom.
(Chad.Hth) RM6 126 EV57
Heathfield Ri, Ruis. HA4 115 BQ59
Heathfield Rd, SW18 180 DC86
Heathfield Rd, W3 158 CP75
Bexleyheath DA6 166 EZ84
Bromley BR1 184 EF94
Bushey WD23 76 BY42
Croydon CR0 220 DR105
Keston BR2 222 EJ106
Sevenoaks TN13 256 FF122
Slough (Burn.) SL1 110 AG62
Walton-on-Thames KT12 214 BY105
Woking GU22 227 BA118
[Sch] Heathfield Sch, Pnr.
HA5 off Beaulieu Dr 116 BX59
Heathfields Cl, Ashtd. KT21 231 CJ118
Heathfields Ct, Houns. TW4
off Frampton Rd 176 BY85
Heathfield S, Twick. TW2 177 CF87
Heathfield Sq, SW18 180 DD87
Heathfield St, W11 6 C10
Heathfield Ter, SE18 165 ET79
W4 158 CQ78
Heathfield Vale, S.Croy. CR2 221 DX109
Heath Gdns, Twick. TW1 177 CF88
Heathgate, NW11 120 DB58
Hertford (Hert.Hth) SG13 32 DV13
Heathgate Pl, NW3
off Agincourt Rd 120 DF64
Heath Gro, SE20
off Maple Rd 182 DW94
Sunbury-on-Thames
TW16 175 BT94
Heath Hill, Dor. RH4 263 CH136
Heath Hurst Rd, NW3 120 DE63
Heathhurst Rd, S.Croy. CR2 220 DS109
Heathland Rd, N16 122 DS60
Heathlands, Tad. KT20 233 CX122
[Sch] Heathland Sch, The, Houns.
TW4 off Wellington Rd S 176 BZ86
Heathlands Cl, Sun. TW16 195 BU96
Twickenham TW1 177 CF89
Woking GU21 210 AY114
Heathlands Dr, St.Alb. AL3 43 CE18
Heathlands Ri, Dart. DA1 187 FH86
[Sch] Heathlands Sch, St.Alb.
AL3 off Heathlands Dr 43 CE17
Heathlands Way, Houns.
TW4 176 BY85
Heath La, SE3 163 ED82
Dartford (Lower) DA1 188 FJ88
Dartford (Upper) DA1 187 FG89
Guildford (Albury) GU5 260 BL141
Hemel Hempstead HP1 40 BJ22
Hertford (Hert.Hth) SG13 32 DW13
Heathlee Rd, SE3 164 EF84
Dartford DA1 187 FE86
Heathley End, Chis. BR7 185 EQ93
Heathmans Rd, SW6 159 CZ81
Heath Mead, SW19 179 CX90
[Sch] Heathmere Prim Sch,
SW15 off Alton Rd 179 CU88
Heath Ms, Wok. GU23
off Portsmouth Rd 228 BH123
Heath Pk Ct, Rom. RM2
off Heath Pk Rd 127 FG57
Heath Pk Dr, Brom. BR1 204 EL97
Heath Pk Rd, Rom. RM2 127 FG57
Heath Pas, NW3 120 DB61
Heath Ridge Grn, Cob. KT11 214 CA113
Heath Ri, SW15 179 CX86
Bromley BR2 204 EF100
Dorking (Westc.) RH4 262 CC138
Virginia Water GU25 192 AX98
Woking (Ripley) GU23 228 BH123
Heath Rd, SW8 161 DH82
Beaconsfield HP9 110 AG55
Bexley DA5 187 FC88
Caterham CR3 236 DR123
Dartford DA1 187 FF86
Grays RM16 171 GG75
Harrow HA1 116 CC59
Hounslow TW3 156 CB84
Leatherhead (Oxshott)
KT22 214 CC112
Potters Bar EN6 64 DA30
Romford RM6 126 EX59
St. Albans AL1 43 CE19
Thornton Heath CR7 202 DQ97
Twickenham TW1, TW2 177 CF88
Uxbridge UB10 135 BQ70
Watford WD19 94 BX45
Weybridge KT13 212 BN106
Woking GU21 227 AZ115
Heathrow, Guil. (Goms.)
GU5 261 BQ139
★ Heathrow Airport, Houns.
TW6 155 BP81
Heathrow Cl, West Dr. UB7 154 BH81
Heathrow Ho, Houns. TW5
off Bath Rd 155 BU81
Heathrow Interchange,
Hayes UB4 136 BW74
Heathrow Int Trd Est, Houns.
TW4 155 BV83
[Sch] Heathrow Prim Sch,
West Dr. UB7
off Harmondsworth La 154 BM79
⇌ Heathrow Terminal 4 175 BP85
⊖ Heathrow Terminal 4 175 BP85
⇌ Heathrow Terminals
1,2,3 155 BP83
⊖ Heathrow Terminals
1,2,3 155 BP83
Heathrow Tunnel App, Houns.
(Hthrw Air.) TW6 155 BP83
Heathrow Vehicle Tunnel,
Houns. (Hthrw Air.) TW6 155 BP81
Heaths Cl, Enf. EN1 82 DS40
Heath Side, NW3 120 DD63
Heathside, Esher KT10 197 CE104
Hounslow TW4 176 BZ87
Heath Side, Orp. BR5 205 EQ102
Heathside, St.Alb. AL1 43 CE18
St. Albans (Coln.Hth) AL4 44 CP23
Weybridge KT13 213 BP106
Heathside Av, Bexh. DA7 166 EY81
Heathside Cl, Esher KT10 197 CE104
Ilford IG2 125 ER57
Northwood HA6 93 BR50
Heathside Ct, Tad. KT20 233 CV123
Heathside Cres, Wok. GU22 227 AZ117
Heathside Gdns, Wok.
GU22 227 BA117
Heathside Pk Rd, Wok.
GU22 227 AZ118
Heathside Pl, Epsom KT18 233 CX118
Heathside Rd, Nthwd. HA6 93 BR49
Woking GU22 227 AZ118
[Sch] Heathside Sch & 6th
Form Cen, Wey. KT13
off Brooklands La 212 BM106
Heathstan Rd, W12 139 CU72
Heath St, NW3 120 DC63
Dartford DA1 188 FK87
Heath Vw, N2 120 DC56
Leatherhead (E.Hors.)
KT24 245 BT125
Heathview Av, Dart. DA1 187 FE86
Heath Vw Cl, N2 120 DC56
Heathview Ct, SW19 179 CX89
Heathview Cres, Dart. DA1 187 FG88
Heathview Dr, SE2 166 EX79
Heathview Gdns, SW15 179 CW87
Heath Vw Gdns, Grays
RM16 170 GC75
Heath Vw Rd, Grays RM16 170 GC75
Heathview Rd, Th.Hth. CR7 201 DN98
Heath Vil, SE18 165 ET78
SW18 off Cargill Rd 180 DC88
Heathville Rd, N19 121 DL59
Heathwall St, SW11 160 DF83
Heathway, SE3 164 EF80
Caterham CR3 252 DQ125
Croydon CR0 203 DZ104
Dagenham RM9, RM10 146 FA66
Heath Way, Erith DA8 167 FC81
Heathway, Iver SL0 133 BD68
Leatherhead (E.Hors.)
KT24 229 BT124
Woodford Green IG8 102 EJ49
Heathway Ind Est, Dag.
RM10
off Manchester Way 127 FB63
Heathwood Gdns, SE7 164 EL77
Swanley BR8 207 FC96
Heathwood Pt, SE23
off Dacres Rd 183 DX90
Heathwood Wk, Bex. DA5 187 FE88
Heaton Av, Rom. RM3 105 FH52
Heaton Cl, E4 101 EC48
Romford RM3 106 FJ52
Heaton Ct, Wal.Cr. (Chsht)
EN8 67 DX29
Heaton Gra Rd, Rom. RM2 105 FF54
Heaton Rd, SE15 162 DU83
Mitcham CR4 180 DG94
Heaton Way, Rom. RM3 106 FJ52
Heavens Lea, B.End SL8 110 AC61
Heaven Tree Cl, N1 5 H2
Heaver Rd, SW11 off Wye St 160 DD83
[Coll] Heavers Fm Cen, SE25
off Selhurst Rd 202 DS99
[Sch] Heavers Fm Prim Sch,
SE25 off Dinsdale Gdns 202 DT99
Heavitree Cl, SE18 165 ER78
Heavitree Rd, SE18 165 ER78
Heayfield, Welw.G.C. AL7 30 DC08
Hebden Ct, E2 5 N8
Hebden Ter, N17
off Commercial Rd 100 DS51
Hebdon Rd, SW17 180 DE90
[Sch] Heber Prim Sch, SE22
off Heber Rd 182 DT86
Heber Rd, NW2 119 CX64
SE22 182 DT86
Hebron Rd, W6 159 CV76
Hecham Cl, E17 101 DY54
Heckets Ct, Esher KT10 214 CC111
Heckfield Pl, SW6
off Fulham Rd 160 DA80
Heckford Cl, Wat. WD18 75 BQ44
Heckford St, E1 13 H9
Hector St, SE18 165 ES77
Heddington Gro, N7 4 A1
Heddon Cl, Islw. TW7 157 CG84
Heddon Ct Av, Barn. EN4 80 DF43
Heddon Ct Par, Barn. EN4
off Cockfosters Rd 80 DG43
Heddon Rd, Barn. EN4 80 DF43
Heddon St, W1 9 J9
Hedgebrooms, Welw.G.C.
AL7 30 DC08
Hedge Hill, Enf. EN2 81 DP39
Hedge La, N13 99 DP48
Hedge Lea, H.Wyc.
(Woob.Grn) HP10 110 AD55
Hedgeley, Ilf. IG4 125 EM56
Hedgemans Rd, Dag. RM9 146 EX66
Hedgemans Way, Dag. RM9 146 EY65
Hedge Pl Rd, Green. DA9 189 FT86
HEDGERLEY, Slou. SL2 111 AR60
Hedgerley Ct, Wok. GU21 226 AW117
Hedgerley Gdns, Grnf. UB6 136 CC68
Hedgerley Grn, Slou. (Hedg.)
SL2 112 AT58
Hedgerley Hill, Slou. (Hedg.)
SL2 111 AR62
Hedgerley La, Beac. HP9 111 AN56
Gerrards Cross SL9 112 AV59
Slough SL2 112 AS58
Hedgerow, Ger.Cr.
(Chal.St.P.) SL9 90 AY51
Hedge Row, Hem.H. HP1 40 BG18
Hedgerow La, Barn. EN5 79 CV43
Hedgerows, Saw. CM21 36 EZ05
Hedgerows, The, Grav.
(Nthflt) DA11 190 GE89
Hedgerow Wk, Wal.Cr. EN8 67 DX30
Hedgers Cl, Loug. IG10
off Newmans La 85 EN42
Hedgers Gro, E9 143 DY65
Hedger St, SE11 20 E7
Hedges, The, St.Alb. AL3 42 CC16
Hedges Cl, Hat. AL10 45 CV17
Hedgeside, Berk. (Pott.End)
HP4 39 BA16
Hedgeside Rd, Nthwd. HA6 93 BQ50
Hedge Wk, SE6 183 EB91
Hedgeway, Guil. GU2 258 AU136
Hedgewood Gdns, Ilf. IG5 125 EN57
[Sch] Hedgewood Sch, Hayes
UB4 off Weymouth Rd 135 BS69
Hedgley St, SE12 184 EF85
Hedingham Cl, N1 4 G6
Horley RH6 269 DJ147
Hedingham Ho, Kings.T.
KT2 off Kingsgate Rd 198 CL95
Hedingham Rd, Dag. RM8 126 EV64
Grays (Chaff.Hun.) RM16 169 FW78
Hornchurch RM11 128 FN60
Hedley Av, Grays RM20 169 FW80
Hedley Cl, Rom. RM1
off High St 127 FE57
Hedley Rd, St.Alb. AL1 43 CH20
Twickenham TW2 176 CA87
Hedley Row, N5 5 K1
Hedley Vw, H.Wyc. (Loud.)
HP10 88 AD54
[Sch] Hedley Walter Sch, The,
Brwd. CM15
off Sawyers Hall La 108 FW45
Hedsor Hill, B.End SL8 110 AC62
Hedsor La, H.Wyc.
(Woob.Grn) HP10 110 AG61
Slough (Burn.) SL1 110 AG61
Hedsor Pk, B.End SL8 110 AD63
Hedworth Av, Wal.Cr. EN8 67 DX33
Heenan Cl, Bark. IG11
off Glenny Rd 145 EQ65
Heene Rd, Enf. EN2 82 DR39
Heideck Gdns, Brwd. (Hutt.)
CM13 off Victors Cres 109 GB47

Heidegger Cres, SW13
off Trinity Ch Rd ... 159 CV79
Heigham Rd, E6 ... 144 EK66
Heighams, Harl. CM19 ... 51 EM18
Heighton Gdns, Croy. CR0 ... 219 DP106
Heights, The, SE7 ... 164 EJ78
Beckenham BR3 ... 183 EC94
Hemel Hempstead HP2
off Saturn Way ... 40 BM18
Loughton IG10 ... 85 EM40
Northolt UB5 ... 116 BZ64
Waltham Abbey (Nazeing)
EN9 ... 68 EH25
Weybridge KT13 ... 212 BN110
Heights Cl, SW20 ... 179 CV94
Banstead SM7 ... 233 CY116
★ Heinz Gall, R.I.B.A., W1 ... 8 E7
Heiron St, SE17 ... 161 DP79
Helby Rd, SW4 ... 181 DK86
Helder Gro, SE12 ... 184 EF87
Helder St, S.Croy. CR2 ... 220 DR107
Heldmann Cl, Houns. TW3 ... 157 CD84
Helegan Cl, Orp. BR6 ... 223 ET105
Helena Cl, Barn. EN4 ... 80 DD38
Helena Ho, Red. RH1 ... 266 DF137
Helena Pl, E9 off Fremont St ... 142 DW67
Helena Rd, E13 ... 144 EF68
E17 ... 123 EA57
NW10 ... 119 CV64
W5 ... 137 CK71
Windsor SL4 ... 151 AR82
Helena Sq, SE16 ... 13 J10
Helen Av, Felt. TW14 ... 175 BV87
Helen Cl, N2
off Thomas More Way ... 120 DC55
Dartford DA1 ... 187 FH87
West Molesey KT8 ... 196 CB98
Helen Rd, Horn. RM11 ... 128 FK55
Helens Gate, Wal.Cr. EN8 ... 67 DZ26
Helensleа Av, NW11 ... 119 CZ60
Helen's Pl, E2 ... 12 E1
Helen St, SE18
off Wilmount St ... 165 EP77
Helford Cl, Ruis. HA4
off Chichester Av ... 115 BS61
Helford Wk, Wok. GU21 ... 226 AU118
Helford Way, Upmin. RM14 ... 129 FR58
Helgiford Gdns, Sun. TW16 ... 175 BS94
Helions Rd, Harl. CM19 ... 51 EP15
Helios Rd, Wall. SM6 ... 200 DG102
Helix Gdns, SW2
off Helix Rd ... 181 DM86
Helix Rd, SW2 ... 181 DM86
Helleborine, Grays
(Bad.Dene) RM17 ... 170 FZ78
Hellen Way, Wat. WD19 ... 94 BX49
Hellings St, E1 ... 22 B2
Hellyer Way, B.End SL8 ... 110 AC60
Helm Cl, Epsom KT19 ... 216 CN112
Helme Cl, SW19 ... 179 CZ92
Helmet Row, EC1 ... 11 H3
Helmore Rd, Bark. IG11 ... 145 ET66
Helmsdale, Wok. GU21
off Winnington Way ... 226 AV118
Helmsdale Cl, Hayes UB4 ... 136 BY70
Romford RM1 ... 105 FE52
Helmsdale Rd, SW16 ... 201 DJ95
Romford RM1 ... 105 FE52
Helmsley Pl, E8 ... 142 DV66
Helperby Rd, NW10
off Mayo Rd ... 138 CS65
Helsinki Sq, SE16 ... 23 K5
Helston Cl, Pnr. HA5 ... 94 BZ52
Helston Gro, Hem.H. HP2 ... 40 BK16
Helston La, Wind. SL4 ... 151 AN81
Helston Pl, Abb.L. WD5
off Shirley Rd ... 59 BT32
Helvellyn Cl, Egh. TW20 ... 173 BB94
Helvetia St, SE6 ... 183 DZ89
Hemans St, SW8 ... 161 DK80
Hemberton Rd, SW9 ... 161 DL83
HEMEL HEMPSTEAD, HP1 -
HP3 ... 40 BK21
⇌ Hemel Hempstead ... 40 BG23
H Hemel Hempstead Gen
Hosp, Hem.H. HP2 ... 40 BK21
Hemel Hempstead Ind Est,
Hem.H. HP2 ... 41 BP17
Hemel Hempstead Rd,
Hem.H. HP3 ... 41 BR22
St. Albans AL3 ... 42 CA21
St. Albans (Redbn) AL3 ... 41 BQ15
Sch Hemel Hempstead Sch,
Hem.H. HP1
off Heath La ... 40 BJ21
Hemery Rd, Grnf. UB6 ... 117 CD64
Hemingford Cl, N12 ... 98 DD50
Hemingford Rd, N1 ... 4 B8
Sutton SM3 ... 217 CW105
Watford WD17 ... 75 BS36
Heming Rd, Edg. HA8 ... 96 CP52
Hemington Av, N11 ... 98 DF50
Hemlock Cl, Tad. (Kgswd)
KT20 ... 233 CY123
Hemlock Rd, W12 ... 139 CT73
Hemmen La, Hayes UB3 ... 135 BT72
Hemming Cl, Hmptn. TW12
off Chandler Cl ... 196 CA95
Hemmings, The, Berk. HP4 ... 38 AT20
Hemmings Cl, Sid. DA14 ... 186 EV89
Hemming St, E1 ... 12 B4
Hemming Way, Slou. SL2 ... 131 AP69
Watford WD25 ... 75 BU35
Hemnall St, Epp. CM16 ... 69 ET31
Hempshaw Av, Bans. SM7 ... 234 DF116
Hempson Av, Slou. SL3 ... 152 AW76
Hempstall, Welw.G.C. AL7
off Linces Way ... 30 DB11
Hempstead Cl, Buck.H. IG9 ... 102 EG47
Hempstead La, Berk.
(Pott.End) HP4 ... 39 BC17
Hempstead Rd, E17 ... 101 ED54
Hemel Hempstead HP3 ... 57 BA27
Kings Langley WD4 ... 58 BM26
Watford WD17 ... 75 BT39
Hemp Wk, SE17 ... 21 K7
Hemsby Rd, Chess. KT9 ... 216 CM107
Hemstal Rd, NW6 ... 140 DA66
Hemsted Rd, Erith DA8 ... 167 FE80
Hemswell Dr, NW9 ... 96 CS53
Hemsworth Ct, N1 ... 5 L8
Hemsworth St, N1 ... 5 L9
Hemus Pl, SW3 ... 18 B10
Hemwood Rd, Wind. SL4 ... 151 AK83
Hen & Chicken Ct, EC4
off Fleet St ... 141 DN72
Henbane Path, Rom. RM3
off Clematis Cl ... 106 FK52
Henbit Cl, Tad. KT20 ... 233 CV119
Henbury Way, Wat. WD19 ... 94 BX48
Henchley Dene, Guil. GU4 ... 243 BD131
Henchman St, W12 ... 139 CT72
Hencroft St N, Slou. SL1 ... 152 AT75
Hencroft St S, Slou. SL1 ... 152 AT76
Hendale Av, NW4 ... 119 CU55
Henderson Av, Guil. GU2 ... 242 AV129
Henderson Cl, NW10 ... 138 CQ65
Hornchurch RM11 ... 127 FH61
St. Albans AL3 ... 42 CC16
Henderson Dr, NW8 ... 7 N3
Dartford DA1 ... 168 FM84
H Henderson Hosp, Sutt.
SM2 ... 218 DB109
Henderson Pl, Abb.L.
(Bedmond) WD5 ... 59 BT27
Hertford SG13
off Church Rd ... 47 DJ21
Henderson Rd, E7 ... 144 EJ65
N9 ... 100 DV46
SW18 ... 180 DE87
Croydon CR0 ... 202 DR100
Hayes UB4 ... 135 BU69
Westerham (Bigg.H.)
TN16 ... 222 EJ112
Hendham Rd, SW17 ... 180 DE89
HENDON, NW4 ... 119 CV56
⇌ Hendon ... 119 CU58
Hendon Av, N3 ... 97 CY53
⊖ Hendon Central ... 119 CW57
Hendon Gdns, Rom. RM5 ... 105 FC51
Hendon Gro, Epsom KT19 ... 216 CN109
Hendon Hall Ct, NW4
off Parson St ... 119 CX55
Hendon La, N3 ... 119 CY55
Hendon Pk Row, NW11 ... 119 CZ58
Sch Hendon Prep Sch,
NW4 off Tenterden Gro ... 119 CX55
Hendon Rd, N9 ... 100 DU47
Sch Hendon Sch, NW4
off Golders Ri ... 119 CX57
Hendon Way, NW2 ... 119 CZ62
NW4 ... 119 CV58
Staines (Stanw.) TW19 ... 174 BK86
Hendon Wd La, NW7 ... 79 CT44
Hendren Cl, Grnf. UB6
off Dimmock Dr ... 117 CD64
Hendre Rd, SE1 ... 21 M8
Hendrick Av, SW12 ... 180 DF86
Heneage Cres, Croy.
(New Adgtn) CR0 ... 221 EC110
Heneage La, EC3 ... 11 M8
Heneage St, E1 ... 11 P5
Henfield Cl, N19 ... 121 DJ60
Bexley DA5 ... 186 FA86
Henfield Rd, SW19 ... 199 CZ95
Henfold La, Dor. RH5 ... 264 CL144
Hengelo Gdns, Mitch. CR4 ... 200 DD98
Hengist Rd, SE12 ... 184 EH87
Erith DA8 ... 167 FB80
Hengist Way, Brom. BR2 ... 204 EE98
Hengrave Rd, SE23 ... 183 DX87
Hengrove Ct, Bex. DA5
off Hurst Rd ... 186 EY88
Hengrove Cres, Ashf. TW15 ... 174 BK90
Henhurst Rd, Grav.
(Cobham) DA12 ... 191 GK94
Henley Av, Sutt. SM3 ... 199 CY104
Henley Bk, Guil. GU2 ... 258 AU136
Henley Cl, Grnf. UB6 ... 136 CC68
Isleworth TW7 ... 157 CF81
Henley Ct, N14 ... 99 DJ45
Woking GU22 ... 227 BB120
Henley Cross, SE3 ... 164 EH83
Henley Deane, Grav. (Nthflt)
DA11 ... 190 GE91
Henley Dr, SE1 ... 21 P7
Kingston upon Thames
KT2 ... 179 CT94
Henley Gdns, Pnr. HA5 ... 115 BV55
Romford RM6 ... 126 EY57
Henley Rd, E16 ... 165 EM75
N18 ... 100 DS49
NW10 ... 139 CW67
Ilford IG1 ... 125 EQ63
Slough SL1 ... 131 AL72
Henley St, SW11 ... 160 DG82
Henley Way, Felt. TW13 ... 176 BX92
Henlow Pl, Rich. TW10
off Sandpits Rd ... 177 CK89
Hennel Cl, SE23 ... 182 DW90
Hennessy Ct, Wok. GU21 ... 211 BC113
Hennessy Rd, N9 ... 100 DW47
Henniker Gdns, E6 ... 144 EK69
Henniker Ms, SW3
off Callow St ... 160 DD79
Henniker Pt, E15 ... 124 EE64
Henniker Rd, E15 ... 123 ED64
Henningham Rd, N17 ... 100 DR53
Henning St, SW11 ... 160 DE81
Sch Henrietta Barnett Sch,
NW11 off Central Sq ... 120 DB57
Henrietta Cl, SE8 ... 163 EA79
Henrietta Ms, WC1 ... 9 P3
Henrietta Pl, W1 ... 8 G8
Henrietta St, E15 ... 123 EC64
WC2 ... 9 P9
Henriques St, E1 ... 12 B7
Henry Addlington Cl, E6 ... 145 EP71
Sch Henry Cavendish Prim Sch,
SW12 off Hydethorpe Rd ... 181 DJ88
Henry Cl, Enf. EN2 ... 82 DS38
Sch Henry Compton Sec Sch,
SW6 off Kingwood Rd ... 159 CY81
Henry Cooper Way, SE9 ... 184 EK90
Henry Darlot Dr, NW7 ... 97 CX50
Henry De Gray Cl, Grays
RM17 ... 170 FZ77
Henry Dent Cl, SE5 ... 162 DR83
Henry Dickens Ct, W11 ... 16 B1
Henry Doulton Dr, SW17 ... 181 DH91
Sch Henry Fawcett Prim Sch,
SE11 off Clayton St ... 161 DN79
Sch Henry Grn Prim Sch, Dag.
RM8 off Green La ... 126 EX61
Henry Jackson Rd, SW15 ... 159 CX83
Henry Macaulay Av, Kings.T.
KT2 ... 197 CK95
Sch Henry Maynard Inf Sch,
E17 off Maynard Rd ... 123 EC57
Sch Henry Maynard Jun Sch,
E17 off Addison Rd ... 123 EC57
Sch Henry Moore Prim Sch,
Harl. CM17 off Kiln La ... 52 EX17
Henry Rd, E6 ... 144 EL68
N4 ... 122 DQ60
Barnet EN4 ... 80 DD43
Slough SL1 ... 151 AR75
Henry's Av, Wdf.Grn. IG8 ... 102 EF50
Henryson Rd, SE4 ... 183 EA85
Henry St, Brom. BR1 ... 204 EH95
Grays RM17
off East Thurrock Rd ... 170 GC79
Hemel Hempstead HP3 ... 40 BK24
Henry's Wk, Ilf. IG6 ... 103 ER52
Henry Tate Ms, SW16 ... 181 DN92
Henry Wells Sq, Hem.H.
HP2 off Aycliffe Dr ... 40 BL16
Hensford Gdns, SE26
off Wells Pk Rd ... 182 DV91
Henshall Pt, E3 ... 14 B1
Henshall St, N1 ... 5 K4
Henshawe Rd, Dag. RM8 ... 126 EX62
Henshaw St, SE17 ... 21 J7
Hensley Pt, E9 off Wick Rd ... 143 DX65
Henslowe Rd, SE22 ... 182 DU85
Henslow Way, Wok. GU21 ... 211 BD114
Henson Av, NW2 ... 119 CW64
Henson Cl, Orp. BR6 ... 205 EP103
Henson Path, Har. HA3 ... 117 CK55
Henson Pl, Nthlt. UB5 ... 136 BW67
Henstridge Pl, NW8 ... 140 DE68
Hensworth Rd, Ashf. TW15 ... 174 BK93
Henty Cl, SW11 ... 160 DE80
Henty Wk, SW15 ... 179 CV85
Henville Rd, Brom. BR1 ... 204 EH95
Sch Henwick Prim Sch,
SE9 off Henwick Rd ... 164 EK83
Henwick Rd, SE9 ... 164 EK83
Henwood Side, Wdf.Grn.
IG8 off Love La ... 103 EM51
Hepburn Cl, Grays
(Chaff.Hun.) RM16 ... 169 FX77
Hepburn Gdns, Brom. BR2 ... 204 EE102
Hepburn Ms, SW11
off Webbs Rd ... 180 DF85
Hepple Cl, Islw. TW7 ... 157 CH82
Hepplestone Cl, SW15
off Dover Pk Dr ... 179 CV86
Hepscott Rd, E9 ... 143 EA66
Hepworth Ct, Bark. IG11 ... 126 EU64
Hepworth Gdns, Bark. IG11 ... 126 EU64
Hepworth Rd, SW16 ... 181 DL94
Hepworth Wk, NW3
off Haverstock Hill ... 120 DE64
Hepworth Way, Walt. KT12 ... 195 BT102
Heracles Cl, Wall. SM6 ... 219 DL108
Herald Gdns, Wall. SM6 ... 201 DH104
Herald's Pl, SE11 ... 20 E7
Herald St, E2 ... 12 D3
Herald Wk, Dart. DA1
off Temple Hill Sq ... 188 FM85
Herbal Hill, EC1 ... 10 D4
Herbert Cres, SW1 ... 18 D5
Woking (Knap.) GU21 ... 226 AS117
Herbert Gdns, NW10 ... 139 CV68
W4 off Magnolia Rd ... 158 CP79
Romford RM6 ... 126 EX59
St. Albans AL2 ... 60 CB29
Herbert Ms, SW2
off Bascombe St ... 181 DN86
Herbert Morrison Ho, SW6
off Clem Attlee Ct ... 159 CZ79
Sch Herbert Morrison Prim Sch,
SW8 off Hartington Rd ... 161 DL80
Herbert Pl, SE18
off Plumstead
Common Rd ... 165 EP79
Herbert Rd, E12 ... 124 EL63
E17 ... 123 DZ59
N11 ... 99 DL52
N15 ... 122 DT57
NW9 ... 119 CU58
SE18 ... 165 EN80
SW19 ... 179 CZ94
Bexleyheath DA7 ... 166 EY82
Bromley BR2 ... 204 EK99
Hornchurch RM11 ... 128 FL59
Ilford IG3 ... 125 ES61
Kingston upon Thames
KT1 ... 198 CM97
Southall UB1 ... 136 BZ74
Swanley BR8 ... 187 FH93
Swanscombe DA10 ... 190 FZ86
Herbert St, E13 ... 144 EG68
NW5 ... 140 DG65
Hemel Hempstead HP2
off St. Mary's Rd ... 40 BK19
Herbert Ter, SE18
off Herbert Rd ... 165 EP79
Herbrand St, WC1 ... 9 N4
Hercies Rd, Uxb. UB10 ... 134 BM66
Hercules Pl, N7
off Hercules St ... 121 DL62
Hercules Rd, SE1 ... 20 B6
Hercules St, N7 ... 121 DL62
Hercules Way, Wat. (Lvsdn)
WD25 ... 59 BT33
Hereford Av, Barn. EN4 ... 98 DF46
Hereford Cl, Epsom KT18 ... 216 CR113
Guildford GU2 ... 242 AT132
Staines TW18 ... 194 BH95
Hereford Copse, Wok. GU22 ... 226 AV119
Hereford Ct, Sutt. SM2
off Worcester Rd ... 218 DA108
Hereford Gdns, SE13
off Longhurst Rd ... 184 EE85
Ilford IG1 ... 124 EL59
Pinner HA5 ... 116 BY57
Twickenham TW2 ... 176 CC88
Hereford Ho, NW6 ... 140 DA68
Hereford Ms, W2 ... 7 H8
Hereford Pl, SE14
off Royal Naval Pl ... 163 DZ80
Hereford Retreat, SE15
off Bird in Bush Rd ... 162 DU80
Hereford Rd, E11 ... 124 EH57
W2 ... 7 H7
W3 ... 138 CP73
W5 ... 157 CJ76
Feltham TW13 ... 176 BW88
Hereford Sq, SW7 ... 17 M8
Hereford St, E2 ... 12 A3
Hereford Way, Chess. KT9 ... 215 CJ106
Herent Dr, Ilf. IG5 ... 124 EL56
Hereward Av, Pur. CR8 ... 219 DN111
Hereward Cl, Wal.Abb. EN9 ... 67 ED32
Sch Hereward Co Prim Sch,
Loug. IG10
off Colebrook La ... 85 EQ39
Hereward Gdns, N13 ... 99 DN50
Hereward Grn, Loug. IG10 ... 85 EQ39
Sch Hereward Ho Sch, NW3
off Strathray Gdns ... 140 DE66
Hereward Rd, SW17 ... 180 DF91
Herga Ct, Har. HA1 ... 117 CE62
Watford WD17 ... 75 BU40
Herga Rd, Har. HA3 ... 117 CF56
Herington Gro, Brwd. (Hutt.)
CM13 ... 109 GA45
Sch Herington Ho Sch, Brwd.
CM13 off Mount Av ... 109 GB44
Heriot Av, E4 ... 101 EA47
Heriot Rd, NW4 ... 119 CW57
Chertsey KT16 ... 194 BG101
Heriots Cl, Stan. HA7 ... 95 CG49
Heritage Cl, SW9 ... 161 DP83
Uxbridge UB8 ... 134 BJ70
Heritage Hill, Kes. BR2 ... 222 EJ106
Sch Heritage Ho Sch, The,
Chesh. HP5
off Cameron Rd ... 54 AR30
Heritage Lawn, Horl. RH6 ... 269 DJ147
Heritage Pl, SW18
off Earlsfield Rd ... 180 DC88
Heritage Vw, Har. HA1 ... 117 CF62
Heritage Wk, Rick. (Chorl.)
WD3 off Chenies Rd ... 73 BE41
Herkomer Cl, Bushey WD23 ... 76 CB44
Herkomer Rd, Bushey WD23 ... 76 CA43
Herlwyn Av, Ruis. HA4 ... 115 BS62
Herlwyn Gdns, SW17 ... 180 DF91
Hermes Cl, W9 ... 6 G4
Hermes St, N1 ... 4 C10
Hermes Wk, Nthlt. UB5
off Hotspur Rd ... 136 CA68
Hermes Way, Wall. SM6 ... 219 DK108
Herm Ho, Enf. EN3
off Eastfield Rd ... 83 DX38
Hermiston Av, N8 ... 121 DL57
Hermitage, The, SE23 ... 182 DW88
SW13 ... 159 CT81
Feltham TW13 ... 175 BT90
Richmond TW10 ... 177 CK85
Uxbridge UB8 ... 134 BL65
Hermitage Cl, E18 ... 124 EF56
SE2 off Felixstowe Rd ... 166 EW76
Enfield EN2 ... 81 DP40
Esher (Clay.) KT10 ... 215 CG107
Shepperton TW17 ... 194 BN98
Slough SL3 ... 152 AW76
Hermitage Ct, E18 ... 124 EG56
NW2 off Hermitage La ... 120 DA62
Potters Bar EN6
off Southgate Rd ... 64 DC33
Hermitage Gdns, NW2 ... 120 DA62
SE19 ... 182 DQ93
Hermitage La, N18 ... 100 DR50
NW2 ... 120 DA62
SE25 ... 202 DU100
SW16 ... 181 DM94
Croydon CR0 ... 202 DU100
Windsor SL4 ... 151 AN83
Hermitage Path, SW16 ... 201 DL95
Sch Hermitage Prim Sch, E1 ... 22 B2
Uxbridge UB8
off Belmont Rd ... 134 BK65
Hermitage Rd, N4 ... 121 DP59
N15 ... 121 DP59
SE19 ... 182 DQ94
Kenley CR8 ... 236 DQ116
Woking GU21 ... 226 AT119
Hermitage Row, E8 ... 122 DU64
Sch Hermitage Sch, The, Wok.
GU21 off Oakwood Rd ... 226 AS119
Hermitage St, W2 ... 7 N6
Hermitage Wk, E18 ... 124 EF56
Hermitage Wall, E1 ... 22 B2
Hermitage Waterside, E1 ... 22 A1
Hermitage Way, Stan. HA7 ... 95 CG53
Hermitage Wds Cres, Wok.
GU21 ... 226 AS119
Hermit Pl, NW6
off Belsize Rd ... 140 DB67
Hermit Rd, E16 ... 15 J5
Hermit St, EC1 ... 10 E1
Hermon Gro, Hayes UB3 ... 135 BU74
Hermon Hill, E11 ... 124 EG57
E18 ... 124 EG57
Herndon Cl, Egh. TW20 ... 173 BA91
Herndon Rd, SW18 ... 180 DC85
Herne Cl, NW10
off North Circular Rd ... 118 CR64
HERNE HILL, SE24 ... 182 DQ85
⇌ Herne Hill ... 181 DP86
Herne Hill, SE24 ... 182 DQ86
Herne Hill Ho, SE24
off Railton Rd ... 181 DP86
Herne Hill Rd, SE24 ... 162 DQ83
Herne Ms, N18
off Lyndhurst Rd ... 100 DU49
Herne Pl, SE24 ... 181 DP85
Herne Rd, Bushey WD23 ... 76 CB44
Surbiton KT6 ... 197 CK103
Hernes Cl, Stai. TW18
off Staines Rd ... 194 BH95
Herneshaw, Hat. AL10
off Hazel Gro ... 45 CT20
Herns La, Welw.G.C. AL7 ... 30 DB08
Herns Way, Welw.G.C. AL7 ... 30 DA07
Heron Cl, E17 ... 101 DZ54
NW10 ... 138 CS65
Buckhurst Hill IG9 ... 102 EG46
Guildford GU2 ... 242 AV131
Hemel Hempstead HP3 ... 58 BM25
Rickmansworth WD3 ... 92 BK47
Sawbridgeworth CM21 ... 36 EX06
Sutton SM1
off Sandpiper Rd ... 217 CZ106
Uxbridge UB8 ... 134 BK65
Heron Ct, Brom. BR2 ... 204 EJ98
Heron Cres, Sid. DA14 ... 185 ES90
Heron Dale, Add. KT15 ... 212 BK106
Herondale, S.Croy. CR2 ... 221 DX109
Herondale Av, SW18 ... 180 DD88
Heron Dr, N4 ... 122 DQ61
Slough SL3 ... 153 BB77
Ware (Stans.Abb.) SG12 ... 33 EC12
Heronfield, Egh. (Eng.Grn)
TW20 ... 172 AV93
Potters Bar EN6 ... 64 DC30
Heron Flight Av, Horn.
RM12 ... 147 FG66
Herongate Rd, E12 ... 124 EJ61
Swanley BR8 ... 187 FE93
Waltham Cross (Chsht)
EN8 ... 67 DY27
Heron Hill, Belv. DA17 ... 166 EZ77
Heron Ms, Ilf. IG1
off Balfour Rd ... 125 EP61
Heron Pl, SE16 ... 23 K1
Uxbridge (Hare.) UB9 ... 92 BG51
Heron Quay, E14 ... 23 N2
DLR Heron Quays ... 23 P2
Heron Rd, SE24 ... 162 DQ84
Croydon CR0
off Tunstall Rd ... 202 DS103
Twickenham TW1 ... 157 CG84
Heronry, The, Walt. KT12 ... 213 BU107
Herons, The, E11 ... 124 EE58
Herons Cft, Wey. KT13 ... 213 BR107
Herons Elm, Berk. HP4 ... 38 AS16
Heronsforde, W13 ... 137 CJ72
HERONSGATE, Rick. WD3 ... 91 BD45
Heronsgate, Edg. HA8 ... 96 CN50
Sch Heronsgate Prim Sch,
SE28 off Whinchat Rd ... 165 ER76
Heronsgate Rd, Rick. (Chorl.)
WD3 ... 73 BB44
Heronslea, Wat. WD25 ... 76 BW36
Heronslea Dr, Stan. HA7 ... 96 CL50
Heron's Pl, Islw. TW7 ... 157 CH83
Heron Sq, Rich. TW9
off Bridge St ... 177 CK85
Herons Ri, Barn. EN4 ... 80 DE42
Herons Way, St.Alb. AL1 ... 43 CG24
Herons Wd, Harl. CM20 ... 35 EP13
Heronswood, Wal.Abb.
EN9 off Roundhills ... 68 EE34
Herons Wd Ct, Horl. RH6
off Tanyard Way ... 269 DH147
Heronswood Pl, Welw.G.C.
AL7 ... 30 DA10
Heronswood Rd, Welw.G.C.
AL7 ... 30 DA09
Heron Trd Est, W3
off Alliance Rd ... 138 CP70
Heron Wk, Nthwd. HA6 ... 93 BS49
Woking GU21
off Blackmore Cres ... 211 BC114
Heronway, Brwd. (Hutt.)
CM13 ... 109 GA46
Heron Way, Felt. TW14 ... 155 BU84
Grays RM20 ... 169 FV78
Harlow (Roydon) CM19
off Roydon Mill Pk ... 34 EG14
Hatfield AL10 ... 45 CU19
Upminster RM14 ... 129 FS60
Heronway, Wdf.Grn. IG8 ... 102 EJ49
Herrick Rd, N5 ... 122 DQ62
Herrick St, SW1 ... 19 M7
Herries St, W10 ... 139 CY68
Sch Herringham Inf Sch,
Grays RM16
off St. Mary's Rd ... 171 GH76
Sch Herringham Jun Sch,
Grays RM16
off St. Mary's Rd ... 171 GH77
Herringham Rd, SE7 ... 164 EJ76
Herrings La, Cher. KT16 ... 194 BG100
Herrongate Cl, Enf. EN1 ... 82 DT40
H Her Royal Highness
Princess Christian's Hosp,
Wind. SL4 ... 151 AQ81
Hersant Cl, NW10 ... 139 CU67
Sch Herschel Gram Sch, Slou.
SL1 off Northampton Av ... 131 AQ73
Herschell Ms, SE5
off Bicknell Rd ... 162 DQ83
Herschell Rd, SE23 ... 183 DY87
Herschel Pk Dr, Slou. SL1 ... 152 AT75
Herschel St, Slou. SL1 ... 152 AT75
HERSHAM, Walt. KT12 ... 214 BX107
⇌ Hersham ... 196 BY104
Hersham Bypass, Walt.
KT12 ... 213 BV106
Hersham Cl, SW15 ... 179 CU87
Hersham Gdns, Walt. KT12 ... 214 BW105
Hersham Rd, Walt. KT12 ... 214 BW105
HERTFORD, SG13 & SG14 ... 31 DP10
Hertford Av, SW14 ... 178 CR85
Hertford Cl, Barn. EN4 ... 80 DD41
H Hertford Co Hosp, Hert.
SG14 ... 31 DP09
⇌ Hertford East ... 32 DS09
HERTFORD HEATH, Hert.
SG13 ... 32 DV12
Sch Hertford Heath Prim Sch,
Hert. SG13
off Woodland Rd ... 32 DW12
★ Hertford Mus, Hert. SG14 ... 32 DR09
⇌ Hertford North ... 31 DP09
Hertford Pl, W1 ... 9 J4
Coll Hertford Regional Coll,
Broxbourne Cen, Brox.
EN10 off High Rd ... 67 DZ25
Ware Cen, Ware SG12
off Scotts Rd ... 33 DX07
Hertford Rd, N1 ... 5 M7
N2 ... 120 DE55
N9 ... 100 DV47
Barking IG11 ... 145 EP66
Barnet EN4 ... 80 DC41
Enfield EN3 ... 82 DW41
Hatfield AL9 ... 45 CW16
Hertford SG14 ... 30 DB06
Hertford (Hert.Hth) SG13 ... 32 DW13
Hertford (Marden Hill)
SG14 ... 30 DG06
Hoddesdon EN11 ... 49 DY15
Ilford IG2 ... 125 ES58
Waltham Cross EN8 ... 83 DX37
Ware SG12 ... 32 DW07
Ware (Gt Amwell) SG12 ... 33 DZ11
Welwyn AL6 ... 30 DB06
Welwyn (Tewin) AL6 ... 30 DE05
Hertford Sq, Mitch. CR4
off Hertford Way ... 201 DL98
Hertford St, W1 ... 18 G1
Hertford Wk, Belv. DA17
off Hoddesdon Rd ... 166 FA78
Hertford Way, Mitch. CR4 ... 201 DL98
HERTINGFORDBURY, Hert.
SG14 ... 31 DL10
Sch Hertingfordbury Cowper
JMI Sch, Hert. SG14
off Birch Grn ... 31 DJ11
Hertingfordbury Rd, Hert.
SG14 ... 31 DL11
Hertslet Rd, N7 ... 121 DM62
Sch Hertsmere Jewish Prim Sch,
Rad. WD7 off Watling St ... 77 CJ38
Hertsmere Rd, E14 ... 13 N10
Sch Hertswood Sch, Borwd.
WD6 off Cowley Hill ... 78 CQ39
Annexe, Borwd. WD6
off Thrift Fm La ... 78 CQ40
Hervey Cl, N3 ... 98 DA53
Hervey Pk Rd, E17 ... 123 DY56
Hervey Rd, SE3 ... 164 EH81
Hervines Ct, Amer. HP6 ... 55 AQ37
Hervines Rd, Amer. HP6 ... 55 AP37
Hesa Rd, Hayes UB3 ... 135 BU72
Hesewall Cl, SW4
off Brayburne Av ... 161 DJ82
Hesiers Hill, Warl. CR6 ... 238 EE117
Hesiers Rd, Warl. CR6 ... 238 EE117
Hesketh Av, Dart. DA2 ... 188 FP88
Hesketh Pl, W11 ... 6 C10
Hesketh Rd, E7 ... 124 EG62
Heslop Rd, SW12 ... 180 DF88
Hesper Ms, SW5 ... 17 J9
Hesperus Cres, E14 ... 24 A8
Hessel Rd, W13 ... 157 CG75
Hessel St, E1 ... 12 C8
Hesselyn Dr, Rain. RM13 ... 147 FH66
Hessle Gro, Epsom KT17 ... 217 CT111
Hestercombe Av, SW6 ... 159 CY82
Hesterman Way, Croy. CR0 ... 201 DL102
Hester Rd, N18 ... 100 DU50
SW11 ... 160 DE80
Hester Ter, Rich. TW9
off Chilton Rd ... 158 CN83
HESTON, Houns. TW5 ... 156 BZ80
Heston Av, Houns. TW5 ... 156 BY80
Sch Heston Comm Sch,
Houns. TW5 off Heston Rd ... 156 CA80
Coll Heston Comm Sch
Adult Ed, Houns. TW5
off Heston Rd ... 156 CA80

Heston Gra La, Houns. TW5 .156 BZ79
Heston Ind Mall, Houns. TW5 .156 BZ80
Heston Inf & Nurs Sch, Houns. TW5 off Heston Rd .156 CA80
Heston Jun Sch, Houns. TW5 off Heston Rd .156 CA80
Heston Rd, Houns. TW5 .156 CA80
Redhill RH1 .266 DF138
Heston St, SE14 .163 DZ81
Heston Wk, Red. RH1 .266 DF138
Heswell Grn, Wat. WD19 off Fairhaven Cres .93 BU48
Hetchleys, Hem.H. HP1 .40 BG17
Hetherington Cl, Slou. SL2 .131 AM69
Hetherington Rd, SW4 .161 DL84
Shepperton TW17 .195 BQ96
Hetherington Way, Uxb. UB10 .114 BL63
Hethersett Cl, Reig. RH2 .250 DC131
Hetley Gdns, SE19 .182 DT94
Hetley Rd, W12 .139 CV74
Heton Gdns, NW4 .119 CU56
Heusden Way, Ger.Cr. SL9 .113 AZ60
Hevelius Cl, SE10 .25 J9
Hever Ct Rd, Grav. DA12 .191 GK93
Hever Cft, SE9 .185 EN91
Hever Gdns, Brom. BR1 .205 EN97
Heverham Rd, SE18 .165 ES77
Hevers Av, Horl. RH6 .268 DF147
Heversham Rd, Bexh. DA7 .166 FA82
Hewens Rd, Hayes UB4 .135 BQ70
Uxbridge UB10 .135 BQ70
Hewer St, W10 .6 B5
Hewers Way, Tad. KT20 .233 CV120
Hewett Cl, Stan. HA7 .95 CH49
Hewett Pl, Swan. BR8 .207 FD98
Hewett Rd, Dag. RM8 .126 EX64
Hewett St, EC2 .11 M4
Hewins Cl, Wal.Abb. EN9 off Broomstick Hall Rd .68 EE33
Hewish Rd, N18 .100 DS49
Hewison St, E3 .143 DZ68
Hewitt Av, N22 .99 DP54
Hewitt Cl, Croy. CR0 .203 EA104
Hewitt Rd, N8 .121 DN57
Hewitts Rd, Orp. BR6 .224 EZ108
Hewlett Rd, E3 .143 DY68
Hexagon, The, N6 .120 DF60
Hexal Rd, SE6 .184 EE90
Hexham Gdns, Islw. TW7 .157 CG80
Hexham Rd, SE27 .182 DQ89
Barnet EN5 .80 DB42
Morden SM4 .200 DB102
HEXTABLE, Swan. BR8 .187 FG94
Hextable Inf Sch, Swan. BR8 off St. Davids Rd .187 FF93
Hextable Jun Sch, Swan. BR8 off Rowhill Rd .187 FF93
Hextable Sch, Swan. BR8 off Egerton Av .207 FF95
Hextalls La, Red. (Bletch.) RH1 .252 DR128
Heybourne Rd, N17 .100 DV52
Heybridge Av, SW16 .181 DL94
Heybridge Ct, Hert. SG14 off The Ridgeway .31 DM08
Heybridge Dr, Ilf. IG6 .103 ER54
Heybridge Way, E10 .123 DY59
Heydons Cl, St.Alb. AL3 .43 CD18
Heyford Av, SW8 .161 DL80
SW20 .199 CZ97
Heyford Rd, Mitch. CR4 .200 DE96
Radlett WD7 .77 CF37
Heyford Ter, SW8 off Heyford Av .161 DL80
Heyford Way, Hat. AL10 .45 CW16
Heygate St, SE17 .20 G8
Heylyn Sq, E3 .13 M1
Heymede, Lthd. KT22 .231 CJ123
Heynes Rd, Dag. RM8 .126 EW63
Heysham Dr, Wat. WD19 .94 BW50
Heysham La, NW3 .120 DB62
Heysham Rd, N15 .122 DR58
Heythorp Cl, Wok. GU21 .226 AT117
Heythorp St, SW18 .179 CZ88
Heythrop Coll, W8 .17 J5
Heythrop Dr, Uxb. (Ickhm) UB10 .114 BM63
Heywood Av, NW9 .96 CS53
Heyworth Rd, E5 .122 DV63
E15 .124 EF64
Hibbert Av, Wat. WD24 .76 BX38
Hibbert Lo, Ger.Cr. (Chal.St.P.) SL9 off Gold Hill E .90 AX54
Hibbert Rd, E17 .123 DZ59
Harrow HA3 .95 CF54
Hibberts All, Wind. SL4 off Bachelors Acre .151 AR81
Hibbert St, SW11 .160 DC83
Hibberts Way, Ger.Cr. SL9 off North Pk .112 AY56
Hibbs Cl, Swan. BR8 .207 FD96
Hibernia Dr, Grav. DA12 .191 GM90
Hibernia Gdns, Houns. TW3 .156 CA84
Hibernia Pt, SE2 off Wolvercote Rd .166 EX75
Hibernia Rd, Houns. TW3 .156 CA84
Hibiscus Cl, Edg. HA8 off Campion Way .96 CQ49
Hichisson Rd, SE15 .182 DW85
Hickin Cl, SE7 .164 EK77
Hickin St, E14 .24 C5
Hickling Rd, Ilf. IG1 .125 EP64
Hickman Av, E4 .101 EC51
Hickman Cl, E16 .144 EK71
Broxbourne EN10 .49 DX20
Hickman Rd, Rom. RM6 .126 EW59
Hickmans Cl, Gdse. RH9 .252 DW132
Hickmore Wk, SW4 .161 DJ83
Hickory Cl, N9 .100 DU45
Hicks Av, Grnf. UB6 .137 CD68
Hicks Cl, SW11 .160 DE83
Hicks St, SE8 .23 J9
Hidalgo Ct, Hem.H. HP2 .40 BM18
Hidcote Cl, Wok. GU22 .227 BB116
Hidcote Gdns, SW20 .199 CV97
Hide, E6 off Downings .145 EN72
Hideaway, The, Abb.L. WD5 .59 BU31
Hide Pl, SW1 .19 L8
Hide Rd, Har. HA1 .117 CD56
Hides, The, Harl. CM20 .35 ER14
Hides St, N7 .4 B3
Hide Twr, SW1 .19 L8
Higgins Rd, Wal.Cr. (Chsht) EN7 .66 DR27
Higgins Wk, Hmptn. TW12 off Abbott Cl .176 BY93
High, The, Harl. CM20 .51 ER15
Highacre, Dor. RH4 .263 CH139
High Acres, Abb.L. WD5 .59 BR32
Enfield EN2 off Old Pk Vw .81 DP41
HIGHAM HILL, E17 .101 DY54
Higham Hill Rd, E17 .101 DY54
Higham Mead, Chesh. HP5 .54 AQ30
Higham Pl, E17 .123 DY55
Higham Rd, N17 .122 DR55
Chesham HP5 .54 AP30
Woodford Green IG8 .102 EG51
Highams Ct, E4 off Friars Cl .101 ED48
Highams Lo Business Cen, E17 .123 DY55
HIGHAMS PARK, E4 .101 ED50
Highams Park .101 ED51
Highams Pk Ind Est, E4 .101 EC51
Highams Pk Sch, E4 off Handsworth Av .101 ED51
Higham Sta Av, E4 .101 EB51
Higham St, E17 .123 DY55
Higham Vw, Epp. (N.Wld Bas.) CM16 .71 FB26
Highbanks Cl, Well. DA16 .166 EV80
Highbanks Rd, Pnr. HA5 .94 CB50
Highbank Way, N8 .121 DN58
HIGH BARNET, Barn. EN5 .79 CX40
High Barnet .80 DA42
High Barn Rd, Dor. RH5 .246 BX133
Leatherhead (Eff.) KT24 .246 BX129
Highbarns, Hem.H. HP3 .58 BN25
Highbarrow Rd, Croy. CR0 .202 DU101
HIGH BEACH, Loug. IG10 .84 EG39
High Beech, S.Croy. CR2 .220 DS108
High Beech C of E Prim Sch, Loug. IG10 off Mott St .84 EG39
High Beeches, Bans. SM7 .217 CX114
Gerrards Cross SL9 .112 AX60
Orpington BR6 .224 EU107
Sidcup DA14 .186 EY92
High Beeches Cl, Pur. CR8 .219 DK110
High Beech Rd, Loug. IG10 .84 EK42
High Bois La, Amer. HP6 .55 AR35
High Br, SE10 .24 F10
Highbridge Ind Est, Uxb. UB8 .134 BJ66
Highbridge Rd, Bark. IG11 .145 EP67
Highbridge St, Wal.Abb. EN9 .67 EA33
High Br Wf, SE10 .24 E10
Highbrook Rd, SE3 .164 EK83
High Broom Cres, W.Wick. BR4 .203 EB101
HIGHBURY, N5 .4 G2
Highbury & Islington .4 D4
Highbury & Islington .4 D4
Highbury Av, Hodd. EN11 .49 EA15
Thornton Heath CR7 .201 DN96
Highbury Cl, N.Mal. KT3 .198 CQ98
West Wickham BR4 .203 EB103
Highbury Cor, N5 .4 E3
Highbury Cres, N5 .4 D2
Highbury Est, N5 .5 H2
Highbury Flds Sch, N5 .4 E1
Highbury Flds Sch Annexe, N5 .4 G1
Highbury Gdns, Ilf. IG3 .125 ES61
Highbury Gra, N5 .121 DP63
Highbury Gro, N5 .4 F3
Highbury Gro Sch, N5 .4 G2
Highbury Hill, N5 .4 F1
Highbury Ms, N7 .4 D3
Highbury New Pk, N5 .4 F3
Highbury Pk, N5 .121 DP62
Highbury Pk Ms, N5 off Highbury Gra .122 DQ63
Highbury Pl, N5 .4 E3
Highbury Quad, N5 .122 DQ62
Highbury Quad Prim Sch, N5 off Highbury New Pk .122 DQ63
Highbury Rd, SW19 .179 CY92
Highbury Sta Rd, N1 .4 D4
Highbury Ter, N5 .4 E2
Highbury Ter Ms, N5 .4 E2
High Canons, Borwd. WD6 .78 CQ37
High Cedar Dr, SW20 .179 CV94
High Clandon, Guil. (E.Clan.) GU4 .244 BL133
Highclere, Guil. GU1 .243 BA132
Highclere Cl, Ken. CR8 .236 DQ115
Highclere Ct, St.Alb. AL1 off Avenue Rd .43 CE19
Highclere Dr, Hem.H. HP3 .41 BP24
Highclere Rd, N.Mal. KT3 .198 CR97
Highclere St, SE26 .183 DY91
Highcliffe Dr, SW15 .179 CT86
Highcliffe Gdns, Ilf. IG4 .124 EL57
High Cl, Rick. WD3 .74 BJ43
Highcombe, SE7 .164 EH79
Highcombe Cl, SE9 .184 EK88
High Coombe Pl, Kings.T. KT2 .178 CR94
High Coppice, Amer. HP7 .55 AQ39
Highcotts La, Guil. GU4 .243 BF126
Woking (Send M.) GU23 .243 BF125
Highcroft, NW9 .118 CR57
Highcroft Av, Wem. HA0 .138 CN67
Highcroft Ct, Lthd. (Bkhm) KT23 .230 CA123
Highcroft Gdns, NW11 .119 CZ58
Highcroft Rd, N19 .121 DL59
Hemel Hempstead (Felden) HP3 .58 BG25
High Cross, Wat. (Ald.) WD25 .77 CD37
High Cross Cen, N15 .122 DU56
High Cross Rd, N17 .122 DU55
Highcross Rd, Grav. (Sthflt) DA13 .189 FX92
Highcross Way, SW15 .179 CU88
Highdaun Dr, SW16 .201 DM98
High Dells, Hat. AL10 .45 CT19
Highdown, Wor.Pk. KT4 .198 CS103
Highdown La, Sutt. SM2 .218 DB111
Highdown Rd, SW15 .179 CV86
High Dr, Cat. (Wold.) CR3 .237 DZ122
Leatherhead (Oxshott) KT22 .215 CD114
New Malden KT3 .198 CQ95
High Elms, Chig. IG7 .103 ES49
Upminster RM14 .129 FS60
Woodford Green IG8 .102 EG50
High Elms Cl, Nthwd. HA6 .93 BR51
High Elms La, Wat. WD25 .59 BV31
High Elms Rd, Orp. BR6 .223 EP110
HIGHER DENHAM, Uxb. UB9 .113 BB59
Higher Dr, Bans. SM7 .217 CX112
Leatherhead KT24 .245 BS127
Purley CR8 .219 DN113
Higher Grn, Epsom KT17 .217 CU113
HIGHFIELD, Hem.H. HP2 .40 BL18
Highfield, Bans. SM7 .234 DE117
Bushey (Bushey Hth) WD23 .95 CE47
Chalfont St. Giles HP8 .90 AX47
Feltham TW13 .175 BU88
Guildford (Shalf.) GU4 .258 AY142
Highfield, Harl. CM18 .52 EU16
Kings Langley WD4 .58 BL28
Watford WD19 .94 BZ48
Highfield Av, NW9 .118 CQ57
NW11 .119 CX59
Erith DA8 .167 FB79
Greenford UB6 .117 CE64
Orpington BR6 .223 ET106
Pinner HA5 .116 BZ57
Wembley HA9 .118 CM62
Highfield Cl, N22 .99 DN53
NW9 .118 CQ57
SE13 .183 ED86
Amersham HP6 .55 AR37
Egham (Eng.Grn) TW20 .172 AW93
Leatherhead (Oxshott) KT22 .215 CD111
Northwood HA6 .93 BS53
Romford RM5 .105 FC51
Surbiton KT6 .197 CJ102
West Byfleet KT14 .212 BG113
Highfield Ct, N14 .81 DJ44
Highfield Cres, Horn. RM12 .128 FM61
Northwood HA6 .93 BS53
Highfield Dr, Brom. BR2 .204 EE98
Broxbourne EN10 .49 DY21
Caterham CR3 .236 DU122
Epsom KT19 .217 CT108
Uxbridge (Ickhm) UB10 .114 BL63
West Wickham BR4 .203 EB103
Highfield Gdns, NW11 .119 CY58
Grays RM16 .170 GD75
Highfield Grn, Epp. CM16 .69 ES31
Highfield Hill, SE19 .182 DR94
Highfield Inf Sch, Brom. BR2 off Highfield Dr .204 EE98
Highfield Jun Sch, Brom. BR2 off South Hill Rd .204 EE98
Highfield La, Hem.H. HP2 .40 BM18
St. Albans (Tytten.) AL4 .44 CL23
Highfield Link, Rom. RM5 .105 FC51
Highfield Manor, St.Alb. AL4 off Highfield La .44 CL24
Highfield Ms, NW6 off Compayne Gdns .140 DB66
Highfield Pk Dr, St.Alb. AL1, AL4 .43 CH23
Highfield Pl, Epp. CM16 .69 ES31
Highfield Prim Sch, N21 off Highfield Rd .99 DP46
Uxbridge UB10 off Charville La W .135 BP69
Highfield Rd, N21 .99 DP47
NW11 .119 CY58
W3 .138 CP71
Berkhamsted HP4 .38 AX20
Bexleyheath DA6 .186 EZ85
Bromley BR1 .205 EM98
Bushey WD23 .76 BY43
Caterham CR3 .236 DU122
Chertsey KT16 .194 BG102
Chesham HP5 .54 AP29
Chislehurst BR7 .205 ET97
Dartford DA1 .188 FK87
Feltham TW13 .175 BU89
Hertford SG13 .32 DR11
Hornchurch RM12 .128 FM61
Isleworth TW7 .157 CF81
Northwood HA6 .93 BS53
Purley CR8 .219 DM110
Romford RM5 .105 FC52
Sunbury-on-Thames TW16 .195 BT98
Surbiton KT5 .198 CQ101
Sutton SM1 .218 DE106
Waltham Cross (Chsht) EN7 .66 DS26
Walton-on-Thames KT12 .195 BU102
West Byfleet KT14 .212 BG113
Westerham (Bigg.H.) TN16 .238 EJ117
Windsor SL4 .151 AM83
Woodford Green IG8 .102 EL52
Highfield Rd S, Dart. DA1 .188 FK87
Highfields, Ashtd. KT21 .231 CK119
Leatherhead (E.Hors.) KT24 .245 BS128
Leatherhead (Fetch.) KT22 .231 CD124
Potters Bar (Cuffley) EN6 .65 DL28
Radlett WD7 .77 CF35
Highfield Sch, SW18 off Trinity Rd .180 DE87
Highfields Gro, N6 .120 DF60
Highfield Twr, Rom. RM5 .105 FD50
Highfield Way, Horn. RM12 .128 FM61
Potters Bar EN6 .64 DB32
Rickmansworth WD3 .74 BH44
High Firs, Rad. WD7 .77 CF35
Swanley BR8 .207 FE98
High Firs Prim Sch, Swan. BR8 off Court Cres .207 FF98
High Foleys, Esher (Clay.) KT10 .215 CH108
High Gables, Loug. IG10 .84 EK43
High Garth, Esher KT10 .214 CC107
HIGHGATE, N6 .120 DG61
Highgate .121 DH58
Highgate Av, N6 .121 DH58
★ Highgate Cem, N6 .120 DG60
Highgate Cl, N6 .120 DG59
Highgate Gro, Saw. CM21 .36 EX05
Highgate High St, N6 .120 DG60
Highgate Hill, N6 .121 DH60
N19 .121 DH60
Highgate Ho, SE26 off Sydenham Hill .182 DU90
Highgate Jun Sch, N6 off Bishopswood Rd .120 DF59
Highgate Mental Health Cen, N19 .121 DH61
Highgate Prim Sch, N6 off North Hill .120 DF58
Highgate Rd, NW5 .121 DH63
Highgate Sch, N6 off North Rd .120 DG59
Highgate Wk, SE23 .182 DW89
Highgate W Hill, N6 .120 DG61
Highgate Wd Sec Sch, N8 off Montenotte Rd .121 DJ57
High Gro, SE18 .165 ER80
Highgrove, Brwd. (Pilg.Hat.) CM15 .108 FV44
High Gro, Brom. BR1 .204 EJ95
St. Albans AL3 .43 CD18
Welwyn Garden City AL8 .29 CW08
Highgrove Cl, N11 off Balmoral Av .98 DG50
Chislehurst BR7 .204 EL95
Highgrove Ms, Cars. SM5 .200 DF104
Grays RM17 .170 GC78
Highgrove Rd, Dag. RM8 .126 EW64
Highgrove Way, Ruis. HA4 .115 BU58
High Hill Est, E5 off Mount Pleasant La .122 DV60
High Hill Ferry, E5 .122 DV60
High Hill Rd, Warl. CR6 .237 EC115
High Holborn, WC1 .9 P7
High Ho La, Grays (Orsett) RM16 .171 GJ75
Tilbury (W.Til.) RM18 .171 GK77
Highland Av, W7 .137 CE72
Brentwood CM15 .108 FW46
Dagenham RM10 .127 FC62
Loughton IG10 .84 EL44
Highland Cotts, Wall. SM6 .219 DH105
Highland Ct, E18 .102 EH53
Highland Cft, Beck. BR3 .183 EB92
Highland Dr, Bushey WD23 .94 CC45
Hemel Hempstead HP3 .41 BP20
Highland Pk, Felt. TW13 .175 BT91
Highland Rd, SE19 .182 DS93
Amersham HP7 .55 AR39
Bexleyheath DA6 .186 FA85
Bromley BR1, BR2 .204 EF95
Northwood HA6 .93 BT54
Purley CR8 .219 DN114
Sevenoaks (Bad.Mt) TN14 .225 FB111
Waltham Abbey EN9 .50 EE22
Highlands, Ashtd. KT21 .231 CJ119
Hatfield AL9 .45 CW15
Slough (Farn.Com.) SL2 .111 AP64
Watford WD19 .94 BW46
Highlands, The, Edg. HA8 .96 CP54
Leatherhead (E.Hors.) KT24 .245 BS125
Potters Bar EN6 .80 DB43
Rickmansworth WD3 .92 BH45
Highlands Av, N21 .81 DM43
W3 .138 CQ73
Leatherhead KT22 .231 CJ122
Highlands Cl, N4 off Mount Vw Rd .121 DL59
Gerrards Cross (Chal.St.P.) SL9 .91 AZ52
Hounslow TW3 .156 CB81
Leatherhead KT22 .231 CH122
Highlands End, Ger.Cr. (Chal.St.P.) SL9 .90 AY52
Highlands Gdns, Ilf. IG1 .125 EM60
Highlands Heath, SW15 .179 CW87
Highlands Hill, Swan. BR8 .207 FG96
Highlands La, Ger.Cr. (Chal.St.P.) SL9 .91 AZ51
Woking GU22 .226 AY122
Highlands Pk, Lthd. KT22 .231 CK123
Sevenoaks (Seal) TN15 .257 FL121
Highlands Prim Sch, Ilf. IG1 off Lennox Gdns .125 EM60
Highlands Rd, Barn. EN5 .80 DA43
Beaconsfield (Seer Grn) HP9 .89 AQ50
Leatherhead KT22 .231 CH122
Orpington BR5 .206 EV101
Reigate RH2 .250 DD133
Highlands Sch, N21 off Worlds End La .81 DN42
High La, W7 .137 CD72
Bishop's Stortford (Sheering) CM22 .37 FE09
Caterham CR3 .237 DZ119
Warlingham CR6 .237 DZ118
HIGH LAVER, Ong. CM5 .53 FH17
High Lawns, Har. HA1 .117 CE62
Highlea Cl, NW9 .96 CS53
High Leigh Barns, Hodd. EN11 off Box La .49 DY17
High Level Dr, SE26 .182 DU91
Highlever Rd, W10 .139 CW71
High March Sch, Beac. HP9 off Ledborough La .89 AK51
Highmead, SE18 .165 ET80
High Mead, Chig. IG7 .103 EQ47
Harrow HA1 .117 CE57
West Wickham BR4 .203 ED103
Highmead Cres, Wem. HA0 .138 CM66
High Meadow Cl, Dor. RH4 .263 CH137
Pinner HA5 off Daymer Gdns .115 BV56
High Meadow Cres, NW9 .118 CR57
High Meadow Pl, Cher. KT16 .193 BF100
High Meadows, Chig. IG7 .103 ER50
High Meads Rd, E16 .144 EK72
Highmoor, Amer. HP7 .55 AR39
Highmore Rd, SE3 .164 EE80
High Mt, NW4 .119 CU58
High Oak Rd, Ware SG12 .33 DX05
High Oaks, Enf. EN2 .81 DM38
St. Albans AL3 .42 CC15
High Oaks Rd, Welw.G.C. AL8 .29 CV08
Highover Pk, Amer. HP7 .55 AR40
High Pk Av, Lthd. (E.Hors.) KT24 .245 BT126
Richmond TW9 .158 CN81
High Pk Rd, Rich. TW9 .158 CN81
High Pastures, B.Stort. (Sheering) CM22 .37 FD06
High Path, SW19 .200 DB95
High Path Rd, Guil. GU1 .243 BC134
High Pewley, Guil. GU1 .258 AY136
High Pine Cl, Wey. KT13 .213 BQ106
High Pines, Warl. CR6 .236 DW119
High Pt, N6 .120 DG59
SE9 .185 EP90
Weybridge KT13 .212 BN106
High Ridge, Pot.B. (Cuffley) EN6 .65 DL27
Highridge Cl, Epsom KT18 .232 CS115
High Ridge Cl, Hem.H. HP3 .58 BK25
Highridge La, Bet. RH3 .264 CP140
High Ridge Rd, Hem.H. HP3 .58 BK25
High Rd, N2 .98 DD53
N11 .99 DH50
N12 .98 DC51
N15 .122 DT58
N17 .100 DT53
N20 .98 DC45
N22 .121 DN55
NW10 (Willesden) .139 CV65
Broxbourne EN10 .49 DZ20
Buckhurst Hill IG9 .102 EH47
Bushey (Bushey Hth) WD23 .95 CD46
Chigwell IG7 .103 EM50
Coulsdon CR5 .234 DF121
Dartford (Wilm.) DA2 .188 FJ90
Epping CM16 .69 ER32
Epping (N.Wld Bas.) CM16 .71 FB27
Epping (Thnwd) CM16 .70 EV28
Harrow (Har.Wld) HA3 .95 CE52
Hatfield (Essen.) AL9 .46 DE17
Ilford IG1 .125 EP62
Ilford (Seven Kings) IG3 .125 ET60
Loughton IG10 .102 EJ45
Pinner HA5 .115 BV56
Reigate RH2 .250 DD126
Romford (Chad.Hth) RM6 .126 EV60
Uxbridge UB8 .134 BJ71
Watford (Lvsdn) WD25 .75 BT35
Wembley HA0, HA9 .117 CK64
High Rd, W. Byf. (Byfleet) KT14 .212 BM112
High Rd Ickenham, Uxb. UB10 .115 BP62
High Rd Leyton, E10 .123 EB60
E15 .123 EC62
High Rd Leytonstone, E11 .124 EE63
E15 .124 EE63
High Rd Turnford, Brox. EN10 .67 DY25
High Rd Woodford Grn, E18 .102 EF52
Woodford Green IG8 .102 EF52
High Rd Wormley, Brox. (Turnf.) EN10 .49 DY24
Highshore Rd, SE15 .162 DT82
Highshore Spec Sch, SE15 off Bellenden Rd .162 DT81
High Silver, Loug. IG10 .84 EK42
High Standing, Cat. CR3 .252 DQ125
Highstead Cres, Erith DA8 .167 FE81
Highstone Av, E11 .124 EG58
High St, E11 .124 EG57
E13 .144 EG68
E15 .143 EC68
E17 .123 DZ57
N8 .121 DL56
N14 .99 DK46
NW7 .97 CV49
NW10 (Harlesden) .139 CT68
SE20 .182 DV93
SE25 (S.Norwood) .202 DT98
W3 .138 CP74
W5 .137 CK73
Abbots Langley WD5 .59 BS31
Abbots Langley (Bedmond) WD5 .59 BT27
Addlestone KT15 .212 BH105
Amersham HP7 .55 AM38
Banstead SM7 .234 DA115
Barnet EN5 .79 CY41
Beckenham BR3 .203 EA96
Berkhamsted HP4 .38 AW19
Borehamwood (Elstree) WD6 .77 CK44
Brentford TW8 .157 CK79
Brentwood CM14 .108 FV47
Bromley BR1 .204 EG96
Bushey WD23 .76 CA44
Carshalton SM5 .218 DG105
Caterham CR3 .236 DS123
Chalfont St. Giles HP8 .90 AW48
Chesham HP5 .54 AQ31
Chislehurst BR7 .185 EP93
Cobham KT11 .213 BV114
Croydon CR0 .202 DQ103
Dartford DA1 .188 FL86
Dartford (Bean) DA2 .189 FV90
Dartford (Eyns.) DA4 .208 FL103
Dartford (Fnghm) DA4 .208 FM100
Dorking RH4 .263 CH136
Edgware HA8 .96 CN51
Egham TW20 .173 BA92
Epping CM16 .69 ET31
Epsom KT19 .216 CR113
Epsom (Ewell) KT17 .217 CT109
Esher KT10 .214 CB105
Esher (Clay.) KT10 .215 CF107
Feltham TW13 .175 BT90
Gerrards Cross (Chal.St.P.) SL9 .90 AY53
Godstone RH9 .252 DV131
Gravesend DA11 .191 GH86
Gravesend (Nthflt) DA11 .190 GB86
Grays RM17 .170 GA79
Greenhithe DA9 .169 FV84
Guildford GU1, GU2 .258 AX135
Hampton TW12 .176 CC93
Harlow CM17 .36 EW11
Harlow (Roydon) CM19 .34 EH14
Harrow HA1, HA2 .117 CE60
Harrow (Wldste) HA3 .117 CE55
Hayes UB3 .155 BS78
Hemel Hempstead HP1 .40 BJ18
Hemel Hempstead (Bov.) HP3 .57 BA27
Hoddesdon EN11 .49 EA19
Horley RH6 .269 DH148
Hornchurch RM11, RM12 .128 FK60
Hounslow TW3 .156 CC83
Hounslow (Cran.) TW5 .155 BV80
Ilford (Barkingside) IG6 .103 EQ54
Iver SL0 .133 BE72
Kings Langley WD4 .58 BN29
Kingston upon Thames KT1 .197 CK96
Kingston upon Thames (Hmptn W.) KT1 .197 CJ95
Leatherhead KT22 .231 CH122
Leatherhead (Bkhm) KT23 .246 CB125
Leatherhead (Oxshott) KT22 .215 CD113
Maidenhead (Bray) SL6 .150 AC75
Maidenhead (Taplow) SL6 .130 AE70
New Malden KT3 .198 CS97
Northwood HA6 .93 BT53
Orpington BR6 .206 EU102
Orpington (Downe) BR6 .223 EN111
Orpington (Farnboro.) BR6 .223 EP106
Orpington (Grn St Grn) BR6 .223 ET108
Orpington (St.M.Cray) BR5 .206 EW98
Oxted RH8 .253 ED130
Oxted (Lmpfld) RH8 .254 EG128
Pinner HA5 .116 BY55
Potters Bar EN6 .64 DC33
Purfleet RM19 off London Rd Purfleet .168 FN78
Purley CR8 .219 DN111
Redhill RH1 .250 DF134
Redhill (Bletch.) RH1 .252 DQ133
Redhill (Merst.) RH1 .251 DH128
Redhill (Nutfld) RH1 .251 DM133
Reigate RH2 .250 DA134
Rickmansworth WD3 .92 BK46
Romford RM1 .127 FE57
Ruislip HA4 .115 BS59
St. Albans AL3 .43 CD20
St. Albans (Coln.Hth) AL4 .44 CP22
St. Albans (Lon.Col.) AL2 .61 CJ25
Sevenoaks TN13 .257 FJ125
Sevenoaks (Chipstead) TN13 .256 FC122
Sevenoaks (Otford) TN14 .241 FF116
Sevenoaks (Seal) TN15 .257 FL121
Sevenoaks (Shore.) TN14 .225 FF110
Shepperton TW17 .195 BP100
Slough SL1 .152 AU75
Slough (Burn.) SL1 .130 AJ69
Slough (Chalvey) SL1 .151 AQ76
Slough (Colnbr.) SL3 .153 BC80
Slough (Datchet) SL3 .152 AV81
Slough (Langley) SL3 .153 AZ78

★ Place of interest | H Hospital | Sch School | Coll College | Uni University | Railway station

High St, S. Ock. (Aveley) RM15 .149 FR74
Southall UB1 .136 BZ74
Staines TW18 .173 BF91
Staines (Stanw.) TW19 .174 BK86
Staines (Wrays.) TW19 .172 AY86
Sutton SM1 .218 DB105
Sutton (Cheam) SM3 .217 CY107
Swanley BR8 .207 FF98
Swanscombe DA10 .190 FZ85
Tadworth KT20 .233 CW123
Teddington TW11 .177 CG92
Thames Ditton KT7 .197 CG101
Thornton Heath CR7 .202 DQ98
Twickenham (Whitton) TW2 .176 CC87
Uxbridge UB8 .134 BK67
Uxbridge (Cowley) UB8 .134 BJ70
Uxbridge (Hare.) UB9 .92 BJ54
Waltham Cross EN8 .67 DY34
Waltham Cross (Chsht) EN8 .67 DX29
Walton-on-Thames KT12 .195 BU102
Ware SG12 .33 DX06
Ware (Hunsdon) SG12 .34 EK06
Ware (Stans.Abb.) SG12 .33 EC11
Watford WD17 .75 BV41
Wembley HA9 .118 CM63
West Drayton (Harm.) UB7 .154 BK79
West Drayton (Yiew.) UB7 .134 BK74
West Molesey KT8 .196 CA98
West Wickham BR4 .203 EB102
Westerham TN16 .255 EQ127
Westerham (Brasted) TN16 .240 EV124
Weybridge KT13 .212 BN105
Windsor SL4 .151 AR81
Windsor (Eton) SL4 .151 AR79
Woking GU21 .226 AY117
Woking (Chobham) GU24 .210 AS111
Woking (Horsell) GU21 .226 AV115
Woking (Old Wok.) GU22 .227 BB121
Woking (Ripley) GU23 .228 BJ121
High St Colliers Wd, SW19 .180 DD94
High St Grn, Hem.H. HP2 .40 BN18
⊖ High Street Kensington .17 J4
High St Ms, SW19 .179 CY92
High St N, E6 .144 EL67
E12 .124 EL64
High St Ponders End, Enf. EN3 .82 DW42
High St S, E6 .145 EM68
High St Wimbledon, SW19 .179 CX92
High Timber St, EC4 .10 G9
High Tor Cl, Brom. BR1 off Babbacombe Rd .184 EH94
High Tree Cl, Add. KT15 .211 BF106
Sawbridgeworth CM21 .36 EX06
High Tree Ct, W7 .137 CE73
High Trees, SW2 .181 DN88
Barnet EN4 .80 DE43
Croydon CR0 .203 DY102
Dartford DA2 .188 FP86
High Trees Cl, Cat. CR3 .236 DT123
High Trees Ct, Brwd. CM14 off Warley Mt .108 FW49
High Trees Rd, Reig. RH2 .266 DD135
Highview, Cat. CR3 .236 DS124
High Vw, Ch.St.G. HP8 .90 AX47
Guildford (Goms.) GU5 .261 BQ139
Hatfield AL10 .45 CT20
Highview, Nthlt. UB5 .136 BY69
High Vw, Pnr. HA5 .116 BW56
Rickmansworth (Chorl.) WD3 .74 BG42
Sutton SM2 .217 CZ111
Watford WD18 .75 BT44
Highview, Wok. (Knap.) GU21 off Mulgrave Way .226 AS117
Highview Av, Edg. HA8 .96 CQ49
High Vw Av, Grays RM17 .170 GC78
Highview Av, Wall. SM6 .219 DM106
High Vw Caravan Pk, Kings L. WD4 .59 BR28
High Vw Cl, SE19 .202 DT96
Loughton IG10 .84 EJ43
Highview Cl, Pot.B. EN6 .64 DC33
Highview Cres, Brwd. (Hutt.) CM13 .109 GC44
Highview Gdns, N3 .119 CY55
N11 .99 DJ50
Edgware HA8 .96 CQ49
High Vw Gdns, Grays RM17 .170 GC78
Highview Gdns, Pot.B. EN6 .64 DC33
St. Albans AL4 .43 CJ15
Upminster RM14 .128 FP61
Highview Ho, Rom. RM6 .126 EY56
Highview Path, Bans. SM7 .234 DA115
Sch High Vw Prim Sch, SW11 off Plough Rd .160 DD84
Wallington SM6 off The Chase .219 DL106
High Vw Rd, E18 .124 EF55
SE19 .182 DR93
Highview Rd, W13 .137 CG71
High Vw Rd, Guil. GU2 .258 AS137
Highview Rd, Sid. DA14 .186 EV91
Highway, The, E1 .12 B10
E14 .12 B10
Beaconsfield HP9 off Station Rd .89 AK52
Orpington BR6 .224 EW106
Stanmore HA7 .95 CF53
Sutton SM2 .218 DC109
Highway Ct, Beac. HP9 off Station Rd .89 AK52
Sch Highway Prim Sch, The, Orp. BR6 off The Highway .224 EW106
High Wickfield, Welw.G.C. AL7 off Amwell Common .30 DC10
Highwold, Couls. CR5 .234 DG118
Highwood, Brom. BR2 .204 EE97
Highwood Av, N12 .98 DC49
Bushey WD23 .76 BZ39
Highwood Cl, Brwd. CM14 .108 FV45
Kenley CR8 .236 DQ117
Orpington BR6 .205 EQ103
Highwood Dr, Orp. BR6 .205 EQ103
Highwood Gdns, Ilf. IG5 .125 EM57
Highwood Gro, NW7 .96 CR50
Highwood Hall La, Hem.H. HP3 .59 BQ25
HIGHWOOD HILL, NW7 .97 CU47
Highwood Hill, NW7 .97 CT47
H Highwood Hosp, Brwd. CM15 .108 FW45
Highwood La, Loug. IG10 .85 EN43
Sch Highwood Prim Sch, Bushey WD23 off Bushey Mill La .76 BY39
Highwood Rd, N19 .121 DL62
High Wd Rd, Hodd. EN11 .49 DZ15
Highwoods, Cat. CR3 .252 DS125
Leatherhead KT22 .231 CJ121
High Worple, Har. HA2 .116 BZ59
Highworth Rd, N11 .99 DK51
HIGH WYCH, Saw. CM21 .36 EV06
Sch High Wych Prim Sch, Saw. CM21 off High Wych Rd .36 EU06
High Wych Rd, Saw. CM21 .36 EV06
Hilary Av, Mitch. CR4 .200 DG97
Hilary Cl, SW6 .160 DB80
Erith DA8 .167 FC81
Hornchurch RM12 .128 FK64
Hilary Rd, W12 .139 CT72
Slough SL3 .152 AY75
Hilbert Rd, Sutt. SM3 .199 CX104
Hilborough Way, Orp. BR6 .223 ER106
Hilbury Cl, Amer. HP6 .55 AQ35
Hilda May Av, Swan. BR8 .207 FE97
Hilda Rd, E6 .144 EK66
E16 .15 H4
Hilda Ter, SW9 .161 DN82
Hilda Vale Cl, Orp. BR6 .223 EP105
Hilda Vale Rd, Orp. BR6 .223 EN105
Hildenborough Gdns, Brom. BR1 .184 EE93
Hilden Dr, Erith DA8 .167 FH80
Hildenlea Pl, Brom. BR2 .204 EE96
Hildenley Cl, Red. RH1 off Malmstone Av .251 DK128
Hildens, The, Dor. (Westc.) RH4 .262 CB138
Hilders, The, Ashtd. KT21 .232 CP117
Hildreth St, SW12 .181 DH88
Hildyard Rd, SW6 .160 DA79
Hiley Rd, NW10 .139 CW69
Hilfield La, Wat. (Ald.) WD25 .77 CD41
Hilfield La S, Bushey WD23 .77 CF44
Hilgay, Guil. GU1 .243 AZ134
Hilgay Cl, Guil. GU1 .243 AZ134
Hilgrove Rd, NW6 .140 DC66
Hiliary Gdns, Stan. HA7 .95 CJ54
Hiljon Cres, Ger.Cr. (Chal.St.P.) SL9 .90 AY53
Hill, The, Cat. CR3 .236 DT124
Gravesend (Nthflt) DA11 .190 GC86
Harlow CM17 .36 EW11
Hillars Heath Rd, Couls. CR5 .235 DL115
Hillary Av, Grav. (Nthflt) DA11 .190 GE90
Hillary Cres, Walt. KT12 .196 BW102
Hillary Dr, Islw. TW7 .157 CF84
Hillary Ri, Barn. EN5 .80 DA42
Hillary Rd, Hem.H. HP2 .40 BN19
Southall UB2 .156 CA76
Hill Av, Amer. HP6 .55 AQ38
Hill Barn, S.Croy. CR2 .220 DS111
Hillbeck Cl, SE15 .162 DW80
Hillbeck Way, Grnf. UB6 .137 CD67
Hillborne Cl, Hayes UB3 .155 BU78
Hillborough Av, Sev. TN13 .257 FK122
Hillborough Cl, SW19 .180 DC94
Hillbrook Gdns, Wey. KT13 .212 BN108
Sch Hillbrook Prim Sch, SW17 off Hillbrook Rd .180 DG91
Hillbrook Rd, SW17 .180 DF90
Hill Brow, Brom. BR1 .204 EK95
Dartford DA1 .187 FF86
Hillbrow, N.Mal. KT3 .199 CT97
Hillbrow Cl, Bex. DA5 .187 FD91
Hillbrow Cotts, Gdse. RH9 .252 DW132
Hillbrow Ct, Gdse. RH9 .252 DW132
Hillbrow Rd, Brom. BR1 .184 EE94
Esher KT10 .214 CC105
Hillbury, Hat. AL10 .45 CT19
Hillbury Av, Har. HA3 .117 CH57
Hillbury Cl, Warl. CR6 .236 DV118
Hillbury Gdns, Warl. CR6 .236 DW118
Hillbury Rd, SW17 .181 DH90
Warlingham CR6 .236 DU117
Whyteleafe CR3 .236 DU117
Hill Cl, NW2 .119 CV62
NW11 .120 DA58
Barnet EN5 .79 CW43
Chislehurst BR7 .185 EP92
Cobham KT11 .214 CA112
Gravesend (Istead Rise) DA13 .190 GE94
Harrow HA1 .117 CE62
High Wycombe (Woob.Grn) HP10 .110 AF56
Purley CR8 .220 DQ113
Stanmore HA7 .95 CH49
Woking GU21 .226 AX115
Hill Common, Hem.H. HP3 .40 BN24
Hillcote Av, SW16 .181 DN94
Hill Ct, Gdmg. GU7 .258 AS144
Northolt UB5 .116 CA64
Hillcourt Av, N12 .98 DB51
Hillcourt Est, N16 .122 DR60
Hillcourt Rd, SE22 .182 DV86
Hill Cres, N20 .98 DB47
Bexley DA5 .187 FC88
Harrow HA1 .117 CG57
Hornchurch RM11 .128 FJ58
Surbiton KT5 .198 CM99
Worcester Park KT4 .199 CW103
Hillcrest, N6 .120 DG59
N21 .99 DP45
Hatfield AL10 .45 CU18
Hill Crest, Pot.B. EN6 .64 DC34
Hillcrest, St.Alb. AL3 .42 CB22
Hill Crest, Sev. TN13 .256 FG122
Sidcup DA15 .186 EU87
Hillcrest, Wey. KT13 .213 BP105
Hillcrest Av, NW11 .119 CY57
Chertsey KT16 .211 BE105
Edgware HA8 .96 CP49
Grays RM20 .169 FU79
Pinner HA5 .116 BX56
Hillcrest Caravan Pk, Tad. (Box H.) KT20 .248 CP131
Hillcrest Cl, SE26 .182 DU91
Beckenham BR3 .203 DZ99
Epsom KT18 .233 CT115
Waltham Cross (Goffs Oak) EN7 .66 DQ29
Hillcrest Ct, Sutt. SM2 off Eaton Rd .218 DD107
Hillcrest Dr, Green. DA9 off Riverview Rd .189 FV85
Hillcrest Gdns, N3 .119 CY56
NW2 .119 CU62
Esher KT10 .197 CF104
Hillcrest Par, Couls. CR5 .219 DH114
Hillcrest Rd, E17 .101 ED54
E18 .102 EF54
W3 .138 CN74
W5 .138 CL71
Bromley BR1 .184 EG92
Dartford DA1 .187 FF87
Guildford GU2 .242 AT133
Hornchurch RM11 .127 FG59
Loughton IG10 .84 EK44
Ongar CM5 .71 FE30
Orpington BR6 .206 EU103
Purley CR8 .219 DM110
Hillcrest Rd, Rad. (Shenley) WD7 .62 CN33
Westerham (Bigg.H.) TN16 .238 EK116
Whyteleafe CR3 .236 DT117
Hillcrest Vw, Beck. BR3 .203 DZ100
Hillcrest Way, Epp. CM16 .70 EU31
Hillcrest Waye, Ger.Cr. SL9 .113 AZ59
Hillcroft, Loug. IG10 .85 EN40
Hillcroft Av, Pnr. HA5 .116 BZ58
Purley CR8 .219 DJ113
Coll Hillcroft Coll, Surb. KT6 off South Bk .198 CL100
Hillcroft Cres, W5 .138 CL72
Ruislip HA4 .116 BX62
Watford WD19 .93 BV46
Wembley HA9 .118 CM63
Sch Hillcroft Prim Sch, Cat. CR3 off Chaldon Rd .236 DS123
Hillcroft Rd, E6 .145 EP71
Chesham HP5 .54 AR29
High Wycombe (Penn) HP10 .88 AC46
Hillcroome Rd, Sutt. SM2 .218 DD107
Hillcross Av, Mord. SM4 .199 CZ99
Sch Hillcross Prim Sch, Mord. SM4 off Ashridge Way .199 CZ98
Hilldale Rd, Sutt. SM1 .217 CZ105
Hilldeane Rd, Pur. CR8 .219 DN109
Hilldene Av, Rom. RM3 .106 FJ51
Hilldene Cl, Rom. RM3 .106 FK50
Sch Hilldene Prim Sch, Rom. RM3 off Grange Rd .106 FJ51
Hilldown Rd, SW16 .181 DL94
Bromley BR2 .204 EE102
Hemel Hempstead HP1 .40 BG18
Hill Dr, NW9 .118 CQ60
SW16 .201 DM97
Hilldrop Cres, N7 .121 DK64
Hilldrop Est, N7 .121 DK64
Hilldrop La, N7 .121 DK64
Hilldrop Rd, N7 .121 DK64
Bromley BR1 .184 EG93
HILL END, Uxb. UB9 .92 BH51
Hillend, SE18 .165 EN81
Hill End, Orp. BR6 off The Approach .205 ET103
Hill End La, St.Alb. AL4 .43 CJ23
Hill End Rd, Uxb. (Hare.) UB9 .92 BH51
Hillersdon, Slou. SL2 .132 AV71
Hillersdon Av, SW13 .159 CU82
Edgware HA8 .96 CM50
Hillery Cl, SE17 .21 K8
Hilley Fld La, Lthd. (Fetch.) KT22 .230 CC122
Hill Fm App, H.Wyc. (Woob.Grn) HP10 .110 AE55
Hill Fm Av, Wat. WD25 .59 BU33
Hill Fm Cl, Wat. WD25 .59 BU33
Hill Fm Ind Est, Wat. WD25 .59 BT33
Hill Fm La, Ch.St.G. HP8 .90 AT46
Hill Fm Rd, W10 .139 CW71
Chesham HP5 .54 AR34
Gerrards Cross (Chal.St.P.) SL9 .90 AY52
Maidenhead (Taplow) SL6 .130 AE68
Uxbridge UB10 off Austin's La .115 BR63
Hillfield, Hat. AL10 .45 CV15
Hillfield Av, N8 .121 DL57
NW9 .118 CS57
Wembley HA0 .138 CL66
Hillfield Cl, Guil. GU1 .243 BC132
Harrow HA2 .116 CC56
Redhill RH1 .250 DG134
Hillfield Ct, NW3 .120 DE64
Hemel Hempstead HP2 .40 BL20
Hillfield Par, Mord. SM4 .200 DE100
Hillfield Pk, N10 .121 DH56
N21 .99 DN47
Hillfield Pk Ms, N10 .121 DH56
Hillfield Rd, NW6 .119 CZ64
Gerrards Cross (Chal.St.P.) SL9 .90 AY52
Hampton TW12 .176 BZ94
Hemel Hempstead HP2 .40 BK20
Redhill RH1 .250 DG134
Sevenoaks (Dunt.Grn) TN13 .241 FE120
Hillfield Sq, Ger.Cr. (Chal.St.P.) SL9 .90 AY52
Hillfoot Av, Rom. RM5 .105 FC53
Hillfoot Rd, Rom. RM5 .105 FC53
Hillford Pl, Red. RH1 .266 DG140
Hillgate Pl, SW12 .181 DH87
W8 .16 G1
Hillgate St, W8 .16 G1
Hill Gate Wk, N6 .121 DJ58
Hill Gro, Felt. TW13 off Watermill Way .176 BZ89
Hillgrove, Ger.Cr. (Chal.St.P.) SL9 .91 AZ53
Hill Gro, Rom. RM1 .127 FE55
Hillgrove Business Pk, Wal.Abb. EN9 .49 EC22
Hill Hall, Epp. (They.Mt) CM16 .86 EZ35
Hillhouse, Wal.Abb. EN9 .68 EF33
Hill Ho Av, Stan. HA7 .95 CF52
Hill Ho Cl, N21 .99 DN45
Gerrards Cross (Chal.St.P.) SL9 off Rickmansworth La .90 AY52
Hill Ho Dr, Hmptn. TW12 .196 CA95
Hillhouse Dr, Reig. RH2 .266 DB136
Hill Ho Dr, Wey. KT13 .212 BN111
Sch Hillhouse Prim Sch, Wal.Abb. EN9 off Ninefields .68 EF33
Hill Ho Rd, SW16 .181 DM92
Hillhouse Rd, Dart. DA2 .188 FQ87
Hillhurst Gdns, Cat. CR3 .236 DS120
Hilliard Rd, Nthwd. HA6 .93 BT53
Hilliards Ct, E1 .22 D1
Hilliards Rd, Uxb. UB8 .134 BK72
Hillier Cl, Barn. EN5 .80 DB44
Hillier Gdns, Croy. CR0 off Crowley Cres .219 DN106
Hillier Pl, Chess. KT9 .215 CJ107
Hillier Rd, SW11 .180 DF86
Guildford GU1 .243 BA134
Hilliers Av, Uxb. UB8 off Harlington Rd .134 BN69
Hilliers La, Croy. CR0 .201 DL104
Hillingdale, West. (Bigg.H.) TN16 .238 EH118
HILLINGDON, Uxb. UB .134 BN69
⊖ Hillingdon .114 BN64
Hillingdon Av, Sev. TN13 .257 FJ121
Staines TW19 .174 BL88
Hillingdon Hill, Uxb. UB10 .134 BL69
H Hillingdon Hosp, Uxb. UB8 .134 BM71
Sch Hillingdon Manor Lwr & Mid Sch, Uxb. UB8 off Harlington Rd .135 BP71
Sch Hillingdon Prim Sch, Uxb. UB10 off Uxbridge Rd .135 BP69
Hillingdon Ri, Sev. TN13 .257 FK122
Hillingdon Rd, Bexh. DA7 .167 FC82
Gravesend DA11 .191 GG89
Uxbridge UB10 .134 BL67
Watford WD25 .59 BU34
Hillingdon St, SE5 .161 DP80
SE17 .161 DP80
Hillington Gdns, Wdf.Grn. IG8 .102 EK54
Hill La, Ruis. HA4 .115 BQ60
Tadworth (Kgswd) KT20 .233 CY121
Hill Ley, Hat. AL10 .45 CT18
Hill Leys, Pot.B. (Cuffley) EN6 .65 DL28
Hillman Cl, Horn. RM11 .128 FK55
Uxbridge UB8 .114 BL64
Hillman Dr, W10 .139 CW70
Hillman St, E8 .142 DV65
Hillmarton Rd, N7 .121 DL64
Hillmead, Berk. HP4 .38 AU20
Hillmead Ct, Maid. (Taplow) SL6 .130 AF71
Hillmead Dr, SW9 .161 DP84
Hill Meadow, Amer. (Colesh.) HP7 .55 AM43
Sch Hill Mead Prim Sch, SW9 off Hillmead Dr .161 DP84
Hillmont Rd, Esher KT10 .197 CE104
Hillmore Gro, SE26 .183 DX92
Hillmount, Wok. GU22 off Constitution Hill .226 AY119
Hill Pk Dr, Lthd. KT22 .231 CF119
Hill Path, SW16 off Valley Rd .181 DM92
Hill Pl, Slou. (Farn.Com.) SL2 .131 AP66
Hillpoint, Rick. (Loud.) WD3 .74 BJ43
Hillreach, SE18 .165 EM78
Hill Ri, N9 .82 DV44
NW11 .120 DB56
SE23 off London Rd .182 DV88
Dartford (Lane End) DA2 .189 FR92
Dorking RH4 .247 CG134
Esher KT10 .197 CH103
Gerrards Cross (Chal.St.P.) SL9 .90 AX54
Greenford UB6 .136 CC66
Potters Bar EN6 .64 DC34
Potters Bar (Cuffley) EN6 .65 DK27
Richmond TW10 .177 CK85
Rickmansworth WD3 .74 BH44
Ruislip HA4 .115 BQ60
Slough SL3 .153 BA79
Upminster RM14 .128 FN61
Hillrise, Walt. KT12 .195 BT101
Hill Rise Av, Wat. WD24 .76 BX38
Hill Ri Cres, Ger.Cr. (Chal.St.P.) SL9 .90 AY54
Hillrise Rd, N19 .121 DL59
Romford RM5 .105 FC51
Hill Rd, N10 .98 DF53
NW8 .140 DC68
Brentwood CM14 .108 FU48
Carshalton SM5 .218 DE107
Dartford DA2 .188 FL89
Epping (They.B.) CM16 .85 ES37
Harrow HA1 .117 CG57
Leatherhead (Fetch.) KT22 .230 CB122
Mitcham CR4 .201 DH95
Northwood HA6 .93 BR51
Pinner HA5 .116 BY57
Purley CR8 .219 DM112
Sutton SM1 .218 DB106
Wembley HA0 .117 CH62
Hillsborough Grn, Wat. WD19 off Ashburnham Dr .93 BU48
Hillsborough Rd, SE22 .182 DS85
Hills Chace, Brwd. CM14 .108 FW49
Hillsgrove, Well. DA16 .166 EW80
Sch Hillsgrove Prim Sch, Well. DA16 off Sidmouth Rd .166 EW80
Hillside, NW9 .118 CR56
NW10 .138 CQ67
SW19 .179 CX93
Banstead SM7 .233 CY115
Barnet EN5 .80 DC43
Chesham HP5 .54 AN28
Dartford (Fnghm) DA4 .208 FM101
Dartford (Lane End) DA2 .189 FS92
Erith DA8 .167 FD77
Grays RM17 .170 GD77
Harlow CM17 .52 EW17
Hatfield AL10 .45 CU18
Hoddesdon EN11 .49 DZ16
Slough SL1 .152 AS75
Uxbridge (Hare.) UB9 .114 BJ57
Virginia Water GU25 .192 AW100
Ware SG12 .32 DW07
Welwyn Garden City AL7 .30 DB12
Woking GU22 .226 AX120
Hillside, The, Orp. BR6 .224 EV109
Hillside Av, N11 .98 DF51
Borehamwood WD6 .78 CP42
Gravesend DA12 .191 GK89
Purley CR8 .219 DP113
Waltham Cross (Chsht) EN8 .67 DX31
Wembley HA9 .118 CM63
Woodford Green IG8 .102 EJ50
Hillside Cl, NW8 .140 DB68
Abbots Langley WD5 .59 BS32
Banstead SM7 .233 CY116
Betchworth (Brock.) RH3 .264 CN135
Chalfont St. Giles HP8 .90 AV48
Gerrards Cross (Chal.St.P.) SL9 .90 AY51
Morden SM4 .199 CY98
Woodford Green IG8 .102 EJ50
Hillside Ct, St.Alb. AL1 off Hillside Rd .43 CE19
Swanley BR8 .207 FG98
Hillside Cres, Enf. EN2 .82 DR38
Harrow HA2 .116 CC60
Northwood HA6 .93 BU53
Waltham Cross (Chsht) EN8 .67 DX31
Ware (Stans.Abb.) SG12 .33 EB11
Watford WD19 .76 BY44
Hillside Dr, Edg. HA8 .96 CN51
Gravesend DA12 .191 GK89
Hillside Est, N15 .122 DT58
Hillside Gdns, E17 .123 ED55
N6 .120 DG58
SW2 .181 DN89
Addlestone KT15 .211 BF107
Barnet EN5 .79 CY42
Berkhamsted HP4 .38 AX20
Betchworth (Brock.) RH3 .248 CN134
Edgware HA8 .96 CM49
Hillside Gdns, Har. HA3 .118 CL59
Northwood HA6 .93 BU52
Wallington SM6 .219 DJ108
Hillside Gate, St.Alb. AL1 .43 CE19
Hillside Gro, N14 .99 DK45
NW7 .97 CU52
Sch Hillside Inf Sch, Nthwd. HA6 off Northwood Way .93 BU52
Sch Hillside Jun Sch, Nthwd. HA6 off Northwood Way .93 BU52
Hillside La, Brom. BR2 .204 EG103
Ware (Gt Amwell) SG12 .33 EA10
Hillside Pas, SW2 .181 DM89
Sch Hillside Prim Sch, Orp. BR5 off Dyke Dr .206 EW101
Hillside Ri, Nthwd. HA6 .93 BU52
Hillside Rd, N15 .122 DS59
SW2 .181 DN89
W5 .138 CL71
Ashtead KT21 .232 CM117
Bromley BR2 .204 EF97
Bushey WD23 .76 BY43
Coulsdon CR5 .235 DM118
Croydon CR0 .219 DP106
Dartford DA1 .187 FG86
Epsom KT17 .217 CW110
Northwood HA6 .93 BU52
Pinner HA5 .93 BV52
Radlett WD7 .77 CH35
Rickmansworth (Chorl.) WD3 .73 BC43
St. Albans AL1 .43 CE19
Sevenoaks TN13 .257 FK123
Southall UB1 .136 CA70
Surbiton KT5 .198 CM99
Sutton SM2 .217 CZ108
Westerham (Tats.) TN16 .238 EL119
Whyteleafe CR3 .236 DU118
Sch Hillside Sch, Borwd. WD6 off Hillside Av .78 CQ41
Hillside Ter, Hert. SG13 .32 DQ11
Hillside Wk, Brwd. CM14 .108 FU48
Hills La, Nthwd. HA6 .93 BS53
Hillsleigh Rd, W8 .16 F1
Hillsmead Way, S.Croy. CR2 .220 DU113
Hills Ms, W5 .138 CL73
Hills Pl, W1 .9 J8
Hillspur Cl, Guil. GU2 .242 AT133
Hillspur Rd, Guil. GU2 .242 AT133
Hills Rd, Buck.H. IG9 .102 EH46
Hillstowe St, E5 .122 DW61
Hill St, W1 .18 F1
Richmond TW9 .177 CK85
St. Albans AL3 .42 CC20
Hillswood Business Pk, Cher. KT16 .211 BC105
Hillswood Dr, Cher. KT16 .211 BC105
HILLTOP, Chesh. HP5 .54 AR28
Hill Top, NW11 .120 DB56
Loughton IG10 .85 EN40
Morden SM4 .200 DA100
Sutton SM3 .199 CZ101
Hilltop Av, NW10 .138 CQ66
Hilltop Cl, Guil. GU3 .242 AT130
Leatherhead KT22 .231 CJ123
Hill Top Cl, Loug. IG10 .85 EN41
Hilltop Cl, Wal.Cr. (Chsht) EN7 .66 DT26
Sch Hilltop First Sch, Wind. SL4 off Clewer Hill Rd .151 AL83
Hilltop Gdns, NW4 .97 CV54
Dartford DA1 .188 FM85
Orpington BR6 .205 ES103
Hilltop La, Cat. CR3 .251 DN126
Redhill RH1 .251 DN126
Hill Top Pl, Loug. IG10 .85 EN41
Hilltop Ri, Lthd. (Bkhm) KT23 .246 CC126
Hilltop Rd, NW6 .140 DA66
Berkhamsted HP4 .38 AW20
Grays RM20 .169 FV79
Kings Langley WD4 .59 BR27
Reigate RH2 .266 DB136
Whyteleafe CR3 .236 DS117
Hill Top Vw, Wdf.Grn. IG8 .103 EM51
Hilltop Wk, Cat. CR3 .237 DY120
Hilltop Way, Stan. HA7 .95 CG48
Hillview, SW20 .179 CV94
Hill Vw, Berk. HP4 .38 AU17
Hillview, Mitch. CR4 .201 DL98
Whyteleafe CR3 .236 DT117
Hillview Av, Har. HA3 .118 CL57
Hornchurch RM11 .128 FJ58
Hillview Cl, Pnr. HA5 .94 BZ51
Purley CR8 .219 DP111
Hill Vw Cl, Tad. KT20 off Shelvers Way .233 CW121
Hillview Cl, Wem. HA9 .118 CM61
Hillview Ct, Wok. GU22 .227 AZ118
Hillview Cres, Guil. GU2 .242 AT132
Ilford IG1 .125 EM58
Hill Vw Cres, Orp. BR6 .205 ET102
Hill Vw Dr, SE28 .145 ES74
Hillview Dr, Red. RH1 .266 DG135
Hill Vw Dr, Well. DA16 .165 ES82
Hillview Gdns, NW4 .119 CX56
Hill Vw Gdns, NW9 .118 CR57
Hillview Gdns, Har. HA2 .116 CA55
Waltham Cross (Chsht) EN8 .67 DX27
Hillview Rd, NW7 .97 CX49
Chislehurst BR7 .185 EN92
Hill Vw Rd, Esher (Clay.) KT10 .215 CG108
Orpington BR6 .205 ET102
Hillview Rd, Pnr. HA5 .94 BZ52
Hill Vw Rd, Stai. (Wrays.) TW19 .172 AX86
Hillview Rd, Sutt. SM1 .200 DC104
Hill Vw Rd, Twick. TW1 .177 CG86
Woking GU22 .227 AZ118
Hillway, N6 .120 DG61
NW9 .118 CS60
Amersham HP7 .55 AP41
Hill Waye, Ger.Cr. SL9 .113 AZ58
Hillwood Cl, Brwd. (Hutt.) CM13 .109 GB46
Hillwood Gro, Brwd. (Hutt.) CM13 .109 GB46
Hillworth Rd, SW2 .181 DN87
Hillyard Rd, W7 .137 CE71
Hillyard St, SW9 .161 DN81
Hillyfield, E17 .101 DY54
Hilly Fld, Harl. CM18 .51 ET19
Hillyfield Cl, E9 off Mabley St .123 DY64
Hillyfields, Loug. IG10 .85 EN40
Welwyn Garden City AL7 .30 DC08
Hilly Flds Cres, SE4 .163 EA83

Hilmay Dr, Hem.H. HP1 .....40 BH21
Hilperton Rd, Slou. SL1 ....152 AS75
Hilsea Pt, SW15
off Wanborough Dr 179 CV88
Hilsea St, E5 ....122 DW63
Hilton Av, N12 ....98 DD50
Hilton Cl, Uxb. UB8 ....134 BH68
Hilton Ct, Horl. RH6
off Clarence Way 269 DK147
Hilton Docklands Nelson Dock Pier 23 L1
Hilton Way, S.Croy. CR2 ....236 DV115
Hilversum Cres, SE22
off East Dulwich Gro 182 DS85
Himalayan Way, Wat. WD18 ..75 BT44
Himley Rd, SW17 ....180 DE92
Hinchley Cl, Esher KT10 ....197 CF104
Hinchley Dr, Esher KT10 ....197 CF104
Hinchley Way, Esher KT10 ..197 CG104
HINCHLEY WOOD, Esher KT10 ....197 CF104
⇌ Hinchley Wood 197 CF104
Sch Hinchley Wd Prim Sch, Esher KT10
off Claygate La 197 CG103
Sch Hinchley Wd Sch & 6th Form Cen, Esher KT10
off Claygate La 197 CG103
Hinckley Rd, SE15 ....162 DU84
Hind Cl, Chig. IG7 ....103 ET50
Hind Ct, EC4 ....10 D8
Hind Cres, Erith DA8 ......167 FD79
Hinde Ms, W1
off Marylebone La 140 DG72
Hindes Rd, Har. HA1 ....117 CD57
Hinde St, W1 ....8 F7
Hind Gro, E14 ....13 N8
Hindhead Cl, N16 ....122 DS60
Uxbridge UB8
off Aldenham Dr 135 BP71
Hindhead Gdns, Nthlt. UB5 .136 BY67
Hindhead Grn, Wat. WD19 ..94 BW50
Hindhead Pt, SW15
off Wanborough Dr 179 CV88
Hindhead Way, Wall. SM6 ..219 DL106
Hind Ho, N7 off Harvist Est .121 DN63
Hindmans Rd, SE22 ....182 DU85
Hindmans Way, Dag. RM9 ..146 EZ70
Hindmarsh Cl, E1 ....12 B9
Hindrey Rd, E5 ....122 DV64
Hindsley's Pl, SE23 ....182 DW89
Hind Ter, Grays RM20
off Mill La 169 FX78
Hine Cl, Couls. CR5 ....235 DJ122
Hinkler Rd, Har. HA3 ....117 CK55
Hinkley Cl, Uxb. (Hare.) UB9 .114 BJ56
Hinksey Cl, Slou. SL3 ......153 BB76
Hinksey Path, SE2 ....166 EX76
Hinstock Rd, SE18 ....165 EQ79
Hinton Av, Houns. TW4 .....156 BX84
Hinton Cl, SE9 ....184 EL88
Hinton Rd, N18 ....100 DS49
SE24 ....161 DP83
Slough SL1 ....131 AL73
Uxbridge UB8 ....134 BJ67
Wallington SM6 ....219 DJ107
Hintons, Harl. CM19 ....51 EM19
Hipkins Pl, Brox. EN10 ......49 DY20
Hipley Ct, Guil. GU1
off Warren Rd 259 BA135
Hipley St, Wok. GU22 ......227 BB121
Hippodrome Ms, W11 ....6 C10
Hippodrome Pl, W11 ....6 D10
Hirst Cres, Wem. HA9
off East La 118 CL62
Hiscocks Ho, NW10 ....138 CQ66
Hitcham La, Maid. (Taplow) SL6 ....130 AG69
Slough (Burn.) SL1 ....130 AG69
Hitcham Rd, E17 ....123 DZ59
Maidenhead (Taplow) SL6 .130 AF72
Slough (Burn.) SL1 ....130 AF70
Hitchcock Cl, Shep. TW17 ..194 BM97
Hitchen Hatch La, Sev. TN13 .256 FG124
Hitchens Cl, Hem.H. HP1 ....39 BF19
Hitchin Cl, Rom. RM3 ....106 FJ49
Hitchings Way, Reig. RH2 ..266 DA138
Hitchin Sq, E3 ....143 DY68
Hitherbaulk, Welw.G.C. AL7 ..29 CY11
Hitherbroom Rd, Hayes UB3 ....135 BU74
Hitherbury Cl, Guil. GU2 ..258 AW137
Hither Fm Rd, SE3 ....164 EJ83
Sch Hitherfield Prim Sch, SW16 off Hitherfield Rd ..181 DN90
Hitherfield Rd, SW16 ....181 DM89
Dagenham RM8 ....126 EY61
HITHER GREEN, SE13 ......184 EE86
⇌ Hither Green 184 EE86
Hither Grn La, SE13 ....183 EC85
Sch Hither Grn Prim Sch, SE13 off Leahurst Rd ...183 ED85
SE13 off Beacon Rd 183 ED86
Hitherlands, SW12 ....181 DH89
Hither Meadow, Ger.Cr. (Chal.St.P.) SL9
off Lower Rd 90 AY53
Hithermoor Rd, Stai. TW19 ..174 BG85
Hitherway, Welw.G.C. AL8 ...29 CY05
Hitherwell Dr, Har. HA3 ......95 CD53
Hitherwood Cl, Horn. RM12 off Swanbourne Dr .128 FK63
Reigate RH2 ....250 DD132
Hitherwood Dr, SE19 ....182 DT91
Hive, The, Grav. (Nthflt) DA11 off Fishermans Hill .190 GB85
Hive Cl, Brwd. CM14 ....108 FU47
Bushey (Bushey Hth) WD23 ....95 CD47
Hive La, Grav. (Nthflt) DA11 .190 GB86
Hive Rd, Bushey (Bushey Hth) WD23 .....95 CD47
Hivings Hill, Chesh. HP5 .....54 AN28
Hivings Pk, Chesh. HP5 .....54 AP28
Hixberry La, St.Alb. AL4 .....43 CK21
★ H.M.S. Belfast, SE1 .....21 M1
★ H.M.S. President, EC4 ...10 D10
★ H.M. Treasury, SW1 .....19 N3
Hoadly Rd, SW16 ....181 DK90
Hobart Cl, N20
off Oakleigh Rd N 98 DE47
Hayes UB4 ....136 BX70
Hobart Dr, Hayes UB4 ......136 BX70
Hobart Gdns, Th.Hth. CR7 ..202 DR97
Hobart La, Hayes UB4 ......136 BX70
Hobart Pl, SW1 ....18 G5
Richmond TW10
off Chisholm Rd 178 CM86
Hobart Rd, Dag. RM9 ....126 EX63
Hobart Rd, Hayes UB4 .....136 BX70
Ilford IG6 ....103 EQ54
Tilbury RM18 ....171 GG81
Worcester Park KT4 ......199 CV104
Hobarts Dr, Uxb. (Denh.) UB9 ....113 BF58
Hobart Wk, St.Alb. AL3
off Valley Rd 43 CF16
Hobbans Fm Chase, Ong. CM5 ....53 FH23
Sch Hobbayne Prim Sch, W7 off Greenford Av ...137 CF72
Hobbayne Rd, W7 ....137 CD72
Hobbes Wk, SW15 ....179 CV85
Hobbs Cl, St.Alb. AL4 ....44 CL21
Waltham Cross (Chsht) EN8 ....67 DX29
West Byfleet KT14 ....212 BH113
Hobbs Cross Rd, Epp. (They.Gar.) CM16 ....86 EW35
Harlow CM17 ....36 EY12
Hobbs Grn, N2 ....120 DC55
Hobbs Hill Rd, Hem.H. HP3 ..40 BL24
Sch Hobbs Hill Wd Prim Sch, Hem.H. HP3
off Peascroft Rd 41 BP22
Hobbs Ms, Ilf. IG3
off Ripley Rd 125 ET61
Hobbs Pl Est, N1 ....5 L8
Hobbs Rd, SE27 ....182 DQ91
Hobbs Way, Welw.G.C. AL8 ..29 CW10
Hobby Horse Cl, Wal.Cr. (Chsht) EN7
off Great Stockwood Rd ..66 DR26
Hobday St, E14 ....14 A6
Hobill Wk, Surb. KT5 ....198 CM100
Hoblands End, Chis. BR7 ...185 ES93
Sch Hobletts Manor Inf & Nurs Sch, Hem.H. HP2
off Adeyfield Rd 40 BN19
Sch Hobletts Manor Jun Sch, Hem.H. HP2
off Adeyfield Rd 40 BN19
Hobletts Rd, Hem.H. HP2 ....40 BM19
Hobsons Cl, Hodd. EN11 ....33 DZ14
Hobsons Pl, E1 ....12 A5
Hobtoe Rd, Harl. CM20 .....35 EN14
Hobury St, SW10 ....160 DC79
Hockenden La, Swan. BR8 ..207 FB96
Hockeridge Bottom, Berk. HP4 ....38 AT21
Hockering Gdns, Wok. GU22 ....227 BA117
Hockering Rd, Wok. GU22 ..227 BA118
Hocker St, E2 ....11 N2
Hockett Cl, SE8 ....23 K7
Hocklands, Welw.G.C. AL7 ...30 DC08
Hockley Av, E6 ....144 EL68
Hockley Ct, E18
off Churchfields 102 EG53
Hockley Dr, Rom. RM2 ......105 FH54
Hockley La, Slou. (Stoke P.) SL2 ....132 AV67
Hockley Ms, Bark. IG11 ....145 ES68
Hocroft Av, NW2 ....119 CZ62
Hocroft Rd, NW2 ....119 CZ63
Hocroft Wk, NW2 ....119 CZ62
Hodder Dr, Grnf. UB6 ......137 CF68
HODDESDON, EN11 ....49 DZ18
Hoddesdon Bypass, Brox. EN10 ....49 DX19
Hertford SG13 ....33 DY14
Hoddesdon EN11 ....33 DY14
Hoddesdon Ind Cen, Hodd. EN11 ....49 EC16
Hoddesdon Rd, Belv. DA17 .166 FA78
Broxbourne EN10 ....67 DX27
Ware (Stans.Abb.) SG12 ...33 EC11
Hodds Wd Rd, Chesh. HP5 ...54 AQ33
Hodford Rd, NW11 ....119 CZ61
Hodgemoor Vw, Ch.St.G. HP8 ....90 AT48
Hodges Cl, Grays (Chaff.Hun.) RM16 ....169 FX78
Hodges Way, Wat. WD18 ....75 BU44
Hodgkin Cl, SE28
off Fleming Way 146 EX73
Hodgkins Ms, Stan. HA7 ....95 CH50
Hodgson Gdns, Guil. GU4
off Sutherland Dr 243 AZ131
Hodings Rd, Harl. CM20 .....35 EP14
Hodister Cl, SE5
off Badsworth Rd 162 DQ80
Hodnet Gro, SE16 ....22 G7
Hodsoll Ct, Orp. BR5 ....206 EX100
Hodson Cl, Har. HA2 ....116 BZ62
Hodson Cres, Orp. BR5 ....206 EX100
Hodson Pl, Enf. EN3 ....83 EA38
HOE, Guil. GU5 ....261 BS143
Hoe, The, Wat. WD19 ....94 BX47
Sch Hoe Br Sch, Wok. GU22
off Old Woking Rd 227 BC119
Hoebrook Cl, Wok. GU22 ...226 AX121
Hoechst, Houns. TW4 ....156 BW83
Hoecroft, Wal.Abb. EN9 .....50 EF22
Hoe La, Dor. (Abin.Ham.) RH5 ....261 BT143
Enfield EN1, EN3 ....82 DU38
Guildford (Peasl.) GU5 ...261 BR144
Romford (Abridge) RM4 ...86 EV43
Waltham Abbey EN9 ....50 EF22
Ware SG12 ....33 DX09
Hoe Meadow, Beac. HP9 .....88 AJ51
Hoestock Rd, Saw. CM21 ....36 EX05
Hoe St, E17 ....123 EA56
Hofland Rd, W14 ....16 B5
Hogan Ms, W2 ....7 N5
Hogan Way, E5
off Geldeston Rd 122 DU61
Hogarth Av, Ashf. TW15 ....175 BQ93
Brentwood CM15 ....108 FY48
Hogarth Business Pk, W4 ...158 CS79
Hogarth Cl, E16 ....144 EK71
W5 ....138 CL71
Slough SL1 ....131 AL73
Sch Hogarth Co Prim Sch, Brwd. CM15
off Riseway 109 FZ48
Hogarth Ct, EC3 ....11 M9
SE19 off Fountain Dr 182 DT91
Bushey WD23
off Steeplands 94 CB45
Hogarth Cres, SW19 ....200 DD95
Croydon CR0 ....202 DQ101
Hogarth Gdns, Houns. TW5 .156 CA80
Hogarth Hill, NW11 ....119 CZ56
Hogarth La, W4 ....158 CS79
Hogarth Pl, SW5 ....17 J8
Hogarth Reach, Loug. IG10 ..85 EM43
Hogarth Rd, SW5 ....17 J8
Dagenham RM8 ....126 EV64
Edgware HA8 ....96 CN54
Hogarth Roundabout, W4 ..159 CT79
Hogarth Roundabout Flyover, W4 off Burlington La ...158 CS79
★ Hogarth's Ho, W4
off Hogarth La 158 CS79
Hogarth Way, Hmptn. TW12 .196 CC95
Hogback Wd Rd, Beac. HP9 ..88 AH51
Hogden La, Dor. (Ran.Com.) RH5 ....246 BZ132
Leatherhead KT23 ....246 CA129
Hogfair La, Slou. (Burn.) SL1 .130 AJ69
Hogg End La, Hem.H. HP2 ...41 BR17
St. Albans AL3 ....41 BT17
Hogges Cl, Hodd. EN11
off Conduit La W 49 EA17
Hogg La, Borwd. (Elstree) WD6 ....77 CG42
Grays RM16, RM17 ....170 GA76
Hog La Roundabout, Grays RM16 ....170 FZ75
Hog Hill Rd, Rom. RM5 .....104 EZ52
Hog Pits, Hem.H. (Flaun.) HP3 ....57 BB32
HOGPITS BOTTOM, Hem.H. HP3 ....57 BA31
Hogpits Bottom, Hem.H. (Flaun.) HP3 ....57 BA32
Hogs Back, Guil. GU3 ......258 AS137
Hogscross La, Couls. CR5 ..234 DF123
Hogsdell La, Hert. (Hert.Hth) SG13 ....32 DV11
Hogshead Pas, E1 ....12 D10
Hogshill La, Cob. KT11 .....214 BX112
Hogs La, Grav. DA11 ....190 GD90
Hogsmill Way, Epsom KT19 .216 CQ106
Hogs Orchard, Swan. BR8 ..207 FH95
Hogtrough Hill, West. (Brasted) TN16 ....239 ET120
Hogtrough La, Gdse. RH9 ..253 EA128
Oxted RH8 ....253 EB128
Redhill RH1 ....267 DJ135
Holbeach Gdns, Sid. DA15 ..185 ES86
Holbeach Ms, SW12
off Harberson Rd 181 DH88
Sch Holbeach Prim Sch, SE6 off Doggett Rd 183 EA87
Holbeach Rd, SE6 ....183 EA87
Holbeck La, Wal.Cr. (Chsht) EN7 ....66 DT26
Holbeck Row, SE15 ....162 DU80
Holbein Gate, Nthwd. HA6 ..93 BS50
Holbein Ms, SW1 ....18 E9
Holbein Pl, SW1 ....18 E8
Holbein Ter, Dag. RM8
off Marlborough Rd 126 EV63
Holberton Gdns, NW10 .....139 CV69
HOLBORN, WC2 ....10 A7
⊖ Holborn 9 P6
Holborn, EC1 ....10 C6
Holborn Circ, EC1 ....10 D6
Holborn Cl, St.Alb. AL4 .....43 CK15
Coll Holborn Coll, SE7
off Woolwich Rd 164 EK77
Holborn Pl, WC1 ....10 A6
Holborn Rd, E13 ....15 N4
Holborn Viaduct, EC1 ....10 D6
Holborn Way, Mitch. CR4 ...200 DF96
Holbreck Pl, Wok. GU22
off Heathside Rd 227 AZ118
Holbrook Cl, N19
off Dartmouth Pk Hill ...121 DH60
Enfield EN1 ....82 DT39
Holbrooke Ct, N7 ....121 DL63
Holbrooke Pl, Rich. TW10
off Hill Ri 177 CK85
Holbrook La, Chis. BR7 ....185 ER94
Holbrook Meadow, Egh. TW20 ....173 BC93
Holbrook Rd, E15 ....144 EF68
Holbrook Way, Brom. BR2 ..205 EM100
Holburne Cl, SE3 ....164 EK81
Holburne Gdns, SE3 ....164 EK81
Holburne Rd, SE3 ....164 EJ81
Holcombe Hill, NW7 ....97 CU48
Holcombe Rd, N17 ....122 DT55
Ilford IG1 ....125 EN59
Holcombe St, W6 ....159 CV78
Holcon Ct, Red. RH1 ....250 DG131
Holcote Cl, Belv. DA17
off Blakemore Way 166 EY76
Holcroft Rd, E9 ....142 DW66
HOLDBROOK, Wal.Cr. EN8 ...67 EA34
Sch Holdbrook JMI Sch, Wal.Cr. EN8 off Longcroft Dr 67 DZ34
Holdbrook N, Wal.Cr. EN8
off Eleanor Way 67 DZ34
Holdbrook S, Wal.Cr. EN8
off Queens Way 67 DZ34
Holdbrook Way, Rom. RM3 .106 FM54
Holden Av, N12 ....98 DB50
NW9 ....118 CQ60
Holdenby Rd, SE4 ....183 DY85
Holden Cl, Dag. RM8 ......126 EV62
Hertford SG13 ....32 DS09
Holden Gdns, Brwd. CM14 ..108 FX50
Holdenhurst Av, N12 ....98 DB52
Holden Pl, Cob. KT11 ....213 BV114
Holden Pt, E15
off Waddington Rd 143 ED65
Holden Rd, N12 ....98 DB50
HOLDENS, Welw.G.C. AL7 ...30 DA06
Holden St, SW11 ....160 DG82
Holden Way, Upmin. RM14 ..129 FR59
Holder Cl, N3 ....98 DB52
Holdernesse Cl, Islw. TW7 ..157 CG81
Holdernesse Rd, SW17 .....180 DF90
Holderness Way, SE27 .....181 DP92
HOLDERS HILL, NW4 ....97 CX54
Holders Hill Av, NW4 ....97 CX54
Holders Hill Circ, NW7
off Dollis Rd 97 CY52
Holders Hill Cres, NW4 .....97 CX54
Holders Hill Dr, NW4 ......119 CX55
Holders Hill Gdns, NW4 ....97 CY54
Holders Hill Rd, NW4 ....97 CX54
NW7 ....97 CX54
Holdings, The, Hat. AL9 .....45 CW16
Holecroft, Wal.Abb. EN9 .....68 EE34
Hole Fm La, Brwd. CM13 ...129 FV55
Holegate St, SE7
off Westmoor St 164 EK76
Hole Hill La, Dor. RH4 .....262 CA135
Holford Ms, WC1 ....4 C10
Holford Pl, WC1 ....10 B1
Holford Rd, NW3 ....120 DC62
Grays RM16 ....171 GK76
Guildford GU1 ....243 BC134
Stanford-le-Hope (Linford) SS17 ....171 GL75
Tilbury RM18 ....171 GK76
Holford St, WC1 ....10 C1
Holford Yd, WC1 ....4 C10
Holgate Av, SW11 ....160 DD83
Holgate Gdns, Dag. RM10 ..126 FA64
Holgate Rd, Dag. RM10 ....126 FA64
HOLLAND, Oxt. RH8 ....254 EG134
Holland Av, SW20 ....199 CT95
Sutton SM2 ....218 DA109
Holland Cl, Barn. EN5 ....98 DD45
Bromley BR2 ....204 EF103
Redhill RH1 ....250 DF134
Romford RM7 ....127 FC57
Stanmore HA7 ....95 CH50
Holland Ct, E17
off Evelyn Rd 123 EC56
NW7 off Page St 97 CU51
Holland Cres, Oxt. RH8 ....254 EG133
Holland Dr, SE23 ....183 DY90
Holland Gdns, W14 ....16 D5
Brentford TW8 ....158 CL79
Egham TW20 ....193 BF96
Watford WD25 ....76 BW35
Holland Gro, SW9 ....161 DN80
★ Holland Ho & Pk, W8 ......16 E4
Sch Holland Ho Sch, Edg. HA8 off Broadhurst Av ...96 CP49
Sch Holland Jun Sch, Oxt. RH8 off Holland Rd 254 EG134
Holland La, Oxt. RH8 ......254 EG133
⊖ Holland Park 16 E2
Holland Pk, W8 ....16 E3
W11 ....16 D2
Holland Pk Av, W11 ....16 B3
Ilford IG3 ....125 ES58
Holland Pk Gdns, W14 ......16 C2
Holland Pk Ms, W11 ....16 D2
Holland Pk Rd, W14 ....16 E6
Holland Pk Roundabout, W11 .16 A3
Sch Holland Pk Sch, W8 ......16 F3
Holland Pas, N1 ....4 G7
Holland Pl, W8 ....17 J3
Holland Rd, E6 ....145 EM67
E15 ....144 EE69
NW10 ....139 CU67
SE25 ....202 DU99
W14 ....16 B3
Oxted RH8 ....254 EG133
Wembley HA0 ....137 CK65
Hollands, The, Felt. TW13 ...176 BX91
Woking GU22
off Montgomery Rd 226 AY118
Worcester Park KT4 ......199 CT102
Hollands Cft, Ware (Hunsdon) SG12 ....34 EK06
Holland St, SE1 ....20 F1
W8 ....17 H4
Holland Vil Rd, W14 ....16 C3
Holland Wk, N19
off Duncombe Rd 121 DK60
W8 ....16 F2
Stanmore HA7 ....95 CG50
Holland Way, Brom. BR2 ...204 EF103
Harlow CM17
off London Rd 36 EW14
Hollar Rd, N16
off Stoke Newington High St 122 DT62
Hollen St, W1 ....9 L7
Holles Cl, Hmptn. TW12 ....176 CA93
Holles St, W1 ....9 H7
Holley Rd, W3 ....158 CS75
Hollickwood Av, N12 ....98 DF51
Sch Hollickwood Prim Sch, N10 off Sydney Rd 99 DH52
Holliday Sq, SW11
off Fowler Cl 160 DD83
Holliday St, Berk. HP4 ......38 AX19
Hollidge Way, Dag. RM10 ..147 FB65
Hollier Ct, Hat. AL10
off Cranborne Rd 45 CV17
Holliers Way, Hat. AL10 .....45 CU18
Hollies, The, E11 ....124 EG57
N20 off Oakleigh Pk N 98 DD46
Gravesend DA12 ....191 GK93
Harrow HA3 ....117 CG56
Hemel Hempstead (Bov.) HP3 ....57 BA29
Welwyn Garden City AL8 ..29 CV13
Hollies Av, Sid. DA15 ......185 ET89
West Byfleet KT14 ....211 BF113
Hollies Cl, SW16 ....181 DN93
Twickenham TW1 ....177 CF89
Hollies Ct, Add. KT15 ......212 BJ106
Hollies End, NW7 ....97 CV50
Hollies Rd, W5 ....157 CJ77
Hollies Way, SW12
off Bracken Av 180 DG87
Potters Bar EN6 ....64 DC31
Holligrave Rd, Brom. BR1 ..204 EG95
Hollingbourne Av, Bexh. DA7 ....166 EZ80
Hollingbourne Gdns, W13 ..137 CH71
Hollingbourne Rd, SE24 ...182 DQ85
Hollingbourne Twr, Orp. BR5 ....206 EX102
Hollingsworth Rd, Croy. CR0 ....220 DV107
Hollington Cres, N.Mal. KT3 .199 CT100
Hollington Rd, E6 ....145 EM69
N17 ....100 DU54
Hollingworth Cl, W.Mol. KT8 ....196 BZ98
Hollingworth Rd, Orp. BR5 .205 EP100
Hollingworth Way, West. TN16 ....255 ER126
Hollis Pl, Grays RM17
off Ward Av 170 GA77
Hollman Gdns, SW16 ......181 DP93
Hollow, The, Wdf.Grn. IG8 ..102 EF49
HOLLOWAY, N7 ....121 DL63
Holloway Cl, West Dr. UB7 ..154 BL78
Holloway Dr, Vir.W. GU25 ..192 AY98
Holloway Hill, Cher. KT16 ..193 BC104
Holloway La, Rick. (Chenies) WD3 ....73 BD36
West Drayton UB7 ....154 BL79
⊖ Holloway Road 4 B1
Holloway Rd, E6 ....145 EM69
E11 ....124 EE62
N7 ....4 D3
N19 ....121 DK61
Sch Holloway Sch, N7
off Hilldrop Rd 121 DK63
Holloways La, Hat. (N.Mymms) AL9 ....45 CX23
Holloway St, Houns. TW3 ...156 CB83
Hollow Cl, Guil. GU2
off Lynwood 258 AV135
Hollow Cotts, Purf. RM19 ..168 FN78
Hollowfield Av, Grays RM17 .170 GD77
Hollowfield Wk, Nthlt. UB5 .136 BY65
Hollow Hill La, Iver SL0 .....133 BB73
Hollow La, Dor. (Wotton) RH5 ....262 BX140
Virginia Water GU25 .....192 AY97
Hollows, The, Brent. TW8
off Kew Br Rd 158 CM79
Hollow Wk, Rich. TW9
off Kew Rd 158 CL80
Hollow Way La, Amer. HP6 ..55 AS35
Chesham HP5 ....55 AS35
Holly Av, Add. (New Haw) KT15 ....212 BG110
Holly Av, Stan. HA7 ....96 CL54
Walton-on-Thames KT12 .196 BX102
Hollybank Cl, Hmptn. TW12 .176 CA92
Hollybank Rd, W.Byf. KT14 .212 BG114
Holly Bk Rd, Wok. GU22 ...226 AV121
Hollyberry La, NW3
off Holly Wk 120 DC63
Hollybrake Cl, Chis. BR7 ...185 ER94
Hollybush Av, St.Alb. AL2 ...42 CA24
Hollybush Cl, E11 ....124 EG57
Berkhamsted (Pott.End) HP4 ....39 BD16
Harrow HA3 ....95 CE53
Sevenoaks TN13 ....257 FJ124
Watford WD19 ....94 BW45
Hollybush Ct, Sev. TN13 ...257 FJ124
Hollybush Gdns, E2 ....12 D1
Hollybush Hill, E11 ....124 EF58
Holly Bush Hill, NW3 ....120 DC63
Hollybush Hill, Slou. (Stoke P.) SL2 ....132 AU66
Hollybush La, Amer. HP6 ....55 AR37
Holly Bush La, Hmptn. TW12 .176 BZ94
Hollybush La, Hem.H. HP1 ..39 BF19
Iver SL0 ....133 BB72
Orpington BR6 ....224 FA107
Holly Bush La, Sev. TN13 ..257 FJ123
Hollybush La, Uxb. (Denh.) UB9 ....113 BE63
Welwyn Garden City AL7 ..29 CZ13
Woking (Ripley) GU23 ...228 BK119
Hollybush Pl, E2 ....12 D1
Sch Hollybush Prim Sch, Hert. SG14 off Fordwich Ri ...31 DN09
Hollybush Rd, Chesh. HP5 ..54 AN27
Gravesend DA12 ....191 GJ89
Kingston upon Thames KT2 ....178 CL92
Holly Bush Steps, NW3
off Heath St 120 DC63
Hollybush St, E13 ....15 P1
Holly Bush Vale, NW3
off Heath St 120 DC63
Hollybush Way, Wal.Cr. EN7 ..66 DU28
Holly Cl, NW10 ....138 CS66
Beckenham BR3 ....203 EC98
Buckhurst Hill IG9 ....102 EK48
Chertsey (Longcr.) KT16 ..192 AU104
Egham (Eng.Grn) TW20 ..172 AV93
Feltham TW13 ....176 BY92
Hatfield AL10 ....45 CT19
Slough (Farn.Com.) SL2 ..111 AQ63
Wallington SM6 ....219 DH108
Woking GU21 ....226 AV119
Hollycombe, Egh. (Eng.Grn) TW20 ....172 AW91
Holly Cottage Ms, Uxb. UB8 off Pield Heath Rd .134 BN71
Holly Ct, Sutt. SM2
off Worcester Rd 218 DA108
Holly Cres, Beck. BR3 ......203 DZ99
Windsor SL4 ....151 AK82
Woodford Green IG8 .....101 ED52
Holly Cft, Hert. SG14 ....31 DN08
Hollycroft Av, NW3 ....120 DA62
Wembley HA9 ....118 CM61
Hollycroft Cl, S.Croy. CR2 ..220 DS106
West Drayton UB7 ....154 BN79
Hollycroft Gdns, West Dr. UB7 ....154 BN79
Holly Cross Rd, Ware SG12 ..33 DZ07
Hollydale Cl, Nthlt. UB5
off Dorchester Rd 116 CB63
Hollydale Dr, Brom. BR2 ..205 EM104
Sch Hollydale Prim Sch, SE15 off Hollydale Rd ..162 DW82
Hollydale Rd, SE15 ....162 DW81
Hollydell, Hert. SG13 ....32 DQ11
Hollydene, SE15 ....162 DV81
Hollydown Way, E11 ....123 ED62
Holly Dr, E4 ....101 EB45
Berkhamsted HP4 ....38 AX20
Brentford TW8 ....157 CG79
Potters Bar EN6 ....64 DB33
South Ockendon RM15 ...149 FX70
Windsor SL4 ....172 AS85
Holly Fm Rd, Sthl. UB2 ....156 BY78
Holly Fld, Harl. CM19 ....51 EQ18
Hollyfield, Hat. AL10 ....45 CU21
Hollyfield Av, N11 ....98 DF50
Hollyfield Rd, Surb. KT5 ....198 CM101
Hollyfields, Brox. EN10 .....67 DY26
Sch Hollyfield Sch & Cen for Cont Ed, The, Surb. KT6
off Surbiton Hill Rd 198 CL99
Holly Gdns, Bexh. DA7 .....167 FC84
West Drayton UB7 ....154 BM75
Holly Grn, Wey. KT13 ....195 BR104
Holly Gro, NW9 ....118 CQ59
SE15 ....162 DT82
Bushey WD23 ....95 CD45
Pinner HA5 ....94 BY53
Holly Gro Rd, Hert. SG14 ...31 DH07
Hollyhedge Rd, Cob. KT11 ..213 BV114
Holly Hedges La, Hem.H. (Bov.) HP3 ....57 BC30
Rickmansworth WD3 ......57 BC30
Holly Hedge Ter, SE13 .....183 ED85
Holly Hill, N21 ....81 DM44
NW3 ....120 DC63
Holly Hill Dr, Bans. SM7 ...234 DA116
Holly Hill Pk, Bans. SM7 ...234 DA117
Holly Hill Rd, Belv. DA17 ..167 FB78
Erith DA8 ....167 FB78
Hollyhock Cl, Hem.H. HP1 ..39 BE18
Holly Ho, Brwd. CM15
off Sawyers Hall La 108 FX46
H Holly Ho Hosp, Buck.H. IG9 ....102 EH47
Holly La, Bans. SM7 ....234 DA116
Holly La E, Bans. SM7 .....234 DA116
Holly La W, Bans. SM7 .....234 DA117
Holly Lea, Guil. GU4 ....242 AX128
Holly Lo Gdns, N6 ....120 DG61
Holly Lo Mobile Home Pk, Tad. KT20 ....249 CY126
Hollymead, Cars. SM5 .....200 DF104
Hollymead Rd, Couls. CR5 ..234 DG118
Hollymeoak Rd, Couls. CR5 .235 DH119
Holly Ms, SW10 ....17 M10
Hollymoor La, Epsom KT19 .216 CR110
Holly Mt, NW3
off Holly Bush Hill 120 DC63
Hollymount Cl, SE10 ....163 EC81
Sch Hollymount Prim Sch, SW20 off Cambridge Rd .199 CW95
Holly Pk, N3 ....119 CZ55
N4 ....121 DM59
Holly Pk Est, N4
off Blythwood Rd 121 DM59
Holly Pk Gdns, N3 ....120 DA55
Sch Holly Pk Prim Sch, N11
off Bellevue Rd 98 DG50
Holly Pk Rd, N11 ....98 DG50
W7 ....137 CF74

Holly Pl, NW3 off Holly Wk .120 DC63
Holly Rd, E11 .124 EF59
W4 off Dolman Rd .158 CR77
Dartford DA1 .188 FK88
Enfield EN3 .83 DX36
Hampton (Hmptn H.)
TW12 .176 CC93
Hounslow TW3 .156 CB84
Orpington BR6 .224 EU108
Reigate RH2 .266 DB136
Twickenham TW1 .177 CG88
Holly St, E8 .5 P5
Holly Ter, N6
off Highgate W Hill .120 DG60
N20 off Swan La .98 DC47
Holly Tree Av, Swan. BR8 .207 FE96
Hollytree Cl, SW19 .179 CX88
Holly Tree Cl, Chesh. (Ley Hill)
HP5 .56 AV31
Hollytree Cl, Ger.Cr.
(Chal.St.P.) SL9 .90 AY50
Holly Tree Rd, Cat. CR3
off Elm Gro .236 DS122
Sch Holly Trees Prim Sch, The,
Brwd. CM14
off Vaughan Williams Way .108 FV49
Holly Vw Cl, NW4 .119 CU58
Holly Village, N6
off Swains La .121 DH61
Holly Wk, NW3 .120 DC63
Enfield EN2 .82 DQ41
Richmond TW9 .158 CL82
Welwyn Garden City AL8 .29 CW05
Holly Way, Mitch. CR4 .201 DK98
Hollywood Ct, Borwd. (Elstree)
WD6 off Deacon's Hill Rd .78 CM42
Hollywood Gdns, Hayes
UB4 .135 BV72
Hollywood Ms, SW10
off Hollywood Rd .160 DC79
Hollywood Rd, E4 .101 DY50
SW10 .17 L10
Hollywoods, Croy. CR0 .221 DZ109
Hollywood Way, Erith DA8 .167 FH81
Woodford Green IG8 .101 ED52
Holman Rd, SW11 .160 DD82
Epsom KT19 .216 CQ106
Holmbank Dr, Shep. TW17 .195 BS98
Holmbridge Gdns, Enf. EN3 .83 DX42
Holmbrook Dr, NW4 .119 CX57
Holmbury Ct, SW17 .180 DF90
SW19 off Cavendish Rd .180 DE94
Holmbury Dr, Dor. (N.Holm.)
RH5 .263 CJ139
Holmbury Gdns, Hayes
UB3 off Church Rd .135 BT74
Holmbury Gro, Croy. CR0 .221 DZ108
Holmbury Pk, Brom. BR1 .184 EL94
Holmbury Vw, E5 .122 DV60
Holmbush Rd, SW15 .179 CY86
Holm Cl, Add. (Wdhm) KT15 .211 BE112
Holmcote Gdns, N5 .4 G2
Holmcroft, Tad. KT20 .249 CV125
Holmcroft Way, Brom. BR2 .205 EM99
Holmdale Cl, Borwd. WD6 .78 CM40
Holmdale Gdns, NW4 .119 CX57
Holmdale Rd, NW6 .120 DA64
Chislehurst BR7 .185 EQ92
Holmdale Ter, N15 .122 DS59
Holmdene Av, NW7 .97 CU51
SE24 .182 DQ85
Harrow HA2 .116 CB55
Holmdene Cl, Beck. BR3 .203 EC96
Holmead Rd, SW6 .160 DB80
Holmebury Cl, Bushey
(Bushey Hth) WD23 .95 CE47
Holme Chase, Wey. KT13 .213 BQ107
Holme Cl, Hat. AL10 .45 CT15
Waltham Cross (Chsht)
EN8 .67 DY31
Holme Ct, Islw. TW7
off Twickenham Rd .157 CG83
Holmedale, Slou. SL2 .132 AW73
Holmefield Ct, NW3 .140 DE65
Holme Lacey Rd, SE12 .184 EF86
Holme Lea, Wat. WD25
off Kingsway .60 BW34
Holme Pk, Borwd. WD6 .78 CM40
Holme Pl, Hem.H. HP2
off Crest Pk .41 BQ19
Holme Rd, E6 .144 EL67
Hatfield AL10 .45 CT15
Hornchurch RM11 .128 FN60
Holmes Av, E17 .123 DZ55
NW7 .97 CY50
Holmes Cl, Wok. GU22 .227 AZ121
Holmesdale, Wal.Cr. EN8 .83 DX35
Holmesdale Av, SW14 .158 CP83
Holmesdale Cl, SE25 .202 DT97
Guildford GU1 .243 BB133
Sch Holmesdale Comm Inf Sch,
Reig. RH2 off Alma Rd .250 DB132
Holmesdale Hill, Dart.
(S.Darenth) DA4 .208 FQ95
Holmesdale Rd, N6 .121 DH59
SE25 .202 DR99
Bexleyheath DA7 .166 EX82
Croydon CR0 .202 DR99
Dartford (S.Darenth) DA4 .208 FQ95
Dorking (N.Holm.) RH5 .263 CH140
Redhill (S.Nutfld) RH1 .267 DM136
Reigate RH2 .250 DA133
Richmond TW9 .158 CM81
Sevenoaks TN13 .257 FJ123
Teddington TW11 .177 CJ93
Holmesdale Ter, Dor. (N.Holm.)
RH5 off Holmesdale Rd .263 CH140
Holmesley Rd, SE23 .183 DY86
Holmes Meadow, Harl.
CM19 .51 EP21
Holmes Pl, SW10
off Fulham Rd .160 DC79
Holmes Rd, NW5 .121 DH64
SW19 .180 DC94
Twickenham TW1 .177 CF89
Holmes Ter, SE1 .20 C3
HOLMETHORPE, Red. RH1 .251 DH132
Holmethorpe Av, Red. RH1 .251 DH131
Holmethorpe Ind Est, Red.
RH1 .251 DH131
Holme Way, Stan. HA7 .95 CF51
Holmewood Gdns, SW2 .181 DM87
Holmewood Rd, SE25 .202 DS97
SW2 .181 DL87
Holmfield Av, NW4 .119 CX57
Holm Gro, Uxb. UB10 .134 BN66
Holmhurst Rd, Belv. DA17 .167 FB78
Holmlea Rd, Slou. (Datchet)
SL3 .152 AX81
Holmlea Wk, Slou. (Datchet)
SL3 .152 AW81
Holmleigh Av, Dart. DA1 .168 FJ84
Sch Holmleigh JMI Sch,
N16 off Dunsmure Rd .122 DT60
Holmleigh Rd, N16 .122 DS60
Holmleigh Rd Est, N16
off Holmleigh Rd .122 DT60
Holm Oak Cl, SW15
off West Hill .179 CZ86
Holm Oak Ms, SW4
off King's Av .181 DL85
Holmsdale Cl, Iver SL0 .133 BF72
Holmsdale Gro, Bexh. DA7 .167 FE82
Holmshaw Cl, SE26 .183 DY91
Holmshill La, Borwd. WD6 .78 CS36
Holmside Ri, Wat. WD19 .93 BV48
Holmside Rd, SW12 .180 DG86
Holmsley Cl, N.Mal. KT3 .199 CT100
Holmsley Ho, SW15
off Tangley Gro .179 CT87
Holms St, E2 .142 DU68
Holmstall Av, Edg. HA8 .118 CQ55
Holm Wk, SE3
off Blackheath Pk .164 EG82
Holmwood Av, Brwd.
(Shenf.) CM15 .109 GA44
South Croydon CR2 .220 DT113
Holmwood Cl, Add. KT15 .212 BG106
Harrow HA2 .116 CC55
Leatherhead (E.Hors.)
KT24 .245 BS128
Northolt UB5 .136 CB65
Sutton SM2 .217 CX109
Holmwood Gdns, N3 .98 DA54
Wallington SM6 .219 DH107
Holmwood Gro, NW7 .96 CR50
Holmwood Rd, Chess. KT9 .215 CK106
Enfield EN3 .83 DX36
Ilford IG3 .125 ES61
Sutton SM2 .217 CW110
Holmwood Vw Rd, Dor.
(Mid Holm.) RH5
off Horsham Rd .263 CH142
Holmwood Vil, SE7 .25 M9
Holne Chase, N2 .120 DC58
Morden SM4 .199 CZ100
Holness Rd, E15 .144 EF65
Holroyd Cl, Esher (Clay.)
KT10 .215 CF109
Holroyd Rd, SW15 .159 CW84
Esher (Clay.) KT10 .215 CF109
Holsart Cl, Tad. KT20 .233 CV122
Holstein Av, Wey. KT13 .212 BN105
Holstein Way, Erith DA18 .166 EY76
Holstock Rd, Ilf. IG1 .125 EQ62
Holsworth Cl, Har. HA2 .116 CC57
Holsworthy Sq, WC1 .10 B4
Holsworthy Way, Chess.
KT9 .215 CJ106
Holt, The, Hem.H. HP2
off Turners Hill .40 BL21
Ilford IG6 .103 EQ51
Wallington SM6 .219 DJ105
Welwyn Garden City AL7 .30 DD10
Holt Cl, N10 .120 DG56
SE28 .146 EV73
Borehamwood (Elstree)
WD6 .78 CM42
Chigwell IG7 .103 ET50
Holt Ct, E15 off Clays La .123 EC64
Holton St, E1 .12 G3
Holt Rd, E16 .144 EL74
Romford RM3 .106 FL52
Wembley HA0 .117 CH62
Holtsmere Cl, Wat. WD25 .76 BW35
Sch Holtsmere End Inf Sch,
Hem.H. HP2
off Shenley Rd .41 BP15
HOLTSPUR, Beac. HP9 .88 AF54
Holtspur Av, H.Wyc.
(Woob.Grn) HP10 .110 AE56
Holtspur Cl, Beac. HP9 .88 AG54
Holtspur La, H.Wyc.
(Woob.Grn) HP10 .110 AE57
Sch Holtspur Sch, Beac.
HP9 off Cherry Tree Rd .88 AG54
Holtspur Top La, Beac. HP9 .88 AG54
Holtspur Way, Beac. HP9 .88 AG54
Holt Way, Chig. IG7 .103 ET50
Holtwhite Av, Enf. EN2 .82 DQ40
Holtwhites Hill, Enf. EN2 .81 DP39
Holtwood Rd, Lthd. (Oxshott)
KT22 .214 CC113
Holwell Caravan Site, Hat.
AL9 .30 DE14
Holwell Hyde, Welw.G.C.
AL7 .30 DC11
Holwell Hyde La, Welw.G.C.
AL7 .30 DC12
Holwell La, Hat. AL9 .30 DE14
Holwell Pl, Pnr. HA5 .116 BY56
Sch Holwell Prim Sch,
Welw.G.C. AL7
off Holwell Rd .29 CZ10
Holwell Rd, Welw.G.C. AL7 .29 CY10
Holwood Cl, Walt. KT12 .196 BW103
Holwood Pk Av, Orp. BR6 .223 EM105
Holwood Pl, SW4 .161 DK84
Holy Acre, Harl. (Roydon)
CM19 off Roydon Mill Pk .34 EG14
Holybourne Av, SW15 .179 CU87
Sch Holy Cross Catholic Prim
Sch, S.Ock. RM15
off Daiglen Dr .149 FV72
Sch Holy Cross Conv Sch,
Ger.Cr. SL9 off Gold Hill E .90 AX53
Holy Cross Hill, Brox. EN10 .48 DU24
Sch Holy Cross Prep Sch,
Kings.T. KT2
off George Rd .178 CQ94
Sch Holy Cross RC Prim Sch,
SE6 off Culverley Rd .183 EB88
SW6 off Basuto Rd .160 DA81
Sch Holy Cross RC Sch for Girls,
N.Mal. KT3 off Sandal Rd .198 CS99
Sch Holy Cross RC (VA) Prim
Sch, Harl. CM18
off Tracyes Rd .52 EU17
Sch Holy Family Coll, E17
off Shernhall St .123 EC55
Wiseman Ho Site, E17
off Shernhall St .123 EC56
Sch Holy Family RC Prim Sch,
E14 .14 A9
SE3 off Tudway Rd .164 EJ84
Slough SL3 off High St .153 AZ78
Welwyn Garden City AL7
off Crookhams .30 DA06
Sch Holy Family RC Prim Sch,
The, Add. KT15
off Ongar Hill .212 BG106
HOLYFIELD, Wal.Abb. EN9 .67 ED28
Holyfield Rd, Wal.Abb. EN9 .67 EC29
Sch Holy Ghost & St. Stephen
RC Prim Sch, The, W12
off Rylett Rd .159 CT75
Sch Holy Ghost RC Prim Sch,
SW12 off Nightingale Sq .180 DG87
Holyhead Cl, E3 .13 P2
E6 off Valiant Way .145 EM71
Holyhead Ms, Slou. SL1
off Bath Rd .131 AL73
Sch Holy Innocents Prim Sch,
Orp. BR6 off Mitchell Rd .205 ET104
Holyoake Av, Wok. GU21 .226 AW117
Holyoake Ct, SE16 .23 K3
Holyoake Cres, Wok. GU21 .226 AW117
Holyoake Ter, Sev. TN13 .256 FG124
Holyoake Wk, N2 .120 DC55
W5 .137 CJ70
Holyoak Rd, SE11 .20 E7
HOLYPORT, Maid. SL6 .150 AC78
Holyport Rd, SW6 .159 CW80
Holyrood Av, Har. HA2 .116 BY63
Holyrood Cres, St.Alb. AL1 .43 CD24
Holyrood Gdns, Edg. HA8 .118 CP55
Grays RM16 .171 GJ77
Holyrood Ms, E16 .25 M1
Sch Holy Rood RC Inf Sch,
Wat. WD17
off Greenbank Rd .75 BR36
Sch Holy Rood RC Jun Sch, Wat.
WD17 off Greenbank Rd .75 BR36
Holyrood Rd, Barn. EN5 .80 DC44
Holyrood St, SE1 .21 L2
Sch Holy Trinity C of E JMI Sch,
E8 .5 N4
Sch Holy Trinity C of E Jun Sch,
Wall. SM6 off Bute Rd .219 DJ105
Sch Holy Trinity C of E Prim Sch,
N2 off Market Pl .120 DD55
SE23 off Dartmouth Rd .182 DW89
Jun, SW1 .18 E7
SW2 off Upper Tulse Hill .181 DM87
Inf, SW3 .18 D7
SW19 off Effra Rd .180 DB93
Dartford DA1
off Chatsworth Rd .188 FJ85
Gravesend DA12
off Trinity Rd .191 GJ87
Northwood HA6
off Rickmansworth Rd .93 BQ51
Richmond TW10
off Carrington Rd .158 CN84
Sidcup DA15
off Burnt Oak La .186 EU88
Sch Holy Trinity Coll, Brom.
BR1 off Plaistow La .184 EJ94
Sch Holy Trinity Coll Prep Sch,
Brom. BR1
off Plaistow La .204 EJ95
Sch Holy Trinity Haverstock Hill
C of E Prim Sch, NW1
off Hartland Rd .141 DH66
Sch Holy Trinity Prim Sch,
NW3 off Trinity Wk .140 DC65
Waltham Cross EN8
off Longlands Cl .67 DX32
Sch Holy Trinity Sch, Guil.
GU1 off Addison Rd .259 AZ136
Holy Wk, Brox. EN10
off St. Catherines Rd .49 EA19
Hoddesdon EN11
off High St .49 EA18
HOLYWELL, Wat. WD18 .75 BS44
Holywell Cl, SE3 .164 EG79
SE16 .22 D9
Orpington BR6 .224 EU105
Staines TW19 .174 BL88
Holywell Hill, St.Alb. AL1 .42 CC21
Holywell Ind Est, Wat. WD18 .75 BR44
Sch Holywell JM & Inf Sch,
Wat. WD18 off Tolpits La .75 BT44
Holywell La, EC2 .11 M3
Holywell Rd, Wat. WD18 .75 BU43
Holywell Row, EC2 .11 L4
Holywell Way, Stai. TW19 .174 BL88
Home Barn Ct, Lthd. (Eff.)
KT24 off The Street .246 BX127
Home Cl, Brox. EN10 .49 DZ24
Carshalton SM5 .200 DF103
Harlow CM20 .51 ET15
Leatherhead (Fetch.)
KT22 .231 CD121
Northolt UB5 .136 BZ69
Virginia Water GU25 .192 AX100
Home Ct, Felt. TW13 .175 BU88
Homecroft Gdns, Loug. IG10 .85 EP42
Homecroft Rd, N22 .100 DQ53
SE26 .182 DW92
Homedean Rd, Sev.
(Chipstead) TN13 .256 FC122
Home Fm, Orp. BR6 .224 EZ106
Home Fm Cl, Bet. RH3 .264 CS135
Chertsey (Ott.) KT16 .211 BA108
Esher KT10 .214 CB107
Shepperton TW17 .195 BS98
Tadworth KT20 .233 CX117
Thames Ditton KT7 .197 CF101
Home Fm Gdns, Walt. KT12 .196 BW103
Home Fm Ind Est, Ware
(Stans.Abb.) SG12 .34 EF10
Homefarm Rd, W7 .137 CE72
Home Fm Rd, Rick. WD3 .92 BN49
Home Fm Way, Slou.
(Stoke P.) SL3 .132 AW67
Home Fld, Berk. (Pott.End)
HP4 .39 BB16
Homefield, Hem.H. (Bov.)
HP3 .57 BB28
Waltham Abbey EN9 .68 EG32
Walton-on-Thames KT12 .214 BX105
Homefield Av, Ilf. IG2 .125 ES57
Homefield Cl, NW10 .138 CQ65
Addlestone (Wdhm) KT15 .211 BE112
Epping CM16 .70 EU30
Hayes UB4 .136 BW70
Horley RH6
off Tanyard Way .269 DH147
Leatherhead KT22 .231 CJ121
Orpington BR5 .206 EV98
Swanley BR8 .207 FF97
Homefield Fm Rd, Dart.
(Sutt.H.) DA4 .208 FM96
Homefield Gdns, N2 .120 DD55
Mitcham CR4 .200 DC96
Tadworth KT20 .233 CW120
Homefield Ms, Beck. BR3 .203 EA95
Homefield Pk, Sutt. SM1 .218 DB107
Homefield Ri, Orp. BR6 .206 EU102
Homefield Rd, SW19 .179 CX93
W4 .159 CT77
Bromley BR1 .204 EJ95
Bushey WD23 .76 CA43
Coulsdon CR5 .235 DP119
Edgware HA8 .96 CR51
Hemel Hempstead HP2 .40 BN20
Radlett WD7 .77 CF37
Rickmansworth (Chorl.)
WD3 .73 BD42
Sevenoaks TN13 .256 FE122
Walton-on-Thames KT12 .196 BY101
Ware SG12 .33 DY05
Warlingham CR6 .236 DW119
Wembley HA0 .117 CG63
Sch Homefield Sch, Sutt.
SM1 off Western Rd .218 DA106
Homefield St, N1 .5 L10
Home Gdns, Dag. RM10 .127 FC62
Dartford DA1 .188 FL86
Home Hill, Swan. BR8 .187 FF94
Homeland Dr, Sutt. SM2 .218 DB109
Homelands, Lthd. KT22 .231 CJ121
Homelands Dr, SE19 .182 DS94
Home Lea, Orp. BR6 .223 ET106
Homeleigh Ct, Wal.Cr. EN8 .66 DV29
Homeleigh Rd, SE15 .183 DX85
Home Ley, Welw.G.C. AL7 .29 CY10
Homemead, SW12 .181 DJ89
Gravesend DA12
off Home Mead Cl .191 GH87
Home Mead, Stan. HA7 .95 CJ53
Home Mead Cl, Grav. DA12 .191 GH87
Home Meadow, Bans. SM7 .234 DA116
Slough (Farn.Royal) SL2 .131 AQ68
Welwyn Garden City AL7 .29 CZ09
Homemead Rd, Brom. BR2 .205 EM99
Croydon CR0 .201 DJ100
★ Home Office, SW1 .19 L4
Home Orchard, Dart. DA1 .188 FL86
Home Pk, Oxt. RH8 .254 EG131
Home Pk Mill Link Rd,
Kings L. WD4 .59 BP31
Home Pk Rd, SW19 .180 DA90
Home Pk Wk, Kings.T. KT1 .197 CK98
Homer Cl, Bexh. DA7 .167 FC81
Homer Dr, E14 .23 N7
Homerfield, Welw.G.C. AL8 .29 CW08
Sch Homer First Sch, Wind.
SL4 off Testwood Rd .151 AK81
Home Rd, SW11 .160 DE82
Homer Rd, E9 .143 DY65
Croydon CR0 .203 DX100
Homer Row, W1 .8 B6
Homersham Rd, Kings.T.
KT1 .198 CN96
Homers Rd, Wind. SL4 .151 AK81
Homer St, W1 .8 B6
Homerswood La, Welw. AL6 .29 CU05
Sch Homerswood Prim Sch,
Welw.G.C. AL8
off Kirklands .29 CX05
HOMERTON, E9 .123 DY64
⇌ Homerton .143 DX65
Sch Homerton Coll of Tech,
E9 off Homerton Row .122 DW64
Homerton Gro, E9 .123 DX64
Homerton High St, E9 .122 DW64
H Homerton Hosp, E9 .123 DX64
Homerton Rd, E9 .123 DY64
Homerton Row, E9 .122 DW64
Homerton Ter, E9
off Morning La .142 DW65
Homesdale Cl, E11 .124 EG57
Homesdale Rd, Brom. BR1,
BR2 .204 EJ98
Caterham CR3 .236 DR123
Orpington BR5 .205 ES101
Homesfield, NW11 .120 DA57
Homestall Rd, SE22 .182 DW85
Homestead, The, N11 .99 DH49
Dartford DA1 .188 FJ86
Homestead Cl, St.Alb.
(Park St) AL2 .60 CC27
Homestead Ct, Welw.G.C.
AL7 .29 CZ11
Homestead Gdns, Esher
(Clay.) KT10 .215 CE106
Homestead La, Welw.G.C.
AL7 .29 CZ12
Homestead Paddock, N14 .81 DH43
Homestead Pk, NW2 .119 CT62
Homestead Rd, SW6 .159 CZ80
Caterham CR3 .236 DR123
Dagenham RM8 .126 EZ61
Hatfield AL10 .45 CU15
Orpington BR6 .224 EV108
Rickmansworth WD3
off Park Rd .92 BK45
Staines TW18 .174 BH93
Homesteads, The, Ware
SG12 off Hunsdon Rd .34 EK07
Homestead Way, Croy.
(New Adgtn) CR0 .221 EC111
Homewaters Av, Sun. TW16 .195 BT95
Home Way, Rick. (Mill End)
WD3 .91 BF46
Homeway, Rom. RM3 .106 FP51
Homewillow Cl, N21 .81 DP44
Homewood, Slou. (Geo.Grn)
SL3 .132 AX72
Homewood Av, Pot.B.
(Cuffley) EN6 .65 DL27
Homewood Cl, Hmptn.
TW12 off Fearnley Cres .176 BZ93
Homewood Cres, Chis. BR7 .185 ES93
Sch Homewood Indep Sch,
St.Alb. AL2 off Hazel Rd .60 CB28
Homewood La, Pot.B. EN6 .65 DJ27
Homewood Rd, St.Alb. AL1 .43 CH17
Homildon Ho, SE26
off Sydenham Hill .182 DU90
Honduras St, EC1 .10 G3
Honeybourne Rd, NW6 .120 DB64
Honeybourne Way, Orp.
BR5 .205 ER102
Honey Brook, Wal.Abb. EN9 .68 EE33
Honeybrook Rd, SW12 .181 DJ87
Honey Cl, Dag. RM10 .147 FB65
Honeycrock La, Red. RH1 .266 DG141
Honeycroft, Loug. IG10 .85 EN42
Welwyn Garden City AL8 .29 CW10
Honeycroft Dr, St.Alb. AL4 .43 CJ22
Honeycroft Hill, Uxb. UB10 .134 BL66
Honeycross Rd, Hem.H. HP1 .39 BE21
Honeyden Rd, Sid. DA14 .186 EY93
Honey Hill, Uxb. UB10 .134 BM66
Honey La, EC2 .11 H8
Hertford SG14 off Fore St .32 DR09
Waltham Abbey EN9 .84 EG35
Honeyman Cl, NW6 .139 CX66
Honeymeade, Saw. CM21 .36 EW08
Honeypot Cl, NW9 .118 CM56
Honeypot La, NW9 .118 CM55
Brentwood CM14 .108 FU48
Stanmore HA7 .118 CM55
Honeypots Rd, Wok. GU22 .226 AX122
Honeysett Rd, N17
off Reform Row .100 DT54
Honeysuckle Bottom, Lthd.
(E.Hors.) KT24 .245 BS134
Honeysuckle Cl, Brwd.
(Pilg.Hat.) CM15 .108 FV43
Hertford SG13 .32 DU09
Horley RH6 off Briars Wd .269 DJ147
Iver SL0 .133 BC72
Romford RM3 .106 FK51
Southall UB1 .136 BY73
Honeysuckle Fld, Chesh.
HP5 .54 AQ30
Honeysuckle Gdns, Croy.
CR0 off Primrose La .203 DX102
Hatfield AL10 .45 CV19
Honeysuckle La, Dor.
(N.Holm.) RH5
off Treelands .263 CJ139
Sch Honeywell Inf Sch,
SW11 off Honeywell Rd .180 DF86
Sch Honeywell Jun Sch,
SW11 off Honeywell Rd .180 DF86
Honeywell Rd, SW11 .180 DF86
Honeywood Cl, Pot.B. EN6 .64 DE33
Honeywood Rd, NW10 .139 CT68
Isleworth TW7 .157 CG84
Honeywood Wk, Cars. SM5 .218 DF105
Sch Honilands Prim Sch,
Enf. EN1 off Lovell Rd .82 DV36
Honister Cl, Stan. HA7 .95 CH53
Honister Gdns, Stan. HA7 .95 CH52
Honister Hts, Pur. CR8 .220 DR114
Honister Pl, Stan. HA7 .95 CH53
Honiton Gdns, NW7 .97 CX52
Honiton Ho, Enf. EN3
off Exeter Rd .83 DX41
Honiton Rd, NW6 .139 CZ68
Romford RM7 .127 FD58
Welling DA16 .165 ET82
Honley Rd, SE6 .183 EB87
Honnor Gdns, Islw. TW7 .157 CD82
Honnor Rd, Stai. TW18 .174 BK94
HONOR OAK, SE23 .182 DW86
HONOR OAK PARK, SE4 .183 DY86
⇌ Honor Oak Park .183 DX86
Honor Oak Pk, SE23 .182 DW86
Honor Oak Ri, SE23 .182 DW86
Honor Oak Rd, SE23 .182 DW88
Hoo, The, Harl. CM17 .36 EW10
Hood Av, N14 .81 DH44
SW14 .178 CQ85
Orpington BR5 .206 EV99
Hood Cl, Croy. CR0
off Parson's Mead .201 DP102
Hoodcote Gdns, N21 .99 DP45
Hood Ct, EC4 .10 D8
Hood Rd, SW20 .179 CT94
Rainham RM13 .147 FE67
Hood Wk, Rom. RM7 .105 FB53
HOOK, Chess. KT9 .216 CL105
Hook, The, Barn. EN5 .80 DD44
Hooke Rd, Lthd. (E.Hors.)
KT24 .245 BT125
Hookers Rd, E17 .123 DX55
Hook Fm Rd, Brom. BR2 .204 EK99
Hookfield, Epsom KT19 .216 CQ113
Harlow CM18 .51 ET17
Hookfields, Grav. (Nthflt)
DA11 .190 GE90
Hook Gate, Enf. EN1 .82 DV36
HOOK GREEN, Dart. DA2 .187 FG91
HOOK GREEN, Grav. DA13 .190 FZ93
Hook Grn La, Dart. DA2 .187 FF90
Hook Grn Rd, Grav. (Sthflt)
DA13 .190 FY94
HOOK HEATH, Wok. GU22 .226 AV120
Hook Heath Av, Wok. GU22 .226 AV119
Hook Heath Gdns, Wok.
GU22 .226 AT121
Hook Heath Rd, Wok. GU22 .226 AW121
Hook Hill, S.Croy. CR2 .220 DS110
Hook Hill La, Wok. GU22 .226 AV121
Hook Hill Pk, Wok. GU22 .226 AV121
Hooking Grn, Har. HA2 .116 CB57
Hook La, Guil. (Shere) GU5 .260 BN141
Potters Bar EN6 .64 DF32
Romford RM4 .86 EZ44
Welling DA16 .185 ET85
Sch Hook La Prim Sch, Well.
DA16 off Faraday Rd .166 EU83
Hook Ri N, Surb. KT6 .198 CN104
Hook Ri S, Surb. KT6 .198 CN104
Hook Ri S Ind Pk, Surb. KT6 .198 CN104
Hook Rd, Chess. KT9 .215 CK106
Epsom KT19 .216 CR111
Surbiton KT6 .198 CL104
Hooks Cl, SE15
off Woods Rd .162 DV81
Hooks Hall Dr, Dag. RM10 .127 FC62
Hookstone Way, Wdf.Grn.
IG8 .102 EK52
Hooks Way, SE22
off Dulwich Common .182 DU88
Hook Wk, Edg. HA8 .96 CQ51
HOOKWOOD, Horl. RH6 .268 DC150
Hookwood Cor, Oxt. RH8
off Hookwood La .254 EH128
Hookwood La, Oxt. RH8 .254 EH128
Hookwood Rd, Orp. BR6 .224 EW111
HOOLEY, Couls. CR5 .234 DG122
Hooley La, Red. RH1 .266 DF135
Hooper Dr, Uxb. UB8 .135 BP71
Hooper Rd, E16 .15 M8
Hooper's Ct, SW3 .18 C4
Hooper's Ms, Bushey WD23 .94 CB46
Hooper St, E1 .12 A9
Hoopers Yd, Sev. TN13 .257 FJ126
Hoop La, NW11 .119 CZ59
Hope Cl, N1 .5 H3
SE12 .184 EH90
Brentford TW8
off Burford Rd .158 CL78
Romford (Chad.Hth) RM6 .126 EW56
Sutton SM1 .218 DC106
Woodford Green IG8
off West Gro .102 EJ51
Hopedale Rd, SE7 .164 EH79
Hopefield Av, NW6 .139 CY68
Hope Grn, Wat. WD25 .59 BU33
Hope Pk, Brom. BR1 .184 EF94
Hope Rd, Swans. DA10 .190 FZ86
Hopes Cl, Houns. TW5
off Old Cote Dr .156 CA79
Hope St, SW11 .160 DD83
Hope Ter, Grays RM20 .169 FX78
Hopetown St, E1 .11 P6
Hopewell Cl, Grays
(Chaff.Hun.) RM16 .169 FX78
Hopewell Dr, Grav. DA12 .191 GM92
Hopewell St, SE5 .162 DR80
Hopewell Yd, SE5
off Hopewell St .162 DR80
Hope Wf, SE16
off St. Marychurch St .162 DW75
Hopfield, Wok. (Horsell)
GU21 .226 AY116
Hopfield Av, W.Byf. (Byfleet)
KT14 .212 BL112
Hopgarden La, Sev. TN13 .256 FG128
Hop Gdns, WC2 .9 N10
Hop Gdn Way, Wat. WD25 .60 BW31

Hopgood St, W12
off Macfarlane Rd 139 CW74
Hopground Cl, St.Alb. AL1 43 CG22
Hopkin Cl, Guil. GU2
off Grange Rd 242 AV130
Hopkins Cl, N10 98 DG52
Romford RM2 128 FJ55
Hopkins Ms,
E15 off West Rd 144 EF67
Hopkinsons Pl, NW1
off Fitzroy Rd 140 DG67
Hopkins St, W1 9 K8
Hoppers Rd, N13 99 DN47
N21 99 DN47
Hoppett Rd, E4 102 EE48
Hoppety, The, Tad. KT20 233 CX122
Hopping La, N1 4 F4
Hoppingwood Av, N.Mal.
KT3 198 CS97
Hoppit Rd, Wal.Abb. EN9 67 EB32
Hoppner Rd, Hayes UB4 135 BQ68
Hop St, SE10 25 K7
Hopton Ct, Guil. GU2
off Park Barn Dr 242 AS134
Hopton Gdns, SE1 20 F1
New Malden KT3 199 CU100
Hopton Rd, SW16 181 DL92
Hopton St, SE1 20 F1
Hoptree Cl, N12
off Woodside Pk Rd 98 DB49
Hopwood Cl, SW17 180 DC90
Watford WD17 75 BR36
Hopwood Rd, SE17 162 DR79
Hopwood Wk, E8
off Wilman Gro 142 DU66
Horace Av, Rom. RM7 127 FC60
Horace Rd, E7 124 EH63
Ilford IG6 125 EQ55
Kingston upon Thames
KT1 198 CM97
Horatio Ct, SE16
off Rotherhithe St 142 DW74
Horatio Pl, E14 24 D3
SW19 off Kingston Rd 180 DA94
Horatio St, E2 142 DT68
Horatius Way, Croy. CR0 219 DM106
Horbury Cres, W11 6 G10
Horbury Ms, W11 6 F10
Horder Rd, SW6 159 CY81
Hordle Gdns, St.Alb. AL1 43 CF22
Hordle Prom E, SE15
off Daniel Gdns 162 DT80
Hordle Prom N, SE15
off Blakes Rd 162 DT80
Hordle Prom S, SE15
off Blakes Rd 162 DT80
Hordle Prom W, SE15
off Blakes Rd 162 DS80
Sch **Horizon Spec Sch**, N16
off Wordsworth Rd 122 DS63
Horizon Way, SE7 25 P8
Horksley Gdns, Brwd. (Hutt.)
CM13 off Bannister Dr 109 GC44
Horle Wk, SE5 161 DP82
HORLEY, RH6 268 DG148
⇌ **Horley** 269 DH149
Coll **Horley Adult Ed Cen**, Horl.
RH6 off Court Lo Rd 268 DE148
Horley Cl, Bexh. DA6 186 FA85
Sch **Horley Inf Sch**, Horl.
RH6 off Lumley Rd 268 DG148
Horley Lo La, Red. RH1 266 DF143
Horley Rd, SE9 184 EL91
Redhill RH1 266 DF136
Horley Row, Horl. RH6 268 DF147
Hormead Rd, W9 6 E4
Hornbeam Av, Upmin.
RM14 128 FN63
Hornbeam Chase, S.Ock.
RM15 149 FX69
Hornbeam Cl, NW7 97 CT48
SE11 20 C7
Borehamwood WD6 78 CN39
Brentwood CM13 109 GB48
Buckhurst Hill IG9
off Hornbeam Rd 102 EK48
Epping (They.B.) CM16 85 ES37
Hertford SG14 31 DP08
Ilford IG1 125 ER64
Northolt UB5 116 BZ64
Hornbeam Cres, Brent. TW8 157 CH80
Hornbeam Gdns, Slou. SL1
off Upton Rd 152 AU76
Hornbeam Gro, E4 102 EE48
Hornbeam La, E4 84 EE43
Bexleyheath DA7 167 FC82
Hatfield (Essen.) AL9 46 DE22
Hornbeam Rd, Buck.H. IG9 102 EK48
Epping (They.B.) CM16 85 ER37
Guildford GU1 242 AW131
Hayes UB4 136 BW71
Reigate RH2 266 DB137
Hornbeams, St.Alb.
(Brick.Wd) AL2 60 BZ30
Hornbeams, The, Harl. CM20 35 EQ13
Hornbeams Av, Enf. EN1 82 DW35
Hornbeam Sq, E3
off Hawthorn Av 143 DZ67
Hornbeams Ri, N11 98 DG51
Hornbeam Ter, Cars. SM5 200 DE102
Hornbeam Wk, Rich. TW10 178 CM90
Walton-on-Thames
(Whiteley Vill.) KT12
off Octagon Rd 213 BT109
Hornbeam Way, Brom. BR2 205 EN100
Waltham Cross EN7 66 DT29
Hornbill Cl, Uxb. UB8 134 BK72
Hornblower Cl, SE16 23 J7
Hornbuckle Cl, Har. HA2 117 CD61
Hornby Cl, NW3 140 DD66
Horncastle Cl, SE12 184 EG87
Horncastle Rd, SE12 184 EG87
HORNCHURCH, RM11 &
RM12 128 FJ61
⊖ **Hornchurch** 128 FK62
Hornchurch Cl, Kings.T. KT2 177 CK91
Hornchurch Hill, Whyt. CR3 236 DT117
Hornchurch Rd, Horn. RM11,
RM12 127 FG60
Horndean Cl, SW15
off Bessborough Rd 179 CU88
Horndon Cl, Rom. RM5 105 FC53
Horndon Grn, Rom. RM5 105 FC53
Horndon Rd, Rom. RM5 105 FC53
Horner La, Mitch. CR4 200 DD96
Horne Rd, Shep. TW17 194 BN98
Hornets, The, Wat. WD18 75 BV42
Horne Way, SW15 159 CW82
Hornfair Rd, SE7 164 EJ79
Hornford Way, Rom. RM7 127 FE59
Hornhatch, Guil. (Chilw.)
GU4 259 BB140
Hornhatch Cl, Guil. (Chilw.)
GU4 259 BB140
Hornhatch La, Guil. GU4 259 BA140
Hornhill Rd, Ger.Cr. SL9 91 BB50
Rickmansworth (Map.Cr.)
WD3 91 BD50
Horniman Dr, SE23 182 DV88
★ **Horniman Mus**, SE23 182 DV88
Sch **Horniman Prim Sch**,
SE23 off Horniman Dr 182 DV88
Horning Cl, SE9 184 EL91
Horn La, SE10 25 L8
W3 138 CQ73
Woodford Green IG8 102 EG51
Horn Link Way, SE10 25 L7
Hornminster Glen, Horn.
RM11 128 FN61
Horn Pk Cl, SE12 184 EH85
Horn Pk La, SE12 184 EH85
Sch **Horn Pk Prim Sch**,
SE12 off Alnwick Rd 184 EH87
Sch **Hornsby Ho Sch**,
SW12 off Hearnville Rd 180 DG88
Hornsby La, Grays (Orsett)
RM16 171 GG75
Horns Cl, Hert. SG13 32 DQ11
Horns Cft Cl, Bark. IG11
off Thornhill Gdns 145 ES66
Horns End Pl, Pnr. HA5 116 BW56
HORNSEY, N8 121 DM55
⇌ **Hornsey** 121 DM56
Hornsey La, N6 121 DH60
N19 121 DJ60
Hornsey La Est, N19
off Hornsey La 121 DK59
Hornsey La Gdns, N6 121 DJ59
Hornsey Pk Rd, N8 121 DM55
Hornsey Ri, N19 121 DK59
Hornsey Ri Gdns, N19 121 DK59
Hornsey Rd, N7 121 DM61
N19 121 DL60
Sch **Hornsey Sch for Girls**,
N8 off Inderwick Rd 121 DM57
Hornsey St, N7 4 B1
Hornsfield, Welw.G.C. AL7 30 DC08
HORNS GREEN, Sev.TN14 239 ES117
Hornshay St, SE15 162 DW79
Horns Mill Rd, Hert. SG13 32 DQ12
Horns Rd, Hert. SG13 32 DQ10
Ilford IG2, IG6 125 EQ57
Hornton Pl, W8 17 J4
Hornton St, W8 17 H3
Horsa Gdns, Hat. AL10
off Mosquito Way 44 CS16
Horsa Rd, SE12 184 EJ87
Erith DA8 167 FC80
Horse & Dolphin Yd, W1 9 M9
Horsebridge Cl, Dag. RM9 146 EY67
Horsecroft, Bans. SM7
off Lyme Regis Rd 233 CZ117
Horsecroft Cl, Orp. BR6 206 EV102
Horsecroft Pl, Harl. CM19 50 EL16
Horsecroft Rd, Edg. HA8 96 CR52
Harlow CM19 50 EL16
Hemel Hempstead HP1 40 BG22
Horse Fair, Kings.T. KT1 197 CK96
Horseferry Pl, SE10 163 EC79
Horseferry Rd, E14 13 J9
SW1 19 L6
Horse Guards Av, SW1 19 N2
★ **Horse Guards Par**, SW1 19 M2
Horse Guards Rd, SW1 19 M2
Horse Hill, Chesh. HP5 56 AX32
Horsehill, Horl. RH6 268 DA146
Horse Leaze, E6 145 EN72
Horselers, Hem.H. HP3 40 BN23
HORSELL, Wok. GU21 226 AY116
Horsell Birch, Wok. GU21 226 AV115
Sch **Horsell C of E Jun Sch**,
Wok. GU21
off Meadway Dr 226 AW116
Horsell Common, Wok.
GU21 210 AX114
Horsell Common Rd, Wok.
GU21 210 AW114
Horsell Ct, Cher. KT16
off Stepgates 194 BH101
Horsell Moor, Wok. GU21 226 AX117
Horsell Pk, Wok. GU21 226 AX116
Horsell Pk Cl, Wok. GU21 226 AX116
Horsell Ri, Wok. GU21 226 AX115
Horsell Ri Cl, Wok. GU21 226 AX115
Horsell Rd, N5 4 C2
Orpington BR5 206 EV95
Horsell Vale, Wok. GU21 226 AY115
Sch **Horsell Village Sch, The**,
Wok. GU21
off Church Hill 226 AX116
Horsell Way, Wok. GU21 226 AW116
Horselydown La, SE1 21 N3
Horseman Side, Brwd.
(Nave.S.) CM14 105 FH45
Horsemans Ride, St.Alb. AL2 60 CA26
Horsemongers Ms, SE1 21 H4
Horsemoor Cl, Slou. SL3
off Parlaunt Rd 153 BA77
Horsenden Av, Grnf. UB6 117 CE64
Horsenden Cres, Grnf. UB6 117 CF64
Horsenden La N, Grnf. UB6 137 CF65
Horsenden La S, Grnf. UB6 137 CG67
Sch **Horsenden Prim Sch**, Grnf.
UB6 off Horsenden La N 137 CE65
Horse Ride, SW1 19 K2
Dorking RH5 263 CD144
Leatherhead KT24 245 BR130
Tadworth KT20 249 CY125
Horse Rd, E7 off Centre Rd 124 EH62
Horseshoe, The, Bans. SM7 233 CZ115
Coulsdon CR5 219 DK113
Hemel Hempstead HP3 41 BQ22
Horseshoe Business Pk, St.Alb.
(Brick.Wd) AL2 60 CA30
Horseshoe Cl, E14 24 C9
NW2 119 CV61
Waltham Abbey EN9 68 EG34
Horse Shoe Ct, EC1
off St. John St 141 DP70
Horseshoe Cres, Beac. HP9 89 AL54
Horse Shoe Cres, Nthlt.
UB5 136 CA68
Horseshoe Dr, Uxb. UB8 134 BN72
Horse Shoe Grn, Sutt. SM1
off Aultone Way 200 DB103
Horseshoe Hill, Slou. (Burn.)
SL1 110 AJ63
Waltham Abbey EN9 68 EJ33
Horseshoe La, N20 97 CX46
Enfield EN2
off Chase Side 82 DQ41
Watford WD25 59 BV32
Horseshoe La E, Guil. GU1 243 BB133
Horseshoe La W, Guil. GU1 243 BB133
Horseshoe Ridge, Wey.
KT13 213 BQ111
Horse Yd, N1 4 F7
Horsfeld Gdns, SE9 184 EL85
Horsfeld Rd, SE9 184 EK85
Horsfield Cl, Dart. DA2 188 FQ87
Horsford Rd, SW2 181 DM85
Horsham Av, N12 98 DE50
Horsham Rd, Bexh. DA6 186 FA85
Dorking RH4 263 CG137
Dorking (N.Holm.) RH5 263 CH140
Dorking (Sutt.Abin.) RH5 261 BT142
Feltham TW14 175 BQ86
Guildford GU4, GU5 258 AY142
Horshams, Harl. CM19
off Little Gro Fld 51 EQ15
⇌ **Horsley** 245 BS125
Horsley Cl, Epsom KT19 216 CR113
Horsleydown Old Stairs,
SE1 21 N2
Horsley Dr, Croy.
(New Adgtn) CR0 221 EC108
Kingston upon Thames
KT2 177 CK92
Horsley Rd, E4 101 EC47
Bromley BR1
off Palace Rd 204 EH95
Cobham KT11 229 BV119
Horsleys, Rick. (Map.Cr.)
WD3 91 BD50
Horsley St, SE17 162 DR79
Horsmonden Cl, Orp. BR6 205 ES101
Horsmonden Rd, SE4 183 DZ85
Hortensia Rd, SW10 160 DC80
Horticultural Pl, W4
off Heathfield Ter 158 CR78
Coll **Horticultural Training Cen**,
N4 off Green Las 121 DP59
HORTON, Epsom KT19 216 CP110
HORTON, Slou. SL3 153 BA83
Horton Av, NW2 119 CY63
Horton Br Rd, West Dr. UB7 134 BM74
Horton Cl, Maid. SL6 130 AC70
West Drayton UB7 134 BM74
★ **Horton Country Pk**,
Epsom KT19 216 CM110
Horton Footpath, Epsom
KT19 216 CQ111
Horton Gdns, Epsom KT19 216 CQ111
Horton Hill, Epsom KT19 216 CQ111
Horton Ind Pk, West Dr. UB7 134 BM74
HORTON KIRBY, Dart. DA4 209 FR98
Sch **Horton Kirby C of E Prim
Sch**, Dart. DA4
off Horton Rd 208 FQ97
Horton La, Epsom KT19 216 CP110
★ **Horton Park Children's Fm**,
Epsom KT19 216 CN110
Horton Rd, E8 142 DV65
Dartford (Hort.Kir.) DA4 208 FQ97
Slough (Colnbr.) SL3 153 BA81
Slough (Datchet) SL3 152 AV80
Slough (Poyle) SL3 153 BE83
Staines TW19 174 BG85
West Drayton UB7 134 BN74
Horton St, SE13 163 EB83
Hortons Way, West. TN16 255 ER126
Horton Way, Croy. CR0 203 DX99
Dartford (Fnghm) DA4 208 FM101
Hortus Rd, E4 101 EC47
Southall UB2 156 BZ75
Horvath Cl, Wey. KT13 213 BR105
Horwood Cl, Rick. WD3
off Thellusson Way 92 BG45
Horwood Ct, Wat. WD24 76 BX37
Hosack Rd, SW17 180 DF89
Hoser Av, SE12 184 EG89
Hosey Common La, West.
TN16 255 ES130
Hosey Common Rd, Eden.
TN8 255 EQ133
Westerham TN16 255 ER130
HOSEY HILL, West. TN16 255 ES127
Hosey Hill, West. TN16 255 ER127
Hosier La, EC1 10 E6
Hoskins Cl, E16 144 EJ72
Hayes UB3
off Cranford Dr 155 BT78
Hoskins Rd, Oxt. RH8 254 EE129
Hoskins St, SE10 24 F10
Hoskins Wk, Oxt. RH8 254 EE129
Hospital Br Rd, Twick. TW2 176 CB87
Hospital Hill, Chesh. HP5 54 AQ32
H **Hospital of St. John &
St. Elizabeth**, NW8 140 DD68
Hospital Rd, E9
off Homerton Row 123 DX64
Hounslow TW3 156 CA83
Sevenoaks TN13 257 FJ121
Hotham Cl, Dart. (Sutt.H.)
DA4 188 FP94
Swanley BR8 207 FH95
West Molesey KT8
off Garrick Gdns 196 CA97
Sch **Hotham Prim Sch**,
SW15 off Charlwood Rd 159 CX84
Hotham Rd, SW15 159 CW83
SW19 180 DC94
Hotham Rd Ms, SW19
off Haydons Rd 180 DC94
Hotham St, E15 144 EE67
Hothfield Pl, SE16 22 F6
Hotspur Rd, Nthlt. UB5 136 CA68
Hotspur St, SE11 20 C9
Houblon Rd, Rich. TW10 178 CL85
Houblons Hill, Epp. (Cooper.)
CM16 70 EW31
Houghton Cl, E8 5 P4
Hampton TW12 176 BY93
Houghton Rd, N15
off West Grn Rd 122 DT57
Houghton St, WC2 10 B8
Houlder Cres, Croy. CR0 219 DP107
Hound Ho Rd, Guil. (Shere)
GU5 260 BN141
Houndsden Rd, N21 81 DM44
Houndsditch, EC3 11 M7
Sch **Houndsfield Prim Sch**,
N9 off Ripon Rd 100 DV45
Houndsfield Rd, N9 100 DV45
HOUNSLOW, TW3 - TW6 156 BZ84
⇌ **Hounslow** 176 CB85
Hounslow Av, Houns. TW3 176 CB85
Hounslow Business Pk,
Houns. TW3
off Alice Way 156 CA84
⊖ **Hounslow Central** 156 CA83
⊖ **Hounslow East** 156 CC82
Hounslow Gdns, Houns.
TW3 176 CB85
★ **Hounslow Heath**, Houns.
TW4 176 BY86
Sch **Hounslow Heath Inf &
Nurs Sch**, Houns. TW4
off Martindale Rd 156 BY83
Sch **Hounslow Heath Jun Sch**,
Houns. TW4
off Selwyn Cl 156 BY83
Coll **Hounslow Manor Adult
Ed Cen**, Houns. TW3
off Prince Regent Rd 156 CC83
Sch **Hounslow Manor Sch**,
Houns. TW3
off Prince Regent Rd 156 CC83
Hounslow Rd, Felt. (Feltham)
TW14 175 BV88
Feltham (Han.) TW13 176 BX91
Twickenham TW2 176 CC86
Sch **Hounslow Town Prim Sch**,
Houns. TW3 off Pears Rd 156 CC83
HOUNSLOW WEST, Houns.
TW4 156 BX83
⊖ **Hounslow West** 156 BY82
Housefield Way, St.Alb. AL4 43 CJ23
★ **Household Cavalry Mus
Combermere Barracks**,
Wind. SL4 151 AQ83
House La, St.Alb. (Sand.)
AL4 43 CK16
Houseman Way, SE5
off Hopewell St 162 DR80
★ **Houses of Parliament**,
SW1 19 P4
Housewood End, Hem.H.
HP1 40 BH17
Houston Pl, Esher KT10
off Lime Tree Av 197 CE102
Houston Rd, SE23 183 DY89
Surbiton KT6 197 CH100
Hove Av, E17 123 DZ57
Hove Cl, Brwd. (Hutt.) CM13 109 GC47
Grays RM17 170 GA79
Hoveden Rd, NW2 119 CY64
Hove Gdns, Sutt. SM1 200 DB102
Hoveton Rd, SE28 146 EW72
Hoveton Way, Ilf. IG6 103 EP52
Howard Agne Cl, Hem.H.
(Bov.) HP3 57 BA27
Howard Av, Bex. DA5 186 EW88
Epsom KT17 217 CU110
Slough SL2 131 AR71
Howard Bldg, SW8
off Queenstown Rd 161 DH79
Howard Business Pk, Wal.Abb.
EN9 off Howard Cl 67 ED33
Howard Cen, The, Welw.G.C.
AL8 29 CX09
Howard Cl, N11 98 DG47
NW2 119 CY63
W3 138 CP72
Ashtead KT21 232 CM118
Bushey (Bushey Hth)
WD23 95 CE45
Hampton TW12 176 CC93
Leatherhead KT22 231 CJ123
Leatherhead (W.Hors.)
KT24 245 BR125
Loughton IG10 84 EL44
St. Albans AL1 43 CJ22
Sunbury-on-Thames
TW16 off Catherine Dr 175 BT93
Tadworth KT20 249 CT125
Waltham Abbey EN9 67 ED34
Watford WD24 75 BU37
Howard Ct, Reig. RH2 250 DC133
Howard Cres, Beac.
(Seer Grn) HP9 89 AQ50
Howard Dr, Borwd. WD6 78 CR42
Howard Gdns, Guil. GU1 243 BA133
Howard Ms, N5
off Hamilton Pk 121 DP63
Slough SL3
off Laburnum Gro 153 BB79
Sch **Howard of Effingham Sch**,
Lthd. KT24 off Lower Rd 246 BX127
Howard Pl, Reig. RH2 250 DA132
Sch **Howard Prim Sch**, Croy.
CR0 off Dering Pl 220 DQ105
Howard Ridge, Guil.
(Burpham) GU4 243 BA130
Howard Rd, E6 145 EM68
E11 124 EE62
E17 123 EA55
N15 122 DS58
N16 122 DR63
NW2 119 CX63
SE20 202 DW95
SE25 202 DU99
Barking IG11 145 ER67
Beaconsfield (Seer Grn)
HP9 89 AQ50
Bromley BR1 184 EG94
Chesham HP5 54 AP28
Coulsdon CR5 235 DJ115
Dartford DA1 188 FN86
Dorking RH4 263 CG136
Dorking (N.Holm.) RH5
off Holmesdale Rd 263 CJ140
Grays (Chaff.Hun.) RM16 169 FW76
Ilford IG1 125 EP63
Isleworth TW7 157 CF83
Leatherhead (Bkhm) KT23 246 CB127
Leatherhead (Eff.Junct.)
KT24 229 BU122
New Malden KT3 198 CS97
Reigate RH2 266 DB135
Southall UB1 136 CB72
Surbiton KT5 198 CM100
Upminster RM14 128 FQ61
Howards Cl, Pnr. HA5 93 BV54
Woking GU22 227 BA120
Howards Crest Cl, Beck.
BR3 203 EC96
Howards Dr, Hem.H. HP1 39 BF17
Howardsgate, Welw.G.C.
AL8 29 CX08
Howards La, SW15 179 CV85
Addlestone KT15 211 BE107
Howards Rd, E13 15 L1
Woking GU22 227 AZ120
Howards Thicket, Ger.Cr.
SL9 112 AW61
Howard St, T.Ditt. KT7 197 CH101
Howards Wd Dr, Ger.Cr. SL9 112 AX61
Howard Wk, N2 120 DC56
Howard Way, Barn. EN5 79 CX43
Harlow CM20 52 EU15
Howarth Ct, E15
off Clays La 123 EC64
Howarth Rd, SE2 166 EU78
Howberry Cl, Edg. HA8 95 CK51
Howberry Rd, Edg. HA8 95 CK51
Stanmore HA7 95 CK51
Thornton Heath CR7 202 DR95
Howbury La, Erith DA8 167 FG82
Howbury Rd, SE15 162 DW83
Howcroft Cres, N3 98 DA52
Howcroft La, Grnf. UB6
off Cowgate Rd 137 CD69
Howden Cl, SE28 146 EX73
Howden Rd, SE25 202 DT96
Howden St, SE15 162 DU83
Howe Cl, Rad. (Shenley)
WD7 62 CL32
Romford RM7 104 FA53
Howe Dell, Hat. AL10 45 CV18
Sch **Howe Dell Prim Sch**, Hat.
AL10 off Old Rectory Dr 45 CV18
Howe Dr, Beac. HP9 89 AK50
Caterham CR3 236 DR122
Howell Cl, Rom. RM6 126 EX57
Howell Hill Cl, Epsom KT17 217 CW111
Howell Hill Gro, Epsom
KT17 217 CW110
Howell Wk, SE1 20 F8
Howe Rd, Hem.H. HP3 40 BN22
Howes Cl, N3 120 DA55
Howfield Grn, Hodd. EN11 33 DZ14
Howfield Pl, N17 122 DT55
Howgate Rd, SW14 158 CR83
Howick Pl, SW1 19 K6
Howicks Grn, Welw.G.C. AL7 30 DA12
Howie St, SW11 160 DE80
Howitt Cl, N16 off Allen Rd 122 DS63
NW3 off Howitt Rd 140 DE65
Howitt Rd, NW3 140 DE65
Howitts Cl, Esher KT10 214 CA107
Howland Est, SE16 22 F5
Howland Garth, St.Alb. AL1 42 CC24
Howland Ms E, W1 9 K5
Howlands, Welw.G.C. AL7 30 DB12
Howlands Ho, Welw.G.C.
AL7 off Howlands 30 DA12
Howland St, W1 9 J5
Howland Way, SE16 23 K4
How La, Couls. CR5 234 DG117
Howletts La, Ruis. HA4 115 BQ57
Howletts Rd, SE24 182 DQ86
Howley Pl, W2 7 M5
Howley Rd, Croy. CR0 201 DP104
Hows Cl, Uxb. UB8
off Hows Rd 134 BJ67
Howse Rd, Wal.Abb. EN9
off Deer Pk Way 83 EB35
Howsman Rd, SW13 159 CU79
Hows Mead, Epp. CM16 53 FD24
Howson Rd, SE4 163 DY84
Howson Ter, Rich. TW10 178 CL86
Hows Rd, Uxb. UB8 134 BJ67
Hows St, E2 5 N9
Howton Pl, Bushey
(Bushey Hth) WD23 95 CD46
HOW WOOD, St.Alb. AL2 60 CC27
⇌ **How Wood** 60 CC28
How Wd, St.Alb. (Park St)
AL2 60 CB28
Sch **How Wd Prim Sch**, St.Alb.
AL2 off Spooners Dr 60 CC27
HOXTON, N1 5 L10
Hoxton Mkt, N1 11 L2
Hoxton Sq, N1 11 L2
Hoxton St, N1 11 M2
Hoylake Cl, Slou. SL1 151 AL75
Hoylake Cres, Uxb. (Ickhm)
UB10 114 BN60
Hoylake Gdns, Mitch. CR4 201 DJ97
Romford RM3 106 FN53
Ruislip HA4 115 BV60
Watford WD19 94 BX49
Hoylake Rd, W3 138 CS72
Hoyland Cl, SE15
off Commercial Way 162 DV80
Hoyle Rd, SW17 180 DE92
Hoy St, E16 15 J8
Hoy Ter, Grays RM20 169 FX78
★ **H.Q.S. Wellington, Master
Mariners' Hall**, WC2 10 C9
Hubbard Dr, Chess. KT9 215 CJ107
Hubbard Rd, SE27 182 DQ91
Hubbards Chase, Horn.
RM11 128 FN57
Hubbards Cl, Horn. RM11 128 FN57
Uxbridge UB8 135 BP72
Hubbard's Hall Est, Harl.
CM17 off Churchgate St 36 EY14
Hubbards Rd, Rick. (Chorl.)
WD3 73 BD43
Hubbard St, E15 144 EE67
Hubbinet Ind Est, Rom.
RM7 127 FC55
Hubert Day Cl, Beac. HP9
off Seeleys Rd 89 AK52
Hubert Gro, SW9 161 DL83
Hubert Rd, E6 144 EK69
Brentwood CM14 108 FV48
Rainham RM13 147 FF69
Slough SL3 152 AX76
Hucknall Cl, Rom. RM3 106 FM51
Huddart St, E3 13 M5
Huddleston Cl, E2 142 DW68
Huddlestone Cres, Red.
RH1 251 DK128
Huddlestone Rd, E7 124 EF63
NW2 139 CV65
Huddleston Rd, N7 121 DK63
Hudson Av, Uxb. (Denh.)
UB9 113 BF58
Hudson Cl, St.Alb. AL1 43 CD23
Watford WD24 75 BT36
Hudson Ct, E14
off Maritime Quay 163 EA78
SW19 180 DB94
Guildford GU2
off Cobbett Rd 242 AT133
Hudson Gdns, Orp. BR6
off Superior Dr 223 ET107
Hudson Palce, Slou. SL3
off Ditton Rd 153 AZ78
Hudson Pl, SE18 165 EQ78
Hudson Rd, Bexh. DA7 166 EZ82
Hayes UB3 155 BR79
Hudsons, Tad. KT20 233 CX121
Hudson's Pl, SW1 19 H7
Hudson Way, N9 100 DW48
NW2 off Gratton Ter 119 CX62
Huggin Ct, EC4 11 H9
Huggin Hill, EC4 11 H9
Huggins La, Hat. (N.Mymms)
AL9 45 CV23
Huggins Pl, SW2
off Roupell Rd 181 DM88
Hughan Rd, E15 123 ED64
Hugh Dalton Av, SW6 159 CZ79
Hughenden Av, Har. HA3 117 CH57
Hughenden Gdns, Nthlt.
UB5 136 BW69
Hughenden Rd, St.Alb. AL4 43 CH17
Slough SL1 131 AR72
Worcester Park KT4 199 CU101
Hughenden Ter, E15
off Westdown Rd 123 EC63
Hughes Cl, N12
off Coleridge Rd 98 DC50
Sch **Hughes Flds Prim Sch**,
SE8 off Benbow St 163 EA79

★ Place of interest H Hospital Sch School Coll College Uni University ⇌ Railway station

Hughes Rd, Ashf. TW15 . . . . 175 BQ94
Grays RM16 . . . . 171 GG76
Hayes UB3 . . . . 135 BV73
Hughes Wk, Croy. CR0
off St. Saviours Rd 202 DQ101
Hugh Gaitskell Cl, SW6 . . . . 159 CZ79
Hugh Ms, SW1 . . . . 19 H8
Sch Hugh Myddelton Jun & Inf Schs, EC1 . . . . 10 D2
Hugh's Twr, Harl. CM20 . . . . 35 ER14
Hugh St, SW1 . . . . 19 H8
Hugo Gdns, Rain. RM13 . . . . 147 FF65
Hugo Gryn Way, Rad. (Shenley) WD7 off Farm Cl 62 CL31
Hugon Rd, SW6 . . . . 160 DB83
Hugo Rd, N19 . . . . 121 DJ63
Huguenot Pl, E1 . . . . 11 P5
SW18 . . . . 180 DC85
Huguenot Sq, SE15
off Scylla Rd 162 DV83
HULBERRY, Swan. BR8 . . . . 207 FG103
Hullbridge Ms, N1 . . . . 5 J7
Hull Cl, SE16 . . . . 23 H3
Slough SL1 . . . . 151 AQ75
Sutton SM2
off Yarbridge Cl 218 DB110
Waltham Cross (Chsht) EN7 . . . . 66 DR26
Hulletts La, Brwd. (Pilg.Hat.) CM15 . . . . 108 FT43
Hull Gro, Harl. CM19 . . . . 51 EN20
Hull Pl, E16
off Fishguard Way 165 EP75
Hull St, EC1 . . . . 10 G2
Hulme Pl, SE1 . . . . 21 H4
Hulse Av, Bark. IG11 . . . . 145 ER65
Romford RM7 . . . . 105 FB53
Hulse Ter, Ilf. IG1
off Buttsbury Rd 125 EQ64
Hulsewood Cl, Dart. DA2 . . . . 187 FH90
Hulton Cl, Lthd. KT22 . . . . 231 CJ123
Hulverston Cl, Sutt. SM2 . . . . 218 DB110
Humber Av, S.Ock. RM15 . . . . 149 FT72
Humber Cl, West Dr. UB7 . . . . 134 BK74
Humber Dr, W10 . . . . 6 A4
Upminster RM14 . . . . 129 FR58
Humber Rd, NW2 . . . . 119 CV61
SE3 . . . . 164 EF79
Dartford DA1 . . . . 188 FK85
Humberstone Rd, E13 . . . . 144 EJ69
Humberton Cl, E9
off Marsh Hill 123 DY64
Humber Way, Slou. SL3 . . . . 153 BA77
Humbolt Cl, Guil. GU2 . . . . 242 AS134
Humbolt Rd, W6 . . . . 159 CY79
Hume Av, Til. RM18 . . . . 171 GG83
Hume Cl, Til. RM18 . . . . 171 GG83
Humes Av, W7 . . . . 157 CE76
Hume Ter, E16
off Prince Regent La 144 EJ72
Hume Way, Ruis. HA4 . . . . 115 BU58
Hummer Rd, Egh. TW20 . . . . 173 BA91
Humphrey Cl, Ilf. IG5 . . . . 103 EM53
Leatherhead (Fetch.) KT22 . . . . 230 CC122
Humphrey St, SE1 . . . . 21 N9
Humphries Cl, Dag. RM9 . . . . 126 EZ63
Hundred Acre, NW9 . . . . 97 CT54
Hundred Acres La, Amer. HP7 . . . . 55 AR40
Hungerdown, E4 . . . . 101 EC46
Hungerford Av, Slou. SL2 . . . . 132 AS71
Hungerford Br, SE1 . . . . 19 P1
WC2 . . . . 19 P1
Hungerford La, WC2 . . . . 19 N1
Sch Hungerford Prim Sch, N7 off Hungerford Rd 141 DK65
Hungerford Rd, N7 . . . . 121 DK64
Hungerford Sq, Wey. KT13
off Rosslyn Pk 213 BR105
Hungerford St, E1 . . . . 12 D7
Hungry Hill, Wok. (Ripley) GU23 off Hungry Hill La 228 BK124
Hungry Hill La, Wok. (Send) GU23 . . . . 228 BK124
HUNSDON, Ware SG12 . . . . 34 EJ06
Hunsdon, Welw.G.C. AL7 . . . . 30 DD09
HUNSDONBURY, Ware SG12 . . . . 34 EJ08
Hunsdon Cl, Dag. RM9 . . . . 146 EY65
Hunsdon Dr, Sev. TN13 . . . . 257 FH123
Sch Hunsdon Prim Sch, Ware SG12 off High St 34 EK06
Hunsdon Rd, SE14 . . . . 163 DX79
Ware (Stans.Abb.) SG12 . . . . 34 EE11
Ware (Widford) SG12 . . . . 34 EE11
Hunslett St, E2
off Royston St 142 DW68
Hunstanton Cl, Slou. (Colnbr.) SL3 . . . . 153 BC80
Hunston Rd, Mord. SM4 . . . . 200 DB102
Hunt Cl, W11 . . . . 16 B1
St. Albans AL4
off Villiers Cres 43 CK17
Hunter Av, Brwd. (Shenf.) CM15 . . . . 109 GA44
Hunter Cl, SE1 . . . . 21 K6
SW12 off Balham Pk Rd 180 DG88
Borehamwood WD6 . . . . 78 CQ43
Potters Bar EN6 . . . . 64 DB33
Wallington SM6 . . . . 219 DL108
Huntercombe Cl, Maid. (Taplow) SL6 . . . . 130 AH72
Huntercombe La N, Maid. (Taplow) SL6 . . . . 130 AJ71
Slough SL1 . . . . 130 AJ71
Huntercombe La S, Maid. (Taplow) SL6 . . . . 130 AH74
H Huntercombe Manor, Maid. SL6 . . . . 130 AJ73
Huntercombe Spur, Slou. SL1 . . . . 130 AJ73
Huntercrombe Gdns, Wat. WD19 . . . . 94 BW50
Hunter Dr, Horn. RM12 . . . . 128 FJ63
Hunter Ho, Felt. TW13 . . . . 175 BU88
Hunter Rd, SW20 . . . . 199 CW95
Guildford GU1 . . . . 258 AY135
Ilford IG1 . . . . 125 EP64
Thornton Heath CR7 . . . . 202 DR97
Hunters, The, Beck. BR3 . . . . 203 EC95
Hunters Cl, Bex. DA5 . . . . 187 FE90
Chesham HP5 . . . . 54 AN30
Epsom KT19
off Marshalls Cl 216 CQ113
Hemel Hempstead (Bov.) HP3 . . . . 57 BA29
Hunters Ct, Rich. TW9
off Friars La 177 CK85
Huntersfield Cl, Reig. RH2 . . . . 250 DB131
Hunters Gate, Red. (Nutfld) RH1 off High St 251 DM133
Watford WD25
off Hunters La 59 BU33
Hunters Gro, Har. HA3 . . . . 117 CJ56
Hunters Gro, Hayes UB3 . . . . 135 BU74
Orpington BR6 . . . . 223 EP105
Romford RM5 . . . . 105 FB50
Sch Hunters Hall Prim Sch, Dag. RM10 off Alibon Rd 126 FA64
Hunters Hall Rd, Dag. RM10 . . . . 126 FA63
Hunters Hill, Ruis. HA4 . . . . 116 BW62
Hunters La, Wat. WD25 . . . . 59 BT33
Hunters Meadow, SE19
off Dulwich Wd Av 182 DS91
Hunters Oak, Hem.H. HP2 . . . . 41 BP15
Hunters Pk, Berk. HP4 . . . . 38 AY18
Hunters Reach, Wal.Cr. EN7 . . . . 66 DT29
Hunters Ride, St.Alb. (Brick.Wd) AL2 . . . . 60 CA31
Hunters Rd, Chess. KT9 . . . . 198 CL104
Hunters Sq, Dag. RM10 . . . . 126 FA63
Hunter St, WC1 . . . . 9 P3
Hunters Wk, Sev. (Knock.) TN14 . . . . 224 EY114
Hunters Way, Croy. CR0 . . . . 220 DS105
Enfield EN2 . . . . 81 DN39
Slough SL1 . . . . 151 AL75
Welwyn Garden City AL7 . . . . 29 CZ12
Hunter Wk, E13 . . . . 144 EG68
Borehamwood WD6
off Hunter Cl 78 CQ43
Hunting Cl, Esher KT10 . . . . 214 CA105
Huntingdon Cl, Brox. EN10 . . . . 49 DY24
Mitcham CR4 . . . . 201 DL97
Huntingdon Gdns, W4 . . . . 158 CQ80
Worcester Park KT4 . . . . 199 CW104
Huntingdon Rd, N2 . . . . 120 DE55
N9 . . . . 100 DW46
Redhill RH1 . . . . 250 DF134
Woking GU21 . . . . 226 AT117
Huntingdon St, E16 . . . . 15 K8
N1 . . . . 4 A6
Huntingfield, Croy. CR0 . . . . 221 DZ108
Huntingfield Rd, SW15 . . . . 159 CU84
Huntingfield Way, Egh. TW20 . . . . 173 BD94
Hunting Gate, Hem.H. HP2 . . . . 40 BL16
Hunting Gate Cl, Enf. EN2 . . . . 81 DN41
Hunting Gate Dr, Chess. KT9 . . . . 216 CL108
Hunting Gate Ms, Sutt. SM1 . . . . 200 DB104
Twickenham TW2
off Colne Rd 177 CE88
Huntings Rd, Dag. RM10 . . . . 146 FA65
Huntland Cl, Rain. RM13 . . . . 147 FH71
Huntley Av, Grav. (Nthflt) DA11 . . . . 190 GB86
H Huntley Cen, WC1 . . . . 9 L4
Huntley Cl, Stai. (Stanw.) TW19
off Cambria Gdns 174 BL87
Huntley Dr, N3 . . . . 98 DA51
Huntley St, WC1 . . . . 9 K4
Huntley Way, SW20 . . . . 199 CU96
Huntly Rd, SE25 . . . . 202 DS98
HUNTON BRIDGE, Kings L. WD4 . . . . 59 BP33
Hunton Br Hill, Kings L. WD4 . . . . 59 BQ33
Coll Hunton Pk Training Cen, Kings L. WD4
off Essex La 59 BR33
Hunton St, E1 . . . . 12 A4
Hunt Rd, Grav. (Nthflt) DA11 . . . . 190 GE90
Southall UB2 . . . . 156 CA76
Hunt's Cl, SE3 . . . . 164 EG82
Hunt's Ct, WC2 . . . . 9 M10
Hunts La, E15 . . . . 143 EC68
Maidenhead (Taplow) SL6 . . . . 130 AE68
Huntsman Cl, Warl. CR6 . . . . 236 DW119
Huntsman Rd, Ilf. IG6 . . . . 104 EU51
Huntsmans Cl, Felt. TW13 . . . . 175 BV91
Leatherhead (Fetch.) KT22 off The Green 231 CD124
Huntsmans Dr, Upmin. RM14 . . . . 128 FQ64
Huntsman St, SE17 . . . . 21 K8
Hunts Mead, Enf. EN3 . . . . 83 DX41
Hunts Mead Cl, Chis. BR7 . . . . 185 EM94
Huntsmill Rd, Hem.H. HP1 . . . . 39 BE21
Huntsmoor Rd, Epsom KT19 . . . . 216 CR106
Huntspill St, SW17 . . . . 180 DC90
Hunts Slip Rd, SE21 . . . . 182 DS90
Huntswood La, Maid. (Taplow) SL6 . . . . 130 AE66
Slough SL1 . . . . 130 AE66
Huntsworth Ms, NW1 . . . . 8 C4
Hunt Way, SE22
off Dulwich Common 182 DU88
Hurdwick Pl, NW1
off Harrington Sq 141 DJ68
Hurley Cl, Walt. KT12 . . . . 195 BV103
Hurley Cres, SE16 . . . . 23 H3
Hurley Gdns, Guil. GU4 . . . . 243 AZ130
Hurley Ho, SE11 . . . . 20 D8
Hurley Rd, Grnf. UB6 . . . . 136 CB72
Hurlfield, Dart. DA2 . . . . 188 FJ90
Hurlford, Wok. GU21 . . . . 226 AU117
Sch Hurlingham & Chelsea Sec Sch, SW6
off Peterborough Rd 160 DA83
Hurlingham Business Pk, SW6 . . . . 160 DA83
Hurlingham Ct, SW6 . . . . 159 CZ83
Hurlingham Gdns, SW6 . . . . 159 CZ83
★ Hurlingham Ho, SW6 . . . . 160 DA83
★ Hurlingham Park, SW6 . . . . 159 CZ82
Hurlingham Retail Pk, SW6
off Carnwath Rd 160 DB83
Hurlingham Rd, SW6 . . . . 159 CZ82
Bexleyheath DA7 . . . . 166 EZ80
Sch Hurlingham Sch, SW15
off Putney Br Rd 159 CZ84
Hurlingham Sq, SW6 . . . . 160 DB83
Hurlock St, N5 . . . . 121 DP62
Hurlstone Rd, SE25 . . . . 202 DR99
Hurn Ct Rd, Houns. TW4
off Renfrew Rd 156 BX82
Hurnford Cl, S.Croy. CR2 . . . . 220 DS110
Huron Cl, Orp. BR6
off Winnipeg Dr 223 ET107
Huron Rd, SW17 . . . . 180 DG89
Uni Huron Uni USA in London, SW7 . . . . 17 P5
Hurren Cl, SE3 . . . . 164 EE83
Hurricane Rd, Wall. SM6 . . . . 219 DL108
Hurricane Way, Abb.L. WD5
off Abbey Dr 59 BU32
Epping (N.Wld Bas.) CM16 . . . . 70 EZ27
Slough SL3 . . . . 153 BB78
Hurry Cl, E15 . . . . 144 EE66
Hursley Rd, Chig. IG7
off Tufter Rd 103 ET50
Hurst Av, E4 . . . . 101 EA49
N6 . . . . 121 DJ58
Hurstbourne, Esher (Clay.) KT10 . . . . 215 CF107
Hurstbourne Gdns, Bark. IG11 . . . . 145 ES65
Hurstbourne Ho, SW15
off Tangley Gro 179 CT86
Hurstbourne Rd, SE23 . . . . 183 DY88
Hurst Cl, E4 . . . . 101 EA48
NW11 . . . . 120 DB58
Bromley BR2 . . . . 204 EF102
Chessington KT9 . . . . 216 CN106
Northolt UB5 . . . . 136 BZ65
Welwyn Garden City AL7 . . . . 30 DC10
Woking GU22 . . . . 226 AW120
Hurstcourt Rd, Sutt. SM1 . . . . 200 DB103
Hurst Cft, Guil. GU1 . . . . 258 AY137
Hurstdene Av, Brom. BR2 . . . . 204 EF102
Staines TW18 . . . . 174 BH93
Hurstdene Gdns, N15 . . . . 122 DS59
Hurst Dr, Tad. KT20 . . . . 249 CU126
Waltham Cross EN8 . . . . 67 DX34
Sch Hurst Dr Prim Sch, Wal.Cr. EN8 off Hurst Dr 67 DX34
Hurst Est, SE2 . . . . 166 EX78
Hurstfield, Brom. BR2 . . . . 204 EG99
Hurstfield Cres, Hayes UB4 . . . . 135 BS70
Hurstfield Dr, Maid. (Taplow) SL6 . . . . 130 AH72
Hurstfield Rd, W.Mol. KT8 . . . . 196 CA97
HURST GREEN, Oxt. RH8 . . . . 254 EG132
⇌ Hurst Green 254 EF132
Hurst Grn Cl, Oxt. RH8 . . . . 254 EG132
Hurst Grn Rd, Oxt. RH8 . . . . 254 EF132
Sch Hurst Grn Sch, Oxt. RH8 off Wolfs Wd 254 EG132
Hurst Gro, Walt. KT12 . . . . 195 BT102
Hurstlands, Oxt. RH8 . . . . 254 EG132
Hurstlands Cl, Horn. RM11 . . . . 128 FJ59
Hurst La, SE2 . . . . 166 EX78
East Molesey KT8 . . . . 196 CC98
Egham TW20 . . . . 193 BA96
Epsom (Headley) KT18 . . . . 232 CQ124
Hurstleigh Cl, Red. RH1 . . . . 250 DF132
Hurstleigh Dr, Red. RH1 . . . . 250 DF132
Hurstleigh Gdns, Ilf. IG5 . . . . 103 EM53
Hurstlings, Welw.G.C. AL7 . . . . 30 DB10
Hurstmead Ct, Edg. HA8 . . . . 96 CP49
Sch Hurstmere Sch, Sid. DA15 off Hurst Rd 186 EW88
Hurst Pk Av, Horn. RM12
off Newmarket Way 128 FL63
Sch Hurst Pk Prim Sch, W.Mol. KT8 off Hurst Rd 196 CA97
Hurst Pl, Nthwd. HA6 . . . . 93 BP53
Sch Hurst Prim Sch, Bex. DA5 off Dorchester Av 186 EX87
Hurst Ri, Barn. EN5 . . . . 80 DA41
Hurst Rd, E17 . . . . 123 EB55
N21 . . . . 99 DN46
Bexley DA5 . . . . 186 EX88
Buckhurst Hill IG9 . . . . 102 EK46
Croydon CR0 . . . . 220 DR106
East Molesey KT8 . . . . 196 CA97
Epsom KT19 . . . . 216 CR111
Epsom (Headley) KT18 . . . . 232 CR123
Erith DA8 . . . . 167 FC80
Horley RH6 . . . . 268 DE147
Sidcup DA15 . . . . 186 EU89
Slough SL1 . . . . 131 AK71
Tadworth KT20 . . . . 232 CR123
Walton-on-Thames KT12 . . . . 196 BW99
West Molesey KT8 . . . . 196 BY97
Hurst Springs, Bex. DA5 . . . . 186 EY88
Hurst St, SE24 . . . . 181 DP86
Hurst Vw Rd, S.Croy. CR2 . . . . 220 DS108
Hurst Way, Sev. TN13 . . . . 257 FJ127
South Croydon CR2 . . . . 220 DS107
Woking (Pyrford) GU22 . . . . 211 BE114
Hurstway Wk, W11 . . . . 6 B9
Hurstwood Av, E18 . . . . 124 EH56
Bexley DA5 . . . . 186 EY88
Bexleyheath DA7 . . . . 167 FE81
Brentwood CM15
off Ongar Rd 108 FV45
Erith DA8 . . . . 167 FE81
Hurstwood Ct, Upmin. RM14 . . . . 128 FQ60
Hurstwood Dr, Brom. BR1 . . . . 205 EM97
Hurstwood Rd, NW11 . . . . 119 CY56
Hurtwood Rd, Walt. KT12 . . . . 196 BZ101
Hurworth Av, Slou. SL3 . . . . 152 AW76
Huson Cl, NW3 . . . . 140 DE66
Hussain Cl, Har. HA1 . . . . 117 CF63
Hussars Cl, Houns. TW4 . . . . 156 BY83
Husseywell Cres, Brom. BR2 . . . . 204 EG102
Hutchingsons Rd, Croy. (New Adgtn) CR0 . . . . 221 EC111
Hutchings Rd, Beac. HP9 . . . . 89 AK50
Hutchings St, E14 . . . . 23 N4
Hutchings Wk, NW11 . . . . 120 DB56
Hutchins Cl, E15
off Gibbins Rd 143 EC66
Hornchurch RM12 . . . . 128 FL62
Hutchinson Ter, Wem. HA9 . . . . 117 CK62
Hutchins Rd, SE28 . . . . 146 EU73
Hutchins Way, Horl. RH6 . . . . 268 DF146
Hutson Ter, Purf. RM19
off London Rd Purfleet 169 FR79
HUTTON, Brwd. CM13 . . . . 109 GD44
Sch Hutton All Saints C of E Prim Sch, Brwd. CM13
off Claughton Way 109 GD44
Hutton Cl, Grnf. UB6
off Mary Peters Dr 117 CD64
Hertford SG14 . . . . 31 DN09
Woodford Green IG8 . . . . 102 EH51
Sch Hutton Co Prim Sch, Brwd. CM13 off Brookfield Cl 109 GD44
Hutton Dr, Brwd. (Hutt.) CM13 . . . . 109 GD45
Hutton Gdns, Har. HA3 . . . . 94 CC52
Hutton Gate, Brwd. (Hutt.) CM13 . . . . 109 GB45
Hutton Gro, N12 . . . . 98 DB50
Hutton La, Har. HA3 . . . . 94 CC52
HUTTON MOUNT, Brwd. CM13 . . . . 109 GB46
Hutton Rd, Brwd. (Shenf.) CM15 . . . . 109 FZ45
Hutton Row, Edg. HA8
off Pavilion Way 96 CQ52
Hutton St, EC4 . . . . 10 D8
Hutton Village, Brwd. (Hutt.) CM13 . . . . 109 GE45
Hutton Wk, Har. HA3 . . . . 94 CC52
Huxbear St, SE4 . . . . 183 DZ85
Huxley Cl, Nthlt. UB5 . . . . 136 BY67
Uxbridge UB8 . . . . 134 BK70
Huxley Dr, Rom. RM6 . . . . 126 EV59
Huxley Gdns, NW10 . . . . 138 CM69
Huxley Par, N18 . . . . 100 DR50
Huxley Pl, N13 . . . . 99 DP49
Huxley Rd, E10 . . . . 123 EC61
N18 . . . . 100 DR49
Guildford (Surr.Res.Pk) GU2 . . . . 258 AS135
Huxley Rd, Well. DA16 . . . . 165 ET83
Huxley Sayze, N18 . . . . 100 DR50
Huxley St, W10 . . . . 6 C2
Huxtable Gdns, Maid. SL6
off Windsor Rd 150 AE79
Hyacinth Cl, Hmptn. TW12
off Gresham Rd 176 CA93
Ilford IG1 . . . . 145 EP65
Hyacinth Ct, Pnr. HA5
off Tulip Ct 116 BW55
Hyacinth Dr, Uxb. UB10 . . . . 134 BL66
Hyacinth Rd, SW15 . . . . 179 CU88
Hyburn Cl, Hem.H. HP3 . . . . 41 BP21
St. Albans (Brick.Wd) AL2 . . . . 60 BZ30
Hycliffe Gdns, Chig. IG7 . . . . 103 EQ49
HYDE, THE, NW9 . . . . 119 CT56
Hyde, The, NW9 . . . . 118 CS57
Ware SG12 . . . . 32 DV05
Hyde Av, Pot.B. EN6 . . . . 64 DB33
Hyde Cl, E13 . . . . 144 EG68
Ashford TW15 off Hyde Ter 175 BS93
Barnet EN5 . . . . 79 CZ41
Grays (Chaff.Hun.) RM16 . . . . 169 FX76
Hyde Ct, N20 . . . . 98 DD48
Waltham Cross EN8
off Parkside 67 DY34
Hyde Cres, NW9 . . . . 118 CS57
Hyde Dr, Orp. BR5 . . . . 206 EV98
Hyde Est Rd, NW9 . . . . 119 CT57
Hyde Fm Ms, SW12
off Telferscot Rd 181 DK88
Hydefield Cl, N21 . . . . 100 DR46
Hydefield Ct, N9 . . . . 100 DS47
Hyde Grn, Beac. HP9 . . . . 89 AM52
Hyde Ho, NW9 . . . . 118 CS57
Hyde La, SW11
off Battersea Br Rd 160 DE81
Hemel Hempstead HP3 . . . . 59 BR26
Hemel Hempstead (Bov.) HP3 . . . . 57 BA27
St. Albans (Frog.) AL2 . . . . 61 CE28
Woking (Ockham) GU23 . . . . 228 BN120
Hyde Mead, Wal.Abb. EN9 . . . . 50 EE23
Hyde Meadows, Hem.H. (Bov.) HP3 . . . . 57 BA28
★ Hyde Park, W2 . . . . 18 A1
Hyde Pk, SW7 . . . . 18 A1
W1 . . . . 18 A1
Hyde Pk Av, N21 . . . . 100 DQ47
⊖ Hyde Park Corner 18 E3
Hyde Pk Cor, W1 . . . . 18 F3
Hyde Pk Cres, W2 . . . . 8 A8
Hyde Pk Gdns, N21 . . . . 100 DQ46
W2 . . . . 7 P9
Hyde Pk Gdns Ms, W2 . . . . 7 P9
Hyde Pk Gate, SW7 . . . . 17 M4
Hyde Pk Gate Ms, SW7 . . . . 17 M4
Hyde Pk Pl, W2 . . . . 8 B9
Hyde Pk Sq, W2 . . . . 8 A8
Hyde Pk Sq Ms, W2 . . . . 8 A8
Hyde Pk St, W2 . . . . 8 A8
Hyderabad Way, E15 . . . . 144 EE66
Hyde Rd, N1 . . . . 5 K8
Bexleyheath DA7 . . . . 166 EZ82
Richmond TW10
off Albert Rd 178 CM85
South Croydon CR2 . . . . 220 DS113
Watford WD17 . . . . 75 BU40
Hyder Rd, Grays RM16 . . . . 171 GJ76
Sch Hyde Sch, The, NW9
off Hyde Cres 119 CT57
Hydeside Gdns, N9 . . . . 100 DT47
Hydes Pl, N1 . . . . 4 E5
Hyde St, SE8
off Deptford High St 163 EA79
Hyde Ter, Ashf. TW15 . . . . 175 BS93
Hydethorpe Av, N9 . . . . 100 DT47
Hydethorpe Rd, SW12 . . . . 181 DJ88
Hyde Vale, SE10 . . . . 163 EC80
Hyde Valley, Welw.G.C. AL7 . . . . 29 CZ11
Hyde Wk, Mord. SM4 . . . . 200 DA101
Hyde Way, N9 . . . . 100 DT47
Hayes UB3 . . . . 155 BT77
Welwyn Garden City AL7 . . . . 29 CY09
Hyland Cl, Horn. RM11 . . . . 127 FH59
Sch Hyland Ho Sch, E17
off Forest Rd 101 ED54
Hylands Cl, Epsom KT18 . . . . 232 CQ115
Hylands Ms, Epsom KT18 . . . . 232 CQ115
Hylands Rd, E17 . . . . 101 ED54
Epsom KT18 . . . . 232 CQ115
Hyland Way, Horn. RM11 . . . . 127 FH59
Coll Hyleford Sch Leavers Unit, Ilf. IG6 off Starch Ho La 103 ER54
Sch Hyleford Spec Sch, Ilf. IG3 off Loxford La 125 ES63
Hylle Cl, Wind. SL4 . . . . 151 AL81
Hylton St, SE18 . . . . 165 ET77
Hyndewood, SE23 . . . . 183 DX90
Hyndford Cres, Green. DA9
off Ingress Pk Av 189 FW85
Hyndman St, SE15 . . . . 162 DV79
Hynton Rd, Dag. RM8 . . . . 126 EW61
Hyperion Ct, Hem.H. HP2 . . . . 40 BM17
Hyperion Pl, Epsom KT19 . . . . 216 CR109
Hyperion Wk, Horl. RH6 . . . . 269 DH150
Hyrons Cl, Amer. HP6 . . . . 55 AS38
Hyrons La, Amer. HP6 . . . . 55 AR38
Hyrstdene, S.Croy. CR2 . . . . 219 DP105
Hyson Rd, SE16 . . . . 22 D9
Hythe, The, Stai. TW18 . . . . 173 BE92
Hythe Av, Bexh. DA7 . . . . 166 EZ80
Hythe Cl, N18 . . . . 100 DU49
Orpington BR5
off Sandway Rd 206 EW98
HYTHE END, Stai. TW19 . . . . 173 BB90
Hythe End Rd, Stai. (Wrays.) TW19 . . . . 173 BA89
Hythe Fld Av, Egh. TW20 . . . . 173 BD93
Hythe Pk Rd, Egh. TW20 . . . . 173 BC92
Hythe Path, Th.Hth. CR7 . . . . 202 DR97
Hythe Rd, NW10 . . . . 139 CU70
Staines TW18 . . . . 173 BD92
Thornton Heath CR7 . . . . 202 DR96
Hythe Rd Ind Est, NW10 . . . . 139 CU69
Sch Hythe Sch, The, Stai. TW18 off Thorpe Rd 173 BD92
Hythe St, Dart. DA1 . . . . 188 FL86
Hythe St Lwr, Dart. DA1 . . . . 188 FL85
Hyver Hill, NW7 . . . . 78 CR44

I

Ian Sq, Enf. EN3
off Lansbury Rd 83 DX39
Ibbetson Path, Loug. IG10 . . . . 85 EP41
Ibbotson Av, E16 . . . . 15 K7
Ibbott St, E1 . . . . 12 F3
Iberian Av, Wall. SM6 . . . . 219 DK105
Ibis La, W4 . . . . 158 CQ81
Ibis Way, Hayes UB4
off Cygnet Way 136 BX72
Ibscott Cl, Dag. RM10 . . . . 147 FC65
Ibsley Gdns, SW15 . . . . 179 CU88
Ibsley Way, Barn. EN4 . . . . 80 DE43
Sch Ibstock Pl Sch, Froebel Sch, SW15 off Clarence La 178 CS86
★ Ice Ho, Holland Pk, W8 . . . . 16 F4
Icehouse Wd, Oxt. RH8 . . . . 254 EE131
Iceland Rd, E3 . . . . 143 EA67
Iceni Ct, E3 off Roman Rd 143 DZ67
Ice Wf, N1 off New Wf Rd 141 DL68
Ice Wf Marina, N1
off New Wf Rd 141 DL68
Ickburgh Est, E5
off Ickburgh Rd 122 DV62
Ickburgh Rd, E5 . . . . 122 DV62
Sch Ickburgh Spec Sch, E5
off Ickburgh Rd 122 DV62
ICKENHAM, Uxb. UB10 . . . . 115 BQ62
⊖ Ickenham 115 BQ63
Ickenham Cl, Ruis. HA4 . . . . 115 BR61
Ickenham Rd, Ruis. HA4 . . . . 115 BR60
Uxbridge (Ickhm) UB10 . . . . 115 BQ61
Ickleton Rd, SE9 . . . . 184 EL91
Icklingham Gate, Cob. KT11 . . . . 214 BW112
Icklingham Rd, Cob. KT11 . . . . 214 BW112
Icknield Cl, St.Alb. AL3 . . . . 42 BZ22
Icknield Dr, Ilf. IG2 . . . . 125 EP57
Ickworth Pk Rd, E17 . . . . 123 DY56
Ida Rd, N15 . . . . 122 DR57
Ida St, E14 . . . . 14 C8
Iden Cl, Brom. BR2 . . . . 204 EE97
Idlecombe Rd, SW17 . . . . 180 DG93
Idmiston Rd, E15 . . . . 124 EF64
SE27 . . . . 182 DQ90
Worcester Park KT4 . . . . 199 CT101
Idmiston Sq, Wor.Pk. KT4 . . . . 199 CT101
Idol La, EC3 . . . . 11 L10
Idonia St, SE8 . . . . 163 DZ80
Iffley Cl, Uxb. UB8 . . . . 134 BK66
Iffley Rd, W6 . . . . 159 CV76
Ifield Cl, Red. RH1 . . . . 266 DE137
Sch Ifield Comm Spec Sch, Grav. DA12 off Cedar Av 191 GJ92
Ifield Rd, SW10 . . . . 160 DB79
Ifield Way, Grav. DA12 . . . . 191 GK93
Ifold Rd, Red. RH1 . . . . 266 DG136
Ifor Evans Pl, E1 . . . . 13 H4
Ightham Rd, Erith DA8 . . . . 166 FA80
Ikea Twr, NW10 . . . . 118 CR64
Ikona Ct, Wey. KT13 . . . . 213 BQ106
Ilbert St, W10 . . . . 6 B2
Ilchester Gdns, W2 . . . . 7 J9
Ilchester Pl, W14 . . . . 16 E5
Ilchester Rd, Dag. RM8 . . . . 126 EV64
Ildersly Gro, SE21 . . . . 182 DR89
Sch Ilderton Prim Sch, SE16 . . . . 22 E10
Ilderton Rd, SE15 . . . . 162 DW80
SE16 . . . . 22 D9
Ilex Cl, Egh. (Eng.Grn) TW20 . . . . 172 AV94
Sunbury-on-Thames TW16 off Oakington Dr 196 BW96
Ilex Ct, Berk. HP4 . . . . 38 AV19
Ilex Ho, N4 . . . . 121 DM59
Ilex Rd, NW10 . . . . 139 CT65
Ilex Way, SW16 . . . . 181 DN92
ILFORD, IG1 - IG6 . . . . 125 EQ62
⇌ Ilford 125 EN62
Sch Ilford Co High Sch, Ilf. IG6 off Fremantle Rd 103 EP54
Ilford Hill, Ilf. IG1 . . . . 125 EN62
Sch Ilford Jewish Prim Sch, Ilf. IG6 off Carlton Dr 125 ER55
Ilford La, Ilf. IG1 . . . . 125 EP62
Sch Ilford Ursuline High Sch, Ilf. IG1 off Morland Rd 125 EP61
Ilfracombe Cres, Horn. RM12 . . . . 128 FJ63
Ilfracombe Gdns, Rom. RM6 . . . . 126 EV59
Ilfracombe Rd, Brom. BR1 . . . . 184 EF90
Iliffe St, SE17 . . . . 20 F9
Iliffe Yd, SE17 . . . . 20 F9
Ilkeston Ct, E5
off Overbury St 123 DX63
Ilkley Cl, SE19 . . . . 182 DR93
Ilkley Rd, E16 . . . . 144 EJ71
Watford WD19 . . . . 94 BX50
Illingworth, Wind. SL4 . . . . 151 AL84
Illingworth Cl, Mitch. CR4 . . . . 200 DD97
Illingworth Way, Enf. EN1 . . . . 82 DS42
Ilmington Rd, Har. HA3 . . . . 117 CK58
Ilminster Gdns, SW11 . . . . 160 DE84
Imber Cl, N14 . . . . 99 DJ45
Esher KT10 off Ember La 197 CD102
Imber Ct Trd Est, E.Mol. KT8 . . . . 197 CD100
Imber Gro, Esher KT10 . . . . 197 CD101
Imber Pk Rd, Esher KT10 . . . . 197 CD102
Imber St, N1 . . . . 5 J8
Imer Pl, T.Ditt. KT7 . . . . 197 CF101
Sch Immanuel & St. Andrew C of E Prim Sch, SW16
off Buckleigh Rd 181 DL93
Coll Immanuel Coll, Bushey WD23 off Elstree Rd 95 CE45
Sch Immanuel Sch, Rom. RM1 off Havering Rd 105 FD50
Imperial Av, N16
off Victorian Rd 122 DT62
Imperial Business Est, Grav. DA11 . . . . 191 GF86
Imperial Cl, Har. HA2 . . . . 116 CA58
Uni Imperial Coll of Science, Tech & Med, Hammersmith Campus, W12 off Du Cane Rd 139 CU72
St. Mary's Campus, W2 . . . . 7 P7
South Kensington Campus, SW7 . . . . 17 N5
Uni Imperial Coll of Science, Tech & Med - Nat Heart & Lung Inst, Royal Brompton Campus, SW3 . . . . 18 A9
Imperial Coll Rd, SW7 . . . . 17 N6
Imperial Cres, SW6
off William Morris Way 160 DC82
Weybridge KT13
off Churchill Dr 195 BQ104
Imperial Dr, Grav. DA12 . . . . 191 GM92
Harrow HA2 . . . . 116 CA59
Imperial Gdns, Mitch. CR4 . . . . 201 DH97
Imperial Ms, E6
off Central Pk Rd 144 EJ68
Imperial Pk, Wat. WD24 . . . . 76 BW39
Imperial Retail Pk, Grav. DA11 . . . . 191 GG86
Imperial Rd, N22 . . . . 99 DL53
SW6 . . . . 160 DB81
Feltham TW14 . . . . 175 BS87
Windsor SL4 . . . . 151 AN83
Imperial Sq, SW6 . . . . 160 DB81
Imperial St, E3 . . . . 14 C2

⊖ London Underground station   DLR Docklands Light Railway station   Tra Tramlink station   Riv Pedestrian ferry landing stage

Imperial Trd Est, Rain. RM13 148 FJ70
★ Imperial War Mus, SE1 20 D6
Imperial Way, Chis. BR7 185 EQ90
Croydon CR0 219 DM107
Harrow HA3 118 CL58
Hemel Hempstead HP3 40 BL24
Watford WD24 76 BW39
Imperial Wf, SW6 160 DC82
Impresa Pk, Hodd. EN11
off Pindar Rd 49 EC16
Imprimo Pk, Loug. IG10 85 ER42
Imre Cl, W12
off Ellerslie Rd 139 CV74
Inca Dr, SE9 185 EP87
Ince Rd, Walt. KT12 213 BS107
Coll Inchbald Sch of Design,
Garden Design Faculty,
SW1 19 H8
Interior Design Faculty,
SW1 18 E7
Inchmery Rd, SE6 183 EB89
Inchwood, Croy. CR0 221 EB105
Indells, Hat. AL10 45 CT19
Sch Independent Jewish
Day Sch, NW4
off Green La 119 CX57
Independent Pl, E8 5 P1
Independents Rd, SE3
off Blackheath Village 164 EF83
Inderwick Rd, N8 121 DM57
Indescon Ct, E14 23 P4
India Pl, WC2 10 A9
India Rd, Slou. SL1 152 AV75
India St, EC3 11 N8
India Way, W12 139 CV73
Indigo Ms, E14 14 D8
N16 122 DR62
Indus Rd, SE7 164 EJ80
Industry Ter, SW9
off Canterbury Cres 161 DN83
Ingal Rd, E13 15 L4
Ingate Pl, SW8 161 DH81
Ingatestone Rd, E12 124 EJ60
SE25 202 DV98
Woodford Green IG8 102 EG52
Ingelow Rd, SW8 161 DH82
Ingels Mead, Epp. CM16 69 ET29
Ingersoll Rd, W12 139 CV74
Enfield EN3 82 DW38
Ingestre Pl, W1 9 K8
Ingestre Rd, E7 124 EG63
NW5 121 DH63
Ingham Cl, S.Croy. CR2 221 DX109
Ingham Rd, NW6 120 DA63
South Croydon CR2 220 DW109
Inglebert St, EC1 10 C1
Ingleboro Dr, Pur. CR8 220 DR113
Ingleborough St, SW9 161 DN82
Ingleby Dr, Har. HA1 117 CD62
Ingleby Gdns, Chig. IG7 104 EV48
Ingleby Rd, N7 off Bryett Rd 121 DL62
Dagenham RM10 147 FB65
Grays RM16 171 GH76
Ilford IG1 125 EP60
Ingleby Way, Chis. BR7 185 EN92
Wallington SM6 219 DK109
Ingle Cl, Pnr. HA5 116 BY55
Ingledew Rd, SE18 165 ER78
Inglefield, Pot.B. EN6 64 DA30
Ingleglen, Horn. RM11 128 FN59
Inglehurst, Add. (New Haw)
KT15 212 BH110
Inglehurst Gdns, Ilf. IG4 125 EM57
Inglemere Rd, SE23 183 DX90
Mitcham CR4 180 DF94
Ingles, Welw.G.C. AL8 29 CX06
Inglesham Wk, E9 143 DZ65
Ingleside, Slou. (Colnbr.)
SL3 153 BE81
Ingleside Cl, Beck. BR3 183 EA94
Ingleside Gro, SE3 164 EF79
Inglethorpe St, SW6 159 CX81
Ingleton Av, Well. DA16 186 EU85
Ingleton Rd, N18 100 DU51
Carshalton SM5 218 DE109
Ingleton St, SW9 161 DN82
Ingleway, N12 98 DD51
Inglewood, Cher. KT16 193 BF104
Croydon CR0 221 DY109
Woking GU21 226 AV118
Inglewood Cl, E14 23 P7
Hornchurch RM12 128 FK63
Ilford IG6 103 ET51
Inglewood Copse, Brom.
BR1 204 EL96
Inglewood Gdns, St.Alb.
AL2 off North Orbital Rd 61 CE25
Inglewood Rd, NW6 120 DA64
Bexleyheath DA7 167 FD84
Inglis Barracks, NW7 97 CX50
Inglis Rd, W5 138 CM73
Croydon CR0 202 DT102
Inglis St, SE5 161 DP81
Ingoldsby Rd, Grav. DA12 191 GL88
Ingram Av, NW11 120 DC59
Ingram Cl, SE11 20 B7
Stanmore HA7 95 CJ50
Ingram Rd, N2 120 DE56
Dartford DA1 188 FL88
Grays RM17 170 GD77
Thornton Heath CR7 202 DQ95
Ingrams Cl, Walt. KT12 214 BW106
Ingram Way, Grnf. UB6 137 CD67
Ingrave Ho, Dag. RM9 146 EV67
Ingrave Rd, Brwd. CM13,
CM15 108 FX47
Romford RM1 127 FD56
Ingrave St, SW11 160 DD83
Ingrebourne Gdns, Upmin.
RM14 128 FQ60
Sch Ingrebourne Jun & Inf Sch,
Rom. RM3
off Taunton Rd 106 FJ49
Ingrebourne Rd, Rain. RM13 147 FH70
Ingrebourne Valley Grn Way,
Horn. RM12 148 FK65
Ingress Gdns, Green. DA9 189 FX85
Ingress Pk Av, Green. DA9 169 FV84
Ingress St, W4
off Devonshire Rd 158 CS78
Ingreway, Rom. RM3 106 FP52
Inholms La, Dor. RH5 263 CH140
Inigo Jones Rd, SE7 164 EL80
Inigo Pl, WC2 9 N9
Inkerman Rd, NW5 141 DH65
St. Albans AL1 43 CE21
Windsor (Eton Wick) SL4 151 AM77
Woking (Knap.) GU21 226 AS118
Inkerman Ter, W8
off Allen St 160 DA76
Chesham HP5 54 AQ33
Inkerman Way, Wok. GU21 226 AS118
Inks Grn, E4 101 EC50
Inkster Ho, SW11
off Ingrave St 160 DE83
Inman Rd, NW10 138 CS67
SW18 180 DC87
Inmans Row, Wdf.Grn. IG8 102 EG49
Inner Circle, NW1 8 E2
Inner Pk Rd, SW19 179 CX88
Inner Ring E, Houns.
(Hthrw Air.) TW6 155 BP83
Inner Ring W, Houns.
(Hthrw Air.) TW6 154 BN83
Inner Temple La, EC4 10 C8
Innes Cl, SW20 199 CY96
Innes Ct, Hem.H. HP3 40 BK22
Innes Gdns, SW15 179 CV86
Innes Yd, Croy. CR0
off Whitgift St 202 DQ104
Inniskilling Rd, E13 144 EJ68
Innova Business Pk, Enf.
EN3 83 DZ36
Innovation Cl, Wem. HA0 138 CL67
Innova Way, Enf. EN3 83 DZ36
Inskip Cl, E10 123 EB61
Inskip Dr, Horn. RM11 128 FL60
Inskip Rd, Dag. RM8 126 EX60
★ Institute of Contemporary
Arts (I.C.A.), SW1 19 M1
Uni Institute of Ed, WC1 9 M4
Institute Pl, E8 122 DV64
Institute Rd, Dor. (Westc.)
RH4 off Guildford Rd 262 CC137
Epping (Cooper.) CM16 70 EX29
Maidenhead (Taplow)
SL6 130 AF72
Instone Rd, Dart. DA1 188 FK87
Integer Gdns, E11 123 ED59
Interchange E Ind Est, E5
off Grosvenor Way 122 DW61
International Av, Houns.
TW5 156 BW78
Sch International Comm Sch,
NW1 8 F4
Sch International Sch of London,
W3 off Gunnersbury Av 158 CN77
Coll International Studies Cen,
W1 9 K7
International Trd Est, Sthl.
UB2 155 BV76
Inveraray Pl, SE18
off Old Mill Rd 165 ER79
Inver Cl, E5 off Theydon Rd 122 DW61
Inverclyde Gdns, Rom. RM6 126 EX56
Inver Ct, W2 7 K8
Inveresk Gdns, Wor.Pk. KT4 199 CT104
Inverforth Cl, NW3
off North End Way 120 DC61
Inverforth Rd, N11 99 DH50
Inverine Rd, SE7 25 P10
Invermore Pl, SE18 165 EQ77
Inverness Av, Enf. EN1 82 DS39
Inverness Dr, Ilf. IG6 103 ES51
Inverness Gdns, W8 17 J2
Inverness Ms, E16 145 EQ74
W2 7 K9
Inverness Pl, W2 7 K9
Inverness Rd, N18
off Aberdeen Rd 100 DV50
Hounslow TW3 156 BZ84
Southall UB2 156 BY77
Worcester Park KT4 199 CX102
Inverness St, NW1 141 DH67
Inverness Ter, W2 7 K9
Inverton Rd, SE15 163 DX84
Invicta Cl, Chis. BR7 185 EN92
Feltham TW14
off Westmacott Dr 175 BT88
Invicta Gro, Nthlt. UB5 136 BZ69
Sch Invicta Inf Sch, SE3
off Invicta Rd 164 EG79
Invicta Plaza, SE1 20 E1
Invicta Rd, SE3 164 EG80
Dartford DA2 188 FP86
Inville Rd, SE17 21 K10
Inwen Ct, SE8 23 K10
Inwood Av, Couls. CR5 235 DN120
Hounslow TW3 156 CC83
Inwood Cl, Croy. CR0 203 DY103
Inwood Ct, Walt. KT12 196 BW103
Inwood Rd, Houns. TW3 156 CB84
Inworth St, SW11 160 DE82
Inworth Wk, N1 4 G7
Iona Cl, SE6 183 EA87
Morden SM4 200 DB101
Iona Cres, Slou. SL1 131 AL72
Ionian Bldg, E14 13 J9
Ionian Way, Hem.H. HP2
off Jupiter Dr 40 BM18
Ionia Wk, Grav. DA12
off Cervia Way 191 GM90
Ion Sq, E2 off Hackney Rd 142 DU68
Ipswich Rd, SW17 180 DG93
Slough SL1 131 AN73
Ireland Cl, E6
off Bradley Stone Rd 145 EM71
Ireland Pl, N22
off Whittington Rd 99 DL52
Ireland Yd, EC4 10 F8
Irene Rd, SW6 160 DA81
Cobham (Stoke D'Ab.)
KT11 214 CA114
Orpington BR6 205 ET101
Ireton Av, Walt. KT12 195 BS103
Ireton Cl, N10 98 DG52
Ireton Pl, Grays RM17
off Russell Rd 170 GA77
Ireton St, E3 13 N3
Iris Av, Bex. DA5 186 EY85
Iris Cl, E6 144 EL70
Brentwood (Pilg.Hat.)
CM15 108 FV43
Croydon CR0 203 DX102
Surbiton KT6 198 CM101
Iris Ct, Pnr. HA5 116 BW55
Iris Cres, Bexh. DA7 166 EZ79
Iris Path, Rom. RM3
off Clematis Cl 106 FJ52
Iris Rd, Epsom (W.Ewell)
KT19 216 CP106
Iris Wk, Edg. HA8 off Ash Cl 96 CQ49
Iris Way, E4 101 DZ51
Irkdale Av, Enf. EN1 82 DT39
Iron Br Cl, NW10 118 CS64
Southall UB2 136 CC74
Iron Br Rd, Uxb. UB11 154 BN75
West Drayton UB7 154 BN75
Iron Dr, Hert. SG13 32 DV08
Iron Mill La, Dart. DA1 167 FE84
Iron Mill Pl, SW18
off Garratt La 180 DB86
Dartford DA1 167 FF84
Iron Mill Rd, SW18 180 DB86
Ironmonger La, EC2 11 J8
Ironmonger Pas, EC1 11 H3
Ironmonger Row, EC1 11 H2
Ironmongers Pl, E14 23 P8
IRONS BOTTOM, Reig. RH2 266 DA142
Ironsbottom, Horl. RH6 268 DA146
Reigate (Sidlow) RH2 266 DB141
Ironside Cl, SE16 22 G3
Irons Way, Rom. RM5 105 FC52
Irvine Av, Har. HA3 117 CG55
Irvine Cl, N20 98 DE47
Irvine Gdns, S.Ock. RM15 149 FT72
Irvine Pl, Vir.W. GU25 192 AY99
Irvine Way, Orp. BR6 205 ET101
Irving Av, Nthlt. UB5 136 BX67
Irving Gro, SW9 161 DM82
Irving Ms, N1 4 G4
Irving Rd, W14 16 B5
Irving St, WC2 9 M10
Irving Wk, Swans. DA10 190 FY87
Irving Way, NW9 119 CT57
Swanley BR8 207 FD96
Irwin Av, SE18 165 ES80
Irwin Cl, Uxb. UB10 114 BN62
Irwin Gdns, NW10 139 CV67
Irwin Rd, Guil. GU2 258 AU135
Isabel Gate, Wal.Cr. (Chsht)
EN8 67 DZ26
Isabel Hill Cl, Hmptn. TW12
off Upper Sunbury Rd 196 CB95
Isabella Cl, N14 99 DJ45
Isabella Ct, Rich. TW10
off Grove Rd 178 CM86
Isabella Dr, Orp. BR6 223 EQ105
Isabella Rd, E9 122 DW64
Isabella St, SE1 20 E2
Isabelle Cl, Wal.Cr.
(Goffs Oak) EN7 66 DQ29
Isabel St, SW9 161 DM81
Isambard Cl, Uxb. UB8 134 BK69
Isambard Ms, E14 24 D6
Isambard Pl, SE16 22 F2
Isbell Gdns, Rom. RM1 105 FE52
Isbells Dr, Reig. RH2 266 DB135
Isel Way, SE22
off East Dulwich Gro 182 DS85
Isenburg Way, Hem.H. HP2 40 BK15
Isham Rd, SW16 201 DL96
Isis Cl, SW15 159 CW84
Ruislip HA4 115 BQ58
Isis Dr, Upmin. RM14 129 FS58
Isis St, SW18 180 DC89
Coll Islamic Coll for Advanced
Studies, NW10
off High Rd 139 CV65
Island, The, Stai. (Wrays.)
TW19 173 BA90
West Drayton UB7 154 BH81
Island Cl, Stai. TW18 173 BE91
Island Fm Av, W.Mol. KT8 196 BZ99
Island Fm Rd, W.Mol. KT8 196 BZ99
DLR Island Gardens 24 C8
Island Rd, Mitch. CR4 180 DF94
Island Row, E14 13 L8
Isla Rd, SE18 165 EQ79
Islay Gdns, Houns. TW4 176 BX85
Islay Wk, N1 5 H4
Isledon Rd, N7 121 DN62
Islehurst Cl, Chis. BR7 205 EN95
Islet Pk Dr, Maid. SL6 130 AC68
Islet Pk Rd, Maid. SL6 130 AC68
ISLEWORTH, TW7 157 CF83
⇌ Isleworth 157 CF82
Sch Isleworth & Syon Sch
for Boys, Islw. TW7
off Ridgeway Rd 157 CE80
Isleworth Business Complex,
Islw. TW7
off St. John's Rd 157 CF82
Isleworth Prom, Twick. TW1 157 CH84
Sch Isleworth Town Prim Sch,
Islw. TW7
off Twickenham Rd 157 CG82
ISLINGTON, N1 4 C8
Sch Islington Arts & Media
Sch, N4 off Turle Rd 121 DM60
Islington Grn, N1 4 E8
Sch Islington Grn Sec Sch, N1 4 G8
Islington High St, N1 4 D10
Islington Pk Ms, N1 4 E5
Islington Pk St, N1 4 D5
Islip Gdns, Edg. HA8 96 CR52
Northolt UB5 136 BY66
Islip Manor Rd, Nthlt. UB5 136 BY66
Islip St, NW5 121 DJ64
Ismailia Rd, E7 144 EH66
★ Ismaili Cen & Zamana
Gall, SW7 17 P7
Ismay Ct, Slou. SL2
off Elliman Av 132 AS73
Isom Cl, E13 15 P2
ISTEAD RISE, Grav. DA13 190 GE94
Istead Ri, Grav. DA13 191 GF94
Sch Italia Conti Acad of Thea
Arts, EC1 10 G5
Itchingwood Common Rd,
Oxt. RH8 254 EJ133
Ivanhoe Cl, Uxb. UB8 134 BK71
Ivanhoe Dr, Har. HA3 117 CG55
Ivanhoe Rd, SE5 162 DT83
Hounslow TW4 156 BX83
Ivatt Pl, W14 16 F10
Ivatt Way, N17 121 DP55
Iveagh Av, NW10 138 CN68
Iveagh Cl, E9 143 DX67
NW10 138 CN68
Northwood HA6 93 BP53
Iveagh Ct, Hem.H. HP2 40 BK19
Iveagh Rd, Guil. GU2 258 AV135
Woking GU21 226 AT118
Iveagh Ter, NW10
off Iveagh Av 138 CN68
Ivedon Rd, Well. DA16 166 EW82
Ive Fm Cl, E10 123 EA61
Ive Fm La, E10 123 EA61
Iveley Rd, SW4 161 DJ82
IVER, SL0 133 BF72
⇌ Iver 153 BF75
Iverdale Cl, Iver SL0 153 BC73
Ivere Dr, Barn. EN5 80 DB44
IVER HEATH, Iver SL0 133 BD69
Sch Iver Heath Inf Sch, Iver
SL0 off Slough Rd 133 BD69
Sch Iver Heath Jun Sch, Iver
SL0 off St. Margarets Cl 133 BD68
Iverhurst Cl, Bexh. DA6 186 EX85
Iver La, Iver SL0 134 BH71
Uxbridge UB8 134 BH71
Iverna Ct, W8 17 H5
Iverna Gdns, W8 17 H5
Feltham TW14 175 BR85
Iver Rd, Brwd. (Pilg.Hat.)
CM15 108 FV44
Iver SL0 134 BG72
Iverson Rd, NW6 139 CZ65
Ivers Way, Croy. (New Adgtn)
CR0 221 EB108
Sch Iver Village Inf Sch, Iver
SL0 off West Sq 133 BF72
Sch Iver Village Jun Sch, Iver
SL0 off High St 133 BE72
Ives Gdns, Rom. RM1
off Sims Cl 127 FF56
Ives Rd, E16 14 G6
Hertford SG14 31 DP08
Slough SL3 153 AZ76
Ives St, SW3 18 B7
Ivestor Ter, SE23 182 DW87
Ivimey St, E2 12 B1
Ivinghoe Cl, Enf. EN1 82 DS40
St. Albans AL4
off Highview Gdns 43 CJ15
Watford WD25 76 BX35
Ivinghoe Rd, Bushey WD23 95 CD45
Dagenham RM8 126 EV64
Rickmansworth (Mill End)
WD3 92 BG45
Ivins Rd, Beac. HP9 88 AG54
Ivor Cl, Guil. GU1 259 AZ135
Ivor Gro, SE9 185 EP88
Ivor Pl, NW1 8 C4
Ivor St, NW1 141 DJ66
Ivory Cl, St.Alb. AL4 43 CJ22
Ivory Ct, Hem.H. HP3 40 BL23
Ivorydown, Brom. BR1 184 EG91
Ivory Sq, SW11
off Gartons Way 160 DC83
Ivy Bower Cl, Green. DA9
off Riverview Rd 189 FV85
Ivybridge, Brox. EN10 49 EA19
Ivybridge Cl, Twick. TW1 177 CG86
Uxbridge UB8 134 BL69
Ivybridge Est, Islw. TW7 177 CF85
Ivybridge La, WC2 9 P10
Sch Ivybridge Prim Sch, Islw.
TW7
off Summerwood Rd 177 CF86
IVY CHIMNEYS, Epp. CM16 69 ES32
Sch Ivy Chimneys Co Prim Sch,
Epp. CM16
off Ivy Chimneys Rd 69 ET32
Ivy Chimneys Rd, Epp.
CM16 69 ES32
Ivychurch Cl, SE20 182 DW94
Ivychurch La, SE17 21 N9
Ivy Cl, Dart. DA1 188 FN87
Gravesend DA12 191 GJ90
Harrow HA2 116 BZ63
Pinner HA5 116 BW59
Sunbury-on-Thames
TW16 196 BW96
Ivy Cotts, E14 14 B9
Ivy Ct, SE16 22 B10
Ivy Cres, W4 158 CQ77
Slough SL1 131 AM73
Sch Ivydale Prim Sch, SE15
off Ivydale Rd 163 DX84
Ivydale Rd, SE15 163 DX83
Carshalton SM5 200 DF103
Ivyday Gro, SW16 181 DM90
Ivydene, W.Mol. KT8 196 BZ99
Ivydene Cl, Red. RH1 267 DH139
Sutton SM1 218 DC105
Ivy Gdns, N8 121 DL58
Mitcham CR4 201 DK97
Ivy Ho La, Berk. HP4 38 AY19
Sevenoaks TN14 241 FD118
Ivyhouse Rd, Dag. RM9 146 EX65
Ivy Ho Rd, Uxb. UB10 115 BP62
Ivy La, Houns. TW4 156 BZ84
Sevenoaks (Knock.) TN14 240 EY116
Woking GU22 227 BB118
Ivy Lea, Rick. WD3
off Springwell Av 92 BG46
Ivy Lo La, Rom. RM3 106 FP53
Ivy Mill Cl, Gdse. RH9 252 DV132
Ivy Mill La, Gdse. RH9 252 DU132
Ivymount Rd, SE27 181 DN90
Ivy Pl, Surb. KT5
off Alpha Rd 198 CM100
Ivy Rd, E16 15 L7
E17 123 EA58
N14 99 DJ45
NW2 119 CW63
SE4 163 DZ84
SW17 off Tooting High St 180 DE92
Hounslow TW3 156 CB84
Surbiton KT6 198 CN102
Ivy St, N1 5 L9
Ivy Ter, Hodd. EN11 49 EC15
Ivy Wk, Dag. RM9 146 EY65
Hatfield AL9 44 CS15
Ixworth Pl, SW3 18 A9
Izane Rd, Bexh. DA6 166 EZ84

J

Jacaranda Cl, N.Mal. KT3 198 CS97
Jacaranda Gro, E8 5 P6
Sch Jack & Jill Sch, Hmptn.
TW12 off Nightingale Rd 176 CA93
Jackass La, Kes. BR2 222 EH107
Oxted (Tand.) RH8 253 DZ131
Jack Barnett Way, N22 99 DM54
Jack Clow Rd, E15 144 EE68
Jack Cornwell St, E12 125 EN63
Jack Dash Way, E6 144 EL70
Jackdaws, Welw.G.C. AL7 30 DC09
Jackets La, Nthwd. HA6 93 BP53
Uxbridge (Hare.) UB9 92 BN52
Jacketts Fld, Abb.L. WD5 59 BT31
Jack Goodchild Way,
Kings.T. KT1
off Kingston Rd 198 CP97
Jacklin Grn, Wdf.Grn. IG8 102 EG49
Sch Jack Lobley Sch, Til.
RM18 off Leicester Rd 171 GF81
Jackman Ms, NW10 118 CS62
Jackmans La, Wok. GU21 226 AU119
Jackman St, E8 142 DV67
Jacks La, Uxb. (Hare.) UB9 92 BG53
Jackson Cl, E9 142 DW66
Epsom KT18 216 CR114
Greenhithe DA9
off Cowley Av 189 FU85
Hornchurch RM11 128 FM56
Uxbridge UB10
off Jackson Rd 134 BL66
Jackson Ct, E11
off Brading Cres 124 EH60
Jackson Rd, N7 121 DM63
Barking IG11 145 ER67
Barnet EN4 80 DE44
Bromley BR2 204 EL103
Uxbridge UB10 134 BL66
Jacksons Dr, Wal.Cr. EN7 66 DU28
Jacksons La, N6 120 DG59
Jacksons Pl, Croy. CR0
off Cross Rd 202 DR102
Jackson St, SE18 165 EN79
Jacksons Way, Croy. CR0 203 EA104
Jackson Way, Epsom KT19
off Lady Harewood Way 216 CN109
Southall UB2 156 CB75
Jack Stevens Cl, Harl. CM17
off Hillside 52 EW17
Sch Jack Taylor Sch, The,
NW8 off Ainsworth Way 140 DC67
Sch Jack Tizard Spec Sch,
SW6 off Finlay St 159 CX81
Jack Walker Ct, N5 121 DP63
Jacob Ho, Erith DA18
off Kale Rd 166 EX75
Jacobs Av, Rom. (Harold Wd)
RM3 106 FL54
Jacobs Cl, Dag. RM10 127 FB63
Windsor SL4 151 AL81
Jacobs Ho, E13 144 EJ69
Jacobs Ladder, Hat. AL9
off The Broadway 45 CW18
Jacobs La, Dart. (Hort.Kir.)
DA4 208 FQ97
Jacob St, SE1 21 P3
JACOBS WELL, Guil. GU4 242 AY129
Jacob's Well Ms, W1 8 F7
Jacob's Well Rd, Guil. GU4 242 AX129
Jacqueline Cl, Nthlt. UB5
off Canford Av 136 BZ67
Jade Cl, E16 144 EK72
NW2 off Marble Dr 119 CX59
Dagenham RM8 126 EW60
Jaffe Rd, Ilf. IG1 125 EQ60
Jaffray Pl, SE27
off Chapel Rd 181 DP91
Jaffray Rd, Brom. BR2 204 EK98
Jaggard Way, SW12 180 DF87
Jagger Cl, Dart. DA2 188 FQ87
Jago Cl, SE18 165 EQ79
Jago Wk, SE5 162 DR80
Jail La, West. (Bigg.H.) TN16 238 EK116
Sch Jamahiriya Sch, SW3
off Glebe Pl 160 DE79
Jamaica Rd, SE1 21 P4
SE16 22 C5
Thornton Heath CR7 201 DP100
Jamaica St, E1 12 F7
Sch James Allen's Girls' Sch,
SE22
off East Dulwich Gro 182 DS85
James Av, NW2 119 CW64
Dagenham RM8 126 EZ60
James Bedford Cl, Pnr. HA5 94 BW54
James Boswell Cl, SW16
off Curtis Fld Rd 181 DN91
James Cl, E13
off Richmond St 144 EG68
NW11 off Woodlands 119 CY58
Bushey WD23
off Aldenham Rd 76 BY43
Romford RM2 127 FG57
James Collins Cl, W9 6 E4
James Ct, N1 5 H6
Sch James Dixon Prim Sch,
SE20
off William Booth Rd 202 DU95
James Dudson Ct, NW10 138 CQ66
Sch James Elliman Prim Sch,
Slou. SL2
off Elliman Av 132 AT73
James Gdns, N22 99 DP52
James Hammett Ho, E2 5 P10
James Joyce Wk, SE24
off Shakespeare Rd 161 DP84
James La, E10 123 ED59
E11 123 ED58
James Lee Sq, Enf. EN3 83 EA38
James Martin Cl, Uxb.
(Denh.) UB9 114 BG58
James Meadow, Slou. SL3
off Ditton Rd 153 AZ79
James Newman Ct, SE9
off Great Harry Dr 185 EN90
Sch James Oglethorpe Prim
Sch, Upmin. RM14
off Ashvale Gdns 129 FT61
Jameson Cl, W3
off Acton La 158 CQ75
Jameson Ct, E2 142 DW68
St. Albans AL1
off Avenue Rd 43 CF19
Jameson St, W8 17 H1
James Pl, N17 100 DT53
James Rd, Dart. DA1 187 FG87
Guildford (Peasm.) GU3 258 AW142
James's Cotts, Rich. TW9
off Kew Rd 158 CN80
James Sinclair Pt, E13 144 EJ67
James St, W1 8 F7
WC2 9 P9
Barking IG11 145 EQ66
Enfield EN1 82 DT43
Epping CM16 69 ET28
Hounslow TW3 157 CD83
Windsor SL4 151 AR81
James Ter, SW14
off Mullins Path 158 CR83
Jamestown Rd, NW1 141 DH67
Jamestown Way, E14 14 F10
James Watt Way, Erith DA8 167 FF79
James Way, Wat. WD19 94 BX49
Sch James Wolfe Inf & Nurs Sch,
SE10 off Randall Pl 163 EC80
Sch James Wolfe Jun Sch,
SE10 off Randall Pl 163 EC80
James Yd, E4 101 ED51
Jamieson Ho, Houns. TW4 176 BZ87
Jamnagar Cl, Stai. TW18 173 BF93
Jamuna Cl, E14 13 K6
Jane Cl, Hem.H. HP2 41 BP15
Jane St, E1 12 C7
Janet St, E14 23 P5
Janeway Pl, SE16 22 C4
Janeway St, SE16 22 B4
Janice Ms, Ilf. IG1
off Oakfield Rd 125 EP62
Janmead, Brwd. (Hutt.)
CM13 109 GB45
Janoway Hill La, Wok. GU21 226 AW119
Jansen Wk, SW11
off Hope St 160 DD84
Janson Cl, E15
off Janson Rd 124 EE64
NW10 118 CR62
Janson Rd, E15 124 EE64
Jansons Rd, N15 122 DS55
Japan Cres, N4 121 DM60
Sch Japanese Sch, W3
off Creffield Rd 138 CN73
Japan Rd, Rom. RM6 126 EX58
Japonica Cl, Wok. GU21 226 AW118
Jardine Rd, E1 13 H9
Jarman Cl, Hem.H. HP3 40 BL22

★ Place of interest   H Hospital   Sch School   Coll College   Uni University   ⇌ Railway station

Jarmans Pk, Hem.H. HP2 40 BM21
Jarman Way, Hem.H. HP2 40 BM21
Jarrah Cotts, Purf. RM19
off London Rd Purfleet 169 FR79
Jarrett Cl, SW2 181 DP88
Jarrow Cl, Mord. SM4 200 DB99
Jarrow Rd, N17 122 DV56
SE16 22 E8
Romford RM6 126 EW58
Jarrow Way, E9 123 DY63
Jarvis Cleys, Wal.Cr. (Chsht)
EN7 66 DT26
Jarvis Cl, Bark. IG11
off Westbury Rd 145 ER67
Barnet EN5 79 CX43
Jarvis Rd, SE22
off Melbourne Gro 162 DS84
South Croydon CR2 220 DR107
Jarvis Way, Rom. (Harold Wd)
RM3 106 FL54
Jasmin Cl, Nthwd. HA6 93 BT53
Jasmine Cl, Ilf. IG1 125 EP64
Orpington BR6 205 EP103
Redhill RH1
off Spencer Way 266 DG139
Southall UB1 136 BY73
Woking GU21 226 AT116
Jasmine Dr, Hert. SG13 32 DU09
Jasmine Gdns, Croy. CR0 203 EB104
Harrow HA2 116 CA61
Hatfield AL10 45 CU16
Jasmine Gro, SE20 202 DV95
Jasmine Rd, Rom. (Rush Grn)
RM7 127 FE61
Jasmine Ter, West Dr. UB7 154 BN75
Jasmine Way, E.Mol. KT8
off Hampton Ct Way 197 CE98
Jasmin Rd, Epsom KT19 216 CP106
Jasmin Way, Hem.H. HP1
off Larkspur Cl 39 BE19
Jason Cl, Brwd. CM14 108 FT49
Redhill RH1 266 DE139
Weybridge KT13 213 BQ106
Jason Ct, W1
off Marylebone La 140 DG72
Jasons Dr, Guil. GU4 243 BC131
Jasons Hill, Chesh. HP5 56 AV30
Jason Wk, SE9 185 EN91
Jasper Cl, Enf. EN3 82 DW38
Jasper Pas, SE19 182 DT93
Jasper Rd, E16 144 EK72
SE19 182 DT92
Jasper Wk, N1 11 J1
Javelin Way, Nthlt. UB5 136 BX69
Jaycroft, Enf. EN2
off The Ridgeway 81 DN39
Jay Gdns, Chis. BR7 185 EM91
Jay Ms, SW7 17 M4
Jays Covert, Couls. CR5 234 DG119
Jazzfern Ter, Wem. HA0
off Maybank Av 117 CG64
Jean Batten Cl, Wall. SM6 219 DM108
Jebb Av, SW2 181 DL86
Jebb St, E3 143 EA68
Jedburgh Rd, E13 144 EJ69
Jedburgh St, SW11 160 DG84
Jeddo Rd, W12 159 CT75
Jefferson Cl, W13 157 CH76
Ilford IG2 125 EP57
Slough SL3 153 BA77
Jefferson Wk, SE18
off Kempt St 165 EN79
Jeffreys Pl, NW1
off Jeffreys St 141 DJ66
Jeffreys Rd, SW4 161 DL82
Enfield EN3 83 DZ41
Jeffreys St, NW1 141 DH66
Jeffreys Wk, SW4 161 DL82
Jeffries Ho, NW10 138 CR67
Jeffries Pas, Guil. GU1
off High St 258 AX135
Jeffries Rd, Lthd. (W.Hors.)
KT24 245 BQ130
Ware SG12 33 DY06
Jeffs Cl, Hmptn. TW12
off Uxbridge Rd 176 CB93
Jeffs Rd, Sutt. SM1 217 CZ105
Coll **Jeff Wooller Coll**, WC1 9 P5
Jeger Av, E2 5 N8
Jeken Rd, SE9 164 EJ84
Jelf Rd, SW2 181 DN85
Jellicoe Av, Grav. DA12 191 GJ90
Jellicoe Av W, Grav. DA12
off Kitchener Av 191 GJ90
Jellicoe Cl, Slou. SL1 151 AP75
Jellicoe Gdns, Stan. HA7 95 CF51
Jellicoe Rd, E13 15 M3
N17 100 DR52
Watford WD18 75 BU44
Jemma Knowles Cl, SW2
off Neil Wates Cres 181 DN88
Jemmett Cl, Kings.T. KT2 198 CP95
Jengar Cl, Sutt. SM1 218 DB105
Jenkins Av, St.Alb. (Brick.Wd)
AL2 60 BY30
Jenkins La, E6 145 EN68
Barking IG11 145 EP68
Jenkins Rd, E13 15 P4
Jenner Av, W3 138 CR71
Jenner Cl, Sid. DA14 186 EU91
Jenner Ho, SE3 164 EE79
Jenner Pl, SW13 159 CV79
Jenner Rd, N16 122 DT61
Guildford GU1 258 AY135
Jenner Way, Epsom KT19
off Monro Pl 216 CN109
Jennery La, Slou. (Burn.)
SL1 130 AJ69
Jennett Rd, Croy. CR0 201 DN104
Jennifer Rd, Brom. BR1 184 EF90
Jennings Cl, Add. (New Haw)
KT15 *off Woodham La* 212 BJ109
Surbiton KT6 197 CJ101
Jennings Fld, H.Wyc. (
Flack.Hth) HP10 110 AC56
Jennings Rd, SE22 182 DT86
St. Albans AL1 43 CG19
Jennings Way, Barn. EN5 79 CW41
Hemel Hempstead HP3 40 BL22
Horley RH6 269 DK148
Jenningtree Rd, Erith DA8 167 FH80
Jenningtree Way, Belv.
DA17 167 FC75
Jenny Hammond Cl, E11
off Newcomen Rd 124 EF62
Sch **Jenny Hammond Prim Sch, The**, E11 *off Worsley Rd* 124 EE63
Jenny Path, Rom. RM3 106 FK52
Jennys Way, Couls. CR5 235 DJ122
Jenson Way, SE19 182 DT94
Jenton Av, Bexh. DA7 166 EY81
Jephson Rd, E7 144 EJ66
Jephson St, SE5
off Grove La 162 DR81
Jephtha Rd, SW18 180 DA86
Jeppos La, Mitch. CR4 200 DF98
Jepps Cl, Wal.Cr. EN7
off Little Gro Av 66 DS27
Jepson Ho, SW6
off Pearscroft Rd 160 DB81
Jerdan Pl, SW6 160 DA80
Jeremiah St, E14 14 A8
Jeremys Grn, N18 100 DV49
Jermyn St, SW1 19 J1
Jerningham Av, Ilf. IG5 103 EP54
Jerningham Rd, SE14 163 DY82
Jerome Cres, NW8 8 A3
Jerome Dr, St.Alb. AL3 42 CA22
Jerome Pl, Kings.T. KT1
off Wadbrook St 197 CK96
Jerome St, E1 11 N5
Jerome Twr, W3 158 CP75
Jerounds, Harl. CM19 51 EP17
Sch **Jerounds Co Inf Sch**, Harl. CM19 *off Pyenest Rd* 51 EP18
Sch **Jerounds Co Jun Sch**, Harl. CM19
off Pyenest Rd 51 EP18
Jerrard St, N1 5 M10
SE13 163 EB83
Jersey Av, Stan. HA7 95 CH54
Jersey Cl, Cher. KT16 193 BF104
Guildford GU4
off Weybrook Dr 243 BB129
Hoddesdon EN11 49 EA16
Jersey Dr, Orp. BR5 205 ER100
JERSEY FARM, St.Alb. AL4 43 CJ15
Jersey Ho, Enf. EN3
off Eastfield Rd 83 DX38
Jersey La, St.Alb. AL4 43 CH18
Jersey Par, Houns. TW5 156 CB81
Jersey Rd, E11 123 ED60
E16 *off Prince Regent La* 144 EJ72
SW17 181 DH93
W7 157 CG75
Hounslow TW3, TW5 156 CB81
Ilford IG1 125 EP63
Isleworth TW7 157 CE79
Rainham RM13 147 FG66
Jersey St, E2 12 D2
Jerusalem Pas, EC1 10 E4
Jervis Av, Enf. EN3 83 DY35
Jervis Ct, W1 9 H8
Jerviston Gdns, SW16 181 DN93
Jesmond Av, Wem. HA9 138 CM65
Jesmond Cl, Mitch. CR4 201 DH97
Jesmond Rd, Croy. CR0 202 DT101
Jesmond Way, Stan. HA7 96 CL50
Jessam Av, E5 122 DV60
Jessamine Pl, Dart. DA2 188 FQ87
Jessamine Rd, W7 137 CE74
Jessamine Ter, Swan. BR8
off Birchwood Rd 207 FC95
Jessamy Rd, Wey. KT13 195 BP103
Jessel Dr, Loug. IG10 85 EQ39
Jesse Rd, E10 123 EC60
Jesses La, Guil. (Peasl.) GU5 261 BQ144
Jessett Cl, Erith DA8
off West St 167 FD77
Jessica Rd, SW18 180 DC86
Jessie Blythe La, N19 121 DL59
Jessiman Ter, Shep. TW17 194 BN99
Jessop Av, Sthl. UB2 156 BZ77
Sch **Jessop Prim Sch**, SE24
off Lowden Rd 162 DQ84
Jessop Rd, SE24
off Milkwood Rd 161 DP84
Jessop Sq, E14
off Heron Quay 143 EA74
Jessops Way, Croy. CR0 201 DJ100
Jessup Cl, SE18 165 EQ77
Jetstar Way, Nthlt. UB5 136 BY69
Jetty Wk, Grays RM17 170 GA79
Jevington Way, SE12 184 EH89
Jewel Rd, E17 123 EA55
Jewels Hill, West. (Bigg.H.)
TN16 222 EG112
★ **Jewel Twr, Hos of Parliament**,
SW1 19 N5
★ **Jewish Mus**, NW1
off Albert St 141 DH67
Jewry St, EC3 11 N8
Jew's Row, SW18 160 DB84
Jews Wk, SE26 182 DV91
Jeymer Av, NW2 119 CV64
Jeymer Dr, Grnf. UB6 136 CC67
Jeypore Pas, SW18
off Jeypore Rd 180 DC86
Jeypore Rd, SW18 180 DC87
Sch **JFS Sch**, Har. HA3
off The Mall 118 CN58
Jillian Cl, Hmptn. TW12 176 CA94
Jim Bradley Cl, SE18
off John Wilson St 165 EN77
Jim Desormeaux Bungalows,
Harl. CM20 *off School La* 35 ES13
Jim Griffiths Ho, SW6
off Clem Attlee Ct 159 CZ79
Jinnings, The, Welw.G.C.
AL7 30 DA12
Sch **J. Menorah Prim Sch**,
NW11 *off Woodstock Av* 119 CY59
Joan Cres, SE9 184 EK87
Joan Gdns, Dag. RM8 126 EY61
Joan Rd, Dag. RM8 126 EY61
Joan St, SE1 20 E2
Jocelyn Rd, Rich. TW9 158 CL83
Jocelyns, Harl. CM17 36 EW11
Jocelyn St, SE15 162 DU81
Jocketts Hill, Hem.H. HP1 39 BF20
Jocketts Rd, Hem.H. HP1 39 BF21
Jockey's Flds, WC1 10 B5
Jodane St, SE8 23 L8
Jodies Ct, St.Alb. AL4 43 CJ18
Jodrell Cl, Islw. TW7 157 CG81
Jodrell Rd, E3 143 DZ67
Jodrell Way, Grays (W.Thur.)
RM20 169 FT78
Joel St, Nthwd. HA6 115 BU55
Pinner HA5 115 BU55
Sch **Johanna Prim Sch**, SE1 20 C4
Johanna St, SE1 20 C4
John Adam St, WC2 9 P10
John Aird Ct, W2 7 M5
John Archer Way, SW18 180 DD86
John Ashby Cl, SW2 181 DL86
John Austin Cl, Kings.T. KT2
off Queen Elizabeth Rd 198 CM95
Sch **John Ball Sch**, SE3
off Southvale Rd 164 EE82
John Barnes Wk, E15 144 EF65
Sch **John Betts Prim Sch**,
W6 *off Paddenswick Rd* 159 CV76
John Bradshaw Rd, N14
off High St 99 DK46
Sch **John Bramston Prim Sch**,
Ilf. IG6 *off Newcastle Av* 104 EU51
John Burns Dr, Bark. IG11 145 ES66
Sch **John Burns Prim Sch**,
SW11 *off Wycliffe Rd* 160 DG82
Johnby Cl, Enf. EN3
off Manly Dixon Dr 83 DY37
John Campbell Rd, N16 5 M2
John Carpenter St, EC4 10 E9
Sch **John Chilton Sch**, Nthlt.
UB5
off Compton Cres 136 BY66
John Cobb Rd, Wey. KT13 212 BN108
John Cornwell VC Ho, E12 125 EN63
John Ct, Hodd. EN11
off Molesworth 33 EA14
Sch **John Donne Prim Sch**,
SE15 *off Woods Rd* 162 DV81
John Drinkwater Cl, E11
off Browning Rd 124 EF59
John Eliot Cl, Wal.Abb. EN9 50 EE21
John Felton Rd, SE16 22 A4
Sch **John Fisher Sch, The**,
Pur. CR8 *off Peaks Hill* 219 DL110
John Fisher St, E1 12 A9
Sch **John F. Kennedy RC Sch**,
Hem.H. HP1
off Hollybush La 39 BF19
Sch **John F. Kennedy Spec Sch**,
E15 *off Pitchford St* 143 ED67
John Gooch Dr, Enf. EN2 81 DP39
John Harrison Way, SE10 25 J6
John Horner Ms, N1 4 G9
H **John Howard Cen**, E9 139 DY65
John Islip St, SW1 19 N8
John Keats Ho, N22 99 DM52
Sch **John Keble C of E Prim Sch**,
NW10 *off Crownhill Rd* 139 CT67
Sch **John Kelly Tech Coll for Boys**,
NW2 *off Crest Rd* 119 CU62
Sch **John Kelly Tech Coll for Girls**,
NW2 *off Crest Rd* 119 CU62
Sch **John Loughborough Sch, The**,
N17 *off Holcombe Rd* 122 DT55
Sch **John Lyon Sch, The**, Har.
HA2 *off Middle Rd* 117 CD60
John Maurice Cl, SE17 21 J7
John McKenna Wk, SE16 22 B5
John Newton Ct, Well.
DA16 166 EV83
John Parker Cl, Dag. RM10 147 FB66
John Parker Sq, SW11
off Thomas Baines Rd 160 DD83
Sch **John Paul II RC Sch**,
SW19 *off Princes Way* 179 CX87
John Penn St, SE13 163 EB81
Sch **John Penrose Sch**, Uxb.
UB9 *off Northwood Way* 92 BK53
John Perrin Pl, Har. HA3 118 CL59
Sch **John Perryn Prim Sch**,
W3 *off Long Dr* 138 CS72
Sch **John Perry Prim Sch**, Dag.
RM10 *off Charles Rd* 147 FD65
John Princes St, W1 9 H7
John Rennie Wk, E1 22 D1
Sch **John Roan Sec Sch, The**,
Lwr Sch, SE3
off Westcombe Pk Rd 164 EF80
Upr Sch, SE3
off Maze Hill 164 EE80
John Roll Way, SE16 22 B5
Sch **John Ruskin Prim Sch**,
SE5 *off John Ruskin St* 162 DQ79
Coll **John Ruskin 6th Form Coll**, S.Croy. CR2
off Selsdon Pk Rd 221 DY108
John Ruskin St, SE5 161 DP80
John Russell Cl, Guil. GU2 242 AU131
Johns Av, NW4 119 CW56
Johns Cl, Ashf. TW15 175 BQ91
John's Ct, Sutt. SM2
off Mulgrave Rd 218 DB107
Sch **John Scurr Prim Sch**, E1 12 E4
Johnsdale, Oxt. RH8 254 EF129
John Silkin La, SE8 23 H8
Johns La, Mord. SM4 200 DC99
John's Ms, WC1 10 B4
John Smith Av, SW6 159 CZ80
John Smith Ms, E14 14 E10
Johnson Cl, E8 142 DU67
Gravesend (Nthflt) DA11 190 GD90
Johnson Ct, Hem.H. HP3 40 BL22
Johnson Rd, NW10 138 CR67
Bromley BR2 204 EK99
Croydon CR0 202 DR101
Hounslow TW5 156 BW80
Johnsons Av, Sev. (Bad.Mt)
TN14 225 FB110
Johnsons Cl, Cars. SM5 200 DF104
Johnson's Ct, EC4
off Fleet St 141 DN72
Johnsons Ct, Sev. (Seal)
TN15 *off School La* 257 FM121
Johnsons Dr, Hmptn. TW12 196 CC95
Johnson's Pl, SW1 19 J10
Johnson St, E1 12 F8
Southall UB2 156 BW76
Johnsons Way, NW10 138 CP70
Greenhithe DA9 189 FW86
Johnsons Yd, Uxb. UB8
off Redford Way 134 BJ66
John Spencer Sq, N1 4 F4
John's Pl, E1 12 D7
Johns Rd, West. (Tats.) TN16 238 EK120
Sch **John Stainer Prim Sch**,
SE4 *off St. Asaph Rd* 163 DY83
John's Ter, Croy. CR0 202 DR102
Romford RM3 106 FP51
Johnston Cl, SW9
off Hackford Rd 161 DM81
Johnstone Rd, E6 145 EM69
Johnston Grn, Guil. GU2 242 AU130
Johnston Rd, Wdf.Grn. IG8 102 EG50
Johnston Ter, NW2
off Kara Way 119 CX62
Johnston Wk, Guil. GU2 242 AU130
John St, E15 144 EF67
SE25 202 DU98
WC1 10 B4
Enfield EN1 82 DT43
Grays RM17 170 GC79
Hounslow TW3 156 BY82
Johns Wk, Whyt. CR3 236 DU119
John Tate Rd, Hert. SG13 32 DT10
John Taylor Ct, Slou. SL1 131 AQ74
John Trundle Ct, EC2
off The Barbican 142 DQ71
John Walsh Twr, E11 124 EF61
Sch **John Warner Sch, The**,
Hodd. EN11
off Stanstead Rd 33 EB14
John Watkin Cl, Epsom
KT19 216 CP109
John William Cl, Grays
(Chaff.Hun.) RM16 169 FX78
John Williams Cl, SE14 163 DX79
Kingston upon Thames
KT2
off Henry Macaulay Av 197 CK95
John Wilson St, SE18 165 EN76
John Woolley Cl, SE13 164 EE84
Joiner's Arms Yd, SE5
off Denmark Hill 162 DR81
Joiners Cl, Chesh. (Ley Hill)
HP5 56 AV30
Gerrards Cross (Chal.St.P.)
SL9 91 AZ52
Joiners La, Ger.Cr. (Chal.St.P.)
SL9 90 AY53
Joiners Pl, N5
off Leconfield Rd 122 DR63
Joiner St, SE1 21 K2
Joiners Way, Ger.Cr.
(Chal.St.P.) SL9 90 AY52
Joiners Yd, N1
off Caledonia St 141 DL68
Joinville Pl, Add. KT15 212 BK105
Jolliffe Rd, Red. RH1 251 DJ126
Jollys La, Har. HA2 117 CD60
Hayes UB4 136 BX71
Jonathan Ct, W4
off Windmill Rd 158 CS77
Jonathan St, SE11 20 A9
Jones Rd, E13 15 P4
Waltham Cross (Chsht)
EN7 65 DP30
Jones St, W1 8 G10
Jones Wk, Rich. TW10
off Pyrland Rd 178 CM86
Jones Way, Slou. (Hedg.)
SL2 111 AR61
Jonquil Cl, Welw.G.C. AL7 30 DB11
Jonquil Gdns, Hmptn.
TW12 *off Partridge Rd* 176 BZ93
Jonson Cl, Hayes UB4 135 BU71
Mitcham CR4 201 DH98
Jordan Cl, Dag. RM10
off Muggeridge Rd 127 FB63
Harrow HA2
off Hamilton Cres 116 BZ62
South Croydon CR2 220 DT111
Watford WD25 75 BT35
Jordan Ct, SW15
off Charlwood Rd 159 CX84
Jordan Rd, Grnf. UB6 137 CH67
JORDANS, Beac. HP9 90 AT52
Jordans Cl, Guil. GU1
off Beatty Av 243 BA133
Isleworth TW7 157 CE81
Redhill RH1
off Spencer Way 266 DG139
Staines (Stanw.) TW19 174 BJ87
Sch **Jordans Co First Sch**,
Beac. HP9 *off Puers La* 90 AT51
Jordans La, Beac. (Jordans)
HP9 90 AS53
Jordans Rd, Rick. WD3 92 BG45
Jordans Way, Beac. (Jordans)
HP9 90 AT51
Rainham RM13 148 FK68
St. Albans (Brick.Wd) AL2 62 BZ30
Joseph Av, W3 138 CR72
Sch **Joseph Clarke Sch**, E4
off Vincent Rd 101 ED51
Joseph Hardcastle Cl, SE14 163 DX80
Sch **Joseph Hood Prim Sch**,
SW20 *off Whatley Av* 199 CY97
Josephine Av, SW2 181 DM85
Tadworth KT20 249 CZ126
Josephine Cl, Tad. KT20 249 CZ127
Sch **Joseph Lancaster Prim Sch**, SE1 21 J6
Joseph Locke Way, Esher
KT10 196 CA103
Joseph Powell Cl, SW12
off Hazelbourne Rd 181 DH86
Joseph Ray Rd, E11 124 EE61
Joseph's Rd, Guil. GU1 242 AW133
Joseph St, E3 13 M4
Joseph Trotter Cl, EC1
off Myddelton St 141 DN69
Joshua Cl, N10 99 DH52
South Croydon CR2 219 DP108
Joshua St, E14 14 C7
Joshua Wk, Wal.Cr. EN8
off Longcroft Dr 67 EA34
Josling Cl, Grays RM17 170 FZ79
Joslin Rd, Purf. RM19 168 FQ78
Joslyn Cl, Enf. EN3 83 EA38
Joubert St, SW11 160 DF82
Journeys End, Slou.
(Stoke P.) SL2 132 AS71
Jowett St, SE15 162 DT80
Joyce Av, N18 100 DT50
Joyce Ct, Wal.Abb. EN9 67 ED34
Joyce Dawson Way, SE28
off Thamesmere Dr 146 EU73
Joyce Dawson Way Shop Arc,
SE28
off Thamesmere Dr 146 EU73
Joyce Grn La, Dart. DA1 168 FL81
Joyce Grn Wk, Dart. DA1 168 FM84
Joyce Page Cl, SE7
off Lansdowne La 164 EK79
Joyce Wk, SW2 181 DN86
JOYDENS WOOD, Bex. DA5 187 FC92
Sch **Joydens Wd Co Inf Sch**,
Bex. DA5 *off Park Way* 187 FE90
Sch **Joydens Wd Co Jun Sch**,
Dart. DA2
off Birchwood Dr 187 FE91
Joydens Wd Rd, Bex. DA5 187 FD91
Joydon Dr, Rom. RM6 126 EV58
Joyes Cl, Rom. RM3 106 FK49
Joyners Cl, Dag. RM9 126 EZ63
Joyners Fld, Harl. CM18 51 EQ19
Joy Rd, Grav. DA12 191 GJ88
Jubb Powell Ho, N15 122 DS58
Jubilee Av, E4 101 EC51
Romford RM7 127 FB57
St. Albans (Lon.Col.) AL2 61 CK26
Twickenham TW2 176 CC88
Ware SG12 33 DZ05
Jubilee Cl, NW9 118 CR58
Greenhithe DA9 189 FW86
Pinner HA5 94 BW54
Romford RM7 127 FB57
Staines (Stanw.) TW19 174 BJ87
Jubilee Ct, Hat. AL10 45 CV15
Staines TW18 *off Leacroft* 174 BG92
Waltham Abbey EN9 68 EF33
Jubilee Cres, E14 24 D6
N9 100 DU46
Addlestone KT15 212 BK106
Gravesend DA12 191 GL89
Jubilee Dr, Ruis. HA4 116 BX63
★ **Jubilee Gdns**, SE1 20 A2
Jubilee Gdns, Sthl. UB1 136 CA72
Sch **Jubilee High Sch**, Add.
KT15 *off School La* 212 BG106
Sch **Jubilee JMI Sch**, N16
off Filey Av 122 DU60
Jubilee Pl, SW3 18 B9
Sch **Jubilee Prim Sch**, SE28
off Crossway 146 EW73
Sch **Jubilee Prim Sch**, SW2
off Tulse Hill 181 DN86
Jubilee Ri, Sev. (Seal) TN15 257 FM121
Jubilee Rd, Grays RM20 169 FV79
Greenford UB6 137 CH67
Orpington BR6 224 FA107
Sutton SM3 217 CX108
Watford WD24 75 BU38
Jubilee St, E1 12 E7
Jubilee Ter, Bet. RH3 264 CQ138
Dorking RH4 263 CH135
Jubilee Wk, Wat. WD19 93 BV49
Jubilee Way, SW19 200 DB95
Chessington KT9 216 CN105
Feltham TW14 175 BT88
Sidcup DA14 186 EU89
Slough SL3
off Montrose Av 152 AW80
Judd St, WC1 9 N2
Jude St, E16 15 K8
Judeth Gdns, Grav. DA12 191 GL92
Judge Heath La, Hayes UB3 135 BQ72
Uxbridge UB8 135 BQ72
Judges Hill, Pot.B. EN6 64 DE29
Judge St, Wat. WD24 75 BV38
Judge Wk, Esher (Clay.)
KT10 215 CE107
Judith Av, Rom. RM5 105 FB51
Juer St, SW11 160 DE80
Jug Hill, West. (Bigg.H.)
TN16 *off Hillcrest Rd* 238 EK116
Juglans Rd, Orp. BR6 206 EU102
Jules Thorn Av, Enf. EN1 82 DT41
Julia Gdns, Bark. IG11 146 EX68
Julia Garfield Ms, E16 25 P1
Juliana Cl, N2 120 DC55
Julian Av, W3 138 CP73
Julian Cl, Barn. EN5 80 DB41
Woking GU21 226 AW118
Julian Hill, Har. HA1 117 CE61
Weybridge KT13 212 BN108
Julian Pl, E14 24 B9
Julian Rd, Orp. BR6 224 EU107
Julians Cl, Sev. TN13 256 FG127
Sch **Julian's Prim Sch**,
SW16 *off Leigham Ct Rd* 181 DN91
Julians Way, Sev. TN13 256 FG127
Julian Taylor Path, SE23 182 DV89
Julia St, NW5
off Oak Village 120 DG63
Julien Rd, W5 157 CJ76
Coulsdon CR5 235 DK115
Juliette Rd, E13 144 EF68
Juliette Way, S.Ock. RM15 168 FM75
Julius Nyerere Cl, N1 4 A8
Junction App, SE13 163 EC83
SW11 160 DE83
Junction Av, W10
off Harrow Rd 139 CW69
Junction Ms, W2 8 A7
Junction Pk, Kings L. WD4 59 BQ33
Junction Pl, W2 8 A7
Junction Rd, E13 144 EH68
N9 100 DU46
N17 122 DU55
N19 121 DJ63
W5 157 CK77
Ashford TW15 175 BQ92
Brentford TW8 157 CK77
Brentwood CM14 108 FW49
Dartford DA1 188 FK86
Dorking RH4 263 CG136
Harrow HA1 117 CE58
Romford RM1 127 FF56
South Croydon CR2 220 DR106
Junction Rd E, Rom. RM6
off Kenneth Rd 126 EY59
Junction Rd W, Rom. RM6 126 EY59
Junction Shop Cen, The,
SW11 *off St. John's Hill* 160 DE84
June Cl, Couls. CR5 219 DH114
June La, Red. RH1 267 DH141
Junewood Cl, Add. (Wdhm)
KT15 211 BF111
Juniper Av, St.Alb.
(Brick.Wd) AL2 60 CA31
Juniper Cl, Barn. EN5 79 CX43
Broxbourne EN10 67 DZ25
Chessington KT9 216 CM107
Guildford GU1 242 AV129
Reigate RH2 266 DC136
Rickmansworth WD3 92 BK48
Wembley HA9 118 CM64
Westerham (Bigg.H.)
TN16 238 EL117
Juniper Ct, Slou. SL1
off Nixey Cl 152 AU75
Juniper Cres, NW1 140 DG66
Juniper Gdns, SW16
off Leonard Rd 201 DJ95
Radlett (Shenley) WD7 62 CL33
Sunbury-on-Thames
TW16 175 BT93
Juniper Gate, Rick. WD3 92 BK47
Juniper Grn, Hem.H. HP1 39 BE20
Juniper Gro, Wat. WD17 75 BU38
Juniper La, E6 144 EL71
High Wycombe
(Woob.Grn) HP10 110 AD56
Juniper Pl, Guil. (Shalf.)
GU4 258 AX141
Juniper Rd, Ilf. IG1 125 EN63
Reigate RH2 266 DC136
Juniper St, E1 12 E9
Juniper Ter, Guil. (Shalf.)
GU4 258 AX141
Juniper Wk, Bet. (Brock.)
RH3 264 CQ136
Swanley BR8 207 FD96
Juniper Way, Hayes UB3 135 BR73
Romford RM3 106 FL53
Juno Rd, Hem.H. HP2
off Saturn Way 40 BM17
Juno Way, SE14 163 DX79
Jupiter Dr, Hem.H. HP2 40 BM18
Sch **Jupiter Dr Prim Sch**,
Hem.H. HP2
off Jupiter Dr 40 BM18
Jupiter Way, N7 4 B3
Jupp Rd, E15 143 ED66
Jupp Rd W, E15 143 EC67
Jurgens Rd, Purf. RM19
off London Rd Purfleet 169 FR79
Jury St, Grav. DA11
off Princes St 191 GH86
Justice Wk, SW3
off Lawrence St 160 DE79
Justin Cl, Brent. TW8 157 CK80
Justin Rd, E4 101 DZ51

⊖ London Underground station   **DLR** Docklands Light Railway station   **Tra** Tramlink station   **Riv** Pedestrian ferry landing stage

Jute La, Enf. EN3 83 DY40
Jutland Cl, N19
off Sussex Way 121 DL60
Jutland Gdns, Couls. CR5 235 DM120
Jutland Pl, Egh. TW20
off Mullens Rd 173 BC92
Jutland Rd, E13 15 M4
SE6 183 EC87
Jutsums Av, Rom. RM7 127 FB58
Jutsums La, Rom. RM7 127 FB58
Juxon Cl, Har. HA3
off Augustine Rd 94 CB53
Juxon St, SE11 20 B7

K

Kaduna Cl, Pnr. HA5 115 BU57
Sch Kaizen Prim Sch, E13 15 N4
Kale Rd, Erith DA18 166 EY75
Kambala Rd, SW11 160 DD82
Kandlewood, Brwd. (Hutt.)
CM13 109 GB45
Kangley Br Rd, SE26 183 DZ92
Kaplan Dr, N21 81 DL43
Karanjia Ct, NW2
off Walm La 139 CW65
Kara Way, NW2 119 CX63
Karen Cl, Brwd. CM15 108 FW45
Rainham RM13 147 FE68
Karen Ct, SE4
off Wickham Rd 163 DZ82
Bromley BR1 off Blyth Rd 204 EF95
Karen Ter, E11
off Montague Rd 124 EF61
Karenza Ct, Wem. HA9
off Lulworth Av 117 CJ59
Kariba Cl, N9 100 DW48
Karina Cl, Chig. IG7 103 ES50
Karoline Gdns, Grnf. UB6
off Oldfield La N 137 CD68
Kashgar Rd, SE18 165 ET78
Kashmir Cl, Add. (New Haw)
KT15 212 BK109
Kashmir Rd, SE7 164 EK80
Kassala Rd, SW11 160 DF81
Katella Trd Est, Bark. IG11 145 ES69
Kates Cl, Barn. EN5 79 CU43
Katescroft, Welw.G.C. AL7 29 CY13
Katharine St, Croy. CR0 202 DQ104
Katherine Cl, SE16 22 G2
Addlestone KT15 212 BG107
Hemel Hempstead HP3 40 BL23
High Wycombe (Penn)
HP10 88 AC47
Katherine Gdns, SE9 164 EK84
Ilford IG6 103 EQ52
Katherine Ms, Whyt. CR3 236 DT117
Katherine Pl, Abb.L. WD5 59 BU32
Katherine Rd, E6 144 EK66
E7 124 EJ64
Twickenham TW1
off London Rd 177 CG88
KATHERINES, Harl. CM19 51 EM18
Sch Katherines GM Prim Sch,
Harl. CM19 off Brookside 51 EN17
Katherines Hatch, Harl.
CM19 off Brookside 51 EN17
Katherine Sq, W11 16 C1
Katherines Way, Harl. CM19 51 EN18
Kathleen Av, W3 138 CQ71
Wembley HA0 138 CL66
Kathleen Rd, SW11 160 DF83
Katrine Sq, Hem.H. HP2 40 BK16
Kavanaghs Rd, Brwd. CM14 108 FU48
Kavanaghs Ter, Brwd. CM14
off Kavanaghs Rd 108 FV48
Kaye Ct, Guil. GU1 242 AW131
Kaye Don Way, Wey. KT13 212 BN111
Kayemoor Rd, Sutt. SM2 218 DE108
Kay Rd, SW9 161 DL82
Kays Ter, E18 off Walpole Rd 102 EF53
Kay St, E2 142 DU68
Welling DA16 166 EV81
Kay Wk, St.Alb. AL4 43 CK19
Kay Way, SE10
off Greenwich High Rd 163 EB80
Kaywood Cl, Slou. SL3 152 AW76
Kean St, WC2 10 A8
Kearton Cl, Ken. CR8 236 DQ117
Keary Rd, Swans. DA10 190 FY87
Keatley Grn, E4 101 DZ51
Keats Av, E16 25 N1
Redhill RH1 250 DG132
Romford RM3 105 FH52
Keats Cl, E11
off Nightingale La 124 EH57
NW3 off Keats Gro 120 DE63
SE1 21 N8
SW19 off North Rd 180 DD93
Chigwell IG7 103 EQ51
Enfield EN3 83 DX43
Hayes UB4 135 BU71
Keats Gdns, Til. RM18 171 GH82
Keats Gro, NW3 120 DD63
★ Keats Ho, NW3 120 DE63
Keats Ho, Beck. BR3 183 EA93
Keats La, Wind. SL4 151 AR79
Keats Pl, EC2 11 J6
Keats Rd, Belv. DA17 167 FC76
Welling DA16 165 ES81
Keats Wk, Brwd. (Hutt.)
CM13 off Byron Rd 109 GD45
Keats Way, Croy. CR0 202 DW100
Greenford UB6 136 CB71
West Drayton UB7 154 BM77
Keble Cl, Nthlt. UB5 116 CC64
Worcester Park KT4 199 CT102
Keble Pl, SW13
off Somerville Av 159 CV79
Sch Keble Prep Sch, N21
off Wades Hill 99 DN45
Keble St, SW17 180 DC91
Keble Ter, Abb.L. WD5 59 BT32
Kechill Gdns, Brom. BR2 204 EG101
Kedelston Ct, E5
off Redwald Rd 123 DX63
Kedeston Ct, Sutt. SM1
off Hurstcourt Rd 200 DB102
Kedleston Dr, Orp. BR5 205 ET100
Kedleston Wk, E2 12 D1
Keedonwood Rd, Brom.
BR1 184 EE92
Keefield, Harl. CM19 51 EP20
Keel Cl, SE16 23 H2
Barking IG11 146 EW68
Keel Dr, Slou. SL1 151 AQ75
Keele Cl, Wat. WD24 76 BW40
Keeler Cl, Wind. SL4 151 AL83
Keeley Rd, Croy. CR0 202 DQ103
Keeley St, WC2 10 A8
Keeling Rd, SE9 184 EK85
Keely Cl, Barn. EN4 80 DE43
Keemor Cl, SE18
off Llanover Rd 165 EN80
Keensacre, Iver SL0 133 BD68
Keens Cl, SW16 181 DK92
Keens La, Guil. GU3 242 AT130
Keens Pk Rd, Guil. GU3 242 AT130
Keens Rd, Croy. CR0 220 DQ105
Sch Keen Students Sch, E1 12 B5
Keens Yd, N1 4 F4
Keep, The, SE3 164 EG82
Kingston upon Thames
KT2 178 CM93
Keepers Cl, Guil. GU4 243 BD131
Keepers Fm Cl, Wind. SL4 151 AL82
Keepers Ms, Tedd. TW11 177 CJ93
Keepers Wk, Vir.W. GU25 192 AX99
Keep La, N11
off Gardeners Cl 98 DG47
Keetons Rd, SE16 22 C5
Keevil Dr, SW19 179 CX87
Keighley Cl, N7 off Penn Rd 121 DL64
Keighley Rd, Rom. RM3 106 FL52
Keightley Dr, SE9 185 EQ88
Keilder Cl, Uxb. UB10
off Charnwood Rd 134 BN68
Keildon Rd, SW11 160 DF84
Keir, The, SW19
off West Side Common 179 CW92
Keir Hardie Est, E5
off Springfield 122 DV60
Keir Hardie Ho, W6
off Lochaline St 159 CW79
Sch Keir Hardie Prim Sch,
E16 15 L6
Keir Hardie Way, Bark. IG11 146 EU66
Hayes UB4 135 BU69
Keith Av, Dart. (Sutt.H.) DA4 188 FP93
Keith Connor Cl, SW8
off Daley Thompson Way 161 DH83
Keith Gro, W12 159 CU75
Keith Pk Cres, West. (Bigg.H.)
TN16 222 EH112
Keith Pk Rd, Uxb. UB10 134 BM66
Keith Rd, E17 101 DZ53
Barking IG11 145 ER68
Hayes UB3 155 BS76
Keiths Rd, Hem.H. HP3 40 BN21
Keith Way, Horn. RM11 128 FL59
Kelbrook Rd, SE3 164 EL83
Kelburn Way, Rain. RM13
off Dominion Way 147 FG69
Kelby Path, SE9 185 EP90
Kelbys, Welw.G.C. AL7 30 DC08
Kelceda Cl, NW2 119 CU61
Kelf Gro, Hayes UB3 135 BT72
Kelfield Gdns, W10 139 CW72
Kelfield Ms, W10 6 A7
Kelland Cl, N8 off Palace Rd 121 DK57
Kelland Rd, E13 15 M3
Kellaway Rd, SE3 164 EJ82
Keller Cres, E12 124 EK63
Kellerton Rd, SE13 184 EE85
Kellett Rd, SW2 161 DN84
Kelling Gdns, Croy. CR0 201 DP101
Kellino St, SW17 180 DF91
Kellner Rd, SE28 165 ET76
Kell St, SE1 20 F5
Kelly Av, SE15 162 DT80
Kelly Cl, NW10 118 CR62
Shepperton TW17 195 BS96
Kelly Ct, Borwd. WD6 78 CQ40
Kelly Ms, W9 6 F4
Kelly Rd, NW7 97 CY51
Kelly St, NW1 141 DH65
Kelly Way, Rom. RM6 126 EY57
Kelman Cl, SW4 161 DK82
Waltham Cross EN8 67 DX31
Kelmore Gro, SE22 162 DU84
Kelmscott Cl, E17 101 DZ54
Watford WD18 75 BU43
Kelmscott Cres, Wat. WD18 75 BU43
Kelmscott Gdns, W12 159 CU76
Kelmscott Rd, SW11 180 DE85
Sch Kelmscott Sec Comp Sch,
E17 off Markhouse Rd 123 DZ58
Kelpatrick Rd, Slou. SL1 131 AK72
Kelross Pas, N5
off Kelross Rd 122 DQ63
Kelross Rd, N5 121 DP63
Kelsall Cl, SE3 164 EH82
Kelsall Ms, Rich. TW9
off Melliss Av 158 CP81
Kelsey Cl, Horl. RH6
off Court Lo Rd 268 DF148
Kelsey Gate, Beck. BR3 203 EB96
Kelsey La, Beck. BR3 203 EA96
Kelsey Pk Av, Beck. BR3 203 EB96
Kelsey Pk Rd, Beck. BR3 203 EA96
Sch Kelsey Pk Sch for Boys,
Beck. BR3 off Manor Way 203 EA97
Kelsey Rd, Orp. BR5 206 EV96
Kelsey Sq, Beck. BR3 203 EA96
Kelsey St, E2 12 B3
Kelsey Way, Beck. BR3 203 EA97
Kelshall, Wat. WD25 76 BY36
Kelshall Ct, N4
off Brownswood Rd 122 DQ61
Kelsie Way, Ilf. IG6 103 ES52
Kelso Dr, Grav. DA12 191 GM91
Kelson Ho, E14 24 D5
Kelso Pl, W8 17 K6
Kelso Rd, Cars. SM5 200 DC101
Kelston Rd, Ilf. IG6 103 EP54
Kelvedon Av, Walt. KT12 213 BS108
Kelvedon Cl, Brwd. (Hutt.)
CM13 109 GE44
Kingston upon Thames
KT2 178 CM93
Kelvedon Ho, SW8 161 DL81
Kelvedon Rd, SW6 159 CZ80
Kelvedon Wk, Rain. RM13
off Ongar Way 147 FE67
Kelvedon Way, Wdf.Grn. IG8 103 EM51
Kelvin Av, N13 99 DM51
Leatherhead KT22 231 CF119
Teddington TW11 177 CE93
Kelvinbrook, W.Mol. KT8 196 CB97
Kelvin Cl, Epsom KT19 216 CN107
Kelvin Cres, Har. HA3 95 CE52
Kelvin Dr, Twick. TW1 177 CH86
Kelvin Gdns, Croy. CR0 201 DL101
Southall UB1 136 CA72
Kelvin Gro, SE26 182 DV90
Chessington KT9 198 CL104
Sch Kelvin Gro Prim Sch,
SE26 off Kirkdale 182 DV90
Kelvington Cl, Croy. CR0 203 DY101
Kelvington Rd, SE15 183 DX85
Kelvin Ind Est, Grnf. UB6 136 CB66
Kelvin Par, Orp. BR6 205 ES102
Kelvin Rd, N5 121 DP63
Tilbury RM18 171 GG82
Welling DA16 166 EU83
Kember St, N1 4 A6
Kemble Cl, Pot.B. EN6 64 DD33
Weybridge KT13 213 BR105
Kemble Cotts, Add. KT15
off Emley Rd 194 BG104
Kemble Dr, Brom. BR2 204 EL104
Kemble Par, Pot.B. EN6
off High St 64 DC32
Kemble Rd, N17 100 DU53
SE23 183 DX88
Croydon CR0 201 DN104
Kembleside Rd, West.
(Bigg.H.) TN16 238 EJ118
Kemble St, WC2 10 A8
Kemerton Rd, SE5 162 DQ83
Beckenham BR3 203 EB96
Croydon CR0 202 DT101
Kemeys St, E9 123 DY64
Kemishford, Wok. GU22 226 AU123
Kemnal Rd, Chis. BR7 185 ER91
Coll Kemnal Tech Coll, Sid.
DA14 off Sevenoaks Way 186 EV94
Kempe Cl, St.Alb. AL1 42 CC24
Slough SL3 153 BC77
Kempe Rd, NW6 139 CX68
Enfield EN1 82 DV36
Kemp Gdns, Croy. CR0
off St. Saviours Rd 202 DQ100
Kempis Way, SE22
off East Dulwich Gro 182 DS85
Kemplay Rd, NW3 120 DD63
Kemp Pl, Bushey WD23 76 CA44
Kemp Rd, Dag. RM8 126 EX60
Kemprow, Wat. (Ald.) WD25 77 CD36
Kemp's Ct, W1 9 K8
Kemps Dr, E14 13 P9
Northwood HA6 93 BT52
Kempsford Gdns, SW5 17 H10
Kempsford Rd, SE11 20 D8
Kemps Gdns, SE13
off Thornford Rd 183 EC85
Kempshott Rd, SW16 181 DK94
Kempson Rd, SW6 160 DA81
Kempthorne Rd, SE8 23 K7
Kempton Av, Horn. RM12 128 FM63
Northolt UB5 136 CA65
Sunbury-on-Thames
TW16 195 BV95
Kempton Cl, Erith DA8 167 FC79
Uxbridge UB10 115 BQ63
Kempton Ct, E1 12 C5
Sunbury-on-Thames
TW16 195 BV95
⇌ Kempton Park
(Race days only) 175 BV94
★ Kempton Park Racecourse,
Sun. TW16 176 BW94
Kempton Rd, E6 145 EM67
Hampton TW12 196 BZ96
Kempton Wk, Croy. CR0 203 DY100
Kempt St, SE18 165 EN79
Kemsing Cl, Bex. DA5 186 EY87
Bromley BR2 204 EF103
Thornton Heath CR7 202 DQ98
Kemsing Rd, SE10 25 L9
Kemsley, SE13 183 EC85
Kemsley Chase, Slou.
(Farn.Royal) SL2 131 AR67
Kemsley Cl, Grav. (Nthflt)
DA11 191 GF91
Greenhithe DA9 189 FV86
Kemsley Rd, West. (Tats.)
TN16 238 EK119
Kenbury Cl, Uxb. UB10 114 BN62
Kenbury Gdns, SE5
off Kenbury St 162 DQ82
Kenbury St, SE5 162 DQ82
Kenchester Cl, SW8 161 DL80
Kencot Cl, Erith DA18 166 EZ75
Kendal Av, N18 100 DR49
W3 138 CN70
Barking IG11 145 ES66
Epping CM16 70 EU31
Kendal Cl, SW9 161 DP80
Feltham TW14
off Ambleside Dr 175 BT88
Hayes UB4 135 BS68
Reigate RH2 250 DD133
Slough SL2 132 AU73
Woodford Green IG8 102 EF47
Kendal Cft, Horn. RM12 127 FG64
Kendal Dr, Slou. SL2 132 AU73
Kendale, Grays RM16 171 GH76
Hemel Hempstead HP3 41 BP21
Kendale Rd, Brom. BR1 184 EE92
Kendal Gdns, N18 100 DR49
Sutton SM1 200 DC103
Kendall Av, Beck. BR3 203 DY96
South Croydon CR2 220 DR109
Kendall Av S, S.Croy. CR2 220 DQ110
Kendall Cl, Welw.G.C. AL7 29 CY13
Kendall Ct, SW19
off Byegrove Rd 180 DD93
Borehamwood WD6
off Gregson Cl 78 CQ39
Kendall Gdns, Grav. DA11 191 GF87
Kendall Pl, W1 8 E6
Kendall Rd, SE18 164 EL81
Beckenham BR3 203 DY96
Isleworth TW7 157 CG82
Kendalmere Cl, N10 99 DH53
Kendal Par, N18
off Great Cambridge Rd 100 DR49
Kendal Pl, SW15 179 CZ85
Kendal Rd, NW10 119 CU63
Waltham Abbey EN9
off Deer Pk Way 83 EC36
Kendals Cl, Rad. WD7 77 CE36
Kendal St, W2 8 B8
Sch Kender Prim Sch, SE14
off Kender St 162 DW81
Kender St, SE14 162 DW80
Kendoa Rd, SW4 161 DK84
Kendon Cl, E11
off The Avenue 124 EH57
Kendor Av, Epsom KT19 216 CQ111
Kendra Hall Rd, S.Croy. CR2 219 DP108
Kendrey Gdns, Twick. TW2 177 CE86
Kendrick Ms, SW7 17 N7
Kendrick Pl, SW7 17 N8
Kendrick Rd, Slou. SL3 152 AV76
Kenelm Cl, Har. HA1 117 CG62
Kenerne Dr, Barn. EN5 79 CY43
Kenford Cl, Wat. WD25 59 BV32
Kenia Wk, Grav. DA12 191 GM90
Kenilford Rd, SW12 181 DH87
Kenilworth Av, E17 101 EA54
SW19 180 DA92
Cobham (Stoke D'Ab.)
KT11 214 CB114
Harrow HA2 116 BZ63
Romford RM3 106 FP50
Kenilworth Cl, Bans. SM7 234 DB116
Borehamwood WD6 78 CQ41
Hemel Hempstead HP2 40 BL21
Slough SL1 152 AT76
Kenilworth Ct, SW15
off Lower Richmond Rd 159 CX83
Watford WD17 75 BU39
Kenilworth Cres, Enf. EN1 82 DS39
Kenilworth Dr, Borwd. WD6 78 CQ41
Rickmansworth (Crox.Grn)
WD3 75 BP42
Walton-on-Thames KT12 196 BX104
Kenilworth Gdns, SE18 165 EP82
Hayes UB4 135 BT71
Hornchurch RM12 128 FJ62
Ilford IG3 125 ET61
Loughton IG10 85 EM44
Southall UB1 136 BZ69
Staines TW18 174 BJ92
Watford WD19 94 BW50
Sch Kenilworth Prim Sch,
Borwd. WD6
off Kenilworth Dr 78 CR41
Kenilworth Rd, E3 143 DY68
NW6 139 CZ67
SE20 203 DX95
W5 138 CL74
Ashford TW15 174 BK90
Edgware HA8 96 CQ48
Epsom KT17 217 CU107
Orpington BR5 205 EQ100
KENLEY, CR8 236 DQ116
⇌ Kenley 220 DQ114
Kenley Av, NW9 96 CS53
Kenley Cl, Barn. EN4 80 DE42
Bexley DA5 186 FA87
Caterham CR3 236 DR120
Chislehurst BR7 205 ES97
Kenley Gdns, Horn. RM12 128 FM61
Thornton Heath CR7 201 DP98
Kenley La, Ken. CR8 220 DQ114
Sch Kenley Prim Sch, Whyt.
CR3 off New Barn La 236 DS116
Kenley Rd, SW19 199 CZ96
Kingston upon Thames
KT1 198 CP96
Twickenham TW1 177 CG86
Kenley Wk, W11 6 C10
Sutton SM3 217 CX105
Kenlor Rd, SW17 180 DD92
Kenmare Dr, N17 100 DT54
Mitcham CR4 180 DF94
Kenmare Gdns, N13 99 DP49
Kenmare Rd, Th.Hth. CR7 201 DN100
Kenmere Gdns, Wem. HA0 138 CN67
Kenmere Rd, Well. DA16 166 EW82
Kenmont Gdns, NW10 139 CV69
Sch Kenmont Prim Sch,
NW10 off Valliere Rd 139 CV69
Kenmore Av, Har. HA3 117 CG56
Kenmore Cl, Rich. TW9
off Kent Rd 158 CN80
Kenmore Cres, Hayes UB4 135 BT69
Kenmore Gdns, Edg. HA8 96 CP54
Sch Kenmore Pk First Sch,
Har. HA3
off Moorhouse Rd 118 CL55
Sch Kenmore Pk Mid Sch,
Har. HA3
off Moorhouse Rd 118 CL55
Kenmore Rd, Har. HA3 117 CK55
Kenley CR8 219 DP114
Kenmure Rd, E8 122 DV64
Kenmure Yd, E8
off Kenmure Rd 122 DV64
Kennacraig Cl, E16 25 M2
Kennard Rd, E15 143 ED66
N11 98 DF50
Kennard St, E16 145 EM74
SW11 160 DG82
Kenneally Cl, Wind. SL4
off Kenneally Row 150 AJ82
Kenneally Pl, Wind. SL4
off Kenneally Row 150 AJ82
Kenneally Rd, Wind. SL4
off Kenneally Row 150 AJ82
Kenneally Row, Wind. SL4 150 AJ82
Kenneally Wk, Wind. SL4
off Kenneally Row 150 AJ82
Kennedy Av, Enf. EN3 82 DW44
Hoddesdon EN11 49 DZ17
Kennedy Cl, E13 144 EG68
Mitcham CR4 200 DG96
Orpington BR5 205 ER102
Pinner HA5 94 BZ51
Slough (Farn.Com.) SL2 131 AQ65
Waltham Cross (Chshh)
EN8 67 DX28
Kennedy Gdns, Sev. TN13 257 FJ123
Kennedy Path, W7
off Harp Rd 137 CF70
Kennedy Rd, W7 137 CE71
Barking IG11 145 ES67
Kennedy Wk, SE17
off Flint St 162 DR77
Kennel Cl, Lthd. (Fetch.)
KT22 230 CC124
Kennel La, Horl. (Hkwd)
RH6 268 DD149
Leatherhead (Fetch.)
KT22 230 CC122
Kennelwood Cres, Croy.
(New Adgtn) CR0 221 ED111
Kennelwood La, Hat. AL10 45 CV17
Kennet Cl, SW11
off Maysoule Rd 160 DD84
Upminster RM14 129 FS58
Kennet Grn, S.Ock. RM15 149 FV73
Kenneth Av, Ilf. IG1 125 EP63
Kenneth Cres, NW2 119 CV64
Kenneth Gdns, Stan. HA7 95 CG51
Kenneth More Rd, Ilf. IG1
off Oakfield Rd 125 EP62
Kenneth Rd, Bans. SM7 234 DD115
Romford RM6 126 EX59
Kenneth Robbins Ho, N17 100 DV52
Kennet Rd, W9 6 F3
Dartford DA1 167 FG83
Isleworth TW7 157 CF83
Kennet Sq, Mitch. CR4 200 DE95
Kennet St, E1 22 B1
Kennett Ct, Swan. BR8 207 FE97
Kennett Dr, Hayes UB4 136 BY71
Kennett Rd, Slou. SL3 153 BB76
Kennet Wf La, EC4 11 H9
Kenninghall, N18 100 DV50
Kenninghall Rd, E5 122 DU62
N18 100 DW50
Kenning Rd, Hodd. EN11 49 EB15
Kenning St, SE16 22 F3
Kennings Way, SE11 20 E9
Kenning Ter, N1 5 L7
KENNINGTON, SE11 161 DN79
⊖ Kennington 20 E9
Kennington Grn, SE11 20 C10
Kennington Gro, SE11
off Oval Way 161 DM79
Kennington La, SE11 20 D9
Kennington Oval, SE11 161 DM79
Kennington Pk, SW9 161 DN80
Kennington Pk Est, SE11
off Harleyford St 161 DN79
Kennington Pk Gdns, SE11 161 DP79
Kennington Pk Pl, SE11 20 D10
Kennington Pk Rd, SE11 161 DN79
Kennington Rd, SE1 20 C5
SE11 20 C6
Sch Kenningtons Prim Sch,
S.Ock. RM15 off Tamar Dr 148 FQ72
Kenny Dr, Cars. SM5 218 DF109
Kenny Rd, NW7 97 CY50
Kenrick Pl, W1 8 E5
Kenrick Sq, Red. (Bletch.)
RH1 252 DS133
KENSAL GREEN, NW10 139 CW69
⇌ Kensal Green 139 CW69
⊖ Kensal Green 139 CW69
★ Kensal Green Cem, W10 139 CW69
KENSAL RISE, NW6 139 CX68
⇌ Kensal Rise 139 CW68
Sch Kensal Ri Prim Sch,
NW6 off Harvist Rd 139 CX68
Kensal Rd, W10 6 D3
KENSAL TOWN, W10 6 B3
Kensal Wf, W10 6 B3
KENSINGTON, W8 16 F2
Coll Kensington & Chelsea Coll,
Hortensia Centre, SW10
off Hortensia Rd 160 DC80
Marlborough Cen, SW3 18 B8
Wornington Cen, W10 6 D5
Kensington Av, E12 144 EL65
Thornton Heath CR7 201 DN95
Watford WD18 75 BT42
Sch Kensington Av Jun & Inf
Sch, Th.Hth. CR7
off Kensington Av 201 DN95
Kensington Ch Ct, W8 17 J4
Kensington Ch St, W8 17 H1
Kensington Ch Wk, W8 17 J4
Kensington Cl, N11 98 DG51
St. Albans AL1 43 CG22
Coll Kensington Coll of
Business, WC2 10 A7
Kensington Ct, NW7
off Grenville Pl 96 CR50
W8 17 K4
Kensington Ct Gdns, W8
off Kensington Ct Pl 160 DB76
Kensington Ct Ms, W8 17 K4
Kensington Ct Pl, W8 17 K5
Kensington Dr, Wdf.Grn.
IG8 102 EK53
★ Kensington Gdns, W2 17 M2
Kensington Gdns, Ilf. IG1 125 EM61
Kingston upon Thames
KT1 off Portsmouth Rd 197 CK97
Kensington Gdns Sq, W2 7 J8
Kensington Gate, W8 17 L5
Kensington Gore, SW7 17 N4
Kensington Hall Gdns, W14 16 E9
Kensington High St, W8 16 G5
W14 16 E6
Kensington Mall, W8 17 H1
⇌ Kensington (Olympia) 16 C5
⊖ Kensington (Olympia) 16 C5
★ Kensington Palace, W8 17 K2
Kensington Palace Gdns, W8 17 J1
Kensington Pk Gdns, W11 6 E10
Kensington Pk Ms, W11 6 E8
Kensington Pk Rd, W11 6 E9
Kensington Pl, W8 16 G2
Sch Kensington Prim Sch,
E12 off Kensington Av 145 EM65
Kensington Rd, SW7 17 P4
W8 17 K4
Brentwood (Pilg.Hat.)
CM15 108 FU44
Northolt UB5 136 CA69
Romford RM7 127 FC58
Kensington Sq, W8 17 J4
Kensington Ter, S.Croy. CR2
off Sanderstead Rd 220 DR108
Kensington Village, W14 16 F8
Kensington Way, Borwd.
WD6 78 CR41
Coll Kensit Mem Coll, N3
off Hendon La 97 CY54
Kent Av, W13 137 CH71
Dagenham RM9 146 FA70
Slough SL1 131 AQ71
Welling DA16 185 ET85
Kent Cl, Borwd. WD6 78 CR38
Mitcham CR4 201 DL98
Orpington BR6 223 ES107
Staines TW18 174 BK93
Uxbridge UB8 134 BJ65
Kent Dr, Barn. EN4 80 DG42
Hornchurch RM12 128 FK63
Teddington TW11 177 CE92
Kentford Way, Nthlt. UB5 136 BY67
Kent Gdns, W13 137 CH71
Ruislip HA4 115 BV58
Kent Gate Way, Croy. CR0 221 EA106
KENT HATCH, Eden. TN8 255 EP131
Kent Hatch Rd, Eden.
(Crock.H.) TN8 255 EM131
Oxted RH8 254 EJ129
⇌ Kent House 203 DY95
Kent Ho La, Beck. BR3 183 DY92
Kent Ho Rd, SE26 203 DX95
Beckenham BR3 183 DY92
Kentish Bldgs, SE1 21 J2
Kentish La, Hat. AL9 64 DC25
Kentish Rd, Belv. DA17 166 FA77
KENTISH TOWN, NW5 141 DJ65
⇌ Kentish Town 121 DJ64
⊖ Kentish Town 121 DJ64
Sch Kentish Town C of E
Prim Sch, NW5
off Islip St 121 DJ64
Kentish Town Rd, NW1 141 DH66
NW5 141 DH66
⇌ Kentish Town West 140 DG65
Kentish Way, Brom. BR1 204 EG96
Kentlea Rd, SE28 165 ES75
Kentmere Rd, SE18 165 ES77
KENTON, Har. HA3 117 CH57
⇌ Kenton 117 CH58
⊖ Kenton 117 CH58
Kenton Av, Har. HA1 117 CF59
Southall UB1 136 CA73
Sunbury-on-Thames
TW16 196 BY96
Kenton Ct, W14 16 E6
Kenton Gdns, Har. HA3 117 CJ57
St. Albans AL1 43 CF21
Kenton La, Har. HA3 117 CJ55
Kenton Pk Av, Har. HA3 117 CK56
Kenton Pk Cl, Har. HA3 117 CJ56

★ Place of interest | H Hospital | Sch School | Coll College | Uni University | ⇌ Railway station

Kenton Pk Cres, Har. HA3 . .**117** CK56
Kenton Pk Rd, Har. HA3 . . . .**117** CJ56
Kenton Rd, E9 . . . .**143** DX65
Harrow HA1, HA3 . . . .**117** CK57
Kentons La, Wind. SL4 . . . . .**151** AL82
Kent St, WC1 . . . .**9** N3
Kenton Way, Hayes UB4
off Exmouth Rd **135** BS69
Woking GU21 . . . .**226** AT117
Kent Pas, NW1 . . . .**8** C3
Kent Rd, N21 . . . .**100** DR46
W4 . . . .**158** CQ76
Dagenham RM10 . . . .**127** FB64
Dartford DA1 . . . .**188** FK86
East Molesey KT8 . . . . . .**196** CC98
Gravesend DA11 . . . .**191** GG88
Grays RM17 . . . .**170** GC79
Kingston upon Thames
KT1 *off The Bittoms* **197** CK97
Longfield DA3 . . . .**209** FX96
Orpington BR5 . . . .**206** EV100
Richmond TW9 . . . .**158** CN80
West Wickham BR4 . . . . .**203** EB102
Woking GU22 . . . .**227** BB116
Kents Av, Hem.H. HP3 . . . . . .**40** BK24
Kents La, Epp. CM16 . . . .**53** FD21
Kents Pas, Hmptn. TW12 . . .**196** BZ95
Kent St, E2 . . . .**5** P9
E13 . . . .**15** P2
Kent Ter, NW1 . . . .**8** B2
Kent Vw, S.Ock. (Aveley)
RM15 . . . .**168** FQ75
Kent Vw Gdns, Ilf. IG3 . . . . . .**125** ES61
Kent Way, Surb. KT6 . . . . . .**198** CL104
Kentwell Cl, SE4 . . . .**163** DY84
Kentwode Grn, SW13 . . . . . .**159** CU80
Coll **Kentwood Cen**, SE20
off Kingsdale Rd **183** DX94
Kentwyns Ri, Red. (S.Nutfld)
RH1 . . . .**267** DM135
Kent Yd, SW7 . . . .**18** B4
Kenver Av, N12 . . . .**98** DD51
Kenward Rd, SE9 . . . .**184** EJ85
Kenway, Rain. RM13 . . . .**148** FJ69
Romford RM5 . . . .**105** FC54
Ken Way, Wem. HA9 . . . .**118** CQ61
Kenway Cl, Rain. RM13
off Kenway **148** FJ69
Kenway Dr, Amer. HP7 . . . . .**72** AV39
Kenway Rd, SW5 . . . .**17** J8
Kenway Wk, Rain. RM13
off Kenway **148** FK69
Kenwood Av, N14 . . . .**81** DK43
SE14 *off Besson St* **163** DX81
Kenwood Cl, NW3 . . . .**120** DD60
West Drayton UB7 . . . .**154** BN79
Kenwood Dr, Beck. BR3 . . . .**203** EC97
Rickmansworth (Mill End)
WD3 . . . .**91** BF47
Walton-on-Thames
KT12 . . . .**213** BV107
Kenwood Gdns, E18 . . . .**124** EH55
Ilford IG2 . . . .**125** EN56
★ **Kenwood Ho (The Iveagh Bequest)**, NW3 . . . .**120** DE60
Kenwood Pk, Wey. KT13 . . .**213** BR107
Kenwood Ridge, Ken. CR8 . .**235** DP117
Kenwood Rd, N6 . . . .**120** DF58
N9 . . . .**100** DU46
Kenworth Cl, Wal.Cr. EN8 . . .**67** DX33
Kenworthy Rd, E9 . . . .**123** DY64
Kenwyn Dr, NW2 . . . .**118** CS62
Kenwyn Rd, SW4 . . . .**161** DK84
SW20 . . . .**199** CW95
Dartford DA1 . . . .**188** FK85
Kenya Rd, SE7 . . . .**164** EK80
Kenyngton Dr, Sun. TW16 . .**175** BU92
Sch **Kenyngton Manor Prim Sch**, Sun. TW16
off Beechwood Av **175** BU93
Kenyngton Pl, Har. HA3 . . . .**117** CJ57
Kenyon Pl, Welw.G.C. AL7
off Twelve Acres **29** CY12
Kenyons, Lthd. (W.Hors.)
KT24 . . . .**245** BP128
Kenyon St, SW6 . . . .**159** CX81
Keogh Rd, E15 . . . .**144** EE65
Kepler Rd, SW4 . . . .**161** DL84
Keppel Rd, E6 . . . .**145** EM66
Dagenham RM9 . . . .**126** EY63
Dorking RH4 . . . .**247** CH134
Keppel Row, SE1 . . . .**20** G2
Keppel Spur, Wind.
(Old Wind.) SL4 . . . .**172** AV87
Keppel St, WC1 . . . .**9** M5
Windsor SL4 . . . .**151** AR82
Kerbela St, E2 . . . .**12** A3
Kerbey St, E14 . . . .**14** B7
Kerdistone Cl, Pot.B. EN6 . . .**64** DB30
Sch **Kerem Sch, The**, N2
off Norrice Lea **120** DD57
Kerfield Cres, SE5 . . . .**162** DR81
Kerfield Pl, SE5 . . . .**162** DR81
Kernow Cl, Horn. RM12 . . . .**128** FL61
Kerri Cl, Barn. EN5 . . . .**79** CW42
Kerridge Ct, N1 . . . .**5** M3
Kerril Cft, Harl. CM20 . . . . . .**35** EN14
Kerrill Av, Couls. CR5 . . . . .**235** DN119
Kerrison Pl, W5 . . . .**137** CK74
Kerrison Rd, E15 . . . .**143** ED67
SW11 . . . .**160** DE83
W5 . . . .**137** CK74
Kerrison Vil, W5
off Kerrison Pl **137** CK74
Kerry Av, S.Ock. (Aveley)
RM15 . . . .**168** FM75
Stanmore HA7 . . . .**95** CK49
Kerry Cl, E16 . . . .**15** N8
N13 . . . .**99** DM47
Upminster RM14 . . . .**129** FT59
Kerry Ct, Stan. HA7 . . . .**95** CK49
Kerry Dr, Upmin. RM14 . . . . .**129** FT59
Kerry Path, SE14 . . . .**163** DZ79
Kerry Rd, SE14 . . . .**163** DZ79
Kerry Ter, Wok. GU21 . . . . . .**227** BB116
Kersey Dr, S.Croy. CR2 . . . .**220** DW112
Kersey Gdns, SE9 . . . .**184** EL91
Romford RM3 . . . .**106** FL53
Kersfield Rd, SW15 . . . .**179** CX86
Kershaw Cl, SW18
off Westover Rd **180** DD86
Grays (Chaff.Hun.) RM16 .**169** FW77
Hornchurch RM11 . . . .**128** FL59
Kershaw Rd, Dag. RM10 . . . .**126** FA62
Kersley Ms, SW11 . . . .**160** DF82
Kersley Rd, N16 . . . .**122** DS62
Kersley St, SW11 . . . .**160** DF82
Kerstin Cl, Hayes UB3
off St. Mary's Rd **135** BT73
Kerswell Cl, N15 . . . .**122** DS57
Kerwick Cl, N7 . . . .**4** A5
Keslake Rd, NW6 . . . .**139** CX68
Kessock Cl, N17 . . . .**122** DV57
Kesters Rd, Chesh. HP5 . . . . .**54** AR32
Kesteven Cl, Ilf. IG6 . . . .**103** ET51

Kestlake Rd, Bex. DA5
off East Rochester Way . .**186** EW86
KESTON, BR2 . . . .**222** EJ106
Keston Av, Add. (New Haw)
KT15 . . . .**212** BG111
Coulsdon CR5 . . . .**235** DN119
Keston BR2 . . . .**222** EJ106
Keston Cl, N18 . . . .**100** DR48
Welling DA16 . . . .**166** EW80
Sch **Keston C of E Prim Sch**, Kes. BR2
off Lakes Rd **222** EK106
Keston Gdns, Kes. BR2 . . . .**222** EJ105
Sch **Keston Inf Sch**, Couls.
CR5 *off Keston Av* **235** DN119
Sch **Keston Jun Sch**, Couls.
CR5 *off Coulsdon Rd* . . .**235** DN119
Keston Ms, Wat. WD17
off Nascot Rd **75** BV40
Keston Pk Cl, Kes. BR2 . . . .**205** EM104
Keston Rd, N17 . . . .**122** DR55
SE15 . . . .**162** DU83
Thornton Heath CR7 . . . . .**201** DN100
Kestral Ct, Wall. SM6
off Carew Rd **219** DJ106
Kestrel Av, E6 *off Swan App* .**144** EL71
SE24 . . . .**181** DP85
Staines TW18 . . . .**173** BF90
Kestrel Cl, NW9 . . . .**96** CS54
NW10 . . . .**118** CR64
Berkhamsted HP4 . . . .**38** AW20
Epsom KT19 . . . .**216** CN111
Guildford GU4 . . . .**243** BD132
Hornchurch RM12 . . . .**147** FH66
Ilford IG6 . . . .**104** EW49
Kingston upon Thames
KT2 . . . .**177** CK91
Watford WD25 . . . .**60** BY34
Kestrel Grn, Hat. AL10 . . . . . .**45** CU19
Kestrel Ho, EC1 . . . .**10** G1
W13 . . . .**137** CF70
Enfield EN3 *off Alma Rd* . . .**83** DX43
Kestrel Path, Slou. SL2 . . . . .**131** AL70
Kestrel Pl, SE14
off Milton Ct Rd **163** DY79
Kestrel Rd, Wal.Abb. EN9 . . . .**68** EG34
Kestrels, The, St.Alb.
(Brick.Wd) AL2 . . . .**60** BZ31
Kestrel Way, Croy.
(New Adgtn) CR0 . . . . .**221** ED109
Hayes UB3 . . . .**155** BR75
Welwyn Garden City AL7 . .**29** CZ07
Keswick Av, SW15 . . . .**178** CS92
SW19 . . . .**200** DA96
Hornchurch RM11 . . . .**128** FK60
Keswick Bdy, SW15
off Upper Richmond Rd . .**179** CY85
Keswick Cl, St.Alb. AL1 . . . . .**43** CH21
Sutton SM1 . . . .**218** DC105
Keswick Ct, Slou. SL2
off Stoke Rd **132** AT73
Keswick Dr, Enf. EN3 . . . .**82** DW36
Keswick Gdns, Ilf. IG4 . . . . . .**124** EL57
Purfleet RM19 . . . .**168** FQ79
Ruislip HA4 . . . .**115** BR58
Wembley HA9 . . . .**118** CL63
Keswick Ms, W5 . . . .**138** CL74
Keswick Rd, SW15 . . . .**179** CY85
Bexleyheath DA7 . . . .**166** FA82
Egham TW20 . . . .**173** BB94
Leatherhead (Fetch.)
KT22, KT23 . . . .**246** CC125
Orpington BR6 . . . .**205** ET102
Twickenham TW2 . . . .**176** CC86
West Wickham BR4 . . . . . .**204** EE103
Kettering Rd, Enf. EN3
off Beaconsfield Rd **83** DX37
Romford RM3 . . . .**106** FL52
Kettering St, SW16 . . . .**181** DJ93
Kett Gdns, SW2 . . . .**181** DM85
Kettlebaston Rd, E10 . . . . . .**123** DZ60
Kettlewell Cl, N11 . . . .**98** DG51
Woking GU21 . . . .**210** AX114
Kettlewell Ct, Swan. BR8 . . .**207** FF96
Kettlewell Dr, Wok. GU21 . . .**210** AY114
Kettlewell Hill, Wok. GU21 . .**210** AY114
Ketton Grn, Red. RH1
off Malmstone Av **251** DK128
Kevan Dr, Wok. (Send)
GU23 . . . .**227** BE124
Kevan Ho, SE5 . . . .**162** DQ80
Kevelioc Rd, N17 . . . .**100** DQ53
Kevin Cl, Houns. TW4 . . . . . .**156** BX82
Kevington Cl, Orp. BR5 . . . . .**205** ET98
Kevington Dr, Chis. BR7 . . . .**205** ET98
Orpington BR5 . . . .**205** ET98
KEW, Rich. TW9 . . . .**158** CN79
⇌ **Kew Bridge** **158** CM78
Kew Br, Brent. TW8 . . . .**158** CM79
Richmond TW9 . . . .**158** CM79
Kew Br Arches, Rich. TW9
off Kew Br **158** CM79
Kew Br Ct, W4 . . . .**158** CN78
Kew Br Rd, Brent. TW8 . . . . .**158** CM79
★ **Kew Bridge Steam Mus**, Brent. TW8 . . . .**158** CM78
Sch **Kew Coll**, Rich. TW9
off Cumberland Rd **158** CN80
Kew Cres, Sutt. SM3 . . . .**199** CY104
Kewferry Dr, Nthwd. HA6 . . . .**93** BP50
Kewferry Rd, Nthwd. HA6 . . . .**93** BQ51
Kew Foot Rd, Rich. TW9 . . . . .**158** CL84
⇌ **Kew Gardens** **158** CM81
⊖ **Kew Gardens** **158** CM81
Kew Gdns Rd, Rich. TW9 . . . .**158** CM80
Kew Grn, Rich. TW9 . . . .**158** CN80
Kew Meadow Path, Rich.
TW9 . . . .**158** CN81
★ **Kew Observatory**, Rich.
TW9 . . . .**157** CH83
★ **Kew Palace, Royal Botanic Gdns**, Rich. TW9 . . . .**158** CL80
Sch **Kew Riverside Prim Sch**, Rich. TW9
off Townmead Rd **158** CP82
Kew Rd, Rich. TW9 . . . .**158** CN79
Keybridge Ho, SW8 . . . .**161** DL79
Key Cl, E1 . . . .**12** D4
Keyes Rd, NW2 . . . .**119** CX64
Dartford DA1 . . . .**168** FM84
Keyfield Ter, St.Alb. AL1 . . . . .**43** CD21
Keymer Cl, West. (Bigg.H.)
TN16 . . . .**238** EK116
Keymer Rd, SW2 . . . .**181** DM89
Keynes Cl, N2 . . . .**120** DF55
Keynsham Av, Wdf.Grn. IG8 .**102** EE49
Keynsham Gdns, SE9 . . . .**184** EL85
Keynsham Rd, SE9 . . . .**184** EK85
Morden SM4 . . . .**200** DB102
Keynsham Wk, Mord. SM4 .**200** DB102
Keynton Cl, Hert. SG14 . . . . . .**31** DM08
Keys, The, Brwd. CM13
off Eagle Way **107** FW51
Keyse Rd, SE1 . . . .**21** N6
Keysers Est, Brox. EN10 . . . . .**49** EB21

Keysers Rd, Brox. EN10 . . . . .**49** EA22
Keysham Av, Houns. TW5
off The Avenue **155** BU81
Keys Ho, Enf. EN3
off Beaconsfield Rd **83** DX37
Sch **Keys Meadow Prim Sch**, Enf. EN3 *off Tysoe Av* **83** DZ36
Keystone Cres, N1
off Caledonian Rd **141** DL68
Keywood Dr, Sun. TW16 . . . .**175** BU93
Keyworth Cl, E5 . . . .**123** DY63
Sch **Keyworth Prim Sch**,
SE17 . . . .**20** E10
Keyworth St, SE1 . . . .**20** F5
Kezia St, SE8 . . . .**23** J10
Khalsa Av, Grav. DA12 . . . . . .**191** GJ87
Khalsa Ct, N22
off Acacia Rd **99** DP53
Khama Rd, SW17 . . . .**180** DE91
Khartoum Pl, Grav. DA12 . . . .**191** GJ86
Khartoum Rd, E13 . . . .**15** N2
SW17 . . . .**180** DD91
Ilford IG1 . . . .**125** EP64
Khyber Rd, SW11 . . . .**160** DE82
Kibes La, Ware SG12 . . . .**33** DX06
Kibworth St, SW8 . . . .**161** DM80
Kidborough Down, Lthd.
(Bkhm) KT23 . . . .**246** CA127
KIDBROOKE, SE3 . . . .**164** EH83
⇌ **Kidbrooke** **164** EH83
Kidbrooke Gdns, SE3 . . . .**164** EG82
Kidbrooke Gro, SE3 . . . .**164** EG81
Kidbrooke La, SE9 . . . .**164** EL84
Kidbrooke Pk Cl, SE3 . . . .**164** EH81
Sch **Kidbrooke Pk Prim Sch**,
SE3 *off Hargood Rd* **164** EJ81
Kidbrooke Pk Rd, SE3 . . . . . .**164** EH81
Sch **Kidbrooke Sch & Arts Coll**,
SE3 *off Corelli Rd* **164** EK82
Kidbrooke Way, SE3 . . . .**164** EH82
Kidderminster Pl, Croy. CR0
off Kidderminster Rd . . .**201** DP102
Kidderminster Rd, Croy.
CR0 . . . .**201** DP102
Slough SL2 . . . .**131** AN69
Kidderpore Av, NW3 . . . .**120** DA63
Kidderpore Gdns, NW3 . . . . .**120** DA63
Kidd Pl, SE7 . . . .**164** EL78
Kidlington Way, NW9 . . . .**96** CS54
Kidman Cl, Rom. (Gidea Pk)
RM2 . . . .**128** FJ55
Kidworth Cl, Horl. RH6 . . . . .**268** DF146
Kielder Cl, Ilf. IG6 . . . .**103** ET51
Kiffen St, EC2 . . . .**11** K3
Kilberry Cl, Islw. TW7 . . . .**157** CD81
Kilbride Ct, Hem.H. HP2
off Aycliffe Dr **40** BL16
KILBURN, NW6 . . . .**140** DA68
⊖ **Kilburn** **139** CZ65
Kilburn Br, NW6
off Kilburn High Rd **140** DA67
Kilburn Gate, NW6
off Kilburn Priory **140** DB68
⇌ **Kilburn High Road** **140** DA67
Kilburn High Rd, NW6 . . . . . .**139** CZ66
Kilburn La, W9 . . . .**6** B2
W10 . . . .**6** B2
⊖ **Kilburn Park** **140** DA68
Sch **Kilburn Pk Jun Sch**,
NW6 *off Malvern Rd* **139** CZ68
Kilburn Pk Rd, NW6 . . . .**6** G2
Kilburn Pl, NW6 . . . .**140** DA67
Kilburn Priory, NW6 . . . .**140** DB67
Kilburn Sq, NW6 . . . .**140** DA67
Kilburn Vale, NW6
off Belsize Rd **140** DB67
Kilby Cl, Wat. WD25 . . . .**76** BX35
Kilcorral Cl, Epsom KT17 . . . .**217** CU114
Kildare Cl, Ruis. HA4 . . . .**116** BW60
Kildare Gdns, W2 . . . .**7** H7
Kildare Rd, E16 . . . .**15** M5
Kildare Ter, W2 . . . .**7** H7
Kildare Wk, E14 . . . .**13** N8
Kildonan Cl, Wat. WD17 . . . . . .**75** BT39
Kildoran Rd, SW2 . . . .**181** DL85
Kildowan Rd, Ilf. IG3 . . . .**126** EU60
Kilfillan Gdns, Berk. HP4 . . . . .**38** AU20
Kilgour Rd, SE23 . . . .**183** DY86
Kilkie St, SW6 . . . .**160** DC82
Killarney Rd, SW18 . . . .**180** DC86
Killasser Ct, Tad. KT20 . . . . .**233** CW123
Killburns Mill Cl, Wall.
SM6 *off London Rd* **219** DH105
Killearn Rd, SE6 . . . .**183** ED88
Killester Gdns, Wor.Pk. KT4 .**217** CV105
Killewarren Way, Orp. BR5 . .**206** EW100
Killick Cl, Sev. (Dunt.Grn)
TN13 . . . .**256** FE121
Killick St, N1 . . . .**4** A9
Killieser Av, SW2 . . . .**181** DL89
Sch **Killigrew Inf Sch**, St.Alb.
AL2 *off West Av* **60** CB25
Sch **Killigrew Jun Sch**,
St.Alb. AL2 *off West Av* . . .**60** CB25
Killip Cl, E16 . . . .**15** K7
Killowen Av, Nthlt. UB5 . . . . .**116** CC64
Killowen Rd, E9 . . . .**143** DX65
Killy Hill, Wok. (Chobham)
GU24 . . . .**210** AS108
Killyon Rd, SW8 . . . .**161** DJ82
Killyon Ter, SW8 . . . .**161** DJ82
Kilmaine Rd, SW6 . . . .**159** CY80
Kilmarnock Gdns, Dag.
RM8 *off Lindsey Rd* **126** EW62
Kilmarnock Pk, Reig. RH2 . . .**250** DB133
Kilmarnock Rd, Wat. WD19 . . .**94** BX49
Kilmarsh Rd, W6 . . . .**159** CW77
Kilmartin Av, SW16 . . . .**201** DM97
Kilmartin Rd, Ilf. IG3 . . . .**126** EU61
Kilmartin Way, Horn. RM12 . .**127** FH64
Kilmeston Way, SE15
off Daniel Gdns **162** DT80
Kilmington Cl, Brwd. (Hutt.)
CM13 . . . .**109** GB47
Kilmington Rd, SW13 . . . .**159** CU79
Kilmiston Av, Shep. TW17 . . .**195** BQ100
Kilmorey Gdns, Twick. TW1 . .**177** CH85
Kilmorey Rd, Twick. TW1 . . . .**157** CH84
Sch **Kilmorie Prim Sch**,
SE23 *off Kilmorie Rd* **183** DY89
Kilmorie Rd, SE23 . . . .**183** DY88
Kiln Av, Amer. HP6 . . . .**72** AW38
Kiln Cl, Berk. HP4
off Water End Rd **39** BB17
Hayes UB3
off Brickfield La **155** BR79
Kiln Ct, Beac. HP9 . . . .**110** AH55
Kilncroft, Hem.H. HP3 . . . .**41** BP22
Kilndown, Grav. DA12 . . . .**191** GK93
Kilner St, E14 . . . .**13** N6
Kilnfield, Welw.G.C. AL7 . . . . . .**29** CZ06
Kiln Flds, H.Wyc.
(Woob.Grn) HP10 . . . .**110** AE61
Kiln Grd, Hem.H. HP3 . . . .**40** BN22
Kiln Ho Cl, Ware SG12 . . . .**33** DY05

Kiln La, Bet. (Brock.) RH3 . . .**264** CP135
Bourne End SL8 . . . .**110** AC60
Chesham (Ley Hill) HP5 . . .**56** AV31
Epsom KT17 . . . .**216** CS111
Harlow (Ch.Lang.) CM17 . .**52** EW16
High Wycombe
(Woob.Grn) HP10 . . . .**110** AC60
Horley RH6 . . . .**268** DG146
Slough (Hedg.) SL2 . . . . . .**111** AQ60
Woking (Ripley) GU23 . . .**228** BH124
Kiln Ms, SW17 . . . .**180** DD92
Kiln Pl, NW5 . . . .**120** DG64
Kiln Rd, Epp. (N.Wld Bas.)
CM16 . . . .**70** FA27
Kilnside, Esher (Clay.) KT10 .**215** CG108
Kiln Wk, Red. RH1 . . . .**266** DG139
Kiln Way, Grays (Bad.Dene)
RM17 . . . .**170** FZ78
Northwood HA6 . . . .**93** BS51
Kilnwood, Sev. (Halst.)
TN14 . . . .**224** EZ113
Kiln Wd La, Rom.
(Hav.at.Bow.) RM4 . . . . . .**105** FD50
Kilpatrick Way, Hayes UB4 . .**136** BY71
Kilravock St, W10 . . . .**6** C2
Kilross Rd, Felt. TW14 . . . . . .**175** BR88
Kilrue La, Walt. KT12 . . . .**213** BT105
Kilrush Ter, Wok. GU21 . . . . .**227** BA116
Kilsby Wk, Dag. RM9
off Rugby Rd **146** EV65
Kilsha Rd, Walt. KT12 . . . . . .**195** BV100
Kilsmore La, Wal.Cr.
(Chsht) EN8 . . . .**67** DX28
Kilvinton Dr, Enf. EN2 . . . .**82** DR38
Kilworth Av, Brwd. (Shenf.)
CM15 . . . .**109** GA44
Kilworth Cl, Welw.G.C. AL7 . .**30** DB11
Kimbell Gdns, SW6 . . . .**159** CY81
Kimbell Pl, SE3
off Tudway Rd **164** EJ84
Kimber Cl, Wind. SL4 . . . .**151** AM83
Kimber Ct, Guil. GU4
off Gilliat Dr **243** BD132
Kimberley Av, E6 . . . .**144** EL68
SE15 . . . .**162** DV82
Ilford IG2 . . . .**125** ER59
Romford RM7 . . . .**127** FC58
Kimberley Cl, Horl. RH6 . . . . .**268** DE148
Slough SL3 . . . .**153** AZ77
Kimberley Dr, Sid. DA14 . . . . .**186** EX89
Kimberley Gdns, N4 . . . .**121** DP57
Enfield EN1 . . . .**82** DT41
Kimberley Gate, Brom. BR1
off Oaklands Rd **184** EF94
Kimberley Ind Est, E17 . . . . . .**101** DZ53
Kimberley Pl, Pur. CR8
off Brighton Rd **219** DN111
Kimberley Ride, Cob. KT11 . .**214** CB113
Kimberley Rd, E4 . . . .**102** EE46
E11 . . . .**123** ED61
E16 . . . .**15** J3
E17 . . . .**101** DZ53
N17 . . . .**100** DU54
N18 . . . .**100** DV51
NW6 . . . .**139** CY67
SW9 . . . .**161** DL82
Beckenham BR3 . . . .**203** DX96
Croydon CR0 . . . .**201** DP100
St. Albans AL3 . . . .**42** CC19
Kimberley Way, E4 . . . .**102** EE46
Kimber Rd, SW18 . . . .**180** DA87
Kimbers Dr, Slou. (Burn.)
SL1 . . . .**131** AK69
Kimble Cl, Wat. WD18 . . . .**75** BS44
Kimble Cres, Bushey WD23 . .**94** CC45
Kimble Rd, SW19 . . . .**180** DD93
Kimbolton Cl, SE12 . . . .**184** EF86
Kimbolton Grn, Borwd. WD6 .**78** CQ42
Kimbolton Row, SW3 . . . .**18** A8
Kimmeridge Gdns, SE9 . . . . .**184** EL91
Kimmeridge Rd, SE9 . . . .**184** EL91
Kimps Way, Hem.H. HP3 . . . . .**40** BN23
Kimpton Av, Brwd. CM15 . . .**108** FV45
Kimpton Cl, Hem.H. HP2 . . . . .**41** BP15
Kimpton Ho, SW15
off Fontley Way **179** CU87
Kimpton Link Business Cen,
Sutt. SM3
off Kimpton Rd **199** CZ103
Kimpton Pl, Wat. WD25 . . . . . .**60** BX34
Kimpton Rd, SE5 . . . .**162** DR81
Sutton SM3 . . . .**199** CZ103
Kimptons Cl, Pot.B. EN6 . . . . .**63** CX33
Kimptons Mead, Pot.B. EN6 . .**63** CX32
Kimpton Trade & Business Cen, Sutt. SM3 . . . .**199** CZ103
Kinburn Dr, Egh. TW20 . . . . . .**172** AY92
Kinburn St, SE16 . . . .**22** G3
Kincaid Rd, SE15 . . . .**162** DV80
Kincardine Gdns, W9 . . . .**6** G4
Kinch Gro, Wem. HA9 . . . .**118** CM59
Kincraig Dr, Sev. TN13 . . . . . .**256** FG124
Kinder Cl, SE28 . . . .**146** EX73
Kinderscout, Hem.H. HP3 . . . . .**40** BN22
Kindersley Way, Abb.L. WD5 . .**59** BQ31
Kinder St, E1 . . . .**12** C8
Kinetic Cres, Enf. EN3 . . . .**83** DZ36
Kinfauns Av, Horn. RM11 . . . .**128** FJ58
Kinfauns Rd, SW2 . . . .**181** DN89
Ilford IG3 . . . .**126** EU60
Kingaby Gdns, Rain. RM13 . . .**147** FG66
King Acre Ct, Stai. TW18
off Moor La **173** BE90
King Alfred Av, SE6 . . . .**183** EA90
King Alfred Rd, Rom. RM3 . . .**106** FM54
Sch **King Alfred Sch, The**,
NW11 *off North End Rd* . .**120** DB60
King & Queen Cl, SE9
off St. Keverne Rd **184** EL91
King & Queen St, SE17 . . . .**21** H8
King Arthur Cl, SE15 . . . .**162** DW80
King Arthur Ct, Wal.Cr. EN8 . . .**67** DX31
Sch **King Athelstan Prim Sch**,
Kings.T. KT1
off Villiers Rd **198** CM97
Coll **King Charles Cen (Surbiton Youth & Comm Cen)**, Surb. KT5
off Hollyfield Rd **198** CM101
King Charles Cres, Surb.
KT5 . . . .**198** CM101
King Charles Rd, Rad.
(Shenley) WD7 . . . .**62** CL32
Surbiton KT5 . . . .**198** CM99
King Charles St, SW1 . . . .**19** M3
King Charles Ter, E1 . . . .**12** D10
King Charles Wk, SW19
off Princes Way **179** CY88
Kingcup Cl, Croy. CR0
off Primrose La **203** DX102
King David La, E1 . . . .**12** E9
Kingdon Rd, NW6 . . . .**140** DA65
King Edward Av, Dart. DA1 . .**188** FK86
Rainham RM13 . . . .**148** FK68
King Edward Ct, Wind. SL4 . .**151** AR81

King Edward Dr, Chess.
KT9 *off Kelvin Gro* **198** CL104
Grays RM16 . . . .**170** GE75
King Edward Ms, SW13 . . . . .**159** CU81
King Edward Rd, E10 . . . .**123** EC60
E17 . . . .**123** DY55
Barnet EN5 . . . .**80** DA42
Brentwood CM14 . . . .**108** FW48
Greenhithe DA9 . . . .**189** FU85
Radlett (Shenley) WD7 . . . .**62** CM33
Romford RM1 . . . .**127** FF58
Waltham Cross EN8 . . . .**67** DY33
Watford WD19 . . . .**76** BY44
King Edward VII Av, Wind.
SL4 . . . .**152** AS80
H **King Edward VII Hosp**,
Wind. SL4 . . . .**151** AQ83
H **King Edward VII's Hosp for Officers**, W1 . . . .**8** F5
King Edward's Gdns, W3 . . . .**138** CN74
King Edwards Gro, Tedd.
TW11 . . . .**177** CH93
King Edward's Pl, W3
off King Edward's Gdns .**138** CN74
King Edwards Rd, E9 . . . .**142** DV67
N9 . . . .**100** DV45
Barking IG11 . . . .**145** ER67
King Edward's Rd, Enf. EN3 . .**83** DX42
King Edwards Rd, Ruis.
HA4 . . . .**115** BR60
Ware SG12 . . . .**33** DY05
King Edward St, EC1 . . . .**10** G7
Hemel Hempstead HP3 . . . .**40** BJ24
Slough SL1 . . . .**151** AR75
King Edward III Ms, SE16 . . . .**22** D4
King Edward Wk, SE1 . . . .**20** D5
Sch **King Fahad Acad**, W5
off Little Ealing La **157** CJ77
Sch **King Fahad Acad, The**,
W3 *off Bromyard Av* **138** CS73
Kingfield Cl, Wok. GU22 . . . .**227** AZ120
Kingfield Dr, Wok. GU22 . . . .**227** AZ120
Kingfield Gdns, Wok. GU22 . .**227** AZ120
Kingfield Grn, Wok. GU22 . . .**227** AZ120
Kingfield Rd, W5 . . . .**137** CK70
Woking GU22 . . . .**226** AY120
Sch **Kingfield Sch**, Wok.
GU22 *off Kingfield Rd* . . .**227** BA120
Kingfield St, E14 . . . .**24** D8
Kingfisher Av, E11
off Eastern Av **124** EH58
Kingfisher Cl, SE28 . . . .**146** EW73
Brentwood (Hutt.) CM13 . .**109** GA45
Harrow (Har.Wld) HA3 . . . . .**95** CF52
Northwood HA6 . . . .**93** BP53
Orpington BR5 . . . .**206** EX98
Walton-on-Thames KT12 . .**214** BY106
Ware (Stans.Abb.) SG12
off Lawrence Av **33** EC12
Kingfisher Ct, SW19
off Queensmere Rd **179** CY89
Enfield EN2
off Mount Vw **81** DM38
Surbiton KT6
off Ewell Rd **198** CM101
Sutton SM1
off Sandpiper Rd **217** CZ106
Woking GU21
off Vale Fm Rd **226** AY117
Woking (Sheer.) GU21
off Blackmore Cres **211** BC114
Kingfisher Dr, Green. DA9 . . .**189** FU86
Guildford GU4 . . . .**243** BC132
Hemel Hempstead HP3 . . . . .**58** BM25
Redhill RH1 . . . .**250** DG131
Richmond TW10 . . . .**177** CH91
Staines TW18 . . . .**173** BF91
Kingfisher Gdns, S.Croy.
CR2 . . . .**221** DX111
Kingfisher Lure, Kings L.
WD4 . . . .**59** BP29
Rickmansworth (Loud.)
WD3 . . . .**74** BH42
Kingfisher Ms, SE13 . . . .**163** EB84
Kingfisher Rd, Upmin.
RM14 . . . .**129** FT60
Kingfisher Sq, SE8 . . . .**163** DZ79
Kingfisher St, E6 . . . .**144** EL71
Kingfisher Wk, NW9
off Eagle Dr **96** CS54
Kingfisher Way, NW10 . . . . . .**118** CR64
Beckenham BR3 . . . .**203** DX99
Harlow (Roydon) CM19
off Roydon Mill Pk **34** EG14
King Frederik IX Twr, SE16 . . .**23** L5
King Gdns, Croy. CR0 . . . .**219** DP106
King George Av, E16 . . . .**144** EK72
Bushey WD23 . . . .**76** CB44
Ilford IG2 . . . .**125** ER57
Walton-on-Thames KT12 . .**196** BX102
King George Cl, Rom. RM7 . .**127** FC55
Sunbury-on-Thames
TW16 . . . .**175** BS92
King George V Rd, Amer.
HP6 . . . .**55** AR38
H **King George Hosp**, Ilf.
IG3 . . . .**126** EV57
King George Rd, Wal.Abb.
EN9 . . . .**67** EC34
Ware SG12 . . . .**33** DY05
King Georges Av, Wat.
WD18 . . . .**75** BS43
King Georges Dr, Add.
(New Haw) KT15 . . . .**212** BG110
Southall UB1 . . . .**136** BZ71
King George VI Av, Mitch.
CR4 . . . .**200** DF98
Westerham TN16 . . . .**238** EK116
King George Sq, Rich.
TW10 . . . .**178** CM86
King Georges Rd, Brwd.
(Pilg.Hat.) CM15 . . . .**108** FV44
King George's Trd Est,
Chess. KT9 . . . .**216** CN105
King George St, SE10 . . . .**163** EC80
Kingham Cl, SW18 . . . .**180** DC87
W11 . . . .**16** C3
Sch **King Harold Sch**,
Wal.Abb. EN9
off Broomstick Hall Rd . . .**68** EE33
King Harolds Way, Bexh.
DA7 . . . .**166** EX80
King Harry La, St.Alb. AL3 . . .**42** CA21
King Harry St, Hem.H. HP2 . . .**40** BK21
King Henry Ms, Orp. BR6
off Osgood Av **223** ET106
King Henry's Ct, Wal.Abb.
EN9 *off Deer Pk Way* **83** EC36
Trm **King Henry's Drive** **221** EB109

⊖ London Underground station DLR Docklands Light Railway station Trm Tramlink station Riv Pedestrian ferry landing stage

King Henry's Dr, Croy. (New Adgtn) CR0 221 EC109
King Henry's Ms, Enf. EN3 83 EA37
King Henry's Reach, W6 159 CW79
King Henry's Rd, NW3 140 DE66
  Kingston upon Thames KT1 198 CP97
King Henry St, N16 5 L1
King Henry's Wk, N1 5 L3
King Henry Ter, E1 12 D10
Kinghorn St, EC1 10 G6
King James Av, Pot.B. (Cuffley) EN6 65 DL29
King James Ct, SE1 20 F4
King James St, SE1 20 F4
King John Ct, EC2 11 M3
King John's Cl, Stai. (Wrays.) TW19 172 AW86
King John St, E1 13 H6
King Johns Wk, SE9 184 EK88
Kinglake Ct, Wok. GU21 off Raglan Rd 226 AS118
Kinglake Est, SE17 21 M9
Kinglake St, SE17 21 L10
Kingly Ct, W1 9 J9
Kingly St, W1 9 J8
Kingsand Rd, SE12 184 EG89
Kings Arbour, Sthl. UB2 156 BY78
Kings Arms Ct, E1 12 A6
Kings Arms Yd, EC2 11 J7
Kingsash Dr, Hayes UB4 136 BY70
Kings Av, N10 120 DG55
  N21 99 DP46
King's Av, SW4 181 DK87
  SW12 181 DK88
Kings Av, W5 137 CK72
  Bromley BR1 184 EF93
  Buckhurst Hill IG9 102 EK47
  Carshalton SM5 218 DE108
  Greenford UB6 136 CB72
  Hemel Hempstead HP3 40 BM24
  Hounslow TW3 156 CB81
  New Malden KT3 198 CS98
  Redhill RH1 266 DE136
  Romford RM6 126 EZ58
  Sunbury-on-Thames TW16 175 BT92
  Watford WD18 75 BT42
  West Byfleet (Byfleet) KT14 212 BK112
  Woodford Green IG8 102 EH51
Sch King's Av Prim Sch, SW4 off King's Av 181 DL85
Sch King's Av Sch Early Years Cen, SW4 off Park Hill 181 DL85
Kings Bench St, SE1 20 F3
Kings Bench Wk, EC4 10 D8
Kingsbridge Av, W3 158 CM75
Kingsbridge Circ, Rom. RM3 106 FL51
Kingsbridge Cl, Rom. RM3 106 FL51
Kingsbridge Ct, E14 off Dockers Tanner Rd 163 EA77
Kingsbridge Cres, Sthl. UB1 136 BZ71
Kingsbridge Dr, NW7 97 CX52
Kingsbridge Rd, W10 139 CW72
  Barking IG11 145 ER68
  Morden SM4 199 CX101
  Romford RM3 106 FL51
  Southall UB2 156 BZ77
  Walton-on-Thames KT12 195 BV101
Kingsbridge Way, Hayes UB4 135 BS69
Kingsbrook, Lthd. KT22 off Ryebrook Rd 231 CG118
KINGSBURY, NW9 118 CP58
⊖ Kingsbury 118 CN57
Kingsbury Av, St.Alb. AL3 42 CC19
Kingsbury Circle, NW9 118 CN57
H Kingsbury Comm Hosp, NW9 118 CN56
Kingsbury Cres, Stai. TW18 173 BD91
Kingsbury Dr, Wind. (Old Wind.) SL4 172 AV86
Sch Kingsbury Grn Prim Sch, NW9 off Old Kenton La 118 CQ57
Sch Kingsbury High Sch, NW9 off Princes Av 118 CP56
  Annexe, NW9 off Bacon La 118 CQ56
Kingsbury Rd, N1 5 M3
  NW9 118 CP57
Sch Kingsbury Spec Sch, NW9 off Grove Pk 118 CQ56
Kingsbury Ter, N1 5 M3
Kingsbury Trd Est, NW9 118 CR58
★ Kingsbury Water Mill Mus, St.Alb. AL3 42 CB19
Kings Butts, SE9 off Strongbow Cres 185 EM85
Kings Chace Vw, Enf. EN2 off Crofton Way 81 DN40
Kings Chase, Brwd. CM14 108 FW48
  East Molesey KT8 196 CC97
Kingsclere Cl, SW15 179 CU87
Kingsclere Ct, Barn. EN5 off Gloucester Rd 80 DC43
Kingsclere Pl, Enf. EN2 off Chase Side 82 DQ40
Kingscliffe Gdns, SW19 179 CZ88
Kings Cl, E10 123 EB59
  NW4 119 CX56
  Beaconsfield HP9 110 AG55
  Chalfont St. Giles HP8 90 AX47
  Dartford DA1 167 FE84
  Kings Langley (Chipper.) WD4 58 BH31
  Northwood HA6 93 BT51
  Staines TW18 174 BK94
  Thames Ditton KT7 197 CG100
  Walton-on-Thames KT12 195 BV102
King's Cl, Wat. WD18 off Lady's Cl 75 BV42
Uni King's Coll - Denmark Hill Campus, SE5 off Champion Hill 162 DR83
Uni King's Coll - Guy's Campus, SE1 21 J5
Uni King's Coll - Half Moon La, SE24 182 DR86
Uni King's Coll - Hampstead Campus, NW3 off Kidderpore Av 120 DA63
Uni King's Coll - Maughan Lib & Information Services Cen, WC2 10 C7
Uni King's Coll - Strand Campus, WC2 10 B9
Uni King's Coll - Waterloo Campus, Franklin-Wilkins Bldg, SE1 20 C2
Uni King's Coll - Waterloo Campus, James Clerk Maxwell Bldg, SE1 20 C2
  Stamford St Apartments, SE1 20 C2
  Waterloo Br Wing, SE1 20 C2
H King's Coll Hosp, SE5 162 DR82
H King's Coll Hospital, Dulwich, SE22 162 DS84
Kings Coll Rd, NW3 140 DE66
  Ruislip HA4 115 BT58
Sch King's Coll Sch, SW19 off Southside Common 179 CW93
Kingscote Rd, W4 158 CR76
  Croydon CR0 202 DV101
  New Malden KT3 198 CR97
Kingscote St, EC4 10 E9
Kings Ct, E13 144 EH67
  W6 off King St 159 CU77
  Berkhamsted HP4 off Lower Kings Rd 38 AW18
  Tadworth KT20 233 CW122
  Wembley HA9 118 CP61
Sch Kings Ct First Sch, Wind. SL4 off Ashbrook Rd 172 AV87
Kingscourt Rd, SW16 181 DK90
Kings Ct S, SW3 off Chelsea Manor Gdns 160 DE78
Kings Cres, N4 122 DQ62
Kings Cres Est, N4 122 DQ61
Kingscroft, Welw.G.C. AL7 30 DB08
Sch Kingscroft Jun Sch, Stai. TW18 off Park Av 174 BG93
Kingscroft Rd, NW2 139 CZ65
  Banstead SM7 234 DD115
  Leatherhead KT22 231 CH120
KING'S CROSS, N1 141 DK67
⇌ King's Cross 141 DL68
King's Cross Br, N1 9 P1
Kings Cross La, Red. (S.Nutfld) RH1 267 DL136
King's Cross Rd, WC1 10 B1
⊖ King's Cross St. Pancras 141 DL68
⇌ King's Cross Thameslink 141 DL68
Kingsdale Ct, Wal.Abb. EN9 off Lamplighters Cl 68 EG34
Kingsdale Gdns, W11 16 B2
Kingsdale Rd, SE18 165 ET80
  SE20 183 DX94
  Berkhamsted HP4 38 AU20
Sch Kingsdale Sec Sch, SE21 off Alleyn Pk 182 DS90
Kingsdene, Tad. KT20 233 CV121
Kingsdon La, Harl. CM17 52 EW16
Kingsdown Av, W3 138 CS73
  W13 157 CH75
  South Croydon CR2 219 DP109
Kingsdown Cl, SE16 22 D10
  W10 6 B8
  Gravesend DA12 off Farley Rd 191 GM88
Kingsdowne Rd, Surb. KT6 198 CL101
Kingsdown Rd, E11 124 EE62
  N19 121 DL61
  Epsom KT17 217 CU113
  Sutton SM3 217 CY106
Kingsdown Way, Brom. BR2 204 EG101
Kings Dr, Edg. HA8 96 CM49
  Gravesend DA12 191 GH90
  Surbiton KT5 198 CN101
  Teddington TW11 177 CD92
  Thames Ditton KT7 197 CH100
  Wembley HA9 118 CP61
Kings Dr, The, Walt. KT12 213 BT110
Kingsend, Ruis. HA4 115 BR60
KINGS FARM, Grav. DA12 191 GJ90
Kings Fm Av, Rich. TW10 158 CN84
Sch King's Fm Prim Sch, Grav. DA12 off Cedar Av 191 GJ91
Kings Fm Rd, Rick. (Chorl.) WD3 73 BD44
Kingsfield, Guil. (Albury) GU5 260 BL144
  Hoddesdon EN11 49 EA15
  Windsor SL4 151 AK81
Kingsfield Av, Har. HA2 116 CB56
Kingsfield Ct, Wat. WD19 94 BX45
Kingsfield Dr, Enf. EN3 83 DX35
Kingsfield Ho, SE9 184 EK90
Kingsfield Rd, Har. HA1 117 CD59
  Watford WD19 94 BX45
Kingsfield Ter, Dart. DA1 off Priory Rd S 188 FK86
Kingsfield Way, Enf. EN3 83 DX35
Sch Kingsford Comm Sch, E6 off Kingsford Way 145 EM72
Kingsford St, NW5 120 DF64
Kingsford Way, E6 145 EM71
Kings Gdns, NW6 off West End La 140 DA66
  Ilford IG1 125 ER60
  Upminster RM14 129 FS59
King's Garth Ms, SE23 off London Rd 182 DW89
Kingsgate, St.Alb. AL3 off King Harry La 42 CB22
  Wembley HA9 118 CQ62
Kingsgate Av, N3 120 DA55
Kingsgate Cl, Bexh. DA7 166 EY81
  Orpington BR5 off Main Rd 206 EW97
Sch Kingsgate Inf & Jun Sch, NW6 off Messina Av 140 DA66
Kingsgate Pl, NW6 140 DA66
Kingsgate Rd, NW6 140 DA66
  Kingston upon Thames KT2 198 CL95
Kings Grn, Loug. IG10 84 EL41
Kingsground, SE9 184 EL87
Kings Gro, SE15 162 DV80
  Romford RM1 127 FG57
Kingshall Ms, SE13 off Lewisham Rd 163 EC83
Kings Hall Rd, Beck. BR3 183 DY94
Kings Head Hill, E4 101 EB45
Kings Head La, W.Byf. (Byfleet) KT14 212 BK111
Kings Head Yd, SE1 21 J2
Kings Highway, SE18 165 ES79
Kings Hill, Loug. IG10 84 EL40
Kingshill Av, Har. HA3 117 CH56
  Hayes UB4 135 BS69
  Northolt UB5 135 BU69
  Romford RM5 105 FC51
  St. Albans AL4 43 CG17
  Worcester Park KT4 199 CU101
Kingshill Cl, Hayes UB4 135 BU69
Kingshill Dr, Har. HA3 117 CH55
Kingshill Way, Berk. HP4 38 AU21
Kingshold Est, E9 off Victoria Pk Rd 142 DW67
Kingshold Rd, E9 142 DW66
Kingsholm Gdns, SE9 164 EK84
Sch King's Ho Sch, Jun Dept, Rich. TW10 off Kings Rd 178 CM85
Sch King's Ho Sch, Sen Dept, Rich. TW10 off Kings Rd 178 CM85
Kingshurst Rd, SE12 184 EG87
Kingside Business Pk, SE18 off Woolwich Ch St 164 EL76
Kings Keep, Kings.T. KT1 off Beaufort Rd 198 CL98
KINGSLAND, N1 5 L4
Kingsland, NW8 off Broxwood Way 140 DE67
  Harlow CM18 51 EQ17
  Potters Bar EN6 63 CZ33
Kingsland Grn, E8 5 M3
Kingsland High St, E8 5 N3
Kingsland Pas, E8 5 M3
Kingsland Rd, E2 11 M1
  E8 5 M7
  E13 144 EJ69
  Hemel Hempstead HP1 40 BG22
Kingsland Shop Cen, E8 5 N3
Kings La, Egh. (Eng.Grn) TW20 172 AU92
  Kings Langley (Chipper.) WD4 58 BG31
  Sutton SM1 218 DD107
KINGS LANGLEY, WD4 58 BM30
⇌ Kings Langley 59 BQ30
Kings Langley Bypass, Hem.H. HP1, HP3 40 BG23
  Kings Langley WD4 58 BK28
Sch Kings Langley Prim Sch, Kings L. WD4 off Common La 58 BM28
Sch Kings Langley Sch, Kings L.WD4 off Love La 58 BL28
Kingslawn Cl, SW15 off Howards La 179 CV85
Kingslea, Lthd. KT22 231 CG120
Kingsleigh Cl, Brent. TW8 off Brook Rd S 157 CK79
Kingsleigh Pl, Mitch. CR4 off Chatsworth Pl 200 DF97
Kingsleigh Wk, Brom. BR2 off Stamford Dr 204 EF98
Kingsley Av, W13 137 CG72
  Banstead SM7 234 DA115
  Borehamwood WD6 78 CM40
  Dartford DA1 188 FN85
  Egham (Eng.Grn) TW20 172 AV93
  Hounslow TW3 156 CC82
  Southall UB1 136 CA73
  Sutton SM1 218 DD105
  Waltham Cross (Chsht) EN8 66 DV29
Kingsley Cl, N2 120 DC57
  Dagenham RM10 127 FB63
  Horley RH6 268 DF146
Kingsley Ct, Edg. HA8 96 CP47
  Welwyn Garden City AL7 29 CZ13
Kingsley Dr, Wor.Pk. KT4 off Badgers Copse 199 CT103
Kingsley Flats, SE1 off Old Kent Rd 162 DS77
Kingsley Gdns, E4 101 EA50
  Hornchurch RM11 128 FK56
Kingsley Gro, Reig. RH2 266 DA137
Sch Kingsley Inf Sch, Croy. CR0 off Thomson Cres 201 DN102
Sch Kingsley Jun Sch, Croy. CR0 off Chapman Rd 201 DN102
Kingsley Ms, E1 12 D10
  W8 17 K6
  Chislehurst BR7 185 EP93
Kingsley Path, Slou. SL2 off Wordsworth Rd 131 AK70
Kingsley Pl, N6 120 DG59
Kingsley Rd, E7 144 EG66
  E17 101 EC54
  N13 99 DN49
  NW6 139 CZ67
  SW19 180 DB92
  Brentwood (Hutt.) CM13 109 GD45
  Croydon CR0 201 DN102
  Harrow HA2 116 CC63
  Horley RH6 268 DF146
  Hounslow TW3 156 CC82
  Ilford IG6 103 EQ53
  Loughton IG10 85 ER41
  Orpington BR6 223 ET108
  Pinner HA5 116 BZ56
Kingsley St, SW11 160 DF83
Kingsley Wk, Grays RM16 171 GG77
Kingsley Way, N2 120 DC58
Kingsley Wd Dr, SE9 185 EM90
Kingslyn Cres, SE19 202 DS95
Kings Lynn Cl, Rom. RM3 off Kings Lynn Dr 106 FK51
Kings Lynn Dr, Rom. RM3 106 FK51
Kings Lynn Path, Rom. RM3 off Kings Lynn Dr 106 FK51
Kings Mall, W6 159 CW77
Sch Kings' Manor Sch, Guil. GU2 off Southway 242 AS134
Kingsman Par, SE18 off Woolwich Ch St 165 EM76
Kingsman St, SE18 165 EM76
Kingsmead, Barn. EN5 80 DA42
Kings Mead, Horl. (Smallfield) RH6 269 DP148
Kingsmead, Pot.B. (Cuffley) EN6 65 DL28
Kings Mead, Red. (S.Nutfld) RH1 267 DL136
Kingsmead, Rich. TW10 178 CM86
  St. Albans AL4 43 CK17
  Sawbridgeworth CM21 36 EY06
  Waltham Cross EN8 67 DX28
  Westerham (Bigg.H.) TN16 238 EK116
Kingsmead Av, N9 100 DV46
  NW9 118 CR59
  Mitcham CR4 201 DJ97
  Romford RM1 127 FE58
  Sunbury-on-Thames TW16 196 BW97
  Surbiton KT6 198 CN103
  Worcester Park KT4 199 CV104
Kingsmead Cl, Epsom KT19 216 CR108
  Harlow (Roydon) CM19 50 EH16
  Sidcup DA15 186 EU89
  Teddington TW11 177 CG93
Kingsmead Dr, Nthlt. UB5 136 BZ66
Kingsmead Est, E9 123 DY64
Kingsmead Hill, Harl. (Roydon) CM19 50 EH16
Kingsmead Ho, E9 off Kingsmead Way 123 DY63
Sch Kingsmead JMI Sch, E9 off Kingsmead Way 123 DY63
Kings Meadow, Kings L. WD4 58 BN28
Kings Mead Pk, Esher (Clay.) KT10 215 CE108
Kingsmead Rd, SW2 181 DN89
Sch Kingsmead Sec Sch, Enf. EN1 off Southbury Rd 82 DU41
Kingsmead Way, E9 123 DY63
Kingsmere Cl, SW15 off Felsham Rd 159 CY83
Kingsmere Pk, NW9 118 CP60
Kingsmere Pl, N16 122 DR60
Kingsmere Rd, SW19 179 CX89
Kings Ms, SW4 off King's Av 181 DL85
King's Ms, WC1 10 B4
Kings Ms, Chig. IG7 103 EQ47
Kingsmill Ct, Hat. AL10 off Drakes Way 45 CV20
Kingsmill Gdns, Dag. RM9 126 EZ64
Kings Mill La, Red. RH1 267 DK138
Kingsmill Rd, Dag. RM9 126 EZ64
Kingsmill Ter, NW8 140 DD68
KINGSMOOR, Harl. CM19 51 EQ20
Sch Kingsmoor Co Inf Sch, Harl. CM18 off Ployters Rd 51 EQ19
Sch Kingsmoor Co Jun Sch, Harl. CM18 off Ployters Rd 51 EQ19
Kingsmoor Rd, Harl. CM19 51 EP18
Kingsnympton Pk, Kings.T. KT2 178 CP93
Kings Oak, Rom. RM7 126 FA55
H King's Oak Private Hosp, Enf. EN2 81 DN38
King's Orchard, SE9 184 EL86
Kings Paddock, Hmptn. TW12 196 CC95
Kings Par, Cars. SM5 off Wrythe La 200 DE104
Kingspark Ct, E18 124 EG55
King's Pas, E11 124 EE59
Kings Pas, Kings.T. KT1 197 CK96
Kings Pl, SE1 20 G4
  W4 158 CQ78
  Buckhurst Hill IG9 102 EJ47
  Loughton IG10 102 EK45
King Sq, EC1 10 G2
King's Reach Twr, SE1 20 D1
Kings Ride Gate, Rich. TW10 158 CN84
Kingsridge, SW19 179 CY89
Kingsridge Gdns, Dart. DA1 188 FK86
Kings Rd, E4 101 ED46
  E6 144 EJ67
  E11 124 EE59
King's Rd, N17 100 DT53
Kings Rd, N18 100 DU50
  N22 99 DM53
  NW10 139 CV66
  SE25 202 DU97
King's Rd, SW1 18 B9
  SW3 18 B9
  SW6 160 DB81
  SW10 160 DB81
Kings Rd, SW14 158 CR83
  SW19 180 DA93
  W5 137 CK71
  Addlestone (New Haw) KT15 212 BH110
  Barking IG11 off North St 145 EQ66
  Barnet EN5 79 CW41
  Berkhamsted HP4 38 AU20
  Brentwood CM14 108 FW48
  Chalfont St. Giles HP8 90 AX47
  Egham TW20 173 BA91
  Feltham TW13 176 BW88
  Guildford GU1 242 AX134
  Guildford (Shalf.) GU4 258 AY141
  Harrow HA2 116 BZ61
King's Rd, Hert. SG13 32 DU08
Kings Rd, Horl. RH6 268 DG148
  Kingston upon Thames KT2 178 CL94
  Mitcham CR4 200 DG97
  Orpington BR6 223 ET105
  Richmond TW10 178 CM85
  Romford RM1 127 FG57
  St. Albans AL3 42 CB19
  St. Albans (Lon.Col.) AL2 61 CJ26
  Slough SL1 152 AS76
  Surbiton KT6 197 CJ102
  Sutton SM2 218 DA110
  Teddington TW11 177 CD92
  Twickenham TW1 177 CH86
King's Rd, Uxb. UB8 134 BK68
Kings Rd, Wal.Cr. EN8 67 DY34
  Walton-on-Thames KT12 195 BV103
  West Drayton UB7 154 BM75
  Westerham (Bigg.H.) TN16 238 EJ116
King's Rd, Wind. SL4 151 AR82
Kings Rd, Wok. GU21 227 BA116
Kings Rd Bungalows, Har. HA2 off Kings Rd 116 BZ62
King's Scholars' Pas, SW1 19 J7
King Stable Ct, Wind. SL4 off King Stable St 151 AR80
King Stable St, Wind. (Eton) SL4 151 AR80
King Stairs Cl, SE16 22 D3
King's Ter, NW1 off Plender St 141 DJ67
Kings Ter, Islw. TW7 off Worple Rd 157 CG83
Kingsthorpe Rd, SE26 183 DX91
⇌ Kingston 198 CL95
Kingston Av, Felt. TW14 175 BS86
  Leatherhead KT22 231 CH121
  Leatherhead (E.Hors.) KT24 245 BS126
  Sutton SM3 199 CY104
  West Drayton UB7 134 BM73
Kingston Br, Kings.T. KT1 197 CK96
Kingston Bypass, SW15 178 CS91
  SW20 178 CS91
  Esher KT10 197 CG104
  New Malden KT3 199 CT95
  Surbiton KT5, KT6 198 CL104
Kingston Cl, Nthlt. UB5 136 BZ67
  Romford RM6 126 EY55
  Teddington TW11 177 CH93
Coll Kingston Coll of Further Ed, Kings.T. KT1 off Kingston Hall Rd 197 CK97
  Annexe, Kings.T. KT2 off Richmond Rd 198 CL95
Kingston Ct, N4 off Wiltshire Gdns 122 DQ58
  Gravesend (Nthflt) DA11 190 GB85
Kingston Cres, Ashf. TW15 174 BJ92
  Beckenham BR3 203 DZ95
Kingston Gdns, Croy. CR0 off Wandle Rd 201 DL104
Sch Kingston Gram Sch, Kings.T. KT2 off London Rd 198 CM96
Kingston Hall Rd, Kings.T. KT1 197 CK97
Kingston Hill, Kings.T. KT2 178 CQ93
Kingston Hill Av, Rom. RM6 126 EY55
Kingston Hill Pl, Kings.T. KT2 178 CQ91
H Kingston Hosp, Kings.T. KT2 198 CP95
Kingston Ho Gdns, Lthd. KT22 off Upper Fairfield Rd 231 CG121
Kingston La, Lthd. KT24 244 BM127
  Teddington TW11 177 CG92
  Uxbridge UB8 134 BL69
  West Drayton UB7 154 BM75
★ Kingston Mus & Heritage Cen, Kings.T. KT1 198 CL96
Kingston Pk Est, Kings.T. KT2 178 CP93
Kingston Pl, Har. HA3 off Richmond Gdns 95 CF52
Kingston Ri, Add. (New Haw) KT15 212 BG110
Kingston Rd, N9 100 DU47
  SW15 179 CU88
  SW19 199 CZ95
  SW20 199 CW96
  Ashford TW15 174 BL93
  Barnet EN4 80 DD43
  Epsom KT17, KT19 216 CS106
  Ilford IG1 125 EP63
  Kingston upon Thames KT1 198 CP97
  Leatherhead KT22 231 CG117
  New Malden KT3 198 CR98
  Romford RM1 127 FF56
  Southall UB2 156 BZ75
  Staines TW18 174 BH93
  Surbiton KT5 198 CP103
  Teddington TW11 177 CH92
  Worcester Park KT4 198 CP103
Kingston Sq, SE19 182 DR92
Uni Kingston Uni, Kingston Hill, Kings.T. KT2 178 CR92
  Kingston Vale, SW15 178 CR91
  Knights Pk, Kings.T. KT1 off Grange Rd 198 CL97
  Penrhyn Rd, Kings.T. KT1 198 CL98
  Roehampton Vale, SW15 off Friars Av 179 CT90
KINGSTON UPON THAMES, KT1 & KT2 198 CL96
KINGSTON VALE, SW15 178 CS91
Kingston Vale, SW15 178 CR91
Kingstown St, NW1 140 DG67
King St, E13 15 L4
  EC2 11 H8
  N2 120 DD55
  N17 100 DT53
  SW1 19 K2
  W3 138 CP74
  W6 159 CU77
  WC2 9 N9
  Chertsey KT16 194 BG102
  Chesham HP5 54 AP32
  Gravesend DA12 191 GH86
  Richmond TW9 177 CK85
  Southall UB2 156 BY76
  Twickenham TW1 177 CG88
  Watford WD18 76 BW42
Kings Wk, Grays RM17 170 GA79
King's Wk, Kings.T. KT2 197 CK95
Kings Wk, S.Croy. CR2 220 DV114
Kings Wk Shop Mall, SW3 off King's Rd 160 DF78
Kings Warren, Lthd. (Oxshott) KT22 214 CC111
Kingswater Pl, SW11 off Battersea Ch Rd 160 DE80
Kingsway, N12 98 DC51
  SW14 158 CP83
  WC2 10 A7
  Croydon CR0 219 DM106
  Enfield EN3 82 DV43
  Gerrards Cross (Chal.St.P.) SL9 112 AY55
Kings Way, Har. HA1 117 CE56
Kingsway, Hayes UB3 135 BQ71
  Iver SL0 off High St 133 BE72
  New Malden KT3 199 CW98
  Orpington BR5 205 ES99
  Potters Bar (Cuffley) EN6 65 DL30
  Slough (Farn.Com.) SL2 131 AP65
  Staines TW19 174 BK88
  Watford WD25 60 BW34
  Wembley HA9 118 CL63
  West Wickham BR4 204 EE104
  Woking GU21 226 AX118
  Woodford Green IG8 102 EJ50
Kingsway, The, Epsom KT17 217 CT111
Kingsway Av, S.Croy. CR2 220 DW109
  Woking GU21 226 AX118
Kingsway Business Pk, Hmptn. TW12 196 BZ95
Kingsway Cres, Har. HA2 116 CC56
Sch Kingsway Inf Sch, Wat. WD25 off North App 59 BU34
Sch Kingsway Jun Sch, Wat. WD25 off Briar Rd 59 BU34
Kingsway Pl, EC1 10 D3
Kingsway Rd, Sutt. SM3 217 CY108
Kingsway Shop Cen, NW3 off Hampstead High St 120 DC63
Kingswear Rd, NW5 121 DH62
  Ruislip HA4 115 BU61
Kingswell Ride, Pot.B. (Cuffley) EN6 65 DL30
Kingswey Business Pk, Wok. GU21 211 BC114
Kings Wf, E8 5 M7
KINGSWOOD, Tad. KT20 233 CY123
KINGSWOOD, Wat. WD25 59 BV34
⇌ Kingswood 233 CZ121
Kingswood Av, NW6 139 CY67
  Belvedere DA17 166 EZ77
  Bromley BR2 204 EE97
  Hampton TW12 176 CB93
  Hounslow TW3 156 BZ81
  South Croydon CR2 236 DV115
  Swanley BR8 207 FF98
  Thornton Heath CR7 201 DN99
Kingswood Cl, N20 80 DC44
  SW8 161 DL80
  Dartford DA1 188 FJ86
  Egham (Eng.Grn) TW20 172 AX91
  Enfield EN1 82 DS43
  Guildford GU1 243 BC133
  New Malden KT3 199 CT100
  Orpington BR6 205 ER101
  Surbiton KT6 198 CL101
  Weybridge KT13 213 BP108
Kingswood Creek, Stai. (Wrays.) TW19 172 AX85
Kingswood Dr, SE19 182 DS91
  Carshalton SM5 200 DF102
  Sutton SM2 218 DB109
Kingswood Est, SE21 off Bowen Dr 182 DS91

★ Place of interest H Hospital Sch School Coll College Uni University ⇌ Railway station

Sch Kingswood Ho Sch, Epsom KT19 off West Hill 216 CQ113
Kingswood La, S.Croy. CR2 220 DW113
Warlingham CR6 236 DW115
Kingswood Ms, N15 off Harringay Rd 121 DP57
Kingswood Pk, N3 97 CZ54
Kingswood Pl, SE13 164 EE84
Sch Kingswood Prim Sch, SE27 off Gipsy Rd 182 DR92
Tadworth KT20 off Buckland Rd 249 CZ128
Kingswood Ri, Egh. (Eng.Grn) TW20 172 AX92
Kingswood Rd, E11 124 EE59
SE20 182 DW93
SW2 181 DL86
SW19 179 CZ94
W4 158 CQ76
Bromley BR2 203 ED98
Ilford IG3 126 EU60
Sevenoaks (Dunt.Grn) TN13 241 FE120
Tadworth KT20 233 CV121
Watford WD25 59 BV34
Wembley HA9 118 CN62
Sch King's Wd Sch, Rom. RM3 off Settle Rd 106 FN49
Kingswood Ter, W4 off Kingswood Rd 158 CQ76
Kingswood Way, S.Croy. CR2 220 DW113
Wallington SM6 219 DL106
Kingsworth Cl, Beck. BR3 203 DY99
Kingsworthy Cl, Kings.T. KT1 198 CM97
King's Yd, SW15 off Stanbridge Rd 159 CW83
Kingthorpe Rd, NW10 138 CR66
Kingthorpe Ter, NW10 138 CR65
Kingwell Rd, Barn. EN4 80 DD38
Kingweston Cl, NW2 off Windmill Dr 119 CY62
King William IV Gdns, SE20 off St. John's Rd 182 DW93
King William La, SE10 24 G10
King William St, EC4 11 K10
King William Wk, SE10 163 EC79
Coll Kingwood City Learning Cen, The, SW6 off Kingwood Rd 159 CY81
Kingwood Rd, SW6 159 CX81
Kinlet Rd, SE18 165 EQ81
Kinloch Dr, NW9 118 CS59
Kinloch St, N7 off Hornsey Rd 121 DM62
Kinloss Ct, N3 off Haslemere Gdns 119 CZ56
Kinloss Gdns, N3 119 CZ56
Kinloss Rd, Cars. SM5 200 DC101
Kinnaird Av, W4 158 CQ80
Bromley BR1 184 EF93
Kinnaird Cl, Brom. BR1 184 EF93
Slough SL1 130 AJ72
Kinnaird Way, Wdf.Grn. IG8 103 EM51
Kinnear Rd, W12 159 CT75
Kinnersley Manor, Reig. RH2 266 DC142
Kinnersley Wk, Reig. RH2 off Castle Dr 266 DB139
Kinnerton Pl N, SW1 18 D4
Kinnerton Pl S, SW1 18 D4
Kinnerton St, SW1 18 E4
Kinnerton Yd, SW1 18 D4
Kinnoul Rd, W6 159 CY79
Kinross Av, Wor.Pk. KT4 199 CU103
Kinross Cl, Edg. HA8 off Tayside Dr 96 CP47
Harrow HA3 118 CM57
Sunbury-on-Thames TW16 175 BT92
Kinross Dr, Sun. TW16 175 BT92
Kinross Ter, E17 101 DZ54
Kinsale Rd, SE15 162 DU83
Kintore Way, SE1 21 N7
Kintyre Cl, SW16 201 DM97
Kinveachy Gdns, SE7 164 EL78
Kinver Rd, SE26 182 DW91
Kipings, Tad. KT20 233 CX122
Kipling Av, Til. RM18 171 GH81
Kipling Dr, SW19 180 DD93
Kipling Est, SE1 21 K4
Kipling Pl, Stan. HA7 off Uxbridge Rd 95 CF51
Kipling Rd, Bexh. DA7 166 EY81
Dartford DA1 188 FP85
Kipling St, SE1 21 K4
Kipling Ter, N9 100 DR48
Kipling Twrs, Rom. RM3 105 FH52
KIPPINGTON, Sev. TN13 256 FG126
Kippington Cl, Sev. TN13 256 FF124
Kippington Dr, SE9 184 EK88
Kippington Ho, Sev. TN13 off Kippington Rd 256 FG126
Kippington Rd, Sev. TN13 256 FG124
Kirby Cl, Epsom KT19 217 CT106
Ilford IG6 103 ES51
Loughton IG10 102 EL45
Northwood HA6 93 BT51
Romford RM3 106 FN50
Kirby Est, SE16 22 C5
Kirby Gro, SE1 21 L3
Kirby Rd, Dart. DA2 188 FQ87
Woking GU21 226 AW117
Kirby St, EC1 10 D5
Kirby Way, Uxb. UB8 off Royal La 134 BM70
Walton-on-Thames KT12 196 BW100
Kirchen Rd, W13 137 CH73
Kirkby Cl, N11 off Coverdale Rd 98 DG51
Kirkcaldy Grn, Wat. WD19 off Trevose Way 94 BW48
Kirk Ct, Sev. TN13 256 FG123
Kirkdale, SE26 182 DV89
Kirkdale Rd, E11 124 EE60
Kirkefields, Guil. GU2 242 AU131
Kirkfield Cl, W13 off Broomfield Rd 137 CH74
Kirkham Rd, E6 144 EL72
Kirkham St, SE18 165 ES79
Kirkland Av, Ilf. IG5 103 EN54
Woking GU21 226 AS116
Kirkland Cl, Sid. DA15 185 ES86
Kirkland Dr, Enf. EN2 81 DP39
Kirklands, Welw.G.C. AL8 29 CX05
Kirkland Wk, E8 5 N4
Kirk La, SE18 165 EQ79
Kirkleas Rd, Surb. KT6 198 CL102
Kirklees Rd, Dag. RM8 126 EW64
Thornton Heath CR7 201 DN99
Kirkley Rd, SW19 200 DA95
Kirkly Cl, S.Croy. CR2 220 DS109
Kirkman Pl, W1 9 L6
Kirkmichael Rd, E14 14 D7
Kirk Ri, Sutt. SM1 200 DB104
Kirk Rd, E17 123 DZ58
Kirkside Rd, SE3 164 EG79
Kirkstall Av, N17 122 DR56
Kirkstall Gdns, SW2 181 DK88
Kirkstall Rd, SW2 181 DK88
Kirkstead Ct, E5 off Mandeville St 123 DY62
Kirksted Rd, Mord. SM4 200 DB102
Kirkstone Way, Brom. BR1 184 EE94
Kirk St, WC1 10 A4
Kirkton Rd, N15 122 DS56
Kirkwall Pl, E2 12 F1
Kirkwall Spur, Slou. SL1 132 AS71
Kirkwood Rd, SE15 162 DV82
Kirn Rd, W13 off Kirchen Rd 137 CH73
Kirrane Cl, N.Mal. KT3 199 CT99
Kirtle Rd, Chesh. HP5 54 AQ31
Kirtley Rd, SE26 183 DY91
Kirtling St, SW8 161 DJ80
Kirton Cl, W4 off Dolman Rd 158 CR77
Hornchurch RM12 148 FJ65
Kirton Gdns, E2 11 P2
Kirton Rd, E13 144 EJ68
Kirton Wk, Edg. HA8 96 CQ52
Kirwyn Way, SE5 161 DP80
Coll Kisharon Coll, NW4 off Parson St 119 CW55
Sch Kisharon Day Sch (Jewish), NW11 off Finchley Rd 119 CZ58
Sch Kisharon Sen Cen (Spec Needs), N3 off Nether St 98 DB51
Kitcat Ter, E3 13 P1
Kitchener Av, Grav. DA12 191 GJ90
Kitchener Cl, St.Alb. AL1 43 CH21
Kitchener Rd, E7 144 EH65
E17 101 EB53
N2 120 DE55
N17 122 DR55
Dagenham RM10 147 FB65
Thornton Heath CR7 202 DR97
Kitcheners Mead, St.Alb. AL3 42 CC20
Kitchenride Cor, Cher. KT16 211 BA105
Kite Fld, Berk. HP4 38 AS16
Kite Pl, E2 12 B1
Kite Yd, SW11 off Cambridge Rd 160 DF81
Kitley Gdns, SE19 202 DT95
Kitsbury Rd, Berk. HP4 38 AV19
Kitsbury Ter, Berk. HP4 38 AV19
Kitsmead La, Cher. (Longcr.) KT16 192 AX103
Kitson Rd, SE5 162 DR80
SW13 159 CU81
Kitson Way, Harl. CM20 35 EQ14
Kitswell Way, Rad. WD7 61 CF33
Kitten La, Ware (Stans.Abb.) SG12 34 EE11
Kitters Grn, Abb.L. WD5 off High St 59 BS31
Kittiwake Cl, S.Croy. CR2 221 DY110
Kittiwake Pl, Sutt. SM1 off Sandpiper Rd 217 CZ106
Kittiwake Rd, Nthlt. UB5 136 BX69
Kittiwake Way, Hayes UB4 136 BX71
Kitto Rd, SE14 163 DX82
KITT'S END, Barn. EN5 79 CY37
Kitt's End Rd, Barn. EN5 79 CX36
Kiver Rd, N19 121 DK61
Kiwi Cl, Twick. TW1 off Crown Rd 177 CH86
Klea Av, SW4 181 DJ86
Knapdale Cl, SE23 182 DV89
Knapmill Rd, SE6 183 EA89
Knapmill Way, SE6 183 EB89
Knapp Cl, NW10 138 CS65
Knapp Rd, E3 13 N4
Ashford TW15 174 BM91
Knapton Ms, SW17 off Seely Rd 180 DG93
Knaresborough Dr, SW18 180 DB88
Knaresborough Pl, SW5 17 J7
Knatchbull Rd, NW10 138 CR67
SE5 162 DQ81
Knaves Beech, H.Wyc. (Loud.) HP10 88 AD53
Knaves Beech Business Cen, H.Wyc. (Loud.) HP10 88 AC54
Knaves Beech Way, H.Wyc. (Loud.) HP10 88 AC54
Knaves Hollow, H.Wyc. HP10 88 AD54
Knebworth Av, E17 101 EA53
Knebworth Path, Borwd. WD6 78 CR42
Knebworth Rd, N16 off Nevill Rd 122 DS63
Knee Hill, SE2 166 EW77
Knee Hill Cres, SE2 166 EW77
Knella Grn, Welw.G.C. AL7 30 DA09
Knella Rd, Welw.G.C. AL7 29 CY10
Kneller Gdns, Islw. TW7 177 CD85
Kneller Rd, SE4 163 DY84
New Malden KT3 198 CS101
Twickenham TW2 176 CC86
Knight Cl, Dag. RM8 126 EW61
Knighten St, E1 22 B2
Knighthead Pt, E14 23 N5
Knightland Rd, E5 122 DV61
Knighton Cl, Rom. RM7 127 FD58
South Croydon CR2 219 DP108
Woodford Green IG8 102 EH49
Knighton Dr, Wdf.Grn. IG8 102 EG49
Knighton Grn, Buck.H. IG9 off High Rd 102 EH47
Knighton La, Buck.H. IG9 102 EH47
Knighton Pk Rd, SE26 183 DX92
Knighton Rd, E7 124 EG62
Redhill RH1 266 DG136
Romford RM7 127 FC58
Sevenoaks (Otford) TN14 241 FF116
Knighton Way La, Uxb. (Denh.) UB9 134 BH65
Knightrider Ct, EC4 off Godliman St 142 DQ73
Knightrider St, EC4 10 G9
Knights Arc, SW1 18 C4
Knights Av, W5 158 CL75
⊖ Knightsbridge 18 C4
Knightsbridge, SW1 18 D4
SW7 18 B4
Knightsbridge Ct, Slou. (Langley) SL3 off High St 153 BA77
Knightsbridge Cres, Stai. TW18 174 BH93
Knightsbridge Gdns, Rom. RM7 127 FD57
Knightsbridge Grn, SW1 18 C4
Knightsbridge Way, Hem.H. HP2 40 BL20
Knights Cl, E9 off Churchill Wk 122 DW64
Egham TW20 173 BD93
Knights Cl, Windsor SL4 151 AK81
Knights Ct, Kings.T. KT1 198 CL97
Romford RM6 126 EY58
Knightsfield, Welw.G.C. AL8 29 CY06
Knights Hill, SE27 181 DP92
Knights Hill Sq, SE27 off Knights Hill 181 DP91
Knights La, N9 100 DU48
Knights Manor Way, Dart. DA1 188 FM86
Sch Knightsmead Sch, S.Ock. RM15 off Fortin Cl 149 FU73
Knights Ms, Sutt. SM2 off York Rd 218 DA108
Knights Orchard, Hem.H. HP1 39 BF18
Knights Pk, Kings.T. KT1 198 CL97
Knights Pl, Red. RH1 off Noke Dr 250 DG133
Knight's Pl, Twick. TW2 off May Rd 177 CE88
Knights Pl, Wind. SL4 off Frances Rd 151 AQ83
Knights Ridge, Orp. BR6 off Stirling Dr 224 EV106
Knights Rd, E16 25 M3
Stanmore HA7 95 CJ49
Knight St, Saw. CM21 36 EY05
Knights Wk, SE11 20 E8
Romford (Abridge) RM4 86 EV41
Knight's Way, Brwd. CM13 109 GA48
Knights Way, Ilf. IG6 103 EQ51
Knightswood, Wok. GU21 226 AT118
Knightswood Cl, Edg. HA8 96 CQ47
Knightswood Rd, Rain. RM13 147 FG68
Knightwood Cl, Reig. RH2 266 DA136
Knightwood Cres, N.Mal. KT3 198 CS100
Knipp Hill, Cob. KT11 214 BZ113
Knivet Rd, SW6 160 DA79
Knobfield, Dor. RH5 261 BT143
Knobs Hill Rd, E15 143 EB67
KNOCKHALL, Green. DA9 189 FW85
Knockhall Chase, Green. DA9 189 FV85
Sch Knockhall Co Prim Sch, Green. DA9 off Eynsford Rd 189 FW85
Knockhall Rd, Green. DA9 189 FW86
KNOCKHOLT, Sev. TN14 240 EU116
⇌ Knockholt 224 EY109
Knockholt Cl, Sutt. SM2 218 DB110
Knockholt Main Rd, Sev. (Knock.) TN14 240 EY115
KNOCKHOLT POUND, Sev. TN14 240 EX115
Knockholt Rd, SE9 184 EK85
Sevenoaks (Halst.) TN14 224 EZ113
Knole, The, SE9 185 EN91
Gravesend (Istead Rise) DA13 190 GE94
Knole Cl, Croy. CR0 off Stockbury Rd 202 DW100
Knole Gate, Sid. DA15 off Woodside Cres 185 ES90
★ Knole Ho & Pk, Sev. TN15 257 FL126
Knole La, Sev. TN13, TN15 257 FJ126
Knole Rd, Dart. DA1 187 FG87
Sevenoaks TN13 257 FK123
Knole Way, Sev. TN13 257 FJ125
Knoll, The, W13 137 CJ71
Beckenham BR3 203 EB95
Bromley BR2 204 EG103
Chertsey KT16 193 BF102
Cobham KT11 214 CA113
Hertford SG13 32 DV08
Leatherhead KT22 231 CJ120
Knoll Ct, SE19 182 DT92
Knoll Cres, Nthwd. HA6 93 BS53
Knoll Dr, N14 98 DG45
Knolles Cres, Hat. AL9 45 CV24
Knollmead, Surb. KT5 198 CQ102
Sch Knollmead Prim Sch, Surb. KT5 off Knollmead 198 CQ103
Knoll Pk Rd, Cher. KT16 193 BF102
Knoll Ri, Orp. BR6 205 ET102
Knoll Rd, SW18 180 DC85
Bexley DA5 186 FA87
Dorking RH4 263 CG138
Sidcup DA14 186 EV92
Knolls, The, Epsom KT17 233 CW116
Knolls Cl, Wor.Pk. KT4 199 CV104
Knollys Cl, SW16 181 DN90
Knollys Rd, SW16 181 DN90
Knolton Way, Slou. SL2 132 AW72
Sch Knotley Sch, W.Wick. BR4 off Springfield Gdns 203 EB103
Knottisford St, E2 12 G1
Knottocks Cl, Beac. HP9 88 AJ50
Knottocks Dr, Beac. HP9 88 AJ50
Knottocks End, Beac. HP9 89 AK50
Knotts Grn Ms, E10 123 EB58
Knotts Grn Rd, E10 123 EB58
Knotts Pl, Sev. TN13 256 FG124
KNOTTY GREEN, Beac. HP9 88 AJ49
Knowland Way, Uxb. (Denh.) UB9 113 BF58
Knowle, The, Hodd. EN11 49 EA18
Tadworth KT20 233 CW121
Knowle Av, Bexh. DA7 166 EY80
Knowle Cl, SW9 161 DN83
Knowle Gdns, W.Byf. KT14 off Madeira Rd 211 BF113
Knowle Grn, Stai. TW18 174 BG92
Knowle Gro, Vir.W. GU25 192 AW101
Knowle Gro Cl, Vir.W. GU25 192 AW101
Knowle Hill, Vir.W. GU25 192 AV101
Knowle Pk, Cob. KT11 230 BY115
Knowle Pk Av, Stai. TW18 174 BH93
Sch Knowle Pk Inf Sch, Stai. TW18 off Knowle Grn 174 BG92
Knowle Rd, Brom. BR2 204 EL103
Twickenham TW2 177 CE88
Knowles Cl, West Dr. UB7 134 BL74
Knowles Hill Cres, SE13 183 ED85
Knowles Ho, SW18 off Neville Gill Cl 180 DB86
Knowles Wk, SW4 161 DJ83
Knowl Hill, Wok. GU22 227 BB119
Knowl Pk, Borwd. (Elstree) WD6 78 CL43
Knowlton Grn, Brom. BR2 204 EF99
Knowl Way, Borwd. (Elstree) WD6 78 CL42
Knowsley Av, Sthl. UB1 136 CA74
Knowsley Rd, SW11 160 DF82
Knoxfield Caravan Pk, Dart. DA2 189 FS90
Knox Rd, E7 144 EF65
Guildford GU2 242 AV130
Knox St, W1 8 C5
Knoyle St, SE14 163 DY79
Knutsford Av, Wat. WD24 76 BX38
Sch Knutsford Prim Sch, Wat. WD24 off Knutsford Av 76 BX38
Sch Kobi Nazrul Prim Sch, E1 12 B7
Kodak Ho, Hem.H. HP1 40 BJ22
Kohat Rd, SW19 180 DB92
Koh-i-noor Av, Bushey WD23 76 CA44
Koonowla Cl, West. (Bigg.H.) TN16 238 EK115
Kooringa, Warl. CR6 236 DV119
Korda Cl, Shep. TW17 194 BM97
Kossuth St, SE10 24 G9
Kotree Way, SE1 22 B8
Kramer Ms, SW5 17 H10
Kreedman Wk, E8 122 DU64
Kreisel Wk, Rich. TW9 158 CM79
Kuala Gdns, SW16 201 DM95
Kuhn Way, E7 off Forest La 124 EG64
Kydbrook Cl, Orp. BR5 205 ER101
Kylemore Cl, E6 off Parr Rd 144 EK68
Kylemore Rd, NW6 140 DA66
Kymberley Rd, Har. HA1 117 CE58
Kyme Rd, Horn. RM11 127 FF58
Kynance Cl, Rom. RM3 106 FJ48
Kynance Gdns, Stan. HA7 95 CJ53
Kynance Ms, SW7 17 L6
Kynance Pl, SW7 17 L6
Kynaston Av, N16 off Dynevor Rd 122 DT62
Thornton Heath CR7 202 DQ99
Kynaston Cl, Har. HA3 95 CD52
Kynaston Cres, Th.Hth. CR7 202 DQ99
Kynaston Rd, N16 122 DS62
Bromley BR1 184 EG92
Enfield EN2 82 DR39
Orpington BR5 206 EV101
Thornton Heath CR7 202 DQ99
Kynaston Wd, Har. HA3 95 CD52
Kynersley Cl, Cars. SM5 off William St 200 DF104
Kyngeshene Gdns, Guil. GU1 off Tangier Rd 259 BA135
Kynock Rd, N18 100 DW49
Kyrle Rd, SW11 180 DG85
Kytes Dr, Wat. WD25 60 BX33
Kytes Est, Wat. WD25 60 BX33
Kyverdale Rd, N16 122 DT61

L

Laburnham Cl, Upmin. RM14 129 FU59
Wembley HA0 off Highcroft Av 138 CN67
Laburnham Gdns, Upmin. RM14 129 FT59
Laburnum Av, N9 100 DS47
N17 100 DR52
Dartford DA1 188 FJ88
Hornchurch RM12 127 FF62
Sutton SM1 200 DE104
Swanley BR8 207 FC97
West Drayton UB7 134 BM73
Laburnum Cl, E4 101 DZ51
N11 98 DG51
SE15 off Clifton Way 162 DW80
Bishop's Stortford (Sheering) CM22 37 FC07
Guildford GU1 242 AW131
Waltham Cross (Chsht) EN8 67 DX31
Laburnum Ct, E2 5 N8
Stanmore HA7 95 CJ49
Laburnum Cres, Sun. TW16 off Batavia Rd 195 BV95
Laburnum Gdns, N21 100 DQ47
Croydon CR0 203 DX101
Laburnum Gro, N21 100 DQ47
NW9 118 CQ59
Gravesend (Nthflt) DA11 190 GD87
Hounslow TW3 156 BZ84
New Malden KT3 198 CR96
Ruislip HA4 115 BR58
St. Albans AL2 60 CB25
Slough SL3 153 BB79
South Ockendon RM15 149 FW69
Southall UB1 136 BZ70
Laburnum Ho, Dag. RM10 off Bradwell Av 126 FA61
Laburnum Pl, Egh. (Eng.Grn) TW20 172 AV93
Laburnum Rd, SW19 180 DC94
Chertsey KT16 194 BG102
Epping (Cooper.) CM16 70 EW29
Epsom KT18 216 CS113
Hayes UB3 155 BT77
Hoddesdon EN11 49 EB15
Mitcham CR4 200 DG96
Woking GU22 226 AX120
Laburnum St, E2 5 N8
Laburnum Wk, Horn. RM12 128 FJ64
Laburnum Way, Brom. BR2 205 EN101
Staines TW19 174 BM88
Waltham Cross (Chsht) EN7 off Millcrest Rd 65 DP28
Lacebark Cl, Sid. DA15 185 ET87
Lacey Av, Couls. CR5 235 DN120
Lacey Cl, N9 100 DU47
Egham TW20 173 BD94
Lacey Dr, Couls. CR5 235 DN120
Dagenham RM8 126 EV63
Edgware HA8 96 CL49
Hampton TW12 196 BZ95
Lacey Grn, Couls. CR5 235 DN120
Lacey Wk, E3 143 EA68
Lackford Rd, Couls. CR5 234 DF118
Lackington St, EC2 11 K5
Lackmore Rd, Enf. EN1 82 DW35
Lacock Cl, SW19 180 DC93
Lacock Ct, W13 off Singapore Rd 137 CG74
Lacon Rd, SE22 162 DU84
Lacy Rd, SW15 159 CX84
Ladas Rd, SE27 182 DQ91
Ladbroke Ct, Red. RH1 250 DG132
Ladbroke Cres, W11 6 D8
Ladbroke Gdns, W11 6 E9
⊖ Ladbroke Grove 6 D7
Ladbroke Gro, W10 6 B3
W11 6 D8
Redhill RH1 250 DG133
Ladbroke Ms, W11 16 D2
Ladbroke Rd, W11 16 D1
Enfield EN1 82 DT44
Epsom KT18 216 CR114
Horley RH6 268 DG146
Redhill RH1 250 DG133
Ladbroke Sq, W11 6 E10
Ladbroke Ter, W11 6 F10
Ladbroke Wk, W11 16 F1
Ladbrook Cl, Pnr. HA5 116 BZ57
Ladbrooke Cl, Pot.B. EN6 off Strafford Gate 64 DA32
Ladbrooke Cres, Sid. DA14 186 EX90
Ladbrooke Dr, Pot.B. EN6 64 DA32
Sch Ladbrooke JMI Sch, Pot.B. EN6 off Watkins Ri 64 DB32
Ladbrooke Rd, Slou. SL1 151 AQ76
Ladbrook Rd, SE25 202 DR97
Ladderstile Ride, Kings.T. KT2 178 CP92
Ladderswood Way, N11 99 DJ50
Ladds Way, Swan. BR8 207 FD98
Ladies Gro, St.Alb. AL3 42 CB18
Lady Aylesford Av, Stan. HA7 95 CH50
Sch Lady Banks Jun Sch, Ruis. HA4 off Dawlish Dr 115 BU61
Lady Booth Rd, Kings.T. KT1 198 CL96
Sch Lady Boswell's C of E Prim Sch, Sev. TN13 off Plymouth Dr 257 FJ125
Ladybower Ct, E5 off Gilpin Rd 123 DY63
Lady Cooper Ct, Berk. HP4 off Frithsden Rd 38 AY17
Ladycroft Gdns, Orp. BR6 223 EQ106
Ladycroft Rd, SE13 163 EB83
Ladycroft Wk, Stan. HA7 95 CK53
Ladycroft Way, Orp. BR6 223 EQ106
Ladyday Pl, Slou. SL1 off Glentworth Pl 131 AQ74
Lady Dock Path, SE16 23 J4
Sch Lady Eden's Sch, W8 17 L5
Ladyegate Cl, Dor. RH5 263 CK135
Ladyegate Rd, Dor. RH5 263 CJ136
Sch Lady Eleanor Holles Jun Sch, The, Hmptn. TW12 off Uxbridge Rd 176 CB92
Sch Lady Eleanor Holles Sch, The, Hmptn. TW12 off Hanworth Rd 176 CB92
Ladyfield Cl, Loug. IG10 85 EP42
Ladyfields, Grav. (Nthflt) DA11 191 GF91
Loughton IG10 85 EP42
Lady Forsdyke Way, Epsom KT19 216 CN109
Ladygate La, Ruis. HA4 115 BP58
Ladygrove, Croy. CR0 221 DY109
Lady Gro, Welw.G.C. AL7 29 CY12
Ladygrove Dr, Guil. GU4 243 BA129
Lady Harewood Way, Epsom KT19 216 CN109
Lady Hay, Wor.Pk. KT4 199 CT103
Sch Lady Margaret Prim Sch, Sthl. UB1 off Lady Margaret Rd 136 BZ71
Lady Margaret Rd, N19 121 DJ63
NW5 121 DJ64
Southall UB1 136 BZ71
Sch Lady Margaret Sec Sch, SW6 off Parsons Grn 160 DA81
Ladymead, Guil. GU1 242 AW133
Ladymeadow, Kings L. WD4 58 BK27
Ladymead Retail Pk, Guil. GU1 242 AW133
Lady's Cl, Wat. WD18 75 BV42
Ladyshot, Harl. CM20 36 EU14
Ladysmith Av, E6 144 EL68
Ilford IG2 125 ER59
Ladysmith Cl, NW7 off Colenso Dr 97 CU52
Ladysmith Rd, E16 15 J2
N17 100 DU54
N18 100 DV50
SE9 185 EN86
Enfield EN1 82 DS41
Harrow HA3 95 CE54
St. Albans AL3 43 CD19
Lady Somerset Rd, NW5 121 DH63
Ladythorpe Cl, Add. KT15 off Church Rd 212 BH105
Ladywalk, Rick. (Map.Cr.) WD3 91 BE50
LADYWELL, SE13 183 EA85
⇌ Ladywell 183 EB85
H Ladywell Cen, SE4 183 EA86
Ladywell Cl, SE4 off Adelaide Av 163 DZ84
Ladywell Hts, SE4 183 DZ86
Ladywell Prospect, Saw. CM21 36 FA06
Ladywell Rd, SE13 183 EA85
Ladywell St, E15 off Plaistow Gro 144 EF67
Ladywood Av, Orp. BR5 205 ES99
Ladywood Cl, Rick. WD3 74 BH41
Ladywood Rd, Dart. (Lane End) DA2 189 FS92
Hertford SG14 31 DM09
Surbiton KT6 198 CN103
Lady Yorke Pk, Iver SL0 133 BD65
Lafone Av, Felt. TW13 off Alfred Rd 176 BW88
Lafone St, SE1 21 N3
Lagado Ms, SE16 23 H2
Lagger, The, Ch.St.G. HP8 90 AV48
Lagger Cl, Ch.St.G. HP8 90 AV48
Laglands Cl, Reig. RH2 250 DC132
Lagonda Av, Ilf. IG6 103 ET51
Lagonda Way, Dart. DA1 168 FJ84
Lagoon Rd, Orp. BR5 206 EV99
Laidlaw Dr, N21 81 DM42
Laidon Sq, Hem.H. HP2 40 BK16
Laing Cl, Ilf. IG6 103 ER51
Laing Dean, Nthlt. UB5 136 BW67
Laings Av, Mitch. CR4 200 DF96
Lainlock Pl, Houns. TW3 off Spring Gro Rd 156 CB81
Lainson St, SW18 180 DA87
Lairdale Cl, SE21 182 DQ88
Laird Av, Grays RM16 170 GD75
Laird Ho, SE5 162 DQ80
Lairs Cl, N7 off Manger Rd 141 DL65
Laitwood Rd, SW12 181 DH88
Lake, The, Bushey (Bushey Hth) WD23 94 CC46
Lake Av, Brom. BR1 184 EG93
Rainham RM13 148 FK68
Slough SL1 131 AR73
Lake Cl, SW19 off Lake Rd 179 CZ92
Dagenham RM8 126 EX62
West Byfleet (Byfleet) KT14 212 BK112
Lakedale Rd, SE18 165 ES79
Lake Dr, Bushey (Bushey Hth) WD23 94 CC47
Lake End Ct, Maid. (Taplow) SL6 off Taplow Rd 130 AH72

Lake End Rd, Maid. (Taplow) SL6 130 AH73
Windsor (Dorney) SL4 150 AH76
Lakefield Cl, SE20 off Limes Av 182 DV94
Lakefield Rd, N22 99 DP54
Lakefields Cl, Rain. RM13 148 FK68
Lake Gdns, Dag. RM10 126 FA64
Richmond TW10 177 CH89
Wallington SM6 201 DH104
Lakehall Gdns, Th.Hth. CR7 201 DP99
Lakehall Rd, Th.Hth. CR7 201 DP99
Lake Ho Rd, E11 124 EG62
Lakehurst Rd, Epsom KT19 216 CS106
Lakeland Cl, Chig. IG7 104 EV49
Harrow HA3 95 CD51
Lake La, Horl. RH6 267 DJ144
Lakenheath, N14 81 DK44
Lake Ri, Grays RM20 169 FU77
Romford RM1 127 FF55
Lake Rd, SW19 179 CZ92
Croydon CR0 203 DZ103
Romford RM6 126 EX56
Virginia Water GU25 192 AV98
Waltham Abbey EN9 50 EE21
Laker Pl, SW15 179 CZ86
Lakers Ri, Bans. SM7 234 DE116
Lakes Cl, Guil. (Chilw.) GU4 259 BB140
Lakeside, N3 98 DB54
W13 off Edgehill Rd 137 CJ72
Beckenham BR3 203 EB97
Enfield EN2 81 DK42
Grays RM20 169 FV77
Rainham RM13 148 FL68
Redhill RH1 250 DG132
Wallington SM6 off Derek Av 201 DH104
Weybridge KT13 195 BS103
Woking GU21 226 AS119
Lakeside Av, SE28 146 EU74
Ilford IG4 124 EK56
Lakeside Cl, SE25 202 DU96
Chigwell IG7 103 ET49
Ruislip HA4 115 BR56
Sidcup DA15 186 EW85
Woking GU21 226 AS119
Lakeside Ct, N4 121 DP61
Borehamwood (Elstree) WD6 off Cavendish Cres 78 CN43
Lakeside Cres, Barn. EN4 80 DF43
Brentwood CM14 108 FX48
Weybridge KT13 off Churchill Dr 195 BQ104
Lakeside Dr, Brom. BR2 204 EL104
Esher KT10 214 CC107
Slough (Stoke P.) SL2 132 AS67
Lakeside Gra, Wey. KT13 195 BQ104
Lakeside Pl, St.Alb. (Lon.Col.) AL2 61 CK27
Lakeside Rd, N13 99 DM49
W14 16 A5
Slough SL3 153 BF80
Waltham Cross (Chsht) EN8 66 DW28
Sch Lakeside Sch, Welw.G.C. AL8 off Lemsford La 29 CV11
Lakeside Way, Wem. HA9 118 CN63
Lakes La, Beac. HP9 89 AM54
Lakes Rd, Kes. BR2 222 EJ106
Lakeswood Rd, Orp. BR5 205 EP100
Lake Vw, Dor. (N.Holm.) RH5 263 CJ139
Edgware HA8 96 CM50
Potters Bar EN6 64 DC33
Lakeview Ct, SW19 off Victoria Dr 179 CY89
Lakeview Rd, SE27 181 DN92
Lake Vw Rd, Sev. TN13 256 FG122
Lakeview Rd, Well. DA16 166 EV84
Lakis Cl, NW3 off Flask Wk 120 DC63
LALEHAM, Stai. TW18 194 BJ97
Laleham Av, NW7 96 CR48
Laleham Cl, Stai. TW18 off Worple Rd 194 BH95
Sch Laleham C of E Prim Sch, Stai. TW18 off The Broadway 194 BJ96
Laleham Ct, Wok. GU21 226 AY116
★ Laleham Heritage Cen, Stai. TW18 194 BJ97
Sch Laleham Lea Prep Sch, Pur. CR8 off Peaks Hill 219 DL110
Laleham Pk, Stai. TW18 194 BJ98
Laleham Reach, Cher. KT16 194 BH96
Laleham Rd, SE6 183 EC86
Shepperton TW17 194 BM98
Staines TW18 173 BF92
Lalor St, SW6 159 CY82
Lambarde Av, SE9 185 EN91
Lambarde Dr, Sev. TN13 256 FG123
Lambarde Rd, Sev. TN13 256 FG122
Lambardes Cl, Orp. BR6 224 EW110
Lamb Cl, Hat. AL10 45 CV19
Northolt UB5 136 BY69
Tilbury RM18 off Coleridge Rd 171 GJ82
Watford WD25 60 BW34
Lamberhurst Cl, Orp. BR5 206 EX102
Lamberhurst Rd, SE27 181 DN91
Dagenham RM8 126 EZ60
Lambert Av, Rich. TW9 158 CP83
Slough SL3 152 AY75
Lambert Cl, West. (Bigg.H.) TN16 238 EK116
Lambert Ct, Bushey WD23 76 BX42
Lambert Jones Ms, EC2 off The Barbican 142 DQ71
Lambert Rd, E16 15 N7
N12 98 DD50
SW2 181 DL85
Banstead SM7 218 DA114
Lamberts Pl, Croy. CR0 202 DR102
Lamberts Rd, Surb. KT5 198 CL99
Lambert St, N1 4 C6
Lambert Wk, Wem. HA9 117 CK62
Lambert Way, N12 off Woodhouse Rd 98 DC50
LAMBETH, SE1 20 A5
Sch Lambeth Acad, SW4 off Elms Rd 181 DJ85
Lambeth Br, SE1 19 P7
SW1 19 P7
Coll Lambeth Coll, Adare Cen, SW16 off Adare Wk 181 DM89
Brixton Cen, SW2 off Brixton Hill 181 DM85
Clapham Cen, SW4 off Clapham Common S Side 181 DJ8
Coll Lambeth Coll, Vauxhall Cen, SW8 off Belmore St 161 DK81
Lambeth High St, SE1 20 A8
Lambeth Hill, EC4 10 G9
⊖ Lambeth North 20 C4
★ Lambeth Palace, SE1 20 A6
Lambeth Palace Rd, SE1 20 A6
Lambeth Rd, SE1 20 B6
SE11 20 B6
Croydon CR0 201 DN101
Sch Lambeth Sec PRU, SE27 off Gipsy Rd 182 DQ91
Lambeth Wk, SE11 20 B7
Lamb La, E8 142 DV66
Lamble St, NW5 120 DG64
Lambley Rd, Dag. RM9 146 EV65
Lambly Hill, Vir.W. GU25 192 AY97
Lambolle Pl, NW3 140 DE65
Lambolle Rd, NW3 140 DE65
Lambourn Chase, Rad. WD7 77 CF36
Lambourn Cl, W7 157 CF75
South Croydon CR2 219 DP109
Lambourne Av, SW19 179 CZ91
Lambourne Cl, Chig. IG7 104 EV48
Sch Lambourne Co Prim Sch, Rom. RM4 off Hoe La 86 EV42
Lambourne Ct, Wdf.Grn. IG8 off Navestock Cres 102 EJ52
Lambourne Cres, Chig. IG7 104 EV47
Woking GU21 211 BD113
Lambourne Dr, Brwd. (Hutt.) CM13 109 GE45
Cobham KT11 230 BX115
LAMBOURNE END, Rom. RM4 86 EX44
Lambourne Gdns, E4 101 EA47
Barking IG11 off Lambourne Rd 145 ET66
Enfield EN1 82 DT40
Hornchurch RM12 128 FK61
Lambourne Gro, Kings.T. KT1 off Kenley Rd 198 CP96
Lambourne Pl, SE3 off Shooter's Hill Rd 164 EH81
Lambourne Rd, E11 123 EC59
Barking IG11 145 ES66
Chigwell IG7 103 ES49
Ilford IG3 125 ES61
Lambourn Rd, SW4 161 DH83
Lambrook Ter, SW6 159 CY81
Lamb's Bldgs, EC1 11 J4
Lambs Cl, Pot.B. (Cuffley) EN6 65 DM29
Lambs Conduit Pas, WC1 10 A5
Lamb's Conduit St, WC1 10 A4
Lambscroft Av, SE9 184 EJ90
Lambscroft Way, Ger.Cr. (Chal.St.P.) SL9 90 AY54
Lambs La N, Rain. RM13 148 FJ70
Lambs La S, Rain. RM13 147 FH71
Lambs Meadow, Wdf.Grn. IG8 102 EK54
Lambs Ms, N1 4 E8
Lamb's Pas, EC1 11 J5
Lambs Ter, N9 100 DR47
Lamb St, E1 11 N5
Lambs Wk, Enf. EN2 82 DQ40
Lambton Av, Wal.Cr. EN8 67 DX32
Lambton Ms, N19 off Lambton Rd 121 DL60
Lambton Pl, W11 6 F9
Lambton Rd, N19 121 DL60
SW20 199 CW95
Lamb Wk, SE1 21 L4
Lambyn Cft, Horl. RH6 269 DJ147
Lamerock Rd, Brom. BR1 184 EF91
Lamerton Rd, Ilf. IG6 103 EP54
Lamerton St, SE8 163 EA79
Lamford Cl, N17 100 DR52
Lamington St, W6 159 CV77
Lamlash St, SE11 20 E7
Lammas Av, Mitch. CR4 200 DG96
Lammas Cl, Stai. TW18 173 BE90
Lammas Ct, Stai. TW19 173 BD89
Windsor SL4 151 AQ82
Lammas Dr, Stai. TW18 173 BD90
Lammas Grn, SE26 182 DV90
Lammas La, Esher KT10 214 CA106
Lammasmead, Brox. EN10 49 DZ23
Lammas Pk, W5 157 CJ75
Lammas Pk Gdns, W5 157 CJ75
Lammas Pk Rd, W5 137 CJ74
Lammas Rd, E9 143 DX66
E10 123 DY61
Richmond TW10 177 CJ91
Slough SL1 131 AK71
Watford WD18 76 BW43
Sch Lammas Sec Sch, The, E10 off Seymour Rd 123 DZ60
Lammas Way, H.Wyc. (Loud.) HP10 88 AC54
Lammermoor Rd, SW12 181 DH87
Lamont Rd, SW10 160 DC79
Lamont Rd Pas, SW10 off Lamont Rd 160 DD79
LAMORBEY, Sid. DA15 185 ET88
Lamorbey Cl, Sid. DA15 185 ET88
Lamorna Av, Grav. DA12 191 GJ90
Lamorna Cl, E17 101 EC53
Orpington BR6 206 EU101
Radlett WD7 61 CH34
Lamorna Gro, Stan. HA7 95 CK53
Lampard Gro, N16 122 DT60
Lampern Sq, E2 12 B1
Lampeter Cl, NW9 118 CS58
Woking GU22 226 AY118
Lampeter Sq, W6 off Humbolt Rd 159 CY79
Lampits, Hodd. EN11 49 EB17
Lamplighter Cl, E1 12 E4
Lamplighters Cl, Dart. DA1 188 FM86
Waltham Abbey EN9 68 EG34
Lampmead Rd, SE12 184 EE85
Lamp Office Ct, WC1 10 A4
Lamport Cl, SE18 165 EM77
LAMPTON, Houns. TW3 156 CB81
Lampton Av, Houns. TW3 156 CB81
Lampton Ho Cl, SW19 179 CX91
Lampton Pk Rd, Houns. TW3 156 CB82
Lampton Rd, Houns. TW3 156 CB82
Sch Lampton Sch, Houns. TW3 off Lampton Av 156 CA81
Lamsey Rd, Hem.H. HP3 40 BK22
Lamson Rd, Rain. RM13 147 FF70
Lanacre Av, NW9 97 CT53
Lanark Cl, W5 137 CJ71
Lanark Ms, W9 7 L2
Lanark Pl, W9 7 M3
Lanark Rd, W9 7 L2
Lanark Sq, E14 24 B5
Lanata Wk, Hayes UB4 off Ramulis Dr 136 BX70
Lanbury Rd, SE15 163 DX84
Lancashire Ct, W1 9 H9
Lancaster Av, E18 124 EH56
SE27 181 DP89
SW19 179 CX92
Barking IG11 145 ES66
Barnet EN4 80 DD38
Guildford GU1 259 AZ136
Mitcham CR4 201 DL99
Slough SL2 131 AQ70
Lancaster Cl, N1 5 M6
N17 off Park La 100 DU52
NW9 97 CT52
Ashford TW15 174 BL91
Brentwood (Pilg.Hat.) CM15 108 FU43
Bromley BR2 204 EF98
Egham TW20 172 AX92
Kingston upon Thames KT2 177 CK92
Staines (Stanw.) TW19 174 BL86
Woking GU21 227 BA116
Lancaster Cotts, Rich. TW10 off Lancaster Pk 178 CL86
Lancaster Ct, SE27 181 DP89
SW6 159 CZ80
W2 7 M10
Banstead SM7 217 CZ114
Walton-on-Thames KT12 195 BU101
Lancaster Dr, E14 24 D2
NW3 140 DE65
Hemel Hempstead (Bov.) HP3 57 AZ27
Hornchurch RM12 127 FH64
Loughton IG10 84 EL44
Lancaster Gdns, SW19 179 CY92
W13 157 CH75
Bromley BR1 204 EL99
Kingston upon Thames KT2 177 CK92
⊖ Lancaster Gate 7 N9
Lancaster Gate, W2 7 M10
Lancaster Gro, NW3 140 DD65
★ Lancaster Ho, SW1 19 J3
Sch Lancasterian Inf & Nurs Sch, N17 off King's Rd 100 DT53
Sch Lancasterian Jun Sch, N17 off King's Rd 100 DT53
Lancaster Ms, SW18 off East Hill 180 DB85
W2 7 M9
Richmond TW10 off Richmond Hill 178 CL86
Lancaster Pk, Rich. TW10 178 CL85
Lancaster Pl, SW19 off Lancaster Rd 179 CX92
WC2 10 A9
Hounslow TW4 156 BW82
Ilford IG1 off Staines Rd 125 EQ64
Twickenham TW1 177 CG86
Lancaster Rd, E7 144 EG66
E11 124 EE61
E17 101 DX54
N4 121 DN59
N11 99 DK51
N18 100 DT50
NW10 119 CT64
SE25 202 DT96
SW19 179 CX92
W11 6 C8
Barnet EN4 80 DD43
Enfield EN2 82 DR39
Epping (N.Wld Bas.) CM16 70 FA26
Grays (Chaff.Hun.) RM16 169 FX78
Harrow HA2 116 CA57
Northolt UB5 136 CC65
St. Albans AL1 43 CF18
Southall UB1 136 BY73
Uxbridge UB8 134 BK65
Lancaster St, SE1 20 F4
Lancaster Ter, W2 7 N9
Lancaster Wk, W2 17 N3
Hayes UB3 135 BQ72
Lancaster Way, Abb.L. WD5 59 BT31
Worcester Park KT4 199 CV101
Lancaster W, W11 off Grenfell Rd 139 CX73
Lancastrian Rd, Wall. SM6 219 DL108
Lancefield St, W10 6 E2
Lancell St, N16 off Stoke Newington Ch St 122 DS61
Lancelot Av, Wem. HA0 117 CK63
Lancelot Cl, Slou. SL1 151 AN75
Lancelot Cres, Wem. HA0 117 CK63
Lancelot Gdns, Barn. EN4 98 DG45
Lancelot Pl, SW7 18 C4
Lancelot Rd, Ilf. IG6 103 ES51
Welling DA16 166 EU84
Wembley HA0 117 CK64
Lance Rd, Har. HA1 116 CC59
Lancer Sq, W8 17 J3
Lancey Cl, SE7 off Cleveley Cl 164 EK77
Lanchester Rd, N6 120 DF57
Lanchester Way, SE14 162 DW81
Lancing Gdns, N9 100 DT46
Lancing Rd, W13 off Drayton Grn Rd 137 CH73
Croydon CR0 201 DM100
Feltham TW13 175 BT89
Ilford IG2 125 ER58
Orpington BR6 206 EU103
Romford RM3 106 FL52
Lancing St, NW1 9 L2
Lancing Way, Rick. (Crox.Grn) WD3 75 BP43
Lancresse Cl, Uxb. UB8 134 BK65
Lancresse Ct, N1 5 L7
Landale Gdns, Dart. DA1 188 FJ87
Landau Way, Brox. EN10 67 DZ26
Erith DA8 168 FK78
Landcroft Rd, SE22 182 DT86
Landells Rd, SE22 182 DT86
Landen Pk, Horl. RH6 268 DE146
Lander Rd, Grays RM17 170 GD78
Landford Cl, Rick. WD3 92 BL47
Landford Rd, SW15 159 CW83
Landgrove Rd, SW19 180 DA92
Landmann Way, SE14 163 DX79
Landmark Hts, E5 123 DY63
Landmead Rd, Wal.Cr. (Chsht) EN8 67 DY29
Landon Pl, SW1 18 C5
Landons Cl, E14 24 D1
Landon Wk, E14 14 B9
Landon Way, Ashf. TW15 off Courtfield Rd 175 BP93
Landor Rd, SW9 161 DL83
Landor Wk, W12 159 CU75
Landport Way, SE15 off Daniel Gdns 162 DT80
Landra Gdns, N21 81 DP44
Landridge Dr, Enf. EN1 82 DV38
Landridge Rd, SW6 159 CZ82
Landrock Rd, N8 121 DL58
Landscape Rd, Warl. CR6 236 DV119
Woodford Green IG8 102 EH52
Landseer Av, E12 125 EN64
Gravesend (Nthflt) DA11 190 GD90
Landseer Cl, SW19 off Brangwyn Cres 200 DC95
Edgware HA8 96 CN54
Hornchurch RM11 127 FH60
Landseer Rd, N19 121 DL62
Enfield EN1 82 DU43
New Malden KT3 198 CR101
Sutton SM1 218 DA107
Lands End, Borwd. (Elstree) WD6 77 CK44
Landstead Rd, SE18 165 ER80
Landway, The, Orp. BR5 206 EW97
Lane, The, NW8 off Marlborough Pl 140 DC68
SE3 164 EG83
Chertsey KT16 194 BG97
Virginia Water GU25 192 AY97
Lane App, NW7 97 CY50
Lane Av, Green. DA9 189 FW86
Lane Cl, NW2 119 CV62
Addlestone KT15 212 BG106
LANE END, Dart. DA2 189 FR92
Lane End, Berk. HP4 38 AT19
Bexleyheath DA7 167 FB83
Epsom KT18 216 CP114
Harlow CM17 52 EY15
Hatfield AL10 45 CT21
Lanefield Wk, Welw.G.C. AL8 29 CW09
Lane Gdns, Bushey (Bushey Hth) WD23 95 CE45
Esher (Clay.) KT10 215 CF108
Lane Ms, E12 off Colchester Av 125 EM62
Lanercost Cl, SW2 181 DN89
Lanercost Gdns, N14 99 DL45
Lanercost Rd, SW2 181 DN89
Lanes Av, Grav. (Nthflt) DA11 191 GG90
Lanesborough Pl, SW1 18 F3
Sch Lanesborough Prep Sch, Guil. GU1 off Maori Rd 243 AZ134
Laneside, Chis. BR7 185 EP92
Edgware HA8 96 CQ50
Laneside Av, Dag. RM8 126 EZ59
Laneway, SW15 179 CV85
Lane Wd Cl, Amer. HP7 72 AT39
Lanfranc Rd, E3 143 DY68
Lanfrey Pl, W14 16 E10
Langaller La, Lthd. KT22 230 CB122
Langbourne Av, N6 120 DG61
Langbourne Pl, E14 24 A9
Sch Langbourne Prim Sch, SE21 off Lyall Av 182 DS90
Langbourne Way, Esher (Clay.) KT10 215 CG107
Langbrook Rd, SE3 164 EK83
Lang Cl, Lthd. (Fetch.) KT22 230 CB123
Langcroft Cl, Cars. SM5 200 DF104
Langdale Av, Mitch. CR4 200 DF97
Langdale Cl, SE17 162 DQ79
SW14 158 CP84
Dagenham RM8 126 EW60
Orpington BR6 off Grasmere Rd 205 EP104
Woking GU21 226 AW116
Langdale Ct, Hem.H. HP2 off Wharfedale 40 BL17
Langdale Cres, Bexh. DA7 166 FA80
Langdale Dr, Hayes UB4 135 BS68
Langdale Gdns, Grnf. UB6 137 CH69
Hornchurch RM12 127 FG64
Waltham Cross EN8 83 DX35
Langdale Rd, SE10 163 EC80
Thornton Heath CR7 201 DN98
Langdale St, E1 12 C8
Langdale Wk, Grav. (Nthflt) DA11 off Landseer Av 190 GE90
Sch Langdon Comp Sch, E6 off Sussex Rd 145 EP67
Langdon Ct, NW10 138 CS67
Langdon Cres, E6 145 EN68
Langdon Dr, NW9 118 CQ60
Langdon Pk, Tedd. TW11 177 CJ94
Langdon Pk Rd, N6 121 DJ59
Sch Langdon Pk Sec Sch, E14 14 B7
Langdon Pl, SW14 off Rosemary La 158 CQ83
Langdon Rd, E6 145 EN67
Bromley BR2 204 EH97
Morden SM4 200 DC99
Langdons Ct, Sthl. UB2 156 CA76
Langdon Shaw, Sid. DA14 185 ET92
Langdon Wk, Mord. SM4 200 DC99
Langdon Way, SE1 22 B8
Langfield Cl, Wal.Abb. EN9 50 EE22
Langford Cl, E8 122 DU64
N15 122 DS58
NW8 off Langford Pl 140 DC68
W3 158 CP75
Langford Ct, NW8 140 DC68
Langford Cres, Barn. EN4 80 DF42
Langford Grn, SE5 162 DS83
Brentwood (Hutt.) CM13 109 GC44
Langford Pl, NW8 140 DC68
Sidcup DA14 186 EU90
Sch Langford Prim Sch, SW6 off Gilstead Rd 160 DB82
Langford Rd, SW6 160 DB82
Barnet EN4 80 DE42
Woodford Green IG8 102 EJ51
Langfords, Buck.H. IG9 102 EK47
Langfords Way, Croy. CR0 221 DY111
Langham Cl, N15 off Langham Rd 121 DP55
St. Albans AL4 43 CK15
Langham Ct, Horn. RM11 128 FK59
Langham Dene, Ken. CR8 235 DP115
Langham Dr, Rom. RM6 126 EV58
Langham Gdns, N21 81 DN43
W13 137 CH73
Edgware HA8 96 CQ52
Richmond TW10 177 CJ91
Wembley HA0 117 CJ61
Langham Ho Cl, Rich. TW10 177 CK91
Langham Pk Pl, Brom. BR2 204 EF98
Langham Pl, N15 121 DP55
W1 9 H6
W4 off Hogarth Roundabout 158 CS79
Egham TW20 173 AZ92
Langham Rd, N15 121 DP55
SW20 199 CW95
Edgware HA8 96 CQ51
Teddington TW11 177 CH92
Langham St, W1 9 H6
Langhedge Cl, N18 off Langhedge La 100 DT51
Langhedge La, N18 100 DT50
Langhedge La Ind Est, N18 100 DT51
Langholm Cl, SW12 off King's Av 181 DK87
Langholme, Bushey WD23 94 CC46
Langhorn Dr, Twick. TW2 177 CE87
Langhorne Rd, Dag. RM10 146 FA66
Langland Ct, Nthwd. HA6 93 BQ52
Langland Cres, Stan. HA7 118 CL55
Langland Dr, Pnr. HA5 94 BY52
Langland Gdns, NW3 120 DB64
Croydon CR0 203 DZ103
Langlands Dr, Dart. (Lane End) DA2 189 FS92
Langlands Ri, Epsom KT19 off Burnet Gro 216 CQ113
Langler Rd, NW10 139 CW68
LANGLEY, Slou. SL3 153 BA76
⇌ Langley 153 BA75
Langley Av, Hem.H. HP3 40 BL23
Ruislip HA4 115 BV60
Surbiton KT6 197 CK102
Worcester Park KT4 199 CX103
Langley Broom, Slou. SL3 153 AZ78
LANGLEYBURY, Kings L. WD4 59 BP34
Langleybury La, Kings L. WD4 75 BP37
Langley Business Cen, Slou. (Langley) SL3 153 BA75
Langley Cl, Epsom KT18 232 CR119
Guildford GU1 242 AW133
Romford RM3 106 FK52
Langley Cor, Slou. (Fulmer) SL3 133 AZ65
Langley Ct, WC2 9 N9
Beckenham BR3 203 EB99
Langley Cres, E11 124 EJ59
Dagenham RM9 146 EW66
Edgware HA8 96 CQ48
Hayes UB3 155 BT80
Kings Langley WD4 58 BN30
St. Albans AL3 42 CC18
Langley Dr, E11 124 EH59
W3 138 CP74
Brentwood CM14 108 FU48
Langley Gdns, Brom. BR2 204 EJ98
Dagenham RM9 146 EW66
Orpington BR5 205 EP100
Sch Langley Gram Sch, Slou. SL3 off Reddington Dr 153 AZ77
Langley Gro, N.Mal. KT3 198 CS96
Langley Hill, Kings L. WD4 58 BM29
Langley Hill Cl, Kings L. WD4 58 BN29
Langley La, SW8 161 DM79
Abbots Langley WD5 59 BT31
Epsom (Headley) KT18 248 CP125
Langley Lo La, Kings L. WD4 58 BN31
Sch Langley Manor Sch, The, Slou. SL3 off St. Mary's Rd 132 AY74
Langley Meadow, Loug. IG10 85 ER40
Langley Oaks Av, S.Croy. CR2 220 DU110
Langley Pk, NW7 96 CS51
★ Langley Park Country Pk, Slou. SL3 133 BA70
Langley Pk Rd, Iver SL0 133 BC72
Slough SL3 153 BA75
Sutton SM1, SM2 218 DC106
Sch Langley Pk Sch for Boys, Beck. BR3 off South Eden Pk Rd 203 EB100
Sch Langley Pk Sch for Girls, Beck. BR3 off South Eden Pk Rd 203 EC100
Langley Quay, Slou. (Langley) SL3 153 BA75
Langley Rd, SW19 199 CZ95
Abbots Langley WD5 59 BS31
Beckenham BR3 203 DY98
Isleworth TW7 157 CF82
Kings Langley (Chipper.) WD4 58 BH30
Slough SL3 152 AW75
South Croydon CR2 221 DX109
Staines TW18 173 BF93
Surbiton KT6 198 CL101
Watford WD17 75 BU39
Welling DA16 166 EW79
Langley Row, Barn. EN5 79 CZ39
Langley St, WC2 9 N8
LANGLEY VALE, Epsom KT18 232 CR120
Langley Vale Rd, Epsom KT18 232 CR118
Langley Wk, Wok. GU22 off Midhope Rd 226 AY119
Langley Way, Wat. WD17 75 BS40
West Wickham BR4 203 ED102
Sch Langleywood Sch, Slou. SL3 off Langley Rd 152 AY76
Langmans La, Wok. GU21 226 AV118
Langmans Way, Wok. GU21 226 AS116
Langmead Dr, Bushey (Bushey Hth) WD23 95 CD46
Langmead St, SE27 off Beadman St 181 DP91
Langmore Ct, Bexh. DA6 off Regency Way 166 EX83
Langport Ct, Walt. KT12 196 BW102
Langridge Ms, Hmptn. TW12 off Oak Av 176 BZ93
Langroyd Rd, SW17 180 DF89
Langshott, Horl. RH6 269 DH146
Langshott Cl, Add. (Wdhm) KT15 211 BE111
Langshott La, Horl. RH6 269 DJ147
Sch Langshott Sch, Horl. RH6 off Smallfield Rd 269 DJ148
Langside Av, SW15 159 CU84
Langside Cres, N14 99 DK48
Langstone Ley, Welw.G.C. AL7 off Black Fan Rd 30 DB10
Langston Hughes Cl, SE24 off Shakespeare Rd 161 DP84
Langston Rd, Loug. IG10 85 EQ43
Lang St, E1 12 E3
Langthorn Ct, EC2 11 J7
Langthorne Cres, Grays RM17 170 GC77
Langthorne Rd, E11 123 ED62
Langthorne St, SW6 159 CX80
Langton Av, E6 145 EN69
N20 98 DC45
Epsom KT17 217 CT111
Langton Cl, WC1 10 B2
Addlestone KT15 194 BH104
Slough SL1 131 AK74
Woking GU21 226 AT117
Langton Gro, Nthwd. HA6 93 BQ50
Langton Ho, SW16 off Colson Way 181 DJ91
Langton Pl, SW18 off Merton Rd 180 DA88
Langton Ri, SE23 182 DV87
Langton Rd, NW2 119 CW62

★ Place of interest | H Hospital | Sch School | Coll College | Uni University | ⇌ Railway station

Langton Rd, SW9 . . . . .161 DP80
Harrow HA3 . . . . .94 CC52
Hoddesdon EN11 . . . . .49 DZ17
West Molesey KT8 . . . . . .196 CC98
Langtons Inf Sch, Horn.
RM11 off Westland Av . .128 FL60
Langtons Jun Sch, Horn.
RM11 off Westland Av . .128 FL60
Langton's Meadow, Slou.
(Farn.Com.) SL2 . . . . . . .131 AQ65
Langton St, SW10 . . . . .160 DC79
Langton Way, SE3 . . . . .164 EF81
Croydon CR0 . . . . .220 DS105
Egham TW20 . . . . .173 BC93
Grays RM16 . . . . .171 GJ77
Langtry Pl, SW6
off Seagrave Rd 160 DA79
Langtry Rd, NW8 . . . . .140 DB67
Northolt UB5 . . . . .136 BX68
Langtry Wk, NW8
off Alexandra Pl 140 DC66
Langwood Chase, Tedd.
TW11 . . . . .177 CJ93
Langwood Cl, Ashtd. KT21 .232 CN117
Langwood Gdns, Wat. WD17 .75 BU39
Langworth Cl, Dart. DA2 . . .188 FK90
Langworth Dr, Hayes UB4 . .135 BU72
Lanhill Rd, W9 . . . . .6 G3
Lanier Rd, SE13 . . . . .183 EC86
Lanigan Dr, Houns. TW3 . . .176 CB85
Lankaster Gdns, N2 . . . . . . .98 DD53
Lankers Dr, Har. HA2 . . . . . .116 BZ58
Lankton Cl, Beck. BR3 . . . . .203 EC95
Lannock Rd, Hayes UB3 . . .135 BS74
Lannoy Rd, SE9 . . . . .185 EQ88
Lanrick Copse, Berk. HP4 . . .38 AY18
Lanrick Rd, E14 . . . . .14 F7
Lanridge Rd, SE2 . . . . .166 EX76
Lansbury Av, N18 . . . . .100 DR50
Barking IG11 . . . . .146 EU66
Feltham TW14 . . . . .175 BV86
Romford RM6 . . . . .126 EY57
Lansbury Cl, NW10 . . . . . . .118 CQ64
Lansbury Cres, Dart. DA1 . . .188 FN85
Lansbury Dr, Hayes UB4 . . .135 BT71
Lansbury Est, E14 . . . . .14 A7
Lansbury Gdns, E14 . . . . . . .14 E7
Tilbury RM18 . . . . .171 GG81
Lansbury Rd, Enf. EN3 . . . . .83 DX39
Lansbury Way, N18 . . . . . . .100 DS50
Lanscombe Wk, SW8 . . . . . .161 DL81
Lansdell Rd, Mitch. CR4 . . . .200 DG96
Lansdown, Guil. GU1 . . . . .243 BA134
Lansdown Cl, Walt. KT12
off St. Johns Dr 196 BW102
Woking GU21 . . . . .226 AT119
Lansdowne Av, Bexh. DA7 . .166 EX80
Orpington BR6 . . . . .205 EP102
Slough SL1 . . . . .132 AS74
Lansdowne Cl, SW20 . . . . . .179 CX94
Surbiton KT5
off Kingston Rd 198 CP103
Twickenham TW1
off Lion Rd 177 CF88
Watford WD25 . . . . .60 BX34
Lansdowne Coll, W2 . . . . . . .7 J10
Lansdowne Copse, Wor.Pk.
KT4 off The Avenue 199 CU103
Lansdowne Ct, Pur. CR8 . . .219 DP110
Slough SL1 . . . . .132 AS74
Worcester Park KT4
off The Avenue 199 CU103
Lansdowne Cres, W11 . . . . . .6 D10
Lansdowne Dr, E8 . . . . .142 DU65
Lansdowne Gdns, SW8 . . . . .161 DL81
Lansdowne Grn, SW8
off Hartington Rd 161 DL81
Lansdowne Gro, NW10 . . . .118 CS63
Lansdowne Hill, SE27 . . . . .181 DP90
Lansdowne La, SE7 . . . . . . .164 EK79
Lansdowne Ms, SE7 . . . . . . .164 EK78
W11 . . . . .16 E1
Lansdowne Pl, SE1 . . . . .21 K6
SE19 . . . . .182 DT94
Lansdowne Prim Sch, Til.
RM18 off Alexandra Rd .171 GF82
Lansdowne Ri, W11 . . . . .6 D10
Lansdowne Rd, E4 . . . . .101 EA47
E11 . . . . .124 EF61
E17 . . . . .123 EA57
E18 . . . . .124 EG55
N3 . . . . .97 CZ52
N10 . . . . .99 DJ54
N17 . . . . .100 DT53
SW20 . . . . .179 CW94
W11 . . . . .6 D9
Bromley BR1 . . . . .184 EG94
Chesham HP5 . . . . .54 AQ29
Croydon CR0 . . . . .202 DR103
Epsom KT19 . . . . .216 CQ108
Harrow HA1 . . . . .117 CE59
Hounslow TW3 . . . . .156 CB83
Ilford IG3 . . . . .125 ET60
Purley CR8 . . . . .219 DN112
Sevenoaks TN13 . . . . .257 FK122
Staines TW18 . . . . .174 BH94
Stanmore HA7 . . . . .95 CJ51
Tilbury RM18 . . . . .171 GF82
Uxbridge UB8 . . . . .135 BP72
Lansdowne Row, W1 . . . . . . .19 H1
Lansdowne Sch, SW9
off Argyll Cl 161 DM83
Lansdowne Sq, Grav.
(Nthflt) DA11 . . . . .191 GF86
Lansdowne Ter, WC1 . . . . . . .9 P4
Lansdowne Wk, W11 . . . . . . .16 D1
Lansdowne Way, SW8 . . . . .161 DK81
Lansdowne Wd Cl, SE27 . . .181 DP90
Lansdown Pl, Grav. (Nthflt)
DA11 . . . . .191 GF88
Lansdown Rd, E7 . . . . .144 EJ66
Gerrards Cross (Chal.St.P.)
SL9 . . . . .90 AX53
Sidcup DA14 . . . . .186 EV90
Lansfield Av, N18 . . . . .100 DU49
Lantern Cl, SW15 . . . . .159 CU84
Wembley HA0 . . . . .117 CK64
Lanterns Ct, E14 . . . . .23 P4
Lantern Way, West Dr. UB7 .154 BL75
Lanthorn Cl, Brox. EN10 . . . .49 DY19
Lant St, SE1 . . . . .20 G3
Lanvanor Rd, SE15 . . . . . . .162 DW82
Lapford Cl, W9 . . . . .6 F3
La Plata Gro, Brwd. CM14 . .108 FV48
Lapponum Wk, Hayes UB4
off Lochan Cl 136 BX71
Lapse Wd Wk, SE23 . . . . . .182 DV88
Lapstone Gdns, Har. HA3 . . .117 CJ58
Lapwing Cl, Erith DA8 . . . . .167 FH80
Hemel Hempstead HP2 . . .40 BL16
South Croydon CR2 . . . . . .221 DY110
Lapwing Ct, Surb. KT6
off Chaffinch Cl 198 CN104
Lapwing Gro, Guil. GU4 . . .243 BD132
Lapwings, The, Grav. DA12 .191 GK89
Lapwing Twr, SE8
off Abinger Gro 163 DZ79
Lapwing Way, Abb.L. WD5 . . .59 BU31
Hayes UB4 . . . . .136 BX72
Lapworth Cl, Orp. BR6 . . . . .206 EW103
Lara Cl, SE13 . . . . .183 EC86
Chessington KT9 . . . . .216 CL108
Larbert Rd, SW16 . . . . .201 DJ95
Larby Pl, Epsom KT17 . . . . .216 CS110
Larch Av, W3 . . . . .138 CS74
Guildford GU1 . . . . .242 AW132
St. Albans (Brick.Wd) AL2 .60 BY30
Larch Cl, E13 . . . . .144 EH70
N11 . . . . .98 DG52
N19 off Bredgar Rd 121 DJ61
SE8 off Clyde St 163 DZ79
SW12 . . . . .181 DH89
High Wycombe (Penn)
HP10 . . . . .88 AC45
Redhill RH1 . . . . .266 DC136
Slough SL2 . . . . .131 AP71
Tadworth KT20 . . . . .234 DC121
Waltham Cross EN7
off The Firs 66 DS27
Warlingham CR6 . . . . .237 DY119
Larch Cres, Epsom KT19 . . .216 CP107
Hayes UB4 . . . . .136 BW70
Larchdene, Orp. BR6 . . . . . .205 EN103
Larch Dr, W4
off Gunnersbury Av 158 CN78
Larches, The, N13 . . . . .100 DQ48
Amersham HP6 . . . . .72 AV38
Bushey WD23 . . . . .76 BY43
Northwood HA6
off Rickmansworth Rd . . .93 BQ51
St. Albans AL4 . . . . .43 CK16
Uxbridge UB10 . . . . .135 BP69
Woking GU21 . . . . .226 AY116
Larches Av, SW14 . . . . .158 CR84
Enfield EN1 . . . . .82 DW35
Larch Grn, NW9
off Clayton Fld 96 CS53
Larch Gro, Sid. DA15 . . . . . .185 ET88
Larchlands, The, H.Wyc.
(Penn) HP10 . . . . .88 AD46
Larch Ri, Berk. HP4 . . . . .38 AU18
Larch Rd, E10 off Walnut Rd .123 EA61
NW2 . . . . .119 CW63
Dartford DA1 . . . . .188 FK87
Larch Tree Way, Croy. CR0 . .203 EA104
Larch Wk, Swan. BR8 . . . . . .207 FD96
Larch Way, Brom. BR2 . . . . .205 EN101
Larchwood Av, Rom. RM5 . . .105 FB51
Larchwood Cl, Bans. SM7 . .233 CY116
Romford RM5 . . . . .105 FC51
Larchwood Dr, Egh.
(Eng.Grn) TW20 . . . . . . .172 AV93
Larchwood Gdns, Brwd.
(Pilg.Hat.) CM15 . . . . . . .108 FU44
Larchwood Prim Sch,
Brwd. CM15
off Larchwood Gdns 108 FU44
Larchwood Rd, SE9 . . . . . . .185 EP89
Hemel Hempstead HP2 . . .40 BM18
Larcombe Cl, Croy. CR0 . . .220 DT105
Larcom St, SE17 . . . . .21 H8
Larden Rd, W3 . . . . .138 CS74
La Retraite RC Girls Sch,
SW12 off Atkins Rd 181 DJ87
Largewood Av, Surb. KT6 . .198 CN103
Largo Wk, Erith DA8
off Selkirk Dr 167 FE81
Larissa St, SE17 . . . . .21 K9
Lark Av, Stai. TW18
off Kestrel Av 173 BF90
Larkbere Rd, SE26 . . . . . . .183 DY91
Lark Cl, Brwd. (Warley)
CM14 . . . . .108 FV49
Larken Cl, Bushey WD23
off Larken Dr 94 CC46
Larken Dr, Bushey WD23 . . .94 CC46
Larkfield, Cob. KT11 . . . . . .213 BU113
Larkfield Av, Har. HA3 . . . . .117 CH55
Larkfield Cl, Brom. BR2 . . . .204 EF103
Larkfield Ct, Horl. (Smallfield)
RH6 off Cooper Cl 269 DN148
Larkfield Rd, Rich. TW9 . . . .158 CL84
Sevenoaks TN13 . . . . .256 FC123
Sidcup DA14 . . . . .185 ET90
Larkfields, Grav. (Nthflt)
DA11 . . . . .190 GE90
Larkhall Cl, Walt. KT12 . . . .214 BW107
Lark Hall Inf & Jun Sch,
SW4 off Smedley St 161 DK82
Larkhall La, SW4 . . . . .161 DK82
Larkhall Ri, SW4 . . . . .161 DJ83
Larkham Cl, Felt. TW13 . . . .175 BS90
Larkhill Ter, SE18 . . . . .165 EN81
Larkin Cl, Brwd. (Hutt.)
CM13 . . . . .109 GC45
Coulsdon CR5 . . . . .235 DM117
Larkings La, Slou. (Stoke P.)
SL2 . . . . .132 AV67
Larkins Rd, Gat. RH6 . . . . .268 DD152
Lark Ri, Hat. AL10 . . . . .45 CU20
Leatherhead (E.Hors.)
KT24 . . . . .245 BS131
Lark Row, E2 . . . . .142 DW67
Larksfield, Egh. (Eng.Grn)
TW20 . . . . .172 AW94
Horley RH6 . . . . .269 DH147
Larksfield Gro, Enf. EN1 . . . .82 DV39
Larks Gro, Bark. IG11
off Thornhill Gdns 145 ES66
Larkshall Ct, Rom. RM7 . . . .105 FC54
Larkshall Cres, E4 . . . . .101 EC49
Larkshall Rd, E4 . . . . .101 EC50
Larkspur Cl, E6 . . . . .144 EL71
N17 off Fryatt Rd 100 DR52
NW9 . . . . .118 CP57
Hemel Hempstead HP1 . . .39 BE19
Orpington BR6 . . . . .206 EW103
Ruislip HA4 . . . . .115 BQ59
South Ockendon RM15 . .149 FW69
Larkspur Gro, Edg. HA8 . . . . .96 CQ49
Larkspur Way, Dor. (N.Holm.)
RH5 . . . . .263 CK139
Epsom KT19 . . . . .216 CQ106
Larks Ri, Chesh. HP5 . . . . . .54 AR33
Larkswood, Harl. CM17 . . . .52 EW17
Larkswood Cl, Erith DA8 . . .167 FG81
Larkswood Ct, E4 . . . . .101 ED50
Larkswood Inf Sch, E4
off New Rd 101 EB49
Larkswood Jun Sch, E4
off New Rd 101 EB49
Larkswood Leisure Pk, E4 . .101 EC49
Larkswood Ri, Pnr. HA5 . . . .116 BW56
St. Albans AL4 . . . . .43 CJ15
Larkswood Rd, E4 . . . . .101 EA49
Lark Way, Cars. SM5 . . . . . .200 DE101
Larkway Cl, NW9 . . . . .118 CR56
Larmans Rd, Enf. EN3 . . . . .82 DW36
Larmenier RC Inf Sch,
W6 . . . . .16 B8
Larnach Rd, W6 . . . . .159 CX79
Larne Rd, Ruis. HA4 . . . . . . .115 BT59
Larner Rd, Erith DA8 . . . . . .167 FE80
La Roche Cl, Slou. SL3 . . . . .152 AW76
Larpent Av, SW15 . . . . .179 CW85
Larsen Dr, Wal.Abb. EN9 . . . .67 ED34
Larwood Cl, Grnf. UB6 . . . . .117 CD64
La Sainte Union Conv
RC Sch, NW5
off Highgate Rd 120 DG62
La Salette RC Prim Sch,
Rain. RM13
off Dunedin Rd 147 FF69
Lascelles Av, Har. HA1 . . . . .117 CD59
Lascelles Cl, E11 . . . . .123 ED61
Brentwood (Pilg.Hat.)
CM15 . . . . .108 FU43
Lascelles Rd, Slou. SL3 . . . .152 AV76
Lascotts Rd, N22 . . . . .99 DM51
Las Palmas Est, Shep. TW17 .195 BQ101
Lassa Rd, SE9 . . . . .184 EL85
Lassell St, SE10 . . . . .24 F10
Lasseter Pl, SE3
off Vanbrugh Hill 164 EF79
Lasswade Rd, Cher. KT16 . . .193 BF101
Latchett Rd, E18 . . . . .102 EH53
Latchford Pl, Chig. IG7
off Manford Way 104 EV49
Latching Cl, Rom. RM3
off Troopers Dr 106 FK49
Latchingdon Ct, E17 . . . . . .123 DX56
Latchingdon Gdns, Wdf.Grn.
IG8 . . . . .102 EL51
Latchmere Cl, Rich. TW10 . . .178 CL92
Latchmere Inf Sch, Kings.T.
KT2 off Latchmere Rd . .178 CM93
Latchmere Jun Sch,
Kings.T. KT2
off Latchmere Rd 178 CM93
Latchmere La, Kings.T. KT2 .178 CM93
Latchmere Pas, SW11
off Cabul Rd 160 DE82
Latchmere Rd, SW11 . . . . . .160 DF82
Kingston upon Thames
KT2 . . . . .178 CL94
Latchmere St, SW11 . . . . . .160 DF82
Latchmoor Av, Ger.Cr.
(Chal.St.P.) SL9 . . . . .112 AX56
Latchmoor Gro, Ger.Cr.
(Chal.St.P.) SL9 . . . . .112 AX56
Latchmoor Way, Ger.Cr.
(Chal.St.P.) SL9 . . . . .112 AX56
Lateward Rd, Brent. TW8 . . .157 CK79
Latham Cl, E6
off Oliver Gdns 144 EL72
Dartford DA2 . . . . .189 FS89
Twickenham TW1 . . . . . . .177 CG87
Westerham (Bigg.H.)
TN16 . . . . .238 EJ116
Latham Ho, E1 . . . . .13 H7
Latham Rd, Bexh. DA6 . . . . .186 FA85
Twickenham TW1 . . . . . . .177 CF87
Lathams Way, Croy. CR0 . . .201 DM102
Lathkill Cl, Enf. EN1 . . . . . . .100 DU45
Lathom Jun Sch, E6
off Lathom Rd 144 EL66
Lathom Rd, E6 . . . . .145 EM66
LATIMER, Chesh. HP5 . . . . . .72 AY36
Latimer, SE17 . . . . .21 L10
Latimer Av, E6 . . . . .145 EM67
Latimer Cl, Amer. HP6 . . . . .72 AW39
Hemel Hempstead HP2 . . .40 BN15
Pinner HA5 . . . . .94 BW53
Watford WD18 . . . . .93 BS45
Woking GU22 . . . . .227 BB116
Worcester Park KT4 . . . . .217 CV105
Latimer Ct, Red. RH1
off Earlswood Rd 266 DF136
Latimer Dr, Horn. RM12 . . . .128 FK62
Latimer Gdns, Pnr. HA5 . . . . .94 BW53
Welwyn Garden City AL7 . .30 DB09
Latimer Ho Day Hosp,
W1 . . . . .9 J5
Latimer Pl, W10 . . . . .139 CW72
Latimer Road 6 A9
Latimer Rd, E7 . . . . .124 EH63
N15 . . . . .122 DS58
SW19 . . . . .180 DB93
W10 . . . . .139 CW72
Barnet EN5 . . . . .80 DB41
Chesham HP5 . . . . .72 AU36
Croydon CR0
off Abbey Rd 201 DP104
Rickmansworth (Chenies)
WD3 . . . . .73 BB38
Teddington TW11 . . . . . . .177 CF92
Latimer Way, Beac.
(Knot.Grn) HP9 . . . . .88 AJ49
Latium Cl, St.Alb. AL1 . . . . . .43 CD21
Latona Dr, Grav. DA12 . . . . .191 GM92
Latona Rd, SE15 . . . . .162 DU79
La Tourne Gdns, Orp. BR6 . .205 EQ104
Lattimer Pl, W4 . . . . .158 CS79
Latton Grn, Harl. CM18 . . . . .51 ET19
Lattimore Rd, St.Alb. AL1 . . .43 CE21
LATTON BUSH, Harl. CM18 . .52 EU19
Latton Cl, Esher KT10 . . . . .214 CB105
Walton-on-Thames KT12 .196 BY101
Latton Common, Harl.
CM17 . . . . .52 EV18
Latton Common Rd, Harl.
CM18 . . . . .52 EU18
Latton Grn, Harl. CM18 . . . . .51 ET19
Latton Grn Co Prim Sch,
Harl. CM18
off Riddings La 51 ET19
Latton Hall Cl, Harl. CM20 . . .36 EU14
Latton Ho, Harl. CM18
off Latton Common Rd . .52 EU18
Latton St, Harl. CM20 . . . . . .36 EU14
Latymer All Saints C of E
Prim Sch, N9
off Hydethorpe Av 100 DT47
Latymer Cl, Wey. KT13 . . . . .213 BQ105
Latymer Ct, W6 . . . . .16 B8
Latymer Rd, N9 . . . . .100 DT46
Latymer Sch, N9
off Haselbury Rd 100 DS47
Latymer Upr Sch, W6
off King St 159 CU77
Latymer Way, N9 . . . . .100 DR47
Lauder Cl, Nthlt. UB5 . . . . .136 BX68
Lauderdale Dr, Rich. TW10 . .177 CK90
Lauderdale Pl, EC2
off Beech St 142 DQ71
Lauderdale Rd, W9 . . . . .7 J2
Kings Langley WD4 . . . . . .59 BQ33
Lauderdale Twr, EC2 . . . . . . .10 G5
Laud St, SE11 . . . . .20 A9
Croydon CR0 . . . . .202 DQ104
Laughton Ct, Borwd. WD6
off Banks Rd 78 CR40
Laughton Rd, Nthlt. UB5 . . .136 BX67
Launcelot Prim Sch, Brom.
BR1 off Launcelot Rd . . .184 EG91
Launcelot Rd, Brom. BR1 . .184 EG91
Launcelot St, SE1 . . . . .20 C4
Launceston Cl, Rom. RM3 . .106 FJ53
Launceston Gdns, Grnf.
UB6 . . . . .137 CJ67
Launceston Pl, W8 . . . . .17 L5
Launceston Rd, Grnf. UB6 . .137 CJ67
Launch St, E14 . . . . .24 C5
Launders La, Rain. RM13 . . .148 FM69
Laundress La, N16 . . . . .122 DU62
Laundry La, N1 . . . . .4 G6
Waltham Abbey EN9 . . . . .68 EE25
Laundry Ms, SE23 . . . . .183 DY87
Laundry Rd, W6 . . . . .159 CY79
Guildford GU1 . . . . .258 AW135
Launton Dr, Bexh. DA6 . . . .166 EX84
Laura Cl, E11 . . . . .124 EJ57
Enfield EN1 . . . . .82 DS43
Lauradale Rd, N2 . . . . .120 DF56
Laura Dr, Swan. BR8 . . . . . .187 FG94
Laurance Haines Prim
Sch, Wat. WD18
off Vicarage Rd 75 BU44
Laura Pl, E5 . . . . .122 DW63
Laureate Way, Hem.H. HP1 . .40 BG18
Laurel Av, Egh. (Eng.Grn)
TW20 . . . . .172 AV92
Gravesend DA12 . . . . . . .191 GJ89
Potters Bar EN6 . . . . .63 CZ32
Slough SL3 . . . . .152 AY75
Twickenham TW1 . . . . . . .177 CF88
Laurel Bk, Hem.H. (Felden)
HP3 . . . . .39 BF23
Laurel Bk Gdns, SW6
off New Kings Rd 159 CZ82
Laurel Bk Rd, Enf. EN2 . . . . .82 DQ39
Laurel Bk Vil, W7
off Lower Boston Rd . . .137 CE74
Laurel Cl, N19
off Hargrave Pk 121 DJ61
SW17 . . . . .180 DE92
Brentwood (Hutt.) CM13 .109 GB43
Dartford DA1
off Willow Rd 188 FJ88
Hemel Hempstead HP2 . . .40 BM19
Ilford IG6 . . . . .103 EQ51
Sidcup DA14 . . . . .186 EU90
Slough (Colnbr.) SL3 . . . .153 BE80
Watford WD19 . . . . .94 BX45
Woking GU21 . . . . .211 BD113
Laurel Ct, Amer. HP6 . . . . . .55 AQ36
Potters Bar (Cuffley)
EN6 off Station Rd 65 DM29
Laurel Cres, Croy. CR0 . . . .203 EA104
Romford RM7 . . . . .127 FE60
Woking GU21 . . . . .211 BC113
Laurel Dr, N21 . . . . .99 DN45
Oxted RH8 . . . . .254 EF131
South Ockendon RM15 . . .149 FX70
Laurel Flds, Pot.B. EN6 . . . . .63 CZ31
Laurel Gdns, E4 . . . . .101 EB45
NW7 . . . . .96 CR48
W7 . . . . .137 CE74
Addlestone (New Haw)
KT15 . . . . .212 BH110
Bromley BR1 . . . . .204 EL98
Hounslow TW4 . . . . .156 BY84
Laurel Gro, SE20 . . . . .182 DV94
SE26 . . . . .183 DX91
Laurel La, Horn. RM12
off Station La 128 FL61
West Drayton UB7 . . . . . .154 BL77
Laurel Lo La, Barn. EN5 . . . . .79 CW36
Laurel Manor, Sutt. SM2
off Devonshire Rd 218 DC108
Laurel Pk, Har. HA3 . . . . .95 CF52
Laurel Rd, SW13 . . . . .159 CU82
SW20 . . . . .199 CV95
Gerrards Cross (Chal.St.P.)
SL9 . . . . .90 AX53
Hampton (Hmptn H.)
TW12 . . . . .177 CD92
St. Albans AL1 . . . . .43 CF20
Laurels, The, Bans. SM7 . . .233 CZ117
Berkhamsted (Pott.End)
HP4 . . . . .39 BB17
Cobham KT11 . . . . .230 BY115
Dartford DA2 . . . . .188 FJ90
Waltham Cross EN7 . . . . . .66 DS27
Weybridge KT13 . . . . .195 BR104
Laurelsfield, St.Alb. AL3 . . . .42 CB23
Laurels Rd, Iver SL0 . . . . . .133 BD68
Laurel St, E8 . . . . .5 P4
Laurel Vw, N12 . . . . .98 DB48
Laurel Way, E18 . . . . .124 EF56
N20 . . . . .98 DA48
Laurence Ms, W12
off Askew Rd 159 CU75
Laurence Pountney Hill, EC4 .11 J9
Laurence Pountney La, EC4 . .11 J9
Laurie Gro, SE14 . . . . .163 DY81
Laurie Rd, W7 . . . . .137 CE71
Laurier Rd, NW5 . . . . .121 DH62
Croydon CR0 . . . . .202 DT101
Lauries Cl, Hem.H. HP1 . . . . .39 BB22
Laurimel Cl, Stan. HA7
off September Way 95 CH51
Laurino Pl, Bushey
(Bushey Hth) WD23 . . . . .94 CC47
Lauriston JMI Sch, E9
off Rutland Rd 143 DX67
Lauriston Rd, E9 . . . . .143 DX67
SW19 . . . . .179 CX93
Lausanne Rd, N8 . . . . .121 DN56
SE15 . . . . .162 DW81
Lauser Rd, Stai. (Stanw.)
TW19 . . . . .174 BJ87
Laustan Cl, Guil. GU1 . . . . .243 BC134
Lavell St, N16 . . . . .122 DR63
Lavender Av, NW9 . . . . .118 CQ60
Brentwood (Pilg.Hat.)
CM15 . . . . .108 FV43
Mitcham CR4 . . . . .200 DE95
Worcester Park KT4 . . . . .199 CW104
Lavender Cl, SW3
off Danvers St 160 DD79
Bromley BR2 . . . . .204 EL100
Carshalton SM5 . . . . .218 DG105
Caterham CR3 . . . . .252 DQ125
Coulsdon CR5 . . . . .235 DJ119
Harlow CM20 . . . . .35 ES14
Hatfield AL9 . . . . .44 CS15
Leatherhead KT22 . . . . . .231 CJ123
Redhill RH1 . . . . .267 DH139
Romford RM3 . . . . .106 FK52
Waltham Cross (Chsht)
EN7 . . . . .66 DT27
Lavender Ct, W.Mol. KT8
off Molesham Way 196 CB97
Lavender Cres, St.Alb. AL3
off Waverley Rd 42 CC19
Lavender Dr, Uxb. UB8 . . . .134 BM71
Lavender Gdns, SW11 . . . . .160 DF84
Enfield EN2 . . . . .81 DP39
Harrow HA3
off Uxbridge Rd 95 CE51
Lavender Gate, Lthd. KT22 .214 CB113
Lavender Gro, E8 . . . . .5 P6
Mitcham CR4 . . . . .200 DE95
Lavender Hill, SW11 . . . . . . .160 DE84
Enfield EN2 . . . . .81 DN39
Swanley BR8 . . . . .207 FD97
Lavender Pk Rd, W.Byf.
KT14 . . . . .212 BG112
Lavender Pl, Ilf. IG1 . . . . . .125 EP64
Lavender Prim Sch, Enf.
EN2 off Lavender Rd 82 DS39
Lavender Ri, West Dr. UB7 . .154 BN75
Lavender Rd, SE16 . . . . .23 J1
SW11 . . . . .160 DD83
Carshalton SM5 . . . . .218 DG105
Croydon CR0 . . . . .201 DM100
Enfield EN2 . . . . .82 DR39
Epsom KT19 . . . . .216 CP106
Sutton SM1 . . . . .218 DD105
Uxbridge UB8 . . . . .134 BM71
Woking GU22 . . . . .227 BB116
Lavender St, E15
off Manbey Gro 144 EE65
Lavender Sweep, SW11 . . . .160 DF84
Lavender Ter, SW11
off Falcon Rd 160 DE83
Lavender Vale, Wall. SM6 . .219 DK107
Lavender Wk, SW11 . . . . . . .160 DF84
Hemel Hempstead HP2 . . .40 BK18
Mitcham CR4 . . . . .200 DG97
Lavender Way, Croy. CR0 . . .203 DX100
Lavengro Rd, SE27 . . . . . . .182 DQ89
Lavenham Rd, SW18 . . . . . .179 CZ89
Lavernock Rd, Bexh. DA7 . . .166 FA82
Laverock Sch, Oxt. RH8
off Bluehouse La 254 EE128
Lavers Rd, N16 . . . . .122 DS62
Laverstoke Gdns, SW15 . . . .179 CU87
Laverton Ms, SW5 . . . . .17 K8
Laverton Pl, SW5 . . . . .17 K8
Lavidge Rd, SE9 . . . . .184 EL89
Lavina Gro, N1 . . . . .4 A9
Lavington Cl, E9
off Beanacre Cl 143 DZ65
Lavington Rd, W13 . . . . . . .137 CH74
Croydon CR0 . . . . .201 DM104
Lavington St, SE1 . . . . .20 F2
Lavinia Av, Wat. WD25 . . . . .60 BX34
Lavinia Rd, Dart. DA1 . . . . .188 FM86
Lavrock La, Rick. WD3 . . . . . .92 BM45
Lawbrook La, Guil. (Peasl.)
GU5 . . . . .261 BQ144
Lawdale Jun Sch, E2 . . . . . .12 B1
Lawdons Gdns, Croy. CR0 . .219 DP105
Lawford Av, Rick. (Chorl.)
WD3 . . . . .73 BC44
Lawford Cl, Horn. RM12 . . . .128 FJ63
Rickmansworth (Chorl.)
WD3 . . . . .73 BC44
Wallington SM6 . . . . .219 DL109
Lawford Gdns, Dart. DA1 . . .188 FJ85
Kenley CR8 . . . . .236 DQ116
Lawford Rd, N1 . . . . .5 L6
NW5 . . . . .141 DJ65
W4 . . . . .158 CQ80
Law Ho, Bark. IG11 . . . . . . .146 EU68
Lawkland, Slou.
(Farn.Royal) SL2 . . . . . . .131 AQ69
Lawless St, E14 . . . . .14 B9
Lawley Rd, N14 . . . . .99 DH45
Lawley St, E5 . . . . .122 DW63
Lawn, The, Harl. CM20 . . . . . .36 EV12
Southall UB2 . . . . .156 CA78
Lawn Av, West Dr. UB7 . . . .154 BJ75
Lawn Cl, N9 . . . . .100 DT45
Bromley BR1 . . . . .184 EH93
New Malden KT3 . . . . . . .198 CS96
Ruislip HA4 . . . . .115 BT62
Slough (Datchet) SL3 . . . .152 AW80
Swanley BR8 . . . . .207 FC96
Lawn Cres, Rich. TW9 . . . . .158 CN82
Lawn Fm Gro, Rom. RM6 . . .126 EY56
Lawnfield, NW2
off Coverdale Rd 139 CX66
Lawn Gdns, W7 . . . . .137 CE74
Lawn Ho Cl, E14 . . . . .24 C3
Lawn La, SW8 . . . . .161 DL79
Hemel Hempstead HP3 . . .40 BK22
Lawn Pk, Sev. TN13 . . . . . .257 FH127
Lawn Prim Sch, Grav.
DA11 off High St 190 GC86
Lawn Rd, NW3 . . . . .120 DF64
Beckenham BR3 . . . . .183 DZ94
Gravesend DA11 . . . . .190 GC86
Guildford GU2 . . . . .258 AW137
Uxbridge UB8
off New Windsor St 134 BJ66
Lawns, The, E4 . . . . .101 EA50
SE3 off Lee Ter 164 EE83
SE19 . . . . .202 DR95
Hemel Hempstead HP1 . . .39 BE19
Pinner HA5 . . . . .94 CB52
Radlett (Shenley) WD7 . . . .62 CL33
St. Albans AL3 . . . . .42 CC19
Sidcup DA14 . . . . .186 EV91
Sutton SM2 . . . . .217 CY108
Welwyn Garden City AL8 . .29 CX06
Lawns Ct, Wem. HA9
off The Avenue 118 CM61
Lawns Cres, Grays RM17 . . .170 GD79
Lawns Dr, The, Brox. EN10 . . .49 DZ21
Lawnside, SE3 . . . . .164 EF84
Lawns Way, Rom. RM5 . . . . .105 FC52
Lawn Ter, SE3 . . . . .164 EE83
Lawn Vale, Pnr. HA5 . . . . . . .94 BX54
Lawrance Gdns, Wal.Cr.
(Chsht) EN8 . . . . .67 DX28
Lawrance Rd, St.Alb. AL3 . . .42 CC16
Lawrence Av, E12 . . . . .125 EN63
E17 . . . . .101 DX53
N13 . . . . .99 DP49
NW7 . . . . .96 CS49
NW10 . . . . .138 CR67
New Malden KT3 . . . . . . .198 CR100
Ware (Stans.Abb.) SG12 . .33 EC11
Lawrence Bldgs, N16 . . . . . .122 DT62
Lawrence Campe Cl, N20
off Friern Barnet La 98 DD48
Lawrence Cl, E3 . . . . .143 EA68
N15 off Lawrence Rd . . .122 DS55
Guildford GU4
off Ladygrove Dr 243 BB129
Hertford SG14 . . . . .31 DL08
Lawrence Ct, NW7 . . . . .96 CS50
Lawrence Cres, Dag. RM10 .127 FB62
Edgware HA8 . . . . .96 CN54
Lawrence Dr, Uxb. UB10 . . . .115 BQ63
Lawrence Gdns, NW7 . . . . . .97 CT48
Tilbury RM18 . . . . .171 GH80

London Underground station · DLR Docklands Light Railway station · Tra Tramlink station · Riv Pedestrian ferry landing stage

Lawrence Hall End, Welw.G.C. AL7 29 CY12
Lawrence Hill, E4 101 EA47
Lawrence Hill Gdns, Dart. DA1 188 FJ86
Lawrence Hill Rd, Dart. DA1 188 FJ86
Lawrence La, EC2 11 H8
Betchworth (Buckland) RH3 249 CV131
Lawrence Moorings, Saw. CM21 36 EZ06
Lawrence Orchard, Rick. (Chorl.) WD3 73 BD43
Lawrence Pl, N1 off Outram Pl 141 DL67
Lawrence Rd, E6 144 EK67
E13 144 EH67
N15 122 DS56
N18 100 DV49
SE25 202 DT98
W5 157 CK77
Erith DA8 167 FB80
Hampton TW12 176 BZ94
Hayes UB4 135 BQ68
Hounslow TW4 156 BW84
Pinner HA5 116 BX57
Richmond TW10 177 CJ91
Romford RM2 127 FH57
West Wickham BR4 222 EG105
Lawrence Sq, Grav. DA11 off Haynes Rd 191 GF90
Lawrence St, E16 15 K6
NW7 97 CT49
SW3 160 DE79
Lawrence Way, NW10 118 CQ62
Slough SL1 131 AK71
Lawrence Weaver Cl, Mord. SM4 off Green La 200 DA100
Lawrie Pk Av, SE26 182 DV92
Lawrie Pk Cres, SE26 182 DV92
Lawrie Pk Gdns, SE26 182 DV91
Lawrie Pk Rd, SE26 182 DV93
Laws Cl, SE25 202 DR98
Lawson Cl, E16 144 EJ71
SW19 179 CX90
Lawson Est, SE1 21 J6
Lawson Gdns, Dart. DA1 188 FK85
Pinner HA5 115 BV55
Lawson Rd, Dart. DA1 168 FK84
Enfield EN3 82 DW39
Southall UB1 136 BZ70
Lawson Wk, Cars. SM5 218 DF110
Law St, SE1 21 K5
Lawton Rd, E3 13 K2
E10 123 EC60
Barnet EN4 80 DD41
Loughton IG10 85 EP41
Laxcon Cl, NW10 118 CQ64
Laxey Rd, Orp. BR6 223 ET107
Laxley Cl, SE5 161 DP80
Laxton Gdns, Rad. (Shenley) WD7 off Porters Pk Dr 62 CL32
Redhill RH1 251 DK128
Laxton Pl, NW1 9 H3
Layard Rd, SE16 22 D7
Enfield EN1 82 DT39
Thornton Heath CR7 202 DR96
Layard Sq, SE16 22 D7
Layborne Av, Rom. RM3 off Cummings Hall La 106 FJ48
Laybrook, St.Alb. AL4 43 CG16
Layburn Cres, Slou. SL3 153 BB79
Sch Laycock Prim Sch, N1 4 E4
Laycock St, N1 4 D4
Layer Gdns, W3 138 CN73
Layfield Cl, NW4 119 CV59
Layfield Cres, NW4 119 CV59
Layfield Rd, NW4 119 CV59
Layhams Rd, Kes. BR2 222 EF106
West Wickham BR4 203 ED104
Layhill, Hem.H. HP2 40 BK18
Laymarsh Cl, Belv. DA17 166 EZ76
Laymead Cl, Nthlt. UB5 136 BY65
Laystall St, EC1 10 C4
Layters Av, Ger.Cr. (Chal.St.P.) SL9 90 AW54
Layters Av S, Ger.Cr. (Chal.St.P.) SL9 90 AW54
Layters Cl, Ger.Cr. (Chal.St.P.) SL9 90 AW54
Layters End, Ger.Cr. (Chal.St.P.) SL9 90 AW54
LAYTER'S GREEN, Ger.Cr. SL9 90 AV54
Layters Grn La, Ger.Cr. (Chal.St.P.) SL9 112 AU55
Layter's Grn Mobile Home Pk, Ger.Cr. (Chal.St.P.) SL9 off Layters Grn La 90 AV54
Layters Way, Ger.Cr. SL9 112 AX56
Layton Ct, Wey. KT13 off Castle Vw Rd 213 BP105
Layton Cres, Croy. CR0 219 DN106
Layton Pl, Rich. TW9 off Station Av 158 CN81
Layton Rd, Brent. TW8 157 CK78
Hounslow TW3 156 CB84
Laytons Bldgs, SE1 21 H3
Laytons La, Sun. TW16 195 BT96
Layton St, Welw.G.C. AL7 29 CY12
Layzell Wk, SE9 off Mottingham La 184 EK88
Lazar Wk, N7 121 DM61
Lazell Gdns, Bet. RH3 264 CQ140
Lea, The, Egh. TW20 193 BB95
Leabank Cl, Har. HA1 117 CE62
Leabank Sq, E9 143 EA65
Leabank Vw, N15 122 DU58
Leabourne Rd, N16 122 DU58
LEA BRIDGE, E5 123 DX62
Lea Br Business Cen, E10 off Burwell Rd 123 DY60
Lea Br Rd, E5 122 DW62
E10 123 DY60
E17 123 ED56
Lea Bushes, Wat. WD25 76 BY35
Leachcroft, Ger.Cr. (Chal.St.P.) SL9 90 AV53
Leach Gro, Lthd. KT22 231 CJ122
Lea Cl, Bushey WD23 76 CB43
Twickenham TW2 176 BZ87
Lea Cres, Ruis. HA4 115 BT63
Leacroft, Stai. TW18 174 BH91
Leacroft Av, SW12 180 DF87
Leacroft Cl, Ken. CR8 236 DQ116
Staines TW18 174 BH91
West Drayton UB7 134 BL72
Leacroft Rd, Iver SL0 133 BD72
Leadale Av, E4 101 EA47
Leadale Rd, N15 122 DU58
N16 122 DU58
Leadbeaters Cl, N11 off Goldsmith Rd 98 DF50
Leadbetter Dr, Wat. WD25 75 BR36
★ Leadenhall Mkt, EC3 11 L8
Leadenhall Pl, EC3 11 L8
Leadenhall St, EC3 11 L8
Leadenham Ct, E3 off Spanby Rd 143 EA70
Leader Av, E12 125 EN64
Leadings, The, Wem. HA9 118 CQ62
Sch Lea Fm Jun Sch, Wat. WD25 off Fourth Av 76 BX35
Leaf Cl, Nthwd. HA6 93 BR52
Thames Ditton KT7 197 CE99
Leaf Gro, SE27 181 DN92
Leafield Cl, SW16 181 DP93
Woking GU21 off Winnington Way 226 AV118
Leafield La, Sid. DA14 186 EZ91
Leafield Rd, SW20 199 CZ97
Sutton SM1 200 DA103
Leaford Cres, Wat. WD24 75 BT37
Leaforis Rd, Wal.Cr. EN7 66 DU28
Leafy Gro, Croy. CR0 221 DY111
Keston BR2 222 EJ106
Leafy Oak Rd, SE12 184 EJ90
Leafy Way, Brwd. (Hutt.) CM13 109 GD46
Croydon CR0 202 DT103
Lea Gdns, Wem. HA9 118 CL63
Leagrave St, E5 122 DW62
Lea Hall Rd, E10 123 EA60
Leahoe Gdns, Hert. SG13 32 DQ10
Leaholme Gdns, Slou. SL1 130 AJ71
Leaholme Way, Ruis. HA4 115 BP58
Leahurst Rd, SE13 183 ED85
Sch Lea Inf Sch, Slou. SL2 off Wexham Rd 132 AV73
Sch Lea Jun Sch, Slou. SL2 off Grasmere Av 132 AV73
Leake St, SE1 20 B3
Lealand Rd, N15 122 DT58
Leamington Av, E17 123 EA57
Bromley BR1 184 EJ92
Morden SM4 199 CZ98
Orpington BR6 223 ES105
Leamington Cl, E12 124 EL64
Bromley BR1 184 EJ92
Hounslow TW3 176 CC85
Romford RM3 106 FM51
Leamington Cres, Har. HA2 116 BY62
Leamington Gdns, Ilf. IG3 125 ET61
Leamington Pk, W3 138 CR71
Leamington Pl, Hayes UB4 135 BT70
Leamington Rd, Rom. RM3 106 FN50
Southall UB2 156 BX77
Leamington Rd Vil, W11 6 F6
Leamore St, W6 159 CV77
Lea Mt, Wal.Cr. EN7 66 DS28
Leamouth Rd, E6 off Remington Rd 144 EL72
E14 14 F8
Leander Ct, SE8 163 EA81
Leander Dr, Grav. DA12 191 GM91
Leander Gdns, Wat. WD25 76 BY37
Leander Rd, SW2 181 DM86
Northolt UB5 136 CA68
Thornton Heath CR7 201 DM98
Leapale La, Guil. GU1 258 AX135
Leapale Rd, Guil. GU1 258 AX135
Learner Dr, Har. HA2 116 CA61
Lea Rd, Beck. BR3 off Fairfield Rd 203 EA96
Enfield EN2 82 DR39
Grays RM16 171 GG78
Hoddesdon EN11 49 EC15
Sevenoaks TN13 257 FJ127
Southall UB2 156 BY77
Waltham Abbey EN9 67 EA34
Learoyd Gdns, E6 145 EN73
Leas, The, Bushey WD23 76 BZ39
Hemel Hempstead HP3 40 BN24
Staines TW18 off Raleigh Ct 174 BG91
Upminster RM14 129 FR59
Leas Cl, Chess. KT9 216 CM108
Leas Dale, SE9 185 EN90
Leas Dr, Iver SL0 133 BE72
Leas Grn, Chis. BR7 185 ET93
Leaside, Hem.H. HP2 41 BQ21
Leatherhead (Bkhm) KT23 230 CA123
Leaside Av, N10 120 DG55
Leaside Ct, Uxb. UB10 off The Larches 135 BP69
Leaside Rd, E5 122 DW60
Leaside Wk, Ware SG12 off East St 33 DX06
Leas La, Warl. CR6 237 DX118
Leaswoes Rd, E10 123 EA60
Lea Sq, E3 off Lefevre Wk 143 DZ67
Leas Rd, Guil. GU1 258 AW135
Warlingham CR6 237 DX118
Leasway, Brwd. CM14 108 FX48
Upminster RM14 128 FQ62
Leathart Cl, Horn. RM12 off Dowding Way 147 FH66
Leatherbottle Grn, Erith DA18 166 EZ76
Leather Bottle La, Belv. DA17 166 EY77
Leather Cl, Mitch. CR4 200 DG96
Leatherdale St, E1 12 F3
Leather Gdns, E15 off Abbey Rd 144 EE67
LEATHERHEAD, KT22 - KT24 231 CF121
⇌ Leatherhead 231 CG121
Leatherhead Bypass Rd, Lthd. KT22 231 CH120
Leatherhead Cl, N16 122 DT60
LEATHERHEAD COMMON, Lthd. KT22 231 CF119
H Leatherhead Hosp, Lthd. KT22 231 CJ122
★ Leatherhead Mus of Local History, Lthd. KT22 231 CH122
Leatherhead Rd, Ashtd. KT21 231 CK121
Chessington KT9 215 CJ111
Leatherhead KT22 231 CK121
Leatherhead (Bkhm) KT22, KT23 246 CB126
Leatherhead (Oxshott) KT22 215 CD114
Leather La, EC1 10 D6
Guildford (Goms.) GU5 261 BQ139
Hornchurch RM11 off North St 128 FK60
★ Leather Mkt Bermondsey, SE1 21 L4
Leathermarket Ct, SE1 21 L4
Leathermarket St, SE1 21 L4
Leathersellers Cl, Barn. EN5 off The Avenue 79 CY42
Leathsail Rd, Har. HA2 116 CB62
Leathwaite Rd, SW11 160 DF84
Leathwell Rd, SE8 163 EB82
Lea Vale, Dart. DA1 167 FD84
Sch Lea Valley High Sch, Enf. EN3 off Bullsmoor La 82 DW35
Sch Lea Valley Prim Sch, N17 off Somerford Gro 100 DU52
Lea Valley Rd, E4 83 DX43
Enfield EN3 83 DX43
Lea Valley Trd Est, N18 101 DX50
Lea Valley Viaduct, E4 101 DX50
N18 101 DX50
Lea Valley Wk, E3 143 EC70
E5 123 DY62
E9 123 DY62
E10 123 DY62
E14 13 N7
E15 143 EC69
E17 100 DW53
N9 100 DY46
N15 122 DU58
N16 122 DU58
N17 100 DW53
N18 100 DW53
Broxbourne EN10 49 EB21
Enfield EN3 83 DZ41
Hatfield AL9 46 DA15
Hertford SG13, SG14 31 DP11
Hoddesdon EN11 49 ED18
Waltham Abbey EN9 67 DZ30
Waltham Cross EN8 67 DZ30
Ware SG12 32 DW06
Welwyn Garden City AL7, AL8 29 CW13
Leaveland Cl, Beck. BR3 203 EA98
Leaver Gdns, Grnf. UB6 137 CD68
Leavesden Ct, Abb.L. WD5 59 BU31
LEAVESDEN GREEN, Wat. WD25 59 BT34
Sch Leavesden Grn Prim Sch, Wat. WD25 off High Rd 59 BU34
Leavesden Rd, Stan. HA7 95 CG51
Watford WD24 75 BV38
Weybridge KT13 213 BP106
LEAVES GREEN, Kes. BR2 222 EK109
Leaves Grn Cres, Kes. BR2 222 EJ111
Leaves Grn Rd, Kes. BR2 222 EK111
Leaview, Wal.Abb. EN9 67 EB33
Lea Vw Hos, E5 off Springfield 122 DV60
Leaway, E10 122 DX60
Leazes Av, Cat. CR3 235 DN123
Leazes La, Cat. CR3 235 DN123
Lebanon Av, Felt. TW13 176 BX92
Lebanon Cl, Wat. WD17 75 BR36
Lebanon Ct, Twick. TW1 177 CH87
Lebanon Dr, Cob. KT11 214 CA113
Lebanon Gdns, SW18 180 DA86
Westerham (Bigg.H.) TN16 238 EK117
Lebanon Pk, Twick. TW1 177 CH87
Trm Lebanon Road 202 DS103
Lebanon Rd, SW18 180 DA85
Croydon CR0 202 DS102
Lebrun Sq, SE3 164 EH83
Lechford Rd, Horl. RH6 268 DG149
Lechmere App, Wdf.Grn. IG8 102 EJ54
Lechmere Av, Chig. IG7 103 EQ49
Woodford Green IG8 102 EK54
Lechmere Rd, NW2 139 CV65
Leckford Rd, SW18 180 DC89
Leckwith Av, Bexh. DA7 166 EY79
Lecky St, SW7 17 N9
Leclair Ho, SE3 off Gallus Sq 164 EH83
Leconfield Av, SW13 159 CT83
Leconfield Rd, N5 122 DR63
Leconfield Wk, Horn. RM12 off Airfield Way 148 FJ65
Le Corte Cl, Kings L. WD4 58 BM29
Lectern La, St.Alb. AL1 60 CD24
Leda Av, Enf. EN3 83 DX39
Leda Rd, SE18 165 EM76
Ledborough Gate, Beac. HP9 89 AM51
Ledborough La, Beac. HP9 89 AK52
Ledborough Wd, Beac. HP9 89 AL51
Ledbury Est, SE15 162 DV80
Ledbury Ms N, W11 6 G9
Ledbury Ms W, W11 6 G9
Ledbury Pl, Croy. CR0 220 DQ105
Ledbury Rd, W11 6 F7
Croydon CR0 220 DQ105
Reigate RH2 249 CZ133
Ledbury St, SE15 162 DU80
Ledger Cl, Guil. GU1 243 BB132
Ledger Dr, Add. KT15 211 BF106
Ledger La, Maid. SL6 150 AD82
Ledgers Rd, Slou. SL1 151 AR75
Warlingham CR6 237 EA116
Ledrington Rd, SE19 182 DU93
Ledway Dr, Wem. HA9 118 CM59
LEE, SE12 164 EE84
⇌ Lee 184 EG86
Lee, The, Nthwd. HA6 93 BT50
Lee Av, Rom. RM6 126 EY58
Lee Br, SE13 163 EC83
Leechcroft Av, Sid. DA15 185 ET85
Swanley BR8 207 FF97
Leechcroft Rd, Wall. SM6 200 DG104
Leech La, Epsom (Headley) KT18 248 CQ126
Leatherhead KT22 248 CQ126
Lee Ch St, SE13 164 EE84
Lee Cl, E17 101 DX53
Barnet EN5 80 DC42
Hertford SG13 32 DQ11
Ware (Stans.Abb.) SG12 33 EC11
Lee Conservancy Rd, E9 123 DZ64
Leecroft Rd, Barn. EN5 79 CY43
Leeds Cl, Orp. BR6 206 EX103
Leeds Pl, N4 off Tollington Pk 121 DM61
Leeds Rd, Ilf. IG1 125 ER60
Slough SL1 132 AS73
Leeds St, N18 100 DU50
Lee Fm Cl, Chesh. HP5 56 AU30
Leefern Rd, W12 159 CU75
Leefe Way, Pot.B. EN6 65 DK28
Lee Gdns Av, Horn. RM11 128 FN60
Leegate, SE12 184 EF85
Leegate Cl, Wok. GU21 off Sythwood 226 AV116
Lee Grn, SE12 off Lee High Rd 184 EF85
Orpington BR5 206 EU99
Lee Grn La, Epsom KT18 232 CP124
Lee Gro, Chig. IG7 103 EN47
Lee High Rd, SE12 163 ED83
SE13 163 ED83
Leeke St, WC1 10 A1
Leeland Rd, W13 137 CG74
Leeland Ter, W13 137 CG74
Leeland Way, NW10 119 CT63
Sch Lee Manor Prim Sch, SE13 off Leahurst Rd 184 EE86
Leeming Rd, Borwd. WD6 78 CM39
Lee Pk, SE3 164 EF84
Lee Pk Way, N9 101 DX49
N18 101 DX49
Leerdam Dr, E14 24 D6
Lee Rd, NW7 97 CX52
SE3 164 EF83
SW19 200 DB95
Enfield EN1 82 DU44
Greenford UB6 137 CJ67
Lees, The, Croy. CR0 203 DZ103
Lees Av, Nthwd. HA6 93 BT53
Leeside, Barn. EN5 79 CY43
Potters Bar EN6 off Wayside 64 DD31
Leeside Ct, SE16 22 G1
Leeside Cres, NW11 119 CZ58
Leeside Rd, N17 100 DV51
Leeson Gdns, Wind. (Eton Wick) SL4 off Victoria Rd 151 AL77
Leeson Rd, SE24 161 DN84
Leesons Hill, Chis. BR7 205 ES97
Orpington BR5 206 EU97
Sch Leesons Prim Sch, Orp. BR5 off Leesons Hill 206 EV97
Leesons Way, Orp. BR5 205 ET96
Lees Pl, W1 8 E9
Lees Rd, Uxb. UB8 135 BP70
Lee St, E8 5 N7
Horley RH6 268 DE148
Lee Ter, SE3 164 EE83
SE13 164 EE83
Lee Valley Cycle Route, Brox. EN10 49 ED20
Harlow CM19 50 EF18
Hoddesdon EN11 34 EE13
Ware SG12 33 EB09
★ Lee Valley Pk, E10 67 DZ31
Lee Valley Pathway, E9 123 DZ62
E10 122 DW59
E17 122 DW59
Waltham Abbey EN9 67 EA31
Lee Valley Technopark, N17 122 DU55
Lee Vw, Enf. EN2 81 DP39
Leeward Gdns, SW19 179 CZ93
Leeway, SE8 23 L9
Leeway Cl, Pnr. HA5 94 BZ52
Leewood Cl, SE12 off Upwood Rd 184 EF86
Leewood Pl, Swan. BR8 207 FD98
Leewood Way, Lthd. (Eff.) KT24 246 BW127
Lefevre Wk, E3 143 DZ67
Lefroy Rd, W12 159 CT75
Legard Rd, N5 121 DP62
Legatt Rd, SE9 184 EK85
Leggatt Rd, E15 143 EC68
Leggatts Cl, Wat. WD24 75 BT36
Leggatts Ri, Wat. WD25 75 BU35
Leggatts Way, Wat. WD24 75 BT36
Leggatts Wd Av, Wat. WD24 75 BV36
Legge St, SE13 183 EC85
Leggfield Ter, Hem.H. HP1 39 BF20
Leghorn Rd, NW10 139 CT68
SE18 165 ER78
Legion Cl, N1 4 D5
Legion Ct, Mord. SM4 200 DA100
Legion Rd, Grnf. UB6 136 CC67
Legion Ter, E3 off Lefevre Wk 143 DZ67
Legion Way, N12 98 DE52
Legon Av, Rom. RM7 127 FC60
Legra Av, Hodd. EN11 49 EA17
Legrace Av, Houns. TW4 156 BX82
Leicester Av, Mitch. CR4 201 DL98
Leicester Cl, Wor.Pk. KT4 217 CW105
Leicester Ct, WC2 9 M9
Leicester Gdns, Ilf. IG3 125 ES59
Leicester Ms, N2 off Leicester Rd 120 DE55
Leicester Pl, WC2 9 M9
Leicester Rd, E11 124 EH57
N2 120 DE55
Barnet EN5 80 DB43
Croydon CR0 202 DS101
Tilbury RM18 171 GF81
⊖ Leicester Square 9 M9
Leicester Sq, WC2 9 M10
Leicester St, WC2 9 M9
LEIGH, Reig. RH2 265 CU141
Leigh, The, Kings.T. KT2 178 CS93
Leigham Av, SW16 181 DL90
Leigham Ct, Wall. SM6 off Stafford Rd 219 DJ107
Leigham Ct Rd, SW16 181 DL89
Leigham Dr, Islw. TW7 157 CE80
Leigham Vale, SW2 181 DM90
SW16 181 DM90
Leigh Av, Ilf. IG4 124 EK56
Coll Leigh City Tech Coll, Dart. DA1 off Green St Grn Rd 188 FP88
Leigh Cl, Add. KT15 211 BF108
New Malden KT3 198 CR98
Leigh Common, Welw.G.C. AL7 29 CY11
Leigh Cor, Cob. KT11 off Leigh Hill Rd 214 BW114
Leigh Ct, SE4 off Lewisham Way 163 EA82
Borehamwood WD6 off Banks Rd 78 CR40
Harrow HA2 117 CE60
Leigh Ct Cl, Cob. KT11 214 BW114
Leigh Cres, Croy. (New Adgtn) CR0 221 EB108
Leigh Dr, Rom. RM3 106 FK49
Leigh Gdns, NW10 139 CW68
Leigh Hill Rd, Cob. KT11 214 BW114
Leigh Hunt Dr, N14 99 DK46
Leigh Hunt St, SE1 20 G3
Leigh Orchard Cl, SW16 181 DM90
Leigh Pk, Slou. (Datchet) SL3 152 AV80
Leigh Pl, EC1 10 C5
Cobham KT11 230 BW115
Dartford DA2 off Hawley Rd 188 FN92
Feltham TW13 176 BW88
Welling DA16 166 EU82
Leigh Pl La, Gdse. RH9 253 DY132
Leigh Pl Rd, Reig. RH2 265 CU140
Leigh Rd, E6 145 EN65
E10 123 EC59
N5 121 DP63
Betchworth RH3 264 CQ140
Cobham KT11 213 BV113
Gravesend DA11 191 GH89
Hounslow TW3 157 CD84
Slough SL1 131 AP73
Leigh Rodd, Wat. WD19 94 BZ48
Leigh Sq, Wind. SL4 151 AK82
Leigh St, WC1 9 N3
Leigh Ter, Orp. BR5 off Saxville Rd 206 EV97
Leighton Av, E12 125 EN64
Pinner HA5 116 BY55
Leighton Buzzard Rd, Hem.H. HP1 40 BJ19
Leighton Cl, Edg. HA8 96 CN54
Leighton Cres, NW5 off Leighton Gro 121 DJ64
Leighton Gdns, NW10 139 CV68
South Croydon CR2 220 DV113
Tilbury RM18 171 GG80
Leighton Gro, NW5 121 DJ64
★ Leighton Ho Mus, W14 16 F5
Leighton Pl, NW5 121 DJ64
Leighton Rd, NW5 121 DK64
W13 157 CG75
Enfield EN1 82 DT43
Harrow (Har.Wld) HA3 95 CD54
Leighton St, Croy. CR0 201 DP102
Leighton Way, Epsom KT18 216 CR114
Leila Parnell Pl, SE7 164 EJ79
Leinster Av, SW14 158 CQ83
Leinster Gdns, W2 7 L8
Leinster Ms, W2 7 L9
Leinster Pl, W2 7 L8
Leinster Rd, N10 121 DH56
Leinster Sq, W2 7 H9
Leinster Ter, W2 7 L9
Leiston Spur, Slou. SL1 132 AS72
Leisure La, W.Byf. KT14 212 BH112
Leisure Way, N12 98 DD52
Leith Cl, NW9 118 CR60
Slough SL1 132 AU74
Leithcote Gdns, SW16 181 DM91
Leithcote Path, SW16 181 DM90
Leith Hill, Orp. BR5 206 EU95
Leith Hill Grn, Orp. BR5 off Leith Hill 206 EU95
Leith Hill La, Dor. (Holm.St.M.) RH5 262 BY144
Leith Pk Rd, Grav. DA12 191 GH88
Leith Rd, N22 99 DP53
Epsom KT17 216 CS112
Leith Vw, Dor. (N.Holm.) RH5 263 CJ140
Leith Yd, NW6 off Quex Rd 140 DA67
Lela Av, Houns. TW4 156 BW82
Lelitia Cl, E8 off Pownall Rd 142 DU67
Leman St, E1 11 P8
Lemark Cl, Stan. HA7 95 CJ50
Le May Av, SE12 184 EH90
Le May Cl, Horl. RH6 268 DG147
Lemmon Rd, SE10 164 EE79
Lemna Rd, E11 124 EE59
Lemonfield Dr, Wat. WD25 60 BY32
Lemonwell Ct, SE9 off Lemonwell Dr 185 EQ85
Lemonwell Dr, SE9 185 EQ85
LEMSFORD, Welw.G.C. AL8 29 CT10
Lemsford Cl, N15 122 DU57
Lemsford Ct, N4 off Brownswood Rd 122 DQ61
Borehamwood WD6 78 CQ42
Lemsford La, Welw.G.C. AL8 29 CV10
Lemsford Rd, Hat. AL10 45 CT17
St. Albans AL1 43 CF20
Welwyn Garden City (Lmsfd) AL8 29 CT10
Lemsford Village, Welw.G.C. (Lmsfd) AL8 29 CU10
Lemuel St, SW18 180 DB86
Lena Cres, N9 100 DW47
Lena Gdns, W6 159 CW76
Sch Lena Gdns Prim Sch, W6 off Lena Gdns 159 CW76
Lena Kennedy Cl, E4 101 EB51
Lenanton Steps, E14 23 P3
Lendal Ter, SW4 161 DK83
Lenelby Rd, Surb. KT6 198 CN102
Len Freeman Pl, SW6 off John Smith Av 159 CZ80
Lenham Rd, SE12 164 EF84
Bexleyheath DA7 166 EZ79
Sutton SM1 218 DB105
Thornton Heath CR7 202 DR96
Lenmore Av, Grays RM17 170 GC76
Lennard Av, W.Wick. BR4 204 EE103
Lennard Cl, W.Wick. BR4 204 EE103
Lennard Rd, SE20 182 DW93
Beckenham BR3 183 DX93
Bromley BR2 205 EM102
Croydon CR0 202 DQ102
Sevenoaks (Dunt.Grn) TN13 241 FE120
Lennard Row, S.Ock. (Aveley) RM15 149 FR74
Lennon Rd, NW2 119 CW64
Lennox Av, Grav. DA11 191 GF86
Lennox Cl, Grays (Chaff.Hun.) RM16 169 FW77
Romford RM1 127 FF58
Lennox Gdns, NW10 119 CT63
SW1 18 C6
Croydon CR0 219 DP105
Ilford IG1 125 EM60
Lennox Gdns Ms, SW1 18 C6
Coll Lennox Lewis Coll, E5 off Theydon Rd 122 DW61
Lennox Rd, E17 123 DZ58
N4 121 DM61
Gravesend DA11 191 GF86
Lennox Rd E, Grav. DA11 191 GG87
Lenor Cl, Bexh. DA6 166 EY84
Lensbury Cl, Wal.Cr. (Chsht) EN8 off Ashdown Cres 67 DY28
Lensbury Way, SE2 166 EW76
Lens Rd, E7 144 EJ66
Lenten Cl, Guil. (Peasl.) GU5 261 BR142
Lent Grn, Slou. (Burn.) SL1 130 AH70
Lent Grn La, Slou. (Burn.) SL1 130 AH70
Lenthall Av, Grays RM17 170 GA75
Lenthall Rd, E8 5 P5
Loughton IG10 85 ER42
Lenthorp Rd, SE10 25 J9
Lentmead Rd, Brom. BR1 184 EF90
Lenton Path, SE18 165 ER79
Lenton Ri, Rich. TW9 off Evelyn Ter 158 CL83
Lenton St, SE18 165 ER77
LENT RISE, Slou. SL1 130 AH71
Sch Lent Ri Comb Sch, Slou. SL1 off Coulson Way 130 AH71
Lent Ri Rd, Maid. (Taplow) SL6 130 AH72
Slough (Burn.) SL1 130 AH72
Coll Leo Baeck Coll, N3 off East End Rd 98 DA54
Leof Cres, SE6 183 EB92
Leominster Rd, Mord. SM4 200 DC100
Leominster Wk, Mord. SM4 200 DC100
Leonard Av, Mord. SM4 200 DC99
Romford RM7 127 FD60

★ Place of interest | H Hospital | Sch School | Coll College | Uni University | ⇌ Railway station

Leonard Av, Sev. (Otford) TN14 .241 FH116
Swanscombe DA10 .190 FY87
Leonard Pl, N16 off Allen Rd .122 DS63
Leonard Rd, E4 .101 EA51
E7 .124 EG63
N9 .100 DT48
SW16 .201 DJ95
Southall UB2 .156 BX76
Leonard Robbins Path, SE28 off Tawney Rd .146 EV73
Leonard St, E16 .144 EL74
EC2 .11 K3
Leonard Way, Brwd. CM14 .108 FS49
Leontine Cl, SE15 .162 DU80
Leopards Ct, EC1 .10 C5
Leopold Av, SW19 .179 CZ92
Leopold Ms, E9 off Fremont St .142 DW67
Sch Leopold Prim Sch, NW10 off Hawkshead Rd .139 CT66
Leopold Rd, E17 .123 EA57
N2 .120 DD55
N18 .100 DV50
NW10 .138 CS66
SW19 .179 CZ91
W5 .138 CM74
Leopold St, E3 .13 M5
Leopold Ter, SW19 off Dora Rd .180 DA92
Leo St, SE15 .162 DV80
Leo Yd, EC1 .10 F4
Le Personne Rd, Cat. CR3 .236 DR122
Leppoc Rd, SW4 .181 DK85
Leret Way, Lthd. KT22 .231 CH121
Leroy St, SE1 .21 L7
Lerwick Dr, Slou. SL1 .132 AS71
Lesbourne Rd, Reig. RH2 .266 DB135
Lescombe Cl, SE23 .183 DY90
Lescombe Rd, SE23 .183 DY90
Lesley Cl, Bex. DA5 .187 FB87
Gravesend (Istead Rise) DA13 .191 GF94
Swanley BR8 .207 FD97
Leslie Gdns, Sutt. SM2 .218 DA108
Leslie Gro, Croy. CR0 .202 DS102
Leslie Gro Pl, Croy. CR0 off Leslie Gro .202 DR102
Leslie Pk Rd, Croy. CR0 .202 DS102
Leslie Rd, E11 .123 EC63
E16 .15 P8
N2 .120 DD55
Dorking RH4 .247 CK134
Woking (Chobham) GU24 .210 AS110
Leslie Smith Sq, SE18 off Nightingale Vale .165 EN79
★ Lesnes Abbey (ruins), Erith DA18 .166 EX77
Lesney Fm Est, Erith DA8 .167 FD80
Lesney Pk, Erith DA8 .167 FD79
Sch Lesney Pk Prim Sch, Erith DA8 off Lesney Pk Rd .167 FD79
Lesney Pk Rd, Erith DA8 .167 FD79
Lessar Av, SW4 .181 DJ85
Lessingham Av, SW17 .180 DF91
Ilford IG5 .125 EN55
Lessing St, SE23 .183 DY87
Lessington Av, Rom. RM7 .127 FC58
Lessness Av, Bexh. DA7 .166 EX80
LESSNESS HEATH, Belv. DA17 .167 FB78
Sch Lessness Heath Prim Sch, Belv. DA17 off Erith Rd .166 FA78
Lessness Pk, Belv. DA17 .166 EZ78
Lessness Rd, Belv. DA17 off Stapley Rd .166 FA78
Morden SM4 .200 DC100
Lester Av, E15 .15 H2
Leston Cl, Rain. RM13 .147 FG69
Leswin Pl, N16 off Leswin Rd .122 DT62
Leswin Rd, N16 .122 DT62
Letchfield, Chesh. (Ley Hill) HP5 .56 AV31
Letchford Gdns, NW10 .139 CU69
Letchford Ms, NW10 off Letchford Gdns .139 CU69
Letchford Ter, Har. HA3 .94 CB53
LETCHMORE HEATH, Wat. WD25 .77 CD38
Letchmore Rd, Rad. WD7 .77 CG36
Letchworth Av, Felt. TW14 .175 BT87
Letchworth Cl, Brom. BR2 .204 EG99
Watford WD19 .94 BX50
Letchworth Dr, Brom. BR2 .204 EG99
Letchworth St, SW17 .180 DF91
Lethbridge Cl, SE13 .163 EC81
Letter Box La, Sev. TN13 .257 FJ129
Letterstone Rd, SW6 off Varna Rd .159 CZ80
Lettice St, SW6 .159 CZ81
Lett Rd, E15 .143 ED66
Lettsom St, SE5 .162 DS82
Lettsom Wk, E13 .144 EG68
LETTY GREEN, Hert. SG14 .31 DH13
Leucha Rd, E17 .123 DY57
Levana Cl, SW19 .179 CY88
Levehurst Way, SW4 .161 DL82
Leven Cl, Wal.Cr. EN8 .67 DX33
Watford WD19 .94 BX50
Levendale Rd, SE23 .183 DY89
Leven Dr, Wal.Cr. EN8 .67 DX33
Leven Rd, E14 .14 D6
Leven Way, Hayes UB3 .135 BS72
Hemel Hempstead HP2 .40 BK16
Leveret Cl, Croy. (New Adgtn) CR0 .221 ED111
Watford WD25 .59 BU34
Leverett St, SW3 .18 B7
Leverholme Gdns, SE9 .185 EN90
Leverson St, SW16 .181 DJ93
Lever Sq, Grays RM16 .171 GG77
LEVERSTOCK GREEN, Hem.H. HP3 .41 BQ21
Sch Leverstock Grn C of E Prim Sch, Hem.H. HP2 off Green La .41 BR21
Leverstock Grn Rd, Hem.H. HP2, HP3 .41 BQ21
Leverstock Grn Way, Hem.H. HP3 .41 BQ20
Lever St, EC1 .10 F2
Sch Leverton Inf Sch, The, Wal.Abb. EN9 off Honey La .68 EF34
Sch Leverton Jun Sch, The, Wal.Abb. EN9 off Honey La .68 EF34
Leverton Pl, NW5 off Leverton St .121 DJ64
Leverton St, NW5 .121 DJ64
Leverton Way, Wal.Abb. EN9 .67 EC33
Leveson Rd, Grays RM16 .171 GH76
Levett Gdns, Ilf. IG3 .125 ET63
Levett Rd, Bark. IG11 .145 ES65
Leatherhead KT22 .231 CH120
Levine Gdns, Bark. IG11 .146 EX68
Levison Way, N19 off Grovedale Rd .121 DK61
Levylsdene, Guil. GU1 .243 BD134
Lewes Cl, Grays RM17 .170 GA79
Northolt UB5 .136 CA65
Lewes Ct, Slou. SL1 off Chalvey Gro .151 AQ75
Lewesdon Cl, SW19 .179 CX88
Lewes Rd, N12 .98 DE50
Bromley BR1 .204 EK96
Romford RM3 .106 FJ49
Leweston Pl, N16 .122 DT59
Lewes Way, Rick. (Crox.Grn) WD3 .75 BQ42
Lewey Ho, E3 .13 M4
Lewgars Av, NW9 .118 CQ58
Lewin Rd, SW14 .158 CR83
SW16 .181 DK93
Bexleyheath DA6 .166 EY84
Lewins Rd, Epsom KT18 .216 CP114
Gerrards Cross (Chal.St.P.) SL9 .112 AX55
Lewins Way, Slou. SL1 .131 AM73
Lewis Av, E17 .101 EA53
Lewis Cl, N14 off Orchid Rd .99 DJ45
Addlestone KT15 .212 BJ105
Brentwood (Shenf.) CM15 .109 FZ45
Uxbridge (Hare.) UB9 .92 BJ54
Lewis Cres, NW10 .118 CQ64
Lewis Gdns, N2 .98 DD54
Lewis Gro, SE13 .163 EC83
LEWISHAM, SE13 .163 EB84
⇌ Lewisham .163 EC83
DLR Lewisham .163 EC83
Sch Lewisham Br Prim Sch, SE13 off Elmira St .163 EB83
Lewisham Cen, SE13 .163 EC83
Coll Lewisham Coll, Deptford Campus, SE8 off Deptford Ch St .163 EA81
Lewisham Way Campus, SE4 off Breakspears Rd .163 EA82
Lewisham High St, SE13 .163 EC83
Lewisham Hill, SE13 .163 EC82
Lewisham Pk, SE13 .183 EB86
Lewisham Rd, SE13 .163 EB81
Lewisham St, SW1 .19 M4
Lewisham Way, SE4 .163 DZ81
SE14 .163 DZ81
Lewis La, Ger.Cr. (Chal.St.P.) SL9 .90 AY53
Lewis Pl, E8 .122 DU64
Lewis Rd, Horn. RM11 .128 FJ58
Mitcham CR4 .200 DD96
Richmond TW10 off Red Lion St .177 CK85
Sidcup DA14 .186 EW90
Southall UB1 .156 BY75
Sutton SM1 .218 DB105
Swanscombe DA10 .190 FY86
Welling DA16 .166 EW83
Lewis St, NW1 .141 DH65
Lewiston Cl, Wor.Pk. KT4 .199 CV101
Lewis Way, Dag. RM10 .147 FB65
Lexden Dr, Rom. RM6 .126 EV58
Lexden Rd, W3 .138 CP73
Mitcham CR4 .201 DK98
Lexham Ct, Grnf. UB6 .137 CD67
Lexham Gdns, W8 .17 J7
Amersham HP6 .55 AQ37
Lexham Gdns Ms, W8 .17 K6
Lexham Ho, Bark. IG11 off St. Margarets .145 ER67
Lexham Ms, W8 .17 H7
Lexham Wk, W8 .17 K6
Lexington, The, EC1 .11 J3
Lexington Cl, Borwd. WD6 .78 CM41
Lexington Ct, Pur. CR8 .220 DQ110
Lexington St, W1 .9 K8
Lexington Way, Barn. EN5 .79 CX42
Upminster RM14 .129 FT58
Lexton Gdns, SW12 .181 DK88
Leybourne Av, W13 .157 CH75
Leybourne Pk, Rich. TW9 .158 CN81
Leybourne Av, W.Byf. (Byfleet) KT14 .212 BM113
Leybourne Cl, Brom. BR2 .204 EG100
West Byfleet (Byfleet) KT14 off Leybourne Av .212 BM113
Leybourne Rd, E11 .124 EF60
NW1 .141 DH66
NW9 .118 CN57
Uxbridge UB10 .135 BQ67
Leybourne St, NW1 off Hawley St .141 DH66
Leybridge Ct, SE12 .184 EG85
Leyburn Cl, E17 off Church La .123 EB56
Leyburn Cres, Rom. RM3 .106 FL52
Leyburn Gdns, Croy. CR0 .202 DS103
Leyburn Gro, N18 .100 DU51
Leyburn Rd, N18 .100 DU51
Romford RM3 .106 FL52
Leycroft Cl, Loug. IG10 .85 EN43
Leycroft Gdns, Erith DA8 .167 FH81
Leydenhatch La, Swan. BR8 .207 FC95
Leyden St, E1 .11 N6
Leydon Cl, SE16 .23 H2
Leyfield, Wor.Pk. KT4 .198 CS102
Leyhill Cl, Swan. BR8 .207 FE99
Sch Ley Hill Co Comb Sch, Chesh. HP5 off Jasons Hill .56 AV30
Ley Hill Rd, Hem.H. (Bov.) HP3 .56 AX30
Leyland Av, Enf. EN3 .83 DY40
St. Albans AL1 .43 CD22
Leyland Cl, Wal.Cr. (Chsht) EN8 .66 DW28
Leyland Gdns, Wdf.Grn. IG8 .102 EJ50
Leyland Rd, SE12 .184 EG85
Leylands La, Stai. TW19 .173 BF85
Leylang Rd, SE14 .163 DX80
Sch Ley Pk Prim Sch, Brox. EN10 off Cozens La E .49 DZ22
Leys, The, N2 .120 DC56
Amersham HP6 .55 AP35
Harrow HA3 .118 CM58
St. Albans AL4 .43 CK17
Leys Av, Dag. RM10 .147 FC66
Leys Cl, Dag. RM10 .147 FC66
Harrow HA1 .117 CD57
Uxbridge (Hare.) UB9 .92 BK53
Leysdown, Welw.G.C. AL7 .30 DD09
Leysdown Av, Bexh. DA7 .167 FC84
Leysdown Rd, SE9 .184 EL89
Leysfield Rd, W12 .159 CU75
Leys Gdns, Barn. EN4 .80 DG43
Sch Leys Prim Sch, Dag. RM10 off Leys Av .147 FC66
Leyspring Rd, E11 .124 EF60
Leys Rd, Hem.H. HP3 .40 BL22
Leatherhead (Oxshott) KT22 .215 CD112
Leys Rd E, Enf. EN3 .83 DY39
Leys Rd W, Enf. EN3 .83 DY39
Ley St, Ilf. IG1, IG2 .125 EP61
Leyswood Dr, Ilf. IG2 .125 ES57
Leythe Rd, W3 .158 CQ75
LEYTON, E11 .123 EB60
⊖ Leyton .123 EC62
Leyton Business Cen, E10 .123 EA61
Leyton Cross Rd, Dart. DA2 .187 FF90
Leyton Gra, E10 off Goldsmith Rd .123 EB60
Leyton Gra Est, E10 .123 EB60
Leyton Grn Rd, E10 .123 EC58
Leyton Ind Village, E10 .123 DX59
⇌ Leyton Midland Road .123 EC60
★ Leyton Orient FC, E10 .123 EB62
Leyton Pk Rd, E10 .123 EC62
Leyton Rd, E15 .123 ED64
SW19 .180 DC94
Coll Leyton 6th Form Coll, E10 off Essex Rd .123 ED58
LEYTONSTONE, E11 .123 ED59
⊖ Leytonstone .124 EE60
⇌ Leytonstone High Road .124 EE61
Leytonstone Rd, E15 .124 EE64
Sch Leytonstone Sch, E11 off Colworth Rd .124 EE58
Ley Wk, Welw.G.C. AL7 .30 DC09
Leywick St, E15 .144 EE68
Leywood Cl, Amer. HP7 .55 AR40
Lezayre Rd, Orp. BR6 .223 ET107
Liardet St, SE14 .163 DY79
Liberia Rd, N5 .4 F3
★ Liberty, W1 .9 J8
Liberty 2 Shop Cen, Rom. RM1 .127 FF57
Liberty Av, SW19 .200 DD95
Liberty Cl, Hert. SG13 .32 DQ11
Liberty Hall Rd, Add. KT15 .212 BG106
Liberty La, Add. KT15 .212 BG106
Liberty Ms, SW12 .181 DH86
Sch Liberty Prim Sch, Mitch. CR4 off Western Rd .200 DE96
Liberty Ri, Add. KT15 .212 BG107
Liberty Shop Cen, Rom. RM1 .127 FE57
Liberty St, SW9 .161 DM81
Libra Rd, E3 .143 DZ67
E13 .144 EG68
Library Hill, Brwd. CM14 off Coptfold Rd .108 FX47
Library Pl, E1 .12 D9
Library St, SE1 .20 E4
Library Way, Twick. TW2 off Nelson Rd .176 CC87
Licenced Victuallers Nat Homes, Uxb. (Denh.) UB9 off Denham Grn La .113 BF58
Lichfield Cl, Barn. EN4 .80 DF41
Lichfield Ct, Rich. TW9 off Sheen Rd .158 CL84
Lichfield Gdns, Rich. TW9 .158 CL84
Lichfield Gro, N3 .98 DA53
Lichfield Pl, St.Alb. AL1 off Avenue Rd .43 CF19
Lichfield Rd, E3 .13 K1
E6 .144 EK69
N9 off Winchester Rd .100 DU47
NW2 .119 CY63
Dagenham RM8 .126 EV63
Hounslow TW4 .156 BW83
Northwood HA6 .115 BU55
Richmond TW9 .158 CM81
Woodford Green IG8 .102 EE49
Lichfield Ter, Upmin. RM14 .129 FS61
Lichfield Way, Brox. EN10 .49 DZ22
South Croydon CR2 .221 DX110
Lichlade Cl, Orp. BR6 .223 ET105
Lidbury Rd, NW7 .97 CY51
Lidcote Gdns, SW9 .161 DN82
Liddall Way, West Dr. UB7 .134 BM74
Liddell Cl, Har. HA3 .117 CK55
Liddell Gdns, NW10 .139 CW68
Liddell Pl, Wind. SL4 off Liddell Way .150 AJ83
Liddell Rd, NW6 .140 DA65
Liddell Sq, Wind. SL4 off Liddell Way .150 AJ83
Liddell Way, Wind. SL4 .150 AJ83
Lidding Rd, Har. HA3 .117 CK57
Liddington Hall Dr, Guil. (Rydes.) GU3 .242 AS131
Liddington New Rd, Guil. (Rydes.) GU3 .242 AS131
Liddington Rd, E15 .144 EF67
Liddon Rd, E13 .15 N2
Bromley BR1 .204 EJ97
Liden Cl, E17 off Hitcham Rd .123 DZ60
Lidfield Rd, N16 .122 DR63
Lidgate Rd, SE15 off Chandler Way .162 DT80
Lidiard Rd, SW18 .180 DC89
Lidlington Pl, NW1 .141 DJ68
Lido Sq, N17 .100 DR54
Lidstone Cl, Wok. GU21 .226 AV117
Lidstone Ct, Slou. SL2 off Uxbridge Rd .132 AX72
Lidyard Rd, N19 .121 DJ60
Lieutenant Ellis Way, Wal.Cr. EN7, EN8 .66 DT31
Coll Lifelong Learning, The Shadwell Cen, E1 .12 G9
★ Lifetimes Mus, Croy. CR0 .202 DQ104
Liffler Rd, SE18 .165 ES78
Liffords Pl, SW13 .159 CT82
Lifford St, SW15 .159 CX84
Lightcliffe Rd, N13 .99 DN49
Lighter Cl, SE16 .23 K7
Lighterman Ms, E1 .13 H7
Lighterman's Ms, Grav. DA11 .190 GE87
Lightermans Rd, E14 .23 P4
Lightermans Way, Green. DA9 .169 FW84
Lightfoot Rd, N8 .121 DL57
Lightley Cl, Wem. HA0 off Stanley Av .138 CM66
Lightswood Cl, Wal.Cr. (Chsht) EN7 .66 DR27
Ligonier St, E2 .11 N3
Lilac Av, Enf. EN1 .82 DW36
Woking GU22 .226 AX120
Lilac Cl, E4 .101 DZ51
Brentwood (Pilg.Hat.) CM15 off Magnolia Way .108 FV43
Guildford GU1 .242 AW130
Waltham Cross (Chsht) EN7 off Greenwood Av .66 DV31
Lilac Ct, Slou. SL2 off Rokesby Rd .131 AM69
Lilac Gdns, W5 .157 CK76
Lilac Gdns, Croydon CR0 .203 EA104
Hayes UB3 .135 BS72
Romford RM7 .127 FE60
Swanley BR8 .207 FD97
Lilac Ms, N8 off Courcy Rd .121 DN55
Lilac Pl, SE11 .20 A8
West Drayton UB7 off Cedar Av .134 BM73
Lilac Rd, Hodd. EN11 .49 EB15
Lilac St, W12 .139 CU73
Lila Pl, Swan. BR8 .207 FE98
Lilbourne Dr, Hert. SG13 .32 DU08
Lilburne Gdns, SE9 .184 EL85
Lilburne Rd, SE9 .184 EL85
Lilburne Wk, NW10 .138 CQ65
Lile Cres, W7 .137 CE71
Lilestone Est, NW8 .7 N4
Lilestone St, NW8 .8 A3
Lilford Rd, SE5 .161 DP82
Lilian Barker Cl, SE12 .184 EG85
Sch Lilian Baylis Sch, SE11 .20 B8
Annexe, SE11 .20 B8
Lilian Board Way, Grnf. UB6 .117 CD64
Lilian Cl, N16 off Barbauld Rd .122 DS62
Lilian Cres, Brwd. (Hutt.) CM13 .109 GC47
Lilian Gdns, Wdf.Grn. IG8 .102 EH53
Lilian Rd, SW16 .201 DJ95
Lillechurch Rd, Dag. RM8 .146 EV65
Lilleshall Rd, Mord. SM4 .200 DD100
Lilley Cl, E1 .22 B2
Brentwood CM14 .108 FT49
Lilley Dr, Tad. (Kgswd) KT20 .234 DB122
Lilley La, NW7 .96 CR50
Lilley Way, Slou. SL1 .131 AL74
Lillian Av, W3 .158 CN75
Lillian Rd, SW13 .159 CU79
Lilliards Cl, Hodd. EN11 .33 EB13
Lillie Rd, SW6 .159 CY80
Westerham (Bigg.H.) TN16 .238 EK118
Lillieshall Rd, SW4 .161 DH83
Lillie Yd, SW6 .160 DA79
Lillingston Ho, N7 off Harvist Est .121 DN63
Lillington Gdns Est, SW1 .19 K8
Lilliots La, Lthd. KT22 off Kingston Rd .231 CG119
Lilliput Av, Nthlt. UB5 .136 BZ67
Lilliput Rd, Rom. RM7 .127 FD59
Lilly La, Hem.H. HP2 .41 BR16
Lily Cl, W14 .16 C8
Lily Dr, West Dr. UB7 .154 BK77
Lily Gdns, Wem. HA0 .137 CJ68
Lily Pl, EC1 .10 D5
Lily Rd, E17 .123 EA58
Lilyville Rd, SW6 .159 CZ81
Limbourne Av, Dag. RM8 .126 EZ59
Limburg Rd, SW11 .160 DF84
Lime Av, Brwd. CM13 .109 FZ48
Gravesend (Nthflt) DA11 .190 GD87
Upminster RM14 .128 FN63
West Drayton UB7 .134 BM73
Windsor SL4 .152 AT80
Limeburner La, EC4 .10 E8
Limebush Cl, Add. (New Haw) KT15 .212 BJ109
Lime Cl, E1 .22 B1
Bromley BR1 .204 EL98
Buckhurst Hill IG9 .102 EK48
Carshalton SM5 .200 DF103
Guildford (W.Clan.) GU4 .244 BH128
Harrow HA3 .95 CF54
Pinner HA5 .115 BT55
Reigate RH2 .266 DB137
Romford RM7 .127 FC56
South Ockendon RM15 .149 FW69
Ware SG12 .33 DY05
Watford WD19 .94 BX45
Lime Ct, Mitch. CR4 off Lewis Rd .200 DD96
Lime Cres, Sun. TW16 .196 BW96
Limecroft Cl, Epsom KT19 .216 CR108
Limedene Cl, Pnr. HA5 .94 BX53
Lime Gro, E4 .101 DZ51
N20 .97 CZ46
W12 .159 CW75
Addlestone KT15 .212 BG105
Guildford GU1 .242 AV130
Guildford (W.Clan.) GU4 .244 BG128
Hayes UB3 .135 BR73
Ilford IG6 .103 ET51
New Malden KT3 .198 CR97
Orpington BR6 .205 EP103
Ruislip HA4 .115 BV59
Sidcup DA15 .185 ET86
Twickenham TW1 .177 CF86
Warlingham CR6 .237 DY118
Woking GU22 .226 AY121
Limeharbour, E14 .24 B4
LIMEHOUSE, E14 .13 K9
⇌ Limehouse .13 J8
DLR Limehouse .13 J8
Limehouse Causeway, E14 .13 M9
Limehouse Flds Est, E14 .13 K6
Limehouse Link, E14 .13 M10
Limekiln Dr, SE7 .164 EH79
Limekiln Pl, SE19 .182 DT94
Lime Meadow Av, S.Croy. CR2 .220 DU113
Lime Pit La, Sev. TN14 .241 FC117
Limerick Cl, SW12 .181 DJ87
Limerick Gdns, Upmin. RM14 .129 FT59
Lime Rd, Epp. CM16 .69 ET31
Richmond TW9 off St. Mary's Gro .158 CM84
Swanley BR8 .207 FD97
Lime Row, Erith DA18 off Northwood Pl .166 EZ76
Limerston St, SW10 .160 DC79
Limes, The, W2 .7 H10
Amersham HP6 .55 AP35
Brentwood CM13 .109 FZ48
Bromley BR2 .204 EL103
Hornchurch RM11 .128 FK55
Purfleet RM19 off Tank Hill Rd .168 FN78
St. Albans AL1 .43 CE18
Welwyn Garden City AL7 .30 DA11
Woking GU21 .226 AX115
Limes Av, E11 .124 EH56
N12 .98 DC49
NW7 .96 CS51
NW11 .119 CY59
SE20 .182 DV94
SW13 .159 CT82
Carshalton SM5 .200 DF102
Chigwell IG7 .103 ER51
Croydon CR0 .201 DN104
Horley RH6 .269 DH150
Limes Av, The, N11 .99 DH50
Limes Cl, Ashf. TW15 .174 BN92
Limes Ct, Brwd. CM15 off Sawyers Hall La .108 FX46
Hoddesdon EN11 off Charlton Way .49 EA17
Limesdale Gdns, Edg. HA8 .96 CQ54
Sch Limes Fm Co Inf Sch, Chig. IG7 off Limes Av .103 ER50
Sch Limes Fm Co Jun Sch, Chig. IG7 off Limes Av .103 ER50
Limes Fld Rd, SW14 off White Hart La .158 CS83
Limesford Rd, SE15 .163 DX84
Limes Gdns, SW18 .180 DA86
Limes Gro, SE13 .163 EC84
Limes Pl, Croy. CR0 .202 DR101
Limes Rd, Beck. BR3 .203 EB96
Croydon CR0 .202 DR100
Egham TW20 .173 AZ92
Waltham Cross (Chsht) EN8 .67 DX32
Weybridge KT13 .212 BN105
Limes Row, Orp. BR6 off Orchard Rd .223 EP106
Limestone Wk, Erith DA18 .166 EX76
Lime St, E17 .123 DY56
EC3 .11 L9
Lime St Pas, EC3 .11 L8
Limes Wk, SE15 .162 DV84
W5 off Chestnut Gro .157 CK75
Lime Ter, W7 off Manor Ct Rd .137 CE73
Lime Tree Av, Esher KT10 .197 CD102
Greenhithe (Bluewater) DA9 .189 FU88
Thames Ditton KT7 .197 CD102
Limetree Cl, SW2 .181 DM88
Lime Tree Cl, Lthd. (Bkhm) KT23 .230 CA124
Lime Tree Gro, Croy. CR0 .203 DZ104
Lime Tree Pl, Mitch. CR4 .201 DH95
St. Albans AL1 .43 CF21
Lime Tree Rd, Houns. TW5 .156 CB81
Limetree Ter, Well. DA16 off Hook La .166 EU83
Limetree Wk, SW17 off Church La .180 DG92
Lime Tree Wk, Amer. HP7 .72 AT39
Bushey (Bushey Hth) WD23 .95 CE46
Enfield EN2 .82 DQ38
Rickmansworth WD3 .74 BH43
Sevenoaks TN13 .257 FH125
Virginia Water GU25 .192 AY98
West Wickham BR4 .222 EF105
Lime Wk, E15 off Church St N .144 EE67
Guildford (Shere) GU5 .260 BM139
Hemel Hempstead HP3 .40 BM22
Uxbridge (Denh.) UB9 .114 BJ64
Sch Lime Wk Prim Sch, Hem.H. HP3 off Lime Wk .40 BM22
Limeway Ter, Dor. RH4 .247 CG134
Limewood Cl, E17 .123 DZ56
W13 off St. Stephens Rd .137 CH72
Beckenham BR3 .203 EC99
Limewood Ct, Ilf. IG4 .125 EM57
Limewood Rd, Erith DA8 .167 FC80
Lime Wks Rd, Red. (Merst.) RH1 .251 DJ126
LIMPSFIELD, Oxt. RH8 .254 EG128
Limpsfield Av, SW19 .179 CX89
Thornton Heath CR7 .201 DM99
LIMPSFIELD CHART, Oxt. RH8 .254 EL130
Sch Limpsfield C of E Inf Sch, Oxt. RH8 off Westerham Rd .254 EJ129
Sch Limpsfield Gra Sch, Oxt. RH8 off Bluehouse La .254 EG127
Limpsfield Rd, S.Croy. CR2 .220 DU112
Warlingham CR6 .236 DW116
Linacre Cl, SE15 .162 DW83
Linacre Ct, W6 .16 B9
Linacre Rd, NW2 .139 CV65
Linberry Wk, SE8 .23 L8
Lince La, Dor. (Westc.) RH4 .263 CD136
Linces Way, Welw.G.C. AL7 .30 DB11
Linchfield Rd, Slou. (Datchet) SL3 .152 AW81
Linchmere Rd, SE12 .184 EF87
Lincoln Av, N14 .99 DJ48
SW19 .179 CX90
Romford RM7 .127 FD60
Twickenham TW2 .176 CB89
Lincoln Cl, SE25 off Woodside Grn .202 DU100
Erith DA8 .167 FF82
Greenford UB6 .136 CC67
Harrow HA2 .116 BZ57
Horley RH6 .268 DG149
Hornchurch RM11 .128 FN57
Welwyn Garden City AL7 .30 DD08
Lincoln Ct, N16 .122 DR59
Berkhamsted HP4 .38 AV19
Borehamwood WD6 .78 CR43
Lincoln Cres, Enf. EN1 .82 DS43
Lincoln Dr, Rick. (Crox.Grn) WD3 .75 BP42
Watford WD19 .94 BW48
Woking GU22 .227 BE115
Lincoln Gdns, Ilf. IG1 .124 EL59
Lincoln Grn Rd, Orp. BR5 .205 ET99
Lincoln Hatch La, Slou. (Burn.) SL1 .130 AJ70
Lincoln Ms, NW6 off Willesden La .139 CZ67
SE21 .182 DR88
Lincoln Pk, Amer. HP7 .55 AS39
Lincoln Rd, E7 .144 EK65
E13 .15 N4
E18 off Grove Rd .102 EG53
N2 .120 DE55
SE25 .202 DV97
Dorking RH4 .247 CJ134
Enfield EN1, EN3 .82 DU43
Erith DA8 .167 FF82
Feltham TW13 .176 BZ90
Gerrards Cross (Chal.St.P.) SL9 .90 AY53
Guildford GU2 .242 AT132
Harrow HA2 .116 BZ57
Mitcham CR4 .201 DL99
New Malden KT3 .198 CQ97
Northwood HA6 .115 BT55
Sidcup DA14 .186 EV92
Wembley HA0 .137 CK65
Worcester Park KT4 .199 CV102
Lincolns, The, NW7 .97 CT48
Lincolns Cl, St.Alb. AL4 .43 CJ15

Lincolns Flds, Epp. CM16 ...69 ET29
Lincolnshott, Grav. (Sthflt) DA13 ...190 GB92
★ Lincoln's Inn, WC2 ...10 B7
Lincoln's Inn Flds, WC2 ...10 A7
Lincoln St, E11 ...124 EE61
SW3 ...18 C8
Lincoln Wk, Epsom KT19 off Hollymoor La ...216 CR110
Lincoln Way, Enf. EN1 ...82 DV43
Rickmansworth (Crox.Grn) WD3 ...75 BP42
Slough SL1 ...131 AK73
Sunbury-on-Thames TW16 ...195 BS95
Lincombe Rd, Brom. BR1 ...184 EF90
Lindal Cres, Enf. EN2 ...81 DL42
Lindale Cl, Vir.W. GU25 ...192 AT98
Lindales, The, N17 off Brantwood Rd ...100 DT51
Lindal Rd, SE4 ...183 DZ85
Lindbergh, Welw.G.C. AL7 ...30 DC09
Lindbergh Rd, Wall. SM6 ...219 DL109
Linden Av, NW10 ...139 CX68
Coulsdon CR5 ...235 DH116
Dartford DA1 ...188 FJ88
Enfield EN1 ...82 DU39
Hounslow TW3 ...176 CB85
Ruislip HA4 ...115 BU60
Thornton Heath CR7 ...201 DP98
Wembley HA9 ...118 CM64
Sch Linden Br Sch, Wor.Pk. KT4 off Grafton Rd ...198 CS104
Linden Chase Rd, Sev. TN13 .257 FH122
Linden Cl, N14 ...81 DJ44
Addlestone (New Haw) KT15 ...212 BG111
Orpington BR6 ...224 EU106
Purfleet RM19 ...168 FQ79
Ruislip HA4 ...115 BU60
Stanmore HA7 ...95 CH50
Tadworth KT20 ...233 CX120
Thames Ditton KT7 ...197 CF101
Waltham Cross EN7 ...66 DV30
Linden Ct, W12 ...139 CW74
Egham (Eng.Grn) TW20 ...172 AV93
Leatherhead KT22 ...231 CH121
Linden Cres, Grnf. UB6 ...137 CF65
Kingston upon Thames KT1 ...198 CM96
St. Albans AL1 ...43 CJ20
Woodford Green IG8 ...102 EH51
Linden Dr, Cat. CR3 ...236 DQ124
Gerrards Cross (Chal.St.P.) SL9 off Woodside Hill ...90 AY54
Slough (Farn.Royal) SL2 .131 AQ66
Lindenfield, Chis. BR7 ...205 EP96
Linden Gdns, W2 ...7 H10
W4 ...158 CR78
Enfield EN1 ...82 DU39
Leatherhead KT22 ...231 CJ121
Linden Glade, Hem.H. HP1 ..40 BG21
Linden Gro, SE15 ...162 DV83
SE26 ...182 DW93
New Malden KT3 ...198 CS97
Teddington TW11 off Waldegrave Rd ...177 CF92
Walton-on-Thames KT12 .195 BT103
Warlingham CR6 ...237 DY118
Linden Ho, Slou. SL3 ...153 BB78
Linden Lawns, Wem. HA9 ..118 CM63
Linden Lea, N2 ...120 DC57
Watford WD25 ...59 BU33
Linden Leas, W.Wick. BR4 .203 ED103
Sch Linden Lo Sch, SW19 off Princes Way ...179 CY88
Linden Ms, N1 ...5 K2
W2 ...7 H10
Linden Pas, W4 off Linden Gdns ...158 CR78
Linden Pit Path, Lthd. KT22 .231 CH121
Linden Pl, Epsom KT17 off East St ...216 CS112
Leatherhead KT24 off Station App ...245 BS126
Mitcham CR4 ...200 DE98
Linden Ri, Brwd. CM14 ...108 FX50
Linden Rd, E17 off High St .123 DZ57
N10 ...121 DH56
N11 ...98 DF47
N15 ...122 DQ56
Guildford GU1 ...242 AX134
Hampton TW12 ...176 CA94
Leatherhead KT22 ...231 CH121
Weybridge KT13 ...213 BQ109
Lindens, The, N12 ...98 DD50
W4 off Hartington Rd ...158 CQ81
Croydon (New Adgtn) CR0 ...221 EC107
Hemel Hempstead HP3 ...39 BF23
Loughton IG10 ...85 EM43
Lindens Cl, Lthd. (Eff.) KT24 off Mount Pleasant ...246 BY128
Linden Sq, Sev. TN13 off London Rd ...256 FE122
Uxbridge (Hare.) UB9 ...92 BG51
Linden St, Rom. RM7 ...127 FD56
Linden Wk, N19 off Hargrave Pk ...121 DJ61
Linden Way, N14 ...81 DJ44
Purley CR8 ...219 DJ110
Shepperton TW17 ...195 BQ99
Woking GU22 ...227 AZ121
Woking (Send M.) GU23 .227 BF124
Lindeth Cl, Stan. HA7 ...95 CH51
Lindfield Gdns, NW3 ...120 DB64
Guildford GU1 ...243 AZ133
Lindfield Rd, W5 ...137 CJ70
Croydon CR0 ...202 DT100
Romford RM3 ...106 FL50
Lindfield St, E14 ...13 P7
Lindhill Cl, Enf. EN3 ...83 DX39
Lindisfarne Cl, Grav. DA12 off St. Benedict's Av ...191 GL89
Lindisfarne Rd, SW20 ...179 CU94
Dagenham RM8 ...126 EW62
Lindisfarne Way, E9 ...123 DY63
Lindley Est, SE15 off Bird in Bush Rd ...162 DU80
Lindley Pl, Rich. TW9 ...158 CN81
Lindley Rd, E10 ...123 EB61
Godstone RH9 ...252 DW130
Walton-on-Thames KT12 .196 BX104
Lindley St, E1 ...12 E5
Lindlings, Hem.H. HP1 ...39 BE21
Lindo Cl, Chesh. HP5 ...54 AP30
Sch Lindon Bennett Sch, Felt. TW13 off Main St ...176 BX92
Lindore Rd, SW11 ...160 DF84
Lindores Rd, Cars. SM5 ...200 DC101
Lindo St, SE15 off Selden Rd ...162 DW82
Lind Rd, Sutt. SM1 ...218 DC106
Lindrop St, SW6 ...160 DC82
Lindsay Cl, Chess. KT9 ...216 CL108
Epsom KT19 ...216 CQ113
Staines (Stanw.) TW19 ...174 BK85
Lindsay Dr, Har. HA3 ...118 CL58
Shepperton TW17 ...195 BR100
Lindsay Pl, Wal.Cr. EN7 ...66 DV30
Lindsay Rd, Add. (New Haw) KT15 ...212 BG110
Hampton (Hmptn H.) TW12 ...176 CB91
Worcester Park KT4 ...199 CV103
Lindsay Sq, SW1 ...19 M9
Lindsell St, SE10 ...163 EC81
Lindsey Cl, Brwd. CM14 ...108 FU49
Bromley BR1 ...204 EK97
Mitcham CR4 ...201 DL98
Lindsey Gdns, Felt. TW14 ...175 BR87
Lindsey Ms, N1 ...5 H5
Lindsey Rd, Dag. RM8 ...126 EW63
Uxbridge (Denh.) UB9 ...114 BG62
Lindsey St, EC1 ...10 F5
Epping CM16 ...69 ER28
Lindsey Way, Horn. RM11 ...128 FJ57
Lind St, SE8 ...163 EB82
Lindum Pl, St.Alb. AL3 ...42 BZ22
Lindum Rd, Tedd. TW11 ...177 CJ94
Lindvale, Wok. GU21 ...226 AY115
Lindway, SE27 ...181 DP92
Lindwood Cl, E6 off Northumberland Rd .144 EL71
Linfield Cl, NW4 ...119 CW55
Walton-on-Thames KT12 .213 BV106
Linfield Ct, Hert. SG14 off The Ridgeway ...31 DM08
Linfields, Amer. HP7 ...72 AW40
LINFORD, S.le H. SS17 ...171 GM75
Linford Cl, Harl. CM19 ...51 EP17
Linford End, Harl. CM19 ...51 EQ17
Linford Rd, E17 ...123 EC55
Grays RM16 ...171 GH78
Tilbury (W.Til.) RM18 ...171 GJ77
Linford St, SW8 ...161 DJ81
Lingards Rd, SE13 ...163 EC84
Lingey Cl, Sid. DA15 ...185 ET89
Lingfield Av, Dart. DA2 ...188 FP87
Kingston upon Thames KT1 ...198 CL98
Upminster RM14 ...128 FM62
Lingfield Cl, Enf. EN1 ...82 DS44
Northwood HA6 ...93 BS52
Lingfield Cres, SE9 ...165 ER84
Lingfield Gdns, N9 ...100 DV45
Coulsdon CR5 ...235 DP119
Lingfield Rd, SW19 ...179 CX92
Gravesend DA12 ...191 GH89
Worcester Park KT4 ...199 CW104
Lingfield Way, Wat. WD17 ...75 BT38
Lingham St, SW9 ...161 DL82
Lingholm Way, Barn. EN5 ...79 CX43
Lingmere Cl, Chig. IG7 ...103 EQ47
Lingmoor Dr, Wat. WD25 ...60 BW33
Ling Rd, E16 ...15 M5
Erith DA8 ...167 FC79
Lingrove Gdns, Buck.H. IG9 off Beech La ...102 EH47
Lings Coppice, SE21 ...182 DR89
Lingwell Rd, SW17 ...180 DE90
Lingwood Gdns, Islw. TW7 .157 CE80
Lingwood Rd, E5 ...122 DU59
Linhope St, NW1 ...8 C3
Linington Av, Chesh. HP5 ...56 AU30
Link, The, SE9 ...185 EN90
W3 ...138 CP72
Enfield EN3 ...83 DY39
Northolt UB5 off Eastcote La ...116 BZ64
Pinner HA5 ...116 BW59
Slough SL2 ...132 AV72
Wembley HA0 off Nathans Rd ...117 CJ60
Link Av, Wok. GU22 ...227 BD115
Link Cl, Hat. AL10 ...45 CV18
Link Dr, Hat. AL10 ...45 CV18
Linkfield, Brom. BR2 ...204 EG100
Welwyn Garden City AL7 ..29 CY13
West Molesey KT8 ...196 CA97
Linkfield Cor, Red. RH1 off Hatchlands Rd ...250 DE133
Linkfield Gdns, Red. RH1 off Hatchlands Rd ...250 DE134
Linkfield La, Red. RH1 ...250 DE133
Linkfield Rd, Islw. TW7 ...157 CF82
Linkfield St, Red. RH1 ...250 DE134
Link La, Wall. SM6 ...219 DK107
Linklea Cl, NW9 ...96 CS52
Sch Link Prim Day Sch, The, Croy. CR0 off Croydon Rd ...219 DL105
Link Rd, N11 ...98 DG49
Addlestone KT15 off Weybridge Rd ...212 BL105
Dagenham RM9 ...147 FB68
Feltham TW14 ...175 BT87
Hemel Hempstead HP1, HP2 ...40 BJ17
Rickmansworth (Chenies) WD3 ...73 BA37
Slough (Datchet) SL3 ...152 AW80
Wallington SM6 ...200 DG102
Watford WD24 ...76 BX40
Links, The, E17 ...123 DY56
Waltham Cross (Chsht) EN8 ...67 DX26
Walton-on-Thames KT12 .195 BU103
Welwyn Garden City AL8 off Applecroft Rd ...29 CV09
Links Av, Hert. SG13 ...32 DV08
Morden SM4 ...200 DA98
Romford RM2 ...105 FH54
Links Brow, Lthd. (Fetch.) KT22 ...231 CE124
Links Cl, Ashtd. KT21 ...231 CJ117
Linkscroft Av, Ashf. TW15 ...175 BP93
Links Dr, N20 ...98 DA46
Borehamwood (Elstree) WD6 ...78 CM41
Radlett WD7 ...61 CF33
Sch Link Sec Day Sch, The, Croy. CR0 off Croydon Rd ...219 DM105
Links Gdns, SW16 ...181 DN94
Links Grn Way, Cob. KT11 ..214 CA114
Linkside, N12 ...97 CZ51
Chigwell IG7 ...103 EQ50
New Malden KT3 ...198 CS96
Linkside Cl, Enf. EN2 ...81 DM41
Linkside Gdns, Enf. EN2 ...81 DM41
Links Pl, Ashtd. KT21 ...231 CK117
Sch Links Prim Sch, SW17 off Frinton Rd ...180 DG93
Links Rd, NW2 ...119 CT61
SW17 ...180 DF93
W3 ...138 CN72
Ashford TW15 ...174 BL92
Ashtead KT21 ...231 CJ118
Epsom KT17 ...217 CU113
Guildford (Bramley) GU5 ..258 AY144
High Wycombe (Flack.Hth) HP10 ...110 AC56
West Wickham BR4 ...203 EC102
Woodford Green IG8 ...102 EG50
Links Side, Enf. EN2 ...81 DN41
Link St, E9 ...142 DW65
Links Vw, N3 ...97 CZ52
Dartford DA1 ...188 FJ88
St. Albans AL3 ...42 CB18
Links Vw Av, Bet. (Brock.) RH3 ...248 CN134
Links Vw Cl, Stan. HA7 ...95 CG51
Links Vw Rd, Croy. CR0 ...203 EA104
Hampton (Hmptn H.) TW12 ...176 CC92
Linksway, NW4 ...97 CX54
Links Way, Beck. BR3 ...203 EA100
Leatherhead (Bkhm) KT23 ...246 BY128
Linksway, Nthwd. HA6 ...93 BQ53
Links Way, Rick. (Crox.Grn) WD3 ...75 BQ41
Linkswood Rd, Slou. (Burn.) SL1 ...130 AJ68
Links Yd, E1 ...12 A5
Link Wk, Hat. AL10 ...45 CV17
Linkway, N4 ...122 DQ59
SW20 ...199 CV97
Link Way, Brom. BR2 ...204 EL101
Linkway, Dag. RM8 ...126 EW63
Guildford GU2 ...242 AT133
Harlow CM20 off North Gate ...35 EQ14
Link Way, Horn. RM11 ...128 FL60
Pinner HA5 ...94 BX53
Linkway, Rich. TW10 ...177 CH89
Link Way, Stai. TW18 ...174 BH93
Uxbridge (Denh.) UB9 ...114 BG58
Linkway, Wok. GU22 ...227 BC117
Linkway, The, Barn. EN5 ...80 DB44
Sutton SM2 ...218 DC109
Link Way Rd, Brwd. CM14 ..108 FT48
Linkwood Wk, NW1 off Maiden La ...141 DK66
Linley Cres, Rom. RM7 ...127 FB55
Linley Rd, N17 ...100 DS54
★ Linley Sambourne Ho, W8 ...17 H4
Linnell Cl, NW11 ...120 DB58
Linnell Dr, NW11 ...120 DB58
Linnell Rd, N18 off Fairfield Rd ...100 DU50
SE5 ...162 DS82
Redhill RH1 ...266 DG135
Linnet Cl, N9 ...101 DX46
SE28 ...146 EW73
Bushey WD23 ...94 CC45
South Croydon CR2 ...221 DX110
Linnet Gro, Guil. GU4 off Partridge Way ...243 BD132
Linnet Ms, SW12 ...180 DG87
Linnet Rd, Abb.L. WD5 ...59 BU31
Linnett Cl, E4 ...101 EC49
Linnet Ter, Ilf. IG5 off Tiptree Cres ...125 EN55
Linnet Wk, Hat. AL10 off Lark Ri ...45 CU20
Linnet Way, Purf. RM19 ...168 FP78
Linom Rd, SW4 ...161 DL84
Linscott Rd, E5 ...122 DW63
Linsdell Rd, Bark. IG11 ...145 EQ67
Linsey Cl, Hem.H. HP3 ...40 BN24
Linsey St, SE16 ...22 A7
Linslade Cl, Houns. TW4 off Frampton Rd ...176 BY85
Pinner HA5 ...115 BV55
Linslade Rd, Orp. BR6 ...224 EU107
Linstead St, NW6 ...140 DA66
Linstead Way, SW18 ...179 CY87
Linsted Ct, SE9 ...185 ES86
Linster Gro, Borwd. WD6 ...78 CQ43
Lintaine Cl, W6 off Moylan Rd ...159 CY79
Linthorpe Av, Wem. HA0 ...137 CJ65
Linthorpe Rd, N16 ...122 DS59
Barnet EN4 ...80 DE41
Linton Av, Borwd. WD6 ...78 CM39
Linton Cl, Mitch. CR4 ...200 DF101
Welling DA16 off Anthony Rd ...166 EV81
Linton Gdns, E6 ...144 EL72
Linton Glade, Croy. CR0 ...221 DY109
Linton Gro, SE27 ...181 DP92
Sch Linton Mead Prim Sch, SE28 off Central Way ...146 EV73
Linton Rd, Bark. IG11 ...145 EQ66
Lintons, The, Bark. IG11 ...145 EQ66
Lintons La, Epsom KT17 ...216 CS112
Linton St, N1 ...5 H8
Lintott Ct, Stai. (Stanw.) TW19 ...174 BK86
Linver Rd, SW6 ...160 DA82
Linwood, Saw. CM21 ...36 EY05
Linwood Cl, SE5 ...162 DT82
Linwood Cres, Enf. EN1 ...82 DU39
Linwood Way, SE15 off Daniel Gdns ...162 DT80
Linzee Rd, N8 ...121 DL56
Lion Av, Twick. TW1 off Lion Rd ...177 CF88
Lion Cl, SE4 ...183 EA86
Shepperton TW17 ...194 BL97
Lion Ct, Borwd. WD6 ...78 CQ39
Lionel Gdns, SE9 ...184 EK85
Lionel Ms, W10 ...6 C5
Lionel Oxley Ho, Grays RM17 off New Rd ...170 GB79
Sch Lionel Prim Sch, Brent. TW8 off Lionel Rd N ...158 CL77
Lionel Rd, SE9 ...184 EK85
Lionel Rd N, Brent. TW8 ...158 CL77
Lionel Rd S, Brent. TW8 ...158 CM78
Lion Gate Gdns, Rich. TW9 .158 CM83
Lion Gate Ms, SW18 off Merton Rd ...180 DA87
Lion Grn Rd, Couls. CR5 ...235 DK115
Lion La, Red. RH1 ...250 DF133
Lion Pk Av, Chess. KT9 ...216 CN105
Lion Plaza, EC2 off Threadneedle St ...142 DR72
Lion Rd, E6 ...145 EM71
N9 ...100 DU47
Bexleyheath DA6 ...166 EZ84
Croydon CR0 ...202 DQ99
Twickenham TW1 ...177 CF88
Lions Cl, SE9 ...184 EJ90
Lion Way, Brent. TW8 ...157 CK80
Lion Wf Rd, Islw. TW7 ...157 CH83
Lion Yd, SW4 off Tremadoc Rd ...161 DK84
Liphook Cl, Horn. RM12 off Petworth Way ...127 FF63
Liphook Cres, SE23 ...182 DW87
Liphook Rd, Wat. WD19 ...94 BX49
Lippitts Hill, Loug. (High Beach) IG10 ...84 EE39
Lipsham Cl, Bans. SM7 ...218 DD113
Lipton Cl, SE28 off Aisher Rd ...146 EW73
Lipton Rd, E1 ...12 G8
Lisbon Av, Twick. TW2 ...176 CC89
Lisbon Cl, E17 ...101 DZ54
Lisburne Rd, NW3 ...120 DF63
Lisford St, SE15 ...162 DT81
Lisgar Ter, W14 ...16 E7
Liskeard Cl, Chis. BR7 ...185 EQ93
Liskeard Gdns, SE3 ...164 EG81
Liskeard Lo, Cat. CR3 ...252 DU126
Lisle Cl, SW17 ...181 DH91
Lisle Pl, Grays RM17 ...170 GA76
Lisle St, WC2 ...9 M9
Lismore, Hem.H. HP3 ...41 BQ22
Lismore Circ, NW5 ...120 DG64
Lismore Cl, Islw. TW7 ...157 CG82
Lismore Pk, Slou. SL2 ...132 AT72
Lismore Rd, N17 ...122 DR55
South Croydon CR2 ...220 DS107
Lismore Wk, N1 ...5 H3
Lissant Cl, Surb. KT6 off Lovelace Rd ...197 CK101
Lissenden Gdns, NW5 ...120 DG63
Lissoms Rd, Couls. CR5 ...234 DG118
Lisson Grn Est, NW8 ...8 A2
LISSON GROVE, NW8 ...7 P4
Lisson Gro, NW1 ...8 A3
NW8 ...7 P2
Lisson St, NW1 ...8 A5
Liss Way, SE15 off Pentridge St ...162 DT80
Lister Av, Rom. RM3 ...106 FK54
Lister Cl, W3 ...138 CR71
Mitcham CR4 ...200 DE95
Sch Lister Comm Sch, E13 off St. Marys Rd ...144 EH68
Lister Ct, NW9 off Pasteur Cl ...96 CS54
Lister Gdns, N18 ...100 DQ50
H Lister Hosp, The, SW1 ...18 G10
Lister Ho, SE3 ...164 EE79
Lister Rd, E11 ...124 EE60
Tilbury RM18 ...171 GG82
Lister Wk, SE28 off Haldane Rd ...146 EX73
Liston Rd, N17 ...100 DU53
SW4 ...161 DJ83
Liston Way, Wdf.Grn. IG8 off Navestock Cres ...102 EJ52
Listowel Cl, SW9 off Mandela St ...161 DN80
Listowel Rd, Dag. RM10 ...126 FA62
Listria Pk, N16 ...122 DS61
Litcham Spur, Slou. SL1 ...131 AR72
Litchfield Av, E15 ...144 EE65
Morden SM4 ...199 CZ101
Litchfield Gdns, NW10 ...139 CU65
Cobham KT11 off Between Sts ...213 BU114
Litchfield Rd, Sutt. SM1 ...218 DC105
Litchfield St, WC2 ...9 M9
Litchfield Way, NW11 ...120 DB57
Guildford GU2 ...258 AT136
Lithos Rd, NW3 ...140 DB65
Little Acre, Beck. BR3 ...203 EA97
St. Albans AL3 ...43 CD17
Little Acres, Ware SG12 ...33 DX07
Little Albany St, NW1 ...9 H3
Little Argyll St, W1 ...9 J8
Little Aston Rd, Rom. RM3 .106 FM52
Little Belhus Cl, S.Ock. RM15 ...149 FU70
Little Benty, West Dr. UB7 ..154 BK78
LITTLE BERKHAMSTED, Hert. SG13 ...47 DH18
Little Berkhamsted La, Hert. SG13 ...47 DH20
Little Birch Cl, Add. (New Haw) KT15 ...212 BK109
Little Birches, Sid. DA15 ...185 ES89
Little Boltons, The, SW5 ...17 K9
SW10 ...17 K9
LITTLE BOOKHAM, Lthd. KT23 ...246 BY125
Little Bookham Common, Lthd. (Bkhm) KT23 ...230 BY122
Little Bookham St, Lthd. (Bkhm) KT23 ...230 BZ124
Little Bornes, SE21 ...182 DS91
Little Borough, Bet. (Brock.) RH3 ...264 CN135
Little Brays, Harl. CM18 ...52 EU16
Little Br Rd, Berk. HP4 ...38 AX19
Little Britain, EC1 ...10 G7
Littlebrook Av, Slou. SL2 ...131 AL70
Littlebrook Cl, Croy. CR0 ...203 DX100
Littlebrook Gdns, Wal.Cr. (Chsht) EN8 ...66 DW30
Littlebrook Manor Way, Dart. DA1 ...188 FN85
Little Brook Rd, Harl. (Roydon) CM19 ...50 EJ15
Little Brownings, SE23 ...182 DV89
Little Buntings, Wind. SL4 ..151 AM83
Little Burrow, Welw.G.C. AL7 .29 CX11
Littlebury Rd, SW4 ...161 DK83
Little Bury St, N9 ...100 DR46
Little Bushey La, Bushey WD23 ...77 CD44
Little Bushey La Footpath, Bushey WD23 off Little Bushey La ...95 CD45
Little Catherells, Hem.H. HP1 ...39 BE18
Little Cattins, Harl. CM19 ...51 EM19
Little Cedars, N12 off Woodside Av ...98 DC49
LITTLE CHALFONT, Amer. HP7 ...72 AW40
LITTLE CHALFONT, Ch.St.G. HP8 ...72 AW40
Sch Little Chalfont Co Comb Sch, Amer. HP6 off Oakington Av ...72 AY39
Little Chapels Way, Slou. SL1 ...151 AN75
Little Chester St, SW1 ...18 F5
Little Cloisters, SW1 off Tufton St ...161 DK76
Little Coll La, EC4 off Upper Thames St ...142 DR73
Little Coll St, SW1 ...19 N5
Little Collins, Red. (Outwood) RH1 ...267 DP144
Littlecombe, SE7 ...164 EH79
Littlecombe Cl, SW15 ...179 CX86
Little Common, Stan. HA7 ...95 CG48
Little Common La, Red. (Bletch.) RH1 ...251 DP132
Littlecote Cl, SW19 ...179 CX87
Littlecote Pl, Pnr. HA5 ...94 BY53
Little Ct, W.Wick. BR4 ...204 EE103
Littlecourt Rd, Sev. TN13 ...256 FG124
Little Cranmore La, Lthd. (W.Hors.) KT24 ...245 BP128
Littlecroft, SE9 ...165 EN83
Gravesend (Istead Rise) DA13 ...190 GE94
Littlecroft Rd, Egh. TW20 ...173 AZ92
Littledale, SE2 ...166 EU79
Dartford DA2 ...188 FQ90
Little Dean's Yd, SW1 ...19 N5
Little Dell, Welw.G.C. AL8 ...29 CX07
Little Dimocks, SW12 ...181 DH89
Little Dormers, Ger.Cr. SL9 .113 AZ56
Little Dorrit Ct, SE1 ...21 H3
Littledown Rd, Slou. SL1 ...132 AT74
Little Dragons, Loug. IG10 ...84 EK42
LITTLE EALING, W5 ...157 CJ77
Little Ealing La, W5 ...157 CJ77
Sch Little Ealing Prim Sch, W5 off Weymouth Av ...157 CJ76
Little E Fld, Couls. CR5 off Blue Leaves Av ...235 DK121
Little Edward St, NW1 ...9 H1
Little Elms, Hayes UB3 ...155 BR80
Little Essex St, WC2 ...10 C9
Little Ferry Rd, Twick. TW1 off Ferry Rd ...177 CH88
Littlefield Cl, N19 off Tufnell Pk Rd ...121 DJ63
Kingston upon Thames KT1 off Fairfield W ...198 CL96
Littlefield Rd, Edg. HA8 ...96 CQ52
Littleford La, Guil. GU4, GU5 ...259 BE142
Little Friday Rd, E4 ...102 EE47
Sch Little Furze JMI Sch, Wat. WD19 off Gosforth La ...93 BV48
Little Ganett, Welw.G.C. AL7 .30 DB11
Little Gaynes Gdns, Upmin. RM14 ...128 FP63
Little Gaynes La, Upmin. RM14 ...128 FM63
Little Gearies, Ilf. IG6 ...125 EP56
Little George St, SW1 ...19 N4
Little Gerpins La, Upmin. RM14 ...148 FM67
Little Gra, Grnf. UB6 off Perivale La ...137 CG69
Little Graylings, Abb.L. WD5 .59 BS33
Little Grn, Rich. TW9 ...157 CK84
Little Greencroft, Chesh. HP5 .54 AN27
Sch Little Grn Jun Sch, Rick. WD3 off Lincoln Dr ...75 BP41
Little Grn La, Cher. KT16 ...193 BE104
Rickmansworth (Crox.Grn) WD3 ...75 BP41
Little Grn St, NW5 off College La ...121 DH63
Little Gregories La, Epp. (They.B.) CM16 ...85 ER35
Littlegrove, Barn. EN4 ...80 DE44
Little Gro, Bushey WD23 ...76 CB42
Little Gro Av, Wal.Cr. (Chsht) EN7 ...66 DS27
Little Gro Fld, Harl. CM19 ...51 EQ15
Little Halliards, Walt. KT12 off Felix Rd ...195 BU100
Little Hardings, Welw.G.C. AL7 ...30 DC08
Little Hayes, Kings L. WD4 ..58 BN29
Little Heath, SE7 ...164 EL79
Romford (Chad.Hth) RM6 .126 EV56
Little Heath La, Berk. HP4 ...39 BB21
Littleheath La, Cob. KT11 ...214 CA114
Little Heath La, Wok. (Chobham) GU24 ...210 AS109
Sch Little Heath Prim Sch, Pot.B. EN6 off School Rd ..64 DC30
Little Heath Rd, Bexh. DA7 .166 EZ81
Littleheath Rd, S.Croy. CR2 .220 DV108
Little Heath Rd, Wok. (Chobham) GU24 ...210 AS109
Sch Little Heath Spec Sch, Rom. RM6 off Hainault Rd ...126 EV56
Little Henleys, Ware SG12 ...34 EK06
Little Hide, Guil. GU1 ...243 BB132
H Little Highwood Hosp, Brwd. CM15 ...108 FV45
Little Hill, Rick. (Herons.) WD3 ...73 BC44
Little Hivings, Chesh. HP5 ...54 AN27
★ Little Holland Ho, Cars. SM5 ...218 DE108
Littlehorse La, Ware SG12 ...33 DX05
Little How Cft, Abb.L. WD5 ..59 BQ31
LITTLE ILFORD, E12 ...124 EL64
Little Ilford La, E12 ...125 EM63
Sch Little Ilford Sec Sch, E12 off Browning Rd ...125 EM64
Littlejohn Rd, W7 ...137 CF72
Orpington BR5 ...206 EU100
Little Julians Hill, Sev. TN13 .256 FG128
Little Kiln, Gdmg. GU7 ...258 AS143
Little Lake, Welw.G.C. AL7 ...30 DB12
Little Ley, Welw.G.C. AL7 ...29 CY12
Little London, Guil. (Albury) GU5 ...260 BL141
Little London Cl, Uxb. UB8 .135 BP71
Little Marlborough St, W1 ...9 J8
Little Martins, Bushey WD23 .76 CB43
Littlemead, Esher KT10 ...215 CD105
Little Mead, Hat. AL10 ...45 CV15
Woking GU21 ...226 AT116
Littlemede, SE9 ...185 EM90
Little Mimms, Hem.H. HP2 ...40 BK19
Littlemoor Rd, Ilf. IG1 ...125 ER62
Littlemore Rd, SE2 ...166 EU75
Little Moreton Cl, W.Byf. KT14 ...212 BH112
Little Moss La, Pnr. HA5 ...94 BY54
Little Mundells, Welw.G.C. AL7 ...29 CZ07
Little Newport St, WC2 ...9 M9
Little New St, EC4 ...10 D7
Little Oaks Cl, Shep. TW17 ..194 BM98
Little Orchard, Add. (Wdhm) KT15 ...211 BF111
Hemel Hempstead HP2 ...40 BN18
Woking GU21 ...211 BA114
Little Orchard Cl, Abb.L. WD5 ...59 BR32
Pinner HA5 off Barrow Pt La ...94 BY54
Little Orchard Way, Guil. (Shalf.) GU4 ...258 AY141
Little Oxhey La, Wat. WD19 .94 BX50
Little Pk, Hem.H. (Bov.) HP3 .57 BA28

★ Place of interest | H Hospital | Sch School | Coll College | Uni University | ⇌ Railway station

Little Pk Dr, Felt. TW13 176 BX89
Little Pk Gdns, Enf. EN2 82 DQ41
LITTLE PARNDON, Harl. CM20 35 EP14
Sch **Little Parndon Co Inf Sch**, Harl. CM20 *off Park Mead* 35 EP14
Sch **Little Parndon Co Jun Sch**, Harl. CM20 *off Park Mead* 35 EP14
Little Pipers Cl, Wal.Cr. (Chsht) EN7 65 DP29
Little Pluckets Way, Buck.H. IG9 102 EJ46
Little Portland St, W1 9 J7
Littleport Spur, Slou. SL1 132 AS72
Little Potters, Bushey WD23 95 CD45
Little Pynchons, Harl. CM18 52 EU18
Little Queens Rd, Tedd. TW11 177 CF93
Little Queen St, Dart. DA1 188 FM87
Sch **Little Reddings Prim Sch**, Bushey WD23 *off Harcourt Rd* 76 CB43
Little Redlands, Brom. BR1 204 EL96
Little Reeves Av, Amer. HP7 72 AT39
Little Ridge, Welw.G.C. AL7 30 DA09
Little Riding, Wok. GU22 227 BB116
Little Rivers, Welw.G.C. AL7 30 DA08
Little Rd, Croy. CR0 *off Lower Addiscombe Rd* 202 DS102
Hayes UB3 155 BT75
Hemel Hempstead HP2 40 BM19
Little Roke Av, Ken. CR8 219 DP114
Little Roke Rd, Ken. CR8 220 DQ114
Littlers Cl, SW19 *off Runnymede* 200 DD95
Little Russell St, WC1 9 N6
Little Russets, Brwd. (Hutt.) CM13 *off Hutton Village* 109 GE45
Little St. James's St, SW1 19 J2
Little St. Leonards, SW14 158 CQ83
Little Sanctuary, SW1 19 M4
Little Shardeloes, Amer. HP7 55 AN39
Little Smith St, SW1 19 M5
Little Somerset St, E1 11 N8
Little Spring, Chesh. HP5 54 AP28
Sch **Little Spring Prim Sch**, Chesh. HP5 *off Greenway* 54 AP28
Sch **Little Stanmore First & Mid Sch**, Edg. HA8 *off St. Davids Dr* 96 CM53
Littlestock Rd, Wal.Cr. (Chsht) EN7 66 DR26
Littlestone Cl, Beck. BR3 *off Abbey La* 183 EA93
Little Strand, NW9 97 CT54
Little Stream Cl, Nthwd. HA6 93 BS50
Little St, Guil. GU2 242 AV130
Waltham Abbey EN9 *off Greenwich Way* 83 EB36
Little Sutton La, Slou. SL3 153 BC78
Little Thistle, Welw.G.C. AL7 30 DC12
Little Thrift, Orp. BR5 205 EQ98
LITTLE THURROCK, Grays RM17 170 GD76
Sch **Little Thurrock Prim Sch**, Grays RM17 *off Rectory Rd* 170 GD76
Little Titchfield St, W1 9 J6
LITTLETON, Guil. GU3 258 AU140
LITTLETON, Shep. TW17 195 BP97
Littleton Av, E4 102 EF46
Sch **Littleton C of E Inf Sch**, Shep. TW17 *off Rectory Cl* 194 BN97
Littleton Cres, Har. HA1 117 CF61
Littleton La, Guil. (Littleton) GU3 258 AU139
Reigate RH2 265 CX136
Shepperton TW17 194 BK101
Littleton Rd, Ashf. TW15 175 BQ94
Harrow HA1 117 CF61
Littleton St, SW18 180 DC89
Little Trinity La, EC4 11 H9
Little Turners Ct, Gdmg. GU7 258 AS144
Little Turnstile, WC1 10 A7
★ **Little Venice (Waterbuses)**, W2 7 L5
Little Wade, Welw.G.C. AL7 29 CZ12
Little Wk, Harl. CM20 51 EQ15
Little Warren Cl, Guil. GU4 259 BB136
Littlewick Rd, Wok. GU21 210 AW114
Little Widbury, Ware SG12 33 DZ06
Little Widbury La, Ware SG12 33 DZ06
Little Windmill Hill, Kings L. (Chipper.) WD4 57 BE32
Littlewood, SE13 183 EC85
Sevenoaks TN13 257 FJ122
Littlewood Cl, W13 157 CH76
Little Wd Cl, Orp. BR5 206 EU95
LITTLE WOODCOTE, Cars. SM5 218 DG111
Little Woodcote Est, Cars. SM5 *off Woodmansterne La* 218 DG111
Wallington SM6 *off Woodmansterne La* 218 DG111
Little Woodcote La, Cars. SM5 219 DH112
Purley CR8 219 DH112
Wallington SM6 219 DH112
Little Woodlands, Wind. SL4 151 AM83
Littleworth Av, Esher KT10 215 CD106
Littleworth Common Rd, Esher KT10 197 CD104
Littleworth La, Esher KT10 215 CD105
Littleworth Pl, Esher KT10 215 CD105
Littleworth Rd, Esher KT10 215 CE105
Slough (Burn.) SL1 111 AK61
Little Youngs, Welw.G.C. AL8 29 CW09
Litton Ct, H.Wyc. (Loud.) HP10 88 AC53
Livermere Rd, E8 5 N7
Liverpool Gro, SE17 21 H10
Liverpool Rd, E10 123 EC58
E16 15 H5
N1 4 D6
N7 4 C3
W5 157 CK75
Kingston upon Thames KT2 178 CN94
St. Albans AL1 43 CE20
Slough SL1 131 AP72
Thornton Heath CR7 202 DQ97
Watford WD18 75 BV43
⇌ **Liverpool Street** 11 L6
⊖ **Liverpool Street** 11 L6
Liverpool St, EC2 11 L6
Livesey Cl, Kings.T. KT1 198 CM97
★ **Livesey Mus**, SE15 162 DV79
Livesey Pl, SE15 *off Peckham Pk Rd* 162 DU79
Livingstone Ct, E10 *off Matlock Rd* 123 EC58
Barnet EN5 *off Christchurch La* 79 CY40
Livingstone Gdns, Grav. DA12 191 GK92
H **Livingstone Hosp**, Dart. DA1 188 FM87
Livingstone Pl, E14 24 C10
Sch **Livingstone Prim Sch**, Barn. EN4 *off Baring Rd* 80 DD41
Livingstone Rd, E15 143 EC67
E17 123 EB58
N13 99 DL51
SW11 *off Winstanley Rd* 160 DD83
Caterham CR3 236 DR122
Gravesend DA12 191 GK92
Hounslow TW3 156 CC84
Southall UB1 136 BX73
Thornton Heath CR7 202 DQ96
Livingstone Ter, Rain. RM13 147 FE67
Livingstone Wk, SW11 160 DD83
Hemel Hempstead HP2 40 BM16
Sch **Livity Sch**, SW2 *off Mandrell Rd* 181 DL85
Livonia St, W1 9 K8
Livsey Cl, SE28 165 EQ76
Lizard St, EC1 11 H2
Lizban St, SE3 164 EH80
Llanbury Cl, Ger.Cr. (Chal.St.P.) SL9 90 AY52
Llanelly Rd, NW2 119 CZ61
Llanover Rd, SE18 165 EN79
Wembley HA9 117 CK62
Llanthony Rd, Mord. SM4 200 DD100
Llanvanor Rd, NW2 119 CZ61
Llewellyn St, SE16 22 B4
Lloyd Av, SW16 201 DL95
Coulsdon CR5 218 DG114
Lloyd Baker St, WC1 10 B2
Lloyd Ct, Pnr. HA5 116 BX57
Lloyd Ms, Enf. EN3 83 EA38
Tra **Lloyd Park** 220 DT105
Lloyd Pk Av, Croy. CR0 220 DT105
Lloyd Rd, E6 145 EM67
E17 123 DX56
Dagenham RM9 146 EZ65
Worcester Park KT4 199 CW104
Lloyd's Av, EC3 11 M8
★ **Lloyds of London**, EC3 11 L8
Lloyds Pl, SE3 164 EE82
Lloyd Sq, WC1 10 C1
Lloyd's Row, EC1 10 D2
Lloyd St, WC1 10 C1
Lloyds Way, Beck. BR3 203 DY99
Sch **Lloyd Williamson Sch**, W10 6 C5
Loampit Hill, SE13 163 EA82
Loampit Vale, SE13 163 EB83
Loanda Cl, E8 5 N7
Loates La, Wat. WD17 76 BW41
Loats Rd, SW2 181 DL86
Lobelia Cl, E6 *off Sorrel Gdns* 144 EL71
Local Board Rd, Wat. WD17 76 BW43
Locarno Rd, W3 138 CQ74
Greenford UB6 136 CC70
Lochaber Rd, SE13 164 EE84
Lochaline St, W6 159 CW79
Lochan Cl, Hayes UB4 136 BY70
Lochinvar Cl, Slou. SL1 151 AP75
Lochinvar St, SW12 181 DH87
Sch **Lochinver Ho Sch**, Pot.B. EN6 *off Heath Rd* 64 DB30
Lochmere Cl, Erith DA8 167 FB79
Lochnagar St, E14 14 D6
Lochnell Rd, Berk. HP4 38 AT17
Lock Av, Maid. SL6 130 AC69
Lockbridge Ct, Maid. SL6 130 AC71
Lock Chase, SE3 164 EE83
Lock Cl, Add. (Wdhm) KT15 211 BE113
Southall UB2 *off Navigator Dr* 156 CC75
Locke Cl, Rain. RM13 147 FF65
Locke Gdns, Slou. SL3 152 AW75
Locke King Cl, Wey. KT13 212 BN108
Locke King Rd, Wey. KT13 212 BN108
Lockers Pk La, Hem.H. HP1 40 BH20
Sch **Lockers Pk Sch**, Hem.H. HP1 *off Lockers Pk La* 40 BH20
Lockesfield Pl, E14 24 B9
Lockesley Dr, Orp. BR5 205 ET100
Lockesley Sq, Surb. KT6 197 CK100
Lockestone, Wey. KT13 212 BM107
Lockestone Cl, Wey. KT13 212 BM107
Locket Rd, Har. HA3 117 CE55
Lockets Cl, Wind. SL4 151 AL81
Locke Way, Wok. GU21 *off The Broadway* 227 AZ117
Lockfield Av, Enf. EN3 83 DY40
Lockfield Dr, Wok. GU21 226 AT118
Lockgate Cl, E9 *off Lee Conservancy Rd* 123 DZ64
Lockhart Cl, N7 4 A3
Enfield EN3 *off Derby Rd* 82 DV43
Lockhart Rd, Cob. KT11 214 BW113
Lockhart St, E3 13 M4
Lockhurstthatch La, Guil. (Far.Grn) GU5 260 BM144
Lockhurst St, E5 123 DX63
Lockie Pl, SE25 202 DU97
Lockier Wk, Wem. HA9 117 CK62
Lockington Rd, SW8 161 DH81
Lock Island, Shep. TW17 194 BN103
Lock La, Wok. GU22 228 BH116
Lockley Cres, Hat. AL10 45 CV16
Lock Mead, Maid. SL6 130 AC69
Lockmead Rd, N15 122 DU58
SE13 163 EC83
Lockner Holt, Guil. (Chilw.) GU4 259 BF141
Lock Path, Wind. (Dorney) SL4 151 AL79
Lock Rd, Guil. GU1 242 AX131
Richmond TW10 177 CJ91
Locks La, Mitch. CR4 200 DF95
Locksley Dr, Wok. GU21 *off Robin Hood Rd* 226 AT118
Locksley Est, E14 13 L7
Locksley St, E14 13 L6
Locksmeade Rd, Rich. TW10 177 CJ91
Lockswood Cl, Barn. EN4 80 DF42
Lockwood Cl, SE26 183 DX91
Lockwood Ind Pk, N17 122 DV55
Lockwood Path, Wok. GU21 211 BD113
Lockwood Sq, SE16 22 C5
Lockwood Way, E17 101 DX54
Chessington KT9 216 CN106
Lockyer Est, SE1 21 K3
Lockyer Rd, Purf. RM19 168 FQ79
Lockyer St, SE1 21 K4
Locomotive Dr, Felt. TW14 175 BU88
Loddiges Rd, E9 142 DW66
Loddon Spur, Slou. SL1 132 AS73
Loder Cl, Wok. GU21 211 BD113
Loder St, SE15 162 DW81
Lodge Av, SW14 158 CS83
Borehamwood (Elstree) WD6 78 CM43
Croydon CR0 201 DN104
Dagenham RM8, RM9 146 EU67
Dartford DA1 188 FJ86
Harrow HA3 118 CL56
Romford RM2 127 FG56
Lodgebottom Rd, Lthd. KT22 248 CM127
Lodge Cl, N18 100 DQ50
Brentwood (Hutt.) CM13 109 GE45
Chigwell IG7 104 EU48
Cobham (Stoke D'Ab.) KT11 230 BZ115
Dorking (N.Holm.) RH5 263 CJ140
Edgware HA8 96 CM51
Egham (Eng.Grn) TW20 172 AX92
Epsom KT17 *off Howell Hill Gro* 217 CW110
Hertford SG14 32 DQ07
Isleworth TW7 157 CH81
Leatherhead (Fetch.) KT22 231 CD122
Orpington BR6 206 EV102
Slough SL1 151 AQ75
Uxbridge UB8 134 BJ70
Wallington SM6 200 DG102
Lodge Ct, Horn. RM12 128 FL61
Wembley HA0 118 CL64
Lodge Cres, Orp. BR6 206 EV102
Waltham Cross EN8 67 DX34
Lodge Dr, N13 99 DN49
Hatfield AL9 45 CX15
Rickmansworth (Loud.) WD3 74 BJ42
Lodge End, Rad. WD7 61 CH34
Rickmansworth (Crox.Grn) WD3 75 BR42
Lodgefield, Welw.G.C. AL7 29 CY06
Lodge Gdns, Beck. BR3 203 DZ99
Lodge Hall, Harl. CM18 51 ES19
Lodge Hill, SE2 166 EV80
Ilford IG4 124 EL56
Purley CR8 235 DN115
Welling DA16 166 EV80
Lodgehill Pk Cl, Har. HA2 116 CB61
Lodge La, N12 98 DC50
Bexley DA5 186 EX86
Chalfont St. Giles HP8 73 AZ41
Croydon (New Adgtn) CR0 221 EA107
Dorking (Holm.) RH5 264 CL144
Grays RM16, RM17 170 GA75
Redhill RH1 266 DE143
Romford RM5 104 FA52
Waltham Abbey EN9 83 ED35
Westerham TN16 255 EQ127
Lodge Pl, Sutt. SM1 218 DB106
Lodge Rd, NW4 119 CW56
NW8 7 P4
Bromley BR1 184 EH94
Croydon CR0 201 DP100
Leatherhead (Fetch.) KT22 230 CC122
Sutton SM1 *off Throwley Way* 218 DB106
Wallington SM6 219 DH106
Lodge Vil, Wdf.Grn. IG8 102 EF52
Lodge Wk, Warl. CR6 237 EA116
Lodge Way, Ashf. TW15 174 BL89
Shepperton TW17 195 BQ96
Windsor SL4 151 AL83
Lodore Gdns, NW9 118 CS57
Lodore Grn, Uxb. UB10 114 BL62
Lodore St, E14 14 C8
Loewen Rd, Grays RM16 171 GG76
Lofthouse Pl, Chess. KT9 215 CJ107
Loftie St, SE16 22 B4
Lofting Rd, N1 4 C6
Loftus Rd, W12 139 CV74
Logan Cl, Enf. EN3 83 DX39
Hounslow TW4 156 BZ83
Logan Ct, Rom. RM1 *off Logan Ms* 127 FE57
Logan Ms, W8 16 G7
Romford RM1 127 FE57
Logan Pl, W8 16 G7
Logan Rd, N9 100 DV47
Wembley HA9 118 CL61
Loggetts, The, SE21 182 DS89
Logmore La, Dor. RH4 262 CB138
Logs Hill, Brom. BR1 184 EL94
Chislehurst BR7 184 EL94
Logs Hill Cl, Chis. BR7 204 EL95
Lois Dr, Shep. TW17 195 BP99
Lolesworth Cl, E1 11 P6
Lollards Cl, Amer. HP6 55 AQ37
Lollard St, SE11 20 B7
Lollesworth La, Lthd. (W.Hors.) KT24 245 BQ126
Loman Path, S.Ock. RM15 149 FT72
Loman St, SE1 20 F3
Lomas Cl, Croy. CR0 221 EC108
Lomas Dr, E8 5 P5
Lomas St, E1 12 B5
Lombard Av, Enf. EN3 82 DW39
Ilford IG3 125 ES60
Lombard Business Pk, SW19 200 DC96
Lombard Ct, EC3 11 K9
W3 *off Crown St* 138 CP74
Lombard La, EC4 10 D8
Lombard Rd, N11 99 DH50
SW11 160 DD82
SW19 200 DB96
Lombards, The, Horn. RM11 128 FM59
Lombard St, EC3 11 K8
Dartford (Hort.Kir.) DA4 208 FQ99
Lombard Wall, SE7 25 N6
Lombardy Cl, Hem.H. HP2 41 BR21
Ilford IG6 *off Hazel La* 103 EP52
Woking GU21 *off Nethercote Av* 226 AT117
Lombardy Dr, Berk. HP4 38 AX20
Lombardy Pl, W2 7 J10
Lombardy Retail Pk, Hayes UB3 135 BV73
Lombardy Way, Borwd. WD6 78 CL39
Lomond Cl, N15 122 DS56
Wembley HA0 138 CM66
Lomond Gdns, S.Croy. CR2 221 DY108
Lomond Gro, SE5 162 DR80
Lomond Rd, Hem.H. HP2 40 BK16
Loncin Mead Av, Add. (New Haw) KT15 212 BJ109
Loncroft Rd, SE5 162 DS79
Londesborough Rd, N16 122 DS63
Coll **London Acad of Computing & Electronics**, SW17 *off Upper Tooting Rd* 180 DF90
★ **London Aquarium**, SE1 20 A3
Coll **London Bible Coll**, Nthwd. HA6 *off Green La* 93 BR51
★ **London Biggin Hill Airport**, West. TN16 222 EK113
★ **London Brass Rubbing Cen, St. Martin-in-the-Fields Ch**, WC2 9 N10
⇌ **London Bridge** 21 L2
⊖ **London Bridge** 21 L2
London Br, EC4 21 K1
SE1 21 K1
Riv **London Bridge City Pier** 21 L1
H **London Br Hosp**, SE1 21 K1
London Br St, SE1 21 J2
London Br Wk, SE1 21 K1
★ **London Broncos R.L.C. (share Griffin Pk with Brentford F.C.)**, Brent. TW8 157 CK79
Coll **London Business Sch**, NW1 8 C3
★ **London Butterfly Ho, Syon Pk**, Brent. TW8 157 CH81
★ **London Canal Mus, The**, N1 *off New Wf Rd* 141 DL68
★ **London Cen Mosque**, NW8 8 B2
H **London Chest Hosp**, E2 142 DW68
★ **London City Airport**, E16 144 EL74
London City Airport, E16 145 EM74
Coll **London City Coll**, SE1 20 C2
H **London Clinic, The**, W1 8 F4
Coll **London Coll of Beauty Therapy**, W1 9 J8
Uni **London Coll of Communication**, Back Hill Site, EC1 10 D4
Elephant & Castle Site, SE1 20 F6
Uni **London Coll of Fashion**, Barrett St, W1 8 F8
Curtain Rd, EC2 11 M3
John Princes St, W1 9 H7
Lime Gro, W12 159 CW75
Mare St, E8 142 DV66
Coll **London Coll of Tech**, Houns. TW3 *off Hanworth Rd* 156 CB84
LONDON COLNEY, St.Alb. AL2 62 CL26
London Colney Bypass, St.Alb. AL2 61 CK25
Sch **London Colney JMI Sch**, St.Alb. AL2 *off Alexander Rd* 61 CK26
★ **London Commodity Exchange**, E1 11 P10
Coll **London Contemporary Dance Sch**, WC1 9 M2
★ **London Dungeon**, SE1 21 K2
Coll **London Electronics Coll**, SW5 17 J9
London End, Beac. HP9 89 AM54
Coll **London Executive Coll, The**, SW17 *off Balham High Rd* 180 DG90
★ **London Eye**, SE1 20 A3
⇌ **London Fields** 142 DV66
London Flds, E8 142 DV66
London Flds E Side, E8 142 DV66
Sch **London Flds JMI Sch**, E8 *off Westgate St* 142 DV67
London Flds W Side, E8 142 DU66
★ **London Fire Brigade Mus**, SE1 20 G3
H **London Foot Hosp & Sch of Podiatric Med, The**, W1 9 J4
★ **London Gatwick Airport**, Gat. RH6 268 DD153
★ **London Heathrow Airport**, Houns. TW6 155 BP81
H **London Indep Hosp**, E1 12 G5
London La, E8 142 DV66
Bromley BR1 184 EF94
Guildford (Shere) GU5 260 BN138
Leatherhead (E.Hors.) KT24 245 BU131
★ **London Met Archives**, EC1 10 D3
Uni **London Met Uni - London City Campus**, Calcutta Ho, E1 11 P7
Central Ho, E1 12 A7
Commercial Rd, E1 12 B7
Jewry St, EC3 11 N8
Moorgate, EC2 11 K6
Students Union, E1 11 P7
Tower Hill, EC3 11 N9
Whitechapel High St, E1 142 DT72
Uni **London Met Uni - London N Campus**, Carleton Gra, N7 *off Carleton Rd* 121 DK63
Eden Gro, N7 4 B1
Grad Cen, N7 *off Holloway Rd* 121 DN64
Harglenis, N7 4 C1
James Leicester Hall of Res, N7 *off Market Rd* 141 DL65
Ladbroke Ho, N5 4 F1
Learning Cen, N7 *off Holloway Rd* 121 DM63
Stapleton Ho, N7 4 B1
The Arc Hall of Res, N7 *off Holloway Rd* 121 DL63
Tower Bldg, N7 4 C1
Tufnell Park Hall of Res, N7 *off Huddleston Rd* 121 DJ62
London Ms, W2 7 P8
Sch **London Nautical Sch**, SE1 20 D1
Sch **London Oratory Sec Sch, The**, SW6 *off Seagrave Rd* 160 DB80
★ **London Palladium**, W1 9 J8
★ **London Peace Pagoda**, SW11 160 DF79
★ **London Regatta Cen**, E16 144 EK73
London Rd, E13 144 EG68
SE1 20 E5
SE23 182 DU88
SW16 201 DM95
SW17 200 DF96
Amersham HP7 55 AQ40
Ashford TW15 174 BH90
Barking IG11 145 EP66
Beaconsfield HP9 89 AM54
Berkhamsted HP4 38 AY20
Borehamwood WD6 62 CN34
Brentford TW8 157 CJ80
Brentwood CM14 108 FT49
Bromley BR1 184 EF94
Bushey WD23 76 BY44
Caterham CR3 236 DR123
Chalfont St. Giles HP8 90 AW47
Croydon CR0 201 DP101
London Rd, Dart. (Cray.) DA1 187 FD85
Dartford (Fnghm) DA4 208 FL100
Dartford (Stone) DA2 188 FP87
Dorking RH4, RH5 247 CJ133
Egham (Eng.Grn) TW20 192 AV95
Enfield EN2 82 DR41
Epping (Thnwd) CM16 52 EV23
Epsom KT17 217 CT109
Feltham TW14 174 BH90
Gatwick RH6 268 DF150
Gravesend (Nthflt) DA11 190 GD86
Grays RM17, RM20 169 FW79
Greenhithe DA9 189 FS86
Guildford GU1, GU4 243 BB129
Harlow (Old Harl.) CM17 52 EV16
Harlow (Pott.St) CM17 52 EW18
Harlow (Thnwd) CM17 52 EV23
Harrow HA1 117 CE61
Hemel Hempstead HP1, HP3 40 BK24
Hertford SG13 32 DT10
High Wycombe HP10, HP11 88 AD54
Hounslow TW3 156 CC83
Isleworth TW7 157 CF82
Kingston upon Thames KT2 198 CM96
Mitcham CR4 200 DF96
Mitcham (Bedd.Cor.) CR4 200 DG101
Morden SM4 200 DA99
Ongar CM5 87 FH36
Radlett (Shenley) WD7 62 CM33
Redhill RH1 250 DG132
Reigate RH2 250 DA134
Rickmansworth WD3 92 BM47
Romford (Abridge) RM4 85 ET42
Romford (Chad.Hth) RM6, RM7 126 FA58
Romford (Stap.Taw.) RM4 87 FC40
St. Albans AL1 43 CH24
Sawbridgeworth CM21 52 EW15
Sevenoaks TN13 256 FF123
Sevenoaks (Halst.) TN14 225 FB112
Sevenoaks (Longford) TN13 241 FD118
Slough SL3 153 AZ78
Slough (Datchet) SL3 152 AV80
South Ockendon (Aveley) RM15 148 FM74
Staines TW18 173 BF91
Stanmore HA7 95 CJ50
Sutton SM3 199 CX104
Swanley BR8 207 FC95
Swanscombe DA10 189 FV85
Thornton Heath CR7 201 DN99
Tilbury RM18 171 GH82
Twickenham TW1 177 CG85
Virginia Water GU25 192 AV95
Wallington SM6 219 DH105
Ware SG12 33 DY07
Wembley HA9 138 CL65
Westerham TN16 239 EQ123
Woking (Send) GU23 243 BC128
London Rd Business Pk, St.Alb. AL1 *off London Rd* 43 CF22
London Rd E, Amer. HP7 72 AT42
⇌ **London Road (Guildford)** 242 AY134
London Rd N, Red. (Merst.) RH1 251 DH125
London Rd Purfleet, Purf. RM19 168 FN78
London Rd S, Red. (Merst.) RH1 250 DG130
London Rd W, Amer. HP7 55 AQ40
London Rd W Thurrock, Grays RM20 169 FS79
Uni **London Sch of Economics & Political Science**, WC2 10 B8
Coll **London Sch of Flying**, Borwd. WD6 *off Hogg La* 77 CF42
Uni **London Sch of Jewish Studies**, NW4 *off Albert Rd* 119 CX56
Londons Cl, Upmin. RM14 128 FQ64
London Shop Pav, W1 9 L10
★ **London Silver Vaults**, WC2 10 C6
Uni **London S Bk Uni**, SE1 20 F5
Caxton Ho, SE1 20 E5
Dante Rd Res, SE11 161 DP77
New Kent Rd Res, SE1 162 DQ76
London Sq, Guil. GU1 242 AY134
London Stile, W4 *off Wellesley Rd* 158 CN78
★ **London Stone**, EC4 11 J9
London St, EC3 11 M9
W2 7 N8
Chertsey KT16 194 BG101
Coll **London Studio Cen**, N1 *off York Way* 141 DL68
★ **London Transport Mus**, WC2 9 P9
London Wall, EC2 11 H6
London Wall Bldgs, EC2 11 K6
Sch **London Welsh Sch**, NW2 *off Willesden La* 139 CW65
★ **London Wildlife Trust**, NW1 141 DK67
★ **London Zoo**, NW1 140 DG68
Londrina Ter, Berk. HP4 38 AX19
Lone Oak, Horl. (Smallfield) RH6 269 DP150
Lonesome La, Reig. RH2 266 DB138
Sch **Lonesome Prim Sch**, Mitch. CR4 *off Grove Rd* 201 DH96
Lonesome Way, SW16 201 DH95
Long Acre, WC2 9 N9
Longacre, Harl. CM17 36 EV11
Long Acre, Orp. BR6 206 EX103
Longacre Pl, Cars. SM5 *off Beddington Gdns* 218 DG107
Longacre Rd, E17 101 ED53
Longacres, St.Alb. AL4 43 CK20
Longaford Way, Brwd. (Hutt.) CM13 109 GB46
Long Arrotts, Hem.H. HP1 40 BH18
Long Banks, Harl. CM18 51 ER19
Long Barn Cl, Wat. WD25 59 BV32
Longbeach Rd, SW11 160 DF83
Longberrys, NW2 119 CZ62
Longboat Row, Sthl. UB1 136 BZ72
Longbottom La, Beac. HP9 89 AR52
Longbourn, Wind. SL4 151 AN83
Longbourne Gm, Gdmg. GU7 *off Barnes Rd* 258 AS143

Longbourne Way, Cher. KT16 193 BF100
Longboyds, Cob. KT11 213 BV114
Longbridge Rd, Bark. IG11 145 EQ66
Dagenham RM8 126 EU63
Gatwick RH6 268 DF150
Horley RH6 268 DF150
Longbridge Roundabout, Horl. RH6 268 DF149
Longbridge Wk, Horl. RH6 268 DF150
Longbridge Way, SE13 183 EC85
Uxbridge UB8 134 BH68
Longbury Cl, Orp. BR5 206 EV97
Longbury Dr, Orp. BR5 206 EV97
Longchamp Cl, Horl. RH6 off Carlton Tye 269 DJ148
Long Chaulden, Hem.H. HP1 39 BE20
Longcliffe Path, Wat. WD19 off Gosforth La 93 BU48
Long Cl, Slou. (Farn.Com.) SL2 131 AP66
Sch Long Cl Sch, Slou. SL3 off Upton Ct Rd 152 AU76
Long Copse Cl, Lthd. (Bkhm) KT23 230 CB123
Long Ct, Purf. RM19 168 FN77
Longcroft, SE9 185 EM90
Watford WD19 93 BV45
Longcroft Av, Bans. SM7 218 DC114
Longcroft Dr, Wal.Cr. EN8 67 DZ34
Longcrofte Rd, Edg. HA8 95 CK52
Longcroft Gdns, Welw.G.C. AL8 29 CX10
Longcroft Grn, Welw.G.C. AL8 off Stanborough Rd 29 CX11
Longcroft La, Hem.H. (Bov.) HP3 57 BC28
Welwyn Garden City AL8 29 CX10
Longcroft Ri, Loug. IG10 85 EN43
Longcroft Rd, Rick. (Map.Cr.) WD3 91 BD50
Longcrofts, Wal.Abb. EN9 off Roundhills 68 EE34
LONGCROSS, Cher. KT16 192 AU104
⇌ Longcross 192 AT102
Longcross Rd, Cher. (Longcr.) KT16 192 AY104
Long Deacon Rd, E4 102 EE46
Longdean Pk, Hem.H. HP3 40 BN24
Sch Longdean Sch, Hem.H. HP3 off Rumballs Rd 41 BP23
LONG DITTON, Surb. KT6 197 CJ102
Sch Long Ditton Inf & Nurs Sch, Surb. KT6 off Ditton Hill Rd 197 CJ102
Sch Long Ditton St. Mary's C of E Jun Sch, T.Ditt. KT7 off Sugden Rd 197 CH102
Longdon Wd, Kes. BR2 222 EL105
Longdown La N, Epsom KT17 217 CU114
Longdown La S, Epsom KT17 217 CU114
Longdown Rd, SE6 183 EA91
Epsom KT17 217 CU114
Guildford GU4 259 BB137
Long Dr, W3 138 CS72
Greenford UB6 136 CB67
Ruislip HA4 116 BX63
Slough (Burn.) SL1 130 AJ69
Long Dyke, Guil. GU1 243 BB132
Long Elmes, Har. HA3 94 CB53
Long Elms, Abb.L. WD5 59 BR33
Long Elms Cl, Abb.L. WD5 off Long Elms 59 BR33
Long Fallow, St.Alb. AL2 60 CA27
Longfellow Dr, Brwd. (Hutt.) CM13 109 GC45
Longfellow Rd, E17 123 DZ58
Worcester Park KT4 199 CU103
Longfellow Way, SE1 21 P8
Long Fld, NW9 96 CS52
Longfield, Brom. BR1 204 EF95
Harlow CM18 52 EU17
Hemel Hempstead HP3 41 BP22
Loughton IG10 84 EJ43
Slough (Hedg.) SL2 111 AR61
Longfield Av, E17 123 DY56
NW7 97 CU52
W5 137 CJ73
Enfield EN3 82 DW37
Hornchurch RM11 127 FF59
Wallington SM6 200 DG102
Wembley HA9 118 CL60
Longfield Cres, SE26 182 DW90
Tadworth KT20 233 CW120
Longfield Dr, SW14 178 CP85
Amersham HP6 55 AP38
Mitcham CR4 180 DE94
Longfield Est, SE1 21 P8
Sch Longfield First Sch, Har. HA2 off Dukes Av 116 CA58
Longfield La, Wal.Cr. (Chsht) EN7 66 DU27
Sch Longfield Mid Sch, Har. HA2 off Dukes Av 116 CA58
Longfield Rd, W5 137 CJ73
Chesham HP5 54 AM29
Dorking RH4 263 CF137
Longfield St, SW18 180 DA87
Longfield Wk, W5 137 CJ72
LONGFORD, Sev. TN13 241 FD120
LONGFORD, West Dr. UB7 154 BH81
Longford Av, Felt. TW14 175 BS86
Southall UB1 136 CA73
Staines TW19 174 BL88
Longford Cl, Hmptn. (Hmptn H.) TW12 176 CA91
Hayes UB4 off Longford Gdns 136 BX73
Sch Longford Comm Sch, Felt. TW14 off Tachbrook Rd 175 BT87
Longford Ct, E5 off Pedro St 123 DX63
NW4 119 CX56
Epsom KT19 216 CQ105
Longford Gdns, Hayes UB4 136 BX73
Sutton SM1 200 DC104
Longford Rd, Twick. TW2 176 CA88
Longford Roundabout, West Dr. UB7 154 BH81
Longford St, NW1 9 H3
Longford Wk, SW2 off Papworth Way 181 DN87
Longford Way, Stai. TW19 174 BL88
Long Furlong Dr, Slou. SL2 131 AN70
Long Gore, Gdmg. GU7 258 AS142
Long Grn, Chig. IG7 103 ES49
Long Gro, Beac. (Seer Grn) HP9 89 AQ51
Long Gro, Rom. (Harold Wd) RM3 106 FL54
Long Gro Cl, Brox. EN10 49 DY19
Long Gro Rd, Epsom KT19 216 CP110
Longhayes Av, Rom. RM6 126 EX56
Longhayes Ct, Rom. RM6 off Longhayes Av 126 EX56
Longheath Gdns, Croy. CR0 202 DW99
Longhedge Ho, SE26 182 DT91
Long Hedges, Houns. TW3 156 CA81
Longhedge St, SW11 160 DG82
Long Hill, Cat. (Wold.) CR3 237 DX121
Longhill Rd, SE6 183 ED89
Longhook Gdns, Nthlt. UB5 135 BU68
Longhope Cl, SE15 162 DS79
Longhouse Rd, Grays RM16 171 GH76
Longhurst Rd, SE13 183 ED85
Croydon CR0 202 DV100
Leatherhead (E.Hors.) KT24 245 BS129
Long John, Hem.H. HP3 40 BM22
Longland Br, B.Stort. (Sheering) CM22 37 FC07
Longland Ct, SE1 22 A9
Longland Dr, N20 98 DB48
LONGLANDS, Chis. BR7 185 EQ90
Longlands, Hem.H. HP2 40 BN20
Longlands Av, Couls. CR5 218 DG114
Longlands Cl, Wal.Cr. (Chsht) EN8 67 DX32
Longlands Ct, W11 6 F9
Mitcham CR4 off Summerhill Way 200 DG95
Longlands Pk Cres, Sid. DA15 185 ES90
Sch Longlands Prim Sch, Brox. EN10 off Nunsbury Dr 67 DZ25
Sidcup DA15 off Woodside Rd 185 ES90
Longlands Rd, Sid. DA15 185 ES90
Welwyn Garden City AL7 29 CY11
Long La, EC1 10 F5
N2 98 DC54
N3 98 DB52
SE1 21 J4
Bexleyheath DA7 166 EX80
Croydon CR0 202 DW99
Grays RM16 170 GA75
Hemel Hempstead (Bov.) HP3 57 AZ31
Rickmansworth (Herons.) WD3 73 BC44
Rickmansworth (Mill End) WD3 91 BF47
Staines (Stanw.) TW19 174 BM87
Uxbridge UB10 134 BN69
Longleat Ms, Orp. BR5 off High St 206 EW98
Longleat Rd, Enf. EN1 82 DS43
Longleat Way, Felt. TW14 175 BR87
Longlees, Rick. (Map.Cr.) WD3 91 BC50
Longleigh La, SE2 166 EW79
Bexleyheath DA7 166 EW79
Longlents Ho, NW10 138 CR67
Long Ley, Harl. CM20 51 ET15
Welwyn Garden City AL7 30 DC09
Longley Av, Wem. HA0 138 CM67
Longley Rd, SW17 180 DE93
Croydon CR0 201 DP101
Harrow HA1 116 CC57
Long Leys, E4 101 EB51
Longley St, SE1 22 A8
Longley Way, NW2 119 CW62
Long Lo Dr, Walt. KT12 196 BW104
Longmans Cl, Wat. WD18 off Byewaters 75 BQ44
Long Mark Rd, E16 off Fulmer Rd 144 EK71
Longmarsh Vw, Dart. (Sutt.H.) DA4 208 FP95
Long Mead, NW9 97 CT53
Longmead, Chis. BR7 205 EN96
Guildford GU1 243 BC134
Hatfield AL10 45 CV15
Windsor SL4 151 AL81
Coll Longmead Adult Ed Cen, Red. RH1 off Holland Cl 250 DF134
Longmead Business Cen, Epsom KT19 216 CR111
Longmead Business Pk, Epsom KT19 216 CS111
Longmead Cl, Brwd. (Shenf.) CM15 108 FY46
Caterham CR3 236 DS122
Longmead Dr, Sid. DA14 186 EX89
Longmeade, Grav. DA12 191 GM88
Longmead La, Slou. SL1 131 AK66
Long Meadow, NW5 off Torriano Av 121 DK64
Brentwood (Hutt.) CM13 109 GC47
Chesham HP5 54 AQ28
Leatherhead (Bkhm) KT23 246 BZ125
Romford (Noak Hill) RM3 106 FJ48
Sevenoaks (Rvrhd) TN13 256 FD121
Long Meadow Cl, W.Wick. BR4 203 EC101
Longmeadow Rd, Sid. DA15 185 ES88
Sch Longmead Prim Sch, West Dr. UB7 off Laurel La 154 BL77
Longmead Rd, SW17 180 DF92
Epsom KT19 216 CR111
Hayes UB3 135 BT73
Thames Ditton KT7 197 CE101
Longmere Gdns, Tad. KT20 233 CW119
Long Mimms, Hem.H. HP2 40 BL19
Longmoor, Wal.Cr. (Chsht) EN8 67 DY29
Longmoore St, SW1 19 J8
Longmoor Pt, SW15 off Norley Vale 179 CV88
Longmore Av, Barn. EN4, EN5 80 DC44
Longmore Cl, Rick. (Map.Cr.) WD3 91 BF49
Longmore Gdns, Welw.G.C. AL7 29 CZ09
Longmore Rd, Walt. KT12 214 BY105
Longnor Rd, E1 13 H2
Long Orchard Dr, H.Wyc. (Penn) HP10 88 AC47
Long Pk, Amer. HP6 55 AQ36
Long Pk Cl, Amer. HP6 55 AQ36
Long Pk Way, Amer. HP6 55 AQ35
Long Pond Rd, SE3 164 EE81
Longport Cl, Ilf. IG6 104 EU51
Long Reach, Lthd. (W.Hors.) KT24 245 BP125
Woking (Ockham) GU23 228 BN123
Long Reach Ct, Bark. IG11 145 ER68
Longreach Rd, Bark. IG11 145 ET70
Erith DA8 167 FH80
Long Readings La, Slou. SL2 131 AP70
Long Ride, The, Hat. AL9 45 CZ18
Longridge Gro, Wok. GU22 off Old Woking Rd 211 BE114
Longridge La, Sthl. UB1 136 CB73
Longridge Rd, SW5 16 G8
Long Ridings Av, Brwd. (Hutt.) CM13 109 GB43
Sch Long Ridings Co Prim Sch, Brwd. CM13 off Long Ridings Av 109 GB43
Long Rd, SW4 161 DH84
Longs Cl, Wok. GU22 228 BG116
Long's Ct, WC2 9 L9
Longs Ct, Rich. TW9 off Crown Ter 158 CM84
Longsdon Way, Cat. CR3 236 DU124
Long Shaw, Lthd. KT22 231 CG119
Sch Longshaw Prim Sch, E4 off Longshaw Rd 101 ED48
Longshaw Rd, E4 101 ED48
Longshore, SE8 23 L8
Longside Cl, Egh. TW20 193 BC95
Long Spring, St.Alb. (Port.Wd) AL3 43 CF16
Longspring, Wat. WD24 75 BV38
Longspring Wd, Sev. TN14 256 FF130
Longstaff Cres, SW18 180 DA86
Longstaff Rd, SW18 180 DA86
Longstone Av, NW10 139 CT66
Longstone Rd, SW17 181 DH92
Iver SL0 133 BC68
Long St, E2 11 N1
Waltham Abbey EN9 68 EL32
Longthornton Rd, SW16 201 DJ96
Longton Av, SE26 182 DU91
Longton Gro, SE26 182 DV91
Longtown Cl, Rom. RM3 106 FJ50
Longtown Rd, Rom. RM3 106 FJ50
Longview, Beac. HP9 110 AF55
Long Vw, Berk. HP4 38 AU17
Longview Way, Rom. RM5 105 FD53
Longville Rd, SE11 20 E7
Long Wk, SE1 21 M5
SE18 165 EP79
SW13 158 CS82
Chalfont St. Giles HP8 72 AX41
Epsom KT18 233 CX119
Leatherhead (W.Hors.) KT24 244 BN128
New Malden KT3 198 CQ97
Waltham Abbey EN9 67 EA30
West Byfleet KT14 212 BJ114
Long Wk, The, Wind. SL4 151 AR83
Longwalk Rd, Uxb. UB11 135 BP74
Longwood, Harl. CM18 51 ER20
Longwood Av, Slou. SL3 off Tamar Way 153 BB78
Longwood Business Pk, Sun. TW16 195 BT99
Longwood Cl, Upmin. RM14 128 FQ64
Longwood Dr, SW15 179 CU86
Long Wd Dr, Beac. (Jordans) HP9 90 AT51
Longwood Gdns, Ilf. IG5, IG6 125 EM56
Longwood La, Amer. HP7 55 AR39
Longwood Rd, Hert. SG14 31 DM08
Kenley CR8 236 DR116
Sch Longwood Sch, Bushey WD23 off Bushey Hall Dr 76 BZ42
Longworth Cl, SE28 146 EX72
Longworth Dr, Maid. SL6 130 AC70
Long Yd, WC1 10 A4
Loning, The, NW9 118 CS56
Enfield EN3 82 DW38
Lonsdale, Hem.H. HP2 40 BL17
Lonsdale Av, E6 144 EK69
Brentwood (Hutt.) CM13 109 GD44
Romford RM7 127 FC58
Wembley HA9 118 CL64
Lonsdale Cl, E6 off Lonsdale Av 144 EL70
SE9 184 EK90
Edgware HA8 off Orchard Dr 96 CM50
Pinner HA5 94 BY52
Uxbridge UB8 off Dawley Av 135 BQ71
Lonsdale Cres, Dart. DA2 188 FQ88
Ilford IG2 125 EP58
Lonsdale Dr, Enf. EN2 81 DL43
Lonsdale Gdns, Th.Hth. CR7 201 DM98
Lonsdale Ms, Rich. TW9 off Elizabeth Cotts 158 CN81
Lonsdale Pl, N1 4 D6
Lonsdale Rd, E11 124 EF59
NW6 139 CZ68
SE25 202 DV98
SW13 159 CU79
W4 159 CT77
W11 6 F8
Bexleyheath DA7 166 EZ82
Dorking RH4 263 CH135
Southall UB2 156 BX76
Weybridge KT13 212 BN108
Lonsdale Sq, N1 4 D6
Lonsdale Way, Maid. SL6 150 AC78
Loobert Rd, N15 122 DS55
Looe Gdns, Ilf. IG6 125 EP55
Loom La, Rad. WD7 77 CG37
Loom Pl, Rad. WD7 77 CG36
Loop Rd, Chis. BR7 185 EQ93
Epsom KT18 off Woodcote Side 232 CQ116
Waltham Abbey EN9 67 EB32
Woking GU22 227 AZ121
Lopen Rd, N18 100 DS49
Loraine Cl, Enf. EN3 82 DW43
Loraine Gdns, Ashtd. KT21 232 CL117
Loraine Rd, N7 121 DM63
W4 158 CP79
Lorane Ct, Wat. WD17 75 BU40
Lord Amory Way, E14 24 C3
Lord Av, Ilf. IG5 125 EM56
Lord Chancellor Wk, Kings.T. KT2 198 CQ95
Lord Chatham's Ride, Sev. TN14 240 EX117
Lordell Pl, SW19 179 CW93
Lorden Wk, E2 12 A2
Lord Gdns, Ilf. IG5 124 EL56
Lord Hills Br, W2 7 K6
Lord Hills Rd, W2 7 K5
Lord Holland La, SW9 off St. Lawrence Way 161 DN81
Lord Knyvett Cl, Stai. (Stanw.) TW19 174 BK86
Lord Knyvetts Ct, Stai. (Stanw.) TW19 off De Havilland Way 174 BL86
Lord Mayors Dr, Slou. (Farn.Com.) SL2 111 AN64
Lord Napier Pl, W6 off Upper Mall 159 CU78
Lord N St, SW1 19 N6
Lord Roberts Ms, SW6 off Moore Pk Rd 160 DB80
Lord Roberts Ter, SE18 165 EN78
★ Lord's, Middlesex County Cricket Club & Mus, NW8 7 P1
Lordsbury Fld, Wall. SM6 219 DJ110
Lord's Cl, SE21 182 DQ89
Lords Cl, Felt. TW13 176 BY89
Radlett (Shenley) WD7 62 CL32
Lordsgrove Cl, Tad. KT20 off Whitegate Way 233 CV120
Lordship Cl, Brwd. (Hutt.) CM13 109 GD46
Lordship Gro, N16 122 DR61
Lordship La, N17 100 DQ53
N22 99 DN54
SE22 182 DT86
Lordship La Est, SE22 182 DU88
Sch Lordship La Prim Sch, N22 off Lordship La 100 DQ53
Lordship Pk, N16 122 DQ61
Lordship Pk Ms, N16 off Allerton Rd 122 DQ61
Lordship Pl, SW3 off Cheyne Row 160 DE79
Lordship Rd, N16 122 DR61
Northolt UB5 136 BY66
Waltham Cross (Chsht) EN7 66 DV30
Lordship Ter, N16 122 DR61
Lordsmead Rd, N17 100 DS53
Lord St, E16 144 EL74
Gravesend DA12 191 GH87
Hoddesdon EN11 48 DV17
Watford WD17 76 BW41
Lord's Vw, NW8 7 P2
Lords Wd, Welw.G.C. AL7 30 DC09
Lordswood Cl, Dart. (Lane End) DA2 189 FS91
Lords Wd Ho, Couls. CR5 235 DK122
Lord Warwick St, SE18 165 EM76
Lorenzo St, WC1 10 A1
Sch Loreto RC Girls' Coll, St.Alb. AL1 off Hatfield Rd 43 CE20
Loretto Gdns, Har. HA3 118 CL56
Lorian Cl, N12 98 DB49
Lorian Dr, Reig. RH2 250 DC133
Loriners Cl, Cob. KT11 213 BU114
Loring Rd, N20 98 DE47
Berkhamsted HP4 38 AW20
Isleworth TW7 157 CF82
Windsor SL4 151 AM81
Loris Rd, W6 159 CW76
Lorn Ct, SW9 161 DN82
Lorne, The, Lthd. (Bkhm) KT23 246 CA126
Lorne Av, Croy. CR0 203 DX101
Lorne Cl, NW8 8 B2
Slough SL1 151 AP76
Lorne Gdns, E11 124 EJ56
W11 16 B3
Croydon CR0 203 DX101
Lorne Rd, E7 124 EH63
E17 123 EA57
N4 121 DM60
Brentwood CM14 108 FW49
Harrow HA3 95 CF54
Richmond TW10 off Albert Rd 178 CM85
Lorn Rd, SW9 161 DM82
Lorraine Chase, S.Ock. RM15 168 FM75
Lorraine Pk, Har. HA3 95 CE52
Lorrimore Rd, SE17 161 DP79
Lorrimore Sq, SE17 161 DP79
Lorton Cl, Grav. DA12 191 GL89
Loseberry Rd, Esher (Clay.) KT10 215 CD106
★ Loseley Ho & Pk, Guil. GU3 258 AS140
Loseley Pk, Guil. (Littleton) GU3 258 AT140
Loseley Rd, Gdmg. GU7 258 AS143
Losfield Rd, Wind. SL4 151 AL81
Lossie Dr, Iver SL0 133 BB73
Lothair Rd, W5 157 CK75
Lothair Rd N, N4 121 DP58
Lothair Rd S, N4 121 DN59
Lothbury, EC2 11 J7
Lothian Av, Hayes UB4 135 BV71
Lothian Cl, Wem. HA0 117 CG63
Lothian Rd, SW9 161 DP81
Lothian Wd, Tad. KT20 233 CV122
Lothrop St, W10 6 C2
Lots Rd, SW10 160 DC80
Lotus Cl, SE21 182 DQ90
Lotus Rd, West. (Bigg.H.) TN16 239 EM118
Loubet St, SW17 180 DF93
Loudhams Rd, Amer. HP7 72 AW39
Loudhams Wd La, Ch.St.G. HP8 72 AX40
Loudoun Av, Ilf. IG6 125 EP57
Loudoun Rd, NW8 140 DC67
Loudoun Rd Ms, NW8 off Loudoun Rd 140 DC67
LOUDWATER, H.Wyc. HP10 88 AD53
LOUDWATER, Rick. WD3 74 BK41
Loudwater Cl, Sun. TW16 195 BU98
Loudwater Dr, Rick. (Loud.) WD3 74 BJ42
Loudwater Hts, Rick. (Loud.) WD3 74 BH41
Loudwater La, Rick. WD3 74 BK42
Loudwater Ridge, Rick. (Loud.) WD3 74 BJ42
Loudwater Rd, Sun. TW16 195 BU98
Loughborough Est, SW9 off Loughborough Rd 161 DP82
⇌ Loughborough Junction 161 DP83
Loughborough Pk, SW9 161 DP84
Sch Loughborough Prim Sch, SW9 off Minet Rd 161 DP82
Loughborough Rd, SW9 161 DN82
Loughborough St, SE11 20 B9
Lough Rd, N7 4 B3
LOUGHTON, IG10 85 EM43
⊖ Loughton 84 EL43
Loughton Ct, Wal.Abb. EN9 68 EH33
Loughton La, Epp. (They.B.) CM16 85 ER38
Loughton Way, Buck.H. IG9 102 EK46
Louisa Cl, E9 off Wetherell Rd 143 DX67
Louisa Gdns, E1 12 G4
Louisa Ho, SW15 158 CS84
Coll Louisa Oakes Cen, E4 off Hall La 101 DZ49
Louisa St, E1 12 G4
Louise Aumonier Wk, N19 off Hillrise Rd 121 DL59
Louise Bennett Cl, SE24 off Shakespeare Rd 161 DP84
Louise Ct, E11 off Grosvenor Rd 124 EH57
Louise Gdns, Rain. RM13 147 FE69
Louise Rd, E15 144 EE65
Louise Wk, Hem.H. (Bov.) HP3 57 BA28
Louis Gdns, Chis. BR7 185 EM91
Louis Ms, N10 99 DH53
Louisville Rd, SW17 180 DG90
Louvaine Rd, SW11 160 DD84
Louvain Rd, Green. DA9 189 FS87
Louvain Way, Wat. WD25 59 BV32
Lovage App, E6 144 EL71
Lovat Cl, NW2 119 CT62
Lovat La, EC3 11 L10
Lovatt Cl, Edg. HA8 96 CP51
Lovatt Dr, Ruis. HA4 115 BU57
Lovatts, Rick. (Crox.Grn) WD3 74 BN42
Lovat Wk, Houns. TW5 off Cranford La 156 BY80
Loveday Rd, W13 137 CH74
Love Grn La, Iver SL0 133 BD71
Lovegrove Dr, Slou. SL2 131 AM70
Lovegrove St, SE1 22 B10
Lovegrove Wk, E14 24 C2
Love Hill La, Slou. SL3 133 BA73
Lovejoy La, Wind. SL4 151 AK82
Lovekyn Cl, Kings.T. KT2 off Queen Elizabeth Rd 198 CM96
Lovelace Av, Brom. BR2 205 EN100
Lovelace Cl, Lthd. (Eff.Junct.) KT24 229 BU123
Lovelace Dr, Wok. GU22 227 BF115
Lovelace Gdns, Bark. IG11 126 EU63
Surbiton KT6 197 CK101
Walton-on-Thames KT12 214 BW106
Lovelace Grn, SE9 165 EM83
Sch Lovelace Prim Sch, Chess. KT9 off Mansfield Rd 215 CJ106
Lovelace Rd, SE21 182 DQ89
Barnet EN4 98 DE45
Surbiton KT6 197 CJ101
Lovelands La, Tad. KT20 250 DB127
Love La, EC2 11 H7
N17 100 DT52
SE18 165 EP77
SE25 202 DV97
Abbots Langley WD5 59 BT30
Bexley DA5 186 EZ86
Godstone RH9 252 DW132
Gravesend DA12 191 GJ87
Iver SL0 133 BD72
Kings Langley WD4 58 BL29
Mitcham CR4 200 DE97
Morden SM4 200 DA101
Pinner HA5 116 BY55
South Ockendon (Aveley) RM15 168 FQ75
Surbiton KT6 197 CK103
Sutton SM3 217 CY106
Tadworth KT20 249 CT126
Woodford Green IG8 103 EM51
Lovel Av, Well. DA16 166 EU82
Lovel Cl, Hem.H. HP1 40 BG20
Lovel End, Ger.Cr. (Chal.St.P.) SL9 90 AW52
Lovelinch Cl, SE15 162 DW79
Lovell Ho, E8 142 DU67
Lovell Pl, SE16 23 K5
Lovell Rd, Enf. EN1 82 DV35
Richmond TW10 177 CJ90
Southall UB1 136 CB72
Lovell Wk, Rain. RM13 147 FG65
Lovel Mead, Ger.Cr. (Chal.St.P.) SL9 90 AW52
Lovelock Cl, Ken. CR8 236 DQ117
Lovel Rd, Ger.Cr. (Chal.St.P.) SL9 90 AW52
Loveridge Ms, NW6 off Loveridge Rd 139 CZ65
Loveridge Rd, NW6 139 CZ65
Lovering Rd, Wal.Cr. (Chsht) EN7 66 DQ26
Lovers La, Green. DA9 169 FX84
Lovers Wk, N3 98 DA52
NW7 97 CZ51
SE10 164 EE79
Lover's Wk, W1 18 E1
Lovet Rd, Harl. CM19 51 EN16
Lovett Dr, Cars. SM5 200 DC101
Lovett Gdns, Maid. SL6 130 AC68
Lovett Rd, St.Alb. (Lon.Col.) AL2 61 CG26
Staines TW18 173 BB91
Uxbridge (Hare.) UB9 114 BJ55
Lovett's Pl, SW18 off Old York Rd 160 DB84
Lovett Way, NW10 118 CQ64
Love Wk, SE5 162 DR82
Lovibonds Av, Orp. BR6 223 EP105
West Drayton UB7 134 BM72
Lowbell La, St.Alb. (Lon.Col.) AL2 62 CL27
Lowbrook Rd, Ilf. IG1 125 EP64
Lowburys, Dor. RH4 263 CH139
Low Cl, Green. DA9 189 FU85
Low Cross Wd La, SE21 182 DT90
Lowdell Cl, West Dr. UB7 134 BL72
Lowden Rd, N9 100 DV46
SE24 161 DP84
Southall UB1 136 BY73
Lowe, The, Chig. IG7 104 EU50
Lowe Av, E16 15 M6
Lowe Cl, Chig. IG7 104 EU50
Lowell St, E14 13 K8
Lowen Rd, Rain. RM13 147 FD68
Lower Addiscombe Rd, Croy. CR0 202 DS102
Lower Addison Gdns, W14 16 B4
Lower Adeyfield Rd, Hem.H. HP2 40 BK19
Lower Alderton Hall La, Loug. IG10 85 EN43
LOWER ASHTEAD, Ashtd. KT21 231 CJ119
Lower Barn, Hem.H. HP3 40 BM23
Lower Barn Rd, Pur. CR8 220 DR112
Lower Bedfords Rd, Rom. RM1 105 FE51
Lower Belgrave St, SW1 18 G6
Lower Bobbingworth Grn, Ong. CM5 53 FG24
LOWER BOIS, Chesh. HP5 54 AR34
Lower Boston Rd, W7 137 CE74
Lower Br Rd, Red. RH1 250 DF134
Lower Britwell Rd, Slou. SL2 131 AK70
Lower Broad St, Dag. RM10 146 FA67
Lower Bury La, Epp. CM16 69 ES31
Lower Camden, Chis. BR7 185 EM94
Lower Ch Hill, Green. DA9 189 FS85

★ Place of interest | H Hospital | Sch School | Coll College | Uni University | ⇌ Railway station

Lower Ch St, Croy. CR0 *off Waddon New Rd* 201 DP103
Lower Cippenham La, Slou. SL1 131 AN74
Lower Clabdens, Ware SG12 33 DZ06
LOWER CLAPTON, E5 123 DX63
Lower Clapton Rd, E5 122 DV64
Lower Clarendon Wk, W11 *off Lancaster Rd* 139 CY72
Lower Common S, SW15 159 CV83
Lower Coombe St, Croy. CR0 220 DQ105
Lower Ct Rd, Epsom KT19 216 CQ111
Lower Cft, Swan. BR8 207 FF98
Lower Dagnall St, St.Alb. AL3 42 CC20
Lower Downs Rd, SW20 199 CX95
Lower Drayton Pl, Croy. CR0 *off Drayton Rd* 201 DP103
Lower Dr, Beac. HP9 89 AK50
Lower Dunnymans, Bans. SM7 *off Basing Rd* 217 CZ114
Lower Edgeborough Rd, Guil. GU1 259 AZ135
LOWER EDMONTON, N9 100 DT46
Lower Emms, Hem.H. HP2 *off Hunters Oak* 41 BQ15
Lower Fm Rd, Lthd. (Eff.) KT24 229 BV124
LOWER FELTHAM, Felt. TW13 175 BS90
Lowerfield, Welw.G.C. AL7 30 DA10
Lower George St, Rich. TW9 *off George St* 177 CK85
Lower Gravel Rd, Brom. BR2 204 EL102
LOWER GREEN, Esher KT10 196 CA103
Lower Grn, Welw. AL6 30 DE05
Lower Grn Gdns, Wor.Pk. KT4 199 CU102
Lower Grn Rd, Esher KT10 196 CB103
Lower Grn W, Mitch. CR4 200 DE97
Lower Grosvenor Pl, SW1 18 G5
Lower Gro Rd, Rich. TW10 178 CM86
Lower Guild Hall, Green. (Bluewater) DA9 *off Bluewater Parkway* 189 FU88
Lower Hall La, E4 101 DY50
Lower Hampton Rd, Sun. TW16 196 BW97
Lower Ham Rd, Kings.T. KT2 177 CK93
Lower Hatfield Rd, Hert. SG13 47 DK15
Lower Higham Rd, Grav. DA12 191 GM88
Lower High St, Wat. WD17 76 BX44
Lower Hill Rd, Epsom KT19 216 CP112
LOWER HOLLOWAY, N7 4 A1
Lower James St, W1 9 K9
Lower John St, W1 9 K9
Lower Kenwood Av, Enf. EN2 81 DK43
Lower Kings Rd, Berk. HP4 38 AW19
Kingston upon Thames KT2 178 CL94
LOWER KINGSWOOD, Tad. KT20 250 DA127
Lower Lea Crossing, E14 14 G9
E16 14 G9
Lower Lees Rd, Slou. SL2 131 AN69
Lower Maidstone Rd, N11 *off Telford Rd* 99 DJ51
Lower Mall, W6 159 CV78
Lower Mardyke Av, Rain. RM13 147 FC68
Lower Marsh, SE1 20 C4
Lower Marsh La, Kings.T. KT1 198 CM98
Lower Mead, Iver SL0 133 BD69
Lower Meadow, Harl. CM18 51 ES19
Waltham Cross EN8 67 DX27
Lower Merton Ri, NW3 140 DE66
Lower Morden La, Mord. SM4 199 CW100
Lower Mortlake Rd, Rich. TW9 158 CL84
LOWER NAZEING, Wal.Abb. EN9 50 EE23
Lower Noke Cl, Brwd. CM14 106 FL47
Lower Northfield, Bans. SM7 217 CZ114
Lower Paddock Rd, Wat. WD19 76 BY44
Lower Pk Rd, N11 99 DJ50
Belvedere DA17 166 FA76
Coulsdon CR5 234 DE118
Loughton IG10 84 EK43
Lower Paxton Rd, St.Alb. AL1 43 CE21
Lower Peryers, Lthd. (E.Hors.) KT24 245 BS128
Lower Pillory Down, Cars. SM5 218 DG113
Lower Plantation, Rick. (Loud.) WD3 74 BJ41
Lower Queens Rd, Buck.H. IG9 102 EK47
Lower Range Rd, Grav. DA12 191 GL87
Lower Richmond Rd, SW14 158 CP83
SW15 159 CW83
Richmond TW9 158 CN83
Lower Riding, Beac. HP9 88 AH53
Lower Rd, SE8 22 E5
SE16 22 G7
Belvedere DA17 166 FA76
Brentwood (Mtnsg) CM13, CM15 109 GD41
Erith DA8 167 FD77
Gerrards Cross SL9 90 AY53
Gravesend (Nthflt) DA11 170 FY84
Harrow HA2 117 CD61
Hemel Hempstead HP3 58 BN25
Kenley CR8 219 DP113
Leatherhead (Fetch.) KT22, KT23, KT24 231 CD123
Loughton IG10 85 EN40
Orpington BR5 206 EV101
Redhill RH1 266 DD136
Rickmansworth (Chorl.) WD3 73 BC42
Sutton SM1 218 DC105
Swanley BR8 187 FF94
Uxbridge (Denh.) UB9 113 BC59
Ware (Gt Amwell) SG12 33 DZ08
Lower Robert St, WC2 *off John Adam St* 141 DL73
Lower Rose Gall, Green. (Bluewater) DA9 *off Bluewater Parkway* 189 FU88
Lower Sales, Hem.H. HP1 39 BF21
Lower Sandfields, Wok. (Send) GU23 227 BD124
Lower Sand Hills, T.Ditt. KT7 197 CJ101
Lower Sawley Wd, Bans. SM7 *off Upper Sawley Wd* 217 CZ114
Lower Shott, Lthd. (Bkhm) KT23 246 CA126
Waltham Cross (Chsht) EN7 66 DT26
Lower Sloane St, SW1 18 E8
Lower Sq, Islw. TW7 157 CH83
Lower Sta Rd, Dart. (Cray.) DA1 187 FE86
Lower Strand, NW9 97 CT54
Lower St, Guil. (Shere) GU5 260 BN139
Lower Sunbury Rd, Hmptn. TW12 196 BZ96
Lower Swaines, Epp. CM16 69 ES30
LOWER SYDENHAM, SE26 183 DX91
⇌ Lower Sydenham 183 DZ92
Lower Sydenham Ind Est, SE26 183 DZ92
Lower Tail, Wat. WD19 94 BY48
Lower Talbot Wk, W11 *off Lancaster Rd* 139 CY72
Lower Teddington Rd, Kings.T. KT1 197 CK95
Lower Ter, NW3 120 DC62
Lower Thames St, EC3 11 K10
Lower Thames Wk, Green. (Bluewater) DA9 *off Bluewater Parkway* 189 FU88
Lower Tub, Bushey WD23 95 CD45
Lower Wd Rd, Esher (Clay.) KT10 215 CG107
Lower Woodside, Hat. AL9 45 CZ22
Lower Yott, Hem.H. HP2 40 BM21
Lowestoft Cl, E5 *off Theydon Rd* 122 DW61
Lowestoft Dr, Slou. SL1 130 AJ72
Lowestoft Ms, E16 165 EP75
Lowestoft Rd, Wat. WD24 75 BV39
Loweswater Cl, Wat. WD25 60 BW33
Wembley HA9 117 CK61
★ Lowewood Mus, Hodd. EN11 49 EA18
Lowfield, Saw. CM21 36 EX06
Lowfield Heath Ind Est, Craw. RH11 268 DE154
Lowfield La, Hodd. EN11 49 EA17
Lowfield Rd, NW6 140 DA66
W3 138 CQ72
Lowfield St, Dart. DA1 188 FL89
Low Hall Cl, E4 101 EA45
Low Hall La, E17 123 DY58
Low Hill Rd, Harl. (Roydon) CM19 50 EF17
Lowick Rd, Har. HA1 117 CE56
Lowlands, Hat. AL9 45 CW15
Lowlands Dr, Stai. (Stanw.) TW19 174 BK85
Lowlands Gdns, Rom. RM7 127 FB58
Lowlands Rd, Har. HA1 117 CE59
Pinner HA5 116 BW59
South Ockendon (Aveley) RM15 148 FP74
Lowman Rd, N7 121 DM63
Lowndes Av, Chesh. HP5 54 AP30
Lowndes Cl, SW1 18 F6
Lowndes Ct, W1 9 J8
Bromley BR1 *off Queens Rd* 204 EG96
Lowndes Pl, SW1 18 E6
Lowndes Sq, SW1 18 D4
Lowndes St, SW1 18 D5
Lowood Ct, SE19 182 DT92
Lowood St, E1 12 D9
Low Rd, Hat. AL9 46 DF15
Lowry Cl, Erith DA8 167 FD77
Lowry Cres, Mitch. CR4 200 DE96
Lowry Rd, Dag. RM8 126 EV63
Lowshoe La, Rom. RM5 105 FB53
Lowson Gro, Wat. WD19 94 BY45
LOW STREET, Til. RM18 171 GM79
Low St La, Til. (E.Til.) RM18 171 GM78
Lowswood Cl, Nthwd. HA6 93 BQ53
Lowther Cl, Borwd. (Elstree) WD6 78 CM43
Lowther Dr, Enf. EN2 81 DL42
Lowther Gdns, SW7 17 P4
Lowther Hill, SE23 183 DY87
Sch Lowther Prim Sch, SW13 *off Stillingfleet Rd* 159 CU79
Lowther Rd, E17 101 DY54
N7 4 C2
SW13 159 CT81
Kingston upon Thames KT2 198 CM95
Stanmore HA7 118 CM55
Lowthorpe, Wok. GU21 *off Shilburn Way* 226 AU118
Lowth Rd, SE5 162 DQ82
LOXFORD, Ilf. IG1 125 EQ64
Loxford Av, E6 144 EK68
Loxford La, Ilf. IG1, IG3 125 EQ64
Loxford Rd, Bark. IG11 145 EP65
Caterham CR3 252 DT125
Sch Loxford Sch of Science & Tech, Ilf. IG1 *off Loxford La* 125 ER64
Loxford Ter, Bark. IG11 *off Fanshawe Av* 145 EQ65
Loxford Way, Cat. CR3 252 DT125
Loxham Rd, E4 101 EA52
Loxham St, WC1 9 P2
Loxley Cl, SE26 183 DX92
Loxley Ct, Ware SG12 33 DY06
Loxley Rd, SW18 180 DD88
Berkhamsted HP4 38 AS17
Hampton TW12 176 BZ91
Loxton Rd, SE23 183 DX88
Loxwood Cl, Felt. TW14 175 BR88
Orpington BR5 206 EX103
Loxwood Rd, N17 122 DS55
Sch Loyola Prep Sch, Buck.H. IG9 *off Palmerston Rd* 102 EJ46
Coll L.S.O. St. Luke's, EC1 11 H3
Sch Lubavitch Ho Sch, Boys', E5 *off Clapton Common* 122 DT59
N16 *off Stamford Hill* 122 DT59
Girls', N16 *off Stamford Hill* 122 DT59
Lubbock Rd, Chis. BR7 185 EM94
Lubbock St, SE14 162 DW80
Lucan Dr, Stai. TW18 174 BK94
Lucan Pl, SW3 18 A8
Lucan Rd, Barn. EN5 79 CY41
Lucas Av, E13 144 EH67
Harrow HA2 116 CA61
Lucas Cl, NW10 *off Pound La* 139 CU66
Lucas Ct, Har. HA2 116 CA60
Waltham Abbey EN9 68 EF33
Lucas Cres, Green. DA9 *off Ingress Pk Av* 189 FW85
Lucas Gdns, N2 98 DC54
Lucas Rd, SE20 182 DW93
Lucas Rd, Grays RM17 170 GA76
Lucas Sq, NW11 *off Hampstead Way* 120 DA58
Lucas St, SE8 163 EA81
Sch Lucas Vale Prim Sch, SE8 *off Thornville St* 163 EA81
Lucern Cl, Wal.Cr. (Chsht) EN7 66 DS27
Lucerne Cl, N13 99 DL49
Woking GU22 *off Claremont Av* 226 AY119
Lucerne Ct, Erith DA18 *off Middle Way* 166 EY76
Lucerne Gro, E17 123 ED56
Lucerne Ms, W8 17 H1
Lucerne Rd, N5 121 DP63
Orpington BR6 205 ET102
Thornton Heath CR7 201 DP99
Lucerne Way, Rom. RM3 106 FK51
Lucey Rd, SE16 22 A6
Lucey Way, SE16 22 B6
Lucie Av, Ashf. TW15 175 BP93
Lucien Rd, SW17 180 DG91
SW19 180 DB89
Lucknow St, SE18 165 ES80
Lucks Hill, Hem.H. HP1 39 BE20
Lucorn Cl, SE12 184 EF86
Lucton Ms, Loug. IG10 85 EP42
Luctons Av, Buck.H. IG9 102 EJ46
Lucy Cres, W3 138 CQ71
Lucy Gdns, Dag. RM8 *off Grafton Rd* 126 EY62
Luddesdon Rd, Erith DA8 166 FA80
Luddington Av, Vir.W. GU25 193 AZ96
Ludford Cl, NW9 96 CS54
Croydon CR0 *off Warrington Rd* 219 DP105
Ludgate Bdy, EC4 10 E8
Ludgate Circ, EC4 10 E8
Ludgate Hill, EC4 10 E8
Ludgate Sq, EC4 10 F8
Ludham Cl, SE28 *off Rollesby Way* 146 EW72
Ilford IG6 103 EP53
Ludlow Cl, Brom. BR2 *off Aylesbury Rd* 204 EG97
Harrow HA2 116 BZ63
Ludlow Mead, Wat. WD19 93 BV48
Ludlow Pl, Grays RM17 170 GB76
Ludlow Rd, W5 137 CJ70
Feltham TW13 175 BU91
Guildford GU2 258 AV135
Ludlow St, EC1 10 G3
Ludlow Way, N2 120 DC56
Rickmansworth (Crox.Grn) WD3 75 BQ42
Ludovick Wk, SW15 158 CS84
Ludwick Cl, Welw.G.C. AL7 29 CZ11
Ludwick Grn, Welw.G.C. AL7 29 CZ10
Ludwick Ms, SE14 163 DY80
Ludwick Way, Welw.G.C. AL7 29 CZ09
Luff Cl, Wind. SL4 151 AL83
Luffield Rd, SE2 166 EV76
Luffman Rd, SE12 184 EH90
Lugard Rd, SE15 162 DV82
Lugg App, E12 125 EN62
Luke Ho, E1 12 C8
Luke St, EC2 11 L3
Lukin Cres, E4 101 ED48
Lukin St, E1 12 F8
Lukintone Cl, Loug. IG10 84 EL44
Lullarook Cl, West. (Bigg.H.) TN16 238 EJ116
Lullingstone Av, Swan. BR8 207 FF97
Lullingstone Cl, Orp. BR5 *off Lullingstone Cres* 186 EV94
Lullingstone Cres, Orp. BR5 186 EU94
Lullingstone La, SE13 183 ED87
Dartford (Eyns.) DA4 208 FJ104
★ Lullingstone Park Visitor Cen, Dart. DA4 225 FG107
Lullingstone Rd, Belv. DA17 166 EZ79
★ Lullingstone Roman Vil, Dart. DA4 207 FH104
Lullington Garth, N12 97 CZ50
Borehamwood WD6 78 CP43
Bromley BR1 184 EE94
Lullington Rd, SE20 182 DU94
Dagenham RM9 146 EY66
Lulot Gdns, N19 121 DH61
Lulworth, SE17 21 J9
Lulworth Av, Houns. TW5 156 CB80
Waltham Cross (Chsht) EN7 65 DP29
Wembley HA9 117 CJ59
Lulworth Cl, Har. HA2 116 BZ62
Lulworth Cres, Mitch. CR4 200 DE96
Lulworth Dr, Pnr. HA5 116 BX59
Romford RM5 105 FB50
Lulworth Gdns, Har. HA2 116 BY61
Lulworth Rd, SE9 184 EL89
SE15 162 DV82
Welling DA16 165 ET82
Lulworth Waye, Hayes UB4 136 BW72
Lumbards, Welw.G.C. AL7 30 DA06
Lumen Rd, Wem. HA9 117 CK61
Lumiere Ct, SW17 180 DG89
Lumley Cl, Belv. DA17 166 FA79
Lumley Ct, WC2 9 P10
Horley RH6 268 DG147
Lumley Gdns, Sutt. SM3 217 CY106
Lumley Rd, Horl. RH6 268 DG147
Sutton SM3 217 CY107
Lumley St, W1 8 F8
Lunar Cl, West. (Bigg.H.) TN16 238 EK116
Luna Rd, Th.Hth. CR7 202 DQ97
Lundin Wk, Wat. WD19 *off Woodhall La* 94 BX49
Lundy Dr, Hayes UB3 155 BS77
Lundy Wk, N1 5 H4
Lunedale Rd, Dart. DA2 188 FQ88
Lunedale Wk, Dart. DA2 *off Lunedale Rd* 188 FP88
Lunghurst Rd, Cat. (Wold.) CR3 237 DZ120
Lunham Rd, SE19 182 DS93
Lupin Cl, SW2 *off Palace Rd* 181 DP89
Croydon CR0 *off Primrose La* 203 DX102
Romford (Rush Grn) RM7 127 FD61
West Drayton UB7 *off Magnolia St* 154 BK78
Lupin Cres, Ilf. IG1 *off Bluebell Way* 125 EP64
Lupino Ct, SE11 20 B8
Luppit Cl, Brwd. (Hutt.) CM13 109 GA46
Lupton Cl, SE12 184 EH90
Lupton St, NW5 121 DJ63
Lupus St, SW1 19 K10
Luralda Gdns, E14 24 D9
Lurgan Av, W6 159 CX79
Lurline Gdns, SW11 160 DG81
Luscombe Ct, Brom. BR2 204 EE96
Luscombe Way, SW8 161 DL80
Lushes Ct, Loug. IG10 *off Lushes Rd* 85 EP43
Lushes Rd, Loug. IG10 85 EP43
Lushington Dr, Cob. KT11 213 BV114
Lushington Rd, NW10 139 CV68
SE6 183 EB92
Lushington Ter, E8 *off Wayland Av* 122 DU64
Lusted Hall La, West. (Tats.) TN16 238 EJ120
Lusted Rd, Sev. TN13 241 FE120
Lusteds Cl, Dor. RH4 *off Glory Mead* 263 CJ139
Luther Cl, Edg. HA8 96 CQ47
Luther King Cl, E17 123 DY58
Luther Ms, Tedd. TW11 *off Luther Rd* 177 CF92
Luther Rd, Tedd. TW11 177 CF92
Luton Pl, SE10 163 EC80
Luton Rd, E17 123 DZ55
Sidcup DA14 186 EW90
Luton St, NW8 7 P4
Lutton Ter, NW3 *off Flask Wk* 120 DD63
Luttrell Av, SW15 179 CV85
Lutwyche Rd, SE6 183 DZ89
Luxborough La, Chig. IG7 102 EL48
Luxborough St, W1 8 E5
Luxembourg Ms, E15 *off Leytonstone Rd* 124 EE64
Luxemburg Gdns, W6 16 A7
Luxfield Rd, SE9 184 EL88
Luxford Pl, Saw. CM21 36 EZ06
Luxford St, SE16 22 G8
Luxmore St, SE4 163 DZ81
Luxor St, SE5 162 DQ83
Luxted Rd, Orp. BR6 223 EN112
Lyall Av, SE21 182 DS90
Lyall Ms, SW1 18 E6
Lyall Ms W, SW1 18 E6
Lyall St, SW1 18 E6
Lyal Rd, E3 143 DY68
Lycaste Cl, St.Alb. AL1 43 CF21
Sch Lycée Français Charles de Gaulle Sch, SW7 17 N7
Lycett Pl, W12 *off Becklow Rd* 159 CU75
Lych Gate, Wat. WD25 60 BX33
Lych Gate Rd, Orp. BR6 206 EU102
Lych Gate Wk, Hayes UB3 135 BT73
Lych Way, Wok. GU21 226 AX116
Lyconby Gdns, Croy. CR0 203 DY101
Lycrome La, Chesh. HP5 54 AR28
Lycrome Rd, Chesh. HP5 54 AS28
Lydd Cl, Sid. DA14 185 ES90
Lydden Ct, SE9 185 ES86
Lydden Gro, SW18 180 DB87
Lydden Rd, SW18 180 DB87
Lydd Rd, Bexh. DA7 166 EZ80
Lydeard Rd, E6 145 EM66
Lydele Cl, Wok. GU21 227 AZ115
Lydford Av, Slou. SL2 131 AR71
Lydford Cl, N16 5 M1
Lydford Rd, N15 122 DR57
NW2 139 CX65
W9 6 F3
Lydhurst Av, SW2 181 DM89
Lydia Ms, Hat. (N.Mymms) AL9 45 CW24
Lydia Rd, Erith DA8 167 FF79
Lydney Cl, SE15 162 DS80
SW19 *off Princes Way* 179 CY89
Lydon Rd, SW4 161 DJ83
Lydsey Cl, Slou. SL2 131 AN69
Lydstep Rd, Chis. BR7 185 EN91
Lye, The, Tad. KT20 233 CW122
LYE GREEN, Chesh. HP5 56 AT27
Lye Grn Rd, Chesh. HP5 56 AR30
Lye La, St.Alb. (Brick.Wd) AL2 60 CA30
Lyell Pl E, Wind. SL4 150 AJ83
Lyell Pl W, Wind. SL4 *off Lyell Pl E* 150 AJ83
Lyell Wk E, Wind. SL4 *off Lyell Pl E* 150 AJ83
Lyell Wk W, Wind. SL4 *off Lyell Pl E* 150 AJ83
Lyfield, Lthd. (Oxshott) KT22 214 CB114
Lyford Rd, SW18 180 DD87
Lygean Av, Ware SG12 33 DY06
Lygon Pl, SW1 18 G6
Lyham Cl, SW2 181 DL86
Lyham Rd, SW2 181 DL85
Lyle Cl, Mitch. CR4 200 DG101
Lyle Pk, Sev. TN13 257 FH123
Lymbourne Cl, Sutt. SM2 218 DA110
Lymden Gdns, Reig. RH2 266 DB135
Lyme Fm Rd, SE12 164 EG84
Lyme Gro, E9 *off St. Thomas's Sq* 142 DW66
Lymer Av, SE19 182 DT92
Lyme Regis Rd, Bans. SM7 233 CZ117
Lyme Rd, Well. DA16 166 EV81
Lymescote Gdns, Sutt. SM1 200 DA103
Lyme St, NW1 141 DJ66
Lyme Ter, NW1 *off Royal Coll St* 141 DJ66
Lyminge Cl, Sid. DA14 185 ET91
Lyminge Gdns, SW18 180 DE88
Lymington Av, N22 99 DN54
Lymington Cl, E6 *off Valiant Way* 145 EM71
SW16 201 DK96
Lymington Dr, Ruis. HA4 115 BR61
Lymington Gdns, Epsom KT19 217 CT106
Lymington Rd, NW6 140 DB65
Dagenham RM8 126 EX60
Lyminster Cl, Hayes UB4 *off West Quay Dr* 136 BY71
Lympstone Gdns, SE15 162 DU80
Lynbridge Gdns, N13 99 DP49
Lynbrook Cl, SE15 *off Blakes Rd* 162 DS80
Rainham RM13 147 FD68
Lynceley Gra, Epp. CM16 70 EU29
Lynch, The, Hodd. EN11 49 EB17
Uxbridge UB8 *off New Windsor St* 134 BJ67
Lynch Cl, Uxb. UB8 *off New Windsor St* 134 BJ66
Lynchen Cl, Houns. TW5 *off The Avenue* 155 BU81
Lynch Hill La, Slou. SL2 131 AL70
Sch Lynch Hill Prim Sch, Slou. SL2 *off Garrard Rd* 131 AM69
Lynchmere Pl, Guil. GU2 *off Peak Rd* 242 AU131
Lynch Wk, SE8 *off Prince St* 163 DZ79
Lyncott Cres, SW4 161 DH84
Lyncroft Av, Pnr. HA5 116 BY57
Lyncroft Gdns, NW6 120 DA64
W13 157 CJ75
Epsom KT17 217 CT109
Lyncroft Gdns, Houns. TW3 156 CC84
Lyndale, NW2 119 CZ63
Lyndale Av, NW2 119 CZ62
Lyndale Cl, SE3 164 EF79
Lyndale Ct, W.Byf. KT14 *off Parvis Rd* 212 BG113
Lyndale Est, Grays RM20 169 FV79
Lyndale Rd, Red. RH1 250 DF131
Lynden Way, Swan. BR8 207 FC97
Lyndhurst Av, N12 98 DF51
NW7 96 CS51
SW16 201 DK96
Pinner HA5 93 BV53
Southall UB1 136 CB74
Sunbury-on-Thames TW16 195 BU97
Surbiton KT5 198 CP102
Twickenham TW2 176 BZ88
Lyndhurst Cl, NW10 118 CR62
Bexleyheath DA7 167 FB83
Croydon CR0 202 DT104
Orpington BR6 223 EP105
Woking GU21 226 AX115
Lyndhurst Ct, E18 *off Churchfields* 102 EG53
Sutton SM2 *off Overton Rd* 218 DA108
Lyndhurst Dr, E10 123 EC59
Hornchurch RM11 128 FJ60
New Malden KT3 198 CS100
Sevenoaks TN13 256 FE124
Lyndhurst Gdns, N3 97 CY53
NW3 120 DD64
Barking IG11 145 ES65
Enfield EN1 82 DS42
Ilford IG2 125 ER58
Pinner HA5 93 BV53
Lyndhurst Gro, SE15 162 DS82
Lyndhurst Ho, SW15 *off Ellisfield Dr* 179 CU87
Sch Lyndhurst Ho Prep Sch, NW3 *off Lyndhurst Gdns* 120 DD64
Sch Lyndhurst Prim Sch, SE5 *off Grove La* 162 DR82
Lyndhurst Ri, Chig. IG7 103 EN49
Lyndhurst Rd, E4 101 EC52
N18 100 DU49
N22 99 DM51
NW3 120 DD64
Bexleyheath DA7 167 FB83
Chesham HP5 54 AP28
Coulsdon CR5 234 DG116
Greenford UB6 136 CB70
Reigate RH2 266 DA137
Thornton Heath CR7 201 DN98
Lyndhurst Sq, SE15 162 DT81
Lyndhurst Ter, NW3 120 DD64
Lyndhurst Way, SE15 162 DT81
Brentwood (Hutt.) CM13 109 GC45
Chertsey KT16 193 BE104
Sutton SM2 218 DA108
Lyndon Av, Pnr. HA5 94 BY51
Sidcup DA15 185 ET85
Wallington SM6 200 DG104
Lyndon Rd, Belv. DA17 166 FA77
Lyndon Yd, SW17 *off Riverside Rd* 180 DC91
Lyndwood Dr, Wind. (Old Wind.) SL4 172 AU86
LYNE, Cher. KT16 193 BA102
Sch Lyne & Long Cross C of E Sch, Cher. KT16 *off Lyne La* 193 BB103
Lyne Cl, Vir.W. GU25 193 AZ100
Lyne Cres, E17 101 DZ53
Lyne Crossing Rd, Cher. (Lyne) KT16 193 BA100
Lynegrove Av, Ashf. TW15 175 BQ92
Lyneham Wk, E5 123 DY64
Pinner HA5 115 BT55
Lyne La, Cher. (Lyne) KT16 193 BA100
Egham TW20 193 BA99
Virginia Water GU25 193 BA100
Lyne Rd, Vir.W. GU25 192 AX100
Lynette Av, SW4 181 DH86
Lynett Rd, Dag. RM8 126 EX61
Lyne Way, Hem.H. HP1 39 BF18
Lynford Cl, Barn. EN5 *off Rowley La* 79 CT43
Edgware HA8 96 CQ52
Lynford Gdns, Edg. HA8 96 CP48
Ilford IG3 125 ET61
Lyngfield Pk, Maid. SL6 *off Windsor Rd* 150 AE79
Lynhurst Cres, Uxb. UB10 135 BQ66
Lynhurst Rd, Uxb. UB10 135 BQ66
Lynmere Rd, Well. DA16 166 EV82
Lyn Ms, E3 13 L2
N16 122 DS63
Lynmouth Av, Enf. EN1 82 DT44
Morden SM4 199 CX101
Lynmouth Dr, Ruis. HA4 115 BV61
Lynmouth Gdns, Grnf. UB6 137 CH67
Hounslow TW5 156 BX81
Lynmouth Ri, Orp. BR5 206 EV98
Lynmouth Rd, E17 123 DY58
N2 120 DF55
N16 122 DT60
Greenford UB6 137 CH67
Welwyn Garden City AL7 29 CZ09
Lynn Cl, Ashf. TW15 *off Goffs Rd* 175 BR92
Harrow HA3 95 CD54
Lynne Cl, Orp. BR6 223 ET107
South Croydon CR2 220 DW111
Lynne Wk, Esher KT10 214 CC106
Lynne Way, NW10 138 CS65
Northolt UB5 136 BX68
Lynn Ms, E11 *off Lynn Rd* 124 EE61
Lynn Rd, E11 124 EE61
SW12 181 DH87
Ilford IG2 125 ER59
Lynn St, Enf. EN2 82 DR39
Lynn Wk, Reig. RH2 266 DB137
Lynross Cl, Rom. RM3 106 FM54
Lynscott Way, S.Croy. CR2 219 DP109
Lynsted Cl, Bexh. DA6 187 FB85
Bromley BR1 204 EJ96
Lynsted Ct, Beck. BR3 *off Churchfields Rd* 203 DY96
Lynsted Gdns, SE9 164 EK83
Lynton Av, N12 98 DD49
NW9 119 CT56
W13 137 CG72
Orpington BR5 206 EV98
Romford RM7 104 FA53
St. Albans AL1 43 CJ21
Lynton Cl, NW10 118 CS64
Chessington KT9 216 CL105

⊖ London Underground station DLR Docklands Light Railway station Tra Tramlink station Riv Pedestrian ferry landing stage

Lynton Cl, Islw. TW7 157 CF84
Lynton Cres, Ilf. IG2 125 EP58
Lynton Crest, Pot.B. EN6 off Strafford Gate 64 DA32
Lynton Est, SE1 22 A8
Lynton Gdns, N11 99 DK51
Enfield EN1 100 DS45
Lynton Mead, N20 98 DA48
Lynton Par, Wal.Cr. EN8 off Turners Hill 67 DX30
Lynton Rd, E4 101 EB50
N8 121 DK57
NW6 139 CZ67
SE1 21 P8
W3 138 CN73
Chesham HP5 54 AP28
Croydon CR0 201 DN100
Gravesend DA11 191 GG88
Harrow HA2 116 BY61
New Malden KT3 198 CR99
Lynton Rd S, Grav. DA11 191 GG88
Lynton Ter, W3 off Lynton Rd 138 CQ72
Lynton Wk, Hayes UB4 135 BS69
Lynwood, Guil. GU2 258 AV135
Lynwood Av, Couls. CR5 235 DH115
Egham TW20 172 AY93
Epsom KT17 217 CT114
Slough SL3 152 AX76
Lynwood Cl, E18 102 EJ53
Harrow HA2 116 BY62
Romford RM5 105 FB51
Woking GU21 211 BD113
Lynwood Dr, Nthwd. HA6 93 BT53
Romford RM5 105 FB51
Worcester Park KT4 199 CU103
Lynwood Gdns, Croy. CR0 219 DM105
Southall UB1 136 BZ72
Lynwood Gro, N21 99 DN46
Orpington BR6 205 ES101
Lynwood Hts, Rick. WD3 74 BH43
Lynwood Rd, SW17 180 DF90
W5 137 CL70
Epsom KT17 217 CT115
Redhill RH1 250 DG132
Thames Ditton KT7 197 CF103
Lynx Hill, Lthd. (E.Hors.) KT24 245 BS128
Lynx Way, E16 off Festoon Way 144 EK73
Lyon Business Pk, Bark. IG11 145 ES68
Lyon Meade, Stan. HA7 95 CJ53
Lyon Pk Av, Wem. HA0 138 CL65
Sch Lyon Pk Inf Sch, Wem. HA0 off Vincent Rd 138 CM66
Sch Lyon Pk Jun Sch, Wem. HA0 off Vincent Rd 138 CM66
Lyon Rd, SW19 200 DC95
Harrow HA1 117 CF58
Romford RM1 127 FF59
Walton-on-Thames KT12 196 BY103
Lyons Ct, Dor. RH4 263 CH136
Lyonsdene, Tad. KT20 249 CZ127
Lyonsdown Av, Barn. EN5 80 DC44
Lyonsdown Rd, Barn. EN5 80 DC44
Sch Lyonsdown Sch (Indep), Barn. EN5 off Richmond Rd 80 DC43
Lyons Dr, Guil. GU2 242 AU129
Lyons Pl, NW8 7 N3
Lyon St, N1 4 A6
Lyons Wk, W14 16 C7
Lyon Way, Grnf. UB6 137 CE67
St. Albans AL4 44 CN20
Lyoth Rd, Orp. BR5 205 EQ103
Lyrical Way, Hem.H. HP1 46 BH18
Lyric Dr, Grnf. UB6 136 CB70
Lyric Ms, SE26 182 DW91
Lyric Rd, SW13 159 CT81
★ Lyric Thea, W6 159 CW77
Lysander Cl, Hem.H. (Bov.) HP3 57 AZ27
Lysander Gdns, Surb. KT6 off Ewell Rd 198 CM100
Lysander Gro, N19 121 DK60
Lysander Ms, N19 off Lysander Gro 121 DJ60
Lysander Rd, Croy. CR0 219 DM107
Ruislip HA4 115 BR61
Lysander Way, Abb.L. WD5 59 BU32
Orpington BR6 205 EQ104
Welwyn Garden City AL7 30 DD08
Lys Hill Gdns, Hert. SG14 31 DP07
Lysias Rd, SW12 180 DG86
Lysia St, SW6 159 CX80
Lysley Pl, Hat. (Brook.Pk) AL9 64 DC27
Lysons Wk, SW15 off Swinburne Rd 179 CU85
Lyster Ms, Cob. KT11 213 BV113
Lytchet Rd, Brom. BR1 184 EH94
Lytchet Way, Enf. EN3 82 DW39
Lytchgate Cl, S.Croy. CR2 220 DS108
Lytcott Dr, W.Mol. KT8 off Freeman Dr 196 BZ97
Lytcott Gro, SE22 182 DT85
Lyte St, E2 off Bishops Way 142 DW68
Lytham Av, Wat. WD19 94 BX50
Lytham Cl, SE28 146 EY72
Lytham Gro, W5 138 CM69
Lytham St, SE17 21 J10
Lyttelton Cl, NW3 140 DE66
Lyttelton Rd, E10 123 EB62
N2 120 DC57
Lyttleton Rd, N8 121 DN55
Lytton Av, N13 99 DN47
Enfield EN3 83 DY38
Lytton Cl, N2 120 DD57
Loughton IG10 85 ER41
Northolt UB5 136 BZ66
Lytton Gdns, Wall. SM6 219 DK105
Welwyn Garden City AL8 29 CX09
Lytton Gro, SW15 179 CX85
Lytton Pk, Cob. KT11 214 BZ112
Lytton Rd, E11 124 EE59
Barnet EN5 80 DC42
Grays RM16 171 GG77
Pinner HA5 94 BY52
Romford RM2 127 FH57
Woking GU22 227 BB116
Lytton Strachey Path, SE28 off Titmuss Av 146 EV73
Lyttons Way, Hodd. EN11 33 EA14
Lyveden Rd, SE3 164 EH80
SW17 180 DE93
Lywood Cl, Tad. KT20 233 CW122

M

Mabbotts, Tad. KT20 233 CX121
Mabbutt Cl, St.Alb. (Brick.Wd) AL2 60 BY30
Mabel Rd, Swan. BR8 187 FG93
Mabel St, Wok. GU21 226 AX117
Maberley Cres, SE19 182 DU94
Maberley Rd, SE19 202 DT95
Beckenham BR3 203 DX97
Mabeys Wk, Saw. (High Wych) CM21 36 EV06
Mabledon Pl, WC1 9 M2
Mablethorpe Rd, SW6 159 CY80
Mabley St, E9 143 DY65
McAdam Cl, Hodd. EN11 49 EA15
McAdam Dr, Enf. EN2 off Rowantree Rd 81 DP40
Macaret Cl, N20 98 DB45
MacArthur Cl, E7 144 EG65
Erith DA8 167 FE78
MacArthur Ter, SE7 164 EL79
Macaulay Av, Esher KT10 197 CE103
Sch Macaulay C of E Prim Sch, SW4 off Victoria Ri 161 DH83
Macaulay Ct, SW4 161 DH83
Macaulay Rd, E6 144 EK68
SW4 161 DH83
Caterham CR3 236 DS122
Macaulay Sq, SW4 161 DH84
Macaulay Way, SE28 off Booth Cl 146 EV73
McAuley Cl, SE1 20 C5
SE9 185 EP85
Macauley Ms, SE13 163 EC82
McAuliffe Dr, Slou. SL2 111 AM63
Macbean St, SE18 165 EN76
Macbeth St, W6 159 CV78
McCall Cl, SW4 off Jeffreys Rd 161 DL82
McCall Cres, SE7 164 EL78
McCarthy Rd, Felt. TW13 176 BX92
Macclesfield Br, NW1 140 DE68
Macclesfield Rd, EC1 10 G1
SE25 202 DV99
Macclesfield St, W1 9 M9
McClintock Pl, Enf. EN3 83 EB38
McCoid Way, SE1 20 G4
McCrone Ms, NW3 off Belsize La 140 DD65
McCudden Rd, Dart. DA1 off Cornwall Rd 168 FM83
McCullum Rd, E3 143 DZ67
McDermott Cl, SW11 160 DE83
McDermott Rd, SE15 162 DU83
Macdonald Av, Dag. RM10 127 FB62
Hornchurch RM11 128 FL56
Macdonald Cl, Amer. HP6 55 AR35
McDonald Ct, Hat. AL10 45 CU20
Macdonald Rd, E7 124 EG63
E17 101 EC54
N11 98 DF50
N19 121 DJ61
Macdonald Way, Horn. RM11 128 FL56
Macdonnell Gdns, Wat. WD25 off High Rd 75 BT35
McDonough Cl, Chess. KT9 216 CL105
McDougall Rd, Berk. HP4 38 AX19
McDowall Cl, E16 15 K6
McDowall Rd, SE5 162 DQ81
Macdowall Rd, Guil. GU2 off Tylehost 242 AV130
Macduff Rd, SW11 160 DG81
Mace Cl, E1 22 C1
Mace Ct, Grays RM17 170 GE79
Mace La, Sev. (Cudham) TN14 223 ER113
McEntee Av, E17 101 DY53
Sch McEntee Sch, E17 off Billet Rd 101 DZ53
Coll McEntree Adult Ed Cen, E17 off Billet Rd 101 DZ53
Macers Ct, Brox. EN10 49 DZ24
Macers La, Brox. EN10 49 DZ24
Mace St, E2 143 DX68
McEwen Way, E15 143 ED67
Macey Ho, SW11 off Surrey La 160 DE81
MacFarlane La, Islw. TW7 157 CF79
Macfarlane Rd, W12 139 CW74
Macfarren Pl, NW1 8 F4
McGrath Rd, E15 124 EF64
McGredy, Wal.Cr. (Chshst) EN7 66 DV29
Macgregor Rd, E16 144 EJ71
McGregor Rd, W11 6 F6
Machell Rd, SE15 162 DW83
McIntosh Cl, Rom. RM1 127 FE55
Wallington SM6 219 DL108
Macintosh Cl, Wal.Cr. EN7 66 DR26
McIntosh Rd, Rom. RM1 127 FE55
Mackay Rd, SW4 161 DH83
McKay Rd, SW20 179 CV94
McKay Trd Est, Slou. (Colnbr.) SL3 153 BE82
McKellar Cl, Bushey (Bushey Hth) WD23 94 CC47
Mackennal St, NW8 140 DE68
Mackenzie Mall, Slou. SL1 off High St 152 AT75
Mackenzie Rd, N7 4 A3
Beckenham BR3 202 DW96
McKenzie Rd, Brox. EN10 49 DZ20
Mackenzie St, Slou. SL1 132 AT74
Mackenzie Wk, E14 23 P2
McKenzie Way, Epsom KT19 216 CN110
Mackenzie Way, Grav. DA12 191 GK93
McKerrell Rd, SE15 162 DU81
Mackeson Rd, NW3 120 DF63
Mackie Rd, SW2 181 DN87
Mackies Hill, Guil. (Peasl.) GU5 261 BR144
Mackintosh La, E9 off Homerton High St 123 DX64
Macklin St, WC2 9 P7
Mackrells, Red. RH1 266 DC137
Mackrow Wk, E14 14 C9
Macks Rd, SE16 22 B7
Mackworth St, NW1 9 J1
Maclaren Ms, SW15 off Clarendon Dr 159 CW84
Maclean Rd, SE23 183 DY86
Maclennan Av, Rain. RM13 148 FK69
Macleod Cl, Grays RM17 170 GD77
Macleod Rd, N21 81 DL43
McLeod Rd, SE2 166 EV77
McLeod's Ms, SW7 17 K6
Macleod St, SE17 21 H10
Maclise Rd, W14 16 C6
McMillan Cl, Grav. DA12 191 GJ91
Macmillan Gdns, Dart. DA1 168 FN84
McMillan St, SE8 163 EA79
Macmillan Way, SW17 181 DH91
McNair Rd, Sthl. UB2 156 CB75
McNeil Rd, SE5 162 DS82
McNicol Dr, NW10 138 CQ68
Macoma Rd, SE18 165 ER79
Macoma Ter, SE18 165 ER79
Maconochies Rd, E14 24 A9
Macon Way, Upmin. RM14 129 FT59
Macquarie Way, E14 24 B8
McRae La, Mitch. CR4 200 DF101
Macroom Rd, W9 6 F1
Mac's Pl, EC4 10 C7
★ Madame Tussaud's, NW1 8 E4
Sch Madani Girls Sch, E1 12 C7
Madan Rd, West. TN16 255 ER125
Madans Wk, Epsom KT18 216 CR114
Mada Rd, Orp. BR6 205 EP104
Maddams St, E3 14 A4
Madden Cl, Swans. DA10 189 FX86
Maddison Cl, Tedd. TW11 177 CF93
Maddocks Cl, Sid. DA14 186 EY92
Maddock Way, SE17 161 DP79
Maddox La, Lthd. (Bkhm) KT23 230 BY123
Maddox Pk, Lthd. (Bkhm) KT23 230 BY123
Maddox Rd, Harl. CM20 35 ES14
Hemel Hempstead HP2 41 BP20
Maddox St, W1 9 H9
Madeira Av, Brom. BR1 184 EE94
Madeira Cl, W.Byf. KT14 off Brantwood Gdns 212 BG113
Madeira Cres, W.Byf. KT14 off Brantwood Gdns 212 BG113
Madeira Gro, Wdf.Grn. IG8 102 EJ51
Madeira Rd, E11 123 ED60
N13 99 DP49
SW16 181 DL92
Mitcham CR4 200 DF98
West Byfleet KT14 211 BF113
Madeira Wk, Brwd. CM15 108 FY48
Reigate RH2 250 DD133
Windsor SL4 151 AR81
Madeley Cl, Amer. HP6 55 AR36
Madeley Rd, W5 138 CL72
Madeline Gro, Ilf. IG1 125 ER64
Madeline Rd, SE20 202 DU95
Madells, Epp. CM16 69 ET31
Madford Retail Pk, Hert. SG13 off Ware Rd 32 DS09
Madge Gill Way, E6 off Ron Leighton Way 144 EL67
Madgeways Cl, Ware (Gt Amwell) SG12 33 DZ09
Madgeways La, Ware (Gt Amwell) SG12 33 DZ10
Madinah Rd, E8 142 DU65
Madingley, Kings.T. KT1 off St. Peters Rd 198 CN96
Madison Cres, Bexh. DA7 166 EW80
Madison Gdns, Bexh. DA7 166 EW80
Bromley BR2 204 EF97
Madison Way, Sev. TN13 256 FF123
Madras Pl, N7 4 C3
Madras Rd, Ilf. IG1 125 EP63
Madresfield Ct, Rad. (Shenley) WD7 off Russet Dr 62 CL32
Madrid Rd, SW13 159 CU81
Guildford GU2 258 AV135
Madrigal La, SE5 161 DP80
Madron St, SE17 21 M9
Maesmaur Rd, West. (Tats.) TN16 238 EK121
Mafeking Av, E6 144 EK68
Brentford TW8 158 CL79
Ilford IG2 125 ER59
Mafeking Rd, E16 15 J3
N17 100 DU54
Enfield EN1 82 DT41
Staines (Wrays.) TW19 173 BB89
Magazine Pl, Lthd. KT22 231 CH122
Magazine Rd, Cat. CR3 235 DP122
Magdala Av, N19 121 DH61
Magdala Rd, Islw. TW7 157 CG83
South Croydon CR2 off Napier Rd 220 DR108
Magdalen Cl, W.Byf. (Byfleet) KT14 212 BL114
Magdalen Cres, W.Byf. (Byfleet) KT14 212 BL114
Magdalene Cl, SE15 off Pilkington Rd 162 DV82
Magdalene Gdns, E6 145 EN70
Magdalene Rd, Shep. TW17 194 BM98
Magdalen Gdns, Brwd. (Hutt.) CM13 109 GE44
Magdalen Gro, Orp. BR6 224 EV105
MAGDALEN LAVER, Ong. CM5 53 FE17
Magdalen Pas, E1 11 P9
Magdalen Rd, SW18 180 DC88
Magdalen St, SE1 21 L2
Magee St, SE11 161 DN79
Magellan Pl, E14 off Maritime Quay 163 EA78
Maggie Blakes Causeway, SE1 off Shad Thames 142 DT74
Magna Carta La, Stai. (Wrays.) TW19 172 AX88
★ Magna Carta Monument, Egh. TW20 172 AX89
Sch Magna Carta Sch, The, Stai. TW18 off Thorpe Rd 173 BD93
Magna Rd, Egh. (Eng.Grn) TW20 172 AV93
Magnaville Rd, Bushey (Bushey Hth) WD23 95 CE45
Magnet Est, Grays RM20 169 FW78
Magnet Rd, Grays RM20 169 FW79
Wembley HA9 117 CK61
Magnin Cl, E8 off Wilde Cl 142 DU67
Magnolia Av, Abb.L. WD5 59 BU32
Magnolia Cl, E10 123 EA61
Hertford SG13 32 DU09
Kingston upon Thames KT2 178 CQ93
St. Albans (Park St) AL2 61 CD27
Magnolia Ct, Har. HA3 118 CM59
Horley RH6 268 DG148
Richmond TW9 off West Hall Rd 158 CP81
Wallington SM6 off Parkgate Rd 219 DH106
Magnolia Dr, West. (Bigg.H.) TN16 238 EK116
Magnolia Gdns, Edg. HA8 96 CQ49
Slough SL3 152 AW76
Magnolia Pl, SW4 181 DL85
W5 off Montpelier Rd 138 CL71
Magnolia Rd, W4 158 CP79
Magnolia St, West Dr. UB7 154 BK77
Magnolia Way, Brwd. (Pilg.Hat.) CM15 108 FV43
Dorking (N.Holm.) RH5 263 CK139
Epsom KT19 216 CQ106
Magnolia Way, H.Wyc. HP10 off Glory Mill La 110 AE56
Magnum Cl, Rain. RM13 148 FJ70
Magpie All, EC4 10 D8
Magpie Cl, E7 124 EF64
NW9 off Eagle Dr 96 CS54
Coulsdon CR5 off Ashbourne Cl 235 DJ118
Enfield EN1 82 DU39
Magpie Hall Cl, Brom. BR2 204 EL100
Magpie Hall La, Brom. BR2 205 EM99
Magpie Hall Rd, Bushey (Bushey Hth) WD23 95 CE47
Magpie La, Amer. (Colesh.) HP7 89 AM45
Brentwood CM13 107 FW54
Magpie Pl, SE14 off Milton Ct Rd 163 DY79
Magpies, The, Epp. CM16 51 EN24
Magpie Wk, Hat. AL10 off Lark Ri 45 CU20
Magpie Way, Slou. SL2 off Pemberton Rd 131 AL70
Magri Wk, E1 12 E6
Maguire Dr, Rich. TW10 177 CJ91
Maguire St, SE1 21 P3
Mahlon Av, Ruis. HA4 115 BV64
Mahogany Cl, SE16 23 K2
Mahon Cl, Enf. EN1 82 DT39
Maida Av, E4 101 EB45
W2 7 M5
MAIDA HILL, W9 6 G3
Maida Rd, Belv. DA17 166 FA76
MAIDA VALE, W9 7 K3
⊖ Maida Vale 7 L2
Maida Vale, W9 7 L2
Maida Vale Rd, Dart. DA1 187 FG85
Maida Way, E4 101 EB45
Maiden Erlegh Av, Bex. DA5 186 EY88
Maidenhead Rd, Wind. SL4 151 AK80
Maidenhead St, Hert. SG14 32 DR09
Maiden La, NW1 141 DK66
SE1 21 H1
WC2 9 P10
Dartford DA1 167 FG83
Maiden Rd, E15 144 EE66
Maidenshaw Rd, Epsom KT19 216 CR112
Maidenstone Hill, SE10 163 EC81
Maids of Honour Row, Rich. TW9 off The Green 177 CK85
Maidstone Av, Rom. RM5 105 FC54
Maidstone Bldgs Ms, SE1 21 H2
Maidstone Ho, E14 14 B7
Maidstone Rd, N11 99 DJ51
Grays RM17 170 GA79
Sevenoaks TN13 256 FE122
Sevenoaks (Seal) TN15 257 FN121
Sidcup DA14 186 EX93
Swanley BR8 207 FB95
Maidstone St, E2 off Audrey St 142 DU68
Main Av, Enf. EN1 82 DT43
Northwood HA6 93 BQ48
Main Dr, Ger.Cr. SL9 112 AW57
Iver SL0 153 BE77
Wembley HA9 117 CK62
Main Par, Rick. (Chorl.) WD3 off Whitelands Av 73 BC42
Main Par Flats, Rick. (Chorl.) WD3 off Whitelands Av 73 BC42
Main Ride, Egh. TW20 172 AS93
Mainridge Rd, Chis. BR7 185 EN91
Main Rd, Dart. (Fnghm) DA4 208 FL100
Dartford (Sutt.H.) DA4 188 FP93
Edenbridge (Crock.H.) TN8 255 EQ134
Longfield DA3 209 FX96
Orpington BR5 206 EW95
Romford RM1, RM2 127 FF56
Sevenoaks (Knock.) TN14 240 EV117
Sevenoaks (Sund.) TN14 240 EX124
Sidcup DA14 185 ES90
Swanley (Crock.) BR8 207 FD100
Swanley (Hext.) BR8 187 FF94
Westerham TN16 222 EJ113
Main St, Felt. TW13 176 BX92
Maisemore St, SE15 off Peckham Pk Rd 162 DU80
Maisie Webster Cl, Stai. (Stanw.) TW19 off Lauser Rd 174 BK87
Maitland Cl, Houns. TW4 156 BZ83
Walton-on-Thames KT12 196 BY103
West Byfleet KT14 212 BG113
Maitland Cl Est, SE10 off Greenwich High Rd 163 EB80
Maitland Pk Est, NW3 140 DF65
Maitland Pk Rd, NW3 140 DF65
Maitland Pk Vil, NW3 140 DF65
Maitland Pl, E5 off Clarence Rd 122 DV63
Maitland Rd, E15 144 EF65
SE26 183 DX93
Maize Cft, Horl. RH6 269 DJ147
Maizey Ct, Brwd. (Pilg.Hat.) CM15 off Danes Way 108 FU43
Majendie Rd, SE18 165 ER78
Majestic Way, Mitch. CR4 200 DF96
Sch Majorie McClure Sch, Chis. BR7 off Hawkwood La 205 EQ96
Major Rd, E15 123 EC64
SE16 22 B5
Majors Fm Rd, Slou. SL3 152 AX80
Makepeace Av, N6 120 DG61
Makepeace Rd, E11 124 EG56
Northolt UB5 136 BY68
Makins St, SW3 18 B8
Malabar St, E14 23 N4
Malacca Fm, Guil. (W.Clan.) GU4 244 BH127
Malam Gdns, E14 14 A9
Malan Cl, West. (Bigg.H.) TN16 238 EL117
Malan Sq, Rain. RM13 147 FH65
Malbrook Rd, SW15 159 CV84
Malcolm Ct, Stan. HA7 95 CJ50
Malcolm Cres, NW4 119 CU58
Malcolm Dr, Surb. KT6 198 CL102
Malcolm Gdns, Horl. (Hkwd) RH6 268 DD150
Malcolm Pl, E2 12 E3
Sch Malcolm Prim Sch, SE20 off Malcolm Rd 182 DW94
Malcolm Rd, E1 12 E3
SE20 182 DW94
SE25 202 DU100
SW19 179 CY93
Coulsdon CR5 235 DK115
Uxbridge UB10 114 BM63
Malcolms Way, N14 81 DJ43
Malcolm Way, E11 124 EG57
Malden Av, SE25 202 DV98
Malden Av, Grnf. UB6 117 CE64
Malden Cl, Amer. HP6 72 AT38
Malden Ct, N.Mal. KT3 off West Barnes La 199 CV97
Malden Cres, NW1 140 DG65
Malden Flds, Bushey WD23 76 BX43
Malden Grn Av, Wor.Pk. KT4 199 CT102
Malden Hill, N.Mal. KT3 199 CT97
Malden Hill Gdns, N.Mal. KT3 199 CT97
⇌ Malden Manor 198 CS101
Sch Malden Manor Prim Sch, N.Mal. KT3 off Lawrence Av 198 CS101
Malden Pk, N.Mal. KT3 199 CT100
Sch Malden Parochial C of E Prim Sch, Wor.Pk. KT4 off The Manor Dr 198 CS102
Malden Pl, NW5 off Grafton Ter 120 DG64
Malden Rd, NW5 120 DG64
Borehamwood WD6 78 CN41
New Malden KT3 198 CS99
Sutton SM3 217 CX105
Watford WD17 75 BU40
Worcester Park KT4 199 CT101
MALDEN RUSHETT, Chess. KT9 215 CH111
Malden Way, N.Mal. KT3 199 CT99
Maldon Cl, E15 off David St 123 ED64
N1 4 G7
SE5 162 DS83
Maldon Ct, Wall. SM6 off Maldon Rd 219 DJ106
Maldon Rd, N9 100 DT48
W3 138 CQ73
Romford RM7 127 FC59
Wallington SM6 219 DH106
Maldon Wk, Wdf.Grn. IG8 102 EJ51
Malet Cl, Egh. TW20 173 BD93
Malet Pl, WC1 9 L4
Malet St, WC1 9 L4
Maley Av, SE27 181 DP89
Malford Ct, E18 102 EG54
Malford Gro, E18 124 EF56
Malfort Rd, SE5 162 DS83
Malham Cl, N11 off Catterick Cl 98 DG51
Malham Rd, SE23 183 DX88
Malins Cl, Barn. EN5 79 CV43
Malkin Dr, Beac. HP9 88 AJ52
Harlow (Ch.Lang.) CM17 52 EY16
Sch Mall, The, Twick. TW2 off Hampton Rd 177 CD90
E15 143 ED66
N14 99 DL48
SW1 19 K3
SW14 178 CQ85
W5 138 CL73
Croydon CR0 202 DQ103
Harrow HA3 118 CM58
Hornchurch RM11 127 FH60
St. Albans (Park St) AL2 60 CC27
Surbiton KT6 197 CK99
Mallams Ms, SW9 off St. James's Cres 161 DP83
Mallard Cl, E9 off Berkshire Rd 143 DZ65
NW6 140 DA68
W7 157 CE75
Barnet EN5 off The Hook 80 DD44
Dartford DA1 188 FM85
Horley RH6 268 DG146
Redhill RH1 250 DG131
Twickenham TW2 off Stephenson Rd 176 CA87
Upminster RM14 129 FT59
Mallard Dr, Slou. SL1 131 AM73
Mallard Path, SE28 165 ER76
Mallard Pl, Twick. TW1 177 CG90
Mallard Pt, E3 14 A2
Mallard Rd, Abb.L. WD5 59 BU31
South Croydon CR2 221 DX110
Mallards, The, Hem.H. HP3 off Kingfisher Dr 58 BM25
Staines TW18 194 BH96
Mallards Reach, Wey. KT13 195 BR103
Mallards Ri, Harl. CM17 52 EX15
Mallards Rd, Bark. IG11 146 EU70
Woodford Green IG8 102 EH52
Mallard Wk, Beck. BR3 203 DX99
Sidcup DA14 186 EW92
Mallard Way, NW9 118 CQ59
Brentwood (Hutt.) CM13 109 GB45
Harlow (Roydon) CM19 off Roydon Mill Pk 34 EG14
Northwood HA6 93 BQ52
Wallington SM6 219 DJ109
Watford WD25 76 BY37
Mallet Dr, Nthlt. UB5 116 BZ64
Mallet Rd, SE13 183 ED86
★ Mall Galleries, SW1 19 M1
Malling, SE13 183 EC85
Malling Cl, Croy. CR0 202 DW100
Malling Gdns, Mord. SM4 200 DC100
Malling Way, Brom. BR2 204 EF101
Mallinson Cl, Horn. RM12 128 FJ64
Mallinson Rd, SW11 180 DE85
Croydon CR0 201 DK104
Mallion Ct, Wal.Abb. EN9 68 EF33
Mallord St, SW3 160 DD79
Mallory Cl, SE4 163 DY84
Mallory Gdns, Barn. EN4 98 DG45
Mallory St, NW8 8 B3
Mallow Cl, Croy. CR0 off Marigold Way 203 DX102
Gravesend (Nthflt) DA11 190 GE91
Tadworth KT20 233 CV119
Mallow Ct, Grays RM17 170 GD79
Mallows Cres, Guil. GU4 243 BB131
Mallow Cft, Hat. AL10 off Oxlease Dr 45 CV19
Mallow Mead, NW7 97 CY52
Mallows, The, Uxb. UB10 115 BP62
Mallows Grn, Harl. CM19 51 EN19
Mallow St, EC1 11 J3
Mallow Wk, Wal.Cr. EN7 66 DR28
Mall Rd, W6 159 CV78
Mallys Pl, Dart. (S.Darenth) DA4 208 FQ95
Malmains Cl, Beck. BR3 203 ED99
Malmains Way, Beck. BR3 203 EC98
Malm Cl, Rick. WD3 92 BK47
Malmesbury Cl, Pnr. HA5 115 BT56
Sch Malmesbury Inf Sch, E3 13 M1
Sch Malmesbury Jun Sch, E3 13 M1
Sch Malmesbury Prim Sch, Mord. SM4 off Malmesbury Rd 200 DC101
Malmesbury Rd, E3 13 L1
E16 15 H5
E18 102 EF53
Morden SM4 200 DC101
Malmesbury Ter, E16 15 J5
Malmescroft, Hem.H. HP3 41 BQ22

★ Place of interest | H Hospital | Sch School | Coll College | Uni University | ⇌ Railway station

Malmsdale, Welw.G.C. AL8 ..29 CX05
Malmsmead Ho, E9
off Kingsmead Way ..123 DY64
Malmstone Av, Red. RH1 ..251 DJ128
Sch Malorees Inf & Jun Sch,
NW6 off Christchurch Av .139 CX66
Sch Malory Sch, Brom. BR1
off Launcelot Rd ..184 EG91
Malpas Dr, Pnr. HA5 ..116 BX57
Malpas Rd, E8 ..142 DV65
SE4 ..163 DZ82
Dagenham RM9 ..146 EX65
Grays RM16 ..171 GJ76
Slough SL2 ..132 AV73
Malta Rd, E10 ..123 EA60
Tilbury RM18 ..171 GF82
Malta St, EC1 ..10 F3
Maltby Cl, Orp. BR6
off Vinson Cl ..206 EU102
Maltby Dr, Enf. EN1 ..82 DV38
Maltby Rd, Chess. KT9 ..216 CN107
Maltby St, SE1 ..21 N4
Malt Hill, Egh. TW20 ..172 AY92
Malt Ho Cl, Wind. (Old Wind.)
SL4 ..172 AV87
Malthouse Dr, W4 ..158 CS79
Feltham TW13 ..176 BX92
Malthouse Pas, SW13
off The Terrace ..158 CS82
Malthouse Pl, Rad. WD7 ..61 CG34
Malthouse Sq, Beac. HP9 ..111 AM55
Malthus Path, SE28
off Owen Cl ..146 EW74
Malting Ho, E14 ..13 L9
Maltings, The, Kings L. WD4 ..59 BQ33
Orpington BR6 ..205 ET102
Oxted RH8 ..254 EF131
Romford RM1 ..127 FF59
St. Albans AL1 ..43 CD20
Sawbridgeworth CM21 ..36 FA05
Staines TW18
off Church St ..173 BE91
Ware SG12 off Roydon Rd .33 ED11
West Byfleet (Byfleet)
KT14 ..212 BM113
Maltings Cl, SW13
off Cleveland Gdns ..158 CS82
Maltings Dr, Epp. CM16
off Palmers Hill ..70 EU29
Maltings La, Epp. CM16 ..70 EU29
Maltings Ms, Amer. HP7 ..55 AP40
Sidcup DA15
off Station Rd ..186 EU90
Maltings Pl, SW6 ..160 DB81
Malting Way, Islw. TW7 ..157 CF83
Malt La, Rad. WD7 ..77 CG35
Sch Maltman's Grn Sch, Ger.Cr.
SL9 off Maltmans La ..112 AW55
Maltmans La, Ger.Cr.
(Chal.St.P.) SL9 ..112 AW55
Malton Av, Slou. SL1 ..131 AP72
Malton Ms, SE18
off Malton St ..165 ES79
W10 off Cambridge Gdns ..139 CY72
Malton Rd, W10 ..6 C7
Malton St, SE18 ..165 ES79
Maltravers St, WC2 ..10 B9
Malt St, SE1 ..162 DU79
Malus Cl, Add. KT15 ..211 BF108
Hemel Hempstead HP2 ..40 BN19
Malus Dr, Add. KT15 ..211 BF107
Malva Cl, SW18
off St. Ann's Hill ..180 DB85
Malvern Av, E4 ..101 ED52
Bexleyheath DA7 ..166 EY80
Harrow HA2 ..116 BY62
Malvern Cl, SE20
off Derwent Rd ..202 DU96
W10 ..6 E6
Bushey WD23 ..76 CC44
Chertsey (Ott.) KT16 ..211 BC107
Hatfield AL10 ..45 CT17
Mitcham CR4 ..201 DJ97
St. Albans AL4 ..43 CH16
Surbiton KT6 ..198 CL102
Uxbridge UB10 ..115 BP61
Malvern Ct, SE14
off Avonley Rd ..162 DW80
SW7 ..17 P8
Slough SL3 off Hill Ri ..153 BA79
Sutton SM2
off Overton Rd ..218 DA108
Malvern Dr, Felt. TW13 ..176 BX92
Ilford IG3 ..125 ET63
Woodford Green IG8 ..102 EJ50
Malvern Gdns, NW2 ..119 CY61
NW6 off Carlton Vale ..139 CZ68
Harrow HA3 ..118 CL55
Loughton IG10 ..85 EM44
Malvern Ms, NW6 ..6 G2
Malvern Pl, NW6 ..6 F1
Malvern Rd, E6 ..144 EL67
E8 ..142 DU66
E11 ..124 EE61
N8 ..121 DM55
N17 ..122 DU55
NW6 ..6 G1
Enfield EN3 ..83 DY37
Grays RM17 ..170 GD77
Hampton TW12 ..176 CA94
Hayes UB3 ..155 BS80
Hornchurch RM11 ..127 FG58
Orpington BR6 ..224 EV105
Surbiton KT6 ..198 CL103
Thornton Heath CR7 ..201 DN98
Malvern Ter, N1 ..4 C7
N9 off Latymer Rd ..100 DT46
Malvern Way, W13
off Templewood ..137 CH71
Hemel Hempstead HP2 ..40 BM18
Rickmansworth (Crox.Grn)
WD3 ..75 BP43
Sch Malvern Way Inf Sch, Rick.
WD3 off Malvern Way ..75 BQ43
Malvina Av, Grav. DA12 ..191 GH89
Malwood Rd, SW12 ..181 DH86
Malyons, The, Shep. TW17
off Gordon Rd ..195 BR100
Malyons Rd, SE13 ..183 EB85
Swanley BR8 ..187 FF94
Malyons Ter, SE13 ..183 EB85
Managers St, E14 ..24 D2
Manan Cl, Hem.H. HP3 ..41 BQ22
Manatee Pl, Wall. SM6
off Croydon Rd ..201 DK104
Manaton Cl, SE15 ..162 DV83
Manaton Cres, Sthl. UB1 ..136 CA72
Manbey Gro, E15 ..144 EE65
Manbey Pk Rd, E15 ..144 EE65
Manbey Rd, E15 ..144 EE65
Manbey St, E15 ..144 EE65
Manbre Rd, W6 ..159 CW79
Manbrough Av, E6 ..145 EM69
Sch Manby Lo Inf Sch, Wey.
KT13 off Princes Rd ..213 BQ105
Manchester Ct, E16 ..15 P8
Manchester Dr, W10 ..6 C4
Manchester Gro, E14 ..24 C9
Manchester Ms, W1 ..8 E6
Manchester Rd, E14 ..24 C9
N15 ..122 DR58
Thornton Heath CR7 ..202 DQ97
Manchester Sq, W1 ..8 E7
Manchester St, W1 ..8 E6
Manchester Way, Dag.
RM10 ..127 FB63
Manchuria Rd, SW11 ..180 DG86
Manciple St, SE1 ..21 J4
Mandalay Rd, SW4 ..181 DJ85
Mandarin St, E14 ..13 N9
Mandarin Way, Hayes UB4 ..136 BX71
Mandela Av, Harl. CM20 ..35 ES13
Mandela Cl, NW10 ..138 CQ66
Mandela Rd, E16 ..15 M8
Mandela St, NW1 ..141 DJ67
SW9 ..161 DN80
Mandela Way, SE1 ..21 M7
Mandelyns, Berk. HP4 ..38 AS16
Coll Mander Portman
Woodward 6th Form
Tutorial Coll, SW7 ..17 N8
Mandeville Cl, SE3
off Vanbrugh Pk ..164 EF80
SW20 ..199 CY95
Broxbourne EN10 ..49 DZ20
Guildford GU2 ..242 AU131
Harlow CM17 ..52 EW17
Hertford SG13 ..32 DQ12
Watford WD17 ..75 BT38
Mandeville Ct, E4 ..101 DY49
Egham TW20 ..173 BA91
Mandeville Dr, St.Alb. AL1 ..43 CD23
Surbiton KT6 ..197 CK102
Sch Mandeville JMI Sch,
E5 off Oswald St ..123 DX62
St. Albans AL1
off Mandeville Dr ..43 CD23
Mandeville Ms, SW4
off Clapham Pk Rd ..161 DL84
Mandeville Pl, W1 ..8 F7
Mandeville Ri, Welw.G.C.
AL8 ..29 CX07
Mandeville Rd, N14 ..99 DH47
Enfield EN3 ..83 DX36
Hertford SG13 ..32 DQ12
Isleworth TW7 ..157 CG82
Northolt UB5 ..136 CA66
Potters Bar EN6 ..64 DC32
Shepperton TW17 ..194 BN99
Sch Mandeville (Spec) Sch,
Nthlt. UB5
off Eastcote La ..136 BZ65
Mandeville St, E5 ..123 DY62
Mandeville Wk, Brwd. (Hutt.)
CM13 ..109 GE44
Mandrake Rd, SW17 ..180 DF90
Mandrake Way, E15 ..144 EE66
Mandrell Rd, SW2 ..181 DL85
Manette St, W1 ..9 M8
Manfield Cl, Slou. SL2 ..131 AN69
Manford Cl, Chig. IG7 ..104 EU49
Manford Cross, Chig. IG7 ..104 EU50
Manford Ind Est, Erith DA8 .167 FG79
Sch Manford Prim Sch, Chig.
IG7 off Manford Way ..103 ET50
Manford Way, Chig. IG7 ..103 ES49
Manfred Rd, SW15 ..179 CZ85
Manger Rd, N7 ..141 DL65
Mangles Rd, Guil. GU1 ..242 AX132
Mangold Way, Erith DA18 ..166 EY76
Mangrove Dr, Hert. SG13 ..32 DS11
Mangrove La, Hert. SG13 ..48 DT16
Mangrove Rd, Hert. SG13 ..32 DS10
Manhattan Wf, E16 ..25 L3
Manilla St, E14 ..23 N3
Manister Rd, SE2 ..166 EU76
Manitoba Ct, SE16
off Renforth St ..162 DW75
Manitoba Gdns, Orp. BR6
off Superior Dr ..223 ET107
Manley Ct, N16
off Stoke Newington
High St ..122 DT62
Manley Rd, Hem.H. HP2
off Knightsbridge Way ..40 BL19
Manley St, NW1 ..140 DG67
Manly Dixon Dr, Enf. EN3 ..83 DY37
Mannamead, Epsom KT18 .232 CS119
Mannamead Cl, Epsom
KT18 off Mannamead ..232 CS119
Mann Cl, Croy. CR0
off Salem Pl ..202 DQ104
Mannicotts, Welw.G.C. AL8 ..29 CV09
Manningford Cl, EC1 ..10 E1
Manning Gdns, Har. HA3 ..117 CK59
Manning Pl, Rich. TW10
off Grove Rd ..178 CM86
Manning Rd, E17
off Southcote Rd ..123 DY57
Dagenham RM10 ..146 FA65
Orpington BR5 ..206 EX99
Manning St, S.Ock. (Aveley)
RM15 ..148 FQ74
Manningtree Cl, SW19 ..179 CY88
Manningtree Rd, Ruis. HA4 .115 BV63
Manningtree St, E1 ..12 A7
Mannin Rd, Rom. RM6 ..126 EV59
Mannock Dr, Loug. IG10 ..85 EQ40
Mannock Ms, E18 ..102 EH53
Mannock Rd, N22 ..121 DP55
Dartford DA1
off Barnwell Rd ..168 FM83
Manns Cl, Islw. TW7 ..177 CF85
Manns Rd, Edg. HA8 ..96 CN51
Manoel Rd, Twick. TW2 ..176 CC89
Manor Av, SE4 ..163 DZ82
Caterham CR3 ..236 DS124
Hemel Hempstead HP3 ..40 BK23
Hornchurch RM11 ..128 FJ57
Hounslow TW4 ..156 BX83
Northolt UB5 ..136 BZ66
Manorbrook, SE3 ..164 EG84
Manor Chase, Wey. KT13 ..213 BP106
Manor Cl, E17 off Manor Rd .101 DY54
NW7 off Manor Dr ..96 CR50
NW9 ..118 CP57
SE28 ..146 EW72
Barnet EN5 ..79 CY42
Berkhamsted HP4 ..38 AW19
Dagenham RM10 ..147 FD65
Dartford (Cray.) DA1 ..167 FD84
Dartford (Wilm.) DA2 ..187 FG90
Hatfield AL10 ..45 CT15
Hertford SG14 ..32 DR07
Horley RH6 ..268 DF148
Leatherhead (E.Hors.)
KT24 ..245 BS128
Romford RM1
off Manor Rd ..127 FG57
Ruislip HA4 ..115 BT60
Manor Cl, S. Ock. (Aveley)
RM15 ..148 FQ74
Warlingham CR6 ..237 DY117
Woking GU22 ..227 BF116
Worcester Park KT4 ..198 CS102
Manor Cl S, S.Ock. (Aveley)
RM15 off Manor Cl ..148 FQ74
Manor Cotts, Nthwd. HA6 ..93 BT53
Manor Cotts App, N2 ..98 DC54
Manor Ct, E10
off Grange Pk Rd ..123 EB60
N2 ..120 DF57
SW6 off Bagley's La ..160 DB81
Enfield EN1 ..82 DV36
Radlett WD7 ..77 CF38
Slough SL1
off Richards Way ..131 AM74
Twickenham TW2 ..176 CC89
Wembley HA9 ..118 CL64
Weybridge KT13 ..213 BP105
Manor Ct Rd, W7 ..137 CE73
Manor Cres, Beac.
(Seer Grn) HP9 ..89 AR51
Epsom KT19 ..216 CN112
Guildford GU2 ..242 AV132
Hornchurch RM11 ..128 FJ57
Surbiton KT5 ..198 CN100
West Byfleet (Byfleet)
KT14 ..212 BM113
Sch Manorcroft Sch, Egh.
TW20 off Wesley Dr ..173 BA93
Manorcrofts Rd, Egh. TW20 .173 BA93
Sch Manor Day Sch, NW10
off Chamberlayne Rd ..139 CW67
Manordene Cl, T.Ditt. KT7 ..197 CG102
Manordene Rd, SE28 ..146 EW72
Manor Dr, N14 ..99 DH45
N20 ..98 DE48
NW7 ..96 CR50
Addlestone (New Haw)
KT15 ..212 BG110
Amersham HP6 ..55 AP36
Epsom KT19 ..216 CS107
Esher KT10 ..197 CF103
Feltham TW13
off Lebanon Av ..176 BX92
Horley RH6 ..268 DF148
St. Albans AL2 ..60 CA27
Sunbury-on-Thames
TW16 ..195 BU96
Surbiton KT5 ..198 CM100
Wembley HA9 ..118 CM63
Manor Dr, The, Wor.Pk. KT4 .198 CS102
Manor Dr N, N.Mal. KT3 ..198 CR101
Worcester Park KT4 ..198 CS102
Manor Est, SE16 ..22 C8
Manor Fm, Dart. (Fnghm)
DA4 ..208 FM101
Manor Fm Av, Shep. TW17 .195 BP100
Manor Fm Cl, Wind. SL4 ..151 AM83
Worcester Park KT4 ..198 CS102
Manor Fm Dr, E4 ..102 EE48
Manor Fm Est, Stai. (Wrays.)
TW19 ..172 AW86
Manor Fm La, Egh. TW20 ..173 BA92
Manor Fm Rd, Enf. EN1 ..82 DV35
Thornton Heath CR7 ..201 DN96
Wembley HA0 ..137 CK68
Manor Fm Way, Beac.
(Seer Grn) HP9
off Orchard Rd ..89 AR51
Manorfield Cl, N19
off Junction Rd ..121 DJ63
Sch Manorfield Prim Sch,
E14 ..14 B5
Manor Flds, SW15 ..179 CX86
Manorfields Cl, Chis. BR7 ..205 ET97
Manor Gdns, N7 ..121 DL62
SW20 ..199 CZ96
W3 ..158 CN77
W4 off Devonshire Rd ..158 CS78
Godalming GU7
off Farncombe St ..258 AS144
Guildford GU2 ..242 AV132
Hampton TW12 ..176 CB94
High Wycombe
(Woob.Grn) HP10 ..110 AE58
Leatherhead (Eff.) KT24 ..246 BX128
Richmond TW9 ..158 CM84
Ruislip HA4 ..116 BW64
South Croydon CR2 ..220 DT107
Sunbury-on-Thames
TW16 ..195 BU96
Manor Gate, Nthlt. UB5 ..136 BY66
Manorgate Rd, Kings.T. KT2 .198 CN95
Manor Grn Rd, Epsom
KT19 ..216 CP113
Manor Gro, SE15 ..162 DW79
Beckenham BR3 ..203 EB96
Maidenhead SL6 ..150 AD80
Richmond TW9 ..158 CN84
Manor Hall Av, NW4 ..97 CW54
Manor Hall Dr, NW4 ..97 CX54
Manorhall Gdns, E10 ..123 EA60
Manor Hatch Cl, Harl. CM18 .52 EV16
⊖ Manor House ..121 DP59
Manor Ho Ct, Epsom KT18 .216 CQ113
Shepperton TW17 ..195 BP101
Manor Ho Dr, NW6 ..139 CX66
Northwood HA6 ..93 BP52
Walton-on-Thames KT12 .213 BT107
Manor Ho Est, Stan. HA7
off Old Ch La ..95 CH51
Manor Ho Gdns, Abb.L. WD5 .59 BR31
Manor Ho La, Lthd. (Bkhm)
KT23 ..246 BY126
Slough (Datchet) SL3 ..152 AV80
Sch Manor Ho Sch, W7
off Golden Manor ..137 CE73
Leatherhead KT23
off Manor Ho La ..246 BY127
Manor Ho Way, Islw. TW7 ..157 CH83
Sch Manor Inf Sch, Bark.
IG11
off Sandringham Rd ..145 ET65
Sch Manor Jun Sch, Bark.
IG11
off Sandringham Rd ..145 ET65
Manor La, SE12 ..184 EE86
SE13 ..164 EE84
Feltham TW13 ..175 BU89
Gerrards Cross SL9 ..112 AX59
Hayes UB3 ..155 BR79
Longfield (Fawk.Grn)
DA3 ..209 FW101
Sevenoaks TN15 ..209 FW103
Sunbury-on-Thames
TW16 ..195 BU96
Sutton SM1 ..218 DC106
Tadworth KT20 ..250 DA129
Manor La Ter, SE13 ..164 EE84
Manor Leaze, Egh. TW20 ..173 BB92
Manor Lo, Guil. GU2 ..242 AV132
Sch Manor Lo Sch, Rad.
WD7 off Rectory La ..62 CQ30
Sch Manor Mead Sch, Shep.
TW17 off Laleham Rd ..195 BP99
Manor Ms, NW6
off Cambridge Av ..140 DA68
SE4 ..163 DZ82
Manor Mt, SE23 ..182 DW88
Sch Manor Oak Prim Sch,
Orp. BR5 off Sweeps La ..206 EX99
Manor Par, NW10
off Station Rd ..139 CT68
Hatfield AL10 ..45 CT15
MANOR PARK, E12 ..124 EL63
MANOR PARK, Slou. SL2 ..131 AQ70
⇌ Manor Park ..124 EK63
Manor Pk, SE13 ..163 ED84
Chislehurst BR7 ..205 ER96
Richmond TW9 ..158 CM84
Staines TW18 ..173 BD90
Manor Pk Cl, W.Wick. BR4 ..203 EB102
Manor Pk Cres, Edg. HA8 ..96 CN51
Manor Pk Dr, Har. HA2 ..116 CB55
Manor Pk Gdns, Edg. HA8 ..96 CN50
Manor Pk Par, SE13
off Lee High Rd ..163 ED84
Sch Manor Pk Prim Sch, Sutt.
SM1 off Greyhound Rd .218 DC106
Manor Pk Rd, E12 ..124 EK63
N2 ..120 DD55
NW10 ..139 CT67
Chislehurst BR7 ..205 EQ95
Sutton SM1 ..218 DC106
West Wickham BR4 ..203 EB102
Manor Pl, SE17 ..20 F10
Chislehurst BR7 ..205 ER95
Dartford DA1
off Highfield Rd S ..188 FL88
Feltham TW14 ..175 BU88
Leatherhead (Bkhm)
KT23 ..246 CA126
Mitcham CR4 ..201 DJ97
Staines TW18 ..174 BH92
Sutton SM1 ..218 DB105
Walton-on-Thames
KT12 off Manor Rd ..195 BT101
Sch Manor Prim Sch, E15
off Richardson Rd ..144 EE68
Romford RM1
off Shaftesbury Rd ..127 FF57
Manor Rd, E10 ..123 EA59
E15 ..144 EE69
E16 ..14 G3
E17 ..101 DY54
N16 ..122 DR61
N17 ..100 DU53
N22 ..99 DL51
SE25 ..202 DU98
SW20 ..199 CZ96
W13 ..137 CG73
Ashford TW15 ..174 BM92
Barking IG11 ..145 ET65
Barnet EN5 ..79 CY43
Beaconsfield (Seer Grn)
HP9 ..89 AR50
Beckenham BR3 ..203 EB96
Bexley DA5 ..187 FB88
Chesham HP5
off Lansdowne Rd ..54 AP29
Chigwell IG7 ..103 EP50
Dagenham RM10 ..147 FC65
Dartford DA1 ..167 FE84
East Molesey KT8 ..197 CD98
Enfield EN2 ..82 DR40
Erith DA8 ..167 FF79
Gravesend DA12 ..191 GH86
Grays RM17 ..170 GC79
Grays (W.Thur.) RM20 ..169 FW79
Guildford GU2 ..242 AV132
Harlow CM17 ..36 EW10
Harrow HA1 ..117 CG58
Hatfield AL10 ..45 CT15
Hayes UB3 ..135 BU72
Hoddesdon EN11 ..49 EA16
Loughton IG10 ..84 EH44
Loughton (High Beach)
IG10 ..84 EH38
Mitcham CR4 ..201 DJ98
Potters Bar EN6 ..63 CZ31
Redhill RH1 ..251 DJ129
Reigate RH2 ..249 CZ132
Richmond TW9 ..158 CM83
Romford RM1 ..127 FG57
Romford (Chad.Hth) RM6 ..126 EX58
Romford (Lamb.End) RM4 .104 EW47
Ruislip HA4 ..115 BR60
St. Albans AL1 ..43 CE19
St. Albans (Lon.Col.) AL2 ..61 CJ26
Sevenoaks (Sund.) TN14 ..240 EX124
Sidcup DA15 ..185 ET90
Sutton SM2 ..217 CZ108
Swanscombe DA10 ..189 FX86
Teddington TW11 ..177 CH92
Tilbury RM18 ..171 GG82
Twickenham TW2 ..176 CC89
Wallington SM6 ..219 DH105
Waltham Abbey EN9 ..67 ED33
Walton-on-Thames KT12 ..195 BT101
Watford WD17 ..75 BV39
West Wickham BR4 ..203 EB103
Westerham (Tats.) TN16 ..238 EL120
Windsor SL4 ..151 AL82
Woking GU21 ..226 AW116
Woking (Send M.) GU23 .227 BF123
Woodford Green IG8 ..103 EM51
Manor Rd N, Esher KT10 ..197 CF104
Thames Ditton KT7 ..197 CG103
Wallington SM6 ..219 DH105
Manor Rd S, Esher KT10 ..215 CE105
Sch Manor Sch, The, W.Byf.
KT14 off Magdalen Cres .212 BL114
Manorside, Barn. EN5 ..79 CY42
Manorside Cl, SE2 ..166 EW77
Sch Manorside Prim Sch,
N3 off Squires La ..98 DC53
Manor Sq, Dag. RM8 ..126 EX61
Manor St, Berk. HP4 ..38 AX19
Manor Vale, Brent. TW8 ..157 CJ78
Manor Vw, N3 ..98 DB54
Manorville Rd, Hem.H. HP3 ..40 BJ24
Manor Wk, Wey. KT13 ..213 BP106
Manor Way, E4 ..101 ED49
NW9 ..118 CS55
SE3 ..164 EF84
SE23 ..182 DW87
SE28 ..146 EW74
Amersham (Colesh.) HP7 ..55 AM44
Banstead SM7 ..234 DF116
Beckenham BR3 ..203 EA96
Bexley DA5 ..186 FA88
Bexleyheath DA7 ..167 FD83
Borehamwood WD6 ..78 CQ42
Brentwood CM14 ..108 FU48
Bromley BR2 ..204 EL100
Chesham HP5 ..54 AR30
Egham TW20 ..173 AZ93
Manorway, Enf. EN1 ..100 DS45
Manor Way, Grays RM17 ..170 GB80
Guildford GU2 ..258 AS137
Harrow HA2 ..116 CB56
Leatherhead (Oxshott)
KT22 ..230 CC115
Mitcham CR4 ..201 DJ97
Orpington BR5 ..205 EQ98
Potters Bar EN6 ..64 DA30
Purley CR8 ..219 DL112
Rainham RM13 ..147 FE71
Rickmansworth
(Crox.Grn) WD3 ..74 BN42
Ruislip HA4 ..115 BS59
South Croydon CR2 ..220 DS107
Southall UB2 ..156 BX77
Swanscombe DA10 ..169 FX84
Waltham Cross (Chsht)
EN8 off Russells Ride ..67 DY31
Woking GU22 ..227 BB121
Manorway, Wdf.Grn. IG8 ..102 EJ50
Manor Way, Wor.Pk. KT4 ..198 CS102
Manor Way, The, Wall. SM6 .219 DH105
Manor Waye, Uxb. UB8 ..134 BK67
Manor Way Ind Est, Grays
RM17 ..170 GC80
Manor Wd Rd, Pur. CR8 ..219 DL113
Manpreet Ct, E12
off Morris Av ..125 EM64
Manresa Rd, SW3 ..18 A10
Mansard Beeches, SW17 ..180 DG92
Mansard Cl, Horn. RM12 ..127 FG61
Pinner HA5 ..116 BX55
Mansards, The, St.Alb.
AL1 off Avenue Rd ..43 CE19
Mansbridge Way, NW7 ..97 CY52
Manscroft Rd, Hem.H. HP1 ..40 BH17
Manse Cl, Hayes UB3 ..155 BR79
Mansel Cl, Guil. GU2 ..242 AV129
Slough SL2 ..132 AV71
Mansel Gro, E17 ..101 EA53
Mansell Cl, Wind. SL4 ..151 AL82
Mansell Rd, W3 ..158 CR75
Greenford UB6 ..136 CB71
Mansell St, E1 ..11 P10
Mansell Way, Cat. CR3 ..236 DR122
Mansel Rd, SW19 ..179 CY93
Mansergh Cl, SE18 ..164 EL80
Manse Rd, N16 ..122 DT62
Manser Rd, Rain. RM13 ..147 FE69
Manse Way, Swan. BR8 ..207 FG98
Mansfield, Saw. (High Wych)
CM21 ..36 EU06
Mansfield Av, N15 ..122 DR56
Barnet EN4 ..80 DF44
Ruislip HA4 ..115 BV60
Mansfield Cl, N9 ..82 DU44
Orpington BR5 ..206 EX101
Weybridge KT13 ..213 BP106
Mansfield Dr, Hayes UB4 ..135 BS70
Redhill RH1 ..251 DK128
Mansfield Gdns, Hert. SG14 .32 DQ07
Hornchurch RM12 ..128 FK61
Mansfield Hill, E4 ..101 EB46
Mansfield Ms, W1 ..8 G6
Mansfield Pl, NW3
off New End ..120 DC63
Mansfield Rd, E11 ..124 EH58
E17 ..123 DZ56
NW3 ..120 DF64
W3 ..138 CP70
Chessington KT9 ..215 CJ106
Ilford IG1 ..125 EN61
South Croydon CR2 ..220 DR107
Swanley BR8 ..187 FE93
Mansfield St, W1 ..8 G6
Mansford St, E2 ..142 DU68
Manship Rd, Mitch. CR4 ..180 DG94
Mansion, The, Berk. HP4
off Frithsden Rd ..38 AY17
Guildford (Albury) GU5 ..260 BL139
Mansion Cl, SW9
off Cowley Rd ..161 DN81
Mansion Gdns, NW3 ..120 DB62
★ Mansion Ho, EC4 ..11 J8
⊖ Mansion House ..11 H9
Mansion Ho Pl, EC4 ..11 J8
Mansion Ho St, EC4 ..11 J8
Mansion La, Iver SL0 ..133 BC74
Manson Ms, SW7 ..17 M8
Manson Pl, SW7 ..17 N8
Manstead Gdns, Rain.
RM13 ..147 FH72
Mansted Gdns, Rom. RM6 .126 EW59
Manston Av, Sthl. UB2 ..156 CA77
Manston Cl, SE20
off Garden Rd ..202 DW95
Waltham Cross (Chsht)
EN8 ..66 DW30
Manstone Rd, NW2 ..119 CY64
Manston Gro, Kings.T. KT2 .177 CK92
Manston Rd, Guil. GU4 ..243 BA130
Harlow CM20 ..51 ES15
Manston Way, Horn. RM12 .147 FH65
St. Albans AL4 ..43 CK21
Manthorp Rd, SE18 ..165 EQ78
Mantilla Rd, SW17 ..180 DG91
Mantle Rd, SE4 ..163 DY83
Mantlet Cl, SW16 ..181 DJ94
Mantle Way, E15
off Romford Rd ..144 EE66
Manton Av, W7 ..157 CF75
Manton Cl, Hayes UB3 ..135 BS73
Manton Rd, SE2 ..166 EU77
Enfield EN3 ..83 EA37
Mantua St, SW11 ..160 DD83
Mantus Cl, E1 ..12 F3
Mantus Rd, E1 ..12 E3
Manus Way, N20
off Blakeney Cl ..98 DC47
Manville Gdns, SW17 ..181 DH89
Manville Rd, SW17 ..180 DG89
Manwood Rd, SE4 ..183 DZ85
Manwood St, E16 ..145 EM74
Manygate La, Shep. TW17 ..195 BQ101
Manygates, SW12 ..181 DH89
Maori Rd, Guil. GU1 ..243 AZ134
Mapesbury Ms, NW4
off Station Rd ..119 CU58
Mapesbury Rd, NW2 ..139 CY65
Mapeshill Pl, NW2 ..139 CW65
Mape St, E2 ..12 C3
Maple Av, E4 ..101 DZ50
W3 ..138 CS74
Harrow HA2 ..116 CB61
St. Albans AL3 ..42 CC16
Upminster RM14 ..128 FP62
West Drayton UB7 ..134 BL73
Maple Cl, N3 ..98 DA51
N16 ..122 DU58

⊖ London Underground station DLR Docklands Light Railway station Tra Tramlink station Riv Pedestrian ferry landing stage

Maple Cl, SW4 181 DK86
Brentwood CM13
off Cherry Av 109 FZ48
Buckhurst Hill IG9 102 EK48
Bushey WD23 76 BY40
Epping (They.B.) CM16
off Loughton La 85 ER37
Hampton TW12 176 BZ93
Hatfield AL10 off Elm Dr 45 CU19
Hayes UB4 136 BX69
Hornchurch RM12 127 FH62
Ilford IG6 103 ES50
Mitcham CR4 201 DH95
Orpington BR5 205 ER99
Ruislip HA4 115 BV58
Swanley BR8 207 FE96
Whyteleafe CR3 236 DT117
Maple Ct, Egh. (Eng.Grn)
TW20 off Ashwood Rd 172 AV93
New Malden KT3 198 CS97
Ware (Stans.Abb.) SG12 33 ED11
Maplecourt Wk, Wind.
SL4 off Common Rd 151 AN77
Maple Cres, Sid. DA15 186 EU86
Slough SL2 132 AV73
Maplecroft Cl, E6
off Allhallows Rd 144 EL72
Maplecroft La, Wal.Abb.
EN9 50 EE21
MAPLE CROSS, Rick. WD3 91 BD49
Maple Cross Ind Est, Rick.
(Map.Cr.) WD3 91 BF49
Sch Maple Cross JMI Sch, Rick.
WD3 off Denham Way 91 BE50
Mapledale Av, Croy. CR0 202 DU103
Mapledene, Chis. BR7
off Kemnal Rd 185 EQ92
Mapledene Rd, E8 5 P5
Sch Mapledown Spec Sch,
NW2 off Claremont Rd 119 CW59
Maple Dr, Lthd. KT23
off Lower Rd 246 CB125
South Ockendon RM15 149 FX70
Maplefield, St.Alb. (Park St)
AL2 60 CB29
Maplefield La, Ch.St.G. HP8 72 AV41
Maple Gdns, Edg. HA8 96 CS52
Staines TW19 174 BL89
Maple Gate, Loug. IG10 85 EN40
Maple Grn, Hem.H. HP1 39 BE18
Maple Gro, NW9 118 CQ59
W5 157 CK76
Brentford TW8 157 CH80
Guildford GU1 242 AX132
Southall UB1 136 BZ71
Watford WD17 75 BU39
Welwyn Garden City AL7 29 CZ06
Woking GU22 226 AY121
Maple Hill, Hem.H. (Bov.)
HP3 off Ley Hill Rd 56 AX30
Maplehurst, Lthd. KT22 231 CD123
Maplehurst Cl, Dart. DA2
off Sandringham Dr 187 FE89
Kingston upon Thames
KT1 198 CL98
Maple Ind Est, Felt. TW13
off Maple Way 175 BU90
Sch Maple Inf Sch, Surb.
KT6 off Maple Rd 197 CK99
Maple Leaf Cl, Abb.L. WD5 59 BU32
Mapleleaf Cl, S.Croy. CR2 221 DX111
Maple Leaf Cl, Ware
(Stans.Abb.) SG12 33 ED12
Westerham (Bigg.H.)
TN16 off Main Rd 238 EK116
Maple Leaf Dr, Sid. DA15 185 ET88
Mapleleafe Gdns, Ilf. IG6 125 EP55
Maple Leaf Sq, SE16 23 H3
Maple Lo Cl, Rick. (Map.Cr.)
WD3 91 BE49
Maple Ms, NW6
off Kilburn Pk Rd 140 DB68
SW16 181 DM92
Maple Pl, W1 9 K4
Banstead SM7 217 CX114
West Drayton UB7
off Maple Av 134 BM73
Sch Maple Prim Sch, St.Alb.
AL1 off Hall Pl Gdns 43 CE19
Maple River Ind Est, Harl.
CM20 36 EV09
Maple Rd, E11 124 EE58
SE20 202 DV95
Ashtead KT21 231 CK119
Dartford DA1 188 FJ88
Gravesend DA12 191 GJ91
Grays RM17 170 GC79
Hayes UB4 136 BW69
Redhill RH1 266 DF138
Surbiton KT6 198 CL99
Whyteleafe CR3 236 DT117
Woking (Ripley) GU23 228 BG124
Maples, The, Bans. SM7 218 DB114
Chertsey (Ott.) KT16 211 BB107
Esher (Clay.) KT10 215 CG108
Harlow CM19 51 EP20
Waltham Cross
(Goffs Oak) EN7 66 DS28
Maplescombe La, Dart.
(Fnghm) DA4 208 FN104
Maples Pl, E1 12 D5
Maple Springs, Wal.Abb.
EN9 68 EG33
Maplestead Rd, SW2 181 DM87
Dagenham RM9 146 EV67
Maple St, W1 9 J5
Romford RM7 127 FC56
Maplethorpe Rd, Th.Hth.
CR7 201 DP98
Mapleton Cl, Brom. BR2 204 EG100
Mapleton Cres, SW18 180 DB86
Enfield EN3 82 DW38
Mapleton Rd, E4 101 EC48
SW18 180 DB86
Edenbridge TN8 255 ET133
Enfield EN1 82 DV40
Westerham TN16 255 ES130
Maple Wk, W10 6 B2
Sutton SM2 218 DB110
Maple Way, Couls. CR5 235 DH121
Feltham TW13 175 BU90
Waltham Abbey EN9
off Breach Barn
Mobile Home Pk 68 EH30
Maplewood Gdns, Beac.
HP9 88 AH54
Maplin Cl, N21 81 DM44
Maplin Ho, SE2
off Wolvercote Rd 166 EX75
Maplin Pk, Slou. SL3 153 BC75
Maplin Rd, E16 15 N7
Maplin St, E3 13 L2
Mapperley Dr, Wdf.Grn. IG8
off Forest Dr 102 EE52
Maran Way, Erith DA18 166 EX75
Marathon Way, SE28 165 ET75
Marban Rd, W9 6 E1
Marbeck Cl, Wind. SL4 151 AK81
★ Marble Arch, W1 8 D9
⊖ Marble Arch 8 D9
Marble Cl, W3 138 CP74
Marble Dr, NW2 119 CX60
Marble Hill Cl, Twick. TW1 177 CH87
Marble Hill Gdns, Twick.
TW1 177 CH87
★ Marble Hill Ho, Twick.
TW1 177 CJ87
Marble Ho, SE18
off Felspar Cl 165 ET78
Marble Quay, E1 22 A1
Marbles Way, Tad. KT20 233 CX119
Marbrook Ct, SE12 184 EJ90
Marcella Rd, SW9 161 DN82
Marcellina Way, Orp. BR6 205 ES104
Marcet Rd, Dart. DA1 188 FJ85
Marchant Rd, E11 123 ED61
Marchant St, SE14 163 DY79
Marchbank Rd, W14 159 CZ79
Marchmant Cl, Horn. RM12 128 FJ62
Marchmont Gdns, Rich.
TW10 off Marchmont Rd 178 CM85
Marchmont Grn, Hem.H.
HP2 off Paston Rd 40 BK18
Marchmont Rd, Rich. TW10 178 CM85
Wallington SM6 219 DJ108
Marchmont St, WC1 9 N3
March Rd, Twick. TW1 177 CG87
Weybridge KT13 212 BN106
Marchside Cl, Houns. TW5
off Springwell Rd 156 BX81
Marchwood Cl, SE5 162 DS80
Marchwood Cres, W5 137 CJ72
Marcia Ct, Slou. SL1
off Richards Way 131 AM74
Marcia Rd, SE1 21 M8
Marcilly Rd, SW18 180 DD85
Marconi Gdns, Brwd.
(Pilg.Hat.) CM15 108 FW43
Marconi Rd, E10 123 EA60
Gravesend (Nthflt) DA11 190 GD90
Marconi Way, St.Alb. AL4 43 CK20
Southall UB1 136 CB72
Marcon Pl, E8 142 DV65
Marco Rd, W6 159 CW76
Marcourt Lawns, W5 138 CL70
Marcus Ct, E15 144 EE67
Marcuse Rd, Cat. CR3 236 DR123
Marcus Garvey Ms, SE22
off St. Aidan's Rd 182 DV85
Marcus Garvey Way, SE24 161 DN84
Marcus Rd, Dart. DA1 187 FG87
Marcus St, E15 144 EF67
SW18 180 DB86
Marcus Ter, SW18 180 DB86
Mardale Dr, NW9 118 CR57
Mardell Rd, Croy. CR0 203 DX99
Marden Av, Brom. BR2 204 EG100
Marden Cl, Chig. IG7 104 EV47
Marden Cres, Bex. DA5 187 FC85
Croydon CR0 201 DM100
Sch Marden Lo Prim Sch,
Cat. CR3 off Croydon Rd 236 DV121
Marden Pk, Cat. (Wold.)
CR3 253 DZ125
Marden Rd, N17 122 DS55
Croydon CR0 201 DM100
Romford RM1 127 FE58
Marden Sq, SE16 22 C6
Marder Rd, W13 157 CG75
Mardyke Cl, Rain. RM13 147 FC68
Mardyke Ho, Rain. RM13
off Lower Mardyke Av 147 FD68
Mardyke Rd, Harl. CM20 36 EU13
Marechal Niel Av, Sid. DA15 185 ER90
Mareschal Rd, Guil. GU2 258 AW136
Marescroft Rd, Slou. SL2 131 AL70
Maresfield, Croy. CR0 202 DS104
Maresfield Gdns, NW3 120 DC64
Mare St, E8 142 DV67
Marfleet Cl, Cars. SM5 200 DE103
Marford Rd, St.Alb. (Wheat.)
AL4 28 CN07
Welwyn Garden City AL8 28 CS10
Margaret Av, E4 83 EB44
Brentwood (Shenf.) CM15 109 FZ45
St. Albans AL3 43 CD18
Margaret Bondfield Av,
Bark. IG11 146 EU66
Margaret Bldgs, N16
off Margaret Rd 122 DT60
Margaret Cl, Abb.L. WD5 59 BT32
Epping CM16
off Margaret Rd 70 EU29
Potters Bar EN6 64 DC33
Romford RM2
off Margaret Rd 127 FH57
Staines TW18
off Charles Rd 174 BK93
Waltham Abbey EN9 67 ED33
Margaret Ct, W1 9 J7
Margaret Dr, Horn. RM11 128 FM60
Margaret Gardner Dr, SE9 185 EM89
Margaret Ingram Cl, SW6
off John Smith Av 159 CZ80
Margaret Lockwood Cl,
Kings.T. KT1 198 CM98
Margaret Rd, N16 122 DT60
Barnet EN4 80 DD42
Bexley DA5 186 EX86
Epping CM16 70 EU29
Guildford GU1 258 AW135
Romford RM2 127 FH57
Sch Margaret Roper RC
Prim Sch, Pur. CR8
off Russell Hill Rd 219 DN110
Margaret Sq, Uxb. UB8 134 BJ67
Margaret St, W1 9 H7
Margaretta Ter, SW3 160 DE79
Margaretting Rd, E12 124 EJ61
Margaret Way, Couls. CR5 235 DP118
Ilford IG4 124 EL58
Sch Margaret Wix Prim Sch,
St.Alb. AL3 off High Oaks 42 CC16
Margate Rd, SW2 181 DL85
Margeholes, Wat. WD19 94 BY47
MARGERY, Tad. KT20 250 DA129
Margery Gro, Tad. KT20 249 CY129
Margery La, Tad. KT20 249 CZ129
Margery Pk Rd, E7 144 EG65
Margery Rd, Dag. RM8 126 EX62
Margery St, WC1 10 C2
Margery Wd, Welw.G.C. AL7 30 DA06
Margery Wd La, Tad. KT20 249 CZ129
Margherita Pl, Wal.Abb. EN9 68 EF34
Margherita Rd, Wal.Abb.
EN9 68 EG34
Margin Dr, SW19 179 CX92
Margravine Gdns, W6 16 B9
Margravine Rd, W6 16 B10
Marham Gdns, SW18 180 DE88
Morden SM4 200 DC100
Maria Cl, SE1 22 C7
Sch Maria Fidelis Conv Sch,
Lwr Sch, NW1 9 K2
Upr Sch, NW1 9 L1
Mariam Gdns, Horn. RM12 128 FM61
Marian Cl, Hayes UB4 136 BX70
Marian Ct, Sutt. SM1 218 DB106
Marian Pl, E2 142 DV68
Marian Rd, SW16 201 DJ95
Marian Sq, E2
off Pritchard's Rd 142 DU68
Marian St, E2
off Hackney Rd 142 DV68
Sch Marian Vian Prim Sch,
Beck. BR3
off Shirley Cres 203 DY99
Marian Way, NW10 139 CT66
Maria Ter, E1 12 G4
Maria Theresa Cl, N.Mal.
KT3 198 CR99
Maricas Av, Har. HA3 95 CD53
Marie Lloyd Gdns, N19
off Hornsey Ri Gdns 121 DL59
Marie Lloyd Wk, E8 5 P4
Marie Manor Way, Dart.
DA2 169 FS84
Mariette Way, Wall. SM6 219 DL109
Marigold All, SE1 10 E10
Marigold Cl, Sthl. UB1
off Lancaster Rd 136 BY73
Marigold Ct, Guil. GU1
off Waterside Rd 242 AY131
Marigold Pl, Harl. CM17
off Broadway Av 36 EV11
Marigold Rd, N17 100 DW52
Marigold St, SE16 22 C4
Marigold Way, E4
off Silver Birch Av 101 DZ51
Croydon CR0 203 DX102
H Marillac Hosp, Brwd.
CM13 107 FX51
Marina App, Hayes UB4 136 BY71
Marina Av, N.Mal. KT3 199 CV99
Marina Cl, Brom. BR2 204 EG97
Chertsey KT16 194 BH102
Marina Dr, Dart. DA1 188 FN88
Gravesend (Nthflt) DA11 191 GF87
Welling DA16 165 ES82
Marina Gdns, Rom. RM7 127 FC58
Waltham Cross (Chsht)
EN8 66 DW30
Marina Way, Iver SL0 133 BF73
Slough SL1 131 AK73
Teddington TW11
off Fairways 177 CK94
Marine Dr, SE18 165 EM77
Barking IG11 146 EV70
Marinefield Rd, SW6 160 DB82
Mariner Gdns, Rich. TW10 177 CJ90
Mariner Rd, E12
off Dersingham Av 125 EM63
Mariners Ct, Green. DA9
off High St 169 FV84
Mariners Ms, E14 24 E7
Mariners Wk, Erith DA8
off Frobisher Rd 167 FF79
Mariner's Way, Grav. DA11 190 GE87
Mariner Way, Hem.H. HP2 40 BN21
Marine St, SE16 22 A5
Marine Twr, SE8
off Abinger Gro 163 DZ79
Marion Av, Shep. TW17 195 BP99
Marion Cl, Bushey WD23 76 BZ39
Ilford IG6 103 ER52
Marion Cres, Orp. BR5 206 EU99
Marion Gro, Wdf.Grn. IG8 102 EE50
Sch Marion Richardson
Prim Sch, E1 12 G8
Marion Rd, NW7 97 CU50
Thornton Heath CR7 202 DQ99
Marion Wk, Hem.H. HP2
off Washington Av 40 BM15
Marischal Rd, SE13 163 ED83
Marisco Cl, Grays RM16 171 GH77
Sch Marish Inf Sch, Slou.
SL3 off Swabey Rd 153 BA76
Sch Marish Jun Sch, The, Slou.
SL3 off Swabey Rd 153 BA76
Marish La, Uxb. (Denh.) UB9 113 BC56
Marish Wf, Slou. (Mdgrn)
SL3 152 AY75
Sch Marist RC Prim Sch, The,
W.Byf. KT14
off Old Woking Rd 211 BF113
Maritime Cl, Green. DA9 189 FV85
Maritime Gate, Grav. DA11 190 GE87
Maritime Ho, Bark. IG11
off Linton Rd 145 EQ66
Maritime Quay, E14 23 P9
Maritime St, E3 13 M4
Marius Pas, SW17
off Marius Rd 180 DG89
Marius Rd, SW17 180 DG89
Marjoram Cl, Guil. GU2 242 AU130
Marjorams Av, Loug. IG10 85 EM40
Marjorie Gro, SW11 160 DF84
Marjorie Ms, E1 12 G8
Sch Marjory Kinnon Sch, Felt.
TW14 off Hatton Rd 175 BS85
Markab Rd, Nthwd. HA6 93 BT50
Mark Av, E4 83 EB44
Mark Cl, Bexh. DA7 166 EY81
Southall UB1
off Longford Av 136 CB74
Mark Dr, Ger.Cr. (Chal.St.P.)
SL9 90 AX49
Marke Cl, Kes. BR2 222 EL105
Markedge La, Couls. CR5 234 DE124
Redhill RH1 250 DF126
Markenfield Rd, Guil. GU1 242 AX134
Markeston Grn, Wat. WD19 94 BX49
Market Ct, W1 9 J7
Market Est, N7 141 DL65
Marketfield Rd, Red. RH1 250 DF134
Marketfield Way, Red. RH1 250 DF134
Market Hill, SE18 165 EN76
Market La, Edg. HA8 96 CQ53
Iver SL0 153 BC75
Slough SL3 153 BC76
Market Link, Rom. RM1 127 FE56
Market Meadow, Orp. BR5 206 EW98
Market Ms, W1 18 G2
Market Oak La, Hem.H. HP3 40 BN24
Market Pl, N2 120 DE55
NW11 120 DC56
SE16 22 B7
W1 9 J7
W3 138 CQ74
Market Pl, Bexh. DA6 166 FA84
Brentford TW8 157 CJ80
Dartford DA1
off Market St 188 FL87
Enfield EN2 off The Town 82 DR41
Gerrards Cross
(Chal.St.P.) SL9 90 AX53
Hatfield AL10
off Dog Kennel La 45 CU17
Hertford SG14 off Fore St 32 DR09
Kingston upon Thames
KT1 197 CK96
Romford RM1 127 FE57
Romford (Abridge) RM4 86 EV41
St. Albans AL3 43 CD20
Tilbury RM18 171 GF82
Market Rd, N7 141 DL65
Richmond TW9 158 CN83
Market Row, SW9
off Atlantic Rd 161 DN84
Market Sq, E14 14 B8
N9 off New Rd 100 DU47
Amersham HP7 off High St 55 AP40
Bromley BR1 204 EG96
Chesham HP5 off High St 54 AP32
Harlow CM20 off East Gate 35 ER14
Staines TW18
off Clarence St 173 BE91
Uxbridge UB8 off High St 134 BJ66
Waltham Abbey EN9
off Leverton Way 67 EC33
Westerham TN16 255 EQ127
Woking GU21
off Cawsey Way 226 AY117
Market St, E6 145 EM68
SE18 165 EN77
Dartford DA1 188 FL87
Guildford GU1 258 AX135
Harlow CM17 36 EW11
Hertford SG14 32 DR09
Watford WD18 75 BV42
Windsor SL4 151 AR81
Market Way, E14 14 B8
Wembley HA0
off Turton Rd 118 CL64
Westerham TN16
off Costell's Meadow 255 ER126
Market Yd Ms, SE1 21 M5
Markfield, Croy. CR0 221 DZ110
Markfield Gdns, E4 101 EB45
Markfield Rd, N15 122 DU56
Caterham CR3 252 DV126
Sch Mark Hall Comp Sch,
Harl. CM17 off First Av 36 EW12
Mark Hall Moors, Harl.
CM20 36 EV12
MARK HALL NORTH, Harl.
CM20 36 EU12
MARK HALL SOUTH, Harl.
CM20 36 EU14
Markham Pl, SW3 18 C9
Markham Rd, Wal.Cr.
(Chsht) EN7 66 DQ26
Markham Sq, SW3 18 C9
Markham St, SW3 18 B9
Markhole Cl, Hmptn. TW12
off Priory Rd 176 BZ94
Markhouse Av, E17 123 DY58
Markhouse Rd, E17 123 DZ57
Markland Ho, W10 6 A9
Mark La, EC3 11 M10
Gravesend DA12 191 GL86
Markmanor Av, E17 123 DY59
Mark Oak La, Lthd. KT22 230 CA122
Mark Rd, N22 99 DP54
Hemel Hempstead HP2 40 BN18
Marksbury Av, Rich. TW9 158 CN83
MARK'S GATE, Rom. RM6 104 EY54
Sch Marks Gate Inf Sch, Rom.
RM6 off Lawn Fm Gro 126 EY55
Sch Marks Gate Jun Sch,
Rom. RM6 off Rose La 126 EY55
Mark Sq, EC2 11 L3
Marks Rd, Rom. RM7 127 FC57
Warlingham CR6 237 DY118
Marks Sq, Grav. (Nthflt)
DA11 191 GF91
Mark St, E15 144 EE66
EC2 11 L3
Reigate RH2 250 DB133
Markville Gdns, Cat. CR3 252 DU125
Markway, Sun. TW16 196 BW96
Mark Way, Swan. BR8 207 FG99
Markwell Cl, SE26
off Longton Gro 182 DV91
Markwell Wd, Harl. CM19 51 EP21
Markyate Rd, Dag. RM8 126 EV64
Marlands Rd, Ilf. IG5 124 EL55
Marlborough, SW3 18 B7
Marlborough Av, E8 142 DU67
N14 99 DJ48
Edgware HA8 96 CP48
Ruislip HA4 115 BQ58
Marlborough Cl, N20
off Marlborough Gdns 98 DF48
SE17 20 F8
SW19 180 DE93
Grays RM16 170 GC75
Orpington BR6
off Aylesham Rd 205 ET101
Upminster RM14 129 FS60
Walton-on-Thames KT12
off Arch Rd 196 BX104
Marlborough Ct, W1 9 J8
W8 16 G7
Dorking RH4
off Marlborough Rd 263 CH136
Wallington SM6
off Cranley Gdns 219 DJ108
Marlborough Cres, W4 158 CR76
Hayes UB3 155 BR80
Sevenoaks TN13 256 FE124
Marlborough Dr, Ilf. IG5 124 EL55
Weybridge KT13 195 BQ104
Sch Marlborough First &
Mid Sch, Har. HA1
off Marlborough Hill 117 CE56
Marlborough Gdns, N20 98 DF48
Upminster RM14 129 FR60
Marlborough Gate, St.Alb.
AL1 43 CE20
Marlborough Gate Ho, W2 7 N9
Marlborough Gro, SE1 22 A10
Marlborough Hill, NW8 140 DC67
Dorking RH4 263 CH136
Harrow HA1 117 CE56
★ Marlborough Ho, SW1 19 K2
Marlborough La, SE7 164 EJ79
Marlborough Ms, Bans.
SM7 234 DA115
Marlborough Pk Av, Sid.
DA15 186 EU87
Marlborough Pl, NW8 140 DC68
Sch Marlborough Prim Sch,
SW3 18 B8
Sch Marlborough Prim Sch,
Islw. TW7 off London Rd 157 CG81
Marlborough Ri, Hem.H.
HP2 40 BL17
Marlborough Rd, E4 101 EA51
E7 144 EJ66
E15 off Borthwick Rd 124 EE63
E18 124 EG55
N9 100 DT46
N19 121 DK61
N22 99 DL52
SW1 19 K2
SW19 180 DD93
W4 158 CQ78
W5 157 CK75
Ashford TW15 174 BK92
Bexleyheath DA7 166 EX83
Brentwood (Pilg.Hat.)
CM15 108 FU44
Bromley BR2 204 EJ98
Dagenham RM8 126 EV63
Dartford DA1 188 FJ86
Dorking RH4 263 CH136
Feltham TW13 176 BX89
Hampton TW12 176 CA93
Isleworth TW7 157 CH81
Richmond TW10 178 CL86
Romford RM7 126 FA56
St. Albans AL1 43 CE20
Slough SL3 152 AX77
South Croydon CR2 220 DQ108
Southall UB2 156 BW76
Sutton SM1 200 DA104
Uxbridge UB10 135 BP70
Watford WD18 75 BV42
Woking GU21 227 BA116
Sch Marlborough Sch, St.Alb.
AL1 off Watling St 43 CC23
Sidcup DA15
off Marlborough Pk Av 186 EU87
Marlborough St, SW3 18 A8
Marlborough Yd, N19 121 DK61
Marld, The, Ashtd. KT21 232 CM118
Marle Gdns, Wal.Abb. EN9 67 EC32
Marler Rd, SE23 183 DY88
Marlescroft Way, Loug. IG10 85 EP43
Marley Av, Bexh. DA7 166 EX79
Marley Cl, N15
off Stanmore Rd 121 DP56
Addlestone KT15 211 BF107
Greenford UB6 136 CA69
Marley Ct, Brox. EN10 49 DZ23
Marley Ri, Dor. RH4 263 CG139
Marley Rd, Welw.G.C. AL7 30 DA11
Marley Wk, NW2
off Lennon Rd 119 CW64
Marl Fld Cl, Wor.Pk. KT4 199 CU102
Marlin Cl, Berk. HP4 38 AT18
Sunbury-on-Thames
TW16 175 BT93
Marlin Copse, Berk. HP4 38 AU20
Marlin End, Berk. HP4 38 AT20
Marlingdene Cl, Hmptn.
TW12 176 CA93
Marlings Cl, Chis. BR7 205 ES98
Whyteleafe CR3 236 DS117
Marlings Pk Av, Chis. BR7 205 ES98
Marling Way, Grav. DA12 191 GL92
Marlins, The, Nthwd. HA6 93 BT51
Marlins Cl, Rick. (Chorl.)
WD3 73 BE40
Sutton SM1
off Turnpike La 218 DC106
Marlins Meadow, Wat.
WD18 75 BR44
Marlin Sq, Abb.L. WD5 59 BT31
Marlins Turn, Hem.H. HP1 40 BH17
Marloes Cl, Wem. HA0 117 CK63
Marloes Rd, W8 17 J6
Marlow Av, Purf. RM19 168 FN77
Marlow Cl, SE20 202 DV97
Marlow Ct, NW6 139 CX66
NW9 119 CT55
Marlow Cres, Twick. TW1 177 CF86
Marlow Dr, Sutt. SM3 199 CX103
Marlowe Cl, Chis. BR7 185 ER93
Ilford IG6 103 EQ53
Marlowe Ct, SE19
off Lymer Av 182 DT92
Marlowe Gdns, SE9 185 EN86
Romford RM3
off Shenstone Gdns 106 FJ53
Marlowe Rd, E17 123 EC56
Marlowes, Hem.H. HP1 40 BK21
Marlowes, The, NW8 140 DD67
Dartford DA1 167 FD84
Marlowes Cen, The, Hem.H.
HP1 40 BK21
Marlowe Sq, Mitch. CR4 201 DJ98
Marlowe Way, Croy. CR0 201 DL103
Marlow Gdns, Hayes UB3 155 BR76
Marlow Rd, E6 145 EM69
SE20 202 DV97
Southall UB2 156 BZ76
Marlow Way, SE16 22 G3
Marlpit Av, Couls. CR5 235 DL117
Marlpit La, Couls. CR5 235 DK116
Marl Rd, SW18 160 DB84
Marl St, SW18 off Marl Rd 160 DC84
Marlton St, SE10 25 K9
Marlwood Cl, Sid. DA15 185 ES89
Marlyns Cl, Guil. GU4 243 BA130
Marlyns Dr, Guil. GU4 243 BA130
Marlyon Rd, Ilf. IG6 104 EV50
Marmadon Rd, SE18 165 ET77
Marmion App, E4 101 EA49
Marmion Av, E4 101 DZ49
Coll Marmion Av Adult Ed
Cen, E4 off Marmion Av 101 EA49
Marmion Cl, E4 101 DZ49
Marmion Ms, SW11
off Taybridge Rd 160 DG83
Marmion Rd, SW11 160 DG84
Marmont Rd, SE15 162 DU81
Marmora Rd, SE22 182 DW86
Marmot Rd, Houns. TW4 156 BX83
Marne Av, N11 99 DH49
Welling DA16 166 EU83
Marnell Way, Houns. TW4 156 BX83
Sch Marner Prim Sch, E3 14 B3
Marne St, W10 6 C1
Marney Rd, SW11 160 DG84
Marneys Cl, Epsom KT18 232 CN115
Marnfield Cres, SW2 181 DM88
Marnham Av, NW2 119 CY63
Marnham Cres, Grnf. UB6 136 CB69
Marnham Ri, Hem.H. HP1 40 BG18
Marnock Rd, SE4 183 DY85
Maroon St, E14 13 J6
Maroons Way, SE6 183 EA92
Marquess Rd, N1 5 J4
Marquis Cl, Wem. HA0 138 CM66
Marquis Rd, N4 121 DM60
N22 99 DM51
NW1 141 DK65

★ Place of interest | H Hospital | Sch School | Coll College | Uni University | ⇌ Railway station

Marrabon Cl, Sid. DA15 ....186 EU88
Marram Ct, Grays RM17
off Medlar Rd 170 GE79
Marrick Cl, SW15 ....159 CU84
Marrilyne Av, Enf. EN3 ......83 DZ38
Marriott Cl, Felt. TW14 .....175 BR86
Marriot Ter, Rick. (Chorl.)
WD3 ....73 BF42
Marriott Lo Cl, Add. KT15 ..212 BJ105
Marriott Rd, E15 ....144 EE67
N4 ....121 DM60
N10 ....98 DF53
Barnet EN5 ....79 CX41
Dartford DA1 ....188 FN87
Marriotts, Harl. CM17
off Old Rd 36 EW10
Marriotts Cl, NW9 ....119 CT58
Marriotts Way, Hem.H. HP3 ..40 BK22
Mar Rd, S.Ock. RM15 ......149 FW70
Marrods Bottom, Beac. HP9 .88 AJ47
Marrowells, Wey. KT13 ....195 BS104
Marryat Cl, Houns. TW4 ....156 BZ84
Marryat Pl, SW19 ....179 CY91
Marryat Rd, SW19 ....179 CX92
Enfield EN1 ....82 DV35
Marryat Sq, SW6 ....159 CY81
Marsala Rd, SE13 ....163 EB84
Marsden Cl, Welw.G.C. AL8 ..29 CV11
Marsden Grn, Welw.G.C.
AL8 ....29 CV10
Marsden Rd, N9 ....100 DV47
SE15 ....162 DT83
Welwyn Garden City AL8 ..29 CV10
Marsden St, NW5 ....140 DG65
Marsden Way, Orp. BR6 ....223 ET105
Marshall Av, St.Alb. AL3 ....43 CE17
Marshall Cl, SW18
off Allfarthing La 180 DC86
Harrow HA1 off Bowen Rd .117 CD59
Hounslow TW4 ....176 BZ85
South Croydon CR2 .....220 DU113
Marshall Dr, Hayes UB4 ...135 BT71
Marshall Path, SE28
off Attlee Rd 146 EV73
Marshall Pl, Add. (New Haw)
KT15 ....212 BJ109
Marshall Rd, E10 ....123 EB62
N17 ....100 DR53
Marshalls Cl, N11 ....99 DH49
Epsom KT19 ....216 CQ113
Marshalls Dr, Rom. RM1 ...127 FE55
Marshall's Gro, SE18 ......164 EL77
[Sch] Marshalls Pk Sch, Rom.
RM1 off Pettits La 105 FE54
Marshalls Pl, SE16 ....21 P6
Marshalls Rd, Rom. RM7 ...127 FD56
Marshall's Rd, Sutt. SM1 ..218 DB105
Marshall St, W1 ....9 K8
Marshals Dr, St.Alb. AL1 ....43 CG17
Marshalsea Rd, SE1 ....21 H3
MARSHALSWICK, St.Alb.
AL1 ....43 CG17
Marshalswick La, St.Alb. AL1 .43 CH17
Marsham Cl, Chis. BR7 ....185 EP92
Marsham La, Ger.Cr. SL9 ..112 AY58
Marsham Lo, Ger.Cr. SL9 ..112 AY58
Marsham St, SW1 ....19 M6
Marsham Way, Ger.Cr. SL9 .112 AY57
Marsh Av, Epsom KT19 ....216 CS110
Mitcham CR4 ....200 DG96
Marshbrook Cl, SE3 ......164 EK83
Marsh Cl, NW7 ....97 CT48
Waltham Cross EN8 ......67 DZ33
Marsh Ct, SW19 ....200 DC95
Marshcroft Dr, Wal.Cr.
(Chsht) EN8 ....67 DY30
Marsh Dr, NW9 ....119 CT58
Marshe Cl, Pot.B. EN6 ......64 DD32
Marsh Fm Rd, Twick. TW2 ..177 CF88
Marshfield, Slou. (Datchet)
SL3 ....152 AW81
[Sch] Marshfields C of E Inf Sch,
Cher. KT16
off Fletcher Cl 211 BE107
Marshfield St, E14 ....24 C5
Marshfoot Rd, Grays RM16,
RM17 ....170 GE78
Marshgate, Harl. CM20
off School La 35 ES12
Marshgate Dr, Hert. SG13 ...32 DS08
Marshgate La, E15 ....143 EB67
Marshgate Path, SE28
off Tom Cribb Rd 165 EQ77
[Sch] Marshgate Prim Sch, Rich.
TW10 off Queens Rd ...158 CM84
Marshgate Sidings, E15 ....143 EB67
Marshgate Trd Est, Maid.
(Taplow) SL6 ....130 AG72
[Sch] Marsh Grn Prim Sch, Dag.
RM10 off South Cl 146 FA67
Marsh Grn Rd, Dag. RM10 ..146 FA67
Marsh Hill, E9 ....123 DY64
Marsh La, E10 ....123 EA61
N17 ....100 DV52
NW7 ....96 CS49
Addlestone KT15 ......212 BH105
Harlow CM17 ....36 EY10
Maidenhead SL6 ......150 AF75
Stanmore HA7 ....95 CJ50
Ware SG12 ....33 DY07
Ware (Stans.Abb.) SG12 ..33 ED12
Windsor (Dorney) SL4 ...150 AF75
Marshmoor Cres, Hat.
(N.Mymms) AL9 ......45 CW22
Marshmoor La, Hat.
(N.Mymms) AL9 ......45 CW22
Marsh Rd, Pnr. HA5 ......116 BY56
Wembley HA0 ....137 CK68
Marshside Cl, N9 ....100 DW46
Marsh St, E14 ....24 A8
Dartford DA1 ....168 FN82
Marsh Ter, Orp. BR5
off Buttermere Rd 206 EX98
Marsh Vw, Grav. DA12 .....191 GM88
Marsh Wall, E14 ....23 N2
Marsh Way, Rain. RM13 ....147 FD70
Marsland Cl, SE17 ....20 F10
Marston, Epsom KT19 ....216 CQ111
Marston Av, Chess. KT9 ...216 CL107
Dagenham RM10 ......126 FA61
Marston Cl, NW6 ....140 DC66
Chesham HP5 ....54 AN27
Dagenham RM10 ......126 FA62
Hemel Hempstead HP3 ..40 BN21
Marston Ct, Walt. KT12
off St. Johns Dr 196 BW102
Marston Dr, Warl. CR6 .....237 DY118
Marston Ho, Grays RM17 ..170 GA79
Marston Rd, Hodd. EN11 ....49 EB16
Ilford IG5 ....102 EL53
Teddington TW11 ......177 CH92
Woking GU21 ....226 AV117
Marston Way, SE19 ......181 DP94
Marsworth Av, Pnr. HA5 ....94 BX53
Marsworth Cl, Hayes UB4 ..136 BY71
Marsworth Cl, Wat. WD18 ...75 BS44
Martaban Rd, N16 ....122 DS61
Martara Ms, SE17 ....20 G10
Martello St, E8 ....142 DV66
Martello Ter, E8 ....142 DV66
Martell Rd, SE21 ....182 DR90
Martel Pl, E8 ....5 P3
Marten Gate, St.Alb. AL4 ....43 CG16
Marten Rd, E17 ....101 EA54
Martens Av, Bexh. DA7 ....167 FC84
Martens Cl, Bexh. DA7 ....167 FC84
Martha Ct, E2 ....142 DV68
Martham Cl, SE28 ....146 EX73
Ilford IG6 ....103 EP53
Martha Rd, E15 ....144 EE65
Martha's Bldgs, EC1 ....11 J3
Martha St, E1 ....12 D8
Marthorne Cres, Har. HA3 ...95 CD54
Martian Av, Hem.H. HP2 ....40 BM17
Martina Ter, Chig. IG7
off Manford Way 103 ET50
Martin Bowes Rd, SE9 .....165 EM83
Martinbridge Trd Est, Enf.
EN1 ....82 DU43
Martin Cl, N9 ....101 DX46
Hatfield AL10 ....45 CU20
South Croydon CR2 .....221 DX111
Uxbridge UB10
off Valley Rd 134 BL68
Warlingham CR6 ......236 DV116
Windsor SL4 ....150 AJ81
Martin Cres, Croy. CR0 ....201 DN102
Martindale, SW14 ....178 CQ85
Iver SL0 ....133 BD70
Martindale Av, E16 ....15 M9
Orpington BR6 ....224 EU106
Martindale Cl, Guil. GU4
off Gilliat Dr 243 BD132
[Sch] Martindale JMI Sch,
Hem.H. HP1
off Boxted Rd 39 BF19
Martindale Rd, SW12 ......181 DH87
Hemel Hempstead HP1 ...39 BF19
Hounslow TW4 ....156 BY83
Woking GU21 ....226 AT118
Martin Dene, Bexh. DA6 ....186 EZ85
Martin Dr, Dart. (Stone) DA2 .188 FQ86
Northolt UB5 ....116 BZ64
Rainham RM13 ....147 FH70
Martineau Cl, Esher KT10 ..215 CD105
Martineau Dr, Dor. RH4 ....263 CH138
Martineau Ms, N5
off Martineau Rd 121 DP63
Martineau Rd, N5 ....121 DP63
Martineau St, E1 ....12 E8
Martinfield, Welw.G.C. AL7 ..29 CZ08
Martingale Cl, Sun. TW16 ..195 BU98
Martingales Cl, Rich. TW10 .177 CK90
Martin Gdns, Dag. RM8 ....126 EW63
Martin Gro, Mord. SM4 ....200 DA97
Martini Dr, Enf. EN3 ....83 EA37
[Sch] Martin Jun & Inf Sch,
N2 off High Rd 98 DE54
Martin La, EC4 ....11 K9
Martin Ri, Bexh. DA6 ......186 EZ85
Martin Rd, Dag. RM8 ......126 EW63
Dartford DA2 ....188 FJ90
Guildford GU2 ....242 AU132
Slough SL1 ....152 AS76
South Ockendon (Aveley)
RM15 ....149 FR73
Martins Cl, Guil. GU1 .....243 BC133
Orpington BR5 ....206 EX97
Radlett WD7 ....77 CE36
West Wickham BR4 .....203 ED102
Martins Ct, St.Alb. AL1
off Cell Barnes La 43 CH23
Martins Dr, Hert. SG13 ....31 DV09
Waltham Cross (Chsht)
EN8 ....67 DY28
Martinsfield Cl, Chig. IG7 ..103 ES49
Martins Mt, Barn. EN5 ......80 DA42
Martins Pl, SE28
off Martin St 145 ES74
Martin's Plain, Slou.
(Stoke P.) SL2 ....132 AT69
Martins Rd, Brom. BR2 ....204 EE96
Martins Shaw, Sev.
(Chipstead) TN13 .....256 FC122
Martinstown Cl, Horn.
RM11 ....128 FN58
Martin St, SE28 ....145 ES74
Martins Wk, N10 ....98 DG53
SE28 ....145 ES74
Borehamwood WD6
off Siskin Cl 78 CN42
Martinsyde, Wok. GU22 ...227 BC117
Martin Way, SW20 ....199 CY97
Morden SM4 ....199 CY97
Woking GU21 ....226 AU118
Martlands Ind Est, Wok.
GU22
off Smarts Heath La ...226 AU123
Martlesham, Welw.G.C. AL7 ..30 DE09
Martlesham Cl, Horn. RM12 .128 FJ64
Martlet Gro, Nthlt. UB5 ....136 BX69
Martlett Ct, WC2 ....9 P8
Martley Dr, Ilf. IG2 ....125 EP57
Martock Cl, Har. HA3 ......117 CG56
Martock Gdns, N11 ....98 DF50
Marton Cl, SE6 ....183 EA90
Marton Rd, N16 ....122 DS61
Martyr Cl, St.Alb. AL1
off Creighton Av 43 CD24
Martyr Rd, Guil. GU1 ......258 AX135
MARTYR'S GREEN, Wok.
KT11 ....229 BR120
Martyrs La, Wok. GU21 ....211 BB112
Martys Yd, NW3
off Hampstead High St .120 DD63
Marunden Grn, Slou. SL2 ..131 AM69
Marvell Av, Hayes UB4 ....135 BU71
Marvels Cl, SE12 ....184 EH89
Marvels La, SE12 ....184 EH89
[Sch] Marvels La Prim Sch,
SE12 off Riddons Rd ...184 EJ91
Marville Rd, SW6 ....159 CZ80
Marvin St, E8
off Sylvester Rd 142 DV65
Marwell, West. TN16 ......255 EP126
Marwell Cl, Rom. RM1 .....127 FG57
West Wickham BR4
off Deer Pk Way 204 EF103
Marwood Cl, Kings L. WD4 ..58 BN29
Welling DA16 ....166 EV83
Marwood Dr, NW7 ....97 CX52
Mary Adelaide Cl, SW15 ...178 CS91
Mary Ann Gdns, SE8 ......163 EA79
Maryatt Av, Har. HA2 ......116 CB61
Marybank, SE18 ....165 EM77
Mary Cl, Stan. HA7 ....118 CM56
Mary Datchelor Cl, SE5 ....162 DR81
Maryfield Cl, Bex. DA5 ....187 FE90
Marygold Wk, Amer. HP6 ....72 AV39
Mary Grn, NW8 ....140 DB67
Maryhill Cl, Ken. CR8 ......236 DQ117
⇌ Maryland 144 EE65
Maryland, Hat. AL10 ....45 CT19
Maryland Conv, St.Alb.
AL3 off Townsend Dr 43 CD18
Maryland Ind Est, E15
off Maryland Rd 123 ED64
Maryland Pk, E15 ....124 EE64
Maryland Pt, E15
off Leytonstone Rd 144 EE65
[Sch] Maryland Prim Sch,
E15 off Gurney Rd 124 EE64
Maryland Rd, E15 ....123 ED64
N22 ....99 DM51
Thornton Heath CR7 ....201 DP95
Maryland Sq, E15 ....124 EE64
Marylands Rd, W9 ....7 H4
Maryland St, E15 ....123 ED64
Maryland Wk, N1 ....4 G7
Maryland Way, Sun. TW16 ..195 BU96
Mary Lawrenson Pl, SE3 ...164 EF80
MARYLEBONE, NW1 ....8 C7
⇌ Marylebone 8 C4
⊖ Marylebone 8 C4
Marylebone Flyover, NW1 ....7 P6
W2 ....7 P6
Marylebone High St, W1 ....8 F5
Marylebone La, W1 ....8 G8
Marylebone Ms, W1 ....8 G6
Marylebone Pas, W1 ....9 K7
Marylebone Rd, NW1 ....8 B5
Marylebone St, W1 ....8 F6
Marylee Way, SE11 ....20 B9
Mary Macarthur Ho, W6
off Field Rd 159 CY79
Mary Morgan Ct, Slou.
SL2 off Douglas Rd 131 AR71
[Sch] Marymount Int Sch,
Kings.T. KT2
off George Rd 178 CQ94
Maryon Gro, SE7 ....164 EL77
Maryon Ms, NW3
off South End Rd 120 DE63
Maryon Rd, SE7 ....164 EL77
SE18 ....164 EL77
Mary Peters Dr, Grnf. UB6 ..117 CD64
Mary Pl, W11 ....6 C10
Mary Rd, Guil. GU1 ......258 AW135
Mary Rose Cl, Grays
(Chaff.Hun.) RM16 .....169 FW77
Hampton TW12
off Ashley Rd 196 CA95
Mary Rose Mall, E6
off Frobisher Rd 145 EN71
Maryrose Way, N20 ....98 DD46
Mary Seacole Cl, E8 ....5 N7
Maryside, Slou. SL3 ......152 AY75
Mary's Ter, Twick. TW1 ....177 CG87
Mary St, E16 ....15 J6
N1 ....5 H8
Mary Ter, NW1 ....141 DH67
[Coll] Mary Ward Adult Ed Cen,
The, WC1 off Queen Sq .141 DL71
Mary Way, Wat. WD19 ......94 BX49
Masbro Rd, W14 ....16 B6
Mascalls Ct, SE7
off Victoria Way 164 EJ79
Mascalls Gdns, Brwd. CM14 .108 FT49
Mascalls La, Brwd. CM14 ...108 FT49
[H] Mascalls Pk, Brwd.
CM14 ....107 FV51
Mascalls Rd, SE7 ....164 EJ79
Mascoll Path, Slou. SL2 ....131 AM69
Mascotte Rd, SW15 ......159 CX84
Mascotts Cl, NW2 ....119 CV62
Masefield Av, Borwd. WD6 ..78 CP43
Southall UB1 ....136 CA73
Stanmore HA7 ....95 CF50
Masefield Cl, Chesh. HP5 ....54 AP28
Erith DA8 ....167 FF81
Romford RM3 ....106 FJ53
Masefield Ct, Brwd. CM14 ..108 FW49
Masefield Cres, N14 ....81 DJ44
Romford RM3 ....106 FJ53
Masefield Dr, Upmin. RM14 .128 FQ59
Masefield Gdns, E6 ....145 EN70
Masefield La, Hayes UB4 ...135 BV70
Masefield Rd, Dart. DA1 ....188 FP85
Gravesend (Nthflt) DA11 .190 GD90
Grays RM16 ....170 GE75
Hampton TW12
off Wordsworth Rd 176 BZ91
Masefield Vw, Orp. BR6 ....205 EQ104
Masefield Way, Stai. TW19 ..174 BM88
Masham Ho, Erith DA18
off Kale Rd 166 EX75
Mashie Rd, W3 ....138 CS72
Mashiters Hill, Rom. RM1 ..105 FD53
Mashiters Wk, Rom. RM1 ..127 FE55
Maskall Cl, SW2 ....181 DN88
Maskani Wk, SW16
off Bates Cres 181 DJ94
Maskell Rd, SW17 ....180 DC90
Maskelyne Cl, SW11 ......160 DE81
Maslen Rd, St.Alb. AL4 ......43 CJ23
Mason Bradbear Ct, N1
off St. Paul's Rd 142 DR65
Mason Cl, E16 ....15 L9
SE16 ....22 B9
SW20 ....199 CX95
Bexleyheath DA7 ......167 FB83
Borehamwood WD6 ......78 CQ40
Hampton TW12 ....196 BZ95
Mason Dr, Rom. (Harold Wd)
RM3 off Whitmore Av ...106 FL54
Masonic Hall Rd, Cher.
KT16 ....193 BF100
Mason Rd, Sutt. SM1
off Manor Pl 218 DB106
Woodford Green IG8 ....102 EE49
Masons Arms Ms, W1 ....9 H8
Masons Av, EC2 ....11 J7
Croydon CR0 ....202 DQ104
Harrow HA3 ....117 CF56
Masons Br Rd, Red. RH1 ...267 DH139
Masons Ct, Slou. SL1 ......131 AL73
Wembley HA9
off Mayfields 118 CN61
Masons Grn La, W3 ....138 CN71
Masons Hill, SE18 ....165 EP77
Bromley BR1, BR2 ......204 EG97
Masons Paddock, Dor. RH4 .247 CG134
Mason's Pl, EC1 ....10 F1
Masons Pl, Mitch. CR4 .....200 DF95
Masons Rd, Enf. EN1 ....82 DW36
Hemel Hempstead HP2 ...41 BP19
Slough SL1 ....131 AL73
Mason St, SE17 ....21 K8
Mason's Yd, SW1 ....19 K1
SW19
off High St Wimbledon ..179 CX92
Mason Way, Wal.Abb. EN9 ..68 EF34
Massetts Rd, Horl. RH6 ....268 DF149
Massey Cl, N11
off Grove Rd 99 DH50
Massey Ct, E6 ....144 EJ67
Massie Rd, E8
off Graham Rd 142 DU65
Massingberd Way, SW17 ...181 DH91
Massinger St, SE17 ....21 L8
Massingham St, E1 ....12 G3
Masson Av, Ruis. HA4 .....136 BW65
Master Cl, Oxt. RH8
off Church La 254 EE129
Master Gunner Pl, SE18 ....164 EL80
Masterman Ho, SE5 ......162 DR80
Masterman Rd, E6 ....144 EL69
Masters Cl, SW16
off Blegborough Rd 181 DJ93
Masters Dr, SE16 ....22 C10
Masters St, E1 ....13 H5
Masthead Cl, Dart. DA2 ....168 FQ84
[Riv] Masthouse Terrace 23 P9
Masthouse Ter, E14 ....23 P8
Mast Leisure Pk, SE16 ......23 H6
Mastmaker Rd, E14 ....23 P4
Maswell Pk Cres, Houns.
TW3 ....176 CC85
Maswell Pk Rd, Houns. TW3 .176 CB85
Matcham Rd, E11 ....124 EE62
Matching Rd, B.Stort.
(Hat.Hth) CM22 ....37 FH06
Harlow (Old Harl.) CM17 ..37 FB11
Ongar CM5 ....53 FH18
MATCHING TYE, Harl. CM17 ..37 FF12
Matchless Dr, SE18 ......165 EN80
Matfield Cl, Brom. BR2 ....204 EG99
Matfield Rd, Belv. DA17 ....166 FA79
Matham Gro, SE22 ....162 DT84
Matham Rd, E.Mol. KT8 ....197 CD99
Matheson Rd, W14 ....16 E8
Mathews Av, E6 ....145 EN68
Mathews Pk Av, E15 ......144 EF65
Mathias Cl, Epsom KT18 ...216 CQ113
[Sch] Mathilda Marks-Kennedy
Jewish Prim Sch &
Kindergarten, NW7
off Hale La 96 CR50
Mathisen Way, Slou.
(Colnbr.) SL3 ....153 BE81
Mathon Ct, Guil. GU1
off Cross Las 243 AZ134
Matilda Cl, SE19
off Elizabeth Way 182 DR94
Matilda St, N1 ....4 B8
Matlock Cl, SE24 ....162 DQ84
Barnet EN5 ....79 CX43
Matlock Ct, SE5
off Denmark Hill Est 162 DR84
Matlock Cres, Sutt. SM3 ...217 CY105
Watford WD19 ....94 BW48
Matlock Gdns, Horn. RM12 .128 FL62
Sutton SM3 ....217 CY105
Matlock Pl, Sutt. SM3 .....217 CY105
Matlock Rd, E10 ....123 EC58
Caterham CR3 ....236 DS121
Matlock St, E14 ....13 J7
Matlock Way, N.Mal. KT3 ...198 CR95
Matrimony Pl, SW8 ....161 DJ82
Matson Ct, Wdf.Grn. IG8
off The Bridle Path 102 EE52
Matthew Arnold Cl, Cob.
KT11 ....213 BU114
Staines TW18
off Elizabeth Av 174 BJ93
[Sch] Matthew Arnold Sch,
The, Stai. TW18
off Kingston Rd 174 BJ93
Matthew Cl, W10 ....6 A4
Matthew Ct, Mitch. CR4 ....201 DK99
Matthew Parker St, SW1 ....19 M4
Matthews Cl, Rom.
(Hav.at.Bow.) RM3
off Oak Rd 106 FM53
Matthews Gdns, Croy.
(New Adgtn) CR0 ......221 ED111
Matthews Rd, Grnf. UB6 ...117 CD64
Matthews St, SW11 ....160 DF82
Reigate RH2 ....266 DA138
Matthews Yd, WC2 ....9 N8
Matthias Rd, N16 ....5 K1
Mattingley Way, SE15
off Daniel Gdns 162 DT80
Mattison Rd, N4 ....121 DN58
Mattock La, W5 ....137 CH74
W13 ....137 CH74
Maud Cashmore Way,
SE18 ....165 EM76
Maude Cres, Wat. WD24 ....75 BV37
Maude Rd, E17 ....123 DY57
SE5 ....162 DS81
Beaconsfield HP9 ....89 AN54
Swanley BR8 ....187 FG93
Maudesville Cotts, W7
off The Broadway 137 CE74
Maude Ter, E17 ....123 DY56
Maud Gdns, E13 ....144 EF67
Barking IG11 ....145 ET68
Maudlin's Grn, E1 ....22 A1
Maud Rd, E10 ....123 EC62
E13 ....144 EF68
Maudslay Rd, SE9 ....165 EM83
[H] Maudsley Hosp, The,
SE5 ....162 DR82
Maudsley Ho, Brent. TW8
off Green Dragon La ...158 CL78
Maud St, E16 ....15 J6
Maud Wilkes Cl, NW5 ......121 DJ64
Mauleverer Rd, SW2 ......181 DL85
Maundeby Wk, NW10
off Neasden La 138 CS65
Maunder Cl, Grays
(Chaff.Hun.) RM16 .....169 FX77
Maunder Rd, W7 ....137 CF74
Maunds Fm, Harl. CM18 ....51 ER20
Maunds Hatch, Harl. CM18 ..51 ER19
Maunsel St, SW1 ....19 L7
Maurice Av, N22 ....99 DP54
Caterham CR3 ....236 DR122
Maurice Brown Cl, NW7 ....97 CX50
Maurice St, W12 ....139 CV72
Maurice Wk, NW11 ....120 DC56
Maurier Cl, Nthlt. UB5 .....136 BW67
Mauritius Rd, SE10 ....25 H8
Maury Rd, N16 ....122 DU61
Mauveine Gdns, Houns.
TW3 ....156 CA84
Mavelstone Cl, Brom. BR1 .204 EL95
Mavelstone Rd, Brom. BR1 .204 EL95
Maverton Rd, E3 ....143 EA67
Mavis Av, Epsom KT19 .....216 CS106
Mavis Cl, Epsom KT19 .....216 CS106
Mavis Gro, Horn. RM12 ....128 FL61
Mavis Wk, E6 ....144 EL71
Mawbey Est, SE1 ....22 A10
Mawbey Pl, SE1 ....21 P10
Mawbey Rd, SE1 ....21 P10
Chertsey (Ott.) KT16 ....211 BD107
Mawbey St, SW8 ....161 DL80
Mawney Cl, Rom. RM7 .....105 FB54
[Sch] Mawney Prim Sch, Rom.
RM7 off Mawney Rd ...127 FD57
Mawney Rd, Rom. RM7 .....127 FC56
Mawson Cl, SW20 ....199 CY96
Mawson La, W4
off Great W Rd 159 CT79
Maxey Gdns, Dag. RM9 .....126 EY63
Maxey Rd, SE18 ....165 EQ77
Dagenham RM9 ....126 EY63
Maxfield Cl, N20 ....98 DC45
Maxilla Gdns, W10 ....6 B7
Maxilla Wk, W10
off Kingsdown Cl 139 CX72
Maximfeldt Rd, Erith DA8 ..167 FE78
Maxim Rd, N21 ....81 DN44
Dartford DA1 ....187 FE85
Erith DA8 ....167 FE77
Maxted Cl, Hem.H. HP2 ....41 BQ18
Maxted Pk, Har. HA1 ......117 CE59
Maxted Rd, SE15 ....162 DT83
Hemel Hempstead HP2 ...41 BP17
Maxwell Cl, Croy. CR0 .....201 DL102
Hayes UB3 ....135 BU73
Rickmansworth (Mill End)
WD3 ....92 BG47
Maxwell Dr, W.Byf. KT14 ...212 BJ111
Maxwell Gdns, Orp. BR6 ...205 ET104
Maxwell Ri, Wat. WD19 ......94 BY45
Maxwell Rd, SW6 ....160 DB80
Ashford TW15 ....175 BQ93
Beaconsfield HP9 ....89 AK52
Borehamwood WD6 ......78 CP41
Northwood HA6 ....93 BR52
St. Albans AL1 ....43 CH21
Welling DA16 ....166 EU84
West Drayton UB7 ......154 BM77
Maxwelton Av, NW7 ....96 CR50
Maxwelton Cl, NW7 ....96 CR50
Maya Angelou Ct, E4
off Bailey Cl 101 EC49
Maya Cl, SE15 ....162 DV82
Mayall Rd, SE24 ....181 DP85
Maya Pl, N11 ....99 DK52
Maya Rd, N2 ....120 DC56
May Av, Grav. (Nthflt) DA11 .191 GF88
Orpington BR5 ....206 EV99
May Av Ind Est, Grav. (Nthflt)
DA11 off May Av 191 GF88
Maybank Av, E18 ....102 EH54
Hornchurch RM12 ......127 FH64
Wembley HA0 ....117 CF64
Maybank Gdns, Pnr. HA5 ...115 BU57
Maybank Lo, Horn. RM12
off Maybank Av 128 FJ64
Maybank Rd, E18 ....102 EH53
May Bate Av, Kings.T. KT2 .197 CK95
Maybells Commercial Est,
Bark. IG11 ....146 EX68
Mayberry Pl, Surb. KT5 ....198 CM101
Maybourne Cl, SE26 ......182 DV92
Maybourne Ri, Wok. GU22 .226 AX124
Maybrick Rd, Horn. RM11 ..128 FJ58
Maybrook Meadow Est,
Bark. IG11 ....146 EU66
MAYBURY, Wok. GU22 .....227 BB117
Maybury Av, Dart. DA2 ....188 FQ88
Waltham Cross (Chsht)
EN8 ....66 DV28
Maybury Cl, Enf. EN1 ......82 DV38
Loughton IG10 ....85 EP42
Orpington BR5 ....205 EP99
Slough SL1 ....131 AK72
Tadworth KT20
off Ballards Grn 233 CY119
Maybury Gdns, NW10 ......139 CV65
Maybury Hill, Wok. GU22 ..227 BB116
[Sch] Maybury Inf Sch, Wok.
GU21 off Walton Rd ...227 BA116
Maybury Ms, N6 ....121 DJ59
Maybury Rd, E13 ....144 EJ70
Barking IG11 ....145 ET68
Woking GU21 ....227 AZ117
Maybury St, SW17 ....180 DE92
Maybush Rd, Horn. RM11 ..128 FL59
Maychurch Cl, Stan. HA7 ....95 CK52
May Cl, Chess. KT9 ......216 CM107
St. Albans AL3 ....43 CD18
Maycock Gro, Nthwd. HA6 ..93 BT51
May Cotts, Wat. WD18 ......76 BW43
May Ct, SW19 ....200 DC95
Grays RM17
off Medlar Rd 170 GE79
Maycroft, Pnr. HA5 ....93 BV54
Maycroft Av, Grays RM17 ..170 GD78
Maycroft Gdns, Grays
RM17 ....170 GD78
Maycroft Rd, Wal.Cr. (Chsht)
EN7 ....66 DS26
Maycross Av, Mord. SM4 ...199 CZ97
Mayday Gdns, SE3 ....164 EL82
[H] Mayday Hosp, Th.Hth.
CR7 ....201 DP100
Mayday Rd, Th.Hth. CR7 ...201 DP100
Maydew Twr, SE16
off Abbeyfield Rd 162 DW77
Maydwell Lo, Borwd. WD6 ..78 CM40
Mayell Cl, Lthd. KT22 ......231 CJ123
Mayerne Rd, SE9 ....184 EK85
Mayer Rd, Wal.Abb. EN9
off Deer Pk Way 83 EB36
Mayesbrook Rd, Bark. IG11 .145 ET67
Dagenham RM8 ....126 EU62
Ilford IG3 ....126 EU62
Mayes Cl, Swan. BR8 ......207 FG98
Warlingham CR6 ......237 DX118
Mayesford Rd, Rom. RM6 ..126 EW59
[Sch] Mayespark Prim Sch, Ilf.
IG3 off Goodmayes La ..126 EU62
Mayes Rd, N22 ....99 DN54
Mayeswood Rd, SE12 ......184 EJ90
MAYFAIR, W1 ....8 G10
Mayfair Av, Bexh. DA7 ....166 EX81
Ilford IG1 ....125 EM61
Romford RM6 ....126 EX58
Twickenham TW2 ......176 CC87
Worcester Park KT4 .....199 CU102
Mayfair Cl, Beck. BR3 .....203 EB95
St. Albans AL4 ....43 CJ15
Surbiton KT6 ....198 CL102
Mayfair Gdns, N17 ....100 DR51
Woodford Green IG8 ....102 EG52
Mayfair Ms, NW1
off Regents Pk Rd 140 DF66
Mayfair Pl, W1 ....19 H1
Mayfair Rd, Dart. DA1 ....188 FK85
Mayfair Ter, N14 ....99 DK45
Mayfare, Rick. (Crox.Grn)
WD3 ....75 BR43
Mayfield, Bexh. DA7 ......166 EZ83

Mayfield, Lthd. KT22 231 CJ121
Waltham Abbey EN9 67 ED34
Welwyn Garden City AL8 29 CW05
Mayfield Av, N12 98 DC49
N14 99 DK47
W4 158 CS77
W13 157 CH76
Addlestone (New Haw) KT15 212 BH110
Gerrards Cross SL9 112 AX56
Harrow HA3 117 CH57
Orpington BR6 205 ET102
Woodford Green IG8 102 EG52
Mayfield Cl, E8 5 N4
SW4 181 DK85
Addlestone (New Haw) KT15 212 BJ110
Ashford TW15 175 BP93
Harlow CM17 36 EZ11
Redhill RH1 *off Brookfield Cl* 266 DG140
Thames Ditton KT7 197 CH102
Uxbridge UB10 135 BP69
Walton-on-Thames KT12 213 BU105
Mayfield Cres, N9 82 DV44
Thornton Heath CR7 201 DM98
Mayfield Dr, Pnr. HA5 116 BZ56
Mayfield Gdns, NW4 119 CX58
W7 137 CD72
Brentwood CM14 108 FV46
Staines TW18 173 BF93
Walton-on-Thames KT12 213 BU105
Sch **Mayfield Inf Sch**, Wal.Cr. EN8 *off Cheshunt Wash* 67 DY27
Mayfield Mans, SW15 *off West Hill* 179 CX87
Mayfield Pk, West Dr. UB7 154 BJ76
Sch **Mayfield Prim Sch**, W7 *off High La* 137 CD72
Mayfield Rd, E4 101 EC47
E8 5 N6
E13 15 K4
E17 101 DY54
N8 121 DM58
SW19 199 CZ95
W3 138 CP73
W12 158 CS75
Belvedere DA17 167 FC77
Bromley BR1 204 EL99
Dagenham RM8 126 EW60
Enfield EN3 83 DX40
Gravesend DA11 191 GF87
High Wycombe (Woob.Grn) HP10 110 AE57
South Croydon CR2 220 DR109
Sutton SM2 218 DD107
Thornton Heath CR7 201 DM98
Walton-on-Thames KT12 213 BU105
Weybridge KT13 212 BM106
Mayfields, Grays RM16 170 GC75
Swanscombe DA10 190 FY86
Wembley HA9 118 CN61
Sch **Mayfield Sch & Coll**, Dag. RM8 *off Mayfield Rd* 126 EW60
Mayfields Cl, Wem. HA9 118 CN61
Mayflower Av, Hem.H. HP2 40 BK20
Mayflower Cl, SE16 23 H7
Hertford SG14 31 DL11
Ruislip HA4 *off Leaholme Way* 115 BQ58
South Ockendon RM15 149 FW70
Waltham Abbey EN9 50 EE22
Mayflower Ct, SE16 *off St. Marychurch St* 162 DW75
Harlow CM19 51 EP19
Sch **Mayflower Prim Sch**, E14 14 A8
Mayflower Rd, SW9 161 DL83
Grays (Chaff.Hun.) RM16 169 FW78
St. Albans (Park St) AL2 60 CB27
Mayflower St, SE16 22 E4
Mayflower Way, Beac. HP9 110 AG55
Slough (Farn.Com.) SL2 111 AQ64
Mayfly Cl, Orp. BR5 206 EX98
Pinner HA5 116 BW59
Mayfly Gdns, Nthlt. UB5 *off Ruislip Rd* 136 BX69
MAYFORD, Wok. GU22 226 AW122
Mayford Cl, SW12 180 DF87
Beckenham BR3 203 DX97
Woking GU22 226 AX122
Mayford Grn, Wok. GU22 *off Smarts Heath Rd* 226 AW122
Mayford Rd, SW12 180 DF87
May Gdns, Borwd. (Elstree) WD6 77 CK44
Wembley HA0 137 CJ68
Maygoods Cl, Uxb. UB8 134 BK71
Maygoods Grn, Uxb. UB8 *off Worcester Rd* 134 BK71
Maygoods La, Uxb. UB8 134 BK71
Maygood St, N1 4 B9
Maygoods Vw, Uxb. UB8 *off Benbow Waye* 134 BJ71
Maygreen Cres, Horn. RM11 127 FG59
Maygrove Rd, NW6 139 CZ65
Mayhall La, Amer. HP6 55 AP35
Mayhew Cl, E4 101 EA48
Mayhill Rd, SE7 164 EH79
Barnet EN5 79 CY44
Mayhurst Av, Wok. GU22 227 BC116
Mayhurst Cl, Wok. GU22 227 BC116
Mayhurst Cres, Wok. GU22 227 BC116
Maylands Av, Hem.H. HP2 41 BP17
Hornchurch RM12 127 FH63
Maylands Dr, Sid. DA14 186 EX90
Uxbridge UB8 134 BK65
Maylands Rd, Wat. WD19 94 BW49
Maylands Way, Rom. RM3 106 FQ51
Maylins Dr, Saw. CM21 36 EX05
Maynard Cl, N15 *off Brunswick Rd* 122 DS56
SW6 *off Cambria St* 160 DB80
Erith DA8 167 FF80
Maynard Ct, Enf. EN3 *off Harston Dr* 83 EA38
Waltham Abbey EN9 68 EF34
Maynard Dr, St.Alb. AL1 43 CD23
Maynard Path, E17 123 EC57
Maynard Pl, Pot.B. EN6 65 DL29
Maynard Rd, E17 123 EC57
Hemel Hempstead HP2 40 BK21
Maynards, Horn. RM11 128 FL59
Maynards Quay, E1 12 E10
Mayne Av, St.Alb. AL3 42 BZ22
Maynooth Gdns, Cars. SM5 200 DF101
Mayo Cl, Wal.Cr. (Chsht) EN8 66 DW28
Mayo Gdns, Hem.H. HP1 *off Anchor La* 40 BH21

Mayola Rd, E5 122 DW63
Mayo Rd, NW10 138 CS65
Croydon CR0 202 DR99
Walton-on-Thames KT12 195 BT101
Mayor's La, Dart. DA2 188 FJ92
Mayow Rd, SE23 183 DX90
SE26 183 DX91
Mayplace Av, Dart. DA1 167 FG84
Mayplace Cl, Bexh. DA7 167 FB83
Mayplace La, SE18 165 EP80
Sch **Mayplace Prim Sch**, Bexh. DA7 *off Woodside Rd* 167 FD84
Mayplace Rd E, Bexh. DA7 167 FB83
Dartford DA1 167 FC83
Mayplace Rd W, Bexh. DA7 166 FA84
MAYPOLE, Orp. BR6 224 EZ106
Sch **Maypole Co Prim Sch**, Bex. DA5 *off Old Bexley La* 187 FE89
Maypole Cres, Erith DA8 168 FK79
Ilford IG6 103 ER52
Maypole Dr, Chig. IG7 104 EU48
Maypole Rd, Grav. DA12 191 GM88
Maidenhead (Taplow) SL6 130 AG71
Orpington BR6 224 EZ106
Maypole St, Harl. CM17 *off London Rd* 36 EW14
May Rd, E4 101 EA51
E13 144 EG68
Dartford (Hawley) DA2 188 FM91
Twickenham TW2 177 CE88
Mayroyd Av, Surb. KT6 198 CN103
May's Bldgs Ms, SE10 *off Crooms Hill* 163 ED80
Mays Cl, Wey. KT13 212 BM110
Mays Ct, WC2 9 N10
Maysfield Rd, Wok. (Send) GU23 227 BD123
MAY'S GREEN, Cob. KT11 229 BT121
Mays Gro, Wok. (Send) GU23 227 BD123
Mays Hill Rd, Brom. BR2 204 EE96
Mays La, E4 101 ED47
Barnet EN5 79 CY43
Maysoule Rd, SW11 160 DD84
Mays Rd, Tedd. TW11 177 CD92
Mayston Ms, SE10 *off Westcombe Hill* 164 EG78
May St, W14 16 F10
Mayswood Gdns, Dag. RM10 147 FC65
Maythorne Cl, Wat. WD18 75 BS42
Mayton St, N7 121 DM62
Maytree Cl, Edg. HA8 96 CQ48
Guildford GU1 242 AV131
Rainham RM13 147 FE68
Maytree Cres, Wat. WD24 75 BT35
Maytree Gdns, W5 *off South Ealing Rd* 157 CK75
May Tree La, Stan. HA7 95 CF52
Maytrees, Rad. WD7 77 CG37
Maytree Wk, SW2 181 DN89
Mayville Est, N16 5 L1
Sch **Mayville Infants' Sch**, E11 *off Lincoln St* 124 EE62
Sch **Mayville Jun Sch**, E11 *off Mayville Rd* 124 EE62
Mayville Rd, E11 124 EE61
Ilford IG1 125 EP64
May Wk, E13 144 EH68
Maywater Cl, S.Croy. CR2 220 DR111
Maywin Dr, Horn. RM11 128 FM60
Maywood Cl, Beck. BR3 183 EB94
⇌ **Maze Hill** 164 EE79
Maze Hill, SE3 164 EE79
SE10 164 EE79
Mazenod Av, NW6 140 DA66
Maze Rd, Rich. TW9 158 CN80
Mead, The, N2 98 DC54
W13 137 CH71
Ashtead KT21 232 CL119
Beaconsfield HP9 89 AL53
Beckenham BR3 203 EC95
Uxbridge UB10 114 BN61
Wallington SM6 219 DK107
Waltham Cross (Chsht) EN8 66 DW29
Watford WD19 94 BY48
West Wickham BR4 203 ED102
Mead Av, Red. RH1 266 DG142
Slough SL3 153 BB75
Mead Business Cen, The, Hert. SG13 32 DS08
Mead Cl, Egh. TW20 173 BB93
Grays RM16 170 GB75
Harrow HA3 95 CD53
Loughton IG10 85 EP40
Redhill RH1 250 DG131
Romford RM2 105 FG54
Slough SL3 153 BB75
Swanley BR8 207 FG99
Uxbridge (Denh.) UB9 114 BG61
Mead Ct, NW9 118 CQ57
Egham TW20 *off Holbrook Meadow* 173 BC93
Waltham Abbey EN9 67 EB34
Woking (Knap.) GU21 226 AS116
Mead Cres, E4 101 EC49
Dartford DA1 *off Beech Rd* 188 FK88
Leatherhead (Bkhm) KT23 246 CA125
Sutton SM1 218 DE105
Meadcroft Rd, SE11 161 DP79
Meade Cl, W4 158 CN79
Meade Ct, Tad. KT20 233 CU124
Mead End, Ashtd. KT21 232 CM116
Meades, The, Wey. KT13 213 BQ107
Meades La, Chesh. HP5 54 AP32
Meadfield, Edg. HA8 96 CP47
Mead Fld, Har. HA2 *off Kings Rd* 116 BZ62
Meadfield Av, Slou. SL3 153 BA76
Meadfield Grn, Edg. HA8 96 CP47
Meadfield Rd, Slou. SL3 153 BA76
Meadfoot Rd, SW16 181 DJ94
Meadgate Av, Wdf.Grn. IG8 102 EL50
Meadgate Rd, Brox. EN10 49 ED20
Harlow CM19 49 ED20
Mead Gro, Rom. RM6 126 EY55
Mead Ho La, Hayes UB4 135 BR70
Meadhurst Rd, Cher. KT16 194 BH102
Mead Ind Pk, Harl. CM20 35 ET11
Sch **Mead Inf Sch, The**, Epsom KT19 *off Newbury Gdns* 217 CT105
Meadlands Dr, Rich. TW10 177 CK89
Sch **Meadlands Prim Sch**, Rich. TW10 *off Broughton Av* 177 CJ91
Mead La, Cher. KT16 194 BH102
Hertford SG13 32 DR08
Meadow, The, Chis. BR7 185 EQ93
Hertford (Hailey) SG13 33 DY13
Meadow Av, Croy. CR0 203 DX100
Meadow Bk, N21 81 DM44
Meadowbank, NW3 140 DF66
SE3 164 EF83

Meadowbank, Kings L. WD4 58 BN30
Surbiton KT5 198 CM100
Watford WD19 94 BW45
Meadow Bk, Lthd. (E.Hors.) KT24 245 BT128
Meadowbank Cl, SW6 159 CW80
Meadowbank Gdns, Houns. TW5 155 BU82
Meadowbank Rd, NW9 118 CR59
Meadowbanks, Barn. EN5 79 CT43
Meadowbrook, Oxt. RH8 253 EC130
Meadowbrook Cl, Slou. (Colnbr.) SL3 153 BF82
Meadowbrook Rd, Dor. RH4 263 CG135
Meadow Bungalows, Guil. (Chilw.) GU4 259 BB140
Meadow Cl, E4 *off Mount Echo Av* 101 EB46
E9 123 DZ64
SE6 183 EA92
SW20 199 CW98
Barnet EN5 79 CZ44
Bexleyheath DA6 186 EZ85
Chesham HP5 *off Little Hivings* 54 AN27
Chislehurst BR7 185 EP92
Enfield EN3 83 DY38
Esher KT10 197 CF104
Godalming GU7 258 AS144
Hatfield AL9 45 CX24
Hertford SG13 32 DT08
Hounslow TW4 176 CA86
Northolt UB5 136 CA68
Purley CR8 219 DK113
Richmond TW10 178 CL88
Ruislip HA4 115 BT58
St. Albans AL4 43 CJ17
St. Albans (Brick.Wd) AL2 60 CA29
St. Albans (Lon.Col.) AL2 61 CK27
Sevenoaks TN13 256 FG123
Sutton SM1 *off Aultone Way* 200 DB103
Walton-on-Thames KT12 214 BZ105
Windsor (Old Wind.) SL4 172 AV86
Meadowcot La, Amer. (Colesh.) HP7 55 AM44
Meadow Cotts, Beac. HP9 89 AL54
Meadow Ct, Epsom KT18 216 CQ113
Harlow CM18 51 ES19
Redhill RH1 251 DK130
Staines TW18 173 BE90
Meadowcourt Rd, SE3 164 EF84
Meadowcroft, Brom. BR1 205 EM97
Bushey WD23 76 CB44
Gerrards Cross (Chal.St.P.) SL9 90 AX54
Meadow Cft, Hat. AL10 45 CT18
Meadowcroft, St.Alb. AL1 43 CG23
Meadowcroft Cl, Horl. RH6 269 DJ151
Sch **Meadowcroft Comm Inf Sch**, Cher. KT16 *off Little Grn La* 193 BF104
Meadowcroft Rd, N13 99 DN47
Meadowcross, Wal.Abb. EN9 68 EE34
Meadow Dell, Hat. AL10 45 CT18
Meadow Dr, N10 121 DH55
NW4 97 CW54
Amersham HP6 55 AS37
Woking (Ripley) GU23 227 BF123
Meadow Gdns, Edg. HA8 96 CP51
Staines TW18 173 BD92
Meadow Garth, NW10 138 CQ65
Meadowgate Cl, NW7 *off Stanhope Gdns* 97 CT50
Sch **Meadowgate Sch**, SE4 *off Revelon Rd* 163 DY83
Meadow Grn, Welw.G.C. AL8 29 CW09
Meadow Hill, Couls. CR5 219 DJ113
New Malden KT3 198 CS100
Purley CR8 219 DJ113
Meadowlands, Cob. KT11 213 BU113
Guildford (W.Clan.) GU4 244 BH130
Hornchurch RM11 128 FL59
Oxted RH8 254 EG134
Meadowlands Pk, Add. KT15 194 BL104
Meadow La, SE12 184 EH90
Beaconsfield HP9 89 AM53
Leatherhead (Fetch.) KT22 230 CC121
Windsor (Eton) SL4 151 AQ80
Meadowlea Cl, West Dr. UB7 154 BK79
Meadow Ms, SW8 161 DM79
Meadow Pl, SW8 161 DL80
W4 *off Edensor Rd* 158 CS80
Meadow Ri, Couls. CR5 219 DK113
Meadow Rd, SW8 161 DM79
SW19 180 DC94
Ashford TW15 175 BR92
Ashtead KT21 232 CL117
Barking IG11 145 ET66
Berkhamsted HP4 38 AU17
Borehamwood WD6 78 CP40
Bromley BR2 204 EE95
Bushey WD23 76 CB43
Dagenham RM9 146 EZ65
Epping CM16 69 ET29
Esher (Clay.) KT10 215 CE107
Feltham TW13 176 BY89
Gravesend DA11 191 GG89
Guildford GU4 243 BA130
Hemel Hempstead HP3 40 BN24
Loughton IG10 84 EL43
Pinner HA5 116 BX57
Romford RM7 127 FC60
Slough SL3 152 AY76
Southall UB1 136 BZ73
Sutton SM1 218 DE106
Virginia Water GU25 192 AS99
Watford WD25 59 BU34
Meadow Row, SE1 20 G6
Meadows, The, Amer. HP7 55 AS39
Guildford GU2 258 AW137
Hemel Hempstead HP1 39 BE19
Orpington BR6 224 EW107
Sawbridgeworth CM21 36 FA05
Sevenoaks (Halst.) TN14 224 EZ113
Warlingham CR6 237 DX117
Welwyn Garden City AL7 30 DC09
Sch **Meadow Sch, The**, Uxb. UB8 *off Royal La* 134 BM69
Meadows Cl, E10 123 EA61
Meadows End, Sun. TW16 195 BU95
Meadowside, SE9 164 EJ84
Beaconsfield (Jordans) HP9 90 AT52
Dartford DA1 188 FK88
Horley RH6 *off Stockfield* 269 DH147
Leatherhead (Bkhm) KT23 230 CA123
Walton-on-Thames KT12 196 BW103
Meadow Side, Wat. WD25 59 BV31
Meadowside Rd, Sutt. SM2 217 CY109

Meadowside Rd, Upmin. RM14 128 FQ64
Meadows Leigh Cl, Wey. KT13 195 BQ104
Sch **Meadows Sch**, H.Wyc. HP10 *off School Rd* 110 AE57
Meadow Stile, Croy. CR0 *off High St* 202 DQ104
Meadowsweet Cl, E16 *off Monarch Dr* 144 EK71
SW20 199 CW99
Meadow Vw, Ch.St.G. HP8 90 AU48
Chertsey KT16 194 BJ102
Harrow HA1 117 CE60
Meadowview, Orp. BR5 206 EW97
Meadow Vw, Sid. DA15 186 EV87
Staines TW19 173 BF85
Meadowview Rd, SE6 183 DZ92
Bexley DA5 186 EY86
Epsom KT19 216 CS109
Meadow Vw Rd, Hayes UB4 135 BQ70
Thornton Heath CR7 201 DP99
Meadow Wk, E18 124 EG56
Dagenham RM9 146 EZ65
Dartford DA2 188 FJ91
Epsom KT17, KT19 216 CS107
High Wycombe (Penn) HP10 88 AC46
Tadworth KT20 233 CV124
Wallington SM6 201 DH104
Meadow Way, NW9 118 CR57
Abbots Langley (Bedmond) WD5 59 BT27
Addlestone KT15 212 BH105
Chessington KT9 216 CL106
Chigwell IG7 103 EQ48
Dartford DA2 188 FQ87
Hemel Hempstead HP3 39 BF23
Kings Langley WD4 58 BN30
Leatherhead (Bkhm) KT23 230 CB123
Leatherhead (W.Hors.) KT24 245 BR125
Maidenhead (Dorney R.) SL6 150 AF75
Maidenhead (Fifield) SL6 150 AD81
Orpington BR6 205 EN104
Potters Bar EN6 64 DA34
Reigate RH2 266 DB138
Rickmansworth WD3 92 BJ45
Ruislip HA4 115 BV58
Sawbridgeworth CM21 36 FA06
Tadworth KT20 233 CY118
Upminster RM14 128 FQ62
Wembley HA9 117 CK63
Windsor (Old Wind.) SL4 172 AV86
Meadow Way, The, Har. HA3 95 CE53
Meadow Waye, Houns. TW5 156 BY79
Sch **Meadow Wd Sch**, Bushey WD23 *off Coldharbour La* 76 CC43
Mead Path, SW17 180 DC92
Mead Pl, E9 142 DW65
Croydon CR0 201 DP102
Rickmansworth WD3 92 BH46
Mead Plat, NW10 138 CQ65
Mead Rd, Cat. CR3 236 DT123
Chislehurst BR7 185 EQ93
Dartford DA1 188 FK88
Edgware HA8 96 CN51
Gravesend DA11 191 GH89
Radlett (Shenley) WD7 62 CM33
Richmond TW10 177 CJ90
Uxbridge UB8 134 BK66
Walton-on-Thames KT12 214 BY105
Sch **Mead Rd Inf Sch**, Chis. BR7 *off Mead Rd* 185 EQ93
Mead Row, SE1 20 C5
Meads, The, Berk. HP4 38 AS17
Edgware HA8 96 CR51
St. Albans (Brick.Wd) AL2 60 BZ29
Sutton SM3 199 CY104
Upminster RM14 129 FS61
Uxbridge UB8 134 BL70
Sch **Mead Sch**, Rom. RM3 *off Amersham Rd* 106 FM51
Sch **Mead Sch, The**, Harl. CM18 *off Tendring Rd* 51 ES17
Meads La, Ilf. IG3 125 ES59
Meads Rd, N22 99 DP54
Enfield EN3 83 DY39
Guildford GU1 243 BA134
Meadsway, Brwd. CM13 107 FV51
Mead Ter, Wem. HA9 *off Meadow Way* 117 CK63
MEAD VALE, Red. RH1 266 DD136
Meadvale Rd, W5 137 CH70
Croydon CR0 202 DT101
Meadview Rd, Ware SG12 33 DX07
Mead Wk, Slou. SL3 153 BB75
Meadway, N14 99 DK47
NW11 120 DB58
SW20 199 CW98
Ashford TW15 174 BN91
Barnet EN5 80 DA42
Beckenham BR3 203 EC95
Berkhamsted HP4 38 AY18
Mead Way, Brom. BR2 204 EF100
Bushey WD23 76 BY40
Coulsdon CR5 235 DL118
Croydon CR0 203 DY103
Meadway, Enf. EN3 82 DW36
Epsom KT19 216 CQ112
Esher KT10 214 CB109
Grays RM17 170 GD77
Mead Way, Guil. GU4 243 BC129
Meadway, Hodd. EN11 49 EA19
Ilford IG3 125 ES63
Leatherhead (Eff.) KT24 246 BY128
Leatherhead (Oxshott) KT22 215 CD114
Romford RM2 105 FG54
Ruislip HA4 115 BR58
St. Albans (Coln.Hth) AL4 44 CR23
Sevenoaks (Halst.) TN14 224 EZ113
Mead Way, Slou. SL1 131 AK71
Meadway, Stai. TW18 174 BG94
Surbiton KT5 198 CQ102
Twickenham TW2 177 CD88
Warlingham CR6 236 DW115
Welwyn Garden City AL7 29 CZ11
Woodford Green IG8 102 EJ50
Meadway, The, SE3 *off Heath La* 163 ED82
Buckhurst Hill IG9 102 EK46
Horley RH6 269 DJ148
Loughton IG10 85 EM44
Orpington BR6 224 EV106
Potters Bar (Cuffley) EN6 65 DM28
Sevenoaks TN13 256 FF122
Meadway Cl, NW11 120 DB58
Barnet EN5 80 DA42
Pinner HA5 *off Highbanks Rd* 94 CB51
Staines TW18 173 BF94
Meadway Ct, NW11 120 DB58

Meadway Dr, Add. KT15 212 BJ108
Woking GU21 226 AW116
Meadway Gdns, Ruis. HA4 115 BR58
Meadway Gate, NW11 120 DA58
Meadway Pk, Ger.Cr. SL9 112 AX60
Meaford Way, SE20 182 DV94
Meakin Est, SE1 21 L5
Meanley Rd, E12 124 EL63
Meard St, W1 9 L8
Meare Cl, Tad. KT20 233 CW123
Meare Est, H.Wyc. (Woob.Grn) HP10 110 AD55
Meath Cl, Orp. BR5 206 EV99
MEATH GREEN, Horl. RH6 268 DE146
Meath Grn Av, Horl. RH6 268 DF146
Sch **Meath Grn Inf Sch**, Horl. RH6 *off Kiln La* 268 DF146
Sch **Meath Grn Jun Sch**, Horl. RH6 *off Greenfields Rd* 268 DF146
Meath Grn La, Horl. RH6 266 DE143
Meath Rd, E15 144 EF68
Ilford IG1 125 EQ62
Sch **Meath Sch**, Cher. KT16 *off Brox Rd* 211 BD108
Meath St, SW11 161 DH81
Meautys, St.Alb. AL3 42 BZ22
Mecklenburgh Pl, WC1 10 A3
Mecklenburgh Sq, WC1 10 A3
Mecklenburgh St, WC1 10 A3
Sch **Mecklenburg PRU**, Kings.T. KT2 *off Dukes Av* 177 CK91
Medburn St, NW1 141 DK68
Medbury Rd, Grav. DA12 191 GM88
Medcalf Rd, Enf. EN3 83 DZ37
Medcroft Gdns, SW14 158 CQ84
Medebourne Cl, SE3 164 EG83
Mede Cl, Stai. (Wrays.) TW19 172 AX88
Mede Fld, Lthd. KT22 231 CD124
Medesenge Way, N13 99 DP51
Medfield St, SW15 179 CV87
Medhurst Cl, E3 *off Arbery Rd* 143 DY68
Woking (Chobham) GU24 210 AT109
Medhurst Cres, Grav. DA12 191 GM90
Medhurst Gdns, Grav. DA12 191 GM90
Medhurst Rd, E3 *off Arbery Rd* 143 DY68
Median Rd, E5 122 DW64
★ **Medici Galleries**, W1 9 H10
Medick Ct, Grays RM17 170 GE79
Medina Av, Esher KT10 197 CE104
Medina Gro, N7 *off Medina Rd* 121 DN62
Medina Ho, Erith DA8 *off Waterhead Cl* 167 FE80
Medina Rd, N7 121 DN62
Grays RM17 170 GD77
Medina Sq, Epsom KT19 216 CN109
Medlake Rd, Egh. TW20 173 BC93
Medland Cl, Wall. SM6 200 DG102
Medland Ho, E14 13 J9
Medlar Cl, Guil. GU1 242 AW132
Northolt UB5 *off Parkfield Av* 136 BY68
Medlar Ct, Slou. SL2 132 AW74
Medlar Rd, Grays RM17 170 GD79
Medlar St, SE5 162 DQ81
Medley Rd, NW6 140 DA65
Medman Cl, Uxb. UB8 *off Chiltern Vw Rd* 134 BJ68
Medora Rd, SW2 181 DM87
Romford RM7 127 FD56
Medow Mead, Rad. WD7 61 CF33
Medusa Rd, SE6 183 EB86
Medway Bldgs, E3 *off Medway Rd* 143 DY68
Medway Cl, Croy. CR0 202 DW100
Ilford IG1 125 EQ64
Watford WD25 60 BW34
Medway Dr, Grnf. UB6 137 CF68
Medway Gdns, Wem. HA0 117 CG63
Medway Ms, E3 *off Medway Rd* 143 DY68
Medway Par, Grnf. UB6 137 CF68
Medway Rd, E3 143 DY68
Dartford DA1 167 FG83
Hemel Hempstead HP2 40 BM15
Medway St, SW1 19 M6
Medwick Ms, Hem.H. HP2 *off Hunters Oak* 41 BP15
Medwin St, SW4 161 DM84
Meerbrook Rd, SE3 164 EJ83
Meeson Rd, E15 144 EF67
Meesons La, Grays RM17 170 FZ77
Meeson St, E5 123 DY63
Meeting Fld Path, E9 *off Chatham Pl* 142 DW65
Meeting Ho All, E1 22 D1
Meeting Ho La, SE15 162 DV81
Megg La, Kings L. (Chipper.) WD4 58 BH29
Mehetabel Rd, E9 142 DW65
Meister Cl, Ilf. IG1 125 ER60
Melancholy Wk, Rich. TW10 177 CJ89
Melanda Cl, Chis. BR7 185 EM92
Melanie Cl, Bexh. DA7 166 EY81
Melba Gdns, Til. RM18 171 GG80
Melba Way, SE13 163 EB81
Melbourne Av, N13 99 DM51
W13 137 CG74
Pinner HA5 116 CB55
Slough SL1 131 AQ72
Melbourne Cl, Orp. BR6 205 ES101
St. Albans AL3 43 CF16
Uxbridge UB10 114 BN63
Wallington SM6 *off Melbourne Rd* 219 DJ106
Melbourne Ct, E5 *off Daubeney Rd* 123 DY63
N10 *off Sydney Rd* 99 DH52
SE20 182 DU94
Welwyn Garden City AL8 29 CV10
Melbourne Gdns, Rom. RM6 126 EY57
Melbourne Gro, SE22 162 DS84
Melbourne Ho, Hayes UB4 136 BW70
Melbourne Ms, SE6 183 EC87
SW9 161 DN81
Melbourne Pl, WC2 10 B9
Melbourne Rd, E6 145 EM67
E10 123 EB59
E17 123 DY56
SW19 200 DA95
Bushey WD23 76 CB44
Ilford IG1 125 EP60
Teddington TW11 177 CJ93
Tilbury RM18 170 GE81
Wallington SM6 219 DH106
Melbourne Sq, SW9 *off Melbourne Ms* 161 DN81
Melbourne Ter, SW6 *off Waterford Rd* 160 DB80
Melbourne Way, Enf. EN1 82 DT44
Melbury Av, Sthl. UB2 156 CB76

★ Place of interest | H Hospital | Sch School | Coll College | Uni University | ⇌ Railway station

Melbury Cl, Cher. KT16 . . . .194 BG101
Chislehurst BR7 . . . . .185 EM93
Esher (Clay.) KT10 . . . . . .215 CH107
West Byfleet KT14 . . . . . . .212 BG114
Melbury Ct, W8 . . . . .16 F5
Melbury Dr, SE5
off Sedgmoor Pl 162 DS80
Melbury Gdns, SW20 . . . . . .199 CV95
Melbury Rd, W14 . . . . .16 E5
Harrow HA3 . . . . .118 CM57
Melcombe Gdns, Har. HA3 . .118 CM58
Melcombe Pl, NW1 . . . . .8 C5
Sch Melcombe Prim Sch, W6
off Fulham Palace Rd . . .159 CX79
Melcombe St, NW1 . . . . .8 D4
Meldex Cl, NW7 . . . . .97 CW51
Meldon Cl, SW6
off Bagley's La 160 DB81
Meldone Cl, Surb. KT5 . . . . .198 CP100
Meldrum Cl, Orp. BR5
off Killewarren Way 206 EW100
Oxted RH8 . . . . .254 EF132
Meldrum Rd, Ilf. IG3 . . . . . .126 EU61
Melfield Gdns, SE6 . . . . . . .183 EB91
Melford Av, Bark. IG11 . . . . .145 ES65
Melford Cl, Chess. KT9 . . . .216 CM106
Melford Rd, E6 . . . . .145 EM70
E11 . . . . .124 EE61
E17 . . . . .123 DY56
SE22 . . . . .182 DU87
Ilford IG1 . . . . .125 ER61
Melfort Av, Th.Hth. CR7 . . . .201 DP97
Melfort Rd, Th.Hth. CR7 . . . .201 DP97
Melgund Rd, N5 . . . . .4 D2
Melina Cl, Hayes UB3
off Middleton Rd 135 BR71
Melina Pl, NW8 . . . . .7 N2
Melina Rd, W12 . . . . .159 CV75
Melings, The, Hem.H. HP2 . . .41 BP15
Melior Pl, SE1 . . . . .21 L3
Melior St, SE1 . . . . .21 K3
Meliot Rd, SE6 . . . . .183 ED89
Melksham Cl, Rom. RM3 . . .106 FL52
Melksham Dr, Rom. RM3
off Melksham Gdns 106 FM52
Melksham Gdns, Rom. RM3 .106 FL52
Melksham Grn, Rom. RM3
off Melksham Gdns 106 FM52
Meller Cl, Croy. CR0 . . . . . .201 DL104
Mellersh Hill Rd, Guil.
(Won.) GU5 . . . . .259 BB144
Melling Dr, Enf. EN1 . . . . . . .82 DU39
Melling St, SE18 . . . . .165 ES79
Mellish Cl, Bark. IG11 . . . . .145 ET67
Mellish Gdns, Wdf.Grn. IG8 .102 EG50
Mellish Ind Est, SE18 . . . . . .164 EL76
Mellish St, E14 . . . . .23 N5
Mellish Way, Horn. RM11 . . .128 FJ57
Mellison Rd, SW17 . . . . . . .180 DE92
Melliss Av, Rich. TW9 . . . . .158 CP81
Mellitus St, W12 . . . . .139 CT72
Mellor Cl, Walt. KT12 . . . . .196 BZ101
Mellor Wk, Wind. SL4
off Bachelors Acre 151 AR81
Mellow Cl, Bans. SM7 . . . . .218 DB114
Mellow La E, Hayes UB4 . . .135 BQ69
Sch Mellow La Sch, Hayes
UB4 off Hewens Rd 135 BQ70
Mellow La W, Uxb. UB10 . . .135 BQ69
Mellows Rd, Ilf. IG5 . . . . . .125 EM55
Wallington SM6 . . . . .219 DK106
Mells Cres, SE9 . . . . .185 EM91
Mell St, SE10 . . . . .24 G10
Melody La, N5 . . . . .4 F1
Melody Rd, SW18 . . . . .180 DC85
Westerham (Bigg.H.)
TN16 . . . . .238 EJ118
Melon Pl, W8 . . . . .17 J3
Melon Rd, E11 . . . . .124 EE62
SE15 . . . . .162 DU81
Melrose Av, N22 . . . . .99 DP53
NW2 . . . . .119 CV64
SW16 . . . . .201 DM97
SW19 . . . . .180 DA89
Borehamwood WD6 . . . . . .78 CP43
Dartford DA1 . . . . .187 FE86
Greenford UB6 . . . . .136 CB68
Mitcham CR4 . . . . .181 DH94
Potters Bar EN6 . . . . .64 DB32
Twickenham TW2 . . . . .176 CB87
Melrose Cl, SE12 . . . . .184 EG88
Greenford UB6 . . . . .136 CB68
Hayes UB4 . . . . .135 BU71
Melrose Ct, W13
off Williams Rd 137 CG74
Melrose Cres, Orp. BR6 . . . .223 ER105
Melrose Dr, Sthl. UB1 . . . . .136 CA74
Melrose Gdns, W6 . . . . .159 CW76
Edgware HA8 . . . . .96 CP54
New Malden KT3 . . . . . . .198 CR97
Walton-on-Thames KT12 .214 BW106
Melrose Pl, Wat. WD17 . . . . . .75 BT38
Melrose Rd, SW13 . . . . .159 CT82
SW18 . . . . .179 CZ86
SW19 . . . . .200 DA96
W3 off Stanley Rd 158 CQ76
Coulsdon CR5 . . . . .235 DH115
Pinner HA5 . . . . .116 BZ56
Westerham (Bigg.H.)
TN16 . . . . .238 EJ116
Weybridge KT13 . . . . .212 BN106
Sch Melrose Sch, Mitch.
CR4 off Church Rd 200 DE97
Melrose Ter, W6 . . . . .159 CW75
Melsa Rd, Mord. SM4 . . . . .200 DC100
Melsted Rd, Hem.H. HP1 . . . .40 BH20
Melstock Av, Upmin. RM14 .128 FQ63
Melthorne Dr, Ruis. HA4 . . .116 BW62
Melthorpe Gdns, SE3 . . . . . .164 EL81
Melton Cl, Ruis. HA4 . . . . . .116 BW60
Melton Ct, SW7 . . . . .17 P8
Sutton SM2 . . . . .218 DC108
Melton Flds, Epsom KT19 . .216 CR109
Melton Gdns, Rom. RM1 . . .127 FF59
Melton Pl, Epsom KT19 . . . .216 CR109
Melton Rd, Red. RH1 . . . . . .251 DJ130
Melton St, NW1 . . . . .9 K2
Melville Av, SW20 . . . . .179 CU94
Greenford UB6 . . . . .117 CF64
South Croydon CR2 . . . . .220 DT106
Melville Cl, Uxb. UB10 . . . .115 BR62
Melville Gdns, N13 . . . . .99 DP50
Melville Pl, N1 . . . . .4 G6
Melville Rd, E17 . . . . .123 DZ55
NW10 . . . . .138 CR66
SW13 . . . . .159 CU81
Rainham RM13 . . . . .147 FG70
Romford RM5 . . . . .105 FB52
Sidcup DA14 . . . . .186 EW89
Melville Vil Rd, W3
off High St 138 CR74
Melvin Rd, SE20 . . . . .202 DW95
Melvinshaw, Lthd. KT22 . . .231 CJ121
Melvyn Cl, Wal.Cr. (Chsht)
EN7 . . . . .65 DP28
Melyn Cl, N7 off Anson Rd .121 DJ63
Memel Ct, EC1 . . . . .10 G4
Memel St, EC1 . . . . .10 G4
Memess Path, SE18 . . . . . . .165 EN79
Memorial Av, E15 . . . . .14 G1
Memorial Cl, Houns. TW5 . . .156 BZ79
H Memorial Hosp, SE18 . .165 EN82
Mendip Cl, SE26 . . . . .182 DW91
Hayes UB3 . . . . .155 BR80
St. Albans AL4 . . . . .43 CJ15
Slough SL3 . . . . .153 BA78
Worcester Park KT4 . . . . .199 CW102
Mendip Dr, NW2 . . . . .119 CX61
Mendip Ho, N9 off New Rd .100 DU48
Mendip Rd, SW11 . . . . .160 DC83
Bexleyheath DA7 . . . . . . .167 FE81
Bushey WD23 . . . . .76 CC44
Hornchurch RM11 . . . . . . .127 FG59
Ilford IG2 . . . . .125 ES57
Mendip Way, Hem.H. HP2 . . .40 BL17
Mendlesham, Welw.G.C. AL7 .30 DE09
Mendora Rd, SW6 . . . . .159 CY80
Mendoza Cl, Horn. RM11 . . .128 FL57
Menelik Rd, NW2 . . . . .119 CY63
Menlo Gdns, SE19 . . . . .182 DR94
Menon Dr, N9 . . . . .100 DV48
Sch Menorah Foundation
Sch, Edg. HA8
off Abbots Rd 96 CQ52
Sch Menorah Gram Sch, Edg.
HA8 off Abbots Rd 96 CQ52
Menotti St, E2 . . . . .12 B3
Sch Mentally Handicapped
Support Cen, Hert.
SG13 off Ware Rd 33 EA13
Menthone Pl, Horn. RM11 . .128 FK59
Mentmore Cl, Har. HA3 . . . .117 CJ58
Mentmore Rd, St.Alb. AL1 . . .43 CD22
Mentmore Ter, E8 . . . . .142 DV66
Meon Cl, Tad. KT20 . . . . . . .233 CV122
Meon Ct, Islw. TW7 . . . . . . .157 CE82
Meon Rd, W3 . . . . .158 CQ75
Meopham Rd, Mitch. CR4 . .201 DJ95
Mepham Cres, Har. HA3 . . . .94 CC52
Mepham Gdns, Har. HA3 . . . .94 CC52
Mepham St, SE1 . . . . .20 B2
Mera Dr, Bexh. DA7 . . . . . . .166 FA84
Merantun Way, SW19 . . . . .200 DC95
Merbury Cl, SE13 . . . . .183 EC85
Merbury Rd, SE28 . . . . .165 ES75
Mercator Pl, E14 . . . . .23 P9
Mercator Rd, SE13 . . . . . . .163 ED84
Mercer Cl, T.Ditt. KT7 . . . . .197 CF101
Merceron St, E1 . . . . .12 C4
Mercer Pl, Pnr. HA5
off Crossway 94 BW54
Mercers, Harl. CM19 . . . . . . .51 EN18
Hemel Hempstead HP2 . . . .40 BL18
Mercers Cl, SE10 . . . . .25 J8
Mercers Pl, W6 . . . . .159 CW77
Mercers Rd, N19 . . . . .121 DK62
Mercers Row, St.Alb. AL1 . . .42 CC22
Mercer St, WC2 . . . . .9 N8
Mercer Wk, Uxb. UB8
off High St 134 BJ66
Merchant Dr, Hert. SG13 . . . .32 DT08
Merchants Cl, SE25
off Clifford Rd 202 DU98
Merchants Ho, SE10
off Hoskins St 163 ED78
Merchant St, E3 . . . . .13 M2
Sch Merchant Taylors' Sch,
Nthwd. HA6
off Sandy Lo La 93 BS46
Merchiston Rd, SE6 . . . . . .183 ED89
Merchland Rd, SE9 . . . . . . .185 EQ88
Mercia Gro, SE13 . . . . .163 EC84
Mercian Way, Slou. SL1 . . . .131 AK74
Mercia Wk, Wok. GU21
off Church St W 227 AZ117
Mercier Rd, SW15 . . . . .179 CY85
Mercury Cen, Felt. TW14 . . .175 BV85
Mercury Gdns, Rom. RM1 . .127 FE56
Mercury Pk, H.Wyc. HP10
off Wycombe La 110 AE56
Mercury Wk, Hem.H. HP2 . . .40 BM17
Mercury Way, SE14 . . . . . . .163 DX79
Mercy Ter, SE13 . . . . .163 EB84
Merebank La, Croy. CR0 . . .219 DM106
Mere Cl, SW15 . . . . .179 CX87
Orpington BR6 . . . . .205 EP103
Meredith Av, NW2 . . . . .119 CW64
Meredith Cl, Pnr. HA5 . . . . . .94 BX52
Meredith Ms, SE4 . . . . .163 DZ84
Meredith Rd, Grays RM16 . .171 GG77
Meredith St, E13 . . . . .15 M2
EC1 . . . . .10 E2
Meredyth Rd, SW13 . . . . . . .159 CU82
Mere End, Croy. CR0 . . . . . .203 DX101
Merefield, Saw. CM21 . . . . . .36 EY06
Merefield Gdns, Tad. KT20 . .233 CX119
Mere Rd, Shep. TW17 . . . . . .195 BP100
Slough SL1 . . . . .152 AT76
Tadworth KT20 . . . . .233 CV124
Weybridge KT13 . . . . .195 BR104
Mere Side, Orp. BR6 . . . . . .205 EN103
Mereside Pl, Vir.W. GU25 . . .192 AX100
Meretone Cl, SE4 . . . . .163 DY84
Merevale Cres, Mord. SM4 . .200 DC100
Mereway Rd, Twick. TW2 . . .177 CD88
Merewood Cl, Brom. BR1 . . .205 EN96
Merewood Rd, Bexh. DA7 . .167 FC82
Mereworth Cl, Brom. BR2 . .204 EF99
Mereworth Dr, SE18 . . . . . .165 EP80
Merganser Gdns, SE28
off Avocet Ms 165 ER76
MERIDEN, Wat. WD25 . . . . . .76 BY35
Meriden Cl, Brom. BR1 . . . .184 EK94
Ilford IG6 . . . . .103 EQ53
Sch Meriden Prim Sch, Wat.
WD25 off Harvest End 76 BX36
Meriden Way, Wat. WD25 . . . .76 BY36
Meridian Gate, E14 . . . . .24 C3
Meridian Gro, Horl. RH6
off Wheatfield Way 269 DJ147
Meridian Pl, E14 . . . . .24 C3
Sch Meridian Prim Sch, SE10 .24 F10
Meridian Rd, SE7 . . . . .164 EK80
Meridian Sq, E15 . . . . .143 ED66
Meridian Trd Est, SE7 . . . . . .25 P7
Meridian Wk, N17
off Commercial Rd 100 DS51
Meridian Way, N9 . . . . .100 DW50
N18 . . . . .100 DW51
Enfield EN3 . . . . .83 DX44
Waltham Abbey EN9
off Sewardstone Rd 83 EB35
Ware (Stans.Abb.) SG12 . .33 EB10
Meriel Wk, Green. DA9
off The Avenue 169 FV84
Merifield Rd, SE9 . . . . .164 EJ84
Merino Cl, E11 . . . . .124 EJ56
Merino Pl, Sid. DA15
off Blackfen Rd 186 EU86
Merivale Rd, SW15 . . . . . . .159 CY84
Merivale Rd, Har. HA1 . . . . .116 CC59
Merland Cl, Tad. KT20 . . . . .233 CW120
Merland Grn, Tad. KT20
off Merland Ri 233 CW120
Merland Ri, Epsom KT18 . . .233 CW119
Tadworth KT20 . . . . .233 CW119
Sch Merland Ri Co Prim Sch,
Epsom KT18
off Merland Ri 233 CW119
Merle Av, Uxb. (Hare.) UB9 . .92 BH54
Merlewood, Sev. TN13 . . . . .257 FH123
Merlewood Cl, Cat. CR3 . . . .236 DR120
Merlewood Dr, Chis. BR7 . .205 EM95
Merley Ct, NW9 . . . . .118 CQ60
Merlin Cl, Croy. CR0 . . . . . .220 DS105
Grays (Chaff.Hun.) RM16 .170 FY76
Ilford IG6 . . . . .104 EW50
Mitcham CR4 . . . . .200 DE97
Northolt UB5 . . . . .136 BW69
Romford RM5 . . . . .105 FD51
Slough SL3 . . . . .153 BB79
Wallington SM6 . . . . .219 DM107
Waltham Abbey EN9 . . . . . .68 EG34
Merlin Ct, Wok. GU21
off Blackmore Cres 211 BC114
Merlin Cres, Edg. HA8 . . . . . .96 CM53
Merlin Gdns, Brom. BR1 . . .184 EG90
Romford RM5 . . . . .105 FD51
Merling Cl, Chess. KT9
off Coppard Gdns 215 CK106
Merling Cft, Berk. HP4 . . . . .38 AS17
Merlin Gro, Beck. BR3 . . . . .203 DZ98
Ilford IG6 . . . . .103 EP52
Merlin Ho, Enf. EN3
off Allington Ct 83 DX43
Sch Merlin Prim Sch, Brom.
BR1 off Ballamore Rd 184 EG90
Merlin Rd, E12 . . . . .124 EJ61
Romford RM5 . . . . .105 FD51
Welling DA16 . . . . .166 EU84
Merlin Rd N, Well. DA16 . . .166 EU84
Merlins Av, Har. HA2 . . . . . .116 BZ62
Sch Merlin Sch, The, SW15
off Carlton Dr 179 CX85
Merlin St, WC1 . . . . .10 C2
Merlin Way, Epp.
(N.Wld Bas.) CM16 . . . . . .70 FA27
Watford (Lvsdn) WD25 . . . .59 BT34
Mermagen Dr, Rain. RM13 . .147 FH66
Mermaid Cl, Grav. DA11 . . . .190 GD87
Mermaid Ct, SE1 . . . . .21 J3
SE16 . . . . .23 L2
Mermaid Twr, SE8
off Abinger Gro 163 DZ79
Mermerus Gdns, Grav.
DA12 . . . . .191 GM91
Merredene St, SW2 . . . . . . .181 DM86
Merriam Av, E9 . . . . .143 DZ65
Merriam Cl, E4 . . . . .101 EC50
Merrick Rd, Sthl. UB2 . . . . .156 BZ75
Merrick Sq, SE1 . . . . .21 H5
Merridale, SE12 . . . . .184 EG85
Merridene, N21 . . . . .81 DP44
Merrielands Cres, Dag.
RM9 . . . . .146 EZ67
Merrilands Rd, Wor.Pk. KT4 .199 CW102
Merrilees Rd, Sid. DA15 . . . .185 ES88
Merrilyn Cl, Esher (Clay.)
KT10 . . . . .215 CG107
Merriman Rd, SE3 . . . . .164 EJ81
Merrington Rd, SW6 . . . . . .160 DA79
Merrin Hill, S.Croy. CR2 . . . .220 DS111
Merrion Av, Stan. HA7 . . . . . .95 CK50
Merrion Wk, SE17
off Dawes St 162 DR78
Merritt Gdns, Chess. KT9 . . .215 CJ107
Merritt Rd, SE4 . . . . .183 DZ85
Merritt Wk, Hat. AL9 . . . . . . .45 CV23
Merrivale, N14 . . . . .81 DK44
Merrivale Av, Ilf. IG4 . . . . . .124 EK56
Merrivale Gdns, Wok. GU21 .226 AW117
MERROW, Guil. GU1 . . . . . . .243 BB133
Merrow Business Cen, Guil.
GU4 off Merrow La 243 BC131
Merrow Chase, Guil. GU1 . .243 BC134
Sch Merrow C of E Inf Sch,
Guil. GU4
off Kingfisher Dr 243 BB132
Merrow Common Rd, Guil.
GU4 . . . . .243 BC131
Merrow Copse, Guil. GU1 . .243 BB133
Merrow Ct, Guil. GU1
off Levylsdene 243 BD134
Merrow Cft, Guil. GU1 . . . . .243 BC133
Merrow Downs, Guil. GU1 . .259 BD135
Merrow Dr, Hem.H. HP1 . . . .39 BE19
Merrow La, Guil. GU4 . . . . .243 BC129
Merrow Pl, Guil. GU4 . . . . . .243 BD132
Merrow Rd, Sutt. SM2 . . . . .217 CX109
Merrows Cl, Nthwd. HA6
off Rickmansworth Rd . . .93 BQ51
Merrow St, SE17 . . . . .162 DQ79
Guildford GU4 . . . . .243 BD132
Merrow Wk, SE17 . . . . .21 K9
Merrow Way, Croy.
(New Adgtn) CR0 . . . . . .221 EC107
Guildford GU1 . . . . .243 BD133
Merrow Wds, Guil. GU1 . . . .243 BB132
Merrydown Way, Chis. BR7 .204 EL95
Merryfield, SE3 . . . . .164 EF82
Merryfield Gdns, Stan. HA7 . .95 CJ50
Merryfield Ho, SE9
off Grove Pk Rd 184 EJ90
Merryfields, St.Alb. AL4
off Firwood Av 44 CL20
Uxbridge UB8
off The Greenway 134 BL68
Merryfields Way, SE6 . . . . .183 EB87
MERRY HILL, Bushey WD23 .94 CA46
Merryhill Cl, E4 . . . . .101 EB45
Sch Merry Hill Ho Sch, Bushey
WD23 off Merry Hill Rd . .94 CA46
Sch Merry Hill Inf Sch, Bushey
WD23 off School La 94 CB45
Merry Hill Mt, Bushey WD23 .94 CB46
Merry Hill Rd, Bushey WD23 .94 CB46
Merryhills Cl, West. (Bigg.H.)
TN16 . . . . .238 EK116
Merryhills Ct, N14 . . . . .81 DJ43
Merryhills Dr, Enf. EN2 . . . . .81 DK42
Sch Merryhills Prim Sch,
Enf. EN2 off Bincote Rd . .81 DM41
Merrylands, Cher. KT16 . . . .193 BE104
Merrylands Rd, Lthd. (Bkhm)
KT23 . . . . .230 BZ123
Merrymeet, Bans. SM7 . . . .218 DF114
Merryweather Cl, Dart. DA1 .188 FM86
Merrywood Gro, Tad. KT20 .249 CX130
Merrywood Pk, Reig. RH2 . .250 DB132
Tadworth (Box H.) KT20 . .248 CP130
Mersea Ho, Bark. IG11 . . . . .145 EP65
Mersey Av, Upmin. RM14 . .129 FR58
Mersey Pl, Hem.H. HP2
off Colne Way 40 BM15
Mersey Rd, E17 . . . . .123 DZ55
Mersey Wk, Nthlt. UB5
off Brabazon Rd 136 CA68
Mersham Dr, NW9 . . . . .118 CN57
Mersham Pl, SE20 . . . . .202 DV95
Mersham Rd, Th.Hth. CR7 . .202 DR97
MERSTHAM, Red. RH1 . . . .251 DJ128
⇌ Merstham 251 DJ128
Sch Merstham Co Prim Sch,
Red. RH1
off London Rd S 251 DJ129
Merstham Rd, Red. RH1 . . .251 DN129
Merten Rd, Rom. RM6 . . . . .126 EY59
Merthyr Ter, SW13 . . . . .159 CV79
MERTON, SW19 . . . . .200 DA95
Sch Merton Abbey Prim Sch,
SW19 off High Path 200 DB95
Coll Merton Adult Coll,
SW20 off Whatley Av . . .199 CY97
Merton Av, W4 . . . . .159 CT77
Northolt UB5 . . . . .116 CC64
Uxbridge UB10 . . . . .135 BP66
Coll Merton Coll, Mord.
SM4 off London Rd 200 DA99
6th Form Cen, Mord.
SM4 off Central Rd 200 DB99
Sch Merton Ct Sch, Sid.
DA14 off Knoll Rd 186 EW91
Merton Gdns, Orp. BR5 . . . .205 EP99
Tadworth KT20
off Marbles Way 233 CX120
Merton Hall Gdns, SW20 . . .199 CY95
Merton Hall Rd, SW19 . . . . .199 CY95
Merton High St, SW19 . . . . .180 DB94
Merton Ind Pk, SW19 . . . . . .200 DC95
Sch Merton Key Stage
Three PRU, SW19
off Brangwyn Cres 200 DD96
Merton La, N6 . . . . .120 DF61
Merton Mans, SW20 . . . . . .199 CX96
MERTON PARK, SW19 . . . . .200 DA96
Tra Merton Park 200 DA95
Merton Pk Par, SW19
off Kingston Rd 199 CZ95
Sch Merton Pk Prim Sch,
SW19 off Church La 200 DA96
Merton Pl, Grays RM16 . . . .171 GG77
Merton Ri, NW3 . . . . .140 DE66
Merton Rd, E17 . . . . .123 EC57
SE25 . . . . .202 DU99
SW18 . . . . .180 DA85
SW19 . . . . .180 DB94
Barking IG11 . . . . .145 ET66
Enfield EN2 . . . . .82 DR38
Harrow HA2 . . . . .116 CC60
Ilford IG3 . . . . .125 ET59
Slough SL1 . . . . .152 AU76
Watford WD18 . . . . .75 BV42
Merton Wk, Lthd. KT22 . . . .231 CG118
Merton Way, Lthd. KT22 . . .231 CG119
Uxbridge UB10 . . . . .135 BP66
West Molesey KT8 . . . . . .196 CB98
Merttins Rd, SE15 . . . . .183 DX85
Meru Cl, NW5 . . . . .120 DG63
Mervan Rd, SW2 . . . . .161 DN84
Mervyn Av, SE9 . . . . .185 EQ90
Mervyn Rd, W13 . . . . .157 CG76
Shepperton TW17 . . . . . . .195 BQ101
Merwin Way, Wind. SL4 . . . .151 AK82
Meryfield Cl, Borwd. WD6 . . .78 CM40
Sch Meryfield Prim Sch, Borwd.
WD6 off Theobald St 78 CM39
Mesne Way, Sev. (Shore.)
TN14 . . . . .225 FF112
Messaline Av, W3 . . . . .138 CQ72
Messant Cl, Rom.
(Harold Wd) RM3 . . . . . .106 FK54
Messent Rd, SE9 . . . . .184 EJ85
Messeter Pl, SE9 . . . . .185 EN86
Messina Av, NW6 . . . . .140 DA66
Metcalf Rd, Ashf. TW15 . . . .175 BP92
Metcalf Wk, Felt. TW13
off Gabriel Cl 176 BY91
Meteor St, SW11 . . . . .160 DG84
Meteor Way, Wall. SM6 . . . .219 DL108
Metford Cres, Enf. EN3 . . . . .83 EA38
Metheringham Way, NW9 . . .96 CS53
Methley St, SE11 . . . . .20 D10
★ Methodist Cen Hall, SW1 19 M4
Methuen Cl, Edg. HA8 . . . . . .96 CN52
Methuen Pk, N10 . . . . .99 DH54
Methuen Rd, Belv. DA17 . . .167 FB77
Bexleyheath DA6 . . . . . . .166 EZ84
Edgware HA8 . . . . .96 CN52
Methwold Rd, W10 . . . . .6 A5
Metro Cen, The, Islw. TW7 . .157 CE82
Metropolis Cen, Borwd.
WD6 . . . . .78 CN41
Metropolitan Cen, The,
Grnf. UB6 . . . . .136 CB67
Metropolitan Cl, E14 . . . . . . .13 P6
Metropolitan Ho, Pot.B.
EN6 . . . . .64 DA32
Coll Metropolitan Pol Cadet
Training Cen, Loug.
IG10 off Lippitts Hill 84 EF40
Coll Metropolitan Pol
Training Sch, E.Mol.
KT8 off Ember La 197 CD100
Meux Cl, Wal.Cr. (Chsht)
EN7 . . . . .66 DU31
Mews, The, N1 . . . . .5 H7
N8 off Turnpike La 121 DN55
Grays RM17 . . . . .170 GC77
Guildford GU1
off Walnut Tree Cl 258 AW135
Harlow CM18
off Commonside Rd 51 ES19
Ilford IG4 . . . . .124 EK57
Romford RM1
off Market Link 127 FE56
Sevenoaks TN13 . . . . .256 FG123
Twickenham TW1
off Bridge Rd 177 CH86
Mews Deck, E1 . . . . .12 D10
Mews End, West. (Bigg.H.)
TN16 . . . . .238 EK118
Mews Pl, Wdf.Grn. IG8 . . . .102 EG49
Mews St, E1 . . . . .22 A1
Mexfield Rd, SW15 . . . . . . .179 CZ85
Meyer Grn, Enf. EN1 . . . . . . .82 DU38
Meyer Rd, Erith DA8 . . . . . .167 FC79
Meymott St, SE1 . . . . .20 E2
Meynell Cres, E9 . . . . .143 DX66
Meynell Gdns, E9 . . . . .143 DX66
Meynell Rd, E9 . . . . .143 DX66
Romford RM3 . . . . .105 FH52
Meyrick Cl, Wok. (Knap.)
GU21 . . . . .226 AS116
Meyrick Rd, NW10 . . . . . . .139 CU65
SW11 . . . . .160 DD83
Mezen Cl, Nthwd. HA6 . . . . .93 BR50
Miah Ter, E1
off Wapping High St 142 DU74
Miall Wk, SE26 . . . . .183 DY91
Micawber Av, Uxb. UB8 . . . .134 BN70
Micawber St, N1 . . . . .11 H1
Michael Cliffe Ho, EC1
off Skinner St 141 DP69
Michael Cres, Horl. RH6 . . . .268 DG150
Michael Faraday Ho, SE17 . . .21 K10
Sch Michael Faraday Prim
Sch, SE17
off Portland St 162 DR79
Michael Gdns, Grav. DA12 . .191 GL92
Hornchurch RM11 . . . . . . .128 FK56
Michael Gaynor Cl, W7 . . . .137 CF74
Michaelmas Cl, SW20 . . . . .199 CW97
Coll Michael Reid Coll, Brwd.
CM14 off Coxtie Grn Rd . .108 FS43
Michael Rd, E11 . . . . .124 EE60
SE25 . . . . .202 DS97
SW6 . . . . .160 DB81
Michaels Cl, SE13 . . . . .164 EE84
Michaels La, Long.
(Fawk.Grn) DA3 . . . . . . .209 FV103
Sevenoaks TN15 . . . . .209 FV103
Sch Michael Sobell Sinai
Sch, Har. HA3
off Shakespeare Dr 118 CN58
Sch Michael Tippett Sch,
SE11 . . . . .20 D7
Micheldever Rd, SE12 . . . . .184 EE86
Michelham Gdns, Tad.
KT20 off Waterfield 233 CW121
Twickenham TW1 . . . . .177 CF90
Michels Row, Rich. TW9
off Kew Foot Rd 158 CL84
Michigan Av, E12 . . . . .124 EL63
Michleham Down, N12 . . . . .97 CZ49
Micholls Av, Ger.Cr. SL9 . . . .90 AY49
Mickleffield Rd, Hem.H. HP2 . .41 BQ20
Sch Micklefield Sch, Reig.
RH2 off Somers Rd 250 DA133
Micklefield Way, Borwd.
WD6 . . . . .78 CL38
MICKLEHAM, Dor. RH5 . . . .247 CJ128
Mickleham Bypass, Dor.
RH5 . . . . .247 CH127
Mickleham Cl, Orp. BR5 . . . .205 ET96
Mickleham Downs, Dor.
(Mick.) RH5 . . . . .247 CK127
Mickleham Dr, Lthd. KT22 . .247 CJ126
Mickleham Gdns, Sutt. SM3 .217 CY107
Mickleham Rd, Orp. BR5 . . .205 ET95
Mickleham Way, Croy.
(New Adgtn) CR0 . . . . . .221 ED108
Micklem Dr, Hem.H. HP1 . . . .39 BF19
Sch Micklem JMI Sch, The,
Hem.H. HP1
off Boxted Rd 40 BG19
Micklethwaite Rd, SW6 . . . .160 DA79
Midas Ind Est, Uxb. UB8 . . .134 BH68
Midas Met Ind Est, The, Mord.
SM4 off Garth Rd 199 CX102
Midcot Way, Berk. HP4 . . . . .38 AT17
Midcroft, Ruis. HA4 . . . . . . .115 BS60
Slough SL2 . . . . .131 AP70
Mid Cross La, Ger.Cr.
(Chal.St.P.) SL9 . . . . .90 AY50
Middle Boy, Rom. (Abridge)
RM4 . . . . .86 EW41
Middle Cl, Amer. HP6 . . . . . .72 AT37
Coulsdon CR5 . . . . .235 DN120
Epsom KT17
off Middle La 216 CS112
Middle Cres, Uxb. (Denh.)
UB9 . . . . .113 BD59
Middle Dene, NW7 . . . . .96 CR48
Middle Dr, Beac. HP9 . . . . . .89 AK50
Middle Fm Cl, Lthd. (Eff.)
KT24 . . . . .246 BX127
Middle Fm Pl, Lthd. (Eff.)
KT24 . . . . .246 BW127
Middle Fld, NW8 . . . . .140 DD67
Middlefield, Hat. AL10 . . . . . .45 CU17
Horley RH6 . . . . .269 DJ147
Welwyn Garden City AL7 . .29 CY13
Middlefield Av, Hodd. EN11 . .49 EA15
Middlefield Cl, Hodd. EN11 . .49 EA15
St. Albans AL4 . . . . .43 CJ17
Middlefielde, W13 . . . . .137 CH71
Middlefield Gdns, Ilf. IG2 . . .125 EP58
Middlefield Rd, Hodd. EN11 . .49 EA15
Middlefields, Croy. CR0 . . . .221 DY109
Middle Furlong, Bushey
WD23 . . . . .76 CB42
Middle Gorse, Croy. CR0 . . .221 DY112
MIDDLE GREEN, Slou. SL3 . .132 AY73
Middle Grn, Bet. (Brock.)
RH3 . . . . .264 CP136
Slough SL3 . . . . .132 AY74
Staines TW18 . . . . .174 BK94
Middle Grn Cl, Surb. KT5
off Alpha Rd 198 CM100
Middlegreen Rd, Slou. SL3 . .132 AX74
Middleham Gdns, N18 . . . . .100 DU51
Middleham Rd, N18 . . . . . . .100 DU51
Middle Hill, Egh. TW20 . . . . .172 AW91
Hemel Hempstead HP1 . . . .39 BE20
Middleknights Hill, Hem.H.
HP1 . . . . .40 BG17
Middle La, N8 . . . . .121 DL57
Epsom KT17 . . . . .216 CS112
Hemel Hempstead (Bov.)
HP3 . . . . .57 BA29
Sevenoaks (Seal) TN15
off Church Rd 257 FM121
Teddington TW11 . . . . . . .177 CF93
Middle La Ms, N8
off Middle La 121 DL57
Middlemead Cl, Lthd.
(Bkhm) KT23 . . . . .246 CA125
Middle Meadow, Ch.St.G.
HP8 . . . . .90 AW48
Middlemead Rd, Lthd.
(Bkhm) KT23 . . . . .246 BZ125
Middle Ope, Wat. WD24 . . . . .75 BV37
Middle Pk Av, SE9 . . . . .184 EK86
Sch Middle Pk JMI Sch,
SE9 off Middle Pk Av . . .184 EK87
Middle Path, Har. HA2
off Middle Rd 117 CD60
Middle Rd, E13
off London Rd 144 EG68
SW16 . . . . .201 DK96
Barnet EN4 . . . . .80 DE44
Berkhamsted HP4 . . . . .38 AV19
Brentwood (Ingrave)
CM13 . . . . .109 GC50
Harrow HA2 . . . . .117 CD61
Leatherhead KT22 . . . . . . .231 CH121
Uxbridge (Denh.) UB9 . . . .113 BC59
Waltham Abbey EN9 . . . . . .67 EB32
Middle Row, W10 . . . . .6 C4

Sch Middle Row Prim Sch, W10 6 C3
Middlesborough Rd, N18 100 DU51
Middlesex Business Cen, Sthl. UB2 156 CA75
Middlesex Cl, Sthl. UB1 136 CB70
Middlesex Ct, W4 off British Gro 159 CT77
★ Middlesex Guildhall, SW1 19 N4
H Middlesex Hosp, W1 9 K6
Middlesex Ho, Wem. HA0 137 CK67
Middlesex Pas, EC1 10 F6
Middlesex Rd, Mitch. CR4 201 DL99
Middlesex St, E1 11 M6
Uni Middlesex Uni, Cat Hill Campus, Barn. EN4 80 DG43
Enfield Campus, Enf. EN3 off Queensway 82 DV43
Hendon Campus, NW4 off The Burroughs 119 CV56
Tottenham Campus, N17 off White Hart La 100 DS51
Trent Park Campus, N14 off Bramley Rd 81 DJ40
Middlesex Wf, E5 122 DW61
Middle St, EC1 10 G5
Betchworth RH3 264 CP136
Croydon CR0 off Surrey St 202 DQ104
Guildford (Shere) GU5 260 BN139
Waltham Abbey EN9 50 EG23
Middle Temple, EC4 10 C9
Middle Temple La, EC4 10 C8
Middleton Av, E4 101 DZ49
Greenford UB6 137 CD68
Sidcup DA14 186 EW93
Middleton Cl, E4 101 DZ48
Middleton Dr, SE16 23 H4
Pinner HA5 115 BU55
Middleton Gdns, Ilf. IG2 125 EP58
Middleton Gro, N7 121 DL64
Middleton Hall La, Brwd. CM15 108 FY47
Middleton Ms, N7 off Middleton Gro 121 DL64
Middleton Pl, W1 9 J6
Middleton Rd, E8 5 P6
NW11 120 DA59
Brentwood (Shenf.) CM15 108 FY46
Carshalton SM5 200 DE101
Cobham (Down.) KT11 229 BV119
Epsom KT19 216 CR110
Hayes UB3 135 BR71
Morden SM4 200 DC100
Rickmansworth (Mill End) WD3 92 BG46
Middleton St, E2 12 C1
Middleton Way, SE13 163 ED84
Middle Wk, Slou. (Burn.) SL1 130 AH69
Woking GU21 off Commercial Way 226 AY117
Middleway, NW11 120 DB57
Middle Way, SW16 201 DK96
Erith DA18 166 EY76
Hayes UB4 136 BW70
Watford WD24 75 BV37
Middle Way, The, Har. HA3 95 CF54
Middle Yd, SE1 21 K1
Middlings, The, Sev. TN13 256 FF125
Middlings Ri, Sev. TN13 256 FF126
Middlings Wd, Sev. TN13 256 FF125
Coll Mid Essex Adult Comm Coll, Bishops Hill, Brwd. CM13 off Rayleigh Rd 109 GB44
Warley Cen, Brwd. CM13 off Essex Way 107 FW51
Midfield Av, Bexh. DA7 167 FC83
Swanley BR8 187 FH93
Midfield Par, Bexh. DA7 167 FC83
Sch Midfield Prim Sch, Orp. BR5 off Grovelands Rd 186 EU94
Midfield Way, Orp. BR5 206 EV95
Midford Pl, W1 9 K4
Midgarth Cl, Lthd. (Oxshott) KT22 214 CC114
Coll Mid Herts Music Cen, Hat. AL10 off Birchwood Av 45 CV16
Midholm, NW11 120 DB56
Wembley HA9 118 CN60
Midholm Cl, NW11 120 DB56
Midholm Rd, Croy. CR0 203 DY103
MID HOLMWOOD, Dor. RH5 263 CJ142
Mid Holmwood La, Dor. (Mid Holm.) RH5 263 CJ142
Midhope Cl, Wok. GU22 226 AY119
Midhope Gdns, Wok. GU22 off Midhope Rd 226 AY119
Midhope Rd, Wok. GU22 226 AY119
Midhope St, WC1 9 P2
Midhurst Av, N10 120 DG55
Croydon CR0 201 DN101
Midhurst Cl, Horn. RM12 127 FG63
Midhurst Gdns, Uxb. UB10 135 BQ66
Midhurst Hill, Bexh. DA6 186 FA86
Midhurst Rd, W13 157 CG75
Midhurst Way, E5 122 DU63
Midland Cres, NW3 off Finchley Rd 140 DC65
Midland Pl, E14 24 C9
Midland Rd, E10 123 EC59
NW1 141 DK68
Hemel Hempstead HP2 40 BK20
Midland Ter, NW2 119 CX62
NW10 138 CS70
Midleton Ind Est, Guil. GU2 242 AV133
Midleton Rd, Guil. GU2 242 AV133
New Malden KT3 198 CQ97
Midlothian Rd, E3 13 L4
Midmoor Rd, SW12 181 DJ88
SW19 199 CX95
Midship Cl, SE16 23 H2
Midship Pt, E14 23 N4
Midstrath Rd, NW10 118 CS63
Mid St, Red. (S.Nutfld) RH1 251 DM134
Midsummer Av, Houns. TW4 156 BZ84
Midway, St.Alb. AL3 42 CB23
Sutton SM3 199 CZ101
Walton-on-Thames KT12 195 BV103
Midway Av, Cher. KT16 194 BG97
Egham TW20 193 BB97
Midway Cl, Stai. TW18 174 BH90
Midwinter Cl, Well. DA16 off Hook La 166 EU83
Midwood Cl, NW2 119 CV62
Miena Way, Ashtd. KT21 231 CK117
Miers Cl, E6 145 EN67
Mighell Av, Ilf. IG4 124 EK57
Mike Spring Ct, Grav. DA12 191 GK91
Milan Rd, Sthl. UB1 156 BZ75
Milborne Gro, SW10 17 M10
Milborne St, E9 142 DW65
Milborough Cres, SE12 184 EE86
Milbourne La, Esher KT10 214 CC107
Sch Milbourne Lo Jun Sch, Esher KT10 off Milbourne La 214 CC106
Sch Milbourne Lo Sen Sch, Esher KT10 off Arbrook La 215 CD107
Milbrook, Esher KT10 214 CC107
Milburn Dr, West Dr. UB7 134 BL73
Milburn Wk, Epsom KT18 232 CS115
Milcombe Cl, Wok. GU21 off Inglewood 226 AV118
Milcote St, SE1 20 E4
Mildenhall Rd, E5 122 DW63
Slough SL1 132 AS72
Mildmay Av, N1 5 K3
Mildmay Gro N, N1 5 K2
Mildmay Gro S, N1 5 K2
Mildmay Pk, N1 5 K1
Mildmay Pl, N16 5 M2
Sevenoaks (Shore.) TN14 225 FF111
Mildmay Rd, N1 5 K1
Ilford IG1 off Winston Way 125 EP62
Romford RM7 127 FC57
Mildmay St, N1 5 K3
Mildred Av, Borwd. WD6 78 CN42
Hayes UB3 155 BR77
Northolt UB5 116 CB64
Watford WD18 75 BT42
Mildred Cl, Dart. DA1 188 FN86
Mildred Rd, Erith DA8 167 FE78
Mile Cl, Wal.Abb. EN9 67 EC33
MILE END, E1 13 J2
⊖ Mile End 13 L3
Mile End, The, E17 101 DX53
MILE END GREEN, Dart. DA2 209 FW96
Mile End Pl, E1 12 G3
Mile End Rd, E1 12 D5
E3 12 D5
Mile Ho Cl, St.Alb. AL1 43 CG23
Mile Ho La, St.Alb. AL1 43 CG23
Mile Path, Wok. GU22 226 AV120
Mile Rd, Wall. SM6 201 DJ102
Miles Cl, Harl. CM19 51 EP16
Sch Miles Coverdale Prim Sch, W12 off Coverdale Rd 159 CW75
Miles Dr, SE28 145 ER74
Miles La, Cob. KT11 214 BY113
Milespit Hill, NW7 97 CV50
Miles Pl, NW1 7 P5
Surbiton KT5 off Villiers Av 198 CM98
Miles Rd, N8 121 DL55
Epsom KT19 216 CR112
Mitcham CR4 200 DE97
Miles St, SW8 161 DL79
Milestone Cl, N9 off Chichester Rd 100 DU47
Sutton SM2 218 DD107
Woking (Ripley) GU23 228 BG122
Milestone Rd, SE19 182 DT93
Dartford DA2 188 FP86
Miles Way, N20 98 DE47
Milfoil St, W12 139 CU73
Milford Cl, SE2 166 EY79
St. Albans AL4 43 CK16
Milford Gdns, Croy. CR0 off Tannery Cl 203 DX99
Edgware HA8 96 CN52
Wembley HA0 117 CK64
Milford Gro, Sutt. SM1 218 DC105
Milford La, WC2 10 B9
Milford Ms, SW16 181 DM90
Milford Rd, W13 137 CH74
Southall UB1 136 CA73
Milford Twrs, SE6 off Thomas La 183 EB87
Milkhouse Gate, Guil. GU1 off High St 258 AX136
Milking La, Kes. BR2 222 EK111
Orpington BR6 222 EL112
Milk St, E16 145 EP74
EC2 11 H8
Bromley BR1 184 EH93
Milkwell Gdns, Wdf.Grn. IG8 102 EH52
Milkwell Yd, SE5 162 DQ81
Milkwood Rd, SE24 181 DP85
Milk Yd, E1 12 E10
Millacres, Ware SG12 off Station Rd 33 DX06
Millais Av, E12 125 EN64
Millais Cres, Epsom KT19 216 CS106
Millais Gdns, Edg. HA8 96 CN54
Millais Pl, Til. RM18 171 GG80
Millais Rd, E11 123 EC63
Enfield EN1 82 DT43
New Malden KT3 198 CS100
Millais Way, Epsom KT19 216 CQ105
Millan Cl, Add. (New Haw) KT15 212 BH110
Milland Ct, Borwd. WD6 78 CR39
Millard Cl, N16 5 M1
Millard Ter, Dag. RM10 off Church Elm La 146 FA65
Mill Av, Uxb. UB8 134 BJ68
Millbank, SW1 19 N6
Hemel Hempstead HP3 40 BK24
Staines TW18 174 BH92
Millbank Millennium Pier 19 P8
Sch Millbank Prim Sch, SW1 19 M8
Millbank Twr, SW1 19 N8
Millbank Way, SE12 184 EG85
Millbourne Rd, Felt. TW13 176 BY91
Millbridge, Hert. SG14 32 DQ09
Millbridge Ms, Hert. SG14 off Millbridge 32 DQ09
Mill Br Pl, Uxb. UB8 134 BH68
Millbro, Swan. BR8 187 FG94
Millbrook, Guil. GU1 258 AX136
Weybridge KT13 213 BS105
Millbrook Av, Well. DA16 165 ER84
Millbrook Ct, Ware SG12 33 DX05
Millbrook Gdns, Rom. (Chad.Hth) RM6 126 EZ58
Romford (Gidea Pk) RM2 105 FE54
Millbrook Pl, NW1 off Hampstead Rd 141 DJ68
Sch Millbrook Prim Sch, Wal.Cr. EN8 off Gews Cor 67 DX29
Millbrook Rd, N9 100 DV46
SW9 161 DP83
Bushey WD23 76 BZ39
Mill Brook Rd, Orp. BR5 206 EW98
Millbrook Way, Slou. (Colnbr.) SL3 153 BE82
Mill Cl, Cars. SM5 200 DG103
Mill Cl, Chesh. HP5 54 AS34
Hemel Hempstead HP3 58 BN25
Hemel Hempstead (Picc.End) HP1 40 BH16
Horley RH6 268 DE147
Leatherhead (Bkhm) KT23 230 CA124
Ware SG12 33 DX06
Welwyn Garden City (Lmsfd) AL8 29 CU10
West Drayton UB7 154 BK76
Mill Cor, Barn. EN5 79 CZ39
Mill Ct, E10 123 EC62
Millcrest Rd, Wal.Cr. (Chsht) EN7 65 DP28
Millcroft Ho, SE6 183 EC91
Millen Ct, Dart. (Hort.Kir.) DA4 208 FQ98
MILL END, Rick. WD3 91 BF46
Millender Wk, SE16 22 F8
Millennium Br, EC4 10 G9
SE1 10 G9
Millennium Cl, E16 15 M7
Uxbridge UB8 134 BH68
Millennium Dr, E14 24 E7
Millennium Harbour, E14 23 M3
Millennium Pl, E2 142 DV68
Millennium Sq, SE1 21 P3
Sch Millennium Village Sch, SE10 25 J6
Millennium Way, SE10 24 G3
Millennium Wf, Rick. WD3 off Wharf La 92 BL45
Miller Av, Enf. EN3 83 EA38
Miller Cl, Mitch. CR4 200 DF101
Pinner HA5 94 BW54
Miller Pl, Ger.Cr. SL9 112 AX57
Miller Rd, SW19 180 DD93
Croydon CR0 201 DM102
Guildford GU4 243 BC131
Miller's Av, E8 5 N1
Millers Cl, NW7 97 CU49
Chigwell IG7 104 EV47
Rickmansworth (Chorl.) WD3 73 BE41
Staines TW18 174 BH92
Millers Copse, Epsom KT18 232 CR119
Redhill RH1 267 DP144
Millers Ct, W4 off Chiswick Mall 159 CT78
Hertford SG14 off Parliament Sq 32 DR10
Millersdale, Harl. CM19 51 EP19
Millers Grn Cl, Enf. EN2 81 DP41
Miller's La, Chig. IG7 104 EV46
Millers La, Ware (Stans.Abb.) SG12 33 EC11
Windsor SL4 172 AT86
Millers Meadow Cl, SE3 off Meadowcourt Rd 184 EF85
Millers Ri, St.Alb. AL1 43 CE21
Miller's Ter, E8 5 N1
Miller St, NW1 141 DJ68
Millers Way, W6 159 CW75
Miller Wk, SE1 20 D2
Millet Rd, Grnf. UB6 136 CB69
Mill Fm Av, Sun. TW16 175 BS94
Mill Fm Cl, Pnr. HA5 94 BW54
Mill Fm Cres, Houns. TW4 176 BY88
Millfield, Berk. HP4 38 AX18
Mill Fld, Harl. CM17 36 EW11
Millfield, Sun. TW16 195 BR95
Welwyn Garden City AL7 30 DC08
Millfield Av, E17 101 DY53
Millfield Dr, Grav. (Nthflt) DA11 190 GE89
Millfield La, N6 120 DF61
Tadworth KT20 249 CZ125
Millfield Pl, N6 120 DG61
Millfield Rd, Edg. HA8 96 CQ54
Hounslow TW4 176 BY88
Millfields, Chesh. HP5 54 AQ33
Millfields Cl, Orp. BR5 206 EV97
Sch Millfields Comm Sch, E5 off Hilsea St 122 DW63
Millfields Cotts, Orp. BR5 off Millfields Cl 206 EV98
Millfields Est, E5 off Denton Way 123 DX62
Millfields Rd, E5 122 DW63
Millfield Wk, Hem.H. HP3 40 BN22
Millford, Wok. GU21 226 AV117
Mill Gdns, SE26 182 DV91
MILL GREEN, Hat. AL9 45 CY15
Mill Grn, Mitch. CR4 off London Rd 200 DG101
Mill Grn Business Pk, Mitch. CR4 off Mill Grn Rd 200 DG101
Mill Grn La, Hat. AL9 45 CY15
★ Mill Green Mus, Hat. AL9 45 CY15
Mill Grn Rd, Mitch. CR4 200 DF101
Welwyn Garden City AL7 29 CY10
Millgrove St, SW11 160 DG82
Millharbour, E14 24 A5
Millhaven Cl, Rom. RM6 126 EV58
Millhedge Cl, Cob. KT11 230 BY116
MILL HILL, NW7 97 CU50
Mill Hill, SW13 off Mill Hill Rd 159 CU82
Brentwood (Shenf.) CM15 108 FY45
≠ Mill Hill Broadway 96 CS51
Mill Hill Circ, NW7 off Watford Way 97 CT50
Sch Mill Hill Co High Sch, NW7 off Worcester Cres 96 CS47
Oakhill Campus, Barn. EN4 off Church Hill Rd 98 DF46
⊖ Mill Hill East 97 CX52
Mill Hill Gro, W3 off Mill Hill Rd 138 CP74
Mill Hill La, Bet. (Brock.) RH3 248 CP134
Mill Hill Rd, SW13 159 CU82
W3 158 CP75
Sch Mill Hill Sch, NW7 off The Ridgeway 97 CV49
Millhoo Ct, Wal.Abb. EN9 68 EF34
Mill Ho Cl, Dart. (Eyns.) DA4 off Mill La 208 FL102
Millhouse La, Abb.L. (Bedmond) WD5 59 BT27
Mill Ho La, Cher. KT16 193 BB98
Egham TW20 193 BB98
Millhouse Pl, SE27 181 DP91
Millhurst Ms, Harl. CM17 36 EY11
Millicent Rd, E10 123 DZ60
Milligan St, E14 13 M10
Milliners Ct, Loug. IG10 off The Croft 85 EN40
Milliners Ho, SW18 off Point Pleasant 160 DA84
Milling Rd, Edg. HA8 96 CR52
Millington Rd, Hayes UB3 155 BS76
Mill La, E4 83 EB41
NW6 119 CZ64
SE18 165 EN78
Mill La, Amer. HP7 55 AN39
Beaconsfield HP9 89 AL54
Broxbourne EN10 49 DZ21
Carshalton SM5 218 DF105
Chalfont St. Giles HP8 90 AU47
Croydon CR0 201 DM104
Dartford (Eyns.) DA4 208 FL102
Dorking RH4 263 CH135
Egham TW20 193 BC98
Epsom KT17 217 CT109
Gerrards Cross SL9 113 AZ58
Grays RM20 169 FX78
Grays (Chaff.Hun.) RM16 169 FX77
Guildford GU1 off Quarry St 258 AX136
Guildford (Chilw.) GU4 259 BF139
Guildford (Peasm.) GU3 258 AV142
Harlow CM17 36 EY11
Horley (Hkwd) RH6 268 DD148
Kings Langley WD4 58 BN29
Leatherhead (Fetch.) KT22 231 CG122
Maidenhead (Taplow) SL6 130 AC71
Ongar (Toot Hill) CM5 71 FE29
Orpington (Downe) BR6 223 EN110
Oxted RH8 254 EF132
Oxted (Lmpfld Cht.) RH8 255 EM131
Redhill RH1 251 DJ131
Rickmansworth (Crox.Grn) WD3 75 BQ44
Romford (Chad.Hth) RM6 126 EY58
Romford (Nave.) RM4 87 FH40
Sevenoaks TN14 257 FJ121
Sevenoaks (Shore.) TN14 225 FF110
Slough (Horton) SL3 153 BB83
Waltham Cross EN8 67 DY28
West Byfleet (Byfleet) KT14 212 BM113
Westerham TN16 255 EQ127
Windsor SL4 151 AN80
Woking (Ripley) GU23 228 BK119
Woodford Green IG8 102 EF50
Mill La Cl, Brox. EN10 49 DZ21
Mill La Trd Est, Croy. CR0 201 DM104
Millman Ms, WC1 10 A4
Millman Pl, WC1 off Millman St 141 DM70
Millman St, WC1 10 A4
Millmark Gro, SE14 163 DY82
Millmarsh La, Enf. EN3 83 DY40
Millmead, Guil. GU2 258 AW136
Mill Mead, Stai. TW18 173 BF91
Millmead, W.Byf. (Byfleet) KT14 212 BM112
Sch Mill Mead Prim Sch, Hert. SG14 off Port Vale 32 DQ09
Mill Mead Rd, N17 122 DV56
Millmead Ter, Guil. GU2 258 AW136
Millmead Way, Hert. SG14 31 DP08
Mill Pk Av, Horn. RM12 128 FL61
Mill Pl, E14 13 K8
Chislehurst BR7 205 EP95
Dartford DA1 167 FG84
Kingston upon Thames KT1 198 CM97
Slough (Datchet) SL3 152 AX82
Mill Pl Caravan Pk, Slou. (Datchet) SL3 152 AW82
Mill Plat, Islw. TW7 157 CG82
Mill Plat Av, Islw. TW7 157 CG82
Mill Pond Cl, SW8 off Crimsworth Rd 161 DK80
Sevenoaks TN14 257 FK121
Millpond Ct, Add. KT15 212 BL106
Millpond Est, SE16 22 C4
Millpond Pl, Cars. SM5 200 DG104
Mill Pond Rd, Dart. DA1 188 FL86
Mill Race, Ware (Stans.Abb.) SG12 33 ED11
Mill Ridge, Edg. HA8 96 CM50
Mill Rd, E16 25 P1
SW19 180 DC94
Cobham KT11 230 BW115
Dartford (Hawley) DA2 188 FM91
Dorking (Holm.) RH5 263 CJ144
Epsom KT17 217 CT112
Erith DA8 167 FC80
Esher KT10 196 CA103
Gravesend (Nthflt) DA11 190 GE87
Hertford SG14 32 DR08
Ilford IG1 125 EN62
Purfleet RM19 168 FP79
Sevenoaks (Dunt.Grn) TN13 256 FE121
South Ockendon (Aveley) RM15 148 FQ73
Tadworth KT20 233 CX123
Twickenham TW2 176 CC89
West Drayton UB7 154 BJ76
Mill Row, N1 5 M8
Mills Cl, Uxb. UB10 134 BN68
Mills Ct, EC2 11 M2
Mills Gro, E14 14 C6
NW4 119 CX55
Mill Shaw, Oxt. RH8 254 EF132
Mill Shot Cl, SW6 159 CW80
Millshot Dr, Amer. HP7 55 AR40
Millside, B.End SL8 110 AC60
Carshalton SM5 200 DF103
Millside Ct, Iver SL0 154 BH75
Millside Ind Est, Dart. DA1 168 FK84
Millside Pl, Islw. TW7 157 CH82
Millsmead Way, Loug. IG10 85 EM40
Millson Cl, N20 98 DD47
Mills Rd, Walt. KT12 214 BW106
Mills Row, W4 158 CR77
Mills Spur, Wind. (Old Wind.) SL4 172 AV87
Millstead Cl, Tad. KT20 233 CV122
Millstone Cl, Dart. (S.Darenth) DA4 208 FQ96
Millstone Ms, Dart. (S.Darenth) DA4 208 FQ95
Millstream Cl, N13 99 DN50
Hertford SG14 31 DP09
Millstream La, Slou. SL1 131 AL74
Millstream Rd, SE1 21 N4
Millstream Way, H.Wyc. HP10 110 AD55
Mill St, SE1 21 P4
W1 9 H9
Berkhamsted HP4 38 AW19
Harlow CM17 52 EY17
Hemel Hempstead HP3 40 BK24
Kingston upon Thames KT1 198 CL97
Redhill RH1 266 DE135
Slough SL2 132 AT74
Slough (Colnbr.) SL3 153 BD80
Westerham TN16 255 ER127
Mills Way, Brwd. (Hutt.) CM13 109 GC46
Millthorne Cl, Rick. (Crox.Grn) WD3 74 BM43
Mill Vale, Brom. BR2 204 EF96
Mill Vw, St.Alb. (Park St) AL2 off Park St 61 CD27
Mill Vw Cl, Epsom (Ewell) KT17 217 CT108
Millview Cl, Reig. RH2 250 DD132
Mill Vw Gdns, Croy. CR0 203 DX104
MILLWALL, E14 24 A7
Millwall Dock Rd, E14 23 N5
★ Millwall FC, SE16 22 F10
Millwards, Hat. AL10 45 CV21
Millway, NW7 96 CS50
Mill Way, Bushey WD23 76 BY40
Feltham TW14 175 BV85
Leatherhead KT22 232 CM124
Millway, Reig. RH2 250 DD134
Mill Way, Rick. (Mill End) WD3 91 BF46
Millway Gdns, Nthlt. UB5 136 BZ65
Millwell Cres, Chig. IG7 103 ER50
Millwood Rd, Houns. TW3 176 CC85
Orpington BR5 206 EW97
Millwood St, W10 6 C6
Millwrights Wk, Hem.H. HP3 off Stephenson Wf 58 BM25
Mill Yd, E1 12 A9
Milman Cl, Pnr. HA5 116 BX55
Milman Rd, NW6 139 CY68
Milman's St, SW10 160 DD79
Milmead Ind Cen, N17 100 DV54
Milne Ct, E18 off Churchfields 102 EG53
Milne Feild, Pnr. HA5 94 CA52
Milne Gdns, SE9 184 EL85
Milne Pk E, Croy. (New Adgtn) CR0 221 ED111
Milne Pk W, Croy. (New Adgtn) CR0 221 ED111
Milner App, Cat. CR3 236 DU121
Milner Cl, Cat. CR3 236 DT121
Watford WD25 59 BV34
Milner Ct, Bushey WD23 76 CB44
Milner Dr, Cob. KT11 214 BZ112
Twickenham TW2 177 CD87
Milner Pl, N1 4 D7
Carshalton SM5 off High St 218 DG105
Milner Rd, E15 14 G2
SW19 200 DB95
Caterham CR3 236 DU122
Dagenham RM8 126 EW61
Kingston upon Thames KT1 197 CK97
Morden SM4 200 DD99
Slough (Burn.) SL1 130 AG71
Thornton Heath CR7 202 DR97
Milner Sq, N1 4 E6
Milner St, SW3 18 C7
Milner Wk, SE9 185 ER89
Milne Way, Uxb. (Hare.) UB9 92 BH53
Milnthorpe Rd, W4 158 CR79
Milo Rd, SE22 182 DT86
Milroy Av, Grav. (Nthflt) DA11 190 GE89
Milroy Wk, SE1 20 E1
Milson Rd, W14 16 B5
MILTON, Grav. DA12 191 GK86
Milton Av, E6 144 EK66
N6 121 DJ59
NW9 118 CQ55
NW10 138 CQ67
Barnet EN5 79 CZ43
Croydon CR0 202 DR101
Dorking (Westc.) RH4 263 CD137
Gerrards Cross (Chal.St.P.) SL9 112 AX56
Gravesend DA12 191 GJ88
Hornchurch RM12 127 FF61
Sevenoaks (Bad.Mt) TN14 225 FB110
Sutton SM1 200 DD104
Milton Cl, N2 120 DC57
SE1 21 N8
Hayes UB4 135 BU72
Slough (Horton) SL3 153 BA83
Sutton SM1 200 DD104
Milton Ct, EC2 11 J5
Romford (Chad.Hth) RM6 off Cross Rd 126 EW59
Uxbridge UB10 115 BP62
Waltham Abbey EN9 67 EC34
Milton Ct La, Dor. RH4 263 CF136
Milton Ct Rd, SE14 163 DY79
Milton Cres, Ilf. IG2 125 EQ59
Milton Dene, Hem.H. HP2 41 BP15
Milton Dr, Borwd. WD6 78 CP43
Shepperton TW17 194 BL98
Milton Flds, Ch.St.G. HP8 90 AV48
Milton Gdn Est, N16 off Milton Gro 122 DS63
Milton Gdns, Epsom KT18 216 CS114
Staines TW19 off Chesterton Dr 174 BM88
Tilbury RM18 171 GH81
Milton Gro, N11 99 DJ50
N16 122 DR63
Milton Hall Rd, Grav. DA12 191 GK88
Milton Hill, Ch.St.G. HP8 90 AV48
Milton Lawns, Amer. HP6 55 AR36
Milton Pk, N6 121 DJ59
Milton Pl, N7 4 C1
Gravesend DA12 191 GJ86
Milton Rd, E17 123 EA56
N6 121 DJ59
N15 121 DP56
NW7 97 CU50
NW9 off West Hendon Bdy 119 CU59
SE24 181 DP86
SW14 158 CR83
SW19 180 DC93
W3 138 CR74
W7 137 CF73
Addlestone KT15 212 BG107
Belvedere DA17 166 FA77
Brentwood CM14 108 FW49
Caterham CR3 236 DR121
Chesham HP5 54 AP29
Croydon CR0 202 DR102
Egham TW20 173 AZ92
Gravesend DA12 191 GJ86
Grays RM17 170 GB78
Hampton TW12 176 CA94
Harrow HA1 117 CE56
Mitcham CR4 180 DG94
Romford RM1 127 FG58
Sevenoaks (Dunt.Grn) TN13 256 FE121
Slough SL2 131 AR70
Sutton SM1 200 DA104
Swanscombe DA10 190 FY86
Uxbridge UB10 114 BN63
Wallington SM6 219 DJ107
Walton-on-Thames KT12 196 BX104
Ware SG12 33 DX05
Welling DA16 165 ET81
★ Milton's Cottage, Ch.St.G. HP8 90 AV48

★ Place of interest | H Hospital | Sch School | Coll College | Uni University | ≠ Railway station

Milton St, EC2 **11** J5
Dorking (Westc.) RH4 **263** CD137
Swanscombe DA10 **189** FX86
Waltham Abbey EN9 **67** EC34
Watford WD24 **75** BV38
Milton Way, Lthd. (Fetch.) KT22 **246** CC125
West Drayton UB7 **154** BM77
Milverton Dr, Uxb. UB10 **115** BQ63
Milverton Gdns, Ilf. IG3 **125** ET61
Milverton Ho, SE23 **183** DY90
Milverton Rd, NW6 **139** CW66
Milverton St, SE11 **20** D10
Milverton Way, SE9 **185** EN91
Milwards, Harl. CM19 **51** EP19
Sch **Milwards Co Prim Sch**, Harl. CM19 *off Paringdon Rd* **51** EP19
Milward St, E1 **12** D6
Milward Wk, SE18 *off Spearman St* **165** EN79
Mimas Rd, Hem.H. HP2 *off Saturn Way* **40** BM17
MIMBRIDGE, Wok. GU24 **210** AV113
Mimms Hall Rd, Pot.B. EN6 **63** CX31
Mimms La, Pot.B. (S.Mimms) EN6 **62** CQ33
Radlett (Shenley) WD7 **62** CN33
Mimosa Cl, Brwd. (Pilg.Hat.) CM15 **108** FV43
Orpington BR6 *off Berrylands* **206** EW104
Romford RM3 **106** FJ52
Mimosa Rd, Hayes UB4 **136** BW71
Mimosa St, SW6 **159** CZ81
Mimram Rd, Hert. SG14 **31** DP10
Mina Av, Slou. SL3 **152** AX75
Minard Rd, SE6 **184** EE87
Mina Rd, SE17 **21** M10
SW19 **200** DA95
Minchenden Cres, N14 **99** DJ48
Minchen Rd, Harl. CM20 **35** ET13
Minchin Cl, Lthd. KT22 **231** CG122
Mincing La, EC3 **11** L9
Woking (Chobham) GU24 **210** AT108
Minden Rd, SE20 **202** DV95
Sutton SM3 **199** CZ103
Minehead Rd, SW16 **181** DM92
Harrow HA2 **116** CA62
Mineral La, Chesh. HP5 **54** AQ32
Mineral St, SE18 **165** ES77
Minera Ms, SW1 **18** F7
Minerva Cl, SW9 **161** DN80
Sidcup DA14 **185** ES90
Staines TW19 **174** BG85
Minerva Dr, Wat. WD24 **75** BS36
Minerva Rd, E4 **101** EB52
NW10 **138** CQ70
Kingston upon Thames KT1 **198** CM96
Minerva St, E2 **142** DV68
Minerva Way, Beac. HP9 **89** AP54
Minet Av, NW10 **138** CS68
Minet Dr, Hayes UB3 **135** BU74
Minet Gdns, NW10 **138** CS68
Hayes UB3 **135** BU74
Sch **Minet Inf Sch**, Hayes UB3 *off Avondale Dr* **135** BV74
Sch **Minet Jun Sch**, Hayes UB3 *off Avondale Dr* **135** BV74
Minet Rd, SW9 **161** DP82
Minford Gdns, W14 **16** A4
Mingard Wk, N7 *off Hornsey Rd* **121** DM61
Ming St, E14 **13** P9
Minims, The, Hat. AL10 **45** CU17
Ministers Gdns, St.Alb. AL2 *off Frogmore* **61** CE28
★ **Ministry of Defence**, SW1 **19** N2
Ministry Way, SE9 **185** EM89
Miniver Pl, EC4 *off Garlick Hill* **142** DQ73
Mink Ct, Houns. TW4 **156** BW83
Minniecroft Rd, Slou. (Burn.) SL1 **130** AH69
Minniedale, Surb. KT5 **198** CM99
Minnow St, SE17 *off East St* **162** DS77
Minnow Wk, SE17 **21** M8
Minoan Dr, Hem.H. HP3 **40** BL24
Minorca Rd, Wey. KT13 **212** BN105
Minories, EC3 **11** N9
Minshull Pl, Beck. BR3 **183** EA94
Minshull St, SW8 *off Wandsworth Rd* **161** DK81
Minson Rd, E9 **143** DX67
Minstead Gdns, SW15 **179** CT87
Minstead Way, N.Mal. KT3 **198** CS100
Minster Av, Sutt. SM1 *off Leafield Rd* **200** DA103
Minster Cl, Hat. AL10 **45** CU20
Minster Ct, EC3 *off Mincing La* **142** DR73
Hornchurch RM11 **128** FN61
St. Albans (Frog.) AL2 **61** CE28
Minster Dr, Croy. CR0 **220** DS105
Minster Gdns, W.Mol. KT8 **196** BZ98
Minsterley Av, Shep. TW17 **195** BS98
Minster Pavement, EC3 *off Mincing La* **142** DR73
Minster Rd, NW2 **119** CY64
Bromley BR1 **184** EH94
Minster Wk, N8 *off Lightfoot Rd* **121** DL56
Minster Way, Horn. RM11 **128** FM60
Slough SL3 **153** AZ75
Minstrel Cl, Hem.H. HP1 **40** BH19
Minstrel Gdns, Surb. KT5 **198** CM98
Mint Business Pk, E16 **15** M6
Mint Cl, Uxb. (Hlgdn) UB10 **135** BP69
Mintern Cl, N13 **99** DP48
Minterne Av, Sthl. UB2 **156** CA77
Minterne Rd, Har. HA3 **118** CM57
Minterne Waye, Hayes UB4 **136** BW72
Mintern St, N1 **5** K9
Mint Gdns, Dor. RH4 *off Church St* **263** CG135
Mint La, Tad. (Lwr Kgswd) KT20 **250** DA129
Minton Ms, NW6 *off Lymington Rd* **140** DB65
Minton Ri, Maid. (Taplow) SL6 **130** AH72
Mint Rd, Bans. SM7 **234** DC116
Wallington SM6 **219** DH105
Mint St, SE1 **20** G3
Mint Wk, Croy. CR0 *off High St* **202** DQ104
Warlingham CR6 **237** DX118
Woking (Knap.) GU21 **226** AS117
Mirabel Rd, SW6 **159** CZ80
Mirador Cres, Slou. SL2 **132** AV73
Miramar Way, Horn. RM12 **128** FK64
Miranda Cl, E1 **12** E6
Miranda Ct, W3 *off Queens Dr* **138** CM72
Miranda Rd, N19 **121** DJ60
Mirfield St, SE7 **164** EK77
Miriam Rd, SE18 **165** ES78
Mirravale Trd Est, Dag. RM8 **126** EZ59
Mirren Cl, Har. HA2 **116** BZ63
Mirrie La, Uxb. (Denh.) UB9 **113** BC57
Mirror Path, SE9 *off Lambscroft Av* **184** EJ90
Misbourne Av, Ger.Cr. (Chal.St.P.) SL9 **90** AY50
Misbourne Cl, Ger.Cr. (Chal.St.P.) SL9 **90** AY50
Misbourne Ct, Slou. SL3 *off High St* **153** BA77
Misbourne Meadows, Uxb. (Denh.) UB9 **113** BC60
Misbourne Rd, Uxb. UB10 **134** BN67
Misbourne Vale, Ger.Cr. (Chal.St.P.) SL9 **90** AX50
Miskin Rd, Dart. DA1 **188** FJ87
Miskin Way, Grav. DA12 **191** GK93
Missden Dr, Hem.H. HP3 **41** BQ22
Missenden Cl, Felt. TW14 **175** BT88
Missenden Gdns, Mord. SM4 **200** DC100
Slough (Burn.) SL1 **130** AH72
Missenden Rd, Chesh. HP5 **54** AL32
Mission Gro, E17 **123** DY57
Sch **Mission Gro Prim Sch**, E17 *off Buxton Rd* **123** DZ56
Mission Pl, SE15 **162** DU81
Mission Sq, Brent. TW8 **158** CL79
Mistletoe Cl, Croy. CR0 *off Marigold Way* **203** DX102
Mistley Gdns, Horl. RH6 *off Reigate Rd* **268** DD149
Mistley Rd, Harl. CM20 **36** EU13
Misty's Fld, Walt. KT12 **196** BW102
Mitali Pas, E1 **12** A8
MITCHAM, CR4 **200** DG97
Tra **Mitcham** **200** DE98
Mitcham Gdn Village, Mitch. CR4 **200** DG99
Mitcham Ind Est, Mitch. CR4 **200** DG95
⇌ **Mitcham Junction** **200** DG99
Tra **Mitcham Junction** **200** DG99
Mitcham La, SW16 **181** DJ93
Mitcham Pk, Mitch. CR4 **200** DF98
Mitcham Rd, E6 **144** EL69
SW17 **180** DF92
Croydon CR0 **201** DL100
Ilford IG3 **125** ET59
Sch **Mitcham Vale Sch**, Mitch. CR4 *off Acacia Rd* **201** DH96
Mitchell Av, Grav. (Nthflt) DA11 **190** GD89
Sch **Mitchell Brook Prim Sch**, NW10 *off Bridge Rd* **138** CR65
Mitchellbrook Way, NW10 **138** CR65
Mitchell Cl, SE2 **166** EW77
Abbots Langley WD5 **59** BU32
Belvedere DA17 **167** FC76
Dartford DA1 **188** FL89
Hemel Hempstead (Bov.) HP3 **57** AZ27
Rainham RM13 **148** FJ68
St. Albans AL1 **43** CD24
Slough SL1 **151** AN75
Welwyn Garden City AL7 **30** DC09
Mitchell Rd, N13 **99** DP50
Orpington BR6 **223** ET105
Mitchells Cl, Guil. (Shalf.) GU4 *off Station Rd* **258** AY140
Mitchell's Pl, SE21 *off Dulwich Village* **182** DS87
Mitchells Row, Guil. (Shalf.) GU4 **258** AY141
Mitchell St, EC1 **10** G3
Mitchell Wk, E6 **144** EL71
Amersham HP6 **55** AS38
Swanscombe DA10 **190** FY87
Mitchell Way, NW10 **138** CQ65
Bromley BR1 **204** EG95
Mitchison Rd, N1 **5** J4
Mitchley Av, Pur. CR8 **220** DQ113
South Croydon CR2 **220** DQ113
Mitchley Gro, S.Croy. CR2 **220** DU113
Mitchley Hill, S.Croy. CR2 **220** DT113
Mitchley Rd, N17 **122** DU55
Mitchley Vw, S.Croy. CR2 **220** DU113
Mitford Cl, Chess. KT9 *off Merritt Gdns* **215** CJ107
Mitford Rd, N19 **121** DL61
Mitre, The, E14 **13** L9
Mitre Av, E17 *off Greenleaf Rd* **123** DZ55
Mitre Cl, Brom. BR2 *off Beckenham La* **204** EF96
Shepperton TW17 **195** BR100
Sutton SM2 **218** DC108
Mitre Ct, EC2 **11** H7
EC4 **10** D8
Mitre Rd, E15 **144** EE68
SE1 **20** D3
Mitre Sq, EC3 **11** M8
Mitre St, EC3 **11** M8
Mitre Way, W10 **139** CV70
Mixbury Gro, Wey. KT13 **213** BR107
Mixnams La, Cher. KT16 **194** BG97
Mizen Cl, Cob. KT11 **214** BX114
Mizen Way, Cob. KT11 **230** BW115
Moat, The, N.Mal. KT3 **198** CS95
Ongar CM5 **71** FF29
Sch **Moatbridge Sch**, SE9 *off Eltham Palace Rd* **184** EK86
Moat Cl, Bushey WD23 **76** CB43
Orpington BR6 **223** ET107
Sevenoaks (Chipstead) TN13 **256** FB123
Moat Ct, Ashtd. KT21 **232** CL117
Moat Cres, N3 **120** DB55
Moat Cft, Well. DA16 **166** EW83
Moat Dr, E13 *off Boundary Rd* **144** EJ68
Harrow HA1 **116** CC56
Ruislip HA4 **115** BS59
Slough SL2 **132** AW71
Moated Fm Dr, Add. KT15 **212** BJ108
Moat Fm Rd, Nthlt. UB5 **136** BZ65
Moatfield Rd, Bushey WD23 **76** CB43
Moat La, Erith DA8 **167** FG81
Moat Pl, SW9 **161** DM83
W3 **138** CP72
Uxbridge (Denh.) UB9 **114** BH63
Moatside, Enf. EN3 **83** DX42
Feltham TW13 **176** BW91
Moats La, Red. (S.Nutfld) RH1 **267** DN140
Moatview Ct, Bushey WD23 **76** CB43
Moatwood Grn, Welw.G.C. AL7 **29** CY10
Moberley Rd, SW4 **181** DK87
Modbury Gdns, NW5 *off Queen's Cres* **140** DG65
Modder Pl, SW15 **159** CX84
Model Cotts, SW14 *off Upper Richmond Rd W* **158** CQ84
Model Fm Cl, SE9 **184** EL90
Modling Ho, E2 **143** DX68
Moelwyn Hughes Ct, N7 *off Hilldrop Cres* **121** DK64
Moelyn Ms, Har. HA1 **117** CG57
Moffat Rd, N13 **99** DL51
SW17 **180** DE91
Thornton Heath CR7 **202** DQ96
Moffats Cl, Hat. AL9 **64** DA26
Moffats La, Hat. AL9 **63** CZ26
MOGADOR, Tad. KT20 **249** CY129
Mogador Cotts, Tad. KT20 *off Mogador Rd* **249** CX128
Mogador Rd, Tad. (Lwr Kgswd) KT20 **249** CX128
Mogden La, Islw. TW7 **177** CE85
Mohmmad Khan Rd, E11 *off Harvey Rd* **124** EF60
Moira Cl, N17 **100** DS54
Moira Rd, SE9 **165** EM84
Moir Cl, S.Croy. CR2 **220** DU109
Moland Mead, SE16 **22** G9
Molash Rd, Orp. BR5 **206** EX98
Molasses Row, SW11 *off Cinnamon Row* **160** DC83
Mole Abbey Gdns, W.Mol. KT8 *off New Rd* **196** CA97
Mole Business Pk, Lthd. KT22 **231** CG121
Mole Ct, Epsom KT19 **216** CQ105
Molember Ct, E.Mol. KT8 **197** CE99
Molember Rd, E.Mol. KT8 **197** CE99
Mole Rd, Lthd. (Fetch.) KT22 **231** CD121
Walton-on-Thames KT12 **214** BX106
Molescroft, SE9 **185** EQ90
Molesey Av, W.Mol. KT8 **196** BZ98
Molesey Cl, Walt. KT12 **214** BY105
Molesey Dr, Sutt. SM3 **199** CY103
Molesey Pk Av, W.Mol. KT8 **196** CB99
Molesey Pk Cl, E.Mol. KT8 **196** CC99
Molesey Pk Rd, E.Mol. KT8 **197** CD99
West Molesey KT8 **196** CB99
Molesey Rd, Walt. KT12 **214** BX106
West Molesey KT8 **196** BY99
Molesford Rd, SW6 **160** DA81
Molesham Cl, W.Mol. KT8 **196** CB97
Molesham Way, W.Mol. KT8 **196** CB97
Moles Hill, Lthd. (Oxshott) KT22 **215** CD111
Molesworth, Hodd. EN11 **33** EA13
Molesworth Rd, Cob. KT11 **213** BU113
Molesworth St, SE13 **183** EC83
Mole Valley Pl, Ashtd. KT21 **231** CK119
Molewood Rd, Hert. SG14 **31** DP08
Mollands La, S.Ock. RM15 **149** FW70
Mollison Av, Enf. EN3 **83** DY43
Mollison Dr, Wall. SM6 **219** DL107
Mollison Ri, Grav. DA12 **191** GL92
Mollison Sq, Wall. SM6 *off Mollison Dr* **219** DL108
Mollison Way, Edg. HA8 **96** CN54
Molloy Ct, Wok. GU21 *off Courtenay Rd* **227** BA116
Molly Huggins Cl, SW12 **181** DJ87
Molteno Rd, Wat. WD17 **75** BU39
Molyneaux Av, Hem.H. (Bov.) HP3 **57** AZ27
Molyneux Dr, SW17 **181** DH91
Molyneux Rd, Gdmg. GU7 **258** AT144
Weybridge KT13 **212** BN106
Molyneux St, W1 **8** B6
Molyns Ms, Slou. SL1 *off Moor Furlong* **131** AL74
Momples Rd, Harl. CM20 **36** EV13
Monahan Av, Pur. CR8 **219** DM112
Monarch Cl, Felt. TW14 **175** BS87
Rainham RM13 *off Whymark Cl* **147** FG68
Tilbury RM18 **171** GH82
West Wickham BR4 **222** EF105
Monarch Dr, E16 **144** EK71
Monarch Ms, E17 **123** EB57
SW16 **181** DN92
Monarch Par, Mitch. CR4 *off London Rd* **200** DF96
Monarch Pl, Buck.H. IG9 **102** EJ47
Monarch Rd, Belv. DA17 **166** FA76
Monarchs Ct, NW7 *off Grenville Pl* **96** CR50
Monarchs Way, Ruis. HA4 **115** BR60
Waltham Cross EN8 **67** DY34
Mona Rd, SE15 **162** DW82
Monastery Gdns, Enf. EN2 **82** DR40
Mona St, E16 **15** K5
Monaveen Gdns, W.Mol. KT8 **196** CA97
Monck St, SW1 **19** M6
Monclar Rd, SE5 **162** DR84
Moncorvo Cl, SW7 **18** A4
Moncrieff Cl, E6 *off Linton Gdns* **144** EL72
Moncrieff Pl, SE15 *off Rye La* **162** DU82
Moncrieff St, SE15 **162** DU82
Mondial Way, Hayes UB3 **155** BQ80
Sch **Monega Prim Sch**, E12 *off Monega Rd* **144** EK65
Monega Rd, E7 **144** EJ65
E12 **144** EK65
Money Av, Cat. CR3 **236** DR122
MONEYHILL, Rick. WD3 **92** BH46
Moneyhill Par, Rick. WD3 *off Uxbridge Rd* **92** BH46
Money Hill Rd, Rick. WD3 **92** BJ46
Money Hole La, Welw.G.C. AL7 **30** DE08
Money La, West Dr. UB7 **154** BK76
Money Rd, Cat. CR3 **236** DR122
Mongers La, Epsom KT17 **217** CT110
Monica Cl, Wat. WD24 **76** BW40
Monier Rd, E3 **143** EA66
Monivea Rd, Beck. BR3 **183** DZ94
Monkchester Cl, Loug. IG10 **85** EN39
Monk Dr, E16 **15** L8
MONKEN HADLEY, Barn. EN5 **79** CZ39
Sch **Monken Hadley C of E Prim Sch**, Barn. EN4 *off Camlet Way* **80** DA39
Monkey Island La, Maid. SL6 **150** AE78
Monkfrith Av, N14 **81** DH44
Monkfrith Cl, N14 **99** DH45
Sch **Monkfrith Prim Sch**, N14 *off Knoll Dr* **98** DG45
Monkfrith Way, N14 **98** DG45
Monkhams Av, Wdf.Grn. IG8 **102** EG50
Monkhams Dr, Wdf.Grn. IG8 **102** EH49
Monkhams La, Buck.H. IG9 **102** EH48
Woodford Green IG8 **102** EG50
Monkleigh Rd, Mord. SM4 **199** CY97
Monk Pas, E16 **15** L9
Monks Av, Barn. EN5 **80** DC44
West Molesey KT8 **196** BZ99
Monksbury, Harl. CM18 **52** EU18
Monks Chase, Brwd. (Ingrave) CM13 **109** GC50
Monks Cl, SE2 **166** EX77
Broxbourne EN10 **49** EA20
Enfield EN2 **82** DQ40
Harrow HA2 **116** CB61
Ruislip HA4 **116** BX63
St. Albans AL1 **43** CE22
Monks Cres, Add. KT15 **212** BH106
Walton-on-Thames KT12 **195** BV102
Monksdene Gdns, Sutt. SM1 **200** DB104
Monks Dr, W3 **138** CN71
Monksfield Way, Slou. SL2 **131** AN69
Monks Grn, Lthd. (Fetch.) KT22 **230** CC121
Monksgrove, Loug. IG10 **85** EN43
Monks Horton Way, St.Alb. AL1 **43** CH18
Monksmead, Borwd. WD6 **78** CQ42
Sch **Monksmead First Sch**, Borwd. WD6 *off Hillside Av* **78** CQ41
MONKS ORCHARD, Croy. CR0 **203** DZ101
Monks Orchard, Dart. DA1 **188** FJ89
Sch **Monks Orchard Prim Sch**, Croy. CR0 *off The Glade* **203** DX99
Monks Orchard Rd, Beck. BR3 **203** EA102
Monks Pk, Wem. HA9 **138** CQ65
Monks Pk Gdns, Wem. HA9 **138** CP65
Monks Pl, Cat. CR3 *off Tillingdown Hill* **236** DU122
Monk's Ridge, N20 **97** CV46
Monks Ri, Welw.G.C. AL8 **29** CX05
Monks Rd, Bans. SM7 **234** DA116
Enfield EN2 **82** DQ40
Virginia Water GU25 **192** AX98
Windsor SL4 **151** AK82
Monk St, SE18 **165** EN77
Monks Wk, Cher. KT16 **193** BE98
Gravesend (Sthflt) DA13 **190** GA93
Monk's Wk, Reig. RH2 **250** DB134
Monks Way, NW11 *off Hurstwood Rd* **119** CZ56
Beckenham BR3 **203** EA99
Orpington BR5 **205** EQ102
Staines TW18 **174** BK94
West Drayton UB7 **154** BL79
Monks Well, Green. DA9 **169** FV84
Monkswell Ct, N10 *off Pembroke Rd* **98** DG53
Monkswell La, Couls. CR5 **234** DB124
Monkswick Rd, Harl. CM20 **35** ET13
Monkswood, Welw.G.C. AL8 **29** CW05
Monkswood Av, Wal.Abb. EN9 **67** ED33
Monkswood Gdns, Borwd. WD6 **78** CR42
Ilford IG5 **125** EN55
Monkton Rd, Well. DA16 **165** ET82
Monkton St, SE11 **20** D7
Monkville Av, NW11 **119** CZ56
Monkwell Sq, EC2 **11** H6
Monkwood Cl, Rom. RM1 **127** FG57
Monmouth Av, E18 **124** EH56
Kingston upon Thames KT1 **177** CJ94
Monmouth Cl, W4 *off Beaumont Rd* **158** CR76
Mitcham CR4 *off Recreation Way* **201** DL98
Welling DA16 **166** EU84
Monmouth Gro, Brent. TW8 *off Sterling Pl* **158** CL77
Monmouth Pl, W2 **7** H8
Monmouth Rd, E6 **145** EM69
N9 **100** DV47
W2 **7** H8
Dagenham RM9 **126** EZ64
Hayes UB3 **155** BS77
Watford WD17 **75** BV41
Monmouth St, WC2 **9** N8
Monnery Rd, N19 **121** DJ62
Monnow Grn, S.Ock. (Aveley) RM15 *off Monnow Rd* **148** FQ73
Monnow Rd, SE1 **22** A9
South Ockendon (Aveley) RM15 **148** FQ73
Mono La, Felt. TW13 **175** BV89
Monoux Gro, E17 **101** EA53
Monro Dr, Guil. GU2 **242** AU131
Monroe Cres, Enf. EN1 **82** DV39
Monroe Dr, SW14 **178** CP85
Monro Gdns, Har. HA3 **95** CE52
Monro Pl, Epsom KT19 **216** CN109
Monro Way, E5 **122** DV63
Monsal Ct, E5 *off Redwald Rd* **123** DX63
Monsell Ct, N4 *off Monsell Rd* **121** DP62
Monsell Gdns, Stai. TW18 **173** BE92
Monsell Rd, N4 **121** DP62
Sch **Monson Prim Sch**, SE14 *off Hunsdon Rd* **163** DX80
Monson Rd, NW10 **139** CU68
SE14 **163** DX80
Broxbourne EN10 **49** DZ20
Redhill RH1 **250** DF130
Mons Wk, Egh. TW20 **173** BC92
Mons Way, Brom. BR2 **204** EL100
Montacute Rd, SE6 **183** DZ87
Bushey (Bushey Hth) WD23 **95** CE45
Croydon (New Adgtn) CR0 **221** EC109
Morden SM4 **200** DD100
Montagu Cres, N18 **100** DV49
Montague Av, SE4 **163** DZ84
W7 **137** CF74
South Croydon CR2 **220** DS112
Montague Cl, SE1 **21** J1
Walton-on-Thames KT12 **195** BU101
Montague Dr, Cat. CR3 *off Drake Av* **236** DQ122
Montague Gdns, W3 **138** CN73
Montague Hall Pl, Bushey WD23 **76** CA44
Montague Pl, WC1 **9** M5
Montague Rd, E8 **122** DU64
E11 **124** EF61
N8 **121** DM57
N15 **122** DU56
SW19 **180** DB94
Montague Rd, W7 **137** CF74
W13 **137** CH72
Berkhamsted HP4 **38** AV19
Croydon CR0 **201** DP102
Hounslow TW3 **156** CB83
Richmond TW10 **178** CL86
Slough SL1 **132** AT73
Slough (Datchet) SL3 **152** AV81
Southall UB2 **156** BY77
Uxbridge UB8 **134** BK66
Montague Sq, SE15 *off Clifton Way* **162** DW80
Montague St, EC1 **10** G6
WC1 **9** N5
Montague Waye, Sthl. UB2 **156** BY76
Montagu Gdns, N18 **100** DV49
Wallington SM6 **219** DJ105
Montagu Mans, W1 **8** D5
Montagu Ms N, W1 **8** D6
Montagu Ms S, W1 **8** D7
Montagu Ms W, W1 **8** D7
Montagu Pl, W1 **8** C6
Montagu Rd, N9 **100** DW49
N18 **100** DV50
NW4 **119** CU58
Montagu Rd Ind Est, N18 **100** DW49
Montagu Row, W1 **8** D6
Montagu Sq, W1 **8** D6
Montagu St, W1 **8** D7
Montaigne Cl, SW1 **19** M7
Montalt Rd, Wdf.Grn. IG8 **102** EF50
Montana Cl, S.Croy. CR2 **220** DR110
Montana Gdns, SE26 **183** DZ92
Sutton SM1 *off Lind Rd* **218** DC106
Montana Rd, SW17 **180** DG91
SW20 **199** CW95
Montayne Rd, Wal.Cr. (Chsht) EN8 **67** DX32
Sch **Montbelle Prim Sch**, SE9 *off Montbelle Rd* **185** EP90
Montbelle Rd, SE9 **185** EP90
Montbretia Cl, Orp. BR5 **206** EW98
Montcalm Cl, Brom. BR2 **204** EG100
Hayes UB4 *off Ayles Rd* **135** BV69
Montcalm Rd, SE7 **164** EK80
Montclare St, E2 **11** N2
Monteagle Av, Bark. IG11 **145** EQ65
Sch **Monteagle Prim Sch**, Dag. RM9 *off Burnham Rd* **146** EV66
Monteagle Way, E5 *off Rendlesham Rd* **122** DU62
SE15 **162** DV83
Montefiore St, SW8 **161** DH82
Montego Cl, SE24 *off Railton Rd* **161** DN84
Sch **Montem First Sch**, Slou. SL1 *off Chalvey Gro* **151** AP75
Sch **Montem Inf & Jun Sch**, N7 *off Hornsey Rd* **121** DM62
Montem La, Slou. SL1 **131** AR74
Sch **Montem Mid Sch**, Slou. SL1 *off Chalvey Gro* **151** AP75
Montem Rd, SE23 **183** DZ87
New Malden KT3 **198** CS98
Montem St, N4 *off Thorpedale Rd* **121** DM60
Montenotte Rd, N8 **121** DJ57
Monterey Cl, Bex. DA5 **187** FC89
Montesole Ct, Pnr. HA5 **94** BW54
Montevetro, SW11 **160** DD81
Montford Pl, SE11 **20** C10
Montford Rd, Sun. TW16 **195** BU98
Montfort Gdns, Ilf. IG6 **103** EQ51
Montfort Pl, SW19 **179** CX88
Montfort Ri, Red. RH1 **266** DF142
Montgolfier Wk, Nthlt. UB5 *off Jetstar Way* **136** BY69
Montgomerie Cl, Berk. HP4 *off Mortain Dr* **38** AU17
Montgomerie Dr, Guil. GU2 **242** AU129
Montgomery Av, Esher KT10 **197** CE104
Hemel Hempstead HP2 **40** BN19
Montgomery Cl, Grays RM16 **170** GC75
Mitcham CR4 **201** DL98
Sidcup DA15 **185** ET86
Montgomery Ct, W4 *off St. Thomas' Rd* **158** CQ79
Montgomery Cres, Rom. RM3 **106** FJ50
Montgomery Dr, Wal.Cr. (Chsht) EN8 **67** DY28
Montgomery Pl, Slou. SL2 **132** AW72
Montgomery Rd, W4 **158** CQ77
Dartford (S.Darenth) DA4 **209** FR95
Edgware HA8 **96** CM51
Woking GU22 **226** AY118
Montgomery St, E14 **24** B2
Montholme Rd, SW11 **180** DF86
Monthope Rd, E1 **12** A6
Montolieu Gdns, SW15 **179** CV85
Montpelier Av, W5 **137** CJ71
Bexley DA5 **186** EX87
Montpelier Cl, Uxb. UB10 **134** BN67
Montpelier Ct, Wind. SL4 *off St. Leonards Rd* **151** AQ82
Montpelier Gdns, E6 **144** EK69
Romford RM6 **126** EW59
Montpelier Gro, NW5 **121** DJ64
Montpelier Ms, SW7 **18** B5
Montpelier Pl, E1 **12** E8
SW7 **18** B5
Sch **Montpelier Prim Sch**, W5 *off Helena Rd* **137** CK71
Montpelier Ri, NW11 **119** CY59
Wembley HA9 **117** CK60
Montpelier Rd, N3 **98** DC53
SE15 **162** DV81
W5 **137** CK71
Purley CR8 **219** DP110
Sutton SM1 **218** DC105
Montpelier Row, SE3 **164** EF82
Twickenham TW1 **177** CH87
Montpelier Sq, SW7 **18** B4
Montpelier St, SW7 **18** B4
Montpelier Ter, SW7 **18** B4
Montpelier Vale, SE3 **164** EF82
Montpelier Wk, SW7 **18** B5
Montpelier Way, NW11 **119** CY59
Montrave Rd, SE20 **182** DW93
Montreal Pl, WC2 **10** A9
Montreal Rd, Ilf. IG1 **125** EQ59
Sevenoaks TN13 **256** FE123
Tilbury RM18 **171** GG82
Montrell Rd, SW2 **181** DL88
Montrose Av, NW6 **139** CY68
Edgware HA8 **96** CQ54
Romford RM2 **106** FJ54

Montrose Av, Sid. DA15 . . . .186 EU87
Slough SL1 . . . . .131 AP72
Slough (Datchet) SL3 . . . .152 AW80
Twickenham TW2 . . . . . . .176 CB87
Welling DA16 . . . . .165 ER83
Montrose Cl, Ashf. TW15 . . . .175 BQ93
Welling DA16 . . . . .165 ET83
Woodford Green IG8 . . . . .102 EG49
Montrose Ct, SW7 . . . . .17 P4
Montrose Cres, N12 . . . . .98 DC51
Wembley HA0 . . . . .138 CL65
Montrose Gdns, Lthd.
(Oxshott) KT22 . . . . .215 CD112
Mitcham CR4 . . . . .200 DF97
Sutton SM1 . . . . .200 DB103
Montrose Pl, SW1 . . . . .18 F4
Montrose Rd, Felt. TW14 . . .175 BR86
Harrow HA3 . . . . .95 CE54
Montrose Wk, Wey. KT13 . . .195 BP104
Montrose Way, SE23 . . . . . .183 DX88
Slough (Datchet) SL3 . . . .152 AX81
Montrouge Cres, Epsom
KT17 . . . . .233 CW116
Montserrat Av, Wdf.Grn.
IG8 . . . . .101 ED52
Montserrat Cl, SE19 . . . . . . .182 DR92
Montserrat Rd, SW15 . . . . . .159 CY84
⊖ Monument 11 K9
★ Monument, The, EC3 . . . . .11 K10
Monument Gdns, SE13 . . . . .183 EC85
Monument Grn, Wey. KT13 .195 BP104
Monument Hill, Wey. KT13 .213 BP105
Monument La, Ger.Cr.
(Chal.St.P.) SL9 . . . . .90 AY51
Monument Rd, Wey. KT13 . .213 BP105
Woking GU21 . . . . .211 BA114
Monument St, EC3 . . . . .11 K9
Monument Way, N17 . . . . . .122 DT55
Monument Way E, Wok.
GU21 . . . . .227 BB115
Monument Way W, Wok.
GU21 . . . . .227 BA115
Monza St, E1 . . . . .12 E10
Moodkee St, SE16 . . . . .22 E5
Moody Rd, SE15 . . . . .162 DT80
Moody St, E1 . . . . .13 H2
Moon Ct, Lthd. KT22
off Pound Cres 231 CD121
Moon La, Barn. EN5 . . . . . . .79 CZ41
Moon St, N1 . . . . .4 E7
Moorcroft Gdns, Brom. BR2
off Southborough Rd 204 EL99
Moorcroft La, Uxb. UB8 . . . .134 BN71
Moorcroft Rd, SW16 . . . . . .181 DL90
Sch Moorcroft Spec Sch, Uxb.
UB8 off Bramble Cl 134 BM72
Moorcroft Way, Pnr. HA5 . . .116 BY57
Moordown, SE18 . . . . .165 EN81
Moore Av, Grays RM20 . . . .170 FY78
Tilbury RM18 . . . . .171 GH82
Moore Cl, SW14
off Little St. Leonards . . .158 CQ83
Addlestone KT15 . . . . . . .212 BH106
Dartford DA2 . . . . .189 FR89
Mitcham CR4 . . . . .201 DH96
Slough SL1 . . . . .151 AP75
Wallington SM6
off Brabazon Av 219 DL109
Moore Cres, Dag. RM9 . . . . .146 EV67
Moorefield Rd, N17 . . . . . . .100 DT54
Moore Gro Cres, Egh. TW20 .172 AY94
Moorehead Way, SE3 . . . . . .164 EH83
Mooreland Rd, Brom. BR1 . . .184 EF94
Moor End, Maid. SL6 . . . . . .150 AC78
Moorend, Welw.G.C. AL7 . . . .30 DA12
Moor End Rd, Hem.H. HP1 . . .40 BJ21
Moore Pk Rd, SW6 . . . . .160 DB80
Moore Rd, SE19 . . . . .182 DQ93
Berkhamsted HP4 . . . . .38 AT17
Swanscombe DA10 . . . . . .190 FY86
Moores La, Wind.
(Eton Wick) SL4 . . . . . . .151 AM77
Moores Pl, Brwd. CM14 . . . .108 FX47
Moores Rd, Dor. RH4 . . . . . .263 CH135
Moore St, SW3 . . . . .18 C7
Moore Wk, E7
off Stracey Rd 124 EG63
Moore Way, SE22
off Lordship La 182 DU88
Sutton SM2 . . . . .218 DA109
Moorey Cl, E15
off Stephen's Rd 144 EF67
Moorfield, Dor. (Holm.) RH5 .263 CK144
Harlow CM18 . . . . .51 EQ20
Moorfield Av, W5 . . . . .137 CK70
Moorfield Rd, Chess. KT9 . . .216 CL106
Enfield EN3 . . . . .82 DW39
Guildford GU1 . . . . .242 AX130
Orpington BR6 . . . . .206 EU101
Uxbridge UB8 . . . . .134 BK72
Uxbridge (Hare.) UB9 . . . .114 BG59
Moorfields, EC2 . . . . .11 J6
Moorfields Cl, Stai. TW18 . . .193 BE95
H Moorfields Eye Hosp,
EC1 . . . . .11 J2
Moorfields Highwalk,
EC2 off Fore St 142 DR71
Sch Moorfields Prim Sch,
EC1 . . . . .11 J3
Moor Furlong, Slou. SL1 . . . .131 AL74
⇌ Moorgate 11 J6
⊖ Moorgate 11 J6
Moorgate, EC2 . . . . .11 J7
Moorgate Pl, EC2 . . . . .11 J7
Moor Hall Rd, Harl. CM17 . . .36 EZ11
Moorhall Rd, Uxb. (Hare.)
UB9 . . . . .114 BH58
Moorhayes Dr, Stai. TW18 . .194 BJ97
Moorhen Cl, Erith DA8 . . . . .167 FH80
Moorhen Way, Harl. (Roydon)
CM19 off Roydon Mill Pk . .34 EG14
Moorholme, Wok. GU22
off Oakbank 226 AY119
MOORHOUSE BANK, West.
TN16 . . . . .255 EM128
Moorhouse Rd, W2 . . . . .6 G7
Harrow HA3 . . . . .117 CK55
Oxted RH8 . . . . .255 EM131
Westerham TN16 . . . . . . .255 EM128
Sch Moor Ho Sch, Oxt. RH8
off Mill La 254 EF132
Moorhurst Av, Wal.Cr.
(Chsht) EN7 . . . . .65 DN29
Moorings, SE28 . . . . .146 EV73
Moorings, The, Lthd. (Bkhm)
KT23 off Church Rd 246 CA125
Windsor SL4
off Straight Rd 172 AW87
Moorland Cl, Rom. RM5 . . . .105 FB52
Moorland Cl, Twick. TW2
off Telford Rd 176 CA87
Moorland Rd, SW9 . . . . . . .161 DP84
Hemel Hempstead HP1 . . .40 BG22
West Drayton UB7 . . . . . .154 BJ79
Moorlands, St.Alb. (Frog.)
AL2 off Frogmore 61 CE28
Welwyn Garden City AL7 . .30 DA12
Moorlands, The, Wok. GU22 .227 AZ121
Moorlands Av, NW7 . . . . .97 CV51
Moorlands Est, SW9 . . . . . .161 DN84
Moorlands Reach, Saw.
CM21 . . . . .36 EZ06
Moor La, EC2 . . . . .11 J6
Chessington KT9 . . . . . . .216 CL105
Rickmansworth WD3 . . . . .92 BM47
Rickmansworth (Sarratt)
WD3 . . . . .73 BE36
Staines TW18, TW19 . . . . .173 BE90
Upminster RM14 . . . . . . .129 FS60
West Drayton UB7 . . . . . .154 BJ79
Woking GU22 . . . . .226 AY122
Moor La Crossing, Wat.
WD18 . . . . .93 BQ46
Sch Moor La Jun Sch, Chess.
KT9 off Moor La 216 CM106
Moormead Dr, Epsom KT19 .216 CS106
Moor Mead Rd, Twick. TW1 .177 CG86
Moormede Cres, Stai. TW18 173 BF91
Moor Mill La, St.Alb.
(Coln.St) AL2 . . . . .61 CE29
MOOR PARK, Nthwd. HA6 . . .93 BQ49
⊖ Moor Park 93 BR48
Moor Pk Est, Nthwd. HA6 . . .93 BQ49
Moor Pk Gdns, Kings.T. KT2 .178 CS94
Moor Pk Ind Est, Wat. WD18 . .93 BQ45
★ Moor Park Mansion,
Rick. WD3 . . . . .92 BN48
Moor Pk Rd, Nthwd. HA6 . . . .93 BR50
Moor Pl, EC2 . . . . .11 J6
Moor Rd, Chesh. HP5 . . . . . .54 AQ32
Moor Rd, The, Sev. TN14 . . .241 FH120
Moors, The, Welw.G.C. AL7 . .30 DA08
Moorside, Hem.H. HP3
off Stratford Way 40 BH23
High Wycombe
(Woob.Grn) HP10 . . . . . .110 AE55
Welwyn Garden City AL7 . .30 DA12
Moorside Rd, Brom. BR1 . . .184 EE90
Moorsom Way, Couls. CR5 .235 DK117
Moorstown Ct, Slou. SL1 . .152 AS75
Moor St, W1 . . . . .9 M8
Moors Wk, Welw.G.C. AL7 . . .30 DC09
Moor Twr, Harl. CM18 . . . . . .51 ET16
Moortown Rd, Wat. WD19 . . .94 BW49
Moor Vw, Wat. WD18 . . . . . . .93 BU45
Moot Ct, NW9 . . . . .118 CN57
Moran Cl, St.Alb. (Brick.Wd)
AL2 . . . . .60 BZ31
Morant Gdns, Rom. RM5 . . .105 FB50
Morant Pl, N22
off Commerce Rd 99 DM53
Morant Rd, Grays RM16 . . .171 GH76
Morants Ct Cross, Sev.
(Dunt.Grn) TN14 . . . . . . .241 FB118
Morants Ct Rd, Sev.
(Dunt.Grn) TN13 . . . . . . .241 FC118
Morant St, E14 . . . . .13 P9
Sch Mora Prim Sch, NW2
off Mora Rd 119 CW63
Mora Rd, NW2 . . . . .119 CW63
Mora St, EC1 . . . . .11 H2
Morat St, SW9 . . . . .161 DM81
Moravian Pl, SW10
off Milman's St 160 DD79
Moravian St, E2 . . . . .142 DW69
Moray Av, Hayes UB3 . . . . .135 BT74
Moray Cl, Edg. HA8
off Pentland Av 96 CP47
Romford RM1 . . . . .105 FE52
Moray Dr, Slou. SL2 . . . . . . .132 AU72
Moray Ms, N7
off Durham Rd 121 DM61
Moray Rd, N4 . . . . .121 DM61
Moray Way, Rom. RM1 . . . . .105 FD52
Morcote Cl, Guil. (Shalf.)
GU4 . . . . .258 AY141
Mordaunt Gdns, Dag. RM9 .146 EY66
Mordaunt Ho, NW10 . . . . . .138 CR67
Mordaunt Rd, NW10 . . . . . .138 CR67
Mordaunt St, SW9 . . . . .161 DM83
MORDEN, SM4 . . . . .200 DA97
⊖ Morden 200 DB97
Morden Cl, Tad. KT20
off Marbles Way 233 CX120
Morden Ct, Mord. SM4 . . . . .200 DB98
Morden Gdns, Grnf. UB6 . . .117 CF64
Mitcham CR4 . . . . .200 DD98
★ Morden Hall Pk N.T.,
Mord. SM4 . . . . .200 DB97
Morden Hall Rd, Mord. SM4 200 DB97
Morden Hill, SE13 . . . . .163 EC82
Morden La, SE13 . . . . .163 EC81
Sch Morden Mt Prim Sch,
SE13 off Lewisham Rd . .163 EB82
MORDEN PARK, Mord. SM4 .199 CY99
Sch Morden Prim Sch, Mord.
SM4 off London Rd 200 DA99
Tra Morden Road 200 DB96
Morden Rd, SE3 . . . . .164 EG82
SW19 . . . . .200 DB95
Mitcham CR4 . . . . .200 DC98
Romford RM6 . . . . .126 EY59
Morden Rd Ms, SE3 . . . . . . .164 EG82
⇌ Morden South 200 DA99
Morden St, SE13 . . . . .163 EB81
Morden Way, Sutt. SM3 . . . .200 DA101
Morden Wf Rd, SE10 . . . . . . .24 G6
Mordon Rd, Ilf. IG3 . . . . . . .125 ET59
Mordred Rd, SE6 . . . . .184 EE89
Moreau Wk, Slou. (Geo.Grn)
SL3 off Alan Way 132 AY72
Morecambe Cl, E1 . . . . .12 G5
Hornchurch RM12 . . . . . .127 FH64
Morecambe Gdns, Stan.
HA7 . . . . .95 CK49
Morecambe St, SE17 . . . . . . .21 H8
Morecambe Ter, N18 . . . . . .100 DR49
More Circle, Gdmg. GU7 . . .258 AS144
More Cl, E16 . . . . .15 K7
W14 . . . . .16 B8
Purley CR8 . . . . .219 DN111
Morecoombe Cl, Kings.T.
KT2 . . . . .178 CP94
Moree Way, N18 . . . . .100 DU49
Sch More Ho Sch, SW1 . . . . . .18 D6
Moreland Av, Grays RM16 . .170 GC75
Slough (Colnbr.) SL3 . . . .153 BC80
Moreland Cl, Slou. (Colnbr.)
SL3
off Moreland Av 153 BC80
Moreland Dr, Ger.Cr. SL9 . . .113 AZ59
Sch Moreland Prim Sch, EC1 .10 F1
Moreland St, EC1 . . . . .10 F1
Moreland Way, E4 . . . . .101 EB48
More La, Esher KT10 . . . . . .196 CB103
Morel Ct, Sev. TN13 . . . . . . .257 FH122
Morella Cl, Vir.W. GU25 . . . .192 AW98
Morella Rd, SW12 . . . . .180 DF87
Morell Cl, Barn. EN5
off Galdana Av 80 DC41
Morello Av, Uxb. UB8 . . . . .135 BP71
Morello Cl, Swan. BR8 . . . . .207 FD98
Morello Dr, Slou. SL3 . . . . . .133 AZ74
Moremead, Wal.Abb. EN9 . . .67 ED33
Moremead Rd, SE6 . . . . .183 DZ91
Morena St, SE6 . . . . .183 EB87
More Rd, Gdmg. GU7 . . . . . .258 AS144
Moresby Av, Surb. KT5 . . . .198 CP101
Moresby Rd, E5 . . . . .122 DV60
Moresby Wk, SW8 . . . . .161 DH82
Moretaine Rd, Ashf. TW15
off Hengrove Cres 174 BK90
MORETON, Ong. CM5 . . . . . .53 FH20
Moreton Av, Islw. TW7 . . . . .157 CE81
Moreton Cl, E5 . . . . .122 DW61
N15 . . . . .122 DR58
NW7 . . . . .97 CW51
SW1 . . . . .19 K9
Swanley BR8
off Bonney Way 207 FE96
Waltham Cross (Chsht)
EN7 . . . . .66 DV27
Moreton Gdns, Wdf.Grn.
IG8 . . . . .102 EL50
Moreton Gate, Ong. CM5
off Pedlars End 53 FH21
Moreton Ind Est, Swan.
BR8 . . . . .207 FH98
Moreton Pl, SW1 . . . . .19 K9
Moreton Rd, N15 . . . . .122 DR58
Ongar (Moreton) CM5 . . . .53 FG24
South Croydon CR2 . . . . .220 DR106
Worcester Park KT4 . . . . .199 CU103
Moreton St, SW1 . . . . .19 K9
Moreton Ter, SW1 . . . . .19 K9
Moreton Ter Ms N, SW1 . . . . .19 K9
Moreton Ter Ms S, SW1 . . . . .19 K9
Moreton Twr, W3 . . . . .138 CP74
Moreton Way, Slou. SL1 . . . .131 AK74
Morewood Cl, Sev. TN13 . . .256 FF123
Morewood Cl Ind Pk, Sev.
TN13 off Morewood Cl .256 FF123
Morford Cl, Ruis. HA4 . . . . .115 BV59
Morford Way, Ruis. HA4 . . . .115 BV59
Morgan Av, E17 . . . . .123 ED56
Morgan Cl, Dag. RM10 . . . . .146 FA66
Northwood HA6 . . . . .93 BT51
Morgan Cres, Epp. (They.B.)
CM16 . . . . .85 ER36
Morgan Dr, Green. DA9 . . . .189 FS87
Morgan Gdns, Wat. (Ald.)
WD25 . . . . .76 CB38
Morgan Rd, N7 . . . . .4 C2
W10 . . . . .6 E5
Bromley BR1 . . . . .184 EG94
Morgans Cl, Hert. SG13 . . . .32 DR11
Morgans La, SE1 . . . . .21 L2
Hayes UB3 . . . . .135 BR71
Morgans Rd, Hert. SG13 . . . .32 DR11
Morgan St, E3 . . . . .13 K2
E16 . . . . .15 K5
Morgans Wk, Hert. SG13 . . . .32 DR12
Sch Morgans Wk JMI Sch, Hert.
SG13 off Morgans Rd . . .32 DR11
Morgan Way, Rain. RM13 . . .148 FJ69
Woodford Green IG8 . . . .102 EL51
Sch Moriah Jewish Day Sch,
Pnr. HA5
off Cannon La 116 BY60
Moriatry Cl, N7 . . . . .121 DL63
Morice Rd, Hodd. EN11 . . . . .49 DZ15
Morie St, SW18 . . . . .180 DB85
Morieux Rd, E10 . . . . .123 DZ60
Moring Rd, SW17 . . . . .180 DG91
Morkyns Wk, SE21 . . . . .182 DS90
Morland Av, Croy. CR0 . . . .202 DS102
Dartford DA1 . . . . .187 FH85
Morland Cl, NW11 . . . . .120 DB60
Hampton TW12 . . . . .176 BZ92
Mitcham CR4 . . . . .200 DE97
Morland Gdns, NW10 . . . . .138 CR66
Southall UB1 . . . . .136 CB74
Morland Ms, N1 . . . . .4 D6
Morland Rd, E17 . . . . .123 DX57
SE20 . . . . .183 DX93
Croydon CR0 . . . . .202 DS102
Dagenham RM10 . . . . . . .146 FA66
Harrow HA3 . . . . .118 CL57
Ilford IG1 . . . . .125 EP61
Sutton SM1 . . . . .218 DC106
H Morland Rd Day Hosp,
Dag. RM10 . . . . .146 FA66
Morland Way, Wal.Cr.
(Chsht) EN8 . . . . .67 DY28
Morley Av, E4 . . . . .101 ED52
N18 . . . . .100 DU49
N22 . . . . .99 DN54
Morley Cl, Orp. BR6 . . . . . . .205 EP103
Slough SL3 . . . . .153 AZ75
Coll Morley Coll, SE1 . . . . . . .20 D5
Morley Cres, Edg. HA8 . . . . . .96 CQ47
Ruislip HA4 . . . . .116 BW61
Morley Cres E, Stan. HA7 . . . .95 CJ54
Morley Cres W, Stan. HA7 . . .95 CJ54
Morley Gro, Harl. CM20 . . . . .35 EQ13
Morley Hill, Enf. EN2 . . . . . . .82 DR38
Morley Rd, E10 . . . . .123 EC60
E15 . . . . .144 EF68
SE13 . . . . .163 EC84
Barking IG11 . . . . .145 ER67
Chislehurst BR7 . . . . .205 EQ95
Romford RM6 . . . . .126 EY57
South Croydon CR2 . . . . .220 DT110
Sutton SM3 . . . . .199 CZ102
Twickenham TW1 . . . . . . .177 CK86
Morley Sq, Grays RM16 . . . .171 GG77
Morley St, SE1 . . . . .20 D5
Morna Rd, SE5 . . . . .162 DQ82
Morning La, E9 . . . . .142 DW65
Morning Ri, Rick. (Loud.)
WD3 . . . . .74 BK41
Sch Morningside JMI Sch,
E9 off Chatham Pl 142 DW65
Morningside Rd, Wor.Pk.
KT4 . . . . .199 CV103
Mornington Av, W14 . . . . . . .16 E8
Bromley BR1 . . . . .204 EJ97
Ilford IG1 . . . . .125 EN59
Mornington Cl, West.
(Bigg.H.) TN16 . . . . .238 EK117
Woodford Green IG8 . . . .102 EG49
Mornington Ct, Bex. DA5 . . .187 FC88
⊖ Mornington Crescent . . .141 DH68
Mornington Cres, NW1 . . . .141 DJ68
Hounslow TW5 . . . . .155 BV81
Mornington Gro, E3 . . . . . . .13 N2
Mornington Ms, SE5 . . . . . .162 DQ81
Mornington Pl, NW1
off Mornington Ter 141 DH68
Mornington Rd, E4 . . . . .101 ED45
E11 . . . . .124 EF60
SE8 . . . . .163 DZ80
Ashford TW15 . . . . .175 BQ92
Greenford UB6 . . . . .136 CB71
Loughton IG10 . . . . .85 EQ41
Radlett WD7 . . . . .61 CG34
Woodford Green IG8 . . . .102 EF49
Morningtons, Harl. CM19 . . . .51 EQ20
Mornington St, NW1 . . . . . .141 DH68
Mornington Ter, NW1 . . . . . .141 DH67
Mornington Wk, Rich. TW10 .177 CK91
Morocco St, SE1 . . . . .21 L4
Morpeth Av, Borwd. WD6 . . .78 CM38
Morpeth Cl, Hem.H. HP2
off York Way 40 BL21
Morpeth Gro, E9 . . . . .143 DX67
Morpeth Rd, E9 . . . . .142 DW67
Sch Morpeth Sch, E2 . . . . . . .12 F2
Annexe, E2 . . . . .12 E2
Morpeth St, E2 . . . . .12 G1
Morpeth Ter, SW1 . . . . .19 J6
Morpeth Wk, N17
off West Rd 100 DV52
Morrab Gdns, Ilf. IG3 . . . . .125 ET62
Morrell Ct, Welw.G.C. AL7 . . .29 CZ08
Morrice Cl, Slou. SL3 . . . . . .153 AZ77
Morris Av, E12 . . . . .125 EM64
Morris Cl, Croy. CR0 . . . . . .203 DY100
Gerrards Cross
(Chal.St.P.) SL9 . . . . .91 AZ53
Orpington BR6 . . . . .205 ES104
Morris Ct, E4 . . . . .101 EB48
Enfield EN3
off Martini Dr 83 EA37
Waltham Abbey EN9 . . . . .68 EF34
Morris Gdns, SW18 . . . . . . .180 DA87
Dartford DA1 . . . . .188 FN85
Morris Ho, Harl. CM18
off Tendring Rd 51 EQ18
Morrish Rd, SW2 . . . . .181 DL87
Morrison Av, E4 . . . . .101 EA51
N17 . . . . .122 DS55
Morrison Rd, Bark. IG11 . . . .146 EY68
Hayes UB4 . . . . .135 BV69
Morrison St, SW11 . . . . .160 DG83
Morris Pl, N4 . . . . .121 DN61
Morris Rd, E14 . . . . .14 A5
E15 . . . . .124 EE63
Dagenham RM8 . . . . .126 EZ61
Isleworth TW7 . . . . .157 CF83
Redhill (S.Nutfld) RH1 . . .267 DL136
Romford RM3 . . . . .105 FH52
Morris St, E1 . . . . .12 D8
Morriston Cl, Wat. WD19 . . . .94 BW50
Morris Way, St.Alb. (Lon.Col.)
AL2 . . . . .62 CL26
Morse Cl, E13 . . . . .15 L2
Uxbridge (Hare.) UB9 . . . . .92 BJ54
Morshead Rd, W9 . . . . .7 H2
Morson Rd, Enf. EN3 . . . . . . .83 DY44
Morston Cl, Tad. KT20
off Waterfield 233 CV120
Morston Gdns, SE9 . . . . . . .185 EM91
Mortain Dr, Berk. HP4 . . . . . .38 AT17
Morten Cl, SW4 . . . . .181 DK86
Morten Gdns, Uxb. (Denh.)
UB9 . . . . .114 BG59
Mortens Wd, Amer. HP7 . . . . .55 AR40
Morteyne Rd, N17 . . . . .100 DR53
Mortgramit Sq, SE18
off Powis St 165 EN76
Mortham St, E15 . . . . .143 ED67
Mortimer Cl, NW2 . . . . .119 CZ62
SW16 . . . . .181 DK89
Bushey WD23 . . . . .76 CB44
Mortimer Cres, NW6 . . . . . .140 DB67
Worcester Park KT4 . . . . .198 CR104
Mortimer Dr, Enf. EN1 . . . . . .82 DR43
Mortimer Est, NW6 . . . . . . .140 DB67
Mortimer Gate, Wal.Cr. EN8 .67 DZ27
Mortimer Ho, W11
off St. Anns Rd 139 CX74
Mortimer Mkt, WC1 . . . . .9 K4
Mortimer Pl, NW6 . . . . .140 DB67
Mortimer Rd, E6 . . . . .145 EM69
N1 .5 M6
NW10 . . . . .139 CW69
W13 . . . . .137 CJ72
Erith DA8 . . . . .167 FD79
Mitcham CR4 . . . . .200 DF95
Orpington BR6 . . . . .206 EU103
Slough SL3 . . . . .152 AX76
Westerham (Bigg.H.)
TN16 . . . . .222 EJ112
Mortimer Sq, W11 . . . . .6 B10
Mortimer St, W1 . . . . .9 J7
Mortimer Ter, NW5
off Gordon Ho Rd 121 DH63
MORTLAKE, SW14 . . . . .158 CQ83
⇌ Mortlake 158 CQ83
Mortlake Cl, Croy. CR0
off Richmond Rd 201 DL104
Mortlake Dr, Mitch. CR4 . . . .200 DE95
Mortlake High St, SW14 . . . .158 CR83
Mortlake Rd, E16 . . . . .15 P7
Ilford IG1 . . . . .125 EQ63
Richmond TW9 . . . . .158 CN80
Mortlake Ter, Rich. TW9
off Kew Rd 158 CN80
Mortlock Cl, SE15
off Cossall Wk 162 DV81
Morton, Tad. KT20
off Hudsons 233 CX121
Morton Cl, Uxb. UB8
off Pield Heath Rd 134 BM70
Wallington SM6 . . . . .219 DM108
Woking GU21 . . . . .226 AW115
Morton Ct, Nthlt. UB5 . . . . .116 CC64
Morton Cres, N14 . . . . .99 DK49
Morton Dr, Slou. SL2 . . . . . .111 AL64
Morton Gdns, Wall. SM6 . . .219 DJ106
Morton Ms, SW5 . . . . .17 J8
Morton Pl, SE1 . . . . .20 C6
Morton Rd, E15 . . . . .144 EF66
N1 .5 H6
Morden SM4 . . . . .200 DD99
Woking GU21 . . . . .226 AW115
Morton Way, N14 . . . . .99 DJ48
Morvale Cl, Belv. DA17 . . . .166 EZ77
Morval Rd, SW2 . . . . .181 DN85
Morven Cl, Pot.B. EN6 . . . . . .64 DC31
Morven Rd, SW17 . . . . .180 DF90
Morville Ho, SW18
off Fitzhugh Gro 180 DD86
Morville St, E3 . . . . .143 EA68
Morwell St, WC1 . . . . .9 M6
Mosbach Gdns, Brwd.
(Hutt.) CM13 . . . . .109 GB47
Moscow Pl, W2 . . . . .7 J9
Moscow Rd, W2 . . . . .7 J9
Moseley Row, SE10 . . . . .25 K7
Moselle Av, N22 . . . . .99 DN54
Moselle Cl, N8
off Miles Rd 121 DM55
Moselle Ho, N17
off William St 100 DT52
Moselle Pl, N17 off High Rd .100 DT52
Moselle Rd, West. (Bigg.H.)
TN16 . . . . .238 EL118
Sch Moselle Spec Sch, The,
N17 off Adams Rd 100 DS54
Moselle St, N17 . . . . .100 DT52
Mosford Cl, Horl. RH6 . . . . .268 DF146
Mospey Cres, Epsom KT17 .233 CT115
Mosquito Way, Hat. AL10 . . . .44 CS17
Moss Bk, Grays RM17 . . . . .170 FZ78
Mossborough Cl, N12 . . . . . .98 DB51
Sch Mossbourne Comm Acad,
E5 off Downs Pk Rd 122 DU64
Mossbury Rd, SW11 . . . . . . .160 DE83
Moss Cl, E1 . . . . .12 B5
Pinner HA5 . . . . .94 BZ54
Rickmansworth WD3 . . . . .92 BK47
Mossdown Cl, Belv. DA17 . .166 FA77
Mossendew Cl, Uxb. (Hare.)
UB9 . . . . .92 BK53
Mossfield, Cob. KT11 . . . . . .213 BU113
Mossford Ct, Ilf. IG6 . . . . . .125 EP55
Mossford Grn, Ilf. IG6 . . . . .125 EP55
Sch Mossford Grn Prim Sch,
Ilf. IG6 off Fairlop Rd 103 EQ54
Mossford La, Ilf. IG6 . . . . . .103 EP54
Mossford St, E3 . . . . .13 L3
Moss Gdns, Felt. TW13 . . . .175 BU89
South Croydon CR2
off Warren Av 221 DX108
Moss Grn, Welw.G.C. AL7 . . .29 CY11
Moss Hall Ct, N12 . . . . .98 DB51
Moss Hall Cres, N12 . . . . . . .98 DB51
Moss Hall Gro, N12 . . . . .98 DB51
Sch Moss Hall Inf Sch, N12
off Moss Hall Gro 98 DB51
Sch Moss Hall Jun Sch, N3
off Nether St 98 DB53
Mossington Gdns, SE16 . . . .22 E8
Moss La, Pnr. HA5 . . . . .116 BZ55
Romford RM1
off Wheatsheaf Rd 127 FF58
Mosslea Rd, SE20 . . . . .182 DW93
Bromley BR2 . . . . .204 EK99
Orpington BR6 . . . . .205 EQ104
Whyteleafe CR3 . . . . .236 DT116
Mossop St, SW3 . . . . .18 B7
Moss Rd, Dag. RM10 . . . . . .146 FA66
South Ockendon RM15 . .149 FW71
Watford WD25 . . . . .59 BV34
Moss Side, St.Alb.
(Brick.Wd) AL2 . . . . .60 BZ30
Mossville Gdns, Mord. SM4 199 CZ97
Moss Way, Beac. HP9 . . . . . .88 AJ51
Dartford (Lane End) DA2 .189 FR91
Moston Cl, Hayes UB3
off Fuller Way 155 BT78
Mostyn Av, Wem. HA9 . . . . .118 CM64
Mostyn Gdns, NW10 . . . . .6 A1
Mostyn Gro, E3 . . . . .143 DZ68
Mostyn Rd, SW9 . . . . .161 DN81
SW19 . . . . .199 CZ95
Bushey WD23 . . . . .76 CC43
Edgware HA8 . . . . .96 CR52
Mostyn Ter, Red. RH1 . . . . .266 DG135
Mosul Way, Brom. BR2 . . . .204 EL100
Mosyer Dr, Orp. BR5 . . . . . .206 EX103
Motcomb St, SW1 . . . . .18 D5
Moth Cl, Wall. SM6 . . . . . . .219 DL108
Mothers' Sq, E5 . . . . .122 DV63
Motherwell Way, Grays
RM20 . . . . .169 FU78
Motley Av, EC2 . . . . .11 L3
Motley St, SW8
off St. Rule St 161 DJ82
MOTSPUR PARK, N.Mal.
KT3 . . . . .199 CU100
⇌ Motspur Park 199 CV99
Motspur Pk, N.Mal. KT3 . . .199 CT100
MOTTINGHAM, SE9 . . . . . . .184 EJ89
⇌ Mottingham 184 EL88
Mottingham Gdns, SE9 . . . .184 EK88
Mottingham La, SE9 . . . . . .184 EJ88
SE12 . . . . .184 EJ88
Sch Mottingham Prim Sch,
SE9 off Ravensworth Rd . .185 EM90
Mottingham Rd, N9 . . . . .83 DX44
SE9 . . . . .184 EL89
Mottisfont Rd, SE2 . . . . . . .166 EU76
Motts Hill La, Tad. KT20 . . . .233 CU123
Mott St, E4 . . . . .83 ED38
Loughton (High Beach)
IG10 . . . . .84 EF39
Mouchotte Cl, West.
(Bigg.H.) TN16 . . . . .222 EH112
Moulins Rd, E9 . . . . .142 DW67
Moulsford Ho, N7 . . . . .121 DK64
Moultain Hill, Swan. BR8 . . .207 FG98
Moulton Av, Houns. TW3 . . .156 BY82
Moultrie Way, Upmin. RM14 .129 FS59
Mound, The, SE9 . . . . .185 EN90
Moundfield Rd, N16 . . . . . . .122 DU58
Moundsfield Way, Slou. SL1 151 AL75
Mount, The, N20 . . . . .98 DC47
NW3 off Heath St 120 DC63
W3 . . . . .138 CP74
Brentwood CM14 . . . . . . .108 FW48
Coulsdon CR5 . . . . .234 DG115
Epsom (Ewell) KT17 . . . . .217 CT110
Esher KT10 . . . . .214 CA107
Guildford GU2 . . . . .258 AV137
Leatherhead (Fetch.)
KT22 . . . . .231 CE123
New Malden KT3 . . . . . . .199 CT97
Potters Bar EN6 . . . . .64 DB30
Rickmansworth WD3 . . . . .74 BJ44
Romford RM3 . . . . .106 FJ48
Tadworth KT20 . . . . .249 CZ126
Virginia Water GU25 . . . . .192 AX100
Waltham Cross (Chsht)
EN7 . . . . .66 DR26
Warlingham CR6 . . . . . . .236 DU119
Wembley HA9 . . . . .118 CP61
Weybridge KT13 . . . . .195 BS103
Woking GU21 . . . . .226 AX118
Woking (St.John's) GU21 .226 AU119
Worcester Park KT4 . . . . .217 CV105
Mountacre Cl, SE26 . . . . . . .182 DT91
Mount Adon Pk, SE22 . . . . .182 DU87
Mountague Pl, E14 . . . . .14 C9
Mountain Ct, Dart. (Eyns.)
DA4 off Pollyhaugh 208 FL103
H Mount Alvernia Hosp,
Guil. GU1 . . . . .258 AY136
Mount Angelus Rd, SW15 . .179 CT87
Mount Ararat Rd, Rich.
TW10 . . . . .178 CL85
Mount Ash Rd, SE26 . . . . . .182 DV90
Mount Av, E4 . . . . .101 EA48
W5 . . . . .137 CK71
Brentwood CM13 . . . . . . .109 GA44
Caterham CR3 . . . . .236 DQ124
Romford RM3 . . . . .106 FQ51

Mount Av, Sthl. UB1 .....136 CA72
Mountbatten Cl, SE18 .....165 ES79
SE19 .....182 DS92
St. Albans AL1 .....43 CH23
Slough SL1 .....152 AU76
Mountbatten Ct, SE16
off Rotherhithe St 142 DW74
Buckhurst Hill IG9 .....102 EK47
Mountbatten Gdns, Beck.
BR3 off Balmoral Av 203 DY98
Mountbatten Ms, SW18
off Inman Rd 180 DC88
Mountbatten Sq, Wind.
SL4 off Alma Rd 151 AQ81
Mountbel Rd, Stan. HA7 .....95 CG53
Sch Mount Carmel RC Prim Sch, W5
off Little Ealing La 157 CJ76
Sch Mount Carmel RC Tech Coll for Girls, N19
off Holland Wk 121 DK60
Mount Cl, W5 .....137 CJ71
Barnet EN4 .....80 DG42
Bromley BR1 .....204 EL95
Carshalton SM5 .....218 DG109
Hemel Hempstead HP1 .....39 BF20
Kenley CR8 .....236 DQ116
Leatherhead (Fetch.)
KT22 .....231 CE123
Sevenoaks TN13 .....256 FF123
Slough (Farn.Com.) SL2 .....111 AQ63
Woking GU22 .....226 AV121
Mount Cl, The, Vir.W. GU25 .....192 AX100
Mountcombe Cl, Surb. KT6 .....198 CL101
Mount Cor, Felt. TW13 .....176 BX89
Mount Ct, SW15
off Weimar St 159 CY83
West Wickham BR4 .....204 EE103
Mount Cres, Brwd. CM14 .....108 FX49
Mount Culver Av, Sid. DA14 .....186 EX93
Mount Dr, Bexh. DA6 .....186 EY85
Harrow HA2 .....116 BZ57
St. Albans (Park St) AL2 .....61 CD25
Wembley HA9 .....118 CQ61
Mount Dr, The, Reig. RH2 .....250 DC132
Mountearl Gdns, SW16 .....181 DM90
Mount Echo Av, E4 .....101 EB47
Mount Echo Dr, E4 .....101 EB46
MOUNT END, Epp. CM16 .....70 EZ32
Mount Ephraim La, SW16 .....181 DK90
Mount Ephraim Rd, SW16 .....181 DK90
Mount Est, The, E5
off Mount Pleasant La 122 DV61
Mount Felix, Walt. KT12 .....195 BT102
Mountfield Cl, SE6 .....183 ED87
Mountfield Rd, E6 .....145 EN68
N3 .....120 DA55
W5 .....137 CK72
Hemel Hempstead HP2 .....40 BL20
Mountfield Way, Orp. BR5 .....206 EW98
Mountford St, E1 .....12 A7
Mountfort Cres, N1 .....4 C5
Mountfort Ter, N1 .....4 C6
Mount Gdns, SE26 .....182 DV90
Mount Grace Rd, Pot.B. EN6 .....64 DA31
Sch Mount Grace Sch, Pot.B.
EN6 off Church Rd 64 DB30
Mount Gro, Edg. HA8 .....96 CQ48
Mountgrove Rd, N5 .....121 DP62
Mount Harry Rd, Sev. TN13 .....256 FG123
MOUNT HERMON, Wok.
GU22 .....226 AX118
Mount Hermon Cl, Wok.
GU22 .....226 AX118
Mount Hermon Rd, Wok.
GU22 .....226 AX119
Mount Hill La, Ger.Cr. SL9 .....112 AV60
Mounthurst Rd, Brom. BR2 .....204 EF101
Mountington Pk Cl, Har.
HA3 .....117 CK58
Mountjoy Cl, SE2 .....166 EV75
Mountjoy Ho, EC2
off The Barbican 142 DQ71
Mount La, Uxb. (Denh.)
UB9 .....113 BD61
Mount Lee, Egh. TW20 .....172 AY92
Mount Ms, Hmptn. TW12 .....196 CB95
Mount Mills, EC1 .....10 F2
Mountnessing Bypass,
Brwd. CM15 .....109 GD41
Mount Nod Rd, SW16 .....181 DM90
Mount Nugent, Chesh. HP5 .....54 AN27
Mount Pk, Cars. SM5 .....218 DG109
Mount Pk Av, Har. HA1 .....117 CD61
South Croydon CR2 .....219 DP109
Mount Pk Cres, W5 .....137 CK72
Mount Pk Rd, W5 .....137 CK71
Harrow HA1 .....117 CD62
Pinner HA5 .....115 BU57
Mount Pl, W3
off High St 138 CP74
Guildford GU2
off The Mount 258 AW136
Mount Pleasant, SE27 .....182 DQ91
WC1 .....10 B4
Barnet EN4 .....80 DE42
Epsom KT17 .....217 CT110
Guildford GU2 .....258 AW136
Hertford (Hert.Hth) SG13 .....32 DW11
Leatherhead (Eff.) KT24 .....246 BY128
Leatherhead (W.Hors.)
KT24 .....245 BP129
Ruislip HA4 .....116 BW61
St. Albans AL3 .....42 CB19
Uxbridge (Hare.) UB9 .....92 BG53
Wembley HA0 .....138 CL67
Westerham (Bigg.H.)
TN16 .....238 EK117
Weybridge KT13 .....194 BN104
Mount Pleasant Av, Brwd.
(Hutt.) CM13 .....109 GE44
Mount Pleasant Cl, Hat. AL9 .....45 CW15
Mount Pleasant Cres, N4 .....121 DM59
Mount Pleasant Hill, E5 .....122 DV61
Mount Pleasant La, E5 .....122 DV61
Hatfield AL9 .....29 CW14
St. Albans (Brick.Wd) AL2 .....60 BY30
Sch Mount Pleasant La JMI Sch, St.Alb. AL2
off Mount Pleasant La 60 BY30
Mount Pleasant Pl, SE18
off Orchard Rd 165 ER77
Mount Pleasant Rd, E17 .....101 DY54
N17 .....100 DS54
NW10 .....139 CW66
SE13 .....183 EB86
W5 .....137 CJ70
Caterham CR3 .....236 DU123
Chigwell IG7 .....103 ER49
Dartford DA1 .....188 FM86
New Malden KT3 .....198 CQ97
Romford RM5 .....105 FD51
Mount Pleasant Vil, N4 .....121 DM59
Mount Pleasant Wk, Bex.
DA5 .....187 FC85
Sch Mount Prim Sch, The,
N.Mal. KT3
off Dickerage La 198 CP97
Mount Ri, Red. RH1 .....266 DD136
Mount Rd, NW2 .....119 CV62
NW4 .....119 CU58
SE19 .....182 DR93
SW19 .....180 DA89
Barnet EN4 .....80 DE43
Bexleyheath DA6 .....186 EX85
Chessington KT9 .....216 CM106
Dagenham RM8 .....126 EZ60
Dartford DA1 .....187 FF86
Epping CM16 .....70 EW32
Feltham TW13 .....176 BY90
Hayes UB3 .....155 BT75
Hertford SG14 .....31 DN10
Ilford IG1 .....125 EP64
Mitcham CR4 .....200 DE96
New Malden KT3 .....198 CR97
Woking GU22 .....226 AV121
Woking (Chobham) GU24 .....210 AV112
Mount Row, W1 .....8 G10
Sch Mount Sch, The, NW7
off Milespit Hill 97 CV50
Mountsfield Cl, Stai. TW19 .....174 BG86
Mountsfield Ct, SE13 .....183 ED86
Mountside, Felt. TW13 .....176 BY90
Guildford GU2 .....258 AV136
Stanmore HA7 .....95 CF53
Mountsorrel, Hert. SG13 .....32 DT08
Mounts Pond Rd, SE3 .....163 ED82
Mount Sq, The, NW3
off Heath St 120 DC62
Mounts Rd, Green. DA9 .....189 FV85
Mount Stewart Av, Har.
HA3 .....117 CK58
Sch Mount Stewart Inf Sch, Har. HA3
off Carlisle Gdns 117 CK59
Sch Mount Stewart Jun Sch, Har. HA3
off Mount Stewart Av 117 CK59
Mount St, W1 .....8 F10
Dorking RH4 .....263 CG136
Mount Ter, E1 .....12 C6
Mount Vernon, NW3 .....120 DC63
H Mount Vernon Hosp,
Nthwd. HA6 .....93 BP51
Mount Vw, NW7 .....96 CR48
W5 .....137 CK70
Enfield EN2 .....81 DM38
Mountview, Nthwd. HA6 .....93 BT51
Mount Vw, Rick. WD3 .....92 BH46
St. Albans (Lon.Col.) AL2 .....62 CL27
Coll Mountview Acad of Thea Arts, Crouch End,
N8 off Crouch Hill 121 DL58
Mountview Cl, NW11 .....120 DB60
Redhill RH1 .....266 DE136
Mountview Ct, N8
off Green Las 121 DP56
Mountview Dr, Red. RH1 .....266 DD136
Mount Vw Rd, E4 .....101 EC45
N4 .....121 DL59
NW9 .....118 CR56
Mountview Rd, Esher (Clay.)
KT10 .....215 CH108
Orpington BR6 .....206 EU101
Waltham Cross (Chsht)
EN7 .....66 DS26
Mount Vil, SE27 .....181 DP90
Mount Way, Cars. SM5 .....218 DG109
Mountway, Pot.B. EN6 .....64 DA30
Welwyn Garden City AL7 .....29 CZ12
Mountway Cl, Welw.G.
AL7 .....29 CZ12
Mountwood, W.Mol. KT8 .....196 CA97
Mountwood Cl, S.Croy. CR2 .....220 DV110
Movers La, Bark. IG11 .....145 ER67
Mowat Ind Est, Wat. WD24 .....76 BW38
Mowatt Cl, N19 .....121 DK60
Mowbray Av, W.Byf. (Byfleet)
KT14 .....212 BL113
Mowbray Cres, Egh. TW20 .....173 BA92
Mowbray Gdns, Dor. RH4 .....247 CH134
Mowbray Rd, NW6 .....139 CY66
SE19 .....202 DT95
Barnet EN5 .....80 DC42
Edgware HA8 .....96 CN49
Harlow CM20 .....35 ET13
Richmond TW10 .....177 CJ90
Mowbrays Cl, Rom. RM5 .....105 FC53
Mowbrays Rd, Rom. RM5 .....105 FC54
Mowbrey Gdns, Loug. IG10 .....85 EQ40
Sch Mowlem Prim Sch,
E2 off Mowlem St 142 DW68
Mowlem St, E2 .....142 DV68
Mowlem Trd Est, N17 .....100 DW52
Mowll St, SW9 .....161 DN80
Moxom Av, Wal.Cr. (Chsht)
EN8 .....67 DY30
Moxon Cl, E13
off Whitelegg Rd 144 EF68
Moxon St, W1 .....8 E6
Barnet EN5 .....79 CZ41
Moye Cl, E2 off Dove Row 142 DU67
Moyers Rd, E10 .....123 EC59
Moylan Rd, W6 .....159 CY79
Moyne Ct, Wok. GU21
off Iveagh Rd 226 AT118
Moyne Pl, NW10 .....138 CN68
Moynihan Dr, N21 .....81 DL43
Moys Cl, Croy. CR0 .....201 DL100
Moyser Rd, SW16 .....181 DH92
Mozart St, W10 .....6 E2
Mozart Ter, SW1 .....18 F8
Muchelney Rd, Mord. SM4 .....200 DC100
Muckhatch La, Egh. TW20 .....193 BB97
MUCKINGFORD, S.le H.
SS17 .....171 GM76
Muckingford Rd, S.le H.
(Linford) SS17 .....171 GM77
Tilbury (W.Til.) RM18 .....171 GL77
DLR Mudchute 24 B7
Muddy La, Slou. SL2 .....132 AS71
Mudlands Ind Est, Rain.
RM13 .....147 FE69
Mud La, W5 .....137 CK71
Muggeridge Cl, S.Croy. CR2 .....220 DR106
Muggeridge Rd, Dag. RM10 .....127 FB63
MUGSWELL, Couls. CR5 .....250 DB125
Muirdown Av, SW14 .....158 CQ84
Muir Dr, SW18 .....180 DD86
Muirfield, W3 .....138 CS72
Muirfield Cl, SE16 .....22 D10
Watford WD19 .....94 BW49
Muirfield Cres, E14 .....24 A5
Muirfield Grn, Wat. WD19 .....94 BW49
Muirfield Rd, Wat. WD19 .....94 BX49
Woking GU21 .....226 AU118
Muirkirk Rd, SE6 .....183 EC88
Muir Rd, E5 .....122 DU63
Muir St, E16 off Newland St 145 EM74
Mulberry Av, Stai. TW19 .....174 BL88
Mulberry Av, Wind. SL4 .....152 AT82
Mulberry Business Cen,
SE16 .....23 H4
Mulberry Cl, E4 .....101 EA47
N8 .....121 DL57
NW3 off Hampstead
High St 120 DD63
NW4 .....119 CW55
SE7 off Charlton Pk Rd 164 EK79
SE22 .....182 DU85
SW3 off Beaufort St 160 DD79
SW16 .....181 DJ91
Amersham HP7 .....72 AT39
Barnet EN4 .....80 DD42
Broxbourne EN10 .....49 DZ24
Northolt UB5
off Parkfield Av 136 BY68
Romford RM2 .....127 FH56
St. Albans (Park St) AL2 .....60 CB28
Watford WD25 .....75 BS36
Weybridge KT13 .....195 BP104
Woking GU21 .....210 AY114
Mulberry Ct, Bark. IG11
off Westrow Dr 145 ET66
Beaconsfield HP9 .....111 AM55
Guildford GU4
off Gilliat Dr 243 BD131
Mulberry Cres, Brent. TW8 .....157 CH80
West Drayton UB7 .....154 BN75
Mulberry Dr, Purf. RM19 .....168 FM77
Slough SL3 .....152 AY78
Mulberry Gdns, Rad.
(Shenley) WD7 .....62 CL33
Mulberry Gate, Bans. SM7 .....233 CZ116
Mulberry Grn, Harl. CM17 .....36 EX11
Mulberry Hill, Brwd. (Shenf.)
CM15 .....109 FZ45
Sch Mulberry Ho Sch, The,
NW2 off Minster Rd 119 CY64
Mulberry La, Croy. CR0 .....202 DT102
Mulberry Mead, Hat. AL10 .....29 CT14
Mulberry Ms, SE14
off Lewisham Way 163 DZ81
Wallington SM6
off Ross Rd 219 DJ107
Mulberry Par, West Dr. UB7 .....154 BN76
Mulberry Pl, W6
off Chiswick Mall 159 CU78
Mulberry Rd, E8 .....5 N5
Gravesend (Nthflt) DA11 .....190 GE90
Sch Mulberry Sch for Girls,
E1 .....12 C8
Coll Mulberry 6th Form Coll,
E1 .....12 C9
Mulberry St, E1 .....12 A7
Mulberry Trees, Shep. TW17 .....195 BQ101
Mulberry Wk, SW3 .....160 DD79
Mulberry Way, E18 .....102 EH54
Belvedere DA17 .....167 FC75
Ilford IG6 .....125 EQ56
Mulgrave Rd, NW10 .....119 CT63
SE18 .....165 EM77
SW6 .....159 CZ79
W5 .....137 CK69
Croydon CR0 .....202 DR104
Harrow HA1 .....117 CG61
Sutton SM2 .....218 DA107
Sch Mulgrave Sch, SE18
off Rectory Pl 165 EN77
Mulgrave Way, Wok. (Knap.)
GU21 .....226 AS118
Mulholland Cl, Mitch. CR4 .....201 DH96
Mulkern Rd, N19 .....121 DK60
Mullards Cl, Mitch. CR4 .....200 DF102
Mullein Ct, Grays RM17 .....170 GD79
Mullens Rd, Egh. TW20 .....173 BB92
Muller Rd, SW4 .....181 DK86
Mullet Gdns, E2 .....12 B1
Mullins Path, SW14 .....158 CR83
Mullion Cl, Har. HA3 .....94 CB53
Mullion Wk, Wat. WD19
off Ormskirk Rd 94 BX49
Mull Wk, N1 .....5 H4
Mulready St, NW8 .....8 A4
Mulready Wk, Hem.H. HP3 .....40 BL24
Multi-way, W3
off Valetta Rd 158 CS75
Multon Rd, SW18 .....180 DD87
Mulvaney Way, SE1 .....21 K4
Mumford Ct, EC2 .....11 H7
Mumford Rd, SE24
off Railton Rd 181 DP85
Mumfords La, Ger.Cr.
(Chal.St.P.) SL9 .....112 AU55
Muncaster Cl, Ashf. TW15 .....174 BN91
Muncaster Rd, SW11 .....180 DF85
Ashford TW15 .....175 BP92
Muncies Ms, SE6 .....183 EC89
Mundania Rd, SE22 .....182 DV86
Munday Rd, E16 .....15 L8
Mundells, Wal.Cr. EN7 .....66 DU27
Welwyn Garden City AL7 .....29 CZ07
Mundells Ct, Welw.G.C. AL7 .....29 CZ07
Munden Dr, Wat. WD25 .....76 BY37
Munden Gro, Wat. WD24 .....76 BW38
Munden St, W14 .....16 C7
Munden Vw, Wat. WD25 .....76 BX36
Mundesley Cl, Wat. WD19 .....94 BW49
Mundesley Spur, Slou. SL1 .....132 AS72
Mundford Rd, E5 .....122 DW61
Mundon Gdns, Ilf. IG1 .....125 ER60
Mund St, W14 .....16 F10
Mundy St, N1 .....11 L1
Munford Dr, Swans. DA10 .....190 FY87
Mungo Pk Cl, Bushey
(Bushey Hth) WD23 .....94 CC47
Mungo Pk Rd, Grav. DA12 .....191 GK92
Rainham RM13 .....147 FG65
Mungo Pk Way, Orp. BR5 .....206 EW101
Munnery Way, Orp. BR6 .....205 EN104
Munnings Gdns, Islw. TW7 .....177 CD85
Munro Dr, N11 .....99 DJ51
Munro Ms, W10 .....6 D5
Munro Rd, Bushey WD23 .....76 CB43
Munro Ter, SW10 .....160 DD80
Munslow Gdns, Sutt. SM1 .....218 DD105
Munstead Vw, Guil. (Art.)
GU3 .....258 AV138
Munster Av, Houns. TW4 .....156 BZ84
Munster Ct, Tedd. TW11 .....177 CJ93
Munster Gdns, N13 .....99 DP49
Munster Ms, SW6
off Lillie Rd 159 CY80
Munster Rd, SW6 .....159 CZ81
Teddington TW11 .....177 CH93
Munster Sq, NW1 .....9 H2
Munton Rd, SE17 .....21 H7
Murchison Av, Bex. DA5 .....186 EX88
Murchison Rd, E10 .....123 EC61
Hoddesdon EN11 .....33 EB14
Murdoch Cl, Stai. TW18 .....174 BG92
Murdock Cl, E16 .....15 K7
Murdock St, SE15 .....162 DV79
Murfett Cl, SW19 .....179 CY89
Murfitt Way, Upmin. RM14 .....128 FN63
Muriel Av, Wat. WD18 .....76 BW43
Muriel St, N1 .....4 B9
Murillo Rd, SE13 .....163 ED84
Murphy St, SE1 .....20 C4
Murray Av, Brom. BR1 .....204 EH96
Hounslow TW3 .....176 CB85
Murray Business Cen, Orp.
BR5 .....206 EV97
Murray Cres, Pnr. HA5 .....94 BX53
Murray Grn, Wok. GU21
off Bunyard Dr 211 BC114
Murray Gro, N1 .....5 H10
Murray Ms, NW1 .....141 DK66
Murray Rd, SW19 .....179 CX93
W5 .....157 CJ77
Berkhamsted HP4 .....38 AV18
Chertsey (Ott.) KT16 .....211 BC107
Northwood HA6 .....93 BS53
Orpington BR5 .....206 EV97
Richmond TW10 .....177 CH89
Murrays La, W.Byf. (Byfleet)
KT14 .....212 BK114
Murray Sq, E16 .....15 M8
Murray St, NW1 .....141 DK66
Murrays Yd, SE18 .....165 EP77
Murray Ter, NW3
off Flask Wk 120 DD63
W5 off Murray Rd 157 CK77
Murrells Wk, Lthd. (Bkhm)
KT23 .....230 CA123
Murreys, The, Ashtd. KT21 .....231 CK118
Mursell Est, SW8 .....161 DM81
Murthering La, Rom. RM4 .....87 FG43
Murton Ct, St.Alb. AL1 .....43 CE19
Murtwell Dr, Chig. IG7 .....103 EQ51
Musard Rd, W6 .....159 CY79
W14 .....159 CY79
Musbury St, E1 .....12 E7
Muscal, W6 .....159 CY79
Muscatel Pl, SE5
off Dalwood St 162 DS81
Sch Muschamp Prim Sch,
Cars. SM5
off Muschamp Rd 200 DE103
Muschamp Rd, SE15 .....162 DT83
Carshalton SM5 .....200 DE103
Muscovy Ho, Erith DA18
off Kale Rd 166 EY75
Muscovy St, EC3 .....11 M10
★ Museum in Docklands,
E14 .....13 P10
★ Museum Interpretative Cen, E6 off Norman Rd 145 EM70
Museum La, SW7 .....17 N6
★ Museum of Artillery, The Rotunda, SE18 .....165 EM78
★ Museum of Gdn History,
SE1 .....20 A6
★ Museum of Harlow,
Harl. CM20 .....36 EV12
★ Museum of Instruments, Royal Coll of Music,
SW7 .....17 N5
★ Museum of London,
EC2 .....10 G6
★ Museum of Richmond,
Rich. TW9 .....177 CK85
★ Museum of St. Albans,
St.Alb. AL1 .....43 CE19
Museum Pas, E2 .....12 E1
Museum St, WC1 .....9 N6
Musgrave Cl, Barn. EN4 .....80 DC39
Waltham Cross EN7
off Allwood Rd 66 DT27
Musgrave Cres, SW6 .....160 DA80
Musgrave Rd, Islw. TW7 .....157 CF81
Musgrove Rd, SE14 .....163 DX81
★ Musical Mus (re-opening 2004), Brent.
TW8 off High St 158 CL79
Musjid Rd, SW11
off Kambala Rd 160 DD82
Muskalls Cl, Wal.Cr. (Chsht)
EN7 .....66 DU27
Musket Cl, Barn. EN4
off East Barnet Rd 80 DD43
Muskham Rd, Harl. CM20 .....36 EU12
Musk Hill, Hem.H. HP1 .....39 BE21
Musleigh Manor, Ware
SG12 .....33 DZ06
Musley Hill, Ware SG12 .....33 DY05
Musley La, Ware SG12 .....33 DY05
Musquash Way, Houns.
TW4 .....156 BW82
Mussenden La, Dart.
(Hort.Kir.) DA4 .....208 FQ99
Longfield (Fawk.Grn)
DA3 .....209 FS101
Mustard Mill Rd, Stai. TW18 .....173 BE91
Muston Rd, E5 .....122 DV61
Mustow Pl, SW6
off Munster Rd 159 CZ82
Muswell Av, N10 .....99 DH54
MUSWELL HILL, N10 .....121 DH55
Muswell Hill, N10 .....121 DH55
Muswell Hill Bdy, N10 .....121 DH55
Muswell Hill Pl, N10 .....121 DH56
Muswell Hill Rd, N6 .....120 DG58
N10 .....120 DG56
Muswell Ms, N10
off Muswell Rd 121 DH55
Sch Muswell Prim Sch,
N10 off Muswell Hill 121 DH55
Muswell Rd, N10 .....121 DH55
Mutchetts Cl, Wat. WD25 .....60 BY33
Mutrix Rd, NW6 .....140 DA67
Mutton La, Pot.B. EN6 .....63 CY31
Mutton Pl, NW1
off Harmood St 141 DH65
Muybridge Rd, N.Mal. KT3 .....198 CQ96
Sch Myatt Gdn Prim Sch,
SE4 off Rokeby Rd 163 DZ82
Myatt Rd, SW9 .....161 DP81
Myatt's Flds N, SW9
off Eythorne Rd 161 DN81
Mycenae Rd, SE3 .....164 EG80
Myddelton Av, Enf. EN1 .....82 DS38
Myddelton Cl, Enf. EN1 .....82 DT39
Myddelton Gdns, N21 .....99 DP45
Myddelton Pk, N20 .....98 DD48
Myddelton Pas, EC1 .....10 D1
Myddelton Rd, N8 .....121 DL56
Myddelton Sq, EC1 .....10 D1
Myddelton St, EC1 .....10 D2
Myddleton Av, N4 .....122 DQ61
Myddleton Ms, N22 .....99 DL52
Myddleton Path, Wal.Cr.
(Chsht) EN7 .....66 DV31
Myddleton Rd, N22 .....99 DL52
Uxbridge UB8 .....134 BJ67
Ware SG12 .....33 DX07
Myers Dr, Slou. SL2 .....111 AP64
Myers La, SE14 .....163 DX79
Mygrove Cl, Rain. RM13 .....148 FK68
Mygrove Gdns, Rain. RM13 .....148 FK68
Mygrove Rd, Rain. RM13 .....148 FK68
Myles Ct, Wal.Cr. EN7 .....66 DQ29
Mylis Cl, SE26 .....182 DV91
Mylius Cl, SE14
off Kender St 162 DW81
Mylne Cl, Wal.Cr. EN8 .....66 DW27
Mylner Ct, Hodd. EN11
off Ditchfield Rd 49 EA15
Mylne St, EC1 .....4 C10
Mylor Cl, Wok. GU21 .....210 AY114
Mymms Dr, Hat. AL9 .....64 DA26
Mynchen Cl, Beac. HP9 .....89 AK49
Mynchen End, Beac. HP9 .....89 AK49
Mynchen Rd, Beac. HP9 .....89 AK50
Mynns Cl, Epsom KT18 .....216 CP114
Mynterne Ct, SW19
off Swanton Gdns 179 CX88
Myra St, SE2 .....166 EU78
Myrdle St, E1 .....12 B6
Myrke, The, Slou. (Datchet)
SL3 .....152 AT77
Myrna Cl, SW19 .....180 DE94
Myron Pl, SE13 .....163 EC83
Myrtle Av, Felt. TW14 .....155 BS84
Ruislip HA4 .....115 BU59
Myrtleberry Cl, E8 .....5 N4
Myrtle Cl, Barn. EN4 .....98 DF46
Erith DA8 .....167 FE81
Slough (Colnbr.) SL3 .....153 BE81
Uxbridge UB8
off Violet Av 134 BM71
West Drayton UB7 .....154 BM76
Myrtle Cres, Slou. SL2 .....132 AT73
Myrtledene Rd, SE2 .....166 EU78
Myrtle Gdns, W7 .....137 CE74
Myrtle Grn, Hem.H. HP1
off Newlands Rd 39 BE20
Myrtle Gro, Enf. EN2 .....82 DR38
New Malden KT3 .....198 CQ96
South Ockendon (Aveley)
RM15 .....168 FQ75
Myrtle Pl, Dart. DA2 .....189 FR87
Myrtle Rd, E6 .....144 EL67
E17 .....123 DY58
N13 .....100 DQ48
W3 .....138 CQ74
Brentwood CM14 .....108 FW49
Croydon CR0 .....203 EA104
Dartford DA1 .....188 FK88
Dorking RH4 .....263 CG135
Hampton (Hmptn H.)
TW12 .....176 CC93
Hounslow TW3 .....156 CC82
Ilford IG1 .....125 EP61
Romford RM3 .....106 FJ51
Sutton SM1 .....218 DC106
Myrtleside Cl, Nthwd. HA6 .....93 BR52
Myrtle Wk, N1 .....5 L10
Mysore Rd, SW11 .....160 DF83
Myton Rd, SE21 .....182 DR90

N

N1 Shop Cen, N1 .....4 D9
Nadine Ct, Wall. SM6
off Woodcote Rd 219 DJ109
Nadine St, SE7 .....164 EJ78
Nafferton Ri, Loug. IG10 .....84 EK43
Nagle Cl, E17 .....101 ED54
Nags Head Cl, Hert. SG13 .....32 DV08
Nag's Head Ct, EC1 .....10 G4
Nags Head La, Brwd. CM14 .....107 FR51
Upminster RM14 .....106 FQ53
Welling DA16 .....166 EV83
Nags Head Rd, Enf. EN3 .....82 DW42
Nags Head Shop Cen, N7 .....121 DM63
Nailsworth Cres, Red. RH1 .....251 DK129
Nailzee Cl, Ger.Cr. SL9 .....112 AY59
Nairn Ct, Til. RM18
off Dock Rd 171 GF82
Nairne Gro, SE24 .....182 DR85
Nairn Grn, Wat. WD19 .....93 BU48
Nairn Rd, Ruis. HA4 .....136 BW65
Nairn St, E14 .....14 D6
Nalders Rd, Chesh. HP5 .....54 AR29
NALDERSWOOD, Reig. RH2 .....265 CW144
Nallhead Rd, Felt. TW13 .....176 BW92
Namba Roy Cl, SW16 .....181 DM91
Namton Dr, Th.Hth. CR7 .....201 DM98
Nan Clark's La, NW7 .....97 CT47
Nancy Downs, Wat. WD19 .....94 BW45
Nankin St, E14 .....13 P8
Nansen Rd, SW11 .....160 DG84
Gravesend DA12 .....191 GK91
Nansen Village, N12 .....98 DB49
Nantes Cl, SW18 .....160 DC84
Nantes Pas, E1 .....11 N5
Nant Rd, NW2 .....119 CZ61
Nant St, E2 .....12 D1
Naoroji St, WC1 .....10 C2
Nap, The, Kings L. WD4 .....58 BN29
Napier Av, E14 .....23 P9
SW6 .....159 CZ83
Napier Cl, SE8
off Amersham Vale 163 DZ80
W14 .....16 E5
Hornchurch RM11 .....127 FH60
St. Albans (Lon.Col.) AL2 .....61 CK25
West Drayton UB7 .....154 BM76
Napier Ct, SW6
off Ranelagh Gdns 159 CZ83
Waltham Cross (Chsht) EN8
off Flamstead End Rd 66 DV28
Napier Dr, Bushey WD23 .....76 BY42
Napier Gdns, Guil. GU1 .....243 BB133
Napier Gro, N1 .....5 H10
Napier Ho, Rain. RM13 .....147 FF69
Napier Pl, W14 .....16 E6
Napier Rd, E6 .....145 EN67
E11 .....124 EE63
E15 .....144 EE68
N17 .....122 DS55
NW10 .....139 CV69
SE25 .....202 DV98
W14 .....16 E6
Ashford TW15 .....175 BR94
Belvedere DA17 .....166 EZ77
Bromley BR2 .....204 EH98
Enfield EN3 .....83 DX43
Gravesend (Nthflt) DA11 .....191 GF88
Hounslow (Hthrw Air.)
TW6 .....154 BK81
Isleworth TW7 .....157 CG84
South Croydon CR2 .....220 DR108
Wembley HA0 .....117 CK64
Napier Ter, N1 .....4 E6
Napier Wk, Ashf. TW15 .....175 BR94

⊖ London Underground station DLR Docklands Light Railway station Tra Tramlink station Riv Pedestrian ferry landing stage

Napoleon Rd, E5 122 DV62
Twickenham TW1 177 CH87
Napsbury Av, St.Alb. (Lon.Col.) AL2 61 CJ26
Napsbury La, St.Alb. AL1 43 CG23
Napton Cl, Hayes UB4 136 BY70
Narbonne Av, SW4 181 DJ85
Narboro Ct, Rom. RM1 *off Manor Rd* 127 FG57
Narborough Cl, Uxb. UB10 *off Aylsham Dr* 115 BQ61
Narborough St, SW6 160 DB82
Narcissus Rd, NW6 120 DA64
Narcot La, Ch.St.G. HP8 90 AU48
Gerrards Cross (Chal.St.P.) SL9 90 AV52
Narcot Rd, Ch.St.G. HP8 90 AU48
Narcot Way, Ch.St.G. HP8 90 AU49
Nare Rd, S.Ock. (Aveley) RM15 148 FQ73
Naresby Fold, Stan. HA7 95 CJ51
Narford Rd, E5 122 DU62
Narrow Boat Cl, SE28 *off Ridge Cl* 165 ER75
Narrow La, Warl. CR6 236 DV119
Narrow St, E14 13 J9
Narrow Way, Brom. BR2 204 EL100
Nascot Pl, Wat. WD17 75 BV39
Nascot Rd, Wat. WD17 75 BV40
Nascot St, W12 139 CW72
Watford WD17 75 BV40
Sch **Nascot Wd Inf Sch**, Wat. WD17 *off Nascot Wd Rd* 75 BU38
Sch **Nascot Wd Jun Sch**, Wat. WD17 *off Nascot Wd Rd* 75 BU38
Nascot Wd Rd, Wat. WD17 75 BT37
Naseberry Ct, E4 *off Merriam Cl* 101 EC50
Naseby Cl, NW6 140 DC66
Isleworth TW7 157 CE81
Naseby Ct, Walt. KT12 *off Clements Rd* 196 BW103
Naseby Rd, SE19 182 DR93
Dagenham RM10 126 FA62
Ilford IG5 103 EM53
Nash Cl, Borwd. (Elstree) WD6 78 CM42
Hatfield (N.Mymms) AL9 45 CX23
Sutton SM1 200 DD104
Nash Ct, E14 24 A2
Nash Cft, Grav. (Nthflt) DA11 190 GE91
Nashdom La, Slou. (Burn.) SL1 130 AG66
Nash Dr, Red. RH1 250 DF132
Nash Gdns, Red. RH1 250 DF132
Nash Grn, Brom. BR1 184 EG93
Hemel Hempstead HP3 58 BM25
Nash La, Kes. BR2 222 EG106
Nashleigh Hill, Chesh. HP5 54 AQ29
Sch **Nash Mills C of E Prim Sch**, Hem.H. HP3 *off Belswains La* 58 BM25
Nash Mills La, Hem.H. HP3 58 BM26
Nash Rd, N9 100 DW47
SE4 163 DX84
Romford RM6 126 EX56
Slough SL3 153 AZ77
Nash St, NW1 9 H2
Nash's Yd, Uxb. UB8 *off Bakers Rd* 134 BK66
Nash Way, Har. HA3 117 CH58
Nasmyth St, W6 159 CV76
Nassau Path, SE28 *off Disraeli Cl* 146 EW74
Nassau Rd, SW13 159 CT81
Nassau St, W1 9 J6
Nassington Rd, NW3 120 DE63
Natalie Cl, Felt. TW14 175 BR87
Natalie Ms, Twick. TW2 *off Sixth Cross Rd* 177 CD90
Natal Rd, N11 99 DL51
SW16 181 DK93
Ilford IG1 125 EP63
Thornton Heath CR7 202 DR97
Nathan Cl, Upmin. RM14 129 FS60
Nathaniel Cl, E1 11 P6
Nathans Rd, Wem. HA0 117 CJ60
Nathan Way, SE28 165 ES77
★ **National Army Mus**, SW3 160 DF79
H **National Blood Service/ Brentwood Transfusion Cen**, Brwd. CM15 109 FZ46
Coll **National Film & Television Sch Beaconsfield Studios**, Beac. HP9 *off Station Rd* 89 AL54
★ **National Gall**, WC2 9 M10
H **National Hosp for Neurology & Neurosurgery, The**, WC1 9 P4
★ **National Maritime Mus**, SE10 163 ED79
★ **National Portrait Gall**, WC2 9 M10
National Ter, SE16 *off Bermondsey Wall E* 162 DV75
Nation Way, E4 101 EC46
★ **Natural History Mus**, SW7 17 N6
Natwoke Cl, Beac. HP9 89 AK50
Naunton Way, Horn. RM12 128 FK62
Naval Row, E14 14 D9
Naval Wk, Brom. BR1 *off High St* 204 EG97
Navarino Gro, E8 142 DU65
Navarino Rd, E8 142 DU65
Navarre Gdns, Rom. RM5 105 FB51
Navarre Rd, E6 144 EL68
Navarre St, E2 11 N3
Navenby Wk, E3 13 P3
Navestock Cl, E4 *off Mapleton Rd* 101 EC48
Navestock Cres, Wdf.Grn. IG8 102 EJ53
Navestock Ho, Bark. IG11 146 EV68
Navigator Dr, Sthl. UB2 156 CC75
Navigator Pk, Sthl. UB2 *off Southall La* 156 BW77
Navy St, SW4 161 DK83
Naxos Bldg, E14 *off Hutchings St* 163 EA75
Nayim Pl, E8 *off Amhurst Rd* 122 DV64
Naylor Gro, Enf. EN3 *off South St* 83 DX43
Naylor Rd, N20 98 DC47
SE15 162 DV80
Naylor Ter, Slou. (Colnbr.) SL3 *off Vicarage Way* 153 BC80
Nazareth Gdns, SE15 162 DV82
NAZEING, Wal.Abb. EN9 50 EJ22
Nazeingbury Cl, Wal.Abb. EN9 49 ED22
Nazeingbury Par, Wal.Abb. EN9 *off Nazeing Rd* 49 ED22
Nazeing Common, Wal.Abb. EN9 50 EH24
Sch **Nazeing Co Prim Sch**, Wal.Abb. EN9 *off Hyde Mead* 50 EE23
NAZEING GATE, Wal.Abb. EN9 68 EJ25
Nazeing New Rd, Brox. EN10 49 EA21
Nazeing Rd, Wal.Abb. EN9 49 EC22
Nazeing Wk, Rain. RM13 *off Ongar Way* 147 FE67
Nazrul St, E2 11 N1
Neagle Cl, Borwd. WD6 *off Balcon Way* 78 CQ39
Neal Av, Sthl. UB1 136 BZ70
Neal Cl, Ger.Cr. SL9 113 BB60
Northwood HA6 93 BU53
Neal Ct, Hert. SG14 32 DQ09
Waltham Abbey EN9 68 EF33
Nealden St, SW9 161 DM83
Neale Cl, N2 120 DC55
Neal St, WC2 9 N8
Watford WD18 76 BW43
Neal's Yd, WC2 9 N8
Near Acre, NW9 97 CT53
NEASDEN, NW2 118 CS62
⊖ **Neasden** 118 CS64
Neasden Cl, NW10 118 CS64
Neasden La, NW10 118 CS63
Neasden La N, NW10 118 CR62
Neasham Rd, Dag. RM8 126 EV64
Neate St, SE5 162 DT79
Neath Gdns, Mord. SM4 200 DC100
Neathouse Pl, SW1 19 J7
Neats Acre, Ruis. HA4 115 BR59
Neatscourt Rd, E6 144 EK71
Neave Cres, Rom. RM3 106 FJ53
Neb La, Oxt. RH8 253 EC131
Nebraska St, SE1 21 J4
Neckinger, SE16 21 P5
Neckinger Est, SE16 21 P5
Neckinger St, SE1 21 P4
Nectarine Way, SE13 163 EB82
Necton Rd, St.Alb. (Wheat.) AL4 28 CL07
Needham Cl, Wind. SL4 151 AL81
Needham Rd, W11 6 G8
Needham Ter, NW2 *off Kara Way* 119 CX62
Needleman St, SE16 22 G4
Needles Bk, Gdse. RH9 252 DV131
Neela Cl, Uxb. UB10 115 BP63
Neeld Cres, NW4 119 CV57
Wembley HA9 118 CN64
Neeld Par, Wem. HA9 *off Harrow Rd* 118 CN64
Neil Cl, Ashf. TW15 175 BQ92
Neil Wates Cres, SW2 181 DN88
Nelgarde Rd, SE6 183 EA87
Nella Rd, W6 159 CX79
Nelldale Rd, SE16 22 E7
Nellgrove Rd, Uxb. UB10 135 BP70
Nell Gwynn Cl, Rad. (Shenley) WD7 62 CL32
Nell Gwynne Av, Shep. TW17 195 BR100
Nell Gwynne Cl, Epsom KT19 216 CN111
Nello James Gdns, SE27 182 DR91
Nelmes Cl, Horn. RM11 128 FM57
Nelmes Cres, Horn. RM11 128 FL57
Sch **Nelmes Prim Sch**, Horn. RM11 *off Wingletye La* 128 FM56
Nelmes Rd, Horn. RM11 128 FL59
Nelmes Way, Horn. RM11 128 FL56
Nelson Av, St.Alb. AL1 43 CH23
Nelson Cl, NW6 6 G1
Brentwood (Warley) CM14 108 FX50
Croydon CR0 201 DP102
Feltham TW14 175 BT88
Romford RM7 105 FB53
Slough SL3 152 AX77
Uxbridge UB10 135 BP69
Walton-on-Thames KT12 195 BV102
Westerham (Bigg.H.) TN16 238 EL117
Nelson Ct, SE16 *off Brunel Rd* 142 DW74
Nelson Gdns, E2 12 B1
Guildford GU1 243 BA133
Hounslow TW3 176 CA86
Nelson Gro Rd, SW19 200 DB95
H **Nelson Hosp**, SW20 199 CZ96
Nelson La, Uxb. UB10 *off Nelson Rd* 135 BP69
Nelson Mandela Cl, N10 98 DG54
Nelson Mandela Rd, SE3 164 EJ83
Nelson Pas, EC1 11 H2
Nelson Pl, N1 4 F10
Sidcup DA14 *off Sidcup High St* 186 EU91
Sch **Nelson Prim Sch**, E6 *off Napier Rd* 145 EN68
Twickenham TW2 *off Nelson Rd* 176 CB87
Nelson Rd, E4 101 EB51
E11 124 EG56
N8 121 DM57
N9 100 DV47
N15 122 DS56
SE10 163 EC79
SW19 180 DB94
Ashford TW15 174 BL92
Belvedere DA17 166 EZ78
Bromley BR2 204 EJ98
Caterham CR3 236 DR123
Dartford DA1 188 FJ86
Enfield EN3 83 DX44
Gravesend (Nthflt) DA11 191 GF89
Harrow HA1 117 CD60
Hounslow TW3, TW4 176 CA86
Hounslow (Hthrw Air.) TW6 154 BM81
New Malden KT3 198 CR99
Rainham RM13 147 FF68
Sidcup DA14 *off Sidcup High St* 186 EU91
South Ockendon RM15 149 FW68
Stanmore HA7 95 CJ51
Twickenham TW2 176 CC86
Uxbridge UB10 135 BP69
Windsor SL4 151 AM83
★ **Nelson's Column**, WC2 19 N1
Nelson Sq, SE1 20 E3
Nelson's Row, SW4 161 DK84
Nelson St, E1 12 C7
E6 145 EM68
E16 15 J9
Nelson St, Hert. SG14 31 DP08
Nelsons Yd, NW1 *off Mornington Cres* 141 DJ68
Nelson Ter, N1 4 F10
Nelson Trd Est, SW19 200 DB95
Nelson Wk, SE16 23 K2
Epsom KT19 216 CN109
Nelwyn Av, Horn. RM11 128 FM57
Nemoure Rd, W3 138 CQ73
Nene Gdns, Felt. TW13 176 BZ89
Nene Rd, Houns. (Hthrw Air.) TW6 155 BP81
Nepaul Rd, SW11 160 DE82
Nepean St, SW15 179 CU86
Neptune Cl, Rain. RM13 147 FF68
Neptune Ct, Borwd. WD6 *off Clarendon Rd* 78 CN41
Neptune Dr, Hem.H. HP2 40 BL18
Neptune Rd, Har. HA1 117 CD58
Hounslow (Hthrw Air.) TW6 155 BR81
Neptune St, SE16 22 E5
Neptune Wk, Erith DA8 167 FD77
Neptune Way, Slou. SL1 *off Hunters Way* 151 AL75
Nero Ct, Brent. TW8 *off Justin Cl* 157 CK80
Nesbit Rd, SE9 164 EK84
Nesbitt Cl, SE3 *off Hurren Cl* 164 EE83
Nesbitts All, Barn. EN5 *off Bath Pl* 79 CZ41
Nesbitt Sq, SE19 *off Coxwell Rd* 182 DS94
Coll **Nescot**, Epsom KT17 *off Reigate Rd* 217 CU111
Nesham St, E1 22 A1
Ness Rd, Erith DA8 168 FK79
Ness St, SE16 22 A5
Nesta Rd, Wdf.Grn. IG8 102 EE51
Nestles Av, Hayes UB3 155 BT76
Neston Rd, Wat. WD24 76 BW37
Nestor Av, N21 81 DP44
Nethan Dr, S.Ock. (Aveley) RM15 148 FQ73
Netheravon Rd, W4 159 CT77
W7 137 CF74
Netheravon Rd S, W4 159 CT78
Netherbury Rd, W5 157 CK76
Netherby Gdns, Enf. EN2 81 DL42
Netherby Pk, Wey. KT13 213 BS106
Netherby Rd, SE23 182 DW87
Nether Cl, N3 98 DA52
Nethercote Av, Wok. GU21 226 AT117
Nethercourt Av, N3 98 DA51
Netherfield Gdns, Bark. IG11 145 ER65
Netherfield La, Ware (Stans.Abb.) SG12 34 EE12
Netherfield Rd, N12 98 DB50
SW17 180 DG90
Netherford Rd, SW4 161 DJ82
Netherhall Gdns, NW3 140 DC65
Netherhall Rd, Harl. (Roydon) CM19 50 EF17
Netherhall Way, NW3 *off Netherhall Gdns* 120 DC64
Netherlands, The, Couls. CR5 235 DJ119
Netherlands Rd, Barn. EN5 80 DD44
Netherleigh Cl, N6 121 DH60
Netherleigh Pk, Red. RH1 267 DL137
Nether Mt, Guil. GU2 258 AV136
Nethern Ct Rd, Cat. (Wold.) CR3 237 EA123
Netherne Dr, Couls. CR5 235 DH121
Netherne La, Couls. CR5 235 DK121
Redhill RH1 235 DJ123
Netherpark Dr, Rom. RM2 105 FF54
Nether St, N3 98 DA53
N12 98 DA52
Netherton Gro, SW10 160 DC79
Netherton Rd, N15 122 DR58
Twickenham TW1 177 CH85
Netherway, St.Alb. AL3 42 CA23
Netherwood, N2 98 DD54
Netherwood Pl, W14 16 A5
Netherwood Rd, W14 16 A5
Beaconsfield HP9 89 AK50
Netherwood St, NW6 139 CZ66
Netley Cl, Croy. (New Adgtn) CR0 221 EC108
Sutton SM3 217 CX106
Netley Dr, Walt. KT12 196 BZ101
Netley Gdns, Mord. SM4 200 DC101
Sch **Netley Prim Sch**, NW1 9 J2
Netley Rd, E17 123 DZ57
Brentford TW8 158 CL79
Hounslow (Hthrw Air.) TW6 155 BR81
Ilford IG2 125 ER57
Morden SM4 200 DC101
Netley St, NW1 9 J2
NETTESWELL, Harl. CM20 35 ES14
Netteswell Orchard, Harl. CM20 35 ER14
Netteswell Rd, Harl. CM20 35 ES12
Netteswell Twr, Harl. CM20 35 ER14
Nettlecombe Cl, Sutt. SM2 218 DB109
Nettlecroft, Hem.H. HP1 40 BH21
Welwyn Garden City AL7 30 DB08
Nettleden Av, Wem. HA9 138 CN65
Nettleden Rd, Berk. HP4 39 BA16
Nettlefold Pl, SE27 181 DP90
Nettlestead Cl, Beck. BR3 *off Copers Cope Rd* 183 DZ94
Nettles Ter, Guil. GU1 242 AX134
Nettleswellbury Fm, Harl. CM18 *off Tendring Rd* 51 ET16
Nettleton Rd, SE14 163 DX81
Hounslow (Hthrw Air.) TW6 155 BP81
Uxbridge UB10 114 BM63
Nettlewood Rd, SW16 181 DK94
Neuchatel Rd, SE6 183 DZ89
Nevada Cl, N.Mal. KT3 *off Georgia Rd* 198 CQ98
Nevada St, SE10 163 EC79
Nevell Rd, Grays RM16 171 GH76
Nevern Pl, SW5 17 H8
Nevern Rd, SW5 16 G8
Nevern Sq, SW5 17 H8
Nevil Cl, Nthwd. HA6 93 BQ50
Neville Av, N.Mal. KT3 198 CR95
Neville Cl, E11 124 EF62
NW1 *off Brill Pl* 141 DK68
NW6 139 CZ68
SE15 162 DU80
W3 *off Acton La* 158 CQ75
Banstead SM7 218 DB114
Esher KT10 214 BZ107
Hounslow TW3 156 CB82
Potters Bar EN6 63 CZ31
Sidcup DA15 185 ET91
Slough (Stoke P.) SL2 132 AT65
Neville Ct, Slou. SL1 *off Dropmore Rd* 130 AJ69
Neville Dr, N2 120 DC58
Neville Gdns, Dag. RM8 126 EX62
Neville Gill Cl, SW18 180 DA86
Neville Pl, N22 99 DM53
Neville Rd, E7 144 EG66
NW6 139 CZ68
W5 137 CK70
Croydon CR0 202 DR101
Dagenham RM8 126 EX61
Ilford IG6 103 EQ53
Kingston upon Thames KT1 198 CN96
Richmond TW10 177 CJ90
Nevilles Ct, NW2 119 CU62
Neville St, SW7 17 N9
Neville Ter, SW7 17 N9
Neville Wk, Cars. SM5 *off Green Wrythe La* 200 DE101
Nevill Gro, Wat. WD24 75 BV39
Nevill Rd, N16 122 DS63
Nevill Way, Loug. IG10 *off Valley Hill* 102 EL45
Nevin Dr, E4 101 EB46
Nevinson Cl, SW18 180 DD86
Nevis Cl, Rom. RM1 105 FE51
Nevis Rd, SW17 180 DG89
New Acres Rd, SE28 165 ES75
NEW ADDINGTON, Croy. CR0 221 ED109
Tra **New Addington** 221 EC110
Newall Rd, Houns. (Hthrw Air.) TW6 155 BQ81
New Arc, Uxb. UB8 *off High St* 134 BK67
Newark Cl, Guil. GU4 *off Dairyman's Wk* 243 BB129
Woking (Ripley) GU23 228 BG121
Newark Cotts, Wok. (Ripley) GU23 228 BG121
Newark Ct, Walt. KT12 196 BW102
Newark Cres, NW10 138 CR69
Newark Grn, Borwd. WD6 78 CR41
Newark Knok, E6 145 EN72
Newark La, Wok. (Ripley) GU23 227 BF118
Newark Par, NW4 *off Greyhound Hill* 119 CU55
Newark Rd, S.Croy. CR2 220 DR107
Newark St, E1 12 C6
Newark Way, NW4 119 CU56
New Ash Cl, N2 *off Oakridge Dr* 120 DD55
NEW ASH GREEN, Long. DA3 209 FX103
New Atlas Wf, E14 23 M6
New Barn Cl, Wall. SM6 219 DM107
New Barnes Av, St.Alb. AL1 43 CG23
NEW BARNET, Barn. EN5 80 DB42
⇌ **New Barnet** 80 DD43
New Barn La, Beac. HP9 90 AS49
Sevenoaks (Cudham) TN14 239 EQ116
Westerham TN16 239 EQ118
Whyteleafe CR3 236 DS117
New Barn Rd, Grav. (Sthflt) DA13 190 GC90
Swanley BR8 207 FE95
New Barns Av, Mitch. CR4 201 DK98
New Barn St, E13 15 M3
New Barns Way, Chig. IG7 103 EP48
New Battlebridge La, Red. RH1 251 DH130
Sch **New Beacon Sch, The**, Sev. TN13 *off Brittains La* 256 FG127
NEW BECKENHAM, Beck. BR3 183 DZ93
⇌ **New Beckenham** 183 DZ94
Newberries Av, Rad. WD7 77 CJ35
Sch **Newberries Prim Sch**, Rad. WD7 *off Newberries Av* 77 CJ36
Newberry Cres, Wind. SL4 151 AK82
New Berry La, Walt. KT12 214 BX106
Newbery Rd, Erith DA8 167 FF81
Newbery Way, Slou. SL1 151 AR75
Newbiggin Path, Wat. WD19 94 BW49
Newbolt Av, Sutt. SM3 217 CW106
Newbolt Rd, Stan. HA7 95 CF51
New Bond St, W1 8 G8
Newborough Grn, N.Mal. KT3 198 CR98
New Brent St, NW4 119 CW57
Sch **New Briars Prim & Nurs Sch**, Hat. AL10 *off Briars La* 45 CU18
Newbridge Pt, SE23 *off Windrush La* 183 DX90
New Br St, EC4 10 E8
New Broad St, EC2 11 L6
New Bdy, W5 137 CJ73
Hampton (Hmptn H.) TW12 *off Hampton Rd* 177 CD92
New Bdy Bldgs, W5 *off New Bdy* 137 CK73
Newburgh Rd, W3 138 CQ74
Grays RM17 170 GD78
Newburgh St, W1 9 J8
New Burlington Ms, W1 9 J9
New Burlington Pl, W1 9 J9
New Burlington St, W1 9 J9
Newburn St, SE11 20 B10
Newbury Av, Enf. EN3 83 DZ38
Newbury Cl, Dart. DA2 *off Lingfield Av* 188 FP87
Northolt UB5 136 BZ65
Romford RM3 106 FK51
Newbury Gdns, Epsom KT19 217 CT105
Romford RM3 106 FK51
Upminster RM14 128 FM62
Newbury Ho, N22 99 DL53
Newbury Ms, NW5 *off Malden Rd* 140 DG65
NEWBURY PARK, Ilf. IG2 125 ER57
⊖ **Newbury Park** 125 ER58
Sch **Newbury Pk Prim Sch**, Ilf. IG2 *off Perrymans Fm Rd* 125 ER58
Newbury Rd, E4 101 EC51
Bromley BR2 204 EG97
Hounslow (Hthrw Air.) TW6 154 BM81
Ilford IG2 125 ER58
Romford RM3 106 FK50
Newbury St, EC1 10 G6
Newbury Wk, Rom. RM3 106 FK50
Newbury Way, Nthlt. UB5 136 BY65
New Butt La, SE8 163 EA80
New Butt La N, SE8 *off Reginald Rd* 163 EA80
Newby Cl, Enf. EN1 82 DS40
Newby Pl, E14 14 C9
Newby St, SW8 161 DH83
New Caledonian Wf, SE16 23 L5
Newcastle Av, Ilf. IG6 104 EU51
Newcastle Cl, EC4 10 E7
Newcastle Pl, W2 7 P6
Newcastle Row, EC1 10 D3
New Causeway, Reig. RH2 266 DB137
New Cavendish St, W1 9 H5
New Change, EC4 10 G8
New Chapel Sq, Felt. TW13 175 BV88
New Charles St, EC1 10 F1
NEW CHARLTON, SE7 164 EJ77
New Ch Ct, SE19 *off Waldegrave Rd* 182 DU94
New Ch Rd, SE5 162 DQ80
Newchurch Rd, Slou. SL2 131 AM71
Sch **New City Prim Sch**, E13 *off New City Rd* 144 EJ69
New City Rd, E13 144 EJ69
New Cl, SW19 200 DC97
Feltham TW13 176 BY92
New Coll Ct, NW3 *off Finchley Rd* 140 DC65
New Coll Ms, N1 4 D5
New Coll Par, NW3 *off Finchley Rd* 140 DD65
Newcombe Gdns, SW16 181 DL91
Hounslow TW4 156 BZ84
Newcombe Pk, NW7 96 CS50
Wembley HA0 138 CM67
Newcombe Ri, West Dr. UB7 134 BL72
Newcombe St, W8 17 H1
Newcomen Rd, E11 124 EF62
SW11 160 DD83
Newcomen St, SE1 21 J3
Newcome Path, Rad. (Shenley) WD7 *off Newcome Rd* 62 CN34
Newcome Rd, Rad. (Shenley) WD7 62 CN34
New Compton St, WC2 9 M8
New Concordia Wf, SE1 22 A3
New Coppice, Wok. GU21 226 AS119
New Cotts, Rain. (Wenn.) RM13 148 FJ72
New Ct, EC4 10 C9
Addlestone KT15 194 BJ104
Newcourt, Uxb. UB8 134 BJ71
Newcourt St, NW8 140 DE68
★ **New Covent Garden Flower Mkt**, SW8 161 DK79
★ **New Covent Garden Mkt**, SW8 161 DK80
New Crane Pl, E1 22 E1
Newcroft Cl, Uxb. UB8 134 BM71
NEW CROSS, SE14 163 DY81
⇌ **New Cross** 163 DZ80
⊖ **New Cross** 163 DZ80
NEW CROSS GATE, SE14 163 DX81
⇌ **New Cross Gate** 163 DY81
⊖ **New Cross Gate** 163 DY81
New Cross Rd, SE14 162 DW80
Guildford GU2 242 AU132
New Cut, Slou. SL1 130 AG70
Newdales Cl, N9 *off Balham Rd* 100 DU47
Newdene Av, Nthlt. UB5 136 BX68
Newdigate Grn, Uxb. (Hare.) UB9 92 BK53
Newdigate Rd, Reig. RH2 264 CS141
Uxbridge (Hare.) UB9 92 BJ53
Newdigate Rd E, Uxb. (Hare.) UB9 92 BK53
Newell Ri, Hem.H. HP3 40 BL23
Newell Rd, Hem.H. HP3 40 BL23
Newell St, E14 13 L8
NEW ELTHAM, SE9 185 EN89
⇌ **New Eltham** 185 EP88
New End, NW3 120 DC63
Sch **New End Prim Sch**, NW3 *off Streatley Pl* 120 DC63
New End Sq, NW3 120 DD63
New England St, St.Alb. AL3 42 CC20
Newenham Rd, Lthd. (Bkhm) KT23 246 CA126
Newent Cl, SE15 162 DS80
Carshalton SM5 200 DF102
New Fm Av, Brom. BR2 204 EG98
New Fm Cl, Stai. TW18 194 BK95
New Fm Dr, Rom. (Abridge) RM4 86 EV41
New Fm La, Nthwd. HA6 93 BS53
New Ferry App, SE18 165 EN76
New Fetter La, EC4 10 D7
Newfield Cl, Hmptn. TW12 *off Percy Rd* 196 CA95
Newfield La, Hem.H. HP2 40 BL20
Sch **Newfield Prim Sch**, NW10 *off Longstone Av* 139 CT66
Newfield Ri, NW2 119 CV62
Newfields, Welw.G.C. AL8 29 CV10
Newfield Way, St.Alb. AL4 43 CJ22
Newford Cl, Hem.H. HP2 41 BP19
New Ford Rd, Wal.Cr. EN8 67 DZ34
New Forest La, Chig. IG7 103 EN51
New Frontiers Science Pk, Harl. CM19 51 EN16
Sch **New Furness Prim Sch, The**, NW10 *off Palermo Rd* 139 CU68
Newgale Gdns, Edg. HA8 96 CM53
New Gdn Dr, West Dr. UB7 *off Drayton Gdns* 154 BL75
Newgate, Croy. CR0 202 DQ102
Newgate Cl, Felt. TW13 176 BY89
St. Albans AL4 43 CK17
NEWGATE STREET, Hert. SG13 47 DK24
Newgate St, E4 102 EF48
EC1 10 F7
Hertford SG13 47 DK22
Newgatestreet Rd, Wal.Cr. (Chsht) EN7 65 DP27
Newgate St Village, Hert. SG13 65 DL25
New Globe Wk, SE1 20 G1
New Goulston St, E1 11 N7
New Grn Pl, SE19 *off Hawke Rd* 182 DS93
NEW GREENS, St.Alb. AL3 42 CC16
New Grns Av, St.Alb. AL3 43 CD15
New Hall Cl, Hem.H. (Bov.) HP3 57 BA27
Newhall Ct, Wal.Abb. EN9 68 EF33
New Hall Dr, Rom. RM3 106 FL53
Newhall Gdns, Walt. KT12 196 BW103
Coll **Newham Acad of Music**, E6 *off Wakefield St* 144 EL67
Coll **Newham Coll of Further Ed**, East Ham Campus, E6 *off High St S* 145 EM68
Little Ilford Cen, E12 *off Browning Rd* 125 EM64
Royal Docks Campus, E16 *off Woolwich Manor Way* 145 EQ74

Coll Newham Coll of Further Ed, Stratford Campus, E15 off Welfare Rd ... 144 EE66
H Newham Gen Hosp, E13 ... 144 EJ70
Coll Newham 6th Form Coll, Main Site, E13 ... 15 P3
Stratford Site, E15 off High St ... 143 ED66
Newhams Row, SE1 ... 21 M4
Newham Way, E6 ... 144 EJ71
E16 ... 15 L6
Newhaven Cl, Hayes UB3 ... 155 BT77
Newhaven Cres, Ashf. TW15 175 BR92
Newhaven Gdns, SE9 ... 164 EK84
Newhaven La, E16 ... 15 K4
Newhaven Rd, SE25 ... 202 DR99
Newhaven Spur, Slou. SL2 . 131 AP70
NEW HAW, Add. KT15 ... 212 BK108
Sch New Haw Co Jun Sch, Add. KT15 off The Avenue ... 212 BG110
New Haw Rd, Add. KT15 ... 212 BJ106
New Heston Rd, Houns. TW5 ... 156 BZ80
New Horizons Ct, Brent. TW8 off Shield Dr ... 157 CG79
Newhouse Av, Rom. RM6 ... 126 EX55
Newhouse Cl, N.Mal. KT3 ... 198 CS101
Newhouse Cres, Wat. WD25 . 59 BV32
New Ho La, Epp. (N.Wld Bas.) CM16 ... 53 FC24
Gravesend DA11 ... 191 GF90
Newhouse La, Ong. CM5 ... 53 FH22
New Ho La, Red. RH1 ... 267 DK142
New Ho Pk, St.Alb. AL1 ... 43 CG23
Newhouse Rd, Hem.H. (Bov.) HP3 ... 57 BA26
Newhouse Wk, Mord. SM4 . 200 DC101
Newick Cl, Bex. DA5 ... 187 FB86
Newick Rd, E5 ... 122 DV62
Newing Grn, Brom. BR1 ... 184 EK94
NEWINGTON, SE1 ... 20 G7
Newington Barrow Way, N7 . 121 DM62
Newington Butts, SE1 ... 20 F8
SE11 ... 20 F8
Newington Causeway, SE1 ... 20 F6
Newington Grn, N1 ... 5 K1
N16 ... 5 K1
Sch Newington Grn Jun & Inf Sch, N16 ... 5 K1
Newington Grn Rd, N1 ... 5 J2
New Inn Bdy, EC2 ... 11 M3
New Inn La, Guil. GU4 ... 243 BB130
New Inn Pas, WC2 ... 10 B8
New Inn Sq, EC2 ... 11 M3
New Inn St, EC2 ... 11 M3
New Inn Yd, EC2 ... 11 M3
New James Ct, SE15 off Nunhead La ... 162 DV83
New Jersey Ter, SE15 off Nunhead La ... 162 DV83
New Jubilee Ct, Wdf.Grn. IG8 off Grange Av ... 102 EG52
New Kent Rd, SE1 ... 20 G6
St. Albans AL1 ... 43 CD20
Sch New King's Prim Sch, SW6 off New Kings Rd . 159 CZ82
New Kings Rd, SW6 ... 159 CZ82
New King St, SE8 ... 163 EA79
Newland Cl, Pnr. HA5 ... 94 BY51
St. Albans AL1 ... 43 CG23
Newland Ct, Wem. HA9 off Forty Av ... 118 CN61
Newland Dr, Enf. EN1 ... 82 DV39
Newland Gdns, W13 ... 157 CG75
Hertford SG13 off Ware Rd ... 32 DS09
Sch Newland Ho Sch, Twick. TW1 off Waldegrave Pk ... 177 CF91
Newland Rd, N8 ... 121 DL55
Newlands, Abb.L. (Bedmond) WD5 ... 59 BT26
Hatfield AL9 ... 45 CW16
Newlands, The, Wall. SM6 ... 219 DJ108
Newlands Av, Rad. WD7 ... 61 CF34
Thames Ditton KT7 ... 197 CE102
Woking GU22 ... 227 AZ121
Newlands Cl, Brwd. (Hutt.) CM13 ... 109 GD45
Edgware HA8 ... 96 CL48
Horley RH6 ... 268 DF146
Southall UB2 ... 156 BY78
Walton-on-Thames KT12 . 214 BY105
Wembley HA0 ... 137 CJ65
Newlands Cor, Guil. GU4 ... 260 BG136
Newlands Ct, SE9 ... 185 EN86
Newlands Cres, Guil. GU1 ... 259 AZ136
Newlands Dr, Slou. (Colnbr.) SL3 ... 153 BE83
Newlands Pk, SE26 ... 183 DX92
Newlands Pl, Barn. EN5 ... 79 CX43
Newlands Quay, E1 ... 12 E10
Newlands Rd, SW16 ... 201 DL96
Hemel Hempstead HP1 ... 39 BE19
Woodford Green IG8 ... 102 EF47
Newland St, E16 ... 144 EL74
Newlands Wk, Wat. WD25 off Trevellance Way ... 60 BX33
Newlands Way, Chess. KT9 . 215 CJ106
Potters Bar EN6 ... 64 DB30
Newlands Wd, Croy. CR0 ... 221 DZ109
New La, Guil. (Sutt.Grn) GU4 ... 226 AY122
Newling Cl, E6 off Porter Rd ... 145 EM72
New Lo Dr, Oxt. RH8 ... 254 EF128
Sch New Lo Sch, Dor. RH4 off Chichester Rd ... 247 CH134
New London St, EC3 ... 11 M9
New Lydenburg St, SE7 ... 164 EJ76
Newlyn Cl, Orp. BR6 ... 223 ET105
St. Albans (Brick.Wd) AL2 ... 60 BY30
Uxbridge UB8 ... 134 BN71
Newlyn Gdns, Har. HA2 ... 116 BZ59
Newlyn Rd, N17 ... 100 DT53
NW2 off Tilling Rd ... 119 CW60
Barnet EN5 ... 79 CZ42
Welling DA16 ... 165 ET82
NEW MALDEN, KT3 ... 198 CR97
⇌ New Malden ... 198 CS97
Newman Cl, Horn. RM11 ... 128 FL57
Newman Pas, W1 ... 9 K6
Newman Rd, E13 ... 15 N2
E17 off Southcote Rd ... 123 DX57
Bromley BR1 ... 204 EG95
Croydon CR0 ... 201 DM102
Hayes UB3 ... 135 BV73
Newmans Cl, Loug. IG10 ... 85 EP41
Newman's Ct, EC3 ... 11 K8
Newmans Dr, Brwd. (Hutt.) CM13 ... 109 GC45
NEWMAN'S END, Harl. CM17 ... 37 FE10
Newmans La, Loug. IG10 ... 85 EN41
Surbiton KT6 ... 197 CK100
Newmans Rd, Grav. (Nthflt) DA11 ... 191 GF89
Newman's Row, WC2 ... 10 B6
Newman St, W1 ... 9 K6
Newmans Way, Barn. EN4 ... 80 DC39
Newman Yd, W1 ... 9 L7
Newmarket Av, Nthlt. UB5 ... 116 CA64
Newmarket Ct, St.Alb. AL3 ... 42 CC19
Newmarket Grn, SE9 off Middle Pk Av ... 184 EK87
Newmarket Way, Horn. RM12 ... 128 FL63
Newmarsh Rd, SE28 ... 145 ET74
New Mill Rd, Orp. BR5 ... 206 EW95
Newminster Rd, Mord. SM4 . 200 DC100
Sch New Monument Prim Sch, Wok. GU22 off Alpha Rd ... 227 BC115
New Mt St, E15 ... 143 ED66
Newnes Path, SW15 off Putney Pk La ... 159 CV84
Newnham Av, Ruis. HA4 ... 116 BW60
Newnham Cl, Loug. IG10 ... 84 EK44
Northolt UB5 ... 116 CC64
Slough SL2 ... 132 AU74
Thornton Heath CR7 ... 202 DQ96
Newnham Gdns, Nthlt. UB5 . 116 CC64
Sch Newnham Inf Sch, Ruis. HA4 off Newnham Av ... 116 BW60
Sch Newnham Jun Sch, Ruis. HA4 off Newnham Av ... 116 BW60
Newnham Ms, N22 off Newnham Rd ... 99 DM53
Newnham Pl, Grays RM16 . 171 GG77
Newnham Rd, N22 ... 99 DM53
Newnhams Cl, Brom. BR1 . 205 EM97
Newnham Ter, SE1 ... 20 C5
Newnham Way, Har. HA3 ... 118 CL57
New N Pl, EC2 ... 11 L4
New N Rd, N1 ... 5 K10
Ilford IG6 ... 103 ER52
Reigate RH2 ... 265 CZ137
New N St, WC1 ... 10 A5
Newnton Cl, N4 ... 122 DR59
New Oak Rd, N2 ... 98 DC54
New Orleans Wk, N19 ... 121 DK59
New Oxford St, WC1 ... 9 M7
New Par, Ashf. TW15 off Church Rd ... 174 BM91
Rickmansworth (Chorl.) WD3 off Whitelands Av ... 73 BC42
Rickmansworth (Crox.Grn) WD3 off The Green ... 74 BM44
New Par Flats, Rick. (Chorl.) WD3 off Whitelands Av ... 73 BC42
New Pk Av, N13 ... 100 DQ48
New Pk Cl, Nthlt. UB5 ... 136 BY65
New Pk Ct, SW2 ... 181 DL87
New Pk Dr, Hem.H. HP2 ... 41 BP19
New Pk Par, SW2 off Doverfield Rd ... 181 DL86
New Pk Rd, SW2 ... 181 DK88
Ashford TW15 ... 175 BQ92
Hertford SG13 ... 47 DK24
Uxbridge (Hare.) UB9 ... 92 BJ53
New Peachey La, Uxb. UB8 . 134 BK72
Newpiece, Loug. IG10 ... 85 EP41
New Pl Gdns, Upmin. RM14 . 129 FR61
New Pl Sq, SE16 ... 22 C5
New Plaistow Rd, E15 ... 144 EE67
New Plymouth Ho, Rain. RM13 ... 147 FF69
New Pond Rd, Gdmg. GU7 . 258 AS142
Guildford GU3 ... 258 AS142
Newport Av, E13 ... 15 P4
E14 ... 14 F9
Newport Cl, Enf. EN3 ... 83 DY37
Newport Ct, WC2 ... 9 M9
Sch Newport Jun & Inf Sch, E10 off Newport Rd ... 123 EC61
Newport Mead, Wat. WD19 off Kilmarnock Rd ... 94 BX49
Newport Pl, WC2 ... 9 M9
Newport Rd, E10 ... 123 EC61
E17 ... 123 DY56
SW13 ... 159 CU81
Hayes UB4 ... 135 BR71
Hounslow (Hthrw Air.) TW6 ... 154 BN81
Slough SL2 ... 131 AL70
Newports, Saw. CM21 ... 36 EW06
Swanley BR8 ... 207 FD101
Newport St, SE11 ... 20 A8
New Printing Ho Sq, WC1 off Gray's Inn Rd ... 141 DM70
New Priory Ct, NW6 off Mazenod Av ... 140 DA66
New Providence Wf, E14 off Blackwall Way ... 143 ED74
Newquay Cres, Har. HA2 ... 116 BY61
Newquay Gdns, Wat. WD19 off Fulford Gro ... 93 BV47
Newquay Rd, SE6 ... 183 EB89
New Quebec St, W1 ... 8 D8
New Ride, SW7 ... 18 C3
New River Av, Ware (Stans.Abb.) SG12 ... 33 EB11
New River Cl, Hodd. EN11 ... 49 EB16
New River Ct, N5 ... 122 DR63
Waltham Cross (Chsht) EN7 off Pengelly Cl ... 66 DV30
New River Cres, N13 ... 99 DP49
New River Head, EC1 ... 10 D1
New River Trd Est, Wal.Cr. (Chsht) EN8 ... 67 DX26
New River Wk, N1 ... 4 G4
New River Way, N4 ... 122 DR59
New Rd, E1 ... 12 C6
E4 ... 101 EB49
N8 ... 121 DL57
N9 ... 100 DU48
N17 ... 100 DT53
N22 ... 100 DQ53
NW7 ... 97 CY52
NW7 (Barnet Gate) ... 97 CT45
SE2 ... 166 EX77
Amersham HP6 ... 55 AS37
Amersham (Colesh.) HP7 . 55 AM42
Berkhamsted HP4 ... 38 AX18
Berkhamsted (Nthch) HP4 . 38 AS17
Borehamwood (Elstree) WD6 ... 77 CK44
Brentford TW8 ... 157 CK79
Brentwood CM14 ... 108 FX47
Broxbourne EN10 ... 49 DZ19
Chalfont St. Giles HP8 ... 72 AY41
Chertsey KT16 ... 193 BF101
Dagenham RM9, RM10 ... 146 FA67
Dartford (S.Darenth) DA4 ... 208 FQ96
Dorking (Forest Grn) RH5 ... 263 CK137
Epping CM16 ... 70 FA32
Esher KT10 ... 196 CC104
Esher (Clay.) KT10 ... 215 CF110
Feltham TW14 ... 175 BV88
Feltham (E.Bed.) TW14 ... 175 BR86
New Rd, Felt. (Han.) TW13 ... 176 BY92
Gravesend DA11 ... 191 GH86
Grays RM17 ... 170 GA79
Grays (Manor Way) RM17 . 170 GB79
Guildford (Albury) GU5 ... 260 BK139
Guildford (Chilw.) GU4 ... 259 BB141
Guildford (E.Clan.) GU4 ... 244 BL131
Guildford (Goms.) GU5 ... 261 BQ139
Guildford (Won.) GU5 ... 259 BB143
Harlow CM17 ... 36 EX11
Harrow HA1 ... 117 CF63
Hayes UB3 ... 155 BQ80
Hertford SG14 ... 32 DQ07
High Wycombe (Penn) HP10 ... 88 AC47
Horley (Smallfield) RH6 ... 269 DP148
Hounslow TW3 off Station Rd ... 156 CB84
Ilford IG3 ... 125 ES61
Kings Langley (Chipper.) WD4 ... 57 BF30
Kingston upon Thames KT2 ... 178 CN94
Leatherhead KT22 ... 215 CF110
Mitcham CR4 ... 200 DF102
Orpington BR6 ... 206 EU101
Oxted (Lmpfld) RH8 ... 254 EH130
Potters Bar (S.Mimms) EN6 ... 63 CU33
Radlett WD7 ... 77 CE36
Radlett (Shenley) WD7 ... 62 CN34
Rainham RM13 ... 147 FG69
Richmond TW10 ... 177 CJ91
Rickmansworth (Ch.End) WD3 ... 73 BF39
Rickmansworth (Crox.Grn) WD3 ... 74 BN43
Romford (Abridge) RM4 ... 86 EX44
Sevenoaks (Sund.) TN14 . 240 EX124
Shepperton TW17 ... 195 BP97
Slough (Datchet) SL3 ... 152 AX81
Slough (Langley) SL3 ... 153 BA76
Staines TW18 ... 173 BC92
Swanley BR8 ... 207 FF97
Swanley (Hext.) BR8 ... 187 FF94
Tadworth KT20 ... 233 CW123
Uxbridge UB8 ... 135 BQ70
Ware SG12 ... 33 DX06
Watford WD17 ... 76 BW42
Watford (Let.Hth) WD25 ... 77 CE39
Welling DA16 ... 166 EV82
Welwyn Garden City (Stanboro.) AL8 ... 29 CU12
West Molesey KT8 ... 196 CA97
Weybridge KT13 ... 213 BQ106
New Rd Hill, Kes. BR2 ... 222 EL109
Orpington BR6 ... 222 EL109
New Row, WC2 ... 9 N9
Newry Rd, Twick. TW1 ... 157 CG84
Newsam Av, N15 ... 122 DR57
Sch New Sch at W Heath, The, Sev. TN13 off Ashgrove Rd ... 257 FH129
★ New Scotland Yd, SW1 ... 19 L5
Newsham Rd, Wok. GU21 ... 226 AT117
Newsholme Dr, N21 ... 81 DM43
NEW SOUTHGATE, N11 ... 99 DK49
⇌ New Southgate ... 99 DH50
New Spring Gdns Wk, SE11 ... 19 P10
New Sq, WC2 ... 10 B7
Feltham TW14 ... 175 BQ88
Slough SL1 ... 152 AT75
New Sq Pas, WC2 off New Sq ... 141 DM72
Sch New Stanford Prim Sch, SW16 off Chilmark Rd ... 201 DK95
Newstead, Hat. AL10 ... 45 CT21
Newstead Av, Orp. BR6 ... 205 ER104
Newstead Ri, Cat. CR3 ... 252 DV126
Newstead Rd, SE12 ... 184 EE87
Newstead Wk, Cars. SM5 ... 200 DC101
Newstead Way, SW19 ... 179 CX91
Sch Newstead Wd Sch for Girls, Orp. BR6 off Avebury Rd ... 205 ER104
New St, EC2 ... 11 M6
Berkhamsted HP4 ... 38 AX19
Staines TW18 ... 174 BG91
Watford WD18 ... 76 BW42
Westerham TN16 ... 255 EQ127
New St Hill, Brom. BR1 ... 184 EH92
New St Sq, EC4 ... 10 D7
New Swan Yd, Grav. DA12 off Bank St ... 191 GH86
Newteswell Dr, Wal.Abb. EN9 ... 67 ED32
Newton Abbot Rd, Grav. (Nthflt) DA11 ... 191 GF89
Newton Av, N10 ... 98 DG53
W3 ... 158 CQ75
Newton Cl, E17 ... 123 DY58
Harrow HA2 ... 116 CA61
Hoddesdon EN11 ... 33 EB13
Slough SL3 ... 153 AZ75
Newton Ct, Wind. (Old Wind.) SL4 ... 172 AU86
Newton Cres, Borwd. WD6 ... 78 CQ42
Newton Dr, Saw. CM21 ... 36 EX06
Sch Newton Fm First & Mid Sch, Har. HA2 off Ravenswood Cres ... 116 BZ61
Newton Gro, W4 ... 158 CS77
Newton Ho, Enf. EN3 off Exeter Rd ... 83 DX41
Newton La, Wind. (Old Wind.) SL4 ... 172 AV86
Newton Pl, E14 ... 23 N7
Sch Newton Prep Sch, SW8 off Battersea Pk Rd . 161 DH81
Newton Rd, E15 ... 123 ED64
N15 ... 122 DT57
NW2 ... 119 CW62
SW19 ... 179 CY94
W2 ... 7 H8
Chigwell IG7 ... 104 EV50
Harrow HA3 ... 95 CE54
Isleworth TW7 ... 157 CF82
Purley CR8 ... 219 DJ112
Tilbury RM18 ... 171 GG82
Welling DA16 ... 166 EU83
Wembley HA0 ... 138 CM66
Newtons Cl, Rain. RM13 ... 147 FF66
Newtons Ct, Dart. DA2 ... 169 FR84
Newtonside Orchard, Wind. SL4 ... 172 AU86
Sch Newtons Prim Sch, Rain. RM13 off Lowen Rd ... 147 FD68
Newton St, WC2 ... 9 P7
Newtons Yd, SW18 off Wandsworth High St . 180 DB85
Newton Wk, Edg. HA8 off North Rd ... 96 CP53
Newton Way, N18 ... 100 DQ50
Newton Wd, Ashtd. KT21 ... 216 CL114
Newton Wd Rd, Ashtd. KT21 ... 232 CM116
NEWTOWN, Chesh. HP5 ... 54 AP30
NEW TOWN, Dart. DA1 ... 188 FN86
Sch Newtown Co First Sch, Chesh. HP5 off Berkhampstead Rd ... 54 AQ29
Newtown Rd, Uxb. (Denh.) UB9 ... 134 BH65
Newtown St, SW11 off Strasburg Rd ... 161 DH81
New Trinity Rd, N2 ... 120 DD55
New Turnstile, WC1 ... 10 A6
New Union Cl, E14 ... 24 D5
New Union St, EC2 ... 11 J6
H New Victoria Hosp, Kings.T. KT2 ... 198 CS95
New Wanstead, E11 ... 124 EF58
New Way La, Harl. (Thres.B.) CM17 ... 53 FB16
New Way Rd, NW9 ... 118 CS56
New Wf Rd, N1 ... 141 DL68
New Wickham La, Egh. TW20 ... 173 BA94
New Windsor St, Uxb. UB8 . 134 BJ67
New Wd, Welw.G.C. AL7 ... 30 DC08
Sch New Woodlands Sch, Brom. BR1 off Shroffold Rd ... 184 EE91
NEWYEARS GREEN, Uxb. UB9 ... 114 BN59
New Years Grn La, Uxb. (Hare.) UB9 ... 114 BL58
New Years La, Orp. BR6 ... 224 EU114
Sevenoaks (Knock.) TN14 . 239 ET116
New Zealand Av, Walt. KT12 ... 195 BT102
New Zealand Way, W12 ... 139 CV73
Rainham RM13 ... 147 FF69
Niagara Av, W5 ... 157 CJ77
Niagara Cl, N1 off Cropley St ... 142 DR68
Waltham Cross (Chsht) EN8 ... 67 DX29
Nibthwaite Rd, Har. HA1 ... 117 CE57
Sch Nicholas Breakspear RC Sch, St.Alb. AL4 off Colney Heath La ... 44 CL21
Nicholas Cl, Grnf. UB6 ... 136 CB68
St. Albans AL3 ... 43 CD17
South Ockendon RM15 ... 149 FW69
Watford WD24 ... 75 BV37
Nicholas Ct, E13 ... 15 P2
Nicholas Gdns, W5 ... 157 CK75
Slough SL1 ... 131 AL74
Woking GU22 ... 227 BE116
Nicholas La, EC4 ... 11 K9
Hertford SG14 off Old Cross ... 32 DQ09
Nicholas Ms, W4 off Short Rd ... 158 CS79
Nicholas Pas, EC4 ... 11 K9
Nicholas Rd, E1 ... 12 F3
Borehamwood (Elstree) WD6 ... 78 CM44
Croydon CR0 ... 219 DL105
Dagenham RM8 ... 126 EZ61
Nicholas Wk, Grays RM16 off Godman Rd ... 171 GH75
Nicholas Way, Hem.H. HP2 ... 40 BM18
Northwood HA6 ... 93 BQ53
Nicholay Rd, N19 ... 121 DK60
Nichol Cl, N14 ... 99 DK46
Nicholes Rd, Houns. TW3 ... 156 CA84
Nichol La, Brom. BR1 ... 184 EG94
Nicholl Rd, Epp. CM16 ... 69 ET31
Nicholls Av, Uxb. UB8 ... 134 BN70
Nicholls Fld, Harl. CM18 ... 52 EV16
Nichollsfield Wk, N7 ... 4 A2
Nicholls Pt, E15 off Park Gro ... 144 EG67
Nicholls Twr, Harl. CM18 ... 52 EU16
Nicholl St, E2 ... 142 DU67
Nicholls Wk, Wind. SL4 ... 150 AJ83
Nichols Cl, N4 off Osborne Rd ... 121 DN60
Chessington KT9 off Merritt Gdns ... 215 CJ107
Nichols Ct, E2 ... 5 N10
Nichols Grn, W5 off Montpelier Rd ... 138 CL71
Nicholson Ms, Egh. TW20 off Nicholson Wk ... 173 BA92
Nicholson Rd, Croy. CR0 ... 202 DT102
Nicholson St, SE1 ... 20 E2
Nicholson Wk, Egh. TW20 ... 173 BA92
Nicholson Way, Sev. TN13 ... 257 FK122
Nickelby Cl, SE28 ... 146 EW72
Uxbridge UB8 off Dickens Av ... 135 BP72
Nickols Wk, SW18 off Jew's Row ... 160 DB84
Nicola Cl, Har. HA3 ... 95 CD54
South Croydon CR2 ... 220 DQ107
Nicola Ms, Ilf. IG6 ... 103 EP52
Nicol Cl, Ger.Cr. (Chal.St.P.) SL9 ... 90 AX53
Twickenham TW1 off Cassilis Rd ... 177 CH86
Nicol End, Ger.Cr. (Chal.St.P.) SL9 ... 90 AW53
Nicoll Pl, NW4 ... 119 CV58
Nicoll Rd, NW10 ... 138 CS67
Nicoll Way, Borwd. WD6 ... 78 CR43
Nicol Rd, Ger.Cr. (Chal.St.P.) SL9 ... 90 AW53
Nicolson Dr, Bushey (Bushey Hth) WD23 ... 94 CC46
Nicolson Rd, Orp. BR5 ... 206 EX101
Nicosia Rd, SW18 ... 180 DE87
Nidderdale, Hem.H. HP2 off Wharfedale ... 40 BM17
Niederwald Rd, SE26 ... 183 DY91
Nield Rd, Hayes UB3 ... 155 BT75
Nield Way, Rick. WD3 ... 91 BF45
Nigel Cl, Nthlt. UB5 off Church Rd ... 136 BY67
Nigel Fisher Way, Chess. KT9 ... 215 CJ108
Nigel Ms, Ilf. IG1 ... 125 EP63
Nigel Playfair Av, W6 off King St ... 159 CV77
Nigel Rd, E7 ... 124 EJ64
SE15 ... 162 DU83
Nigeria Rd, SE7 ... 164 EJ80
Nightingale Av, E4 ... 102 EE50
Harrow HA1 ... 117 CH59
Leatherhead (W.Hors.) KT24 ... 229 BR124
Upminster RM14 ... 129 FT60
Nightingale Cl, E4 ... 102 EE49
W4 off Grove Pk Ter ... 158 CQ79
Abbots Langley WD5 ... 59 BU31
Carshalton SM5 ... 200 DG103
Cobham KT11 ... 214 BX111
Epsom KT19 ... 216 CN112
Nightingale Cl, Grav. (Nthflt) DA11 ... 190 GE91
Pinner HA5 ... 116 BW57
Radlett WD7 ... 77 CF36
Westerham TN16 off Main Rd ... 238 EK115
Nightingale Ct, E11 off Nightingale La ... 124 EH57
Hertford SG14 ... 32 DQ09
Slough SL1 off St. Laurence Way ... 152 AU76
Nightingale Cres, Lthd. (W.Hors.) KT24 ... 229 BQ124
Romford RM3 off Lister Av ... 106 FL54
Nightingale Dr, Epsom KT19 ... 216 CP107
Nightingale Est, E5 ... 122 DU62
Nightingale Gro, SE13 ... 183 ED85
Dartford DA1 ... 168 FN84
Nightingale Hts, SE18 off Nightingale Vale ... 165 EP79
Sch Nightingale JMI Sch, E5 off Rendlesham Rd ... 122 DU63
Nightingale La, E11 ... 124 EG57
N6 ... 120 DE60
N8 ... 121 DL56
SW4 ... 180 DF87
SW12 ... 180 DF87
Bromley BR1 ... 204 EJ96
Richmond TW10 ... 178 CL87
St. Albans AL1 ... 43 CJ24
Sevenoaks (Ide Hill) TN14 . 256 FB130
Nightingale Ms, E3 off Chisenhale Rd ... 143 DY68
E11 ... 124 EG57
SE11 ... 20 D7
Kingston upon Thames KT1 off South La ... 197 CK97
Nightingale Pk, Slou. (Farn.Com.) SL2 ... 131 AM66
Nightingale Pl, SE18 ... 165 EN79
SW10 off Fulham Rd ... 160 DC79
Rickmansworth WD3 off Nightingale Rd ... 92 BK45
Sch Nightingale Prim Sch, E18 off Ashbourne Av ... 124 EJ56
N22 off Bounds Grn Rd ... 99 DM53
SE18 off Bloomfield Rd ... 165 EP78
Nightingale Rd, E5 ... 122 DV62
N1 ... 5 H4
N9 ... 82 DW44
N22 ... 99 DL53
NW10 ... 139 CT68
W7 ... 137 CF74
Bushey WD23 ... 76 CA43
Carshalton SM5 ... 200 DF104
Chesham HP5 ... 54 AP29
Esher KT10 ... 214 BZ106
Guildford GU1 ... 242 AX134
Hampton TW12 ... 176 CA92
Leatherhead (E.Hors.) KT24 ... 245 BT125
Orpington BR5 ... 205 EQ100
Rickmansworth WD3 ... 92 BJ46
South Croydon CR2 ... 221 DX111
Waltham Cross (Chsht) EN7 ... 66 DQ25
Walton-on-Thames KT12 . 195 BV101
West Molesey KT8 ... 196 CB99
Nightingales, Harl. CM17 ... 52 EW17
Waltham Abbey EN9 off Roundhills ... 68 EE34
Nightingales, The, Stai. TW19 ... 174 BM87
Nightingales Cor, Amer. HP7 off Chalfont Sta Rd ... 72 AW40
Nightingale Shott, Egh. TW20 ... 173 AZ93
Nightingales La, Ch.St.G. HP8 ... 90 AX46
Nightingale Sq, SW12 ... 180 DG87
Nightingale Vale, SE18 ... 165 EN79
Nightingale Wk, SW4 ... 181 DH86
Windsor SL4 ... 151 AQ83
Nightingale Way, E6 ... 144 EL71
Redhill (Bletch.) RH1 ... 252 DS134
Swanley BR8 ... 207 FE97
Uxbridge (Denh.) UB9 ... 113 BF59
Nile Cl, N16 off Evering Rd ... 122 DT62
Nile Dr, N9 ... 100 DW47
Nile Path, SE18 off Jackson St ... 165 EN79
Nile Rd, E13 ... 144 EJ68
Nile St, N1 ... 11 H1
Nile Ter, SE15 ... 21 N10
Nimbus Rd, Epsom KT19 ... 216 CR110
Nimegen Way, SE22 ... 182 DS85
Nimmo Dr, Bushey (Bushey Hth) WD23 ... 95 CD45
Nimrod Cl, Nthlt. UB5 ... 136 BX69
St. Albans AL4 ... 43 CJ18
Nimrod Dr, Hat. AL10 off Mosquito Way ... 44 CR17
Nimrod Pas, N1 ... 5 M4
Nimrod Rd, SW16 ... 181 DH93
Nina Mackay Cl, E15 off Arthingworth St ... 144 EE67
Nine Acre La, Hat. AL10 off Bishops Ri ... 45 CT19
Nine Acres, Slou. SL1 ... 131 AM74
Nine Acres Cl, E12 ... 124 EL64
Nineacres Way, Couls. CR5 . 235 DL116
Nine Ashes, Ware SG12 off Acorn St ... 34 EK08
NINE ELMS, SW8 ... 161 DH80
Nine Elms Av, Uxb. UB8 ... 134 BK71
Nine Elms Cl, Felt. TW14 ... 175 BT88
Uxbridge UB8 ... 134 BK72
Nine Elms Gro, Grav. DA11 . 191 GG87
Nine Elms La, SW8 ... 161 DJ80
Ninefields, Wal.Abb. EN9 ... 68 EF33
Ninehams Cl, Cat. CR3 ... 236 DR120
Ninehams Gdns, Cat. CR3 ... 236 DR120
Ninehams Rd, Cat. CR3 ... 236 DR121
Westerham (Tats.) TN16 ... 238 EJ121
Nine Stiles Cl, Uxb. (Denh.) UB9 ... 134 BH65
Nineteenth Rd, Mitch. CR4 . 201 DL98
Ninhams Wd, Orp. BR6 ... 223 EN105
Ninian Rd, Hem.H. HP2 ... 40 BL15
Ninnings Rd, Ger.Cr. (Chal.St.P.) SL9 ... 91 AZ52
Ninnings Way, Ger.Cr. (Chal.St.P.) SL9 ... 91 AZ52
Ninth Av, Hayes UB3 ... 135 BU73
Nisbet Ho, E9 off Homerton High St ... 123 DX64
Nita Rd, Brwd. CM14 ... 108 FW50

Nithdale Rd, SE18 ....165 EP80
Nithsdale Gro, Uxb. UB10
off Tweeddale Gro 115 BQ62
Niton Cl, Barn. EN5 ....79 CX44
Niton Rd, Rich. TW9 ....158 CN83
Niton St, SW6 ....159 CX80
Niven Cl, Borwd. WD6 ....78 CQ39
Nixey Cl, Slou. SL1 ....152 AU75
N.L.A. Twr, Croy. CR0 ....202 DR103
NOAK HILL, Rom. RM4 ....106 FK47
Noak Hill Rd, Rom. RM3 ....106 FJ49
Nobel Dr, Hayes UB3 ....155 BR80
Nobel Rd, N18 ....100 DW50
Noble St, EC2 ....10 G7
Walton-on-Thames KT12 ....195 BV104
Nobles Way, Egh. TW20 ....172 AY93
NOEL PARK, N22 ....99 DN54
Sch **Noel Pk Prim Sch**, N22
off Gladstone Av 99 DN54
Noel Pk Rd, N22 ....99 DN54
Noel Rd, E6 ....144 EL70
N1 ....4 E9
W3 ....138 CP72
Noel Sq, Dag. RM8 ....126 EW63
Noel St, W1 ....9 K8
Noel Ter, SE23
off Dartmouth Rd 182 DW89
Noke Dr, Red. RH1 ....250 DG133
Noke Fm Barns, Couls. CR5 ....234 DF122
Noke La, St.Alb. AL2 ....60 BY26
Nokes, The, Hem.H. HP1 ....40 BG18
Noke Side, St.Alb. AL2 ....60 CA27
Nolan Way, E5 ....122 DU63
Nolton Pl, Edg. HA8 ....96 CM53
Nonsuch Cl, Ilf. IG6 ....103 EP51
Nonsuch Ct Av, Epsom
KT17 ....217 CV110
Sch **Nonsuch High Sch for Girls**, Sutt. SM3
off Ewell Rd 217 CX108
Nonsuch Ind Est, Epsom
KT17 ....216 CS111
★ **Nonsuch Mansion Ho**, Sutt. SM3 ....217 CW107
Sch **Nonsuch Prim Sch**, Epsom
KT17 *off Chadacre Rd* 217 CV106
Nonsuch Wk, Sutt. SM2 ....217 CW110
Nook, The, Ware (Stans.Abb.) SG12 33 EB11
Noons Cor Rd, Dor. RH5 ....262 BZ143
Nora Gdns, NW4 ....119 CX56
NORBITON, Kings.T. KT2 ....198 CP96
⇌ **Norbiton** 198 CN95
Norbiton Av, Kings.T. KT1 ....198 CN96
Norbiton Common Rd,
Kings.T. KT1 ....198 CP97
Norbiton Rd, E14 ....13 L7
Norbreck Gdns, NW10
off Lytham Gro 138 CM69
Norbreck Par, NW10
off Lytham Gro 138 CM69
Norbroke St, W12 ....139 CT73
Norburn St, W10 ....6 C6
NORBURY, SW16 ....201 DN95
⇌ **Norbury** 201 DM95
Norbury Av, SW16 ....201 DM95
Hounslow TW3 ....177 CD85
Thornton Heath CR7 ....201 DN96
Watford WD24 ....76 BW39
Norbury Cl, SW16 ....201 DN95
Norbury Ct Rd, SW16 ....201 DL97
Norbury Cres, SW16 ....201 DM95
Norbury Cross, SW16 ....201 DL97
Sch **Norbury First & Mid Sch**, Har. HA1
off Welldon Cres 117 CE57
Norbury Gdns, Rom. RM6 ....126 EX57
Norbury Gro, NW7 ....96 CS48
Norbury Hill, SW16 ....181 DN94
Sch **Norbury Manor Girls' High Sch**, Th.Hth. CR7
off Kensington Av 201 DN95
Sch **Norbury Manor Prim Sch**, SW16
off Abingdon Rd 201 DL95
Norbury Pk, Dor. (Mick.)
RH5 ....247 CF127
Norbury Ri, SW16 ....201 DL97
Norbury Rd, E4 ....101 EA50
Feltham TW13
off Bedfont Rd 175 BT90
Reigate RH2 ....249 CZ134
Thornton Heath CR7 ....202 DQ96
Norbury Way, Lthd. (Bkhm)
KT23 ....246 CC125
Norcombe Gdns, Har. HA3 ....117 CJ58
Norcott Cl, Hayes UB4 ....136 BW70
Norcott Rd, N16 ....122 DU61
Norcroft Gdns, SE22 ....182 DU87
Norcutt Rd, Twick. TW2 ....177 CE88
Nordenfeldt Rd, Erith DA8 ....167 FD78
Nordmann Pl, S.Ock. RM15 ....149 FX70
Norelands Dr, Slou. (Burn.)
SL1 ....130 AJ68
Norfield Rd, Dart. DA2 ....187 FC91
Norfolk Av, N13 ....99 DP51
N15 ....122 DT58
Slough SL1 ....131 AQ71
South Croydon CR2 ....220 DU110
Watford WD24 ....76 BW38
Norfolk Cl, N2 *off Park Rd* 120 DE55
N13 ....99 DP51
Barnet EN4 ....80 DG42
Dartford DA1 ....188 FN86
Horley RH6 ....268 DF149
Twickenham TW1
off Cassilis Rd 177 CH86
Norfolk Ct, Dor. RH5 ....263 CK139
Norfolk Cres, W2 ....8 B7
Sidcup DA15 ....185 ES87
Norfolk Fm Cl, Wok. GU22 ....227 BD116
Norfolk Fm Rd, Wok. GU22 ....227 BD115
Norfolk Gdns, Bexh. DA7 ....166 EZ81
Borehamwood WD6 ....78 CR42
Norfolk Ho, SE3 ....164 EE79
Norfolk Ho Rd, SW16 ....181 DK90
Norfolk La, Dor. (Mid Holm.)
RH5 ....263 CH142
Norfolk Ms, W10 ....6 D6
Norfolk Pl, W2 ....7 P7
Grays (Chaff.Hun.) RM16 ....169 FW78
Welling DA16 ....166 EU82
Norfolk Rd, E6 ....145 EM67
E17 ....101 DX54
NW8 ....140 DD67
NW10 ....138 CS66
SW19 ....180 DE94
Barking IG11 ....145 ES66
Barnet EN5 ....80 DA41
Norfolk Rd, Dag. RM10 ....127 FB64
Dorking RH4 ....263 CG136
Dorking (S.Holm.) RH5 ....263 CJ144
Enfield EN3 ....82 DV44
Esher (Clay.) KT10 ....215 CE106
Feltham TW13 ....176 BW88
Gravesend DA12 ....191 GK86
Harrow HA1 ....116 CB57
Ilford IG3 ....125 ES60
Rickmansworth WD3 ....92 BL46
Romford RM7 ....127 FC58
Thornton Heath CR7 ....202 DQ97
Upminster RM14 ....128 FN62
Uxbridge UB8 ....134 BK65
Norfolk Row, SE1 ....20 A7
Norfolk Sq, W2 ....7 P8
Norfolk Sq Ms, W2 ....7 P8
Norfolk St, E7 ....124 EG63
Norfolk Ter, W6 ....16 C10
Norgrove Pk, Ger.Cr. SL9 ....112 AY56
Norgrove St, SW12 ....180 DG87
Norheads La, Warl. CR6 ....238 EG119
Westerham (Bigg.H.)
TN16 ....238 EJ116
Norhyrst Av, SE25 ....202 DT97
NORK, Bans. SM7 ....233 CY115
Nork Gdns, Bans. SM7 ....217 CY114
Nork Ri, Bans. SM7 ....233 CX116
Nork Way, Bans. SM7 ....233 CY115
Norland Ho, W11 ....16 B2
Norland Pl, W11 ....16 D2
Sch **Norland Pl Sch**, W11 ....16 C2
Norland Rd, W11 ....16 B2
Norlands Cres, Chis. BR7 ....205 EP95
Norlands Gate, Chis. BR7 ....205 EP95
Norlands La, Egh. TW20 ....193 BE97
Norland Sq, W11 ....16 D2
Norley Vale, SW15 ....179 CU88
Norlington Rd, E10 ....123 EC60
E11 ....123 EC60
Sch **Norlington Sch**, E10
off Norlington Rd 123 ED60
Norman Av, N22 ....99 DP53
Epsom KT17 ....217 CT112
Feltham TW13 ....176 BY89
South Croydon CR2 ....220 DQ110
Southall UB1 ....136 BY73
Twickenham TW1 ....177 CH87
Normanby Cl, SW15
off Manfred Rd 179 CZ85
Normanby Rd, NW10 ....119 CT63
Norman Cl, Epsom KT18 ....233 CV119
Orpington BR6 ....205 EQ104
Romford RM5 ....105 FB54
Waltham Abbey EN9 ....67 ED33
Norman Ct, Ilf. IG2 ....125 ER59
Potters Bar EN6 ....64 DC30
Woodford Green IG8
off Monkhams Av 102 EH50
Norman Cres, Brwd. CM13 ....109 GA48
Hounslow TW5 ....156 BX81
Pinner HA5 ....94 BW53
Normand Gdns, W14
off Greyhound Rd 159 CY79
Normand Ms, W14
off Normand Rd 159 CY79
Sch **Normand Pk Prim Sch**,
SW6 *off Lillie Rd* 159 CZ79
Normand Rd, W14 ....159 CZ79
Normandy Av, Barn. EN5 ....79 CZ43
Normandy Cl, SE26 ....183 DY90
Normandy Ct, Hem.H. HP2 ....40 BK19
Normandy Dr, Berk. HP4 ....38 AV17
Hayes UB3 ....135 BQ72
Sch **Normandy Prim Sch**,
Bexh. DA7
off Fairford Av 167 FD81
Normandy Rd, SW9 ....161 DN81
St. Albans AL3 ....43 CD18
Normandy Ter, E16 ....15 N8
Normandy Wk, Egh. TW20
off Mullens Rd 173 BC92
Normandy Way, Erith DA8 ....167 FE81
Hoddesdon EN11 ....49 EC16
Norman Gro, E3 ....143 DY68
Normanhurst, Ashf. TW15 ....174 BN92
Brentwood (Hutt.) CM13 ....109 GC44
Normanhurst Av, Bexh.
DA7 ....166 EX81
Normanhurst Dr, Twick.
TW1 *off St. Margarets Rd* 177 CH85
Normanhurst Rd, SW2 ....181 DM89
Orpington BR5 ....206 EV96
Walton-on-Thames KT12 ....196 BX103
Sch **Normanhurst Sch**, E4
off Station Rd 101 ED45
Norman Rd, E6 ....145 EM70
E11 ....123 ED61
N15 ....122 DT57
SE10 ....163 EB80
SW19 ....180 DC94
Ashford TW15 ....175 BR93
Belvedere DA17 ....167 FB76
Dartford DA1 ....188 FL88
Hornchurch RM11 ....127 FG59
Ilford IG1 ....125 EP64
Sutton SM1 ....218 DA106
Thornton Heath CR7 ....201 DP99
Normans, The, Slou. SL2 ....132 AV72
Norman's Bldgs, EC1
off Ironmonger Row 142 DQ69
Normans Cl, NW10 ....138 CR65
Gravesend DA11 ....191 GG87
Uxbridge UB8 ....134 BL71
Normansfield Av, Tedd.
TW11 ....177 CJ94
Normansfield Cl, Bushey
WD23 ....94 CB45
Normanshire Av, E4 ....101 EC49
Normanshire Dr, E4 ....101 EA49
Normans Mead, NW10 ....138 CR65
Norman St, EC1 ....10 G2
Normanton Av, SW19 ....180 DA89
Normanton Pk, E4 ....102 EE48
Normanton Rd, S.Croy. CR2 ....220 DS107
Normanton St, SE23 ....183 DX89
Norman Way, N14 ....99 DL47
W3 ....138 CP71
Normington Cl, SW16 ....181 DN92
Norrels Dr, Lthd. (E.Hors.)
KT24 ....245 BT126
Norrels Ride, Lthd. (E.Hors.)
KT24 ....245 BT125
Norrice Lea, N2 ....120 DD57
Norris Gro, Brox. EN10 ....49 DY20
Norris La, Hodd. EN11 ....49 EA16
Norris Ri, Hodd. EN11 ....49 DZ16
Norris Rd, Hodd. EN11 ....49 EA17
Staines TW18 ....173 BF91
Norris St, SW1 ....9 L10
Norris Way, Dart. DA1 ....167 FF83
Norroy Rd, SW15 ....159 CX84
Norrys Cl, Barn. EN4 ....80 DF43
Norrys Rd, Barn. EN4 ....80 DF42
Norseman Cl, Ilf. IG3 ....126 EV60
Norseman Way, Grnf. UB6
off Olympic Way 136 CB67
Norstead Pl, SW15 ....179 CU89
Norsted La, Orp. BR6 ....224 EU110
North Access Rd, E17 ....123 DX58
North Acre, NW9 ....96 CS53
Banstead SM7 ....233 CZ116
NORTH ACTON, W3 ....138 CR70
⊖ **North Acton** 138 CR70
North Acton Rd, NW10 ....138 CR69
Northallerton Way, Rom.
RM3 ....106 FK50
Northall Rd, Bexh. DA7 ....167 FC82
Northampton Av, Slou. SL1 ....131 AQ72
Northampton Gro, N1 ....5 J2
Northampton Pk, N1 ....5 H3
Northampton Rd, EC1 ....10 D3
Croydon CR0 ....202 DU103
Enfield EN3 ....83 DY42
Northampton Row, EC1 ....10 D2
Northampton Sq, EC1 ....10 E2
Northampton St, N1 ....4 G5
Coll **North & W Essex Adult Comm Coll**, Rivermill
Cen, Harl. CM20
off Hodings Rd 35 EQ13
Northanger Rd, SW16 ....181 DL93
North App, Nthwd. HA6 ....93 BQ47
Watford WD25 ....75 BT35
North Arc, Croy. CR0
off North End 202 DQ103
North Audley St, W1 ....8 E8
North Av, N18 ....100 DU49
W13 ....137 CH72
Brentwood CM14 ....107 FR45
Carshalton SM5 ....218 DF108
Harrow HA2 ....116 CB58
Hayes UB3 ....135 BU73
Radlett (Shenley) WD7 ....62 CL32
Richmond TW9
off Sandycombe Rd 158 CN81
Southall UB1 ....136 BZ73
Walton-on-Thames
(Whiteley Vill.) KT12 ....213 BS109
NORTHAW, Pot.B. EN6 ....64 DF30
Northaw Cl, Hem.H. HP2 ....41 BP15
Sch **Northaw C of E Prim Sch**, Pot.B. EN6
off Vineyards Rd 64 DG30
Northaw Pl, Pot.B. EN6 ....64 DD30
Northaw Rd E, Pot.B.
(Cuffley) EN6 ....65 DK31
Northaw Rd W, Pot.B. EN6 ....64 DG30
North Bk, NW8 ....7 P2
Northbank Rd, E17 ....101 EC54
North Barn, Brox. EN10 ....49 EA21
NORTH BECKTON, E6 ....144 EL70
Sch **North Beckton Prim Sch**,
E6 *off Harrier Way* 145 EM71
North Birkbeck Rd, E11 ....123 ED62
Northborough Rd, SW16 ....201 DK97
Slough SL2 ....131 AN70
Northbourne, Brom. BR2 ....204 EG101
Godalming GU7 ....258 AT143
Northbourne Rd, SW4 ....161 DK84
North Branch Av, W10
off Harrow Rd 139 CW69
Sch **North Br Ho Jun Sch**,
NW1 *off Gloucester Av* 141 DH67
Sch **North Br Ho Sch**, NW3
off Netherhall Gdns 120 DC64
Sch **North Br Ho Sen Sch**,
NW1 *off Gloucester Av* 141 DH67
Northbridge Rd, Berk. HP4 ....38 AT17
Sch **Northbrook C of E Sch**,
SE12 *off Taunton Rd* 184 EF85
Northbrook Dr, Nthwd. HA6 ....93 BS53
Northbrook Rd, N22 ....99 DL52
SE13 ....183 ED85
Barnet EN5 ....79 CY44
Croydon CR0 ....202 DR99
Ilford IG1 ....125 EN61
Northbrooks, Harl. CM19 ....51 EQ15
Northburgh St, EC1 ....10 F3
North Burnham Cl, Slou.
(Burn.) SL1
off Wyndham Cres 130 AH68
Sch **Northbury Jun & Inf Sch**, Bark. IG11
off North St 145 EQ65
North Carriage Dr, W2 ....8 A9
NORTH CHEAM, Sutt. SM3 ....199 CW104
NORTHCHURCH, Berk. HP4 ....38 AT17
Northchurch, SE17 ....21 K9
Northchurch Rd, N1 ....5 J5
Wembley HA9 ....138 CM65
Sch **Northchurch St. Mary's C of E First Sch**, Berk.
HP4 *off New Rd* 38 AS17
Northchurch Ter, N1 ....5 L6
North Circular Rd, E4 (A406) 101 DZ52
E6 (A406) 145 EP68
E11 (A406) 102 EJ54
E12 (A406) 125 EN64
E17 (A406) 101 DZ52
E18 (A406) 102 EJ54
N3 (A406) 120 DB55
N11 (A406) 98 DD53
N12 (A406) 98 DD53
N13 (A406) 99 DN50
N18 (A406) 100 DS50
NW2 (A406) 118 CS62
NW10 (A406) 138 CP66
NW11 (A406) 119 CY56
W3 (A406) 158 CM75
W4 (A406) 158 CM75
W5 (A406) 158 CM75
Barking (A406) IG11 ....145 EP68
Ilford (A406) IG1, IG4 ....124 EL60
Northcliffe Cl, Wor.Pk. KT4 ....198 CS104
Northcliffe Dr, N20 ....97 CZ46
North Cl, Barn. EN5 ....79 CW43
Bexleyheath DA6 ....166 EX84
Chigwell IG7 ....104 EU50
Dagenham RM10 ....146 FA67
Dorking (N.Holm.) RH5 ....263 CJ140
Feltham TW14
off North Rd 175 BR86
Morden SM4 ....199 CY98
St. Albans AL2 ....60 CB25
Windsor SL4 ....151 AM81
North Colonnade, E14 ....23 P1
North Common, Wey. KT13 ....213 BP105
North Common Rd, W5 ....138 CL73
Uxbridge UB8 ....114 BK64
Northcote, Add. KT15 ....212 BK105
Leatherhead (Oxshott)
KT22 ....214 CC114
Pinner HA5 ....94 BW54
Northcote Av, W5 ....138 CL73
Isleworth TW7 ....177 CG85
Southall UB1 ....136 BY73
Surbiton KT5 ....198 CN101
Northcote Cl, Lthd.
(W.Hors.) KT24 ....245 BQ125
Northcote Cres, Lthd.
(W.Hors.) KT24 ....245 BQ125
Sch **Northcote Lo Sch**, SW11
off Bolingbroke Gro 180 DF86
Northcote Ms, SW11
off Northcote Rd 160 DE84
Northcote Rd, E17 ....123 DY56
NW10 ....138 CS66
SW11 ....160 DE84
Croydon CR0 ....202 DR100
Gravesend DA11 ....191 GF88
Leatherhead (W.Hors.)
KT24 ....245 BQ125
New Malden KT3 ....198 CQ97
Sidcup DA14 ....185 ES91
Twickenham TW1 ....177 CG85
North Cotts, St.Alb.
(Lon.Col.) AL2 ....61 CG25
Northcott Av, N22 ....99 DL53
Northcotts, Abb.L. WD5
off Long Elms 59 BR33
Hatfield AL9 ....45 CW17
North Countess Rd, E17 ....101 DZ54
Northcourt, Rick. (Mill End)
WD3 *off Springwell Av* 92 BG46
NORTH CRAY, Sid. DA14 ....186 FA90
North Cray Rd, Bex. DA5 ....186 EZ90
Sidcup DA14 ....186 EY93
North Cres, E16 ....14 F3
N3 ....97 CZ54
WC1 ....9 L5
Northcroft, H.Wyc.
(Woob.Grn) HP10 ....110 AE56
Slough SL2 ....131 AP70
Northcroft Cl, Egh. (Eng.Grn)
TW20 ....172 AV92
Northcroft Gdns, Egh.
(Eng.Grn) TW20 ....172 AV92
Northcroft Rd, W13 ....157 CH75
Egham (Eng.Grn) TW20 ....172 AV92
Epsom KT19 ....216 CR108
Northcroft Ter, W13
off Northcroft Rd 157 CH75
Northcroft Vil, Egh.
(Eng.Grn) TW20 ....172 AV92
North Cross Rd, SE22 ....182 DT85
Ilford IG6 ....125 EQ56
North Dene, NW7 ....96 CR48
Northdene, Chig. IG7 ....103 ER50
North Dene, Houns. TW3 ....156 CB81
Northdene Gdns, N15 ....122 DT58
North Down, S.Croy. CR2 ....220 DS111
Northdown Cl, Ruis. HA4 ....115 BT62
Northdown Gdns, Ilf. IG2 ....125 ES57
Northdown La, Guil. GU1 ....258 AY137
Northdown Rd, Cat. (Wold.)
CR3 ....237 EA123
Gerrards Cross (Chal.St.P.)
SL9 ....90 AY51
Hatfield AL10 ....45 CU21
Hornchurch RM11 ....127 FH59
Longfield DA3 ....209 FX96
Sutton SM2 ....218 DA110
Welling DA16 ....166 EV82
North Downs Cres, Croy.
(New Adgtn) CR0 ....221 EB110
H **North Downs Private Hosp, The**, Cat. CR3 ....252 DT125
North Downs Rd, Croy.
(New Adgtn) CR0 ....221 EB110
Northdown St, N1 ....141 DM68
North Downs Way, Bet.
RH3 ....249 CU130
Caterham CR3 ....251 DN126
Dorking RH5 ....247 CE133
Godstone RH9 ....253 DY128
Guildford GU3, GU4 ....258 AT138
Oxted RH8 ....254 EE126
Redhill RH1 ....250 DG128
Reigate RH2 ....250 DD130
Sevenoaks TN13, TN14 ....241 FD118
Tadworth KT20 ....249 CX130
Westerham TN16 ....239 ER121
North Dr, SW16 ....181 DJ91
Beaconsfield HP9 ....110 AG55
Hounslow TW3 ....156 CC82
Orpington BR6 ....223 ES105
Romford RM2 ....128 FJ55
Ruislip HA4 ....115 BS59
St. Albans (Oakl.) AL4 ....44 CL18
Slough SL2 ....132 AS69
Virginia Water GU25 ....192 AS100
⇌ **North Dulwich** 182 DR85
⊖ **North Ealing** 138 CM72
Sch **North Ealing Prim Sch**,
W5 *off Pitshanger La* 137 CH70
North End, NW3 ....120 DC61
Northend, Brwd. CM14 ....108 FW50
North End, Buck.H. IG9 ....102 EJ45
Croydon CR0 ....202 DQ103
Northend, Hem.H. HP3 ....41 BP22
North End, Rom. (Noak Hill)
RM3 ....106 FJ47
North End Av, NW3 ....120 DC61
Northend Cl, H.Wyc.
(Flack.Hth) HP10 ....110 AC56
North End Cres, W14 ....16 E8
North End Ho, W14 ....16 D8
North End La, Orp. BR6 ....223 EN110
North End Par, W14 ....16 D8
Sch **Northend Prim Sch**, Erith
DA8 *off Peareswood Rd* 167 FF81
North End Rd, NW11 ....120 DA60
SW6 ....159 CZ79
W14 ....16 E9
Northend Rd, Dart. DA1 ....167 FF80
Erith DA8 ....167 FF80
North End Rd, Wem. HA9 ....118 CN62
Northend Trd Est, Erith DA8 ....167 FE81
North End Way, NW3 ....120 DC61
Northern Av, N9 ....100 DT47
Northernhay Wk, Mord.
SM4 ....199 CY98
Northern Perimeter Rd,
Houns. (Hthrw Air.) TW6 ....155 BQ81
Northern Perimeter Rd W,
Houns. (Hthrw Air.) TW6 ....154 BK81
Northern Relief Rd, Bark.
IG11 ....145 EP66
Northern Rd, E13 ....144 EH67
Slough SL2 ....131 AR70
Northern Service Rd, Barn.
EN5 ....79 CY41
Northern Wds, H.Wyc.
(Flack.Hth) HP10 ....110 AC56
Northey Av, Sutt. SM2 ....217 CZ110
North Eyot Gdns, W6 ....159 CU78
Northey St, E14 ....13 K9
Northfield, Guil. (Shalf.)
GU4 ....258 AY142
Hatfield AL10
off Longmead 45 CV15
Loughton IG10 ....84 EK42
Northfield Av, W5 ....157 CH75
W13 ....157 CH75
Northfield Av, Orp. BR5 ....206 EW100
Pinner HA5 ....116 BX56
Northfield Cl, Brom. BR1 ....204 EL95
Hayes UB3 ....155 BT76
Northfield Ct, Stai. TW18 ....194 BH95
Northfield Cres, Sutt. SM3 ....217 CY105
Northfield Fm Ms, Cob.
KT11 *off Portsmouth Rd* 213 BU114
Northfield Gdns, Dag. RM9
off Northfield Rd 126 EZ63
Watford WD24 ....76 BW37
Northfield Ind Est, NW10 ....138 CN69
Northfield Pk, Hayes UB3 ....155 BT76
Northfield Path, Dag. RM9 ....126 EZ62
Northfield Pl, Wey. KT13 ....213 BP108
Northfield Rd, E6 ....145 EM66
N16 ....122 DS59
W13 ....157 CH75
Barnet EN4 ....80 DE41
Borehamwood WD6 ....78 CP39
Cobham KT11 ....213 BU113
Dagenham RM9 ....126 EZ63
Enfield EN3 ....82 DV43
Hounslow TW5 ....156 BX79
Staines TW18 ....194 BH95
Waltham Cross EN8 ....67 DY32
Windsor (Eton Wick) SL4 ....151 AM77
⊖ **Northfields** 157 CH76
Northfields, SW18 ....160 DA84
Ashtead KT21 ....232 CL119
Grays RM17 ....170 GC77
Northfields Ind Est, Wem.
HA0 ....138 CN67
Northfields Rd, W3 ....138 CP71
NORTH FINCHLEY, N12 ....98 DD50
NORTHFLEET, Grav. DA10 ....190 GD86
⇌ **Northfleet** 190 GA86
NORTHFLEET GREEN, Grav.
DA13 ....190 GC92
Northfleet Grn Rd, Grav.
DA13 ....190 GC93
Sch **Northfleet Sch for Boys**,
Grav. DA11
off Colyer Rd 190 GD88
Sch **Northfleet Sch for Girls**,
Grav. DA11
off Hall Rd 190 GD89
North Flockton St, SE16 ....22 A3
North Gdn, E14
off Westferry Circ 143 DZ74
North Gdns, SW19 ....180 DD94
Northgate, Gat. RH6 ....268 DF151
North Gate, Harl. CM20 ....35 EQ14
Northgate, Nthwd. HA6 ....93 BQ52
Northgate Dr, NW9 ....118 CS58
Northgate Ind Pk, Rom.
RM5 ....104 EZ54
Northgate Path, Borwd.
WD6 ....78 CM39
North Glade, The, Bex. DA5 ....186 EZ87
North Gower St, NW1 ....9 K2
North Grn, NW9
off Clayton Fld 96 CS52
Slough SL1 ....132 AS73
⊖ **North Greenwich** 24 G3
North Gro, N6 ....120 DG59
N15 ....122 DR57
Chertsey KT16 ....193 BF100
Harlow CM18 ....52 EU16
Sch **North Harringay Inf Sch**,
N8 *off Falkland Rd* 121 DN56
Sch **North Harringay Jun Sch**,
N8 *off Falkland Rd* 121 DN56
NORTH HARROW, Har. HA2 ....116 CA58
⊖ **North Harrow** 116 CA57
North Hatton Rd, Houns.
(Hthrw Air.) TW6 ....155 BR81
North Hill, N6 ....120 DF58
Rickmansworth WD3 ....73 BE40
North Hill Av, N6 ....120 DG58
North Hill Dr, Rom. RM3 ....106 FK48
North Hill Grn, Rom. RM3 ....106 FK49
NORTH HILLINGDON, Uxb.
UB10 ....135 BQ66
NORTH HOLMWOOD, Dor.
RH5 ....263 CH141
North Ho, Harl. CM18
off Tilegate Rd 51 ET17
NORTH HYDE, Sthl. UB2 ....156 BY77
North Hyde Gdns, Hayes
UB3 ....155 BU77
North Hyde La, Houns. TW5 ....156 BY78
Southall UB2 ....156 BY78
North Hyde Rd, Hayes UB3 ....155 BT76
Northiam, N12 ....98 DA48
Northiam St, E9 ....142 DV67
Northington St, WC1 ....10 A4
NORTH KENSINGTON, W10 ....6 B6
North Kent Av, Grav. (Nthflt)
DA11 ....190 GC86
Coll **North Kingston Cen**,
Kings.T. KT2
off Richmond Rd 178 CL93
Northlands, Pot.B. EN6 ....64 DD31
Northlands Av, Orp. BR6 ....223 ES105
Northlands St, SE5 ....162 DQ82
North La, Tedd. TW11 ....177 CF93
North Lo Cl, SW15
off Westleigh Av 179 CX85
H **North London Blood Transfusion Cen**, NW9 ....96 CR54
Sch **North London Collegiate Sch**, Edg. HA8
off Canons Dr 96 CL50
H **North London Nuffield Hosp**, Enf. EN2 ....81 DN40
NORTH LOOE, Epsom KT17 ....217 CW113
North Mall, N9
off St. Martins Rd 100 DV47
North Mead, Red. RH1 ....250 DF131
Sch **Northmead Co Jun Sch**,
Guil. GU2
off Grange Rd 242 AV131
Northmead Rd, Slou. SL2 ....131 AM70
North Ms, WC1 ....10 B4
H **North Middlesex Hosp**,
N18 ....100 DS50
North Moors, Guil. GU1 ....242 AY130
North Mymms Pk, Hat. AL9 ....63 CT25
NORTH OCKENDON, Upmin.
RM14 ....129 FV64
Northolm, Edg. HA8 ....96 CR49
Northolme Cl, Grays RM16
off Premier Av 170 GC76
Northolme Gdns, Edg. HA8 ....96 CN53
Northolme Ri, Orp. BR6 ....205 ES103
Northolme Rd, N5 ....122 DQ63
NORTHOLT, UB5 ....136 BZ66
⊖ **Northolt** 136 CA66
★ **Northolt Aerodrome**,
Ruis. HA4 ....135 BT65
Northolt Av, Ruis. HA4 ....115 BV64
Northolt Gdns, Grnf. UB6 ....117 CF64
Sch **Northolt High Sch**, Nthlt.
UB5 *off Eastcote La* 136 BZ65

★ Place of interest   H Hospital   Sch School   Coll College   Uni University   ⇌ Railway station

⇌ Northolt Park 116 CB63
Sch Northolt Pk Inf Sch, Nthlt.
UB5 off Newmarket Av ..116 CB64
Sch Northolt Prim Sch, Nthlt.
UB5 off Compton Cres ..136 BY66
Northolt Rd, Har. HA2 ....116 CB63
Hounslow (Hthrw Air.)
TW6 ....154 BK81
Northolt Way, Horn. RM12 ..148 FJ65
North Orbital Commercial
Pk, St.Alb. AL1 ....43 CG24
North Orbital Rd, Hat. AL10 ..29 CV14
Rickmansworth WD3 ....91 BE52
St. Albans AL1, AL2, AL4 ..61 CK25
Uxbridge (Denh.) UB9 ..113 BF60
Watford WD25 ....59 BU34
Northover, Brom. BR1 ....184 EF90
North Par, Chess. KT9 ....216 CL106
North Pk, SE9 ....185 EM86
Gerrards Cross SL9 ....112 AY56
Iver SL0 ....153 BC76
North Pk La, Gdse. RH9 ...252 DU129
North Pas, SW18 ....160 DA84
North Peckham Est, SE15 ..162 DT80
North Perimeter Rd, Uxb.
UB8 off Kingston La 134 BL69
North Pl, Guil. GU1 ....258 AX135
Mitcham CR4 ....180 DF94
Teddington TW11 ....177 CF93
Waltham Abbey EN9
off Highbridge St 67 EB33
Northpoint, Brom. BR1
off Sherman Rd 204 EG95
North Pole La, Kes. BR2 ...222 EF107
North Pole Rd, W10 ....139 CW71
Northport St, N1 ....5 K8
Sch North Prim Sch, Sthl.
UB1 off Meadow Rd 136 BZ73
North Ride, W2 ....8 A10
Northridge Rd, Grav. DA12 .191 GJ90
Northridge Way, Hem.H. HP1 .39 BF21
North Riding, St.Alb.
(Brick.Wd) AL2 ....60 CA30
North Rd, N6 ....120 DG59
N7 ....141 DL65
N9 ....100 DV46
SE18 ....165 ES77
SW19 ....180 DC93
W5 ....157 CK76
Amersham (Chesh.B.) HP6 .55 AQ36
Belvedere DA17 ....167 FB76
Berkhamsted HP4 ....38 AV19
Brentford TW8 ....158 CL79
Brentwood CM14 ....108 FW46
Bromley BR1 ....204 EH95
Dartford DA1 ....187 FF86
Edgware HA8 ....96 CP53
Feltham TW14 ....175 BR86
Guildford GU2 ....242 AV131
Hayes UB3 ....135 BR71
Hertford SG14 ....32 DQ09
Hoddesdon EN11 ....49 EA16
Ilford IG3 ....125 ES61
Purfleet RM19 ....169 FR77
Reigate RH2 ....265 CZ137
Richmond TW9 ....158 CN83
Rickmansworth (Chorl.)
WD3 ....73 BD43
Romford (Chad.Hth) RM6 .126 EY57
Romford (Hav.at.Bow.)
RM4 ....105 FE48
South Ockendon RM15 ..149 FW68
Southall UB1 ....136 CA73
Surbiton KT6 ....197 CK100
Waltham Cross EN8 ....67 DY33
Walton-on-Thames KT12 .214 BW106
West Drayton UB7 ....154 BM76
West Wickham BR4 ....203 EB102
Woking GU21 ....227 BA116
North Rd Av, Brwd. CM14 ..108 FW46
Hertford SG14 ....31 DN08
North Rd Gdns, Hert. SG14 ..31 DP09
Northrop Rd, Houns.
(Hthrw Air.) TW6 ....155 BS81
North Row, W1 ....8 D9
North Several, SE3
off Orchard Rd 163 ED82
NORTH SHEEN, Rich. TW9 ..158 CN82
⇌ North Sheen 158 CN84
Sch Northside Prim Sch,
N12 off Albert St 98 DC50
Northside Rd, Brom. BR1
off Mitchell Way 204 EG95
North Side Wandsworth
Common, SW18 ....180 DC85
Northspur Rd, Sutt. SM1 ..200 DA104
North Sq, N9
off St. Martins Rd 100 DV47
NW11 ....120 DA57
North Sta App, Red.
(S.Nutfld) RH1 ....267 DM136
Northstead Rd, SW2 ....181 DN89
North St, E13 ....144 EG68
NW4 ....119 CW57
SW4 ....161 DJ83
Barking IG11 ....145 EP65
Bexleyheath DA7 ....166 FA84
Bromley BR1 ....204 EG95
Carshalton SM5 ....200 DF104
Dartford DA1 ....188 FK87
Dorking RH4 ....263 CG136
Dorking (Westc.) RH4
off Guildford Rd 262 CC137
Egham TW20 ....173 AZ92
Godalming GU7
off Station Rd 258 AT144
Gravesend DA12
off South St 191 GH87
Guildford GU1 ....258 AX135
Hornchurch RM11 ....128 FK59
Isleworth TW7 ....157 CG83
Leatherhead KT22 ....231 CG121
Redhill RH1 ....250 DF133
Romford RM1, RM5 ....127 FD55
Waltham Abbey EN9 ....50 EE22
North St Pas, E13 ....144 EH68
North Tenter St, E1 ....11 P8
North Ter, SW3 ....18 A6
Windsor SL4
off The Long Wk 151 AR80
Northumberland All, EC3 ....11 M8
Northumberland Av, E12 ..124 EJ60
WC2 ....19 N1
Enfield EN1 ....82 DV39
Hornchurch RM11 ....128 FJ57
Isleworth TW7 ....157 CF81
Welling DA16 ....165 ER84
Northumberland Cl, Erith
DA8 ....167 FC80
Staines (Stanw.) TW19 ..174 BL86
Northumberland Cres, Felt.
TW14 ....175 BS86
Northumberland Gdns, N9 .100 DT48
Bromley BR1 ....205 EN98
Isleworth TW7 ....157 CG80
Northumberland Gdns, Mitch.
CR4 ....201 DK99
Northumberland Gro, N17 ..100 DV52
NORTHUMBERLAND HEATH,
Erith DA8 ....167 FC80
Sch Northumberland Heath
Prim Sch, Erith DA8
off Byron Dr 167 FB80
⇌ Northumberland Park 100 DV53
Northumberland Pk, N17 ...100 DT52
Erith DA8 ....167 FC80
Sch Northumberland Pk
Comm Sch, N17
off Trulock Rd 100 DU52
Northumberland Pl, W2 ....6 G7
Richmond TW10 ....177 CK85
Northumberland Rd, E6 ...144 EL72
E17 ....123 EA59
Barnet EN5 ....80 DC44
Gravesend (Istead Rise)
DA13 ....191 GF94
Harrow HA2 ....116 BZ57
Northumberland Row, Twick.
TW2
off Colne Rd 177 CE88
Northumberland St, WC2 ...19 N1
Northumberland Way, Erith
DA8 ....167 FC81
Northumbria St, E14 ....14 P7
North Verbena Gdns, W6
off St. Peter's Sq 159 CU78
Northview, N7 ....121 DL62
North Vw, SW19 ....179 CV92
W5 ....137 CJ70
Northview, Hem.H. HP1
off Winkwell 39 BD22
North Vw, Ilf. IG6 ....104 EU52
Pinner HA5 ....116 BW59
Northview, Swan. BR8 ....207 FE96
North Vw Av, Til. RM18 ...171 GG81
Northview Cres, NW10 ...119 CT63
North Vw Cres, Epsom
KT18 ....233 CV117
North Vw Dr, Wdf.Grn. IG8 .102 EK54
Sch Northview Prim Sch,
NW10
off Northview Cres 119 CT64
North Vw Rd, N8 ....121 DK55
Sevenoaks TN14
off Seal Rd 257 FJ121
North Vil, NW1 ....141 DK65
North Wk, W2 ....7 L10
Croydon (New Adgtn)
CR0 ....221 EB106
NORTH WATFORD, Wat.
WD24 ....75 BV37
North Way, N9 ....100 DW47
N11 ....99 DJ51
NW9 ....118 CP55
Northway, NW11 ....120 DB57
Guildford GU2 ....242 AU132
Morden SM4 ....199 CY97
North Way, Pnr. HA5 ....116 BW55
Northway, Rick. WD3 ....92 BK45
North Way, Uxb. UB10 ....134 BL66
Northway, Wall. SM6 ....219 DJ105
Welwyn Garden City AL7
off Nursery Hill 29 CZ06
Northway Circ, NW7 ....96 CR49
Northway Cres, NW7 ....96 CR49
Northway Ho, N20 ....98 DC46
Northway Rd, SE5 ....162 DQ83
Croydon CR0 ....202 DT100
Sch Northway Sch, NW7
off The Fairway 96 CR48
Northways Par, NW3
off Finchley Rd 140 DD66
North Weald Airfield, Epp.
(N.Wld Bas.) CM16 ....70 EZ26
NORTH WEALD BASSETT,
Epp. CM16 ....71 FB27
North Weald Cl, Horn.
RM12 off Airfield Way ..147 FH65
Northweald La, Kings.T.
KT2 ....177 CK92
NORTH WEMBLEY, Wem.
HA0 ....117 CH61
⇌ North Wembley 117 CK62
⊖ North Wembley 117 CK62
North Western Av, Wat.
WD24, WD25 ....76 BW36
Coll North W Kent Coll, Grav.
DA12
off Dering Way 191 GM88
Dartford Campus, Dart.
DA1
off Oakfield La 188 FJ89
Sch North W London Jewish
Prim Sch, NW6
off Willesden La 139 CY66
Sch North Westminster
Comm Sch, W2 ....7 P6
Sch North Westminster
Comm Sch (Lwr), NW1
(Marylebone Lwr Ho) 8 A5
W9 (Paddington Lwr Ho) ..7 H3
Northwest Pl, N1 ....4 D9
North Wf Rd, W2 ....7 N6
Northwick Av, Har. HA3 ...117 CG58
Northwick Circle, Har. HA3 .117 CJ58
Northwick Cl, NW8 ....7 N3
Harrow HA1
off Nightingale Av 117 CH59
⊖ Northwick Park 117 CG59
H Northwick Pk Hosp, Har.
HA1 ....117 CH59
Northwick Pk Rd, Har. HA1 .117 CF58
Northwick Rd, Wat. WD19 ..94 BW49
Wembley HA0 ....137 CK67
Northwick Ter, NW8 ....7 N3
Northwick Wk, Har. HA1 ..117 CF59
Northwold Dr, Pnr. HA5
off Cuckoo Hill 116 BW55
Northwold Est, E5 ....122 DU61
Sch Northwold JMI Sch,
E5 off Northwold Rd ..122 DU61
Northwold Rd, E5 ....122 DT61
N16 ....122 DT61
NORTHWOOD, HA6 ....93 BR51
⊖ Northwood 93 BS52
Northwood, Grays RM16 ..171 GH75
Welwyn Garden City AL7 ..30 DD09
Coll Northwood Adult
Ed Cen, Nthwd. HA6
off Potter St 93 BV53
H Northwood & Pinner
Comm Hosp, Nthwd.
HA6 ....93 BU53
Northwood Av, Horn. RM12 .127 FG63
Purley CR8 ....219 DN113
Northwood Cl, Wal.Cr. EN7 ..66 DT27
Sch Northwood Coll, Nthwd.
HA6 off Maxwell Rd 93 BR52
North Wd Ct, SE25
off Regina Rd 202 DU97
Northwood Gdns, N12 ....98 DD50
Greenford UB6 ....117 CF64
Ilford IG5 ....125 EN56
Northwood Hall, N6 ....121 DJ59
NORTHWOOD HILLS,
Nthwd. HA6 ....93 BT54
⊖ Northwood Hills 93 BU54
Northwood Ho, SE27 ....182 DR91
Northwood Pl, Erith DA18 ..166 EZ76
Sch Northwood Prep Sch, Rick.
WD3 off Sandy Lo Rd ...93 BQ47
Sch Northwood Prim Sch, Erith
DA18 off Northwood Pl .166 EZ76
Northwood Rd, N6 ....121 DH59
SE23 ....183 DZ88
Carshalton SM5 ....218 DG107
Hounslow (Hthrw Air.)
TW6 ....154 BK81
Thornton Heath CR7 ....201 DP96
Uxbridge (Hare.) UB9 ....92 BJ53
Sch Northwood Sch, Nthwd.
HA6 off Potter St 93 BU53
Northwood Twr, E17 ....123 EC56
Northwood Way, SE19
off Roman Ri 182 DR93
Northwood HA6 ....93 BU52
Uxbridge (Hare.) UB9 ....92 BK53
NORTH WOOLWICH, E16 ..164 EL75
⇌ North Woolwich 165 EN75
North Woolwich Rd, E16 ...25 K1
North Woolwich
Roundabout, E16
off North Woolwich Rd ..144 EK74
★ North Woolwich Sta
Mus, E16 ....165 EN75
North Worple Way, SW14 ..158 CR83
Nortoft Rd, Ger.Cr.
(Chal.St.P.) SL9 ....91 AZ51
Norton Av, Surb. KT5 ....198 CP101
Norton Cl, E4 ....101 EA50
Borehamwood WD6 ....78 CN39
Enfield EN1 off Brick La ..82 DV40
Norton Folgate, E1 ....11 M5
Norton Gdns, SW16 ....201 DL96
Norton La, Cob. KT11 ....229 BT119
Norton Rd, E10 ....123 DZ60
Dagenham RM10 ....147 FD65
Uxbridge UB8 ....134 BK69
Wembley HA0 ....137 CK65
Norval Rd, Wem. HA0 ....117 CH61
Norvic Ho, Erith DA8
off Waterhead Cl 167 FF80
Norway Dr, Slou. SL2 ....132 AV71
Norway Gate, SE16 ....23 K5
Norway Pl, E14 ....13 L8
Norway St, SE10 ....163 EB79
Norway Wk, Rain. RM13
off The Glen 148 FJ70
Sch Norwegian Sch in
London, The, SW20
off Arterberry Rd 179 CW94
Norwich Ho, E14 ....14 B7
Norwich Ms, Ilf. IG3
off Ashgrove Rd 126 EU60
Norwich Pl, Bexh. DA6 ....166 FA84
Norwich Rd, E7 ....124 EG64
Dagenham RM9 ....146 FA68
Greenford UB6 ....136 CB67
Northwood HA6 ....115 BT55
Thornton Heath CR7 ....202 DQ97
Norwich St, EC4 ....10 C7
Norwich Wk, Edg. HA8 ....96 CQ52
Norwich Way, Rick.
(Crox.Grn) WD3 ....75 BP41
NORWOOD, SE19 ....182 DS93
Norwood Av, Rom. RM7 ...127 FE59
Wembley HA0 ....138 CM67
Norwood Cl, NW2 ....119 CY62
Hertford SG14 ....31 DM08
Leatherhead (Eff.) KT24 .246 BY128
Southall UB2 ....156 CA77
Twickenham TW2
off Fourth Cross Rd 177 CD89
Norwood Ct, Amer. HP7 ....55 AP40
Norwood Cres, Houns.
(Hthrw Air.) TW6 ....155 BQ81
Norwood Dr, Har. HA2 ....116 BZ58
Norwood Fm La, Cob. KT11 .213 BU111
Norwood Gdns, Hayes UB4 .136 BW70
Southall UB2 ....156 BZ77
NORWOOD GREEN, Sthl.
UB2 ....156 CA77
Sch Norwood Grn Inf &
Nurs Sch, Sthl. UB2
off Thorncliffe Rd 156 BZ78
Sch Norwood Grn Jun Sch,
Sthl. UB2
off Thorncliffe Rd 156 BY78
Norwood Grn Rd, Sthl. UB2 .156 CA77
Norwood High St, SE27 ...181 DP90
⇌ Norwood Junction 202 DT98
Norwood La, Iver SL0 ....133 BD70
NORWOOD NEW TOWN,
SE19 ....182 DQ93
Norwood Pk Rd, SE27 ....182 DQ92
Norwood Rd, SE24 ....181 DP88
SE27 ....181 DP89
Leatherhead (Eff.) KT24 .246 BY128
Southall UB2 ....156 BZ77
Waltham Cross (Chsht)
EN8 ....67 DY30
Sch Norwood Sch, SE19
off Crown Dale 182 DQ92
Norwood Ter, Sthl. UB2
off Tentelow La 156 CB77
Notley End, Egh. (Eng.Grn)
TW20 ....172 AW93
Notley St, SE5 ....162 DR80
Notre Dame Est, SW4 ....161 DJ84
Sch Notre Dame Prep Sch, Cob.
KT11 off Burwood Pk ..213 BT111
Sch Notre Dame RC Prim
Sch, SE18
off Eglinton Rd 165 EP79
Sch Notre Dame Sch, SE1 ..20 E5
Sch Notre Dame Sen Sch, Cob.
KT11 off Burwood Pk ..213 BT111
Notson Rd, SE25 ....202 DV98
Notting Barn Rd, W10 ....6 A4
Nottingdale Sq, W11 ....6 C10
Nottingham Av, E16 ....144 EJ71
Nottingham Cl, Wat. WD25 ..59 BU33
Woking GU21 ....226 AT118
Nottingham Ct, WC2 ....9 N8
Woking GU21
off Nottingham Cl 226 AT118
Nottingham Pl, W1 ....8 E4
Nottingham Rd, E10 ....123 EC58
SW17 ....180 DF88
Isleworth TW7 ....157 CF82
Rickmansworth (Herons.)
WD3 ....91 BC45
South Croydon CR2 ....220 DQ105
Nottingham St, W1 ....8 E5
Nottingham Ter, NW1 ....8 E4
NOTTING HILL, W11 ....6 D9
Sch Notting Hill & Ealing
High Sch, W13
off Cleveland Rd 137 CH71
⊖ Notting Hill Gate 6 G10
Notting Hill Gate, W11 ....16 G1
Nova Ms, Sutt. SM3 ....199 CY102
Novar Cl, Orp. BR6 ....205 ET101
Nova Rd, Croy. CR0 ....201 DP101
Novar Rd, SE9 ....185 EQ88
Novello St, SW6 ....160 DA81
Novello Way, Borwd. WD6 ...78 CR39
Nowell Rd, SW13 ....159 CU79
Nower, The, Sev. TN14 ....239 ET119
Nower Hill, Pnr. HA5 ....116 BZ56
Sch Nower Hill High Sch, Pnr.
HA5 off George V Av ...116 CA56
Nower Rd, Dor. RH4 ....263 CG136
Noyna Rd, SW17 ....180 DF90
Nuding Cl, SE13 ....163 EA83
Nuffield Rd, Swan. BR8 ....187 FG93
H Nuffield Speech &
Language Unit, W5 ....137 CJ71
Nugent Ind Pk, Orp. BR5 ..206 EW99
Nugent Rd, N19 ....121 DL60
SE25 ....202 DT97
Nugents Ct, Pnr. HA5
off St. Thomas' Dr 94 BY53
Nugents Pk, Pnr. HA5 ....94 BY53
Nugent Ter, NW8 ....140 DC68
Numa Ct, Brent. TW8
off Justin Cl 157 CK80
★ No. 2 Willow Rd, NW3 ..120 DE63
Nunappleton Way, Oxt.
RH8 ....254 EG132
Nun Ct, EC2 ....11 J7
Nuneaton Rd, Dag. RM9 ...146 EX66
Nunfield, Kings L. (Chipper.)
WD4 ....58 BH31
NUNHEAD, SE15 ....162 DW83
⇌ Nunhead 162 DW82
Nunhead Cres, SE15 ....162 DV83
Nunhead Est, SE15 ....162 DV84
Nunhead Grn, SE15 ....162 DV83
Uxbridge (Denh.) UB9 ...113 BF58
Nunhead Gro, SE15 ....162 DV83
Nunhead La, SE15 ....162 DV83
Nunhead Pas, SE15
off Peckham Rye 162 DU83
Nunnery Cl, St.Alb. AL1 ....43 CD22
Nunnery Stables, St.Alb.
AL1 ....43 CD22
Nunnington Cl, SE9 ....184 EL90
Nunns Rd, Enf. EN2 ....82 DQ40
Nunns Way, Grays RM17 ...170 GD77
Nunsbury Dr, Brox. EN10 ...67 DY25
Nuns La, St.Alb. AL1 ....43 CE24
Nuns Wk, Vir.W. GU25 ....192 AX99
NUPER'S HATCH, Rom.
RM4 ....105 FE45
Nupton Dr, Barn. EN5 ....79 CW44
Nurseries Rd, St.Alb.
(Wheat.) AL4 ....28 CL08
Nursery, The, Erith DA8 ....167 FF80
Nursery Av, N3 ....98 DC54
Bexleyheath DA7 ....166 EZ83
Croydon CR0 ....203 DX103
Nursery Cl, SE4 ....163 DZ82
SW15 ....159 CX84
Addlestone (Wdhm) KT15 .211 BF110
Amersham HP7 ....55 AS39
Croydon CR0 ....203 DX103
Dartford DA2 ....188 FQ87
Enfield EN3 ....83 DX39
Epsom KT17 ....216 CS110
Feltham TW14 ....175 BV87
High Wycombe (Penn)
HP10 ....88 AC47
Orpington BR6 ....206 EU101
Romford RM6 ....126 EX58
Sevenoaks TN13 ....257 FJ122
South Ockendon RM15 ..149 FW70
Swanley BR8 ....207 FC96
Tadworth KT20 ....249 CU125
Woking GU21 ....226 AW116
Woodford Green IG8 ....102 EH50
Nursery Ct, N17
off Nursery St 100 DT52
Nursery Flds, Saw. CM21 ...36 EX05
Nursery Gdns, Chis. BR7 ..185 EP93
Enfield EN3 ....83 DX39
Guildford (Chilw.) GU4 ..259 BB140
Hounslow TW4 ....176 BZ85
Staines TW18 ....174 BH94
Sunbury-on-Thames
TW16 ....195 BT96
Waltham Cross EN7 ....66 DR28
Ware SG12 ....33 DY06
Welwyn Garden City AL7 ..29 CY06
Nursery Hill, Welw.G.C. AL7 ..29 CY06
Nursery La, E2 ....5 N8
E7 ....144 EG65
W10 ....139 CW71
High Wycombe (Penn)
HP10 ....88 AC47
Horley (Hkwd) RH6 ....268 DD149
Slough SL3 ....132 AW74
Uxbridge UB8 ....134 BK70
Nurserymans Rd, N11 ....98 DG47
Nursery Pl, Sev. TN13 ....256 FD122
Windsor SL4
off Gregory Dr 172 AV86
Nursery Rd, E9
off Morning La 142 DW65
N2 ....98 DD53
N14 ....99 DJ45
SW9 ....161 DM84
Broxbourne EN10 ....67 DY25
Godalming GU7 ....258 AT144
Hoddesdon EN11 ....33 EB14
Loughton IG10 ....84 EJ43
Loughton (High Beach)
IG10 ....84 EH39
Maidenhead (Taplow)
SL6 ....130 AH72
Pinner HA5 ....116 BW55
Sunbury-on-Thames
TW16 ....195 BS96
Sutton SM1 ....218 DC105
Tadworth KT20 ....249 CU125
Thornton Heath CR7 ....202 DR98
Waltham Abbey EN9 ....49 ED22
Nursery Rd Merton, SW19 ..200 DB96
Nursery Rd Mitcham, Mitch.
CR4 ....200 DE97
Nursery Rd Wimbledon,
SW19 off Worple Rd 179 CY94
Nursery Row, SE17 ....21 J8
Barnet EN5
off St. Albans Rd 79 CY41
Nursery St, N17 ....100 DT52
Nursery Ter, Berk. (Pott.End)
HP4 off The Front 39 BB16
Nursery Wk, NW4 ....119 CV55
Romford RM7 ....127 FD59
Nursery Way, Stai. (Wrays.)
TW19 ....172 AX86
Nursery Waye, Uxb. UB8 ...134 BK67
Nurstead Rd, Erith DA8 ...166 FA80
Nutberry Av, Grays RM16 ..170 GA75
Nutberry Cl, Grays RM16
off Long La 170 GA75
Nutbourne St, W10 ....6 C1
Nutbrook St, SE15 ....162 DU83
Nutbrowne Rd, Dag. RM9 ..146 EZ67
Nutcombe La, Dor. RH4 ....263 CF136
Nutcroft Gro, Lthd. (Fetch.)
KT22 ....231 CE121
Nutcroft Rd, SE15 ....162 DV80
NUTFIELD, Red. RH1 ....251 DM133
⇌ Nutfield 267 DL136
Nutfield, Welw.G.C. AL7 ....30 DA06
Sch Nutfield Ch Prim Sch,
Red. RH1 off Mid St 267 DM135
Nutfield Cl, N18 ....100 DU51
Carshalton SM5 ....200 DE104
Nutfield Gdns, Ilf. IG3 ....125 ET61
Northolt UB5 ....136 BW68
Nutfield Marsh Rd, Red.
(Nutfld) RH1 ....251 DJ130
Nutfield Rd, E15 ....123 EC63
NW2 ....119 CU61
SE22 ....182 DT85
Coulsdon CR5 ....234 DG116
Redhill RH1 ....250 DG134
Redhill (S.Merst.) RH1 ...251 DJ129
Thornton Heath CR7 ....201 DP98
Nutfield Way, Orp. BR6 ....205 EN103
Nutford Pl, W1 ....8 B7
Nut Gro, Welw.G.C. AL8 ....29 CX06
Nuthatch Cl, Stai. TW19 ...174 BM88
Nuthatch Gdns, SE28 ....165 ER75
Reigate RH2 ....266 DC138
Nuthurst Av, SW2 ....181 DM89
Nutkins Way, Chesh. HP5 ...54 AQ29
Nutkin Wk, Uxb. UB8
off Park Rd 134 BL66
Nutley Cl, Swan. BR8 ....207 FF95
Nutley Ct, Reig. RH2
off Nutley La 249 CZ134
Nutley La, Reig. RH2 ....249 CZ133
Nutley Ter, NW3 ....140 DC65
Nutmead Cl, Bex. DA5 ....187 FC88
Nutmeg Cl, E16 ....15 H3
Nutmeg La, E14 ....14 E8
Nuttall St, N1 ....5 M9
Nutter La, E11 ....124 EJ58
Nuttfield Cl, Rick.
(Crox.Grn) WD3 ....75 BP44
Nutt Gro, Edg. HA8 ....95 CK47
Nut Tree Cl, Orp. BR6 ....206 EX104
Nutt St, SE15 ....162 DT80
Nutty La, Shep. TW17 ....195 BQ98
Nutwell St, SW17 ....180 DE92
Nutwood Av, Bet. (Brock.)
RH3 ....264 CQ135
Nutwood Cl, Bet. (Brock.)
RH3 ....264 CQ135
Nutwood Gdns, Wal.Cr.
(Chsht) EN7
off Great Stockwood Rd ...66 DS26
Nuxley Rd, Belv. DA17 ....166 EZ79
Nyall Ct, Rom. (Gidea Pk)
RM2 ....128 FJ55
Nyanza St, SE18 ....165 ER79
Nye Bevan Est, E5 ....123 DX62
Nyefield Pk, Tad. KT20 ....249 CU126
Nye Way, Hem.H. (Bov.)
HP3 ....57 BA28
Nylands Av, Rich. TW9 ....158 CN81
Nymans Gdns, SW20
off Hidcote Gdns 199 CV97
Nynehead St, SE14 ....163 DY80
Nyon Gro, SE6 ....183 DZ89
Nyssa Cl, Wdf.Grn. IG8
off Gwynne Pk Av 103 EM51
Nyth Cl, Upmin. RM14 ....129 FR58
Nyton Cl, N19
off Courtauld Rd 121 DL60

O

O2 Shop Cen, NW3
off Finchley Rd 140 DC65
Oakapple Cl, S.Croy. CR2 ..220 DV114
Oak Apple Ct, SE12 ....184 EG89
Oak Av, N8 ....121 DL56
N10 ....99 DH52
N17 ....100 DR52
Croydon CR0 ....203 EA103
Egham TW20 ....173 BC94
Enfield EN2 ....81 DM38
Hampton TW12 ....176 BY92
Hounslow TW5 ....156 BX80
St. Albans (Brick.Wd) AL2 ..60 CA30
Sevenoaks TN13 ....257 FH128
Upminster RM14 ....128 FP62
Uxbridge UB10 ....115 BP61
West Drayton UB7 ....154 BN76
Oakbank, Brwd. (Hutt.)
CM13 ....109 GE43
Oak Bk, Croy. (New Adgtn)
CR0 ....221 EC107
Oakbank, Lthd. (Fetch.)
KT22 ....230 CC123
Woking GU22 ....226 AY119
Oakbank Av, Walt. KT12 ...196 BZ101
Oakbank Gro, SE24 ....162 DQ84
Oakbrook Cl, Brom. BR1 ...184 EH91
Oakbury Rd, SW6 ....160 DB82
Oak Cl, N14 ....99 DH45
Dartford DA1 ....167 FE84
Godalming GU7 ....258 AS143
Hemel Hempstead HP3 ...40 BM24
Sutton SM1 ....200 DC103
Tadworth (Box H.) KT20 ..248 CP130
Waltham Abbey EN9 ....67 ED34
Oakcombe Cl, N.Mal. KT3
off Traps La 198 CS95
Oak Cottage Cl, SE6 ....184 EF88
Oak Cres, E16 ....15 H6
Oakcroft Cl, Pnr. HA5 ....93 BV54
West Byfleet KT14 ....211 BF114
Oakcroft Rd, SE13 ....163 ED82
Chessington KT9 ....216 CM105
West Byfleet KT14 ....211 BF114
Oakcroft Vil, Chess. KT9 ..216 CM105
Oakdale, N14 ....99 DH46
Welwyn Garden City AL8 ..29 CW05
Oakdale Av, Har. HA3 ....118 CL57
Northwood HA6 ....93 BU54
Oakdale Cl, Wat. WD19 ....94 BW49

Oakdale Gdns, E4 ....**101** EC50
Sch **Oakdale Inf Sch**, E18
off Woodville Rd **102** EH54
Sch **Oakdale Jun Sch**, E18
off Oakdale Rd **102** EH54
Oakdale La, Eden.
(Crock.H.) TN8 ....**255** EP133
Oakdale Rd, E7 ....**144** EH66
E11 ....**123** ED61
E18 ....**102** EH54
N4 ....**122** DQ58
SE15 ....**162** DW83
SW16 ....**181** DL92
Epsom KT19 ....**216** CR109
Watford WD19 ....**94** BW48
Weybridge KT13 ....**194** BN104
Oakdale Way, Mitch. CR4
off Wolseley Rd **200** DG101
Oakdene, SE15
off Carlton Gro **162** DV81
Oak Dene, W13
off The Dene **137** CH71
Oakdene, Beac. HP9 ....**89** AL52
Romford RM3 ....**106** FM54
Tadworth KT20 ....**233** CY120
Waltham Cross (Chsht)
EN8 ....**67** DY30
Woking (Chobham) GU24 .**210** AT110
Oakdene Av, Chis. BR7 ....**185** EN92
Erith DA8 ....**167** FC79
Thames Ditton KT7 .....**197** CG102
Oakdene Cl, Bet. (Brock.)
RH3 ....**264** CQ136
Hornchurch RM11 ....**127** FH58
Leatherhead (Bkhm) KT23 .**246** CC127
Pinner HA5 ....**94** BZ52
Oakdene Dr, Surb. KT5 ....**198** CQ101
Oakdene Ms, Sutt. SM3 ....**199** CZ102
Oakdene Par, Cob. KT11
off Anyards Rd **213** BV114
Oakdene Pk, N3 ....**97** CZ52
Oakdene Rd, Bet. (Brock.)
RH3 ....**264** CQ136
Cobham KT11 ....**213** BV114
Guildford (Peasm.) GU3 ..**258** AW142
Hemel Hempstead HP3 ....**40** BM24
Leatherhead (Bkhm) KT23 .**230** BZ124
Orpington BR5 ....**205** ET99
Redhill RH1 ....**250** DE134
Sevenoaks TN13 ....**256** FG122
Uxbridge UB10 ....**135** BP68
Watford WD24 ....**75** BV36
Oakdene Way, St.Alb. AL1 ...**43** CJ20
Oakden St, SE11 ....**20** D7
Oak Dr, Berk. HP4 ....**38** AX20
Sawbridgeworth CM21 ...**36** EW07
Tadworth (Box H.) KT20 ..**248** CP130
Oake Ct, SW15 ....**179** CY85
Oaken Coppice, Ashtd.
KT21 ....**232** CN119
Oak End, Harl. CM18 ....**51** ET17
Oak End Dr, Iver SL0 ......**133** BC68
Oaken Dr, Esher (Clay.)
KT10 ....**215** CF107
Oak End Way, Add. (Wdhm)
KT15 ....**211** BE112
Gerrards Cross SL9 .....**113** AZ57
Oakengate Wd, Tad. KT20
off Boxhill Rd **248** CQ131
Oaken Gro, Welw.G.C. AL7 ...**29** CY11
Oakenholt Ho, SE2
off Hartslock Dr **166** EX75
Oaken La, Esher (Clay.)
KT10 ....**215** CE106
Oakenshaw Cl, Surb. KT6 ..**198** CL101
Oakes Cl, E6
off Savage Gdns **145** EM72
Oakeshott Av, N6 ....**120** DG61
Oakey La, SE1 ....**20** C5
Oak Fm, Borwd. WD6 ......**78** CQ43
Sch **Oak Fm Inf Sch**, Uxb.
UB10 *off Windsor Av* ...**135** BP67
Sch **Oak Fm Jun Sch**, Uxb.
UB10 *off Windsor Av* ...**135** BP67
Oakfield, E4 ....**101** EB50
Oak Fld, Chesh. HP5 ....**54** AP30
Oakfield, Rick. (Mill End)
WD3 ....**91** BF45
Woking GU21 ....**226** AS116
Oakfield Av, Har. HA3 ....**117** CH55
Slough SL1 ....**131** AP74
Oakfield Cl, Amer. HP6 ......**55** AQ37
New Malden KT3
off Blakes La **199** CT99
Potters Bar EN6 ....**63** CZ31
Ruislip HA4 ....**115** BT58
Weybridge KT13 ....**213** BQ105
Sch **Oakfield Co Prim Sch**,
Inf Dept, Dart. DA1
off Oakfield La **188** FL89
Jun Dept, Dart. DA1
off Oakfield La **188** FK89
Oakfield Ct, N8 ....**121** DL59
NW2 *off Hendon Way* **119** CX59
Borehamwood WD6 ....**78** CP41
Oakfield Dr, Reig. RH2 .....**250** DA132
Sch **Oakfield First Sch**, Wind.
SL4 *off Imperial Rd* **151** AP82
Oakfield Gdns, N18 ....**100** DS49
SE19 ....**182** DS92
Beckenham BR3 ....**203** EA99
Carshalton SM5 ....**200** DE102
Greenford UB6 ....**137** CD70
Oakfield Glade, Wey. KT13 ..**213** BQ105
Sch **Oakfield Jun Sch**, Lthd.
KT22 *off Bell La* **231** CD123
Oakfield La, Bex. DA5 ....**187** FE89
Dartford DA1, DA2 ....**187** FG89
Keston BR2 ....**222** EJ105
Oakfield Pk Rd, Dart. DA1 ..**188** FK89
Oakfield Pl, Dart. DA1 .....**188** FK89
Sch **Oakfield Prep Sch**,
SE21 *off Thurlow Pk Rd* ..**182** DR88
Oakfield Rd, E6 ....**144** EL67
E17 ....**101** DY54
N3 ....**98** DB53
N4 ....**121** DN58
N14 ....**99** DL48
SE20 ....**182** DV94
SW19 ....**179** CX90
Ashford TW15 ....**175** BP92
Ashtead KT21 ....**231** CK117
Cobham KT11 ....**213** BV113
Croydon CR0 ....**202** DQ102
Ilford IG1 ....**125** EP61
Orpington BR6
off Goodmead Rd **206** EU101
Oakfields, Guil. GU3 ....**242** AS132
Sevenoaks TN13 ....**257** FH126
Oakfields, Walt. KT12 .....**195** BU102
West Byfleet KT14 ......**212** BH114
Sch **Oakfield Sch**, Wok.
GU22 *off Coldharbour Rd* .**227** BF115
Oakfields Rd, NW11 ....**119** CY58
Oakfield St, SW10 ....**160** DC79
Oakford Rd, NW5 ....**121** DJ63
Oak Gdns, Croy. CR0 ......**203** EA103
Edgware HA8 ....**96** CQ54
Oak Glade, Epp. (Cooper.)
CM16
off Coopersale Common ..**70** EX29
Epsom KT19
off Christ Ch Rd **216** CN112
Northwood HA6 ....**93** BP53
Oak Glen, Horn. RM11 .....**128** FL55
Oak Gra Rd, Guil. (W.Clan.)
GU4 ....**244** BH128
Oak Grn, Abb.L. WD5 ....**59** BS32
Oak Grn Way, Abb.L. WD5 ...**59** BS32
Oak Gro, NW2 ....**119** CY63
Hatfield AL10 ....**45** CT18
Hertford SG13 ....**32** DS11
Ruislip HA4 ....**115** BV59
Sunbury-on-Thames
TW16 ....**175** BV94
West Wickham BR4 .....**203** EC103
Oak Gro Rd, SE20 ....**202** DW95
Oakhall Ct, E11 ....**124** EH58
Oakhall Dr, Sun. TW16 .....**175** BT92
Oak Hall Rd, E11 ....**124** EH58
Oakham Cl, SE6
off Rutland Wk **183** DZ89
Barnet EN4 ....**80** DF41
Oakham Dr, Brom. BR2 ....**204** EF98
Oakhampton Rd, NW7 ......**97** CX52
Oak Hill, Epsom KT18 .....**232** CR116
Oakhill, Esher (Clay.) KT10 ..**215** CG107
Oak Hill, Guil. (Burpham)
GU4 ....**243** BC129
Surbiton KT6 ....**198** CL101
Woodford Green IG8 .....**101** ED52
Oakhill Av, NW3 ....**120** DB63
Pinner HA5 ....**94** BY54
Oakhill Cl, Ashtd. KT21 .....**231** CJ118
Rickmansworth (Map.Cr.)
WD3 ....**91** BE49
Oak Hill Cl, Wdf.Grn. IG8 ...**101** ED52
Coll **Oak Hill Coll**, N14
off Chase Side **80** DG44
Oakhill Ct, SW19 ....**179** CX94
Oak Hill Cres, Surb. KT6 ....**198** CL101
Woodford Green IG8 .....**101** ED52
Oakhill Dr, Surb. KT6 ......**198** CL101
Oakhill Gdns, Wey. KT13 ...**195** BS103
Oak Hill Gdns, Wdf.Grn. IG8 .**102** EE53
Oakhill Gro, Surb. KT6 .....**198** CL100
Oak Hill Pk, NW3 ....**120** DB63
Oak Hill Pk Ms, NW3 ....**120** DC63
Oakhill Path, Surb. KT6 ....**198** CL100
Oakhill Pl, SW15
off Oakhill Rd **180** DA85
Sch **Oakhill Prim Sch**,
Wdf.Grn. IG8
off Alders Av **102** EE51
Oakhill Rd, SW15 ....**179** CZ85
SW16 ....**201** DL95
Addlestone KT15 ....**211** BF107
Ashtead KT21 ....**231** CJ118
Beckenham BR3 ....**203** EC96
Orpington BR6 ....**205** ET102
Purfleet RM19 ....**168** FP78
Reigate RH2 ....**266** DB135
Rickmansworth (Map.Cr.)
WD3 ....**91** BD49
Oak Hill Rd, Rom.
(Stap.Abb.) RM4 ....**105** FD45
Sevenoaks TN13 ....**256** FG124
Surbiton KT6 ....**198** CL100
Oakhill Rd, Sutt. SM1 ......**200** DB104
Oak Hill Way, NW3 ....**120** DC63
Oakhouse Rd, Bexh. DA6 ....**186** FA85
Oakhurst, Wok. (Chobham)
GU24 ....**210** AS109
Oakhurst Av, Barn. EN4 .....**98** DE45
Bexleyheath DA7 ....**166** EY80
Oakhurst Cl, E17 ....**124** EE56
Chislehurst BR7 ....**205** EM95
Ilford IG6 ....**103** EQ53
Teddington TW11 ....**177** CE92
Oakhurst Gdns, E4 ....**102** EF46
E17 ....**124** EE56
Bexleyheath DA7 ....**166** EY80
Oakhurst Gro, SE22 ....**162** DU84
Oakhurst Pl, Wat. WD18
off Cherrydale **75** BT42
Oakhurst Ri, Cars. SM5 .....**218** DE110
Oakhurst Rd, Enf. EN3 ....**83** DX36
Epsom KT19 ....**216** CQ107
Sch **Oakhyrst Gra**, Cat. CR3
off Stanstead Rd **252** DR126
Oakington, Welw.G.C. AL7 ...**30** DD08
Oakington Av, Amer. HP6 ....**72** AY39
Harrow HA2 ....**116** CA59
Hayes UB3 ....**155** BR77
Wembley HA9 ....**118** CM62
Oakington Dr, Sun. TW16 ...**196** BW96
Oakington Manor Dr, Wem.
HA9 ....**118** CN64
Sch **Oakington Manor Prim
Sch**, Wem. HA9
off Oakington Manor Dr .**118** CP64
Oakington Rd, W9 ....**7** H3
Oakington Way, N8 ....**121** DL58
Oakland Gdns, Brwd. (Hutt.)
CM13 ....**109** GC43
Oakland Pl, Buck.H. IG9 ....**102** EG47
Oakland Rd, E15 ....**123** ED63
Oaklands, N21 ....**99** DM47
Berkhamsted HP4 ....**38** AU19
Horley RH6 ....**269** DJ148
Kenley CR8 ....**220** DQ114
Leatherhead (Fetch.)
KT22 ....**231** CD124
Twickenham TW2 ....**176** CC87
Oaklands Av, N9 ....**82** DV44
Esher KT10 ....**197** CD102
Hatfield AL9 ....**63** CY27
Isleworth TW7 ....**157** CF79
Romford RM1 ....**127** FE55
Sidcup DA15 ....**185** ET87
Thornton Heath CR7 .....**201** DN98
Watford WD19 ....**93** BV46
West Wickham BR4 .....**203** EB104
Oaklands Cl, Bexh. DA6 ....**186** EZ85
Chessington KT9 ....**215** CJ105
Guildford (Shalf.) GU4 ...**258** AY142
Orpington BR5 ....**205** ES100
Coll **Oaklands Coll**,
Borehamwood Campus,
Borwd. WD6
off Elstree Way **78** CQ40
St. Albans City Campus,
St.Alb. AL1
off St. Peters Rd **43** CE20
Coll **Oaklands Coll**, St. Alb.
Smallford Campus, St.Alb.
AL4 *off Hatfield Rd* **44** CL19
Welwyn Garden City
Campus, Welw.G.C.
AL8 *off The Campus* **29** CX08
Oaklands Ct, Add. KT15 .....**194** BH104
Watford WD17 ....**75** BU39
Wembley HA0 ....**117** CK64
Oaklands Dr, Harl. CM17 ....**52** EW16
Redhill RH1 ....**267** DH136
South Ockendon RM15 ..**149** FW71
Twickenham TW2 ....**176** CC87
Oaklands Est, SW4 ....**181** DJ86
Oaklands Gdns, Ken. CR8 ...**220** DQ114
Oaklands Gate, Nthwd.
HA6 *off Green La* **93** BS51
Oaklands Gro, W12 ....**139** CU74
Broxbourne EN10 ....**49** DY24
Sch **Oaklands Inf Sch**, West.
TN16 *off Norheads La* ...**238** EJ116
Sch **Oaklands Jun Sch**,
West. TN16
off Oaklands La **238** EJ116
Oaklands La, Barn. EN5 .....**79** CV42
St. Albans (Smallford) AL4 ..**44** CL18
Westerham (Bigg.H.)
TN16 ....**222** EH113
Oaklands Pk Av, Ilf. IG1
off High Rd **125** ER61
Oaklands Pl, SW4
off St. Alphonsus Rd **161** DJ84
Sch **Oaklands Prim Sch**,
W7 *off Oaklands Rd* **157** CF75
Oaklands Rd, N20 ....**97** CZ45
NW2 ....**119** CX63
SW14 ....**158** CR83
W7 ....**157** CF75
Bexleyheath DA6 ....**166** EZ84
Bromley BR1 ....**184** EE94
Dartford DA2 ....**188** FP88
Gravesend (Nthflt) DA11 ..**191** GF91
Waltham Cross (Chsht)
EN7 ....**66** DS26
Sch **Oaklands Sch**, Islw.
TW7 *off Woodlands Rd* ..**157** CD83
Loughton IG10
off Albion Hill **84** EK43
Sch **Oaklands Sec Sch**, E2 ....**12** C1
Oaklands Way, Tad. KT20 ...**233** CW122
Wallington SM6 ....**219** DK108
Oaklands Wd, Hat. AL10 .....**45** CU18
Oakland Way, Epsom KT19 ..**216** CR107
Oak La, E14 ....**13** L9
N2 ....**98** DD54
N11 ....**99** DK51
Egham (Eng.Grn) TW20 ..**172** AW90
Isleworth TW7 ....**157** CE84
Potters Bar (Cuffley) EN6 ..**65** DM28
Sevenoaks TN13 ....**256** FG127
Twickenham TW1 ....**177** CG87
Windsor SL4 ....**151** AN81
Woking GU22
off Beaufort Rd **227** BC116
Woodford Green IG8 .....**102** EF49
Oaklawn Rd, Lthd. KT22 ....**231** CE118
Oak Leaf Cl, Epsom KT19 ...**216** CQ112
Oakleafe Gdns, Ilf. IG6 .....**125** EP55
Oaklea Pas, Kings.T. KT1 ...**197** CK97
Oakleigh Av, N20 ....**98** DD47
Edgware HA8 ....**96** CP54
Surbiton KT6 ....**198** CN102
Oakleigh Cl, N20 ....**98** DF48
Swanley BR8 ....**207** FE97
Oakleigh Ct, Barn. EN4
off Church Hill Rd **80** DE44
Edgware HA8 ....**96** CQ54
Oakleigh Cres, N20 ....**98** DE47
Oakleigh Dr, Rick. (Crox.Grn)
WD3 ....**75** BQ44
Oakleigh Gdns, N20 ....**98** DC46
Edgware HA8 ....**96** CM50
Orpington BR6 ....**223** ES105
Oakleigh Ms, N20
off Oakleigh Rd N **98** DC47
OAKLEIGH PARK, N20 ....**98** DD46
⇌ **Oakleigh Park** **98** DD45
Oakleigh Pk Av, Chis. BR7 ..**205** EN95
Oakleigh Pk N, N20 ....**98** DD46
Oakleigh Pk S, N20 ....**98** DE47
Oakleigh Ri, Epp. CM16
off Bower Hill **70** EU32
Oakleigh Rd, Pnr. HA5 ....**94** BZ51
Uxbridge UB10 ....**135** BQ66
Oakleigh Rd N, N20 ....**98** DD47
Oakleigh Rd S, N11 ....**98** DG48
Sch **Oakleigh Spec Sch**,
N20 *off Oakleigh Rd N* ...**98** DF48
Oakleigh Way, Mitch. CR4 ...**201** DH95
Surbiton KT6 ....**198** CN102
Oakley Av, W5 ....**138** CN73
Barking IG11 ....**145** ET66
Croydon CR0 ....**219** DL105
Oakley Cl, E4 ....**101** EC48
E6
off Northumberland Rd .**144** EL72
W7 ....**137** CE73
Addlestone KT15 ....**212** BK105
Grays RM20 ....**169** FW79
Isleworth TW7 ....**157** CD81
Oakley Ct, Loug. IG10
off Hillyfields **85** EN40
Mitcham CR4
off London Rd **200** DG102
Oakley Cres, EC1 ....**4** F10
Slough SL1 ....**132** AS73
Oakley Dell, Guil. GU4 .....**243** BC132
Oakley Dr, SE9 ....**185** ER88
SE13 ....**183** ED86
Bromley BR2 ....**204** EL104
Romford RM3 ....**106** FN50
Oakley Gdns, N8 ....**121** DM57
SW3 ....**160** DE79
Banstead SM7 ....**234** DB115
Betchworth RH3 ....**264** CQ140
OAKLEY GREEN, Wind. SL4 .**150** AH82
Oakley Grn Rd, Wind.
(Oakley Grn) SL4 ....**150** AG82
Oakley Pk, Bex. DA5 ....**186** EW87
Oakley Pl, SE1 ....**21** N10
Oakley Rd, N1 ....**5** J5
SE25 ....**202** DV99
Bromley BR2 ....**204** EL104
Harrow HA1 ....**117** CE58
Warlingham CR6 ....**236** DU118
Oakley Sq, NW1 ....**141** DJ68
Oakley St, SW3 ....**160** DE79
Oakley Wk, W6 ....**159** CX79
Oakley Yd, E2 ....**11** P3
Oak Lo Av, Chig. IG7 ....**103** ER50
Oak Lo Cl, Stan. HA7
off Dennis La **95** CJ50
Walton-on-Thames KT12 ..**214** BW106
Oak Lo Dr, Red. RH1 ....**266** DG142
West Wickham BR4 .....**203** EB101
Oak Lo La, West. TN16 .....**255** ER125
Sch **Oak Lo Prim Sch**,
W.Wick. BR4
off Chamberlain Cres ...**203** EB102
Sch **Oak Lo Spec Sch**, N2
off Heath Vw **120** DC56
SW12 *off Nightingale La* .**180** DG87
Oak Manor Dr, Wem. HA9
off Oakington Manor Dr .**118** CM64
Oakmead Av, Brom. BR2 ...**204** EG100
Oakmeade, Pnr. HA5 ....**94** CA51
Oakmead Gdns, Edg. HA8 ...**96** CR49
Oakmead Grn, Epsom KT18 .**232** CP115
Oakmead Pl, Mitch. CR4 ....**200** DE95
Oakmead Rd, SW12 ....**180** DG88
Croydon CR0 ....**201** DK100
Oakmere Av, Pot.B. EN6 ....**64** DC33
Oakmere Cl, Pot.B. EN6 .....**64** DD31
Oakmere La, Pot.B. EN6 .....**64** DC32
Sch **Oakmere Prim Sch**, Pot.B.
EN6 *off Chace Av* **64** DD32
Oakmere Rd, SE2 ....**166** EU79
Oakmoor Way, Chig. IG7 ....**103** ES50
Oakmount Pl, Orp. BR6 ......**205** ER102
Oak Pk, W.Byf. KT14 ....**211** BE113
Oak Pk Gdns, SW19 ....**179** CX87
Oak Pk Ms, E5
off Brooke Rd **122** DT62
Oak Path, Bushey WD23
off Ashfield Av **76** CB44
Oak Piece, Epp. (N.Wld Bas.)
CM16 ....**71** FC25
Oak Pl, SW18 *off East Hill* ..**180** DB85
Oak Ridge, Dor. RH4 ....**263** CH139
Oakridge, St.Alb. (Brick.Wd)
AL2 ....**60** BZ29
Oakridge Av, Rad. WD7 .....**61** CF34
Oakridge Dr, N2 ....**120** DD55
Oakridge La, Brom. BR1
off Downham Way **183** ED92
Radlett WD7 ....**61** CF33
Watford (Ald.) WD25 ......**77** CD35
Oakridge Rd, Brom. BR1 ...**183** ED91
Oak Ri, Buck.H. IG9 ....**102** EK48
Oak Rd, W5
off The Broadway **137** CK73
Caterham CR3 ....**236** DS122
Cobham KT11 ....**230** BX115
Epping CM16 ....**69** ET30
Erith (Northumb.Hth) DA8 .**167** FC80
Erith (Slade Grn) DA8 ....**167** FG81
Gravesend DA12 ....**191** GJ90
Grays RM17 ....**170** GC79
Greenhithe DA9 ....**189** FS86
Leatherhead KT22 ....**231** CG118
New Malden KT3 ....**198** CR96
Orpington BR6 ....**224** EU108
Reigate RH2 ....**250** DB133
Romford RM3 ....**106** FM53
Westerham TN16 ....**255** ER125
Oak Row, SW16 ....**201** DJ96
Oakroyd Av, Pot.B. EN6 .....**63** CZ33
Oakroyd Cl, Pot.B. EN6 ......**63** CZ34
Oaks, The, N12 ....**98** DB49
SE18 ....**165** EQ78
Berkhamsted HP4 ....**38** AU19
Dartford DA2 ....**188** FP86
Dorking RH4
off Oak Ridge **263** CH139
Epsom KT18 ....**217** CT114
Hayes UB4
off Charville La **135** BQ68
Ruislip HA4 ....**115** BS59
Staines TW18
off Moormede Cres **173** BF91
Swanley BR8 ....**207** FE96
Tadworth KT20 ....**233** CW123
Watford WD19 ....**94** BW46
West Byfleet KT14 ......**212** BG113
Woodford Green IG8 ....**102** EE51
Oaks Av, SE19 ....**182** DS92
Feltham TW13 ....**176** BY89
Romford RM5 ....**105** FC54
Worcester Park KT4 .....**199** CV104
Oaks Cl, Lthd. KT22 ....**231** CG121
Radlett WD7 ....**77** CF35
Oaksford Av, SE26 ....**182** DV90
Oaks Gro, E4 ....**102** EE47
Oakshade Rd, Brom. BR1 ...**183** ED91
Leatherhead (Oxshott)
KT22 ....**214** CC114
Oakshaw, Oxt. RH8 ....**253** ED127
Oakshaw Rd, SW18 ....**180** DB87
Oakside, Uxb. (Denh.) UB9 .**134** BH65
Oakside Ct, Horl. RH6
off Oakside La **269** DJ147
Oakside La, Horl. RH6 ......**269** DJ147
Oaks La, Croy. CR0 ....**202** DW104
Dorking (Mid Holm.) RH5 .**263** CH143
Ilford IG2 ....**125** ES57
Sch **Oaks Pk High Sch**,
Ilf. IG2 *off Oaks La* **125** ES57
Oak Sq, Sev. TN13
off High St **257** FJ126
Oaks Rd, Croy. CR0 ....**220** DV106
Kenley CR8 ....**219** DP114
Reigate RH2 ....**250** DC133
Staines (Stanw.) TW19 ...**174** BK86
Woking GU21 ....**226** AY117
Oaks Track, Cars. SM5 ......**218** DF111
Wallington SM6 ....**219** DH110
Oak St, Hem.H. HP3 ....**40** BM24
Romford RM7 ....**127** FC57
Oak Stubbs La, Maid.
(Dorney R.) SL6 ....**150** AF75
Oaks Way, Cars. SM5 ....**218** DF108
Epsom KT18
off Epsom La N **233** CV119
Kenley CR8 ....**220** DQ114
Surbiton KT6 ....**197** CK103
Sch **Oakthorpe Prim Sch**,
N13 *off Tile Kiln La* **100** DQ50
Oakthorpe Rd, N13 ....**99** DN50
Oaktree Av, N13 ....**99** DP48
Oak Tree Av, Green.
(Bluewater) DA9 ....**189** FT87
Oak Tree Cl, W5
off Pinewood Gro **137** CJ72
Abbots Langley WD5 ......**59** BR32
Oaktree Cl, Brwd. CM13
off Hawthorn Av **109** FZ49
Oak Tree Cl, Guil. (Burpham)
GU4 ....**243** BB129
Guildford (Jacobs Well)
GU4 ....**242** AW128
Hatfield AL10 ....**45** CU17
Hertford (Hert.Hth) SG13 ..**32** DW12
Loughton IG10 ....**85** EQ39
Stanmore HA7 ....**95** CJ52
Virginia Water GU25 .....**192** AX101
Oaktree Cl, Wal.Cr. EN7 .....**65** DP28
Oak Tree Ct, Borwd. (Elstree)
WD6 *off Barnet La* **77** CK44
Oak Tree Dell, NW9 ....**118** CQ57
Oak Tree Dr, N20 ....**98** DB46
Egham (Eng.Grn) TW20 ..**172** AW92
Oak Tree Dr, Guil. GU1 .....**242** AW130
Slough SL3
off Tamar Way **153** BB78
Oak Tree Gdns, Brom. BR1 ..**184** EH92
Oaktree Garth, Welw.G.C.
AL7 ....**29** CY10
Oaktree Gro, Ilf. IG1 ....**125** ER64
Oak Tree Rd, NW8 ....**7** P2
Sch **Oaktree Sch**, N14
off Chase Side **80** DG44
Sch **Oaktree Sch, The**, Wok.
GU21 *off Gorsewood Rd* .**226** AS119
Oaktree Wk, Cat. CR3
off Essendene Rd **236** DS123
Oak Vw, Wat. WD18
off Gade Av **75** BS41
Oakview Cl, Wal.Cr. EN7 .....**66** DV28
Watford WD19 ....**76** BW44
Oakview Gdns, N2 ....**120** DD56
Oakview Gro, Croy. CR0 ....**203** DY102
Oakview Rd, SE6 ....**183** EB92
Sch **Oak Vw Sch**, Orp. BR5
off Crockenhill Rd **206** EY99
Oak Village, NW5 ....**120** DG63
Oak Wk, Saw. CM21 ....**36** EX07
Wallington SM6
off Helios Rd **200** DG102
Oak Warren, Sev. TN13
off Oak La **256** FG129
Oak Way, N14 ....**99** DH45
Oakway, SW20 ....**199** CW98
Oak Way, W3 ....**138** CS74
Oakway, Amer. HP6 ....**55** AP35
Oak Way, Ashtd. KT21 ......**232** CN116
Oakway, Brom. BR2 ....**203** ED96
Oak Way, Croy. CR0 ....**203** DX100
Feltham TW14 ....**175** BS88
Reigate RH2 ....**266** DD135
Oakway, Wok. GU21 ....**226** AS119
Oakway Cl, Bex. DA5 ......**186** EY86
Oakway Pl, Rad. WD7
off Watling St **61** CG34
Oakways, SE9 ....**185** EP86
Oakwell Dr, Pot.B. EN6 .....**65** DH32
OAKWOOD, N14 ....**81** DK44
⊖ **Oakwood** **81** DJ43
Oakwood, Berk. HP4 ....**38** AT20
Guildford GU2 ....**242** AU129
Wallington SM6 ....**219** DH109
Waltham Abbey EN9
off Roundhills **83** ED35
Oakwood Av, N14 ....**99** DK45
Beckenham BR3 ....**203** EC96
Borehamwood WD6 ....**78** CP42
Brentwood (Hutt.) CM13 ..**109** GE44
Bromley BR2 ....**204** EH97
Epsom KT19 ....**216** CP109
Mitcham CR4 ....**200** DD96
Purley CR8 ....**219** DP112
Southall UB1 ....**136** CA73
Oakwood Chase, Horn.
RM11 ....**128** FM58
Oakwood Cl, N14 ....**81** DJ44
Chislehurst BR7 ....**185** EM93
Dartford DA1 ....**188** FP88
Leatherhead (E.Hors.)
KT24 ....**245** BS127
Redhill RH1 ....**250** DG134
Redhill (S.Nutfld) RH1
off The Avenue **267** DM136
Woodford Green IG8
off Green Wk **102** EL51
Oakwood Ct, W14 ....**16** E5
Oakwood Cres, N21 ....**81** DL44
Greenford UB6 ....**137** CG65
Oakwood Dr, SE19 ....**182** DR93
Bexleyheath DA7 ....**167** FD84
Edgware HA8 ....**96** CQ51
Leatherhead (E.Hors.)
KT24 ....**245** BS127
St. Albans AL4 ....**43** CJ19
Sevenoaks TN13 ....**257** FH123
Oakwood Gdns, Ilf. IG3 .....**125** ET61
Orpington BR6 ....**205** EQ103
Sutton SM1 ....**200** DA103
Oakwood Hill, Loug. IG10 ...**85** EM44
Oakwood Hill Ind Est, Loug.
IG10 ....**85** EQ43
Oakwood La, W14 ....**16** E5
Oakwood Ms, Harl. CM17
off Station Rd **36** EW11
Oakwood Pk Rd, N14 ....**99** DK45
Oakwood Pl, Croy. CR0 .....**201** DN100
Sch **Oakwood Prim Sch**, St.Alb.
AL4 *off Oakwood Dr* **43** CJ19
Oakwood Ri, Cat. CR3 ......**252** DS125
Oakwood Rd, NW11 ....**120** DB57
SW20 ....**199** CU95
Croydon CR0 ....**201** DN100
Horley RH6 ....**268** DG147
Orpington BR6 ....**205** EQ103
Pinner HA5 ....**93** BV54
Redhill (Merst.) RH1 .....**251** DN129
St. Albans (Brick.Wd) AL2 ..**60** BY29
Virginia Water GU25 .....**192** AW99
Woking GU21 ....**226** AS119
Sch **Oakwood Sch**, Bexh.
DA7 *off Woodside Rd* ...**167** FD84
Horley RH6
off Balcombe Rd **269** DJ148
Purley CR8
off Godstone Rd **219** DP113
Oakwood Vw, N14 ....**81** DK44
Oakworth Rd, W10 ....**139** CW71
Oarsman Pl, E.Mol. KT8 .....**197** CE98
Oast Ho Cl, Stai. (Wrays.)
TW19 ....**172** AY87
Oasthouse Way, Orp. BR5 ..**206** EV98
Oast Rd, Oxt. RH8 ....**254** EF131
Oates Cl, Brom. BR2 ....**203** ED97
Oates Rd, Rom. RM5 ....**105** FB50
Oatfield Ho, N15
off Bushey Rd **122** DS58
Oatfield Rd, Orp. BR6 ......**205** ET102
Tadworth KT20 ....**233** CV120
Oatland Ri, E17 ....**101** DY54
Oatlands, Horl. RH6 ....**269** DH147
Oatlands Av, Wey. KT13 .....**213** BR106
Oatlands Chase, Wey. KT13 ..**195** BS104
Oatlands Cl, Wey. KT13 .....**213** BQ105
Oatlands Dr, Slou. SL1 .....**131** AR72
Weybridge KT13 ....**195** BR104
Oatlands Grn, Wey. KT13 ...**195** BR104
Sch **Oatlands Inf Sch**, Wey.
KT13
off St. Marys Rd **213** BR105
Oatlands Mere, Wey. KT13 ..**195** BR104
OATLANDS PARK, Wey.
KT13 ....**213** BR105
Oatlands Rd, Enf. EN3 ....**82** DW39
Tadworth KT20 ....**233** CY119
Oat La, EC2 ....**10** G7
Oban Cl, E13 ....**144** EJ70
Oban Ct, Slou. SL1
off Montem La **151** AR75

Oban Ho, Bark. IG11 off Wheelers Cross 145 ER68
Oban Rd, E13 144 EJ69
SE25 202 DR98
Oban St, E14 14 F7
Obelisk Ride, Egh. TW20 172 AS93
Oberon Cl, Borwd. WD6 78 CQ39
Oberon Way, Shep. TW17 194 BL97
Oberstein Rd, SW11 160 DD84
Oborne Cl, SE24 181 DP85
Observatory Gdns, W8 17 H3
Observatory Ms, E14 24 E7
Observatory Rd, SW14 158 CQ84
Observatory Shop Cen, Slou. SL1 152 AU75
Observatory Wk, Red. RH1 off Lower Br Rd 250 DF134
Occupation La, SE18 165 EP81
W5 157 CK77
Occupation Rd, SE17 20 G9
W13 157 CH75
Watford WD18 75 BV43
Ocean Est, E1 13 H4
Ocean St, E1 13 H5
Ocean Wf, E14 23 N4
Ockenden Cl, Wok. GU22 off Ockenden Rd 227 AZ118
Ockenden Gdns, Wok. GU22 off Ockenden Rd 227 AZ118
Ockenden Rd, Wok. GU22 227 AZ118
⇌ Ockendon 149 FX69
Ockendon Ms, N1 5 J4
Ockendon Rd, N1 5 J4
Upminster RM14 128 FQ64
Sch Ockendon Sch, The, S.Ock. RM15 off Erriff Dr 149 FU71
OCKHAM, Wok. GU23 228 BN121
Ockham Dr, Lthd. (W.Hors.) KT24 229 BR124
Orpington BR5 186 EU94
Ockham La, Cob. KT11 229 BT118
Woking (Ockham) GU23 229 BP120
Ockham Rd N, Lthd. KT24 229 BQ124
Woking (Ockham) GU23 228 BN121
Ockham Rd S, Lthd. (E.Hors.) KT24 245 BS126
Ockley Ct, Guil. GU4 off Cotts Wd Dr 243 BB129
Sutton SM1 off Oakhill Rd 218 DC105
Ockley Rd, SW16 181 DL90
Croydon CR0 201 DM101
Ockleys Mead, Gdse. RH9 252 DW129
Octagon Arc, EC2 11 L6
Octagon Rd, Walt. (Whiteley Vill.) KT12 213 BS109
Octavia Cl, Mitch. CR4 200 DE99
Octavia Ms, W9 6 E3
Octavia Rd, Islw. TW7 157 CF82
Octavia St, SW11 160 DE81
Octavia Way, SE28 off Booth Cl 146 EV73
Staines TW18 174 BG93
Octavius St, SE8 163 EA80
Odard Rd, W.Mol. KT8 off Down St 196 CA98
Oddesey Rd, Borwd. WD6 78 CP39
Odds Fm Est, H.Wyc. HP10 off Wooburn Common Rd 110 AH59
Odell Cl, Bark. IG11 145 ET66
Odencroft Rd, Slou. SL2 131 AN69
Odeon, The, Bark. IG11 off Longbridge Rd 145 ER66
Sch Odessa Inf Sch, E7 off Wellington Rd 124 EG64
Odessa Rd, E7 124 EF62
NW10 139 CU68
Odessa St, SE16 23 L4
Odger St, SW11 160 DF82
Odhams Wk, WC2 9 P8
Odyssey Business Pk, Ruis. HA4 115 BV64
Offa Rd, St.Alb. AL3 42 CC20
Offa's Mead, E9 off Lindisfarne Way 123 DY63
Offenbach Ho, E2 143 DX68
Offenham Rd, SE9 185 EM91
Offers Ct, Kings.T. KT1 off Winery La 198 CM97
Offerton Rd, SW4 161 DJ83
Offham Slope, N12 97 CZ50
Offley Pl, Islw. TW7 157 CD82
Offley Rd, SW9 161 DN80
Offord Cl, N17 100 DU52
Offord Rd, N1 4 A5
Offord St, N1 4 B5
Ogard Rd, Hodd. EN11 49 EC15
Ogilby St, SE18 165 EM77
Oglander Rd, SE15 162 DT84
Ogle St, W1 9 J5
Oglethorpe Rd, Dag. RM10 126 EZ62
Ohio Rd, E13 15 K4
Oil Mill La, W6 159 CU78
Okeburn Rd, SW17 180 DG92
Okehampton Cl, N12 98 DD50
Okehampton Cres, Well. DA16 166 EV81
Okehampton Rd, NW10 139 CW67
Romford RM3 106 FJ51
Okehampton Sq, Rom. RM3 106 FJ51
Okemore Gdns, Orp. BR5 206 EW98
Olaf St, W11 6 B10
Old Acre, Wok. GU22 212 BG114
Oldacre Ms, SW12 off Balham Gro 181 DH87
★ Old Admiralty Bldgs (M.o.D.), SW1 19 M2
Old Amersham Rd, Ger.Cr. SL9 113 BB60
Old Av, W.Byf. KT14 211 BE113
Weybridge KT13 213 BR107
Old Av Cl, W.Byf. KT14 211 BE113
Old Bailey, EC4 10 F8
Old Bakery Ms, Guil. (Albury) GU5 260 BH139
Old Barge Ho All, SE1 off Upper Grd 141 DN74
Old Barn Cl, Sutt. SM2 217 CY108
Old Barn La, Ken. CR8 236 DT116
Rickmansworth (Crox.Grn) WD3 74 BM43
Old Barn Ms, Rick. (Crox.Grn) WD3 off Old Barn La 74 BM43
Old Barn Rd, Epsom KT18 232 CQ117
Old Barn Way, Bexh. DA7 167 FD83
Old Barrack Yd, SW1 18 E3
Old Barrowfield, E15 off New Plaistow Rd 144 EE67
Old Bath Rd, Slou. (Colnbr.) SL3 153 BE81
Old Beaconsfield Rd, Slou. (Farn.Com.) SL2 131 AQ65
Old Bell Ct, Hem.H. HP2 off George St 40 BK19
Old Bellgate Pl, E14 23 N6
Oldberry Rd, Edg. HA8 96 CR51
Old Bethnal Grn Rd, E2 12 A1
OLD BEXLEY, Bex. DA5 187 FB87
Sch Old Bexley C of E Prim Sch, Bex. DA5 off Hurst Rd 186 EZ88
Old Bexley La, Bex. DA5 187 FD89
Dartford DA1 187 FF88
Old Billingsgate Wk, EC3 off Lower Thames St 142 DS72
Old Bishop's Palace, Hat. AL9 45 CX18
Old Bond St, W1 9 J10
Oldborough Rd, Wem. HA0 117 CJ61
Old Brewers Yd, WC2 9 N8
Old Brewery Ms, NW3 off Hampstead High St 120 DD63
Old Br Cl, Nthlt. UB5 136 CA68
Old Br St, Kings.T. (Hmptn W.) KT1 197 CK96
Old Broad St, EC2 11 K8
Old Bromley Rd, Brom. BR1 183 ED92
Old Brompton Rd, SW5 17 H10
SW7 17 H10
Old Bldgs, WC2 10 C7
Old Burlington St, W1 9 J9
Oldbury Cl, Cher. KT16 off Oldbury Rd 193 BE101
Orpington BR5 206 EX98
Oldbury Gro, Beac. HP9 89 AK50
Oldbury Pl, W1 8 F5
Oldbury Rd, Cher. KT16 193 BE101
Enfield EN1 82 DU40
Old Canal Ms, SE15 21 P10
Old Carriageway, The, Sev. TN13 256 FC123
Old Castle St, E1 11 N6
Old Cavendish St, W1 8 G7
Old Change Ct, EC4 off Carter La 142 DQ72
Old Chapel Rd, Swan. BR8 207 FC101
Old Charlton Rd, Shep. TW17 195 BQ99
Old Char Wf, Dor. RH4 263 CF135
Old Chelsea Ms, SW3 off Danvers St 160 DD79
Old Chertsey Rd, Wok. (Chobham) GU24 210 AV110
Old Chestnut Av, Esher KT10 214 CA107
Old Chorleywood Rd, Rick. WD3 off Chorleywood Rd 74 BK44
Oldchurch Gdns, Rom. RM7 127 FD59
H Oldchurch Hosp, Rom. RM7 127 FE58
Old Ch La, NW9 118 CQ61
Brentwood (Mtnsg) CM13 109 GE42
Greenford UB6 off Perivale La 137 CG69
Stanmore HA7 95 CJ52
Old Ch Path, Esher KT10 off High St 214 CB105
Oldchurch Ri, Rom. RM7 127 FD59
Old Ch Rd, E1 13 G7
E4 101 EA49
Oldchurch Rd, Rom. RM7 127 FD59
Old Ch St, SW3 17 P10
Old Claygate La, Esher (Clay.) KT10 215 CG107
Old Clem Sq, SE18 off Kempt St 165 EN79
Old Coach Rd, Cher. KT16 193 BD99
Old Coach Rd, The, Hert. (Cole Grn) SG14 30 DF12
Old Coal Yd, SE28 off Pettman Cres 165 ER77
Old Common Rd, Cob. KT11 213 BU112
Rickmansworth WD3 off Common Rd 73 BD42
Old Compton St, W1 9 L9
Old Cote Dr, Houns. TW5 156 CA79
OLD COULSDON, Couls. CR5 235 DN119
Old Ct, Ashtd. KT21 232 CL119
Old Ct Grn, Berk. (Pott.End) HP4 off Hempstead La 39 BC17
Old Ct Pl, W8 17 J3
Old Ct Rd, Guil. GU2 258 AU135
Old Crabtree La, Hem.H. HP2 40 BL21
Old Cross, Hert. SG14 32 DQ09
★ Old Curiosity Shop, WC2 10 A7
Old Dairy Ms, SW12 off Chestnut Gro 180 DG87
Old Dartford Rd, Dart. (Fnghm) DA4 208 FM100
Old Dean, Hem.H. (Bov.) HP3 57 BA27
Old Deer Pk Gdns, Rich. TW9 158 CL83
Old Devonshire Rd, SW12 181 DH87
Old Dock App Rd, Grays RM17 170 GE77
Old Dock Cl, Rich. TW9 off Watcombe Cotts 158 CN79
Old Dover Rd, SE3 164 EG80
Old Dr, The, Welw.G.C. AL8 29 CV10
Olden La, Pur. CR8 219 DN112
Old Esher Cl, Walt. KT12 214 BX106
Old Esher Rd, Walt. KT12 214 BX106
Old Farleigh Rd, S.Croy. CR2 220 DW110
Warlingham CR6 221 DY113
Old Fm Av, N14 99 DJ45
Sidcup DA15 185 ER88
Old Fm Cl, Beac. (Knot.Grn) HP9 88 AJ50
Hounslow TW4 156 BZ84
Old Fm Gdns, Swan. BR8 207 FF97
Old Farmhouse Dr, Lthd. (Oxshott) KT22 231 CD115
Old Fm Pas, Hmptn. TW12 196 CC95
Old Fm Rd, N2 98 DD53
Guildford GU1 242 AX131
Hampton TW12 176 BZ93
West Drayton UB7 154 BK75
Old Fm Rd E, Sid. DA15 186 EU89
Old Fm Rd W, Sid. DA15 185 ET89
Old Fm Yd, The, B.Stort. (Sheering) CM22 37 FC07
Old Ferry Dr, Stai. (Wrays.) TW19 172 AW86
Old Fld Cl, Amer. HP6 72 AY39
Oldfield Cl, Brom. BR1 205 EM98
Greenford UB6 117 CE64
Horley RH6 off Oldfield Rd 268 DF150
Stanmore HA7 95 CG50
Waltham Cross (Chsht) EN8 67 DY28
Oldfield Dr, Wal.Cr. (Chsht) EN8 67 DY28
Oldfield Fm Gdns, Grnf. UB6 137 CD67
Oldfield Gdns, Ashtd. KT21 231 CK119
Oldfield Gro, SE16 22 G8
Sch Oldfield Ho Unit, Hmptn. TW12 off Oldfield Rd 196 BZ95
Oldfield La N, Grnf. UB6 137 CE65
Oldfield La S, Grnf. UB6 136 CC70
Oldfield Ms, N6 121 DJ59
Sch Oldfield Prim Sch, Grnf. UB6 off Oldfield La N 137 CD68
Oldfield Rd, N16 122 DS62
NW10 139 CT66
SW19 179 CY93
W3 off Valetta Rd 159 CT75
Bexleyheath DA7 166 EY82
Bromley BR1 205 EM98
Hampton TW12 196 BZ95
Hemel Hempstead HP1 39 BE21
Horley RH6 268 DF150
St. Albans (Lon.Col.) AL2 61 CK25
Oldfields Circ, Nthlt. UB5 136 CC65
Oldfields Rd, Sutt. SM1 199 CZ104
Oldfields Trd Est, Sutt. SM1 200 DA104
Oldfield Wd, Wok. GU22 off Maybury Hill 227 BB117
Old Fishery La, Hem.H. HP1 39 BF22
Old Fish St Hill, EC4 10 G9
Old Fives Ct, Slou. (Burn.) SL1 130 AH69
Old Fleet La, EC4 10 E7
Old Fold Cl, Barn. EN5 off Old Fold La 79 CZ39
Old Fold La, Barn. EN5 79 CZ39
Old Fold Vw, Barn. EN5 79 CW41
OLD FORD, E3 143 DZ66
Sch Old Ford Prim Sch, E3 off Wrights Rd 143 DZ68
Old Ford Rd, E2 12 D1
E3 143 DY68
Old Forge Cl, Stan. HA7 95 CG49
Watford WD25 59 BU33
Welwyn Garden City AL7 29 CZ05
Old Forge Cres, Shep. TW17 195 BP100
Old Forge Ms, W12 off Goodwin Rd 159 CV75
Old Forge Rd, Enf. EN1 82 DT38
High Wycombe (Loud.) HP10 88 AC53
Old Forge Way, Sid. DA14 186 EV91
Old Fox Cl, Cat. CR3 235 DP121
Old Fox Footpath, S.Croy. CR2 off Essenden Rd 220 DS108
Old French Horn La, Hat. AL10 45 CW17
Old Gannon Cl, Nthwd. HA6 93 BQ50
Old Gdn, The, Sev. TN13 256 FD123
Old Gdn Ct, St.Alb. AL3 42 CC20
Old Gloucester St, WC1 9 P5
Old Gro Cl, Wal.Cr. (Chsht) EN7 66 DR26
Old Hall Cl, Pnr. HA5 94 BY53
Old Hall Dr, Pnr. HA5 94 BY53
Old Hall Ri, Harl. CM17 52 EY15
Old Hall St, Hert. SG14 32 DR09
Oldham Ter, W3 138 CQ74
OLD HARLOW, Harl. CM17 36 EX11
Old Harpenden Rd, St.Alb. AL3 43 CE17
Old Harrow La, West. TN16 239 EQ119
Old Hatch Manor, Ruis. HA4 115 BT59
OLD HATFIELD, Hat. AL9 45 CX17
Old Herns La, Welw.G.C. AL7 off Herns La 30 DC07
Old Hertford Rd, Hat. AL9 45 CW16
Old Highway, Hodd. EN11 33 EB14
Old Hill, Chis. BR7 205 EN95
Orpington BR6 223 ER107
Woking GU22 226 AX120
Oldhill St, N16 122 DU60
Old Homesdale Rd, Brom. BR2 204 EJ98
Old Hosp Cl, SW12 180 DF88
Old Ho Cl, SW19 179 CY92
Epsom KT17 217 CT110
Old Ho Ct, Hem.H. HP2 40 BM20
Oldhouse Cft, Harl. CM20 35 ES13
Old Ho Gdns, Twick. TW1 177 CJ85
Old Ho La, Harl. (Roydon) CM19 50 EK18
Kings Langley WD4 74 BL35
Waltham Abbey EN9 50 EF23
Old Ho Rd, Hem.H. HP2 40 BM20
Old Howlett's La, Ruis. HA4 115 BQ58
Old Jamaica Rd, SE16 22 A5
Old James St, SE15 162 DV83
Old Jewry, EC2 11 J8
Old Kenton La, NW9 118 CP57
Old Kent Rd, SE1 21 K6
SE15 162 DS77
Old Kiln La, Bet. (Brock.) RH3 264 CQ135
Old Kiln Rd, H.Wyc. (Penn) HP10 88 AC45
Old Kingston Rd, Wor.Pk. KT4 198 CQ104
Old La, Cob. KT11 229 BP117
Westerham (Tats.) TN16 238 EK121
Old La Gdns, Cob. KT11 229 BT122
Old Leys, Hat. AL10 45 CU22
Old Lo Dr, Beac. HP9 89 AL54
Old Lo La, Ken. CR8 219 DM114
Purley CR8 219 DM114
Old Lo Pl, Twick. TW1 off St. Margarets Rd 177 CH86
Old Lo Way, Stan. HA7 95 CG50
Old London Rd, Dor. (Mick.) RH5 247 CJ127
Epsom KT18 233 CU118
Hertford SG13 32 DS09
Kingston upon Thames KT2 198 CL96
Leatherhead (E.Hors.) KT24 245 BU126
St. Albans AL1 43 CD21
Sevenoaks (Bad.Mt) TN14 224 FA110
Sevenoaks (Knock.P.) TN14 240 EY115
Old Long Gro, Beac. HP9 89 AQ51
Old Maidstone Rd, Sid. DA14 186 EZ94
OLD MALDEN, Wor.Pk. KT4 198 CR102
Old Malden La, Wor.Pk. KT4 198 CR103
Old Malt Way, Wok. GU21 226 AX117
Old Manor Dr, Grav. DA12 191 GJ88
Isleworth TW7 176 CC86
Old Manor Gdns, Guil. (Chilw.) GU4 259 BD140
Old Manor Ho Ms, Shep. TW17 off Squires Br Rd 194 BN97
Old Manor La, Guil. (Chilw.) GU4 259 BC140
Old Manor Rd, Sthl. UB2 156 BX77
Old Manor Way, Bexh. DA7 167 FD82
Chislehurst BR7 185 EM92
Old Manor Yd, SW5 17 H9
Old Mkt Sq, E2 11 N1
Old Marsh La, Maid. (Taplow) SL6 150 AF75
Old Marylebone Rd, NW1 8 B6
Old Mead, Ger.Cr. (Chal.St.P.) SL9 90 AY51
Old Meadow Cl, Berk. HP4 38 AU21
Old Merrow St, Guil. GU4 243 BC131
Old Ms, Har. HA1 off Hindes Rd 117 CE57
Old Mill Cl, Dart. (Eyns.) DA4 208 FL102
Old Mill Ct, E18 124 EJ55
Old Mill Gdns, Berk. HP4 off London Rd 38 AX20
Old Mill La, Maid. SL6 150 AD75
Redhill RH1 251 DH128
Uxbridge UB8 134 BH72
Old Mill Pl, Rom. RM7 127 FD58
Old Mill Rd, SE18 165 ER79
Kings Langley WD4 59 BQ33
Uxbridge (Denh.) UB9 114 BG62
Old Mitre Ct, EC4 off Fleet St 141 DN72
Old Montague St, E1 12 A6
Old Moor La, H.Wyc. HP10 110 AE55
Old Nazeing Rd, Brox. EN10 49 EA21
Old Nichol St, E2 11 N3
Old N St, WC1 10 A5
Old Nurs Ct, Slou. (Hedg.) SL2 111 AQ61
Old Nurs Pl, Ashf. TW15 off Park Rd 175 BP92
Old Oak, St.Alb. AL1 off Cottonmill La 43 CE23
Old Oak Av, Couls. CR5 234 DE119
Old Oak Cl, Chess. KT9 216 CM105
Cobham KT11 213 BV113
OLD OAK COMMON, NW10 139 CT71
Old Oak Common La, NW10 138 CS71
W3 138 CS71
Old Oak La, NW10 138 CS69
Sch Old Oak Prim Sch, W12 off Mellitus St 139 CT72
Old Oak Rd, W3 139 CT73
Old Oaks, Wal.Abb. EN9 68 EE32
★ Old Operating Thea Mus & Herb Garret, SE1 21 K2
Old Orchard, Harl. CM18 51 ER17
St. Albans (Park St) AL2 60 CC26
Sunbury-on-Thames TW16 196 BW96
West Byfleet (Byfleet) KT14 212 BM112
Old Orchard, The, NW3 off Nassington Rd 120 DF63
Old Orchard Cl, Barn. EN4 80 DD38
Uxbridge UB8 134 BN72
Old Orchard Ms, Berk. HP4 38 AW20
Old Otford Rd, Sev. TN14 241 FH117
Old Palace La, Rich. TW9 177 CJ85
Sch Old Palace Prim Sch, E3 14 B1
Old Palace Rd, Croy. CR0 201 DP104
Guildford GU2 258 AU135
Weybridge KT13 195 BP104
Sch Old Palace Sch of John Whitgift, Croy. CR0 off Old Palace Rd 201 DP104
Old Palace Ter, Rich. TW9 off King St 177 CK85
Old Palace Yd, SW1 19 N5
Richmond TW9 177 CJ85
Old Papermill Cl, H.Wyc. HP10 off Glory Mill La 110 AE56
Old Paradise St, SE11 20 A7
Old Pk Av, SW12 180 DG86
Enfield EN2 82 DQ42
Old Parkbury La, St.Alb. (Coln.St) AL2 61 CF30
Old Pk Gro, Enf. EN2 82 DQ42
Old Pk La, W1 18 F2
Old Pk Ms, Houns. TW5 156 BZ80
Old Pk Ride, Wal.Cr. EN7 66 DT33
Old Pk Ridings, N21 81 DP44
Old Pk Rd, N13 99 DM49
SE2 166 EU78
Enfield EN2 81 DP41
Old Pk Rd S, Enf. EN2 81 DP42
Old Pk Vw, Enf. EN2 81 DN41
Old Parvis Rd, W.Byf. KT14 212 BK112
Old Perry St, Chis. BR7 185 ES94
Gravesend (Nthflt) DA11 190 GE89
Old Polhill, Sev. TN14 241 FD115
Old Portsmouth Rd, Gdmg. GU7 258 AV142
Guildford GU3 258 AV142
Old Pottery Cl, Reig. RH2 266 DB136
Old Pound Cl, Islw. TW7 157 CG81
Old Priory, Uxb. (Hare.) UB9 115 BP59
Old Pye St, SW1 19 L5
Old Quebec St, W1 8 D8
Old Queen St, SW1 19 M4
Old Rectory Cl, Tad. KT20 233 CU124
Old Rectory Dr, Hat. AL10 45 CV18
Old Rectory Gdns, Edg. HA8 96 CN51
Old Rectory La, Lthd. (E.Hors.) KT24 245 BS126
Uxbridge (Denh.) UB9 113 BE59
Old Redding, Har. HA3 94 CC49
Old Redstone Dr, Red. RH1 266 DG135
Old Reigate Rd, Bet. RH3 248 CP134
Dorking RH4 248 CL134
Oldridge Rd, SW12 180 DG87
Old River Lea Towpath, E15 off City Mill River Towpath 143 EB66
Old Rd, SE13 164 EE84
Addlestone KT15 211 BF108
Betchworth (Buckland) RH3 248 CR134
Dartford DA1 167 FD84
Enfield EN3 82 DW39
Harlow CM17 36 EX11
Old Rd E, Grav. DA12 191 GH88
Old Rd W, Grav. DA11 191 GF88
Old Rope Wk, Sun. TW16 off The Avenue 195 BV97
Old Royal Free Pl, N1 off Liverpool Rd 141 DN67
Old Royal Free Sq, N1 4 D9
Old Ruislip Rd, Nthlt. UB5 136 BX68
Old St. Mary's, Lthd. (W.Hors.) KT24 off Ripley La 245 BP129
Olds App, Wat. WD18 93 BP46
Old Savill's Cotts, Chig. IG7 off The Chase 103 EQ49
Old Sch Cl, SE10 25 H6
SW19 200 DA96
Beckenham BR3 203 DX96
Guildford GU1 off Markenfield Rd 242 AX134
Old Sch Ct, Stai. (Wrays.) TW19 172 AY87
Old Sch Cres, E7 144 EF65
Old Sch La, Bet. (Brock.) RH3 264 CN138
Old Sch Ms, Egh. TW20 173 BD92
Weybridge KT13 213 BR105
Old Sch Pl, Croy. CR0 219 DN105
Woking GU22 226 AY121
Old Sch Rd, Uxb. UB8 134 BM70
Old Schs La, Epsom KT17 217 CT109
Old Sch Sq, E14 13 N8
Thames Ditton KT7 197 CF100
Olds Cl, Wat. WD18 93 BP46
Old Seacoal La, EC4 10 E7
Old Shire La, Ger.Cr. SL9 91 BA46
Rickmansworth (Chorl.) WD3 73 BB44
Waltham Abbey EN9 84 EG35
Old Slade La, Iver SL0 153 BE76
Old Solesbridge La, Rick. (Chorl.) WD3 74 BG41
Old Sopwell Gdns, St.Alb. AL1 43 CE22
Old S Cl, Pnr. HA5 94 BX53
Old S Lambeth Rd, SW8 161 DL80
★ Old Spitalfields Mkt, E1 11 N5
Old Sq, WC2 10 B7
Old Sta App, Lthd. KT22 231 CG121
Old Sta Rd, Hayes UB3 155 BT76
Loughton IG10 84 EL43
Old Sta Way, H.Wyc. (Woob.Grn) HP10 110 AE58
Old Sta Yd, Brom. BR2 off Bourne Way 204 EF102
Oldstead Rd, Brom. BR1 183 ED91
Old Stockley Rd, West Dr. UB7 155 BP75
⇌ Old Street 11 J2
⊖ Old Street 11 J2
Old St, E13 144 EH68
EC1 10 G3
Old Swan Yd, Cars. SM5 218 DF105
Old Tilburstow Rd, Gdse. RH9 252 DW134
Old Town, SW4 161 DJ83
Croydon CR0 201 DP104
Old Town Cl, Beac. HP9 89 AL54
★ Old Town Hall Arts Cen, Hem.H. HP1 40 BJ19
Old Tram Yd, SE18 off Lakedale Rd 165 ES77
Old Tye Av, West. (Bigg.H.) TN16 238 EL116
Old Uxbridge Rd, Rick. (Map.Cr.) WD3 91 BE53
Sch Old Vicarage Sch, Rich. TW10 off Richmond Hill 178 CL86
Old Vicarage Way, H.Wyc. (Woob.Grn) HP10 110 AE59
Old Wk, The, Sev. (Otford) TN14 241 FH117
Old Watery La, H.Wyc. (Woob.Grn) HP10 110 AE55
Old Watford Rd, St.Alb. (Brick.Wd) AL2 60 BY30
Old Watling St, Grav. DA11 191 GG92
Oldway La, Slou. SL1 151 AK75
Old Westhall Cl, Warl. CR6 236 DW119
Old Wf Way, Wey. KT13 off Weybridge Rd 212 BM105
OLD WINDSOR, Wind. SL4 172 AU86
Old Windsor Lock, Wind. (Old Wind.) SL4 172 AW85
OLD WOKING, Wok. GU22 227 BA121
Old Woking Rd, W.Byf. KT14 211 BF113
Woking GU22 227 BE116
Old Woolwich Rd, SE10 163 ED79
Old Yd, The, West. TN16 240 EW124
Old York Rd, SW18 180 DB85
Oleander Cl, Orp. BR6 223 ER106
O'Leary Sq, E1 12 E5
Sch Olga Prim Sch, E3 off Lanfranc Rd 143 DY68
Olga St, E3 143 DY68
Olinda Rd, N16 122 DT58
Oliphant St, W10 6 B1
Olive Cl, St.Alb. AL1 off Burnside 43 CH22
Oliver Av, SE25 202 DT97
Oliver Cl, W4 158 CP79
Addlestone KT15 212 BG105
Grays RM20 169 FT80
Hemel Hempstead HP3 40 BL24
Hoddesdon EN11 49 EB15
St. Albans (Park St) AL2 61 CD27
Oliver Cres, Dart. (Fnghm) DA4 208 FM101
Oliver Gdns, E6 144 EL72
Oliver-Goldsmith Est, SE15 162 DU81
Sch Oliver Goldsmith Prim Sch, NW9 off Coniston Gdns 118 CR57
SE5 off Peckham Rd 162 DT81
Oliver Gro, SE25 202 DT98
Oliver Ms, SE15 162 DU82
Olive Rd, E13 144 EJ69
NW2 119 CW63
SW19 off Norman Rd 180 DC94
W5 157 CK76
Dartford DA1 188 FK88
Oliver Ri, Hem.H. HP3 40 BL24
Oliver Rd, E10 123 EB61
E17 123 EC57
NW10 138 CQ68
Brentwood (Shenf.) CM15 109 GA43
Grays RM20 169 FT81
Hemel Hempstead HP3 40 BL24
New Malden KT3 198 CQ96
Rainham RM13 147 FF67
Sutton SM1 218 DD105
Swanley BR8 207 FD97
Olivers Cl, Berk. (Pott.End) HP4 39 BC16
Olivers Yd, EC1 11 K3
Olive St, Rom. RM7 127 FD57
Olivette St, SW15 159 CX83
Olivia Dr, Slou. SL3 off Ditton Rd 153 AZ78
Olivia Gdns, Uxb. (Hare.) UB9 92 BJ53
Ollards Gro, Loug. IG10 84 EK42
Olleberrie La, Rick. (Sarratt) WD3 57 BD32
Ollerton Grn, E3 143 DZ67
Ollerton Rd, N11 99 DK50
Olley Cl, Wall. SM6 219 DL108
Ollgar Cl, W12 139 CT74
Olliffe St, E14 24 D6
Olmar St, SE1 162 DU79
Olney Rd, SE17 161 DP79

Olron Cres, Bexh. DA6 . . . . . 186 EX85
Olven Rd, SE18 . . . . 165 EQ80
Olveston Wk, Cars. SM5 . . . 200 DD100
Olwen Ms, Pnr. HA5 . . . . 94 BX54
Olyffe Av, Well. DA16 . . . . . 166 EU82
Olyffe Dr, Beck. BR3 . . . . . . 203 EC95
★ Olympia, W14 . . . . 16 D6
Olympia Ms, W2 . . . . 7 K10
Olympia Way, W14 . . . . 16 D6
Olympic Way, Grnf. UB6 . . . 136 CB67
Wembley HA9 . . . . 118 CN63
Olympus Sq, E5
off Nolan Way 122 DU63
Oman Av, NW2 . . . . 119 CW63
O'Meara St, SE1 . . . . 21 H2
Omega Cl, E14 . . . . 24 A5
Omega Ct, Ware SG12
off Crib St 33 DX06
Omega Pl, N1
off Caledonian Rd 141 DL68
Omega Rd, Wok. GU21 . . . . 227 BA115
Omega St, SE14 . . . . 163 EA81
Ommaney Rd, SE14 . . . . 163 DX81
Omnibus Way, E17 . . . . 101 EA54
Ondine Rd, SE15 . . . . 162 DT84
Onega Gate, SE16 . . . . 23 J5
O'Neill Path, SE18
off Kempt St 165 EN79
One Pin La, Slou.
(Farn.Com.) SL2 . . . . 111 AQ63
One Tree Cl, SE23 . . . . 182 DW86
One Tree Hill Rd, Guil. GU4 . 259 BB135
One Tree La, Beac. HP9 . . . . . 89 AL52
Ongar Cl, Add. KT15 . . . . . . 211 BF107
Romford RM6 . . . . 126 EW57
Ongar Hill, Add. KT15 . . . . . 212 BG107
Ongar Pl, Add. KT15 . . . . . . 212 BG107
Sch Ongar Pl Inf Sch, Add.
KT15 off Milton Rd 212 BG107
Ongar Rd, SW6 . . . . 160 DA79
Addlestone KT15 . . . . . . 212 BG106
Brentwood CM15 . . . . 108 FV45
Romford RM4 . . . . 86 EW40
Ongar Way, Rain. RM13 . . . . 147 FE67
Onra Rd, E17 . . . . 123 EA59
Onslow Av, Rich. TW10 . . . . 178 CL85
Sutton SM2 . . . . 217 CZ110
Onslow Cl, E4 . . . . 101 EC47
Hatfield AL10 . . . . 45 CV18
Thames Ditton KT7 . . . . . . 197 CE102
Woking GU22 . . . . 227 BA117
Sch Onslow Co Inf Sch, Guil.
GU2 off Powell Cl 258 AT136
Onslow Cres, Chis. BR7 . . . . 205 EP95
Woking GU22 . . . . 227 BA117
Onslow Dr, Sid. DA14 . . . . . . 186 EX89
Onslow Gdns, E18 . . . . 124 EH55
N10 . . . . 121 DH57
N21 . . . . 81 DN43
SW7 . . . . 17 N8
South Croydon CR2 . . . . . 220 DU112
Thames Ditton KT7 . . . . . . 197 CE102
Wallington SM6 . . . . 219 DJ107
Onslow Ms, Cher. KT16 . . . . 194 BG100
Onslow Ms E, SW7 . . . . 17 N8
Onslow Ms W, SW7 . . . . 17 N8
Onslow Rd, Croy. CR0 . . . . . 201 DM101
Guildford GU1 . . . . 242 AX134
New Malden KT3 . . . . 199 CU98
Richmond TW10 . . . . 178 CL85
Walton-on-Thames KT12 . . 213 BT105
Sch Onslow St. Audrey's Sch,
Hat. AL10
off Old Rectory Dr 45 CV18
Onslow Sq, SW7 . . . . 17 P7
Onslow St, EC1 . . . . 10 D4
Guildford GU1 . . . . 258 AW135
ONSLOW VILLAGE, Guil.
GU2 . . . . 258 AS136
Onslow Way, T.Ditt. KT7 . . . . 197 CE102
Woking GU22 . . . . 227 BF115
Ontario Cl, Brox. EN10 . . . . . 67 DY25
Horley (Smallfield) RH6 . . 269 DN149
Ontario St, SE1 . . . . 20 F6
Ontario Way, E14 . . . . 13 N10
On The Hill, Wat. WD19 . . . . . 94 BY47
Opal Cl, E16 . . . . 144 EK72
Opal Ct, Slou. (Wexham)
SL3 off Wexham St 132 AV70
Opal Ms, NW6
off Priory Pk Rd 139 CZ67
Ilford IG1 off Ley St 125 EP61
Opal St, SE11 . . . . 20 E8
Opecks Cl, Slou. SL2
off Church La 132 AV70
Opendale Rd, Slou. (Burn.)
SL1 . . . . 130 AH71
Openshaw Rd, SE2 . . . . 166 EV77
Uni Open Uni in London, The,
NW1 off Hawley Cres . . . 141 DH66
Openview, SW18 . . . . 180 DC88
Ophelia Gdns, NW2
off Hamlet Sq 119 CY62
Ophir Ter, SE15 . . . . 162 DU81
Opossum Way, Houns. TW4 . 156 BW82
Oppenheim Rd, SE13 . . . . . 163 EC82
Oppidans Ms, NW3
off Meadowbank 140 DF66
Oppidans Rd, NW3 . . . . 140 DF66
Optima Business Pk, Hodd.
EN11 . . . . 49 EC16
Oram Pl, Hem.H. HP3 . . . . . . 40 BK23
Orange Ct, E1 . . . . 22 B2
Orange Ct La, Orp. BR6 . . . . 223 EN109
Orange Gro, E11 . . . . 124 EE62
Chigwell IG7 . . . . 103 EQ51
Orange Hill Rd, Edg. HA8 . . . . 96 CQ52
Orange Pl, SE16 . . . . 22 F6
Orangery, The, Rich. TW10 . . 177 CJ89
Orangery La, SE9 . . . . 185 EM85
Orange Sq, SW1 . . . . 18 F8
Orange St, WC2 . . . . 9 L10
Orange Tree Hill, Rom.
(Hav.at.Bow.) RM4 . . . . . 105 FD50
Orange Yd, W1 . . . . 9 M8
Oransay Rd, N1 . . . . 5 H4
Oransay Wk, N1
off Clephane Rd 142 DQ65
Oratory La, SW3 . . . . 17 P9
Sch Oratory RC Prim Sch,
SW3 . . . . 18 A9
Orbain Rd, SW6 . . . . 159 CY80
Orbel St, SW11 . . . . 160 DE81
Orbital Cres, Wat. WD25 . . . . 75 BT35
Orbital One, Dart. DA1 . . . . . 188 FP89
Orb St, SE17 . . . . 21 J8
Orchard, The, N14 . . . . 81 DH43
N21 . . . . 82 DR44
NW11 . . . . 120 DA57
Orchard, The, SE3 . . . . 163 ED82
W4 . . . . 158 CR77
W5 . . . . 137 CK71
Banstead SM7 . . . . 234 DA115
Dorking (N.Holm.) RH5 . . 263 CJ140
Epsom KT17 . . . . 217 CT108
Epsom (Ewell) KT17
off Tayles Hill Dr 217 CT110
Hertford SG14 . . . . 32 DQ06
Hounslow TW3 . . . . 156 CC82
Kings Langley WD4 . . . . . . 58 BN29
Rickmansworth (Crox.Grn)
WD3 off Green La 74 BM43
Sevenoaks (Dunt.Grn)
TN13 . . . . 241 FE120
Swanley BR8 . . . . 207 FD96
Virginia Water GU25 . . . . 192 AY99
Welwyn Garden City AL8 . . 29 CX07
Weybridge KT13 . . . . 213 BP105
Woking GU22 . . . . 226 AY122
Orchard Av, N3 . . . . 120 DA55
N14 . . . . 81 DJ44
N20 . . . . 98 DD47
Addlestone (Wdhm) KT15 . 211 BF111
Ashford TW15 . . . . 175 BQ93
Belvedere DA17 . . . . 166 EY79
Berkhamsted HP4 . . . . 38 AU19
Brentwood CM13 . . . . 109 FZ48
Croydon CR0 . . . . 203 DY101
Dartford DA1 . . . . 187 FH87
Feltham TW14 . . . . 175 BR85
Gravesend DA11 . . . . 191 GH92
Hounslow TW5 . . . . 156 BY80
Mitcham CR4 . . . . 200 DG102
New Malden KT3 . . . . 198 CS96
Rainham RM13 . . . . 148 FJ70
Slough SL1 . . . . 131 AK71
Southall UB1 . . . . 136 BY74
Thames Ditton KT7 . . . . . 197 CG102
Watford WD25 . . . . 59 BV32
Windsor SL4 . . . . 151 AN81
Orchard Bungalow Caravan
Site, Slou. SL2 . . . . 131 AM66
Orchard Cl, E4
off Chingford Mt Rd 101 EA49
E11 . . . . 124 EH56
N1 off Morton Rd 142 DQ66
NW2 . . . . 119 CU62
SE23 off Brenchley Gdns . 182 DW86
SW20 off Grand Dr 199 CW98
W10 . . . . 6 D5
Ashford TW15 . . . . 175 BQ93
Banstead SM7 . . . . 218 DB114
Beaconsfield HP9
off Seeleys Rd 89 AK52
Bexleyheath DA7 . . . . 166 EY81
Bishop's Stortford
(Sheering) CM22 . . . . 37 FC07
Borehamwood (Elstree)
WD6 . . . . 78 CM42
Bushey (Bushey Hth)
WD23 . . . . 95 CD46
Edgware HA8 . . . . 96 CL51
Egham TW20 . . . . 173 BB92
Epsom (W.Ewell) KT19 . . 216 CP107
Guildford GU1 . . . . 243 BB134
Hemel Hempstead HP2 . . . 40 BM18
Hertford SG13 . . . . 47 DJ19
Horley RH6 . . . . 268 DF147
Leatherhead KT22 . . . . . . 231 CF119
Leatherhead (E.Hors.)
KT24 . . . . 229 BT124
Leatherhead (Fetch.)
KT22 . . . . 231 CD122
Northolt UB5 . . . . 116 CC64
Potters Bar (Cuffley) EN6 . . 65 DL28
Radlett WD7 . . . . 77 CE37
Rickmansworth (Chorl.)
WD3 . . . . 73 BD42
Ruislip HA4 . . . . 115 BQ59
St. Albans AL1 . . . . 43 CF21
South Ockendon RM15 . . 149 FW70
Surbiton KT6 . . . . 197 CH101
Uxbridge (Denh.) UB9 . . . 134 BH65
Walton-on-Thames KT12 . 195 BV101
Ware SG12 . . . . 33 DX05
Ware (Stans.Abb.) SG12 . . 33 EC11
Watford WD17 . . . . 75 BT40
Wembley HA0 . . . . 138 CL67
Woking GU22 . . . . 227 BB116
Orchard Ct, Hem.H. (Bov.)
HP3 . . . . 57 BA27
Isleworth TW7
off Thornbury Av 157 CD81
Twickenham TW2 . . . . 177 CD89
Wallington SM6
off Parkgate Rd 219 DH106
Worcester Park KT4 . . . . . 199 CU102
Orchard Cres, Edg. HA8 . . . . 96 CQ50
Enfield EN1 . . . . 82 DT39
Orchard Cft, Harl. CM20 . . . . 36 EU13
Orchard Dr, SE3
off Orchard Rd 164 EE82
Ashtead KT21 . . . . 231 CK120
Edgware HA8 . . . . 96 CM50
Epping (They.B.) CM16 . . . . 85 ES36
Grays RM17 . . . . 170 GA75
High Wycombe
(Woob.Grn) HP10 . . . . . . 110 AD59
Rickmansworth (Chorl.)
WD3 . . . . 73 BC41
St. Albans (Park St) AL2 . . . 60 CB27
Uxbridge UB8 . . . . 134 BK70
Watford WD17 . . . . 75 BT39
Woking GU21 . . . . 227 AZ115
Orchard End, Cat. CR3 . . . . . 236 DS122
Leatherhead (Fetch.) KT22 . 230 CC124
Weybridge KT13 . . . . 195 BS103
Orchard End Av, Amer. HP7 . . 72 AT39
Orchard Est, Wdf.Grn. IG8 . . 102 EJ52
Orchard Fm Mobile Home
Pk, Red. RH1 . . . . 267 DM143
Orchard Fld Rd, Gdmg.
GU7 . . . . 258 AT144
Orchard Gdns, Chess. KT9 . . 216 CL105
Epsom KT18 . . . . 216 CQ114
Leatherhead (Eff.) KT24 . . 246 BY128
Sutton SM1 . . . . 218 DA106
Waltham Abbey EN9 . . . . . . 67 EC34
Orchard Gate, NW9 . . . . 118 CS56
Esher KT10 . . . . 197 CD102
Greenford UB6 . . . . 137 CH65
Slough (Farn.Com.) SL2 . . 111 AQ64
Orchard Grn, Orp. BR6 . . . . . 205 ES103
Orchard Gro, SE20 . . . . 182 DU94
Croydon CR0 . . . . 203 DY101
Edgware HA8 . . . . 96 CN53
Gerrards Cross (Chal.St.P.)
SL9 . . . . 90 AW53
Harrow HA3 . . . . 118 CM57
Orpington BR6 . . . . 205 ET103
Orchard Hill, SE13
off Coldbath St 163 EB82
Carshalton SM5 . . . . 218 DF106
Dartford DA1 . . . . 187 FE85
Orchard Ho, Erith DA8
off Northend Rd 167 FF81
Sch Orchard Inf & Nurs Sch,
The, Houns. TW4
off Orchard Rd 176 CA85
Sch Orchard Inf Sch, Reig.
RH2 off Alexander Rd . . . 266 DA137
Sch Orchard JMI Sch, E9
off Holcroft Rd 142 DW66
Sch Orchard Jun Sch, The,
Houns. TW4
off Orchard Rd 176 CA85
Orchard La, SW20 . . . . 199 CV95
Amersham HP6 . . . . 55 AR38
Brentwood (Pilg.Hat.)
CM15 . . . . 108 FT43
East Molesey KT8 . . . . . . 197 CD100
Woodford Green IG8 . . . . 102 EJ49
Orchard Lea Cl, Wok. GU22 . 227 BE115
ORCHARD LEIGH, Chesh.
HP5 . . . . 56 AV28
Orchard Leigh, Chesh. HP5 . . 56 AU28
Orchardleigh, Lthd. KT22 . . . 231 CH122
Orchardleigh Av, Enf. EN3 . . . 82 DW40
Sch Orchard Lo (Spec Residential
Resource Cen), SE20
off William Booth Rd 202 DU95
Orchard Mains, Wok. GU22 . 226 AW119
Orchard Mead, Hat. AL10
off Days Mead 45 CT18
Orchardmede, N21 . . . . 82 DR44
Orchard Ms, N1 . . . . 5 K6
Beaconsfield (Seer Grn)
HP9 off Orchard Rd 89 AQ50
Orchard Path, Slou. SL3 . . . 133 BA72
Orchard Pl, E5 . . . . 122 DV64
E14 . . . . 14 G9
N17 . . . . 100 DT52
Keston BR2 . . . . 222 EJ109
Sevenoaks (Sund.) TN14 . . 240 EY124
Waltham Cross (Chsht)
EN8 off Turners Hill 67 DX30
Sch Orchard Prim Sch, Sid.
DA14 off Oxford Rd 186 EV92
Watford WD24
off Gammons La 75 BT36
Orchard Ri, Croy. CR0 . . . . . 203 DY102
Kingston upon Thames
KT2 . . . . 198 CQ95
Pinner HA5 . . . . 115 BT55
Richmond TW10 . . . . 158 CP84
Orchard Ri E, Sid. DA15 . . . . 185 ET85
Orchard Ri W, Sid. DA15 . . . 185 ES85
Orchard Rd, N6 . . . . 121 DH59
SE3 . . . . 164 EE82
SE18 . . . . 165 ER77
Barnet EN5 . . . . 79 CZ42
Beaconsfield HP9 . . . . 89 AM54
Beaconsfield (Seer Grn)
HP9 . . . . 89 AQ50
Belvedere DA17 . . . . 166 FA77
Brentford TW8 . . . . 157 CJ79
Bromley BR1 . . . . 204 EJ95
Chalfont St. Giles HP8 . . . . 90 AW47
Chessington KT9 . . . . 216 CL105
Dagenham RM10 . . . . 146 FA67
Dorking RH4 . . . . 263 CH137
Enfield EN3 . . . . 82 DW43
Gravesend (Nthflt) DA11 . . 190 GC89
Guildford (Burpham) GU4 . 243 BB130
Guildford (Ons.Vill.) GU2 . 258 AT136
Guildford (Shalf.) GU4 . . . 258 AY140
Guildford (Shere) GU5 . . . 260 BN139
Hampton TW12 . . . . 176 BZ94
Hayes UB3 . . . . 135 BT73
Horley (Smallfield) RH6 . . 269 DP148
Hounslow TW4 . . . . 176 BZ85
Kingston upon Thames
KT1 . . . . 198 CL96
Mitcham CR4 . . . . 200 DG102
Orpington (Farnboro.) BR6 . 223 EP106
Orpington (Pr.Bot.) BR6 . . 224 EW110
Reigate RH2 . . . . 250 DB134
Richmond TW9 . . . . 158 CN83
Romford RM7 . . . . 105 FB53
Sevenoaks (Otford) TN14 . 241 FF116
Sevenoaks (Rvrhd) TN13 . 256 FE122
Sidcup DA14 . . . . 185 ES91
South Croydon CR2 . . . . . 220 DV114
South Ockendon RM15 . . . 149 FW70
Sunbury-on-Thames TW16
off Hanworth Rd 175 BV94
Sutton SM1 . . . . 218 DA106
Swanscombe DA10 . . . . . . 190 FY85
Twickenham TW1 . . . . 177 CG85
Welling DA16 . . . . 166 EV83
Windsor (Old Wind.) SL4 . 172 AV86
Orchards, The, Epp. CM16 . . . 70 EU32
Sawbridgeworth CM21 . . . . 36 EY05
Orchards Business Cen,
Red. RH1 . . . . 267 DH143
Sch Orchard Sch, The, E.Mol.
KT8 off Bridge Rd 197 CD99
Orchards Cl, W.Byf. KT14 . . . 212 BG114
Orchardson St, NW8 . . . . 7 N4
Orchard Sq, W14 . . . . 16 E10
Broxbourne EN10 . . . . 49 DZ24
Orchards Residential Pk, The,
Slou. SL3 . . . . 133 AZ74
Orchards Shop Cen, Dart.
DA1 . . . . 188 FL86
Orchard St, E17 . . . . 123 DY56
W1 . . . . 8 E8
Dartford DA1 . . . . 188 FL86
Hemel Hempstead HP3 . . . . 40 BK24
St. Albans AL3 . . . . 42 CC21
Orchard Ter, Enf. EN1
off Great Cambridge Rd . . 82 DU44
Orchard Vw, Cher. KT16 . . . . 194 BG100
Uxbridge UB8 . . . . 134 BK70
Orchard Vil, Sid. DA14 . . . . . 186 EW93
Orchardville, Slou. (Burn.)
SL1 . . . . 130 AH70
Orchard Way, Add. KT15 . . . . 212 BH106
Ashford TW15 . . . . 174 BM89
Beckenham BR3 . . . . 203 DY99
Chigwell IG7 . . . . 104 EU48
Croydon CR0 . . . . 203 DY102
Dartford DA2 . . . . 188 FK90
Dorking RH4 . . . . 263 CH137
Enfield EN1 . . . . 82 DS41
Esher KT10 . . . . 214 CC107
Hemel Hempstead (Bov.)
HP3 . . . . 57 BA28
Oxted RH8 . . . . 254 EG133
Potters Bar EN6 . . . . 64 DB28
Reigate RH2 . . . . 266 DB138
Rickmansworth (Mill End)
WD3 . . . . 92 BG45
Slough SL3 . . . . 132 AY74
Sutton SM1 . . . . 218 DD105
Tadworth KT20 . . . . 249 CZ126
Waltham Cross (Chsht)
EN7 . . . . 65 DP27
Woking (Send) GU23 . . . . 243 BC125
Orchard Waye, Uxb. UB8 . . . 134 BK68
Sch Orchard Way Prim Sch,
Croy. CR0
off Orchard Way 203 DY101
Orchehill Av, Ger.Cr. SL9 . . . 112 AX56
Orchehill Ct, Ger.Cr. SL9 . . . 112 AY57
Orchehill Ri, Ger.Cr. SL9 . . . 112 AY57
Orchid Cl, E6 . . . . 144 EL71
Chessington KT9 . . . . 215 CJ108
Hatfield AL10 . . . . 29 CT14
Romford (Abridge) RM4 . . . 86 EV41
Southall UB1 . . . . 136 BY72
Waltham Cross
(Goffs Oak) EN7 . . . . 66 DQ30
Orchid Ct, Egh. TW20 . . . . . 173 BB91
Romford RM7 . . . . 127 FE61
Orchid Rd, N14 . . . . 99 DJ45
Orchid St, W12 . . . . 139 CU73
Orchis Gro, Grays
(Bad.Dene) RM17 . . . . . . 170 FZ78
Orchis Way, Rom. RM3 . . . . . 106 FM51
Orde Hall St, WC1 . . . . 10 A4
Ordell Rd, E3 . . . . 143 DZ68
Ordnance Cl, Felt. TW13 . . . . 175 BU90
Ordnance Cres, SE10 . . . . 24 F3
Ordnance Hill, NW8 . . . . 140 DD67
Ordnance Ms, NW8
off St. Ann's Ter 140 DD68
Ordnance Rd, E16 . . . . 15 J5
SE18 . . . . 165 EN79
Enfield EN3 . . . . 83 DX37
Gravesend DA12 . . . . 191 GJ86
Oregano Cl, West Dr. UB7
off Camomile Way 134 BM72
Oregano Dr, E14 . . . . 14 F8
Oregano Way, Guil. GU2 . . . 242 AU129
Oregon Av, E12 . . . . 125 EM63
Oregon Cl, N.Mal. KT3
off Georgia Rd 198 CQ98
Oregon Sq, Orp. BR6 . . . . . . 205 ER102
Orestan La, Lthd. (Eff.) KT24 . 245 BV127
Orestes Ms, NW6
off Aldred Rd 120 DA64
Oreston Rd, Rain. RM13 . . . . 148 FK69
Orewell Gdns, Reig. RH2 . . . 266 DB136
Orford Ct, SE27 . . . . 181 DP89
Orford Gdns, Twick. TW1 . . . 177 CF89
Orford Rd, E17 . . . . 123 EA57
E18 . . . . 124 EH55
SE6 . . . . 183 EB90
Organ Hall Rd, Borwd. WD6 . . 78 CL39
Organ La, E4 . . . . 101 EC47
Oriel Cl, Mitch. CR4 . . . . 201 DK98
Oriel Ct, NW3 off Heath St . . 120 DC63
Oriel Dr, SW13 . . . . 159 CV79
Oriel Gdns, Ilf. IG5 . . . . 125 EM55
Oriel Pl, NW3 off Heath St . . 120 DC63
Sch Oriel Prim Sch, Felt.
TW13 off Hounslow Rd . . 176 BY90
Oriel Rd, E9 . . . . 143 DX65
Oriel Way, Nthlt. UB5 . . . . . 136 CB66
Oriental Cl, Wok. GU22
off Oriental Rd 227 BA117
Oriental Rd, E16 . . . . 144 EK74
Woking GU22 . . . . 227 BA117
Oriental St, E14 . . . . 13 P9
Orient Cl, St.Alb. AL1 . . . . . . 43 CE22
Orient Ind Pk, E10 . . . . 123 EA61
Orient St, SE11 . . . . 20 E7
Orient Way, E5 . . . . 123 DX62
E10 . . . . 123 DY61
Oriole Cl, Abb.L. WD5 . . . . . . 59 BU31
Oriole Way, SE28 . . . . 146 EV73
Sch Orion, The, NW9
off Lanacre Av 97 CT53
Orion Rd, N11 . . . . 99 DH51
Orion Way, Nthwd. HA6 . . . . . 93 BT49
Orissa Rd, SE18 . . . . 165 ES78
Orkney Ct, Maid. (Taplow)
SL6 . . . . 130 AE66
Orkney St, SW11 . . . . 160 DG82
Orlando Gdns, Epsom KT19 . 216 CR110
Orlando Rd, SW4 . . . . 161 DJ83
Orleans Cl, Esher KT10 . . . . 197 CD103
★ Orleans Ho Gall, Twick.
TW1 . . . . 177 CH88
Sch Orleans Inf Sch, Twick.
TW1 off Hartington Rd . . 177 CH87
Sch Orleans Pk Sch, Twick.
TW1 off Richmond Rd . . . 177 CH87
Orleans Rd, SE19 . . . . 182 DR93
Twickenham TW1 . . . . 177 CH87
Orlestone Gdns, Orp. BR6 . . 224 EY106
Orleston Ms, N7 . . . . 4 D4
Orleston Rd, N7 . . . . 4 D3
Orley Fm Rd, Har. HA1 . . . . 117 CE62
Sch Orley Fm Sch, Har. HA1
off South Hill Av 117 CD62
Orlop St, SE10 . . . . 24 G10
Ormanton Rd, SE26 . . . . 182 DU91
Orme Ct, W2 . . . . 7 J10
Orme Ct Ms, W2 . . . . 7 K10
Orme La, W2 . . . . 7 J10
Ormeley Rd, SW12 . . . . 181 DH88
Orme Rd, Kings.T. KT1 . . . . . 198 CP96
Sutton SM1 off Grove Rd . 218 DB107
Ormerod Gdns, Mitch. CR4 . 200 DG96
Ormesby Cl, SE28
off Wroxham Rd 146 EX73
Ormesby Dr, Pot.B. EN6 . . . . . 63 CX32
Ormesby Way, Har. HA3 . . . . 118 CM58
Orme Sq, W2 . . . . 7 J10
Ormiston Gro, W12 . . . . 139 CV74
Ormiston Rd, SE10 . . . . 25 L10
Ormond Av, Hmptn. TW12 . . 196 CB95
Richmond TW10
off Ormond Rd 177 CK85
Ormond Cl, WC1 . . . . 9 P5
Romford (Harold Wd)
RM3 off Chadwick Dr . . . 106 FK54
Ormond Cres, Hmptn. TW12 196 CB95
Ormond Dr, Hmptn. TW12 . . 176 CB94
Ormonde Av, Epsom KT19 . . 216 CR109
Orpington BR6 . . . . 205 EQ103
Ormonde Gate, SW3 . . . . 18 D10
Ormonde Pl, SW1 . . . . 18 E8
Ormonde Ri, Buck.H. IG9 . . . 102 EJ46
Ormonde Rd, SW14 . . . . 158 CP83
Northwood HA6 . . . . 93 BR49
Woking GU21 . . . . 226 AW116
Ormonde Ter, NW8 . . . . 140 DF67
Ormond Ms, WC1 . . . . 9 P4
Ormond Rd, N19 . . . . 121 DL60
Richmond TW10 . . . . 177 CK85
Ormond Yd, SW1 . . . . 19 K1
Ormsby, Sutt. SM2
off Grange Rd 218 DB108
Ormsby Gdns, Grnf. UB6 . . . 136 CC68
Ormsby Pl, N16
off Victorian Gro 122 DT62
Ormsby Pt, SE18 off Troy Ct . 165 EP77
Ormsby St, E2 . . . . 5 N9
Ormside St, SE15 . . . . 162 DW79
Ormside Way, Red. RH1 . . . . 251 DH130
Ormskirk Rd, Wat. WD19 . . . . 94 BX49
Oman Rd, NW3 . . . . 120 DE64
Oronsay, Hem.H. HP3
off Northend 41 BP22
Orpen Wk, N16 . . . . 122 DS62
Orphanage Rd, Wat. WD17,
WD24 . . . . 76 BW40
Orpheus St, SE5 . . . . 162 DR81
ORPINGTON, BR5 & BR6 . . . 205 ES102
⇌ Orpington 205 ET103
Orpington Bypass, Orp.
BR6 . . . . 206 EV103
Sevenoaks TN14 . . . . 224 FA109
Coll Orpington Coll of Further
Ed, Orp. BR6
off The Walnuts 206 EU102
Orpington Gdns, N18 . . . . . . 100 DS48
H Orpington Hosp, Orp.
BR6 . . . . 223 ET105
Orpington Rd, N21 . . . . 99 DP46
Chislehurst BR7 . . . . 205 ES97
Orpin Rd, Red. RH1 . . . . 251 DH130
Orpwood Cl, Hmptn. TW12 . . 176 BZ92
ORSETT HEATH, Grays
RM16 . . . . 171 GG75
Orsett Heath Cres, Grays
RM16 . . . . 171 GG76
Orsett Rd, Grays RM17 . . . . 170 GA78
Orsett St, SE11 . . . . 20 B9
Orsett Ter, W2 . . . . 7 K7
Woodford Green IG8 . . . . 102 EJ53
Orsman Rd, N1 . . . . 5 L8
Orton Cl, St.Alb. AL4 . . . . 43 CG16
Orton St, E1 . . . . 22 A2
Orville Rd, SW11 . . . . 160 DD82
Orwell Cl, Hayes UB3 . . . . . 135 BS73
Rainham RM13 . . . . 147 FD71
Windsor SL4 . . . . 151 AR83
Orwell Ct, N5 . . . . 122 DQ63
Orwell Rd, E13 . . . . 144 EJ68
Osbaldeston Rd, N16 . . . . . . 122 DU61
Osberton Rd, SE12 . . . . 184 EG85
Osbert St, SW1 . . . . 19 L8
Osborn Cl, E8 . . . . 142 DU67
Osborne Av, Stai. TW19 . . . . 174 BL88
Osborne Cl, Barn. EN4 . . . . . . 80 DF41
Beckenham BR3 . . . . 203 DY98
Feltham TW13 . . . . 176 BX92
Hornchurch RM11 . . . . 127 FH58
Osborne Ct, Pot.B. EN6 . . . . . 64 DB29
Windsor SL4
off Osborne Rd 151 AQ82
Osborne Gdns, Pot.B. EN6 . . . 64 DB30
Thornton Heath CR7 . . . . . 202 DQ96
Osborne Gro, E17 . . . . 123 DZ56
N4 . . . . 121 DN60
Osborne Ms, E17
off Osborne Gro 123 DZ56
Windsor SL4 . . . . 151 AQ82
Osborne Pl, Sutt. SM1 . . . . . 218 DD106
Osborne Rd, E7 . . . . 124 EH64
E9 . . . . 143 DZ65
E10 . . . . 123 EB62
N4 . . . . 121 DM60
N13 . . . . 99 DN48
NW2 . . . . 139 CV65
W3 . . . . 158 CP76
Belvedere DA17 . . . . 166 EZ78
Brentwood (Pilg.Hat.)
CM15 . . . . 108 FU44
Broxbourne EN10 . . . . 49 EA19
Buckhurst Hill IG9 . . . . . . 102 EH46
Dagenham RM9 . . . . 126 EZ64
Egham TW20 . . . . 173 AZ93
Enfield EN3 . . . . 83 DY40
Hornchurch RM11 . . . . 127 FH58
Hounslow TW3 . . . . 156 BZ83
Kingston upon Thames
KT2 . . . . 178 CL94
Potters Bar EN6 . . . . 64 DB30
Redhill RH1 . . . . 250 DG131
Southall UB1 . . . . 136 CC72
Thornton Heath CR7 . . . . . 202 DQ96
Uxbridge UB8
off Oxford Rd 134 BJ66
Waltham Cross (Chsht)
EN8 . . . . 67 DY27
Walton-on-Thames KT12 . 195 BU102
Watford WD24 . . . . 76 BW38
Windsor SL4 . . . . 151 AQ82
Osborne Sq, Dag. RM9 . . . . . 126 EZ63
Osborne St, Slou. SL1 . . . . . 152 AT75
Osborne Ter, SW17
off Church La 180 DG92
Osborne Way, Chess. KT9
off Bridge Rd 216 CM106
Osborn Gdns, NW7 . . . . 97 CX52
Osborn La, SE23 . . . . 183 DY87
Osborn St, E1 . . . . 11 P6
Osborn Ter, SE3 off Lee Rd . 164 EF84
Osborn Way, Welw.G.C. AL8 . 29 CX10
Osborn Way Tunnel, Welw.G.C.
AL8 off Osborn Way 29 CX09
Osbourne Av, NW7 . . . . 97 CX52
Kings Langley WD4 . . . . . . 58 BM28
Osbourne Hts, Brwd.
(Warley) CM14 . . . . 108 FV49
Osbourne Rd, Dart. DA2 . . . 188 FP86
Oscar Faber Pl, N1 . . . . 5 M6
Oscar St, SE8 . . . . 163 EA81
Oseney Cres, NW5 . . . . 141 DJ65
Osgood Av, Orp. BR6 . . . . . 223 ET106
Osgood Gdns, Orp. BR6 . . . 223 ET106
OSIDGE, N14 . . . . 99 DH46
Osidge La, N14 . . . . 98 DG46
Sch Osidge Prim Sch, N14
off Chase Side 99 DJ46
Osier Cres, N10 . . . . 98 DF53
Osier La, SE10 . . . . 25 K6
Osier Ms, W4 . . . . 159 CT79
Osier Pl, Egh. TW20 . . . . . . 173 BC93
Osiers Rd, SW18 . . . . 160 DA84
Osier St, E1 . . . . 12 F4
Osier Way, E10 . . . . 123 EB62
Banstead SM7 . . . . 217 CY114
Mitcham CR4 . . . . 200 DE99
Oslac Rd, SE6 . . . . 183 EB92
Oslo Ct, NW8
off Greenberry St 140 DE68
Oslo Sq, SE16 . . . . 23 K5
Osman Cl, N15
off Tewkesbury Rd 122 DR58
Sch Osmani Prim Sch, E1 . . . . 12 B5
Osman Rd, N9 . . . . 100 DU48
W6 off Batoum Gdns 159 CW76
Osmond Cl, Har. HA2 . . . . . . 116 CC61
Osmond Gdns, Wall. SM6 . . 219 DJ106
Osmund St, W12
off Braybrook St 139 CT72
Osnaburgh St, NW1 . . . . 9 H4
NW1 (north section) 9 H2
Osnaburgh Ter, NW1 . . . . 9 H3
Osney Ho, SE2
off Hartslock Dr 166 EX75
Osney Wk, Cars. SM5 . . . . . 200 DD100
Osney Way, Grav. DA12 . . . . 191 GM89

Osprey Cl, E6
off Dove App 144 EL71
E11 124 EG56
E17 101 DY52
Leatherhead (Fetch.) KT22 230 CC122
Sutton SM1
off Sandpiper Rd 217 CZ106
Watford WD25 60 BY34
West Drayton UB7 154 BK75
Osprey Ct, Wal.Abb. EN9 68 EG34
Osprey Gdns, S.Croy. CR2 221 DX110
Osprey Hts, SW11
off Bramlands Cl 160 DE83
Osprey Ms, Enf. EN3 82 DV43
Osprey Rd, Wal.Abb. EN9 68 EG34
Ospringe Cl, SE20 182 DW94
Ospringe Ct, SE9
off Alderwood Rd 185 ER86
Ospringe Rd, NW5 121 DJ63
Osram Ct, W6 off Lena Gdns 159 CW76
Osram Rd, Wem. HA9 117 CK62
Osric Path, N1 5 L10
Ossian Ms, N4 121 DM59
Ossian Rd, N4 121 DM59
Ossington Bldgs, W1 8 E5
Ossington Cl, W2 7 H10
Ossington St, W2 7 H10
Ossory Rd, SE1 22 A10
Ossulston St, NW1 141 DK69
Ossulton Pl, N2
off East End Rd 120 DC55
Ossulton Way, N2 120 DC56
Ostade Rd, SW2 181 DM87
Ostell Cres, Enf. EN3 83 EA38
Osten Ms, SW7 17 K6
Osterberg Rd, Dart. DA1 168 FM84
OSTERLEY, Islw. TW7 156 CC80
⊖ Osterley 157 CD80
Osterley Av, Islw. TW7 157 CD80
Osterley Cl, Orp. BR5
off Leith Hill 206 EU95
Osterley Ct, Islw. TW7 157 CD81
Osterley Cres, Islw. TW7 157 CE81
Osterley Gdns, Th.Hth. CR7 202 DQ96
Osterley Ho, E14 14 A7
Osterley La, Islw. TW7 157 CE78
Southall UB2 156 CA78
Osterley Pk, Islw. TW7 157 CD78
★ Osterley Park Ho, Islw. TW7 156 CC78
Osterley Pk Rd, Sthl. UB2 156 BZ76
Osterley Pk Vw Rd, W7 157 CE75
Osterley Rd, N16 122 DS63
Isleworth TW7 157 CE80
Osterley Views, Sthl. UB2
off West Pk Rd 136 CC74
Oster St, St.Alb. AL3 42 CC19
Oster Ter, E17
off Southcote Rd 123 DX57
Ostlers Dr, Ashf. TW15 175 BQ92
Ostliffe Rd, N13 100 DQ50
Oswald Cl, Lthd. (Fetch.) KT22 230 CC122
Oswald Rd, Lthd. (Fetch.) KT22 230 CC122
St. Albans AL1 43 CE21
Southall UB1 136 BY74
Oswald's Mead, E9
off Lindisfarne Way 123 DY63
Oswald St, E5 123 DX62
Oswald Ter, NW2
off Temple Rd 119 CW62
Osward, Croy. CR0 221 DZ109
Osward Pl, N9 100 DV47
Osward Rd, SW17 180 DF89
Oswell Ho, E1 32 D1
Oswin St, SE11 20 F7
Oswyth Rd, SE5 162 DS82
OTFORD, Sev. TN14 241 FG116
Otford Cl, SE20 202 DW95
Bexley DA5
off Southwold Rd 187 FB86
Bromley BR1 205 EN97
Otford Cres, SE4 183 DZ86
Otford La, Sev. (Halst.) TN14 224 EZ112
Sch Otford Prim Sch, Sev. TN14 off High St 241 FH116
Otford Rd, Sev. TN14 241 FH118
Othello Cl, SE11 20 E9
Otho Ct, Brent. TW8 157 CK80
Otis St, E3 14 C1
Otley App, Ilf. IG2 125 EP58
Otley Dr, Ilf. IG2 125 EP57
Otley Rd, E16 144 EJ72
Otley Ter, E5 123 DX61
Otley Way, Wat. WD19 94 BW48
Otlinge Rd, Orp. BR5 206 EX98
Ottawa Ct, Brox. EN10 67 DY25
Ottawa Gdns, Dag. RM10 147 FD66
Ottawa Rd, Til. RM18 171 GG82
Ottaway St, E5
off Stellman Cl 122 DU62
Ottenden Cl, Orp. BR6
off Southfleet Rd 223 ES105
Otterbourne Rd, E4 101 ED48
Croydon CR0 202 DQ103
Otterburn Gdns, Islw. TW7 157 CG80
Otterburn Ho, SE5 162 DQ80
Otterburn St, SW17 180 DF93
Otter Cl, E15 143 EC67
Chertsey (Ott.) KT16 211 BB107
Otterden St, SE6 183 EA91
Otterfield Rd, West Dr. UB7 134 BL73
Otter Gdns, Hat. AL10 45 CV19
Ottermead La, Cher. (Ott.) KT16 211 BC107
Otter Meadow, Lthd. KT22 231 CF119
Otter Rd, Grnf. UB6 136 CC70
Otters Cl, Orp. BR5 206 EX98
OTTERSHAW, Cher. KT16 211 BC106
Otterspool La, Wat. WD25 76 BY38
Otterspool Service Rd, Wat. WD25 76 BZ39
Otterspool Way, Wat. WD25 76 BY37
Otto Cl, SE26 182 DV90
Ottoman Ter, Wat. WD17
off Ebury Rd 76 BW41
Otto St, SE17 161 DP79
Ottways Av, Ashtd. KT21 231 CK119
Ottways La, Ashtd. KT21 231 CK120
Otway Gdns, Bushey WD23 95 CE45
Otways Cl, Pot.B. EN6 64 DB32
Oulton Cl, E5
off Mundford Rd 122 DW61
SE28 off Rollesby Way 146 EW72
Oulton Cres, Bark. IG11 145 ET65
Potters Bar EN6 63 CX32
Oulton Rd, N15 122 DR57
Oulton Way, Wat. WD19 94 BY49
Oundle Av, Bushey WD23 76 CC44
Sch Our Lady & St. John's RC Prim Sch, Brent. TW8
off Boston Pk Rd 157 CJ78
Sch Our Lady & St. Joseph JMI Sch, N1 5 L4
Sch Our Lady & St. Philip Neri RC Prim Sch, SE26
off Sydenham Rd 183 DY91
Annexe, SE23
off Mayow Rd 183 DX90
Sch Our Lady Immaculate RC Prim Sch, Surb. KT6 off Ewell Rd 198 CP102
Sch Our Lady of Dolours RC Prim Sch, W2 7 J5
Sch Our Lady of Grace RC Inf Sch, NW2
off Dollis Hill Av 119 CW61
Sch Our Lady of Grace RC JM & Inf Sch, SE7
off Charlton Rd 164 EH79
Sch Our Lady of Grace RC Jun Sch, NW2
off Dollis Hill La 119 CV62
Sch Our Lady of Lourdes RC Prim Sch, E11
off Chestnut Dr 124 EG58
N11 off The Limes Avenue 99 DJ50
N12 off Bow La 98 DC53
NW10 off Wesley Rd 138 CQ67
SE13 off Belmont Hill 163 ED83
Sch Our Lady of Muswell RC Prim Sch, N10
off Pages La 120 DG55
Sch Our Lady of Peace Catholic Inf & Nurs Sch, Slou. SL1 off Derwent Dr 130 AJ71
Sch Our Lady of Peace Catholic Jun Sch, Slou. SL1
off Derwent Dr 130 AJ71
Sch Our Lady of the Rosary RC Prim Sch, Sid. DA15
off Holbeach Gdns 185 ES86
Staines TW18 off Park Av 174 BG93
Sch Our Lady of the Visitation RC Prim Sch, Grnf. UB6
off Greenford Rd 136 CC70
Sch Our Lady of Victories RC Prim Sch, SW7 17 M8
SW15 off Clarendon Dr 159 CX84
Sch Our Lady Prim Sch, E14 13 M8
Sch Our Lady Queen of Heaven RC Prim Sch, SW19
off Victoria Dr 179 CX87
Sch Our Lady's Conv High Sch, N16 off Amhurst Pk 122 DS59
Sch Our Lady's RC Comb Sch, Amer. HP6
off Amersham Rd 55 AP35
Sch Our Lady's RC Prim Sch, NW1 off Pratt St 141 DJ67
Dartford DA1
off King Edward Av 188 FK86
Welwyn Garden City AL7
off Woodhall La 29 CY11
Ousden Cl, Wal.Cr. (Chsht) EN8 67 DY30
Ousden Dr, Wal.Cr. (Chsht) EN8 67 DY30
Ouseley Rd, SW12 180 DF88
Staines (Wrays.) TW19 172 AW87
Windsor (Old Wind.) SL4 172 AW87
Outdowns, Lthd. (Eff.) KT24 245 BV129
Outer Circle, NW1 8 E4
Outfield Rd, Ger.Cr. (Chal.St.P.) SL9 90 AX52
Outgate Rd, NW10 139 CT66
Outlook Dr, Ch.St.G. HP8 90 AX48
Outram Pl, N1 141 DL67
Weybridge KT13 213 BQ106
Outram Rd, E6 144 EL67
N22 99 DK53
Croydon CR0 202 DT102
Outwich St, EC3 11 M7
OUTWOOD, Red. RH1 267 DP143
Outwood La, Couls. CR5 234 DF118
Tadworth (Kgswd) KT20 234 DB122
★ Oval, The, Surrey County Cricket Club, SE11 161 DM79
⊖ Oval 161 DN79
Oval, The, E2 142 DV68
Banstead SM7 218 DA114
Broxbourne EN10 67 DY25
Godalming GU7 258 AT144
Guildford GU2 258 AU135
Sidcup DA15 186 EU87
Oval Gdns, Grays RM17 170 GC76
Oval Pl, SW8 161 DM80
Sch Oval Prim Sch, Croy. CR0
off Cherry Orchard Rd 202 DS102
Oval Rd, NW1 141 DH67
Croydon CR0 202 DS102
Oval Rd N, Dag. RM10 147 FB67
Oval Rd S, Dag. RM10 147 FB68
Oval Way, SE11 20 B10
Gerrards Cross SL9 112 AY56
Ovenden Rd, Sev. (Sund.) TN14 240 EX120
Overbrae, Beck. BR3 183 EA93
Overbrook, Lthd. (W.Hors.) KT24 245 BP129
Overbrook Wk, Edg. HA8 96 CN52
Overbury Av, Beck. BR3 203 EB97
Overbury Cres, Croy. (New Adgtn) CR0 221 EC110
Overbury Rd, N15 122 DR58
Overbury St, E5 123 DX63
Overcliffe, Grav. DA11 191 GG86
Overcliff Rd, SE13 163 EA83
Grays RM17 170 GD78
Overcourt Cl, Sid. DA15 186 EV86
Overdale, Ashtd. KT21 232 CL115
Dorking RH5 263 CJ135
Redhill (Bletch.) RH1 252 DQ133
Overdale Av, N.Mal. KT3 198 CQ96
Overdale Rd, W5 157 CJ76
Chesham HP5 54 AP28
Overdown Rd, SE6 183 EA91
Overhill, Warl. CR6 236 DW119
Overhill Rd, SE22 182 DU87
Purley CR8 219 DN109
Overhill Way, Beck. BR3 203 ED99
Overlea Rd, E5 122 DU59
Overlord Cl, Brox. EN10 49 DY20
Overmead, Sid. DA15 185 ER87
Swanley BR8 207 FE99
Oversley Ho, W2 7 H5
Overstand Cl, Beck. BR3 203 EA99
Overstone Gdns, Croy. CR0 203 DZ101
Overstone Rd, W6 159 CW76
Overstrand Ho, Horn. RM12 off Sunrise Av 127 FH61
Overstream, Rick. (Loud.) WD3 74 BH42
Over The Misbourne, Ger.Cr. SL9 113 BA58
Uxbridge (Denh.) UB9 113 BC58
Overthorpe Cl, Wok. (Knap.) GU21 226 AS117
Overton Cl, NW10 138 CQ65
Overton Cl, Islw. TW7
off Avenue Rd 157 CF81
Overton Ct, E11 124 EG59
Overton Dr, E11 124 EH59
Romford RM6 126 EW59
Sch Overton Gra Sch, Sutt. SM2 off Stanley Rd 218 DB109
Overton Ho, SW15
off Tangley Gro 179 CT87
Overton Rd, E10 123 DY60
N14 81 DL43
SE2 166 EW76
SW9 161 DN82
Sutton SM2 218 DA107
Overton Rd E, SE2 166 EX76
Overtons Yd, Croy. CR0 202 DQ104
Overy St, Dart. DA1 188 FL86
Ovesdon Av, Har. HA2 116 BZ60
Oveton Way, Lthd. (Bkhm) KT23 246 CA126
Ovett Cl, SE19 182 DS93
Ovex Cl, E14 24 D4
Ovington Ct, Wok. GU21
off Roundthorn Way 226 AT116
Ovington Gdns, SW3 18 B6
Ovington Ms, SW3 18 B6
Ovington Sq, SW3 18 B6
Ovington St, SW3 18 B6
Owen Cl, SE28 146 EW74
Croydon CR0 202 DR100
Hayes UB4 135 BV69
Romford RM5 105 FB51
Slough SL3 off Parish La 153 AZ78
Owen Gdns, Wdf.Grn. IG8 102 EL51
Owenite St, SE2 166 EV77
Owen Pl, Lthd. KT22
off Church Rd 231 CH122
Owen Rd, N13 100 DQ50
Hayes UB4 135 BV69
Owen's Ct, EC1 10 E1
Owen's Row, EC1 10 E1
Owen St, EC1 4 E10
Owens Way, SE23 183 DY87
Rickmansworth (Crox.Grn) WD3 74 BN43
Owen Wk, SE20
off Sycamore Gro 182 DU94
Owen Waters Ho, Ilf. IG5 103 EM53
Owen Way, NW10 138 CQ65
Owgan Cl, SE5
off Benhill Rd 162 DR80
Owl Cl, S.Croy. CR2 221 DX110
Owlets Hall Cl, Horn. RM11 off Prospect Rd 128 FM55
Owl Pk, Loug. (High Beach) IG10 84 EF40
Owlsears Cl, Beac. HP9 89 AK51
Ownstead Gdns, S.Croy. CR2 220 DT111
Ownsted Hill, Croy. (New Adgtn) CR0 221 EC110
Oxberry Av, SW6 159 CY82
Oxdowne Cl, Cob. (Stoke D'Ab.) KT11 214 CB114
Oxenden Dr, Hodd. EN11 49 EA18
Oxenden Wd Rd, Orp. BR6 224 EV107
Oxendon St, SW1 9 L10
Oxenford St, SE15 162 DT83
Oxenholme, NW1 141 DJ68
Oxenpark Av, Wem. HA9 118 CL59
Oxestalls Rd, SE8 23 K9
Oxfield Cl, Berk. HP4 38 AU20
Oxford Av, SW20 199 CY96
Grays RM16 171 GG77
Hayes UB3 155 BT80
Hornchurch RM11 128 FN56
Hounslow TW5 156 CA78
St. Albans AL1 43 CJ21
Slough SL1 131 AM71
Slough (Burn.) SL1 130 AG68
★ Oxford Circ, W1 9 J7
⊖ Oxford Circus 9 J7
Oxford Circ Av, W1 9 J8
Oxford Cl, N9 100 DV47
Ashford TW15 175 BQ94
Gravesend DA12 191 GM89
Mitcham CR4 201 DJ97
Northwood HA6 93 BQ49
Waltham Cross (Chsht) EN8 67 DX29
Oxford Ct, EC4 11 J9
W3 138 CN72
Brentwood (Warley) CM14 108 FX49
Feltham TW13
off Oxford Way 176 BX91
Oxford Cres, N.Mal. KT3 198 CR100
Oxford Dr, SE1 21 L2
Ruislip HA4 116 BW61
Oxford Gdns, N20 98 DD46
N21 100 DQ45
W4 158 CN78
W10 6 D6
Uxbridge (Denh.) UB9 113 BF62
Sch Oxford Gdns Prim Sch, W10 6 A7
Oxford Gate, W6 16 B7
Oxford Ms, Bex. DA5 186 FA87
Oxford Pl, NW10
off Neasden La N 118 CR62
Hatfield AL10
off Mosquito Way 44 CS16
Oxford Rd, E15 143 ED65
N4 121 DN60
N9 100 DV47
NW6 140 DA68
SE19 182 DR93
SW15 159 CY84
W5 137 CK73
Beaconsfield HP9 111 AP55
Beaconsfield (Holt.) HP9 88 AE54
Carshalton SM5 218 DE107
Enfield EN3 82 DV43
Gerrards Cross SL9 113 BA60
Guildford GU1 258 AX136
Harrow HA1 116 CC58
Harrow (Wldste) HA3 117 CF55
High Wycombe HP10 88 AE54
Ilford IG1 125 EQ63
Redhill RH1 250 DE133
Romford RM3 106 FM51
Sidcup DA14 186 EV92
Teddington TW11 177 CD92
Uxbridge UB8, UB9 134 BJ65
Wallington SM6 219 DJ106
Windsor SL4 151 AQ81
Woodford Green IG8 102 EJ50
Oxford Rd E, Wind. SL4 151 AQ81
Oxford Rd N, W4 158 CP78
Oxford Rd S, W4 158 CN78
Oxford Sq, W2 8 B8
Oxford St, W1 9 K7
Watford WD18 75 BV43
Oxford Ter, Guil. GU1
off Pewley Hill 258 AX136
Oxford Wk, Sthl. UB1 136 BZ74
Oxford Way, Felt. TW13 176 BX91
Oxgate Gdns, NW2 119 CV62
Oxgate La, NW2 119 CV61
Oxhawth Cres, Brom. BR2 205 EN99
OXHEY, Wat. WD19 76 BW44
Oxhey Av, Wat. WD19 94 BX45
Oxhey Dr, Nthwd. HA6 93 BV50
Watford WD19 94 BW48
Oxhey Dr S, Nthwd. HA6 93 BV50
Sch Oxhey Inf Sch, Bushey WD23 off Aldenham Rd 76 BY43
Oxhey La, Har. HA3 94 CA50
Pinner HA5 94 CA50
Watford WD19 94 BZ47
Oxhey Ridge Cl, Nthwd. HA6 93 BU50
Oxhey Rd, Wat. WD19 76 BW44
Sch Oxhey Wd Prim Sch, Wat. WD19 off Oxhey Dr 94 BW48
Ox La, Epsom KT17
off Church St 217 CU109
Oxleas, E6 145 EP72
Oxleas Cl, Well. DA16 165 ER82
OXLEASE, Hat. AL10 45 CV19
Oxlease Dr, Hat. AL10 45 CV19
Oxleay Ct, Har. HA2 116 CA60
Oxleay Rd, Har. HA2 116 CA60
Oxleigh Cl, N.Mal. KT3 198 CS99
Oxley Cl, SE1 21 P9
Romford RM2 106 FJ54
Oxleys, The, Harl. CM17 36 EY11
Oxleys Rd, NW2 119 CV62
Waltham Abbey EN9 68 EG32
Oxlip Cl, Croy. CR0
off Marigold Way 203 DX102
Oxlow La, Dag. RM9, RM10 126 FA63
Oxonian St, SE22 162 DT84
Oxo Twr Wf, SE1 10 D10
OXSHOTT, Lthd. KT22 215 CD113
⇌ Oxshott 214 CC113
Oxshott Ri, Cob. KT11 214 BX113
Oxshott Rd, Lthd. KT22 231 CE115
Oxshott Way, Cob. KT11 230 BY115
OXTED, RH8 253 ED129
⇌ Oxted 254 EE129
Oxted Cl, Mitch. CR4 200 DD97
Oxted Rd, Gdse. RH9 252 DW130
Sch Oxted Sch, Oxt. RH8
off Bluehouse La 254 EF128
Oxtoby Way, SW16 201 DK96
Oyster Catchers Cl, E16 15 N7
Oyster Catcher Ter, Ilf. IG5
off Tiptree Cres 125 EN55
Oysterfields, St.Alb. AL3 42 CB19
Oyster La, W.Byf. (Byfleet) KT14 212 BK110
Oyster Row, E1 12 F8
Oyster Wf, SW11
off Lombard Rd 160 DD82
Ozolins Way, E16 15 L7

P

Pablo Neruda Cl, SE24
off Shakespeare Rd 161 DP84
Paceheath Cl, Rom. RM5 105 FD51
Pace Pl, E1 12 D8
PACHESHAM PARK, Lthd. KT22 231 CG116
Pachesham Pk, Lthd. KT22 231 CG117
Pacific Cl, Felt. TW14 175 BT88
Swanscombe DA10 190 FY85
Pacific Rd, E16 15 L7
Packet Boat La, Uxb. UB8 134 BH72
Packham Cl, Orp. BR6
off Berrylands 206 EW104
Packham Ct, Wor.Pk. KT4
off Lavender Av 199 CW104
Packham Rd, Grav. (Nthflt) DA11 191 GF90
Packhorse Cl, St.Alb. AL4 43 CJ17
Packhorse La, Borwd. WD6 78 CS37
Potters Bar (Ridge) EN6 62 CR31
Packhorse Rd, Ger.Cr. (Chal.St.P.) SL9 112 AY58
Sevenoaks TN13 256 FC123
Packington Rd, W3 158 CQ76
Packington Sq, N1 4 G8
Packington St, N1 4 F7
Packmores Rd, SE9 185 ER85
Padbrook, Oxt. RH8 254 EG129
Padbrook Cl, Oxt. RH8 254 EH128
Padbury, SE17 21 L10
Padbury Cl, Felt. TW14 175 BR88
Padbury Ct, E2 11 P2
Padcroft Rd, West Dr. UB7 134 BK74
Padden Ct, NW7
off Bittacy Hill 97 CY52
Paddenswick Rd, W6 159 CU76
Paddick Cl, Hodd. EN11 49 DZ16
PADDINGTON, W2 7 L6
⇌ Paddington 7 N7
⊖ Paddington 7 N7
Paddington Cl, Hayes UB4 136 BX70
Paddington Grn, W2 7 P5
Sch Paddington Grn Prim Sch, W2 7 N4
Paddington St, W1 8 E5
Paddock, The, Brox. EN10 49 EA20
Dorking (Westc.) RH4 262 CB137
Gerrards Cross (Chal.St.P.) SL9 90 AY50
Guildford GU1 243 BD133
Hatfield AL10 45 CU16
Slough (Datchet) SL3 152 AV81
Uxbridge (Ickhm) UB10 115 BP63
Westerham TN16 255 EQ126
Paddock Cl, SE3 164 EG82
SE26 183 DX91
Dartford (S.Darenth) DA4 208 FQ95
Northolt UB5 136 CA68
Orpington BR6
off State Fm Av 223 EP105
Oxted RH8 254 EF131
Ware SG12 34 EK06
Watford WD19 76 BY44
Worcester Park KT4 198 CS102
Paddock Gdns, SE19
off Westow St 182 DS93
Paddock Mead, Harl. CM18 51 EQ20
Paddock Rd, NW2 119 CU62
Bexleyheath DA6 166 EY84
Ruislip HA4 116 BX62
Paddocks, The, NW7 97 CY51
Addlestone (New Haw) KT15 212 BH110
Barnet EN4 80 DF41
Hertford (Hert.Hth) SG13 32 DV12
Leatherhead (Bkhm) KT23
off Leatherhead Rd 246 CB126
Rickmansworth (Chorl.) WD3 73 BF42
Romford (Stap.Abb.) RM4 87 FF44
Paddock, The, Sev. TN13 257 FK124
Virginia Water GU25 192 AY100
Welwyn Garden City AL7 30 DB08
Wembley HA9 118 CP61
Weybridge KT13 195 BS104
Sch Paddock Sch, SW15
off Priory La 159 CT84
Paddocks Cl, Ashtd. KT21 232 CL118
Cobham KT11 214 BW114
Harrow HA2 116 CB63
Orpington BR5 206 EX103
Paddocks Mead, Wok. GU21 226 AS116
Paddocks Retail Pk, Wey. KT13 212 BL111
Paddocks Rd, Guil. GU4 243 BA130
Paddocks Way, Ashtd. KT21 232 CL118
Chertsey KT16 194 BH102
Paddock Wk, Warl. CR6 236 DV119
Paddock Way, SW15 179 CW87
Chislehurst BR7 185 ER94
Hemel Hempstead HP1 39 BE20
Oxted RH8 254 EF131
Woking GU21 211 BB114
Padfield Ct, Wem. HA9
off Forty Av 118 CM62
Padfield Rd, SE5 162 DQ83
Padgets, The, Wal.Abb. EN9 67 ED34
Padley Cl, Chess. KT9 216 CM106
Padnall Ct, Rom. RM6
off Padnall Rd 126 EX55
Padnall Rd, Rom. RM6 126 EX56
Padstow Cl, Orp. BR6 223 ET105
Slough SL3 152 AY76
Padstow Rd, Enf. EN2 81 DP40
Padstow Wk, Felt. TW14 175 BT88
Padua Rd, SE20 202 DW95
Pagden St, SW8 161 DH81
Pageant Av, NW9 96 CR53
Pageant Cl, Til. RM18 171 GJ81
Pageant Cres, SE16 23 K1
Pageantmaster Ct, EC4 10 E8
Pageant Rd, St.Alb. AL1 43 CD21
Pageant Wk, Croy. CR0 202 DS104
Page Av, Wem. HA9 118 CQ62
Page Cl, Dag. RM9 126 EY64
Dartford (Bean) DA2 189 FW90
Hampton TW12 176 BY93
Harrow HA3 118 CM58
Page Cres, Croy. CR0 219 DN106
Erith DA8 167 FF80
Page Grn Rd, N15 122 DU57
Page Grn Ter, N15 122 DT57
Page Heath La, Brom. BR1 204 EK97
Page Heath Vil, Brom. BR1 204 EK97
Page Hill, Ware SG12 32 DV05
Pagehurst Rd, Croy. CR0 202 DV101
Page Meadow, NW7 97 CU52
Page Rd, Felt. TW14 175 BR86
Hertford SG13 32 DU09
Pages Cft, Berk. HP4 38 AU17
Pages Hill, N10 98 DG54
Pages La, N10 98 DG54
Romford RM3 106 FP54
Uxbridge UB8 134 BJ65
Page St, NW7 97 CU53
SW1 19 M7
Pages Wk, SE1 21 L7
Pages Yd, W4 off Church St 158 CS79
Paget Av, Sutt. SM1 200 DD104
Paget Cl, Hmptn. TW12 177 CD91
Paget Gdns, Chis. BR7 205 EP95
Paget La, Islw. TW7 157 CD83
Paget Pl, Kings.T. KT2 178 CQ93
Thames Ditton KT7
off Brooklands Rd 197 CG102
Paget Ri, SE18 165 EN80
Paget Rd, N16 122 DR60
Ilford IG1 125 EP63
Slough SL3 153 AZ77
Uxbridge UB10 135 BQ70
Paget St, EC1 10 E1
Paget Ter, SE18 165 EN79
Pagette Way, Grays (Bad.Dene) RM17 170 GA77
Pagitts Gro, Barn. EN4 80 DB39
Paglesfield, Brwd. (Hutt.) CM13 109 GC44
Pagnell St, SE14 163 DZ80
Pagoda Av, Rich. TW9 158 CM83
Pagoda Gdns, SE3 163 ED82
Pagoda Vista, Rich. TW9 158 CM82
Paignton Rd, N15 122 DS58
Ruislip HA4 115 BU62
Paines Brook Rd, Rom. RM3
off Paines Brook Way 106 FM51
Paines Brook Way, Rom. RM3 106 FM51
Paines Cl, Pnr. HA5 116 BY55
Paines La, Pnr. HA5 94 BY53
Pains Cl, Mitch. CR4 201 DH96
Pains Hill, Oxt. RH8 254 EJ132
★ Painshill Park, Cob. KT11 213 BS114
Painsthorpe Rd, N16
off Oldfield Rd 122 DS62
Painters Ash La, Grav. (Nthflt) DA11 190 GD90
Sch Painters Ash Prim Sch, Grav. DA11
off Masefield Rd 190 GD90
Painters La, Enf. EN3 83 DY35
Painters Ms, SE16
off Macks Rd 162 DU77
Painters Rd, Ilf. IG2 125 ET55
Paisley Rd, N22 99 DP53
Carshalton SM5 200 DD102
Sch Pakeman Prim Sch, N7 off Hornsey Rd 121 DM62
Pakeman St, N7 121 DM62
Pakenham Cl, SW12
off Balham Pk Rd 180 DG88
Pakenham St, WC1 10 B2
Pakes Way, Epp. (They.B.) CM16 85 ES37
Palace Av, W8 17 K2
Palace Cl, Kings L. WD4 58 BM30
Slough SL1 131 AM74
Palace Ct, NW3 120 DB64
W2 7 J9
Bromley BR1
off Palace Gro 204 EH95
Harrow HA3 118 CL58
Palace Ct Gdns, N10 121 DJ55
Palace Dr, Wey. KT13 195 BP104
Palace Gdns, Buck.H. IG9 102 EK46
Palace Gdns Ms, W8 17 H1
Palace Gdns Prec, Enf. EN2
off Sydney Rd 82 DR41
Palace Gdns Ter, W8 17 H1

Palace Gate, W8 17 L4
Palace Gates Rd, N22 99 DK53
Palace Grn, W8 17 K3
Croydon CR0 221 DZ108
Palace Gro, SE19 182 DT94
Bromley BR1 204 EH95
Palace Ms, E17 123 DZ56
SW1 18 F8
SW6 *off Hartismere Rd* 159 CZ80
Palace of Industry, Wem. HA9 118 CN63
Palace Par, E17 123 EA56
Palace Pl, SW1 19 J5
Palace Rd, N8 121 DK57
N11 99 DL52
SE19 182 DT94
SW2 181 DM88
Bromley BR1 204 EH95
East Molesey KT8 197 CD97
Kingston upon Thames KT1 197 CK98
Ruislip HA4 116 BY63
Westerham TN16 239 EN121
Palace Rd Est, SW2 181 DM88
Palace Sq, SE19 182 DT94
Palace St, SW1 19 J5
Palace Vw, SE12 184 EG89
Bromley BR1 204 EG97
Croydon CR0 221 DZ105
Palace Vw Rd, E4 101 EB50
Palace Way, Wey. KT13 *off Palace Dr* 195 BP104
Palamos Rd, E10 123 EA60
Palatine Av, N16 *off Stoke Newington Rd* 122 DT63
Palatine Rd, N16 122 DS63
Palermo Rd, NW10 139 CU68
Palestine Gro, SW19 200 DD95
Palewell Cl, Orp. BR5 206 EV96
Palewell Common Dr, SW14 178 CR85
Palewell Pk, SW14 178 CR85
Paley Gdns, Loug. IG10 85 EP41
Palfrey Cl, St.Alb. AL3 43 CD18
Palfrey Pl, SW8 161 DM80
Palgrave Av, Sthl. UB1 136 CA73
Palgrave Gdns, NW1 8 B3
Palgrave Rd, W12 159 CT76
Palissy St, E2 11 N2
Palladino Ho, SW17 *off Laurel Cl* 180 DE92
Pallant Way, Orp. BR6 205 EN104
Pallas Rd, Hem.H. HP2 40 BM18
Pallet Way, SE18 164 EL81
Palliser Dr, Rain. RM13 147 FG71
Palliser Rd, W14 16 C9
Chalfont St. Giles HP8 90 AU48
Pallister Ter, SW15 *off Roehampton Vale* 179 CT90
Pall Mall, SW1 19 K2
Pall Mall E, SW1 19 M1
Palmar Cres, Bexh. DA7 166 FA83
Palmar Rd, Bexh. DA7 166 FA82
Palmarsh Rd, Orp. BR5 *off Wotton Grn* 206 EX98
Palm Av, Sid. DA14 186 EX93
Palm Cl, E10 123 EB62
Palmeira Rd, Bexh. DA7 166 EX83
Palmer Av, Bushey WD23 76 CB43
Gravesend DA12 191 GK91
Sutton SM3 217 CW105
Palmer Cl, Hert. SG14 32 DQ07
Horley RH6 268 DF145
Hounslow TW5 156 CA81
Redhill RH1 266 DG135
West Wickham BR4 203 ED104
Palmer Cres, Cher. (Ott.) KT16 211 BD107
Kingston upon Thames KT1 198 CL97
Palmer Gdns, Barn. EN5 79 CX43
Palmer Pl, N7 4 C2
Palmer Rd, E13 15 P4
Dagenham RM8 126 EX60
Hertford SG14 32 DR07
Palmers Av, Grays RM17 170 GC78
[Coll] Palmer's Coll, Grays RM17 *off Chadwell Rd* 170 GE77
Palmers Dr, Grays RM17 170 GC77
Palmersfield Rd, Bans. SM7 218 DA114
PALMERS GREEN, N13 99 DN48
⇌ Palmers Green 99 DM49
[Sch] Palmers Grn High Sch, N21 *off Hoppers Rd* 99 DN47
Palmers Gro, Wal.Abb. EN9 50 EF22
West Molesey KT8 196 CA98
Palmers Hill, Epp. CM16 70 EU29
Palmers La, Enf. EN1, EN3 82 DV39
Palmer's Lo, Guil. GU2 *off Old Palace Rd* 258 AU135
Palmers Moor La, Iver SL0 134 BG70
Palmers Orchard, Sev. (Shore.) TN14 225 FF111
Palmers Pas, SW14 *off Palmers Rd* 158 CQ83
Palmers Rd, E2 143 DX68
N11 99 DJ50
SW14 158 CQ83
SW16 201 DM96
Borehamwood WD6 78 CP39
Palmerston Av, Slou. SL3 152 AV76
Palmerston Cl, Red. RH1 *off Reed Dr* 266 DG137
Welwyn Garden City AL8 29 CW09
Woking GU21 211 AZ114
Palmerston Cres, N13 99 DM50
SE18 165 EQ79
Palmerstone Ct, Vir.W. GU25 *off Sandhills La* 192 AY99
Palmerston Gdns, Grays RM20 169 FX78
Palmerston Gro, SW19 180 DA94
Palmerston Rd, E7 124 EH64
E17 123 DZ56
N22 99 DM52
NW6 140 DA66
SW14 158 CQ84
SW19 180 DA94
W3 158 CQ76
Buckhurst Hill IG9 102 EH47
Carshalton SM5 218 DF105
Croydon CR0 202 DR99
Grays RM20 169 FX78
Harrow HA3 117 CF55
Hounslow TW3 156 CC81
Orpington BR6 223 EQ105
Rainham RM13 148 FJ68
Sutton SM1 *off Vernon Rd* 218 DC106
Twickenham TW2 177 CF86

Palmerston Way, SW8 *off Bradmead* 161 DH80
Palmer St, SW1 19 L4
Palmers Way, Wal.Cr. (Chsht) EN8 67 DY29
Palm Gro, W5 158 CL76
Guildford GU1 242 AW129
Palm Rd, Rom. RM7 127 FC57
Pamela Av, Hem.H. HP3 40 BM23
Pamela Gdns, Pnr. HA5 115 BV57
Pamela Wk, E8 *off Marlborough Av* 142 DU67
Pampisford Rd, Pur. CR8 219 DN111
South Croydon CR2 219 DP108
Pams Way, Epsom KT19 216 CR106
Pancake La, Hem.H. HP2 41 BR21
Pancras La, EC4 11 H8
Pancras Rd, NW1 141 DK68
Pancroft, Rom. (Abridge) RM4 86 EV41
Pandora Rd, NW6 140 DA65
Panfield Ms, Ilf. IG2 *off Cranbrook Rd* 125 EN58
Panfield Rd, SE2 166 EU76
Pangbourne Av, W10 139 CW71
Pangbourne Dr, Stan. HA7 95 CK50
Pangbourne Ho, N7 121 DL64
Panhard Pl, Sthl. UB1 136 CB73
Pank Av, Barn. EN5 80 DC43
Pankhurst Av, E16 25 P1
Pankhurst Cl, SE14 *off Briant St* 163 DX80
Isleworth TW7 157 CF83
Pankhurst Rd, Walt. KT12 196 BW101
Panmuir Rd, SW20 199 CV95
Panmure Cl, N5 121 DP63
Panmure Rd, SE26 182 DV90
Pannells Cl, Cher. KT16 193 BF102
Pannells Ct, Guil. GU1 258 AX135
PANSHANGER, Welw.G.C. AL7 30 DB09
Panshanger Dr, Welw.G.C. AL7 30 DB09
Panshanger La, Hert. SG14 30 DF10
[Sch] Panshanger Prim Sch, Welw.G.C. AL7 *off Daniells* 30 DA08
Pansy Gdns, W12 139 CU73
Panters, Swan. BR8 187 FF94
Panther Dr, NW10 118 CR64
Pantile Rd, Wey. KT13 213 BR105
Pantile Row, Slou. SL3 153 BA77
Pantiles, The, NW11 *off Willifield Way* 119 CZ57
Bexleyheath DA7 166 EZ80
Bromley BR1 204 EL97
Bushey (Bushey Hth) WD23 95 CD45
Pantiles Cl, N13 99 DP50
Woking GU21 226 AV118
Pantile Wk, Uxb. UB8 *off High St* 134 BJ66
Panton St, SW1 9 L10
Panxworth Rd, Hem.H. HP3 40 BL22
Panyer All, EC4 10 G8
Papercourt La, Wok. (Ripley) GU23 227 BF122
Paper Ms, Dor. RH4 263 CH135
Papermill Cl, Cars. SM5 218 DG105
Papillons Wk, SE3 164 EG82
Papworth Gdns, N7 4 B2
Papworth Way, SW2 181 DN87
Parade, The, SW11 160 DF80
Brentwood CM14 *off Kings Rd* 108 FW48
Dartford DA1 *off Crayford Way* 187 FF85
Epsom KT18 216 CR113
Epsom (Epsom Com.) KT18 *off Spa Dr* 216 CN114
Esher (Clay.) KT10 215 CE107
Hampton TW12 *off Hampton Rd* 177 CD92
Romford RM3 106 FP51
South Ockendon (Aveley) RM15 168 FQ75
Sunbury-on-Thames TW16 175 BT94
Virginia Water GU25 192 AX100
Watford WD17 75 BV41
Watford (Carp.Pk) WD19 94 BY48
Watford (S.Oxhey) WD19 *off Prestwick Rd* 94 BX48
Windsor SL4 151 AK81
Parade Ms, SE27 *off Norwood Rd* 181 DP89
Paradise, Hem.H. HP2 40 BK21
Paradise Cl, Wal.Cr. (Chsht) EN7 66 DV28
Paradise Pas, N7 4 C2
Paradise Path, SE28 *off Birchdene Dr* 146 EU74
Paradise Pl, SE18 *off Woodhill* 164 EL77
Paradise Rd, SW4 161 DL82
Richmond TW9 177 CK85
Waltham Abbey EN9 67 EC34
Paradise Row, E2 12 D1
Paradise St, SE16 22 C4
Paradise Wk, SW3 160 DF79
Paragon, The, SE3 164 EF82
Paragon Cl, E16 15 L7
Paragon Gro, Surb. KT5 198 CM100
Paragon Ms, SE1 21 K7
Paragon Pl, SE3 164 EF82
Surbiton KT5 *off Berrylands Rd* 198 CM100
Paragon Rd, E9 142 DW65
[Sch] Parayhouse Sch, SW10 *off King's Rd* 160 DC80
Parbury Ri, Chess. KT9 216 CL107
Parbury Rd, SE23 183 DY86
Parchment Cl, Amer. HP6 55 AS37
Parchmore Rd, Th.Hth. CR7 201 DP96
Parchmore Way, Th.Hth. CR7 201 DP96
[Sch] Pardes Ho Gram Sch, N3 *off Hendon La* 97 CZ54
Pardoner St, SE1 21 K5
Pardon St, EC1 10 F3
Pares Cl, Wok. GU21 226 AX116
Parfett St, E1 12 B6
Parfitt Cl, NW3 *off North End* 120 DC61
Parfour Dr, Ken. CR8 236 DQ116
Parfrey St, W6 159 CW79
Parham Dr, Ilf. IG2 125 EP58
Parham Way, N10 99 DJ54
Paringdon Rd, Harl. CM18, CM19 51 EP19
Paris Gdn, SE1 20 E1
[Sch] Parish Ch C of E Inf & Jun Sch, Croy. CR0 *off Warrington Rd* 201 DP104
Parish Cl, Horn. RM11 127 FH61

Parish Cl, Wat. WD25 *off Crown Ri* 60 BX34
[Sch] Parish C of E Prim Sch, Brom. BR1 *off London La* 184 EG94
Parish Gate Dr, Sid. DA15 185 ES86
Parish La, SE20 183 DX93
Slough (Farn.Com.) SL2 111 AP61
Parish Ms, SE20 183 DX94
Parish Wf, SE18 *off Woodhill* 164 EL77
Park, The, N6 120 DG58
NW11 120 DB60
SE19 182 DS94
SE23 *off Park Hill* 182 DV88
W5 137 CK74
Carshalton SM5 218 DF106
Leatherhead (Bkhm) KT23 230 CA123
St. Albans AL1 43 CG18
Sidcup DA14 185 ET92
Park App, Well. DA16 166 EV84
Park Av, E6 145 EN67
E15 144 EE65
N3 98 DB53
N13 99 DN48
N18 100 DU49
N22 99 DL54
NW2 139 CV65
NW10 138 CM69
NW11 120 DB60
SW14 158 CR84
Barking IG11 145 EQ65
Brentwood (Hutt.) CM13 109 GC46
Bromley BR1 184 EF93
Bushey WD23 76 BZ40
Carshalton SM5 218 DG107
Caterham CR3 236 DS124
Egham TW20 173 BC93
Enfield EN1 82 DS44
Gravesend DA12 191 GJ88
Gravesend (Perry St) DA11 190 GE88
Grays RM20 169 FU79
Harlow CM17 52 EW18
Hounslow TW3 176 CB86
Ilford IG1 125 EN61
Mitcham CR4 181 DH94
Orpington BR6 206 EU103
Orpington (Farnboro.) BR6 205 EM104
Potters Bar EN6 64 DC34
Radlett WD7 61 CH33
Redhill RH1 266 DF142
Rickmansworth (Chorl.) WD3 74 BG43
Ruislip HA4 115 BR58
St. Albans AL1 43 CG19
Southall UB1 136 CA74
Staines TW18 173 BF93
Staines (Wrays.) TW19 172 AX85
Upminster RM14 129 FS59
Watford WD18 75 BU42
West Wickham BR4 203 EC103
Woodford Green IG8 102 EH50
Park Av E, Epsom KT17 217 CU107
Park Av Ms, Mitch. CR4 *off Park Av* 181 DH94
Park Av N, N8 121 DK55
NW10 119 CV64
Park Av Rd, N17 100 DV52
Park Av S, N8 121 DK56
Park Av W, Epsom KT17 217 CU107
PARK BARN, Guil. GU2 242 AS133
Park Barn Dr, Guil. GU2 242 AS132
Park Barn E, Guil. GU2 242 AT133
Park Boul, Rom. RM2 105 FF53
Park Chase, Guil. GU1 242 AY134
Wembley HA9 118 CM63
Park Cl, E9 142 DW67
NW2 119 CV62
NW10 138 CM69
SW1 18 C4
W4 158 CR78
W14 16 F5
Addlestone (New Haw) KT15 212 BH110
Betchworth (Strood Grn) RH3 264 CP139
Bushey WD23 76 BX41
Carshalton SM5 218 DF107
Epping (N.Wld Bas.) CM16 70 FA27
Esher KT10 214 BZ107
Hampton TW12 196 CC95
Harrow HA3 95 CE53
Hatfield AL9 45 CW17
Hatfield (Brook.Pk) AL9 63 CZ26
Hounslow TW3 176 CC85
Kingston upon Thames KT2 198 CN95
Leatherhead (Fetch.) KT22 231 CD124
Oxted RH8 254 EF128
Rickmansworth WD3 93 BP49
Walton-on-Thames KT12 195 BT103
Windsor SL4 151 AR82
Park Copse, Dor. RH5 263 CK136
Park Cor, St.Alb. (Coln.Hth) AL4 44 CP23
Windsor SL4 151 AL83
Park Cor Dr, Lthd. (E.Hors.) KT24 245 BS128
Park Cor Rd, Grav. (Sthflt) DA13 190 FZ91
Park Ct, SE26 182 DV93
Harlow CM20 35 ER14
Kingston upon Thames (Hmptn W.) KT1 197 CJ95
Leatherhead (Bkhm) KT23 *off Church Rd* 246 CA125
New Malden KT3 198 CR98
Wembley HA9 118 CL64
West Byfleet KT14 212 BG113
Woking GU22 *off Park Dr* 227 AZ118
Park Cres, N3 98 DB52
W1 8 G4
Borehamwood (Elstree) WD6 78 CM41
Enfield EN2 82 DR42
Erith DA8 167 FC79
Harrow HA3 95 CE53
Hornchurch RM11 127 FG59
Twickenham TW2 177 CD88
Park Cres Ms E, W1 9 H4
Park Cres Ms W, W1 8 G5
Park Cres Rd, Erith DA8 167 FD79
Park Cft, Edg. HA8 96 CQ53
Parkcroft Rd, SE12 184 EF87
Park Dale, N11 99 DK51
Parkdale Cres, Wor.Pk. KT4 198 CR104
Parkdale Rd, SE18 165 ES78
Park Dr, N21 82 DQ44
NW11 120 DB60
SE7 164 EL79
SW14 158 CR84
W3 158 CN76
Ashtead KT21 232 CN118

Park Dr, B. Stort. (Hat.Hth) CM22 37 FH05
Dagenham RM10 127 FC62
Harrow (Har.Wld) HA3 95 CE51
Harrow (N.Har.) HA2 116 CA59
Potters Bar EN6 64 DA31
Romford RM1 127 FD56
Upminster RM14 128 FQ63
Weybridge KT13 213 BP106
Woking GU22 227 AZ118
Park Dr Cl, SE7 164 EL78
Park End, NW3 *off South Hill Pk* 120 DE63
Bromley BR1 204 EF95
Park End Rd, Rom. RM1 127 FE56
Parker Av, Hert. SG14 32 DR07
Tilbury RM18 171 GJ81
Parker Cl, E16 144 EL74
Carshalton SM5 218 DF107
Parker Ms, WC2 9 P7
Parke Rd, SW13 159 CU81
Sunbury-on-Thames TW16 195 BU98
Parker Rd, Croy. CR0 220 DQ105
Grays RM17 170 FZ78
Parkers Cl, Ashtd. KT21 232 CL119
Parkers Hill, Ashtd. KT21 232 CL119
Parkers La, Ashtd. KT21 232 CL119
Parkers Row, SE1 21 P4
Parker St, E16 144 EL74
WC2 9 P7
Watford WD24 75 BV39
Parkes Rd, Chig. IG7 103 ES50
Park Fm Cl, N2 120 DC55
Pinner HA5 *off Field End Rd* 115 BV57
Park Fm Rd, Brom. BR1 204 EK95
Kingston upon Thames KT2 178 CL94
Upminster RM14 128 FM64
Parkfield, Rick. (Chorl.) WD3 73 BF42
Sevenoaks TN15 257 FM123
Parkfield Av, SW14 158 CS84
Amersham HP6 55 AR37
Feltham TW13 175 BU90
Harrow HA2 94 CC54
Northolt UB5 136 BX68
Uxbridge (Hlgdn) UB10 135 BP69
Parkfield Cl, Edg. HA8 96 CP51
Northolt UB5 136 BY68
Parkfield Cres, Felt. TW13 175 BU90
Harrow HA2 94 CC54
Ruislip HA4 116 BY62
Parkfield Dr, Nthlt. UB5 136 BX68
Parkfield Gdns, Har. HA2 116 CB55
[Sch] Parkfield JMI Sch, NW4 *off Park Rd* 119 CV59
Parkfield Rd, NW10 139 CU66
SE14 163 DZ81
Feltham TW13 175 BU90
Harrow HA2 116 CC62
Northolt UB5 136 BY68
Uxbridge (Ickhm) UB10 115 BP61
Parkfields, SW15 159 CW84
Croydon CR0 203 DZ102
Harlow (Roydon) CM19 50 EH16
Leatherhead (Oxshott) KT22 215 CD111
Welwyn Garden City AL8 29 CX09
Parkfields Av, NW9 118 CR60
SW20 199 CV95
Parkfields Cl, Cars. SM5 *off Devonshire Rd* 218 DG105
Parkfields Rd, Kings.T. KT2 178 CM92
Parkfield St, N1 4 D9
Parkfield Vw, Pot.B. EN6 64 DB32
Parkfield Way, Brom. BR2 205 EM100
Park Gdns, NW9 118 CP55
Erith DA8 *off Valley Rd* 167 FD77
Kingston upon Thames KT2 178 CM92
Park Gate, N2 120 DD55
N21 99 DM45
Parkgate, SE3 164 EF83
Park Gate, W5 137 CK71
Parkgate, Slou. (Burn.) SL1 130 AJ70
Parkgate Av, Barn. EN4 80 DC39
Parkgate Cl, Kings.T. KT2 *off Warboys App* 178 CP93
Parkgate Cres, Barn. EN4 80 DC40
Parkgate Gdns, SW14 178 CR85
[Sch] Parkgate Inf Sch, Wat. WD24 *off Northfield Gdns* 76 BW37
[Sch] Parkgate Jun Sch, Wat. WD24 *off Southwold Rd* 76 BW37
Parkgate Ms, N6 *off Stanhope Rd* 121 DJ59
Parkgate Rd, SW11 160 DE80
Orpington BR6 225 FB105
Reigate RH2 266 DB135
Wallington SM6 218 DG106
Watford WD24 76 BW37
Park Gates, Har. HA2 116 CA63
Park Gra Gdns, Sev. TN13 *off Solefields Rd* 257 FJ127
Park Grn, Lthd. (Bkhm) KT23 230 CA124
Park Gro, E15 144 EG67
N11 99 DK52
Bexleyheath DA7 167 FC84
Bromley BR1 204 EH95
Chalfont St. Giles HP8 72 AX41
Edgware HA8 96 CM50
Park Gro Rd, E11 124 EE61
Park Hall Rd, N2 120 DE56
SE21 182 DQ90
Reigate RH2 250 DA132
Parkham Ct, Brom. BR2 204 EE96
Parkham St, SW11 160 DE81
[Sch] Park High Sch, Stan. HA7 *off Thistlecroft Gdns* 95 CK54
Park Hill, SE23 182 DV89
SW4 181 DK85
W5 137 CK71
Bromley BR1 204 EL98
Carshalton SM5 218 DE107
Harlow CM17 36 EV12
Loughton IG10 84 EK43
Richmond TW10 178 CM86
Park Hill Cl, Cars. SM5 218 DE106
Parkhill Cl, Horn. RM12 128 FJ62
Park Hill Ct, SW17 *off Beeches Rd* 180 DF90
[Sch] Park Hill Inf Sch, Croy. CR0 *off Stanhope Rd* 202 DS104
[Sch] Parkhill Inf Sch, Ilf. IG5 *off Lord Av* 125 EN55
[Sch] Park Hill Jun Sch, Croy. CR0 *off Stanhope Rd* 202 DS104
[Sch] Parkhill Jun Sch, Ilf. IG5 *off Lord Av* 125 EN55
Park Hill Ri, Croy. CR0 202 DS103
Parkhill Rd, E4 101 EC46
NW3 120 DF64
Bexley DA5 186 EZ87

Park Hill Rd, Brom. BR2 204 EE96
Croydon CR0 202 DS103
Epsom KT17 217 CT111
Parkhill Rd, Hem.H. HP1 40 BH20
Sidcup DA15 185 ER90
Park Hill Rd, Wall. SM6 219 DH108
[Sch] Park Hill Sch, Kings.T. KT2 *off Queens Rd* 178 CN94
Parkhill Wk, NW3 120 DF64
Parkholme Rd, E8 5 P3
Park Horsley, Lthd. (E.Hors.) KT24 245 BU129
Park Ho, N21 99 DM45
Park Ho Dr, Reig. RH2 265 CZ136
Park Ho Gdns, Twick. TW1 177 CJ86
Parkhouse St, SE5 162 DR80
Parkhurst, Epsom KT19 216 CQ110
Parkhurst Gdns, Bex. DA5 186 FA87
Parkhurst Gro, Horl. RH6 268 DE147
[Sch] Parkhurst Inf Sch, N17 *off Parkhurst Rd* 100 DU54
Parkhurst Rd, E12 125 EN63
E17 123 DY56
N7 121 DL63
N11 98 DG49
N17 100 DU54
N22 99 DM52
Bexley DA5 186 FA87
Guildford GU2 242 AU133
Hertford SG14 31 DP08
Horley RH6 268 DE147
Sutton SM1 218 DD105
Park Ind Est, St.Alb. (Frog.) AL2 61 CE27
Parkland Av, Rom. RM1 127 FE55
Slough SL3 152 AX77
Upminster RM14 128 FP64
Parkland Cl, Chig. IG7 103 EQ48
Hoddesdon EN11 33 EB14
Sevenoaks TN13 257 FJ129
Parkland Dr, St.Alb. AL3 43 CA21
Parkland Gdns, SW19 179 CX88
Parkland Gro, Ashf. TW15 174 BN91
Parkland Rd, N22 99 DM54
Ashford TW15 174 BN91
Woodford Green IG8 102 EG52
Parklands, N6 121 DH59
Addlestone KT15 212 BJ106
Chigwell IG7 103 EQ48
Dorking (N.Holm.) RH5 263 CH140
Epping (Cooper.) CM16 70 EX29
Guildford GU2 *off Grange Rd* 242 AV130
Hemel Hempstead HP1 39 BF18
Leatherhead (Bkhm) KT23 230 CA123
Oxted RH8 254 EE131
Surbiton KT5 198 CM99
Waltham Abbey EN9 67 ED32
Parklands Cl, SW14 178 CQ85
Barnet EN4 80 DD38
Ilford IG2 125 EQ59
Parklands Ct, Houns. TW5 156 BX82
Parklands Dr, N3 119 CY55
[Sch] Parklands Inf Sch, Rom. RM1 *off Havering Rd* 105 FD54
[Sch] Parklands Jun Sch, Rom. RM1 *off Havering Rd* 127 FD55
Parklands Pl, Guil. GU1 243 BB134
Parklands Rd, SW16 181 DH92
Parklands Way, Wor.Pk. KT4 198 CS104
Parkland Wk, N4 121 DM59
N6 121 DK59
N10 121 DH56
Park La, E15 *off High St* 143 ED67
N9 100 DT48
N17 100 DU52
W1 18 F2
Ashtead KT21 232 CM118
Banstead SM7 234 DD118
Beaconsfield HP9 89 AM54
Broxbourne EN10 49 DY19
Broxbourne (Wormley) EN10 48 DV22
Carshalton SM5 218 DG105
Coulsdon CR5 235 DK121
Croydon CR0 202 DR104
Guildford GU4 243 BC131
Harlow CM20 35 ER13
Harrow HA2 116 CB62
Hayes UB4 135 BS71
Hemel Hempstead HP1, HP2 40 BK21
Hornchurch RM11 127 FG58
Hornchurch (Elm Pk) RM12 147 FH65
Hounslow TW5 155 BU80
Reigate RH2 265 CY135
Richmond TW9 157 CK84
Romford (Chad.Hth) RM6 126 EX58
St. Albans (Coln.Hth) AL4 44 CP23
Sevenoaks TN13 257 FJ124
Sevenoaks (Seal) TN15 257 FN121
Slough SL3 152 AV76
Slough (Burn.) SL1 111 AL64
Slough (Horton) SL3 153 BA83
South Ockendon (Aveley) RM15 149 FR74
Stanmore HA7 95 CG48
Sutton SM3 217 CY107
Swanley BR8 208 FJ96
Teddington TW11 177 CF93
Uxbridge (Hare.) UB9 92 BG53
Wallington SM6 218 DG105
Waltham Cross EN8 66 DW33
Waltham Cross (Chsht) EN7 66 DU26
Wembley HA9 118 CL64
Park La Cl, N17 100 DU52
Park La E, Reig. RH2 266 DA136
Park La Paradise, Wal.Cr. (Chsht) EN7 48 DU24
[Sch] Park La Prim Sch, Wem. HA9 *off Park La* 118 CL63
PARK LANGLEY, Beck. BR3 203 EC99
Park Lawn, Slou. (Farn.Royal) SL2 131 AQ69
Parklawn Av, Epsom KT18 216 CP113
Horley RH6 268 DF146
Park Lawn Rd, Wey. KT13 213 BQ105
Park Lawns, Wem. HA9 118 CM63
Parklea Cl, NW9 96 CS53
Parkleigh Rd, SW19 200 DB96
Park Ley Rd, Cat. (Wold.) CR3 237 DX120
Parkleys, Rich. TW10 177 CK91
Parkmead, SW15 179 CV86
Park Mead, Harl. CM20 35 EP14
Harrow HA2 116 CB62
Parkmead, Loug. IG10 85 EN43
Park Mead, Sid. DA15 186 EV85
Parkmead Gdns, NW7 97 CT51
Park Meadow, Hat. AL9 45 CW17
Park Ms, SE24 *off Croxted Rd* 182 DQ86

★ Place of interest [H] Hospital [Sch] School [Coll] College [Uni] University ⇌ Railway station

Park Ms, Chis. BR7 185 EP93
East Molesey KT8 196 CC98
Hampton (Hmptn H.)
TW12 off Park Rd 176 CC92
Hatfield AL9 45 CW16
Rainham RM13
off Sowrey Av 147 FG65
Parkmore Cl, Wdf.Grn. IG8 102 EG49
Park Nook Gdns, Enf. EN2 82 DR37
Parkpale La, Bet. RH3 264 CN139
Park Par, NW10 139 CT68
Park Pl, E14 23 N1
SW1 19 J2
W3 158 CN77
W5 137 CK74
Amersham HP6 72 AT38
Beaconsfield (Seer Grn)
HP9 89 AR50
Gravesend DA12 191 GJ86
Hampton (Hmptn H.)
TW12 176 CC93
St. Albans (Park St) AL2 61 CD27
Sevenoaks TN13 256 FD123
Wembley HA9 118 CM63
Woking GU22 off Park Dr 227 AZ118
Park Pl Vil, W2 7 M5
Park Prim Sch, E15
off Mathews Pk Av 144 EF66
Park Ridings, N8 121 DN55
Park Ri, SE23 183 DY88
Berkhamsted HP4 38 AS17
Harrow HA3 95 CE53
Leatherhead KT22 231 CH121
Park Ri Cl, Lthd. KT22 231 CH121
Park Ri Rd, SE23 183 DY88
Park Rd, E6 144 EJ67
E10 123 EA60
E12 124 EH60
E15 144 EG67
E17 123 DZ57
N2 120 DD55
N8 121 DJ56
N11 99 DK52
N14 99 DK45
N15 121 DP56
N18 100 DT49
NW1 8 A1
NW4 119 CU59
NW8 8 A1
NW9 118 CR59
NW10 138 CS67
SE25 202 DS98
SW19 180 DD93
W4 158 CQ80
W7 137 CF73
Amersham HP6 72 AT37
Ashford TW15 175 BP92
Ashtead KT21 232 CL118
Banstead SM7 234 DB115
Barnet EN5 79 CZ42
Barnet (New Barn.) EN4 80 DE42
Beckenham BR3 183 DZ94
Brentwood CM14 108 FV46
Bromley BR1 204 EH95
Bushey WD23 76 CA44
Caterham CR3 236 DS123
Chesham HP5 54 AP31
Chislehurst BR7 185 EP93
Dartford DA1 188 FN87
East Molesey KT8 196 CC98
Egham TW20 173 BA91
Enfield EN3 83 DY36
Esher KT10 214 CB105
Feltham TW13 176 BX91
Gravesend DA11 191 GH88
Grays RM17 170 GB78
Guildford GU1 242 AX134
Guildford (Albury) GU5 260 BL140
Hampton (Hmptn H.)
TW12 176 CB91
Hayes UB4 135 BS71
Hemel Hempstead HP1 40 BJ22
Hertford SG13 32 DS09
Hoddesdon EN11 49 EA17
Hounslow TW3 156 CC84
Ilford IG1 125 ER62
Isleworth TW7 157 CH81
Kenley CR8 235 DP115
Kingston upon Thames
KT2 178 CM92
Kingston upon Thames
(Hmptn W.) KT1 197 CJ95
New Malden KT3 198 CR98
Orpington BR5 206 EW99
Oxted RH8 254 EF128
Potters Bar EN6 64 DG30
Radlett WD7 77 CG35
Redhill RH1 250 DF132
Richmond TW10 178 CM86
Rickmansworth WD3 92 BK45
Shepperton TW17 194 BN102
Slough SL2 131 AQ68
Staines (Stanw.) TW19 174 BH86
Sunbury-on-Thames
TW16 175 BV94
Surbiton KT5 198 CM99
Sutton SM3 217 CY107
Swanley BR8 207 FF97
Swanscombe DA10 190 FY86
Teddington TW11 177 CF93
Twickenham TW1 177 CJ86
Uxbridge UB8 134 BL66
Wallington SM6 219 DH106
Wallington (Hackbr.) SM6 201 DH103
Waltham Cross EN8 67 DX33
Ware SG12 32 DV05
Warlingham CR6 222 EE114
Watford WD17 75 BU39
Wembley HA0 138 CL65
Woking GU22 227 BA117
Park Rd E, W3 158 CP75
Uxbridge UB10
off Hillingdon Rd 134 BK68
Park Rd N, W3 158 CP75
W4 158 CR78
Park Row, SE10 163 ED79
PARK ROYAL, NW10 138 CN69
⊖ Park Royal 138 CN70
Park Royal Cen for
Mental Health, NW10 138 CQ68
Park Royal Rd, NW10 138 CQ69
W3 138 CQ69
Park Sch, The, Wok.
GU22 off Onslow Cres 227 BA117
Park Sch for Girls, Ilf. IG1
off Park Av 125 EP60
Parkshot, Rich. TW9 158 CL84
Parkside, N3 98 DB53
NW2 119 CU62
NW7 97 CU51
SE3 164 EF80
SW19 179 CX91
Addlestone (New Haw)
KT15 212 BH110
Buckhurst Hill IG9 102 EH47
Parkside, Ger. Cr. (Chal.St.P.)
SL9 off Lower Rd 113 AZ56
Grays RM16 170 GE76
Hampton (Hmptn H.)
TW12 177 CD92
Harlow (Match.Tye) CM17 37 FE12
Potters Bar EN6
off High St 64 DC32
Sevenoaks (Halst.) TN14 224 EZ113
Sidcup DA14 186 EV89
Sutton SM3 217 CY107
Waltham Cross EN8 67 DY34
Watford WD19 76 BW44
Parkside Av, SW19 179 CX92
Bexleyheath DA7 167 FD82
Bromley BR1 204 EL98
Romford RM1 127 FD55
Tilbury RM18 171 GH82
Parkside Business Est,
SE8 off Rolt St 163 DY79
Parkside Cl, SE20 182 DW94
Leatherhead (E.Hors.)
KT24 245 BT125
Parkside Comm Prim
Sch, Borwd. WD6
off Aycliffe Rd 78 CM38
Parkside Ct, Wey. KT13 212 BN105
Parkside Cres, N7 121 DN62
Surbiton KT5 198 CQ100
Parkside Cross, Bexh. DA7 167 FE82
Parkside Dr, Edg. HA8 96 CN48
Watford WD17 75 BS40
Parkside Est, E9
off Rutland Rd 142 DW67
Parkside Gdns, SW19 179 CX91
Barnet EN4 98 DF46
Coulsdon CR5 235 DH117
Parkside Hosp, SW19 179 CX90
Parkside Ho, Dag. RM10 127 FC62
Parkside Pl, Lthd. (E.Hors.)
KT24 245 BS125
Staines TW18 174 BG93
Parkside Rd, SW11 160 DG81
Belvedere DA17 167 FC77
Hounslow TW3 176 CB85
Northwood HA6 93 BT50
Warlingham CR6 237 EA116
Parkside Sch, Cob.
KT11 off Stoke Rd 230 CA118
Parkside Ter, N18
off Great Cambridge Rd 100 DR49
Orpington BR6
off Willow Wk 205 EP104
Parkside Wk, SE10 24 G6
Slough SL1 152 AU76
Parkside Way, Har. HA2 116 CB56
Park S, SW11 off Austin Rd 160 DG81
Park Sq, Esher KT10
off Park Rd 214 CB105
Romford (Abridge) RM4 86 EY44
Park Sq E, NW1 8 G3
Park Sq Ms, NW1 8 G4
Park Sq W, NW1 8 G3
Parkstead Rd, SW15 179 CU85
Parkstone Av, N18 100 DT50
Hornchurch RM11 128 FK58
Parkstone Rd, E17 123 EC55
SE15 off Rye La 162 DU82
PARK STREET, St.Alb. AL2 61 CD26
⇌ Park Street 61 CD26
Park St, SE1 20 G1
W1 8 E9
Berkhamsted HP4 38 AV18
Croydon CR0 202 DQ103
Guildford GU1 258 AW136
Hatfield AL9 45 CW17
St. Albans AL2 61 CD26
Slough SL1 152 AT76
Slough (Colnbr.) SL3 153 BD80
Teddington TW11 177 CE93
Windsor SL4 151 AR81
Park St C of E JMI Sch,
St.Alb. AL2 off Branch Rd 61 CD27
Park St La, St.Alb. (Park St)
AL2 60 CB30
Park Ter, Green. DA9 189 FV85
Sevenoaks (Sund.) TN14
off Main Rd 240 EX124
Worcester Park KT4 199 CU102
Parkthorne Cl, Har. HA2 116 CB58
Parkthorne Dr, Har. HA2 116 CA58
Parkthorne Rd, SW12 181 DK87
Park Vw, N21 99 DM45
W3 138 CQ71
Hatfield AL9 45 CW16
Hoddesdon EN11 49 EA18
Horley RH6
off Brighton Rd 268 DG148
Leatherhead (Bkhm) KT23 246 CA125
New Malden KT3 199 CT97
Pinner HA5 94 BZ53
Potters Bar EN6 64 DC33
Parkview, St.Alb. AL1 43 CG21
Park Vw, S.Ock. (Aveley)
RM15 149 FR74
Wembley HA9 118 CP64
Park Vw Acad, N15
off Langham Rd 122 DQ56
Parkview Chase, Slou. SL1 131 AL72
Park Vw Cl, St.Alb. AL1 43 CG21
Parkview Ct, SW18
off Broomhill Rd 180 DA86
Park Vw Ct, Ilf. IG2
off Brancaster Rd 125 ES58
Woking GU22 226 AY119
Park Vw Cres, N11 99 DH49
Parkview Dr, Mitch. CR4 200 DD96
Park Vw Est, E2 143 DX68
N5 122 DQ63
Park Vw Gdns, NW4 119 CW57
Grays RM17 170 GB78
Ilford IG4 125 EM56
Park Vw Ho, SE24
off Hurst St 181 DP86
Parkview Ho, Horn. RM12
off Sunrise Av 127 FH61
Park Vw Ms, SW9 161 DM82
Park Vw Rd, N3 98 DB53
N17 122 DU55
NW10 119 CT63
Parkview Rd, SE9 185 EP89
Park Vw Rd, W5 138 CL71
Berkhamsted HP4 38 AV19
Caterham (Wold.) CR3 237 DY122
Parkview Rd, Croy. CR0 202 DU102
Park Vw Rd, Pnr. HA5 93 BV52
Redhill RH1 266 DG141
Southall UB1 136 CA74
Uxbridge UB8 134 BN72
Welling DA16 166 EW83
Park Vw Rd Est, N17 100 DV54
Parkview Vale, Guil. GU4
off Foxglove Gdns 243 BC132
Park Village E, NW1 141 DH68
Park Village W, NW1 141 DH68
Park Vil, Rom. RM6 126 EX58
Parkville Rd, SW6 159 CZ80
Park Vista, SE10 163 ED79
Park Wk, N6 off North Rd 120 DG59
SE10 off Crooms Hill 163 ED80
SW10 160 DC79
Ashtead KT21
off Rectory La 232 CM119
Park Wk Prim Sch,
SW10 off Park Wk 160 DD79
Parkway, N14 99 DL47
Park Way, N20 98 DF49
Parkway, NW1 141 DH67
Park Way, NW11 119 CY57
Parkway, SW20 199 CX98
Park Way, Bex. DA5 187 FE90
Brentwood (Shenf.) CM15 109 FZ46
Parkway, Croy. (New Adgtn)
CR0 221 EC109
Dorking RH4 263 CG135
Park Way, Edg. HA8 96 CP53
Enfield EN2 81 DN40
Parkway, Erith DA18 166 EY76
Park Way, Felt. TW14 175 BV87
Parkway, Guil. GU1 242 AY133
Park Way, Horl. RH6 268 DG148
Parkway, Ilf. IG3 125 ET62
Park Way, Lthd. (Bkhm)
KT23 230 CA123
Parkway, Rain. RM13
off Upminster Rd S 147 FG70
Park Way, Rick. WD3 92 BJ46
Parkway, Rom. RM2 127 FF55
Park Way, Ruis. HA4 115 BU60
Parkway, Saw. CM21 36 EY06
Uxbridge UB10 134 BN66
Welwyn Garden City AL8 29 CW11
Park Way, W.Mol. KT8 196 CB97
Parkway, Wey. KT13 213 BR105
Woodford Green IG8 102 EJ50
Parkway, The, Hayes UB3,
UB4 136 BW72
Hounslow (Cran.) TW4,
TW5 155 BV82
Iver SL0 133 BC68
Northolt UB5 136 BX69
Southall UB2 155 BU78
Parkway Cl, Welw.G.C. AL8 29 CW09
Parkway Ct, St.Alb. AL1 43 CH23
Parkway Gdns, Welw.G.C.
AL8 29 CW10
Parkway Prim Sch, Erith
DA18 off Alsike Rd 166 EY76
Parkway Trd Est, Houns.
TW5 156 BW79
Park W, W2 8 B8
Park W Pl, W2 8 B7
Parkwood, N20 98 DF48
Beckenham BR3 203 EA95
Parkwood Av, Esher KT10 196 CC102
Parkwood Cl, Bans. SM7 233 CX115
Broxbourne EN10 49 DZ19
Parkwood Dr, Hem.H. HP1 39 BF20
Parkwood Gro, Sun. TW16 195 BU97
Parkwood Hall Sch, Swan.
BR8 off Beechenlea La 207 FH97
Parkwood JMI Sch, N4
off Queens Dr 121 DP61
Parkwood Ms, N6 121 DH58
Parkwood Rd, SW19 179 CZ92
Banstead SM7 233 CX115
Bexley DA5 186 EZ87
Isleworth TW7 157 CF81
Redhill (Nutfld) RH1 251 DL133
Westerham (Tats.) TN16 238 EL121
Parkwood Vw, Bans. SM7 233 CW116
Park Wks Rd, Red. RH1 251 DM133
Parlaunt Pk Prim Sch, Slou.
SL3 off Kennett Rd 153 BB76
Parlaunt Rd, Slou. SL3 153 BA77
Parley Dr, Wok. GU21 226 AW117
Parliament Ct, E1
off Sandy's Row 142 DS71
Parliament Hill, NW3 120 DE63
Parliament Hill Sch,
NW5 off Highgate Rd 120 DG63
Parliament La, Slou. (Burn.)
SL1 130 AF66
Parliament Ms, SW14
off Thames Bk 158 CQ82
Parliament Sq, SW1 19 N4
Hertford SG14 32 DR09
Parliament St, SW1 19 N4
Parliament Vw Apartments,
SE1 20 A7
Parma Cres, SW11 160 DF84
Parmiter's Sch, Wat.
WD25 off High Elms La 60 BW31
Parmiter St, E2 142 DV68
Parmoor Ct, EC1 10 G3
Parnall Rd, Harl. CM18 51 ER18
Parndon Mill La, Harl. CM20 35 EP12
Parndon Wd Rd, Harl. CM19 51 EQ20
Parnell Cl, W12 159 CV76
Abbots Langley WD5 59 BT30
Edgware HA8 96 CP49
Grays (Chaff.Hun.) RM16 169 FW78
Parnell Gdns, Wey. KT13 212 BN111
Parnell Rd, E3 143 DZ67
Parnel Rd, Ware SG12 33 DZ05
Parnham St, E14 13 K7
Parolles Rd, N19 121 DJ60
Paroma Rd, Belv. DA17 166 FA76
Parr Av, Epsom KT17 217 CV109
Parr Cl, N9 100 DV49
N18 100 DV49
Grays (Chaff.Hun.) RM16 169 FW77
Leatherhead KT22 231 CF120
Parr Ct, N1 5 J9
Feltham TW13 176 BW91
Parr Cres, Hem.H. HP2 41 BP15
Parris Cft, Dor. RH4
off Goodwyns Rd 263 CJ139
Parrock, The, Grav. DA12 191 GJ88
Parrock Av, Grav. DA12 191 GJ88
PARROCK FARM, Grav.
DA12 191 GK91
Parrock Rd, Grav. DA12 191 GJ88
Parrock St, Grav. DA12 191 GH87
Parrotts Cl, Rick. (Crox.Grn)
WD3 74 BN42
Parrotts Fld, Hodd. EN11 49 EB16
Parr Pl, W4
off Chiswick High Rd 159 CT77
Parr Rd, E6 144 EK67
Stanmore HA7 95 CK53
Parrs Cl, S.Croy. CR2
off Florence Rd 220 DR109
Parrs Pl, Hmptn. TW12 176 CA94
Parr St, N1 5 J9
Parry Av, E6 145 EM72
Parry Cl, Epsom KT17 217 CU108
Parry Dr, Wey. KT13 212 BN110
Parry Grn N, Slou. SL3 153 AZ77
Parry Grn S, Slou. SL3 153 AZ77
Parry Pl, SE18 165 EP77
Parry Rd, SE25 202 DS97
W10 6 D1
Parry St, SW8 161 DL79
Parsifal Rd, NW6 120 DA64
Parsley Gdns, Croy. CR0
off Primrose La 203 DX102
Parsloe Rd, Epp. (Epp.Grn)
CM16 51 EN21
Harlow CM19 51 EP20
Parsloes Av, Dag. RM9 126 EX63
Parsloes Prim Sch, Dag.
RM9 off Spurling Rd 146 EZ65
Parsonage Cl, Abb.L. WD5 59 BS30
Dorking (Westc.) RH4
off Parsonage La 262 CC138
Hayes UB3 135 BT72
Warlingham CR6 237 DY116
Parsonage Fm Inf Sch,
Rain. RM13 off Farm Rd 148 FJ69
Parsonage Fm Jun Sch,
Rain. RM13 off Farm Rd 148 FJ69
Parsonage Gdns, Enf. EN2 82 DQ40
Parsonage La, Chesh. HP5
off Blucher St 54 AP31
Dartford (Sutt.H.) DA4 188 FP93
Dorking (Westc.) RH4 262 CC137
Enfield EN1, EN2 82 DR40
Hatfield (N.Mymms) AL9 45 CV23
Sidcup DA14 186 EZ91
Slough (Farn.Com.) SL2 131 AQ68
Windsor SL4 151 AN81
Parsonage Leys, Harl. CM20 51 ET15
Parsonage Manorway, Belv.
DA17 166 FA79
Parsonage Rd, Ch.St.G. HP8 90 AV48
Egham (Eng.Grn) TW20 172 AX92
Grays RM20 169 FW79
Hatfield (N.Mymms) AL9 45 CV23
Rainham RM13 148 FJ69
Rickmansworth WD3 92 BK45
Parsonage Sq, Dor. RH4 263 CG135
Parsonage St, E14 24 D8
Parsons Cl, Horl. RH6
off Baden Dr 268 DE147
Sutton SM1 200 DB104
Parsons Cres, Edg. HA8 96 CN48
Parsonsfield Cl, Bans. SM7 233 CX115
Parsonsfield Rd, Bans. SM7 233 CX116
PARSONS GREEN, SW6 160 DA81
⊖ Parsons Green 159 CZ81
Parsons Grn, SW6 160 DA81
Guildford GU1
off Bellfields Rd 242 AX132
Parsons Grn Ct, Guil. GU1
off Bellfields Rd 242 AX132
Parsons Grn La, SW6 160 DA81
Parsons Gro, Edg. HA8 96 CN48
Parsons Ho, SW2
off New Pk Rd 181 DL87
Parson's Ho, W2 7 N4
Parsons La, Dart. DA2 187 FH90
Parson's Mead, Croy. CR0 201 DP102
Parsons Mead, E.Mol. KT8 196 CC97
Parsons Mead Sch, Ashtd.
KT21 off Ottways La 232 CL119
Parsons Pightle, Couls. CR5 235 DN120
Parsons Rd, E13 off Old St 144 EJ68
Slough SL3 off Ditton Rd 153 AZ78
Parson St, NW4 119 CW56
Parsons Wd, Slou.
(Farn.Com.) SL2 131 AQ65
Parthenia Rd, SW6 160 DA81
Parthia Cl, Tad. KT20 233 CV119
Partingdale La, NW7 97 CX50
Partington Cl, N19 121 DK60
Partridge Cl, E16
off Fulmer Rd 144 EK71
Barnet EN5 79 CW44
Bushey WD23 94 CB46
Chesham HP5 54 AS28
Stanmore HA7 96 CL49
Partridge Ct, EC1
off Percival St 141 DP70
Harlow CM18 51 ES17
Partridge Dr, Orp. BR6 205 EQ104
Partridge Grn, SE9 185 EN90
Partridge Knoll, Pur. CR8 219 DP112
Partridge Mead, Bans. SM7 233 CW116
Partridge Rd, Hmptn. TW12 176 BZ93
Harlow CM18 51 ER17
St. Albans AL3 43 CD16
Sidcup DA14 185 ES90
Partridge Sq, E6
off Nightingale Way 144 EL71
Partridge Way, N22 99 DL53
Guildford GU4 243 BD132
Parvills, Wal.Abb. EN9 67 ED32
Parvin St, SW8 161 DK81
Parvis Rd, W.Byf. KT14 212 BG113
Pasadena Cl, Hayes UB3 155 BV75
Pasadena Cl Trd Est, Hayes
UB3 off Pasadena Cl 155 BV75
Pascal St, SW8 161 DK80
Pascoe Rd, SE13 183 ED85
Pasfield, Wal.Abb. EN9 67 ED33
Pasley Cl, SE17 20 G10
Pasquier Rd, E17 123 DY55
Passey Pl, SE9 185 EM86
Passfield Dr, E14 14 B5
Passfield Path, SE28
off Booth Cl 146 EV73
Passing All, EC1 10 F4
Passmore Gdns, N11 99 DK51
PASSMORES, Harl. CM18 51 ER17
Passmores Comp Sch,
Harl. CM18
off Tendring Rd 51 ER17
Passmore St, SW1 18 E8
★ Passport Office, SW1 19 H7
Pastens Rd, Oxt. RH8 254 EJ131
Pasteur Cl, NW9 96 CS54
Pasteur Dr, Rom.
(Harold Wd) RM3 106 FK54
Pasteur Gdns, N18 99 DP50
Paston Cl, E5
off Caldecott Way 123 DX62
Wallington SM6 201 DJ104
Paston Cres, SE12 184 EH87
Paston Rd, Hem.H. HP2 40 BK18
Pastoral Way, Brwd.
(Warley) CM14 108 FV50
Pastor St, SE11 20 F7
Pasture Cl, Bushey WD23 94 CC45
Wembley HA0 117 CH62
Pasture Rd, SE6 184 EF88
Dagenham RM9 126 EZ63
Wembley HA0 117 CH61
Pastures, The, N20 97 CZ46
Hatfield AL10 45 CV19
Hemel Hempstead HP1 39 BE19
St. Albans AL2 42 CA24
Watford WD19 94 BW45
Welwyn Garden City AL7 30 DB11
Pastures Mead, Uxb. UB10 134 BN65
Patch, The, Sev. TN13 256 FE122
Patcham Ct, Sutt. SM2 218 DC109
Patcham Ter, SW8 161 DH81
Patch Cl, Uxb. UB10 134 BM67
PATCHETTS GREEN, Wat.
WD25 76 CC39
Patching Way, Hayes UB4 136 BY71
Paternoster Cl, Wal.Abb.
EN9 68 EF33
Paternoster Hill, Wal.Abb.
EN9 68 EF32
Paternoster Row, EC4 10 G8
Romford (Noak Hill) RM4 106 FJ47
Paternoster Sq, EC4 10 F8
Paterson Rd, Ashf. TW15 174 BK92
Pater St, W8 16 G6
Pates Manor Dr, Felt. TW14 175 BR87
Path, The, SW19 200 DB95
Pathfield Rd, SW16 181 DK93
Pathfields, Guil. (Shere)
GU5 260 BN140
Pathway, The, Rad. WD7 77 CF36
Watford WD19
off Anthony Cl 94 BX46
Woking (Send) GU23 243 BF125
Patience Rd, SW11 160 DE82
Patio Cl, SW4 181 DK86
Patmore Est, SW8 161 DJ81
Patmore La, Walt. KT12 213 BT107
Patmore Link Rd, Hem.H.
HP2 41 BQ20
Patmore Rd, Wal.Abb. EN9 68 EE34
Patmore St, SW8 161 DJ81
Patmore Way, Rom. RM5 105 FB50
Patmos Rd, SW9 161 DP80
Paton Cl, E3 13 P1
Paton St, EC1 10 G2
Patricia Cl, Slou. SL1 131 AL73
Patricia Ct, Chis. BR7
off Manor Pk Rd 205 ER95
Welling DA16 166 EV80
Patricia Dr, Horn. RM11 128 FL60
Patricia Gdns, Sutt. SM2
off The Crescent 218 DA111
Patrick Connolly Gdns, E3 14 B2
Patrick Gro, Wal.Abb. EN9
off Beaulieu Dr 67 EB33
Patrick Rd, E13 144 EJ69
Patrington Cl, Uxb. UB8
off Boulmer Rd 134 BJ69
Patriot Sq, E2 142 DV68
Patrol Pl, SE6 183 EB86
Patrons Dr, Uxb. (Denh.)
UB9 113 BF58
Patshull Pl, NW5
off Patshull Rd 141 DJ65
Patshull Rd, NW5 141 DJ65
Patten All, Rich. TW10
off The Hermitage 177 CK85
Pattenden Rd, SE6 183 DZ88
Patten Rd, SW18 180 DE87
Patterdale Cl, Brom. BR1 184 EF93
Patterdale Rd, SE15 162 DW80
Dartford DA2 189 FR88
Patterson Ct, SE19 182 DT94
Dartford DA1 188 FN85
High Wycombe HP10
off Glory Mill La 110 AE56
Patterson Rd, SE19 182 DT93
Chesham HP5 54 AP28
Pattina Wk, SE16 23 K2
Pattison Pt, E16 15 M6
Pattison Rd, NW2 120 DA62
Pattison Wk, SE18 165 EQ78
Paul Cl, E15 144 EE66
Paulet Rd, SE5 161 DP82
Paul Gdns, Croy. CR0 202 DT103
Paulhan Rd, Har. HA3 117 CK56
Paulin Dr, N21 99 DN45
Pauline Cres, Twick. TW2 176 CC88
Paulinus Cl, Orp. BR5 206 EW96
Paul Julius Cl, E14 14 E10
Paul Robeson Cl, E6
off Eastbourne Rd 145 EN69
Pauls Grn, Wal.Cr. EN8
off Eleanor Rd 67 DY33
Pauls Hill, H.Wyc. (Penn)
HP10 88 AF48
Pauls La, Hodd. EN11
off Taverners Way 49 EA17
Paul's Pl, Ashtd. KT21 232 CP119
Paul St, E15 143 ED67
EC2 11 K4
Paul's Wk, EC4 10 F9
Paultons Sq, SW3 160 DD79
Paultons St, SW3 160 DD79
Pauntley St, N19 121 DJ60
Paved Ct, Rich. TW9 177 CK85
Paveley Dr, SW11 160 DE80
Paveley St, NW8 8 B3
Pavement, The, SW4 161 DJ84
W5 off Popes La 158 CL76
Pavement Ms, Rom. RM6
off Clarissa Rd 126 EX59
Pavement Sq, Croy. CR0 202 DU102
Pavet Cl, Dag. RM10 147 FB65
Pavilion Gdns, Stai. TW18 174 BH94
Pavilion La, Beck. BR3 183 DZ93
Pavilion Ms, N3
off Windermere Av 98 DA54
Pavilion Rd, SW1 18 D6
Ilford IG1 125 EM59
Pavilions, The, Epp.
(N.Wld Bas.) CM16 71 FC25
Uxbridge UB8 134 BJ66
Pavilion Shop Cen, The,
Wal.Cr. EN8 67 DX34
Pavilion Sq, SW17 180 DF90
Pavilion St, SW1 18 D6
Pavilion Ter, E.Mol. KT8 197 CF98
Ilford IG2
off Southdown Cres 125 ES57
Pavilion Way, Amer. HP6 72 AW39
Edgware HA8 96 CP52
Ruislip HA4 116 BW61
Pawleyne Cl, SE20 182 DW94
Pawsey Cl, E13
off Plashet Rd 144 EG67
Pawson's Rd, Croy. CR0 202 DQ100
Paxford Rd, Wem. HA0 117 CH61
Paxton Av, Slou. SL1 151 AQ76
Paxton Cl, Rich. TW9 158 CM82
Walton-on-Thames KT12 196 BW101
Paxton Gdns, Wok. GU21 211 BE112
Paxton Pl, SE27 182 DS91
Paxton Prim Sch,
SE19 off Woodland Rd 182 DS93
Paxton Rd, N17 100 DT52

Paxton Rd, SE23 .. 183 DY90
W4 .. 158 CS79
Berkhamsted HP4 .. 38 AX19
Bromley BR1 .. 184 EG94
St. Albans AL1 .. 43 CE21
Paxton Ter, SW1 .. 161 DH79
Paycock Rd, Harl. CM19 .. 51 EN17
Payne Cl, Bark. IG11 .. 145 ES66
Paynell Ct, SE3 off Lawn Ter .. 164 EE83
Payne Rd, E3 .. 143 EB68
Paynesfield Av, SW14 .. 158 CR83
Paynesfield Rd, Bushey
(Bushey Hth) WD23 .. 95 CF45
Westerham (Tats.) TN16 .. 238 EK119
Paynes La, Wal.Abb. EN9 .. 49 EC24
Payne St, SE8 .. 163 DZ79
Paynes Wk, W6 .. 159 CY79
Peabody Av, SW1 .. 18 G9
Peabody Cl, SE10
off Devonshire Dr .. 163 EB81
SW1 .. 19 H10
Croydon CR0
off Shirley Rd .. 202 DW102
Peabody Ct, Enf. EN3
off Martini Dr .. 83 EA37
Peabody Dws, WC1 .. 9 N3
Peabody Est, EC1 .. 11 H4
N1 (Islington) .. 4 G6
N17 .. 100 DS53
SE1 .. 20 D2
SE24 .. 182 DQ87
SW3 off Margaretta Ter .. 160 DE79
W6 off The Square .. 159 CW78
W10 .. 139 CW71
Peabody Hill, SE21 .. 181 DP88
Peabody Hill Est, SE21 .. 181 DP87
Peabody Sq, SE1 .. 20 E4
Peabody Twr, EC1
off Golden La .. 142 DQ70
Peabody Trust, SE1 .. 20 G2
Peabody Yd, N1 .. 4 G7
Peace Cl, N14 .. 81 DH43
SE25 .. 202 DS98
Waltham Cross EN7
off Goffs La .. 66 DU29
Peace Dr, Wat. WD17 .. 75 BU41
Peace Gro, Wem. HA9 .. 118 CP62
Peace Prospect, Wat. WD17 .. 75 BU41
Peace Rd, Iver SL0 .. 133 AZ69
Slough SL3 .. 133 BA68
Peace St, SE18
off Nightingale Vale .. 165 EP79
Peach Cft, Grav. (Nthflt)
DA11 .. 190 GE90
Peaches Cl, Sutt. SM2 .. 217 CY108
Peachey Cl, Uxb. UB8 .. 134 BK72
Peachey La, Uxb. UB8 .. 134 BK71
Peach Rd, W10 .. 6 B1
Peach Tree Av, West Dr. UB7
off Pear Tree Av .. 134 BM72
Peachum Rd, SE3 .. 164 EF79
Peachwalk Ms, E3
off Grove Rd .. 143 DX68
Peacock Av, Felt. TW14 .. 175 BR88
Peacock Cl, Horn. RM11 .. 128 FL56
Peacock Gdns, S.Croy. CR2 .. 221 DY110
Peacocks, Harl. CM19 .. 51 EM17
Peacocks Cen, The, Wok.
GU21 .. 226 AY117
Peacocks Cl, Berk. HP4 .. 38 AT17
Peacock St, SE17 .. 20 F8
Gravesend DA12 .. 191 GJ87
Peacock Wk, E16 .. 15 P7
Abbots Langley WD5 .. 59 BU31
Dorking RH4 off Rose Hill .. 263 CG137
Peacock Yd, SE17 .. 20 F8
Peak, The, SE26 .. 182 DW90
Peakes La, Wal.Cr. (Chsht)
EN7 .. 66 DT27
Peakes Way, Wal.Cr. (Chsht)
EN7 .. 66 DT27
Peaketon Av, Ilf. IG4 .. 124 EK56
Peak Hill, SE26 .. 182 DW91
Peak Hill Av, SE26 .. 182 DW91
Peak Hill Gdns, SE26 .. 182 DW91
Peak Rd, Guil. GU2 .. 242 AU131
Peaks Hill, Pur. CR8 .. 219 DK110
Peaks Hill Ri, Pur. CR8 .. 219 DL110
Pea La, Upmin. RM14 .. 149 FU66
Peal Gdns, W13
off Ruislip Rd E .. 137 CG70
Peall Rd, Croy. CR0 .. 201 DM100
Pearce Cl, Mitch. CR4 .. 200 DG96
Pearcefield Av, SE23 .. 182 DW88
Pearce Rd, Chesh. HP5 .. 54 AP29
West Molesey KT8 .. 196 CB97
Pearces Wk, St.Alb. AL1
off Albert St .. 43 CD21
Pear Cl, NW9 .. 118 CR56
SE14
off Southerngate Way .. 163 DY80
Pearcroft Rd, E11 .. 123 ED61
Pearcy Cl, Rom. (Harold Hill)
RM3 .. 106 FL52
Peardon St, SW8 .. 161 DH82
Peareswood Gdns, Stan.
HA7 .. 95 CK53
Peareswood Rd, Erith DA8 .. 167 FF81
Pearfield Rd, SE23 .. 183 DY90
Pearl Cl, E6 .. 145 EN72
NW2 off Marble Dr .. 119 CX59
Pearl Ct, Wok. GU21
off Langmans Way .. 226 AS116
Pearl Gdns, Slou. SL1 .. 131 AP74
Pearl Rd, E17 .. 123 EA55
Pearl St, E1 .. 22 D1
Pearmain Cl, Shep. TW17 .. 195 BP99
Pearman St, SE1 .. 20 D5
Pear Pl, SE1 .. 20 C3
Pear Rd, E11 .. 123 ED62
Pearscroft Ct, SW6 .. 160 DB81
Pearscroft Rd, SW6 .. 160 DB81
Pearse St, SE15
off Dragon Rd .. 162 DS79
Pearson Av, Hert. SG13 .. 32 DQ11
Pearson Cl, SE5
off Medlar St .. 162 DQ81
Hertford SG13
off Pearson Av .. 32 DQ11
Purley CR8 .. 219 DP111
Pearson Ms, SW4
off Edgeley Rd .. 161 DK83
Pearsons Av, SE14
off Tanners Hill .. 163 EA81
Pearson St, E2 .. 5 M9
Pearson Way, Dart. DA1 .. 188 FM89
Pears Rd, Houns. TW3 .. 156 CC83
PEARTREE, Welw.G.C. AL7 .. 29 CZ09
Peartree Av, SW17 .. 180 DC90
Pear Tree Av, West Dr. UB7 .. 134 BM72
Pear Tree Cl, E2 .. 5 N8
Addlestone KT15
off Pear Tree Rd .. 212 BG106
Amersham HP7
off Orchard End Av .. 72 AT39
Beaconsfield (Seer Grn)
HP9 .. 89 AQ51
Chessington KT9 .. 216 CN106
Peartree Cl, Erith DA8 .. 167 FD81
Hemel Hempstead HP1 .. 40 BG19
Pear Tree Cl, Mitch. CR4 .. 200 DE96
Slough SL1 .. 131 AM74
Peartree Cl, S.Croy. CR2 .. 220 DV114
South Ockendon RM15 .. 149 FW68
Pear Tree Cl, Swan. BR8 .. 207 FD96
Peartree Cl, Welw.G.C. AL7 .. 29 CY09
Peartree Ct, E18
off Churchfields .. 102 EH53
Pear Tree Ct, EC1 .. 10 D4
Peartree Ct, Welw.G.C. AL7 .. 29 CY10
Peartree Fm, Welw.G.C. AL7 .. 29 CY09
Peartree Gdns, Dag. RM8 .. 126 EV63
Romford RM7 .. 105 FB54
Pear Tree Hill, Red. (Salf.)
RH1 .. 266 DG143
Peartree La, E1 .. 12 F10
Welwyn Garden City AL7 .. 29 CY10
Pear Tree Mead, Harl. CM18 .. 52 EU18
[Sch] Pear Tree Mead Co Prim
Sch, Harl. CM18
off Trotters Rd .. 52 EU18
[Sch] Peartree Prim Sch,
Welw.G.C. AL7
off Peartree La .. 29 CY10
Pear Tree Rd, Add. KT15 .. 212 BG106
Ashford TW15 .. 175 BQ92
Peartree Rd, Enf. EN1 .. 82 DS41
Hemel Hempstead HP1 .. 40 BG19
Pear Tree St, EC1 .. 10 F3
Pear Tree Wk, Wal.Cr. (Chsht)
EN7 .. 66 DR26
Peartree Way, SE10 .. 25 L7
Peary Pl, E2 .. 12 F1
Peascod Pl, Wind. SL4
off Peascod St .. 151 AR81
Peascod St, Wind. SL4 .. 151 AR81
Peascroft Rd, Hem.H. HP3 .. 40 BN23
Pease Cl, Horn. RM12
off Dowding Way .. 147 FH66
PEASMARSH, Guil. GU3 .. 258 AW142
Peatfield Cl, Sid. DA15
off Woodside Rd .. 185 ES90
Peatmore Av, Wok. GU22 .. 228 BG116
Peatmore Cl, Wok. GU22 .. 228 BG116
Pebble Cl, Tad. KT20 .. 248 CS128
PEBBLE COOMBE, Tad.
KT20 .. 248 CS128
Pebble Hill, Lthd. KT24 .. 245 BQ133
Pebble Hill Rd, Bet. RH3 .. 248 CS131
Tadworth KT20 .. 248 CS131
Pebble La, Epsom KT18 .. 232 CN121
Leatherhead KT22 .. 248 CL125
Pebble Way, W3 .. 138 CP74
Pebworth Rd, Har. HA1 .. 117 CG61
Peckarmans Wd, SE26 .. 182 DU90
Peckett Sq, N5
off Highbury Gra .. 122 DQ63
Peckford Pl, SW9 .. 161 DN82
PECKHAM, SE15 .. 162 DU81
Peckham Gro, SE15 .. 162 DS80
Peckham High St, SE15 .. 162 DU81
Peckham Hill St, SE15 .. 162 DU80
Peckham Pk Rd, SE15 .. 162 DU80
[Sch] Peckham Pk Sch,
SE15 off Friary Rd .. 162 DU80
Peckham Rd, SE5 .. 162 DS81
SE15 .. 162 DS81
⇌ Peckham Rye .. 162 DU82
Peckham Rye, SE15 .. 162 DU83
SE22 .. 162 DU84
[Sch] Peckham Rye Prim Sch,
SE15 off Whorlton Rd .. 162 DV83
Pecks Hill, Wal.Abb. EN9 .. 50 EE21
Pecks Yd, E1 .. 11 N5
Peckwater St, NW5 .. 121 DJ64
Pedham Pl Ind Est, Swan.
BR8 .. 207 FG99
Pedlars End, Ong. CM5 .. 53 FH21
Pedlars Wk, N7 .. 141 DL65
Pedley Rd, Dag. RM8 .. 126 EW60
Pedley St, E1 .. 11 P4
PEDNORMEAD END,
Chesh. HP5 .. 54 AN32
Pednormead End, Chesh.
HP5 .. 54 AP32
Pednor Rd, Chesh. HP5 .. 54 AM30
Pedro St, E5 .. 123 DX62
Pedworth Gdns, SE16 .. 22 E8
Peek Cres, SW19 .. 179 CX92
Peeks Brook La, Horl. RH6 .. 269 DM150
[Coll] Peel Cen (Met Pol Training
& Driving Sch), NW9
off Aerodrome Rd .. 119 CT55
Peel Cl, E4 .. 101 EB47
N9 off Plevna Rd .. 100 DU48
Windsor SL4 .. 151 AP83
Peel Ct, Slou. SL1
off Farnburn Av .. 131 AQ71
Peel Cres, Hert. SG14 .. 31 DP07
Peel Dr, NW9 .. 119 CT55
Ilford IG5 .. 124 EL55
Peel Gro, E2 .. 142 DW68
Peel Pas, W8 .. 16 G2
Peel Pl, Ilf. IG5 .. 102 EL54
Peel Prec, NW6 .. 140 DA68
Peel Rd, E18 .. 102 EF53
NW6 .. 6 F1
Harrow (Wldste) HA3 .. 117 CF55
Orpington BR6 .. 223 EQ106
Wembley HA9 .. 117 CK62
Peel St, W8 .. 16 G2
Peel Way, Rom. RM3 .. 106 FM54
Uxbridge UB8 .. 134 BL71
Peerage Way, Horn. RM11 .. 128 FL59
Peerless Dr, Uxb. (Hare.)
UB9 .. 114 BJ57
Peerless St, EC1 .. 11 J2
Pegamoid Rd, N18 .. 100 DW48
Pegasus Cl, N16
off Green Las .. 122 DR63
Pegasus Ct, Abb.L. WD5
off Furtherfield .. 59 BT32
Gravesend DA12 .. 191 GJ90
Pegasus Pl, SE11
off Clayton St .. 161 DN79
SW6 off Ackmar Rd .. 160 DA81
St. Albans AL3
off Waverley Rd .. 43 CD18
Pegasus Rd, Croy. CR0 .. 219 DN107
Pegasus Way, N11 .. 99 DH51
Pegelm Gdns, Horn. RM11 .. 128 FM59
Peggotty Way, Uxb. UB8
off Dickens Av .. 135 BP72
Pegg Rd, Houns. TW5 .. 156 BX80
Pegley Gdns, SE12 .. 184 EG89
Pegmire La, Wat. (Ald.)
WD25 .. 76 CC39
Pegrams Rd, Harl. CM18 .. 51 EQ18
Pegrum Dr, St.Alb.
(Lon.Col.) AL2 .. 61 CH26
Pegs La, Hert. SG13 .. 32 DR11
Pegwell St, SE18 .. 165 ES80
Peket Cl, Stai. TW18 .. 193 BE95
Pekin Cl, E14 .. 13 P8
Pekin St, E14 .. 13 P8
Peldon Ct, Rich. TW9 .. 158 CM84
Peldon Pas, Rich. TW10
off Worple Way .. 158 CM84
Peldon Rd, Harl. CM19 .. 51 EN17
Peldon Wk, N1 .. 4 F7
Pelham Av, Bark. IG11 .. 145 ET67
Pelham Cl, SE5 .. 162 DS82
Pelham Ct, Hem.H. HP2 .. 41 BQ20
Welwyn Garden City AL7
off Amwell Common .. 30 DC10
Pelham Cres, SW7 .. 18 A8
Pelham Pl, SW7 .. 18 A8
W13 off Ruislip Rd E .. 137 CF70
[Sch] Pelham Prim Sch,
SW19 off Southey Rd .. 180 DA94
Bexleyheath DA7
off Pelham Rd .. 166 FA83
Pelham Rd, E18 .. 124 EH55
N15 .. 122 DT56
N22 .. 99 DN54
SW19 .. 180 DA94
Beckenham BR3 .. 202 DW96
Bexleyheath DA7 .. 166 FA83
Gravesend DA11 .. 191 GF87
Ilford IG1 .. 125 ER61
Pelham Rd S, Grav. DA11 .. 191 GF88
Pelhams, The, Wat. WD25 .. 76 BX35
Pelhams Cl, Esher KT10 .. 214 CA105
Pelham St, SW7 .. 17 P7
Pelhams Wk, Esher KT10 .. 196 CA104
Pelham Ter, Grav. DA11
off Campbell Rd .. 191 GF87
Pelham Way, Lthd. (Bkhm)
KT23 .. 246 CB126
Pelican Est, SE15 .. 162 DT81
Pelican Pas, E1 .. 12 E3
Pelier St, SE17
off Langdale Cl .. 162 DQ79
Pelinore Rd, SE6 .. 184 EE89
Pellant Rd, SW6 .. 159 CY80
Pellatt Gro, N22 .. 99 DN53
Pellatt Rd, SE22 .. 182 DT85
Wembley HA9 .. 117 CK61
Pellerin Rd, N16 .. 5 M1
Pelling Hill, Wind.
(Old Wind.) SL4 .. 172 AV87
Pelling St, E14 .. 13 N7
Pellipar Cl, N13 .. 99 DN48
Pellipar Gdns, SE18 .. 165 EM78
Pelly Ct, Epp. CM16 .. 69 ET31
Pelly Rd, E13 .. 144 EG68
Pelter St, E2 .. 11 N1
Pelton Av, Sutt. SM2 .. 218 DB110
Pelton Rd, SE10 .. 24 G9
Pembar Av, E17 .. 123 DY55
Pemberley Chase, Epsom
(W.Ewell) KT19 .. 216 CP106
Pemberley Cl, Epsom
(W.Ewell) KT19 .. 216 CP106
Pember Rd, NW10 .. 6 A2
Pemberton Av, Rom. RM2 .. 127 FH55
Pemberton Cl, St.Alb. AL1 .. 43 CD23
Pemberton Gdns, N19 .. 121 DJ62
Romford RM6 .. 126 EY57
Swanley BR8 .. 207 FE97
Pemberton Ho, SE26
off High Level Dr .. 182 DU91
Pemberton Pl, E8
off Mare St .. 142 DV66
Esher KT10
off Carrick Gate .. 196 CC104
Pemberton Rd, N4 .. 121 DN57
East Molesey KT8 .. 196 CC98
Slough SL2 .. 131 AL70
Pemberton Row, EC4 .. 10 D7
Pemberton Ter, N19 .. 121 DJ62
Pembrey Way, Horn. RM12 .. 148 FJ65
Pembridge Av, Twick. TW2 .. 176 BZ88
Pembridge Chase, Hem.H.
(Bov.) HP3
off Pembridge Cl .. 57 BA28
Pembridge Cl, Hem.H.
(Bov.) HP3 .. 57 AZ28
Pembridge Cres, W11 .. 6 G9
Pembridge Gdns, W2 .. 6 G10
[Sch] Pembridge Hall Sch, W2 .. 7 H10
Pembridge La, Brox. EN10 .. 48 DR21
Hertford (Brickendon)
SG13 .. 48 DQ19
Pembridge Ms, W11 .. 6 G9
Pembridge Pl, SW15 .. 180 DA85
W2 .. 7 H9
Pembridge Rd, W11 .. 6 G10
Hemel Hempstead (Bov.)
HP3 .. 57 BA28
Pembridge Sq, W2 .. 6 G10
Pembridge Vil, W2 .. 6 G9
W11 .. 6 G9
Pembroke Av, N1 .. 141 DL67
Enfield EN1 .. 82 DV38
Harrow HA3 .. 117 CG55
Pinner HA5 .. 116 BX60
Surbiton KT5 .. 198 CP99
Walton-on-Thames KT12 .. 214 BX105
Pembroke Cl, SW1 .. 18 F4
Banstead SM7 .. 234 DB117
Broxbourne EN10 .. 49 DY23
Erith DA8
off Pembroke Rd .. 167 FD77
Hornchurch RM11 .. 128 FM56
Pembroke Cotts, W8
off Pembroke Sq .. 160 DA76
Pembroke Dr, Wal.Cr.
(Chsht) EN7 .. 65 DP29
Pembroke Gdns, W8 .. 16 F7
Dagenham RM10 .. 127 FB62
Woking GU22 .. 227 BA118
Pembroke Gdns Cl, W8 .. 16 F6
Pembroke Ms, E3 .. 13 K1
N10 off Pembroke Rd .. 98 DG53
W8 .. 16 G6
Sevenoaks TN13
off Pembroke Rd .. 257 FH125
Pembroke Pl, W8 .. 16 G6
Dartford (Sutt.H.) DA4 .. 208 FP95
Edgware HA8 .. 96 CN52
Isleworth TW7
off Thornbury Rd .. 157 CE82
Pembroke Rd, E6 .. 145 EM71
E17 .. 123 EB57
N8 .. 121 DL56
N10 .. 98 DG53
N13 .. 100 DQ48
N15 .. 122 DT57
Pembroke Rd, SE25 .. 202 DS98
W8 .. 16 G7
Bromley BR1 .. 204 EJ96
Erith DA8 .. 167 FC78
Greenford UB6 .. 136 CB70
Ilford IG3 .. 125 ET60
Mitcham CR4 .. 200 DG96
Northwood HA6 .. 93 BQ48
Ruislip HA4 .. 115 BS60
Sevenoaks TN13 .. 257 FH125
Wembley HA9 .. 117 CK62
Woking GU22 .. 227 BA118
Pembroke Sq, W8 .. 16 G6
Pembroke St, N1 .. 141 DL66
Pembroke Studios, W8 .. 16 F6
Pembroke Vil, W8 .. 16 G7
Richmond TW9 .. 157 CK84
Pembroke Wk, W8 .. 16 G7
Pembroke Way, Hayes UB3 .. 155 BQ76
Pembry Cl, SW9 .. 161 DN81
Pembury Av, Wor.Pk. KT4 .. 199 CU101
Pembury Cl, Brom. BR2 .. 204 EF101
Coulsdon CR5 .. 218 DG114
Pembury Ct, Hayes UB3 .. 155 BR79
Pembury Cres, Sid. DA14 .. 186 EY89
Pembury Pl, E5 .. 122 DV64
Pembury Rd, E5 .. 122 DV64
N17 .. 100 DT54
SE25 .. 202 DU98
Bexleyheath DA7 .. 166 EY80
Pemdevon Rd, Croy. CR0 .. 201 DN101
Pemell Cl, E1 .. 12 F3
Pemerich Cl, Hayes UB3 .. 155 BT78
Pempath Pl, Wem. HA9 .. 117 CK61
Pemsel Ct, Hem.H. HP3
off Crabtree La .. 40 BK22
Penally Pl, N1 .. 5 K7
Penang St, E1 .. 22 D1
Penard Rd, Sthl. UB2 .. 156 CA76
Penarth St, SE15 .. 162 DW79
Penates, Esher KT10 .. 215 CD105
Penberth Rd, SE6 .. 183 EC89
Penbury Rd, Sthl. UB2 .. 156 BZ77
Pencombe Ms, W11 .. 6 F9
Pencraig Way, SE15 .. 162 DV79
Pencroft Dr, Dart. DA1
off Shepherds La .. 188 FJ87
Pendall Cl, Barn. EN4 .. 80 DE42
Penda Rd, Erith DA8 .. 167 FB80
Pendarves Rd, SW20 .. 199 CW95
Penda's Mead, E9
off Lindisfarne Way .. 123 DY63
Pendell Av, Hayes UB3 .. 155 BT80
Pendell Ct, Red. (Bletch.)
RH1 .. 251 DP131
Pendell Rd, Red. (Bletch.)
RH1 .. 251 DP131
Pendennis Cl, W.Byf. KT14 .. 212 BG114
Pendennis Rd, N17 .. 122 DR55
SW16 .. 181 DL91
Orpington BR6 .. 206 EW103
Sevenoaks TN13 .. 257 FH123
Penderel Rd, Houns. TW3 .. 176 CA85
Penderry Ri, SE6 .. 183 ED89
Penderyn Way, N7 .. 121 DK63
Pendle Rd, SW16 .. 181 DH93
Pendlestone Rd, E17 .. 123 EA57
Pendleton Cl, Red. RH1 .. 266 DF136
Pendleton Rd, Red. RH1 .. 266 DE136
Reigate RH2 .. 266 DC137
Pendragon Rd, Brom. BR1 .. 184 EF90
[Sch] Pendragon Sec Sch, Brom.
BR1 off Pendragon Rd .. 184 EG90
Pendragon Wk, NW9 .. 118 CS58
Pendrell Rd, SE4 .. 163 DY82
Pendrell St, SE18 .. 165 ER80
Pendula Dr, Hayes UB4 .. 136 BX70
Pendulum Ms, E8 .. 5 N2
Penerley Rd, SE6 .. 183 EB88
Rainham RM13 .. 147 FH71
Penfold Cl, Croy. CR0
off Epsom Rd .. 201 DN104
Penfold La, Bex. DA5 .. 186 EX89
Penfold Pl, NW1 .. 7 P5
Penfold Rd, N9 .. 101 DX46
Penfold St, NW1 .. 7 P4
NW8 .. 7 P4
Penford Gdns, SE9 .. 164 EK83
Penford St, SE5 .. 161 DP82
Pengarth Rd, Bex. DA5 .. 186 EX85
PENGE, SE20 .. 182 DW94
⇌ Penge East .. 182 DW93
Penge Ho, SW11 off Wye St .. 160 DD83
Penge La, SE20 .. 182 DW94
Pengelly Cl, Wal.Cr.
(Chsht) EN7 .. 66 DV30
Penge Rd, E13 .. 144 EJ66
SE20 .. 202 DU97
SE25 .. 202 DU97
⇌ Penge West .. 182 DV93
Penhale Cl, Orp. BR6 .. 224 EU105
Penhall Rd, SE7 .. 164 EK77
Penhill Rd, Bex. DA5 .. 186 EW87
Penhurst, Wok. GU21 .. 211 AZ114
Penhurst Pl, SE1 .. 20 B6
Penhurst Rd, Ilf. IG6 .. 103 EP52
Penifather La, Grnf. UB6 .. 137 CD69
Peninsula Apartments, W2
off Praed St .. 140 DD71
Peninsula Hts, SE1
off Albert Embk .. 161 DL78
Peninsular Cl, Felt. TW14 .. 175 BR86
Peninsular Pk Rd, SE7 .. 25 M8
Penistone Rd, SW16 .. 181 DL94
Penistone Wk, Rom. RM3
off Okehampton Rd .. 106 FJ51
Penketh Dr, Har. HA1 .. 117 CD62
Penlow Rd, Harl. CM18 .. 51 EQ18
Penman Cl, St.Alb. AL2 .. 60 CA27
Penman's Grn, Kings L. WD4 .. 57 BF32
Penmon Rd, SE2 .. 166 EU76
PENN, H.Wyc. HP10 .. 88 AE48
Pennack Rd, SE15 .. 162 DT79
Pennant Ms, W8 .. 17 J7
Pennant Ter, E17 .. 101 DZ54
Pennard Rd, W12 .. 159 CW75
Pennards, The, Sun. TW16 .. 196 BW96
Penn Av, Chesh. HP5 .. 54 AN30
Penn Bottom, H.Wyc.
(Penn) HP10 .. 88 AG47
Penn Cl, Grnf. UB6 .. 136 CB68
Harrow HA3 .. 117 CJ56
Rickmansworth (Chorl.)
WD3 .. 73 BD44
Uxbridge UB8 .. 134 BK70
Penn Dr, Uxb. (Denh.) UB9 .. 113 BF58
Penne Cl, Rad. WD7 .. 61 CF34
Penner Cl, SW19 .. 179 CY89
Penners Gdns, Surb. KT6 .. 198 CL101
Pennethorne Cl, E9
off Victoria Pk Rd .. 142 DW67
Pennethorne Ho, SW11
off Wye St .. 160 DD83
Pennethorne Rd, SE15 .. 162 DV80
Penney Cl, Dart. DA1 .. 188 FK87
Penn Gdns, Chis. BR7 .. 205 EP96
Romford RM5 .. 104 FA52
Penn Gaskell La, Ger.Cr.
(Chal.St.P.) SL9 .. 91 AZ50
Penn Grn, Beac. HP9 .. 89 AK51
Pennine Dr, NW2 .. 119 CY61
Pennine Ho, N9
off Plevna Rd .. 100 DU48
Pennine La, NW2
off Pennine Dr .. 119 CY61
Pennine Rd, Slou. SL2 .. 131 AN71
Pennine Way, Bexh. DA7 .. 167 FE81
Gravesend (Nthflt) DA11 .. 190 GE90
Hayes UB3 .. 155 BR80
Hemel Hempstead HP2 .. 40 BM17
Pennings Av, Guil. GU2 .. 242 AT132
Pennington Cl, SE27
off Hamilton Rd .. 182 DR91
Romford RM5 .. 104 FA50
Pennington Dr, N21 .. 81 DL43
Weybridge KT13 .. 195 BS104
Pennington Rd, Beac. HP9 .. 110 AH55
Gerrards Cross
(Chal.St.P.) SL9 .. 90 AX52
Penningtons, The, Amer.
HP6 .. 55 AS37
Pennington St, E1 .. 12 B10
Pennington Way, SE12 .. 184 EH89
Pennis La, Long.
(Fawk.Grn) DA3 .. 209 FX100
Penniston Cl, N17 .. 100 DQ54
Penn La, Bex. DA5 .. 186 EX85
Penn Meadow, Slou.
(Stoke P.) SL2 .. 132 AT67
Penn Pl, Rick. WD3
off Northway .. 92 BK45
Penn Rd, N7 .. 121 DL64
Beaconsfield HP9 .. 88 AJ48
Gerrards Cross
(Chal.St.P.) SL9 .. 90 AX53
Rickmansworth (Mill End)
WD3 .. 91 BF46
St. Albans (Park St) AL2 .. 60 CC27
Slough SL2 .. 131 AR70
Slough (Datchet) SL3 .. 152 AX81
Watford WD24 .. 75 BV39
[Sch] Penn Sch, Penbury Gro
Site, H.Wyc. HP10
off Church Rd .. 88 AG49
Rayners Site, H.Wyc.
HP10 off Church Rd .. 88 AD48
Penn St, N1 .. 5 K8
Penn Way, Rick. (Chorl.) WD3 .. 73 BD44
Penny Cl, Rain. RM13 .. 147 FH69
Pennycroft, Croy. CR0 .. 221 DY109
Pennyfather La, Enf. EN2 .. 82 DQ40
Pennyfield, Cob. KT11 .. 213 BU113
Pennyfields, E14 .. 13 P9
Brentwood CM14 .. 108 FW49
Penny La, Shep. TW17 .. 195 BS101
Pennylets Grn, Slou.
(Stoke P.) SL2 .. 132 AT66
Pennymead, Harl. CM20 .. 36 EU14
Pennymead Dr, Lthd.
(E.Hors.) KT24 .. 245 BT127
Pennymead Ri, Lthd.
(E.Hors.) KT24 .. 245 BT127
Pennymead Twr, Harl. CM20 .. 52 EU15
Penny Ms, SW12
off Caistor Rd .. 181 DH87
Pennymoor Wk, W9 .. 6 F3
Penny Rd, NW10 .. 138 CP69
Pennyroyal Av, E6 .. 145 EN72
Pennys La, Saw.
(High Wych) CM21 .. 35 ER05
Penpoll Rd, E8 .. 142 DV65
Penpool La, Well. DA16 .. 166 EV83
Penrhyn Av, E17 .. 101 DZ53
Penrhyn Cl, Cat. CR3
off Buxton La .. 236 DR120
Penrhyn Cres, E17 .. 101 EA53
SW14 .. 158 CQ84
Penrhyn Gdns, Kings.T.
KT1 off Surbiton Rd .. 197 CK98
Penrhyn Gro, E17 .. 101 EA53
Penrhyn Rd, Kings.T. KT1 .. 198 CL97
Penrith Cl, SW15 .. 179 CY85
Beckenham BR3
off Albemarle Rd .. 203 EB95
Reigate RH2 .. 250 DE133
Uxbridge UB8
off Chippendale Waye .. 134 BK66
Penrith Cres, Rain. RM13 .. 127 FG64
Penrith Pl, SE27
off Harpenden Rd .. 181 DP89
Penrith Rd, N15 .. 122 DR57
Ilford IG6 .. 103 ET51
New Malden KT3 .. 198 CR98
Romford RM3 .. 106 FN51
Thornton Heath CR7 .. 202 DQ96
Penrith St, SW16 .. 181 DJ93
Penrose Av, Wat. WD19 .. 94 BX47
Penrose Ct, Hem.H. HP2 .. 40 BL16
Penrose Dr, Epsom KT19 .. 216 CN111
Penrose Gro, SE17 .. 20 G10
Penrose Ho, SE17 .. 20 G10
Penrose Rd, Lthd. (Fetch.)
KT22 .. 230 CC122
Penrose St, SE17 .. 20 G10
Penryn St, NW1 .. 141 DK68
Penry St, SE1 .. 21 M8
Pensbury Pl, SW8 .. 161 DJ82
Pensbury St, SW8 .. 161 DJ82
Penscroft Gdns, Borwd.
WD6 .. 78 CR42
Pensford Av, Rich. TW9 .. 158 CN82
Penshurst, Harl. CM17 .. 36 EV12
Penshurst Av, Sid. DA15 .. 186 EU86
Penshurst Cl, Ger.Cr.
(Chal.St.P.) SL9 .. 90 AX54
Penshurst Gdns, Edg. HA8 .. 96 CP50
Penshurst Grn, Brom. BR2 .. 204 EF99
Penshurst Rd, E9 .. 143 DX66
N17 .. 100 DT52
Bexleyheath DA7 .. 166 EZ81
Potters Bar EN6 .. 64 DD31
Thornton Heath CR7 .. 201 DP99
Penshurst Wk, Brom. BR2
off Hayesford Pk Dr .. 204 EF99
Penshurst Way, Orp. BR5
off Star La .. 206 EW98
Sutton SM2 .. 218 DA108
Pensilver Cl, Barn. EN4 .. 80 DE42
Pensons La, Ong. CM5 .. 71 FG28
Penstemon Cl, N3 .. 98 DA52
Penstemon Dr, Swans.
DA10 .. 189 FX85
Penstock Footpath, N22 .. 121 DL55
Pentavia Retail Pk, NW7
off Bunns La .. 97 CT52
Pentelow Gdns, Felt. TW14 .. 175 BU86
Pentire Cl, Upmin. RM14 .. 129 FS58
Pentire Rd, E17 .. 101 ED53
Pentland, Hem.H. HP2
off Mendip Way .. 40 BM17

Pentland Av, Edg. HA8 96 CP47
Shepperton TW17 194 BN99
Pentland Cl, N9 100 DW47
NW11 119 CY61
Pentland Gdns, SW18
off St. Ann's Hill 180 DC86
Pentland Pl, Nthlt. UB5 136 BY67
Pentland Rd, Bushey WD23 76 CC44
Slough SL2 131 AN71
Pentlands Cl, Mitch. CR4 201 DH97
Pentland St, SW18 180 DC86
Pentland Way, Uxb. UB10 115 BQ62
Pentley Cl, Welw.G.C. AL8 29 CX06
Pentley Pk, Welw.G.C. AL8 29 CX06
Pentlow St, SW15 159 CW83
Pentlow Way, Buck.H. IG9 102 EL45
Pentney Rd, E4 101 ED46
SW12 181 DJ88
SW19 off Midmoor Rd 199 CY95
Penton Av, Stai. TW18 173 BF94
Penton Dr, Wal.Cr. (Chsht)
EN8 67 DX29
Penton Gro, N1 4 C10
Penton Hall Dr, Stai.TW18 194 BG95
Penton Hook Rd, Stai.TW18 174 BG94
Penton Ho, SE2
off Hartslock Dr 166 EX75
Penton Pk, Cher. KT16 194 BG97
Penton Pl, SE17 20 F9
Penton Ri, WC1 10 B1
Penton Rd, Stai.TW18 173 BF94
Penton St, N1 4 C9
PENTONVILLE, N1 4 C10
Pentonville Rd, N1 4 A10
Pentreath Av, Guil. GU2 258 AT135
Pentrich Av, Enf. EN1 82 DU38
Pentridge St, SE15 162 DT80
Pentyre Av, N18 100 DR50
Penwerris Av, Islw. TW7 156 CC80
Penwith Rd, SW18 180 DB89
Penwith Wk, Wok. GU22
off Wych Hill Pk 226 AX119
Penwood End, Wok. GU22 226 AV121
Penwood Ho, SW15
off Tunworth Cres 179 CT86
Sch Penwortham Prim Sch,
SW16
off Penwortham Rd 181 DH93
Penwortham Rd, SW16 181 DH93
South Croydon CR2 220 DQ110
Penylan Pl, Edg. HA8 96 CN52
Penywern Rd, SW5 17 H9
Penzance Cl, Uxb. (Hare.)
UB9 92 BK53
Penzance Gdns, Rom. RM3 106 FN51
Penzance Pl, W11 16 C1
Penzance Rd, Rom. RM3 106 FN51
Penzance Spur, Slou. SL2 131 AP70
Penzance St, W11 16 C1
Peony Cl, Brwd. (Pilg.Hat.)
CM15 108 FV44
Peony Ct, Wdf.Grn. IG8
off The Bridle Path 102 EE52
Peony Gdns, W12 139 CU73
Pepler Ms, SE5
off Cobourg Rd 162 DT79
Pepler Way, Slou. SL1
off Gore Rd 130 AH69
Peplins Cl, Hat. AL9 63 CY26
Peplins Way, Hat. AL9 63 CY25
Peploe Rd, NW6 139 CX68
Peplow Cl, West Dr. UB7
off Tavistock Rd 134 BK74
Pepper All, Loug.
(High Beach) IG10 84 EG39
Pepper Cl, E6 145 EM71
Caterham CR3 252 DS125
Peppercorn Cl, Th.Hth. CR7 202 DR96
Pepper Hill, Grav. (Nthflt)
DA11 190 GC90
Ware (Gt Amwell) SG12 33 DZ10
Pepperhill La, Grav. (Nthflt)
DA11 190 GC90
Peppermead Sq, SE13 183 EA85
Peppermint Cl, Croy. CR0 201 DL101
Peppermint Pl, E11
off Birch Gro 124 EE62
Pepper St, E14 24 A5
SE1 20 G3
Peppie Cl, N16
off Bouverie Rd 122 DS61
Pepys Cl, Ashtd. KT21 232 CN117
Dartford DA1 168 FN84
Gravesend (Nthflt) DA11 190 GD90
Slough SL3 153 BB79
Tilbury RM18 171 GJ81
Uxbridge UB10 115 BP63
Pepys Cres, E16 25 M1
Barnet EN5 79 CW43
Pepys Ri, Orp. BR6 205 ET102
Pepys Rd, SE14 163 DX81
SW20 199 CW95
Pepys St, EC3 11 M9
Perceval Av, NW3 120 DE64
Percheron Cl, Islw. TW7 157 CG83
Percheron Rd, Borwd. WD6 78 CR44
Perch St, E8 122 DT63
Percival Ct, Lthd. KT22 214 CB111
Percival Ct, N17 off High Rd 100 DT52
Northolt UB5 116 CA64
★ Percival David Foundation
of Chinese Art, WC1
off Gordon Sq 9 M3
Percival Gdns, Rom. RM6 126 EW58
Percival Rd, SW14 158 CQ84
Enfield EN1 82 DT42
Feltham TW13 175 BT89
Hornchurch RM11 128 FJ58
Orpington BR6 205 EP103
Percival St, EC1 10 E3
Percival Way, Epsom KT19 216 CQ105
Percy Av, Ashf. TW15 174 BN92
Percy Bryant Rd, Sun.TW16 175 BS94
Percy Bush Rd, West Dr.
UB7 154 BM76
Percy Circ, WC1 10 B1
Percy Gdns, Enf. EN3 83 DX43
Hayes UB4 135 BS69
Isleworth TW7 157 CG82
Worcester Park KT4 198 CR102
Percy Ms, W1 9 L6
Percy Pas, W1 9 K6
Percy Pl, Slou. (Datchet) SL3 152 AV81
Percy Rd, E11 124 EE59
E16 15 H5
N12 98 DC50
N21 100 DQ45
SE20 203 DX95
SE25 202 DU99
W12 159 CU75
Bexleyheath DA7 166 EY82
Guildford GU2 242 AV132
Hampton TW12 176 CA94
Ilford IG3 126 EU59
Isleworth TW7 157 CG84
Percy Rd, Mitch. CR4 200 DG101
Romford RM7 127 FB55
Twickenham TW2 176 CB88
Watford WD18 75 BV42
Percy St, W1 9 L6
Grays RM17 170 GC79
Percy Way, Twick. TW2 176 CC88
Percy Yd, WC1 10 B1
Peregrine Cl, NW10 118 CR64
Watford WD25 60 BY34
Peregrine Ct, SW16
off Leithcote Gdns 181 DM91
Welling DA16 165 ET81
Peregrine Gdns, Croy. CR0 203 DY103
Peregrine Ho, EC1 10 F1
Peregrine Rd, Ilf. IG6 104 EV50
Sunbury-on-Thames
TW16 195 BT96
Waltham Abbey EN9 68 EG34
Peregrine Wk, Horn. RM12
off Heron Flight Av 147 FH65
Peregrine Way, SW19 179 CW94
Perham Rd, W14 16 D10
Perham Way, St.Alb.
(Lon.Col.) AL2 61 CK26
Peridot St, E6 144 EL71
Perifield, SE21 182 DQ88
Perimeade Rd, Grnf. UB6 137 CJ68
Perimeter Rd E, Gat. RH6 268 DG154
Perimeter Rd N, Gat. RH6 268 DF151
Perimeter Rd S, Gat. RH6 268 DC154
Periton Rd, SE9 164 EK84
PERIVALE, Grnf. UB6 137 CJ67
⊖ Perivale 137 CG68
Perivale Gdns, W13
off Bellevue Rd 137 CH70
Watford WD25 59 BV34
Perivale Gra, Grnf. UB6 137 CG69
Perivale Ind Pk, Grnf. UB6 137 CH68
Perivale La, Grnf. UB6 137 CG69
Perivale New Business Cen,
Grnf. UB6 137 CH68
Sch Perivale Prim Sch, Grnf.
UB6 off Federal Rd 137 CJ68
Perkin Cl, Houns. TW3 156 CB84
Wembley HA0 117 CH64
Perkins Cl, Green. DA9 189 FT85
Perkins Ct, Ashf. TW15 174 BM92
Perkin's Rents, SW1 19 L5
Perkins Rd, Ilf. IG2 125 ER57
Perkins Sq, SE1 21 H1
Perks Cl, SE3 off Hurren Cl 164 EE83
Perleybrooke La, Wok.
GU21 off Bampton Way 226 AU117
Permain Cl, Rad. (Shenley)
WD7 61 CK33
Perpins Rd, SE9 185 ES86
Perram Cl, Brox. EN10 67 DY26
Perran Rd, SW2
off Christchurch Rd 181 DP89
Perran Wk, Brent. TW8 158 CL78
Perren St, NW5
off Ryland Rd 141 DH65
Perrers Rd, W6 159 CV77
Perrin Cl, Ashf. TW15
off Fordbridge Rd 174 BM92
Perrin Ct, Wok. GU21
off Blackmore Cres 227 BB115
Perrin Rd, Wem. HA0 117 CG63
Perrins Ct, NW3
off Hampstead High St 120 DC63
Perrins La, NW3 120 DC63
Perrin's Wk, NW3 120 DC63
Perrior Rd, Gdmg. GU7 258 AS144
Perriors Cl, Wal.Cr. (Chsht)
EN7 66 DU27
Perrott St, SE18 165 EQ77
Perry Av, W3 138 CR72
Perry Cl, Rain. RM13
off Lowen Rd 147 FD68
Uxbridge UB8
off Harlington Rd 135 BQ72
Perry Ct, E14 off Napier Av 163 EA78
N15 off Albert Rd 122 DS58
Perry Cft, Wind. SL4 151 AL83
Perryfields Way, Slou.
(Burn.) SL1 130 AH70
Perryfield Way, NW9 119 CT58
Richmond TW10 177 CH89
Perry Gdns, N9
off Deansway 100 DS48
Perry Garth, Nthlt. UB5 136 BW67
Perry Gro, Dart. DA1 168 FN84
Perry Hall Cl, Orp. BR6 206 EU101
Sch Perry Hall Prim Sch, Orp.
BR6 off Perry Hall Rd 205 ET100
Perry Hall Rd, Orp. BR6 205 ET100
Perry Hill, SE6 183 DZ90
Guildford (Worp.) GU3 242 AS128
Waltham Abbey EN9 50 EF23
Perry Ho, SW2
off Tierney Rd 181 DL87
Rainham RM13
off Lowen Rd 147 FD68
Perry How, Wor.Pk. KT4 199 CT102
Perrylands La, Horl.
(Smallfield) RH6 269 DM149
Perryman Ho, Bark. IG11 145 EQ67
Perrymans Fm Rd, Ilf. IG2 125 ER58
Perryman Way, Slou. SL2 131 AM69
Perry Mead, Bushey WD23 94 CB45
Enfield EN2 81 DP40
Perrymead St, SW6 160 DA81
Sch Perrymount Prim Sch,
SE23 off Sunderland Rd 183 DX89
Perryn Rd, SE16 22 C5
W3 138 CR73
Perry Ri, SE23 183 DY90
Perry Rd, Dag. RM9 146 EZ70
Harlow CM18 51 EQ18
Perrysfield Rd, Wal.Cr.
(Chsht) EN8 67 DY27
Perrys La, Sev. (Knock.)
TN14 224 EV113
Perrys Pl, W1 9 L7
Perry Spring, Harl. CM17 52 EX17
PERRY STREET, Grav. DA11 190 GE88
Perry St, Chis. BR7 185 ER93
Dartford DA1 167 FE84
Gravesend (Nthflt) DA11 190 GE88
Perry St Gdns, Chis. BR7
off Old Perry St 185 ES93
Perry Vale, SE23 182 DW89
Perry Way, S.Ock. (Aveley)
RM15 148 FQ73
Perrywood Business Pk,
Red. RH1 267 DH142
Persant Rd, SE6 184 EE89
Perseverance Cotts, Wok.
(Ripley) GU23 228 BJ121
Perseverance Pl, SW9 161 DN80
Richmond TW9
off Shaftesbury Rd 158 CL83
Persfield Cl, Epsom KT17 217 CU110
Pershore Cl, Ilf. IG2 125 EP57
Pershore Gro, Cars. SM5 200 DD100
Pert Cl, N10 99 DH52
Perth Av, NW9 118 CR59
Hayes UB4 136 BW70
Slough SL1 131 AP72
Perth Cl, SW20
off Huntley Way 199 CU96
Perth Rd, E10 123 DY60
E13 144 EH68
N4 121 DN60
N22 99 DP53
Barking IG11 145 ER68
Beckenham BR3 203 EC96
Ilford IG2 125 EN58
Perth Ter, Ilf. IG2 125 EQ59
Perwell Av, Har. HA2 116 BZ60
Perwell Ct, Har. HA2 116 BZ60
Pescot Hill, Hem.H. HP1 40 BH18
Peter Av, NW10 139 CV66
Oxted RH8 253 ED129
Peterboat Cl, SE10 25 H7
Sch Peterborough & St.
Margarets Sch, Stan.
HA7 off Common Rd 95 CE48
Peterborough Av, Upmin.
RM14 129 FS60
Peterborough Gdns, Ilf. IG1 124 EL59
Peterborough Ms, SW6 160 DA82
Sch Peterborough Prim Sch,
SW6 off Clancarty Rd 160 DA82
Peterborough Rd, E10 123 EC57
SW6 160 DA82
Carshalton SM5 200 DE100
Guildford GU2 242 AT132
Harrow HA1 117 CE60
Peterborough Vil, SW6 160 DB81
Peterchurch Ho, SE15
off Commercial Way 162 DV79
Petergate, SW11 160 DC84
Peterhead Ms, Slou. SL3
off Grampian Way 153 BA78
Peter Heathfield Ho, E15
off High St 143 ED67
Peterhill Cl, Ger.Cr.
(Chal.St.P.) SL9 90 AY50
Sch Peter Hills with St. Mary's
& St. Paul's C of E Prim
Sch, SE16 23 H1
Peterhouse Gdns, SW6
off Bagley's La 160 DB81
Peter James Business Cen,
Hayes UB3 155 BU75
Peterlee Ct, Hem.H. HP2 40 BM16
Peterley Business Cen, E2
off Hackney Rd 142 DV68
★ Peter Pan Statue, W2 17 N1
Peters Av, St.Alb. (Lon.Col.)
AL2 61 CJ26
Peters Cl, Dag. RM8 126 EX60
Stanmore HA7 95 CK51
Welling DA16 165 ES82
Petersfield Av, Rom. RM3 106 FL51
Slough SL2 132 AU74
Staines TW18 174 BJ92
Petersfield Cl, N18 100 DQ50
Romford RM3 106 FN51
Petersfield Cres, Couls. CR5 235 DL115
Petersfield Ri, SW15 179 CV88
Petersfield Rd, W3 158 CQ75
Staines TW18 174 BJ92
PETERSHAM, Rich. TW10 178 CL88
Petersham Av, W.Byf.
(Byfleet) KT14 212 BL112
Petersham Cl, Rich. TW10 177 CK89
Sutton SM1 218 DA106
West Byfleet (Byfleet)
KT14 212 BL112
Petersham Dr, Orp. BR5 205 ET96
Petersham Gdns, Orp. BR5 205 ET96
Petersham La, SW7 17 L5
Petersham Ms, SW7 17 L6
Petersham Pl, SW7 17 L5
Petersham Rd, Rich. TW10 178 CL86
Petersham Ter, Croy. CR0
off Richmond Grn 201 DL104
Peters Hill, EC4 10 G9
Peter's La, EC1 10 F5
Peterslea, Kings L. WD4 59 BP29
Petersmead Cl, Tad. KT20 233 CW123
Peters Path, SE26 182 DV91
Peterstone Rd, SE2 166 EV76
Peterstow Cl, SW19 179 CY89
Peter St, W1 9 K9
Gravesend DA12 191 GH87
Peterswood, Harl. CM18 51 ER19
Sch Peterswood Co Inf Sch,
Harl. CM18
off Paringdon Rd 51 ER19
Sch Peterswood Co Jun Sch,
Harl. CM18
off Paringdon Rd 51 ER19
Peters Wd Hill, Ware SG12 33 DX07
Peterwood Way, Croy. CR0 201 DM103
Petherton Rd, N5 5 H2
Petley Rd, W6 159 CW79
Peto Pl, NW1 9 H3
Peto St N, E16 15 J9
Petridge Rd, Red. RH1 266 DF139
Petridgewood Common,
Red. RH1 266 DF140
Petrie Cl, NW2 139 CY65
★ Petrie Mus of Egyptian
Archaeology, WC1
off Malet Pl 9 L4
Pett Cl, Horn. RM11 127 FH61
Petten Cl, Orp. BR5 206 EX102
Petten Gro, Orp. BR5 206 EW102
Petters Rd, Ashtd. KT21 232 CM116
★ Petticoat La (Market), E1 11 M6
Petticoat Sq, E1 11 N7
Petticoat Twr, E1
off Petticoat Sq 142 DT72
Pettits Boul, Rom. RM1 105 FE53
Pettits Cl, Rom. RM1 105 FE54
Pettits La, Rom. RM1 105 FE54
Pettits La N, Rom. RM1 105 FD53
Pettits Pl, Dag. RM10 126 FA64
Pettits Rd, Dag. RM10 126 FA64
Pettiward Cl, SW15 159 CW84
Pettley Gdns, Rom. RM7 127 FD57
Pettman Cres, SE28 165 ER76
Pettsgrove Av, Wem. HA0 117 CJ64
Petts Hill, Nthlt. UB5 116 CB64
Petts La, Shep. TW17 194 BN98
Pett St, SE18 164 EL77
PETTS WOOD, Orp. BR5 205 ER99
⇌ Petts Wood 205 EQ99
Petts Wd Rd, Orp. BR5 205 EQ99
Petty Cross, Slou. SL1
off Suffolk Cl 131 AL72
Petty France, SW1 19 K5
Pettys Cl, Wal.Cr. (Chsht)
EN8 67 DX28
Petty Wales, EC3
off Lower Thames St 142 DS73
Petworth Cl, Couls. CR5 235 DJ119
Northolt UB5 136 BZ66
Petworth Ct, Wind. SL4 151 AP81
Petworth Gdns, SW20
off Hidcote Gdns 199 CV97
Uxbridge UB10 135 BQ67
Petworth Rd, N12 98 DE50
Bexleyheath DA6 186 FA85
Petworth St, SW11 160 DE81
Petworth Way, Horn. RM12 127 FF63
Petyt Pl, SW3 off Old Ch St 160 DE79
Petyward, SW3 18 B8
Pevensey Av, N11 99 DK50
Enfield EN1 82 DR40
Pevensey Cl, Islw. TW7 156 CC80
Pevensey Rd, E7 124 EF63
SW17 180 DD91
Feltham TW13 176 BY88
Slough SL2 131 AN71
Peverel, E6 off Downings 145 EN72
Peverel Ho, Dag. RM10 126 FA61
Peveret Cl, N11
off Woodland Rd 99 DH50
Peveril Dr, Tedd. TW11 177 CD92
Pewley Bk, Guil. GU1 258 AY136
Sch Pewley Down Inf Sch,
Guil. GU1
off Semaphore Rd 258 AY136
Pewley Hill, Guil. GU1 258 AX136
Pewley Pt, Guil. GU1 258 AY136
Pewley Way, Guil. GU1 258 AY136
Pewsey Cl, E4 101 EA50
Peyton Pl, SE10 163 EC80
Peyton's Cotts, Red. RH1 251 DM132
Pharaoh Cl, Mitch. CR4 200 DF101
Pharaoh's Island, Shep.
TW17 194 BM103
Pheasant Cl, E16 15 M7
Berkhamsted HP4 38 AW20
Purley CR8
off Partridge Knoll 219 DP113
Pheasant Hill, Ch.St.G. HP8 90 AW47
Pheasant Ri, Chesh. HP5 54 AR33
Pheasants Way, Rick. WD3 92 BH45
Pheasant Wk, Ger.Cr.
(Chal.St.P.) SL9 90 AX49
Phelips Rd, Harl. CM19 51 EN20
Phelp St, SE17 162 DR79
Phelps Way, Hayes UB3 155 BT77
Phene St, SW3 160 DE79
Philanthropic Rd, Red. RH1 266 DG135
Philan Way, Rom. RM5 105 FD51
Philbeach Gdns, SW5 16 F9
Phil Brown Pl, SW8
off Daley Thompson Way 161 DH82
Philbye Ms, Slou. SL1 151 AM75
Philchurch Pl, E1 12 B8
Philimore Cl, SE18 165 ES78
Philip Av, Rom. RM7 127 FD60
Swanley BR8 207 FD98
Philip Cl, Brwd. CM15 108 FV44
Romford RM7
off Philip Av 127 FD60
Philip Dr, H.Wyc. (Flack.Hth)
HP10 110 AC56
Philip Gdns, Croy. CR0 203 DZ103
Philip La, N15 122 DR56
Philipot Path, SE9 185 EM86
Philippa Gdns, SE9 184 EK85
Philippa Way, Grays RM16 171 GH77
Philip Rd, Rain. RM13 147 FE69
Staines TW18 174 BK93
Philips Cl, Cars. SM5 200 DG102
Sch Philip Southcote Sch,
Add. KT15
off Addlestone Moor 194 BJ103
Philip St, E13 15 L3
Philip Sydney Rd, Grays
RM16 169 FX78
Philip Wk, SE15 162 DU83
Phillida Rd, Rom. RM3 106 FN54
Phillimore Gdns, NW10 139 CW67
W8 16 G4
Phillimore Gdns Cl, W8 16 G5
Phillimore Pl, W8 16 G4
Radlett WD7 77 CE36
Phillimore Wk, W8 16 G5
Phillipers, Wat. WD25 76 BY35
Phillipp St, N1 5 L8
Phillips Cl, Dart. DA1 187 FH86
Phillips Hatch, Guil. (Won.)
GU5 259 BC143
Philpot La, EC3 11 L9
Woking (Chobham) GU24 210 AV113
Philpot Path, Ilf. IG1
off Sunnyside Rd 125 EQ62
Philpots Cl, West Dr. UB7 134 BK73
Philpot Sq, SW6
off Peterborough Rd 160 DB83
Philpot St, E1 12 D7
Phineas Pett Rd, SE9 164 EL83
Tra Phipps Bridge 200 DC97
Phipps Br Rd, SW19 200 DC96
Mitcham CR4 200 DC96
Phipps Hatch La, Enf. EN2 82 DQ38
Phipp's Ms, SW1 19 H6
Phipps Rd, Slou. SL1 131 AK71
Phipp St, EC2 11 L3
Phoebe Rd, Hem.H. HP2 40 BM17
Phoebeth Rd, SE4 183 EA85
Phoenix Cl, E8 5 N7
E17 101 DZ54
Epsom KT19 216 CN112
Northwood HA6 93 BT49
West Wickham BR4 204 EE103
Phoenix Ct, Guil. GU1
off High St 258 AX136
Phoenix Dr, Kes. BR2 204 EK104
Sch Phoenix High Sch,
W12 off The Curve 139 CU73
Phoenix Pk, Brent. TW8 157 CK78
Phoenix Pl, WC1 10 B3
Dartford DA1 188 FK87
Phoenix Rd, NW1 9 L1
SE20 182 DW93
Sch Phoenix Sch, E3 13 M1
NW3 off College Cres 140 DC65
Coll Phoenix Sch of Int
Languages & Business
Studies, Beck. BR3
off Croydon Rd 203 DY97
Phoenix St, WC2 9 M8
Phoenix Way, Houns. TW5 156 BW79
Phoenix Wf, SE10 25 J3
Phoenix Wf Rd, SE1 21 P4
Phoenix Yd, WC1 10 B2
★ Photographers' Gall,
WC2 9 M9
Phygtle, The, Ger.Cr.
(Chal.St.P.) SL9 90 AY51
Phyllis Av, N.Mal. KT3 199 CV99
★ Physical Energy Statue,
W2 17 M2
Physic Pl, SW3
off Royal Hosp Rd 160 DF79
Piazza, The, WC2
off Covent Gdn 141 DL73
Picardy Manorway, Belv.
DA17 167 FB76
Picardy Rd, Belv. DA17 166 FA77
Picardy St, Belv. DA17 166 FA76
Piccadilly, W1 19 H2
Piccadilly Arc, SW1 19 J1
⊖ Piccadilly Circus 9 K10
Piccadilly Circ, W1 9 L10
Piccadilly Pl, W1 9 K10
Piccards, The, Guil. GU2
off Chestnut Av 258 AW138
PICCOTTS END, Hem.H.
HP2 40 BJ16
Piccotts End La, Hem.H.
HP2 40 BJ17
Piccotts End Rd, Hem.H.
HP1 40 BJ18
Pickard St, EC1 10 F1
Pickering Av, E6 145 EN68
Pickering Cl, E9
off Cassland Rd 143 DX66
Pickering Gdns, N11 98 DG51
Croydon CR0 202 DT100
Pickering Ms, W2 7 K7
Pickering Pl, SW1 19 K2
Guildford GU2
off Aldershot Rd 242 AU132
Pickering St, N1 4 F7
Pickets Cl, Bushey
(Bushey Hth) WD23 95 CD46
Pickets St, SW12 181 DH87
Pickett Cft, Stan. HA7 95 CK53
Picketts, Welw.G.C. AL8 29 CX06
Picketts La, Red. RH1 267 DJ144
Picketts Lock La, N9 100 DW47
Pickford Cl, Bexh. DA7 166 EY82
Pickford Dr, Slou. SL3 133 AZ74
Pickford Gdn, Slou. SL1
off Stoke Poges La 132 AS74
Pickford La, Bexh. DA7 166 EY82
Pickford Rd, Bexh. DA7 166 EY83
St. Albans AL1 43 CH20
Pickfords Wf, N1 4 G10
Pick Hill, Wal.Abb. EN9 68 EF32
Pickhurst Grn, Brom. BR2 204 EF101
Sch Pickhurst Inf Sch, W.Wick.
BR4 off Pickhurst La 204 EF100
Sch Pickhurst Jun Sch, W.Wick.
BR4 off Pickhurst La 204 EF100
Pickhurst La, Brom. BR2 204 EF102
West Wickham BR4 204 EE100
Pickhurst Mead, Brom. BR2 204 EF101
Pickhurst Pk, Brom. BR2 204 EE99
Pickhurst Ri, W.Wick. BR4 203 EC101
Pickins Piece, Slou. (Horton)
SL3 153 BA82
Pickle Herring St, SE1
off Tooley St 142 DS74
Pickmoss La, Sev. (Otford)
TN14 241 FH116
Pickwick Cl, Houns. TW4
off Dorney Way 176 BY85
Pickwick Ct, SE9
off West Pk 184 EL88
Pickwick Gdns, Grav.
(Nthflt) DA11 190 GD90
Pickwick Ms, N18 100 DS50
Pickwick Pl, Har. HA1 117 CE59
Pickwick Rd, SE21 182 DR87
Pickwick St, SE1 20 G4
Pickwick Ter, Slou. SL2
off Maple Cres 132 AV73
Pickwick Way, Chis. BR7 185 EQ93
Pickworth Cl, SW8
off Kenchester Cl 161 DL80
Picquets Way, Bans. SM7 233 CY116
Picton Pl, W1 8 F8
Surbiton KT6 198 CN102
Picton St, SE5 162 DR80
Piedmont Rd, SE18 165 ER78
Pield Heath Av, Uxb. UB8 134 BN70
Sch Pield Heath Ho Sch, Uxb.
UB8 off Pield Heath Rd 134 BL70
Pield Heath Rd, Uxb. UB8 134 BM71
Piercing Hill, Epp. (They.B.)
CM16 85 ER35
Pier Head, E1 22 C2
Pierian Spring, Hem.H. HP1 40 BH18
Piermont Grn, SE22 182 DV85
Piermont Pl, Brom. BR1 204 EL96
Piermont Rd, SE22 182 DV85
Pier Par, E16 off Pier Rd 145 EN74
Pierrepoint Arc, N1
off Islington High St 141 DP68
Pierrepoint Rd, W3 138 CP73
Pierrepoint Row, N1 4 E9
Pier Rd, E16 165 EM75
Erith DA8 167 FE79
Feltham TW14 175 BV85
Gravesend (Nthflt) DA11 191 GF86
Greenhithe DA9 169 FV84
Pierson Rd, Wind. SL4 151 AK82
Pier St, E14 24 D7
Pier Ter, SW18
off Jew's Row 160 DC84
Pier Wk, Grays RM17 170 GA80
Pier Way, SE28 165 ER76
Pigeonhouse La, Couls. CR5 250 DC125
Pigeon La, Hmptn. TW12 176 CA91
Piggotts End, Amer. HP7 55 AP40
Piggotts Orchard, Amer.
HP7 55 AP40
Piggs Cor, Grays RM17 170 GC76
Piggy La, Rick. (Chorl.) WD3 73 BB44
Pigott St, E14 13 N8
Pike Cl, Brom. BR1 184 EH92
Uxbridge UB10 134 BM67
Pike La, Upmin. RM14 129 FT64
Pike Rd, NW7
off Ellesmere Av 96 CR49
Pikes End, Pnr. HA5 115 BV56
Pikes Hill, Epsom KT17 216 CS113
Pikestone Cl, Hayes UB4
off Berrydale Rd 136 BY70
Pike Way, Epp. (N.Wld Bas.)
CM16 70 FA27
Pilgrimage St, SE1 21 J4
Pilgrim Cl, Mord. SM4 200 DB101
St. Albans (Park St) AL2 60 CC27
Pilgrim Hill, SE27 182 DQ91
Orpington BR5 206 EY96
Pilgrims Cl, N13 99 DM49
Brentwood (Pilg.Hat.)
CM15 108 FT43
Dorking (Westh.) RH5 246 CG131
Guildford (Shere) GU5 260 BN139
Northolt UB5 116 CC64

⊖ London Underground station DLR Docklands Light Railway station Tra Tramlink station Riv Pedestrian ferry landing stage

Pilgrims Cl, Wat. WD25
off Kytes Dr 60 BX33
Pilgrims Ct, SE3 164 EG81
Dartford DA1 188 FN85
PILGRIM'S HATCH, Brwd.
CM15 108 FU42
Pilgrim's La, NW3 120 DD63
Pilgrims La, Cat. CR3 251 DM125
Grays (N.Stfd) RM16 149 FW74
Oxted (Titsey) RH8 254 EH125
Westerham TN16 238 EL123
Pilgrims Ms, E14
off Blackwall Way 143 EC73
Pilgrims Pl, NW3
off Hampstead High St 120 DD63
Reigate RH2 250 DA132
Pilgrims Ri, Barn. EN4 80 DE43
Pilgrims Rd, Swans. DA10 170 FY84
Pilgrim St, EC4 10 E8
Pilgrims Vw, Green. DA9 189 FW86
Pilgrims Way, E6
off High St N 144 EL67
N19 121 DK60
Pilgrims' Way, Bet. RH3 249 CY131
Caterham CR3 251 DN126
Pilgrims Way, Dart. DA1 188 FN88
Pilgrims' Way, Dor. RH4 247 CE134
Pilgrims Way, Dor. (Westh.)
RH5 247 CH131
Guildford GU4 258 AX138
Pilgrims' Way, Guil. (Albury)
GU5 260 BK138
Pilgrims Way, Guil. (Shere)
GU5 260 BN139
Pilgrims' Way, Red. RH1 251 DJ127
Pilgrims Way, Reig. RH2 250 DA131
Sevenoaks (Chev.) TN14 240 EV121
South Croydon CR2 220 DT106
Pilgrim's Way, Wem. HA9 118 CP60
Pilgrims Way, West. TN16 239 EM123
Sch **Pilgrims' Way Prim Sch**,
SE15 *off Manor Gro* 162 DW79
Pilgrims Way W, Sev. (Otford)
TN14 241 FD116
Pilkington Rd, SE15 162 DV82
Orpington BR6 205 EQ103
Pilkingtons, Harl. CM17 52 EX15
Pillions La, Hayes UB4 135 BR70
Pilot Cl, SE8 163 DZ79
Pilots Pl, Grav. DA12 191 GJ86
Pilsdon Cl, SW19
off Inner Pk Rd 179 CX88
Piltdown Rd, Wat. WD19 94 BX49
Pilton Est, The, Croy.
(Pitlake) CR0 *off Pitlake* 201 DP103
Pilton Pl, SE17 21 H9
Pimento Ct, W5 *off Olive Rd* 157 CK76
PIMLICO, SW1 19 J9
⊖ **Pimlico** 19 L9
Pimlico Rd, SW1 18 E9
Sch **Pimlico Sch**, SW1 19 K10
Pimlico Wk, N1 11 L1
Pimms Cl, Guil. GU4 243 BA130
Pimpernel Way, Rom. RM3 106 FK51
Pinceybrook Rd, Harl. CM18 51 EQ19
Pinchbeck Rd, Orp. BR6 223 ET107
Pinchfield, Rick. (Map.Cr.)
WD3 91 BE50
Pinchin St, E1 12 B9
Pincott La, Lthd. KT24 245 BP129
Pincott Pl, SE4 163 DX84
Pincott Rd, SW19 180 DC94
Bexleyheath DA6 186 FA85
Pindar Rd, Hodd. EN11 49 EC16
Pindar St, EC2 11 L5
PINDEN, Dart. DA2 209 FW96
Pindock Ms, W9 7 K4
Pineapple Ct, SW1 19 J5
Pineapple Rd, Amer. HP7 72 AT39
Pine Av, E15 123 ED64
Gravesend DA12 191 GK88
West Wickham BR4 203 EB102
Pine Cl, E10 *off Walnut Rd* 123 EB61
N14 99 DJ45
N19 *off Hargrave Pk* 121 DJ61
SE20 202 DW95
Addlestone (New Haw)
KT15 212 BH111
Berkhamsted HP4 38 AV19
Kenley CR8 236 DR117
Stanmore HA7 95 CH49
Swanley BR8 207 FF98
Waltham Cross (Chsht)
EN8 67 DX28
Woking GU21 226 AW117
Pine Coombe, Croy. CR0 221 DX105
Pine Ct, Upmin. RM14 128 FN63
Pine Cres, Brwd. (Hutt.)
CM13 109 GD43
Carshalton SM5 218 DD111
Pinecrest Gdns, Orp. BR6 223 EP105
Pinecroft, Brwd. (Hutt.)
CM13 109 GB45
Hemel Hempstead HP3 40 BM24
Romford (Gidea Pk) RM2 128 FJ56
Pinecroft Cres, Barn. EN5
off Hillside Gdns 79 CY42
Pine Dean, Lthd. (Bkhm)
KT23 246 CB125
Pinedene, SE15
off Meeting Ho La 162 DV81
Pinefield Cl, E14 13 N9
Pine Gdns, Horl. RH6 268 DG149
Ruislip HA4 115 BV60
Surbiton KT5 198 CN100
Pine Glade, Orp. BR6 223 EM105
Pine Gro, N4 121 DL61
N20 97 CZ46
SW19 179 CZ92
Bushey WD23 76 BZ40
Hatfield (Brook.Pk) AL9 64 DB25
St. Albans (Brick.Wd) AL2 60 BZ30
Weybridge KT13 213 BP106
Pine Gro Ms, Wey. KT13 213 BQ106
Pine Hill, Epsom KT18 232 CR115
Pinehurst, Sev. TN14 257 FL121
Pinehurst Cl, Abb.L. WD5 59 BS32
Tadworth (Kgswd) KT20 234 DA122
Pinehurst Wk, Orp. BR6 205 ES102
Pinelands Cl, SE3
off St. John's Pk 164 EF80
Pinel Cl, Vir.W. GU25 192 AY98
Pinemartin Cl, NW2 119 CW62
Pine Ms, NW10
off Clifford Gdns 139 CX68
Pineneedle La, Sev. TN13 257 FH123
Pine Pl, Bans. SM7 217 CX114
Hayes UB4 135 BT70
Pine Ridge, Cars. SM5 218 DG109
Pine Rd, N11 98 DG47
NW2 119 CW63
Woking GU22 226 AW120
Pines, The, N14 81 DJ43
Borehamwood WD6
off Anthony Rd 78 CM40
Coulsdon CR5 235 DH118
Dorking RH4 *off South Ter* 263 CH137
Hemel Hempstead HP3 39 BF24
Purley CR8 219 DP113
Sunbury-on-Thames
TW16 195 BU97
Woking GU21 211 AZ114
Woodford Green IG8 102 EG48
Pines Av, Enf. EN1 82 DV36
Pines Cl, Amer. HP6 55 AP36
Northwood HA6 93 BS51
Sch **Pines JMI & Nurs Sch**,
The, Hert. SG13
off Divot Pl 32 DV08
Pines Rd, Brom. BR1 204 EL96
Pine St, EC1 10 C3
Pinetree Cl, Ger.Cr.
(Chal.St.P.) SL9 90 AW52
Pine Tree Cl, Hem.H. HP2
off Christchurch Rd 40 BK19
Hounslow TW5 155 BV81
Pinetree Gdns, Hem.H. HP3 40 BL22
Pine Tree Hill, Wok. GU22 227 BD116
Pine Trees Dr, Uxb. UB10 114 BL63
Pine Vw Cl, Guil. (Chilw.)
GU4 259 BF140
Pine Vw Manor, Epp. CM16 70 EU30
Pine Wk, Bans. SM7 234 DF117
Bromley BR1 204 EJ95
Carshalton SM5 218 DD110
Caterham CR3 236 DT122
Cobham KT11 214 BX114
Pinewalk, Lthd. (Bkhm)
KT23 246 CB125
Pine Wk, Lthd. (E.Hors.)
KT24 245 BT128
Surbiton KT5 198 CN100
Pine Way, Egh. (Eng.Grn)
TW20 *off Ashwood Rd* 172 AV93
Pine Wd, Sun. TW16 195 BU95
Pinewood, Welw.G.C. AL7 29 CY11
Pinewood Av, Add.
(New Haw) KT15 212 BJ109
Pinner HA5 94 CB51
Rainham RM13 147 FH70
Sevenoaks TN14 257 FK121
Sidcup DA15 185 ES88
Uxbridge UB8 134 BM72
Pinewood Cl, Borwd. WD6 78 CR39
Croydon CR0 203 DY104
Gerrards Cross SL9
off Dukes Wd Av 112 AY59
Harlow CM17 52 EW16
Iver SL0 133 BC66
Northwood HA6 93 BV50
Orpington BR6 205 ER102
Pinner HA5 94 CB51
St. Albans AL4 43 CJ20
Watford WD17 75 BU39
Woking GU21 211 BA114
Pinewood Dr, Orp. BR6 223 ES106
Potters Bar EN6 63 CZ31
Staines TW18
off Cotswold Cl 174 BG92
Pinewood Gdns, Hem.H.
HP1 40 BH20
Pinewood Grn, Iver SL0 133 BC66
Pinewood Gro, W5 137 CJ72
Addlestone (New Haw)
KT15 212 BH110
Pinewood Ms, Stai. (Stanw.)
TW19 174 BK86
Pinewood Pk, Add.
(New Haw) KT15 212 BH111
Pinewood Pl, Dart. DA2 187 FE89
Sch **Pinewood Prim Sch**, Rom.
RM5 *off Thistledene Av* 105 FB50
Pinewood Ride, Iver SL0 133 BA68
Slough SL3 133 BA68
Pinewood Rd, SE2 166 EX79
Bromley BR2 204 EG98
Feltham TW13 175 BV90
Iver SL0 133 BB67
Romford (Hav.at.Bow.)
RM4 105 FC49
Virginia Water GU25 192 AU98
Sch **Pinewood Sch**, Ware
SG12 *off Hoe La* 33 DX08
Pinewood Way, Brwd. (Hutt.)
CM13 109 GD43
Pinfold Rd, SW16 181 DL91
Bushey WD23 76 BZ40
Pinglestone Cl, West Dr.
UB7 154 BL80
Pinkcoat Cl, Felt. TW13
off Tanglewood Way 175 BV90
Pinkerton Pl, SW16
off Riggindale Rd 181 DK91
Pinkham Way, N11 98 DG52
Pink La, Slou. (Burn.) SL1 130 AH68
Pinkneys Ct, Maid. (Taplow)
SL6 130 AG72
Pinks Hill, Swan. BR8 207 FE99
Coll **Pinkwell Adult Ed Cen**,
Hayes UB3
off Pinkwell La 155 BR77
Pinkwell Av, Hayes UB3 155 BR77
Sch **Pinkwell Inf Sch**, Hayes
UB3 *off Pinkwell La* 155 BQ77
Sch **Pinkwell Jun Sch**, Hayes
UB3 *off Pinkwell La* 155 BQ77
Pinkwell La, Hayes UB3 155 BQ77
Pinley Gdns, Dag. RM9
off Stamford Rd 146 EV67
Pinnacle Hill, Bexh. DA7 167 FB84
Pinnacle Hill N, Bexh. DA7 167 FB83
PINNACLES, Harl. CM19 51 EN15
Pinnacles, Wal.Abb. EN9 68 EE34
Pinnate Pl, Welw.G.C. AL7 29 CY13
Pinn Cl, Uxb. UB8
off High Rd 134 BK72
Pinnell Rd, SE9 164 EK84
PINNER, HA5 116 BY56
⊖ **Pinner** 116 BY56
Pinner Ct, Pnr. HA5 116 CA56
PINNER GREEN, Pnr. HA5 94 BW53
Pinner Grn, Pnr. HA5 94 BW54
Pinner Gro, Pnr. HA5 116 BY56
Pinner Hill, Pnr. HA5 94 BW53
Pinner Hill Rd, Pnr. HA5 94 BW54
Pinner Pk, Pnr. HA5 94 CA53
Pinner Pk Av, Har. HA2 116 CB55
Sch **Pinner Pk First Sch**, Pnr.
HA5 *off Melbourne Av* 116 CB55
Pinner Pk Gdns, Har. HA2 94 CC54
Sch **Pinner Pk Mid Sch**, Pnr.
HA5 *off Melbourne Av* 116 CB55
Pinner Rd, Har. HA1, HA2 116 CB57
Northwood HA6 93 BT53
Pinner Rd, Pnr. HA5 116 BZ56
Watford WD19 76 BX44
Pinner Vw, Har. HA1, HA2 116 CC58
Sch **Pinner Wd First Sch**, Pnr.
HA5 *off Latimer Gdns* 94 BW53
Sch **Pinner Wd Mid Sch**, Pnr.
HA5 *off Latimer Gdns* 94 BW53
PINNERWOOD PARK, Pnr.
HA5 94 BW52
Pinnocks Av, Grav. DA11 191 GH88
Pinn Way, Ruis. HA4 115 BS59
Pinstone Way, Ger.Cr. SL9 113 BB61
Pintail Cl, E6 *off Swan App* 144 EL71
Pintail Rd, Wdf.Grn. IG8 102 EH52
Pintail Way, Hayes UB4 136 BX71
Pinter Ho, SW9
off Grantham Rd 161 DL82
Pinto Cl, Borwd. WD6
off Percheron Rd 78 CR44
Pinto Way, SE3 164 EH84
Pioneer Pl, Croy. CR0 221 EA109
Pioneers Ind Pk, Croy. CR0 201 DL102
Pioneer St, SE15 162 DU81
Pioneer Way, W12
off Du Cane Rd 139 CV72
Swanley BR8 207 FE97
Watford WD18 75 BT44
Piper Cl, N7 4 A3
Piper Rd, Kings.T. KT1 198 CN97
Pipers Cl, Cob. KT11 230 BX115
Slough (Burn.) SL1 130 AJ69
Pipers End, Hert. SG14 31 DJ13
Virginia Water GU25 192 AX97
Piper's Gdns, Croy. CR0 203 DY101
Pipers Grn, NW9 118 CQ57
Pipers Grn La, Edg. HA8 96 CL48
Pipewell Rd, Cars. SM5 200 DE100
Pippbrook, Dor. RH4 263 CH135
Pippbrook Gdns, Dor. RH4
off London Rd 263 CH135
Pippens, Welw.G.C. AL8 29 CY06
Pippin Cl, NW2 119 CV62
Croydon CR0 203 DZ102
Radlett (Shenley) WD7 61 CK33
Pippins, The, Slou. SL3
off Pickford Dr 133 AZ74
Watford WD25 60 BW34
Pippins Cl, West Dr. UB7 154 BK76
Pippins Ct, Ashf. TW15 175 BP93
Sch **Pippins Sch**, Slou. SL3
off Raymond Cl 153 BF81
Piquet Rd, SE20 202 DW96
Pirbright Cres, Croy.
(New Adgtn) CR0 221 EC107
Pirbright Rd, SW18 179 CZ88
Pirie Cl, SE5
off Denmark Hill 162 DR83
Pirie St, E16 25 P2
Pirrip Cl, Grav. DA12 191 GM89
Pirton Cl, St.Alb. AL4 43 CJ15
Pishiobury Dr, Saw. CM21 36 EW07
Pishiobury Ms, Saw. CM21 36 EX08
Pitcairn Cl, Rom. RM7 126 FA56
Pitcairn Rd, Mitch. CR4 180 DF94
Pitcairn's Path, Har. HA2
off Eastcote Rd 116 CC62
Pitchfont La, Oxt. RH8 238 EF124
Pitchford St, E15 143 ED66
PITCH PLACE, Guil. GU3 242 AT129
Pitch Pond Cl, Beac.
(Knot.Grn) HP9 88 AH50
Pit Fm Rd, Guil. GU1 243 BA134
Pitfield Cres, SE28 146 EU74
Pitfield Est, N1 11 K1
Pitfield St, N1 11 L2
Pitfield Way, NW10 138 CQ65
Enfield EN3 82 DW39
Pitfold Cl, SE12 184 EG86
Pitfold Rd, SE12 184 EG86
Pitlake, Croy. CR0 201 DP103
Pitman Ho, SE8
off Tanners Hill 163 EA81
Pitman St, SE5 162 DQ80
Pitmaston Ho, SE13
off Lewisham Rd 163 EC82
Pitmaston Rd, SE13
off Morden Hill 163 EC82
Pitsea Pl, E1 13 H8
Pitsea St, E1 13 H8
Pitsfield, Welw.G.C. AL8 29 CX06
Pitshanger La, W5 137 CH70
★ **Pitshanger Manor & Gall**,
W5 137 CJ74
Pitshanger Pk, W13 137 CJ69
Pitson Cl, Add. KT15 212 BK105
Pitstone Cl, St.Alb. AL4
off Highview Gdns 43 CJ15
Pitt Cres, SW19 180 DB91
Pitt Dr, St.Alb. AL4 43 CJ23
Pittman Cl, Brwd. (Ingrave)
CM13 109 GC50
Pittman Gdns, Ilf. IG1 125 EQ64
Pittmans Fld, Harl. CM20 35 ET14
Pitt Pl, Epsom KT17 216 CS114
Pitt Rd, Croy. CR0 202 DQ99
Epsom KT17 216 CS114
Orpington BR6 223 EQ105
Thornton Heath CR7 202 DQ99
Pitt's Head Ms, W1 18 F2
Pittsmead Av, Brom. BR2 204 EG101
Pitts Rd, Slou. SL1 131 AQ74
Pitt St, W8 17 H3
Pittville Gdns, SE25 202 DU97
Pittwood, Brwd. (Shenf.)
CM15 109 GA46
Pitwood Grn, Tad. KT20 233 CW120
Pitwood Pk Ind Est, Tad.
KT20 *off Waterfield* 233 CV120
Pix Fm La, Hem.H. HP1 39 BB21
Pixfield Ct, Brom. BR2
off Beckenham La 204 EF96
PIXHAM, Dor. RH4 247 CJ133
Pixham La, Dor. RH4 247 CJ133
Pixholme Gro, Dor. RH4 247 CJ134
Pixies Hill Cres, Hem.H. HP1 39 BF22
Sch **Pixies Hill JMI Sch**, Hem.H.
HP1 *off Hazeldell Rd* 39 BF21
Pixies Hill Rd, Hem.H. HP1 39 BF21
Pixley St, E14 13 M7
Pixton Way, Croy. CR0 221 DY109
Place Fm Av, Orp. BR6 205 ER102
Place Fm Rd, Red. (Bletch.)
RH1 252 DR130
Placehouse La, Couls. CR5 235 DM119
Plackett Way, Slou. SL1 131 AK74
Plain, The, Epp. CM16 70 EV29
Plaines Cl, Slou. SL1 131 AM74
PLAISTOW, E13 15 J1
PLAISTOW, Brom. BR1 184 EF93
⊖ **Plaistow** 144 EF68
Plaistow Gro, E15 144 EF67
Bromley BR1 184 EH94
H **Plaistow Hosp**, E13 144 EJ68
Plaistow La, Brom. BR1 184 EH94
Plaistow Pk Rd, E13 144 EH68
Sch **Plaistow Prim Sch**, E13
off Junction Rd 144 EH68
Plaistow Rd, E13 144 EF67
E15 144 EF67
Plaitford Cl, Rick. WD3 92 BL47
Plane Av, Grav. (Nthflt) DA11 190 GD87
Planes, The, Cher. KT16 194 BJ101
Plane St, SE26 182 DV90
★ **Planetarium**, NW1 8 D4
Plane Tree Cres, Felt. TW13 175 BV90
Plane Tree Wk, N2 120 DD55
SE19 *off Central Hill* 182 DS93
Plantaganet Pl, Wal.Abb.
EN9 67 EB33
Plantagenet Cl, Wor.Pk. KT4 216 CR105
Plantagenet Gdns, Rom.
RM6 126 EX59
Plantagenet Pl, Rom. RM6
off Broomfield Rd 126 EX59
Plantagenet Rd, Barn. EN5 80 DC42
Plantain Gdns, E11
off Hollydown Way 123 ED62
Plantain Pl, SE1 21 J3
Plantation, The, SE3 164 EG82
Plantation Cl, Green. DA9 189 FT86
Plantation Dr, Orp. BR5 206 EX102
Plantation La, Warl. CR6 237 DY119
Plantation Rd, Amer. HP6 55 AS37
Erith DA8 167 FG81
Swanley BR8 187 FG94
Plantation Wk, Hem.H. HP1 40 BG17
Plantation Way, Amer. HP6 55 AS37
Plantation Wf, SW11 160 DC83
Plasel Ct, E13
off Plashet Rd 144 EG67
Sch **Plashet Comp Sch**, E6
off Plashet Gro 144 EK66
Plashet Gdns, Brwd. CM13 109 GA49
Plashet Gro, E6 144 EJ67
Plashet Rd, E13 144 EG67
Plashets, B.Stort. (Sheering)
CM22 37 FC06
Plassy Rd, SE6 183 EB87
Platford Grn, Horn. RM11 128 FL56
Platina St, EC2 11 K3
Plato Rd, SW2 161 DL84
Platt, The, SW15 159 CX83
Amersham HP7 55 AP40
Platt Meadow, Guil. GU4
off Eustace Rd 243 BD131
Platts Av, Wat. WD17 75 BV41
Platt's Eyot, Hmptn. TW12 196 CA96
Platt's La, NW3 120 DA63
Platts Rd, Enf. EN3 82 DW39
Platt St, NW1 141 DK68
Plawsfield Rd, Beck. BR3 203 DX95
Plaxtol Cl, Brom. BR1 204 EJ95
Plaxtol Rd, Erith DA8 166 FA80
Plaxton Ct, E11
off Woodhouse Rd 124 EF62
Playfair St, W6
off Winslow Rd 159 CW78
Playfield Av, Rom. RM5 105 FC53
Playfield Cres, SE22 182 DT85
Playfield Rd, Edg. HA8 96 CQ54
Playford Rd, N4 121 DM61
Playgreen Way, SE6 183 EA91
Playground Cl, Beck. BR3
off Churchfields Rd 203 DX96
Playhouse Ct, SE1
off Southwark Br Rd 162 DQ75
Playhouse Sq, Harl. CM20
off College Gate 51 EQ15
Playhouse Yd, EC4 10 E8
Plaza Par, NW6
off Kilburn High Rd 140 DB68
Plaza Shop Cen, The, W1 9 K7
Plaza W, Houns. TW3 156 CB81
Pleasance, The, SW15 159 CV84
Pleasance Rd, SW15 179 CV85
Orpington BR5 206 EV96
Pleasant Gro, Croy. CR0 203 DZ104
Pleasant Pl, N1 4 F6
Rickmansworth (Map.Cr.)
WD3 91 BE52
Walton-on-Thames KT12 214 BW107
Pleasant Ri, Hat. AL9 45 CW15
Pleasant Row, NW1 141 DH67
Pleasant Vw, Erith DA8 167 FE78
Pleasant Vw Pl, Orp. BR6
off High St 223 EP106
Pleasant Way, Wem. HA0 137 CJ68
Pleasure Pit Rd, Ashtd.
KT21 232 CP118
Plender St, NW1 141 DJ67
Pleshey Rd, N7 121 DK63
Plesman Way, Wall. SM6 219 DL109
Plevna Cres, N15 122 DS58
Plevna Rd, N9 100 DU48
Hampton TW12 196 CB95
Plevna St, E14 24 C5
Pleydell Av, SE19 182 DT94
W6 159 CT77
Pleydell Ct, EC4 10 D8
Pleydell Est, EC1
off Radnor St 142 DQ69
Pleydell St, EC4 10 D8
Plimsoll Cl, E14 14 A8
Plimsoll Rd, N4 121 DN62
Plough Ct, EC3 11 K9
Plough Fm Cl, Ruis. HA4 115 BR58
Plough Hill, Pot.B. (Cuffley)
EN6 65 DL28
Plough Ind Est, Lthd. KT22 231 CG120
Plough La, SE22 182 DT86
SW17 180 DB92
SW19 180 DB92
Berkhamsted (Pott.End)
HP4 39 BB16
Cobham (Down.) KT11 229 BU116
Purley CR8 219 DL109
Rickmansworth (Sarratt)
WD3 57 BF33
Slough (Stoke P.) SL2 132 AV67
Teddington TW11 177 CG92
Uxbridge (Hare.) UB9 92 BJ51
Wallington SM6 219 DL105
Plough La Cl, Wall. SM6 219 DL106
Ploughlees La, Slou. SL1 132 AS73
Ploughmans Cl, NW1
off Crofters Way 141 DK67
Ploughmans End, Islw. TW7 177 CD85
Welwyn Garden City AL7 30 DC10
Ploughmans Wk, N2
off Long La 98 DC54
Plough Ms, SW11
off Plough Ter 160 DD84
Plough Pl, EC4 10 D7
Plough Ri, Upmin. RM14 129 FS59
Plough Rd, SW11 160 DD83
Epsom KT19 216 CR109
Horley (Smallfield) RH6 269 DP148
Plough St, E1 12 A7
Plough Ter, SW11 160 DD84
Plough Way, SE16 23 H7
Plough Yd, EC2 11 M4
Plover Cl, Berk. HP4 38 AW20
Staines TW18
off Waters Dr 173 BF90
Plover Gdns, Upmin. RM14 129 FT60
Plover Way, SE16 23 J5
Hayes UB4 136 BX72
Plowden Bldgs, EC4
off Middle Temple La 141 DN72
Plowman Cl, N18 100 DR50
Plowman Way, Dag. RM8 126 EW60
Ployters Rd, Harl. CM18 51 EQ18
Plumbers Row, E1 12 A6
Plumbridge St, SE10
off Blackheath Hill 163 EC81
Plum Cl, Felt. TW13
off Highfield Rd 175 BU88
Sch **Plumcroft Prim Sch**,
SE18 *off Plum La* 165 EQ79
Plum Garth, Brent. TW8 157 CK77
Plum La, SE18 165 EP80
Plummer La, Mitch. CR4 200 DF96
Plummer Rd, SW4 181 DK87
Plummers Cft, Sev.
(Dunt.Grn) TN13 256 FE121
Plumpton Av, Horn. RM12 128 FL63
Plumpton Cl, Nthlt. UB5 136 CA65
Plumpton Rd, Hodd. EN11 49 EC15
Plumpton Way, Cars. SM5 200 DE104
PLUMSTEAD, SE18 165 ES78
⇌ **Plumstead** 165 ER77
Plumstead Common Rd,
SE18 165 EP79
Plumstead High St, SE18 165 ES77
Sch **Plumstead Manor Sch**,
SE18 *off Old Mill Rd* 165 ER79
Plumstead Rd, SE18 165 EP77
Plumtree Cl, Dag. RM10 147 FB65
Wallington SM6 219 DK108
Plumtree Ct, EC4 10 D7
Plumtree Mead, Loug. IG10 85 EN41
Pluto Cl, Slou. SL1 151 AL75
Pluto Ri, Hem.H. HP2 40 BL18
Plymouth Dr, Sev. TN13 257 FJ124
Plymouth Pk, Sev. TN13 257 FJ124
Plymouth Rd, E16 15 L6
Bromley BR1 204 EH95
Grays (Chaff.Hun.) RM16 169 FW77
Slough SL1 131 AL71
Plymouth Wf, E14 24 E7
Plympton Av, NW6 139 CZ66
Plympton Cl, Belv. DA17
off Halifield Dr 166 EY76
Plympton Pl, NW8 8 A4
Plympton Rd, NW6 139 CZ66
Plympton St, NW8 8 A4
Plymstock Rd, Well. DA16 166 EW80
Pocket Hill, Sev. TN13
off Hopgarden La 256 FG128
Pocketsdell La, Hem.H.
(Bov.) HP3 56 AX28
Pocklington Cl, NW9 96 CS54
Pocock Av, West Dr. UB7 154 BM76
Pococks La, Wind. (Eton)
SL4 152 AS78
Pocock St, SE1 20 E3
Podmore Rd, SW18 160 DC84
Poets Chase, Hem.H. HP1
off Laureate Way 40 BH18
Poets Gate, Wal.Cr. EN7 66 DS28
Poets Rd, N5 5 J1
Poets Way, Har. HA1
off Blawith Rd 117 CE56
Point, The, Ruis. HA4
off Bedford Rd 115 BU63
Pointalls Cl, N3 98 DC54
Point Cl, SE10
off Point Hill 163 EC81
Pointer Cl, SE28 146 EX72
Pointers, The, Ashtd. KT21 232 CL120
Sch **Pointer Sch, The**, SE3
off Stratheden Rd 164 EG80
Pointers Cl, E14 24 A9
Pointers Hill, Dor. (Westc.)
RH4 262 CC138
Pointers Rd, Cob. KT11 229 BQ116
Point Hill, SE10 163 EC80
Point of Thomas Path, E1 12 F10
Point Pl, Wem. HA9 138 CP66
Point Pleasant, SW18 160 DA84
Point Wf La, Brent. TW8
off High St 158 CL79
Poland Ho, E15 143 ED67
Poland St, W1 9 K8
Polayn Garth, Welw.G.C.
AL8 29 CW08
Polebrook Rd, SE3 164 EJ83
Pole Cat All, Brom. BR2 204 EF103
Polecroft La, SE6 183 DZ89
Polehamptons, The, Hmptn.
TW12 *off High St* 176 CC94
Polehanger La, Hem.H. HP1 39 BE18
Pole Hill Rd, E4 101 EC45
Hayes UB4 135 BQ69
Uxbridge UB10 135 BQ69
Pole La, Ong. CM5 53 FE17
Polesden Gdns, SW20 199 CV96
Polesden Lacey, Dor. RH5 246 CA130
★ **Polesden Lacey, Ho &**
Gdn, Dor. RH5 246 CA130
Polesden La, Wok. (Send M.)
GU23 227 BF122
Polesden Rd, Lthd. (Bkhm)
KT23 246 CB129
Polesden Vw, Lthd. (Bkhm)
KT23 246 CB127
Poles Hill, Chesh. HP5 54 AN29
Rickmansworth (Sarratt)
WD3 57 BE33
Polesteeple Hill, West.
(Bigg.H.) TN16 238 EK117
Polesworth Ho, W2 7 H5
Polesworth Rd, Dag. RM9 146 EX66
Polhill, Sev. (Halst.) TN14 241 FC115
Police Sta La, Bushey WD23
off Sparrows Herne 94 CB45
Police Sta Rd, Walt. KT12 214 BW107
★ **Polish Inst & Sikorski Mus**,
SW7 *off Princes Gate* 17 P4
Pollard Av, Uxb. (Denh.) UB9 113 BF58
Pollard Cl, E16 15 L9
N7 4 B1
Chigwell IG7 104 EU50
Windsor (Old Wind.) SL4 172 AV85
Pollard Hatch, Harl. CM19 51 EP18
Pollard Rd, N20 98 DE47
Morden SM4 200 DD99
Woking GU22 227 BB116
Pollard Row, E2 12 B1
Pollards, Rick. (Map.Cr.) WD3 91 BD50
Pollards Cl, Loug. IG10 84 EJ43
Waltham Cross (Chsht)
EN7 66 DQ29
Pollards Cres, SW16 201 DL97
Pollards Hill E, SW16 201 DM97

★ Place of interest | H Hospital | Sch School | Coll College | Uni University | ⇌ Railway station

Pollards Hill N, SW16 ... 201 DL97
Pollards Hill S, SW16 ... 201 DL97
Pollards Hill W, SW16 ... 201 DL97
Pollards Oak Cres, Oxt. RH8 254 EG132
Pollards Oak Rd, Oxt. RH8 . 254 EG132
Pollard St, E2 ... 12 B1
Pollards Wd Hill, Oxt. RH8 . 254 EH130
Pollards Wd Rd, SW16 ... 201 DL96
Oxted RH8 ... 254 EH131
Pollard Wk, Sid. DA14 ... 186 EW93
Pollen St, W1 ... 9 H8
Pollicott Cl, St.Alb. AL4 ... 43 CJ15
Pollitt Dr, NW8 ... 7 N3
★ Pollock's Toy Mus, W1 ... 9 K5
Pollyhaugh, Dart. (Eyns.)
DA4 ... 208 FL104
Polperro Cl, Orp. BR6
off Cotswold Ri ... 205 ET100
Polperro Ms, SE11 ... 20 D7
Polsted Rd, SE6 ... 183 DZ87
Polsten Ms, Enf. EN3
off Martini Dr ... 83 EA37
Polthorne Est, SE18 ... 165 ER77
Polthorne Gro, SE18 ... 165 EQ77
Poltimore Rd, Guil. GU2 ... 258 AU136
Polworth Rd, SW16 ... 181 DL92
Polygon, The, SW4
off Old Town ... 161 DJ84
Polygon Rd, NW1 ... 141 DK68
Polytechnic St, SE18 ... 165 EN77
Pomell Way, E1 ... 11 P7
Pomeroy Cl, Amer. HP7 ... 55 AR40
Pomeroy Cres, Wat. WD24 ... 75 BV36
Pomeroy St, SE14 ... 162 DW81
Pomfret Rd, SE5
off Flaxman Rd ... 161 DP83
Pomoja La, N19 ... 121 DK61
Pompadour Cl, Brwd. CM14
off Queen St ... 108 FW50
Pond Cl, N12
off Summerfields Av ... 98 DE51
SE3 ... 164 EF82
Ashtead KT21 ... 232 CL117
Uxbridge (Hare.) UB9 ... 92 BJ54
Walton-on-Thames KT12 . 213 BU107
Pond Cottage La, W.Wick.
BR4 ... 203 EA102
Pond Cotts, SE21 ... 182 DS88
Pond Cft, Hat. AL10 ... 45 CT18
Pondcroft, Welw.G.C. AL7 ... 29 CZ10
PONDERS END, Enf. EN3 ... 82 DW43
⇌ Ponders End ... 83 DX43
Ponders End Ind Est, Enf.
EN3 ... 83 DZ42
Pond Fm Cl, Tad. KT20 ... 233 CU124
Pond Fld, Welw.G.C. AL7 ... 30 DA06
Pondfield Cres, St.Alb. AL4 ... 43 CH16
Pond Fld End, Loug. IG10 ... 102 EJ45
Pondfield La, Brwd. CM13 ... 109 GA49
Pondfield Rd, Brom. BR2 ... 204 EE102
Dagenham RM10 ... 127 FB64
Godalming GU7 ... 258 AT144
Kenley CR8 ... 235 DP116
Orpington BR6 ... 205 EP104
Pond Grn, Ruis. HA4 ... 115 BS61
Pond Hill Gdns, Sutt. SM3 ... 217 CY107
Pond La, Ger.Cr. (Chal.St.P.)
SL9 ... 90 AV53
Guildford (Peasl.) GU5 ... 261 BQ144
Pond Lees Cl, Dag. RM10
off Leys Av ... 147 FD66
Pond Mead, SE21 ... 182 DR86
Pond Meadow, Guil. GU2 ... 242 AS134
Sch Pond Meadow Sch, Guil.
GU2 off Pond Meadow . 242 AS133
Pond Pk Rd, Chesh. HP5 ... 54 AP29
Pond Path, Chis. BR7
off Heathfield La ... 185 EP93
Pond Piece, Lthd. (Oxshott)
KT22 ... 214 CB114
Pond Pl, SW3 ... 18 A8
Pond Rd, E15 ... 144 EE68
SE3 ... 164 EF82
Egham TW20 ... 173 BC93
Hemel Hempstead HP3 ... 58 BN25
Woking GU22 ... 226 AU120
Ponds, The, Wey. KT13
off Ellesmere Rd ... 213 BS107
Pondside Cl, Hayes UB3
off Providence La ... 155 BR80
Ponds La, Guil. (Alb.Hth)
GU5 ... 260 BL142
Pond Sq, N6 off South Gro . 120 DG60
Pond St, NW3 ... 120 DE64
Pond Wk, Upmin. RM14 ... 129 FS61
Pond Way, Tedd. TW11
off Holmesdale Rd ... 177 CJ93
Pondwicks, Amer. HP7 ... 55 AP39
Pondwicks Cl, St.Alb. AL1 ... 42 CC21
Pondwood Ri, Orp. BR6 ... 205 ES101
Ponler St, E1 ... 12 C8
Ponsard Rd, NW10 ... 139 CV69
Ponsbourne Pk, Hert. SG13 ... 47 DL23
Sch Ponsbourne St. Mary's C of E Prim Sch, Hert. SG13
off Newgate St Village ... 47 DL24
Ponsford St, E9 ... 142 DW65
Ponsonby Pl, SW1 ... 19 M9
Ponsonby Rd, SW15 ... 179 CV87
Ponsonby Ter, SW1 ... 19 M9
Pontefract Rd, Brom. BR1 ... 184 EF92
Pontoise Cl, Sev. TN13 ... 256 FF122
Ponton Rd, SW8 ... 161 DK79
Pont St, SW1 ... 18 C6
Pont St Ms, SW1 ... 18 C6
Pontypool Pl, SE1 ... 20 E3
Pontypool Wk, Rom. RM3 ... 106 FJ51
Pony Chase, Cob. KT11 ... 214 BZ113
Pool Cl, Beck. BR3 ... 183 EA92
West Molesey KT8 ... 196 BZ99
Pool Ct, SE6 ... 183 EA89
Poole Cl, Ruis. HA4
off Chichester Av ... 115 BS61
Poole Ct Rd, Houns. TW4
off Vicarage Fm Rd ... 156 BY82
Poole Ho, Grays RM16 ... 171 GJ75
Pool End Cl, Shep. TW17 ... 194 BN99
Poole Rd, E9 ... 143 DX65
Epsom KT19 ... 216 CR107
Hornchurch RM11 ... 128 FM59
Woking GU21 ... 226 AY117
Pooles Bldgs, EC1 ... 10 C4
Pooles La, SW10 off Lots Rd . 160 DC80
Dagenham RM9 ... 146 EY68
Pooles Pk, N4
off Seven Sisters Rd ... 121 DN61
Sch Pooles Pk Inf & Jun Sch,
N4 off Lennox Rd ... 121 DM61
Poole St, N1 ... 5 J8
Poole Way, Hayes UB4 ... 135 BR69
Pooley Av, Egh. TW20 ... 173 BB92
POOLEY GREEN, Egh. TW20 . 173 BC92
Pooley Grn Cl, Egh. TW20 ... 173 BB92
Pooley Grn Rd, Egh. TW20 ... 173 BB92
Pooleys La, Hat. AL9 ... 45 CV23
Pool Gro, Croy. CR0 ... 221 DY112
Pool La, Slou. SL1 ... 132 AS73
Poolmans Rd, Wind. SL4 ... 151 AK83
Poolmans St, SE16 ... 22 G3
Pool Rd, Har. HA1 ... 117 CD59
West Molesey KT8 ... 196 BZ100
Poolsford Rd, NW9 ... 118 CS56
Poonah St, E1 ... 12 F8
Pootings Rd, Eden.
(Crock.H.) TN8 ... 255 ER134
Pope Cl, SW19 ... 180 DD93
Feltham TW14 ... 175 BT88
Sch Pope John RC Prim Sch,
W12
off Commonwealth Av ... 139 CV73
Sch Pope Paul RC Prim Sch,
Pot.B. EN6 off Baker St ... 63 CZ33
Pope Rd, Brom. BR2 ... 204 EK99
Popes Av, Twick. TW2 ... 177 CE89
Popes Cl, Amer. HP6 ... 72 AT37
Slough (Colnbr.) SL3 ... 153 BB80
Popes Dr, N3 ... 98 DA53
Popes Gro, Croy. CR0 ... 203 DZ104
Twickenham TW1, TW2 ... 177 CF89
Pope's Head All, EC3
off Cornhill ... 142 DR72
Popes La, W5 ... 157 CK76
Oxted RH8 ... 254 EE134
Watford WD24 ... 75 BV37
Popes Rd, SW9 ... 161 DN83
Abbots Langley WD5 ... 59 BS31
Pope St, SE1 ... 21 M4
Popham Cl, Felt. TW13 ... 176 BZ90
Popham Gdns, Rich. TW9
off Lower Richmond Rd . 158 CN83
Popham Rd, N1 ... 4 G8
Popham St, N1 ... 4 F7
POPLAR, E14 ... 24 A1
DLR Poplar ... 14 A10
Poplar Av, Amer. HP7 ... 72 AT39
Gravesend DA12 ... 191 GJ91
Leatherhead KT22 ... 231 CH122
Mitcham CR4 ... 200 DF95
Orpington BR6 ... 205 EP103
Southall UB2 ... 156 CB76
West Drayton UB7 ... 134 BM73
Poplar Bath St, E14 ... 14 B9
Poplar Business Pk, E14 ... 14 C10
Poplar Cl, E9
off Lee Conservancy Rd . 123 DZ64
Chesham HP5 ... 54 AQ28
Pinner HA5 ... 94 BX53
Slough (Colnbr.) SL3 ... 153 BE81
South Ockendon RM15 ... 149 FX70
Poplar Ct, SW19 ... 180 DA92
Poplar Cres, Epsom KT19 ... 216 CQ107
Poplar Dr, Bans. SM7 ... 217 CX114
Brentwood (Hutt.) CM13 ... 109 GC44
Poplar Fm Cl, Epsom KT19 . 216 CQ107
Poplar Gdns, N.Mal. KT3 ... 198 CR96
Poplar Gro, N11 ... 98 DG51
W6 ... 159 CW75
New Malden KT3 ... 198 CR97
Wembley HA9 ... 118 CQ62
Woking GU22 ... 226 AY119
Poplar High St, E14 ... 14 A9
Poplar Mt, Belv. DA17 ... 167 FB77
Poplar Pl, SE28 ... 146 EW73
W2 ... 7 J9
Hayes UB3
off Central Av ... 135 BU73
Sch Poplar Prim Sch,
SW19 off Poplar Rd S ... 200 DA97
Poplar Rd, SE24 ... 162 DQ84
SW19 ... 200 DA96
Ashford TW15 ... 175 BQ92
Guildford (Shalf.) GU4 ... 258 AY141
High Wycombe HP10
off Glory Mill La ... 110 AE56
Leatherhead KT22 ... 231 CH122
Sutton SM3 ... 199 CZ102
Uxbridge (Denh.) UB9 ... 114 BJ64
Poplar Rd S, SW19 ... 200 DA97
Poplar Row, Epp. (They.B.)
CM16 ... 85 ES37
Poplars, Welw.G.C. AL7 ... 30 DB08
Poplars, The, N14 ... 81 DH43
Gravesend DA12 ... 191 GL87
Hemel Hempstead HP1 ... 40 BH21
Romford (Abridge) RM4
off Hoe La ... 86 EV41
St. Albans AL1 ... 43 CH24
Waltham Cross (Chsht)
EN7 ... 66 DS26
Poplars Av, NW10 ... 139 CW65
Hatfield AL10 ... 44 CR18
Poplars Cl, Hat. AL10 ... 44 CQ18
Ruislip HA4 ... 115 BS60
Watford WD25 ... 59 BV32
Poplar Shaw, Wal.Abb. EN9 . 68 EF33
Poplars Rd, E17 ... 123 EB58
Poplar St, Rom. RM7 ... 127 FC56
Poplar Vw, Wem. HA9
off Magnet Rd ... 117 CK61
Poplar Wk, SE24 ... 162 DQ84
Caterham CR3 ... 236 DS123
Croydon CR0 ... 202 DQ103
Poplar Way, Felt. TW13 ... 175 BU90
Ilford IG6 ... 125 EQ56
Poppins Ct, EC4 ... 10 E8
Poppleton Rd, E11 ... 124 EE58
Poppy Cl, Belv. DA17 ... 167 FB76
Brentwood (Pilg.Hat.)
CM15 ... 108 FV43
Hemel Hempstead HP1 ... 39 BE19
Northolt UB5 ... 136 BZ65
Wallington SM6 ... 200 DG102
★ Poppy Factory Mus, The,
Rich. TW10 ... 177 CK86
Poppyfields, Welw.G.C. AL7 ... 30 DC09
Poppy La, Croy. CR0 ... 202 DW101
Poppy Wk, Hat. AL9 ... 45 CT15
Waltham Cross EN7 ... 66 DR28
Porchester Cl, SE5 ... 162 DQ84
Hornchurch RM11 ... 128 FL58
Porchester Gdns, W2 ... 7 J9
Porchester Gdns Ms, W2 ... 7 K8
Porchester Mead, Beck. BR3 . 183 EB93
Porchester Ms, W2 ... 7 K7
Porchester Pl, W2 ... 8 B8
Porchester Rd, W2 ... 7 J7
Kingston upon Thames
KT1 ... 198 CP96
Porchester Sq, W2 ... 7 K7
Porchester Ter, W2 ... 7 L8
Porchester Ter N, W2 ... 7 K7
Porchfield Cl, Grav. DA12 ... 191 GJ89
Sutton SM2 ... 218 DB110
Porch Way, N20 ... 98 DF48
Porcupine Cl, SE9 ... 184 EL89
Porden Rd, SW2 ... 161 DM84
Porlock Av, Har. HA2 ... 116 CC60
Porlock Rd, W10 ... 6 B4
Enfield EN1 ... 100 DT45
Porlock St, SE1 ... 21 J3
Porridge Pot All, Guil. GU2
off Bury Flds ... 258 AW136
Porrington Cl, Chis. BR7 ... 205 EM95
Portal Cl, SE27 ... 181 DN90
Ruislip HA4 ... 115 BU63
Uxbridge UB10 ... 134 BL66
Port Av, Green. DA9 ... 189 FV86
Portbury Cl, SE15
off Clayton Rd ... 162 DU81
Port Cres, E13 ... 15 N4
★ Portcullis Ho, SW1 ... 19 N3
Portcullis Lo Rd, Enf. EN2 ... 82 DR41
Portelet Ct, N1 ... 5 K7
Portelet Rd, E1 ... 12 G2
Porten Rd, W14 ... 16 C6
Porter Cl, Grays RM20 ... 169 FW79
Porter Rd, E6 ... 145 EM72
Porters Av, Dag. RM8, RM9 . 146 EV65
Porters Cl, Brwd. CM14 ... 108 FU46
Portersfield Rd, Enf. EN1 ... 82 DS42
Porters Pk Dr, Rad.
(Shenley) WD7 ... 61 CK33
Porter Sq, N19
off Hornsey Rd ... 121 DL60
Porter St, SE1 ... 21 H1
W1 ... 8 D5
Porters Wk, E1 ... 12 D10
Porters Way, West Dr. UB7 ... 154 BM76
Porters Wd, St.Alb. AL3 ... 43 CE16
Porteus Rd, W2 ... 7 M6
Portgate Cl, W9 ... 6 F3
Porthallow Cl, Orp. BR6
off Sevenoaks Rd ... 223 ET105
Porthcawe Rd, SE26 ... 183 DY91
Port Hill, Hert. SG14 ... 32 DQ09
Orpington BR6 ... 224 EV112
Porthkerry Av, Well. DA16 ... 166 EU84
Portia Way, E3 ... 13 L4
Portinscale Rd, SW15 ... 179 CY85
Portland Av, N16 ... 122 DT59
Gravesend DA12 ... 191 GH89
New Malden KT3 ... 199 CT101
Sidcup DA15 ... 186 EU86
Portland Cl, Rom. RM6 ... 126 EY57
Slough SL2 ... 131 AK70
Worcester Park KT4 ... 199 CV101
Portland Cres, SE9 ... 184 EL89
Feltham TW13 ... 175 BR91
Greenford UB6 ... 136 CB70
Stanmore HA7 ... 95 CK54
Portland Dr, Enf. EN2 ... 82 DS38
Redhill RH1 ... 251 DK129
Waltham Cross (Chsht)
EN7 ... 66 DU31
Portland Gdns, N4 ... 121 DP58
Romford RM6 ... 126 EX57
Portland Gro, SW8 ... 161 DM81
Portland Hts, Nthwd. HA6 ... 93 BT49
H Portland Hosp for Women
& Children, The, W1 ... 9 H4
Portland Ho, Red. RH1 ... 251 DK129
Portland Ms, W1 ... 9 K8
Portland Pk, Ger.Cr. SL9 ... 112 AX58
Portland Pl, W1 ... 9 H6
Epsom KT17 ... 216 CS112
Hertford (Hert.Hth) SG13 ... 32 DW11
Portland Ri, N4 ... 121 DP60
Portland Ri Est, N4 ... 122 DQ60
Portland Rd, N15 ... 122 DT56
SE9 ... 184 EL89
SE25 ... 202 DU98
W11 ... 16 D1
Ashford TW15 ... 174 BL90
Bromley BR1 ... 184 EJ91
Dorking RH4 ... 263 CG135
Gravesend DA12 ... 191 GH88
Hayes UB4 ... 135 BS69
Kingston upon Thames
KT1 ... 198 CL97
Mitcham CR4 ... 200 DE96
Southall UB2 ... 156 BZ76
Portland Sq, E1 ... 22 C1
Portland St, SE17 ... 21 J9
St. Albans AL3 ... 42 CC20
Portland Ter, Rich. TW9 ... 157 CK84
Portland Wk, SE17
off Portland St ... 162 DR79
Portley La, Cat. CR3 ... 236 DS121
Portley Wd Rd, Whyt. CR3 ... 236 DT120
Portman Av, SW14 ... 158 CR83
Portman Cl, W1 ... 8 D7
Bexley DA5 ... 187 FE88
Bexleyheath DA7
off Queen Anne's Gate ... 166 EX83
St. Albans AL4 ... 43 CJ15
Portman Dr, Wdf.Grn. IG8 ... 102 EK54
Portman Gdns, NW9 ... 96 CR54
Uxbridge UB10 ... 134 BN66
Portman Gate, NW1 ... 8 B4
Portman Hall, Har. HA3 ... 95 CD49
Portman Ho, St.Alb. AL3 ... 43 CD17
Portman Ms S, W1 ... 8 E8
Portman Pl, E2 ... 12 F2
Portman Rd, Kings.T. KT1 ... 198 CM96
Portman Sq, W1 ... 8 D7
Portman St, W1 ... 8 E8
Portmeadow Wk, SE2 ... 166 EX75
Portmeers Cl, E17
off Lennox Rd ... 123 DZ58
Portmore Gdns, Rom. RM5 . 104 FA50
Portmore Pk Rd, Wey. KT13 . 212 BN105
Portmore Quays, Wey.
KT13 off Weybridge Rd . 212 BM105
Portmore Way, Wey. KT13 ... 194 BN104
Portnall Dr, Vir.W. GU25 ... 192 AT99
Portnall Ri, Vir.W. GU25 ... 192 AT99
Portnall Rd, W9 ... 6 E3
Virginia Water GU25 ... 192 AT99
Portnalls Cl, Couls. CR5 ... 235 DH116
Portnalls Ri, Couls. CR5 ... 235 DH116
Portnalls Rd, Couls. CR5 ... 235 DH118
Portnoi Cl, Rom. RM1 ... 105 FD54
Portobello Cl, Chesh. HP5 ... 54 AN29
Portobello Ct, W11 ... 6 F8
Portobello Ms, W11 ... 6 G10
Portobello Rd, W10 ... 6 E7
W11 ... 6 F9
Porton Ct, Surb. KT6 ... 197 CJ100
Portpool La, EC1 ... 10 C5
Portree Cl, N22
off Nightingale Rd ... 99 DM52
Portree St, E14 ... 14 F7
Portsdown, Edg. HA8
off Rectory La ... 96 CN50
Portsdown Av, NW11 ... 119 CZ58
Portsdown Ms, NW11 ... 119 CZ58
Portsea Ms, W2 ... 8 B8
Portsea Pl, W2 ... 8 B8
Portsea Rd, Til. RM18 ... 171 GJ81
Portslade Rd, SW8 ... 161 DJ82
Portsmouth Av, T.Ditt. KT7 ... 197 CG101
Portsmouth Ct, Slou. SL1 ... 132 AS73
Portsmouth Ms, E16 ... 25 P1
Portsmouth Rd, SW15 ... 179 CV87
Cobham KT11 ... 213 BU114
Portsmouth Rd, Esher KT10 . 214 CC105
Guildford GU2, GU3 ... 258 AW138
Kingston upon Thames
KT1 ... 197 CJ99
Surbiton KT6 ... 197 CJ99
Thames Ditton KT7 ... 197 CE103
Woking (Ripley) GU23 ... 228 BM119
Portsmouth St, WC2 ... 10 A8
Portsoken St, E1 ... 11 N9
Portugal Gdns, Twick. TW2
off Fulwell Pk Av ... 176 CC89
Portugal Rd, Wok. GU21 ... 227 BA116
Portugal St, WC2 ... 10 A8
Port Vale, Hert. SG14 ... 31 DP08
Portway, E15 ... 144 EF67
Epsom KT17 ... 217 CU110
Rainham RM13 ... 147 FG67
Portway Cres, Epsom KT17 . 217 CU109
Portway Gdns, SE18
off Shooter's Hill Rd ... 164 EK80
Sch Portway Prim Sch,
E15 off Park Rd ... 144 EG67
Postern Grn, Enf. EN2 ... 81 DN40
Postfield, Welw.G.C. AL7 ... 30 DA06
Post Ho La, Lthd. (Bkhm)
KT23 ... 246 CA125
Post La, Twick. TW2 ... 177 CD88
Post Meadow, Iver SL0 ... 133 BD69
Postmill Cl, Croy. CR0 ... 203 DX104
Post Office App, E7 ... 124 EH64
Post Office Ct, EC3 ... 11 K8
Post Office La, Beac. HP9 ... 89 AK52
Slough (Geo.Grn) SL3 ... 132 AX72
Post Office Rd, Harl. CM20 ... 35 EQ14
Post Office Row, Oxt. RH8 ... 254 EL131
Post Office Wk, Harl. CM20 ... 35 ER14
Post Office Way, SW8 ... 161 DK80
Post Rd, Sthl. UB2 ... 156 CB76
Postway Ms, Ilf. IG1
off Clements Rd ... 125 EP62
Postwood Grn, Hert.
(Hert.Hth) SG13 ... 32 DW12
Post Wd Rd, Ware SG12 ... 33 DY08
Potier St, SE1 ... 21 K6
Potkiln La, Beac. (Jordans)
HP9 ... 111 AQ55
POTTEN END, Berk. HP4 ... 39 BC16
Sch Potten End First Sch,
Berk. HP4 off Church Rd ... 39 BB17
Potten End Hill, Berk.
(Pott.End) HP4 ... 39 BD16
Hemel Hempstead HP1 ... 39 BD16
Porter Cl, Mitch. CR4 ... 201 DH96
Potterells, Hat. (N.Mymms)
AL9 ... 63 CX25
Potteries, The, Cher. KT16 ... 211 BE107
Potterne Cl, SW19 ... 179 CX87
POTTERS BAR, EN6 ... 64 DA32
⇌ Potters Bar ... 64 DA32
H Potters Bar Comm Hosp,
Pot.B. EN6 ... 64 DC34
★ Potters Bar Mus, The
Wyllyotts Cen, Pot.B.
EN6 ... 63 CZ32
Potters Cl, Croy. CR0 ... 203 DY102
Loughton IG10 ... 84 EL40
Potters Ct, Pot.B. EN6 ... 64 DA32
Potters Cross, Iver SL0 ... 133 BE69
POTTERS CROUCH, St.Alb.
AL2 ... 60 BX25
Potters Fld, Harl. CM17 ... 52 EX17
St. Albans AL3 ... 43 CE16
Potters Flds, SE1 ... 21 M2
Potters Gro, N.Mal. KT3 ... 198 CQ98
Potters Hts Cl, Pnr. HA5 ... 93 BV52
Potters La, SW16 ... 181 DK93
Barnet EN5 ... 80 DA42
Borehamwood WD6 ... 78 CQ39
Woking (Send) GU23 ... 227 BB123
Potters Ms, Borwd. (Elstree)
WD6
off Elstree Hill N ... 77 CK44
Potters Rd, SW6 ... 160 DC82
Barnet EN5 ... 80 DB42
POTTER STREET, Harl.
CM17 ... 52 EW17
Potter St, Harl. CM17 ... 52 EW16
Northwood HA6 ... 93 BU53
Pinner HA5 ... 93 BV53
Sch Potter St Co Prim Sch,
Harl. CM17 off Potter St ... 52 EW17
Potter St Hill, Pnr. HA5 ... 93 BV51
Potters Way, Reig. RH2 ... 266 DC138
Pottery La, W11 ... 6 C10
Pottery Rd, Bex. DA5 ... 187 FC89
Brentford TW8 ... 158 CL79
Pottery St, SE16 ... 22 C4
Pottiphere Pl, Brwd. (Warley)
CM14 ... 108 FV49
Pott St, E2 ... 12 D2
Pouchen End La, Hem.H.
HP1 ... 39 BD21
Poulcott, Stai. (Wrays.)
TW19 ... 172 AY86
Poulett Gdns, Twick. TW1 ... 177 CG88
Poulett Rd, E6 ... 145 EM68
Poulner Way, SE15
off Daniel Gdns ... 162 DT80
Poulters Wd, Kes. BR2 ... 222 EK106
Poultney Cl, Rad. (Shenley)
WD7 ... 62 CM32
Poulton Av, Sutt. SM1 ... 200 DD104
Poulton Cl, E8
off Spurstowe Ter ... 122 DV64
Poultry, EC2 ... 11 J8
Pound, The, Slou. (Burn.)
SL1 off Hogfair La ... 130 AJ70
Pound Cl, Orp. BR6 ... 205 ER103
Surbiton KT6 ... 197 CJ102
Waltham Abbey EN9 ... 50 EE23
Pound Ct, Ashtd. KT21 ... 232 CM118
Pound Ct Dr, Orp. BR6 ... 205 ER103
Pound Cres, Lthd. (Fetch.)
KT22 ... 231 CD121
Pound Fm Cl, Esher KT10 ... 197 CD102
Pound Fld, Guil. GU1 ... 242 AX133
Poundfield, Wat. WD25
off Ashfields ... 75 BT35
Poundfield Ct, Wok. GU22
off High St ... 227 BC121
Poundfield Gdns, Wok.
GU22 ... 227 BC120
Poundfield Rd, Loug. IG10 ... 85 EN43
Pound La, NW10 ... 139 CU65
Epsom KT19 ... 216 CR112
Radlett (Shenley) WD7 ... 62 CM33
Sevenoaks TN13 ... 240 FX115
Sevenoaks (Knock.P.)
TN14 ... 257 FH124
Pound Pk Rd, SE7 ... 164 EK77
Pound Pl, SE9 ... 185 EN86
Guildford (Shalf.) GU4 ... 259 AZ140
Pound Pl Cl, Guil. (Shalf.)
GU4 ... 259 AZ140
Pound Rd, Bans. SM7 ... 233 CZ117
Pound Rd, Cher. KT16 ... 194 BH101
Pound St, Cars. SM5 ... 218 DF106
Pound Way, Chis. BR7
off Royal Par ... 185 EQ94
Poundwell, Welw.G.C. AL7 ... 30 DA10
Pounsley Rd, Sev.
(Dunt.Grn) TN13 ... 256 FE121
Pountney Rd, SW11 ... 160 DG83
POVEREST, Orp. BR5 ... 205 ET99
Sch Poverest Prim Sch, Orp.
BR5
off Tillingbourne Grn ... 206 EU99
Poverest Rd, Orp. BR5 ... 205 ET99
Povey Cross Rd, Horl. RH6 ... 268 DD150
Powder Mill La, Dart. DA1 ... 188 FL89
Twickenham TW2 ... 176 BZ88
Powdermill La, Wal.Abb.
EN9 ... 67 EB33
Powdermill Ms, Wal.Abb.
EN9 off Powdermill La ... 67 EB33
Powdermill Way, Wal.Abb.
EN9 ... 67 EB32
Powell Cl, Chess. KT9
off Coppard Gdns ... 215 CK106
Dartford DA2 ... 189 FS89
Edgware HA8 ... 96 CM51
Guildford GU2 ... 258 AT136
Horley RH6 off Baden Dr ... 268 DE147
Wallington SM6 ... 219 DK108
Sch Powell Corderoy Prim
Sch, Dor. RH4
off Longfield Rd ... 263 CF137
Powell Gdns, Dag. RM10 ... 126 FA63
Powell Rd, E5 ... 122 DV62
Buckhurst Hill IG9 ... 102 EJ45
Powells Cl, Dor. RH4
off Goodwyns Rd ... 263 CJ139
Powell's Wk, W4 ... 158 CS79
Power Cl, Guil. GU1
off Woodbridge Rd ... 242 AW133
Power Dr, Enf. EN3 ... 83 DZ36
Powergate Business Pk,
NW10 ... 138 CR69
Power Ind Est, Erith DA8 ... 167 FG81
Power Rd, W4 ... 158 CN77
Powers Ct, Twick. TW1 ... 177 CK87
Powerscroft Rd, E5 ... 122 DW63
Sidcup DA14 ... 186 EW93
Powis Ct, Pot.B. EN6 ... 64 DC34
Powis Gdns, NW11 ... 119 CZ59
W11 ... 6 F7
Powis Ms, W11 ... 6 F7
Powis Pl, WC1 ... 9 P4
Powis Rd, E3 ... 14 B2
Powis Sq, W11 ... 6 F7
Powis St, SE18 ... 165 EN76
Powis Ter, W11 ... 6 F7
Powle Ter, Ilf. IG1
off Oaktree Gro ... 125 EQ64
Powlett Pl, NW1
off Harmood St ... 141 DH65
Pownall Gdns, Houns. TW3 ... 156 CB84
Pownall Rd, E8 ... 5 P8
Hounslow TW3 ... 156 CB84
Pownsett Ter, Ilf. IG1
off Buttsbury Rd ... 125 EQ64
Powster Rd, Brom. BR1 ... 184 EH92
Powys Cl, Bexh. DA7 ... 166 EX79
Powys Ct, Borwd. WD6
off Kensington Way ... 78 CR41
Powys La, N13 ... 99 DL50
N14 ... 99 DL49
POYLE, Slou. SL3 ... 153 BE81
Poyle La, Slou. (Burn.) SL1 ... 130 AH67
Poyle Pk, Slou. (Colnbr.)
SL3 ... 153 BE83
Poyle Rd, Guil. GU1 ... 258 AY136
Slough (Colnbr.) SL3 ... 153 BE83
Poyle Tech Cen, Slou. SL3 ... 153 BE82
Poyle Ter, Guil. GU1
off Sydenham Rd ... 258 AX136
Poynder Rd, Til. RM18 ... 171 GH81
Poynders Ct, SW4
off Poynders Rd ... 181 DJ86
Poynders Gdns, SW4 ... 181 DJ87
Poynders Hill, Hem.H. HP2 ... 41 BQ21
Poynders Rd, SW4 ... 181 DJ86
Poynes Rd, Horl. RH6 ... 268 DE146
Poynings, The, Iver SL0 ... 153 BF77
Poynings Cl, Orp. BR6 ... 206 EW103
Poynings Rd, N19 ... 121 DJ62
Poynings Way, N12 ... 98 DA50
Romford RM3
off Arlington Gdns ... 106 FL53
Poyntell Cres, Chis. BR7 ... 205 ER95
Poynter Ho, W11 ... 16 B1
Poynter Rd, Enf. EN1 ... 82 DU43
Poynton Rd, N17 ... 100 DU54
Poyntz Rd, SW11 ... 160 DF82
Poyser St, E2 ... 142 DV68
Prae, The, Wok. GU22 ... 227 BF118
Prae Cl, St.Alb. AL3 ... 42 CB19
Praed Ms, W2 ... 7 P7
Praed St, W2 ... 8 A6
Praetorian Ct, St.Alb. AL1 ... 42 CC23
Sch Prae Wd Prim Sch, St.Alb.
AL3 off King Harry La ... 42 CA22
Pragel St, E13 ... 144 EH68
Pragnell Rd, SE12 ... 184 EH89
Prague Pl, SW2 ... 181 DL85
Prah Rd, N4 ... 121 DN61
Prairie Cl, Add. KT15 ... 194 BH104
Prairie Rd, Add. KT15 ... 194 BH104
Prairie St, SW8 ... 160 DG82
Pratt Ms, NW1 off Pratt St ... 141 DJ67
PRATT'S BOTTOM, Orp.
BR6 ... 224 EV110
Sch Pratt's Bottom Prim Sch,
Orp. BR6
off Hookwood Rd ... 224 EW111
Pratts La, Walt. KT12
off Molesey Rd ... 214 BX105
Pratts Pas, Kings.T. KT1
off Eden St ... 198 CL96
Pratt St, NW1 ... 141 DJ67
Pratt Wk, SE11 ... 20 B7
Prayle Gro, NW2 ... 119 CX60
Prebend Gdns, W4 ... 159 CT76
W6 ... 159 CT76
Prebend St, N1 ... 4 G8
Precinct, The, Egh. TW20
off High St ... 173 BA92
West Molesey KT8
off Victoria Av ... 196 CB97
Precinct Rd, Hayes UB3 ... 135 BU73
Precincts, The, Mord. SM4
off Green La ... 200 DA100
Slough (Burn.) SL1 ... 130 AH70
Premier Av, Grays RM16 ... 170 GC75

Premier Cor, W9
off Kilburn La 139 CZ68
Premiere Pl, E14 13 N10
Premier Pk, NW10 138 CP67
Premier Pk Rd, NW10 138 CP68
Premier Pl, SW15
off Putney High St 159 CY84
Prendergast Rd, SE3 164 EE83
Sch Prendergast Sec Sch, VA Sch for Girls, SE4
off Adelaide Av 163 EA84
Prentice Pl, Harl. CM17 52 EW17
Prentis Rd, SW16 181 DK91
Prentiss Ct, SE7 164 EK77
Presburg Rd, N.Mal. KT3 198 CS99
Presburg St, E5 off Glyn Rd 123 DX62
Prescelly Pl, Edg. HA8 96 CM53
Prescot St, E1 11 P9
Prescott Av, Orp. BR5 205 EP100
Prescott Cl, SW16 181 DL94
Prescott Grn, Loug. IG10 85 EQ41
Prescott Ho, SE17
off Hillingdon St 161 DP79
Prescott Pl, SW4 161 DK83
Prescott Rd, Slou. (Colnbr.)
SL3 153 BE82
Waltham Cross (Chsht)
EN8 67 DY27
Presdales Ct, Ware SG12
off Presdales Dr 33 DY07
Presdales Dr, Ware SG12 33 DX07
Sch Presdales Sch, Ware
SG12
off Hoe La 33 DX08
Presentation Ms, SW2
off Palace Rd 181 DM88
President Dr, E1 22 C1
President St, EC1 10 G1
Prespa Cl, N9
off Hudson Way 100 DW47
Press Rd, NW10 118 CR62
Uxbridge UB8 134 BK65
Prestage Way, E14 14 D9
Prestbury Ct, Wok. GU21
off Muirfield Rd 226 AU118
Prestbury Cres, Bans. SM7 234 DF116
Prestbury Rd, E7 144 EJ66
Prestbury Sq, SE9 185 EM91
Prested Rd, SW11
off St. John's Hill 160 DE84
Prestige Way, NW4
off Heriot Rd 119 CW57
PRESTON, Wem. HA9 117 CK59
Preston Av, E4 101 ED51
Preston Cl, SE1 21 L7
Twickenham TW2 177 CE90
Preston Ct, Walt. KT12
off St. Johns Dr 196 BW102
Preston Cross, Lthd. KT23 246 BZ126
Preston Dr, E11 124 EJ57
Bexleyheath DA7 166 EX81
Epsom KT19 216 CS107
Preston Gdns, NW10
off Church Rd 138 CS65
Enfield EN3 83 DY37
Ilford IG1 124 EL58
Preston Gro, Ashtd. KT21 231 CJ117
Preston Hill, Chesh. HP5 54 AR29
Harrow HA3 118 CM58
Preston La, Tad. KT20 233 CV121
Sch Preston Manor High Sch,
Wem. HA9
off Carlton Av E 118 CM61
Sch Preston Pk Prim Sch, Wem.
HA9 off College Rd 117 CK60
Preston Pl, NW2 139 CU65
Richmond TW10 178 CL85
⊖ Preston Road 118 CL60
Preston Rd, E11 124 EE58
SE19 181 DP93
SW20 179 CT94
Gravesend (Nthflt) DA11 190 GE88
Harrow HA3 118 CL59
Romford RM3 106 FK49
Shepperton TW17 194 BN99
Slough SL2 132 AW73
Wembley HA9 118 CL61
Prestons Rd, E14 24 D3
Bromley BR2 204 EG104
Preston Waye, Har. HA3 118 CL60
Prestwick Cl, Sthl. UB2
off Ringway 156 BY78
Prestwick Rd, Wat. WD19 94 BX50
Prestwood, Slou. SL2 132 AV72
Prestwood Av, Har. HA3 117 CH56
Prestwood Cl, SE18 166 EU80
Harrow HA3 117 CJ56
Prestwood Dr, Rom. RM5 105 FC50
Prestwood Gdns, Croy. CR0 202 DQ101
Prestwood St, N1 5 H10
Pretoria Av, E17 123 DY56
Pretoria Cl, N17
off Pretoria Rd 100 DT52
Pretoria Cres, E4 101 EC46
Pretoria Ho, Erith DA8
off Waterhead Cl 167 FE80
Pretoria Rd, E4 101 EC46
E11 123 ED60
E16 15 J3
N17 100 DT52
SW16 181 DH93
Chertsey KT16 193 BF102
Ilford IG1 125 EP64
Romford RM7 127 FC56
Watford WD18 75 BU42
Pretoria Rd N, N18 100 DT51
Pretty La, Couls. CR5 235 DJ121
Prevost Rd, N11 98 DG47
Prey Heath, Wok. GU22 226 AV123
Prey Heath Cl, Wok. GU22 226 AW124
Prey Heath Rd, Wok. GU22 226 AV124
Price Cl, NW7 97 CY51
SW17 180 DF90
Price Rd, Croy. CR0 219 DP106
Price's Ct, SW11 160 DD83
Prices La, Reig. RH2 266 DA137
Price's St, SE1 20 F2
Price's Yd, N1 4 B7
Price Way, Hmptn. TW12
off Victors Dr 176 BY93
Pricklers Hill, Barn. EN5 80 DB44
Prickley Wd, Brom. BR2 204 EF102
Priddy's Yd, Croy. CR0
off Church St 202 DQ103
Prideaux Pl, W3
off Friars Pl La 138 CR73
WC1 10 B1
Prideaux Rd, SW9 161 DL83
Pridham Rd, Th.Hth. CR7 202 DR98
Priest Ct, EC2 10 G7
Priestfield Rd, SE23 183 DY90
Priest Hill, Egh. TW20 172 AW90
Windsor (Old Wind.) SL4 172 AW90
Priestland Gdns, Berk. HP4
off Frithsden Rd 38 AY17
Priestlands Cl, Horl. RH6 268 DF147
Priestlands Pk Rd, Sid.
DA15 185 ET90
Priestley Cl, N16
off Ravensdale Rd 122 DT59
Priestley Gdns, Rom. RM6 126 EV58
Priestley Rd, Mitch. CR4 200 DG96
Priestley Way, E17 123 DX55
NW2 119 CU60
Priestly Gdns, Wok. GU22 227 BA120
Priestman Pt, E3 14 A2
Sch Priestmead First Sch, Har.
HA3 off Hartford Av 117 CH55
Sch Priestmead Mid Sch, Har.
HA3 off Hartford Av 117 CH55
Priest Pk Av, Har. HA2 116 CA61
Priests Av, Rom. RM1 105 FD54
Priests Br, SW14 158 CS84
SW15 158 CS84
Priests Fld, Brwd. (Ingrave)
CM13 109 GC50
Priests La, Brwd. CM15 108 FY47
Prima Rd, SW9 161 DN80
Primley La, B.Stort.
(Sheering) CM22 37 FC06
Primrose Av, Enf. EN2 82 DR39
Horley RH6 269 DH150
Romford RM6 126 EV59
Primrose Cl, SE6 183 EC92
Harrow HA2 116 BZ63
Hatfield AL10 45 CV19
Hemel Hempstead HP1 39 BE21
Wallington SM6 201 DH102
Primrose Dr, Hert. SG13 32 DV09
West Drayton UB7 154 BK77
Primrose Fld, Harl. CM18 51 ET18
Primrose Gdns, NW3 140 DE65
Bushey WD23 94 CB45
Ruislip HA4 116 BW64
Primrose Glen, Horn. RM11 128 FL56
PRIMROSE HILL, NW8 140 DF67
Primrose Hill, EC4 10 D8
Brentwood CM14 108 FW48
Kings Langley WD4 59 BP28
Primrose Hill Ct, NW3 140 DF66
Sch Primrose Hill Prim Sch,
NW1 off Princess Rd 140 DG67
Primrose Hill Rd, NW3 140 DE66
Primrose Hill Studios, NW1
off Fitzroy Rd 140 DG67
Primrose La, Croy. CR0 203 DX102
Primrose Ms, NW1
off Sharpleshall St 140 DF66
SE3 164 EH80
W5 off St. Mary's Rd 157 CK75
Primrose Path, Wal.Cr.
(Chsht) EN7 66 DU31
Primrose Rd, E10 123 EB60
E18 102 EH54
Walton-on-Thames KT12 214 BW106
Primrose Sq, E9 142 DW66
Primrose St, EC2 11 L5
Primrose Wk, SE14
off Alexandra St 163 DY80
Epsom KT17 217 CT108
Primrose Way, Wem. HA0 137 CK68
Primula St, W12 139 CU72
Prince Albert Rd, NW1 140 DE68
NW8 140 DE68
Prince Albert Sq, Red. RH1 266 DF139
Prince Alberts Wk, Wind.
SL4 152 AU81
Prince Arthur Ms, NW3
off Perrins La 120 DC63
Prince Arthur Rd, NW3 120 DC64
Prince Charles Av, Dart.
(S.Darenth) DA4 209 FR96
Prince Charles Dr, NW4 119 CW59
Prince Charles Rd, SE3 164 EF81
Prince Charles Way, Wall.
SM6 201 DH104
Prince Consort Cotts, Wind.
SL4 151 AR82
Prince Consort Dr, Chis.
BR7 205 ER95
Prince Consort Rd, SW7 17 M5
Princedale Rd, W11 16 D1
Prince Edward Rd, E9 143 DZ65
Prince Edward St, Berk. HP4 38 AW19
Prince George Av, N14 81 DJ42
Prince George Duke of Kent
Ct, Chis. BR7
off Holbrook La 185 ER94
Prince George Rd, N16 122 DS63
Prince George's Av, SW20 199 CW96
Prince George's Rd, SW19 200 DD95
Prince Henry Rd, SE7 164 EK80
★ Prince Henry's Room,
EC4 10 C8
Prince Imperial Rd, SE18 165 EM81
Chislehurst BR7 185 EP94
Prince John Rd, SE9 184 EL85
Princelet St, E1 11 P5
Prince of Orange La, SE10
off Greenwich High Rd 163 EC80
Prince of Wales Cl, NW4
off Church Ter 119 CV56
Prince of Wales Dr, SW8 161 DH80
SW11 160 DF81
Prince of Wales Footpath,
Enf. EN3 83 DY38
Prince of Wales Gate, SW7 18 A3
Prince of Wales Pas, NW1 9 J2
Sch Prince of Wales Prim Sch,
Enf. EN3
off Salisbury Rd 83 DZ37
Prince of Wales Rd, NW5 140 DG65
SE3 164 EF81
Redhill (Outwood) RH1 267 DN143
Sutton SM1 200 DD103
Prince of Wales Ter, W4 158 CS78
W8 17 K4
Prince Pk, Hem.H. HP1 40 BG21
DLR Prince Regent 144 EJ73
Prince Regent La, E13 144 EH69
E16 144 EJ71
Prince Regent Ms, NW1 9 J2
Prince Regent Rd, Houns.
TW3 156 CC83
Prince Rd, SE25 202 DS99
Prince Rupert Rd, SE9 165 EM84
Prince's Arc, SW1 19 K1
Princes Av, N3 98 DA53
N10 120 DG55
N13 99 DN50
N22 99 DK53
NW9 118 CP56
W3 158 CN76
Carshalton SM5 218 DF108
Princes Av, Dart. DA2 188 FP88
Enfield EN3 83 DY36
Greenford UB6 136 CB72
Orpington BR5 205 ES99
South Croydon CR2 236 DV115
Surbiton KT6 198 CN102
Watford WD18 75 BT43
Woodford Green IG8 102 EH49
Princes Cl, N4 121 DP60
NW9 118 CN56
SW4 off Old Town 161 DJ83
Berkhamsted HP4 38 AU17
Edgware HA8 96 CN50
Epping (N.Wld Bas.)
CM16 71 FC25
Sidcup DA14 186 EX90
South Croydon CR2 236 DV115
Teddington TW11 177 CD91
Windsor (Eton Wick) SL4 151 AM78
Princes Ct, E1 12 D10
SE16 23 L6
Hemel Hempstead HP3
off Roughdown Rd 40 BH23
Wembley HA9 118 CL64
Princes Dr, Har. HA1 117 CE55
Prince's Dr, Lthd. (Oxshott)
KT22 215 CE112
Princesfield Rd, Wal.Abb.
EN9 68 EH33
Coll Prince's Foundation, The,
EC2 11 L3
Princes Gdns, SW7 17 P5
W3 138 CN71
W5 137 CJ70
Princes Gate, SW7 18 A4
Harlow CM20 35 ES12
Princes Gate Ct, SW7 17 P4
Princes Gate Ms, SW7 17 P5
Princes La, N10 121 DH55
Princes Ms, W2 7 J9
Princes Par, Pot.B. EN6
off High St 64 DC32
Princes Pk, Rain. RM13 147 FG66
Princes Pk Av, NW11 119 CY58
Hayes UB3 135 BR73
Princes Pk Circle, Hayes
UB3 135 BR73
Princes Pk Cl, Hayes UB3 135 BR73
Princes Pk La, Hayes UB3 135 BR73
Princes Pk Par, Hayes UB3 135 BR73
Princes Pl, SW1 19 K1
W11 16 C1
Princes Plain, Brom. BR2 204 EL101
Sch Princes Plain Prim Sch,
Brom. BR2 off Church La 204 EL101
Princes Ri, SE13 163 EC82
Princes Riverside Rd, SE16 22 G1
Princes Rd, N18 100 DW49
SE20 183 DX93
SW14 158 CR83
SW19 180 DA93
W13 off Broomfield Rd 137 CH74
Ashford TW15 174 BM92
Bourne End SL8 110 AC60
Buckhurst Hill IG9 102 EJ47
Dartford DA1, DA2 187 FG86
Egham TW20 173 AZ93
Feltham TW13 175 BT89
Gravesend DA12 191 GJ90
Ilford IG6 125 ER56
Kingston upon Thames
KT2 178 CN94
Redhill RH1 266 DF136
Richmond TW10 178 CM85
Richmond (Kew) TW9 158 CM80
Romford RM1 127 FG57
Swanley BR8 187 FG93
Teddington TW11 177 CD91
Weybridge KT13 213 BP106
H Princess Alexandra Hosp,
Harl. CM20 35 EQ14
Princess Alice Way, SE28 165 ER75
Princess Av, Wem. HA9 118 CL61
Windsor SL4 151 AP83
Princess Cl, SE28
off Redbourne Dr 146 EX72
Princess Cres, N4 121 DP61
Princess Diana Dr, St.Alb.
AL4 43 CK21
Princesses Wk, Rich. TW9
off Kew Rd 158 CL80
Sch Princess Frederica C of E
Prim Sch, NW10
off College Rd 139 CW68
Princess Gdns, Wok. GU22 227 BB116
H Princess Grace Hosp,
The, W1 8 E4
Princess La, Ruis. HA4 115 BS60
Princess Louise Cl, W2 7 P5
H Princess Louise Hosp,
W10 6 A6
H Princess Margaret Hosp,
Wind. SL4 151 AR82
Sch Princess Margaret Royal
Free Sch, The, Wind.
SL4 off Bourne Av 151 AQ83
Princess Mary Cl, Guil.
GU2 off Tylehost 242 AU130
Princess Mary's Rd, Add.
KT15 212 BJ105
Sch Princess May Prim Sch,
N16 5 N1
Princess May Rd, N16 122 DS63
Princess Ms, NW3
off Belsize Cres 140 DD65
Kingston upon Thames
KT1 198 CM97
Princess Par, Orp. BR6
off Crofton Rd 205 EN104
Princess Pk Manor, N11 98 DG50
Princess Prec, Horl. RH6
off High St 269 DH148
Princess Sq, W2 7 J9
Princess Rd, NW1 140 DG67
NW6 140 DA68
Croydon CR0 202 DQ100
Woking GU22 227 BB116
H Princess Royal Uni Hosp,
The, Orp. BR6 205 EN104
Princess St, SE1 20 F6
Princes St, EC2 11 J7
N17 off Queen St 100 DS51
W1 9 H8
Bexleyheath DA7 166 EZ84
Gravesend DA11 191 GH86
Richmond TW9
off Sheen Rd 178 CL85
Slough SL1 152 AV75
Sutton SM1 218 DD105
Ware SG12 33 DX05
Princess Way, Red. RH1 250 DG133
Princes Ter, E13 144 EH67
Prince St, SE8 163 DZ79
Watford WD17 76 BW41
Princes Vw, Dart. DA1 188 FN88
Princes Way, SW19 179 CX87
Brentwood (Hutt.) CM13 109 GA46
Buckhurst Hill IG9 102 EJ47
Croydon CR0 219 DM106
Ruislip HA4 116 BY63
West Wickham BR4 222 EF105
Princes Yd, W11 16 D2
Princethorpe Ho, W2 7 J5
Princethorpe Rd, SE26 183 DX91
Princeton Ct, SW15
off Felsham Rd 159 CX83
Princeton St, WC1 10 A5
Principal Sq, E9
off Chelmer Rd 123 DX64
Pringle Gdns, SW16 181 DJ91
Purley CR8 219 DM110
Sch Prins Willem Alexander
Sch, Wok. GU22
off Old Woking Rd 227 BC117
Printers Inn Ct, EC4 10 C7
Printers Ms, E3 143 DY67
Printer St, EC4 10 D7
Printers Way, Harl. CM20 36 EU10
Printing Ho La, Hayes UB3 155 BS75
Printing Ho Yd, E2 11 M1
Print Village, SE15
off Chadwick Rd 162 DT82
Priolo Rd, SE7 164 EJ78
Prior Av, Sutt. SM2 218 DE108
Prior Bolton St, N1 4 F4
Prior Chase, Grays
(Bad.Dene) RM17 170 FZ77
Prioress Cres, Green. DA9 169 FW84
Prioress Rd, SE27 181 DP90
Prioress St, SE1 21 K6
Prior Gro, Chesh. HP5 54 AQ30
Prior Rd, Ilf. IG1 125 EN62
Priors, The, Ashtd. KT21 231 CK119
Priors Cl, Hert. (Hert.Hth)
SG13 32 DV12
Slough SL1 152 AU76
Priors Ct, Wok. GU21 226 AU118
Priors Cft, E17 101 DY54
Woking GU22 227 BA120
Priors Fm La, Nthlt. UB5 136 BZ65
Priors Fld, Nthlt. UB5
off Arnold Rd 136 BY65
Priorsford Av, Orp. BR5 206 EU98
Priors Gdns, Ruis. HA4 116 BW64
Priors Mead, Enf. EN1 82 DS39
Leatherhead (Bkhm)
KT23 246 CC125
Priors Pk, Horn. RM12 128 FJ62
Priors Rd, Wind. SL4 151 AK83
Priors Shop Cen, The, N12
off High Rd 98 DC50
Prior St, SE10 163 EC80
Priors Wd Rd, Hert. (Hert.Hth)
SG13 32 DW12
Sch Prior Weston Prim Sch,
EC1 11 H4
Priory, The, SE3 164 EF84
Godstone RH9 252 DV131
Priory Av, E4 101 DZ48
E17 123 EA57
N8 121 DK56
W4 158 CS77
Harlow CM17 36 EW10
Orpington BR5 205 ER100
Sutton SM3 217 CX105
Uxbridge (Hare.) UB9 114 BJ56
Wembley HA0 117 CF63
Priory Cl, E4 101 DZ48
E18 102 EG53
N3 off Church Cres 97 CZ53
N14 81 DH43
N20 97 CZ45
SW19 off High Path 200 DB95
Beckenham BR3 203 DY97
Brentwood (Pilg.Hat.)
CM15 108 FU43
Broxbourne EN10
off High Rd Turnford 49 DY24
Chislehurst BR7 205 EM95
Dartford DA1 188 FJ85
Dorking RH4 263 CG138
Hampton TW12
off Priory Gdns 196 BZ95
Hayes UB3 135 BV73
Hoddesdon EN11 49 EA18
Horley RH6 268 DF147
Ruislip HA4 115 BT60
Stanmore HA7 95 CF48
Sunbury-on-Thames
TW16 off Staines Rd E 175 BU94
Uxbridge (Denh.) UB9 114 BG62
Uxbridge (Hare.) UB9 114 BH56
Walton-on-Thames KT12 195 BU104
Wembley (Sudbury) HA0 117 CF63
Woking GU21 211 BD113
Sch Priory C of E Prim Sch, The,
SW19 off Queens Rd 180 DB92
Sch Priory C of E VA Sch, The,
Dor. RH4 off West Bk 263 CF137
Priory Ct, E17 123 DZ55
EC4 off Carter La 141 DP72
SW8 161 DK81
Berkhamsted HP4 38 AW19
Bushey WD23
off Sparrows Herne 94 CC46
Epsom KT17
off Old Schs La 217 CT109
Guildford GU2
off Portsmouth Rd 258 AW137
Harlow CM18
off Southern Way 52 EV18
Priory Ct Est, E17
off Priory Ct 101 DZ54
Priory Cres, SE19 182 DQ94
Sutton SM3 217 CX105
Wembley HA0 117 CG62
Priory Dr, SE2 166 EX78
Reigate RH2 266 DA136
Stanmore HA7 95 CF48
Priory Fld Dr, Edg. HA8 96 CP49
Priory Flds, Dart. (Fnghm)
DA4 208 FM103
Priory Gdns, N6 121 DH58
SE25 202 DT98
SW13 159 CT83
W4 158 CS77
W5 off Hanger La 138 CL69
Ashford TW15 175 BR92
Berkhamsted HP4 38 AW19
Dartford DA1 188 FK85
Hampton TW12 176 BZ94
Uxbridge (Hare.) UB9 114 BJ56
Wembley HA0 117 CG63
Priory Gate, Wal.Cr. EN8 67 DZ27
Priory Grn, Stai. TW18 174 BH92
Priory Grn Est, N1 4 B9
Priory Gro, SW8 161 DL81
Barnet EN5 80 DA43
Romford RM3 106 FL48
Priory Hill, Dart. DA1 188 FK85
Priory Hill, Wem. HA0 117 CG63
H Priory Hosp, The, N14 99 DL46
Priory La, SW15 178 CS86
Dartford (Fnghm) DA4 208 FM102
Richmond TW9
off Forest Rd 158 CN80
West Molesey KT8 196 CA98
Priory Ms, SW8 161 DK81
Hornchurch RM11 127 FH60
Staines TW18
off Chestnut Manor Cl 174 BH92
Priory Pk, SE3 164 EF83
Priory Pk Rd, NW6 139 CZ67
Wembley HA0 117 CG63
Priory Path, Rom. RM3 106 FL48
Priory Pl, Dart. DA1 188 FK86
Walton-on-Thames KT12 195 BU104
Priory Rd, E6 144 EK67
N8 121 DK56
NW6 140 DB67
SW19 180 DD94
W4 158 CR76
Barking IG11 145 ER66
Chessington KT9 198 CL104
Croydon CR0 201 DN101
Gerrards Cross (Chal.St.P.)
SL9 112 AX55
Hampton TW12 176 BZ94
Hounslow TW3 176 CC85
Loughton IG10 84 EL42
Reigate RH2 266 DA136
Richmond TW9 158 CN79
Romford RM3 106 FL48
Slough SL1 130 AJ71
Sutton SM3 217 CX105
Priory Rd N, Dart. DA1 168 FK84
Priory Rd S, Dart. DA1 188 FK85
Sch Priory Sch, Slou. SL1
off Orchard Av 131 AK71
Sch Priory Sch, The,
Bans. SM7
off Bolters La 234 DA115
Orpington BR5
off Tintagel Rd 206 EW102
Priory Shop Cen, Dart. DA1 188 FL86
Priory St, E3 14 B1
Hertford SG14 32 DR09
Ware SG12 32 DW06
Priory Ter, NW6 140 DB67
Sunbury-on-Thames
TW16 off Staines Rd E 175 BU94
Priory Vw, Bushey
(Bushey Hth) WD23 95 CE45
Priory Wk, SW10 17 M10
St. Albans AL1 43 CE23
Priory Way, Ger.Cr.
(Chal.St.P.) SL9 112 AX55
Harrow HA2 116 CB56
Slough (Datchet) SL3 152 AV80
Southall UB2 156 BX76
West Drayton UB7 154 BL79
Priory Wf, Hert. SG14
off Priory St 32 DR09
Priscilla Cl, N15
off Conway Rd 122 DQ57
Pritchard's Rd, E2 142 DU67
Pritchett Cl, Enf. EN3 83 EA37
Priter Rd, SE16 22 B6
Priter Way, SE16
off Dockley Rd 162 DU76
Sch Private Jewish Sch,
NW9 off Edgware Rd 118 CR55
Private Rd, Enf. EN1 82 DS43
Probert Rd, SW2 181 DN85
Probyn Rd, SW2 181 DP89
Procter St, WC1 10 A6
Proctor Cl, Mitch. CR4 200 DG95
Proctor Gdns, Lthd. (Bkhm)
KT23 246 CB125
Proctors Cl, Felt. TW14 175 BU88
Profumo Rd, Walt. KT12 214 BX106
Progress Business Pk, Croy.
CR0 201 DM103
Progress Way, N22 99 DN53
Croydon CR0 201 DM103
Enfield EN1 82 DU43
Promenade, The, W4 158 CS81
Promenade App Rd, W4 158 CS80
Promenade de Verdun, Pur.
CR8 219 DK111
Promenade Mans, Edg.
HA8 off Hale La 96 CP50
Prospect Business Pk, Loug.
IG10 85 EQ42
Prospect Cl, SE26 182 DV91
Belvedere DA17 166 FA77
Hounslow TW3 156 BZ81
Ruislip HA4 116 BX59
Prospect Cotts, SW18
off Point Pleasant 160 DA84
Prospect Cres, Twick. TW2 176 CC86
Prospect Gro, Grav. DA12 191 GK87
Prospect Hill, E17 123 EB56
Prospect La, Egh. (Eng.Grn)
TW20 172 AT92
Prospect Pl, E1 22 E1
N2 120 DD56
N7 off Parkhurst Rd 121 DL63
N17 100 DS53
NW2 off Ridge Rd 119 CZ62
NW3 off Holly Wk 120 DC63
W4 off Chiswick High Rd 158 CR78
Bromley BR2 204 EH97
Epsom KT17
off Clayton Rd 216 CS113
Gravesend DA12 191 GK87
Grays RM17 170 GB79
Romford RM5 105 FC54
Staines TW18 173 BF92
Prospect Pl Shop Pk, Dart.
DA1 188 FL86
Prospect Quay, SW18 160 DA84
Prospect Ring, N2 120 DD55
Prospect Rd, NW2 119 CZ62
Barnet EN5 80 DA43
Hornchurch RM11 128 FM55
St. Albans AL1 43 CD22
Sevenoaks TN13 257 FJ123
Surbiton KT6 197 CJ100
Waltham Cross (Chsht)
EN8 66 DW29
Woodford Green IG8 102 EJ50
Prospect St, SE16 22 D5
Prospect Vale, SE18 164 EL77
Prospect Way, Brwd. (Hutt.)
CM13 109 GE42
Prospero Rd, N19 121 DJ60
Prossers, Tad. KT20
off Croffets 233 CX121
Protea Cl, E16 15 J3
Prothero Gdns, NW4 119 CV57
Prothero Ho, NW10 138 CR66
Prothero Rd, SW6 159 CY80
Prout Gro, NW10 118 CS63
Prout Rd, E5 122 DV62

★ Place of interest | H Hospital | Sch School | Coll College | Uni University | ⇌ Railway station

Provence St, N1
off St. Peters St 142 DQ68
Providence Cl, E9
off Wetherell Rd 143 DX67
Providence Ct, W1 ....8 F9
Providence La, Hayes UB3 ..155 BR80
Providence Pl, N1 ....4 E7
Epsom KT17 ....216 CS112
Romford RM5 ....104 EZ54
Woking GU22 ....212 BG114
Providence Rd, West Dr.
UB7 ....134 BL74
Providence Row, N1
off Pentonville Rd 141 DM68
Providence Row Cl, E2
off Ainsley St 142 DV69
Providence Sq, SE1
off Jacob St 162 DT75
Providence St, N1
off St. Peters St 142 DQ68
Greenhithe DA9 ....189 FU85
Providence Yd, E2 ....12 A1
Provident Ind Est, Hayes
UB3 ....155 BU75
Provost Est, N1 ....11 J1
Provost Rd, NW3 ....140 DF66
Provost St, N1 ....11 J2
Prowse Av, Bushey
(Bushey Hth) WD23 .....94 CC47
Prowse Pl, NW1
off Bonny St 141 DH66
Pruden Cl, N14 ....99 DJ47
Prudent Pas, EC2 ....11 H7
Prune Hill, Egh. (Eng.Grn)
TW20 ....172 AX94
Prusom St, E1 ....22 D2
Pryor Cl, Abb.L. WD5 ....59 BT32
Pryors, The, NW3 ....120 DD62
★ P.S. Tattershall Castle,
SW1 ....19 P2
H Public Health Laboratory
Service HQ, NW9 ......118 CS55
★ Public Record Office,
Rich. TW9 ....158 CP80
Puck La, Wal.Abb. EN9 ......67 ED29
Pucknells Cl, Swan. BR8 ....207 FC95
Puddenhole Cotts, Bet. RH3 .248 CN133
Pudding La, EC3 ....11 K10
Chigwell IG7 ....103 ET46
Hemel Hempstead HP1 ...40 BG18
Sevenoaks (Seal) TN15
off Church St 257 FN121
DLR Pudding Mill Lane 143 EB67
Pudding Mill La, E15 ....143 EB67
Puddingstone Dr, St.Alb.
AL4 ....43 CJ22
Puddle Dock, EC4 ....10 F9
Puddledock La, Dart. DA2 ..187 FE92
Westerham TN16 ....255 ET133
Puers La, Beac. (Jordans)
HP9 ....90 AS51
Puffin Cl, Bark. IG11 ....146 EV69
Beckenham BR3 ....203 DX99
Puffin Ter, Ilf. IG5
off Tiptree Cres 125 EN55
Pulborough Rd, SW18 .....179 CZ87
Pulborough Way, Houns.
TW4 ....156 BW84
Pulford Rd, N15 ....122 DR58
Pulham Av, N2 ....120 DC56
Broxbourne EN10 ....49 DX21
Puller Rd, Barn. EN5 ....79 CY40
Hemel Hempstead HP1 ...40 BG21
Pulleyns Av, E6 ....144 EL69
Pulleys Cl, Hem.H. HP1 .....39 BF19
Pulleys La, Hem.H. HP1 .....39 BF19
Pullfields, Chesh. HP5 ......54 AN30
Pullman Cl, St.Alb. AL1
off Ramsbury Rd 43 CE22
Pullman Ct, SW2 ....181 DL88
Pullman Gdns, SW15 ......179 CW86
Pullman Pl, SE9 ....184 EL85
Pullmans Pl, Stai. TW18 ....174 BG92
Pulpit Cl, Chesh. HP5 ......54 AN29
Pulross Rd, SW9 ....161 DM83
Pulteney Cl, E3 ....143 DZ67
Isleworth TW7
off Gumley Gdns 157 CG83
Pulteney Gdns, E18
off Pulteney Rd 124 EH55
Pulteney Rd, E18 ....124 EH55
Pulteney Ter, N1 ....4 B8
Pulton Pl, SW6 ....160 DA80
Puma Ct, E1 ....11 N5
Pump All, Brent. TW8 ......157 CK80
Pump Cl, Nthlt. UB5
off Union Rd 136 CA68
Pump Ct, EC4 ....10 C8
Pumphandle Path, N2
off Tarling Rd 98 DC54
Pump Hill, Loug. IG10 ....85 EM40
Pump Ho Cl, SE16 ....22 F4
Bromley BR2 ....204 EF96
Pump Ho Ms, E1 ....12 A9
Pumping Sta Rd, W4 ....158 CS80
Pumpkin Hill, Slou. (Burn.)
SL1 ....131 AL65
Pump La, SE14 ....162 DW80
Chesham HP5 ....54 AS32
Epping (Epp.Grn) CM16 ...51 EP24
Hayes UB3 ....155 BV75
Orpington BR6 ....225 FB106
Pump Pail N, Croy. CR0
off Old Town 202 DQ104
Pump Pail S, Croy. CR0
off Southbridge Rd 202 DQ104
Punch Bowl La, Chesh. HP5
off Red Lion St 54 AQ32
Punchbowl La, Dor. RH5 ...263 CK135
Punch Bowl La, Hem.H. HP2 .41 BR17
St. Albans AL3 ....41 BT16
Pundersons Gdns, E2 ....12 D1
Punjab La, Sthl. UB1
off Herbert Rd 136 BZ74
Purbeck Av, N.Mal. KT3 ....199 CT100
Purbeck Cl, Red. RH1 ......251 DK128
Purbeck Ct, Guil. GU2
off Egerton Rd 242 AS134
Purbeck Dr, NW2 ....119 CY61
Woking GU21 ....211 AZ114
Purbeck Rd, Horn. RM11 ...127 FG60
Purberry Gro, Epsom KT17 .217 CT110
Purbrock Av, Wat. WD25 ....76 BW36
Purbrook Est, SE1 ....21 M4
Purbrook St, SE1 ....21 M5
Purcell Cl, Borwd. WD6 .....77 CK39
Kenley CR8 ....220 DR114
Purcell Cres, SW6 ....159 CY80
Purcell Ms, NW10
off Suffolk Rd 138 CS66
Purcell Rd, Grnf. UB6 ......136 CB71
Purcells Av, Edg. HA8 ....96 CN50
Sch Purcell Sch, The, Bushey
WD23
off Aldenham Rd 76 CA41

Purcells Cl, Ashtd. KT21
off Albert Rd 232 CM118
Purcell St, N1 ....5 L9
Purchese St, NW1 ....141 DK68
Purdom Rd, Welw.G.C. AL7 ..29 CY12
Purdy St, E3 ....14 A3
Purelake Ms, SE13 ....163 ED83
PURFLEET, RM19 ....168 FP77
⇌ Purfleet 168 FN78
Purfleet Bypass, Purf. RM19 .168 FP77
Purfleet Ind Pk, S.Ock.
(Aveley) RM15 ....168 FM75
Sch Purfleet Prim Sch, Purf.
RM19 off Tank Hill Rd ...168 FN77
Purfleet Rd, S.Ock. (Aveley)
RM15 ....168 FN75
Purfleet Thames Terminal,
Purf. RM19 ....168 FQ80
Purford Grn, Harl. CM18 .....52 EU16
Sch Purford Grn Co Inf Sch,
Harl. CM18
off Purford Grn 52 EU17
Sch Purford Grn Co Jun Sch,
Harl. CM18
off Purford Grn 52 EU17
Purkis Cl, Uxb. UB8
off Dawley Rd 135 BQ72
Purkiss Rd, Hert. SG13 ......32 DQ12
Purland Cl, Dag. RM8 ......126 EZ60
Purland Rd, SE28 ....165 ET75
Purleigh Av, Wdf.Grn. IG8 ..102 EL51
PURLEY, CR8 ....219 DM111
⇌ Purley 219 DP112
H Purley & District War
Mem Hosp, Pur. CR8 ...219 DN111
Purley Av, NW2 ....119 CY62
Purley Bury Av, Pur. CR8 ...220 DQ110
Purley Bury Cl, Pur. CR8 ...220 DQ111
Purley Cl, Ilf. IG5 ....103 EN54
Purley Downs Rd, Pur. CR8 .220 DQ110
South Croydon CR2 .....220 DR111
Purley Hill, Pur. CR8 ......219 DP112
Purley Knoll, Pur. CR8 .....219 DM111
⇌ Purley Oaks 220 DQ109
Sch Purley Oaks Prim Sch,
S.Croy. CR2
off Bynes Rd 220 DR108
Purley Oaks Rd, S.Croy.
CR2 ....220 DR109
Purley Par, Pur. CR8
off High St 219 DN111
Purley Pk Rd, Pur. CR8 .....219 DP110
Purley Pl, N1 ....4 E5
Purley Ri, Pur. CR8 ....219 DM112
Purley Rd, N9 ....100 DR48
Purley CR8 ....219 DN111
South Croydon CR2 .....220 DR108
Purley Vale, Pur. CR8 ......219 DP113
Purley Way, Croy. CR0 .....201 DM101
Purley CR8 ....219 DN108
Purley Way Cres, Croy. CR0
off Purley Way 201 DM101
Purlieu Way, Epp. (They.B.)
CM16 ....85 ES35
Purlings Rd, Bushey WD23 ..76 CB43
Purneys Rd, SE9 ....164 EK84
Purrett Rd, SE18 ....165 ET78
Pursers Ct, Slou. SL2
off Elliman Av 132 AS72
Purser's Cross Rd, SW6 ....159 CZ81
Pursers La, Guil. (Peasl.)
GU5 ....261 BR142
Pursewardens Cl, W13 .....137 CJ74
Pursley Gdns, Borwd. WD6 ..78 CN38
Pursley Rd, NW7 ....97 CV52
Purton Ct, Slou. (Farn.Royal)
SL2 ....131 AQ66
Purton La, Slou. (Farn.Royal)
SL2 ....131 AQ66
Purves Rd, NW10 ....139 CW68
Puteaux Ho, E2 ....143 DX68
PUTNEY, SW15 ....159 CY84
⇌ Putney 159 CY84
⊖ Putney Bridge 159 CY83
Putney Br, SW6 ....159 CY83
SW15 ....159 CY83
Putney Br App, SW6 ....159 CY83
Putney Br Rd, SW15 ....159 CY84
SW18 ....159 CY84
Putney Common, SW15 ....159 CW83
Putney Ex Shop Cen, SW15 .159 CX84
Putney Gdns, Rom.
(Chad.Hth) RM6
off Heathfield Pk Dr 126 EV58
PUTNEY HEATH, SW15 ....179 CW86
Putney Heath, SW15 ....179 CW86
Putney Heath La, SW15 ....179 CX86
Sch Putney High Sch,
SW15 off Putney Hill ...179 CX85
Putney High St, SW15 .....159 CX84
Putney Hill, SW15 ....179 CX86
H Putney Hosp, SW15 .....159 CW82
Putney Pk Av, SW15 ....159 CU84
Putney Pk La, SW15 ....159 CV84
Sch Putney Pk Sch, SW15
off Woodborough Rd ...159 CV84
Putney Rd, Enf. EN3 ....83 DX36
Coll Putney Sch of Art & Design,
SW15 off Oxford Rd 159 CY84
PUTNEY VALE, SW15 ....179 CT90
Putney Wf Twr, SW15 .....159 CY83
Puttenham Cl, Wat. WD19 ...94 BW48
Putters Cft, Hem.H. HP2 .....40 BM15
Puttocks Cl, Hat. AL9 ....45 CW23
Puttocks Dr, Hat. AL9 ....45 CW23
Pycroft Way, N9 ....100 DU49
Pyebush La, Beac. HP9 .....111 AN56
Pye Cl, Cat. CR3
off St. Lawrence Way ...236 DR123
Pyecombe Cor, N12 ....97 CZ49
PYE CORNER, Harl. CM20 ....35 ER10
Pyenest Rd, Harl. CM19 ......51 EP18
Pyghtle, The, Uxb. (Denh.)
UB9 ....114 BG60
Pylbrook Rd, Sutt. SM1 ....200 DA104
Pyle Hill, Wok. GU22 ....226 AX124
Pylon Way, Croy. CR0 ......201 DL102
Pym Cl, Barn. EN4 ....80 DD43
Pymers Mead, SE21 ....182 DQ88
Pymmes Cl, N13 ....99 DM50
N17 ....100 DV53
Pymmes Gdns N, N9 ....100 DT48
Pymmes Gdns S, N9 ....100 DT48
Pymmes Grn Rd, N11 ....99 DH49
Pymmes Rd, N13 ....99 DL51
Pymms Brook Dr, Barn. EN4 .80 DE42
Pym Orchard, West. (Brasted)
TN16 ....240 EW124
Pym Pl, Grays RM17 ....170 GA77
Pynchester Cl, Uxb. UB10 ..114 BN61
Pyne Rd, Surb. KT6 ....198 CN102
Pynest Grn La, Wal.Abb.
EN9 ....84 EG38
Pyne Ter, SW19
off Windlesham Gro 179 CX88

Pynfolds, SE16 ....22 D4
Pynham Cl, SE2 ....166 EU76
Pynnacles Cl, Stan. HA7 .....95 CH50
Pypers Hatch, Harl. CM20 ....35 ET14
Sch Pyrcroft Gra Prim Sch,
Cher. KT16
off Pyrcroft Rd 193 BE100
Pyrcroft La, Wey. KT13 .....213 BP106
Pyrcroft Rd, Cher. KT16 ....193 BF101
PYRFORD, Wok. GU22 ......227 BE115
Sch Pyrford Cen, Wok.
GU22 off Engliff La 227 BF116
Sch Pyrford C of E Prim Sch,
Wok. GU22
off Coldharbour Rd 228 BG116
Pyrford Common Rd, Wok.
GU22 ....227 BD116
★ Pyrford Ct, Wok. GU22 ..227 BE117
PYRFORD GREEN, Wok.
GU22 ....228 BH117
Pyrford Heath, Wok. GU22 ..227 BF116
Pyrford Lock, Wok. (Wisley)
GU23 ....228 BJ116
Pyrford Rd, W.Byf. KT14 ....212 BG113
Woking GU22 ....212 BG114
PYRFORD VILLAGE, Wok.
GU22 ....228 BG118
Pyrford Wds Cl, Wok. GU22 .227 BF115
Pyrford Wds Rd, Wok. GU22 .227 BE115
Sch Pyrgo Priory Prim Sch,
Rom. RM3
off Dagnam Pk Dr 106 FN50
Pyrland Rd, N5 ....5 J1
Richmond TW10 ....178 CM86
Pyrles Grn, Loug. IG10 ......85 EP39
Pyrles La, Loug. IG10 ....85 EP40
Pyrmont Gro, SE27 ....181 DP90
Pyrmont Rd, W4 ....158 CN79
Ilford IG1 off High Rd ...125 EQ61
Pytchley Cres, SE19 ....182 DQ93
Pytchley Rd, SE22 ....162 DS83
Pytt Fld, Harl. CM17 ....52 EV16

Q

Quadrangle, The, W2 ....8 A7
Guildford GU2
off The Oval 258 AU135
Welwyn Garden City AL8 ..29 CW08
Quadrangle Cl, SE1 ....21 L7
Quadrangle Ms, Stan. HA7 ...95 CJ52
Quadrant, The, SE24
off Herne Hill 182 DQ85
SW20 ....199 CY95
Bexleyheath DA7 ....166 EX80
Epsom KT17 ....216 CS113
Purfleet RM19 ....168 FQ77
Richmond TW9 ....158 CL84
St. Albans AL4 ....43 CH17
Sutton SM2 ....218 DC107
Quadrant Arc, W1 ....9 K10
Romford RM1 ....127 FE57
Quadrant Cl, NW4
off The Burroughs 119 CV57
Quadrant Gro, NW5 ....120 DF64
Quadrant Ho, Sutt. SM2 ....218 DC107
Quadrant Rd, Rich. TW9 ....157 CK84
Thornton Heath CR7 .....201 DP98
Quadrant Way, Wey. KT13
off Weybridge Rd 212 BM105
Quad Rd, Wem. HA9
off Courtenay Rd 117 CK62
Quaggy Wk, SE3 ....164 EG84
Quail Gdns, S.Croy. CR2 ...221 DY110
Sch Quainton Hall Sch, Har.
HA1 off Hindes Rd 117 CE57
Quainton St, NW10 ....118 CR62
Quaker Cl, Sev. TN13 ......257 FK123
Quaker Ct, E1 ....11 N4
Quaker La, Sthl. UB2 ....156 CA76
Waltham Abbey EN9 .....67 EC34
Quakers Course, NW9 ....97 CT53
Quakers Hall La, Sev. TN13 .257 FJ122
Quakers La, Islw. TW7 ......157 CG81
Potters Bar EN6 ....64 DB30
Quaker's Pl, E7 ....124 EK64
Quaker St, E1 ....11 N4
Quakers Wk, N21 ....82 DR44
Quality Ct, WC2 ....10 C7
Quality St, Red. RH1 ....251 DH128
Quantock Cl, Hayes UB3 ...155 BR80
St. Albans AL4 ....43 CJ16
Slough SL3 ....153 BA78
Quantock Dr, Wor.Pk. KT4 ..199 CW103
Quantock Gdns, NW2 ......119 CX61
Quantock Rd, Bexh. DA7
off Cumbrian Av 167 FE82
Quantocks, Hem.H. HP2 .....40 BM17
Quarles Cl, Rom. RM5 ......104 FA52
Quarley Way, SE15
off Daniel Gdns 162 DT80
Quarrendon Rd, Amer. HP7 ..55 AR40
Quarrendon St, SW6 ....160 DA82
Quarr Rd, Cars. SM5 ....200 DD100
Quarry, The, Bet. RH3
off Station Rd 248 CS132
Quarry Cl, Lthd. KT22 ......231 CK121
Oxted RH8 ....254 EE130
Quarry Cotts, Sev. TN13 ....256 FG123
Quarry Gdns, Lthd. KT22 ...231 CK121
Quarry Hill, Grays RM17 ....170 GA78
Sevenoaks TN15 ....257 FK123
Sch Quarry Hill Inf Sch,
Grays RM17
off Dell Rd 170 GB78
Sch Quarry Hill Jun Sch, Grays
RM17 off Bradleigh Av ..170 GB78
Quarry Hill Pk, Reig. RH2 ...250 DC131
Quarry Ms, Purf. RM19 .....168 FN77
Quarry Pk Rd, Sutt. SM1 ....217 CZ107
Quarry Ri, Sutt. SM1 ....217 CZ107
Quarry Rd, SW18 ....180 DC86
Godstone RH9 ....252 DW128
Oxted RH8 ....254 EE130
Quarryside Business Pk,
Red. RH1 ....251 DH130
Quarry Spring, Harl. CM20 ...52 EU15
Quarry St, Guil. GU1 ....258 AX136
Quarterdeck, The, E14 ......23 N4
Quartermaine Av, Wok.
GU22 ....227 AZ122
Quartermass Cl, Hem.H.
HP1
off Quartermass Rd 40 BG19
Quartermass Rd, Hem.H.
HP1 ....40 BG19
Quarter Mile La, E10 ....123 EB63
Quaves Rd, Slou. SL3 ......152 AV76
Quay La, Green. DA9 ....169 FV84
Quayside Wk, Kings.T. KT1
off Bishop's Hall 197 CK96
Quay W, Tedd. TW11 ......177 CH92
Quebec Av, West. TN16 ....255 ER126

Quebec Cl, Horl. (Smallfield)
RH6 off Alberta Dr 269 DN148
★ Quebec Ho (Wolfe's Ho),
West. TN16 ....255 ER126
Quebec Ms, W1 ....8 D8
Quebec Rd, Hayes UB4 ....136 BW73
Ilford IG1, IG2 ....125 EP59
Tilbury RM18 ....171 GG82
Quebec Sq, West. TN16 ....255 ER126
Quebec Way, SE16 ....23 H4
Queen Adelaide Rd, SE20 ..182 DW93
Queen Alexandra's Ct,
SW19 ....179 CZ92
Queen Alexandra's Way,
Epsom KT19 ....216 CN112
Queen Anne Av, N15
off Suffield Rd 122 DT57
Bromley BR2 ....204 EF97
Queen Anne Dr, Esher
(Clay.) KT10 ....215 CE108
Queen Anne Ms, W1 ....9 H6
Queen Anne Rd, E9 ....143 DX65
Sch Queen Anne Royal Free
First Sch, The, Wind.
SL4 off Chaucer Cl 151 AR83
Queen Anne's Cl, Twick. TW2 .177 CD90
Queen Anne's Gdns, W4 ....158 CS76
Queen Annes Gdns, W5 .....158 CL75
Enfield EN1 ....82 DS44
Leatherhead KT22
off Upper Fairfield Rd ..231 CH121
Queen Anne's Gdns, Mitch.
CR4 ....200 DF97
Queen Anne's Gate, SW1 ...19 L4
Bexleyheath DA7 ....166 EX83
Queen Anne's Gro, W4 .....158 CS76
Queen Annes Gro, W5 ......158 CL75
Enfield EN1 ....100 DR45
Queen Anne's Ms, Lthd.
KT22 off Fairfield Rd ...231 CH121
Queen Annes Pl, Enf. EN1 ...82 DS44
Queen Annes Rd, Wind.
SL4 ....151 AQ84
Queen Annes Ter, Lthd.
KT22
off Upper Fairfield Rd ..231 CH121
Queen Anne St, W1 ....8 G7
Queen Anne's Wk, WC1
off Guilford St 141 DL70
Queen Anne Ter, E1 ....12 D10
Queenborough Gdns, Chis.
BR7 ....185 ER93
Ilford IG2 ....125 EN56
Queen Caroline Est, W6 ....159 CW78
Queen Caroline St, W6 .....159 CW77
H Queen Charlotte's &
Chelsea Hosp, W12 ....139 CU72
Queen Charlotte St, Wind.
SL4 off High St 151 AR81
Queendale Ct, Wok. GU21
off Roundthorn Way 226 AT116
Sch Queen Eleanor's C of E
Jun Sch, Guil. GU2
off Queen Eleanor's Rd .258 AU135
Queen Eleanor's Rd, Guil.
GU2 ....258 AT135
Queen Elizabeth Ct, Brox.
EN10 off Groom Rd 67 DZ26
Waltham Abbey EN9
off Greenwich Way 83 EC36
Queen Elizabeth Gdns,
Mord. SM4 ....200 DA98
★ Queen Elizabeth Hall &
Purcell Room, SE1 ......20 A1
H Queen Elizabeth Hosp,
SE18 ....164 EL80
Queen Elizabeth Rd, E17 ...123 DY55
Kingston upon Thames
KT2 ....198 CM95
Queen Elizabeths Cl, N16 ..122 DR61
Queen Elizabeths Dr, N14 ...99 DL46
Queen Elizabeth's Dr, Croy.
(New Adgtn) CR0 ......221 ED110
Queen Elizabeth II Br, Dart.
DA1 ....169 FR82
Purfleet RM19 ....169 FR82
★ Queen Elizabeth II Conf
Cen, SW1 ....19 M4
H Queen Elizabeth II Hosp,
Welw.G.C. AL7 ....30 DA13
Sch Queen Elizabeth II
Jubilee Sch, W9 ....6 F3
Sch Queen Elizabeth's
Foundation Dev Cen,
Lthd. KT22
off Oaklawns Rd 231 CE117
Sch Queen Elizabeth's
Foundation Training Coll,
Lthd. KT22
off Woodlands Rd 231 CD117
Queen Elizabeth's Gdns,
Croy. (New Adgtn) CR0
off Queen Elizabeth's Dr .221 ED110
Sch Queen Elizabeth's Girls'
Sch, Barn. EN5
off Barnet Hill 79 CZ42
★ Queen Elizabeth's
Hunting Lo, Epping Forest,
E4 ....102 EF45
Sch Queen Elizabeth's Sch
for Boys, Barn. EN5
off Queens Rd 79 CX41
Queen Elizabeth St, SE1 ....21 M3
Queen Elizabeths Wk, N16 .122 DR61
Queen Elizabeth's Wk, Wall.
SM6 ....219 DK105
Queen Elizabeth Wk, SW13 .159 CV81
Windsor SL4 ....152 AS82
Queen Elizabeth Way, Wok.
GU22 ....227 AZ119
Queenhill Rd, S.Croy. CR2 ..220 DV110
Queenhithe, EC4 ....11 H9
Queenhythe Rd, Guil. GU4 .242 AX128
Queen Margaret's Gro, N1 ....5 L2
Uni Queen Mary, E1 ....13 J3
Halls of Res, E18
off High Rd
Woodford Grn 102 EG53
Uni Queen Mary - Barts &
The London Sch of Med
& Dentistry, EC1 ....10 F4
Royal London Hosp, E1
off Turner St 142 DV71
Queen Mary Av, Mord. SM4 .199 CX99
Queen Mary Cl, Rom. RM1 ..127 FF58
Surbiton KT6 ....198 CN104
Woking GU22 ....227 BC116
Queen Mary Ct, Stai. TW19
off Long La 174 BL88
Queen Mary Rd, SE19 ......181 DP93
Shepperton TW17 ......195 BQ96
Queen Mary's Av, Cars.
SM5 ....218 DF108
Queen Marys Av, Wat.
WD18 ....75 BS42

Queen Marys Ct, Wal.Abb.
EN9 off Greenwich Way ...83 EC35
Queen Marys Dr, Add.
(New Haw) KT15 ....211 BF110
★ Queen Mary's Gdns, NW1 .8 E2
H Queen Mary's Hosp,
NW3 ....120 DC62
Sidcup DA14 ....186 EU93
H Queen Mary's Hosp for
Children, Cars. SM5 ....200 DC102
H Queen Mary's Uni Hosp
(Roehampton), SW15 ....179 CU86
Queen Mother's Dr, Uxb.
(Denh.) UB9 ....113 BF58
Queen of Denmark Ct, SE16 ..23 L5
Queens Acre, Sutt. SM3 ....217 CX108
Windsor SL4 ....151 AR84
Queens All, Epp. CM16 ......69 ET31
Queens Av, N3 ....98 DC52
N10 ....120 DG55
N20 ....98 DD47
Queen's Av, N21 ....99 DP46
Queens Av, Felt. TW13 .....176 BW91
Greenford UB6 ....136 CB72
Stanmore HA7 ....117 CJ55
Watford WD18 ....75 BT42
West Byfleet (Byfleet)
KT14 ....212 BK112
Woodford Green IG8 ....102 EH50
Queensberry Ms W, SW7 ....17 N7
Queensberry Pl, E12 ....124 EK64
SW7 ....17 N7
Richmond TW9
off Friars La 177 CK85
Queensberry Way, SW7 .....17 N7
Queensborough Ms, W2 .....7 L9
Queensborough Pas, W2 .....7 L9
Queensborough S Bldgs,
W2 off Porchester Ter ...140 DC73
Queensborough Studios,
W2 ....7 L9
Queensborough Ter, W2 .....7 K9
Sch Queensbridge Inf Sch,
E8 ....5 P6
Queensbridge Pk, Islw. TW7 .177 CE85
Queensbridge Rd, E2 ....5 P7
E8 ....5 P4
QUEENSBURY, Har. HA3 ...117 CK55
⊖ Queensbury 118 CM55
Queensbury Circle Par, Har.
HA3 off Streatfield Rd ..118 CL55
Stanmore HA7
off Streatfield Rd 118 CL55
Queensbury Rd, NW9 ......118 CR59
Wembley HA0 ....138 CM68
Queensbury Sta Par, Edg.
HA8 ....118 CM55
Queensbury St, N1 ....5 H6
Queen's Circ, SW8
off Queenstown Rd 161 DH80
SW11 off Queenstown Rd .161 DH80
Queens Cl, Edg. HA8 ....96 CN50
Tadworth KT20 ....233 CU124
Wallington SM6
off Queens Rd 219 DH106
Windsor (Old Wind.) SL4 .172 AU85
★ Queens Club (Tennis Cen),
W14 ....16 C10
Queens Club Gdns, W14 ....159 CY79
Sch Queen's C of E JMI Sch,
The, Rich. TW9
off Cumberland Rd 158 CN80
Sch Queen's Coll, W1 ....8 G6
Queens Ct, SE23 ....182 DW88
Broxbourne EN10 ....49 DZ24
Hertford SG13
off Queens Rd 32 DR10
Richmond TW10 ....178 CM86
St. Albans AL1
off Hatfield Rd 43 CH20
Slough SL1 ....132 AT73
Queenscourt, Wem. HA9 ...118 CL63
Queens Ct, Wey. KT13 .....213 BR106
Woking GU22
off Hill Vw Rd 227 AZ118
Queens Ct Ride, Cob. KT11 .213 BU113
Queen's Cres, NW5 ....140 DG65
Queens Cres, Rich. TW10 ...178 CM85
St. Albans AL4 ....43 CH17
Queenscroft Rd, SE9 ....184 EK85
Queensdale Cres, W11 ....16 B1
Queensdale Pl, W11 ....16 C1
Queensdale Rd, W11 ....16 B2
Queensdale Wk, W11 ....16 C2
Queensdown Rd, E5 ....122 DV63
Queens Dr, E10 ....123 EA59
N4 ....121 DP61
W3 ....138 CM72
W5 ....138 CM72
Abbots Langley WD5 .....59 BT32
Guildford GU2 ....242 AU131
Leatherhead (Oxshott)
KT22 ....214 CC111
Queen's Dr, Slou. SL3 ......133 AZ66
Queens Dr, Surb. KT5 ......198 CN101
Thames Ditton KT7 .....197 CG101
Waltham Cross EN8 ......67 EA34
Queens Dr, The, Rick.
(Mill End) WD3 ....91 BF45
Queens Elm Par, SW3
off Old Ch St 160 DD78
Queen's Elm Sq, SW3 ....17 P10
Queensferry Wk, N17
off Jarrow Rd 122 DV56
★ Queen's Gall, The, SW1 ...19 H4
Queens Gdns, NW4 ....119 CW57
W2 ....7 L9
W5 ....137 CJ70
Dartford DA2 ....188 FP88
Queen's Gdns, Houns. TW5 .156 BY81
Queens Gdns, Rain. RM13 ..147 FD68
Upminster RM14 ....129 FT58
Queen's Gate, SW7 ....17 M4
Queensgate, Cob. KT11 .....214 BX112
Queen's Gate, Gat. RH6 ....268 DG152
Queensgate, Wal.Cr. EN8 ....67 DZ34
Queensgate Cen, Harl.
CM20 ....35 ET11
Queen's Gate Gdns, SW7 ...17 M6
Queens Gate Gdns, SW15
off Upper Richmond Rd ..159 CV84
Queensgate Gdns, Chis.
BR7 ....205 ER95
Queen's Gate Ms, SW7 ......17 M4
Queensgate Pl, NW6 ....140 DA66
Queen's Gate Pl, SW7 ....17 M6
Queen's Gate Pl Ms, SW7 ...17 M6
Sch Queen's Gate Sch, SW7 ..17 N7
Queen's Gate Ter, SW7 ......17 L5

⊖ London Underground station   DLR Docklands Light Railway station   Tra Tramlink station   Riv Pedestrian ferry landing stage

Queen's Gro, NW8 140 DD67
Queen's Gro Ms, NW8 140 DD67
Queens Gro Rd, E4 101 ED46
Queen's Head Pas, EC4 10 G7
Queen's Head St, N1 4 F8
Queens Head Wk, Brox.
EN10
off High Rd Wormley 49 DY23
Queens Head Yd, SE1 21 J2
Queens Ho, Tedd. TW11 177 CF93
★ Queen's Ice Rink, W2 7 K10
Queenside Ms,
Horn. RM12 128 FL61
Queensland Av, N18 100 DQ51
SW19 200 DB95
Queensland Cl, E17 101 DZ54
Queensland Ho, E16
off Rymill St 145 EN74
Queens La, N10 121 DH55
Ashford TW15
off Clarendon Rd 174 BM91
Queen's Manor Prim Sch,
SW6 off Lysia St 159 CX80
Queens Mkt, E13
off Green St 144 EJ67
Queensmead, NW8 140 DD67
Leatherhead KT22 214 CC111
Slough (Datchet) SL3 152 AV81
Queensmead Av, Epsom
KT17 217 CV110
Queensmead Rd, Brom.
BR2 204 EF96
Queensmead Sch, Ruis.
HA4 off Queens Wk 116 BX63
Queensmere Cl, SW19 179 CX89
Queensmere Rd, SW19 179 CX89
Slough SL1
off Wellington St 152 AU75
Queensmere Shop Cen,
Slou. SL1 152 AT75
Queens Ms, W2 7 K9
Queensmill Rd, SW6 159 CX80
Queens Par, N11
off Colney Hatch La 98 DF50
W5 138 CM72
Queens Par Cl, N11
off Colney Hatch La 98 DF50
⇌ Queen's Park 139 CY68
⊖ Queen's Park 139 CY68
Queens Pk Comm Sch,
NW6 off Aylestone Av 139 CX67
Queens Pk Ct, W10 6 B2
Queens Pk Gdns, Felt.
TW13 off Vernon Rd 175 BU90
Queen's Pk Prim Sch,
W10 6 D3
★ Queens Park Rangers FC,
W12 139 CV74
Queens Pk Rd, Cat. CR3 236 DS123
Romford RM3 106 FM53
Queens Pas, Chis. BR7
off High St 185 EP93
Queens Pl, Mord. SM4 200 DA98
Watford WD17 76 BW41
Queen's Prom, Kings.T. KT1
off Portsmouth Rd 197 CK97
Queen Sq, WC1 9 P4
Queen Sq Pl, WC1 9 P4
Queens Reach, E.Mol. KT8 197 CE98
Queens Ride, SW13 159 CU83
SW15 159 CU83
Queen's Ride, Rich. TW10 178 CP88
Queen's Ri, Rich. TW10 178 CM86
Queens Rd, E11 123 ED59
E13 144 EH67
Queen's Rd, E17 123 DZ58
Queens Rd, N3 98 DC53
N9 100 DV48
Queen's Rd, N11 99 DL52
Queens Rd, NW4 119 CW57
SE14 162 DV81
SE15 162 DV81
SW14 158 CR83
SW19 179 CZ93
W5 138 CL72
Barking IG11 145 EQ66
Barnet EN5 79 CX41
Beckenham BR3 203 DY96
Berkhamsted HP4 38 AU18
Brentwood CM14 108 FW48
Bromley BR1 204 EG96
Buckhurst Hill IG9 102 EH47
Chesham HP5 54 AQ30
Chislehurst BR7 185 EP93
Queen's Rd, Croy. CR0 201 DP100
Queens Rd, Egh. TW20 173 AZ93
Enfield EN1 82 DS42
Epping (N.Wld Bas.)
CM16 71 FB26
Queen's Rd, Erith DA8 167 FE79
Queens Rd, Felt. TW13 175 BV88
Gravesend DA12 191 GJ90
Guildford GU1 242 AX134
Hampton (Hmptn H.)
TW12 176 CB91
Hayes UB3 135 BS72
Hertford SG13, SG14 32 DR11
Horley RH6 268 DG148
Queen's Rd, Houns. TW3 156 CB83
Queens Rd, Kings.T. KT2 178 CN94
Loughton IG10 84 EL41
Mitcham CR4 200 DD97
Morden SM4 200 DA98
New Malden KT3 199 CT98
Richmond TW10 178 CM85
Queen's Rd, Slou. SL1 132 AT73
Queens Rd, Slou. (Datchet)
SL3 152 AU81
Southall UB2 156 BX75
Sutton SM2 218 DA110
Queen's Rd, Tedd. TW11 177 CE93
Thames Ditton KT7 197 CF99
Queens Rd, Twick. TW1 177 CF88
Queens Rd, Uxb. UB8 134 BJ69
Queens Rd, Wall. SM6 219 DH106
Waltham Cross EN8 67 DY34
Walton-on-Thames KT12 213 BV106
Ware SG12 33 DZ05
Watford WD17 76 BW42
Queen's Rd, Well. DA16 166 EV82
Queens Rd, West Dr. UB7 154 BM75
Weybridge KT13 213 BQ105
Windsor SL4 151 AQ82
Windsor (Eton Wick) SL4 151 AL78
⇌ Queens Road Peckham 162 DW81
Queens Rd W, E13 144 EG68
Queen's Row, SE17 162 DR79
Queen's Sch, Bushey
WD23 off Aldenham Rd 76 BZ41
Queen's Sq, The, Hem.H.
HP2 40 BM20
Queens Ter, E13 144 EH67
Queen's Ter, NW8 140 DD68
Queens Ter, Islw. TW7 157 CG84
Queens Ter Cotts, W7
off Boston Rd 157 CE75
Queensthorpe Rd, SE26 183 DX91
★ Queen's Twr, SW7 17 N5
Queenstown Gdns, Rain.
RM13 147 FF69
Queenstown Ms, SW8
off Queenstown Rd 161 DH82
Queenstown Rd, SW8 161 DH79
⇌ Queenstown Road
(Battersea) 161 DH81
Queen St, EC4 11 H9
N17 100 DS51
W1 18 G1
Bexleyheath DA7 166 EZ83
Brentwood (Warley)
CM14 108 FW50
Chertsey KT16 194 BG102
Croydon CR0 220 DQ105
Erith DA8 167 FE79
Gravesend DA12 191 GH86
Guildford (Goms.) GU5 261 BQ139
Kings Langley (Chipper.)
WD4 58 BG32
Romford RM7 127 FD58
St. Albans AL3 42 CC20
Queen St Pl, EC4 11 H10
Queensville Rd, SW12 181 DK87
Queens Wk, E4
off The Green Wk 101 ED46
NW9 118 CQ61
Queen's Wk, SE1 20 A2
SW1 19 J2
Queens Wk, W5 137 CJ70
Ashford TW15 174 BK91
Queen's Wk, Har. HA1 117 CE56
Queens Wk, Ruis. HA4 116 BX62
⊖ Queensway 7 K10
Queens Way, NW4 119 CW57
Queensway, W2 7 K8
Queens Way, Croy. CR0 219 DM107
Queensway, Enf. EN3 82 DV42
Queens Way, Felt. TW13 176 BW91
Queensway, Hat. AL10 45 CU18
Hemel Hempstead HP1,
HP2 40 BM18
Orpington BR5 205 EQ99
Queens Way, Rad. (Shenley)
WD7 62 CL32
Queensway, Red. RH1 250 DF133
Sunbury-on-Thames TW16 195 BV96
Queens Way, Wal.Cr. EN8 67 DZ34
Queensway, W.Wick. BR4 204 EE104
Queensway, The, Ger.Cr.
(Chal.St.P.) SL9 112 AX55
Queensway N, Walt. KT12
off Robinsway 214 BW105
Queensway S, Walt. KT12
off Trenchard Cl 214 BW106
Queenswell Av, N20 98 DE48
Queenswell Inf Sch,
N20 off Sweets Way 98 DD47
Queenswell Jun Sch,
N20 off Sweets Way 98 DD47
Queenswood Av, E17 101 EC53
Brentwood (Hutt.) CM13 109 GD43
Hampton TW12 176 CB93
Hounslow TW3 156 BZ82
Thornton Heath CR7 201 DN99
Wallington SM6 219 DK105
Queenswood Cres, Wat.
WD25 59 BU33
Queenswood Gdns, E11 124 EG60
Queenswood Pk, N3 97 CY54
Queen's Wd Rd, N10 121 DH58
Queenswood Rd, SE23 183 DX90
Sidcup DA15 185 ET85
Queenswood Sch, Hat.
AL9 off Shepherds Way 64 DD28
Queens Yd, WC1 9 K4
Queen Victoria Av, Wem.
HA0 137 CK66
★ Queen Victoria Mem,
SW1 19 J3
Queen Victoria St, EC4 10 F9
Queen Victoria's Wk, Wind.
SL4 152 AS81
Queen Victoria Ter, E1 12 D10
Quemerford Rd, N7 4 A1
Quendell Wk, Hem.H. HP2 40 BL20
Quendon Dr, Wal.Abb. EN9 67 ED33
Quennell Cl, Ashtd. KT21
off Parkers La 232 CL119
Quennel Way, Brwd. (Hutt.)
CM13 109 GC45
Quentin Pl, SE13 164 EE83
Quentin Rd, SE13 164 EE83
Quentins Dr, West.
(Berry's Grn) TN16 239 EP116
Quentins Wk, West.
(Berry's Grn) TN16
off St. Anns Way 239 EP116
Quentin Way, Vir.W. GU25 192 AV98
Quernmore Cl, Brom. BR1 184 EG93
Quernmore Rd, N4 121 DN58
Bromley BR1 184 EG93
Querrin St, SW6 160 DC82
Quex Ms, NW6 off Quex Rd 140 DA67
Quex Rd, NW6 140 DA67
Quickbeams, Welw.G.C. AL7 30 DA06
Quickberry Pl, Amer. HP7 55 AR39
Quickley La, Rick. (Chorl.)
WD3 73 BB44
Quickley Ri, Rick. (Chorl.)
WD3 73 BC44
Quickmoor La, Kings L.
WD4 58 BH33
Quick Rd, W4 158 CS78
Quicks Rd, SW19 180 DB94
Quick St, N1 4 F10
Quick St Ms, N1 4 E10
Quickswood, NW3
off King Henry's Rd 140 DE66
Quickwood Cl, Rick. WD3 74 BG44
Quiet Cl, Add. KT15 212 BG105
Quiet Nook, Brom. BR2
off Croydon Rd 204 EK104
Quill Hall La, Amer. HP6 72 AT37
Quill La, SW15 159 CX84
Quillot, The, Walt. KT12 213 BT106
Quill St, N4 121 DN62
W5 138 CL69
Quilp St, SE1 20 G3
Quilter Gdns, Orp. BR5 206 EW102
Quilter Rd, Orp. BR5 206 EW102
Quilter St, E2 12 A1
SE18 165 ET78
Quilting Ct, SE16
off Poolmans St 163 DX75
Quinbrookes, Slou. SL2 132 AW72
Quince Rd, SE13 163 EB82
Quinces Cft, Hem.H. HP1 40 BG18
Quince Tree Cl, S.Ock. RM15 149 FW70
Quincy Rd, Egh. TW20 173 BA92
Quinta Dr, Barn. EN5 79 CV43
Quintin Av, SW20 199 CZ95
Quintin Cl, Pnr. HA5
off High Rd 115 BV57
Quintin Kynaston Sch,
NW8
off Marlborough Hill 140 DD67
Quinton Cl, Beck. BR3 203 EC97
Hounslow TW5 155 BV80
Wallington SM6 219 DH105
Quinton Rd, T.Ditt. KT7 197 CG102
Quinton St, SW18 180 DC89
Quintrell Cl, Wok. GU21 226 AV117
Quixley St, E14 14 E9
Quorn Rd, SE22 162 DS84

R

Raans Rd, Amer. HP6 72 AT38
Rabbit La, Walt. KT12 213 BU108
Rabbit Row, W8 17 H1
Rabbits Rd, E12 124 EL63
Dartford (S.Darenth) DA4 209 FR96
Rabbsfarm Prim Sch,
West Dr. UB7
off Gordon Rd 134 BL73
Rabbs Mill Ho, Uxb. UB8 134 BK68
Rabies Heath Rd, Gdse.
RH9 252 DU134
Redhill (Bletch.) RH1 252 DS133
Rabournmead Dr, Nthlt.
UB5 116 BY64
Raby Rd, N.Mal. KT3 198 CR98
Raby St, E14 13 J7
Raccoon Way, Houns. TW4 156 BW82
Racecourse Way, Gat. RH6 268 DF151
Rachel Cl, Ilf. IG6 125 ER55
Rachel Pt, E5 off Muir Rd 122 DU63
Rachels Way, Chesh. HP5
off Cresswell Rd 54 AR34
Rackham Cl, Well. DA16 166 EV82
Rackham Ms, SW16
off Westcote Rd 181 DJ93
Racks Ct, Guil. GU1 258 AX136
Racton Rd, SW6 160 DA79
Radbourne Av, W5 157 CJ77
Radbourne Cl, E5
off Overbury St 123 DX63
Radbourne Cres, E17 101 ED54
Radbourne Rd, SW12 181 DJ87
Radburn Cl, Harl. CM18 52 EU19
Radcliffe Av, NW10 139 CU68
Enfield EN2 82 DQ39
Radcliffe Gdns, Cars. SM5 218 DE108
Radcliffe Ms, Hmptn.
(Hmptn H.) TW12
off Taylor Cl 176 CC92
Radcliffe Path, SW8
off Robertson St 161 DH82
Radcliffe Rd, N21 99 DP46
SE1 21 M5
Croydon CR0 202 DT103
Harrow HA3 95 CG54
Radcliffe Sq, SW15 179 CX86
Radcliffe Way, Nthlt. UB5 136 BX69
Radcot Av, Slou. SL3 153 BB76
Radcot Pt, SE23 183 DX90
Radcot St, SE11 20 D10
Raddington Rd, W10 6 D6
Radfield Way, Sid. DA15 185 ER87
Radford Rd, SE13 183 EC86
Radford Way, Bark. IG11 145 ET69
Radipole Rd, SW6 159 CZ81
Radius Pk, Felt. TW14 155 BT84
Radland Rd, E16 15 K8
Rad La, Dor. (Abin.Ham.)
RH5 off Horsham Rd 261 BS142
Guildford (Peasl.) GU5 261 BS140
Radlet Av, SE26 182 DV90
RADLETT, WD7 77 CH35
⇌ Radlett 77 CG35
Radlett Cl, E7 144 EF65
Radlett La, Rad. (Shenley)
WD7 77 CK35
Radlett Lo Sch, Rad.
WD7 off Harper La 61 CH31
Radlett Pk Rd, Rad. WD7 61 CG34
Radlett Pl, NW8 140 DE67
Radlett Prep Sch, Rad.
WD7 off Watling St 77 CJ38
Radlett Rd, St.Alb. AL2 61 CE28
Watford WD17, WD24 76 BW41
Watford (Ald.) WD25 76 CB39
Radley Av, Ilf. IG3 125 ET63
Radley Cl, Felt. TW14 175 BT88
Radley Ct, SE16 23 H3
Radley Gdns, Har. HA3 118 CL56
Radley Ho, SE2
off Wolvercote Rd 166 EX75
Radley Ms, W8 17 H6
Radley Rd, N17 100 DS54
Radley's La, E18 102 EG54
Radleys Mead, Dag. RM10 147 FB65
Radley Sq, E5
off Dudlington Rd 122 DW61
Radlix Rd, E10 123 EA60
Radnor Av, Har. HA1 117 CE57
Welling DA16 186 EV85
Radnor Cl, Chis. BR7
off Homewood Cres 185 ES93
Mitcham CR4 201 DL98
Radnor Cres, SE18 166 EU79
Ilford IG4 125 EM57
Radnor Gdns, Enf. EN1 82 DS39
Twickenham TW1 177 CF89
Radnor Gro, Uxb. UB10
off Charnwood Rd 134 BN68
Radnor La, Dor. (Holm.St.M.)
RH5 261 BU144
Radnor Ms, W2 7 P8
Radnor Pl, W2 8 A8
Radnor Rd, NW6 139 CY67
SE15 162 DU80
Harrow HA1 117 CD57
Twickenham TW1 177 CF89
Weybridge KT13 194 BN104
Radnor St, EC1 11 H2
Radnor Ter, W14 16 E7
Radnor Wk, E14 23 P7
SW3 18 B10
Croydon CR0 203 DZ100
Radnor Way, NW10 138 CP70
Slough SL3 152 AY77
Radolphs, Tad. KT20
off Heathcote 233 CX122
Radstock Av, Har. HA3 117 CG55
Radstock Cl, N11
off Martock Gdns 98 DG51
Radstock St, SW11 160 DE80
Radstock Way, Red. RH1 251 DK128
Radstone Ct, Wok. GU22 227 AZ118
Radwell Path, Borwd. WD6
off Cromwell Rd 78 CL39
Radzan Cl, Dart. DA2 187 FE89
Raebarn Gdns, Barn. EN5 79 CV43
Raeburn Av, Dart. DA1 187 FH85
Surbiton KT5 198 CP100
Raeburn Cl, NW11 120 DC58
Kingston upon Thames
KT1 177 CK94
Raeburn Ct, Wok. GU21
off Martin Way 226 AU118
Raeburn Rd, Edg. HA8 96 CN54
Hayes UB4 135 BR68
Sidcup DA15 185 ES86
Raeburn St, SW2 161 DL84
Raeside Cl, Beac. (Seer Grn)
HP9 89 AQ51
Rafford Way, Brom. BR1 204 EH96
Raft Rd, SW18
off North Pas 160 DA84
Ragged Hall La, St.Alb. AL2 42 BZ24
★ Ragged Sch Mus, E3 13 K5
Raggleswood, Chis. BR7 205 EN95
Rag Hill Cl, West. (Tats.)
TN16 238 EL121
Rag Hill Rd, West. (Tats.)
TN16 238 EK121
Raglan Av, Wal.Cr. EN8 67 DX34
Raglan Cl, Houns. TW4
off Vickers Way 176 BY85
Reigate RH2 250 DC132
Raglan Ct, SE12 184 EG85
South Croydon CR2 219 DP106
Wembley HA9 118 CM63
Raglan Gdns, Wat. WD19 93 BV46
Raglan Inf Sch, Enf.
EN1 off Wellington Rd 100 DS45
Raglan Jun Sch, Enf.
EN1 off Raglan Rd 100 DS45
Raglan Prec, Cat. CR3 236 DS122
Raglan Prim Sch, Brom.
BR2 off Raglan Rd 204 EJ98
Raglan Rd, E17 123 EC57
SE18 165 EQ78
Belvedere DA17 166 EZ77
Bromley BR2 204 EJ98
Enfield EN1 100 DS45
Reigate RH2 250 DB131
Woking (Knap.) GU21 226 AS118
Raglan St, NW5 141 DH65
Raglan Ter, Har. HA2 116 CB63
Raglan Way, Nthlt. UB5 136 CC65
Ragley Cl, W3 off Church Rd 158 CQ75
Rags La, Wal.Cr. (Chsht) EN7 66 DS27
Ragstone Rd, Slou. SL1 151 AR76
Ragwort Ct, SE26 182 DV92
Rahn Rd, Epp. CM16 70 EU31
Raider Cl, Rom. RM7 104 FA53
Raikes Hollow, Dor.
(Abin.Ham.) RH5 261 BV142
Raikes La, Dor. (Abin.Ham.)
RH5 261 BV141
Railey Ms, NW5 121 DJ64
Railpit La, Warl. CR6 238 EE115
Railshead Rd, Islw. TW7 157 CH84
Railton Rd, SE24 161 DN84
Guildford GU2
off Grange Rd 242 AV130
Railway App, N4
off Wightman Rd 121 DN58
SE1 21 K1
Harrow HA3 117 CF56
Hertford SG14 32 DQ09
Twickenham TW1 177 CG87
Wallington SM6 219 DH107
Railway Av, SE16 22 F3
Railway Children Wk,
SE12 off Baring Rd 184 EG89
Bromley BR1
off Reigate Rd 184 EG89
Railway Cotts, Rad. WD7
off Shenley Hill 77 CH35
Watford WD24 75 BV39
Railway Ms, E3 13 N2
W10 6 D7
Railway Pas, Tedd. TW11
off Victoria Rd 177 CG93
Railway Pl, SW19
off Hartfield Rd 179 CZ93
Belvedere DA17 166 FA76
Gravesend DA12
off Stone St 191 GH86
Hertford SG13 32 DS09
Railway Ri, SE22
off Grove Vale 162 DS84
Railway Rd, Tedd. TW11 177 CF91
Waltham Cross EN8 67 DY33
Railway Side, SW13 158 CS83
Railway Sq, Brwd. CM14
off Fairfield Rd 108 FW48
Railway St, N1 141 DL68
Gravesend (Nthflt) DA11 190 GA85
Hertford SG13, SG14 32 DR09
Romford RM6 126 EW60
Railway Ter, SE13
off Ladywell Rd 183 EB85
Feltham TW13 175 BU88
Kings Langley WD4 58 BN27
Slough SL2 132 AT74
Staines TW18 173 BD92
Westerham TN16 255 ER125
Rainborough Cl, NW10 138 CQ65
Rainbow Av, E14 24 A9
Rainbow Ct, Wat. WD19
off Oxhey Rd 76 BW44
Woking GU21
off Langmans Way 226 AS116
Rainbow Ind Est, West Dr.
UB7 134 BK73
Rainbow Quay, SE16 23 K6
Rainbow Rd, Grays
(Chaff.Hun.) RM16 169 FW77
Harlow CM17 37 FE12
Rainbow St, SE5 162 DS80
Rainer Cl, Wal.Cr. (Chsht)
EN8 67 DX29
Raines Ct, N16
off Northwold Rd 122 DT61
Raine's Foundation Sch,
E2 off Approach Rd 142 DW68
Lwr Sch, E2 12 D1
Raine St, E1 22 D1
RAINHAM, RM13 147 FG69
⇌ Rainham 147 FF70
Rainham Cl, SE9 185 ER86
SW11 180 DE86
★ Rainham Hall, Rain.
RM13 147 FG70
Rainham Prim Sch,
Rain. RM13
off Upminster Rd S 147 FG70
Rainham Rd, NW10 139 CW69
Rainham RM13 147 FE66
Rainham Rd N, Dag. RM10 127 FB61
Rainham Rd S, Dag. RM10 127 FB63
Rainhill Way, E3 13 P1
Rainsborough Av, SE8 23 J8
Rainsford Cl, Stan. HA7
off Coverdale Cl 95 CJ50
Rainsford Rd, NW10 138 CP69
Rainsford St, W2 8 A7
Rainsford Way, Horn. RM12 127 FG60
Rainton Rd, SE7 25 M9
Rainville Rd, W6 159 CW79
Raisins Hill, Pnr. HA5 116 BW55
Raith Av, N14 99 DK48
Raleana Rd, E14 24 D1
Raleigh Av, Hayes UB4 135 BV71
Wallington SM6 219 DK105
Raleigh Cl, NW4 119 CW57
Erith DA8 167 FF79
Pinner HA5 116 BX59
Ruislip HA4 115 BT61
Slough SL1 131 AN74
Raleigh Ct, SE16
off Rotherhithe St 143 DX74
SE19 off Lymer Av 182 DT92
Beckenham BR3 203 EB95
Staines TW18 174 BG91
Wallington SM6 219 DH107
Raleigh Dr, N20 98 DE48
Esher (Clay.) KT10 215 CD106
Horley (Smallfield) RH6 269 DN148
Surbiton KT5 198 CQ102
Raleigh Gdns, SW2
off Brixton Hill 181 DM86
Mitcham CR4 200 DF96
Raleigh Ms, N1
off Queen's Head St 141 DP67
Orpington BR6
off Osgood Av 223 ET106
Raleigh Rd, N8 121 DN56
SE20 183 DX94
Enfield EN2 82 DR42
Feltham TW13 175 BT90
Richmond TW9 158 CM83
Southall UB2 156 BY78
Raleigh Sch, The, Ltdhd.
KT24 off Northcote Cres 245 BQ125
Raleigh St, N1 4 F8
Raleigh Way, N14 99 DK46
Feltham TW13 176 BW92
Ralliwood Rd, Ashtd. KT21 232 CN119
Ralph Ct, W2 7 K7
Ralph Perring Ct, Beck. BR3 203 EA98
Ralston St, SW3 18 C10
Ralston Way, Wat. WD19 94 BX47
Rama Cl, SW16 181 DK94
Rama Ct, Har. HA1 117 CE61
Ramac Way, SE7 25 N8
Rama La, SE19 182 DT94
Rambert Sch of Ballet &
Contemporary Dance,
Twickenham Campus,
Twick. TW1
off St. Margarets Rd 157 CH84
Rambler Cl, SW16 181 DJ91
Maidenhead (Taplow) SL6 130 AH72
Rambler La, Slou. SL3 152 AW76
Ramblers Way, Welw.G.C.
AL7 30 DB10
Rambling Way, Berk.
(Pott.End) HP4 39 BC17
Rame Cl, SW17 180 DG92
Ram Gorse, Harl. CM20 35 EP13
Ramilles Cl, SW2 181 DL86
Ramillies Pl, W1 9 J8
Ramillies Rd, NW7 96 CS47
W4 158 CR77
Sidcup DA15 186 EV86
Ramillies St, W1 9 J8
Ramin Ct, Guil. GU1
off Rowan Cl 242 AW131
Ramney Dr, Enf. EN3 83 DY37
Ramornie Cl, Walt. KT12 214 BZ106
Ramparts, The, St.Alb. AL3 42 CB21
Rampart St, E1 12 C8
Ram Pas, Kings.T. KT1
off High St 197 CK96
Rampayne St, SW1 19 L9
Ram Pl, E9 off Chatham Pl 142 DW65
Rampton Cl, E4 101 EA48
Ramsay Cl, Brox. EN10 49 DY21
Ramsay Gdns, Rom. RM3 106 FJ53
Ramsay Ms, SW3
off King's Rd 160 DE79
Ramsay Pl, Har. HA1 117 CE60
Ramsay Rd, E7 124 EE63
W3 158 CQ76
Ramsbury Rd, St.Alb. AL1 43 CE21
Ramscote La, Chesh. (Bell.)
HP5 54 AN25
Ramscroft Cl, N9 100 DS45
Ramsdale Rd, SW17 180 DG92
RAMSDEN, Orp. BR5 206 EW102
Ramsden Cl, Orp. BR5 206 EW102
Ramsden Dr, Rom. RM5 104 FA52
Ramsden Rd, N11 98 DF50
SW12 180 DG86
Erith DA8 167 FD80
Orpington BR5, BR6 206 EV101
Ramsey Cl, NW9 119 CT58
Greenford UB6 116 CC64
Hatfield (Brook.Pk) AL9 64 DD27
Horley RH6 268 DF148
St. Albans AL1 43 CG22
Ramsey Ct, Slou. SL2
off Lower Britwell Rd 131 AK70
Ramsey Ho, Wem. HA9 138 CL65
Ramsey Lo Ct, St.Alb. AL1 43 CE19
Ramsey Ms, N4
off Monsell Rd 121 DP62
Ramsey Rd, Th.Hth. CR7 201 DM100
Ramsey St, E2 12 B3
Ramsey Wk, N1 5 J4
Ramsey Way, N14 99 DJ45
Ramsgate Cl, E16 25 N2
Ramsgate St, E8 5 P3
Ramsgill App, Ilf. IG2 125 ET56
Ramsgill Dr, Ilf. IG2 125 ET57
Rams Gro, Rom. RM6 126 EY56
Ramson Ri, Hem.H. HP1 39 BE21
Ram St, SW18 180 DB85
Ramulis Dr, Hayes UB4 136 BX70
Ramus Wd Av, Orp. BR6 223 ES106
Rancliffe Gdns, SE9 164 EL84
Rancliffe Rd, E6 144 EL68
Randal Cremer JMI Sch,
E2 5 N9
Randal Cres, Reig. RH2 266 DA136
Randall Av, NW2 119 CT62
Randall Cl, SW11 160 DE81
Erith DA8 167 FC79
Slough SL3 153 AZ78
Randall Ct, NW7 off Page St 97 CU52
Randall Dr, Horn. RM12 128 FJ63
Randall Pl, SE10 163 EC80
Randall Rd, SE11 20 A9

★ Place of interest | Hospital | School | College | University | ⇌ Railway station

Randall Row, SE11 20 A8
Randalls Cres, Lthd. KT22 231 CG120
Randalls Dr, Brwd. (Hutt.) CM13 109 GE44
Randalls Pk Av, Lthd. KT22 231 CG120
Randalls Pk Dr, Lthd. KT22 off Randalls Rd 231 CG121
Randalls Ride, Hem.H. HP2 40 BK18
Randalls Rd, Lthd. KT22 231 CE119
Randall's Wk, St.Alb. AL2 60 BZ30
Randalls Way, Lthd. KT22 231 CG121
Randell's Rd, N1 141 DL67
Randle Rd, Rich. TW10 177 CJ91
Randlesdown Rd, SE6 183 EA91
Randles La, Sev. (Knock.) TN14 240 EX115
Randolph App, E16 144 EK72
Randolph Av, W9 7 M3
Randolph Cl, Bexh. DA7 167 FC83
Cobham (Stoke D'Ab.) KT11 230 CA115
Kingston upon Thames KT2 178 CQ92
Woking (Knap.) GU21 off Creston Av 226 AS117
Randolph Cres, W9 7 L4
Randolph Gdns, NW6 140 DB68
Randolph Gro, Rom. RM6 off Donald Dr 126 EW57
Randolph Ho, Croy. CR0 202 DQ102
Randolph Ms, W9 7 M4
Randolph Rd, E17 123 EB57
W9 7 L4
Bromley BR2 205 EM102
Epsom KT17 217 CT114
Slough SL3 152 AY76
Southall UB1 156 BZ75
Randolph's La, West. TN16 255 EP126
Randolph St, NW1 141 DJ66
Randon Cl, Har. HA2 94 CB54
Ranelagh Av, SW6 159 CZ83
SW13 159 CU82
Ranelagh Br, W2 off Gloucester Ter 140 DB71
Ranelagh Cl, Edg. HA8 96 CN49
Ranelagh Dr, Edg. HA8 96 CN49
Twickenham TW1 177 CH85
★ Ranelagh Gdns, SW3 18 E10
Ranelagh Gdns, E11 124 EJ57
SW6 159 CZ83
W4 off Grove Pk Gdns 158 CQ80
W6 159 CT76
Gravesend (Nthflt) DA11 191 GF87
Ilford IG1 125 EN60
Ranelagh Gdns Mans, SW6 off Ranelagh Gdns 159 CY83
Ranelagh Gro, SW1 18 F9
Ranelagh Ms, W5 off Ranelagh Rd 157 CK75
Ranelagh Pl, N.Mal. KT3 198 CS99
[Sch] Ranelagh Prim Sch, E15 off Corporation St 144 EE68
Ranelagh Rd, E6 145 EN67
E11 124 EE63
E15 144 EE67
N17 122 DS55
N22 99 DM53
NW10 139 CT68
SW1 19 K10
W5 157 CK75
Hemel Hempstead HP2 41 BP20
Redhill RH1 250 DE134
Southall UB1 136 BX74
Wembley HA0 117 CK64
Ranfurly Rd, Sutt. SM1 200 DA103
[Sch] Rangefield Prim Sch, Brom. BR1 off Glenbow Rd 184 EE92
Rangefield Rd, Brom. BR1 184 EE92
Rangemoor Rd, N15 122 DT57
Range Rd, Grav. DA12 191 GL87
Rangers Rd, E4 102 EE45
Loughton IG10 102 EE45
Rangers Sq, SE10 163 ED81
Ranger Wk, Add. KT15 off Monks Cres 212 BH106
Range Way, Shep. TW17 194 BN101
Rangeworth Pl, Sid. DA15 off Priestlands Pk Rd 185 ET90
Rangoon St, EC3 11 N8
Rank Ho, Harl. CM20 51 EQ15
Rankin Cl, NW9 118 CS55
Ranleigh Gdns, Bexh. DA7 166 EZ80
Ranmere St, SW12 off Ormeley Rd 181 DH88
Ranmoor Cl, Har. HA1 117 CD56
Ranmoor Gdns, Har. HA1 117 CD56
Ranmore Av, Croy. CR0 202 DT104
Ranmore Cl, Red. RH1 250 DG131
★ Ranmore Common, Dor. RH5 246 CB133
Ranmore Common, Dor. RH5 246 CC133
Ranmore Common Rd, Dor. (Westh.) RH5 247 CD133
Leatherhead KT24 245 BU134
Ranmore Path, Orp. BR5 206 EU98
Ranmore Rd, Dor. RH4 246 CC134
Sutton SM2 217 CX109
Rannoch Cl, Edg. HA8 96 CP47
Rannoch Rd, W6 159 CW79
Rannoch Wk, Hem.H. HP2 40 BK16
Rannock Av, NW9 118 CS59
Ranskill Rd, Borwd. WD6 78 CN39
Ransom Cl, Wat. WD19 94 BW45
Ransome's Dock Business Cen, SW11 off Parkgate Rd 160 DE80
Ransom Rd, SE7 off Floyd Rd 164 EJ78
Ransom Wk, SE7 off Woolwich Rd 164 EJ78
Ranston Cl, Uxb. (Denh.) UB9 off Nightingale Way 113 BF58
Ranston St, NW1 8 A5
Rant Meadow, Hem.H. HP3 40 BN22
Ranulf Cl, Harl. CM17 36 EW09
Ranulf Rd, NW2 119 CZ63
Ranwell Cl, E3 off Beale Rd 143 DZ67
Ranwell St, E3 143 DZ67
Ranworth Av, Hodd. EN11 33 EB13
Ranworth Cl, Erith DA8 167 FE82
Hemel Hempstead HP3 off Panxworth Rd 40 BK22
Ranworth Rd, N9 100 DW47
Ranyard Cl, Chess. KT9 198 CM104
Raphael Av, Rom. RM1 127 FF55
Tilbury RM18 171 GG80
Raphael Cl, Rad. (Shenley) WD7 62 CL32
Raphael Dr, T.Ditt. KT7 197 CF101
Watford WD24 76 BX40
[Sch] Raphael Indep Sch, Horn. RM11 off Park La 127 FG59
Raphael Rd, Grav. DA12 191 GK87
Raphael St, SW7 18 C4
Rapier Cl, Purf. RM19 168 FN77
Rasehill Cl, Rick. WD3 74 BJ43
Rashleigh St, SW8 off Peardon St 161 DH82
Rashleigh Way, Dart. (Hort.Kir.) DA4 208 FQ98
Rasper Rd, N20 98 DC47
Rastell Av, SW2 181 DK89
Ratcliffe Cl, SE12 184 EG87
Uxbridge UB8 134 BK69
Ratcliffe Cross St, E1 13 H8
Ratcliffe La, E14 13 J8
Ratcliffe Orchard, E1 13 H9
Ratcliff Rd, E7 124 EJ64
Rathbone Mkt, E16 15 J6
Rathbone Pl, W1 9 L7
Rathbone Pt, E5 off Nolan Way 122 DU63
Rathbone St, E16 15 J6
W1 9 K6
Rathcoole Av, N8 121 DM56
Rathcoole Gdns, N8 121 DM57
[Sch] Rathfern Prim Sch, SE6 off Rathfern Rd 183 DZ88
Rathfern Rd, SE6 183 DZ88
Rathgar Av, W13 137 CH74
Rathgar Cl, N3 97 CZ54
Redhill RH1 266 DG139
Rathgar Rd, SW9 off Coldharbour La 161 DP83
Rathlin, Hem.H. HP3 41 BP22
Rathmell Dr, SW4 181 DK86
Rathmore Rd, SE7 25 P9
Gravesend DA11 191 GH87
Rathwell Path, Borwd. WD6 78 CL39
Rats La, Loug. (High Beach) IG10 84 EH38
Rattray Rd, SW2 161 DN84
Ratty's La, Hodd. EN11 49 ED17
Raul Rd, SE15 162 DU81
Raveley St, NW5 121 DJ63
Ravel Gdns, S.Ock. (Aveley) RM15 148 FQ72
Ravel Rd, S.Ock. (Aveley) RM15 148 FQ72
Raven Cl, NW9 off Eagle Dr 96 CS54
Rickmansworth WD3 92 BJ45
Raven Ct, E5 off Stellman Cl 122 DU62
Hatfield AL10 45 CU19
Ravencroft, Grays RM16 off Alexandra Cl 171 GH75
Ravendale Rd, Sun. TW16 195 BT96
Ravenet St, SW11 off Strasburg Rd 161 DH81
Ravenfield, Egh. (Eng.Grn) TW20 172 AW93
Ravenfield Rd, SW17 180 DF90
Welwyn Garden City AL7 29 CZ09
Ravenhill Rd, E13 144 EJ68
Ravenna Rd, SW15 179 CX85
Ravenoak Way, Chig. IG7 103 ES50
Ravenor Pk Rd, Grnf. UB6 136 CB69
[Sch] Ravenor Prim Sch, Grnf. UB6 off Rosedene Av 136 CA69
Raven Rd, E18 102 EJ54
Raven Row, E1 12 D5
⇌ Ravensbourne 183 ED94
Ravensbourne Av, Beck. BR3 183 ED94
Bromley BR2 183 ED94
Staines TW19 174 BL88
[Coll] Ravensbourne Cen (Adult Ed), The, Brom. BR1 off Nightingale La 204 EJ97
[Coll] Ravensbourne Coll of Design & Communication, Chis. BR7 off Walden Rd 185 EM92
Ravensbourne Cres, Rom. RM3 128 FM55
Ravensbourne Gdns, W13 137 CH71
Ilford IG5 103 EN53
Ravensbourne Pk, SE6 183 EA87
Ravensbourne Pk Cres, SE6 183 DZ87
Ravensbourne Pl, SE13 163 EB82
Ravensbourne Rd, SE6 183 DZ87
Bromley BR1 204 EG97
Dartford DA1 167 FG83
Twickenham TW1 177 CJ86
[Sch] Ravensbourne Sch, Rom. RM3 off Neave Cres 106 FK53
[Sch] Ravensbourne Sch, The, Brom. BR2 off Hayes La 204 EH98
Ravensbury Av, Mord. SM4 200 DC99
Ravensbury Ct, Mitch. CR4 off Ravensbury Gro 200 DD98
Ravensbury Gro, Mitch. CR4 200 DD98
Ravensbury La, Mitch. CR4 200 DD98
Ravensbury Path, Mitch. CR4 200 DD98
Ravensbury Rd, SW18 180 DA89
Orpington BR5 205 ET98
Ravensbury Ter, SW18 180 DB89
Ravenscar Rd, Brom. BR1 184 EE91
Surbiton KT6 198 CM103
Ravens Cl, Brom. BR2 204 EF96
Chessington KT9 197 CK100
Enfield EN1 82 DS40
Redhill RH1 250 DF132
Ravens Ct, Berk. HP4 off Frithsden Rd 38 AY17
Ravenscourt, Sun. TW16 195 BT95
Ravenscourt Av, W6 159 CU77
Ravenscourt Cl, Horn. RM12 off Ravenscourt Dr 128 FL62
Ruislip HA4 115 BQ59
Ravenscourt Dr, Horn. RM12 128 FL62
Ravenscourt Gdns, W6 159 CU77
Ravenscourt Gro, Horn. RM12 128 FL61
⊖ Ravenscourt Park 159 CU77
Ravenscourt Pk, W6 159 CU76
Ravenscourt Pl, W6 159 CV77
Ravenscourt Rd, W6 159 CV77
Orpington BR5 206 EU97
Ravenscourt Sq, W6 159 CU76
Ravenscraig Rd, N11 99 DH49
Ravenscroft, Wat. WD25 60 BY34
Ravenscroft Av, NW11 119 CZ59
Wembley HA9 118 CM60
Ravenscroft Cl, E16 15 L5
Ravenscroft Cres, SE9 185 EM90
Ravenscroft Pk, Barn. EN5 79 CX42
Ravenscroft Pt, E9 off Kenton Rd 143 DX65
[Sch] Ravenscroft Prim Sch, E16 15 M4
Ravenscroft Rd, E16 15 M5
W4 158 CQ77
Beckenham BR3 202 DW96
Weybridge KT13 213 BQ111
[Sch] Ravenscroft Sec Sch, N20 off Barnet La 97 CZ45
Ravenscroft St, E2 5 P10
Ravensdale Av, N12 98 DC49
Ravensdale Gdns, SE19 182 DR94
Ravensdale Rd, Houns. TW4 156 BY83
Ravensdale Ms, Stai. TW18 off Worple Rd 174 BH93
Ravensdale Rd, N16 122 DT59
Hounslow TW4 156 BY83
Ravensdell, Hem.H. HP1 39 BF19
Ravensdon St, SE11 20 D10
Ravensfield, Slou. SL3 152 AX75
Ravensfield Cl, Dag. RM9 126 EX63
Ravensfield Gdns, Epsom KT19 216 CS106
Ravenshaw St, NW6 119 CZ64
Ravenshead Cl, S.Croy. CR2 220 DW111
Ravenshill, Chis. BR7 205 EP95
Ravenshurst Av, NW4 119 CW56
Ravenside Cl, N18 101 DX51
Ravenside Retail Pk, N18 101 DX50
Ravens La, Berk. HP4 38 AX19
Ravenslea Rd, SW12 180 DF87
Ravensmead, Ger.Cr. (Chal.St.P.) SL9 91 AZ50
Ravensmead Rd, Brom. BR2 183 ED94
Ravensmede Way, W4 159 CT77
Ravensmere, Epp. CM16 70 EU31
Ravens Ms, SE12 off Ravens Way 184 EG85
Ravenstone, SE17 21 M10
[Sch] Ravenstone Prim Sch, SW12 off Ravenstone St 181 DH88
Ravenstone Rd, N8 121 DN55
NW9 off West Hendon Bdy 119 CT58
Ravenstone St, SW12 180 DG88
Ravens Way, SE12 184 EG85
Ravens Wf, Berk. HP4 38 AX19
Ravenswold, Ken. CR8 236 DQ115
Ravenswood, Bex. DA5 186 EY88
Ravenswood Av, Surb. KT6 198 CM103
West Wickham BR4 203 EC102
Ravenswood Cl, Cob. KT11 230 BX115
Romford RM5 105 FB50
Ravenswood Ct, Kings.T. KT2 178 CP93
Woking GU22 227 AZ118
Ravenswood Cres, Har. HA2 116 BZ61
West Wickham BR4 203 EC102
Ravenswood Gdns, Islw. TW7 157 CE81
Ravenswood Pk, Nthwd. HA6 93 BU51
Ravenswood Rd, E17 123 EB56
SW12 181 DH87
Croydon CR0 201 DP104
[Sch] Ravens Wd Sch for Boys, Brom. BR2 off Oakley Rd 204 EK104
Ravensworth Rd, NW10 139 CV69
SE9 185 EM91
Slough SL2 off Wentworth Av 131 AN69
Ravey St, EC2 11 L3
Ravine Gro, SE18 165 ES79
Rav Pinter Cl, N16 122 DS59
Rawdon Dr, Hodd. EN11 49 EA18
Rawlings Cl, Beck. BR3 off Creswell Dr 203 EB99
Orpington BR6 223 ET106
Rawlings Cres, Wem. HA9 118 CP62
Rawlings La, Beac. (Seer Grn) HP9 89 AQ48
Rawlings St, SW3 18 C7
Rawlins Cl, N3 119 CY55
South Croydon CR2 221 DY108
Rawlyn Cl, Grays (Chaff.Hun.) RM16 169 FW78
Rawnsley Av, Mitch. CR4 200 DD99
Rawreth Wk, N1 5 H7
Rawson St, SW11 off Strasburg Rd 160 DG81
Rawsthorne Cl, E16 off Kennard St 145 EM74
Rawstone Wk, E13 144 EG68
Rawstorne Pl, EC1 10 E1
Rawstorne St, EC1 10 E1
Raybarn Rd, Hem.H. HP1 40 BG18
Rayburn Rd, Horn. RM11 128 FN59
Ray Cl, Chess. KT9 off Merritt Gdns 215 CJ107
Raydean Rd, Barn. EN5 80 DB43
Raydon Rd, Wal.Cr. (Chsht) EN8 67 DX32
Raydons Gdns, Dag. RM9 126 EY64
Raydons Rd, Dag. RM9 126 EY64
Raydon St, N19 121 DH61
Rayfield, Epp. CM16 70 EU30
Welwyn Garden City AL8 29 CX06
Rayfield Cl, Brom. BR2 204 EL100
Rayford Av, SE12 184 EF87
Rayford Cl, Dart. DA1 188 FJ85
Ray Gdns, Bark. IG11 146 EU68
Stanmore HA7 95 CH50
Ray Lamb Way, Erith DA8 167 FH79
Raylands Mead, Ger.Cr. SL9 off Bull La 112 AW57
Rayleas Cl, SE18 165 EP81
Rayleigh Av, Tedd. TW11 177 CE93
Rayleigh Cl, N13 off Rayleigh Rd 100 DR48
Brentwood (Hutt.) CM13 109 GC44
Rayleigh Ct, Kings.T. KT1 198 CM96
Rayleigh Ri, S.Croy. CR2 220 DS107
Rayleigh Rd, E16 25 P1
N13 100 DQ48
SW19 199 CZ95
Brentwood (Hutt.) CM13 109 GB44
Woodford Green IG8 102 EJ51
Rayley La, Epp. (N.Wld Bas.) CM16 52 FA24
[Sch] Ray Lo Prim Sch, Wdf.Grn. IG8 off Snakes La E 102 EK51
Ray Lo Rd, Wdf.Grn. IG8 102 EJ51
Ray Massey Way, E6 off Ron Leighton Way 144 EL67
Raymead, NW4 off Tenterden Gro 119 CW56
Raymead Av, Th.Hth. CR7 201 DN99
Raymead Cl, Lthd. (Fetch.) KT22 231 CE122
Ray Mead Ct, Maid. SL6 off Boulters La 130 AC70
Raymead Pas, Th.Hth. CR7 off Raymead Av 201 DN99
Ray Mead Rd, Maid. SL6 130 AC72
Raymead Way, Lthd. (Fetch.) KT22 231 CE122
Raymer Cl, St.Alb. AL1 43 CE19
Raymere Gdns, SE18 165 ER80
Raymer Wk, Horl. RH6 269 DJ147
Raymond Av, E18 124 EF55
W13 157 CG76
Raymond Bldgs, WC1 10 B5
Raymond Cl, SE26 182 DW92
Abbots Langley WD5 59 BR32
Slough (Colnbr.) SL3 153 BE81
Raymond Ct, N10 off Pembroke Rd 98 DG52
Raymond Ct, Pot. B. EN6 off St. Francis Cl 64 DC34
Sutton SM2 off Mulgrave Rd 218 DB107
Raymond Cres, Guil. GU2 258 AT135
Raymond Gdns, Chig. IG7 104 EV48
Raymond Rd, E13 144 EJ66
SW19 179 CY93
Beckenham BR3 203 DY98
Ilford IG2 125 ER59
Slough SL3 153 BA76
Raymonds Cl, Welw.G.C. AL7 29 CY11
Raymonds Plain, Welw.G.C. AL7 29 CY11
Raymond Way, Esher (Clay.) KT10 215 CG107
Raymouth Rd, SE16 22 D7
Rayne Ct, E18 124 EF56
[Sch] Raynehurst Jun Sch, Grav. DA12 off Cerne Rd 191 GM90
Rayners Cl, H.Wyc. (Loud.) HP10 88 AC52
Slough (Colnbr.) SL3 153 BC80
Wembley HA0 117 CK64
Rayners Ct, Grav. DA11 190 GB86
Harrow HA2 116 CA60
Rayners Cres, Nthlt. UB5 135 BV69
Rayners Gdns, Nthlt. UB5 135 BV68
RAYNERS LANE, Har. HA2 116 BZ60
⊖ Rayners Lane 116 BZ59
Rayners La, Har. HA2 116 CB61
Pinner HA5 116 BZ58
Rayners Rd, SW15 179 CY85
Rayner Twr, E10 123 EA59
Raynes Av, E11 124 EJ59
RAYNES PARK, SW20 199 CV97
⇌ Raynes Park 199 CW96
[Sch] Raynes Pk High Sch, SW20 off Bushey Rd 199 CV97
Raynham Av, N18 100 DU51
[Sch] Raynham Prim Sch, N18 off Raynham Av 100 DU50
Raynham Rd, N18 100 DU50
W6 159 CV77
Raynham St, Hert. SG13 32 DS08
Raynham Ter, N18 100 DU50
Raynor Cl, Sthl. UB1 136 BZ74
Raynor Pl, N1 5 H6
Raynsford Rd, Ware SG12 33 DY06
Raynton Cl, Har. HA2 116 BY60
Hayes UB4 135 BT70
Raynton Dr, Hayes UB4 135 BT70
Raynton Rd, Enf. EN3 83 DX37
Ray Rd, Rom. RM5 105 FB50
West Molesey KT8 196 CB99
Rays Av, N18 100 DW49
Windsor SL4 151 AM80
Rays Hill, Dart. (Hort.Kir.) DA4 208 FQ98
Rays La, H.Wyc. (Penn) HP10 88 AC47
Rays Rd, N18 100 DW49
West Wickham BR4 203 EC101
Ray St, EC1 10 D4
Ray St Br, EC1 10 D4
Ray Wk, N7 off Andover Rd 121 DM61
Raywood Cl, Hayes UB3 155 BQ80
Reachview Cl, NW1 off Baynes St 141 DJ66
Read Cl, T.Ditt. KT7 197 CG101
Read Ct, Wal.Abb. EN9 68 EG33
Reade Ct, Slou. (Farn.Com.) SL2 off Victoria Rd 131 AQ65
Readens, The, Bans. SM7 234 DF116
Reade Wk, NW10 off Denbigh Cl 138 CS66
Reading Arch Rd, Red. RH1 250 DF134
Reading La, E8 142 DV65
Reading Rd, Nthlt. UB5 116 CB64
Sutton SM1 218 DC106
Readings, The, Harl. CM18 51 ET18
Rickmansworth (Chorl.) WD3 73 BF41
Reading Way, NW7 97 CX50
Read Rd, Ashtd. KT21 231 CK117
Reads Cl, Ilf. IG1 off Chapel Rd 125 EP62
Reads Rest La, Tad. KT20 233 CZ119
Read Way, Grav. DA12 191 GK92
Reapers Cl, NW1 off Crofters Way 141 DK67
Reapers Way, Islw. TW7 off Hall Rd 177 CD85
Reardon Ct, N21 off Cosgrove Cl 100 DQ47
Reardon Path, E1 22 D2
Reardon St, E1 22 C1
Reaston St, SE14 162 DW80
[Sch] Reay Prim Sch, SW9 off Hackford Rd 161 DM80
Reckitt Rd, W4 158 CS78
Record St, SE15 162 DW79
Recovery St, SW17 180 DE92
Recreation Av, Rom. RM7 127 FC57
Romford (Harold Wd) RM3 106 FM54
Recreation Rd, SE26 183 DX91
Bromley BR2 204 EF96
Guildford GU1 242 AW134
Sidcup DA15 off Woodside Rd 185 ES90
Southall UB2 156 BY77
Recreation Way, Mitch. CR4 201 DK97
Rector St, N1 4 G8
Rectory Chase, Brwd. (Lt.Warley) CM13 129 FX56
Rectory Cl, E4 101 EA48
N3 97 CZ53
SW20 199 CW97
Ashtead KT21 232 CM119
Dartford DA1 167 FE84
Guildford GU4 243 BD132
Hatfield AL9 46 DF17
Shepperton TW17 194 BN97
Sidcup DA14 186 EV91
Slough (Farn.Royal) SL2 131 AQ69
Stanmore HA7 95 CH51
Surbiton KT6 197 CJ102
Ware SG12 34 EK07
West Byfleet (Byfleet) KT14 212 BL113
Windsor SL4 151 AN81
Rectory Cres, E11 124 EJ58
Rectory Fm Rd, Enf. EN2 81 DM38
Rectory Fld, Harl. CM19 51 EP17
Rectory Fld Cres, SE7 164 EJ80
Rectory Gdns, N8 121 DL56
SW4 off Fitzwilliam Rd 161 DJ83
Chalfont St. Giles HP8 90 AV48
Hatfield AL10 45 CV18
Northolt UB5 136 BZ67
Upminster RM14 129 FR61
Rectory Grn, Beck. BR3 203 DZ95
Rectory Gro, SW4 161 DJ83
Rectory Gro, Croy. CR0 201 DP103
Hampton TW12 176 BZ91
Rectory Hill, Amer. HP6, HP7 55 AP39
Rectory La, SW17 180 DG93
Ashtead KT21 232 CM118
Banstead SM7 218 DF114
Berkhamsted HP4 38 AW19
Betchworth (Buckland) RH3 249 CT131
Edgware HA8 96 CN51
Guildford (Shere) GU5 260 BM139
Harlow CM19 51 EP17
Kings Langley WD4 58 BN28
Leatherhead (Bkhm) KT23 246 BZ126
Loughton IG10 85 EN40
Radlett (Shenley) WD7 62 CN33
Rickmansworth WD3 92 BK46
Sevenoaks TN13 257 FJ126
Sidcup DA14 186 EV91
Stanmore HA7 95 CH50
Surbiton KT6 197 CH102
Wallington SM6 219 DJ105
West Byfleet (Byfleet) KT14 212 BL113
Westerham TN16 238 EL123
Westerham (Brasted) TN16 240 EW123
Rectory Meadow, Grav. (Sthflt) DA13 190 GA93
Rectory Orchard, SW19 179 CY91
[Sch] Rectory Paddock Sch & Research Unit, Orp. BR5 off Main Rd 206 EW96
Rectory Pk, S.Croy. CR2 220 DS113
Rectory Pk Av, Nthlt. UB5 136 BZ69
Rectory Pl, SE18 165 EN77
⇌ Rectory Road 122 DT62
Rectory Rd, E12 125 EM64
E17 123 EB55
N16 122 DT62
SW13 159 CU82
W3 138 CP74
Beckenham BR3 203 EA95
Coulsdon CR5 250 DD125
Dagenham RM10 146 FA66
Grays RM17 170 GD76
Hayes UB3 135 BU72
Hounslow TW4 155 BV81
Keston BR2 222 EK108
Maidenhead (Taplow) SL6 130 AD70
Rickmansworth WD3 92 BK46
Southall UB2 156 BZ76
Sutton SM1 200 DA104
Swanscombe DA10 190 FY87
Tilbury (W.Til.) RM18 171 GK79
Welwyn Garden City AL8 29 CV06
Rectory Sq, E1 13 H5
Rectory Way, Amer. HP7 55 AP39
Uxbridge UB10 115 BP62
Rectory Wd, Harl. CM20 35 EQ14
Reculver Ms, N18 off Lyndhurst Rd 100 DU49
Reculver Rd, SE16 22 G9
Red Anchor Cl, SW3 off Old Ch St 160 DE79
Redan Pl, W2 7 J8
Redan St, W14 16 B5
Redan Ter, SE5 off Flaxman Rd 162 DQ82
Redbarn Cl, Pur. CR8 off Whytecliffe Rd S 219 DP111
Red Barracks Rd, SE18 165 EM77
Redberry Gro, SE26 182 DW90
Redbourne Av, N3 98 DA53
Redbourne Dr, SE28 146 EX72
Redbourn Rd, Hem.H. HP2 40 BN16
St. Albans AL3 42 CA18
REDBRIDGE, Ilf. IG 125 EM58
⊖ Redbridge 124 EK58
[Coll] Redbridge Coll, Rom. RM6 off Little Heath 126 EV57
[Coll] Redbridge Drama Cen, E18 off Churchfields 102 EG53
Redbridge Enterprise Cen, Ilf. IG1 125 EQ61
Redbridge Gdns, SE5 162 DS80
[Sch] Redbridge Inf Sch, Ilf. IG4 off College Gdns 124 EL57
[Coll] Redbridge Inst of Adult Ed, Gearies Cen, Ilf. IG2 off Gaysham Av 125 EP57
Valentines Cen, Ilf. IG2 off Cranbrook Rd 125 EN58
[Sch] Redbridge Jun Sch, Ilf. IG4 off College Gdns 124 EL57
Redbridge La E, Ilf. IG4 124 EK58
Redbridge La W, E11 124 EH58
[Coll] Redbridge Music Sch, John Savage Cen, Ilf. IG6 off Fencepiece Rd 103 EQ52
Redburn St, SW3 160 DF79
Redbury Cl, Rain. RM13 off Deri Av 147 FH70
Redcar Cl, Nthlt. UB5 116 CB64
Redcar Rd, Rom. RM3 106 FM50
Redcar St, SE5 162 DQ80
Redcastle Cl, E1 12 E9
Red Cedars Rd, Orp. BR6 205 ES101
Redchurch St, E2 11 N3
Redcliffe Cl, SW5 off Warwick Rd 160 DB78
Redcliffe Gdns, SW5 17 K10
SW10 17 K10
W4 158 CP80
Ilford IG1 125 EN60
Redcliffe Ms, SW10 17 K10
Redcliffe Pl, SW10 160 DC79
Redcliffe Rd, SW10 17 L10
[Sch] Redcliffe Sch, SW10 off Redcliffe Gdns 160 DC79
Redcliffe Sq, SW10 17 K10
Redcliffe St, SW10 160 DB79
Redclose Av, Mord. SM4 200 DA99
Redclyffe Rd, E6 144 EJ67
Redcote Pl, Dor. RH4 247 CK134
Red Cottage Ms, Slou. SL3 152 AW76
Red Ct, Slou. SL1 132 AS74
Redcourt, Wok. GU22 227 BD115
Redcroft Rd, Sthl. UB1 136 CC73
Redcross Way, SE1 21 H3
Redden Ct Rd, Rom. RM3 128 FL55
[Sch] Redden Ct Sch, Rom. RM3 off Cotswold Rd 128 FM55
Redding Cl, Dart. DA2 189 FS89
Redding Dr, Amer. HP6 55 AN37
Reddings, Hem.H. HP3 40 BM22

Reddings, Welw. G. C. AL8 ... 29 CW08
Reddings, The, NW7 ... 97 CT48
Borehamwood WD6 ... 78 CM41
Reddings Av, Bushey WD23 .. 76 CB43
Reddings Cl, NW7 ... 97 CT49
Sch **Reddings Prim Sch**, Hem.H. HP3
off Bennetts End Rd ... 40 BN22
Reddington Cl, S.Croy. CR2 .220 DR109
Reddington Dr, Slou. SL3 .. 152 AY76
Reddins Rd, SE15 ... 162 DU79
Redditch Ct, Hem.H. HP2 ... 40 BM16
Reddons Rd, Beck. BR3 ... 183 DY94
Reddown Rd, Couls. CR5 .. 235 DK118
Reddy Rd, Erith DA8 ... 167 FF79
Rede Ct, Wey. KT13
off Old Palace Rd ... 195 BP104
Redehall Rd, Horl. (Smallfield) RH6 ... 269 DP148
Redenham Ho, SW15
off Tangley Gro ... 179 CT87
Rede Pl, W2 ... 7 H8
Redesdale Gdns, Islw. TW7 .157 CG80
Redesdale St, SW3 ... 160 DF79
Redfern Av, Houns. TW4 ... 176 CA87
Redfern Cl, Uxb. UB8 ... 134 BJ67
Redfern Gdns, Rom. RM2 .. 106 FK54
Redfern Rd, NW10 ... 138 CS66
SE6 ... 183 EC87
Redfield La, SW5 ... 17 H7
Redfield Ms, SW5 ... 17 H7
Redford Av, Couls. CR5 ... 219 DH114
Thornton Heath CR7 ... 201 DM98
Wallington SM6 ... 219 DL107
Redford Cl, Felt. TW13 ... 175 BT89
H **Redford Lo Psychiatric Hosp**, N9 ... 100 DU47
Redford Rd, Wind. SL4 ... 151 AK81
Redford Wk, N1 ... 4 F7
Redford Way, Uxb. UB8 ... 134 BJ66
Redgate Dr, Brom. BR2 ... 204 EH103
Sch **Redgates Sch**, Croy.
CR0 *off Purley Way* ... 219 DN106
Redgate Ter, SW15
off Lytton Gro ... 179 CX86
Redgrave Cl, Croy. CR0 ... 202 DT100
Redgrave Rd, SW15 ... 159 CX83
Redhall Cl, Hat. AL10 ... 45 CT21
Redhall Ct, Cat. CR3 ... 236 DR123
Redhall Dr, Hat. AL10 ... 45 CT22
Redhall La, Rick. WD3 ... 74 BL39
Redheath Cl, Wat. WD25 ... 75 BT35
REDHILL, RH1 ... 250 DG134
⇌ **Redhill** ... 250 DG133
Red Hill, Chis. BR7 ... 185 EN92
Uxbridge (Denh.) UB9 ... 113 BD61
Coll **Redhill Coll (Royal Nat Inst for the Blind)**, Red.
RH1 *off Philanthropic Rd* .267 DH136
Redhill Common, Red. RH1 .266 DE135
Redhill Dr, Edg. HA8 ... 96 CQ54
Sch **Red Hill Prim Sch**, Chis.
BR7 *off Red Hill* ... 185 EP92
Redhill Rd, Cob. KT11 ... 213 BP113
Red Hills, Hodd. EN11 ... 48 DV19
Redhill St, NW1 ... 9 H1
Red Ho Cl, Beac. (Knot.Grn)
HP9 ... 88 AH51
Ware SG12 ... 33 DY07
Red Ho La, Bexh. DA6 ... 166 EX84
Walton-on-Thames KT12 .195 BU103
Redhouse Rd, Croy. CR0 ... 201 DK100
Westerham (Tats.) TN16 .238 EJ120
Red Ho Sq, N1 ... 5 H4
★ **Red Ho (William Morris Ho)**,
The, Bexh. DA6 ... 166 EY84
Redington Gdns, NW3 ... 120 DB63
Redington Rd, NW3 ... 120 DB63
Redland Gdns, W.Mol. KT8
off Dunstable Rd ... 196 BZ98
Redlands, Couls. CR5 ... 235 DL116
Sch **Redlands C of E Prim Sch**,
The, Dor. RH4
off Goodwyns Rd ... 263 CH139
Redlands Ct, Brom. BR1 ... 184 EF94
Redlands La, Dor. RH5 ... 263 CG142
Sch **Redlands Prim Sch**, E1 ... 12 F5
Redlands Rd, Enf. EN3 ... 83 DY39
Sevenoaks TN13 ... 256 FF124
Redlands Way, SW2 ... 181 DM87
Red La, Dor. RH5 ... 264 CL142
Esher (Clay.) KT10 ... 215 CG107
Oxted RH8 ... 254 EH133
Redleaf Cl, Belv. DA17 ... 166 FA79
Red Leaf Cl, Slou. SL3
off Pickford Dr ... 133 AZ74
Redleaves Av, Ashf. TW15 ... 175 BP93
Redlees Cl, Islw. TW7 ... 157 CG84
Red Leys, Uxb. UB8
off Park Rd ... 134 BL66
Red Lion Cl, SE17
off Red Lion Row ... 162 DQ79
Orpington BR5 ... 206 EW100
Red Lion Ct, EC4 ... 10 D7
Red Lion Cres, Harl. CM17 ... 52 EW17
Red Lion Hill, N2 ... 98 DD54
Red Lion La, SE18 ... 165 EN80
Harlow CM17 ... 52 EW17
Hemel Hempstead HP3 ... 58 BM26
Rickmansworth (Sarratt)
WD3 ... 74 BG35
Woking (Chobham) GU24 .210 AS109
Red Lion Pl, SE18
off Shooter's Hill Rd ... 165 EN81
Red Lion Rd, Surb. KT6 ... 198 CM103
Woking (Chobham) GU24 .210 AS109
Red Lion Row, SE17 ... 162 DQ79
Red Lion Sq, SW18
off Wandsworth High St .180 DA85
WC1 ... 10 A6
Red Lion St, WC1 ... 10 A5
Chesham HP5 ... 54 AP32
Richmond TW9 ... 177 CK85
Red Lion Way, H.Wyc.
(Woob.Grn) HP10 ... 110 AE57
Red Lion Yd, W1 ... 18 F1
Watford WD17 *off High St* .. 76 BW42
Red Lo Cres, Bex. DA5 ... 187 FD90
Red Lo Gdns, Berk. HP4 ... 38 AU20
Red Lo Rd, Beck. BR3 ... 203 ED100
Bexley DA5 ... 187 FD90
West Wickham BR4 ... 203 EC102
Redman Cl, Nthlt. UB5 ... 136 BW68
Redmans La, Sev. (Shore.)
TN14 ... 225 FE107
Redman's Rd, E1 ... 12 E5
Redmead La, E1 ... 22 A2
Redmead Rd, Hayes UB3 ... 155 BS77
Redmore Rd, W6 ... 159 CV77
Red Oak Cl, Orp. BR6 ... 205 EP104
Red Oaks Mead, Epp.
(They.B.) CM16 ... 85 ER37
Red Path, E9 ... 143 DZ65
Red Pl, W1 ... 8 E9
Redpoll Way, Erith DA18 ... 166 EX76
Red Post Hill, SE21 ... 182 DR85
SE24 ... 162 DR84
Redricks La, Saw. CM21 ... 35 ES09
Redriffe Rd, E13 ... 144 EF67
Redriff Est, SE16 ... 23 L5
Sch **Redriff Prim Sch**, SE16 ... 23 K3
Redriff Rd, SE16 ... 23 H6
Romford RM7 ... 105 FB54
Red Rd, Borwd. WD6 ... 78 CM41
Brentwood CM14 ... 108 FV49
Redroofs Cl, Beck. BR3 ... 203 EB95
Redruth Cl, N22
off Palmerston Rd ... 99 DM52
Redruth Gdns, Rom. RM3 .. 106 FM50
Redruth Rd, E9 ... 143 DX67
Romford RM3 ... 106 FM50
Redruth Wk, Rom. RM3 ... 106 FN50
Red Sq, N16 ... 122 DR62
Redstart Cl, E6
off Columbine Av ... 144 EL71
SE14
off Southerngate Way .. 163 DY80
Croydon (New Adgtn) CR0 .221 ED110
Redstone Hill, Red. RH1 ... 250 DG134
Redstone Hollow, Red. RH1 .266 DG135
Redstone Manor, Red. RH1 .250 DG134
Redstone Pk, Red. RH1 ... 250 DG134
Redstone Rd, Red. RH1 ... 266 DG135
Redston Rd, N8 ... 121 DK56
REDSTREET, Grav. DA13 ... 190 GB93
Red St, Grav. (Sthflt) DA13 .190 GA93
Redvers Rd, N22 ... 99 DN54
Warlingham CR6 ... 236 DW118
Redvers St, N1 ... 11 M1
Redwald Rd, E5 ... 123 DX63
Redway Dr, Twick. TW2 ... 176 CC87
Red Willow, Harl. CM19 ... 51 EM18
Redwing Cl, S.Croy. CR2 ... 221 DX111
Redwing Gdns, W.Byf. KT14 .212 BH112
Redwing Gro, Abb.L. WD5 ... 59 BU31
Redwing Path, SE28 ... 165 ER75
Redwing Ri, Guil. GU4 ... 243 BD132
Redwing Rd, Wall. SM6 ... 219 DL108
Redwood, Egh. TW20 ... 193 BE96
Slough (Burn.) SL1 ... 130 AG68
Redwood Chase, S.Ock.
RM15 ... 149 FW70
Redwood Cl, E3 ... 143 EA68
N14 *off The Vale* ... 99 DK45
SE16 ... 23 K2
Buckhurst Hill IG9
off Beech La ... 102 EH47
Kenley CR8 ... 220 DQ114
Sidcup DA15 ... 186 EU87
Uxbridge UB10
off The Larches ... 135 BP68
Watford WD19 ... 94 BW49
Redwood Ct, NW6
off The Avenue ... 139 CY66
Redwood Dr, Hem.H. HP3 ... 40 BL22
Redwood Est, Houns. TW5 .155 BV79
Redwood Gdns, E4 ... 83 EB44
Chigwell IG7 ... 104 EU50
Slough SL1
off Godolphin Rd ... 131 AR73
Redwood Gro, Guil. (Chilw.)
GU4 ... 259 BC140
Redwood Ms, SW4
off Hannington Rd ... 161 DH83
Ashford TW15
off Napier Wk ... 175 BR94
Redwood Mt, Reig. RH2 ... 250 DA131
Redwood Ri, Borwd. WD6 ... 78 CN37
Redwoods, SW15 ... 179 CU88
Addlestone KT15 ... 212 BG107
Hertford SG14 ... 32 DQ08
Redwoods, The, Wind. SL4 .151 AR83
Redwood Wk, Surb. KT6 ... 197 CK102
Redwood Way, Barn. EN5 ... 79 CX43
Reece Ms, SW7 ... 17 N7
Reed Av, Orp. BR6 ... 205 ES104
Reed Cl, E16 ... 15 L6
SE12 ... 184 EG85
Iver SL0 ... 133 BE72
St. Albans (Lon.Col.) AL2 . 61 CK27
Reed Dr, Red. RH1 ... 266 DG137
Reede Gdns, Dag. RM10 ... 127 FB64
Reede Rd, Dag. RM10 ... 146 FA65
Reede Way, Dag. RM10 ... 147 FB65
⇌ **Reedham** ... 219 DM113
Reedham Cl, N17 ... 122 DV56
St. Albans (Brick.Wd) AL2 . 60 CA29
Reedham Dr, Pur. CR8 ... 219 DN113
Reedham Pk Av, Pur. CR8 .. 235 DN116
Reedham Rd, Slou. SL1
off Hogfair La ... 130 AJ69
Reedham St, SE15 ... 162 DU82
Reedholm Vil, N16
off Winston Rd ... 122 DR63
Reed Pl, Shep. TW17 ... 194 BM102
West Byfleet KT14 ... 211 BE113
Reed Pond Wk, Rom. RM2 .. 105 FF54
Reed Rd, N17 ... 100 DT54
Reeds, The, Welw.G.C. AL7 .. 29 CX10
Reeds Cres, Wat. WD24 ... 76 BW40
Reedsfield Cl, Ashf. TW15
off The Yews ... 175 BP91
Reedsfield Rd, Ashf. TW15 .. 175 BP91
Reeds Pl, NW1
off Royal Coll St ... 141 DJ66
Sch **Reed's Sch**, Cob. KT11
off Sandy La ... 214 CA112
Reeds Wk, Wat. WD24 ... 76 BW40
Reedworth St, SE11 ... 20 D8
Ree La Cotts, Loug. IG10
off Englands La ... 85 EN40
Reenglass Rd, Stan. HA7 ... 95 CK49
Rees Dr, Stan. HA7 ... 96 CL49
Rees Gdns, Croy. CR0 ... 202 DT100
Reesland Cl, E12 ... 145 EN65
Rees St, N1 ... 5 H8
Reets Fm Cl, NW9 ... 118 CS58
Reeve Rd, Reig. RH2 ... 266 DC138
Reeves Av, NW9 ... 118 CR59
Uni **Reeves Corner** ... 201 DP103
Reeves Cor, Croy. CR0
off Roman Way ... 201 DP103
Reeves Cres, Swan. BR8 ... 207 FD97
Reeves La, Harl. (Roydon)
CM19 ... 50 EJ19
Reeves Ms, W1 ... 8 E10
Reeves Rd, E3 ... 14 A3
SE18 ... 165 EP79
Reflection, The, E16
off Woolwich Manor Way .165 EP75
Reform Row, N17 ... 100 DT54
Reform St, SW11 ... 160 DF82
Regal Cl, E1 ... 12 B5
W5 ... 137 CK71
Regal Ct, N18 *off College Cl* .100 DT50
Regal Cres, Wall. SM6 ... 201 DH104
Regal Dr, N11 ... 99 DH50
Regalfield Cl, Guil. GU2 ... 242 AU130
Regal La, NW1
off Regents Pk Rd ... 140 DG67
Regal Pl, E3 ... 13 M2
SW6 *off Maxwell Rd* ... 160 DB80
Regal Row, SE15
off Astbury Rd ... 162 DW81
Regal Way, Har. HA3 ... 118 CL58
Watford WD24 ... 76 BW38
Regan Cl, Guil. GU2 ... 242 AV129
Regan Way, N1 ... 5 L10
Regarder Rd, Chig. IG7 ... 104 EU50
Regarth Av, Rom. RM1 ... 127 FE58
Regatta Ho, Tedd. TW11
off Twickenham Rd ... 177 CG91
Regency Cl, W5 ... 138 CL72
Chigwell IG7 ... 103 EQ50
Hampton TW12 ... 176 BZ92
Regency Ct, Brwd. CM14 ... 108 FW47
Broxbourne EN10
off Berners Way ... 49 DZ23
Harlow CM18 ... 52 EU18
Hemel Hempstead HP2
off Alexandra Rd ... 40 BK20
Sutton SM1
off Brunswick Rd ... 218 DB105
Regency Cres, NW4 ... 97 CX54
Regency Dr, Ruis. HA4 ... 115 BS60
West Byfleet KT14 ... 211 BF113
Regency Gdns, Horn. RM11 .128 FJ59
Walton-on-Thames KT12 .196 BW102
Regency Ho, SW6
off The Boulevard ... 160 DC81
Regency Lo, Buck.H. IG9 ... 102 EK47
Regency Ms, NW10
off High Rd ... 139 CU65
SW9 *off Lothian Rd* ... 161 DP80
Beckenham BR3 ... 203 EC95
Isleworth TW7
off Queensbridge Pk ... 177 CE85
Regency Pl, SW1 ... 19 M7
Regency St, SW1 ... 19 L7
Regency Ter, SW7
off Fulham Rd ... 160 DD78
Regency Wk, Croy. CR0 ... 203 DY100
Richmond TW10
off Grosvenor Rd ... 178 CL85
Regency Way, Bexh. DA6 ... 166 EX83
Woking GU22 ... 227 BD115
Regent Av, Uxb. UB10 ... 135 BP66
Regent Cl, N12 *off Nether St* . 98 DC50
Addlestone (New Haw)
KT15 ... 212 BK109
Grays RM16 ... 170 GC75
Harrow HA3 ... 118 CL58
Hounslow TW4 ... 155 BV81
Redhill RH1 ... 251 DJ129
St. Albans AL4 ... 43 CJ16
Regent Ct, Slou. SL1
off Stoke Poges La ... 132 AS72
Windsor SL4 ... 151 AR81
Regent Cres, Red. RH1 ... 250 DF132
Regent Gdns, Ilf. IG3 ... 126 EU58
Regent Gate, Wal.Cr. EN8 ... 67 DY34
Regent Pk, Lthd. KT22 ... 231 CG118
Regent Pl, SW19
off Haydons Rd ... 180 DB92
W1 ... 9 K9
Croydon CR0 *off Grant Rd* .202 DT102
Regent Rd, SE24 ... 181 DP86
Epping CM16 ... 69 ET30
Surbiton KT5 ... 198 CM99
Regents Av, N13 ... 99 DM50
Regents Br Gdns, SW8 ... 161 DL80
Regents Cl, Hayes UB4
off Park Rd ... 135 BS71
Radlett WD7 ... 61 CG34
South Croydon CR2 ... 220 DS107
Whyteleafe CR3 ... 236 DS118
Coll **Regent's Coll**, NW1 ... 8 E3
Regents Dr, Kes. BR2 ... 222 EK106
Woodford Green IG8 ... 103 EN52
Regents Ms, NW8
off Langford Pl ... 140 DC68
Horley RH6
off Victoria Rd ... 268 DG148
REGENT'S PARK, NW1 ... 141 DH69
★ **Regent's Park**, NW1 ... 8 C1
⊖ **Regent's Park** ... 8 G4
Regent's Pk Est, NW1 ... 9 J2
Regents Pk Rd, N3 ... 119 CZ55
NW1 ... 140 DF67
Regents Pk Ter, NW1
off Oval Rd ... 141 DH67
Regent's Pl, SE3 ... 164 EG82
Regents Pl, Loug. IG10 ... 102 EK45
Regent Sq, E3 ... 14 A2
WC1 ... 9 P2
Belvedere DA17 ... 167 FB77
Regents Row, E8 ... 142 DU67
Regent St, NW10 ... 6 B2
SW1 ... 9 L10
W1 ... 9 H7
W4 ... 158 CN78
Watford WD24 ... 75 BV38
Regents Wf, N1 ... 4 A9
Regina Cl, Barn. EN5 ... 79 CX41
Sch **Regina Coeli Catholic Prim Sch**, S.Croy. CR2
off Pampisford Rd ... 219 DP108
Reginald Ms, Harl. CM17
off London Rd ... 36 EW14
Reginald Rd, E7 ... 144 EG66
SE8 ... 163 EA80
Northwood HA6 ... 93 BT53
Romford RM3 ... 106 FN53
Reginald Sq, SE8 ... 163 EA80
Regina Pt, SE16 ... 22 F5
Regina Rd, N4 ... 121 DM60
SE25 ... 202 DU97
W13 ... 137 CG74
Southall UB2 ... 156 BY77
Regina Ter, W13 ... 137 CG74
Regis Pl, SW2 ... 161 DM84
Regis Rd, NW5 ... 121 DH64
Regius Ct, H.Wyc. (Penn)
HP10 ... 88 AD47
Regnart Bldgs, NW1 ... 9 K3
Reid Av, Cat. CR3 ... 236 DR121
Reid Cl, Couls. CR5 ... 235 DH116
Pinner HA5 ... 115 BU56
Reidhaven Rd, SE18 ... 165 ES77
REIGATE, RH2 ... 250 DA134
⇌ **Reigate** ... 250 DA133
Reigate Av, Sutt. SM1 ... 200 DA102
Reigate Business Ms, Reig.
RH2 *off Albert Rd N* ... 249 CZ133
Coll **Reigate Coll**, Reig. RH2
off Castlefield Rd ... 250 DB134
Sch **Reigate Gram Sch**, Reig.
RH2 *off Reigate Rd* ... 250 DC134
Reigate Heath, Reig. RH2 .. 265 CX135
Reigate Hill, Reig. RH2 ... 250 DB130
Reigate Hill Cl, Reig. RH2 .. 250 DA131
Sch **Reigate Parish Ch Sch**,
Reig. RH2
off Blackborough Rd .. 250 DC134
Sch **Reigate Priory Jun Sch**,
Reig. RH2 *off Bell St* ... 250 DA134
Reigate Rd, Bet. RH3 ... 248 CS132
Bromley BR1 ... 184 EF90
Dorking RH4 ... 263 CJ135
Epsom KT17, KT18 ... 217 CT110
Horley (Hkwd) RH6 ... 268 DC146
Ilford IG3 ... 125 ET61
Leatherhead KT22 ... 231 CJ123
Redhill RH1 ... 250 DB134
Reigate RH2 ... 250 DB134
Reigate (Sidlow) RH2 ... 266 DB141
Tadworth KT20 ... 233 CX117
Sch **Reigate St. Mary's Prep & Choir Sch**, Reig.
RH2 *off Chart La* ... 250 DB134
Sch **Reigate Sch**, Reig. RH2
off Pendleton Rd ... 266 DC137
Reigate Way, Wall. SM6 ... 219 DL106
Reighton Rd, E5 ... 122 DU62
Reindorp Cl, Guil. GU2
off Old Ct Rd ... 258 AU135
Reinickendorf Av, SE9 ... 185 EQ85
Reizel Cl, N16 ... 122 DT60
Relay Rd, W12 ... 139 CW73
Relf Rd, SE15 ... 162 DU83
Reliance Sq, EC2 ... 11 M3
Relko Ct, Epsom KT19 ... 216 CR110
Relko Gdns, Sutt. SM1 ... 218 DD106
Relton Ms, SW7 ... 18 B5
Rembrandt Cl, E14 ... 24 E6
SW1 ... 18 E8
Rembrandt Ct, Epsom KT19 .217 CT107
Rembrandt Dr, Grav. (Nthflt)
DA11 ... 190 GD90
Rembrandt Rd, SE13 ... 164 EE84
Edgware HA8 ... 96 CN54
Rembrandt Way, Walt. KT12 .195 BV104
Remington Rd, E6 ... 144 EL72
N15 ... 122 DR58
Remington St, N1 ... 4 F10
Remnant St, WC2 ... 10 A7
Remus Cl, St.Alb. AL1 ... 43 CD24
Remus Rd, E3 *off Monier Rd* .143 EA66
Renaissance Wk, SE10 ... 25 K5
Rendle Cl, Croy. CR0 ... 202 DT99
Rendlesham Av, Rad. WD7 ... 77 CF37
Rendlesham Cl, Ware SG12 .. 32 DV05
Rendlesham Rd, E5 ... 122 DU63
Enfield EN2 ... 81 DP39
Rendlesham Way, Rick.
(Chorl.) WD3 ... 73 BC44
Renforth St, SE16 ... 22 F4
Renfree Way, Shep. TW17 .. 194 BM101
Renfrew Cl, E6 ... 145 EN73
Renfrew Rd, SE11 ... 20 F7
Hounslow TW4 ... 156 BX82
Kingston upon Thames
KT2 ... 178 CP94
Renmans, The, Ashtd. KT21 .232 CM116
Renmuir St, SW17 ... 180 DF93
Rennell St, SE13 ... 163 EC83
Rennels Way, Islw. TW7
off St. John's Rd ... 157 CE82
Renness Rd, E17 ... 123 DY55
Rennets Cl, SE9 ... 185 ES85
Rennets Wd Rd, SE9 ... 185 ER85
Rennie Cl, Ashf. TW15 ... 174 BK90
Rennie Est, SE16 ... 22 D8
Rennie St, SE1 ... 20 E1
Rennie Ter, Red. RH1 ... 266 DG135
Rennison Cl, Wal.Cr. EN7
off Allwood Rd ... 66 DT27
Renovation, The, E16
off Woolwich Manor Way .165 EP75
Renown Cl, Croy. CR0 ... 201 DP102
Romford RM7 ... 104 FA53
Rensburg Rd, E17 ... 123 DX57
Renshaw Cl, Belv. DA17
off Grove Rd ... 166 EZ79
Renters Av, NW4 ... 119 CW58
Renton Dr, Orp. BR5 ... 206 EX101
Renwick Ind Est, Bark. IG11 .146 EV67
Renwick Rd, Bark. IG11 ... 146 EV70
Repens Way, Hayes UB4
off Stipularis Dr ... 136 BX70
Rephidim St, SE1 ... 21 L6
Replingham Rd, SW18 ... 179 CZ88
Reporton Rd, SW6 ... 159 CY81
Repository Rd, SE18 ... 165 EM79
Repton Av, Hayes UB3 ... 155 BR77
Romford RM2 ... 127 FG55
Wembley HA0 ... 117 CJ63
Repton Cl, Cars. SM5 ... 218 DE106
Repton Ct, Beck. BR3 ... 203 EB95
Ilford IG5 *off Repton Gro* .103 EM53
Repton Dr, Rom. RM2 ... 127 FG56
Repton Gdns, Rom. RM2 ... 127 FG55
Repton Grn, St.Alb. AL3 ... 43 CD16
Repton Gro, Ilf. IG5 ... 103 EM53
Repton Pl, Amer. HP7 ... 72 AU39
Repton Rd, Har. HA3 ... 118 CM56
Orpington BR6 ... 206 EU104
Repton St, E14 ... 13 K7
Repton Way, Rick. (Crox.Grn)
WD3 ... 75 BN43
Repulse Cl, Rom. RM5 ... 105 FB53
Reservoir Cl, Green. DA9 .. 189 FW86
Thornton Heath CR7 ... 202 DR98
Reservoir Rd, N14 ... 81 DJ43
SE4 ... 163 DY82
Ruislip HA4 ... 115 BQ57
Resham Cl, Sthl. UB2 ... 156 BW76
Resolution Wk, SE18 ... 165 EM76
Resolution Way, SE8
off Deptford High St ... 163 EA80
Reson Way, Hem.H. HP1 ... 40 BH21
Restavon Pk, West.
(Berry's Grn) TN16 ... 239 EP116
Restell Cl, SE3 ... 164 EE79
Restmor Way, Wall. SM6 ... 200 DG103
Reston Cl, Borwd. WD6 ... 78 CN38
Reston Path, Borwd. WD6 ... 78 CN38
Reston Pl, SW7 ... 17 L4
Restons Cres, SE9 ... 185 ER86
Restormel Cl, Houns. TW3 .. 176 CA85
Retcar Cl, N19
off Dartmouth Pk Hill ... 121 DH61
Retcar Pl, N19 ... 121 DH61
Retford Cl, Borwd. WD6
off The Campions ... 78 CN38
Romford RM3 ... 106 FN51
Retford Path, Rom. RM3 ... 106 FN51
Retford Rd, Rom. RM3 ... 106 FM51
Retford St, N1 ... 5 M10
Retingham Way, E4 ... 101 EB47
Retreat, The, NW9 ... 118 CR57
SW14
off South Worple Way .. 158 CS83
Addlestone KT15 ... 212 BK106
Retreat, The, Amer. HP6 ... 72 AY39
Brentwood CM14
off Costead Manor Rd .. 108 FV46
Brentwood (Hutt.) CM13 .109 GB44
Egham TW20 ... 172 AX92
Grays RM17 ... 170 GB79
Harrow HA2 ... 116 CA59
Kings Langley WD4 ... 59 BQ31
Maidenhead (Fifield) SL6 .150 AD80
Orpington BR6 ... 224 EV107
Surbiton KT5 ... 198 CM100
Thornton Heath CR7 ... 202 DR98
Worcester Park KT4 ... 199 CV103
Retreat Cl, Har. HA3 ... 117 CJ57
Retreat Pl, E9 ... 142 DW65
Retreat Rd, Rich. TW9 ... 177 CK85
Retreat Way, Chig. IG7 ... 104 EV48
Reubens Rd, Brwd. (Hutt.)
CM13 ... 109 GB44
Reunion Row, E1 ... 12 D10
Reveley Sq, SE16 ... 23 K4
Revell Cl, Lthd. (Fetch.)
KT22 ... 230 CB122
Revell Dr, Lthd. (Fetch.)
KT22 ... 230 CB122
Revell Ri, SE18 ... 165 ET79
Revell Rd, Kings.T. KT1 ... 198 CP95
Sutton SM1 ... 217 CZ107
Revelon Rd, SE4 ... 163 DY84
Revel Rd, H.Wyc. (Woob.Grn)
HP10 ... 110 AD55
Revels Cl, Hert. SG14 ... 32 DR07
Revels Rd, Hert. SG14 ... 32 DR07
Revelstoke Rd, SW18 ... 179 CZ89
Reventlow Rd, SE9 ... 185 EQ88
Reverdy Rd, SE1 ... 22 A8
Reverend Cl, Har. HA2 ... 116 CB62
Revesby Rd, Cars. SM5 ... 200 DD100
Review Rd, NW2 ... 119 CT61
Dagenham RM10 ... 147 FB67
Rewell St, SW6 ... 160 DC80
Rewley Rd, Cars. SM5 ... 200 DD100
Rex Av, Ashf. TW15 ... 174 BN93
Rex Cl, Rom. RM5 ... 105 FB52
Rex Pl, W1 ... 8 F10
Reydon Av, E11 ... 124 EJ58
Reynard Cl, SE4
off Foxwell St ... 163 DY83
Bromley BR1 ... 205 EM97
Reynard Dr, SE19 ... 182 DT94
Reynard Pl, SE14
off Milton Ct Rd ... 163 DY79
Reynardson Rd, N17 ... 100 DQ52
Reynards Way, St.Alb.
(Brick.Wd) AL2 ... 60 BZ29
Reynard Way, Hert. SG13 ... 32 DU09
Reynolah Gdns, SE7 ... 25 P9
Reynolds Av, E12 ... 125 EN64
Chessington KT9 ... 216 CL108
Romford RM6 ... 126 EW59
Reynolds Cl, NW11 ... 120 DB59
SW19 ... 200 DD95
Carshalton SM5 ... 200 DF102
Hemel Hempstead HP1 ... 40 BG19
Reynolds Ct, E11
off Cobbold Rd ... 124 EF62
Romford RM6 ... 126 EX55
Reynolds Cres, St.Alb.
(Sand.) AL4 ... 43 CH15
Reynolds Dr, Edg. HA8 ... 118 CM55
Reynolds Pl, SE3 ... 164 EH80
Richmond TW10
off Cambrian Rd ... 178 CM86
Reynolds Rd, SE15 ... 182 DW85
W4 ... 158 CQ76
Beaconsfield HP9 ... 88 AJ52
Hayes UB4 ... 136 BW70
New Malden KT3 ... 198 CR101
Reynolds Wk, Chesh. HP5
off Great Hivings ... 54 AN27
Reynolds Way, Croy. CR0 ... 220 DS105
Rheidol Ms, N1 ... 4 G9
Rheidol Ter, N1 ... 4 F9
Rheingold Way, Wall. SM6 .. 219 DL109
Rheola Cl, N17 ... 100 DT53
Rhoda St, E2 ... 11 P3
Rhodes Av, N22 ... 99 DJ53
Sch **Rhodes Av Prim Sch**,
N22 *off Rhodes Av* ... 99 DJ53
Rhodes Cl, Egh. TW20
off Mullens Rd ... 173 BC92
Rhodesia Rd, E11 ... 123 ED61
SW9 ... 161 DL82
Rhodes Moorhouse Ct,
Mord. SM4 ... 200 DA100
Rhodes St, N7 ... 4 B2
Rhodes Way, Wat. WD24 ... 76 BX40
Rhodeswell Rd, E14 ... 13 K5
Rhododendron Ride, Egh.
TW20 ... 172 AT94
Slough SL3 ... 133 AZ69
Rhodrons Av, Chess. KT9 ... 216 CL106
Rhondda Gro, E3 ... 13 K2
Sch **Rhyl Prim Sch**, NW5
off Rhyl St ... 140 DG65
Rhyl Rd, Grnf. UB6 ... 137 CF68
Rhyl St, NW5 ... 140 DG65
Rhymes, The, Hem.H. HP1 ... 40 BH18
Rhys Av, N11 ... 99 DK52
Rialto Rd, Mitch. CR4 ... 200 DG96
Ribble Cl, Wdf.Grn. IG8
off Prospect Rd ... 102 EJ51
Ribbledale, St.Alb. (Lon.Col.)
AL2 ... 62 CM27
Ribblesdale, Dor. RH4
off Roman Rd ... 263 CH138
Hemel Hempstead HP2 ... 40 BL17
Ribblesdale Av, N11 ... 98 DG51
Northolt UB5 ... 136 CB65
Ribblesdale Rd, N8 ... 121 DM56
SW16 ... 181 DH93
Dartford DA2 ... 188 FQ88
Ribbon Dance Ms, SE5
off Camberwell Gro ... 162 DR81
Ribchester Av, Grnf. UB6 ... 137 CF69
Ribston Cl, Brom. BR2 ... 205 EM102
Radlett (Shenley) WD7
off Wayside ... 61 CK33
Rib Vale, Hert. SG14 ... 32 DR06
Ricardo Path, SE28
off Byron Cl ... 146 EW74
Ricardo Rd, Wind. (Old Wind.)
SL4 ... 172 AV86
Ricardo St, E14 ... 14 A8
Sch **Ricards Lo High Sch**,
SW19 *off Lake Rd* ... 179 CZ92
Ricards Rd, SW19 ... 179 CZ92
Ricebridge La, Reig. RH2 .. 265 CV137
Rice Cl, Hem.H. HP2 ... 40 BM19
Rices Cor, Guil. (Shalf.)
GU4 ... 259 BA141
Sch **Richard Alibon Prim Sch**,
Dag. RM10 *off Alibon Rd* .126 FA64
Sch **Richard Atkins Prim Sch**,
SW2 *off New Pk Rd* ... 181 DL87

Sch Richard Challoner Sch, N.Mal. KT3 off Manor Dr N 198 CR101
Richard Cl, SE18 164 EL77
Sch Richard Cloudesley Sch, EC1 10 G4
Sch Richard Cobden Prim Sch, NW1 off Camden St 141 DJ68
Richard Fell Ho, E12 off Walton Rd 125 EN63
Richard Foster Cl, E17 123 DZ59
Sch Richard Hale Sch, Hert. SG13 off Hale Rd 32 DR10
Richard Ho Dr, E16 144 EK72
Richards Av, Rom. RM7 127 FC57
Richards Cl, Bushey WD23 95 CD45
Harrow HA1 117 CG57
Hayes UB3 155 BR79
Uxbridge UB10 134 BN67
Richards Fld, Epsom KT19 216 CR109
Richardson Cl, E8 5 N7
Greenhithe DA9 off Steele Av 189 FU85
St. Albans (Lon.Col.) AL2 62 CL27
Richardson Cres, Wal.Cr. (Chsht) EN7 65 DP25
Richardson Pl, St.Alb. (Coln.Hth) AL4 44 CP22
Richardson Rd, E15 144 EE68
Richardson's Ms, W1 9 J4
Richards Pl, E17 123 EA55
SW3 18 B7
Richards Rd, Cob. (Stoke D'Ab.) KT11 214 CB114
Richards St, Hat. AL10 off Mosquito Way 44 CR16
Richard Stagg Cl, St.Alb. AL1 43 CJ22
Richard St, E1 12 C8
Richards Way, Slou. SL1 131 AN74
Richbell Cl, Ashtd. KT21 231 CK118
Richbell Pl, WC1 10 A5
Richborne Ter, SW8 161 DM80
Richborough Cl, Orp. BR5 206 EX98
Richborough Rd, NW2 119 CX63
Richens Cl, Houns. TW3 157 CD82
Riches Rd, Ilf. IG1 125 EQ61
Richfield Rd, Bushey WD23 94 CC45
Richford Rd, E15 144 EF67
Richford St, W6 159 CW75
RICHINGS PARK, Iver SL0 153 BE75
Richings Way, Iver SL0 153 BF76
Richland Av, Couls. CR5 218 DG114
Richlands Av, Epsom KT17 217 CU105
Rich La, SW5 17 J10
Richmer Rd, Erith DA8 167 FG80
RICHMOND, TW9 & TW10 178 CL86
⇌ Richmond 158 CL84
⊖ Richmond 158 CL84
Coll Richmond Adult Comm Coll, Clifden, Twick. TW1 off Clifden Rd 177 CF88
Parkshot, Rich. TW9 off Parkshot 157 CK84
Shaftesbury, Rich. TW9 off Kew Rd 158 CL84
Richmond Av, E4 101 ED50
N1 4 A7
NW10 139 CW65
SW20 199 CY95
Feltham TW14 175 BS86
Uxbridge UB10 135 BP65
Richmond Br, Rich. TW9 177 CK86
Twickenham TW1 177 CK86
Richmond Bldgs, W1 9 L8
Richmond Cl, E17 123 DZ58
Amersham HP6 72 AT38
Borehamwood WD6 78 CR43
Epsom KT18 216 CS114
Leatherhead (Fetch.) KT22 230 CC124
Waltham Cross (Chsht) EN8 66 DW29
Westerham (Bigg.H.) TN16 238 EH119
Richmond Ct, Brox. EN10 49 DZ20
Hatfield AL10 off Cooks Way 45 CV20
Potters Bar EN6 64 DC31
Richmond Cres, E4 101 ED50
N1 4 B7
N9 100 DU46
Slough SL1 132 AU74
Staines TW18 173 BF92
Richmond Dr, Grav. DA12 191 GL89
Shepperton TW17 195 BQ100
Watford WD17 75 BS39
Woodford Green IG8 103 EN52
Richmond Gdns, NW4 119 CU57
Harrow HA3 95 CF51
Richmond Grn, Croy. CR0 201 DL104
Richmond Gro, N1 4 E6
Surbiton KT5 198 CM100
Richmond Hill, Rich. TW10 178 CL86
Richmond Hill Ct, Rich. TW10 178 CL86
Sch Richmond Ho Sch, Hmptn. TW12 off Buckingham Rd 176 BZ92
Richmond Ms, W1 9 L8
Teddington TW11 off Broad St 177 CF93
★ Richmond Palace (remains), Rich. TW9 177 CJ85
★ Richmond Park, Rich. TW10 178 CN88
Richmond Pk, Kings.T. KT2 178 CN88
Loughton IG10 off Fallow Flds 102 EJ45
Richmond TW10 178 CN88
Richmond Pk Rd, SW14 178 CQ85
Kingston upon Thames KT2 178 CL94
Richmond Pl, SE18 165 EQ77
Richmond Rd, E4 101 ED46
E7 124 EH64
E8 5 N5
E11 123 ED61
N2 98 DC54
N11 99 DL51
N15 122 DS58
SW20 199 CV95
W5 158 CL75
Barnet EN5 80 DB43
Coulsdon CR5 235 DH115
Croydon CR0 201 DL104
Grays RM17 170 GC79
Ilford IG1 125 EQ62
Isleworth TW7 157 CG83
Kingston upon Thames KT2 177 CK92
Potters Bar EN6 64 DC31
Romford RM1 127 FF58
Staines TW18 173 BF92
Thornton Heath CR7 201 DP97
Twickenham TW1 177 CJ86
Richmond St, E13 144 EG68
Richmond Ter, SW1 19 N3
Richmond Ter Ms, SW1 off Parliament St 161 DL75
Uni Richmond Uni - The American Int Uni In London, Kensington Campus, W8 17 K5
Richmond Hill Campus, Rich. TW10 off Queens Rd 178 CL87
Coll Richmond upon Thames Coll, Twick. TW2 off Egerton Rd 177 CE87
Richmond Wk, St.Alb. AL4 43 CK16
Richmond Way, E11 124 EG61
W12 16 B4
W14 16 B5
Leatherhead (Fetch.) KT22 230 CB123
Rickmansworth (Crox.Grn) WD3 75 BQ42
Richmount Gdns, SE3 164 EG83
Rich St, E14 13 M9
Rickard Cl, NW4 119 CV56
SW2 181 DM88
West Drayton UB7 154 BK76
Rickards Cl, Surb. KT6 198 CL102
Ricketts Hill Rd, West. (Tats.) TN16 238 EK118
Rickett St, SW6 160 DA79
Rickfield Cl, Hat. AL10 45 CU20
Rickman Cres, Add. KT15 194 BH104
Rickman Hill, Couls. CR5 235 DH118
Rickman Hill Rd, Couls. CR5 235 DH118
Rickmans La, Slou. (Stoke P.) SL2 112 AS64
Rickman St, E1 12 F3
RICKMANSWORTH, WD3 92 BL45
⇌ Rickmansworth 92 BK45
⊖ Rickmansworth 92 BK45
Rickmansworth La, Ger.Cr. (Chal.St.P.) SL9 91 AZ50
Rickmansworth Pk, Rick. WD3 92 BK45
Sch Rickmansworth Pk JMI Sch, Rick. WD3 off Park Rd 92 BL45
Sch Rickmansworth PNEU Sch, Rick. WD3 off The Drive 74 BJ44
Rickmansworth Rd, Amer. HP6 55 AQ37
Northwood HA6 93 BR52
Pinner HA5 93 BV54
Rickmansworth (Chorl.) WD3 73 BE41
Uxbridge (Hare.) UB9 92 BJ53
Watford WD17, WD18 75 BS42
Sch Rickmansworth Sch, Rick. WD3 off Scots Hill 74 BM44
Rick Roberts Way, E15 143 EC67
Ricksons La, Lthd. (W.Hors.) KT24 245 BP127
Rickthorne Rd, N19 off Landseer Rd 121 DL61
Rickwood, Horl. RH6 off Woodhayes 269 DH147
Rickyard Path, SE9 164 EL84
Ridding La, Grnf. UB6 117 CF64
Riddings, The, Cat. CR3 252 DT125
Riddings La, Harl. CM18 51 ET19
⇌ Riddlesdown 220 DR113
Riddlesdown Av, Pur. CR8 220 DQ112
Sch Riddlesdown High Sch, Pur. CR8 off Dunmail Dr 220 DS114
Riddlesdown Rd, Pur. CR8 220 DQ111
Riddons Rd, SE12 184 EJ90
Ride, The, Brent. TW8 157 CH78
Enfield EN3 82 DW41
Ride La, Guil. (Far.Grn) GU5 260 BK144
Rideout St, SE18 165 EM77
Rider Cl, Sid. DA15 185 ES86
Riders Way, Gdse. RH9 252 DW131
Ridgdale St, E3 143 EB68
RIDGE, Pot.B. EN6 62 CS34
Ridge, The, Bex. DA5 186 EZ87
Caterham (Wold.) CR3 253 EB126
Coulsdon CR5 219 DL114
Epsom KT18 232 CP117
Leatherhead (Fetch.) KT22 231 CD124
Orpington BR6 205 ER103
Purley CR8 219 DJ110
Surbiton KT5 198 CN99
Twickenham TW2 177 CD87
Woking GU22 227 BB117
Ridge Av, N21 100 DQ45
Dartford DA1 187 FF86
Ridgebank, Slou. SL1 131 AM73
Ridgebrook Rd, SE3 164 EJ84
Ridge Cl, NW4 97 CX54
NW9 118 CR56
SE28 165 ER75
Betchworth (Strood Grn) RH3 264 CP138
Woking GU22 226 AV121
Ridge Crest, Enf. EN2 81 DM39
Ridgecroft Cl, Bex. DA5 187 FC88
Ridgefield, Wat. WD17 75 BS37
Ridgegate Cl, Reig. RH2 250 DD132
RIDGE GREEN, Red. RH1 267 DL137
Ridge Grn, Red. (S.Nutfld) RH1 267 DL137
Ridge Grn Cl, Red. (S.Nutfld) RH1 267 DL137
RIDGEHILL, Rad. WD7 62 CQ30
Ridge Hill, NW11 119 CY60
Ridgehurst Av, Wat. WD25 59 BT34
Ridgelands, Lthd. (Fetch.) KT22 231 CD124
Ridge La, Wat. WD17 75 BS38
Ridge Langley, S.Croy. CR2 220 DU109
Ridge Lea, Hem.H. HP1 39 BF20
Ridgemead Rd, Egh. (Eng.Grn) TW20 172 AU90
Ridgemont Gdns, Edg. HA8 96 CQ49
Ridgemount, Guil. GU2 258 AV135
Weybridge KT13 off Oatlands Dr 195 BS103
Ridgemount Av, Couls. CR5 235 DH117
Croydon CR0 203 DX102
Ridgemount Cl, SE20 182 DV94
Ridgemount End, Ger.Cr. (Chal.St.P.) SL9 90 AY50
Ridgemount Gdns, Enf. EN2 81 DP40
Ridgemount Way, Red. RH1 266 DE136
Ridge Pk, Pur. CR8 219 DK110
Ridge Rd, N8 121 DM58
N21 100 DQ46
NW2 119 CZ62
Mitcham CR4 181 DH94
Sutton SM3 199 CY102
Ridges, The, Guil. (Art.) GU3 258 AW139
Ridge St, Wat. WD24 75 BV38
Ridgeview Cl, Barn. EN5 79 CX44
Ridgeview Lo, St.Alb. (Lon.Col.) AL2 62 CM28
Ridgeview Rd, N20 98 DB48
Ridge Way, SE19 off Central Hill 182 DS93
Ridgeway, SE28 off Pettman Cres 165 ER77
Berkhamsted HP4 38 AT19
Brentwood (Hutt.) CM13 109 GB46
Bromley BR2 204 EG103
Ridge Way, Dart. (Cray.) DA1 187 FF86
Ridgeway, Dart. (Lane End) DA2 189 FS92
Epsom KT19 216 CQ112
Ridge Way, Felt. TW13 176 BY90
Ridgeway, Grays RM17 170 GE77
Ridge Way, Iver SL0 133 BE74
Ridgeway, Rick. WD3 92 BH45
Virginia Water GU25 192 AY99
Welwyn Garden City AL7 30 DA09
Woking (Horsell) GU21 226 AX115
Woodford Green IG8 102 EJ49
Ridgeway, The, E4 101 EB47
N3 98 DB52
N11 98 DF49
N14 99 DL47
NW7 97 CU49
NW9 118 CS56
NW11 119 CZ60
W3 158 CN76
Amersham HP7 55 AR40
Croydon CR0 201 DM104
Enfield EN2 81 DN39
Gerrards Cross (Chal.St.P.) SL9 112 AY55
Guildford GU1 259 BA135
Harrow (Kenton) HA3 117 CJ58
Harrow (N.Har.) HA2 116 CA58
Hertford SG14 31 DM08
Horley RH6 268 DG150
Leatherhead (Fetch.) KT22 231 CD123
Leatherhead (Oxshott) KT22 214 CC114
Potters Bar EN6 64 DD34
Potters Bar (Cuffley) EN6 64 DE28
Radlett WD7 77 CF37
Romford (Gidea Pk) RM2 127 FG56
Romford (Harold Wd) RM3 106 FL53
Ruislip HA4 115 BU59
St. Albans AL4 43 CH17
South Croydon CR2 220 DS110
Stanmore HA7 95 CJ51
Walton-on-Thames KT12 195 BT102
Watford WD17 75 BS37
Ridgeway Av, Barn. EN4 80 DF44
Gravesend DA12 191 GH90
Ridgeway Cl, Chesh. HP5 54 AP28
Dorking RH4 263 CG138
Hemel Hempstead HP3 off London Rd 58 BM26
Leatherhead (Oxshott) KT22 214 CC114
Woking GU21 226 AX116
Ridgeway Ct, Red. RH1 266 DF135
Ridgeway Cres, Orp. BR6 205 ES104
Ridgeway Cres Gdns, Orp. BR6 205 ES103
Ridgeway Dr, Brom. BR1 184 EH91
Dorking RH4 263 CG139
Ridgeway E, Sid. DA15 185 ET85
Ridgeway Est, The, Iver SL0 133 BF74
Ridgeway Gdns, N6 121 DJ59
Ilford IG4 124 EL57
Woking GU21 226 AX115
Sch Ridgeway Inf Sch, S.Croy. CR2 off Southcote Rd 220 DS110
Sch Ridgeway Jun Sch, S.Croy. CR2 off Southcote Rd 220 DS110
Ridgeway Rd, SW9 161 DP83
Chesham HP5 54 AN28
Dorking RH4 263 CG139
Isleworth TW7 157 CE80
Redhill RH1 250 DE134
Ridgeway Rd N, Islw. TW7 157 CE79
Ridgeways, Harl. CM17 52 EY15
Ridgeway Wk, Nthlt. UB5 off Fortunes Mead 136 BY65
Ridgeway W, Sid. DA15 185 ES85
Ridgewell Cl, N1 5 H7
SE26 183 DZ91
Dagenham RM10 147 FB67
Ridgewell Gro, Horn. RM12 off Airfield Way 147 FH65
Ridgmont Rd, St.Alb. AL1 43 CE21
Ridgmount Gdns, WC1 9 L4
Ridgmount Pl, WC1 9 L5
Ridgmount Rd, SW18 180 DB85
Ridgmount St, WC1 9 L5
Ridgway, SW19 179 CX93
Woking (Pyrford) GU22 227 BF115
Ridgway, The, Sutt. SM2 218 DD108
Ridgway Gdns, SW19 179 CX94
Ridgway Pl, SW19 179 CY93
Ridgway Rd, Wok. (Pyrford) GU22 227 BF115
Ridgwell Rd, E16 144 EJ71
Riding, The, NW11 off Golders Grn Rd 119 CZ59
Woking GU21 211 BB114
Riding Ct Rd, Slou. (Datchet) SL3 152 AW80
Riding Hill, S.Croy. CR2 220 DU113
Riding Ho St, W1 9 J6
Riding La, Beac. HP9 88 AF53
Ridings, The, E11 off Malcolm Way 124 EG57
W5 138 CM70
Addlestone KT15 211 BF107
Amersham HP6 55 AR35
Ashtead KT21 231 CK117
Chesham HP5 72 AX36
Chigwell IG7 off Manford Way 104 EV49
Cobham KT11 214 CA112
Epsom KT18 232 CS115
Epsom (Ewell) KT17 217 CT109
Hertford SG14 31 DN10
Iver SL0 153 BF77
Leatherhead (E.Hors.) KT24 245 BS125
Reigate RH2 250 DD131
Sunbury-on-Thames TW16 195 BU95
Surbiton KT5 198 CN99
Tadworth KT20 233 CZ120
Westerham (Bigg.H.) TN16 238 EL117
Woking (Ripley) GU23 228 BG123
Ridings Av, N21 81 DP42
Ridings Cl, N6 off Hornsey La Gdns 121 DJ59
Ridings La, Wok. GU23 228 BN123
Ridlands Gro, Oxt. RH8 254 EL130
Ridlands La, Oxt. RH8 254 EK130
Ridlands Ri, Oxt. RH8 254 EL130
Ridler Rd, Enf. EN1 82 DS38
Ridley Av, W13 157 CH76
Ridley Cl, Bark. IG11 145 ET66
Romford RM3 105 FH53
Ridley Rd, E7 124 EJ63
E8 5 N2
NW10 139 CU68
SW19 180 DB94
Bromley BR2 204 EF97
Warlingham CR6 236 DW118
Welling DA16 166 EV81
Ridsdale Rd, SE20 202 DV95
Woking GU21 226 AV117
Riefield Rd, SE9 165 EQ84
Riesco Dr, Croy. CR0 220 DW107
Riffel Rd, NW2 119 CW64
Riffhams, Brwd. CM13 109 GB48
Rifle Butts All, Epsom KT18 233 CT115
Rifle Pl, SE11 161 DN79
Rifle St, E14 14 B6
Rigault Rd, SW6 159 CY82
Rigby Cl, Croy. CR0 201 DN104
Rigby Gdns, Grays RM16 171 GH77
Rigby La, Hayes UB3 155 BR75
Rigby Ms, Ilf. IG1 off Cranbrook Rd 125 EP61
Rigby Pl, Enf. EN3 83 EA37
Rigden St, E14 14 A8
Rigeley Rd, NW10 139 CU69
Rigg App, E10 123 DX60
Rigge Pl, SW4 161 DK84
Riggindale Rd, SW16 181 DK92
Riley Rd, SE1 21 M5
Enfield EN3 82 DW38
Riley St, SW10 160 DD79
Rinaldo Rd, SW12 181 DH87
Ring, The, W2 8 A9
Ring Cl, Brom. BR1 off Garden Rd 184 EH94
Ringcroft St, N7 4 C2
Ringers Rd, Brom. BR1 204 EG97
Ringford Rd, SW18 179 CZ85
Ringlet Cl, E16 15 N6
Ringlewell Cl, Enf. EN1 off Central Av 82 DV40
Ringley Av, Horl. RH6 268 DG148
Ringley Pk Av, Reig. RH2 266 DD135
Ringley Pk Rd, Reig. RH2 250 DC134
Ringmer Av, SW6 159 CY81
Ringmer Gdns, N19 off Sussex Way 121 DL61
Ringmer Pl, N21 82 DR43
Ringmer Way, Brom. BR1 205 EM99
Ringmore Dr, Guil. GU4 243 BC131
Ringmore Ri, SE23 182 DV87
Ringmore Rd, Walt. KT12 196 BW104
Ring Rd, W12 139 CW73
Ring Rd N, Gat. RH6 269 DH152
Ring Rd S, Gat. RH6 269 DH152
Ringshall Rd, Orp. BR5 206 EU97
Ringslade Rd, N22 99 DM54
Ringstead Rd, SE6 183 EB87
Sutton SM1 218 DD105
Ringway, N11 99 DJ51
Southall UB2 156 BY78
Ringway Rd, St.Alb. (Park St) AL2 60 CB27
Ringwold Cl, Beck. BR3 183 DY94
Ringwood Av, N2 98 DF54
Croydon CR0 201 DL101
Hornchurch RM12 128 FK61
Orpington BR6 224 EW110
Redhill RH1 250 DF131
Ringwood Cl, Pnr. HA5 116 BW55
Ringwood Gdns, E14 23 P7
SW15 179 CU89
Ringwood Rd, E17 123 DZ58
Ringwood Way, N21 99 DP46
Hampton (Hmptn H.) TW12 176 CA91
RIPLEY, Wok. GU23 228 BJ122
Ripley Av, Egh. TW20 172 AY93
Ripley Bypass, Wok. GU23 228 BK122
Ripley Cl, Brom. BR1 off Ringmer Way 205 EM99
Croydon (New Adgtn) CR0 221 EC107
Slough SL3 152 AY77
Sch Ripley C of E Inf Sch, Wok. GU23 off Georgelands 228 BH121
Sch Ripley Ct Sch, Wok. GU23 off Rose La 228 BJ122
Ripley Gdns, SW14 158 CR83
Sutton SM1 218 DC105
Ripley La, Lthd. (W.Hors.) KT24 244 BN125
Woking GU23 228 BL123
Ripley Ms, E11 off Wadley Rd 124 EE59
Ripley Rd, E16 144 EJ72
Belvedere DA17 166 FA77
Enfield EN2 82 DQ39
Guildford (E.Clan.) GU4 244 BJ127
Hampton TW12 176 CA94
Ilford IG3 125 ET61
Woking (Send) GU23 244 BJ127
RIPLEY SPRINGS, Egh. TW20 172 AY93
Ripley Vw, Loug. IG10 85 EP38
Ripley Vil, W5 off Castlebar Rd 137 CJ72
Ripley Way, Epsom KT19 216 CN111
Hemel Hempstead HP1 39 BE19
Waltham Cross (Chsht) EN7 66 DV30
Riplington Ct, SW15 off Longwood Dr 179 CU87
Ripon Cl, Guil. GU2 242 AT132
Northolt UB5 116 CA64
Ripon Gdns, Chess. KT9 215 CK106
Ilford IG1 124 EL58
Ripon Rd, N9 100 DV45
N17 122 DR55
SE18 165 EP79
Ripon Way, Borwd. WD6 78 CQ43
St. Albans AL4 43 CK16
Rippersley Rd, Well. DA16 166 EU81
Sch Ripple Jun & Inf Sch, Bark. IG11 off Suffolk Rd 145 ES66
Ripple Rd, Bark. IG11 145 EQ66
Dagenham RM9 146 EV67
Rippleside Commercial Est, Bark. IG11 146 EW68
Ripplevale Gro, N1 4 B6
Rippolson Rd, SE18 165 ET78
Ripston Rd, Ashf. TW15 175 BR92
Risborough Dr, Wor.Pk. KT4 199 CU101
Risborough St, SE1 20 F3
Risdens, Harl. CM18 51 EQ19
Risdon St, SE16 22 F4
Rise, The, E11 124 EG57
N13 99 DN49
NW7 97 CT51
NW10 118 CR63
Amersham HP7 55 AQ39
Bexley DA5 186 EW87
Rise, The, Borwd. (Elstree) WD6 78 CM43
Buckhurst Hill IG9 102 EK45
Dartford DA1 167 FF84
Edgware HA8 96 CP50
Epsom KT17 217 CT110
Gravesend DA12 191 GL91
Greenford UB6 117 CG64
Leatherhead (E.Hors.) KT24 245 BS126
St. Albans (Park St) AL2 61 CD25
Sevenoaks TN13 257 FJ129
South Croydon CR2 220 DW109
Tadworth KT20 233 CW121
Uxbridge UB10 134 BM68
Waltham Abbey EN9 off Breach Barn Mobile Home Pk 68 EH30
Risebridge Chase, Rom. RM1 105 FF52
Risebridge Rd, Rom. RM2 105 FF54
Rise Cotts, Ware SG12 off Widford Rd 34 EK05
Risedale Cl, Hem.H. HP3 off Risedale Hill 40 BL23
Risedale Hill, Hem.H. HP3 40 BL23
Risedale Rd, Bexh. DA7 167 FB83
Hemel Hempstead HP3 40 BL23
Riseldine Rd, SE23 183 DY86
Rise Pk Boul, Rom. RM1 105 FF53
Sch Rise Pk Inf Sch, Rom. RM1 off Annan Way 105 FD53
Sch Rise Pk Jun Sch, Rom. RM1 off Annan Way 105 FD53
Rise Pk Par, Rom. RM1 105 FE54
Riseway, Brwd. CM15 108 FY48
Sch Rish Hall Spec Sch, Ilf. IG2 off Aldborough Rd N 125 ET57
Rising Hill Cl, Nthwd. HA6 off Ducks Hill Rd 93 BQ51
Risinghill St, N1 4 C9
Risingholme Cl, Bushey WD23 94 CB45
Harrow HA3 95 CE53
Risingholme Rd, Har. HA3 95 CE54
Risings, The, E17 123 ED56
Rising Sun Ct, EC1 10 F6
Risley Av, N17 100 DQ53
Sch Risley Av Prim Sch, N17 off The Roundway 100 DS53
Rita Rd, SW8 161 DM80
Ritches Rd, N15 122 DQ57
Ritchie Rd, Croy. CR0 202 DV100
Ritchie St, N1 4 D9
Ritchings Av, E17 123 DY56
Ritcroft Cl, Hem.H. HP3 41 BP21
Ritcroft Dr, Hem.H. HP3 41 BP21
Ritcroft St, Hem.H. HP3 41 BP21
Ritherdon Rd, SW17 180 DG89
Ritson Rd, E8 5 P3
Ritter St, SE18 165 EN79
Ritz Ct, Pot.B. EN6 64 DA31
Ritz Par, W5 off Connell Cres 138 CM70
Rivaz Pl, E9 142 DW65
Rivenhall End, Welw.G.C. AL7 30 DC09
Rivenhall Gdns, E18 124 EF56
River Ash Est, Shep. TW17 195 BT101
River Av, N13 99 DP48
Hoddesdon EN11 49 EB16
Thames Ditton KT7 197 CG101
River Bk, N21 100 DQ45
East Molesey KT8 197 CE97
Riverbank, Stai. TW18 173 BF93
River Bk, T.Ditt. KT7 197 CF99
West Molesey KT8 196 BZ97
Riverbank Way, Brent. TW8 157 CJ79
River Barge Cl, E14 24 D4
River Brent Business Pk, W7 157 CE76
River Cl, E11 124 EJ58
Rainham RM13 147 FH71
Ruislip HA4 115 BT58
Southall UB2 156 CC75
Surbiton KT6 off Catherine Rd 197 CK99
Waltham Cross EN8 67 EA34
River Ct, Shep. TW17 195 BQ101
Woking GU21 227 BC115
River Ct Flats, Maid. (Taplow) SL6 off River Rd 130 AC72
Rivercourt Rd, W6 159 CV77
River Crane Wk, Felt. TW13 176 BX88
Hounslow TW4 176 BX88
River Crane Way, Felt. TW13 off Watermill Way 176 BZ89
Riverdale, SE13 off Lewisham High St 163 EC83
Riverdale Cl, Bark. IG11 146 EV70
Riverdale Dr, SW18 off Strathville Rd 180 DB88
Woking GU22 227 AZ121
Riverdale Gdns, Twick. TW1 177 CJ86
Riverdale Rd, SE18 165 ET78
Bexley DA5 186 EZ87
Erith DA8 167 FB78
Feltham TW13 176 BY91
Twickenham TW1 177 CJ86
Riverdene, Edg. HA8 96 CQ48
Riverdene Rd, Ilf. IG1 125 EN62
River Dr, Upmin. RM14 128 FQ58
Riverfield Rd, Stai. TW18 173 BF93
River Front, Enf. EN1 82 DR41
River Gdns, Cars. SM5 200 DG103
Feltham TW14 175 BV85
Maidenhead SL6 150 AD75
River Gro Pk, Beck. BR3 203 DZ95
RIVERHEAD, Sev. TN13 256 FD122
Riverhead Cl, E17 101 DX54
Riverhead Dr, Sutt. SM2 218 DA110
Sch Riverhead Inf Sch, Sev. TN13 off Worships Hill 256 FE123
River Hill, Cob. KT11 229 BV115
Riverhill, Sev. TN15 257 FL130
Riverholme Dr, Epsom KT19 216 CR109
River Island Cl, Lthd. (Fetch.) KT22 231 CD121
River La, Lthd. KT22 231 CD120
Richmond TW10 177 CK88
Rivermead, E.Mol. KT8 196 CC97
West Byfleet (Byfleet) KT14 212 BM113
Rivermead Cl, Add. KT15 212 BJ108
Teddington TW11 177 CH92
Rivermead Ct, SW6 159 CZ83
Rivermead Ho, E9 off Kingsmead Way 123 DY64

Rivermead Rd, N18 ....101 DX51
River Meads, Ware
(Stans.Abb.) SG12 ......33 EC10
Rivermeads Av, Twick. TW2 .176 CA90
Rivermill, SW1
off Grosvenor Rd 161 DK78
Harlow CM20 ....35 EQ13
Rivermount, Walt. KT12 ....195 BT101
Rivermount Gdns, Guil.
GU2 ....258 AW137
Rivernook Cl, Walt. KT12 ...196 BW99
River Pk, Berk. HP4 ....38 AU18
Hemel Hempstead HP1 ....40 BG22
River Pk Av, Stai. TW18 ....173 BD91
River Pk Gdns, Brom. BR2 ..183 ED94
River Pk Rd, N22 ....99 DM54
River Pl, N1 ....4 G6
River Reach, Tedd. TW11 ....177 CJ92
River Rd, Bark. IG11 ....145 ES68
Brentwood CM14 ....108 FS49
Buckhurst Hill IG9 ....102 EL46
Maidenhead (Taplow) SL6 .130 AC73
Staines TW18 ....193 BF95
River Rd Business Pk, Bark.
IG11 ....145 ET69
Riversdale, Grav. (Nthflt)
DA11 ....190 GE89
[Sch] Riversdale Prim Sch,
SW18 *off Merton Rd* ...180 DA88
Riversdale Rd, N5 ....121 DP62
Romford RM5 ....105 FB52
Thames Ditton KT7 .....197 CG99
Riversdell Cl, Cher. KT16 ...193 BF101
Riversend Rd, Hem.H. HP3 ..40 BJ23
Riversfield Rd, Enf. EN1 .....82 DS41
[H] Rivers Hosp, The, Saw.
CM21 ....36 EW06
Riverside, NW4 ....119 CV59
SE7 ....25 N6
Chertsey KT16 ....194 BG97
Dartford (Eyns.) DA4 ....208 FK103
Dorking RH4 ....247 CK134
Egham (Runny.) TW20 ...173 BA90
Guildford GU1 ....242 AX132
Horley RH6 ....268 DG150
St. Albans (Lon.Col.) AL2 ..62 CL27
Shepperton TW17 ....195 BS101
Staines TW18 ....193 BF95
Staines (Wrays.) TW19 ...172 AW87
Twickenham TW1 ....177 CH88
Ware (Stans.Abb.) SG12 ..33 EC11
Riverside, The, E.Mol. KT8 ..197 CD97
Riverside Av, Brox. EN10 ....49 EA22
East Molesey KT8 ......197 CD99
Riverside Business Cen,
SW18 ....180 DB88
Riverside Cl, E5 ....122 DW60
W7 ....137 CE70
Kings Langley WD4 ......59 BP29
Kingston upon Thames
KT1 ....198 CK98
Orpington BR5 ....206 EW96
St. Albans AL1
off Riverside Rd 43 CE21
Staines TW18 ....193 BF95
Wallington SM6 ....201 DH104
Riverside Ct, E4
off Chelwood Cl 83 EB44
SW8 ....161 DK79
Harlow CM17 ....36 EW09
St. Albans AL1 ....43 CE22
Riverside Dr, NW11 ....119 CY58
W4 ....158 CR80
Esher KT10 ....214 CA105
Guildford (Bramley) GU5 .259 BA144
Mitcham CR4 ....200 DE99
Richmond TW10 ....177 CH89
Rickmansworth WD3 .....92 BK46
Staines (Egh.H.) TW18 ...173 BE92
Riverside Gdns, N3 ....119 CY55
W6 ....159 CV78
Berkhamsted HP4 ....38 AU18
Enfield EN2 ....82 DQ40
Wembley HA0 ....138 CL68
Woking (Old Wok.) GU22 .227 BB121
Riverside Ind Est, Bark.
IG11 ....146 EU69
Dartford DA1 ....188 FL85
Enfield EN3 ....83 DY44
Riverside Mans, E1 ....12 E10
Riverside Ms, Croy. CR0
off Wandle Rd 201 DL104
Riverside Pk, Wey. KT13 ....212 BL106
Riverside Path, Wal.Cr.
(Chsht) EN8
off Dewhurst Rd 67 DY29
Riverside Pl, Stai. (Stanw.)
TW19 ....174 BK86
[Sch] Riverside Prim Sch,
SE16 ....22 B4
Riverside Retail Pk, Sev.
TN14 ....241 FH119
Riverside Rd, E15 ....143 EC68
N15 ....122 DU58
SW17 ....180 DB91
St. Albans AL1 ....43 CE21
Sidcup DA14 ....186 EY90
Staines TW18 ....173 BF94
Staines (Stanw.) TW19 ...174 BK85
Walton-on-Thames KT12 .214 BX105
Watford WD19 ....75 BV44
Riverside Twr, SW6 ....160 DC82
Riverside Wk, Bex. DA5 ....186 EW87
Isleworth TW7 ....157 CE83
Kingston upon Thames
KT1 *off High St* 197 CK96
Loughton IG10 ....85 EP44
West Wickham BR4
off The Alders 203 EB102
Riverside Way, Dart. DA1 ...188 FL85
St. Albans AL2 ....61 CD32
Uxbridge UB8 ....134 BH67
Riverside W, SW18
off Smugglers Way 160 DB84
Riverside Yd, SW17
off Riverside Rd 180 DC91
Riversmead, Hodd. EN11 ....49 EA18
Riversmeet, Hert. SG14 .....31 DP10
[Sch] Riverston Sch, SE12
off Eltham Rd 184 EG85
River St, EC1 ....10 C1
Ware SG12 ....33 DY06
Windsor SL4 ....151 AR80
River Ter, W6 *off Crisp Rd* ..159 CW78
Riverton Cl, W9 ....6 F2
River Vw, Enf. EN2
off Chase Side 82 DQ41
Grays RM16 ....171 GG77
Welwyn Garden City AL7 ..29 CZ05
[Sch] Riverview C of E Prim Sch
& Nurs, Epsom KT19
off Riverview Rd 216 CR105
Riverview Gdns, SW13 ....159 CV79
Cobham KT11 ....213 BU113
Twickenham TW1 ....177 CF89
Riverview Gro, W4 ....158 CP79
River Vw Hts, SE16 ....22 A3
[Sch] Riverview Inf Sch, Grav.
DA12 *off Cimba Wd* 191 GL91
[Sch] Riverview Jun Sch, Grav.
DA12 *off Cimba Wd* 191 GL91
RIVERVIEW PARK, Grav.
DA12 ....191 GK92
Riverview Pk, SE6 ....183 EA89
Riverview Rd, W4 ....158 CP79
Epsom KT19 ....216 CQ105
Greenhithe DA9 ....189 FU85
River Wk, Uxb. (Denh.) UB9 .114 BJ64
Walton-on-Thames KT12 .195 BU100
Riverway, N13 ....99 DN50
River Way, Epsom KT19 ....216 CR106
Harlow CM20 ....36 EU10
Loughton IG10 ....85 EN44
Riverway, Stai. TW18 ......194 BH95
River Way, Twick. TW2 .....176 CB89
Riverway Est, Guil. (Peasm.)
GU3 ....258 AW142
River Wey Navigation, Guil.
GU1 ....242 AX132
Woking GU23 ....227 BB122
Riverwood La, Chis. BR7 ...205 ER95
Rivett-Drake Cl, Guil. GU2
off Tylehost 242 AV130
Rivett Drake Rd, Guil. GU2 .242 AU130
Rivey Cl, W.Byf. KT14 ......211 BF114
Rivington Av, Wdf.Grn. IG8 .102 EK54
Rivington Ct, NW10 ....139 CU67
Rivington Cres, NW7 ....97 CT52
Rivington Pl, EC2 ....11 M2
Rivington St, EC2 ....11 L2
Rivington Wk, E8
off Wilde Cl 142 DU67
Rivulet Rd, N17 ....100 DQ52
Rixon Cl, Slou. (Geo.Grn)
SL3 ....132 AY72
Rixon Ho, SE18
off Barnfield Rd 165 EP79
Rixon St, N7 ....121 DN62
Rixsen Rd, E12 ....124 EL64
[Sch] R.J. Mitchell Prim Sch,
Horn. RM12
off Tangmere Cres 147 FH65
Roach Rd, E3 ....143 EA66
Roads Pl, N19
off Hornsey Rd 121 DL61
Roakes Av, Add. KT15 .....194 BH103
Roan St, SE10 ....163 EC79
Roasthill La, Wind. (Dorney)
SL4 ....151 AK79
Robarts Cl, Pnr. HA5
off Field End Rd 115 BV57
Robb Rd, Stan. HA7 ....95 CG51
Robbs Cl, Hem.H. HP1 ......40 BG17
Robe End, Hem.H. HP1 .....39 BF18
Robert Adam St, W1 ....8 E7
Roberta St, E2 ....12 A1
Robert Av, St.Alb. AL1 ......42 CB24
[Sch] Robert Blair Prim Sch,
N7 *off Brewery Rd* 141 DL65
[Sch] Robert Browning Prim
Sch, SE17 ....21 J9
Robert Burns Ms, SE24
off Mayall Rd 181 DP85
[Sch] Robert Clack Comp Sec
Sch, Lwr Sch, Dag.
RM8 *off Green La* 126 EX61
[Sch] Robert Clack Sch,
Upr Sch, Dag. RM8
off Gosfield Rd 126 FA61
Robert Cl, W9 ....7 M4
Chigwell IG7 ....103 ET50
Potters Bar EN6 ....63 CY33
Walton-on-Thames KT12 .213 BV106
Robert Dashwood Way,
SE17 ....20 G8
Robert Keen Cl, SE15
off Cicely Rd 162 DU81
Robert Lowe Cl, SE14 ......163 DX80
Roberton Dr, Brom. BR1 ....204 EJ95
Robert Owen Ho, SW6 ......159 CX81
Robert Rd, Slou. (Hedg.)
SL2 ....111 AR61
Robertsbridge Rd, Cars.
SM5 ....200 DC102
Roberts Cl, SE9 ....185 ER88
SE16 ....23 H4
Orpington BR5 ....206 EW99
Romford RM3 ....105 FH53
Staines (Stanw.) TW19 ...174 BJ86
Sutton SM3 ....217 CX108
Thornton Heath CR7
off Kitchener Rd 202 DR97
Waltham Cross (Chsht)
EN8 *off Norwood Rd* 67 DY30
West Drayton UB7 ......134 BL74
Roberts La, Ger.Cr.
(Chal.St.P.) SL9 ....91 BA50
Roberts Ms, SW1 ....18 E6
Orpington BR6 ....206 EU102
Robertson Cl, Brox. EN10 ....67 DY26
Robertson Ct, Wok. GU21
off Raglan Rd 226 AS118
Robertson Rd, E15 ....143 EC67
Berkhamsted HP4 ....38 AX19
Robertson St, SW8 ....161 DH83
Robert's Pl, EC1 ....10 D3
Roberts Rd, E17 ....101 EB53
NW7 ....97 CY51
Belvedere DA17 ....166 FA78
Watford WD18
off Tucker St 76 BW43
Robert St, E16 ....145 EP74
NW1 ....9 H2
SE18 ....165 ER77
WC2 ....9 P10
Croydon CR0 *off High St* .202 DQ104
Roberts Way, Egh. (Eng.Grn)
TW20 ....172 AW94
Hatfield AL10 ....45 CT19
[Sch] Robertswood Comb Sch,
Ger.Cr. SL9
off Denham La 91 AZ52
Roberts Wd Dr, Ger.Cr.
(Chal.St.P.) SL9 ....91 AZ50
Robeson St, E3 ....13 M5
Robeson Way, Borwd. WD6 ..78 CQ39
Robina Cl, Bexh. DA6 ......166 EX84
Northwood HA6 ....93 BT53
Robin Cl, NW7 ....96 CS48
Addlestone KT15 ....212 BK106
Hampton TW12 ....176 BY92
Romford RM5 ....105 FD52
Ware (Stans.Abb.) SG12 ..33 EC12
Robin Ct, SE16 ....22 A7
Robin Ct, Wall. SM6
off Carew Rd 219 DJ107
Robin Cres, E6 ....144 EK71
Robin Gdns, Red. RH1 .....250 DG131
Robin Gro, N6 ....120 DG61
Brentford TW8 ....157 CJ79
Harrow HA3 ....118 CM58
Robin Hill, Berk. HP4 ....38 AW20
Robin Hill Dr, Chis. BR7 ....184 EL93
Robinhood Cl, Mitch. CR4 ..201 DJ97
Robin Hood Cl, Slou. SL1 ...131 AL74
Woking GU21 ....226 AT118
Robin Hood Cres, Wok.
(Knap.) GU21 ....226 AS117
Robin Hood Dr, Bushey
WD23 ....76 BZ39
Harrow HA3 ....95 CF52
Robin Hood Gdns, E14 ......14 D9
Robin Hood Grn, Orp. BR5 ..206 EU99
[Sch] Robin Hood Inf Sch, Sutt.
SM1 *off Robin Hood La* ..218 DA106
[Sch] Robin Hood Jun Sch, Sutt.
SM1 *off Thorncroft Rd* ..218 DB106
Robin Hood La, E14 ....14 D9
SW15 ....178 CS91
Bexleyheath DA6 ....186 EY85
Guildford (Sutt.Grn) GU4 .227 AZ124
Hatfield AL10 ....45 CU17
Robinhood La, Mitch. CR4 ..201 DJ97
Robin Hood La, Sutt. SM1 ..218 DA106
Robin Hood Meadow,
Hem.H. HP2 ....40 BM15
[Sch] Robin Hood Prim Sch,
SW15 *off Bowness Cres* ..178 CS92
Robin Hood Rd, SW19 ......179 CV92
Brentwood CM15 ....108 FV45
Woking GU21 ....226 AT118
Robin Hood Way, SW15 .....178 CS91
SW20 ....178 CS91
Greenford UB6 ....137 CF65
Robin Ho, NW8
off Newcourt St 140 DE68
Robinia Av, Grav. (Nthflt)
DA11 ....190 GD87
Robinia Cl, SE20
off Sycamore Gro 202 DU95
Ilford IG6 ....103 ES51
Robinia Cres, E10 ....123 EB61
Robin Mead, Welw.G.C. AL7 .30 DA06
Robins Cl, St.Alb. (Lon.Col.)
AL2 *off High St* 62 CL27
Uxbridge UB8
off Newcourt 134 BJ71
Robins Ct, SE12 ....184 EJ90
Robinscroft Ms, SE10
off Sparta St 163 EB81
Robinsfield, Hem.H. HP1 ....40 BG20
[Sch] Robinsfield Inf Sch,
NW8 *off Ordnance Hill* ..140 DE68
Robins Gro, W.Wick. BR4 ...204 EG104
Robins La, Epp. (They.B.)
CM16 ....85 EQ36
Robins Nest Hill, Hert. SG13 .47 DJ19
Robinson Av, Wal.Cr. (Chsht)
EN7 ....65 DP28
Robinson Cl, E11 ....124 EE62
Hornchurch RM12 ....147 FH66
Robinson Cres, Bushey
(Bushey Hth) WD23 .....94 CC46
Robinson Rd, E2 ....142 DW68
SW17 ....180 DE93
Dagenham RM10 ....126 FA63
Robinsons Cl, W13 ....137 CG71
Robinson St, SW3
off Christchurch St 160 DF79
Robins Orchard, Ger.Cr.
(Chal.St.P.) SL9 ....90 AY51
Robins Rd, Hem.H. HP3 .....40 BN22
Robins Way, Hat. AL10 ......45 CT21
Robinsway, Wal.Abb. EN9
off Roundhills 68 EE34
Walton-on-Thames KT12 .214 BW105
Robinswood Cl, Beac. HP9 ..88 AJ50
Robin Way, Guil. GU2 ......242 AV130
Orpington BR5 ....206 EV97
Potters Bar (Cuffley) EN6 ..65 DL28
Staines TW18 ....173 BF90
Robin Willis Way, Wind.
(Old Wind.) SL4 ....172 AU86
Robinwood Gro, Uxb. UB8 .134 BM70
Robinwood Pl, SW15 ....178 CR91
Roborough Wk, Horn. RM12 .148 FJ65
Robsart St, SW9 ....161 DM82
Robson Av, NW10 ....139 CU67
Robson Cl, E6
off Linton Gdns 144 EL72
Enfield EN2 ....81 DP40
Gerrards Cross (Chal.St.P.)
SL9 ....90 AY50
Robson Rd, SE27 ....181 DP90
Robsons Cl, Wal.Cr. EN8 ....66 DW29
Robyns Cft, Grav. (Nthflt)
DA11 ....190 GE90
Robyns Way, Sev. TN13 ....256 FF122
Roch Av, Edg. HA8 ....96 CM54
Rochdale Rd, E17 ....123 EA59
SE2 ....166 EV78
Rochdale Way, SE8
off Octavius St 163 EA80
Rochelle Cl, SW11 ....160 DD84
Rochelle St, E2 ....11 N2
Rochemont Wk, E8 ....5 P8
Roche Rd, SW16 ....201 DM95
[Sch] Roche Sch, The,
SW18 *off Frogmore* 180 DA85
Rochester Av, E13 ....144 EJ67
Bromley BR1 ....204 EH96
Feltham TW13 ....175 BT89
Rochester Cl, SW16 ....181 DL94
Enfield EN1 ....82 DS39
Sidcup DA15 ....186 EV86
Rochester Dr, Bex. DA5 ....186 EZ86
Pinner HA5 ....116 BX57
Watford WD25 ....60 BW34
Rochester Gdns, Cat. CR3 ..236 DS122
Croydon CR0 ....202 DS104
Ilford IG1 ....125 EM59
Rochester Ms, NW1 ....141 DJ66
Rochester Pl, NW1 ....141 DJ65
Rochester Rd, NW1 ....141 DJ65
Carshalton SM5 ....218 DF105
Dartford DA1 ....188 FN87
Gravesend DA12 ....191 GL87
Hornchurch RM12
off Airfield Way 147 FH65
Northwood HA6 ....115 BT55
Staines TW18 ....173 BD92
Rochester Row, SW1 ....19 K7
Rochester Sq, NW1 ....141 DJ66
Rochester St, SW1 ....19 L6
Rochester Ter, NW1 ....141 DJ65
Rochester Wk, SE1 ....21 J1
Reigate RH2 *off Castle Dr* .266 DB139
Rochester Way, SE3 ....164 EH81
SE9 ....165 EM83
Rochester Way, Dart. DA1 ..187 FD87
Rickmansworth (Crox.Grn)
WD3 ....75 BP42
Rochester Way Relief Rd,
SE3 ....164 EH81
SE9 ....164 EL84
Roche Wk, Cars. SM5 .....200 DD100
Rochford Av, Brwd. (Shenf.)
CM15 ....109 GA43
Loughton IG10 ....85 EQ41
Romford RM6 ....126 EW57
Waltham Abbey EN9 .....67 ED33
Rochford Cl, E6
off Boleyn Rd 144 EK68
Broxbourne EN10 ....67 DY26
Hornchurch RM12 ......147 FH65
Rochford Grn, Loug. IG10 ...85 EQ41
Rochfords Gdns, Slou. SL2 .132 AW74
Rochford St, NW5 ....120 DF64
Rochford Wk, E8
off Wilman Gro 142 DU66
Rochford Way, Croy. CR0 ...201 DL100
Maidenhead (Taplow) SL6 .130 AG73
Rockall Ct, Slou. SL3 ......153 BB76
Rock Av, SW14
off South Worple Way ..158 CR83
Rockbourne Rd, SE23 ......183 DX88
Rockchase Gdns, Horn.
RM11 ....128 FL58
★ Rock Circ, W1 ....9 L10
[Sch] Rockcliffe Manor Prim Sch,
SE18 *off Bassant Rd* 165 ET79
Rockdale Rd, Sev. TN13 ....257 FH125
Rockells Pl, SE22 ....182 DV86
Rockfield Cl, Oxt. RH8 .....254 EF131
Rockfield Rd, Oxt. RH8 .....254 EF129
Rockford Av, Grnf. UB6 ....137 CG68
Rock Gdns, Dag. RM10 .....127 FB64
Rock Gro Way, SE16 ....22 B7
Rockhall Rd, NW2 ....119 CX63
Rockhall Way, NW2
off Midland Ter 119 CX62
Rockhampton Cl, SE27
off Rockhampton Rd ...181 DN91
Rockhampton Rd, SE27 .....181 DN91
South Croydon CR2 .....220 DS107
Rock Hill, SE26 ....182 DT91
Orpington BR6 ....224 FA107
Rockingham Av, Horn.
RM11 ....127 FH58
Rockingham Cl, SW15 .....159 CT84
Uxbridge UB8 ....134 BJ67
Rockingham Est, SE1 ....20 G6
Rockingham Par, Uxb. UB8 .134 BJ66
Rockingham Pl, Beac. HP9 ..89 AM54
Rockingham Rd, Uxb. UB8 .134 BH67
Rockingham St, SE1 ....20 G6
Rockland Rd, SW15 ....159 CY84
Rocklands Dr, Stan. HA7 ....95 CH54
Rockleigh Ct, Brwd. (Shenf.)
CM15 *off Hutton Rd* 109 GA45
Rockley Rd, W14 ....16 A4
Rockliffe Av, Kings L. WD4 ..58 BN30
[Sch] Rockmount Prim Sch,
SE19 *off Hermitage Rd* ..182 DR93
Rockmount Rd, SE18 ....165 ET78
SE19 ....182 DR93
Rockshaw Rd, Red. RH1 ....251 DM127
Rocks La, SW13 ....159 CU81
Rock St, N4 ....121 DN61
Rockware Av, Grnf. UB6 ....137 CD67
Rockways, Barn. EN5 ....79 CT44
Rockwell Gdns, SE19 ......182 DS92
Rockwell Rd, Dag. RM10 ....127 FB64
Rockwood Pl, W12 ....159 CW75
Rocky La, Reig. RH2 ....250 DF128
Rocliffe St, N1 ....4 F10
Rocombe Cres, SE23 ....182 DW87
Rocque La, SE3 ....164 EF83
Rodborough Rd, NW11 ......120 DA60
Roden Cl, Harl. CM17 ....36 EZ11
Roden Ct, N6
off Hornsey La 121 DK59
Roden Gdns, Croy. CR0 ....202 DS100
Rodenhurst Rd, SW4 ....181 DJ86
Roden St, N7 ....121 DM62
Ilford IG1 ....125 EN62
Rodeo Cl, Erith DA8 ....167 FH81
Roderick Rd, NW3 ....120 DF63
Rodgers Cl, Borwd. (Elstree)
WD6 ....77 CK44
Roding Av, Wdf.Grn. IG8 ...102 EL51
Roding Gdns, Loug. IG10 ....84 EL44
Roding La, Buck.H. IG9 .....102 EL46
Chigwell IG7 ....103 EN46
Roding La N, Wdf.Grn. IG8 .102 EK54
Roding La S, Ilf. IG4 ....124 EK56
Woodford Green IG8 .....124 EK56
Roding Ms, E1 ....22 B1
[Sch] Roding Prim Sch, Dag.
RM8 *off Hewett Rd* 126 EX63
Woodford Green IG8
off Roding La N 102 EL52
Roding Rd, E5 ....123 DX63
E6 ....145 EP71
Loughton IG10 ....84 EL43
Rodings, The, Upmin. RM14 .129 FR58
Woodford Green IG8 ....102 EJ51
Rodings Row, Barn. EN5
off Leecroft Rd 79 CY43
Roding Trd Est, Bark. IG11 ..145 EP66
⊖ Roding Valley 102 EK49
[Sch] Roding Valley High Sch,
Loug. IG10
off Alderton Hill 84 EL43
Annexe, Loug. IG10
off Roding Rd 84 EL43
Roding Vw, Buck.H. IG9 ....102 EK46
Roding Way, Rain. RM13 ....148 FK68
Rodmarton St, W1 ....8 D6
Rodmell Cl, Hayes UB4 .....136 BY70
Rodmell Slope, N12 ....97 CZ50
Rodmere St, SE10 ....25 H10
Rodmill La, SW2 ....181 DL87
Rodney Av, St.Alb. AL1 ......43 CG22
Rodney Cl, Croy. CR0 ......201 DP102
New Malden KT3 ....198 CS99
Pinner HA5 ....116 BY59
Walton-on-Thames KT12 .196 BW102
Rodney Ct, W9 ....7 M3
Rodney Cres, Hodd. EN11 ...49 EA15
Rodney Gdns, Pnr. HA5 .....115 BV57
West Wickham BR4 .....222 EG105
Rodney Grn, Walt. KT12 ....196 BW103
Rodney Pl, E17 ....101 DY54
SE17 ....21 H7
SW19 ....200 DC95
Rodney Rd, E11 ....124 EH56
SE17 ....21 H7
Mitcham CR4 ....200 DE96
New Malden KT3 ....198 CS99
Twickenham TW2 ....176 CA86
Walton-on-Thames KT12 .196 BW103
Rodney St, N1 ....4 B9
Rodney Way, Guil. GU1 ....243 BA133
Rodney Way, Rom. RM7 ....104 FA53
Slough (Colnbr.) SL3 ....153 BE81
Rodona Rd, Wey. KT13 .....213 BR111
Rodway Rd, SW15 ....179 CU87
Bromley BR1 ....204 EH95
Rodwell Cl, Ruis. HA4 ......116 BW60
Rodwell Ct, Add. KT15
off Garfield Rd 212 BJ105
Rodwell Pl, Edg. HA8
off Whitchurch La 96 CN51
Rodwell Rd, SE22 ....182 DT86
Roebourne Way, E16 ....165 EN75
Roebuck Cl, Ashtd. KT21 ...232 CL120
Feltham TW13 ....175 BV91
Hertford SG13 ....32 DU09
Reigate RH2 ....250 DB134
Roebuck Grn, Slou. SL1 ....131 AL74
Roebuck La, N17
off High Rd 100 DT51
Buckhurst Hill IG9 ....102 EJ45
Roebuck Rd, Chess. KT9 ...216 CN106
Ilford IG6 ....104 EV50
Roedean Av, Enf. EN3 ....82 DW39
Roedean Cl, Enf. EN3 ....82 DW39
Orpington BR6 ....224 EV105
Roedean Cres, SW15 ....178 CS86
Roedean Dr, Rom. RM1 .....127 FE56
Roe End, NW9 ....118 CQ56
Roefields Cl, Hem.H.
(Felden) HP3 ....40 BG24
ROE GREEN, Hat. AL10 .....45 CU18
Roe Grn, NW9 ....118 CQ57
Roe Grn Cl, Hat. AL10 ......44 CS19
Roe Grn La, Hat. AL10 ......45 CT18
[Sch] Roe Grn Prim Sch,
NW9 *off Princes Av* 118 CP56
ROEHAMPTON, SW15 ....179 CU85
Roehampton Cl, SW15 .....159 CU84
Gravesend DA12 ....191 GL87
[Sch] Roehampton C of E Prim
Sch, SW15
off Roehampton La 179 CV87
Roehampton Dr, Chis. BR7 .185 EQ93
Roehampton Gate, SW15 ...178 CS86
Roehampton High St,
SW15 ....179 CV87
Roehampton La, SW15 .....159 CU84
[H] Roehampton Priory Hosp,
The, SW15 ....159 CT84
Roehampton Vale, SW15 ....178 CS90
Roe Hill Cl, Hat. AL10 ......44 CT19
Roehyde Way, Hat. AL10 ....44 CS20
Roe La, NW9 ....118 CP56
ROESTOCK, St.Alb. AL4 .....44 CR23
Roestock Gdns, St.Alb.
(Coln.Hth) AL4 ....44 CS22
Roestock La, St.Alb.
(Coln.Hth) AL4 ....44 CR23
Roe Way, Wall. SM6 ....219 DL107
Rofant Rd, Nthwd. HA6 .....93 BS51
Roffes La, Cat. CR3 ....236 DR124
Roffey Cl, Horl. RH6
off Court Lo Rd 268 DF148
Purley CR8 ....235 DP116
Roffey St, E14 ....24 C4
Roffords, Wok. GU21 ......226 AV117
Rogate Ho, E5 *off Muir Rd* ..122 DU62
[Sch] Roger Ascham Prim Sch, E17
off Wigton Rd 101 DZ53
Roger Dowley Ct, E2 ....142 DW68
Rogers Cl, Cat. CR3
off Tillingdown Hill 236 DV122
Coulsdon CR5 ....235 DP118
Waltham Cross (Chsht)
EN7 ....66 DR26
Rogers Ct, Swan. BR8 ......207 FG98
Rogers Gdns, Dag. RM10 ...126 FA64
Rogers La, Slou. (Stoke P.)
SL2 ....132 AT67
Warlingham CR6 ....237 DZ118
Rogers Mead, Gdse. RH9
off Ivy Mill La 252 DV132
Rogers Rd, E16 ....15 K8
SW17 ....180 DD91
Dagenham RM10 ....126 FA64
Grays RM17 ....170 GC77
Rogers Ruff, Nthwd. HA6 ....93 BQ53
Roger St, WC1 ....10 B4
Rogers Wk, N12
off Brook Meadow 98 DB48
Rojack Rd, SE23 ....183 DX88
Rokeby Ct, Wok. GU21 .....226 AT117
Rokeby Gdns, Wdf.Grn. IG8 .102 EG53
Rokeby Pl, SW20 ....179 CV94
Rokeby Rd, SE4 ....163 DZ82
[Sch] Rokeby Sch, Kings.T.
KT2 *off George Rd* 178 CQ94
[Sch] Rokeby Sec Sch, E15
off Pitchford St 143 ED66
Rokeby St, E15 ....144 EE67
Roke Cl, Ken. CR8 ....220 DQ114
Rokefield, Dor. RH4 ....262 CB136
Roke Lo Rd, Ken. CR8 ......219 DP113
[Sch] Roke Prim Sch, Ken.
CR8 *off Little Roke Rd* ..220 DQ114
Roke Rd, Ken. CR8 ....236 DQ115
Roker Pk Av, Uxb. UB10 ....114 BL63
Rokesby Cl, Well. DA16 ....165 ER82
Rokesby Pl, Wem. HA0 .....117 CK64
Rokesby Rd, Slou. SL2 .....131 AM69
Rokesly Av, N8 ....121 DL57
[Sch] Rokesly Inf Sch, N8
off Hermiston Av 121 DL57
[Sch] Rokesly Jun Sch, N8
off Rokesly Av 121 DL57
Rokewood Ms, Ware SG12 ...33 DX05
Roland Gdns, SW7 ....17 M9
Feltham TW13 ....176 BY90
Roland Ms, E1 ....12 G5
Roland Rd, E17 ....123 ED56
Roland St, St.Alb. AL1 ......43 CG20
Roland Way, SE17 ....21 K10
SW7 ....17 M9
Worcester Park KT4 .....199 CT103
Roles Gro, Rom. RM6 ......126 EX56
Rolfe Cl, Barn. EN4 ....80 DE42
Beaconsfield HP9 ....89 AL54
Rolinsden Way, Kes. BR2 ...222 EK105
Rollesby Rd, Chess. KT9 ...216 CN107
Rollesby Way, SE28 ....146 EW73
Rolleston Av, Orp. BR5 ....205 EP100
Rolleston Cl, Orp. BR5 .....205 EP101
Rolleston Rd, S.Croy. CR2 ..220 DR108
Roll Gdns, Ilf. IG2 ....125 EN57
Rollins St, SE15 ....162 DW79
Rollit Cres, Houns. TW3 ....176 CA85
Rollit St, N7 ....4 C1
Rollo Rd, Swan. BR8 ....187 FF94
Rolls Bldgs, EC4 ....10 C7
Rollscourt Av, SE24 ....182 DQ85
Rolls Pk Av, E4 ....101 EA51
Rolls Pk Rd, E4 ....101 EB50
Rolls Pas, EC4 ....10 C7
Rolls Rd, SE1 ....21 P9
Rollswood, Welw.G.C. AL7 ..29 CY12

★ Place of interest [H] Hospital [Sch] School [Coll] College [Uni] University ⇌ Railway station

Rolt St, SE8 ... 163 DY79
Rolvenden Gdns, Brom.
BR1 ... 184 EK94
Rolvenden Pl, N17
off Manor Rd ... 100 DU53
★ **Roman Bath**, WC2
off Strand La ... 10 B9
Romanby Ct, Red. RH1
off Mill St ... 266 DF135
Roman Cl, W3
off Avenue Gdns ... 158 CP75
Feltham TW14 ... 176 BW85
Rainham RM13 ... 147 FD68
Uxbridge (Hare.) UB9 ... 92 BH53
Romanfield Rd, SW2 ... 181 DM87
Roman Gdns, Kings L. WD4 . 59 BP30
Roman Ho, Rain. RM13
off Roman Cl ... 147 FD68
Romanhurst Av, Brom. BR2 . 204 EE98
Romanhurst Gdns, Brom.
BR2 ... 204 EE98
Roman Ind Est, Croy. CR0 . 202 DS101
Roman Ms, Hodd. EN11
off North Rd ... 49 EA16
Roman Ri, SE19 ... 182 DR93
Sawbridgeworth CM21 ... 36 EX05
Roman Rd, E2 ... 12 E2
E3 ... 143 DY68
E6 ... 144 EL70
N10 ... 99 DH52
NW2 ... 119 CW62
W4 ... 158 CS77
Brentwood CM15 ... 109 GA41
Dorking RH4 ... 263 CG138
Gravesend (Nthflt) DA11 . 190 GC90
Ilford IG1 ... 145 EP65
Roman Rd Prim Sch,
E6 *off Roman Rd* ... 144 EK70
Romans End, St.Alb. AL3 ... 42 CC22
Roman Sq, SE28 ... 146 EU74
Roman St, Hodd. EN11 ... 49 EA16
Romans Way, Wok. GU22 . 228 BG115
Roman Vale, Harl. CM17 ... 36 EW10
Roman Vil Rd, Dart.
(S.Darenth) DA2, DA4 . 188 FQ92
Roman Way, N7 ... 4 B4
SE15 *off Clifton Way* ... 162 DW80
Carshalton SM5 ... 218 DF109
Croydon CR0 ... 201 DP103
Dartford DA1 ... 187 FE85
Enfield EN1 ... 82 DT43
Waltham Abbey EN9 ... 83 EB35
Roman Way Ind Est, N1
off Offord St ... 141 DM66
Romany Ct, Hem.H. HP2
off Wood End Cl ... 41 BQ19
Romany Gdns, E17
off McEntee Av ... 101 DY53
Sutton SM3 ... 200 DA101
Romany Ri, Orp. BR5 ... 205 EQ102
Roma Read Cl, SW15
off Bessborough Rd ... 179 CV87
Roma Rd, E17 ... 123 DY55
Romberg Rd, SW17 ... 180 DG90
Romborough Gdns, SE13 . 183 EC85
Romborough Way, SE13 ... 183 EC85
Rom Cres, Rom. RM7 ... 127 FF59
Romeland, Borwd. (Elstree)
WD6 ... 77 CK44
St. Albans AL3 ... 42 CC20
Waltham Abbey EN9 ... 67 EC33
Romeland Hill, St.Alb. AL3 . 42 CC20
Romero Cl, SW9
off Stockwell Rd ... 161 DM83
Romero Sq, SE3 ... 164 EJ84
Romeyn Rd, SW16 ... 181 DM90
ROMFORD, RM1 - RM7 ... 127 FF57
⇌ **Romford** ... 127 FE58
Romford Rd, E7 ... 124 EH64
E12 ... 124 EL63
E15 ... 144 EE66
Chigwell IG7 ... 104 EU48
Romford RM5 ... 104 EY52
South Ockendon (Aveley)
RM15 ... 148 FQ73
Romford St, E1 ... 12 B6
Romilly Dr, Wat. WD19 ... 94 BY49
Romilly Rd, N4 ... 121 DP61
Romilly St, W1 ... 9 L9
Rommany Rd, SE27 ... 182 DR91
Romney Chase, Horn. RM11 . 128 FM58
Romney Cl, N17 ... 100 DV53
NW11 ... 120 DC60
SE14 *off Kender St* ... 162 DW80
Ashford TW15 ... 175 BQ92
Chessington KT9 ... 216 CL105
Harrow HA2 ... 116 CA59
Romney Dr, Brom. BR1 ... 184 EK94
Harrow HA2 ... 116 CA59
Romney Gdns, Bexh. DA7 . 166 EZ81
Romney Lock, Wind. SL4 ... 152 AS79
Romney Lock Rd, Wind.
SL4 ... 151 AR80
Romney Ms, W1 ... 8 E5
Romney Par, Hayes UB4
off Romney Rd ... 135 BR68
Romney Rd, SE10 ... 163 EC79
Gravesend (Nthflt) DA11 . 190 GE90
Hayes UB4 ... 135 BR68
New Malden KT3 ... 198 CR100
Romney Row, NW2
off Brent Ter ... 119 CX61
Romney St, SW1 ... 19 M6
Romola Rd, SE24 ... 181 DP88
Romsey Cl, Orp. BR6 ... 223 EP105
Slough SL3 ... 153 AZ76
Romsey Dr, Slou.
(Farn.Com.) SL2 ... 111 AR62
Romsey Gdns, Dag. RM9 ... 146 EX67
Romsey Rd, W13 ... 137 CG73
Dagenham RM9 ... 146 EX67
Romside Pl, Rom. RM7
off Brooklands La ... 127 FD56
Romulus Ct, Brent. TW8
off Justin Cl ... 157 CK80
Rom Valley Way, Rom. RM7 . 127 FE59
Ronald Av, E15 ... 15 H2
Ronald Cl, Beck. BR3 ... 203 DZ98
Ronald Ct, St.Alb. AL2 ... 60 BY29
Ronald Ho, SE3
off Cambert Way ... 164 EJ84
Ronald Rd, Beac. HP9 ... 89 AM53
Romford RM3 ... 106 FN53
Ronald Ross Prim Sch,
SW19
off Castlecombe Dr ... 179 CY87
Ronaldsay Spur, Slou. SL1 . 132 AS71
Ronalds Rd, N5 ... 4 D2
Bromley BR1 ... 204 EG95
Ronaldstone Rd, Sid. DA15 . 185 ES86
Ronald St, E1 ... 12 F8
Rona Rd, NW3 ... 120 DG63
Ronart St, Har. (Wldste)
HA3 *off Stuart Rd* ... 117 CF55
Rona Wk, N1 ... 5 J4
Rondu Rd, NW2 ... 119 CY64
Ronelean Rd, Surb. KT6 ... 196 CM104
Roneo Cor, Horn. RM12 ... 127 FF60
Roneo Link, Horn. RM12 ... 127 FF60
Ronfearn Av, Orp. BR5 ... 206 EX99
Ron Leighton Way, E6 ... 144 EL67
Ronneby Cl, Wey. KT13 ... 195 BS104
Ronnie La, E12
off Walton Rd ... 125 EN63
Ronsons Way, St.Alb. AL4 ... 43 CF17
Ronson Way, Lthd. KT22 ... 231 CG121
Ronver Rd, SE12 ... 184 EF87
Rood La, EC3 ... 11 L9
Roof of the World Caravan Pk,
Tad. (Box H.) KT20 ... 248 CP132
Rookby Ct, N21
off Carpenter Gdns ... 99 DP47
Rook Cl, Horn. RM12 ... 147 FG66
Wembley HA9 ... 118 CP62
Rookdean, Sev. (Chipstead)
TN13 ... 256 FC122
Rookeries Cl, Felt. TW13 ... 175 BV90
Rookery, The, Dor. (Westc.)
RH4 ... 262 CA138
Grays RM20 ... 169 FU79
Rookery Cl, NW9 ... 119 CT57
Leatherhead (Fetch.)
KT22 ... 231 CE124
Rookery Ct, Grays RM20 ... 169 FU79
Rookery Cres, Dag. RM10 ... 147 FB66
Rookery Dr, Chis. BR7 ... 205 EN95
Dorking (Westc.) RH4 ... 262 CA138
Rookery Gdns, Orp. BR5 ... 206 EW99
Rookery Hill, Ashtd. KT21 . 232 CN118
Redhill (Outwood) RH1 . 289 DN145
Rookery La, Brom. BR2 ... 204 EK100
Grays RM17 ... 170 GD78
Horley (Smallfield) RH6 . 269 DN146
Rookery Mead, Couls. CR5
off Blue Leaves Av ... 235 DK122
Rookery Rd, SW4 ... 161 DJ84
Orpington BR6 ... 223 EM110
Staines TW18 ... 174 BH92
Rookery Vw, Grays RM17 . 170 GD78
Rookery Way, NW9 ... 119 CT57
Tadworth (Lwr Kgswd)
KT20 ... 249 CZ127
Rookes All, Hert. SG13
off Mangrove Rd ... 32 DR09
Rookesley Rd, Orp. BR5 ... 206 EX101
Rooke Way, SE10 ... 25 J9
Rookfield Av, N10 ... 121 DJ56
Rookfield Cl, N10
off Cranmore Way ... 121 DJ56
Rook La, Cat. CR3 ... 235 DM124
Rookley Cl, Sutt. SM2 ... 218 DB110
Rook Rd, H.Wyc. (Woob.Grn)
HP10 ... 110 AD59
Rooks Cl, Welw.G.C. AL8 ... 29 CX10
Rooks Heath High Sch,
Har. HA2
off Eastcote La ... 116 CA62
Rooks Hill, Rick. (Loud.)
WD3 ... 74 BK42
Welwyn Garden City AL8 . 29 CW10
Rooksmead Rd, Sun. TW16 . 195 BT96
Rooks Nest, Gdse. RH9
off Godstone Bypass ... 253 DY130
Rookstone Rd, SW17 ... 180 DF92
Rook Wk, E6
off Allhallows Rd ... 144 EL72
Rookwood Av, Loug. IG10 ... 85 EQ41
New Malden KT3 ... 199 CU98
Wallington SM6 ... 219 DK105
Rookwood Cl, Grays RM17 . 170 GB77
Redhill RH1 ... 251 DH129
Rookwood Ct, Guil. GU2 ... 258 AW137
Rookwood Gdns, E4
off Whitehall Rd ... 102 EF46
Loughton IG10 ... 85 EQ41
Rookwood Ho, Bark. IG11
off St. Marys ... 145 ER68
Rookwood Rd, N16 ... 122 DT59
★ **Roosevelt Mem**, W1 ... 8 F9
Roosevelt Way, Dag. RM10 . 147 FD65
Rootes Dr, W10 ... 6 A5
Roothill La, Bet. RH3 ... 264 CN140
Ropemaker Rd, SE16 ... 23 J4
Ropemakers Flds, E14 ... 13 L10
Ropemaker St, EC2 ... 11 J5
Roper La, SE1 ... 21 M4
Ropers Av, E4 ... 101 EC50
Ropers Orchard, SW3
off Danvers St ... 160 DE79
Roper St, SE9 ... 185 EM86
Ropers Wk, SW2
off Brockwell Pk Gdns . 181 DN87
Roper Way, Mitch. CR4 ... 200 DG96
Ropery St, E3 ... 13 L4
Rope St, SE16 ... 23 K6
Rope Wk, Sun. TW16 ... 196 BW97
Rope Wk Gdns, E1 ... 12 B8
Ropewalk Ms, E8
off Middleton Rd ... 142 DT66
Rope Yd Rails, SE18 ... 165 EP76
Ropley St, E2 ... 142 DU68
Rosa Alba Ms, N5
off Kelross Rd ... 122 DQ63
Rosa Av, Ashf. TW15 ... 174 BN91
Rosaline Rd, SW6 ... 159 CY80
Rosamond St, SE26 ... 182 DV90
Rosamund Cl, S.Croy. CR2 . 220 DR105
Rosamun St, Sthl. UB2 ... 156 BY77
Rosary, The, Egh. TW20 ... 193 BD96
Rosary Cl, Houns. TW3 ... 156 BY82
Rosary Ct, Pot.B. EN6 ... 64 DB30
Rosary Gdns, SW7 ... 17 M8
Ashford TW15 ... 175 BP91
Bushey WD23 ... 95 CE45
Rosary RC Inf & Jun Sch,
NW3 *off Haverstock Hill* . 120 DE64
Rosary RC Inf & Nurs Sch,
The, Houns. TW5
off Heston Rd ... 156 CA79
Rosary RC Jun Sch, The,
Houns. TW5
off The Green ... 156 CA79
Rosaville Rd, SW6 ... 159 CZ80
Roscoe St, EC1 ... 11 H4
Roscoff Cl, Edg. HA8 ... 96 CQ53
Roseacre, Oxt. RH8 ... 254 EG134
Roseacre Cl, W13
off Middlefielde ... 137 CH71
Hornchurch RM11 ... 128 FM60
Shepperton TW17 ... 194 BN99
Roseacre Gdns, Guil. (Chilw.)
GU4 ... 259 BF140
Welwyn Garden City AL7 . 30 DC09
Roseacre Rd, Well. DA16 ... 166 EV83
Rose All, EC2
off Bishopsgate ... 142 DS71
SE1 ... 21 H1
Rose & Crown Ct, EC2 ... 10 G7
Rose & Crown Yd, SW1 ... 19 K1
Roseary Cl, West Dr. UB7 . 154 BK77
Rose Av, E18 ... 102 EH54
Gravesend DA12 ... 191 GL88
Mitcham CR4 ... 200 DF95
Morden SM4 ... 200 DC99
Rosebank, SE20 ... 182 DV94
Rose Bk, Brwd. CM14 ... 108 FX48
Rosebank, Epsom KT18 ... 216 CQ114
Waltham Abbey EN9 ... 68 EE33
Rosebank Av, Horn. RM12 . 128 FJ64
Wembley HA0 ... 117 CF63
Rosebank Cl, N12 ... 98 DE50
Teddington TW11 ... 177 CG93
Rose Bk Cotts, Wok. GU22 . 226 AY122
Rosebank Gdns, E3 ... 143 DZ68
Gravesend (Nthflt) DA11 . 190 GE88
Rosebank Gro, E17 ... 123 DZ55
Rosebank Rd, E17 ... 123 EB58
W7 ... 157 CE75
Rosebank Vil, E17 ... 123 EA56
Rosebank Wk, NW1
off Maiden La ... 141 DK66
SE18 *off Woodhill* ... 164 EL77
Rosebank Way, W3 ... 138 CR72
Rose Bates Dr, NW9 ... 118 CN56
Roseberry Cl, Upmin. RM14 . 129 FT58
Roseberry Ct, Wat. WD17
off Grandfield Av ... 75 BU39
Roseberry Gdns, N4 ... 121 DP58
Dartford DA1 ... 188 FJ87
Orpington BR6 ... 205 ES104
Upminster RM14 ... 129 FT59
Roseberry Pl, E8 ... 5 N4
Roseberry St, SE16 ... 22 C8
Rosebery Av, E12 ... 144 EL65
EC1 ... 10 C4
N17 ... 100 DU54
Epsom KT17 ... 216 CS114
Harrow HA2 ... 116 BZ63
New Malden KT3 ... 199 CT96
Sidcup DA15 ... 185 ES87
Thornton Heath CR7 ... 202 DQ96
Rosebery Cl, Mord. SM4 ... 199 CX100
Rosebery Ct, EC1
off Rosebery Av ... 141 DN70
Gravesend (Nthflt) DA11 . 191 GF88
Rosebery Cres, Wok. GU22 . 227 AZ121
Rosebery Gdns, N8 ... 121 DL57
W13 ... 137 CG72
Sutton SM1 ... 218 DB105
Rosebery Ms, N10 ... 99 DJ54
SW2 *off Rosebery Rd* ... 181 DL86
Rosebery Rd, N9 ... 100 DU48
N10 ... 99 DJ54
SW2 ... 181 DL86
Bushey WD23 ... 94 CB45
Epsom KT18 ... 232 CR119
Grays RM17 ... 170 FY79
Hounslow TW3 ... 176 CC85
Kingston upon Thames
KT1 ... 198 CP96
Sutton SM1 ... 217 CZ107
Rosebery Sch, Epsom
KT18 *off White Horse Dr* . 216 CQ114
Rosebery Sq, EC1 ... 10 C4
Kingston upon Thames
KT1 ... 198 CN96
Rosebine Av, Twick. TW2 ... 177 CD87
Rosebriar Cl, Wok. GU22 ... 228 BG116
Rosebriars, Cat. CR3 ... 236 DS120
Esher KT10 ... 214 CC106
Rosebriar Wk, Wat. WD24 ... 75 BT36
Rose Bruford Coll, Lamorbey
Pk Campus, Sid. DA15
off Burnt Oak La ... 186 EV88
Rosebury Rd, SW6 ... 160 DB82
Rosebury Sq, Wdf.Grn. IG8 . 103 EN52
Rosebury Vale, Ruis. HA4 ... 115 BT60
Rose Bushes, Epsom KT17 . 233 CV116
Rose Ct, E1 ... 11 N6
Pinner HA5
off Nursery Rd ... 116 BW55
Waltham Cross EN7 ... 66 DU27
Rosecourt Rd, Croy. CR0 ... 201 DM100
Rosecroft Av, NW3 ... 120 DA62
Rosecroft Cl, Orp. BR5 ... 206 EW100
Westerham (Bigg.H.)
TN16 *off Lotus Rd* ... 239 EM118
Rosecroft Dr, Wat. WD17 ... 75 BS36
Rosecroft Gdns, NW2 ... 119 CU62
Twickenham TW2 ... 177 CD88
Rosecroft Rd, Sthl. UB1 ... 136 CA70
Rosecroft Wk, Pnr. HA5 ... 116 BX57
Wembley HA0 ... 117 CK64
Rosedale, Ashtd. KT21 ... 231 CJ118
Caterham CR3 ... 236 DS123
Rose Dale, Orp. BR6 ... 205 EP103
Rosedale, Welw.G.C. AL7 ... 29 CZ05
Rosedale Av, Hayes UB3 ... 135 BR71
Waltham Cross (Chsht)
EN7 ... 66 DT29
Rosedale Cl, SE2
off Finchale Rd ... 166 EV76
W7 *off Boston Rd* ... 157 CF75
Dartford DA2 ... 188 FP87
St. Albans (Brick.Wd) AL2 . 60 BY30
Stanmore HA7 ... 95 CH51
Rosedale Ct, N5 ... 121 DP63
Rosedale Gdns, Dag. RM9 . 146 EV66
Rosedale Pl, Croy. CR0 ... 203 DX101
Rosedale Rd, E7 ... 124 EJ64
Dagenham RM9 ... 146 EV66
Epsom KT17 ... 217 CU106
Grays RM17 ... 170 GD78
Richmond TW9 ... 158 CL84
Romford RM1 ... 105 FC54
Rosedale Ter, W6
off Dalling Rd ... 159 CV76
Rosedale Way, Wal.Cr.
(Chsht) EN7 ... 66 DU29
Rosedene, NW6 ... 139 CX67
Rosedene Av, SW16 ... 181 DM90
Croydon CR0 ... 201 DM101
Greenford UB6 ... 136 CA69
Morden SM4 ... 200 DA99
Rosedene Ct, Dart. DA1
off Shepherds La ... 188 FJ87
Ruislip HA4 ... 115 BS60
Rosedene Gdns, Ilf. IG2 ... 125 EN56
Rosedene Ter, E10 ... 123 EB61
Rosedew Rd, W6 ... 159 CX79
Rose Dr, Chesh. HP5 ... 54 AS32
Rose End, Wor.Pk. KT4 ... 199 CX102
Rosefield, Sev. TN13 ... 256 FG124
Rosefield Cl, Cars. SM5 ... 218 DE106
Rosefield Gdns, E14 ... 13 N9
Chertsey (Ott.) KT16 ... 211 BD107
Rosefield Rd, Stai. TW18 ... 174 BG91
Roseford Ct, W12 ... 16 A4
Rose Gdn Cl, Edg. HA8 ... 96 CL51
Rose Gdns, W5 ... 157 CK76
Feltham TW13 ... 175 BU89
Southall UB1 ... 136 CA70
Staines (Stanw.) TW19
off Diamedes Av ... 174 BK87
Watford WD18 ... 75 BU43
Rose Glen, NW9 ... 118 CR56
Romford RM7 ... 127 FE60
Rosehart Ms, W11 ... 6 G8
Rosehatch Av, Rom. RM6 ... 126 EX55
Roseheath, Hem.H. HP1 ... 39 BE19
Roseheath Rd, Houns. TW4 . 176 BZ85
ROSE HILL, Dor. RH4 ... 263 CG136
ROSEHILL, Sutt. SM1 ... 200 DB102
Rose Hill, Dor. RH4 ... 263 CH136
Rosehill, Esher (Clay.) KT10 . 215 CG107
Hampton TW12 ... 196 CA95
Rose Hill, Slou. (Burn.) SL1 . 130 AG66
Sutton SM1 ... 200 DB104
Rosehill Av, Sutt. SM1 ... 200 DC102
Woking GU21 ... 226 AW116
Rosehill Cl, Hodd. EN11 ... 49 DZ17
Rosehill Ct, Hem.H. HP1
off Green End Rd ... 40 BG22
Slough SL1
off Yew Tree Rd ... 152 AU76
Rosehill Fm Meadow, Bans.
SM7 *off The Tracery* ... 234 DB115
Rosehill Gdns, Abb.L. WD5 . 59 BQ32
Greenford UB6 ... 117 CF64
Sutton SM1 ... 200 DB103
Rosehill Pk W, Sutt. SM1 ... 200 DC102
Rosehill Rd, SW18 ... 180 DC86
Westerham (Bigg.H.)
TN16 ... 238 EJ117
Roseland Cl, N17
off Cavell Rd ... 100 DR52
Roselands Av, Hodd. EN11 ... 49 DZ15
Roselands Prim Sch, Hodd.
EN11 *off High Wd Rd* ... 33 DZ14
Rose La, Rom. RM6 ... 126 EX55
Woking (Ripley) GU23 ... 228 BJ121
Rose Lawn, Bushey
(Bushey Hth) WD23 ... 94 CC46
Roseleigh Av, N5 ... 121 DP63
Roseleigh Cl, Twick. TW1 ... 177 CK86
Roseley Cotts, Harl. CM20 ... 35 EP11
Rosemary Av, N3 ... 98 DB54
N9 ... 100 DV46
Enfield EN2 ... 82 DR39
Hounslow TW4 ... 156 BX82
Romford RM1 ... 127 FF55
West Molesey KT8 ... 196 CA97
Rosemary Cl, Croy. CR0 ... 201 DL100
Harlow CM17 ... 36 EW11
Oxted RH8 ... 254 EG133
South Ockendon RM15 ... 149 FW69
Uxbridge UB8 ... 134 BN71
Rosemary Ct, Horl. RH6 ... 268 DE147
Rosemary Cres, Guil. GU2 . 242 AT130
Rosemary Dr, E14 ... 14 E8
Ilford IG4 ... 124 EK57
Rosemary Gdns, SW14
off Rosemary La ... 158 CQ83
Chessington KT9 ... 216 CL105
Dagenham RM8 ... 126 EZ60
Rosemary La, SW14 ... 158 CQ83
Egham TW20 ... 193 BB97
Horley RH6 ... 269 DH149
Rosemary Rd, SE15 ... 162 DT80
SW17 ... 180 DC90
Welling DA16 ... 165 ET81
Rosemary St, N1 ... 5 J7
Rosemead, NW9 ... 119 CT59
Chertsey KT16 ... 194 BH101
Potters Bar EN6 ... 64 DC30
Rosemead Av, Felt. TW13 ... 175 BT89
Mitcham CR4 ... 201 DJ96
Wembley HA9 ... 118 CL64
Rosemead Cl, Red. RH1 ... 266 DD136
Rosemead Gdns, Brwd.
(Hutt.) CM13 ... 109 GD42
Rosemead Prep Sch,
SE21 *off Thurlow Pk Rd* . 182 DQ89
Rosemont Av, N12 ... 98 DC51
Rosemont Rd, NW3 ... 140 DC65
W3 ... 138 CP73
New Malden KT3 ... 198 CQ97
Richmond TW10 ... 178 CL86
Wembley HA0 ... 138 CL67
Rosemoor Cl, Welw.G.C.
AL7 *off Salisbury Rd* ... 29 CZ10
Rosemoor St, SW3 ... 18 C8
Rosemount, Harl. CM19 ... 51 EP18
Rosemount Av, W.Byf. KT14 . 212 BG113
Rosemount Cl, Wdf.Grn.
IG8
off Chapelmount Rd ... 103 EM51
Rosemount Dr, Brom. BR1 . 205 EM98
Rosemount Pt, SE23
off Dacres Rd ... 183 DX90
Rosemount Rd, W13 ... 137 CG72
Rosenau Cres, SW11 ... 160 DE81
Rosenau Rd, SW11 ... 160 DE81
Rosendale Prim Sch,
SE21 *off Rosendale Rd* . 182 DQ87
Rosendale Rd, SE21 ... 182 DQ87
SE24 ... 182 DQ87
Roseneath Av, N21 ... 99 DP46
Roseneath Cl, Orp. BR6 ... 224 EW108
Roseneath Rd, SW11 ... 180 DG86
Roseneath Wk, Enf. EN1 ... 82 DS42
Rosens Wk, Edg. HA8 ... 96 CP48
Rosenthal Rd, SE6 ... 183 EB86
Rosenthorpe Rd, SE15 ... 183 DX85
Rose Pk Cl, Hayes UB4 ... 136 BW70
Rosepark Ct, Ilf. IG5 ... 103 EM54
Roserton St, E14 ... 24 C4
Rosery, The, Croy. CR0 ... 203 DX100
Roses, The, Wdf.Grn. IG8 ... 102 EF52
Roses La, Wind. SL4 ... 151 AL82
Rose Sq, SW3 ... 17 P9
Rose St, EC4 ... 10 F7
WC2 ... 9 N9
Gravesend (Nthflt) DA11 . 190 GB86
Rosethorn Cl, SW12 ... 181 DJ87
Rosetrees, Guil. GU1 ... 259 BA135
Rosetta Cl, SW8 ... 161 DL80
Rosetta Prim Sch, E16 ... 15 P6
Rosetti Ter, Dag. RM8
off Marlborough Rd ... 126 EV63
Rose Vale, Hodd. EN11 ... 49 EA17
Rose Valley, Brwd. CM14 ... 108 FW48
Roseveare Rd, SE12 ... 184 EJ91
Rose Vil, Dart. DA1 ... 188 FP87
Roseville Av, Houns. TW3 ... 176 CA85
Roseville Rd, Hayes UB3 ... 155 BU78
Rosevine Rd, SW20 ... 199 CW95
Rose Wk, Pur. CR8 ... 219 DK111
St. Albans AL4 ... 43 CJ18
Slough SL2 *off Birch Gro* . 131 AP71
Surbiton KT5 ... 198 CP99
West Wickham BR4 ... 203 ED103
Rose Wk, The, Rad. WD7 ... 77 CH37
Rosewarne Cl, Wok. GU21
off Muirfield Rd ... 226 AU118
Rose Way, SE12 ... 184 EG85
Roseway, SE21 ... 182 DR86
Rose Way, Edg. HA8 ... 96 CQ49
Rosewell Cl, SE20 ... 182 DV94
Rosewood, Dart. DA2 ... 187 FE91
Rosewood, Esher KT10 ... 197 CG103
Sutton SM2 ... 218 DC110
Woking GU22 ... 227 BA119
Rosewood Av, Grnf. UB6 ... 117 CG64
Hornchurch RM12 ... 127 FG64
Rosewood Cl, Sid. DA14 ... 186 EW90
Rosewood Ct, Brom. BR1 ... 204 EJ95
Hemel Hempstead HP1 ... 39 BE19
Romford RM6 ... 126 EW57
Rosewood Dr, Enf. EN2 ... 81 DN35
Shepperton TW17 ... 194 BM99
Rosewood Gdns, SE13
off Morden Hill ... 163 EC82
Wallington SM6 *(see note)*
Rosewood Gro, Sutt. SM1 . 200 DC103
Rosewood Sq, W12
off Primula St ... 139 CU72
Rosewood Ter, SE20
off Laurel Gro ... 182 DW94
Rosewood Way, Slou.
(Farn.Com.) SL2 ... 111 AQ64
Rosher Cl, E15 ... 143 ED66
ROSHERVILLE, Grav. DA11 . 191 GF85
**Rosherville C of E Prim
Sch**, Grav. DA11
off London Rd ... 190 GD86
Rosherville Way, Grav. DA11 . 190 GE87
Rosina St, E9 ... 123 DX64
Roskell Rd, SW15 ... 159 CX83
Rosken Gro, Slou.
(Farn.Royal) SL2 ... 131 AP68
Roslin Rd, W3 ... 158 CP76
Roslin Sq, W3 ... 158 CP76
Roslin Way, Brom. BR1 ... 184 EG92
Roslyn Cl, Brox. EN10 ... 49 DY21
Mitcham CR4 ... 200 DD96
Roslyn Ct, Wok. GU21
off St. John's Rd ... 226 AU118
Roslyn Gdns, Rom. RM2 ... 105 FF54
Roslyn Rd, N15 ... 122 DR57
Rosmead Rd, W11 ... 6 D9
Rosoman Pl, EC1 ... 10 D3
Rosoman St, EC1 ... 10 D2
Rossall Cl, Horn. RM11 ... 127 FG58
Rossall Cres, NW10 ... 138 CM69
Ross Av, NW7 ... 97 CY50
Dagenham RM8 ... 126 EZ61
Ross Cl, Har. HA3 ... 94 CC52
Hatfield AL10
off Homestead Rd ... 45 CU15
Hayes UB3 ... 155 BR77
Northolt UB5 ... 117 CD63
Ross Ct, SW15 ... 179 CX87
Ross Cres, Wat. WD25 ... 75 BU35
Rossdale, Sutt. SM1 ... 218 DE106
Rossdale Dr, N9 ... 82 DW44
NW9 ... 118 CQ60
Rossdale Rd, SW15 ... 159 CW84
Rosse Ms, SE3 ... 164 EH81
Rossendale St, E5 ... 122 DV61
Rossendale Way, NW1 ... 141 DJ66
Rossetti Gdns, Couls. CR5 . 235 DM118
Rossetti Rd, SE16 ... 22 C9
Rossgate, Hem.H. HP1
off Galley Hill ... 40 BG18
Rossgate Prim Sch,
Hem.H. HP1
off Galley Hill ... 40 BG18
Rossignol Gdns, Cars. SM5 . 200 DG103
Rossindel Rd, Houns. TW3 ... 176 CA85
Rossington Av, Borwd. WD6 . 78 CL38
Rossington Cl, Enf. EN1 ... 82 DV38
Rossington St, E5 ... 122 DU61
Rossiter Cl, Slou. SL3 ... 152 AY77
Rossiter Flds, Barn. EN5 ... 79 CY44
Rossiter Rd, SW12 ... 181 DH88
Rossland Cl, Bexh. DA6 ... 187 FB85
Rosslare Cl, West. TN16 ... 255 ER125
Rosslyn Av, E4 ... 102 EF47
SW13 ... 158 CS83
Barnet EN4 ... 80 DE44
Dagenham RM8 ... 126 EZ59
Feltham TW14 ... 175 BU86
Romford RM3 ... 106 FM54
Rosslyn Cl, Hayes UB3
off Morgans La ... 135 BR71
Sunbury-on-Thames
TW16 *off Cadbury Rd* ... 175 BS93
West Wickham BR4 ... 204 EF104
Rosslyn Cres, Har. HA1 ... 117 CF57
Wembley HA9 ... 118 CL63
Rosslyn Gdns, Wem. HA9
off Rosslyn Cres ... 118 CL62
Rosslyn Hill, NW3 ... 120 DD63
Rosslyn Ms, NW3
off Rosslyn Hill ... 120 DD63
Rosslyn Pk, Wey. KT13 ... 213 BR105
Rosslyn Pk Ms, NW3
off Lyndhurst Rd ... 120 DD64
Rosslyn Rd, E17 ... 123 EC56
Barking IG11 ... 145 ER66
Twickenham TW1 ... 177 CJ86
Watford WD18 ... 75 BV41
Rossmore Ct, NW1 ... 8 C3
Rossmore Rd, NW1 ... 8 B4
Ross Par, Wall. SM6 ... 219 DH107
Ross Rd, SE25 ... 202 DR97
Cobham KT11 ... 214 BW113
Dartford DA1 ... 187 FG86
Twickenham TW2 ... 176 CB88
Wallington SM6 ... 219 DJ106
Ross Way, SE9 ... 164 EL83
Northwood HA6 ... 93 BT49
Rossway Dr, Bushey WD23 ... 76 CC43
Rosswood Gdns, Wall. SM6 . 219 DJ107
Rostella Rd, SW17 ... 180 DD91
Rostrevor Av, N15 ... 122 DT58
Rostrevor Gdns, Hayes UB3 . 135 BS74
Iver SL0 ... 133 BD68
Southall UB2 ... 156 BY78
Rostrevor Ms, SW6 ... 159 CZ81
Rostrevor Rd, SW6 ... 159 CZ81
SW19 ... 180 DA92
Roswell Cl, Wal.Cr. (Chsht)
EN8 ... 67 DY30
Rotary St, SE1 ... 20 E5
Rothbury Av, Rain. RM13 ... 147 FH71
Rothbury Gdns, Islw. TW7 . 157 CG80
Rothbury Rd, E9 ... 143 DZ66
Rothbury Wk, N17 ... 100 DU52
Roth Dr, Brwd. (Hutt.) CM13 . 109 GB47
Rother Cl, Wat. WD25 ... 60 BW34
**Rotherfield Jun & Inf
Sch**, N1 ... 5 H7
Rotherfield Rd, Cars. SM5 . 218 DG105
Enfield EN3 ... 83 DX37
Rotherfield St, N1 ... 5 H6
Rotherham Wk, SE1 ... 20 E2
Rotherhill Av, SW16 ... 181 DK93
ROTHERHITHE, SE16 ... 22 G5

A B C D E F G H I J K L M N O P Q R S T U V W X Y Z

⊖ Rotherhithe 22 F3
★ Rotherhithe Heritage Mus, SE16 23 K1
Rotherhithe New Rd, SE16 22 B10
Rotherhithe Old Rd, SE16 22 G6
Sch Rotherhithe Prim Sch, SE16 22 G7
Rotherhithe St, SE16 22 F3
Rotherhithe Tunnel, E1 22 G1
Rotherhithe Tunnel App, E14 13 J9
SE16 22 E4
Rothermere Rd, Croy. CR0 219 DM106
Rothervale, Horl. RH6 268 DF145
Rotherwick Hill, W5 138 CM70
Rotherwick Rd, NW11 120 DA59
Rotherwood Cl, SW20 199 CY95
Rotherwood Rd, SW15 159 CX83
Rothery St, N1 4 E7
Rothery Ter, SW9 161 DP80
Rothesay Av, SW20 199 CY96
Greenford UB6 137 CD65
Richmond TW10 158 CP84
Rothesay Rd, SE25 202 DS98
Rothes Rd, Dor. RH4 263 CH135
Rothsay Rd, E7 144 EJ65
Rothsay St, SE1 21 L5
Rothsay Wk, E14 23 P7
Rothschild Rd, W4 158 CQ77
Rothschild St, SE27 181 DP91
Roth Wk, N7 off Durham Rd 121 DM62
Rothwell Gdns, Dag. RM9 146 EW66
Rothwell Rd, Dag. RM9 146 EW67
Rothwell St, NW1 140 DF67
Rotten Row, SW1 18 E3
SW7 18 A3
Rotterdam Dr, E14 24 D6
Rouel Rd, SE16 22 A6
Rouge La, Grav. DA12 191 GH88
Rougemont Av, Mord. SM4 200 DA100
Roughdown Av, Hem.H. HP3 40 BG23
Roughdown Rd, Hem.H. HP3 40 BH23
Roughdown Vil Rd, Hem.H. HP3 40 BG23
Roughetts La, Gdse. RH9 252 DS129
Redhill RH1 252 DS129
Roughlands, Wok. GU22 227 BE115
Rough Rew, Dor. RH4 263 CH139
Roughs, The, Nthwd. HA6 93 BT48
Roughtallys, Epp. (N.Wld Bas.) CM16 70 EZ27
Roughwood Cl, Wat. WD17 75 BS38
Roughwood La, Ch.St.G. HP8 90 AY45
Roundacre, SW19 off Inner Pk Rd 179 CX89
Roundaway Rd, Ilf. IG5 103 EM54
ROUND BUSH, Wat. WD25 76 CC38
Roundcroft, Wal.Cr. (Chsht) EN7 66 DT26
Roundel Cl, SE4 off Adelaide Av 163 DZ84
Round Gro, Croy. CR0 203 DX101
Roundhay Cl, SE23 183 DX89
Roundheads End, Beac. (Forty Grn) HP9 88 AH51
Roundhedge Way, Enf. EN2 81 DM38
Round Hill, SE26 182 DW89
Roundhill, Wok. GU22 227 BB119
Roundhill Dr, Enf. EN2 81 DM42
Woking GU22 227 BB118
Roundhills, Wal.Abb. EN9 68 EE34
Roundhill Way, Cob. KT11 214 CB111
Guildford GU2 242 AT134
Roundings, The, Hert. (Hert.Hth) SG13 32 DV14
Roundlyn Gdns, Orp. (St.M.Cray) BR5 off Lynmouth Ri 206 EV98
Roundmead Av, Loug. IG10 85 EN41
Roundmead Cl, Loug. IG10 85 EN41
Roundmoor Dr, Wal.Cr. (Chsht) EN8 67 DX29
Round Oak Rd, Wey. KT13 212 BM105
Roundshaw Cen, Wall. SM6 off Meteor Way 219 DL108
Roundtable Rd, Brom. BR1 184 EF90
Roundthorn Way, Wok. GU21 226 AT116
Roundtree Rd, Wem. HA0 117 CH64
Roundway, Egh. TW20 173 BC92
Westerham (Bigg.H.) TN16 off Norheads La 238 EK116
Roundway, The, N17 100 DQ53
Esher (Clay.) KT10 215 CF106
Watford WD18 75 BT44
Roundways, Ruis. HA4 115 BT62
Roundwood, Chis. BR7 205 EP96
Kings Langley WD4 58 BL26
Roundwood Av, Brwd. (Hutt.) CM13 109 GA46
Uxbridge UB11 135 BQ74
Roundwood Cl, Ruis. HA4 115 BR59
Roundwood Dr, Welw.G.C. AL8 29 CW07
Roundwood Gro, Brwd. (Hutt.) CM13 109 GB45
Roundwood Lake, Brwd. (Hutt.) CM13 109 GB46
Roundwood Rd, NW10 139 CT65
Amersham HP6 55 AS38
Roundwood Vw, Bans. SM7 233 CX115
Roundwood Way, Bans. SM7 233 CX115
Rounton Rd, E3 13 P3
Waltham Abbey EN9 68 EE33
Roupell Rd, SW2 181 DM88
Roupell St, SE1 20 D2
Rousden St, NW1 141 DJ66
Rousebarn La, Rick. WD3 75 BQ41
Rouse Gdns, SE21 182 DS91
Rous Rd, Buck.H. IG9 102 EL46
Routemaster Cl, E13 15 N1
Routh Ct, Felt. TW14 off Loxwood Cl 175 BS88
Routh Rd, SW18 180 DE87
Routh St, E6 145 EM71
Routledge Cl, N19 121 DK60
Rover Av, Ilf. IG6 103 ET51
Rowallan Rd, SW6 159 CY80
Rowan Av, E4 101 DZ51
Egham TW20 173 BC92
Rowan Cl, SW16 201 DJ95
W5 158 CL75
Beaconsfield HP9 88 AH54
Guildford GU1 242 AV131
Ilford IG1 125 ER64
New Malden KT3 198 CS96
Radlett (Shenley) WD7 off Juniper Gdns 62 CL33
Rowan Cl, Reig. RH2 266 DC136
St. Albans AL4 44 CL20
St. Albans (Brick.Wd) AL2 60 CA31
Stanmore HA7 off Woodlands Dr 95 CF51
Wembley HA0 117 CG62
Rowan Ct, Borwd. WD6 off Theobald St 78 CL39
Rowan Cres, SW16 201 DJ95
Dartford DA1 188 FJ88
Rowan Dr, NW9 119 CU56
Broxbourne EN10 67 DZ25
Rowan Gdns, Croy. CR0 off Radcliffe Rd 202 DT104
Iver SL0 133 BC68
Rowan Grn, Wey. KT13 213 BR105
Rowan Grn E, Brwd. CM13 109 FZ48
Rowan Grn W, Brwd. CM13 109 FZ49
Rowan Gro, Couls. CR5 235 DH121
South Ockendon (Aveley) RM15 148 FQ73
Rowanhurst Dr, Slou. (Farn.Com.) SL2 111 AQ64
Rowan Pl, Amer. HP6 72 AT38
Hayes UB3 off West Av 135 BT73
Sch Rowan Prep Sch, Esher KT10 off Fitzalan Rd 215 CF108
Esher KT10 off Gordon Rd 215 CE108
Rowan Rd, SW16 201 DJ96
W6 16 A8
Bexleyheath DA7 166 EY83
Brentford TW8 157 CH80
Swanley BR8 207 FD97
West Drayton UB7 154 BK77
Rowans, Welw.G.C. AL7 30 DA06
Rowans, The, N13 99 DP48
Gerrards Cross (Chal.St.P.) SL9 112 AX55
Hemel Hempstead HP1 40 BG20
South Ockendon (Aveley) RM15 off Purfleet Rd 148 FQ74
Sunbury-on-Thames TW16 175 BT92
Woking GU22 226 AY118
Rowans Cl, Long. DA3 209 FX96
Sch Rowans Prim Sch, Welw.G.C. AL7 off Rowans 30 DA06
Sch Rowans Sch, The, SW20 off Drax Av 179 CU94
Rowans Way, Loug. IG10 85 EM42
Rowan Ter, SE20 off Sycamore Gro 202 DU95
W6 16 A8
Rowantree Cl, N21 100 DR46
Rowantree Rd, N21 100 DR46
Enfield EN2 81 DP40
Rowan Wk, N2 120 DC58
N19 off Bredgar Rd 121 DJ61
W10 6 C3
Barnet EN5 off Station Rd 80 DB43
Bromley BR2 205 EM104
Hatfield AL10 45 CU21
Hornchurch RM11 128 FK56
Rowan Way, Rom. RM6 126 EW55
Slough SL2 131 AP71
South Ockendon RM15 149 FX70
Rowanwood Av, Sid. DA15 186 EU88
Rowanwood Ms, Enf. EN2 81 DP40
Rowbarns Way, Lthd. (E.Hors.) KT24 245 BT130
Rowben Cl, N20 98 DB46
Rowberry Cl, SW6 159 CW80
Rowbury, Gdmg. GU7 258 AU143
Rowcroft, Hem.H. HP1 39 BE21
Rowcross St, SE1 21 N9
Rowdell Rd, Nthlt. UB5 136 CA67
Rowden Pk Gdns, E4 off Rowden Rd 101 EA51
Rowden Rd, E4 101 EA51
Beckenham BR3 203 DY95
Epsom KT19 216 CP105
Rowditch La, SW11 160 DG82
Rowdon Av, NW10 139 CV66
Rowdown Cres, Croy. (New Adgtn) CR0 221 ED109
Sch Rowdown Inf Sch, Croy. CR0 off Calley Down Cres 221 ED110
Sch Rowdown Jun Sch, Croy. CR0 off Calley Down Cres 221 ED110
Rowdowns Rd, Dag. RM9 146 EZ67
Rowe Gdns, Bark. IG11 145 ET68
Rowe La, E9 122 DW64
Rowena Cres, SW11 160 DE82
Rowe Wk, Har. HA2 116 CA62
Rowfant Rd, SW17 180 DG88
Rowhedge, Brwd. CM13 109 GA48
Row Hill, Add. KT15 211 BF107
Rowhill Rd, E5 122 DV63
Dartford DA2 187 FF93
Swanley BR8 187 FF93
Sch Rowhill Sch, Dart. DA2 off Stock La 188 FJ91
Rowhurst Av, Add. KT15 212 BH107
Leatherhead KT22 231 CF117
Rowington Cl, W2 7 J5
Rowland Av, Har. HA3 117 CJ56
Rowland Cl, Wind. SL4 151 AK83
Rowland Ct, E16 15 J3
Rowland Cres, Chig. IG7 103 ES49
Rowland Gro, SE26 off Dallas Rd 182 DV90
Rowland Hill Av, N17 100 DQ52
Rowland Hill St, NW3 120 DE64
Rowlands Av, Pnr. HA5 94 CA51
Rowlands Cl, N6 off North Hill 120 DG58
NW7 97 CU52
Waltham Cross (Chsht) EN8 67 DX30
Rowlands Flds, Wal.Cr. (Chsht) EN8 67 DX29
Rowlands Rd, Dag. RM8 126 EZ61
Rowland Wk, Rom. (Hav.at.Bow.) RM4 105 FE48
Rowland Way, SW19 off Hayward Cl 200 DB95
Ashford TW15 off Littleton Rd 175 BQ94
Rowlatt Cl, Dart. DA2 188 FJ91
Rowlatt Ct, St.Alb. AL1 off Hillside Rd 43 CE19
Rowlatt Dr, St.Alb. AL3 42 CA22
Rowlatt Rd, Dart. DA2 off Whitehead Cl 188 FJ91
Rowley Av, Sid. DA15 186 EV87
Rowley Cl, Wat. WD19 off Lower Paddock Rd 76 BY44
Wembley HA0 138 CM66
Woking (Pyrford) GU22 228 BG116
Rowley Ct, Cat. CR3 236 DQ122
Rowley Gdns, N4 122 DQ59
Waltham Cross (Chsht) EN8 off Warwick Dr 67 DX28
ROWLEY GREEN, Barn. EN5 79 CT42
Rowley Grn Rd, Barn. EN5 79 CT43
Rowley Ind Pk, W3 158 CP76
Rowley La, Barn. EN5 79 CT43
Borehamwood WD6 78 CR39
Slough (Wexham) SL3 132 AW67
Rowley Mead, Epp. (Thnwd) CM16 70 EW25
Rowley Rd, N15 122 DQ57
Rowleys Rd, Hert. SG13 32 DT08
Rowley Wk, Hem.H. HP2 41 BQ15
Rowley Way, NW8 140 DB67
Rowlheys Pl, West Dr. UB7 154 BL76
Rowlls Rd, Kings.T. KT1 198 CM97
Rowmarsh Cl, Grav. (Nthflt) DA11 190 GD91
Rowney Gdns, Dag. RM9 146 EW65
Sawbridgeworth CM21 36 EW07
Rowney Rd, Dag. RM9 146 EV65
Rowney Wd, Saw. CM21 36 EW06
Rowntree Clifford Cl, E13 15 N3
Rowntree Path, SE28 off Booth Cl 146 EV73
Rowntree Rd, Twick. TW2 177 CE88
Rows, The, Harl. CM20 off East Gate 35 ER14
Rowse Cl, E15 143 EC66
Rowsley Av, NW4 119 CW55
Rowstock Gdns, N7 121 DK64
Rowton Rd, SE18 165 EQ80
ROWTOWN, Add. KT15 211 BF108
Rowtown, Add. KT15 211 BF108
Rowzill Rd, Swan. BR8 187 FF93
Roxborough Av, Har. HA1 117 CD59
Isleworth TW7 157 CF80
Roxborough Pk, Har. HA1 117 CE59
Roxborough Rd, Har. HA1 117 CD57
Roxbourne Cl, Nthlt. UB5 136 BX65
Sch Roxbourne First Sch, Har. HA2 off Torbay Rd 116 BY61
Sch Roxbourne Mid Sch, Har. HA2 off Torbay Rd 116 BY61
Roxburgh Av, Upmin. RM14 128 FQ62
Roxburgh Rd, SE27 181 DP92
Roxburn Way, Ruis. HA4 115 BT62
Roxby Pl, SW6 160 DA79
ROXETH, Har. HA2 117 CD61
Roxeth Ct, Ashf. TW15 174 BN92
Sch Roxeth First & Mid Sch, Har. HA2 off Brickfields 117 CD61
Roxeth Grn Av, Har. HA2 116 CB62
Roxeth Gro, Har. HA2 116 CB63
Roxeth Hill, Har. HA2 117 CD61
Sch Roxeth Manor First Sch, Har. HA2 off Eastcote La 116 CA62
Sch Roxeth Manor Mid Sch, Har. HA2 off Eastcote La 116 CA62
Roxford Cl, Shep. TW17 195 BS99
Roxley Rd, SE13 183 EB86
Roxton Gdns, Croy. CR0 221 EA106
Roxwell Cl, Slou. SL1 131 AL74
Roxwell Gdns, Brwd. (Hutt.) CM13 109 GC43
Roxwell Rd, W12 159 CU75
Barking IG11 146 EU68
Roxwell Trd Pk, E10 123 DY59
Roxwell Way, Wdf.Grn. IG8 102 EJ52
Roxy Av, Rom. RM6 126 EW59
★ Royal Acad of Arts, W1 9 J10
Coll Royal Acad of Dance, SW11 off Battersea Sq 160 DD81
★ Royal Acad of Dramatic Art (R.A.D.A.), WC1 9 L5
Uni Royal Acad of Music, NW1 8 F4
H Royal Air Force, Headley Ct, Epsom KT18 232 CP123
★ Royal Air Force Museums, NW9 97 CU54
DLR Royal Albert 144 EL73
Royal Albert Dock, E16 145 EM73
★ Royal Albert Hall, SW7 17 N4
Royal Albert Roundabout, E16 off Royal Albert Way 144 EL73
Royal Albert Way, E16 144 EK73
Sch Royal Alexandra & Albert Jun Sch, Reig. RH2 off Rocky La 250 DE129
Sch Royal Alexandra & Albert Sec Sch, Reig. RH2 off Rocky La 250 DE129
Royal Arc, W1 9 J10
Royal Artillery Barracks, SE18 off Repository Rd 165 EN78
Royal Av, SW3 18 C9
Waltham Cross EN8 67 DY33
Worcester Park KT4 198 CS103
Sch Royal Ballet Sch, The, Lwr Sch, Rich. TW10 off Richmond Pk 178 CR88
Upper Sch, WC2 9 P8
★ Royal Botanic Gdns, Kew, Rich. TW9 158 CL80
H Royal Brompton Hosp, SW3 18 A9
H Royal Brompton Hosp Annexe, SW3 17 P9
Royal Circ, SE27 181 DN90
Royal Cl, N16 off Manor Rd 122 DS60
SE8 163 DZ79
SW19 179 CX89
Ilford IG3 126 EU59
Orpington BR6 223 EP105
Uxbridge UB8 134 BM72
Worcester Park KT4 198 CS103
Coll Royal Coll of Anaesthetists, The, WC1 9 N5
Uni Royal Coll of Art, SW7 17 M4
Coll Royal Coll of Defence Studies, SW1 18 F5
Coll Royal Coll of Music, SW7 17 N5
Coll Royal Coll of Nursing, W1 8 G7
Coll Royal Coll of Obstetricians & Gynaecologists, NW1 8 C3
Coll Royal Coll of Physicians, NW1 9 H3
Coll Royal Coll of Surgeons of England, WC2 10 B7
Royal Coll St, NW1 141 DJ66
Royal Ct, EC3 off Cornhill 142 DR72
SE16 23 L5
Hemel Hempstead HP3 40 BL23
★ Royal Courts of Justice, WC2 10 B8
Royal Cres, W11 16 B2
Ruislip HA4 116 BY63
Royal Cres Ms, W11 16 B2
Sch Royal Docks Comm Sch, The, E16 off Prince Regent La 144 EJ72
Royal Docks Rd, E6 145 EP72
Royal Dr, N11 98 DG50
Epsom KT18 233 CV118
Royal Duchess Ms, SW12 off Dinsmore Rd 181 DH87
Royal Earlswood Pk, Red. RH1 266 DG138
Royale Leisure Pk, W3 138 CN70
★ Royal Exchange, EC3 11 K8
Royal Ex Av, EC3 11 K8
Royal Ex Bldgs, EC3 11 K8
Royal Ex Steps, EC3 off Cornhill 142 DR72
★ Royal Festival Hall, SE1 20 A1
Uni Royal Free & Uni Coll Med Sch, Royal Free Campus, NW3 off Rowland Hill St 120 DE64
H Royal Free Hosp, The, NW3 120 DE64
Royal Gdns, W7 157 CG76
★ Royal Geographical Society, SW7 17 N4
Sch Royal Gram Sch, Guil. GU1 off High St 258 AY135
Royal Herbert Pavilions, SE18 165 EM81
Royal Hill, SE10 163 EC80
Uni Royal Holloway Coll, Egh. TW20 off Egham Hill 172 AX93
Inst for Environmental Research, Vir.W. GU25 off Callow Hill 192 AW96
Kingswood, Egh. TW20 off Coopers Hill La 172 AX91
Royal Horticultural Society Cotts, Wok. (Wisley) GU23 off Wisley La 228 BL116
★ Royal Horticultural Society Gdns, Wisley, Wok. GU22 228 BL118
★ Royal Horticultural Society (Lawrence Hall), SW1 19 L6
★ Royal Horticultural Society (Lindley Hall), SW1 19 L7
★ Royal Hosp Chelsea & Mus, SW3 18 E10
H Royal Hosp for Neuro-disability, SW15 179 CY86
H Royal Hosp (Richmond), Rich. TW9 158 CL83
Royal Hosp Rd, SW3 160 DF79
Sch Royal Kent C of E Prim Sch, The, Lthd. KT22 off Oakshade Rd 214 CC114
Royal La, Uxb. UB8 134 BM69
West Drayton UB7 134 BM72
Sch Royal Liberty Sch, The, Rom. RM2 off Upper Brentwood Rd 128 FJ55
Royal London Est, The, N17 100 DV51
H Royal London Homoeopathic Hosp, WC1 9 P5
H Royal London Hosp, The, Mile End, E1 13 H3
St. Clements, E3 13 M2
Whitechapel, E1 12 C6
H Royal Marsden Hosp, The, Sutt. SM2 218 DC110
H Royal Marsden Hosp (Fulham), The, SW3 17 P9
Sch Royal Masonic Sch, The, Rick. WD3 off Chorleywood Rd 74 BK44
★ Royal Mews, The, SW1 19 H5
Coll Royal Military Acad, SE18 off Red Lion La 165 EN80
Coll Royal Military Sch of Music, Twick. TW2 off Kneller Rd 177 CD86
Royal Mint Ct, EC3 11 P10
Royal Mint Pl, E1 11 P9
Royal Mint St, E1 11 P9
Royal Mt Ct, Twick. TW2 177 CE90
H Royal Nat Ear, Nose & Throat Hosp, WC1 10 A1
Sch Royal Nat Inst for the Blind Sunshine Ho Sch, Nthwd. HA6 off Dene Rd 93 BS51
H Royal Nat Orthopaedic Hosp, W1 9 H4
Stanmore HA7 95 CJ47
★ Royal Nat Thea, SE1 20 B1
Royal Naval Pl, SE14 163 DZ80
⊖ Royal Oak 7 K6
Royal Oak Ct, N1 off Pitfield St 142 DS69
Royal Oak Pl, SE22 182 DV86
Royal Oak Rd, E8 142 DV65
Bexleyheath DA6 186 EZ85
Woking GU21 226 AW118
Royal Oak Yd, SE1 21 M4
Royal Opera Arc, SW1 19 L1
★ Royal Opera Ho, WC2 9 P8
Royal Orchard Cl, SW18 179 CY87
Royal Par, SE3 164 EE82
SW6 off Dawes Rd 159 CY80
W5 off Western Av 138 CL69
Chislehurst BR7 185 EQ94
Richmond TW9 off Station App 158 CN81
Royal Par Ms, SE3 off Royal Par 164 EF82
Chislehurst BR7 185 EQ94
Sch Royal Pk Prim Sch, Sid. DA14 off Riverside Rd 186 EY90
Royal Pier Ms, Grav. DA12 off Royal Pier Rd 191 GH86
Royal Pier Rd, Grav. DA12 191 GH86
Royal Pl, SE10 163 EC80
Royal Quarter, Kings.T. KT2 off Seven Kings Way 198 CL95
Royal Rd, E16 144 EK72
SE17 161 DP79
Dartford (Darenth) DA2 188 FN92
St. Albans AL1 43 CH20
Sidcup DA14 186 EX90
Teddington TW11 177 CD92
Royal Route, Wem. HA9 118 CM63
Sch Royal Russell Jun Sch, Croy. CR0 off Coombe La 220 DV106
Sch Royal Russell Sen Sch, Croy. CR0 off Coombe La 220 DV107
Sch Royal Sch Hampstead, The, NW3 off Rosslyn Hill 120 DD63
Coll Royal Sch of Church Music, The, Dor. RH5 off Westhumble St 247 CH131
Coll Royal Sch of Needlework, E.Mol. KT8 off Hampton Ct Palace 197 CF98
Royal St, SE1 20 B5
H Royal Surrey Co Hosp, Guil. GU2 242 AS134
Royalty Ms, W1 9 L8
Uni Royal Vet Coll - Camden Campus, Beaumont Animals' Hosp, NW1 off Royal Coll St 141 DJ67
Royal College St, NW1 off Royal Coll St 141 DK67
Uni Royal Vet Coll - Hawkshead Campus, Hat. AL9 off Hawkshead La 63 CX28
Boltons Pk, Pot.B. EN6 off Hawkshead Rd 64 DA29
DLR Royal Victoria 15 L9
Royal Victoria Dock, E16 15 N10
Royal Victoria Pl, E16 25 P1
Royal Victoria Sq, E16 15 N10
Royal Victor Pl, E3 143 DX68
Royal Wk, Wall. SM6 off Prince Charles Way 201 DH104
Royce Cl, Brox. EN10 49 DZ21
Royce Gro, Wat. (Lvsdn) WD25 59 BT34
Roycraft Av, Bark. IG11 145 ET68
Roycraft Cl, Bark. IG11 145 ET68
Roycroft Cl, E18 102 EH53
SW2 181 DN88
Roydene Rd, SE18 165 ES79
ROYDON, Harl. CM19 50 EH15
⇌ Roydon 34 EG13
Roydonbury Ind Est, Harl. CM19 50 EL15
Roydon Cl, SW11 off Reform St 160 DF82
Loughton IG10 102 EL45
Sch Roydon Co Prim Sch, Harl. CM19 off Epping Rd 50 EH15
Roydon Ct, Walt. KT12 213 BU105
ROYDON HAMLET, Harl. CM19 50 EJ19
Roydon Lo Chalet Est, Harl. (Roydon) CM19 34 EJ14
Roydon Mill Pk, Harl. (Roydon) CM19 34 EG14
Roydon Rd, Harl. CM19 34 EL14
Ware (Stans.Abb.) SG12 34 EE11
Roydon St, SW11 off Southolm St 161 DH81
Roy Gdns, Ilf. IG2 125 ES56
Roy Gro, Hmptn. TW12 176 CB93
Royle Cl, Ger.Cr. (Chal.St.P.) SL9 91 AZ52
Romford RM2 127 FH57
Royle Cres, W13 137 CG70
Roy Rd, Nthwd. HA6 93 BT52
Roy Sq, E14 13 K9
Royston Av, E4 101 EA50
Sutton SM1 200 DD104
Wallington SM6 219 DK105
West Byfleet (Byfleet) KT14 212 BL112
Royston Cl, Hert. SG14 31 DP09
Hounslow TW5 155 BV81
Walton-on-Thames KT12 195 BU102
Royston Ct, SE24 off Burbage Rd 182 DQ86
Richmond TW9 off Lichfield Rd 158 CM81
Surbiton KT6 off Hook Ri N 198 CN104
Royston Gdns, Ilf. IG1 124 EK58
Royston Gro, Pnr. HA5 94 BZ51
Royston Par, Ilf. IG1 124 EK58
Royston Pk Rd, Pnr. HA5 94 BZ51
Sch Royston Prim Sch, SE20 off High St 203 DX95
Royston Rd, SE20 203 DX95
Dartford DA1 187 FF86
Richmond TW10 178 CL85
Romford RM3 106 FN52
St. Albans AL1 43 CH21
West Byfleet (Byfleet) KT14 212 BL112
Roystons, The, Surb. KT5 198 CP99
Royston St, E2 142 DW68
Royston Way, Slou. SL1 130 AJ71
Rozel Ct, N1 5 L7
Rozel Rd, SW4 161 DJ82
Rubastic Rd, Sthl. UB2 155 BV76
Rubens Pl, SW4 off Dolman St 161 DM84
Rubens Rd, Nthlt. UB5 136 BW68
Rubens St, SE6 183 DZ89
Rubin Pl, Enf. EN3 83 EA37
Ruby Cl, Slou. SL1 151 AN75
Ruby Ms, E17 off Ruby Rd 123 EA55
Ruby Rd, E17 123 EA55
Ruby St, NW10 off Diamond St 138 CR66
SE15 162 DV79
Ruby Triangle, SE15 off Sandgate St 162 DV79
Ruckholt Cl, E10 123 EB62
Ruckholt Rd, E10 123 EA63
Rucklers La, Kings L. WD4 58 BK27
Ruckles Way, Amer. HP7 55 AQ40
Rucklidge Av, NW10 139 CT68
Rudall Cres, NW3 off Willoughby Rd 120 DD63
Ruddington Cl, E5 123 DY63
Ruddlesway, Wind. SL4 151 AK81
Ruddock Cl, Edg. HA8 96 CQ52
Ruddstreet Cl, SE18 165 EP77
Ruden Way, Epsom KT17 233 CV116
Rudge Ri, Add. KT15 211 BF106
Rudgwick Ter, NW8 off Avenue Rd 140 DE67
Rudland Rd, Bexh. DA7 167 FB83
Rudloe Rd, SW12 181 DJ87
Rudolf Pl, SW8 off Miles St 161 DL79
Sch Rudolf Steiner Sch, Kings L. WD4 off Langley Hill 58 BM29
Rudolph Ct, SE22 182 DU87
Rudolph Rd, E13 144 EF68
NW6 140 DA68
Bushey WD23 76 CA44
Rudsworth Cl, Slou. (Colnbr.) SL3 153 BD80
Rudyard Gro, NW7 96 CQ51
Rue de St. Lawrence, Wal.Abb. EN9 off Quaker La 67 EC34
Ruffets Wd, Grav. DA12 191 GJ93
Ruffetts, The, S.Croy. CR2 220 DV108
Ruffetts Cl, S.Croy. CR2 220 DV108
Ruffetts Way, Tad. KT20 233 CY118
Ruffle Cl, West Dr. UB7 154 BL75
Rufford Cl, Har. HA3 117 CG58
Watford WD17 75 BT37
Rufford St, N1 141 DL67
Rufford Twr, W3 138 CP74
Rufus Cl, Ruis. HA4 116 BY62
Rufus St, N1 11 L2
Rugby Av, N9 100 DT46
Greenford UB6 137 CD65
Wembley HA0 117 CH64
Rugby Cl, Har. HA1 117 CE57

★ Place of interest H Hospital Sch School Coll College Uni University ⇌ Railway station

★ Rugby Football Union Twickenham, Twick. TW2 177 CE86
Rugby Gdns, Dag. RM9 146 EW65
Rugby La, Sutt. SM2 off Nonsuch Wk 217 CX109
Rugby Rd, NW9 118 CP56
W4 158 CS75
Dagenham RM9 146 EV66
Twickenham TW1 177 CE86
Rugby St, WC1 10 A4
Rugby Way, Rick. (Crox.Grn) WD3 75 BP43
Rugged La, Wal.Abb. EN9 68 EK33
Ruggles-Brise Rd, Ashf. TW15 174 BK92
Rugg St, E14 13 N9
RUISLIP, HA4 115 BS59
⊖ Ruislip 115 BS60
Ruislip Cl, Grnf. UB6 136 CB70
RUISLIP COMMON, Ruis. HA4 115 BR57
Ruislip Ct, Ruis. HA4 off Courtfield Gdns 115 BT61
RUISLIP GARDENS, Ruis. HA4 115 BS63
⊖ Ruislip Gardens 115 BU63
Sch Ruislip Gdns Prim Sch, Ruis. HA4 off Stafford Rd 115 BT63
RUISLIP MANOR, Ruis. HA4 115 BU61
⊖ Ruislip Manor 115 BU60
Ruislip Rd, Grnf. UB6 136 CA69
Northolt UB5 136 BX68
Southall UB1 136 CA69
Ruislip Rd E, W7 137 CD70
W13 137 CD70
Greenford UB6 137 CD70
Ruislip St, SW17 180 DF91
Rumania Wk, Grav. DA12 191 GM90
Rumballs Cl, Hem.H. HP3 40 BN23
Rumballs Rd, Hem.H. HP3 40 BN23
Rumbold Rd, SW6 160 DB80
Hoddesdon EN11 49 EC15
Rum Cl, E1 12 E10
Rumsey Cl, Hmptn. TW12 176 BZ93
Rumsey Ms, N4 off Monsell Rd 121 DP62
Rumsey Rd, SW9 161 DM83
Rumsley, Wal.Cr. EN7 66 DU27
Runbury Circle, NW9 118 CR61
Runcie Cl, St.Alb. AL4 43 CG16
Runciman Cl, Orp. BR6 224 EW110
Runcorn Cl, N17 122 DV56
Runcorn Cres, Hem.H. HP2 40 BM16
Runcorn Pl, W11 6 C9
Rundell Cres, NW4 119 CV57
Rundells, Harl. CM18 52 EU19
Runes Cl, Mitch. CR4 200 DD98
Runham Rd, Hem.H. HP3 40 BL22
Runnel Fld, Har. HA1 117 CE62
Runnemede Rd, Egh. TW20 173 BA91
Running Horse Yd, Brent. TW8 off Pottery Rd 158 CL79
Running Waters, Brwd. CM13 109 GA49
Runnymede, SW19 200 DD95
Runnymede Cl, Twick. TW2 176 CB86
Runnymede Ct, Croy. CR0 202 DT103
Egham TW20 173 BA91
Runnymede Cres, SW16 201 DK95
Runnymede Gdns, Grnf. UB6 137 CD68
Twickenham TW2 176 CB86
H Runnymede Hosp, Cher. KT16 193 BD104
Runnymede Ho, E9 off Kingsmead Way 123 DY63
Runnymede Rd, Twick. TW2 176 CB86
Coll Runnymede Staff Dev Cen, Add. KT15 off Chertsey Rd 194 BH103
Runrig Hill, Amer. HP6 55 AS35
Runsley, Welw.G.C. AL7 29 CZ06
Runtley Wd La, Guil. (Sutt.Grn) GU4 243 AZ125
Runway, The, Hat. AL10 off Mosquito Way 44 CS17
Ruislip HA4 115 BV64
Rupack St, SE16 22 E4
Rupert Av, Wem. HA9 118 CL64
Rupert Ct, W1 9 L9
West Molesey KT8 off St. Peter's Rd 196 CA98
Rupert Gdns, SW9 161 DP82
Rupert Rd, N19 off Holloway Rd 121 DK62
NW6 139 CZ68
W4 158 CS76
Guildford GU2 258 AV135
Rupert St, W1 9 L9
Rural Cl, Horn. RM11 127 FH60
Rural Vale, Grav. (Nthflt) DA11 190 GE87
Rural Way, SW16 181 DH94
Redhill RH1 250 DG134
Rusbridge Cl, E8 off Amhurst Rd 122 DU64
Ruscoe Dr, Wok. GU22 off Pembroke Rd 227 BA117
Ruscoe Rd, E16 15 J7
Ruscombe Dr, St.Alb. (Park St) AL2 60 CB26
Ruscombe Gdns, Slou. (Datchet) SL3 152 AU80
Ruscombe Way, Felt. TW14 175 BT87
Rush, The, SW19 off Kingston Rd 199 CZ95
Rusham Pk Av, Egh. TW20 173 AZ93
Rusham Rd, SW12 180 DF86
Egham TW20 173 AZ93
Rushbrook Cres, E17 101 DZ53
Rushbrook Rd, SE9 185 EQ89
Rushburn, H.Wyc. (Woob.Grn) HP10 110 AF57
Rush Cl, Ware (Stans.Abb.) SG12 33 EC11
Rush Common Ms, SW2 181 DM87
Rush Cft, Gdmg. GU7 258 AU143
Rushcroft Rd, E4 101 EA52
SW2 161 DN84
Sch Rush Cft Sec Sch, E4 off Rushcroft Rd 101 EB52
Rushden Cl, SE19 182 DR94
Rushdene, SE2 166 EX76
Rushdene Av, Barn. EN4 98 DE45
Rushdene Cl, Nthlt. UB5 136 BW69
Rushdene Cres, Nthlt. UB5 136 BW68
Rushdene Rd, Brwd. CM15 108 FW45
Pinner HA5 116 BX58
Rushdene Wk, West. (Bigg.H.) TN16 238 EK117
Rushden Gdns, NW7 97 CW51
Ilford IG5 125 EN55
Rushdon Cl, Grays RM17 170 GA76
Romford RM1 127 FG57
Rush Dr, Wal.Abb. EN9 83 EC36
Rushen Dr, Hert. (Hert.Hth) SG13 32 DW12
Rushen Wk, Cars. SM5 off Paisley Rd 200 DD102
Rushes Mead, Harl. CM18 51 ES17
Uxbridge UB8 off Frays Waye 134 BJ67
Rushet Rd, Orp. BR5 206 EU96
Rushett Cl, T.Ditt. KT7 197 CH102
Rushett Dr, Dor. RH4 263 CH139
Rushett La, Chess. KT9 215 CJ111
Epsom KT18 215 CJ111
Rushett Rd, T.Ditt. KT7 197 CH101
Rushetts Rd, Reig. RH2 266 DC138
Rushey Cl, N.Mal. KT3 198 CR98
Rushey Grn, SE6 183 EB87
Sch Rushey Grn Prim Sch, SE6 off Culverley Rd 183 EC88
Rushey Hill, Enf. EN2 81 DM42
Rushey Mead, SE4 183 EA85
Rushfield, Pot.B. EN6 63 CX33
Sawbridgeworth CM21 36 EY05
Rushford Rd, SE4 183 DZ86
RUSH GREEN, Rom. RM7 127 FC59
Rush Grn Gdns, Rom. RM7 127 FC60
Sch Rush Grn Inf Sch, Rom. RM7 off Dagenham Rd 127 FD60
Sch Rush Grn Jun Sch, Rom. RM7 off Dagenham Rd 127 FE60
Rush Grn Rd, Rom. RM7 127 FC60
Rushgrove Av, NW9 119 CT57
Rush Gro St, SE18 165 EM77
Sch Rush Hall Sch, Ilf. IG6 off Fencepiece Rd 103 EQ52
Rush Hill Ms, SW11 off Rush Hill Rd 160 DG83
Rush Hill Rd, SW11 160 DG83
Rushleigh Av, Wal.Cr. (Chsht) EN8 67 DX31
Rushley Cl, Kes. BR2 222 EK105
Rushmead, E2 12 C2
Richmond TW10 177 CH90
Rushmead Cl, Croy. CR0 220 DT105
Rushmere Av, Upmin. RM14 128 FQ62
Rushmere Ct, Wor.Pk. KT4 off The Avenue 199 CU103
Rushmere Ho, SW15 off Fontley Way 179 CU88
Rushmere La, Chesh. (Orch.L.) HP5 56 AU28
Rushmere Pl, SW19 179 CX92
Egham TW20 172 AY92
Rushmoor Cl, Guil. GU2 242 AT131
Pinner HA5 115 BV56
Rickmansworth WD3 92 BK47
Rushmore Cl, Brom. BR1 204 EL97
Rushmore Cres, E5 off Rushmore Rd 123 DX63
Rushmore Hill, Orp. BR6 224 EW110
Sevenoaks (Knock.) TN14 224 EX112
Sch Rushmore Inf Sch, E5 off Rushmore Rd 123 DX63
Sch Rushmore Prim Sch, E5 off Elderfield Rd 123 DX63
Rushmore Rd, E5 122 DW63
Rusholme Av, Dag. RM10 126 FA62
Rusholme Gro, SE19 182 DS92
Rusholme Rd, SW15 179 CX86
Rushout Av, Har. HA3 117 CH58
Rushton Av, Wat. WD25 75 BU35
Rushton Gro, Harl. CM17 52 EX15
Rushton St, N1 5 K9
Rushworth Av, NW4 off Rushworth Gdns 119 CU55
Rushworth Gdns, NW4 119 CU56
Rushworth Rd, Reig. RH2 250 DA133
Rushworth St, SE1 20 F3
Rushy Meadow La, Cars. SM5 200 DE103
Sch Rushy Meadow Prim Sch, Cars. SM5 off Rushy Meadow La 200 DE104
Ruskin Av, E12 144 EL65
Feltham TW14 175 BT86
Richmond TW9 158 CN80
Upminster RM14 128 FQ59
Waltham Abbey EN9 68 EE34
Welling DA16 166 EU83
Ruskin Cl, NW11 120 DB58
Waltham Cross (Chsht) EN7 66 DS26
Ruskin Dr, Orp. BR6 205 ES104
Welling DA16 166 EU83
Worcester Park KT4 199 CV103
Ruskin Gdns, W5 137 CK70
Harrow HA3 118 CM56
Romford RM3 105 FH52
Ruskin Gro, Dart. DA1 188 FN85
Welling DA16 166 EU82
Ruskin Pk Ho, SE5 162 DR83
Ruskin Rd, N17 100 DT53
Belvedere DA17 166 FA77
Carshalton SM5 218 DF106
Croydon CR0 201 DP103
Grays RM16 171 GG77
Isleworth TW7 157 CF83
Southall UB1 136 BY73
Staines TW18 173 BF94
Ruskin Wk, N9 off Durham Rd 100 DU47
SE24 182 DQ85
Bromley BR2 205 EM100
Ruskin Way, SW19 200 DD95
Rusland Av, Orp. BR6 205 ER104
Rusland Hts, Har. HA1 off Rusland Pk Rd 117 CE56
Rusland Pk Rd, Har. HA1 117 CE56
Rusper Cl, NW2 119 CW62
Stanmore HA7 95 CJ49
Rusper Rd, N22 100 DQ54
Dagenham RM9 146 EW65
Russell Av, N22 99 DP54
St. Albans AL3 43 CD20
Russell Cl, NW10 138 CQ66
SE7 164 EJ80
W4 159 CT79
Amersham HP6 72 AX39
Beckenham BR3 203 EB97
Bexleyheath DA7 166 FA84
Brentwood CM15 108 FV45
Dartford DA1 167 FG83
Northwood HA6 93 BQ50
Ruislip HA4 116 BW61
Tadworth KT20 249 CU125
Woking GU21 226 AW115
Russell Ct, SW1 19 K2
Chesham HP5 54 AR29
Guildford GU1 off Rowan Cl 242 AW131
Leatherhead KT22 231 CH122
St. Albans AL2 60 CA30
Russell Cres, Wat. WD25 off High Rd 75 BT35
Russellcroft Rd, Welw.G.C. AL8 29 CW08
Russell Dr, Stai. (Stanw.) TW19 174 BK86
Russell Gdns, N20 98 DE47
NW11 119 CY58
W14 16 C5
Richmond TW10 177 CJ89
West Drayton UB7 154 BN78
Russell Gdns Ms, W14 16 C4
Russell Grn Cl, Pur. CR8 219 DN110
Russell Gro, NW7 96 CS50
SW9 161 DN80
Russell Hill, Pur. CR8 219 DM110
Russell Hill Pl, Pur. CR8 219 DN111
Russell Hill Rd, Pur. CR8 219 DN110
Russell Kerr Cl, W4 off Burlington La 158 CQ80
Russell La, N20 98 DE47
Watford WD17 75 BR36
Russell Mead, Har. (Har.Wld) HA3 95 CF53
Russell Par, NW11 off Golders Grn Rd 119 CY58
Russell Pl, NW3 off Aspern Gro 120 DE64
SE16 23 J6
Dartford (Sutt.H.) DA4 208 FN95
Hemel Hempstead HP3 40 BH23
Sch Russell Prim Sch, The, Rich. TW10 off Petersham Rd 177 CK88
Russell Rd, E4 101 DZ49
E10 123 EB58
E16 15 N7
E17 123 DZ55
N8 121 DK58
N13 99 DM51
N15 122 DS57
N20 98 DE47
NW9 119 CT58
SW19 180 DA94
W14 16 C5
Buckhurst Hill IG9 102 EH46
Enfield EN1 82 DT38
Gravesend DA12 191 GK86
Grays RM17 170 GA77
Mitcham CR4 200 DE97
Northolt UB5 116 CC64
Northwood HA6 93 BQ49
Shepperton TW17 195 BQ101
Tilbury RM18 170 GE81
Twickenham TW2 177 CF86
Walton-on-Thames KT12 195 BU100
Woking GU21 226 AW115
Russells, Tad. KT20 233 CX122
Sch Russell Sch, The, Rick. WD3 off Brushwood Dr 73 BB42
Russells Cres, Horl. RH6 268 DG149
Russell's Footpath, SW16 181 DL92
⊖ Russell Square 9 N4
Russell Sq, WC1 9 N4
Longfield DA3 off Cavendish Sq 209 FX97
Russells Ride, Wal.Cr. (Chsht) EN8 67 DX31
Russell St, WC2 9 P9
Hertford SG14 32 DQ09
Windsor SL4 151 AR81
Russell Wk, Rich. TW10 off Park Hill 178 CM86
Russell Way, Sutt. SM1 218 DA106
Watford WD19 93 BV45
Russet Cl, Horl. RH6 off Carlton Tye 269 DJ148
Staines TW19 173 BF86
Uxbridge UB10 off Uxbridge Rd 135 BQ70
Walton-on-Thames KT12 196 BX104
Russet Cres, N7 4 A1
Russet Dr, Croy. CR0 203 DY102
Radlett (Shenley) WD7 62 CL32
St. Albans AL4 43 CJ21
Sch Russet Ho Sch, Enf. EN1 off Autumn Cl 82 DV39
Russets, The, Ger.Cr. (Chal.St.P.) SL9 off Austenwood Cl 90 AX54
Russets Cl, E4 off Larkshall Rd 101 ED49
Russett Cl, Orp. BR6 224 EV106
Waltham Cross EN7 66 DS26
Russett Ct, Cat. CR3 252 DU125
Russett Hill, Ger.Cr. (Chal.St.P.) SL9 112 AY55
Russetts, Horn. RM11 128 FL56
Russetts Cl, Wok. GU21 227 AZ115
Russett Way, SE13 163 EB82
Swanley BR8 207 FD96
Russett Wd, Welw.G.C. AL7 30 DD10
Russet Way, Dor. (N.Holm.) RH5 263 CK140
Russia Ct, EC2 11 H7
Russia Dock Rd, SE16 23 K2
Russia La, E2 142 DW68
Russia Row, EC2 11 H8
Russia Wk, SE16 23 J4
Russington Rd, Shep. TW17 195 BR100
Rusthall Av, W4 158 CR77
Rusthall Cl, Croy. CR0 202 DW100
Rustic Av, SW16 181 DH94
Rustic Cl, Upmin. RM14 129 FS60
Rustic Pl, Wem. HA0 117 CK63
Rustic Wk, E16 15 N7
Rustington Wk, Mord. SM4 199 CZ101
Ruston Av, Surb. KT5 198 CP101
Ruston Gdns, N14 off Farm La 80 DG44
Ruston Ms, W11 6 C8
Ruston Rd, SE18 164 EL76
Ruston St, E3 143 DZ67
Rust Sq, SE5 162 DR80
Rutford Rd, SW16 181 DL92
Ruth Cl, Stan. HA7 118 CM56
Ruthen Cl, Epsom KT18 216 CP114
Rutherford Cl, Borwd. WD6 78 CQ40
Sutton SM2 218 DD107
Uxbridge UB8 134 BM70
Windsor SL4 151 AM81
Sch Rutherfords Sch, S.Croy. CR2 off Melville Av 220 DT106
Rutherford St, SW1 19 L7
Rutherford Twr, Sthl. UB1 136 CB72
Rutherford Way, Bushey (Bushey Hth) WD23 95 CD46
Wembley HA9 118 CN63
Rutherglen Rd, SE2 166 EU79
Rutherwick Cl, Horl. RH6 268 DF148
Rutherwick Ri, Couls. CR5 235 DL117
Rutherwyke Cl, Epsom KT17 217 CU107
Rutherwyk Rd, Cher. KT16 193 BE101
Ruthin Cl, NW9 118 CS58
Ruthin Rd, SE3 164 EG79
Ruthven Av, Wal.Cr. EN8 67 DX33
Ruthven St, E9 off Lauriston Rd 143 DX67
Rutland App, Horn. RM11 128 FN57
Rutland Av, Sid. DA15 186 EU87
Slough SL1 131 AR71
Rutland Cl, SW14 158 CQ83
SW19 off Rutland Rd 180 DE94
Ashtead KT21 232 CL117
Bexley DA5 186 EX88
Chessington KT9 216 CM107
Dartford DA1 188 FK87
Epsom KT19 216 CR110
Redhill RH1 250 DF133
Rutland Ct, Enf. EN3 82 DW43
Rutland Dr, Horn. RM11 128 FN57
Morden SM4 199 CZ100
Richmond TW10 177 CK88
Rutland Gdns, N4 121 DP58
SW7 18 B4
W13 137 CG71
Croydon CR0 220 DS105
Dagenham RM8 126 EW64
Hemel Hempstead HP2 40 BM19
Rutland Gdns Ms, SW7 18 B4
Rutland Gate, SW7 18 B4
Belvedere DA17 167 FB78
Bromley BR2 204 EF98
Rutland Gate Ms, SW7 18 A4
Rutland Gro, W6 159 CV78
Rutland Ms, NW8 off Boundary Rd 140 DB67
Rutland Ms E, SW7 18 A5
Rutland Ms S, SW7 18 A5
Rutland Ms W, SW7 off Ennismore St 160 DE76
Rutland Pk, NW2 139 CW65
SE6 183 DZ89
Rutland Pk Gdns, NW2 off Rutland Pk 139 CW65
Rutland Pk Mans, NW2 off Walm La 139 CW65
Rutland Pl, EC1 10 G4
Bushey (Bushey Hth) WD23 off The Rutts 95 CD46
Rutland Rd, E7 144 EK66
E9 142 DW67
E11 124 EH57
E17 123 EA58
SW19 180 DE94
Harrow HA1 116 CC58
Hayes UB3 155 BR77
Ilford IG1 125 EP63
Southall UB1 136 CA71
Twickenham TW2 177 CD89
Rutland St, SW7 18 B5
Rutland Wk, SE6 183 DZ89
Rutland Way, Orp. BR5 206 EW100
Rutley Cl, SE17 off Royal Rd 161 DP79
Romford (Harold Wd) RM3 off Pasteur Dr 106 FK54
Rutlish Rd, SW19 200 DA95
Sch Rutlish Sch, SW20 off Watery La 199 CZ96
Rutson Rd, W.Byf. (Byfleet) KT14 212 BM114
Rutter Gdns, Mitch. CR4 200 DC98
Rutters Cl, West Dr. UB7 154 BN75
Rutts, The, Bushey (Bushey Hth) WD23 95 CD46
Rutts Ter, SE14 163 DX81
Ruvigny Gdns, SW15 159 CX83
Ruxbury Rd, Cher. KT16 193 BC100
Ruxley Cl, Epsom KT19 216 CP106
Sidcup DA14 186 EX93
Ruxley Cor Ind Est, Sid. DA14 186 EX93
Ruxley Cres, Esher (Clay.) KT10 215 CH107
Ruxley Gdns, Shep. TW17 195 BQ99
Ruxley La, Epsom KT19 216 CR106
Sch Ruxley Manor Prim Sch, SE9 off Milverton Way 185 EN91
Ruxley Ms, Epsom KT19 216 CP106
Ruxley Ridge, Esher (Clay.) KT10 215 CG108
Ruxton Cl, Swan. BR8 207 FE97
Ryall Cl, St.Alb. (Brick.Wd) AL2 60 BY29
Ryalls Ct, N20 98 DF48
Ryan Cl, SE3 164 EJ84
Ruislip HA4 115 BV60
Ryan Dr, Brent. TW8 157 CG79
Ryan Way, Wat. WD24 76 BW39
Ryarsh Cres, Orp. BR6 223 ES105
Rybrook Dr, Walt. KT12 196 BW103
Rycott Path, SE22 off Lordship La 182 DU87
Rycroft La, Sev. TN14 256 FE130
Rycroft Way, N17 122 DT55
Ryculff Sq, SE3 164 EF82
Rydal Cl, NW4 97 CY53
Purley CR8 220 DR113
Rydal Ct, Wat. WD25 off Grasmere Cl 59 BV32
Rydal Cres, Grnf. UB6 137 CH69
Rydal Dr, Bexh. DA7 166 FA81
West Wickham BR4 204 EE103
Rydal Gdns, NW9 118 CS57
SW15 178 CS92
Hounslow TW3 176 CB86
Wembley HA9 117 CJ60
Rydal Rd, SW16 181 DK91
Rydal Way, Egh. TW20 173 BB94
Enfield EN3 82 DW44
Ruislip HA4 116 BW63
RYDE, THE, Hat. AL9 45 CW15
Ryde, The, Hat. AL9 45 CW16
Staines TW18 194 BH95
Ryde Cl, Wok. (Ripley) GU23 228 BJ121
Ryde Heron, Wok. (Knap.) GU21 off Robin Hood Rd 226 AS117
RYDENS, Walt. KT12 196 BW103
Rydens Av, Walt. KT12 195 BV103
Rydens Cl, Walt. KT12 196 BW103
Rydens Gro, Walt. KT12 214 BX105
Rydens Pk, Walt. KT12 off Rydens Rd 196 BX103
Rydens Rd, Walt. KT12 196 BX103
Sch Rydens Sch, Walt. KT12 off Hersham Rd 214 BW105
Rydens Way, Wok. GU22 227 BA120
Ryde Pl, Twick. TW1 177 CJ86
Sch Ryde Prim Sch, The, Hat. AL9 off Pleasant Ri 45 CW15
Ryder Av, Hat. AL10 44 CS20
Ryder Cl, Brom. BR1 184 EH92
Bushey WD23 76 CB44
Hemel Hempstead (Bov.) HP3 57 BA28
Hertford SG13 32 DV08
Ryder Ct, SW1 19 K1
Ryder Dr, SE16 22 C10
Ryder Gdns, Rain. RM13 147 FF65
Ryder Ms, E9 off Homerton High St 122 DW64
Ryder Seed Ms, St.Alb. AL1 off Pageant Rd 43 CD21
Ryders Ter, NW8 off Blenheim Ter 140 DC68
Ryder St, SW1 19 K1
Ryder Yd, SW1 19 K1
Rydes Av, Guil. GU2 242 AT131
Rydes Cl, Wok. GU22 227 BC120
RYDESHILL, Guil. GU3 242 AS131
Rydes Hill Cres, Guil. GU2 242 AT130
Sch Rydes Hill Prep Sch, Guil. GU2 off Aldershot Rd 242 AT132
Rydes Hill Rd, Guil. GU2 242 AT132
Ryde Vale Rd, SW12 181 DH89
Rydings, Wind. SL4 151 AM83
Rydon Business Cen, Lthd. KT22 231 CH119
Rydons Cl, SE9 164 EL83
Rydon's La, Couls. CR5 236 DQ120
Rydon St, N1 5 H7
Rydon's Wd Cl, Couls. CR5 236 DQ120
Rydston Cl, N7 4 A5
Rye, The, N14 99 DJ45
Ryebridge Cl, Lthd. KT22 231 CG118
Ryebrook Rd, Lthd. KT22 231 CG118
Rye Cl, Bex. DA5 187 FB86
Guildford GU2 242 AS132
Hornchurch RM12 128 FJ64
Ryecotes Mead, SE21 182 DS88
Rye Ct, Slou. SL1 off Alpha St S 152 AU76
Rye Cres, Orp. BR5 206 EW102
Ryecroft, Grav. DA12 191 GL92
Harlow CM19 51 EP15
Hatfield AL10 off Hazel Gro 45 CT20
Windsor SL4 151 AM83
Ryecroft Av, Ilf. IG5 103 EP54
Twickenham TW2 176 CB87
Ryecroft Cl, Hem.H. HP2 off Poynders Hill 41 BQ21
Ryecroft Ct, St.Alb. AL4 44 CL20
Ryecroft Cres, Barn. EN5 79 CV43
Ryecroft Rd, SE13 183 EC85
SW16 181 DN93
Chesham HP5 54 AN32
Orpington BR5 205 ER100
Sevenoaks (Otford) TN14 241 FG116
Ryecroft St, SW6 160 DB81
Ryedale, SE22 182 DV86
Ryedale Ct, Sev. TN13 off London Rd 256 FE121
Rye Fld, Ashtd. KT21 231 CK117
Orpington BR5 206 EX102
Ryefield Av, Uxb. UB10 135 BP66
Ryefield Cl, Hodd. EN11 33 EC13
Ryefield Ct, Nthwd. HA6 off Ryefield Cres 93 BU54
Ryefield Cres, Nthwd. HA6 93 BU54
Ryefield Par, Nthwd. HA6 off Ryefield Cres 93 BU54
Ryefield Path, SW15 179 CU88
Sch Ryefield Prim Sch, Uxb. UB10 off Ryefield Av 135 BQ67
Ryefield Rd, SE19 182 DQ93
Ryegates, SE15 off Caulfield Rd 162 DV82
Rye Hill Pk, SE15 162 DW84
Rye Hill Rd, Epp. (Thnwd) CM16 52 EU23
Harlow CM18 51 ES22
⇌ Rye House 49 EC15
Ryeland Cl, West Dr. UB7 134 BL72
Ryelands, Horl. RH6 269 DJ147
Welwyn Garden City AL7 29 CZ12
Ryelands Cl, Cat. CR3 236 DS121
Ryelands Ct, Lthd. KT22 231 CG118
Ryelands Cres, SE12 184 EJ86
Ryelands Pl, Wey. KT13 195 BS104
Sch Ryelands Prim Sch, SE25 off Albert Rd 202 DV99
Hoddesdon EN11 off Essex Rd 49 EB16
Rye La, SE15 162 DU81
Sevenoaks TN14 241 FG117
RYE PARK, Hodd. EN11 49 EB16
Rye Pk Ind Est, Hodd. EN11 off Salisbury Rd 49 EC15
Rye Pas, SE15 162 DU83
Rye Rd, SE15 163 DX84
Hoddesdon EN11 49 EB15
Rye Wk, SW15 off Chartfield Av 179 CX85
Rye Way, Edg. HA8 off Canons Dr 96 CM51
Ryfold Rd, SW19 180 DA90
Ryhope Rd, N11 99 DH49
Rykens La, Bet. RH3 264 CQ139
Rykhill, Grays RM16 171 GH76
Ryland Cl, Felt. TW13 175 BT91
Rylandes Rd, NW2 119 CU62
South Croydon CR2 220 DV109
Ryland Ho, Croy. CR0 202 DQ104
Ryland Rd, NW5 141 DH65
Rylett Cres, W12 159 CT76
Rylett Rd, W12 159 CT75
Rylston Rd, N13 100 DR48
SW6 159 CZ79
Rymer Rd, Croy. CR0 202 DS101
Rymer St, SE24 181 DP86
Rymill Cl, Hem.H. (Bov.) HP3 57 BA28
Rymill St, E16 145 EN74
Rysbrack St, SW3 18 C5
Rysted La, West. TN16 255 EQ126
Rythe Cl, Chess. KT9 off Nigel Fisher Way 215 CJ108
Rythe Ct, T.Ditt. KT7 197 CG101
Rythe Rd, Esher (Clay.) KT10 215 CD106
Sch Ryvers Comb Sch, Slou. SL3 off Trelawney Av 152 AX76
Ryvers Rd, Slou. SL3 153 AZ76

S

★ Saatchi Gall, SE1 20 A4
Sabah Ct, Ashf. TW15 174 BN91
Sabbarton St, E16 15 J8
Sabella Ct, E3 143 DZ68
Sabina Rd, Grays RM16 171 GJ77
Sabine Rd, SW11 160 DF83
Sable Cl, Houns. TW4 156 BW83
Sable St, N1 4 F5
Sach Rd, E5 122 DV61
Sackville Av, Brom. BR2 204 EG102

Sackville Cl, Har. HA2 ......117 CD62
Sevenoaks TN13 ....257 FH122
Sackville Cl, Rom. RM3
off Sackville Cres 106 FL53
Sackville Cres, Rom. RM3 ..106 FL53
Sackville Est, SW16 ......181 DL90
Sackville Gdns, Ilf. IG1 .....125 EM60
Sackville Rd, Dart. DA2 ....188 FK89
Sutton SM2 ....218 DA108
Sackville St, W1 ....9 K10
Sackville Way, SE22
off Dulwich Common ...182 DU88
Sacombe Rd, Hem.H. HP1 ..39 BF18
Sch Sacred Heart High Sch,
Har. HA3 off High St 95 CE54
Sch Sacred Heart of Mary
Girls Sch, Upmin. RM14
off St. Mary's La 128 FP61
Sch Sacred Heart RC High
Sch, W6 ....16 B8
Sch Sacred Heart RC Jun
Sch, W6 ....16 B8
Sch Sacred Heart RC Prim
Sch, N7 ....4 B2
N20 off Oakleigh Pk S 98 DE47
SW11 off Este Rd 160 DE82
SW15 off Roehampton La .179 CU85
New Malden KT3
off Burlington Rd 199 CU98
Ruislip HA4
off Herlwyn Av 115 BS61
Teddington TW11
off St. Mark's Rd 177 CH94
Ware SG12
off Broadmeads 33 DX06
Sch Sacred Heart RC Prim
Sch, The, Bushey WD23
off Merry Hill Rd 76 BZ44
Sch Sacred Heart RC Sec Sch,
SE5
off Camberwell New Rd ..162 DQ81
Saddington St, Grav. DA12 .191 GH87
Saddlebrook Pk, Sun.TW16 .175 BS94
Saddlers Cl, Barn. (Arkley)
EN5 ....79 CV43
Borehamwood WD6
off Farriers Way 78 CR44
Pinner HA5 ....94 CA51
Saddlers Ms, SW8
off Portland Gro 161 DM81
Kingston upon Thames
(Hmptn W.) KT1 ....197 CJ95
Wembley HA0
off The Boltons 117 CF63
Saddler's Pk, Dart. (Eyns.)
DA4 ....208 FK104
Saddlers Path, Borwd. WD6 .78 CR43
Saddlers Way, Epsom KT18 .232 CR119
Saddlescombe Way, N12 ...98 DA50
Saddleworth Rd, Rom. RM3 .106 FJ51
Saddleworth Sq, Rom. RM3 .106 FJ51
Saddle Yd, W1 ....18 G1
Sadleir Rd, St.Alb. AL1 .....43 CE22
Sadler Cl, Mitch. CR4 .....200 DF96
Waltham Cross (Chsht)
EN7 off Markham Rd ...66 DQ25
Sadlers Cl, Guil. GU4 .....243 BD133
Sadlers Mead, Harl. CM18 ..52 EU16
Sadlers Ride, W.Mol. KT8 ..196 CC96
Sadlers Way, Hert. SG14 ....31 DN09
★ Sadler's Wells Thea, EC1 .10 E1
Saffron Av, E14 ....14 E9
Saffron Cl, NW11 ....119 CZ57
Croydon CR0 ....201 DL100
Hoddesdon EN11 ....49 DZ16
Slough (Datchet) SL3 ....152 AV81
Saffron Ct, Felt. TW14
off Staines Rd 175 BQ87
Sch Saffron Grn First Sch,
Borwd. WD6
off Nicoll Way 78 CR42
Saffron Hill, EC1 ....10 D4
Saffron La, Hem.H. HP1 ....40 BH19
Saffron Platt, Guil. GU2 ...242 AU130
Saffron Rd, Grays
(Chaff.Hun.) RM16 .....169 FW77
Romford RM5 ....105 FC54
Saffron St, EC1 ....10 D5
Saffron Way, Surb. KT6 ...197 CK102
Sage Cl, E6
off Bradley Stone Rd ...145 EM71
Sage Ms, SE22
off Lordship La 182 DT85
Sage St, E1 ....12 E9
Sage Way, WC1 ....10 A2
Saigasso Cl, E16
off Royal Rd 144 EK72
Sailmakers Ct, SW6
off William Morris Way ..160 DC83
Sail St, SE11 ....20 B7
Sainfoin Rd, SW17 ....180 DG89
Sainsbury Rd, SE19 ....182 DS92
Sch St. Adrian's RC Prim Sch,
St.Alb. AL1
off Watling Vw 42 CC23
St. Agatha's Dr, Kings.T.
KT2 ....178 CM93
St. Agathas Gro, Cars. SM5 .200 DF102
Sch St. Agatha's RC Prim Sch,
Kings.T. KT2
off St. Agatha's Dr 178 CM93
St. Agnells Ct, Hem.H. HP2 ..40 BN16
St. Agnells La, Hem.H. HP2 ..40 BM15
St. Agnes Cl, E9
off Gore Rd 142 DW67
St. Agnes Pl, SE11 ....161 DN79
Sch St. Agnes RC Prim Sch,
E3 ....14 A1
Sch St. Agnes' RC Prim Sch,
NW2 off Thorverton Rd ..119 CY62
St. Agnes Well, EC1
off Old St 142 DR70
St. Aidans Ct, W13
off St. Aidans Rd 157 CH75
Barking IG11
off Choats Rd 146 EV69
Sch St. Aidan's Prim Sch,
N4 off Albany Rd 121 DN59
Sch St. Aidan's RC Prim Sch,
Couls. CR5
off Portnalls Rd 235 DJ116
Ilford IG1
off Benton Rd 125 ER60
St. Aidan's Rd, SE22 ......182 DV86
St. Aidans Rd, W13 ....157 CH75
St. Aidan's Way, Grav. DA12 .191 GL90
Sch St. Alban & Stephen RC
Inf Sch, St.Alb. AL1
off Vanda Cres 43 CF21
Sch St. Alban & Stephen RC
Jun Sch, St.Alb. AL1
off Cecil Rd 43 CG20
ST. ALBANS, AL1 - AL4 .....43 CE20
⇌ St. Albans Abbey 43 CD22
St. Albans Av, E6 ....145 EM69
St. Alban's Av, W4 ....158 CR77
St. Albans Av, Felt. TW13 ..176 BX92
Upminster RM14 ....129 FS60
Weybridge KT13 ....194 BN104
★ St. Albans Cath, St.Alb.
AL3 ....42 CC20
Sch St. Alban's Catholic Prim
Sch, E.Mol. KT8
off Beauchamp Rd 196 CC99
⇌ St. Albans City 43 CE20
H St. Albans City Hosp,
St.Alb. AL3 ....42 CC18
Mid Herts Wing, St.Alb.
AL3 ....42 CC19
St. Albans Cl, NW11 ....120 DA60
Gravesend DA12 ....191 GK90
Sch St. Alban's C of E Prim
Sch, EC1 ....10 C5
St. Albans Ct, EC2 ....11 H7
St. Albans Cres, N22 ....99 DN53
St. Alban's Cres, Wdf.Grn.
IG8 ....102 EG52
St. Albans Gdns, Grav.
DA12 ....191 GK90
St. Alban's Gdns, Tedd.
TW11 ....177 CG92
Sch St. Albans Girls' Sch,
St.Alb. AL3
off Sandridgebury La 43 CE16
St. Albans Gro, W8 ....17 K5
St. Alban's Gro, Cars. SM5 .200 DE101
Sch St. Albans High Sch for
Girls, St.Alb. AL1
off Townsend Av 43 CE19
St. Albans Hill, Hem.H. HP3 ..40 BL23
St. Albans La, NW11
off West Heath Dr 120 DA60
Abbots Langley
(Bedmond) WD5 ....59 BT26
Sch St. Albans Music Sch,
St.Alb. AL3
off Townsend Dr 43 CD17
★ St. Albans Organ Mus,
St.Alb. AL1 off Camp Rd ..43 CH21
St. Alban's Pl, N1 ....4 E8
Sch St. Albans RC Prim Sch,
Harl. CM20 off First Av ...35 ET13
Sch St. Alban's RC Prim Sch,
Horn. RM12
off Heron Flight Av 147 FG66
St. Albans Rd, NW5 ....120 DG62
NW10 ....138 CS67
Barnet EN5 ....79 CX39
Dartford DA1 ....188 FM87
Epping (Cooper.) CM16 ...70 EX29
Hemel Hempstead HP2,
HP3 ....40 BN21
Ilford IG3 ....125 ET60
St. Alban's Rd, Kings.T. KT2 .178 CL93
St. Albans Rd, Pot.B.
(Dance.H.) EN6 ....79 CV35
Potters Bar (S.Mimms)
EN6 ....63 CV34
Radlett (Shenley) WD7 ....62 CQ30
Reigate RH2 ....250 DA133
St. Albans (Lon.Col.) AL2 ..62 CN28
St. Albans (Sand.) AL4 ....43 CF17
St. Alban's Rd, Sutt. SM1 ..217 CZ105
St. Albans Rd, Wat. WD17,
WD24, WD25 ....75 BV40
St. Alban's Rd, Wdf.Grn. IG8 .102 EG52
Sch St. Albans Rd Co Inf Sch,
Dart. DA1
off St. Albans Rd 188 FM86
St. Albans Rd E, Hat. AL10 ...45 CV17
St. Albans Rd W, Hat. AL10 ..44 CR18
Hatfield (Roe Grn) AL10 ...45 CT17
Sch St. Albans Sch, St.Alb.
AL3 off Abbey Gateway ...42 CC20
St. Albans St, SW1 ....9 L10
St. Alban's St, Wind. SL4 ...151 AR81
St. Albans Ter, W6
off Margravine Rd 159 CY79
St. Alban's Vil, NW5
off Highgate Rd 120 DG62
Sch St. Albert the Gt RC Prim
Sch, Hem.H. HP3
off Acorn Rd 40 BN21
St. Alfege Pas, SE10 ....163 EC79
St. Alfege Rd, SE7 ....164 EK79
Sch St. Alfege with St. Peters
C of E Prim Sch, SE10
off Creek Rd 163 EC79
Sch St. Aloysius Coll, N6
off Hornsey La 121 DJ60
Sch St. Aloysius RC Inf Sch,
NW1 ....9 L1
Sch St. Aloysius RC Jun Sch,
NW1 off Aldenham St ..141 DJ68
St. Alphage Gdns, EC2 .....11 H6
St. Alphage Highwalk, EC2 ..11 J6
St. Alphage Wk, Edg. HA8 ...96 CQ54
St. Alphege Rd, N9 ....100 DW45
St. Alphonsus Rd, SW4 .....161 DJ84
St. Amunds Cl, SE6 ....183 EA91
Sch St. Andrew & St. Francis
C of E Prim Sch, NW2
off Belton Rd 139 CU65
St. Andrew Ms, Hert. SG14 ..32 DQ09
Sch St. Andrew's & St. Mark's
C of E Jun Sch, Surb.
KT6 off Maple Rd 197 CK99
H St. Andrew's at Harrow,
Har. HA1 ....117 CE61
St. Andrews Av, Horn.
RM12 ....127 FG64
Wembley HA0 ....117 CG63
Windsor SL4 ....151 AM82
St. Andrew's Cl, N12
off Woodside Av 98 DC49
St. Andrews Cl, NW2 ......119 CV62
SE16 ....22 D10
SE28 ....146 EX72
Epping CM16 ....53 FC24
St. Andrew's Cl, Islw. TW7 ..157 CD81
St. Andrews Cl, Reig. RH2
off St. Marys Rd 266 DB135
Ruislip HA4 ....116 BX61
St. Andrew's Cl, Shep. TW17 195 BR98
Staines (Wrays.) TW19 ...172 AY87
St. Andrews Cl, Stan. HA7 ...95 CJ54
Thames Ditton KT7 .....197 CH102
St. Andrew's Cl, Wind.
(Old Wind.) SL4 ....172 AU86
St. Andrews Cl, Wok. GU21
off St. Mary's Rd 226 AW117
Sch St. Andrews C of E High
Sch, Croy. CR0
off Warrington Rd 219 DP105
Sch St. Andrew's C of E Prim
Sch, N1 ....4 B7
N14 off Chase Rd 99 DK45
N20
off Totteridge Village 97 CZ47
SW9 off Kay Rd 161 DL82
Cobham KT11
off Lockhart Rd 214 BW113
Enfield EN1
off Churchbury La 82 DS40
Sch St. Andrew's C of E (VA)
Prim Sch, Uxb. UB8
off Nursery Waye 134 BK67
Sch St. Andrews C of E (VC)
Prim Sch, Epp. CM16
off School Grn La 71 FC25
St. Andrew's Ct, SW18
off Waynflete St 180 DC89
St. Andrews Ct, Slou.
(Colnbr.) SL3
off High St 153 BD80
Watford WD17 ....75 BV39
St. Andrews Cres, Wind.
SL4 ....151 AM82
St. Andrews Dr, Orp. BR5 ..206 EV100
Stanmore HA7 ....95 CJ53
St. Andrews Gdns, Cob.
KT11 ....214 BW113
Sch St. Andrew's Greek Sch,
NW5 off Kentish Town Rd .141 DJ65
St. Andrew's Gro, N16 .....122 DR60
St. Andrew's Hill, EC4 ......10 F9
H St. Andrew's Hosp, E3 ....14 B3
Sch St. Andrew's JMI Sch,
Ware SG12 off Mill Race ..33 ED11
St. Andrews Meadow, Harl.
CM18 ....51 ET16
St. Andrew's Ms, N16 .....122 DS60
St. Andrews Ms, SE3
off Mycenae Rd 164 EG80
Sch St. Andrew's Montessori
Prep Sch, Wat. WD25
off High Elms La 60 BW31
St. Andrews Pl, NW1 ....9 H3
Brentwood (Shenf.) CM15 .109 FZ47
Sch St. Andrew's Prim Sch,
Hert. SG14 off Calton Av ..31 DM08
Sch St. Andrew's RC Prim
Sch, SW16
off Polworth Rd 181 DL92
Sch St. Andrew's RC Sch,
Hillfield, Lthd. KT22
off Grange Rd 231 CK120
The Gra, Lthd. KT22
off Grange Rd 231 CK120
St. Andrews Rd, E11 ....124 EE58
E13 ....15 N2
E17 ....101 DX54
N9 ....100 DW45
NW9 ....118 CR60
NW10 ....139 CV65
NW11 ....119 CZ58
W3 ....138 CS73
W7 off Churchfield Rd ...157 CE75
W14 ....159 CY79
Carshalton SM5 ....200 DE104
Coulsdon CR5 ....234 DG116
Croydon CR0
off Lower Coombe St ..220 DQ105
Enfield EN1 ....82 DR41
St. Andrew's Rd, Grav.
DA12 ....191 GJ87
St. Andrews Rd, Hem.H.
HP3 off West Valley Rd ..40 BJ24
Ilford IG1 ....125 EM59
Romford RM7 ....127 FD58
Sidcup DA14 ....186 EX90
St. Andrew's Rd, Surb. KT6 .197 CK100
St. Andrews Rd, Til. RM18 ..170 GE81
Uxbridge UB10 ....134 BM66
Watford WD19 ....94 BX48
St. Andrews Sq, W11 ....6 C8
St. Andrew's Sq, Surb. KT6 .197 CK100
St. Andrews Twr, Sthl. UB1 .136 CC73
St. Andrew St, EC4 ....10 D6
Hertford SG14 ....32 DQ09
St. Andrews Wk, Cob. KT11 .229 BV115
St. Andrews Way, E3 ....14 A4
Oxted RH8 ....254 EL130
Slough SL1 ....131 AK73
Sch St. Angela's Ursuline
Conv Sch, E7
off St. Georges Rd 144 EH65
St. Anna Rd, Barn. EN5
off Sampson Av 79 CX43
St. Annes Av, Stai. (Stanw.)
TW19 ....174 BK87
St. Annes Boul, Red. RH1 ..251 DH132
St. Anne's Cl, N6
off Highgate W Hill 120 DG62
St. Annes Cl, Wal.Cr. (Chsht)
EN7 ....66 DU28
St. Anne's Cl, Wat. WD19 ....94 BW49
Sch St. Anne's C of E Prim
Sch, SW18
off St. Ann's Hill 180 DB85
St. Anne's Ct, W1 ....9 L8
St. Anne's Dr, Red. RH1 ...250 DG133
St. Annes Dr N, Red. RH1 ..250 DG132
St. Annes Gdns, NW10 .....138 CM69
St. Anne's Mt, Red. RH1 ...250 DG133
St. Annes Pk, Brox. EN10 ...49 EA20
St. Annes Pas, E14 ....13 L8
Sch St. Anne's Prim Sch, E1 ..12 A4
Staines TW19
off Clare Rd 174 BL87
Sch St. Anne's RC Prim Sch,
SE11 off Durham St 161 DM79
Banstead SM7
off Court Rd 234 DA116
Chertsey KT16
off Free Prae Rd 194 BG102
Sch St. Anne's RC Sch for
Girls (Lwr), Enf. EN2
off London Rd 82 DR42
Sch St. Anne's RC Sch for Girls
(Upr), N13 (Palmers Green)
off Oakthorpe Rd 99 DN49
St. Annes Ri, Red. RH1 ....250 DG133
St. Annes Rd, E11 ....123 ED61
St. Anne's Rd, St.Alb.
(Lon.Col.) AL2 ....61 CK27
Uxbridge (Hare.) UB9 ....114 BJ55
Wembley HA0 ....117 CK64
St. Anne's Row, E14 ....13 M8
St. Anne St, E14 ....13 M8
St. Anne's Way, Red. RH1
off St. Anne's Dr 250 DG133
St. Ann's, Bark. IG11 ....145 EQ67
St. Anns Cl, Cher. KT16 ....193 BF100
Sch St. Ann's C of E Prim Sch,
N15 off Avenue Rd 122 DR57
St. Ann's Cres, SW18 ......180 DC86
St. Ann's Gdns, NW5
off Queen's Cres 140 DG65
Sch St. Ann's Heath Co Jun
Sch, Vir.W. GU25
off Sandhills La 192 AY99
St. Ann's Hill, SW18 ....180 DB85
St. Anns Hill Rd, Cher. KT16 .193 BC100
H St. Ann's Hosp, N15 ....122 DQ57
St. Ann's La, SW1 ....19 M5
St. Ann's Pk Rd, SW18 .....180 DC86
St. Ann's Pas, SW13 ....158 CS83
St. Anns Rd, N9 ....100 DT47
St. Ann's Rd, N15 ....121 DP57
SW13 ....159 CT82
St. Anns Rd, W11 ....6 B10
St. Ann's Rd, Bark. IG11
off Axe St 145 EQ67
St. Anns Rd, Cher. KT16 ...193 BF100
St. Ann's Rd, Har. HA1 .....117 CE58
Sch St. Ann's Sch, Mord.
SM4 off Bordesley Rd ..200 DB99
St. Ann's Shop Cen, Har.
HA1 ....117 CE58
Sch St. Ann's (Spec) Sch,
W7 off Springfield Rd ..137 CE74
St. Ann's St, SW1 ....19 M5
St. Ann's Ter, NW8 ....140 DD68
St. Anns Vil, W11 ....16 B2
St. Anns Way, S.Croy. CR2 ..219 DP107
Westerham (Berry's Grn)
TN16 ....239 EP116
St. Anselm's Pl, W1 ....8 G8
Sch St. Anselm's RC First &
Mid Sch, Har. HA1
off Roxborough Pk 117 CE59
Sch St. Anselm's RC Prim Sch,
SW17 off Tooting Bec Rd .180 DG90
Dartford DA1
off Littlebrook
Manor Way 188 FN85
Sch St. Anselms RC Prim Sch,
Sthl. UB2
off Church Av 156 BZ76
St. Anselms Rd, Hayes UB3 .155 BT75
St. Anthonys Av, Hem.H.
HP3 ....41 BP22
Woodford Green IG8 ....102 EJ51
St. Anthonys Cl, E1 ....22 A1
SW17 off College Gdns ..180 DE89
St. Anthonys Ct, Beac. HP9
off Walkwood Ri 110 AJ55
H St. Anthony's Hosp,
Sutt. SM3 ....199 CX102
Sch St. Anthony's Prep Sch,
NW3 off Fitzjohn's Av ..120 DD64
Sch St. Anthony's RC Prim Sch,
SE20 off Genoa Rd 202 DV95
SE22 off Etherow St 182 DU86
Slough SL2
off Farnham Rd 131 AQ70
Watford WD18
off Croxley Vw 75 BS43
Woodford Green IG8
off Mornington Rd 102 EG49
St. Anthony's Way, Felt.
TW14 ....155 BT84
Sch St. Antony's RC Prim Sch,
E7 off Upton Av 144 EH66
St. Antony's Rd, E7 ....144 EH66
St. Arvans Cl, Croy. CR0 ....202 DS104
St. Asaph Rd, SE4 ....163 DX83
St. Aubyn's Av, SW19 ......179 CZ92
St. Aubyns Av, Houns. TW3 .176 CA85
St. Aubyns Cl, Orp. BR6 ....205 ET104
St. Aubyns Gdns, Orp. BR6 .205 ET103
St. Aubyn's Rd, SE19 ....182 DT93
Sch St. Aubyn's Sch, Wdf.Grn.
IG8 off Bunces La 102 EF52
St. Audrey Av, Bexh. DA7 ...166 FA82
St. Audreys Cl, Hat. AL10 ....45 CV21
St. Audreys Grn, Welw.G.C.
AL7 ....29 CZ10
Sch St. Augustine RC Prim
Sch, W6
off Disbrowe Rd 159 CY79
St. Augustine Rd, Grays
RM16 ....171 GH77
St. Augustine's Av, W5 .....138 CL68
St. Augustines Av, Brom.
BR2 ....204 EL99
St. Augustine's Av, S.Croy.
CR2 ....220 DQ107
St. Augustines Av, Wem.
HA9 ....118 CL62
St. Augustines Cl, Brox.
EN10 ....49 DZ20
Sch St. Augustine's C of E
Sec Sch, NW6
off Oxford Rd 140 DA68
St. Augustines Dr, Brox.
EN10 ....49 DZ19
St. Augustine's Path, N5
off Highbury New Pk ...122 DQ63
Sch St. Augustine's Prim Sch,
NW6 off Kilburn Pk Rd ..140 DB68
Belvedere DA17
off St. Augustine's Rd ...166 EZ76
Sch St. Augustine's Priory Sch,
W5 off Hillcrest Rd 138 CM71
Sch St. Augustine's RC Prim
Sch, SE6 off Dunfield Rd .183 EC92
Hoddesdon EN11
off Riversmead 49 EA17
Ilford IG2
off Cranbrook Rd 125 EP57
St. Augustines Rd, NW1 ....141 DK66
St. Augustine's Rd, Belv.
DA17 ....166 EZ77
St. Austell Cl, Edg. HA8 .....96 CM54
St. Austell Rd, SE13 ....163 EC82
St. Awdry's Rd, Bark. IG11 ..145 ER66
St. Awdry's Wk, Bark. IG11
off Station Par 145 EQ66
Sch St. Barnabas & St. Philip
C of E Prim Sch, W8 .....16 G6
St. Barnabas Cl, SE22
off East Dulwich Gro ...182 DS85
Beckenham BR3 ....203 EC96
Sch St. Barnabas C of E Prim
Sch, SW1 ....18 F9
St. Barnabas Ct, Har. HA3 ...94 CC53
St. Barnabas Gdns, W.Mol.
KT8 ....196 CA99
St. Barnabas Rd, E17 ......123 EA58
Mitcham CR4 ....180 DG94
Sutton SM1 ....218 DD106
Woodford Green IG8 ....102 EH53
St. Barnabas St, SW1 ....18 F9
St. Barnabas Ter, E9 ....123 DX64
St. Barnabas Vil, SW8 ......161 DL81
Sch St. Bartholomew RC Prim
Sch, Swan. BR8
off Sycamore Dr 207 FE97
St. Bartholomews Cl, SE26 .182 DW91
Sch St. Bartholomew's C of E
Prim Sch, SE26
off The Peak 182 DW91
St. Bartholomews Ct, Guil.
GU1 ....259 AZ135
H St. Bartholomew's Hosp,
EC1 ....10 F6
St. Bartholomew's Rd, E6 ..144 EL67
★ St. Bartholomew-the-Great
Ch, EC1 ....10 F6
St. Bart's Cl, St.Alb. AL4 ....43 CK21
Sch St. Bede's C of E & RC Sch,
Red. RH1 off Carlton Rd ..250 DE131
Sch St. Bede's C of E Jun Sch,
Wok. GU23
off Bush La 227 BD124
Sch St. Bede's RC Inf Sch,
SW12 off Thornton Rd ..181 DK88
Sch St. Bede's RC Prim Sch,
Rom. RM6 off Canon Av .126 EW57
St. Benedict's Av, Grav.
DA12 ....191 GK89
St. Benedict's Cl, SW17
off Church La 180 DG92
Sch St. Benedict's Jun Sch,
W5 off Montpelier Av ...137 CJ71
Sch St. Benedict's Sch, W5
off Eaton Ri 137 CK71
St. Benet's Cl, SW17
off College Gdns 180 DE89
St. Benet's Gro, Cars. SM5 .200 DC101
St. Benet's Pl, EC3 ....11 K9
St. Benjamins Dr, Orp. BR6 .224 EW109
Sch St. Bernadette's RC First
& Mid Sch, Har. HA3
off Clifton Rd 118 CM56
Sch St. Bernadette's RC Jun
Sch, SW12
off Atkins Rd 181 DJ87
Sch St. Bernadette's RC Prim
Sch, St.Alb. AL2
off Walsingham Way 61 CK27
Uxbridge UB10
off Long La 135 BP67
St. Bernards, Croy. CR0 ....202 DS104
St. Bernard's Cl, SE27
off St. Gothard Rd 182 DR91
Sch St. Bernard's Conv Sch,
Slou. SL3
off Langley Rd 152 AW75
H St. Bernard's Hosp, Sthl.
UB1 ....157 CD75
Sch St. Bernard's Prep Sch,
Slou. SL1
off Hawtrey Cl 152 AV75
St. Bernard's Rd, E6 ....144 EK67
St. Bernards Rd, St.Alb. AL3 .43 CD19
Slough SL3 ....152 AW76
St. Blaise Av, Brom. BR1 ...204 EH96
Sch St. Bonaventure's RC Sch,
E7 off Boleyn Rd 144 EG66
Sch St. Boniface RC Prim Sch,
SW17 off Undine St 180 DF92
St. Botolph Rd, Grav. DA11 .190 GC90
St. Botolph Row, EC3 ....11 N8
St. Botolph's Av, Sev. TN13 .256 FG124
Sch St. Botolph's C of E Prim
Sch, Grav. DA11
off Dover Rd 190 GD87
St. Botolph's Rd, Sev. TN13 .256 FG124
St. Botolph St, EC3 ....11 N8
St. Brelades Cl, Dor. RH4 ...263 CG138
St. Brelades Pl, St.Alb. AL4
off Harvesters 43 CK16
St. Brides Av, EC4 ....10 E8
Edgware HA8 ....96 CM53
★ St. Bride's Ch & Crypt
Mus, EC4 ....10 E8
St. Brides Cl, Erith DA18
off St. Katherines Rd ...166 EX75
St. Bride's Pas, EC4 ....10 E8
St. Bride St, EC4 ....10 E7
Sch St. Catherine of Siena
RC JMI Sch, Wat. WD25
off Horseshoe La 60 BX33
St. Catherines, Wok. GU22 .226 AW119
Sch St. Catherine's Bletchingley
Village Sch, Red. RH1
off Coneybury 252 DS133
Sch St. Catherine's Catholic
Sch, Twick. TW1
off Cross Deep 177 CG89
St. Catherines Cl, SW17
off College Gdns 180 DE89
Sch St. Catherine's C of E
Prim Sch, Hodd. EN11
off Haslewood Av 49 EA17
Hoddesdon EN11
off Haslewood Av 49 EB17
St. Catherines Cross, Red.
(Bletch.) RH1 ....252 DS134
St. Catherines Dr, SE14
off Kitto Rd 163 DX82
Guildford GU2 ....258 AV138
St. Catherines Fm Ct, Ruis.
HA4 ....115 BQ58
St. Catherines Hill, Guil.
GU2 off Portsmouth Rd ..258 AW138
St. Catherine's Ms, SW3 .....18 C7
St. Catherines Pk, Guil. GU1 259 AZ136
Sch St. Catherine's Prim Sch,
Ware SG12 off Park Rd ...32 DV05
Sch St. Catherine's RC Prim
Sch, Barn. EN5
off Vale Dr 80 DA42
West Drayton UB7
off Money La 154 BK75
Sch St. Catherine's RC Sch for
Girls, Bexh. DA6
off Watling St 167 FB84
St. Catherines Rd, E4 ....101 EA47
Broxbourne EN10 ....49 EA19
Ruislip HA4 ....115 BR57
Sch St. Catherine's Sch, Guil.
GU5 off Station Rd 259 AZ144
St. Catherines Twr, E10
off Kings Cl 123 EB59
St. Cecilia Rd, Grays RM16 .171 GH77
St. Cecilia's Cl, Sutt. SM3 ..199 CY102
Sch St. Cecilia's RC Prim Sch,
Sutt. SM3
off London Rd 199 CX103
Sch St. Ceilia's C of E Seconday
Sch, SW18
off Sutherland Gro 179 CZ87
St. Chads Cl, Surb. KT6 ....197 CJ101
St. Chad's Dr, Grav. DA12 ..191 GL90
St. Chad's Gdns, Rom. RM6 126 EY59
St. Chad's Pl, WC1 ....9 P1
Sch St. Chad's RC Prim Sch,
SE25
off Alverston Gdns 202 DS99
St. Chad's Rd, Rom. RM6 ...126 EY58
Tilbury RM18 ....171 GG80
St. Chad's St, WC1 ....9 P1
Sch St. Charles Borromeo
Catholic Prim Sch, Wey.
KT13 off Portmore Way ..194 BN104

★ Place of interest | H Hospital | Sch School | Coll College | Uni University | ⇌ Railway station

St. Charles Catholic 6th Form Coll, W10 6 B6
St. Charles Ct, Wey. KT13 212 BN106
St. Charles Hosp, W10 6 B5
St. Charles Pl, W10 6 C6
Weybridge KT13 212 BN106
St. Charles RC Prim Sch, W10 6 B5
St. Charles Rd, Brwd. CM14 108 FV46
St. Charles Sq, W10 6 C5
St. Christina's Sch, NW8 off St. Edmunds Ter 140 DE68
St. Christopher Rd, Uxb. UB8 134 BK71
St. Christopher's Cl, Islw. TW7 157 CE81
St. Christopher's Dr, Hayes UB3 135 BV73
St. Christophers Gdns, Th.Hth. CR7 201 DN97
St. Christophers Ms, Wall. SM6 219 DJ106
St. Christopher's Pl, W1 8 F7
St. Christopher's Sch, NW3 off Belsize La 120 DD64
Beckenham BR3 off Bromley Rd 203 EC96
Epsom KT18 off Downs Rd 216 CS114
Wembley HA9 off Wembley Pk Dr 118 CM62
St. Clair Cl, Oxt. RH8 253 EC130
Reigate RH2 250 DC134
St. Clair Dr, Wor.Pk. KT4 199 CV104
St. Clair Rd, E13 144 EH68
St. Clair's Rd, Croy. CR0 202 DS103
St. Clare Business Pk, Hmptn. TW12 176 CC93
St. Clare Cl, Ilf. IG5 103 EM54
St. Clare St, EC3 11 N8
St. Clement Cl, Uxb. UB8 134 BK72
★ St. Clement Danes Ch, WC2 10 B8
St. Clement Danes C of E Prim Sch, WC2 10 A8
St. Clement Danes Sch, Rick. WD3 off Chenies Rd 73 BD40
St. Clements & St. James C of E Prim Sch, W11 16 C1
St. Clements Av, Grays RM20 169 FU79
St. Clement's Catholic Prim Sch, Epsom KT17 off Fennells Mead 217 CT109
St. Clement's Cl, Grav. (Nthflt) DA11 off Coldharbour Rd 191 GF90
St. Clements C of E Jun Sch, Wal.Cr. EN8 off Cheshunt Wash 67 DY27
St. Clements Ct, EC4 off Clements La 142 DR73
N7 4 C4
Purfleet RM19 168 FN77
St. Clements Hts, SE26 182 DU90
St. Clement's La, WC2 10 B8
St. Clements Rd, Grays RM20 169 FW80
St. Clements St, N7 4 C4
St. Clements Way, Grays RM20 169 FT79
Greenhithe DA9 189 FU85
St. Clements Yd, SE22 off Archdale Rd 182 DT85
St. Cloud Rd, SE27 182 DQ91
St. Columba's Cl, Grav. DA12 191 GL90
St. Columba's Coll, St.Alb. AL3 off King Harry La 42 CC22
St. Columba's Coll Prep Sch, St.Alb. AL3 off King Harry La 42 CB22
St. Columba's RC Sec Sch for Boys, Bexh. DA6 off Halcot Av 187 FB85
St. Crispins Cl, NW3 120 DE63
Southall UB1 136 BZ72
St. Crispins Way, Cher. (Ott.) KT16 211 BC109
St. Cross Ct, Hodd. EN11 49 EA19
St. Cross RC Prim Sch, Hodd. EN11 off Upper Marsh La 49 EA19
St. Cross St, EC1 10 D5
St. Cuthbert Mayne RC Jun Sch, Hem.H. HP1 off Clover Way 40 BH19
St. Cuthberts Cl, Egh. TW20 172 AX92
St. Cuthberts Gdns, Pnr. HA5 off Westfield Pk 94 BZ52
St. Cuthbert's RC Prim Sch, Egh. TW20 off Bagshot Rd 172 AW94
St. Cuthberts Rd, N13 99 DN51
NW2 139 CZ65
Hoddesdon EN11 33 EC14
St. Cuthbert with St. Matthias C of E Prim Sch, SW5 17 J9
St. Cyprian's Greek Orthodox Prim Sch, Th.Hth. CR7 off Springfield Rd 202 DQ95
St. Cyprian's St, SW17 180 DF91
St. David Cl, Uxb. UB8 134 BK71
St. Davids, Couls. CR5 235 DM117
St. Davids Cl, SE16 22 D10
Hemel Hempstead HP3 41 BR21
Iver SL0 133 BD67
St. David's Cl, Reig. RH2 250 DC133
St. Davids Cl, Wem. HA9 118 CQ62
St. David's Cl, W.Wick. BR4 203 EB101
St. David's Coll, W.Wick. BR4 off Beckenham Rd 203 DX95
St. David's Ct, E17 123 EC55
St. David's Cres, Grav. DA12 191 GK91
St. David's Dr, Brox. EN10 49 DZ19
St. Davids Dr, Edg. HA8 96 CM53
St. David's Dr, Egh. (Eng.Grn) TW20 172 AW94
St. Davids Ms, E3 off Morgan St 143 DY69
St. Davids Pl, NW4 119 CV59
St. Davids Rd, Swan. BR8 187 FF93
St. David's Sch, Ashf. TW15 off Church Rd 174 BM90
St. Davids Sch, Pur. CR8 off Woodcote Valley Rd 219 DM111
St. Davids Sq, E14 24 B9
St. Denis Rd, SE27 182 DR91
St. Dionis Rd, SW6 159 CZ82
St. Dominic's RC Prim Sch, NW5 off Southampton Rd 120 DF64
St. Dominic's RC Sch, E9 off Ballance Rd 143 DY65
St. Dominic's 6th Form Coll, Har. HA1 off Mount Pk Av 117 CE61
St. Donatts Rd, SE14 163 DZ81
St. Dunstan's All, EC3 11 L9
St. Dunstans Av, W3 138 CR73
St. Dunstan's, Cheam, C of E Prim Sch, Sutt. SM3 off Anne Boleyn's Wk 217 CY108
St. Dunstans Cl, Hayes UB3 155 BT77
St. Dunstan's Coll, SE6 off Stanstead Rd 183 EA88
St. Dunstan's Ct, EC4 off Fleet St 141 DN72
St. Dunstan's Dr, Grav. DA12 191 GL91
St. Dunstans Gdns, W3 off St. Dunstans Av 138 CR73
St. Dunstan's Hill, EC3 11 L10
Sutton SM1 217 CY106
St. Dunstan's La, EC3 11 L10
Beckenham BR3 203 EC100
St. Dunstan's RC Prim Sch, Wok. GU22 off Onslow Cres 227 BA117
St. Dunstan's Rd, E7 144 EJ65
St. Dunstans Rd, SE25 202 DT98
W6 16 A10
W7 157 CE75
St. Dunstan's Rd, Felt. TW13 175 BT90
St. Dunstans Rd, Houns. TW4 156 BW82
Ware (Hunsdon) SG12 34 EK07
St. Ebba's Hosp, Epsom KT19 216 CQ109
St. Edith Cl, Epsom KT18 off St. Elizabeth Dr 216 CQ114
St. Edmunds, Berk. HP4 38 AW20
St. Edmunds Av, Ruis. HA4 115 BR58
St. Edmunds Cl, NW8 off St. Edmunds Ter 140 DF67
SW17 off College Gdns 180 DE89
Erith DA18 off St. Katherines Rd 166 EX75
St. Edmunds Dr, Stan. HA7 95 CG53
St. Edmund's La, Twick. TW2 176 CB87
St. Edmund's RC Prim Sch, E14 23 P7
N9 off Hertford Rd 100 DV46
Twickenham TW2 off Nelson Rd 176 CB87
St. Edmunds Rd, N9 100 DU45
Dartford DA1 168 FM84
Ilford IG1 125 EM58
St. Edmunds Sq, SW13 159 CW79
St. Edmunds Ter, NW8 140 DE67
St. Edmunds Wk, St.Alb. AL4 43 CJ21
St. Edmunds Way, Harl. CM17 36 EW11
St. Edwards Cl, NW11 120 DA58
Croydon (New Adgtn) CR0 221 ED111
St. Edward's C of E Comp Sch, Rom. RM7 off London Rd 126 FA58
St. Edward's C of E Prim Sch, Rom. RM1 off Havering Dr 127 FE56
St. Edward's RC First Sch, Wind. SL4 off Parsonage La 151 AN81
St. Edward's RC Prim Sch, E13 off Green St 144 EJ67
NW1 8 B4
St. Edward's Royal Free Ecumenical Mid Sch, Wind. SL4 off Parsonage La 151 AN81
St. Edwards Way, Rom. RM1 127 FD57
St. Egberts Way, E4 101 EC46
St. Elizabeth Dr, Epsom KT18 216 CQ114
St. Elizabeth RC Prim Sch, E2 off Bonner Rd 142 DW68
St. Elizabeth's Catholic Prim Sch, Rich. TW10 off Queens Rd 178 CM86
St. Elmo Cl, Slou. SL2 off St. Elmo Cres 131 AR70
St. Elmo Cres, Slou. SL2 131 AR70
St. Elmo Rd, W12 139 CT74
St. Elmos Rd, SE16 23 J3
St. Elphege's RC Inf & Jun Schs, Wall. SM6 off Mollison Dr 219 DL107
St. Erkenwald Ms, Bark. IG11 off St. Erkenwald Rd 145 ER67
St. Erkenwald Rd, Bark. IG11 145 ER67
St. Ermin's Hill, SW1 19 L5
St. Ervans Rd, W10 6 D5
St. Ethelbert's RC Prim Sch, Slou. SL2 off Wexham Rd 132 AV72
St. Ethelredas Dr, Hat. AL10 45 CW18
St. Eugene de Mazenod RC Prim Sch, NW6 off Mazenod Av 140 DA66
St. Faiths Cl, Enf. EN2 82 DQ39
St. Faith's C of E Prim Sch, SW18 off Alma Rd 180 DC85
St. Faith's Rd, SE21 181 DP88
St. Fidelis RC Prim Sch, Erith DA8 off Bexley Rd 167 FC79
St. Fidelis Rd, Erith DA8 167 FD77
St. Fillans Rd, SE6 183 EC88
St. Francesca Cabrini RC Prim Sch, SE23 off Honor Oak Pk 182 DW86
St. Francis Av, Grav. DA12 191 GL91
St. Francis Cl, Orp. BR5 205 ES100
Potters Bar EN6 64 DC33
Watford WD19 93 BV46
St. Francis de Sales RC Inf Sch, N17 off Brereton Rd 100 DT52
St. Francis de Sales RC Jun Sch, N17 off Brereton Rd 100 DT52
St. Francis of Assisi RC Prim Sch, W11 6 B10
St. Francis RC Prim Sch, E15 off Maryland Pk 124 EE64
SE15 off Friary Rd 162 DU80
Caterham CR3 off Whyteleafe Rd 236 DT121
St. Francis Rd, SE22 162 DS84
Erith DA8 off West St 167 FD77
Uxbridge (Denh.) UB9 113 BF58
St. Francis Way, Grays RM16 171 GJ77
Ilford IG1 125 ES63
St. Francis Xavier 6th Form Coll, SW12 off Malwood Rd 181 DH86
St. Frideswides Ms, E14 14 C8
St. Gabriel's Cl, E11 124 EH61
St. Gabriel's C of E Prim Sch, SW1 19 J10
St. Gabriels Rd, NW2 119 CX64
St. Georges Av, E7 144 EH66
N7 121 DK63
NW9 118 CQ56
St. George's Av, W5 157 CK75
St. Georges Av, Grays RM17 170 GC77
Hornchurch RM11 128 FM59
Southall UB1 136 BZ73
St. George's Av, Wey. KT13 213 BP107
St. George's Bickley C of E Prim Sch, Brom. BR1 off Tylney Rd 204 EK96
St. George's Catholic School, Westminster, W9 off Lanark Rd 140 DB68
St. George's Cen, Grav. DA11 191 GH86
St. Georges Cen, Har. HA1 off St. Ann's Rd 117 CE58
St. Georges Circ, SE1 20 E5
St. Georges Cl, NW11 119 CZ58
SE28 off Redbourne Dr 146 EX72
St. George's Cl, SW8 off Patmore St 161 DJ81
St. Georges Cl, Horl. RH6 269 DH148
Wembley HA0 117 CG62
St. George's Cl, Wey. KT13 213 BQ106
Windsor SL4 151 AL81
St. George's C of E First Sch, Amer. HP7 off White Lion Rd 72 AT39
St. George's C of E Prim Sch, SE5 off Coleman Rd 162 DS80
SW8 off Corunna Rd 161 DJ80
St. George's C of E Sch, Grav. DA11 off Meadow Rd 191 GG89
St. George's Coll, Add. KT15 off Weybridge Rd 194 BK104
St. George's Coll Jun Sch, Wey. KT13 off Thames St 195 BP104
St. Georges Ct, E6 145 EM70
EC4 10 E7
SW7 17 L5
St. Georges Cres, Grav. DA12 191 GK91
St. George's Cres, Slou. SL1 131 AK73
St. George's Dr, SW1 19 J9
St. Georges Dr, Uxb. UB10 114 BM62
Watford WD19 94 BY48
St. Georges Flds, W2 8 B8
St. Georges Gdns, Epsom KT17 217 CT114
St. George's Gdns, Surb. KT6 off Hamilton Av 198 CP103
St. Georges Gro, SW17 180 DD90
St. Georges Gro Est, SW17 180 DD90
St. George's Hanover Sq Prim Sch, W1 8 F10
ST. GEORGE'S HILL, Wey. KT13 213 BQ110
St. George's Hosp, SW17 180 DD92
Hornchurch RM12 128 FK63
St. George's Hosp Med Sch, SW17 off Cranmer Ter 180 DD92
St. Georges Ind Est, Kings.T. KT2 off Richmond Rd 177 CK92
St. Georges La, EC3 11 L9
St. George's Lo, Wey. KT13 213 BR106
St. Georges Ms, NW1 off Regents Pk Rd 140 DF66
SE1 20 D5
St. Georges Pl, Twick. TW1 off Church St 177 CG88
St. George's Prim Sch, SE1 20 E5
St. George's RC First & Mid Sch, Har. HA1 off Sudbury Hill 117 CF62
St. George's RC Prim Sch, Enf. EN2 off Gordon Rd 82 DR40
St. Georges Rd, E7 144 EH65
E10 123 EC62
N9 100 DU48
N13 99 DM48
NW11 119 CZ58
SE1 20 D5
St. George's Rd, SW19 179 CZ93
St. Georges Rd, W4 158 CS75
W7 137 CF74
Addlestone KT15 212 BJ105
St. George's Rd, Beck. BR3 203 EB95
St. Georges Rd, Brom. BR1 205 EM96
Dagenham RM9 126 EY64
Enfield EN1 82 DT38
St. George's Rd, Felt. TW13 176 BX91
St. Georges Rd, Hem.H. HP3 40 BJ24
Ilford IG1 125 EM59
St. George's Rd, Kings.T. KT2 178 CN94
Mitcham CR4 201 DH97
Orpington BR5 205 ER100
St. Georges Rd, Red. RH1 267 DK142
Richmond TW9 158 CM83
St. George's Rd, Sev. TN13 257 FH122
Sidcup DA14 186 EX93
St. Georges Rd, Swan. BR8 207 FF98
Twickenham TW1 177 CH85
Wallington SM6 219 DH106
Watford WD24 75 BV38
St. George's Rd, Wey. KT13 213 BR107
St. Georges Rd W, Brom. BR1 204 EL95
St. George's Sch, Wind. SL4 off Windsor Castle 151 AR80
St. Georges Sq, E7 144 EH66
E14 13 J9
SE8 23 L7
St. George's Sq, SW1 19 L9
New Malden KT3 off High St 198 CS97
St. George's Sq Ms, SW1 19 L10
St. Georges Ter, NW1 off Regents Pk Rd 140 DF66
St. George St, W1 9 H8
St. Georges Wk, Croy. CR0 202 DQ104
St. Georges Way, SE15 162 DS79
St. George the Martyr C of E Prim Sch, WC1 10 A4
St. George Wf, SW8 19 N10
St. Gerards Cl, SW4 181 DJ85
St. German's Pl, SE3 164 EG81
St. Germans Rd, SE23 183 DY88
St. Gilda's RC Jun Sch, N8 off Oakington Way 121 DL59
St. Giles Av, Dag. RM10 147 FB66
Potters Bar EN6 63 CV32
Uxbridge UB10 115 BQ63
St. Giles Cl, Dag. RM10 off St. Giles Av 147 FB66
Orpington BR6 223 ER106
St. Giles C of E Aided Prim Sch, Ashtd. KT21 off Dene Rd 232 CM118
St. Giles' C of E Prim Sch, Pot.B. EN6 off Blanche La 63 CU32
St. Giles Coll, London Cen, WC1 off Southampton Row 141 DL71
London Highgate, N6 off Shepherds Hill 121 DJ58
St. Giles Ct, WC2 off St. Giles High St 141 DL72
St. Giles High St, WC2 9 M7
St. Giles Pas, WC2 9 M8
St. Giles Rd, SE5 162 DS80
St. Giles Sch, S.Croy. CR2 off Pampisford Rd 219 DP107
St. Gilles Ho, E2 143 DX68
St. Godric's Coll, NW3 off Arkwright Rd 120 DC64
St. Gothard Rd, SE27 182 DR91
St. Gregory Cl, Ruis. HA4 116 BW63
St. Gregorys Cres, Grav. DA12 191 GL89
St. Gregory's RC High Sch, Har. HA3 off Donnington Rd 117 CK57
St. Gregory's RC Prim Sch, W5 off Woodfield Rd 137 CK71
St. Helena Rd, SE16 22 G8
St. Helena St, WC1 10 C2
St. Helens Cl, Uxb. UB8 134 BK72
St. Helen's Coll, Uxb. UB10 off Parkway 135 BP66
St. Helens Ct, Epp. CM16 off Hemnall St 70 EU30
Rainham RM13 147 FG70
St. Helens Cres, SW16 off St. Helens Rd 201 DM95
St. Helens Gdns, W10 6 A6
St. Helens Pl, EC3 11 L7
St. Helen's RC Inf Sch, Brwd. CM14 off Queens Rd 108 FX47
E17 off Shernhall St 123 EC57
St. Helen's RC Jun Sch, Brwd. CM15 off Sawyers Hall La 108 FX45
St. Helen's RC Prim Sch, E13 15 L3
SW9 off Knowle Cl 161 DN83
St. Helens Rd, SW16 201 DM95
St. Helen's Rd, W13 off Dane Rd 137 CH74
St. Helens Rd, Erith DA18 166 EX75
Ilford IG1 125 EM58
St. Helen's Sch, Nthwd. HA6 off Eastbury Rd 93 BS51
ST. HELIER, Cars. SM5 200 DD101
St. Helier 200 DA100
St. Helier Av, Mord. SM4 200 DC101
St. Helier Hosp, Cars. SM5 200 DC102
St. Helier Rd, St.Alb. (Sand.) AL4 43 CH15
St. Heliers Av, Houns. TW3 176 CA85
St. Heliers Rd, E10 123 EC58
St. Hildas Av, Ashf. TW15 174 BL92
St. Hildas Cl, NW6 139 CX66
SW17 180 DE89
Horley RH6 269 DH148
St. Hilda's Rd, SW13 159 CV79
St. Hilda's Sch, Bushey WD23 off High St 94 CB45
St. Hilda's Way, Grav. DA12 191 GK91
St. Huberts Cl, Ger.Cr. SL9 112 AY60
St. Huberts La, Ger.Cr. SL9 113 AZ61
St. Hughe's Cl, SW17 off College Gdns 180 DE89
St. Hughs Rd, SE20 off Ridsdale Rd 202 DV95
St. Ignatious RC Prim Sch, N15 off St. Ann's Rd 122 DT58
St. Ignatius Coll, Enf. EN1 off Turkey St 82 DV37
St. Ignatius RC Prim Sch, Sun. TW16 off Green St 195 BU95
St. Ives Cl, Rom. RM3 106 FM52
St. Ivians Dr, Rom. RM2 127 FG55
St. James' & St. Michael's C of E Prim Sch, W2 7 M9
St. James Av, N20 98 DE48
W13 137 CG74
Epsom KT17 217 CT111
Sutton SM1 218 DA106
St. James Catholic High Sch, NW9 off Great Strand 97 CT53
St. James Cl, N20 98 DE48
SE18 off Congleton Gro 165 EQ78
Barnet EN4 80 DD42
Epsom KT18 216 CS114
New Malden KT3 199 CT99
Ruislip HA4 116 BW61
Woking GU21 226 AU118
St. James' C of E Jun Sch, E7 off Tower Hamlets Rd 124 EG64
St. James C of E Prim Sch, N10 off Woodside Av 120 DG56
St. James' C of E Prim Sch, Enf. EN3 off Frederick Cres 82 DW40
Harlow CM18 off Paringdon Rd 51 ER19
St. James C of E Prim Sch, Wey. KT13 off Grotto Rd 195 BQ104
St. James Ct, Green. DA9 189 FT86
St. James Gdns, Rom. (Lt.Hth) RM6 126 EV56
Wembley HA0 137 CK66
St. James Gate, NW1 off St. Paul's Cres 141 DK66
St. James Gro, SW11 off Reform St 160 DF82
St. James Indep Sch, Sen Girls Sch, W14 16 D7
Sen Boys, Twick. TW1 off Cross Deep 177 CG89
St. James La, Green. DA9 189 FS88
St. James Ms, E14 24 D6
E17 off St. James's St 123 DY57
St. James Ms, Wey. KT13 213 BP105
St. James Oaks, Grav. DA11 191 GG87
St. James Pl, Dart. DA1 off Spital St 188 FK86
Slough SL1 off Greenfern Av 130 AJ72
St. James' RC Prim Sch, Orp. BR5 off Maybury Cl 205 EP99
St. James Rd, E15 124 EF64
N9 off Queens Rd 100 DV47
Brentwood CM14 108 FW48
Carshalton SM5 200 DE104
Kingston upon Thames KT1 198 CL96
Mitcham CR4 180 DG94
Purley CR8 219 DP113
Sevenoaks TN13 257 FH122
Surbiton KT6 197 CK100
Sutton SM1 218 DA106
Waltham Cross (Chsht) EN7 66 DQ28
Watford WD18 75 BV43
ST. JAMES'S, SW1 19 K2
St. James's, SE14 163 DY81
St. James's & Lucie Clayton Coll, SW5 17 L8
St. James's Av, E2 142 DW68
Beckenham BR3 203 DY97
Gravesend DA11 191 GG87
Hampton (Hmptn H.) TW12 176 CC92
St. James's Cl, SW17 off St. James's Dr 180 DF89
St. James's C of E Prim Sch, SE16 22 A5
St. James's Cotts, Rich. TW9 off Paradise Rd 177 CK85
St. James's Ct, SW1 19 K5
St. James's Cres, SW9 161 DN83
St. James's Dr, SW12 180 DF88
SW17 180 DF88
St. James's Gdns, W11 16 C1
St. James's Hatcham C of E Prim Sch, SE14 off St. James's 163 DY81
St. James's La, N10 121 DH56
St. James's Mkt, SW1 9 L10
★ St. James's Palace, SW1 19 K3
★ St. James's Park, SW1 19 L3
St. James's Park 19 L5
St. James's Pk, Croy. CR0 202 DQ101
St. James's Pas, EC3 11 M8
St. James's Pl, SW1 19 J2
St. James's RC Prim Sch, Twick. TW2 off Stanley Rd 177 CD90
St. James's Rd, SE1 22 B9
SE16 22 B5
Croydon CR0 201 DP101
Gravesend DA11 191 GG86
Hampton (Hmptn H.) TW12 176 CB92
St. James's Sq, SW1 19 K1
St. James's St, E17 123 DY57
SW1 19 J1
Gravesend DA11 191 GG86
St. James's Ter, NW8 off Prince Albert Rd 140 DF68
St. James's Ter Ms, NW8 140 DF67
St. James Street 123 DY57
St. James St, W6 159 CW78
St. James's Wk, EC1 10 E3
St. James the Gt RC Prim Sch, SE15 off Peckham Rd 162 DT81
Thornton Heath CR7 off Windsor Rd 201 DP96
St. James Wk, Iver SL0 153 BE75
St. James Way, Sid. DA14 186 EY92
St. Jeromes Gro, Hayes UB3 135 BQ72
St. Joachim's RC Prim Sch, E16 off Shipman Rd 144 EJ72
St. Joan of Arc RC Prim Sch, N5 off Northolme Rd 122 DQ63
St. Joan of Arc RC Sch, Rick. WD3 off High St 92 BL45
St. Joans Rd, N9 100 DT46
St. John & St. James Prim Sch, E9 off Mehetabel Rd 122 DW64
St. John Evangelist RC Prim Sch, N1 4 E9
St. John Fisher RC First & Mid Sch, Pnr. HA5 off Melrose Rd 116 CA56
St. John Fisher RC JMI Sch, St.Alb. AL4 off Hazelmere Rd 43 CJ17
St. John Fisher RC Prim Sch, SW20 off Grand Dr 199 CX99
Erith DA18 off Kale Rd 166 EY76
Inf Dept, Grnf. UB6 off Sarsfield Rd 137 CJ68
Jun Dept, Grnf. UB6 off Thirlmere Av 137 CJ69
Loughton IG10 off Burney Dr 85 EQ40
St. John Fisher Rd, Erith DA18 166 EX76
St. John of Jerusalem C of E JMI Sch, E9 off Ainsworth Rd 142 DW66
St. John Rigby Catholic Coll, W.Wick. BR4 off Layhams Rd 221 ED105
ST. JOHN'S, SE8 163 EA82
ST. JOHN'S, Wok. GU21 226 AV118
St. John's 163 EA82
St. Johns, Dor. (N.Holm.) RH5 263 CH140
St. John's, Red. RH1 266 DE136
St. John's & St. Clement's C of E Prim Sch, SE15 off Adys Rd 162 DU83
St. Johns & St. James C of E Prim Sch, N18 off Grove St 100 DT50
St. John's (Angell Town) C of E Prim Sch, SW9 off Angell Rd 161 DN82
St. Johns Av, N11 98 DF50
St. John's Av, NW10 139 CT67
SW15 179 CX85
St. Johns Av, Brwd. CM14 108 FX49
St. John's Av, Epsom KT17 217 CT112
Harlow CM17 36 EW11

London Underground station | Docklands Light Railway station | Tramlink station | Pedestrian ferry landing stage

St. Johns Av, Lthd. KT22 231 CH121
Sch St. John's Beaumont Prep Sch, Wind. SL4
off Priest Hill 172 AV89
St. John's Ch Rd, E9 122 DW64
Dorking (Wotton) RH5
off Coast Hill 262 BZ139
St. Johns Cl, N14
off Chase Rd 81 DJ44
St. John's Cl, SW6
off Dawes Rd 160 DA80
Guildford GU2
off St. John's Rd 258 AU135
St. Johns Cl, Hem.H. HP1
off Anchor La 40 BH22
Leatherhead KT22 231 CJ120
St. John's Cl, Pot.B. EN6 64 DC33
St. Johns Cl, Rain. RM13 147 FG66
St. John's Cl, Uxb. UB8 134 BH67
Wembley HA9 118 CL64
St. Johns Cl, West. (Berry's Grn) TN16
off St. Johns Ri 239 EP116
Sch St. John's C of E Inf Sch, NW4 off Prothero Gdns 119 CV57
Sch St. John's C of E Jun Sch, Cat. CR3
off Markfield Rd 252 DV125
Sch St. John's C of E Mid Sch, Stan. HA7 off Green La 95 CG49
Sch St. John's C of E Prim Sch, N11 off Crescent Rd 98 DF49
N20 off Swan La 98 DC47
SE20 off Maple Rd 182 DW94
SW6 off Filmer Rd 159 CY81
Buckhurst Hill IG9
off High Rd 102 EH46
Croydon CR0
off Spring Pk Rd 203 DX104
Enfield EN2
off Theobalds Pk Rd 81 DP37
Kingston upon Thames KT1 off Portland Rd 198 CL97
Sevenoaks TN13
off Bayham Rd 257 FK123
Sch St. John's C of E (VA) First Sch, Stan. HA7
off Embry Way 95 CH49
St. John's Cotts, SE20
off Maple Rd 182 DW94
St. Johns Cotts, Rich. TW9
off Kew Foot Rd 158 CL84
Sch St. John's Co Prim Sch, Red. RH1
off Pendleton Rd 266 DE136
St. Johns Ct, Buck.H. IG9 102 EH46
St. John's Ct, Egh. TW20 173 BA92
St. Johns Ct, Hert. SG14
off St. John's St 32 DR09
St. John's Ct, Islw. TW7 157 CF82
St. Johns Ct, Nthwd. HA6
off Murray Rd 93 BS53
St. Albans AL1 43 CH19
St. John's Ct, Wok. GU21
off St. Johns Hill Rd 226 AU119
St. John's Cres, SW9 161 DN83
St. Johns Dr, SW18 180 DB88
Walton-on-Thames KT12 196 BW102
Windsor SL4 151 AM82
St. John's Est, N1 5 K10
SE1 21 N3
St. John's Gdns, W11 6 E10
★ St. John's Gate & Mus of the Order of St. John, EC1 10 E4
St. Johns Gro, N19 121 DJ61
SW13 off Terrace Gdns 159 CT82
Richmond TW9
off Kew Foot Rd 158 CL84
Sch St. John's Highbury Vale C of E Prim Sch, N5
off Conewood St 121 DP62
St. John's Hill, SW11 160 DD84
Coulsdon CR5 235 DN117
Purley CR8 235 DN116
Sevenoaks TN13 257 FJ123
St. John's Hill Gro, SW11 160 DD84
St. Johns Hill Rd, Wok. GU21 226 AU119
Sch St. John's Inf Sch, Rad. WD7 off Gills Hill La 77 CF36
★ St. John's Jerusalem, Dart. DA4 188 FP94
St. John's La, EC1 10 E4
Ware (Gt Amwell) SG12 33 EA09
St. John's Lye, Wok. GU21 226 AT119
St. John's Ms, W11 6 G8
Woking GU21 226 AU119
St. Johns Par, Sid. DA14 186 EU91
St. John's Pk, SE3 164 EF80
St. John's Pas, SW19
off Ridgway Pl 179 CY93
St. John's Path, EC1 10 E4
St. Johns Pathway, SE23
off Devonshire Rd 182 DW88
St. John's Pl, EC1 10 E4
Sch St. John's Prep Sch, Pot.B. EN6 off The Ridgeway 64 DE34
Sch St. John's Prim Sch, E2
off Peel Gro 142 DW68
W13 off Felix Rd 137 CG73
Woking GU21
off Victoria Rd 226 AS118
Sch St. John's RC Comp Sch, Grav. DA12
off Rochester Rd 191 GK88
Sch St. John's RC Prim Sch, SE16 23 J4
Gravesend DA12
off Rochester Rd 191 GK87
Rickmansworth WD3
off Berry La 92 BH46
St. Johns Ri, West. (Berry's Grn) TN16 239 EP116
Woking GU21 226 AV119
St. John's Rd, E4 101 EB48
E6 off Ron Leighton Way 144 EL67
St. Johns Rd, E16 15 L7
St. John's Rd, E17 101 EB54
N15 122 DS58
St. Johns Rd, NW11 119 CZ58
St. John's Rd, SE20 182 DW94
SW11 160 DE84
SW19 179 CY94
Barking IG11 145 ES67
Carshalton SM5 200 DE104
St. Johns Rd, Croy. CR0
off Sylverdale Rd 201 DP104
St. John's Rd, Dart. DA2 188 FQ87
St. John's Rd, Dor. (Westc.) RH4 262 CC137
St. Johns Rd, E.Mol. KT8 197 CD98
St. John's Rd, Epp. CM16 69 ET30
St. Johns Rd, Erith DA8 167 FD78
St. John's Rd, Felt. TW13 176 BY91
St. Johns Rd, Grav. DA12 191 GK87
Grays RM16 171 GH78
St. John's Rd, Guil. GU2 258 AT135
Harrow HA1 117 CF58
St. Johns Rd, Hem.H. HP1 40 BG22
Ilford IG2 125 ER59
St. John's Rd, Islw. TW7 157 CE82
Kingston upon Thames (Hmptn W.) KT1 197 CJ96
St. Johns Rd, Lthd. KT22 231 CJ121
Loughton IG10 85 EM40
New Malden KT3 198 CQ97
St. John's Rd, Orp. BR5 205 ER100
Redhill RH1 266 DF136
Richmond TW9 158 CL84
St. Johns Rd, Rom. RM5 105 FC50
St. John's Rd, Sev. TN13 257 FH121
St. Johns Rd, Sid. DA14 186 EV91
Slough SL2 132 AU74
Southall UB2 156 BY76
Sutton SM1 200 DA103
Uxbridge UB8 134 BH67
Watford WD17 75 BV40
St. John's Rd, Well. DA16 166 EV83
Wembley HA9 117 CK63
St. Johns Rd, Wind. SL4 151 AN82
St. John's Rd, Wok. GU21 226 AV118
Sch St. John's Sch, Lthd. KT22 off Epsom Rd 231 CH121
Northwood HA6
off Wieland Rd 93 BV51
Woodford Green IG8
off Turpins La 103 EN50
Coll St. John's Seminary, Guil. GU5 off Cranleigh Rd 259 BC144
Sch St. John's Sen Sch, Enf. EN2 off The Ridgeway 80 DG35
St. John's Sq, EC1 10 E4
St. John's St, Gdmg. GU7 258 AT144
Hertford SG14 32 DR09
St. Johns Ter, E7 144 EH65
SE18 165 EQ79
SW15 off Kingston Vale 178 CR91
W10 6 B3
St. John's Ter, Enf. EN2 82 DR37
Redhill RH1
off St. John's Ter Rd 266 DF136
St. John's Ter Rd, Red. RH1 266 DF136
St. John St, EC1 10 F4
Sch St. John's Upr Holloway C of E Prim Sch, N19
off Pemberton Gdns 121 DK61
St. Johns Vale, SE8 163 EA82
Sch St. John's (VC) C of E Sch, Epp. CM16 off Tower Rd 69 ES30
St. Johns Vil, N19 121 DK61
St. John's Vil, W8 17 K6
Sch St. John's VA C of E Prim Sch, Welw. AL6
off Hertford Rd 29 CZ05
Welwyn Garden City AL8
off Lemsford Village 29 CT10
St. Johns Wk, Harl. CM17 36 EW11
Sch St. John's Walworth C of E Prim Sch, SE17 21 H8
St. John's Waterside, Wok. GU21 off Copse Rd 226 AU118
St. Johns Way, N19 121 DK60
St. Johns Well Ct, Berk. HP4 38 AV18
St. Johns Well La, Berk. HP4 38 AV18
ST. JOHN'S WOOD, NW8 7 N1
⊖ St. John's Wood 140 DD68
St. John's Wd Ct, NW8 7 P2
St. John's Wd High St, NW8 140 DD68
St. John's Wd Pk, NW8 140 DD67
St. John's Wd Rd, NW8 7 N3
St. John's Wd Ter, NW8 140 DD68
Sch St. John the Baptist C of E Jun Sch, Kings.T. KT1
off Lower Teddington Rd 177 CK94
Sch St. John the Baptist C of E Prim Sch, Ware SG12
off Hillside La 33 EA10
Sch St. John the Baptist Hoxton C of E JMI Sch, N1 5 L10
Sch St. John the Baptist RC Jun Sch, E2
off Waterloo Gdns 142 DW68
Sch St. John the Baptist Sch, Wok. GU22
off Elmbridge La 227 BA119
Sch St. John the Baptist Southend C of E Prim Sch, Brom. BR1
off Beachborough Rd 183 EC91
Sch St. John the Divine C of E Prim Sch, SE5
off Warham St 161 DP80
Sch St. John Vianney RC Prim Sch, N15 off Stanley Rd 121 DP56
Sch St. Joseph's Acad, SE3
off Lee Ter 164 EE83
Sch St. Joseph's Catholic High Sch, Slou. SL2
off Shaggy Calf La 132 AU73
Sch St. Joseph's Catholic Prim Sch, Epsom KT18
off Rosebank 216 CQ114
St. Josephs Cl, W10 6 D6
St. Joseph's Cl, Orp. BR6 223 ET105
Coll St. Joseph's Coll, NW7
off Lawrence St 97 CT49
SE19 off Beulah Hill 181 DP93
Sch St. Joseph's Conv Prep Sch, Grav. DA12
off Old Rd E 191 GJ89
Sch St. Joseph's Conv Sch, E11 off Cambridge Pk 124 EG58
St. Joseph's Ct, SE7 164 EH79
St. Josephs Dr, Sthl. UB1 136 BY74
St. Joseph's Gro, NW4 119 CV56
Sch St. Joseph's in the Pk, Hert. SG14 off St. Mary's La 31 DN11
St. Joseph's Ms, Beac. HP9 89 AM53
Sch St. Joseph's Prim Sch, SW3 18 C8
Sch St. Joseph's RC Comb Sch, Ger.Cr. SL9
off Priory Rd 112 AW55
Sch St. Joseph's RC First & Mid Sch, Har. HA3
off Dobbin Cl 95 CG54
Sch St. Joseph's RC Inf & Jun Sch, SE5 off Pitman St 162 DQ80
Sch St. Joseph's RC Inf Sch, E10 off Marsh La 123 EA61
NW4 off Watford Way 119 CV56
SE19 off Crown Dale 182 DQ93
Sch St. Joseph's RC Inf Sch, Wem. HA9
off Waverley Av 118 CM64
Sch St. Joseph's RC JM Sch, SE19 off Woodend 182 DQ93
Sch St. Joseph's RC Jun Sch, E10 off Vicarage Rd 123 EB60
NW4 off Watford Way 119 CV56
Guildford GU2
off Aldershot Rd 242 AT132
Wembley HA9
off Chatsworth Av 118 CM64
Sch St. Joseph's RC Prim Sch, N19 off Highgate Hill 121 DH60
NW10 off Goodson Rd 138 CS66
SE1 21 H3
SE8 off Crossfield St 163 EA80
SE10 25 H9
SE16 (Bermondsey) 22 A4
SE16 (Rotherhithe) 22 F6
SW15 off Oakhill Rd 180 DA85
W7 off York Av 137 CE74
W9 7 L2
WC2 9 P7
Bark. IG11
off Broadway 145 EQ67
Dag. RM9
off Connor Rd 126 EZ63
Dartford DA1 off Old Rd 167 FE84
Dorking RH4
off Norfolk Rd 263 CG136
Gravesend DA11
off Springhead Rd 190 GD87
Hertford SG14
off North Rd 31 DN08
Kingston upon Thames KT1 off Fairfield S 198 CM96
Redhill RH1
off Linkfield La 250 DE133
Upminster RM14
off St. Mary's La 128 FP61
Waltham Cross EN8
off Royal Av 67 DY32
Watford WD19
off Ainsdale Rd 94 BW48
Sch St. Joseph's RC (VA) Prim Sch, Brom. BR1
off Plaistow La 184 EH94
St. Josephs Rd, N9 100 DV45
St. Joseph's Rd, Wal.Cr. EN8 67 DY33
St. Josephs St, SW8
off Battersea Pk Rd 161 DH81
St. Joseph's Vale, SE3 163 ED82
Sch St. Joseph the Worker RC Prim Sch, Brwd.
CM13 off Highview Cres 109 GC44
Sch St. Jude's & St. Paul's C of E Prim Sch, N1 5 L3
St. Judes Cl, Egh. TW20 172 AW92
Sch St. Jude's C of E Prim Sch, SE1 20 E5
SE24 off Regent Rd 181 DP85
Sch St. Jude's C of E Sch, Egh. TW20 off Bagshot Rd 172 AW93
St. Jude's Rd, E2 142 DV68
Egham TW20 172 AW90
St. Jude St, N16 5 M2
ST. JULIANS, St.Alb. AL1 43 CD23
St. Julians, Sev. TN15 257 FN128
St. Julian's Cl, SW16 181 DN91
St. Julian's Fm Rd, SE27 181 DN91
St. Julian's Rd, NW6 139 CZ66
St. Julians Rd, St.Alb. AL1 43 CD22
St. Justin Cl, Orp. BR5 206 EX97
★ St. Katharine's Dock, E1 11 P10
Riv St. Katharine's Pier 21 N1
St. Katharines Prec, NW1
off Outer Circle 141 DH68
St. Katharine's Way, E1 21 P1
Sch St. Katherine's Knockholt C of E Prim Sch, Sev.
TN14 off Main Rd 240 EV117
St. Katherines Rd, Cat. CR3 252 DU125
Erith DA18 166 EX75
St. Katherine's Row, EC3 11 M8
St. Katherine's Wk, W11 16 B1
St. Katherines Way, Berk. HP4 38 AT16
St. Keverne Rd, SE9 184 EL91
St. Kilda Rd, W13 137 CG74
Orpington BR6 205 ET102
St. Kilda's Rd, N16 122 DR60
Brentwood CM15 108 FV45
Harrow HA1 117 CE58
St. Kitts Ter, SE19 182 DS92
St. Laurence Cl, NW6 139 CX67
Orpington BR5 206 EX97
Uxbridge UB8 134 BJ71
Sch St. Laurence C of E Jun Sch, Uxb. UB8
off Worcester Rd 134 BK71
St. Laurence Dr, Brox. EN10 49 DZ23
St. Laurence Way, Slou. SL1 152 AU76
St. Lawrence Cl, Abb.L. WD5 59 BS30
Edgware HA8 96 CM52
Hemel Hempstead (Bov.) HP3 57 BA27
Sch St. Lawrence C of E (Aided) Jun Sch, E.Mol. KT8
off Church Rd 196 CC97
St. Lawrence Dr, Pnr. HA5 115 BV58
★ St. Lawrence Jewry Ch, EC2 11 H7
Sch St. Lawrence Prim Sch, Felt. TW13
off Victoria Rd 175 BV88
Leatherhead KT24
off Lower Rd 246 BX127
St. Lawrence Rd, Upmin. RM14 128 FQ61
St. Lawrence St, E14 24 D1
St. Lawrence's Way, Reig. RH2 off Church St 250 DA134
St. Lawrence Ter, W10 6 C5
St. Lawrence Way, SW9 161 DN81
Caterham CR3 236 DQ123
St. Albans (Brick.Wd) AL2 60 BZ30
St. Leonards Av, E4 101 ED51
Harrow HA3 117 CJ56
Windsor SL4 151 AQ82
St. Leonards Cl, Bushey WD23 76 BY42
Grays RM17 170 FZ79
Hertford SG14 32 DS07
St. Leonard's Cl, Well. DA16 off Hook La 166 EU83
Sch St. Leonard's C of E Prim Sch, SW16
off Mitcham La 181 DK92
St. Leonards Ct, N1 11 H1
St. Leonard's Gdns, Houns. TW5 156 BY80
St. Leonards Gdns, Ilf. IG1 125 EQ64
St. Leonards Hill, Wind. SL4 151 AK84
St. Leonards Ri, Orp. BR6 223 ES105
St. Leonards Rd, E14 14 B6
NW10 138 CR70
St. Leonard's Rd, SW14 158 CP83
St. Leonards Rd, W13 137 CJ73
Amersham HP6 55 AS35
Croydon CR0 201 DP104
Epsom KT18 233 CW119
Esher (Clay.) KT10 215 CF107
Hertford SG14 32 DR07
St. Leonard's Rd, Surb. KT6 197 CK99
St. Leonards Rd, T.Ditt. KT7 197 CG100
Waltham Abbey EN9 68 EE25
Windsor SL4 151 AQ82
St. Leonards Sq, NW5 140 DG65
St. Leonard's Sq, Surb. KT6
off St. Leonard's Rd 197 CK99
St. Leonards St, E3 14 B1
St. Leonard's Ter, SW3 18 C10
St. Leonards Wk, SW16 181 DM94
Iver SL0 153 BF76
St. Leonards Way, Horn. RM11 127 FH61
St. Loo Av, SW3 160 DE79
St. Louis Rd, SE27 182 DQ91
St. Loy's Rd, N17 100 DS54
St. Lucia Dr, E15 144 EF67
St. Luke Cl, Uxb. UB8 134 BK72
ST. LUKE'S, EC1 11 H3
St. Luke's Av, SW4 161 DK84
St. Lukes Av, Enf. EN2 82 DR38
St. Luke's Av, Ilf. IG1 125 EP64
St. Luke's Cl, EC1 11 H3
SE25 202 DV100
St. Lukes Cl, Dart. (Lane End) DA2 189 FS92
Swanley BR8 207 FD96
Sch St. Luke's C of E Prim Sch, EC1 11 H2
SE27 off Linton Gro 182 DQ92
W9 6 E1
Kingston upon Thames KT2 off Acre Rd 198 CM95
Sch St. Luke's C of E (VA) Prim Sch, E16 15 K7
St. Luke's Est, EC1 11 J2
H St. Luke's Hosp for the Clergy, W1 9 J4
Sch St. Luke's Ho Sch, Rich. TW9
off Sandycombe Rd 158 CN82
St. Lukes Ms, W11 6 F7
Sch St. Luke's Prim Sch, E14 24 E8
Sch St. Luke's RC Prim Sch, Harl. CM19
off Pyenest Rd 51 EQ17
St. Lukes Rd, W11 6 F6
Uxbridge UB10 134 BL66
Whyteleafe CR3
off Whyteleafe Hill 236 DT118
Windsor (Old Wind.) SL4 172 AU86
Sch St. Luke's Sch, Loug. IG10 off Borders La 85 EN42
St. Lukes Sq, E16 15 K8
Guildford GU1 259 AZ135
St. Luke's St, SW3 18 A9
H St. Luke's Woodside Hosp, N10 120 DG56
St. Luke's Yd, W9 139 CZ68
St. Malo Av, N9 100 DW48
Sch St. Margaret Clitherow RC Prim Sch, NW10
off Quainton St 118 CR63
SE28 off Cole Cl 146 EV74
St. Margaret Dr, Epsom KT18 216 CR114
ST. MARGARETS, Twick. TW1 177 CG85
ST. MARGARETS, Ware SG12 33 EB10
⇌ St. Margarets (Twick. TW1) 177 CH86
⇌ St. Margarets (Ware SG12) 33 EC11
St. Margarets, Bark. IG11 145 ER67
Guildford GU1 243 AZ133
St. Margarets Av, N15 121 DP56
N20 98 DC47
Ashford TW15 175 BP92
Harrow HA2 116 CC62
Sidcup DA15 185 ER90
St. Margaret's Av, Sutt. SM3 199 CY104
St. Margarets Av, Uxb. UB8 134 BN70
Westerham (Berry's Grn) TN16 off Berry's Grn Rd 239 EP116
St. Margarets Cl, EC2
off Lothbury 142 DR72
Berkhamsted HP4 38 AX20
Dartford DA2 189 FR89
High Wycombe (Penn) HP10 88 AC47
Iver SL0
off St. Margarets Gate 133 BD68
Orpington BR6 224 EV105
Sch St. Margaret's C of E Prim Sch, SE18
off St. Margaret's Gro 165 EQ78
Barking IG11 off North St 145 EQ66
St. Margaret's Ct, SE1 21 H2
St. Margaret's Cres, SW15 179 CV85
Gravesend DA12 191 GL90
St. Margaret's Dr, Twick. TW1 177 CH85
St. Margarets Gate, Iver SL0 133 BD68
St. Margaret's Gro, E11 124 EF62
SE18 165 EQ79
St. Margarets Gro, Twick. TW1 177 CG86
H St. Margaret's Hosp, Epp. CM16 70 EV29
St. Margarets La, W8 17 J6
Sch St. Margaret's Lee C of E Prim Sch, SE13
off Lee Ch St 164 EE84
St. Margarets Pas, SE13
off Church Ter 164 EE83
St. Margarets Path, SE18 165 EQ78
St. Margarets Rd, E12 124 EJ61
St. Margaret's Rd, N17 122 DS55
NW10 139 CW69
St. Margarets Rd, SE4 163 DZ84
W7 157 CE75
Coulsdon CR5 235 DH121
Dartford (S.Darenth) DA2, DA4 189 FS93
Edgware HA8 96 CP50
St. Margaret's Rd, Grav. (Nthflt) DA11 190 GE89
St. Margarets Rd, Islw. TW7 157 CH84
St. Margaret's Rd, Ruis. HA4 115 BR58
St. Margarets Rd, Twick. TW1 157 CH84
St. Margaret's Rd, Ware SG12 33 EA13
Sch St. Margaret's Sch, NW3
off Kidderpore Gdns 120 DB63
Bushey WD23
off Merry Hill Rd 94 CA45
Tadworth KT20
off Tadworth Ct 233 CX121
St. Margarets Sq, SE4
off Adelaide Av 163 DZ84
St. Margaret's St, SW1 19 N4
St. Margaret's Ter, SE18 165 EQ78
St. Margarets Way, Hem.H. HP2 41 BR20
St. Marks Av, Grav. (Nthflt) DA11 191 GF87
Sch St. Mark's Catholic Sch, Houns. TW3
off Bath Rd 156 BZ83
St. Marks Cl, SE10
off Ashburnham Gro 163 EC80
SW6 off Ackmar Rd 160 DA81
W11 6 C8
St. Mark's Cl, Barn. EN5 80 DB41
St. Marks Cl, Har. HA1
off Nightingale Av 117 CH59
St. Albans (Coln.Hth) AL4 44 CP22
Sch St. Mark's C of E Prim Sch, N19 off Sussex Way 121 DL61
SE11 off Harleyford Rd 161 DM79
SE25 off Albert Rd 202 DU98
Bromley BR2
off Aylesbury Rd 204 EG97
St. Marks Cres, NW1 140 DG67
St. Mark's Gate, E9
off Cadogan Ter 143 DZ66
St. Mark's Gro, SW10 160 DB79
St. Mark's Hill, Surb. KT6 198 CL100
St. Mark's Pl, SW19
off Wimbledon Hill Rd 179 CZ93
St. Marks Pl, W11 6 D8
Windsor SL4 151 AQ82
Sch St. Mark's Prim Sch, W7
off Lower Boston Rd 157 CE75
Mitcham CR4
off St. Marks Rd 200 DF96
St. Marks Ri, E8 5 P2
St. Marks Rd, SE25
off Coventry Rd 202 DU98
St. Mark's Rd, W5
off The Common 138 CL74
St. Marks Rd, W7 157 CE75
W10 6 B7
W11 6 C8
Bromley BR2 204 EH97
Enfield EN1 82 DT44
St. Mark's Rd, Epsom KT18 233 CW118
St. Marks Rd, Mitch. CR4 200 DF96
St. Mark's Rd, Tedd. TW11 177 CH94
St. Marks Rd, Wind. SL4 151 AQ82
St. Marks Sq, NW1 140 DG67
St. Mark St, E1 11 P8
Sch St. Mark's W Essex Catholic Sch, Harl.
CM18 off Tripton Rd 51 ES16
St. Martha's Av, Wok. GU22 227 AZ121
Sch St. Martha's Conv Jun Sch (Indep), Barn. EN5
off Wood St 79 CY42
Sch St. Martha's Conv Sch, Barn. EN4
off Camlet Way 80 DA39
St. Martin Cl, Uxb. UB8 134 BK72
★ St. Martin-in-the-Fields Ch, WC2 9 N10
Sch St. Martin-in-the-Fields High Sch for Girls, SW2
off Tulse Hill 181 DN86
Sch St. Martin of Porres RC Prim Sch, N11
off Blake Rd 99 DJ51
St. Martins, Nthwd. HA6 93 BR50
St. Martins App, Ruis. HA4 115 BS59
St. Martins Av, E6 144 EK68
Epsom KT18 216 CS114
St. Martins Cl, NW1 141 DJ67
Enfield EN1 82 DV39
Epsom KT17
off Church Rd 216 CS113
Erith DA18
off St. Helens Rd 166 EX75
Leatherhead (E.Hors.) KT24 245 BS129
St. Martin's Cl, Wat. WD19
off Muirfield Rd 94 BW49
West Drayton UB7
off St. Martin's Rd 154 BK76
Sch St. Martin's C of E Inf Sch, Epsom KT18
off Worple Rd 232 CR115
Sch St. Martin's C of E Jun Sch, Epsom KT18
off Ashley Rd 232 CR115
Sch St. Martin's C of E Prim Sch, Dor. RH4
off Pixham La 247 CJ134
, Dor. RH4
off Ranmore Rd 263 CG135
Coll St. Martin's Coll, Tower Hamlets Professional Dev Cen, E3 13 L4
St. Martin's Ct, WC2
off St. Martin's La 141 DK73
Ashford TW15 174 BJ92
St. Martins Dr, Walt. KT12 196 BW104
St. Martins Est, SW2 181 DN88
St. Martin's La, WC2 9 N9
St. Martins La, Beck. BR3 203 EB99
St. Martin's-le-Grand, EC1 10 G7
St. Martins Meadow, West. (Brasted) TN16 240 EW123
St. Martin's Ms, WC2 9 N10
St. Martins Ms, Dor. RH4
off Church St 263 CG136
Woking (Pyrford) GU22 228 BG116
St. Martin's Pl, WC2 9 N10
St. Martins Rd, N9 100 DV47
St. Martin's Rd, SW9 161 DM82
St. Martins Rd, Dart. DA1 188 FM86
St. Martin's Rd, West Dr. UB7 154 BJ76
Sch St. Martin's Sch, Brwd. CM13
off Hanging Hill La 109 GC46
Northwood HA6
off Moor Pk Rd 93 BR50
St. Martin's St, WC2 9 M10
St. Martins Ter, N10
off Pages La 98 DG54
St. Martins Wk, Dor. RH4
off High St 263 CH136
St. Martins Way, SW17 180 DC90
Sch St. Mary Abbots C of E Prim Sch, W8 17 J4
St. Mary Abbots Pl, W8 16 F6
St. Mary Abbots Ter, W14 16 F6

★ Place of interest | H Hospital | Sch School | Coll College | Uni University | ⇌ Railway station

St. Mary & All Saints C of E Prim Sch, Beac. HP9 off Maxwell Rd 89 AL52
St. Mary & St. Joseph's RC Sec Sch, Sid. DA14 off Chislehurst Rd 186 EU92
St. Mary & St. Michael Prim Sch, E1 12 E8
St. Mary & St. Pancras C of E Prim Sch, NW1 off Polygon Rd 141 DK68
St. Mary at Hill, EC3 11 L10
★ St. Mary at Hill Ch, EC3 11 L10
St. Mary Av, Wall. SM6 200 DG104
St. Mary Axe, EC3 11 L8
St. Marychurch St, SE16 22 E4
ST. MARY CRAY, Orp. BR5 206 EW99
St. Mary Cray 206 EU98
St. Mary Cray Prim Sch, Orp. BR5 off High St 206 EW100
St. Marylebone C of E Sch, W1 8 F5
★ St. Mary-le-Bow Ch, EC2 11 H8
St. Mary Magdalene C of E Prim Sch, N7 4 C3
SE15 off Godman Rd 162 DV82
St. Mary Magdalene's C of E Prim Sch, W2 7 J5
St. Mary Magdalene's RC Prim Sch, SW14 off Worple St 158 CR83
St. Mary Magdalen's RC Jun Sch, NW2 off Linacre Rd 139 CV65
St. Mary Magdalen's RC Prim Sch, SE4 off Howson Rd 163 DY84
St. Mary of the Angels RC Prim Sch, W2 6 G7
St. Mary Rd, E17 123 EA56
St. Marys, Bark. IG11 145 ER67
St. Mary's & St. Peter's C of E Prim Sch, Tedd. TW11 off Somerset Rd 177 CF92
St. Marys App, E12 125 EM64
St. Marys Av, E11 124 EH58
St. Mary's Av, N3 97 CY54
St. Marys Av, Brwd. (Shenf.) CM15 109 GA43
St. Mary's Av, Brom. BR2 204 EE97
Northwood HA6 93 BS50
Staines (Stanw.) TW19 174 BK87
Teddington TW11 177 CF93
St. Mary's Av Cen, Sthl. UB2 156 CB77
St. Mary's Av N, Sthl. UB2 156 CB77
St. Mary's Av S, Sthl. UB2 156 CB77
St. Mary's Bryanston Sq C of E Prim Sch, W1 8 C5
St. Mary's CE High Sch, NW4 off Downage 119 CW55
St. Mary's Cl, N17 off Kemble Rd 100 DT53
St. Marys Cl, Chess. KT9 216 CM108
Epsom KT17 217 CU108
St. Mary's Cl, Grav. DA12 191 GJ89
St. Marys Cl, Grays RM17 off Dock Rd 170 GD79
St. Mary's Cl, Lthd. (Fetch.) KT22 231 CD123
St. Marys Cl, Orp. BR5 206 EV96
St. Mary's Cl, Oxt. RH8 254 EE129
Staines (Stanw.) TW19 174 BK87
Sunbury-on-Thames TW16 off Green Way 195 BU98
Uxbridge (Hare.) UB9 114 BH55
St. Marys Cl, Wat. WD18 off King St 75 BV42
St. Mary's C of E Comb Sch, Amer. HP7 off School La 55 AP39
St. Mary's C of E High Sch, Wal.Cr. EN8 off Churchgate 66 DV30
St. Mary's C of E Inf Sch, N8 off Church La 121 DM56
Leatherhead KT22 off Fortyfoot Rd 231 CJ122
St. Mary's C of E Jun Sch, N8 off Rectory Gdns 121 DL56
NW4 off Prothero Gdns 119 CV57
Oxted RH8 off Silkham Rd 254 EE128
Staines TW19 off Clare Rd 174 BL86
St. Mary's C of E Prim Sch, E17 off The Drive 123 EB56
N1 4 F7
N3 off Dollis Pk 97 CZ52
NW10 off Garnet Rd 138 CS65
SE13 off Lewisham High St 183 EC85
SE18 off Kingsman St 165 EN77
SW15 off Felsham Rd 159 CX83
Barnet EN4 off Littlegrove 80 DE44
Brentwood CM15 off Hall La 109 FZ44
Chessington KT9 off Church La 216 CL107
Rickmansworth WD3 off Stockers Fm Rd 92 BK48
Slough SL1 off Yew Tree Rd 152 AU76
St. Mary's C. of E Prim Sch, Swan. BR8 off St. Marys Rd 207 FE98
St. Mary's C of E Prim Sch, Twick. TW1 off Amyand Pk Rd 177 CG87
West Byfleet KT14 off Hart Rd 212 BL113
St. Mary's Conv Sch, NW3 off Fitzjohn's Av 120 DD64
St. Mary's Copse, Wor.Pk. KT4 198 CS103
St. Marys Ct, E6 145 EM70
St. Mary's Ct, SE7 164 EK80
W5 off St. Mary's Rd 157 CK75
St. Mary's Cres, NW4 119 CV55
Hayes UB3 135 BT73
St. Marys Cres, Islw. TW7 157 CD80
St. Mary's Cres, Stai. (Stanw.) TW19 174 BK87
St. Marys Dr, Felt. TW14 175 BQ87
St. Mary's Dr, Sev. TN13 256 FE123
St. Mary's Gdns, SE11 20 D7
St. Mary's Gate, W8 17 J6
St. Marys Grn, N2 off Thomas More Way 120 DC55
Westerham (Bigg.H.) TN16 238 EJ118
St. Mary's Gro, N1 4 F4
SW13 159 CV83
W4 158 CP79
Richmond TW9 158 CM84
St. Marys Gro, West. (Bigg.H.) TN16 238 EJ118
St. Mary's Hare Pk Jun Sch, Rom. RM2 off South Dr 128 FJ55
St. Mary's Hosp, W2 7 P7
St. Mary's Jun & Sen Sch, Ger.Cr. SL9 off Packhorse Rd 112 AY56
St. Mary's JMI Sch, Hat. AL9 off Dellsome La 45 CV23
St. Mary's Kilburn C of E Prim Sch, NW6 off Quex Rd 140 DA66
St. Mary's La, Hert. SG14 31 DM11
Upminster RM14 128 FN61
St. Marys Mans, W2 7 N5
St. Mary's Ms, NW6 off Priory Rd 140 DB66
Richmond TW10 177 CJ89
St. Mary's Mt, Cat. CR3 236 DT124
St. Marys Path, N1 4 F7
St. Mary's Pl, SE9 off Eltham High St 185 EN86
W5 off St. Mary's Rd 157 CK75
W8 17 J6
St. Mary's RC High Sch, Croy. CR0 off Woburn Rd 202 DQ102
St. Mary's RC Inf & Jun Sch, Annexe, NW6 off Carlton Vale 140 DA68
St. Mary's RC Inf Sch, N15 off Hermitage Rd 122 DR58
NW6 off Canterbury Rd 140 DA68
Croydon CR0 off Bedford Pk 202 DR102
Carshalton SM5 off West St 218 DF105
St. Mary's RC JMI Sch, Horn. RM12 off Hornchurch Rd 127 FG60
St. Mary's RC Jun Sch, E17 off Shernhall St 123 EC55
N15 off Hermitage Rd 122 DR57
NW6 off Canterbury Rd 140 DA68
Carshalton SM5 off Shorts Rd 218 DF106
Croydon CR0 off Sydenham Rd 202 DR102
St. Mary's RC Prim Sch, E4 off Station Rd 101 ED46
SE9 off Glenure Rd 185 EN85
SW4 off Crescent La 161 DJ84
SW8 off Lockington Rd 161 DH81
SW19 off Russell Rd 180 DA94
W4 off Duke Rd 158 CS78
W10 6 C4
W14 16 B6
Enfield EN3 off Durants Rd 83 DX42
Islw. TW7 off South St 157 CG83
Tilbury RM18 off Calcutta Rd 171 GF82
Uxbridge UB8 off Rockingham Cl 134 BJ67
St. Mary's RC (VA) Prim Sch, Beck. BR3 off Westgate Rd 183 EC94
St. Marys Rd, E10 123 EC62
E13 144 EH68
N8 off High St 121 DL56
N9 100 DW46
St. Mary's Rd, NW10 138 CS67
St. Marys Rd, NW11 119 CY59
St. Mary's Rd, SE15 162 DW81
SE25 202 DS97
SW19 (Wimbledon) 179 CY92
W5 157 CK75
Barnet EN4 98 DF45
Bexley DA5 187 FC88
St. Marys Rd, E.Mol. KT8 197 CD99
St. Mary's Rd, Grays RM16 171 GH77
Greenhithe DA9 189 FS85
Hayes UB3 135 BT73
Hemel Hempstead HP2 40 BK19
St. Marys Rd, Ilf. IG1 125 EQ61
Leatherhead KT22 231 CH122
Reigate RH2 266 DB135
St. Mary's Rd, Slou. SL3 132 AY74
South Croydon CR2 220 DR110
St. Marys Rd, Surb. KT6 197 CK100
Surbiton (Long Dit.) KT6 197 CJ101
Swanley BR8 207 FD98
St. Mary's Rd, Uxb. (Denh.) UB9 113 BF58
Uxbridge (Hare.) UB9 114 BH56
Waltham Cross (Chsht) EN8 66 DW29
Watford WD18 75 BV42
St. Marys Rd, Wey. KT13 213 BR105
St. Mary's Rd, Wok. GU21 226 AW117
Worcester Park KT4 198 CS103
St. Marys Sq, W2 7 N5
St. Mary's Sq, W5 off St. Mary's Rd 157 CK75
St. Mary's Stoke Newington C of E JMI Sch, N16 off Lordship Rd 122 DS61
St. Marys Ter, W2 7 N5
St. Mary's Twr, EC1 off Fortune St 142 DQ70
St. Mary St, SE18 165 EM77
St. Mary's Uni Coll, Twick. TW1 off Waldegrave Rd 177 CF90
St. Marys Vw, Har. HA3 117 CJ57
St. Mary's Vw, Wat. WD18 off King St 76 BW42
St. Mary's Wk, SE11 20 D7
Hayes UB3 off St. Mary's Rd 135 BT73
Redhill (Bletch.) RH1 252 DR133
St. Marys Wk, St.Alb. AL4 43 CH16
St. Mary's Way, Chesh. HP5 54 AP31
Chigwell IG7 103 EN50
Gerrards Cross (Chal.St.P.) SL9 90 AX54
Guildford GU2 242 AS132
St. Matthew Cl, Uxb. UB8 134 BK72
St. Matthew's Av, Surb. KT6 198 CL102
St. Matthews Cl, Rain. RM13 147 FG66
Watford WD19 76 BX44
St. Matthew's C of E (Aided) Inf Sch, Cob. KT11 off Downside Rd 229 BV118
St. Matthew's C of E Prim Sch, SW1 19 M5
Enfield EN3 off South St 82 DW43
St. Matthews C of E Prim Sch, Red. RH1 off Linkfield La 250 DF132
St. Matthew's C of E Prim Sch, Surb. KT6 off Langley Rd 198 CL101
West Drayton UB7 off High St 134 BL74
St. Matthew's Dr, Brom. BR1 205 EM97
St. Matthews Prim Sch, SW20 off Cottenham Pk Rd 199 CU95
St. Matthew's Rd, SW2 161 DM84
St. Matthews Rd, W5 off The Common 138 CL74
St. Matthew's Rd, Red. RH1 250 DF133
St. Matthew's Row, E2 12 A2
St. Matthew St, SW1 19 L6
St. Matthias Cl, NW9 119 CT57
St. Matthias C of E JMI Sch, N16 5 L1
St. Matthias C of E Prim Sch, E2 11 P3
St. Maur Rd, SW6 159 CZ81
St. Mellion Cl, SE28 off Redbourne Dr 146 EX72
St. Merryn Cl, SE18 165 ER80
St. Meryl JMI Sch, Wat. WD19 off The Mead 94 BY48
St. Michael at Bowes C of E Jun Sch, N13 off Tottenhall Rd 99 DN51
St. Michael's All, EC3 11 K8
St. Michael's & St. Martin's RC Prim Sch, Houns. TW4 off Belgrave Rd 156 BZ83
St. Michaels Av, N9 100 DW45
Hemel Hempstead HP3 41 BP21
St. Michael's Av, Wem. HA9 138 CN65
St. Michael's Camden Town C of E Prim Sch, NW1 off Camden St 141 DJ67
St. Michael's Catholic Gram Sch, N12 off Nether St 98 DC50
St. Michael's Catholic High Sch, Wat. WD25 off High Elms La 60 BX32
St. Michaels Cl, E16 off Fulmer Rd 144 EK71
St. Michael's Cl, N3 97 CZ54
St. Michaels Cl, N12 98 DE50
Bromley BR1 204 EL97
Erith DA18 off St. Helens Rd 166 EX75
Harlow CM20 35 ES14
South Ockendon (Aveley) RM15 148 FQ73
Walton-on-Thames KT12 196 BW103
Worcester Park KT4 199 CT103
St. Michael's C of E First Sch, Dor. RH5 off School La 247 CJ127
St. Michael's C of E JMI Sch, St.Alb. AL3 off St. Michaels St 42 CB20
St. Michael's C of E Prim Sch, N6 off North Rd 120 DG59
N22 off Bounds Grn Rd 99 DM53
SE26 off Champion Rd 183 DY91
SW18 off Granville Rd 179 CZ87
Enfield EN2 off Brigadier Hill 82 DQ39
St. Michael's C of E (VA) Prim Sch, Well. DA16 off Wrotham Rd 166 EW81
St. Michael's Ct, Slou. SL2 131 AK70
St. Michaels Cres, Pnr. HA5 116 BY58
St. Michaels Dr, Wat. WD25 59 BV33
St. Michaels Gdns, W10 6 C6
St. Michael's Grn, Beac. HP9 89 AL52
St. Michael's RC Prim Sch, E6 off Arthur Rd 145 EM68
Ashford TW15 off Feltham Hill Rd 174 BN92
St. Michael's RC Sch, SE16 22 A4
St. Michaels Rd, NW2 119 CW63
St. Michael's Rd, SW9 161 DM82
Ashford TW15 174 BN92
St. Michaels Rd, Brox. EN10 49 DZ20
Caterham CR3 236 DR122
Croydon CR0 202 DQ102
Grays RM16 171 GH78
Wallington SM6 219 DJ107
Welling DA16 166 EV83
St. Michael's Rd, Wok. GU21 211 BD114
St. Michaels St, W2 7 P7
St. Albans AL3 42 CB20
St. Michaels Ter, N22 99 DL54
St. Michaels Way, Pot.B. EN6 64 DB30
St. Mildred's Ct, EC2 off Poultry 142 DR72
St. Mildreds Rd, SE12 184 EE87
Guildford GU1 243 AZ133
St. Monica's RC Prim Sch, N1 11 L1
N14 off Cannon Rd 99 DL48
St. Monica's Rd, Tad. KT20 233 CZ121
St. Nazaire Cl, Egh. TW20 off Mullens Rd 173 BC92
St. Neots Cl, Borwd. WD6 78 CN38
St. Neots Rd, Rom. RM3 106 FM52
St. Nicholas Av, Horn. RM12 127 FG62
Leatherhead (Bkhm) KT23 246 CB125
St. Nicholas Cen, Sutt. SM1 off St. Nicholas Way 218 DB105
St. Nicholas Cl, Amer. HP7 72 AV39
Borehamwood (Elstree) WD6 77 CK44
Uxbridge UB8 134 BK72
St. Nicholas' C of E Comb Sch, Maid. SL6 off Rectory Rd 130 AE70
St. Nicholas C of E Prim Sch, Shep. TW17 off Manor Fm Av 195 BP100
St. Nicholas Cres, Wok. (Pyrford) GU22 228 BG116
St. Nicholas Dr, Sev. TN13 257 FH126
Shepperton TW17 194 BN101
St. Nicholas Elstree C of E Prim Sch, Borwd. WD6 off St. Nicholas Cl 77 CK44
St. Nicholas Glebe, SW17 180 DG93
St. Nicholas Grn, Harl. CM17 off London Rd 36 EW14
St. Nicholas Gro, Brwd. (Ingrave) CM13 109 GC50
St. Nicholas Hill, Lthd. KT22 231 CH122
St. Nicholas Mt, Hem.H. HP1 39 BF20
St. Nicholas Pl, Loug. IG10 85 EN42
St. Nicholas Prep Sch, SW7 17 P4
St. Nicholas Rd, SE18 165 ET78
Sutton SM1 218 DB106
Thames Ditton KT7 197 CF100
St. Nicholas Sch, Harl. CM17 off Hobbs Cross Rd 36 EY12
Purley CR8 off Old Lo La 219 DN113
Redhill RH1 off Taynton Dr 251 DK129
St. Nicholas St, SE8 off Lucas St 163 EA81
St. Nicholas Way, Sutt. SM1 218 DB105
St. Nicolas C of E Inf Sch, Guil. GU2 off Portsmouth Rd 258 AW136
St. Nicolas La, Chis. BR7 204 EL95
St. Ninian's Ct, N20 98 DF48
St. Norbert Grn, SE4 163 DY84
St. Norbert Rd, SE4 163 DY84
St. Normans Way, Epsom KT17 217 CU110
St. Olaf's Rd, SW6 159 CY80
St. Olaves Cl, Stai. TW18 173 BF94
St. Olaves Ct, EC2 11 J8
St. Olave's Est, SE1 21 M3
St. Olaves Gdns, SE11 20 C7
St. Olave's Prep Sch, SE9 off Southwood Rd 185 EP89
St. Olaves Rd, E6 145 EN67
St. Olave's Sch & St. Saviour's Gram Sch, Orp. BR6 off Goddington La 206 EV104
St. Olave's Wk, SW16 201 DJ96
St. Olav's Sq, SE16 22 E5
St. Omer Ridge, Guil. GU1 259 BA135
St. Omer Rd, Guil. GU1 259 BA135
St. Osmund's RC Prim Sch, SW13 off Church Rd 159 CT81
St. Oswald's Pl, SE11 20 A10
St. Oswald's Rd, SW16 201 DP95
St. Oswulf St, SW1 19 M8
ST. PANCRAS, WC1 9 N2
St. Pancras 9 N1
St. Pancras Hosp, NW1 141 DK67
St. Pancras Way, NW1 141 DJ66
St. Patrick's Ct, Wdf.Grn. IG8 102 EE52
St. Patrick's Gdns, Grav. DA12 191 GK90
St. Patricks Pl, Grays RM16 171 GJ77
St. Patrick's RC Prim Sch, E1 22 C2
Inf, E1 22 D1
E17 off Longfield Av 123 DY56
NW5 off Raglan St 141 DH65
SE18 off Griffin Rd 165 ER77
Romford RM5 off Lowshoe La 105 FB53
St. Paul Cl, Uxb. UB8 134 BK71
St. Paulinus C of E Prim Sch, Dart. DA1 off Iron Mill La 167 FE84
St. Paul's 10 G7
St. Paul's All, EC4 off St. Paul's Chyd 141 DP72
St. Paul's & All Hallows C.E. Inf Sch, N17 off Park La 100 DU52
St. Paul's & All Hallows C.E. Jun Sch, N17 off Worcester Av 100 DU52
St. Paul's Av, NW2 139 CV65
SE16 23 H1
St. Pauls Av, Har. HA3 118 CM57
Slough SL2 132 AT73
★ St. Paul's Cath, EC4 10 G8
St. Paul's Cath Choir Sch, EC4 10 G8
St. Paul's Catholic Coll, Sun. TW16 off Green St 195 BU95
St. Paul's Chyd, EC4 10 F8
St. Paul's Cl, SE7 164 EK78
W5 158 CM75
St. Pauls Cl, Add. KT15 212 BG106
St. Paul's Cl, Ashf. TW15 175 BQ92
Carshalton SM5 200 DE102
St. Pauls Cl, Chess. KT9 215 CK105
Hayes UB3 155 BR78
St. Paul's Cl, Houns. TW3 156 BY82
St. Pauls Cl, S.Ock. (Aveley) RM15 148 FQ73
Swanscombe DA10 off Swanscombe St 190 FY87
St. Paul's C of E Comb Sch, H.Wyc. HP10 off Stratford Dr 110 AD59
St. Paul's C of E Jun Sch, Kings.T. KT2 off Princes Rd 178 CN94
St. Paul's C of E Prim Sch, N11 off The Avenue 99 DH50
N21 off Ringwood Way 99 DP45
NW3 off Elsworthy Rd 140 DF66
NW7 off The Ridgeway 97 CV49
SE17 20 G10
St. Paul's C of E Prim Sch, W6 off Worlidge St 159 CW78
St. Paul's C of E Prim Sch, Add. KT15 off School La 212 BG105
Brentford TW8 off St. Paul's Rd 157 CK79
St. Pauls C of E Prim Sch, Chess. KT9 off Orchard Rd 216 CL105
St. Paul's C of E Prim Sch, Kings L. WD4 off Langleybury La 59 BQ34
Swanley BR8 off School La 207 FH95
St. Paul's C of E (VA) Prim Sch, Dor. RH4 off St. Paul's Rd W 263 CH137
St. Paul's Ct, W14 16 B8
St. Pauls Ctyd, SE8 off Deptford High St 163 EA80
ST. PAUL'S CRAY, Orp. BR5 206 EU96
St. Paul's Cray C of E Prim Sch, Orp. BR5 off Buttermere Rd 206 EX97
St. Pauls Cray Rd, Chis. BR7 205 ER95
St. Paul's Cres, NW1 141 DK66
St. Pauls Dr, E15 123 ED64
St. Paul's Girls Sch, W6 16 A7
St. Paul's Ms, NW1 off St. Paul's Cres 141 DK66
Dorking RH4 off St. Paul's Rd W 263 CH137
St. Paul's Pl, N1 5 J3
St. Pauls Pl, St.Alb. AL1 43 CG20
South Ockendon (Aveley) RM15 148 FQ73
St. Paul's Prep Sch, SW13 off Lonsdale Rd 159 CU78
St. Paul's Prim Sch, E1 12 B9
Kings Langley WD4 off The Common 58 BG31
St. Paul's RC (Aided) Prim Sch, T.Ditt. KT7 off Hampton Ct Way 197 CE101
St. Paul's RC Prim Sch, N2 off Bradley Rd 99 DM54
Waltham Cross EN7 off Park La 66 DV27
St. Paul's RC SM Sch, SE2 off Wickham La 166 EU79
St. Pauls Ri, N13 99 DP51
St. Paul's Rd, N1 4 E4
N17 100 DU52
Barking IG11 145 EQ67
Brentford TW8 157 CK79
Erith DA8 167 FC80
St. Pauls Rd, Hem.H. HP2 40 BK19
St. Paul's Rd, Rich. TW9 158 CM83
Staines TW18 173 BD92
Thornton Heath CR7 202 DQ97
St. Pauls Rd, Wok. GU22 227 BA117
St. Paul's Rd E, Dor. RH4 263 CH137
St. Paul's Rd W, Dor. RH4 263 CG137
St. Paul's Sch, SW13 off Lonsdale Rd 159 CU78
St. Paul's Shrubbery, N1 5 J3
St. Pauls Sq, Brom. BR2 204 EG96
St. Paul's Ter, SE17 off Westcott Rd 161 DP79
St. Pauls Twr, E10 123 EB59
St. Paul St, N1 4 G8
St. Pauls Wk, Kings.T. KT2 off Alexandra Rd 178 CN94
St. Pauls Way, E3 13 L6
E14 13 L6
St. Paul's Way, N3 98 DB52
St. Pauls Way, Wal.Abb. EN9 off Rochford Av 67 ED33
Watford WD24 76 BW40
St. Paul's Way Comm Sch, E3 13 N5
St. Paul's with St. Luke's Prim Sch, E3 13 M5
St. Paul's with St. Michael's C of E Prim Sch, E8 off Wilde Cl 142 DU67
St. Pauls Wd Hill, Orp. BR5 205 ES96
St. Peter & St. Paul Catholic Sch, Orp. BR5 off St. Pauls Wd Hill 205 ES96
St. Peter & St. Paul C of E Prim Sch, Cat. CR3 off Rook La 251 DN125
St. Peter & St. Paul RC Prim Sch, Mitch. CR4 off Cricket Grn 200 DF98
St. Peter Chanel RC Prim Sch, Sid. DA14 off Baugh Rd 186 EW92
St. Peter in Chains RC Inf Sch, N8 off Elm Gro 121 DL58
St. Peter's All, EC3 11 K8
St. Peter's & St. Paul's RC JMI Sch, EC1 10 F3
St. Peter's & St. Paul's RC Prim Sch, Ilf. IG1 off Gordon Rd 125 ER62
St. Peter's Av, E2 off St. Peter's Cl 142 DU68
E17 124 EE56
St. Peters Av, N18 100 DU49
Westerham (Berry's Grn) TN16 239 EP116
St. Petersburgh Ms, W2 7 J9
St. Petersburgh Pl, W2 7 J9
St. Peter's Catholic Comp Sch, Guil. GU1 off Horseshoe La E 243 BC133
St. Peter's Catholic Prim Sch, Lthd. KT22 off Grange Rd 231 CJ120
St. Peter's Cl, E2 142 DU68
St. Peters Cl, SW17 off College Gdns 180 DE89
St. Peter's Cl, Barn. EN5 79 CV43
St. Peters Cl, Bushey (Bushey Hth) WD23 95 CD46
Chislehurst BR7 185 ER94
Gerrards Cross (Chal.St.P.) SL9 off Lewis La 90 AY53
Hatfield AL10 45 CU17
Ilford IG2 125 ES56
Rickmansworth (Mill End) WD3 92 BH46
St. Peter's Cl, Ruis. HA4 116 BX61
St. Peters Cl, St.Alb. AL1 43 CD19
St. Peter's Cl, Slou. SL1 130 AH70
St. Peters Cl, Stai. TW18 173 BF93
Swanscombe DA10 190 FZ87
Windsor (Old Wind.) SL4 off Church Rd 172 AU85
Woking GU22 227 BC120
St. Peter's C of E Comb Sch, Slou. SL1 off Minniecroft Rd 130 AH69
St. Peter's C of E Inf Sch, Oxt. RH8 off Tandridge La 253 EA133
St. Peter's C of E Mid Sch, Wind. SL4 off Crimp Hill Rd 172 AT86
St. Peter's C of E Prim Sch, SE17 21 J10
W6 off St. Peter's Gro 159 CU77
W9 6 G4
Brentwood CM14 off Wigley Bush La 108 FS47
St. Peter's C of E (VA) Sch, Rick. WD3 off Church La 92 BH46
St. Peter's Ct, NW4 119 CW57
St. Peters Ct, SE3 off Eltham Rd 164 EF84
SE4 off Wickham Rd 163 DZ82
Gerrards Cross (Chal.St.P.) SL9 off High St 90 AY53
West Molesey KT8 196 CA98
St. Peter's Eaton Sq C of E Prim Sch, SW1 19 H6
St. Peter's Gdns, SE27 181 DN90
St. Peter's Gro, W6 159 CU77
St. Peter's Hosp, Cher. KT16 193 BD104
St. Peters La, Orp. BR5 206 EU96
St. Peter's Pl, W9 7 J4
St. Peter's Prim Sch, E1 22 E1

St. Peter's Prim Sch, St. Alb. AL1 off Cottonmill La 43 CE21
South Croydon CR2 off Normanton Rd 220 DS107
St. Peter's RC Prim Sch, SE18 off Crescent Rd 165 EP78
Dagenham RM9 off Goresbrook Rd 146 EZ67
Romford RM1 off Dorset Av 127 FE55
St. Peters Rd, N9 100 DW46
St. Peter's Rd, W6 159 CU78
St. Peters Rd, Brwd. CM14 off Crescent Rd 108 FV49
St. Peter's Rd, Croy. CR0 220 DR105
Grays RM16 171 GH77
St. Peters Rd, Kings.T. KT1 198 CN96
St. Albans AL1 43 CE20
Southall UB1 136 CA71
Twickenham TW1 177 CH85
Uxbridge UB8 134 BK71
St. Peter's Rd, W.Mol. KT8 196 CA98
St. Peters Rd, Wok. GU22 227 BB121
St. Peter's Sq, E2 off St. Peter's Cl 142 DU68
W6 159 CU78
St. Peters St, N1 4 F8
St. Albans AL1 43 CD20
St. Peter's St, S.Croy. CR2 220 DR106
St. Peters Ter, SW6 159 CY80
St. Peter's Vil, W6 159 CU77
St. Peter's Way, N1 5 M6
St. Peters Way, W5 137 CK71
St. Peter's Way, Add. KT15 194 BG104
Chertsey KT16 211 BD105
St. Peters Way, Hayes UB3 155 BR78
Rickmansworth (Chorl.) WD3 73 BB43
St. Philip Howard RC Prim Sch, Hat. AL10 off Woods Av 45 CV18
St. Philip's Av, Wor.Pk. KT4 199 CV103
St. Philips Gate, Wor.Pk. KT4 199 CV103
St. Philip Sq, SW8 161 DH82
St. Philip's Rd, E8 142 DU65
St. Philips Rd, Surb. KT6 197 CK100
St. Philip's Sch, SW7 17 M8
Chessington KT9 off Harrow Cl 215 CK108
St. Philip St, SW8 161 DH82
St. Philip's Way, N1 5 H7
St. Philomena's RC Prim Sch, Orp. BR5 off Chelsfield Rd 206 EW101
St. Philomena's Sch, Cars. SM5 off Pound St 218 DF106
St. Pinnock Av, Stai. TW18 194 BG95
St. Quentin Ho, SW18 off Fitzhugh Gro 180 DD86
St. Quentin Rd, Well. DA16 165 ET83
St. Quintin Av, W10 139 CW71
St. Quintin Gdns, W10 139 CW71
St. Quintin Rd, E13 144 EH68
St. Raphaels Ct, St.Alb. AL1 off Avenue Rd 43 CE19
St. Raphael's RC Prim Sch, Nthlt. UB5 off Hartfield Av 135 BV68
St. Raphael's Way, NW10 118 CQ64
St. Regis Cl, N10 99 DH54
St. Richard's with St. Andrew's C of E Prim Sch, Rich. TW10 off Ashburnham Rd 177 CH90
St. Robert Southwell Sch, NW9 off Slough La 118 CQ58
St. Ronan's Cl, Barn. EN4 80 DD38
St. Ronans Cres, Wdf.Grn. IG8 102 EG52
St. Rose's RC Inf Sch, Hem.H. HP1 off Green End Rd 40 BG22
St. Rule St, SW8 161 DJ82
St. Saviour's & St. Olave's C of E Sch, SE1 21 K6
St. Saviour's C of E Inf Sch, W5 off The Grove 137 CK74
St. Saviour's C of E Prim Sch, E17 off Verulam Av 123 DZ59
SE24 off Herne Hill Rd 162 DQ83
W9 7 K4
St. Saviour's Est, SE1 21 N5
St. Saviours Pl, Guil. GU1 off Leas Rd 242 AW134
St. Saviour's Prim Sch, E14 14 A6
St. Saviour's RC Prim Sch, SE13 off Bonfield Rd 163 EC84
St. Saviour's Rd, SW2 181 DM85
St. Saviours Rd, Croy. CR0 202 DQ100
St. Saviours Vw, St.Alb. AL1 off Summerhill Ct 43 CF19
St. Scholastica's RC JMI Sch, E5 off Kenninghall Rd 122 DU62
Saints Cl, SE27 off Wolfington Rd 181 DP91
Saints Dr, E7 124 EK64
St. Silas Pl, NW5 140 DG65
St. Silas St Est, NW5 140 DG65
St. Simon's Av, SW15 179 CW85
ST. STEPHENS, St.Alb. AL3 42 CC22
St. Stephens Av, E17 123 EC57
W12 159 CV75
W13 137 CH72
St. Stephen's Av, Ashtd. KT21 232 CL116
St. Stephens Av, St.Alb. AL3 42 CB22
St. Stephens Cl, E17 123 EB57
NW8 off Avenue Cl 140 DE67
St. Albans AL3 42 CB23
Southall UB1 136 CA71
St. Stephen's C of E Jun Sch, Twick. TW1 off Winchester Rd 177 CH86
St. Stephen's C of E Prim Sch, SE8 off Albyn Rd 163 EA82
SW8 off Dorset Rd 161 DM80
W2 7 H6
W12 off Uxbridge Rd 159 CW75
St. Stephens Cres, W2 7 H7
Brentwood CM13 109 GA49
Thornton Heath CR7 201 DN97
St. Stephens Gdn Est, W2 6 G7
St. Stephens Gdns, SW15 off Manfred Rd 179 CZ85
W2 7 H6
St. Stephens Gdns, Twick. TW1 177 CJ86
St. Stephens Gro, SE13 163 EC83
St. Stephens Hill, St.Alb. AL1 42 CC22
St. Stephens Ms, W2 7 H6
St. Stephen's Par, E7 off Green St 144 EJ66
St. Stephen's Pas, Twick. TW1 off Richmond Rd 177 CJ86
St. Stephen's Prim Sch, E6 off Whitfield Rd 144 EJ66
St. Stephen's RC Prim Sch, Well. DA16 off Deepdene Rd 166 EU82
St. Stephen's Rd, E3 143 DZ68
St. Stephens Rd, E6 144 EJ66
St. Stephen's Rd, E17 off Grove Rd 123 EB57
St. Stephens Rd, W13 137 CH72
St. Stephen's Rd, Barn. EN5 79 CX43
St. Stephens Rd, Enf. EN3 83 DX37
Hounslow TW3 176 CA86
St. Stephen's Rd, West Dr. UB7 134 BK74
St. Stephens Row, EC4 11 J8
St. Stephens Ter, SW8 161 DM80
St. Stephen's Wk, SW7 17 L7
Saints Wk, Grays RM16 171 GJ77
St. Swithin's La, EC4 11 J9
St. Swithun's Rd, SE13 183 ED85
St. Swithun Wells RC Prim Sch, Ruis. HA4 off Hunters Hill 116 BX62
St. Teresa RC Prim Sch, The, Dag. RM8 off Bowes Rd 126 EW63
St. Teresa's Prep Sch, Lthd. KT24 off Guildford Rd 246 BX128
St. Teresa's RC First & Mid Sch, Har. HA3 off Long Elmes 94 CC53
St. Teresa's RC Prim Sch, Borwd. WD6 off Brook Rd 78 CP40
Morden SM4 off Montacute Rd 200 DD100
St. Teresa Wk, Grays RM16 171 GH76
St. Theresa Cl, Epsom KT18 216 CQ114
St. Theresa's RC Prim Sch, N3 off East End Rd 120 DB55
St. Theresa's Rd, Felt. TW14 155 BT84
St. Thomas Becket RC Prim Sch, SE25 off Becket Cl 202 DU100
St. Thomas' Cl, Surb. KT6 198 CM102
St. Thomas Cl, Wok. GU21 off St. Mary's Rd 226 AW117
St. Thomas C of E JMI Sch, N16 off Lynmouth Rd 122 DU60
St. Thomas C of E Prim Sch, W10 6 D4
St. Thomas Ct, Bex. DA5 186 FA87
St. Thomas Dr, Guil. (E.Clan.) GU4 off The Street 244 BL131
Orpington BR5 205 EQ102
St. Thomas' Dr, Pnr. HA5 94 BY53
St. Thomas Gdns, Ilf. IG1 145 EQ65
St. Thomas' Hosp, SE1 20 A5
St. Thomas' Med Sch & The Nightingale Sch, SE1 20 A6
St. Thomas More Prim Sch, SE9 off Appleton Rd 164 EL83
St. Thomas More RC Prim Sch, Berk. HP4 off Greenway 38 AU19
Bexleyheath DA7 off Sheldon Rd 166 EZ82
St. Thomas More RC Sch, N22 off Glendale Av 99 DN52
St. Thomas More RC Sec Sch, SE9 off Footscray Rd 185 EN86
St. Thomas More Sec Sch, SW3 18 C8
St. Thomas of Canterbury Catholic Prim Sch, Grays RM17 off Ward Av 170 GB77
St. Thomas of Canterbury Inf Sch, Brwd. CM15 off Sawyers Hall La 108 FX45
St. Thomas of Canterbury Jun Sch, Brwd. CM15 off Sawyers Hall La 108 FX45
St. Thomas of Canterbury RC Prim Sch, Guil. GU1 off Horseshoe La W 243 BB134
St. Thomas of Canterbury RC Sch, Mitch. CR4 off Commonside E 200 DG97
St. Thomas Pl, NW1 off Maiden La 141 DK66
St. Thomas RC Prim Sch, SW6 off Estcourt Rd 159 CZ80
St. Thomas' RC Prim Sch, Sev. TN13 off South Pk 257 FH125
St. Thomas Rd, E16 15 L7
N14 99 DK45
St. Thomas' Rd, W4 158 CQ79
St. Thomas Rd, Belv. DA17 167 FC75
Brentwood CM14 108 FX47
Gravesend (Nthflt) DA11 off St. Margaret's Rd 190 GE89
St. Thomas's Av, Grav. DA11 191 GH88
St. Thomas's Cl, Wal.Abb. EN9 68 EH33
St. Thomas's Gdns, NW5 off Queen's Cres 140 DG65
St. Thomas's Ms, Guil. GU1 off St. Catherines Pk 259 AZ136
St. Thomas's Pl, E9 142 DW66
St. Thomas's Rd, N4 121 DN61
NW10 138 CS67
St. Thomas's Sq, E9 142 DV66
St. Thomas St, SE1 21 J2
St. Thomas's Way, SW6 159 CZ80
St. Thomas the Apostle Sch, SE15 off Hollydale Rd 162 DW82
St. Thomas Wk, Slou. (Colnbr.) SL3 153 BD80
St. Thomas à Becket RC Prim Sch, SE2 off Mottisfont Rd 166 EU76
St. Timothy's Ms, Brom. BR1 off Wharton Rd 204 EH95
St. Ursula Gro, Pnr. HA5 116 BX57
St. Ursula Rd, Sthl. UB1 136 CA72
St. Ursula's Conv Sec Sch, SE10 off Crooms Hill 163 ED80
St. Ursula's Inf Sch, Rom. RM3 off Straight Rd 106 FJ51
St. Ursula's Jun Sch, Rom. RM3 off Straight Rd 105 FH51
St. Vincent Cl, SE27 181 DP92
St. Vincent de Paul RC Prim Sch, SW1 19 J6
St. Vincent Dr, St.Alb. AL1 43 CG23
St. Vincent Rd, Twick. TW2 176 CC86
Walton-on-Thames KT12 195 BV104
St. Vincents Av, Dart. DA1 188 FN85
ST. VINCENT'S HAMLET, Brwd. CM14 106 FP46
St. Vincent's RC Prim Sch, NW7 off The Ridgeway 97 CW50
SE9 off Harting Rd 184 EL91
W1 8 F6
W3 off Pierrepoint Rd 138 CP73
Dagenham RM8 off Burnside Rd 126 EW61
St. Vincents Rd, Dart. DA1 188 FN86
St. Vincent St, W1 8 F6
St. Vincents Way, Pot.B. EN6 64 DC33
St. Wilfrids Cl, Barn. EN4 80 DE43
St. Wilfrids Rd, Barn. EN4 80 DD43
St. William of York RC Prim Sch, SE23 off Brockley Pk 183 DY88
St. Winefride's Av, E12 125 EM64
St. Winefride's RC Prim Sch, E12 off Church Rd 125 EM64
St. Winifreds, Ken. CR8 236 DQ115
St. Winifreds Cl, Chig. IG7 103 EQ50
St. Winifred's Inf, SE12 off Effingham Rd 184 EE85
St. Winifred's Juniors, SE12 off Newstead Rd 184 EF86
St. Winifred's Rd, Tedd. TW11 177 CH93
Westerham (Bigg.H.) TN16 239 EM118
St. Yon Ct, St.Alb. AL4 43 CK20
Sakins Cft, Harl. CM18 51 ET18
Saladin Dr, Purf. RM19 168 FN77
Sala Ho, SE3 off Pinto Way 164 EH84
Salamanca Pl, SE1 20 A8
Salamanca St, SE1 19 P8
Salamander Cl, Kings.T. KT2 177 CJ92
Salamander Quay, Uxb. (Hare.) UB9 92 BG52
Salamons Way, Rain. RM13 147 FE72
Salbrook Rd, Red. (Salf.) RH1 266 DG142
Salcombe Dr, Mord. SM4 199 CX102
Romford RM6 126 EZ58
Salcombe Gdns, NW7 97 CW51
Salcombe Pk, Loug. IG10 84 EK43
Salcombe Prep Sch, N14 off Chase Side 99 DH45
Salcombe Rd, E17 123 DZ59
N16 5 M1
Ashford TW15 174 BL91
Salcombe Way, Hayes UB4 off Portland Rd 135 BS69
Ruislip HA4 115 BU61
Salcot Cres, Croy. (New Adgtn) CR0 221 EC110
Salcote Rd, Grav. DA12 191 GL92
Salcott Rd, SW11 180 DE85
Croydon CR0 201 DL104
Salehurst Cl, Har. HA3 118 CL57
Salehurst Rd, SE4 183 DZ86
Salem Pl, Croy. CR0 202 DQ104
Gravesend (Nthflt) DA11 190 GD87
Salem Rd, W2 7 K9
Sale Pl, W2 8 A6
Salesian Coll, SW11 off Surrey La 160 DE81
Salesian Gdns, Cher. KT16 194 BG102
Salesian RC Sch, Cher. KT16 off Guildford Rd 193 BE103
Annexe, Cher. KT16 off Highfield Rd 194 BG102
Sale St, E2 12 A3
Salford Rd, SW2 181 DK88
SALFORDS, Red. RH1 266 DF142
⇌ Salfords 266 DG142
Salfords Co Prim Sch, Red. RH1 off Copsleigh Av 266 DG140
Salfords Ind Est, Red. RH1 267 DH143
Salfords Way, Red. RH1 266 DG142
Salhouse Cl, SE28 off Rollesby Way 146 EW72
Salisbury Av, N3 119 CZ55
Barking IG11 145 ES66
St. Albans AL1 43 CH19
Slough SL2 131 AQ70
Sutton SM1 217 CZ107
Swanley BR8 207 FG98
Salisbury Cl, SE17 21 J7
Amersham HP7 55 AS39
Potters Bar EN6 64 DC32
Upminster RM14 off Canterbury Av 129 FT61
Worcester Park KT4 199 CT104
Salisbury Ct, EC4 10 E8
Salisbury Cres, Wal.Cr. (Chsht) EN8 67 DX32
Salisbury Gdns, SW19 179 CY94
Buckhurst Hill IG9 102 EK47
Welwyn Garden City AL7 29 CZ10
Salisbury Hall Gdns, E4 101 EA51
Salisbury Hill Dr, Hat. AL10 off Mosquito Way 44 CS16
Salisbury Ho, E14 14 A7
Salisbury Ms, SW6 off Dawes Rd 159 CZ80
Bromley BR2 off Salisbury Rd 204 EL99
Salisbury Pl, SW9 161 DP80
W1 8 C5
West Byfleet KT14 212 BJ111
Salisbury Prim Sch, E12 off Romford Rd 124 EL64
Salisbury Rd, E4 101 EA48
E7 144 EG65
E10 123 EC61
E12 124 EK64
E17 123 EC57
N4 121 DP57
N9 100 DU48
N22 99 DP53
SE25 202 DU100
SW19 179 CY94
W13 157 CG75
Banstead SM7 218 DB114
Barnet EN5 79 CY41
Bexley DA5 186 FA88
Bromley BR2 204 EL99
Carshalton SM5 218 DF107
Dagenham RM10 147 FB65
Dartford DA2 188 FQ88
Enfield EN3 83 DZ37
Feltham TW13 176 BW88
Godstone RH9 252 DW131
Gravesend DA11 191 GF88
Grays RM17 170 GC79
Harrow HA1 117 CD57
Hoddesdon EN11 49 EC15
Hounslow TW4 156 BW83
Salisbury Rd, Houns. (Hthrw Air.) TW6 175 BQ85
Ilford IG3 125 ES61
New Malden KT3 198 CR97
Pinner HA5 115 BU56
Richmond TW9 158 CL84
Romford RM2 127 FH57
Southall UB2 156 BY77
Uxbridge UB8 134 BH68
Watford WD24 75 BV38
Welwyn Garden City AL7 29 CZ10
Woking GU22 226 AY119
Worcester Park KT4 199 CT104
Salisbury Sch, Lwr Sch, N9 off Turin Rd 100 DW45
Upr Sch, N9 off Nightingale Rd 100 DW45
Salisbury Sq, EC4 10 D8
Hatfield AL9 off Park St 45 CW17
Hertford SG14 off Railway St 32 DR09
Salisbury St, NW8 7 P4
W3 158 CQ75
Salisbury Ter, SE15 162 DW83
Salisbury Wk, N19 121 DJ61
Salix Cl, Lthd. (Fetch.) KT22 230 CB123
Sunbury-on-Thames TW16 off Oak Gro 175 BV94
Salix Rd, Grays RM17 170 GD79
Salliesfield, Twick. TW2 177 CD86
Sally Murrey Cl, E12 off Grantham Rd 125 EN63
Salmen Rd, E13 144 EF68
Salmon Cl, Welw.G.C. AL7 30 DA06
Salmond Cl, Stan. HA7 off Robb Rd 95 CG51
Salmonds Gro, Brwd. (Ingrave) CM13 109 GC50
Salmon La, E14 13 J7
Salmon Meadow Footpath, Hem.H. HP3 40 BK24
Salmon Rd, Belv. DA17 166 FA78
Dartford DA1 168 FM83
Salmons La, Whyt. CR3 236 DU119
Salmons La W, Cat. CR3 236 DS120
Salmons Rd, N9 100 DU46
Chessington KT9 215 CK107
Leatherhead (Eff.) KT24 245 BV129
Salmon St, E14 13 L7
NW9 118 CP60
Salomons Rd, E13 off Chalk Rd 144 EJ71
Salop Rd, E17 123 DX58
Saltash Cl, Sutt. SM1 217 CZ105
Saltash Rd, Ilf. IG6 103 ER52
Welling DA16 166 EW81
Salt Box Hill, West. TN16 222 EH113
Salt Box Rd, Guil. GU3, GU4 242 AT129
Saltcoats Rd, W4 158 CS75
Saltcote Cl, Dart. DA1 187 FE86
Saltcroft Cl, Wem. HA9 118 CP60
Salter Cl, Har. HA2 116 BZ62
Salterford Rd, SW17 180 DG93
Salter Rd, SE16 22 G2
Salters Cl, Berk. HP4 38 AT17
Rickmansworth WD3 92 BL46
Salters Gdns, Wat. WD17 75 BU39
Salters Hall Ct, EC4 11 J9
Salters Hill, SE19 182 DR92
Salters Rd, E17 123 ED56
W10 6 A4
Salter St, E14 13 N9
NW10 139 CU69
Salterton Rd, N7 121 DL62
Saltford Cl, Erith DA8 167 FE78
Salt Hill Av, Slou. SL1 131 AQ74
Salthill Cl, Uxb. UB8 114 BL64
Salt Hill Dr, Slou. SL1 131 AQ74
Salt Hill Way, Slou. SL1 131 AQ74
Saltley Cl, E6 off Dunnock Rd 144 EL72
Saltoun Rd, SW2 161 DN84
Saltram Cl, N15 122 DT56
Saltram Cres, W9 6 F1
Saltwell St, E14 13 P9
Saltwood Cl, Orp. BR6 224 EW105
Saltwood Gro, SE17 21 J10
Salusbury Prim Sch, NW6 off Salusbury Rd 139 CZ67
Salusbury Rd, NW6 139 CY67
Salutation Rd, SE10 25 H7
Salvation Army Avalon Training Cen, The, Chis. BR7 off Summer Hill 205 EN96
Salvatorian Coll, Har. HA3 off High St 95 CE54
Salvia Gdns, Grnf. UB6 off Selborne Gdns 137 CG68
Salvin Rd, SW15 159 CX83
Salway Cl, Wdf.Grn. IG8 102 EF52
Salway Pl, E15 off Broadway 144 EE65
Salway Rd, E15 off Great Eastern Rd 143 ED65
Salwey Cres, Brox. EN10 49 DZ20
Samantha Cl, E17 123 DZ59
Samantha Ms, Rom. (Hav.at.Bow.) RM4 105 FE48
Sam Bartram Cl, SE7 164 EJ78
Sambruck Ms, SE6 183 EB88
Samels Ct, W6 off South Black Lion La 159 CU78
Samford St, NW8 7 P4
Samian Gate, St.Alb. AL3 off Mayne Av 42 BZ22
Samira Cl, E17 off Colchester Rd 123 EA58
Samos Rd, SE20 202 DV96
Samphire Ct, Grays RM17 off Salix Rd 170 GE80
Sample Oak La, Guil. (Chilw.) GU4 259 BE140
Sampson Av, Barn. EN5 79 CX43
Sampson Cl, Belv. DA17 off Carrill Way 166 EX76
Sampsons Ct, Shep. TW17 off Linden Way 195 BQ99
Sampsons Grn, Slou. SL2 131 AM69
Sampson St, E1 22 B2
Samson St, E13 144 EJ68
Samuel Cl, E8 5 P7
SE14 163 DX79
SE18 164 EL77
Samuel Gray Gdns, Kings.T. KT2 197 CK95
Samuel Johnson Cl, SW16 off Curtis Fld Rd 181 DN91
Samuel Lewis Trust Dws, E8 off Amhurst Rd 122 DU63
N1 4 D4
SW3 18 A8
SW6 160 DA80
Samuel Rhodes Sch, N1 4 C7
Samuels Cl, W6 off South Black Lion La 159 CU78
Samuel Sq, St.Alb. AL1 off Pageant Rd 43 CD21
Samuel St, SE15 162 DT80
SE18 165 EM77
Sancroft Cl, NW2 119 CV62
Sancroft Rd, Har. HA3 95 CF54
Sancroft St, SE11 20 B9
Sanctuary, The, SW1 19 M4
Bexley DA5 186 EX86
Morden SM4 200 DA100
Sanctuary Cl, Dart. DA1 188 FJ86
Uxbridge (Hare.) UB9 92 BJ52
Sanctuary Rd, Houns. (Hthrw Air.) TW6 174 BN86
Sanctuary St, SE1 21 H4
Sandale Cl, N16 off Stoke Newington Ch St 122 DR62
Sandall Cl, W5 138 CL70
Sandall Rd, NW5 141 DJ65
W5 138 CL70
Sandalls Spring, Hem.H. HP1 39 BF18
Sandal Rd, N18 100 DU50
New Malden KT3 198 CR99
Sandal St, E15 144 EE67
Sandalwood, Guil. GU2 258 AV135
Sandalwood Av, Cher. KT16 193 BD104
Sandalwood Cl, E1 13 J4
Sandalwood Dr, Ruis. HA4 115 BQ59
Sandalwood Rd, Felt. TW13 175 BV90
Sanday Cl, Hem.H. HP3 41 BP22
Sandbach Pl, SE18 165 EQ77
Sandbanks, Felt. TW14 175 BT88
Sandbanks Hill, Dart. (Bean) DA2 189 FV93
Sandbourne Av, SW19 200 DB97
Sandbourne Rd, SE4 163 DY82
Sandbrook Cl, NW7 96 CR51
Sandbrook Rd, N16 122 DS62
Sandby Grn, SE9 164 EL83
Sandcliff Rd, Erith DA8 167 FD77
Sandcroft Cl, N13 99 DP51
Sandcross Jun Sch, Reig. RH2 off Sandcross La 265 CZ137
Sandcross La, Reig. RH2 265 CZ137
Sandells Av, Ashf. TW15 175 BQ91
Sandell St, SE1 20 C3
Sandels Way, Beac. HP9 89 AK51
Sandelswood End, Beac. HP9 89 AK50
Sandeman Gdns, Ware SG12 off Homefield Rd 33 DY05
Sanderling Way, Green. DA9 189 FU85
Sanders Cl, Hmptn. (Hmptn H.) TW12 176 CC92
Hemel Hempstead HP3 40 BM24
St. Albans (Lon.Col.) AL2 61 CK27
Sanders Draper Sch, The, Horn. RM12 off Suttons La 128 FK63
Sandersfield Gdns, Bans. SM7 234 DA115
Sandersfield Rd, Bans. SM7 234 DB115
Sanders La, NW7 97 CX52
Sanderson Av, Sev. (Bad.Mt) TN14 224 FA110
Sanderson Cl, NW5 121 DH63
Sanderson Rd, Uxb. UB8 134 BJ65
Sanders Rd, Hem.H. HP3 40 BM23
SANDERSTEAD, S.Croy. CR2 220 DT111
⇌ Sanderstead 220 DR109
Sanderstead Av, NW2 119 CY61
Sanderstead Cl, SW12 off Atkins Rd 181 DJ87
Sanderstead Ct Av, S.Croy. CR2 220 DU113
Sanderstead Hill, S.Croy. CR2 220 DS111
Sanderstead Rd, E10 123 DY60
Orpington BR5 206 EV100
South Croydon CR2 220 DR108
Sanders Way, N19 off Sussex Way 121 DK60
Sandes Pl, Lthd. KT22 231 CG118
Sandfield Co Prim Sch, Guil. GU1 off York Rd 258 AX135
Sandfield Gdns, Th.Hth. CR7 201 DP97
Sandfield Pas, Th.Hth. CR7 202 DQ97
Sandfield Rd, St.Alb. AL1 43 CG20
Thornton Heath CR7 201 DP97
Sandfields, Wok. (Send) GU23 227 BD124
Sandfield Ter, Guil. GU1 258 AX135
Sandford Av, N22 100 DQ52
Loughton IG10 85 EQ41
Sandford Cl, E6 145 EM70
Sandford Ct, N16 122 DS60
Sandford Rd, E6 144 EL70
Bexleyheath DA7 166 EY84
Bromley BR2 204 EG98
Sandford St, SW6 off King's Rd 160 DB80
Sandgate Cl, Rom. RM7 127 FD59
Sandgate La, SW18 180 DE88
Sandgate Rd, Well. DA16 166 EW80
Sandgates, Cher. KT16 off Guildford Rd 193 BE102
Sandgate St, SE15 162 DV79
Sandham Pt, SE18 off Troy Ct 165 EP77
Sandhills, Wall. SM6 219 DK105
Sandhills La, Vir.W. GU25 192 AY99
Sandhills Meadow, Shep. TW17 195 BQ101
Sandhills Rd, Reig. RH2 266 DA136
Sandhurst Av, Har. HA2 116 CB58
Surbiton KT5 198 CP101
Sandhurst Cl, NW9 118 CN55
South Croydon CR2 220 DS109
Sandhurst Dr, Ilf. IG3 125 ET63
Sandhurst Inf, SE6 off Sandhurst Rd 184 EE88
Sandhurst Rd, N9 82 DW44
NW9 118 CN55
SE6 183 ED88
Bexley DA5 186 EX85
Orpington BR6 206 EU104
Sidcup DA15 185 ET90
Tilbury RM18 171 GJ82
Sandhurst Way, S.Croy. CR2 220 DS108
Sandifer Dr, NW2 119 CX62
Sandifield, Hat. AL10 45 CU21
Sandiford Rd, Sutt. SM3 199 CZ103
Sandiland Cres, Brom. BR2 204 EF103
Sandilands 202 DT103
Sandilands, Croy. CR0 202 DU103
Sevenoaks TN13 256 FD122

Sandilands Rd, SW6 160 DB81
Sandison St, SE15 162 DT83
Sandlands Gro, Tad. KT20 233 CU123
Sandlands Rd, Tad. KT20 233 CU123
Sandland St, WC1 10 B6
Sandlers End, Slou. SL2 131 AP70
Sandling Ri, SE9 185 EN90
Sandlings, The, N22 99 DN54
Sandlings Cl, SE15 *off Pilkington Rd* 162 DV82
Sandmartin Way, Wall. SM6 200 DG102
Sandmere Cl, Hem.H. HP2 *off St. Albans Rd* 40 BN21
Sandmere Rd, SW4 161 DL84
Sandon Cl, Esher KT10 197 CD101
Sandon Rd, Wal.Cr. (Chsht) EN8 66 DW30
Sandow Cres, Hayes UB3 155 BT76
Sandown Av, Dag. RM10 147 FC65
Esher KT10 214 CC106
Hornchurch RM12 128 FK61
Sandown Cl, Houns. TW5 155 BU81
Sandown Ct, Sutt. SM2 *off Grange Rd* 218 DB108
Sandown Dr, Cars. SM5 218 DG109
Sandown Gate, Esher KT10 196 CC104
Sandown Ind Pk, Esher KT10 196 CA103
★ **Sandown Park Racecourse**, Esher KT10 196 CB104
Sandown Rd, SE25 202 DV99
Coulsdon CR5 234 DG116
Esher KT10 214 CC105
Gravesend DA12 191 GJ93
Slough SL2 131 AM71
Watford WD24 76 BW38
Sandown Way, Nthlt. UB5 136 BY65
Sandpiper Cl, E17 101 DX53
SE16 23 L3
Greenhithe DA9 189 FU86
Sandpiper Dr, Erith DA8 167 FH80
Sandpiper Rd, S.Croy. CR2 221 DX111
Sutton SM1 217 CZ106
Sandpipers, The, Grav. DA12 191 GK89
Sandpiper Way, Orp. BR5 206 EX98
Sandpit Hall Rd, Wok. (Chobham) GU24 210 AU112
Sandpit La, Brwd. (Pilg.Hat.) CM14, CM15 108 FT46
St. Albans AL1, AL4 43 CJ18
Sandpit Pl, SE7 164 EL78
Sandpit Rd, Brom. BR1 184 EE92
Dartford DA1 168 FJ84
Redhill RH1 266 DE135
Welwyn Garden City AL7 29 CY11
Sandpits La, H.Wyc. (Penn) HP10 88 AC48
Sandpits Rd, Croy. CR0 221 DX105
Richmond TW10 177 CK89
Sandra Cl, N22 *off New Rd* 100 DQ53
Hounslow TW3 176 CB85
Sandridgebury La, St.Alb. AL3 43 CE16
Sandridge Cl, Har. HA1 117 CE56
Sandridge Rd, St.Alb. AL1 43 CE18
Sandridge St, N19 121 DJ61
Sandringham Av, SW20 199 CY96
Harlow CM19 50 EL15
Sandringham Cl, SW19 179 CX88
Enfield EN1 82 DS40
Ilford IG6 125 EQ55
Woking GU22 228 BG116
Sandringham Ct, W9 7 M2
Slough SL1 131 AK72
Sandringham Cres, Har. HA2 116 CA61
St. Albans AL4 43 CJ15
Sandringham Dr, Ashf. TW15 174 BK91
Dartford DA2 187 FE89
Welling DA16 165 ES82
Sandringham Gdns, N8 121 DL58
N12 98 DC51
Hounslow TW5 155 BU81
Ilford IG6 125 EQ55
West Molesey KT8 *off Rosemary Av* 196 CA98
Sch **Sandringham Inf Sch**, E7 *off Sandringham Rd* 124 EJ64
Sch **Sandringham Jun Sch**, E7 *off Sandringham Rd* 124 EJ64
Sandringham Ms, W5 *off High St* 137 CK73
Hampton TW12 *off Oldfield Rd* 196 BZ95
Sandringham Pk, Cob. KT11 214 BZ112
Sandringham Rd, E7 124 EJ64
E8 5 N2
E10 123 ED58
N22 122 DQ55
NW2 139 CV65
NW11 119 CY59
Barking IG11 145 ET65
Brentwood (Pilg.Hat.) CM15 108 FV43
Bromley BR1 184 EG92
Hounslow (Hthrw Air.) TW6 174 BL85
Northolt UB5 136 CA66
Potters Bar EN6 64 DB30
Thornton Heath CR7 202 DQ99
Watford WD24 76 BW37
Worcester Park KT4 199 CU104
Sch **Sandringham Sch**, St.Alb. AL4 *off The Ridgeway* 43 CH16
Sandringham Way, Wal.Cr. EN8 67 DX34
Sandrock Pl, Croy. CR0 221 DX105
Sandrock Rd, SE13 163 EA83
Dorking (Westc.) RH4 262 CB138
Sandroyd Way, Cob. KT11 214 CA113
SANDS END, SW6 160 DC81
Sand's End La, SW6 160 DB81
Sands Fm Dr, Slou. (Burn.) SL1 130 AJ70
Sandstone La, E16 15 N9
Sandstone Pl, N19 121 DH61
Sandstone Rd, SE12 184 EH89
Sands Way, Wdf.Grn. IG8 102 EL51
Sandtoft Rd, SE7 164 EH79
Sandway Path, Orp. BR5 *off Okemore Gdns* 206 EW98
Sandway Rd, Orp. BR5 206 EW98
Sandwell Cres, NW6 140 DA65
Sandwich St, WC1 9 N2
Sandwick Cl, NW7 *off Sebergham Gro* 97 CU52
Sandy Bk Rd, Grav. DA12 191 GH88
Sandy Bury, Orp. BR6 205 ER104
Sandy Cl, Hert. SG14 31 DP09
Woking GU22 *off Sandy La* 227 BB117
Sandycombe Rd, Felt. TW14 175 BU88
Richmond TW9 158 CN83
Sandycoombe Rd, Twick. TW1 177 CJ86
Sandycroft, SE2 166 EU79
Epsom KT17 217 CW110
Sandycroft Rd, Amer. HP6 72 AV39
Sandy Dr, Cob. KT11 214 CA111
Feltham TW14 175 BS88
Sandy Hill Av, SE18 165 EP78
Sandy Hill Rd, SE18 165 EP78
Sandyhill Rd, Ilf. IG1 125 EP63
Sandy Hill Rd, Wall. SM6 219 DJ109
Sandy La, Bet. RH3 264 CS135
Bushey WD23 76 CC41
Cobham KT11 214 CA112
Dartford (Bean) DA2 189 FW89
Grays (Chad.St.M.) RM16 171 GH79
Grays (W.Thur.) RM20 *off London Rd W Thurrock* 169 FV79
Guildford GU3 258 AU139
Guildford (Alb.Hth) GU5 260 BJ141
Guildford (Shere) GU5 260 BN139
Harrow HA3 118 CM58
Kingston upon Thames KT1 177 CG94
Leatherhead KT22 214 CA112
Mitcham CR4 200 DG95
Northwood HA6 93 BU50
Orpington BR6 206 EU101
Orpington (St.P.Cray) BR5 206 EX95
Oxted RH8 253 EC129
Oxted (Lmpfld) RH8 254 EH127
Redhill (Bletch.) RH1 251 DP132
Redhill (Nutfld) RH1 267 DK135
Reigate RH2 265 CW135
Richmond TW10 177 CJ89
Sevenoaks TN13 257 FJ123
Sidcup DA14 186 EX94
South Ockendon (Aveley) RM15 148 FM73
Sutton SM2 217 CY108
Tadworth (Kgswd) KT20 233 CZ124
Teddington TW11 177 CG94
Virginia Water GU25 192 AY98
Walton-on-Thames KT12 195 BV100
Watford WD25 76 CC41
Westerham TN16 255 ER125
Woking GU22 227 BC116
Woking (Chobham) GU24 210 AS109
Woking (Pyrford) GU22 227 BF117
Woking (Send) GU23 227 BC123
Sandy La Est, Rich. TW10 177 CK89
Sandy La N, Wall. SM6 219 DK107
Sandy La S, Wall. SM6 219 DK107
Sandy Lo La, Nthwd. HA6 93 BR47
Sandy Lo Rd, Rick. WD3 93 BP47
Sandy Lo Way, Nthwd. HA6 93 BS50
Sandy Mead, Epsom KT19 216 CN109
Maidenhead SL6 150 AC78
Sandymount Av, Stan. HA7 95 CJ50
Sandy Ridge, Chis. BR7 185 EN93
Sandy Ri, Ger.Cr. (Chal.St.P.) SL9 90 AY53
Sandy Rd, NW3 120 DB62
Addlestone KT15 212 BG107
Sandy's Row, E1 11 M6
Sandy Way, Cob. KT11 214 CA112
Croydon CR0 203 DZ104
Walton-on-Thames KT12 195 BT102
Woking GU22 227 BC117
Sanfoin End, Hem.H. HP2 40 BN18
Sanford La, N16 *off Lawrence Bldgs* 122 DT61
Sanford St, SE14 163 DY79
Sanford Ter, N16 122 DT62
Sanford Wk, N16 *off Sanford Ter* 122 DT61
SE14 *off Cold Blow La* 163 DY79
Sanger Av, Chess. KT9 216 CL106
Sanger Dr, Wok. (Send) GU23 227 BC123
Sangers Dr, Horl. RH6 268 DF148
Sch **Sangers Jun Sch**, Horl. RH6 *off Sangers Dr* 268 DF148
Sangers Wk, Horl. RH6 *off Sangers Dr* 268 DF148
Sangley Rd, SE6 183 EB87
SE25 202 DS98
Sangora Rd, SW11 160 DD84
San Juan Dr, Grays (Chaff.Hun.) RM16 169 FW77
San Luis Dr, Grays (Chaff.Hun.) RM16 169 FX77
San Marcos Dr, Grays (Chaff.Hun.) RM16 169 FW77
Sansom Rd, E11 124 EE61
Sansom St, SE5 162 DR80
Sans Wk, EC1 10 D3
Santers La, Pot.B. EN6 63 CY33
Santiago Way, Grays (Chaff.Hun.) RM16 169 FX78
Santley St, SW4 161 DM84
Santos Rd, SW18 180 DA85
Santway, The, Stan. HA7 95 CE50
Sanway Cl, W.Byf. (Byfleet) KT14 212 BL114
Sanway Rd, W.Byf. (Byfleet) KT14 212 BL114
Sapcote Trd Cen, NW10 119 CT64
Saperton Wk, SE11 20 B7
Sapho Pk, Grav. DA12 191 GM91
Saphora Cl, Orp. BR6 *off Oleander Cl* 223 ER106
Sappers Cl, Saw. CM21 36 EZ05
Sapperton Ct, EC1 10 G3
Sapphire Cl, E6 145 EN72
Dagenham RM8 126 EW60
Sapphire Rd, SE8 23 K8
Sappho Ct, Wok. GU21 *off Langmans Way* 226 AS116
Saracen Cl, Croy. CR0 202 DR100
Saracen Ind Area, Hem.H. HP2 41 BP18
Saracens Head, Hem.H. HP2 *off Adeyfield Rd* 40 BN19
Saracen's Head Yd, EC3 11 M8
★ **Saracens R.F.C. (share Vicarage Rd with Watford F.C.)**, Wat. WD18 75 BV43
Saracen St, E14 13 P8
Sara Ct, Beck. BR3 *off Albemarle Rd* 203 EB95
Sara Cres, Green. DA9 169 FU84
Sch **Sarah Bonnell Sec Sch**, E15 *off Deanery Rd* 144 EE65
Sarah Ho, SW15 159 CT84
Sara Ho, Erith DA8 *off Larner Rd* 167 FE80
Sara Pk, Grav. DA12 191 GL91
Saratoga Rd, E5 122 DW63
Sardinia St, WC2 10 A8
Sarel Way, Horl. RH6 269 DH146
Sargeant Cl, Uxb. UB8 *off Ratcliffe Cl* 134 BK69
Sarita Cl, Har. HA3 95 CD54
Sarjant Path, SW19 *off Queensmere Rd* 179 CX89
Sark Cl, Houns. TW5 156 CA80
Sark Ho, Enf. EN3 *off Eastfield Rd* 83 DX38
Sark Wk, E16 15 P7
Sarnesfield Ho, SE15 *off Pencraig Way* 162 DV79
Sarnesfield Rd, Enf. EN2 *off Church St* 82 DR41
SARRATT, Rick. WD3 74 BG35
Sarratt Bottom, Rick. (Sarratt) WD3 73 BE36
Sch **Sarratt C of E Sch**, Rick. WD3 *off The Green* 74 BG36
Sarratt La, Rick. WD3 74 BH40
Sarratt Rd, Rick. WD3 74 BM41
Sarre Av, Horn. RM12 148 FJ65
Sarre Rd, NW2 119 CZ64
Orpington BR5 206 EW99
Sarsby Dr, Stai. TW19 173 BA89
Sarsen Av, Houns. TW3 156 BZ82
Sarsfeld Rd, SW12 180 DF88
Sarsfield Rd, Grnf. UB6 137 CH68
Sartor Rd, SE15 163 DX84
Sarum Complex, Uxb. UB8 134 BH68
Sarum Grn, Wey. KT13 195 BS104
Sch **Sarum Hall Sch**, NW3 *off Eton Av* 140 DE66
Sarum Pl, Hem.H. HP2 40 BL16
Sarum Ter, E3 13 L4
Satanita Cl, E16 *off Fulmer Rd* 144 EK72
Satchell Mead, NW9 97 CT53
Satchwell Rd, E2 12 A2
Satinwood Ct, Hem.H. HP3 40 BL22
Satis Ct, Epsom KT17 *off Windmill Av* 217 CT111
Sattar Ms, N16 *off Clissold Rd* 122 DR62
Saturn Way, Hem.H. HP2 40 BM18
Sauls Grn, E11 *off Napier Rd* 124 EE62
Saunder Cl, Wal.Cr. EN8 *off Welsummer Way* 67 DX27
Saunders Cl, E14 13 M10
Gravesend (Nthflt) DA11 190 GE89
Saunders Copse, Wok. GU22 226 AV122
Saunders La, Wok. GU22 226 AS122
Saunders Ness Rd, E14 24 D9
Saunders Rd, SE18 165 ET78
Uxbridge UB10 134 BM66
Saunders St, SE11 20 C7
Saunders Way, SE28 *off Oriole Way* 146 EV73
Dartford DA1 188 FM89
Saunderton Rd, Wem. HA0 117 CH64
Saunton Av, Hayes UB3 155 BT80
Saunton Rd, Horn. RM12 127 FG61
Savage Gdns, E6 145 EM72
EC3 11 M9
Savay Cl, Uxb. (Denh.) UB9 114 BG59
Savay La, Uxb. (Denh.) UB9 114 BG58
Savernake Rd, N9 82 DU44
NW3 120 DF63
Savery Dr, Surb. KT6 197 CJ101
Savile Cl, N.Mal. KT3 198 CS99
Thames Ditton KT7 197 CF102
Savile Gdns, Croy. CR0 202 DT103
Savile Row, W1 9 J9
Savill Cl, Wal.Cr. (Chsht) EN7 *off Markham Rd* 66 DQ25
Coll **Saville & Holdsworth Ltd Management Training Cen**, Esher KT10 *off Woodstock La S* 197 CJ103
Saville Cres, Ashf. TW15 175 BR93
Saville Rd, E16 144 EL74
W4 158 CR76
Romford RM6 126 EZ58
Twickenham TW1 177 CF88
Saville Row, Brom. BR2 204 EF102
Enfield EN3 83 DX40
Savill Gdns, SW20 *off Bodnant Gdns* 199 CU97
Savill Ms, Egh. TW20 *off Armstrong Rd* 172 AX93
Savill Row, Wdf.Grn. IG8 102 EF51
Savona Cl, SW19 179 CY94
Savona Est, SW8 161 DJ80
Savona St, SW8 161 DJ80
Savoy Av, Hayes UB3 155 BS78
Savoy Bldgs, WC2 10 A10
Savoy Cl, E15 *off Arthingworth St* 144 EE67
Edgware HA8 96 CN50
Uxbridge (Hare.) UB9 92 BK54
Savoy Ct, WC2 9 P10
Savoy Hill, WC2 10 A10
Riv **Savoy Pier** 10 A10
Savoy Pl, WC2 9 P10
Savoy Rd, Dart. DA1 188 FK85
Savoy Row, WC2 10 A9
Savoy Steps, WC2 *off Savoy St* 141 DM73
Savoy St, WC2 10 A9
Savoy Way, WC2 10 A10
Savoy Wd, Harl. CM19 51 EN20
Sawbill Cl, Hayes UB4 136 BX71
SAWBRIDGEWORTH, CM21 36 EW05
Sawells, Brox. EN10 49 DZ21
Sawkins Cl, SW19 179 CY89
Sawley Rd, W12 139 CT74
Sawmill Yd, E3 143 DY67
Sawpit La, Guil. (E.Clan.) GU4 244 BL131
Sawtry Cl, Cars. SM5 200 DE101
Sawtry Way, Borwd. WD6 78 CN38
Sawyer Cl, N9 *off Lion Rd* 100 DU47
Sawyers Chase, Rom. (Abridge) RM4 86 EV41
Sawyers Cl, Dag. RM10 147 FC65
Windsor SL4 151 AL80
Sawyers Gro, Brwd. CM15 108 FX46
Sawyers Hall La, Brwd. CM15 108 FW45
Sawyer's Hill, Rich. TW10 178 CP87
Sawyers La, Borwd. (Elstree) WD6 77 CH40
Potters Bar EN6 63 CX34
Sawyers Lawn, W13 137 CF72
Sawyer St, SE1 20 G3
Sawyers Way, Hem.H. HP2 40 BM20
Saxby Rd, SW2 181 DL87
Saxham Rd, Bark. IG11 145 ES68
Saxley, Horl. RH6 *off Ewelands* 269 DJ147
Saxlingham Rd, E4 101 ED48
Saxon Av, Felt. TW13 176 BZ89
Saxonbury Av, Sun. TW16 195 BV97
Saxonbury Cl, Mitch. CR4 200 DD97
Saxonbury Gdns, Surb. KT6 197 CJ102
Saxon Cl, E17 123 EA59
Amersham HP6 55 AS38
Brentwood CM13 109 GA48
Gravesend (Nthflt) DA11 190 GC90
Romford RM3 106 FM54
Sevenoaks (Otford) TN14 241 FF117
Slough SL3 153 AZ75
Surbiton KT6 197 CK100
Uxbridge UB8 134 BM71
Saxon Ct, Borwd. WD6 78 CL40
Saxon Dr, W3 138 CP72
Saxonfield Cl, SW2 181 DM87
Saxon Gdns, Maid. (Taplow) SL6 130 AD70
Southall UB1 *off Saxon Rd* 136 BY73
Saxon Pl, Dart. (Hort.Kir.) DA4 208 FQ99
Sch **Saxon Prim Sch**, Shep. TW17 *off Briar Rd* 194 BN99
Saxon Rd, E3 143 DZ68
E6 145 EM70
N22 99 DP53
SE25 202 DR99
Ashford TW15 175 BR93
Bromley BR1 184 EF94
Dartford (Hawley) DA2 188 FL91
Ilford IG1 145 EP65
Kingston upon Thames KT2 198 CL95
Southall UB1 136 BY74
Walton-on-Thames KT12 196 BX104
Wembley HA9 118 CQ62
Saxons, Tad. KT20 233 CX121
Saxon Shore Way, Grav. DA12 191 GM86
Saxon Wk, Sid. DA14 186 EW93
Saxon Way, N14 81 DK44
Reigate RH2 249 CZ133
Waltham Abbey EN9 67 EC33
West Drayton UB7 154 BJ79
Windsor (Old Wind.) SL4 172 AV86
Saxony Par, Hayes UB3 135 BQ71
Saxton Cl, SE13 163 ED83
Saxton Ms, Wat. WD17 75 BU40
Saxville Rd, Orp. BR5 206 EV97
Sayer Cl, Green. DA9 189 FU85
Sayers Cl, Lthd. (Fetch.) KT22 230 CC124
Sayers Gdns, Berk. HP4 38 AU16
Sayers Wk, Rich. TW10 *off Stafford Pl* 178 CM87
Sayesbury La, N18 100 DU50
Sayesbury Rd, Saw. CM21 36 EX05
Sayes Ct, SE8 *off Sayes Ct St* 163 DZ78
Addlestone KT15 212 BJ106
Sayes Ct Fm Dr, Add. KT15 212 BH106
Sch **Sayes Ct Jun Sch**, Add. KT15 *off Sayes Ct Fm Dr* 212 BH106
Sayes Ct Rd, Orp. BR5 206 EU98
Sayes Ct St, SE8 163 DZ79
Sayes Gdns, Saw. CM21 36 EZ05
Sayward Cl, Chesh. HP5 54 AR29
Scadbury Pk, Chis. BR7 185 ET93
Scads Hill Cl, Orp. BR6 205 ET100
Scafell Rd, Slou. SL2 131 AM71
Scala St, W1 9 K5
Scales Rd, N17 122 DT55
Scammel Way, Wat. WD18 75 BT44
Scampston Ms, W10 6 B7
Scampton Rd, Houns. (Hthrw Air.) TW6 *off Southampton Rd* 174 BM86
Scandrett St, E1 22 C2
Scarba Wk, N1 5 J4
Scarborough Cl, Sutt. SM2 217 CZ111
Westerham (Bigg.H.) TN16 238 EJ118
Scarborough Rd, E11 123 ED60
N4 121 DN59
N9 100 DW45
Hounslow (Hthrw Air.) TW6 *off Southern Perimeter Rd* 175 BQ86
Scarborough St, E1 11 P8
Scarborough Way, Slou. SL1 151 AP75
Scarbrook Rd, Croy. CR0 202 DQ104
Sch **Scargill Inf Sch**, Rain. RM13 *off Mungo Pk Rd* 147 FG65
Sch **Scargill Jun Sch**, Rain. RM13 *off Mungo Pk Rd* 147 FG65
Scarle Rd, Wem. HA0 137 CK65
Scarlet Cl, Orp. BR5 206 EV98
Scarlet Rd, SE6 184 EE90
Scarlett Cl, Wok. GU21 *off Bingham Dr* 226 AT118
Scarlette Manor Way, SW2 *off Papworth Way* 181 DN87
Scarsbrook Rd, SE3 164 EK83
Scarsdale Pl, W8 17 J5
Scarsdale Rd, Har. HA2 116 CC62
Scarsdale Vil, W8 17 H6
Scarth Rd, SW13 159 CT83
Scatterdells La, Kings L. (Chipper.) WD4 57 BF30
Scawen Cl, Cars. SM5 218 DG105
Scawen Rd, SE8 23 J10
Scawfell St, E2 5 P10
Scaynes Link, N12 98 DA50
Sceaux Est, SE5 162 DS81
Sceptre Rd, E2 12 F2
Uni **Schiller Int Uni**, SE1 20 C2
Schofield Wk, SE3 *off Dornberg Cl* 164 EH80
Scholars Ms, Welw.G.C. AL8 29 CX07
Scholars Pl, N16 *off Oldfield Rd* 122 DS62
Scholars Rd, E4 101 EC46
SW12 181 DJ88
Scholars Wk, Ger.Cr. (Chal.St.P.) SL9 90 AY51
Guildford GU2 258 AV135
Hatfield AL10 45 CU21
Slough SL3 *off Station Rd* 153 BA75
Scholars Way, Amer. HP6 72 AT38
Scholefield Rd, N19 121 DK60
Schonfeld Sq, N16 122 DR61
Schoolbank Rd, SE10 25 J7
Schoolbell Ms, E3 *off Arbery Rd* 143 DY68
School Cl, Guil. GU1 242 AX132
Hatfield (Essen.) AL9 *off School La* 46 DF17
School Cres, Dart. (Cray.) DA1 167 FF84
Schoolfield Rd, Grays RM20 169 FU79
School Gdns, Berk. (Pott.End) HP4 39 BB17
School Grn La, Epp. (N.Wld Bas.) CM16 71 FC25
School Hill, Red. RH1 251 DJ128
Schoolhouse Gdns, Loug. IG10 85 EP42
Schoolhouse La, E1 12 G9
School Ho La, Tedd. TW11 177 CH94
School La, Add. KT15 212 BG105
Amersham (Amer.O.T.) HP7 55 AM39
Beaconsfield (Seer Grn) HP9 89 AR51
Bushey WD23 94 CB45
Caterham CR3 252 DT126
Chalfont St. Giles HP8 90 AV47
Chigwell IG7 103 ET49
Dartford (Bean) DA2 189 FW90
Dartford (Hort.Kir.) DA4 208 FQ98
Dorking (Mick.) RH5 247 CJ127
Dorking (Westc.) RH4 263 CD137
Egham TW20 173 BA92
Gerrards Cross (Chal.St.P.) SL9 90 AX54
Guildford (E.Clan.) GU4 244 BL131
Harlow CM20 35 ES12
Hatfield AL10 45 CV17
Hatfield (Essen.) AL9 46 DE17
Kingston upon Thames KT1 *off School Rd* 197 CJ95
Leatherhead (Fetch.) KT22 231 CD122
Leatherhead (W.Hors.) KT24 245 BP129
Longfield DA3 209 FT100
Ongar (Magd.Lav.) CM5 53 FD17
Pinner HA5 116 BY56
St. Albans (Brick.Wd) AL2 60 CA31
Sevenoaks (Seal) TN15 257 FM121
Shepperton TW17 195 BP100
Slough SL2 132 AT73
Slough (Stoke P.) SL2 132 AV67
Surbiton KT6 198 CN102
Swanley BR8 207 FH95
Tadworth KT20 *off Chequers La* 249 CU125
Welling DA16 166 EV83
Welwyn (Tewin) AL6 30 DE06
Woking (Ockham) GU23 229 BP122
School Mead, Abb.L. WD5 59 BS32
Coll **School of Economic Science**, W1 8 F7
Coll **School of Nursing & Midwifery**, Sid. DA14 *off Frognal Pl* 186 EU93
Uni **School of Oriental & African Studies**, Russell Sq Campus, WC1 9 M4
Vernon Sq Campus, WC1 141 DM69
Uni **School of Pharmacy**, WC1 9 P3
School Pas, Kings.T. KT1 198 CM96
Southall UB1 136 BZ74
School Rd, E12 *off Sixth Av* 125 EM63
NW10 138 CR70
Ashford TW15 175 BP93
Chislehurst BR7 205 EQ95
Dagenham RM10 146 FA67
East Molesey KT8 197 CD98
Hampton (Hmptn H.) TW12 176 CC93
High Wycombe (Penn) HP10 88 AC47
High Wycombe (Woob.Grn) HP10 110 AE57
Hounslow TW3 156 CC83
Kingston upon Thames KT1 197 CJ95
Ongar CM5 71 FG32
Potters Bar EN6 64 DC30
West Drayton UB7 154 BK79
School Rd Av, Hmptn. (Hmptn H.) TW12 176 CC93
School Row, Hem.H. HP1 39 BF21
School Wk, Horl. RH6 *off Thornton Cl* 268 DE148
Slough SL2 *off Grasmere Av* 132 AV73
Sunbury-on-Thames TW16 195 BT98
School Way, N12 *off High Rd* 98 DC49
Schoolway, N12 (Woodhouse Rd) 98 DD51
School Way, Dag. RM8 126 EW62
Schooner Cl, E14 24 E6
SE16 22 G3
Barking IG11 146 EV69
Schooner Ct, Dart. DA2 168 FQ84
Schroder Ct, Egh. (Eng.Grn) TW20 172 AV92
Schubert Rd, SW15 179 CZ85
Borehamwood (Elstree) WD6 77 CK44
★ **Science Mus**, SW7 17 P6
Scilla Ct, Grays RM17 170 GD79
Scillonian Rd, Guil. GU2 258 AU135
Scimitar Pk, Harl. CM18 35 EM14
Sclater St, E1 11 N3
Scoble Pl, N16 *off Amhurst Rd* 122 DT63
Scoles Cres, SW2 181 DN88
Scope Way, Kings.T. KT1 198 CL98
Scoresby St, SE1 20 E2
Scorton Av, Grnf. UB6 137 CG68
Scotch Common, W13 137 CG71
Scoter Cl, Wdf.Grn. IG8 *off Mallards Rd* 102 EH52
Scot Gro, Pnr. HA5 94 BX52
Scotia Rd, SW2 181 DN87
Scotland Br Rd, Add. (New Haw) KT15 212 BG111
Scotland Grn, N17 100 DT54
Scotland Grn Rd, Enf. EN3 83 DX43
Scotland Grn Rd N, Enf. EN3 83 DX42
Scotland Pl, SW1 19 N1
Scotland Rd, Buck.H. IG9 102 EJ46
Scotlands Dr, Slou. (Farn.Com.) SL2 131 AP65
Scotney Cl, Orp. BR6 223 EN105
Scotney Wk, Horn. RM12 *off Bonington Rd* 128 FK64
Scotscraig, Rad. WD7 77 CF35
Scotsdale Cl, Orp. BR5 205 ES98
Sutton SM3 217 CY108
Scotsdale Rd, SE12 184 EH85
Scotshall La, Warl. CR6 221 EC114
Scots Hill, Rick. (Crox.Grn) WD3 74 BM44

⊖ London Underground station DLR Docklands Light Railway station Tra Tramlink station Riv Pedestrian ferry landing stage

Scots Hill Cl, Rick. (Crox.Grn) WD3 74 BM44
Scotsmill La, Rick. (Crox.Grn) WD3 74 BM44
Scotswood Cl, Beac. HP9 89 AK50
Scotswood St, EC1 10 D3
Scotswood Wk, N17 100 DU52
Scott Av, Ware (Stans.Abb.) SG12 33 EB11
Scott Cl, SW16 201 DM95
Epsom KT19 216 CQ106
Guildford GU2 242 AU132
Slough (Farn.Com.) SL2 111 AQ64
West Drayton UB7 154 BM77
Scott Ct, W3 off Petersfield Rd 158 CQ75
Scott Cres, Erith DA8 off Cloudesley Rd 167 FF81
Harrow HA2 116 CB60
Scott Ellis Gdns, NW8 7 N2
Scottes La, Dag. RM8 off Valence Av 126 EX60
Scott Fm Cl, T.Ditt. KT7 197 CH102
Scott Gdns, Houns. TW5 156 BX80
Scott Ho, E13 off Queens Rd W 144 EG68
N18 100 DU50
Scott Lidgett Cres, SE16 22 A4
Scott Rd, Grav. DA12 191 GK92
Grays RM16 171 GG77
Scott Russell Pl, E14 24 A9
Scotts Av, Brom. BR2 203 ED96
Sunbury-on-Thames TW16 175 BS94
Scotts Cl, Horn. RM12 off Rye Cl 128 FJ64
Staines TW19 174 BK88
Ware SG12 33 DX07
Scotts Dr, Hmptn. TW12 176 CB94
Scotts Fm Rd, Epsom KT19 216 CQ107
Scotts La, Brom. BR2 203 ED97
Walton-on-Thames KT12 214 BX105
Sch Scotts Pk Prim Sch, Brom. BR1 off Orchard Rd 204 EJ95
Sch Scotts Prim Sch, Horn. RM12 off Bonington Rd 128 FJ64
Scotts Rd, E10 123 EC60
W12 159 CV75
Bromley BR1 184 EG94
Southall UB2 156 BW76
Ware SG12 33 DX07
Scott St, E1 12 C4
Scotts Vw, Welw.G.C. AL8 29 CW10
Scotts Way, Sev. TN13 256 FE122
Sunbury-on-Thames TW16 175 BS93
Scottswood Cl, Bushey WD23 off Scottswood Rd 76 BY40
Scottswood Rd, Bushey WD23 76 BY40
Scott Trimmer Way, Houns. TW3 156 BY82
Scottwell Dr, NW9 119 CT57
Sch Scott Wilkie Prim Sch, E16 off Hoskins Cl 144 EK72
Scoulding Rd, E16 15 K7
Scouler St, E14 14 E10
Scout App, NW10 118 CS63
Scout La, SW4 off Old Town 161 DJ83
Scout Way, NW7 96 CR49
Scovell Cres, SE1 20 G4
Scovell Rd, SE1 20 G4
Scratchers La, Long. (Fawk.Grn) DA3 209 FR103
Scrattons Ter, Bark. IG11 146 EX68
Scriveners Cl, Hem.H. HP2 40 BL20
Scriven St, E8 5 P7
Scrooby St, SE6 183 EB86
Scrubbitts Pk Rd, Rad. WD7 77 CG35
Scrubbitts Sq, Rad. WD7 off The Dell 77 CG36
Scrubs La, NW10 139 CU69
W10 139 CU69
Scrutton Cl, SW12 181 DK87
Scrutton St, EC2 11 L4
Scudamore La, NW9 118 CQ55
Scudders Hill, Long. (Fawk.Grn) DA3 209 FV100
Scutari Rd, SE22 182 DW85
Scylla Cres, Houns. (Hthrw Air.) TW6 175 BP87
Scylla Pl, Wok. (St.John's) GU21 off Church Rd 226 AU119
Scylla Rd, SE15 162 DV83
Hounslow (Hthrw Air.) TW6 175 BP86
Seaborough Rd, Grays RM16 171 GJ76
Sch Seabright JMI Sch, E2 off Audrey St 142 DU68
Seabright St, E2 12 C2
Seabrook Dr, W.Wick. BR4 204 EE103
Seabrooke Ri, Grays RM17 170 GB79
Seabrook Gdns, Rom. RM7 126 FA59
Seabrook Rd, Dag. RM8 126 EX62
Kings Langley WD4 59 BR27
Seaburn Cl, Rain. RM13 147 FE68
Seacole Cl, W3 138 CR71
Seacon Twr, E14 off Hutchings St 163 EA75
Seacourt Rd, SE2 166 EX75
Slough SL3 153 BB77
Seacroft Gdns, Wat. WD19 94 BX48
Seafield Rd, N11 99 DK49
Seaford Cl, Ruis. HA4 115 BR61
Seaford Rd, E17 123 EB55
N15 122 DR57
W13 137 CH74
Enfield EN1 82 DS42
Hounslow (Hthrw Air.) TW6 174 BK85
Seaford St, WC1 9 P2
Seaforth Av, N.Mal. KT3 199 CV99
Seaforth Cl, Rom. RM1 105 FE52
Seaforth Cres, N5 4 G1
Seaforth Dr, Wal.Cr. EN8 67 DX34
Seaforth Gdns, N21 99 DM45
Epsom KT19 217 CT105
Woodford Green IG8 102 EJ50
Seaforth Pl, SW1 off Buckingham Gate 161 DJ76
Seagrave Rd, SW6 160 DA79
Beaconsfield HP9 88 AJ51
Seagry Rd, E11 124 EG58
Seagull Cl, Bark. IG11 146 EU69
Seagull La, E16 15 M9
SEAL, Sev. TN15 257 FN121
Sealand Rd, Houns. (Hthrw Air.) TW6 174 BN86
Sealand Wk, Nthlt. UB5 off Wayfarer Rd 136 BY69
Seal Dr, Sev. (Seal) TN15 257 FM121
Seale Hill, Reig. RH2 266 DA136
Seal Hollow Rd, Sev. TN13, TN15 257 FJ124
Seal Rd, Sev. TN14, TN15 257 FJ121
Seal St, E8 122 DT63
Seaman Cl, St.Alb. (Park St) AL2 61 CD25
Searches La, Abb.L. (Bedmond) WD5 59 BV28
Searchwood Rd, Warl. CR6 236 DV118
Searle Pl, N4 off Evershot Rd 121 DM60
Searles Cl, SW11 160 DE80
Searles Dr, E6 145 EP71
Searles Rd, SE1 21 K7
Sears St, SE5 162 DR80
Seasprite Cl, Nthlt. UB5 136 BX69
Seaton Av, Ilf. IG3 125 ES64
Seaton Cl, E13 15 M4
SE11 20 D9
SW15 179 CV88
Twickenham TW2 177 CD86
Seaton Dr, Ashf. TW15 174 BL89
Seaton Gdns, Ruis. HA4 115 BU62
Sch Seaton Ho Sch, Sutt. SM2 off Banstead Rd S 218 DD110
Seaton Pt, E5 off Nolan Way 122 DV63
Seaton Rd, Dart. DA1 187 FG87
Hayes UB3 155 BR77
Hemel Hempstead HP3 40 BK23
Mitcham CR4 200 DE96
St. Albans (Lon.Col.) AL2 61 CK26
Twickenham TW2 176 CC86
Welling DA16 166 EW80
Wembley HA0 138 CL68
Seaton Sq, NW7 off Tavistock Av 97 CX52
Seaton St, N18 100 DU50
Sebastian Av, Brwd. (Shenf.) CM15 109 GA44
Sebastian St, EC1 10 F2
Sebastopol Rd, N9 100 DU49
Sebbon St, N1 4 F6
Sebergham Gro, NW7 97 CU52
Sebert Rd, E7 124 EH64
Sebright Pas, E2 off Hackney Rd 142 DU68
Sebright Rd, Barn. EN5 79 CX40
Hemel Hempstead HP1 40 BG21
Secker Cres, Har. HA3 94 CC53
Secker St, SE1 20 C2
Second Av, E12 124 EL63
E13 15 L1
E17 123 EA57
N18 100 DW49
NW4 119 CX56
SW14 158 CS83
W3 139 CT74
W10 6 D3
Dagenham RM10 147 FB67
Enfield EN1 82 DT43
Grays RM20 169 FU79
Harlow CM18 51 ER15
Hayes UB3 135 BT74
Romford RM6 126 EW57
Waltham Abbey EN9 off Breach Barn Mobile Home Pk 68 EH30
Walton-on-Thames KT12 195 BV100
Watford WD25 76 BX35
Wembley HA9 117 CK61
Second Cl, W.Mol. KT8 196 CC98
Second Cres, Slou. SL1 131 AQ71
Second Cross Rd, Twick. TW2 177 CE89
Second Way, Wem. HA9 118 CP63
Sedan Way, SE17 21 L9
Sedcombe Cl, Sid. DA14 off Knoll Rd 186 EV91
Sedcote Rd, Enf. EN3 82 DW43
Sedding St, SW1 18 E7
Seddon Highwalk, EC2 off Beech St 142 DQ71
Seddon Ho, EC2 off The Barbican 142 DQ71
Seddon Rd, Mord. SM4 200 DD99
Seddon St, WC1 10 B2
Sedgebrook Rd, SE3 164 EK82
Sedgecombe Av, Har. HA3 117 CJ57
Sedge Ct, Grays RM17 170 GE80
Sedgefield Cl, Rom. RM3 106 FM49
Sedgefield Cres, Rom. RM3 106 FM49
Sedgeford Rd, W12 139 CT74
Sedge Grn, Harl. (Roydon) CM19 50 EE20
Waltham Abbey EN9 50 EE20
Sedgehill Rd, SE6 183 EA91
Sch Sedgehill Sch, SE6 off Sedgehill Rd 183 EB92
Sedgemere Av, N2 120 DC55
Sedgemere Rd, SE2 166 EW76
Sedgemoor Dr, Dag. RM10 126 FA63
Sedge Rd, N17 100 DW52
Sedgeway, SE6 184 EF88
Sedgewick Av, Uxb. UB10 135 BP66
Sedgewood Cl, Brom. BR2 204 EF101
Sedgmoor Pl, SE5 162 DS80
Sedgwick Rd, E10 123 EC61
Sedgwick St, E9 123 DX64
Sedleigh Rd, SW18 179 CZ86
Sedlescombe Rd, SW6 159 CZ79
Sedley, Grav. (Sthflt) DA13 190 GA93
Sedley Cl, Enf. EN1 82 DV38
Sedley Gro, Uxb. (Hare.) UB9 114 BJ56
Sedley Pl, W1 8 G8
Sedley Ri, Loug. IG10 85 EM40
Sch Sedley's C of E First Sch, Grav. DA13 off Church St 190 GA92
Sedum Cl, NW9 118 CP57
Seeley Dr, SE21 182 DS91
Seeleys, Harl. CM17 36 EW12
Seeleys Cl, Beac. HP9 88 AJ51
Seeleys La, Beac. HP9 off Seeleys Wk 89 AK52
Seeleys Rd, Beac. HP9 88 AJ50
Seeleys Wk, Beac. HP9 88 AJ52
Seelig Av, NW9 119 CU59
Seely Rd, SW17 180 DG93
SEER GREEN, Beac. HP9 89 AR52
⇌ Seer Green 89 AR52
Sch Seer Grn C of E Comb Sch, Beac. HP9 off School La 89 AQ51
Seer Grn La, Beac. (Jordans) HP9 90 AS52
Seer Mead, Beac. (Seer Grn) HP9 89 AR52
Seething La, EC3 11 M10
Seething Wells La, Surb. KT6 197 CJ100
Sefton Av, NW7 96 CR50
Harrow HA3 95 CD53
Sefton Cl, Orp. BR5 205 ET98
St. Albans AL1 off Blenheim Rd 43 CF19
Slough (Stoke P.) SL2 132 AT66
Sefton Paddock, Slou. (Stoke P.) SL2 132 AU66
Sefton Pk, Slou. (Stoke P.) SL2 132 AU66
Sefton Rd, Croy. CR0 202 DU102
Epsom KT19 216 CR110
Orpington BR5 205 ET98
Sefton St, SW15 159 CW82
Sefton Way, Uxb. UB8 134 BJ72
Segal Cl, SE23 183 DY87
Segrave Cl, Wey. KT13 212 BN108
Sekforde St, EC1 10 E4
Sekhon Ter, Felt. TW13 176 CA90
Selah Dr, Swan. BR8 207 FC95
Selan Gdns, Hayes UB4 135 BV71
Selbie Av, NW10 119 CT64
Selborne Av, E12 off Walton Rd 125 EN63
Bexley DA5 186 EY88
Selborne Gdns, NW4 119 CU56
Greenford UB6 137 CG67
Sch Selborne Prim Sch, Grnf. UB6 off Conway Cres 137 CF68
Selborne Rd, E17 123 DZ57
N14 99 DL48
N22 99 DM53
SE5 off Denmark Hill 162 DR82
Croydon CR0 202 DS104
Ilford IG1 125 EN61
New Malden KT3 198 CS96
Sidcup DA14 186 EV91
Selbourne Av, E17 123 DZ56
Addlestone (New Haw) KT15 212 BH110
Surbiton KT6 198 CM103
Selbourne Cl, Add. (New Haw) KT15 212 BH109
Selbourne Rd, Guil. GU4 243 BA131
Selbourne Sq, Gdse. RH9 252 DW130
Selbourne Wk, E17 off Selbourne Wk Shop Cen 123 DZ56
Selbourne Wk Shop Cen, E17 123 DZ56
Selby Av, St.Alb. AL3 43 CD20
Selby Chase, Ruis. HA4 115 BV61
Selby Cl, E6 off Linton Gdns 144 EL71
Chessington KT9 216 CL108
Chislehurst BR7 185 EN93
Selby Gdns, Sthl. UB1 136 CA70
Selby Grn, Cars. SM5 200 DE101
Selby Rd, E11 124 EE62
E13 15 P5
N17 100 DS51
SE20 202 DU96
W5 137 CH70
Ashford TW15 175 BQ93
Carshalton SM5 200 DE101
Selby St, E1 12 B4
Selby Wk, Wok. GU21 off Wyndham Rd 226 AV118
Selcroft Rd, Pur. CR8 219 DP112
Selden Hill, Hem.H. HP2 40 BK21
Selden Rd, SE15 162 DW82
Selden Wk, N7 off Durham Rd 121 DM61
Sele Rd, Hert. SG14 31 DP09
Sch Sele Sch, The, Hert. SG14 off Welwyn Rd 31 DM09
★ Selfridges, W1 8 F8
SELHURST, SE25 202 DS100
⇌ Selhurst 202 DS99
Selhurst Cl, SW19 179 CX88
Woking GU21 227 AZ115
Sch Selhurst High Sch for Boys, Croy. CR0 off The Crescent 202 DR99
Selhurst New Rd, SE25 202 DS100
Selhurst Pl, SE25 202 DS100
Selhurst Rd, N9 100 DR48
SE25 202 DS99
Selinas La, Dag. RM8 126 EY59
Selkirk Dr, Erith DA8 167 FE81
Selkirk Rd, SW17 180 DE91
Twickenham TW2 176 CC89
Sell Cl, Wal.Cr. (Chsht) EN7 off Gladding Rd 65 DP26
Sellers Cl, Borwd. WD6 78 CQ39
Sellers Hall Cl, N3 98 DA52
Sch Sellincourt Prim Sch, SW17 off Sellincourt Rd 180 DE93
Sellincourt Rd, SW17 180 DE92
Sellindge Cl, Beck. BR3 183 DZ94
Sellons Av, NW10 139 CT67
Sells Cl, Guil. GU1 259 AZ136
Sells Rd, Ware SG12 33 DZ05
Sellwood Dr, Barn. EN5 79 CX43
Sellwood St, SW2 off Tulse Hill 181 DN87
SELSDON, S.Croy. CR2 220 DW110
Selsdon Av, S.Croy. CR2 220 DR107
Selsdon Cl, Rom. RM5 105 FC53
Surbiton KT6 198 CL99
Selsdon Cres, S.Croy. CR2 220 DW109
Sch Selsdon High Sch, S.Croy. CR2 off Farnborough Av 221 DX108
Selsdon Pk Rd, S.Croy. CR2 221 DX109
Sch Selsdon Prim Sch, S.Croy. CR2 off Addington Rd 220 DW109
Selsdon Rd, E11 124 EG59
E13 144 EJ67
NW2 119 CT61
SE27 181 DP90
Addlestone (New Haw) KT15 212 BG111
South Croydon CR2 220 DR106
Selsdon Rd Ind Est, S.Croy. CR2 off Selsdon Rd 220 DR107
Selsdon Way, E14 24 B6
Selsea Pl, N16 5 M1
Selsey Cres, Well. DA16 166 EX81
Selsey St, E14 13 N6
Selvage La, NW7 96 CR50
Selway Cl, Pnr. HA5 115 BV56
Selwood Cl, Stai. (Stanw.) TW19 174 BJ86
Selwood Gdns, Stai. (Stanw.) TW19 174 BJ86
Selwood Pl, SW7 17 N9
Selwood Rd, Brwd. CM14 108 FT48
Chessington KT9 215 CK105
Croydon CR0 202 DV103
Sutton SM3 199 CZ102
Woking GU22 227 BB120
Selwood Ter, SW7 17 N9
Selworthy Cl, E11 124 EG57
Selworthy Ho, SW11 160 DD81
Selworthy Rd, SE6 183 DZ90
Selwyn Av, E4 101 EC51
Hatfield AL10 44 CR19
Ilford IG3 125 ES58
Selwyn Av, Rich. TW9 158 CL83
Selwyn Cl, Houns. TW4 156 BY84
Selwyn Ct, SE3 164 EE83
Edgware HA8 off Camrose Av 96 CP52
Selwyn Cres, Hat. AL10 44 CS18
Welling DA16 166 EV84
Selwyn Dr, Hat. AL10 44 CR18
Sch Selwyn Inf Sch, E4 off Selwyn Av 101 EC51
Sch Selwyn Jun Sch, E4 off Cavendish Rd 101 EC51
Selwyn Pl, Orp. BR5 206 EV97
Sch Selwyn Prim Sch, E13 off Cecil Rd 144 EG67
Selwyn Rd, E3 143 DZ68
E13 144 EH67
NW10 138 CR66
New Malden KT3 198 CR99
Tilbury RM18 off Dock Rd 171 GF82
Semaphore Rd, Guil. GU1 258 AY136
Semley Pl, SW1 18 F8
Semley Rd, SW16 201 DL96
Semper Cl, Wok. (Knap.) GU21 226 AS117
Semper Rd, Grays RM16 171 GJ75
Semphill Rd, Hem.H. HP3 40 BL23
Senate St, SE15 162 DW82
Senator Wk, SE28 off Broadwater Rd 165 ER76
SEND, Wok. GU23 227 BC124
Sendall Ct, SW11 160 DD83
Send Barns La, Wok. (Send) GU23 227 BD124
Send Cl, Wok. (Send) GU23 227 BC123
Sch Send C of E GM First Sch, Wok. GU23 off Send Barns La 227 BE124
SENDGROVE, Wok. GU23 243 BC126
Send Hill, Wok. (Send) GU23 243 BC125
SEND MARSH, Wok. GU23 227 BF124
Send Marsh Rd, Wok. (Ripley) GU23 227 BF123
Send Par Cl, Wok. (Send) GU23 off Send Rd 227 BC123
Send Rd, Wok. (Send) GU23 227 BB122
Seneca Rd, Th.Hth. CR7 202 DQ98
Senga Rd, Wall. SM6 200 DG102
Senhouse Rd, Sutt. SM3 199 CX104
Senior St, W2 7 J5
Senlac Rd, SE12 184 EH88
Sennen Rd, Enf. EN1 100 DT45
Sennen Wk, SE9 184 EL90
Senrab St, E1 12 G7
Sentinel Cl, Nthlt. UB5 136 BY70
Sentinel Sq, NW4 119 CW56
Sentis Ct, Nthwd. HA6 off Carew Rd 93 BS51
September Way, Stan. HA7 95 CH51
Sequoia Cl, Bushey (Bushey Hth) WD23 off Giant Tree Hill 95 CD46
Sequoia Gdns, Orp. BR6 205 ET101
Sequoia Pk, Pnr. HA5 94 CB51
Serbin Cl, E10 123 EC59
Serenaders Rd, SW9 161 DN82
Sergeants Grn La, Wal.Abb. EN9 68 EJ33
Sergeants Pl, Cat. CR3 off Coulsdon Rd 236 DQ122
Sergehill La, Abb.L. (Bedmond) WD5 59 BT27
Serjeants Inn, EC4 10 D8
Serle St, WC2 10 B7
Sermed Ct, Slou. SL2 132 AW74
Sermon Dr, Swan. BR8 207 FC97
Sermon La, EC4 10 G8
★ Serpentine, The, W2 18 A2
Serpentine Ct, Sev. TN13 257 FK122
★ Serpentine Gall, W2 17 P2
Serpentine Grn, Red. RH1 off Malmstone Av 251 DK129
Serpentine Rd, W2 18 C2
Sevenoaks TN13 257 FJ123
Service Rd, The, Pot.B. EN6 64 DA32
Serviden Dr, Brom. BR1 204 EK95
Sch Servite RC Prim Sch, SW10 off Fulham Rd 160 DC79
Setchell Rd, SE1 21 N7
Setchell Way, SE1 21 N7
Seth St, SE16 22 F4
Seton Gdns, Dag. RM9 146 EW66
Settle Pt, E13 off London Rd 144 EG68
Settle Rd, E13 off London Rd 144 EG68
Romford RM3 106 FN49
Settles St, E1 12 B6
Settrington Rd, SW6 160 DB82
Seven Acres, Cars. SM5 200 DE103
Northwood HA6 93 BU51
Swanley BR8 207 FD100
Seven Arches App, Wey. KT13 212 BM108
Seven Arches Rd, Brwd. CM14 108 FX48
Seven Hills Cl, Walt. KT12 213 BS109
Seven Hills Rd, Cob. KT11 213 BS111
Iver SL0 133 BC65
Walton-on-Thames KT12 213 BS109
Seven Hills Rd S, Cob. KT11 213 BS113
SEVEN KINGS, Ilf. IG3 125 ES59
⇌ Seven Kings 125 ES60
Sch Seven Kings High Sch, Ilf. IG2 off Ley St 125 ER59
Seven Kings Rd, Ilf. IG3 125 ET61
Seven Kings Way, Kings.T. KT2 198 CL95
Sch Seven Mills Prim Sch, E14 23 P4
SEVENOAKS, TN13 - TN15 257 FJ125
⇌ Sevenoaks 256 FG124
Coll Sevenoaks Adult Ed Cen, Sev. TN13 off Bradbourne Rd 257 FH122
Sevenoaks Business Cen, Sev. TN14 257 FJ121
Sevenoaks Bypass, Sev. TN14 256 FC123
Sevenoaks Cl, Bexh. DA7 167 FC84
Romford RM3 106 FJ49
Sutton SM2 218 DA110
SEVENOAKS COMMON, Sev. TN13 257 FH129
Sevenoaks Ct, Nthwd. HA6 93 BQ52
H Sevenoaks Hosp, Sev. TN13 257 FJ121
Sevenoaks Ho, SE25 202 DU97
★ Sevenoaks Mus, Sev. TN13 257 FJ125
Sch Sevenoaks Prep Sch, Sev. TN15 off Fawke Common Rd 257 FN126
Sch Sevenoaks Prim Sch, Sev. TN13 off Bradbourne Pk Rd 256 FG123
Sevenoaks Rd, SE4 183 DY86
Orpington BR6 223 ET106
Orpington (Grn St Grn) BR6 223 ET108
Sevenoaks (Otford) TN14 241 FH116
Sch Sevenoaks Sch, Sev. TN13 off High St 257 FJ126
Sevenoaks Way, Orp. BR5 186 EW94
Sidcup DA14 186 EW94
⇌ Seven Sisters 122 DS57
⊖ Seven Sisters 122 DS57
Sch Seven Sisters Prim Sch, N15 off South Gro 122 DR57
Seven Sisters Rd, N4 121 DM62
N7 121 DM62
N15 122 DQ59
Seven Stars Cor, W12 off Goldhawk Rd 159 CU76
Seven Stars Yd, E1 11 P5
Seventh Av, E12 125 EM63
Hayes UB3 135 BU74
Severalls Av, Chesh. HP5 54 AQ30
Severnake Cl, E14 23 P7
Severn Av, Rom. RM2 127 FH55
Severn Cres, Slou. SL3 153 BB78
Severn Dr, Enf. EN1 82 DU38
Esher KT10 197 CG103
Upminster RM14 129 FR58
Walton-on-Thames KT12 196 BX103
Severnmead, Hem.H. HP2 40 BL17
Severn Rd, S.Ock. (Aveley) RM15 148 FQ72
Severns Fld, Epp. CM16 70 EU29
Severnvale, St.Alb. (Lon.Col.) AL2 off Thamesdale 62 CM27
Severn Way, NW10 119 CT64
Watford WD25 60 BW34
Severus Rd, SW11 160 DE84
Seville Ms, N1 5 L6
Seville St, SW1 18 D4
Sevington Rd, NW4 119 CV58
Sevington St, W9 7 J4
Seward Rd, W7 157 CG75
Beckenham BR3 203 DX96
SEWARDSTONE, E4 83 EC39
SEWARDSTONEBURY, E4 84 EE42
Sewardstone Gdns, E4 83 EB43
Sewardstone Grn, E4 84 EE42
Sewardstone Rd, E2 142 DW68
E4 101 EB45
Waltham Abbey EN9 83 EC38
Sewardstone Roundabout, Wal.Abb. EN9 83 EC35
Sewardstone St, Wal.Abb. EN9 67 EC34
Seward St, EC1 10 F3
Sewdley St, E5 123 DX62
Sewell Cl, Grays (Chaff.Hun.) RM16 169 FW78
St. Albans AL4 44 CL20
Sewell Harris Cl, Harl. CM20 35 ET13
Sewell Rd, SE2 166 EU76
Sewells, Welw.G.C. AL8 29 CY05
Sewell St, E13 15 M1
Sextant Av, E14 24 E7
Sexton Cl, Rain. RM13 off Blake Cl 147 FF67
Waltham Cross (Chsht) EN7 off Shambrook Rd 66 DQ25
Sexton Rd, Til. RM18 171 GF81
Seymer Rd, Rom. RM1 127 FD55
Seymour Av, N17 100 DU54
Caterham CR3 236 DQ123
Epsom KT17 217 CV109
Morden SM4 199 CX101
Seymour Cl, E.Mol. KT8 196 CC99
Loughton IG10 84 EL44
Pinner HA5 94 BZ53
Seymour Ct, E4 102 EF47
Seymour Cres, Hem.H. HP2 40 BL20
Seymour Dr, Brom. BR2 205 EM102
Seymour Gdns, SE4 163 DY83
Feltham TW13 176 BW91
Ilford IG1 125 EM60
Ruislip HA4 116 BX60
Surbiton KT5 198 CM99
Twickenham TW1 177 CH87
Seymour Ms, W1 8 E7
Sawbridgeworth CM21 36 EY08
Seymour Pl, SE25 202 DV98
W1 8 C6
Hornchurch RM11 128 FK59
Seymour Rd, E4 101 EB46
E6 144 EK68
E10 123 DZ60
N3 98 DB52
N8 121 DN57
N9 100 DV47
SW18 179 CZ87
SW19 179 CX89
W4 158 CQ77
Berkhamsted HP4 38 AS17
Carshalton SM5 218 DG106
Chalfont St. Giles HP8 90 AW49
East Molesey KT8 196 CC99
Gravesend (Nthflt) DA11 191 GF88
Hampton (Hmptn H.) TW12 176 CC92
Kingston upon Thames KT1 197 CK95
Mitcham CR4 200 DG101
St. Albans AL3 43 CE17
Slough SL1 151 AR75
Tilbury RM18 171 GF81
Seymours, Harl. CM19 51 EM18
Seymours, The, Loug. IG10 85 EN39
Seymour St, SE18 165 EQ76
W1 8 C8
W2 8 C8
Seymour Ter, SE20 202 DV95
Seymour Vil, SE20 202 DV95
Seymour Wk, SW10 160 DC79
Swanscombe DA10 190 FY87
Seymour Way, Sun. TW16 175 BS93
Seyssel St, E14 24 D7
Shaa Rd, W3 138 CR73
Shacklands Rd, Sev. (Bad.Mt) TN14 225 FB111
Shackleford Rd, Wok. GU22 227 BA121
Shacklegate La, Tedd. TW11 177 CE91
Shackleton Cl, SE23 off Featherstone Av 182 DV89
Shackleton Ct, E14 off Maritime Quay 163 EA78
W12 159 CV75
Shackleton Rd, Slou. SL1 132 AT73
Southall UB1 136 BZ73
Shackleton Wk, Guil. GU2 off Humbolt Cl 242 AT134
Shackleton Way, Abb.L. WD5 off Lysander Way 59 BU32
Welwyn Garden City AL7 30 DD09
SHACKLEWELL, N16 122 DT63
Shacklewell Grn, E8 122 DT63

★ Place of interest | H Hospital | Sch School | Coll College | Uni University | ⇌ Railway station

Sch Shacklewell JMI Sch,
E8 off Shacklewell Row 122 DT63
Shacklewell La, E8 5 N1
Shacklewell Rd, N16 122 DT63
Shacklewell Row, E8 122 DT63
Shacklewell St, E2 11 P3
Shadbolt Av, E4 101 DY50
Shadbolt Cl, Wor.Pk. KT4 199 CT103
Shad Thames, SE1 21 N2
SHADWELL, E1 12 E10
⊖ Shadwell 12 D9
DLR Shadwell 12 D9
Shadwell Ct, Nthlt. UB5
off Shadwell Dr 136 BZ68
Shadwell Dr, Nthlt. UB5 136 BZ69
Shadwell Gdns Est, E1 12 E9
Shadwell Pierhead, E1 12 F10
Shadwell Pl, E1 12 E9
Shady Bush Cl, Bushey
WD23 94 CC45
Shady La, Wat. WD17 75 BV40
Shaef Way, Tedd. TW11 177 CG94
Shafter Rd, Dag. RM10 147 FC65
Shaftesbury, Loug. IG10 84 EK41
Shaftesbury Av, W1 9 L9
WC2 9 L9
Barnet EN5 80 DC42
Enfield EN3 83 DX40
Feltham TW14 175 BU86
Harrow HA2 116 CB60
Harrow (Kenton) HA3 117 CK58
Southall UB2 156 CA77
Shaftesbury Circle, Har.
HA2 off Shaftesbury Av 116 CC60
Shaftesbury Ct, N1
off Shaftesbury St 142 DR68
Shaftesbury Cres, Stai.
TW18 174 BK94
Shaftesbury Gdns, NW10 138 CS70
Shaftesbury La, Dart. DA1 168 FP84
Shaftesbury Ms, SW4
off Clapham Common
S Side 181 DJ85
W8 17 H6
Sch Shaftesbury Pk Prim Sch,
SW11 off Ashbury Rd 160 DG82
Shaftesbury Pl, W14
off Warwick Rd 159 CZ77
Shaftesbury Pt, E13
off High St 144 EH68
Sch Shaftesbury Prim Sch,
E7 off Shaftesbury Rd 144 EJ66
Shaftesbury Quay, Hert.
SG14 off Railway St 32 DR09
Shaftesbury Rd, E4 101 ED46
E7 144 EJ66
E10 123 EA60
E17 123 EB58
N18 100 DS51
N19 121 DL60
Beckenham BR3 203 DZ96
Carshalton SM5 200 DD101
Epping CM16 69 ET29
Richmond TW9 158 CL83
Romford RM1 127 FF58
Watford WD17 76 BW41
Woking GU22 227 BA117
Shaftesburys, The, Bark.
IG11 145 EQ67
Sch Shaftesbury Sch, Har.
HA3 off Headstone La 94 CB53
Shaftesbury St, N1 5 H10
Shaftesbury Way, Kings L.
WD4 59 BQ28
Twickenham TW2 177 CD90
Shaftesbury Waye, Hayes
UB4 135 BV71
Shafto Ms, SW1 18 C6
Shafton Rd, E9 143 DX67
Shaggy Calf La, Slou. SL2 132 AU73
Shakespeare Av, N11 99 DJ50
NW10 138 CR67
Feltham TW14 175 BU86
Hayes UB4 135 BV70
Tilbury RM18 171 GH82
Shakespeare Cres, E12 145 EM65
NW10 138 CR67
Shakespeare Dr, Har. HA3 118 CM58
Shakespeare Gdns, N2 120 DF56
Shakespeare Ho, N14
off High St 99 DK47
Shakespeare Rd, E17 101 DX54
N3 off Popes Dr 98 DA53
NW7 97 CT49
SE24 181 DP85
W3 138 CQ74
W7 137 CF73
Addlestone KT15 212 BK105
Bexleyheath DA7 166 EY81
Dartford DA1 168 FN84
Romford RM1 127 FF58
★ Shakespeare's Globe Thea,
SE1 10 G10
Shakespeare Sq, Ilf. IG6 103 EQ51
Shakespeare St, Wat. WD24 75 BV38
Shakespeare Twr, EC2 11 H5
Shakespeare Way, Felt.
TW13 176 BW91
Shakspeare Ms, N16
off Shakspeare Wk 122 DS63
Shakspeare Wk, N16 122 DS63
Shalbourne Sq, E9 143 DZ65
Shalcomb St, SW10 160 DC79
Shalcross Dr, Wal.Cr. (Chsht)
EN8 67 DZ30
Shalden Ho, SW15
off Tunworth Cres 179 CT86
Shaldon Dr, Mord. SM4 199 CY99
Ruislip HA4 116 BW62
Shaldon Rd, Edg. HA8 96 CM53
Shaldon Way, Walt. KT12 196 BW104
Shale Grn, Red. RH1
off Bletchingley Rd 251 DK129
Shalfleet Dr, W10 6 A9
SHALFORD, Guil. GU4 258 AX141
⇌ Shalford 258 AY140
Shalford Cl, Orp. BR6 223 EQ105
Sch Shalford Co Inf Sch, Guil.
GU4 off Station Row 258 AY140
Shalford Rd, Guil. GU1,
GU4 258 AX137
Shalimar Gdns, W3 138 CQ73
Shalimar Rd, W3
off Hereford Rd 138 CQ73
Shallcross Cres, Hat. AL10 45 CU21
Shallons Rd, SE9 185 EP91
Shalstone Rd, SW14 158 CP83
Shalston Vil, Surb. KT6 198 CM100
Shambrook Rd, Wal.Cr.
(Chsht) EN7 65 DP25
Shamrock Cl, Lthd. (Fetch.)
KT22 231 CD121
Shamrock Ho, SE26
off Talisman Sq 182 DU91
Shamrock Rd, Croy. CR0 201 DM100
Shamrock Rd, Grav. DA12 191 GL87
Shamrock St, SW4 161 DK83
Shamrock Way, N14 99 DH46
Shandon Rd, SW4 181 DJ86
Shand St, SE1 21 L3
Shandy St, E1 13 H4
Shanklin Cl, Wal.Cr. EN7
off Hornbeam Way 66 DT29
Shanklin Gdns, Wat. WD19 94 BW49
Shanklin Rd, N8 121 DK57
N15 122 DU56
Shanklin Way, SE15
off Pentridge St 162 DT80
Shannon Cl, NW2 119 CX62
Southall UB2 156 BX78
Shannon Gro, SW9 161 DM84
Shannon Pl, NW8
off Allitsen Rd 140 DE68
Shannon Way, Beck. BR3 183 EB93
South Ockendon (Aveley)
RM15 148 FQ73
Shantock Hall La, Hem.H.
(Bov.) HP3 56 AY29
Shantock La, Hem.H. (Bov.)
HP3 56 AX30
Shap Cres, Cars. SM5 200 DF102
Shapland Way, N13 99 DM50
Sch Shapla Prim Sch, E1 12 A9
Shapwick Cl, N11
off Friern Barnet Rd 98 DF50
Shardcroft Av, SE24 181 DP85
Shardeloes Rd, SE4 163 DZ83
SE14 163 DZ83
Sharland Cl, Th.Hth. CR7
off Dunheved Rd N 201 DN100
Sharland Rd, Grav. DA12 191 GJ89
Sharman Ct, Sid. DA14 186 EU91
Sharman Row, Slou. SL3
off Ditton Rd 153 AZ78
Sharnbrooke Cl, Well. DA16 166 EW83
Sharney Av, Slou. SL3 153 BB76
Sharon Cl, Epsom KT19 216 CQ113
Leatherhead (Bkhm) KT23 230 CA124
Surbiton KT6 197 CK102
Sharon Gdns, E9 142 DW67
Sharon Rd, W4 158 CR78
Enfield EN3 83 DY40
Sharpcroft, Hem.H. HP2 40 BK18
Sharpe Cl, W7
off Templeman Rd 137 CF71
Sharpecroft, Harl. CM19 51 EQ15
Sharpes La, Hem.H. HP1 39 BB21
Sharpleshall St, NW1 140 DF66
Sharpness Cl, Hayes UB4 136 BY71
Sharps La, Ruis. HA4 115 BR60
Sharp Way, Dart. DA1 168 FM83
Sharratt St, SE15 162 DW79
Sharsted St, SE17 20 E10
Sharvel La, Nthlt. UB5 135 BU67
Shavers Pl, SW1 9 L10
Shaw Av, Bark. IG11 146 EY68
Shawbridge, Harl. CM19 51 EQ18
Shawbrooke Rd, SE9 184 EJ85
Shawbury Rd, SE22 182 DT85
Shaw Cl, SE28 146 EV74
Bushey (Bushey Hth)
WD23 95 CE47
Chertsey (Ott.) KT16 211 BC107
Epsom KT17 217 CT111
Hornchurch RM11 127 FH60
South Croydon CR2 220 DT112
Waltham Cross (Chsht)
EN8 66 DW28
Shaw Ct, SW11 160 DD83
Windsor SL4 172 AU85
Shaw Cres, Brwd. (Hutt.)
CM13 109 GD43
South Croydon CR2 220 DT112
Tilbury RM18 171 GH81
Shaw Dr, Walt. KT12 196 BW101
Shawfield Ct, West Dr. UB7 154 BL76
Shawfield Pk, Brom. BR1 204 EK96
Shawfield St, SW3 19 B10
Shawford Ct, SW15 179 CU87
Shawford Rd, Epsom KT19 216 CR107
Shaw Gdns, Bark. IG11 146 EY68
Slough SL3 off Ditton Rd 153 AZ78
Sch Shawley Comm Prim Sch,
Epsom KT18
off Shawley Way 233 CW118
Shawley Cres, Epsom KT18 233 CW118
Shawley Way, Epsom KT18 233 CV118
Sch Shaw Prim Sch, S.Ock.
RM15 off Avon Grn 149 FV72
Shaw Rd, SE22 162 DS84
Bromley BR1 184 EF90
Enfield EN3 83 DX39
Westerham (Tats.) TN16 238 EJ120
Shaws, The, Welw.G.C. AL7 30 DC10
Shaws Cotts, SE23 183 DY90
Shaw Sq, E17 101 DY53
Shaw Way, Wall. SM6 219 DL108
Shaxton Cres, Croy.
(New Adgtn) CR0 221 EC109
Sheares Hoppit, Ware
(Hunsdon) SG12 34 EK05
Shearing Dr, Cars. SM5
off Stavordale Rd 200 DC101
Shearling Way, N7 141 DL65
Shearman Rd, SE3 164 EF84
Shears Ct, Sun. TW16
off Staines Rd W 175 BS94
Sch Shears Grn Inf Sch, Grav.
DA11 off Packham Rd 191 GF90
Sch Shears Grn Jun Sch, Grav.
DA11 off White Av 191 GF90
Shearsmith Ho, E1 12 B9
Shearwater Cl, Bark. IG11 146 EU69
Shearwater Rd, Sutt. SM1 217 CZ106
Shearwater Way, Hayes
UB4 136 BX72
Shearwood Cres, Dart. DA1 167 FF83
Sheath's La, Lthd. KT22 214 CB113
Sheaveshill Av, NW9 118 CS56
Sheehy Way, Slou. SL2 132 AV73
Sheen Common Dr, Rich.
TW10 158 CN84
Sheen Ct, Rich. TW10 158 CN84
Sheen Ct Rd, Rich. TW10 158 CN84
Sheendale Rd, Rich. TW9 158 CM84
Sheenewood, SE26 182 DV92
Sheen Gate Gdns, SW14 158 CQ84
Sheen Gro, N1 4 C7
Sheen La, SW14 158 CQ83
Sch Sheen Mt Prim Sch, SW14
off West Temple Sheen 178 CP85
Sheen Pk, Rich. TW9 158 CM84
Sheen Rd, Orp. BR5 205 ET98
Richmond TW9, TW10 178 CL85
Sch Sheen Sec Sch, SW14
off Park Av 158 CS84
Sheen Way, Wall. SM6 219 DM106
Sheen Wd, SW14 178 CQ85
Sheepbarn La, Warl. CR6 222 EF112
Sheepcot Dr, Wat. WD25 60 BW34
Sheepcote, Welw.G.C. AL7 30 DA12
Sheepcote Cl, Beac. HP9 88 AJ51
Hounslow TW5 155 BU80
Sheepcote Gdns, Uxb.
(Denh.) UB9 114 BG58
Sheepcote La, SW11 160 DF82
High Wycombe
(Woob.Grn) HP10 110 AG61
Orpington BR5 206 EZ99
St. Albans (Wheat.) AL4 28 CL07
Slough (Burn.) SL1 110 AF62
Swanley BR8 206 EZ98
Sheepcote Rd, Har. HA1 117 CF58
Hemel Hempstead HP2 40 BM20
Windsor SL4 151 AL82
Windsor (Eton Wick) SL4 151 AM78
Sheepcotes Rd, Rom. RM6 126 EX56
Sheepcot La, Wat. WD25 59 BV34
Sheepfold La, Amer. HP7 55 AR39
Sheepfold Rd, Guil. GU2 242 AT131
Sheephouse Grn, Dor.
(Wotton) RH5 262 BZ140
Sheephouse La, Dor.
(Wotton) RH5 262 BZ139
Sheephouse Rd, Hem.H.
HP3 40 BM22
Sheephouse Way, N.Mal.
KT3 198 CS101
Sheeplands Av, Guil. GU1 243 BC132
Sheep La, E8 142 DV67
Sheep Wk, Epsom KT18 232 CR122
Reigate RH2 249 CY131
Shepperton TW17 194 BM101
Sheep Wk, The, Wok. GU22 227 BE118
Sheepwalk La, Lthd.
(E.Hors.) KT24 245 BT134
Sheep Wk Ms, SW19 179 CX93
SHEERING, B.Stort. CM22 37 FC07
Sch Sheering C of E VC Prim
Sch, B.Stort. CM22
off The Street 37 FD06
Sheering Dr, Harl. CM17 36 EX12
Sheering Lwr Rd, Harl.
CM17 36 EZ09
Sawbridgeworth CM21 36 FA06
Sheering Mill La, Saw.
CM21 36 EZ05
Sheering Rd, B.Stort.
(Hat.Hth) CM22 37 FF05
Harlow CM17 36 EY11
Sheerness Ms, E16 165 EP75
SHEERWATER, Wok. GU21 211 BC113
Sheerwater Av, Add.
(Wdhm) KT15 211 BE112
Sheerwater Rd, E16 144 EK71
Addlestone (Wdhm)
KT15 211 BE112
West Byfleet KT14 211 BE112
Sheethanger La, Hem.H.
(Felden) HP3 40 BG24
Sheet St, Wind. SL4 151 AR82
Sheffield Dr, Rom. RM3 106 FN50
Sheffield Gdns, Rom. RM3 106 FN50
Sheffield Rd, Houns. (Hthrw Air.)
TW6 off Southern
Perimeter Rd 175 BR85
Slough SL1 131 AQ72
Sheffield Sq, E3 13 M1
Sheffield St, WC2 10 A8
Sheffield Ter, W8 16 G2
Shefton Ri, Nthwd. HA6 93 BU52
Sheila Cl, Rom. RM5 105 FB52
Sheila Rd, Rom. RM5 105 FB52
Sheilings, The, Horn. RM11 128 FM57
Shelbourne Cl, Pnr. HA5 116 BZ55
Shelbourne Pl, Beck. BR3 183 DZ94
Shelbourne Rd, N17 100 DV54
Shelburne Dr, Houns. TW4
off Hanworth Rd 176 CA86
Shelburne Rd, N7 121 DM63
Shelbury Cl, Sid. DA14 186 EU90
Shelbury Rd, SE22 182 DV85
Sheldon Av, N6 120 DE59
Ilford IG5 103 EP54
Sheldon Cl, SE12 184 EH85
SE20 202 DV95
Harlow CM17 52 EY15
Reigate RH2 266 DB135
Waltham Cross (Chsht)
EN7 66 DS26
Sheldon Ct, Guil. GU1
off Lower
Edgeborough Rd 259 AZ135
Sheldon Rd, N18 100 DS49
NW2 119 CX63
Bexleyheath DA7 166 EZ81
Dagenham RM9 146 EY66
Sheldon Sq, W2 7 M6
Sheldon St, Croy. CR0 202 DQ104
Sheldrake Cl, E16 145 EM74
Sheldrake Pl, W8 16 G3
Sheldrick Cl, SW19 200 DD96
Shelduck Cl, E15 124 EF64
Sheldwich Ter, Brom. BR2 204 EL100
Shelford Pl, N16
off Stoke Newington
Ch St 122 DR62
Shelford Ri, SE19 182 DT94
Shelford Rd, Barn. EN5 79 CW44
Shelgate Rd, SW11 180 DE85
Shellbank La, Dart. (Bean)
DA2 189 FU93
★ Shell Cen, SE1 20 B2
Shell Cl, Brom. BR2 205 EM100
Shellduck Cl, NW9
off Swan Dr 96 CS54
Shelley Av, E12 144 EL65
Greenford UB6 137 CD69
Hornchurch RM12 127 FF61
Shelley Cl, SE15 162 DV82
Banstead SM7 233 CX115
Coulsdon CR5 235 DM117
Edgware HA8 96 CN49
Greenford UB6 137 CD69
Hayes UB4 135 BU71
High Wycombe HP10
off Falcons Cft 110 AE55
Northwood HA6 93 BT50
Orpington BR6 205 ES104
Slough SL3 153 AZ78
Shelley Cres, Houns. TW5 156 BX82
Southall UB1 136 BZ72
Shelley Dr, Well. DA16 165 ES81
Shelley Gdns, Wem. HA0 117 CJ61
Shelley Gro, Loug. IG10 85 EM42
Shelley La, Uxb. (Hare.) UB9 92 BG53
Shelley Pl, Til. RM18
off Kipling Av 171 GH81
Shelley Rd, NW10 138 CR67
Brentwood (Hutt.) CM13 109 GD45
Chesham HP5 54 AP29
Shelleys La, Sev. (Knock.)
TN14 239 ET116
Shelley Way, SW19 180 DD93
Shellfield Cl, Stai. TW19 174 BG85
Shellgrove Est, N16 5 M1
Shellness Rd, E5 122 DV64
Shell Rd, SE13 163 EB83
Shellwood Dr, Dor.
(N.Holm.) RH5 263 CJ140
Shellwood Rd, SW11 160 DF82
Reigate (Leigh) RH2 264 CQ141
Shelmerdine Cl, E3 13 N5
Shelson Av, Felt. TW13 175 BT90
Shelton Av, Warl. CR6 236 DW117
Shelton Cl, Guil. GU2 242 AU129
Warlingham CR6 236 DW117
Shelton Ct, Slou. SL3
off London Rd 152 AW76
Shelton Rd, SW19 200 DA95
Shelton St, WC2 9 N8
Shelvers Grn, Tad. KT20 233 CW121
Shelvers Hill, Tad. KT20
off Ashurst Rd 233 CW121
Shelvers Spur, Tad. KT20 233 CW121
Shelvers Way, Tad. KT20 233 CW121
Shenden Cl, Sev. TN13 257 FJ128
Shenden Way, Sev. TN13 257 FJ128
Shendish Edge, Hem.H. HP3
off London Rd 58 BM25
SHENFIELD, Brwd. CM15 109 GA45
⇌ Shenfield 109 GA45
Shenfield Cl, Couls. CR5
off Woodfield Cl 235 DJ119
Shenfield Common, Brwd.
CM15 108 FY48
Shenfield Cres, Brwd.
CM15 108 FY47
Shenfield Gdns, Brwd.
(Hutt.) CM13 109 GB44
Shenfield Grn, Brwd.
(Shenf.) CM15
off Hutton Rd 109 GA45
Sch Shenfield High Sch,
Brwd. CM15
off Alexander La 109 GA43
Shenfield Ho, SE18
off Shooter's Hill Rd 164 EK80
Shenfield Pl, Brwd.
(Shenf.) CM15 108 FY45
Shenfield Rd, Brwd. CM15 108 FX46
Woodford Green IG8 102 EH52
Shenfield St, N1 5 M10
SHENLEY, Rad. WD7 62 CN33
Shenley Av, Ruis. HA4 115 BT61
Shenleybury, Rad.
(Shenley) WD7 62 CL30
Shenleybury Cotts, Rad.
(Shenley) WD7 62 CL31
Shenley Hill, Rad. WD7 77 CG35
Shenley La, St.Alb.
(Lon.Col.) AL2 61 CJ27
Shenley Manor, Rad.
(Shenley) WD7 61 CK33
Sch Shenley Prim Sch,
Rad. WD7
off London Rd 62 CM34
Shenley Rd, SE5 162 DS81
Borehamwood WD6 78 CN42
Dartford DA1 188 FN86
Hounslow TW5 156 BY81
Radlett WD7 61 CH34
Shenstone Cl, Dart. DA1 167 FD84
Shenstone Dr, Slou.
(Burn.) SL1 131 AK70
Shenstone Gdns, Rom.
RM3 106 FJ53
Shenstone Hill, Berk. HP4 38 AX18
Sch Shenstone Sch,
Dart. DA1
off Old Rd 167 FD84
Shepcot Ho, N14 81 DJ44
Shepherd Cl, W1
off Lees Pl 140 DG73
Abbots Langley WD5 59 BT30
Feltham (Han.) TW13 176 BY91
Shepherdess Pl, N1 11 H1
Shepherdess Wk, N1 5 H9
Sch Shepherd JMI & Nurs Sch,
Rick. WD3
off Shepherds La 92 BG46
Shepherd Mkt, W1 18 G1
SHEPHERD'S BUSH, W12 139 CW74
⊖ Shepherd's Bush 159 CW75
Shepherds Bush Grn, W12 159 CW75
Shepherds Bush Mkt, W12 159 CW75
Shepherds Bush Pl, W12 16 A3
Shepherds Bush Rd, W6 159 CW77
Shepherds Cl, N6 121 DH58
Beaconsfield HP9 89 AM54
Leatherhead KT22 232 CL124
Orpington BR6
off Stapleton Rd 205 ET104
Romford RM6 126 EX57
Shepperton TW17 195 BP100
Stanmore HA7 95 CH50
Uxbridge (Cowley) UB8
off High St 134 BJ70
Shepherds Ct, W12 16 A3
Hertford SG14 32 DQ06
Shepherds Grn, Chis. BR7 185 ER94
Hemel Hempstead HP1 39 BE21
Shepherds Hill, N6 121 DH58
Guildford GU2 242 AU132
Redhill RH1 251 DJ126
Romford RM3 106 FN54
Shepherds La, E9 123 DX64
Beaconsfield HP9 89 AM54
Shepherd's La, Brwd. CM14 108 FS45
Shepherds La, Dart. DA1 187 FG88
Guildford GU2 242 AT131
Rickmansworth WD3 91 BF45
Shepherds Path, Nthlt. UB5
off Fortunes Mead 136 BY65
Shepherd's Pl, W1 8 E9
Shepherds Rd, Wat. WD18 75 BT41
Shepherd St, W1 18 G2
Gravesend (Nthflt) DA11 190 GD87
Shepherds Wk, NW2 119 CU61
NW3 120 DD64
Bushey (Bushey Hth)
WD23 95 CD47
Shepherds' Wk, Epsom
KT18 232 CP121
Shepherds Way, Chesh. HP5 54 AR33
Guildford (Shalf.) GU4 258 AY138
Hatfield (Brook.Pk) AL9 64 DC27
Rickmansworth WD3 92 BH45
South Croydon CR2 221 DX108
Shepiston La, Hayes UB3 155 BR77
West Drayton UB7 155 BQ77
Shepley Cl, Cars. SM5 200 DG104
Shepley Ms, Enf. EN3 83 EA37
Sheppard Cl, Enf. EN1 82 DV39
Kingston upon Thames
KT1 off Beaufort Rd 198 CL98
Sheppard Dr, SE16 22 C9
Sheppards, Harl. CM19
off Heighams 51 EM18
Sheppards Cl, St.Alb. AL3 43 CE17
Sheppard St, E16 15 K3
SHEPPERTON, TW17 194 BN101
⇌ Shepperton 195 BQ99
Shepperton Business Pk,
Shep. TW17 195 BQ99
Shepperton Cl, Borwd. WD6 78 CR39
Shepperton Ct, Shep. TW17 195 BP100
Shepperton Ct Dr, Shep.
TW17 195 BP99
Shepperton Rd, N1 5 H7
Orpington BR5 205 EQ100
Staines TW18 194 BJ97
Sheppey Cl, Erith DA8 167 FH80
Sheppey Gdns, Dag. RM9
off Sheppey Rd 146 EW66
Sheppey Rd, Dag. RM9 146 EV66
Sheppeys La, Abb.L.
(Bedmond) WD5 59 BS28
Sheppey Wk, N1 5 H5
Sheppy Pl, Grav. DA12 191 GH87
Sherard Ct, N7
off Manor Gdns 121 DL62
Sherard Rd, SE9 184 EL85
Sherards Orchard, Harl.
CM19 51 EP17
Sheraton Business Cen,
Grnf. UB6 137 CH68
Sheraton Cl, Borwd.
(Elstree) WD6 78 CM43
Sheraton Dr, Epsom KT19 216 CQ113
Sheraton Ms, Wat. WD18 75 BS42
Sheraton St, W1 9 L8
Sherborne Av, Enf. EN3 82 DW40
Southall UB2 156 CA77
Sherborne Cl, Epsom KT18 233 CW117
Hayes UB4 136 BW72
Slough (Colnbr.) SL3 153 BE81
Sherborne Cres, Cars. SM5 200 DE101
Sherborne Gdns, NW9 118 CN55
W13 137 CH72
Romford RM5 104 FA50
Sherborne La, EC4 11 J9
Sherborne Pl, Nthwd. HA6 93 BR51
Sherborne Rd, Chess. KT9 216 CL106
Feltham TW14 175 BR87
Orpington BR5 205 ET98
Sutton SM3 200 DA103
Sherborne St, N1 5 J7
Sherborne Wk, Lthd. KT22
off Windfield 231 CJ121
Sherborne Way, Rick.
(Crox.Grn) WD3 75 BP42
Sherboro Rd, N15
off Ermine Rd 122 DT58
Sherbourne, Guil. (Albury)
GU5 260 BK139
Sherbourne Cl, Hem.H.
HP2 40 BL21
Sherbourne Cotts, Guil.
(Albury) GU5 260 BL138
Watford WD18
off Watford Fld Rd 76 BW43
Sherbourne Dr, Wind. SL4 151 AM84
Sherbourne Gdns, Shep.
TW17 195 BS101
Sherbourne Pl, Stan. HA7 95 CG51
Sherbourne Wk, Slou.
(Farn.Com.) SL2 111 AQ63
Sherbrooke Cl, Bexh. DA6 166 FA84
Sherbrooke Rd, SW6 159 CZ80
Sherbrooke Way, Wor.Pk.
KT4 199 CV101
Sherbrook Gdns, N21 99 DP45
SHERE, Guil. GU5 260 BN139
Shere Av, Sutt. SM2 217 CW110
Shere Cl, Chess. KT9 215 CK106
Dorking (N.Holm.) RH5 263 CJ140
Sch Shere C of E Inf Sch,
Guil. GU5
off Gomshall La 260 BN139
Sheredan Rd, E4 101 ED50
Sheredes Dr, Hodd. EN11 49 DZ19
Sch Sheredes Prim Sch,
Hodd. EN11
off Benford Rd 49 DZ19
Sch Sheredes Sch, Hodd.
EN11
off Cock La 49 DZ18
Shere La, Guil. (Shere)
GU5 260 BN139
★ Shere Mus, Guil. GU5 260 BN139
Shere Rd, Guil. GU4, GU5 260 BN138
Ilford IG2 125 EN57
Leatherhead (W.Hors.)
KT24 245 BP130
Sherfield Av, Rick. WD3 92 BK47
Sherfield Cl, N.Mal. KT3 198 CP98
Sherfield Gdns, SW15 179 CT86
Sherfield Rd, Grays RM17 170 GB79
Sheridan Cl, Hem.H. HP1 40 BH21
Romford RM3 105 FH52
Swanley BR8
off Willow Av 207 FF97
Uxbridge UB10
off Alpha Rd 135 BQ70
Sheridan Ct, Houns. TW4
off Vickers Way 176 BZ85
Northolt UB5 116 CB64
Sheridan Cres, Chis. BR7 205 EP96
Sheridan Dr, Reig. RH2 250 DB132
Sheridan Gdns, Har. HA3 117 CK58
Sheridan Ms, E11
off Woodbine Pl 124 EG58
Sheridan Pl, SW13
off Brookwood Av 159 CT82
Hampton TW12 196 CB95
Sheridan Rd, E7 124 EF62
E12 124 EL64
SW19 199 CZ95
Belvedere DA17 166 FA77
Bexleyheath DA7 166 EY83
Richmond TW10 177 CJ90
Watford WD19 94 BX45
Sheridans Rd, Lthd. (Bkhm)
KT23 246 CC126
Sheridan St, E1 12 D8
Sheridan Ter, Nthlt. UB5
off Whitton Av W 116 CB64
Sheridan Wk, NW11 120 DA58
Broxbourne EN10 49 DY20
Carshalton SM5
off Carshalton Pk Rd 218 DF106
Sheridan Way, Beck. BR3
off Turners Meadow Way 203 DZ95
Sheriff Way, Wat. WD25 59 BU33
Sch Sheringdale Prim Sch,
SW18 off Standen Rd 179 CZ88
Sheringham Av, E12 125 EM63
N14 81 DK43

Sheringham Av, Felt. TW13 175 BU90
Romford RM7 127 FC58
Twickenham TW2 176 BZ88
Sheringham Dr, Bark. IG11 125 ET64
Sch Sheringham Jun Sch, E12 off Sheringham Av 125 EM63
Sheringham Rd, N7 4 B3
SE20 202 DV97
Sheringham Twr, Sthl. UB1 136 CB73
Sherington Av, Pnr. HA5 94 CA52
Sch Sherington Jun Sch, SE7 off Sherington Rd 164 EH79
Sherington Rd, SE7 164 EH79
Sherland Rd, Twick. TW1 177 CF88
Sherlies Av, Orp. BR6 205 ES103
★ Sherlock Holmes Mus, NW1 8 D4
Sherlock Ms, W1 8 E5
Sherman Rd, Brom. BR1 204 EG95
Slough SL1 132 AS71
Shernbroke Rd, Wal.Abb. EN9 68 EF34
Shernhall St, E17 123 EC57
Sherpa Rd, Hem.H. HP2 40 BN19
Sherrard Rd, E7 144 EJ65
E12 144 EK65
Sherrards, Welw.G.C. AL8 29 CV06
Sherrards Mansion, Welw.G.C. AL8 off Sherrards 29 CV06
Sherrards Ms, Welw.G.C. AL8 off Sherrards 29 CV06
SHERRARDSPARK, Welw.G.C. AL8 29 CV07
Sherrardspark Rd, Welw.G.C. AL8 29 CW07
Sherrards Way, Barn. EN5 80 DA43
Sherrick Grn Rd, NW10 119 CV64
Sherriff Rd, NW6 140 DA65
Sherringham Av, N17 100 DU54
Sherrin Rd, E10 123 EA63
Sherrock Gdns, NW4 119 CU56
Sherry Ms, Bark. IG11 off Cecil Av 145 ER66
Sherwin Rd, SE14 163 DX81
Sherwood Av, E18 124 EH55
SW16 181 DK94
Greenford UB6 137 CE65
Hayes UB4 135 BV70
Potters Bar EN6 63 CY32
Ruislip HA4 115 BS58
St. Albans AL4 43 CH17
Sherwood Cl, SW13 off Lower Common S 159 CV83
W13 137 CH74
Bexley DA5 186 EW86
Leatherhead (Fetch.) KT22 230 CC122
Slough SL3 152 AY76
Sherwood Ct, Slou. (Colnbr.) SL3 off High St 153 BD80
Watford WD25 off High Rd 59 BU34
Sherwood Cres, Reig. RH2 266 DB138
Sherwood Gdns, E14 23 P7
SE16 22 B10
Barking IG11 145 ER66
Sherwood Pk Av, Sid. DA15 186 EU87
Sch Sherwood Pk Prim Sch, Sid. DA15 off Sherwood Pk Av 186 EV86
Sherwood Pk Rd, Mitch. CR4 201 DJ98
Sutton SM1 218 DA106
Sch Sherwood Pk Sch, Wall. SM6 off Streeters La 201 DK104
Sherwood Pl, Hem.H. HP2 off Turnpike Grn 40 BM16
Sherwood Rd, NW4 119 CW55
SW19 179 CZ94
Coulsdon CR5 235 DJ116
Croydon CR0 202 DV101
Hampton (Hmptn H.) TW12 176 CC92
Harrow HA2 116 CC61
Ilford IG6 125 ER56
Welling DA16 165 ES82
Woking (Knap.) GU21 226 AS117
Sch Sherwood Sch, The, Mitch. CR4 off Abbotts Rd 201 DJ98
Sherwoods Rd, Wat. WD19 94 BY45
Sherwood St, N20 98 DD48
W1 9 K9
Sherwood Ter, N20 off Green Rd 98 DD48
Sherwood Way, W.Wick. BR4 203 EB103
Shetland Cl, Borwd. WD6 off Percheron Rd 78 CR44
Guildford GU4 off Weybrook Dr 243 BB129
Shetland Rd, E3 143 DZ68
Shevon Way, Brwd. CM14 108 FT49
Shewens Rd, Wey. KT13 213 BR105
Shey Copse, Wok. GU22 227 BC117
Shield Dr, Brent. TW8 157 CG79
Shieldhall St, SE2 166 EW77
Shield Rd, Ashf. TW15 175 BQ91
Shifford Path, SE23 183 DX90
Shilburn Way, Wok. GU21 226 AU118
Shillibeer Pl, W1 8 B5
Shillibeer Wk, Chig. IG7 103 ET48
Shillingford Cl, NW7 97 CX52
Shillingford St, N1 4 F6
Shillitoe Av, Pot.B. EN6 63 CX32
Shimmings, The, Guil. GU1 243 BA133
Shinfield St, W12 139 CW72
Shingle Ct, Wal.Abb. EN9 68 EG33
Shinglewell Rd, Erith DA8 166 FA80
Shinners Cl, SE25 202 DU99
Ship All, W4 off Thames Rd 158 CN79
Ship & Mermaid Row, SE1 21 K3
Shipfield Cl, West. (Tats.) TN16 238 EJ121
Ship Hill, H.Wyc. HP10 111 AL60
Westerham (Tats.) TN16 238 EJ121
Shipka Rd, SW12 181 DH88
Ship La, SW14 158 CQ82
Brentwood (Mtnsg) CM13 109 GF41
Dartford (Sutt.H.) DA4 208 FK95
Purfleet RM19 169 FS76
South Ockendon (Aveley) RM15 169 FR75
Swanley BR8 208 FK95
Ship La Caravan Site, S.Ock. RM15 169 FR76
Shipman Rd, E16 15 P8
SE23 183 DX89
Ship St, SE8 163 EA81
Ship Tavern Pas, EC3 11 L9
Shipton Cl, Dag. RM8 126 EX62
Shipton St, E2 11 P1
Shipwright Rd, SE16 23 J4
Shipwright Yd, SE1 21 L2
Ship Yd, E14 24 A9
Weybridge KT13 off High St 213 BP105
Shirburn Cl, SE23 off Tyson Rd 182 DW87
Shirbutt St, E14 14 A9
Shirebrook Rd, SE3 164 EK83
Shire Cl, Brox. EN10 off Groom Rd 67 DZ26
Shire Ct, Epsom KT17 217 CT108
Erith DA18 off St. John Fisher Rd 166 EX76
Shirehall Cl, NW4 119 CX58
Shirehall Gdns, NW4 119 CX58
Shirehall La, NW4 119 CX58
Shirehall Pk, NW4 119 CX58
Shirehall Rd, Dart. DA2 188 FK92
Shire Horse Way, Islw. TW7 157 CF83
Shire La, Ger.Cr. (Chal.St.P.) SL9 91 BD54
Keston BR2 223 EM108
Orpington BR6 223 ER107
Rickmansworth (Chorl.) WD3 73 BB43
Uxbridge (Denh.) UB9 113 BE55
Shiremeade, Borwd. (Elstree) WD6 78 CM43
Shire Pk, Welw.G.C. AL7 29 CY07
Shire Pl, SW18 off Swaffield Rd 180 DB87
Redhill RH1 266 DF136
Shires, The, Rich. TW10 178 CL91
Watford WD25 59 BV31
Shires Cl, Ashtd. KT21 231 CK118
Shires Ho, W.Byf. (Byfleet) KT14 off Eden Gro Rd 212 BL113
Shirland Ms, W9 6 F2
Shirland Rd, W9 6 G2
SHIRLEY, Croy. CR0 203 DX104
Shirley Av, Bex. DA5 186 EX87
Coulsdon CR5 235 DP119
Croydon CR0 202 DW102
Redhill RH1 266 DF139
Sutton SM1 218 DE105
Sutton (Cheam) SM2 217 CZ109
Windsor SL4 151 AM81
Shirley Ch Rd, Croy. CR0 203 DX104
Shirley Cl, E17 off Addison Rd 123 EB57
Broxbourne EN10 49 DZ24
Dartford DA1 168 FJ84
Hounslow TW3 176 CC85
Waltham Cross (Chsht) EN8 66 DW29
Shirley Ct, Croy. CR0 203 DX104
Shirley Cres, Beck. BR3 203 DY98
Shirley Dr, Houns. TW3 176 CC85
Shirley Gdns, W7 137 CF74
Barking IG11 145 ES65
Hornchurch RM12 128 FJ61
Shirley Gro, N9 100 DW45
SW11 160 DG83
Shirley Hts, Wall. SM6 219 DJ109
Sch Shirley High Sch, Croy. CR0 off Shirley Ch Rd 203 DX104
Shirley Hills Rd, Croy. CR0 221 DX106
Shirley Ho Dr, SE7 164 EJ80
H Shirley Oaks Hosp, Croy. CR0 202 DW101
Shirley Oaks Rd, Croy. CR0 203 DX102
Shirley Pk Rd, Croy. CR0 202 DV102
Shirley Rd, E15 144 EE66
W4 158 CR75
Abbots Langley WD5 59 BT32
Croydon CR0 202 DV101
Enfield EN2 82 DQ41
St. Albans AL1 43 CF21
Sidcup DA15 185 ES90
Wallington SM6 219 DJ109
Shirley St, E16 15 J7
Shirley Way, Croy. CR0 203 DY104
Shirlock Rd, NW3 120 DF63
Shirwell Cl, NW7 97 CX52
Shobden Rd, N17 100 DR53
Shobroke Cl, NW2 119 CW62
Shoebury Rd, E6 145 EM66
Shoe La, EC4 10 D7
Harlow CM17 52 EZ16
Sholden Gdns, Orp. BR5 206 EW99
Sholto Rd, Houns. (Hthrw Air.) TW6 174 BM85
Shonks Mill Rd, Rom. (Nave.) RM4 87 FG37
Shooters Av, Har. HA3 117 CJ56
Shooters Dr, Wal.Abb. EN9 50 EE22
SHOOTER'S HILL, SE18 165 EQ81
Shooter's Hill, SE18 165 EN81
Welling DA16 165 EN81
Coll Shooters Hill Post 16 Campus, SE18 off Red Lion La 165 EN81
Shooter's Hill Rd, SE3 164 EF81
SE10 163 ED81
SE18 164 EH80
Shooters Rd, Enf. EN2 81 DP39
Shootersway, Berk. HP4 38 AU20
Shootersway La, Berk. HP4 38 AT20
Shootersway Pk, Berk. HP4 38 AT20
Shoot Up Hill, NW2 119 CY64
Shophouse La, Guil. (Albury) GU5 260 BK144
Shoplands, Welw.G.C. AL8 29 CX05
Shord Hill, Ken. CR8 236 DR116
Shore, The, Grav. (Nthflt) DA11 190 GC85
Gravesend (Rosh.) DA11 191 GF86
Shore Cl, Felt. TW14 175 BU87
Hampton TW12 off Stewart Cl 176 BY92
Shorediche Cl, Uxb. UB10 114 BM62
SHOREDITCH, E1 11 N4
⊖ Shoreditch 11 P4
Shoreditch High St, E1 11 M4
Shoreditch Ho, N1 11 K2
Shore Gro, Felt. TW13 176 CA89
SHOREHAM, Sev. TN14 225 FG111
⇌ Shoreham 225 FG111
Shoreham Cl, SW18 off Ram St 180 DB85
Bexley DA5 186 EX88
Croydon CR0 202 DW100
Shoreham La, Orp. BR6 224 FA107
Sevenoaks TN13 256 FF122
Sevenoaks (Halst.) TN14 224 EZ112
Shoreham Pl, Sev. (Shore.) TN14 225 FG112
Shoreham Ri, Slou. SL2 off Lower Britwell Rd 131 AK70
Shoreham Rd, Orp. BR5 206 EV95
Sevenoaks (Otford) TN14 225 FH111
Shoreham Rd E, Houns. (Hthrw Air.) TW6 174 BL85
Shoreham Rd W, Houns. (Hthrw Air.) TW6 174 BL85
Sch Shoreham Village Sch, Sev. TN14 off Church St 225 FF111
Shoreham Way, Brom. BR2 204 EG100
Shore Pl, E9 142 DW66
Shore Rd, E9 142 DW66
Shores Rd, Wok. GU21 210 AY114
Shorncliffe Rd, SE1 21 N9
Shorndean St, SE6 183 EC88
Shorne Cl, Orp. BR5 206 EX98
Sidcup DA15 186 EV86
Shornefield Cl, Brom. BR1 205 EN97
Shornells Way, SE2 off Willrose Cres 166 EW78
Shorrolds Rd, SW6 159 CZ80
Shortacres, Red. RH1 251 DM133
Shortcroft Rd, Epsom KT17 217 CT108
Shortcrofts Rd, Dag. RM9 146 EZ65
Shorter Av, Brwd. (Shenf.) CM15 109 FZ44
Shorter St, E1 11 N9
Shortfern, Slou. SL2 132 AW72
Shortgate, N12 97 CZ49
Short Hedges, Houns. TW3, TW5 156 CB81
Short Hill, Har. HA1 off High St 117 CE60
SHORTLANDS, Brom. BR1 204 EE97
⇌ Shortlands 204 EE96
Shortlands, W6 16 A8
Hayes UB3 155 BR79
Shortlands Cl, N18 100 DR48
Belvedere DA17 166 EZ76
Shortlands Gdns, Brom. BR2 204 EE96
Shortlands Grn, Welw.G.C. AL7 29 CZ10
Shortlands Gro, Brom. BR2 203 ED97
Shortlands Rd, E10 123 EB59
Bromley BR2 203 ED97
Kingston upon Thames KT2 178 CM94
Short La, Oxt. RH8 254 EH132
St. Albans (Brick.Wd) AL2 60 BZ30
Staines TW19 174 BM88
Shortmead Dr, Wal.Cr. (Chsht) EN8 67 DY31
Short Path, SE18 off Westdale Rd 165 EP79
Short Rd, E11 124 EE61
E15 143 ED67
W4 158 CS79
Hounslow (Hthrw Air.) TW6 174 BL86
Shorts Cft, NW9 118 CP56
Shorts Gdns, WC2 9 N8
Shorts Rd, Cars. SM5 218 DE105
Short St, NW4 off New Brent St 119 CW56
SE1 20 D3
Short Wall, E15 14 D1
Shortway, N12 98 DE51
Short Way, SE9 164 EL83
Shortway, Amer. HP6 55 AR37
Chesham HP5 54 AP29
Short Way, Twick. TW2 176 CC87
Shortwood Av, Stai. TW18 174 BH90
Shortwood Common, Stai. TW18 174 BH91
Sch Shortwood Inf Sch, Stai. TW18 off Stanwell New Rd 174 BH90
Shotfield, Wall. SM6 219 DH107
Shothanger Way, Hem.H. (Bov.) HP3 57 BC26
Shott Cl, Sutt. SM1 off Turnpike La 218 DC106
Shottendane Rd, SW6 160 DA81
Shottery Cl, SE9 184 EL90
Shottfield Av, SW14 158 CS84
Shoulder of Mutton All, E14 13 K9
Shouldham St, W1 8 B6
Showers Way, Hayes UB3 135 BU74
Shrapnel Cl, SE18 164 EL80
Shrapnel Rd, SE9 165 EM83
SHREDING GREEN, Iver SL0 133 BB72
Shrewsbury Av, SW14 158 CQ84
Harrow HA3 118 CL56
Shrewsbury Cl, Surb. KT6 216 CL103
Shrewsbury Ct, EC1 off Whitecross St 142 DQ70
Shrewsbury Cres, NW10 138 CR67
Sch Shrewsbury Ho Sch, Surb. KT6 off Ditton Rd 198 CL103
Shrewsbury La, SE18 165 EP81
Shrewsbury Ms, W2 6 G6
Shrewsbury Rd, E7 124 EK64
N11 99 DJ51
W2 6 G7
Beckenham BR3 203 DY97
Carshalton SM5 200 DE100
Hounslow (Hthrw Air.) TW6 175 BQ86
Redhill RH1 250 DE134
Shrewsbury St, W10 139 CW70
Shrewsbury Wk, Islw. TW7 off South St 157 CG83
Shrewton Rd, SW17 180 DF94
Shrimpton Cl, Beac. HP9 89 AK49
Shrimpton Rd, Beac. HP9 89 AK49
Shroffold Rd, Brom. BR1 184 EE91
Shropshire Cl, Mitch. CR4 201 DL98
Shropshire Ho, N18 off Cavendish Rd 100 DV50
Shropshire Pl, WC1 9 K4
Shropshire Rd, N22 99 DM52
Shroton St, NW1 8 A5
Shrubberies, The, E18 102 EG54
Chigwell IG7 103 EQ50
Shrubbery, The, E11 124 EH57
Hemel Hempstead HP1 39 BE19
Upminster RM14 128 FQ62
Shrubbery Cl, N1 5 H8
Shrubbery Gdns, N21 99 DP45
Shrubbery Rd, N9 100 DU48
SW16 181 DL91
Dartford (S.Darenth) DA4 209 FR95
Gravesend DA12 191 GH88
Southall UB1 136 BZ74
Shrubhill Rd, Hem.H. HP1 39 BF21
Shrubland Gro, Wor.Pk. KT4 199 CW104
Shrubland Rd, E8 5 P7
E10 123 EA59
Shrubland Rd, E17 123 EA57
Banstead SM7 233 CZ116
Shrublands, Hat. AL9 64 DB26
Shrublands, The, Pot.B. EN6 63 CY33
Shrublands Av, Berk. HP4 38 AU19
Croydon CR0 221 EA105
Shrublands Cl, N20 98 DD46
SE26 182 DW90
Chigwell IG7 103 EQ51
Shrublands Rd, Berk. HP4 38 AU18
Shrubsall Cl, SE9 184 EL88
Shrubs Rd, Rick. WD3 92 BM51
Shuna Wk, N1 off St. Paul's Rd 142 DR65
Shurland Av, Barn. EN4 80 DD44
Shurland Gdns, SE15 off Rosemary Rd 162 DT80
Shurlock Av, Swan. BR8 207 FD96
Shurlock Dr, Orp. BR6 223 EQ105
Shuters Sq, W14 16 E10
Shuttle Cl, Sid. DA15 185 ET87
Shuttlemead, Bex. DA5 186 EZ87
Shuttle Rd, Dart. DA1 167 FG83
Shuttle St, E1 12 A4
Shuttleworth Rd, SW11 160 DE82
Siamese Ms, N3 off Station Rd 98 DA53
Sibella Rd, SW4 161 DK82
Sibley Cl, Bexh. DA6 186 EY85
Bromley BR1 off Southborough Rd 204 EL99
Sibley Gro, E12 144 EL66
Sibneys Grn, Harl. CM18 51 ES20
Sibthorpe Rd, SE12 184 EH86
Hatfield (N.Mymms) AL9 45 CX24
Sibton Rd, Cars. SM5 200 DE101
Sicilian Av, WC1 9 P6
Sicklefield Cl, Wal.Cr. (Chsht) EN7 66 DT26
Sidbury St, SW6 159 CY81
SIDCUP, DA14 & DA15 185 ET91
⇌ Sidcup 186 EU89
Coll Sidcup Arts & Adult Ed Cen, Sid. DA14 off Alma Rd 186 EV90
Sidcup Bypass, Chis. BR7 185 ES91
Orpington BR5 186 EX94
Sidcup DA14 185 ES91
Sidcup High St, Sid. DA14 186 EU91
Sidcup Hill, Sid. DA14 186 EV91
Sidcup Hill Gdns, Sid. DA14 off Sidcup Hill 186 EW92
Sidcup Pl, Sid. DA14 186 EU92
Sidcup Rd, SE9 184 EK87
SE12 184 EH85
Sidcup Tech Cen, Sid. DA14 186 EX92
Siddeley Dr, Houns. TW4 156 BY83
Siddons La, NW1 8 D4
Siddons Rd, N17 100 DU53
SE23 183 DY89
Croydon CR0 201 DN104
Side Rd, E17 123 DZ57
Uxbridge (Denh.) UB9 113 BD59
Sideways La, Horl. (Hkwd) RH6 268 DD149
Sidewood Rd, SE9 185 ER88
Sidford Cl, Hem.H. HP1 39 BF20
Sidford Pl, SE1 20 B6
Sidings, The, E11 123 EC60
Hatfield AL10 44 CS19
Loughton IG10 84 EL44
Staines TW18 174 BH91
Sidings Ms, N7 121 DN62
Siding Way, St.Alb. (Lon.Col.) AL2 61 CH26
SIDLOW, Reig. RH2 266 DB141
Sch Sidlow Br Cen, Reig. RH2 off Ironsbottom 266 DB141
Sidmouth Av, Islw. TW7 157 CE82
Sidmouth Cl, Wat. WD19 93 BV47
Sidmouth Dr, Ruis. HA4 115 BU62
Sidmouth Par, NW2 off Sidmouth Rd 139 CW66
Sidmouth Rd, E10 123 EC62
NW2 139 CW66
Orpington BR5 206 EV99
Welling DA16 166 EW80
Sidmouth St, WC1 9 P2
Sidney Av, N13 99 DM50
Sidney Cl, Uxb. UB8 134 BJ66
Sidney Elson Way, E6 off Edwin Av 145 EN68
Sidney Gdns, Brent. TW8 157 CJ79
Sidney Gro, EC1 4 E10
Sidney Rd, E7 124 EG62
N22 99 DM52
SE25 202 DU99
SW9 161 DM82
Beckenham BR3 203 DY96
Epping (They.B.) CM16 85 ER36
Harrow HA2 116 CC55
Staines TW18 174 BG91
Twickenham TW1 177 CG86
Walton-on-Thames KT12 195 BU101
Windsor SL4 150 AJ83
Sidney Sq, E1 12 E6
Sidney St, E1 12 E7
Sidworth St, E8 142 DV66
Siebert Rd, SE3 164 EG79
Siemens Rd, SE18 164 EK76
Sigdon Rd, E8 122 DU64
Sigers, The, Pnr. HA5 115 BV58
Signmakers Yd, NW1 off Delancey St 141 DH67
Sigrist Sq, Kings.T. KT2 198 CL95
Silbury Av, Mitch. CR4 200 DE95
Silbury Ho, SE26 off Sydenham Hill 182 DU90
Silbury St, N1 11 J1
Sch Silchester Ho Sch, Maid. SL6 off Bath Rd 130 AD72
Silchester Rd, W10 6 B8
Silecroft Rd, Bexh. DA7 166 FA81
Silent Pool Junct, Guil. GU5 off Shere Rd 260 BL138
Silesia Bldgs, E8 off London La 142 DV66
Silex St, SE1 20 F4
Silk Cl, SE12 184 EG85
Silkfield Rd, NW9 118 CS57
Silkham Rd, Oxt. RH8 253 ED127
Silkin Ho, Wat. WD19 94 BW48
Silk Mill Ct, Wat. WD19 off Silk Mill Rd 93 BV45
Silk Mill Rd, Wat. WD19 93 BV45
Silk Mills Cl, Sev. TN14 257 FJ121
Silk Mills Pas, SE13 off Russett Way 163 EB82
Silk Mills Path, SE13 off Lewisham Rd 163 EC82
Silk Mills Sq, E9 143 DZ65
Silkmore La, Lthd. (W.Hors.) KT24 244 BN125
Silkstream Rd, Edg. HA8 96 CQ53
Silk St, EC2 11 H5
Silo Cl, Gdmg. GU7 258 AT143
Silo Dr, Gdmg. GU7 258 AT143
Silo Rd, Gdmg. GU7 258 AT143
Silsden Cres, Ch.St.G. HP8 off London Rd 90 AX48
Silsoe Rd, N22 99 DM54
Silver Birch Av, E4 101 DZ51
Epping (N.Wld Bas.) CM16 70 EY27
Silver Birch Cl, N11 98 DG51
SE6 183 DZ90
SE28 146 EU74
Addlestone (Wdhm) KT15 211 BE112
Dartford DA2 187 FE91
Uxbridge UB10 114 BL63
Silver Birch Ct, Wal.Cr. (Chsht) EN8 67 DX31
Silver Birches, Brwd. (Hutt.) CM13 109 GA46
Silver Birch Gdns, E6 145 EM70
Silver Birch Ms, Ilf. IG6 off Fencepiece Rd 103 EQ51
Silverbirch Wk, NW3 off Queen's Cres 140 DG65
Silvercliffe Gdns, Barn. EN4 80 DE42
Silver Cl, SE14 off Southerngate Way 163 DY80
Harrow HA3 95 CD52
Tadworth (Kgswd) KT20 233 CY124
Silver Cres, W4 158 CP77
Silverdale, SE26 182 DW91
Enfield EN2 81 DL42
Silverdale Av, Ilf. IG3 125 ES57
Leatherhead (Oxshott) KT22 214 CC114
Walton-on-Thames KT12 195 BT104
Silverdale Cl, W7 137 CE74
Betchworth (Brock.) RH3 264 CP138
Northolt UB5 116 BZ64
Sutton SM1 217 CZ105
Silverdale Ct, Stai. TW18 off Leacroft 174 BH91
Silverdale Dr, SE9 184 EL89
Hornchurch RM12 127 FH64
Sunbury-on-Thames TW16 195 BV96
Silverdale Gdns, Hayes UB3 155 BU75
Silverdale Rd, E4 101 ED51
Bexleyheath DA7 167 FB82
Bushey WD23 76 BY43
Hayes UB3 155 BU75
Orpington (Petts Wd) BR5 205 EQ98
Orpington (St.P.Cray) BR5 206 EU97
Silver Dell, Wat. WD24 75 BT35
Silverfield, Brox. EN10 49 DZ22
Silvergate, Epsom KT19 216 CQ106
Silverglade Business Pk, Chess. KT9 215 CJ112
Silverhall St, Islw. TW7 157 CG83
Silver Hill, Ch.St.G. HP8 90 AV47
Silverholme Cl, Har. HA3 117 CK59
Silver Jubilee Way, Houns. TW4 155 BV82
Silverland St, E16 145 EM74
Silver La, Pur. CR8 219 DK112
West Wickham BR4 203 ED103
Silverlea Gdns, Horl. RH6 269 DJ149
Silverleigh Rd, Th.Hth. CR7 201 DM98
Silverlocke Rd, Grays RM17 170 GD79
Silvermead, E18 off Churchfields 102 EG52
Silvermere Av, Rom. RM5 105 FB51
Silvermere Dr, N18 101 DX51
Silvermere Rd, SE6 183 EB86
Silver Pl, W1 9 K9
Silver Rd, SE13 163 EB83
W12 6 A10
Gravesend DA12 191 GL89
Silversmiths Way, Wok. GU21 226 AW118
Silver Spring Cl, Erith DA8 167 FB79
Silverstead La, West. TN16 239 ER121
Silverstone Cl, Red. RH1 off Goodwood Rd 250 DF132
Silverston Way, Stan. HA7 95 CJ51
⇌ Silver Street 100 DT50
Silver St, N18 100 DS49
Enfield EN1 82 DR41
Romford (Abridge) RM4 86 EV41
Waltham Abbey EN9 67 EC34
Waltham Cross (Goffs Oak) EN7 66 DR30
Silverthorn Dr, Hem.H. HP3 41 BP24
Silverthorne Rd, SW8 161 DH82
Silverthorn Gdns, E4 101 EA47
Silverton Rd, W6 159 CX79
SILVERTOWN, E16 164 EJ75
⇌ Silvertown & London City Airport 144 EK74
Silvertown Way, E16 15 H7
Silver Tree Cl, Walt. KT12 195 BU104
Silvertree La, Grnf. UB6 off Cowgate Rd 137 CD69
Silver Trees, St.Alb. (Brick.Wd) AL2 60 BZ30
Silver Wk, SE16 23 L2
Silver Way, Rom. RM7 127 FB55
Uxbridge UB10 off Oakdene Rd 135 BP68
Silverwood Cl, Beck. BR3 183 EA94
Croydon CR0 221 DZ109
Northwood HA6 93 BQ53
Silverwood Cotts, Guil. (Shere) GU5 off Shere Rd 260 BM138
Silvester Rd, SE22 182 DT85
Silvesters, Harl. CM19 51 EM17
Silvester St, SE1 21 H4
Silvocea Way, E14 14 F8
Silwood Est, SE16 22 F8
Silwood St, SE16 22 F8
Simla Ho, SE1 21 K4
Simmil Rd, Esher (Clay.) KT10 215 CE106
Simmonds Ri, Hem.H. HP3 40 BK22
Simmons Cl, N20 98 DE46
Chessington KT9 215 CJ108
Slough SL3 off Common Rd 153 BA77
Simmons Gate, Esher KT10 214 CC106
Simmons La, E4 101 ED47
Simmons Pl, Stai. TW18 off Chertsey La 173 BE92
Simmons Rd, SE18 165 EP78
Simmons Way, N20 98 DE47
Simms Cl, Cars. SM5 200 DE103
Simms Gdns, N2 98 DC54
Simms Rd, SE1 22 A8
Simnel Rd, SE12 184 EH87
Sch Simon Balle Sch, Hert. SG13 off Mangrove Rd 32 DS10

★ Place of interest | H Hospital | Sch School | Coll College | Uni University | ⇌ Railway station

Simon Cl, W11 ... 6 F9
Simon Dean, Hem.H. (Bov.)
HP3 ... 57 BA27
Simonds Rd, E10 ... 123 EA61
Simone Cl, Brom. BR1 ... 204 EK95
Simone Dr, Ken. CR8 ... 236 DQ116
Sch Simon Marks Jewish JMI Sch, N16
off Cazenove Rd ... 122 DT61
Simons Cl, Cher. (Ott.) KT16 ... 211 BC107
Simons Wk, E15
off Waddington Rd ... 123 ED64
Egham (Eng.Grn) TW20 ... 172 AW94
Simplemarsh Ct, Add. KT15
off Simplemarsh Rd ... 212 BH105
Simplemarsh Rd, Add. KT15 ... 212 BG105
Simpson Cl, N21
off Macleod Rd ... 81 DL43
Simpson Dr, W3 ... 138 CR72
Simpson Rd, Houns. TW4 ... 176 BZ86
Rainham RM13 ... 147 FF65
Richmond TW10 ... 177 CJ91
Simpsons Rd, E14 ... 14 B10
Bromley BR2 ... 204 EG97
Simpson St, SW11 ... 160 DE82
Simpsons Way, Slou. SL1
off Stoke Poges La ... 132 AS74
Simrose Ct, SW18
off Wandsworth High St ... 180 DA85
Sims Cl, Rom. RM1 ... 127 FF56
Sims Wk, SE3 ... 164 EF84
Sinclair Ct, Beck. BR3 ... 183 EA94
Sinclair Dr, Sutt. SM2 ... 218 DB109
Sinclair Gdns, W14 ... 16 B4
Sinclair Gro, NW11 ... 119 CX58
Sinclair Pl, SE4 ... 183 EA86
Sinclair Rd, E4 ... 101 DZ50
W14 ... 16 B4
Sinclair Way, Dart.
(Lane End) DA2 ... 189 FR91
Sinclare Cl, Enf. EN1 ... 82 DT39
Sincots Rd, Red. RH1
off Lower Br Rd ... 250 DF134
Sinderby Cl, Borwd. WD6 ... 78 CL39
Singapore Rd, W13 ... 137 CG74
Singer St, EC2 ... 11 K2
Sch Singlegate Prim Sch,
SW19 off South Gdns ... 180 DD94
Singles Cross La, Sev.
(Knock.) TN14 ... 224 EW114
SINGLE STREET, West.
TN16 ... 239 EN115
Single St, West.
(Berry's Grn) TN16 ... 239 EP115
Singleton Cl, SW17 ... 180 DF94
Croydon CR0
off St. Saviours Rd ... 202 DQ101
Hornchurch RM12
off Carfax Rd ... 127 FF63
Singleton Rd, Dag. RM9 ... 126 EZ64
Singleton Scarp, N12 ... 98 DA50
SINGLEWELL, Grav. DA12 ... 191 GK93
Sch Singlewell Prim Sch,
Grav. DA12
off Mackenzie Way ... 191 GK93
Singlewell Rd, Grav. DA11 ... 191 GH89
Singret Pl, Uxb.
(Cowley) UB8 off High St ... 134 BJ70
Sinnott Rd, E17 ... 101 DX53
Sch Sion Manning RC Sch,
The, W10 ... 6 C6
Sion Rd, Twick. TW1 ... 177 CH88
SIPSON, West Dr. UB7 ... 154 BN79
Sipson Cl, West Dr. UB7 ... 154 BN79
Sipson La, Hayes UB3 ... 154 BN79
West Drayton UB7 ... 154 BN79
Sipson Rd, West Dr. UB7 ... 154 BN78
Sipson Way, West Dr. UB7 ... 154 BN80
Sir Alexander Cl, W3 ... 139 CT74
Sir Alexander Rd, W3 ... 139 CT74
Sir Cyril Black Way, SW19 ... 180 DA94
Sch Sir Cyril Burt Sch,
Beck. BR3
off Monks Orchard Rd ... 203 EA102
Sirdar Rd, N22 ... 121 DP55
W11 ... 6 B10
Mitcham CR4
off Grenfell Rd ... 180 DG93
Sirdar Strand, Grav. DA12 ... 191 GM92
Sch Sir Francis Drake Prim
Sch, SE8 ... 23 J10
Sir Francis Way, Brwd.
CM14 ... 108 FV47
Sch Sir Frederic Osborn Sch,
Welw.G.C. AL7
off Herns La ... 30 DB08
Coll Sir George Monoux Coll,
E17 off Chingford Rd ... 101 EB54
Sir Henry Peek's Dr, Slou.
SL2 ... 131 AN65
Coll Siri Guru Nanak Ed Cen,
Grav. DA12 off Trinity Rd ... 191 GJ87
Sirinham Pt, SW8 ... 161 DM79
Sirius Rd, Nthwd. HA6 ... 93 BU50
Sch Sir James Barrie Prim
Sch, SW8 off Condell Rd ... 161 DJ81
Sch Sir John Cass's Foundation
& Redcoat Sch, E1 ... 13 H6
Sch Sir John Cass's Foundation
C of E Prim Sch, EC3 ... 11 N8
Sch Sir John Heron Prim Sch,
E12 off School Rd ... 125 EM63
Sir John Kirk Cl, SE5
off Bethwin Rd ... 162 DQ80
Sch Sir John Lillie Prim Sch,
SW6 off Lillie Rd ... 159 CY79
Sir John Newsom Way,
Welw.G.C. AL7 ... 29 CY12
★ Sir John Soane's Mus,
WC2 off Lincoln's Inn Flds ... 10 A7
Sir Robert Ms, Slou. SL3
off Cheviot Rd ... 153 BA78
Sch Sir Thomas Abney JMI
Sch, N16 off Fairholt Rd ... 122 DR60
Sir Thomas More Est, SW3
off Beaufort St ... 160 DD79
Sch Sir William Burrough Prim
Sch, E14 ... 13 K7
Sch Sir William Perkin's Sch,
Cher. KT16
off Guildford Rd ... 193 BF102
Sch Sir Winston Churchill Schs
for the Deaf, E18
off Churchfields ... 102 EG53
Sise La, EC4 ... 11 J8
Siskin Cl, Borwd. WD6 ... 78 CN42
Bushey WD23 ... 76 BY42
Sisley Rd, Bark. IG11 ... 145 ES67
Sispara Gdns, SW18 ... 179 CZ86
Sissinghurst Rd, Croy. CR0 ... 202 DU101
Sissulu Ct, E6 ... 144 EJ67
Sister Mabel's Way, SE15
off Radnor Rd ... 162 DU80
Sisters Av, SW11 ... 160 DF84
Sistova Rd, SW12 ... 181 DH88
Sisulu Pl, SW9 ... 161 DN83
Sittingbourne Av, Enf. EN1 ... 82 DR44
Sitwell Gro, Stan. HA7 ... 95 CF50
Siverst Cl, Nthlt. UB5 ... 136 CB65
Sivill Ho, E2 ... 11 P1
Siviter Way, Dag. RM10 ... 147 FB66
Siward Rd, N17 ... 100 DR53
SW17 ... 180 DC90
Bromley BR2 ... 204 EH97
Six Acres, Hem.H. HP3 ... 40 BN23
Six Acres Est, N4 ... 121 DN61
Six Bells La, Sev. TN13 ... 257 FJ126
Six Bridges Trd Est, SE1 ... 22 B10
Sixth Av, E12 ... 125 EM63
W10 ... 6 C2
Hayes UB3 ... 135 BT74
Watford WD25 ... 76 BX35
Sixth Cross Rd, Twick. TW2 ... 176 CC90
Skardu Rd, NW2 ... 119 CY64
Skarnings Ct, Wal.Abb. EN9 ... 68 EG33
Skeena Hill, SW18 ... 179 CY87
Skeet Hill La, Orp. BR5,
BR6 ... 206 EY103
Skeffington Rd, E6 ... 144 EL67
Skeffington St, SE18 ... 165 EQ76
Skelbrook St, SW18 ... 180 DB89
Skelgill Rd, SW15 ... 159 CZ84
Skelley Rd, E15 ... 144 EF66
Skelton Cl, E8 ... 5 P4
Beaconsfield HP9 ... 110 AG55
Skelton Rd, E7 ... 144 EG65
Skeltons La, E10 ... 123 EB59
Skelwith Rd, W6 ... 159 CW79
Skenfrith Ho, SE15
off Commercial Way ... 162 DV79
Skerne Rd, Kings.T. KT2 ... 197 CK95
Skerne Wk, Kings.T. KT2 ... 197 CK95
Skerries Ct, Slou.
(Langley) SL3
off Blacksmith Row ... 153 BA77
Sketchley Gdns, SE16 ... 22 G9
Sketty Rd, Enf. EN1 ... 82 DS41
Skibbs La, Orp. BR5, BR6 ... 206 EZ103
Skid Hill La, Warl. CR6 ... 222 EF113
Skidmore Way, Rick. WD3 ... 92 BL46
Skiers St, E15 ... 144 EE67
Skiffington Cl, SW2 ... 181 DN88
Skillet Hill, Wal.Abb. EN9 ... 84 EH35
Skimpans Cl, Hat. AL9 ... 45 CX24
Skinner Ct, E2
off Parmiter St ... 142 DV68
Skinner Pl, SW1 ... 18 E8
Sch Skinner's Company's Sch
for Girls, The, Lwr Sch, E5
off Mount Pleasant La ... 122 DV60
Upr Sch, N16
off Stamford Hill ... 122 DT59
★ Skinners' Hall, EC4
off Dowgate Hill ... 11 J9
Skinners La, EC4 ... 11 H9
Ashtead KT21 ... 231 CK118
Hounslow TW5 ... 156 CB81
Skinner St, EC1 ... 10 D2
Skinney La, Dart. (Hort.Kir.)
DA4 ... 208 FQ97
Skip La, Uxb. (Hare.) UB9 ... 114 BL60
Skippers Cl, Green. DA9 ... 189 FV85
Skips Cor, Epp. (N.Wld Bas.)
CM16 ... 71 FD25
Skipsea Ho, SW18
off Fitzhugh Gro ... 180 DD86
Skipsey Av, E6 ... 145 EM69
Skipton Cl, N11
off Ribblesdale Av ... 98 DG51
Skipton Dr, Hayes UB3 ... 155 BQ76
Skipton Way, Horl. RH6 ... 269 DH145
Skipworth Rd, E9 ... 142 DW67
Skomer Wk, N1
off Ashby Gro ... 142 DQ65
Skydmore Path, Slou. SL2
off Umberville Way ... 131 AM69
Skylark Rd, Uxb. (Denh.)
UB9 ... 113 BC60
Skylines Village, E14 ... 24 C4
Sky Peals Rd, Wdf.Grn. IG8 ... 101 ED53
Skyport Dr, West Dr. UB7 ... 154 BK80
Sch Skyswood Prim Sch,
St.Alb. AL4
off Chandlers Rd ... 43 CJ16
Skys Wd Rd, St.Alb. AL4 ... 43 CH16
Slacksbury Hatch,
Harl. CM19
off Helions Rd ... 51 EP15
Slade, The, SE18 ... 165 ES79
Sladebrook Rd, SE3 ... 164 EK83
Slade Ct, Cher. (Ott.) KT16 ... 211 BD107
Radlett WD7 ... 77 CG35
Sladedale Rd, SE18 ... 165 ES78
Slade End, Epp. (They.B.)
CM16 ... 85 ES36
Slade Gdns, Erith DA8 ... 167 FF81
⇌ Slade Green ... 167 FG81
Sch Slade Grn Inf Sch,
Erith DA8
off Slade Grn Rd ... 167 FG80
Sch Slade Grn Jun Sch,
Erith DA8
off Slade Grn Rd ... 167 FG80
Slade Grn Rd, Erith DA8 ... 167 FG80
Slade Ho, Houns. TW4 ... 176 BZ86
Slade Oak La, Ger.Cr. SL9 ... 113 BB55
Uxbridge (Denh.) UB9 ... 113 BD59
Slade Rd, Cher. (Ott.) KT16 ... 211 BD107
Slades Cl, Enf. EN2 ... 81 DN41
Slades Dr, Chis. BR7 ... 185 EQ90
Slades Gdns, Enf. EN2 ... 81 DN40
Slades Hill, Enf. EN2 ... 81 DN41
Slades Ri, Enf. EN2 ... 81 DN41
Slade Twr, E10 ... 123 EB61
Slade Wk, SE17 off Heiron St ... 161 DP79
Slagrove Pl, SE13 ... 183 EA85
Slaidburn St, SW10 ... 160 DC79
Slaithwaite Rd, SE13 ... 163 EC84
Slaney Pl, N7 ... 4 C1
Slaney Rd, Rom. RM1 ... 127 FE57
Slapleys, Wok. GU22 ... 226 AX120
Slater Cl, SE18
off Woolwich New Rd ... 165 EN78
Slattery Rd, Felt. TW13 ... 176 BW88
Sleaford Grn, Wat. WD19 ... 94 BX48
Sleaford Ho, E3
off Chiltern Rd ... 143 EA70
Sleaford St, SW8 ... 161 DJ80
Sleapcross Gdns, St.Alb.
(Smallford) AL4 ... 44 CP21
SLEAPSHYDE, St.Alb. AL4 ... 44 CP21
Sleapshyde La, St.Alb.
(Smallford) AL4 ... 44 CP21
Sledmere Ct, Felt. TW14
off Kilross Rd ... 175 BS88
Sleepers Fm Rd, Grays
RM16 ... 171 GH75
Sleets End, Hem.H. HP1 ... 40 BH18
Slewins Cl, Horn. RM11 ... 128 FJ57
Slewins La, Horn. RM11 ... 128 FJ57
Slievemore Cl, SW4
off Voltaire Rd ... 161 DK83
Slimmons Dr, St.Alb. AL4 ... 43 CG16
Slines Oak Rd, Cat. (Wold.)
CR3 ... 237 EA123
Warlingham CR6 ... 237 EA119
Slingsby Pl, WC2 ... 9 N9
Slip, The, West. TN16 ... 255 EQ126
Slipe La, Brox. EN10 ... 49 DZ24
Slippers Hill, Hem.H. HP2 ... 40 BK19
Slippers Pl, SE16 ... 22 D5
Slipshatch Rd, Reig. RH2 ... 265 CX138
Slipshoe St, Reig. RH2
off West St ... 249 CZ134
Sloane Av, SW3 ... 18 A7
Sloane Ct E, SW3 ... 18 E9
Sloane Ct W, SW3 ... 18 E9
Sloane Gdns, SW1 ... 18 E8
Orpington BR6 ... 205 EQ104
H Sloane Hosp, Beck. BR3 ... 203 ED95
⊖ Sloane Square ... 18 E8
Sloane Sq, SW1 ... 18 E8
Sloane St, SW1 ... 18 D5
Sloane Ter, SW1 ... 18 D7
Sloane Wk, Croy. CR0 ... 203 DZ100
Sloansway, Welw.G.C. AL7 ... 29 CZ06
Slocock Hill, Wok. GU21 ... 226 AW117
Slocum Cl, SE28 ... 146 EW73
SLOUGH, SL1 - SL3 ... 132 AS74
⇌ Slough ... 132 AT74
Sch Slough & Eton C of E Sch,
Slou. SL1
off Ragstone Rd ... 151 AR76
Sch Slough Gram Sch,
Slou. SL3
off Lascelles Rd ... 152 AV76
Slough La, NW9 ... 118 CQ58
Betchworth (Buckland)
RH3 ... 249 CU133
Epping CM16 ... 53 FD24
Epsom (Headley) KT18 ... 248 CQ125
★ Slough Mus, Slou. SL1 ... 152 AU75
Slough Retail Pk, Slou. SL1
off Twinches La ... 131 AP74
Slough Rd, Iver SL0 ... 133 BE68
Slough (Datchet) SL3 ... 152 AU78
Windsor (Eton) SL4 ... 151 AR78
Slough Trd Est, Slou. SL1 ... 131 AP72
Slowmans Cl, St.Alb.
(Park St) AL2 ... 60 CC28
Slyfield Ct, Guil. GU1
off Slyfield Grn ... 242 AY130
Slyfield Grn, Guil. GU1 ... 242 AX130
Slyfield Ind Est, Guil. GU1 ... 242 AY130
Sly St, E1 ... 12 C8
Smaldon Cl, West Dr. UB7
off Walnut Av ... 154 BN76
Small Acre, Hem.H. HP1 ... 39 BF20
Smallberry Av, Islw. TW7 ... 157 CF82
Sch Smallberry Grn Prim Sch,
Islw. TW7
off Turnpike Way ... 157 CG81
Smallbrook Ms, W2 ... 7 N8
Smallcroft, Welw.G.C. AL7 ... 30 DB08
Smalley Cl, N16 ... 122 DT62
Smalley Rd Est, N16
off Smalley Cl ... 122 DT62
SMALLFIELD, Horl. RH6 ... 269 DP149
Smallfield Rd, Horl. RH6 ... 269 DH148
SMALLFORD, St.Alb. AL4 ... 44 CP19
Smallford La, St.Alb.
(Smallford) AL4 ... 44 CP21
Small Grains, Long.
(Fawk.Grn) DA3 ... 209 FV104
Smallholdings Rd, Epsom
KT17 ... 217 CW114
Smallmead, Horl. RH6 ... 269 DH148
Small's Hill Rd, Reig.
(Leigh) RH2 ... 265 CU141
Smallwood Cl, St.Alb.
(Wheat.) AL4 ... 28 CL08
Sch Smallwood Prim Sch,
SW17 off Smallwood Rd ... 180 DD91
Smallwood Rd, SW17 ... 180 DD91
Smardale Rd, SW18
off Alma Rd ... 180 DC85
Smarden Cl, Belv. DA17
off Essenden Rd ... 166 FA78
Smarden Gro, SE9 ... 185 EM91
Smart Cl, Rom. RM3 ... 105 FH53
Smarts Grn, Wal.Cr. (Chsht)
EN7 ... 66 DT27
Smarts Heath La, Wok.
GU22 ... 226 AU123
Smarts Heath Rd, Wok.
GU22 ... 226 AT123
Smarts La, Loug. IG10 ... 84 EK42
Smarts Pl, N18 off Fore St ... 100 DU50
Smart's Pl, WC2 ... 9 P7
Smarts Rd, Grav. DA12 ... 191 GH89
Smart St, E2 ... 12 G1
Smeaton Cl, Chess. KT9
off Merritt Gdns ... 215 CK107
Waltham Abbey EN9 ... 68 EE32
Smeaton Rd, SW18 ... 180 DA87
Enfield EN3 ... 83 EA37
Woodford Green IG8 ... 103 EM50
Smeaton St, E1 ... 22 C1
Smedley St, SW4 ... 161 DK82
SW8 ... 161 DK82
Smeed Rd, E3 ... 143 EA66
Coll Smerdon Adult Training
Cen, Belv. DA17
off Lumley Cl ... 166 FA78
Smiles Pl, SE13 ... 163 EC82
⇌ Smitham ... 235 DL115
Smitham Bottom La, Pur.
CR8 ... 219 DJ111
Smitham Downs Rd, Pur.
CR8 ... 219 DK113
Sch Smitham Prim Sch,
Couls. CR5
off Portnalls Rd ... 235 DJ116
Smithbarn Cl, Horl. RH6
off Tanyard Way ... 269 DH147
Smith Cl, SE16 ... 22 G2
Smithers, The, Bet. (Brock.)
RH3 ... 264 CP136
Smithfield, Hem.H. HP2 ... 40 BK18
★ Smithfield Cen Mkt, EC1 ... 10 F6
Smithfield St, EC1 ... 10 E6
Smithies Ct, E15 ... 123 EC64
Smithies Rd, SE2 ... 166 EV77
Smith Rd, Reig. RH2 ... 265 CZ137
Smiths Caravan Site, Iver
SL0 ... 133 BC74
Smith's Ct, W1 ... 9 K9
Smiths Ct, Epp. (Thnwd)
CM16 ... 70 EW25
Smiths Cres, St.Alb.
(Smallford) AL4 ... 44 CP21
Smiths Fm Est, Nthlt. UB5 ... 136 CA68
Smiths La, Eden. (Crock.H.)
TN8 ... 255 EQ133
Smiths La, Wal. Cr. (Chsht)
EN7 ... 66 DR26
Windsor SL4 ... 151 AL82
Smithson Rd, N17 ... 100 DR53
Smiths Pt, E13
off Brooks Rd ... 144 EG67
Smith Sq, SW1 ... 19 N6
Smith St, SW3 ... 18 C9
Surbiton KT5 ... 198 CM100
Watford WD18 ... 76 BW42
Smiths Yd, SW18
off Summerley St ... 180 DC89
Smith's Yd, Croy. CR0
off St. Georges Wk ... 202 DQ104
Smith Ter, SW3 ... 18 C10
Smithwood Cl, SW19 ... 179 CY88
Smithy Cl, Tad. (Lwr Kgswd)
KT20 ... 249 CZ126
Smithy La, Tad. (Lwr Kgswd)
KT20 ... 249 CZ127
Smithy St, E1 ... 12 E5
Sch Smithy St Prim Sch, E1 ... 12 F5
Smock Wk, Croy. CR0 ... 202 DQ100
Smokehouse Yd, EC1 ... 10 F5
Smoke La, Reig. RH2 ... 266 DB136
SMOKY HOLE, Guil. GU5 ... 261 BR144
Smugglers Wk, Green. DA9 ... 189 FV85
Smugglers Way, SW18 ... 160 DB84
Smug Oak Grn Business Cen,
St.Alb. AL2 ... 60 CB30
Smug Oak La, St.Alb.
(Brick.Wd) AL2 ... 60 CB30
Smyrks Rd, SE17 ... 21 M10
Smyrna Rd, NW6 ... 140 DA66
Smythe Rd, Dart. (Sutt.H.)
DA4 ... 208 FN95
Smythe St, E14 ... 14 B9
Snag La, Sev. (Cudham)
TN14 ... 223 ES109
Snakeley Cl, H.Wyc. (Loud.)
HP10 ... 88 AC54
Snakes La, Barn. EN4 ... 80 DH41
Snakes La E, Wdf.Grn. IG8 ... 102 EJ51
Snakes La W, Wdf.Grn. IG8 ... 102 EG51
Snape Spur, Slou. SL1 ... 132 AS72
SNARESBROOK, E11 ... 124 EE57
⊖ Snaresbrook ... 124 EG57
Sch Snaresbrook Coll, E18
off Woodford Rd ... 124 EG55
Snaresbrook Dr, Stan. HA7 ... 95 CK49
Sch Snaresbrook Prim Sch,
E18 off Meadow Wk ... 124 EG56
Snaresbrook Rd, E11 ... 124 EE56
Snarsgate St, W10 ... 139 CW71
Snatts Hill, Oxt. RH8 ... 254 EF129
Sneath Av, NW11 ... 119 CZ59
Snelling Av, Grav. (Nthflt)
DA11 ... 190 GE89
Snellings Rd, Walt. KT12 ... 214 BW106
Snells La, Amer. HP7 ... 72 AV39
Snells Pk, N18 ... 100 DT51
Snells Wd Ct, Amer. HP7 ... 72 AW40
Sneyd Rd, NW2 ... 119 CW63
Snipe Cl, Erith DA8 ... 167 FH80
Snodland Cl, Orp. BR6
off Mill La ... 223 EN110
Snowberry Cl, E15 ... 123 ED63
Snowbury Rd, SW6 ... 160 DB82
Snowden Av, Uxb. UB10 ... 135 BP68
Snowden St, EC2 ... 11 L4
Snowdon Cl, Wind. SL4 ... 151 AK83
Snowdon Cres, Hayes UB3 ... 155 BQ76
Snowdon Dr, NW9 ... 118 CS58
Snowdon Rd, Houns.
(Hthrw Air.) TW6
off Southern Perimeter Rd ... 175 BQ85
Snowdown Cl, SE20 ... 203 DX95
Snowdrop Cl, Hmptn. TW12
off Gresham Rd ... 176 CA93
Snowdrop Path, Rom. RM3 ... 106 FK52
Snowerhill Rd, Bet. RH3 ... 264 CS136
Snow Hill, EC1 ... 10 E6
Snowhill Cotts, Chesh. HP5 ... 38 AT24
Snow Hill Ct, EC1 ... 10 F7
Snowman Ho, NW6 ... 140 DB67
Snowsfields, SE1 ... 21 K3
Sch Snowsfields Prim Sch,
SE1 ... 21 L3
Snowshill Rd, E12 ... 124 EL64
Snowy Fielder Waye, Islw.
TW7 ... 157 CH82
Soames St, SE15 ... 162 DT83
Soames Wk, N.Mal. KT3 ... 198 CS95
Soane Cl, W5 ... 157 CK75
Soap Ho La, Brent. TW8 ... 158 CL80
Socket La, Brom. BR2 ... 204 EH100
SOCKETT'S HEATH, Grays
RM16 ... 170 GD76
Soham Rd, Enf. EN3 ... 83 DZ37
SOHO, W1 ... 9 L9
Soho Cres, H.Wyc.
(Woob.Grn) HP10 ... 110 AD59
Soho Mills Ind Est, H.Wyc.
(Woob.Grn) HP10 ... 110 AD59
Sch Soho Parish Sch, W1 ... 9 L9
Soho Sq, W1 ... 9 L7
Soho St, W1 ... 9 L7
Sojourner Truth Cl, E8
off Richmond Rd ... 142 DV65
Solander Gdns, E1 ... 12 E9
Solar Way, Enf. EN3 ... 83 DZ36
Solebay St, E1 ... 13 J4
Solecote, Lthd. (Bkhm)
KT23 ... 246 CA125
Sole Fm Av, Lthd. (Bkhm)
KT23 ... 246 BZ125
Sole Fm Cl, Lthd. (Bkhm)
KT23 ... 230 BZ124
Sole Fm Rd, Lthd. (Bkhm)
KT23 ... 246 BZ125
Solefields Rd, Sev. TN13 ... 257 FH128
Sch Solefields Sch,
Sev. TN13
off Solefields Rd ... 257 FJ126
Solent Ri, E13 ... 15 L2
Solent Rd, NW6 ... 120 DA64
Hounslow (Hthrw Air.)
TW6 ... 174 BM86
Soleoak Dr, Sev. TN13 ... 257 FH127
Solesbridge Cl, Rick. (Chorl.)
WD3 ... 73 BF41
Solesbridge La, Rick. WD3 ... 74 BG40
Soley Ms, WC1 ... 10 C1
Solna Av, SW15 ... 179 CW85
Solna Rd, N21 ... 100 DR46
Solomon Av, N9 ... 100 DU49
Solomons Hill, Rick. WD3
off Northway ... 92 BK45
Solomon's Pas, SE15 ... 162 DV84
Solom's Ct Rd, Bans. SM7 ... 234 DE117
Solon New Rd, SW4 ... 161 DL84
Solon New Rd Est, SW4
off Solon New Rd ... 161 DL84
Solon Rd, SW2 ... 161 DL84
Solway, Hem.H. HP2 ... 40 BM18
Solway Cl, E8 ... 5 P4
Hounslow TW4 ... 156 BY83
Solway Rd, N22 ... 99 DP53
SE22 ... 162 DU84
Somaford Gro, Barn. EN4 ... 80 DD44
Somali Rd, NW2 ... 119 CZ63
Somborne Ho, SW15
off Fontley Way ... 179 CU87
Somerby Cl, Brox. EN10 ... 49 EA21
Somerby Rd, Bark. IG11 ... 145 ER66
Somercoates Cl, Barn. EN4 ... 80 DE41
Somerden Rd, Orp. BR5 ... 206 EX101
Somerfield Cl, Tad. KT20 ... 233 CY119
Somerfield Rd, N4 ... 121 DP61
Somerford Cl, Pnr. HA5 ... 115 BU56
Somerford Gro, N16 ... 122 DT63
N17 ... 100 DU52
Somerford Gro Est, N16
off Somerford Gro ... 122 DT63
Somerford Pl, Beac. HP9 ... 89 AK52
Somerford St, E1 ... 12 C4
Somerford Way, SE16 ... 23 J4
Somerhill Av, Sid. DA15 ... 186 EV87
Somerhill Rd, Well. DA16 ... 166 EV82
Someries Rd, Hem.H. HP1 ... 39 BF18
Somerleyton Pas, SW9 ... 161 DP84
Somerleyton Rd, SW9 ... 161 DN84
Somersby Gdns, Ilf. IG4 ... 125 EM57
Somers Cl, NW1
off Platt St ... 141 DK68
Reigate RH2 ... 250 DA133
Somers Cres, W2 ... 8 A8
Somerset Av, SW20 ... 199 CV96
Chessington KT9 ... 215 CK105
Welling DA16 ... 185 ET85
Somerset Cl, N17 ... 100 DR54
Epsom KT19 ... 216 CS109
New Malden KT3 ... 198 CS100
Walton-on-Thames KT12
off Queens Rd ... 213 BV106
Woodford Green IG8 ... 102 EG53
Somerset Est, SW11 ... 160 DD81
Somerset Gdns, N6 ... 120 DG59
N17 ... 100 DS52
SE13 ... 163 EB82
SW16 ... 201 DM97
Hornchurch RM11 ... 128 FN60
Teddington TW11 ... 177 CE92
★ Somerset Ho, WC2 ... 10 A9
Somerset Ho, SW19 ... 179 CX90
Somerset Rd, E17 ... 123 EA57
N17 ... 122 DT55
N18 ... 100 DT50
NW4 ... 119 CW56
SW19 ... 179 CY91
W4 ... 158 CR76
W13 ... 137 CH74
Barnet EN5 ... 80 DB43
Brentford TW8 ... 157 CJ79
Dartford DA1 ... 187 FH86
Enfield EN3 ... 83 EA38
Harrow HA1 ... 116 CC57
Kingston upon Thames
KT1 ... 198 CM96
Orpington BR6 ... 206 EU101
Redhill RH1 ... 266 DD136
Southall UB1 ... 136 BZ71
Teddington TW11 ... 177 CE92
Somerset Sq, W14 ... 16 D4
Somerset Way, Iver SL0 ... 153 BF75
Somerset Waye, Houns.
TW5 ... 156 BY79
Somersham, Welw.G.C.
AL7 ... 30 DD09
Somersham Rd, Bexh.
DA7 ... 166 EY82
Sch Somers Heath Co Prim
Sch, S.Ock. RM15
off Foyle Dr ... 149 FU73
Somers Ms, W2 ... 8 A8
Somers Pl, SW2 ... 181 DM87
Reigate RH2 ... 250 DA133
Somers Rd, E17 ... 123 DZ56
SW2 ... 181 DM86
Hatfield AL9 ... 45 CW24
Reigate RH2 ... 249 CZ133
Somers Sq, Hat. AL9 ... 45 CW23
SOMERS TOWN, NW1 ... 9 M1
Somers Way, Bushey WD23 ... 94 CC45
Somerswey, Guil. (Shalf.)
GU4 ... 258 AY142
Somerton Av, Rich. TW9 ... 158 CP83
Somerton Cl, Pur. CR8 ... 235 DN115
Somerton Rd, NW2 ... 119 CY62
SE15 ... 162 DV84
Somertons Cl, Guil. GU2 ... 242 AU131
Somertrees Av, SE12 ... 184 EH89
Somervell Rd, Har. HA2 ... 116 BZ64
Somerville Av, SW13 ... 159 CV79
Somerville Rd, SE20 ... 183 DX94
Cobham KT11 ... 214 CA114
Dartford DA1 ... 188 FM86
Romford RM6 ... 126 EW58
Windsor (Eton) SL4 ... 151 AQ78
Sommer's Ct, Ware SG12
off Sutton Ct ... 33 DY07
Sonderburg Rd, N7 ... 121 DM61
Sondes Pl Dr, Dor. RH4 ... 263 CF136
Sondes St, SE17 ... 162 DR79
Sonia Cl, Wat. WD19 ... 94 BW45
Sonia Ct, Har. HA1 ... 117 CF58
Sonia Gdns, N12
off Woodside Av ... 98 DC49
NW10 ... 119 CT63
Hounslow TW5 ... 156 CA80
Sonic Ct, Guil. GU1
off Woodbridge Rd ... 242 AW133
Sonnets, The, Hem.H. HP1 ... 40 BH19
Sonnet Wk, West. (Bigg.H.)
TN16 off Kings Rd ... 238 EH118
Sonning Gdns, Hmptn.
TW12 ... 176 BY93
Sonning Rd, SE25 ... 202 DU100
Soothouse Spring, St.Alb.
AL3 ... 43 CF16
Soper Cl, E4 ... 101 DZ50
SE23 ... 183 DX88
Soper Dr, Cat. CR3
off Hambledon Rd ... 236 DR123
Soper Ms, Enf. EN3
off Harston Dr ... 83 EA38
Soper Sq, Harl. CM17
off London Rd ... 36 EW14
Sopers Rd, Pot.B. (Cuffley)
EN6 ... 65 DM29
Sophia Cl, N7 ... 4 A3
Sophia Rd, E10 ... 123 EB60
E16 ... 15 N7
Sophia Sq, SE16 ... 13 J10

⊖ London Underground station   DLR Docklands Light Railway station   Tra Tramlink station   Riv Pedestrian ferry landing stage

Sophie Gdns, Slou. SL3 off Downs Rd 152 AX75
Sopwell La, St.Alb. AL1 43 CD21
Sopwith Av, Chess. KT9 216 CL106
Sopwith Cl, Kings.T. KT2 178 CM92
Westerham (Bigg.H.) TN16 238 EK116
Sopwith Dr, W.Byf. KT14 212 BL111
Weybridge KT13 212 BL111
Sopwith Rd, Houns. TW5 156 BW80
Sopwith Way, SW8 161 DH80
Kingston upon Thames KT2 198 CL95
Sorbie Cl, Wey. KT13 213 BR107
Sorrel Bk, Croy. CR0 221 DY110
Sorrel Cl, SE28 146 EU74
Sorrel Ct, Grays RM17 off Salix Rd 170 GD79
Sorrel Gdns, E6 144 EL71
Sorrel La, E14 14 F8
Sorrell Cl, SE14 off Southerngate Way 163 DY80
Sorrel Wk, Rom. RM1 127 FF55
Sorrel Way, Grav. (Nthflt) DA11 190 GE91
Sorrento Rd, Sutt. SM1 200 DB104
Sospel Ct, Slou. (Farn.Royal) SL2 131 AQ68
Sotheby Rd, N5 121 DP62
Sotheran Cl, E8 142 DU67
Sotheron Rd, SW6 160 DB80
Watford WD17 76 BW40
Soudan Rd, SW11 160 DF81
Souldern Rd, W14 16 B6
Souldern St, Wat. WD18 75 BU43
Sounds Lo, Swan. BR8 207 FC100
South Access Rd, E17 123 DY59
Southacre Way, Pnr. HA5 94 BW53
SOUTH ACTON, W3 158 CN76
⇌ South Acton 158 CQ76
South Acton Est, W3 158 CP75
South Africa Rd, W12 139 CV74
South Albert Rd, Reig. RH2 249 CZ133
SOUTHALL, UB1 & UB2 136 BX74
⇌ Southall 156 BZ75
Coll Southall & W London Coll, Sthl. UB1 off Beaconsfield Rd 136 BY74
Southall Cl, Ware SG12 33 DX05
Southall La, Houns. TW5 155 BV79
Southall UB2 155 BV79
Southall Pl, SE1 21 J4
Southall Way, Brwd. CM14 108 FT49
Southampton Bldgs, WC2 10 C7
Southampton Gdns, Mitch. CR4 201 DL99
Southampton Ms, E16 25 N1
Southampton Pl, WC1 9 P6
Southampton Rd, NW5 120 DF64
Hounslow (Hthrw Air.) TW6 174 BN86
Southampton Row, WC1 9 P5
Southampton St, WC2 9 P9
Southampton Way, SE5 162 DR80
Southam St, W10 6 D4
South App, Nthwd. HA6 93 BR48
South Audley St, W1 8 F10
South Av, E4 101 EB45
Carshalton SM5 218 DF108
Egham TW20 173 BC93
Richmond TW9 off Sandycombe Rd 158 CN82
Southall UB1 136 BZ73
Walton-on-Thames (Whiteley Vill.) KT12 213 BS110
South Av Gdns, Sthl. UB1 136 BZ73
South Bk, Chis. BR7 185 EQ91
Surbiton KT6 198 CL100
Southbank, T.Ditt. KT7 197 CH101
South Bk, West. TN16 255 ER126
Southbank Business Cen, SW8 161 DK79
Sch Southbank Int Sch, NW3 off Netherhall Gdns 140 DC65
W11 6 G10
South Bk Rd, Berk. HP4 38 AT17
South Bk Ter, Surb. KT6 198 CL100
SOUTH BEDDINGTON, Wall. SM6 219 DK107
⇌ South Bermondsey 22 E9
South Birkbeck Rd, E11 123 ED62
South Black Lion La, W6 159 CU78
South Bolton Gdns, SW5 17 K9
Sch South Bookham Sch, Lthd. KT23 off Oakdene Cl 246 CC127
South Border, The, Pur. CR8 219 DK111
SOUTHBOROUGH, Brom. BR2 205 EM100
Southborough Cl, Surb. KT6 197 CK102
Southborough La, Brom. BR2 204 EL99
Sch Southborough Prim Sch, Brom. BR2 off Southborough La 205 EN99
Southborough Rd, E9 142 DW67
Bromley BR1 204 EL97
Surbiton KT6 198 CL102
Sch Southborough Sch, Surb. KT6 off Hook Rd 198 CL104
Southbourne, Brom. BR2 204 EG101
Southbourne Av, NW9 96 CQ54
Southbourne Cl, Pnr. HA5 116 BY59
Southbourne Cres, NW4 119 CY56
Southbourne Gdns, SE12 184 EH85
Ilford IG1 125 EQ64
Ruislip HA4 115 BV60
Southbridge Pl, Croy. CR0 220 DQ105
Southbridge Rd, Croy. CR0 220 DQ105
Southbridge Way, Sthl. UB2 156 BY75
Southbrook, Saw. CM21 36 EY06
Southbrook Dr, Wal.Cr. (Chsht) EN8 67 DX28
Southbrook Ms, SE12 184 EF86
Southbrook Rd, SE12 184 EF86
SW16 201 DL95
⇌ Southbury 82 DV42
Southbury Av, Enf. EN1 82 DU43
Southbury Cl, Horn. RM12 128 FK64
Sch Southbury Prim Sch, Enf. EN3 off Swansea Rd 82 DW42
Southbury Rd, Enf. EN1, EN3 82 DR41
Coll South Camden City Learning Cen, NW1 off Charrington St 141 DK68
Sch South Camden Comm Sch, NW1 off Charrington St 141 DK68
South Carriage Dr, SW1 18 C3
SW7 17 P4
SOUTH CHINGFORD, E4 101 DZ50
Southchurch Rd, E6 145 EM68
South Circular Rd, SE6 (A205) 183 ED87
SE9 (A205) 165 EM83
SE12 (A205) 184 EH86
SE18 (A205) 165 EN79
SE21 (A205) 182 DS88
SE22 (A205) 182 DV88
SE23 (A205) 183 DZ88
SW2 (A205) 181 DN88
SW4 (A205) 180 DG85
SW11 (A3) 180 DE85
SW12 (A205) 181 DN88
SW14 (A205) 158 CS84
SW15 (A205) 159 CW84
SW18 (A3) 180 DE85
W4 (A205) 158 CN78
Brentford (A205) TW8 158 CN78
Richmond (A205) TW9 158 CP82
Southcliffe Dr, Ger.Cr. (Chal.St.P.) SL9 90 AY50
South Cl, N6 121 DH58
Barnet EN5 79 CZ41
Bexleyheath DA6 166 EX84
Dagenham RM10 146 FA67
Morden SM4 200 DA100
Pinner HA5 116 BZ59
St. Albans AL2 60 CB25
Slough SL1 off St. George's Cres 131 AK73
Twickenham TW2 176 CA90
West Drayton UB7 154 BM76
Woking GU21 226 AW116
South Cl Grn, Red. RH1 251 DH129
South Colonnade, E14 23 P1
Southcombe St, W14 16 C7
South Common Rd, Uxb. UB8 134 BL65
Southcote, Wok. GU21 226 AX115
Southcote Av, Felt. TW13 175 BT89
Surbiton KT5 198 CP101
Southcote Ri, Ruis. HA4 115 BR59
Southcote Rd, E17 123 DX57
N19 121 DJ63
SE25 202 DV100
Redhill RH1 251 DJ129
South Croydon CR2 220 DS110
South Cottage Dr, Rick. (Chorl.) WD3 73 BF43
South Cottage Gdns, Rick. (Chorl.) WD3 73 BF43
Southcott Ms, NW8 off Allitsen Rd 140 DE68
South Countess Rd, E17 123 DZ55
South Cres, E16 14 E4
WC1 9 L6
South Cft, Egh. (Eng.Grn) TW20 172 AV92
Southcroft, Slou. SL2 131 AP70
Southcroft Av, Well. DA16 165 ES83
West Wickham BR4 203 EC103
Southcroft Rd, SW16 180 DG93
SW17 180 DG93
Orpington BR6 205 ES104
South Cross Rd, Ilf. IG6 125 EQ57
South Croxted Rd, SE21 182 DR90
SOUTH CROYDON, CR2 220 DQ107
⇌ South Croydon 220 DR106
Southdale, Chig. IG7 103 ER51
SOUTH DARENTH, Dart. DA4 209 FR95
Southdean Gdns, SW19 179 CZ89
South Dene, NW7 96 CR48
Southdene, Sev. (Halst.) TN14 224 EY113
Southdown Av, W7 157 CG76
Southdown Ct, Hat. AL10 45 CV21
Southdown Cres, Har. HA2 116 CB60
Ilford IG2 125 ES57
Southdown Dr, SW20 off Crescent Rd 179 CX94
Southdown Rd, SW20 199 CX95
Carshalton SM5 218 DG109
Caterham (Wold.) CR3 237 DZ122
Hatfield AL10 45 CU21
Hornchurch RM11 127 FH59
Walton-on-Thames KT12 214 BY105
Southdowns, Dart. (S.Darenth) DA4 209 FR96
South Dr, Bans. SM7 218 DE113
Beaconsfield HP9 110 AH55
Brentwood CM14 108 FX49
Coulsdon CR5 235 DK115
Dorking RH5 263 CJ136
Orpington BR6 223 ES106
Potters Bar (Cuffley) EN6 65 DL30
Romford RM2 128 FJ55
Ruislip HA4 115 BS60
St. Albans AL4 43 CK20
Sutton SM2 217 CY110
Virginia Water GU25 192 AU102
⊖ South Ealing 157 CJ76
South Ealing Rd, W5 157 CK75
South Eastern Av, N9 100 DT48
Coll South E London Coll, SE4 off Shardeloes Rd 163 DY83
South Eaton Pl, SW1 18 F7
South Eden Pk Rd, Beck. BR3 203 EB100
South Edwardes Sq, W8 16 F6
SOUTHEND, SE6 183 EB91
South End, W8 17 K5
Croydon CR0 220 DQ105
Leatherhead (Bkhm) KT23 246 CB126
Southend Arterial Rd, Brwd. CM13 129 FV57
Hornchurch RM11 127 FK54
Romford RM2, RM3 106 FK54
Upminster RM14 129 FR57
South End Cl, NW3 120 DE63
Southend Cl, SE9 185 EP86
Southend Cres, SE9 185 EN86
South End Grn, NW3 off South End Rd 120 DE63
Southend La, SE6 183 DZ91
SE26 183 DZ91
Waltham Abbey EN9 68 EH34
Southend Rd, E4 101 DY50
E6 145 EM66
E17 101 EB53
E18 102 EG53
South End Rd, NW3 120 DE63
Southend Rd, Beck. BR3 183 EA94
Grays RM17 170 GC77
South End Rd, Horn. RM12 147 FH65
Rainham RM13 147 FG67
Southend Rd, Wdf.Grn. IG8 102 EJ54
South End Row, W8 17 K5
Southerland Cl, Wey. KT13 213 BQ105
Southern Av, SE25 202 DT97
Feltham TW14 175 BU88
Southern Av, Red. RH1 266 DG141
Southern Dr, Loug. IG10 85 EM44
Southerngate Way, SE14 163 DY80
Southern Gro, E3 13 L3
Southernhay, Loug. IG10 84 EK43
Southern Lo, Harl. CM19 51 EQ18
Southern Perimeter Rd, Houns. (Hthrw Air.) TW6 175 BR85
Southern Pl, Swan. BR8 207 FD98
Southern Rd, E13 144 EH68
N2 120 DF56
Sch Southern Rd Prim Sch, E13 off Southern Rd 144 EH68
Southern Row, W10 6 C4
Southerns La, Couls. CR5 250 DC125
Southern St, N1 4 A9
Southern Way, SE10 25 K7
Harlow CM17, CM18 51 EN18
Romford RM7 126 FA58
Southernwood Cl, Hem.H. HP2 40 BN19
Southerton Rd, W6 159 CW76
Southerton Way, Rad. (Shenley) WD7 62 CL33
South Esk Rd, E7 144 EJ65
Southey Ms, E16 25 M1
Southey Rd, N15 122 DS57
SW9 161 DN81
SW19 180 DA94
Southey St, SE20 183 DX94
Southey Wk, Til. RM18 171 GH81
Southfield, Barn. EN5 79 CX44
Welwyn Garden City AL7 29 CX11
Southfield Av, Wat. WD24 76 BW38
Southfield Cl, Uxb. UB8 134 BN69
Windsor (Dorney) SL4 150 AJ76
Southfield Cotts, W7 off Oaklands Rd 157 CF75
Southfield Gdns, Slou. (Burn.) SL1 130 AH71
Twickenham TW1 177 CF91
Southfield Pk, Har. HA2 116 CB56
Southfield Pl, Wey. KT13 213 BP108
Sch Southfield Prim Sch, W4 off Southfield Rd 158 CS75
Southfield Rd, N17 off The Avenue 100 DS54
W4 158 CS76
Chislehurst BR7 205 ET97
Enfield EN3 82 DV44
Hoddesdon EN11 49 EA15
Waltham Cross EN8 67 DY32
SOUTHFIELDS, SW18 180 DA88
⊖ Southfields 179 CZ88
Southfields, NW4 119 CU55
East Molesey KT8 197 CE100
Swanley BR8 187 FE94
Southfields Av, Ashf. TW15 175 BP93
Sch Southfield Sch, Hat. AL10 off Travellers La 45 CV21
Coll Southfields Comm Coll, SW18 off Merton Rd 180 DA88
Southfields Ct, SW19 179 CY88
Sutton SM1 off Sutton Common Rd 200 DA103
Southfields Ms, SW18 off Southfields Rd 180 DA86
Southfields Pas, SW18 180 DA86
Southfields Rd, SW18 180 DA86
Caterham (Wold.) CR3 237 EB123
Southfield Way, St.Alb. AL4 43 CK18
SOUTHFLEET, Grav. DA13 190 GB93
Southfleet Rd, Dart. (Bean) DA2 189 FW91
Gravesend (Nthflt) DA11 191 GF89
Orpington BR6 205 ES104
Swanscombe DA10 190 FZ87
South Gdns, SW19 180 DD94
SOUTHGATE, N14 99 DJ47
⊖ Southgate 99 DJ46
South Gate, Harl. CM20 51 ER15
Southgate, Purf. RM19 168 FQ77
Southgate Av, Felt. TW13 175 BR91
Southgate Circ, N14 off The Bourne 99 DK46
Coll Southgate Coll, N14 off High St 99 DK46
Minchenden Complex, N14 off High St 99 DK47
Southgate Gro, N1 5 K6
Southgate Rd, N1 5 K7
Potters Bar EN6 64 DC33
Sch Southgate Sch, Barn. EN4 off Sussex Way 81 DH43
South Gipsy Rd, Well. DA16 166 EX83
South Glade, The, Bex. DA5 186 EZ88
South Grn, NW9 off Clayton Fld 96 CS53
Slough SL1 132 AS73
⇌ South Greenford 137 CE69
South Gro, E17 123 DZ57
N6 120 DG60
N15 122 DR57
Chertsey KT16 193 BF100
South Gro Ho, N6 off Highgate W Hill 120 DG60
Sch South Gro Prim Sch, E17 off Ringwood Rd 123 DZ58
SOUTH HACKNEY, E9 142 DW66
South Hall Cl, Dart. (Fnghm) DA4 208 FM101
South Hall Dr, Rain. RM13 147 FH71
SOUTH HAMPSTEAD, NW6 140 DB66
⇌ South Hampstead 140 DC66
Sch South Hampstead High Sch, NW3 off Maresfield Gdns 140 DC65
SOUTH HAREFIELD, Uxb. UB9 114 BJ56
Sch South Harringey Inf Sch, N4 off Pemberton Rd 121 DP57
Sch South Harringey Jun Sch, N4 off Mattison Rd 121 DP57
SOUTH HARROW, Har. HA2 116 CB62
⊖ South Harrow 116 CC62
SOUTH HATFIELD, Hat. AL10 45 CU20
South Hill, Chis. BR7 185 EM93
Guildford GU1 258 AX136
South Hill Av, Har. HA1, HA2 116 CC62
Sch South Hill Co Prim Sch, Hem.H. HP1 off Heath La 40 BJ21
South Hill Gro, Har. HA1 117 CE63
South Hill Pk, NW3 120 DE63
South Hill Pk Gdns, NW3 120 DE63
South Hill Rd, Brom. BR2 204 EE97
Gravesend DA12 191 GH88
Hemel Hempstead HP1 40 BJ20
Southholme Cl, SE19 202 DS95
SOUTH HOLMWOOD, Dor. RH5 263 CJ144
SOUTH HORNCHURCH, Rain. RM13 147 FE67
South Huxley, N18 100 DR50
Southill La, Pnr. HA5 115 BU56
Southill Rd, Chis. BR7 184 EL94
Southill St, E14 14 B7
South Island Pl, SW9 161 DM80
SOUTH KENSINGTON, SW7 17 L8
⊖ South Kensington 17 P7
South Kensington Sta Arc, SW7 off Pelham St 160 DD77
South Kent Av, Grav. (Nthflt) DA11 190 GC86
⇌ South Kenton 117 CJ60
⊖ South Kenton 117 CJ60
SOUTH LAMBETH, SW8 161 DL81
South Lambeth Pl, SW8 161 DL79
South Lambeth Rd, SW8 161 DL79
Southland Rd, SE18 165 ET80
Southlands Av, Horl. RH6 268 DF147
Orpington BR6 223 ER105
Southlands Cl, Couls. CR5 235 DM117
Southlands Dr, SW19 179 CX89
Southlands Gro, Brom. BR1 204 EL97
Southlands La, Oxt. (Tand.) RH8 253 EB134
Southlands Rd, Brom. BR1, BR2 204 EJ99
Iver SL0 113 BF64
Uxbridge (Denh.) UB9 113 BF63
Southland Way, Houns. TW3 177 CD85
South La, Kings.T. KT1 197 CK97
New Malden KT3 198 CR98
South La W, N.Mal. KT3 198 CR98
SOUTHLEA, Slou. SL3 152 AV82
Southlea Rd, Slou. (Datchet) SL3 152 AV81
Windsor SL4 152 AU84
South Ley, Welw.G.C. AL7 29 CY12
South Ley Ct, Welw.G.C. AL7 off South Ley 29 CY12
South Lo Av, Mitch. CR4 201 DL98
South Lo Cres, Enf. EN2 81 DK42
South Lo Dr, N14 81 DL43
South Lo Rd, Walt. KT12 213 BU109
H South London & Maudsley NHS Trust - Landor Rd Unit, SW9 161 DL83
★ South London Art Gall, SE5 162 DS81
Southly Cl, Sutt. SM1 200 DA104
South Mall, N9 off Edmonton Grn Shop Cen 100 DU48
South Mead, NW9 97 CT53
Epsom KT19 216 CS108
Redhill RH1 250 DF131
Southmead Cres, Wal.Cr. (Chsht) EN8 67 DY30
South Meadow La, Wind. (Eton) SL4 151 AQ80
South Meadows, Wem. HA9 118 CM64
Sch Southmead Prim Sch, SW19 off Princes Way 179 CY88
Southmead Rd, SW19 179 CY88
SOUTH MERSTHAM, Red. RH1 251 DJ130
⇌ South Merton 199 CZ97
SOUTH MIMMS, Pot.B. EN6 63 CT32
South Molton La, W1 8 G8
South Molton Rd, E16 15 M7
South Molton St, W1 8 G8
Southmont Rd, Esher KT10 197 CE103
Southmoor Way, E9 143 DZ65
South Mundells, Welw.G.C. AL7 29 CZ08
SOUTH NORWOOD, SE25 202 DT97
South Norwood Hill, SE25 202 DS96
Sch South Norwood Prim Sch, SE25 off Crowther Rd 202 DU98
SOUTH NUTFIELD, Red. RH1 267 DL136
South Oak Rd, SW16 181 DM91
SOUTH OCKENDON, RM15 149 FW70
Southold Ri, SE9 185 EM90
Southolm St, SW11 161 DH81
South Ordnance Rd, Enf. EN3 83 EA37
Southover, N12 98 DA49
Bromley BR1 184 EG92
SOUTH OXHEY, Wat. WD19 94 BW48
South Par, SW3 17 P9
W4 158 CR77
Waltham Abbey EN9 off Sun St 67 EC33
SOUTH PARK, Reig. RH2 265 CZ138
South Pk, SW6 160 DA82
Gerrards Cross SL9 113 AZ57
Sevenoaks TN13 257 FH125
South Pk Av, Rick. (Chorl.) WD3 73 BF43
South Pk Cres, SE6 184 EF88
Gerrards Cross SL9 112 AY56
Ilford IG1 125 ER62
South Pk Dr, Bark. IG11 125 ES63
Gerrards Cross SL9 112 AY56
Ilford IG3 125 ES63
South Pk Gdns, Berk. HP4 38 AV18
South Pk Gro, N.Mal. KT3 198 CQ98
South Pk Hill Rd, S.Croy. CR2 220 DR106
South Pk Ms, SW6 160 DB83
Sch South Pk Prim Sch, Ilf. IG3 off Water La 125 ES62
South Pk Rd, SW19 180 DA93
Ilford IG1 125 ER62
South Pk Ter, Ilf. IG1 125 ER62
South Pk Vw, Ger.Cr. SL9 113 AZ56
South Pk Way, Ruis. HA4 136 BW65
South Path, Wind. SL4 151 AQ81
South Penge Pk Est, SE20 202 DV96
South Perimeter Rd, Uxb. UB8 off Kingston La 134 BL69
South Pier Rd, Gat. RH6 269 DH152
South Pl, EC2 11 K5
Enfield EN3 82 DW43
Harlow CM20 36 EU12
Surbiton KT5 198 CM101
South Pl Ms, EC2 11 K6
Southport Rd, SE18 165 ER77
DLR South Quay 24 A3
South Quay Plaza, E14 off Marsh Wall 163 EB75
South Ridge, Wey. KT13 213 BP110
Southridge Pl, SW20 179 CX94
South Riding, St.Alb. (Brick.Wd) AL2 60 CA30
South Ri, Cars. SM5 218 DE109
Sch South Ri Prim Sch, SE18 off Brewery Rd 165 ER78
South Ri Way, SE18 165 ER78
South Rd, N9 100 DU46
SE23 183 DX89
SW19 180 DC93
South Rd, W5 157 CK77
Amersham HP6 55 AQ36
Edgware HA8 96 CP53
Egham (Eng.Grn) TW20 172 AW93
Erith DA8 167 FF79
Feltham TW13 176 BX92
Guildford GU2 242 AV132
Hampton TW12 176 BY93
Harlow CM20 36 EU12
Reigate RH2 266 DB135
Rickmansworth (Chorl.) WD3 73 BC43
Romford (Chad.Hth) RM6 126 EY58
Romford (Lt.Hth) RM6 126 EW57
South Ockendon RM15 149 FW72
Southall UB1 156 BZ75
Twickenham TW2 177 CD90
West Drayton UB7 154 BM76
Weybridge KT13 213 BQ106
Weybridge (St.Geo.H.) KT13 213 BP109
Woking GU21 210 AX114
South Row, SE3 164 EF82
SOUTH RUISLIP, Ruis. HA4 116 BW63
⇌ South Ruislip 116 BW63
⊖ South Ruislip 116 BW63
Southsea Av, Wat. WD18 75 BU42
Southsea Rd, Kings.T. KT1 198 CL98
South Sea St, SE16 23 L5
South Side, W6 159 CT76
Southside, Ger.Cr. (Chal.St.P.) SL9 112 AX55
Southside Common, SW19 179 CW93
Southspring, Sid. DA15 185 ER87
South Sq, NW11 120 DB58
WC1 10 C6
South Sta App, Red. (S.Nutfld) RH1 267 DL136
SOUTH STIFFORD, Grays RM20 169 FW78
SOUTH STREET, West. TN16 239 EM119
South St, W1 18 F1
Brentwood CM14 108 FW47
Bromley BR1 204 EG96
Dorking RH4 263 CG137
Enfield EN3 83 DX43
Epsom KT18 216 CR113
Gravesend DA12 191 GH87
Hertford SG14 32 DR09
Isleworth TW7 157 CG83
Rainham RM13 147 FC68
Romford RM1 127 FF58
Staines TW18 173 BF92
Ware (Stans.Abb.) SG12 33 EC11
South Tenter St, E1 11 P9
South Ter, SW7 18 A7
Dorking RH4 263 CH137
Surbiton KT6 198 CL100
Coll South Thames Coll, SW17 off Tooting High St 180 DE92
Putney Cen, SW15 off Putney Hill 179 CX85
Roehampton Cen, SW15 off Roehampton La 179 CU86
Wandsworth Cen, SW18 off Wandsworth High St 180 DB85
SOUTH TOTTENHAM, N15 122 DS57
⇌ South Tottenham 122 DT57
South Vale, SE19 182 DS93
Harrow HA1 117 CE63
Southvale Rd, SE3 164 EE82
South Vw, Brom. BR1 204 EH96
Epsom KT19 216 CN109
Southview Av, NW10 119 CT64
South Vw Av, Til. RM18 171 GG81
Southview Cl, SW17 180 DG92
Bexley DA5 186 EZ86
Swanley BR8 207 FF98
Waltham Cross (Chsht) EN7 66 DS26
South Vw Ct, Wok. GU22 off Constitution Hill 226 AY118
Southview Cres, Ilf. IG2 125 EP58
South Vw Dr, E18 124 EH55
Upminster RM14 128 FN62
Southview Gdns, Wall. SM6 219 DJ108
South Vw Rd, N8 121 DK55
Ashtead KT21 231 CK119
Southview Rd, Brom. BR1 183 ED91
Caterham (Wold.) CR3 237 EB124
South Vw Rd, Dart. DA2 188 FK90
Gerrards Cross SL9 112 AX56
Grays RM20 169 FW79
Loughton IG10 85 EM44
Pinner HA5 93 BV51
Southview Rd, Warl. CR6 236 DU119
Southviews, S.Croy. CR2 221 DX109
South Vil, NW1 141 DK65
Southville, SW8 161 DK81
Southville Cl, Epsom KT19 216 CR109
Feltham TW14 175 BS88
Southville Cres, Felt. TW14 175 BS88
Sch Southville Inf & Nurs Sch, Felt. TW14 off Bedfont La 175 BT88
Sch Southville Jun Sch, Felt. TW14 off Bedfont La 175 BT88
Southville Rd, Felt. TW14 175 BS88
Thames Ditton KT7 197 CH101
South Wk, Hayes UB3 off Middleton Rd 135 BR71
Reigate RH2 off Church St 250 DB134
West Wickham BR4 204 EE104
SOUTHWARK, SE1 20 F2
⊖ Southwark 20 E2
Coll Southwark Adult Ed, Nunhead Cen, SE15 off Whorlton Rd 162 DV83
Thomas Calton Cen, SE15 off Alpha St 162 DU82
Southwark Br, EC4 21 H1
SE1 21 H1
Southwark Br Rd, SE1 20 F5
★ Southwark Cath, SE1 21 J1
Coll Southwark Coll, Bermondsey Cen, SE16 22 C5
Camberwell Cen, SE5 off Southampton Way 162 DS80
Grange Cen, SE1 21 M6
Waterloo Cen, SE1 20 E3
Southwark Pk Est, SE16 22 D7
Sch Southwark Pk Prim Sch, SE16 22 D6
Southwark Pk Rd, SE16 21 P7
Southwark Pl, Brom. BR1 off St. Georges Rd 205 EM97
Southwark St, SE1 20 F1
Southwater Cl, E14 13 L7
Beckenham BR3 183 EB94
South Way, N9 100 DW47
N11 off Ringway 99 DJ51
Southway, N20 98 DA47
NW11 120 DB58

★ Place of interest | H Hospital | Sch School | Coll College | Uni University | ⇌ Railway station

Southway, SW20 ... 199 CW98
South Way, Abb.L. WD5 ... 59 BT33
Beaconsfield HP9 ... 110 AG55
Bromley BR2 ... 204 EG101
Southway, Cars. SM5 ... 218 DD110
South Way, Croy. CR0 ... 203 DY104
Southway, Guil. GU2 ... 242 AT134
South Way, Har. HA2 ... 116 CA56
Southway, Hat. AL10 ... 45 CU22
South Way, Purf. RM19 ... 169 FS76
Southway, Wall. SM6 ... 219 DJ105
South Way, Wem. HA9 ... 118 CN64
Southway Ct, Guil. GU2 ... 242 AS134
SOUTH WEALD, Brwd. CM14 ... 108 FS47
South Weald Dr, Wal.Abb. EN9 ... 67 ED33
South Weald Rd, Brwd. CM14 ... 108 FU48
Southwell Av, Nthlt. UB5 ... 136 CA65
Southwell Cl, Grays (Chaff.Hun.) RM16 ... 169 FW78
Southwell Gdns, SW7 ... 17 L7
Southwell Gro Rd, E11 ... 124 EE61
Southwell Rd, SE5 ... 162 DQ83
Croydon CR0 ... 201 DN100
Harrow HA3 ... 117 CK58
South Western Rd, Twick. TW1 ... 177 CG86
Southwest Rd, E11 ... 123 ED60
South Wf Rd, W2 ... 7 N7
Southwick Ms, W2 ... 7 P7
Southwick Pl, W2 ... 8 A8
Southwick St, W2 ... 8 A7
SOUTH WIMBLEDON, SW19 ... 180 DB94
⊖ South Wimbledon ... 180 DB94
Southwold Dr, Bark. IG11 ... 126 EU64
Sch Southwold JMI Sch, E5 off Detmold Rd ... 122 DW61
Southwold Rd, E5 ... 122 DV61
Bexley DA5 ... 187 FB86
Watford WD24 ... 76 BW38
Southwold Spur, Slou. SL3 ... 153 BC75
Southwood Av, N6 ... 121 DH59
Chertsey (Ott.) KT16 ... 211 BC108
Coulsdon CR5 ... 235 DJ115
Kingston upon Thames KT2 ... 198 CQ95
Southwood Cl, Brom. BR1 ... 205 EM98
Worcester Park KT4 ... 199 CX102
Southwood Dr, Surb. KT5 ... 198 CQ101
SOUTH WOODFORD, E18 ... 102 EF54
⊖ South Woodford ... 102 EG54
South Woodford to Barking Relief Rd, E11 ... 124 EJ56
E12 ... 125 EN62
E18 ... 124 EJ56
Barking IG11 ... 125 EN62
Ilford IG1, IG4 ... 125 EN62
Southwood Gdns, Esher KT10 ... 197 CG104
Ilford IG2 ... 125 EP56
H Southwood Hosp, N6 ... 120 DG59
Sch Southwood Inf Sch, Dag. RM9 off Keppel Rd ... 126 EY63
Sch Southwood Jun Sch, Dag. RM9 off Keppel Rd ... 126 EY63
Southwood La, N6 ... 120 DG59
Southwood Lawn Rd, N6 ... 120 DG59
Southwood Rd, SE9 ... 185 EP89
SE28 ... 146 EV74
Southwood Smith St, N1 ... 4 E8
South Worple Av, SW14 ... 158 CS83
South Worple Way, SW14 ... 158 CR83
Soval Ct, Nthwd. HA6 off Maxwell Rd ... 93 BR52
Sovereign Cl, E1 ... 12 D10
W5 ... 137 CJ71
Barnet EN4 ... 80 DF41
Purley CR8 ... 219 DM110
Ruislip HA4 ... 115 BS60
Sovereign Ct, Harl. CM19 off Rosemount ... 51 EP18
West Molesey KT8 ... 196 BZ98
Sovereign Cres, SE16 ... 13 J10
Sovereign Gro, Wem. HA0 ... 117 CK62
Sovereign Ms, E2 ... 5 N9
Barnet EN4 off Bournwell Cl ... 80 DF41
Sovereign Hts, Slou. SL3 off Majors Fm Rd ... 153 BA79
Sovereign Pk, NW10 ... 138 CP70
Sovereign Pl, Har. HA1 ... 117 CF57
Kings Langley WD4 ... 58 BN29
Sovereign Rd, Bark. IG11 ... 146 EW69
Sowerby Cl, SE9 ... 184 EL85
Sowrey Av, Rain. RM13 ... 147 FF65
Soyer Ct, Wok. GU21 off Raglan Rd ... 226 AS118
Space Waye, Felt. TW14 ... 175 BU85
Spackmans Way, Slou. SL1 ... 151 AQ76
Spa Cl, SE25 ... 202 DS95
Spa Dr, Epsom KT18 ... 216 CN114
Spafield St, EC1 ... 10 C3
Spa Grn Est, EC1 ... 10 D1
Spa Hill, SE19 ... 202 DR95
Spalding Cl, Edg. HA8 off Blundell Rd ... 96 CS52
Spalding Rd, NW4 ... 119 CW58
SW17 ... 181 DH92
Spalt Cl, Brwd. (Hutt.) CM13 ... 109 GB47
Spanby Rd, E3 ... 13 P4
Spaniards Cl, NW11 ... 120 DD60
Spaniards End, NW3 ... 120 DC60
Spaniards Rd, NW3 ... 120 DC61
Spanish Pl, W1 ... 8 F7
Spanish Rd, SW18 ... 180 DC85
Spareleaze Hill, Loug. IG10 ... 85 EM43
Sparepenny La, Dart. (Eyns.) DA4 ... 208 FL102
Sparkbridge Rd, Har. HA1 ... 117 CE56
Sparkford Gdns, N11 off Friern Barnet Rd ... 98 DG50
Sparkford Ho, SW11 ... 160 DD81
Sparks Cl, W3 off Joseph Av ... 138 CR72
Dagenham RM8 ... 126 EX61
Hampton TW12 off Victors Dr ... 176 BY93
Spa Rd, SE16 ... 21 N6
Sparrow Cl, Hmptn. TW12 ... 176 BY93
Sparrow Dr, Orp. BR5 ... 205 EQ102
Sch Sparrow Fm Comm Jun Sch, Epsom KT17 off Sparrow Fm Rd ... 217 CV105
Sparrow Fm Dr, Felt. TW14 ... 176 BX87
Sch Sparrow Fm Inf & Nurs Sch, Felt. TW14 off Denham Rd ... 176 BW87
Sch Sparrow Fm Jun Sch, Felt. TW14 off Sparrow Fm Dr ... 176 BW87
Sparrow Fm Rd, Epsom KT17 ... 217 CU105
Sparrow Grn, Dag. RM10 ... 127 FB62
Sparrows Herne, Bushey WD23 ... 94 CB45
Sparrows La, SE9 ... 185 EQ87
Sparrows Mead, Red. RH1 ... 250 DG131
Sparrows Way, Bushey WD23 off Sparrows Herne ... 94 CC46
Sparrowswick Ride, St.Alb. AL3 ... 42 CC15
Sparsholt Rd, N19 ... 121 DM60
Barking IG11 ... 145 ES67
Sparta St, SE10 ... 163 EB81
Sch Spa Spec Sch, SE1 ... 22 A8
★ Speaker's Cor, W2 ... 8 D9
Speaker's Ct, Croy. CR0 off St. James's Rd ... 202 DR102
Spearman St, SE18 ... 165 EN79
Spear Ms, SW5 ... 17 H8
Spearpoint Gdns, Ilf. IG2 ... 125 ET56
Spears Rd, N19 ... 121 DL60
Speart La, Houns. TW5 ... 156 BY80
Spedan Cl, NW3 ... 120 DB62
Speechly Ms, E8 ... 5 P1
Speedbird Way, West Dr. UB7 ... 154 BH80
Speedgate Hill, Long. (Fawk.Grn) DA3 ... 209 FU103
Speed Highwalk, EC2 off Beech St ... 142 DQ71
Speed Ho, EC2 ... 11 J5
Speedwell Cl, Guil. GU4 ... 243 BB131
Hemel Hempstead HP1 off Campion Rd ... 39 BE21
Speedwell Ct, Grays RM17 ... 170 GE80
Speedwell St, SE8 off Comet St ... 163 EA80
Speedy Pl, WC1 ... 9 N2
Speer Rd, T.Ditt. KT7 ... 197 CF99
Speirs Cl, N.Mal. KT3 ... 199 CT100
Spekehill, SE9 ... 185 EM90
Speke Ho, SE5 ... 162 DQ80
Speke Rd, Th.Hth. CR7 ... 202 DR96
Speldhurst Cl, Brom. BR2 ... 204 EF99
Speldhurst Rd, E9 ... 143 DX66
W4 ... 158 CR76
Spellbrook Wk, N1 ... 5 H7
Spelman St, E1 ... 12 A5
Coll Spelthorne Coll, Ashf. TW15 off Church Rd ... 174 BM91
Spelthorne Gro, Sun. TW16 ... 175 BT94
Sch Spelthorne Inf & Nurs Sch, Ashf. TW15 off Chertsey Rd ... 175 BS93
Sch Spelthorne Jun Sch, Ashf. TW15 off Feltham Hill Rd ... 175 BR93
Spelthorne La, Ashf. TW15 ... 195 BQ95
Spence Av, W.Byf. (Byfleet) KT14 ... 212 BL114
Spence Cl, SE16 ... 23 L4
Spencer Av, N13 ... 99 DM51
Hayes UB4 ... 135 BU71
Waltham Cross (Chsht) EN7 ... 66 DS26
Spencer Cl, N3 ... 97 CZ54
NW10 ... 138 CM69
Epsom KT18 ... 232 CS119
Orpington BR6 ... 205 ES103
Uxbridge UB8 ... 134 BJ69
Woking GU21 ... 211 BC113
Woodford Green IG8 ... 102 EJ50
H Spencer Cl Mental Hosp, Epp. CM16 ... 70 EV29
Spencer Ct, NW8 off Marlborough Pl ... 140 DC68
Spencer Dr, N2 ... 120 DC58
Spencer Gdns, SE9 ... 185 EM85
SW14 ... 178 CQ85
Egham (Eng.Grn) TW20 ... 172 AX92
Spencer Gate, St.Alb. AL1 ... 43 CE18
Spencer Hill, SW19 ... 179 CY93
Spencer Hill Rd, SW19 ... 179 CY94
★ Spencer Ho, SW1 ... 19 J2
Sch Spencer JM Sch, St.Alb. AL3 off Watson Av ... 43 CE17
Spencer Ms, SW8 off Lansdowne Way ... 161 DM81
W6 off Greyhound Rd ... 159 CY79
Spencer Pk, SW18 ... 180 DD85
Spencer Pas, E2 off Pritchard's Rd ... 142 DV68
Spencer Pl, N1 ... 4 E5
Croydon CR0 off Gloucester Rd ... 202 DR101
Spencer Ri, NW5 ... 121 DH63
Spencer Rd, E6 ... 144 EK67
E17 ... 101 EC53
N8 ... 121 DM57
N11 ... 99 DH49
N17 ... 100 DU53
SW18 ... 160 DD84
SW20 ... 199 CV95
W3 ... 138 CQ74
W4 ... 158 CQ80
Bromley BR1 ... 184 EE94
Caterham CR3 ... 236 DR121
Cobham KT11 ... 229 BV115
East Molesey KT8 ... 196 CC99
Harrow HA3 ... 95 CE54
Ilford IG3 ... 125 ET60
Isleworth TW7 ... 157 CD81
Mitcham CR4 ... 200 DG97
Mitcham (Bedd.Cor.) CR4 ... 200 DG101
Rainham RM13 ... 147 FD69
Slough SL3 ... 153 AZ76
South Croydon CR2 ... 220 DS106
Twickenham TW2 ... 177 CE90
Wembley HA0 ... 117 CJ61
Spencers Cft, Harl. CM18 ... 52 EV17
Spencer St, EC1 ... 10 E2
Gravesend DA11 ... 191 GG87
Hertford SG13 ... 32 DS08
St. Albans AL3 ... 43 CD20
Southall UB2 ... 156 BX75
Spencer Wk, NW3 ... 120 DD63
SW15 ... 159 CX84
Rickmansworth WD3 ... 74 BJ43
Tilbury RM18 ... 171 GG82
Spencer Way, Hem.H. HP1 ... 40 BG17
Redhill RH1 ... 266 DG139
Spencer Yd, SE3 off Blackheath Village ... 164 EF82
Spenser Av, Wey. KT13 ... 212 BN108
Spenser Cres, Upmin. RM14 ... 128 FQ59
Spenser Gro, N16 ... 122 DS63
Spenser Ms, SE21 off Croxted Rd ... 182 DR88
Spenser Rd, SE24 ... 181 DN85
Spenser St, SW1 ... 19 K5
Spensley Wk, N16 off Clissold Rd ... 122 DR62
Speranza St, SE18 ... 165 ET78
Sperling Rd, N17 ... 100 DS54
Spert St, E14 ... 13 J9
Speyhawk Pl, Pot.B. EN6 ... 64 DB30
Speyside, N14 ... 81 DJ44
Spey St, E14 ... 14 C6
Spey Way, Rom. RM1 ... 105 FE52
Spezia Rd, NW10 ... 139 CU68
Sphere Ind Est, St.Alb. AL1 ... 43 CG21
Spice Quay Hts, SE1 ... 21 P2
Spicer Cl, SW9 ... 161 DP82
Walton-on-Thames KT12 ... 196 BW100
Spicers Fld, Lthd. (Oxshott) KT22 ... 215 CD113
Spicersfield, Wal.Cr. (Chsht) EN7 ... 66 DU27
Spicers La, Harl. CM17 off Wayre St ... 36 EW11
Spicer St, St.Alb. AL3 ... 42 CC20
Spice's Yd, Croy. CR0 ... 220 DQ105
Spielman Rd, Dart. DA1 ... 168 FM84
Spiers Way, Horl. RH6 ... 269 DH150
Spigurnell Rd, N17 ... 100 DR53
Spikes Br Moorings, Hayes UB4 ... 136 BY72
Spikes Br Rd, Sthl. UB1 ... 136 BY72
Spilsby Cl, NW9 off Kenley Av ... 96 CS54
Spilsby Rd, Rom. RM3 ... 106 FK52
Spindle Cl, SE18 ... 164 EL76
Spindles, Til. RM18 ... 171 GG80
Spindlewood Gdns, Croy. CR0 ... 220 DS105
Spindlewoods, Tad. KT20 ... 233 CV122
Spindrift Av, E14 ... 24 A7
Spinel Cl, SE18 ... 165 ET78
Spingate Cl, Horn. RM12 ... 128 FK64
Spinnaker Cl, Bark. IG11 ... 146 EV69
Spinnells Rd, Har. HA2 ... 116 BZ60
Spinners Wk, Wind. SL4 ... 151 AQ81
Spinney, Slou. SL1 ... 131 AP74
Spinney, The, N21 ... 99 DN45
SW16 ... 181 DK90
Barnet EN5 ... 80 DB40
Beaconsfield HP9 ... 111 AK55
Berkhamsted HP4 ... 38 AT20
Brentwood (Hutt.) CM13 ... 109 GC44
Broxbourne EN10 ... 49 DZ19
Chesham HP5 ... 54 AR29
Epsom KT18 ... 233 CV119
Hertford SG13 ... 32 DT09
Horley RH6 ... 268 DG146
Leatherhead (Bkhm) KT23 ... 230 CB124
Leatherhead (Oxshott) KT22 ... 214 CC112
Potters Bar EN6 ... 64 DD31
Purley CR8 ... 219 DP111
Sidcup DA14 ... 186 EY92
Stanmore HA7 ... 96 CL49
Sunbury-on-Thames TW16 ... 195 BU95
Sutton SM3 ... 217 CW105
Swanley BR8 ... 207 FE96
Watford WD17 ... 75 BU39
Welwyn Garden City AL7 ... 29 CY10
Wembley HA0 ... 117 CG62
Woking (Send) GU23 ... 244 BJ127
Spinney Cl, Beck. BR3 ... 203 EB98
Cobham KT11 ... 214 CA111
New Malden KT3 ... 198 CS99
Rainham RM13 ... 147 FE68
West Drayton UB7 off Yew Av ... 134 BL73
Worcester Park KT4 ... 199 CT104
Sch Spinney Co Inf Sch, The, Harl. CM20 off Cooks Spinney ... 36 EU14
Sch Spinney Co Jun Sch, The, Harl. CM20 off Cooks Spinney ... 36 EU14
Spinneycroft, Lthd. KT22 ... 231 CD115
Spinney Dr, Felt. TW14 ... 175 BQ87
Spinney Gdns, SE19 ... 182 DT92
Dagenham RM9 ... 126 EY64
Spinney Hill, Add. KT15 ... 211 BE106
Spinney Oak, Brom. BR1 ... 204 EL96
Chertsey (Ott.) KT16 ... 211 BD107
Spinneys, The, Brom. BR1 ... 205 EM96
Spinneys Dr, St.Alb. AL3 ... 42 CB22
Spinney St, Hert. SG13 ... 32 DU09
Spinney Way, Sev. (Cudham) TN14 ... 223 ER111
Spinning Wk, The, Guil. (Shere) GU5 ... 260 BN139
Spinning Wheel Mead, Harl. CM18 ... 52 EU18
Spire Cl, Grav. DA12 ... 191 GH88
Spire Grn Cen, Harl. CM19 ... 50 EL16
Spire Ho, W2 off Lancaster Gate ... 140 DC73
Spires, The, Dart. DA1 ... 188 FK89
Spires Shop Cen, The, Barn. EN5 ... 79 CY41
Spirit Quay, E1 ... 22 B1
SPITALBROOK, Hodd. EN11 ... 49 EA19
★ Spitalfields Comm Fm, E1 ... 12 A4
Spital Heath, Dor. RH4 ... 263 CJ135
Spital La, Brwd. CM14 ... 108 FT48
Spital Sq, E1 ... 11 M5
Spital St, E1 ... 12 A5
Dartford DA1 ... 188 FK86
Spital Yd, E1 ... 11 M5
Spitfire Cl, Slou. SL3 off Common Rd ... 153 BA77
Spitfire Est, Houns. TW5 ... 156 BW78
Spitfire Rd, Wall. SM6 ... 219 DL108
Spitfire Way, Houns. TW5 ... 156 BW78
Spode Wk, NW6 off Lymington Rd ... 140 DB65
Spondon Rd, N15 ... 122 DU56
Spook Hill, Dor. (N.Holm.) RH5 ... 263 CH141
Spoonbill Way, Hayes UB4 off Cygnet Way ... 136 BX71
Spooners Dr, St.Alb. (Park St) AL2 ... 60 CC27
Spooners Ms, W3 off Churchfield Rd ... 138 CR74
Spooner Wk, Wall. SM6 ... 219 DK106
Sporle Ct, SW11 ... 160 DD83
Sportsbank St, SE6 ... 183 EC87
Spotted Dog Path, E7 off Upton La ... 144 EG65
Spottons Gro, N17 off Gospatrick Rd ... 100 DQ53
Spout Hill, Croy. CR0 ... 221 EA106
Spout La, Eden. (Crock.H.) TN8 ... 255 EQ134
Staines TW19 ... 174 BG85
Spout La N, Stai. TW19 ... 154 BH84
Spratt Hall Rd, E11 ... 124 EG58
Spratts All, Cher. (Ott.) KT16 ... 211 BE107
Spratts La, Cher. (Ott.) KT16 ... 211 BE107
Spray La, Twick. TW2 ... 177 CE86
Spray St, SE18 ... 165 EP77
Spread Eagle Wk Shop Cen, Epsom KT19 off High St ... 216 CR113
Spreighton Rd, W.Mol. KT8 ... 196 CB98
Spriggs Oak, Epp. CM16 off Palmers Hill ... 70 EU29
Sprimont Pl, SW3 ... 18 C9
Springall St, SE15 ... 162 DV80
Springate Fld, Slou. SL3 ... 152 AY75
Spring Av, Egh. TW20 ... 172 AY93
Springbank, N21 ... 81 DM44
Springbank Av, Horn. RM12 ... 128 FJ64
Springbank Rd, SE13 ... 183 ED86
Springbank Wk, NW1 off St. Paul's Cres ... 141 DK66
Spring Bottom La, Red. (Bletch.) RH1 ... 251 DN127
Springbourne Ct, Beck. BR3 ... 203 EC95
Spring Br Ms, W5 off Spring Br Rd ... 137 CK73
Spring Br Rd, W5 ... 137 CK73
Spring Cl, Barn. EN5 ... 79 CX43
Borehamwood WD6 ... 78 CN39
Chesham (Latimer) HP5 ... 72 AX36
Dagenham RM8 ... 126 EX60
Godalming GU7 ... 258 AS143
Uxbridge (Hare.) UB9 ... 92 BK53
Springclose La, Sutt. SM3 ... 217 CY107
Springcopse Rd, Reig. RH2 ... 266 DC135
Spring Cotts, Surb. KT6 off St. Leonard's Rd ... 197 CK99
Spring Ct, Guil. GU2 off Dayspring ... 242 AV130
Sidcup DA15 off Station Rd ... 186 EU90
Spring Ct Rd, Enf. EN2 ... 81 DN38
Springcroft Av, N2 ... 120 DF56
Spring Cfts, Bushey WD23 ... 76 CA43
Springdale Ms, N16 off Springdale Rd ... 122 DR63
Springdale Rd, N16 ... 122 DR63
Spring Dr, Maid. SL6 ... 130 AE65
Pinner HA5 off Eastcote Rd ... 115 BU58
Spring Fm Cl, Rain. RM13 ... 148 FK69
Springfield, E5 ... 122 DV60
Bushey (Bushey Hth) WD23 ... 95 CD46
Epping CM16 ... 69 ET32
Oxted RH8 ... 253 ED130
Springfield Av, N10 ... 121 DJ55
SW20 ... 199 CZ97
Brentwood (Hutt.) CM13 ... 109 GE45
Hampton TW12 ... 176 CB93
Swanley BR8 ... 207 FF98
Springfield Cl, N12 ... 98 DB50
Chesham HP5 ... 54 AQ33
Potters Bar EN6 ... 64 DD31
Rickmansworth (Crox.Grn) WD3 ... 75 BP43
Stanmore HA7 ... 95 CG48
Windsor SL4 ... 151 AP82
Woking (Knap.) GU21 ... 226 AS118
Sch Springfield Co Prim Sch, Sun. TW16 off Nursery Rd ... 195 BT96
Springfield Ct, Wall. SM6 off Springfield Rd ... 219 DH106
Springfield Dr, Ilf. IG2 ... 125 EQ58
Leatherhead KT22 ... 231 CE119
Springfield Gdns, E5 ... 122 DV60
NW9 ... 118 CR57
Bromley BR1 ... 205 EM98
Ruislip HA4 ... 115 BV60
Upminster RM14 ... 128 FQ62
West Wickham BR4 ... 203 EB103
Woodford Green IG8 ... 102 EJ52
Springfield Gro, SE7 ... 164 EJ79
Sunbury-on-Thames TW16 ... 195 BT95
Springfield La, NW6 ... 140 DB67
Weybridge KT13 ... 213 BP105
Springfield Meadows, Wey. KT13 ... 213 BP105
Springfield Mt, NW9 ... 118 CS57
Springfield Pl, N.Mal. KT3 ... 198 CQ98
Springfield Ri, SE26 ... 182 DV90
Springfield Rd, E4 ... 102 EE46
E6 ... 145 EM66
E15 ... 15 H1
E17 ... 123 DZ58
N11 ... 99 DH50
N15 ... 122 DU56
NW8 ... 140 DC67
SE26 ... 182 DV92
SW19 ... 179 CZ92
W7 ... 137 CE74
Ashford TW15 ... 174 BM92
Berkhamsted HP4 ... 38 AT16
Bexleyheath DA7 ... 167 FB83
Bromley BR1 ... 205 EM98
Chesham HP5 ... 54 AQ33
Dorking (Westc.) RH4 ... 262 CB137
Epsom KT17 ... 217 CW110
Grays RM16 ... 170 GD75
Guildford GU1 ... 258 AY135
Harrow HA1 ... 117 CE58
Hayes UB4 ... 136 BW74
Hemel Hempstead HP2 ... 40 BM19
Kingston upon Thames KT1 ... 198 CL97
St. Albans AL1 ... 43 CG21
St. Albans (Smallford) AL4 ... 44 CP20
Slough SL3 ... 153 BB80
Teddington TW11 ... 177 CG92
Thornton Heath CR7 ... 202 DQ95
Twickenham TW2 ... 176 CA88
Wallington SM6 ... 219 DH106
Waltham Cross (Chsht) EN8 ... 67 DY32
Watford WD25 off Haines Way ... 59 BV33
Welling DA16 ... 166 EV83
Windsor SL4 ... 151 AP82
Springfields, Brox. EN10 ... 49 DZ19
Waltham Abbey EN9 ... 68 EE34
Welwyn Garden City AL8 ... 29 CV11
Springfields Cl, Cher. KT16 ... 194 BH102
H Springfield Uni Hosp, SW17 ... 180 DE89
Springfield Wk, NW6 ... 140 DB67
Orpington BR6 off Place Fm Av ... 205 ER102
Spring Gdns, N5 ... 4 G2
SW1 ... 19 M1
Dorking RH4 ... 263 CG136
High Wycombe (Woob.Grn) HP10 off Watery La ... 110 AE55
Hornchurch RM12 ... 127 FH63
Orpington BR6 ... 224 EV107
Romford RM7 ... 127 FC57
Wallington SM6 ... 219 DJ106
Watford WD25 ... 76 BW35
West Molesey KT8 ... 196 CC99
Westerham (Bigg.H.) TN16 ... 238 EJ118
Spring Gdns, Wdf.Grn. IG8 ... 102 EJ52
Spring Gdns Ind Est, Rom. RM7 ... 127 FC57
Spring Glen, Hat. AL10 ... 45 CT19
SPRING GROVE, Islw. TW7 ... 157 CF81
Spring Gro, SE19 off Alma Pl ... 182 DT94
W4 ... 158 CN78
Godalming GU7 ... 258 AS143
Gravesend DA12 ... 191 GH88
Hampton TW12 off Plevna Rd ... 196 CB95
Leatherhead (Fetch.) KT22 ... 230 CB123
Loughton IG10 ... 84 EK44
Mitcham CR4 ... 200 DG95
Spring Gro Cres, Houns. TW3 ... 156 CC81
Sch Spring Gro Prim Sch, Islw. TW7 off Star Rd ... 157 CD82
Spring Gro Rd, Houns. TW3 ... 156 CB81
Isleworth TW7 ... 156 CB81
Richmond TW10 ... 178 CM85
Springhall La, Saw. CM21 ... 36 EY07
Sch Springhallow Sch, W13 off Compton Cl ... 137 CG72
Springhall Rd, Saw. CM21 ... 36 EY05
Springhaven Cl, Guil. GU1 ... 243 BA134
Springhead Enterprise Pk, Grav. DA11 ... 190 GC88
Springhead Rd, Erith DA8 ... 167 FF79
Gravesend (Nthflt) DA11 ... 190 GC87
Spring Hill, E5 ... 122 DU59
SE26 ... 182 DW91
Springhill Cl, SE5 ... 162 DR83
Spring Hills, Harl. CM20 ... 35 EN14
Springholm Cl, West. (Bigg.H.) TN16 ... 238 EJ118
Springhurst Cl, Croy. CR0 ... 221 DZ105
Spring Lake, Stan. HA7 ... 95 CH49
Spring La, E5 ... 122 DV60
N10 ... 120 DG55
SE25 ... 202 DV100
Hemel Hempstead HP1 ... 39 BF18
Oxted RH8 ... 253 ED131
Slough SL1 ... 131 AM74
Slough (Farn.Com.) SL2 ... 131 AP66
Springle La, Hert. (Hailey) SG13 ... 33 DZ12
Sch Springmead JMI Sch, Welw.G.C. AL7 off Hillyfields ... 30 DC08
Spring Ms, W1 ... 8 D5
Epsom KT17 off Old Schs La ... 217 CT109
Richmond TW9 off Rosedale Rd ... 158 CL84
Spring Pk Av, Croy. CR0 ... 203 DX103
Spring Pk Dr, N4 ... 122 DQ60
Springpark Dr, Beck. BR3 ... 203 EC97
Sch Spring Pk Inf Sch, Croy. CR0 off Bridle Rd ... 203 EA104
Sch Spring Pk Jun Sch, Croy. CR0 off Bridle Rd ... 203 EA104
Spring Pk Rd, Croy. CR0 ... 203 DX103
Spring Pas, SW15 off Embankment ... 159 CX83
Spring Path, NW3 ... 120 DD64
Spring Pl, N3 off Windermere Av ... 98 DA54
NW5 ... 121 DH64
Springpond Rd, Dag. RM9 ... 126 EY64
Springrice Rd, SE13 ... 183 EC86
Spring Ri, Egh. TW20 ... 172 AY93
Spring Rd, Felt. TW13 ... 175 BT90
Springs, The, Brox. EN10 ... 67 DY25
Hertford SG13 ... 32 DT08
Springshaw Cl, Sev. TN13 ... 256 FD123
Spring Shaw Rd, Orp. BR5 ... 206 EU95
Springside Ct, Guil. GU1 ... 242 AW133
Spring St, W2 ... 7 N8
Epsom KT17 ... 217 CT109
Spring Ter, Rich. TW9 ... 178 CL85
Springtide Cl, SE15 off Staffordshire St ... 162 DU81
Spring Vale, Bexh. DA7 ... 167 FB84
Greenhithe DA9 ... 189 FW86
Springvale Av, Brent. TW8 ... 157 CK78
Springvale Cl, Lthd. KT23 off Leatherhead Rd ... 246 CB126
Spring Vale Cl, Swan. BR8 ... 207 FF95
Springvale Est, W14 ... 16 C6
Spring Vale N, Dart. DA1 ... 188 FK87
Springvale Retail Pk, Orp. BR5 ... 206 EW97
Spring Vale S, Dart. DA1 ... 188 FK87
Springvale Ter, W14 ... 16 B6
Springvale Way, Orp. BR5 ... 206 EW97
Spring Vw Rd, Ware SG12 ... 32 DW07
Spring Vil Rd, Edg. HA8 ... 96 CN52
Spring Wk, E1 ... 12 A5
Broxbourne EN10 ... 48 DW22
Horley RH6 off Court Lo Rd ... 268 DF148
Springwater Cl, SE18 ... 165 EN81
Springway, Har. HA1 ... 117 CD59
Spring Way, Hem.H. HP2 ... 41 BP18
Springwell Av, NW10 ... 139 CT67
Rickmansworth (Mill End) WD3 ... 92 BG47
Springwell Cl, SW16 off Etherstone Rd ... 181 DN91
Springwell Ct, Houns. TW4 ... 156 BX82
Springwell Hill, Uxb. (Hare.) UB9 ... 92 BH51
Sch Springwell Inf & Nurs Sch, Houns. TW5 off Speart La ... 156 BY80
Sch Springwell Jun Sch, Houns. TW5 off Vicarage Fm Rd ... 156 BY80
Springwell La, Rick. WD3 ... 92 BG49
Uxbridge (Hare.) UB9 ... 92 BG49
Springwell Rd, SW16 ... 181 DN91
Hounslow TW4, TW5 ... 156 BX81
Springwood, Wal.Cr. (Chsht) EN7 ... 66 DU26
Springwood Cl, Uxb. (Hare.) UB9 ... 92 BK53
Springwood Cres, Edg. HA8 ... 96 CP47
Springwood Pl, Wey. KT13 ... 213 BP108
Spring Wds, Vir.W. GU25 ... 192 AV98
Springwood Wk, St.Alb. AL4 ... 43 CK17
Springwood Way, Rom. RM1 ... 127 FG57
Sprowston Ms, E7 ... 144 EG65
Sprowston Rd, E7 ... 124 EG64
Spruce Cl, Red. RH1 ... 250 DF133
Spruce Ct, W5 off Elderberry Rd ... 158 CL76

⊖ London Underground station DLR Docklands Light Railway station Tra Tramlink station Riv Pedestrian ferry landing stage

Sprucedale Cl, Swan. BR8 . 207 FE96
Sprucedale Gdns, Croy.
CR0 . 221 DX105
Wallington SM6 . 219 DK109
Spruce Hill, Harl. CM18 . 51 ES20
Spruce Hills Rd, E17 . 101 EC54
Spruce Pk, Brom. BR2
off Cumberland Rd . 204 EF98
Spruce Rd, West. (Bigg.H.)
TN16 . 238 EK116
Spruce Way, St.Alb.
(Park St) AL2 . 60 CB27
Sprules Rd, SE4 . 163 DY82
Spur, The, Slou. SL1 . 131 AK71
Waltham Cross (Chsht)
EN8 off Welsummer Way . 67 DX28
Spur Cl, Abb.L. WD5 . 59 BR33
Romford (Abridge) RM4 . 86 EV41
Spurfield, W.Mol. KT8 . 196 CB97
Spurgate, Brwd. (Hutt.)
CM13 . 109 GA47
Spurgeon Av, SE19 . 202 DR95
Spurgeon Rd, SE19 . 202 DR95
Coll Spurgeons Coll (Theological), SE25
off South Norwood Hill . 202 DS96
Spurgeon St, SE1 . 21 J6
Spurling Rd, SE22 . 162 DT84
Dagenham RM9 . 146 EZ65
Spurrell Av, Bex. DA5 . 187 FD91
Spur Rd, N15 off Philip La . 122 DR56
SE1 . 20 C3
SW1 . 19 J4
Barking IG11 . 145 EQ68
Edgware HA8 . 96 CL49
Feltham TW14 . 175 BV85
Isleworth TW7 . 157 CH80
Orpington BR6 . 206 EU103
Spur Rd Est, Edg. HA8 . 96 CM49
Spurstowe Rd, E8
off Marcon Pl . 142 DV65
Spurstowe Ter, E8 . 122 DV64
Squadrons App, Horn.
RM12 . 148 FJ65
Square, The, W6 . 159 CW78
Berkhamsted (Pott.End)
HP4 . 39 BB16
Broxbourne EN10
off High Rd Wormley . 49 DY23
Carshalton SM5 . 218 DG106
Guildford GU2
off Orchard Rd . 258 AT136
Guildford (Shere) GU5 . 260 BN139
Hayes UB3 . 135 BR74
Ilford IG1 . 125 EN59
Richmond TW9 . 177 CK85
Sawbridgeworth CM21 . 36 EY05
Sevenoaks TN13
off Amherst Hill . 256 FE122
Swanley BR8 . 207 FD97
Watford WD24
off The Harebreaks . 75 BV37
West Drayton UB7 . 154 BH81
Westerham (Tats.) TN16 . 238 EJ120
Weybridge KT13 . 213 BQ105
Woking (Wisley) GU23 . 228 BL116
Woodford Green IG8 . 102 EG50
Square Rigger Row, SW11
off York Pl . 160 DC83
Square St, Harl. CM17
off London Rd . 36 EW14
Squarey St, SW17 . 180 DC90
★ Squerryes Ct, West.
TN16 . 255 EQ128
Squerryes Mede, West.
TN16 . 255 EQ127
Squire Gdns, NW8 . 7 N2
Squires, The, Rom. RM7 . 127 FC58
Squires Br Rd, Shep. TW17 . 194 BM98
Squires Ct, SW19 . 180 DA91
Chertsey KT16
off Springfields Cl . 194 BH102
Squires Fld, Swan. BR8 . 207 FF95
Squires La, N3 . 98 DB54
Squires Mt, NW3
off East Heath Rd . 120 DD62
Squires Rd, Shep. TW17 . 194 BM98
Squire's Wk, Ashf. TW15 . 175 BR94
Squires Way, Dart. DA2 . 187 FD91
Squires Wd Dr, Chis. BR7 . 184 EL94
Squirrel Chase, Hem.H. HP1 . 39 BE19
Squirrel Cl, Houns. TW4 . 156 BW82
Squirrel Keep, W.Byf. KT14 . 212 BH112
Squirrel Ms, W13 . 137 CG73
Squirrels, The, SE13
off Belmont Hill . 163 ED83
Bushey WD23 . 77 CD44
Hertford SG13 . 32 DU09
Pinner HA5 . 116 BZ55
Welwyn Garden City AL7 . 30 DC10
Squirrels Chase, Grays
(Orsett) RM16
off Hornsby La . 171 GG75
Squirrels Cl, N12
off Woodside Av . 98 DC49
Uxbridge UB10 . 134 BN66
Squirrels Grn, Lthd. (Bkhm)
KT23 . 230 CA123
Worcester Park KT4 . 199 CT102
Squirrels Heath Av, Rom.
RM2 . 127 FH55
Sch Squirrels Heath Jun & Inf Sch, Rom. RM2
off Salisbury Rd . 127 FH57
Squirrels Heath La, Horn.
RM11 . 128 FJ56
Romford RM2 . 128 FJ56
Squirrels Heath Rd, Rom.
RM3 . 128 FL55
Squirrels La, Buck.H. IG9 . 102 EK48
Squirrels Trd Est, The, Hayes
UB3 . 155 BU76
Squirrels Way, Epsom KT18 . 232 CR115
Squirrel Wd, W.Byf. KT14 . 212 BH112
Squirries St, E2 . 12 B1
Stable Cl, Epsom KT18
off Beaconsfield Rd . 232 CS119
Northolt UB5 . 136 CA68
Stable La, Beac. (Seer Grn)
HP9 . 89 AQ51
Stable Ms, Twick. TW1 . 177 CF88
Stables, The, Buck.H. IG9 . 102 EJ45
Cobham KT11 . 214 BZ114
Guildford GU1
off Old Fm Rd . 242 AX131
Swanley BR8 . 207 FH95
Stables End, Orp. BR6 . 205 EQ104
Stables Ms, SE27 . 182 DQ92
Stables Way, SE11 . 20 C9
Stable Wk, N1
off Wharfdale Rd . 141 DL68
N2 off Old Fm Rd . 98 DD53
Stable Way, W10
off Latimer Rd . 139 CW72
Stable Yd, SW1 . 19 J3
SW9 off Broomgrove Rd . 161 DM82
SW15 off Danemere St . 159 CW83
Stable Yd Rd, SW1 . 19 J2
Stacey Av, N18 . 100 DW49
Stacey Cl, E10
off Halford Rd . 123 ED57
Gravesend DA12 . 191 GL92
Stacey St, N7 . 121 DN62
WC2 . 9 M8
Stackfield, Harl. CM20 . 36 EU12
Stackhouse St, SW3 . 18 C5
Stacklands, Welw.G.C. AL8 . 29 CV11
Stack Rd, Dart. (Hort.Kir.)
DA4 . 209 FR97
Stacy Path, SE5 off Harris St . 162 DS80
Stadium Business Cen, Wem. HA9 . 118 CP62
Stadium Retail Pk, Wem.
HA9 off Wembley Pk Dr . 118 CN62
Stadium Rd, NW2 . 119 CV59
SE18 . 164 EL80
Stadium Rd E, NW2 . 119 CW59
Stadium St, SW10 . 160 DC80
Stadium Way, Dart. DA1 . 187 FE85
Harlow CM19 . 35 EM14
Wembley HA9 . 118 CM63
Staffa Rd, E10 . 123 DY60
Stafford Av, Horn. RM11 . 128 FK55
Slough SL2 . 131 AQ70
Stafford Cl, E17 . 123 DZ58
N14 . 81 DJ43
NW6 . 6 G2
Caterham CR3 . 236 DT123
Grays (Chaff.Hun.) RM16 . 169 FW77
Greenhithe DA9 . 189 FT85
Maidenhead (Taplow) SL6 . 130 AH72
Sutton SM3 . 217 CY107
Waltham Cross (Chsht)
EN8 . 66 DV29
Stafford Ct, W8 . 16 G5
Stafford Cross, Croy. CR0 . 219 DM106
Stafford Dr, Brox. EN10 . 49 EA20
Stafford Gdns, Croy. CR0 . 219 DM106
Stafford Pl, SW1 . 19 J5
Richmond TW10 . 178 CM87
Stafford Rd, E3 . 143 DZ68
E7 . 144 EJ66
NW6 . 6 G1
Caterham CR3 . 236 DT122
Croydon CR0 . 219 DN105
Harrow HA3 . 94 CC52
New Malden KT3 . 198 CQ97
Ruislip HA4 . 115 BT63
Sidcup DA14 . 185 ES91
Wallington SM6 . 219 DJ107
Staffords, Harl. CM17 . 36 EY11
Staffordshire St, SE15 . 162 DU81
Staffords Pl, Horl. RH6 . 269 DH150
Stafford Sq, Wey. KT13
off Rosslyn Pk . 213 BR105
Stafford St, W1 . 19 J1
Stafford Ter, W8 . 16 G5
Stafford Way, Sev. TN13 . 257 FJ127
Staff St, EC1 . 11 K2
Stagbury Av, Couls. CR5 . 234 DE118
Stagbury Cl, Couls. CR5 . 234 DE119
Stag Cl, Edg. HA8 . 96 CP54
Staggart Grn, Chig. IG7 . 103 ET51
Stagg Hill, Barn. EN4 . 80 DD35
Potters Bar EN6 . 80 DD35
Stag Grn Av, Hat. AL9 . 45 CW16
STAG HILL, Guil. GU2 . 258 AU135
Stag Hill, Guil. GU2 . 258 AU135
Stag La, NW9 . 118 CQ55
SW15 . 179 CT89
Berkhamsted HP4 . 38 AU18
Buckhurst Hill IG9 . 102 EH47
Edgware HA8 . 96 CP54
Rickmansworth (Chorl.) WD3 . 73 BC44
Sch Stag La First Sch,
Edg. HA8 off Collier Dr . 96 CN54
Sch Stag La Mid Sch,
Edg. HA8 off Collier Dr . 96 CN54
Stag Leys, Ashtd. KT21 . 232 CL120
Stag Leys Cl, Bans. SM7 . 234 DD115
Stag Pl, SW1 . 19 J5
Stag Ride, SW19 . 179 CT90
Stags Way, Islw. TW7 . 157 CF79
Stainash Cres, Stai. TW18 . 174 BH92
Stainash Par, Stai. TW18
off Kingston Rd . 174 BH92
Stainbank Rd, Mitch. CR4 . 201 DH97
Stainby Cl, West Dr. UB7 . 154 BL76
Stainby Rd, N15 . 122 DT56
Stainer Ho, SE3 off Ryan Cl . 164 EJ84
Stainer Rd, Borwd. WD6 . 77 CK39
Stainer St, SE1 . 21 K2
STAINES, TW18 & TW19 . 174 BG91
⇌ Staines . 174 BG92
Staines Av, Sutt. SM3 . 199 CX103
Staines Br, Stai. TW18 . 173 BE92
Staines Bypass, Ashf. TW15 . 174 BH91
Staines TW18, TW19 . 174 BH91
Staines Grn, Hert. SG14 . 31 DK11
Staines La, Cher. KT16 . 193 BF99
Staines La Cl, Cher. KT16 . 193 BF100
Sch Staines Prep Sch, Stai.
TW18 off Gresham Rd . 174 BG92
Staines Rd, Cher. KT16 . 193 BF97
Feltham TW14 . 175 BR87
Hounslow TW3, TW4 . 156 CB83
Ilford IG1 . 125 EQ63
Staines TW18 . 194 BH95
Staines (Wrays.) TW19 . 172 AY87
Twickenham TW2 . 176 CA90
Staines Rd E, Sun. TW16 . 175 BU94
Staines Rd W, Ashf. TW15 . 175 BP93
Sunbury-on-Thames
TW16 . 175 BP93
Staines Wk, Sid. DA14
off Evry Rd . 186 EW93
Stainford Cl, Ashf. TW15 . 175 BR92
Stainforth Rd, E17 . 123 EA56
Ilford IG2 . 125 ER59
Staining La, EC2 . 11 H7
Stainmore Cl, Chis. BR7 . 205 ER95
Stainsbury St, E2
off Royston St . 142 DW68
Stainsby Pl, E14 . 13 N7
Stainsby Rd, E14 . 13 N7
Stains Cl, Wal.Cr. (Chsht)
EN8 . 67 DY28
Stainton Rd, SE6 . 183 ED86
Enfield EN3 . 82 DW39
Stainton Wk, Wok. GU21
off Inglewood . 226 AW118
Stairfoot La, Sev.
(Chipstead) TN13 . 256 FC122
Staithes Way, Tad. KT20 . 233 CV120
Stakescorner Rd, Guil.
(Littleton) GU3 . 258 AU142
Stalbridge St, NW1 . 8 B5
Stalham St, SE16 . 22 D6
Stalham Way, Ilf. IG6 . 103 EP53
Stalisfield Pl, Orp. BR6
off Mill La . 223 EN110
Stambourne Way, SE19 . 182 DS94
West Wickham BR4 . 203 EC104
⊖ Stamford Brook . 159 CT77
Stamford Brook Av, W6 . 159 CT76
Stamford Brook Gdns, W6
off Stamford Brook Rd . 159 CT76
Stamford Brook Rd, W6 . 159 CT76
Stamford Cl, N15 . 122 DU56
Harrow HA3 . 95 CE52
Potters Bar EN6 . 64 DD32
Southall UB1 . 136 CA73
Stamford Cotts, SW10
off Billing St . 160 DB80
Stamford Ct, W6
off Goldhawk Rd . 159 CT77
Stamford Dr, Brom. BR2 . 204 EF98
Stamford Gdns, Dag. RM9 . 146 EW66
Sch Stamford Grn Prim Sch,
Epsom KT19
off Christ Ch Mt . 216 CP112
Stamford Grn Rd, Epsom
KT18 . 216 CP113
Stamford Gro E, N16
off Oldhill St . 122 DU60
Stamford Gro W, N16
off Oldhill St . 122 DU60
STAMFORD HILL, N16 . 122 DS60
⇌ Stamford Hill . 122 DS59
Stamford Hill, N16 . 122 DT61
Stamford Hill Est, N16 . 122 DT60
Sch Stamford Hill Prim Sch,
N15 off Berkeley Rd . 122 DR58
H Stamford Hosp, W6 . 159 CU77
Stamford Rd, E6 . 144 EL67
N1 . 5 M5
N15 . 122 DU57
Dagenham RM9 . 146 EV67
Walton-on-Thames KT12
off Kenilworth Dr . 196 BX104
Watford WD17 . 75 BV40
Stamford St, SE1 . 20 C2
Stamp Pl, E2 . 11 N1
Stanard Cl, N16 . 122 DS59
STANBOROUGH, Welw.G.C.
AL8 . 29 CT12
Stanborough Av, Borwd.
WD6 . 78 CN37
Stanborough Cl, Borwd.
WD6 . 78 CN38
Hampton TW12 . 176 BZ93
Welwyn Garden City AL8 . 29 CW10
Stanborough Grn, Welw.G.C.
AL8 . 29 CW11
Stanborough La Cycle Path,
Welw.G.C. AL8 . 29 CV12
Stanborough Ms, Welw.G.C.
AL8 . 29 CX11
Stanborough Pk, Wat. WD25 . 75 BV35
Stanborough Pas, E8 . 5 N3
Sch Stanborough Prim Sch,
Wat. WD25
off Appletree Wk . 76 BW35
Stanborough Rd, Houns.
TW3 . 157 CD83
Welwyn Garden City AL8 . 29 CV12
Sch Stanborough Sch, Wat.
WD25 off Stanborough Pk . 75 BV35
Welwyn Garden City
AL8 off Lemsford La . 29 CV11
Stanbridge Pl, N21 . 99 DP47
Stanbridge Rd, SW15 . 159 CW83
Stanbrook Rd, SE2 . 166 EV75
Gravesend DA11 . 191 GF88
Sch Stanburn First Sch, Stan.
HA7 off Abercorn Rd . 95 CJ52
Sch Stanburn Mid Sch, Stan.
HA7 off Abercorn Rd . 95 CJ52
Stanbury Av, Wat. WD17 . 75 BS37
Stanbury Rd, SE15 . 162 DV81
Stancroft, NW9 . 118 CS56
Standale Gro, Ruis. HA4 . 115 BQ57
Standard Ind Est, E16 . 165 EM75
Standard Pl, EC2 . 11 M2
Standard Rd, NW10 . 138 CQ70
Belvedere DA17 . 166 FA78
Bexleyheath DA6 . 166 EY84
Enfield EN3 . 83 DY38
Hounslow TW4 . 156 BY83
Orpington BR6 . 223 EN110
Standen Av, Horn. RM12 . 128 FK62
Standen Rd, SW18 . 179 CZ87
Standfield, Abb.L. WD5 . 59 BS31
Standfield Gdns, Dag. RM10
off Standfield Rd . 146 FA65
Standfield Rd, Dag. RM10 . 126 FA64
Standingford, Harl. CM19 . 51 EP20
Standish Ho, SE3
off Elford Cl . 164 EJ84
Standish Rd, W6 . 159 CU77
Standlake Pt, SE23 . 183 DX90
Standring Ri, Hem.H. HP3 . 40 BH23
Stane Cl, SW19
off Hayward Cl . 200 DB95
Stane St, Dor. (Ockley) RH5 . 247 CK127
Leatherhead KT22 . 231 CL126
Stane Way, SE18 . 164 EK80
Epsom KT17 . 217 CU110
Stanfield Rd, E3 . 143 DY68
Stanford Cl, Hmptn. TW12 . 176 BZ93
Romford RM7 . 127 FB58
Ruislip HA4 . 115 BQ58
Woodford Green IG8 . 102 EL50
Stanford Ct, SW6
off Bagley's La . 160 DB81
Waltham Abbey EN9 . 68 EG33
Stanford Gdns, S.Ock.
(Aveley) RM15 . 149 FR74
Stanford Ho, Bark. IG11 . 146 EV68
Stanford Pl, SE17 . 21 L8
Stanford Rd, N11 . 98 DF50
SW16 . 201 DK96
W8 . 17 K5
Grays RM16 . 170 GD76
Stanford St, SW1 . 19 L8
Stanford Way, SW16 . 201 DK96
Stangate Cres, Borwd. WD6 . 78 CS43
Stangate Gdns, Stan. HA7 . 95 CH49
Stanger Rd, SE25 . 202 DU98
Stanham Pl, Dart. DA1
off Crayford Way . 167 FG84
Stanham Rd, Dart. DA1 . 188 FJ85
Stanhope Av, N3 . 119 CZ55
Bromley BR2 . 204 EF102
Harrow HA3 . 95 CD53
Stanhope Cl, SE16 . 23 H3
Stanhope Gdns, N4 . 121 DP58
N6 . 121 DH58
NW7 . 97 CT50
Stanhope Gdns, SW7 . 17 M7
Dagenham RM8 . 126 EZ62
Ilford IG1 . 125 EM60
Stanhope Gate, W1 . 18 F1
Stanhope Gro, Beck. BR3 . 203 DZ99
Stanhope Heath, Stai.
(Stanw.) TW19 . 174 BJ86
Stanhope Ms E, SW7 . 17 M7
Stanhope Ms S, SW7 . 17 M8
Stanhope Ms W, SW7 . 17 M7
Stanhope Par, NW1 . 9 J1
Stanhope Pk Rd, Grnf. UB6 . 136 CC70
Stanhope Pl, W2 . 8 C8
Sch Stanhope Prim Sch,
Grnf. UB6
off Mansell Rd . 136 CC70
Stanhope Rd, E17 . 123 EB57
N6 . 121 DJ58
N12 . 98 DC50
Barnet EN5 . 79 CW44
Bexleyheath DA7 . 166 EY82
Carshalton SM5 . 218 DG108
Croydon CR0 . 202 DS104
Dagenham RM8 . 126 EZ61
Greenford UB6 . 136 CC71
Rainham RM13 . 147 FG68
St. Albans AL1 . 43 CF21
Sidcup DA15 . 186 EU91
Slough SL1 . 131 AK72
Swanscombe DA10 . 190 FZ85
Waltham Cross EN8 . 67 DY33
Stanhope Row, W1 . 18 G2
Stanhopes, Oxt. RH8 . 254 EH128
Stanhope St, NW1 . 9 J2
Stanhope Ter, W2 . 7 P9
Stanhope Way, Sev. TN13 . 256 FD122
Staines (Stanw.) TW19 . 174 BJ86
Stanier Cl, W14 . 16 F10
Stanier Ri, Berk. HP4 . 38 AT16
Staniland Dr, Wey. KT13 . 212 BM110
Stanlake Ms, W12 . 139 CW74
Stanlake Rd, W12 . 139 CV74
Stanlake Vil, W12 . 139 CV74
Stanley Av, Bark. IG11 . 145 ET68
Beckenham BR3 . 203 EC96
Chesham HP5 . 54 AP31
Dagenham RM8 . 126 EZ60
Greenford UB6 . 136 CC67
New Malden KT3 . 199 CU99
Romford RM2 . 127 FG56
St. Albans AL2 . 60 CA25
Wembley HA0 . 138 CL66
Stanley Cl, SW8 . 161 DM79
Coulsdon CR5 . 235 DM117
Greenhithe DA9 . 189 FS85
Hornchurch RM12
off Stanley Rd . 128 FJ61
Romford RM2 . 127 FG56
Uxbridge UB8 . 134 BK67
Wembley HA0 . 138 CL66
Stanley Cotts, Slou. SL2 . 132 AT74
Stanley Ct, Cars. SM5
off Stanley Pk Rd . 218 DG108
Stanley Cres, W11 . 6 E9
Gravesend DA12 . 191 GK92
Stanleycroft Cl, Islw. TW7 . 157 CE81
Stanley Dr, Hat. AL10 . 45 CV20
Stanley Gdns, NW2 . 119 CW64
W3 . 138 CS74
W11 . 6 E9
Borehamwood WD6 . 78 CL39
Mitcham CR4
off Ashbourne Rd . 180 DG93
South Croydon CR2 . 220 DU112
Wallington SM6 . 219 DJ107
Walton-on-Thames KT12 . 214 BW107
Stanley Gdns Ms, W11 . 6 F9
Stanley Gdns Rd, Tedd.
TW11 . 177 CE92
Stanley Grn E, Slou. SL3 . 153 AZ77
Stanley Grn W, Slou. SL3 . 153 AZ77
Stanley Gro, SW8 . 160 DG82
Croydon CR0 . 201 DN100
Stanley Hill, Amer. HP7 . 55 AR40
Stanley Hill Av, Amer. HP7 . 55 AR39
Sch Stanley Inf & Nurs Sch,
Tedd. TW11
off Strathmore Rd . 177 CE91
Sch Stanley Jun Sch, Tedd.
TW11 off Stanley Rd . 177 CE91
Stanley Pk Dr, Wem. HA0 . 138 CM66
Sch Stanley Pk High Sch, Cars.
SM5 off Stanley Pk Rd . 218 DG107
Sch Stanley Pk Inf Sch, Cars.
SM5 off Stanley Pk Rd . 218 DF108
Sch Stanley Pk Jun Sch,
Cars. SM5
off Stanley Pk Rd . 218 DF108
Stanley Pk Rd, Cars. SM5 . 218 DF108
Wallington SM6 . 219 DH107
Stanley Rd, E4 . 101 ED46
E10 . 123 EB58
E12 . 124 EL64
E15 . 143 ED67
E18 . 102 EF53
N2 . 120 DD55
N9 . 100 DT46
N10 . 99 DH52
N11 . 99 DK51
N15 . 121 DP56
NW9 off West Hendon Bdy . 119 CU59
SW14 . 158 CP84
SW19 . 180 DA94
W3 . 158 CQ76
Ashford TW15 . 174 BL92
Bromley BR2 . 204 EH98
Carshalton SM5 . 218 DG108
Croydon CR0 . 201 DN101
Enfield EN1 . 82 DS41
Gravesend (Nthflt) DA11 . 190 GE88
Grays RM17 . 170 GB78
Harrow HA2 . 116 CC61
Hertford SG13 . 32 DS09
Hornchurch RM12 . 128 FJ61
Hounslow TW3 . 156 CC84
Ilford IG1 . 125 ER61
Mitcham CR4 . 180 DG94
Morden SM4 . 200 DA98
Northwood HA6 . 93 BU53
Orpington BR6 . 206 EU102
Sidcup DA14 . 186 EU90
Southall UB1 . 136 BY73
Sutton SM2 . 218 DB107
Swanscombe DA10 . 190 FZ86
Teddington TW11 . 177 CE91
Twickenham TW2 . 177 CD90
Watford WD17 . 76 BW41
Wembley HA9 . 138 CM65
Woking GU21 . 227 AZ116
Stanley Rd N, Rain. RM13 . 147 FE67
Stanley Rd S, Rain. RM13 . 147 FF68
Stanley Sq, Cars. SM5 . 218 DF109
Stanley St, SE8 . 163 DZ80
Caterham CR3
off Coulsdon Rd . 236 DQ122
Sch Stanley Tech Boys' High Sch, SE25
off South Norwood Hill . 202 DT97
Stanley Ter, N19 . 121 DL61
Stanley Way, Orp. BR5 . 206 EV99
Stanmer St, SW11 . 160 DE81
STANMORE, HA7 . 95 CG50
⊖ Stanmore . 95 CK50
Stanmore Chase, St.Alb.
AL4 . 43 CK21
Coll Stanmore Coll, Stan.
HA7 off Elm Pk . 95 CJ51
Stanmore Gdns, Rich. TW9 . 158 CM83
Sutton SM1 . 200 DC104
Stanmore Hall, Stan. HA7 . 95 CH48
Stanmore Hill, Stan. HA7 . 95 CG48
Stanmore Pl, NW1
off Arlington Rd . 141 DH67
Stanmore Rd, E11 . 124 EF60
N15 . 121 DP56
Belvedere DA17 . 167 FC77
Richmond TW9 . 158 CM83
Watford WD24 . 75 BV39
Stanmore St, N1 . 4 A7
Stanmore Ter, Beck. BR3 . 203 EA96
Stanmore Way, Loug. IG10 . 85 EN39
Stanmount Rd, St.Alb. AL2 . 60 CA25
Stannard Ms, E8 . 142 DU65
Stannard Rd, E8 . 142 DU65
Stannary Pl, SE11 . 20 D10
Stannary St, SE11 . 161 DN79
Stannet Way, Wall. SM6 . 219 DJ105
Stannington Path, Borwd.
WD6 . 78 CN39
Stansfeld Rd, E6 . 144 EK71
Stansfield Rd, SW9 . 161 DM83
Hounslow TW4 . 155 BV82
Stansgate Rd, Dag. RM10 . 126 FA61
STANSTEAD ABBOTTS,
Ware SG12 . 33 ED11
Stanstead Cl, Brom. BR2 . 204 EF99
Stanstead Dr, Hodd. EN11 . 49 EB15
Stanstead Gro, SE6
off Stanstead Rd . 183 DZ88
Stanstead Manor, Sutt.
SM1 . 218 DA107
Stanstead Rd, E11 . 124 EH57
SE6 . 183 DX88
SE23 . 183 DX88
Caterham CR3 . 252 DR125
Hertford SG13 . 32 DT08
Hoddesdon EN11 . 49 EB16
Hounslow (Hthrw Air.)
TW6 . 174 BM86
Ware SG12 . 32 DW09
Stansted Cl, Horn. RM12 . 147 FH65
Stansted Cres, Bex. DA5 . 186 EX88
Stanswood Gdns, SE5 . 162 DS80
Stanthorpe Cl, SW16 . 181 DL92
Stanthorpe Rd, SW16 . 181 DL92
Stanton Av, Tedd. TW11 . 177 CE92
Stanton Cl, Epsom KT19 . 216 CP106
Orpington BR5 . 206 EW101
St. Albans AL4 . 43 CK16
Worcester Park KT4 . 199 CX102
Stanton Ho, SE16 . 23 L3
Stanton Rd, SE26
off Stanton Way . 183 DZ91
SW13 . 159 CT82
SW20 . 199 CX96
Croydon CR0 . 202 DQ101
Stantons, Harl. CM20 . 51 EP15
Stanton Sq, SE26
off Stanton Way . 183 DZ91
Stantons Wf, Guil. (Bramley)
GU5 . 259 BA144
Stanton Way, SE26 . 183 DZ91
Slough SL3 . 152 AY77
Stanway Cl, Chig. IG7 . 103 ES50
Stanway Ct, N1 . 5 M10
Stanway Gdns, W3 . 138 CN74
Edgware HA8 . 96 CQ50
Stanway Rd, Wal.Abb. EN9 . 68 EG33
Stanway St, N1 . 5 M9
STANWELL, Stai. TW19 . 174 BL87
Stanwell Cl, Stai. (Stanw.)
TW19 . 174 BK86
Stanwell Gdns, Stai.
(Stanw.) TW19 . 174 BK86
STANWELL MOOR, Stai.
TW19 . 174 BG85
Stanwell Moor Rd, Stai.
TW19 . 174 BH85
West Drayton UB7 . 154 BH81
Stanwell New Rd, Stai.
TW18 . 174 BH90
Stanwell Rd, Ashf. TW15 . 174 BL89
Feltham TW14 . 175 BQ87
Slough (Horton) SL3 . 153 BA83
Stanwick Rd, W14 . 16 E8
Stanworth St, SE1 . 21 N4
Stanwyck Dr, Chig. IG7 . 103 EQ50
Stanwyck Gdns, Rom. RM3 . 105 FH50
Stapenhill Rd, Wem. HA0 . 117 CH62
Staple Cl, Bex. DA5 . 187 FD90
Staplefield Cl, SW2 . 181 DL88
Pinner HA5 . 94 BY52
Stapleford, Welw.G.C. AL7 . 30 DC09
STAPLEFORD ABBOTTS,
Rom. RM4 . 87 FC43
Sch Stapleford Abbotts Co Prim Sch, Rom. RM4
off Stapleford Rd . 87 FB43
★ Stapleford Airfield, Rom.
RM4 . 86 EZ40
Stapleford Av, Ilf. IG2 . 125 ES57
Stapleford Cl, E4 . 101 EC48
SW19 . 179 CY87
Kingston upon Thames KT1 . 198 CN97
Stapleford Ct, Sev. TN13 . 256 FF123
Stapleford Gdns, Rom.
RM5 . 104 FA51
Stapleford Rd, Rom. RM4 . 87 FB42
Wembley HA0 . 137 CK66
STAPLEFORD TAWNEY, Rom.
RM4 . 87 FC37
Stapleford Way, Bark. IG11 . 146 EV69
Staple Hill Rd, Wok.
(Chob.Com.) GU24 . 210 AS105
Staplehurst Cl, Reig. RH2 . 266 DC138
Staplehurst Rd, SE13 . 184 EE85
Carshalton SM5 . 218 DE108
Reigate RH2 . 266 DC138
Staple Inn, WC1 . 10 C6
Staple Inn Bldgs, WC1 . 10 C6
Staple La, Guil. (Shere) GU5 . 244 BK132
Staples Cl, SE16 . 23 J1
Staples Cor, NW2 . 119 CV60
Staples Cor Business Pk,
NW2 . 119 CV60
Staples Rd, Loug. IG10 . 84 EL41
Sch Staples Rd Co Inf Sch,
Loug. IG10 off Staples Rd . 84 EL41
Sch Staples Rd Co Jun Sch,
Loug. IG10 off Staples Rd . 84 EL41

★ Place of interest | H Hospital | Sch School | Coll College | Uni University | ⇌ Railway station

Staple St, SE1 . . . 21 K4
Stapleton Cl, Pot.B. EN6 . . . 64 DD31
Stapleton Cres, Rain. RM13 . . . 147 FG65
Stapleton Gdns, Croy. CR0 . . . 219 DN106
Stapleton Hall Rd, N4 . . . 121 DM59
Stapleton Rd, SW17 . . . 180 DG90
Bexleyheath DA7 . . . 166 EZ80
Borehamwood WD6 . . . 78 CN38
Orpington BR6 . . . 205 ET104
Staple Tye Shop Ms, Harl. CM18 off Perry Rd . . . 51 EQ18
Stapley Rd, Belv. DA17 . . . 166 FA78
St. Albans AL3 . . . 43 CD19
Stapylton Rd, Barn. EN5 . . . 79 CY41
Star All, EC3 . . . 11 M9
Star & Garter Hill, Rich. TW10 . . . 178 CL88
Starboard Av, Green. DA9 . . . 189 FV86
Starboard Way, E14 . . . 23 P5
Starch Ho La, Ilf. IG6 . . . 103 ER54
Starcross St, NW1 . . . 9 K2
Starfield Rd, W12 . . . 159 CU75
Star Hill, Dart. DA1 . . . 187 FE85
Woking GU22 . . . 226 AW119
Star Hill Rd, Sev. (Dunt.Grn) TN14 . . . 240 EZ116
Star Home Ct, Ware SG12 . . . 33 DY06
Sch Starhurst Sch, Dor. RH5 off Chart La S . . . 263 CJ138
Starkey Cl, Wal.Cr. (Chsht) EN7 off Shambrook Rd . . . 66 DQ25
Star La, E16 . . . 14 G4
Coulsdon CR5 . . . 234 DG122
Epping CM16 . . . 70 EU30
Orpington BR5 . . . 206 EW98
Starlight Way, St.Alb. AL4 . . . 43 CJ22
Starling Cl, Buck.H. IG9 . . . 102 EG46
Pinner HA5 . . . 116 BW55
Starling La, Pot.B. (Cuffley) EN6 . . . 65 DM28
Starlings, The, Lthd. (Oxshott) KT22 . . . 214 CC113
Starling Wk, Hmptn. TW12 off Oak Av . . . 176 BY93
Starmans Cl, Dag. RM9 . . . 146 EY67
Star Path, Nthlt. UB5 off Brabazon Rd . . . 136 CA68
Star Pl, E1 . . . 21 P10
Sch Star Prim Sch, E16 . . . 15 H4
Star Rd, W14 . . . 159 CZ79
Isleworth TW7 . . . 157 CD82
Uxbridge UB10 . . . 135 BQ70
Starrock La, Couls. (Chipstead) CR5 . . . 234 DF120
Starrock Rd, Couls. CR5 . . . 235 DH119
Star St, E16 . . . 15 K5
W2 . . . 7 P7
Ware SG12 . . . 33 DY06
Starts Cl, Orp. BR6 . . . 205 EN104
Starts Hill Av, Orp. BR6 . . . 223 EP105
Starts Hill Rd, Orp. BR6 . . . 205 EN104
Starveall Cl, West Dr. UB7 . . . 154 BM76
Starwood Cl, W.Byf. KT14 . . . 212 BJ111
Starwood Ct, Slou. SL3 off London Rd . . . 152 AW76
Star Yd, WC2 . . . 10 C7
State Fm Av, Orp. BR6 . . . 223 EP105
Staten Gdns, Twick. TW1 . . . 177 CF88
Statham Gro, N16 off Green Las . . . 122 DQ63
N18 . . . 100 DS50
Station App, E4 (Highams Pk) off The Avenue . . . 101 ED51
E7 off Woodford Rd . . . 124 EH63
E11 (Snaresbrook) off High St . . . 124 EG57
N11 off Friern Barnet Rd . . . 99 DH50
N12 (Woodside Pk) . . . 98 DB49
N16 (Stoke Newington) off Stamford Hill . . . 122 DT61
NW10 off Station Rd . . . 139 CT69
SE1 . . . 20 B2
SE3 off Kidbrooke Pk Rd . . . 164 EH83
SE9 (Mottingham) . . . 185 EM88
SE26 (Lwr Sydenham) off Worsley Br Rd . . . 183 DZ92
SE26 (Sydenham) off Sydenham Rd . . . 182 DW91
SW6 . . . 159 CY83
SW16 . . . 181 DK92
W7 . . . 137 CE74
Amersham HP6 . . . 55 AQ38
Amersham (Lt.Chal.) HP7 off Chalfont Sta Rd . . . 72 AX39
Ashford TW15 . . . 174 BL91
Barnet EN5 . . . 80 DC42
Bexley DA5 off Bexley High St . . . 186 FA87
Bexleyheath DA7 off Avenue Rd . . . 166 EY82
Bexleyheath (Barne.) DA7 . . . 167 FC82
Bromley (Hayes) BR2 . . . 204 EG102
Buckhurst Hill IG9 off Cherry Tree Ri . . . 102 EK49
Chislehurst BR7 . . . 205 EN95
Chislehurst (Elm.Wds) BR7 . . . 184 EL93
Coulsdon CR5 . . . 235 DK116
Coulsdon (Chipstead) CR5 . . . 234 DF118
Dartford DA1 . . . 188 FL86
Dartford (Cray.) DA1 . . . 187 FF86
Dorking RH4 . . . 247 CJ134
Epping (They.B.) CM16 off Coppice Row . . . 85 ES36
Epsom KT18 . . . 216 CR113
Epsom (Ewell E.) KT17 . . . 217 CV110
Epsom (Ewell W.) KT19 off Chessington Rd . . . 217 CT109
Epsom (Stoneleigh) KT19 . . . 217 CU106
Esher (Hinch.Wd) KT10 . . . 197 CF104
Gerrards Cross SL9 . . . 112 AY57
Grays RM17 . . . 170 GA79
Greenford UB6 . . . 137 CD66
Guildford GU1 . . . 258 AY135
Hampton TW12 off Milton Rd . . . 196 CA95
Harlow CM20 . . . 36 EW10
Harrow HA1 . . . 117 CE59
Hayes UB3 . . . 155 BT75
Hemel Hempstead HP3 . . . 40 BG23
Horley RH6 . . . 269 DH148
Kenley CR8 off Hayes La . . . 220 DQ114
Kingston upon Thames KT1 . . . 198 CN95
Leatherhead KT22 . . . 231 CG121
Leatherhead (E.Hors.) KT24 . . . 245 BS126
Leatherhead (Oxshott) KT22 . . . 214 CC113
Loughton IG10 . . . 84 EL43
Loughton (Debden) IG10 . . . 85 EQ42
Northwood HA6 . . . 93 BS52
Orpington BR6 . . . 205 ET103
Orpington (Chels.) BR6 . . . 224 EV106
Orpington (St.M.Cray) BR5 . . . 206 EV98
Oxted RH8 . . . 254 EE128
Station App, Pnr. HA5 . . . 116 BY55
Pinner (Hatch End) HA5 off Uxbridge Rd . . . 94 CA52
Purley CR8 off Whytecliffe Rd S . . . 219 DN111
Radlett WD7 off Shenley Hill . . . 77 CG35
Richmond TW9 . . . 158 CN81
Rickmansworth (Chorl.) WD3 . . . 73 BC42
Ruislip HA4 . . . 115 BS60
Ruislip (S.Ruis.) HA4 . . . 115 BV64
Shepperton TW17 . . . 195 BQ100
South Croydon CR2 off Sanderstead Rd . . . 220 DR109
Staines TW18 . . . 174 BG92
Sunbury-on-Thames TW16 . . . 195 BU95
Sutton (Belmont) SM2 off Brighton Rd . . . 218 DB110
Sutton (Cheam) SM2 . . . 217 CY108
Swanley BR8 . . . 207 FE98
Upminster RM14 . . . 128 FQ61
Uxbridge (Denh.) UB9 off Middle Rd . . . 113 BD59
Virginia Water GU25 . . . 192 AX98
Waltham Cross EN8 . . . 67 DY34
Waltham Cross (Chsht) EN8 . . . 67 DZ30
Watford WD18 off Cassiobury Pk Av . . . 75 BT41
Watford (Carp.Pk) WD19 off Prestwick Rd . . . 94 BX48
Welling DA16 . . . 165 ET82
Wembley HA0 . . . 137 CH65
West Byfleet KT14 . . . 212 BG112
West Drayton UB7 . . . 134 BL74
Weybridge KT13 . . . 212 BN107
Whyteleafe CR3 . . . 236 DU117
Woking GU22 . . . 227 AZ117
Worcester Park KT4 . . . 199 CU102
Station App E, Red. (Earls.) RH1 off Earlsbrook Rd . . . 266 DF136
Station App N, Sid. DA15 . . . 186 EU89
Station App Path, SE9 off Glenlea Rd . . . 185 EM85
Station App Rd, W4 . . . 158 CQ80
Coulsdon CR5 . . . 235 DK115
Gatwick RH6 off London Rd . . . 269 DH152
Tadworth KT20 . . . 233 CW122
Station App W, Red. (Earls.) RH1 off Earlswood Rd . . . 266 DF136
Station Av, SW9 off Coldharbour La . . . 161 DP83
Caterham CR3 . . . 236 DU124
Epsom KT19 . . . 216 CS109
New Malden KT3 . . . 198 CS97
Richmond TW9 . . . 158 CN81
Walton-on-Thames KT12 . . . 213 BU105
Station Cl, N3 . . . 98 DA53
N12 (Woodside Pk) . . . 98 DB49
Hampton TW12 . . . 196 CB95
Hatfield AL9 off Station Rd . . . 63 CY26
Potters Bar EN6 . . . 63 CZ31
Station Ct, SW6 off Townmead Rd . . . 160 DC81
Station Cres, N15 . . . 122 DR56
SE3 . . . 25 L10
Ashford TW15 . . . 174 BK90
Wembley HA0 . . . 137 CH65
Stationers Hall Ct, EC4 off Ludgate Hill . . . 141 DP72
Station Est, Beck. BR3 off Elmers End Rd . . . 203 DX98
Station Est Rd, Felt. TW14 . . . 175 BV88
Station Footpath, Kings L. WD4 . . . 59 BP31
Station Gar Ms, SW16 off Estreham Rd . . . 181 DK93
Station Gdns, W4 . . . 158 CQ80
Station Gro, Wem. HA0 . . . 138 CL65
Station Hill, Brom. BR2 . . . 204 EG103
Station Ho Ms, N9 off Fore St . . . 100 DU49
Station La, Horn. RM12 . . . 128 FK62
Station Par, E11 . . . 124 EG57
N14 off High St . . . 99 DK46
NW2 . . . 139 CW65
SW12 off Balham High Rd . . . 180 DG88
W3 . . . 138 CN72
Ashford TW15 off Woodthorpe Rd . . . 174 BM91
Barking IG11 . . . 145 EQ66
Barnet EN4 off Cockfosters Rd . . . 80 DG42
Beaconsfield HP9 . . . 89 AK52
Feltham TW14 . . . 175 BV87
Hornchurch RM12 off Rosewood Av . . . 127 FH63
Leatherhead KT24 off Ockham Rd S . . . 245 BS126
Richmond TW9 . . . 158 CN81
Sevenoaks TN13 off London Rd . . . 256 FG124
Uxbridge (Denh.) UB9 . . . 114 BG59
Virginia Water GU25 . . . 192 AX98
Station Pas, E18 off Maybank Rd . . . 102 EH54
SE15 . . . 162 DW81
Station Path, E8 off Amhurst Rd . . . 142 DV65
Staines TW18 . . . 173 BF91
Station Pl, N4 off Seven Sisters Rd . . . 121 DN61
Godalming GU7 off Summers Rd . . . 258 AT144
Station Ri, SE27 off Norwood Rd . . . 181 DP89
Station Rd, E4 (Chingford) . . . 101 ED46
E7 . . . 124 EG63
E12 . . . 124 EK63
E17 . . . 123 DY58
N3 . . . 98 DA53
N11 . . . 99 DH50
N17 . . . 122 DU55
N19 . . . 121 DJ62
N21 . . . 99 DP46
N22 . . . 99 DM54
NW4 . . . 119 CU58
NW7 . . . 96 CS50
NW10 . . . 139 CT68
SE13 . . . 163 EC83
SE20 . . . 182 DW93
SE25 (Norwood Junct.) . . . 202 DT98
SW13 . . . 159 CU83
SW19 . . . 200 DC95
W5 . . . 138 CM72
W7 (Hanwell) . . . 137 CE74
Addlestone KT15 . . . 212 BJ105
Amersham HP6, HP7 . . . 55 AQ38
Ashford TW15 . . . 174 BM91
Barnet EN5 . . . 80 DB43
Beaconsfield HP9 . . . 89 AK52
Belvedere DA17 . . . 166 FA76
Station Rd, Berk. HP4 . . . 38 AW18
Betchworth RH3 . . . 248 CS131
Bexleyheath DA7 . . . 166 EY83
Borehamwood WD6 . . . 78 CN42
Brentford TW8 . . . 157 CJ79
Bromley BR1 . . . 204 EG95
Bromley (Short.) BR2 . . . 204 EE96
Broxbourne EN10 . . . 49 DZ20
Carshalton SM5 . . . 218 DF105
Caterham (Wold.) CR3 . . . 237 DZ123
Chertsey KT16 . . . 193 BF102
Chesham HP5 . . . 54 AP31
Chessington KT9 . . . 216 CL106
Chigwell IG7 . . . 103 EP48
Cobham (Stoke D'Ab.) KT11 . . . 230 BY117
Croydon (E.Croy.) CR0 . . . 202 DR103
Croydon (W.Croy.) CR0 . . . 202 DQ102
Dartford (Cray.) DA1 . . . 187 FF86
Dartford (Eyns.) DA4 . . . 208 FK104
Dartford (S.Darenth) DA4 . . . 208 FP96
Dorking RH4 . . . 263 CG135
Edgware HA8 . . . 96 CN51
Egham TW20 . . . 173 BA92
Epping CM16 . . . 70 EU31
Epping (N.Wld Bas.) CM16 . . . 71 FB27
Esher KT10 . . . 197 CD103
Esher (Clay.) KT10 . . . 215 CD106
Gerrards Cross SL9 . . . 112 AY57
Godalming (Farnc.) GU7 . . . 258 AT144
Gravesend (Betsham) DA13 . . . 190 GA91
Gravesend (Nthflt) DA11 . . . 190 GB86
Greenhithe DA9 . . . 169 FU84
Guildford (Bramley) GU5 . . . 259 AZ144
Guildford (Goms.) GU5 . . . 261 BS139
Guildford (Shalf.) GU4 . . . 258 AY140
Hampton TW12 . . . 196 CA95
Harlow CM17 . . . 36 EW11
Harrow HA1 . . . 117 CF59
Harrow (N.Har.) HA2 . . . 116 CB57
Hatfield (Brook.Pk) AL9 . . . 63 CX25
Hayes UB3 . . . 155 BT76
Hemel Hempstead HP1 . . . 40 BH22
Hertford (Letty Grn) SG14 . . . 30 DG12
High Wycombe (Loud.) HP10 . . . 88 AC53
Horley RH6 . . . 269 DH148
Hounslow TW3 . . . 156 CB84
Ilford IG1 . . . 125 EP62
Ilford (Barkingside) IG6 . . . 125 ER55
Kenley CR8 . . . 220 DQ114
Kings Langley WD4 . . . 59 BP29
Kingston upon Thames KT2 . . . 198 CN95
Kingston upon Thames (Hmptn W.) KT1 . . . 197 CJ95
Leatherhead KT22 . . . 231 CG121
Loughton IG10 . . . 84 EL42
Maidenhead (Taplow) SL6 . . . 130 AF72
New Malden (Mots.Pk) KT3 . . . 199 CV99
Orpington BR6 . . . 205 ET103
Orpington (St.P.Cray) BR5 . . . 206 EW98
Potters Bar (Cuffley) EN6 . . . 65 DM29
Radlett WD7 . . . 77 CG35
Redhill RH1 . . . 250 DG133
Redhill (Merst.) RH1 . . . 251 DJ128
Rickmansworth WD3 . . . 92 BK45
Romford (Chad.Hth) RM6 . . . 126 EX59
Romford (Gidea Pk) RM2 . . . 127 FH56
Romford (Harold Wd) RM3 . . . 106 FM53
St. Albans (Brick.Wd) AL2 . . . 60 CA31
St. Albans (Smallford) AL4 . . . 44 CP19
Sevenoaks (Dunt.Grn) TN13 . . . 241 FE120
Sevenoaks (Halst.) TN14 . . . 224 EZ111
Sevenoaks (Otford) TN14 . . . 241 FH116
Sevenoaks (Shore.) TN14 . . . 225 FG111
Shepperton TW17 . . . 195 BQ99
Sidcup DA15 . . . 186 EU91
Slough (Cipp.) SL1 . . . 131 AL72
Slough (Langley) SL3 . . . 153 BA76
Staines (Wrays.) TW19 . . . 173 AZ86
Sunbury-on-Thames TW16 . . . 175 BU94
Sutton (Belmont) SM2 . . . 218 DA110
Swanley BR8 . . . 207 FE98
Teddington TW11 . . . 177 CF92
Thames Ditton KT7 . . . 197 CF101
Twickenham TW1 . . . 177 CF88
Upminster RM14 . . . 128 FQ61
Uxbridge UB8 . . . 134 BJ70
Waltham Cross EN8 . . . 67 EA34
Ware SG12 . . . 33 DX06
Ware (Stans.Abb.) SG12 . . . 33 EA11
Watford WD17 . . . 75 BV40
West Byfleet KT14 . . . 212 BG112
West Drayton UB7 . . . 134 BK74
West Wickham BR4 . . . 203 EC102
Westerham (Brasted) TN16 . . . 240 EV123
Whyteleafe CR3 . . . 236 DT118
Woking (Chobham) GU24 . . . 210 AT111
Station Rd E, Oxt. RH8 . . . 254 EE128
Station Rd N, Belv. DA17 . . . 167 FB76
Egham TW20 . . . 173 BA92
Redhill (Merst.) RH1 . . . 251 DJ128
Station Rd S, Red. (Merst.) RH1 . . . 251 DJ128
Station Rd W, Oxt. RH8 . . . 254 EE129
Station Row, Guil. (Shalf.) GU4 . . . 258 AY140
Station Sq, Orp. (Petts Wd) BR5 . . . 205 EQ99
Romford RM2 . . . 127 FH56
Station St, E15 . . . 143 ED66
E16 . . . 145 EP74
Station Ter, NW10 . . . 139 CX68
SE5 . . . 162 DQ81
Dorking RH4 off Chalkpit La . . . 263 CG135
St. Albans (Park St) AL2 off Park St . . . 61 CD26
Station Vw, Grnf. UB6 . . . 137 CD67
Guildford GU1 . . . 258 AW135
Station Way, Buck.H. (Rod.Val.) IG9 . . . 102 EJ49
Epsom (Epsom) KT19 . . . 216 CR113
Esher (Clay.) KT10 . . . 215 CE107
St. Albans AL1 . . . 43 CF20
Sutton (Cheam) SM3 . . . 217 CY107
Station Yd, Twick. TW1 . . . 177 CG87
Staunton Rd, Kings.T. KT2 . . . 178 CL93
Slough SL2 . . . 131 AR71
Staunton St, SE8 . . . 163 DZ79
★ Stave Hill Ecological Pk, SE16 . . . 23 J3
Staveley Cl, E9 off Churchill Wk . . . 122 DW64
N7 off Penn Rd . . . 121 DL63
SE15 off Asylum Rd . . . 162 DV81
Staveley Gdns, W4 . . . 158 CR81
Staveley Rd, W4 . . . 158 CR80
Ashford TW15 . . . 175 BR93
Staveley Way, Wok. (Knap.) GU21 . . . 226 AS117
Staverton Rd, NW2 . . . 139 CW66
Hornchurch RM11 . . . 128 FK58
Stave Yd Rd, SE16 . . . 23 J2
Stavordale Rd, N5 . . . 121 DP63
Stavordale Rd, Cars. SM5 . . . 200 DC101
Stayne End, Vir.W. GU25 . . . 192 AU98
Stayner's Rd, E1 . . . 12 G3
Stayton Rd, Sutt. SM1 . . . 200 DA104
Steadfast Rd, Kings.T. KT1 . . . 197 CK95
Stead St, SE17 . . . 21 J8
Steam Fm La, Felt. TW14 . . . 155 BT84
Stean St, E8 . . . 5 N7
Stebbing Ho, W11 . . . 16 B1
Stebbing Way, Bark. IG11 . . . 146 EU68
Stebondale St, E14 . . . 24 D8
Sch Stebon Prim Sch, E14 . . . 13 N6
Stedham Pl, WC1 . . . 9 N7
Stedman Cl, Bex. DA5 . . . 187 FE90
Uxbridge UB10 . . . 114 BN62
Steed Cl, Horn. RM11 . . . 127 FH61
Steedman St, SE17 . . . 20 G8
Steeds Rd, N10 . . . 98 DF53
Steeds Way, Loug. IG10 . . . 84 EL41
Steele Av, Green. DA9 . . . 189 FT85
Steele Rd, E11 . . . 124 EE63
N17 . . . 122 DS55
NW10 . . . 138 CQ68
W4 . . . 158 CQ76
Isleworth TW7 . . . 157 CG84
Steeles Ms N, NW3 off Steeles Rd . . . 140 DF65
Steeles Ms S, NW3 off Steeles Rd . . . 140 DF65
Steeles Rd, NW3 . . . 140 DF65
Steele Wk, Erith DA8 . . . 167 FB79
Steel's La, E1 . . . 12 F8
Steels La, Lthd. (Oxshott) KT22 . . . 214 CB114
Steelyard Pas, EC4 off Upper Thames St . . . 142 DR73
Steen Way, SE22 off East Dulwich Gro . . . 182 DS85
Steep Cl, Orp. BR6 . . . 223 ET107
Steep Hill, SW16 . . . 181 DK90
Croydon CR0 . . . 220 DS105
Steeplands, Bushey WD23 . . . 94 CB45
Steeple Cl, SW6 . . . 159 CY82
SW19 . . . 179 CY92
Steeple Ct, E1 . . . 12 D3
Steeple Gdns, Add. KT15 off Weatherall Cl . . . 212 BH106
Steeple Hts Dr, West. (Bigg.H.) TN16 . . . 238 EK117
Steeplestone Cl, N18 . . . 100 DQ50
Steeple Wk, N1 . . . 5 H7
Steerforth St, SW18 . . . 180 DB89
Steer Pl, Red. RH1 off Bonehurst Rd . . . 266 DG143
Steers Mead, Mitch. CR4 . . . 200 DF95
Steers Way, SE16 . . . 23 K4
Stella Cl, Uxb. UB8 . . . 135 BP71
Sch Stella Mann Sch, NW3 off Finchley Rd . . . 120 DB64
Stellar Ho, N17 . . . 100 DT51
Stella Rd, SW17 . . . 180 DF93
Stelling Rd, Erith DA8 . . . 167 FD80
Stellman Cl, E5 . . . 122 DU62
Stembridge Rd, SE20 . . . 202 DV96
Sten Cl, Enf. EN3 . . . 83 EA37
Stents La, Cob. KT11 . . . 230 BZ120
Stepbridge Path, Wok. GU21 off Goldsworth Rd . . . 226 AX117
Stepgates, Cher. KT16 . . . 194 BH101
Stepgates Cl, Cher. KT16 . . . 194 BH101
Sch Stepgates Prim Sch, Cher. KT16 off Stepgates . . . 194 BH101
Stephan Cl, E8 . . . 142 DU67
Stephen Av, Rain. RM13 . . . 147 FG65
Stephen Cl, Egh. TW20 . . . 173 BC93
Orpington BR6 . . . 205 ET104
Stephendale Rd, SW6 . . . 160 DB82
Sch Stephen Hawking Sch, E14 . . . 13 K10
Stephen Ms, W1 . . . 9 L6
Stephen Pl, SW4 off Rectory Gro . . . 161 DJ83
Stephen Rd, Bexh. DA7 . . . 167 FC83
Stephens Cl, Rom. RM3 . . . 106 FJ50
Stephenson Av, Til. RM18 . . . 171 GG81
Stephenson Dr, Wind. SL4 . . . 151 AP80
Stephenson Rd, E17 . . . 123 DY57
W7 . . . 137 CF72
Twickenham TW2 . . . 176 CA87
Stephenson St, E16 . . . 14 G4
NW10 . . . 138 CS69
Stephenson Way, NW1 . . . 9 K3
Watford WD24 . . . 76 BX41
Stephenson Wf, Hem.H. HP3 . . . 58 BM25
Stephen's Rd, E15 . . . 144 EE67
Stephen St, W1 . . . 9 L6
Stephyns Chambers, Hem.H. HP1 off Waterhouse St . . . 40 BJ21
STEPNEY, E1 . . . 12 G6
Stepney Causeway, E1 . . . 13 H8
⊖ Stepney Green . . . 12 G4
Stepney Grn, E1 . . . 12 F5
Sch Stepney Greencoat C of E Prim Sch, E14 . . . 13 L7
Sch Stepney Grn Sch, E1 . . . 13 H6
Stepney High St, E1 . . . 13 H6
Stepney Way, E1 . . . 12 C6
Sterling Av, Edg. HA8 . . . 96 CM49
Waltham Cross EN8 . . . 67 DX34
Sterling Cl, N9 . . . 100 DW46
NW10 . . . 139 CU65
Sterling Gdns, SE14 . . . 163 DY79
Sterling Ho, SE3 off Cambert Way . . . 164 EH84
Sterling Ind Est, Dag. RM10 . . . 127 FB63
Sterling Pl, W5 . . . 158 CL77
Weybridge KT13 off Oatlands Av . . . 213 BS105
Sterling Rd, Enf. EN2 . . . 82 DR38
Sterling St, SW7 . . . 18 B5
Sterling Way, N18 . . . 100 DR50
★ Sternberg Cen, N3 . . . 98 DB54
Stern Cl, Bark. IG11 . . . 146 EW68
Sterndale Rd, W14 . . . 16 A6
Dartford DA1 . . . 188 FM87
Sterne St, W12 . . . 16 A3
Sternhall La, SE15 . . . 162 DU83
Sternhold Av, SW2 . . . 181 DK89
Sterry Cres, Dag. RM10 off Alibon Rd . . . 126 FA64
Sterry Dr, Epsom KT19 . . . 216 CS105
Thames Ditton KT7 . . . 197 CE100
Sterry Gdns, Dag. RM10 . . . 146 FA65
Sterry Rd, Bark. IG11 . . . 145 ET67
Dagenham RM10 . . . 126 FA63
Sterry St, SE1 . . . 21 J4
Steucers La, SE23 . . . 183 DY87
Steve Biko La, SE6 . . . 183 EA91
Steve Biko Rd, N7 . . . 121 DN62
Steve Biko Way, Houns. TW3 . . . 156 CA83
Stevedale Rd, Well. DA16 . . . 166 EW82
Stevedore St, E1 . . . 22 C1
Stevenage Cres, Borwd. WD6 . . . 78 CL39
Stevenage Ri, Hem.H. HP2 . . . 40 BM16
Stevenage Rd, E6 . . . 145 EN65
SW6 . . . 159 CX80
Stevens Av, E9 . . . 142 DW65
Stevens Cl, Beck. BR3 . . . 183 EA93
Bexley DA5 . . . 187 FD91
Steven's Cl, Dart. (Lane End) DA2 . . . 189 FS92
Stevens Cl, Epsom KT17 off Upper High St . . . 216 CS113
Hampton TW12 . . . 176 BY93
Pinner HA5 off Bridle Rd . . . 116 BW57
Stevens Grn, Bushey (Bushey Hth) WD23 . . . 94 CC46
Stevens La, Esher (Clay.) KT10 . . . 215 CG108
Stevenson Cl, Barn. EN5 . . . 80 DD44
Erith DA8 . . . 167 FH80
Stevenson Cres, SE16 . . . 22 B9
Stevenson Rd, Slou. (Hedg.) SL2 . . . 111 AR61
Stevens Pl, Pur. CR8 . . . 219 DP113
Stevens Rd, Dag. RM8 . . . 126 EV62
Stevens St, SE1 . . . 21 M5
Steven's Wk, Croy. CR0 . . . 221 DY111
Stevens Way, Chig. IG7 . . . 103 ES49
Steventon Rd, W12 . . . 139 CT73
Steward Cl, Wal.Cr. (Chsht) EN8 . . . 67 DY30
STEWARDS, Harl. CM18 . . . 51 ER19
Stewards Cl, Epp. CM16 . . . 70 EU33
Stewards Grn La, Epp. CM16 . . . 70 EV32
Stewards Grn Rd, Epp. CM16 . . . 70 EU33
Stewards Holte Wk, N11 off Coppies Gro . . . 99 DH49
Sch Stewards Sch, Harl. CM18 off Parnall Rd . . . 51 ER19
Steward St, E1 . . . 11 M6
Stewart, Tad. KT20 . . . 233 CX121
Stewart Av, Shep. TW17 . . . 194 BN98
Slough SL1 . . . 132 AT71
Upminster RM14 . . . 128 FP62
Stewart Cl, NW9 . . . 118 CQ58
Abbots Langley WD5 . . . 59 BT32
Chislehurst BR7 . . . 185 EP92
Hampton TW12 . . . 176 BY92
Maidenhead (Fifield) SL6 . . . 150 AD81
Woking GU21 off Nethercote Av . . . 226 AT117
Sch Stewart Fleming Prim Sch, SE20 off Witham Rd . . . 202 DW97
Sch Stewart Headlam Prim Sch, E1 . . . 12 C3
Stewart Rainbird Ho, E12 . . . 125 EN64
Stewart Rd, E15 . . . 123 EC63
Stewartsby Cl, N18 . . . 100 DQ50
Stewart's Dr, Slou. (Farn.Com.) SL2 . . . 111 AP64
Stewart's Gro, SW3 . . . 17 P9
Stewart's Rd, SW8 . . . 161 DJ80
Stewart St, E14 . . . 24 D4
Stew La, EC4 . . . 10 G9
Steyne Rd, W3 . . . 138 CQ74
Steyning Cl, Ken. CR8 . . . 235 DP116
Steyning Gro, SE9 . . . 185 EM91
Steynings Way, N12 . . . 98 DA50
Steyning Way, Houns. TW4 . . . 156 BW84
Steynton Av, Bex. DA5 . . . 186 EX89
Stickland Rd, Belv. DA17 off Picardy Rd . . . 166 FA77
Stickleton Cl, Grnf. UB6 . . . 136 CB69
Stifford Hill, Grays (N.Stfd) RM16 . . . 149 FX74
South Ockendon RM15 . . . 149 FW73
Sch Stifford Prim Sch, Grays RM17 off Parker Rd . . . 170 FY78
Stifford Rd, S.Ock. RM15 . . . 149 FR74
Stilecroft, Harl. CM18 . . . 52 EU17
Stilecroft Gdns, Wem. HA0 . . . 117 CH62
Stile Hall Gdns, W4 . . . 158 CN78
Stile Hall Par, W4 off Chiswick High Rd . . . 158 CN78
Stile Meadow, Beac. HP9 off Maxwell Rd . . . 89 AL52
Stile Path, Sun. TW16 . . . 195 BU98
Stile Rd, Slou. SL3 . . . 152 AX76
Stiles Cl, Brom. BR2 . . . 205 EM100
Erith DA8 off Riverdale Rd . . . 167 FB78
Stillingfleet Rd, SW13 . . . 159 CU79
Stillington St, SW1 . . . 19 K7
Sch Stillness Inf, SE23 off Brockley Ri . . . 183 DY86
Sch Stillness Juniors, SE23 off Brockley Ri . . . 183 DY86
Stillness Rd, SE23 . . . 183 DY86
Stilton Path, Borwd. WD6 . . . 78 CN38
Stilwell Dr, Uxb. UB8 . . . 134 BM70
Stilwell Roundabout, Uxb. UB8 . . . 134 BN73
Stipularis Dr, Hayes UB4 . . . 136 BX70
Stirling Av, Pnr. HA5 . . . 116 BY59
Wallington SM6 . . . 219 DL108
Stirling Cl, SW16 . . . 201 DJ95
Banstead SM7 . . . 233 CZ117
Rainham RM13 . . . 147 FH69
Uxbridge UB8 off Ferndale Cres . . . 134 BJ69
Windsor SL4 . . . 151 AK82
Stirling Cor, Barn. EN5 . . . 78 CR44
Borehamwood WD6 . . . 78 CR44
Stirling Dr, Orp. BR6 . . . 224 EV106
Stirling Gro, Houns. TW3 . . . 156 CC82
Stirling Rd, E13 . . . 144 EH68
E17 . . . 123 DY55
N17 . . . 100 DU53
N22 . . . 99 DP53
SW9 . . . 161 DL82
W3 . . . 158 CP76
Harrow HA3 . . . 117 CF55
Hayes UB3 . . . 135 BV73
Hounslow (Hthrw Air.) TW6 . . . 174 BM86
Slough SL1 . . . 131 AP72
Twickenham TW2 . . . 176 CA87
Stirling Rd Path, E17 . . . 123 DY55
Stirling Wk, N.Mal. KT3 . . . 198 CQ99
Surbiton KT5 . . . 198 CP100
Stirling Way, Abb.L. WD5 . . . 59 BU32
Borehamwood WD6 . . . 78 CR44
Croydon CR0 . . . 201 DL101
Welwyn Garden City AL7 . . . 30 DE09
Stites Hill Rd, Couls. CR5 . . . 235 DP120
Stiven Cres, Har. HA2 . . . 116 BZ62
Stoat Cl, Hert. SG13 . . . 32 DQ09
Stoats Nest Rd, Couls. CR5 . . . 219 DL114
Stoats Nest Village, Couls. CR5 . . . 235 DL115

⊖ London Underground station   DLR Docklands Light Railway station   Tra Tramlink station   Riv Pedestrian ferry landing stage

Stockbreach Cl, Hat. AL10 ..45 CU17
Stockbreach Rd, Hat. AL10 ..45 CU17
Stockbury Rd, Croy. CR0 ..202 DW100
Stockdale Rd, Dag. RM8 ..126 EZ61
Stockdales Rd, Wind.
(Eton Wick) SL4 ..151 AM77
Stockdove Way, Grnf. UB6 ..137 CF69
Stocker Gdns, Dag. RM9 ..146 EW66
Stockers Fm Rd, Rick. WD3 ..92 BK48
Stockers La, Wok. GU22 ..227 AZ120
★ Stock Exchange, EC2 ..10 F7
Stockfield, Horl. RH6 ..269 DH147
Stockfield Av, Hodd. EN11 ..49 EA15
Stockfield Rd, SW16 ..181 DM90
Esher (Clay.) KT10 ..215 CE106
Stockham's Cl, S.Croy. CR2 .220 DR111
Stock Hill, West. (Bigg.H.)
TN16 ..238 EK116
Stockholm Ho, E1 ..12 C9
Stockholm Rd, SE16 ..22 F10
Stockholm Way, E1 ..22 A1
Stockhurst Cl, SW15 ..159 CW82
Stocking La, Hert. (Bayford)
SG13 ..47 DN18
Stockings La, Hert. (Lt.Berk.)
SG13 ..47 DK18
Stockingswater La, Enf.
EN3 ..83 DY41
Stockland Rd, Rom. RM7 ..127 FD58
Stock La, Dart. DA2 ..188 FJ91
Stockley Cl, West Dr. UB7 ..155 BP75
Stockley Fm Rd, West Dr.
UB7 off Stockley Rd ..155 BP76
Stockley Pk, Uxb. UB11 ..135 BP74
Stockley Pk Roundabout,
Uxb. UB11 ..135 BP74
Stockley Rd, Uxb. UB8 ..135 BP73
West Drayton UB7 ..155 BP77
Stock Orchard Cres, N7 ..4 A1
Stock Orchard St, N7 ..4 A2
Stockport Rd, SW16 ..201 DK95
Rickmansworth (Herons.)
WD3 ..91 BC45
Stocks Cl, Horl. RH6 ..269 DH149
Stocksfield Rd, E17 ..123 EC55
Stocks Meadow, Hem.H. HP2 .40 BN19
Stocks Pl, E14 ..13 M9
Stock St, E13 ..144 EG68
Stockton Cl, Barn. EN5 ..80 DC42
Stockton Gdns, N17
off Stockton Rd ..100 DQ52
NW7 ..96 CS48
Stockton Rd, N17 ..100 DQ52
N18 ..100 DU51
Reigate RH2 ..266 DA137
STOCKWELL, SW9 ..161 DM81
⊖ Stockwell ..161 DL81
Stockwell Av, SW9 ..161 DM83
Stockwell Cl, Brom. BR1 ..204 EH96
Edgware HA8
off Burnt Oak Bdy ..96 CQ54
Waltham Cross (Chsht) EN7 ..66 DU28
Stockwell Gdns, SW9 ..161 DM82
Stockwell Gdns Est, SW9 ..161 DL82
Stockwell Grn, SW9 ..161 DM82
Stockwell La, SW9 ..161 DM82
Waltham Cross (Chsht)
EN7 ..66 DU28
Stockwell Ms, SW9
off Stockwell Rd ..161 DM82
Stockwell Pk Cres, SW9 ..161 DM82
Stockwell Pk Est, SW9 ..161 DM82
Stockwell Pk Rd, SW9 ..161 DM81
Sch Stockwell Pk SM Sch,
SW9 off Stockwell Pk Rd .161 DM81
Stockwell Pk Wk, SW9 ..161 DM83
Sch Stockwell Prim Sch,
SW9 off Stockwell Rd ..161 DM83
Stockwell Rd, SW9 ..161 DM82
Stockwells, Maid. (Taplow)
SL6 ..130 AD70
Stockwell St, SE10 ..163 EC79
Stockwell Ter, SW9 ..161 DM81
Stocton Cl, Guil. GU1 ..242 AW133
Stocton Rd, Guil. GU1 ..242 AW133
Stodart Rd, SE20 ..202 DW95
Stofield Gdns, SE9
off Aldersgrove Av ..184 EK90
Stoford Cl, SW19 ..179 CY87
Stoke Av, Ilf. IG6 ..104 EU51
Stoke Cl, Cob. (Stoke D'Ab.)
KT11 ..230 BZ116
Stoke Common Rd, Slou.
(Fulmer) SL3 ..112 AU63
Stoke Ct Dr, Slou. (Stoke P.)
SL2 ..132 AS67
STOKE D'ABERNON, Cob.
KT11 ..230 BZ116
Stoke Flds, Guil. GU1
off Stoke Rd ..258 AX135
Stoke Gdns, Slou. SL1 ..132 AS74
STOKE GREEN, Slou. SL2 ..132 AU70
Stoke Grn, Slou. (Stoke P.)
SL2 ..132 AU70
Stoke Gro, Guil. GU1
off Stoke Rd ..242 AX134
Sch Stoke Hill Co Prim Sch,
Guil. GU1 off Hazel Av .242 AW131
Stoke Ms, Guil. GU1
off Stoke Rd ..258 AX135
Stokenchurch St, SW6 ..160 DB81
STOKE NEWINGTON, N16 ..122 DS61
⇌ Stoke Newington ..122 DT61
Stoke Newington Ch St,
N16 ..122 DR62
Stoke Newington Common,
N16 ..122 DT62
Stoke Newington High St,
N16 ..122 DT62
Stoke Newington Rd, N16 ..5 N1
Sch Stoke Newington Sec
Sch, N16 off Clissold Rd .122 DR62
Stoke Pk Av, Slou.
(Farn.Royal) SL2 ..131 AQ69
Stoke Pl, NW10 ..139 CT69
STOKE POGES, Slou. SL2 ..132 AT66
Stoke Poges La, Slou. SL1,
SL2 ..132 AS72
Sch Stoke Poges Sch, Slou.
SL2 off Rogers La ..132 AT66
Stoke Rd, Cob. KT11 ..230 BW115
Guildford GU1 ..242 AX133
Kingston upon Thames
KT2 ..178 CQ94
Rainham RM13 ..148 FK68
Slough SL2 ..132 AT71
Walton-on-Thames KT12 .196 BW104
Stokers Cl, Gat. RH6 ..268 DE151
Stokesay, Slou. SL2 ..132 AT73
Stokesby Rd, Chess. KT9 ..216 CM107
Stokesheath Rd, Lthd.
(Oxshott) KT22 ..214 CC111
Stokesley Ri, H.Wyc.
(Woob.Grn) HP10 ..110 AE55
Stokesley St, W12 ..139 CT72
Stokes Ridings, Tad. KT20 ..233 CX123
Stokes Rd, E6 ..144 EL70
Croydon CR0 ..203 DX100
Stoke Wd, Slou. (Stoke P.)
SL2 ..112 AT63
Stoll Cl, NW2 ..119 CW62
Stompond La, Walt. KT12 ..195 BU103
Stomp Rd, Slou. (Burn.) SL1 .130 AJ71
Stonard Rd, N13 ..99 DN48
Dagenham RM8 ..126 EV64
Stonards Hill, Epp. CM16 ..70 EW31
Loughton IG10 ..85 EM44
Stondon Pk, SE23 ..183 DY87
Stondon Wk, E6 ..144 EK68
STONE, Green. DA9 ..189 FT85
Stonebank, Welw.G.C. AL8
off Stonehills ..29 CX08
Stonebanks, Walt. KT12 ..195 BU101
STONEBRIDGE, NW10 ..138 CP67
STONEBRIDGE, Dor. RH5 ..264 CL139
Stonebridge Common, E8 ..5 N6
Stonebridge Fld, Wind.
(Eton) SL4 ..151 AP78
Stonebridge Flds, Guil.
(Shalf.) GU4 ..258 AX141
⇌ Stonebridge Park ..138 CN66
⊖ Stonebridge Park ..138 CN66
Stonebridge Pk, NW10 ..138 CR66
Sch Stonebridge Prim Sch,
The, NW10
off Shakespeare Av ..138 CQ67
Stonebridge Rd, N15 ..122 DS57
Gravesend (Nthflt) DA11 .190 GA85
Stonebridge Way, Wem. HA9 .138 CP65
Stonebridge Wf, Guil.
(Shalf.) GU4 ..258 AX141
Stone Bldgs, WC2 ..10 B6
Stonechat Sq, E6
off Peridot St ..144 EL71
Stone Cl, SW4
off Larkhall Ri ..161 DJ82
Dagenham RM8 ..126 EZ61
West Drayton UB7 ..154 BM74
Sch Stone C of E Prim Sch,
Green. DA9 off Hayes Rd .189 FS87
Stonecot Cl, Sutt. SM3 ..199 CY102
Stonecot Hill, Sutt. SM3 ..199 CY102
Stonecourt Cl, Horl. RH6 ..269 DJ148
Stone Cres, Felt. TW14 ..175 BT87
Stonecroft Av, Iver SL0 ..133 BE72
Stonecroft Cl, Barn. EN5 ..79 CV42
Stonecroft Rd, Erith DA8 ..167 FC80
Stonecroft Way, Croy. CR0 ..201 DL101
Stonecrop Cl, NW9 ..118 CR55
Stonecrop Rd, Guil. GU4
off Chatfield Dr ..243 BC132
Stone Cross, Harl. CM20
off Post Office Rd ..35 ER14
Stonecross, St.Alb. AL1 ..43 CE19
Stonecross Cl, St.Alb. AL1
off Stonecross ..43 CE19
⇌ Stone Crossing ..189 FS85
Stonecross Rd, Hat. AL10 ..45 CV16
Stonecutter Ct, EC4
off Stonecutter St ..141 DP72
Stonecutter St, EC4 ..10 E7
Stonefield Cl, Bexh. DA7 ..166 FA83
Ruislip HA4 ..116 BY64
Stonefield St, N1 ..4 D7
Stonefield Way, SE7
off Greenbay Rd ..164 EK80
Ruislip HA4 ..116 BY63
Stonegate Cl, Orp. BR5
off Main Rd ..206 EW97
Stonegrove, Edg. HA8 ..96 CL49
Stonegrove Est, Edg. HA8 ..96 CM49
Stonegrove Gdns, Edg. HA8 .96 CM50
Stonehall Av, Ilf. IG1 ..124 EL58
Stone Hall Gdns, W8 ..17 J6
Stone Hall Pl, W8 ..17 J6
Stone Hall Rd, N21 ..99 DM45
Stoneham Rd, N11 ..99 DJ51
STONEHILL, Cher. KT16 ..210 AY107
Stonehill Cl, SW14 ..178 CR85
Leatherhead (Bkhm) KT23 .246 CA125
Stonehill Cres, Cher. (Ott.)
KT16 ..210 AY107
Stonehill Grn, Dart. DA2 ..187 FC94
Stonehill Rd, SW14 ..178 CQ85
W4 off Wellesley Rd ..158 CN78
Chertsey (Ott.) KT16 ..211 BA105
Woking (Chobham) GU24 .210 AW108
Stonehills, Welw.G.C. AL8 ..29 CX09
Stonehills Business Pk, N18
off Silvermere Dr ..101 DX51
Stonehills Ct, SE21 ..182 DS90
Stonehill Wds Pk, Sid.
DA14 ..187 FB93
Stonehorse Rd, Enf. EN3 ..82 DW43
Stone Ho Ct, EC3 ..11 L7
Stonehouse Gdns, Cat. CR3 .252 DS125
H Stone Ho Hosp, Dart.
DA2 ..188 FQ86
Stonehouse La, Purf. RM19 .169 FS79
Sevenoaks (Halst.) TN14 ..224 EX109
Stonehouse Rd, Sev. (Halst.)
TN14 ..224 EW110
Stoneings La, Sev. (Knock.)
TN14 ..239 ET118
Stone Lake Retail Pk, SE7 ..25 P8
Stonelea Rd, Hem.H. HP3 ..40 BM23
STONELEIGH, Epsom KT17 .217 CU106
⇌ Stoneleigh ..217 CU106
Stoneleigh Av, Enf. EN1 ..82 DV39
Worcester Park KT4 ..217 CU105
Stoneleigh Bdy, Epsom
KT17 ..217 CU106
Stoneleigh Cl, Wal.Cr. EN8 ..67 DX33
Stoneleigh Cres, Epsom
KT19 ..217 CT106
Stoneleigh Dr, Hodd. EN11 ..33 EB14
Stoneleigh Ms, E3
off Stanfield Rd ..143 DY68
Stoneleigh Pk, Wey. KT13 ..213 BQ106
Stoneleigh Pk Av, Croy.
CR0 ..203 DX100
Stoneleigh Pk Rd, Epsom
KT19 ..217 CT107
Stoneleigh Pl, W11 ..6 B10
Stoneleigh Rd, N17 ..122 DT55
Carshalton SM5 ..200 DE101
Ilford IG5 ..124 EL55
Oxted RH8 ..254 EL130
Stoneleigh St, W11 ..6 B9
Stoneleigh Ter, N19 ..121 DH61
Stonells Rd, SW11
off Chatham Rd ..180 DF85
Stonemasons Cl, N15 ..122 DR56
Stone Ness Rd, Grays RM20 .169 FV79
Stonenest St, N4 ..121 DM60
Stone Pk Av, Beck. BR3 ..203 EA98
Stone Pl, Wor.Pk. KT4 ..199 CU103
Stone Pl Rd, Green. DA9 ..189 FS85
Stone Rd, Brom. BR2 ..204 EF99
Stones All, Wat. WD18 ..75 BV42
Stones Cross Rd, Swan.
BR8 ..207 FC99
Stones End St, SE1 ..20 G4
Stones La, Dor. (Westc.) RH4 .262 CC137
Stones Rd, Epsom KT17 ..216 CS112
Stone St, Croy. CR0 ..219 DN106
Gravesend DA11 ..191 GH86
Stoneswood Rd, Oxt. RH8 ..254 EH130
Stonewall, E6 ..145 EN71
Stonewood, Dart. (Bean)
DA2 ..189 FW90
Stonewood Rd, Erith DA8 ..167 FE78
Stoney All, SE18 ..165 EN82
Stoneyard La, E14 ..14 A10
Stoney Br Rd, Wal.Abb. EN9 ..68 EG34
Stoney Brook, Guil. GU2 ..242 AS133
Stoney Cft, Couls. CR5 ..235 DJ122
Stoneycroft, Hem.H. HP1 ..40 BG20
Welwyn Garden City AL7 ..30 DA08
Stoneycroft Cl, SE12 ..184 EF87
Stoneycroft Rd, Wdf.Grn.
IG8 ..102 EL51
Stoneydeep, Tedd. TW11
off Twickenham Rd ..177 CG91
Stoneydown, E17 ..123 DY56
Stoneydown Av, E17 ..123 DY56
Sch Stoneydown Pk Prim Sch,
E17 off Pretoria Av ..123 DY56
Stoneyfield Rd, Couls. CR5 .235 DM117
Stoneyfields Gdns, Edg. HA8 .96 CQ49
Stoneyfields La, Edg. HA8 ..96 CQ50
Stoney Gro, Chesh. HP5 ..54 AR30
Stoneylands Ct, Egh. TW20 .173 AZ92
Stoneylands Rd, Egh. TW20 .173 AZ92
Stoney La, E1 ..11 M7
SE19 off Church Rd ..182 DT93
Hemel Hempstead HP1 ..39 BB23
Hemel Hempstead (Bov.)
HP3 ..57 BB27
Kings Langley (Chipper.)
WD4 ..57 BE30
Slough (E.Burn.) SL2 ..131 AN67
Stoney Meade, Slou. SL1
off Weekes Dr ..131 AP74
Stoney St, SE1 ..21 J1
Stonhouse St, SW4 ..161 DK83
Stony Cft, Ashtd. KT21 ..232 CM117
Stonycroft Cl, Enf. EN3
off Brimsdown Av ..83 DY40
Sch Stony Dean Sch, Amer.
HP7 off Orchard End Av ..72 AT39
Stony La, Amer. HP6 ..72 AY38
Stony Path, Loug. IG10 ..85 EM40
Stonyrock La, Dor. RH5 ..246 BY131
Stonyshotts, Wal.Abb. EN9 ..68 EE34
Stony Wd, Harl. CM18 ..51 ES16
Stoop Ct, W.Byf. KT14 ..212 BH112
Stopes St, SE15 ..162 DT80
Stopford Rd, E13 ..144 EG67
SE17 ..20 F10
Store Rd, E16 ..165 EN75
Storers Quay, E14 ..24 E8
Store St, E15 ..123 ED64
WC1 ..9 L6
Sch Storey Prim Sch, E16
off Woodman St ..145 EP74
Storey Rd, E17 ..123 DZ56
N6 ..120 DF58
Storey's Gate, SW1 ..19 M4
Storey St, E16 ..145 EN74
Hemel Hempstead HP3 ..40 BK24
Stories Ms, SE5 ..162 DS82
Stories Rd, SE5 ..162 DS83
Stork Rd, E7 ..144 EF65
Storksmead Rd, Edg. HA8 ..96 CS52
Storks Rd, SE16 ..22 B6
Sch Stormont Ho Spec Sch,
E5 off Downs Pk Rd ..122 DV63
Stormont Rd, N6 ..120 DF59
SW11 ..160 DG83
Sch Stormont Sch, Pot.B.
EN6 off The Causeway ..64 DD31
Stormont Way, Chess. KT9 .215 CJ106
Stormount Dr, Hayes UB3 ..155 BQ75
Stornaway Rd, Slou. SL3 ..153 BC77
Stornaway Strand, Grav.
DA12 ..191 GM91
Stornoway, Hem.H. HP3 ..41 BP22
Storr Gdns, Brwd. (Hutt.)
CM13 ..109 GD43
Storrington Rd, Croy. CR0 ..202 DT102
Stortford Rd, Hodd. EN11 ..49 EB16
Stort Mill, Harl. CM20 ..36 EV09
Stort Twr, Harl. CM20 ..35 ET13
Story St, N1 ..4 A6
Stothard Pl, EC2
off Bishopsgate ..142 DS71
Stothard St, E1 ..12 E3
Stott Cl, SW18 ..180 DD86
STOUGHTON, Guil. GU2 ..242 AV131
Stoughton Av, Sutt. SM3 ..217 CX106
Stoughton Cl, SE11 ..20 B8
SW15
off Bessborough Rd ..179 CU88
Sch Stoughton Gra Co Jun
Sch, Guil. GU2
off Grange Rd ..242 AV131
Sch Stoughton Inf Sch,
Guil. GU2
off Stoughton Rd ..242 AV131
Stoughton Rd, Guil. GU1,
GU2 ..242 AU131
Stour Av, Sthl. UB2 ..156 CA76
Stourcliffe St, W1 ..8 C8
Stour Cl, Kes. BR2 ..222 EJ105
Slough SL1 ..151 AP76
Stourhead Cl, SW19
off Castlecombe Dr ..179 CX87
Stourhead Gdns, SW20 ..199 CU97
Stour Rd, E3 ..143 EA66
Dagenham RM10 ..126 FA61
Dartford DA1 ..167 FG83
Grays RM16 ..171 GG78
Stourton Av, Felt. TW13 ..176 BZ91
Stour Way, Upmin. RM14 ..129 FS58
Stovell Rd, Wind. SL4 ..151 AP80
Stow, The, Harl. CM20 ..35 ET13
Stowage, SE8 ..163 EA79
Stow Cres, E17 ..101 DY52
Stowe Ct, Dart. DA2 ..188 FQ87
Stowe Cres, Ruis. HA4 ..115 BP58
Stowe Gdns, N9 ..100 DT46
Stowell Av, Croy.
(New Adgtn) CR0 ..221 ED110
Stowe Pl, N15 ..122 DS55
Stowe Rd, W12 ..159 CV75
Orpington BR6 ..224 EV105
Slough SL1 ..131 AL73
Coll Stowford Coll, Sutt. SM2
off Brighton Rd ..218 DC108
Stowting Rd, Orp. BR6 ..223 ES105
Stox Mead, Har. HA3 ..95 CD53
Stracey Rd, E7 ..124 EG63
NW10 ..138 CR67
Strachan Pl, SW19
off Woodhayes Rd ..179 CW93
Stradbroke Dr, Chig. IG7 ..103 EN51
Stradbroke Gro, Buck.H. IG9 .102 EK46
Ilford IG5 ..124 EL55
Stradbroke Pk, Chig. IG7 ..103 EP51
Stradbroke Rd, N5 ..122 DQ63
Stradbrook Cl, Har. HA2
off Stiven Cres ..116 BZ62
Stradella Rd, SE24 ..182 DQ86
Strafford Av, Ilf. IG5 ..103 EN54
Strafford Cl, Pot.B. EN6
off Strafford Gate ..64 DA32
Strafford Gate, Pot.B. EN6 ..64 DA32
Strafford Rd, W3 ..158 CQ75
Barnet EN5 ..79 CY41
Hounslow TW3 ..156 BZ83
Twickenham TW1 ..177 CG87
Strafford St, E14 ..23 N3
Strahan Rd, E3 ..13 K1
Straight, The, Sthl. UB1 ..156 BX75
Straight Bit, H.Wyc.
(Flack.Hth) HP10 ..110 AC55
Straight Rd, Rom. RM3 ..106 FJ52
Windsor (Old Wind.) SL4 .172 AU85
Straightsmouth, SE10 ..163 EC80
Strait Rd, E6 ..144 EL73
Straker's Rd, SE22 ..162 DV84
STRAND, WC2 ..9 N9
Strand, WC2 ..9 N10
Strand Cl, Epsom KT18 ..232 CR119
Strand Ct, SE18
off Strandfield Cl ..165 ES78
Strand Dr, Rich. TW9
off Bessant Dr ..158 CP80
Strandfield Cl, SE18 ..165 ES78
Strand La, WC2 ..10 B9
Strand on the Grn, W4 ..158 CN79
Sch Strand-on-the-Green
Inf & Nurs Sch, W4
off Thames Rd ..158 CN79
Sch Strand-on-the-Green
Jun Sch, W4
off Thames Rd ..158 CN79
Strand Pl, N18 ..100 DR49
Strand Sch App, W4
off Thames Rd ..158 CN79
Strangeways, Wat. WD17 ..75 BS36
Strangways Ter, W14 ..16 E6
Stranraer Gdns, Slou. SL1 ..132 AS74
Stranraer Rd, Houns.
(Hthrw Air.) TW6 ..174 BL86
Stranraer Way, N1 ..4 A6
Strasburg Rd, SW11 ..161 DH81
Stratfield Dr, Brox. EN10 ..49 DY19
Stratfield Pk Cl, N21 ..99 DP45
Stratfield Rd, Borwd. WD6 ..78 CN41
Slough SL1 ..152 AU75
STRATFORD, E15 ..143 EC65
⇌ Stratford ..143 EC65
⊖ Stratford ..143 EC66
DLR Stratford ..143 EC66
Stratford Av, W8 ..17 H6
Uxbridge UB10 ..134 BM68
Stratford Cen, The, E15 ..143 ED66
Stratford Cl, Bark. IG11 ..146 EU66
Dagenham RM10 ..147 FC66
Slough SL2 ..131 AK70
Stratford Ct, N.Mal. KT3
off Kingston Rd ..198 CR98
Stratford Dr, H.Wyc.
(Woob.Grn) HP10 ..110 AD59
Stratford Gro, SW15 ..159 CX84
Stratford Ho Av, Brom. BR1 .204 EL97
Stratford Pl, W1 ..8 G8
Stratford Rd, E13 ..144 EF67
NW4 ..119 CX56
W8 ..17 H7
Hayes UB4 ..135 BV70
Hounslow (Hthrw Air.) TW6 .175 BP86
Southall UB2 ..156 BY77
Thornton Heath CR7 ..201 DN98
Watford WD17 ..75 BU40
Sch Stratford Sch, E7
off Upton La ..144 EG66
Stratford Vil, NW1 ..141 DJ66
Stratford Way, Hem.H. HP3 ..40 BH23
St. Albans (Brick.Wd) AL2 .60 BZ29
Watford WD17 ..75 BT40
Strathan Cl, SW18 ..179 CY86
Strathaven Rd, SE12 ..184 EH86
Strathblaine Rd, SW11 ..160 DD84
Strathbrook Rd, SW16 ..181 DM94
Strathcona Av, Lthd. (Bkhm)
KT23 ..246 BY128
Strathcona Cl, H.Wyc.
(Flack.Hth) HP10 ..110 AC56
Strathcona Rd, Wem. HA9 ..117 CK61
Strathcona Way, H.Wyc.
(Flack.Hth) HP10 ..110 AC56
Strathdale, SW16 ..181 DM92
Strathdon Dr, SW17 ..180 DD90
Strathearn Av, Hayes UB3 ..155 BT80
Twickenham TW2 ..176 CB88
Strathearn Pl, W2 ..7 P9
Strathearn Rd, SW19 ..180 DA92
Sutton SM1 ..218 DA106
Stratheden Par, SE3
off Stratheden Rd ..164 EG80
Stratheden Rd, SE3 ..164 EG81
Strathfield Gdns, Bark. IG11 145 ER65
Strathleven Rd, SW2 ..181 DL85
Strathmore Cl, Cat. CR3 ..236 DS121
Strathmore Gdns, N3 ..98 DB53
W8 ..17 H1
Edgware HA8 ..96 CP54
Hornchurch RM12 ..127 FF60
Strathmore Rd, SW19 ..180 DA90
Croydon CR0 ..202 DQ101
Teddington TW11 ..177 CE91
Sch Strathmore Sch, Rich.
TW10 off Meadlands Dr .177 CK89
Strathnairn St, SE1 ..22 B8
Strathray Gdns, NW3 ..140 DE65
Strath Ter, SW11 ..160 DE84
Strathville Rd, SW18 ..180 DB89
Strathyre Av, SW16 ..201 DN97
Stratton Av, Enf. EN2 ..82 DR37
Wallington SM6 ..219 DK109
Stratton Chase Dr, Ch.St.G.
HP8 ..90 AU47
Stratton Cl, SW19 ..200 DA96
Bexleyheath DA7 ..166 EY83
Edgware HA8 ..96 CM51
Hounslow TW3 ..156 BZ81
Walton-on-Thames KT12
off St. Johns Dr ..196 BW102
Strattondale St, E14 ..24 C5
Stratton Dr, Bark. IG11 ..125 ET64
Stratton Gdns, Sthl. UB1 ..136 BZ72
Stratton Rd, SW19 ..200 DA96
Beaconsfield HP9 ..88 AH53
Bexleyheath DA7 ..166 EY83
Romford RM3 ..106 FN50
Sunbury-on-Thames TW16 .195 BT96
Stratton St, W1 ..19 H1
Stratton Ter, West. TN16
off High St ..255 EQ127
Stratton Wk, Rom. RM3 ..106 FN50
Strauss Rd, W4 ..158 CR75
Strawberry Fld, Hat. AL10 ..45 CU21
Strawberry Flds, Swan. BR8 .207 FE95
Ware SG12 ..32 DV05
STRAWBERRY HILL, Twick.
TW1 ..177 CE90
⇌ Strawberry Hill ..177 CE90
Strawberry Hill, Twick. TW1 .177 CF90
Strawberry Hill Cl, Twick.
TW1 ..177 CF90
Strawberry Hill Rd, Twick.
TW1 ..177 CF90
Strawberry La, Cars. SM5 ..200 DF104
Strawberry Vale, N2 ..98 DD53
Twickenham TW1 ..177 CG90
Straw Cl, Cat. CR3 ..236 DQ123
Strawfields, Welw.G.C. AL7 ..30 DB08
Strawmead, Hat. AL10
off Cob Mead ..45 CV16
Strawson Ct, Horl. RH6
off Charlesfield Rd ..268 DF147
Strayfield Rd, Enf. EN2 ..81 DP37
Streakes Fld Rd, NW2 ..119 CU61
Stream Cl, W.Byf. (Byfleet)
KT14 ..212 BK112
Streamdale, SE2 ..166 EU79
Stream La, Edg. HA8 ..96 CP50
Streamline Ms, SE22 ..182 DU88
Streamside, Slou. SL1
off Warner Cl ..131 AL74
Streamside Cl, N9 ..100 DT46
Bromley BR2 ..204 EG98
Streamway, Belv. DA17 ..166 FA79
Sch Stream Wds JMI Sch,
Hat. AL10 off Woods Av ..45 CV19
Streatfield Av, E6 ..145 EM67
Streatfield Rd, Har. HA3 ..117 CK55
STREATHAM, SW16 ..181 DL91
⇌ Streatham ..181 DL92
Coll Streatham & Tooting
Adult Ed Inst, Tooting
Health Clinic, SW17
off Bevill Allen Cl ..180 DF93
Streatham Cl, SW16 ..181 DL89
⇌ Streatham Common ..181 DK94
Streatham Common N,
SW16 ..181 DL92
Streatham Common S,
SW16 ..181 DL93
Streatham Ct, SW16 ..181 DL90
Streatham High Rd, SW16 ..181 DL92
STREATHAM HILL, SW2 ..181 DM87
⇌ Streatham Hill ..181 DL89
Streatham Hill, SW2 ..181 DL89
Sch Streatham Hill &
Clapham High Sch, SW16
off Abbotswood Rd ..181 DK90
Sch Streatham Hill &
Clapham High Sch
Jun, SW2
off Wavertree Rd ..181 DM88
STREATHAM PARK, SW16 ..181 DJ91
Streatham Pl, SW2 ..181 DL87
Streatham Rd, SW16 ..200 DG95
Mitcham CR4 ..200 DG95
Streatham St, WC1 ..9 M7
STREATHAM VALE, SW16 ..181 DK94
Streatham Vale, SW16 ..181 DJ94
Sch Streatham Wells Prim
Sch, SW2 off Palace Rd .181 DN89
Streathbourne Rd, SW17 ..180 DG89
Streatley Pl, NW3
off New End Sq ..120 DC63
Streatley Rd, NW6 ..139 CZ66
Street, The, Ashtd. KT21 ..232 CL119
Betchworth RH3 ..264 CS135
Bishop's Stortford
(Sheering) CM22 ..37 FC07
Dartford (Hort.Kir.) DA4 ..208 FP98
Guildford (Albury) GU5 ..260 BH139
Guildford (E.Clan.) GU4 ..244 BK131
Guildford (Shalf.) GU4 ..258 AY139
Guildford (W.Clan.) GU4 ..244 BH131
Guildford (Won.) GU5 ..259 BA144
Kings Langley (Chipper.)
WD4 ..58 BG31
Leatherhead (Eff.) KT24 ..246 BX127
Leatherhead (Fetch.)
KT22 ..231 CD122
Leatherhead (W.Hors.)
KT24 ..245 BP129
Sch Streete Ct Sch, Gdse.
RH9 off Rooks Nest ..253 DY130
Streeters La, Wall. SM6 ..201 DK104
Streetfield Ms, SE3 ..164 EG83
Streimer Rd, E15 ..143 EC68
Strelley Way, W3 ..138 CS73
Stretton Mans, SE8 ..23 P10
Stretton Pl, Amer. HP6 ..72 AT38
Stretton Rd, Croy. CR0 ..202 DS101
Richmond TW10 ..177 CJ89
Stretton Way, Borwd. WD6 ..78 CL38
Strickland Av, Dart. DA1 ..168 FL83
Strickland Row, SW18 ..180 DD87
Strickland St, SE8 ..163 EA82
Strickland Way, Orp. BR6 ..223 ET105
Stride Rd, E13 ..144 EF68
Strides Ct, Cher. KT16
off Brox Rd ..211 BC107
Strimon Cl, N9 ..100 DW47
Stringers Av, Guil. GU4 ..242 AX128
Stringer's Common, Guil.
GU1 ..242 AW129
Stringhams Copse, Wok.
(Ripley) GU23 ..227 BF124
Stripling Way, Wat. WD18 ..75 BU44
Strode Cl, N10
off Pembroke Rd ..98 DG52
Strode Rd, E7 ..124 EG63
N17 ..100 DS54
NW10 ..139 CU65
SW6 ..159 CX80
Sch Strodes Coll, Egh. TW20
off High St ..173 AZ92
Strodes Coll La, Egh. TW20 .173 AZ92
Strodes Cres, Stai. TW18 ..174 BJ92
Strode St, Egh. TW20 ..173 BA91
Stroma Cl, Hem.H. HP3 ..41 BQ22
Stroma Ct, Slou. SL1
off Lincoln Way ..131 AK73
Strone Rd, E7 ..144 EJ65
E12 ..144 EK65
Strone Way, Hayes UB4 ..136 BY70
Strongbow Cres, SE9 ..185 EM85
Strongbow Rd, SE9 ..185 EM85

Strongbridge Cl, Har. HA2 116 CA60
Stronsa Rd, W12 159 CT75
Stronsay Cl, Hem.H. HP3
off Northend 41 BQ22
Strood Av, Rom. RM7 127 FD60
STROOD GREEN, Bet. RH3 264 CP138
Stroud Cl, Wind. SL4 151 AK83
Stroud Cres, SW15 179 CU90
STROUDE, Vir.W. GU25 193 AZ96
Stroude Rd, Egh. TW20 173 BA93
Virginia Water GU25 192 AY98
Stroudes Cl, Wor.Pk. KT4 198 CS101
Stroud Fld, Nthlt. UB5 136 BY65
Stroud Gate, Har. HA2 116 CB63
STROUD GREEN, N4 121 DM58
Stroud Grn Gdns, Croy. CR0 202 DW101
Sch Stroud Grn Prim Sch, N4
off Woodstock Rd 121 DN60
Stroud Grn Rd, N4 121 DM60
Stroud Grn Way, Croy. CR0 202 DV101
Stroudley Wk, E3 14 A1
Stroud Rd, SE25 202 DU100
SW19 180 DA90
Strouds Cl, Rom. (Chad.Hth)
RM6 126 EV57
Stroudwater Pk, Wey. KT13 213 BP107
Stroud Way, Ashf. TW15
off Courtfield Rd 175 BP93
Strouts Pl, E2 11 N1
Struan Gdns, Wok. GU21 226 AY115
Strutton Grd, SW1 19 L5
Struttons Av, Grav. (Nthflt)
DA11 191 GF89
Strype St, E1 11 N6
Stuart Av, NW9 119 CU59
W5 138 CM74
Bromley BR2 204 EG102
Harrow HA2 116 BZ62
Walton-on-Thames KT12 195 BV102
Stuart Cl, Brwd. (Pilg.Hat.)
CM15 108 FV43
Swanley BR8 187 FF94
Uxbridge UB10 134 BN65
Windsor SL4 151 AM82
Stuart Ct, Borwd. (Elstree)
WD6 off High St 77 CK44
Stuart Cres, N22 99 DM53
Croydon CR0 203 DZ104
Hayes UB3 135 BQ72
Reigate RH2 266 DA137
Stuart Evans Cl, Well. DA16 166 EW83
Stuart Gro, Tedd. TW11 177 CE92
Stuart Mantle Way, Erith
DA8 167 FD80
Stuart Pl, Mitch. CR4 200 DF95
Stuart Rd, NW6 6 G2
SE15 162 DW84
SW19 180 DA90
W3 138 CQ74
Barking IG11 145 ET66
Barnet EN4 98 DE45
Gravesend DA11 191 GG86
Grays RM17 170 GB78
Harrow HA3 95 CF54
Reigate RH2 266 DA137
Richmond TW10 177 CH89
Thornton Heath CR7 202 DQ98
Warlingham CR6 236 DV120
Welling DA16 166 EV81
Stuarts Cl, Hem.H. HP3
off Marriotts Way 40 BK22
Stuart Twr, W9 7 L2
Stuart Way, Stai. TW18 174 BH93
Virginia Water GU25 192 AU97
Waltham Cross (Chsht)
EN7 66 DV31
Windsor SL4 151 AL82
Stubbers La, Upmin. RM14 149 FR65
Stubbins Hall La, Wal.Abb.
EN9 67 EB28
Stubbs Cl, NW9 118 CQ57
Stubbs Dr, SE16 22 C9
Stubbs End Cl, Amer. HP6 55 AS37
Stubbs Hill, Sev. (Knock.)
TN14 224 EW113
Stubbs La, Tad. (Lwr Kgswd)
KT20 249 CZ128
Stubbs Ms, Dag. RM8
off Marlborough Rd 126 EV63
Stubbs Pt, E13 15 N4
Stubbs Way, SW19
off Brangwyn Cres 200 DD95
Stubbs Wd, Amer. HP6 55 AS36
Stubs Cl, Dor. RH4
off Stubs Hill 263 CJ138
Stubs Hill, Dor. RH4 263 CJ138
Stucley Pl, NW1
off Hawley Cres 141 DH66
Stucley Rd, Houns. TW5 156 CC80
Studdridge St, SW6 160 DA82
Studd St, N1 4 E7
Stud Grn, Wat. WD25 59 BV32
Studholme Ct, NW3 120 DA63
Studholme St, SE15 162 DV80
Studio Pl, SW1 18 D4
Studios, The, Bushey WD23 76 CA44
Studios Rd, Shep. TW17 194 BM97
Studio Way, Borwd. WD6 78 CQ40
Studland, SE17 21 J9
Studland Cl, Sid. DA15 185 ET90
Studland Rd, SE26 183 DX92
W7 137 CD72
Kingston upon Thames
KT2 178 CL93
West Byfleet (Byfleet)
KT14 212 BM113
Studland St, W6 159 CV77
Studley Av, E4 101 ED52
Studley Cl, E5 123 DY64
Studley Ct, Sid. DA14 186 EV92
Studley Dr, Ilf. IG4 124 EK58
Studley Est, SW4 161 DL81
Studley Gra Rd, W7 157 CE75
Studley Rd, E7 144 EH65
SW4 161 DL81
Dagenham RM9 146 EX66
Sch Study Prep Sch, The,
Spencer Ho, SW19
off Peek Cres 179 CX92
Wilberforce Ho, SW19
off Camp Rd 179 CW92
Sch Study Sch, The, N.Mal.
KT3 off Thetford Rd 198 CS99
Stukeley Rd, E7 144 EH66
Stukeley St, WC2 9 P7
Stump Rd, Epp. CM16 70 EW27
Stumps Hill La, Beck. BR3 183 EA93
Stumps La, Whyt. CR3 236 DS117
Stumpwell La, H.Wyc.
(Penn) HP10 88 AD48
Sturdy Rd, SE15 162 DV82
Sturge Av, E17 101 EB54
Sturgeon Rd, SE17 20 G10
Sturges Fld, Chis. BR7 185 ER93
Sturgess Av, NW4 119 CV59
Sturge St, SE1 20 G3
Sturla Cl, Hert. SG14
off Millmead Way 31 DP08
Sturlas Way, Wal.Cr. EN8 67 DX33
Sturmer Cl, St.Alb. AL4 43 CJ21
Sturmer Way, N7 4 A1
Sturminster Cl, Hayes UB4 136 BW72
Sturrock Cl, N15 122 DR56
Sturry St, E14 14 B8
Sturt Ct, Guil. GU4 243 BB132
Sturts La, Tad. KT20 249 CT127
Sturt St, N1 5 H10
Stutfield St, E1 12 B8
Stychens Cl, Red. (Bletch.)
RH1 252 DQ133
Stychens La, Red. (Bletch.)
RH1 252 DQ132
Stylecroft Rd, Ch.St.G. HP8 90 AX47
Styles End, Lthd. (Bkhm)
KT23 246 CB127
Styles Gdns, SW9 161 DP83
Styles Way, Beck. BR3 203 EC98
Styventon Pl, Cher. KT16 193 BF101
Subrosa Dr, Red. RH1 251 DH130
Succombs Hill, Warl. CR6 236 DV120
Whyteleafe CR3 236 DV120
Succombs Pl, Warl. CR6 236 DV120
Sch Sudbourne Prim Sch,
SW2 off Hayter Rd 181 DM85
Sudbourne Rd, SW2 181 DL85
Sudbrooke Rd, SW12 180 DF86
Sudbrook Gdns, Rich. TW10 177 CK90
Sudbrook La, Rich. TW10 178 CL88
SUDBURY, Wem. HA0 117 CG64
Sudbury, E6
off Newark Knok 145 EN72
⇌ Sudbury & Harrow Road 117 CH64
Sudbury Av, Wem. HA0 117 CK62
Sudbury Ct Dr, Har. HA1 117 CF62
Sudbury Ct Rd, Har. HA1 117 CF62
Sudbury Cres, Brom. BR1 184 EG93
Wembley HA0 117 CH64
Sudbury Cft, Wem. HA0 117 CF63
Sudbury Gdns, Croy. CR0 220 DS105
Sudbury Hts Av, Grnf. UB6 117 CF64
⊖ Sudbury Hill 117 CE63
Sudbury Hill, Har. HA1 117 CE61
Sudbury Hill Cl, Wem. HA0 117 CF63
⇌ Sudbury Hill Harrow 117 CE63
Sudbury Ho, SW18
off Wandsworth High St 180 DB85
Sch Sudbury Prim Sch, Wem.
HA0 off Watford Rd 117 CH63
Sudbury Rd, Bark. IG11 125 ET64
⊖ Sudbury Town 137 CH65
Sudeley St, N1 4 F10
Sudicamps Ct, Wal.Abb. EN9 68 EG33
Sudlow Rd, SW18 160 DA84
Sudrey St, SE1 20 G4
Suez Av, Grnf. UB6 137 CF68
Suez Rd, Enf. EN3 83 DY42
Suffield Cl, S.Croy. CR2 221 DX112
Suffield Rd, E4 101 EB48
N15 122 DT57
SE20 202 DW96
Suffolk Cl, Borwd. WD6
off Clydesdale Cl 78 CR43
Horley RH6 268 DG149
St. Albans (Lon.Col.) AL2 61 CJ25
Slough SL1 131 AL72
Suffolk Ct, E10 123 EA59
Ilford IG3 125 ES58
Suffolk Dr, Guil. GU4 243 BB129
Suffolk La, EC4 11 J9
Suffolk Pk Rd, E17 123 DY56
Suffolk Pl, SW1 19 M1
Suffolk Rd, E13 15 K2
N15 122 DR58
NW10 138 CS66
SE25 202 DT98
SW13 159 CT80
Barking IG11 145 ER66
Dagenham RM10 127 FC64
Dartford DA1 188 FL86
Enfield EN3 82 DV43
Gravesend DA12 191 GK86
Harrow HA2 116 BZ58
Ilford IG3 125 ES58
Potters Bar EN6 63 CY32
Sidcup DA14 186 EW93
Worcester Park KT4 199 CT103
Sch Suffolks Prim Sch, Enf.
EN1 off Brick La 82 DV40
Suffolk St, E7 124 EG64
SW1 19 M1
Suffolk Way, Horn. RM11 128 FN56
Sevenoaks TN13 257 FJ125
Sugar Bakers Ct, EC3
off Creechurch La 142 DS72
Sugar Ho La, E15 143 EC68
Sugar La, Berk. HP4 39 AZ22
Hemel Hempstead HP1 39 BB22
Sugar Loaf Wk, E2 12 E1
Sugar Quay Wk, EC3 11 M10
Sugden Rd, SW11 160 DG83
Thames Ditton KT7 197 CH102
Sugden Way, Bark. IG11 145 ET68
Sulgrave Gdns, W6
off Sulgrave Rd 159 CW75
Sulgrave Rd, W6 159 CW75
Sulina Rd, SW2 181 DL87
Sulivan Ct, SW6 160 DA83
Sch Sulivan Prim Sch, SW6
off Peterborough Rd 160 DA82
Sulivan Rd, SW6 160 DA83
Sullivan Av, E16 144 EK71
Sullivan Cl, SW11 160 DE83
Dartford DA1 187 FH86
Hayes UB4 136 BW71
West Molesey KT8
off Victoria Av 196 CA97
Sullivan Cres, Uxb. (Hare.)
UB9 92 BK54
Sullivan Rd, SE11 20 D7
Tilbury RM18 171 GG81
Sullivans Reach, Walt. KT12 195 BT101
Sullivan Way, Borwd.
(Elstree) WD6 77 CJ44
Sultan Rd, E11 124 EH56
Sultan St, SE5 162 DQ80
Beckenham BR3 203 DX96
Sultan Ter, N22
off Vincent Rd 99 DN54
Sumatra Rd, NW6 120 DA64
Sumburgh Rd, SW12 180 DG86
Sumburgh Way, Slou. SL1 132 AS71
Summer Av, E.Mol. KT8 197 CE99
Summer Ct, Hem.H. HP2
off Townsend 40 BK18
Summercourt Rd, E1 12 F7
Summerdale, Welw.G.C.
AL8 29 CX05
Summerene Cl, SW16 181 DJ94
Summerfield, Ashtd. KT21 231 CK119
Hatfield AL10 45 CU21
Summerfield Av, NW6 139 CY68
Summerfield Cl, Add. KT15
off Spinney Hill 211 BF106
St. Albans (Lon.Col.) AL2 61 CJ26
Summerfield La, Surb. KT6 197 CK103
Summerfield Pl, Cher. (Ott.)
KT16 off Crawshaw Rd 211 BD107
Summerfield Rd, W5 137 CH70
Loughton IG10 84 EK44
Watford WD25 75 BU35
Summerfields Av, N12 98 DE51
Summerfield St, SE12 184 EF87
Summer Gdns, E.Mol. KT8 197 CE99
Summer Gro, Borwd.
(Elstree) WD6 77 CK44
Summerhayes Cl, Wok.
GU21 210 AY114
Summerhays, Cob. KT11 214 BX113
Summer Hill, Borwd.
(Elstree) WD6 78 CN43
Chislehurst BR7 205 EN96
Summerhill Cl, Orp. BR6 205 ES104
Summerhill Ct, St.Alb. AL1 43 CF19
Summerhill Gro, Enf. EN1 82 DS44
Summerhill Rd, N15 122 DR56
Dartford DA1 188 FK87
Summer Hill Vil, Chis. BR7 205 EN95
Summerhill Way, Mitch. CR4 200 DG95
Summerhouse Av, Houns.
TW5 156 BY81
Summerhouse Dr, Bex. DA5 187 FD91
Dartford DA2 187 FD91
Summerhouse La, Uxb.
(Hare.) UB9 92 BG52
Watford (Ald.) WD25 76 CC40
West Drayton UB7 154 BK79
Summerhouse Rd, N16 122 DS61
Summerhouse Way, Abb.L.
WD5 59 BT30
Summerland Gdns, N10 121 DH55
Summerlands Av, W3 138 CQ73
Summerlands Rd, St.Alb.
AL4 43 CJ16
Summerlay Cl, Tad. KT20 233 CY120
Summerlea, Slou. SL1 131 AP74
Summerlee Av, N2 120 DF56
Summerlee Gdns, N2 120 DF56
Summerley St, SW18 180 DB89
Summerly Av, Reig. RH2
off Burnham Dr 250 DA133
Summer Rd, E.Mol. KT8 197 CE99
Thames Ditton KT7 197 CF99
Summersbury Dr, Guil.
(Shalf.) GU4 258 AY142
Summersby Rd, N6 121 DH58
Summers Cl, Sutt. SM2
off Overton Rd 218 DA108
Wembley HA9 118 CP60
Weybridge KT13 212 BN111
Sch Summerside JMI Sch,
N12 off Crossway 98 DD51
Summerskille Cl, N9
off Plevna Rd 100 DV47
Summers La, N12 98 DD52
Summers Rd, Gdmg. GU7 258 AT144
Slough (Burn.) SL1 130 AJ69
Summers Row, N12 98 DE51
SUMMERSTOWN, SW17 180 DB90
Summerstown, SW17 180 DC90
Summer St, EC1 10 C4
Summerswood Cl, Ken.
CR8 off Longwood Rd 236 DR116
Summerswood La, Borwd.
WD6 62 CS34
Sch Summerswood Prim
Sch, Borwd. WD6
off Furzehill Rd 78 CP42
Summerton Way, SE28 146 EX72
Summer Trees, Sun. TW16
off The Avenue 195 BV95
Summerville Gdns, Sutt.
SM1 217 CZ107
Summerwood Rd, Islw. TW7 177 CF85
Summit, The, Loug. IG10 85 EM39
Summit Av, NW9 118 CR57
Summit Cl, N14 99 DJ47
NW9 118 CR56
Edgware HA8 96 CN52
Summit Ct, NW2 119 CY64
Summit Dr, Wdf.Grn. IG8 102 EK54
Summit Est, N16 122 DU59
Summit Pl, Wey. KT13
off Caenshill Rd 212 BN108
Summit Rd, E17 123 EB56
Northolt UB5 136 CA66
Potters Bar EN6 63 CY30
Summit Way, N14 99 DH47
SE19 182 DS94
Sumner Av, SE15
off Peckham Rd 162 DT81
Sumner Cl, Lthd. (Fetch.)
KT22 231 CD124
Orpington BR6 223 EQ105
Sumner Est, SE15 162 DT80
Sumner Gdns, Croy. CR0 201 DN102
Sumner Pl, SW7 17 P8
Addlestone KT15 212 BG106
Sumner Pl Ms, SW7 17 P8
Sumner Rd, SE15 162 DT80
Croydon CR0 201 DN102
Harrow HA1 116 CC59
Sumner Rd S, Croy. CR0 201 DN102
SUMNERS, Harl. CM19 51 EN19
Sch Sumners Co Prim Sch, Harl.
CM19 off Broadley Rd 51 EN19
Sumners Fm Cl, Harl. CM19 51 EN20
Sumner St, SE1 20 F1
Sumpter Cl, NW3 140 DC65
Sumpter Yd, St.Alb. AL1 43 CD20
Sun All, Rich. TW9 off Kew Rd 158 CL84
Sunbeam Cres, W10 139 CW70
Sunbeam Rd, NW10 138 CQ70
SUNBURY, Sun. TW16 213 BV107
⇌ Sunbury 195 BT95
Sunbury Av, NW7 96 CR50
SW14 158 CR84
Sunbury Cl, Walt. KT12 195 BU100
Sunbury Ct, Sun. TW16 196 BX96
Sunbury Ct Island, Sun.
TW16 196 BX97
Sunbury Ct Ms, Sun. TW16
off Lower Hampton Rd 196 BX96
Sunbury Ct Rd, Sun. TW16 196 BW96
Sunbury Cres, Felt. TW13
off Ryland Cl 175 BT91
Sunbury Cross Cen, Sun.
TW16 175 BT94
Sunbury Gdns, NW7 96 CR50
Sunbury La, SW11 160 DD81
Walton-on-Thames KT12 195 BU100
Sunbury Lock Ait, Walt.
KT12 195 BV98
Sch Sunbury Manor Sch,
Sun. TW16
off Nursery Rd 195 BT95
Sunbury Rd, Felt. TW13 175 BT90
Sutton SM3 199 CX104
Windsor (Eton) SL4 151 AR79
Sunbury St, SE18 165 EM76
Coll Sunbury Training Cen
(Met Pol), Sun. TW16
off Thames St 195 BU98
Sunbury Way, Felt. TW13 176 BW92
Sun Ct, EC3 11 K8
Erith DA8 167 FF82
Suncroft Pl, SE26 182 DW90
Sundale Av, S.Croy. CR2 220 DW110
Sunderland Av, St.Alb. AL1 43 CG18
Sunderland Ct, SE22 182 DU87
Sunderland Gro, Wat.
(Lvsdn) WD25 59 BT34
Sunderland Mt, SE23
off Sunderland Rd 183 DX89
Sunderland Rd, SE23 183 DX88
W5 157 CK76
Sunderland Ter, W2 7 J7
Sunderland Way, E12 124 EK61
Sundew Av, W12 139 CU73
Sundew Ct, Grays RM17
off Salix Rd 170 GD79
Sundew Rd, Hem.H. HP1 39 BE21
Sundial Av, SE25 202 DT97
Sundon Cres, Vir.W. GU25 192 AV99
Sundorne Rd, SE7 164 EH78
Sundown Av, S.Croy. CR2 220 DT111
Sundown Rd, Ashf. TW15 175 BQ92
Sundra Wk, E1 12 G4
SUNDRIDGE, Brom. BR1 184 EJ93
SUNDRIDGE, Sev. TN14 240 EZ124
Sundridge Av, Brom. BR1 204 EK95
Chislehurst BR7 184 EK94
Welling DA16 165 ER82
Sundridge Cl, Dart. DA1 188 FN86
Sundridge Ho, Brom. BR1
off Burnt Ash La 184 EH92
Sundridge La, Sev. (Knock.)
TN14 240 EV117
⇌ Sundridge Park 184 EH94
Sundridge Pl, Croy. CR0
off Inglis Rd 202 DU102
Sundridge Rd, Croy. CR0 202 DT101
Sevenoaks (Dunt.Grn)
TN14 240 FA120
Woking GU22 227 BA119
Sunfields Pl, SE3 164 EH80
Sunflower Way, Rom. RM3 106 FK53
Sun Hill, Long. (Fawk.Grn)
DA3 209 FU104
Woking GU22 226 AU121
Sunken Rd, Croy. CR0 220 DW106
Sunkist Way, Wall. SM6 219 DL109
Sunland Av, Bexh. DA6 166 EY84
Sun La, SE3 164 EH80
Gravesend DA12 191 GJ89
Sunleigh Rd, Wem. HA0 138 CL67
Sunley Gdns, Grnf. UB6 137 CG67
Sunlight Cl, SW19 180 DC93
Sunlight Sq, E2 12 D2
Sunmead Cl, Lthd. (Fetch.)
KT22 231 CF122
Sunmead Rd, Hem.H. HP2 40 BK18
Sunbury-on-Thames TW16 195 BU97
Sunna Gdns, Sun. TW16 195 BV96
Sunningdale, N14
off Wilmer Way 99 DK50
Sunningdale Av, W3 138 CS73
Barking IG11 145 ER67
Feltham TW13 176 BY89
Rainham RM13 147 FH70
Ruislip HA4 116 BW60
Sunningdale Cl, E6 145 EM69
SE16 22 C10
SE28 146 EY72
Stanmore HA7 95 CG52
Surbiton KT6
off Culsac Rd 198 CL103
Sunningdale Gdns, NW9 118 CQ57
W8 17 H6
Sunningdale Ms, Welw.G.C.
AL7 29 CY05
Sunningdale Rd, Brom. BR1 204 EL98
Rainham RM13 147 FG66
Sutton SM1 217 CZ105
Sunningfields Cres, NW4 97 CV54
Sunningfields Rd, NW4 97 CV54
Sunning Hill, Grav. (Nthflt)
DA11 190 GE89
Sunninghill Rd, SE13 163 EB82
Sunnings La, Upmin. RM14 148 FQ65
Sunningvale Av, West.
(Bigg.H.) TN16 238 EJ115
Sunningvale Cl, West.
(Bigg.H.) TN16 238 EK116
Sunny Bk, SE25 202 DU97
Sunnybank, Epsom KT18 232 CQ116
Sunny Bk, Warl. CR6 237 DY117
Sch Sunny Bk Prim Sch, Pot.B.
EN6 off Field Vw Rd 64 DA34
Sunnybank Rd, Pot.B. EN6 64 DA33
Sunnybank Vil, Red. RH1 252 DT132
Sunny Cres, NW10 138 CQ66
Sunny Cft, Harl. CM18 51 ET18
Sunnycroft Gdns, Upmin.
RM14 129 FT59
Sunnycroft Rd, SE25 202 DU97
Hounslow TW3 156 CB82
Southall UB1 136 CA71
Sunnydale, Orp. BR6 205 EN103
Sunnydale Gdns, NW7 96 CR51
Sunnydale Rd, SE12 184 EH85
Sunnydell, St.Alb. AL2 60 CB26
Sunnydene Av, E4 101 ED50
Ruislip HA4 115 BU61
Sunnydene Cl, Rom. RM3 106 FM52
Sunnydene Gdns, Wem.HA0 137 CJ65
Sunnydene Rd, Pur. CR8 219 DP113
Sunnydene St, SE26 183 DY91
Sch Sunnydown Sch, Cat.
CR3 off Whyteleafe Rd 236 DT121
Sunnyfield, NW7 97 CT49
Hatfield AL9 45 CX15
Sunnyfield Rd, Chis. BR7 206 EU97
Sch Sunnyfields Prim Sch,
NW4 off Hatchcroft 119 CV55
Sunny Gdns Par, NW4
off Great N Way 97 CW54
Sunny Gdns Rd, NW4 97 CV54
Sunny Hill, NW4 119 CV55
Sunnyhill Cl, E5 123 DY63
Sch Sunnyhill Prim Sch,
SW16 off Sunnyhill Rd 181 DM91
Sunnyhill Rd, SW16 181 DL91
Hemel Hempstead HP1 40 BH20
Rickmansworth (Map.Cr.)
WD3 91 BD51
Sunnyhurst Cl, Sutt. SM1 200 DA104
Sunnymead Av, Mitch. CR4 201 DJ97
Sunnymead Rd, NW9 118 CR59
SW15 179 CV85
SUNNYMEADS, Stai. TW19 152 AY84
⇌ Sunnymeads 152 AY83
Sunnymede, Chig. IG7 104 EV48
Sunnymede Av, Cars. SM5 218 DD111
Chesham HP5 54 AS28
Epsom KT19 216 CS109
Sunnymede Dr, Ilf. IG6 125 EP56
Sunny Ms, Rom. RM5 105 FC52
Sunny Nook Gdns, S.Croy.
CR2 220 DR107
Sunny Ri, Cat. CR3 236 DR124
Sunny Rd, The, Enf. EN3 83 DX39
Sunnyside, NW2 119 CZ62
SW19 179 CY93
Waltham Abbey EN9 50 EF22
Walton-on-Thames KT12 196 BW99
Sunnyside Cotts, Chesh. HP5 56 AU26
Sunnyside Dr, E4 101 EC45
Sunnyside Gdns, Upmin.
RM14 128 FQ61
Sunnyside Pas, SW19 179 CY93
Sunnyside Pl, SW19
off Sunnyside 179 CY93
Sunnyside Rd, E10 123 EA60
N19 121 DK59
W5 137 CK74
Chesham HP5 54 AP30
Epping CM16 69 ET32
Ilford IG1 125 EQ62
Teddington TW11 177 CD91
Sunnyside Rd E, N9 100 DU48
Sunnyside Rd N, N9 100 DT48
Sunnyside Rd S, N9 100 DT48
Sunnyside Ter, NW9
off Edgware Rd 118 CR55
Sunny Vw, NW9 118 CR57
Sunny Way, N12 98 DE52
Sun Pas, SE16 22 A5
Windsor SL4
off Bachelors Acre 151 AR81
Sunray Av, SE24 162 DR84
Brentwood (Hutt.) CM13 109 GE44
Bromley BR2 204 EL100
Surbiton KT5 198 CP103
West Drayton UB7 154 BK75
Sunrise Av, Horn. RM12 128 FJ62
Sunrise Cl, Felt. TW13
off Exeter Rd 176 BZ90
Sunrise Cres, Hem.H. HP3 40 BL23
Sun Rd, W14 16 E10
Swanscombe DA10 190 FZ86
Sunset Av, E4 101 EB46
Woodford Green IG8 102 EF49
Sunset Cl, Erith DA8 167 FH81
Sunset Ct, Wdf.Grn. IG8
off Navestock Cres 102 EJ52
Sunset Dr, Rom.
(Hav.at.Bow.) RM4 105 FH50
Sunset Gdns, SE25 202 DT96
Sunset Ms, Rom. RM5 105 FC51
Sunset Rd, SE5 162 DQ84
SE28 166 EU75
Sunset Vw, Barn. EN5 79 CY40
Sunshine Way, Mitch. CR4 200 DF96
Sun Sq, Hem.H. HP1
off High St 40 BK19
Sunstone Gro, Red. RH1 251 DL129
Sun St, EC2 11 L6
Sawbridgeworth CM21 36 EZ06
Waltham Abbey EN9 67 EC33
Sun St Pas, EC2 11 L6
Sun Wk, E1 12 A10
Sunwell Cl, SE15
off Cossall Wk 162 DV81
Superior Dr, Orp. BR6 223 ET107
SURBITON, KT5 & KT6 198 CM101
⇌ Surbiton 197 CK100
Surbiton Ct, Surb. KT6 197 CJ100
Surbiton Cres, Kings.T. KT1 198 CL98
H Surbiton Gen Hosp, 198 CL100
Surb. KT6
Surbiton Hall Cl, Kings.T.
KT1 198 CL98
Sch Surbiton High Jun Girls'
Sch, Kings.T. KT1
off Surbiton Rd 198 CL98
Sch Surbiton High Sch, Kings.T.
KT1 off Surbiton Cres 198 CL98
Boys' Prep, Surb. KT6
off Avenue Elmers 198 CL99
Surbiton Hill Pk, Surb. KT5 198 CN99
Surbiton Hill Rd, Surb. KT6 198 CL98
Surbiton Par, Surb. KT6
off St. Mark's Hill 198 CL100
Surbiton Rd, Kings.T. KT1 198 CL98
Surlingham Cl, SE28 146 EX73
Surly Hall Wk, Wind. SL4 151 AM81
Surma Cl, E1 12 C4
Surman Cres, Brwd. (Hutt.)
CM13 109 GC45
Surmans Cl, Dag. RM9 146 EW67
Surrendale Pl, W9 7 H4
Surrey Av, Slou. SL2 131 AQ71
Surrey Canal Rd, SE14 162 DW79
SE15 162 DW79
Surrey Cres, W4 158 CN78
★ Surrey Docks City Fm,
SE16 23 L4
Surrey Dr, Horn. RM11 128 FN56
Surrey Gdns, N4
off Finsbury Pk Av 122 DQ58
Leatherhead (Eff.Junct.)
KT24 229 BT123
Surrey Gro, SE17 21 L10
Sutton SM1 200 DD104
Surrey Hills, Tad. (Box H.)
KT20 248 CP130
Surrey Hills Av, Tad. (Box H.)
KT20 248 CQ130
Coll Surrey Inst of Adult Ed,
Epsom KT17
off Church St 216 CS113
Surrey La, SW11 160 DE81
Surrey La Est, SW11 160 DE81
Surrey Lo, SE1 20 C6
Surrey Ms, SE27
off Hamilton Rd 182 DS91
Surrey Mt, SE23 182 DV88
⊖ Surrey Quays 22 G7
Surrey Quays Retail Cen,
SE16 22 G6
Surrey Quays Rd, SE16 22 F5
Surrey Rd, SE15 183 DX85
Barking IG11 145 ES67
Dagenham RM10 127 FB64
Harrow HA1 116 CC57
West Wickham BR4 203 EB102
Surrey Row, SE1 20 E3
Surrey Sq, SE17 21 L9
Sch Surrey Sq Inf Sch, SE17 21 L9

Sch Surrey Sq Jun Sch, SE17 .21 L9
Surrey St, E13 .15 P2
WC2 .10 B9
Croydon CR0 .202 DQ104
Surrey Ter, SE17 .21 M9
Surrey Twrs, Add. KT15
off Garfield Rd .212 BJ106
Surrey Water Rd, SE16 .23 H2
Surridge Cl, Rain. RM13 .148 FJ69
Surridge Gdns, SE19
off Hancock Rd .182 DR93
Surr St, N7 .121 DL64
Sury Basin, Kings.T. KT2 .198 CL95
Susan Cl, Rom. RM7 .127 FC55
Susan Lawrence Ho, E12
off Walton Rd .125 EN63
Sch Susan Lawrence Inf & Jun Sch, E14 .14 A8
Susannah St, E14 .14 C8
Susan Rd, SE3 .164 EH82
Susan Wd, Chis. BR7 .205 EN95
Sussex Av, Islw. TW7 .157 CE83
Romford RM3 .106 FM52
Sussex Border Path, Horl. RH6 .268 DF150
Sussex Cl, N19
off Cornwallis Rd .121 DL61
Chalfont St. Giles HP8 .90 AV47
Hoddesdon EN11
off Roman St .49 EA16
Ilford IG4 .125 EM58
New Malden KT3 .198 CS98
Reigate RH2 .266 DD135
Slough SL1 .152 AV75
Twickenham TW1
off Westmorland Cl .177 CH86
Sussex Cres, Nthlt. UB5 .136 CA65
Sussex Gdns, N4 .122 DQ57
N6 off Great N Rd .120 DF57
W2 .7 N9
Chessington KT9 .215 CK107
Sch Sussex Ho Prep Sch, SW1 .18 C7
Sussex Keep, Slou. SL1
off Sussex Cl .152 AV75
Sussex Ms, SE6
off Ravensbourne Pk .183 EA87
Sussex Ms E, W2 .7 P8
Sussex Ms W, W2 .7 P9
Sussex Pl, NW1 .8 C2
W2 .7 P8
W6 .159 CW78
Erith DA8 .167 FB80
New Malden KT3 .198 CS98
Slough SL1 .152 AV75
Sussex Ring, N12 .98 DA50
Sussex Rd, E6 .145 EN67
Brentwood CM14 .108 FV49
Carshalton SM5 .218 DF107
Dartford DA1 .188 FN87
Erith DA8 .167 FB80
Harrow HA1 .116 CC57
Mitcham CR4
off Lincoln Rd .201 DL99
New Malden KT3 .198 CS98
Orpington BR5 .206 EW100
Sidcup DA14 .186 EV92
South Croydon CR2 .220 DR107
Southall UB2 .156 BX76
Uxbridge UB10 .115 BQ63
Watford WD24 .75 BU38
West Wickham BR4 .203 EB102
Sussex Sq, W2 .7 P9
Sussex St, E13 .15 P2
SW1 .19 H10
Sussex Way, N7 .121 DL61
N19 .121 DL60
Barnet EN4 .80 DG43
Uxbridge (Denh.) UB9 .113 BF57
Sutcliffe Cl, NW11 .120 DB57
Bushey WD23 .76 CC42
Sutcliffe Ho, Hayes UB3 .135 BU72
Sutcliffe Rd, SE18 .165 ES79
Welling DA16 .166 EW82
Sutherland Av, W9 .7 L2
W13 .137 CH72
Guildford (Jacobs Well) GU4 .242 AX128
Hayes UB3 .155 BU77
Orpington BR5 .205 ET100
Potters Bar (Cuffley) EN6 .65 DK28
Sunbury-on-Thames TW16 .195 BT96
Welling DA16 .165 ES84
Westerham (Bigg.H.) TN16 .238 EK117
Sutherland Cl, Barn. EN5 .79 CY42
Greenhithe DA9 .189 FT85
Sutherland Ct, NW9 .118 CP57
Welwyn Garden City AL7 .29 CZ08
Sutherland Dr, SW19 .200 DD95
Guildford (Burpham) GU4 .243 AZ131
Sutherland Gdns, SW14 .158 CS83
Sunbury-on-Thames TW16
off Sutherland Av .195 BT96
Worcester Park KT4 .199 CV102
Sutherland Gro, SW18 .179 CY86
Teddington TW11 .177 CE92
Sutherland Pl, W2 .6 G7
Sutherland Rd, E17 .101 DX54
N9 .100 DU46
N17 .100 DU52
W4 .158 CS79
W13 .137 CG72
Belvedere DA17 .166 FA76
Croydon CR0 .201 DN101
Enfield EN3 .83 DX43
Southall UB1 .136 BZ72
Sutherland Rd Path, E17 .123 DX55
Sutherland Row, SW1 .19 H9
Sutherland Sq, SE17 .20 G10
Sutherland St, SW1 .18 G9
Sutherland Wk, SE17 .21 H10
Sutherland Way, Pot.B. (Cuffley) EN6 .65 DK28
Sutlej Rd, SE7 .164 EJ80
Sutterton St, N7 .4 A4
SUTTON, SM1 - SM3 .218 DB107
⇌ Sutton .218 DC107
SUTTON ABINGER, Dor. RH5 .261 BU143
Coll Sutton Adult Sch & Inst, Sutt. SM1
off Benhill Av .218 DC105
SUTTON AT HONE, Dart. DA4 .208 FN95
Sch Sutton at Hone C of E Prim Sch, Dart. DA4
off Church Rd .188 FN94
Sutton Av, Slou. SL3 .152 AW75
Woking GU21 .226 AS119
Sutton Cl, Beck. BR3
off Albemarle Rd .203 EB95
Broxbourne EN10 .49 DY19
Loughton IG10 .102 EL45
Pinner HA5 .115 BU57
Coll Sutton Coll of Learning for Adults, Sutton Cen, Sutt. SM1
off St. Nicholas Way .218 DB106
Sutton W Cen, Sutt. SM1
off Robin Hood La .218 DA106
⇌ Sutton Common .200 DB103
Sutton Common Rd, Sutt. SM1, SM3 .199 CZ101
Sutton Ct, W4 .158 CQ79
Sutton SM2 .218 DC107
Ware SG12 .33 DY07
Sutton Ct Rd, E13 .144 EJ69
W4 .158 CQ80
Sutton SM1 .218 DC107
Uxbridge UB10 .135 BP67
Sutton Cres, Barn. EN5 .79 CX43
Sutton Dene, Houns. TW3 .156 CB81
Sutton Est, SW3 .18 B9
W10 .139 CW71
Sutton Est, The, N1 .4 E5
Sutton Gdns, Bark. IG11
off Sutton Rd .145 ES67
Croydon CR0 .202 DT99
Redhill RH1 .251 DK129
Sch Sutton Gram Sch for Boys, Sutt. SM1 off Manor La .218 DC106
SUTTON GREEN, Guil. GU4 .243 AZ125
Sutton Grn, Bark. IG11
off Sutton Rd .145 ES67
Sutton Grn Rd, Guil. (Sutt.Grn) GU4 .242 AY126
Sutton Gro, Sutt. SM1 .218 DD105
Sutton Hall Rd, Houns. TW5 .156 CA80
★ Sutton Heritage Cen, Cars. SM5 .218 DF105
Sch Sutton High Sch, Sutt. SM1
off Cheam Rd .218 DB107
H Sutton Hosp, Sutt. SM2 .218 DB110
★ Sutton Ho, E9 .122 DW64
Sutton Ho, Hem.H. HP2 .40 BL16
Sutton La, EC1 .10 F4
Banstead SM7 .234 DB115
Dorking (Abin.Com.) RH5 .261 BV143
Hounslow TW3 .156 BZ83
Slough SL3 .153 BC78
Sutton SM2 .218 DB111
Sutton La N, W4 .158 CQ78
Sutton La S, W4 .158 CQ79
Sutton Par, NW4
off Church Rd .119 CW56
Sutton Pk, Guil. (Sutt.Grn) GU4 .243 AZ127
Sutton Pk Rd, Sutt. SM1 .218 DB107
Sutton Path, Borwd. WD6
off Stratfield Rd .78 CN40
★ Sutton Pl, Guil. GU4 .243 BA127
Sutton Pl, E9 .122 DW64
Dartford DA4 .188 FN92
Dorking (Abin.Ham.) RH5 .261 BT143
Slough SL3 .153 BB79
Sutton Rd, E13 .15 K4
E17 .101 DX53
N10 .98 DG54
Barking IG11 .145 ES68
Hounslow TW5 .156 CA81
St. Albans AL1 .43 CH21
Watford WD17 .76 BW41
Sutton Row, W1 .9 M7
Suttons Av, Horn. RM12 .128 FJ62
Suttons Gdns, Horn. RM12 .128 FK62
Suttons La, Horn. RM12 .128 FK64
Sch Suttons Prim Sch, Horn. RM12 off Suttons La .128 FK63
Sutton Sq, E9 off Urswick Rd .122 DW64
Hounslow TW5 .156 BZ81
Sutton St, E1 .12 E9
Sutton's Way, EC1 .11 H4
Sutton Wk, SE1 .20 B2
Sutton Way, W10 .139 CW71
Hounslow TW5 .156 BZ81
Swabey Rd, Slou. SL3 .153 BA77
Swaby Rd, SW18 .180 DC88
Swaffham Way, N22
off White Hart La .99 DP52
Sch Swaffield Prim Sch, SW18 off St. Ann's Hill .180 DC86
Swaffield Rd, SW18 .180 DB87
Sevenoaks TN13 .257 FJ122
Swain Cl, SW16 .181 DH93
Swain Rd, Th.Hth. CR7 .202 DQ99
Swains Cl, West Dr. UB7 .154 BL75
Swains La, N6 .120 DG62
Swainson Rd, W3 .159 CT75
Swains Rd, SW17 .180 DF94
Swain St, NW8 .8 A3
Swaisland Dr, Dart. (Cray.) DA1 .187 FF85
Swaisland Rd, Dart. DA1 .187 FH85
Swakeleys Dr, Uxb. UB10 .114 BM63
Swakeleys Rd, Uxb. (Ickhm) UB10 .114 BM62
Sch Swakeleys Sch, Uxb. UB10 off Clifton Gdns .135 BP68
Swale Cl, S.Ock. (Aveley) RM15 .148 FQ72
Swaledale Cl, N11
off Ribblesdale Av .98 DG51
Swaledale Rd, Dart. DA2 .188 FQ88
Swale Rd, Dart. DA1 .167 FG83
Swallands Rd, SE6 .183 EA90
Swallow Cl, SE14 .162 DW81
Bushey WD23 .94 CC46
Erith DA8 .167 FE81
Grays (Chaff.Hun.) RM16 .169 FW77
Greenhithe DA9 .189 FT85
Rickmansworth WD3 .92 BJ45
Staines TW18 .173 BF91
Swallow Ct, Hert. SG14 .32 DQ09
Swallowdale, Iver SL0 .133 BD69
South Croydon CR2 .221 DX109
Swallowdale La, Hem.H. HP2 .41 BP17
Sch Swallow Dell Prim Sch, Welw.G.C. AL7
off Blackthorn Rd .30 DA10
Swallow Dr, NW10
off Kingfisher Way .138 CR65
Northolt UB5 .136 CA68
Swallow End, Welw.G.C. AL7 .29 CZ09
Swallowfield, Egh. (Eng.Grn) TW20 off Heronfield .172 AV93
Swallowfield Rd, SE7 .25 P10
Swallowfields, Grav. (Nthflt) DA11 off Hillary Av .190 GE90
Welwyn Garden City AL7 .29 CZ09
Swallowfield Way, Hayes UB3 .155 BR75
Swallow Gdns, SW16 .181 DK92
Hatfield AL10 .45 CU20
Swallow Ho, NW8
off Allitsen Rd .140 DE68
Swallow La, Dor. (Mid Holm.) RH5 .263 CH142
St. Albans AL1 .43 CH23
Swallow Oaks, Abb.L. WD5 .59 BT31
Swallow Pas, W1 .9 H8
Swallow Pl, W1 .9 H8
Swallows, Harl. CM17
off Station Rd .36 EW11
Swallows, The, Welw.G.C. AL7 .29 CZ05
Swallow St, E6 .144 EL71
W1 .9 K10
Iver SL0 .133 BD69
Swallowtail Cl, Orp. BR5 .206 EX98
Swallow Wk, Horn. RM12
off Heron Flight Av .147 FH65
Swanage Rd, E4 .101 EC52
SW18 .180 DC86
Swanage Waye, Hayes UB4 .136 BW72
Swan & Pike Rd, Enf. EN3 .83 EA38
Swan App, E6 .144 EL71
Swan Av, Upmin. RM14 .129 FT60
Swanbourne Dr, Horn. RM12 .128 FJ64
Swanbridge Rd, Bexh. DA7 .166 FA81
Swan Business Pk, Dart. DA1 .168 FK84
Swan Cl, E17 .101 DY53
Chesham HP5 .54 AP27
Croydon CR0 .202 DS101
Feltham TW13 .176 BY91
Orpington BR5 .206 EU97
Rickmansworth WD3
off Parsonage Rd .92 BK45
Sch Swancombe High Sch, Swan. BR8
off St. Marys Rd .207 FE97
Swan Ct, SW3 .18 B10
Guildford GU1 .242 AX132
Hemel Hempstead HP1
off Waterhouse St .40 BJ21
Swandon Way, SW18 .160 DB84
Swan Dr, NW9 .96 CS54
Swanfield Rd, Wal.Cr. EN8 .67 DY33
Swanfield St, E2 .11 N2
Swanhill, Welw.G.C. AL7 .30 DA06
Swanland Rd, Hat. (N.Mymms) AL9 .63 CV28
Potters Bar (S.Mimms) EN6 .63 CV33
Swan La, EC4 .11 J10
N20 .98 DC48
Dartford DA1 .187 FF87
Guildford GU1 .258 AX135
Loughton IG10 .102 EJ45
SWANLEY, BR8 .207 FE98
⇌ Swanley .207 FD98
Swanley Bar La, Pot.B. EN6 .64 DB28
Swanley Bypass, Sid. DA14 .207 FC97
Swanley BR8 .207 FC97
Swanley Cen, Swan. BR8 .207 FE97
Swanley Cres, Pot.B. EN6 .64 DB29
Swanley La, Swan. BR8 .207 FF97
Swanley Rd, Well. DA16 .166 EW81
Sch Swanley Sch, Swan. BR8 off St. Marys Rd .207 FE97
Sch Swanley Sec Sch, E1 .12 C4
SWANLEY VILLAGE, Swan. BR8 .208 FJ95
Swanley Village Rd, Swan. BR8 .207 FH95
Swan Mead, SE1 .21 L6
Hemel Hempstead HP3 .58 BM25
Swan Mill Gdns, Dor. RH4 .247 CJ134
Swanns Meadow, Lthd. (Bkhm) KT23 .246 CA126
Swan Pas, E1
off Cartwright St .142 DT73
Swan Path, E10 off Jesse Rd .123 EC60
Swan Pl, SW13 .159 CT82
Swan Rd, SE16 .22 F3
SE18 .164 EK76
Feltham TW13 .176 BY92
Iver SL0 .133 BF72
Southall UB1 .136 CB72
West Drayton UB7 .154 BK75
Swans Cl, St.Alb. AL4 .44 CL21
SWANSCOMBE, DA10 .190 FZ86
⇌ Swanscombe .190 FZ85
Sch Swanscombe Co Inf Sch, Swans. DA10
off Keary Rd .190 FZ87
Swanscombe Ho, W11
off St. Anns Rd .139 CX74
Swanscombe Rd, W4 .158 CS78
W11 .16 B2
Swanscombe St, Swans. DA10 .190 FY87
Swansea Ct, E16
off Fishguard Way .145 EP74
Swansea Rd, Enf. EN3 .82 DW42
Hounslow (Hthrw Air.) TW6
off Southern Perimeter Rd .175 BQ86
Swanshope, Loug. IG10 .85 EP40
Swansland Gdns, E17
off McEntee Av .101 DY53
Sch Swansmere Inf Sch, Walt. KT12 off Ambleside Av .196 BW102
Swanston Path, Wat. WD19 .94 BW48
Swan St, SE1 .21 H5
Isleworth TW7 .157 CH83
Swan Ter, Wind. SL4
off Mill La .151 AP80
Swanton Gdns, SW19 .179 CX88
Swanton Rd, Erith DA8 .167 FB80
Sch Swan Valley Comm Sch, Swans. DA10
off Southfleet Rd .190 FZ87
Swan Wk, SW3 .160 DF79
Shepperton TW17 .195 BS101
Swan Way, Enf. EN3 .83 DX40
Swanwick Cl, SW15 .179 CT87
Swanworth La, Dor. (Mick.) RH5 .247 CH128
Swan Yd, N1 .4 E4
Sward Rd, Orp. BR5 .206 EU100
Swaton Rd, E3 .13 P4
Swaylands Rd, Belv. DA17 .166 FA79
Swaynesland Rd, Eden. (Crock.H.) TN8 .255 EM134
Swaynes La, Guil. GU1 .243 BE134
Swaythling Cl, N18 .100 DV49
Swaythling Ho, SW15
off Tunworth Cres .179 CT86
Swedenborg Gdns, E1 .12 B9
Sweden Gate, SE16 .23 J6
Sch Swedish Sch, The, SW13
off Lonsdale Rd .159 CT79
Sweeney Cres, SE1 .21 P4
Sweeps Ditch Cl, Stai. TW18 .194 BG95
Sweeps La, Egh. TW20 .173 AZ92
Orpington BR5 .206 EX99
Sweet Briar, Welw.G.C. AL7 .30 DA11
Sweetbriar Cl, Hem.H. HP1 .40 BG17
Sweet Briar Grn, N9 .100 DT48
Sweet Briar Gro, N9 .100 DT48
Sweet Briar La, Epsom KT18 .216 CR114
Sweet Briar Wk, N18 .100 DT49
Sweetcroft La, Uxb. UB10 .134 BN66
Sweet La, Guil. (Peasl.) GU5 .261 BR143
Sweetmans Av, Pnr. HA5 .116 BX55
Sweets Way, N20 .98 DD47
Swetenham Wk, SE18
off Sandbach Pl .165 EQ78
Swete St, E13 .144 EG68
Sch Sweyne Co Jun Sch, The, Swans. DA10
off Keary Rd .190 FZ87
Sweyne Rd, Swans. DA10 .190 FY86
Sweyn Pl, SE3 .164 EG82
Sweyns, Harl. CM17 .52 EX17
Swievelands Rd, West. (Bigg.H.) TN16 .238 EH119
Swift Cl, E17 .101 DY52
Harrow HA2 .116 CB61
Hayes UB3 off Church Rd .135 BT72
Upminster RM14 .129 FS60
Ware (Stans.Abb.) SG12 .33 EC12
Swiftfields, Welw.G.C. AL7 .29 CZ08
Swift Rd, Felt. TW13 .176 BY90
Southall UB2 .156 BZ76
Swiftsden Way, Brom. BR1 .184 EE93
Swift St, SW6 .159 CZ81
Swiftsure Rd, Grays (Chaff.Hun.) RM16 .169 FW77
SWILLET, THE, Rick. WD3 .73 BB44
Swinbrook Rd, W10 .6 D5
Swinburne Ct, SE5
off Basingdon Way .162 DR84
Swinburne Cres, Croy. CR0 .202 DW100
Swinburne Gdns, Til. RM18 .171 GH82
Swinburne Rd, SW15 .159 CU84
Swinderby Rd, Wem. HA0 .138 CL65
Swindon Cl, Ilf. IG3
off Salisbury Rd .125 ES61
Romford RM3 .106 FM50
Swindon Gdns, Rom. RM3 .106 FM50
Swindon La, Rom. RM3 .106 FM50
Swindon Rd, Houns. (Hthrw Air.) TW6 .175 BQ85
Swindon St, W12 .139 CV74
Swinfield Cl, Felt. TW13 .176 BY91
Swinford Gdns, SW9 .161 DP83
Swingate La, SE18 .165 ES79
Sch Swing Gate First Sch, Berk. HP4 off Swing Gate La .38 AX20
Swing Gate La, Berk. HP4 .38 AX22
Swinnerton St, E9 .123 DY64
Swinton Cl, Wem. HA9 .118 CP60
Swinton Pl, WC1 .10 A1
Swinton St, WC1 .10 A1
Swires Shaw, Kes. BR2 .222 EK105
Swiss Av, Wat. WD18 .75 BS42
Swiss Cl, Wat. WD18 .75 BS41
⊖ Swiss Cottage .140 DD66
Sch Swiss Cottage Sch, NW8 off Avenue Rd .140 DD66
Swiss Ct, W1 .9 M10
Swiss Ter, NW6 .140 DD66
Switch Ho, E14 .14 F9
Swithland Gdns, SE9 .185 EN91
Sword Cl, Brox. EN10 .49 DX20
Swyncombe Av, W5 .157 CH77
Swynford Gdns, NW4
off Handowe Cl .119 CU56
Sch Sybil Elgar Sch, The, W5 off Florence Rd .138 CL73
Sybil Ms, N4
off Lothair Rd N .121 DP58
Sybil Phoenix Cl, SE8 .23 H9
Sch Sybourn Inf Sch, E17
off Sybourn St .123 DZ59
Sch Sybourn Jun Sch, E17
off Sybourn St .123 DZ59
Sybourn St, E17 .123 DZ59
Sycamore App, Rick. (Crox.Grn) WD3 .75 BQ43
Sycamore Av, E3 .143 DZ67
W5 .157 CK76
Hatfield AL10 .45 CU19
Hayes UB3 .135 BS73
Sidcup DA15 .185 ET86
Upminster RM14 .128 FN62
Sycamore Cl, E16 .14 G4
N9 off Pycroft Way .100 DU49
SE9 .184 EL89
W3 off Bromyard Av .138 CS74
Amersham HP6 .55 AR37
Barnet EN4 .80 DD44
Bushey WD23 .76 BY40
Carshalton SM5 .218 DF105
Chalfont St. Giles HP8 .90 AU48
Edgware HA8 off Ash Cl .96 CQ49
Feltham TW13 .175 BU90
Gravesend DA12 .191 GK87
Leatherhead (Fetch.) KT22 .231 CE123
Loughton IG10
off Cedar Dr .85 EP40
Northolt UB5 .136 BY67
South Croydon CR2 .220 DS106
Waltham Cross EN7 .66 DT27
Watford WD25 .75 BV35
West Drayton UB7
off Whitethorn Av .134 BM73
Sycamore Ct, Surb. KT6
off Penners Gdns .198 CL101
Sycamore Dene, Chesh. HP5 .54 AR28
Sycamore Dr, Brwd. CM14
off Copperfield Gdns .108 FW46
St. Albans (Park St) AL2 .61 CD27
Swanley BR8 .207 FE97
Sycamore Fld, Harl. CM19 .51 EN19
Sycamore Gdns, W6 .159 CV75
Mitcham CR4 .200 DD96
Sycamore Gro, NW9 .118 CQ59
SE6 .183 EC86
SE20 .182 DU94
New Malden KT3 .198 CR97
Sycamore Hill, N11 .98 DG51
Sycamore Ms, SW4 .161 DJ83
Sycamore Ri, Bans. SM7 .217 CX114
Berkhamsted HP4 .38 AX20
Chalfont St. Giles HP8 .90 AU48
Sycamore Rd, SW19 .179 CW93
Amersham HP6 .55 AR37
Chalfont St. Giles HP8 .90 AU48
Dartford DA1 .188 FK88
Guildford GU1 .242 AX134
Rickmansworth (Crox.Grn) WD3 .75 BQ43
Sycamores, The, Hem.H. HP3 .39 BF23
Leatherhead KT23
off Lower Rd .230 CC124
Radlett WD7
off The Avenue .61 CH34
South Ockendon (Aveley) RM15 off Dacre Av .149 FR74
Sycamore St, EC1 .10 G4
Sycamore Wk, W10 .6 C3
Egham (Eng.Grn) TW20 .172 AV93
Ilford IG6 off Civic Way .125 EQ56
Sycamore Wk, Reigate RH2 .266 DC137
Slough (Geo.Grn) SL3 .132 AY72
Sycamore Way, S.Ock. RM15 .149 FX70
Teddington TW11 .177 CJ93
Thornton Heath CR7 .201 DN99
SYDENHAM, SE26 .182 DW92
⇌ Sydenham .182 DW91
Sydenham Av, N21
off Fleming Dr .81 DM43
SE26 .182 DV92
Sydenham Cl, Rom. RM1 .127 FF56
Sydenham Cotts, SE12 .184 EJ89
Sch Sydenham High Sch, SE26 off Westwood Hill .182 DV92
Sch Sydenham High Sch Jun Dept, SE26
off Westwood Hill .182 DV91
⇌ Sydenham Hill .182 DT90
Sydenham Hill, SE23 .182 DV88
SE26 .182 DU90
Sydenham Hill Est, SE26 .182 DU90
Sydenham Pk, SE26 .182 DW90
Sydenham Pk Rd, SE26 .182 DW90
Sydenham Ri, SE23 .182 DV89
Sydenham Rd, SE26 .182 DW92
Croydon CR0 .202 DR101
Guildford GU1 .258 AX136
Sch Sydenham Sch, SE26
off Dartmouth Rd .182 DV90
Sydmons Ct, SE23 .182 DW87
Sydner Ms, N16
off Sydner Rd .122 DT63
Sydner Rd, N16 .122 DT63
Sydney Av, Pur. CR8 .219 DM112
Sydney Cl, SW3 .17 P8
Sydney Cres, Ashf. TW15 .175 BP93
Sydney Gro, NW4 .119 CW57
Slough SL1 .131 AQ72
Sydney Ms, SW3 .17 P8
Sydney Pl, SW7 .17 P8
Guildford GU1 .259 AZ135
Sydney Rd, E11
off Mansfield Rd .124 EH58
N8 .121 DN56
N10 .98 DG53
SE2 .166 EW76
SW20 .199 CX96
W13 .137 CG74
Bexleyheath DA6 .166 EX84
Enfield EN2 .82 DR42
Feltham TW14 .175 BU88
Guildford GU1 .259 AZ135
Ilford IG6 .103 EQ54
Richmond TW9 .158 CL84
Sidcup DA14 .185 ES91
Sutton SM1 .218 DA105
Teddington TW11 .177 CF92
Tilbury RM18 .171 GG82
Watford WD18 .75 BS43
Woodford Green IG8 .102 EG49
Sch Sydney Russell Comp Sch, Dag. RM9 off Parsloes Av .126 EX64
Sydney St, SW3 .18 A9
Syke Cluan, Iver SL0 .153 BE75
Syke Ings, Iver SL0 .153 BE76
Sykes Dr, Stai. TW18 .174 BH92
Sykes Rd, Slou. SL1 .131 AP72
Sylvana Cl, Uxb. UB10 .134 BM67
Sylvan Av, N3 .98 DA54
N22 .99 DM52
NW7 .97 CT51
Hornchurch RM11 .128 FL58
Romford RM6 .126 EZ58
Sylvan Cl, Grays (Chaff.Hun.) RM16 .170 FY77
Hemel Hempstead HP3 .40 BN21
Oxted RH8 .254 EH129
South Croydon CR2 .220 DV110
Woking GU22 .227 BB117
Sylvan Ct, N12 off Holden Rd .98 DB49
Sylvandale, Welw.G.C. AL7 .30 DC10
Sylvan Est, SE19 .202 DT95
Sylvan Gdns, Surb. KT6 .197 CK101
Sylvan Gro, NW2 .119 CX63
SE15 .162 DV80
Sylvan Hill, SE19 .202 DS95
Sylvan Ms, Green. DA9
off Watermans Way .169 FV84
Sylvan Rd, E7 .144 EG65
E11 .124 EG57
E17 .123 EA57
SE19 .202 DT95
Ilford IG1
off Hainault St .125 EQ61
Sylvan Wk, Brom. BR1 .205 EM97
Sylvan Way, Chig. IG7 .104 EV48
Dagenham RM8 .126 EV62
Redhill RH1 .266 DG135
Welwyn Garden City AL7 .30 DC10
West Wickham BR4 .222 EE105
Sylverdale Rd, Croy. CR0 .201 DP104
Purley CR8 .219 DP113
Sylvester Av, Chis. BR7 .185 EM93
Sylvester Gdns, Ilf. IG6 .104 EV50
Sylvester Path, E8
off Sylvester Rd .142 DV65
Sylvester Rd, E8 .142 DV65
E17 .123 DZ59
N2 .98 DC54
Wembley HA0 .117 CJ64
Sylvestres, Sev. (Rvrhd) TN13 .256 FD121
Sylvestrus Cl, Kings.T. KT1 .198 CN95
Sylvia Av, Brwd. (Hutt.) CM13 .109 GC47
Pinner HA5 .94 BZ51
Sylvia Ct, Wem. HA9
off Harrow Rd .138 CP66
Sylvia Gdns, Wem. HA9 .138 CP66
Sch Sylvia Young Thea Sch, NW1 .8 B4
Symes Ms, NW1
off Camden High St .141 DJ68
Symington Ms, E9
off Coopersale Rd .123 DX64
Symister Ms, N1 .11 L2
Symonds Ct, Wal.Cr. (Chsht) EN8 off High St .67 DX28
Symons St, SW3 .18 D8
Symphony Ms, W10 .6 D1
Syon Gate Way, Brent. TW8 .157 CG80
★ Syon Ho & Pk, Brent. TW8 .157 CJ81
⇌ Syon Lane .157 CG80
Syon La, Islw. TW7 .157 CH80
Syon Pk Gdns, Islw. TW7 .157 CF80
Sch Syon Pk Sch, Islw. TW7
off Twickenham Rd .157 CH81
Syon Vista, Rich. TW9 .157 CK81
Syracuse Av, Rain. RM13 .148 FL69
Uni Syracuse Uni, W11 .6 E10
Syringa Ct, Grays RM17 .170 GD80
Sythwood, Wok. GU21 .226 AV117
Sch Sythwood Prim Sch, Wok. GU21
off Sythwood .226 AV116

★ Place of interest | H Hospital | Sch School | Coll College | Uni University | ⇌ Railway station

T

Tabard Cen, SE1
off Prioress St .162 DR76
Tabard Gdn Est, SE1 .21 K4
Tabard St, SE1 .21 J4
Tabarin Way, Epsom KT17 .233 CW116
Tabernacle Av, E13 .15 L4
Tabernacle St, EC2 .11 K4
Tableer Av, SW4 .181 DK85
Tabley Rd, N7 .121 DL63
Tabor Gdns, Sutt. SM3 .217 CZ107
Tabor Gro, SW19 .179 CY94
Tabor Rd, W6 .159 CV76
Tabors Ct, Brwd. (Shenf.)
CM15 off Shenfield Rd .109 FZ45
Tabrums Way, Upmin. RM14 .129 FS59
Tachbrook Est, SW1 .19 M10
Tachbrook Ms, SW1 .19 J7
Tachbrook Rd, Felt. TW14 .175 BT87
Southall UB2 .156 BX77
Uxbridge UB8 .134 BJ68
Tachbrook St, SW1 .19 K8
Tack Ms, SE4 .163 EA83
Tadema Rd, SW10 .160 DC80
Tadlows Cl, Upmin. RM14 .128 FP64
Tadmor Cl, Sun. TW16 .195 BT98
Tadmor St, W12 .16 A2
Tadorne Rd, Tad. KT20 .233 CW121
TADWORTH, KT20 .233 CV121
⇌ Tadworth .233 CW122
Tadworth Av, N.Mal. KT3 .199 CT99
Tadworth Cl, Tad. KT20 .233 CX122
Tadworth Par, Horn. RM12
off Maylands Av .127 FH63
Sch Tadworth Prim Sch, Tad.
KT20 off Tadworth St .233 CX122
Tadworth Rd, NW2 .119 CU61
Tadworth St, Tad. KT20 .233 CW123
Taeping St, E14 .24 A7
Taffy's How, Mitch. CR4 .200 DE97
Taft Way, E3 .14 B1
Tagalie Pl, Rad. (Shenley)
WD7 off Porters Pk Dr .62 CL32
Tagg's Island, Hmptn. TW12 .197 CD96
Tailworth St, E1 .12 A6
Tait Rd, Croy. CR0 .202 DS101
Takeley Cl, Rom. RM5 .105 FD54
Waltham Abbey EN9 .67 ED33
Takhar Ms, SW11
off Cabul Rd .160 DE82
Talacre Rd, NW5 .140 DG65
Talbot Av, N2 .120 DD55
Slough SL3 .153 AZ76
Watford WD19 .94 BY45
Talbot Cl, N15 .122 DT56
Reigate RH2 .266 DB135
Talbot Ct, EC3 .11 K9
Hemel Hempstead HP3
off Crabtree La .40 BK22
Talbot Cres, NW4 .119 CU57
Talbot Gdns, Ilf. IG3 .126 EU61
Talbot Ho, E14 .14 A7
N7 off Harvist Est .121 DN62
Talbot Pl, SE3 .164 EE82
Slough (Datchet) SL3 .152 AW81
Talbot Rd, E6 .145 EN68
E7 .124 EG63
N6 .120 DG58
N15 .122 DT56
N22 .99 DJ54
SE22 .162 DS84
W2 .7 H7
W11 .6 F7
W13 .137 CG73
Ashford TW15 .174 BK92
Bromley BR2
off Masons Hill .204 EH98
Carshalton SM5 .218 DG106
Dagenham RM9 .146 EZ65
Harrow HA3 .95 CF54
Hatfield AL10 .45 CU15
Isleworth TW7 .157 CG84
Rickmansworth WD3 .92 BL46
Southall UB2 .156 BY77
Thornton Heath CR7 .202 DR98
Twickenham TW2 .177 CE88
Wembley HA0 .117 CK64
Talbot Roundabout, Epp.
(N.Wld Bas.) CM16 .71 FD25
Talbot Sq, W2 .7 P8
Talbot St, Hert. SG13 .32 DS09
Talbot Wk, NW10
off Garnet Rd .138 CS65
W11 .6 C8
Talbot Yd, SE1 .21 J2
Talbrook, Brwd. CM14 .108 FT48
Taleworth Cl, Ashtd. KT21 .231 CK120
Taleworth Pk, Ashtd. KT21 .231 CK120
Taleworth Rd, Ashtd. KT21 .231 CK119
Talfourd Pl, SE15 .162 DT81
Talfourd Rd, SE15 .162 DT81
Talfourd Way, Red. RH1
off Royal Earlswood Pk .266 DG137
Talgarth Rd, W6 .159 CY78
W14 .16 B9
Talgarth Wk, NW9 .118 CS57
Talisman Cl, Ilf. IG3 .126 EV60
Talisman Sq, SE26 .182 DU91
Talisman Way, Epsom KT17 .233 CW116
Wembley HA9 .118 CM62
Tallack Cl, Har. HA3
off College Hill Rd .95 CE52
Tallack Rd, E10 .123 DZ60
Tall Elms Cl, Brom. BR2 .204 EF99
Tallents Cl, Dart. (Sutt.H.)
DA4 .188 FP94
Tallis Cl, E16 .15 N8
Tallis Ct, Rom. (Gidea Pk)
RM2 .128 FJ55
Tallis Gro, SE7 .164 EH79
Tallis St, EC4 .10 D9
Tallis Vw, NW10 .138 CR65
Tallis Way, Borwd. WD6 .77 CK39
Brentwood (Warley) CM14 .108 FV50
Tall Oaks, Amer. HP6 .55 AR37
Tallon Rd, Brwd. (Hutt.) CM13 .109 GE43
Tall Trees, SW16 .201 DM97
Slough (Colnbr.) SL3 .153 BE81
Tall Trees Cl, Horn. RM11 .128 FK58
Tally Ho Cor, N12 .98 DC50
Tally Rd, Oxt. RH8 .254 EL131
Talma Gdns, Twick. TW2 .177 CE86
Talmage Cl, SE23
off Tyson Rd .182 DW87
Talman Gro, Stan. HA7 .95 CK51
Talma Rd, SW2 .161 DN84
Sch Talmud Torah Machikei
Hadass Sch, E5
off Clapton Common .122 DU59
Talus Cl, Purf. RM19 .169 FR77
Talwin St, E3 .14 B2
Tamar Cl, E3 off Lefevre Wk .143 DZ67
Tamar Cl, Upmin. RM14 .129 FS58
Tamar Dr, S.Ock. (Aveley)
RM15 .148 FQ72
Tamar Grn, Hem.H. HP2 .40 BM15
Tamarind Cl, Guil. GU2 .242 AU129
Tamarind Yd, E1 .22 B1
Tamarisk Cl, St.Alb. AL3
off New Grns Av .43 CD16
South Ockendon RM15 .149 FW70
Tamarisk Rd, S.Ock. RM15 .149 FW69
Tamarisk Sq, W12 .139 CT73
Tamarisk Way, Slou. SL1 .151 AN75
Tamar Sq, Wdf.Grn. IG8 .102 EH51
Tamar St, SE7
off Woolwich Rd .164 EL76
Tamar Way, N17 .122 DU55
Slough SL3 .153 BB78
Tamerton Sq, Wok. GU22 .226 AY119
Tamesis Gdns, Wor.Pk. KT4 .198 CS102
Tamesis Strand, Grav. DA12 .191 GL92
Tamian Way, Houns. TW4 .156 BW84
Tamworth Av, Wdf.Grn. IG8 .102 EE51
Tamworth La, Mitch. CR4 .201 DH96
Sch Tamworth Manor High Sch,
Mitch. CR4 off Wide Way .201 DK97
Tamworth Pk, Mitch. CR4 .201 DH98
Tamworth Pl, Croy. CR0 .202 DQ103
Tamworth Rd, Croy. CR0 .201 DP103
Hertford SG13 .32 DS08
Tamworth St, SW6 .160 DA79
Tancred Rd, N4 .121 DP58
Tandem Cen, SW19
off Prince George's Rd .200 DD95
Tandem Way, SW19 .200 DD95
TANDRIDGE, Oxt. RH8 .253 EA133
Tandridge Ct, Cat. CR3 .236 DU122
Tandridge Dr, Orp. BR6 .205 ER102
Tandridge Gdns, S.Croy. CR2 .220 DT113
Tandridge Hill La, Gdse. RH9 .253 DZ128
Tandridge La, Oxt. (Tand.)
RH8 .253 EA131
Tandridge Pl, Orp. BR6
off Tandridge Dr .205 ER101
Tandridge Rd, Warl. CR6 .237 DX119
Tanfield Av, NW2 .119 CT63
Tanfield Cl, Wal.Cr. EN7 .66 DU27
Tanfield Rd, Croy. CR0 .220 DQ105
Tangent Link, Rom.
(Harold Hill) RM3 .106 FK53
Tangent Rd, Rom. RM3
off Ashton Rd .106 FK53
Tangier La, Wind. (Eton) SL4 .151 AR79
Tangier Rd, Guil. GU1 .259 BA135
Richmond TW10 .158 CP83
Tangier Way, Tad. KT20 .233 CY117
Tangier Wd, Tad. KT20 .233 CY118
Tanglebury Cl, Brom. BR1 .205 EM98
Tangle Tree Cl, N3 .98 DB54
Tanglewood Cl, Cher.
(Longcr.) KT16 .192 AV104
Croydon CR0 .202 DW104
Stanmore HA7 .95 CE47
Uxbridge UB10 .134 BN69
Woking GU22 .227 BD116
Tanglewood Way, Felt. TW13 .175 BV90
Tangley Gro, SW15 .179 CT87
Tangley La, Guil. GU3 .242 AT130
Tangley Pk Rd, Hmptn. TW12 .176 BZ93
Tanglyn Av, Shep. TW17 .195 BP99
Tangmere Cres, Horn. RM12 .147 FH65
Tangmere Gdns, Nthlt. UB5 .136 BW68
Tangmere Gro, Kings.T. KT2 .177 CK92
Tangmere Way, NW9 .96 CS54
Tanhouse Rd, Oxt. RH8 .253 ED132
Tanhurst Wk, SE2
off Alsike Rd .166 EX76
Tankerton Rd, Surb. KT6 .198 CM103
Tankerton St, WC1 .9 P2
Tankerville Rd, SW16 .181 DK93
Tank Hill Rd, Purf. RM19 .168 FN78
Tank La, Purf. RM19 .168 FN77
Tankridge Rd, NW2 .119 CV61
Tanner Pt, E13 off Pelly Rd .144 EG67
Tanners Cl, St.Alb. AL3 .42 CC19
Walton-on-Thames KT12 .195 BV100
Tanners Cres, Hert. SG13 .32 DQ11
Tanners Dean, Lthd. KT22 .231 CJ122
Tanners End La, N18 .100 DS49
Tannersfield, Guil. (Shalf.)
GU4 .258 AY142
Tanners Hill, SE8 .163 DZ81
Abbots Langley WD5 .59 BT31
Tanners La, Ilf. IG6 .125 EQ55
Tanners Meadow, Bet.
(Brock.) RH3 .264 CP138
Tanner St, SE1 .21 M4
Barking IG11 .145 EQ65
Tanners Way, Ware SG12 .34 EJ06
Tanners Wd Cl, Abb.L. WD5
off Tanners Wd La .59 BS32
Sch Tanners Wd JMI Sch, Abb.L.
WD5 off Hazelwood La .59 BS32
Tanners Wd La, Abb.L. WD5 .59 BS32
Tannery, The, Red. RH1
off Oakdene Rd .250 DE134
Tannery Cl, Beck. BR3 .203 DX99
Dagenham RM10 .127 FB62
Tannery La, Guil. (Bramley)
GU5 .258 AY144
Woking (Send) GU23 .227 BF122
Tannington Ter, N5 .121 DN62
Tannsfeld Rd, SE26 .183 DX92
Tannsfield Dr, Hem.H. HP2 .40 BM18
Tannsmore Cl, Hem.H. HP2 .40 BM18
Tansley Cl, N7
off Hilldrop Rd .121 DK64
Tanswell Est, SE1 .20 D4
Tanswell St, SE1 .20 C4
Tansy Cl, E6 .145 EN72
Guildford GU4 .243 BC132
Romford RM3 .106 FL51
Tansycroft, Welw.G.C. AL7 .30 DB08
Tantallon Rd, SW12 .180 DG88
Tant Av, E16 .15 J7
Tantony Gro, Rom. RM6 .126 EX55
Tanworth Cl, Nthwd. HA6 .93 BQ51
Tanworth Gdns, Pnr. HA5 .93 BV54
Tanyard La, Bex. DA5 .186 FA87
Tanyard Way, Horl. RH6 .269 DH146
Tanys Dell, Harl. CM20 .36 EU12
Sch Tany's Dell Co Prim Sch,
Harl. CM20
off Mowbray Rd .36 EU12
Tanza Rd, NW3 .120 DF63
Tapestry Cl, Sutt. SM2 .218 DB108
TAPLOW, Maid. SL6 .130 AE70
⇌ Taplow .130 AF72
Taplow, NW3 .140 DD66
SE17 .21 L10
Taplow Common Rd, Slou.
(Burn.) SL1 .130 AG67
Taplow Rd, N13 .100 DQ49
Maidenhead (Taplow) SL6 .130 AG71
Taplow St, N1 .5 H10
Tapners Rd, Bet. RH3 .265 CT139
Tapners Rd, Reig. (Leigh)
RH2 .265 CT139
Tappesfield Rd, SE15 .162 DW83
Tapp St, E1 .12 C3
Tapster St, Barn. EN5 .79 CZ42
Tara Ms, N8 off Edison Rd .121 DK58
Taransay, Hem.H. HP3 .41 BP22
Taransay Wk, N1 .5 J3
Tarbay La, Wind.
(Oakley Grn) SL4 .150 AH82
Tarbert Ms, N15
off Roslyn Rd .122 DS57
Tarbert Rd, SE22 .182 DS85
Tarbert Wk, E1 .12 E9
Target Cl, Felt. TW14 .175 BS86
Tarham Cl, Horl. RH6 .268 DE146
Tariff Cres, SE8 .23 L7
Tariff Rd, N17 .100 DU51
Tarleton Gdns, SE23 .182 DV88
Tarling Cl, Sid. DA14 .186 EV90
Tarling Rd, E16 .15 K8
N2 .98 DC54
Tarling St, E1 .12 E8
Tarling St Est, E1 .12 E8
Tarmac Way, West Dr. UB7 .154 BH80
Tarnbank, Enf. EN2 .81 DL43
Tarn St, SE1 .20 G6
Tarnwood Pk, SE9 .185 EM88
Tarnworth Rd, Rom. RM3 .106 FN50
Tarpan Way, Brox. EN10 .67 DZ26
Tarquin Ho, SE26 .182 DU91
Tarragon Cl, SE14 .163 DY80
Tarragon Dr, Guil. GU2 .242 AU129
Tarragon Gro, SE26 .183 DX93
Tarrant Pl, W1 .8 C6
Tarrington Cl, SW16 .181 DK90
Tartar Rd, Cob. KT11 .214 BW113
Tarver Rd, SE17 .20 F10
Tarves Way, SE10 .163 EB80
Tash Pl, N11
off Woodland Rd .99 DH50
Sch Tasis England, Egh.
TW20 off Coldharbour La .193 BC97
Tasker Cl, Hayes UB3 .155 BQ80
Tasker Ho, Bark. IG11
off Dovehouse Mead .145 ER68
Tasker Rd, NW3 .120 DF64
Grays RM16 .171 GH76
Tasman Ct, E14
off Westferry Rd .163 EB77
Sunbury-on-Thames TW16 .175 BS94
Tasmania Ho, Til. RM18
off Hobart Rd .171 GG81
Tasmania Ter, N18 .100 DQ51
Tasman Rd, SW9 .161 DL83
Tasman Wk, E16 off Royal Rd .144 EK72
Tasso Rd, W6 .159 CY79
Tatam Rd, NW10 .138 CQ66
Tatchbury Ho, SW15
off Tunworth Cres .179 CT86
Tate & Lyle Jetty, E16 .164 EL75
★ Tate Britain, SW1 .19 N8
Tate Cl, Lthd. KT22 .231 CJ123
Tate Gdns, Bushey WD23 .95 CE45
★ Tate Modern, SE1 .20 F1
Tate Rd, E16 off Newland St .145 EM74
Gerrards Cross
(Chal.St.P.) SL9 .91 AZ50
Sutton SM1 .218 DA106
Tatham Pl, NW8
off Acacia Rd .140 DD68
TATLING END, Ger.Cr. SL9 .113 BB61
Tatnell Rd, SE23 .183 DY86
TATSFIELD, West. TN16 .238 EL120
Tatsfield App Rd, West.
(Tats.) TN16 .238 EH123
Tatsfield Av, Wal.Abb. EN9 .49 ED23
Tatsfield La, West. (Tats.)
TN16 .239 EM121
Sch Tatsfield Prim Sch, West.
TN16 off Church La .238 EK121
TATTENHAM CORNER,
Epsom KT18 .233 CV118
⇌ Tattenham Corner .233 CV118
Tattenham Cor Rd, Epsom
KT18 .233 CT117
Tattenham Cres, Epsom
KT18 .233 CU118
Tattenham Gro, Epsom KT18 .233 CV118
Tattenham Way, Tad. KT20 .233 CX118
Tattersall Cl, SE9 .184 EL85
Tattle Hill, Hert. SG14 .31 DL05
Tatton Cres, N16
off Clapton Common .122 DT59
Tatton St, Harl. CM17
off London Rd .36 EW14
Tatum St, SE17 .21 K8
Tauber Cl, Borwd. (Elstree)
WD6 .78 CM42
Tauheed Cl, N4 .122 DQ61
Taunton Av, SW20 .199 CV96
Caterham CR3 .236 DT123
Hounslow TW3 .156 CC82
Taunton Cl, Bexh. DA7 .167 FD82
Ilford IG6 .103 ET51
Sutton SM3 .200 DA102
Taunton Dr, N2 .98 DC54
Enfield EN2 .81 DN41
Taunton La, Couls. CR5 .235 DN119
Taunton Ms, NW1 .8 C4
Taunton Pl, NW1 .8 C3
Taunton Rd, SE12 .184 EE85
Gravesend (Nthflt) DA11 .190 GA85
Greenford UB6 .136 CB67
Romford RM3 .106 FJ49
Taunton Vale, Grav. DA12 .191 GK90
Taunton Way, Stan. HA7 .118 CL55
Tavern Cl, Cars. SM5 .200 DE101
Taverners, Hem.H. HP2 .40 BL18
Taverners Cl, W11 .16 C2
Taverner Sq, N5
off Highbury Gra .122 DQ63
Taverners Way, E4
off Douglas Rd .102 EE46
Hoddesdon EN11 .49 EA17
Tavern La, SW9 .161 DN82
Tavistock Av, E17 .123 DY55
NW7 .97 CX52
Greenford UB6 .137 CG68
St. Albans AL1 .42 CC23
Tavistock Cl, N16 .5 M2
Potters Bar EN6 .64 DD31
Romford RM3 .106 FK53
St. Albans AL1 .43 CD24
Staines TW18 .174 BK94
Tavistock Ct, WC2
off Tavistock St .141 DL73
Tavistock Cres, W11 .6 F6
Mitcham CR4 .201 DL98
Tavistock Gdns, Ilf. IG3 .125 ES63
Tavistock Gate, Croy. CR0 .202 DR102
Tavistock Gro, Croy. CR0 .202 DR101
Tavistock Ms, E18
off Avon Way .124 EG56
W11 off Lancaster Rd .139 CZ72
Tavistock Pl, E18
off Avon Way .124 EG55
N14 off Chase Side .99 DH45
WC1 .9 M3
Tavistock Rd, E7 .124 EF63
E15 .144 EF65
E18 .124 EG55
N4 .122 DR58
NW10 .139 CT68
W11 .6 E7
Bromley BR2 .204 EF98
Carshalton SM5 .200 DD102
Croydon CR0 .202 DR102
Edgware HA8 .96 CN53
Uxbridge UB10 .115 BQ64
Watford WD24 .76 BX39
Welling DA16 .166 EW81
West Drayton UB7 .134 BK74
Tavistock Sq, WC1 .9 M3
Tavistock St, WC2 .9 P9
Tavistock Ter, N19 .121 DK62
Tavistock Twr, SE16 .23 J6
Tavistock Wk, Cars. SM5
off Tavistock Rd .200 DD102
Taviton St, WC1 .9 L3
Tavy Cl, SE11 .20 D9
Tawney Common, Epp.
(They.Mt) CM16 .70 FA32
Tawney La, Ong. CM5 .71 FC32
Romford (Stap.Taw.) RM4 .87 FD35
Tawney Rd, SE28 .146 EV73
Tawneys Rd, Harl. CM18 .51 ES16
Tawny Av, Upmin. RM14 .128 FP64
Tawny Cl, W13 .137 CH74
Feltham TW13
off Chervil Cl .175 BU90
Tawny Way, SE16 .23 H7
Tayben Av, Twick. TW2 .177 CE86
Taybridge Rd, SW11 .160 DG83
Tayburn Cl, E14 .14 C7
Tayfield Cl, Uxb. UB10 .115 BQ62
Tayler Cotts, Pot.B. EN6
off Crossoaks La .63 CT34
Tayles Hill, Epsom KT17
off Tayles Hill Dr .217 CT110
Tayles Hill Dr, Epsom KT17 .217 CT110
Taylifers, Harl. CM19 .51 EN20
Taylor Av, Rich. TW9 .158 CP82
Taylor Cl, N17 .100 DU52
SE8 .163 DZ79
Epsom KT19 .216 CN111
Hampton (Hmptn H.) TW12 .176 CC92
Hounslow TW3 .156 CC81
Orpington BR6 .223 ET105
Romford RM5 .104 FA52
St. Albans AL4 .43 CG16
Uxbridge (Hare.) UB9
off High St .92 BJ53
Taylor Ct, E15 off Clays La .123 EC64
Taylor Rd, Ashtd. KT21 .231 CK117
Mitcham CR4 .180 DE94
Wallington SM6 .219 DH106
Taylor Row, Dart. DA2 .188 FJ90
Romford (Noak Hill) RM3
off Cummings Hall La .106 FJ48
Taylors Av, Hodd. EN11 .49 EA18
Taylors Bldgs, SE18
off Spray St .165 EP77
Taylors Cl, Sid. DA14 .185 ET91
Taylors Grn, W3 off Long Dr .138 CS72
Taylors La, NW10 .138 CS66
SE26 .182 DV91
Barnet EN5 .79 CZ39
Taylors Rd, Chesh. HP5 .54 AR29
Taymount Ri, SE23 .182 DW89
Taynton Dr, Red. RH1 .251 DK129
Tayport Cl, N1 .4 A6
Tayside Dr, Edg. HA8 .96 CP48
Tay Way, Rom. RM1 .105 FF53
Taywood Rd, Nthlt. UB5 .136 BZ69
Teak Cl, SE16 .23 K2
Teal Av, Orp. BR5 .206 EX98
Teal Cl, E16 off Fulmer Rd .144 EK71
South Croydon CR2 .221 DX111
Teal Ct, Wall. SM6
off Carew Rd .219 DJ107
Teal Dr, Nthwd. HA6 .93 BQ52
Teale St, E2 .142 DU68
Tealing Dr, Epsom KT19 .216 CR105
Teal Pl, Sutt. SM1
off Sandpiper Rd .217 CZ106
Teal St, SE10 .25 K5
Teal Way, Hem.H. HP3 .58 BM25
Teardrop Ind Est, Swan. BR8 .207 FH99
Teasel Cl, Croy. CR0 .203 DX102
Teasel Cres, SE28 .145 ES74
Teasel Way, E15 .14 G1
Teazle Meade, Epp. (Thnwd)
CM16 .70 EV25
Teazle Wd Hill, Lthd. KT22 .231 CE117
Teazlewood Pk, Lthd. KT22 .231 CG117
Tebworth Rd, N17 .100 DT52
Teck Cl, Islw. TW7 .157 CG82
Tedder Cl, Chess. KT9 .215 CJ106
Ruislip HA4
off West End Rd .115 BV64
Uxbridge UB10 .134 BM66
Tedder Rd, Hem.H. HP2 .40 BN19
South Croydon CR2 .220 DW108
TEDDINGTON, TW11 .177 CG93
⇌ Teddington .177 CG93
Teddington Cl, Epsom KT19 .216 CR110
Teddington Lock, Tedd. TW11 .177 CH91
H Teddington Mem Hosp,
Tedd. TW11 .177 CE93
Teddington Pk, Tedd. TW11 .177 CF92
Teddington Pk Rd, Tedd.
TW11 .177 CF91
Sch Teddington Sch, Tedd.
TW11 off Broom Rd .177 CJ93
Tedworth Gdns, SW3 .18 C10
Tedworth Sq, SW3 .18 C10
Tee, The, W3 .138 CS72
Tees Av, Grnf. UB6 .137 CE68
Tees Cl, Upmin. RM14 .129 FR59
Teesdale, Hem.H. HP2 .40 BL17
Teesdale Av, Islw. TW7 .157 CG81
Teesdale Cl, E2 .142 DV68
Teesdale Gdns, SE25 .202 DS96
Isleworth TW7 .157 CG81
Teesdale Rd, E11 .124 EF58
Dartford DA2 .188 FQ88
Slough SL2 .131 AM71
Teesdale St, E2 .142 DV68
Teesdale Yd, E2
off Teesdale St .142 DV68
Tees Dr, Rom. RM3 .106 FK48
Tee Side, Hert. SG13 .32 DV08
Teeswater Ct, Erith DA18
off Middle Way .166 EX76
Teevan Cl, Croy. CR0 .202 DU101
Teevan Rd, Croy. CR0 .202 DU101
Teggs La, Wok. GU22 .227 BF116
Teignmouth Cl, SW4 .161 DK84
Edgware HA8 .96 CM54
Teignmouth Gdns, Grnf.
UB6 .137 CF68
Teignmouth Rd, NW2 .119 CX64
Welling DA16 .166 EW82
Sch Teikyo Sch U.K., Slou.
SL2 off Framewood Rd .132 AX66
Telcote Way, Ruis. HA4
off Woodlands Av .116 BW59
★ Telecom Twr, W1 .9 J5
Telegraph Hill, NW3 .120 DB62
Telegraph La, Esher (Clay.)
KT10 .215 CF107
Telegraph Ms, Ilf. IG3 .126 EU60
Telegraph Path, Chis. BR7 .185 EP92
Telegraph Pl, E14 .24 A7
Telegraph Rd, SW15 .179 CV87
Telegraph St, EC2 .11 J7
Telegraph Track, Cars. SM5 .218 DG110
Telemann Sq, SE3 .164 EH83
Telephone Pl, SW6
off Lillie Rd .159 CZ79
Telfer Cl, W3 off Church Rd .158 CQ75
Sch Telferscot Prim Sch,
SW12 off Telferscot Rd .181 DK88
Telferscot Rd, SW12 .181 DK88
Telford Av, SW2 .181 DL88
Telford Cl, E17 .123 DY59
SE19 off St. Aubyn's Rd .182 DT93
Watford WD25 .76 BX35
Telford Ct, Guil. GU1
off Clandon Rd .258 AY135
St. Albans AL1 .43 CE21
Telford Dr, Slou. SL1 .151 AN75
Walton-on-Thames KT12 .196 BW101
Telford Rd, N11 .99 DJ51
NW9 off West Hendon Bdy .119 CU58
SE9 .185 ER89
W10 .6 C5
St. Albans (Lon.Col.) AL2 .61 CJ27
Southall UB1 .136 CB73
Twickenham TW2 .176 CA87
Telfords Yd, E1 .12 B10
Telford Ter, SW1 .161 DJ79
Telford Way, W3 .138 CS71
Hayes UB4 .136 BY71
Telham Rd, E6 .145 EN68
Tell Gro, SE22 .162 DT84
Tellisford, Esher KT10 .214 CB105
Tellson Av, SE18 .164 EL81
Telscombe Cl, Orp. BR6 .205 ES103
Telston La, Sev. (Otford) TN14 .241 FF117
Temeraire St, SE16 .22 F4
Temperance St, St.Alb. AL3 .42 CC20
Temperley Rd, SW12 .180 DG87
Tempest Av, Pot.B. EN6 .64 DC32
Tempest Mead, Epp.
(N.Wld Bas.) CM16 .71 FB27
Tempest Rd, Egh. TW20 .173 BC93
Tempest Way, Rain. RM13 .147 FG65
Templar Dr, SE28 .146 EX72
Gravesend DA11 .191 GG92
Templar Ho, NW2
off Shoot Up Hill .139 CZ65
Rainham RM13
off Chantry Way .147 FD68
Templar Pl, Hmptn. TW12 .176 CA94
Templars Av, NW11 .119 CZ58
Templars Cres, N3 .98 DA54
Templars Dr, Har. HA3 .95 CD51
Templar St, SE5 .161 DP82
⊖ Temple .10 B9
Temple, EC4 .141 DN73
★ Temple, The, EC4 .10 C9
Temple Av, EC4 .10 D9
N20 .98 DD45
Croydon CR0 .203 DZ103
Dagenham RM8 .126 FA60
Temple Bk, Harl. CM20 .36 EV09
★ Temple Bar, EC4 .10 C8
Temple Bar Rd, Wok. GU21 .226 AT119
Temple Cl, E11 off Wadley Rd .124 EE59
N3 off Cyprus Rd .97 CZ54
SE28 .165 EQ76
Epsom KT19 .216 CR112
Waltham Cross (Chsht)
EN7 .66 DU31
Watford WD17 .75 BT40
Templecombe Ms, Wok.
GU22 off Dorchester Ct .227 BA116
Templecombe Rd, E9 .142 DW67
Templecombe Way, Mord.
SM4 .199 CY99
Temple Ct, E1 off Rectory Sq .143 DX71
Hertford SG14 .32 DR06
Potters Bar EN6 .63 CY31
Templecroft, Ashf. TW15 .175 BR93
Templedene Av, Stai. TW18 .174 BH94
Templefield Cl, Add. KT15 .212 BH107
Temple Flds, Hert. SG14 .32 DR06
Templefields Enterprise Cen,
Harl. CM20 .36 EU11
Temple Fortune Hill, NW11 .120 DA57
Temple Fortune La, NW11 .120 DA58
Temple Fortune Par, NW11
off Finchley Rd .119 CZ57
Temple Gdns, N21
off Barrowell Grn .99 DP47
NW11 .119 CZ58
Dagenham RM8 .126 EX62
Rickmansworth WD3 .93 BP49
Staines TW18 .193 BF95
Temple Gro, NW11 .120 DA58
Enfield EN2 .81 DP41
Temple Hill, Dart. DA1 .188 FM86
Sch Temple Hill Co Prim Sch,
Dart. DA1
off St. Edmunds Rd .188 FN85
Temple Hill Sq, Dart. DA1 .188 FM85
Templehof Av, NW2 .119 CW59
Temple La, EC4 .10 D8
Templeman Cl, Pur. CR8
off Croftleigh Av .235 DP116
Templeman Rd, W7 .137 CF71
Temple Mead, Harl.
(Roydon) CM19 .50 EH15
Hemel Hempstead HP2 .40 BK18
Templemead Cl, W3 .138 CS72
Temple Mead Cl, Stan. HA7 .95 CH51
Templemead Ho, E9
off Kingsmead Way .123 DY63
Templemere, Wey. KT13 .195 BR104
Temple Mill La, E15 .123 EB63
★ Temple of Mithras, EC4
off Queen Victoria St .11 J8
Templepan La, Rick. WD3 .74 BL37
Temple Pk, Uxb. UB8 .134 BN69
Temple Pl, WC2 .10 B9
Temple Av, Grays RM16 .171 GG77
Temple Rd, E6 .144 EL67

⊖ London Underground station DLR Docklands Light Railway station Tra Tramlink station Riv Pedestrian ferry landing stage

Temple Rd, N8 121 DM56
NW2 119 CW63
W4 158 CQ76
W5 157 CK76
Croydon CR0 220 DR105
Epsom KT19 216 CR112
Hounslow TW3 156 CB84
Richmond TW9 158 CM83
Westerham (Bigg.H.) TN16 238 EK117
Windsor SL4 151 AQ82
Temple Sheen, SW14 178 CQ85
Temple Sheen Rd, SW14 158 CP84
Temple St, E2 142 DV68
Templeton Av, E4 101 EA49
Templeton Cl, N16 5 M1
SE19 202 DR95
Templeton Ct, NW7
off Kingsbridge Dr 97 CX52
Templeton Pl, SW5 17 H8
Templeton Rd, N15 122 DR58
Temple Vw, St.Alb. AL3 42 CC18
Temple Way, Slou.
(Farn.Com.) SL2 111 AQ64
Sutton SM1 200 DD104
Temple W Ms, SE11 20 E6
Templewood, W13 137 CH71
Welwyn Garden City AL8 29 CX06
Templewood Av, NW3 120 DB62
Temple Wd Dr, Red. RH1 250 DF130
Templewood Gdns, NW3 120 DB62
Templewood La, Slou. SL2 112 AS63
Templewood Pk, Slou. SL2 112 AT63
Templewood Pt, NW2
off Granville Rd 119 CZ61
Sch Templewood Prim Sch,
Welw.G.C. AL8
off Pentley Pk 29 CX07
Tempsford, Welw.G.C. AL7 30 DD09
Tempsford Av, Borwd. WD6 78 CR42
Tempsford Cl, Enf. EN2
off Gladbeck Way 82 DQ41
Temsford Cl, Har. HA2 94 CC54
Ten Acre, Wok. GU21
off Abercorn Way 226 AU118
Ten Acre La, Egh. TW20 193 BC96
Ten Acres, Lthd. (Fetch.) KT22 231 CD124
Ten Acres Cl, Lthd. (Fetch.)
KT22 231 CD124
Tenbury Cl, E7
off Romford Rd 124 EK64
Tenbury Ct, SW2 181 DK88
Tenby Av, Har. HA3 95 CH54
Tenby Cl, N15 off Hanover Rd 122 DT56
Romford RM6 126 EY58
Tenby Gdns, Nthlt. UB5 136 CA65
Tenby Rd, E17 123 DY57
Edgware HA8 96 CM53
Enfield EN3 82 DW41
Romford RM6 126 EY58
Welling DA16 166 EX81
Tenchleys La, Oxt. RH8 254 EK131
Tench St, E1 22 C2
Tenda Rd, SE16 22 C8
Tendring Ms, Harl. CM18
off Tendring Rd 51 ES16
Tendring Rd, Harl. CM18 51 EQ17
Tendring Way, Rom. RM6 126 EW57
Tenham Av, SW2 181 DK88
Tenison Ct, W1 9 J9
Tenison Way, SE1 20 C2
Tennand Cl, Wal.Cr. (Chsht)
EN7 66 DT26
Tenniel Cl, W2 7 L8
Guildford GU2 242 AV132
Tennis Ct La, E.Mol. KT8
off Hampton Ct Way 197 CF97
Tennison Av, Borwd. WD6 78 CP43
Tennison Cl, Couls. CR5 235 DP120
Tennison Rd, SE25 202 DT98
Tennis St, SE1 21 J3
Tenniswood Rd, Enf. EN1 82 DT39
Tennyson Av, E11 124 EG59
E12 144 EL66
NW9 118 CQ55
Grays RM17 170 GB76
New Malden KT3 199 CV99
Twickenham TW1 177 CF88
Waltham Abbey EN9 68 EE34
Tennyson Cl, Enf. EN3 83 DX43
Feltham TW14 175 BT86
Welling DA16 165 ES81
Tennyson Rd, E10 123 EB61
E15 144 EE66
E17 123 DZ58
NW6 139 CZ67
NW7 97 CU50
SE20 183 DX94
SW19 180 DC93
W7 137 CF73
Addlestone KT15 212 BL105
Ashford TW15 174 BL92
Brentwood (Hutt.) CM13 109 GC45
Dartford DA1 188 FN85
Hounslow TW3 156 CC82
Romford RM3 106 FJ52
St. Albans AL2 60 CA26
Tennyson St, SW8 161 DH82
Tennyson Wk, Grav. (Nthflt)
DA11 190 GD90
Tilbury RM18 171 GH82
Tennyson Way, Horn. RM12 127 FF61
Slough SL2
off Wordsworth Rd 131 AL70
Tensing Av, Grav. (Nthflt)
DA11 190 GE90
Tensing Rd, Sthl. UB2 156 CA76
Tentelow La, Sthl. UB2 156 CA78
Tenterden Cl, NW4 119 CX55
SE9 185 EM91
Tenterden Dr, NW4 119 CX55
Tenterden Gdns, NW4 119 CX55
Croydon CR0 202 DU101
Tenterden Gro, NW4 119 CX56
Tenterden Rd, N17 100 DT52
Croydon CR0 202 DU101
Dagenham RM8 126 EZ61
Tenterden St, W1 9 H8
Tenter Grd, E1 11 N6
Tenter Pas, E1 11 P8
Tent Peg La, Orp. BR5 205 EQ99
Tent St, E1 12 C3
Tenzing Rd, Hem.H. HP2 40 BN20
Terborch Way, SE22
off East Dulwich Gro 182 DS85
Tercel Path, Chig. IG7 104 EV49
Teredo St, SE16 23 H6
Terence Cl, Grav. DA12 191 GM88
Terence Ct, Belv. DA17
off Nuxley Rd 166 EZ79
Teresa Gdns, Wal.Cr. EN8 66 DW34
Teresa Ms, E17 123 EA56
Teresa Wk, N10
off Connaught Gdns 121 DH57
Terling Cl, E11 124 EF62
Terling Rd, Dag. RM8 126 FA61
Terlings, The, Brwd. CM14 108 FU48
Terling Wk, N1 4 G7
Terminus Ho, Harl. CM20 35 ER14
Terminus Pl, SW1 19 H6
Terminus St, Harl. CM20 35 ER14
Tern Gdns, Upmin. RM14 129 FS60
Tern Way, Brwd. CM14 108 FS49
Terrace, The, E4
off Chingdale Rd 102 EE48
N3 off Hendon La 97 CZ54
NW6 140 DA67
SW13 158 CS82
Addlestone KT15 212 BL106
Dorking RH5 263 CJ137
Gravesend DA12 191 GH86
Maidenhead SL6 150 AC76
Sevenoaks TN13 256 FD122
Woodford Green IG8
off Broadmead Rd 102 EG51
Terrace Gdns, SW13 159 CT82
Watford WD17 75 BV40
Terrace La, Rich. TW10 178 CL86
Terrace Rd, E9 142 DW66
E13 144 EG67
Walton-on-Thames KT12 195 BU101
Terraces, The, Dart. DA2 188 FQ87
Terrace St, Grav. DA12 191 GH86
Terrace Wk, Dag. RM9 126 EY64
Terrapin Rd, SW17 181 DH90
Terretts Pl, N1 4 E6
Terrick Rd, N22 99 DL53
Terrick St, W12 139 CV72
Terrilands, Pnr. HA5 116 BZ55
Terront Rd, N15 122 DQ57
Tersha St, Rich. TW9 158 CM84
Tessa Sanderson Pl, SW8 161 DH83
Tessa Sanderson Way, Grnf.
UB6 off Lilian Board Way 117 CD64
Testard Rd, Guil. GU2 258 AW136
Testers Cl, Oxt. RH8 254 EH131
Testerton Wk, W11 6 B9
Testwood Rd, Wind. SL4 151 AK81
Tetbury Pl, N1 4 E8
Tetcott Rd, SW10 160 DC80
Tetherdown, N10 120 DG55
Coll Tetherdown Adult Ed Cen,
N10 off Tetherdown 120 DG55
Sch Tetherdown Prim Sch,
N10 off Grand Av 120 DG56
Tethys Rd, Hem.H. HP2 40 BM17
Tetty Way, Brom. BR2 204 EG96
Teversham La, SW8 161 DL81
Teviot Av, S.Ock. (Aveley)
RM15 148 FQ72
Teviot Cl, Guil. GU2 242 AU131
Welling DA16 166 EV81
Teviot St, E14 14 C5
TEWIN, Welw. AL6 30 DE05
Tewin Cl, St.Alb. AL4 43 CJ16
Tewin Ct, Welw.G.C. AL7 29 CZ08
Sch Tewin Cowper C of E VA
Prim Sch, Welw. AL6
off Cannons Meadow 30 DE05
Tewin Rd, Hem.H. HP2 41 BQ20
Welwyn Garden City AL7 29 CZ09
Tewkesbury Av, SE23 182 DV88
Pinner HA5 116 BY57
Tewkesbury Cl, N15
off Tewkesbury Rd 122 DR58
Barnet EN4
off Approach Rd 80 DD42
Loughton IG10 84 EL44
West Byfleet (Byfleet) KT14 212 BK111
Tewkesbury Gdns, NW9 118 CP55
Tewkesbury Rd, N15 122 DR58
W13 137 CG73
Carshalton SM5 200 DD102
Tewkesbury Ter, N11 99 DJ51
Tewson Rd, SE18 165 ES78
Teynham Av, Enf. EN1 82 DR44
Teynham Grn, Brom. BR2 204 EG99
Teynton Ter, N17 100 DQ53
Thackeray Av, N17 100 DU54
Tilbury RM18 171 GH81
Thackeray Cl, SW19 179 CX94
Harrow HA2 116 CA60
Isleworth TW7 157 CG82
Uxbridge UB8
off Dickens Av 135 BP72
Thackeray Dr, Rom. RM6 126 EU59
Thackeray Rd, E6 144 EK68
SW8 161 DH82
Thackeray St, W8 17 K4
Thakeham Cl, SE26 182 DV92
Thalia Cl, SE10 163 ED79
Thalmassing Cl, Brwd. (Hutt.)
CM13 109 GB47
Thame Rd, SE16 23 H3
Thames Av, SW10 160 DC81
Chertsey KT16 194 BG97
Dagenham RM9 147 FB70
Greenford UB6 137 CF68
Hemel Hempstead HP2 40 BM15
Windsor SL4 151 AR80
Thames Bk, SW14 158 CQ82
Thamesbank Pl, SE28 146 EW72
Thames Circle, E14 24 P7
Thames Cl, Cher. KT16 194 BH101
Hampton TW12 196 CB96
Rainham RM13 147 FH72
Thames Ct, W.Mol. KT8 196 CB96
Thames Cres, W4
off Corney Rd 158 CS80
Thamesdale, St.Alb.
(Lon.Col.) AL2 62 CM27
THAMES DITTON, KT7 197 CF100
⇌ Thames Ditton 197 CF101
Sch Thames Ditton Inf Sch,
T.Ditt. KT7 off Speer Rd 197 CF100
Thames Ditton Island, T.Ditt.
KT7 197 CG99
Sch Thames Ditton Jun Sch,
T.Ditt. KT7 off Mercer Cl 197 CF101
Thames Dr, Grays RM16 171 GG78
Ruislip HA4 115 BQ58
Thames Edge Ct, Stai. TW18
off Clarence St 173 BE91
Thames Europort, Dart. DA2 169 FS84
Thamesfield Ct, Shep. TW17 195 BQ101
★ Thames Flood Barrier &
Visitors Cen, SE18 164 EK75
Thames Gate, Dart. DA1
off St. Edmunds Rd 168 FN84
Thamesgate Cl, Rich. TW10
off Locksmeade Rd 177 CH91
Thames Gateway, Dag. RM9 146 EZ68
Rainham RM13 147 FG72
South Ockendon RM15 168 FP75
Thameshill Av, Rom. RM5 105 FC54
★ Thames Ho, SW1 19 N7
Thameside, Tedd. TW11 177 CK94
Thameside Ind Est, E16 164 EL75
Sch Thameside Inf Sch, Grays
RM17 off Manor Rd 170 GC79
Sch Thameside Jun Sch, Grays
RM17 off Manor Rd 170 GC79
Thameside Wk, SE28 145 ET72
THAMESMEAD, SE28 145 ET74
Thamesmead, Walt. KT12 195 BU101
Thames Mead, Wind. SL4 151 AL81
Coll Thamesmead Cen, Erith
DA18 off Yarnton Way 166 EY75
THAMESMEAD NORTH, SE28 146 EW72
Thames Meadow, Shep. TW17 195 BR102
West Molesey KT8 196 CA96
Sch Thamesmead Sch,
Shep. TW17
off Manygate La 195 BQ100
Thamesmead Spine Rd, Belv.
DA17 167 FB75
THAMESMEAD WEST, SE18 165 EP76
Thamesmere Dr, SE28 146 EU73
Thames Pl, SW15 159 CX83
Thames Pt, SW6
off The Boulevard 160 DC81
Thames Quay, SW10
off Harbour Av 160 DC81
Thames Rd, E16 144 EK74
W4 158 CN79
Barking IG11 145 ET69
Dartford DA1 167 FF82
Grays RM17 170 GB80
Slough SL3 153 BA77
Thames Side, Cher. KT16 194 BJ100
Kingston upon Thames KT1 197 CK95
Staines TW18 194 BH96
Windsor SL4 151 AR80
Thames St, SE10 163 EB79
Hampton TW12 196 CB95
Kingston upon Thames KT1 197 CK96
Staines TW18 173 BE91
Sunbury-on-Thames TW16 195 BV98
Walton-on-Thames KT12 195 BT101
Weybridge KT13 195 BP103
Windsor SL4 151 AR81
Thamesvale Cl, Houns. TW3 156 CA83
H Thames Valley Nuffield
Hosp, Slou. SL2 132 AW67
Uni Thames Valley Uni -
Ealing Campus, W5
off St. Mary's Rd 137 CK74
Grove Ho, W5
off The Grove 137 CK74
London Coll of Music, W5
off Ranelagh Rd 157 CK75
Walpole Ho, W5
off Bond St 137 CK73
Westel Ho, W5
off Uxbridge Rd 137 CJ73
Uni Thames Valley Uni -
Faculty of Health &
Human Sciences, Wexham
Pk Hosp, Slou. SL2
off Wexham St 132 AV70
Uni Thames Valley Uni -
Slough Campus, Slou.
SL1 off Wellington St 132 AS74
Thames Vw, Grays RM16 171 GG78
Sch Thames Vw Inf Sch, Bark.
IG11 off Bastable Av 146 EU68
Sch Thames Vw Jun Sch, Bark.
IG11 off Bastable Av 145 ET68
Sch Thamesview Sch, Grav.
DA12 off Thong La 191 GM90
Thames Village, W4 158 CQ81
Thames Way, Grav. DA11 190 GD88
Thames Wf, E16 25 J1
Thamley, Purf. RM19 168 FN77
Thanescroft Gdns, Croy. CR0 202 DS104
Thanet Dr, Kes. BR2
off Phoenix Dr 204 EK104
Thanet Pl, Croy. CR0 220 DQ105
Thanet Rd, Bex. DA5 186 FA87
Erith DA8 167 FE80
Thanet St, WC1 9 N2
Thane Vil, N7 121 DM62
Thane Wks, N7 121 DM62
Thanington Ct, SE9 185 ES86
Thanstead Copse, H.Wyc.
(Loud.) HP10 88 AC53
Thanstead Ct, H.Wyc.
(Loud.) HP10 88 AC53
Thant Cl, E10 123 EB62
Tharp Rd, Wall. SM6 219 DK106
Thatcham Gdns, N20 98 DC45
Thatcher Cl, West Dr. UB7
off Classon Cl 154 BL75
Thatcher Ct, Dart. DA1
off Heath St 188 FK87
Thatchers Cl, Horl. RH6
off Wheatfield Way 269 DH146
Loughton IG10 85 EQ40
Thatchers Cft, Hem.H. HP2 40 BL16
Thatchers Way, Islw. TW7 177 CD85
Thatches Gro, Rom. RM6 126 EY56
Thavies Inn, EC1 10 D7
Thaxted Ct, N1 5 J10
Thaxted Grn, Brwd. (Hutt.)
CM13 109 GC43
Thaxted Ho, Dag. RM10 147 FB66
Thaxted Pl, SW20 179 CX94
Thaxted Rd, SE9 185 EQ89
Buckhurst Hill IG9 102 EL45
Thaxted Wk, Rain. RM13
off Ongar Way 147 FF67
Thaxted Way, Wal.Abb. EN9 67 ED33
Thaxton Rd, W14 159 CZ79
Thayers Fm Rd, Beck. BR3 203 DY95
Thayer St, W1 8 F6
Thaynesfield, Pot.B. EN6 64 DD31
★ Theatre Mus, WC2
off Russell St 9 P9
★ Theatre Royal, WC2 9 P8
Theatre Sq, E15
off Great Eastern Rd 143 ED65
Theatre St, SW11 160 DF83
Theberton St, N1 4 D7
Theed St, SE1 20 C2
Thele Av, Ware (Stans.Abb.)
SG12 33 ED11
Theleway Cl, Hodd. EN11 33 EB14
Thellusson Way, Rick. WD3 91 BF45
Thelma Cl, Grav. DA12 191 GM92
Thelma Gdns, SE3 164 EK81
Feltham TW13 176 BY90
Thelma Gro, Tedd. TW11 177 CG93
Theobald Cres, Har. HA3 94 CB53
Theobald Rd, E17 123 DZ59
Croydon CR0 201 DP103
Theobalds Av, N12 98 DC49
Grays RM17 170 GC78
Theobalds Cl, Pot.B. (Cuffley)
EN6 65 DM30
Theobalds Ct, N4
off Queens Dr 122 DQ61
⇌ Theobalds Grove 67 DX32
Theobalds La, Wal.Cr. (Chsht)
EN8 66 DV32
Theobalds Pk Rd, Enf. EN2 81 DP35
Theobald's Rd, WC1 10 A5
Theobalds Rd, Pot.B. (Cuffley)
EN6 65 DL30
Theobald St, SE1 21 J6
Borehamwood WD6 78 CM40
Radlett WD7 77 CH36
Theodora Way, Pnr. HA5 115 BT55
Theodore Rd, SE13 183 EC86
Thepps Cl, Red. (S.Nutfld)
RH1 267 DM137
Therapia Lane 201 DL101
Therapia La, Croy. CR0 201 DL100
Therapia Rd, SE22 182 DW86
Theresa Rd, W6 159 CU77
Theresas Wk, S.Croy. CR2
off Sanderstead Rd 220 DR110
Therfield Ct, N4
off Brownswood Rd 122 DQ61
Therfield Rd, St.Alb. AL3 43 CD16
Sch Therfield Sch, Lthd. KT22
off Dilston Rd 231 CG119
Thermopylae Gate, E14 24 B8
Theseus Wk, N1 4 F10
Thesiger Rd, SE20 183 DX94
Thessaly Rd, SW8 161 DJ80
Thetford Cl, N13 99 DP51
Thetford Gdns, Dag. RM9 146 EX66
Thetford Rd, Ashf. TW15 174 BL91
Dagenham RM9 146 EX67
New Malden KT3 198 CR100
Thetis Ter, Rich. TW9
off Kew Grn 158 CN79
THEYDON BOIS, Epp. CM16 85 ET37
⊖ Theydon Bois 85 ET36
Sch Theydon Bois Co Prim Sch,
Epp. CM16 off Orchard Dr 85 ES36
Theydon Bower, Epp. CM16 70 EU31
Theydon Ct, Wal.Abb. EN9 68 EG33
Theydon Gdns, Rain. RM13 147 FE66
THEYDON GARNON, Epp.
CM16 86 EW35
Theydon Gate, Epp. (They.B.)
CM16 off Coppice Row 85 ES37
Theydon Gro, Epp. CM16 70 EU30
Woodford Green IG8 102 EJ51
THEYDON MOUNT, Epp.
CM16 70 FA34
Theydon Pk Rd, Epp.
(They.B.) CM16 85 ES39
Theydon Pl, Epp. CM16 69 ET31
Theydon Rd, E5 122 DW61
Epping CM16 69 ER34
Theydon St, E17 123 DZ59
Thicket, The, West Dr. UB7 134 BL72
Thicket Cres, Sutt. SM1 218 DC105
Thicket Gro, SE20
off Anerley Rd 182 DU94
Dagenham RM9 146 EW65
Thicket Rd, SE20 182 DU94
Sutton SM1 218 DC105
Thicketts, Sev. TN13 257 FJ123
Thickthorne La, Stai. TW18 174 BJ94
Thieves La, Hert. SG14 31 DM10
Ware SG12 32 DW08
Third Av, E12 124 EL63
E13 15 M1
E17 123 EA57
W3 139 CT74
W10 6 D3
Dagenham RM10 147 FB67
Enfield EN1 82 DT43
Grays RM20 169 FU79
Harlow CM18, CM19 51 EM16
Hayes UB3 135 BT74
Romford RM6 126 EW58
Waltham Abbey EN9
off Breach Barn Mobile
Home Pk 68 EH30
Watford WD25 76 BX35
Wembley HA9 117 CK61
Third Cl, W.Mol. KT8 196 CB98
Third Cres, Slou. SL1 131 AQ71
Third Cross Rd, Twick. TW2 177 CD89
Third Way, Wem. HA9 118 CP63
Thirkleby Cl, Slou. SL1 131 AQ74
Thirleby Rd, SW1 19 K6
Edgware HA8 96 CR53
Thirlmere Av, Grnf. UB6 137 CJ69
Slough SL1 130 AJ71
Thirlmere Cl, Egh. TW20
off Keswick Rd 173 BB94
Thirlmere Dr, St.Alb. AL1 43 CH22
Thirlmere Gdns, Nthwd. HA6 93 BQ51
Wembley HA9 117 CJ60
Thirlmere Ho, Islw. TW7
off Summerwood Rd 177 CF85
Thirlmere Ri, Brom. BR1 184 EF93
Thirlmere Rd, N10 99 DH53
SW16 181 DK91
Bexleyheath DA7 167 FC82
Thirlstane, St.Alb. AL1 43 CE19
Thirsk Cl, Nthlt. UB5 136 CA65
Thirsk Rd, SE25 202 DR98
SW11 160 DG83
Borehamwood WD6 78 CN37
Mitcham CR4 180 DG94
Thirston Path, Borwd. WD6 78 CN40
Thirza Rd, Dart. DA1 188 FM86
Thistlebrook, SE2 166 EW76
Thistlebrook Ind Est, SE2 166 EW75
Thistle Cl, Hem.H. HP1 39 BE21
Thistlecroft, Hem.H. HP1 40 BH21
Thistlecroft Gdns, Stan. HA7 95 CK53
Thistlecroft Rd, Walt. KT12 214 BW105
Thistledene, T.Ditt. KT7 197 CE100
West Byfleet KT14 211 BF113
Thistledene Av, Har. HA2 116 BY62
Romford RM5 105 FB50
Thistledown, Grav. DA12 191 GK93
Thistle Dr, Hat. AL9 45 CT15
Thistlefield Cl, Bex. DA5 186 EX88
Thistle Gro, SW10 17 M9
Welwyn Garden City AL7 30 DC12
Thistlemead, Chis. BR7 205 EP96
Thistle Mead, Loug. IG10 85 EN41
Thistle Rd, Grav. DA12 191 GL87
Thistles, The, Hem.H. HP1 40 BH19
Thistlewaite Rd, E5 122 DV62
Thistlewood Cl, N7 121 DM61
Thistlewood Cres, Croy.
(New Adgtn) CR0 221 ED112
Thistleworth Cl, Islw. TW7 157 CD80
Thistley Cl, N12
off Summerfields Av 98 DE51
Thistley Ct, SE8
off Glaisher St 163 EB79
Thomas a'Beckett Cl, Wem.
HA0 117 CF63
Sch Thomas Arnold Prim Sch,
Dag. RM9
off Rowdowns Rd 146 EZ66
Thomas Av, Cat. CR3 236 DQ121
Thomas Baines Rd, SW11 160 DD83
Sch Thomas Buxton Inf & Jun
Sch, E1 12 B4
Thomas Cl, Brwd. CM15 108 FY48
Sch Thomas Coram Sch, The,
Berk. HP4
off Swing Gate La 38 AX21
Thomas Cribb Ms, E6 145 EM72
Thomas Darby Ct, W11 6 C8
Thomas Dean Rd, SE26
off Kangley Br Rd 183 DZ91
Thomas Dinwiddy Rd, SE12 184 EH89
Thomas Doyle St, SE1 20 E5
Thomas Dr, Grav. DA12 191 GK89
Sch Thomas Fairchild JMI Sch,
N1 5 H9
Sch Thomas Gamuel Prim Sch,
E17 off Colchester Rd 123 EA58
Sch Thomas Harding Mid Sch,
Chesh. HP5
off Fullers Hill 54 AP32
Thomas Hardy Ho, N22 99 DM52
Sch Thomas Jones Prim Sch,
W11 6 C8
Thomas La, SE6 183 EA87
Thomas More Ho, EC2
off The Barbican 142 DQ71
Sch Thomas More RC Sch, Pur.
CR8 off Russell Hill Rd 219 DN110
Thomas More St, E1 12 A10
Thomas More Way, N2 120 DC55
Thomas Pl, W8 17 J6
Thomas Rd, E14 13 M7
High Wycombe
(Woob.Grn) HP10 110 AD59
Thomas Rochford Way,
Wal.Cr. EN8 67 DZ27
Thomas Sims Ct, Horn. RM12 127 FH64
Sch Thomas's Prep Sch,
SW11 (Battersea)
off Battersea High St 160 DD81
SW11 (Clapham)
off Broomwood Rd 180 DF86
W8 (Kensington) 17 K5
Thomas St, SE18 165 EN77
Sch Thomas Tallis Sec Sch,
SE3 off Kidbrooke Pk Rd 164 EH83
Thomas Wall Cl, Sutt. SM1
off Clarence Rd 218 DB106
Sch Thomas Willingale Co
Prim Sch, The, Loug.
IG10 off The Broadway 85 EQ41
Thompkins La, Slou.
(Farn.Royal) SL2 131 AM66
Thompson Av, Rich. TW9 158 CN83
Thompson Cl, Ilf. IG1
off High Rd 125 EQ61
Slough SL3 153 BA77
Sutton SM1
off Barrington Rd 200 DA102
Thompson Rd, SE22 182 DT86
Dagenham RM9 126 EZ62
Hounslow TW3 156 CB84
Uxbridge UB10 134 BL66
Thompson's Av, SE5 162 DQ80
Thompsons Cl, Wal.Cr. EN7 66 DT29
Thompson's La, Loug.
(High Beach) IG10 84 EF39
Thompson Way, Rick. WD3 92 BG45
Thomson Cres, Croy. CR0 201 DN102
Thomson Rd, Har. HA3 117 CE55
Thong La, Grav. DA12 191 GM90
Thorburn Sq, SE1 22 A8
Thorburn Way, SW19 200 DC95
Thoresby St, N1 11 H1
Thorkhill Gdns, T.Ditt. KT7 197 CG102
Thorkhill Rd, T.Ditt. KT7 197 CH101
Thorley Cl, W.Byf. KT14 212 BG114
Thorley Gdns, Wok. GU22 212 BG114
Thornaby Gdns, N18 100 DU51
Thornaby Pl, H.Wyc. (Woob.Grn)
HP10 off Wootton Dr 110 AE55
Thornash Cl, Wok. GU21 226 AW115
Thornash Rd, Wok. GU21 226 AW115
Thornash Way, Wok. GU21 226 AW115
Thorn Av, Bushey
(Bushey Hth) WD23 94 CC46
Thorn Bk, Guil. GU2 258 AU136
Thornbank Cl, Stai. TW19 174 BG85
Thornberry Way, Guil. GU1 243 AZ130
Thornbridge Rd, Iver SL0 133 BC67
Thornbrook, Epp. (Thnwd)
CM16 70 EX25
Thornbury Av, Islw. TW7 157 CD80
Thornbury Cl, N16 5 M1
NW7 off Kingsbridge Dr 97 CX52
Hoddesdon EN11 33 EB13
Thornbury Gdns, Borwd. WD6 78 CQ42
Thornbury Rd, SW2 181 DL86
Isleworth TW7 157 CD81
Thornbury Sq, N6 121 DJ60
Thornby Rd, E5 122 DW62
Sch Thornchace Sch, Guil.
GU1 off Grove Rd 243 BC134
Thorncliffe Rd, SW2 181 DL86
Southall UB2 156 BZ78
Thorn Cl, Brom. BR2 205 EN100
Northolt UB5 136 BZ69
Thorncombe Rd, SE22 182 DS85
Thorncroft, Egh. (Eng.Grn)
TW20 172 AW94
Hemel Hempstead HP3 41 BP22
Hornchurch RM11 127 FH58
Thorncroft Cl, Couls. CR5
off Waddington Av 235 DN120
Thorncroft Dr, Lthd. KT22 231 CH123
Thorncroft Rd, Sutt. SM1 218 DB105
Thorncroft St, SW8 161 DL80
Thorndales, Brwd. CM14 108 FX49
Thorndean St, SW18 180 DC89
Thorndene Av, N11 98 DG46
Thorndike, Slou. SL2 131 AN71
Thorndike Av, Nthlt. UB5 136 BX67
Thorndike Cl, SW10 160 DC80
Thorndike Rd, N1 5 H4
Thorndike St, SW1 19 L9
Thorndon Cl, Orp. BR5 205 ET96
Thorndon Ct, Brwd.
(Gt Warley) CM13 107 FW51
Thorndon Gdns, Epsom KT19 216 CS105
Thorndon Gate, Brwd.
(Ingrave) CM13 109 GC50
Thorndon Rd, Orp. BR5 205 ET96
Thorn Dr, Slou. (Geo.Grn)
SL3 132 AY72
Thorndyke Ct, Pnr. HA5
off Westfield Pk 94 BZ52
Thorne Cl, E11 124 EE63
E16 15 L7
Ashford TW15 175 BQ94
Erith DA8 167 FC79
Hemel Hempstead HP1
off St. Johns Rd 40 BH22
Thorneloe Gdns, Croy. CR0 219 DN106
Thorne Pas, SW13 158 CS82
Thorne Rd, SW8 161 DL80
Thornes Cl, Beck. BR3 203 EC97
Thorne St, E16 15 K7
SW13 158 CS83
Thornet Wd Rd, Brom. BR1 205 EN97
THORNEY, Iver SL0 154 BH76
Thorney Cres, SW11 160 DD80
Thorneycroft Cl, Walt. KT12 196 BW100
Thorneycroft Dr, Enf. EN3 83 EA37
Thorney Hedge Rd, W4 158 CP77
Thorney La N, Iver SL0 133 BF74
Thorney La S, Iver SL0 153 BF75
Thorney Mill Rd, Iver SL0 154 BG76
West Drayton UB7 154 BG76
Thorney St, SW1 19 N7
Thornfield Av, NW7 97 CY53
Thornfield Rd, W12 159 CV75
Banstead SM7 234 DA117
Thornford Rd, SE13 183 EC85
Thorngate Rd, W9 7 H3
Thorngrove Rd, E13 144 EH67
Thornham Gro, E15 123 ED64
Thornham St, SE10 163 EB79
Thornhaugh Ms, WC1 9 M4
Thornhaugh St, WC1 9 M5
Thornhill, Epp. (N.Wld Bas.)
CM16 71 FC26
Thornhill Av, SE18 165 ES80
Surbiton KT6 198 CL103
Thornhill Br Wf, N1 4 A8
Thornhill Cl, Amer. HP7 55 AP40
Thornhill Cres, N1 4 A6
Thornhill Gdns, E10 123 EB61
Barking IG11 145 ES66
Thornhill Gro, N1 4 B6
Sch Thornhill Prim Sch, N1 4 C6
Thornhill Rd, E10 123 EB61
N1 4 C5

★ Place of interest | H Hospital | Sch School | Coll College | Uni University | ⇌ Railway station

Thornhill Rd, Croy. CR0 .....202 DQ101
Northwood HA6 .....93 BQ49
Surbiton KT6 .....198 CL103
Uxbridge UB10 .....114 BM63
Thornhill Sq, N1 .....4 B6
Thornhill Way, Shep. TW17 ..194 BN99
Thorn Ho, Beck. BR3 .....203 DY95
Thorn La, Rain. RM13 .....148 FK68
Thornlaw Rd, SE27 .....181 DN91
Thornleas Pl, Lthd. (E.Hors.)
KT24 off Station App 245 BS126
Thornley Cl, N17 .....100 DU52
Thornley Dr, Har. HA2 .....116 CB61
Thornley Pl, SE10 .....24 G10
Thornridge, Brwd. CM14 .....108 FV45
Thornsbeach Rd, SE6 .....183 EC88
Thornsett Pl, SE20 .....202 DV96
Thornsett Rd, SE20 .....202 DV96
SW18 .....180 DB89
Thornside, Edg. HA8
off High St 96 CN51
Thorns Meadow, West.
(Brasted) TN16 .....240 EW123
Thorn Ter, SE15
off Nunhead Gro 162 DW83
Thornton Av, SW2 .....181 DK88
W4 .....158 CS77
Croydon CR0 .....201 DM100
West Drayton UB7 .....154 BM76
Thornton Cl, Guil. GU2 .....244 AU130
Horley RH6 .....268 DE148
West Drayton UB7 .....154 BM76
Thornton Ct, SW20 .....199 CX99
Thornton Cres, Couls. CR5 ..235 DN119
Thornton Dene, Beck. BR3 ..203 EA96
Thornton Gdns, SW12 .....181 DK88
Thornton Gro, Pnr. HA5 .....94 CA51
THORNTON HEATH, CR7 .....201 DP98
⇌ Thornton Heath 202 DQ98
Thornton Hill, SW19 .....179 CY94
Thornton Pl, W1 .....8 D5
Horley RH6 .....268 DE148
Thornton Rd, E11 .....123 ED61
N18 .....100 DW48
SW12 .....181 DK87
SW14 .....158 CR83
SW19 .....179 CX93
Barnet EN5 .....79 CY41
Belvedere DA17 .....167 FB77
Bromley BR1 .....184 EG92
Carshalton SM5 .....200 DD102
Croydon CR0 .....201 DM101
Ilford IG1 .....125 EP63
Potters Bar EN6 .....64 DC30
Thornton Heath CR7 .....201 DM101
Thornton Rd E, SW19
off Thornton Rd 179 CX93
Thornton Rd Retail Pk, Croy.
CR0 .....201 DM100
Thornton Row, Th.Hth. CR7
off London Rd 201 DN99
Thorntons Fm Av, Rom. RM7 .127 FD60
Thornton St, SW9 .....161 DN82
Hertford SG14 .....32 DR09
St. Albans AL3 .....42 CC19
Thornton Wk, Horl. RH6
off Thornton Pl 268 DE148
Thornton Way, NW11 .....120 DB57
Sch Thorntree Inf Sch, SE7
off Thorntree Rd 164 EK78
Thorntree Rd, SE7 .....164 EK78
Thornville Gro, Mitch. CR4 ...200 DC96
Thornville St, SE8 .....163 EA81
THORNWOOD, Epp. CM16 .....70 EW25
Thornwood Cl, E18 .....102 EH54
Thornwood Rd, SE13 .....184 EE85
Epping CM16 .....70 EV29
Thorogood Gdns, E15 .....124 EE64
Thorogood Way, Rain. RM13 .147 FE67
Thorold Cl, S.Croy. CR2 .....221 DX110
Thorold Rd, N22 .....99 DL52
Ilford IG1 .....125 EP61
Thoroughfare, The, Tad. KT20 .249 CU125
Thorparch Rd, SW8 .....161 DK81
THORPE, Egh. TW20 .....193 BC97
Thorpebank Rd, W12 .....139 CU74
Thorpe Bypass, Egh. TW20 ..193 BB96
Thorpe Cl, W10 .....6 D7
Croydon (New Adgtn) CR0 221 EC111
Orpington BR6 .....205 ES103
Sch Thorpe C of E Inf Sch, Egh.
TW20 off The Bence 193 BB97
H Thorpe Coombe Hosp,
E17 .....123 EC55
Thorpe Cres, E17 .....101 DZ54
Watford WD19 .....94 BW45
Thorpedale Gdns, Ilf. IG2, IG6 .125 EN56
Thorpedale Rd, N4 .....121 DL60
Thorpefield Cl, St.Alb. AL4 ...43 CK17
THORPE GREEN, Egh. TW20 .193 BA98
Sch Thorpe Hall Prim Sch,
E17 off Hale End Rd 101 EC53
Thorpe Hall Rd, E17 .....101 EC53
Sch Thorpe Ho Sch, Ger.Cr.
SL9 off Oval Way 112 AY56
Thorpe Ind Est, Egh. TW20 ..193 BC96
THORPE LEA, Egh. TW20 .....173 BB93
Sch Thorpe Lea Prim Sch, Egh.
TW20
off Huntingfield Way 173 BD93
Thorpe Lea Rd, Egh. TW20 ..173 BB93
Thorpe Lo, Horn. RM11 .....128 FL59
★ Thorpe Park, Cher. KT16 .193 BE98
Thorpe Rd, E6 .....145 EM67
E7 .....124 EF63
E17 .....101 EC54
N15 .....122 DS58
Barking IG11 .....145 ER66
Chertsey KT16 .....193 BD99
Kingston upon Thames KT2 .178 CL94
St. Albans AL1 .....43 CD21
Staines TW18 .....173 BD93
Thorpes Cl, Guil. GU2 .....242 AU131
Thorpeside Cl, Stai. TW18 ..193 BE96
Thorpe Wk, Grnf. UB6 .....137 CE68
Thorpewood Av, SE26 .....182 DV89
Thorpland Av, Uxb. UB10 .....115 BQ62
Thorsden Cl, Wok. GU22 .....226 AY118
Thorsden Ct, Wok. GU22
off Guildford Rd 226 AY118
Thorsden Way, SE19
off Oaks Av 182 DS91
Thorverton Rd, NW2 .....119 CY62
Thoydon Rd, E3 .....143 DY68
Thrale Rd, SW16 .....181 DJ92
Thrale St, SE1 .....21 H2
Thrasher Cl, E8 .....5 N7
Thrawl St, E1 .....11 P6
Threadneedle St, EC2 .....11 K8
Three Arches Pk, Red. RH1 ..266 DF138
Three Arch Rd, Red. RH1 .....266 DF138
Three Barrels Wk, EC4 .....11 H9
Sch Three Bridges Prim Sch,
Sthl. UB2 off Melbury Av ..156 CB76
Three Cherry Trees La, Hem.H.
HP2 .....41 BP16
Three Cl La, Berk. HP4 .....38 AW20
Three Colts Cor, E2 .....12 A3
Three Colts La, E2 .....12 C3
Three Colt St, E14 .....13 M8
Three Cors, Bexh. DA7 .....167 FB82
Hemel Hempstead HP3 .....40 BN22
Three Cups Yd, WC1 .....10 B6
Three Forests Way, Chig. IG7 .104 EW48
Epping CM16 .....51 EM23
Harlow CM19 .....50 EH18
Harlow (Mark Hall N.) CM20 .36 EU10
Loughton IG10 .....84 EK38
Romford RM4 .....104 EW48
Waltham Abbey EN9 .....84 EK36
Waltham Abbey
(Broad.Com.) EN9 .....50 EL21
Ware SG12 .....34 EL12
Three Gates, Guil. GU1 .....243 BC133
Three Gates Rd, Long.
(Fawk.Grn) DA3 .....209 FU102
Three Horseshoes Rd, Harl.
CM19 .....51 EP17
Three Households, Ch.St.G.
HP8 .....90 AT49
Three Kings Rd, Mitch. CR4 ..200 DG97
Three Kings Yd, W1 .....8 G9
Three Mill La, E3 .....14 C1
Three Oak La, SE1 .....21 N3
Three Oaks Cl, Uxb. UB10 ...114 BM62
Three Pears Rd, Guil. GU1 ...243 BD134
Three Quays Wk, EC3 .....11 M10
Three Valleys Way, Bushey
WD23 .....76 BY43
THRESHERS BUSH, Harl.
CM17 .....53 FB16
Threshers Bush, Harl. CM17 ..53 FA14
Threshers Pl, W11 .....6 C9
Thriffwood, SE26 .....182 DW90
Thrift, The, Dart. (Bean) DA2 .189 FW90
Thrift Fm La, Borwd. WD6 .....78 CP40
Thriftfield, Hem.H. HP2 .....40 BK18
Thrift Grn, Brwd. CM13
off Knight's Way 109 GA48
Thrift La, Sev. (Cudham) TN14 .239 ER117
Thrifts Hall Fm Ms, Epp.
(They.B.) CM16 .....85 ET37
Thrifts Mead, Epp. (They.B.)
CM16 .....85 ES37
Thrift Vale, Guil. GU4 .....243 BD131
Thrigby Rd, Chess. KT9 .....216 CM107
Throckmorten Rd, E16 .....15 P8
Throgmorton Av, EC2 .....11 K7
Throgmorton St, EC2 .....11 K7
Throwley Cl, SE2 .....166 EW76
Throwley Rd, Sutt. SM1 .....218 DB106
Throwley Way, Sutt. SM1 .....218 DB105
Thrums, The, Wat. WD24 .....75 BV37
Thrupp Cl, Mitch. CR4 .....201 DH96
Thrupps Av, Walt. KT12 .....214 BX106
Thrupps La, Walt. KT12 .....214 BX106
Thrush Av, Hat. AL10 .....45 CU20
Thrush Grn, Har. HA2 .....116 CA56
Rickmansworth WD3 .....92 BJ45
Thrush La, Pot.B. (Cuffley) EN6 ..65 DL28
Thrush St, SE17 .....20 G9
Thruxton Way, SE15
off Daniel Gdns 162 DT80
Thumbswood, Welw.G.C. AL7 ..30 DA12
Thumpers, Hem.H. HP2 .....40 BL18
Thundercourt, Ware SG12 .....33 DX05
Thunderer Rd, Dag. RM9 .....146 EY70
Thundridge Cl, Welw.G.C. AL7
off Amwell Common 30 DB10
Thurbarn Rd, SE6 .....183 EB92
Thurgood Rd, Hodd. EN11 .....49 EA15
Thurland Rd, SE16 .....22 A5
Thurlby Cl, Har. HA1
off Gayton Rd 117 CG58
Woodford Green IG8 .....103 EM50
Thurlby Rd, SE27 .....181 DN91
Wembley HA0 .....137 CK65
Thurleigh Av, SW12 .....180 DG86
Thurleigh Rd, SW12 .....180 DG86
Thurleston Av, Mord. SM4 ...199 CY99
Thurlestone Av, N12 .....98 DF51
Ilford IG3 .....125 ET63
Thurlestone Cl, Shep. TW17 ..195 BQ100
Thurlestone Rd, SE27 .....181 DN90
Thurloe Cl, SW7 .....18 A7
Thurloe Gdns, Rom. RM1 .....127 FF58
Thurloe Pl, SW7 .....17 P7
Thurloe Pl Ms, SW7 .....17 P7
Thurloe Sq, SW7 .....18 A7
Thurloe St, SW7 .....17 P7
Thurloe Wk, Grays RM17 .....170 GA76
Thurlow Cl, E4
off Higham Sta Av 101 EB51
Thurlow Gdns, Ilf. IG6 .....103 ER51
Wembley HA0 .....117 CK64
Thurlow Hill, SE21 .....182 DQ88
Thurlow Pk Rd, SE21 .....181 DP88
Sch Thurlow Pk Sch, SE27
off Elmcourt Rd 181 DP89
Thurlow Rd, NW3 .....120 DD64
W7 .....157 CG75
Thurlow St, SE17 .....21 K9
Thurlow Ter, NW5 .....120 DG64
Thurlstone Rd, Ruis. HA4 .....115 BU62
Thurlton Ct, Wok. GU21
off Chobham Rd 226 AY116
Thurnby Ct, Twick. TW2 .....177 CE90
Thurnham Way, Tad. KT20 ...233 CW120
Thurrock Pk Way, Til. RM18 ..170 GD80
Coll Thurrock Tech Coll, Grays
RM16 off Woodview 171 GF77
Thursby Rd, Wok. GU21 .....226 AU118
Thursland Rd, Sid. DA14 .....186 EY92
Thursley Cres, Croy.
(New Adgtn) CR0 .....221 ED108
Thursley Gdns, SW19 .....179 CX89
Thursley Rd, SE9 .....185 EM90
Thurso Cl, Rom. RM3 .....106 FP51
Thurso St, SW17 .....180 DD91
Thurstan Rd, SW20 .....179 CV94
Thurstans, Harl. CM19 .....51 EQ20
Thurston Rd, SE13 .....163 EB82
Slough SL1 .....132 AS72
Southall UB1 .....136 BZ72
Thurston Rd Ind Est, SE13
off Jerrard St 163 EB83
Thurtle Rd, E2 .....5 P8
Thwaite Cl, Erith DA8 .....167 FC79
Thyer Cl, Orp. BR6
off Isabella Dr 223 EQ105
Thyme Cl, SE3
off Nelson Mandela Rd ..164 EJ83
Thyme Ct, Guil. GU4
off Mallow Cres 243 BB131
Thyra Gro, N12 .....98 DB51
Tibbatts Rd, E3 .....14 A3
Tibbenham Pl, SE6 .....183 EA89
Tibbenham Wk, E13 .....144 EF68
Tibberton Sq, N1 .....4 G6
Tibbets Cl, SW19 .....179 CX88
Tibbet's Cor, SW15 .....179 CX87
Tibbet's Cor Underpass,
SW15 off West Hill 179 CX87
Tibbet's Ride, SW15 .....179 CX87
Tibbles Cl, Wat. WD25 .....76 BY35
Tibbs Hill Rd, Abb.L. WD5 .....59 BT30
Tiber Gdns, N1
off Copenhagen St 141 DM67
Ticehurst Cl, Orp. BR5
off Grovelands Rd 186 EU94
Ticehurst Rd, SE23 .....183 DY89
Tichborne, Rick. (Map.Cr.) WD3 .91 BD50
Tichmarsh, Epsom KT19 .....216 CQ110
Tickenhall Dr, Harl. CM17 .....52 EX15
Tickford Cl, SE2
off Ampleforth Rd 166 EW75
Tidal Basin Rd, E16 .....15 K10
Sch Tidemill Prim Sch, SE8
off Frankham St 163 EA80
Tidenham Gdns, Croy. CR0 ..202 DS104
Tideswell Rd, SW15 .....179 CW85
Croydon CR0 .....203 EA104
Tideway Cl, Rich. TW10
off Locksmeade Rd 177 CH91
Tideway Ind Est, SW8 .....161 DJ79
Tideway Wk, SW8
off Cringle St 161 DJ80
Tidey St, E3 .....13 P5
Tidford Rd, Well. DA16 .....165 ET82
Tidworth Rd, E3 .....13 N3
Tidy's La, Epp. CM16 .....70 EV29
Tiepigs La, Brom. BR2 .....204 EE103
West Wickham BR4 .....204 EE103
Tierney Rd, SW2 .....181 DL88
Sch Tiffin Girl's Sch, The,
Kings.T. KT2
off Richmond Rd 178 CL93
Sch Tiffin Sch for Boys,
Kings.T. KT2
off Queen Elizabeth Rd ..198 CM96
Tiger La, Brom. BR2 .....204 EH98
Tiger Moth Way, Hat. AL10
off Mosquito Way 44 CR17
Tiger Way, E5 .....122 DV63
Tigris Cl, N9 .....100 DW47
Tilbrook Rd, SE3 .....164 EJ83
Tilburstow Hill Rd, Gdse. RH9 .252 DW132
TILBURY, RM18 .....171 GG81
Tilbury Cl, SE15
off Sumner Rd 162 DT80
Orpington BR5 .....206 EV96
Tilbury Docks, Til. RM18 .....170 GE84
Coll Tilbury Energy &
Environment Cen, Til.
RM18 off Fort Rd 171 GK83
★ Tilbury Fort, Til. RM18 .....171 GJ84
Sch Tilbury Manor Inf Sch,
Til. RM18 off Dickens Av .171 GH80
Sch Tilbury Manor Jun Sch,
Til. RM18
off Dickens Av 171 GH80
Tilbury Mead, Harl. CM18 .....52 EU17
Tilbury Rd, E6 .....145 EM68
E10 .....123 EC59
⇌ Tilbury Town 170 GE82
Tilbury Wk, Slou. SL3 .....153 BB76
Tildesley Rd, SW15 .....179 CW86
Tilecroft, Welw.G.C. AL8 .....29 CX06
Tile Fm Rd, Orp. BR6 .....205 ER104
Tilegate Rd, Harl. CM18 .....51 ET17
Ongar CM5 .....53 FC19
Tilehouse Cl, Borwd. WD6 .....78 CM41
Sch Tilehouse Comb Sch, Uxb.
UB9 off Nightingale Way .113 BF58
Tilehouse La, Ger.Cr. SL9 .....91 BE53
Rickmansworth (Map.Cr.)
WD3 .....91 BE53
Uxbridge (Denh.) UB9 .....113 BE58
Tilehouse Rd, Guil. GU4 .....258 AY138
Tilehouse Way, Uxb. (Denh.)
UB9 .....113 BF59
Tilehurst La, Dor. RH5 .....264 CL137
Tilehurst Pt, SE2
off Yarnton Way 166 EW75
Tilehurst Rd, SW18 .....180 DD88
Sutton SM3 .....217 CY106
Tile Kiln Cl, Hem.H. HP3 .....41 BP21
Tilekiln Cl, Wal.Cr. EN7 .....66 DT29
Tile Kiln Cres, Hem.H. HP3 .....41 BP21
Tile Kiln La, N6
off Winchester Rd 121 DH60
N13 .....100 DQ50
Bexley DA5 .....187 FC89
Hemel Hempstead HP3 .....40 BN21
Uxbridge (Hare.) UB9 .....115 BP59
Tilers Cl, Red. RH1
off Nutfield Rd 251 DJ131
Tiler's Wk, Reig. RH2 .....266 DC138
Tiler's Way, Reig. RH2 .....266 DC138
Tile Yd, E14 .....13 M8
Tileyard Rd, N7 .....141 DL66
Tilford Av, Croy. (New Adgtn)
CR0 .....221 EC109
Tilford Gdns, SW19 .....179 CX89
Tilia Cl, Sutt. SM1 .....217 CZ106
Tilia Rd, E5 off Clarence Rd ..122 DV63
Tilia Wk, SW9
off Moorland Rd 161 DP84
Till Av, Dart. (Fnghm) DA4 ..208 FM102
Tiller Rd, E14 .....23 N5
Tillett Cl, NW10 .....138 CQ65
Tillett Sq, SE16 .....23 K4
Tillett Way, E2 .....12 A1
Tilley La, Epsom (Headley)
KT18 .....232 CQ123
Tillgate Common, Red. RH1 .252 DQ133
Sch Tillingbourne Co Jun Sch,
Guil. GU4 off New Rd ..259 BB141
Tillingbourne Gdns, N3 .....119 CZ55
Tillingbourne Grn, Orp. BR5 .206 EU98
Tillingbourne Rd, Guil.
(Shalf.) GU4 .....258 AY140
Tillingbourne Way, N3
off Tillingbourne Gdns 119 CZ55
Tillingdown Hill, Cat. CR3 ..236 DU122
Tillingdown La, Cat. CR3 .....236 DV124
Tillingham Ct, Wal.Abb. EN9 ..68 EG33
Tillingham Way, N12 .....98 DA49
Tilling Rd, NW2 .....119 CW60
Tilling Way, Wem. HA9 .....117 CK61
Tillman St, E1 .....12 D8
Tilloch St, N1 .....4 A6
Tillotson Rd, N9 .....100 DT47
Harrow HA3 .....94 CB52
Ilford IG1 .....125 EN59
Tillwicks Rd, Harl. CM18 .....52 EU17
Tilly's La, Stai. TW18 .....173 BF91
Tilmans Mead, Dart. (Fnghm)
DA4 .....208 FM101
Tilney Ct, EC1 .....11 H3
Tilney Dr, Buck.H. IG9 .....102 EG47
Tilney Gdns, N1 .....5 K4
Tilney Rd, Dag. RM9 .....146 EZ65
Southall UB2 .....156 BW77
Tilney St, W1 .....18 F1
Tilson Gdns, SW2 .....181 DL87
Tilson Ho, SW2
off Tilson Gdns 181 DL87
Tilson Rd, N17 .....100 DU53
Tilston Cl, E11
off Matcham Rd 124 EF62
Tilstone Av, Wind. (Eton Wick)
SL4 .....151 AL78
Tilstone Cl, Wind. (Eton Wick)
SL4 .....151 AL78
Tilsworth Rd, Beac. HP9 .....110 AJ55
Tilsworth Wk, St.Alb. AL4
off Sandringham Cres 43 CJ15
Tilt Cl, Cob. KT11 .....230 BY116
Tilthams Cor Rd, Gdmg. GU7 .258 AV143
Tilthams Grn, Gdmg. GU7 .....258 AV143
Tilt Meadow, Cob. KT11 .....230 BY116
Tilton St, SW6 .....159 CY79
Tilt Rd, Cob. KT11 .....230 BW115
Tiltwood, The, W3
off Acacia Rd 138 CQ73
Tilt Yd App, SE9 .....185 EM86
Timber Cl, Chis. BR7 .....205 EN96
Leatherhead (Bkhm) KT23 .246 CC126
Timber Cl, Wok. GU22
off Hacketts La 211 BF114
Timber Ct, Grays RM17
off Columbia Wf Rd 170 GA79
Timbercroft, Epsom KT19 ...216 CS105
Welwyn Garden City AL7 .....29 CZ06
Timbercroft La, SE18 .....165 ES79
Sch Timbercroft Prim Sch,
SE18 off Timbercroft La ..165 ES80
Timberdene, NW4 .....97 CX54
Timberdene Av, Ilf. IG6 .....103 EP53
Timberham Fm Rd, Gat. RH6 .268 DD151
Timberham Way, Horl. RH6 ..268 DE152
Timberhill, Ashtd. KT21
off Ottways La 232 CL119
Timber Hill Cl, Cher. KT16 ...211 BC108
Timber Hill Rd, Cat. CR3 .....236 DU124
Timberland Cl, SE15
off Peckham Hill St 162 DU80
Timberland Rd, E1 .....12 D8
Timber La, Cat. CR3
off Timber Hill Rd 236 DU124
Timberling Gdns, S.Croy.
CR2 off Sanderstead Rd ..220 DR109
Timber Mill Way, SW4 .....161 DK83
Timber Orchard, Hert. SG14 ...31 DN05
Timber Pond Rd, SE16 .....23 H2
Timber Ridge, Rick. (Loud.)
WD3 .....74 BK42
Timberslip Dr, Wall. SM6 .....219 DK109
Timber St, EC1 .....10 G3
Timbertop Rd, West.
(Bigg.H.) TN16 .....238 EJ118
Timberwharf Rd, N16 .....122 DU58
Timberwood, Slou. SL2 .....111 AR62
Timbrell Pl, SE16 .....23 L2
Time Sq, E8 .....5 N2
Times Sq, Sutt. SM1 .....218 DB106
Times Sq Shop Cen, Sutt.
SM1 off High St 218 DB106
Timothy Cl, SW4 off Elms Rd .181 DJ85
Bexleyheath DA6 .....186 EY85
Timothy Ho, Erith DA18
off Kale Rd 166 EY75
Timothy Rd, E3 .....13 L6
Timperley Gdns, Red. RH1 ..250 DE132
Timplings Row, Hem.H. HP1 ..40 BH18
Timsbury Wk, SW15 .....179 CU88
Timsway, Stai. TW18 .....173 BF92
Tindale Cl, S.Croy. CR2 .....220 DR111
Tindall Cl, Rom. RM3 .....106 FM54
Tindal St, SW9 .....161 DP81
Tinderbox All, SW14 .....158 CR83
Tine Rd, Chig. IG7 .....103 ES50
Tingeys Top La, Enf. EN2 .....81 DN36
Tinkers La, Wind. SL4 .....151 AK82
Tinniswood Cl, N5
off Drayton Pk 121 DN64
Tinsey Cl, Egh. TW20 .....173 BB92
Tinsley Rd, E1 .....12 F5
Tintagel Cl, Epsom KT17 .....217 CT114
Hemel Hempstead HP2 .....40 BK15
Tintagel Cres, SE22 .....162 DT84
Tintagel Dr, Stan. HA7 .....95 CK49
Tintagel Gdns, SE22
off Oxonian St 162 DT84
Tintagel Rd, Orp. BR5 .....206 EW103
Tintagel Way, Wok. GU22 .....227 BA116
Tintells La, Lthd. (W.Hors.)
KT24 .....245 BP128
Tintern Av, NW9 .....118 CP55
Tintern Cl, SW15 .....179 CY85
SW19 .....180 DC94
Slough SL1 .....151 AQ76
Tintern Ct, W13
off Green Man La 137 CG73
Tintern Gdns, N14 .....99 DL45
Tintern Path, NW9
off Ruthin Cl 118 CS58
Tintern Rd, N22 .....100 DQ53
Carshalton SM5 .....200 DD102
Tintern St, SW4 .....161 DL84
Tintern Way, Har. HA2 .....116 CB60
Tinto Rd, E16 .....15 M4
Tinwell Ms, Borwd. WD6
off Cranes Way 78 CQ43
Tinworth St, SE11 .....19 P9
Tippendell La, St.Alb.
(Park St) AL2 .....60 CB26
Tippetts Cl, Enf. EN2 .....82 DQ39
Tipthorpe Rd, SW11 .....160 DG83
Tipton Cotts, Add. KT15
off Oliver Cl 212 BG105
Tipton Dr, Croy. CR0 .....220 DS105
Tiptree Cl, E4
off Mapleton Rd 101 EC48
Hornchurch RM11 .....128 FN60
Tiptree Cres, Ilf. IG5 .....125 EN55
Tiptree Dr, Enf. EN2 .....82 DR42
Tiptree Est, Ilf. IG5 .....125 EN55
Tiptree Rd, Ruis. HA4 .....115 BV63
Tiree Cl, Hem.H. HP3 .....41 BP22
Tirlemont Rd, S.Croy. CR2 ...220 DQ108
Tirrell Rd, Croy. CR0 .....202 DQ100
Tisbury Ct, W1 off Rupert St .141 DK73
Tisbury Rd, SW16 .....201 DL96
Tisdall Pl, SE17 .....21 K8
Titan Rd, Grays RM17 .....170 GA78
Hemel Hempstead HP2 .....40 BM17
Titchborne Row, W2 .....8 B8
Titchfield Rd, NW8 .....140 DF67
Carshalton SM5 .....200 DD102
Enfield EN3 .....83 DY37
Titchfield Wk, Cars. SM5
off Titchfield Rd 200 DD101
Titchwell Rd, SW18 .....180 DD87
Tite Hill, Egh. TW20 .....172 AX92
Tite St, SW3 .....28 C10
★ Tithe Barn Agricultural &
Folk Mus, The, Upmin.
RM14 .....129 FR59
Tithe Barn Cl, Kings.T. KT2 ..198 CM95
St. Albans AL1 .....42 CC23
Tithe Barn Ct, Abb.L. WD5
off Dairy Way 59 BT29
Tithe Barn Dr, Maid. SL6 .....150 AE78
Tithe Barn Est, St.Alb. AL1 ...42 CC24
Tithebarns La, Wok. (Send)
GU23 .....244 BG126
Tithe Barn Way, Nthlt. UB5 ..135 BV69
Tithe Cl, NW7 .....97 CU53
Hayes UB4 off Gledwood Dr .135 BT71
Maidenhead SL6 .....150 AC78
Virginia Water GU25 .....192 AX100
Walton-on-Thames KT12 ..195 BV100
Tithe Ct, Slou. SL3 .....153 BA77
Tithe Fm Av, Har. HA2 .....116 CA62
Tithe Fm Cl, Har. HA2 .....116 CA62
Tithelands, Harl. CM19 .....51 EM18
Tithe La, Stai. (Wrays.) TW19 .173 BA86
Tithe Meadow, Wat. WD18 .....75 BR44
Tithe Meadows, Vir.W. GU25 .192 AW100
Tithepit Shaw La, Warl. CR6 .236 DV115
Tithe Wk, NW7 .....97 CU53
Titian Av, Bushey
(Bushey Hth) WD23 .....95 CE45
Titley Cl, E4 .....101 EA50
Titmus Cl, Uxb. UB8 .....135 BQ72
Titmuss Av, SE28 .....146 EV73
Titmuss St, W12
off Goldhawk Rd 159 CW75
TITSEY, Oxt. RH8 .....254 EH125
Titsey Hill, Oxt. (Titsey) RH8 .238 EF123
Titsey Rd, Oxt. RH8 .....254 EH125
Tiverton Av, Ilf. IG5 .....125 EN55
Tiverton Cl, Croy. CR0
off Exeter Rd 202 DT101
Tiverton Dr, SE9 .....185 EQ88
Tiverton Gro, Rom. RM3 .....106 FN50
Tiverton Ho, Enf. EN3 .....83 DX41
Sch Tiverton Prim Sch, N15
off Pulford Rd 122 DR58
Tiverton Rd, N15 .....122 DR58
N18 .....100 DS50
NW10 .....139 CX67
Edgware HA8 .....96 CM54
Hounslow TW3 .....156 CC82
Potters Bar EN6 .....64 DD31
Ruislip HA4 .....115 BU62
Thornton Heath CR7
off Willett Rd 201 DN99
Wembley HA0 .....138 CL68
Tiverton St, SE1 .....20 G6
Tiverton Way, NW7 .....97 CX52
Chessington KT9 .....215 CJ106
Tivoli Ct, SE16 .....23 L3
Tivoli Gdns, SE18 .....164 EL77
Tivoli Rd, N8 .....121 DK57
SE27 .....182 DQ92
Hounslow TW4 .....156 BY84
Toad La, Houns. TW4 .....156 BZ84
Tobacco Dock, E1 .....12 C10
Tobacco Quay, E1 .....12 C10
Tobago St, E14 .....23 N3
Tobin Cl, NW3 .....140 DE66
Toby La, E1 .....13 J4
Toby Way, Surb. KT5 .....198 CP103
Tockley Rd, Slou. (Burn.) SL1 .130 AH69
Toddbrook, Harl. CM19
off Harberts Rd 51 EP16
Todd Cl, Rain. RM13 .....148 FK70
Todds Cl, Horl. RH6 .....268 DE146
Todds Wk, N7 off Andover Rd .121 DM61
Toft Av, Grays RM17 .....170 GD77
Tokenhouse Yd, EC2 .....11 J7
Token Yd, SW15
off Montserrat Rd 159 CY84
TOKYNGTON, Wem. HA9 .....138 CP65
Tokyngton Av, Wem. HA9 .....138 CN65
Toland Sq, SW15 .....179 CU85
Tolcarne Dr, Pnr. HA5 .....115 BV55
Toldene Ct, Couls. CR5 .....235 DM120
Toley Av, Wem. HA9 .....118 CL59
Toll Bar Ct, Sutt. SM2 .....218 DB109
Tollbridge Cl, W10 .....6 D3
Tolldene Cl, Wok. (Knap.)
GU21 off Robin Hood Rd ..226 AS117
Tollers La, Couls. CR5 .....235 DM119
Tollesbury Gdns, Ilf. IG6 .....125 ER55
Tollet St, E1 .....12 G3
Tollgate, Guil. GU1 .....243 BD133
Tollgate Av, Red. RH1 .....266 DF139
Tollgate Cl, Rick. (Chorl.) WD3 ..73 BF41
Tollgate Dr, SE21 .....182 DS89
Hayes UB4 .....136 BX73
Tollgate Gdns, NW6 .....140 DB68
Sch Tollgate Prim Sch, E13
off Barclay Rd 144 EJ70
Croydon CR0 off Malling Cl .202 DW100
Tollgate Rd, E6 .....144 EK71
E16 .....144 EJ71
Dartford DA2 .....189 FR87
Dorking RH4 .....263 CH139
Hatfield AL9 .....44 CS24
St. Albans (Coln.Hth) AL4 ..44 CS24
Waltham Cross EN8 .....83 DX35
Tollhouse La, Wall. SM6 .....219 DJ109
Tollhouse Way, N19 .....121 DJ61
Tollington Pk, N4 .....121 DM61
Tollington Pl, N4 .....121 DM61
Tollington Rd, N7 .....121 DM63
Tollington Way, N7 .....121 DL62
Tollpit End, Hem.H. HP1 .....40 BG17
Tolmers Av, Pot.B. (Cuffley)
EN6 .....65 DL28
Tolmers Gdns, Pot.B.
(Cuffley) EN6 .....65 DL29
Tolmers Ms, Hert.
(Newgate St) SG13 .....65 DL25
Tolmers Pk, Hert.
(Newgate St) SG13 .....65 DL25
Tolmers Rd, Pot.B. (Cuffley)
EN6 .....65 DL27
Tolmers Sq, NW1 .....9 K3
Tolpits Cl, Wat. WD18 .....75 BT43
Tolpits La, Wat. WD18 .....75 BT44
Tolpuddle Av, E13
off Rochester Av 144 EJ67
Tolpuddle St, N1 .....4 C9
Tolsford Rd, E5 .....122 DV64
Tolson Rd, Islw. TW7 .....157 CG83
Tolvaddon, Wok. GU21
off Cardingham 226 AU117
Tolverne Rd, SW20 .....199 CW95
TOLWORTH, Surb. KT6 .....198 CN103
⇌ Tolworth 198 CP103
Tolworth Bdy, Surb. KT6 .....198 CP102
Tolworth Cl, Surb. KT6 .....198 CP102
Tolworth Gdns, Rom. RM6 .....126 EX57
Sch Tolworth Girls' Sch &
Cen for Cont Ed,
Surb. KT6
off Fullers Way N 198 CM104
H Tolworth Hosp, Surb.
KT6 .....198 CN103
Sch Tolworth Inf Sch, Surb.
KT6 off School La 198 CM102
Sch Tolworth Jun Sch, Surb.
KT6 off Douglas Rd 198 CM102
Tolworth Pk Rd, Surb. KT6 ..198 CM103
Tolworth Ri N, Surb. KT5
off Elmbridge Av 198 CQ101
Tolworth Ri S, Surb. KT5
off Warren Dr S 198 CQ102
Tolworth Rd, Surb. KT6 .....198 CL103
Tolworth Twr, Surb. KT6 .....198 CP103
Tomahawk Gdns, Nthlt.
UB5 off Javelin Way 136 BX69
Tom Coombs Cl, SE9
off Well Hall Rd 164 EL84
Tom Cribb Rd, SE28 .....165 EQ76
Tom Gros Cl, E15
off Maryland St 123 ED64
Tom Hood Cl, E15
off Maryland St 123 ED64
Sch Tom Hood Sec Sch, E11
off Terling Cl 124 EF62
Tom Jenkinson Rd, E16 .....25 M1
Tomkins Cl, Borwd. WD6
off Tallis Way 78 CL39
Tomkyns La, Upmin. RM14 ..129 FR56
Tomlin Cl, Epsom KT19 .....216 CR111
Tomlin Rd, Slou. SL2 .....131 AL70
Tomlins Gro, E3 .....13 P1
Tomlinson Cl, E2 .....11 P2
W4 .....158 CP78
Tomlins Orchard, Bark. IG11 ..145 EQ67
Tomlins Ter, E14 .....13 K7
Tomlins Wk, N7
off Briset Way 121 DM61

Tomlyns Cl, Brwd. (Hutt.) CM13 109 GE44
Tom Mann Cl, Bark. IG11 145 ES67
Tom Nolan Cl, E15 144 EE68
Tomo Ind Est, Uxb. UB8 134 BJ72
Tompion St, EC1 10 E2
Toms Cft, Hem.H. HP2 40 BL21
Tomsfield, Hat. AL10 44 CS19
Toms Hill, Kings L. WD4
off Bucks Hill 58 BJ33
Rickmansworth WD3 74 BL36
Toms La, Abb.L. (Bedmond) WD5 59 BR28
Kings Langley WD4 59 BP29
Tom Smith Cl, SE10
off Maze Hill 164 EE79
Tomswood Ct, Ilf. IG6 103 EQ53
Tomswood Hill, Ilf. IG6 103 EP52
Tomswood Rd, Chig. IG7 103 EN51
Tom Thumbs Arch, E3
off Malmesbury Rd 143 EA68
Tom Williams Ho, SW6
off Clem Attlee Ct 159 CZ79
Tonbridge Cl, Bans. SM7 218 DF114
Tonbridge Cres, Har. HA3 118 CL56
Tonbridge Ho, SE25 202 DU97
Tonbridge Rd, Rom. RM3 106 FK52
Sevenoaks TN13 257 FJ127
West Molesey KT8 196 BY98
Tonbridge St, WC1 9 N1
Tonbridge Wk, WC1
off Tonbridge St 141 DL69
Tonfield Rd, Sutt. SM3 199 CZ102
Tonge Cl, Beck. BR3 203 EA99
Tonsley Hill, SW18 180 DB85
Tonsley Pl, SW18 180 DB85
Tonsley Rd, SW18 180 DB85
Tonsley St, SW18 180 DB85
Tonstall Rd, Epsom KT19 216 CR110
Mitcham CR4 200 DG96
Tony Cannell Ms, E3 13 L2
Tooke Cl, Pnr. HA5 94 BY53
Tookey Cl, Har. HA3 118 CM59
Took's Ct, EC4 10 C7
Tooley St, SE1 21 K1
Gravesend (Nthflt) DA11 190 GD87
Toorack Rd, Har. HA3 95 CD54
TOOT HILL, Ong. CM5 71 FF30
Toot Hill Rd, Ong. CM5 71 FF29
⇌ Tooting 180 DG93
⊖ Tooting Bec 180 DF90
Tooting Bec Gdns, SW16 181 DK91
Tooting Bec Rd, SW16 180 DG90
SW17 180 DG90
⊖ Tooting Broadway 180 DE92
TOOTING GRAVENEY, SW17 180 DE93
Tooting Gro, SW17 180 DE92
Tooting High St, SW17 180 DE93
Tootswood Rd, Brom. BR2 204 EE99
Tooveys Mill Cl, Kings L. WD4 58 BN28
Topaz Cl, Slou. SL1
off Pearl Gdns 131 AP74
Topaz Wk, NW2
off Marble Dr 119 CX59
Topcliffe Dr, Orp. BR6 223 ER105
Top Dartford Rd, Dart. DA2 187 FF94
Swanley BR8 187 FF94
Top Fm Cl, Beac. HP9 88 AG54
Topham Sq, N17 100 DQ53
Topham St, EC1 10 C3
Top Ho Ri, E4
off Parkhill Rd 101 EC45
Topiary, The, Ashtd. KT21 232 CL120
Topiary Sq, Rich. TW9 158 CM83
Topland Rd, Ger.Cr. (Chal.St.P.) SL9 90 AX52
Toplands Av, S.Ock. (Aveley) RM15 148 FP74
Topley St, SE9 164 EK84
Topmast Pt, E14 23 N4
Top Pk, Beck. BR3 204 EE99
Gerrards Cross SL9 112 AW58
Topping La, Uxb. UB8 134 BK69
Topp Wk, NW2 119 CW61
Topsfield Cl, N8
off Wolseley Rd 121 DK57
Topsfield Par, N8
off Tottenham La 121 DL57
Topsfield Rd, N8 121 DL57
Topsham Rd, SW17 180 DF90
Torbay Rd, NW6 139 CZ66
Harrow HA2 116 BY61
Torbay St, NW1
off Hawley Rd 141 DH66
Torbitt Way, Ilf. IG2 125 ET57
Torbridge Cl, Edg. HA8 96 CL52
Torbrook Cl, Bex. DA5 186 EY86
Torcross Dr, SE23 182 DW89
Torcross Rd, Ruis. HA4 115 BV62
Tor Gdns, W8 16 G3
Tor Gro, SE28 145 ES74
Torin Ct, Egh. (Eng.Grn) TW20 172 AW92
Torland Dr, Lthd. (Oxshott) KT22 215 CD114
Tor La, Wey. KT13 213 BQ111
Tormead Cl, Sutt. SM1 218 DA107
Tormead Rd, Guil. GU1 243 AZ134
Sch Tormead Sch, Guil. GU1
off Cranley Rd 243 AZ134
Guildford GU1
off Cranley Rd 243 AZ134
Tormount Rd, SE18 165 ES79
Toronto Av, E12 125 EM63
Toronto Dr, Horl. (Smallfield) RH6 269 DN148
Toronto Rd, E11 123 ED63
Ilford IG1 125 EP60
Tilbury RM18 171 GG82
Torquay Gdns, Ilf. IG4 124 EK56
Torquay Spur, Slou. SL2 131 AP70
Torquay St, W2 7 J6
Torrance Cl, SE7 164 EK79
Hornchurch RM11 127 FH60
Torrens Cl, Guil. GU2 242 AU131
Torrens Rd, E15 144 EF65
SW2 181 DM85
Torrens Sq, E15 144 EE65
Torrens St, EC1 4 D10
Torrens Wk, Grav. DA12 191 GL92
Torres Sq, E14
off Maritime Quay 163 EA78
Torre Wk, Cars. SM5 200 DE102
Torrey Dr, SW9
off Overton Rd 161 DN82
Torriano Av, NW5 121 DK64
Torriano Cotts, NW5
off Torriano Av 121 DJ64
Sch Torriano Inf Sch, NW5
off Torriano Av 141 DK65
Sch Torriano Jun Sch, NW5
off Torriano Av 121 DK64
Torriano Ms, NW5
off Torriano Av 121 DK64
Torridge Gdns, SE15 162 DW84
Torridge Rd, Slou. SL3 153 BB79
Thornton Heath CR7 201 DP99
Torridge Wk, Hem.H. HP2
off The Dee 40 BM15
Torridon Cl, Wok. GU21 226 AV117
Sch Torridon Inf Sch, SE6
off Torridon Rd 183 ED89
Sch Torridon Jun Sch, SE6
off Hazelbank Rd 183 ED89
Torridon Rd, SE6 183 ED88
SE13 183 ED87
Torrington Av, N12 98 DD50
Torrington Cl, N12 98 DD49
Esher (Clay.) KT10 215 CE107
Torrington Dr, Har. HA2 116 CB63
Loughton IG10 85 EQ42
Potters Bar EN6 64 DD32
Torrington Gdns, N11 99 DJ51
Greenford UB6 137 CJ66
Loughton IG10 85 EQ42
Torrington Gro, N12 98 DE50
Torrington Pk, N12 98 DC50
Torrington Pl, E1 22 B1
WC1 9 K5
Torrington Rd, E18 124 EG55
Berkhamsted HP4 38 AV19
Dagenham RM8 126 EZ60
Esher (Clay.) KT10 215 CE107
Greenford UB6 137 CJ67
Ruislip HA4 115 BT62
Torrington Sq, WC1 9 M4
Croydon CR0
off Tavistock Gro 202 DR101
Torrington Way, Mord. SM4 202 DA100
Tor Rd, Well. DA16 166 EW81
Torr Rd, SE20 183 DX94
Tortoiseshell Way, Berk. HP4 38 AT17
Torver Rd, Har. HA1 117 CE56
Torver Way, Orp. BR6 205 ER104
Torwood Cl, Berk. HP4 38 AT19
Torwood La, Whyt. CR3 236 DT120
Torwood Rd, SW15 179 CU85
Torworth Rd, Borwd. WD6 78 CM39
Tothill St, SW1 19 L4
Totnes Rd, Well. DA16 166 EV80
Totnes Wk, N2 120 DD56
Tottan Ter, E1 13 H7
Sch Tottenhall Inf Sch, N13
off Tottenhall Rd 99 DN51
Tottenhall Rd, N13 99 DN51
TOTTENHAM, N17 100 DS53
⊖ Tottenham Court Road 9 L7
Tottenham Ct Rd, W1 9 K4
Tottenham Grn E, N15 122 DT56
TOTTENHAM HALE, N17 122 DV55
⇌ Tottenham Hale 122 DV55
⊖ Tottenham Hale 122 DV55
Tottenham Hale Retail Pk, N15 122 DU56
★ Tottenham Hotspur FC, N17 100 DT52
Tottenham La, N8 121 DL57
Tottenham Ms, W1 9 K5
Tottenham Rd, N1 5 L4
Tottenham St, W1 9 K6
Totterdown St, SW17 180 DF91
TOTTERIDGE, N20 97 CY46
⊖ Totteridge & Whetstone 98 DB47
Totteridge Common, N20 97 CU47
Totteridge Grn, N20 98 DA47
Totteridge Ho, SW11 160 DD82
Totteridge La, N20 98 DA47
Totteridge Rd, Enf. EN3 83 DX37
Totteridge Village, N20 97 CY46
Totternhoe Cl, Har. HA3 117 CJ57
Totton Rd, Th.Hth. CR7 201 DN97
Toulmin Dr, St.Alb. AL3 42 CC16
Toulmin St, SE1 20 G4
Toulon St, SE5 162 DQ80
Tournay Rd, SW6 159 CZ80
Tours Pas, SW11 160 DD84
Toussaint Wk, SE16 22 B5
Tovey Av, Hodd. EN11 49 EA15
Tovey Cl, St.Alb. (Lon.Col.) AL2 61 CK26
Waltham Abbey EN9 50 EE23
Tovil Cl, SE20 202 DU96
Towcester Rd, E3 14 B4
Tower, The, Couls. CR5 235 DK122
Tower 42, EC2 11 L7
Tower Br, E1 21 N2
SE1 21 N2
Tower Br App, E1 21 N1
★ Tower Br Experience, SE1 21 N2
Tower Br Piazza, SE1 21 N2
Sch Tower Br Prim Sch, SE1 21 N3
Tower Br Rd, SE1 21 L6
Tower Br Wf, E1 22 A2
Tower Cen, Hodd. EN11 49 EA17
Tower Cl, NW3
off Lyndhurst Rd 120 DD64
SE20 182 DV94
Berkhamsted HP4 38 AU20
Epping CM16 53 FD24
Gravesend DA12 191 GL92
High Wycombe (Flack.Hth) HP10 110 AC56
Horley RH6 268 DF148
Ilford IG6 103 EP51
Orpington BR6 205 ET103
Woking GU21 226 AX117
Tower Ct, WC2 9 N8
Brentwood CM14 108 FV47
Tower Cft, Dart. (Eyns.) DA4
off High St 208 FL103
Tower Gdns, Esher (Clay.) KT10 215 CG108
Tower Gdns Rd, N17 100 DQ53
Towergate Cl, Uxb. UB8 114 BL64
DLR Tower Gateway 11 P9
Tower Gro, Wey. KT13 195 BS103
Coll Tower Hamlets Coll,
Arbour Sq Cen, E1 12 G7
Bethnal Green Cen, E2 12 A2
East India Dock Rd, E14 14 B8
Poplar Cen, E14 14 A10
Tower Hamlets Rd, E7 124 EF63
E17 123 EA55
Tower Hts, Hodd. EN11
off Amwell St 49 EA17
TOWER HILL, Dor. RH4 263 CH138
⊖ Tower Hill 11 N9
Tower Hill, EC3 11 M10
Brentwood CM14 108 FW47
Dorking RH4 263 CH138
Guildford (Goms.) GU5 261 BQ140
Kings Langley (Chipper.) WD4 57 BE29
Tower Hill La, Guil. (Goms.) GU5 261 BQ140
St. Albans (Sand.) AL4 28 CM10
Tower Hill Ri, Guil. (Goms.) GU5 261 BQ140
Tower Hill Rd, Dor. RH4 263 CH138
Tower Hill Ter, EC3
off Tower Hill 142 DS73
Sch Tower Ho Sch, SW14
off Sheen La 158 CQ84
Tower La, Wem. HA9
off Main Dr 117 CK62
Tower Ms, E17 123 EA56
★ Tower Millennium Pier, EC3 21 M1
Tower Mill Rd, SE15
off Wells Way 162 DS79
★ Tower of London, EC3 11 N10
Tower Pk Rd, Dart. DA1 187 FF85
Tower Pl, EC3 11 M10
Warlingham CR6 237 EA115
Tower Pt, Enf. EN2 82 DR42
Tower Retail Pk, Dart. DA1 187 FF85
Tower Ri, Rich. TW9
off Jocelyn Rd 158 CL83
Tower Rd, NW10 139 CU66
Amersham (Colesh.) HP7 55 AN43
Belvedere DA17 167 FC77
Bexleyheath DA7 167 FB84
Dartford DA1 188 FJ86
Epping CM16 69 ES30
Orpington BR6 205 ET103
Tadworth KT20 233 CW123
Twickenham TW1 177 CF90
Ware SG12 33 DY05
Tower Royal, EC4 11 H9
Towers, The, Ken. CR8 236 DQ115
Towers Av, Uxb. (Hlgdn) UB10 135 BQ69
Sch Towers Inf Sch, Horn. RM11 off Osborne Rd 128 FJ59
Sch Towers Jun Sch, Horn. RM11 off Windsor Rd 128 FJ59
Towers Pl, Rich. TW9
off Eton St 178 CL85
Towers Rd, Grays RM17 170 GC78
Hemel Hempstead HP2 40 BL19
Pinner HA5 94 BY53
Southall UB1 136 CA70
Tower St, WC2 9 M8
Hertford SG14 32 DQ07
Towers Wk, Wey. KT13 213 BP107
Towers Wd, Dart. (S.Darenth) DA4 209 FR95
Tower Ter, N22 off Mayes Rd 99 DM54
SE4 off Foxberry Rd 163 DY84
Tower Vw, Croy. CR0 203 DX101
Towfield Rd, Felt. TW13 176 BZ89
Towing Path, Guil. GU1 258 AW138
Towing Path Wk, N1
off York Way 141 DL67
Town, The, Enf. EN2 82 DR41
Town Br Ct, Chesh. HP5
off Water Meadow 54 AP32
Town Cen, Hat. AL10 45 CU17
Towncourt Cres, Orp. BR5 205 EQ99
Towncourt La, Orp. BR5 205 ER100
Town Ct Path, N4 122 DQ60
Town End, Cat. CR3 236 DS122
Town End Cl, Cat. CR3 236 DS122
Towney Mead, Nthlt. UB5 136 BZ68
Towney Mead Ct, Nthlt. UB5
off Towney Mead 136 BZ68
Sch Town Fm Prim Sch, Stai. TW19 off St. Mary's Cres 174 BK87
Town Fm Way, Stai. (Stanw.) TW19 off Town La 174 BK87
Townfield, Chesh. HP5 54 AP32
Rickmansworth WD3 92 BJ45
Townfield Cor, Grav. DA12 191 GJ88
Townfield Ct, Dor. RH4
off Horsham Rd 263 CG137
Town Fld La, Ch.St.G. HP8 90 AW48
Townfield Rd, Dor. RH4 263 CG137
Hayes UB3 135 BT74
Townfields, Hat. AL10 45 CU17
Townfield Sq, Hayes UB3 135 BT74
Town Fld Way, Islw. TW7 157 CG82
Towngate, Cob. KT11 230 BY115
Town Hall App, N16
off Milton Gro 122 DS63
Town Hall App Rd, N15 122 DT56
Town Hall Av, W4 158 CR78
Town Hall Rd, SW11 160 DF83
Townholm Cres, W7 157 CF76
Town La, H.Wyc. (Woob.Grn) HP10 110 AD59
Staines (Stanw.) TW19 174 BK86
Townley Ct, E15 144 EF65
Sch Townley Gram Sch for Girls, Bexh. DA6
off Townley Rd 186 EZ85
Townley Rd, SE22 182 DS85
Bexleyheath DA6 186 EZ85
Townley St, SE17 21 J9
Townmead, Red. RH1 252 DR133
Townmead Business Cen, SW6
off William Morris Way 160 DC83
Town Meadow, Brent. TW8 157 CK80
Townmead Rd, SW6 160 DC82
Richmond TW9 158 CP82
Waltham Abbey EN9 67 EC34
Town Mill Ms, Hert. SG14
off Millbridge 32 DQ09
Town Path, Egh. TW20 173 BA92
Town Pier, Grav. DA11
off West St 191 GH86
Town Quay, Bark. IG11 145 EP67
Town Rd, N9 100 DV47
TOWNSEND, St.Alb. AL3 43 CD17
Townsend, Hem.H. HP2 40 BK18
Townsend Av, N14 99 DK49
St. Albans AL1 43 CE19
Sch Townsend C of E Sch, St.Alb. AL3
off Sparrowswick Ride 42 CC15
Townsend Dr, St.Alb. AL3 43 CD18
Townsend Ind Est, NW10 138 CR68
Townsend La, NW9 118 CR59
Woking GU22
off St. Peters Rd 227 BB121
Sch Townsend Prim Sch, SE17 21 L7
Townsend Rd, N15 122 DT57
Ashford TW15 174 BL92
Chesham HP5 54 AP30
Southall UB1 136 BY74
Townsend St, SE17 21 K8
Townsend Way, Nthwd. HA6 93 BT52
Townsend Yd, N6 121 DH60
Townshend Cl, Sid. DA14 186 EV93
Townshend Est, NW8 140 DE68
Townshend Rd, NW8 140 DE67
Chislehurst BR7 185 EP92
Richmond TW9 158 CM84
Townshend St, Hert. SG13 32 DS09
Townshend Ter, Rich. TW9 158 CM84
Townshott Cl, Lthd. (Bkhm) KT23 246 CA126
Townslow La, Wok. (Wisley) GU23 228 BJ116
Townson Av, Nthlt. UB5 135 BU69
Townson Way, Nthlt. UB5
off Townson Av 135 BU68
Town Sq, Erith DA8
off Pier Rd 167 FE79
Woking GU21
off Church St E 227 AZ117
Town Sq Cres, Green. (Bluewater) DA9 189 FT87
Town Tree Rd, Ashf. TW15 174 BN92
Towpath, Shep. TW17 194 BM103
Towpath Rd, N18 101 DX51
Towpath Wk, E9 123 DZ64
Towpath Way, Croy. CR0 202 DT100
Towton Rd, SE27 182 DQ89
Toynbec Cl, Chis. BR7
off Beechwood Ri 185 EP91
★ Toynbee Hall, E1 11 P6
Toynbee Rd, SW20 199 CY95
Toynbee St, E1 11 N6
Toyne Way, N6 off Gaskell Rd 120 DF58
Tozer Wk, Wind. SL4 151 AK83
Tracery, The, Bans. SM7 234 DB115
Tracey Av, NW2 119 CW64
Tracious Cl, Wok. GU21
off Sythwood 226 AV116
Tracious La, Wok. GU21 226 AV116
Tracy Av, Slou. SL3
off Ditton Rd 153 AZ79
Tracy Ct, Stan. HA7 95 CJ52
Tracyes Rd, Harl. CM18 52 EV17
Trade Cl, N13 99 DN49
Trader Rd, E6 145 EP72
Tradescant Rd, SW8 161 DL80
Trading Est Rd, NW10 138 CQ70
Trafalgar Av, N17 100 DS51
SE15 21 P10
Broxbourne EN10 49 DZ21
Worcester Park KT4 199 CX102
Trafalgar Business Cen, Bark. IG11 145 ET70
Trafalgar Cl, SE16 23 J7
Trafalgar Ct, E1 12 F10
Cobham KT11 213 BU113
Trafalgar Dr, Walt. KT12 195 BU104
Trafalgar Gdns, E1 13 H5
W8 17 K5
Trafalgar Gro, SE10 163 ED79
Sch Trafalgar Inf Sch, Twick. TW2 ,off Elmsleigh Rd 177 CD89
Sch Trafalgar Jun Sch, Twick. TW2 off Elmsleigh Rd 177 CD89
Trafalgar Ms, E9 143 DZ65
Trafalgar Pl, E11 124 EG56
N18 100 DU50
Trafalgar Rd, SE10 163 ED79
SW19 180 DB94
Dartford DA1 188 FL89
Gravesend DA11 191 GG87
Rainham RM13 147 FF68
Twickenham TW2 177 CD89
Trafalgar Sq, SW1 19 M1
WC2 19 M1
Trafalgar St, SE17 21 J9
Trafalgar Ter, Har. HA1
off Nelson Rd 117 CE60
Trafalgar Way, E14 24 C1
Croydon CR0 201 DM103
Trafford Cl, E15 123 EB64
Ilford IG6 103 ET51
Radlett (Shenley) WD7 62 CL32
Trafford Rd, Th.Hth. CR7 201 DM99
Tralee Ct, SE16 22 D9
Tramsheds Ind Est, Croy. CR0 201 DK101
Tramway Av, E15 144 EE66
N9 100 DV45
Tramway Cl, SE20 202 DW95
Tramway Path, Mitch. CR4 200 DF99
Tranby Pl, E9
off Homerton High St 123 DX64
Tranley Ms, NW3 off Fleet Rd 120 DE64
Tranmere Rd, N9 100 DT45
SW18 180 DC89
Twickenham TW2 176 CB87
Tranquil Dale, Bet. (Buckland) RH3 249 CT132
Tranquil Pas, SE3
off Tranquil Vale 164 EF82
Tranquil Ri, Erith DA8
off West St 167 FE78
Tranquil Vale, SE3 164 EE82
Transept St, NW1 8 A6
Transmere Cl, Orp. BR5 205 EQ100
Transmere Rd, Orp. BR5 205 EQ100
Transom Cl, SE16 23 K7
Transom Sq, E14 24 A8
Transport Av, Brent. TW8 157 CG78
Tranton Rd, SE16 22 B5
Trapps La, Chesh. HP5 54 AR32
Traps Hill, Loug. IG10 85 EM41
Traps La, N.Mal. KT3 198 CS95
Trapstyle Rd, Ware SG12 32 DU05
Trasher Mead, Dor. RH4 263 CJ139
Travellers Cl, Hat. AL9 45 CW23
Travellers La, Hat. AL10 45 CU19
Hatfield (Wel.Grn) AL9 45 CW22
Travellers Way, Houns. TW4 156 BW82
Travers Cl, E17 101 DX53
Travers Rd, N7 121 DN62
Travic Rd, Slou. SL2 131 AM69
Travis Ct, Slou. (Farn.Royal) SL2 131 AP69
Treachers Cl, Chesh. HP5 54 AP31
Treacy Cl, Bushey (Bushey Hth) WD23 94 CC47
Treadgold St, W11 6 B9
Treadway St, E2 142 DV68
Treadwell Rd, Epsom KT18 232 CS115
Treasury Cl, Wall. SM6 219 DK106
Treaty Cen, Houns. TW3 156 CB83
Treaty Rd, Houns. TW3
off Hanworth Rd 156 CB83
Treaty St, N1 4 A8
Trebble Rd, Swans. DA10 190 FY86
Trebeck St, W1 18 G1
Trebellan Dr, Hem.H. HP2 40 BM19
Trebovir Rd, SW5 17 H9
Treby St, E3 13 L4
Trecastle Way, N7
off Carleton Rd 121 DK63
Tredegar Ms, E3 13 L1
Tredegar Rd, E3 143 DZ68
N11 99 DK52
Dartford DA2 187 FG89
Tredegar Sq, E3 13 L1
Tredegar Ter, E3 13 L1
Trederwen Rd, E8 142 DU67
Tredown Rd, SE26 182 DW92
Tredwell Cl, SW2
off Hillside Rd 181 DM89
Bromley BR2 204 EL98
Tredwell Rd, SE27 181 DP91
Treebourne Rd, West. (Bigg.H.) TN16 238 EJ117
Treebys Av, Guil. GU4 242 AX128
Tree Cl, Rich. TW10 177 CK88
Treelands, Dor. (N.Holm.) RH5 263 CJ139
Treemount Ct, Epsom KT17 216 CS113
Treen Av, SW13 159 CT83
Tree Rd, E16 144 EJ72
Treeside Cl, West Dr. UB7 154 BK77
Tree Tops, Brwd. CM15 108 FW46
Treetops, Grav. DA12 191 GH92
Whyteleafe CR3 236 DU118
Treetops Cl, SE2 166 EY78
Northwood HA6 93 BR50
Sch Treetops Sch, Grays RM17 off Dell Rd 170 GB77
Treetops Vw, Loug. IG10 102 EK45
Treeview Cl, SE19 202 DS95
Treewall Gdns, Brom. BR1 184 EH91
Tree Way, Reig. RH2 250 DB131
Trefgarne Rd, Dag. RM10 126 FA61
Trefil Wk, N7 121 DL63
Trefoil Ho, Erith DA18
off Kale Rd 166 EY75
Trefoil Rd, SW18 180 DC85
Trefusis Wk, Wat. WD17 75 BS39
Tregaron Av, N8 121 DL58
Tregaron Gdns, N.Mal. KT3
off Avenue Rd 198 CS98
Tregarthen Pl, Lthd. KT22 231 CJ121
Tregarth Pl, Wok. GU21 226 AT117
Tregarvon Rd, SW11 160 DG84
Tregelles Rd, Hodd. EN11 33 EA14
Tregenna Av, Har. HA2 116 BZ63
Tregenna Cl, N14 81 DJ43
Tregenna Ct, Har. HA2 116 CA63
Tregony Rd, Orp. BR6 223 ET105
Trego Rd, E9 143 EA66
Tregothnan Rd, SW9 161 DL83
Tregunter Rd, SW10 160 DC79
Trehaven Par, Reig. RH2
off Hornbeam Rd 266 DB137
Trehearn Rd, Ilf. IG6 103 ER52
Treherne Ct, SW9
off Eythorne Rd 161 DN81
SW17 180 DG91
Trehern Rd, SW14 158 CR83
Trehurst St, E5 123 DY64
Trelawn Cl, Cher. (Ott.) KT16 211 BC108
Trelawney Av, Slou. SL3 152 AX76
Trelawney Cl, E17
off Orford Rd 123 EB56
Trelawney Est, E9 142 DW65
Trelawney Gro, Wey. KT13 212 BN107
Trelawney Rd, Ilf. IG6 103 ER52
Trelawn Rd, E10 123 EC62
SW2 181 DN85
Trellick Twr, W10 6 E4
Trellis Sq, E3 13 M1
Treloar Gdns, SE19
off Hancock Rd 182 DR93
Tremadoc Rd, SW4 161 DK84
Tremaine Cl, SE4 163 EA82
Tremaine Gro, Hem.H. HP2 40 BL16
Tremaine Rd, SE20 202 DV96
Trematon Pl, Tedd. TW11 177 CJ94
Tremlett Gro, N19 121 DJ62
Tremlett Ms, N19 121 DJ62
Trenance, Wok. GU21
off Cardingham 226 AU117
Trenance Gdns, Ilf. IG3 126 EU62
Trenchard Av, Ruis. HA4 115 BV63
Trenchard Cl, NW9
off Fulbeck Dr 96 CS53
Stanmore HA7 95 CG51
Walton-on-Thames KT12 214 BW106
Trenchard Ct, Mord. SM4
off Green La 200 DA100
Trenchard St, SE10 24 F10
Trenches La, Slou. SL3 133 BA73
Trenchold St, SW8 161 DL79
Trenear Cl, Orp. BR6 224 EU105
Trenham Dr, Warl. CR6 236 DW116
Trenholme Cl, SE20 182 DV94
Trenholme Ct, Cat. CR3 236 DU122
Trenholme Rd, SE20 182 DV94
Trenholme Ter, SE20 182 DV94
Trenmar Gdns, NW10 139 CV69
Trent Av, W5 157 CJ76
Upminster RM14 129 FR58
Trentbridge Cl, Ilf. IG6 103 ET51
Trent Cl, Rad. (Shenley) WD7
off Edgbaston Dr 62 CL32
Sch Trent C of E Prim Sch, Barn. EN4 off Church Way 80 DF42
Trent Gdns, N14 81 DH44
Trentham Cres, Wok. GU22 227 BA121
Trentham Dr, Orp. BR5 206 EU98
Trentham Rd, Red. RH1 266 DF136
Trentham St, SW18 180 DA88
★ Trent Park Country Pk, Barn. EN4 81 DH40
Trent Rd, SW2 181 DM85
Buckhurst Hill IG9 102 EH46
Slough SL3 153 BB79
Trent Way, Hayes UB4 135 BS68
Worcester Park KT4 199 CW104
Trentwood Side, Enf. EN2 81 DM41
Treport St, SW18 180 DB87
Tresco Cl, Brom. BR1 184 EE93
Trescoe Gdns, Har. HA2 116 BY59
Romford RM5 105 FC50
Tresco Gdns, Ilf. IG3 126 EU61
Tresco Rd, SE15 162 DV84
Berkhamsted HP4 38 AT19
Tresham Cres, NW8 8 A3
Tresham Rd, Bark. IG11 145 ET66
Tresham Wk, E9
off Churchill Wk 122 DW64
Tresilian Av, N21 81 DM43
Tresilian Sq, Hem.H. HP2 40 BM15
Tresillian Way, Wok. GU21 226 AU116
Tressell Cl, N1 4 F6
Tressillian Cres, SE4 163 EA83
Tressillian Rd, SE4 163 DZ84
Tresta Wk, Wok. GU21 226 AU115
Trestis Cl, Hayes UB4
off Jollys La 136 BY71
Treston Ct, Stai. TW18 173 BF92
Treswell Rd, Dag. RM9 146 EY67
Tretawn Gdns, NW7 96 CS49
Tretawn Pk, NW7 96 CS49
Trevalga Way, Hem.H. HP2 40 BL16
Trevanion Rd, W14 16 D9
Treve Av, Har. HA1 116 CC59
Trevellance Way, Wat. WD25 60 BW33
Trevelyan Av, E12 125 EM63
Trevelyan Cl, Dart. DA1 168 FM84
Trevelyan Cres, Har. HA3 117 CK59
Trevelyan Gdns, NW10 139 CW67
Sch Trevelyan Mid Sch, The, Wind. SL4
off St. Leonards Rd 151 AQ84
Trevelyan Rd, E15 124 EE63
SW17 180 DE92
Trevelyan Way, Berk. HP4 38 AV17
Trevera Ct, Wal.Cr. EN8
off Eleanor Rd 67 DY33
Trevereux Hill, Oxt. RH8 255 EM131
Treveris St, SE1 20 E2
Treverton St, W10 6 B4
Treves Cl, N21 81 DM43
Treville St, SW15 179 CV87
Treviso Rd, SE23
off Farren Rd 183 DX89
Trevithick Cl, Felt. TW14 175 BT88
Trevithick Dr, Dart. DA1 168 FM84
Trevithick St, SE8 163 EA78
Trevone Gdns, Pnr. HA5 116 BY58
Trevor Cl, Barn. EN4 80 DD43
Bromley BR2 204 EF101
Harrow HA3 off Kenton La 95 CF52
Isleworth TW7 177 CF85
Northolt UB5 136 BW68
Trevor Cres, Ruis. HA4 115 BT63
Trevor Gdns, Edg. HA8 96 CR53
Northolt UB5 136 BW68
Ruislip HA4
off Clyfford Rd 115 BU63
Trevor Pl, SW7 18 B4
Trevor Rd, SW19 179 CY94
Edgware HA8 96 CR53
Hayes UB3 155 BS75
Woodford Green IG8 102 EG52
Trevor Sq, SW7 18 C4
Trevor St, SW7 18 B4
Trevor Wk, SW7 off Trevor Sq 160 DF75
Trevose Av, W.Byf. KT14 211 BF114
Trevose Rd, E17 101 ED53
Trevose Way, Wat. WD19 94 BW48
Trewarden Av, Iver SL0 133 BD68
Trewenna Dr, Chess. KT9 215 CK106
Potters Bar EN6 64 DD32
Trewince Rd, SW20 199 CW95
Trewint St, SW18 180 DC89

★ Place of interest   H Hospital   Sch School   Coll College   Uni University   ⇌ Railway station

Trewsbury Ho, SE2
 off Hartslock Dr ...166 EX75
Trewsbury Rd, SE26 ...183 DX92
Triandra Way, Hayes UB4 ...136 BX71
Triangle, The, EC1 ...10 F3
 N13 off Lodge Dr ...99 DN49
 Barking IG11
 off Tanner St ...145 EQ65
 Hampton TW12 off High St ...196 CC95
 Kingston upon Thames KT1
 off Kenley Rd ...198 CQ96
 Woking GU21 ...226 AW118
Triangle Business Cen, NW10
 off Enterprise Way ...139 CU69
Triangle Ct, E16
 off Tollgate Rd ...144 EK71
Triangle Est, SE11 ...20 C10
Triangle Pas, Barn. EN4
 off Station App ...80 DC42
Triangle Pl, SW4 ...161 DK84
Triangle Rd, E8 ...142 DV67
Trident Cen, Wat. WD24 ...76 BW39
Trident Gdns, Nthlt. UB5
 off Jetstar Way ...136 BX69
Trident Ind Est, Hodd. EN11 ...49 EC17
 Slough (Colnbr.) SL3 ...153 BE83
Trident Rd, Wat. WD25 ...59 BT34
Trident St, SE16 ...23 H7
Trident Way, Sthl. UB2 ...155 BV76
Trigg's Cl, Wok. GU22 ...226 AX119
Trigg's La, Wok. GU21, GU22 ...226 AW118
Trig La, EC4 ...10 G9
Trigo Ct, Epsom KT19
 off Blakeney Cl ...216 CR111
Trigon Rd, SW8 ...161 DM80
Trilby Rd, SE23 ...183 DX89
Trimmer Wk, Brent. TW8 ...158 CL79
Trim St, SE14 ...163 DZ79
Trinder Gdns, N19
 off Trinder Rd ...121 DL60
Trinder Ms, Tedd. TW11 ...177 CG92
Trinder Rd, N19 ...121 DL60
 Barnet EN5 ...79 CW43
Trindles Rd, Red. (S.Nutfld)
 RH1 ...267 DM136
Tring Av, W5 ...138 CM74
 Southall UB1 ...136 BZ72
 Wembley HA9 ...138 CN65
Tring Cl, Ilf. IG2 ...125 EQ57
 Romford RM3 ...106 FM49
Tring Gdns, Rom. RM3 ...106 FL49
Tring Grn, Rom. RM3 ...106 FM49
Tringham Cl, Cher. (Ott.) KT16 ...211 BC107
Tring Wk, Rom. RM3
 off Tring Gdns ...106 FL49
Trinidad Gdns, Dag. RM10 ...147 FD66
Trinidad St, E14 ...13 M9
Trinity Av, N2 ...120 DD55
 Enfield EN1 ...82 DT44
Trinity Buoy Wf, E14 ...15 J10
Trinity Ch Pas, SW13 ...159 CV79
Trinity Ch Rd, SW13 ...159 CV79
Trinity Ch Sq, SE1 ...21 H5
Trinity Chyd, Guil. GU1
 off High St ...258 AX136
Trinity Cl, E8 ...5 P3
 E11 ...124 EE61
 NW3 off Hampstead High St ...120 DD63
 SE13 off Wisteria Rd ...163 ED84
 SW4 off The Pavement ...161 DJ84
 Bromley BR2 ...204 EL102
 Hounslow TW4 ...156 BY84
 Northwood HA6 ...93 BS51
 South Croydon CR2 ...220 DS109
 Staines (Stanw.) TW19 ...174 BJ86
Coll **Trinity Coll of Music**,
 SE10 off King William Wk ...163 EC79
Trinity Cotts, Rich. TW9
 off Trinity Rd ...158 CM83
Trinity Ct, N1 ...5 L7
 NW2 off Anson Rd ...119 CW64
 SE7 off Charlton La ...164 EK77
Trinity Cres, SW17 ...180 DF89
Trinity Dr, Uxb. UB8 ...135 BQ72
Trinity Gdns, E16
 off Cliff Wk ...144 EF70
 SW9 ...161 DM84
 Dartford DA1
 off Summerhill Rd ...188 FK86
Trinity Gro, SE10 ...163 EC81
 Hertford SG14 ...32 DQ07
Trinity Hall Cl, Wat. WD24 ...76 BW41
★ **Trinity Ho**, EC3 ...11 M9
Trinity La, Wal.Cr. EN8 ...67 DY32
Trinity Ms, SE20 ...202 DV95
 W10 ...6 B7
 Hemel Hempstead HP2 ...41 BR21
Trinity Path, SE26 ...182 DW90
Trinity Pl, EC3 ...11 N10
 Bexleyheath DA6 ...166 EZ84
 Windsor SL4 ...151 AQ82
Sch **Trinity RC High Sch**,
 Lwr Sch, Wdf.Grn. IG8
 off Sydney Rd ...102 EG49
 Upr Sch, Wdf.Grn. IG8
 off Mornington Rd ...102 EG49
Trinity Ri, SW2 ...181 DN88
Trinity Rd, N2 ...120 DD55
 N22 ...99 DL53
 SW17 ...180 DF89
 SW18 ...180 DD85
 SW19 ...180 DA93
 Gravesend DA12 ...191 GJ87
 Hertford (Hert.Hth) SG13 ...32 DW12
 Ilford IG6 ...125 EQ55
 Richmond TW9 ...158 CM83
 Southall UB1 ...136 BY74
 Ware SG12 ...33 DY05
Sch **Trinity St. Mary's Prim Sch**,
 SW12 off Balham Pk Rd ...180 DG88
Sch **Trinity St. Stephen C of E First Sch**, Wind. SL4
 off Vansittart Rd ...151 AP81
Sch **Trinity Sch**, Belv. DA17
 off Erith Rd ...167 FC77
 Bentry Site, Dag. RM10
 off Heathway ...126 FA63
Sch **Trinity Sch of John Whitgift**,
 Croy. CR0 off Shirley Rd ...202 DW103
Trinity Sq, EC3 ...11 M10
Trinity St, E16 ...15 L6
 SE1 ...21 H4
 Enfield EN2 ...82 DQ40
Trinity Wk, NW3 ...140 DC65
 Hemel Hempstead HP2
 off Pancake La ...41 BR21
 Hertford (Hert.Hth) SG13 ...32 DW12
Trinity Way, E4 ...101 DZ51
 W3 ...138 CS73
Trio Pl, SE1 ...21 H4
Tripps Hill, Ch.St.G. HP8 ...90 AU48
Tripps Hill Cl, Ch.St.G. HP8 ...90 AU48
Tripton Rd, Harl. CM18 ...51 ES16
Tristan Sq, SE3 ...164 EE83
Tristram Cl, E17 ...123 ED55
Tristram Dr, N9
 off Barbot Cl ...100 DU48
Tristram Rd, Brom. BR1 ...184 EF91
Triton Sq, NW1 ...9 J3
Triton Way, Hem.H. HP2 ...40 BM18
Tritton Av, Croy. CR0 ...219 DL105
Tritton Rd, SE21 ...182 DR90
Trittons, Tad. KT20 ...233 CW121
Triumph Cl, Grays
 (Chaff.Hun.) RM16 ...169 FW77
 Hayes UB3 ...155 BQ80
Triumph Ho, Bark. IG11 ...146 EV69
Triumph Rd, E6 ...145 EM72
Trivett Cl, Green. DA9 ...189 FU85
★ **Trocadero Cen**, W1 ...9 L10
Trodd's La, Guil. GU1 ...259 BF135
Trojan Ct, NW6
 off Willesden La ...139 CY66
Trojan Way, Croy. CR0 ...201 DM104
Trolling Down Hill, Dart. DA2 ...188 FP89
Troon Cl, SE16 ...22 D9
 SE28 off Fairway Dr ...146 EX72
Troon St, E1 ...13 J7
Troopers Dr, Rom. RM3 ...106 FK49
Trosley Av, Grav. DA11 ...191 GH89
Trosley Rd, Belv. DA17 ...166 FA79
Trossachs Rd, SE22 ...182 DS85
Trothy Rd, SE1 ...22 B7
Trotsworth Av, Vir.W. GU25 ...192 AX98
Trotsworth Ct, Vir.W. GU25 ...192 AY98
Trotters Bottom, Barn. EN5 ...79 CU37
Trotters Gap, Ware
 (Stans.Abb.) SG12 ...33 ED11
Trotters La, Wok. (Mimbr.)
 GU24 ...210 AV112
Trotters Rd, Harl. CM18 ...52 EU17
Trotter Way, Epsom KT19 ...216 CP112
Trott Rd, N10 ...98 DF52
Trotts La, West. TN16 ...255 EQ127
Trott St, SW11 ...160 DE81
Trotwood, Chig. IG7 ...103 ER51
Trotwood Cl, Brwd. (Shenf.)
 CM15
 off Middleton Rd ...108 FY46
Troughton Rd, SE7 ...25 N9
Troutbeck Cl, Slou. SL2 ...132 AU73
Troutbeck Rd, SE14 ...163 DY81
Trout La, West Dr. UB7 ...134 BJ73
Trout Ri, Rick. (Loud.) WD3 ...74 BH41
Trout Rd, West Dr. UB7 ...134 BK74
Troutstream Way, Rick.
 (Loud.) WD3 ...74 BH42
Trouvere Pk, Hem.H. HP1 ...40 BH18
Trouville Rd, SW4 ...181 DJ86
Trowbridge Est, E9
 off Osborne Rd ...143 DZ65
Trowbridge Rd, E9 ...143 DZ65
 Romford RM3 ...106 FK51
Trowers Way, Red. RH1 ...251 DH131
Trowley Ri, Abb.L. WD5 ...59 BS31
Trowlock Av, Tedd. TW11 ...177 CJ93
Trowlock Island, Tedd. TW11 ...177 CK92
Trowlock Way, Tedd. TW11 ...177 CK93
Troy Cl, Tad. KT20 ...233 CV120
Troy Ct, SE18 ...165 EP77
Troy Rd, SE19 ...182 DR93
Troy Town, SE15 ...162 DU83
Trubshaw Rd, Sthl. UB2
 off Havelock Rd ...156 CB76
Truesdale Dr, Uxb. (Hare.)
 UB9 ...114 BJ57
Truesdale Rd, E6 ...145 EM72
Trulock Ct, N17 ...100 DU52
Trulock Rd, N17 ...100 DU52
Truman Cl, Edg. HA8
 off Pavilion Way ...96 CP52
Truman's Rd, N16 ...5 M1
Trumpers Way, W7 ...157 CE76
Trumper Way, Slou. SL1 ...131 AM74
 Uxbridge UB8 ...134 BJ67
Trumpets Hill Rd, Reig. RH2 ...265 CU135
Trumpington Dr, St.Alb. AL1 ...43 CD23
Trumpington Rd, E7 ...124 EF63
Trumps Grn Av, Vir.W. GU25 ...192 AX100
Trumps Grn Cl, Vir.W. GU25
 off Trumps Grn Rd ...192 AY99
Sch **Trumps Grn Inf Sch**, Vir.W.
 GU25 off Crown Rd ...192 AX100
Trumps Grn Rd, Vir.W. GU25 ...192 AX100
Trumps Mill La, Vir.W. GU25 ...193 AZ100
Trump St, EC2 ...11 H8
Trundlers Way, Bushey
 (Bushey Hth) WD23 ...95 CE46
Trundle St, SE1 ...20 G3
Trundleys Rd, SE8 ...23 H9
Trundleys Ter, SE8 ...23 H8
Trunks All, Swan. BR8 ...207 FB96
Trunley Heath Rd, Guil.
 (Bramley) GU5 ...258 AW144
Truro Gdns, Ilf. IG1 ...124 EL59
Truro Rd, E17 ...123 DZ56
 N22 ...99 DL52
 Gravesend DA12 ...191 GK90
Truro St, NW5 ...140 DG65
Truro Wk, Rom. RM3 ...106 FJ51
Truro Way, Hayes UB4
 off Portland Rd ...135 BS69
Truslove Rd, SE27 ...181 DN92
Trussley Rd, W6 ...159 CW76
Trustees Way, Uxb. (Denh.)
 UB9 ...113 BF57
Trustons Gdns, Horn. RM11 ...127 FG59
Trust Rd, Wal.Cr. EN8 ...67 DY34
Trust Wk, SE21
 off Peabody Hill ...181 DP88
Tryfan Cl, Ilf. IG4 ...124 EK57
Tryon Cres, E9 ...142 DW67
Tryon St, SW3 ...18 C9
Trys Hill, Cher. (Lyne) KT16 ...193 AZ103
Trystings Cl, Esher (Clay.)
 KT10 ...215 CG107
Tuam Rd, SE18 ...165 ER79
Tubbenden Cl, Orp. BR6 ...205 ES103
Tubbenden Dr, Orp. BR6 ...223 ER105
Sch **Tubbenden Inf Sch**, Orp.
 BR6 off Sandy Bury ...205 ER104
Sch **Tubbenden Jun Sch**, Orp.
 BR6 off Sandy Bury ...205 ER104
Tubbenden La, Orp. BR6 ...205 ES104
Tubbenden La S, Orp. BR6 ...223 ER106
Tubbs Rd, NW10 ...139 CT68
Tubs Hill Par, Sev. TN13 ...256 FG124
Tubwell Rd, Slou. (Stoke P.)
 SL2 ...132 AV67
Tucker Rd, Cher. (Ott.) KT16 ...211 BD107
Tucker St, Wat. WD18 ...76 BW43
Tuckey Gro, Wok. (Ripley)
 GU23 ...227 BF124
Tuck Rd, Rain. RM13 ...147 FG65
Tudor Av, Hmptn. TW12 ...176 CA93
 Romford RM2 ...127 FG55
 Waltham Cross (Chsht) EN7 ...66 DU31
 Watford WD24 ...76 BX38
 Worcester Park KT4 ...199 CV104
Tudor Circle, Gdmg. GU7 ...258 AS144
Tudor Cl, N6 ...121 DJ59
 NW3 ...120 DE64
 NW7 ...97 CU51
 NW9 ...118 CQ61
 SW2 off Elm Pk ...181 DM86
 Ashford TW15 ...174 BL91
 Banstead SM7 ...233 CY115
 Brentwood (Shenf.) CM15 ...109 FZ44
 Chessington KT9 ...216 CL106
 Chigwell IG7 ...103 EN49
 Chislehurst BR7 ...205 EM95
 Cobham KT11 ...214 BZ113
 Coulsdon CR5 ...235 DN118
 Dartford DA1 ...187 FH86
 Epsom KT17 ...217 CT110
 Gravesend (Nthflt) DA11 ...190 GE88
Tudor Cl, Hat. AL10 ...44 CS21
 Horley (Smallfield) RH6 ...269 DP148
 Leatherhead (Bkhm) KT23 ...230 CA124
 Pinner HA5 ...115 BU57
 South Croydon CR2 ...236 DV115
 Sutton SM3 ...217 CX106
 Wallington SM6 ...219 DJ108
 Waltham Cross (Chsht) EN7 ...66 DV31
 Ware SG12 ...34 EK07
 Woking GU22 ...227 BA117
 Woodford Green IG8 ...102 EH50
Tudor Ct, E17 ...123 DY59
 Borehamwood WD6 ...78 CL40
 Feltham TW13 ...176 BW91
 Swanley BR8 ...207 FC101
Tudor Ct N, Wem. HA9 ...118 CN64
Sch **Tudor Ct Prim Sch**, Grays
 RM16 off Bark Burr Rd ...170 FZ75
Tudor Ct S, Wem. HA9 ...118 CN64
Tudor Cres, Enf. EN2 ...81 DP39
 Ilford IG6 ...103 EP51
Tudor Dr, H.Wyc. (Woob.Grn)
 HP10 ...110 AD55
 Kingston upon Thames KT2 ...178 CL92
 Morden SM4 ...199 CX100
 Romford RM2 ...127 FG56
 Walton-on-Thames KT12 ...196 BX102
 Watford WD24 ...76 BX38
Tudor Est, NW10 ...138 CP68
Tudor Gdns, NW9 ...118 CQ61
 SW13 off Treen Av ...158 CS83
 W3 ...138 CN72
 Harrow HA3 off Tudor Rd ...95 CD54
 Romford RM2 ...127 FG56
 Slough SL1 ...130 AJ72
 Twickenham TW1 ...177 CF88
 Upminster RM14 ...128 FQ61
 West Wickham BR4 ...203 EC104
Tudor Gro, E9 ...142 DW66
 N20 off Church Cres ...98 DE48
Tudor Ho, Surb. KT6
 off Lenelby Rd ...198 CN102
Tudor La, Wind. (Old Wind.)
 SL4 ...172 AW87
Tudor Manor Gdns, Wat.
 WD25 ...60 BX32
Tudor Ms, Rom. RM1
 off Eastern Rd ...127 FF57
Tudor Par, Rick. WD3
 off Berry La ...92 BG45
Tudor Pk, Amer. HP6 ...55 AR37
Tudor Pl, Mitch. CR4 ...180 DE94
Sch **Tudor Prim Sch**, N3
 off Queens Rd ...98 DC53
 Hemel Hempstead HP3
 off Redwood Dr ...40 BL22
 Southall UB1 off Tudor Rd ...136 BY73
Tudor Ri, Brox. EN10 ...49 DY21
Tudor Rd, E4 ...101 EB51
 E6 ...144 EJ67
 E9 ...142 DV67
 N9 ...100 DV45
 SE19 ...182 DT94
 SE25 ...202 DV99
 Ashford TW15 ...175 BR93
 Barking IG11 ...145 ET67
 Barnet EN5 ...80 DA41
 Beckenham BR3 ...203 EB97
 Godalming GU7 ...258 AS144
 Hampton TW12 ...176 CA94
 Harrow HA3 ...95 CD54
 Hayes UB3 ...135 BR72
 High Wycombe (Haz.) HP15 ...88 AC45
 Hounslow TW3 ...157 CD84
 Kingston upon Thames KT2 ...178 CN94
 Pinner HA5 ...94 BW54
 St. Albans AL3 ...43 CE16
 St. Albans (Wheat.) AL4 ...28 CL07
 Southall UB1 ...136 BY73
Tudors, The, Reig. RH2 ...250 DC131
Tudor Sq, Hayes UB3 ...135 BR71
Tudor St, EC4 ...10 D9
Tudor Wk, Bex. DA5 ...186 EY86
Tudorwalk, Grays RM17
 off Thurloe Wk ...170 GA76
Tudor Wk, Lthd. KT22 ...231 CF120
 Watford WD24 ...76 BX37
 Weybridge KT13
 off West Palace Gdns ...195 BP104
Tudor Way, N14 ...99 DK46
 W3 ...158 CN75
 Hertford SG14 ...31 DN09
 Orpington BR5 ...205 ER100
 Rickmansworth (Mill End)
 WD3 ...92 BG46
 Uxbridge UB10 ...134 BN65
 Waltham Abbey EN9 ...67 ED33
 Windsor SL4 ...151 AL81
Tudor Well Cl, Stan. HA7 ...95 CH50
Tudway Rd, SE3 ...164 EH83
Tufnail Rd, Dart. DA1 ...188 FM86
TUFNELL PARK, N7 ...121 DK63
⊖ **Tufnell Park** ...121 DJ63
Sch **Tufnell Pk Prim Sch**, N7
 off Dalmeny Rd ...121 DK63
Tufnell Pk Rd, N7 ...121 DJ63
 N19 ...121 DJ63
Tufter Rd, Chig. IG7 ...103 ET50
Tufton Gdns, W.Mol. KT8 ...196 CB96
Tufton Rd, E4 ...101 EA49
Tufton St, SW1 ...19 M5
Tugboat St, SE28 ...165 ES75
Tugela Rd, Croy. CR0 ...202 DR100
Tugela St, SE6 ...183 DZ89
Tugmutton Cl, Orp. BR6
 off Acorn Way ...223 EP105
Tugwood Cl, Couls. CR5
 off Netherne Dr ...235 DK121
Tuilerie St, E2 ...142 DU68
Coll **Tuition Cen, The**, NW4
 off Lodge Rd ...119 CW56
Sch **Tuke Sch**, SE15
 off Woods Rd ...162 DV81
Tulip Cl, E6
 off Bradley Stone Rd ...145 EM71
 Brentwood (Pilg.Hat.) CM15
 off Poppy Cl ...108 FV43
 Croydon CR0 ...203 DX102
 Hampton TW12
 off Partridge Rd ...176 BZ93
 Romford RM3 ...106 FK51
 Southall UB2 off Chevy Rd ...156 CC75
Tulip Ct, Pnr. HA5 ...116 BW55
Tulip Gdns, Ilf. IG1 ...145 EP65
Tulip Tree Ct, Sutt. SM2
 off The Crescent ...218 DA111
Tulip Way, West Dr. UB7 ...154 BK77
Tull St, Mitch. CR4 ...200 DF101
Tulse Cl, Beck. BR3 ...203 EC97
TULSE HILL, SE21 ...182 DQ88
⇌ **Tulse Hill** ...181 DP89
Tulse Hill, SW2 ...181 DN86
Tulse Hill Est, SW2 ...181 DN86
Tulsemere Rd, SE27 ...182 DQ89
Tulyar Cl, Tad. KT20 ...233 CV120
Tumber St, Epsom (Headley)
 KT18 ...248 CQ125
Tumbler Rd, Harl. CM18 ...52 EU17
Tumblewood Rd, Bans. SM7 ...233 CY116
Tumbling Bay, Walt. KT12 ...195 BU100
Tummons Gdns, SE25 ...202 DS96
Tuncombe Rd, N18 ...100 DS49
Tunfield Rd, Hodd. EN11 ...33 EB14
Tunis Rd, W12 ...139 CV74
Tunley Grn, E14
 off Burdett Rd ...143 DZ71
Tunley Rd, NW10 ...138 CS67
 SW17 ...180 DG88
Tunmarsh La, E13 ...15 P1
Sch **Tunmarsh Spec Sch & Cen**,
 E13 off Tunmarsh La ...144 EJ69
Tunmers End, Ger.Cr.
 (Chal.St.P.) SL9 ...90 AW53
Tunnan Leys, E6 ...145 EN72
Tunnel Av, SE10 ...24 F7
Tunnel Est, Grays RM20 ...169 FT77
Tunnel Gdns, N11 ...99 DJ52
Tunnel Rd, SE16 ...22 E3
 Reigate RH2 off Church St ...250 DA133
Tunnel Wd Cl, Wat. WD17 ...75 BT37
Tunnel Wd Rd, Wat. WD17 ...75 BT37
Tunnmeade, Harl. CM20 ...36 EU14
Tunsgate, Guil. GU1 ...258 AX136
Tunsgate Sq Shop Cen, Guil.
 GU1 off High St ...258 AX136
Tuns La, Slou. SL1 ...151 AQ76
Tunstall Av, Ilf. IG6 ...104 EU51
Tunstall Cl, Orp. BR6 ...223 ES105
Tunstall Rd, SW9 ...161 DM84
 Croydon CR0 ...202 DS102
Tunstall Wk, Brent. TW8 ...158 CL79
Tunstock Way, Belv. DA17 ...166 EY76
Tunworth Cl, NW9 ...118 CQ58
Tunworth Cres, SW15 ...179 CT86
Tun Yd, SW8 off Peardon St ...161 DH82
Tupelo Rd, E10 ...123 EB61
Tuppers Ct, Guil. (Albury)
 GU5 ...260 BJ139
Tupsy St, SE28 ...165 EQ76
Tupwood Ct, Cat. CR3 ...252 DU125
Tupwood La, Cat. CR3 ...252 DU125
Tupwood Scrubbs Rd, Cat.
 CR3 ...252 DU128
Turenne Cl, SW18 ...160 DC84
Turfhouse La, Wok.
 (Chobham) GU24 ...210 AS109
Turin Rd, N9 ...100 DW45
Turin St, E2 ...12 A2
Turkey Oak Cl, SE19 ...202 DS95
⇌ **Turkey Street** ...82 DW37
Turkey St, Enf. EN1, EN3 ...82 DV37
Turks Cl, Uxb. UB8
 off Harlington Rd ...134 BN69
Turk's Head Yd, EC1 ...10 E5
Turks Row, SW3 ...18 D9
Turle Rd, N4 ...121 DM60
 SW16 ...201 DL96
Turlewray Cl, N4 ...121 DM60
Turley Cl, E15 ...144 EE67
Turmore Dale, Welw.G.C. AL8 ...29 CW10
Turnagain La, EC4 ...10 E7
 Dartford DA2 ...187 FG90
Turnage Rd, Dag. RM8 ...126 EY60
Turnberry Cl, NW4 ...97 CX54
 SE16 ...22 D10
Turnberry Ct, Wat. WD19 ...94 BW48
Turnberry Dr, St.Alb.
 (Brick.Wd) AL2 ...60 BY30
Turnberry Quay, E14 ...24 B5
Turnberry Way, Orp. BR6 ...205 ER102
Turnbull Cl, Green. DA9 ...189 FS87
Turnbury Cl, SE28 ...146 EX72
Turnchapel Ms, SW4
 off Cedars Rd ...161 DH83
Turner Av, N15 ...122 DS56
 Mitcham CR4 ...200 DF95
 Twickenham TW2 ...176 CC90
Turner Cl, NW11 ...120 DB58
 SW9 ...161 DP81
 Guildford GU4 ...243 AZ131
 Hayes UB4
 off Charville La ...135 BQ68
 Wembley HA0 ...117 CK64
Turner Ct, Dart. DA1 ...188 FJ85
Turner Dr, NW11 ...120 DB58
Turner Pl, SW11
 off Cairns Rd ...180 DE85
Turner Rd, E17 ...123 EC55
 Bushey WD23 ...76 CC42
 Dartford (Bean) DA2 ...189 FV90
 Edgware HA8 ...118 CM55
 Hornchurch RM12 ...127 FF61
 New Malden KT3 ...198 CR101
 Slough SL3 ...152 AW75
 Westerham (Bigg.H.) TN16 ...222 EJ112
Turners Cl, Stai. TW18 ...174 BH92
Turners Ct, Rom. (Abridge)
 RM4 ...86 EV41
Turners Gdns, Sev. TN13 ...257 FJ128
Turners Hill, Hem.H. HP2 ...40 BL21
 Waltham Cross (Chsht)
 EN8 ...67 DX30
Turners La, Walt. KT12 ...213 BV107
Turners Meadow Way, Beck.
 BR3 ...203 DZ95
Turners Rd, E3 ...13 L6
Turner St, E1 ...12 C6
 E16 ...15 K8
Turners Way, Croy. CR0 ...201 DN103
Turners Wd, NW11 ...120 DC59
Turners Wd Dr, Ch.St.G. HP8 ...90 AX48
Turneville Rd, W14 ...159 CZ79
Turney Grn, E14
 off Wallwood St ...143 DZ71
Sch **Turney Prim & Sec Sch**,
 SE21 off Turney Rd ...182 DQ87
Turney Rd, SE21 ...182 DR87
Turneys Orchard, Rick.
 (Chorl.) WD3 ...73 BD43
TURNFORD, Brox. EN10 ...67 DZ26
Sch **Turnford Sec Sch**, Wal.Cr.
 EN8 off Mill La ...67 DY28
Turnham Cl, Guil. GU2 ...258 AW138
⊖ **Turnham Green** ...158 CS77
Turnham Grn Ter, W4 ...158 CS77
Turnham Grn Ter Ms, W4
 off Turnham Grn Ter ...158 CS77
Sch **Turnham Prim**, SE4
 off Turnham Rd ...163 DY84
Turnham Rd, SE4 ...183 DY85
Turnmill St, EC1 ...10 D4
Turnoak Av, Wok. GU22 ...226 AY120
Turnoak La, Wok. GU22
 off Wych Hill La ...226 AY119
Turnoak Pk, Wind. SL4 ...151 AL84
Turnors, Harl. CM20 ...51 EQ15
Turnpike Cl, SE8
 off Amersham Vale ...163 DZ80
Turnpike Dr, Orp. BR6 ...224 EW109
Turnpike Grn, Hem.H. HP2 ...40 BL16
Turnpike Ho, EC1 ...10 F2
⊖ **Turnpike Lane** ...121 DN55
Turnpike La, N8 ...121 DM56
 Sutton SM1 ...218 DC106
 Tilbury (W.Til.) RM18 ...171 GK78
 Uxbridge UB10 ...134 BL69
Turnpike Link, Croy. CR0 ...202 DS103
Turnpike Way, Islw. TW7 ...157 CG81
Turnpin La, SE10 ...163 EC79
Turnstone Cl, E13 ...15 L2
 NW9 off Kestrel Cl ...96 CS54
 South Croydon CR2 ...221 DY110
 Uxbridge (Ickhm) UB10 ...115 BP64
Turnstones, The, Grav. DA12 ...191 GK89
 Watford WD25 ...76 BY36
Turp Av, Grays RM16 ...170 GC75
Turpentine La, SW1 ...19 H9
Turpin Av, Rom. RM5 ...104 FA52
Turpin Cl, Enf. EN3
 off Burton Dr ...83 EA37
Turpington Cl, Brom. BR2 ...204 EL100
Turpington La, Brom. BR2 ...204 EL101
Turpin La, Erith DA8 ...167 FG80
Turpin Rd, Felt. TW14
 off Staines Rd ...175 BT86
Turpins Cl, Hert. SG14 ...31 DM09
Turpins La, Wdf.Grn. IG8 ...103 EM50
Turpin Way, N19
 off Elthorne Rd ...121 DK61
 Wallington SM6 ...219 DH108
Turquand St, SE17 ...21 H8
Turret Gro, SW4 ...161 DJ83
Turton Rd, Wem. HA0 ...118 CL64
Turton Way, Slou. SL1 ...151 AR76
Turville Ct, Lthd. (Bkhm)
 KT23 off Proctor Gdns ...246 CB125
Turville St, E2 ...11 N3
Tuscan Rd, SE18 ...165 ER78
Tuskar St, SE10 ...24 G10
Tussauds Cl, Rick. (Crox.Grn)
 WD3 ...74 BN43
Tustin Est, SE15 ...162 DW79
Tuttlebee La, Buck.H. IG9 ...102 EG47
Tuxford Cl, Borwd. WD6 ...78 CL38
Twankhams All, Epp. CM16
 off Hemnall St ...70 EU30
Tweedale Ct, E15 ...123 EC64
Tweed Cl, Berk. HP4 ...38 AV18
Tweeddale Gro, Uxb. UB10 ...115 BQ62
Sch **Tweeddale Inf Sch**, Cars.
 SM5 off Paisley Rd ...200 DD101
Sch **Tweeddale Jun Sch**, Cars.
 SM5 off Tweeddale Rd ...200 DD101
Tweeddale Rd, Cars. SM5 ...200 DD102
Tweed Glen, Rom. RM1 ...105 FD52
Tweed Grn, Rom. RM1 ...105 FE52
Tweed La, Bet. (Strood Grn)
 RH3 ...264 CP139
Tweedmouth Rd, E13 ...144 EH68
Tweed Rd, Slou. SL3 ...153 BA79
Tweed Way, Rom. RM1 ...105 FD52
Tweedy Cl, Enf. EN1 ...82 DT43
Tweedy Rd, Brom. BR1 ...204 EF95
Tweenways, Chesh. HP5 ...54 AR30
Tweezer's All, WC2 ...10 C9
Twelve Acre Cl, Lthd. (Bkhm)
 KT23 ...230 BZ124
Twelve Acre Ho, E12
 off Grantham Rd ...125 EN62
Twelve Acres, Welw.G.C. AL7 ...29 CY11
Twelvetrees Cres, E3 ...14 C3
Twentyman Cl, Wdf.Grn. IG8 ...102 EG50
TWICKENHAM, TW1 & TW2 ...177 CG89
⇌ **Twickenham** ...177 CF87
Twickenham Br, Rich. TW9 ...177 CJ85
 Twickenham TW1 ...177 CJ85
Twickenham Cl, Croy. CR0 ...201 DM104
Twickenham Gdns, Grnf.
 UB6 ...117 CG64
 Harrow HA3 ...95 CE52
Sch **Twickenham Prep Sch**,
 Hmptn. TW12 off High St ...196 CC95
Twickenham Rd, E11 ...123 ED61
 Feltham TW13 ...176 BZ90
 Isleworth TW7 ...157 CG83
 Richmond TW9 ...157 CJ84
 Teddington TW11 ...177 CG92
Twickenham Trd Est, Twick.
 TW1 ...177 CF86
Twig Folly Cl, E2
 off Roman Rd ...143 DX68
Twigg Cl, Erith DA8 ...167 FE80
Twilley St, SW18 ...180 DB87
Twinches La, Slou. SL1 ...131 AP74
Twine Cl, Bark. IG11
 off Thames Rd ...146 EV69
Twine Ct, E1 ...12 E9
Twineham Grn, N12
 off Tillingham Way ...98 DA49
Twine Ter, E3 off Ropery St ...143 DZ70
Twining Av, Twick. TW2 ...176 CC90
Twinn Rd, NW7 ...97 CY51
Twinoaks, Cob. KT11 ...214 CA113
Twin Tumps Way, SE28 ...146 EU73
Twisden Rd, NW5 ...121 DH63
Twisleton Ct, Dart. DA1
 off Priory Hill ...188 FK86
Twitchells La, Beac.
 (Jordans) HP9 ...90 AT51
TWITTON, Sev. TN14 ...241 FF116
Twitton La, Sev. (Otford)
 TN14 ...241 FD115
Twitton Meadows, Sev.
 (Otford) TN14 ...241 FE116
Two Acres, Welw.G.C. AL7 ...29 CZ11
Two Dells La, Chesh.
 (Ash.Grn) HP5 ...38 AT24
Two Mile Dr, Slou. SL1 ...131 AK74
Two Rivers Retail Pk, Stai.
 TW18 ...173 BE91
Sch **Two Waters Prim Sch**,
 Hem.H. HP3
 off High Ridge Cl ...58 BK25
Two Waters Rd, Hem.H. HP3 ...40 BJ24
Twybridge Way, NW10 ...138 CQ66
Twycross Ms, SE10 ...25 H8
Twyford Abbey Rd, NW10 ...138 CM69
Twyford Av, N2 ...120 DF55
 W3 ...138 CN73
Sch **Twyford C of E High Sch**,
 W3 off Twyford Cres ...138 CP74
Twyford Cres, W3 ...138 CN74
Twyford Ho, N15
 off Chisley Rd ...122 DS58
Twyford Pl, WC2 ...10 A7
Twyford Rd, Cars. SM5 ...200 DD102
 Harrow HA2 ...116 CB60
 Ilford IG1 ...125 EQ64
 St. Albans AL4 ...43 CJ16
Twyford St, N1 ...4 A7
Twyner Cl, Horl. RH6 ...269 DK147
Twysdens Ter, Hat. AL9
 off Dellsome La ...45 CW24
Tyas Rd, E16 ...15 J4
Tybenham Rd, SW19 ...200 DA97
Tyberry Rd, Enf. EN3 ...82 DV41
Tyburn La, Har. HA1 ...117 CE59
Tyburns, The, Brwd. (Hutt.)
 CM13 ...109 GC47
Tyburn Way, W1 ...8 D9
Tycehurst Hill, Loug. IG10 ...85 EM42
Tychbourne Dr, Guil. GU4 ...243 BC131
Tydcombe Rd, Warl. CR6 ...236 DW119
TYE GREEN, Harl. CM18 ...51 ET17
Sch **Tye Grn Sch**, Harl.
 CM18 off Tendring Rd ...51 ES17
Tye Grn Village, Harl. CM18 ...51 ET18
Tye La, Epsom (Headley)
 KT18 ...248 CR127
 Orpington BR6 ...223 EQ106
 Tadworth KT20
 off Dorking Rd ...249 CT128
Tyers Est, SE1 ...21 L3

⊖ London Underground station DLR Docklands Light Railway station Tra Tramlink station Riv Pedestrian ferry landing stage

Tyers Gate, SE1 21 L3
Tyers St, SE11 20 A9
Tyers Ter, SE11 20 A10
Tyeshurst Cl, SE2 166 EY78
Tyfield Cl, Wal.Cr. (Chsht) EN8 66 DW30
Tykeswater La, Borwd. (Elstree) WD6 77 CJ39
Tylecroft Rd, SW16 201 DL96
Tyle Grn, Horn. RM11 128 FL56
Tylehost, Guil. GU2 242 AU130
Tylehurst Gdns, Ilf. IG1 125 EQ64
Tyle Pl, Wind. (Old Wind.) SL4 172 AU85
Tyler Cl, E2 5 N9
Erith DA8 off Brook St 167 FB80
Tyler Gdns, Add. KT15 212 BJ105
Tyler Gro, Dart. DA1 off Spielman Rd 168 FM84
Tyler Rd, Sthl. UB2 off McNair Rd 156 CB76
TYLERS CAUSEWAY, Hert. SG13 47 DK22
Tylers Causeway, Hert. (Newgate St) SG13 47 DH23
Tylers Cl, Gdse. RH9 252 DV130
Kings Langley WD4 58 BL28
Loughton IG10 102 EL45
Tyler's Ct, W1 9 L8
Tylers Cres, Horn. RM12 128 FJ64
Tylersfield, Abb.L. WD5 59 BT31
Tylers Gate, Har. HA3 118 CL58
Tylers Grn First Sch, H.Wyc. HP10 off School Rd 88 AD47
Tylers Grn Rd, Swan. BR8 207 FC100
Tylers Hill Rd, Chesh. HP5 56 AT30
Tylers Path, Cars. SM5 off Rochester Rd 218 DF105
Tylers Rd, Harl. (Roydon) CM19 50 EJ19
Tyler St, SE10 25 H10
Tylers Way, Wat. WD25 77 CD42
Tyler Wk, Slou. SL3 off Ditton Rd 153 AZ78
Tyler Way, Brwd. CM14 108 FV46
Tylney Av, SE19 182 DT92
Tylney Cft, Harl. CM19 51 EP17
Tylney Rd, E7 124 EJ63
Bromley BR1 204 EK96
Tylsworth Cl, Amer. HP6 55 AR38
Tymperley Ct, SW19 off Windlesham Gro 179 CY88
Tynan Cl, Felt. TW14 off Sandycombe Rd 175 BU88
Tyndale Ct, E14 24 A9
Tyndale La, N1 4 E5
Tyndale Ter, N1 4 E5
Tyndall Rd, E10 123 EC61
Welling DA16 165 ET83
Tyne Cl, Upmin. RM14 129 FR58
Tynedale, St.Alb. (Lon.Col.) AL2 off Thamesdale 62 CM27
Tynedale Cl, Dart. DA2 189 FR88
Tynedale Rd, Bet. (Strood Grn) RH3 264 CP138
Tyne Gdns, S.Ock. (Aveley) RM15 148 FQ73
Tyneham Cl, SW11 off Shirley Gro 160 DG83
Tyneham Rd, SW11 160 DG82
Tynemouth Cl, E6 off Covelees Wall 145 EP72
Tynemouth Dr, Enf. EN1 82 DU38
Tynemouth Rd, N15 122 DT56
SE18 165 ET78
Mitcham CR4 180 DG94
Tynemouth St, SW6 160 DC82
Tyne St, E1 11 P7
Tynley Gro, Guil. GU4 242 AX128
Tynsdale Rd, NW10 off Mayo Rd 138 CS65
Tynwald Ho, SE26 off Sydenham Hill 182 DU90
Type St, E2 143 DX68
Typleden Cl, Hem.H. HP2 40 BK18
Tyrawley Rd, SW6 160 DB81
Tyre La, NW9 off Sheaveshill Av 118 CS56
Tyrell Cl, Har. HA1 117 CE63
Tyrell Ct, Cars. SM5 218 DF105
Tyrell Gdns, Wind. SL4 151 AM83
Tyrell Ri, Brwd. CM14 108 FW50
Tyrells Cl, Upmin. RM14 128 FN61
Tyrols Rd, SE23 off Wastdale Rd 183 DX88
Tyrone Rd, E6 145 EM68
Tyron Way, Sid. DA14 185 ES91
Tyrrell Av, Well. DA16 186 EU85
Tyrrell Rd, SE22 162 DU84
Tyrrells Hall Cl, Grays RM17 170 GD79
Tyrrell Sq, Mitch. CR4 200 DE95
TYRRELL'S WOOD, Lthd. KT22 232 CM123
Tyrrel Way, NW9 119 CT59
Tyrwhitt Av, Guil. GU2 242 AV130
Tyrwhitt Ct, Guil. GU2 off Grange Rd 242 AV130
Tyrwhitt Rd, SE4 163 EA83
Tysea Cl, Harl. CM18 51 ET18
Tysea Hill, Rom. (Stap.Abb.) RM4 105 FF45
Tysea Rd, Harl. CM18 51 ET18
Tysoe Av, Enf. EN3 83 DZ36
Tysoe St, EC1 10 C2
Tyson Rd, SE23 182 DW87
Tyssen JMI Sch, N16 off Oldhill St 122 DU60
Tyssen Pas, E8 5 N3
Tyssen Pl, S.Ock. RM15 149 FW69
Tyssen Rd, N16 122 DT62
Tyssen St, E8 5 P3
N1 5 M9
Tythebarn Cl, Guil. GU4 off Dairyman's Wk 243 BB129
Tytherton Rd, N19 121 DK62
TYTTENHANGER, St.Alb. AL4 43 CK23
Tyttenhanger Grn, St.Alb. (Tytten.) AL4 43 CK23

U

Uamvar St, E14 14 B5
Uckfield Gro, Mitch. CR4 200 DG95
Uckfield Rd, Enf. EN3 83 DX37
Udall Gdns, Rom. RM5 104 FA51
Udall St, SW1 19 K8
Udney Pk Rd, Tedd. TW11 177 CG92
Uffington Rd, NW10 139 CU67
SE27 181 DN91
Ufford Cl, Har. HA3 off Ufford Rd 94 CB52
Ufford Rd, Har. HA3 94 CB52
Ufford St, SE1 20 D3
Ufton Gro, N1 5 K5
Ufton Rd, N1 5 K6
Uhura Sq, N16 122 DS62
Ujima Ct, SW16 off Sunnyhill Rd 181 DL91
Ullathorne Rd, SW16 181 DJ91
Ulleswater Rd, N14 99 DL49
Ullin St, E14 14 C6
Ullswater Business Pk, Couls. CR5 235 DL116
Ullswater Cl, SW15 178 CR91
Bromley BR1 184 EE93
Hayes UB4 135 BS68
Slough SL1 off Buttermere Av 130 AJ71
Ullswater Ct, Har. HA2 off Oakington Av 116 CA59
Ullswater Cres, SW15 178 CR91
Coulsdon CR5 235 DL116
Ullswater Rd, SE27 181 DP89
SW13 159 CU80
Hemel Hempstead HP3 41 BQ22
Ullswater Way, Horn. RM12 127 FG64
Ulstan Cl, Cat. (Wold.) CR3 237 EA123
Ulster Gdns, N13 100 DQ49
Ulster Pl, NW1 8 G4
Ulster Ter, NW1 8 G3
Ulundi Rd, SE3 164 EE79
Ulva Rd, SW15 off Ravenna Rd 179 CX85
Ulverscroft Rd, SE22 182 DT85
Ulverstone Rd, SE27 181 DP89
Ulverston Rd, E17 101 ED54
Ulwin Av, W.Byf. (Byfleet) KT14 212 BL113
Ulysses Rd, NW6 119 CZ64
Umberstones, Vir.W. GU25 off Furnival Cl 192 AX100
Umberston St, E1 12 C7
Umberville Way, Slou. SL2 131 AM70
Umbria St, SW15 179 CU86
Umfreville Rd, N4 121 DP58
Underacres Cl, Hem.H. HP2 40 BN19
Undercliff Rd, SE13 163 EA83
UNDERHILL, Barn. EN5 80 DA43
Underhill, Barn. EN5 80 DA43
Underhill Inf Sch, Barn. EN5 off Mays La 79 CY43
Underhill Jun Sch, Barn. EN5 off Mays La 79 CY43
Underhill Pk Rd, Reig. RH2 250 DA131
Underhill Pas, NW1 off Camden High St 141 DH67
Underhill Rd, SE22 182 DV86
Underhill St, NW1 off Camden High St 141 DH67
Underne Av, N14 99 DH47
UNDERRIVER, Sev. TN15 257 FN130
Underriver Ho Rd, Sev. (Undrvr) TN15 257 FP130
Undershaft, EC3 11 L8
Undershaw Rd, Brom. BR1 184 EE90
Underwood, Croy. (New Adgtn) CR0 221 EC106
Underwood, The, SE9 185 EM89
Underwood Rd, E1 12 A4
E4 101 EB50
Caterham CR3 252 DS126
Woodford Green IG8 102 EK52
Underwood Row, N1 11 H1
Underwood St, N1 11 H1
Undine Rd, E14 24 B7
Undine St, SW17 180 DF92
Uneeda Dr, Grnf. UB6 137 CD67
Unicorn Ho, Brom. BR1 off Elmfield Rd 204 EG97
Unicorn Prim Sch, Beck. BR3 off Creswell Dr 203 EB99
Unicorn Sch, Rich. TW9 off Kew Rd 158 CM81
Unicorn Wk, Green. DA9 189 FT85
Union Cl, E11 123 ED63
Union Cotts, E15 off Welfare Rd 144 EE66
Union Ct, EC2 11 L7
Richmond TW9 off Eton St 178 CL85
Union Dr, E1 13 K3
Union Grn, Hem.H. HP2 off Church St 40 BK19
Union Gro, SW8 161 DK82
Union Jack Club, SE1 off Sandell St 161 DN75
Union Rd, N11 99 DK51
SW4 161 DK82
SW8 161 DK82
Bromley BR2 204 EK99
Croydon CR0 202 DQ101
Northolt UB5 136 CA68
Wembley HA0 138 CL65
Union Sq, N1 5 H8
Union St, E15 143 EC67
SE1 20 F2
Barnet EN5 79 CY42
Kingston upon Thames KT1 197 CK96
Union Wk, E2 11 M1
Union Wf, N1 4 G10
United Elizabeth Garrett Anderson Hosp & Hosp for Women, The, NW1 9 M2
Unity Cl, NW10 139 CU65
SE19 off Crown Dale 182 DQ92
Croydon (New Adgtn) CR0 221 EB109
Unity Rd, Enf. EN3 82 DW37
Unity Ter, Har. HA2 off Scott Cres 116 CB61
Unity Trd Est, Wdf.Grn. IG8 124 EK55
Unity Way, SE18 164 EK76
Unity Wf, SE1 21 P3
University Cl, NW7 97 CT52
Bushey WD23 76 CA42
University Coll Hosp, WC1 9 K4
Obstetric Hosp, WC1 9 K4
Out-Patients, W1 9 K3
Private Wing, WC1 9 K4
University Coll Jun Sch, NW3 off Holly Hill 120 DC63
University Coll London, Main Site, WC1 9 L3
Arthur Stanley Ho, W1 9 K5
Eastman Dental Inst, WC1 10 A2
John Astor Ho, W1 9 J5
Prankerd Ho, NW1 9 K3
Ramsay Hall, W1 off Maple St 141 DJ70
The Inst of Neurology, WC1 9 P4
Wolfson Ho, NW1 9 K2
University Coll London - Maternity Wing, WC1 9 K4
University Coll Sch, NW3 off Frognal 120 DC64
University Gdns, Bex. DA5 186 EZ87
University Hosp Lewisham, SE13 183 EB85
University of E London - Barking Campus, Dag. RM8 off Longbridge Rd 126 EU63
University of E London - London Docklands Campus, E16 off University Way 145 EN73
University of E London - Stratford Campus, Duncan Ho, E15 off High St 143 ED67
Uni Ho, E15 off Romford Rd 144 EE65
University of Greenwich - Avery Hill Campus, Mansion Site, SE9 off Bexley Rd 185 EQ86
Southwood Site, SE9 off Avery Hill Rd 185 EQ85
University of Greenwich - Maritime Greenwich Campus, Cooper Bldg, SE10 off King William Wk 163 ED79
Old Royal Naval Coll, SE10 off Park Row 163 ED79
University of Hertfordshire, Bayfordbury Fld Sta & Observatory, Hert. SG13 off Lower Hatfield Rd 31 DN14
de Havilland Campus, Hat. AL10 off Mosquito Way 44 CR18
Fielder Cen, Hat. AL10 off Manor Rd 44 CR15
Hatfield Campus, Hat. AL10 off College La 45 CT20
St. Albans Campus, St.Alb. AL1 off Hatfield Rd 43 CE19
★ University of London, WC1 9 M4
University of London, Senate Ho, WC1 9 M5
University of Surrey, Guil. GU2 off Gill Av 258 AS135
European Inst of Health & Med Sciences, Guil. GU2 off Alresford Rd 242 AV134
Guildford Park, Guil. GU2 off Alresford Rd 242 AV134
Post Grad Med Sch, Guil. GU2 off Gill Av 258 AS135
University of Surrey Roehampton - Digby Stuart Coll, SW15 off Roehampton La 179 CU85
University of Surrey Roehampton - Froebel Coll, SW15 off Roehampton La 179 CT86
Halls of Res, SW15 off Minstead Gdns 179 CT87
University of Surrey Roehampton - Southlands Coll, SW15 off Roehampton La 179 CU85
University of Surrey Roehampton - Whitelands Coll, Parkstead Ho, SW15 off Holybourne Av 179 CU87
University of the Arts, W1 8 G8
University of Westminster - Cavendish Campus, W1 9 J5
University of Westminster - Euston Cen, NW1 9 J3
University of Westminster - Harrow Campus, Har. HA1 off Watford Rd 117 CG59
University of Westminster - Marylebone Campus, NW1 8 E5
University of Westminster - Regent Campus, W1 9 H7
Great Portland St, W1 9 H5
Little Titchfield St, W1 9 J6
Riding Ho St, W1 9 J6
University Pl, Erith DA8 off Belmont Rd 167 FB80
University Rd, SW19 180 DD93
University St, WC1 9 K4
University Way, E16 145 EN73
Dartford DA1 168 FP84
Unstead La, Guil. (Bramley) GU5 258 AW144
Unstead Wd, Guil. (Peasm.) GU3 258 AW142
Unwin Av, Felt. TW14 175 BS85
Unwin Cl, SE15 162 DU79
Unwin Rd, SW7 17 P5
Isleworth TW7 157 CE83
Upbrook Ms, W2 7 M8
Upcerne Rd, SW10 160 DC80
Upchurch Cl, SE20 182 DV94
Up Cor, Ch.St.G. HP8 90 AW47
Up Cor Cl, Ch.St.G. HP8 90 AV47
Upcroft, Wind. SL4 151 AP83
Upcroft Av, Edg. HA8 96 CQ50
Updale Cl, Pot.B. EN6 63 CY33
Updale Rd, Sid. DA14 185 ET91
Upfield, Croy. CR0 202 DV103
Horley RH6 268 DG149
Upfield Cl, Horl. RH6 268 DG150
Upfield Rd, W7 137 CF70
Upfolds Grn, Guil. GU4 243 BC130
Upgrove Manor Way, SW2 off Trinity Ri 181 DN87
Uphall Prim Sch, Ilf. IG1 off Uphall Rd 125 EP64
Uphall Rd, Ilf. IG1 125 EP64
Upham Pk Rd, W4 158 CS77
Uphavering Ho, Horn. RM12 off Parkhill Cl 128 FJ61
Uphill Dr, NW7 96 CS50
NW9 118 CQ57
Uphill Gro, NW7 96 CS49
Uphill Rd, NW7 96 CS49
Upland Av, Chesh. HP5 54 AP28
Upland Ct Rd, Rom. RM3 106 FM54
Upland Dr, Hat. AL9 64 DB25
Upland Ms, SE22 off Upland Rd 182 DU85
Upland Prim Sch, Bexh. DA7 off Church Rd 166 EZ83
Upland Rd, E13 15 K3
SE22 182 DU85
Bexleyheath DA7 166 EZ83
Caterham CR3 237 EB120
Epping CM16 69 ET25
South Croydon CR2 220 DR106
Sutton SM2 218 DD108
Uplands, Ashtd. KT21 231 CK120
Beckenham BR3 203 EA96
Rickmansworth (Crox.Grn) WD3 74 BM44
Ware SG12 33 DZ05
Welwyn Garden City AL8 29 CW05
Uplands, The, Ger.Cr. SL9 112 AY60
Loughton IG10 85 EM41
Ruislip HA4 115 BU60
St. Albans (Brick.Wd) AL2 60 BY30
Uplands Av, E17 off Blackhorse La 101 DX54
Uplands Business Pk, E17 101 DX54
Uplands Cl, SW14 off Monroe Dr 178 CP85
Gerrards Cross SL9 112 AY60
Sevenoaks TN13 256 FF123
Uplands Dr, Lthd. (Oxshott) KT22 215 CD113
Uplands End, Wdf.Grn. IG8 102 EL52
Uplands Pk Rd, Enf. EN2 81 DN41
Uplands Rd, N8 121 DM57
Barnet EN4 98 DG46
Brentwood (Warley) CM14 108 FY50
Kenley CR8 236 DQ116
Orpington BR6 206 EV102
Romford RM6 126 EX55
Woodford Green IG8 102 EL52
Uplands Way, N21 81 DN43
Uplands Way, Sev. TN13 256 FF123
Upland Way, Epsom KT18 233 CW118
UPMINSTER, RM14 128 FQ62
⇌ Upminster 128 FQ61
⊖ Upminster 128 FQ61
⊖ Upminster Bridge 128 FN61
Upminster Inf Sch, Upmin. RM14 off St. Mary's La 128 FQ62
Upminster Jun Sch, Upmin. RM14 off St. Mary's La 128 FQ62
Upminster Rd, Horn. RM11, RM12 128 FM61
Upminster RM14 128 FM61
Upminster Rd N, Rain. RM13 148 FJ69
Upminster Rd S, Rain. RM13 147 FG70
Upminster Trd Pk, Upmin. RM14 129 FX59
⊖ Upney 145 ET66
Upney Cl, Horn. RM12 off Tylers Cres 128 FJ64
Upney La, Bark. IG11 145 ES65
Upnor Way, SE17 21 M9
Uppark Dr, Ilf. IG2 125 EQ58
Upper Abbey Rd, Belv. DA17 166 EZ77
Upper Addison Gdns, W14 16 C3
Upper Ashlyns Rd, Berk. HP4 38 AV20
Upper Bk St, E14 24 A2
Upper Bardsey Wk, N1 off Clephane Rd 142 DQ65
Upper Barn, Hem.H. HP3 40 BM23
Upper Belgrave St, SW1 18 F5
Upper Belmont Rd, Chesh. HP5 54 AP28
Upper Berkeley St, W1 8 C8
Upper Beulah Hill, SE19 202 DS95
Upper Bourne End La, Hem.H. HP1 57 BA25
Upper Bray Rd, Maid. SL6 150 AC77
Upper Brentwood Rd, Rom. RM2 128 FJ56
Upper Br Rd, Red. RH1 250 DE134
Upper Brighton Rd, Surb. KT6 197 CK100
Upper Brockley Rd, SE4 163 DZ82
Upper Brook St, W1 8 E10
Upper Butts, Brent. TW8 157 CJ79
Upper Caldy Wk, N1 off Clephane Rd 142 DQ65
Upper Camelford Wk, W11 off Lancaster Rd 139 CY72
Upper Cavendish Av, N3 120 DA55
Upper Cheyne Row, SW3 160 DE79
Upper Ch Hill, Green. DA9 189 FS85
Upper Clabdens, Ware SG12 33 DZ05
UPPER CLAPTON, E5 122 DV60
Upper Clapton Rd, E5 122 DV60
Upper Clarendon Wk, W11 off Lancaster Rd 139 CY72
Upper Cornsland, Brwd. CM14 108 FX48
Upper Ct Rd, Cat. (Wold.) CR3 237 EA123
Epsom KT19 216 CQ111
Upper Culver Rd, St.Alb. AL1 43 CE18
Upper Dagnall St, St.Alb. AL3 43 CD20
Upper Dengie Wk, N1 off Popham Rd 142 DQ67
Upper Dr, Beac. HP9 89 AK50
Westerham (Bigg.H.) TN16 238 EJ118
Upper Dunnymans, Bans. SM7 off Basing Rd 217 CZ114
Upper Edgeborough Rd, Guil. GU1 259 AZ135
UPPER EDMONTON, N18 100 DU51
UPPER ELMERS END, Beck. BR3 203 DZ100
Upper Elmers End Rd, Beck. BR3 203 DY98
Upper Fairfield Rd, Lthd. KT22 231 CH121
Upper Fm Rd, W.Mol. KT8 196 BZ98
Upperfield Rd, Welw.G.C. AL7 29 CZ11
Upper Forecourt, Gat. RH6 269 DH152
Upper Fosters, NW4 off New Brent St 119 CW57
Upper George St, Chesh. HP5 off Frances St 54 AQ30
Upper Gladstone Rd, Chesh. HP5 54 AQ30
Upper Grn E, Mitch. CR4 200 DF97
Upper Grn Rd, Welw. (Tewin) AL6 30 DE05
Upper Grn W, Mitch. CR4 off London Rd 200 DF97
Upper Grenfell Wk, W11 off Whitchurch Rd 139 CX73
Upper Grosvenor St, W1 8 E10
Upper Grotto Rd, Twick. TW1 177 CF89
Upper Grd, SE1 20 C1
Upper Gro, SE25 202 DS98
Upper Gro Rd, Belv. DA17 166 EZ79
Upper Guild Hall, Green. (Bluewater) DA9 off Bluewater Parkway 189 FU88
Upper Guildown Rd, Guil. GU2 258 AV137
Upper Gulland Wk, N1 off Clephane Rd 142 DQ65
UPPER HALLIFORD, Shep. TW17 195 BS97
⇌ Upper Halliford 195 BS96
Upper Halliford Bypass, Shep. TW17 195 BS99
Upper Halliford Grn, Shep. TW17 off Holmbank Dr 195 BS98
Upper Halliford Rd, Shep. TW17 195 BS96
Upper Hall Pk, Berk. HP4 38 AX20
Upper Ham Rd, Kings.T. KT2 177 CK91
Richmond TW10 177 CK91
Upper Handa Wk, N1 off Clephane Rd 142 DR65
Upper Hawkwell Wk, N1 off Popham Rd 142 DQ67
Upper Heath Rd, St.Alb. AL1 43 CF18
Upper High St, Epsom KT17 216 CS113
Upper Highway, Abb.L. WD5 59 BR33
Kings Langley WD4 59 BQ32
Upper Hill Ri, Rick. WD3 74 BH44
Upper Hitch, Wat. WD19 94 BY46
UPPER HOLLOWAY, N19 121 DJ62
⇌ Upper Holloway 121 DK61
Upper Holly Hill Rd, Belv. DA17 167 FB78
Upper Hook, Harl. CM18 51 ES17
Upper James St, W1 9 K9
Upper John St, W1 9 K9
Upper Lattimore Rd, St.Alb. AL1 43 CE20
Upper Lees Rd, Slou. SL2 131 AP69
Upper Lismore Wk, N1 off Clephane Rd 142 DQ65
Upper Lo Way, Couls. CR5 off Netherne Dr 235 DK122
Upper Mall, W6 159 CU78
Upper Manor Rd, Gdmg. GU7 258 AS144
Upper Marlborough Rd, St.Alb. AL1 43 CE20
Upper Marsh, SE1 20 B5
Upper Marsh La, Hodd. EN11 49 EA18
Upper Mealines, Harl. CM18 52 EU18
Upper Montagu St, W1 8 C5
Upper Mulgrave Rd, Sutt. SM2 217 CY108
Upper N St, E14 13 P9
UPPER NORWOOD, SE19 182 DR94
Upper Paddock Rd, Wat. WD19 76 BY44
Upper Palace Rd, E.Mol. KT8 196 CC97
Upper Pk, Harl. CM20 35 EP14
Loughton IG10 84 EK42
Upper Pk Rd, N11 99 DH50
NW3 120 DF64
Belvedere DA17 167 FB77
Bromley BR1 204 EH95
Kingston upon Thames KT2 178 CN93
Upper Phillimore Gdns, W8 16 G4
Upper Pillory Down, Cars. SM5 218 DG113
Upper Pines, Bans. SM7 234 DF117
Upper Rainham Rd, Horn. RM12 127 FF63
Upper Ramsey Wk, N1 off Clephane Rd 142 DR65
Upper Rawreth Wk, N1 off Popham Rd 142 DQ67
Upper Richmond Rd, SW15 159 CY84
Upper Richmond Rd W, SW14 158 CP84
Richmond TW10 158 CN84
Upper Riding, Beac. HP9 88 AG54
Upper Rd, E13 15 L1
Uxbridge (Denh.) UB9 113 BD59
Wallington SM6 219 DK106
Upper Rose Gall, Green. (Bluewater) DA9 off Bluewater Parkway 189 FU88
Upper Rose Hill, Dor. RH4 263 CH137
Upper Ryle, Brwd. CM14 106 FV45
Upper St. Martin's La, WC2 9 N9
Upper Sales, Hem.H. HP1 39 BF21
Upper Sawley Wd, Bans. SM7 217 CZ114
Upper Selsdon Rd, S.Croy. CR2 220 DT108
Upper Sheppey Wk, N1 off Clephane Rd 142 DQ66
Upper Sheridan Rd, Belv. DA17 off Coleman Rd 166 FA77
Upper Shirley Rd, Croy. CR0 202 DW103
Upper Shot, Welw.G.C. AL7 30 DA08
Upper Shott, Wal.Cr. (Chsht) EN7 66 DT26
Upper Sq, Islw. TW7 157 CG83
Upper Sta Rd, Rad. WD7 77 CG35
Upper Stonyfield, Harl. CM19 51 EP15
Upper St, N1 4 D9
Guildford (Shere) GU5 260 BM139
Upper Sunbury Rd, Hmptn. TW12 196 BY95
Upper Sutton La, Houns. TW5 156 CA80
Upper Swaines, Epp. CM16 69 ET30
UPPER SYDENHAM, SE26 182 DU91
Upper Tachbrook St, SW1 19 J7
Upper Tail, Wat. WD19 94 BY48
Upper Talbot Wk, W11 off Lancaster Rd 139 CY72
Upper Teddington Rd, Kings.T. KT1 197 CJ95
Upper Ter, NW3 120 DC62
Upper Thames St, EC4 10 F9
Upper Thames Wk, Green. (Bluewater) DA9 off Bluewater Parkway 189 FU88
Upper Tollington Pk, N4 121 DN60
Upperton Rd, Guil. GU2 258 AW136
Sidcup DA14 185 ET92
Upperton Rd E, E13 off Inniskilling Rd 144 EJ69
Upperton Rd W, E13 144 EJ69
UPPER TOOTING, SW17 180 DE90
Upper Tooting Indep High Sch, SW17 off Trinity Rd 180 DF89
Upper Tooting Pk, SW17 180 DF89
Upper Tooting Rd, SW17 180 DF91
Upper Town Rd, Grnf. UB6 136 CB70
Upper Tulse Hill, SW2 181 DM87
Upper Vernon Rd, Sutt. SM1 218 DD106
Upper Wk, Vir.W. GU25 192 AY98
UPPER WALTHAMSTOW, E17 123 EB56
Upper Walthamstow Rd, E17 123 ED56
⇌ Upper Warlingham 236 DU118
Upper W St, Reig. RH2 249 CZ134
Upper Wickham La, Well. DA16 166 EV80
Upper Wimpole St, W1 8 G5
Upper Woburn Pl, WC1 9 M2
Upper Woodcote Village, Pur. CR8 219 DK112
Uppingham Av, Stan. HA7 95 CH53
Upsdell Av, N13 99 DN51
UPSHIRE, Wal.Abb. EN9 68 EJ32
Upshirebury Grn, Wal.Abb. EN9 off Horseshoe Hill 68 EK33
Upshire Prim Sch, Wal.Abb. EN9 off Upshire Rd 68 EH33
Upshire Rd, Wal.Abb. EN9 68 EF32
Upshott La, Wok. GU22 227 BF117
Upstall St, SE5 161 DP81
UPTON, E7 144 EH66
UPTON, Slou. SL1 152 AU76
Upton, Wok. GU21 226 AV117
Upton Av, E7 144 EG66
St. Albans AL3 43 CD19
Upton Cl, NW2 off Somerton Rd 119 CY62
Bexley DA5 186 EZ86
St. Albans (Park St) AL2 61 CD25
Slough SL1 152 AT76
Upton Ct, SE20 off Blean Gro 182 DW94
Upton Ct Rd, Slou. SL3 152 AU76
Upton Cross Prim Sch, E13 off Churston Av 144 EH67
Upton Dene, Sutt. SM2 218 DB108
Upton Gdns, Har. HA3 117 CH57
Upton Hosp, Slou. SL1 152 AT76
Upton Ho Sch, Wind. SL4 off St. Leonards Rd 151 AQ82
Upton La, E7 144 EG66
Upton Lo Cl, Bushey WD23 94 CC45
UPTON PARK, E6 144 EJ67
UPTON PARK, Slou. SL1 152 AT76
⊖ Upton Park 144 EH67
Upton Pk, Slou. SL1 152 AT76
Upton Pk Rd, E7 144 EH66
Upton Prim Sch, Bexh. DA6 off Upton Rd 186 EZ85
Upton Rd, N18 100 DU50
SE18 165 EQ79
Bexley DA5 186 EZ86
Bexleyheath DA6 166 EY84
Hounslow TW3 156 CA83
Slough SL1 152 AU76
Thornton Heath CR7 202 DR96
Watford WD18 75 BV42
Upton Rd S, Bex. DA5 186 EZ86
Upway, N12 98 DE52
Gerrards Cross (Chal.St.P.) SL9 91 AZ53
Upwood Rd, SE12 184 EF86
SW16 201 DL95
Uranus Rd, Hem.H. HP2 40 BL18
Urban Av, Horn. RM12 128 FJ62

★ Place of interest | Hospital | School | College | University | ⇌ Railway station

Coll Urban Learning Foundation,
E14 .... 13 N9
Urlwin St, SE5 .... 162 DQ79
Urlwin Wk, SW9 .... 161 DN82
Urmston Dr, SW19 .... 179 CY88
Ursula Ms, N4
off Portland Ri 122 DQ60
Ursula St, SW11 .... 160 DE81
Sch Ursuline Conv Prep Sch,
SW20 off The Downs 199 CX95
Sch Ursuline High Sch, SW20
off Crescent Rd 199 CX95
Urswick Gdns, Dag. RM9
off Urswick Rd 146 EY66
Urswick Rd, E9 .... 122 DW64
Dagenham RM9 .... 146 EX66
Usborne Ms, SW8 .... 161 DM80
Usher Rd, E3 .... 143 DZ68
Usherwood Cl, Tad. (Box H.)
KT20 .... 248 CP131
Usk Rd, SW11 .... 160 DC84
South Ockendon (Aveley)
RM15 .... 148 FQ72
Usk St, E2 .... 12 G1
Utopia Village, NW1
off Chalcot Rd 140 DG67
Uvedale Cl, Croy. (New Adgtn)
CR0 off Uvedale Cres 221 ED111
Uvedale Cres, Croy.
(New Adgtn) CR0 .... 221 ED111
Uvedale Rd, Dag. RM10 .... 126 FA62
Enfield EN2 .... 82 DR43
Oxted RH8 .... 254 EF129
Uverdale Rd, SW10 .... 160 DC80
UXBRIDGE, UB8 - UB11 .... 134 BK66
⊖ Uxbridge 134 BK66
Coll Uxbridge Coll, Hayes
Comm Campus, Hayes
UB3 off Coldharbour La 135 BU73
Uxbridge Campus, Uxb.
UB8 off Park Rd 134 BL65
Uxbridge Gdns, Felt. TW13
off Marlborough Rd 176 BX89
Sch Uxbridge High Sch, Uxb.
UB8 off The Greenway 134 BK68
UXBRIDGE MOOR, Iver SL0 .... 134 BG67
UXBRIDGE MOOR, Uxb. UB8 .... 134 BG67
Uxbridge Rd, W3 .... 138 CL73
W5 .... 137 CJ73
W5 (Ealing Com.) 138 CL73
W7 .... 137 CE74
W12 .... 139 CU74
W13 .... 137 CH74
Feltham TW13 .... 176 BW89
Hampton (Hmptn H.) TW12 .... 176 CA91
Harrow HA3 .... 94 CC52
Hayes UB4 .... 136 BW73
Iver SL0 .... 133 AY71
Kingston upon Thames KT1 .... 197 CK98
Pinner HA5 .... 94 CB52
Rickmansworth WD3 .... 91 BF47
Slough SL1, SL2, SL3 .... 152 AU75
Southall UB1 .... 136 CA74
Stanmore HA7 .... 95 CF51
Uxbridge UB10 .... 134 BN69
Uxbridge St, W8 .... 16 G1
Uxendon Cres, Wem. HA9 .... 118 CL60
Uxendon Hill, Wem. HA9 .... 118 CM60
Sch Uxendon Manor JMI Sch,
Har. HA3 off Vista Way 118 CL57

V

Vache La, Ch.St.G. HP8 .... 90 AW47
Vache Ms, Ch.St.G. HP8 .... 90 AX46
Vaillant Rd, Wey. KT13 .... 213 BQ105
Valance Av, E4 .... 102 EF46
Valan Leas, Brom. BR2 .... 204 EE97
Vale, The, N10 .... 98 DG53
N14 .... 99 DK45
NW11 .... 119 CX62
SW3 .... 160 DD79
W3 .... 138 CR74
Brentwood CM14 .... 108 FW46
Coulsdon CR5 .... 219 DK114
Croydon CR0 .... 203 DX103
Feltham TW14 .... 175 BV86
Gerrards Cross (Chal.St.P.)
SL9 .... 90 AX53
Hounslow TW5 .... 156 BY79
Ruislip HA4 .... 116 BW63
Sunbury-on-Thames TW16
off Ashridge Way 175 BU93
Woodford Green IG8 .... 102 EG52
Vale Av, Borwd. WD6 .... 78 CP43
Vale Border, Croy. CR0 .... 221 DX111
Vale Cl, N2 off Church Vale 120 DF55
W9 .... 7 L2
Brentwood (Pilg.Hat.) CM15 .... 108 FT43
Gerrards Cross (Chal.St.P.)
SL9 .... 90 AX53
Orpington BR6 .... 223 EN105
Weybridge KT13 .... 195 BR104
Woking GU21 .... 226 AY116
Vale Cotts, SW15
off Kingston Vale 178 CR91
Vale Ct, W9 .... 7 L2
Weybridge KT13 .... 195 BR104
Vale Cres, SW15 .... 178 CS90
Vale Cft, Esher (Clay.) KT10 .... 215 CE108
Pinner HA5 .... 116 BY57
Vale Dr, Barn. EN5 .... 79 CZ42
Vale End, SE22
off Grove Vale 162 DS84
Vale Fm Rd, Wok. GU21 .... 226 AX117
Vale Gro, N4 .... 122 DQ59
W3 off The Vale 138 CR74
Slough SL1 .... 152 AS76
Vale Ind Est, Wat. WD18 .... 93 BQ46
Vale La, W3 .... 138 CN71
Valence Av, Dag. RM8 .... 126 EX62
Valence Circ, Dag. RM8 .... 126 EX62
Valence Dr, Wal.Cr. (Chsht)
EN7 .... 66 DU28
★ Valence Ho Mus, Dag.
RM8 .... 126 EY61
Sch Valence Inf Sch, Dag.
RM8 off Bonham Rd 126 EX61
Sch Valence Jun Sch, Dag.
RM8 off Bonham Rd 126 EX61
Valence Rd, Erith DA8 .... 167 FD80
Sch Valence Sch, West. TN16
off Westerham Rd 255 ET126
Valence Wd Rd, Dag. RM8 .... 126 EX62
Valencia Rd, Stan. HA7 .... 95 CJ49
Valency Cl, Nthwd. HA6 .... 93 BT49
Valentia Pl, SW9
off Brixton Sta Rd 161 DN84
Valentine Av, Bex. DA5 .... 186 EY89
Valentine Ct, SE23 .... 183 DX89
Valentine Pl, SE1 .... 20 E3
Valentine Rd, E9 .... 143 DX65
Harrow HA2 .... 116 CC62
Valentine Row, SE1 .... 20 E4
Sch Valentines High Sch, Ilf.
IG2 off Cranbrook Rd 125 EN58
Valentines Rd, Ilf. IG1 .... 125 EP60
Valentines Way, Rom. RM7 .... 127 FE61
Valentine Way, Ch.St.G. HP8 .... 90 AX48
Valentyne Cl, Croy.
(New Adgtn) CR0 .... 222 EE111
Vale of Health, NW3
off East Heath Rd 120 DD62
Vale Par, SW15
off Kingston Vale 178 CR91
Sch Vale Prim Sch, The, Epsom
KT18 off Beaconsfield Rd 232 CS119
Valerian Way, E15 .... 15 H2
Valerie Cl, St.Alb. AL1 .... 43 CH20
Valerie Ct, Bushey WD23 .... 94 CC45
Sutton SM2 off Stanley Rd 218 DB108
Vale Ri, NW11 .... 119 CZ60
Chesham HP5 .... 54 AQ28
Vale Rd, E7 .... 144 EH65
N4 .... 122 DQ59
Bromley BR1 .... 205 EN96
Bushey WD23 .... 76 BY43
Chesham HP5 .... 54 AQ27
Dartford DA1 .... 187 FH88
Epsom KT19 .... 217 CT105
Esher (Clay.) KT10 .... 215 CE109
Gravesend (Nthflt) DA11 .... 190 GD87
Mitcham CR4 .... 201 DK97
Sutton SM1 .... 218 DB105
Weybridge KT13 .... 195 BR104
Windsor SL4 .... 151 AM80
Worcester Park KT4 .... 217 CT105
Vale Rd N, Surb. KT6 .... 198 CL103
Vale Rd S, Surb. KT6 .... 198 CL103
Vale Row, N5
off Gillespie Rd 121 DP62
Vale Royal, N7 .... 141 DL66
Valery Pl, Hmptn. TW12 .... 176 CA94
Sch Vale Sch, The, SW7 .... 17 L6
Valeside, Hert. SG14 .... 31 DN10
Vale St, SE27 .... 182 DR90
Valeswood Rd, Brom. BR1 .... 184 EF92
Vale Ter, N4 .... 122 DQ58
Valetta Gro, E13 .... 144 EG68
Valetta Rd, W3 .... 158 CS75
Valette St, E9 .... 142 DV65
Valiant Cl, Nthlt. UB5
off Ruislip Rd 136 BX69
Romford RM7 .... 104 FA54
Valiant Ho, SE7 .... 164 EJ78
Valiant Path, NW9
off Blundell Rd 96 CS52
Valiant Way, E6 .... 145 EM71
Vallance Rd, E1 .... 12 B2
E2 .... 12 B2
N22 .... 99 DJ54
Vallentin Rd, E17 .... 123 EC56
Valley, The, Guil. GU2
off Portsmouth Rd 258 AW138
Valley Av, N12 .... 98 DD49
Valley Cl, Dart. DA1 .... 187 FF86
Hertford SG13 .... 32 DR10
Loughton IG10 .... 85 EM44
Pinner HA5
off Alandale Dr 93 BV54
Waltham Abbey EN9 .... 67 EC32
Ware SG12 .... 32 DV05
Valley Ct, Cat. CR3
off Beechwood Gdns 236 DU122
Kenley CR8 off Hayes La 220 DQ114
Valley Dr, NW9 .... 118 CN58
Gravesend DA12 .... 191 GK91
Sevenoaks TN13 .... 257 FH125
Valleyfield Rd, SW16 .... 181 DM92
Valley Flds Cres, Enf. EN2 .... 81 DN40
Valley Gdns, SW19 .... 180 DD94
Wembley HA0 .... 138 CM66
★ Valley Gdns, The, Egh.
TW20 .... 192 AS96
Valley Grn, The, Welw.G.C.
AL8 .... 29 CW08
Valley Gro, SE7 .... 164 EJ78
Valley Hill, Loug. IG10 .... 102 EL45
Valley Link Ind Est, Enf. EN3 .... 83 DY44
Valley Ms, Twick. TW1
off Cross Deep 177 CG89
Sch Valley Prim Sch, Brom.
BR2 off Beckenham La 204 EF96
Valley Ri, Wat. WD25 .... 59 BV33
Valley Rd, SW16 .... 181 DM91
Belvedere DA17 .... 167 FB77
Berkhamsted HP4 .... 38 AT17
Bromley BR2 .... 204 EE96
Dartford DA1 .... 187 FF86
Erith DA8 .... 167 FD77
Kenley CR8 .... 236 DR115
Longfield (Fawk.Grn) DA3 .... 209 FV102
Orpington BR5 .... 206 EV95
Rickmansworth WD3 .... 74 BG43
St. Albans AL3 .... 43 CE15
Uxbridge UB10 .... 134 BL68
Welwyn Garden City AL8 .... 29 CV10
Valley Side, E4 .... 101 EA47
Valleyside, Hem.H. HP1 .... 39 BF20
Valley Side Par, E4
off Valley Side 101 EA47
Valley Vw, Barn. EN5 .... 79 CY44
Chesham HP5 .... 54 AN29
Greenhithe DA9 .... 189 FV86
Waltham Cross (Chsht)
EN7 .... 66 DQ28
Westerham (Bigg.H.) TN16 .... 238 EJ118
Valley Vw Gdns, Ken. CR8
off Godstone Rd 236 DS115
Valley Wk, Croy. CR0 .... 202 DW103
Rickmansworth (Crox.Grn)
WD3 .... 75 BQ43
Valley Way, Ger.Cr. SL9 .... 112 AW58
Valliere Rd, NW10 .... 139 CV69
Valliers Wd Rd, Sid. DA15 .... 185 ER88
Vallis Way, W13 .... 137 CG71
Chessington KT9 .... 215 CK105
Valmar Rd, SE5 .... 162 DQ81
Val McKenzie Av, N7
off Parkside Cres 121 DN62
Valnay St, SW17 .... 180 DF92
Valognes Av, E17 .... 101 DY53
Valonia Gdns, SW18 .... 179 CZ86
Vambery Rd, SE18 .... 165 EQ79
Vanbrough Cres, Nthlt. UB5 .... 136 BW67
Vanbrugh Cl, E16
off Fulmer Rd 144 EK71
Vanbrugh Dr, Walt. KT12 .... 196 BW101
Vanbrugh Flds, SE3 .... 164 EF80
Vanbrugh Hill, SE3 .... 164 EF78
SE10 .... 25 H10
Vanbrugh Pk, SE3 .... 164 EF80
Vanbrugh Pk Rd, SE3 .... 164 EF80
Vanbrugh Pk Rd W, SE3 .... 164 EF80
Vanbrugh Rd, W4 .... 158 CR76
Vanbrugh Ter, SE3 .... 164 EF81
Vanburgh Cl, Orp. BR6 .... 205 ES102
Vancouver Cl, Epsom KT19 .... 216 CQ111
Orpington BR6 .... 223 ET105
Vancouver Ct, Horl.
(Smallfield) RH6 .... 269 DN148
Vancouver Rd, SE23 .... 183 DY89
Broxbourne EN10 .... 67 DY25
Edgware HA8 .... 96 CP53
Hayes UB4 .... 135 BV70
Richmond TW10 .... 177 CJ91
Vanda Cres, St.Alb. AL1 .... 43 CF21
Vanderbilt Rd, SW18 .... 180 DC88
Vanderville Gdns, N2
off Tarling Rd 98 DC54
Vandome Cl, E16 .... 15 N8
Vandon Pas, SW1 .... 19 K5
Vandon St, SW1 .... 19 K5
Van Dyck Av, N.Mal. KT3 .... 198 CR101
Vandyke Cl, SW15 .... 179 CX87
Redhill RH1 .... 250 DF131
Vandyke Cross, SE9 .... 184 EL85
Vandy St, EC2 .... 11 L4
Vane Cl, NW3 .... 120 DD63
Harrow HA3 .... 118 CM58
Vanessa Cl, Belv. DA17 .... 166 FA78
Vanessa Wk, Grav. DA12 .... 191 GM92
Vanessa Way, Bex. DA5 .... 187 FD90
Vane St, SW1 .... 19 K7
Van Gogh Cl, Islw. TW7
off Twickenham Rd 157 CG83
Vanguard Cl, E16 .... 15 M6
Croydon CR0 .... 201 DP102
Romford RM7 .... 105 FB54
Vanguard St, SE8 .... 163 EA81
Vanguard Way, Cat. CR3
off Slines Oak Rd 237 EB121
Wallington SM6 .... 219 DL108
Warlingham CR6 .... 237 EB121
Vanneck Sq, SW15 .... 179 CU85
Vanner Pt, E9 off Wick Rd 143 DX65
Vanners Par, W.Byf. (Byfleet)
KT14 off Brewery La 212 BL113
Vanoc Gdns, Brom. BR1 .... 184 EG90
Vanquisher Wk, Grav. DA12 .... 191 GM90
Vansittart Est, Wind. SL4 .... 151 AQ81
Vansittart Rd, E7 .... 124 EF63
Windsor SL4 .... 151 AP80
Vansittart St, SE14 .... 163 DY80
Vanston Pl, SW6 .... 160 DA80
Vantage Ms, E14 .... 24 D2
Vantage Pl, W8 .... 17 H6
Vantage Rd, Slou. SL1
off Summerlea 131 AP74
Vantorts Cl, Saw. CM21 .... 36 EY05
Vantorts Rd, Saw. CM21 .... 36 EY06
Vant Rd, SW17 .... 180 DF92
Varcoe Rd, SE16 .... 22 D10
Vardens Rd, SW11 .... 160 DD84
Varden St, E1 .... 12 C7
Vardon Cl, W3 .... 138 CR72
Varley Par, NW9 .... 118 CS56
Varley Rd, E16 .... 15 P7
Varley Way, Mitch. CR4 .... 200 DD96
Varna Rd, SW6 .... 159 CY80
Hampton TW12 .... 196 CB95
Varndell St, NW1 .... 9 J1
Varney Cl, Hem.H. HP1 .... 39 BF20
Waltham Cross (Chsht) EN7 .... 66 DU27
Varney Rd, Hem.H. HP1 .... 39 BF20
Varnishers Yd, N1
off Caledonian Rd 141 DL68
Varsity Dr, Twick. TW1 .... 177 CE85
Varsity Row, SW14
off William's La 158 CQ82
Vartry Rd, N15 .... 122 DR58
Vassall Rd, SW9 .... 161 DN80
Vauban Est, SE16 .... 21 P6
Vauban St, SE16 .... 21 P6
Vaughan Av, NW4 .... 119 CU57
W6 .... 159 CT77
Hornchurch RM12 .... 128 FK63
Vaughan Cl, Hmptn. TW12
off Oak Av 176 BY93
Vaughan Ct, Guil. GU2
off Grange Rd 242 AV130
Sch Vaughan First & Mid Sch,
Har. HA1
off Vaughan Rd 116 CC58
Vaughan Gdns, Ilf. IG1 .... 125 EM59
Windsor (Eton Wick) SL4
off Eton Wick Rd 151 AM77
Vaughan Rd, E15 .... 144 EF65
SE5 .... 162 DQ83
Harrow HA1 .... 116 CC59
Thames Ditton KT7 .... 197 CH101
Welling DA16 .... 165 ET82
Vaughan St, SE16 .... 23 L4
Vaughan Way, E1 .... 12 A10
Dorking RH4 .... 263 CG136
Slough SL2 .... 131 AL70
Vaughan Williams Cl, SE8
off Watson's St 163 EA80
Vaughan Williams Way,
Brwd. (Warley) CM14 .... 107 FU51
Vaux Cres, Walt. KT12 .... 213 BV107
VAUXHALL, SE11 .... 19 P10
⇌ Vauxhall 161 DL79
⊖ Vauxhall 161 DL79
Vauxhall Br, SE1 .... 19 N10
SW1 .... 19 N10
Vauxhall Br Rd, SW1 .... 19 K7
Vauxhall Cl, Grav. (Nthflt)
DA11 .... 191 GF87
Vauxhall Gdns, S.Croy. CR2 .... 220 DQ107
Vauxhall Gdns Est, SE11 .... 20 B10
Vauxhall Gro, SW8 .... 161 DL79
Vauxhall Pl, Dart. DA1 .... 188 FL87
Sch Vauxhall Prim Sch, SE11 .... 20 B9
Vauxhall Rd, Hem.H. HP2 .... 40 BN20
Vauxhall St, SE11 .... 20 B10
Vauxhall Wk, SE11 .... 20 A9
Vawdrey Cl, E1 .... 12 E4
Veals Mead, Mitch. CR4 .... 200 DE95
Vectis Gdns, SW17
off Vectis Rd 181 DH93
Vectis Rd, SW17 .... 181 DH93
Veda Rd, SE13 .... 163 EA84
Vega Cres, Nthwd. HA6 .... 93 BT50
Vegal Cres, Egh. (Eng.Grn)
TW20 .... 172 AW92
Vega Rd, Bushey WD23 .... 94 CC45
Veitch Cl, Felt. TW14 .... 175 BT88
Veldene Way, Har. HA2 .... 116 BZ62
Velde Way, SE22
off East Dulwich Gro 182 DS85
Velizy Av, Harl. CM20 .... 51 ER15
Velletri Ho, E2 .... 143 DX68
Vellum Dr, Cars. SM5 .... 200 DG104
Venables Cl, Dag. RM10 .... 127 FB63
Venables St, NW8 .... 7 P5
Vencourt Pl, W6 .... 159 CU78
Venetian Rd, SE5 .... 162 DQ82
Venetia Rd, N4 .... 121 DP58
W5 .... 157 CK75
Venette Cl, Rain. RM13 .... 147 FH71
Venner Rd, SE26 .... 182 DW93
Venners Cl, Bexh. DA7 .... 167 FE82
Venn St, SW4 .... 161 DJ84
Ventnor Av, Stan. HA7 .... 95 CH53
Ventnor Dr, N20 .... 98 DB48
Ventnor Gdns, Bark. IG11 .... 145 ES65
Ventnor Rd, SE14 .... 163 DX80
Sutton SM2 .... 218 DB108
Venton Cl, Wok. GU21 .... 226 AV117
Ventura Pk, St.Alb. AL2 .... 61 CF29
Venture Cl, Bex. DA5 .... 186 EY87
Venue St, E14 .... 14 B5
Venus Hill, Hem.H. (Bov.) HP3 .... 57 BA31
Venus Rd, SE18 .... 165 EM76
Veny Cres, Horn. RM12 .... 128 FK64
Vera Av, N21 .... 81 DN43
Vera Ct, Wat. WD19 .... 94 BX45
Vera Lynn Cl, E7
off Dames Rd 124 EG63
Vera Rd, SW6 .... 159 CY81
Verbena Cl, E16 .... 15 J3
South Ockendon RM15 .... 149 FW72
West Drayton UB7
off Magnolia St 154 BK78
Verbena Gdns, W6 .... 159 CU78
Verdant La, SE6 .... 184 EE88
Verdayne Av, Croy. CR0 .... 203 DX102
Verdayne Gdns, Warl. CR6 .... 236 DW116
Verderers Rd, Chig. IG7 .... 104 EU50
Verdun Rd, SE18 .... 166 EU79
SW13 .... 159 CU79
Verdure Cl, Wat. WD25 .... 60 BY32
Vereker Dr, Sun. TW16 .... 195 BU97
Vereker Rd, W14 .... 16 D10
Vere Rd, Loug. IG10 .... 85 EQ42
Vere St, W1 .... 8 G8
Verity Cl, W11 .... 6 C8
Veritys, Hat. AL10 .... 45 CU18
Vermeer Gdns, SE15
off Elland Rd 162 DW84
Vermont Cl, Enf. EN2 .... 81 DP42
Vermont Rd, SE19 .... 182 DR93
SW18 .... 180 DB86
Slough SL2 .... 131 AM70
Sutton SM1 .... 200 DB104
Verney Cl, Berk. HP4 .... 38 AT18
Verney Gdns, Dag. RM9 .... 126 EY63
Verney Rd, SE16 .... 162 DU79
Dagenham RM9 .... 126 EY64
Slough SL3 .... 153 BA77
Verney St, NW10 .... 118 CR62
Verney Way, SE16 .... 22 C10
Vernham Rd, SE18 .... 165 EQ79
Vernon Av, E12 .... 125 EM63
SW20 .... 199 CX96
Enfield EN3 .... 83 DY36
Woodford Green IG8 .... 102 EH52
Vernon Cl, Cher. (Ott.) KT16 .... 211 BD107
Epsom KT19 .... 216 CQ107
Orpington BR5 .... 206 EV97
St. Albans AL1 .... 43 CD21
Staines TW19 off Long La 174 BL88
Vernon Ct, Stan. HA7
off Vernon Dr 95 CH53
Vernon Cres, Barn. EN4 .... 80 DG44
Brentwood CM13 .... 109 GA48
Vernon Dr, Cat. CR3 .... 236 DQ122
Stanmore HA7 .... 95 CG53
Uxbridge (Hare.) UB9 .... 92 BJ53
Sch Vernon Ho Sch, NW10
off Drury Way 118 CR64
Vernon Ms, E17
off Vernon Rd 123 DZ56
W14 .... 16 D8
Vernon Pl, WC1 .... 9 P6
Vernon Ri, WC1 .... 10 B1
Greenford UB6 .... 117 CD64
Vernon Rd, E3 .... 143 DZ68
E11 .... 124 EE60
E15 .... 144 EE66
E17 .... 123 DZ57
N8 .... 121 DN55
SW14 .... 158 CR83
Bushey WD23 .... 76 BY43
Feltham TW13 .... 175 BT89
Ilford IG3 .... 125 ET60
Romford RM5 .... 105 FC50
Sutton SM1 .... 218 DC106
Swanscombe DA10 .... 190 FZ86
Vernon Sq, WC1 .... 10 B1
Vernon St, W14 .... 16 C8
Vernon Wk, Tad. KT20 .... 233 CX120
Vernon Way, Guil. GU2 .... 242 AT133
Vernon Yd, W11 .... 6 E9
Veroan Rd, Bexh. DA7 .... 166 EY82
Verona Cl, Uxb. UB8 .... 134 BJ72
Verona Ct, W4
off Chiswick La 158 CS78
Verona Dr, Surb. KT6 .... 198 CL103
Verona Gdns, Grav. DA12 .... 191 GL91
Verona Ho, Erith DA8
off Waterhead Cl 167 FF80
Verona Rd, E7 off Upton La 144 EG66
Veronica Cl, Rom. RM3 .... 106 FJ52
Veronica Gdns, SW16 .... 201 DJ95
Veronica Rd, SW17 .... 181 DH90
Veronique Gdns, Ilf. IG6 .... 125 EP57
Verralls, Wok. GU22 .... 227 BB117
Verran Rd, SW12
off Balham Gro 181 DH87
Ver Rd, St.Alb. AL3 .... 42 CC20
Versailles Rd, SE20 .... 182 DU94
Verulam Av, E17 .... 123 DZ58
Purley CR8 .... 219 DJ112
Verulam Bldgs, WC1 .... 10 B5
Verulam Cl, Welw.G.C. AL7 .... 29 CZ09
Verulam Ind Est, St.Alb. AL1
off London Rd 43 CF22
★ Verulamium Mus & Pk,
St.Alb. AL3 .... 42 CB20
Verulam Pas, Wat. WD17 .... 75 BV40
Verulam Rd, Grnf. UB6 .... 136 CA70
St. Albans AL3 .... 42 CB19
Sch Verulam Sch, St.Alb. AL1
off Brampton Rd 43 CG19
Verulam St, WC1 .... 10 C5
Verwood Dr, Barn. EN4 .... 80 DF41
Verwood Rd, Har. HA2 .... 94 CC54
Veryan, Wok. GU21 .... 226 AU117
Veryan Cl, Orp. BR5 .... 206 EW98
Vesey Path, E14 .... 14 B8
Vespan Rd, W12 .... 159 CU75
Vesta Av, St.Alb. AL1 .... 42 CC23
Vesta Rd, SE4 .... 163 DY82
Hemel Hempstead HP2
off Saturn Way 40 BM18
Vestris Rd, SE23 .... 183 DX89
Vestry Ms, SE5 .... 162 DS81
Vestry Rd, E17 .... 123 EB56
SE5 .... 162 DS81
Vestry St, N1 .... 11 J1
Vevers Rd, Reig. RH2 .... 266 DB137
Vevey St, SE6 .... 183 DZ89
Vexil Cl, Purf. RM19 .... 169 FR77
Veysey Cl, Hem.H. HP1
off Halwick Cl 40 BH22
Veysey Gdns, Dag. RM10 .... 126 FA62
Viaduct Pl, E2 .... 12 C2
Viaduct Rd, Ware SG12 .... 33 DY06
Viaduct St, E2 .... 12 C2
Viaduct Way, Welw.G.C. AL7 .... 29 CZ06
Vian Av, Enf. EN3 .... 83 DY35
Vian St, SE13 .... 163 EB83
Vibart Gdns, SW2 .... 181 DM87
Vibart Wk, N1 off Outram Pl 141 DL67
Vicarage Av, SE3 .... 164 EG81
Egham TW20 .... 173 BB93
Vicarage Causeway, Hert.
(Hert.Hth) SG13 .... 32 DV11
Vicarage Cl, Beac. (Seer Grn)
HP9 .... 89 AQ52
Brentwood CM14 .... 108 FS49
Erith DA8 .... 167 FC79
Hemel Hempstead HP1 .... 40 BJ22
Leatherhead (Bkhm) KT23 .... 246 CA125
Northolt UB5 .... 136 BZ66
Potters Bar EN6 .... 64 DF30
Ruislip HA4 .... 115 BR59
St. Albans AL1 .... 42 CC23
Tadworth KT20 .... 233 CY124
Worcester Park KT4 .... 198 CS102
Vicarage Ct, W8 .... 17 J3
Egham TW20 .... 173 BB93
Feltham TW14 .... 175 BQ87
Vicarage Cres, SW11 .... 160 DD81
Egham TW20 .... 173 BB92
Vicarage Dr, SW14 .... 178 CR85
Barking IG11 .... 145 EQ66
Beckenham BR3 .... 203 EA95
Vicarage Dr, Grav. (Nthflt)
DA11 .... 190 GC86
Maidenhead (Bray) SL6 .... 150 AC75
Vicarage Fm Rd, Houns
TW3, TW5 .... 156 BY82
Vicarage Flds, Walt. KT12 .... 196 BW100
Vicarage Fld Shop Cen, Bark.
IG11 .... 145 EQ66
Vicarage Gdns, SW14
off Vicarage Rd 178 CQ85
W8 .... 17 H2
Berkhamsted (Pott.End)
HP4 .... 39 BB16
Mitcham CR4 .... 200 DE97
Vicarage Gate, W8 .... 17 J3
Guildford GU2 .... 258 AU136
Vicarage Gate Ms, Tad. KT20 .... 233 CY124
Vicarage Gro, SE5 .... 162 DR81
Vicarage Hill, West. TN16 .... 255 ER126
Vicarage La, E6 .... 145 EM69
E15 .... 144 EE66
Chigwell IG7 .... 103 EQ47
Epping (N.Wld Bas.) CM16 .... 52 FA24
Epsom KT17 .... 217 CU109
Hemel Hempstead (Bov.)
HP3 .... 57 BB26
Horley RH6 .... 268 DF147
Ilford IG1 .... 125 ER60
Kings Langley WD4 .... 58 BM29
Leatherhead KT22 .... 231 CH122
Sevenoaks (Dunt.Grn)
TN13 off London Rd 241 FD119
Staines (Laleham) TW18 .... 194 BH97
Staines (Wrays.) TW19 .... 172 AY88
Woking (Send) GU23 .... 243 BC126
Vicarage Pk, SE18 .... 165 EQ78
Vicarage Path, N8 .... 121 DL59
Vicarage Pl, Slou. SL1 .... 152 AU76
Sch Vicarage Prim Sch, E6
off Vicarage La 145 EM69
Vicarage Rd, E10 .... 123 EB60
E15 .... 144 EF66
N17 .... 100 DU52
NW4 .... 119 CU58
SE18 .... 165 EQ78
SW14 .... 178 CQ85
Berkhamsted (Pott.End)
HP4 .... 39 BA16
Bexley DA5 .... 187 FB88
Croydon CR0 .... 201 DN104
Dagenham RM10 .... 147 FB65
Egham TW20 .... 173 BB93
Epping (Cooper.) CM16 .... 70 EW29
Hornchurch RM12 .... 127 FG60
Kingston upon Thames
KT1 .... 197 CK96
Kingston upon Thames
(Hmptn W.) KT1 .... 197 CJ95
Staines TW18 .... 173 BE91
Sunbury-on-Thames TW16 .... 175 BT92
Sutton SM1 .... 218 DB105
Teddington TW11 .... 177 CG92
Twickenham TW2 .... 177 CE89
Twickenham (Whitton) TW2 .... 176 CC86
Ware SG12 .... 33 DY06
Watford WD18 .... 75 BU44
Woking GU22 .... 227 AZ121
Woodford Green IG8 .... 102 EL52
Vicarage Sq, Grays RM17 .... 170 GA79
Vicarage Wk, SW11
off Battersea Ch Rd 160 DD81
Reigate RH2 off Chartway 250 DB134
Vicarage Way, NW10 .... 118 CR62
Gerrards Cross SL9 .... 113 AZ58
Harrow HA2 .... 116 CA59
Slough (Colnbr.) SL3 .... 153 BC80
Vicarage Wd, Harl. CM20 .... 36 EU14
Vicars Br Cl, Wem. HA0 .... 138 CL68
Vicars Cl, E9
off Northiam St 142 DW67
E15 .... 144 EG67
Enfield EN1 .... 82 DS40
Sch Vicar's Grn Prim Sch,
Wem. HA0 off Lily Gdns 137 CJ68
Vicars Hill, SE13 .... 163 EB84
Vicars Moor La, N21 .... 99 DN45
Vicars Oak Rd, SE19 .... 182 DS93
Vicars Rd, NW5 .... 120 DG64
Vicars Wk, Dag. RM8 .... 126 EV62
Viceroy Cl, N2 off Market Pl 120 DE56
Viceroy Ct, NW8
off Prince Albert Rd 140 DE68
Viceroy Par, N2 off High Rd 120 DE55
Viceroy Rd, SW8 .... 161 DL81
Vickers Cl, Wall. SM6 .... 219 DM108
Vickers Dr N, Wey. KT13 .... 212 BL110
Vickers Dr S, Wey. KT13 .... 212 BL111
Vickers Rd, Erith DA8 .... 167 FD78
Vickers Way, Houns. TW4 .... 176 BY85
Victor App, Horn. RM12
off Abbs Cross Gdns 128 FK60
Victor Cl, Horn. RM12 .... 128 FK60
Victor Ct, Horn. RM12 .... 128 FK60
Rainham RM13
off Askwith Rd 147 FD68
Victor Gdns, Horn. RM12 .... 128 FK60
Victor Gro, Wem. HA0 .... 138 CL66
⇌ Victoria 19 H7
⊖ Victoria 19 H7
★ Victoria & Albert Mus,
SW7 .... 17 P6
Victoria Arc, SW1
off Terminus Pl 161 DH76
Victoria Av, E6 .... 144 EK67
EC2 .... 11 M6
N3 .... 97 CZ53
Barnet EN4 .... 80 DD42
Gravesend DA12
off Sheppy Pl 191 GH87
Grays RM16 .... 170 GC75
Hounslow TW3 .... 176 BZ85
Romford RM5 .... 105 FB51
South Croydon CR2 .... 220 DQ110
Surbiton KT6 .... 197 CK101
Uxbridge UB10 .... 135 BP66
Wallington SM6 .... 200 DG104
Wembley HA9 .... 138 CP65
West Molesey KT8 .... 196 CA97
Coll Victoria Cen for Adult Ed,
Grav. DA11 off Darnley Rd 191 GG86
Victoria Cl, Barn. EN4 .... 80 DD42
Grays RM16 .... 170 GC75
Hayes UB3
off Commonwealth Av 135 BR72
Horley RH6 .... 268 DG148
Rickmansworth WD3
off Nightingale Rd 92 BK45
Waltham Cross EN8 .... 67 DX30
West Molesey KT8
off Victoria Av 196 CA97
Weybridge KT13 .... 195 BR104
★ Victoria Coach Sta, SW1 .... 18 G8
Victoria Cotts, Rich. TW9 .... 158 CM81
Victoria Ct, Red. RH1 .... 266 DG137
Wembley HA9 .... 138 CN65
Victoria Cres, N15 .... 122 DS57
SE19 .... 182 DS93

⊖ London Underground station · DLR Docklands Light Railway station · Tra Tramlink station · Riv Pedestrian ferry landing stage

Victoria Cres, SW19 179 CZ94
Iver SL0 134 BG73
Victoria Dock Rd, E16 15 P9
Victoria Dr, SW19 179 CX87
Dartford (S.Darenth) DA4 209 FR96
Slough SL1, SL2 131 AL65
Victoria Embk, EC4 10 A10
SW1 19 P3
WC2 10 A10
★ **Victoria Embankment Gdns**, WC2 9 P10
Sch **Victoria First Sch**, Berk. HP4
off Prince Edward St 38 AW19
Victoria Gdns, W11 16 G1
Hounslow TW5 156 BY81
Westerham (Bigg.H.) TN16 238 EJ115
Victoria Gate, Harl. CM17 52 EW15
Victoria Gro, N12 98 DC50
W8 17 L5
Victoria Gro Ms, W2 7 H10
Victoria Hill Rd, Swan. BR8 207 FF95
H **Victoria Hosp**, Rom. RM1 127 FF56
Victoria Ind Est, NW10 138 CS69
Victoria Ind Pk, Dart. DA1 188 FL85
Sch **Victoria Jun Sch**, Felt. TW13
off Victoria Rd 175 BV88
Victoria La, Barn. EN5 79 CZ42
Hayes UB3 155 BQ78
Victoria Ms, E8
off Dalston La 122 DU64
NW6 140 DA67
SW4 *off Victoria Ri* 161 DH84
SW18 180 DC88
Victorian Gro, N16 122 DS62
Victorian Rd, N16 122 DS62
★ **Victoria Park**, E9 143 DY66
Victoria Pk Rd, E9 142 DW67
Victoria Pk Sq, E2 12 E1
Victoria Pas, NW8 7 N3
Watford WD18 75 BV42
Victoria Pl, SE22
off Underhill Rd 182 DU85
SW1 19 H7
Epsom KT17 216 CS112
Richmond TW9 177 CK85
Victoria Pt, E13
off Victoria Rd 144 EG68
Victoria Retail Pk, Ruis. HA4 116 BY64
Victoria Ri, SW4 161 DH83
Victoria Rd, E4 102 EE46
E11 124 EE63
E13 144 EG68
E17 101 EC54
E18 102 EH54
N4 121 DM59
N9 100 DT49
N15 122 DU56
N18 100 DT49
N22 99 DJ53
NW4 119 CW56
NW6 139 CZ67
NW7 97 CT50
NW10 138 CR71
SW14 158 CR83
W3 138 CR71
W5 137 CH71
W8 17 L6
Addlestone KT15 212 BK105
Barking IG11 145 EP65
Barnet EN4 80 DD42
Berkhamsted HP4 38 AW20
Bexleyheath DA6 166 FA84
Brentwood (Warley) CM14 108 FW49
Bromley BR2 204 EK99
Buckhurst Hill IG9 102 EK47
Bushey WD23 94 CB46
Chesham HP5 54 AQ31
Chislehurst BR7 185 EN92
Coulsdon CR5 235 DK115
Dagenham RM10 127 FB64
Dartford DA1 188 FK85
Erith DA8 167 FE79
Feltham TW13 175 BV88
Gravesend (Nthflt) DA11 191 GF88
Guildford GU1 242 AY134
Horley RH6 268 DG148
Kingston upon Thames KT1 198 CM96
Mitcham CR4 180 DE94
Redhill RH1 266 DG135
Romford RM1 127 FE58
Ruislip HA4 116 BW64
Sevenoaks TN13 257 FH125
Sidcup DA15 185 ET90
Slough SL2 132 AV74
Slough (Farn.Com.) SL2 131 AQ65
Southall UB2 156 BZ76
Staines TW18 173 BE90
Surbiton KT6 197 CK100
Sutton SM1 218 DD106
Teddington TW11 177 CG93
Twickenham TW1 177 CG87
Uxbridge UB8
off New Windsor St 134 BJ66
Waltham Abbey EN9 67 EC34
Watford WD24 75 BV38
Weybridge KT13 195 BR104
Windsor (Eton Wick) SL4 151 AM78
Woking GU22 226 AY117
Victoria Scott Ct, Dart. DA1 167 FE83
Victoria Sq, SW1 19 H5
Victoria Steps, Brent. TW8
off Kew Br Rd 158 CM79
Victoria St, E15 144 EE66
SW1 19 J6
Belvedere DA17 166 EZ78
Egham (Eng.Grn) TW20 172 AW93
St. Albans AL1 43 CD20
Slough SL1 152 AT75
Windsor SL4 151 AQ81
Victoria Ter, N4 121 DN60
NW10 *off Old Oak La* 138 CS69
Dorking RH4 *off South St* 263 CG136
Harrow HA1 117 CE60
★ **Victoria Twr**, SW1 19 N5
Victoria Vil, Rich. TW9 158 CM83
Victoria Way, SE7 25 N9
Weybridge KT13 195 BR104
Woking GU21 226 AY117
Victoria Wf, E14 13 K10
Victoria Yd, E1
off Fairclough St 142 DU72
Victor Rd, NW10 139 CV69
SE20 183 DX94
Harrow HA2 116 CC55
Teddington TW11 177 CE91
Windsor SL4 151 AQ83
Victors Cres, Brwd. (Hutt.) CM13 109 GB47
Victors Dr, Hmptn. TW12 176 BY93
Sch **Victor Seymour Inf Sch**, Cars. SM5
off Denmark Rd 218 DF105
Victor Smith Ct, St.Alb. (Brick.Wd) AL2 60 CA31
Victors Way, Barn. EN5 79 CZ41
Victor Vil, N9 100 DR48
Victor Wk, NW9 96 CS53
Hornchurch RM12
off Abbs Cross Gdns 128 FK60
Victory Av, Mord. SM4 200 DC99
Victory Business Cen, Islw. TW7 157 CF83
Victory Cl, Grays (Chaff.Hun.) RM16 169 FW77
Staines TW19 *off Long La* 174 BL88
Victory Pk Rd, Add. KT15 212 BJ105
Victory Pl, E14 13 K9
SE17 21 H7
SE19 *off Westow St* 182 DS93
Sch **Victory Prim Sch**, SE17 21 H7
Victory Rd, E11 124 EH56
SW19 180 DC94
Berkhamsted HP4
off Gossoms End 38 AU18
Chertsey KT16 194 BG102
Rainham RM13 147 FG68
Victory Rd Ms, SW19
off Victory Rd 180 DC94
Victory Wk, SE8 *off Ship St* 163 EA81
Victory Way, SE16 23 K4
Dartford DA2 168 FQ84
Hounslow TW5 156 BW78
Romford RM7 105 FB54
Vidler Cl, Chess. KT9
off Merritt Gdns 215 CJ107
Vienna Cl, Ilf. IG5 124 EK55
View, The, SE2 166 EY78
View Cl, N6 120 DF59
Chigwell IG7 103 ER50
Harrow HA1 117 CD56
Westerham (Bigg.H.) TN16 238 EJ116
Viewfield Cl, Har. HA3 118 CL59
Viewfield Rd, SW18 179 CZ86
Bexley DA5 186 EW88
Viewland Rd, SE18 165 ET78
Viewlands Av, West. TN16 239 ES120
View Rd, N6 120 DF59
Potters Bar EN6 64 DC32
Viga Rd, N21 81 DN44
Vigerons Way, Grays RM16 171 GH77
Viggory La, Wok. GU21 226 AW115
Vigilant Cl, SE26 182 DU91
Vigilant Way, Grav. DA12 191 GL92
Vignoles Rd, Rom. RM7 126 FA59
Vigors Cft, Hat. AL10 45 CT19
Vigo St, W1 9 J10
Viking Cl, E3 *off Selwyn Rd* 143 DY68
Viking Ct, SW6 160 DA79
Viking Gdns, E6
off Jack Dash Way 144 EL70
Viking Pl, E10 123 DZ60
Sch **Viking Prim Sch**, Nthlt. UB5 *off Radcliffe Way* 136 BX69
Viking Rd, Grav. (Nthflt) DA11 190 GC90
Southall UB1 136 BY73
Viking Way, Brwd. (Pilg.Hat.) CM15 108 FV45
Erith DA8 167 FC76
Rainham RM13 147 FG70
Villa Ct, Dart. DA1
off Greenbanks 188 FL89
Villacourt Rd, SE18 166 EU80
Village, The, SE7 164 EJ79
Greenhithe (Bluewater) DA9 189 FT87
Village Arc, E4
off Station Rd 101 ED46
Village Cl, E4 101 EC50
NW3 *off Belsize La* 120 DD64
Hoddesdon EN11 49 ED15
Weybridge KT13 195 BR104
Village Ct, E17 *off Eden Rd* 123 EB57
Village Gdns, Epsom KT17 217 CT110
Village Grn Av, West. (Bigg.H.) TN16 238 EL117
Village Grn Rd, Dart. DA1 167 FG84
Village Grn Way, West. (Bigg.H.) TN16
off Main Rd 238 EL117
Village Hts, Wdf.Grn. IG8 102 EF50
Sch **Village Inf Sch**, Dag. RM10 *off Ford Rd* 146 FA66
Village La, Slou. (Hedg.) SL2 111 AR60
Village Ms, NW9 118 CR61
Village Pk Cl, Enf. EN1 82 DS44
Village Rd, N3 97 CY53
Amersham (Colesh.) HP7 55 AM44
Egham TW20 193 BC97
Enfield EN1 82 DS44
Uxbridge (Denh.) UB9 113 BF61
Windsor (Dorney) SL4 150 AH76
Village Row, Sutt. SM2 218 DA108
Village Sq, The, Couls. CR5
off Netherne Dr 235 DK122
Village Way, NW10 118 CR63
SE21 182 DR86
Amersham HP7 72 AX40
Ashford TW15 174 BM91
Beckenham BR3 203 EA96
Pinner HA5 116 BY59
South Croydon CR2 220 DU113
Village Way E, Har. HA2 116 BZ59
Villa Rd, SW9 161 DN83
Villas Rd, SE18 165 EQ77
Villa St, SE17 21 K10
Villier Ct, Uxb. UB8
off Villier St 134 BK68
Villiers, The, Wey. KT13 213 BR107
Villiers Av, Surb. KT5 198 CM99
Twickenham TW2 176 BZ88
Villiers Cl, E10 123 EA61
Surbiton KT5 198 CM98
Villiers Ct, N20
off Buckingham Av 98 DC45
Villiers Cres, St.Alb. AL4 43 CK17
Villiers Gro, Sutt. SM2 217 CX109
Sch **Villiers High Sch**, Sthl. UB1 *off Boyd Av* 136 BZ74
Villiers Path, Surb. KT5 198 CL99
Villiers Rd, NW2 139 CU65
Beckenham BR3 203 DX96
Isleworth TW7 157 CE82
Kingston upon Thames KT1 198 CM97
Slough SL2 131 AR71
Southall UB1 136 BZ74
Watford WD19 76 BY44
Villiers St, WC2 9 N10
Hertford SG13 32 DS09
Villier St, Uxb. UB8 134 BK68
Vincam Cl, Twick. TW2 176 CA87
Vincent Av, Cars. SM5 218 DD111
Croydon CR0 221 DY111
Surbiton KT5 198 CP102
Vincent Cl, SE16 23 J4
Barnet EN5 80 DA41
Bromley BR2 204 EH98
Chertsey KT16 193 BE101
Esher KT10 196 CB104
Ilford IG6 103 EQ51
Leatherhead (Fetch.) KT22 230 CB123
Sidcup DA15 185 ES88
Waltham Cross (Chsht) EN8 67 DY28
West Drayton UB7 154 BN79
Vincent Dr, Dor. RH4 263 CG137
Shepperton TW17 195 BS97
Uxbridge UB10
off Birch Cres 134 BM67
Vincent Gdns, NW2 119 CT62
Vincent Grn, Couls. CR5
off High Rd 234 DF120
Vincent La, Dor. RH4 263 CG136
Vincent Ms, E3 143 EA68
Vincent Rd, E4 101 ED51
N15 122 DQ56
N22 99 DN54
SE18 165 EP77
W3 158 CQ76
Chertsey KT16 193 BE101
Cobham (Stoke D'Ab.) KT11 230 BY116
Coulsdon CR5 235 DJ116
Croydon CR0 202 DS101
Dagenham RM9 146 EY66
Dorking RH4 263 CG136
Hounslow TW4 156 BX82
Isleworth TW7 157 CD81
Kingston upon Thames KT1 198 CN97
Rainham RM13 148 FJ70
Wembley HA0 138 CM66
Vincent Row, Hmptn. (Hmptn H.) TW12 176 CC93
Vincent's Cl, Couls. CR5 234 DF120
Vincents Dr, Dor. RH4
off Nower Rd 263 CG137
Vincents La, NW7 97 CW49
Vincents Path, Nthlt. UB5
off Arnold Rd 136 BY65
Vincent Sq, SW1 19 K7
Westerham (Bigg.H.) TN16 222 EJ113
Vincent St, E16 15 K6
SW1 19 L7
Vincents Wk, Dor. RH4
off Arundel Rd 263 CG136
Vincent Ter, N1 4 E9
Vincent Wks, Dor. RH4 263 CG136
Vincenzo Cl, Hat. AL9 45 CW23
Vince St, EC1 11 K2
Vine, The, Sev. TN13 257 FH124
Vine Av, Sev. TN13 257 FH124
Vine Cl, Stai. TW19 174 BG85
Surbiton KT5 198 CM100
Sutton SM1 200 DC104
Welwyn Garden City AL8 29 CY07
West Drayton UB7 154 BN77
Vine Ct, E1 12 B6
Harrow HA3 118 CL58
Vine Ct Rd, Sev. TN13 257 FJ124
Vinegar All, E17 123 EB56
Vine Gdns, Ilf. IG1 125 EQ64
Vinegar St, E1 22 C1
Vinegar Yd, SE1 21 L3
Vine Gate, Slou. (Farn.Com.) SL2 131 AQ65
Vine Gro, Harl. CM20 35 ER10
Uxbridge UB10 134 BN66
Vine Hill, EC1 10 C4
Vine La, SE1 21 M2
Uxbridge UB10 134 BM67
Vine Pl, W5 *off The Common* 138 CL74
Hounslow TW3 156 CB84
Viner Cl, Walt. KT12 196 BW100
Vineries, The, N14 81 DJ44
Enfield EN1 82 DS41
Vineries Bk, NW7 97 CV50
Vineries Cl, Dag. RM9
off Heathway 146 FA65
West Drayton UB7 154 BN79
Vine Rd, E15 144 EF66
SW13 159 CT83
East Molesey KT8 196 CC98
Orpington BR6 223 ET107
Slough (Stoke P.) SL2 132 AT65
Vines Av, N3 98 DB53
Vine Sq, W14 16 F10
Sch **Vines Sch, The**, SW11
off Forthbridge Rd 160 DG84
Vine St, EC3 11 N9
W1 9 K10
Romford RM7 127 FC57
Uxbridge UB8 134 BK67
Vine St Br, EC1 10 D4
Vine Way, Brwd. CM14 108 FW46
Vine Yd, SE1 21 H3
Vineyard, The, Rich. TW10 178 CL85
Ware SG12 33 EA05
Welwyn Garden City AL8 29 CX07
Vineyard Av, NW7 97 CY52
Vineyard Cl, SE6 183 EA88
Kingston upon Thames KT1 198 CM97
Vineyard Gro, N3 98 DB53
Vineyard Hill, Pot.B. (Northaw) EN6 64 DG29
Vineyard Hill Rd, SW19 180 DA91
Vineyard Pas, Rich. TW9
off Paradise Rd 178 CL85
Vineyard Path, SW14 158 CR83
Sch **Vineyard Prim Sch**, Rich. TW10
off Friars Stile Rd 178 CL86
Vineyard Rd, Felt. TW13 175 BU90
Vineyard Row, Kings.T. (Hmptn W.) KT1 197 CJ95
Vineyards Rd, Pot.B. EN6 64 DF30
Vineyard Wk, EC1 10 C3
Viney Bk, Croy. CR0 221 DZ109
Viney Rd, SE13 163 EB83
Vining St, SW9 161 DN84
Vinlake Av, Uxb. UB10 114 BM62
★ **Vinopolis**, SE1 21 H1
Vinson Cl, Orp. BR6 206 EU102
Vintners Ct, EC4 11 H9
Vintry Ms, E17
off Cleveland Pk Cres 123 EA56
Viola Av, SE2 166 EV77
Feltham TW14 176 BW86
Staines TW19 174 BK88
Viola Cl, S.Ock. RM15 149 FW69
Viola Sq, W12 139 CT73
Violet Av, Enf. EN2 82 DR38
Uxbridge UB8 134 BM71
Violet Cl, E16 15 H4
SE8 *off Dorking Cl* 163 DZ79
Sutton SM3 199 CY102
Wallington SM6 201 DH102
Violet Gdns, Croy. CR0 219 DP106
Violet Hill, NW8 140 DC68
Violet La, Croy. CR0 219 DP106
Violet Rd, E3 14 A4
E17 123 EA58
E18 102 EH54
Violet St, E2 12 D3
Violet Way, Rick. (Loud.) WD3 74 BJ42
Virgil Dr, Brox. EN10 49 DZ23
Virgil Pl, W1 8 C6
Virgil St, SE1 20 B5
Virginia Av, Vir.W. GU25 192 AW99
Virginia Beeches, Vir.W. GU25 192 AW97
Virginia Cl, Ashtd. KT21
off Skinners La 231 CK118
New Malden KT3
off Willow Rd 198 CQ98
Romford RM5 105 FC52
Staines TW18
off Blacksmiths La 194 BJ97
Weybridge KT13 213 BQ107
Virginia Dr, Vir.W. GU25 192 AW99
Virginia Gdns, Ilf. IG6 103 EQ54
Virginia Pl, Cob. KT11 213 BU114
Sch **Virginia Prim Sch**, E2 11 N2
Virginia Rd, E2 11 N2
Virginia Rd, Th.Hth. CR7 201 DP95
Virginia St, E1 12 B10
Virginia Wk, SW2 181 DM86
Gravesend DA12 191 GK93
VIRGINIA WATER, GU25 192 AX99
⇌ **Virginia Water** 192 AY99
Sch **Virgo Fidelis Conv Jun Sch**, SE19 *off Central Hill* 182 DR93
Sch **Virgo Fidelis Conv Sen Sch**, SE19 *off Central Hill* 182 DR93
Viscount Cl, N11 99 DH50
Viscount Dr, E6 145 EM71
Viscount Gdns, W.Byf. KT14 212 BL112
Viscount Gro, Nthlt. UB5 136 BX69
Viscount Rd, Stai. (Stanw.) TW19 174 BK88
Viscount St, EC1 10 G4
Viscount Way, Houns. (Hthrw Air.) TW6 155 BS84
Vista, The, SE9 184 EK86
Sidcup DA14
off Langdon Shaw 185 ET92
Vista Av, Enf. EN3 83 DX40
Vista Dr, Ilf. IG4 124 EK57
Vista Way, Har. HA3 118 CL58
Sch **Vita et Pax Sch**, N14
off Priory Cl 81 DH43
Sch **Vittoria Prim Sch**, N1 4 C9
Viveash Cl, Hayes UB3 155 BT76
Vivian Av, NW4 119 CV57
Wembley HA9 118 CN64
Vivian Cl, Wat. WD19 93 BU46
Vivian Comma Cl, N4
off Blackstock Rd 121 DP62
Vivian Gdns, Wat. WD19 93 BU46
Wembley HA9 118 CN64
Vivian Rd, E3 143 DY68
Vivian Sq, SE15
off Scylla Rd 162 DV83
Vivian Way, N2 120 DD57
Vivien Cl, Chess. KT9 216 CL108
Vivienne Cl, Twick. TW1 177 CJ86
Vixen Ct, Hat. AL10
off Foxhollows 45 CV16
Vixen Dr, Hert. SG13 32 DU09
Voce Rd, SE18 165 ER80
Voewood Cl, N.Mal. KT3 199 CT100
Vogan Cl, Reig. RH2 266 DB137
Volta Cl, N9 *off Hudson Way* 100 DW48
Voltaire Rd, SW4 161 DK83
Voltaire Way, Hayes UB3
off Judge Heath La 135 BS73
Volt Av, NW10 138 CR69
Volta Way, Croy. CR0 201 DM102
Voluntary Pl, E11 124 EG58
Vorley Rd, N19 121 DJ61
Voss Ct, SW16 181 DL93
Voss St, E2 12 B2
Voyagers Cl, SE28 146 EW72
Voysey Cl, N3 119 CY55
Vulcan Cl, E6 145 EN72
Vulcan Gate, Enf. EN2 81 DN40
Vulcan Rd, SE4 163 DZ82
Vulcan Sq, E14 23 P8
Vulcan Ter, SE4 163 DZ82
Vulcan Way, N7 4 B3
Croydon (New Adgtn) CR0 222 EE110
Vyne, The, Bexh. DA7 167 FB83
Vyner Rd, W3 138 CR73
Sch **Vyners Sch**, Uxb. UB10
off Warren Rd 114 BM63
Vyner St, E2 142 DV67
Vyners Way, Uxb. UB10 114 BN64
Vyse Cl, Barn. EN5 79 CW42

W

Wacketts, Wal.Cr. (Chsht) EN7 *off Spicersfield* 66 DU27
Wadbrook St, Kings.T. KT1 197 CK96
Wadding St, SE17 21 J8
Waddington Av, Couls. CR5 235 DN120
Waddington Cl, Couls. CR5 235 DP119
Enfield EN1 82 DS42
Waddington Rd, E15 123 ED64
St. Albans AL3 43 CD20
Waddington St, E15 143 ED65
Waddington Way, SE19 182 DQ94
WADDON, Croy. CR0 201 DN103
⇌ **Waddon** 219 DN105
Waddon Cl, Croy. CR0 201 DN104
Waddon Ct Rd, Croy. CR0 219 DN105
Sch **Waddon Inf Sch**, Croy. CR0 *off Purley Way* 219 DN106
Tram **Waddon Marsh** 201 DM102
Waddon Marsh Way, Croy. CR0 201 DM102
Waddon New Rd, Croy. CR0 201 DP104
Waddon Pk Av, Croy. CR0 219 DN105
Waddon Rd, Croy. CR0 201 DN104
Waddon Way, Croy. CR0 219 DP107
Wade, The, Welw.G.C. AL7 29 CZ12
Wade Av, Orp. BR5 206 EX101
Wade Dr, Slou. SL1 131 AN74
Wades, The, Hat. AL10 45 CU21
Wades Gro, N21 99 DN45
Wades Hill, N21 81 DN44
Wades La, Tedd. TW11
off High St 177 CG92
Wades Ms, N21
off Wades Hill 99 DN45
Wadesmill Rd, Hert. SG14 32 DQ06
Ware (Chap.End) SG12 32 DQ06
Wadeson St, E2 142 DV68
Wades Pl, E14 14 A9
Wadeville Av, Rom. RM6 126 EZ59
Wadeville Cl, Belv. DA17 166 FA79
Wadham Av, E17 101 EB52
Wadham Cl, Shep. TW17 195 BQ101
Wadham Gdns, NW3 140 DE67
Greenford UB6 137 CD65
Wadham Rd, E17 101 EB53
SW15 159 CY84
Abbots Langley WD5 59 BT31
Wadhurst Cl, SE20 202 DV96
Wadhurst Rd, SW8 161 DJ81
W4 158 CR76
Wadley Cl, Hem.H. HP2
off White Hart Dr 40 BM21
Wadley Rd, E11 124 EE59
Wadsworth Business Cen, Grnf. UB6 137 CJ68
Wadsworth Cl, Enf. EN3 83 DX43
Greenford UB6 137 CJ68
Wadsworth Rd, Grnf. UB6 137 CH68
Wager St, E3 13 L5
Waggon Cl, Guil. GU2 242 AS133
Waggon Ms, N14
off Chase Side 99 DJ46
Waggon Rd, Barn. EN4 80 DC37
Waghorn Rd, E13 144 EJ67
Harrow HA3 117 CK55
Waghorn St, SE15 162 DU83
Wagner St, SE15 162 DW80
Wagon Rd, Barn. EN4 80 DB36
Wagon Way, Rick. (Loud.) WD3 74 BJ41
Wagstaff Gdns, Dag. RM9 146 EW66
Wagtail Cl, NW9 *off Swan Dr* 96 CS54
Wagtail Gdns, S.Croy. CR2 221 DY110
Wagtail Wk, Beck. BR3 203 EC99
Wagtail Way, Orp. BR5 206 EX98
Waid Cl, Dart. DA1 188 FM86
Waight Cl, Hat. AL10
off Mosquito Way 44 CS16
Waights Ct, Kings.T. KT2 198 CL95
Wain Cl, Pot.B. EN6 64 DB29
Wainfleet Av, Rom. RM5 105 FC54
Wainford Cl, SW19
off Windlesham Gro 179 CX88
Wainwright Av, Brwd. (Hutt.) CM13 109 GD44
Wainwright Gro, Islw. TW7 157 CD84
Waite Davies Rd, SE12 184 EF87
Waite St, SE15 162 DT79
Waithman St, EC4 10 E8
Wakefield Cl, W.Byf. (Byfleet) KT14 212 BL112
Wakefield Cres, Slou. (Stoke P.) SL2 132 AT66
Wakefield Gdns, SE19 182 DS94
Ilford IG1 124 EL58
Wakefield Ms, WC1 9 P2
Wakefield Rd, N11 99 DK50
N15 122 DT57
Greenhithe DA9 189 FW85
Richmond TW10 177 CK85
Wakefield St, E6 144 EK67
N18 100 DU50
WC1 9 P3
Wakefield Wk, Wal.Cr. (Chsht) EN8 67 DY31
Wakeford Cl, SW4
off Clapham Common S Side 181 DJ85
Wakehams Hill, Pnr. HA5 116 BZ55
Wakeham St, N1 5 J4
Wakehurst Path, Wok. GU21 211 BC114
Wakehurst Rd, SW11 180 DE85
Wakeling Rd, W7 137 CF71
Wakeling St, E14 13 J8
Wakelin Rd, E15 144 EE68
Wakely Cl, West. (Bigg.H.) TN16 238 EJ118
Wakeman Rd, NW10 6 A1
Wakemans Hill Av, NW9 118 CR57
Wakerfield Cl, Horn. RM11 128 FM57
Wakering Rd, Bark. IG11 145 EQ65
Wakerley Cl, E6
off Truesdale Rd 145 EM72
Wake Rd, Loug. (High Beach) IG10 84 EJ38
Wakley St, EC1 10 E1
Walberswick St, SW8 161 DL80
Walbrook, EC4 11 J9
Walbrook Ho, N9 100 DW46
Walbrook Wf, EC4
off Upper Thames St 142 DQ73
Walburgh St, E1 12 C8
Walburton Rd, Pur. CR8 219 DJ113
Walcorde Av, SE17 21 H8
Walcot Rd, Enf. EN3 83 DZ40
Walcot Sq, SE11 20 D7
Walcott St, SW1 19 K7
Waldair Ct, E16
off Barge Ho Rd 165 EP75
Waldair Wf, E16 165 EP75
Waldeck Gro, SE27 181 DP90
Waldeck Rd, N15 121 DP56
SW14
off Lower Richmond Rd 158 CQ83
W4 158 CN79
W13 137 CH72
Dartford DA1 188 FM86
Waldeck Ter, SW14
off Lower Richmond Rd 158 CQ83
Waldegrave Av, Tedd. TW11
off Waldegrave Rd 177 CF92
Sch **Waldegrave Comp Sch**, Twick. TW2
off Fifth Cross Rd 177 CD90
Waldegrave Ct, Upmin. RM14 128 FP60
Waldegrave Gdns, Twick. TW1 177 CF89
Upminster RM14 128 FP60
Waldegrave Pk, Twick. TW1 177 CF91
Waldegrave Rd, N8 121 DN55
SE19 182 DT94
W5 138 CM72
Bromley BR1 204 EL98
Dagenham RM8 126 EW61
Teddington TW11 177 CF91
Twickenham TW1 177 CF91
Waldegrove, Croy. CR0 202 DT104
Waldemar Av, SW6 159 CY81
W13 137 CJ74
Waldemar Rd, SW19 180 DA92
Walden Av, N13 100 DQ49
Chislehurst BR7 185 EM91
Rainham RM13 147 FD68
Walden Cl, Belv. DA17 166 EZ78
Walden Gdns, Th.Hth. CR7 201 DM97
Waldenhurst Rd, Orp. BR5 206 EX101
Walden Par, Chis. BR7
off Walden Rd 185 EM93
Walden Pl, Welw.G.C. AL8 29 CX07
Walden Rd, N17 100 DR53
Chislehurst BR7 185 EM93
Hornchurch RM11 128 FK58
Welwyn Garden City AL8 29 CX07
Waldens Cl, Orp. BR5 206 EX101
Waldenshaw Rd, SE23 182 DW88
Waldens Pk Rd, Wok. GU21 226 AW116
Waldens Rd, Orp. BR5 206 EY101
Woking GU21 226 AX117
Walden St, E1 12 C7
Walden Way, NW7 97 CX51
Hornchurch RM11 128 FK58
Ilford IG6 103 ES52
Waldo Cl, SW4 181 DJ85
Waldo Pl, Mitch. CR4 180 DE94
Waldorf Cl, S.Croy. CR2 219 DP109
Waldo Rd, NW10 139 CU69
Bromley BR1 204 EK97
Waldram Cres, SE23 182 DW88
Waldram Pk Rd, SE23 183 DX88
Waldram Pl, SE23
off Waldram Cres 182 DW88
Waldrist Way, Erith DA18 166 EZ75
Waldron Gdns, Brom. BR2 203 ED97
Waldronhyrst, S.Croy. CR2 219 DP105
Waldron Ms, SW3
off Old Ch St 160 DD79
Waldron Rd, SW18 180 DC90
Harrow HA1, HA2 117 CE60
Waldrons, The, Croy. CR0 219 DP105
Oxted RH8 254 EF131
Waldrons Path, S.Croy. CR2 220 DQ105
Waldstock Rd, SE28 146 EU73
Waleran Cl, Stan. HA7 95 CF51
Walerand Rd, SE13 163 EC82
Waleran Flats, SE1
off Old Kent Rd 162 DS77
Wales Av, Cars. SM5 218 DF106
Wales Cl, SE15 162 DV80
Wales Fm Rd, W3 138 CR71
Waleton Acres, Wall. SM6 219 DJ107
Waley St, E1 13 H5
Walfield Av, N20 98 DB45
Walford Cl, Harl. CM17 36 EW12
Walford Rd, N16 122 DS63
Dorking (N.Holm.) RH5 263 CH140
Uxbridge UB8 134 BJ68
Walfrey Gdns, Dag. RM9 146 EY66
WALHAM GREEN, SW6 160 DB80

Walham Grn Ct, SW6
off Waterford Rd 160 DB80
Walham Gro, SW6 160 DA80
Walham Ri, SW19 179 CY93
Walham Yd, SW6
off Walham Gro 160 DA80
Walk, The, Horn. RM11 128 FM61
Oxted (Tand.) RH8 253 EA133
Potters Bar EN6 64 DA32
Sunbury-on-Thames TW16 175 BT94
Windsor (Eton Wick) SL4 151 AN78
Walkden Rd, Chis. BR7 185 EN92
Walker Cl, N11 99 DJ49
SE18 165 EQ77
W7 137 CE74
Dartford DA1 167 FF83
Feltham TW14
off Westmacott Dr 175 BT87
Hampton TW12
off Fearnley Cres 176 BZ93
Walker Cres, Slou. SL3
off Ditton Rd 153 AZ78
Walker Ms, SW2
off Effra Rd 181 DN85
Sch Walker Prim Sch, N14
off Waterfall Rd 99 DK47
Walkers Ct, E8
off Wilton Way 142 DU65
W1 9 L9
Walkerscroft Mead, SE21 182 DQ88
Walkers Pl, SW15
off Felsham Rd 159 CY83
Walkfield Dr, Epsom KT18 233 CV117
Walkford Way, SE15
off Daniel Gdns 162 DT80
Walkley Rd, Dart. DA1 187 FH85
Walks, The, N2 120 DD55
Walkwood End, Beac. HP9 88 AJ54
Walkwood Ri, Beac. HP9 110 AJ55
Walkynscroft, SE15
off Firbank Rd 162 DV82
Wallace Cl, SE28
off Haldane Rd 146 EX73
Shepperton TW17 195 BR98
Uxbridge UB10
off Grays Rd 134 BL68
★ Wallace Collection, W1 8 E7
Wallace Cres, Cars. SM5 218 DF106
Wallace Flds, Epsom KT17 217 CT112
Sch Wallace Flds Inf Sch, Epsom KT17
off Wallace Flds 217 CU113
Sch Wallace Flds Jun Sch, Epsom KT17
off Dorling Dr 217 CU112
Wallace Gdns, Swans. DA10 190 FY86
Wallace Rd, N1 5 H3
Grays RM17 170 GA76
Wallace Sq, Couls. CR5
off Cayton Rd 235 DK122
Wallace Wk, Add. KT15 212 BJ105
Wallace Way, N19
off Giesbach Rd 121 DK61
Romford RM1 105 FD53
Wallasey Cres, Uxb. UB10 114 BN61
Wallbutton Rd, SE4 163 DY82
Wallcote Av, NW2 119 CX60
Walled Gdn, The, Bet. RH3 264 CR135
Tadworth KT20
off Heathcote 233 CX122
Wall End Rd, E6 145 EM66
Wallenger Av, Rom. RM2 127 FH55
Waller Dr, Nthwd. HA6 93 BU54
Waller La, Cat. CR3 236 DT123
Waller Rd, SE14 163 DX81
Beaconsfield HP9 89 AM53
Wallers Cl, Dag. RM9 146 EY67
Woodford Green IG8 103 EM51
Wallers Hoppit, Loug. IG10 84 EL40
Wallers Way, Hodd. EN11 33 EB14
Waller Way, SE10
off Greenwich High Rd 163 EB80
Wallfield All, Hert. SG13 32 DQ10
Wallflower St, W12 139 CT73
Wallgrave Rd, SW5 17 J7
Wallhouse Rd, Erith DA8 167 FH80
Wallingford Av, W10 6 A6
Wallingford Rd, Uxb. UB8 134 BH68
Wallingford Wk, St.Alb. AL1 43 CD23
WALLINGTON, SM6 219 DJ106
≠ Wallington 219 DH107
Wallington Cl, Ruis. HA4 115 BQ58
Wallington Cor, Wall. SM6
off Manor Rd N 219 DH105
Sch Wallington Co Gram Sch, Wall. SM6
off Croydon Rd 219 DH105
Sch Wallington High Sch for Girls, Wall. SM6
off Woodcote Rd 219 DH109
Wallington Rd, Chesh. HP5 54 AP30
Ilford IG3 125 ET59
Wallington Sq, Wall. SM6
off Woodcote Rd 219 DH107
Wallis All, SE1 21 H3
Wallis Cl, SW11 160 DD83
Dartford DA2 187 FF90
Hornchurch RM11 127 FH60
Wallis Ct, Slou. SL1
off Nixey Cl 152 AU76
Wallis Ms, N22
off Brampton Pk Rd 121 DN55
Leatherhead (Fetch.) KT22 231 CG122
Wallis Pk, Grav. (Nthflt) DA11 190 GB85
Wallis Rd, E9 143 DZ65
Southall UB1 136 CB72
Wallis's Cotts, SW2 181 DL87
Wallman Pl, N22
off Bounds Grn Rd 99 DM53
Wallorton Gdns, SW14 158 CR84
Wallside, EC2 11 H6
Wall St, N1 5 K4
Wallwood Rd, E11 123 ED60
Wallwood St, E14 13 M6
Walmar Cl, Barn. EN4 80 DD39
Walmer Cl, E4 101 EB47
Orpington BR6
off Tubbenden La S 223 ER105
Romford RM7 105 FB54
Walmer Gdns, W13 157 CG75
Walmer Ho, N9 100 DT45
Walmer Pl, W1 8 C5
Walmer Rd, W10
off Latimer Rd 139 CW72
W11 6 C9
Walmer St, W1 8 C5
Walmer Ter, SE18 165 EQ77
Walmgate Rd, Grnf. UB6 137 CH67
Walmington Fold, N12 98 DA51
Walm La, NW2 119 CX64
Walmsley Ho, SW16
off Colson Way 181 DJ91
Walney Wk, N1 5 H3
Walnut Av, West Dr. UB7 154 BN76
Walnut Cl, SE8 off Clyde St 163 DZ79
Carshalton SM5 218 DF106
Dartford (Eyns.) DA4 208 FK104
Epsom KT18 233 CT115
Hayes UB3 135 BS73
Ilford IG6 off Civic Way 125 EQ56
St. Albans (Park St) AL2 60 CB27
Walnut Ct, W5 158 CL75
Welwyn Garden City AL7 29 CY12
Walnut Dr, Tad. (Kgswd) KT20
off Warren Lo Dr 233 CY124
Walnut Gdns, E15
off Burgess Rd 124 EE63
Walnut Grn, Bushey WD23 76 BZ40
Walnut Gro, Bans. SM7 217 CX114
Enfield EN1 82 DR43
Harlow CM20
off Hamstel Rd 35 EP14
Hemel Hempstead HP2 40 BK20
High Wycombe (Woob.Grn)
HP10 off Holtspur La 110 AE57
Hornchurch RM12 128 FK60
Welwyn Garden City AL7 29 CY12
Walnut Ms, Sutt. SM2 218 DC108
Walnut Rd, E10 123 EA61
Walnuts, The, Orp. BR6
off High St 206 EU102
Walnut Shop Cen, Orp. BR6 206 EU102
Walnuts Rd, Orp. BR6 206 EU102
Walnut Tree Av, Dart. DA1 188 FL89
Mitcham CR4
off De'Arn Gdns 200 DE97
Walnut Tree Cl, SW13 159 CT81
Banstead SM7 217 CY112
Chislehurst BR7 205 EQ95
Guildford GU1 242 AW134
Hoddesdon EN11 49 EA17
Waltham Cross (Chsht) EN8 67 DX31
Walnut Tree Cotts, SW19
off Church Rd 179 CY91
Walnut Tree La, W.Byf.
(Byfleet) KT14 212 BK112
Walnut Tree Pk, Guil. GU1 242 AW134
Walnut Tree Rd, SE10 25 H10
Brentford TW8 158 CL79
Dagenham RM8 126 EX61
Erith DA8 167 FE78
Hounslow TW5 156 BZ79
Shepperton TW17 195 BQ96
Walnut Tree Wk, SE11 20 C7
Ware SG12 33 DX09
Sch Walnut Tree Wk Prim Sch, SE11 20 C7
Walnut Way, Buck.H. IG9 102 EK48
Ruislip HA4 136 BW65
Swanley BR8 207 FD96
Walpole Av, Couls. CR5 234 DF118
Richmond TW9 158 CM82
Walpole Cl, W13 157 CJ75
Grays RM17 off Palmers Dr 170 GC77
Pinner HA5 94 CA51
Walpole Cres, Tedd. TW11 177 CF92
Walpole Gdns, W4 158 CQ78
Twickenham TW2 177 CE89
Walpole Ms, NW8
off Queen's Gro 140 DD67
SW19 off Walpole Rd 180 DD93
Walpole Pk, W5 137 CJ74
Weybridge KT13 212 BN108
Walpole Pl, SE18
off Brookhill Rd 165 EP77
Teddington TW11 177 CF92
Walpole Rd, E6 144 EJ66
E17 123 DY56
E18 102 EF53
N17 (Downhills Way) 122 DQ55
N17 (Lordship La) 100 DQ54
SW19 180 DD93
Bromley BR2 204 EK99
Croydon CR0 202 DR103
Slough SL1 131 AK72
Surbiton KT6 198 CL100
Teddington TW11 177 CF92
Twickenham TW2 177 CE89
Windsor (Old Wind.) SL4 172 AV87
Walpole St, SW3 18 C9
Walrond Av, Wem. HA9 118 CL64
Walsham Cl, N16
off Braydon Rd 122 DU59
SE28 146 EX73
Walsham Rd, SE14 163 DX82
Feltham TW14 175 BV87
Walsh Cres, Croy.
(New Adgtn) CR0 222 EE112
Walshford Way, Borwd. WD6 78 CN38
Walsingham Cl, Hat. AL10 45 CT17
Walsingham Gdns, Epsom
KT19 216 CS105
Walsingham Pk, Chis. BR7 205 ER96
Walsingham Pl, SW4
off Clapham Common
W Side 160 DF84
SW11 180 DG86
Walsingham Rd, E5 122 DU62
W13 137 CG74
Croydon (New Adgtn) CR0 221 EC110
Enfield EN2 82 DR42
Mitcham CR4 200 DF99
Orpington BR5 206 EV95
Walsingham Wk, Belv. DA17 166 FA79
Walsingham Way, St.Alb.
(Lon.Col.) AL2 61 CJ27
Walter Hurford Par, E12
off Walton Rd 125 EN63
Walter Rodney Cl, E6
off Stevenage Rd 145 EM65
Walters Cl, SE17 21 H8
Hayes UB3
off St. Anselms Rd 155 BT75
Waltham Cross (Chsht) EN7 65 DP25
Walters Ho, SE17 off Otto St 161 DP79
Walters Mead, Ashtd. KT21 232 CL117
Walters Rd, SE25 202 DS98
Enfield EN3 82 DW43
Walter St, E2 12 G2
Kingston upon Thames
KT2 off Sopwith Way 198 CL95
Walters Way, SE23 183 DX86
Walters Yd, Brom. BR1 204 EG96
Walter Ter, E1 13 H7
Walterton Rd, W9 6 F4
Walter Wk, Edg. HA8 96 CQ51
WALTHAM ABBEY, EN9 84 EF35
★ Waltham Abbey (ruins), Wal.Abb. EN9 67 EC33
Waltham Av, NW9 118 CN58
Guildford GU2 242 AV131
Hayes UB3 155 BQ76
Waltham Cl, Brwd. (Hutt.)
CM13 off Bannister Dr 109 GC44
Dartford DA1 187 FG86
Orpington BR5 206 EX102
WALTHAM CROSS, EN7 & EN8 67 DZ33
≠ Waltham Cross 67 DY34
Waltham Dr, Edg. HA8 96 CN54
Coll Waltham Forest Coll,
E17 off Forest Rd 123 EB55
Waltham Gdns, Enf. EN3 82 DW36
Waltham Gate, Wal.Cr. EN8 67 DZ26
Sch Waltham Holy Cross Co Inf Sch, Wal.Abb. EN9
off Quendon Dr 67 ED33
Sch Waltham Holy Cross Co Jun Sch, Wal.Abb. EN9
off Quendon Dr 67 ED33
Waltham Pk Way, E17 101 EA53
Waltham Rd, Cars. SM5 200 DD101
Caterham CR3 236 DV122
Southall UB2 156 BY76
Waltham Abbey EN9 68 EF26
Woodford Green IG8 102 EL51
WALTHAMSTOW, E17 101 EB54
Coll Walthamstow Adult Ed Cen, E17
off Greenleaf Rd 123 DZ55
Walthamstow Av, E4 101 EA52
Walthamstow Business Cen,
E17 101 EC54
≠ Walthamstow Central 123 EA56
⊖ Walthamstow Central 123 EA56
Sch Walthamstow Hall, Sev.
TN13 off Holly Bush La 257 FJ123
Sch Walthamstow Hall Jun Sch, Sev. TN13
off Bradbourne Pk Rd 257 FH122
≠ Walthamstow Queens Road 123 DZ57
Sch Walthamstow Sch for Girls,
E17 off Church Hill 123 EB56
Waltham Way, E4 101 DZ49
Waltheof Av, N17 100 DR53
Waltheof Gdns, N17 100 DR53
Walton Av, Har. HA2 116 BZ64
New Malden KT3 199 CT98
Sutton SM3 199 CZ104
Wembley HA9 118 CP62
Walton Br, Shep. TW17 195 BS101
Walton-on-Thames KT12
off Bridge St 195 BS101
Walton Br Rd, Shep. TW17 195 BS101
Walton Cl, E5 off Orient Way 123 DX62
NW2 119 CV61
SW8 161 DL80
Harrow HA1 117 CD56
H Walton Comm Hosp,
Walt. KT12 195 BV103
Walton Ct, Wok. GU21 227 BA116
Walton Cres, Har. HA2 116 BZ63
Walton Dr, NW10
off Mitchellbrook Way 138 CR65
Harrow HA1 117 CD56
Walton Gdns, W3 138 CP71
Brentwood (Hutt.) CM13 109 GC43
Feltham TW13 175 BT91
Waltham Abbey EN9 67 EB33
Wembley HA9 118 CL61
Walton Grn, Croy.
(New Adgtn) CR0 221 EC108
Walton La, Shep. TW17 195 BR101
Slough (Farn.Royal) SL2 131 AL69
Walton-on-Thames KT12 195 BQ102
Weybridge KT13 195 BP103
Sch Walton Leigh Sch, Walt.
KT12 off Queens Rd 213 BT105
WALTON-ON-THAMES, KT12 195 BT103
≠ Walton-on-Thames 213 BU105
WALTON ON THE HILL, Tad.
KT20 249 CT125
Sch Walton-on-the-Hill Co Prim Sch, Tad. KT20
off Walton St 233 CV124
Walton Pk, Walt. KT12 196 BX103
Walton Pk La, Walt. KT12 196 BX103
Walton Pl, SW3 18 C5
Walton Rd, E12 125 EN63
E13 144 EJ68
N15 122 DT57
Bushey WD23 76 BX42
East Molesey KT8 196 CA98
Epsom (Epsom Downs)
KT18 233 CT117
Epsom (Headley) KT18 232 CQ121
Harrow HA1 117 CD56
Hoddesdon EN11 49 EB15
Romford RM5 104 EZ52
Sidcup DA14 186 EW89
Walton-on-Thames KT12 196 BW99
Ware SG12 33 DX07
West Molesey KT8 196 BY99
Woking GU21 227 AZ116
Walton St, SW3 18 B7
Enfield EN2 82 DR39
St. Albans AL1 43 CF19
Tadworth KT20 233 CU124
Walton Ter, Wok. GU21 227 BB115
Walton Way, W3 138 CP71
Mitcham CR4 201 DJ98
Walt Whitman Cl, SE24
off Shakespeare Rd 161 DP84
Walverns Cl, Wat. WD19 76 BW44
WALWORTH, SE17 20 G9
★ Walworth Garden Fm - Horticultural Training Cen,
SE17 20 F10
Sch Walworth Lwr Sch, SE17 21 K9
Walworth Pl, SE17 21 H10
Walworth Rd, SE1 20 G7
SE17 20 G7
Sch Walworth Sch, SE1 21 M10
Walwyn Av, Brom. BR1 204 EK97
Wambrook Cl, Brwd. (Hutt.)
CM13 109 GC46
Wanborough Dr, SW15 179 CV88
Wanderer Dr, Bark. IG11 146 EV69
Wandle Bk, SW19 180 DD93
Croydon CR0 201 DL104
Wandle Ct, Epsom KT19 216 CQ105
Wandle Ct Gdns, Croy. CR0 219 DL105
Tra Wandle Park 201 DN103
Wandle Rd, SW17 180 DE89
Croydon CR0 202 DQ104
Croydon (Waddon) CR0 201 DL104
Morden SM4 200 DC98
Wallington SM6 201 DH103
Wandle Side, Croy. CR0 201 DM104
Wallington SM6 201 DH104
Wandle Tech Pk, Mitch. CR4
off Goat Rd 200 DF101
Wandle Trd Est, Mitch. CR4
off Budge La 200 DF101
Sch Wandle Valley Sch, Cars.
SM5 off Welbeck Rd 200 DE101
Wandle Way, SW18 180 DB88
Mitcham CR4 200 DF99
Wandon Rd, SW6 160 DB80
WANDSWORTH, SW18 179 CZ85
Wandsworth Br, SW6 160 DB83
SW18 160 DB83
Wandsworth Br Rd, SW6 160 DB81
≠ Wandsworth Common 180 DF88
Wandsworth Common,
SW12 180 DE86
Wandsworth Common W Side,
SW18 180 DC85
Wandsworth High St, SW18 180 DA85
★ Wandsworth Mus,
SW18 off Garratt La 180 DB85
Wandsworth Plain, SW18 180 DB85
≠ Wandsworth Road 161 DJ82
Wandsworth Rd, SW8 161 DK80
Wandsworth Shop Cen,
SW18 180 DB86
≠ Wandsworth Town 160 DB84
Wangey Rd, Rom. RM6 126 EX59
Wanless Rd, SE24 162 DQ83
Wanley Rd, SE5 162 DR84
Wanlip Rd, E13 15 N3
Wanmer Ct, Reig. RH2
off Birkheads Rd 250 DA133
Wannions Cl, Chesh. HP5 56 AU30
Wannock Gdns, Ilf. IG6 103 EP52
Wansbeck Rd, E3 143 DZ66
E9 143 DZ66
Wansbury Way, Swan. BR8 207 FG99
Wansdown Pl, SW6
off Fulham Rd 160 DB80
Wansey St, SE17 20 G8
Coll Wansfell Coll, Epp.
CM16 off Piercing Hill 85 ER35
Wansford Cl, Brwd. CM14 108 FT48
Wansford Grn, Wok. GU21
off Kenton Way 226 AT117
Wansford Pk, Borwd. WD6 78 CS42
Wansford Rd, Wdf.Grn. IG8 102 EJ53
WANSTEAD, E11 124 EH59
⊖ Wanstead 124 EH58
Sch Wanstead Ch Prim Sch,
E11 off Church Path 124 EG57
Wanstead Cl, Brom. BR1 204 EJ96
Sch Wanstead High Sch,
E11 off Redbridge La W 124 EJ58
Wanstead La, Ilf. IG1 124 EK58
≠ Wanstead Park 124 EH63
Wanstead Pk, E11 124 EK59
Wanstead Pk Av, E12 124 EK61
Wanstead Pk Rd, Ilf. IG1 125 EM60
Wanstead Pl, E11 124 EG58
Wanstead Rd, Brom. BR1 204 EJ96
Wansunt Rd, Bex. DA5 187 FC88
Wantage Rd, SE12 184 EF85
Wantz La, Rain. RM13 147 FH70
Wantz Rd, Dag. RM10 127 FB63
Waplings, The, Tad. KT20 233 CV124
WAPPING, E1 22 B1
⊖ Wapping 22 E2
Wapping Dock St, E1 22 D2
Wapping High St, E1 22 A2
Wapping La, E1 12 D10
Wapping Wall, E1 22 E1
Wapseys La, Slou. (Hedg.)
SL2 112 AS58
Wapshott Rd, Stai. TW18 173 BE93
Warbank Cl, Croy.
(New Adgtn) CR0 222 EE111
Warbank Cres, Croy.
(New Adgtn) CR0 222 EE110
Warbank La, Kings.T. KT2 179 CT94
Warbeck Rd, W12 139 CV74
Warberry Rd, N22 99 DM54
Warblers Grn, Cob. KT11 214 BZ114
Warboys App, Kings.T. KT2 178 CP93
Warboys Cres, E4 101 EC50
Warboys Rd, Kings.T. KT2 178 CP93
Warburton Cl, N1 5 L3
Harrow HA3 95 CD51
Warburton Rd, E8 142 DV66
Twickenham TW2 176 CB88
Warburton St, E8
off Warburton Rd 142 DV67
Warburton Ter, E17 101 EB54
War Coppice Rd, Cat. CR3 252 DR127
Wardalls Gro, SE14 162 DW80
Ward Av, Grays RM17 170 GA77
Ward Cl, Erith DA8 167 FD79
Iver SL0 133 BF72
South Croydon CR2 220 DS106
Waltham Cross (Chsht)
EN7 off Spicersfield 66 DU27
Ware SG12 32 DW05
Wardell Cl, NW7 96 CS52
Wardell Fld, NW9 96 CS53
Warden Av, Har. HA2 116 BZ60
Romford RM5 105 FC50
Warden Rd, NW5 140 DG65
Wardens Fld Cl, Orp. BR6 223 ES107
Wardens Gro, SE1 20 G2
Ward Gdns, Rom. (Harold Wd)
RM3 off Whitmore Av 106 FK54
Slough SL1 131 AL73
Ward Hatch, Harl. CM20
off Mowbray Rd 36 EU12
Ward La, Warl. CR6 236 DW116
Wardle St, E9 123 DX64
Wardley St, SW18
off Garratt La 180 DB87
Wardo Av, SW6 159 CY81
Wardour Ms, W1 9 K8
Wardour St, W1 9 L9
Ward Pl, Amer. HP7 55 AP40
Ward Rd, E15 143 ED67
N19 121 DJ62
Wardrobe Pl, EC4
off Carter La 141 DP72
Wardrobe Ter, EC4 10 F8
Ward Royal, Wind. SL4 151 AQ81
Wards La, Borwd. (Elstree)
WD6 77 CG40
Ward's Pl, Egh. TW20 173 BC93
Wards Rd, Ilf. IG2 125 ER59
Ward St, Guil. GU1
off Martyr Rd 258 AX135
Wards Wf App, E16 164 EK75
WARE, SG12 33 DZ06
≠ Ware 33 DY07
Wareham Cl, Houns. TW3 156 CB84
Warehams La, Hert. SG14 32 DQ10
Waremead Rd, Ilf. IG2 125 EP57
★ Ware Mus, Ware SG12 33 DX06
Warenford Way, Borwd. WD6 78 CN39
Warenne Hts, Red. RH1 266 DD136
Warenne Rd, Lthd. (Fetch.)
KT22 230 CC122
Ware Pk Rd, Hert. SG14 32 DR07
Ware Pt Dr, SE28 165 ER75
Ware Rd, Hert. SG13 32 DS09
Hertford (Hailey) SG13 33 EA12
Hoddesdon EN11 49 EA15
Ware SG12 33 EC05
Ware (Chad.Spr.) SG12 32 DU08
Warescot Cl, Brwd. CM15 108 FV45
Warescot Rd, Brwd. CM15 108 FV45
Wareside Cl, Welw.G.C. AL7 30 DB10
Warfield Rd, NW10 6 A2
Feltham TW14 175 BS87
Hampton TW12 196 CB95
Warfield Yd, NW10 6 A2
Wargrave Av, N15 122 DT58
Wargrave Rd, Har. HA2 116 CC62
Warham Rd, N4 121 DN57
Harrow HA3 95 CF54
Sevenoaks (Otford) TN14 241 FH116
South Croydon CR2 220 DQ106
Warham St, SE5 161 DP80
Waring Cl, Orp. BR6 223 ET107
Waring Dr, Orp. BR6 223 ET107
Waring Rd, Sid. DA14 186 EW93
Waring St, SE27 182 DQ91
Warkworth Gdns, Islw. TW7 157 CG80
Warkworth Rd, N17 100 DR52
Warland Rd, SE18 165 ER80
WARLEY, Brwd. CM14 108 FV50
Warley Av, Dag. RM8 126 EZ59
Hayes UB4 135 BU71
Warley Cl, E10
off Millicent Rd 123 DZ60
Sch Warley Co Prim Sch, Brwd.
CM14 off Chindits La 108 FW50
Warley Gap, Brwd.
(Lt.Warley) CM13 107 FV52
Warley Hill, Brwd. CM13,
CM14 107 FV51
Warley Mt, Brwd. CM14 108 FW49
Warley Rd, N9 100 DW47
Brentwood CM13 107 FT54
Hayes UB4 135 BU72
Ilford IG5 103 EN53
Upminster RM14 106 FQ54
Warley Rd, Wdf.Grn. IG8 102 EH52
Warley St, E2 12 G1
Brentwood (Gt Warley)
CM13 129 FW58
Upminster RM14 129 FW58
Warley St Flyover, Brwd.
CM13 129 FX57
Warley Wds Cres, Brwd.
CM14 108 FV49
WARLINGHAM, CR6 237 DX118
Sch Warlingham Co Sec Sch, Warl. CR6
off Tithepit Shaw La 236 DV116
Sch Warlingham Pk Sch, Warl. CR6
off Chelsham
Common Rd 237 EA116
Warlingham Rd, Th.Hth. CR7 201 DP98
Warlock Rd, W9 6 G3
Warlow Cl, Enf. EN3 83 EA37
Warlters Cl, N7
off Warlters Rd 121 DL63
Warlters Rd, N7 121 DL63
Warltersville Rd, N19 121 DL59
Warltersville Way, Horl. RH6 269 DJ150
Warmark Rd, Hem.H. HP1 39 BE18
Warmington Cl, E5
off Orient Way 123 DX62
Warmington Rd, SE24 182 DQ86
Warmington St, E13 15 M3
Warminster Gdns, SE25 202 DU96
Warminster Rd, SE25 202 DT96
Warminster Sq, SE25 202 DU96
Warminster Way, Mitch. CR4 201 DH95
Warndon St, SE16 22 F8
Warneford Pl, Wat. WD19 76 BY44
Warneford Rd, Har. HA3 117 CK55
Warneford St, E9 142 DV67
Warne Pl, Sid. DA15
off Westerham Dr 186 EV86
Warner Av, Sutt. SM3 199 CY103
Warner Cl, E15 124 EE64
NW9 119 CT59
Hampton TW12
off Tangley Pk Rd 176 BZ92
Hayes UB3 155 BR80
Slough SL1 131 AL74
Warner Ho, SE13
off Conington Rd 163 EB82
Warner Par, Hayes UB3 155 BR80
Warner Pl, E2 142 DU68
Warner Rd, E17 123 DY56
N8 121 DK56
SE5 162 DQ81
Bromley BR1 184 EF94
Ware SG12 32 DW07
Warners Av, Hodd. EN11 49 DZ19
Warners Cl, Wdf.Grn. IG8 102 EG50
WARNERS END, Hem.H. HP1 39 BE19
Warners End Rd, Hem.H. HP1 40 BG20
Warners La, Guil. (Albury)
GU5 260 BL141
Kingston upon Thames KT2 177 CK91
Warners Path, Wdf.Grn. IG8 102 EG50
Warner St, EC1 10 C4
Warner Ter, E14 14 A6
Warner Yd, EC1 10 C4
Warnford Ho, SW15
off Tunworth Cres 179 CT86
Warnford Ind Est, Hayes UB3 155 BS75
Warnford Rd, Orp. BR6 223 ET106
Warnham Ct Rd, Cars. SM5 218 DF108
Warnham Rd, N12 98 DE50
Warple Ms, W3
off Warple Way 158 CS75
Warple Way, W3 138 CS74
Warren, The, E12 124 EL63
Ashtead KT21 232 CL119
Carshalton SM5 218 DD109
Chesham HP5 54 AL28
Gerrards Cross (Chal.St.P.)
SL9 91 AZ52
Gravesend DA12 191 GK91
Hayes UB4 135 BU72
Hounslow TW5 156 BZ80
Leatherhead (E.Hors.)
KT24 245 BT130
Leatherhead (Oxshott)
KT22 214 CC112
Radlett WD7 61 CG33
Tadworth (Kgswd) KT20 233 CY123
Worcester Park KT4 216 CR105
Warren Av, E10 123 EC62
Bromley BR1 184 EE94
Orpington BR6 223 ET106
Richmond TW10 158 CP84
South Croydon CR2 221 DX108
Sutton SM2 217 CZ110
Warren Cl, N9 101 DX45
SE21 off Lairdale Cl 182 DQ87
Bexleyheath DA6 186 FA85
Esher KT10 214 CB105
Hatfield AL10 45 CV15
Hayes UB4 136 BW71
Slough SL3 152 AY76
Wembley HA9 117 CK61
Sch Warren Comp Sch, Rom.
RM6 off Whalebone La N 126 EZ57
Warren Ct, Chig. IG7 103 ER49
Sevenoaks TN13 257 FJ125
Weybridge KT13 212 BN106
Warren Cres, N9 100 DT45
Warren Cutting, Kings.T. KT2 178 CR94
Warren Dale, Welw.G.C. AL8 29 CX06
Sch Warren Dell Prim Sch, Wat.
WD19 off Gosforth La 94 BW48
Sch Warrender Prim Sch, Ruis.
HA4 off Old Hatch Manor 115 BT59
Warrender Rd, N19 121 DJ62
Chesham HP5 54 AS29
Warrender Way, Ruis. HA4 115 BU59
Warren Dr, Grnf. UB6 136 CB70
Hornchurch RM12 127 FG62
Orpington BR6 224 EV106
Ruislip HA4 116 BX59
Tadworth (Kgswd) KT20 233 CZ122
Warren Dr, The, E11 124 EJ59
Warren Dr N, Surb. KT5 198 CP102
Warren Dr S, Surb. KT5 198 CQ102
Warreners La, Wey. KT13 213 BR109
Warren Fld, Epp. CM16 70 EU32
Iver SL0 133 BC68
Warrenfield Cl, Wal.Cr. (Chsht)
EN7 off Portland Dr 66 DU31
Warren Flds, Stan. HA7
off Valencia Rd 95 CJ49
Warren Footpath, Twick. TW1 177 CJ88
Warren Gdns, E15
off Ashton Rd 123 ED64
Orpington BR6 224 EU106
Warrengate La, Pot.B. EN6 63 CW31
Warrengate Rd, Hat.
(N.Mymms) AL9 63 CW28
Warren Grn, Hat. AL10 45 CV15
Warren Gro, Borwd. WD6 78 CR42
Warren Hastings Ct, Grav.
DA11 off Pier Rd 191 GF86

Warren Hts, Grays (Chaff.Hun.) RM16 170 FY77
Loughton IG10 84 EJ43
Warren Hill, Epsom KT18 232 CR116
Loughton IG10 84 EJ44
Warren Ho, E3 14 A1
Warrenhyrst, Guil. GU1 off Warren Rd 259 BA135
Sch Warren Jun Sch, Rom. RM6 off Gordon Rd 126 EZ57
Warren La, SE18 165 EP76
Grays RM16 169 FW77
Guildford (Albury) GU5 260 BJ139
Leatherhead (Oxshott) KT22 214 CC111
Oxted RH8 254 EF134
Stanmore HA7 95 CF48
Woking GU22 228 BH118
Warren La Gate, SE18 165 EP76
Warren Lo Dr, Tad. (Kgswd) KT20 233 CY124
Warren Mead, Bans. SM7 233 CW115
Sch Warren Mead Inf Sch, Bans. SM7 off Partridge Mead 233 CX115
Sch Warren Mead Jun Sch, Bans. SM7 off Roundwood Way 233 CX115
Warren Ms, W1 9 J4
Warrenne Rd, Bet. (Brock.) RH3 264 CP136
Warrenne Way, Reig. RH2 250 DA134
Warren Pk, Kings.T. KT2 178 CQ93
Tadworth (Box H.) KT20 248 CQ131
Warlingham CR6 237 DX118
Warren Pk Rd, Hert. SG14 32 DQ08
Sutton SM1 218 DD107
Warren Pond Rd, E4 102 EF46
Sch Warren Prim Sch, Grays RM16 off Gilbert Rd 169 FW76
Warren Ri, N.Mal. KT3 198 CR95
Warren Rd, E4 101 EC47
E10 123 EC62
E11 124 EJ60
NW2 119 CT61
SW19 180 DE93
Addlestone (New Haw) KT15 212 BG110
Ashford TW15 175 BS94
Banstead SM7 217 CW114
Bexleyheath DA6 186 FA85
Bromley BR2 204 EG103
Bushey (Bushey Hth) WD23 94 CC46
Croydon CR0 202 DS102
Dartford DA1 188 FK90
Godalming GU7 258 AS144
Gravesend (Sthflt) DA13 190 GB92
Guildford GU1 259 AZ135
Ilford IG6 125 ER57
Kingston upon Thames KT2 178 CQ93
Orpington BR6 223 ET106
Purley CR8 219 DP112
Reigate RH2 250 DB133
St. Albans AL1 42 CC24
Sidcup DA14 186 EW90
Twickenham TW2 176 CC86
Uxbridge UB10 114 BL63
Sch Warren Rd Prim Sch, Orp. BR6 off Warren Rd 223 ET106
Warrens Shawe La, Edg. HA8 96 CP46
⊖ Warren Street 9 K3
Warren St, W1 9 H4
Warren Ter, Grays RM16 off Arterial Rd W Thurrock 169 FX75
Hertford SG14 32 DR07
Romford RM6 126 EX56
Warren Wk, SE7 164 EJ79
Warren Way, NW7 97 CY51
Weybridge KT13 213 BQ106
Warren Wd Cl, Brom. BR2 204 EF103
Warriner Av, Horn. RM12 128 FK61
Warriner Dr, N9 100 DU48
Warriner Gdns, SW11 160 DF81
Warrington Av, Slou. SL1 131 AQ72
Warrington Cres, W9 7 L4
Warrington Gdns, W9 7 L4
Hornchurch RM11 128 FJ58
Warrington Pl, E14 24 D1
Warrington Rd, Croy. CR0 201 DP104
Dagenham RM8 126 EX61
Harrow HA1 117 CE57
Richmond TW10 177 CK85
Warrington Spur, Wind. (Old Wind.) SL4 172 AV87
Warrington Sq, Dag. RM8 126 EX61
Warrior Av, Grav. DA12 191 GJ91
Warrior Sq, E12 125 EN63
Warsaw Cl, Ruis. HA4 off Glebe Av 135 BV65
Warsdale Dr, NW9 off Mardale Dr 118 CR57
Warspite Rd, SE18 164 EL76
Warton Rd, E15 143 EC66
Warwall, E6 145 EP72
⊖ Warwick Avenue 7 L4
Warwick Av, W2 7 L4
W9 7 L4
Edgware HA8 96 CP48
Egham TW20 193 BC95
Harrow HA2 116 BZ63
Potters Bar (Cuffley) EN6 65 DK27
Slough SL2 131 AQ70
Staines TW18 174 BJ93
Warwick Bldg, SW8 off Queenstown Rd 161 DH79
Warwick Cl, Barn. EN4 80 DD43
Bexley DA5 186 EZ87
Bushey (Bushey Hth) WD23 off Magnaville Rd 95 CE45
Dorking (Holm.) RH5 263 CH144
Hampton TW12 176 CC94
Hertford SG13 32 DQ11
Hornchurch RM11 off Wiltshire Av 128 FM56
Orpington BR6 206 EU104
Potters Bar (Cuffley) EN6 65 DK27
Warwick Ct, SE15 162 DU82
WC1 10 B6
Rickmansworth (Chorl.) WD3 73 BF41
Surbiton KT6 off Hook Rd 198 CL103
Warwick Cres, W2 7 L5
Hayes UB4 135 BT70
Warwick Deeping, Cher. (Ott.) KT16 211 BC106
Warwick Dene, W5 138 CL74
Warwick Dr, SW15 159 CV83
Waltham Cross (Chsht) EN8 67 DX28
Warwick Est, W2 7 K6
Warwick Gdns, N4 122 DQ57
W14 16 F6
Ashtead KT21 231 CJ117
Barnet EN5 off Great N Rd 79 CZ38
Ilford IG1 125 EP60
Romford RM2 128 FJ55
Thames Ditton KT7 197 CF99
Warwick Gro, E5 122 DV60
Surbiton KT5 198 CM101
Warwick Ho St, SW1 19 M1
Warwick La, EC4 10 F8
Rainham RM13 148 FM68
Warwick La, Upmin. RM14 148 FP68
Woking GU21 226 AU119
Warwick Ms, Rick. (Crox.Grn) WD3 74 BN44
Warwick Pas, EC4 10 F7
Warwick Pl, W5 off Warwick Rd 157 CK75
W9 7 L5
Gravesend (Nthflt) DA11 190 GB85
Uxbridge UB8 134 BJ66
Warwick Pl N, SW1 19 J8
Warwick Quad Shop Mall, Red. RH1 off London Rd 250 DG133
Warwick Rd, E4 101 EA50
E11 124 EH57
E12 124 EL64
E15 144 EF65
E17 101 DZ53
N11 99 DK51
N18 100 DS49
SE20 202 DV97
SW5 16 E7
W5 157 CK75
W14 16 E7
Ashford TW15 174 BL92
Barnet EN5 80 DB42
Beaconsfield HP9 89 AK52
Borehamwood WD6 78 CR41
Coulsdon CR5 219 DJ114
Enfield EN3 83 DZ37
Hounslow TW4 155 BV83
Kingston upon Thames KT1 197 CJ95
New Malden KT3 198 CQ97
Rainham RM13 148 FJ70
Redhill RH1 250 DF133
St. Albans AL1 43 CF18
Sidcup DA14 186 EV92
Southall UB2 156 BZ76
Sutton SM1 218 DC105
Thames Ditton KT7 197 CF99
Thornton Heath CR7 201 DN97
Twickenham TW2 177 CE88
Welling DA16 166 EW83
West Drayton UB7 154 BL75
Warwick Row, SW1 19 H5
Warwicks Bench, Guil. GU1 258 AX136
Warwicks Bench La, Guil. GU1 258 AY137
Warwicks Bench Rd, Guil. GU1 258 AY137
Sch Warwick Sch, The, Red. RH1 off Noke Dr 250 DG133
Sch Warwick Sch for Boys, N Site, E17 off Barrett Rd 123 EC56
S Site, E17 off Brooke Rd 123 EC56
Warwickshire Path, SE8 163 DZ80
Warwick Sq, EC4 10 F7
SW1 19 J9
Warwick Sq Ms, SW1 19 J8
Warwick St, W1 9 K9
Warwick Ter, SE18 165 ER79
Warwick Way, SW1 19 J8
Dartford DA1 188 FL89
Rickmansworth (Crox.Grn) WD3 75 BQ42
WARWICK WOLD, Red. RH1 251 DN129
Warwick Wold Rd, Red. RH1 251 DN128
Warwick Yd, EC1 11 H4
Wash, The, Hert. SG14 32 DR09
Wash Hill, H.Wyc. (Woob.Grn) HP10 110 AE60
Wash Hill Lea, H.Wyc. (Woob.Grn) HP10 110 AD59
Washington Av, E12 124 EL63
Hemel Hempstead HP2 40 BM15
Washington Cl, Reig. RH2 250 DA131
Washington Dr, Slou. SL1 131 AK73
Windsor SL4 151 AL83
Washington Rd, E6 off St. Stephens Rd 144 EJ66
E18 102 EF54
SW13 159 CU80
Kingston upon Thames KT1 198 CN96
Worcester Park KT4 199 CV103
Washington Row, Amer. HP7 off London Rd W 55 AQ40
Wash La, Pot.B. EN6 63 CV33
Washneys Rd, Orp. BR6 224 EV113
Washpond La, Warl. CR6 237 EC118
Wash Rd, Brwd. (Hutt.) CM13 109 GD44
Wasp Grn La, Red. (Outwood) RH1 267 DP143
Wastdale Rd, SE23 183 DX88
Watchfield Ct, W4 158 CQ78
Watchgate, Dart. (Lane End) DA2 189 FR91
Watchlytes, Welw.G.C. AL7 30 DC09
Sch Watchlytes Prim Sch, Welw.G.C. AL7 off Watchlytes 30 DC09
Watchmead, Welw.G.C. AL7 30 DA09
Watcombe Cotts, Rich. TW9 158 CN79
Watcombe Pl, SE25 off Albert Rd 202 DV99
Watcombe Rd, SE25 202 DV99
Waterbank Rd, SE6 183 EB90
Waterbeach, Welw.G.C. AL7 30 DD08
Waterbeach Cl, Slou. SL1 131 AR72
Waterbeach Rd, Dag. RM9 146 EW65
Slough SL1 131 AR72
Waterbrook La, NW4 119 CW57
Water Circ, Green. (Bluewater) DA9 189 FT88
Watercress Pl, N1 5 M6
Watercress Rd, Wal.Cr. (Chsht) EN7 66 DR26
Watercress Way, Wok. GU21 226 AV117
Watercroft Rd, Sev. (Halst.) TN14 224 EZ110
Waterdale, Hert. SG13 32 DQ11
Waterdale Rd, SE2 166 EU79
Waterdales, Grav. (Nthflt) DA11 190 GD88
Waterdell Pl, Rick. WD3 off Uxbridge Rd 92 BG47
Waterden Cl, Guil. GU1 259 AZ135
Waterden Rd, E15 123 EA64
Guildford GU1 258 AY135
WATER END, Hat. AL9 63 CV26
Waterend La, St.Alb. (Wheat.) AL4 28 CQ07
Welwyn AL6 28 CQ07
Water End Rd, Berk. (Pott.End) HP4 39 BB17
Waterer Gdns, Tad. KT20 233 CX118
Waterer Ri, Wall. SM6 219 DK107
Waterfall Cl, N14 99 DJ48
Virginia Water GU25 192 AU97
Waterfall Cotts, SW19 180 DD93
Waterfall Rd, N11 99 DH49
N14 99 DJ48
SW19 180 DD93
Waterfall Ter, SW17 180 DE93
Waterfield, Rick. (Herons.) WD3 91 BC45
Tadworth KT20 233 CV119
Welwyn Garden City AL7 30 DB08
Waterfield Cl, SE28 146 EV74
Belvedere DA17 166 FA76
Waterfield Dr, Warl. CR6 236 DW119
Waterfield Gdns, SE25 202 DS99
Waterfield Grn, Tad. KT20 233 CW120
Waterfields, Lthd. KT22 231 CH119
Waterfields Shop Pk, Wat. WD17 76 BX42
Waterfields Way, Wat. WD17 76 BX42
WATERFORD, Hert. SG14 31 DM05
Waterford Cl, Cob. KT11 214 BY111
Waterford Common, Hert. SG14 31 DP05
Waterford Grn, Welw.G.C. AL7 30 DB09
Waterford Rd, SW6 160 DB81
Waterfront Studios Business Cen, E16 off Dock Rd 144 EF74
Water Gdns, Stan. HA7 95 CH51
Water Gdns, The, W2 8 B7
Harlow CM20 off South Gate 51 ER15
Watergardens, The, Kings.T. KT2 178 CQ93
Watergate, EC4 10 E9
Watergate, The, Wat. WD19 94 BX47
Sch Watergate Sch, SE6 off Lushington Rd 163 EB84
Watergate St, SE8 163 EA79
Watergate Wk, WC2 19 P1
Waterglade Ind Pk, Grays RM20 169 FT78
Waterhall Av, E4 102 EE49
Waterhall Cl, E17 101 DX53
Waterhead Cl, Erith DA8 167 FE80
Waterhouse Cl, E16 144 EK71
NW3 off Lyndhurst Rd 120 DD64
W6 16 B9
Waterhouse La, Ken. CR8 236 DQ119
Redhill (Bletch.) RH1 252 DT132
Tadworth (Kgswd) KT20 233 CY121
Waterhouse Moor, Harl. CM18 51 ET16
Waterhouse Sq, EC1 10 C6
Waterhouse St, Hem.H. HP1 40 BJ20
Wateridge Cl, E14 23 N6
Wateringbury Cl, Orp. BR5 206 EV97
Water La, E15 144 EE65
EC3 11 L10
N9 100 DV46
NW1 off Kentish Town Rd 141 DH66
SE14 162 DW80
Berkhamsted HP4 38 AW19
Chesham HP5 54 AP32
Cobham KT11 230 BY115
Dorking (Abin.Ham.) RH5 261 BV143
Guildford (Albury) GU5 260 BH137
Harlow CM19 50 EL19
Hemel Hempstead (Bov.) HP3 57 BA29
Hertford SG14 32 DQ10
Ilford IG3 125 ES62
Kings Langley WD4 59 BP29
Kingston upon Thames KT1 197 CK95
Leatherhead (Bkhm) KT23 246 BY125
Oxted (Titsey) RH8 254 EG126
Purfleet RM19 168 FN77
Redhill RH1 251 DP130
Richmond TW9 177 CK85
Sevenoaks (Shore.) TN14 225 FF112
Sidcup DA14 186 EZ89
Twickenham TW1 off The Embankment 177 CG88
Watford WD17 76 BW42
Westerham TN16 255 ER127
Water Lily Cl, Sthl. UB2 off Navigator Dr 156 CC75
⇌ Waterloo 20 C3
⊖ Waterloo 20 C3
Waterloo Br, SE1 10 A10
WC2 10 A10
Waterloo Cl, E9 off Churchill Wk 122 DW64
Feltham TW14 175 BT88
⇌ Waterloo East 20 C2
Waterloo Est, E2 142 DW68
Waterloo Gdns, E2 142 DW68
N1 4 E6
Romford RM7 127 FD58
⇌ Waterloo International 20 B3
Riv Waterloo Millennium Pier 20 A3
Waterloo Pas, NW6 139 CZ66
Waterloo Pl, SW1 19 L1
Richmond TW9 off Sheen Rd 178 CL85
Richmond (Kew) TW9 158 CN79
Waterloo Rd, E6 144 EJ66
E7 off Wellington Rd 124 EF64
E10 123 EA59
NW2 119 CU60
SE1 20 C3
Brentwood CM14 108 FW46
Epsom KT19 216 CR112
Ilford IG6 103 EQ54
Romford RM7 127 FE57
Sutton SM1 218 DD106
Uxbridge UB8 134 BJ67
Waterloo St, Grav. DA12 191 GJ87
Waterloo Ter, N1 4 E6
Waterlow Ct, NW11 off Heath Cl 120 DB59
Waterlow Rd, N19 121 DJ60
Reigate RH2 266 DC135
Waterman Cl, Wat. WD19 75 BV44
Waterman Ct, Slou. SL1 131 AL74
★ Watermans Art Cen, Brent. TW8 158 CL79
Waterman's Cl, Kings.T. KT2 off Woodside Rd 178 CL94
Waterman St, SW15 159 CX83
Watermans Wk, SE16 23 J5
Watermans Way, Epp. (N.Wld Bas.) CM16 70 FA27
Greenhithe DA9 169 FV84
Waterman Way, E1 22 C1
Watermark Way, Hert. SG13 32 DT09
Water Mead, Couls. CR5 off Outwood La 234 DF117
Watermead, Felt. TW14 175 BS88
Tadworth KT20 233 CV120
Woking GU21 226 AT116
Watermead Ho, E9 off Kingsmead Way 123 DY64
Watermead La, Cars. SM5 off Middleton Rd 200 DF101
Water Meadow, Chesh. HP5 54 AP32
Watermeadow Cl, Erith DA8 167 FH81
Watermeadow La, SW6 160 DC82
Watermead Rd, SE6 183 EC91
Watermead Way, N17 122 DV55
Watermen's Sq, SE20 182 DW94
Water Ms, SE15 162 DW84
Watermill Cl, Rich. TW10 177 CJ90
Watermill La, N18 100 DS50
Hertford SG14 32 DR06
Watermill La N, Hert. SG14 32 DQ06
Watermill Way, SW19 200 DC95
Water Mill Way, Dart. (S.Darenth) DA4 208 FP96
Watermill Way, Felt. TW13 176 BZ89
Watermint Cl, Orp. BR5 off Wagtail Way 206 EX98
Watermint Quay, N16 122 DU59
Waterperry La, Wok. (Chobham) GU24 210 AT110
Water Rd, Wem. HA0 138 CM67
Water Row, Ware SG12 33 DX06
Waters Dr, Rick. WD3 92 BL46
Staines TW18 173 BF90
Watersedge, Epsom KT19 216 CQ105
Waters Edge Ct, Erith DA8 off Erith High St 167 FF78
Watersfield Way, Edg. HA8 95 CK52
Waters Gdns, Dag. RM10 126 FA64
WATERSIDE, Chesh. HP5 54 AR32
Waterside, Beck. BR3 203 EA95
Berkhamsted HP4 off Holliday St 38 AX19
Chesham HP5 54 AQ32
Dartford DA1 187 FE85
Gravesend DA11 190 GE87
High Wycombe (Woob.Grn) HP10 110 AE56
Horley RH6 268 DG146
Water Side, Kings L. WD4 58 BN29
Waterside, Rad. WD7 61 CH34
St. Albans (Lon.Col.) AL2 62 CL27
Uxbridge UB8 134 BJ71
Welwyn Garden City AL7 30 DA07
Waterside Av, Beck. BR3 off Creswell Dr 203 EB99
Waterside Cl, E3 143 DZ67
SE16 22 B4
Barking IG11 126 EU63
Northolt UB5 136 BZ69
Romford (Harold Wd) RM3 106 FN52
Surbiton KT6 off Culsac Rd 198 CL103
Sch Waterside Co Comb Sch, Chesh. HP5 off Black Horse Av 54 AR33
Waterside Ct, SE13 off Weardale Rd 163 ED84
Kings Langley WD4 off Water Side 59 BP29
Waterside Dr, Slou. (Langley) SL3 153 AZ75
Walton-on-Thames KT12 195 BU99
Waterside Ms, Guil. GU1 242 AW132
Uxbridge (Hare.) UB9 92 BG51
Waterside Path, SW18 off Smugglers Way 160 DB84
Waterside Pl, NW1 off Princess Rd 140 DG67
Sawbridgeworth CM21 36 FA05
Waterside Pt, SW11 160 DE80
Sch Waterside Prim Sch, SE18 off Robert St 165 ER78
Waterside Rd, Guil. GU1 242 AX131
Southall UB2 156 CA76
Waterside Twr, SW6 160 DC81
Waterside Trd Cen, W7 157 CE76
Waterside Way, SW17 180 DC91
Woking GU21 off Winnington Way 226 AV118
Watersmeet, Harl. CM19 51 EP19
Watersmeet Cl, Guil. GU4 off Cotts Wd Dr 243 BA129
Watersmeet Way, SE28 146 EW72
Waterson Rd, Grays RM16 171 GH77
Waterson St, E2 11 M1
Waters Pl, SW15 off Danemere St 159 CW82
Watersplash Cl, Kings.T. KT1 198 CL97
Watersplash La, Hayes UB3 155 BU77
Hounslow TW5 155 BV78
Watersplash Rd, Shep. TW17 194 BN98
Waters Rd, SE6 184 EE90
Kingston upon Thames KT1 198 CP96
Waters Sq, Kings.T. KT1 198 CP97
Water St, WC2 10 B9
Waterton Av, Grav. DA12 191 GL87
Water Twr Cl, Uxb. UB8 114 BL64
Water Twr Hill, Croy. CR0 220 DR105
Water Twr Pl, N1 4 E8
Water Twr Rd, Brwd. (Gt Warley) CM14 108 FW50
Water Vw, Horl. RH6 off Carlton Tye 269 DJ148
Waterview Ho, E14 13 K6
Waterway Rd, Lthd. KT22 231 CG122
Waterworks Cor, E18 102 EE54
Waterworks Cotts, Brox. EN10 49 DY22
Waterworks La, E5 123 DX61
Waterworks Rd, SW2 181 DM86
Waterworks Yd, Croy. CR0 off Surrey St 202 DQ104
Watery La, SW20 199 CZ96
Chertsey (Lyne) KT16 193 BD101
Hatfield AL10 44 CS19
High Wycombe (Woob.Grn) HP10 88 AE54
Northolt UB5 136 BW68
St. Albans (Flam.) AL3 61 CK28
Sidcup DA14 186 EV93
Wates Way, Brwd. CM15 108 FX46
Mitcham CR4 200 DF100
Wates Way Ind Est, Mitch. CR4 off Wates Way 200 DF100
Wateville Rd, N17 100 DQ53
WATFORD, WD17 - WD19; WD24 & WD25 75 BT41
⊖ Watford 75 BT41
Watford Arches Trd Est, Wat. WD17 76 BX43
Watford Business Pk, Wat. WD18 75 BS44
Watford Bypass, Borwd. WD6 95 CG45
Watford Cl, SW11 off Petworth St 160 DE81
Guildford GU1 243 AZ134
Watford Fld Rd, Wat. WD18 76 BW43
★ Watford FC, Wat. WD18 75 BV43
H Watford Gen Hosp, Wat. WD18 75 BV43
Sch Watford Gram Sch for Boys, Wat. WD18 off Rickmansworth Rd 75 BT42
Sch Watford Gram Sch for Girls, Wat. WD18 off Lady's Cl 76 BW43
WATFORD HEATH, Wat. WD19 94 BY46
Watford Heath, Wat. WD19 94 BX45
⇌ Watford High Street 76 BW42
⇌ Watford Junction 76 BW40
★ Watford Mus, Wat. WD17 76 BW43
⇌ Watford North 76 BW37
Watford Rd, E16 15 M6
Borehamwood (Elstree) WD6 77 CJ44
Harrow HA1 117 CG61
Kings Langley WD4 59 BP32
Northwood HA6 93 BT52
Radlett WD7 77 CE36
Rickmansworth (Crox.Grn) WD3 75 BQ43
St. Albans AL1, AL2 60 CA27
Wembley HA0 117 CG61
Coll Watford Sch of Music, Wat. WD17 off Nascot Wd Rd 75 BU38
⇌ Watford Stadium Halt (closed) 75 BU44
Watford Way, NW4 119 CU56
NW7 119 CU56
⇌ Watford West (closed) 75 BT43
Wathen Rd, Dor. RH4 263 CH135
Watkin Rd, Wem. HA9 118 CP62
Watkins Cl, Nthwd. HA6 off Chestnut Av 93 BT53
Watkinson Rd, N7 4 A3
Watkins Ri, Pot.B. EN6 off The Walk 64 DB32
Watling Av, Edg. HA8 96 CR52
Watling Cl, Hem.H. HP2 40 BL17
Watling Ct, EC4 11 H8
Borehamwood WD6 77 CK44
Watling Fm Cl, Stan. HA7 95 CJ46
Watling Gdns, NW2 139 CY65
Watling Knoll, Rad. WD7 61 CF33
Watlings Cl, Croy. CR0 203 DY100
Watling St, EC4 10 G8
SE15 off Dragon Rd 162 DS79
Bexleyheath DA6 167 FB84
Borehamwood (Elstree) WD6 77 CJ40
Dartford DA1, DA2 188 FP87
Gravesend DA11, DA12, DA13 190 GC90
Radlett WD7 61 CF32
St. Albans AL1, AL2 60 CC25
Watling St Caravan Site (Travellers), St.Alb. (Park St) AL2 60 CC25
Watlington Gro, SE26 183 DY92
Watlington Rd, Harl. CM17 36 EX11
Watling Vw, St.Alb. AL1 42 CC24
Sch Watling Vw Sch, St.Alb. AL1 off Watling Vw 43 CD24
Watney Mkt, E1 12 D8
Watney Rd, SW14 158 CQ83
Watneys Rd, Mitch. CR4 201 DK99
Watney St, E1 12 D8
Watson Av, E6 145 EN66
St. Albans AL3 43 CF17
Sutton SM3 199 CY103
Watson Cl, N16 5 K1
SW19 180 DE93
Grays RM20 169 FU81
Watson Gdns, Rom. (Harold Wd) RM3 106 FK54
Watson Rd, Dor. (Westc.) RH4 262 CC137
Watson's Ms, W1 8 B6
Watsons Rd, N22 99 DM53
Watson's St, SE8 163 EA80
Watson St, E13 144 EH68
Watsons Wk, St.Alb. AL1 43 CE21
Watsons Yd, NW2 off North Circular Rd 119 CT61
Sch Wattenden Prim Sch, Pur. CR8 off Old Lo La 235 DP116
Wattendon Rd, Ken. CR8 235 DP116
Wattisfield Rd, E5 122 DW62
Wattleton Rd, Beac. HP9 89 AK54
Watton Rd, Ware SG12 32 DW05
Watts Cl, N15 off Seaford Rd 122 DS57
Tadworth KT20 233 CX122
Watts Cres, Purf. RM19 168 FQ77
Watts Fm Par, Wok. (Chobham) GU24 off Barnmead 210 AT110
Watts Gro, E3 14 A5
Watts La, Chis. BR7 205 EP95
Tadworth KT20 233 CX122
Teddington TW11 177 CG92
Watts Mead, Tad. KT20 233 CX122
Watts Rd, T.Ditt. KT7 197 CG101
Watts St, E1 22 D1
SE15 162 DT81
Watts Way, SW7 17 P5
Wat Tyler Rd, SE3 163 EC82
SE10 163 EC82
Wauthier Cl, N13 99 DP50
Wavell Cl, Wal.Cr. (Chsht) EN8 67 DY27
Wavell Dr, Sid. DA15 185 ES86
Wavell Gdns, Slou. SL2 131 AM69
Wavell Rd, Beac. HP9 89 AP54
Wavel Ms, N8 121 DK56
NW6 off Acol Rd 140 DB66
Wavel Pl, SE26 off Sydenham Hill 182 DT91
Wavendene Av, Egh. TW20 173 BB94
Wavendon Av, W4 158 CR78
Waveney, Hem.H. HP2 40 BM15
Waveney Av, SE15 162 DV84
Waveney Cl, E1 22 B1
Waverley Av, E4 101 DZ49
E17 123 ED55
Kenley CR8 236 DS116
Surbiton KT5 198 CP100
Sutton SM1 200 DB103
Twickenham TW2 176 BZ88
Wembley HA9 118 CM64
Waverley Cl, E18 102 EJ53
Bromley BR2 204 EK99
Hayes UB3 155 BR77
West Molesey KT8 196 CA99
Waverley Ct, Wok. GU22 226 AY118
Waverley Cres, SE18 165 ER78
Romford RM3 106 FJ52
Waverley Dr, Cher. KT16 193 BD104
Virginia Water GU25 192 AU97
Waverley Gdns, E6 off Oliver Gdns 144 EL71
NW10 138 CM69
Barking IG11 145 ES68
Grays RM16 170 GA75
Ilford IG6 103 EQ54
Northwood HA6 93 BU53
Waverley Gro, N3 119 CY55
Waverley Ind Est, Har. HA1 117 CD55
Waverley Pl, N4 off Adolphus Rd 121 DP61
NW8 140 DD68
Leatherhead KT22 off Church Rd 231 CH122
Waverley Rd, E17 123 EC55
E18 102 EJ53
N8 121 DK58
N17 100 DV52
SE18 165 EQ78
SE25 202 DV98
Cobham (Stoke D'Ab.) KT11 214 CB114
Enfield EN2 81 DP42
Epsom KT17 217 CV106
Harrow HA2 116 BZ60
Leatherhead (Oxshott) KT22 214 CB114
Rainham RM13 147 FH69
St. Albans AL3 43 CD18
Slough SL1 131 AQ71
Southall UB1 136 CA73
Weybridge KT13 212 BN106
Sch Waverley Sch, Enf. EN3 off The Ride 82 DW42
Sch Waverley Sec Sch, SE22 off Homestall Rd 182 DW85
Waverley Vil, N17 100 DT54
Waverley Wk, W2 7 H5
Waverley Way, Cars. SM5 218 DE107
Waverton Ho, E3 143 DZ67
Waverton Rd, SW18 180 DC87
Waverton St, W1 18 F1
Wavertree Ct, SW2 off Streatham Hill 181 DM88
Wavertree Rd, E18 102 EG54
SW2 181 DL88
Waxlow Cres, Sthl. UB1 136 CA72
Waxlow Rd, NW10 138 CQ68
Waxwell Cl, Pnr. HA5 94 BX54
Waxwell La, Pnr. HA5 94 BX54
Way, The, Reig. RH2 250 DD133
Wayborne Gro, Ruis. HA4 115 BQ58
Waycross Rd, Upmin. RM14 129 FS58
Waye Av, Houns. TW5 155 BU81
Wayfarer Rd, Nthlt. UB5 136 BX70

★ Place of interest | H Hospital | Sch School | Coll College | Uni University | ⇌ Railway station

Wayfarers Pk, Berk. HP4 38 AT19
Wayfaring Grn, Grays (Bad.Dene) RM17 off Curling La 170 FZ78
Wayfield Link, SE9 185 ER86
Wayford St, SW11 160 DE82
Wayland Av, E8 122 DU64
Waylands, Hayes UB3 135 BR71
Staines (Wrays.) TW19 172 AY86
Swanley BR8 207 FF98
Waylands Cl, Sev. (Knock.) TN14 240 EY115
Waylands Mead, Beck. BR3 203 EB95
Wayleave, The, SE28 146 EV73
Waylett Pl, SE27 181 DP90
Wembley HA0 117 CK63
Wayman Ct, E8 142 DV65
Wayne Cl, Orp. BR6 205 ET104
Wayneflete Twr Av, Esher KT10 196 CA104
Waynflete Av, Croy. CR0 201 DP104
Waynflete Sq, W10 6 A9
Waynflete St, SW18 180 DC89
Wayre, The, Harl. CM17 36 EW11
Wayre St, Harl. CM17 36 EW11
Wayside, NW11 119 CY60
SW14 178 CQ85
Croydon CR0 off Field Way 221 EB107
Kings Langley (Chipper.) WD4 58 BH30
Potters Bar EN6 64 DD33
Radlett (Shenley) WD7 61 CK33
Wayside, The, Hem.H. HP3 41 BQ21
Wayside Av, Bushey WD23 77 CD44
Hornchurch RM12 128 FK61
Wayside Cl, N14 81 DJ44
Romford RM1 127 FF55
Wayside Commercial Est, Bark. IG11 146 EU67
Wayside Ct, Twick. TW1 177 CJ86
Wembley HA9 off Oakington Av 118 CN62
Woking GU21 off Langmans Way 226 AS116
Wayside Gdns, SE9 off Wayside Gro 185 EM91
Dagenham RM10 126 FA64
Gerrards Cross SL9 112 AX59
Wayside Gro, SE9 185 EM91
Wayside Ms, Ilf. IG2 off Gaysham Av 125 EN57
Wayville Rd, Dart. DA1 188 FP87
Way Volante, Grav. DA12 191 GL91
Weald, The, Chis. BR7 185 EM93
Weald Br Rd, Epp. (N.Wld Bas.) CM16 53 FD24
Weald Cl, SE16 22 C9
Brentwood CM14 108 FU48
Bromley BR2 204 EL103
Gravesend (Istead Rise) DA13 190 GE94
Guildford (Shalf.) GU4 off Station Rd 258 AY140
★ Weald Country Pk, Brwd. CM14 108 FS45
Sch Weald First Sch, Har. HA3 off Robin Hood Dr 95 CF52
Weald Hall La, Epp. (Thnwd) CM16 70 EW25
Weald La, Har. HA3 95 CD54
Sch Weald Mid Sch, Har. HA3 off Robin Hood Dr 95 CF52
Wealdon Ct, Guil. GU2 off Humbolt Cl 242 AT134
Weald Pk Way, Brwd. (S.Wld) CM14 108 FS48
Weald Ri, Har. HA3 95 CF52
Weald Rd, Brwd. CM14 107 FR46
Sevenoaks TN13 257 FH129
Uxbridge UB10 134 BN68
Weald Sq, E5 off Rossington St 122 DV61
WEALDSTONE, Har. HA3 117 CF55
Wealdstone Rd, Sutt. SM3 199 CZ103
Weald Way, Cat. CR3 252 DS128
Wealdway, Grav. DA13 191 GH93
Weald Way, Hayes UB4 135 BS69
Reigate RH2 266 DC138
Romford RM7 127 FB58
Wealdwood Gdns, Pnr. HA5 off Highbanks Rd 94 CB51
Weale Rd, E4 101 ED48
Weall Cl, Pur. CR8 219 DM112
Weall Grn, Wat. WD25 59 BV32
Weardale Av, Dart. DA2 188 FQ89
Weardale Gdns, Enf. EN2 82 DR39
Weardale Rd, SE13 163 ED84
Wear Pl, E2 12 C2
Wearside Rd, SE13 163 EB84
Weasdale Ct, Wok. GU21 off Roundthorn Way 226 AT116
Weatherall Cl, Add. KT15 212 BH106
Weatherhill Cl, Horl. RH6 269 DM148
Weatherhill Common, Horl. (Smallfield) RH6 269 DM147
Weatherhill Rd, Horl. (Smallfield) RH6 269 DM148
Weatherley Cl, E3 13 M5
Weaver Cl, E6 off Trader Rd 145 EP73
Croydon CR0 220 DT105
Weavers Cl, Grav. DA11 191 GG88
Isleworth TW7 157 CE84
Weavers La, Sev. TN14 257 FJ121
Weavers Orchard, Grav. (Sthflt) DA13 190 GA93
Weavers Ter, SW6 160 DA79
Weaver St, E1 12 A4
Weavers Way, NW1 141 DK67
Weaver Wk, SE27 181 DP91
Webb Cl, W10 139 CW70
Chesham HP5 54 AP30
Slough SL3 152 AX77
Webber Cl, Borwd. (Elstree) WD6 off Rodgers Cl 77 CK44
Erith DA8 167 FH80
Webber Row, SE1 20 D5
Webber St, SE1 20 D3
Webb Est, E5 122 DU59
Webb Gdns, E13 15 M3
Webb Pl, NW10 off Old Oak La 139 CT69
Webb Rd, SE3 164 EF79
Webb's All, Sev. TN13, TN15 257 FJ125
Webbscroft Rd, Dag. RM10 127 FB63
Webbs Rd, SW11 180 DF85
Hayes UB4 135 BV69
Webb St, SE1 21 L6
Webheath Est, NW6 139 CZ66
Webley Ct, Enf. EN3 off Sten Cl 83 EA37
Webster Cl, Horn. RM12 128 FK62
Leatherhead (Oxshott) KT22 214 CB114
Waltham Abbey EN9 68 EG33
Webster Gdns, W5 137 CK74
Webster Rd, E11 123 EC62
SE16 22 B6
Websters Cl, Wok. GU22 226 AU120
Wedderburn Rd, NW3 120 DD64
Barking IG11 145 ER67
Wedgewood Cl, Epp. CM16 off Theydon Gro 70 EU30
Northwood HA6 93 BQ51
Wedgewood Dr, Harl. CM17 52 EX16
Wedgewoods, West. (Tats.) TN16 off Westmore Rd 238 EJ121
Wedgewood Wk, NW6 off Lymington Rd 120 DB64
Wedgwood Ms, W1 9 M8
Wedgwood Pl, Cob. KT11 213 BU114
Wedgwood Way, SE19 182 DQ94
Wedhey, Harl. CM19 51 EQ15
Wedlake Cl, Horn. RM11 128 FL60
Wedlake St, W10 6 D3
Wedmore Av, Ilf. IG5 103 EN53
Wedmore Gdns, N19 121 DK61
Wedmore Ms, N19 off Wedmore St 121 DK62
Wedmore Rd, Grnf. UB6 137 CD69
Wedmore St, N19 121 DK62
Wednesbury Gdns, Rom. RM3 106 FM52
Wednesbury Grn, Rom. RM3 off Wednesbury Gdns 106 FM52
Wednesbury Rd, Rom. RM3 106 FM52
Weech Rd, NW6 120 DA63
Weedington Rd, NW5 120 DG64
Weedon Cl, Ger.Cr. (Chal.St.P.) SL9 90 AV53
Weedon La, Amer. HP6 55 AN36
Weekes Dr, Slou. SL1 131 AP74
Weekley Sq, SW11 off Thomas Baines Rd 160 DD83
Weigall Rd, SE12 164 EG84
Weighhouse St, W1 8 F8
Weighton Rd, SE20 202 DV96
Harrow HA3 95 CD53
Weihurst Gdns, Sutt. SM1 218 DD106
Weimar St, SW15 159 CY83
Weind, The, Epp. (They.B.) CM16 85 ES36
Weirdale Av, N20 98 DF47
Weir Est, SW12 181 DJ87
Weir Hall Av, N18 100 DR51
Weir Hall Gdns, N18 100 DR50
Weir Hall Rd, N17 100 DR50
N18 100 DR50
Weir Pl, Stai. TW18 193 BE95
Weir Rd, SW12 181 DJ87
SW19 180 DB90
Bexley DA5 187 FB87
Chertsey KT16 194 BH101
Walton-on-Thames KT12 195 BU100
Weirside Gdns, West Dr. UB7 134 BK74
Weir's Pas, NW1 9 M1
Weiss Rd, SW15 159 CX83
Welbeck Av, Brom. BR1 184 EG91
Hayes UB4 135 BV70
Sidcup DA15 186 EU88
Welbeck Cl, N12 off Torrington Pk 98 DD50
Borehamwood WD6 78 CN41
Epsom KT17 217 CU108
New Malden KT3 199 CT99
Welbeck Rd, E6 144 EK69
Barnet EN4 80 DD44
Carshalton SM5 200 DE102
Harrow HA2 116 CB60
Sutton SM1 200 DD103
Welbeck St, W1 8 G7
Welbeck Wk, Cars. SM5 off Welbeck Rd 200 DE102
Welbeck Way, W1 8 G7
Sch Welbourne Prim Sch, N17 off High Cross Rd 122 DU55
Welby St, SE5 161 DP81
Welch Ho, Enf. EN3 off Beaconsfield Rd 83 DX37
Welch Pl, Pnr. HA5 94 BW53
Welclose St, St.Alb. AL3 42 CC20
Welcomes Rd, Ken. CR8 236 DQ116
Welcote Dr, Nthwd. HA6 93 BR51
Welden, Slou. SL2 132 AW72
Welders La, Beac. (Jordans) HP9 90 AT52
Gerrards Cross (Chal.St.P.) SL9 90 AT52
Weldon Cl, Ruis. HA4 135 BV65
Weldon Dr, W.Mol. KT8 196 BZ98
Weldon Way, Red. RH1 251 DK129
Weld Pl, N11 99 DH50
Welfare Rd, E15 144 EE66
Welford Cl, E5 off Denton Way 123 DX62
Welford Pl, SW19 179 CY91
Welham Cl, Hat. AL9 45 CW24
Welham Ct, Hat. AL9 off Dixons Hill Rd 45 CW24
WELHAM GREEN, Hat. AL9 45 CV23
⇌ Welham Green 45 CX23
Welham Manor, Hat. AL9 45 CW24
Welham Rd, SW16 180 DG92
SW17 180 DG92
Welhouse Rd, Cars. SM5 200 DE102
Welkin Grn, Hem.H. HP2 off Wood End Cl 41 BQ19
Wellacre Rd, Har. HA3 117 CH58
Wellan Cl, Sid. DA15 186 EV85
Welland Cl, Slou. SL3 153 BA79
Welland Gdns, Grnf. UB6 137 CF68
Welland Ms, E1 22 B1
Wellands, Hat. AL10 45 CU16
Wellands Cl, Brom. BR1 205 EM96
Welland St, SE10 163 EC79
Well App, Barn. EN5 79 CW43
Wellbank, Maid. (Taplow) SL6 off Rectory Rd 130 AE70
Wellbrook Rd, Orp. BR6 223 EN105
Wellbury Ter, Hem.H. HP2 41 BQ20
Well Cl, SW16 181 DM91
Ruislip HA4 off Parkfield Cres 116 BY62
Woking GU21 226 AW117
Wellclose Sq, E1 12 B9
Wellclose St, E1 12 B10
Wellcome Av, Dart. DA1 168 FM84
Coll Wellcome Trust, NW1 9 L3
Well Cottage Cl, E11 124 EJ59
Well Ct, EC4 11 H8
SW16 181 DM91
Well Cft, Hem.H. HP1 off Gadebridge Rd 40 BH19
Wellcroft Cl, Welw.G.C. AL7 30 DA11
Wellcroft Rd, Slou. SL1 131 AP74
Welwyn Garden City AL7 30 DA11
Welldon Cres, Har. HA1 117 CE58
Sch Welldon Pk First Sch, Har. HA2 off Kingsley Rd 116 CC63
Sch Welldon Pk Mid Sch, Har. HA2 off Wyvenhoe Rd 116 CC63
WELL END, Borwd. WD6 78 CR38
Well End Rd, Borwd. WD6 78 CQ37
Wellen Ri, Hem.H. HP3 40 BL23
Weller Cl, Amer. HP6 55 AS37
Weller Rd, Amer. HP6 55 AS37
Wellers Cl, West. TN16 255 EQ127
Wellers Ct, Guil. (Shere) GU5 260 BN139
Wellers Gro, Wal.Cr. (Chsht) EN7 66 DU28
Weller St, SE1 20 G3
Wellesford Cl, Bans. SM7 233 CZ117
Wellesley, Harl. CM19 51 EN20
Wellesley Av, W6 159 CV76
Iver SL0 153 BF76
Northwood HA6 93 BT50
Wellesley Cl, SE7 off Wellington Gdns 164 EJ78
Wellesley Ct, W9 7 L1
Wellesley Ct Rd, Croy. CR0 202 DR103
Wellesley Cres, Pot.B. EN6 63 CY33
Twickenham TW2 177 CE89
Wellesley Gro, Croy. CR0 202 DR103
Wellesley Pk Ms, Enf. EN2 81 DP40
Wellesley Pas, Croy. CR0 off Wellesley Rd 202 DQ103
Wellesley Path, Slou. SL1 off Wellesley Rd 152 AU75
Wellesley Pl, NW1 9 L2
Trm Wellesley Road 202 DQ103
Wellesley Rd, E11 124 EG57
E17 123 EA58
N22 99 DN54
NW5 120 DG64
W4 158 CN78
Brentwood CM14 108 FW46
Croydon CR0 202 DQ102
Harrow HA1 117 CE57
Ilford IG1 125 EP61
Slough SL1 152 AU75
Sutton SM2 218 DC107
Twickenham TW2 177 CD90
Wellesley St, E1 12 G6
Wellesley Ter, N1 11 H1
Welley Av, Stai. (Wrays.) TW19 152 AY84
Welley Rd, Slou. (Horton) SL3 152 AY84
Staines (Wrays.) TW19 172 AX85
Well Fm Rd, Warl. CR6 236 DU119
Wellfield Av, N10 121 DH55
Wellfield Cl, Hat. AL10 45 CU17
Wellfield Gdns, Cars. SM5 218 DE109
Wellfield Rd, SW16 181 DL91
Hatfield AL10 45 CU16
Wellfields, Loug. IG10 85 EN41
Wellfield Wk, SW16 181 DM92
Wellfit St, SE24 off Hinton Rd 161 DP83
Wellgarth, Grnf. UB6 137 CH65
Welwyn Garden City AL7 29 CY10
Wellgarth Rd, NW11 120 DB60
Well Gro, N20 98 DC45
Well Hall Par, SE9 off Well Hall Rd 165 EM84
Well Hall Rd, SE9 165 EM83
WELL HILL, Orp. BR6 225 FB107
Well Hill, Orp. BR6 225 FB107
Well Hill La, Orp. BR6 225 FB108
Well Hill Rd, Sev. TN14 225 FC107
Wellhouse La, Barn. EN5 79 CW42
Betchworth RH3 264 CQ138
Wellhouse Rd, Beck. BR3 203 DZ98
WELLING, DA16 166 EU83
⇌ Welling 166 EU82
Welling High St, Well. DA16 166 EV83
Sch Welling Sch, Well. DA16 off Elsa Rd 166 EV81
Wellings Ho, Hayes UB3 135 BV74
★ Wellington Arch, W1 18 F3
Wellington Av, E4 101 EA47
N9 100 DV48
N15 122 DT58
Hounslow TW3 176 CA85
Pinner HA5 94 BZ53
Sidcup DA15 186 EU86
Virginia Water GU25 192 AV99
Worcester Park KT4 217 CW105
Wellington Bldgs, SW1 18 F10
Wellington Cl, SE14 off Rutts Ter 163 DX81
W11 6 G8
Dagenham RM10 147 FC66
Walton-on-Thames KT12 off Hepworth Way 195 BT102
Watford WD19 off Highfield 94 BZ48
Wellington Cotts, Lthd. (E.Hors.) KT24 245 BS129
Wellington Ct, NW8 off Wellington Rd 140 DD68
Ashford TW15 off Wellington Rd 174 BL92
Staines TW19 off Clare Rd 174 BL87
Wellington Cres, N.Mal. KT3 198 CQ97
Wellington Dr, Dag. RM10 147 FC66
Purley CR8 219 DM110
Welwyn Garden City AL7 30 DC09
Wellington Gdns, SE7 164 EJ79
Twickenham TW2 177 CD91
Wellington Gro, SE10 off Crooms Hill 163 ED80
Wellington Hill, Loug. (High Beach) IG10 84 EG37
H Wellington Hosp, NW8 140 DD68
Wellington Ho, Rom. (Gidea Pk) RM2 off Kidman Cl 128 FJ55
Wellingtonia Av, Rom. (Hav.at.Bow.) RM4 105 FE48
Wellington Ms, SE7 164 EJ79
SE22 off Peckham Rye 162 DU84
SW16 off Woodbourne Av 181 DK90
Wellington Pk Est, NW2 119 CU61
Wellington Pas, E11 off Wellington Rd 124 EG57
Wellington Pl, N2 off Great N Rd 120 DE57
NW8 7 P1
Brentwood CM14 108 FW50
Broxbourne EN10 48 DW23
Cobham KT11 214 BZ112
Sch Wellington Prim Sch, E3 13 N2
E4 off Wellington Av 101 EB47
Hounslow TW3 off Sutton La 156 BZ82
Wellington Rd, E6 145 EM68
E7 124 EF63
E10 123 DY60
E11 124 EG57
E17 123 DY55
NW8 140 DD68
NW10 6 B2
SW19 180 DA89
W5 157 CJ76
Ashford TW15 174 BL92
Belvedere DA17 166 EZ78
Bexley DA5 186 EX85
Bromley BR2 204 EJ98
Caterham CR3 236 DQ122
Croydon CR0 201 DP101
Dartford DA1 188 FJ86
Enfield EN1 82 DS42
Epping (N.Wld Bas.) CM16 70 FA27
Feltham TW14 175 BS85
Hampton TW12 177 CD92
Harrow HA3 117 CE55
Orpington BR5 206 EV100
Pinner HA5 94 BZ53
St. Albans AL1 43 CH21
St. Albans (Lon.Col.) AL2 61 CK26
Tilbury RM18 171 GG83
Twickenham TW2 177 CD92
Uxbridge UB8 134 BJ67
Watford WD17 75 BV40
Wellington Rd N, Houns. TW4 156 BZ83
Wellington Rd S, Houns. TW4 156 BZ84
Wellington Row, E2 11 P1
Wellington Sq, SW3 18 C9
Wellington St, SE18 165 EN77
WC2 9 P9
Barking IG11 off Axe St 145 EQ67
Gravesend DA12 191 GJ87
Hertford SG14 31 DP08
Slough SL1 152 AT75
Wellington Ter, E1 22 C1
W2 off Notting Hill Gate 140 DB73
Harrow HA1 off West St 117 CD60
Woking (Knap.) GU21 off Victoria Rd 226 AS118
Wellington Way, E3 13 N2
Horley RH6 268 DF146
Weybridge KT13 212 BN110
Welling Way, SE9 165 ER83
Welling DA16 165 ER83
Well La, SW14 178 CQ85
Brentwood (Pilg.Hat.) CM15 108 FT41
Harlow CM19 35 EN14
Woking GU21 226 AW117
Wellmeade Dr, Sev. TN13 257 FH127
Wellmeadow Rd, SE6 184 EE87
SE13 184 EE86
W7 157 CG77
Wellow Wk, Cars. SM5 200 DD102
Well Pas, NW3 120 DD62
Well Path, Wok. GU21 off Well La 226 AW117
Well Rd, NW3 120 DD62
Barnet EN5 79 CW43
Potters Bar (Northaw) EN6 64 DE28
Well Row, Hert. SG13 47 DM17
Wells, The, N14 99 DK45
Wells Cl, Lthd. KT23 230 CB124
Northolt UB5 off Yeading La 136 BW69
St. Albans AL3 off Artisan Cres 42 CC19
South Croydon CR2 220 DS106
Waltham Cross (Chsht) EN7 off Bloomfield Rd 66 DQ25
Windsor SL4 151 AN81
Wells Ct, Rom. RM1 off Regarth Av 127 FE58
Wells Dr, NW9 118 CR60
Wells Gdns, Dag. RM10 127 FB64
Ilford IG1 124 EL59
Rainham RM13 147 FF65
Wells Ho Rd, NW10 138 CS71
Wellside Cl, Barn. EN5 79 CW42
Wellside Gdns, SW14 off Well La 178 CQ85
Wells Ms, W1 9 K6
Wellsmoor Gdns, Brom. BR1 205 EN97
Wells Pk Rd, SE26 182 DU90
Sch Wells Pk Sch & Training Cen, Chig. IG7 off Lambourne Rd 103 ET49
Wells Path, Hayes UB4 135 BS69
Wells Pl, SW18 180 DC87
Redhill RH1 251 DH130
Westerham TN16 off High St 255 EQ127
Sch Wells Prim Sch, Wdf.Grn. IG8 off Barclay Oval 102 EG49
Wells Ri, NW8 140 DF67
Wells Rd, W12 159 CW75
Bromley BR1 205 EM96
Epsom KT18 216 CN114
Guildford GU4 243 BC131
Wells Sq, WC1 10 A2
Wells St, W1 9 J6
Wellstead Av, N9 100 DW45
Wellstead Rd, E6 145 EN68
Wells Ter, N4 121 DN61
Wellstones, Wat. WD17 75 BV41
Wellstones Yd, Wat. WD17 off Wellstones 75 BV41
Well St, E9 142 DV66
E15 144 EE65
Wells Way, SE5 162 DR79
SW7 17 N5
Wellswood Cl, Hem.H. HP2 41 BP19
Wells Yd S, N7 4 C1
Well Wk, NW3 120 DD63
Well Way, Epsom KT18 232 CN115
Wellwood Cl, Couls. CR5 off The Vale 219 DL114
Wellwood Rd, Ilf. IG3 126 EU60
Welmar Ms, SW4 off Clapham Pk Rd 161 DK84
Welsford St, SE1 22 A9
Welsh Cl, E13 15 L2
Welshpool Ho, E8 off Benjamin Cl 142 DU67
Welshpool St, E8 off Broadway Mkt 142 DV67
Welshside Wk, NW9 off Fryent Gro 118 CS58
Welstead Way, W4 159 CT77
Welsummer Way, Wal.Cr. EN8 67 DX27
Weltje Rd, W6 159 CU78
Welton Rd, SE18 165 ES80
Welwyn Av, Felt. TW14 175 BT86
Welwyn Ct, Hem.H. HP2 40 BM16
WELWYN GARDEN CITY, AL7 & AL8 29 CX09
⇌ Welwyn Garden City 29 CY09
Welwyn Rd, Hert. SG14 30 DG08
Welwyn St, E2 12 F1
Welwyn Way, Hayes UB4 135 BS70
WEMBLEY, HA0 & HA9 118 CL64
⇌ Wembley Central 118 CL64
⊖ Wembley Central 118 CL64
Wembley Commercial Cen, Wem. HA9 117 CK61
★ Wembley Conf Cen, Wem. HA9 118 CM63
Sch Wembley High Sch, Wem. HA9 off East La 117 CJ62
Wembley Hill Rd, Wem. HA9 118 CM64
Sch Wembley Manor Jun & Inf Sch, Wem. HA9 off East La 118 CL62
WEMBLEY PARK, Wem. HA9 118 CM61
⊖ Wembley Park 118 CN62
Wembley Pk Business Cen, Wem. HA9 118 CP62
Wembley Pk Dr, Wem. HA9 118 CM62
Wembley Pt, Wem. HA9 138 CP66
Wembley Rd, Hmptn. TW12 176 CA94
★ Wembley Stadium (under redevelopment), Wem. HA9 118 CN63
⇌ Wembley Stadium 118 CM64
Wembley Way, Wem. HA9 118 CP65
Wemborough Rd, Stan. HA7 95 CJ52
Wembury Ms, N6 off Wembury Rd 121 DH59
Wembury Rd, N6 121 DH59
Wemyss Rd, SE3 164 EF82
Wend, The, Couls. CR5 219 DK114
Croydon CR0 221 DZ111
Wendela Cl, Wok. GU22 227 AZ118
Wendela Ct, Har. HA1 117 CE62
Sch Wendell Pk Prim Sch, W12 off Cobbold Rd 159 CT75
Wendell Rd, W12 159 CT75
Wendle Ct, SW8 161 DL79
Wendley Dr, Add. (New Haw) KT15 211 BF110
Wendling Rd, Sutt. SM1 200 DD102
Wendon St, E3 143 DZ67
Wendover, SE17 21 L10
Wendover Cl, Hayes UB4 136 BY70
St. Albans AL4 off Highview Gdns 43 CJ15
Wendover Dr, N.Mal. KT3 199 CT100
Wendover Gdns, Brwd. CM13 109 GB47
Wendover Pl, Stai. TW18 173 BD92
Wendover Rd, NW10 139 CT68
SE9 164 EK83
Bromley BR2 204 EH97
Slough (Burn.) SL1 130 AH71
Staines TW18 173 BC92
Wendover Way, Bushey WD23 76 CC44
Hornchurch RM12 128 FJ64
Orpington BR6 off Glendower Cres 206 EU100
Welling DA16 186 EU85
Wendron Cl, Wok. GU21 off Shilburn Way 226 AU118
Wendy Cl, Enf. EN1 82 DT44
Wendy Cres, Guil. GU2 242 AU132
Wendy Way, Wem. HA0 138 CL67
Wengeo La, Ware SG12 32 DV05
Wenham Gdns, Brwd. (Hutt.) CM13 off Bannister Dr 109 GC44
Wenham Pl, Hat. AL10 off Wellfield Rd 45 CU17
Wenlack Cl, Uxb. (Denh.) UB9 off Lindsey Rd 114 BG62
Wenlock Ct, N1 5 K10
Wenlock Gdns, NW4 off Rickard Cl 119 CU56
Wenlock Rd, N1 4 G9
Edgware HA8 96 CP52
Wenlock St, N1 5 H10
WENNINGTON, Rain. RM13 148 FK73
Wennington Rd, E3 143 DX68
Rainham RM13 147 FG70
Wensley Av, Wdf.Grn. IG8 102 EF52
Wensley Cl, N11 off Pickering Gdns 98 DG51
SE9 185 EM86
Romford RM5 104 FA50
Wensleydale, Hem.H. HP2 40 BM17
Wensleydale Av, Ilf. IG5 102 EL54
Wensleydale Gdns, Hmptn. TW12 176 CB94
Wensleydale Pas, Hmptn. TW12 196 CA95
Wensleydale Rd, Hmptn. TW12 176 CA93
Wensley Rd, N18 100 DV51
Wensum Way, Rick. WD3 92 BK46
Wentbridge Path, Borwd. WD6 78 CN38
Wentland Cl, SE6 183 ED89
Wentland Rd, SE6 183 ED89
WENTWORTH, Vir.W. GU25 192 AS100
Wentworth Av, N3 98 DA52
Borehamwood (Elstree) WD6 78 CM43
Slough SL2 131 AN68
Wentworth Cl, N3 98 DB52
SE28 146 EX72
Ashford TW15 off Reedsfield Rd 175 BP91
Bromley BR2 off Hillside La 204 EG103
Gravesend DA11 191 GG92
Morden SM4 200 DA101
Orpington BR6 223 ES106
Potters Bar EN6 off Strafford Gate 64 DA31
Surbiton KT6 197 CK103
Watford WD17 75 BT38
Woking (Ripley) GU23 228 BH121
Wentworth Cotts, Brox. EN10 49 DY22
Sch Wentworth Co Jun & Inf Sch, Dart. DA1 off Wentworth Dr 187 FG87
Wentworth Ct, Surb. KT6 off Culsac Rd 198 CL103
Wentworth Cres, SE15 162 DU80
Hayes UB3 155 BR76
Wentworth Dene, Wey. KT13 213 BP106
Wentworth Dr, Dart. DA1 187 FG86
Pinner HA5 115 BU57
Virginia Water GU25 192 AT98
Wentworth Gdns, N13 99 DP49
★ Wentworth Golf Course, Vir.W. GU25 192 AT100
Wentworth Hill, Wem. HA9 118 CM60
Wentworth Ms, E3 13 K3
Wentworth Pk, N3 98 DA52
Wentworth Pl, Grays RM16 170 GD76
Stanmore HA7 off Greenacres Dr 95 CH51
Wentworth Rd, E12 124 EK63
NW11 119 CZ58
Barnet EN5 79 CX41
Croydon CR0 201 DN101
Hertford SG13 32 DQ12
Southall UB2 156 BW77
Wentworth St, E1 11 N7
Wentworth Way, Pnr. HA5 116 BX56
Rainham RM13 147 FH69
South Croydon CR2 220 DU114
Wenvoe Av, Bexh. DA7 167 FB82
Wepham Cl, Hayes UB4 136 BX71
Wernbrook St, SE18 165 EQ79
Werndee Rd, SE25 202 DU98
Werneth Hall Rd, Ilf. IG5 125 EM55
Werrington St, NW1 141 DJ68
Werter Rd, SW15 159 CY84
Wescott Way, Uxb. UB8 134 BJ68
Wesleyan Pl, NW5 off Gordon Ho Rd 121 DH63
Wesley Av, E16 25 N1
NW10 138 CR69
Hertford SG13 off Hale Rd 32 DR10
Hounslow TW3 156 BY82
Wesley Cl, N7 121 DM61
SE17 20 F8
Harrow HA2 116 CC61
Horley RH6 268 DG146
Orpington BR5 206 EW97
Reigate RH2 265 CZ135
Waltham Cross (Chsht) EN7 66 DQ28
Wesley Dr, Egh. TW20 173 BA93
Wesley Hill, Chesh. HP5 54 AP30
Wesley Rd, E10 123 EC59
NW10 138 CQ67
Hayes UB3 135 BU73
★ Wesley's Ho, EC1 11 K3
Wesley Sq, W11 6 C8
Wesley St, W1 8 F6
Wessels, Tad. KT20 233 CX121
Wessex Av, SW19 200 DA96
Wessex Cl, Ilf. IG3 125 ES58
Kingston upon Thames KT1 off Gloucester Rd 198 CP95

⊖ London Underground station   DLR Docklands Light Railway station   Trm Tramlink station   Riv Pedestrian ferry landing stage

Wessex Cl, T.Ditt. KT7 ....197 CF103
Wessex Ct, Wem. HA9
off The Avenue 118 CM61
Wessex Dr, Erith DA8 ....167 FE81
Pinner HA5 ....94 BY52
Wessex Gdns, NW11 ....119 CY60
Sch Wessex Gdns Jun & Inf Schs, NW11
off Wessex Gdns 119 CY60
Wessex La, Grnf. UB6 ....137 CD68
Wessex St, E2 ....12 F2
Wessex Wk, Dart. DA2
off Sandringham Dr 187 FE89
Wessex Way, NW11 ....119 CY59
West 12 Shop Cen, W12 ....16 A3
Westacott, Hayes UB4 ....135 BS71
Westacott Cl, N19 ....121 DK60
West Acres, Amer. HP7 ....55 AR40
Westacres, Esher KT10 ....214 BZ108
WEST ACTON, W3 ....138 CN72
⊖ West Acton 138 CN72
Sch West Acton Prim Sch, W3 off Noel Rd 138 CP72
Westall Cl, Hert. SG13 ....32 DQ10
Westall Ms, Hert. SG13
off West St 32 DQ10
Westall Rd, Loug. IG10 ....85 EP41
Westanley Av, Amer. HP7 ....55 AR39
West App, Orp. BR5 ....205 EQ99
West Arbour St, E1 ....12 G7
Sch West Ashtead Prim Sch, Ashtd. KT21
off Taleworth Rd 232 CL120
West Av, E17 ....123 EB56
N3 ....98 DA51
NW4 ....119 CX57
Hayes UB3 ....135 BT73
High Wycombe (Penn) HP10 ....88 AC46
Pinner HA5 ....116 BZ58
Redhill RH1 ....266 DG140
St. Albans AL2 ....60 CB25
Southall UB1 ....136 BZ73
Wallington SM6 ....219 DL106
Walton-on-Thames (Whiteley Vill.) KT12 ....213 BS109
West Av Rd, E17 ....123 EA56
West Bk, N16 ....122 DS59
Barking IG11
off Highbridge Rd 145 EP67
Dorking RH4 ....263 CF137
Enfield EN2 ....82 DQ40
Westbank Rd, Hmptn. (Hmptn H.) TW12 ....176 CC93
WEST BARNES, N.Mal. KT3 ....199 CU99
West Barnes La, SW20 ....199 CV97
New Malden KT3 ....199 CV97
Westbeech Rd, N22 ....121 DN55
Westbere Dr, Stan. HA7 ....95 CK49
Westbere Rd, NW2 ....119 CY63
Sch Westborough Co Prim Sch, Guil. GU2
off Southway 242 AT133
Westbourne Av, W3 ....138 CR72
Sutton SM3 ....199 CY103
Westbourne Br, W2 ....7 L6
Westbourne Cl, Hayes UB4 ....135 BV70
Westbourne Cres, W2 ....7 N9
Westbourne Cres Ms, W2 ....7 N9
Westbourne Dr, SE23 ....183 DX89
Brentwood CM14 ....108 FT49
Westbourne Gdns, W2 ....7 J7
WESTBOURNE GREEN, W2 ....6 G6
Westbourne Gro, W2 ....6 H8
W11 ....6 F9
Westbourne Gro Ms, W11 ....6 G8
Westbourne Gro Ter, W2 ....7 J7
Westbourne Ms, St.Alb. AL1
off London Rd 43 CD20
⊖ Westbourne Park 6 F5
Westbourne Pk Ms, W2 ....7 J7
Westbourne Pk Pas, W2 ....7 H6
Westbourne Pk Rd, W2 ....7 H6
W11 ....6 D8
Westbourne Pk Vil, W2 ....7 H6
Westbourne Pl, N9
off Eastbournia Av 100 DV48
Sch Westbourne Prim Sch, Sutt. SM1 off Anton Cres 200 DA104
Westbourne Rd, N7 ....4 C4
SE26 ....183 DX93
Bexleyheath DA7 ....166 EY80
Croydon CR0 ....202 DT100
Feltham TW13 ....175 BT90
Staines TW18 ....174 BH94
Uxbridge UB8 ....135 BP70
Westbourne St, W2 ....7 N9
Westbourne Ter, SE23
off Westbourne Dr 183 DX89
W2 ....7 M7
Westbourne Ter Ms, W2 ....7 L7
Westbourne Ter Rd, W2 ....7 L6
Sch Westbridge Prim Sch, SW11 off Westbridge Rd 160 DE81
Westbridge Rd, SW11 ....160 DD81
WEST BROMPTON, SW10 ....160 DB79
⇌ West Brompton 17 H10
⊖ West Brompton 17 H10
Westbrook, Maid. SL6 ....150 AE78
Westbrook Av, Hmptn. TW12 ....176 BZ94
Westbrook Cl, Barn. EN4 ....80 DD41
Westbrook Cres, Barn. EN4 ....80 DD41
Westbrook Dr, Orp. BR5 ....206 EW102
Westbrooke Cres, Well. DA16 ....166 EW83
Westbrooke Rd, Sid. DA15 ....185 ER89
Welling DA16 ....166 EV83
Sch Westbrooke Sch, Well. DA16
off South Gipsy Rd 166 EX83
Sch Westbrook Hay Prep Sch, Hem.H. HP1
off London Rd 39 BD24
Westbrook Rd, SE3 ....164 EH81
Hounslow TW5 ....156 BZ80
Staines TW18 off South St 173 BF92
Thornton Heath CR7 ....202 DR95
Westbrook Sq, Barn. EN4
off Westbrook Cres 80 DD41
West Burrowfield, Welw.G.C. AL7 ....29 CX11
Westbury Av, N22 ....121 DP55
Esher (Clay.) KT10 ....215 CF107
Southall UB1 ....136 CA70
Wembley HA0 ....138 CL66
Westbury Cl, Ruis. HA4 ....115 BU59
Shepperton TW17
off Burchetts Way 195 BP100
Whyteleafe CR3
off Beverley Rd 236 DS116
Westbury Dr, Brwd. CM14 ....108 FV47
Westbury Gro, N12 ....98 DA51
Sch Westbury Ho Sch (Prep), N.Mal. KT3
off Westbury Rd 198 CR99
Westbury La, Buck.H. IG9 ....102 EJ47
Westbury Lo Cl, Pnr. HA5 ....116 BX55
Westbury Par, SW12
off Balham Hill 181 DH86
Westbury Pl, Brent. TW8 ....157 CK79
Westbury Ri, Harl. CM17 ....52 EX16
Westbury Rd, E7 ....124 EH64
E17 ....123 EA56
N11 ....99 DL51
N12 ....98 DA51
SE20 ....203 DX95
W5 ....138 CL72
Barking IG11 ....145 ER67
Beckenham BR3 ....203 DY97
Brentwood CM14 ....108 FW47
Bromley BR1 ....204 EK95
Buckhurst Hill IG9 ....102 EJ47
Croydon CR0 ....202 DR100
Feltham TW13 ....176 BX88
Ilford IG1 ....125 EM61
New Malden KT3 ....198 CR98
Northwood HA6 ....93 BS49
Waltham Cross (Chsht) EN8 off Turners Hill 67 DX30
Watford WD18 ....75 BV43
Wembley HA0 ....138 CL66
Westbury St, SW8 ....161 DJ82
Westbury Ter, E7 ....144 EH65
Upminster RM14 ....129 FS61
Westerham TN16 ....255 EQ127
Westbush Cl, Hodd. EN11 ....33 DZ14
WEST BYFLEET, KT14 ....212 BH113
⇌ West Byfleet 212 BG112
Sch West Byfleet Co Inf Sch, W.Byf. KT14
off Camphill Rd 212 BH112
Sch West Byfleet Co Jun Sch, W.Byf. KT14
off Camphill Rd 212 BH112
Westcar La, Walt. KT12 ....213 BV107
West Carriage Dr, W2 ....17 P2
West Cen St, WC1 ....9 N7
West Cen Av, W10
off Harrow Rd 139 CV69
West Chantry, Har. HA3
off Chantry Rd 94 CB53
Westchester Dr, NW4 ....119 CX55
WEST CLANDON, Guil. GU4 ....244 BH129
Westcliffe Apartments, W2
off Praed St 140 DD71
West Cl, N9 ....100 DT48
Ashford TW15 ....174 BL91
Barnet EN5 ....79 CV43
Barnet (Cockfos.) EN4 ....80 DG42
Greenford UB6 ....136 CC68
Hampton TW12 off Oak Av 176 BY93
Hoddesdon EN11 ....49 EA16
Rainham RM13 ....147 FH70
Wembley HA9 ....118 CM60
Westcombe Av, Croy. CR0 ....201 DL100
Westcombe Ct, SE3
off Westcombe Pk Rd 164 EF80
Westcombe Dr, Barn. EN5 ....80 DA43
Westcombe Hill, SE3 ....164 EG78
SE10 ....25 L10
Westcombe Lo Dr, Hayes UB4 ....135 BR71
⇌ Westcombe Park 25 M10
Westcombe Pk Rd, SE3 ....164 EE79
West Common, Ger.Cr. SL9 ....112 AX57
West Common Cl, Ger.Cr. SL9 ....112 AY57
West Common Rd, Brom. BR2 ....204 EG103
Keston BR2 ....222 EH105
Uxbridge UB8 ....114 BK64
Westcoombe Av, SW20 ....199 CT95
Westcote Ri, Ruis. HA4 ....115 BQ59
Westcote Rd, SW16 ....181 DJ92
WESTCOTT, Dor. RH4 ....262 CC138
Westcott, Welw.G.C. AL7 ....30 DD08
West Cotts, NW6 ....120 DA64
Westcott Av, Grav. (Nthflt) DA11 ....191 GG90
Westcott Cl, N15
off Ermine Rd 122 DT58
Bromley BR1
off Ringmer Way 204 EL99
Croydon (New Adgtn) CR0 off Castle Hill Av 221 EB109
Sch Westcott C of E Aided First Sch, Dor. RH4
off School La 263 CD137
Westcott Cres, W7 ....137 CE72
Westcott Rd, SE17 ....161 DP79
Dorking RH4 ....263 CE137
Westcott St, Dor. (Westc.) RH4 ....262 CB137
Westcott Way, Sutt. SM2 ....217 CW110
WESTCOURT, Grav. DA12 ....191 GL89
West Ct, SE18
off Prince Imperial Rd 165 EM81
Westcourt, Sun. TW16 ....195 BV96
West Ct, Wem. HA0 ....117 CJ61
Coll Westcourt Cen, The, Grav. DA12 off Jubilee Cres 191 GL89
Sch Westcourt Prim Sch, Grav. DA12 off Silver Rd 191 GL89
West Cres, Wind. SL4 ....151 AM81
West Cres Rd, Grav. DA12 ....191 GH86
Westcroft, Slou. SL2 ....131 AP70
Westcroft Cl, NW2 ....119 CY63
Enfield EN3 ....82 DW38
Westcroft Ct, Brox. EN10 ....49 EA19
Westcroft Gdns, Mord. SM4 ....199 CZ97
Westcroft Rd, Cars. SM5 ....218 DG105
Wallington SM6 ....218 DG105
Westcroft Sq, W6 ....159 CU77
Westcroft Way, NW2 ....119 CY63
West Cromwell Rd, SW5 ....16 G8
W14 ....16 E9
West Cross Cen, Brent. TW8 ....157 CG79
West Cross Route, W10 ....6 A9
W11 ....6 A9
West Cross Way, Brent. TW8 ....157 CH79
⇌ West Croydon 202 DQ102
Tram West Croydon 202 DQ102
Westdale Pas, SE18 ....165 EP79
Westdale Rd, SE18 ....165 EP79
Westdean Av, SE12 ....184 EH88
Westdean Cl, SW18 ....180 DB86
West Dene, Sutt. SM3
off Park La 217 CY107
West Dene Dr, Rom. RM3 ....106 FK50
Sch West Dene Sch, Pur. CR8 off Brighton Rd 219 DM114
Westdene Way, Wey. KT13 ....195 BS104
West Down, Lthd. (Bkhm) KT23 ....246 CB127
Westdown Rd, E15 ....123 EC63
SE6 ....183 EA87
WEST DRAYTON, UB7 ....154 BK76
⇌ West Drayton 134 BL74
West Drayton Pk Av, West Dr. UB7 ....154 BL76
Sch West Drayton Prim Sch, West Dr. UB7
off Kingston La 154 BL75
West Drayton Rd, Uxb. UB8 ....134 BM72
Uxbridge (Hayes End) UB8 ....135 BP71
West Dr, SW16 ....181 DJ91
Carshalton SM5 ....218 DD110
Harrow HA3 ....95 CD51
Sutton (Cheam) SM2 ....217 CX109
Tadworth KT20 ....233 CX118
Virginia Water GU25 ....192 AT101
Watford WD25 ....75 BV36
West Dr Gdns, Har. HA3 ....95 CD51
WEST DULWICH, SE21 ....182 DR90
⇌ West Dulwich 182 DR88
⇌ West Ealing 137 CH73
West Eaton Pl, SW1 ....18 E7
West Eaton Pl Ms, SW1 ....18 E7
Wested La, Swan. BR8 ....207 FG101
West Ella Rd, NW10 ....138 CS66
WEST END, Esher KT10 ....214 BZ107
WEST END, Hat. AL9 ....46 DC18
West End Av, E10 ....123 EC57
Pinner HA5 ....116 BX56
West End Cl, NW10 ....138 CQ66
West End Ct, Pnr. HA5 ....116 BX56
Slough (Stoke P.) SL2 ....132 AT67
West End Gdns, Esher KT10 ....214 BZ106
Northolt UB5
off Edward Cl 136 BW68
West End La, NW6 ....140 DA66
Barnet EN5 ....79 CX42
Esher KT10 ....214 BZ107
Hatfield (Essen.) AL9 ....46 DC18
Hayes UB3 ....155 BQ80
Pinner HA5 ....116 BX55
Slough (Stoke P.) SL2 ....132 AS67
West End Rd, Brox. EN10 ....48 DS23
Northolt UB5 ....136 BW66
Ruislip HA4 ....115 BV64
Southall UB1 ....136 BY74
Westerdale, Hem.H. HP2 ....40 BL17
Westerdale Rd, SE10 ....25 L10
Westerfield Rd, N15 ....122 DT57
Westerfolds Cl, Wok. GU22 ....227 BC116
Westergate Rd, SE2 ....166 EY78
WESTERHAM, TN16 ....255 EQ126
Westerham Av, N9 ....100 DR48
Westerham Cl, Add. KT15 ....212 BJ107
Sutton SM2 ....218 DA110
Westerham Dr, Sid. DA15 ....186 EV86
Westerham Hill, West. TN16 ....239 EN121
Westerham Rd, E10 ....123 EB59
Keston BR2 ....222 EK107
Oxted RH8 ....254 EF129
Sevenoaks TN13 ....256 FC123
Westerham TN16 ....255 EM128
Westerham (Brasted) TN16 ....255 ET125
Westerley Cres, SE26 ....183 DZ92
Westerley Ware, Rich. TW9
off Kew Grn 158 CN79
Westermain, Add. (New Haw) KT15 ....212 BJ110
Western Av, NW11 ....119 CX58
W3 ....138 CR71
W5 ....138 CM69
Brentwood CM14 ....108 FW46
Chertsey KT16 ....194 BG97
Dagenham RM10 ....147 FC65
Egham TW20 ....193 BB97
Epping CM16 ....69 ET32
Grays RM20 ....169 FT78
Greenford UB6 ....137 CF69
Northolt UB5 ....136 BZ67
Romford RM2 ....106 FJ54
Ruislip HA4 ....135 BP65
Uxbridge (Denh.) UB9 ....114 BJ63
Uxbridge (Ickhm) UB10 ....135 BP65
Western Av Business Pk, W3
off Mansfield Rd 138 CP70
Western Av Underpass, W5
off Western Av 138 CM69
Western Beach Apartments, E16 ....25 L1
Western Cl, Cher. KT16
off Western Av 194 BG97
Western Ct, N3
off Huntley Dr 98 DA51
Western Cross Cl, Green. DA9 off Johnsons Way 189 FW86
Western Dr, H.Wyc. (Woob.Grn) HP10 ....110 AE58
Shepperton TW17 ....195 BR100
H Western Eye Hosp, NW1 ....8 C5
Western Gdns, W5 ....138 CN73
Brentwood CM14 ....108 FW47
Western Gateway, E16 ....15 L10
H Western Ho Hosp, Ware SG12 ....33 DX05
Sch Western Ho Sch, Slou. SL1 off Brook Path 131 AM73
Western La, SW12 ....180 DG87
Western Ms, W9 ....6 F4
Western Par, Barn. EN5
off Great N Rd 80 DA43
Reigate RH2 off Prices La 266 DA137
Western Pathway, Horn. RM12 ....148 FJ65
Western Perimeter Rd, Houns. (Hthrw Air.) TW6 ....154 BH83
Western Pl, SE16 ....22 F3
Western Rd, E13 ....144 EJ67
E17 ....123 EC57
N2 ....120 DF56
N22 ....99 DM54
NW10 ....138 CQ70
SW9 ....161 DN83
SW19 ....200 DD95
W5 ....137 CK73
Brentwood CM14 ....108 FW47
Epping CM16 ....69 ET32
Mitcham CR4 ....200 DD95
Romford RM1 ....127 FE57
Southall UB2 ....156 BX76
Sutton SM1 ....218 DA106
Waltham Abbey EN9 ....50 EE22
Western Ter, W6
off Chiswick Mall 159 CU78
Western Trd Est, NW10 ....138 CQ70
Western Vw, Hayes UB3 ....155 BT75
Westernville Gdns, Ilf. IG2 ....125 EQ59
Western Way, SE28 ....165 ER76
Barnet EN5 ....98 DA44
WEST EWELL, Epsom KT19 ....216 CS108
Sch West Ewell Inf Sch, Epsom KT19
off Ruxley La 216 CR106
West Fm Av, Ashtd. KT21 ....231 CJ118
West Fm Cl, Ashtd. KT21 ....231 CJ119
West Fm Dr, Ashtd. KT21 ....231 CK119
DLR Westferry 13 N9
Westferry Circ, E14 ....23 N1
Westferry Rd, E14 ....23 M1
WESTFIELD, Wok. GU22 ....227 AZ122
Westfield, Ashtd. KT21 ....232 CM118
Dorking (Abin.Ham.) RH5 ....261 BS143
Harlow CM18 ....51 ES16
Hatfield AL9 ....46 DA23
Loughton IG10 ....84 EJ43
Reigate RH2 ....250 DB131
Sevenoaks TN13 ....257 FJ122
Welwyn Garden City AL7 ....30 DA08
Westfield Av, S.Croy. CR2 ....220 DR113
Watford WD24 ....76 BW37
Woking GU22 ....226 AY121
Westfield Cl, NW9 ....118 CQ55
SW10 ....160 DC80
Enfield EN3 ....83 DY41
Gravesend DA12 ....191 GJ93
Sutton SM1 ....217 CZ105
Waltham Cross EN8 ....67 DZ31
Westfield Common, Wok. GU22 ....226 AY122
Sch Westfield Comm Tech Coll, Wat. WD18 off Tolpits La 75 BT44
Sch Westfield Co Prim Sch, Hodd. EN11
off Westfield Rd 49 DZ16
Westfield Ct, St.Alb. AL4 ....43 CK17
Westfield Dr, Har. HA3 ....117 CK57
Leatherhead (Bkhm) KT23 ....230 CA122
Westfield Gdns, Dor. RH4
off Westcott Rd 263 CG136
Harrow HA3 ....117 CK56
Westfield Gro, Wok. GU22 ....227 AZ120
Westfield La, Har. HA3 ....117 CK56
Slough (Geo.Grn) SL3 ....132 AX73
Westfield Par, Add. (New Haw) KT15 ....212 BK110
Westfield Pk, Pnr. HA5 ....94 BZ52
Westfield Pk Dr, Wdf.Grn. IG8 ....102 EL51
Sch Westfield Prim Sch, Wok. GU22 off Bonsey La 226 AY121
Westfield Rd, NW7 ....96 CR48
W13 ....137 CG74
Beaconsfield HP9 ....88 AJ54
Beckenham BR3 ....203 DZ96
Berkhamsted HP4 ....38 AS17
Bexleyheath DA7 ....167 FC82
Croydon CR0 ....201 DP103
Dagenham RM9 ....126 EY63
Guildford GU1 ....242 AY130
Hertford SG14 ....31 DP07
Hoddesdon EN11 ....49 DZ16
Mitcham CR4 ....200 DF96
Slough SL2 ....131 AP70
Surbiton KT6 ....197 CK99
Sutton SM1 ....217 CZ105
Walton-on-Thames KT12 ....196 BY101
Woking GU22 ....226 AX122
Westfields, SW13 ....159 CT83
St. Albans AL3 ....42 CA22
Westfields Av, SW13 ....158 CS83
Westfields Rd, W3 ....138 CP71
Westfield St, SE18 ....164 EK76
Westfield Wk, Wal.Cr. EN8
off Westfield Cl 67 DZ31
Westfield Way, E1 ....13 J2
Ruislip HA4 ....115 BS62
Woking GU22 ....226 AY122
⊖ West Finchley 98 DB51
West Gdn Pl, W2 ....8 B8
West Gdns, E1 ....12 D10
SW17 ....180 DE93
Epsom KT17 ....216 CS110
West Gate, W5 ....138 CL69
Harlow CM20 ....51 EQ15
Westgate Cl, Epsom KT18
off Chalk La 232 CR115
Sch Westgate Co Prim Sch, Dart. DA1
off Summerhill Rd 188 FK87
Westgate Ct, Wal.Cr. EN8
off Holmesdale 83 DX35
Westgate Cres, Slou. SL1 ....131 AM73
Westgate Ho, Brent. TW8 ....157 CK78
Westgate Retail Pk, Slou. SL1 ....131 AN73
Westgate Rd, SE25 ....202 DV98
Beckenham BR3 ....203 EB96
Dartford DA1 ....188 FK86
Sch Westgate Sec Sch, Slou. SL1 off Cippenham La 131 AN74
Westgate St, E8 ....142 DV67
Westgate Ter, SW10 ....17 K10
Westglade Ct, Har. HA3 ....117 CK57
West Gorse, Croy. CR0 ....221 DY112
WEST GREEN, N15 ....122 DQ55
West Grn Pl, Grnf. UB6
off Uneeda Dr 137 CD67
Sch West Grn Prim Sch, N15
off Woodlands Pk Rd 122 DQ56
West Grn Rd, N15 ....121 DP56
West Gro, SE10 ....163 EC81
Walton-on-Thames KT12 ....213 BV105
Woodford Green IG8 ....102 EJ51
Westgrove La, SE10 ....163 EC81
Sch West Gro Prim Sch, N14
off Chase Rd 99 DK45
West Halkin St, SW1 ....18 E5
West Hallowes, SE9 ....184 EK88
Westhall Pk, Warl. CR6 ....236 DW119
West Hall Rd, Rich. TW9 ....158 CP81
Westhall Rd, Warl. CR6 ....236 DV119
WEST HAM, E15 ....144 EF66
⇌ West Ham 14 G1
⊖ West Ham 15 H1
Sch West Ham Ch Prim Sch, E15 off Portway 144 EF67
West Ham La, E15 ....144 EE66
West Ham Pk, E7 ....144 EG66
WEST HAMPSTEAD, NW6 ....120 DB64
⇌ West Hampstead 140 DA65
⊖ West Hampstead 140 DA65
West Hampstead Ms, NW6 ....140 DB65
⇌ West Hampstead (Thameslink) 140 DA65
★ West Ham United FC, E13 ....144 EJ68
West Harding St, EC4 ....10 D7
West Harold, Swan. BR8 ....207 FD97
WEST HARROW, Har. HA1 ....116 CC59
⊖ West Harrow 116 CC58
Sch West Hatch High Sch, Chig. IG7 off High Rd 103 EM50
West Hatch Manor, Ruis. HA4 ....115 BT60
Westhay Gdns, SW14 ....178 CP85
WEST HEATH, SE2 ....166 EX79
West Heath, Oxt. RH8 ....254 EG130
West Heath Av, NW11 ....120 DA60
West Heath Cl, NW3 ....120 DA62
Dartford DA1
off West Heath Rd 187 FF86
West Heath Dr, NW11 ....120 DA60
West Heath Gdns, NW3 ....120 DA62
West Heath La, Sev. TN13 ....257 FH128
West Heath Rd, NW3 ....120 DA61
SE2 ....166 EX79
Dartford DA1 ....187 FF86
WEST HENDON, NW9 ....118 CS59
West Hendon Bdy, NW9 ....119 CT58
Coll West Herts Coll, Cassio Campus, Wat. WD17
off Langley Rd 75 BU38
Dacorum Campus, Hem.H. HP1 off Marlowes 40 BJ19
Leggatts Campus, Wat. WD24 off Leggatts Way 75 BU36
Park Av Campus, Bushey WD23 ....76 BX41
Sch of Art and Design, Wat. WD24 off Ridge St 75 BV38
Watford Campus, Wat. WD17 off Hempstead Rd 75 BU41
West Herts Management Cen, Kings L. WD4
off Bucks Hill 74 BK35
William St Annexe, Bushey WD23 ....76 BX41
West Hill, SW15 ....179 CX87
SW18 ....180 DA85
Dartford DA1 ....188 FK86
Epsom KT19 ....216 CQ113
Harrow HA2 ....117 CE61
Orpington BR6 ....223 EM112
Oxted RH8 ....253 ED130
South Croydon CR2 ....220 DS110
West Hill, Wem. HA9 ....118 CM60
West Hill Av, Epsom KT19 ....216 CQ112
West Hill Bk, Oxt. RH8 ....253 ED130
Westhill Cl, Grav. DA12
off Leith Pk Rd 191 GH88
Sch West Hill Co Prim Sch, Dart. DA1 off Dartford Rd 188 FJ86
West Hill Ct, N6 ....120 DG62
West Hill Dr, Dart. DA1 ....188 FJ86
West Hill Pk, N6
off Merton La 120 DF61
Sch West Hill Prim Sch, SW18
off Merton Rd 180 DA85
West Hill Ri, Dart. DA1 ....188 FK86
West Hill Rd, SW18 ....180 DA86
Westhill Rd, Hodd. EN11 ....49 DZ16
West Hill Rd, Wok. GU22 ....226 AX119
Sch West Hill Sch, Lthd. KT22
off Kingston Rd 231 CG118
West Hill Way, N20 ....98 DB46
Westholm, NW11 ....120 DB56
West Holme, Erith DA8 ....167 FC81
Westholme, Orp. BR6 ....205 ES101
Westholme Gdns, Ruis. HA4 ....115 BU60
Westhorne Av, SE9 ....184 EJ86
SE12 ....184 EG87
Westhorpe Gdns, NW4 ....119 CW55
Westhorpe Rd, SW15 ....159 CW83
WEST HORSLEY, Lthd. KT24 ....245 BP127
West Ho Cl, SW19 ....179 CY88
WESTHUMBLE, Dor. RH5 ....247 CG131
Westhumble St, Dor. (Westh.) RH5 ....247 CH131
Westhurst Dr, Chis. BR7 ....185 EP92
West Hyde La, Ger.Cr. (Chal.St.P.) SL9 ....91 AZ52
West India Av, E14 ....23 N1
West India Dock Rd, E14 ....13 M8
DLR West India Quay 14 A10
⊖ West Kensington 16 E9
West Kent Av, Grav. (Nthflt) DA11 ....190 GC86
West Kent Cold Storage, Sev. (Dunt.Grn) TN14 ....241 FF120
WEST KILBURN, W9 ....6 E1
Westlake Cl, N13 ....99 DN48
Hayes UB4 off Lochan Cl 136 BY70
Westlake Rd, Wem. HA9 ....117 CK61
Westland Av, Horn. RM11 ....128 FL60
Westland Cl, Stai. (Stanw.) TW19 ....174 BL86
Watford (Lvsdn) WD25 ....59 BT34
Westland Dr, Brom. BR2 ....204 EF103
Hatfield AL9 ....63 CY27
Westland Ho, E16
off Rymill St 145 EN74
Westland Pl, N1 ....11 J1
Westland Rd, Wat. WD17 ....75 BV40
Westlands Av, Slou. SL1 ....130 AJ72
Westlands Cl, Hayes UB3
off Granville Rd 155 BU77
Slough SL1
off Westlands Av 130 AJ72
Westlands Ct, Epsom KT18 ....232 CQ115
Westlands Ter, SW12
off Gaskarth Rd 181 DJ86
Westlands Way, Oxt. RH8 ....253 ED127
West La, SE16 ....22 C4
Dorking (Abin.Ham.) RH5 ....262 BX139
Westlea Av, Wat. WD25 ....76 BY37
Westlea Cl, Brox. EN10 ....49 DZ24
Westlea Rd, W7 ....157 CG76
Broxbourne EN10 ....49 DZ23
Westleas, Horl. RH6 ....268 DE146
Sch West Lea Sch, N9
off Haselbury Rd 100 DS48
Westlees Cl, Dor. (N.Holm.) RH5 off Wildcroft Dr 263 CK139
Westleigh Av, SW15 ....179 CV85
Coulsdon CR5 ....234 DG116
Westleigh Dr, Brom. BR1 ....204 EL95
Westleigh Gdns, Edg. HA8 ....96 CN53
Westlinks, Wem. HA0
off Alperton La 137 CK69
Westlinton Cl, NW7 ....97 CY51
West Lo Av, W3 ....138 CN74
Sch West Lo First Sch, Pnr. HA5 off West End La 116 BX56
Sch West Lo Mid Sch, Pnr. HA5 off West End La 116 BX56
Sch West Lo Sch Ltd, Sid. DA15 off Station Rd 186 EU90
Sch West London Acad, The, Nthlt. UB5
off Bengarth Rd 136 BY67
Coll West London Coll, W1 ....8 F8
Westlyn Cl, Rain. RM13 ....148 FJ69
Westly Wd, Welw.G.C. AL7 ....30 DA08
Westmacott Dr, Felt. TW14 ....175 BT88
West Mall, W8 ....17 H1
West Malling Way, Horn. RM12 ....128 FJ64
Westmark Pt, SW15
off Norley Vale 179 CV88
Westmead, SW15 ....179 CV86
West Mead, Epsom KT19 ....216 CS107
Ruislip HA4 ....116 BW63
Welwyn Garden City AL7 ....30 DB12
Westmead, Wind. SL4 ....151 AP83
Woking GU21 ....226 AV117
Westmead Cor, Cars. SM5
off Colston Av 218 DE105
Westmead Dr, Red. RH1 ....266 DG142
Westmeade Cl, Wal.Cr. (Chsht) EN7 ....66 DV29
Westmead Rd, Sutt. SM1 ....218 DD105
West Meads, Guil. GU2 ....258 AT135
Horley RH6 ....269 DJ148
Westmede, Chig. IG7 ....103 EQ51
Westmere Dr, NW7 ....96 CR48
West Mersea Cl, E16 ....25 N2
West Ms, N17 ....100 DV51
SW1 ....19 H8
H West Middlesex Uni Hosp, Islw. TW7 ....157 CG82
West Mill, Grav. DA11 ....191 GF86
Westmill Ct, N4
off Brownswood Rd 122 DQ61
WESTMINSTER, SW1 ....19 J5
⊖ Westminster 19 P4
★ Westminster Abbey, SW1 ....19 N5
Sch Westminster Abbey Choir Sch, SW1 ....19 M5
★ Westminster Abbey Mus, SW1 ....19 N5
Coll Westminster Adult Ed Service, Amberley Rd Cen, W9 ....7 J4
Frith St Cen, W1 ....141 DK72
Westminster Av, Th.Hth. CR7 ....201 DP96
Westminster Br, SE1 ....19 P4
SW1 ....19 P4
Westminster Br Rd, SE1 ....20 B4
★ Westminster Cath, SW1 ....19 J6
Sch Westminster Cath Choir Sch, SW1 ....19 K6
Sch Westminster Cath RC Prim Sch, SW1 ....19 M9
Sch Westminster City C of E Sch, SW1 ....19 K5
★ Westminster City Hall, SW1 ....19 K5
Westminster Cl, Felt. TW14 ....175 BU88

★ Place of interest | H Hospital | Sch School | Coll College | Uni University | ⇌ Railway station

Westminster Cl, Ilf. IG6 103 ER54
Teddington TW11 177 CG92
St.Alb. AL1 42 CC22
Westminster Dr, N13 99 DL50
Westminster Gdns, E4 102 EE46
SW1 19 N7
Barking IG11 145 ES68
Ilford IG6 103 EQ54
[Coll] Westminster Kingsway Coll, Battersea Pk Cen, SW11
off Battersea Pk Rd 160 DG81
Castle La Cen, SW1 19 K5
Gray's Inn Cen, WC1 10 A2
Kentish Town Cen, NW5
off Holmes Rd 141 DH65
Lucas-Tooth Gymnasium, WC1 10 A2
Peter St Cen, W1 9 L9
Regent's Park Cen, NW1 9 J3
Vincent Sq Cen, SW1 19 L7
★ Westminster Millennium Pier, SW1 19 P3
[Riv] Westminster Millennium Pier 19 P3
Westminster Rd, N9 100 DV46
W7 137 CE74
Sutton SM1 200 DD103
[Sch] Westminster Sch, SW1 19 N5
[Sch] Westminster Under Sch, SW1 19 L8
Westmoat Cl, Beck. BR3 183 EC94
WEST MOLESEY, KT8 196 BZ99
[H] West Molesey Hosp, W.Mol. KT8 196 CA99
Westmoor Rd, Esher KT10 197 CE103
Westmoor Gdns, Enf. EN3 83 DX40
Westmoor Rd, Enf. EN3 83 DX40
Westmoor St, SE7 164 EJ76
Westmore Grn, West. (Tats.) TN16 238 EJ121
Westmoreland Av, Horn. RM11 128 FJ57
Welling DA16 165 ES83
Westmoreland Bldgs, EC1 off Bartholomew Cl 142 DQ71
Westmoreland Dr, Sutt. SM2 218 DB109
Westmoreland Pl, SW1 19 H10
W5 137 CK71
Bromley BR1 204 EG97
Westmoreland Rd, NW9 118 CN56
SE17 162 DQ79
SW13 159 CT81
Bromley BR1, BR2 204 EE99
Westmoreland St, W1 8 F6
Westmoreland Ter, SW1 19 H10
Westmoreland Wk, SE17 162 DR79
Westmore Rd, West. (Tats.) TN16 238 EJ121
Westmorland Cl, E12 124 EK61
Epsom KT19 216 CS110
Twickenham TW1 177 CH86
Westmorland Rd, E17 123 EA58
Harrow HA1 116 CB57
Westmorland Sq, Mitch. CR4 off Westmorland Way 201 DL99
Westmorland Ter, SE20 182 DV94
Westmorland Way, Mitch. CR4 201 DK98
West Mt, Guil. GU2 off The Mount 258 AW136
Westmount Av, Amer. HP7 55 AQ39
Westmount Rd, SE9 165 EM82
WEST NORWOOD, SE27 182 DQ90
⇌ West Norwood 181 DP90
West Oak, Beck. BR3 203 ED95
Westoe Rd, N9 100 DV47
Weston Av, Add. KT15 212 BG105
Grays RM20 169 FT77
Thames Ditton KT7 197 CE101
West Molesey KT8 196 BY97
Weston Cl, Brwd. (Hutt.) CM13 109 GC45
Coulsdon CR5 235 DM120
Godalming GU7 258 AS144
Potters Bar EN6 63 CZ32
Weston Ct, N4 off Queens Dr 122 DQ62
N20 off Farnham Cl 98 DC45
Weston Dr, Cat. CR3 off Coulsdon Rd 236 DQ122
Stanmore HA7 95 CH53
West One Shop Cen, W1 8 F8
Westonfields, Guil. (Albury) GU5 260 BJ139
Weston Gdns, Islw. TW7 157 CD81
Woking GU22 227 BE116
WESTON GREEN, T.Ditt. KT7 197 CF102
Weston Grn, Dag. RM9 126 EZ63
Thames Ditton KT7 197 CE102
Weston Grn Rd, Esher KT10 197 CD102
Thames Ditton KT7 197 CE102
Weston Gro, Brom. BR1 204 EF95
Weston Lea, Lthd. (W.Hors.) KT24 245 BR125
Weston Pk, N8 121 DL58
Kingston upon Thames KT1 off Fairfield W 198 CL96
Thames Ditton KT7 197 CE102
Weston Pk Cl, T.Ditt. KT7 off Weston Pk 197 CE102
[Sch] Weston Pk Prim Sch, N8 off Denton Rd 121 DM57
Weston Ri, WC1 4 B10
Weston Rd, W4 158 CQ76
Bromley BR1 184 EF94
Dagenham RM9 126 EY63
Enfield EN2 82 DR39
Epsom KT17 216 CS111
Guildford GU2 242 AV133
Slough SL1 131 AM71
Thames Ditton KT7 197 CE102
Weston St, SE1 21 K5
Weston Wk, E8 off Mare St 142 DV66
Weston Way, Wok. GU22 227 BE116
Weston Yd, Guil. (Albury) GU5 260 BJ139
Westover Cl, Sutt. SM2 218 DB109
Westover Hill, NW3 120 DA61
Westover Rd, SW18 180 DC86
Westow Hill, SE19 182 DS93
Westow St, SE19 182 DS93
West Palace Gdns, Wey. KT13 195 BP104
West Pk, SE9 184 EL89
West Pk Av, Rich. TW9 158 CN81
West Pk Cl, Houns. TW5 off Heston Gra La 156 BZ79
Romford RM6 126 EX57
West Pk Hill, Brwd. CM14 108 FU48
[H] West Pk Hosp, Epsom KT19 216 CM112
West Pk Rd, Epsom KT19 216 CM112
Richmond TW9 158 CN81
Southall UB2 136 CC74
West Parkside, SE10 25 K6
Warlingham CR6 237 EA115
West Pier, E1 22 C2
West Pl, SW19 179 CW92
West Pt, Slou. SL1 131 AK74
Westpoint Trd Est, W3 138 CP71
Westpole Av, Barn. EN4 80 DG42
Westport Rd, E13 15 N4
Westport St, E1 13 H7
West Poultry Av, EC1 10 E6
West Quarters, W12 139 CU72
West Quay Dr, Hayes UB4 136 BY71
West Ramp, Houns. (Hthrw Air.) TW6 154 BN81
Westray, Hem.H. HP3 41 BQ22
Westridge Cl, Hem.H. HP1 39 BF20
West Ridge Gdns, Grnf. UB6 136 CC68
West Riding, St.Alb. (Brick.Wd) AL2 60 BZ30
West Rd, E15 144 EF67
N17 100 DV51
SW3 18 D10
SW4 181 DK85
W5 138 CL71
Barnet EN4 98 DG46
Berkhamsted HP4 38 AU18
Chessington KT9 215 CJ112
Feltham TW14 175 BR86
Guildford GU1 258 AY135
Harlow CM20 36 EU11
Kingston upon Thames KT2 198 CQ95
Reigate RH2 266 DB135
Romford (Chad.Hth) RM6 126 EX58
Romford (Rush Grn) RM7 127 FD59
South Ockendon RM15 149 FV69
West Drayton UB7 154 BM76
Weybridge KT13 213 BP109
Westrow, SW15 179 CW85
West Row, W10 6 C3
Westrow Dr, Bark. IG11 145 ET65
Westrow Gdns, Ilf. IG3 125 ET61
⇌ West Ruislip 115 BQ61
⊖ West Ruislip 115 BQ61
West Shaw, Long. DA3 209 FX96
West Sheen Vale, Rich. TW9 158 CM84
Westside, NW4 97 CV54
West Side, Brox. EN10 off High Rd Turnford 67 DY25
West Side Common, SW19 179 CW92
West Smithfield, EC1 10 E6
West Spur Rd, Uxb. UB8 134 BK69
West Sq, SE11 20 E6
Harlow CM20 35 EQ14
Iver SL0 off High St 133 BF72
West St, E2 142 DV68
E11 124 EE62
E17 off Grove Rd 123 EB57
WC2 9 M8
Bexleyheath DA7 166 EZ84
Brentford TW8 157 CJ79
Bromley BR1 204 EG95
Carshalton SM5 200 DF104
Croydon CR0 220 DQ105
Dorking RH4 263 CG136
Epsom KT18 216 CR113
Epsom (Ewell) KT17 216 CS110
Erith DA8 167 FD77
Gravesend DA11 191 GG86
Grays RM17 170 GA79
Harrow HA1 117 CD60
Hertford SG13 32 DQ10
Reigate RH2 249 CY133
Sutton SM1 218 DB106
Ware SG12 33 DX06
Watford WD17 75 BV40
Woking GU21 off Church St E 227 AZ117
West St La, Cars. SM5 218 DF105
⇌ West Sutton 218 DA105
West Temple Sheen, SW14 158 CP84
West Tenter St, E1 11 P8
[Coll] West Thames Coll, Islw. TW7 off London Rd 157 CE81
West Thamesmead Business Pk, SE28 165 ET76
[Sch] West Thornton Prim Sch, Croy. CR0 off Rosecourt Rd 201 DM100
WEST THURROCK, Grays RM20 169 FU78
[Sch] West Thurrock Prim Sch, Grays RM20 off The Rookery 169 FU79
West Thurrock Way, Grays RM20 169 FT77
WEST TILBURY, Til. RM18 171 GL79
West Twrs, Pnr. HA5 116 BX58
[Sch] West Twyford Prim Sch, NW10 off Twyford Abbey Rd 138 CN68
Westvale Ms, W3 138 CS74
West Valley Rd, Hem.H. HP3 58 BJ25
West Vw, NW4 119 CW56
Chesham HP5 54 AR29
Feltham TW14 175 BQ87
Hatfield AL10 45 CU16
Loughton IG10 85 EM41
West Vw Av, Whyt. CR3 off Station Rd 236 DU118
Westview Cl, NW10 119 CT64
W7 137 CE72
W10 139 CW72
Rainham RM13 148 FJ69
Redhill RH1 266 DE136
West Vw Ct, Borwd. (Elstree) WD6 off High St 77 CK44
Westview Cres, N9 100 DS45
Westview Dr, Wdf.Grn. IG8 102 EK54
West Vw Gdns, Borwd. (Elstree) WD6 off High St 77 CK44
Westview Ri, Hem.H. HP2 40 BK19
West Vw Rd, Dart. DA1 188 FM86
St. Albans AL3 43 CD19
Swanley BR8 207 FG98
Swanley (Crock.) BR8 207 FD100
Westview Rd, Warl. CR6 236 DV119
Westville Rd, W12 159 CU75
Thames Ditton KT7 197 CG102
West Wk, W5 138 CL71
Barnet EN4 98 DG45
Harlow CM20 35 EQ14
Hayes UB3 135 BU74
West Walkway, The, Sutt. SM1 off Cheam Rd 218 DB106
Westward Ho, Guil. GU1 243 AZ132
[Sch] Westward Prep Sch, Walt. KT12 off Hersham Rd 195 BV103
Westward Rd, E4 101 DZ50
Westward Way, Har. HA3 118 CL58
West Warwick Pl, SW1 19 J8
WEST WATFORD, Wat. WD18 75 BU42
West Way, N18 100 DR49
NW10 118 CR62
Westway, SW20 199 CV97
W2 6 G5
W9 6 G5
W10 6 D7
W12 139 CU73
West Way, Beac. HP9 89 AF54
Brentwood CM14 108 FU48
Carshalton SM5 218 DD110
Westway, Cat. CR3 236 DR122
West Way, Croy. CR0 203 DY103
Edgware HA8 96 CP51
Westway, Gat. RH6 269 DH152
Guildford GU2 242 AT132
West Way, Houns. TW5 156 BZ81
Westway, Orp. BR5 205 ER99
West Way, Pnr. HA5 116 BX56
Rickmansworth WD3 92 BH46
Ruislip HA4 115 BT60
Shepperton TW17 195 BR100
West Way, W.Wick. BR4 203 ED100
Westway Cl, SW20 199 CV97
Westway Cross Shop Pk, Grnf. UB6 137 CE67
West Way Gdns, Croy. CR0 203 DX103
Westway Gdns, Red. RH1 250 DG131
Westways, Epsom KT19 217 CT105
Westerham TN16 255 EQ126
Westwell Cl, Orp. BR5 206 EX102
Westwell Rd, SW16 181 DL93
Westwell Rd App, SW16 off Westwell Rd 181 DL93
Westwick Cl, Hem.H. HP2 41 BR21
Westwick Gdns, W14 16 A4
Hounslow TW4 155 BV82
WEST WICKHAM, BR4 203 EC103
⇌ West Wickham 203 EC101
Westwick Pl, Wat. WD25 60 BW34
Westwick Row, Hem.H. HP2 41 BR20
[Sch] West Wimbledon Prim Sch, SW20 off West Barnes La 199 CV97
Westwood Av, SE19 202 DQ95
Addlestone (Wdhm) KT15 211 BF112
Brentwood CM14 108 FU49
Harrow HA2 116 CB63
Westwood Cl, Amer. HP6 72 AX39
Bromley BR1 204 EK97
Esher KT10 196 CC104
Potters Bar EN6 64 DA30
Ruislip HA4 115 BP58
Westwood Ct, Guil. GU2 off Hillcrest Rd 242 AT133
Westwood Dr, Amer. HP6 72 AX39
Westwood Gdns, SW13 159 CT83
[Sch] Westwood Girls' High Sch, SE19 off Spurgeon Rd 182 DR94
Westwood Hill, SE26 182 DU92
[Sch] Westwood Inf Sch, Well. DA16 off Northumberland Av 165 ES84
[Sch] Westwood Jun Sch, Well. DA16 off The Grove 165 ES84
Westwood La, Sid. DA15 186 EU85
Welling DA16 165 ET83
Westwood Pk, SE23 182 DV87
[Sch] Westwood Pk Co Prim Sch, Guil. GU2 off Southway 242 AS134
Westwood Pl, SE26 182 DU91
Westwood Rd, E16 25 N2
SW13 159 CT83
Coulsdon CR5 235 DK118
Gravesend (Sthflt) DA13 190 FY93
Ilford IG3 125 ET60
[Sch] Westwood Sec Sch, Well. DA16 off The Green 165 ES84
West Woodside, Bex. DA5 186 EY87
Westwood Way, Sev. TN13 256 FF122
West World, W5 138 CL69
West Yoke, Sev. (Ash) TN15 209 FX103
Wetheral Dr, Stan. HA7 95 CH53
Wetherby Cl, Nthlt. UB5 136 CB65
Wetherby Gdns, SW5 17 L8
Wetherby Ms, SW5 17 J9
Wetherby Pl, SW7 17 L8
Wetherby Rd, Borwd. WD6 78 CL39
Enfield EN2 82 DQ39
Wetherby Way, Chess. KT9 216 CL108
Wetherden St, E17 123 DZ59
Wethered Dr, Slou. (Burn.) SL1 130 AH71
Wetherell Rd, E9 143 DX67
Wetherill Rd, N10 98 DG53
Wetherly Cl, Harl. CM17 off Moor Hall Rd 36 EZ11
★ Wetland Cen, The, SW13 159 CV80
Wettern Cl, S.Croy. CR2 off Purley Oaks Rd 220 DS110
Wetton Pl, Egh. TW20 173 AZ92
Wexfenne Gdns, Wok. GU22 228 BH116
Wexford Rd, SW12 180 DF87
[Sch] Wexham Ct Prim Sch, Slou. SL3 off Church La 132 AW71
[H] Wexham Pk Hosp, Slou. SL2 132 AW70
Wexham Pk La, Slou. (Wexham) SL3 132 AW70
Wexham Pl, Slou. (Wexham) SL2 132 AX65
Wexham Rd, Slou. SL1, SL2 132 AV71
[Sch] Wexham Sch, Slou. SL2 off Norway Dr 132 AW71
Wexham Springs, Slou. SL2 off Framewood Rd 132 AW66
WEXHAM STREET, Slou. SL3 132 AW67
Wexham St, Slou. (Wexham) SL2, SL3 132 AW67
Wexham Wds, Slou. (Wexham) SL3 132 AW71
Wey Av, Cher. KT16 194 BG97
Weybank, Wok. (Wisley) GU23 228 BL116
Wey Barton, W.Byf. (Byfleet) KT14 212 BM113
Weybourne Pl, S.Croy. CR2 220 DR110
Weybourne St, SW18 180 DC89
WEYBRIDGE, KT13 212 BN105
⇌ Weybridge 212 BN107
Weybridge Business Pk, Add. KT15 212 BL105
Weybridge Ct, SE16 22 B10
[H] Weybridge Hosp, Wey. KT13 212 BN105
Weybridge Pk, Wey. KT13 213 BP106
Weybridge Pt, SW11 160 DG82
Weybridge Rd, Add. KT15 194 BK104
Thornton Heath CR7 201 DN98
Weybridge KT13 194 BL104
Weybridge Trd Est, Add. KT15 212 BL105
Weybrook Dr, Guil. GU4 243 BB129
Wey Cl, W.Byf. KT14 off Broadoaks Cres 212 BH113
Wey Ct, Add. (New Haw) KT15 212 BK109
Epsom KT19 216 CQ105
Weydown Cl, SW19 179 CY88
Guildford GU2 242 AU129
Weydown La, Guil. GU2 off Cumberland Av 242 AU129
[Sch] Weyfield Prim Sch, Guil. GU1 off School Cl 242 AX131
Weyhill Rd, E1 12 B7
[Sch] Wey Ho Sch, Guil. GU5 off Horsham Rd 258 AY143
Weylands Cl, Walt. KT12 196 BZ102
Weylands Pk, Wey. KT13 213 BR107
Wey La, Chesh. HP5 54 AP32
Weylea Av, Guil. GU4 243 BA131
Weylond Rd, Dag. RM8 126 EZ62
Wey Manor Rd, Add. (New Haw) KT15 212 BK109
Weyman Rd, SE3 164 EJ81
Weymead Cl, Cher. KT16 194 BJ102
Wey Meadows, Wey. KT13 212 BL106
Weymede, W.Byf. (Byfleet) KT14 212 BM112
Weymouth Av, NW7 96 CS50
W5 157 CJ76
Weymouth Cl, E6 off Covelees Wall 145 EP72
Weymouth Ct, Sutt. SM2 218 DA108
Weymouth Ms, W1 8 G5
Weymouth Rd, Hayes UB4 135 BS69
Weymouth St, W1 8 F6
Hemel Hempstead HP3 40 BK24
Weymouth Ter, E2 5 P9
Weymouth Wk, Stan. HA7 95 CG51
Wey Rd, Wey. KT13 194 BM104
Weyside Cl, W.Byf. (Byfleet) KT14 212 BM112
Weyside Gdns, Guil. GU1 242 AV132
Weyside Rd, Guil. GU1 242 AV132
Weystone Rd, Add. KT15 off Weybridge Rd 212 BM105
Weyver Ct, St.Alb. AL1 off Avenue Rd 43 CE19
Weyview Cl, Guil. GU1 242 AW132
Wey Vw Ct, Guil. GU1 off Walnut Tree Cl 258 AW135
Whadcote St, N4 off Seven Sisters Rd 121 DN61
Whalebone Av, Rom. RM6 126 EZ58
Whalebone Ct, EC2 11 K7
Whalebone Gro, Rom. RM6 126 EZ58
Whalebone La, E15 off West Ham La 144 EE66
Whalebone La N, Rom. RM6 126 EY57
Whalebone La S, Dag. RM8 126 EZ59
Romford RM6 126 EZ59
Whaley Rd, Pot.B. EN6 64 DC33
Wharfdale Cl, N11 off Ribblesdale Av 98 DG51
Wharfdale Ct, E5 off Rushmore Rd 123 DX63
Wharfdale Rd, N1 141 DL68
Wharfedale, Hem.H. HP2 40 BL17
Wharfedale Gdns, Th.Hth. CR7 201 DM98
Wharfedale Rd, Dart. DA2 188 FQ88
Wharfedale St, SW10 17 J10
Wharf La, Rick. WD3 92 BL46
Twickenham TW1 177 CG88
Woking (Ripley) GU23 228 BJ118
Woking (Send) GU23 227 BC123
Wharf Pl, E2 142 DU67
Wharf Rd, E15 143 ED67
N1 4 G9
Brentwood CM14 108 FW48
Broxbourne EN10 49 DZ23
Enfield EN3 83 DY44
Gravesend DA12 191 GL86
Grays RM17 170 FZ79
Guildford GU1 242 AW134
Hemel Hempstead HP1 40 BH22
Staines (Wrays.) TW19 172 AW87
Wharf Rd S, Grays RM17 170 FZ79
Wharfside Cl, Erith DA8 167 FF78
Wharfside Rd, E16 14 G6
Wharf St, E16 14 G6
[Sch] Wharf Study Cen, SW6 off Fulham High St 159 CY82
Wharley Hook, Harl. CM18 51 ET18
Wharncliffe Dr, Sthl. UB1 137 CD74
Wharncliffe Gdns, SE25 202 DS96
Wharncliffe Rd, SE25 202 DS96
Wharton Cl, NW10 138 CS65
Wharton Cotts, WC1 off Wharton St 141 DM69
Wharton Rd, Brom. BR1 204 EH95
Wharton St, WC1 10 B2
Whateley Cl, Guil. GU2 off Grange Rd 242 AV129
Whateley Rd, SE20 183 DX94
SE22 182 DT85
Guildford GU2 242 AV129
Whatley Av, SW20 199 CY97
Whatman Rd, SE23 183 DX87
Whatmore Cl, Stai. TW19 174 BG86
Wheatash Rd, Add. KT15 194 BH103
Wheatbarn, Welw.G.C. AL7 30 DB08
Wheatbutts, The, Wind. (Eton Wick) SL4 151 AM77
Wheat Cl, St.Alb. (Sand.) AL4 43 CG16
Wheatcroft, Wal.Cr. (Chsht) EN7 66 DV28
[Sch] Wheatcroft JMI Sch, Hert. SG13 off Stanstead Rd 32 DU08
Wheatfield, Hat. AL10 off Crop Common 45 CV17
Hemel Hempstead HP2 40 BK18
Wheatfields, E6 off Oxleas 145 EP72
Enfield EN3 83 DY40
Harlow CM17 36 EW09
[Sch] Wheatfields Inf Sch, St.Alb. AL4 off Downes Rd 43 CH16
[Sch] Wheatfields Jun Sch, St.Alb. AL4 off Downes Rd 43 CH16
Wheatfield Way, Horl. RH6 269 DH147
Kingston upon Thames KT1 198 CL96
WHEATHAMPSTEAD, St.Alb. AL4 28 CL06
Wheathill Rd, SE20 202 DV97
Wheat Knoll, Ken. CR8 236 DQ116
Wheatlands, Houns. TW5 156 CA79
Wheatlands Rd, SW17 off Stapleton Rd 180 DG90
Slough SL3 152 AW76
Wheatley Cl, NW4 97 CU54
Greenhithe DA9 off Steele Av 189 FU85
Hornchurch RM11 128 FK57
Sawbridgeworth CM21 36 EW06
Welwyn Garden City AL7 30 DA11
Wheatley Cres, Hayes UB3 135 BU73
Wheatley Dr, Wat. WD25 60 BW34
Wheatley Gdns, N9 100 DS47
Wheatley Ho, SW15 off Tangley Gro 179 CU87
Wheatley Rd, Islw. TW7 157 CF83
Welwyn Garden City AL7 29 CZ10
Wheat Leys, St.Alb. AL4 43 CJ18
Wheatley's Ait, Sun. TW16 195 BU99
Wheatley St, W1 8 F6
Wheatley Ter Rd, Erith DA8 167 FF79
Wheatley Way, Ger.Cr. (Chal.St.P.) SL9 90 AY51
Wheat Sheaf Cl, E14 24 A7
Wheatsheaf Cl, Cher. (Ott.) KT16 211 BD107
Northolt UB5 116 BY64
Woking GU21 226 AY116
Wheatsheaf Hill, Sev. (Halst.) TN14 224 EZ109
Wheatsheaf La, SW6 159 CW80
SW8 161 DL80
Staines TW18 173 BF94
Wheatsheaf Rd, Rom. RM1 127 FF58
Ware SG12 34 EK06
Wheatsheaf Ter, SW6 159 CZ80
Wheatstone Cl, Mitch. CR4 200 DE95
Slough SL3 off Upton Ct Rd 152 AU76
Wheatstone Rd, W10 6 D5
Wheeler Av, H.Wyc. (Penn) HP10 88 AC47
Oxted RH8 253 ED129
Wheeler Cl, Wdf.Grn. IG8 off Chigwell Rd 103 EM50
Wheeler Gdns, N1 off Outram Pl 141 DL67
Wheelers, Epp. CM16 69 ET29
Wheelers Cl, Wal.Abb. EN9 50 EE22
Wheelers Cross, Bark. IG11 145 ER68
Wheelers Dr, Ruis. HA4 off Wallington Cl 115 BQ58
Wheelers Fm Gdns, Epp. (N.Wld Bas.) CM16 71 FB26
Wheelers La, Bet. (Brock.) RH3 264 CP136
Epsom KT18 216 CP113
Hemel Hempstead HP3 40 BL22
Horley (Smallfield) RH6 269 DN149
Wheelers Orchard, Ger.Cr. (Chal.St.P.) SL9 90 AY51
Wheel Fm Dr, Dag. RM10 127 FC62
Wheelock Cl, Erith DA8 167 FB80
Wheelwright Cl, Bushey WD23 off Ashfield Av 76 CB44
Wheelwright St, N7 4 A5
Whelan Way, Wall. SM6 201 DK104
Wheler St, E1 11 N4
Whellock Rd, W4 158 CS76
WHELPLEY HILL, Chesh. HP5 56 AX26
Whelpley Hill Pk, Chesh. (Whel.Hill) HP5 56 AX26
Whenman Av, Bex. DA5 187 FC89
Whernside Cl, SE28 146 EW73
Wherwell Rd, Guil. GU2 258 AW136
WHETSTONE, N20 98 DB47
Whetstone Cl, N20 off Oakleigh Rd N 98 DD47
Whetstone Pk, WC2 10 A7
Whetstone Rd, SE3 164 EJ82
Whewell Rd, N19 121 DL61
Whichcote Gdns, Chesh. HP5 54 AR33
Whichcote St, SE1 20 C2
Whichert Cl, Beac. (Knot.Grn) HP9 88 AJ49
Whidborne Cl, SE8 off Cliff Ter 163 EA82
Whidborne St, WC1 9 P2
Whielden Cl, Amer. HP7 55 AP40
Whielden Gate, Amer. (Winch.Hill) HP7 55 AL43
Whielden Grn, Amer. HP7 55 AP40
Whielden La, Amer. HP7 55 AL43
Whielden St, Amer. HP7 55 AN41
Whieldon Gra, Harl. (Ch.Lang.) CM17 52 EY16
Whiffins Orchard, Epp. (Cooper.) CM16 70 EX29
Whimbrel Cl, SE28 146 EW73
South Croydon CR2 220 DR111
Whimbrel Way, Hayes UB4 136 BX72
Whinchat Rd, SE28 165 ER76
Whinfell Cl, SW16 181 DK92
Whinfell Way, Grav. DA12 191 GM91
Whinneys Rd, H.Wyc. (Loud.) HP10 88 AC52
Whinyates Rd, SE9 164 EL83
Whipley Cl, Guil. GU4 off Weybrook Dr 243 BB129
Whippendell Cl, Orp. BR5 206 EV95
Whippendell Hill, Kings L. WD4 58 BJ30
Whippendell Rd, Wat. WD18 75 BU43
Whippendell Way, Orp. BR5 206 EV95
[H] Whipps Cross Hosp, E11 123 ED58
Whipps Cross Rd, E11 123 ED57
Whiskin St, EC1 10 E2
Whisperwood, Rick. (Loud.) WD3 74 BH41
Whisperwood Cl, Har. HA3 95 CE52
Whistler Gdns, Edg. HA8 96 CM54
Whistler Ms, SE15 off Kelly Av 162 DT80
Dagenham RM8 off Fitzstephen Rd 126 EV64
Whistlers Av, SW11 160 DD80
Whistler St, N5 4 E1
Whistler Wk, SW10 off World's End Est 160 DD80
Whiston Rd, E2 5 N9
Whitacre Ms, SE11 off Stannary St 161 DN78
Whitakers Way, Loug. IG10 85 EM39
Whitbread Cl, N17 100 DU53
Whitbread Rd, SE4 163 DY84
Whitburn Rd, SE13 163 EB84
Whitby Av, NW10 138 CP69
Whitby Cl, Green. DA9 189 FU85
Westerham (Bigg.H.) TN16 238 EH119
Whitby Gdns, NW9 118 CN55
Sutton SM1 200 DD103
Whitby Rd, SE18 165 EM77
Harrow HA2 116 CC62
Ruislip HA4 115 BV62
Slough SL1 131 AQ73
Sutton SM1 200 DD103
Whitby St, E1 11 N3
Whitcher Cl, SE14 163 DY79
Whitcher Pl, NW1 off Rochester Rd 141 DJ66
Whitchurch Av, Edg. HA8 96 CM52
Whitchurch Cl, Edg. HA8 96 CM51
[Sch] Whitchurch First Sch, Stan. HA7 off Wemborough Rd 95 CK52
Whitchurch Gdns, Edg. HA8 96 CM51
Whitchurch La, Edg. HA8 95 CK52
Whitchurch Rd, W11 6 B9
Romford RM3 106 FK49
Whitcomb Ct, WC2 off Whitcomb St 141 DK73
Whitcombe Ms, Rich. TW9 158 CP81
Whitcomb St, WC2 9 M10
Whiteadder Way, E14 24 B7
Whitear Wk, E15 143 ED65
White Av, Grav. (Nthflt) DA11 191 GF90
Whitebarn La, Dag. RM10 146 FA67
Whitebeam Av, Brom. BR2 205 EN100
Whitebeam Cl, SW9 off Clapham Rd 161 DM80
Radlett (Shenley) WD7 off Mulberry Gdns 62 CM33
Waltham Cross EN7 off The Laurels 66 DS26
Whitebeam Dr, Reig. RH2 266 DB137
South Ockendon RM15 149 FW69
Whitebeams, Hat. AL10 45 CU21
White Beams, St.Alb. (Park St) AL2 60 CC28
White Beam Way, Tad. KT20 233 CU121
White Bear Pl, NW3 off New End Sq 120 DD63
Whiteberry Rd, Dor. RH5 262 CB143
White Br Av, Mitch. CR4 200 DD98
Whitebridge Cl, Felt. TW14 175 BT86
[Sch] White Br Co Inf Sch, The, Loug. IG10 off Greensted Rd 102 EL45
[Sch] White Br Co Jun Sch, The, Loug. IG10 off Greensted Rd 102 EL45
Whitebroom Rd, Hem.H. HP1 39 BE18
WHITE BUSHES, Red. RH1 267 DH139
White Butts Rd, Ruis. HA4 116 BX62
WHITECHAPEL, E1 12 A8
⊖ Whitechapel 12 C5
★ Whitechapel Art Gall, E1 11 P7
Whitechapel High St, E1 11 P7
Whitechapel Rd, E1 12 A7
White Ch La, E1 12 A7

Whitechurch Mid Sch, Stan. HA7
off Wemborough Rd 95 CK52
White Ch Pas, E1 12 A7
⊖ White City 139 CW73
White City Cl, W12 139 CW73
White City Est, W12 139 CV73
White City Rd, W12 139 CV73
White Cl, Slou. SL1 131 AR74
White Conduit St, N1 4 D9
Whitecote Rd, Sthl. UB1 136 CB72
White Craig Cl, Pnr. HA5 94 CA50
Whitecroft, Horl. RH6
off Woodhayes 269 DH147
St. Albans AL1 43 CH23
Swanley BR8 207 FE96
Whitecroft Cl, Beck. BR3 203 ED98
Whitecroft Way, Beck. BR3 203 EC99
Whitecross Pl, EC2 11 K5
Whitecross St, EC1 11 H3
White Down Rd, Dor. RH5 262 BW135
Whitefield Av, NW2 119 CW59
Purley CR8 235 DN116
Whitefield Cl, SW15 179 CY86
Orpington BR5 206 EW97
Whitefield Sch, NW2
off Claremont Rd 119 CX59
Whitefield Sch & Cen, The, E17
off Macdonald Rd 101 ED54
Whitefields Rd, Wal.Cr.
(Chsht) EN8 66 DW28
Whitefoot La, Brom. BR1 183 EC91
Whitefoot Ter, Brom. BR1 184 EE90
Whiteford Rd, Slou. SL2 132 AS71
White Friars, Sev. TN13 256 FG127
Whitefriars Av, Har. HA3 95 CE54
Whitefriars Dr, Har. HA3 95 CD54
Whitefriars First & Mid Sch, Har. HA3
off Whitefriars Av 95 CE54
Whitefriars St, EC4 10 D8
White Gdns, Dag. RM10 146 FA65
Whitegate Gdns, Har. HA3 95 CF52
White Gates, Horn. RM12 128 FJ61
Whitegates, Whyt. CR3
off Court Bushes Rd 236 DU119
Woking GU22 off Loop Rd 227 AZ120
Whitegates Cl, Rick.
(Crox.Grn) WD3 74 BN42
Whitegate Way, Tad. KT20 233 CV120
Whitehall, SW1 19 N1
White Hall, Rom. (Abridge)
RM4 off Market Pl 86 EV41
Whitehall Cl, Chig. IG7 104 EU48
Uxbridge UB8 134 BJ67
Waltham Abbey EN9 50 EE22
Whitehall Ct, SW1 19 N2
Whitehall Cres, Chess. KT9 215 CK106
Whitehall Fm La, Vir.W. GU25 192 AY96
Whitehall Gdns, E4 102 EE46
SW1 19 N2
W3 138 CN74
W4 158 CP79
Whitehall Inf Sch, Uxb.
UB8 off Cowley Rd 134 BJ67
Whitehall Jun Sch, Uxb.
UB8 off Cowley Rd 134 BJ68
Whitehall La, Buck.H. IG9 102 EG47
Egham TW20 173 AZ94
Erith DA8 167 FF82
Grays RM17 170 GC78
Reigate (S.Park) RH2 265 CZ138
Staines (Wrays.) TW19 173 BA86
Whitehall Pk, N19 121 DJ60
Whitehall Pk Rd, W4 158 CP79
Whitehall Pl, E7
off Station Rd 124 EG64
SW1 19 N2
Wallington SM6
off Bernard Rd 219 DH105
Whitehall Prim Sch, E4
off Normanton Pk 102 EE47
Whitehall Rd, E4 102 EE47
W7 157 CG75
Bromley BR2 204 EK99
Grays RM17 170 GC77
Harrow HA1 117 CE59
Thornton Heath CR7 201 DN99
Uxbridge UB8 134 BK67
Woodford Green IG8 102 EE47
Whitehall St, N17 100 DT52
Whitehands Cl, Hodd. EN11 49 DZ17
White Hart Cl, Ch.St.G. HP8 90 AU48
Sevenoaks TN13 257 FJ128
White Hart Ct, EC2
off Bishopsgate 142 DS72
Woking (Ripley) GU23 228 BJ121
White Hart Dr, Hem.H. HP2 40 BM21
⇌ White Hart Lane 100 DT52
White Hart La, N17 100 DR52
N22 99 DN53
NW10 off Church Rd 139 CT65
SW13 158 CS83
Romford RM7 104 FA53
White Hart La Sch, N22
off White Hart La 99 DP52
White Hart Meadow, Beac.
HP9 89 AL54
White Hart Meadows, Wok.
(Ripley) GU23 228 BJ121
White Hart Rd, SE18 165 ES77
Hemel Hempstead HP2 40 BN21
Orpington BR6 206 EU101
Slough SL1 151 AR76
White Hart Row, Cher.
KT16 off Heriot Rd 194 BG101
White Hart Slip, Brom.
BR1 off Market Sq 204 EG96
White Hart St, EC4 10 F7
SE11 20 D9
White Hart Wd, Sev. TN13 257 FJ129
White Hart Yd, SE1 21 J2
Whitehaven, Slou. SL1 132 AT73
Whitehaven Cl, Brom. BR2 204 EG98
Waltham Cross (Goffs Oak)
EN7 66 DS28
Whitehaven St, NW8 8 A4
Whitehead Cl, N18 100 DR50
SW18 180 DC87
Dartford DA2 188 FJ90
Whitehead's Gro, SW3 18 B9
Whiteheart Av, Uxb. UB8 135 BQ71
Whiteheath Av, Ruis. HA4 115 BQ59
Whiteheath Inf Sch, Ruis.
HA4 off Ladygate La 115 BP58
Whiteheath Jun Sch, Ruis.
HA4 off Whiteheath Av 115 BP58
White Hedge Dr, St.Alb. AL3 42 CC19
White Heron Ms, Tedd. TW11 177 CF93
White Hill, Beac. HP9 110 AG55
Whitehill, Berk. HP4 38 AX18
White Hill, Chesh. HP5 54 AQ31
Coulsdon (Chipstead) CR5 234 DC124
Hemel Hempstead HP1 39 BF21
Northwood HA6 92 BN51
Rickmansworth WD3 92 BN51
White Hill, S.Croy. CR2
off St. Mary's Rd 220 DR109
Welwyn AL6 29 CU05
Whitehill Cl, Berk. HP4
off Whitehill 38 AX18
White Hill Cl, Chesh. HP5 54 AQ30
White Hill Ct, Berk. HP4
off Whitehill 38 AX18
Whitehill Inf Sch, Grav.
DA12 off Sun La 191 GJ90
Whitehill Jun Sch, Grav.
DA12 off Sun La 191 GJ90
Whitehill La, Grav. DA12 191 GK90
Redhill (Bletch.) RH1 252 DR127
Woking (Ockham) GU23 229 BQ123
Whitehill Par, Grav. DA12 191 GJ90
Whitehill Pl, Vir.W. GU25 192 AY99
White Hill Rd, Berk. HP4 38 AV21
Chesham HP5 56 AX26
Whitehill Rd, Dart. DA1 187 FG85
Gravesend DA12 191 GJ89
Gravesend (Hook Grn)
DA13 209 FX96
Longfield DA3 209 FX96
Whitehills Rd, Loug. IG10 85 EN41
White Horse All, EC1 10 E5
White Horse Dr, Epsom KT18 216 CQ114
Whitehorse Hill, Chis. BR7 185 EN91
White Horse La, E1 12 G4
Whitehorse La, SE25 202 DR98
White Horse La, St.Alb.
(Lon.Col.) AL2 62 CL25
Woking (Ripley) GU23 228 BJ121
Whitehorse Manor Jun & Inf Sch, Th.Hth. CR7
off Whitehorse Rd 202 DR98
White Horse Ms, SE1 20 D5
White Horse Rd, E1 13 J8
E6 145 EM69
Whitehorse Rd, Croy. CR0 202 DR100
Thornton Heath CR7 202 DR100
White Horse Rd, Wind. SL4 151 AK83
White Horse St, W1 18 G2
White Horse Yd, EC2 11 J7
Whitehouse Av, Borwd. WD6 78 CP41
White Ho Cl, Ger.Cr.
(Chal.St.P.) SL9 90 AY52
Whitehouse Cl, H.Wyc.
(Woob.Grn) HP10 88 AE54
White Ho Dr, Guil. GU1 243 BB134
Stanmore HA7 95 CJ49
Whitehouse La, Abb.L.
(Bedmond) WD5 59 BV26
Enfield EN2
off Brigadier Hill 82 DQ39
White Ho La, Guil.
(Jacobs Well) GU4 242 AX129
Whitehouse La, H.Wyc.
(Woob.Grn) HP10 88 AE54
White Ho La, Sev. TN14 256 FF130
White Ho Rd, Sev. TN14 256 FF130
Whitehouse Way, N14 99 DH47
Iver SL0 133 BD69
Slough SL3 152 AW76
Whitehurst Dr, N18 101 DX50
White Kennett St, E1 11 M7
White Knights Rd, Wey.
KT13 213 BQ108
White Knobs Way, Cat. CR3 252 DU125
Whitelands Av, Rick. (Chorl.)
WD3 73 BC42
Whitelands Way, Rom. RM3 106 FK54
White La, Guil. GU4, GU5 259 BC136
Oxted RH8 238 EH123
Warlingham CR6 238 EH123
Whiteleaf Rd, Hem.H. HP3 40 BJ23
Whiteledges, W13 137 CJ72
Whitelegg Rd, E13 144 EF68
Whiteley, Wind. SL4 151 AL80
Whiteley Rd, SE19 182 DR92
Whiteleys Shop Cen, W2 7 J8
Whiteleys Way, Felt. TW13 176 CA90
WHITELEY VILLAGE, Walt.
KT12 213 BS110
White Lion Cl, Amer. HP7 72 AU39
White Lion Ct, EC3 11 L8
White Lion Gate, Cob. KT11
off Virginia Pl 213 BU114
White Lion Hill, EC4 10 F9
White Lion Hos, Hat. AL10
off Robin Hood La 45 CU17
White Lion Rd, Amer. HP7 72 AT38
White Lion Sq, Hat. AL10
off Robin Hood La 45 CU17
White Lion St, N1 4 C10
Hemel Hempstead HP3 40 BK24
White Lion Wk Shop Cen,
Guil. GU1 off High St 258 AX136
White Lo, SE19 181 DP94
White Lo Cl, N2 120 DD58
Isleworth TW7 157 CG82
Sevenoaks TN13 257 FH123
Sutton SM2 218 DC108
White Lo Gdns, Red. RH1 266 DG142
White Lyon Ct, EC2
off Fann St 142 DQ70
White Lyons Rd, Brwd. CM14 108 FW47
Whitemore Rd, Guil. GU1 242 AX130
White Oak Business Pk,
Swan. BR8
off London Rd 207 FE97
White Oak Dr, Beck. BR3 203 EC96
White Oak Gdns, Sid. DA15 185 ET87
White Oak Prim Sch,
Swan. BR8
off Hilda May Av 207 FE96
White Oaks, Bans. SM7 218 DB113
Whiteoaks La, Grnf. UB6 137 CD68
White Orchards, N20 97 CZ45
Stanmore HA7 95 CG50
Whitepit La, H.Wyc.
(Flack.Hth) HP10 110 AE57
White Post Fld, Saw. CM21 36 EX05
White Post Hill, Dart. (Fnghm)
DA4 208 FN101
Whitepost Hill, Red. RH1 250 DE134
White Post La, E9 143 DZ66
SE13 163 EA83
White Post St, SE15 162 DW80
White Rd, E15 144 EE66
Betchworth RH3 248 CN133
Tadworth (Box H.) KT20 248 CN133
White Rose La, Wok. GU22 227 AZ117
Whites Av, Ilf. IG2 125 ES58
Whites Cl, Green. DA9 189 FW86
Whites Grds, SE1 21 M4
Whites Grds Est, SE1 21 M3
White Shack La, Rick. WD3 74 BM37
Whites La, Slou. (Datchet)
SL3 152 AV79
White's Row, E1 11 N6
White's Sq, SW4
off Nelson's Row 161 DK84
Whitestile Rd, Brent. TW8 157 CJ78
Whitestone La, NW3
off Heath St 120 DC62
Whitestone Wk, NW3
off North End Way 120 DC62
Hemel Hempstead HP1
off Fennycroft Rd 40 BG17
White St, Sthl. UB1 156 BX75
White Stubbs La, Brox. EN10 47 DP21
Hertford SG13 47 DK21
White Swan Ms, W4
off Bennett St 158 CS79
Whitethorn, Welw.G.C. AL7 30 DB10
Whitethorn Av, Couls. CR5 234 DG115
West Drayton UB7 134 BL73
Whitethorn Gdns, Croy. CR0 202 DV103
Enfield EN2 82 DR43
Hornchurch RM11 128 FJ58
Whitethorn Pl, West Dr.
UB7 off Whitethorn Av 134 BM74
Whitethorn St, E3 13 P4
Whitewaits, Harl. CM20 35 ES14
White Way, Lthd. (Bkhm)
KT23 246 CB126
Whiteways Ct, Stai. TW18
off Pavilion Gdns 174 BH94
Whitewebbs La, Enf. EN2 82 DS35
Whitewebbs Pk, Enf. EN2 82 DQ35
Whitewebbs Rd, Enf. EN2 81 DP35
Whitewebbs Way, Orp. BR5 205 ET95
Whitewood Cotts, West.
(Tats.) TN16 238 EJ120
Whitewood Rd, Berk. HP4 38 AU19
Whitfield Cl, Guil. GU2 242 AU131
Whitfield Pl, W1 9 J4
Whitfield Rd, E6 144 EJ66
SE3 163 ED81
Bexleyheath DA7 166 EZ80
Whitfield St, W1 9 L6
Whitfield Way, Rick. (Mill End)
WD3 91 BF46
Whitford Gdns, Mitch. CR4 200 DF97
Whitgift Av, S.Croy. CR2 220 DQ106
Whitgift Cen, Croy. CR0 202 DQ103
Whitgift Ho, SW11
off Westbridge Rd 160 DE81
Whitgift Sch, S.Croy.
CR2 off Haling Pk Rd 220 DQ106
Whitgift St, SE11 20 A7
Croydon CR0 202 DQ104
Whit Hern Ct, Wal.Cr. EN8
off College Rd 66 DW30
Whiting Av, Bark. IG11 145 EP66
Whitings, Ilf. IG2 125 ER57
Whitings Hill Prim Sch,
Barn. EN5
off Whitings Rd 79 CW43
Whitings Rd, Barn. EN5 79 CW43
Whitings Way, E6 145 EN71
Whitland Rd, Cars. SM5 200 DD102
Whitlars Dr, Kings L. WD4 58 BM28
Whitley Cl, Abb.L. WD5 59 BU32
Staines (Stanw.) TW19 174 BL86
Whitley Rd, N17 100 DS54
Hoddesdon EN11 49 EB15
Whitlock Dr, SW19 179 CY87
Whitman Rd, E3 13 K3
Whitmead Cl, S.Croy. CR2 220 DS107
Whitmoor Common, Guil.
(Worp.) GU3 242 AV127
Whitmoor La, Guil. GU4 242 AX126
Whitmore Av, Rom.
(Harold Wd) RM3 106 FL54
Whitmore Cl, N11 99 DH50
Whitmore Est, N1 5 M8
Whitmore Gdns, NW10 139 CW68
Whitmore High Sch, Har.
HA2 off Porlock Av 116 CC60
Whitmore JMI Sch, N1 5 K8
Whitmore Rd, N1 5 L8
Beckenham BR3 203 DZ97
Harrow HA1 116 CC59
Whitmores Cl, Epsom KT18 232 CQ115
Whitmore's Wd, Hem.H. HP2 41 BP19
Whitmore Way, Horl. RH6 268 DE147
Whitnell Way, SW15 179 CX85
Whitney Av, Ilf. IG4 124 EK56
Whitney Rd, E10 123 EB59
Whitney Wk, Sid. DA14 186 EY93
Whitstable Cl, Beck. BR3 203 DZ95
Ruislip HA4
off Chichester Av 115 BS61
Whitstable Ho, W10 6 B8
Whitstable Pl, Croy. CR0 220 DQ105
Whitstone La, Beck. BR3 203 EB99
Whittaker Av, Rich. TW9
off Hill St 177 CK85
Whittaker Rd, E6 144 EJ66
Slough SL2 131 AK70
Sutton SM3 199 CZ104
Whittaker St, SW1 18 E8
Whittaker Way, SE1 22 B8
Whitta Rd, E12 124 EK63
Whittell Gdns, SE26 182 DW90
Whittenham Cl, Slou. SL2 132 AU74
Whittingham Comm Prim Sch, E17
off Higham Hill Rd 101 DY53
Whittingstall Rd, SW6 159 CZ81
Whittington Av, EC3 11 L8
Hayes UB4 135 BT71
Whittington Ct, N2 120 DF57
Whittington Hosp, N19 121 DJ61
Whittington Ms, N12
off Fredericks Pl 98 DC49
Whittington Rd, N22 99 DL52
Brentwood (Hutt.) CM13 109 GC44
Whittington Way, Pnr. HA5 116 BY57
Whittlebury Cl, Cars. SM5 218 DF108
Whittle Cl, E17 123 DY58
Southall UB1 136 CB72
Watford (Lvsdn) WD25 59 BT34
Whittle Parkway, Slou. SL1 131 AK72
Whittle Rd, Houns. TW5 156 BW80
Southall UB2 off Post Rd 156 CB75
Whittlesea Cl, Har. HA3 94 CC52
Whittlesea Path, Har. HA3 94 CC53
Whittlesea Rd, Har. HA3 94 CC53
Whittlesea Sch, Har.
HA3 off Whittlesea Rd 94 CC52
Whittlesey St, SE1 20 C2
WHITTON, Twick. TW2 176 CB87
⇌ Whitton 176 CC87
Whitton Av E, Grnf. UB6 117 CE64
Whitton Av W, Grnf. UB6 116 CC64
Northolt UB5 116 CC64
Whitton Cl, Grnf. UB6 137 CH65
Whitton Dene, Houns. TW3 176 CB85
Isleworth TW7 177 CD85
Whitton Dr, Grnf. UB6 137 CG65
Whitton Manor Rd, Islw. TW7 176 CC85
Whitton Rd, Houns. TW3 156 CB84
Twickenham TW1, TW2 177 CF86
Whitton Sch, Twick.
TW2 off Percy Rd 176 CB89
Whitton Wk, E3 13 N1
Whitton Waye, Houns. TW3 176 CA86
Whitwell Rd, E13 15 L2
Watford WD25 76 BX35
Whitworth Cres, Enf.
EN3 off Martini Dr 83 EA37
Whitworth Pl, SE18 165 EP77
Whitworth Rd, SE18 165 EN80
SE25 202 DS97
Whitworth St, SE10 25 H9
Whopshott Av, Wok. GU21 226 AW116
Whopshott Cl, Wok. GU21 226 AW116
Whopshott Dr, Wok. GU21 226 AW116
Whorlton Rd, SE15 162 DV83
Whybridge Cl, Rain. RM13 147 FE67
Whybridge Inf Sch, Rain.
RM13 off Ford La 147 FG67
Whybridge Jun Sch, Rain.
RM13 off Blacksmiths La 147 FF67
Whybrow Gdns, Berk. HP4
off Frithsden Rd 38 AY17
Whychcote Pt, NW2
off Claremont Rd 119 CW59
Whymark Av, N22 121 DN55
Whymark Cl, Rain. RM13 147 FF68
Whytebeam Vw, Whyt. CR3 236 DT118
Whytecliffe Rd N, Pur. CR8 219 DP111
Whytecliffe Rd S, Pur. CR8 219 DN111
Whytecroft, Houns. TW5 156 BX80
WHYTELEAFE, Cat. CR3 236 DS118
⇌ Whyteleafe 236 DT117
Whyteleafe Business Village,
Whyt. CR3
off Whyteleafe Hill 236 DT118
Whyteleafe Hill, Whyt. CR3 236 DT118
Whyteleafe Rd, Cat. CR3 236 DS120
Whyteleafe Sch, Whyt.
CR3 off Whyteleafe Hill 236 DT118
⇌ Whyteleafe South 236 DU119
Whyteville Rd, E7 144 EH65
Wichling Cl, Orp. BR5 206 EX102
Wick, The, Hert. SG14 31 DP06
Wickenden Rd, Sev. TN13 257 FJ122
Wicken's Meadow, Sev.
(Dunt.Grn) TN14 241 FF119
Wickersley Rd, SW11 160 DG82
Wickers Oake, SE19 182 DT91
Wicker St, E1 12 C8
Wicket, The, Croy. CR0 221 EA106
Wicket Rd, Grnf. UB6 137 CG69
Wickets, The, Ashf. TW15 174 BL91
Wickets End, Rad. (Shenley)
WD7 62 CL33
Wickets Way, Ilf. IG6 103 ET51
Wickford Cl, Rom. RM3
off Wickford Dr 106 FM50
Wickford Dr, Rom. RM3 106 FM50
Wickford St, E1 12 E3
Wickford Way, E17 123 DX56
Wickham Av, Croy. CR0 203 DY103
Sutton SM3 217 CW106
Wickham Chase, W.Wick.
BR4 203 ED101
Wickham Cl, E1 12 F6
Enfield EN3 82 DV41
Horley RH6 268 DF147
New Malden KT3 199 CT99
Uxbridge (Hare.) UB9 92 BK53
Wickham Common Prim Sch, W.Wick. BR4
off Gates Grn Rd 222 EG105
Wickham Ct, St.Alb. AL1 43 CH18
Wickham Ct Rd, W.Wick. BR4 203 EC103
Wickham Ct Sch, W.Wick.
BR4 off Layhams Rd 222 EE105
Wickham Cres, W.Wick. BR4 203 EC103
Wickham Fld, Sev. (Otford)
TN14 241 FF116
Wickham Gdns, SE4 163 DZ83
Wickham La, SE2 166 EU78
Egham TW20 173 BA94
Welling DA16 166 EU78
Wickham Ms, SE4 163 DZ82
Wickham Rd, E4 101 EC52
SE4 163 DZ84
Beckenham BR3 203 EB96
Croydon CR0 203 DX103
Grays RM16 171 GJ75
Harrow HA3 95 CD54
Wickham St, SE11 20 A9
Welling DA16 165 ES82
Wickham Way, Beck. BR3 203 EC98
Wicklands Rd, Ware
(Hunsdon) SG12 34 EK07
Wick La, E3 143 EA68
Egham (Eng.Grn) TW20 172 AT92
Wickliffe Av, N3 97 CY54
Wickliffe Gdns, Wem. HA9 118 CP61
Wicklow St, WC1 10 A1
Wick Rd, E9 143 DX65
Egham (Eng.Grn) TW20 172 AV94
Teddington TW11 177 CH94
Wicks Cl, SE9 184 EK91
Wicksteed Cl, Bex. DA5 187 FD90
Wicksteed Ho, Brent. TW8
off Green Dragon La 158 CM78
Wick Way, St.Alb. AL1 43 CH17
Wickwood St, SE5 161 DP82
Widbury Gdns, Ware SG12 33 DZ06
Widbury Hill, Ware SG12 33 DZ06
Wid Cl, Brwd. (Hutt.) CM13 109 GD43
Widdecombe Av, Har. HA2 116 BY61
Widdenham Rd, N7 121 DM63
Widdin St, E15 143 ED66
Widecombe Cl, Rom. RM3 106 FK53
Widecombe Gdns, Ilf. IG4 124 EL56
Widecombe Rd, SE9 184 EL90
Widecombe Way, N2 120 DD57
Widecroft Rd, Iver SL0 133 BE72
Widegate St, E1 11 M6
Widenham Cl, Pnr. HA5
off Bridle Rd 116 BW57
Wide Way, Mitch. CR4 201 DK97
Widewing Cl, Tedd. TW11 177 CH94
Widford Rd, Ware (Hunsdon)
SG12 34 EK05
Welwyn Garden City AL7 30 DB09
Widgeon Cl, E16 15 N7
Widgeon Rd, Erith DA8 167 FH80
Widgeon Way, Wat. WD25 76 BY36
Widley Rd, W9 7 H2
Widmoor, H.Wyc. (Woob.Grn)
HP10 110 AE60
WIDMORE, Brom. BR1 204 EH97
Widmore Dr, Hem.H. HP2 40 BN18
WIDMORE GREEN, Brom.
BR1 204 EJ95
Widmore Lo Rd, Brom. BR1 204 EK96
Widmore Rd, Brom. BR1 204 EG96
Uxbridge UB8 135 BP70
Widworthy Hayes, Brwd.
(Hutt.) CM13 109 GB46
Wieland Rd, Nthwd. HA6 93 BU52
Wigan Ho, E5
off Warwick Gro 122 DV60
Wigeon Path, SE28 165 ER76
Wigeon Way, Hayes UB4 136 BX72
Wiggenhall Rd, Wat. WD18 75 BV43
Wiggie La, Red. RH1 250 DG132
Wiggins La, Rich. TW10 177 CJ89
Wiggins Mead, NW9 97 CT52
Wigginton Av, Wem. HA9 138 CP65
Wigham Ho, Bark. IG11 145 EQ66
Wightman Rd, N4 121 DN57
N8 121 DN56
Wigley Bush La, Brwd.
(S.Wld) CM14 108 FS47
Wigley Rd, Felt. TW13 176 BX88
Wigmore Ct, W13
off Singapore Rd 137 CG74
Wigmore Pl, W1 8 G7
Wigmore Rd, Cars. SM5 200 DD103
Wigmores N, Welw.G.C. AL8 29 CX08
Wigmores S, Welw.G.C. AL8 29 CX09
Wigmore St, W1 8 E8
Wigmore Wk, Cars. SM5 200 DD103
Wigram Rd, E11 124 EJ58
Wigram Sq, E17 101 EC54
Wigston Cl, N18 100 DS50
Wigston Rd, E13 15 N3
Wigton Gdns, Stan. HA7 96 CL53
Wigton Pl, SE11 20 D10
Wigton Rd, E17 101 DZ53
Romford RM3 106 FL49
Wigton Way, Rom. RM3 106 FL49
Wilberforce Prim Sch,
W10 6 D1
Wilberforce Rd, N4 121 DP61
NW9 119 CU58
Wilberforce Way, SW19 179 CX93
Gravesend DA12 191 GK92
Wilbraham Pl, SW1 18 D7
Wilbury Av, Sutt. SM2 217 CZ110
Wilbury Prim Sch, N18
off Wilbury Way 100 DR50
Wilbury Rd, Wok. GU21 226 AX117
Wilbury Way, N18 100 DR50
Wilby Ms, W11 16 F1
Wilcon Way, Wat. WD25 60 BX34
Wilcot Av, Wat. WD19 94 BY45
Wilcot Cl, Wat. WD19
off Wilcot Av 94 BY45
Wilcox Cl, SW8 161 DL80
Borehamwood WD6 78 CQ39
Wilcox Gdns, Shep. TW17 194 BM97
Wilcox Pl, SW1 19 K6
Wilcox Rd, SW8 161 DL80
Sutton SM1 218 DB105
Teddington TW11 177 CD91
Wildacres, Nthwd. HA6 93 BT49
West Byfleet KT14 212 BJ111
Wildbank Ct, Wok. GU22
off White Rose La 227 AZ118
Wild Ct, WC2 10 A7
Wildcroft Dr, Dor. (N.Holm.)
RH5 263 CK139
Wildcroft Gdns, Edg. HA8 95 CK51
Wildcroft Rd, SW15 179 CW87
Wilde Cl, E8 142 DU67
Tilbury RM18
off Coleridge Rd 171 GJ82
Wilde Pl, N13
off Medesenge Way 99 DP51
SW18 off Heathfield Rd 180 DD87
Wilder Cl, Ruis. HA4 115 BV60
Wilderness, The, Berk. HP4 38 AW19
East Molesey KT8 196 CC99
Hampton (Hmptn H.)
TW12 off Park Rd 176 CB91
WILDERNESSE, Sev. TN15 257 FL122
Wildernesse Av, Sev. (Seal)
TN15 257 FL122
Wildernesse Mt, Sev. TN13 257 FK122
Wildernesse Sch for Boys,
Sev. TN13
off Seal Hollow Rd 257 FL121
Wilderness Ms, SW4
off The Chase 161 DH84
Wilderness Rd, Chis. BR7 185 EP94
Guildford GU2 258 AT135
Oxted RH8 254 EE130
Wilde Rd, Erith DA8 167 FB80
Wilders Cl, Wok. GU21 226 AW118
Wilderton Rd, N16 122 DS59
Wildfell Rd, SE6 183 EB87
Wild Goose Dr, SE14 162 DW81
Wild Grn N, Slou. SL3
off Verney Rd 153 BA77
Wild Grn S, Slou. SL3
off Swabey Rd 153 BA77
Wild Hatch, NW11 120 DA58
WILDHILL, Hat. AL9 46 DD21
Wildhill Rd, Hat. AL9 45 CY23
Wild Oaks Cl, Nthwd. HA6 93 BT51
Wild's Rents, SE1 21 L5
Wild St, WC2 9 P8
Wildwood, Nthwd. HA6 93 BR51
Wildwood Av, St.Alb.
(Brick.Wd) AL2 60 BZ30
Wildwood Cl, SE12 184 EF87
Leatherhead (E.Hors.) KT24 245 BT125
Woking GU22 227 BF115
Wildwood Ct, Ken. CR8 236 DR115
Wildwood Gro, NW3
off North End Way 120 DC60
Wildwood Ri, NW11 120 DC60
Wildwood Rd, NW11 120 DC59
Wildwood Ter, NW3 120 DC60
Wilford Cl, Enf. EN2 82 DR41
Northwood HA6 93 BR52
Wilford Rd, Slou. SL3 153 AZ77
Wilfred Av, Rain. RM13 147 FG71
Wilfred Owen Cl, SW19
off Tennyson Rd 180 DC93
Wilfred St, SW1 19 J5
Gravesend DA12 191 GH86
Woking GU21 226 AX118
Wilfred Turney Est, W6
off Hammersmith Gro 159 CW76
Wilfrid Gdns, W3 138 CQ71
Wilhelmina Av, Couls. CR5 235 DJ119
Wilkes Rd, Brent. TW8 158 CL79
Brentwood (Hutt.) CM13 109 GD43
Wilkes St, E1 11 P5
Wilkie Way, SE22
off Lordship La 182 DU88
Wilkins Cl, Hayes UB3 155 BT78
Mitcham CR4 200 DE95
WILKIN'S GREEN, Hat. AL10 44 CQ19
Wilkins Grn La, Hat. AL10 44 CQ19
St. Albans (Smallford) AL4 44 CP20
Wilkins Gro, Welw.G.C. AL8 29 CX10
Wilkinson Cl, Dart. DA1 168 FM84
Uxbridge UB10 135 BP67
Waltham Cross (Chsht) EN7 66 DQ26
Wilkinson Rd, E16 144 EJ72
Wilkinson St, SW8 161 DM80
Wilkinson Way, W4 158 CR75
Wilkin St, NW5 141 DH65
Wilkin St Ms, NW5
off Wilkin St 141 DH65
Wilkins Way, West. (Brasted)
TN16 240 EV124
Wilks Av, Dart. DA1 188 FM89
Wilks Gdns, Croy. CR0 203 DY102
Wilks Pl, N1 5 M10
Willan Rd, N17 100 DR54
Willan Wall, E16 15 J9
Willard St, SW8 161 DH83
Willats Cl, Cher. KT16 194 BG100
Willcocks Cl, Chess. KT9 198 CL104
Willcott Rd, W3 138 CP74
Will Crooks Gdns, SE9 164 EJ84
Willen Fld Rd, NW10 138 CQ68
Willenhall Av, Barn. EN5 80 DC44
Willenhall Dr, Hayes UB3 135 BS73
Willenhall Rd, SE18 165 EP78
Willersley Av, Orp. BR6 205 ER104
Sidcup DA15 185 ET88
Willersley Cl, Sid. DA15 185 ET88
WILLESDEN, NW10 139 CT65
Willesden Comm Hosp,
NW10 139 CU66
WILLESDEN GREEN, NW10 139 CV66
⊖ Willesden Green 139 CW65
⇌ Willesden Junction 139 CT69
⊖ Willesden Junction 139 CT69
Willesden La, NW2 139 CX65
NW6 139 CX65
Willes Rd, NW5 141 DH65
Willett Cl, Nthlt. UB5
off Broomcroft Av 136 BW69
Orpington BR5 205 ES100

Willett Ho, E13
off Queens Rd W 144 EG68
Willett Pl, Th.Hth. CR7
off Willett Rd 201 DN99
Willett Rd, Th.Hth. CR7 201 DN99
Willetts La, Uxb. (Denh.) UB9 113 BF63
Willetts Ms, Hodd. EN11 49 EA16
Willett Way, Orp. BR5 205 ER99
Willey Broom La, Cat. CR3 251 DN125
Willey Fm La, Cat. CR3 252 DQ126
Willey La, Cat. CR3 252 DR125
William Barefoot Dr, SE9 185 EN91
Sch William Bellamy Inf Sch,
Dag. RM10
off Frizlands La 126 FA61
Sch William Bellamy Jun Sch,
Dag. RM10
off Frizlands La 126 FA61
William Bonney Est, SW4 161 DK84
Coll William Booth Coll, SE5
off Champion Hill 162 DR82
William Booth Rd, SE20 202 DU95
Sch William Byrd Prim Sch,
Hayes UB3 off Victoria La 155 BR79
William Carey Way, Har. HA1 117 CE59
Sch William C. Harvey Spec
Sch, N17 off Adams Rd 100 DR54
William Cl, N2 off King St 120 DD55
SE13 163 EC82
Romford RM5 105 FC53
Southall UB2
off Windmill Av 156 CC75
William Cory Prom, Erith
DA8 167 FE78
William Ct, Hem.H. HP3
off King Edward St 40 BK24
William Covell Cl, Enf. EN2 81 DM38
Sch William Davies Prim Sch,
E7 off Stafford Rd 144 EK65
Sch William Davis Prim Sch,
E2 12 A3
William Dr, Stan. HA7 95 CH50
William Dunbar Ho, NW6 139 CZ68
William Dyce Ms, SW16
off Babington Rd 181 DK91
Sch William Ellis Boys' Sch,
NW5 off Highgate Rd 120 DG62
William Ellis Cl, Wind.
(Old Wind.) SL4 172 AU85
William Ellis Way, SE16 22 B6
William Evans Rd, Epsom
KT19 216 CN111
William Evelyn Ct, Dor.
(Wotton) RH5 262 BZ139
Sch William Ford C of E Jun
Sch, Dag. RM10
off Ford Rd 146 FA66
William IV St, WC2 9 N10
William Gdns, SW15 179 CV85
William Guy Gdns, E3 14 B2
William Harvey Ho, SW19
off Whitlock Dr 179 CY88
William Henry Wk, SW8
off Nine Elms La 161 DK79
Sch William Hogarth Sch, The,
W4 off Duke Rd 158 CS78
William Hunter Way, Brwd.
CM14 108 FW47
William Margrie Cl, SE15
off Moncrieff St 162 DU82
Sch William Martin C of E Inf
Sch, Harl. CM18
off Tawneys Rd 51 ES17
Sch William Martin C of E
Jun Sch, Harl. CM18
off Tawneys Rd 51 ET17
William Ms, SW1 18 D4
William Morley Cl, E6 144 EK67
Sch William Morris Acad, W6 16 A8
William Morris Cl, E17 123 DZ55
★ William Morris Gall, Lloyd
Pk, E17 123 EA55
Sch William Morris Prim Sch,
Mitch. CR4
off Recreation Way 201 DK97
Sch William Morris Sch, E17
off Folly La 101 DY53
William Morris Way, SW6 160 DC83
William Moulder Ct, Chesh.
HP5 54 AP28
William Nash Ct, Orp. BR5
off Brantwood Way 206 EW97
Sch William Patten JMI Sch,
N16 off Stoke Newington
Ch St 122 DT61
Sch William Penn Sch, The,
Slou. SL2 off Penn Rd 131 AR70
William Perkin Ct, Grnf. UB6
off Greenford Rd 137 CE65
William Pl, E3 off Roman Rd 143 DZ68
William Rd, NW1 9 H2
SW19 179 CY94
Caterham CR3 236 DR122
Guildford GU1 242 AW134
Sutton SM1 218 DC106
William Russell Ct, Wok.
GU21 off Raglan Rd 226 AS118
Williams Av, E17 101 DZ53
William Saville Ho, NW6 139 CZ68
Williams Bldgs, E2 12 E3
Williams Cl, N8
off Coolhurst Rd 121 DK58
SW6 off Pellant Rd 159 CY80
Addlestone KT15
off Monks Cres 212 BH106
Williams Dr, Houns. TW3 156 CA84
Williams Gro, N22 99 DN53
Surbiton KT6 197 CJ100
William's La, SW14 158 CQ83
Williams La, Mord. SM4 200 DC99
Williamson Cl, SE10 25 J9
Williamson Rd, N4 121 DP58
Williamson St, N7 121 DL63
Williamson Way, NW7 97 CY51
Rickmansworth WD3 92 BG46
William Sq, SE16 13 K10
Williams Rd, W13 137 CG73
Southall UB2 156 BY77
Williams Ter, Croy. CR0 219 DN107
William St, E10 123 EB58
N17 100 DT52
SW1 18 D4
Barking IG11 145 EQ66
Berkhamsted HP4 38 AX19
Bushey WD23 76 BX41
Carshalton SM5 200 DE104
Gravesend DA12 191 GH87
Grays RM17 170 GB79
Slough SL1 132 AT74
Windsor SL4 151 AR81
Williams Wk, Guil. GU2
off Grange Rd 242 AV130
Williams Way, Dart. DA2 187 FD89
Radlett WD7 77 CJ35
William Swayne Pl, Guil.
GU1 off Station App 258 AY135
Sch William Torbitt Prim Sch,
Ilf. IG2 off Eastern Av 125 ET57
Sch William Tyndale Prim Sch,
N1 4 F5
Willifield Way, NW11 119 CZ56
Willingale Cl, Brwd. (Hutt.)
CM13 off Fairview Av 109 GE44
Willingale Cl, Loug. IG10
off Willingale Rd 85 EQ40
Woodford Green IG8 102 EK51
Willingale Rd, Loug. IG10 85 EQ41
Willingdon Rd, N22 99 DP54
Willinghall Cl, Wal.Abb. EN9 67 ED32
Willingham Cl, NW5
off Leighton Rd 121 DJ64
Willingham Ter, NW5
off Leighton Rd 121 DJ64
Willingham Way, Kings.T. KT1 198 CN97
Willington Ct, E5
off Mandeville St 123 DY62
Willington Rd, SW9 161 DL83
Sch Willington Sch, SW19
off Worcester Rd 179 CZ92
Willis Av, Sutt. SM2 218 DE107
Willis Cl, Epsom KT18 216 CP113
Willis Ho, E12
off Grantham Rd 125 EN62
Willis Rd, E15 144 EF67
Croydon CR0 202 DQ101
Erith DA8 167 FC77
Willis St, E14 14 B8
Willmore End, SW19 200 DB95
Willoners, Slou. SL2 131 AN70
Willoughby Av, Croy. CR0 219 DM105
Willoughby Cl, Brox. EN10 49 DY21
Willoughby Ct, St.Alb.
(Lon.Col.) AL2 61 CK26
Willoughby Dr, Rain. RM13 147 FE66
Willoughby Gro, N17 100 DV52
Sch Willoughby Hall Sch,
NW3 off Willoughby Rd 120 DD63
Willoughby Ho, EC2
off The Barbican 142 DQ71
Willoughby La, N17 100 DV52
Willoughby Ms, SW4
off Wixs La 161 DH84
Willoughby Pk Rd, N17 100 DV52
Willoughby Pas, E14 23 N1
Willoughby Rd, N8 121 DN55
NW3 120 DD63
Kingston upon Thames KT2 198 CM95
Slough SL3 153 BA76
Twickenham TW1 177 CK86
Willoughbys, The, SW14
off Upper Richmond
Rd W 158 CS84
Willoughby St, WC1 9 N6
Willoughby Way, SE7 25 N7
Willow Av, SW13 159 CT82
Sidcup DA15 186 EU86
Swanley BR8 207 FF97
Uxbridge (Denh.) UB9 114 BJ64
West Drayton UB7 134 BM73
Willow Bk, SW6 159 CY83
Richmond TW10 177 CH90
Woking GU22 226 AY122
Willowbank Gdns, Tad. KT20 233 CV122
Willowbank Pl, Pur. CR8
off Kingsdown Av 219 DP109
Willowbay Cl, Barn. EN5
off Chesterfield Rd 79 CX44
Willow Brean, Horl. RH6 268 DE147
Willow Br Rd, N1 4 G4
Willowbrook, Wind. (Eton)
SL4 151 AR77
Willowbrook Est, SE15
off Sumner Rd 162 DT80
Willowbrook Rd, SE15 162 DT79
Southall UB2 156 CA76
Staines TW19 174 BL89
Willow Business Cen, Mitch.
CR4 off Willow La 200 DF99
Willow Cl, Add. (Wdhm) KT15 211 BF111
Bexley DA5 186 EZ86
Brentford TW8 157 CJ79
Brentwood (Hutt.) CM13 109 GB44
Bromley BR2 205 EM99
Buckhurst Hill IG9 102 EK48
Erith DA8 off Willow Rd 167 FG81
High Wycombe (Flack.Hth)
HP10 110 AC57
Hornchurch RM12 127 FH62
Orpington BR5 206 EV101
Slough (Colnbr.) SL3 153 BC80
Thornton Heath CR7 201 DP100
Waltham Cross (Chsht) EN7 66 DS26
Willow Cor, Hert. SG13 47 DM18
Willow Cotts, Mitch. CR4 201 DJ97
Richmond TW9
off Kew Grn 158 CN79
Willow Ct, EC2 11 L3
Edgware HA8 96 CL49
Horley RH6 269 DH145
Willowcourt Av, Har. HA3 117 CH57
Willow Cres, St.Alb. AL1 43 CJ20
Willow Cres E, Uxb. (Denh.)
UB9 114 BJ64
Willow Cres W, Uxb. (Denh.)
UB9 114 BJ64
Willowdene, N6
off Denewood Rd 120 DF59
Brentwood (Pilg.Hat.) CM15 108 FT43
Willow Dene, Bushey
(Bushey Hth) WD23 95 CE45
Pinner HA5 94 BX54
Willowdene, Wal.Cr. EN8 67 DY27
Willowdene Cl, Twick. TW2 176 CC87
Willowdene Ct, Brwd. CM14 108 FW49
Willow Dr, Barn. EN5 79 CY42
Woking (Ripley) GU23 228 BG124
Willow Edge, Kings L. WD4 58 BN29
Willow End, N20 98 DA47
Northwood HA6 93 BU51
Surbiton KT6 198 CL102
Willow Fm La, SW15
off Queens Ride 159 CV83
Willowfield, Harl. CM18 51 ER17
Willowfield Cl, SE18 165 ES78
Sch Willowfield Sch, SE24
off Heron Rd 162 DQ84
Sch Willowfield Sec Sch, E17
off Clifton Av 123 DX55
Willow Gdns, Houns. TW3 156 CA81
Ruislip HA4 115 BT61
Willow Glade, Reig. RH2
off Hornbeam Rd 266 DB137
Willow Grn, NW9
off Clayton Fld 96 CS53
Borehamwood WD6 78 CR43
Dorking (N.Holm.) RH5
off Holmesdale Rd 263 CH140
Willow Gro, E13
off Libra Rd 144 EG68
Chislehurst BR7 185 EN93
Ruislip HA4 115 BT61
Willowhayne Dr, Walt. KT12 195 BV101
Willowhayne Gdns, Wor.Pk.
KT4 199 CW104
Willowherb Wk, Rom. RM3
off Clematis Cl 106 FJ52
Willow La, SE18 165 EM77
Amersham HP7 72 AT41
Guildford GU1
off Boxgrove Rd 243 BA133
Mitcham CR4 200 DF99
Watford WD18 75 BU43
Willow Mead, Chig. IG7 104 EU48
Dorking RH4
off Portland Rd 263 CG135
Willowmead, Hert. SG14 31 DN10
Willow Mead, Saw. CM21 36 EY06
Willowmead, Stai. TW18 194 BH95
Willowmead Cl, W5 137 CK71
Woking GU21 226 AU116
Willowmere, Esher KT10 214 CC105
Willow Mt, Croy. CR0
off Langton Way 202 DS104
Willow Pk, Sev. (Otford) TN14 241 FF117
Slough (Stoke P.) SL2 132 AU66
Willow Path, Wal.Abb. EN9 68 EE34
Willow Pl, SW1 19 K7
Harlow CM17 52 EZ19
Windsor (Eton) SL4 151 AQ78
Willow Rd, NW3 120 DD63
W5 158 CL75
Dartford DA1 188 FJ88
Enfield EN1 82 DS41
Erith DA8 167 FG81
Godalming GU7 258 AT143
New Malden KT3 198 CQ98
Redhill RH1 266 DC137
Romford RM6 126 EY58
Slough (Colnbr.) SL3 153 BE82
Wallington SM6 219 DH108
Willows, The, Amer. HP6 55 AP35
Buckhurst Hill IG9 102 EK48
Esher (Clay.) KT10 215 CE107
Grays RM17 170 GE79
Guildford GU4
off Collier Way 243 BD132
Rickmansworth (Mill End)
WD3 off Uxbridge Rd 92 BG47
St. Albans AL1 43 CH24
Watford WD19
off Brookside Rd 93 BV45
West Byfleet (Byfleet) KT14 212 BL113
Weybridge KT13 194 BN104
Willows Av, Mord. SM4 200 DB99
Willows Cl, Pnr. HA5 94 BW54
Willowside, St.Alb. (Lon.Col.)
AL2 62 CL27
Willows Path, Epsom KT18 216 CP114
Windsor SL4 150 AJ81
Willows Riverside Pk, Wind.
SL4 150 AJ80
Sch Willows Sch, The, Hayes
UB4 off Stipularis Dr 136 BX70
Willow St, E4 101 ED45
EC2 11 L3
Romford RM7 127 FC56
Willow Tree Cl, E3
off Birdsfield La 143 DZ67
SW18 off Cargill Rd 180 DB88
Hayes UB4 136 BW70
Romford (Abridge) RM4 86 EV41
Uxbridge UB10 115 BQ62
Willow Tree La, Hayes UB4 136 BW70
Willowtree Marina, Hayes
UB4 136 BY72
Sch Willow Tree Prim Sch,
Nthlt. UB5 off Arnold Rd 136 BY65
Willow Tree Wk, Brom. BR1 204 EH95
Willowtree Way, Th.Hth.
CR7 off Kensington Av 201 DN95
Willow Vale, W12 139 CU74
Chislehurst BR7 185 EP93
Leatherhead (Fetch.) KT22 230 CB123
Willow Vw, SW19 200 DD95
Ware SG12 33 DY07
Willow Wk, E17 123 DZ57
N2 98 DD54
N15 121 DP56
N21 81 DM44
SE1 21 M7
Chertsey KT16 194 BG101
Dartford DA1 188 FJ85
Egham (Eng.Grn) TW20 172 AW92
Guildford (Shere) GU5 260 BN139
Orpington BR6 205 EP104
Redhill RH1 off Ash Dr 267 DH136
Sutton SM3 199 CZ104
Tadworth (Box H.) KT20
off Oak Dr 248 CQ130
Upminster RM14 129 FS60
Willow Way, N3 98 DB52
SE26 182 DV90
W11 6 B10
Epsom KT19 216 CR107
Godstone RH9 252 DV132
Guildford GU1 242 AV130
Hatfield AL10 45 CT21
Hemel Hempstead HP1 40 BH18
Potters Bar EN6 64 DB33
Radlett WD7 77 CE36
Romford RM3 106 FP51
St. Albans AL2 60 CA27
Sunbury-on-Thames TW16 195 BU98
Tadworth (Box H.) KT20
off Oak Dr 248 CP130
Twickenham TW2 176 CB89
Wembley HA0 117 CG62
West Byfleet KT14 212 BJ111
Woking GU22 226 AX121
Willow Wd Cl, Slou. (Burn.)
SL1 130 AH68
Willow Wd Cres, SE25 202 DS100
Willrose Cres, SE2 166 EW78
Wills Cres, Houns. TW3 176 CB86
Wills Gro, NW7 97 CU50
Willson Rd, Egh. (Eng.Grn)
TW20 172 AV92
Wilman Gro, E8 142 DU66
Wilmar Cl, Hayes UB4 135 BR70
Uxbridge UB8 134 BK66
Wilmar Gdns, W.Wick. BR4 203 EB102
Wilmcote Ho, W2 7 J5
Wilmer Cl, Kings.T. KT2 178 CM92
Wilmer Cres, Kings.T. KT2 178 CM92
Wilmer Gdns, N1 5 L8
Wilmerhatch La, Epsom
KT18 232 CP118
Wilmer Lea Cl, E15 143 EC66
Wilmer Pl, N16
off Stoke Newington
Ch St 122 DT61
Wilmer Way, N14 99 DK50
WILMINGTON, Dart. DA2 188 FK91
Wilmington Av, W4 158 CR80
Orpington BR6 206 EW103
Sch Wilmington Co Prim Sch,
Dart. DA2 off Common La 187 FH90
Wilmington Ct Rd, Dart. DA2 187 FG90
Wilmington Gdns, Bark. IG11 145 ER65
Sch Wilmington Gram Sch for
Boys, Dart. DA2
off Common La 187 FH90
Sch Wilmington Gram Sch for
Girls, Dart. DA2
off Parsons La 187 FH90
Sch Wilmington Hall Sch, Dart.
DA2 off Common La 187 FH90
Wilmington Sq, WC1 10 C2
Wilmington St, WC1 10 C2
Wilmot Cl, N2 98 DC54
SE15 162 DU80
Wilmot Grn, Brwd.
(Gt Warley) CM13 107 FW51
Wilmot Pl, NW1 141 DJ66
W7 off Boston Rd 137 CE74
Wilmot Rd, E10 123 EB61
N17 122 DR55
Carshalton SM5 218 DF106
Dartford DA1 187 FH85
Wilmot Rd, Pur. CR8 219 DN112
Slough (Burn.) SL1 130 AH69
Wilmots Cl, Reig. RH2 250 DC133
Wilmot St, E2 12 C3
Wilmot Way, Bans. SM7 218 DA114
Wilmount St, SE18 165 EP77
Wilna Rd, SW18 180 DC87
Wilsham St, W11 16 B1
Wilshaw Cl, NW4 119 CU55
Wilshaw St, SE14 163 EA81
Wilshere Av, St.Alb. AL1 42 CC23
Wilsman Rd, S.Ock. RM15 149 FW68
Wilsmere Dr, Har. HA3 95 CF52
Northolt UB5 136 BY65
Wilson Av, Mitch. CR4 180 DE94
Wilson Cl, S.Croy. CR2
off Bartlett St 220 DR106
Wembley HA9 118 CM59
Wilson Dr, Cher. (Ott.) KT16 211 BB106
Wembley HA9 118 CM59
Wilson Gdns, Har. HA1 116 CC59
Wilson Gro, SE16 22 C4
Wilson La, Dart. DA4 209 FT96
Wilson Rd, E6 144 EK69
SE5 162 DS81
Chessington KT9 216 CM107
Ilford IG1 125 EM59
Wilsons, Tad. KT20
off Heathcote 233 CX121
Wilsons Pl, E14 13 L8
Wilsons Rd, W6 16 B9
Sch Wilson's Sch, Wall.
SM6 off Mollison Dr 219 DL107
Wilson St, E17 123 EC57
EC2 11 K5
N21 99 DN45
Wilson Way, Wok. GU21 226 AX116
Wilstone Cl, Hayes UB4 136 BY70
Wilstone Dr, St.Alb. AL4 43 CJ15
Wilthorne Gdns, Dag.
RM10 off Acre Rd 147 FB66
Wilton Av, W4 158 CS78
Wilton Cl, West Dr. UB7 154 BK79
Wilton Cres, SW1 18 E4
SW19 199 CZ95
Beaconsfield HP9 89 AL52
Hertford SG13 32 DQ12
Windsor SL4 151 AK84
Wilton Dr, Rom. RM5 105 FC52
Wilton Gdns, Walt. KT12 196 BX102
West Molesey KT8 196 CA97
Wilton Gro, SW19 199 CZ95
New Malden KT3 199 CT100
Wilton La, Beac. (Jordans)
HP9 89 AR52
Wilton Ms, SW1 18 F5
Wilton Par, Felt. TW13
off Highfield Rd 175 BU89
Wilton Pk, Beac. HP9 89 AP53
Wilton Pk Ct, SE18
off Prince Imperial Rd 165 EN81
Wilton Pl, SW1 18 E4
Addlestone (New Haw)
KT15 212 BK109
Wilton Rd, N10 98 DG54
SE2 166 EW76
SW1 19 H6
SW19 180 DE94
Barnet (Cockfos.) EN4 80 DF42
Beaconsfield HP9 89 AL51
Hounslow TW4 156 BX83
Ilford IG1 off Ilford La 125 EP62
Redhill RH1 266 DF135
Wilton Row, SW1 18 E4
Wilton Sq, N1 5 J7
Wilton St, SW1 18 G5
Wilton Ter, SW1 18 E5
Wilton Vil, N1 5 J8
Wilton Way, E8 142 DU65
Hertford SG13 32 DQ11
Wiltshire Av, Horn. RM11 128 FM56
Slough SL2 131 AQ70
Wiltshire Cl, NW7 97 CT50
SW3 18 C7
Dartford DA2 189 FR87
Wiltshire Gdns, N4 122 DQ58
Twickenham TW2 176 CC88
Wiltshire La, Pnr. HA5 115 BT55
Wiltshire Rd, SW9 161 DN83
Orpington BR6 206 EU101
Thornton Heath CR7 201 DN97
Wiltshire Row, N1 5 J8
Wilverley Cres, N.Mal. KT3 198 CS100
Wimbart Rd, SW2 181 DM87
WIMBLEDON, SW19 179 CY93
⇌ Wimbledon 179 CZ93
⊖ Wimbledon 179 CZ93
Tra Wimbledon 179 CZ93
★ Wimbledon (All England
Tenn & Croquet Club),
SW19 179 CY91
Wimbledon Br, SW19 179 CZ93
⇌ Wimbledon Chase 199 CY96
Sch Wimbledon Chase Prim
Sch, SW19
off Merton Hall Rd 199 CY95
Sch Wimbledon Coll, SW19
off Edge Hill 179 CX94
The Campion Cen, SW20
off Grand Dr 199 CW99
Sch Wimbledon Coll Prep Sch
(Donhead Lo), SW19
off Edge Hill 179 CX94
★ Wimbledon Common,
SW19 179 CT91
Wimbledon Common, SW19 179 CU91
Sch Wimbledon High Sch,
SW19 off Mansel Rd 179 CZ93
Wimbledon Hill Rd, SW19 179 CY93
Sch Wimbledon Ho Sch,
SW19 off Dorset Rd 200 DA95
WIMBLEDON PARK, SW19 179 CZ90
⊖ Wimbledon Park 180 DA90
Wimbledon Pk, SW19 179 CZ89
Wimbledon Pk Est, SW19 179 CY88
Sch Wimbledon Pk Prim Sch,
SW19 off Havana Rd 180 DB89
Wimbledon Pk Rd, SW18 179 CZ87
SW19 179 CZ88
Wimbledon Pk Side, SW19 179 CX89
Wimbledon Rd, SW17 180 DC91
Coll Wimbledon Sch of Art,
SW19 off Merton Hall Rd 199 CY95
Annexe, SW19
off Palmerston Rd 180 DA94
Wimbledon Stadium Business
Cen, SW17
off Riverside Rd 180 DB90
★ Wimbledon Windmill Mus,
SW19 179 CV89
Wimbolt St, E2 12 A1
Wimborne Av, Hayes UB4 135 BV72
Redhill RH1 266 DF139
Southall UB2 156 CA77
Wimborne Cl, SE12 184 EF85
Buckhurst Hill IG9 102 EH47
Epsom KT17 216 CS113
Sawbridgeworth CM21 36 EX05
Worcester Park KT4 199 CW102
Wimborne Dr, NW9 118 CN55
Pinner HA5 116 BX59
Wimborne Gdns, W13 137 CH72
Wimborne Gro, Wat. WD17 75 BS37
Wimborne Rd, N9 100 DU47
N17 100 DS54
Wimborne Way, Beck. BR3 203 DX97
Wimbourne Av, Chis. BR7 205 ET98
Orpington BR5 205 ET98
Wimbourne Ct, N1 5 J9
Wimbourne St, N1 5 J9
Wimpole Cl, Brom. BR2 204 EJ98
Kingston upon Thames
KT1 198 CM96
Wimpole Ms, W1 8 G5
Wimpole Rd, West Dr. UB7 134 BK74
Wimpole St, W1 8 G7
Wimshurst Cl, Croy. CR0 201 DL102
Winans Wk, SW9 161 DN82
Wincanton Cres, Nthlt. UB5 116 CA64
Wincanton Gdns, Ilf. IG6 125 EP55
Wincanton Rd, SW18 179 CZ87
Romford RM3 106 FK48
Winchcombe Rd, Cars. SM5 200 DD101
Winchcomb Gdns, SE9 164 EK83
Winchdells, Hem.H. HP3 40 BN23
Winchelsea Av, Bexh. DA7 166 EZ80
Winchelsea Cl, SW15 179 CX85
Winchelsea Rd, E7 124 EG62
N17 122 DS55
NW10 138 CR67
Winchelsey Ri, S.Croy. CR2 220 DT107
Winchendon Rd, SW6 159 CZ80
Teddington TW11 177 CD91
Winches Fm Dr, St.Alb. AL4 43 CK19
Winchester Av, NW6 139 CY67
NW9 118 CN55
Hounslow TW5 156 BZ79
Upminster RM14 129 FT60
Winchester Cl, E6
off Boultwood Rd 144 EL72
SE17 20 F8
Amersham HP7 55 AS39
Bromley BR2 204 EF97
Enfield EN1 82 DS43
Esher KT10 214 CA105
Kingston upon Thames KT2 178 CP94
Slough (Colnbr.) SL3 153 BE81
Waltham Abbey EN9
off Highbridge St 67 EB33
Winchester Ct, E17
off Billet Rd 101 DY53
Winchester Cres, Grav. DA12 191 GK90
Winchester Dr, Pnr. HA5 116 BX57
Winchester Gro, Sev. TN13 257 FH123
Winchester Ho, SE18
off Shooter's Hill Rd 164 EK80
Winchester Ms, NW3
off Winchester Rd 140 DD66
Winchester Pk, Brom. BR2 204 EF97
Winchester Pl, E8 5 N2
N6 121 DH60
W3 off Avenue Rd 158 CQ75
Winchester Rd, E4 101 EC52
N6 121 DH60
N9 100 DU46
NW3 140 DD66
Bexleyheath DA7 166 EX82
Bromley BR2 204 EF97
Feltham TW13 176 BZ90
Harrow HA3 118 CL56
Hayes UB3 155 BS80
Ilford IG1 125 ER62
Northwood HA6 115 BT55
Orpington BR6 224 EW105
Twickenham TW1 177 CH86
Walton-on-Thames KT12 195 BU102
Winchester Sq, SE1 21 J1
Winchester St, SW1 19 H9
W3 138 CQ74
Winchester Wk, SE1 21 J1
Winchester Way, Rick.
(Crox.Grn) WD3 75 BP43
Winchet Wk, Croy. CR0 202 DW100
Winchfield Cl, Har. HA3 117 CJ58
Winchfield Ho, SW15
off Highcliffe Dr 179 CT86
Winchfield Rd, SE26 183 DY92
Winchfield Way, Rick. WD3 92 BJ45
Winchilsea Cres, W.Mol. KT8 196 CC96
WINCHMORE HILL, N21 99 DM45
WINCHMORE HILL, Amer.
HP7 88 AJ45
⇌ Winchmore Hill 99 DN46
Winchmore Hill Rd, N14 99 DK46
N21 99 DK46
Sch Winchmore Sec Sch,
N21 off Laburnum Gro 100 DQ47
Winchstone Cl, Shep. TW17 194 BM98
Winckley Cl, Har. HA3 118 CM57
Wincott St, SE11 20 D7
Wincrofts Dr, SE9 165 ER84
Windall Cl, SE19 202 DU95
Windborough Rd, Cars. SM5 218 DG108
Windermere Av, N3 120 DA55
NW6 139 CY67
SW19 200 DB97
Harrow HA3 117 CJ59
Hornchurch RM12 127 FG64
Ruislip HA4 116 BW59
St. Albans AL1 43 CH22
Wembley HA9 117 CJ59
Windermere Cl, Dart. DA1 187 FH88
Egham TW20
off Derwent Rd 173 BB94
Feltham TW14 175 BT88
Hemel Hempstead HP3 41 BQ21
Orpington BR6 205 EP104
Rickmansworth (Chorl.)
WD3 73 BC43
Staines TW19 off Viola Av 174 BL88
Windermere Ct, SW13 159 CT79
Kenley CR8 235 DP115
Wembley HA9
off Windermere Av 117 CJ59
Windermere Gdns, Ilf. IG4 124 EL57
Windermere Gro, Wem. HA9
off Windermere Av 117 CJ60
Windermere Ho, Islw. TW7
off Summerwood Rd 177 CF85
Sch Windermere JM & Inf Sch,
St.Alb. AL1
off Windermere Av 43 CH22
Windermere Pt, SE15
off Ilderton Rd 162 DW80
Windermere Rd, N10 99 DH53
N19 off Holloway Rd 121 DJ61
SW15 178 CS91
SW16 201 DJ95
W5 157 CJ76
Bexleyheath DA7 167 FC82
Coulsdon CR5 235 DL115
Croydon CR0 202 DT102
Southall UB1 136 BZ71
West Wickham BR4 204 EE103
Windermere Way, Reig. RH2 250 DD133
Slough SL1 130 AJ71
West Drayton UB7
off Providence Rd 134 BM74
Winders Rd, SW11 160 DE82
Windfield, Lthd. KT22 231 CH121

Windfield Cl, SE26 183 DX91
Windgates, Guil. GU4
off Tychbourne Dr 243 BC131
Windham Av, Croy.
(New Adgtn) CR0 221 ED110
Windham Rd, Rich. TW9 158 CM83
Wind Hill, Ong. (Magd.Lav.)
CM5 53 FF20
Windhill, Welw.G.C. AL7 30 DA08
Windhover Way, Grav. DA12 191 GL91
Windings, The, S.Croy. CR2 220 DT111
Winding Shot, Hem.H. HP1 40 BG19
Winding Way, Dag. RM8 126 EW62
Harrow HA1 117 CE63
Windlass Pl, SE8 23 K8
Windlesham Gro, SW19 179 CX88
Windley Cl, SE23 182 DW89
Windmill All, W4
off Windmill Rd 158 CS77
Windmill Av, Epsom KT17 217 CT111
St. Albans AL4 43 CJ16
Southall UB2 156 CC75
Windmill Br Ho, Croy. CR0 202 DS102
Windmill Cl, SE1 22 B7
SE13 163 EC82
Caterham CR3 236 DQ121
Epsom KT17 217 CT112
Horley RH6 269 DH148
Sunbury-on-Thames TW16 175 BS94
Surbiton KT6 197 CH102
Upminster RM14 128 FN61
Waltham Abbey EN9 68 EE34
Windsor SL4 151 AP82
Windmill Ct, NW2 139 CY65
Windmill Dr, NW2 119 CY62
SW4 181 DJ85
Keston BR2 222 EJ105
Leatherhead KT22 231 CJ123
Reigate RH2 250 DD132
Rickmansworth (Crox.Grn)
WD3 74 BM44
Windmill End, Epsom KT17 217 CT112
Windmill Fld, Ware SG12 33 DX07
Windmill Flds, Harl. CM17 36 EZ11
Windmill Gdns, Enf. EN2 81 DN41
Windmill Grn, Shep. TW17 195 BS101
Windmill Gro, Croy. CR0 202 DQ101
WINDMILL HILL, Grav. DA11 191 GG88
Windmill Hill, NW3 120 DC62
Amersham (Colesh.) HP7 89 AM45
Enfield EN2 81 DP41
Kings Langley (Chipper.)
WD4 57 BF32
Ruislip HA4 115 BT59
Windmill Ho, E14 23 N7
Windmill La, E15 143 ED65
Barnet EN5 79 CT44
Bushey (Bushey Hth) WD23 95 CE46
Epsom KT17 217 CT112
Greenford UB6 136 CC71
Isleworth TW7 157 CE77
Southall UB2 156 CC76
Surbiton KT6 197 CH100
Waltham Cross (Chsht) EN8 67 DX30
Windmill Ms, W4
off Windmill Rd 158 CS77
Windmill Pas, W4 158 CS77
Windmill Ri, Kings.T. KT2 178 CP94
Windmill Rd, N18 100 DR49
SW18 180 DD86
SW19 179 CV88
W4 158 CS77
W5 157 CJ77
Brentford TW8 157 CK78
Croydon CR0 202 DQ101
Gerrards Cross (Chal.St.P.)
SL9 90 AX52
Hampton (Hmptn H.) TW12 176 CB92
Hemel Hempstead HP2 40 BL21
Mitcham CR4 201 DJ99
Sevenoaks TN13 257 FH130
Slough SL1 131 AR74
Slough (Fulmer) SL3 112 AX64
Sunbury-on-Thames TW16 195 BS95
Windmill Rd W, Sun. TW16 195 BS96
Windmill Row, SE11 20 C10
Windmill Shott, Egh. TW20
off Rusham Rd 173 AZ93
Windmill St, W1 9 L6
Bushey (Bushey Hth) WD23 95 CE46
Gravesend DA12 191 GH86
Windmill Wk, SE1 20 D2
Windmill Way, Reig. RH2 250 DD132
Ruislip HA4 115 BT60
Windmill Wd, Amer. HP6 55 AN37
Windmore Av, Pot.B. EN6 63 CW31
Windmore Cl, Wem. HA0 117 CG64
Windover Av, NW9 118 CR56
Windridge Cl, St.Alb. AL3 42 CA22
Windrose Cl, SE16 22 G3
Windrush, N.Mal. KT3 198 CP98
Windrush Av, Slou. SL3 153 BB76
Windrush Cl, SW11
off Maysoule Rd 160 DD84
W4 158 CQ81
Uxbridge UB10 114 BM63
Windrush La, SE23 183 DX90
Sch Windrush Prim Sch,
SE28 *off Bentham Rd* 146 EV74
Windrush Rd, NW10 138 CR67
Windrush Sq, SW2
off Rushcroft Rd 161 DN84
Winds End Cl, Hem.H. HP2 40 BN18
Windsock Cl, SE16 23 L7
WINDSOR, SL4 152 AS82
⇌ Windsor & Eton Central 151 AR81
Windsor & Eton Relief Rd,
Wind. SL4 151 AP80
⇌ Windsor & Eton Riverside 151 AR80
Windsor Av, E17 101 DY54
SW19 200 DC95
Edgware HA8 96 CP49
Grays RM16 170 GB75
New Malden KT3 198 CQ99
Sutton SM3 199 CY104
Uxbridge UB10 135 BP67
West Molesey KT8 196 CA97
Sch Windsor Boys' Sch, The,
Wind. SL4
off Maidenhead Rd 151 AP81
★ Windsor Castle, Wind.
SL4 152 AS81
Windsor Cen, The, SE27
off Advance Rd 182 DQ91
Windsor Cl, N3 97 CY54
SE27 182 DQ91
Borehamwood WD6 78 CN39
Brentford TW8 157 CH79
Chislehurst BR7 185 EP92
Guildford GU2 258 AT136
Harrow HA2 116 CA62
Hemel Hempstead HP2 40 BL22
Hemel Hempstead (Bov.)
HP3 57 BA28
Northwood HA6 93 BU54
Waltham Cross (Chsht)
EN7 66 DU30
Windsor Ct, N14 99 DJ45
Sunbury-on-Thames TW16
off Windsor Rd 175 BU93
Windsor Ct Rd, Wok.
(Chobham) GU24 210 AS109
Windsor Cres, Har. HA2 116 CA63
High Wycombe (Loud.)
HP10 88 AC53
Wembley HA9 118 CP62
Windsor Dr, Ashf. TW15 174 BK91
Barnet EN4 80 DF44
Dartford DA1 187 FG86
Hertford SG14 31 DM09
Orpington BR6 224 EU107
Windsor End, Beac. HP9 111 AM55
Windsor Gdns, W9 6 G5
Croydon CR0
off Richmond Rd 201 DL104
Hayes UB3 155 BR76
Sch Windsor Girls' Sch, Wind.
SL4 *off Imperial Rd* 151 AN83
★ Windsor Great Pk, Ascot,
Egh. & Wind. 172 AS93
Windsor Gro, SE27 182 DQ91
Windsor Hill, H.Wyc.
(Woob.Grn) HP10 110 AF58
Windsor La, H.Wyc.
(Woob.Grn) HP10 110 AE58
Slough (Burn.) SL1 130 AJ70
Windsor Ms, SE6 183 EC88
SE23 183 DY88
Windsor Pk Rd, Hayes UB3 155 BT80
Windsor Pl, SW1 19 K6
Chertsey KT16
off Windsor St 194 BG100
Harlow CM20
off River Way 36 EU11
★ Windsor Racecourse
(Royal), Wind. SL4 151 AM79
Windsor Rd, E4
off Chivers Rd 101 EB49
E7 124 EH64
E10 123 EB61
E11 124 EG60
N3 97 CY54
N7 121 DL62
N13 99 DN48
N17 100 DU54
NW2 139 CV65
W5 138 CL73
Barnet EN5 79 CY44
Beaconsfield HP9 111 AN57
Bexleyheath DA6 166 EY84
Brentwood (Pilg.Hat.)
CM15 108 FV44
Chesham HP5 54 AP28
Dagenham RM8 126 EY62
Egham (Eng.Grn) TW20 173 AZ90
Enfield EN3 83 DX36
Gerrards Cross SL9 112 AW60
Gravesend DA12 191 GH90
Harrow HA3 95 CD53
Hornchurch RM11 128 FJ59
Hounslow TW4 155 BV82
Ilford IG1 125 EP63
Kingston upon Thames
KT2 178 CL94
Maidenhead SL6 150 AF79
Richmond TW9 158 CM82
Slough SL1 152 AS76
Slough (Datchet) SL3 152 AT80
Slough (Stoke P.) SL2 112 AU63
Southall UB2 156 BZ76
Staines (Wrays.) TW19 172 AY86
Sunbury-on-Thames TW16 175 BU93
Teddington TW11 177 CD92
Thornton Heath CR7 201 DP96
Watford WD24 76 BW38
Windsor (Eton) SL4 151 AR79
Windsor (Wat.Oak.) SL4 150 AF79
Woking (Chobham) GU24 210 AS109
Worcester Park KT4 199 CU103
Windsor Royal Sta, Wind.
SL4 151 AR81
Windsors, The, Buck.H. IG9 102 EL47
Windsor St, N1 4 F7
Chertsey KT16 194 BG100
Uxbridge UB8 134 BJ66
Windsor Ter, N1 11 H1
Windsor Wk, SE5 162 DR82
Walton-on-Thames KT12
off King George Av 196 BX102
Weybridge KT13 213 BP106
Windsor Way, W14 16 B7
Rickmansworth WD3 92 BG46
Woking GU22 227 BC116
Windsor Wf, E9 123 DZ64
Windsor Wd, Wal.Abb. EN9
off Monkswood Av 68 EE33
Windspoint Dr, SE15
off Ethnard Rd 162 DV79
Winds Ridge, Wok. (Send)
GU23 243 BC125
Windus Rd, N16 122 DT60
Windus Wk, N16 122 DT60
Windward Cl, Enf. EN3
off Bullsmoor La 83 DX35
Windycroft Cl, Pur. CR8 219 DK113
Windy Hill, Brwd. (Hutt.)
CM13 109 GC46
Windy Ridge, Brom. BR1 204 EL95
Windyridge Cl, SW19 179 CX92
Wine Cl, E1 12 E10
Wine Office Ct, EC4 10 D7
Winern Glebe, W.Byf. (Byfleet)
KT14 212 BK113
Winery La, Kings.T. KT1 198 CM97
Winey Cl, Chess. KT9
off Nigel Fisher Way 215 CJ108
Winfield Mobile Home Pk,
Wat. WD25 76 CB39
Winford Dr, Brox. EN10 49 DZ22
Winford Ho, E3 143 DZ66
Winford Par, Sthl. UB1
off Telford Rd 136 CB72
Winforton St, SE10 163 EC81
Winfrith Rd, SW18 180 DC87
Wingate Cres, Croy. CR0 201 DK100
Wingate Rd, W6 159 CV76
Ilford IG1 125 EP64
Sidcup DA14 186 EW92
Wingate Trd Est, N17 100 DU52
Wingate Way, St.Alb. AL1 43 CG21
Wing Cl, Epp. (N.Wld Bas.)
CM16 *off Epping Rd* 70 FA27
Wingfield, Grays (Bad.Dene)
RM17 170 FZ78
Wingfield Bk, Grav. (Nthflt)
DA11 190 GC89
Wingfield Cl, Add. (New Haw)
KT15 212 BH110
Brentwood CM13
off Pondfield La 109 GA48
Wingfield Gdns, Upmin.
RM14 129 FT58
Wingfield Ms, SE15
off Wingfield St 162 DU83
Sch Wingfield Prim Sch,
SE3 *off Moorehead Way* 164 EH83
Wingfield Rd, E15 124 EE64
E17 123 EB57
Gravesend DA12 191 GH87
Kingston upon Thames KT2 178 CN93
Wingfield St, SE15 162 DU83
Wingfield Way, Ruis. HA4 135 BV65
Wingford Rd, SW2 181 DL86
Wingletye La, Horn. RM11 128 FM60
Wingmore Rd, SE24 162 DQ83
Wingrave Cres, Brwd. CM14 108 FS49
Wingrave Rd, W6 159 CW79
Wingrove Dr, Purf. RM19 168 FP78
Wingrove Rd, SE6 184 EE89
Wings Cl, Sutt. SM1 218 DA105
Wing Way, Brwd. CM14
off Geary Dr 108 FW46
Winifred Av, Horn. RM12 128 FK63
Winifred Cl, Barn. EN5 79 CT44
Winifred Gro, SW11 160 DF84
Winifred Pl, N12 *off High Rd* 98 DC50
Winifred Rd, SW19 200 DA95
Coulsdon CR5 234 DG116
Dagenham RM8 126 EY61
Dartford DA1 187 FH85
Erith DA8 167 FE78
Hampton (Hmptn H.) TW12 176 CA91
Hemel Hempstead HP3 40 BK24
Winifred St, E16 145 EM74
Winifred Ter, E13
off Victoria Rd 144 EG68
Enfield EN1
off Great Cambridge Rd 100 DT45
Winkers Cl, Ger.Cr.
(Chal.St.P.) SL9 91 AZ53
Winkers La, Ger.Cr.
(Chal.St.P.) SL9 91 AZ53
Winkfield Rd, E13 144 EH68
N22 99 DN53
Winkley St, E2 142 DV68
Winkwell, Hem.H. HP2 39 BD22
Winkworth Pl, Bans. SM7
off Bolters La 217 CZ114
Winkworth Rd, Bans. SM7 217 CZ114
Winlaton Rd, Brom. BR1 183 ED91
Winmill Rd, Dag. RM8 126 EZ62
Winnards, Wok. GU21
off Abercorn Way 226 AV118
Winn Common Rd, SE18 165 ES79
Winnett St, W1 9 L9
Winningales Ct, Ilf. IG5
off Vienna Cl 124 EL55
Winnings Wk, Nthlt. UB5
off Arnold Rd 136 BY65
Winnington Cl, N2 120 DD58
Winnington Rd, N2 120 DD59
Enfield EN3 82 DW38
Winnington Way, Wok. GU21 226 AV118
Winnipeg Dr, Orp. BR6 223 ET107
Winnipeg Way, Brox. EN10 67 DY25
Winnock Rd, West Dr. UB7 134 BK74
Winn Rd, SE12 184 EG88
Winns Av, E17 123 DY55
Winns Ms, N15
off Grove Pk Rd 122 DS56
Sch Winns Prim Sch, The,
E17 *off Fleeming Rd* 101 DZ54
Winns Ter, E17 101 EA54
Winsbeach, E17 123 ED55
Winscombe Cres, W5 137 CK70
Winscombe St, N19 121 DH61
Winscombe Way, Stan. HA7 95 CG50
Winsford Rd, SE6 183 DZ90
Winsford Ter, N18 100 DR50
Winsham Gro, SW11 180 DG85
Winslade Rd, SW2 181 DL85
Winslade Way, SE6
off Rushey Grn 183 EB87
Winsland Ms, W2 7 N7
Winsland St, W2 7 N7
Winsley St, W1 9 J7
Winslow, SE17 21 L10
Winslow Cl, NW10
off Neasden La N 118 CS62
Pinner HA5 115 BV58
Winslow Gro, E4 102 EE47
Winslow Rd, W6 159 CW79
Winslow Way, Felt. TW13 176 BX90
Walton-on-Thames KT12 196 BW104
Sch Winsor Prim Sch, E6
off East Ham Manor Way 145 EN72
Winsor Ter, E6 145 EN71
Winsor Ter Roundabout, E6
off Royal Docks Rd 145 EP71
Winstanley Cl, Cob. KT11 213 BV114
Winstanley Est, SW11 160 DD83
Winstanley Rd, SW11 160 DD83
Winstanley Wk, Cob. KT11
off Winstanley Cl 213 BU114
Winstead Gdns, Dag. RM10 127 FC64
Winston Av, NW9 118 CS59
Sch Winston Churchill Sch,
The, Wok. GU21
off Hermitage Rd 226 AT118
Winston Churchill Way, Wal.Cr.
(Chsht) EN8 66 DW33
Winston Cl, Green. DA9 189 FT85
Harrow HA3 95 CF51
Romford RM7 127 FB56
Winston Ct, Har. HA3 94 CB52
Winston Dr, Cob.
(Stoke D'Ab.) KT11 230 BY116
Winstone Cl, Amer. HP6 54 AP34
Winston Gdns, Berk. HP4 38 AT19
Winston Rd, N16 5 K1
Winston Wk, W4
off Beaconsfield Rd 158 CR77
Winston Way, Ilf. IG1 125 EP62
Potters Bar EN6 64 DA34
Woking (Old Wok.) GU22 227 BB120
Winstre Rd, Borwd. WD6 78 CN39
Winter Av, E6 144 EL67
Winterborne Av, Orp. BR6 205 ER104
Winterbourne Gro, Wey.
KT13 213 BQ107
Sch Winterbourne Inf Sch,
Th.Hth. CR7
off Winterbourne Rd 201 DN98
Sch Winterbourne Jun Boys'
Sch, Th.Hth. CR7
off Winterbourne Rd 201 DN98
Sch Winterbourne Jun Girls'
Sch, Th.Hth. CR7
off Winterbourne Rd 201 DN98
Winterbourne Rd, SE6 183 DZ88
Dagenham RM8 126 EW61
Thornton Heath CR7 201 DN97
Winter Box Wk, Rich. TW10 158 CM84
Winterbrook Rd, SE24 182 DQ86
Winterburn Cl, N11 98 DG51
Winterdown Gdns, Esher
KT10 214 BZ107
Winterdown Rd, Esher KT10 214 BZ107
Winterfold Cl, SW19 179 CY89
Wintergarden, Green.
(Bluewater) DA9
off Bluewater Parkway 189 FU88
Winter Gdn Cres, Green.
(Bluewater) DA9 189 FU87
Wintergreen Cl, E6
off Yarrow Cres 144 EL71
Winterhill Way, Guil. GU4 243 BB130
Winters Cft, Grav. DA12 191 GK93
Winterscroft Rd, Hodd. EN11 49 DZ16
Wintersells Rd, W.Byf.
(Byfleet) KT14 212 BK110
Winters Rd, T.Ditt. KT7 197 CH101
Winterstoke Gdns, NW7 97 CU50
Winterstoke Rd, SE6 183 DZ88
Winters Way, Wal.Abb. EN9 68 EG33
Winterton Ho, E1 12 D8
Winterton Pl, SW10
off Park Wk 160 DC79
Winterwell Rd, SW2 181 DL85
Winthorpe Rd, SW15 159 CY84
Winthrop St, E1 12 C5
Winthrop Wk, Wem. HA9
off Everard Way 118 CL62
Winton App, Rick. (Crox.Grn)
WD3 75 BQ43
Winton Av, N11 99 DJ52
Winton Cl, N9 101 DX45
Winton Cres, Rick. (Crox.Grn)
WD3 75 BP43
Winton Dr, Rick. (Crox.Grn)
WD3 75 BP44
Waltham Cross (Chsht)
EN8 67 DY29
Winton Gdns, Edg. HA8 96 CM52
Sch Winton Prim Sch, N1 4 A10
Winton Rd, Orp. BR6 223 EP105
Ware SG12 33 DZ06
Winton Way, SW16 181 DN92
Wintoun Path, Slou. SL2 131 AL70
Winvale, Slou. SL1 152 AS76
Winwood, Slou. SL2 132 AW72
Wireless Rd, West. (Bigg.H.)
TN16 238 EK115
Wirrall Ho, SE26
off Sydenham Hill 182 DU90
Wisbeach Rd, Croy. CR0 202 DR99
Wisborough Rd, S.Croy. CR2 220 DT109
Wisdom Dr, Hert. SG13
off Park Rd 32 DS09
Wisdons Cl, Dag. RM10 127 FB60
Wise La, NW7 97 CV51
West Drayton UB7 154 BK77
Wiseman Ct, SE19 182 DS92
Wiseman Rd, E10 123 EA61
Wisemans Gdns, Saw.
CM21
off High Wych Rd 36 EW06
Wise Rd, E15 143 ED67
Wise's La, Hat. AL9 63 CW27
Wiseton Rd, SW17 180 DE88
Wishart Rd, SE3 164 EK81
Wishbone Way, Wok. GU21 226 AT116
Wishford Ct, Ashtd. KT21
off The Marld 232 CM118
Sch Wishmore Cross Sch,
Wok. GU24
off Alpha Rd 210 AT110
WISLEY, Wok. GU23 228 BL116
Wisley Common, Wok.
GU23 228 BN117
Wisley Ct, S.Croy. CR2
off Sanderstead Rd 220 DS110
Wisley La, Wok. (Wisley)
GU23 228 BL116
Wisley Rd, SW11 180 DG85
Orpington BR5 186 EU94
Wissants, Harl. CM19 51 EP19
Wistaria Cl, Brwd.
(Pilg.Hat.) CM15 108 FW43
Wistaria Dr, St.Alb.
(Lon.Col.) AL2 61 CH26
Wisteria Cl, NW7 97 CT51
Ilford IG1 125 EP64
Orpington BR6 205 EP103
Wisteria Gdns, Swan. BR8 207 FD96
Wisteria Rd, SE13 163 ED84
Wistlea Cres, St.Alb.
(Coln.Hth) AL4 44 CP22
Witan St, E2 12 D2
Witches La, Sev. TN13 256 FD122
Witchford, Welw.G.C. AL7 30 DD09
Witham Cl, Loug. IG10 84 EL44
Witham Rd, SE20 202 DW97
W13 137 CG74
Dagenham RM10 126 FA64
Isleworth TW7 157 CD81
Romford RM2 127 FH57
Withens Cl, Orp. BR5 206 EW98
Witherby Cl, Croy. CR0 220 DS106
Wither Dale, Horl. RH6 268 DE147
Witheridge La, Beac.
(Knot.Grn) HP9 88 AF48
High Wycombe (Penn) HP10 88 AF48
Witherings, The, Horn. RM11 128 FL57
Witherington Rd, N5 4 D2
Withers Cl, Chess. KT9
off Coppard Gdns 215 CJ107
Withers Mead, NW9 97 CT53
Witherston Way, SE9 185 EN89
Withey Brook, Horl. (Hkwd)
RH6 268 DD150
Withey Cl, Wind. SL4 151 AL81
Witheygate Av, Stai. TW18 174 BH93
Withey Meadows, Horl.
(Hkwd) RH6 268 DD150
Withies, The, Lthd. KT22 231 CH120
Woking (Knap.) GU21 226 AS117
Withybed Cor, Tad. KT20 233 CV123
Withycombe Rd, SW19 179 CX87
Withycroft, Slou. (Geo.Grn)
SL3 132 AY72
Withy La, Ruis. HA4 115 BQ57
Withy Mead, E4 101 ED48
Withy Pl, St.Alb. (Park St) AL2 60 CC28
Witley Cres, Croy.
(New Adgtn) CR0 221 EC107
Witley Gdns, Sthl. UB2 156 BZ77
Witley Pt, SW15
off Wanborough Dr 179 CV88
Witley Rd, N19
off Holloway Rd 121 DJ61
Witney Cl, Pnr. HA5 94 BZ51
Uxbridge UB10 114 BM63
Witney Path, SE23 183 DX90
Wittenham Way, E4 101 ED48
Wittering Cl, Kings.T. KT2 177 CK92
Wittering Wk, Horn. RM12 148 FJ65
Wittersham Rd, Brom. BR1 184 EF92
Wivenhoe Cl, SE15 162 DV83
Wivenhoe Ct, Houns. TW3 156 BZ84
Wivenhoe Rd, Bark. IG11 146 EU68
Wiverton Rd, SE26 182 DW93
Wix Hill, Lthd. (W.Hors.) KT24 245 BP130
Wix Hill Cl, Lthd. (W.Hors.)
KT24 245 BP131
Wixom Ho, SE3
off Romero Sq 164 EJ84
Sch Wix Prim Sch, SW4
off Wixs La 161 DH83
Wix Rd, Dag. RM9 146 EX67
Wixs La, SW4 161 DH84
Woburn Av, Epp. (They.B.)
CM16 85 ES37
Hornchurch RM12 127 FG63
Purley CR8 *off High St* 219 DN111
Woburn Cl, SE28
off Summerton Way 146 EX72
SW19 *off Tintern Cl* 180 DC93
Bushey WD23 76 CC43
Woburn Ct, SE16
off Masters Dr 162 DV78
Woburn Hill, Add. KT15 194 BJ103
Woburn Pl, WC1 9 M3
Woburn Rd, Cars. SM5 200 DE102
Croydon CR0 202 DQ102
Woburn Sq, WC1 9 M4
Woburn Wk, WC1 9 M2
Wodehouse Av, SE5 162 DT81
Wodehouse Rd, Dart. DA1 168 FN84
Wodeland Av, Guil. GU2 258 AV136
Woffington Cl, Kings.T. KT1 197 CJ95
Wokindon Rd, Grays RM16 171 GH76
WOKING, GU21 - GU24 227 AZ118
⇌ Woking 227 AZ117
Coll Woking Adult Learning
Cen, Highlands, Wok.
GU22 *off Bonsey La* 226 AX121
Woking Business Pk, Wok.
GU21 227 BB115
Woking Cl, SW15 159 CT84
Coll Woking Coll,
Wok. GU22
off Rydens Way 227 BA120
H Woking Comm Hosp,
Wok. GU22 227 AZ118
Sch Woking High Sch, Wok.
GU21 *off Morton Rd* 226 AX115
H Woking Nuffield Hosp,
The, Wok. GU21 210 AY114
Woking Rd, Guil. GU1, GU4 242 AX130
Wold, The, Cat. (Wold.) CR3 237 EA122
Woldham Pl, Brom. BR2 204 EJ98
Woldham Rd, Brom. BR2 204 EJ98
WOLDINGHAM, Cat. CR3 237 EB122
⇌ Woldingham 237 DX122
WOLDINGHAM GARDEN
VILLAGE, Cat. CR3 237 DY121
Woldingham Rd, Cat. (Wold.)
CR3 236 DV120
Sch Woldingham Sch, Cat.
CR3 *off Marden Pk* 253 DY125
Wolds Dr, Orp. BR6 223 EN105
Wolfe Cl, Brom. BR2 204 EG100
Hayes UB4 *off Ayles Rd* 135 BV69
Wolfe Cres, SE7 164 EK78
SE16 22 G4
Wolferton Rd, E12 125 EM63
Wolffe Gdns, E15 144 EF65
Sch Wolf Flds Prim Sch, Sthl.
UB2 *off Norwood Rd* 156 BZ77
Wolffram Cl, SE13 184 EE85
Wolfington Rd, SE27 181 DP91
Wolf La, Wind. SL4 151 AK83
Wolfs Hill, Oxt. RH8 254 EG131
Sch Wolfson Hillel Prim Sch,
N14 *off Chase Rd* 81 DK44
H Wolfson Med Rehab Cen,
SW20 179 CV94
Wolf's Row, Oxt. RH8 254 EH130
Wolfs Wd, Oxt. RH8 254 EG132
Wolftencroft Cl, SW11 160 DD83
Wollaston Cl, SE1 20 G7
Wolmer Cl, Edg. HA8 96 CP49
Wolmer Gdns, Edg. HA8 96 CN48
Wolseley Av, SW19 180 DA89
Wolseley Gdns, W4 158 CP79
Wolseley Rd, E7 144 EH66
N8 121 DK58
N22 99 DM53
W4 158 CQ77
Harrow HA3 117 CE55
Mitcham CR4 200 DG101
Romford RM7 127 FD59
Wolseley St, SE1 21 P4
Wolsey Av, E6 145 EN69
E17 123 DZ55
Thames Ditton KT7 197 CF99
Waltham Cross (Chsht) EN7 66 DT29
Wolsey Business Pk, Wat.
WD18 93 BR45
Wolsey Cl, SW20 179 CV94
Hounslow TW3 156 CC84
Kingston upon Thames KT2 198 CP95
Southall UB2 156 CC76
Worcester Park KT4 217 CU105
Wolsey Cres, Croy.
(New Adgtn) CR0 221 EC109
Morden SM4 199 CY101
Wolsey Dr, Kings.T. KT2 178 CL92
Walton-on-Thames KT12 196 BX102
Wolsey Gdns, Ilf. IG6 103 EQ51
Wolsey Gro, Edg. HA8 96 CR52
Esher KT10 214 CB105
Sch Wolsey Jun Sch, Croy.
CR0 *off King Henry's Dr* 221 EC108
Wolsey Ms, NW5 141 DJ65
Orpington BR6
off Osgood Av 223 ET106
Wolsey Pl Shop Cen, Wok.
GU21
off Commercial Way 226 AY117
Wolsey Rd, N1 5 K2
Ashford TW15 174 BL91
East Molesey KT8 197 CD98
Enfield EN1 82 DV40
Esher KT10 214 CB105
Hampton (Hmptn H.) TW12 176 CB93
Hemel Hempstead HP2 40 BK21
Northwood HA6 93 BQ47
Sunbury-on-Thames TW16 175 BT94
Wolsey St, E1 12 E6
Wolsey Wk, Wok. GU21 226 AY117
Wolsey Way, Chess. KT9 216 CN106
Wolsley Cl, Dart. DA1 187 FE85
Wolstan Cl, Uxb. (Denh.)
UB9 *off Lindsey Rd* 114 BG62
Wolstonbury, N12 98 DA50
Wolvens La, Dor. RH4, RH5 262 CA140
Wolvercote Rd, SE2 166 EX75
Wolverley St, E2 12 C2
Wolverton, SE17 21 K9
Wolverton Av, Kings.T. KT2 198 CN95
Wolverton Cl, Horl. RH6 268 DF150
Wolverton Gdns, W5 138 CM73
W6 16 A7
Horley RH6 268 DF149
Wolverton Rd, Stan. HA7 95 CH51
Wolverton Way, N14 81 DJ43
Wolves La, N13 99 DN52
N22 99 DN52
Wombwell Gdns, Grav.
(Nthflt) DA11 190 GE89
WOMBWELL PARK, Grav.
DA11 190 GD89
Womersley Rd, N8 121 DM58
WONERSH, Guil. GU5 259 BB144
Wonersh Common, Guil.
(Won.) GU5 259 BB141
Wonersh Common Rd, Guil.
(Won.) GU5 259 BB142
Wonersh Way, Sutt. SM2 217 CX109
Wonford Cl, Kings.T. KT2 198 CS95
Tadworth KT20 249 CU126
Wonham La, Bet. RH3 264 CS135
Wonham Way, Guil. (Goms.)
GU5 261 BR139
Wontford Rd, Pur. CR8 235 DN115
Wontner Cl, N1 4 G6
Wontner Rd, SW17 180 DF89
WOOBURN, H.Wyc. HP10 110 AD58
Wooburn Cl, Uxb. UB8
off Aldenham Dr 135 BP70
Wooburn Common, H.Wyc.
(Woob.Grn) HP10 110 AH59
Wooburn Common Rd, H.Wyc.
(Woob.Grn) HP10 110 AH61
Slough SL1 110 AH61
Wooburn Gra, H.Wyc.
(Woob.Grn) HP10 110 AD60

★ Place of interest H Hospital Sch School Coll College Uni University ⇌ Railway station

WOOBURN GREEN, H.Wyc. HP10 110 AF56
Wooburn Grn La, Beac. HP9 110 AG56
Wooburn Ind Pk, H.Wyc. (Woob.Grn) HP10 110 AD59
Wooburn Manor Pk, H.Wyc. (Woob.Grn) HP10 110 AE58
Wooburn Mead, H.Wyc. HP10 off Wycombe La 110 AE57
Wooburn Ms, H.Wyc. (Woob.Grn) HP10 110 AE58
Wooburn Town, H.Wyc. (Woob.Grn) HP10 110 AD59
Sch Woodacre Sch, S.Ock. RM15 off Erriff Dr 149 FU71
Woodall Cl, E14 14 B9
Chessington KT9 215 CK107
Woodall Rd, Enf. EN3 83 DX44
Wood Av, Purf. RM19 168 FQ77
Woodbank, Rick. WD3 74 BJ44
Woodbank Av, Ger.Cr. SL9 112 AX58
Woodbank Dr, Ch.St.G. HP8 90 AX48
Woodbank Rd, Brom. BR1 184 EF90
Woodbastwick Rd, SE26 183 DX92
Woodberry Av, N21 99 DN47
Harrow HA2 116 CB56
Woodberry Cl, NW7 97 CX52
Sunbury-on-Thames TW16 off Ashridge Way 175 BU93
Woodberry Cres, N10 121 DH55
Woodberry Down, N4 122 DQ59
Epping CM16 70 EU29
Woodberry Down Est, N4 122 DQ59
Sch Woodberry Down Inf & Jun Sch, N4 off Woodberry Gro 122 DQ59
Woodberry Gdns, N12 98 DC51
Woodberry Gro, N4 122 DQ59
N12 98 DC51
Bexley DA5 187 FD90
Woodberry Way, E4 101 EC46
N12 98 DC51
Woodbine Cl, Harl. CM19 off Linford End 51 EQ17
Twickenham TW2 177 CD89
Waltham Abbey EN9 84 EJ35
Woodbine Gro, SE20 182 DV94
Enfield EN2 82 DR38
Woodbine La, Wor.Pk. KT4 199 CW104
Woodbine Pl, E11 124 EG58
Woodbine Rd, Sid. DA15 185 ES88
Woodbines Av, Kings.T. KT1 197 CK97
Woodbine Ter, E9 off Morning La 142 DW65
Woodborough Rd, SW15 159 CV84
Woodbourne Av, SW16 181 DK90
Woodbourne Cl, SW16 off Woodbourne Av 181 DL90
Woodbourne Dr, Esher (Clay.) KT10 215 CF107
Woodbourne Gdns, Wall. SM6 219 DH108
Woodbridge Av, Lthd. KT22 231 CG118
Woodbridge Business Pk, Guil.GU1 off Woodbridge Rd 242 AW133
Woodbridge Cl, N7 121 DM61
NW2 119 CU62
Romford RM3 106 FK49
Woodbridge Ct, Wdf.Grn. IG8 102 EL52
Woodbridge Gro, Lthd. KT22 231 CG118
Sch Woodbridge High Sch, Wdf.Grn. IG8 off St. Barnabas Rd 102 EH52
WOODBRIDGE HILL, Guil. GU2 242 AU132
Woodbridge Hill, Guil. GU2 242 AV133
Woodbridge Hill Gdns, Guil. GU2 242 AU133
Woodbridge La, Rom. RM3 106 FK48
Woodbridge Meadows, Guil. GU1 242 AW133
Woodbridge Rd, Bark. IG11 125 ET64
Guildford GU1 242 AW133
Woodbridge St, EC1 10 E3
Woodbrook Gdns, Wal.Abb. EN9 68 EE33
Woodbrook Rd, SE2 166 EU79
Sch Woodbrook Spec Sch, Beck. BR3 off Hayne Rd 203 DZ95
Woodburn Cl, NW4 119 CX57
Woodbury, B.End SL8 110 AC59
Woodbury Cl, E11 124 EH56
Croydon CR0 202 DT103
Westerham (Bigg.H.) TN16 239 EM118
Woodbury Dr, Sutt. SM2 218 DC110
Woodbury Hill, Loug. IG10 84 EL41
Woodbury Hollow, Loug. IG10 84 EL40
Woodbury Pk Rd, W13 137 CH70
Woodbury Rd, E17 123 EB56
Westerham (Bigg.H.) TN16 239 EM118
Woodbury St, SW17 180 DE92
Woodchester Pk, Beac. (Knot.Grn) HP9 88 AJ50
Woodchester Sq, W2 7 J5
Woodchurch Cl, Sid. DA14 185 ER90
Woodchurch Dr, Brom. BR1 184 EK94
Woodchurch Rd, NW6 140 DA66
Wood Cl, E2 12 A3
NW9 118 CR59
Bexley DA5 187 FE90
Harrow HA1 117 CD59
Hatfield AL10 45 CV18
Redhill RH1 266 DG143
Windsor SL4 151 AQ84
Woodclyffe Dr, Chis. BR7 205 EN96
Woodcock Ct, Har. HA3 118 CL59
Woodcock Dell Av, Har. HA3 117 CK59
Woodcock Hill, Berk. HP4 38 AS18
Harrow HA3 117 CK59
Rickmansworth WD3 92 BL50
St. Albans (Sand.) AL4 44 CN15
Woodcocks, E16 144 EJ71
Woodcombe Cres, SE23 182 DW88
Wood Common, Hat. AL10 45 CV15
WOODCOTE, Epsom KT18 232 CQ116
WOODCOTE, Pur. CR8 219 DK111
Woodcote, Guil. GU2 258 AV138
Horley RH6 off The Fieldings 269 DJ147
Woodcote Av, NW7 97 CW51
Hornchurch RM12 127 FG63
Thornton Heath CR7 201 DP98
Wallington SM6 219 DH108
Woodcote Cl, Enf. EN3 82 DW44
Epsom KT18 216 CR114
Kingston upon Thames KT2 178 CM92
Waltham Cross (Chsht) EN8 66 DW30
Woodcote Dr, Orp. BR6 205 ER102
Purley CR8 219 DK110
Woodcote End, Epsom KT18 232 CR115
Woodcote Grn, Wall. SM6 219 DJ109
Woodcote Grn Rd, Epsom KT18 232 CQ116
Woodcote Gro, Couls. CR5 219 DH112
Woodcote Gro Rd, Couls. CR5 235 DK115
Sch Woodcote High Sch, Couls. CR5 off Meadow Ri 219 DK113
Woodcote Hurst, Epsom KT18 232 CQ116
Sch Woodcote Jun & Inf Sch, Couls. CR5 off Dunsfold Ri 219 DK114
Woodcote La, Pur. CR8 219 DK111
Woodcote Lawns, Chesh. HP5 off Little Hivings 54 AN27
Woodcote Ms, Loug. IG10 102 EK45
Wallington SM6 219 DH107
Woodcote Pk Av, Pur. CR8 219 DJ112
Woodcote Pk Rd, Epsom KT18 232 CQ116
Woodcote Pl, SE27 181 DP92
Woodcote Rd, E11 124 EG59
Epsom KT18 216 CR114
Purley CR8 219 DJ109
Wallington SM6 219 DH107
Woodcote Side, Epsom KT18 232 CP115
Woodcote Valley Rd, Pur. CR8 219 DK113
Woodcott Ho, SW15 off Ellisfield Dr 179 CU87
Wood Cres, Hem.H. HP3 40 BK21
Woodcrest Rd, Pur. CR8 219 DL113
Woodcrest Wk, Reig. RH2 250 DE132
Woodcroft, N21 99 DM46
SE9 185 EM90
Greenford UB6 137 CG65
Harlow CM18 51 ER17
Woodcroft Av, NW7 96 CS52
Stanmore HA7 95 CF53
Ware (Stans.Abb.) SG12 33 ED11
Woodcroft Cres, Uxb. UB10 135 BP67
Sch Woodcroft Infants' Sch, Edg. HA8 off Goldbeaters Gro 96 CS52
Sch Woodcroft Jun Sch, Edg. HA8 off Goldbeaters Gro 96 CS52
Woodcroft Ms, SE8 23 J8
Woodcroft Rd, Chesh. HP5 54 AR28
Thornton Heath CR7 201 DP99
Sch Woodcroft Spec Sch, Loug. IG10 off Whitakers Way 85 EM39
Woodcutters Av, Grays RM16 170 GC75
Wood Dr, Chis. BR7 184 EL93
Sevenoaks TN13 256 FF126
Woodedge Cl, E4 102 EF46
Woodend, SE19 182 DQ93
Esher KT10 196 CC103
Wood End, Hayes UB3 135 BS72
Woodend, Lthd. KT22 247 CJ125
Wood End, St.Alb. (Park St) AL2 60 CC28
Woodend, Sutt. SM1 200 DC103
Woodend, The, Wall. SM6 219 DH109
Wood End Av, Har. HA2 116 CB63
Wood End Cl, Hem.H. HP2 41 BQ19
Northolt UB5 117 CD64
Slough (Farn.Com.) SL2 111 AR62
Woodend Cl, Wok. GU21 226 AU119
Woodend Gdns, Enf. EN2 81 DL42
Wood End Gdns, Nthlt. UB5 116 CC64
Wood End Grn Rd, Hayes UB3 135 BR71
Sch Wood End Inf Sch, Nthlt. UB5 off Whitton Av W 117 CD64
Sch Wood End Jun Sch, Grnf. UB6 off Vernon Ri 117 CD64
Wood End La, Nthlt. UB5 136 CB65
Woodend Pk, Cob. KT11 230 BX115
Sch Wood End Pk Comm Sch, Hayes UB3 off Judge Heath La 135 BQ73
Woodend Rd, E17 101 EC54
Wood End Rd, Har. HA1 117 CD63
Wood End Way, Nthlt. UB5 116 CC64
Wooder Gdns, E7 124 EF63
Wooderson Cl, SE25 202 DS98
Woodfall Av, Barn. EN5 79 CZ43
Woodfall Dr, Dart. DA1 167 FE84
Woodfall Rd, N4 121 DN60
Woodfall St, SW3 18 C10
Wood Fm Rd, Hem.H. HP2 40 BL20
Woodfarrs, SE5 162 DR84
Woodfield, Ashtd. KT21 231 CK117
Woodfield Av, NW9 118 CS56
SW16 181 DK90
W5 137 CJ70
Carshalton SM5 218 DG107
Gravesend DA11 191 GH88
Northwood HA6 93 BS49
Wembley HA0 117 CJ62
Sch Woodfield Cen, SW16 off Dingley La 181 DK89
Woodfield Cl, SE19 182 DQ94
Ashtead KT21 231 CK117
Coulsdon CR5 235 DJ119
Enfield EN1 82 DS42
Redhill RH1 250 DE133
Woodfield Cres, W5 137 CJ70
Woodfield Dr, Barn. EN4 98 DG46
Hemel Hempstead HP3 41 BR22
Romford RM2 127 FG56
Woodfield Gdns, W9 6 F5
Hemel Hempstead HP3 41 BQ22
New Malden KT3 199 CT99
Woodfield Gro, SW16 181 DK90
Woodfield Hill, Couls. CR5 235 DH119
Woodfield La, SW16 181 DK90
Ashtead KT21 232 CL116
Hatfield AL9 46 DD23
Hertford SG13 46 DD23
Woodfield Pk, Amer. HP6 55 AN36
Woodfield Pl, W9 6 F4
Woodfield Ri, Bushey WD23 95 CD45
Woodfield Rd, W5 137 CJ70
W9 6 F5
Ashtead KT21 231 CK117
Hounslow TW4 155 BV82
Radlett WD7 77 CG36
Thames Ditton KT7 197 CF103
Welwyn Garden City AL7 29 CZ09
Woodfields, Sev. TN13 256 FD122
Woodfields, The, S.Croy. CR2 220 DT111
Sch Woodfield Sch, NW9 off Glenwood Av 118 CS60
Redhill RH1 off Sunstone Gro 251 DL129
Sch Woodfield Spec Sch, Hem.H. HP3 off Malmescroft 41 BQ22
Woodfield Ter, Epp. (Thnwd) CM16 off High Rd 70 EW25
Uxbridge (Hare.) UB9 92 BH54
Woodfield Way, N11 99 DK52
Hornchurch RM12 128 FK60
Redhill RH1 250 DE132
St. Albans AL4 43 CJ17
Woodfines, The, Horn. RM11 128 FK58
WOODFORD, Wdf.Grn. IG8 102 EH51
⊖ Woodford 102 EH51
Woodford Av, Ilf. IG2, IG4 125 EM57
Woodford Green IG8 124 EK55
WOODFORD BRIDGE, Wdf.Grn. IG8 103 EM52
Woodford Br Rd, Ilf. IG4 124 EK55
Sch Woodford Co High Sch for Girls, Wdf.Grn. IG8 off High Rd Woodford Grn 102 EF51
Woodford Ct, W12 16 A3
Waltham Abbey EN9 68 EG33
Woodford Cres, Pnr. HA5 93 BV54
WOODFORD GREEN, IG8 102 EF49
Sch Woodford Grn Prep Sch, Wdf.Grn. IG8 off Glengall Rd 102 EG51
Sch Woodford Grn Prim Sch, Wdf.Grn. IG8 off Sunset Av 102 EG50
Woodford New Rd, E17 124 EE56
E18 102 EE53
Woodford Green IG8 102 EE53
Woodford Pl, Wem. HA9 118 CL60
Woodford Rd, E7 124 EH63
E18 124 EG56
Watford WD17 75 BV40
Woodford Way, Slou. SL2 131 AN69
WOODFORD WELLS, Wdf.Grn. IG8 102 EH49
Woodgate, Wat. WD25 59 BV33
Woodgate Av, Chess. KT9 215 CK106
Potters Bar EN6 65 DH33
Woodgate Cres, Nthwd. HA6 93 BU51
Woodgate Dr, SW16 181 DK94
Woodgavil, Bans. SM7 233 CZ116
Woodger Cl, Guil. GU4 off Chatfield Dr 243 BC132
Woodger Rd, W12 off Goldhawk Rd 159 CW75
Woodgers Gro, Swan. BR8 207 FF96
Woodget Cl, E6 off Remington Rd 144 EL72
Woodgrange Av, N12 98 DD51
W5 138 CN74
Enfield EN1 82 DU44
Harrow HA3 117 CJ57
Woodgrange Cl, Har. HA3 117 CK57
Woodgrange Gdns, Enf. EN1 82 DU44
Sch Woodgrange Inf Sch, E7 off Sebert Rd 124 EH63
⇌ Woodgrange Park 124 EK64
Woodgrange Rd, E7 124 EH63
Woodgrange Ter, Enf. EN1 off Great Cambridge Rd 82 DU44
WOOD GREEN, N22 99 DL53
⊖ Wood Green 99 DM54
Woodgreen Rd, Wal.Abb. EN9 84 EJ35
Wood Grn Shop City, N22 99 DN54
Wood Grn Way, Wal.Cr. (Chsht) EN8 67 DY31
WOODHALL, Welw.G.C. AL7 29 CY11
Woodhall Av, SE21 182 DT90
Pinner HA5 94 BY54
Woodhall Cl, Hert. SG14 32 DQ07
Uxbridge UB8 114 BK64
Woodhall Ct, Welw.G.C. AL7 29 CY10
Woodhall Cres, Horn. RM11 128 FM59
Woodhall Dr, SE21 182 DT90
Pinner HA5 94 BX53
Woodhall Gate, Pnr. HA5 94 BX52
Woodhall Ho, SW18 off Fitzhugh Gro 180 DD86
Sch Woodhall JMI Sch, Wat. WD19 off Woodhall La 94 BY49
Woodhall La, Hem.H. HP2 40 BL19
Radlett (Shenley) WD7 78 CL35
Watford WD19 94 BX49
Welwyn Garden City AL7 29 CY10
Woodhall Par, Welw.G.C. AL7 29 CZ11
Woodhall Rd, Pnr. HA5 94 BX52
WOODHAM, Add. KT15 211 BF111
Woodham Ct, E18 124 EF56
Woodham La, Add. (New Haw) KT15 212 BG110
Woking GU21 211 BB114
Woodham Pk Rd, Add. (Wdhm) KT15 211 BF109
Woodham Pk Way, Add. (Wdhm) KT15 211 BF111
Woodham Ri, Wok. GU21 211 AZ114
Woodham Rd, SE6 183 EC90
Woking GU21 226 AY115
Woodham Way, Ware (Stans.Abb.) SG12 33 EC11
Woodham Waye, Wok. GU21 211 BB113
WOODHATCH, Reig. RH2 266 DC137
Woodhatch Cl, E6 off Remington Rd 144 EL72
Woodhatch Rd, Red. RH1 266 DB137
Reigate RH2 266 DB137
Woodhatch Spinney, Couls. CR5 235 DL116
Woodhaven Gdns, Ilf. IG6 off Brandville Gdns 125 EQ55
Woodhaw, Egh. TW20 173 BB91
Woodhayes, Horl. RH6 269 DH147
Woodhayes Rd, SW19 179 CW94
Woodhead Dr, Orp. BR6 off Sherlies Av 205 ES103
Woodheyes Rd, NW10 118 CR64
Woodhill, SE18 164 EL77
Harlow CM18 51 ES18
Woking (Send) GU23 243 BE125
Woodhill Av, Ger.Cr. SL9 113 BA58
Woodhill Cres, Har. HA3 117 CK58
Sch Woodhill Prim Sch, SE18 off Woodhill 164 EL77
Wood Ho, SW17 off Laurel Cl 180 DE92
Woodhouse Av, Grnf. UB6 137 CF68
Woodhouse Cl, Grnf. UB6 137 CF68
Hayes UB3 155 BS76
Coll Woodhouse Coll, N12 off Woodhouse Rd 98 DD51
Woodhouse Eaves, Nthwd. HA6 93 BU50
Woodhouse Gro, E12 144 EL65
Wood Ho La, Brox. EN10 48 DT21
Woodhouse La, Dor. (Holm.St.M.) RH5 261 BU143
Woodhouse Rd, E11 124 EF62
N12 98 DD51
Woodhurst Av, Orp. BR5 205 EQ100
Watford WD25 76 BX35
Woodhurst Dr, Uxb. (Denh.) UB9 113 BF57
Woodhurst La, Oxt. RH8 254 EE130
Woodhurst Pk, Oxt. RH8 254 EE130
Woodhurst Rd, SE2 166 EU78
W3 138 CQ73
Woodhyrst Gdns, Ken. CR8 off Firs Rd 235 DP115
Wooding Gro, Harl. CM19 51 EP15
Woodington Cl, SE9 185 EN86
Woodknoll Dr, Chis. BR7 205 EM95
Woodland App, Grnf. UB6 137 CG65
Woodland Av, Brwd. (Hutt.) CM13 109 GC43
Hemel Hempstead HP1 40 BH21
Slough SL1 131 AR73
Windsor SL4 151 AM84
Woodland Cl, NW9 118 CQ58
SE19 off Woodland Hill 182 DS93
Brentwood (Hutt.) CM13 109 GC43
Epsom KT19 216 CS107
Hemel Hempstead HP1 40 BH21
Uxbridge (Ickhm) UB10 115 BP61
Weybridge KT13 off Woodland Gro 213 BR105
Woodford Green IG8 102 EH48
Woodland Ct, Oxt. RH8 253 ED128
Woodland Cres, SE10 164 EE79
SE16 22 G4
Woodland Dr, Lthd. (E.Hors.) KT24 245 BT127
St. Albans AL4 43 CJ18
Watford WD17 75 BT39
Woodland Gdns, N10 121 DH57
Epsom KT18 233 CW117
Isleworth TW7 157 CE82
South Croydon CR2 220 DW111
Woodland Glade, Slou. (Farn.Com.) SL2 111 AR62
Woodland Gro, SE10 24 G10
Epping CM16 70 EU31
Weybridge KT13 213 BR105
Woodland Hill, SE19 182 DS93
Woodland La, Rick. (Chorl.) WD3 73 BD41
Woodland Ms, SW16 181 DL89
Woodland Mt, Hert. SG13 32 DT09
Woodland Pl, Hem.H. HP1 40 BH21
Rickmansworth (Chorl.) WD3 73 BF42
Woodland Ri, N10 121 DH56
Greenford UB6 137 CG65
Oxted RH8 254 EE130
Sevenoaks TN15 257 FL123
Welwyn Garden City AL8 29 CW07
Woodland Rd, E4 101 EC46
N11 99 DH50
SE19 182 DS92
Hertford (Hert.Hth) SG13 32 DV12
Loughton IG10 84 EL41
Rickmansworth (Map.Cr.) WD3 91 BD50
Thornton Heath CR7 201 DN98
WOODLANDS, Islw. TW7 157 CE82
Woodlands, NW11 119 CY58
SW20 199 CW98
Gerrards Cross SL9 113 AZ57
Harrow HA2 116 CA56
Hatfield AL9 64 DB26
Horley RH6 269 DJ147
Radlett WD7 61 CG34
St. Albans (Park St) AL2 60 CC27
Woking GU22 off Constitution Hill 226 AY118
Woodlands, The, N14 99 DH46
SE13 183 ED87
SE19 182 DQ94
Amersham HP6 55 AQ35
Beckenham BR3 203 EC95
Esher KT10 196 CC103
Guildford GU1 off Laustan Cl 243 BC133
Horley (Smallfield) RH6 269 DP148
Isleworth TW7 157 CF82
Orpington BR6 224 EV107
Wallington SM6 219 DH109
Woodlands Av, E11 124 EH60
N3 98 DC52
W3 138 CP74
Berkhamsted HP4 38 AW20
Hornchurch RM11 128 FK57
New Malden KT3 198 CQ95
Redhill RH1 266 DF135
Romford RM6 126 EY58
Ruislip HA4 116 BW60
Sidcup DA15 185 ES88
West Byfleet KT14 211 BF113
Worcester Park KT4 199 CT103
Woodlands Cl, NW11 119 CY57
Borehamwood WD6 78 CP42
Bromley BR1 205 EM96
Chertsey (Ott.) KT16 211 BB110
Esher (Clay.) KT10 215 CF108
Gerrards Cross SL9 113 BA58
Grays RM16 170 GE76
Hoddesdon EN11 49 EA18
Leatherhead (E.Hors.) KT24 245 BT127
Swanley BR8 207 FF97
Woodlands Copse, Ashtd. KT21 231 CK116
Woodlands Ct, Wok. GU22 off Constitution Hill 226 AY119
Woodlands Dr, Beac. HP9 88 AJ51
Hoddesdon EN11 49 EA19
Kings Langley WD4 59 BQ28
Stanmore HA7 95 CF51
Sunbury-on-Thames TW16 196 BW96
Woodlands Glade, Beac. HP9 88 AJ51
Woodlands Gro, Couls. CR5 234 DG117
Isleworth TW7 157 CE82
Woodlands Hill, Beac. HP9 111 AL58
Sch Woodlands Inf Sch, Ilf. IG1 off Loxford La 125 ER64
Sch Woodlands Jun Sch, Ilf. IG1 off Loxford La 125 ER64
Woodlands La, Cob. (Stoke D'Ab.) KT11 230 CA117
Woodlands Par, Ashf. TW15 175 BQ93
Woodlands Pk, Add. KT15 211 BF106
Bexley DA5 187 FC91
Guildford GU1 243 BB132
Tadworth (Box H.) KT20 248 CP131
Woking GU21 off Blackmore Cres 211 BC114
Sch Woodlands Pk Inf Sch, N15 off St. Ann's Rd 122 DQ57
Sch Woodlands Pk Jun Sch, N15 off St. Ann's Rd 122 DQ57
Woodlands Pk Rd, N15 121 DP57
SE10 164 EE79
Sch Woodlands Prep Sch, Upmin. RM14 off Warley St 129 FX56
Sch Woodlands Prim Sch, Borwd. WD6 off Alban Cres 78 CN39
Woodlands Ri, Swan. BR8 207 FF96
Woodlands Rd, E11 124 EE61
E17 123 EC55
N9 100 DW46
SW13 159 CT83
Bexleyheath DA7 166 EY83
Bromley BR1 204 EL96
Bushey WD23 76 BY43
Enfield EN2 82 DR39
Epsom KT18 232 CN115
Guildford GU1 242 AX130
Harrow HA1 117 CF57
Hemel Hempstead HP3 58 BN27
Hertford SG13 32 DT09
Ilford IG1 125 EQ62
Isleworth TW7 157 CE82
Leatherhead KT22 231 CD117
Leatherhead (Eff.) KT23 246 BY128
Orpington BR6 224 EU107
Redhill RH1 266 DF136
Romford RM1 127 FF55
Romford (Harold Wd) RM3 106 FN53
Southall UB1 136 BX74
Surbiton KT6 197 CK101
Virginia Water GU25 192 AW98
West Byfleet KT14 211 BF114
Woodlands Rd E, Vir.W. GU25 192 AW98
Woodlands Rd W, Vir.W. GU25 192 AW97
Sch Woodlands Sch, Lthd. KT22 off Fortyfoot Rd 231 CJ122
Woodlands St, SE13 183 ED87
Woodland St, E8 5 P3
Woodlands Vw, Dor. RH5 263 CH142
Woodlands Vw, Sev. (Bad.Mt) TN14 224 FA110
Woodlands Way, SW15 off Oakhill Rd 179 CZ85
Ashtead KT21 232 CN116
Tadworth (Box H.) KT20 248 CQ130
Woodland Ter, SE7 164 EL77
Woodland Vw, Chesh. HP5 54 AR32
Godalming GU7 258 AS142
Woodland Wk, NW3 120 DE64
SE10 25 H10
Bromley BR1 184 EE91
Epsom KT19 216 CN107
Woodland Way, N21 99 DN47
NW7 96 CS51
SE2 166 EX77
Abbots Langley (Bedmond) WD5 59 BT27
Caterham CR3 252 DS128
Croydon CR0 203 DY102
Epping (They.B.) CM16 85 ER35
Greenhithe DA9 169 FU84
Mitcham CR4 180 DG94
Morden SM4 199 CZ98
Orpington BR5 205 EQ98
Purley CR8 219 DN113
Surbiton KT5 198 CP103
Tadworth (Kgswd) KT20 233 CY122
Waltham Cross (Chsht) EN7 65 DP28
West Wickham BR4 221 EB105
Weybridge KT13 213 BR106
Woodford Green IG8 102 EH48
Wood La, N6 121 DH58
NW9 118 CS59
W12 139 CW72
Caterham CR3 236 DR124
Dagenham RM8, RM9, RM10 126 EW63
Dartford (Lane End) DA2 189 FR91
Hemel Hempstead HP2 40 BK21
Hornchurch RM12 127 FG64
Isleworth TW7 157 CF80
Iver SL0 133 BC71
Ruislip HA4 115 BR60
Slough SL1 151 AM76
Stanmore HA7 95 CG48
Tadworth KT20 233 CZ116
Ware SG12 33 EA05
Weybridge KT13 213 BQ109
Woodford Green IG8 102 EF50
Wood La Cl, Iver SL0 133 BB69
Wood La End, Hem.H. HP2 40 BN19
Sch Woodlane Sch, W12 off Du Cane Rd 139 CV72
Woodlawn Cl, SW15 179 CZ85
Woodlawn Cres, Twick. TW2 176 CB89
Woodlawn Dr, Felt. TW13 176 BX89
Woodlawn Gro, Wok. GU21 227 AZ115
Woodlawn Rd, SW6 159 CX80
Sch Woodlea Co Prim Sch, Cat. CR3 off Long Hill 237 EA122
Woodlea Dr, Brom. BR2 204 EE99
Woodlea Gro, Nthwd. HA6 93 BQ51
Woodlea Rd, N16 122 DS62
Woodlee Cl, Vir.W. GU25 192 AW96
Woodleigh, E18 off Churchfields 102 EG53
Woodleigh Av, N12 98 DE51
Woodleigh Gdns, SW16 181 DL90
Woodley Cl, SW17 off Arnold Rd 180 DF94
Woodley Hill, Chesh. HP5 54 AR34
Woodley La, Cars. SM5 200 DD104
Woodley Rd, Orp. BR6 206 EW103
Ware SG12 33 DZ05
Wood Lo Gdns, Brom. BR1 184 EL94
Wood Lo La, W.Wick. BR4 203 EC104
Woodmancote Gdns, W.Byf. KT14 212 BG113
Woodman La, E4 84 EE43
Woodman Path, Ilf. IG6 103 ES51
Woodman Rd, Brwd. (Warley) CM14 108 FW50
Coulsdon CR5 235 DJ115
Hemel Hempstead HP3 40 BL22
Woodmans Gro, NW10 119 CT64
Woodmans Ms, W12 139 CV71
WOODMANSTERNE, Bans. SM7 234 DD115
⇌ Woodmansterne 235 DH116
Woodmansterne La, Bans. SM7 234 DB115
Carshalton SM5 218 DF112
Wallington SM6 219 DH111
Sch Woodmansterne Prim Sch, SW16 off Stockport Rd 201 DK95
Banstead SM7 off Carshalton Rd 218 DF114
Woodmansterne Rd, SW16 201 DK95
Carshalton SM5 218 DE109
Coulsdon CR5 235 DJ115
Woodmansterne St, Bans. SM7 234 DE115
Woodman St, E16 145 EN74
Wood Meads, Epp. CM16 70 EU29
Woodmere, SE9 185 EM88
Woodmere Av, Croy. CR0 203 DX101
Watford WD24 76 BX38
Woodmere Cl, SW11 off Lavender Hill 160 DG83
Croydon CR0 203 DX101
Woodmere Gdns, Croy. CR0 203 DX101
Woodmere Way, Beck. BR3 203 ED99
Woodmill Ms, Hodd. EN11 off Whittingstall Rd 49 EB15
Woodmount, Swan. BR8 207 FC101
Woodnook Rd, SW16 181 DH92
Woodpecker Cl, N9 82 DV44
Bushey WD23 94 CC46
Cobham KT11 214 BY112
Harrow HA3 95 CF53
Hatfield AL10 45 CT21
Woodpecker Mt, Croy. CR0 221 DY109
Woodpecker Rd, SE14 163 DY79
SE28 146 EW73
Woodpecker Way, Wok. GU22 226 AX123
Woodplace Cl, Couls. CR5 235 DJ119
Woodplace La, Couls. CR5 235 DJ118
Wood Pt, E16 15 M6
Wood Pond Cl, Beac. (Seer Grn) HP9 89 AQ51
Woodquest Av, SE24 182 DQ85
Woodredon Cl, Harl. (Roydon) CM19 off Epping Rd 50 EH16
Woodredon Fm La, Wal.Abb. EN9 84 EK35
Wood Retreat, SE18 165 ER80
Woodridden Hill, Wal.Abb. EN9 84 EK35
Wood Ride, Barn. EN4 80 DD39
Orpington BR5 205 ER98
Woodridge Cl, Enf. EN2 81 DN39
Woodridge Way, Nthwd. HA6 93 BS51
Wood Riding, Wok. GU22 off Pyrford Wds Rd 227 BF115
Woodridings Av, Pnr. HA5 94 BZ53

⊖ London Underground station — DLR Docklands Light Railway station — Tra Tramlink station — Riv Pedestrian ferry landing stage

Woodridings Cl, Pnr. HA5 . . . 94 BY52
Woodriffe Rd, E11 . . . 123 ED59
Sch Woodringe Prim Sch,
N12 *off Southover* . . . 98 DA48
Wood Ri, Guil. GU3 . . . 242 AS132
Pinner HA5 . . . 115 BU57
Wood Rd, NW10 . . . 138 CQ66
Godalming GU7 . . . 258 AT144
Shepperton TW17 . . . 194 BN98
Westerham (Bigg.H.) TN16 . 238 EJ118
Woodrow, SE18 . . . 165 EM77
Woodrow Av, Hayes UB4 . . . 135 BT71
Woodrow Cl, Grnf. UB6 . . . 137 CH66
Woodrow Ct, N17
off Heybourne Rd . . . 100 DV52
Woodroyd Av, Horl. RH6 . . . 268 DF149
Woodroyd Gdns, Horl. RH6 . 268 DF150
Woodruff Av, Guil. GU1 . . . 243 BA131
Woodrush Cl, SE14
off Southerngate Way . . . 163 DY80
Woodrush Way, Rom. RM6 . 126 EX56
Woods, The, Nthwd. HA6 . . . 93 BU50
Radlett WD7 . . . 61 CH34
Uxbridge UB10 . . . 115 BP63
Woods Av, Hat. AL10 . . . 45 CU18
Wood's Bldgs, E1 . . . 12 C5
Woods Dr, Slou. SL2 . . . 111 AM64
Woodseer St, E1 . . . 11 P5
Woodsford, SE17 . . . 21 J10
Woodsford Sq, W14 . . . 16 D4
Woodshire Rd, Dag. RM10 . . 127 FB62
Woodshore Cl, Vir.W. GU25 . 192 AV100
Woodshots Meadow, Wat.
WD18 . . . 75 BR44
WOODSIDE, Croy. CR0 . . . 202 DU100
WOODSIDE, Wat. WD25 . . . 59 BU33
Tra Woodside . . . 202 DV100
Woodside, NW11 . . . 120 DA57
SW19 . . . 179 CZ93
Borehamwood (Elstree)
WD6 . . . 78 CM42
Buckhurst Hill IG9 . . . 102 EJ47
Epping (Thnwd) CM16 . . . 70 EX27
Hertford (Hert.Hth) SG13 . . 32 DW12
High Wycombe (Flack.Hth)
HP10 . . . 110 AC57
Leatherhead (Fetch.) KT22 . 230 CB122
Leatherhead (W.Hors.)
KT24 . . . 245 BQ126
Orpington BR6 . . . 224 EU106
Tadworth (Lwr Kgswd)
KT20 . . . 249 CZ128
Waltham Cross (Chsht)
EN7 . . . 66 DU31
Walton-on-Thames KT12
off Ashley Rd . . . 195 BU102
Watford WD24 . . . 75 BU36
Woodside Av, N6 . . . 120 DF57
N10 . . . 120 DF57
N12 . . . 98 DC49
SE25 . . . 202 DV100
Amersham HP6 . . . 55 AR36
Beaconsfield HP9 . . . 88 AJ52
Chislehurst BR7 . . . 185 EQ92
Esher KT10 . . . 197 CE101
High Wycombe (Flack.Hth)
HP10 . . . 110 AC57
Walton-on-Thames KT12 . . 213 BV105
Wembley HA0 . . . 138 CL67
Woodside Cl, Amer. HP6 . . . 55 AR37
Beaconsfield HP9 . . . 88 AJ52
Bexleyheath DA7 . . . 167 FD84
Brentwood (Hutt.) CM13 . . 109 GD43
Caterham CR3 . . . 236 DS124
Gerrards Cross (Chal.St.P.)
SL9 . . . 90 AY54
Rainham RM13 . . . 148 FJ70
Stanmore HA7 . . . 95 CH50
Surbiton KT5 . . . 198 CQ101
Wembley HA0 . . . 138 CL67
Woodside Commercial Est,
Epp. (Thnwd) CM16 . . . 70 EX26
Woodside Ct, N12
off Woodside Av . . . 98 DC49
Woodside Ct Rd, Croy. CR0 . 202 DU101
Woodside Cres, Horl.
(Smallfield) RH6 . . . 269 DN148
Sidcup DA15 . . . 185 ES90
Woodside Dr, Dart. DA2 . . . 187 FE91
Woodside End, Wem. HA0 . . 138 CL67
Woodside Gdns, E4 . . . 101 EB50
N17 . . . 100 DS54
Woodside Gra Rd, N12 . . . 98 DB49
Woodside Grn, SE25 . . . 202 DV100
Woodside Gro, N12 . . . 98 DC48
Woodside Hill, Ger.Cr.
(Chal.St.P.) SL9 . . . 90 AY54
Sch Woodside Inf Sch, E17
off Wood St . . . 123 EC55
Sch Woodside Jun & Inf Sch,
Croy. CR0
off Morland Rd . . . 202 DU101
Sch Woodside Jun Sch, E17
off Wood St . . . 123 EC55
Woodside La, N12 . . . 98 DB48
Bexley DA5 . . . 186 EX86
Hatfield AL9 . . . 45 CZ21
Woodside Ms, SE22
off Heber Rd . . . 182 DT86
Sch Woodside Mid Sch,
Amer. HP6
off Mitchell Wk . . . 55 AS38
⊖ Woodside Park . . . 98 DB49
Woodside Pk, SE25 . . . 202 DU99
Woodside Pk Av, E17 . . . 123 ED56
Woodside Pk Rd, N12 . . . 98 DB49
Sch Woodside Pk Sch, N11
off Friern Barnet Rd . . . 98 DF50
N12 *off Woodside La* . . . 98 DC48
Woodside Pl, Hat. AL9
off Wildhill Rd . . . 46 DA21
Wembley HA0 . . . 138 CL67
Sch Woodside Prim Sch,
Grays RM16
off Grangewood Av . . . 171 GF76
Waltham Cross EN7
off Jones Rd . . . 65 DP30
Woodside Rd, E13 . . . 144 EJ70
N22 . . . 99 DM52
SE25 . . . 202 DV100
Abbots Langley WD5 . . . 59 BV31
Amersham HP6 . . . 55 AR37
Beaconsfield HP9 . . . 88 AJ52
Bexleyheath DA7 . . . 167 FD84
Bromley BR1 . . . 204 EL99
Cobham KT11 . . . 214 CA113
Guildford GU2 . . . 242 AT133
Kingston upon Thames KT2 . 178 CL94
New Malden KT3 . . . 198 CR96
Northwood HA6 . . . 93 BT52
Purley CR8 . . . 219 DK113
St. Albans (Brick.Wd) AL2 . . 60 BZ30
Sevenoaks TN13 . . . 256 FG123
Sevenoaks (Sund.) TN14 . . 240 EX124
Sidcup DA15 . . . 185 ES90
Sutton SM1 . . . 200 DC104
Watford WD25 . . . 59 BV31
Woodside Rd, Wdf.Grn. IG8 . . 102 EG49
Sch Woodside Sch,
Belv. DA17
off Halt Robin Rd . . . 167 FB77
Woodside Way, Croy. CR0 . . 202 DV100
High Wycombe (Penn)
HP10 . . . 88 AC46
Mitcham CR4 . . . 201 DH95
Redhill RH1 . . . 266 DG135
Redhill (White Bushes)
RH1 . . . 266 DG140
Virginia Water GU25 . . . 192 AV97
Woods Ms, W1 . . . 8 D9
Woodsome Lo, Wey. KT13 . . 213 BQ107
Woodsome Rd, NW5 . . . 120 DG62
Woods Pl, SE1 . . . 21 M6
Woodspring Rd, SW19 . . . 179 CY89
Woods Rd, SE15 . . . 162 DV81
Woodstead Gro, Edg. HA8 . . 96 CL51
Woodstock, Guil. (W.Clan.)
GU4 . . . 244 BH128
Woodstock Av, NW11 . . . 119 CY59
W13 . . . 157 CG76
Isleworth TW7 . . . 177 CG85
Romford RM3 . . . 106 FP50
Slough SL3 . . . 152 AX77
Southall UB1 . . . 136 BZ69
Sutton SM3 . . . 199 CZ101
Woodstock Cl, Bex. DA5 . . . 186 EZ88
Hertford (Hert.Hth) SG13
off Hogsdell La . . . 32 DV11
Stanmore HA7 . . . 96 CL54
Woking GU21 . . . 226 AY116
Woodstock Ct, SE12 . . . 184 EG86
Woodstock Cres, N9 . . . 82 DV44
Woodstock Dr, Uxb. UB10 . . 114 BL63
Woodstock Gdns, Beck. BR3 . 203 EB95
Hayes UB4 . . . 135 BT71
Ilford IG3 . . . 126 EU61
Woodstock Gro, W12 . . . 16 B3
Woodstock La N, Surb. KT6 . 197 CJ103
Woodstock La S, Chess. KT9 . 215 CJ105
Esher (Clay.) KT10 . . . 215 CH106
Woodstock Ms, W1 . . . 8 F6
Woodstock Ri, Sutt. SM3 . . 199 CZ101
Woodstock Rd, E7 . . . 144 EJ66
E17 . . . 101 ED54
N4 . . . 121 DN60
NW11 . . . 119 CZ59
W4 . . . 158 CS76
Broxbourne EN10 . . . 49 DY19
Bushey (Bushey Hth) WD23 . . 95 CE45
Carshalton SM5 . . . 218 DG106
Coulsdon CR5
off Chipstead Valley Rd . . 235 DH116
Croydon CR0 . . . 202 DR104
Wembley HA0 . . . 138 CM66
Woodstock Rd N, St.Alb. AL1 . 43 CH18
Woodstock Rd S, St.Alb. AL1 . 43 CH20
Woodstock St, W1 . . . 8 G8
Woodstock Ter, E14 . . . 14 B9
Woodstock Way, Mitch. CR4 . 201 DH96
Woodstone Av, Epsom KT17 . 217 CU106
⇌ Wood Street . . . 123 EC56
Wood St, E17 . . . 123 EC55
EC2 . . . 11 H8
W4 . . . 158 CS78
Barnet EN5 . . . 79 CW42
Grays RM17 . . . 170 GC79
Kingston upon Thames KT1 . 197 CK95
Mitcham CR4 . . . 200 DG101
Redhill RH1 . . . 251 DJ129
Swanley BR8 . . . 208 FJ96
Woodsway, Lthd. (Oxshott)
KT22 . . . 215 CE114
Woodsyre, SE26 . . . 182 DT91
Woodthorpe Rd, SW15 . . . 159 CV84
Ashford TW15 . . . 174 BL91
Woodtree Cl, NW4
off Ashley La . . . 97 CW54
Wood Vale, N10 . . . 121 DJ57
SE23 . . . 182 DV88
Hatfield AL10 . . . 45 CV18
Woodvale Av, SE25 . . . 202 DT97
Wood Vale Est, SE23 . . . 182 DW86
Woodvale Wk, SE27
off Elder Rd . . . 182 DQ92
Woodvale Way, NW11
off The Vale . . . 119 CX62
Woodview, Chess. KT9 . . . 215 CJ111
Grays RM16, RM17 . . . 170 GE76
Wood Vw, Hem.H. HP1 . . . 40 BH18
Potters Bar (Cuffley) EN6 . . 65 DL27
Woodview Av, E4 . . . 101 EC49
Woodview Cl, N4 . . . 121 DP59
SW15 . . . 178 CR91
Orpington BR6
off Crofton Rd . . . 205 EQ103
South Croydon CR2 . . . 220 DV114
Woodview Rd, Swan. BR8 . . 207 FC96
Woodville, SE3 . . . 164 EH81
Woodville Cl, SE12 . . . 184 EG85
Teddington TW11 . . . 177 CG91
Sch Woodville Co Jun Sch,
Lthd. KT22
off Woodville Rd . . . 231 CH120
Woodville Ct, Wat. WD17 . . . 75 BU40
Woodville Gdns, NW11 . . . 119 CX59
W5 . . . 138 CL72
Ilford IG6 . . . 125 EP55
Ruislip HA4 . . . 115 BQ59
Woodville Gro, Well. DA16 . . 166 EU83
Woodville Pl, Cat. CR3 . . . 236 DQ121
Gravesend DA12 . . . 191 GH87
Woodville Rd, E11 . . . 124 EF60
E17 . . . 123 DY56
E18 . . . 102 EH54
N16 . . . 5 L2
NW6 . . . 139 CZ68
NW11 . . . 119 CX59
W5 . . . 137 CK72
Barnet EN5 . . . 80 DB41
Leatherhead KT22 . . . 231 CH120
Morden SM4 . . . 200 DA98
Richmond TW10 . . . 177 CH90
Thornton Heath CR7 . . . 202 DQ98
Woodville St, SE18
off Woodhill . . . 164 EL77
Wood Wk, Rick. (Chorl.) WD3 . 73 BE40
Woodward Av, NW4 . . . 119 CU57
Woodward Cl, Esher (Clay.)
KT10 . . . 215 CF107
Grays RM17 . . . 170 GB77
Woodwarde Rd, SE22 . . . 182 DS86
Woodward Gdns, Dag. RM9
off Woodward Rd . . . 146 EW66
Stanmore HA7 . . . 95 CF52
Woodward Hts, Grays RM17 . 170 GB77
Woodward Rd, Dag. RM9 . . . 146 EV66
Woodwards, Harl. CM19 . . . 51 EQ17
Woodward Ter, Green. DA9 . . 189 FS86
Wood Way, Beac. HP9 . . . 88 AF54
Woodway, Brwd. CM13,
CM15 . . . 109 GA46
Guildford GU1 . . . 243 BB133
Wood Way, Orp. BR6 . . . 205 EN103
Woodway Cres, Har. HA1 . . . 117 CG58
Woodwaye, Wat. WD19 . . . 94 BW45
Woodwell St, SW18
off Huguenot Pl . . . 180 DC85
Wood Wf, SE10 . . . 163 EB79
Woodwicks, Rick. (Map.Cr.)
WD3 . . . 91 BD50
Woodyard, The, Epp. CM16 . . 70 EW28
Woodyard Cl, NW5
off Gillies St . . . 120 DG64
Woodyard La, SE21 . . . 182 DS87
Woodyates Rd, SE12 . . . 184 EG86
Woodyers Cl, Guil. (Won.)
GU5 . . . 259 BB144
Woolacombe Rd, SE3 . . . 164 EJ81
Woolacombe Way, Hayes
UB3 . . . 155 BS77
Woolborough La, Red.
(Outwood) RH1 . . . 267 DM143
Woolbrook Rd, Dart. DA1 . . 187 FE86
Wooler St, SE17 . . . 21 J10
Woolf Cl, SE28 . . . 146 EV74
Woolf Ms, WC1 . . . 9 M3
Woolf Wk, Til. RM18
off Coleridge Rd . . . 171 GJ82
Woolhampton Way, Chig.
IG7 . . . 104 EV48
Woolhams, Cat. CR3 . . . 252 DT126
Woollam Cres, St.Alb. AL3 . . 42 CC16
Woollard St, Wal.Abb. EN9 . . 67 EC34
Woollaston Rd, N4 . . . 121 DP58
WOOLLENSBROOK, Hodd.
EN11 . . . 49 DX15
Woollett Cl, Dart. (Cray.) DA1 . 167 FG84
Woolmans Cl, Brox. EN10 . . . 49 DZ22
Woolmead Av, NW9 . . . 119 CU59
Woolmer Cl, Borwd. WD6 . . . 78 CN38
Woolmerdine Ct, Bushey
WD23 . . . 76 BX41
Woolmer Dr, Hem.H. HP2 . . . 41 BQ20
Woolmer Gdns, N18 . . . 100 DU50
Woolmer Rd, N18 . . . 100 DU50
Woolmers La, Hert. SG14 . . . 31 DH13
Woolmers Pk, Hert. SG14 . . . 31 DH14
Sch Woolmore Prim Sch, E14 . 14 D9
Woolmore St, E14 . . . 14 C9
Woolneigh St, SW6 . . . 160 DB83
Woolpack Ho, Enf. EN3 . . . 83 DX37
Wool Rd, SW20 . . . 179 CV93
Woolstaplers Way, SE16 . . . 22 A6
Woolston Cl, E17
off Riverhead Cl . . . 101 DX54
Woolstone Rd, SE23 . . . 183 DY89
WOOLWICH, SE18 . . . 165 EN78
⇌ Woolwich Arsenal . . . 165 EP77
Woolwich Ch St, SE18 . . . 164 EL76
★ Woolwich Common, SE18 . 165 EM80
Woolwich Common, SE18 . . 165 EN79
⇌ Woolwich Dockyard . . . 165 EM77
Woolwich Ferry Pier, E16 . . . 165 EN75
Woolwich Foot Tunnel, E16 . 165 EN75
SE18 . . . 165 EN75
Woolwich Garrison, SE18 . . . 165 EM79
Woolwich High St, SE18 . . . 165 EN76
Woolwich Ind Est, SE28
off Hadden Rd . . . 165 ES76
Woolwich Manor Way, E6 . . 145 EM70
E16 . . . 145 EP73
Woolwich Mkt, SE18 . . . 165 EP77
Woolwich New Rd, SE18 . . . 165 EN78
Sch Woolwich Poly Sch,
SE28
off Hutchins Rd . . . 146 EU74
**Coll Woolwich Residential
Training Sch**, Chis. BR7
off Kemnal Rd . . . 185 ER92
Woolwich Rd, SE2 . . . 166 EX79
SE7 . . . 164 EG78
SE10 . . . 25 J9
Belvedere DA17 . . . 166 EX79
Bexleyheath DA7 . . . 166 FA84
Wooster Gdns, E14 . . . 14 E7
Wooster Ms, Har. HA2
off Fairfield Dr . . . 116 CC55
Wooster Pl, SE1 . . . 21 K7
Wooster Rd, Beac. HP9 . . . 88 AJ51
Wootton Cl, Epsom KT18 . . . 233 CT115
Hornchurch RM11 . . . 128 FK57
Wootton Dr, Hem.H. HP2 . . . 41 BM15
High Wycombe (Woob.Grn)
HP10 . . . 110 AE55
Wootton Gro, N3 . . . 98 DA53
Wootton St, SE1 . . . 20 D3
Worbeck Rd, SE20 . . . 202 DV96
Worcester Av, N17 . . . 100 DU52
Upminster RM14 . . . 129 FT61
Worcester Cl, NW2
off Newfield Ri . . . 119 CV62
Croydon CR0 . . . 203 DZ103
Gravesend (Istead Rise)
DA13 . . . 191 GF94
Greenhithe DA9 . . . 169 FV84
Mitcham CR4 . . . 200 DG96
Worcester Ct, Walt. KT12
off Rodney Cl . . . 196 BW102
Worcester Cres, NW7 . . . 96 CS48
Woodford Green IG8 . . . 102 EH50
Worcester Dr, W4 . . . 158 CS75
Ashford TW15 . . . 175 BP93
Worcester Gdns, SW11
off Grandison Rd . . . 180 DF85
Greenford UB6 . . . 136 CC65
Ilford IG1 . . . 124 EL59
Slough SL1 . . . 151 AR75
Worcester Park KT4 . . . 198 CS104
Worcester Ms, NW6
off Lymington Rd . . . 140 DB65
WORCESTER PARK, KT4 . . . 199 CT103
⇌ Worcester Park . . . 199 CU102
Worcester Pk Rd, Wor.Pk.
KT4 . . . 198 CQ104
Worcester Rd, E12 . . . 125 EM63
E17 . . . 101 DX54
SW19 . . . 179 CZ92
Guildford GU2 . . . 242 AT132
Hatfield AL10 . . . 45 CT17
Reigate RH2 . . . 250 DA133
Sutton SM2 . . . 218 DB107
Uxbridge UB8 . . . 134 BJ71
Worcesters Av, Enf. EN1 . . . 82 DU38
Sch Worcesters Prim Sch,
Enf. EN1
off Goat La . . . 82 DT38
Wordsworth Av, E12 . . . 144 EL65
E18 . . . 124 EF55
Greenford UB6 . . . 137 CD68
Kenley CR8 *off Valley Rd* . . 236 DR115
Wordsworth Cl, Rom. RM3 . . 106 FJ53
Tilbury RM18 . . . 171 GJ82
Wordsworth Dr, Sutt. SM3 . . 217 CW105
Wordsworth Mead, Red. RH1 . 250 DG132
Wordsworth Rd, N16 . . . 5 M1
SE1 . . . 21 N8
SE20 . . . 183 DX94
Addlestone KT15 . . . 212 BK105
Hampton TW12 . . . 176 BZ91
Slough SL2 . . . 131 AK70
Wallington SM6 . . . 219 DJ107
Welling DA16 . . . 165 ES81
Wordsworth Wk, NW11 . . . 120 DA56
Wordsworth Way, Dart. DA1 . 168 FN84
West Drayton UB7 . . . 154 BL77
Worfield St, SW11 . . . 160 DE80
Worgan St, SE11 . . . 20 A9
SE16 . . . 23 H6
Workers Rd, Harl. CM17 . . . 53 FB16
Ongar CM5 . . . 53 FD17
**Coll Working Men's Coll,
The**, NW1
off Crowndale Rd . . . 141 DJ68
Worland Rd, E15 . . . 144 EE66
WORLD'S END, Enf. EN2 . . . 81 DN41
World's End, Cob. KT11 . . . 213 BU114
World's End Est, SW10 . . . 160 DD80
Worlds End La, N21 . . . 81 DM43
Enfield EN2 . . . 81 DM43
Orpington BR6 . . . 223 ET107
World's End Pas, SW10
off Riley St . . . 160 DD80
World's End Pl, SW10
off King's Rd . . . 160 DC80
Worley Rd, St.Alb. AL3 . . . 42 CC19
Worlidge St, W6 . . . 159 CW78
Worlingham Rd, SE22 . . . 162 DT84
Sch Wormholt Pk Prim Sch,
W12 *off Bryony Rd* . . . 139 CU73
Wormholt Rd, W12 . . . 139 CU73
WORMLEY, Brox. EN10 . . . 49 DY24
Wormley Ct, Wal.Abb. EN9
off Winters Way . . . 68 EG33
Wormley Lo Cl, Brox. EN10 . . 49 DZ23
Sch Wormley Prim Sch,
Brox. EN10
off St. Laurence Dr . . . 49 DY23
WORMLEY WEST END, Brox.
EN10 . . . 48 DS22
Wormwood St, EC2 . . . 11 L7
Wormyngford Ct,
Wal.Abb. EN9
off Ninefields . . . 68 EG33
Wornington Rd, W10 . . . 6 C4
Woronzow Rd, NW8 . . . 140 DD67
Worple, The, Stai. (Wrays.)
TW19 . . . 173 AZ86
Worple Av, SW19 . . . 179 CX94
Isleworth TW7 . . . 177 CG85
Staines TW18 . . . 174 BH93
Worple Cl, Har. HA2 . . . 116 BZ60
Sch Worple Prim Sch,
Islw. TW7
off Queens Ter . . . 157 CG84
Worple Rd, SW19 . . . 179 CZ93
SW20 . . . 199 CW96
Epsom KT18 . . . 216 CS114
Isleworth TW7 . . . 157 CG84
Leatherhead KT22 . . . 231 CH123
Staines TW18 . . . 174 BH94
Worple Rd Ms, SW19 . . . 179 CZ93
⇌ Worplesdon . . . 226 AV124
Worplesdon Rd, Guil. GU2,
GU3 . . . 242 AT129
Worple St, SW14 . . . 158 CR83
Worple Way, Har. HA2 . . . 116 BZ60
Richmond TW10 . . . 178 CL85
Worrin Cl, Brwd. (Shenf.)
CM15 . . . 109 FZ46
Worrin Rd, Brwd. (Shenf.)
CM15 . . . 109 FZ47
Worsfold Cl, Wok. (Send)
GU23 . . . 227 BB123
Worships Hill, Sev. TN13 . . . 256 FE123
Worship St, EC2 . . . 11 K4
Worslade Rd, SW17 . . . 180 DD91
Sch Worsley Br Jun Sch,
Beck. BR3
off Brackley Rd . . . 183 EA94
Worsley Br Rd, SE26 . . . 183 DZ91
Beckenham BR3 . . . 183 DZ92
Worsley Gra, Chis. BR7
off Kemnal Rd . . . 185 EQ93
Worsley Gro, E5 . . . 122 DU63
Worsley Rd, E11 . . . 124 EE63
Worsopp Dr, SW4 . . . 181 DJ85
Worsted Grn, Red. RH1 . . . 251 DJ129
Worth Cl, Orp. BR6 . . . 223 ES105
Worthfield Cl, Epsom KT19 . . 216 CR108
Worth Gro, SE17 . . . 21 J10
Worthies, The, Amer. HP7 . . . 55 AP40
Worthing Cl, E15
off Mitre Rd . . . 144 EE68
Grays RM20 . . . 170 FY79
Worthing Rd, Houns. TW5 . . 156 BZ79
Worthington Cl, Mitch. CR4 . 201 DH97
Worthington Rd, Surb. KT6 . 198 CM102
Worthy Down Ct, SE18
off Prince Imperial Rd . . . 165 EN81
Wortley Rd, E6 . . . 144 EK66
Croydon CR0 . . . 201 DN101
Worton Gdns, Islw. TW7 . . . 157 CD82
Worton Hall Ind Est, Islw.
TW7 . . . 157 CE84
Worton Rd, Islw. TW7 . . . 157 CE83
Worton Way, Houns. TW3 . . 157 CD82
Isleworth TW7 . . . 156 CC81
WOTTON, Dor. RH5 . . . 262 BZ139
Wotton Dr, Dor. RH5 . . . 262 BZ139
Wotton Grn, Orp. BR5 . . . 206 EX98
Wotton Rd, NW2 . . . 119 CW63
SE8 . . . 163 DZ79
Wotton Way, Sutt. SM2 . . . 217 CW110
Wouldham Rd, E16 . . . 15 J7
Grays RM20 . . . 170 FY79
Wrabness Way, Stai. TW18 . . 194 BH95
Wragby Rd, E11 . . . 124 EE62
Wrampling Pl, N9 . . . 100 DU46
Wrangley Ct, Wal.Abb. EN9 . . 68 EG33
Wrangthorn Wk, Croy. CR0
off Epsom Rd . . . 219 DN105
Wray Av, Ilf. IG5 . . . 125 EN55
Wray Cl, Horn. RM11 . . . 128 FJ59
Wray Common, Reig. RH2 . . 250 DD132
**Sch Wray Common Co Prim
Sch**, Reig. RH2
off Kendal Cl . . . 250 DD133
Wray Common Rd, Reig.
RH2 . . . 250 DC133
Wray Cres, N4 . . . 121 DL61
Wrayfield Av, Reig. RH2 . . . 250 DC133
Wrayfield Rd, Sutt. SM3 . . . 199 CX104
Wraylands Dr, Reig. RH2 . . . 250 DD132
Wray La, Reig. RH2 . . . 250 DC130
Wray Mill Pk, Reig. RH2 . . . 250 DD132
Wray Pk Rd, Reig. RH2 . . . 250 DB133
Wray Rd, Sutt. SM2 . . . 217 CZ109
WRAYSBURY, Stai. TW19 . . . 173 AZ86
⇌ Wraysbury . . . 173 BA86
Wraysbury Cl, Houns. TW4 . . 176 BY85
Sch Wraysbury Comb Sch,
Stai. TW19
off Welley Rd . . . 172 AY86
Wraysbury Gdns, Stai. TW19 . 173 BE91
Wraysbury Rd, Stai. TW18,
TW19 . . . 173 BC90
Wrays Way, Hayes UB4
off Balmoral Dr . . . 135 BS70
Wrekin Rd, SE18 . . . 165 EQ80
Wren Av, NW2 . . . 119 CW64
Southall UB2 . . . 156 BZ77
Wren Cl, E16 . . . 15 K7
N9 *off Chaffinch Cl* . . . 101 DX46
Orpington BR5 . . . 206 EX97
South Croydon CR2 . . . 221 DX109
Wren Ct, Slou. SL3
off New Rd . . . 153 BA76
Wren Cres, Add. KT15 . . . 212 BK106
Bushey WD23 . . . 94 CC46
Wren Dr, Wal.Abb. EN9 . . . 68 EG34
West Drayton UB7 . . . 154 BK76
Wren Gdns, Dag. RM9 . . . 126 EX64
Hornchurch RM12 . . . 127 FF60
Wren Landing, E14 . . . 23 P1
Wren Ms, SE13
off Lee High Rd . . . 164 EE84
Wren Path, SE28 . . . 165 ER76
Wren Pl, Brwd. CM14 . . . 108 FX48
Wren Rd, SE5 . . . 162 DR81
Dagenham RM9 . . . 126 EX64
Sidcup DA14 . . . 186 EW91
Wrens, The, Harl. CM19 . . . 51 EP15
Wrens Av, Ashf. TW15 . . . 175 BQ92
Wrens Cft, Grav. (Nthflt) DA11 . 190 GE91
Wrensfield, Hem.H. HP1 . . . 40 BG21
Wrens Hill, Lthd. (Oxshott)
KT22 . . . 230 CC115
Wren St, WC1 . . . 10 B3
Wren Ter, Ilf. IG5
off Tiptree Cres . . . 125 EN55
Wrentham Av, NW10 . . . 139 CX68
Wrenthorpe Rd, Brom. BR1 . . 184 EE91
Wren Wk, Til. RM18 . . . 171 GH80
Wren Wd, Welw.G.C. AL7 . . . 30 DA08
Wrenwood Way, Pnr. HA5 . . . 115 BV56
Wrestlers Cl, Hat. AL10 . . . 45 CW15
Wrestlers Ct, EC3
off Camomile St . . . 142 DS72
Wrexham Rd, E3 . . . 143 EA68
Romford RM3 . . . 106 FK48
Wricklemarsh Rd, SE3 . . . 164 EH81
Wrigglesworth St, SE14 . . . 163 DX80
Wright Cl, Swans. DA10 . . . 189 FX86
Wright Gdns, Shep. TW17
off Laleham Rd . . . 194 BN99
Wright Rd, N1 . . . 5 M3
Hounslow TW5 . . . 156 BW80
Wrights All, SW19 . . . 179 CW93
Wrightsbridge Rd, Brwd.
CM14 . . . 106 FN46
Wrights Cl, SE13
off Wisteria Rd . . . 163 ED84
Dagenham RM10 . . . 127 FB62
Wrights Grn, SW4
off Nelson's Row . . . 161 DK84
Wrights La, W8 . . . 17 J5
Wrights Pl, NW10
off Mitchell Way . . . 138 CQ65
Wright Sq, Wind. SL4
off Wright Way . . . 150 AJ83
Wrights Rd, E3 . . . 143 DZ68
SE25 . . . 202 DS97
Wrights Row, Wall. SM6 . . . 219 DH105
Wrights Wk, SW14 . . . 158 CR83
Wright Way, Wind. SL4 . . . 150 AJ83
Wrigley Cl, E4 . . . 101 ED50
Wriotsley Way, Add. KT15
off Coombelands La . . . 212 BG107
Writtle Wk, Rain. RM13 . . . 147 FF67
★ Wrotham Pk, Barn. EN5 . . 79 CZ36
Wrotham Rd, NW1
off Agar Pl . . . 141 DJ66
W13 *off Mattock La* . . . 137 CH74
Barnet EN5 . . . 79 CY40
Gravesend DA11, DA13 . . . 191 GG88
Welling DA16 . . . 166 EW81
Sch Wrotham Rd Prim Sch,
Grav. DA11
off Wrotham Rd . . . 191 GH87
Wroths Path, Loug. IG10 . . . 85 EM39
Wrottesley Rd, NW10 . . . 139 CU68
SE18 . . . 165 EQ79
Wroughton Rd, SW11 . . . 180 DF86
Wroughton Ter, NW4 . . . 119 CW56
Wroxall Rd, Dag. RM9 . . . 146 EW65
Sch Wroxham, The,
Pot.B. EN6
off Wroxham Gdns . . . 63 CX31
Wroxham Av, Hem.H. HP3 . . . 40 BK22
Wroxham Gdns, N11 . . . 99 DJ52
Enfield EN2 . . . 81 DN35
Potters Bar EN6 . . . 63 CX31
Wroxham Rd, SE28 . . . 146 EX73
Wroxham Way, Ilf. IG6 . . . 103 EP53
Wroxton Rd, SE15 . . . 162 DV82
WRYTHE, THE, Cars. SM5 . . . 200 DE103
Wrythe Grn, Cars. SM5
off Wrythe Grn Rd . . . 200 DF104
Wrythe Grn Rd, Cars. SM5 . . 200 DF104
Wrythe La, Cars. SM5 . . . 200 DC102
Wulfstan St, W12 . . . 139 CT72
Wulstan Pk, Pot.B. EN6
off Tempest Av . . . 64 DD32
Wyatt Cl, SE16 . . . 23 L4
Bushey (Bushey Hth) WD23 . 95 CE45
Feltham TW13 . . . 176 BW88
Hayes UB4 . . . 135 BU71
Wyatt Dr, SW13 . . . 159 CW80
Wyatt Pk Rd, SW2 . . . 181 DL89
Wyatt Rd, E7 . . . 144 EG65
N5 . . . 122 DQ62
Dartford DA1 . . . 167 FF83
Staines TW18 . . . 174 BG92
Windsor SL4 . . . 151 AK83
Wyatts Cl, Rick. (Chorl.) WD3 . 74 BG41
Wyatt's Covert Caravan Site,
Uxb. (Denh.) UB9 . . . 113 BE56
Wyatts La, E17 . . . 123 EC55
Wyatts Rd, Rick. (Chorl.)
WD3 . . . 73 BF42
Wybert St, NW1 . . . 9 H3
Sch Wyborne Prim Sch, SE9
off Footscray Rd . . . 185 EP88
Wyborne Way, NW10 . . . 138 CQ66
Wyburn Av, Barn. EN5 . . . 79 CZ41
Wyche Gro, S.Croy. CR2 . . . 220 DQ108
Wych Elm, Harl. CM20 . . . 35 EQ14
Wych Elm Cl, Horn. RM11 . . . 128 FN59
Wych Elm Dr, Brom. BR1
off London La . . . 184 EF94
Wych Elm Pas, Kings.T. KT2 . 178 CM94
Wych Elm Ri, Guil. GU1 . . . 258 AY137
Wych Elm Rd, Horn. RM11 . . 128 FN58
Wych Elms, St.Alb. (Park St)
AL2 . . . 60 CB28
Wycherley Cl, SE3 . . . 164 EF80
Wycherley Cres, Barn. EN5 . . 80 DB44
Wychford Dr, Saw. CM21 . . . 36 EW06
Wych Hill, Wok. GU22 . . . 226 AW119
Wych Hill La, Wok. GU22 . . . 226 AY119
Wych Hill Pk, Wok. GU22 . . . 226 AX119
Wych Hill Ri, Wok. GU22 . . . 226 AW119
Wych Hill Way, Wok. GU22 . . 226 AX120
Wychwood Av, Edg. HA8 . . . 95 CK51
Thornton Heath CR7 . . . 202 DQ97
Wychwood Cl, Edg. HA8 . . . 95 CK51
Sunbury-on-Thames TW16 . 175 BU93
Wychwood End, N6 . . . 121 DJ59
Wychwood Gdns, Ilf. IG5 . . . 125 EM56
Wychwood Way, SE19
off Roman Ri . . . 182 DR93
Northwood HA6 . . . 93 BT52
Wycliffe Cl, Well. DA16 . . . 165 ET81
Wycliffe Ct, Abb.L. WD5 . . . 59 BS32
Wycliffe Rd, SW11 . . . 160 DG82
SW19 . . . 180 DB93
Wycliffe Row, Grav. (Nthflt)
DA11 . . . 191 GF88
Wyclif St, EC1 . . . 10 E2
Wycombe End, Beac. HP9 . . 111 AK55
Wycombe Gdns, NW11 . . . 120 DA61
Wycombe La, H.Wyc.
(Woob.Grn) HP10 . . . 110 AE56
Wycombe Pl, SW18 . . . 180 DC86
Wycombe Rd, N17 . . . 100 DU53
Ilford IG2 . . . 125 EM57
Wembley HA0 . . . 138 CN67
Wycombe Sq, W8
off Aubrey Wk . . . 140 DA74

★ Place of interest | H Hospital | Sch School | Coll College | Uni University | ⇌ Railway station

Wycombe Way, St.Alb. AL4 ...43 CJ17
Wyddial Grn, Welw.G.C. AL7
off Widford Rd ...30 DB09
Wydehurst Rd, Croy. CR0 ...202 DU101
Wydell Cl, Mord. SM4 ...199 CW100
Wydeville Manor Rd, SE12 ...184 EH91
Wye, The, Hem.H. HP2 ...40 BN15
Wyecliffe Gdns, Red. RH1 ...251 DJ130
Wye Cl, Ashf. TW15 ...175 BP91
Orpington BR6 ...205 ET101
Ruislip HA4 ...115 BQ58
Wyedale, St.Alb. (Lon.Col.)
AL2 ...62 CM27
Wyemead Cres, E4 ...102 EE47
Wye Rd, Grav. DA12 ...191 GK89
High Wycombe (Woob.Grn)
HP10 ...110 AD55
Wye St, SW11 ...160 DD82
Wyeth's Ms, Epsom KT17 ...217 CT113
Wyeths Rd, Epsom KT17 ...217 CT113
Wyevale Cl, Pnr. HA5 ...115 BU55
Wyfields, Ilf. IG5
off Ravensbourne Gdns ...103 EP53
Wyfold Ho, SE2
off Wolvercote Rd ...166 EX75
Wyfold Rd, SW6 ...159 CY80
Wyhill Wk, Dag. RM10 ...147 FC65
Wyke Cl, Islw. TW7 ...157 CF79
Wyke Gdns, W7 ...157 CG76
Wykeham Av, Dag. RM9 ...146 EW65
Hornchurch RM11 ...128 FK58
Wykeham Cl, Grav. DA12 ...191 GL93
West Drayton UB7 ...154 BN78
Wykeham Grn, Dag. RM9 ...146 EW65
Wykeham Hill, Wem. HA9 ...118 CM60
Sch **Wykeham Inf Sch**,
Horn. RM12
off Rainsford Way ...127 FG60
Sch **Wykeham Jun Sch**,
Horn. RM12
off Rainsford Way ...127 FG60
Sch **Wykeham Prim Sch**,
NW10 *off Aboyne Rd* ...118 CS62
Wykeham Ri, N20 ...97 CY46
Wykeham Rd, NW4 ...119 CW57
Guildford GU1 ...243 BD133
Harrow HA3 ...117 CH56
Wykeridge Cl, Chesh. HP5 ...54 AP27
Wyke Rd, E3 ...143 EA66
SW20 ...199 CW96
Wylands Rd, Slou. SL3 ...153 BA77
Wylchin Cl, Pnr. HA5 ...115 BT56
Wyldes Cl, NW11
off Wildwood Rd ...120 DC60
Wyldfield Gdns, N9 ...100 DT47
Wyld Way, Wem. HA9 ...138 CP65
Wyldwood Cl, Harl. CM17 ...36 EW09
Wyleu St, SE23 ...183 DY87
Wylie Rd, Sthl. UB2 ...156 CA76
Wyllen Cl, E1 ...12 E4
Wyllyotts Cl, Pot.B. EN6 ...63 CZ32
Wyllyotts La, Pot.B. EN6 ...63 CZ32
Wyllyotts Pl, Pot.B. EN6 ...63 CZ32
Wylo Dr, Barn. EN5 ...79 CU44
Wymering Rd, W9 ...7 H2
Wymers Cl, Slou. (Burn.)
SL1 ...130 AH68
Wymers Wd Rd, Slou.
(Burn.) SL1 ...130 AG67
Wymond St, SW15 ...159 CW83
Wynan Rd, E14 ...24 A9
Wynash Gdns, Cars. SM5 ...218 DE106
Wynaud Ct, N22
off Palmerston Rd ...99 DM51
Wyncham Av, Sid. DA15 ...185 ES88
Wynchgate, N14 ...99 DK46
N21 ...99 DL46
Harrow HA3 ...95 CE52
Wynchlands Cres, St.Alb.
AL4 ...43 CK20
Wyncote Way, S.Croy. CR2 ...221 DX109
Wyncroft Cl, Brom. BR1 ...205 EM97
Wyndale Av, NW9 ...118 CN58
Wyndcliff Rd, SE7 ...25 N10
Wyndcroft Cl, Enf. EN2 ...81 DP41
Wyndham Av, Cob. KT11 ...213 BU113
Wyndham Cl, Orp. BR6 ...205 EQ102
Sutton SM2 ...218 DA108
Wyndham Cres, N19 ...121 DJ62
Hounslow TW4 ...176 CA86
Slough (Burn.) SL1 ...130 AH69
Wyndham Est, SE5 ...162 DQ80
Wyndham Ms, W1 ...8 C6
Wyndham Pl, W1 ...8 C6
Wyndham Rd, E6 ...144 EK66
SE5 ...161 DP80
W13 ...157 CH76
Barnet EN4 ...98 DF46
Kingston upon Thames
KT2 ...178 CM94
Woking GU21 ...226 AV118
Wyndhams End, Welw.G.C.
AL7 ...29 CZ13
Wyndham St, W1 ...8 C5
Wyndham Yd, W1 ...8 C6
Wyneham Rd, SE24 ...182 DR85
Wynell Rd, SE23 ...183 DX90
Wynford Gro, Orp. BR5 ...206 EV97
Wynford Pl, Belv. DA17 ...166 FA79
Wynford Rd, N1 ...4 A9
Wynford Way, SE9 ...185 EM90
Wyngrave Pl, Beac.
(Knot.Grn) HP9 ...88 AJ50
Wynlie Gdns, Pnr. HA5 ...93 BV54
Wynn Br Cl, Wdf.Grn. IG8
off Chigwell Rd ...102 EJ53
Wynndale Rd, E18 ...102 EH53
Wynne Rd, SW9 ...161 DN82
Wynns Av, Sid. DA15 ...186 EU85
Wynnstay Gdns, W8 ...17 H5
Wynnstow Pk, Oxt. RH8 ...254 EF131
Wynnswick Rd, Beac.
(Seer Grn) HP9 ...89 AQ50
Wynter St, SW11 ...160 DC84
Wynton Gdns, SE25 ...202 DT99
Wynton Gro, Walt. KT12 ...195 BU104
Wynton Pl, W3 ...138 CP72
Wynyard Cl, Rick. (Sarratt)
WD3 ...74 BG36
Wynyard Ter, SE11 ...20 B9
Wynyatt St, EC1 ...10 E2
Wyre Gro, Edg. HA8 ...96 CP48
Hayes UB3 ...155 BU77
Wyresdale Cres, Grnf. UB6 ...137 CF69
Wysemead, Horl. RH6 ...269 DJ147
Wyteleaf Cl, Ruis. HA4 ...115 BQ58
Wythburn Pl, W1 ...8 C8
Wythenshawe Rd, Dag.
RM10 ...126 FA62
Wythens Wk, SE9 ...185 EP86
Wythes Cl, Brom. BR1 ...205 EM96
Wythes Rd, E16 ...144 EL74
Wythfield Rd, SE9 ...185 EM86
Wyton, Welw.G.C. AL7 ...30 DD09
Wyvenhoe Rd, Har. HA2 ...116 CC62
Wyvern Cl, Dart. DA1 ...188 FJ87
Orpington BR6 ...206 EV104
Wyvern Est, N.Mal. KT3 ...199 CU98
Wyvern Gro, Hayes UB3 ...155 BP80
Wyvern Pl, Add. KT15
off Green La ...212 BH105
Wyvern Rd, Pur. CR8 ...219 DP110
Wyvern Way, Uxb. UB8 ...134 BH66
Wyvil Est, SW8
off Luscombe Way ...161 DL80
Sch **Wyvil Prim Sch**, SW8
off Wyvil Rd ...161 DL80
Wyvil Rd, SW8 ...161 DL79
Wyvis St, E14 ...14 B5

Y

Yabsley St, E14 ...24 D1
Yaffle Rd, Wey. KT13 ...213 BQ110
Yalding Gro, Orp. BR5 ...206 EX98
Yalding Rd, SE16 ...22 A6
Yale Cl, Houns. TW4 ...176 BZ85
Yale Way, Horn. RM12 ...127 FG63
Yaohan Plaza, NW9 ...118 CR55
Yarborough Rd, SW19 ...200 DD95
Yarbridge Cl, Sutt. SM2 ...218 DB110
Yardley Cl, E4 ...83 EB43
Reigate RH2 ...250 DB132
Yardley Ct, Sutt. SM3
off Hemingford Rd ...217 CW105
Yardley La, E4 ...83 EB43
Sch **Yardley Prim Sch**, E4
off Hawkwood Cres ...83 EC43
Yardley St, WC1 ...10 C2
Yard Mead, Egh. TW20 ...173 BA90
Yarm Cl, Lthd. KT22 ...231 CJ123
Yarm Ct Rd, Lthd. KT22 ...231 CJ123
Yarmouth Cres, N17 ...122 DV57
Yarmouth Pl, W1 ...18 G2
Yarmouth Rd, Slou. SL1 ...131 AQ73
Watford WD24 ...76 BW38
Yarm Way, Lthd. KT22 ...231 CJ123
Yarnfield Sq, SE15
off Clayton Rd ...162 DU81
Yarnton Way, SE2 ...166 EX75
Erith DA18 ...166 EZ76
Yarrow Cres, E6 ...144 EL71
Yarrowfield, Wok. GU22 ...226 AX123
Yarrowside, Amer. HP7 ...72 AV41
Yateley St, SE18 ...164 EK76
Yates Ct, NW2 ...139 CX65
Yattendon Rd, Horl. RH6 ...269 DH148
Sch **Yattendon Sch**,
Horl. RH6
off Oakwood Rd ...268 DG147
YEADING, Hayes UB4 ...135 BV69
Yeading Av, Har. HA2 ...116 BY61
Yeading Fork, Hayes UB4 ...136 BW71
Yeading Gdns, Hayes UB4 ...135 BV71
Sch **Yeading Inf Sch**,
Hayes UB4
off Carlyon Rd ...136 BW71
Sch **Yeading Jun Sch**,
Hayes UB4
off Carlyon Rd ...136 BW71
Yeading La, Hayes UB4 ...135 BV72
Northolt UB5 ...136 BW69
Yeames Cl, W13 ...137 CG72
Yearling Cl, Ware (Gt Amwell)
SG12 ...33 DZ09
Yeate St, N1 ...5 J6
Yeatman Rd, N6 ...120 DF58
Yeats Cl, NW10 ...138 CS65
Redhill RH1 ...266 DC137
Yeats Ct, N15
off Tynemouth Rd ...122 DT56
Ye Cor, Wat. WD19 ...76 BY44
Yeend Cl, W.Mol. KT8 ...196 CA98
Sch **Yehudi Menuhin Sch**,
Cob. KT11
off Cobham Rd ...230 CA119
Sch **Yeishiva Gedolah
Lubavitch**, N2
off Kingsley Way ...120 DC57
Yeldham Rd, W6 ...16 A10
Yellow Hammer Ct, NW9
off Eagle Dr ...96 CS54
Yellowpine Way, Chig. IG7 ...104 EV49
Yelverton Cl, Rom. RM3 ...106 FK53
Yelverton Rd, SW11 ...160 DD82
Ye Meads, Maid. (Taplow)
SL6 ...130 AE73
Yenston Cl, Mord. SM4 ...200 DA100
Yeoman Cl, E6
off Ferndale St ...145 EP73
SE27 ...181 DP90
Yeoman Dr, Stai. TW19
off Long La ...174 BL88
Yeoman Rd, Nthlt. UB5 ...136 BY66
Yeomanry Cl, Epsom KT17
off Dirdene Gdns ...217 CT112
Yeomans Acre, Ruis. HA4 ...115 BU58
Yeomans Ct, Hert. SG13 ...32 DS09
Yeomans Cft, Lthd. (Bkhm)
KT23
off Vicarage Cl ...246 CA125
Yeomans Keep, Rick. (Chorl.)
WD3
off Rickmansworth Rd ...73 BF41
Yeomans Meadow, Sev.
TN13 ...256 FG126
Yeoman's Ms, Islw. TW7
off Queensbridge Pk ...177 CE85
Yeoman's Row, SW3 ...18 B6
Yeoman St, SE8 ...23 J7
Yeomans Way, Enf. EN3 ...82 DW40
Yeomans Yd, E1 ...11 P9
Yeoman Way, Red. RH1 ...267 DH139
Yeomen Way, Ilf. IG6 ...103 EQ51
Yeo St, E3 ...14 A5
Yeoveney Cl, Stai. TW19 ...173 BD89
Yeovil Cl, Orp. BR6 ...205 ES103
Yeovil Rd, Slou. SL1 ...131 AL72
Yeovilton Pl, Kings.T. KT2 ...177 CJ92
Sch **Yerbury Prim Sch**, N19
off Foxham Rd ...121 DK62
Yerbury Rd, N19 ...121 DK62
Sch **Yesodey Hatorah
Commercial Rd Talmud
Torah Sch**, N16
off Stamford Hill ...122 DT59
Yester Dr, Chis. BR7 ...184 EL94
Yester Pk, Chis. BR7 ...185 EM94
Yester Rd, Chis. BR7 ...185 EM94
Yevele Way, Horn. RM11 ...128 FL59
Yew Av, West Dr. UB7 ...134 BL73
Yewbank Cl, Ken. CR8 ...236 DR115
Yew Cl, Buck.H. IG9 ...102 EK47
Waltham Cross EN7 ...66 DS27
Yewdale Cl, Brom. BR1 ...184 EE93
Yewdells Cl, Bet. (Buckland)
RH3 ...249 CU133
Yewfield Rd, NW10 ...139 CT66
Yew Gro, NW2 ...119 CX63
Welwyn Garden City AL7 ...30 DC10
Yewlands, Hodd. EN11 ...49 EA18
Sawbridgeworth CM21 ...36 EZ06
Yewlands Cl, Bans. SM7 ...234 DC115
Yewlands Dr, Hodd. EN11 ...49 EA18
Yew Pl, Wey. KT13 ...195 BT104
Yews, The, Ashf. TW15 ...175 BP91
Gravesend DA12 ...191 GK88
Yews Av, Enf. EN1 ...82 DV36
Yew Tree Bottom Rd, Epsom
KT17, KT18 ...233 CV116
Yew Tree Cl, N21 ...99 DN45
Yewtree Cl, N22 ...99 DJ53
Yew Tree Cl, Beac. HP9 ...89 AM54
Brentwood (Hutt.) CM13 ...109 GB44
Yew Tree Cl, Chesh. (Ley Hill)
HP5 *off Botley Rd* ...56 AU30
Coulsdon CR5 ...234 DF119
Yewtree Cl, Har. HA2 ...116 CB56
Yew Tree Cl, Hem.H. HP1
off Fishery Rd ...40 BG22
Horley RH6 ...268 DF147
Sevenoaks TN13 ...256 FD123
Welling DA16 ...166 EU81
Worcester Park KT4 ...198 CS102
Yew Tree Ct, Borwd.
(Elstree) WD6
off Barnet La ...77 CK44
Yew Tree Dr, Cat. CR3 ...252 DT125
Guildford GU1 ...242 AW130
Hemel Hempstead (Bov.)
HP3 ...57 BB28
Yewtree End, St.Alb.
(Park St) AL2 ...60 CB27
Yew Tree Gdns, Epsom KT18 ...232 CP115
Romford RM7 ...127 FD57
Romford (Chad.Hth) RM6 ...126 EY57
Yew Tree La, Reig. RH2 ...250 DB131
Yew Tree Rd, W12 ...139 CT73
Yewtree Rd, Beck. BR3 ...203 DZ97
Yew Tree Rd, Dor. RH4 ...247 CG134
Slough SL1 ...152 AU76
Uxbridge UB10 ...134 BM67
Yew Trees, Egh. TW20 ...193 BC97
Shepperton TW17
off Laleham Rd ...194 BM98
Yew Tree Wk, Houns. TW4 ...176 BZ85
Leatherhead (Eff.) KT24 ...246 BX127
Maidenhead SL6 ...110 AD63
Purley CR8 ...220 DQ110
Yew Tree Way, Croy. CR0 ...221 DY110
Yew Wk, Har. HA1 ...117 CE60
Hoddesdon EN11 ...49 EA18
YIEWSLEY, West Dr. UB7 ...134 BL74
Yoakley Rd, N16 ...122 DS61
Yoke Cl, N7 *off Ewe Cl* ...141 DL65
Yolande Gdns, SE9 ...184 EL85
Yonge Pk, N4 ...121 DN62
York Av, SW14 ...178 CQ85
W7 ...137 CE74
Hayes UB3 ...135 BQ71
Sidcup DA15 ...185 ES89
Slough SL1 ...131 AQ72
Stanmore HA7 ...95 CH53
Windsor SL4 ...151 AP82
York Br, NW1 ...8 E3
York Bldgs, WC2 ...9 P10
York Cl, E6
off Boultwood Rd ...145 EM72
W7 *off York Av* ...137 CE74
Amersham HP7 ...72 AT39
Brentwood (Shenf.) CM15 ...109 FZ45
Kings Langley WD4 ...58 BN29
Morden SM4 ...200 DB98
West Byfleet (Byfleet)
KT14 ...212 BL112
York Cres, Borwd. WD6 ...78 CR40
Loughton IG10 ...84 EL41
Yorke Gdns, Reig. RH2 ...250 DA133
Yorke Gate Rd, Cat. CR3 ...236 DR122
Sch **Yorke Mead Prim Sch**,
Rick. WD3
off Dulwich Way ...74 BN43
Yorke Rd, Reig. RH2 ...249 CZ133
Rickmansworth (Crox.Grn)
WD3 ...74 BN44
Yorkes, Harl. CM18 ...51 ET18
York Gdns, Walt. KT12 ...196 BX103
York Gate, N14 ...99 DL45
NW1 ...8 E4
York Gro, SE15 ...162 DW81
York Hill, SE27 ...181 DP90
Loughton IG10 ...84 EL41
York Hill Est, SE27 ...181 DP90
York Ho, Wem. HA9 ...118 CM63
York Ho Pl, W8 ...17 J3
Sch **York Ho Sch**, Rick. WD3
off Sarratt Rd ...74 BM40
Yorkland Av, Well. DA16 ...165 ET83
York Ms, NW5
off Kentish Town Rd ...121 DH64
Ilford IG1 *off York Rd* ...125 EN62
York Par, Brent. TW8 ...157 CK78
York Pl, SW11 ...160 DD83
WC2 ...9 P10
Dagenham RM10 ...147 FC65
Ilford IG1 *off York Rd* ...125 EN61
York Ri, NW5 ...121 DH62
Orpington BR6 ...205 ES102
York Rd, E4 ...101 EA50
E7 ...144 EG65
E10 ...123 EC62
E17 ...123 DX57
N11 ...99 DK51
N18 ...100 DV51
N21 ...100 DR45
SE1 ...20 B3
SW11 ...160 DC84
SW18 ...160 DC84
SW19 ...180 DC93
W3 ...138 CQ72
W5 ...157 CJ76
Barnet EN5 ...80 DD43
Brentford TW8 ...157 CK78
Brentwood (Shenf.) CM15 ...109 FZ45
Croydon CR0 ...201 DN101
Dartford DA1 ...188 FM87
Epping (N.Wld Bas.)
CM16 ...70 FA27
Gravesend DA12 ...191 GJ90
Gravesend (Nthflt) DA11 ...190 GD87
Guildford GU1 ...258 AX135
Hounslow TW3 ...156 CB83
Ilford IG1 ...125 EN62
Kingston upon Thames
KT2 ...178 CM94
Northwood HA6 ...93 BU54
Rainham RM13 ...147 FD66
Richmond TW10
off Albert Rd ...178 CM85
St. Albans AL1 ...43 CF19
South Croydon CR2 ...221 DX110
Sutton SM2 ...218 DA107
Teddington TW11 ...177 CE91
Uxbridge UB8 ...134 BK66
Waltham Cross EN8 ...67 DY34
Watford WD18 ...76 BW43
West Byfleet (Byfleet)
KT14 ...212 BK112
Westerham (Bigg.H.) TN16 ...238 EH119
Weybridge KT13 ...213 BQ105
Windsor SL4 ...151 AP82
Woking GU22 ...226 AY118
Sch **York Rd Co Jun Sch**,
Dart. DA1
off York Rd ...188 FM87
Yorkshire Cl, N16 ...122 DS62
Yorkshire Gdns, N18 ...100 DV50
Yorkshire Grey Pl, NW3
off Heath St ...120 DC63
Yorkshire Grey Yd, WC1 ...10 A6
Yorkshire Rd, E14 ...13 J8
Mitcham CR4 ...201 DL99
York Sq, E14 ...13 J8
York St, W1 ...8 D5
Barking IG11
off Abbey Rd ...145 EQ67
Mitcham CR4 ...200 DG101
York St, Twick. TW1 ...177 CG88
York Ter, Enf. EN2 ...82 DQ38
Erith DA8 ...167 FC81
York Ter E, NW1 ...8 F4
York Ter W, NW1 ...8 E4
Yorkton St, E2 ...142 DU68
York Way, N1 ...141 DL67
N7 ...141 DK65
N20 ...98 DF48
Borehamwood WD6 ...78 CR40
Chessington KT9 ...216 CL108
Feltham TW13 ...176 BZ90
Hemel Hempstead HP2 ...40 BL21
Watford WD25 ...76 BX36
York Way Ct, N1 ...141 DL67
York Way Est, N7
off York Way ...141 DL65
Youngfield Rd, Hem.H. HP1 ...39 BF19
Youngmans Cl, Enf. EN2 ...82 DQ39
Young Rd, E16 ...144 EJ72
Young's Bldgs, EC1 ...11 H3
★ **Young's Ram Brewery**,
SW18 ...180 DB85
Youngs Ri, Welw.G.C. AL8 ...29 CV09
Youngs Rd, Ilf. IG2 ...125 ER57
Young St, W8 ...17 J4
Leatherhead (Fetch.) KT22 ...247 CE125
Youngstroat La, Wok. GU21,
GU24 ...210 AY110
Yoxley App, Ilf. IG2 ...125 EQ58
Yoxley Dr, Ilf. IG2 ...125 EQ58
Yukon Rd, SW12 ...181 DH87
Broxbourne EN10 ...67 DY25
Yule Cl, St.Alb. (Brick.Wd)
AL2 ...60 BZ30
Yuletide Cl, NW10 ...138 CS66
Yunus Khan Cl, E17 ...123 EA57

Z

Zambezie Dr, N9 ...100 DW48
Zampa Rd, SE16 ...22 E10
Zander Ct, E2
off St. Peter's Cl ...142 DU68
Zangwill Rd, SE3 ...164 EK81
Zealand Av, West Dr. UB7 ...154 BK80
Zealand Rd, E3 ...143 DY68
Zelah Rd, Orp. BR5 ...206 EV101
Zeland Cl, NW2 ...119 CW60
Zennor Rd, SW12 ...181 DJ88
Zenoria St, SE22 ...162 DT84
Zermatt Rd, Th.Hth. CR7 ...202 DQ98
Zetland St, E14 ...14 B6
Zig Zag Rd, Dor. RH5 ...247 CK130
Kenley CR8 ...236 DQ116
Tadworth (Box H.) KT20 ...247 CK132
Zion Pl, Grav. DA12 ...191 GH87
Thornton Heath CR7 ...202 DR98
Zion Rd, Th.Hth. CR7 ...202 DR98
Zion St, Sev. (Seal) TN15
off Church Rd ...257 FM121
Zoar St, SE1 ...20 G1
Zodiac Business Pk, Uxb.
(Cowley) UB8 ...134 BK72
Zoffany St, N19 ...121 DK61

466 London Connections map

Aylesbury, Banbury and Birmingham
Aylesbury
Milton Keynes, Northampton, Rugby, Coventry, Birmingham and The North West
Luton Bedford, Wellingborough, Leicester, Kettering, Nottingham, Derby and Sheffield
Stevenage, Letchworth, Cambridge, Kings Lynn, Huntingdon, Peterborough and The North East
Welwyn Garden City
Hatfield
Welham Green
Brookmans Park
Potters Bar
Hadley Wood
New Barnet
Oakleigh Park
HIGH WYCOMBE
Beaconsfield
Seer Green
Gerrards Cross
Denham Golf Club
Denham
Chesham
Amersham
Chalfont & Latimer
Chorleywood
Rickmansworth
Watford
Croxley
Moor Park
Northwood
Northwood Hills
Pinner
North Harrow
Airport coach link
Watford North
Bricket Wood
St Albans Abbey
Garston
How Wood
Park Street
WATFORD JUNCTION
Watford High Street
Bushey
Carpenders Park
Hatch End
Headstone Lane
Harrow & Wealdstone
Kenton
ST ALBANS
Radlett
Elstree & Borehamwood
Mill Hill Broadway
Stanmore
Edgware
Canons Park
Burnt Oak
Queensbury
Colindale
Kingsbury
Hendon
Hendon Central
Brent Cross
Golders Green
High Barnet
Totteridge & Whetstone
Woodside Park
Mill Hill East
West Finchley
Finchley Central
East Finchley
Highgate
Archway
Upper Holloway
West Ruislip
Uxbridge
Hillingdon
Ickenham
Ruislip
Ruislip Manor
Eastcote
Rayners Lane
West Harrow
Harrow-on-the-Hill
Northwick Park
Preston Road
WEMBLEY PARK
Neasden
Dollis Hill
Willesden Green
Kilburn
Cricklewood
Hampstead
West Hampstead
Hampstead Heath
Gospel Oak
Tufnell Park
Ruislip Gardens
South Ruislip
South Harrow
South Kenton
North Wembley
Wembley Stadium
Northolt
Northolt Park
Sudbury Hill Harrow
Sudbury & Harrow Road
Sudbury Hill
Sudbury Town
Wembley Central
Stonebridge Park
Harlesden
Willesden Junction
Brondesbury
Brondesbury Park
Kensal Rise
Kensal Green
Queens Park
Finchley Road & Frognal
Kentish Town West
Kentish Town
No Thameslink train connection 11th September to May 2005
Holloway Road
Caledonian Road
Greenford
South Greenford
Perivale
Alperton
Hanger Lane
Park Royal
Castle Bar Park
Kilburn Park
Kilburn High Road
South Hampstead
Finchley Road
Swiss Cottage
St John's Wood
Belsize Park
Chalk Farm
Camden Town
Camden Road
Mornington Crescent
ST PANCRAS
KING'S CROSS
EUSTON
King's Cross Thameslink
Maida Vale
Warwick Avenue
Royal Oak
MARYLEBONE
Great Portland Street
North Ealing
Drayton Green
West Acton
North Acton
PADDINGTON
Edgware Road
Baker Street
Regents Park
Warren Street
Euston Square
Goodge Street
King's Cross St Pancras
Russell Square
Farringdon
Reading, Oxford, Swindon, Bath, Bristol, West of England and South Wales
Langley
West Drayton
Hayes & Harlington
Southall
Hanwell
West Ealing
Ealing Broadway
Acton Main Line
East Acton
Westbourne Park
Ladbroke Grove
Latimer Road
Shepherds Bush
Bayswater
Holland Park
Notting Hill Gate
Lancaster Gate
Bond Street
Tottenham Court Road
Holborn
SLOUGH
Iver
White City
Shepherds Bush
Queensway
Marble Arch
Oxford Circus
Acton Central
Goldhawk Road
High Street Kensington
Hyde Park Corner
Green Park
Piccadilly Circus
Covent Garden
Leicester Square
City Thameslink
Kensington Olympia
Knightsbridge
Ealing Common
Railair coach link with Reading
Central WINDSOR & ETON Riverside
Osterley
Northfields
Hounslow East
Boston Manor
South Ealing
Acton Town
South Acton
Chiswick Park
Turnham Green
Stamford Brook
Ravenscourt Park
Hammersmith
Barons Court
West Kensington
Earls Court
Gloucester Road
South Kensington
Sloane Square
VICTORIA
Westminster
St. James's Park
CHARING CROSS
BLACKFRIARS
Temple
Embankment
Hounslow Central
Hounslow West
Heathrow Terminals 1, 2, 3
Hatton Cross
Heathrow Central
HEATHROW AIRPORT
Heathrow Terminal 4
West Brompton
New stations at Imperial Wharf and Shepherd's Bush opening summer 2005.
Pimlico
Southwark
WATERLOO
Waterloo East
Lambeth North
Battersea Park
Vauxhall
Elephant & Castle
Kennington
Oval
Stockwell
Datchet
Gunnersbury
Brentford
Kew Bridge
Fulham Broadway
Parsons Green
Imperial Wharf
Putney Bridge
Sunnymeads
Wraysbury
bus link
Railair coach link
Syon Lane
Isleworth
Hounslow
Chiswick
Kew Gardens
Barnes Bridge
Queenstown Road (Battersea)
Wandsworth Road
Clapham High Street
Loughborough Junction
Denmark Hill
Ascot, Bracknell and Reading
Virginia Water
Egham
Staines
Ashford
Feltham
Whitton
Twickenham
St Margarets
RICHMOND
North Sheen
Mortlake
Barnes
Putney
Wandsworth Town
CLAPHAM JUNCTION
Clapham North
Clapham Common
Brixton
East Putney
Earlsfield
Wandsworth Common
Balham
Clapham South
Southfields
Strawberry Hill
Tooting Bec
Tooting Broadway
Streatham Hill
Herne Hill
Tulse Hill
Wimbledon Park
Shepperton
Sunbury
Hampton
Upper Halliford
Kempton Park (race days only)
Fulwell
Haydons Road
Tooting
Streatham
WIMBLEDON
Dundonald Road
Merton Park
Colliers Wood
South Wimbledon
Chertsey
Teddington
Raynes Park
Wimbledon Chase
Morden Road
Morden
West Norwood
Gipsy Hill
Hampton Wick
New Malden
Motspur Park
Belgrave Walk
Streatham Common
Crystal Palace
Railair coach link
RIVER THAMES
Kingston
Norbiton
South Merton
Morden South
Phipps Bridge
Mitcham
Mitcham Junction
Norbury
Addlestone
Hampton Court
Berrylands
Malden Manor
Tolworth
St Helier
Hackbridge
Beddington Lane
Therapia Lane
Thornton Heath
Thames Ditton
Worcester Park
Sutton Common
Ampere Way
Waddon Marsh
Selhurst
Walton-on-Thames
Stoneleigh
West Sutton
Chessington North
Ewell West
Sutton
Carshalton
Wandle Park
Woking
West Byfleet
Byfleet & New Haw
Weybridge
Hersham
Esher
Surbiton
Chessington South
WEST CROYDON
Aldershot, Basingstoke, Salisbury, Exeter, Southampton, Bournemouth, Poole and Weymouth
Hinchley Wood
Claygate
Oxshott
Ewell East
Cheam
Carshalton Beeches
Wallington
Waddon
Reeves Corner
George Street
Belmont
Epsom
Cobham & Stoke D'Abernon
Ashtead
Banstead
Church Street
Effingham Junction
Bookham
Leatherhead
Epsom Downs
Tattenham Corner
Kingswood
Woodmansterne
Reedham
Guildford, Havant, Portsmouth and Isle of Wight
Guildford
Dorking and Horsham
Tadworth
Chipstead
Smitham
Gatwick Airport, Brighton, Eastbourne and